Discovering Computers and Microsoft® Office 2010:

A Fundamental Combined Approach
CSCI 1101: Columbus State Community College

Gary B. Shelly | Misty E. Vermaat

CENGAGE Learning®

Australia • Brazil • Japan • Korea • Mexico • Singapore • Spain • United Kingdom • United States

CENGAGE Learning

Discovering Computers and Microsoft® Office 2010: A Fundamental Combined Approach, CSCI 1101: Columbus State Community College

Executive Editors:
Maureen Staudt
Michael Stranz

Senior Project Development Manager:
Linda deStefano

Marketing Specialist:
Courtney Sheldon

Senior Production/Manufacturing Manager:
Donna M. Brown

Production Editorial Manager:
Kim Fry

Sr. Rights Acquisition Account Manager:
Todd Osborne

Printed in the United States of America

Discovering Computers and Microsoft® Office 2010: A Fundamental Combined Approach
Gary B. Shelly | Misty E. Vermaat

ISBN-13: 978-1-285-12217-5

ISBN-10: 1-285-12217-8

Cengage Learning
5191 Natorp Boulevard
Mason, Ohio 45040
USA
Cengage Learning is a leading provider of customized learning solutions with office locations around the globe, including Singapore, the United Kingdom, Australia, Mexico, Brazil, and Japan. Locate your local office at:
international.cengage.com/region.

Cengage Learning products are represented in Canada by Nelson Education, Ltd.
For your lifelong learning solutions, visit **www.cengage.com/custom.**
Visit our corporate website at **www.cengage.com.**

SEMESTERS PLAN OF STUDY

Computer Science

COLUMBUS STATE Community College

Computer Science Associate of Applied Science Degree
- **Game Developer Track**
- **MIS/Project Management Track**
- **Network Administrator Track**
- **Network Security Track**
- **Software Developer Track**
- **Web Developer Track**

Cisco Certified Network Administrator (CCNA) Discovery Certificate
Computer Literacy Certificate
Database Specialist Certificate
Network Security Certificate
Management Information Systems (MIS) Certificate
Network Administrator Certificate
Software Developer Certificate
System Z Certificate

The **Computer Science** curriculum provides graduates with a foundation in logic, programming, operating systems, applications, systems analysis, and networking through a core set of courses. Learners may choose to specialize in Game Developer, Network Administrator, Network Security, Software Developer, or Web Developer. CSCI offers a number of industry subject-specific certificates in database, networking, hardware/software, and applications.

Upon completion of the Associate Degree in Computer Science, the graduate will be able to:
- Participate in collaborative projects utilizing the Systems Development Life Cycle (SDLC).
- Determine project requirements.
- Create project documentation using computer based applications software.
- Develop applications using programming languages.
- Create a multiple-page, multiple presentation Web site.
- Perform operating systems fundamentals for effective file management.
- Identify and apply networking concepts. Identify and apply programming logic concepts.
- Identify and apply relevant social networking applications.
- Demonstrate team project skills using effective technical communication.

The **Cisco Certified Network Administrator (CCNA) Discovery Certificate** is a curriculum that provides foundational networking knowledge, practical experience, and soft-skills development to prepare students for entry-level careers in IT and networking. The curriculum focuses on networking for simple home or small office networks to complex enterprise networks. Students are introduced to advanced technologies such as voice, video, wireless and security and gain hands-on experience with switches, routers, cables and other networking technologies. The Cisco Discovery Certificate curriculum prepares students for two different Cisco certification exams, Cisco Certified Entry Network Technician (CCENT), and Cisco Certified Network Associate (CCNA).

In working toward the Computer Literacy Certificate, the student will learn the fundamental components and terminology of personal computer hardware and software basic concepts. This certificate is designed for beginning computer users to develop computer literacy skills.

Upon completion of the **Computer Literacy Certificate**, the student will be able to:
- Use the Windows operating system to manage files and folders, including creating, renaming, copying, deleting, and moving
- Demonstrate proficiency within the Blackboard environment
- Navigate and explore the Internet and the World Wide Web utilizing Microsoft Internet Explorer
- Utilize the Internet as an effective research tool
- Describe the basic elements and terminology of the Windows operating system
- Create and edit Word documents including a research paper, a resume, and a business letter
- Create and format an Excel worksheet with embedded charts, formulas, and functions
- Perform a What-if Analysis in Excel
- Create and use an Access database including tables, queries, and reports
- Create a slide show in PowerPoint
- Integrate Microsoft Office applications.

In addition to many of the Computer Science competencies, a graduate with a **Database Specialist Certificate** will be able to:
- Prepare a systems design utilizing a database management system
- Design and implement an Access, Oracle and Microsoft SQL server database
- Perform basic administration functions of a database management system
- Understand data warehousing systems
- Use the Visual Basic.NET language to interface with a database management system.

In addition to many of the Computer Science competencies, a graduate with a **Security Network Certificate** will be able to:
- Describe and analyze security threats
- Protect an organization's system and data

- Design disaster recovery strategies for the enterprise
- Design and implement computer forensics strategies
- Assess network vulnerabilities
- Recognize and respond to security threats
- Design and develop security audits for an organization
- Understand the ethical issues related to network security
- Design and implement wireless networks
- Work with VPNs and firewalls
- Protect Internet connections and intranets as well as critical data from attacks
- Learn how to carry out and implement secure communications across unsecured networks.

In addition to many of the Computer Science competencies, a graduate with a **Management Information Systems (MIS) Certificate** will be able to:
- Define project goals clearly
- Design and produce a UML requirement model
- Implement a UML design in IT Project
- Determine task dependencies and schedules
- Assign and optimize resources
- Produce the implementation plan
- Manage and respond to change
- Measure and present results effectively
- Apply practical aspects learned in the classroom by managing or assisting in managing IT projects.

In addition to many of the Computer Science competencies, a graduate with a **Network Administrator Certificate** will be able to:
- Describe the various types of distributed processing systems and operating systems
- Design, create, and operate a distributed DBMS
- Use at least one major LAN operating system
- Design, create, and implement a distributed processing system to support the information processing requirements for a large information management organization to include installing a DBMS.

In addition to many of the Computer Science competencies, a graduate with a **Software Developer Certificate** will be able to:
- Demonstrate techniques of object analysis and object design
- Design and code programs in C# and Visual Basic.NET
- Debug a C# or Visual Basic.NET program
- Develop Web front-end applications
- Utilize a database for a web application.

The **System Z Certificate** was developed to address industry's continuing need for skilled professionals with mainframe skills. This certificate was designed by area companies and IBM Corporation, which will provide access to hardware/software, course materials/speaker notes, student textbooks, etc. The System Z Certificate is a four-course sequence focused on the basics of enterprise networking, and it is designed for individuals with significant IT working experience or for current students with instructor's permission.

Software/Hardware Requirements

Students taking courses in this curriculum may need to own or have access to hardware/software to pursue this degree. This is particularly important for students who are enrolled in online/distance learning (DL) sections of a particular course. Check with the program advisor to discuss specific course needs and options.

NOTE: Some courses may require prerequisites; please make sure to fulfill required prerequisites or meet with your program advisor to discuss them.

Computer Science Associate Degree, Game Developer Track

COURSE		CR
Semester 1		
CSCI 1101	Computer Concepts & Applications	3
CSCI 1103	Introduction to Programming Logic	3
MATH 1148	College Algebra	4
CSCI 1511	Python Programming	3
IMM 1115	Survey of Gaming Industry	3
COLS 1100	First Year Experience Seminar	1
TOTAL CREDIT HOURS		**17**
Semester 2		
CSCI 1551	Concepts of 3 D Games Engines	3
CSCI XXXX	Technical Elective	3
ENGL 1100	Composition I	3
CSCI 1151	Operating Systems	2
CSCI 1152	Networking Concepts	2
MATH 1149	Trigonometry	4
TOTAL CREDIT HOURS		**17**
Summer Semester		
PHYS 1200	Introductory Algebra-Based Physics I	5
COMM 2204	Technical Writing	3
ECON 2200	Principles of Microeconomics	3
TOTAL CREDIT HOURS		**11**
Semester 3		
CSCI 2551	Graphics in 3D Games Engines	4
CSCI 2541	Foundations of 2-D Game Programming	3
CSCI 2521	C++ Programming	3
IMM 1201	3D Modeling I	3
TOTAL CREDIT HOURS		**13**
Semester 4		
CSCI 2556	3-D Game Project	3
CSCI 2546	2-D Game Project	3
MKTG 1110	Marketing Principles **or**	
MKTG 1020	Branding	3
HIST XXXX	1111, 1112, 1151, **or** 1152	3
TOTAL CREDIT HOURS		**12**
TOTAL DEGREE CREDIT HOURS		**70**

Technical Electives

The following courses are approved for technical elective requirements:

CSCI 1531	Game Programming Language	3
CSCI 2325	Expert Access	3
CSCI 2467	Java Programming	3

Computer Science Associate Degree, MIS/Project Management Track

COURSE		CR
Semester 1		
CSCI 1101	Computer Concepts & Applications	3
CSCI 1103	Introduction to Programming Logic	3
MATH 1148	College Algebra	4
ENGL 1100	Composition I	3
HUM XXXX	Refer to approved GE - HUM list	3
COLS 1100	First Year Experience Seminar	1
TOTAL CREDIT HOURS		**17**
Semester 2		
CSCI 1151	Operating Systems	2
CSCI 1152	Networking Concepts	2
CSCI 1610	Object Oriented Analysis & UML	3
CSCI 1145	HTML	3
CSCI 1620	Visual Basic I	3
COMM 2200	Business Communication	3
TOTAL CREDIT HOURS		**16**
Summer Semester		
CSCI 1275	Systems Analysis	3
TOTAL CREDIT HOURS		**3**
Semester 3		
ACCT 1211	Financial Accounting	3
ECON 2200	Principles of Microeconomics	3
CSCI 2330	Project Management Fundamentals & Case Studies	4
CSCI XXXX	Technical Elective I	3
NAT XXXX	Refer to approved GE - NAT list	4
TOTAL CREDIT HOURS		**17**
Semester 4		
CSCI XXXX	Technical Elective II	3
CSCI 2370	Database Systems Programming	3
SCM 1501	Information Technology in Logistics	3
CSCI 2802	CSCI Seminar	1
CSCI 2902	CSCI Practicum	3
MKTG 1110	Marketing Principles	3
TOTAL CREDIT HOURS		**16**
TOTAL DEGREE CREDIT HOURS		**69**

Technical Electives

The following courses are approved for technical elective requirements:

CSCI 1001	Computer Fundamentals	1
CSCI 1630	C# Programming I	4
CSCI 1772	Networking I	3
CSCI 2371	Database Administration & Data Mining	4
CSCI 2412	Web Database Development	4
CSCI 2620	Visual Basic II	4

Approved General Education (GE) List

NAT

GE-NATURAL/PHYSICAL SCIENCES REQUIREMENT (SELECT ONE)

		CR
ASTR 1141	Life in the Universe	3
ASTR 1161	The Solar System	3
ASTR 1162	Stars and Galaxies	3
ASTR 1400	Astronomy Laboratory	1
BIO 1112	Introduction to Biology I	4
BIO 1113	Biological Sciences I	4
BIO 1114	Biological Sciences II	4
BIO 1125	Human Biology	4
BIO 1127	Plant Biology	4
BIO 2215	Introduction to Microbiology	4
BIO 2232	Human Physiology	4
CHEM 1110	Chemistry and Society	5

Approved General Education (GE) List (continued)

CHEM 1111	Elementary Chemistry I	4
CHEM 1112	Elementary Chemistry II	4
CHEM 1171	General Chemistry I	5
CHEM 1172	General Chemistry II	5
GEOL 1101	Introduction to Earth Science	4
GEOL 1105	Geology and the National Parks	3
GEOL 1121	Physical Geology	4
GEOL1122	Historical Geology	4
GEOL 1151	Natural Disasters	3
PHYS 1103	World of Energy	3
PHYS 1106	Physics by Inquiry: Properties & Motion	5
PHYS 1200	Introductory Algebra-Based Physics I	5
PHYS 1201	Algebra-Based Physics II	5
PHYS 1250	Calculus-Based Physics I	5
PHYS 1251	Calculus-Based Phys II	5

HUM

GE-ART/HUMANITIES REQUIREMENT (SELECT ONE)

		CR
HART 1201	History of Art I	3
HART 1202	History of Art II	3
HIST 1111	European History to 1648	3
HIST 1112	European History since 1648	3
HIST 1151	American History to 1877	3
HIST 1152	American History since 1877	3
HIST 1181	World Civ I: Non-Western/Non-Amer to 1500	3
HIST 1182	World Civ II: Non-Western/Non-Amer since 1500	3
HIST 2223	African-American History I: 1451-1876	3
HIST 2224	African-American History II: 1877-Present	3
HUM 1100	Introduction to Humanities	3
HUM 1270	Comparative Religions	3
MUS 1251	Survey of Music History	3
PHIL 1101	Introduction to Philosophy	3
PHIL 1130	Ethics	3

Computer Science Associate Degree, Network Administrator Track

COURSE		CR
Semester 1		
CSCI 1101	Computer Concepts & Applications	3
CSCI 1103	Introduction to Programming Logic	3
MATH 1148	College Algebra	4
CSCI 1151	Operating Systems	2
CSCI 1152	Networking Concepts	2
COLS 1100	First Year Experience Seminar	1
TOTAL CREDIT HOURS		**15**
Semester 2		
CSCI 1145	HTML	3
ENGL 1100	Composition I	3
ECON 2200	Principles of Microeconomics	3
PHYS 1200	Introductory Algebra-Based Physics I	5
CSCI 1772	Networking I	3
TOTAL CREDIT HOURS		**17**
Summer Semester		
CSCI 1275	Systems Analysis	3
ACCT 1211	Financial Accounting	3
MKTG 1110	Marketing Principles	3
BMGT 2250	Project Management Principles	3
TOTAL CREDIT HOURS		**12**

Semester 3

CSCI 2774	Networking II	4
CSCI 2770	Network Communication & TCP/IP	3
CSCI 2790	Linux Administration	3
HIST XXXX	1111, 1112, 1151, **or** 1152	3
CSCI 2778	Wireless, Voice, & Mobile Communications	3
TOTAL CREDIT HOURS		**16**

Semester 4

CSCI 2792	Virtualization	3
CSCI XXXX	Technical Elective	1-4
CSCI 2802	CSCI Seminar	1
CSCI 2902	CSCI Practicum	3
IMM 1120	Fundamentals of Interactive Media	3
TOTAL CREDIT HOURS		**11-14**
TOTAL DEGREE CREDIT HOURS		**71-74**

Technical Electives

The following courses are approved for technical elective requirements:

CSCI 2371	Database Administration & Data Mining	4
CSCI 2776	Network & Cyber Security	3
CSCI 2780	Computer Forensics	3
CSCI 2782	Information Security Audit	3
CSCI 2784	Business Continuity & Disaster Recovery	3
CSCI 2994	CSCI Current Topics	1 - 3

Computer Science Associate Degree, Network Security Track

COURSE		CR
Semester 1		
CSCI 1101	Computer Concepts & Applications	3
CSCI 1103	Introduction to Programming Logic	3
MATH 1148	College Algebra	4
ENGL 1100	Composition I	3
COLS 1100	First Year Experience Seminar	1
TOTAL CREDIT HOURS		**14**
Semester 2		
CSCI 1145	HTML	3
CSCI 1151	Operating Systems	2
CSCI 1152	Networking Concepts	2
BMGT 2250	Project Management Principles	3
ECON 2200	Principles of Microeconomics	3
PHIL 1150	Introduction to Logic or	
PHIL 1130	Ethics	3
TOTAL CREDIT HOURS		**16**
Summer Semester		
CSCI 1275	Systems Analysis	3
HIST XXXX	1111, 1112, 1151, **or** 1152	3
MKTG 1110	Marketing Principles	3
CHEM 1111	Elementary Chemistry I	4
TOTAL CREDIT HOURS		**13**
Semester 3		
CSCI 2750	Networking for Home & Small Businesses	3
CSCI 2752	Working at a Small to Medium Business or ISP	3
CSCI 2780	Computer Forensics	3
CSCI XXXX	Technical Elective	3
TOTAL CREDIT HOURS		**12**
Semester 4		
CSCI 2790	Linux Administration	3
CSCI 2776	Network & Cybersecurity	3
CSCI 2802	CSCI Seminar	1
CSCI 2902	CSCI Practicum	3
CSCI 2786	Security Practice & Management	3
IMM 1120	Fundamentals of Interactive Media	3
TOTAL CREDIT HOURS		**16**
TOTAL DEGREE CREDIT HOURS		**71**

Technical Electives

The following courses are approved for technical elective requirements:

CSCI 2754	Intro Routing & Switching in Enterprise	3
CSCI 2756	Designing & Supporting Computer Network	3
CSCI 1445	Content Management & Integration	3
CSCI 2760	CCNA Voice	3
CSCI 2762	CCNA Security	3
CSCI 2764	CCNA Wireless	3

Computer Science Associate Degree, Software Developer Track

COURSE		CR
Semester 1		
CSCI 1101	Computer Concepts & Applications	3
CSCI 1103	Introduction to Programming Logic	3
MATH 1148	College Algebra	4
ENGL 1100	Composition I	3
PHIL 1150	Introduction to Logic	3
COLS 1100	First Year Experience Seminar	1
TOTAL CREDIT HOURS		**17**
Semester 2		
CSCI 1620	Visual Basic I	3
CSC I 1151	Operating Systems	2
CSCI 1152	Networking Concepts	2
CSCI 1145	HTML	3
CSCI 1610	Object Oriented Analysis & UML	3
CSCI 1630	C# Programming I	4
TOTAL CREDIT HOURS		**17**
Summer Semester		
CSCI 1275	Systems Analysis	3
ECON 2200	Principles of Microeconomics	3
PHYS 1200	Introductory Algebra-Based Physics I	5
TOTAL CREDIT HOURS		**11**
Semester 3		
CSCI 2467	Java Programming I	3
CSCI 2447	JavaScript Fundamentals	3
SCM 1190	International Business	2
MKTG 1110	Marketing Principles	3
CSCI 2370	Database Systems Programming	3
TOTAL CREDIT HOURS		**14**
Semester 4		
CSCI XXXX	Technical Elective	1-4
BMGT 1111	Management	3
HIST XXXX	1111, 1112, 1151, **or** 1152	3
CSCI 2802	CSCI Seminar	1
CSCI 2902	CSCI Practicum	3
TOTAL CREDIT HOURS		**11-14**
TOTAL DEGREE CREDIT HOURS		**70-73**

Technical Electives

The following courses are approved for technical elective requirements:

CSCI 2412	Web Database Development	4
CSCI 2469	Java Programming II	3
CSCI 2620	Visual Basic II	4
CSCI 2630	C# Programming II	3
CSCI 2994	CSCI Current Topics	1 – 3

Computer Science Associate Degree, Web Developer Track

COURSE		CR
Semester 1		
CSCI 1101	Computer Concepts & Applications	3
CSCI 1103	Introduction to Programming Logic	3
MATH 1148	College Algebra	4
ENGL 1100	Composition I	3
HIST XXXX	1111, 1112, 1151, **or** 1152	3
COLS 1100	First Year Experience Seminar	1
TOTAL CREDIT HOURS		**17**
Semester 2		
CSCI 1102	Intermediate Excel & Access	3
CSCI 1151	Operating Systems	2
CSCI 1152	Networking Concepts	2
CSCI 1145	HTML	3
ACCT 1211	Financial Accounting	3
ECON 2200	Principles of Microeconomics	3
TOTAL CREDIT HOURS		**16**
Summer Semester		
CSCI 1275	System Analysis	3
TOTAL CREDIT HOURS		**3**
Semester 3		
CSCI 2467	Java Programming I	3
CSCI 2412	Web Database Development	4
CSCI 2447	JavaScript Fundamentals	3
IMM 2620	Website Design Creation	3
COMM 2204	Technical Writing	3
TOTAL CREDIT HOURS		**16**
Semester 4		
CSCI 2489	Mobile Software Development	3
CSCI XXXX	Technical Elective	3
MKTG 1110	Marketing Principles	3
CHEM 1111	Elementary Chemistry I	4
CSCI 2802	CSCI Seminar	1
CSCI 2902	CSCI Practicum	3
TOTAL CREDIT HOURS		**17**
TOTAL DEGREE CREDIT HOURS		**69**

Technical Electives

The following courses are approved for technical elective requirements:

CSCI 1620	Visual Basic I	3
CSCI 1630	C# Programming I	4
CSCI 2241	Introduction to Mainframe-Z/OS Basics	3
CSCI 2251	Intro to Mainframe Large Scale Commercial Computing	2
CSCI 2261	Introduction to Mainframe-Networking	2
CSCI 2271	Introduction to the Mainframe-Security	3
CSCI 2370	Database Systems Programming	3
CSCI 2371	Database Administration & Data Mining	4
CSCI 2479	Advanced Web Programming	3

CCNA Discovery Certificate

COURSE		CR
Semester 1		
CSCI 2750	Networking for Home and Small Businesses	3
CSCI 2752	Working at a Small to Medium Business or ISP	3
TOTAL CREDIT HOURS		**6**
Semester 2		
CSCI 2754	Introducing to Routing & Switching in Enterprise	3
CSCI 2756	Designing & Supporting Computer Network	3
TOTAL CREDIT HOURS		**6**
TOTAL CERTIFICATE CREDIT HOURS		**12**

Computer Literacy Certificate

COURSE		CR
Semester 1		
CSCI 1001	Computer Fundamentals	1
TOTAL CREDIT HOURS		**1**
Semester 2		
CSCI 1101	Computer Concepts & Applications	3
TOTAL CREDIT HOURS		**3**
Semester 3		
CSCI 1102	Intermediate Excel & Access	3
TOTAL CREDIT HOURS		**3**
TOTAL CERTIFICATE CREDIT HOURS		**7**

Database Specialist Certificate

COURSE		CR
Semester 1		
CSCI 1275	Systems Analysis	3
CSCI 2325	Expert Access	3
TOTAL CREDIT HOURS		**6**
Semester 2		
CSCI 2370	Database Systems Programming	3
CSCI 2412	Web Database Development	4
TOTAL CREDIT HOURS		**7**
Semester 3		
CSCI 2371	Database Administration & Data Mining	4
CSCI 1620	Visual Basic I	3
TOTAL CREDIT HOURS		**7**
TOTAL CERTIFICATE CREDIT HOURS		**20**

Management Information Systems (MIS) Certificate

COURSE		CR
Semester 1		
CSCI 1103	Introduction to Programming Logic	3
CSCI 2330	Project Management Fundamentals & Case Studies	4
TOTAL CREDIT HOURS		**7**
Semester 2		
CSCI 1275	Systems Analysis	3
CSCI 1610	Object Oriented Analysis & UML	3
TOTAL CREDIT HOURS		**6**
TOTAL CERTIFICATE CREDIT HOURS		**13**

Network Administrator Certificate

COURSE		CR
Semester 1		
CSCI 1772	Networking I	3
CSCI 2770	Network Communication & TCP/IP	3
TOTAL CREDIT HOURS		**6**
Semester 2		
CSCI 2774	Networking II	4
CSCI 2790	Linux Administration	3
TOTAL CREDIT HOURS		**7**
Semester 3		
CSCI 2792	Virtualization	3
CSCI 2778	Wireless, Voice, & Mobile Communications	3
CSCI XXXX	Technical Elective	3 - 4
TOTAL CREDIT HOURS		**9 - 10**

Semester 4

CSCI 2786	Security Practice & Management	3
CSCI 2750	Networking for Home & Small Businesses	3
TOTAL CREDIT HOURS		**6**
TOTAL CERTIFICATE CREDIT HOURS		**28 - 29**

Technical Electives

The following courses are approved for technical elective requirements:

CSCI 2370	Database Systems Programming	3
CSCI 2371	Database Administration & Data Mining	4
CSCI 2776	Network & Cyber Security	3
CSCI 2780	Computer Forensics	3
CSCI 2782	Information Security Audit	3
CSCI 2784	Business Continuity & Disaster Recovery	3

Network Security Certificate

COURSE		CR
Semester 1		
CSCI 1151	Operating Systems	2
CSCI 1152	Networking Concepts	2
CSCI 1275	System Analysis	3
TOTAL CREDIT HOURS		**7**
Semester 2		
CSCI 2750	Networking for Home & Small Businesses	3
CSCI 2752	Working at a Small-to- Medium Business or ISP	3
TOTAL CREDIT HOURS		**6**
Semester 3		
CSCI 2780	Computer Forensics	3
CSCI XXXX	Technical Elective	3
TOTAL CREDIT HOURS		**6**
Semester 4		
CSCI 2776	Network & Cybersecurity	3
CSCI 2790	Linux Administration	3
CSCI 2786	Security Practice & Management	3
TOTAL CREDIT HOURS		**9**
TOTAL CERTIFICATE CREDIT HOURS		**28**

Technical Electives

The following courses are approved for technical elective requirements:

CSCI 1445	Content Management & Integration	3
CSCI 2782	Information Security Audit	3
CSCI 2784	Business Continuity & Disaster Recovery	3
CSCI 2760	CCNA Voice	3
CSCI 2762	CCNA Security	3
CSCI 2764	CCNA Wireless	3

Software Developer Certificate

COURSE		CR
Semester 1		
CSCI 2467	Java Programming I	3
CSCI 1145	HTML	3
CSCI 1630	C# Programming I	4
TOTAL CREDIT HOURS		**10**
Semester 2		
CSCI 1620	Visual Basic I	3
CSCI 2370	Database Systems Programming	3
CSCI 2447	JavaScript Fundamentals	3
TOTAL CREDIT HOURS		**9**
TOTAL CERTIFICATE CREDIT HOURS		**19**

System Z Certificate

COURSE		CR
Semester 1		
CSCI 2241	Introduction to the Mainframe Z/OS Basics	3
TOTAL CREDIT HOURS		**3**
Semester 2		
CSCI 2251	Intro to Mainframe-Large Scale Commercial Computing	2
CSCI 2261	Introduction to Mainframe Networking	2
CSCI 2271	Introduction to Mainframe Security	3
TOTAL CREDIT HOURS		**7**
TOTAL CERTIFICATE CREDIT HOURS		**10**

Course Descriptions

CSCI 1000 Introduction to HTML (A, SP) **1 credit**

Learn the most important topics of HTML, including creating an HTML document; viewing an HTML file in a Web browser; working with tag text elements; inserting special characters, lines, and graphics; creating hypertext links; working with color and images; creating text and graphical tables; using tables to enhance page design; creating and working with frames; and, controlling the behavior of hyperlinks on a page with frames. 8wk term course.

Lab: 2 hours Lab fee: $2.00

CSCI 1001 Computer Fundamentals (A, SP, SU) **2 credits**

CSCI 1001 introduces the inexperienced user of computers to fundamentals of computer terminology, hardware, software, windows operating system, directories, folders, files, copy paste functions, naming conventions and setting passwords. Additional topics covered include the World Wide Web, the Internet, search engines and Blackboard.

Lecture: 1 hour - Lab: 2 hours Lab fee: $6.00

CSCI 1052 Networking Terminology (SP) **1 credit**

This course is designed to provide students a solid understanding of computer networking terminology and the technologies in the field of computer networking. Students will learn and gain an in-depth analysis of data mobility including the hardware infrastructure (wires, wireless, and devices supporting them), the ISO Open Systems Interconnection (OSI) stack, standards, Internet protocols, enterprise architecture models, OSI model, privacy, confidentiality, network security, topologies, and other technologies associated with computer networking. Note: Computer Science (CSCI) students will not be given credit for this course towards their required Computer Science (CSCI) degree or Networking/Security certificate requirements.

Lab: 2 hours Lab fee: $1.00

CSCI 1100 Essential Computer Topics (SP) **1 credit**

For students without an IT background, provides a basic overview of computer architecture; networking and data communication; the Internet and WWW; computer security; social impact of computing. Basic terminology of computing is covered.

Lab: 2 hours Lab fee: $1.00

CSCI 1101 Computer Concepts & Applications (A, SP, SU) **3 credits**

CSCI 1101 is designed to provide students with a working knowledge of computer concepts and essential skills necessary for work and communication in today's society. Topics include, social networking, computer security, safety, ethics, privacy, operating systems and utility programs, communications and networks, input, output, system units, storage, word processing, spreadsheets, databases and presentation software.

Lecture: 2 hours - Lab: 2 hours
Prerequisite: ENGL 0190 or placement into ENGL 1100
Lab fee: $6.00

CSCI 1102 Intermediate Excel & Access (SP) 3 credits
CSCI 1102 is a continuation of CSCI 1101, incorporating Intermediate concepts and techniques used in spreadsheets and database software. Examples: financial functions, data tables, amortization schedules, working with multiple worksheets, macros, database queries, reports, switchboards, pivot tables and charts, and using SQL. Project management and HTML concepts will be introduced. Students will learn how to use these tools for analysis and decision making.
Lecture: 2 hours - Lab: 2 hours
Prerequisite: CSCI 1101 Lab fee: $2.00

CSCI 1103 Intro Programming Logic (A, SP, SU) 3 credits
CSCI 1103 introduces concepts of programming logic through algorithmic solutions applied to problem-domain scenarios and examples of these scenarios are Computer Science disciplines such as: programming languages, networking, operating systems, databases, and other ones. The course covers the basic units of logic: sequence, selection, and loop. Students repair faulty algorithmic solutions. The course also uses basic UML (Unified Modeling Language) notation to model problem-domain objects, via classes.
Lecture: 2 hours - Lab: 2 hours
Prerequisite: MATH 1030 Lab fee: $27.00

CSCI 1145 HTML (A, SP) 3 credits
CSCI 1145 will teach students the dynamics of the Web environment while pursuing an in-depth study of the most recent version of both Hypertext Markup Language (HTML) and Cascading Style Sheets (CSS). Throughout the course, students will create a real website using HMTL and CSS on a live server environment. Students will learn other important topics such as FTP, TCP/IP, and HTTP.
Lecture: 2 hours - Lab: 3 hours
Prerequisite: CSCI 1103 Lab fee: $4.00

CSCI 1151 Operating Systems (A, SP) 2 credits
CSCI 1151 introduces relevant concepts related to PC Operating Systems such as Windows, MAC OS, and Linux. Students investigate operating systems used in portable devices. The course also uses desktop virtualization to run different operating systems on a single PC. The course uses a hands-on approach to exercise tasks like: installation of operating systems, software installation, system troubleshooting, remote assistance, remote desktop, SOHO networking, and system security.
Lecture: 1 hour - Lab: 2 hours
Prerequisite: CSCI 1103 Lab fee: $4.00

CSCI 1152 Networking Concepts (A, SP) 2 credits
CSCI 1152 is designed for students to learn popular networking and security concepts using Windows and Linux in a hands on lab environment. Students will learn concepts geared towards an industry certification. Students will complete a series of assignments and be able to demonstrate network administration for both wired and wireless networks in a LAN environment using hardware, software, and virtualization.
Lecture: 1 hour - Lab: 2 hours Lab fee: $3.00

CSCI 1275 Systems Analysis (A, SU) 3 credits
CSCI 1275 is an introduction to the fundamentals of traditional and object systems analysis, design, and project management. Emphasis will be placed on the Systems Development Life Cycle (SDLC), various flow diagrams, system requirements, project scheduling and managing analysis, and design activities. In addition, students will produce various flow diagrams, project schedules, and timetables. They will also explore object-oriented design and unified modeling language (UML) in this class. Students will work in teams to learn to prepare and present a systems proposal and how to implement and complete a software project.
Lecture: 2 hours - Lab: 3 hours
Prerequisite: CSCI 1103 Lab fee: $4.00

CSCI 1445 Content Mgt & Integration (SP) 3 credits
The internet contains a massive amount of data which is constantly being served all over the world. Managing this data server-side is no small task. In CSCI 1445, students will explore methods and techniques to managing large amounts of information and learn ways to organize and deliver this information in a meaningful manner. In addition to implementing several examples as projects, students will also learn about the ethics and inherent security concerns of online content.
Lecture: 2 hours - Lab: 3 hours
Prerequisites: CSCI 1103, CSCI 1145 Lab fee: $2.00

CSCI 1511 Python Programming (A, SP) 3 credits
CSCI 1511 introduces basic concepts of game design and programming. Students learn the Python programming language constructs to write programs that integrate classes, class methods, and class instances, built upon basic structures such as: input method handling, 2D sprite manipulation and animation, collision detection, game physics and basic artificial intelligence.
Lecture: 2 hours - Lab: 3 hours
Prerequisite: CSCI 1103 Lab fee: $2.00

CSCI 1531 Game Programming Language (SP) 3 credits
CSCI 1531 introduces the concepts of ANSI C programming. In addition to covering basic syntax and semantics, the course emphasizes problem solving methodology and modular programming techniques. Lab problems are directed by game programming applications. Computer lab projects will provide hands-on experience in developing programs with an ANSI C compiler environment including debugging techniques.
Lecture: 2 hours - Lab: 3 hours
Prerequisite: CSCI 1103

CSCI 1551 Concepts of 3D Games Engines (SP) 3 credits
CSCI 1551 is an introductory course in how a 3D, multiplayer, networked game engine would build platforms and control game logic. The game engine is Panda3D, developed by Disney. Panda3D is a framework for 3D rendering and game development for Python and C++ programs. Panda3D is Open Source and free for any purpose. Game development with Panda3D will consist of writing a Python program that controls the Panda3D library. Computer lab projects will provide hands-on experience investigating the various components of a network game.
Lecture: 2 hours - Lab: 3 hours
Prerequisite: CSCI 1511 Lab fee: $2.00

CSCI 1610 Object Oriented Analysis and UML (A, SP) 3 credits
CSCI 1610 is an introduction to object oriented programming concepts and techniques, and system modeling using Unified Modeling Language. It teaches all of the major UML diagram types and the basic notation involved in creating and deciphering them. Students will learn to read, draw, and use visual modeling language to create clear and effective blueprints for software development projects.
Lecture: 2 hours - Lab: 3 hours
Prerequisite: CSCI 1103 Lab fee: $2.00

CSCI 1620 Visual Basic I (A, SP) 3 credits
CSCI 1620 emphasizes the essential aspects of creating the graphical user interface of a Visual Basic Windows program. The student also will learn fundamental aspects of coding a VB.NET program, along with more advanced topics such as manipulating MS Access databases, sequential file processing, error handling, and data validation. Software is provided to students.
Lecture: 2 hours - Lab: 3 hours
Prerequisite: CSCI 1103 Lab fee: $2.00

CSCI 1630 C# Programming I (A, SP, SU) 4 credits
CSCI 1630 uses the Visual C# programming language as the programming tool for learning principles of object-oriented programming. The course covers implementation of classes that support static and instance methods, concrete vs. abstract classes, class inheritance, polymorphism, exception handling, and object serialization. The course demonstrates the implementation of event handler methods through GUI form containers. Students learn basic use of the LINQ interface to retrieve data from a SQL database for display on a GUI form. Students apply debugging techniques to repair faulty Visual C# code.
Lecture: 2 hours - Lab: 4 hours
Prerequisite: CSCI 1103 Lab fee: $4.00

CSCI 1772 Networking I (SP) 3 credits
CSCI 1772 is designed for students to learn advanced computer networking concepts and how they can be applied to support enterprise-wide information management of a large organization. The student will learn to install and configure network servers.
Lecture: 2 hours - Lab: 3 hours
Prerequisite: CSCI 1152 Lab fee: $2.00

CSCI 2241 Intro Mainframe Z/Os-Basic (A, SP) 3 credits
CSCI 2241 provides students the background, knowledge and skills necessary to begin using the basic facilities of a mainframe computer. Topics covered include: the mainframe in business today, including mainframe job roles; mainframe interfaces; Job Control Language; mainframe hardware and architecture; middleware for the mainframe, application programming on the mainframe; networking, and security topics. This course is designed for someone with prior programming experience or education.
Lecture: 2 hours - Lab: 3 hours
Prerequisite: CSCI 1103 Lab fee: $2.00

CSCI 2251 Intro Mainframe Large Scale (A, SP) 2 credits
CSCI 2251 helps students gain an understanding of the reasons companies chose mainframe system to run (and grow) their large-scale computing environments. Topics include capacity, scalability, integrity and security, availability, access to large amounts of date, systems management and autonomic capabilities. This course is designed for someone with prior programming experience or education. Term course
Lecture: 1 hour - Lab: 2 hours
Prerequisite: CSCI 2241 Lab fee: $2.00

CSCI 2261 Intro Mainframe Networking (A, SP) 2 credits
CSCI 2261 provides the background, knowledge and skills necessary to begin using the basic communication facilities of a mainframe system. Students will be given a broad understanding of networking principles and the hardware and software components necessary to allow the mainframe to participate in a high volume data communications networks. Topics covered include: overview of the importance of the mainframe environment, TCP/IP, SNA, SNA/IP implementation on the mainframe, networking operations, security and problem determination. Term course
Lecture: 1 hour - Lab: 2 hours
Prerequisite: CSCI 2241 Lab fee: $2.00

CSCI 2271 Intro Mainframe Security (A, SP) 3 credits
CSCI 2271 provides the background, knowledge and skills necessary to begin using the basic security facilities of a mainframe system. Students will have a broad understanding of both the security principles and the hardware and software components needed to insure that the mainframe resources and environment are secure. Topics covered include elements of security, systems architecture and virtualization, cryptography, as well as security in operating systems, networks, middleware and applications.
Lecture: 2 hours - Lab: 3 hours
Prerequisite: CSCI 2241 Lab fee: $2.00

CSCI 2325 Expert Access (A, SP, SU) 3 credits
CSCI 2325 covers advanced features of Microsoft Access database application software and the skill set required for Microsoft certification.
Lecture: 2 hours - Lab: 3 hours
Prerequisite: CSCI 1102 Lab fee: $10.00

CSCI 2330 Project Mgt Fundamentals & Case Studies (A)4 credits
CSCI 2330 teaches the genesis of project management and its importance to improving the success of information technology projects. The student will demonstrate knowledge of project management terms and techniques such as the triple constraint of project management and the project life cycle using project management industry tools and techniques. Further, through the use of case studies, students will analyze and implement the concepts and techniques using appropriate project management documentation. This course satisfies PMI's 35-hour education requirement to sit for the Project Management Professional (PMP) Exam.
Lecture: 2 hours – Lab: 4 hours Lab fee: $4.00

CSCI 2370 Database Systems Programming (A, SU) 3 credits
CSCI 2370 presents database systems theory and application. Including functional dependencies, normalization, data modeling and entity relationship model, entity relationship diagrams and structured query language. Students will design, build databases and write database programs.
Lecture: 2 hours - Lab: 3 hours
Prerequisites: CSCI 1103, CSCI 2325 Lab fee: $4.00

CSCI 2371 DB Admin & Data Mining (SP, SU) 4 credits
CSCI 2371 provides the background, knowledge and skills necessary to identify and perform tasks involved in the administration and management of a database system. Topics include user rights and responsibilities, concurrency security, reliability, backup and recovery. The second part of this course will cover data design, data extraction and transformation, data quality, OLAP processing , processing for business intelligence, reporting systems, data mining applications, data warehouses and data marts.
Lecture: 2 hours - Lab: 4 hours
Prerequisite: CSCI 2370 Lab fee: $4.00

CSCI 2412 Web Database Development (SP) 4 credits
Databases are now an integral part of the Internet and many web sites use databases in the background to control their content. This course shows how to design and use databases for the Web using MySQL and PHP. No previous knowledge of MySQL or PHP is required. The focal point of the class is a semester-long web site development project. The student will design an e-commerce site from the ground up, focusing on not only the technical issues but the business aspects, as well.
Lecture: 2 hours - Lab: 4 hours
Prerequisite: CSCI 1145 Lab fee: $4.00

CSCI 2447 JavaScript Fundamentals (A) 3 credits
CSCI 2447 provides an in-depth study of scripting languages that add interactivity to websites. Scripting languages such as JavaScript and PHP work with Hypertext Markup Language (HTML) to extend its functionality. In recent years, several libraries have been created to reduce development time. Students will be introduced to the several scripting languages and use them to complete multiple real-world tasks. Students will also learn how to work with several popular libraries and through multiple exercises.
Lecture: 2 hours - Lab: 3 hours
Prerequisite: CSCI 1145 Lab fee: $2.00

CSCI 2467 Java Programming I (A, SP) 3 credits
CSCI 2467 is an introduction to the art of computer programming in Java. Included are features needed to construct Java Applets, Windows and Frames, and Dialog boxes. Students will learn to program in an object-oriented environment, using classes, objects, interfaces and listeners. This first course will concentrate on data manipulation, decision making,

loops and arrays, and action and item events. Students will learn how to write, compile and debug programs in in-class (solo and group) and take home labs.
Lecture: 2 hours - Lab: 3 hours
Prerequisite: CSCI 1103 Lab fee: $2.00

CSCI 2469 Java Programming II (A, SP) 3 credits
CSCI 2469 is a continuation of Java Programming 1. More advanced work in Java applets, applications, structures, methods, and arrays will be included. In addition, students will learn the Java Database Connectivity (JDBC) environment using mySQL and Access as the background database. They will also create servlets using Apache TomCat. Program debugging will continue to be emphasized.
Lecture: 2 hours - Lab: 3 hours
Prerequisite: CSCI 2467 Lab fee: $2.00

CSCI 2479 Advanced Web Programming (SP) 3 credits
CSCI 2479 is an introduction to advanced programming techniques for web sites and web site management. Students will explore scripting/compiled languages, as well as integrate popular preexisting libraries and extensions into web sites they create. Several projects will be given throughout the semester which will focus on combining local and internet-based technologies to create a seamless, functional end product.
Lecture: 2 hours - Lab: 3 hours
Prerequisites: CSCI 1145, CSCI 2447 Lab fee: $2.00

CSCI 2489 Mobile Software Development (SP) 3 credits
CSCI 2489 is an introduction to developing software for mobile platforms, such as smart phones and other mobile devices. Students will learn the basics of developing software for popular platforms through multiple in-class lab exercises. Topics include an overview of popular platforms, developing applications with graphical user interfaces and 2D/3D interactive graphics.
Lecture: 2 hours - Lab: 3 hours
Prerequisite: CSCI 2467 Lab fee: $2.00

CSCI 2521 C++ Programming (A, SU) 3 credits
CSCI 2521 uses the C++ programming language as the programming tool for learning principles of object-oriented programming. The course covers implementation of classes that support static and instance methods, method and operator overloading, concrete vs. abstract classes, class inheritance, polymorphism, exception handling, and function templates. The course demonstrates storing of objects in data files. Students apply debugging techniques to repair faulty C++ code.
Lecture: 2 hours - Lab: 3 hours
Prerequisite: CSCI 1103 Lab fee: $4.00

CSCI 2541 Foundations of 2-D Game Program (A) 3 credits
CSCI 2541 provides students with an introduction to and many opportunities for applied game prototyping. Students learn about the theory and methods of creating game prototypes for design and development of original game concepts. Topics covered include: breakthrough game design, proof of concept and iterative prototyping, and prototype QA testing and documentation. Lab activities are designed to foster critical thinking and problem solving skills through the development of an understanding of the development process as well as interactive programming techniques through the creation of working interactive programs in a high-level programming language.
Lecture: 2 hours - Lab: 3 hours
Prerequisite: CSCI 1511 Lab fee: $4.00

CSCI 2546 2-D Game Project (SP) 3 credits
CSCI 2546 will address the issue of developing a level for an existing game. Students, individually or in groups, will design their own levels for a game that has an open design. Concepts introduced in the prerequisite course, CSCI 2541, will be continued in the design phase of this course. Students will develop their own assets, or will adopt assets from a library of public domain assets. The course will also discuss the process of porting games to mobile devices, Wii, iPhone, droid, Xbox, etc.
Lecture: 2 hours - Lab: 3 hours
Prerequisite: CSCI 2541 Lab fee: $4.00

CSCI 2551 Graphics in 3-D Game Engines (A) 4 credits
CSCI 2551 is a study in the basic elements of a 3D network game. The material will cover environments and terrain, character animation, texture mapping, modeling, physical dynamics, particles and other selected topics. Students will include these issues while investigating the development of a level for one of the current, popular, game engines.
Lecture: 2 hours - Lab: 4 hours
Prerequisite: CSCI 1551 Lab fee: $4.00

CSCI 2556 3-D Game Project (SP) 3 credits
CSCI 2556 will address the issue of developing a level for an existing multi-player, network game. Students, individually or in groups, will design their own levels for a game that has an open design. Concepts introduced in the prerequisite course, CSCI 2551, will be continued in the design phase of this course. Students will develop their own assets, as well as adopt assets from a public library, and dynamics. The course will continue discussions concerning networking.
Lecture: 2 hours - Lab: 3 hours
Prerequisite: CSCI 2551 Lab fee: $4.00

CSCI 2620 Visual Basic II (SP) 4 credits
CSCI 2620 is a continuation of CSCI 1620. Emphasizes advanced topics in VB. NET such as object-oriented programming, database programming, including SQL and Active X controls, and multi-tiered approach to applications. Advanced topics include deploying Web forms that utilize a database. Advanced features of Visual Studio.NET are explored and applied as they relate to connectivity with SQL Server, Oracle, and other databases.
Lecture: 2 hours - Lab: 4 hours
Prerequisite: CSCI 1620 Lab fee: $4.00

CSCI 2630 C# Programming II (SP) 3 credits
CSCI 2630 is a continuation of C# Programming I (CSCI 1630), and offers an additional level of specialization in the Visual C# programming language. The course covers generics (generic methods), LINQ to SQL database access (retrieve, insert, update, and delete operations) in an n-tier application, Web applications with ASP .NET, and collections.
Lecture: 2 hours - Lab: 3 hours
Prerequisites: CSCI 1630, CSCI 2370 Lab fee: $4.00

CSCI 2750 Networking Home & Small Businesses (A) 3 credits
CSCI 2750 is designed to teach students the fundamentals of networking while gaining the skills needed to obtain entry-level home and small business network installation jobs. Students gain knowledge in networking theory and obtain hands-on experience in networking, PC configuration, Internet connectivity, wireless connectivity, and file/print sharing. Recommended basic computer skills: file systems, web browsing, etc. 1st term course. CISCO
Lecture: 2 hours - Lab: 3 hours Lab fee: $2.00

CSCI 2752 Working Small-Medium Business or ISP (A) 3 credits
CSCI 2752 is designed to teach students the basics of routing and remote access, addressing, and security. Students will gain hands-on experience with servers that provide e-mail services. Web spaces and authenticated access, network monitoring. Students will also learn troubleshooting skills as well as the necessary soft skills required for interacting with customers. 2nd term course.
Lecture: 2 hours - Lab: 3 hours
Prerequisite: CSCI 2750 Lab fee: $20.00

CSCI 2754 Introducing Routing/ Switch Enterprise (SP) 3 credits
CSCI 2754 is designed for students to learn the equipment applications and

protocols installed in enterprise networks with an emphasis on switched networks, IP Telephony requirements and security. This course introduces advanced routing protocols such as Enhanced Interior Gateway Routing Protocol (EIGRP) and Open Shortest Path First (OSPF) Protocol. The hands-on exercises include configuration, installation and troubleshooting. 1st term course
Lecture: 2 hours - Lab: 3 hours
Prerequisite: CSCI 2752 Lab fee: $20.00

CSCI 2756 Design/Support Computer Network (SP) 3 credits
CSCI 2756 is designed for students to learn basic network design, how to gather user requirements, establish proof-of-concept, and perform project management tasks. Students learn lifecycle services such as system upgrades, competitive analysis and system integration. 2nd term course
Lecture: 2 hours - Lab: 3 hours
Prerequisite: CSCI 2754 Lab fee: $20.00

CSCI 2760 CCNA Voice (On Demand) 3 credits
CSCI 2760 covers basic IP telephony installation, configuration, and maintenance skills. Students will implement and configure small- to medium sized IP Telephony solutions using Cisco Unified Communications Manager Express, Cisco Unity Express, and the UC500 Smart Business Communications System solutions.
Lecture: 2 hours - Lab: 3 hours
Prerequisite: CSCI 2756 Lab fee: $2.00

CSCI 2762 CCNA Security (On Demand) 3 credits
CSCI 2762 equips students with the knowledge and skills needed to prepare for entry-level security specialist careers. This course is a hands-on, career-oriented e-learning solution that emphasizes practical experience. CCNA Security is a blended curriculum with both online and classroom learning.
Lecture: 2 hours - Lab: 3 hours
Prerequisite: CSCI 2756 Lab fee: $2.00

CSCI 2770 Network Comm & TCP/IP (A) 3 credits
CSCI 2770 is designed for students to learn data communications, basic communication theory as applied to digital, analog, wireless, and voice networks and the OSI layered network model. The concepts of TCP/IP are thoroughly covered in this course such as TCP/IP history, security, protocols, IP addressing, bridging, and routing/DHCP, sub-netting, Windows domains and name services and Linux.
Lecture: 2 hours - Lab: 3 hours
Prerequisite: CSCI 1772 Lab fee: $4.00

CSCI 2774 Networking II (A) 4 credits
CSCI 2774 is designed for students to learn advanced concepts of the Microsoft Windows Server environment to support small and enterprise-wide information management systems. Students will learn and apply management of data storage, design and develop a security needs analysis, and administer Windows security. Students will apply client/server technologies used in designing and implementing Web services such as network address translators, proxy servers, firewalls, and Internet Information Services. Students will complete a series of laboratory assignments using the Windows Server environment.
Lecture: 2 hours - Lab: 4 hours
Prerequisite: CSCI 2770 Lab fee: $4.00

CSCI 2776 Network & Cybersecurity (A) 3 credits
CSCI 2776 will introduce network security theory and practice in areas of cryptography, security architecture, firewalls, VPNs, IP Security. Intranet/Internet security vulnerabilities and methods of protection will also be introduced.
Lecture: 2 hours - Lab: 3 hours
Prerequisite: CSCI 1151 Lab fee: $6.00

CSCI 2778 Wireless, Voice, & Mobile Comm. (A) 3 credits
CSCI 2778 is designed to provide students and network administrators with an in-depth knowledge of the risk of threats to security and the need to secure wireless, voice over IP (VoIP), and mobile communication networks. Students will learn to configure and install wireless networks, design mixed networks to carry voice, video, and data traffic and define policies to secure mobile networks. Students will learn and apply the concepts of IEEE 802.11, Wi-Fi, Bluetooth, WiMax technologies, encryption techniques, site surveys, securing wireless, VoIP, and mobile networks, troubleshooting, monitoring, and managing these networks, while preparing the students for an industry certification.
Lecture: 2 hours - Lab: 3 hours
Prerequisite: CSCI 1772 Lab fee: $20.00

CSCI 2780 Computer Forensics (A) 3 credits
CSCI 2780 is designed for students and systems administrators involved in responding to security incidents and applying computer forensics skills. This course focuses on the latest technologies in computer forensics techniques in order to recognize and respond to security threats.
Lecture: 2 hours - Lab: 3 hours
Prerequisite: CSCI 2776 Lab fee: $2.00

CSCI 2782 Info Security Audit (On Demand) 3 credits
CSCI 2782 is designed for students, web developers, and network administrators who want to gain knowledge related to information and database security focusing on the areas of security, auditing, and implementation.
Lecture: 2 hours - Lab: 3 hours
Prerequisite: CSCI 2776 Lab fee: $2.00

CSCI 2784 Bus Continuity & Disaster (On Demand) 3 credits
CSCI 2784 is designed for students and network administrators who need to obtain knowledge and experience for disaster recovery. This course will provide methods used to identify vulnerabilities and take appropriate countermeasures to prevent and mitigate failure risks for an organization. This course takes an enterprise-wide approach to developing a disaster recovery plan.
Lecture: 2 hours - Lab: 3 hours
Prerequisite: CSCI 2782 Lab fee: $2.00

CSCI 2786 Security Practice & Mgt (SP) 3 credits
CSCI 2786 is designed to introduce students to introduce practical security applications including penetration testing and modern attack methods such as social engineering. The student will also be expected to understand a management perspective of security including the ten domains identified by (ISC) 2.
Lecture: 2 hours - Lab: 3 hours
Prerequisite: CSCI 2776 Lab fee: $2.00

CSCI 2790 Linux Administration (A) 3 credits
CSCI 2790 is designed to provide students with the knowledge and skills required to build, and manage and Linux servers. Students will apply and demonstrate hands-on administration to install, configure and support Linux servers for reliability, functionality and performance. Students will also configure file, print and network services for both Linux and Windows clients. Students will create, edit and search Linux files, control permissions and ownership, process and format text data, and use learn to write shell scripts to automate routine tasks.
Lecture: 2 hours - Lab: 3 hours
Prerequisite: CSCI 1772 Lab fee: $1.00

CSCI 2792 Virtualization (SP) 3 credits
CSCI 2792 is designed to teach students the knowledge and skills required to install, configure and manage virtual servers and workstations. Students will learn how to use VMware and Microsoft virtual machine (VM) technologies, migrate from physical to virtual machines, combine

Windows and Linux workstations and servers on a single platform, and manage virtual machines using VMWare and Microsoft Hyper-V.
Lecture: 2 hours - Lab: 3 hours
Prerequisite: CSCI 2790 Lab fee: $4.00

CSCI 2802 CSCI Seminar (On Demand) 1 credit
CSCI 2802 seminar offers an opportunity for supervised, on-the-job application of knowledge and skills acquired in the classroom. Student must be a Computer Science major who has completed 12 hours in the technology and has permission of the instructor.
Seminar: 1 hour
Instructor permission required
Corequisite: CSCI 2902 Lab fee: $1.00

CSCI 2902 CSCI Practicum (On Demand) 3 credits
CSCI 2902 practicum offers an opportunity for supervised, on-the-job application of knowledge and skills acquired in the classroom. Student must be a Computer Science major who has completed 12 hours in the technology and has permission of the instructor.
Practicum: 21 hours
Instructor permission required
Corequisite: CSCI 2802 Lab fee: $1.00

CSCI 2994 CSCI Current Topics (On Demand) 1-3 credits
CSCI 2994 course is a detailed examination of a selected current topic in Computer Science. This course can be repeated.
Lecture: 1 hour

CSCI 2999 CSCI Capstone (SP) 3 credits
CSCI majors will work in groups to create a computer based integrated solution for a business organization. Students will apply and demonstrate technical expertise in the areas of software application programming, network administration and web technologies. Students will formally present their project results to faculty and management. Student must be a Computer Science major who has completed 12 hours in the technology and has permission of the instructor.
Lecture: 2 hours - Lab: 3 hours
Instructor permission required Lab fee: $4.00

COLUMBUS STATE
Community
College

614/287-5353
www.cscc.edu

DISCOVERING COMPUTERS & Microsoft® OFFICE 2010

A Fundamental Combined Approach

Table of Contents at a Glance

Discovering Computers—Selected Chapters from Fundamentals, 2012 Edition

Chapter 1
Introduction to Computers 1

Special Feature 1
Living Digitally 37

Chapter 2
The Internet and World Wide Web 43

Special Feature 2
Making Use of the Web 79

Chapter 3
Application Software 95

Special Feature 3
Digital Video Technology 129

Chapter 4
Operating Systems and Utility Programs 135

Special Feature 4
Digital Communications 167

Chapter 5
Computer Security and Safety, Ethics, and Privacy 181

Special Feature 5
Buyer's Guide: How to Purchase Computers and Mobile Devices 217

Quiz Yourself Answers 229

Microsoft Office 2010 and Windows 7

Office 2010 and Windows 7: Essential Concepts and Skills . . . . . OFF 1

Microsoft Windows Internet Explorer 8
Introduction to Internet Explorer . . . . . IE 1

Microsoft Word 2010
Chapter 1
Creating, Formatting, and Editing a Word Document with Pictures . . . . . WD 1

Chapter 2
Creating a Research Paper with Citations and References . . . . . WD 65

Chapter 3
Creating a Business Letter with a Letterhead and Table . . WD 137

Microsoft PowerPoint 2010
Chapter 1
Creating and Editing a Presentation with Clip Art . . . . . PPT 1

Chapter 2
Enhancing a Presentation with Pictures, Shapes, and WordArt . . . . . PPT 73

Chapter 3
Reusing a Presentation and Adding Media . . . . . PPT 137

Microsoft Excel 2010
Chapter 1
Creating a Worksheet and an Embedded Chart . . . . . EX 1

Chapter 2
Formulas, Functions, and Formatting . . . . . EX 65

Chapter 3
What-If Analysis, Charting, and Working with Large Worksheets . . . . . EX 137

Microsoft Access 2010
Chapter 1
Databases and Database Objects: An Introduction . . . . . AC 1

Chapter 2
Querying a Database . . . . . AC 73

DISCOVERING COMPUTERS & Microsoft® OFFICE 2010
A Fundamental Combined Approach

Table of Contents

CHAPTER 1
Introduction to Computers 1
A WORLD OF COMPUTERS 2
WHAT IS A COMPUTER? 3
Data and Information 4
Information Processing Cycle 4
THE COMPONENTS OF A COMPUTER 4
Input Devices 4
Output Devices 5
System Unit 6
Storage Devices 6
Communications Devices 6
ADVANTAGES AND DISADVANTAGES OF USING COMPUTERS . . . 7
Advantages of Using Computers 7
Disadvantages of Using Computers 7
NETWORKS AND THE INTERNET 8
COMPUTER SOFTWARE 11
System Software 11
Application Software 12
Installing and Running Programs 12
Software Development 13
CATEGORIES OF COMPUTERS 14
PERSONAL COMPUTERS 15
Desktop Computers 16
MOBILE COMPUTERS AND MOBILE DEVICES 16
Notebook Computers 16
Mobile Devices 16
GAME CONSOLES 18
SERVERS 19
MAINFRAMES 19
SUPERCOMPUTERS 19
EMBEDDED COMPUTERS 19
EXAMPLES OF COMPUTER USAGE 20
Home User 20
Small Office/Home Office User 22
Mobile User 22
Power User 23
Enterprise User 23
COMPUTER APPLICATIONS IN SOCIETY 24
Education 24
Finance 25
Government 25
Health Care 25
Science 26
Publishing 27
Travel 27
Manufacturing 27
CHAPTER SUMMARY 28
COMPANIES ON THE CUTTING EDGE 29
Apple 29
Amazon 29
TECHNOLOGY TRAILBLAZERS 29
Bill Gates 29
Tom Anderson 29
CHAPTER REVIEW 30
KEY TERMS 31
CHECKPOINT 32
PROBLEM SOLVING 33
LEARN HOW TO 34
LEARN IT ONLINE 35
WEB RESEARCH 36

Special Feature 1
Living Digitally 37

CHAPTER 2
The Internet and World Wide Web 43
THE INTERNET 44
Connecting to the Internet 45
Access Providers 46
How Data and Information Travel the Internet 47
Internet Addresses 48
THE WORLD WIDE WEB 49
Browsing the Web 49
Web Addresses 51
Navigating Web Pages 52
Searching the Web 53
Types of Web Sites 55
Evaluating a Web Site 58
Multimedia on the Web 58
Web Publishing 62
E-Commerce 62
OTHER INTERNET SERVICES 63
E-Mail 63
Mailing Lists 66
Instant Messaging 66
Chat Rooms 67
VoIP 68
FTP 68
Newsgroups and Message Boards 68
NETIQUETTE 69
CHAPTER SUMMARY 70
COMPANIES ON THE CUTTING EDGE 71
Google 71
eBay 71
TECHNOLOGY TRAILBLAZERS 71
Tim Berners-Lee 71
Mark Zuckerberg 71
CHAPTER REVIEW 72
KEY TERMS 73
CHECKPOINT 74
PROBLEM SOLVING 75
LEARN HOW TO 76
LEARN IT ONLINE 77
WEB RESEARCH 78

Special Feature 2
Making Use of the Web 79

CHAPTER 3
Application Software 95
APPLICATION SOFTWARE 96
The Role of System Software 97
Working with Application Software 98
BUSINESS SOFTWARE 100
Word Processing Software 101
Developing a Document 102
Spreadsheet Software 103
Database Software 104
Presentation Software 105
Note Taking Software 106
Business Software Suite 106
Project Management Software 106
Personal Information Manager Software 106
Business Software for Phones 106
Accounting Software 107
Document Management Software 107
Enterprise Computing Software 107
GRAPHICS AND MULTIMEDIA SOFTWARE 108
Computer Aided Design 109
Desktop Publishing Software (for the Professional) 109
Paint/Image Editing Software (for the Professional) 109
Video and Audio Editing Software (for the Professional) 110
Multimedia Authoring Software 110
Web Page Authoring Software 110
SOFTWARE FOR HOME, PERSONAL, AND EDUCATIONAL USE 111
Personal Finance Software 112
Legal Software 113
Tax Preparation Software 113
Desktop Publishing Software (for Personal Use) 113
Paint/Image Editing Software (for Personal Use) 114
Clip Art/Image Gallery 114
Video and Audio Editing Software (for Personal Use) 114
Home Design/Landscaping Software 115
Travel and Mapping Software 115
Reference and Educational Software 115
Entertainment Software 116
WEB APPLICATIONS 116
APPLICATION SOFTWARE FOR COMMUNICATIONS 118
LEARNING TOOLS FOR APPLICATION SOFTWARE 119
Web-Based Training 119
CHAPTER SUMMARY 120
COMPANIES ON THE CUTTING EDGE 121
Adobe Systems 121
Microsoft 121
TECHNOLOGY TRAILBLAZERS 121
Dan Bricklin 121
Masayoshi Son 121
CHAPTER REVIEW 122
KEY TERMS 123
CHECKPOINT 124
PROBLEM SOLVING 125
LEARN HOW TO 126
LEARN IT ONLINE 127
WEB RESEARCH 128

Special Feature 3
Digital Video Technology 129

CHAPTER 4
Operating Systems and Utility Programs 135
SYSTEM SOFTWARE 136
OPERATING SYSTEMS 137
OPERATING SYSTEM FUNCTIONS 138
Starting and Shutting Down a Computer 138
Providing a User Interface 138
Managing Programs 139
Managing Memory 141
Coordinating Tasks 141
Configuring Devices 142
Establishing an Internet Connection 142
Monitoring Performance 143
Providing File Management and Other Utilities 143
Updating Software Automatically 143
Controlling a Network 143
Administering Security 144
TYPES OF OPERATING SYSTEMS 145
STAND-ALONE OPERATING SYSTEMS 146
Windows 7 146
Mac OS X 147
UNIX 147
Linux 148
SERVER OPERATING SYSTEMS 148
EMBEDDED OPERATING SYSTEMS 149
UTILITY PROGRAMS 150
File Manager 151
Search Utility 151
Uninstaller 151
Image Viewer 151
Disk Cleanup 152
Disk Defragmenter 152
Backup and Restore Utilities 152
Screen Saver 153
Personal Firewall 153
Antivirus Programs 154
Spyware and Adware Removers 155
Internet Filters 155
File Compression 156
Media Player 156
Disc Burning 157
Personal Computer Maintenance 157
CHAPTER SUMMARY 158
COMPANIES ON THE CUTTING EDGE 159
VeriSign 159
Research in Motion (RIM) 159
TECHNOLOGY TRAILBLAZERS 159
Steve Wozniak 159
Linus Torvalds 159
CHAPTER REVIEW 160
KEY TERMS 161
CHECKPOINT 162
PROBLEM SOLVING 163
LEARN HOW TO 164
LEARN IT ONLINE 165
WEB RESEARCH 166

Special Feature 4
Digital Communications 167

CHAPTER 5
Computer Security and Safety, Ethics, and Privacy . . . 181
COMPUTER SECURITY RISKS . . . 182
INTERNET AND NETWORK ATTACKS . . . 184
Computer Viruses, Worms, Trojan Horses, and Rootkits . . . 184
Safeguards against Computer Viruses and Other Malware . . . 185
Botnets . . . 187
Denial of Service Attacks . . . 187
Back Doors . . . 188
Spoofing . . . 188
Safeguards against Botnets, DoS Attacks, Back Doors, and Spoofing . . . 188
Firewalls . . . 188
Intrusion Detection Software . . . 189
UNAUTHORIZED ACCESS AND USE . . . 189
Safeguards against Unauthorized Access and Use . . . 189
Identifying and Authenticating Users . . . 189
Digital Forensics . . . 192
HARDWARE THEFT AND VANDALISM . . . 193
Safeguards against Hardware Theft and Vandalism . . . 193
SOFTWARE THEFT . . . 193
Safeguards against Software Theft . . . 193
INFORMATION THEFT . . . 195
Safeguards against Information Theft . . . 195
Encryption . . . 195
SYSTEM FAILURE . . . 196
Safeguards against System Failure . . . 196
BACKING UP — THE ULTIMATE SAFEGUARD . . . 196
WIRELESS SECURITY . . . 197
HEALTH CONCERNS OF COMPUTER USE . . . 198
Computers and Health Risks . . . 198
Ergonomics and Workplace Design . . . 199
Computer Addiction . . . 199
ETHICS AND SOCIETY . . . 199
Information Accuracy . . . 200
Intellectual Property Rights . . . 201
Green Computing . . . 201
INFORMATION PRIVACY . . . 202
Electronic Profiles . . . 203
Cookies . . . 203
Spyware and Adware . . . 204
Spam . . . 204
Phishing . . . 205
Social Engineering . . . 205
Privacy Laws . . . 206
Employee Monitoring . . . 207
Content Filtering . . . 207
CHAPTER SUMMARY . . . 208
COMPANIES ON THE CUTTING EDGE . . . 209
McAfee . . . 209
Symantec . . . 209
TECHNOLOGY TRAILBLAZERS . . . 209
Richard Stallman . . . 209
Gene Spafford . . . 209
CHAPTER REVIEW . . . 210
KEY TERMS . . . 211
CHECKPOINT . . . 212
PROBLEM SOLVING . . . 213
LEARN HOW TO . . . 214
LEARN IT ONLINE . . . 215
WEB RESEARCH . . . 216

Special Feature 5
Buyer's Guide: How to Purchase Computers and Mobile Devices . . . 217

Quiz Yourself Answers . . . 229

Office 2010 and Windows 7
Office 2010 and Windows 7: Essential Concepts and Skills . . . OFF 1
OBJECTIVES . . . OFF 1
OFFICE 2010 AND WINDOWS 7 . . . OFF 2
Overview . . . OFF 2
INTRODUCTION TO THE WINDOWS 7 OPERATING SYSTEM OFF 2
Using a Mouse . . . OFF 2
Scrolling . . . OFF 4
Shortcut Keys . . . OFF 4
Starting Windows 7 . . . OFF 5
To Log On to the Computer . . . OFF 6
The Windows 7 Desktop . . . OFF 7
INTRODUCTION TO MICROSOFT OFFICE 2010 . . . OFF 7
Microsoft Office 2010 Programs . . . OFF 8
Microsoft Office 2010 Suites . . . OFF 8
STARTING AND USING A PROGRAM . . . OFF 9
Word . . . OFF 9
To Start a Program Using the Start Menu . . . OFF 10
To Maximize a Window . . . OFF 12
The Word Document Window, Ribbon, and Elements Common to Office Programs . . . OFF 12
To Display a Different Tab on the Ribbon . . . OFF 16
To Minimize, Display, and Restore the Ribbon . . . OFF 17
To Display and Use a Shortcut Menu . . . OFF 18
To Customize the Quick Access Toolbar . . . OFF 19
To Enter Text in a Document . . . OFF 20
SAVING AND ORGANIZING FILES . . . OFF 21
Organizing Files and Folders . . . OFF 21
To Create a Folder . . . OFF 22
Folder Windows . . . OFF 24
To Create a Folder within a Folder . . . OFF 24
To Expand a Folder, Scroll through Folder Contents, and Collapse a Folder . . . OFF 26
To Switch from One Program to Another . . . OFF 27
To Save a File in a Folder . . . OFF 27
Navigating in Dialog Boxes . . . OFF 30
To Minimize and Restore a Window . . . OFF 30
SCREEN RESOLUTION . . . OFF 31
To Change the Screen Resolution . . . OFF 33
To Quit an Office Program with One Document Open . . . OFF 35
ADDITIONAL MICROSOFT OFFICE PROGRAMS . . . OFF 36
PowerPoint . . . OFF 36
To Start a Program Using the Search Box . . . OFF 37
The PowerPoint Window and Ribbon . . . OFF 39
To Enter Content in a Title Slide . . . OFF 40
To Create a New Office Document from the Backstage View . . . OFF 41
To Enter Content in a Title Slide of a Second PowerPoint Presentation . . . OFF 43
To Close an Office File Using the Backstage View . . . OFF 44
To Open a Recent Office File Using the Backstage View . . . OFF 45
Excel . . . OFF 46
To Create a New Blank Office Document from Windows Explorer . . . OFF 47

To Start a Program from Windows Explorer and Open a File . . . OFF 48
Unique Features of Excel . . . OFF 49
To Enter a Worksheet Title . . . OFF 50
To Save an Existing Office Document with the Same File Name . . . OFF 51
Access . . . OFF 53
Unique Elements in Access . . . OFF 54
To Create an Access Database . . . OFF 55
To Open an Existing Office File . . . OFF 57
OTHER OFFICE PROGRAMS . . . OFF 58
Outlook . . . OFF 58
Publisher . . . OFF 59
OneNote . . . OFF 61
MOVING, RENAMING, AND DELETING FILES . . . OFF 62
To Rename a File . . . OFF 63
To Move a File . . . OFF 64
To Delete a File . . . OFF 64
MICROSOFT OFFICE AND WINDOWS HELP . . . OFF 66
To Open the Help Window in an Office Program . . . OFF 66
Moving and Resizing Windows . . . OFF 66
To Move a Window by Dragging . . . OFF 66
To Resize a Window by Dragging . . . OFF 67
Using Office Help . . . OFF 68
To Obtain Help Using the 'Type words to search for' Text Box . . . OFF 68
To Obtain Help Using the Help Links . . . OFF 70
To Obtain Help Using the Help Table of Contents . . . OFF 71
Obtaining Help while Working in an Office Program . . . OFF 72
Using Windows Help and Support . . . OFF 73
To Start Windows Help and Support . . . OFF 73
CHAPTER SUMMARY . . . OFF 74
LEARN IT ONLINE . . . OFF 75
APPLY YOUR KNOWLEDGE . . . OFF 76
EXTEND YOUR KNOWLEDGE . . . OFF 76
MAKE IT RIGHT . . . OFF 77
IN THE LAB . . . OFF 78
CASES AND PLACES . . . OFF 80

Microsoft Windows Internet Explorer 8
Introduction to Internet Explorer . . . IE 1
OBJECTIVES . . . IE 1
INTRODUCTION . . . IE 2
Overview . . . IE 2
THE INTERNET . . . IE 3
THE WORLD WIDE WEB . . . IE 5
Security Concerns on the Internet . . . IE 6
Web Address . . . IE 7
Hypertext Markup Language . . . IE 9
Home Pages . . . IE 10
Web Browsers . . . IE 10
WHAT IS INTERNET EXPLORER 8? . . . IE 10
Starting Internet Explorer . . . IE 11
To Start Internet Explorer . . . IE 11
The Internet Explorer Window . . . IE 12
Command Bar . . . IE 14
BROWSING THE WORLD WIDE WEB . . . IE 15
To Browse the Web by Entering a Web Address . . . IE 16
Stopping the Transfer of a Page . . . IE 20
Refreshing a Web Page . . . IE 20
To Refresh a Web Page . . . IE 21
Finding a Previously Displayed Web Page . . . IE 21
Finding a Recently Displayed Web Page Using the Navigation Buttons . . . IE 22
To Use the Navigation Buttons to Find Recently Displayed Web Pages . . . IE 23
To Display a Web Page Using the Recent Pages List . . . IE 25
Using the History List to Display Web Pages . . . IE 26
To Display a Web Page Using the History List . . . IE 27
KEEPING TRACK OF FAVORITE WEB PAGES . . . IE 30
To Add a Web Page to the Favorites Center . . . IE 30
To Display the Home Page Using the Home Button . . . IE 32
To Display a Web Page Using the Favorites Center . . . IE 33
To Remove a Web Page from the Favorites Center . . . IE 34
SAVING INFORMATION OBTAINED WITH INTERNET EXPLORER . . . IE 35
To Save a Web Page . . . IE 36
To Save a Picture on a Web Page . . . IE 37
Copying and Pasting Using the Clipboard . . . IE 39
To Start WordPad . . . IE 39
To Display the Yellowstone National Park Web Page . . . IE 41
To Copy and Paste Text from a Web Page into a WordPad Document . . . IE 42
To Copy and Paste a Picture from a Web Page into a WordPad Document . . . IE 44
To Save the WordPad Document and Quit WordPad . . . IE 46
PRINTING A WEB PAGE IN INTERNET EXPLORER . . . IE 47
To Print a Web Page . . . IE 48
INTERNET EXPLORER HELP . . . IE 49
To Access Internet Explorer Help . . . IE 49
QUITTING INTERNET EXPLORER . . . IE 52
To Quit Internet Explorer . . . IE 52
CHAPTER SUMMARY . . . IE 53
LEARN IT ONLINE . . . IE 54
APPLY YOUR KNOWLEDGE . . . IE 54
EXTEND YOUR KNOWLEDGE . . . IE 58
IN THE LAB . . . IE 59
CASES AND PLACES . . . IE 69

Microsoft Word 2010
CHAPTER 1
Creating, Formatting, and Editing a Word Document with Pictures . . . WD 1
OBJECTIVES . . . WD 1
INTRODUCTION . . . WD 2
PROJECT — FLYER WITH PICTURES . . . WD 2
Overview . . . WD 4
ENTERING TEXT . . . WD 5
To Type Text . . . WD 6
To Display Formatting Marks . . . WD 7
To Insert a Blank Line . . . WD 7
Wordwrap . . . WD 8
To Wordwrap Text as You Type . . . WD 8
Spelling and Grammar Check . . . WD 9
To Check Spelling and Grammar as You Type . . . WD 9
Navigating a Document . . . WD 11
FORMATTING PARAGRAPHS AND CHARACTERS . . . WD 12
To Center a Paragraph . . . WD 14
Formatting Single versus Multiple Paragraphs and Characters . . . WD 15
To Select a Line . . . WD 15
To Change the Font Size of Selected Text . . . WD 16
To Change the Font of Selected Text . . . WD 17

To Change the Case of Selected Text .... WD 18
To Apply a Text Effect to Selected Text .... WD 19
To Shade a Paragraph .... WD 20
To Select Multiple Lines .... WD 21
To Bullet a List of Paragraphs .... WD 22
To Undo and Redo an Action .... WD 23
To Italicize Text .... WD 24
To Color Text .... WD 25
To Use the Mini Toolbar to Format Text .... WD 26
To Select a Group of Words .... WD 27
To Underline Text .... WD 27
To Bold Text .... WD 28
To Change Theme Colors .... WD 28
Selecting Text .... WD 30

INSERTING AND FORMATTING PICTURES IN A WORD DOCUMENT .... WD 30
To Insert a Picture .... WD 31
To Zoom the Document .... WD 33
To Resize a Graphic .... WD 34
To Resize a Graphic by Entering Exact Measurements .... WD 36
To Apply a Picture Style .... WD 37
To Apply Picture Effects .... WD 38

ENHANCING THE PAGE .... WD 40
To View One Page .... WD 40
To Add a Page Border .... WD 41
To Change Spacing before and after a Paragraph .... WD 43

CORRECTING ERRORS AND REVISING A DOCUMENT .... WD 44
Types of Changes Made to Documents .... WD 44
To Insert Text in an Existing Document .... WD 46
Deleting Text from a Document .... WD 47
To Delete Text .... WD 47
To Move Text .... WD 47

CHANGING DOCUMENT PROPERTIES .... WD 49
To Change Document Properties .... WD 49

PRINTING A DOCUMENT .... WD 51
To Print a Document .... WD 51

CHAPTER SUMMARY .... WD 53
LEARN IT ONLINE .... WD 54
APPLY YOUR KNOWLEDGE .... WD 54
EXTEND YOUR KNOWLEDGE .... WD 56
MAKE IT RIGHT .... WD 57
IN THE LAB .... WD 58
CASES AND PLACES .... WD 63

CHAPTER 2
Creating a Research Paper with Citations and References .... WD 65

OBJECTIVES .... WD 65
INTRODUCTION .... WD 66
PROJECT — RESEARCH PAPER .... WD 66
Overview .... WD 68
MLA Documentation Style .... WD 69

CHANGING DOCUMENT SETTINGS .... WD 69
Styles .... WD 70
To Modify a Style .... WD 70
Adjusting Line and Paragraph Spacing .... WD 72
To Change Line Spacing .... WD 73
To Remove Space after a Paragraph .... WD 74
To Update a Style to Match a Selection .... WD 74
Headers and Footers .... WD 75
To Switch to the Header .... WD 75
To Right-Align a Paragraph .... WD 76
To Insert a Page Number .... WD 77
To Close the Header .... WD 78

TYPING THE RESEARCH PAPER TEXT .... WD 78
To Click and Type .... WD 80
Shortcut Keys .... WD 81
To Display the Rulers .... WD 82
To First-Line Indent Paragraphs .... WD 83
To AutoCorrect as You Type .... WD 85
To Use the AutoCorrect Options Button .... WD 85
To Create an AutoCorrect Entry .... WD 86
The AutoCorrect Dialog Box .... WD 87
Citations .... WD 88
To Change the Bibliography Style .... WD 89
To Insert a Citation and Create Its Source .... WD 90
To Edit a Citation .... WD 91
Footnotes .... WD 93
To Insert a Footnote Reference Mark .... WD 93
To Insert a Citation Placeholder .... WD 94
Footnote Text Style .... WD 95
To Modify a Style Using a Shortcut Menu .... WD 95
To Edit a Source .... WD 97
Working with Footnotes and Endnotes .... WD 100
To Count Words .... WD 101
Automatic Page Breaks .... WD 101

CREATING AN ALPHABETICAL WORKS CITED PAGE .... WD 105
To Page Break Manually .... WD 106
To Apply a Style .... WD 106
To Create the Bibliographical List .... WD 108
To Modify a Source and Update the Bibliographical List .... WD 109
To Convert a Field to Regular Text .... WD 110

PROOFING AND REVISING THE RESEARCH PAPER .... WD 112
To Scroll Page by Page through a Document .... WD 112
Copying, Cutting, and Pasting .... WD 113
To Copy and Paste .... WD 113
To Display the Paste Options Menu .... WD 114
To Find Text .... WD 115
To Replace Text .... WD 116
Find and Replace Dialog Box .... WD 117
To Go to a Page .... WD 117
To Find and Insert a Synonym .... WD 118
To Check Spelling and Grammar at Once .... WD 118
The Main and Custom Dictionaries .... WD 120
To Use the Research Task Pane to Look Up Information .... WD 120
Research Task Pane Options .... WD 122
To Print Document Properties .... WD 123
To Preview the Document and Then Print It .... WD 124

CHAPTER SUMMARY .... WD 125
LEARN IT ONLINE .... WD 126
APPLY YOUR KNOWLEDGE .... WD 126
EXTEND YOUR KNOWLEDGE .... WD 128
MAKE IT RIGHT .... WD 129
IN THE LAB .... WD 130
CASES AND PLACES .... WD 136

CHAPTER 3
Creating a Business Letter with a Letterhead and Table .... WD 137

OBJECTIVES .... WD 137
INTRODUCTION .... WD 138

PROJECT — BUSINESS LETTER WITH A LETTERHEAD AND TABLE . . . WD 138
Overview . . . WD 138
To Change Margin Settings . . . WD 141
CREATING A LETTERHEAD . . . WD 142
To Insert a Shape . . . WD 142
To Apply a Shape Style . . . WD 144
To Add Text to a Shape . . . WD 145
To Use the Grow Font Button to Increase Font Size . . . WD 146
Floating versus Inline Objects . . . WD 147
To Change an Object's Text Wrapping . . . WD 148
To Insert Clip Art . . . WD 148
To Resize a Graphic to a Percent of the Original WD 150
To Change the Color of a Graphic . . . WD 151
To Set a Transparent Color in a Graphic . . . WD 152
To Adjust the Brightness and Contrast of a Graphic . . . WD 153
To Change the Border Color on a Graphic . . . WD 154
To Move a Graphic . . . WD 155
To Use Paste Options . . . WD 156
To Flip a Graphic . . . WD 157
To Insert a Symbol from the Symbol Dialog Box WD 158
To Insert a Symbol from the Symbol Gallery . . . WD 159
To Bottom Border a Paragraph . . . WD 160
To Clear Formatting . . . WD 161
AutoFormat as You Type . . . WD 162
To Convert a Hyperlink to Regular Text . . . WD 163
CREATING A BUSINESS LETTER . . . WD 164
To Create a New File from an Existing File . . . WD 165
To Apply a Quick Style . . . WD 166
Using Tab Stops to Align Text . . . WD 168
To Set Custom Tab Stops . . . WD 169
To Insert the Current Date in a Document . . . WD 170
To Create a Building Block . . . WD 171
To Modify a Building Block . . . WD 173
To Insert a Building Block . . . WD 174
Building Blocks versus AutoCorrect . . . WD 174
To Insert a Nonbreaking Space . . . WD 175
Tables . . . WD 176
To Insert an Empty Table . . . WD 176
To Enter Data in a Table . . . WD 177
To Apply a Table Style . . . WD 179
To Resize Table Columns to Fit Table Contents . . . WD 180
Selecting Table Contents . . . WD 181
To Align Data in Cells . . . WD 182
To Center a Table . . . WD 183
To Insert a Row in a Table . . . WD 184
Deleting Table Data . . . WD 185
To Merge Cells . . . WD 185
To Bullet a List as You Type . . . WD 186
ADDRESSING AND PRINTING ENVELOPES AND MAILING LABELS . . . WD 189
To Address and Print an Envelope . . . WD 189
Envelopes and Labels . . . WD 189
CHAPTER SUMMARY . . . WD 190
LEARN IT ONLINE . . . WD 191
APPLY YOUR KNOWLEDGE . . . WD 191
EXTEND YOUR KNOWLEDGE . . . WD 192
MAKE IT RIGHT . . . WD 194
IN THE LAB . . . WD 195
CASES AND PLACES . . . WD 199

Microsoft PowerPoint 2010

CHAPTER 1
Creating and Editing a Presentation with Clip Art . . . PPT 1
OBJECTIVES . . . PPT 1
INTRODUCTION . . . PPT 2
PROJECT — PRESENTATION WITH BULLETED LISTS AND CLIP ART . . . PPT 2
Overview . . . PPT 4
CHOOSING A DOCUMENT THEME . . . PPT 5
To Choose a Document Theme . . . PPT 5
CREATING A TITLE SLIDE . . . PPT 7
To Enter the Presentation Title . . . PPT 7
Correcting a Mistake When Typing . . . PPT 8
Paragraphs . . . PPT 8
To Enter the Presentation Subtitle Paragraph . . . PPT 9
FORMATTING CHARACTERS IN A PRESENTATION . . . PPT 10
Fonts and Font Styles . . . PPT 10
To Select a Paragraph . . . PPT 10
To Italicize Text . . . PPT 11
To Increase Font Size . . . PPT 11
To Select a Word . . . PPT 12
To Change the Text Color . . . PPT 13
ADDING A NEW SLIDE TO A PRESENTATION . . . PPT 14
To Add a New Text Slide with a Bulleted List . . . PPT 14
CREATING A TEXT SLIDE WITH A MULTI-LEVEL BULLETED LIST . . . PPT 15
To Enter a Slide Title . . . PPT 16
To Select a Text Placeholder . . . PPT 16
To Type a Multi-Level Bulleted List . . . PPT 17
To Select a Group of Words . . . PPT 19
To Bold Text . . . PPT 19
ADDING NEW SLIDES AND CHANGING THE SLIDE LAYOUTS . . . PPT 21
To Add a Slide with the Title Only Layout . . . PPT 21
To Add a New Slide and Enter a Slide Title and Headings . . . PPT 23
POWERPOINT VIEWS . . . PPT 24
To Move to Another Slide in Normal View . . . PPT 25
INSERTING CLIP ART AND PHOTOGRAPHS INTO SLIDES . . . PPT 26
The Clip Art Task Pane . . . PPT 26
To Insert a Clip from the Clip Organizer into the Title Slide . . . PPT 27
To Insert a Clip from the Clip Organizer into a Content Placeholder . . . PPT 30
PHOTOGRAPHS AND THE CLIP ORGANIZER . . . PPT 31
RESIZING CLIP ART AND PHOTOGRAPHS . . . PPT 33
To Resize Clip Art . . . PPT 33
To Move Clips . . . PPT 36
ENDING A SLIDE SHOW WITH A CLOSING SLIDE . . . PPT 38
To Duplicate a Slide . . . PPT 38
To Arrange a Slide . . . PPT 39
MAKING CHANGES TO SLIDE TEXT CONTENT . . . PPT 40
Replacing Text in an Existing Slide . . . PPT 41
Deleting Text . . . PPT 41
To Delete Text in a Placeholder . . . PPT 41
ADDING A TRANSITION . . . PPT 43
To Add a Transition between Slides . . . PPT 43
CHANGING DOCUMENT PROPERTIES . . . PPT 45
To Change Document Properties . . . PPT 46
VIEWING THE PRESENTATION IN SLIDE SHOW VIEW . . . PPT 47
To Start Slide Show View . . . PPT 47
To Move Manually through Slides in a Slide Show . . . PPT 49

PRINTING A PRESENTATION . . . PPT 51
To Print a Presentation . . . PPT 51
CHAPTER SUMMARY . . . PPT 54
LEARN IT ONLINE . . . PPT 55
APPLY YOUR KNOWLEDGE . . . PPT 55
EXTEND YOUR KNOWLEDGE . . . PPT 57
MAKE IT RIGHT . . . PPT 58
IN THE LAB . . . PPT 59
CASES AND PLACES . . . PPT 70

CHAPTER 2
Enhancing a Presentation with Pictures, Shapes, and WordArt . . . PPT 73
OBJECTIVES . . . PPT 73
INTRODUCTION . . . PPT 74
PROJECT — PRESENTATION WITH PICTURES, SHAPES, AND WORDART . . . PPT 74
Overview . . . PPT 74
STARTING POWERPOINT . . . PPT 76
CREATING SLIDES AND CHANGING FONT COLORS AND BACKGROUND STYLE . . . PPT 77
Presentation Template Color Scheme . . . PPT 80
To Change the Presentation Theme Colors . . . PPT 81
INSERTING AND FORMATTING PICTURES IN A PRESENTATION . . . PPT 82
To Insert a Picture . . . PPT 83
To Insert a Picture into a Slide without a Content Placeholder . . . PPT 85
To Correct a Picture . . . PPT 86
To Apply a Picture Style . . . PPT 87
To Apply Picture Effects . . . PPT 89
To Add a Picture Border . . . PPT 91
To Change a Picture Border Color . . . PPT 92
To Resize a Graphic by Entering Exact Measurements . . . PPT 93
FORMATTING SLIDE BACKGROUNDS . . . PPT 95
To Insert a Texture Fill . . . PPT 95
To Insert a Picture to Create a Background . . . PPT 97
To Format the Background Picture Fill Transparency . . . PPT 98
To Format the Background Texture Fill Transparency . . . PPT 99
To Choose a Background Style . . . PPT 99
FORMATTING TITLE AND CONTENT TEXT . . . PPT 101
To Change the Subtitle and Caption Font . . . PPT 101
To Shadow Text . . . PPT 103
Format Painter . . . PPT 105
To Format Text Using the Format Painter . . . PPT 105
ADDING AND FORMATTING A SHAPE . . . PPT 106
To Add a Shape . . . PPT 106
To Resize a Shape . . . PPT 107
To Copy and Paste a Shape . . . PPT 108
To Add Other Shapes . . . PPT 109
To Apply a Shape Style . . . PPT 110
To Add Formatted Text to a Shape . . . PPT 112
USING WORDART . . . PPT 113
To Insert WordArt . . . PPT 114
To Change the WordArt Shape . . . PPT 115
To Apply a WordArt Text Fill . . . PPT 117
To Change the Weight of the WordArt Outline . . . PPT 118
To Change the Color of the WordArt Outline . . . PPT 118
CHAPTER SUMMARY . . . PPT 122
LEARN IT ONLINE . . . PPT 123
APPLY YOUR KNOWLEDGE . . . PPT 123
EXTEND YOUR KNOWLEDGE . . . PPT 126
MAKE IT RIGHT . . . PPT 129
IN THE LAB . . . PPT 130
CASES AND PLACES . . . PPT 136

CHAPTER 3
Reusing a Presentation and Adding Media . . . PPT 137
OBJECTIVES . . . PPT 137
INTRODUCTION . . . PPT 138
PROJECT — PRESENTATION WITH VIDEO, AUDIO, AND PICTURES WITH EFFECTS . . . PPT 138
Overview . . . PPT 138
STARTING POWERPOINT . . . PPT 140
INSERTING PICTURES AND ADDING EFFECTS . . . PPT 141
Adjusting Picture Colors . . . PPT 142
To Color a Picture . . . PPT 143
To Add an Artistic Effect to a Picture . . . PPT 144
To Change the Stacking Order . . . PPT 146
MODIFYING PLACEHOLDERS AND DELETING A SLIDE . . . PPT 148
To Resize a Placeholder . . . PPT 148
To Move a Placeholder . . . PPT 148
To Align Paragraph Text . . . PPT 150
To Delete a Slide . . . PPT 152
Changing Views . . . PPT 153
To Change Views . . . PPT 153
COPYING AND MODIFYING A CLIP . . . PPT 154
To Copy a Clip from One Slide to Another . . . PPT 155
To Zoom a Slide . . . PPT 156
To Ungroup a Clip . . . PPT 157
To Change the Color of a Clip Object . . . PPT 158
To Delete a Clip Object . . . PPT 161
To Regroup Objects . . . PPT 162
ADDING MEDIA TO SLIDES . . . PPT 163
To Insert a Video File . . . PPT 163
To Trim a Video File . . . PPT 164
To Add Video Options . . . PPT 166
To Insert an Audio File . . . PPT 167
To Add Audio Options . . . PPT 170
To Add a Video Style . . . PPT 172
To Resize a Video . . . PPT 174
To Insert a Movie Clip . . . PPT 174
REVIEWING AND REVISING INDIVIDUAL SLIDES . . . PPT 176
Replace Dialog Box . . . PPT 176
To Find and Replace Text . . . PPT 176
To Find and Insert a Synonym . . . PPT 178
To Add Notes . . . PPT 179
Checking Spelling . . . PPT 180
To Check Spelling . . . PPT 181
To Insert a Slide Number . . . PPT 182
To Preview and Print a Handout . . . PPT 184
To Print Speaker Notes . . . PPT 187
CHAPTER SUMMARY . . . PPT 190
LEARN IT ONLINE . . . PPT 190
APPLY YOUR KNOWLEDGE . . . PPT 191
EXTEND YOUR KNOWLEDGE . . . PPT 192
MAKE IT RIGHT . . . PPT 194
IN THE LAB . . . PPT 195
CASES AND PLACES . . . PPT 200

Microsoft Excel 2010

CHAPTER 1

Creating a Worksheet and an Embedded Chart . . . . . EX 1

OBJECTIVES . . . EX 1
INTRODUCTION . . . EX 2
PROJECT — WORKSHEET WITH AN EMBEDDED CHART . . . EX 2
Overview . . . EX 4
SELECTING A CELL . . . EX 7
ENTERING TEXT . . . EX 7
To Enter the Worksheet Titles . . . EX 8
AutoCorrect . . . EX 9
To Enter Column Titles . . . EX 10
To Enter Row Titles . . . EX 12
ENTERING NUMBERS . . . EX 13
To Enter Numbers . . . EX 13
CALCULATING A SUM . . . EX 15
To Sum a Column of Numbers . . . EX 15
USING THE FILL HANDLE TO COPY A CELL TO ADJACENT CELLS . . . EX 16
To Copy a Cell to Adjacent Cells in a Row . . . EX 17
To Determine Multiple Totals at the Same Time . . . EX 18
FORMATTING THE WORKSHEET . . . EX 20
Font, Style, Size, and Color . . . EX 22
To Change a Cell Style . . . EX 22
To Change the Font . . . EX 24
To Bold a Cell . . . EX 25
To Increase the Font Size of a Cell Entry . . . EX 26
To Change the Font Color of a Cell Entry . . . EX 27
To Center Cell Entries Across Columns by Merging Cells . . . EX 28
To Format Column Titles and the Total Row . . . EX 29
To Format Numbers in the Worksheet . . . EX 31
To Adjust the Column Width . . . EX 33
USING THE NAME BOX TO SELECT A CELL . . . EX 34
To Use the Name Box to Select a Cell . . . EX 34
Other Ways to Select Cells . . . EX 35
ADDING A CLUSTERED CYLINDER CHART TO THE WORKSHEET . . . EX 36
To Add a Clustered Cylinder Chart to the Worksheet . . . EX 38
CHANGING THE WORKSHEET NAMES . . . EX 42
To Change the Worksheet Names . . . EX 42
CHANGING DOCUMENT PROPERTIES . . . EX 43
To Change Document Properties . . . EX 43
PREVIEWING AND PRINTING A WORKSHEET . . . EX 45
To Preview and Print a Worksheet in Landscape Orientation . . . EX 46
STARTING EXCEL AND OPENING A WORKBOOK . . . EX 47
AUTOCALCULATE . . . EX 48
To Use the AutoCalculate Area to Determine a Maximum . . . EX 49
CORRECTING ERRORS . . . EX 49
Correcting Errors While You Are Typing Data into a Cell . . . EX 49
Correcting Errors After Entering Data into a Cell . . . EX 50
Undoing the Last Cell Entry . . . EX 51
Clearing a Cell or Range of Cells . . . EX 52
Clearing the Entire Worksheet . . . EX 52
CHAPTER SUMMARY . . . EX 53
LEARN IT ONLINE . . . EX 54
APPLY YOUR KNOWLEDGE . . . EX 54
EXTEND YOUR KNOWLEDGE . . . EX 56
MAKE IT RIGHT . . . EX 57
IN THE LAB . . . EX 58
CASES AND PLACES . . . EX 63

CHAPTER 2

Formulas, Functions, and Formatting . . . . . EX 65

OBJECTIVES . . . EX 65
INTRODUCTION . . . EX 66
PROJECT — WORKSHEET WITH FORMULAS AND FUNCTIONS . . . EX 66
Overview . . . EX 68
ENTERING THE TITLES AND NUMBERS INTO THE WORKSHEET . . . EX 71
ENTERING FORMULAS . . . EX 74
To Enter a Formula Using the Keyboard . . . EX 75
Arithmetic Operations . . . EX 76
Order of Operations . . . EX 77
To Enter Formulas Using Point Mode . . . EX 77
To Copy Formulas Using the Fill Handle . . . EX 80
OPTION BUTTONS . . . EX 82
USING THE AVERAGE, MAX, AND MIN FUNCTIONS . . . EX 84
To Determine the Average of a Range of Numbers Using the Keyboard and Mouse . . . EX 84
To Determine the Highest Number in a Range of Numbers Using the Insert Function Box . . . EX 86
To Determine the Lowest Number in a Range of Numbers Using the Sum Menu . . . EX 87
To Copy a Range of Cells Across Columns to an Adjacent Range Using the Fill Handle . . . EX 89
VERIFYING FORMULAS USING RANGE FINDER . . . EX 91
To Verify a Formula Using Range Finder . . . EX 91
FORMATTING THE WORKSHEET . . . EX 92
To Change the Workbook Theme . . . EX 94
To Change the Background Color and Apply a Box Border to the Worksheet Title and Subtitle . . . EX 96
To Format Dates and Center Data in Cells . . . EX 98
Formatting Numbers Using the Ribbon . . . EX 100
To Apply an Accounting Number Format and Comma Style Format Using the Ribbon . . . EX 100
To Apply a Currency Style Format with a Floating Dollar Sign Using the Format Cells Dialog Box . . . EX 102
To Apply a Percent Style Format and Use the Increase Decimal Button . . . EX 103
Conditional Formatting . . . EX 104
To Apply Conditional Formatting . . . EX 104
Conditional Formatting Operators . . . EX 107
Changing the Widths of Columns and Heights of Rows . . . EX 107
To Change the Widths of Columns . . . EX 107
To Change the Heights of Rows . . . EX 110
CHECKING SPELLING . . . EX 112
To Check Spelling on the Worksheet . . . EX 112
Additional Spell Checker Considerations . . . EX 113
PREPARING TO PRINT THE WORKSHEET . . . EX 114
To Change the Worksheet's Margins, Header, and Orientation in Page Layout View . . . EX 114
PRINTING THE WORKSHEET . . . EX 117
To Print a Section of the Worksheet . . . EX 118

DISPLAYING AND PRINTING THE FORMULAS VERSION OF THE WORKSHEET . . . . . EX 119
To Display the Formulas in the Worksheet and Fit the Printout on One Page . . . . . EX 119
CHAPTER SUMMARY . . . . . EX 121
LEARN IT ONLINE . . . . . EX 122
APPLY YOUR KNOWLEDGE . . . . . EX 122
EXTEND YOUR KNOWLEDGE . . . . . EX 124
MAKE IT RIGHT . . . . . EX 125
IN THE LAB . . . . . EX 126
CASES AND PLACES . . . . . EX 134

CHAPTER 3
What-If Analysis, Charting, and Working with Large Worksheets . . . . EX 137
OBJECTIVES . . . . . EX 137
INTRODUCTION . . . . . EX 138
PROJECT — FINANCIAL PROJECTION WORKSHEET WITH WHAT-IF ANALYSIS AND CHART . . . . . EX 138
Overview . . . . . EX 141
ROTATING TEXT AND USING THE FILL HANDLE TO CREATE A SERIES . . . . . EX 144
To Rotate Text and Use the Fill Handle to Create a Series of Month Names . . . . . EX 145
Using the Auto Fill Options Menu . . . . . EX 148
To Increase Column Widths . . . . . EX 149
To Enter Row Titles . . . . . EX 150
COPYING A RANGE OF CELLS TO A NONADJACENT DESTINATION AREA . . . . . EX 151
To Copy a Range of Cells to a Nonadjacent Destination Area . . . . . EX 151
Using the Paste Options Menu . . . . . EX 152
Using Drag and Drop to Move or Copy Cells . . . . . EX 153
Using Cut and Paste to Move Cells . . . . . EX 154
INSERTING AND DELETING CELLS IN A WORKSHEET . . . . . EX 154
To Insert a Row . . . . . EX 154
Inserting Columns . . . . . EX 156
Inserting Single Cells or a Range of Cells . . . . . EX 156
Deleting Columns and Rows . . . . . EX 156
To Enter Numbers with Format Symbols . . . . . EX 156
To Freeze Column and Row Titles . . . . . EX 157
To Enter and Format the System Date . . . . . EX 159
ABSOLUTE VERSUS RELATIVE ADDRESSING . . . . . EX 162
To Enter a Formula Containing Absolute Cell References . . . . . EX 162
MAKING DECISIONS — THE IF FUNCTION . . . . . EX 164
To Enter an IF Function . . . . . EX 165
To Copy Formulas with Absolute Cell References Using the Fill Handle . . . . . EX 168
Nested Forms of the IF Function . . . . . EX 170
ADDING AND FORMATTING SPARKLINE CHARTS . . . . . EX 170
To Add a Sparkline Chart to the Worksheet . . . . . EX 170
To Format and Copy the Sparkline Chart . . . . . EX 171
FORMATTING THE WORKSHEET . . . . . EX 173
To Assign Formats to Nonadjacent Ranges . . . . . EX 174
To Format the Worksheet Titles . . . . . EX 176
To Copy a Cell's Format Using the Format Painter Button . . . . . EX 178
ADDING A 3-D PIE CHART TO THE WORKBOOK . . . . . EX 180
To Draw a 3-D Pie Chart on a Separate Chart Sheet . . . . . EX 182
To Insert a Chart Title and Data Labels . . . . . EX 183
To Rotate the 3-D Pie Chart . . . . . EX 186
To Apply a 3-D Format to the Pie Chart . . . . . EX 188
To Explode the 3-D Pie Chart and Change the Color of a Slice . . . . . EX 190
RENAMING AND REORDERING THE SHEETS AND COLORING THEIR TABS . . . . . EX 193
To Reorder the Sheet Tabs . . . . . EX 194
CHANGING THE VIEW OF THE WORKSHEET . . . . . EX 196
To Shrink and Magnify the View of a Worksheet or Chart . . . . . EX 196
To Split a Window into Panes . . . . . EX 198
WHAT-IF ANALYSIS . . . . . EX 199
To Analyze Data in a Worksheet by Changing Values . . . . . EX 200
To Goal Seek . . . . . EX 200
Goal Seeking . . . . . EX 202
CHAPTER SUMMARY . . . . . EX 203
LEARN IT ONLINE . . . . . EX 204
APPLY YOUR KNOWLEDGE . . . . . EX 204
EXTEND YOUR KNOWLEDGE . . . . . EX 206
MAKE IT RIGHT . . . . . EX 208
IN THE LAB . . . . . EX 209
CASES AND PLACES . . . . . EX 221

Microsoft Access 2010
CHAPTER 1
Databases and Database Objects: An Introduction . . . . AC 1
OBJECTIVES . . . . . AC 1
INTRODUCTION . . . . . AC 2
PROJECT — DATABASE CREATION . . . . . AC 2
Overview . . . . . AC 4
DESIGNING A DATABASE . . . . . AC 6
Database Requirements . . . . . AC 6
Naming Tables and Fields . . . . . AC 8
Identifying the Tables . . . . . AC 8
Determining the Primary Keys . . . . . AC 8
Determining Additional Fields . . . . . AC 8
Determining and Implementing Relationships Between the Tables . . . . . AC 9
Determining Data Types for the Fields . . . . . AC 9
Identifying and Removing Redundancy . . . . . AC 10
CREATING A DATABASE . . . . . AC 13
THE ACCESS WINDOW . . . . . AC 15
Navigation Pane and Access Work Area . . . . . AC 15
CREATING A TABLE . . . . . AC 15
To Modify the Primary Key . . . . . AC 16
To Define the Remaining Fields in a Table . . . . . AC 19
Making Changes to the Structure . . . . . AC 20
To Save a Table . . . . . AC 21
To View the Table in Design View . . . . . AC 21
Checking the Structure in Design View . . . . . AC 22
To Close the Table . . . . . AC 23
To Add Records to a Table . . . . . AC 23
Making Changes to the Data . . . . . AC 25
Starting Access and Opening a Database . . . . . AC 27
To Add Additional Records to a Table . . . . . AC 28
To Resize Columns in a Datasheet . . . . . AC 29
PREVIEWING AND PRINTING THE CONTENTS OF A TABLE . . . . . AC 30
To Preview and Print the Contents of a Table . . . . . AC 31

CREATING ADDITIONAL TABLES . . . . AC 32
To Create a Table in Design View . . . . AC 33
Correcting Errors in the Structure . . . . AC 37
IMPORTING DATA FROM OTHER APPLICATIONS TO ACCESS . . . . AC 38
To Import an Excel Worksheet . . . . AC 38
ADDITIONAL DATABASE OBJECTS . . . . AC 42
To Use the Simple Query Wizard to Create a Query . . . . AC 43
Using Queries . . . . AC 45
To Use a Criterion in a Query . . . . AC 46
To Print the Results of a Query . . . . AC 48
Creating and Using Forms . . . . AC 48
To Create a Form . . . . AC 48
Using a Form . . . . AC 50
Creating and Printing Reports . . . . AC 51
To Create a Report . . . . AC 52
Using Layout View in a Report . . . . AC 53
To Modify Column Headings and Resize Columns . . . . AC 54
To Add Totals to a Report . . . . AC 57
DATABASE PROPERTIES . . . . AC 58
To Change Database Properties . . . . AC 59
SPECIAL DATABASE OPERATIONS . . . . AC 60
Backup and Recovery . . . . AC 60
Compacting and Repairing a Database . . . . AC 61
Additional Operations . . . . AC 62
CHAPTER SUMMARY . . . . AC 63
LEARN IT ONLINE . . . . AC 63
APPLY YOUR KNOWLEDGE . . . . AC 64
EXTEND YOUR KNOWLEDGE . . . . AC 65
MAKE IT RIGHT . . . . AC 66
IN THE LAB . . . . AC 66
CASES AND PLACES . . . . AC 72

CHAPTER 2
Querying a Database . . . . AC 73
OBJECTIVES . . . . AC 73
INTRODUCTION . . . . AC 74
PROJECT — QUERYING A DATABASE . . . . AC 74
Overview . . . . AC 76
CREATING QUERIES . . . . AC 77
To Create a Query in Design View . . . . AC 78
To Add Fields to the Design Grid . . . . AC 79
Determining Criteria . . . . AC 80
To Use Text Data in a Criterion . . . . AC 80
Using Saved Queries . . . . AC 82
To Use a Wildcard . . . . AC 83
To Use Criteria for a Field Not Included in the Results . . . . AC 85
Creating a Parameter Query . . . . AC 86
To Create and View a Parameter Query . . . . AC 87
To Use a Parameter Query . . . . AC 89
To Use a Number in a Criterion . . . . AC 90
To Use a Comparison Operator in a Criterion . . . . AC 91
Using Compound Criteria . . . . AC 92
To Use a Compound Criterion Involving AND . . . . AC 92
To Use a Compound Criterion Involving OR . . . . AC 93
Special Criteria . . . . AC 94
SORTING . . . . AC 94
To Clear the Design Grid . . . . AC 95
To Sort Data in a Query . . . . AC 96
To Omit Duplicates . . . . AC 97
To Sort on Multiple Keys . . . . AC 98
To Create a Top-Values Query . . . . AC 99
JOINING TABLES . . . . AC 100
To Join Tables . . . . AC 102
To Change Join Properties . . . . AC 105
To Create a Report Involving a Join . . . . AC 106
CREATING A FORM FOR A QUERY . . . . AC 108
To Create a Form for a Query . . . . AC 109
Using a Form . . . . AC 110
EXPORTING DATA FROM ACCESS TO OTHER APPLICATIONS . . . . AC 110
To Export Data to Excel . . . . AC 111
Text Files . . . . AC 113
ADDING CRITERIA TO A JOIN QUERY . . . . AC 114
To Restrict the Records in a Join . . . . AC 115
CALCULATIONS . . . . AC 115
To Use a Calculated Field in a Query . . . . AC 116
To Change a Caption . . . . AC 118
To Calculate Statistics . . . . AC 119
To Use Criteria in Calculating Statistics . . . . AC 121
To Use Grouping . . . . AC 122
CROSSTAB QUERIES . . . . AC 123
To Create a Crosstab Query . . . . AC 124
To Customize the Navigation Pane . . . . AC 127
CHAPTER SUMMARY . . . . AC 128
LEARN IT ONLINE . . . . AC 129
APPLY YOUR KNOWLEDGE . . . . AC 129
EXTEND YOUR KNOWLEDGE . . . . AC 130
MAKE IT RIGHT . . . . AC 131
IN THE LAB . . . . AC 132
CASES AND PLACES . . . . AC 135

Appendix A
Project Planning Guidelines . . . . APP 1
USING PROJECT PLANNING GUIDELINES . . . . APP 1
Determine the Project's Purpose . . . . APP 1
Analyze Your Audience . . . . APP 1
Gather Possible Content . . . . APP 2
Determine What Content to Present to Your Audience . . . . APP 2
SUMMARY . . . . APP 2

Appendix B
Publishing Office 2010 Web Pages Online . . . . APP 3
Using an Office Program to Publish Office 2010 Web Pages . . . . APP 3

Appendix C
Saving to the Web Using Windows Live SkyDrive . . . . APP 5
INTRODUCTION . . . . APP 5
To Save a File to Windows Live SkyDrive . . . . APP 6
Web Apps . . . . APP 8
To Download a File from Windows Live SkyDrive . . . . APP 9
Collaboration . . . . APP 12

INDEX . . . . IND 1
CREDITS . . . . IND 31
QUICK REFERENCE SUMMARY . . . . QR 1

Preface

The Shelly Cashman Series® offers the finest textbooks in computer education. This book is intended to provide instructors and students with a singular textbook that meets the needs of the combined computer concepts and Microsoft Office 2010 application course.

The early chapters of *Discovering Computers & Microsoft Office 2010: A Fundamental Combined Approach* present introductory computer subjects in an educationally sound, highly visual, and easy-to-follow pedagogy. The computer concepts chapters are followed by an introduction to Microsoft Office 2010 with the Shelly Cashman's step-by-step, screen-by-screen, project-oriented approach. This combination of concepts and applications coverage designed by the renowned Shelly Cashman Series author team provides the ultimate solution for the introductory computing course.

Objectives of This Textbook

Discovering Computers & Microsoft Office 2010: A Fundamental Combined Approach is intended for a full-semester, introductory course that includes an introduction to both computer concepts and Microsoft Office 2010. No experience with a computer is assumed, and no mathematics beyond the high school freshman level is required. The objectives of this book are:

- To provide a concise introduction to computers
- To present the most up-to-date technology in an ever-changing discipline

- To teach the fundamentals of computers and computer nomenclature, particularly with respect to personal computers, software, and the Web
- To present the material in a visually appealing and exciting manner that motivates students to learn
- To present strategies for purchasing a desktop computer, notebook computer, smart phone, portable media player, and digital camera
- To offer an introduction to the following Microsoft products: Windows 7, Internet Explorer 8, Word 2010, PowerPoint 2010, Excel 2010, and Access 2010
- To expose students to practical examples of the computer as a useful tool
- To acquaint students with the proper procedures to use a computer; interact with the Web; and create documents, presentations, worksheets, and databases suitable for coursework, professional purposes, and personal use
- To help students discover the underlying functionality of Microsoft Office 2010 so that they can become more productive
- To develop an exercise-oriented approach that allows learning by doing
- To offer alternative learning techniques and reinforcement via the Web
- To offer distance-education providers a textbook with a meaningful and exercise-rich MS Office 2010 and Concepts CourseMate solution

The Shelly Cashman Approach

To date, more than six million students have learned about computers using a *Discovering Computers* textbook. Our series of Microsoft Office 4.3, Microsoft Office 95, Microsoft Office 97, Microsoft Office 2000, Microsoft Office XP, Microsoft Office 2003, Microsoft Office 2007, and Microsoft Office 2010 textbooks have been the most widely used books in education. Features of this book include:

- **A Proven Pedagogy** Careful explanations of computer concepts and applications, educationally-sound elements, and reinforcement highlight this proven method of presentation.
- **A Visually Appealing Book that Maintains Student Interest** The latest technology, pictures, drawings, and text are combined artfully to produce a visually appealing and easy-to-understand book. Many of the figures include a step-by-step presentation, which simplifies the more complex computer concepts and application techniques.
- **Extensive End-of-Chapter Student Assignments** A notable strength of this book is the extensive student assignments and activities at the end of each chapter. Well-structured student assignments can make the difference between students merely participating in a class and students retaining the information they learn.

DISTINGUISHING FEATURES OF DISCOVERING COMPUTERS—SELECTED CHAPTERS FROM FUNDAMENTALS, 2012 EDITION

- **Innovative Computing** Innovative Computing boxes engage students with examples of how particular technologies are used in creative ways, and Computer Usage @ Work boxes describe how computers are utilized in five different professional industries.
- **At the Movies videos** CNET At the Movies videos highlight current technology events of interest to students, involving them in the constant evolution of the computing world.

- **Learn It Online** The Learn It Online end-of-chapter exercises, which include online videos, practice tests, interactive labs, learning games, and Web-based activities, offer a wealth of online reinforcement.
- **Problem Solving** The Problem Solving and Collaboration end-of-chapter exercises tackle everyday computer problems and put the information presented in each chapter to practical use.

DISTINGUISHING FEATURES OF MICROSOFT OFFICE 2010

- **Project Orientation** Each chapter in the book presents a project with a practical problem and complete solution using an easy-to-understand approach.
- **Step-by-Step, Screen-by-Screen Instructions** Each of the tasks required to complete a project is clearly identified throughout the chapter. Now, the step-by-step instructions provide a context beyond point-and-click. Each step explains why students are performing a task, or the result of performing a certain action. Found on the screens accompanying each step, call-outs give students the information they need to know when they need to know it. We have used color to distinguish the content in the call-outs. The Explanatory call-outs (in black) summarize what is happening on the screen, and the Navigational call-outs (in red) show students where to click.
- **Learn It Online** Every chapter features a Learn It Online section that is comprised of six exercises. These exercises include True/False, Multiple Choice, and Short Answer; Flash Cards; Practice Test; Who Wants To Be a Computer Genius?; Wheel of Terms; and Crossword Puzzle Challenge.
- **Make It Right** This exercise requires students to analyze a document, identify errors and issues, and correct those errors and issues using skills learned in the chapter.
- **In the Lab** Three in-depth assignments per chapter require students to utilize the chapter concepts and techniques to solve problems on a computer.
- **NEW! Expanded Office 2010 Coverage** This edition includes additional coverage of Word 2010, PowerPoint 2010, and Excel 2010—an extra chapter for each of these three applications.

NEW! MS Office 2010 and Concepts CourseMate

The content in the MS Office 2010 and Concepts CourseMate Web site for *Discovering Computers & Microsoft Office 2010* is integrated into each page of the text. It gives students easy access to current information on important topics, reinforcement activities, and alternative learning techniques. Integrating this digital solution into the classroom keeps today's students engaged and involved in the learning experience. For each computer concepts chapter in the text, students can access a variety of interactive Quizzes and Learning Games, Exercises, Web Links, Videos, and other features that specifically reinforce and build on the concepts presented in the chapter. For each Microsoft Office chapter, students can practice the skills they have learned with the Learn It Online exercises, including chapter reinforcement, practice tests, flash cards, learning games, and more. Additionally, students can view 380 Microsoft Office 2010 videos that dynamically illustrate the step-by-step instructions found in the text. The interactive e-book and hands-on activities encourage students to take learning into their own hands and explore related content in which they are especially interested. With all of these resources, the MS Office 2010 and Concepts CourseMate enables students to get more comfortable using technology and applications. For instructors, it allows easy assessment of students' knowledge through Engagement Tracker reports.

Book Resources

- Additional Faculty Files
- Blackboard Testbank
- Data Files
- Instructor's Manual
- Lecture Success System
- PowerPoint Presentations
- Solutions to Exercises
- Syllabus
- Test Bank and Test Engine
- WebCT Testbank

Chapter Reinforcement Exercises
Student Downloads

Instructor Resources

The Instructor Resources include both teaching and testing aids and can be accessed via CD-ROM or at login.cengage.com.

INSTRUCTOR'S MANUAL Includes lecture notes summarizing the chapter sections, figures and boxed elements found in every chapter, teacher tips, classroom activities, lab activities, and quick quizzes in Microsoft Word files.

LECTURE SUCCESS SYSTEM Includes intermediate files that correspond to certain figures in the book, which allow you to step through the creation of a project in a chapter during a lecture without entering large amounts of data.

SYLLABUS Contains easily customizable sample syllabi that cover policies, assignments, exams, and other course information.

FIGURE FILES Illustrations for every figure in the textbook are available in electronic form. Figures are provided both with and without callouts.

POWERPOINT PRESENTATIONS A one-click-per-slide presentation system provides PowerPoint slides for every subject in each chapter. Several computer-related video clips are available for optional presentation. Presentations are based on chapter objectives.

SOLUTIONS TO EXERCISES Includes solutions for all end-of-chapter exercises. Also includes Tip Sheets, which are suggested starting points for the Problem Solving exercises in the concepts chapters, and chapter reinforcement solutions for the Microsoft Office 2010 chapters.

RUBRICS AND ANNOTATED SOLUTION FILES Grading rubrics provide a customizable framework for assigning point values to the laboratory exercises. Annotated solution files correspond to the grading rubrics to make it easy for you to compare students' results with the correct solutions whether you receive their homework as hard copy or via e-mail.

TEST BANK AND TEST ENGINE Test Banks include 112 questions for every chapter, featuring objective-based and critical-thinking question types, and include page number references and figure references, when appropriate. Also included is the test engine, ExamView, the ultimate tool for your objective-based testing needs.

PRINTED TEST BANK A Rich Text Format (.rtf) version of the test bank you can print.

LAB TESTS/TEST OUT Parallel to the Microsoft Office 2010 In the Lab assignments, these can be used for testing students in the laboratory on the chapter material or for testing students out of the course.

DATA FILES FOR STUDENTS Includes all the files that are required by students to complete the exercises.

ADDITIONAL ACTIVITIES FOR STUDENTS Consists of Chapter Reinforcement Exercises for the Microsoft Office 2010 chapters, which are true/false, multiple-choice, and short answer questions that help students gain confidence in the material learned.

Content for Online Learning

Course Technology has partnered with the leading distance learning solution providers and class-management platforms today. To access this material, instructors will visit our password-protected instructor resources available at login.cengage.com. Instructor resources include the following: additional case projects, sample syllabi, PowerPoint presentations per chapter, and more. For additional information or for an instructor user name and password, please contact your sales representative. For students to access this material, they must have purchased a WebTutor PIN-code specific to this title and your campus platform. The resources for students may include (based on instructor preferences), but are not limited to: topic review, review questions, and practice tests.

SAM: Skills Assessment Manager

SAM 2010 is designed to help bring students from the classroom to the real world. It allows students to train on and test important computer skills in an active, hands-on environment.

SAM's easy-to-use system includes powerful interactive exams, training, and projects on the most commonly used Microsoft Office applications. SAM simulates the Microsoft Office 2010 application environment, allowing students to demonstrate their knowledge and think through the skills by performing real-world tasks such as bolding word text or setting up slide transitions. Add in live-in-the-application projects, and students are on their way to truly learning and applying skills to business-centric documents.

Designed to be used with the Shelly Cashman Series, SAM includes handy page references so that students can print helpful study guides that match the Shelly Cashman textbooks used in class. For instructors, SAM also includes robust scheduling and reporting features.

CourseNotes

Course Technology's CourseNotes are six-panel quick reference cards that reinforce the most important and widely used features of a software application in a visual and user-friendly format. CourseNotes serve as a great reference tool during and after the student completes the course. CourseNotes are available for software applications such as Microsoft Office 2010, Word 2010, Excel 2010, Access 2010, PowerPoint 2010, and Windows 7. Topic-based CourseNotes are available for Best Practices in Social Networking, Hot Topics in Technology, and Web 2.0. Visit www.cengagebrain.com to learn more!

course|notes™
quick reference guide

A Guided Tour

Add excitement and interactivity to your classroom with "*A Guided Tour*" product line. Play one of the brief mini-movies to spice up your lecture and spark classroom discussion. Or, assign a movie for homework and ask students to complete the correlated assignment that accompanies each topic. "*A Guided Tour*" product line takes the prep work out of providing your students with information about new technologies and applications and helps keep students engaged with content relevant to their lives—all in under an hour!

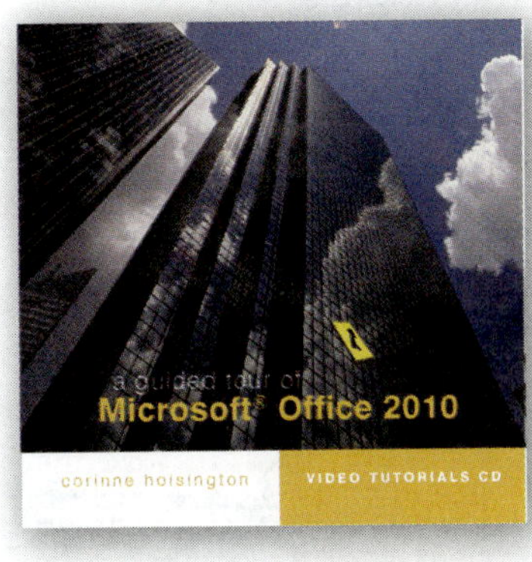

About Our Covers

The Shelly Cashman Series is continually updating our approach and content to reflect the way today's students learn and experience new technology. This focus on student success is reflected on our covers, which feature real students from Bryant University using the Shelly Cashman Series in their courses, and reflect the varied ages and backgrounds of the students learning with our books. When you use the Shelly Cashman Series, you can be assured that you are learning computer skills using the most effective courseware available.

Discovering Computers—Selected Chapters from Fundamentals, 2012 Edition

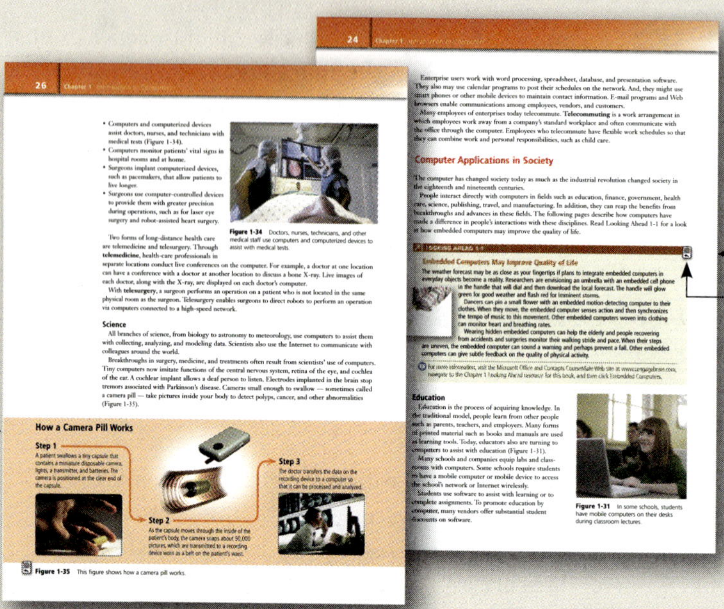

Figure 1-34
Figure 1-31
Figure 1-35 This figure shows how a camera pill works.

Looking Ahead boxes offer a glimpse of the latest advances in computer technology that will be available, usually within five years.

Interactive e-Book Activity Icon Several elements in each chapter are interactive learning activities in the e-book and are identified by this icon.

Step Figures present the more complex computer concepts using a step-by-step pedagogy.

Figure 1-20
Figure 1-21

Web Links provide current information and a different perspective about key terms and concepts by visiting the Web Links found in the margins throughout the book.

Innovative Computing boxes present different and innovative ways of using various technologies and help students learn how computing is applied creatively to solve problems.

CourseMate Icon Visit the MS Office 2010 and Concepts CourseMate Web site for access to many of the interactive chapter elements.

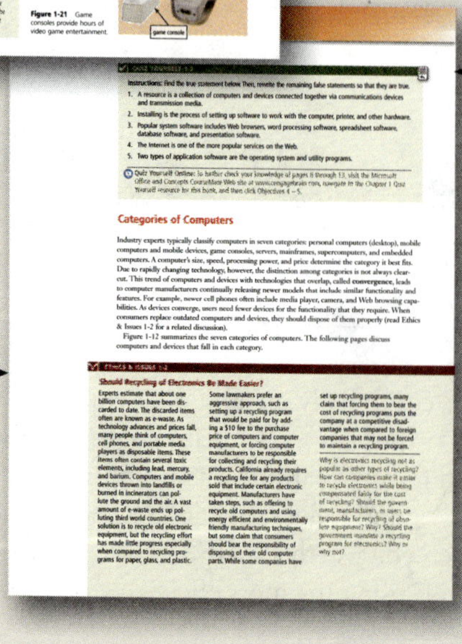

Ethics & Issues boxes raise controversial, computer-related topics of the day, challenging readers to consider closely general concerns of computers in society.

Quiz Yourself boxes help ensure retention by reinforcing sections of the chapter material, rather than waiting for the end of chapter to test. Use the Quiz Yourself boxes for a quick check of the answers, and access additional Quiz Yourself quizzes via the Microsoft Office and Concepts CourseMate Web site.

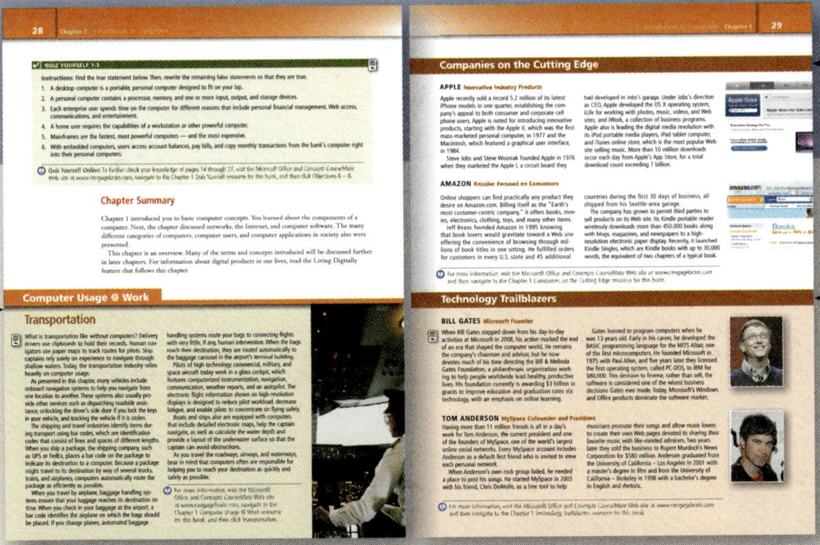

Companies on the Cutting Edge

Computer Usage @ Work

Technology Trailblazers

Companies on the Cutting Edge and Technology Trailblazers at the end of every chapter present the key computer-related companies and the more famous leaders of the computer industry.

Computer Usage @ Work boxes explain how computers are used in five different professional industries, including transportation, entertainment, construction, education, and national and local security.

Learn It Online exercises, which include At the Movies online CNET videos, practice test, interactive labs, learning games, and Web-based activities, offer a wealth of online reinforcement.

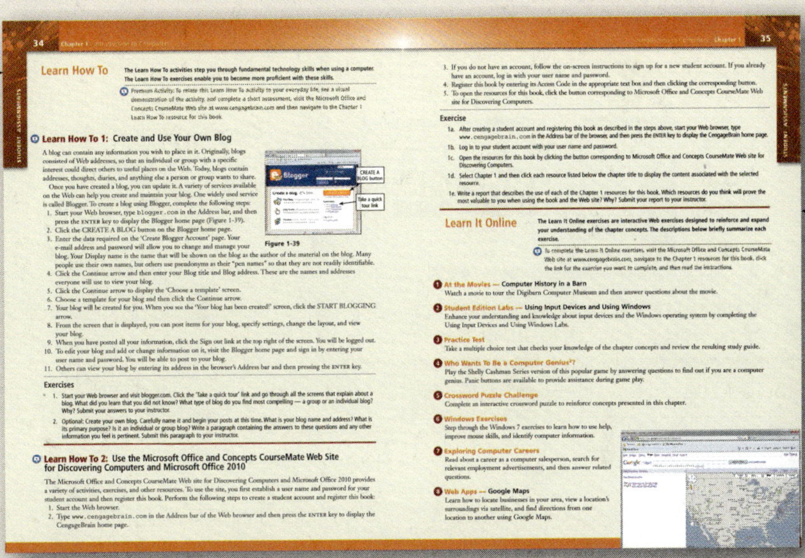

Learn How To

Learn It Online

Learn How To end-of-chapter activities allow students to apply the concepts in the chapter to everyday life with hands-on activities. Learn how the Learn How To activities fit into your life with relevant scenarios, visual demonstrations, and practice questions via the Microsoft Office and Concepts CourseMate Web site.

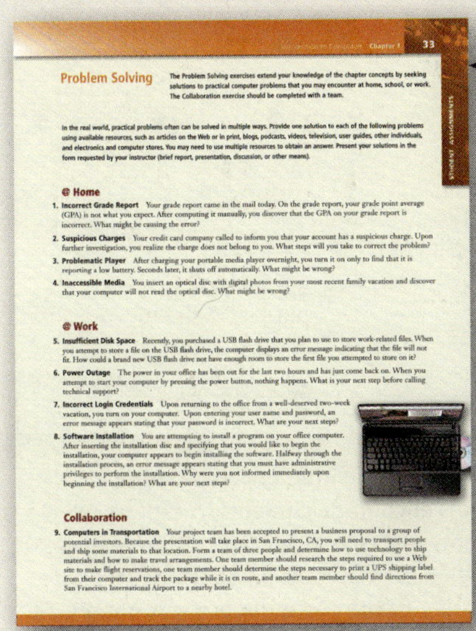

Problem Solving

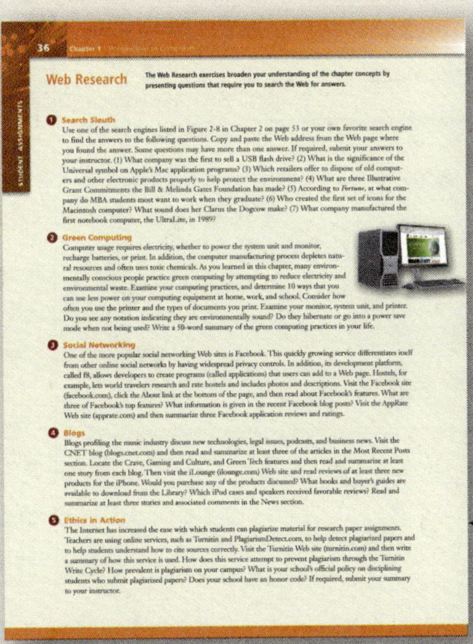

Web Research

Problem Solving and Collaboration exercises tackle everyday computer problems and put the information presented in each chapter to practical use. Students work as a team to solve the Collaboration exercise.

Web Research exercises require follow-up research on the Web and suggest writing a short article or presenting the findings of the research to the class.

Textbook Walk-Through

Microsoft Office 2010

Plan Ahead boxes prepare students to create successful projects by encouraging them to think strategically about what they are trying to accomplish before they begin working.

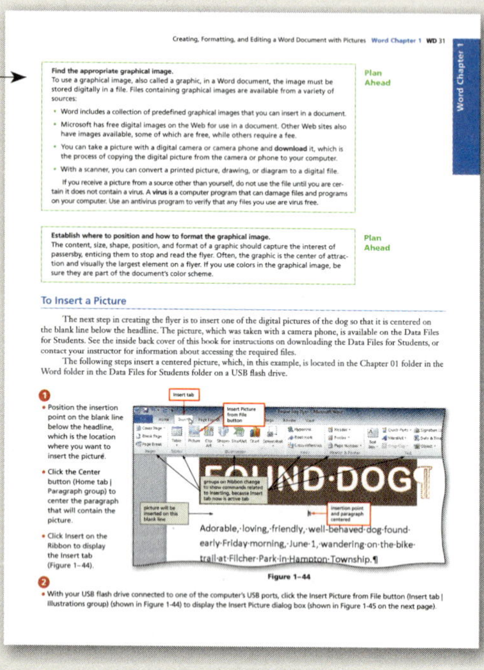

Step-by-step instructions now provide a context beyond the point-and-click. Each step provides information on why students are performing each task or what will occur as a result.

Navigational callouts in red show students where to click.

Explanatory callouts in black summarize what is happening on screen.

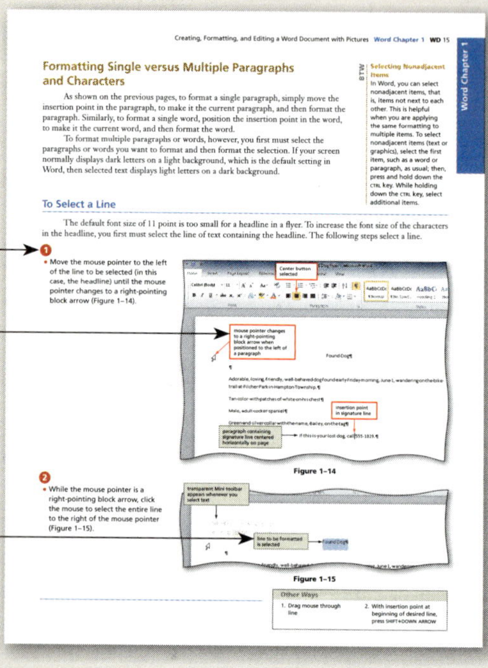

Q&A boxes offer questions students may have when working through the steps and provide additional information about what they are doing right where they need it.

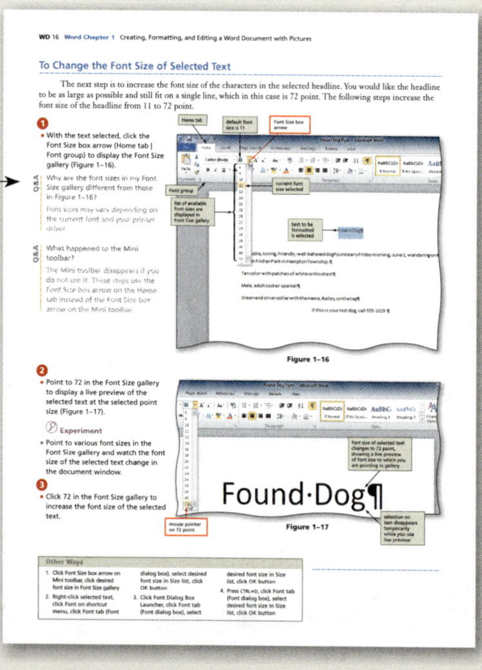

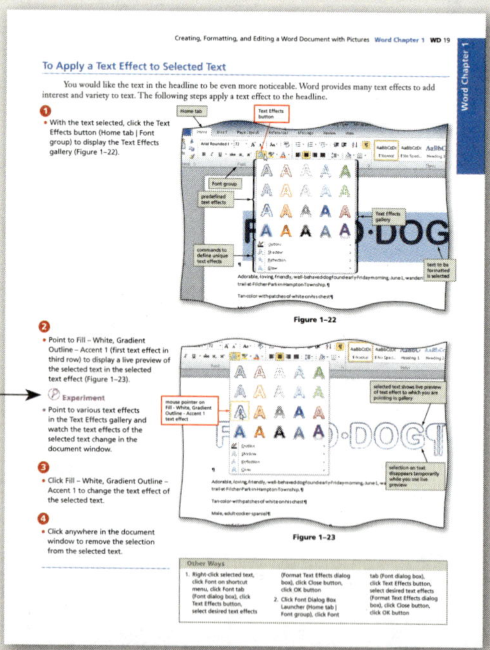

Experiment steps within our step-by-step instructions encourage students to explore, experiment, and take advantage of the features of the Office 2010 user interface. These steps are not necessary to complete the projects but are designed to increase confidence with the software and build problem solving skills.

Break Points identify logical breaks in the chapter if students need to stop before completing the project.

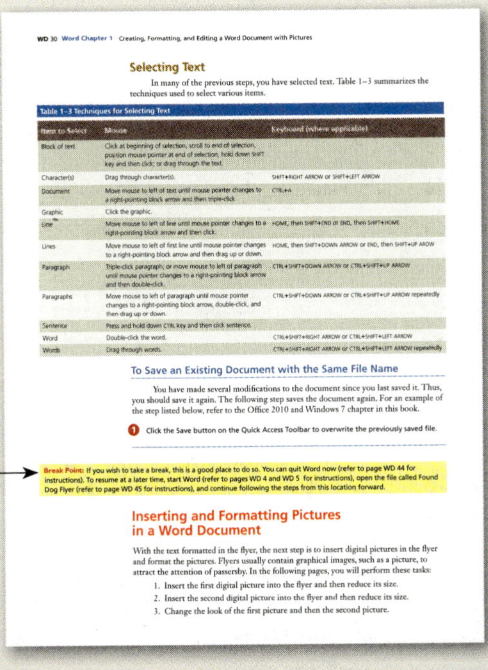
WD 30 Word Chapter 1 Creating, Formatting, and Editing a Word Document with Pictures

Selecting Text

In many of the previous steps, you have selected text. Table 1–3 summarizes the techniques used to select various items.

Table 1-3 Techniques for Selecting Text

Item to Select	Mouse	Keyboard (where applicable)
Block of text	Click at beginning of selection, scroll to end of selection, position mouse pointer at end of selection, hold down SHIFT key and then click; or drag through the text.	
Character(s)	Drag through character(s).	SHIFT+RIGHT ARROW or SHIFT+LEFT ARROW
Document	Move mouse to left of text until mouse pointer changes to a right-pointing block arrow and then triple-click.	CTRL+A
Graphic	Click the graphic.	
Line	Move mouse to left of line until mouse pointer changes to a right-pointing block arrow and then click.	HOME, then SHIFT+END or END, then SHIFT+HOME
Lines	Move mouse to left of first line until mouse pointer changes to a right-pointing block arrow and then drag up or down.	HOME, then SHIFT+DOWN ARROW or END, then SHIFT+UP AROW
Paragraph	Triple-click paragraph; or move mouse to left of paragraph until mouse pointer changes to a right-pointing block arrow and then double-click.	CTRL+SHIFT+DOWN ARROW or CTRL+SHIFT+UP ARROW
Paragraphs	Move mouse to left of paragraph until mouse pointer changes to a right-pointing block arrow, double-click, and then drag up or down.	CTRL+SHIFT+DOWN ARROW or CTRL+SHIFT+UP ARROW repeatedly
Sentence	Press and hold down CTRL key and then click sentence.	
Word	Double-click the word.	CTRL+SHIFT+RIGHT ARROW or CTRL+SHIFT+LEFT ARROW
Words	Drag through words.	CTRL+SHIFT+RIGHT ARROW or CTRL+SHIFT+LEFT ARROW repeatedly

To Save an Existing Document with the Same File Name

You have made several modifications to the document since you last saved it. Thus, you should save it again. The following step saves the document again. For an example of the step listed below, refer to the Office 2010 and Windows 7 chapter in this book.

1 Click the Save button on the Quick Access Toolbar to overwrite the previously saved file.

Break Point: If you wish to take a break, this is a good place to do so. You can quit Word now (refer to page WD 44 for instructions). To resume at a later time, start Word (refer to pages WD 4 and WD 5 for instructions), open the file called Found Dog Flyer (refer to page WD 45 for instructions), and continue following the steps from this location forward.

Inserting and Formatting Pictures in a Word Document

With the text formatted in the flyer, the next step is to insert digital pictures in the flyer and format the pictures. Flyers usually contain graphical images, such as a picture, to attract the attention of passersby. In the following pages, you will perform these tasks:

1. Insert the first digital picture into the flyer and then reduce its size.
2. Insert the second digital picture into the flyer and then reduce its size.
3. Change the look of the first picture and then the second picture.

Extend Your Knowledge projects at the end of each chapter allow students to extend and expand on the skills learned within the chapter. Students use critical thinking to experiment with new skills in order to complete each project.

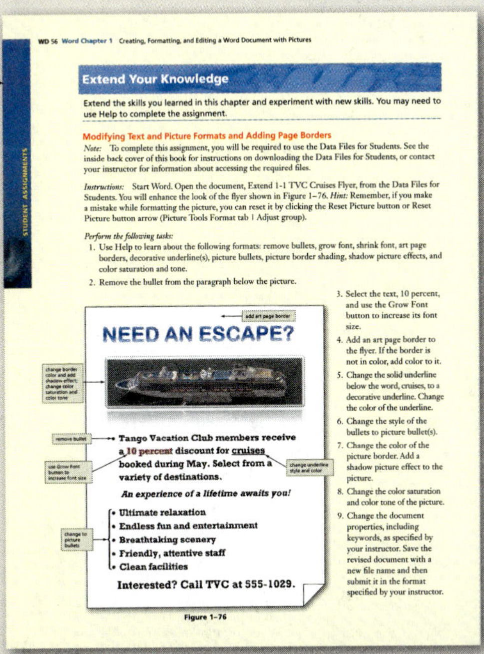
WD 56 Word Chapter 1 Creating, Formatting, and Editing a Word Document with Pictures

STUDENT ASSIGNMENTS

Extend Your Knowledge

Extend the skills you learned in this chapter and experiment with new skills. You may need to use Help to complete the assignment.

Modifying Text and Picture Formats and Adding Page Borders

Note: To complete this assignment, you will be required to use the Data Files for Students. See the inside back cover of this book for instructions on downloading the Data Files for Students, or contact your instructor for information about accessing the required files.

Instructions: Start Word. Open the document, Extend 1-1 TVC Cruises Flyer, from the Data Files for Students. You will enhance the look of the flyer shown in Figure 1–76. *Hint:* Remember, if you make a mistake while formatting the picture, you can reset it by clicking the Reset Picture button or Reset Picture button arrow (Picture Tools Format tab | Adjust group).

Perform the following tasks:

1. Use Help to learn about the following formats: remove bullets, grow font, shrink font, art page borders, decorative underline(s), picture bullets, picture border shading, shadow picture effects, and color saturation and tone.
2. Remove the bullet from the paragraph below the picture.
3. Select the text, 10 percent, and use the Grow Font button to increase its font size.
4. Add an art page border to the flyer. If the border is not in color, add color to it.
5. Change the solid underline below the word, cruises, to a decorative underline. Change the color of the underline.
6. Change the style of the bullets to picture bullet(s).
7. Change the color of the picture border. Add a shadow picture effect to the picture.
8. Change the color saturation and color tone of the picture.
9. Change the document properties, including keywords, as specified by your instructor. Save the revised document with a new file name and then submit it in the format specified by your instructor.

Figure 1–76

Make It Right projects call on students to analyze a file, discover errors in it, and fix them using the skills they learned in the chapter.

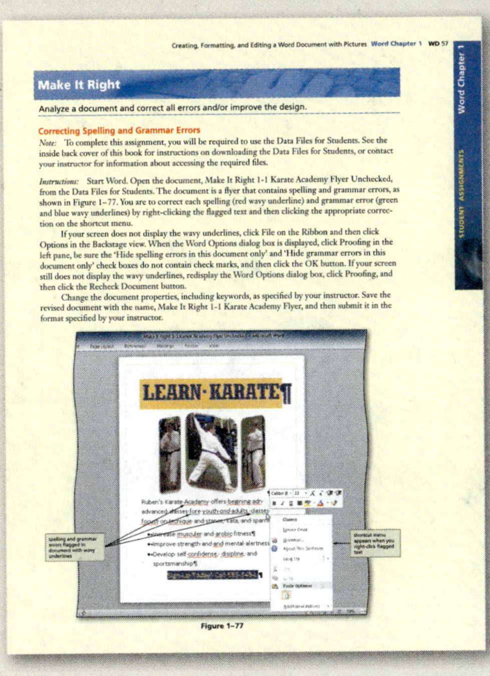
Creating, Formatting, and Editing a Word Document with Pictures Word Chapter 1 WD 57

Word Chapter 1 STUDENT ASSIGNMENTS

Make It Right

Analyze a document and correct all errors and/or improve the design.

Correcting Spelling and Grammar Errors

Note: To complete this assignment, you will be required to use the Data Files for Students. See the inside back cover of this book for instructions on downloading the Data Files for Students, or contact your instructor for information about accessing the required files.

Instructions: Start Word. Open the document, Make It Right 1-1 Karate Academy Flyer Unchecked, from the Data Files for Students. The document is a flyer that contains spelling and grammar errors, as shown in Figure 1–77. You are to correct each spelling (red wavy underline) and grammar error (green and blue wavy underlines) by right-clicking the flagged text and then clicking the appropriate correction on the shortcut menu.

If your screen does not display the wavy underlines, click File on the Ribbon and then click Options in the Backstage view. When the Word Options dialog box is displayed, click Proofing in the left pane, be sure the 'Hide spelling errors in this document only' and 'Hide grammar errors in this document only' check boxes do not contain check marks, and then click the OK button. If your screen still does not display the wavy underlines, redisplay the Word Options dialog box, click Proofing, and then click the Recheck Document button.

Change the document properties, including keywords, as specified by your instructor. Save the revised document with the name, Make It Right 1-1 Karate Academy Flyer, and then submit it in the format specified by your instructor.

Figure 1–77

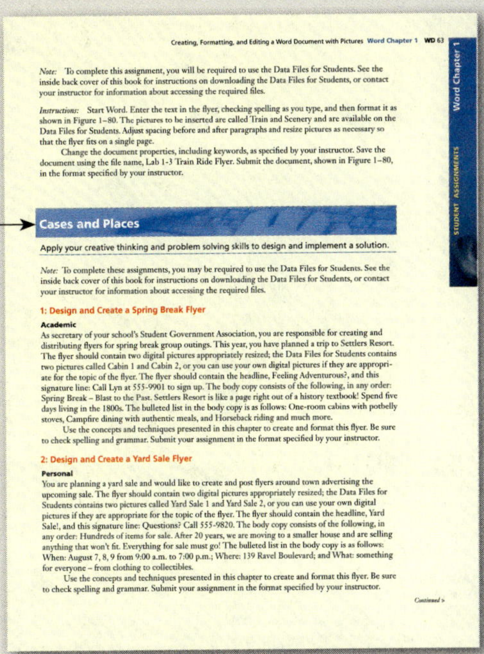
Creating, Formatting, and Editing a Word Document with Pictures Word Chapter 1 WD 63

Word Chapter 1 STUDENT ASSIGNMENTS

Note: To complete this assignment, you will be required to use the Data Files for Students. See the inside back cover of this book for instructions on downloading the Data Files for Students, or contact your instructor for information about accessing the required files.

Instructions: Start Word. Enter the text in the flyer, checking spelling as you type, and then format it as shown in Figure 1–80. The pictures to be inserted are called Train and Scenery and are available on the Data Files for Students. Adjust spacing before and after paragraphs and resize pictures as necessary so that the flyer fits on a single page.

Change the document properties, including keywords, as specified by your instructor. Save the document using the file name, Lab 1-3 Train Ride Flyer. Submit the document, shown in Figure 1–80, in the format specified by your instructor.

Cases and Places

Apply your creative thinking and problem solving skills to design and implement a solution.

Note: To complete these assignments, you may be required to use the Data Files for Students. See the inside back cover of this book for instructions on downloading the Data Files for Students, or contact your instructor for information about accessing the required files.

1: Design and Create a Spring Break Flyer

Academic

As secretary of your school's Student Government Association, you are responsible for creating and distributing flyers for spring break group outings. This year, you have planned a trip to Settlers Resort. The flyer should contain two digital pictures appropriately resized; the Data Files for Students contains two pictures called Cabin 1 and Cabin 2, or you can use your own digital pictures if they are appropriate for the topic of the flyer. The flyer should contain the headline, Feeling Adventurous?, and this signature line: Call Lyn at 555-9901 to sign up. The body copy consists of the following, in any order: Spring Break – Blast to the Past. Settlers Resort is like a page right out of a history textbook! Spend five days living in the 1800s. The bulleted list in the body copy is as follows: One-room cabins with potbelly stoves, Campfire dining with authentic meals, and Horseback riding and much more.

Use the concepts and techniques presented in this chapter to create and format this flyer. Be sure to check spelling and grammar. Submit your assignment in the format specified by your instructor.

2: Design and Create a Yard Sale Flyer

Personal

You are planning a yard sale and would like to create and post flyers around town advertising the upcoming sale. The flyer should contain two digital pictures appropriately resized; the Data Files for Students contains two pictures called Yard Sale 1 and Yard Sale 2, or you can use your own digital pictures if they are appropriate for the topic of the flyer. The flyer should contain the headline, Yard Sale!, and this signature line: Questions? Call 555-9820. The body copy consists of the following, in any order: Hundreds of items for sale. After 20 years, we are moving to a smaller house and are selling anything that won't fit. Everything for sale must go! The bulleted list in the body copy is as follows: When: August 7, 8, 9 from 9:00 a.m. to 7:00 p.m.; Where: 139 Ravel Boulevard; and What: something for everyone – from clothing to collectibles.

Use the concepts and techniques presented in this chapter to create and format this flyer. Be sure to check spelling and grammar. Submit your assignment in the format specified by your instructor.

Continued >

Cases & Places exercises call on students to create open-ended projects that reflect academic, personal, and business settings.

Discovering Computers—Selected Chapters from Fundamentals, 2012 Edition

Chapter One

Introduction to Computers

Objectives

After completing this chapter, you will be able to:

1. Explain why computer literacy is vital to success in today's world
2. Describe the five components of a computer: input devices, output devices, system unit, storage devices, and communications devices
3. Discuss the advantages and disadvantages that users experience when working with computers
4. Discuss the uses of the Internet and World Wide Web
5. Distinguish between system software and application software
6. Differentiate among types, sizes, and functions of computers in each of these categories: personal computers (desktop), mobile computers and mobile devices, game consoles, servers, mainframes, supercomputers, and embedded computers
7. Explain how home users, small office/home office users, mobile users, power users, and enterprise users each interact with computers
8. Discuss how society uses computers in education, finance, government, health care, science, publishing, travel, and manufacturing

A World of Computers

Computers are everywhere: at work, at school, and at home (Figure 1-1). Mobile devices, such as many cell phones, often are classified as computers. Computers are a primary means of local and global communication for billions of people. Employees correspond with clients, students with classmates and teachers, and family with friends and other family members.

Through computers, society has instant access to information from around the globe. Local and national news, weather reports, sports scores, airline schedules, telephone directories, maps and directions, job listings, credit reports, and countless forms of educational material always are accessible. From the computer, you can make a telephone call, meet new friends, share photos and videos, share opinions, shop, book flights, file taxes, take a course, receive alerts, and automate your home.

In the workplace, employees use computers to create correspondence such as e-mail messages, memos, and letters; manage calendars; calculate payroll; track inventory; and generate invoices. At school, teachers use computers to assist with classroom instruction. Students use computers to complete assignments and research. Instead of attending class on campus, some students take entire classes directly from their computer.

Figure 1-1 People use all types and sizes of computers in their daily activities.

People also spend hours of leisure time using a computer. They play games, listen to music or radio broadcasts, watch or compose videos and movies, read books and magazines, share stories, research genealogy, retouch photos, and plan vacations.

Many people believe that computer literacy is vital to success. **Computer literacy**, also known as **digital literacy**, involves having a current knowledge and understanding of computers and their uses. Because the requirements that determine computer literacy change as technology changes, you must keep up with these changes to remain computer literate.

This book presents the knowledge you need to be computer literate today. As you read this first chapter, keep in mind it is an overview. Many of the terms and concepts introduced in this chapter will be discussed in more depth later in the book.

What Is a Computer?

A **computer** is an electronic device, operating under the control of instructions stored in its own memory, that can accept data, process the data according to specified rules, produce results, and store the results for future use.

Data and Information

Computers process data into information. **Data** is a collection of unprocessed items, which can include text, numbers, images, audio, and video. **Information** conveys meaning and is useful to people.

As shown in Figure 1-2, for example, computers process several data items to print information in the form of a cash register receipt.

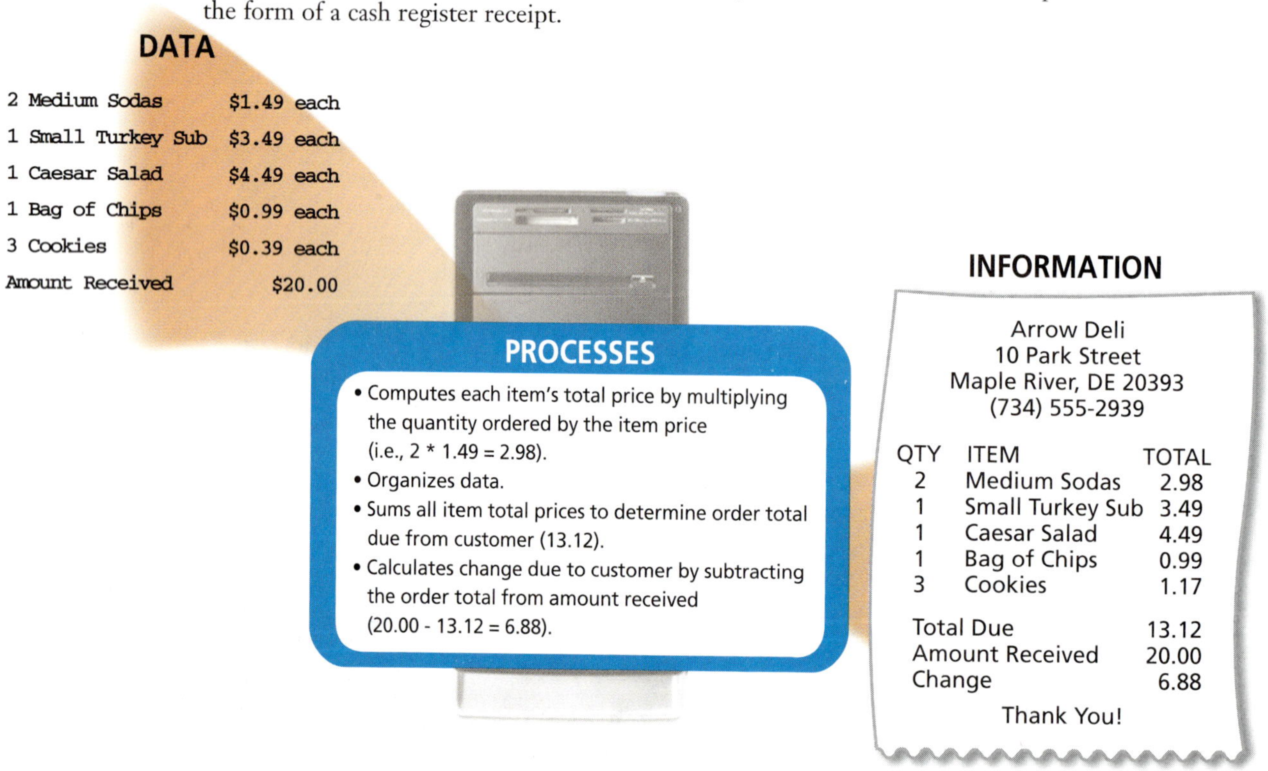

Figure 1-2 A computer processes data into information. In this simplified example, the item ordered, item price, quantity ordered, and amount received all represent data. The computer processes the data to produce the cash register receipt (information).

Information Processing Cycle

Computers process data (input) into information (output). Computers carry out processes using instructions, which are the steps that tell the computer how to perform a particular task. A collection of related instructions organized for a common purpose is referred to as software. A computer often holds data, information, and instructions in storage for future use. Some people refer to the series of input, process, output, and storage activities as the **information processing cycle**. Recently, communications also has become an essential element of the information processing cycle.

The Components of a Computer

A computer contains many electric, electronic, and mechanical components known as **hardware**. These components include input devices, output devices, a system unit, storage devices, and communications devices. Figure 1-3 shows some common computer hardware components.

Input Devices

An **input device** is any hardware component that allows you to enter data and instructions into a computer. Five widely used input devices are the keyboard, mouse, microphone, scanner, and Web cam (Figure 1-3).

A computer keyboard contains keys you press to enter data into the computer. A mouse is a small handheld device. With the mouse, you control movement of a small symbol on the screen, called the pointer, and you make selections from the screen.

A microphone allows a user to speak into the computer. A scanner converts printed material (such as text and pictures) into a form the computer can use.

A Web cam is a digital video camera that allows users to create movies or take pictures and store them on the computer instead of on tape or film.

Output Devices

An **output device** is any hardware component that conveys information to one or more people. Three commonly used output devices are a printer, a monitor, and speakers (Figure 1-3).

A printer produces text and graphics on a physical medium such as paper. A monitor displays text, graphics, and videos on a screen. Speakers allow you to hear music, voice, and other audio (sounds).

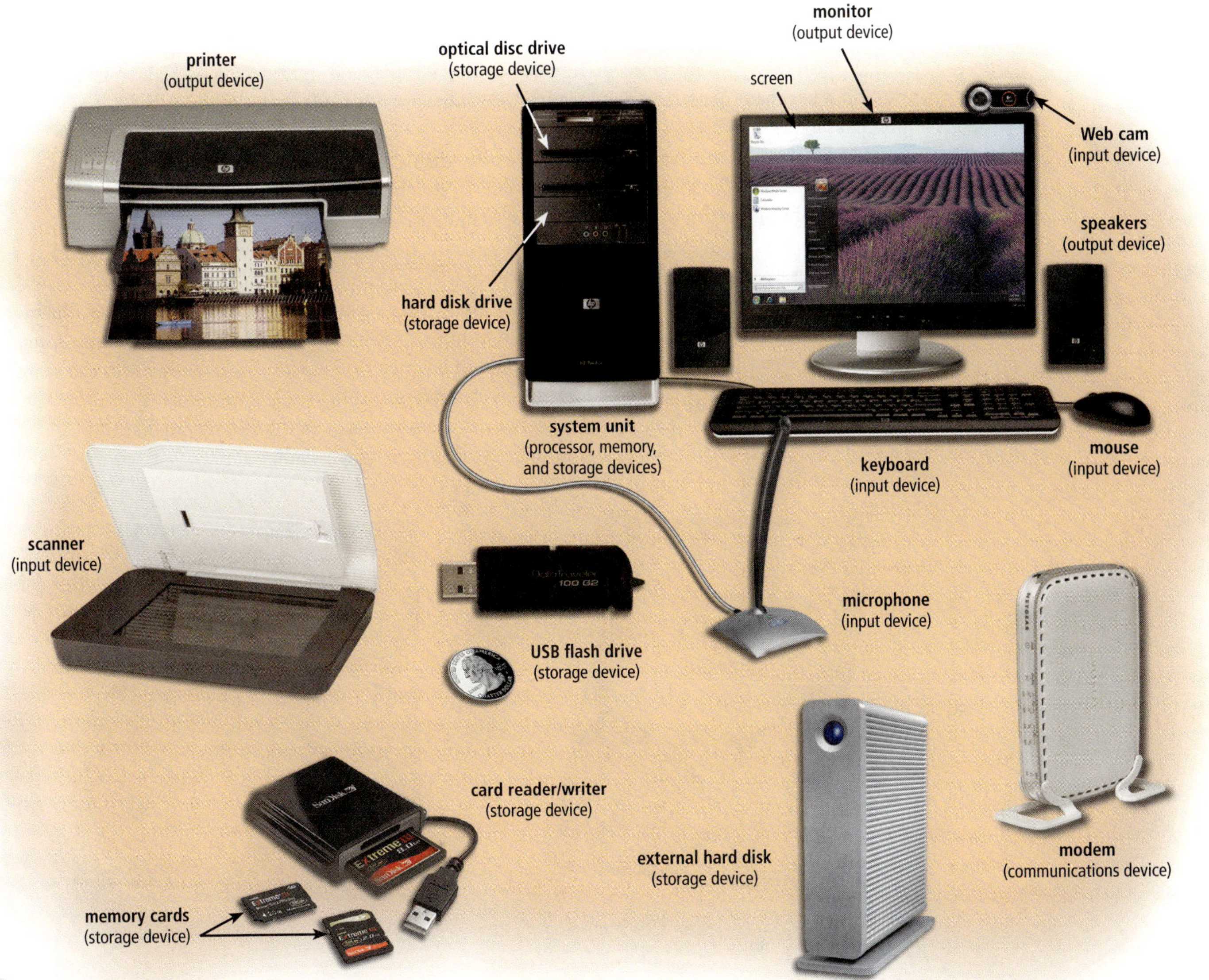

Figure 1-3 Common computer hardware components include the keyboard, mouse, microphone, scanner, Web cam, printer, monitor, speakers, system unit, hard disk drive, external hard disk, optical disc drive(s), USB flash drive, card reader/writer, memory cards, and modem.

System Unit

The **system unit** is a case that contains electronic components of the computer that are used to process data (Figure 1-3 on the previous page). The circuitry of the system unit usually is part of or is connected to a circuit board called the motherboard.

Two main components on the motherboard are the processor and memory. The **processor**, also called the **CPU** (**central processing unit**), is the electronic component that interprets and carries out the basic instructions that operate the computer. **Memory** consists of electronic components that store instructions waiting to be executed and data needed by those instructions. Most memory keeps data and instructions temporarily, which means its contents are erased when the computer is shut off.

Storage Devices

Storage holds data, instructions, and information for future use. For example, computers can store hundreds or millions of customer names and addresses. Storage holds these items permanently.

A computer keeps data, instructions, and information on **storage media**. Examples of storage media are USB flash drives, hard disks, optical discs, and memory cards. A **storage device** records (writes) and/or retrieves (reads) items to and from storage media. Storage devices often function as a source of input because they transfer items from storage to memory.

A USB flash drive is a portable storage device that is small and lightweight enough to be transported on a keychain or in a pocket (Figure 1-3). The average USB flash drive can hold about 4 billion characters.

A hard disk provides much greater storage capacity than a USB flash drive. The average hard disk can hold more than 320 billion characters. Hard disks are enclosed in an airtight, sealed case. Although some are portable, most are housed inside the system unit (Figure 1-4). Portable hard disks are either external or removable. An external hard disk is a separate, freestanding unit, whereas you insert and remove a removable hard disk from the computer or a device connected to the computer.

An optical disc is a flat, round, portable metal disc with a plastic coating. CDs, DVDs, and Blu-ray Discs are three types of optical discs. A CD can hold from 650 million to 1 billion characters. Some DVDs can store two full-length movies or 17 billion characters (Figure 1-5). Blu-ray Discs can store about 46 hours of standard video, or 100 billion characters.

Some mobile devices, such as digital cameras, use memory cards as the storage media. You can use a card reader/writer (Figure 1-3) to transfer stored items, such as digital photos, from the memory card to a computer or printer.

Figure 1-4 Most hard disks are housed inside the system unit.

Figure 1-5 A DVD in a DVD drive.

Communications Devices

A **communications device** is a hardware component that enables a computer to send (transmit) and receive data, instructions, and information to and from one or more computers or mobile devices. A widely used communications device is a modem (Figure 1-3).

Communications occur over cables, telephone lines, cellular radio networks, satellites, and other transmission media. Some transmission media, such as satellites and cellular radio networks, are wireless, which means they have no physical lines or wires.

Advantages and Disadvantages of Using Computers

Society has reaped many benefits from using computers. A **user** is anyone who communicates with a computer or utilizes the information it generates. Both business and home users can make well-informed decisions because they have instant access to information from anywhere in the world. Students, another type of user, have more tools to assist them in the learning process.

Advantages of Using Computers

The benefits from using computers are possible because computers have the advantages of speed, reliability, consistency, storage, and communications.

- **Speed:** When data, instructions, and information flow along electronic circuits in a computer, they travel at incredibly fast speeds. Many computers process billions or trillions of operations in a single second.
- **Reliability:** The electronic components in modern computers are dependable and reliable because they rarely break or fail.
- **Consistency:** Given the same input and processes, a computer will produce the same results — consistently. Computers generate error-free results, provided the input is correct and the instructions work.
- **Storage:** Computers store enormous amounts of data and make this data available for processing anytime it is needed.
- **Communications:** Most computers today can communicate with other computers, often wirelessly. Computers allow users to communicate with one another.

Disadvantages of Using Computers

Some disadvantages of computers relate to the violation of privacy, public safety, the impact on the labor force, health risks, and the impact on the environment.

- **Violation of Privacy:** In many instances, where personal and confidential records stored on computers were not protected properly, individuals have found their privacy violated and identities stolen.
- **Public Safety:** Adults, teens, and children around the world are using computers to share publicly their photos, videos, journals, music, and other personal information. Some of these unsuspecting, innocent computer users have fallen victim to crimes committed by dangerous strangers.
- **Impact on Labor Force:** Although computers have improved productivity and created an entire industry with hundreds of thousands of new jobs, the skills of millions of employees have been replaced by computers. Thus, it is crucial that workers keep their education up-to-date. A separate impact on the labor force is that some companies are outsourcing jobs to foreign countries instead of keeping their homeland labor force employed.
- **Health Risks:** Prolonged or improper computer use can lead to health injuries or disorders. Computer users can protect themselves from health risks through proper workplace design, good posture while at the computer, and appropriately spaced work breaks. Two behavioral health risks are computer addiction and technology overload. Computer addiction occurs when someone becomes obsessed with using a computer. Individuals suffering from technology overload feel distressed when deprived of computers and mobile devices.
- **Impact on Environment:** Computer manufacturing processes and computer waste are depleting natural resources and polluting the environment. **Green computing** involves reducing the electricity consumed and environmental waste generated when using a computer. Strategies that support green computing include recycling, regulating manufacturing processes, extending the life of computers, and immediately donating or properly disposing of replaced computers.

Green Computing
For more information, visit the Microsoft Office and Concepts CourseMate Web site at www.cengagebrain.com, navigate to the Chapter 1 Web Link resource for this book, and then click Green Computing.

QUIZ YOURSELF 1-1

Instructions: Find the true statement below. Then, rewrite the remaining false statements so that they are true.

1. A computer is a motorized device that processes output into input.
2. A storage device records (reads) and/or retrieves (writes) items to and from storage media.
3. An output device is any hardware component that allows you to enter data and instructions into a computer.
4. Computer literacy involves having a current knowledge and understanding of computers and their uses.
5. Three commonly used input devices are a printer, a monitor, and speakers.

Quiz Yourself Online: To further check your knowledge of pages 2 through 7, visit the Microsoft Office and Concepts CourseMate Web site at www.cengagebrain.com, navigate to the Chapter 1 Quiz Yourself resource for this book, and then click Objectives 1 – 3.

Networks and the Internet

A **network** is a collection of computers and devices connected together, often wirelessly, via communications devices and transmission media. When a computer connects to a network, it is **online**. Networks allow computers to share **resources**, such as hardware, software, data, and information. Sharing resources saves time and money.

The Internet
For more information, visit the Microsoft Office and Concepts CourseMate Web site at www.cengagebrain.com, navigate to the Chapter 1 Web Link resource for this book, and then click The Internet.

The **Internet** is a worldwide collection of networks that connects millions of businesses, government agencies, educational institutions, and individuals (Figure 1-6). More than one billion people around the world use the Internet daily for a variety of reasons, including the following: to communicate with and meet other people; to conduct research and access a wealth of information and news; to shop for goods and services; to bank and invest; to participate in online training; to engage in entertaining activities, such as planning vacations, playing online games, listening to music, watching or editing videos, and books and magazines; to share information, photos, and videos; to download music and videos; and to access and interact with Web applications. Figure 1-7 shows examples in each of these areas.

Figure 1-6 The Internet is the largest computer network, connecting millions of computers and devices around the world.

Figure 1-7 Home and business users access the Internet for a variety of reasons.

People connect to the Internet to exchange information with others around the world. E-mail allows you to send and receive messages to and from other users (read Ethics & Issues 1-1 for a related discussion). With instant messaging, you can have a live conversation with another connected user. In a chat room, you can communicate with multiple users at the same time — much like a group discussion. You also can use the Internet to make a telephone call.

Businesses, called access providers, offer access to the Internet free or for a fee. By subscribing to an access provider, you can use your computer and a modem to connect to the many services of the Internet.

The **Web**, short for World Wide Web, is one of the more popular services on the Internet. The Web contains billions of documents called Web pages. A **Web page** can contain text, graphics, animation, audio, and video. The nine screens shown in Figure 1-7 on the previous page are examples of Web pages.

Web pages often have built-in connections, or links, to other documents, graphics, other Web pages, or Web sites. A **Web site** is a collection of related Web pages. Some Web sites allow users to access music and videos that can be downloaded, or transferred to storage media in a computer or portable media player. Once downloaded, you can listen to the music through speakers, headphones, or earbuds, or view the videos on a display device.

Anyone can create a Web page and then make it available, or publish it, on the Internet for others to see. Millions of people worldwide join online communities, each called a **social networking Web site** or **online social network**, that encourage members to share their interests, ideas, stories, photos, music, and videos with other registered users. Hundreds of thousands of people today also use blogs to publish their thoughts on the Web. A **blog** is an informal Web site consisting of time-stamped articles in a diary or journal format, usually listed in reverse chronological order. As others read the articles in a blog, they reply with their own thoughts (to learn more about creating and using blogs, complete the Learn How To 1 activity on page 34). Podcasts are a popular way people verbally share information on the Web. A **microblog**, such as Twitter, allows users to publish short messages, usually between 100 and 200 characters, for others to read. A **podcast** is recorded audio stored on a Web site that can be downloaded to a computer or a portable media player such as an iPod.

A **Web application** is a Web site that allows users to access and interact with software from any computer or device that is connected to the Internet. Examples of software available as Web applications include those that allow you to send and receive e-mail messages, prepare your taxes, organize digital photos, create documents, and play games.

Web sites such as social networking Web sites, blogs, and Web applications are categorized as Web 2.0 sites. The term **Web 2.0** refers to Web sites that provide a means for users to share personal information (such as social networking Web sites), allow users to modify the Web site contents (such as some blogs), and/or have software built into the site for users to access (such as Web applications).

Ethics & Issues

For the complete text of the Ethics & Issues boxes found in this chapter, visit the Microsoft Office and Concepts CourseMate Web site at www.cengagebrain.com and then navigate to the Chapter 1 Ethics & Issues resource for this book.

ETHICS & ISSUES 1-1

What Should Be Done about Identity Theft?

Using e-mail and other techniques on the Internet, scam artists are employing a technique known as phishing to try to steal your personal information, such as credit card numbers, banking information, and passwords. For example, an e-mail message may appear to be a request from your bank to verify your Social Security number and online banking password. Instead, the information you submit ends up in the hands of the scammer, who then uses the information for a variety of unethical and illegal acts. Sadly, the result often is identity theft. You can help to deter identity theft in several ways: 1) shred your financial documents before discarding them, 2) do not click links in unsolicited e-mail messages, and 3) enroll in a credit monitoring service. Consumer advocates often blame credit card companies and credit bureaus for lax security standards. Meanwhile, the companies blame consumers for being too gullible and forthcoming with private information. Both sides blame the government for poor privacy laws and light punishments for identity thieves. But while the arguments go on, law enforcement agencies bear the brunt of the problem by spending hundreds of millions of dollars responding to complaints and finding and processing the criminals.

Who should be responsible for protecting the public from online identity theft? Why? Should laws be changed to stop it, or should consumers change behavior? What is an appropriate punishment for identity thieves? Given the international nature of the Internet, how should foreign identity thieves be handled? Why?

FAQ 1-1

What U.S. Web sites are visited most frequently?

A recent survey found that Google's Web site is visited most frequently, with Microsoft and Yahoo! not far behind. The chart to the right shows the five most frequently visited Web sites, as well as the approximate number of unique visitors per month.

For more information, visit the Microsoft Office and Concepts CourseMate Web site at www.cengagebrain.com, navigate to the Chapter 1 FAQ resource for this book, and then click Top Web Sites.

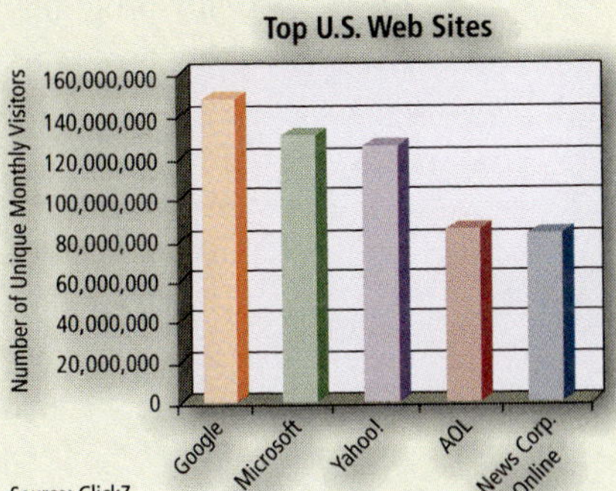

Source: ClickZ

An **FAQ** (frequently asked question) helps you find answers to commonly asked questions.

Computer Software

Software, also called a **program**, is a series of related instructions, organized for a common purpose, that tells the computer what task(s) to perform and how to perform them. You interact with a program through its user interface. Software today often has a graphical user interface. With a **graphical user interface** (**GUI** pronounced gooey), you interact with the software using text, graphics, and visual images such as icons. An icon is a miniature image that represents a program, an instruction, or some other object. You can use the mouse to select icons that perform operations such as starting a program.

The two categories of software are system software and application software. Figure 1-8 shows an example of each of these categories of software, which are explained in the following sections.

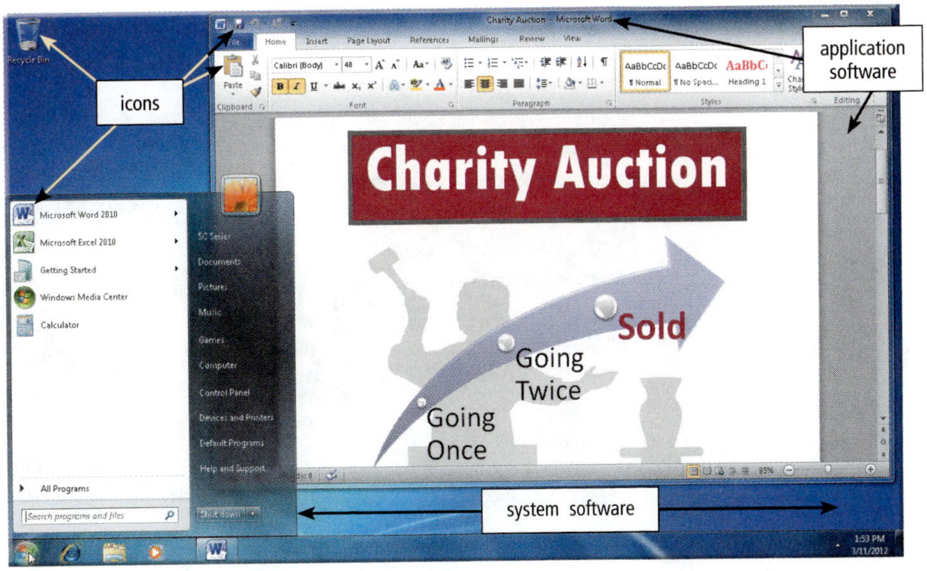

Figure 1-8 Today's system software and application software usually have a graphical user interface.

System Software

System software consists of the programs that control or maintain the operations of the computer and its devices. System software serves as the interface between the user, the application software, and the computer's hardware. Two types of system software are the operating system and utility programs.

Operating System An **operating system** is a set of programs that coordinates all the activities among computer hardware devices. It provides a means for users to communicate with the computer and other software. Many of today's computers use Microsoft's Windows, the latest version of which is shown in Figure 1-8, or Mac OS, Apple's operating system.

When a user starts a computer, portions of the operating system are copied into memory from the computer's hard disk. These parts of the operating system remain in memory while the computer is on.

Windows

For more information, visit the Microsoft Office and Concepts CourseMate Web site at www.cengagebrain.com, navigate to the Chapter 1 Web Link resource for this book, and then click Windows.

Utility Program A **utility program** allows a user to perform maintenance-type tasks usually related to managing a computer, its devices, or its programs. For example, you can use a utility program to transfer digital photos to an optical disc. Most operating systems include several utility programs for managing disk drives, printers, and other devices and media. You also can buy utility programs that allow you to perform additional computer management functions.

Application Software

Application software consists of programs designed to make users more productive and/or assist them with personal tasks. A widely used type of application software related to communications is a Web browser, which allows users with an Internet connection to access and view Web pages or access programs. Other popular application software includes word processing software, spreadsheet software, database software, and presentation software.

Many other types of application software exist that enable users to perform a variety of tasks. These include personal information management, note taking, project management, accounting, document management, computer-aided design, desktop publishing, paint/image editing, audio and video editing, multimedia authoring, Web page authoring, personal finance, legal, tax preparation, home design/landscaping, travel and mapping, education, reference, and entertainment (e.g., games or simulations).

Software is available at stores that sell computer products (Figure 1-9) and also online at many Web sites.

Figure 1-9 Stores that sell computer products have shelves stocked with software for sale.

Installing and Running Programs

When purchasing software from a retailer, you typically receive a box that includes an optical disc(s) that contains the program. If you acquire software from a Web site on the Internet, you may be able to download the program; that is, the program transfers from the Web site to the hard disk in your computer.

The instructions in software are placed on storage media, either locally or online. To use software that is stored locally, such as on a hard disk or optical disc, you usually need to install the software. Web applications that are stored online, by contrast, usually do not need to be installed.

Installing is the process of setting up software to work with the computer, printer, and other hardware. When you buy a computer, it usually has some software preinstalled on its hard disk. This enables you to use the computer the first time you turn it on. To begin installing additional software from an optical disc, insert the program disc in an optical disc drive. To install downloaded software, the Web site typically provides instructions for how to install the program on your hard disk.

Once installed, you can run the program. When you instruct the computer to **run** an installed program, the computer loads it, which means the program is copied from storage to memory. Once in memory, the computer can carry out, or **execute**, the instructions in the program so that you can use the program. Figure 1-10 illustrates the steps that occur when a user installs and runs a program.

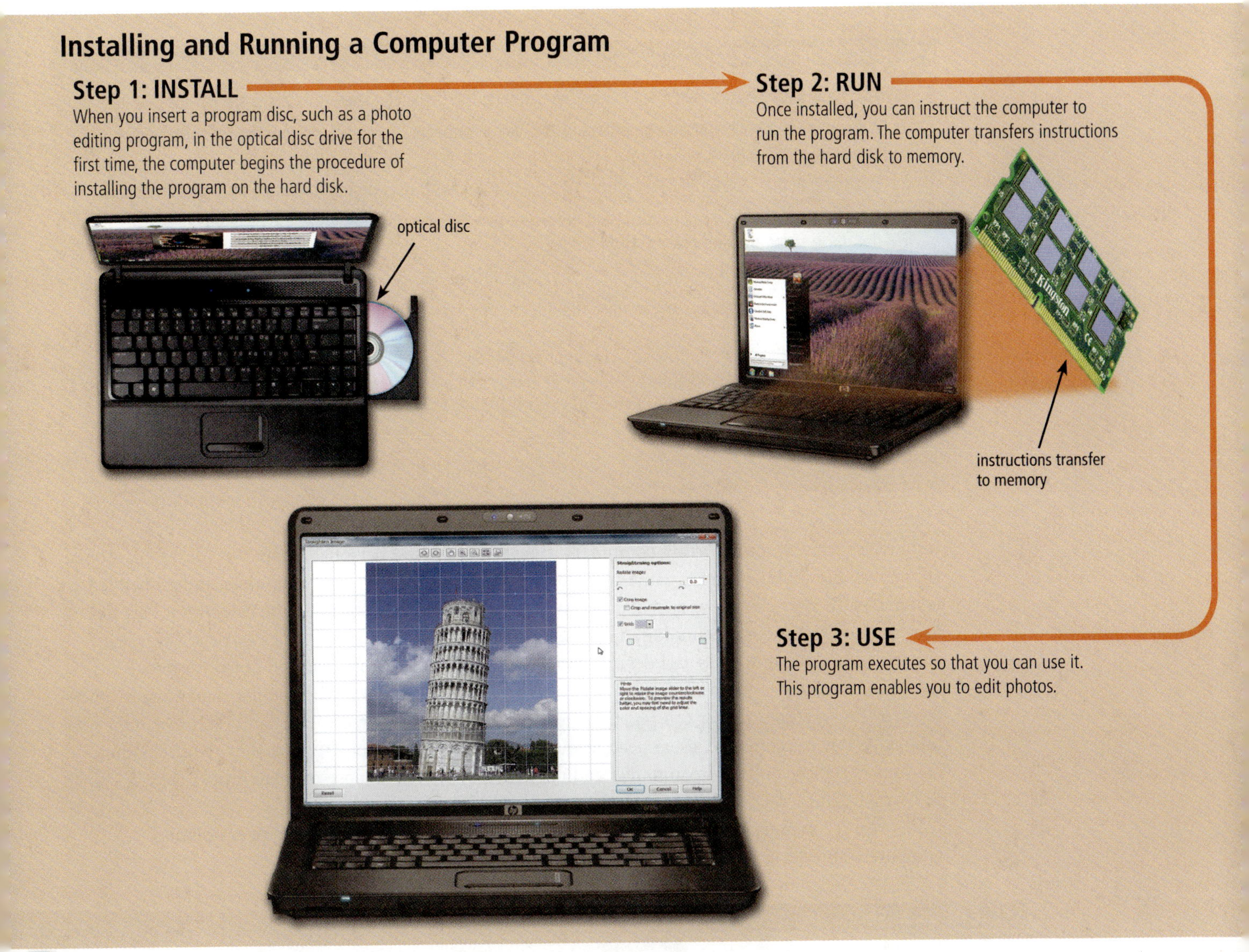

Figure 1-10 This figure shows how to install and run a computer program.

Software Development

A **programmer**, sometimes called a **developer**, is someone who develops software or writes the instructions that direct the computer to process data into information. Complex programs can require thousands to millions of instructions.

Programmers use a programming language or program development tool to create computer programs. Popular programming languages include C++, Visual C#, Visual Basic, JavaScript, and Java. Figure 1-11 shows a simple Visual Basic program.

```
Public Class frmPayrollInformation

    Private Sub btnCalculatePay_Click(ByVal sender As System.Object, ByVal e As System.
    EventArgs) Handles btnCalculatePay.Click
        'This procedure executes when the user clicks the
        'Calculate Pay button. It calculates regular
        'and overtime pay and displays it in the window.

        ' Declare variables
        Dim strHoursWorked As String
        Dim strHourlyRate As String
        Dim decHoursWorked As Decimal
        Dim decHourlyRate As Decimal
        Dim decRegularPay As Decimal
        Dim decOvertimeHours As Decimal
        Dim decOvertimePay As Decimal
        Dim decTotalPay As Decimal

        ' Calculate and display payroll information
        strHoursWorked = Me.txtHoursWorked.Text
        strHourlyRate = Me.txtHourlyRate.Text
        decHoursWorked = Convert.ToDecimal(strHoursWorked)
        decHourlyRate = Convert.ToDecimal(strHourlyRate)

        If decHoursWorked > 40 Then
            decRegularPay = 40 * decHourlyRate
            Me.txtRegularPay.Text = decRegularPay.ToString("C")
            decOvertimeHours = decHoursWorked - 40
            decOvertimePay = (1.5 * decOvertimeHours) * decHourlyRate
            Me.txtOvertimePay.Text = decOvertimePay.ToString("C")
            decTotalPay = decRegularPay + decOvertimePay
            Me.txtTotalPay.Text = decTotalPay.ToString("C")
        Else
            decRegularPay = decHoursWorked * decHourlyRate
            Me.txtRegularPay.Text = decRegularPay.ToString("C")
            Me.txtOvertimePay.Text = "$0.00"
            Me.txtTotalPay.Text = decRegularPay.ToString("C")
        End If
    End Sub
End Class
```

Figure 1-11 Some of the instructions in a program.

QUIZ YOURSELF 1-2

Instructions: Find the true statement below. Then, rewrite the remaining false statements so that they are true.

1. A resource is a collection of computers and devices connected together via communications devices and transmission media.
2. Installing is the process of setting up software to work with the computer, printer, and other hardware.
3. Popular system software includes Web browsers, word processing software, spreadsheet software, database software, and presentation software.
4. The Internet is one of the more popular services on the Web.
5. Two types of application software are the operating system and utility programs.

Quiz Yourself Online: To further check your knowledge of pages 8 through 13, visit the Microsoft Office and Concepts CourseMate Web site at www.cengagebrain.com, navigate to the Chapter 1 Quiz Yourself resource for this book, and then click Objectives 4 – 5.

Categories of Computers

Industry experts typically classify computers in seven categories: personal computers (desktop), mobile computers and mobile devices, game consoles, servers, mainframes, supercomputers, and embedded computers. A computer's size, speed, processing power, and price determine the category it best fits. Due to rapidly changing technology, however, the distinction among categories is not always clear-cut. This trend of computers and devices with technologies that overlap, called **convergence**, leads to computer manufacturers continually releasing newer models that include similar functionality and features. For example, newer cell phones often include media player, camera, and Web browsing capabilities. As devices converge, users need fewer devices for the functionality that they require. When consumers replace outdated computers and devices, they should dispose of them properly (read Ethics & Issues 1-2 for a related discussion).

Figure 1-12 summarizes the seven categories of computers. The following pages discuss computers and devices that fall in each category.

ETHICS & ISSUES 1-2

Should Recycling of Electronics Be Made Easier?

Experts estimate that about one billion computers have been discarded to date. The discarded items often are known as e-waste. As technology advances and prices fall, many people think of computers, cell phones, and portable media players as disposable items. These items often contain several toxic elements, including lead, mercury, and barium. Computers and mobile devices thrown into landfills or burned in incinerators can pollute the ground and the air. A vast amount of e-waste ends up polluting third world countries. One solution is to recycle old electronic equipment, but the recycling effort has made little progress especially when compared to recycling programs for paper, glass, and plastic. Some lawmakers prefer an aggressive approach, such as setting up a recycling program that would be paid for by adding a $10 fee to the purchase price of computers and computer equipment, or forcing computer manufacturers to be responsible for collecting and recycling their products. California already requires a recycling fee for any products sold that include certain electronic equipment. Manufacturers have taken steps, such as offering to recycle old computers and using energy efficient and environmentally friendly manufacturing techniques, but some claim that consumers should bear the responsibility of disposing of their old computer parts. While some companies have set up recycling programs, many claim that forcing them to bear the cost of recycling programs puts the company at a competitive disadvantage when compared to foreign companies that may not be forced to maintain a recycling program.

Why is electronics recycling not as popular as other types of recycling? How can companies make it easier to recycle electronics while being compensated fairly for the cost of recycling? Should the government, manufacturers, or users be responsible for recycling of obsolete equipment? Why? Should the government mandate a recycling program for electronics? Why or why not?

Categories of Computers

Category	Physical Size	Number of Simultaneously Connected Users	General Price Range
Personal computers (desktop)	Fits on a desk	Usually one (can be more if networked)	Several hundred to several thousand dollars
Mobile computers and mobile devices	Fits on your lap or in your hand	Usually one	Less than a hundred dollars to several thousand dollars
Game consoles	Small box or handheld device	One to several	Several hundred dollars or less
Servers	Small cabinet	Two to thousands	Several hundred to a million dollars
Mainframes	Partial room to a full room of equipment	Hundreds to thousands	$300,000 to several million dollars
Supercomputers	Full room of equipment	Hundreds to thousands	$500,000 to several billion dollars
Embedded computers	Miniature	Usually one	Embedded in the price of the product

Figure 1-12 This table summarizes some of the differences among the categories of computers. These should be considered general guidelines only because of rapid changes in technology.

Personal Computers

A **personal computer** is a computer that can perform all of its input, processing, output, and storage activities by itself. A personal computer contains a processor, memory, and one or more input, output, and storage devices. Personal computers also often contain a communications device.

Two popular architectures of personal computers are the PC (Figure 1-13) and the Apple (Figure 1-14). The term, PC-compatible, refers to any personal computer based on the original IBM personal computer design. Companies such as Dell and Toshiba sell PC-compatible computers. PC and PC-compatible computers usually use a Windows operating system. Apple computers usually use a Macintosh operating system (Mac OS).

Two types of personal computers are desktop computers and notebook computers.

? FAQ 1-2

Are PCs or Apple computers more popular?

While PCs still are more popular than Apple computers, Apple computer sales have been rising consistently during the past few years. In fact, Apple computer sales now account for more than 20 percent of all computer sales in the United States, with that number estimated to grow for the foreseeable future.

For more information, visit the Microsoft Office and Concepts CourseMate Web site at www.cengagebrain.com, navigate to the Chapter 1 FAQ resource for this book, and then click Personal Computer Sales.

Figure 1-13 PC and PC-compatible computers usually use a Windows operating system.

Figure 1-14 Apple computers, such as the iMac, usually use a Macintosh operating system.

Desktop Computers

A **desktop computer** is designed so that the system unit, input devices, output devices, and any other devices fit entirely on or under a desk or table. In some models, the monitor sits on top of the system unit, which is placed on the desk. The more popular style of system unit is the tall and narrow tower, which can sit on the floor vertically.

Mobile Computers and Mobile Devices

A **mobile computer** is a personal computer you can carry from place to place. Similarly, a **mobile device** is a computing device small enough to hold in your hand. The most popular type of mobile computer is the notebook computer.

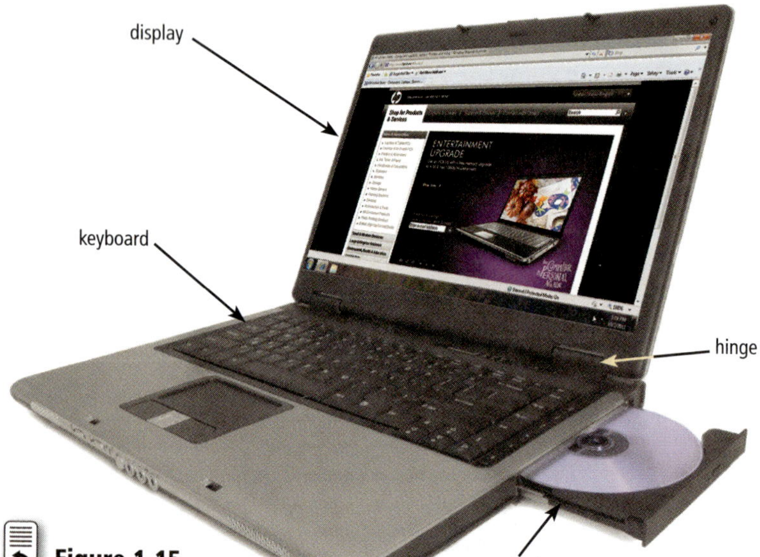

Figure 1-15
On a typical notebook computer, the keyboard is on top of the system unit, and the display attaches to the system unit with hinges.

Notebook Computers

A **notebook computer**, also called a **laptop computer**, is a portable, personal computer often designed to fit on your lap. Notebook computers are thin and lightweight, yet can be as powerful as the average desktop computer. A **netbook**, which is a type of notebook computer, is smaller, lighter, and often not as powerful as a traditional notebook computer. Most netbooks cost less than traditional notebook computers, usually only a few hundred dollars. Some notebook computers have touch screens, allowing you to interact with the device by touching the screen, usually with the tip of a finger.

On a typical notebook computer, the keyboard is on top of the system unit, and the display attaches to the system unit with hinges (Figure 1-15). These computers weigh on average from 2.5 to more than 10 pounds (depending on configuration), which allows users easily to transport the computers from place to place. Most notebook computers can operate on batteries or a power supply or both.

Tablet PCs Resembling a letter-sized slate, the **Tablet PC**, or tablet computer, is a special type of notebook computer that you can interact with by touching the screen with your finger or a digital pen. One design of Tablet PC, called a convertible tablet, has an attached keyboard. Another design, which does not include a keyboard, is called a slate tablet (Figure 1-16) and provides other means for typing. Tablet PCs are useful especially for taking notes in locations where the standard notebook computer is not practical.

Figure 1-16
The iPad is a widely used slate tablet.

Mobile Devices

Mobile devices, which are small enough to carry in a pocket, usually store programs and data permanently on memory inside the system unit or on small storage media such as memory cards. You often can connect a mobile device to a personal computer to exchange information. Some mobile devices are **Internet-enabled**, meaning they can connect to the Internet wirelessly. Because of their reduced size, the screens on handheld computers are small.

Popular types of mobile devices are smart phones and PDAs, e-book readers, handheld computers, portable media players, and digital cameras.

Smart Phones and PDAs Offering the convenience of one-handed operation, a **smart phone** (Figure 1-17) is an Internet-enabled phone that usually also provides personal information management functions such as a calendar, an appointment book, an address book, a calculator, and a notepad. In addition to basic phone capabilities, a smart phone allows you to send and receive e-mail messages and access the Web — usually for an additional fee. Many models also function as a portable media player and include built-in digital cameras so that you can share photos or videos. Many smart phones also offer a variety ofapplication software such as word processing, spreadsheet, and games.

Figure 1-17 Some smart phones have touch screens; others have mini keyboards.

Many smart phones have keypads that contain both numbers and letters so that you can use the same keypad to dial phone numbers and enter messages. Others have a built-in mini keyboard. Some have touch screens, and some include a stylus. Instead of calling someone's smart phone or cell phone, users often send messages to others by pressing buttons on their phone's keypad, keys on the mini keyboard, or images on an on-screen keyboard. Types of messages users send with smart phones include text messages, instant messages, picture messages, and video messages.

- A **text message** is a short note, typically fewer than 300 characters, sent to or from a smart phone or other mobile device.
- An **instant message** is a real-time Internet communication, where you exchange messages with other connected users.
- A **picture message** is a photo or other image, sometimes along with sound and text, sent to or from a smart phone or other mobile device. A phone that can send picture messages often is called a **camera phone**.
- A **video message** is a short video clip, usually about 30 seconds, sent to or from a smart phone or other mobile device. A phone that can send video messages often is called a **video phone**.

A **PDA** (personal digital assistant), which often looks like a smart phone, provides personal information management functions such as a calendar, an appointment book, an address book, a calculator, and a notepad. A PDA differs from a smart phone in that it usually does not provide phone capabilities and may not be Internet-enabled, support voice input, have a built-in camera, or function as a portable media player.

Figure 1-18 An e-book reader.

E-Book Readers An **e-book reader** (short for electronic book reader), or e-reader, is a handheld device that is used primarily for reading e-books (Figure 1-18). An **e-book**, or digital book, is an electronic version of a printed book, readable on computers and other digital devices. Most e-book readers have a touch screen and are Internet-enabled.

Handheld Computers A **handheld computer**, sometimes referred to as an **Ultra-Mobile PC (UMPC)**, is a computer small enough to fit in one hand. Industry-specific handheld computers serve mobile employees, such as parcel delivery people, whose jobs require them to move from place to place.

Portable Media Players A **portable media player** is a mobile device on which you can store, organize, and play digital media (Figure 1-19). For example, you can listen to music; watch videos, movies, and television shows; and view photos on the device's screen. With most, you download the digital media from a computer to the portable media player or to media that you insert in the device.

Figure 1-19 The iPod, shown here, is a popular portable media player.

Portable media players usually include a set of earbuds, which are small speakers that rest inside each ear canal. Some portable media players have a touch screen; others have a touch-sensitive pad that you operate with a thumb or finger, to navigate through digital media, adjust volume, and customize settings.

Digital Cameras A **digital camera** is a device that allows users to take pictures and store the photographed images digitally, instead of on traditional film (Figure 1-20). Although digital cameras usually have some amount of internal storage to hold images, most users store images on small storage media such as memory cards. Digital cameras typically allow users to review, and sometimes modify, images while they are in the camera.

Often users prefer to download images from the digital camera to the computer. Or, you can remove the storage media such as a memory card from the digital camera and insert it in a card reader in or attached to the computer.

Figure 1-20 With a digital camera, users can view photographed images immediately through a small screen on the camera to see if the picture is worth keeping.

Digital Cameras
For more information, visit the Microsoft Office and Concepts CourseMate Web site at www.cengagebrain.com, navigate to the Chapter 1 Web Link resource for this book, and then click Digital Cameras.

INNOVATIVE COMPUTING 1-1

Wii a Welcome Medical Skill Builder

A patient awaiting laparoscopic procedures may be less tense knowing that the surgeons have honed their dexterity and coordination using a Nintendo Wii. Preliminary studies have found that doctors can improve their fine motor control by playing video games that emphasize subtle hand movements used in minimally invasive surgeries. Researchers are developing Wii surgery simulators that will allow doctors to practice their skills at home or in break rooms at hospitals.

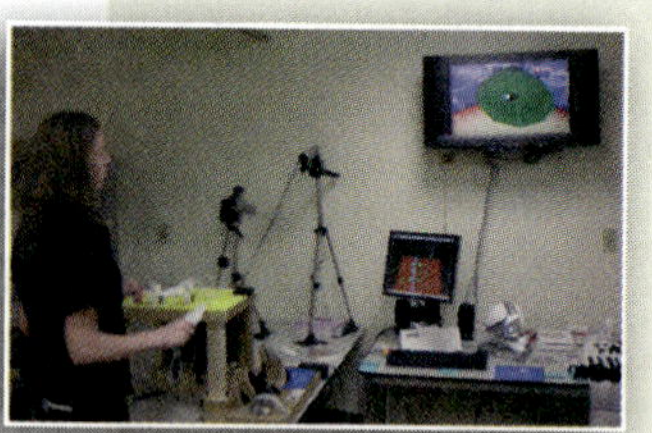

The Wii game system is finding a medical home in other nontraditional places. Physical therapists urge arthritic patients to use Wiihabilitation to build endurance and increase their range of motion. Therapeutic recreation with the Wii's sports games may help patients recovering from strokes, fractures, and combat injuries.

Researchers in a testing lab in California are experimenting with using the Wii's motion-activated controls in non-gaming applications, such as allowing doctors to explain X-ray images to patients.

For more information, visit the Microsoft Office and Concepts CourseMate Web site at www.cengagebrain.com, navigate to the Chapter 1 Innovative Computing resource for this book, and then click Medical Wii.

Game Consoles

A **game console** is a mobile computing device designed for single-player or multiplayer video games (Figure 1-21). Standard game consoles use a handheld controller(s) as an input device(s); a television screen as an output device; and hard disks, optical discs, and/or memory cards for storage. The compact size and light weight of game consoles make them easy to use at home, in the car, in a hotel, or any location that has an electrical outlet. Three popular models are Microsoft's Xbox 360, Nintendo's Wii (pronounced wee), and Sony's PlayStation 3. Read Innovative Computing 1-1 for a look at how Nintendo Wii applications are being used in the medical field.

A handheld game console is small enough to fit in one hand. With the handheld game console, the controls, screen, and speakers are built into the device. Some models use cartridges to store games; others use a memory card or a miniature optical disc. Many handheld game consoles can communicate wirelessly with other similar consoles for multiplayer gaming. Two popular models are Nintendo DS Lite and Sony's PlayStation Portable (PSP).

In addition to gaming, many game console models allow users to listen to music, watch movies, keep fit, and connect to the Internet.

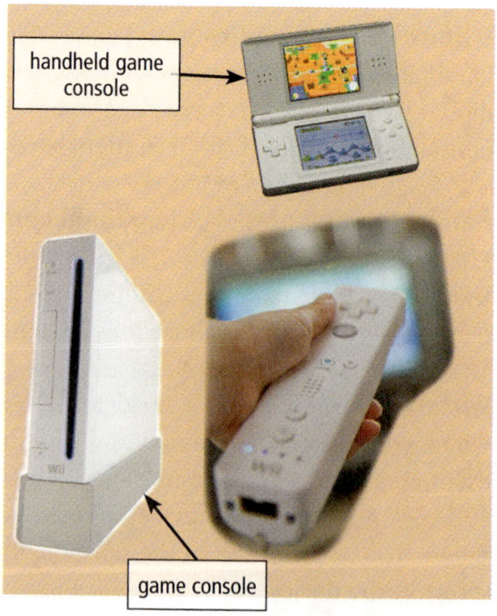

Figure 1-21 Game consoles provide hours of video game entertainment.

Servers

Figure 1-22 A server controls access to resources on a network.

A **server** controls access to the hardware, software, and other resources on a network and provides a centralized storage area for programs, data, and information (Figure 1-22). Servers support from two to several thousand connected computers at the same time.

People use personal computers or terminals to access data, information, and programs on a server. A terminal is a device with a monitor, keyboard, and memory.

Mainframes

Figure 1-23 Mainframe computers can handle thousands of connected computers and process millions of instructions per second.

A **mainframe** is a large, expensive, powerful computer that can handle hundreds or thousands of connected users simultaneously (Figure 1-23). Mainframes store huge amounts of data, instructions, and information. Most major corporations use mainframes for business activities. With mainframes, enterprises are able to bill millions of customers, prepare payroll for thousands of employees, and manage thousands of items in inventory. One study reported that mainframes process more than 83 percent of transactions around the world.

Servers and other mainframes can access data and information from a mainframe. People also can access programs on the mainframe using terminals or personal computers.

Supercomputers

Figure 1-24 This supercomputer, IBM's Roadrunner, can process more than one quadrillion instructions in a single second.

A **supercomputer** is the fastest, most powerful computer — and the most expensive (Figure 1-24). The fastest supercomputers are capable of processing more than one quadrillion instructions in a single second.

Applications requiring complex, sophisticated mathematical calculations use supercomputers. Large-scale simulations and applications in medicine, aerospace, automotive design, online banking, weather forecasting, nuclear energy research, and petroleum exploration use a supercomputer.

Embedded Computers

An **embedded computer** is a special-purpose computer that functions as a component in a larger product. A variety of everyday products contain embedded computers:

- Consumer electronics
- Home automation devices
- Automobiles
- Process controllers and robotics
- Computer devices and office machines

Because embedded computers are components in larger products, they usually are small and have limited hardware. Embedded computers perform various functions, depending on the requirements of the product in which they reside. Embedded computers in printers, for example, monitor the amount of paper in the tray, check the ink or toner level, signal if a paper jam has occurred, and so on. Figure 1-25 shows some of the many embedded computers in cars.

Figure 1-25 Some of the embedded computers designed to improve your safety, security, and performance in today's automobiles.

Examples of Computer Usage

Every day, people around the world rely on different types of computers for a variety of applications. To illustrate the range of uses for computers, this section takes you on a visual and narrative tour of five categories of users: a home user, a small office/home office (SOHO) user, a mobile user, a power user, and an enterprise user.

Home User

In an increasing number of homes, the computer is a basic necessity. Each family member, or **home user**, spends time on the computer for different reasons. These include personal financial management, Web access, communications, and entertainment (Figure 1-26).

On the Internet, home users access a huge amount of information, conduct research, take college classes, pay bills, manage investments, shop, listen to the radio, watch movies, read books, file taxes, book airline reservations, make telephone calls, and play games. They also communicate with others around the world through e-mail, blogs, instant messages, and chat rooms. Home users share ideas, interests, photos, music, and videos on social networking Web sites.

With a digital camera, home users take photos and then send the electronic images to others. Many home users have a portable media player, so that they can listen to downloaded music and/or podcasts at a later time through earbuds attached to the player. They also usually have one or more game consoles to play video games.

Today's homes typically have one or more desktop computers. Some home users network multiple desktop computers throughout the house, often wirelessly. These small networks allow family members to share an Internet connection and a printer.

Home users have a variety of software. They type letters, homework assignments, and other documents with word processing software. Personal finance software helps the home user with personal finances, investments, and family budgets. Other software assists with preparing taxes, keeping a household inventory, setting up maintenance schedules, and protecting computers against threats and unauthorized intrusions.

Reference software, such as encyclopedias, medical dictionaries, or a road atlas, provides valuable information for everyone in the family. With entertainment software, the home user can play games, compose music, research genealogy, or create greeting cards. Educational software helps adults learn to speak a foreign language and youngsters to read, write, count, and spell.

FAQ 1-3

How many households do not use the Internet or related technologies?

A recent survey estimates that 18 percent of U.S. households have no Internet access. Furthermore, about 20 percent of U.S. heads of households have never sent an e-mail message. The chart to the right illustrates the lack of experience with computer and Internet technology.

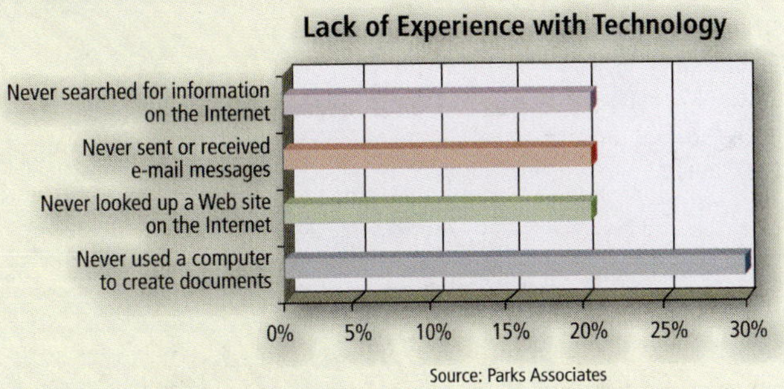

For more information, visit the Microsoft Office and Concepts CourseMate Web site at www.cengagebrain.com, navigate to the Chapter 1 FAQ resource for this book, and then click Experience with Technology.

Figure 1-26 The home user spends time on a computer for a variety of reasons.

Small Office/Home Office User

Computers assist small business and home office users in managing their resources effectively. A **small office/home office (SOHO)** includes any company with fewer than 50 employees, as well as the self-employed who work from home. Small offices include local law practices, accounting firms, travel agencies, and florists. SOHO users typically use a desktop computer. Many also use smart phones.

SOHO users access the Internet — often wirelessly — to look up information such as addresses, directions, postal codes, flights (Figure 1-27a), and package shipping rates or to send and receive e-mail messages, or make telephone calls. Many have entered the e-commerce arena and conduct business on the Web. Their Web sites advertise products and services and may provide a means for taking orders.

To save money on hardware and software, small offices often network their computers. For example, the small office connects one printer to a network for all employees to share.

SOHO users often work with basic business software such as word processing and spreadsheet programs that assist with document preparation and finances (Figure 1-27b). They are likely to use other industry-specific types of software. An auto parts store, for example, will have software that allows for looking up parts, taking orders and payments, and updating inventory.

Figure 1-27a (Web access)

Figure 1-27b (spreadsheet program)

Figure 1-27 People with a home office and employees in small offices typically use a personal computer for some or all of their duties.

Mobile User

Today, businesses and schools are expanding to serve people across the country and around the world. Thus, increasingly more employees and students are **mobile users**, who work on a mobile computer or device while away from a main office, home office, or school (Figure 1-28). Some examples of mobile users are sales representatives, real estate agents, insurance agents, meter readers, package delivery people, journalists, and students.

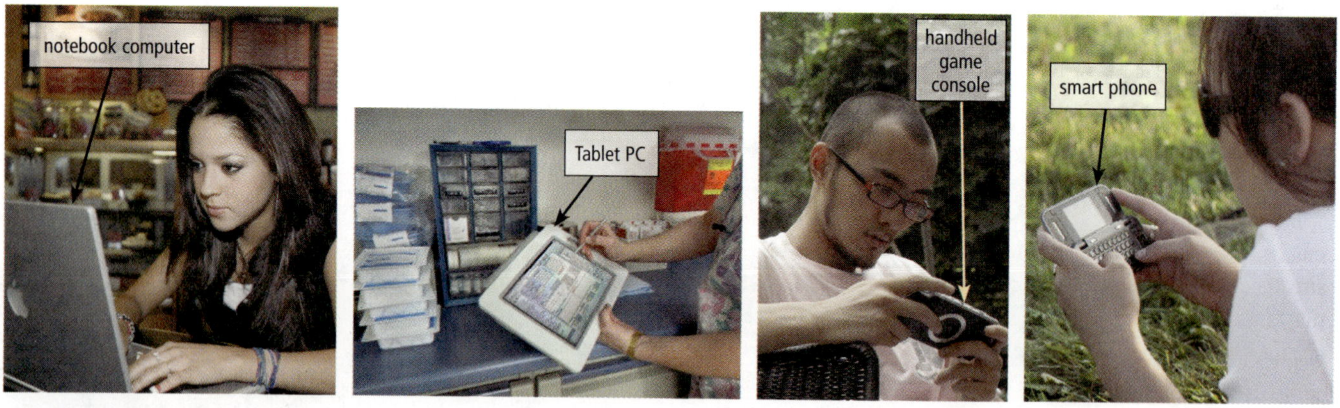

Figure 1-28 Mobile users have a variety of computers and devices so that they can work, do homework, send messages, connect to the Internet, or play games while away from a wired connection.

Mobile users often have a mobile computer and/or mobile device. With these computers and devices, the mobile user can connect to other computers on a network or the Internet, often wirelessly accessing services such as e-mail and the Web. Mobile users can transfer information between their mobile devices and another computer. For entertainment, the mobile user plays video games on a handheld game console and listens to music or watches movies on a portable media player.

The mobile user works with basic business software such as word processing and spreadsheet software. With presentation software, the mobile user can create and deliver presentations to a large audience by connecting a mobile computer or device to a video projector that displays the presentation on a full screen.

Power User

Another category of user, called a **power user**, requires the capabilities of a powerful desktop computer, called a workstation. Examples of power users include engineers, scientists, architects, desktop publishers, and graphic artists (Figure 1-29). Power users typically work with multimedia, combining text, graphics, audio, and video into one application. These users need computers with extremely fast processors because of the nature of their work.

The power user's workstation contains industry-specific software. For example, engineers and architects use software to draft and design floor plans, mechanical assemblies, or vehicles. A desktop publisher uses software to prepare marketing literature. A graphic artist uses software to create sophisticated drawings. This software usually is expensive because of its specialized design.

Power users exist in all types of businesses. Some also work at home. Their computers typically have network connections and Internet access.

Figure 1-29 This graphic artist uses a powerful computer to develop computer games.

Enterprise User

An enterprise has hundreds or thousands of employees or customers that work in or do business with offices across a region, the country, or the world. Each employee or customer who uses a computer in the enterprise is an **enterprise user** (Figure 1-30).

Many large companies use the words, **enterprise computing**, to refer to the huge network of computers that meets their diverse computing needs. The network facilitates communications among employees at all locations. Users access the network through desktop computers, mobile computers, and mobile devices.

Enterprises use computers and the computer network to process high volumes of transactions in a single day. Although they may differ in size and in the products or services offered, all generally use computers for basic business activities. For example, they bill millions of customers or prepare payroll for thousands of employees. Some enterprises use blogs to open communications among employees and/or customers.

Enterprises typically have e-commerce Web sites, allowing customers and vendors to conduct business online. The Web site showcases products, services, and other company information. Customers, vendors, and other interested parties can access this information on the Web.

The marketing department in an enterprise uses desktop publishing software to prepare marketing literature. The accounting department uses software for accounts receivable, accounts payable, billing, general ledger, and payroll activities.

Figure 1-30 An enterprise can have hundreds or thousands of users in offices across a region, the country, or the world.

Enterprise Computing

For more information, visit the Microsoft Office and Concepts CourseMate Web site at www.cengagebrain.com, navigate to the Chapter 1 Web Link resource for this book, and then click Enterprise Computing.

Enterprise users work with word processing, spreadsheet, database, and presentation software. They also may use calendar programs to post their schedules on the network. And, they might use smart phones or other mobile devices to maintain contact information. E-mail programs and Web browsers enable communications among employees, vendors, and customers.

Many employees of enterprises today telecommute. **Telecommuting** is a work arrangement in which employees work away from a company's standard workplace and often communicate with the office through the computer. Employees who telecommute have flexible work schedules so that they can combine work and personal responsibilities, such as child care.

Computer Applications in Society

The computer has changed society today as much as the industrial revolution changed society in the eighteenth and nineteenth centuries.

People interact directly with computers in fields such as education, finance, government, health care, science, publishing, travel, and manufacturing. In addition, they can reap the benefits from breakthroughs and advances in these fields. The following pages describe how computers have made a difference in people's interactions with these disciplines. Read Looking Ahead 1-1 for a look at how embedded computers may improve the quality of life.

LOOKING AHEAD 1-1

Embedded Computers May Improve Quality of Life

The weather forecast may be as close as your fingertips if plans to integrate embedded computers in everyday objects become a reality. Researchers are envisioning an umbrella with an embedded cell phone in the handle that will dial and then download the local forecast. The handle will glow green for good weather and flash red for imminent storms.

Dancers can pin a small flower with an embedded motion-detecting computer to their clothes. When they move, the embedded computer senses action and then synchronizes the tempo of music to this movement. Other embedded computers woven into clothing can monitor heart and breathing rates.

Wearing hidden embedded computers can help the elderly and people recovering from accidents and surgeries monitor their walking stride and pace. When their steps are uneven, the embedded computer can sound a warning and perhaps prevent a fall. Other embedded computers can give subtle feedback on the quality of physical activity.

For more information, visit the Microsoft Office and Concepts CourseMate Web site at www.cengagebrain.com, navigate to the Chapter 1 Looking Ahead resource for this book, and then click Embedded Computers.

Education

Education is the process of acquiring knowledge. In the traditional model, people learn from other people such as parents, teachers, and employers. Many forms of printed material such as books and manuals are used as learning tools. Today, educators also are turning to computers to assist with education (Figure 1-31).

Figure 1-31 In some schools, students have mobile computers on their desks during classroom lectures.

Many schools and companies equip labs and classrooms with computers. Some schools require students to have a mobile computer or mobile device to access the school's network or Internet wirelessly.

Students use software to assist with learning or to complete assignments. To promote education by computer, many vendors offer substantial student discounts on software.

Sometimes, the delivery of education occurs at one place while the learning occurs at other locations. For example, students can take a class on the Web. More than 70 percent of colleges offer distance learning classes. A few even offer entire degrees online.

Finance

Many people and companies use computers to help manage their finances. Some use finance software to balance checkbooks, pay bills, track personal income and expenses, manage investments, and evaluate financial plans. This software usually includes a variety of online services. For example, computer users can track investments and do online banking. With **online banking**, users access account balances, pay bills, and copy monthly transactions from the bank's computer right into their computers (Figure 1-32).

Investors often use **online investing** to buy and sell stocks and bonds — without using a broker. With online investing, the transaction fee for each trade usually is much less than when trading through a broker.

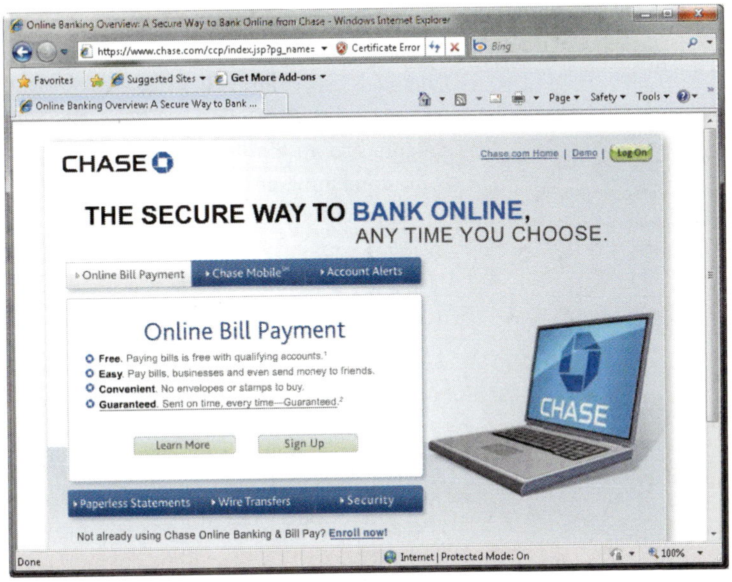

Figure 1-32 An online banking Web site.

Government

A government provides society with direction by making and administering policies. To provide citizens with up-to-date information, most government offices have Web sites. People access government Web sites to file taxes, apply for permits and licenses, pay parking tickets, buy stamps, report crimes, apply for financial aid, and renew vehicle registrations and driver's licenses.

Employees of government agencies use computers as part of their daily routine. Military and other agency officials use the U.S. Department of Homeland Security's network of information about domestic security threats to help protect our nation. Law enforcement officers have online access to the FBI's National Crime Information Center (NCIC) through in-vehicle computers, fingerprint readers, and mobile devices (Figure 1-33). The NCIC contains more than 52 million missing persons and criminal records, including names, fingerprints, parole/probation records, mug shots, and other information.

Figure 1-33 Law enforcement officials have in-vehicle computers and mobile devices to access emergency, missing person, and criminal records in computer networks in local, state, and federal agencies.

Health Care

Nearly every area of health care uses computers. Whether you are visiting a family doctor for a regular checkup, having lab work or an outpatient test, or being rushed in for emergency surgery, the medical staff around you will be using computers for various purposes:

- Doctors use the Web and medical software to assist with researching and diagnosing health conditions.
- Doctors use e-mail to correspond with patients.
- Pharmacists use computers to file insurance claims.
- Robots deliver medication to nurse stations in hospitals.
- Hospitals and doctors use computers and mobile devices to maintain and access patient records.

- Computers and computerized devices assist doctors, nurses, and technicians with medical tests (Figure 1-34).
- Computers monitor patients' vital signs in hospital rooms and at home.
- Surgeons implant computerized devices, such as pacemakers, that allow patients to live longer.
- Surgeons use computer-controlled devices to provide them with greater precision during operations, such as for laser eye surgery and robot-assisted heart surgery.

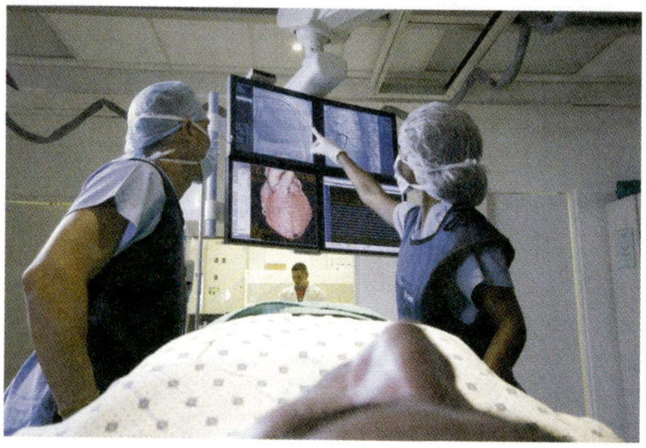

Figure 1-34 Doctors, nurses, technicians, and other medical staff use computers and computerized devices to assist with medical tests.

Two forms of long-distance health care are telemedicine and telesurgery. Through **telemedicine**, health-care professionals in separate locations conduct live conferences on the computer. For example, a doctor at one location can have a conference with a doctor at another location to discuss a bone X-ray. Live images of each doctor, along with the X-ray, are displayed on each doctor's computer.

With **telesurgery**, a surgeon performs an operation on a patient who is not located in the same physical room as the surgeon. Telesurgery enables surgeons to direct robots to perform an operation via computers connected to a high-speed network.

Science

All branches of science, from biology to astronomy to meteorology, use computers to assist them with collecting, analyzing, and modeling data. Scientists also use the Internet to communicate with colleagues around the world.

Breakthroughs in surgery, medicine, and treatments often result from scientists' use of computers. Tiny computers now imitate functions of the central nervous system, retina of the eye, and cochlea of the ear. A cochlear implant allows a deaf person to listen. Electrodes implanted in the brain stop tremors associated with Parkinson's disease. Cameras small enough to swallow — sometimes called a camera pill — take pictures inside your body to detect polyps, cancer, and other abnormalities (Figure 1-35).

How a Camera Pill Works

Step 1
A patient swallows a tiny capsule that contains a miniature disposable camera, lights, a transmitter, and batteries. The camera is positioned at the clear end of the capsule.

Step 2
As the capsule moves through the inside of the patient's body, the camera snaps about 50,000 pictures, which are transmitted to a recording device worn as a belt on the patient's waist.

Step 3
The doctor transfers the data on the recording device to a computer so that it can be processed and analyzed.

Figure 1-35 This figure shows how a camera pill works.

Publishing

Publishing is the process of making works available to the public. These works include books, magazines, newspapers, music, film, and video. Special software assists graphic designers in developing pages that include text, graphics, and photos; artists in composing and enhancing songs; filmmakers in creating and editing film; and journalists and mobile users in capturing and modifying video clips.

Many publishers make their works available online (Figure 1-36). Some Web sites allow you to copy the work, such as a book or music, to your desktop computer, mobile computer, smart phone, or other mobile device.

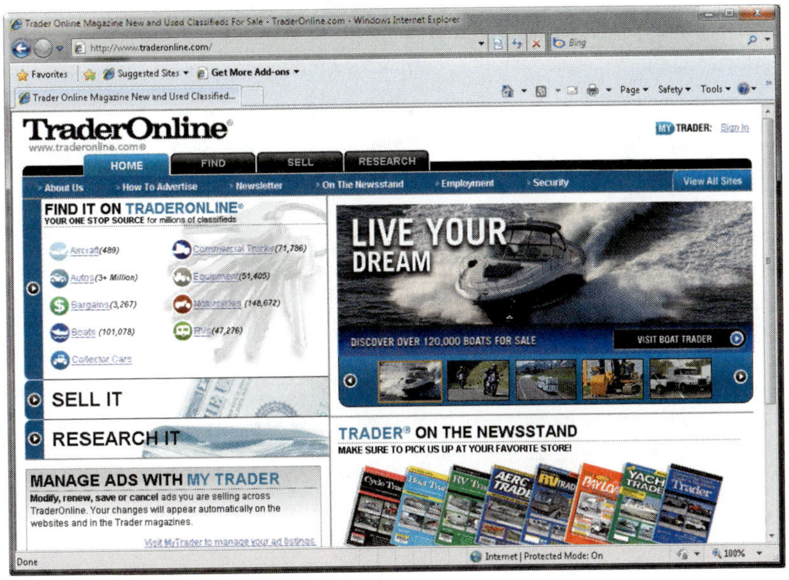

Figure 1-36 Many magazine and newspaper publishers make the content of their publications available online.

Travel

Many vehicles manufactured today include some type of onboard navigation system. Some mobile users prefer to carry specialized handheld navigation devices (Figure 1-37).

In preparing for a trip, you may need to reserve a car, hotel, or flight. Many Web sites offer these services to the public. For example, you can order airline tickets on the Web. If you plan to drive somewhere and are unsure of the road to take to your destination, you can print directions and a map from the Web.

Figure 1-37 This handheld navigation device gives users turn-by-turn voice-prompted directions to a destination.

Manufacturing

Computer-aided manufacturing (CAM) refers to the use of computers to assist with manufacturing processes such as fabrication and assembly. Often, robots carry out processes in a CAM environment. CAM is used by a variety of industries, including oil drilling, power generation, food production, and automobile manufacturing. Automobile plants, for example, have an entire line of industrial robots that assemble a car (Figure 1-38).

Figure 1-38 Automotive factories use industrial robots to weld car bodies.

✔ QUIZ YOURSELF 1-3

Instructions: Find the true statement below. Then, rewrite the remaining false statements so that they are true.

1. A desktop computer is a portable, personal computer designed to fit on your lap.
2. A personal computer contains a processor, memory, and one or more input, output, and storage devices.
3. Each enterprise user spends time on the computer for different reasons that include personal financial management, Web access, communications, and entertainment.
4. A home user requires the capabilities of a workstation or other powerful computer.
5. Mainframes are the fastest, most powerful computers — and the most expensive.
6. With embedded computers, users access account balances, pay bills, and copy monthly transactions from the bank's computer right into their personal computers.

Quiz Yourself Online: To further check your knowledge of pages 14 through 27, visit the Microsoft Office and Concepts CourseMate Web site at www.cengagebrain.com, navigate to the Chapter 1 Quiz Yourself resource for this book, and then click Objectives 6 – 8.

Chapter Summary

Chapter 1 introduced you to basic computer concepts. You learned about the components of a computer. Next, the chapter discussed networks, the Internet, and computer software. The many different categories of computers, computer users, and computer applications in society also were presented.

This chapter is an overview. Many of the terms and concepts introduced will be discussed further in later chapters. For information about digital products in our lives, read the Living Digitally feature that follows this chapter.

Computer Usage @ Work

Transportation

What is transportation like without computers? Delivery drivers use clipboards to hold their records. Human navigators use paper maps to track routes for pilots. Ship captains rely solely on experience to navigate through shallow waters. Today, the transportation industry relies heavily on computer usage.

As presented in this chapter, many vehicles include onboard navigation systems to help you navigate from one location to another. These systems also usually provide other services such as dispatching roadside assistance, unlocking the driver's side door if you lock the keys in your vehicle, and tracking the vehicle if it is stolen.

The shipping and travel industries identify items during transport using bar codes, which are identification codes that consist of lines and spaces of different lengths. When you ship a package, the shipping company, such as UPS or FedEx, places a bar code on the package to indicate its destination to a computer. Because a package might travel to its destination by way of several trucks, trains, and airplanes, computers automatically route the package as efficiently as possible.

When you travel by airplane, baggage handling systems ensure that your luggage reaches its destination on time. When you check in your baggage at the airport, a bar code identifies the airplane on which the bags should be placed. If you change planes, automated baggage handling systems route your bags to connecting flights with very little, if any, human intervention. When the bags reach their destination, they are routed automatically to the baggage carousel in the airport's terminal building.

Pilots of high-technology commercial, military, and space aircraft today work in a glass cockpit, which features computerized instrumentation, navigation, communication, weather reports, and an autopilot. The electronic flight information shown on high-resolution displays is designed to reduce pilot workload, decrease fatigue, and enable pilots to concentrate on flying safely.

Boats and ships also are equipped with computers that include detailed electronic maps, help the captain navigate, as well as calculate the water depth and provide a layout of the underwater surface so that the captain can avoid obstructions.

As you travel the roadways, airways, and waterways, bear in mind that computers often are responsible for helping you to reach your destination as quickly and safely as possible.

For more information, visit the Microsoft Office and Concepts CourseMate Web site at www.cengagebrain.com, navigate to the Chapter 1 Computer Usage @ Work resource for this book, and then click Transportation.

Companies on the Cutting Edge

APPLE Innovative Industry Products

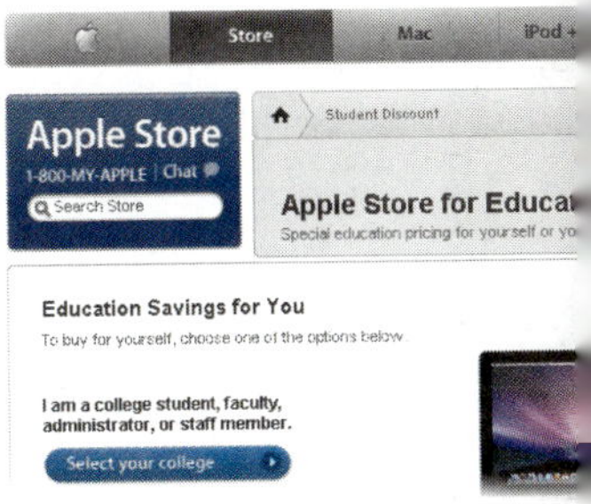

Apple recently sold a record 5.2 million of its latest iPhone models in one quarter, establishing the company's appeal to both consumer and corporate cell phone users. Apple is noted for introducing innovative products, starting with the Apple II, which was the first mass-marketed personal computer, in 1977 and the Macintosh, which featured a graphical user interface, in 1984.

Steve Jobs and Steve Wozniak founded Apple in 1976 when they marketed the Apple I, a circuit board they had developed in Jobs's garage. Under Jobs's direction as CEO, Apple developed the OS X operating system; iLife for working with photos, music, videos, and Web sites; and iWork, a collection of business programs. Apple also is leading the digital media revolution with its iPod portable media players, iPad tablet computer, and iTunes online store, which is the most popular Web site selling music. More than 10 million downloads occur each day from Apple's App Store, for a total download count exceeding 7 billion.

AMAZON Retailer Focused on Consumers

Online shoppers can find practically any product they desire on Amazon.com. Billing itself as the "Earth's most customer-centric company," it offers books, movies, electronics, clothing, toys, and many other items.

Jeff Bezos founded Amazon in 1995 knowing that book lovers would gravitate toward a Web site offering the convenience of browsing through millions of book titles in one sitting. He fulfilled orders for customers in every U.S. state and 45 additional countries during the first 30 days of business, all shipped from his Seattle-area garage.

The company has grown to permit third parties to sell products on its Web site. Its Kindle portable reader wirelessly downloads more than 450,000 books along with blogs, magazines, and newspapers to a high-resolution electronic paper display. Recently, it launched Kindle Singles, which are Kindle books with up to 30,000 words, the equivalent of two chapters of a typical book.

For more information, visit the Microsoft Office and Concepts CourseMate Web site at www.cengagebrain.com and then navigate to the Chapter 1 Companies on the Cutting Edge resource for this book.

Technology Trailblazers

BILL GATES Microsoft Founder

When Bill Gates stepped down from his day-to-day activities at Microsoft in 2008, his action marked the end of an era that shaped the computer world. He remains the company's chairman and advisor, but he now devotes much of his time directing the Bill & Melinda Gates Foundation, a philanthropic organization working to help people worldwide lead healthy, productive lives. His foundation currently is awarding $3 billion in grants to improve education and graduation rates via technology, with an emphasis on online learning.

Gates learned to program computers when he was 13 years old. Early in his career, he developed the BASIC programming language for the MITS Altair, one of the first microcomputers. He founded Microsoft in 1975 with Paul Allen, and five years later they licensed the first operating system, called PC-DOS, to IBM for $80,000. This decision to license, rather than sell, the software is considered one of the wisest business decisions Gates ever made. Today, Microsoft's Windows and Office products dominate the software market.

TOM ANDERSON MySpace Cofounder and President

Having more than 11 million friends is all in a day's work for Tom Anderson, the current president and one of the founders of MySpace, one of the world's largest online social networks. Every MySpace account includes Anderson as a default first friend who is invited to view each personal network.

When Anderson's own rock group failed, he needed a place to post his songs. He started MySpace in 2003 with his friend, Chris DeWolfe, as a free tool to help musicians promote their songs and allow music lovers to create their own Web pages devoted to sharing their favorite music with like-minded admirers. Two years later they sold the business to Rupert Murdoch's News Corporation for $580 million. Anderson graduated from the University of California – Los Angeles in 2001 with a master's degree in film and from the University of California – Berkeley in 1998 with a bachelor's degree in English and rhetoric.

For more information, visit the Microsoft Office and Concepts CourseMate Web site at www.cengagebrain.com and then navigate to the Chapter 1 Technology Trailblazers resource for this book.

Chapter Review

The Chapter Review reinforces the main concepts presented in this chapter.

To listen to an audio version of this Chapter Review, visit the Microsoft Office and Concepts CourseMate Web site at www.cengagebrain.com and then navigate to the Chapter 1 Chapter Review resource for this book.

1. **Why Is Computer Literacy Vital to Success in Today's World?** **Computer literacy**, also called digital literacy, involves having current knowledge and understanding of computers and their uses. As computers become an increasingly important part of daily living, many people believe that computer literacy is vital to success. Because the requirements that determine computer literacy change as technology changes, you must keep up with these changes to remain computer literate.

2. **List and Describe the Five Components of a Computer.** A **computer** is an electronic device, operating under the control of instructions stored in its own memory, that can accept data, process the data according to specified rules, produce results, and store the results for future use. The electric, electronic, and mechanical components of a computer, or **hardware**, include input devices, output devices, a system unit, storage devices, and communications devices. An **input device** allows you to enter data or instructions into a computer. An **output device** conveys information to one or more people. The **system unit** is a case that contains the electronic components of a computer that are used to process data. A **storage device** records and/or retrieves items to and from **storage media**. A **communications device** enables a computer to send and receive data, instructions, and information to and from one or more computers.

3. **What Are the Advantages and Disadvantages That Users Experience When Working with Computers?** A **user** is anyone who communicates with a computer or utilizes the information it generates. Advantages of using a computer include speed, reliability, consistency, storage, and communications. The disadvantages include violation of privacy, public safety, impact on the labor force, health risks, and impact on the environment.

Visit the Microsoft Office and Concepts CourseMate Web site at www.cengagebrain.com, navigate to the Chapter 1 Quiz Yourself resource for this book, and then click Objectives 1 – 3.

4. **How Are the Internet and World Wide Web Used?** The Internet is a worldwide collection of networks that connects millions of businesses, government agencies, educational institutions, and individuals. People use the Internet to communicate with and meet other people; conduct research and access information and news; shop for goods and services; bank and invest; participate in online training; engage in entertaining activities; download music and videos; share information, photos, and videos; and to access and interact with Web applications. The **Web**, short for World Wide Web, contains billions of documents called Web pages.

5. **What Are the Differences between System Software and Application Software?** **Software**, also called a **program**, is a series of related instructions, organized for a common purpose, that tells the computer what tasks to perform and how to perform them. The two categories of software are system software and application software. **System software** consists of the programs that control or maintain the operations of a computer and its devices. Two types of system software are the **operating system**, which coordinates activities among computer hardware devices, and **utility programs**, which perform maintenance-type tasks usually related to managing a computer, its devices, or its programs. **Application software** consists of programs designed to make users more productive and/or assist them with personal tasks. Popular application software includes a Web browser, word processing software, spreadsheet software, database software, and presentation software.

Visit the Microsoft Office and Concepts CourseMate Web site at www.cengagebrain.com, navigate to the Chapter 1 Quiz Yourself resource for this book, and then click Objectives 4 – 5.

6. **What Are the Differences among the Types, Sizes, and Functions in the Following Categories: Personal Computers (Desktop), Mobile Computers and Mobile Devices, Game Consoles, Servers, Mainframes, Supercomputers, and Embedded Computers?** A **personal computer** is a computer that can perform all of its input, processing, output, and storage activities by itself. A **mobile computer** is a personal computer that you can carry from place to place, and a **mobile device** is a computing device small enough to hold in your hand. A game console is a mobile computing device designed for single-player or multiplayer video games. A **server** controls access to the hardware, software, and other resources on a network and provides a centralized storage area for programs, data, and information. A **mainframe** is a large, expensive, powerful computer that can handle hundreds or thousands of connected users simultaneously and can store huge amounts of data, instructions, and information. A **supercomputer** is the fastest, most powerful, and most expensive computer and is used for applications requiring complex, sophisticated mathematical calculations. An **embedded computer** is a special-purpose computer that functions as a component in a larger product.

7. How Do the Various Types of Computer Users Interact with Computers? Computer users can be separated into five categories: home user, small office/home office user, mobile user, power user, and enterprise user. A **home user** is a family member who uses a computer for a variety of reasons, such as personal financial management, Web access, communications, and entertainment. A **small office/home office** (**SOHO**) includes any company with fewer than 50 employees or a self-employed individual who works from home and uses basic business software and sometimes industry-specific software. **Mobile users** are employees and students who work on a computer while away from a main office, home office, or school. A **power user** can exist in all types of businesses and uses powerful computers to work with industry-specific software. An **enterprise user** works in or interacts with a company with many employees and uses a computer and computer network that processes high volumes of transactions in a single day.

8. How Does Society Use Computers in Education, Finance, Government, Health Care, Science, Publishing, Travel, and Manufacturing? In education, students use computers and software to assist with learning or take distance learning classes. In finance, people use computers for **online banking** to access information and **online investing** to buy and sell stocks and bonds. Government offices have Web sites to provide citizens with up-to-date information, and government employees use computers as part of their daily routines. In health care, computers are used to maintain patient records, assist doctors with medical tests and research, file insurance claims, provide greater precision during operations, and as implants. All branches of science use computers to assist with collecting, analyzing, and modeling data and to communicate with scientists around the world. Publishers use computers to assist in developing pages and make their works available online. Many vehicles use some type of online navigation system to help people travel more quickly and safely. Manufacturers use **computer-aided manufacturing** (**CAM**) to assist with manufacturing processes.

Visit the Microsoft Office and Concepts CourseMate Web site at www.cengagebrain.com, navigate to the Chapter 1 Quiz Yourself resource for this book, and then click Objectives 6 – 8.

Key Terms

You should know the Key Terms. The list below helps focus your study.

To see an example of and a definition for each term, and to access current and additional information from the Web, visit the Microsoft Office and Concepts CourseMate Web site at www.cengagebrain.com and then navigate to the Chapter 1 Key Terms resource for this book.

application software (12)
blog (10)
camera phone (17)
communications device (6)
computer (3)
computer literacy (3)
computer-aided manufacturing (CAM) (27)
convergence (14)
CPU (central processing unit) (6)
data (4)
desktop computer (16)
developer (13)
digital camera (18)
digital literacy (3)
e-book (17)
e-book reader (17)
embedded computer (19)
enterprise computing (23)
enterprise user (23)
execute (12)
FAQ (11)
game console (18)
graphical user interface (GUI) (11)
green computing (7)
handheld computer (17)
hardware (4)
home user (20)
information (4)
information processing cycle (4)
input device (4)
installing (12)
instant message (17)
Internet (8)
Internet-enabled (16)
laptop computer (16)
mainframe (19)
memory (6)
microblog (10)
mobile computer (16)
mobile device (16)
mobile users (22)
netbook (16)
network (8)
notebook computer (16)
online (8)
online banking (25)
online investing (25)
online social network (10)
operating system (11)
output device (5)
PDA (17)
personal computer (15)
picture message (17)
podcast (10)
portable media player (17)
power user (23)
processor (6)
program (11)
programmer (13)
resources (8)
run (12)
server (19)
small office/home office (SOHO) (22)
smart phone (17)
social networking Web site (10)
software (11)
storage device (6)
storage media (6)
supercomputer (19)
system software (11)
system unit (6)
Tablet PC (16)
telecommuting (24)
telemedicine (26)
telesurgery (26)
text message (17)
Ultra-Mobile PC (UMPC) (17)
user (7)
utility program (12)
video message (17)
video phone (17)
Web (10)
Web 2.0 (10)
Web application (10)
Web page (10)
Web site (10)

Checkpoint

The Checkpoint exercises test your knowledge of the chapter concepts. The page number containing the answer appears in parentheses after each exercise.

To complete the Checkpoint exercises interactively, visit the Microsoft Office and Concepts CourseMate Web site at www.cengagebrain.com and then navigate to the Chapter 1 Checkpoint resource for this book.

Multiple Choice Select the best answer.

1. Computer literacy, also known as digital literacy, involves having a current knowledge and understanding of _______. (3)
   a. computer programming
   b. computers and their uses
   c. computer repair
   d. all of the above
2. _______ is/are a collection of unprocessed items, which can include text, numbers, images, audio, and video. (4)
   a. Data b. Instructions
   c. Programs d. Information
3. Millions of people worldwide join online communities, each called _______, that encourage members to share their interests, ideas, stories, photos, music, and videos with other registered users. (10)
   a. a podcast
   b. enterprise computing
   c. a social networking Web site or online social network
   d. a blog
4. _______ consists of the programs that control or maintain the operations of the computer and its devices. (11)
   a. A graphical user interface (GUI)
   b. A communications device
   c. System software
   d. Application software
5. Two types of _______ are desktop computers and notebook computers. (15)
   a. servers
   b. supercomputers
   c. mainframe computers
   d. personal computers
6. Five popular types of _______ are smart phones, PDAs, handheld computers, portable media players, and digital cameras. (17)
   a. mobile devices
   b. notebook computers
   c. desktop computers
   d. tower computers
7. A(n) _______ message is a real-time Internet communication, where you exchange messages with other connected users. (17)
   a. text b. instant
   c. picture d. video
8. Many large companies use the word(s), _______, to refer to the huge network of computers that meets their diverse computing needs. (23)
   a. information technology
   b. telecommuting
   c. enterprise computing
   d. multimedia

Matching Match the terms with their definitions.

_______ 1. information processing cycle (4)
_______ 2. processor (6)
_______ 3. storage device (6)
_______ 4. portable media player (17)
_______ 5. digital camera (18)

a. records (writes) and/or retrieves (reads) items to and from storage media
b. mobile device on which you can store, organize, and play digital media
c. fastest, most powerful computer — and the most expensive
d. electronic component that interprets and carries out the basic instructions for a computer
e. series of input, process, output, and storage activities
f. device that allows users to take pictures and store the photographed images digitally, instead of on traditional film

Short Answer Write a brief answer to each of the following questions.

1. What does it mean to be computer literate? _______ What is a computer? _______
2. Describe two health risks posed by computers. _______ How might computers have a negative effect on the environment? _______
3. What are five common storage devices? _______ How are they different? _______
4. What is a Web application? _______ What are some features of a Web 2.0 site? _______
5. How is hardware different from software? _______ What are two types of system software and how are they used? _______
6. How do computers benefit individuals' health care? _______ How does telesurgery differ from telemedicine? _______

Problem Solving

The Problem Solving exercises extend your knowledge of the chapter concepts by seeking solutions to practical computer problems that you may encounter at home, school, or work. The Collaboration exercise should be completed with a team.

In the real world, practical problems often can be solved in multiple ways. Provide one solution to each of the following problems using available resources, such as articles on the Web or in print, blogs, podcasts, videos, television, user guides, other individuals, and electronics and computer stores. You may need to use multiple resources to obtain an answer. Present your solutions in the form requested by your instructor (brief report, presentation, discussion, or other means).

@ Home

1. **Incorrect Grade Report** Your grade report came in the mail today. On the grade report, your grade point average (GPA) is not what you expect. After computing it manually, you discover that the GPA on your grade report is incorrect. What might be causing the error?
2. **Suspicious Charges** Your credit card company called to inform you that your account has a suspicious charge. Upon further investigation, you realize the charge does not belong to you. What steps will you take to correct the problem?
3. **Problematic Player** After charging your portable media player overnight, you turn it on only to find that it is reporting a low battery. Seconds later, it shuts off automatically. What might be wrong?
4. **Inaccessible Media** You insert an optical disc with digital photos from your most recent family vacation and discover that your computer will not read the optical disc. What might be wrong?

@ Work

5. **Insufficient Disk Space** Recently, you purchased a USB flash drive that you plan to use to store work-related files. When you attempt to store a file on the USB flash drive, the computer displays an error message indicating that the file will not fit. How could a brand new USB flash drive not have enough room to store the first file you attempted to store on it?
6. **Power Outage** The power in your office has been out for the last two hours and has just come back on. When you attempt to start your computer by pressing the power button, nothing happens. What is your next step before calling technical support?
7. **Incorrect Login Credentials** Upon returning to the office from a well-deserved two-week vacation, you turn on your computer. Upon entering your user name and password, an error message appears stating that your password is incorrect. What are your next steps?
8. **Software Installation** You are attempting to install a program on your office computer. After inserting the installation disc and specifying that you would like to begin the installation, your computer appears to begin installing the software. Halfway through the installation process, an error message appears stating that you must have administrative privileges to perform the installation. Why were you not informed immediately upon beginning the installation? What are your next steps?

Collaboration

9. **Computers in Transportation** Your project team has been accepted to present a business proposal to a group of potential investors. Because the presentation will take place in San Francisco, CA, you will need to transport people and ship some materials to that location. Form a team of three people and determine how to use technology to ship materials and how to make travel arrangements. One team member should research the steps required to use a Web site to make flight reservations, one team member should determine the steps necessary to print a UPS shipping label from their computer and track the package while it is en route, and another team member should find directions from San Francisco International Airport to a nearby hotel.

Learn How To

The Learn How To activities step you through fundamental technology skills when using a computer. The Learn How To exercises enable you to become more proficient with these skills.

Premium Activity: To relate this Learn How To activity to your everyday life, see a visual demonstration of the activity, and complete a short assessment, visit the Microsoft Office and Concepts CourseMate Web site at www.cengagebrain.com and then navigate to the Chapter 1 Learn How To resource for this book.

Learn How To 1: Create and Use Your Own Blog

A blog can contain any information you wish to place in it. Originally, blogs consisted of Web addresses, so that an individual or group with a specific interest could direct others to useful places on the Web. Today, blogs contain addresses, thoughts, diaries, and anything else a person or group wants to share.

Once you have created a blog, you can update it. A variety of services available on the Web can help you create and maintain your blog. One widely used service is called Blogger. To create a blog using Blogger, complete the following steps:

Figure 1-39

1. Start your Web browser, type `blogger.com` in the Address bar, and then press the ENTER key to display the Blogger home page (Figure 1-39).
2. Click the CREATE A BLOG button on the Blogger home page.
3. Enter the data required on the 'Create Blogger Account' page. Your e-mail address and password will allow you to change and manage your blog. Your Display name is the name that will be shown on the blog as the author of the material on the blog. Many people use their own names, but others use pseudonyms as their "pen names" so that they are not readily identifiable.
4. Click the Continue arrow and then enter your Blog title and Blog address. These are the names and addresses everyone will use to view your blog.
5. Click the Continue arrow to display the 'Choose a template' screen.
6. Choose a template for your blog and then click the Continue arrow.
7. Your blog will be created for you. When you see the 'Your blog has been created!' screen, click the START BLOGGING arrow.
8. From the screen that is displayed, you can post items for your blog, specify settings, change the layout, and view your blog.
9. When you have posted all your information, click the Sign out link at the top right of the screen. You will be logged out.
10. To edit your blog and add or change information on it, visit the Blogger home page and sign in by entering your user name and password. You will be able to post to your blog.
11. Others can view your blog by entering its address in the browser's Address bar and then pressing the ENTER key.

Exercises

1. Start your Web browser and visit blogger.com. Click the 'Take a quick tour' link and go through all the screens that explain about a blog. What did you learn that you did not know? What type of blog do you find most compelling — a group or an individual blog? Why? Submit your answers to your instructor.
2. Optional: Create your own blog. Carefully name it and begin your posts at this time. What is your blog name and address? What is its primary purpose? Is it an individual or group blog? Write a paragraph containing the answers to these questions and any other information you feel is pertinent. Submit this paragraph to your instructor.

Learn How To 2: Use the Microsoft Office and Concepts CourseMate Web Site for Discovering Computers and Microsoft Office 2010

The Microsoft Office and Concepts CourseMate Web site for Discovering Computers and Microsoft Office 2010 provides a variety of activities, exercises, and other resources. To use the site, you first establish a user name and password for your student account and then register this book. Perform the following steps to create a student account and register this book:

1. Start the Web browser.
2. Type `www.cengagebrain.com` in the Address bar of the Web browser and then press the ENTER key to display the CengageBrain home page.

3. If you do not have an account, follow the on-screen instructions to sign up for a new student account. If you already have an account, log in with your user name and password.
4. Register this book by entering its Access Code in the appropriate text box and then clicking the corresponding button.
5. To open the resources for this book, click the button corresponding to Microsoft Office and Concepts CourseMate Web site for Discovering Computers.

Exercise

1a. After creating a student account and registering this book as described in the steps above, start your Web browser, type `www.cengagebrain.com` in the Address bar of the browser, and then press the ENTER key to display the CengageBrain home page.

1b. Log in to your student account with your user name and password.

1c. Open the resources for this book by clicking the button corresponding to Microsoft Office and Concepts CourseMate Web site for Discovering Computers.

1d. Select Chapter 1 and then click each resource listed below the chapter title to display the content associated with the selected resource.

1e. Write a report that describes the use of each of the Chapter 1 resources for this book. Which resources do you think will prove the most valuable to you when using the book and the Web site? Why? Submit your report to your instructor.

Learn It Online

The Learn It Online exercises are interactive Web exercises designed to reinforce and expand your understanding of the chapter concepts. The descriptions below briefly summarize each exercise.

To complete the Learn It Online exercises, visit the Microsoft Office and Concepts CourseMate Web site at www.cengagebrain.com, navigate to the Chapter 1 resources for this book, click the link for the exercise you want to complete, and then read the instructions.

1 At the Movies — Computer History in a Barn
Watch a movie to tour the Digibarn Computer Museum and then answer questions about the movie.

2 Student Edition Labs — Using Input Devices and Using Windows
Enhance your understanding and knowledge about input devices and the Windows operating system by completing the Using Input Devices and Using Windows Labs.

3 Practice Test
Take a multiple choice test that checks your knowledge of the chapter concepts and review the resulting study guide.

4 Who Wants To Be a Computer Genius^2?
Play the Shelly Cashman Series version of this popular game by answering questions to find out if you are a computer genius. Panic buttons are available to provide assistance during game play.

5 Crossword Puzzle Challenge
Complete an interactive crossword puzzle to reinforce concepts presented in this chapter.

6 Windows Exercises
Step through the Windows 7 exercises to learn how to use help, improve mouse skills, and identify computer information.

7 Exploring Computer Careers
Read about a career as a computer salesperson, search for relevant employment advertisements, and then answer related questions.

8 Web Apps — Google Maps
Learn how to locate businesses in your area, view a location's surroundings via satellite, and find directions from one location to another using Google Maps.

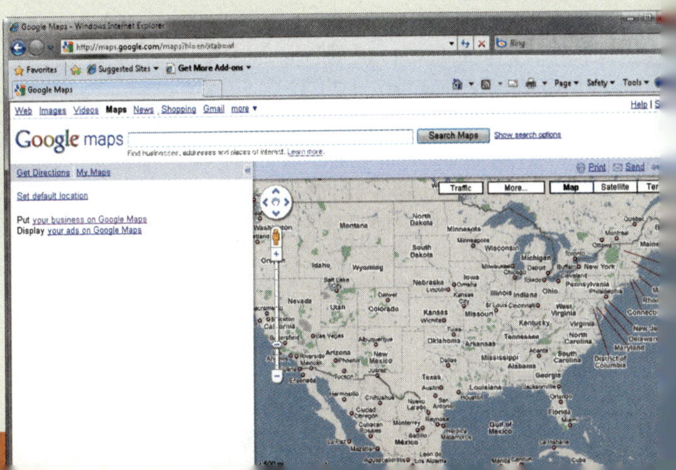

Web Research

The Web Research exercises broaden your understanding of the chapter concepts by presenting questions that require you to search the Web for answers.

1 Search Sleuth

Use one of the search engines listed in Figure 2-8 in Chapter 2 on page 53 or your own favorite search engine to find the answers to the following questions. Copy and paste the Web address from the Web page where you found the answer. Some questions may have more than one answer. If required, submit your answers to your instructor. (1) What company was the first to sell a USB flash drive? (2) What is the significance of the Universal symbol on Apple's Mac application programs? (3) Which retailers offer to dispose of old computers and other electronic products properly to help protect the environment? (4) What are three Illustrative Grant Commitments the Bill & Melinda Gates Foundation has made? (5) According to *Fortune*, at what company do MBA students most want to work when they graduate? (6) Who created the first set of icons for the Macintosh computer? What sound does her Clarus the Dogcow make? (7) What company manufactured the first notebook computer, the UltraLite, in 1989?

2 Green Computing

Computer usage requires electricity, whether to power the system unit and monitor, recharge batteries, or print. In addition, the computer manufacturing process depletes natural resources and often uses toxic chemicals. As you learned in this chapter, many environmentally conscious people practice green computing by attempting to reduce electricity and environmental waste. Examine your computing practices, and determine 10 ways that you can use less power on your computing equipment at home, work, and school. Consider how often you use the printer and the types of documents you print. Examine your monitor, system unit, and printer. Do you see any notation indicating they are environmentally sound? Do they hibernate or go into a power save mode when not being used? Write a 50-word summary of the green computing practices in your life.

3 Social Networking

One of the more popular social networking Web sites is Facebook. This quickly growing service differentiates itself from other online social networks by having widespread privacy controls. In addition, its development platform, called f8, allows developers to create programs (called applications) that users can add to a Web page. Hostels, for example, lets world travelers research and rate hostels and includes photos and descriptions. Visit the Facebook site (facebook.com), click the About link at the bottom of the page, and then read about Facebook's features. What are three of Facebook's top features? What information is given in the recent Facebook blog posts? Visit the AppRate Web site (apprate.com) and then summarize three Facebook application reviews and ratings.

4 Blogs

Blogs profiling the music industry discuss new technologies, legal issues, podcasts, and business news. Visit the CNET blog (blogs.cnet.com) and then read and summarize at least three of the articles in the Most Recent Posts section. Locate the Crave, Gaming and Culture, and Green Tech features and then read and summarize at least one story from each blog. Then visit the iLounge (ilounge.com) Web site and read reviews of at least three new products for the iPhone. Would you purchase any of the products discussed? What books and buyer's guides are available to download from the Library? Which iPod cases and speakers received favorable reviews? Read and summarize at least three stories and associated comments in the News section.

5 Ethics in Action

The Internet has increased the ease with which students can plagiarize material for research paper assignments. Teachers are using online services, such as Turnitin and PlagiarismDetect.com, to help detect plagiarized papers and to help students understand how to cite sources correctly. Visit the Turnitin Web site (turnitin.com) and then write a summary of how this service is used. How does this service attempt to prevent plagiarism through the Turnitin Write Cycle? How prevalent is plagiarism on your campus? What is your school's official policy on disciplining students who submit plagiarized papers? Does your school have an honor code? If required, submit your summary to your instructor.

Living Digitally

OUR DIGITAL LIVES are filled with a variety of products. We listen on portable media players to audio files we create or download. We record and view video content that matches our viewing interests. We play recorded files wherever and whenever we desire. We play games solo or with multiple friends across the globe. Our home networks link security, energy monitoring, and leisure activities throughout the house. Wherever we go in our lives, technology is a pervasive part of our daily existence.

Microsoft Xbox 360

PSPgo

3-D video display

avatar

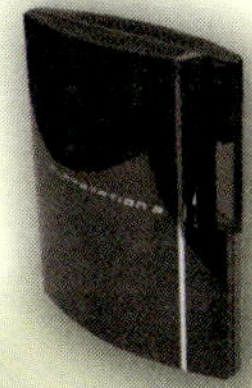
Sony PlayStation 3

Slingbox

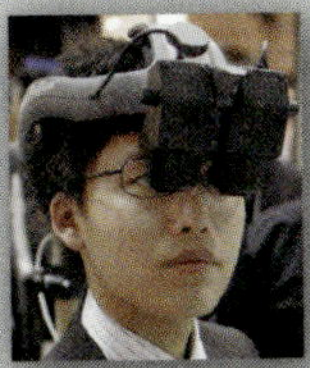
head-mounted display

flat-screen TV

Nintendo Wii

Rock Band

iPod/iPod touch

TiVo

Nintendo DSi

video camera

speakers

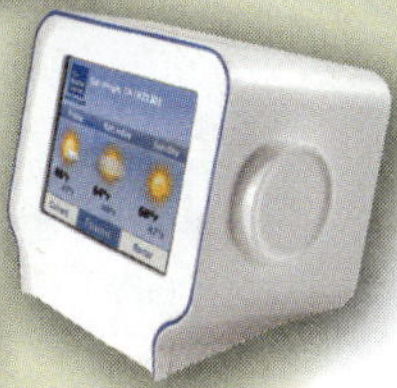
chumby

smart phone

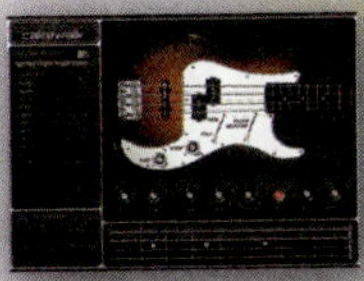
Studio Instruments software

Nero optical disc burning software

combination drive

Dolby logo

digital frames

Netflix

home automation dashboard

multi-room audio system

docking station

Digital products in our lives often include features that overlap in various entertainment and home automation categories.

- Audio
- Video
- Recording
- Gaming
- Digital Home

Audio

THE MUSIC INDUSTRY is a major part of our everyday lives, and digital music sales generate more than $10 billion each year. Audio files can be played on iPods and other portable media players and mobile devices. Musicians of all skill levels can create their own music with Rock Band and Guitar Hero handheld instruments.

Figure 1 Apple has sold hundreds of millions of iPods. The iPod accessory market has grown to a billion-dollar industry, with inventors developing earbuds, cases, and docking stations.

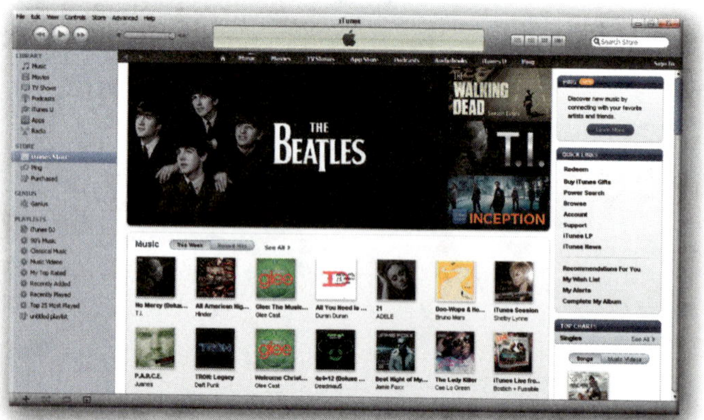

Figure 2 Music downloading services allow you to purchase individual tracks or entire albums and then download the music to a computer or portable media player. More than 500 downloading services are available; Apple iTunes and Amazon MP3 are the sales leaders.

Figure 3 Rock the night away playing set lists from some of the biggest artists and bands of all times. Customize the concert experience by selecting venues and original band members or your own personalized superstars.

Figure 4 Ray Dolby founded Dolby Laboratories in 1965. His company has become the world leader in defining high-quality products, including audio and surround sound in theaters, home entertainment systems, and broadcasting.

Video

WHETHER IN A COMFY CHAIR or on the go, watching television and movies has changed dramatically. Viewers download content and then watch the programs when and where they desire on devices ranging from large flat-screen display devices to compact smart phones. Glasses and 3-D displays add a new dimension to the viewing experience.

Figure 5 A multitude of video streaming devices is infiltrating the marketplace as companies expand their services to add subscribers and bring movies and television programs to homes via a broadband Internet connection. Apple TV takes control of your home theater system by streaming HD movies, television programs, iTunes music, podcasts, and photos to display devices.

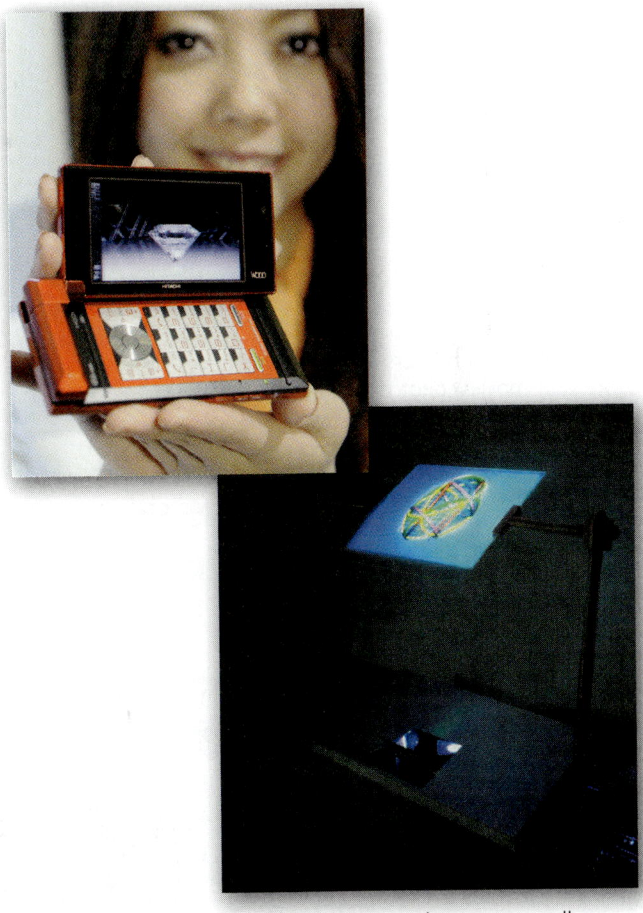

Figure 8 True 3-D video images can be seen on cell phones and video displays without special glasses or goggles. Applications include medical imaging, CAD drawings, mapping, and entertainment.

Figure 6 Experience a private video viewing with a personal head-mounted display (HMD). Video glasses can be connected to a DVD player, iPod, or game console.

Figure 9 High-definition (HD) digital video recorders (DVRs), such as the TiVo, let you locate and record current and off-air digital broadcasts, pause and rewind live television programs, and create your own instant replays with slow motion.

Figure 7 View your favorite television programs anywhere in the world as long as you have a broadband connection and a Slingbox. This device streams video and audio from your home to any Internet-connected device.

Recording

WHETHER YOU ARE WORKING OUT at the gym or driving to Grandma's house for dinner, you might want to download or record your favorite audio, video, and photos to transport them from one location to another or upload them to share with friends and family. You also can record movies or television programs when you are not at home and then play them at your convenience on a home entertainment system or portable media player.

Figure 10
Use optical disc burning software to create optical discs quickly and easily with multiformat burners and rewritable drives to store your movies, photos, music, and digital data.

Figure 11
Capture video using your video camera and then, with the press of a button, upload recorded clips to social networking Web sites. Each minute, more than 20 hours of video are uploaded to YouTube.

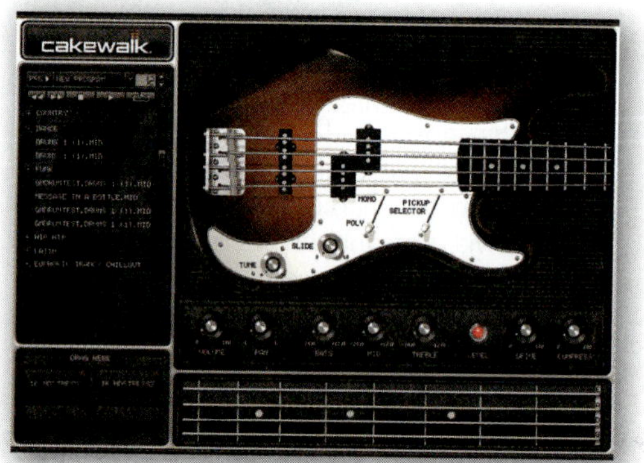

Figure 12 Turn your computer into a virtual bass guitar, drum set, electric piano, or string section with Cakewalk's Studio Instruments software. Then, record, edit, and mix your songs created with these virtual and real instruments and create streaming music players and playlists on your Web site.

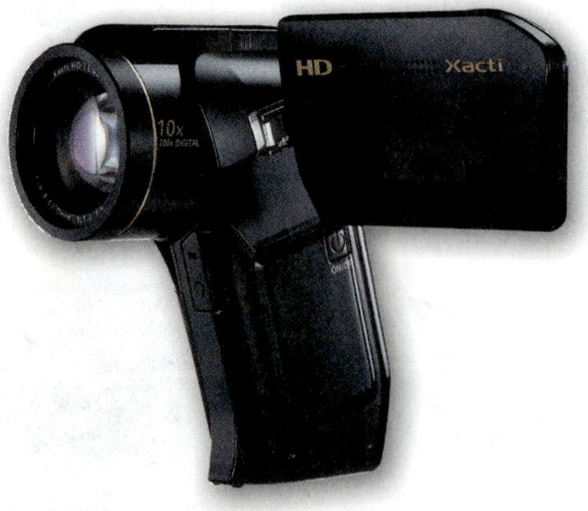

Figure 13 Capture video of friends and family, upload the clips to your computer, and use video editing software to rearrange the sequence of events, add music and titles, and record narration.

Gaming

REVENUE GENERATED BY THE VIDEO GAMING INDUSTRY quickly is approaching $100 billion. The areas experiencing the fastest growth are online and mobile gaming as new game consoles and advanced networking become mainstream.

Figure 14 The three gaming consoles — Nintendo Wii, Sony PlayStation 3, and Microsoft Xbox 360 — offer a variety of game titles.

Figure 16 In a computer role-playing game (CRPG), players interact with one another and generally attempt to accomplish a quest. Massively multiplayer online games (MMOGs) unite millions of gamers worldwide.

Figure 17 Handheld game consoles have large, high-resolution screens and incredible sound to play audio and video files and can display photos. Bluetooth and Wi-Fi technology allows networked gaming and synchronizing with other handheld units or personal computers.

Figure 15 Gaming reaches all generations. The Wii game console's interactive quality appeals to players of all ages. The iPod touch's accelerometer, which detects movement and changes the display accordingly, and 3-D graphics immerse players in the action.

Figure 18 Outdoor treasure hunters use their GPS receivers and navigational skills to create and locate hidden caches throughout the world.

Digital Home

THE AVERAGE HOUSEHOLD has 21 consumer electronics devices, and many of them are linked via home networks and broadband connections that simplify our lives and provide entertainment in innovative ways. Digital music and video are recorded and streamed to multiple devices. Meanwhile, automation systems monitor security, energy usage, and room temperatures to provide optimal conditions.

Figure 19 Set-top boxes stream movies from the Web to your televisions, computers, and mobile devices. On average, Netflix ships approximately two million DVDs each day.

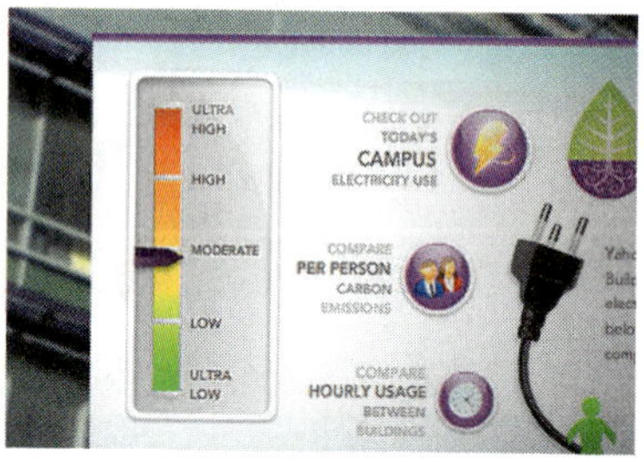

Figure 21 LED screens provide information about home electricity, gas, and water use, and they compare the rates with previous consumption.

Figure 22 Digital picture frames, some as large as 40 inches wide, are among the more popular consumer electronic devices; more than 3 million are sold each year. They provide a convenient method of displaying the billions of digital photos taken each day and may play songs and Web broadcasts.

Figure 20 Program an entire home to fit your lifestyle and needs. A home automation system can set room temperatures, open and close window shades, water the grass, watch for intruders, and play music to wake you or relax you to sleep.

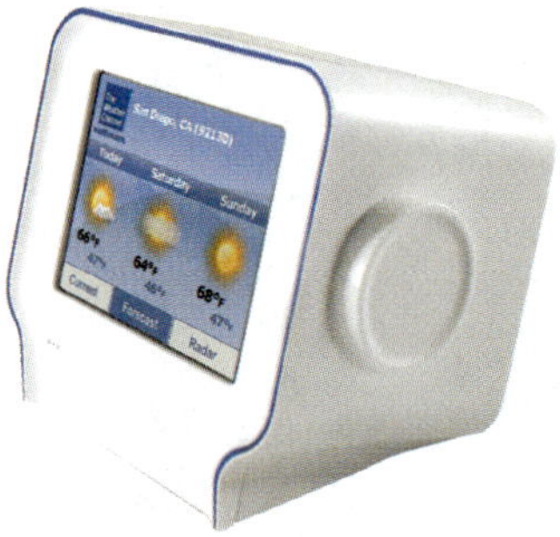

Figure 23 The wireless chumby connects to the Internet and streams news, entertainment, sports scores, video clips, interactive games, photos, and hundreds of favorite widgets.

Computer technology impacts virtually every facet of our lives. From the largest media rooms to the smallest portable media players, we can watch our favorite television programs and movies any place at any time. We can browse the Web, play games with partners on the other side of the world, listen to music we created with handheld instruments, and have fun wherever life takes us. No matter where we are, our digital lives are filled with information and entertainment.

Chapter Two

The Internet and World Wide Web

Objectives

After completing this chapter, you will be able to:

1 Identify and briefly describe various broadband Internet connections

2 Describe the types of Internet access providers: Internet service providers, online service providers, and wireless Internet service providers

3 Explain the purpose of a Web browser and identify the components of a Web address

4 Describe how to use a search engine to search for information on the Web

5 Describe the types of Web sites: portal, news, informational, business/marketing, blog, wiki, online social network, educational, entertainment, advocacy, Web application, content aggregator, and personal

6 Recognize how Web pages use graphics, animation, audio, video, virtual reality, and plug-ins

7 Identify the steps required for Web publishing

8 Explain how e-mail, mailing lists, instant messaging, chat rooms, VoIP, FTP, and newsgroups and message boards work

9 Identify the rules of netiquette

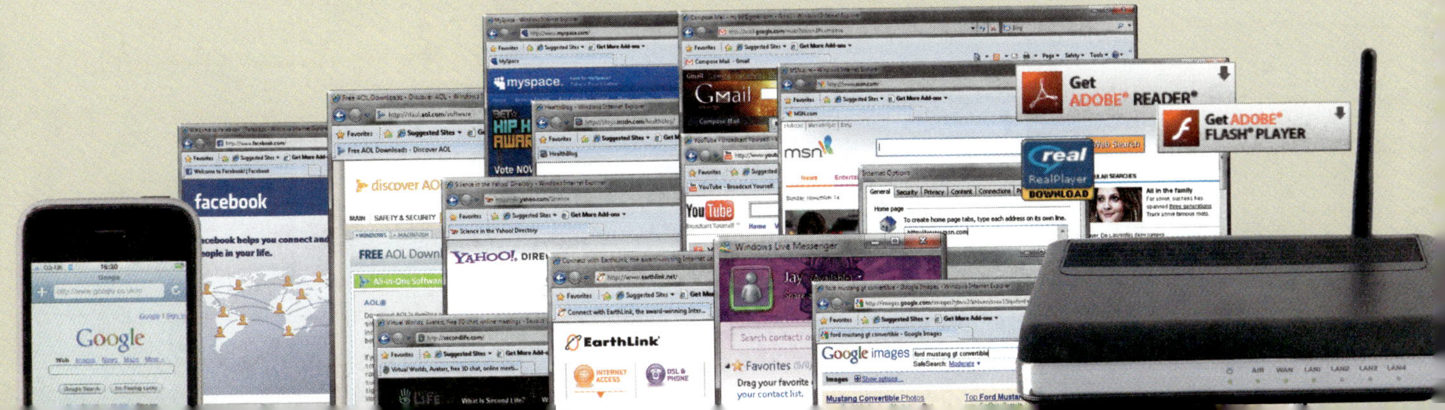

The Internet

One of the major reasons business, home, and other users purchase computers is for Internet access. The **Internet**, also called the **Net**, is a worldwide collection of networks that links millions of businesses, government agencies, educational institutions, and individuals. The Internet is a widely used research tool, providing society with access to global information and instant communications.

Today, more than one billion home and business users around the world access a variety of services on the Internet, some of which are shown in Figure 2-1. The World Wide Web, or simply the Web, and e-mail are two of the more widely used Internet services. Other services include chat rooms, instant messaging, and VoIP (Voice over Internet Protocol).

The Internet has its roots in a networking project started by an agency of the U.S. Department of Defense. The goal was to build a network that (1) allowed scientists at different locations to share information and work together on military and scientific projects and (2) could function even if part of the network were disabled or destroyed by a disaster such as a nuclear attack. That network, called ARPANET, became functional in September 1969, linking scientific and academic researchers across the United States.

The original ARPANET consisted of four main computers, one each located at the University of California at Los Angeles, the University of California at Santa Barbara, the Stanford Research Institute, and the University of Utah. Each of these computers served as a host on the network. A host or server is any computer that provides services and connections to other computers on a network. By 1984, ARPANET had more than 1,000 individual computers linked as hosts. Today, more than 550 million hosts connect to this network, which is known now as the Internet.

Figure 2-1 People around the world use a variety of Internet services in daily activities. Internet services allow home and business users to access the Web for activities such as conducting research, reading blogs, or sharing videos; to send e-mail messages; or to converse with others using chat rooms, instant messaging, or VoIP.

The Internet consists of many local, regional, national, and international networks. Both public and private organizations own networks on the Internet. These networks, along with telephone companies, cable and satellite companies, and the government, all contribute toward the internal structure of the Internet.

Each organization on the Internet is responsible only for maintaining its own network. No single person, company, institution, or government agency controls or owns the Internet. The World Wide Web Consortium (W3C), however, oversees research and sets standards and guidelines for many areas of the Internet. More than 350 organizations from around the world are members of the W3C.

Connecting to the Internet

Many home and small business users connect to the Internet via high-speed **broadband** Internet service. With broadband Internet service, your computer or mobile device usually is connected to the Internet the entire time it is powered on. Examples of broadband Internet service include the following:

- **Cable Internet service** provides high-speed Internet access through the cable television network via a cable modem.
- **DSL** (digital subscriber line) provides high-speed Internet connections using regular telephone lines.
- **Fiber to the Premises (FTTP)** uses fiber-optic cable to provide high-speed Internet access to home and business users.
- **Fixed wireless** provides high-speed Internet connections using a dish-shaped antenna on your house or business to communicate with a tower location via radio signals.
- A **Wi-Fi** (wireless fidelity) network uses radio signals to provide high-speed Internet connections to wireless computers and devices.

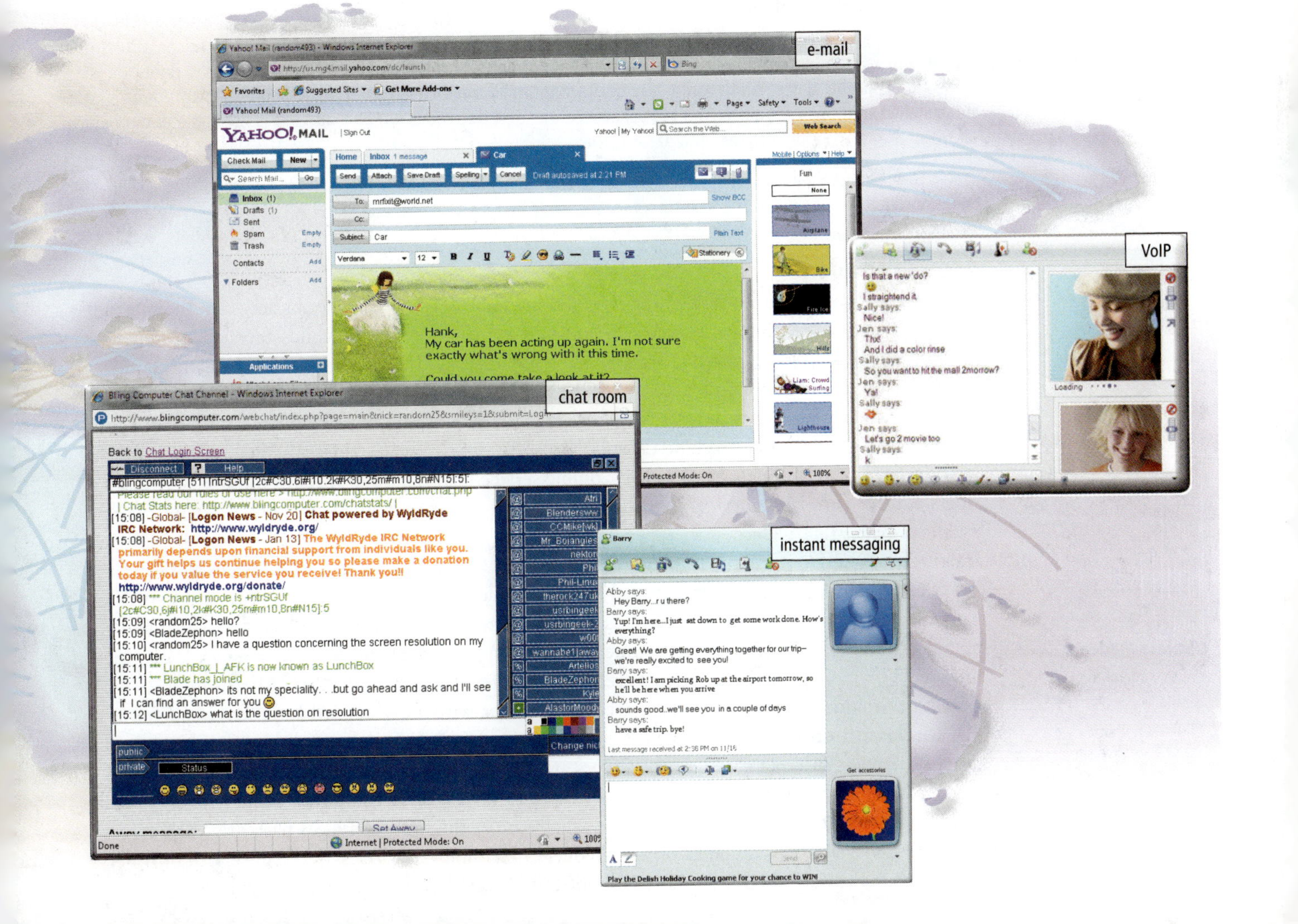

- A **cellular radio network** offers high-speed Internet connections to devices with built-in compatible technology or computers with wireless modems.
- **Satellite Internet service** provides high-speed Internet connections via satellite to a satellite dish that communicates with a satellite modem.

Employees and students typically connect their computers to the Internet through a business or school network. The business or school network connects to a high-speed broadband Internet service.

Mobile users access the Internet using a variety of services. Most hotels and airports provide wired or wireless Internet connections. Wireless Internet services such as Wi-Fi networks, allow mobile users to connect easily to the Internet with notebook computers, smart phones, and other mobile devices while away from a telephone, cable, or other wired connection. Many public locations, such as airports, hotels, schools, and coffee shops, are **hot spots** that provide Wi-Fi Internet connections to users with mobile computers or devices.

Many home users set up a Wi-Fi network, which sends signals to a communications device that is connected to a high-speed Internet service such as cable or DSL. Instead of using broadband Internet service, however, some home users connect to the Internet via dial-up access, which is a slower-speed technology. **Dial-up access** takes place when the modem in your computer connects to the Internet via a standard telephone line that transmits data and information using an analog (continuous wave pattern) signal. Users may opt for dial-up access because of its lower price or because broadband access is not available in their area.

? FAQ 2-1

How popular is broadband?

According to a study performed by Pew Internet & American Life Project, 63 percent of American adults have broadband Internet connections at home. Adoption of broadband connections increases during good economic times, while some may hesitate to make the switch during an economic downturn. It is believed that once the price of a broadband connection decreases, and broadband is available in more rural areas, its popularity will increase further.

For more information, visit the Microsoft Office and Concepts CourseMate Web site at www.cengagebrain.com, navigate to the Chapter 2 FAQ resource for this book, and then click Broadband.

Access Providers

An **access provider** is a business that provides individuals and organizations access to the Internet free or for a fee. For example, some Wi-Fi networks provide free access while others charge a per use fee. Other access providers often charge a fixed amount for an Internet connection, usually about $5 to $24 per month for dial-up access and $13 to $120 for higher-speed access. Many Internet access providers offer services such as news, weather, financial data, games, travel guides, e-mail, photo communities, and online storage to hold digital photos and other files. (A file is a named unit of storage.)

Access providers are categorized as ISPs, online service providers, and wireless Internet service providers. An **ISP (Internet service provider)** is a regional or national access provider. A regional ISP usually provides Internet access to a specific geographic area. A national ISP is a business that provides Internet access in cities and towns nationwide. National ISPs usually offer more services and have a larger technical support staff than regional ISPs. Examples of national ISPs are AT&T and EarthLink.

In addition to providing Internet access, an **online service provider (OSP)** also has many members-only features such as instant messaging or their own customized version of a Web browser. The two more popular OSPs are AOL (America Online) and MSN (Microsoft Network). AOL also provides free access to its services to any user with a high-speed Internet connection.

A **wireless Internet service provider**, sometimes called a wireless data provider, is a company that provides wireless Internet access to computers and mobile devices, such as smart phones and portable media players with built-in wireless capability (such as Wi-Fi) or to computers using wireless modems or wireless access devices. Wireless modems usually are in the form of a USB flash drive or a card that inserts in a slot in a computer or mobile device. Examples of wireless Internet service providers include AT&T, Boingo Wireless, Sprint Broadband Direct, T-Mobile, and Verizon Wireless.

Wireless Modems

For more information, visit the Microsoft Office and Concepts CourseMate Web site at www.cengagebrain.com, navigate to the Chapter 2 Web Link resource for this book, and then click Wireless Modems.

How Data and Information Travel the Internet

Computers connected to the Internet work together to transfer data and information around the world using various wired and wireless transmission media. Several main transmission media carry the heaviest amount of traffic on the Internet. These major carriers of network traffic are known collectively as the **Internet backbone.**

In the United States, the transmission media that make up the Internet backbone exchange data and information at several different major cities across the country. That is, they transfer data and information from one network to another until reaching the final destination (Figure 2-2).

FAQ 2-2

What types of Web sites do mobile Internet users visit?

More than 87 million individuals subscribe to a wireless Internet service provider. Mobile Internet users most frequently visit weather, entertainment, and e-mail Web sites. The chart to the right illustrates various types of Web sites and their associated increase in traffic resulting from mobile Internet users.

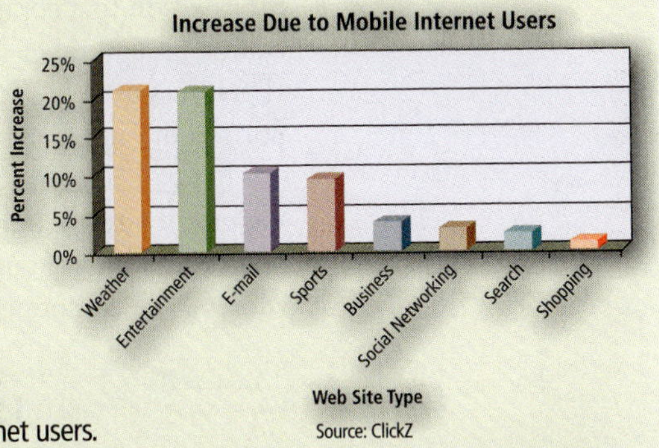

For more information, visit the Microsoft Office and Concepts CourseMate Web site at www.cengagebrain.com, navigate to the Chapter 2 FAQ resource for this book, and then click Mobile Internet.

How a Home User's Data and Information Might Travel the Internet Using a Cable Modem Connection

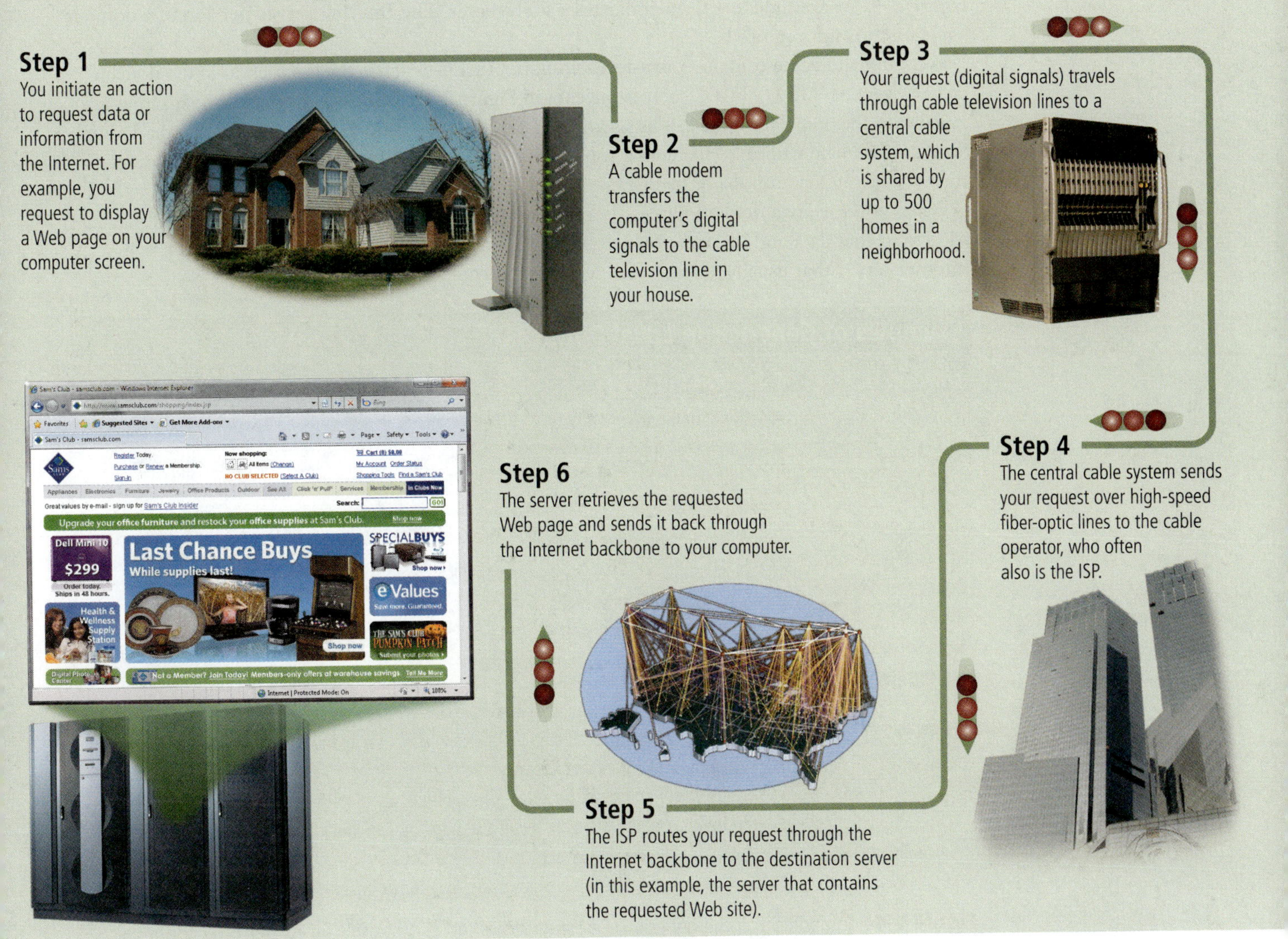

Figure 2-2 This figure shows how a home user's data and information might travel the Internet using a cable modem connection.

Internet Addresses

The Internet relies on an addressing system much like the postal service to send data and information to a computer at a specific destination. An **IP address**, short for Internet Protocol address, is a number that uniquely identifies each computer or device connected to the Internet. The IP address usually consists of four groups of numbers, each separated by a period. In general, the first portion of each IP address identifies the network and the last portion identifies the specific computer.

These all-numeric IP addresses are difficult to remember and use. Thus, the Internet supports the use of a text name that represents one or more IP addresses. A **domain name** is the text version of an IP address. Figure 2-3 shows an IP address and its associated domain name. As with an IP address, the components of a domain name are separated by periods.

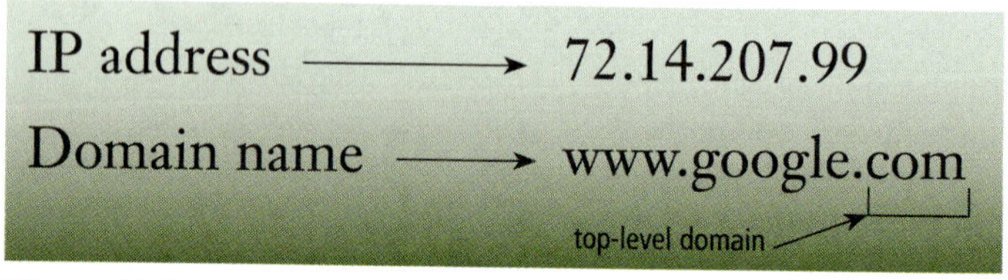

Figure 2-3 The IP address and domain name for the Google Web site.

The text in the domain name up to the first period identifies the type of Internet server. In Figure 2-3, for example, the www indicates a Web server. The Internet server portion of a domain name often is not required.

Every domain name contains a **top-level domain (TLD)**, which is the last section of the domain name. A generic TLD (gTLD), such as the com in Figure 2-3, identifies the type of organization associated with the domain. Figure 2-4 lists some gTLDs. For international Web sites outside the United States, the domain name also includes a country code TLD (ccTLD), which is a two-letter country code, such as au for Australia or fr for France.

When you specify a domain name, a server translates the domain name to its associated IP address so that data and information can be routed to the correct computer. This server is an Internet server that usually is associated with an Internet access provider.

Examples of Generic Top-Level Domains

Generic TLD	Intended Purpose
aero	Aviation community members
biz	Businesses of all sizes
cat	Catalan cultural community
com	Commercial organizations, businesses, and companies
coop	Business cooperatives such as credit unions and rural electric co-ops
edu	Educational institutions
gov	Government agencies
info	Business organizations or individuals providing general information
jobs	Employment or human resource businesses

Generic TLD	Intended Purpose
mil	Military organizations
mobi	Delivery and management of mobile Internet services
museum	Accredited museums
name	Individuals or families
net	Network providers or commercial companies
org	Nonprofit organizations
pro	Certified professionals such as doctors, lawyers, and accountants
tel	Internet communications
travel	Travel industry

Figure 2-4 In addition to the generic TLDs listed in this table, proposals for newer TLDs continually are evaluated.

QUIZ YOURSELF 2-1

Instructions: Find the true statement below. Then, rewrite the remaining false statements so that they are true.

1. An access provider is a business that provides individuals and organizations access to the Internet free or for a fee.
2. A wireless Internet service provider is a number that uniquely identifies each computer or device connected to the Internet.
3. An IP address, such as www.google.com, is the text version of a domain name.
4. Satellite Internet service provides high-speed Internet access through the cable television network via a cable modem.

Quiz Yourself Online: To further check your knowledge of pages 44 through 48, visit the Microsoft Office and Concepts CourseMate Web site at www.cengagebrain.com, navigate to the Chapter 2 Quiz Yourself resource for this book, and then click Objectives 1 – 2.

The World Wide Web

The **World Wide Web** (**WWW**), or **Web**, a widely used service on the Internet, consists of a worldwide collection of electronic documents. Each electronic document on the Web, called a **Web page**, can contain text, graphics, animation, audio, and video. Additionally, Web pages usually have built-in connections to other documents. A **Web site** is a collection of related Web pages and associated items, such as documents and pictures, stored on a Web server. A **Web server** is a computer that delivers requested Web pages to your computer. Some industry experts use the term **Web 2.0** to refer to Web sites that provide a means for users to share personal information (such as social networking Web sites), allow users to modify Web site content (such as wikis, which are discussed later in this chapter), and have application software built into the site for visitors to use (such as e-mail and word processing programs). Read Looking Ahead 2-1 for a look at Web 3.0.

Browsing the Web

A **Web browser**, or **browser**, is application software that allows users to access and view Web pages or access Web 2.0 programs. To browse the Web, you need a computer or mobile device that is connected to the Internet and that has a Web browser. The more widely used Web browsers for personal computers are Internet Explorer, Firefox, Opera, Safari, and Google Chrome.

LOOKING AHEAD 2-1

Web 3.0 to Reinvent the Virtual World

When Tim Berners-Lee developed the World Wide Web 20 years ago, he envisioned a service that allowed users to exchange information seamlessly. The Web has evolved through versions 1.0 and 2.0, and work is underway to develop Web 3.0, also known as the Semantic Web.

This next generation of the Web is predicted to perform practically any imaginable task, according to some researchers. For example, your computer will be able to scan a Web page much as you do to look for specific useful information. If you need the location of the nearest eye doctor and the time when your brother's flight from Chicago actually will land, Web 3.0 will provide those facts and then search your calendar to see if you can fit the doctor's appointment in your schedule in time to pick up your brother at the airport. In essence, the Web will become one huge searchable database, and automated agents of every type will retrieve the data we need to live productive lives.

For more information, visit the Microsoft Office and Concepts CourseMate Web site at www.cengagebrain.com, navigate to the Chapter 2 Looking Ahead resource for this book, and then click Web 3.0.

FAQ 2-3

Which Web browser currently has the highest market share?

Windows Internet Explorer (IE) currently is the most popular browser, with approximately 68 percent of the market share. The chart to the right illustrates the market share of the more popular Web browsers.

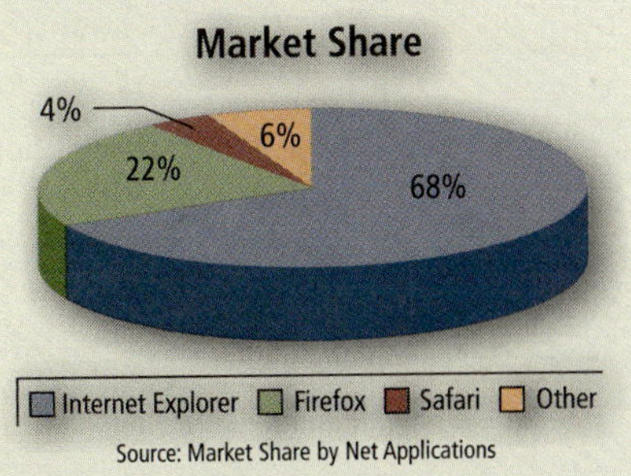

For more information, visit the Microsoft Office and Concepts CourseMate Web site at www.cengagebrain.com, navigate to the Chapter 2 FAQ resource for this book, and then click Browser Market Share.

With an Internet connection established, you start a Web browser. The browser retrieves and displays a starting Web page, sometimes called the browser's home page. Figure 2-5 shows how a Web browser displays a home page.

Another use of the term, **home page**, refers to the first page that a Web site displays. Similar to a book cover or a table of contents for a Web site, the home page provides information about the Web site's purpose and content. Often it provides connections to other documents, Web pages, or Web sites, which can be downloaded to a computer or mobile device. **Downloading** is the process of a computer or device receiving information, such as a Web page, from a server on the Internet.

How a Web Browser Displays a Home Page

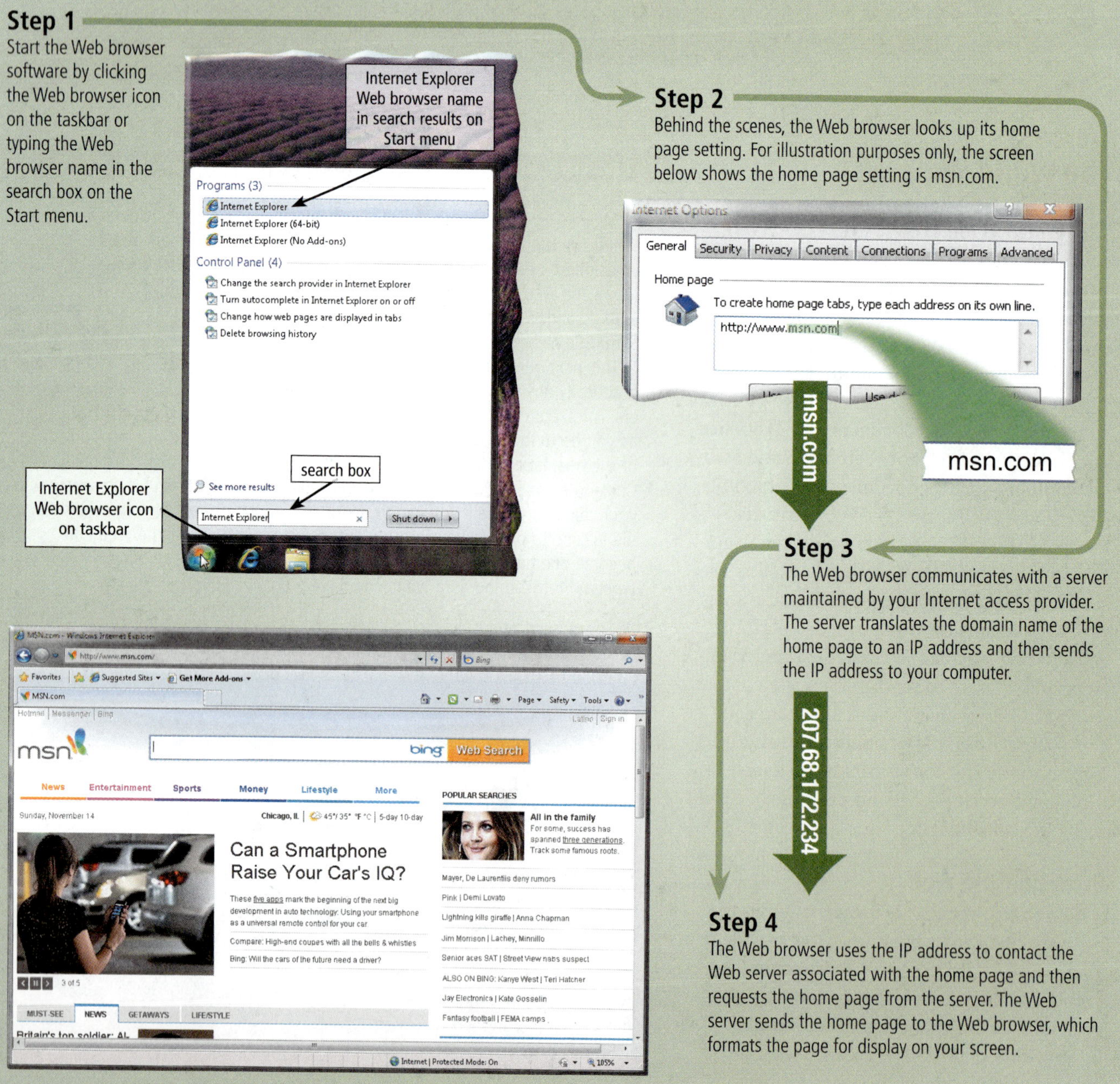

Figure 2-5 This figure shows how a Web browser displays a home page.

Web Addresses

A Web page has a unique address, which is called a **URL** (Uniform Resource Locator) or **Web address**. For example, the home page for the United States National Park Service Web site has a Web address of http://www.nps.gov. A Web browser retrieves a Web page using its Web address.

If you know the Web address of a Web page, you can type it in the Address bar at the top of the browser window. If you type http://www.nps.gov/grsm/planyourvisit/wildlifeviewing.htm as the Web address in the Address bar and then press the ENTER key, the browser downloads and displays the Web page shown in Figure 2-6.

A Web address consists of a protocol, domain name, and sometimes the path to a specific Web page or location on a Web page. Many Web page addresses begin with http://. The http, which stands for Hypertext Transfer Protocol, is a set of rules that defines how pages transfer on the Internet. To help minimize errors, many browsers and Web sites do not require you enter the http:// and www portions of the Web address.

When you enter the Web address, http://www.nps.gov/grsm/planyourvisit/wildlifeviewing.htm in the Web browser, it sends a request to the Web server that contains the nps.com Web site. The server then retrieves the Web page that is named wildlifeviewing.htm in the grsm/planyourvisit path and delivers it to your browser, which then displays the Web page on the screen.

To save time, many users create bookmarks for their frequently visited Web pages. A **bookmark**, or **favorite**, is a saved Web address that you access by clicking the bookmark name in a list. That is, instead of entering a Web address to display a Web page, you can click a previously saved bookmark.

For information about useful Web sites and their associated Web addresses, read the Making Use of the Web feature that follows this chapter.

Figure 2-6 After entering http://www.nps.gov/grsm/planyourvisit/wildlifeviewing.htm as the Web address in the Address bar, this Web page at the United States National Park Service Web site is displayed.

Navigating Web Pages

Most Web pages contain links. A **link**, short for **hyperlink**, is a built-in connection to another related Web page or part of a Web page. Links allow you to obtain information in a nonlinear way. That is, instead of accessing topics in a specified order, you move directly to a topic of interest.

Branching from one related topic to another in a nonlinear fashion is what makes links so powerful. Some people use the phrase, **surfing the Web**, to refer to the activity of using links to explore the Web.

A link can be text or an image. Text links may be underlined and/or displayed in a color different from other text on the Web page. Pointing to, or positioning the pointer on, a link on the screen typically changes the shape of the pointer to a small hand with a pointing index finger. Pointing to a link also sometimes causes the link to change in appearance or play a sound. The Web page shown in Figure 2-7 contains a variety of link types, with the pointer on one of the links.

Each link on a Web page corresponds to a Web address or document. To activate a link, you **click** it, that is, point to the link and then press the left mouse button. Clicking a link causes the Web page or document associated with the link to be displayed on the screen. The linked object might be on the same Web page, a different Web page at the same Web site, or a separate Web page at a different Web site in another city or country.

Tabbed Browsing

For more information, visit the Microsoft Office and Concepts CourseMate Web site at www.cengagebrain.com, navigate to the Chapter 2 Web Link resource for this book, and then click Tabbed Browsing.

Most current Web browsers support **tabbed browsing**, where the top of the browser displays a tab (similar to a file folder tab) for each Web page you open. To move from one open Web page to another, you click the tab in the Web browser.

Because some Web sites attempt to track your browsing habits or gather personal information, some current Web browsers include a feature that allows you to disable and/or more tightly control the dissemination of your browsing habits and personal information. Read Ethics & Issues 2-1 for a related discussion.

Figure 2-7 This browser window has several open tabs. The current tab shows a Web page that has various types of links.

ETHICS & ISSUES 2-1

Should the Government Allow You to Sign Up for a Do-Not-Track List?

When you visit a Web site that includes an advertisement, someone probably is recording the fact that you visited that Web site and viewed the advertisement with your browser. Over time, companies that specialize in tracking who views which online advertisements can amass an enormous amount of information about your online Web surfing habits. Through tracking the Web sites a user visits, the products they buy, and the articles they read, a company may attempt to profile the visitor's beliefs, associations, and habits. Although a user may think he or she is anonymous while navigating the Web, the company can attempt through various means to link the user's true identity with the user's online profile. The company can sell online profiles, with or without the user's true identity, to other advertisers or organizations. Some privacy groups have called for the government to allow consumers to sign up for a do-not-track list modeled after the popular do-not-call list.

Should organizations be allowed to track your Web surfing habits? Why or why not? Should organizations be allowed to associate your real identity with your online identity and profit from the information? Should the government force companies to give you the option of not being tracked? Why or why not? What are the benefits and dangers of online tracking?

Searching the Web

The Web is a worldwide resource of information. A primary reason that people use the Web is to search for specific information, including text, pictures, music, and video. The first step in successful searching is to identify the main idea or concept in the topic about which you are seeking information. Determine any synonyms, alternate spellings, or variant word forms for the topic. Then, use a search tool to locate the information.

Two types of search tools are search engines and subject directories. A **search engine** is a program that finds Web sites, Web pages, images, videos, news, maps, and other information related to a specific topic. A **subject directory** classifies Web pages in an organized set of categories or groups, such as sports or shopping, and related subcategories.

Some Web sites offer the functionality of both a search engine and a subject directory. Google and Yahoo!, for example, are widely used search engines that also provide a subject directory. To use Google or Yahoo!, you enter the Web address (google.com or yahoo.com) in the Address bar in a browser window. The table in Figure 2-8 lists the Web addresses of several popular general-purpose search engines and subject directories.

Ethics & Issues

For the complete text of the Ethics & Issues boxes found in this chapter, visit the Microsoft Office and Concepts CourseMate Web site at www.cengagebrain.com and then navigate to the Chapter 2 Ethics & Issues resource for this book.

Widely Used Search Tools

Search Tool	Web Address	Search Engine	Subject Directory
A9	a9.com	X	
AlltheWeb	alltheweb.com	X	
AltaVista	altavista.com	X	
AOL Search	search.aol.com	X	
Ask	ask.com	X	
Bing	bing.com	X	
Cuil (pronounced cool)	cuil.com	X	
Dogpile	dogpile.com	X	
Excite	excite.com	X	X
Gigablast	gigablast.com	X	X
Google	google.com	X	X
Lycos	lycos.com	X	
MSN	msn.com	X	X
Open Directory Project	dmoz.org	X	X
WebCrawler	webcrawler.com	X	
Yahoo!	yahoo.com	X	X

Figure 2-8 Popular search engines and subject directories.

Search Engines A search engine is helpful in locating information for which you do not know an exact Web address or are not seeking a particular Web site. Some search engines look through Web pages for all types of information. Others can restrict their searches to a specific type of information, such as images, videos, audio, news, maps, people or businesses, and blogs.

Search engines require that you enter a word or phrase, called **search text**, that describes the item you want to find. Your search text can be broad, such as spring break destinations, or more specific, such as Walt Disney World. Figure 2-9 shows one way to use the Google search engine to search for the phrase, Aspen Colorado ski resorts. The results shown in Step 3 include nearly 150,000 links to Web pages, called hits, that reference Aspen Colorado ski resorts. Each hit in the list has a link that, when clicked, displays an associated Web site or Web page. Most search engines sequence the hits based on how close the words in the search text are to one another in the titles and descriptions of the hits. Thus, the first few links probably contain more relevant information.

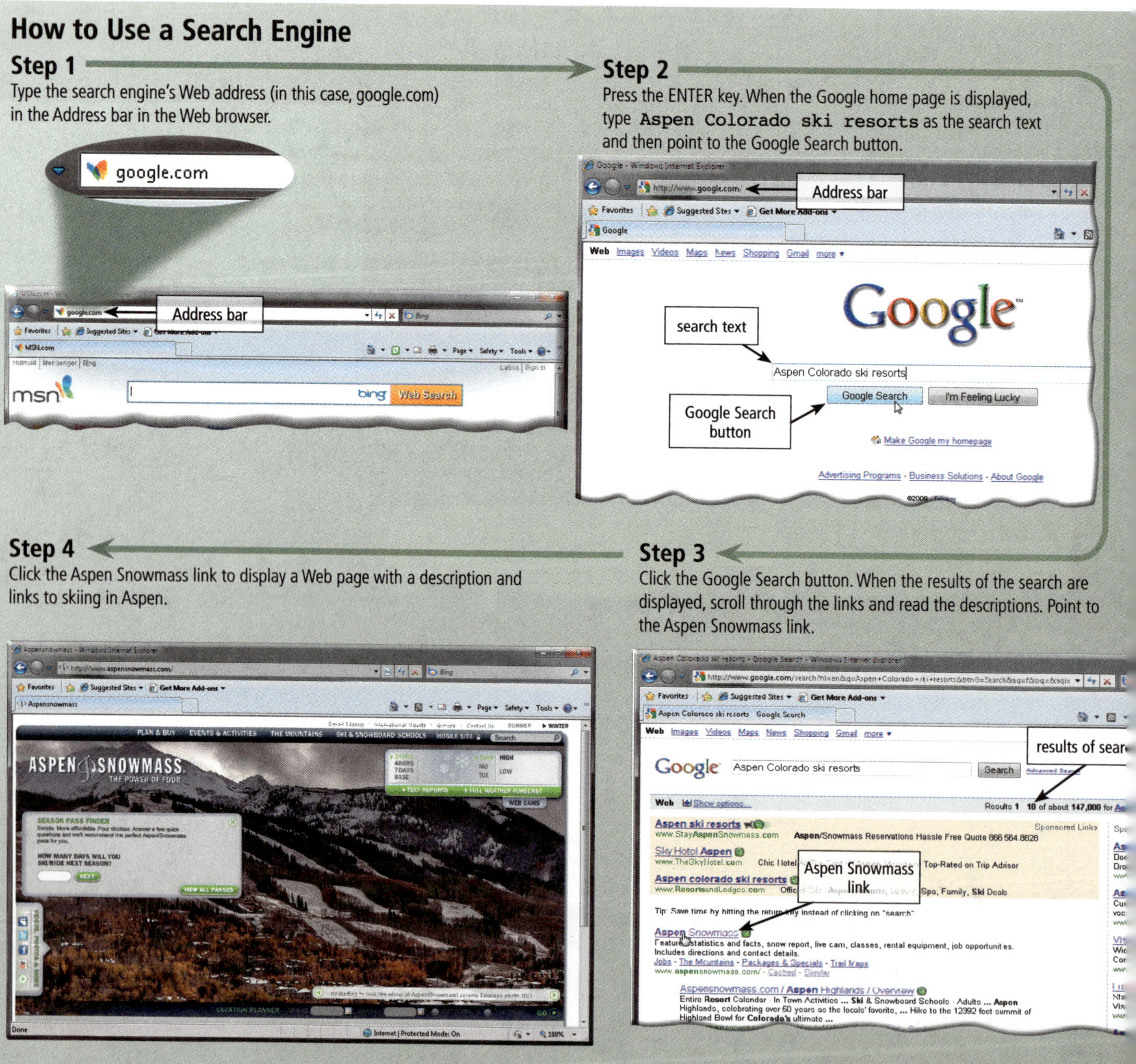

Figure 2-9 This figure shows how to use a search engine.

Some Web browsers contain an Instant Search box that, when filled in, uses a predefined or default search engine to perform searches. Using the Instant Search box eliminates the steps of displaying the search engine's Web page prior to entering the search text.

If you enter a phrase with spaces between the words in the search text, most search engines display results (hits) that include all of the words. The following list identifies techniques you can use to improve your searches. To learn more about searching for information, complete the Learn How To 2 activity on pages 76 and 77.

- Use specific nouns.
- Put the most important terms first in the search text.
- Use the asterisk (*) to substitute characters in words. For example, retriev* displays hits containing retrieves, retrieval, retriever, and any other variation.
- Use quotation marks to create phrases so that the search engine finds an exact sequence of words.
- List all possible spellings, for example, email, e-mail.
- Before using a search engine, read its Help information.
- If the search is unsuccessful with one search engine, try another.

Subject Directories A subject directory provides categorized lists of links arranged by subject (Figure 2-10). Using this search tool, you locate a particular topic by clicking links through different levels, moving from the general to the specific.

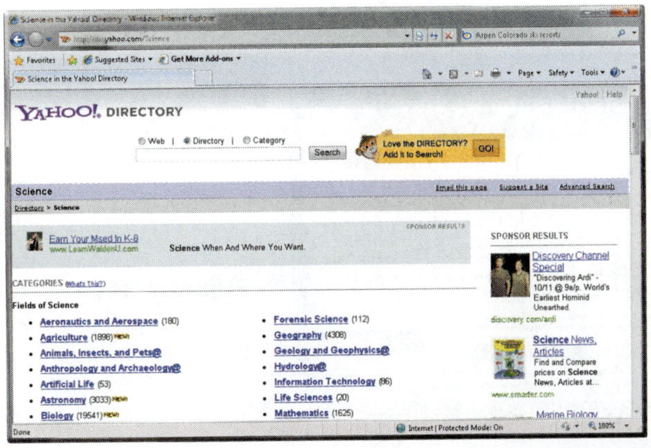

Figure 2-10 A subject directory provides categorized lists of links.

Types of Web Sites

Thirteen types of Web sites are portal, news, informational, business/marketing, blog, wiki, online social network, educational, entertainment, advocacy, Web application, content aggregator, and personal. Many Web sites fall into more than one of these categories.

Portal A **portal** is a Web site that offers a variety of Internet services from a single, convenient location (Figure 2-11a). Most portals offer these free services: search engine; news; sports and weather; Web publishing; reference tools such as yellow pages, stock quotes, and maps; shopping; and e-mail communications services. Popular portals include AltaVista, AOL, Excite, GO.com, iGoogle, Lycos, MSN, and Yahoo!.

News A news Web site contains newsworthy material including stories and articles relating to current events, life, money, sports, and the weather (Figure 2-11b). Newspapers and television and radio stations are some of the media that maintain news Web sites.

Figure 2-11a (portal)

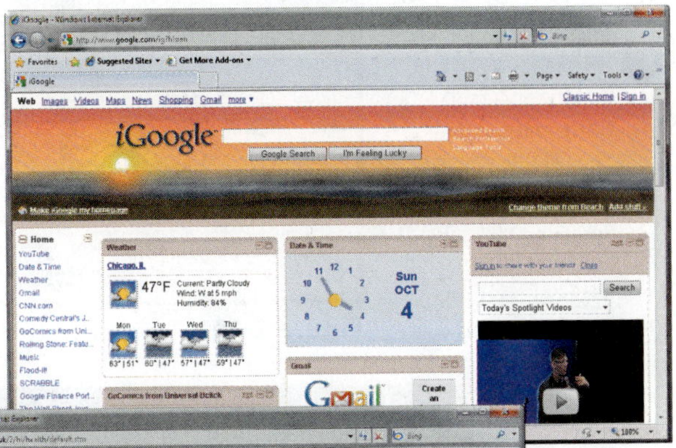

Figure 2-11b (news)

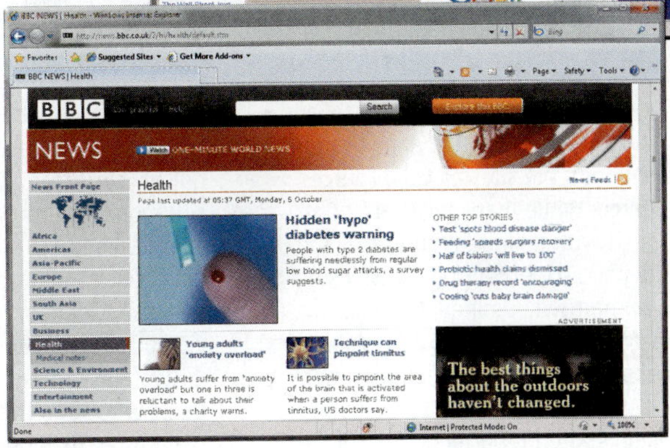

Figure 2-11 Types of Web sites. *(continued on next page)*

Figure 2-11c (informational)

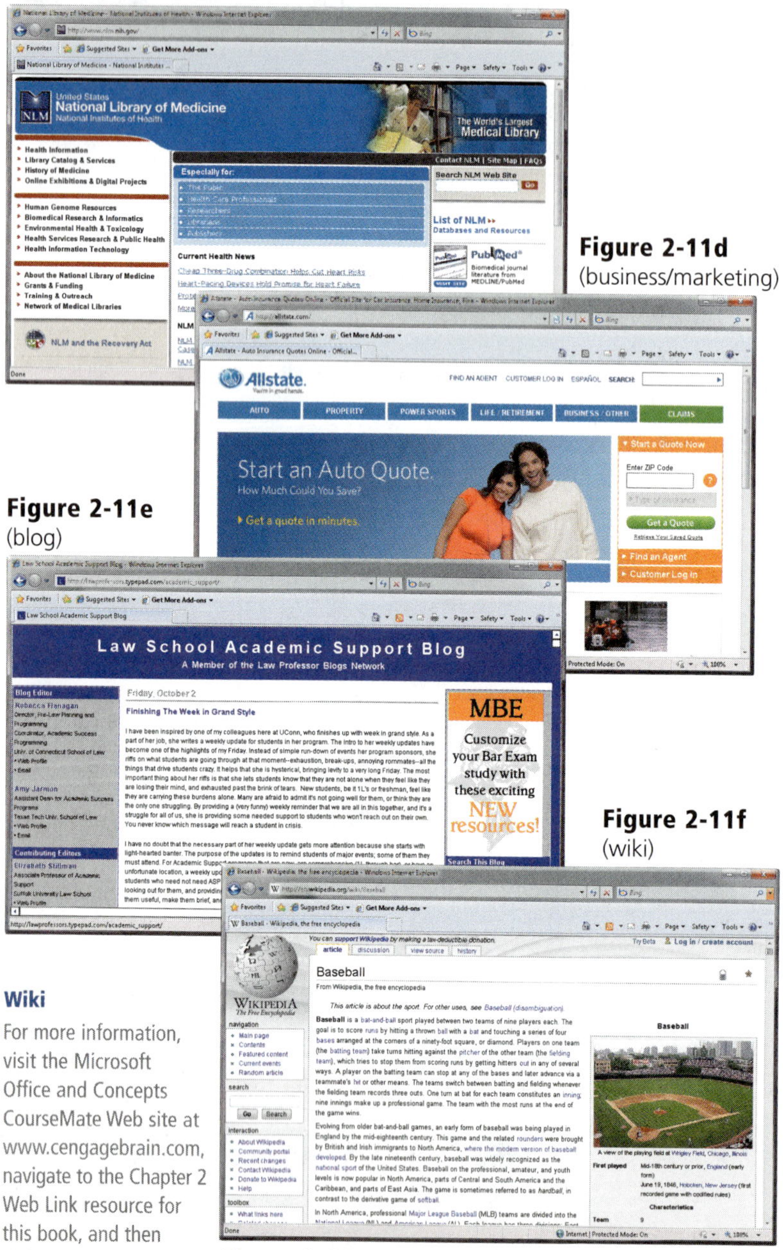

Figure 2-11d (business/marketing)

Figure 2-11e (blog)

Figure 2-11f (wiki)

Figure 2-11 Types of Web sites. *(continued)*

Wiki

For more information, visit the Microsoft Office and Concepts CourseMate Web site at www.cengagebrain.com, navigate to the Chapter 2 Web Link resource for this book, and then click Wiki.

Informational An informational Web site contains factual information (Figure 2-11c). Many United States government agencies have informational Web sites providing information such as census data, tax codes, and the congressional budget. Other organizations provide information such as public transportation schedules and published research findings.

Business/Marketing A business/marketing Web site contains content that promotes or sells products or services (Figure 2-11d). Nearly every enterprise has a business/marketing Web site. Many companies also allow you to purchase their products or services online.

Blog A **blog**, short for Weblog, is an informal Web site consisting of time-stamped articles, or posts, in a diary or journal format, usually listed in reverse chronological order (Figure 2-11e). A blog that contains video clips is called a **video blog** or **vlog**. A **microblog** allows users to publish short messages, usually between 100 and 200 characters, for others to read. Twitter is a popular microblog. The term **blogosphere** refers to the worldwide collection of blogs, and the **vlogosphere** refers to all vlogs worldwide. Blogs reflect the interests, opinions, and personalities of the author and sometimes site visitors. Blogs have become an important means of worldwide communications.

Wiki A **wiki** is a collaborative Web site that allows users to create, add to, modify, or delete the Web site content via their Web browser. Most wikis are open to modification by the general public. Wikis usually collect recent edits on a Web page so that someone can review them for accuracy. The difference between a wiki and a blog is that users cannot modify original posts made by the blogger. A popular wiki is Wikipedia, a free Web encyclopedia (Figure 2-11f). Read Ethics & Issues 2-2 for a related discussion.

ETHICS & ISSUES 2-2

Should You Trust a Wiki for Academic Research?

As wikis have grown in number, size, and popularity, some educators and librarians have shunned the sites as valid sources of research. While many wikis are tightly controlled with a limited number of contributors and expert editors, these usually focus on narrowly-defined, specialized topics. Most large wikis, such as Wikipedia, often involve thousands of editors, many of whom remain anonymous. Recently, television station reporters purposefully vandalized entries on Wikipedia for John Lennon and Elvis Presley in an attempt either to discredit Wikipedia or to test how quickly corrections are made. Editors quickly corrected the information. In other situations, rival political factions falsified or embellished wiki entries in an attempt to give their candidate an advantage. Some wiki supporters argue that most wikis provide adequate controls to correct false or misleading content quickly and to punish those who submit it. One popular wiki now requires an experienced editor to verify changes made to certain types of articles. Some propose that wikis should be used as a starting point for researching a fact, but that the fact should be verified using traditional sources.

Should wikis be allowed as valid sources for academic research? Why or why not? Would you submit a paper to your instructor that cites a wiki as a source? An encyclopedia? Why or why not? What policies could wikis enforce that could garner more confidence from the public? If a wiki provided verification of the credentials of the author, would you trust the wiki more? Why or why not?

Online Social Networks An **online social network**, also called a **social networking Web site**, is a Web site that encourages members in its online community to share their interests, ideas, stories, photos, music, and videos with other registered users (Figure 2-11g). Popular social networking Web sites include MySpace and Facebook, with Facebook alone boasting more than 300 million active users. A **media sharing Web site** is a specific type of online social network that enables members to share media such as photos, music, and videos. Flickr, Fotki, and Webshots are popular photo sharing communities; PixelFish and YouTube are popular video sharing communities.

Educational An educational Web site offers exciting, challenging avenues for formal and informal teaching and learning (Figure 2-11h). For a more structured learning experience, companies provide online training to employees; and colleges offer online classes and degrees. Instructors often use the Web to enhance classroom teaching by publishing course materials, grades, and other pertinent class information.

Entertainment An entertainment Web site offers an interactive and engaging environment (Figure 2-11i). Popular entertainment Web sites offer music, videos, sports, games, ongoing Web episodes, sweepstakes, chat rooms, and more.

Advocacy An advocacy Web site contains content that describes a cause, opinion, or idea (Figure 2-11j). These Web sites usually present views of a particular group or association.

Web Application A **Web application**, or **Web app**, is a Web site that allows users to access and interact with software through a Web browser on any computer or device that is connected to the Internet. Some Web applications provide free access to their software (Figure 2-11k). Others offer part of their software free and charge for access to more comprehensive features or when a particular action is requested. Examples of Web applications include Google Docs (word processing, spreadsheets, presentations), TurboTax Online (tax preparation), and Windows Live Hotmail (e-mail).

Figure 2-11g
(online social network)

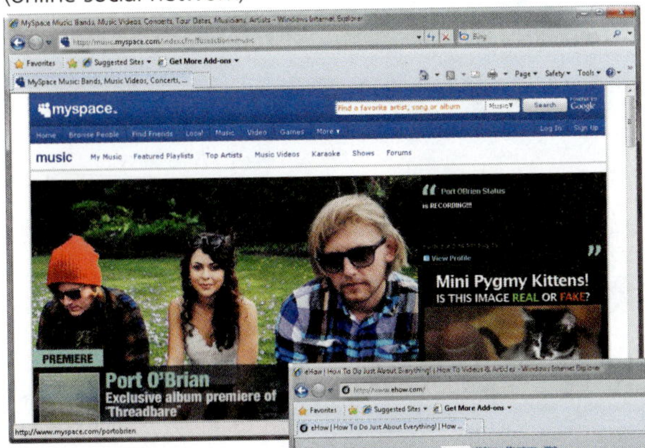

Figure 2-11h
(educational)

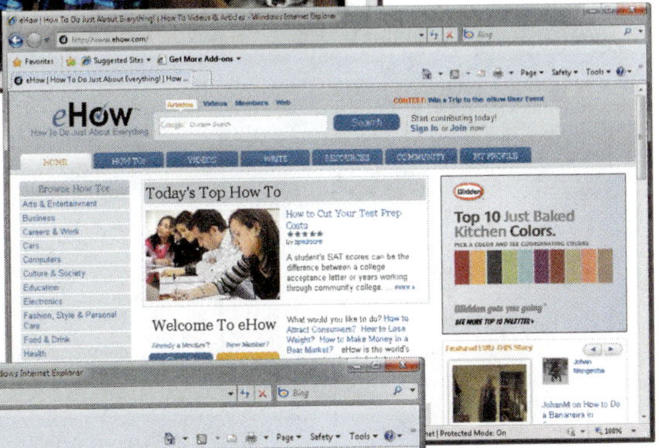

Figure 2-11i
(entertainment)

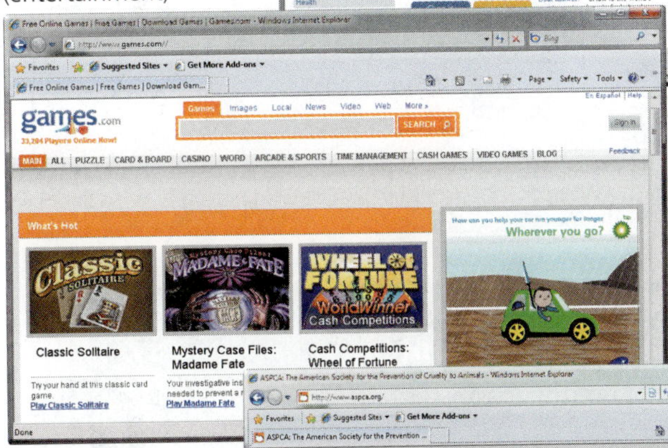

Figure 2-11j
(advocacy)

Figure 2-11k
(Web application)

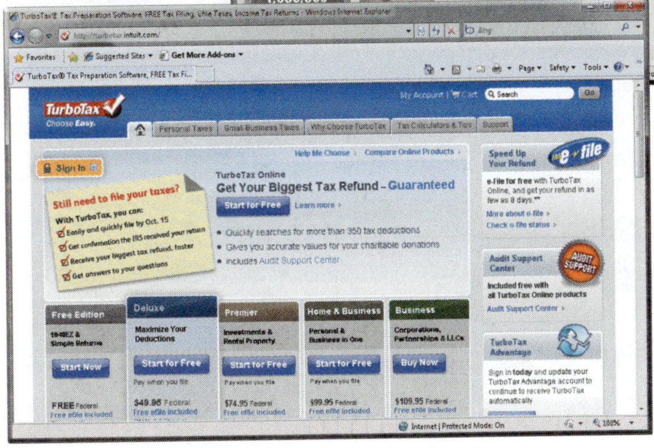

Figure 2-11 Types of Web sites. *(continued on next page)*

Figure 2-11l (content aggregator)

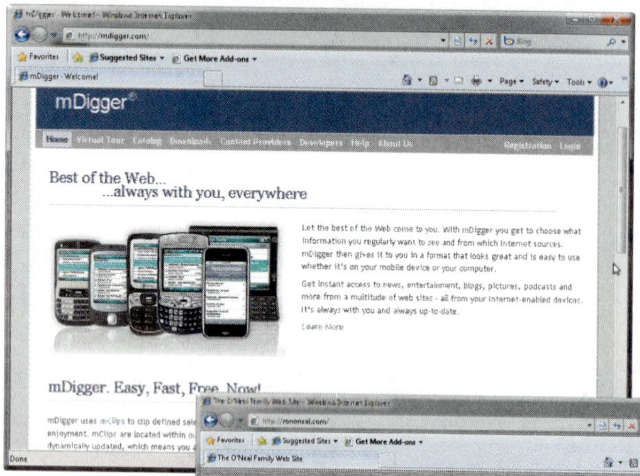

Figure 2-11m (personal)

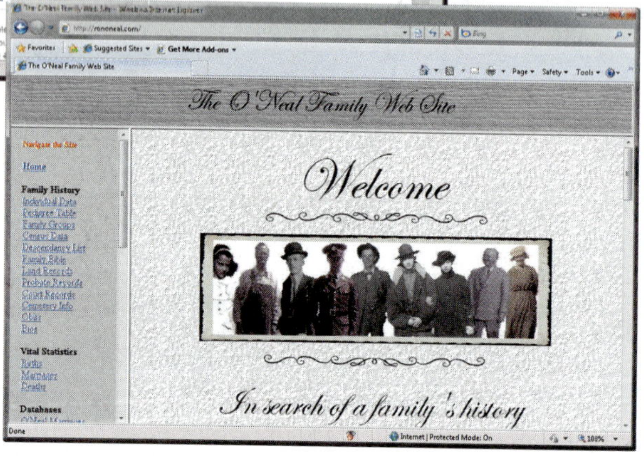

Figure 2-11 Types of Web sites. *(continued)*

Criteria for Evaluating a Web Site's Content

Evaluation Criteria	Reliable Web Sites
Affiliation	A reputable institution should support the Web site without bias in the information.
Audience	The Web site should be written at an appropriate level.
Authority	The Web site should list the author and the appropriate credentials.
Content	The Web site should be well organized and the links should work.
Currency	The information on the Web page should be current.
Design	The pages at the Web site should download quickly, be visually pleasing, and easy to navigate.
Objectivity	The Web site should contain little advertising and be free of preconceptions.

Figure 2-12 Criteria for evaluating a Web site's content.

Content Aggregator A **content aggregator** is a business that gathers and organizes Web content and then distributes, or feeds, the content to subscribers for free or a fee (Figure 2-11l). Examples of distributed content include news, music, video, and pictures. Subscribers select content in which they are interested. Whenever this content changes, it is downloaded automatically (pushed) to the subscriber's computer or mobile device. **RSS 2.0**, which stands for Really Simple Syndication, is a specification that content aggregators use to distribute content to subscribers.

Personal A private individual or family not usually associated with any organization may maintain a personal Web site (Figure 2-11m). People publish personal Web pages for a variety of reasons. Some are job hunting. Others simply want to share life experiences with the world.

Evaluating a Web Site

Do not assume that information presented on the Web is correct or accurate. Any person, company, or organization can publish a Web page on the Internet. No one oversees the content of these Web pages. Figure 2-12 lists guidelines for assessing the value of a Web site or Web page before relying on its content.

Multimedia on the Web

Most Web pages include more than just formatted text and links. The more exciting Web pages use multimedia. **Multimedia** refers to any application that combines text with graphics, animation, audio, video, and/or virtual reality. Multimedia Web pages often require specific hardware and software and take more time to download because they contain large graphics files or video or audio clips. The sections that follow discuss how the Web uses graphics, animation, audio, video, and virtual reality.

Graphics A **graphic**, or graphical image, is a digital representation of nontext information such as a drawing, chart, or photo. Many Web pages use colorful graphical designs and images to convey messages (Figure 2-13). Read Innovative Computing 2-1 to find out how astronomers share graphics of the universe.

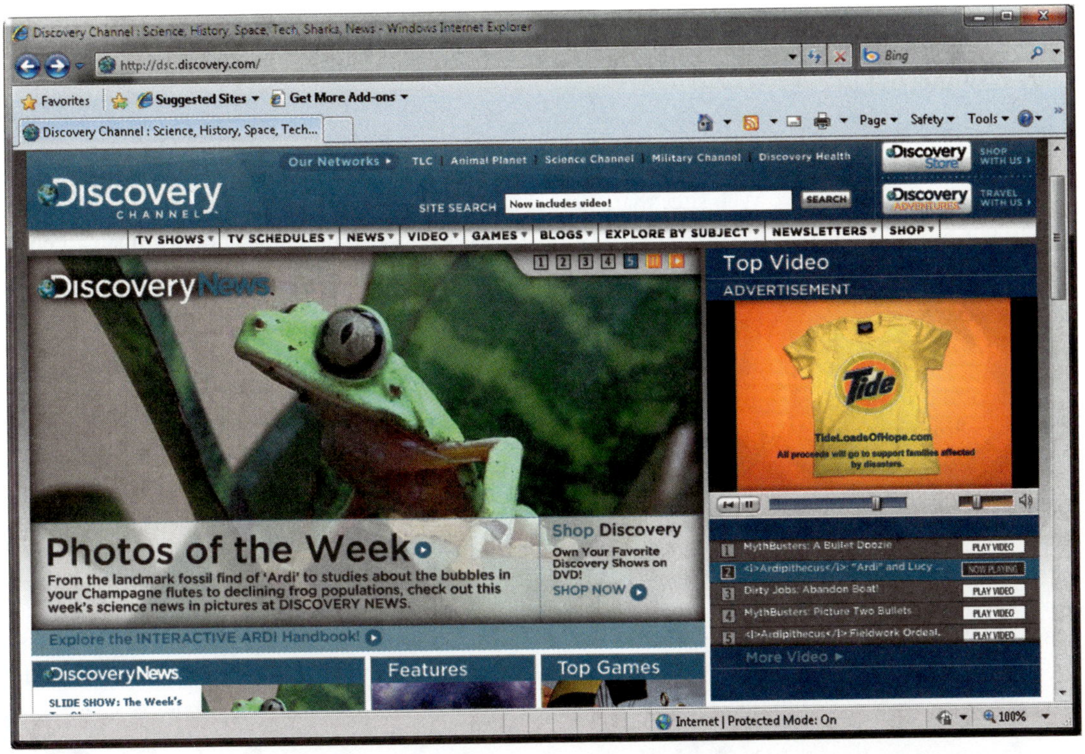

Figure 2-13 This Web page uses colorful graphical designs and images to convey its messages.

INNOVATIVE COMPUTING 2-1

View the Wonders of Space through the WorldWide Telescope

The phrase, reach for the stars, takes on a new meaning when using Microsoft's WorldWide Telescope. Users can access the Telescope from a Web browser or download free software. They then can view a variety of multimedia, including high-resolution graphics from telescopes located on Earth and in space, with Web 2.0 services to allow people to explore the final frontier from their computers.

Users can pan and zoom around the night sky by looking through a specific telescope, such as the Hubble Space Telescope, and view the universe in the past, present, or future. In addition, they can browse graphics of a specific planet, the Milky Way Galaxy, black holes, and other celestial bodies in our solar system, galaxy, and beyond. They also can select different wavelengths, such as X-ray or visible light, to search for objects. Astronomers and educators also have created narrated tours of the sky to help interpret the images.

For more information, visit the Microsoft Office and Concepts CourseMate Web site at www.cengagebrain.com, navigate to the Chapter 2 Innovative Computing resource for this book, and then click WorldWide Telescope.

Of the graphics formats that exist on the Web, the two more common are JPEG and GIF formats. JPEG (pronounced JAY-peg) is a format that compresses graphics to reduce their file size, which means the file takes up less storage space. The goal with JPEG graphics is to reach a balance between image quality and file size. Digital photos often use the JPEG format. GIF (pronounced jiff) graphics also use compression techniques to reduce file sizes. The GIF format works best for images that have only a few distinct colors, such as company logos.

Some Web sites use thumbnails on their pages because graphics can be time-consuming to display. A **thumbnail** is a small version of a larger graphic. You usually can click a thumbnail to display a larger image.

Animation Many Web pages use **animation**, which is the appearance of motion created by displaying a series of still images in sequence. Animation can make Web pages more visually interesting or draw attention to important information or links.

Audio On the Web, you can listen to audio clips and live audio. **Audio** includes music, speech, or any other sound. Simple applications on the Web consist of individual audio files available for download to a computer or device. Once downloaded, you can play (listen to) the contents of these files. Audio files are compressed to reduce their file sizes. For example, the **MP3** format reduces an audio file to about one-tenth its original size, while preserving much of the original quality of the sound.

Some music publishers have Web sites that allow users to download sample tracks free to persuade them to buy all the songs contained on the CD. Others allow a user to purchase and download an entire CD (Figure 2-14). It is legal to download copyrighted music only if the song's copyright holder has granted permission for users to download and play the song.

To listen to an audio file on your computer, you need special software called a **player**. Most current operating systems contain a player, for example, Windows Media Player. Some audio files, however, might require you to download a player. Players available for download include iTunes and RealPlayer.

Some applications on the Web use streaming audio. **Streaming** is the process of transferring data in a continuous and even flow. Streaming allows users to access and use a file while it is transmitting. For example, streaming audio enables you to listen to music as it downloads to your computer.

Podcasting is another popular method of distributing audio. A **podcast** is recorded audio, usually an MP3 file, stored on a Web site that can be downloaded to a computer or a portable media player such as an iPod. Examples of podcasts include music, radio shows, news stories, classroom lectures, political messages, and television commentaries. Podcasters register their podcasts with content aggregators. Subscribers select podcast feeds they want to be downloaded automatically whenever they connect. Most smart phone users who subscribe to a wireless Internet service provider can listen to streaming audio and podcasts.

Figure 2-14 This figure shows how to purchase and download music using iTunes.

Video On the Web, you can view video clips or watch live video. **Video** consists of images displayed in motion. Most video also has accompanying audio. You can use the Internet to watch live and prerecorded coverage of your favorite television programs or enjoy a live performance of your favorite vocalist. You can upload, share, or view video clips at a video sharing Web site such as YouTube. Educators, politicians, and businesses are using video blogs and video podcasts to engage students, voters, and consumers.

Video files often are compressed because they are quite large in size. These clips also are quite short in length, usually less than 10 minutes, because they can take a long time to download. The Moving Pictures Experts Group (MPEG) defines a popular video compression standard, a widely used one called MPEG-4 or **MP4**. Another popular video format is Adobe Flash. As with streaming audio, streaming video allows you to view longer or live video images as they download to your computer.

? FAQ 2-4

How are social networking Web sites and Internet video affecting Internet traffic?

A report from Cisco Systems states that Internet traffic will double every two years until 2012. The volume of Internet traffic is increasing mostly because of Internet videos and social networking. In addition, the increased use of video conferencing by business users accounts for the increase in traffic.

For more information, visit the Microsoft Office and Concepts CourseMate Web site at www.cengagebrain.com, navigate to the Chapter 2 FAQ resource for this book, and then click Internet Traffic.

Virtual Reality **Virtual reality (VR)** is the use of computers to simulate a real or imagined environment that appears as a three-dimensional (3-D) space. VR involves the display of 3-D images that users explore and manipulate interactively. A VR Web site, for example, might show a house for sale. Potential buyers walk through rooms in the VR house by moving an input device forward, backward, or to the side.

Plug-ins Most Web browsers have the capability of displaying basic multimedia elements on a Web page. Sometimes, a browser might need an additional program, called a plug-in. A **plug-in**, or **add-on**, is a program that extends the capability of a browser. You can download many plug-ins at no cost from various Web sites (Figure 2-15).

Popular Plug-Ins

Plug-In Application	Description	Web Address
Acrobat Reader	View, navigate, and print Portable Document Format (PDF) files — documents formatted to look just as they look in print	adobe.com
Flash Player	View dazzling graphics and animation, hear outstanding sound and music, display Web pages across an entire screen	adobe.com
Java	Enable Web browser to run programs written in Java, which add interactivity to Web pages	java.com
QuickTime	View animation, music, audio, video, and VR panoramas and objects directly on a Web page	apple.com
RealPlayer	Listen to live and on-demand near-CD-quality audio and newscast-quality video, stream audio and video content for faster viewing, play MP3 files, create music CDs	real.com
Shockwave Player	Experience dynamic interactive multimedia, 3-D graphics, and streaming audio	adobe.com
Silverlight	Experience high-definition video, high-resolution interactive multimedia, and streaming audio and video	microsoft.com
Windows Media Player	Listen to live and on-demand audio, play or edit WMA and MP3 files, burn CDs, and watch DVD movies	microsoft.com

Figure 2-15 Most plug-ins can be downloaded free from the Web.

Web Publishing

Before the World Wide Web, the means to share opinions and ideas with others easily and inexpensively was limited to the media, classroom, work, or social environments. Today, businesses and individuals convey information to millions of people by creating their own Web pages.

Web publishing is the development and maintenance of Web pages. To develop a Web page, you do not have to be a computer programmer. For the small business or home user, Web publishing is fairly easy as long as you have the proper tools.

The five major steps to Web publishing are as follows:

1. Plan a Web site: Think about issues that could affect the design of the Web site.
2. Analyze and design a Web site: Design the layout of elements of the Web site such as links, text, graphics, animation, audio, video, and virtual reality.
3. Create a Web site: Use a word processing program to create basic Web pages or Web page authoring software to create more sophisticated Web sites.
4. Deploy a Web site: Transfer the Web pages from your computer to a Web server.
5. Maintain a Web site: Ensure the Web site contents remain current and all links work properly.

Web Page Authoring Software

For more information, visit the Microsoft Office and Concepts CourseMate Web site at www.cengagebrain.com, navigate to the Chapter 2 Web Link resource for this book, and then click Web Page Authoring Software.

E-Commerce

E-commerce, short for electronic commerce, is a business transaction that occurs over an electronic network such as the Internet. Anyone with access to a computer or mobile device, an Internet connection, and a means to pay for purchased goods or services can participate in e-commerce.

Three types of e-commerce are business-to-consumer, consumer-to-consumer, and business-to-business. Business-to-consumer (B2C) e-commerce consists of the sale of goods and services to the general public. For example, Apple has a B2C Web site. Instead of visiting a retail store to purchase an iPod, for example, customers can order one directly from Apple's Web site.

E-retail, short for electronic retail, occurs when businesses use the Web to sell products (Figure 2-16). A customer (consumer) visits an online business through an **electronic storefront**, which contains product

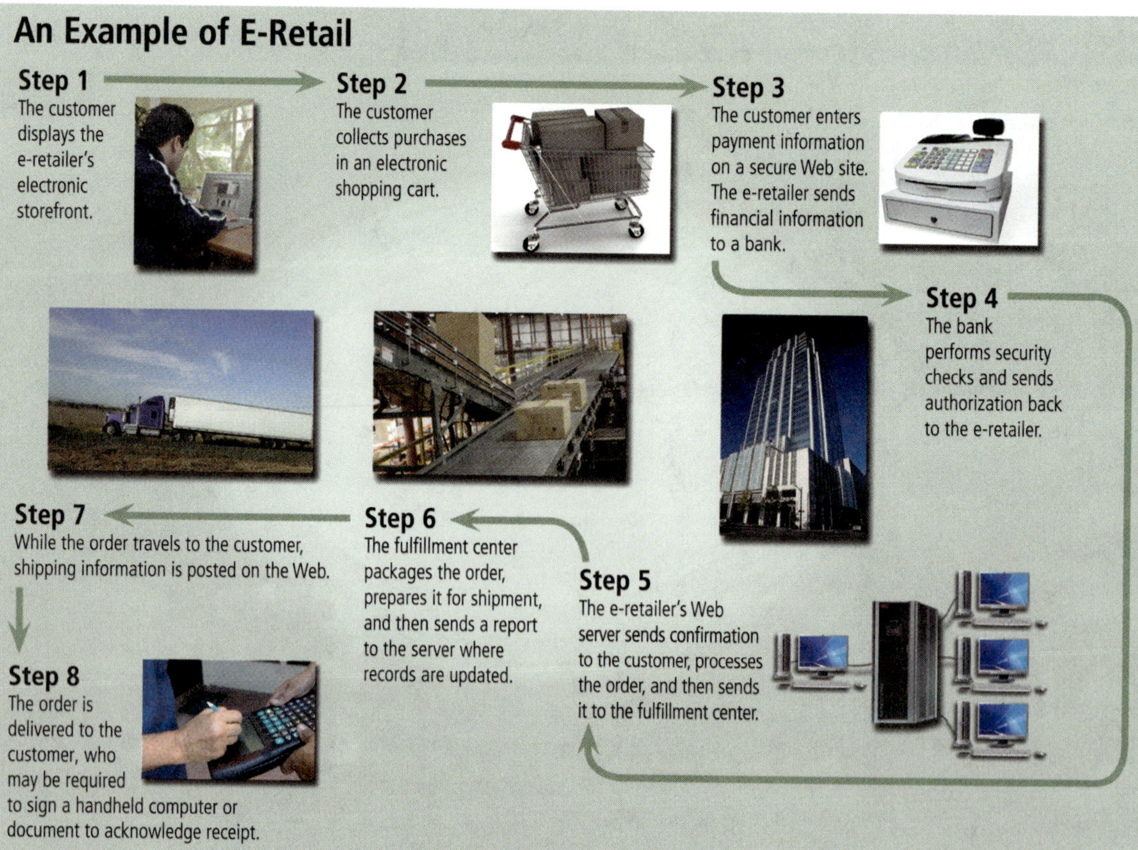

Figure 2-16 This figure shows an example of e-retail.

descriptions, images, and a shopping cart. The **shopping cart** allows the customer to collect purchases. When ready to complete the sale, the customer enters personal data and the method of payment, which should be through a secure Internet connection.

Consumer-to-consumer (C2C) e-commerce occurs when one consumer sells directly to another, such as in an online auction. With an **online auction**, users bid on an item being sold by someone else. The highest bidder at the end of the bidding period purchases the item. eBay is one of the more popular online auction Web sites.

As an alternative to entering credit card, bank account, or other financial information online, some shopping and auction Web sites allow consumers to use an online payment service such as PayPal or Google Checkout. To use an online payment service, you create an account that is linked to your credit card or funds at a financial institution. When you make a purchase, you use your online payment service account, which transfers money for you without revealing your financial information.

Google Checkout
For more information, visit the Microsoft Office and Concepts CourseMate Web site at www.cengagebrain.com, navigate to the Chapter 2 Web Link resource for this book, and then click Google Checkout.

Most e-commerce, though, actually takes place between businesses, which is called business-to-business (B2B) e-commerce. Many businesses provide goods and services to other businesses, such as online advertising, recruiting, credit, sales, market research, technical support, and training.

QUIZ YOURSELF 2-2

Instructions: Find the true statement below. Then, rewrite the remaining false statements so that they are true.

1. A blog is a Web site that uses a regularly updated journal format to reflect the interests, opinions, and personalities of the author and sometimes site visitors.
2. A Web browser classifies Web pages in an organized set of categories and related subcategories.
3. Business-to-consumer e-commerce occurs when one consumer sells directly to another, such as in an online auction.
4. The more widely used search engines for personal computers are Internet Explorer, Firefox, Opera, Safari, and Google Chrome.
5. To develop a Web page, you have to be a computer programmer.

Quiz Yourself Online: To further check your knowledge of pages 49 through 63, visit the Microsoft Office and Concepts CourseMate Web site at www.cengagebrain.com, navigate to the Chapter 2 Quiz Yourself resource for this book, and then click Objectives 3 – 7.

Other Internet Services

The Web is only one of the many services on the Internet. The Web and other Internet services have changed the way we communicate. We use computers and mobile devices to send e-mail messages to the president, have a discussion with experts about the stock market, chat with someone in another country about genealogy, and talk about homework assignments with classmates via instant messages. Many times, these communications take place completely in writing — without the parties ever meeting each other.

The following pages discuss these Internet services: e-mail, mailing lists, instant messaging, chat rooms, VoIP (Voice over IP), FTP (File Transfer Protocol), and newsgroups and message boards.

E-Mail

E-mail (short for electronic mail) is the transmission of messages and files via a computer network. Today, e-mail is a primary communications method for both personal and business use.

You use an **e-mail program** to create, send, receive, forward, store, print, and delete e-mail messages. Outlook and Windows Live Mail are two popular desktop e-mail programs.

The steps in Figure 2-17 illustrate how to send an e-mail message using Outlook; Gmail and Windows Live Hotmail are two popular free e-mail Web applications. The message can be simple text or can include an attachment such as a word processing document, a graphic, an audio clip, or a video clip. To learn more about how to attach a file to an e-mail message, complete the Learn How To 1 activity on page 76.

Just as you address a letter when using the postal system, you address an e-mail message with the e-mail address of your intended recipient. Likewise, when someone sends you a message, he or she must have your e-mail address. An **e-mail address** is a combination of a user name and a domain name that

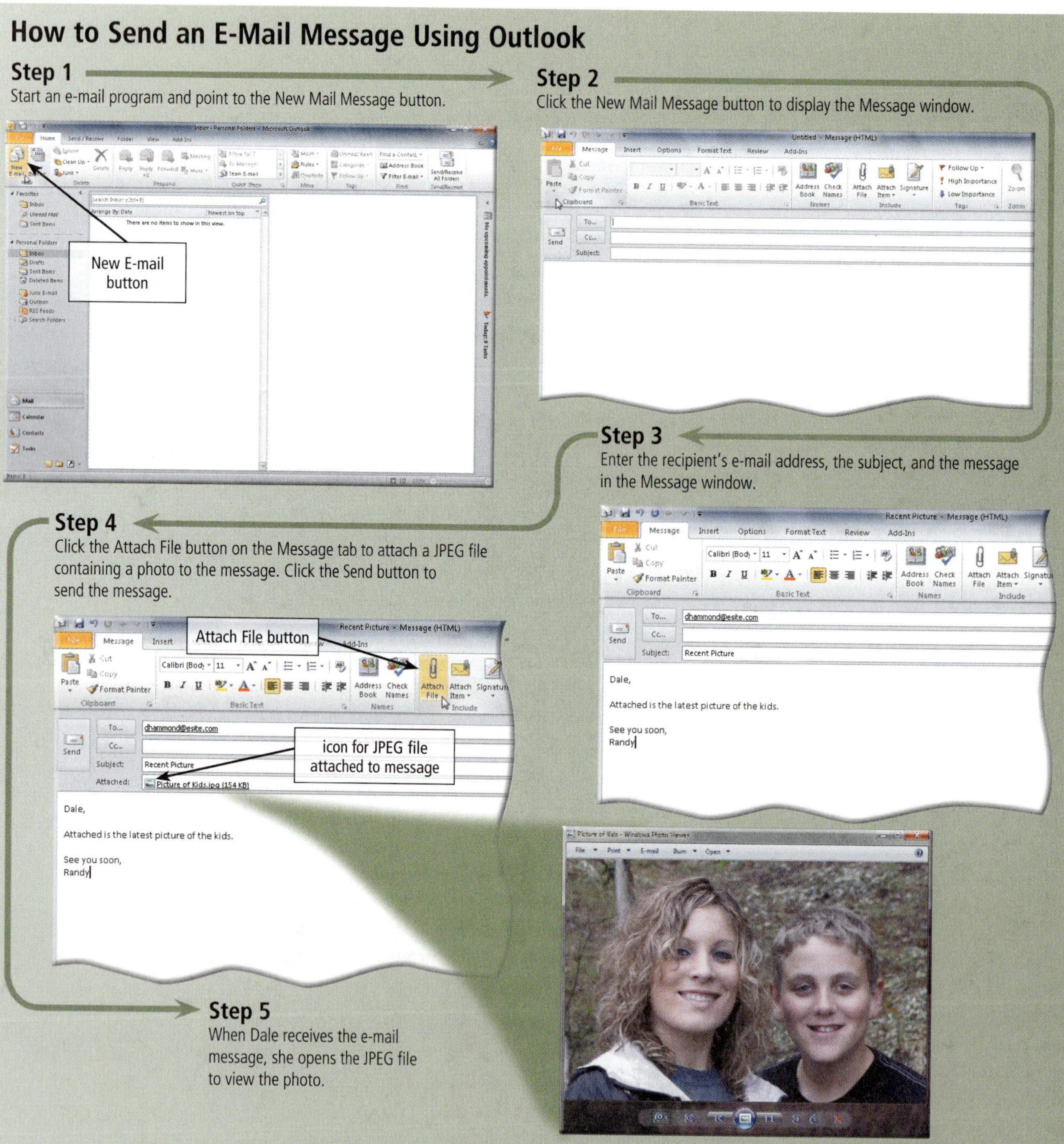

Figure 2-17 This figure shows how to send an e-mail message using Outlook.

identifies a user so that he or she can receive Internet e-mail. A **user name** is a unique combination of characters, such as letters of the alphabet and/or numbers, that identifies a specific user.

In an Internet e-mail address, an @ (pronounced at) symbol separates the user name from the domain name. Your service provider supplies the domain name. A possible e-mail address for Kiley Barnhill would be kbarnhill@esite.com, which would be read as follows: K Barnhill at e site dot com. Most e-mail programs allow you to create an **address book**, or contacts folder, which contains a list of names and e-mail addresses.

When you send an e-mail message, an outgoing mail server that is operated by your Internet access provider determines how to route the message through the Internet and then sends the message. As you receive e-mail messages, an incoming mail server — also operated by your Internet access provider — holds the messages in your mailbox until you use your e-mail program to retrieve them. Most e-mail programs have a mail notification alert that informs you via a message and/or sound when you receive new mail. Figure 2-18 illustrates how an e-mail message may travel from a sender to a receiver using a desktop e-mail program.

E-Mail

For more information, visit the Microsoft Office and Concepts CourseMate Web site at www.cengagebrain.com, navigate to the Chapter 2 Web Link resource for this book, and then click E-Mail.

? FAQ 2-5

Can my computer get a virus through e-mail?

Yes. A virus is a computer program that can damage files and the operating system. One way that virus authors attempt to spread a virus is by sending virus-infected e-mail attachments. If you receive an e-mail attachment, you should use an antivirus program to verify that it is virus free.

For more information, read the section about viruses and antivirus programs in Chapter 4, and visit the Microsoft Office and Concepts CourseMate Web site at www.cengagebrain.com, navigate to the Chapter 2 FAQ resource for this book, and then click Viruses.

Figure 2-18 This figure shows how an e-mail message may travel from a sender to a receiver.

Mailing Lists

A **mailing list**, also called an e-mail list or distribution list, is a group of e-mail names and addresses given a single name. When a message is sent to a mailing list, every person on the list receives a copy of the message in his or her mailbox. For example, your credit card company may add you to its mailing list in order to send you special offers. To add your e-mail name and address to a mailing list, you **subscribe** to it. To remove your name, you **unsubscribe** from the mailing list.

Thousands of mailing lists exist about a variety of topics in areas of entertainment, business, computers, society, culture, health, recreation, and education.

Instant Messaging

Instant messaging (IM) is a real-time Internet communications service that notifies you when one or more people are online and then allows you to exchange messages or files or join a private chat room with them (Figure 2-19). **Real time** means that you and the people with whom you are conversing are online at the same time. Some IM services support voice and video conversations. For IM to work, both parties must be online at the same time. Also, the receiver of a message must be willing to accept messages.

An Example of Instant Messaging

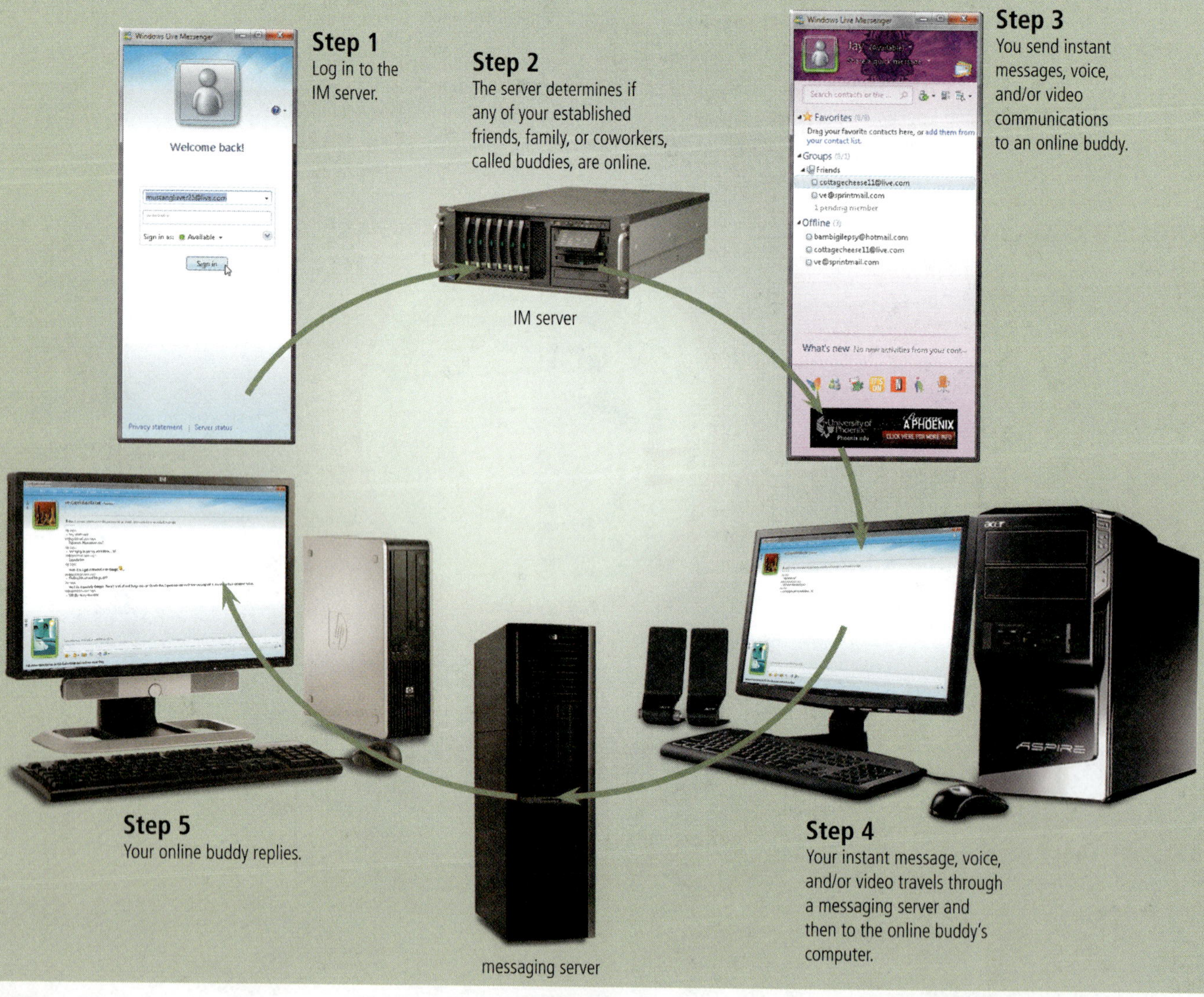

Figure 2-19 This figure shows an example of instant messaging.

To use IM, you may have to install instant messenger software on the computer or device, such as a smart phone, you plan to use. Some operating systems, such as Windows, include an instant messenger. Few IM programs follow IM standards. To ensure successful communications, all individuals on the contact list need to use the same or a compatible instant messenger.

Chat Rooms

A **chat** is a real-time typed conversation that takes place on a computer. A **chat room** is a location on an Internet server that permits users to chat with each other. Anyone in the chat room can participate in the conversation, which usually is specific to a particular topic.

As you type on your keyboard, a line of characters and symbols is displayed on the computer screen. Others connected to the same chat room server also see what you type (Figure 2-20). Some chat rooms support voice chats and video chats, in which people hear or see each other as they chat.

To start a chat session, you connect to a chat server through a program called a chat client. Today's browsers usually include a chat client. If yours does not, you can download a chat client from the Web. Once you have installed a chat client, you can create or join a conversation on the chat server to which you are connected.

Chat Rooms

For more information, visit the Microsoft Office and Concepts CourseMate Web site at www.cengagebrain.com, navigate to the Chapter 2 Web Link resource for this book, and then click Chat Rooms.

Figure 2-20 As you type, the words and symbols you enter are displayed on the computer screens of other people in the same chat room. To save time many chat and IM users type abbreviations and acronyms for phrases, such as 'r u there?', which stands for 'Are You There?'.

VoIP

VoIP (Voice over IP, or Internet Protocol), also called Internet telephony, enables users to speak to other users over the Internet (instead of the public switched telephone network).

To place an Internet telephone call, you need a high-speed Internet connection (e.g., via cable or DSL modem); Internet telephone service; a microphone or telephone, depending on the Internet telephone service; and Internet telephone software or VoIP router, or a telephone adapter, depending on the Internet telephone service (Figure 2-21). VoIP services also are available on some mobile devices that have wireless Internet service. Calls to other parties with the same Internet telephone service often are free, while calls that connect to the telephone network typically cost about $15 to $35 per month.

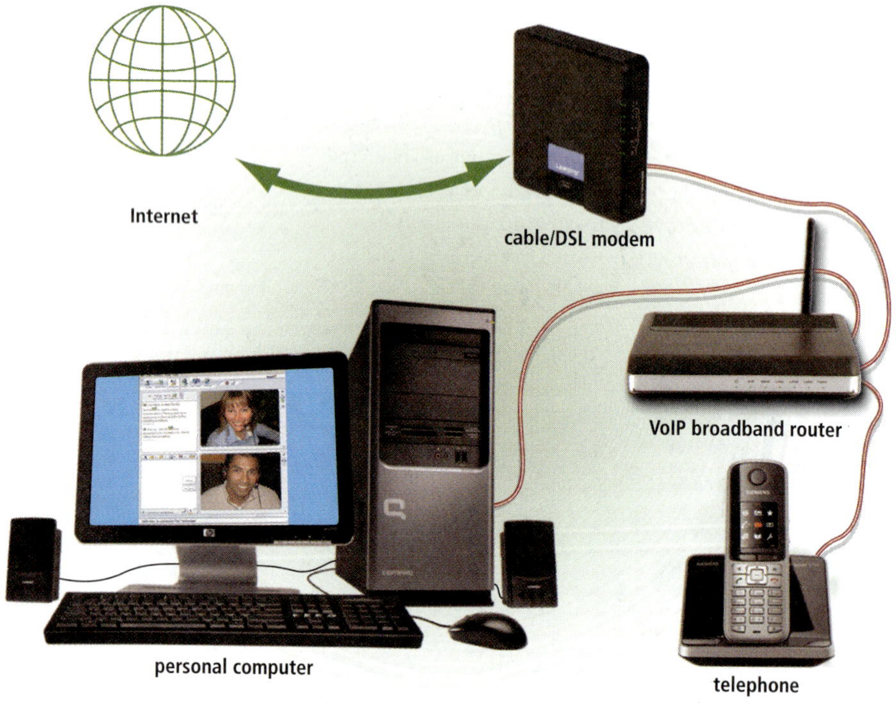

Figure 2-21 One type of equipment configuration for a user making a call via VoIP.

FTP

FTP (File Transfer Protocol) is an Internet standard that permits the process of file uploading and downloading with other computers on the Internet. Uploading is the opposite of downloading; that is, **uploading** is the process of transferring documents, graphics, and other objects from your computer to a server on the Internet.

Many operating systems include FTP capabilities. An FTP site is a collection of files including text, graphics, audio clips, video clips, and program files that reside on an FTP server. Many FTP sites have anonymous FTP, whereby anyone can transfer some, if not all, available files. Some FTP sites restrict file transfers to those who have authorized accounts (user names and passwords) on the FTP server.

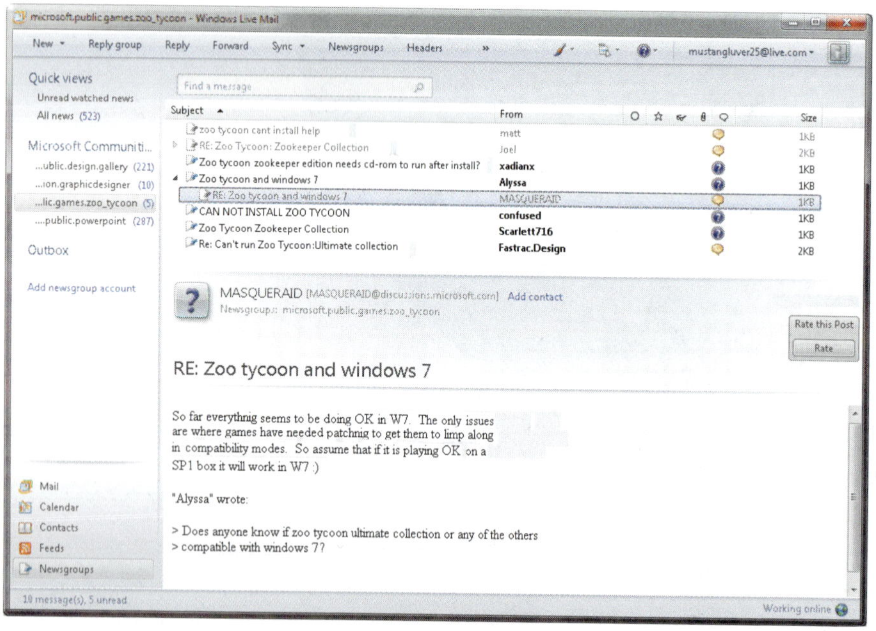

Figure 2-22 Users in a newsgroup read and reply to other users' messages.

Newsgroups and Message Boards

A **newsgroup** is an online area in which users have written discussions about a particular subject (Figure 2-22). To participate in a discussion, a user sends a message to the newsgroup, and other users in the newsgroup read and reply to the message.

Some newsgroups require you to enter a user name and password to participate in the discussion. For example, a newsgroup for students taking a college course may require a user name and password to access the newsgroup. This ensures that only students in the course participate in the discussion. To participate in a newsgroup, typically you use a program called a newsreader.

A popular Web-based type of discussion group that does not require a newsreader is a **message board**. Many Web sites use message boards instead of newsgroups because they are easier to use.

Netiquette

Netiquette, which is short for Internet etiquette, is the code of acceptable behaviors users should follow while on the Internet; that is, it is the conduct expected of individuals while online. Netiquette includes rules for all aspects of the Internet, including the World Wide Web, e-mail, instant messaging, chat rooms, FTP, and newsgroups and message boards. Figure 2-23 outlines some of the rules of netiquette. Read Ethics & Issues 2-3 for a related discussion.

NETIQUETTE — Golden Rule: Treat others as you would like them to treat you.

1. In e-mail, chat rooms, and newsgroups:
   - Keep messages brief. Use proper grammar, spelling, and punctuation.
   - Be careful when using sarcasm and humor, as it might be misinterpreted.
   - Be polite. Avoid offensive language.
   - Read the message before you send it.
   - Use meaningful subject lines.
   - Avoid sending or posting flames, which are abusive or insulting messages. Do not participate in flame wars, which are exchanges of flames.
   - Avoid sending spam, which is the Internet's version of junk mail. Spam is an unsolicited e-mail message or newsgroup posting sent to many recipients or newsgroups at once.
   - Do not use all capital letters, which is the equivalent of SHOUTING!
   - Use **emoticons** to express emotion. Popular emoticons include

:)	Smile	:|	Indifference	:o	Surprised
:(	Frown	:\	Undecided		

   - Use abbreviations and acronyms for phrases:

btw	by the way
imho	in my humble opinion
fyi	for your information
ttfn	ta ta for now
fwiw	for what it's worth
tyvm	thank you very much

   - Clearly identify a spoiler, which is a message that reveals a solution to a game or ending to a movie or program.
2. Read the FAQ (frequently asked questions), if one exists. Many newsgroups and Web pages have an FAQ.
3. Do not assume material is accurate or up-to-date. Be forgiving of other's mistakes.
4. Never read someone's private e-mail.

Figure 2-23 Some of the rules of netiquette.

ETHICS & ISSUES 2-3

Would Banning Anonymous Comments Reduce Cyberbullying?

Recently, several high-profile cases highlighted the issue of cyberbullying. Cyberbullying is the harassment of computer users, often teens and preteens, through various forms of Internet communications. The behavior typically occurs via e-mail, instant messaging, and chat rooms, and can result in a traumatic experience for the recipient. The bullying may be in the form of threats, spreading of rumors, or humiliation. Usually, the perpetrators of cyberbullying remain anonymous. Many people believe that the anonymous nature of the Internet directly leads to this unscrupulous behavior. Some government officials and advocacy groups have asked for laws that would ban anonymous comments in chat rooms and require that Internet access providers verify and record the true identity of all users. Others have proposed that it be illegal to sign up for an e-mail account or instant messaging account with a fake screen name. Opponents of such plans claim that anonymity and privacy are too important to give up. They state, for example, that the right to be critical of the government in an anonymous forum is a basic right. The rights of everyone should not be infringed upon due to bad behavior of a small group of people.

Would banning anonymous comments reduce cyberbullying? Why or why not? What are the positive and negative aspects of the freedom to remain anonymous on the Internet? What other measures can be taken to reduce cyberbullying? What role can parents play in reducing cyberbullying?

✔ QUIZ YOURSELF 2-3

Instructions: Find the true statement below. Then, rewrite the remaining false statements so that they are true.

1. A chat room is a location on an Internet server that permits users to chat with each other.
2. An e-mail address is a combination of a user name and an e-mail program that identifies a user so that he or she can receive Internet e-mail.
3. FTP uses the Internet (instead of the public switched telephone network) to connect a calling party to one or more called parties.
4. Netiquette is the code of unacceptable behaviors while on the Internet.
5. VoIP enables users to subscribe to other users over the Internet.

Quiz Yourself Online: To further check your knowledge of pages 63 through 69, visit the Microsoft Office and Concepts CourseMate Web site at www.cengagebrain.com, navigate to the Chapter 2 Quiz Yourself resource for this book, and then click Objectives 8 – 9.

Chapter Summary

This chapter presented the history and structure of the Internet. It discussed the World Wide Web at length, including topics such as browsing, navigating, searching, Web publishing, and e-commerce. It also introduced other services available on the Internet, such as e-mail, mailing lists, instant messaging, chat rooms, VoIP, FTP, and newsgroups and message boards. Finally, the chapter listed rules of netiquette.

Computer Usage @ Work

Entertainment

Do you wonder how music on the radio sounds so perfectly in tune, how animated motion pictures are created, or how one controls lighting during a concert? Not only does the entertainment industry rely on computers to advertise and sell their services on the Internet, computers also assist in other aspects, including audio and video composition, lighting control, computerized animation, and computer gaming.

As mentioned in this chapter, entertainment Web sites provide music and movies you can purchase and download to your computer or mobile device; live news broadcasts, performances, and sporting events; games you can play with other online users; and much more.

As early as 1951, computers were used to record and play music. Today, computers play a much larger role in the music industry. For example, if you are listening to a song on the radio and notice that not one note is out of tune, it is possible that software was used to change individual notes without altering the rest of the song.

Many years ago, creating cartoons or animated motion pictures was an extremely time-consuming task because artists were responsible for sketching thousands of drawings by hand. Currently, artists use computers to create these drawings in a fraction of the time, which significantly can reduce the time and cost of development.

Computers also are used in the game industry. While some game developers create games from scratch, others might use game engines that simplify the development process. For example, LucasArts created the GrimE game engine, which is designed to create adventure games.

During a concert, lighting technicians use computer programs to turn lights off and on, change color, or change location at specified intervals. In fact, once a performance begins, the technicians often merely are standing by, monitoring the computer as it performs most of the work. A significant amount of time and effort, however, is required to program the computer to perform its required tasks during a live show.

The next time you listen to a song, watch a movie, play a game, or attend a concert, think about the role computers play in contributing to your entertainment.

For more information, visit the Microsoft Office and Concepts CourseMate Web site at www.cengagebrain.com, navigate to the Chapter 2 Computer Usage @ Work resource for this book, and then click Entertainment.

Companies on the Cutting Edge

GOOGLE Popular Search Engine and Services

Google founders Sergey Brin and Larry Page have done very little advertising, but their Web site has become a household word, largely on favorable word-of-mouth reviews. They launched the Web site in 1998 in a friend's garage with the goal of providing the best possible experience for their loyal users who are looking for information presented clearly and quickly.

Google regularly scans more than one trillion Web pages in search of unique phrases and terms. Its thousands of connected computers deliver organized search results for the hundreds of millions of queries users input daily. Recently, the company updated its Google Earth product to allow users to explore the Moon, and also updated its popular advertising product, AdWords. Among its other services are Google Docs and YouTube.

eBAY World's Largest Online Marketplace

Millions of products are traded daily on eBay auctions, whether it is across town or across the globe. The more than 88 million registered worldwide shoppers generate at least $1.8 billion in annual revenue through purchases on the main Web site, eBay, along with items on Shopping.com, tickets on StubHub, classifieds on Kijiji, and other e-commerce venues.

The shoppers likely pay for their merchandise using PayPal, another eBay service. This merchant service allows buyers to transfer money from savings accounts or use their credit card without having to expose the account number to the seller. Other eBay companies are Rent.com, which offers listings for apartments and houses, and Shopping.com, which allows consumers to find and compare products. Recently, eBay introduced a program to more easily identify its top-rated sellers. It also invited buyers and sellers to become members of the eBay Green Team, which encourages and promotes environmentally friendly business practices.

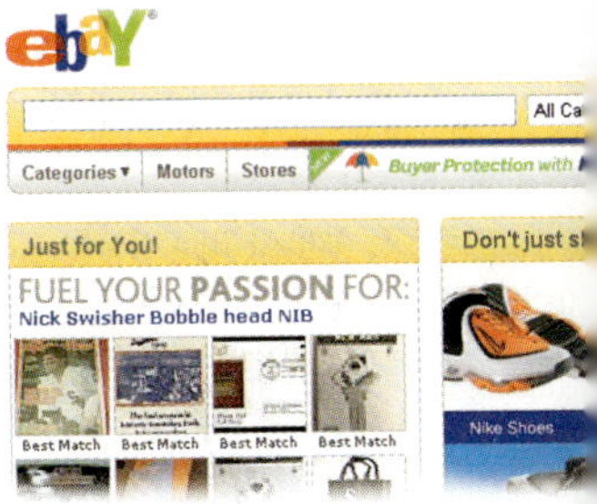

For more information, visit the Microsoft Office and Concepts CourseMate Web site at www.cengagebrain.com and then navigate to the Chapter 2 Companies on the Cutting Edge resource for this book.

Technology Trailblazers

TIM BERNERS-LEE Creator of the World Wide Web

Being the creator of the World Wide Web is an impressive item on any resume, and it certainly helped Tim Berners-Lee become the 3Com Founders Professor of Engineering at the Massachusetts Institute of Technology in 2008. As a professor in the electrical engineering and computer science departments, he researches social and technical collaboration on the Internet.

Berners-Lee's interest in sharing information via Web servers, browsers, and Web addresses developed in 1989 while working at CERN, the European Organization for Nuclear Research, in Geneva, Switzerland. He continued to improve his design of a program that tracked random associations for several years and then became the director of the World Wide Web Consortium (W3C), a forum to develop Web standards, in 1994.

Recently, Queen Elizabeth bestowed the Order of Merit – the highest civilian honor – upon the British-born Berners-Lee.

MARK ZUCKERBERG Facebook Founder and CEO

As one of the youngest self-made billionaires in history, Mark Zuckerberg could have his choice of the finest things in life. Instead, he lives very modestly and walks to Facebook's Palo Alto headquarters.

Both Microsoft and AOL had recruited Zuckerberg during his senior year in high school in New Hampshire. He declined their job offers and decided to attend Harvard. In college, he and some friends developed several projects, laying the foundation that led to Facebook's eventual start. Harvard administrators claimed these Web sites violated students' privacy. He, however, had instant success launching Facebook from his dorm room, and the Web site's popularity quickly spread to other Ivy League and Boston-area colleges and then worldwide. He left his studies at Harvard University in 2004 and moved to California.

Today, Zuckerberg says he spends the majority of his time running the $15 billion company on very little sleep.

For more information, visit the Microsoft Office and Concepts CourseMate Web site at www.cengagebrain.com and then navigate to the Chapter 2 Technology Trailblazers resource for this book.

Chapter Review

The Chapter Review reinforces the main concepts presented in this chapter.

To listen to an audio version of this Chapter Review, visit the Microsoft Office and Concepts CourseMate Web site at www.cengagebrain.com and then navigate to the Chapter 2 Chapter Review resource for this book.

1. **What Are the Various Broadband Internet Connections?** The **Internet** is a worldwide collection of networks that links millions of businesses, government agencies, educational institutions, and individuals. Many home and small business users connect to the Internet via high-speed **broadband** Internet service. **Cable Internet service** provides high-speed Internet access through the cable television network via a cable modem. **DSL** (digital subscriber line) provides high-speed Internet connections using regular telephone lines. **Fiber to the Premises (FTTP)** uses fiber-optic cable to provide high-speed Internet access. **Fixed wireless** high-speed Internet connections use a dish-shaped antenna to communicate via radio signals. A **Wi-Fi** network uses radio signals to provide Internet connections to wireless computers and devices. A **cellular radio network** offers high-speed Internet connections to devices with built-in compatible technology or computers with wireless modems. **Satellite Internet service** communicates with a satellite dish to provide high-speed Internet connections. Some home and small businesses connect to the Internet with **dial-up access**, which uses a modem in the computer and a standard telephone line.

2. **What Are the Types of Internet Access Providers?** An **access provider** is a business that provides access to the Internet free or for a fee. An **ISP (Internet service provider)** is a regional or national access provider. An **online service provider (OSP)** provides Internet access in addition to members-only features, such as instant messaging or customized Web browsers. A **wireless Internet service provider** provides wireless Internet access to computers and mobile devices with built-in wireless capability (such as Wi-Fi) or to computers using wireless modems or wireless access devices.

Visit the Microsoft Office and Concepts CourseMate Web site at www.cengagebrain.com, navigate to the Chapter 2 Quiz Yourself resource for this book, and then click Objectives 1 – 2.

3. **What Is the Purpose of a Web Browser, and What Are the Components of a Web Address?** A **Web browser**, or **browser**, is application software that allows users to access and view Web pages or access Web 2.0 programs. A **Web address** is the unique address for each **Web page** and consists of a protocol, a domain name, and sometimes the path to a specific Web page or location on a Web page.

4. **How Do You Use a Search Engine to Search for Information on the Web?** A **search engine** is a program that finds Web sites, Web pages, images, videos, news, maps, and other information related to a specific topic. A search engine is helpful in locating information for which you do not know an exact Web address or are not seeking a particular Web site. Search engines require **search text** that describes the item you want to find. After performing the search, the search engine returns a list of hits, each one a **link** to an associated Web page.

5. **What Are the Types of Web Sites?** A **portal** is a Web site that offers a variety of Internet services from a single location. A news Web site contains newsworthy material. An informational Web site contains factual information. A business/marketing Web site promotes or sells products or services. A **blog** is an informal Web site consisting of time-stamped articles, or posts, in a diary or journal format, usually listed in reverse chronological order. A **wiki** is a collaborative Web site that allows users to create, add to, modify, or delete the Web site content via their Web browser. An **online social network**, or **social networking Web site**, encourages members to share their interests, ideas, stories, photos, music, and videos with other registered users. An educational Web site offers avenues for teaching and learning. An entertainment Web site offers an interactive and engaging environment. An advocacy Web site describes a cause, opinion, or idea. A **Web application**, or **Web app**, is a Web site that allows users to access and interact with software through a Web browser on any computer connected to the Internet. A **content aggregator** is a business that gathers and organizes Web content and then distributes, or feeds, the content to subscribers for free or a fee. A personal Web site is maintained by a private individual or family.

6. **How Do Web Pages Use Graphics, Animation, Audio, Video, Virtual Reality, and Plug-Ins?** More exciting Web sites use **multimedia**, which refers to any application that combines text with graphics, animation, video, and/or virtual reality. A **graphic**, or graphical image, is a digital representation of nontext information such as a drawing, chart, or photo. **Animation** is the appearance of motion created by displaying a series of still images in sequence. **Audio** includes music, speech, or any other sound. **Video** consists of full-motion images that are played back at various speeds. **Virtual reality (VR)** is the use of computers to simulate a real or imagined environment as a 3-D space. A **plug-in** is a program that extends the capability of a browser.

7. **What Are the Steps Required for Web Publishing?** **Web publishing** is the development and maintenance of Web pages. The five major steps to Web publishing are: (1) plan a Web site, (2) analyze and design a Web site, (3) create a Web site, (4) deploy a Web site, and (5) maintain a Web site.

Visit the Microsoft Office and Concepts CourseMate Web site at www.cengagebrain.com, navigate to the Chapter 2 Quiz Yourself resource for this book, and then click Objectives 3 – 7.

8. **How Do E-Mail, Mailing Lists, Instant Messaging, Chat Rooms, VoIP, FTP, and Newsgroups and Message Boards Work?** E-mail (short for electronic mail) is the transmission of messages and files via a computer network. A **mailing list** is a group of e-mail names and addresses given a single name, so that everyone on the list receives a message sent to the list. **Instant messaging (IM)** is a **real-time** Internet communications service that notifies you when one or more people are online. A **chat room** is a location on an Internet server that permits users to **chat**, or conduct real-time typed conversations. **VoIP** (Voice over IP, or Internet Protocol) enables users to speak to other users over the Internet instead of the public switched telephone network. **FTP** (File Transfer Protocol) is an Internet standard that permits file **uploading** and **downloading** with other computers on the Internet. A **newsgroup** is an online area in which users have written discussions about a particular subject. A **message board** is a popular Web-based type of discussion group that is easier to use than a newsgroup.

9. **What Are the Rules of Netiquette?** **Netiquette**, which is short for Internet etiquette, is the code of acceptable behaviors users should follow while on the Internet. Keep messages short. Be polite. Use **emoticons**. Read the FAQ if one exists. Do not assume material is accurate or up-to-date, and never read someone's private e-mail.

Visit the Microsoft Office and Concepts CourseMate Web site at www.cengagebrain.com, navigate to the Chapter 2 Quiz Yourself resource for this book, and then click Objectives 8 – 9.

Key Terms

You should know the Key Terms. The list below helps focus your study.

To see an example of and a definition for each term, and to access current and additional information from the Web, visit the Microsoft Office and Concepts CourseMate Web site at www.cengagebrain.com and then navigate to the Chapter 2 Key Terms resource for this book.

access provider (46)
add-on (61)
address book (65)
animation (59)
audio (60)
blog (56)
blogosphere (56)
bookmark (51)
broadband (45)
browser (49)
cable Internet service (45)
cellular radio network (46)
c hat (67)
c hat room (67)
click (52)
content aggregator (58)
dial-up access (46)
domain name (48)
downloading (50)
DSL (45)
e-commerce (62)
electronic storefront (62)
e-mail address (64)
e-mail program (63)
emoticons (69)
favorite (51)
Fiber to the Premises (FTTP) (45)
fixed wireless (45)
FTP (68)
graphic (58)
home page (50)
hot spots (46)
hyperlink (52)
instant messaging (IM) (66)
Internet (44)
Internet backbone (47)
IP address (48)
ISP (Internet service provider) (46)
link (52)
mailing list (66)
media sharing Web site (57)
message board (69)
microblog (56)
MP3 (60)
MP4 (61)
multimedia (58)
Net (44)
netiquette (69)
newsgroup (68)
online auction (63)
online service provider (OSP) (46)
online social network (57)
player (60)
plug-in (61)
podcast (60)
portal (55)
real time (66)
RSS 2.0 (58)
satellite Internet service (46)
search engine (53)
search text (54)
shopping cart (63)
social networking Web site (57)
streaming (60)
subject directory (53)
subscribe (66)
surfing the Web (52)
tabbed browsing (52)
thumbnail (59)
top-level domain (TLD) (48)
unsubscribe (66)
uploading (68)
URL (51)
user name (65)
video (61)
video blog (56)
virtual reality (VR) (61)
vlog (56)
vlogosphere (56)
VoIP (68)
Web (49)
Web 2.0 (49)
Web address (51)
Web app (57)
Web application (57)
Web browser (49)
Web page (49)
Web publishing (62)
Web server (49)
Web site (49)
Wi-Fi (45)
wiki (56)
wireless Internet service provider (46)
World Wide Web (WWW) (49)

Checkpoint

The Checkpoint exercises test your knowledge of the chapter concepts. The page number containing the answer appears in parentheses after each exercise.

To complete the Checkpoint exercises interactively, visit the Microsoft Office and Concepts CourseMate Web site at www.cengagebrain.com and then navigate to the Chapter 2 Checkpoint resource for this book.

Multiple Choice

Select the best answer.

1. _____ offers high-speed Internet connections to devices with built-in compatible technology or computers with wireless modems. (46)
   a. Cable Internet service
   b. A digital subscriber line
   c. A cellular radio network
   d. Fiber to the Premises (FTTP)
2. Instead of using broadband Internet service some home users connect to the Internet via _____, which is a slower-speed technology. (46)
   a. satellite Internet service
   b. cable Internet service
   c. DSL
   d. dial-up access
3. _____ is the process of a computer or device receiving information, such as a Web page, from a server on the Internet. (50)
   a. Uploading
   b. Social networking
   c. Downloading
   d. Blogging
4. A _____ is a Web site that allows users to post short text updates, usually between 100 and 200 characters. (56)
   a. podcast
   b. wiki
   c. microblog
   d. portal
5. A _____ is a specific type of online social network that enables members to share photos, music, and videos. (57)
   a. blog
   b. wiki
   c. podcast
   d. media sharing Web site
6. A(n) _____ is a small version of a larger graphic. (59)
   a. thumbnail
   b. wiki
   c. MP3
   d. portal
7. In _____ e-commerce, one consumer sells directly to another. (63)
   a. consumer-to-business
   b. business-to-business
   c. consumer-to-consumer
   d. business-to-consumer
8. The _____ standard permits uploading and downloading of files on the Internet. (68)
   a. FTP
   b. newsgroup
   c. message board
   d. mailing list

Matching

Match the terms with their definitions.

_____ 1. home page (50)
_____ 2. search engine (53)
_____ 3. MP3 (60)
_____ 4. e-mail address (64)
_____ 5. emoticons (69)

a. used to express emotions in e-mail, chat rooms, and newsgroups
b. the first page that a Web site displays
c. combination of a user name and a domain name that identifies an Internet user
d. program that finds Web sites, Web pages, images, videos, news, maps, and other information related to a specific topic
e. built-in connection to a related Web page or part of a Web page
f. format that reduces an audio file to about one-tenth its original size

Short Answer

Write a brief answer to each of the following questions.

1. Describe three different types of broadband Internet services. _________ What is the difference between a regional ISP and a national ISP? _________
2. How is a Web page different from a Web site? _________ How can you use a Web address to display a Web page? _________
3. What are the differences between blogs, wikis, and podcasts? _________ When might you use each? _________
4. What is a Web application? _________ What are some features and examples of Web applications? _________
5. What is one specification used by content aggregators to distribute content? _________ How might you evaluate the accuracy of a Web site? _________

Problem Solving

The Problem Solving exercises extend your knowledge of the chapter concepts by seeking solutions to practical computer problems that you may encounter at home, school, or work. The Collaboration exercise should be completed with a team.

In the real world, practical problems often can be solved in multiple ways. Provide one solution to each of the following problems using available resources, such as articles on the Web or in print, blogs, podcasts, videos, television, user guides, other individuals, and electronics and computer stores. You may need to use multiple resources to obtain an answer. Present your solutions in the form requested by your instructor (brief report, presentation, discussion, or other means).

@ Home

1. **Slow Internet Connection** You just installed VoIP telephone service in your house. Each time you are on the telephone, however, you notice that your Internet connection slows down significantly. What could be causing this?
2. **No Wireless Connection** When you return home to visit your parents and turn on your new notebook computer, it does not connect automatically to their wireless network. What is your next step?
3. **Incorrect Search Engine** A class project requires that you conduct research on the Web. After typing the Web address for Google's home page and pressing the ENTER key, your Web browser redirects you to a different search engine. What could be wrong?
4. **New Browser Windows** While browsing the Web, each time you click a link, the link's destination opens in a new browser window. You prefer to have each link open in a new tab so that your taskbar does not become cluttered. How will you resolve this?

@ Work

5. **Access Denied** During your lunch hour, you decide to search the Web for possible vacation destinations. After visiting several airline and hotel Web sites, you attempt to visit the Web site for a Caribbean resort. Much to your surprise, the Web browser informs you that the Web site has been blocked. Why might this happen?
6. **Sporadic E-Mail Message Delivery** The e-mail program on your computer has been delivering new messages only every hour, on the hour. Historically, new e-mail messages would arrive and be displayed immediately upon being sent by the sender. Furthermore, your coworkers claim that they sometimes do not receive your e-mail messages until hours after they are sent. What might be the problem?

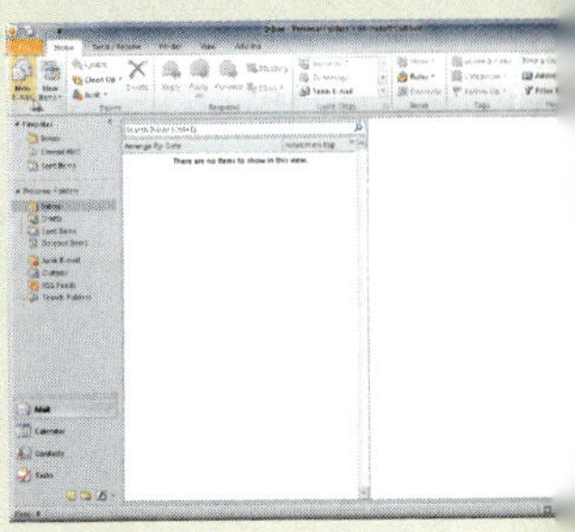

7. **E-Mail Message Formatting** A friend sent an e-mail message containing a photo to your e-mail account at work. Upon receiving the e-mail message, the photo does not display. You also notice that e-mail messages never display any formatting, such as different fonts, font sizes, and font colors. What might be causing this?
8. **Automatic Response** When you return from vacation, a colleague informs you that when she sent e-mail messages to your e-mail address, she would not always receive your automatic response stating that you were out of the office. Why might your e-mail program not respond automatically to every e-mail message received?

Collaboration

9. **Computers in Entertainment** The drama department at a local high school is considering developing a movie and has asked for your help. The drama teacher would like to incorporate technology wherever possible, in hopes that it would decrease the costs of the movie's production. Form a team of three people to help determine what technology can be used to assist in the movie's production. One team member should research the type of technology that can be used during the filming process. Another team member should research the types of hardware and software available for editing footage, and the third team member should research the hardware and software requirements for creating the media to distribute the finished product.

Learn How To

The Learn How To activities step you through fundamental technology skills when using a computer. The Learn How To exercises enable you to become more proficient with these skills.

Premium Activity: To relate this Learn How To activity to your everyday life, see a visual demonstration of the activity, and complete a short assessment, visit the Microsoft Office and Concepts CourseMate Web site at www.cengagebrain.com and then navigate to the Chapter 2 Learn How To resource for this book.

Learn How To 1: Attach a File to an E-Mail Message

When you send an e-mail message, it sometimes is necessary to attach a file to supplement the body of the e-mail message. Most e-mail programs allow you to attach a file to your e-mail messages easily, but many do not allow you to attach files exceeding a specified size limit (which varies by your e-mail service). You can attach a file to an e-mail message by completing the following steps:

1. Start your e-mail program and compose a new e-mail message to your recipient. Make sure that you have a descriptive subject and that you explain in the e-mail message that you are attaching a file.
2. To attach a file, locate and click the Attach File button or link. If you are unable to locate this button, you may find an icon with a picture of a paperclip or a menu command to attach a file. Some e-mail programs also may have a text box in the new message window with an adjacent Browse button. In this case, click the Browse button.
3. Locate and click the file you wish to attach and then click the Open (or Insert or Select) button (Figure 2-24).
4. Verify that your e-mail message contains the attachment and then click the Send button.

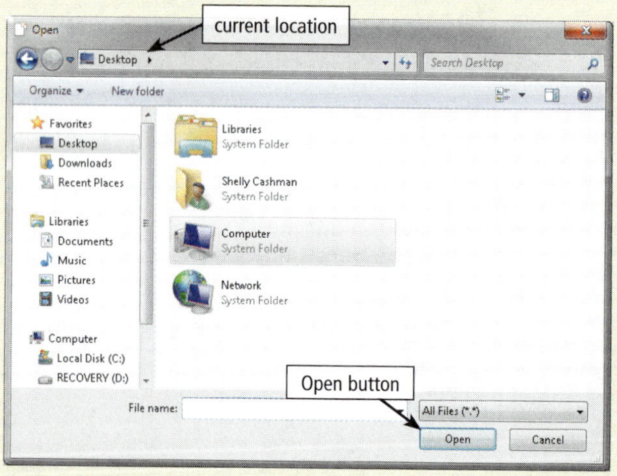

Figure 2-24

When the recipient opens the e-mail message, he or she also will be able to open the attachment.

Exercises

1. Start your e-mail program. Compose a new e-mail message to your instructor, and attach a file containing your current course schedule. Verify that your message has been received and then close your e-mail program.
2. Locate three free e-mail Web applications. How many file attachments do these e-mail programs allow you to attach to one e-mail message? Is a maximum file size specified for an e-mail attachment? Can you pay to upgrade your e-mail account so that these restrictions are lifted? Submit these answers to your instructor.

Learn How To 2: Search the Web for Driving Directions, Addresses, and Telephone Numbers

In addition to searching the Web for information using search engines such as Google and Yahoo!, some Web sites are designed specifically to search for other information such as driving directions, addresses, and telephone numbers.

Search for Driving Directions

1. Start your Web browser, type `mapquest.com` in the Address bar, press the ENTER key to display the MapQuest home page, and then click the Directions tab.
2. Type the starting address (or intersection), city, state, and ZIP code (if you know it) in the appropriate text boxes in the Starting Location area of the Directions page.
3. Type the ending address (or intersection), city, state, and ZIP code (if you know it) in the appropriate text boxes in the Ending Location area of the Directions page.
4. Click the Get Directions button to display the driving directions.

Search for the Address and Telephone Number of a Business

1. If necessary, start your Web browser. Type `yellowpages.com` in the Address bar, and then press the ENTER key to display the Yellow Pages Local Directory home page.

2. Type the name of the business in the Find text box, and type the city, state, and ZIP (if you know it) in the Location text box.
3. Click the FIND button to display the search results.
4. Close your Web browser.

Exercises

1. If necessary, start Internet Explorer by clicking the Start button, and then click Internet Explorer on the Start menu. Type `mapquest.com` in the Address bar, and then press the ENTER key. Search for driving directions between your address and the address of a friend or family member. How many miles are between the two addresses? How long would it take you to drive from your address to the other address? Write a paragraph explaining whether you would or would not use MapQuest to retrieve driving directions. Submit this paragraph to your instructor.
2. Use the Web to search for another Web site that provides driving directions. Use the Web site to search for directions between the same two locations from Exercise 1. Are the driving directions the same as the ones that MapQuest provided? If not, why might they be different? Which Web site did you use? Do you prefer this Web site to MapQuest? Why or why not? Write a paragraph with your answers and submit it to your instructor.
3. Think about a company for which you would like to work. In your Web browser, display the Yellow Pages Web page (yellowpages.com) and then search for the address and telephone number of this company. If Yellow Pages does not display the desired information, what other Web sites might you be able to use to search for the address and telephone number for a company?

Learn It Online

The Learn It Online exercises are interactive Web exercises designed to reinforce and expand your understanding of the chapter concepts. The descriptions below briefly summarize each exercise.

To complete the Learn It Online exercises, visit the Microsoft Office and Concepts CourseMate Web site at www.cengagebrain.com, navigate to the Chapter 2 resources for this book, click the link for the exercise you want to complete, and then read the instructions.

1 At the Movies — Tell Your Stories via Vlog
Watch a movie to learn about how to post your thoughts to a vlog and then answer questions about the movie.

2 Student Edition Labs — Connecting to the Internet, Getting the Most out of the Internet, and E-mail
Enhance your understanding and knowledge about the Internet and e-mail by completing the Connecting to the Internet, Getting the Most out of the Internet, and E-mail Labs.

3 Practice Test
Take a multiple choice test that checks your knowledge of the chapter concepts and review the resulting study guide.

4 Who Wants To Be a Computer Genius²?
Play the Shelly Cashman Series version of this popular game by answering questions to find out if you are a computer genius. Panic buttons are available to provide assistance during game play.

5 Crossword Puzzle Challenge
Complete an interactive crossword puzzle to reinforce concepts presented in this chapter.

6 Windows Exercises
Step through the Windows 7 exercises to learn about Internet properties, dial-up networking connections, and using Help to understand the Internet.

7 Exploring Computer Careers
Read about a career as a Web developer, search for related employment advertisements, and then answer related questions.

8 Web Apps — Windows Live Hotmail
Learn how to sign up for a free e-mail account, add a contact to your address book, and send an e-mail message.

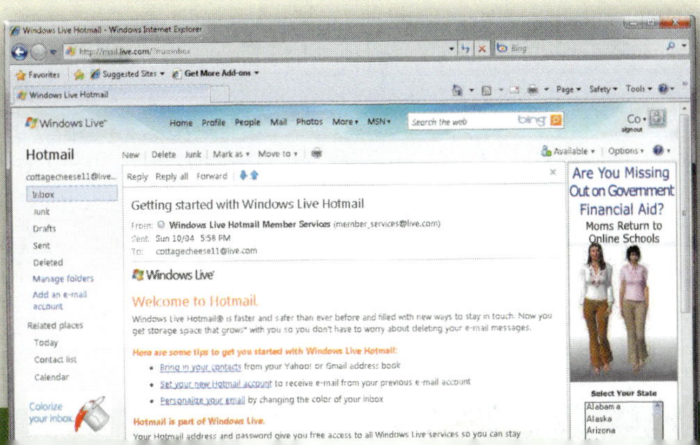

Web Research

The Web Research exercises broaden your understanding of the chapter concepts by presenting questions that require you to search the Web for answers.

1 Search Sleuth

Use one of the search engines listed in Figure 2-8 in Chapter 2 on page 53 or your own favorite search engine to find the answers to the following questions. Copy and paste the Web address from the Web page where you found the answer. Some questions may have more than one answer. If required, submit your answers to your instructor. (1) What were the title, date of publication, and purpose of the Internet Engineering Task Force's RFC 1 document? (2) What is the mission of the World Wide Web Consortium (W3C)? (3) What topic does the film *Adina's Deck* address? (4) What are the current figures on the Reporters Without Borders' Press Freedom Barometer? (5) What was eBay's original name, and what was the first item offered for auction? (6) Why did ConnectU sue Facebook in 2008 and 2004? (7) What is the cost to use Google's 411 service?

2 Green Computing

EcoSearch is a search engine dedicated to supporting the Earth's natural resources. Visit this Web site (ecosearch.org), use your word processing program to answer the following questions, and then, if required, submit your answers to your instructor. (1) From what company do the search results come? (2) Click the Learn More link on the page. What charities does EcoSearch support? (3) How can you get involved to help EcoSearch? (4) Click the EcoSearch Home link at the bottom of the page to return to the EcoSearch home page. In the text box, type `ecosearch donate profits` and then click the Search button. Click several of the resulting links and review the information. Write a 50-word summary of the information, including what percent of EcoSearch proceeds is donated to charities and how much money EcoSearch expects to donate each year.

3 Social Networking

MySpace is considered one of the pioneering Web sites that helped popularize the online social networking phenomenon. Calling itself "a place for friends," it allows the millions of registered members to create profiles for free and then invite friends to join their networks. The growth of this Web site has helped it emerge as one of the more popular search engines. Visit the MySpace site (myspace.com), type the name of your favorite musical artist or group in the search text box, and then click the Search button. How many search results were found? Visit some of these profiles. Which music videos, playlists, and ringtones are featured? How do you create and edit your own playlists and add a song to your profile? Then click the Safety Tips link at the bottom of the page and read the guidelines for posting information and reporting inappropriate content. Summarize the music profiles you viewed and the guidelines. If required, submit your summary to your instructor.

4 Blogs

Many of the best blogs in the blogosphere have received awards for their content and design. For example, loyal blogging fans nominate and vote for their favorite blogs by visiting the Blogger's Choice Awards Web site (bloggerschoiceawards.com). Visit this Web site, click the Best Blog Design, Best Blog About Blogging, and Best Education Blog links, and view some of the blogs receiving the largest number of votes. Then visit other award sites, including the Interactive Media Awards (interactivemediaawards.com), Bloggies (bloggies.com), and the Best of Blogs (thebestofblogs.com). Which blogs, if any, received multiple awards on the different Web sites? Who casts the votes? What criteria are used to judge these blogs?

5 Ethics in Action

Some Internet access providers have admitted they monitored their users' Web surfing activities without giving notice of this eavesdropping practice. Embarq and Charter Communications secretly tested advertising technology to gather data about specific Web searches and then display advertisements relating to these searches. Privacy experts claim these Internet access providers' practices violate federal privacy laws, including the wiretapping statute. Locate news articles discussing the Internet access providers' Web eavesdropping. Then locate Web sites that oppose this practice. Summarize the views of the advertisers and the privacy proponents. If required, submit your summary to your instructor.

Special Feature

Making Use of the Web

INFORMATION LITERACY IS DEFINED as having the practical skills needed to evaluate information critically from print and electronic resources and to use this information accurately in daily life. Locating Web sites may be profitable for your educational and professional careers, as the resources may help you research class assignments and make your life more fulfilling and manageable.

Because the Web does not have an organizational structure to assist you in locating reliable material, you may need additional resources to guide you in searching. To help you find useful Web sites, this Special Feature describes specific information about a variety of Web pages, and it includes tables of Web addresses so that you can get started. The material is organized in several areas of interest.

Web Exercises at the end of each area will reinforce the material and help you discover Web sites that may add a treasure trove of knowledge to your life.

Areas of Interest	
Fun and Entertainment	Shopping and Auctions
Research	Weather, Sports, and News
Blogs	Learning
Online Social Networks and Media Sharing	Science
Travel	Health
Environment	Careers
Finance	Literature and Arts
Government	

Fun and Entertainment

That's Entertainment

Rock 'n' Roll on the Web

Consumers place great significance on buying entertainment products for fun and recreation. Nearly 10 percent of the United States's economy is spent on attending concerts and buying optical discs, reading materials, sporting goods, and toys.

Many Web sites supplement our cravings for fun and entertainment. For example, you can see and hear the musicians inducted into the Rock and Roll Hall of Fame and Museum. If you need an update on your favorite reality-based television program or a preview of an upcoming movie, E! Online and Entertainment Weekly provide the latest features about actors and actresses. The Internet Movie Database contains reviews of more than one million titles (Figure 1).

Watch the surfers riding the waves and romp with pandas at the San Diego Zoo. Web cams can display live video on Web pages, taking armchair travelers across the world for views of natural attractions, monuments, and cities. Many Web sites featuring Web cams are listed in the table in Figure 2.

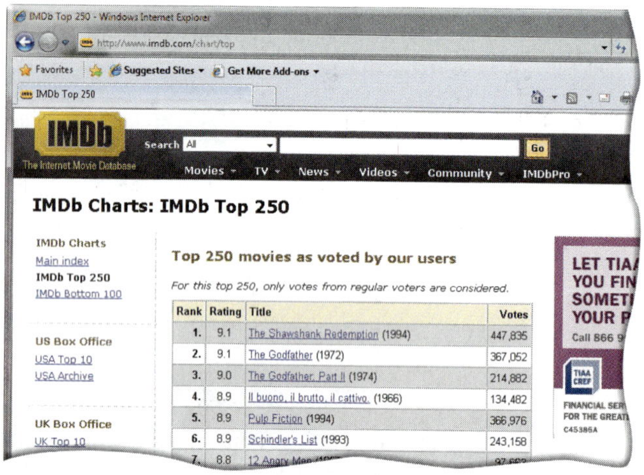

Figure 1 Visitors exploring the Internet Movie Database will find the latest news about their favorite television programs and movies.

Fun and Entertainment Web Sites

Entertainment	Web Address
allmusic	allmusic.com
E! Online	eonline.com
Entertainment Weekly's EW	ew.com/ew
Games.com	games.com
Internet Movie Database	imdb.com
Old Time Radio (OTR) — Radio Days: A Radio History	otr.com
Rock and Roll Hall of Fame and Museum	rockhall.com
World Radio Network	wrn.org
Yahoo! Entertainment	entertainment.yahoo.com
Web Cams	**Web Address**
Camvista	camvista.com
Discovery Kids — Live Cams	kids.discovery.com/cams/cams.html
EarthCam — Webcam Network	earthcam.com
ESRL/GMD Mauna Loa Live Camera	esrl.noaa.gov/gmd/obop/mlo/livecam/index.html
Gatorland	gatorland.com/gatorcam.php
Geocaching — The Official Global GPS Cache Hunt Site	geocaching.com
Panda Cam San Diego Zoo	sandiegozoo.org/zoo/ ex_panda_station.html
WebCam Central	camcentral.com
Wild Birds Unlimited Bird FeederCam	wbu.com/feedercam_home.html

For more information about fun and entertainment Web sites, visit the Microsoft Office and Concepts CourseMate Web site at www.cengagebrain.com and then navigate to the Making Use of the Web Feature resource for this book.

Figure 2 When you visit Web sites offering fun and entertainment resources, you can be both amused and informed.

Fun and Entertainment Web Exercises

1. **Visit the Geocaching site listed in Figure 2.** Find the geocaches within five miles of your home or school and then print a map showing their locations. Then, visit the Discovery Kids — Live Cams Web site and view one of the animal cams in the Live Cams. What do you observe? Visit another Web site listed in Figure 2 and describe the view. What are the benefits of having Web cams at these locations throughout the world?

2. **What are your favorite movies?** Use the Internet Movie Database Web site listed in Figure 2 to search for information about two films, and write a brief description of the biographies of the major stars and director for each movie. Then, visit one of the entertainment Web sites and describe three of the featured stories. At the Rock and Roll Hall of Fame and Museum Web site, view the information about The Beatles and one of your favorite musicians. Write a paragraph describing the information available about these rock stars.

Research

Search and Ye Shall Find

Information on the Web

A recent Web Usability survey conducted by the Nielsen Norman Group found that 88 percent of people who connect to the Internet use a search engine as their first online action. Search engines require users to type words and phrases that characterize the information being sought. Bing (Figure 3), Google, and AltaVista are some of the more popular search engines. The key to effective searching on the Web is composing search queries that narrow the search results and place the more relevant Web sites at the top of the results list.

Keep up with the latest computer and related product developments by viewing online dictionaries and encyclopedias that add to their collections on a regular basis. Shopping for a new computer can be a daunting experience, but many online guides can help you select the components that best fit your needs and budget. If you are not confident in your ability to solve a problem alone, turn to online technical support. Hardware and software reviews, price comparisons, shareware, technical questions and answers, and breaking technology news are found on comprehensive portals. Figure 4 lists popular research Web sites.

Figure 3 The Bing Web site provides a search engine for images, videos, shopping, news, maps, and travel.

Research Web Sites

Research	Web Address
A9.com	a9.com
AccessMyLibrary	accessmylibrary.com
AltaVista	altavista.com
Answers.com	answers.com
Ask	ask.com
Bing	bing.com
ChaCha	chacha.com
CNET	cnet.com
eHow	ehow.com
Google	google.com
HotBot	hotbot.com
Librarians' Internet Index	lii.org
PC911	pcnineoneone.com
Switchboard	switchboard.com
Webopedia	webopedia.com
ZDNet	zdnet.com

For more information about research Web sites, visit the Microsoft Office and Concepts CourseMate Web site at www.cengagebrain.com and then navigate to the Making Use of the Web Feature resource for this book.

Figure 4 Web users can find information by using research Web sites.

Research Web Exercises

1. **Visit two of the research Web sites listed in Figure 4** to find three Web sites that review the latest digital cameras from Kodak and Canon. Make a table listing the research Web sites, the located Web site names, and the cameras' model numbers, suggested retail price, and features.

2. **Visit the Webopedia Web site.** Search this site for five terms of your choice. Create a table with two columns: one for the term and one for the Web definition. Then, create a second table listing five recently added or updated words and their definitions on this Web site. Next, visit the CNET Web site to choose the components you would buy if you were building a customized desktop computer and notebook computer. Create a table for both computers, listing the computer manufacturer, processor model name or number and manufacturer, clock speed, RAM, cache, number of expansion slots, and number of bays.

Blogs

Express Yourself

Blogosphere Growing Swiftly

Internet users are feeling the need to publish their views, and they are finding Weblogs, or blogs for short, the ideal vehicle. The blogosphere began as an easy way for individuals to express their opinions on the Web. Today, this communications vehicle has become a powerful tool, for individuals, groups, and corporations are using blogs to promote their ideas and advertise their products. It is not necessary to have a background in Web design to be able to post to a blog.

Bloggers generally update their Web sites frequently to reflect their views. Their posts range from a paragraph to an entire essay and often contain links to other Web sites. The more popular blogs discuss politics, lifestyles, and technology.

Individuals easily may set up a blog free or for a fee, using Web sites such as Blogger, Bloglines (Figure 5), and TypePad. In addition, online social networks may have a built-in blogging feature. Be cautious of the information you post on your blog, especially if it is accessible to everyone online.

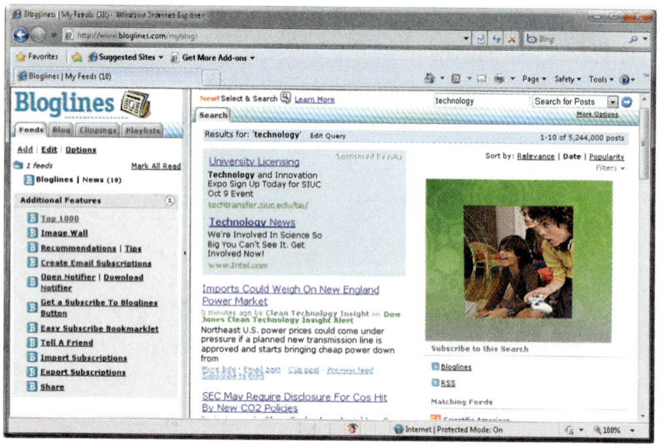

Figure 5 Bloglines keeps readers abreast of the latest technology, entertainment, and political news in the blogosphere.

Corporate blogs, such as The GM FastLane Blog, discuss all aspects of the company's products, whereas all-encompassing blogs, such as the MetaFilter Community Weblog and others in Figure 6, are designed to keep general readers entertained and informed.

Blogs are affecting the manner in which people communicate, and some experts predict they will one day become our primary method of sharing information.

Blogs Web Sites

Blog	Web Address
A List Apart	alistapart.com
Blog.com	blog.com
Blog Flux	topsites.blogflux.com
Blogger	blogger.com
Bloglines	bloglines.com
Blogstream	blogstream.com
Davenetics*Remote Control Revolutionary	davenetics.com
Geek News Central	geeknewscentral.com
GM FastLane Blog	fastlane.gmblogs.com
kottke.org	kottke.org
MetaFilter Community Weblog	metafilter.com
Rocketboom	rocketboom.com
TreeHugger	treehuggertv.com
Twitter	twitter.com
TypePad	typepad.com

For more information about blogs Web sites, visit the Microsoft Office and Concepts CourseMate Web site at www.cengagebrain.com and then navigate to the Making Use of the Web Feature resource for this book.

Figure 6 These blogs offer information about technology, news, politics, and entertainment.

Blogs Web Exercises

1. **Visit three of the blog Web sites listed in Figure 6.** Make a table listing the blog name, its purpose, the author, its audience, and advertisers, if any, who sponsor the blog. Then, write a paragraph that describes the information you found on each of these blogs.

2. **Many Internet users read the technology blogs to keep abreast of the latest developments.** Visit the Geek News Central and Bloglines blogs listed in Figure 6 and write a paragraph describing the top story in each blog. Read the posted comments, if any. Then, write another paragraph describing two other stories found on these blogs that cover material you have discussed in this course. Write a third paragraph discussing which one is more interesting to you. Would you add reading blogs to your list of Internet activities? Why or why not?

Online Social Networks and Media Sharing

Check Out My New Photos

Online Social Networks and Media Sharing Web Sites Gain Popularity

Do you ever wonder what your friends are doing? What about your friends' friends? The popularity of online social networks has increased dramatically in recent years. Online social networks, such as those listed in Figure 7, allow you to create a personalized profile that others are able to view online. These profiles may include information about you such as your hometown, your age, your hobbies, and pictures. You also may create links to your friends' pages, post messages for individual friends, or bulletins for all of your friends to see. Online social networks are great places to keep in touch with your friends and to network with professionals for business purposes.

If you would like to post pictures and videos and do not require the full functionality of an online social network, you might consider a media sharing Web site, which is a type of online social network. Media sharing Web sites such as YouTube and Phanfare (Figure 8) allow you to post media, including photos and videos, for others to view, print, and/or download. Media sharing Web sites, which may be free or charge a fee, provide a quick, efficient way to share photos of your last vacation or videos of your family reunion.

Online Social Networks and Media Sharing

Online Social Networks	Web Address
Club Penguin	clubpenguin.com
Facebook	facebook.com
LinkedIn	linkedin.com
MySpace — a place for friends	myspace.com
orkut	orkut.com
Windows Live Spaces	spaces.live.com
Media Sharing	**Web Address**
flickr	flickr.com
Phanfare	phanfare.com
Photobucket	photobucket.com
Picasa	picasa.com
Shutterfly	shutterfly.com
Yahoo! Video	video.yahoo.com
YouTube	youtube.com

For more information about online social networks and media sharing Web sites, visit the Microsoft Office and Concepts CourseMate Web site at www.cengagebrain.com and then navigate to the Making Use of the Web Feature resource for this book.

Figure 7 Online social networks and media sharing Web sites are popular ways to keep in touch with friends, meet new people, and share media.

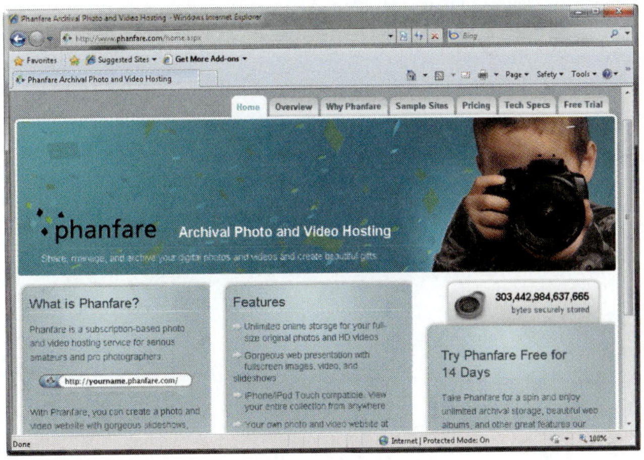

Figure 8 The Phanfare Web site allows users to share their photo and video files with people throughout the world.

Online Social Networks and Media Sharing Web Exercises

1. **Many individuals now use online social networks.** Visit two online social networks listed in Figure 7. (If you are attempting to access an online social network from your classroom and are unable to do so, your school may have restricted use of social networking Web sites.) Compare and contrast these two sites by performing the following actions and recording your findings. First, create a profile on each of these sites. If you find a Web site that charges a fee to sign up, choose another Web site. How easy is the sign-up process? Does either Web site ask for any personal information you are uncomfortable sharing? If so, what information? Once you sign up, make a list of five of your closest friends, and search for their profiles on each of these two sites. Which site contains more of your friends? Browse each site and make a list of its features. In your opinion, which site is better? Explain why.

2. **Media sharing Web sites make it easy to share photos and videos with friends, family, and colleagues.** Before choosing a media sharing Web site to use, do some research. Visit two media sharing Web sites in Figure 7. Is there a fee to post media to these Web sites? If so, how much? Are these Web sites supported by advertisements? Locate the instructions for posting media to these Web sites. Are the instructions straightforward? Do these Web sites impose a limit on the number and/or size of media files you can post? Summarize your responses to these questions in two or three paragraphs.

Travel

Get Packing!

Explore the World without Leaving Home

When you are ready to arrange your next travel adventure or just want to explore destination possibilities, the Internet provides ample resources to set your plans in motion.

To discover exactly where your destination is on this planet, cartography Web sites, including MapQuest and Yahoo! Maps, allow you to pinpoint your destination. View your exact destination using satellite imagery with Google Maps and Bing Maps (Figure 9).

Some excellent starting places are general travel Web sites such as Expedia Travel, Cheap Tickets, Orbitz, and Travelocity. Many airline Web sites allow you to reserve hotel rooms, activities, and rental cars while booking a flight. These all-encompassing Web sites, including those in Figure 10, have tools to help you find the lowest prices and details about flights, car rentals, cruises, and hotels. Comprehensive online guidebooks can provide useful details about maximizing your vacation time while saving money.

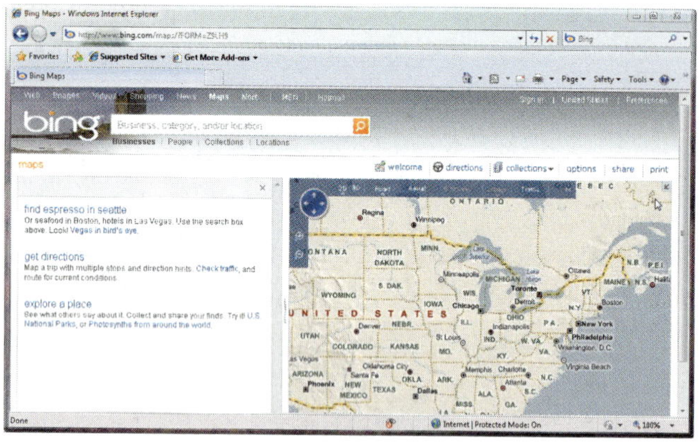

Figure 9 Bing Maps provides location information and satellite imagery for many regions on this planet.

Travel Web Sites

General Travel	Web Address
CheapTickets	cheaptickets.com
Expedia Travel	expedia.com
Kayak	kayak.com
Orbitz	orbitz.com
SideStep	sidestep.com
Travelocity	travelocity.com
Cartography	**Web Address**
Bing Maps	bing.com/maps
Google Maps	maps.google.com
MapQuest	mapquest.com
Maps.com	maps.com
Yahoo! Maps	maps.yahoo.com
Travel and City Guides	**Web Address**
Frommer's Travel Guides	frommers.com
GoPlanit	goplanit.com
U.S.-Parks US National Parks Travel Guide	www.us-parks.com
Virtual Tourist	virtualtourist.com

For more information about travel Web sites, visit the Microsoft Office and Concepts CourseMate Web site at www.cengagebrain.com and then navigate to the Making Use of the Web Feature resource for this book.

Figure 10 These travel resources Web sites offer travel information to exciting destinations throughout the world.

Travel Web Exercises

1. **Visit one of the cartography Web sites listed in Figure 10** and obtain the directions from your campus to one of these destinations: the Washington Monument in Washington, D.C.; the Statue of Liberty on Ellis Island in New York; Disneyland in Anaheim, California; or the Grand Old Opry in Nashville, Tennessee. How many miles is it to your destination? What is the estimated driving time? Use the Google Maps Web site to obtain an overhead image of this destination. Then, visit one of the general travel Web sites listed in the table and plan a flight from the nearest major airport to one of the four destinations for the week after finals and a return trip one week later. Which airline, flight numbers, and departure and arrival times did you select?

2. **Visit one of the travel and city guides Web sites listed in Figure 10,** and choose a destination for a getaway this coming weekend. Write a one-page paper giving details about this location, such as popular hotels and lodging, expected weather, population, local colleges and universities, parks and recreation, ancient and modern history, and tours. Include a map or satellite photo of this place. Why did you select this destination? How would you travel there and back? What is the breakdown of expected costs for this weekend, including travel expenditures, meals, lodging, and tickets to events and activities? Which Web addresses did you use to complete this exercise?

Environment

The Future of the Planet

Making a Difference for Earth

From the rain forests of Africa to the marine life in the Pacific Ocean, the fragile ecosystem is under extreme stress. Many environmental groups have developed informative Web sites, including those listed in Figure 11, in attempts to educate worldwide populations and to increase resource conservation. The Environmental Defense Fund Web site (Figure 12) contains information for people who would like to help safeguard the environment.

On an international scale, the Environmental Sites on the Internet Web page developed by the Royal Institute of Technology in Stockholm, Sweden, has been rated as one of the better ecological Web sites. Its comprehensive listing of environmental concerns range from aquatic ecology to wetlands.

The U.S. federal government has a number of Web sites devoted to specific environmental concerns. For example, the U.S. Environmental Protection Agency (EPA) provides pollution data, including ozone levels and air pollutants, for specific areas. Its AirData Web site displays air pollution emissions and monitoring data from the entire United States and is the world's most extensive collection of air pollution data.

Environment Web Sites

Name	Web Address
Central African Regional Program for the Environment (CARPE)	carpe.umd.edu
Earthjustice	earthjustice.org
EarthTrends: Environmental Information	earthtrends.wri.org
Environmental Defense Fund	edf.org
Environmental Sites on the Internet	www.ima.kth.se/im/envsite/envsite.htm
EPA AirData — Access to Air Pollution Data	epa.gov/air/data
Global Warming	globalwarming.org
Green Computing Impact Organization	gcio.org
GreenNet	gn.apc.org
New American Dream	newdream.org
University of Wisconsin — Milwaukee Environmental Health and Safety Resources	uwm.edu/Dept/EHSRM/EHSLINKS
USGS Branch of Quality Systems	bqs.usgs.gov/acidrain

For more information about environment Web sites, visit the Microsoft Office and Concepts CourseMate Web site at www.cengagebrain.com and then navigate to the Making Use of the Web Feature resource for this book.

Figure 11 Environment Web sites provide vast resources for ecological data and action groups.

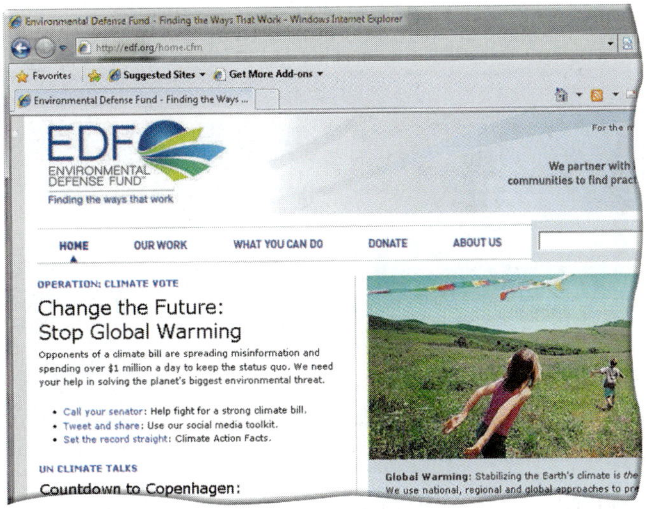

Figure 12 A visit to the Environmental Defense Fund Web site provides practical advice about protecting the environment.

Environment Web Exercises

1. **The New American Dream Web site encourages consumers to reduce the amount of junk mail sent to their homes.** Using the table in Figure 11, visit the Web site to learn how many trees are leveled each year to provide paper for these mailings and how many garbage trucks are needed to haul this waste. Read the letters used to eliminate names from bulk mail lists. To whom would you mail these letters? How long does it take to stop these unsolicited letters?

2. **Visit the EPA AirData Web site.** What is the highest ozone level recorded in your state this past year? Where are the nearest air pollution monitoring Web sites, and what are their levels? Where are the nearest sources of air pollution? Read two reports about two different topics, such as acid rain and air quality, and summarize their findings. Include information about who sponsored the research, who conducted the studies, when the data was collected, and the impact of this pollution on the atmosphere, water, forests, and human health. Whom would you contact for further information regarding the data and studies?

Finance

Money Matters

Cashing In on Financial Advice

You can manage your money with advice from financial Web sites that offer online banking, tax help, personal finance, and small business and commercial services.

If you do not have a personal banker or a financial planner, consider a Web adviser to guide your investment decisions. The MSN Money Web site (Figure 13) provides financial news and investment information.

If you are ready to ride the ups and downs of the Dow and the NASDAQ, an abundance of Web sites listed in Figure 14, including Reuters and Morningstar, can help you select companies that fit your interests and financial needs.

Claiming to be the fastest, easiest tax publication on the planet, the Internal Revenue Service Web site contains procedures for filing tax appeals and contains IRS forms, publications, and legal regulations.

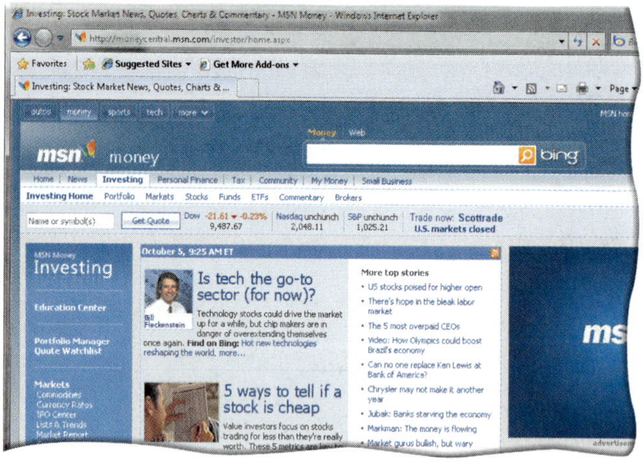

Figure 13 The MSN Money Web site contains features and information related to college and family finances.

Finance Web Sites

Advice and Education	Web Address
Bankrate	bankrate.com
ING Direct	ingdirect.com
LendingTree	lendingtree.com
Loan.com	loan.com
The Motley Fool	fool.com
MSN Money	moneycentral.msn.com
Wells Fargo	wellsfargo.com
Yahoo! Finance	finance.yahoo.com
Stock Market	**Web Address**
E*TRADE	us.etrade.com
Financial Engines	financialengines.com
Merrill Lynch	ml.com
Morningstar	morningstar.com
Reuters	reuters.com/investing
Valic	valic.com
Vanguard	vanguard.com
Taxes	**Web Address**
H&R Block	hrblock.com
Internal Revenue Service	www.irs.gov
Jackson Hewitt	jacksonhewitt.com
Liberty Tax Service	libertytax.com

For more information about finance Web sites, visit the Microsoft Office and Concepts CourseMate Web site at www.cengagebrain.com and then navigate to the Making Use of the Web Feature resource for this book.

Figure 14 Financial resources Web sites offer general information, stock market analyses, and tax advice, as well as guidance and money-saving tips.

Finance Web Exercises

1. **Visit three advice and education Web sites listed in Figure 14** and read their top business world reports. Write a paragraph about each, summarizing these stories. Which stocks or mutual funds do these Web sites predict as being sound investments today? What are the current market indexes for the DJIA (Dow Jones Industrial Average), S&P 500, and NASDAQ, and how do these figures compare with the previous day's numbers?

2. **Using two of the stock market Web sites listed in Figure 14,** search for information about Microsoft, Apple, and one other software vendor. Write a paragraph about each of these stocks describing the revenues, net incomes, total assets for the previous year, current stock price per share, highest and lowest prices of each stock during the past year, and other relevant investment information.

Government

Stamp of Approval

Making a Federal Case for Useful Information

When it is time to buy stamps to mail your correspondence, you no longer need to wait in long lines at your local post office. The U.S. Postal Service has authorized several organizations to sell stamps online.

You can recognize U.S. Government Web sites on the Internet by their gov top-level domain. For example, the Library of Congress Web site is loc.gov (Figure 15). Government and military Web sites offer a wide range of information. The Time Service Department Web site will provide you with the correct time. If you are looking for a federal document, FedWorld lists thousands of documents distributed by the government on its Web site. For access to the names of your congressional representatives, visit the extensive HG.org Web site. Figure 16 shows some of the more popular U.S. Government Web sites.

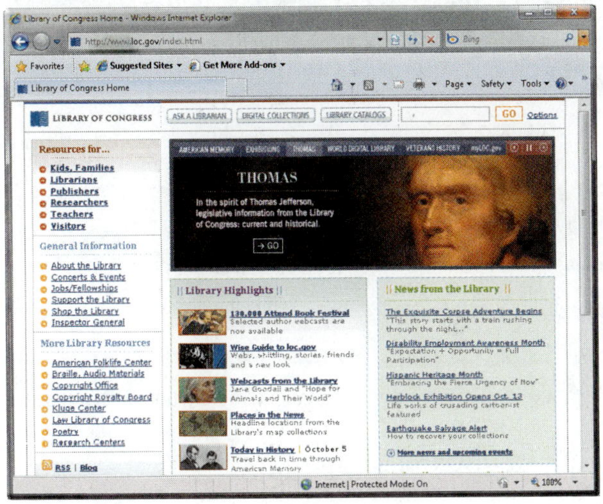

Figure 15 The Library of Congress Web site has resources about American history, world culture, and digital preservation.

Government Resources Web Sites

Postage	Web Address
Endicia	endicia.com
Pitney Bowes	pb.com
Stamps.com	stamps.com
Government	**Web Address**
FedWorld	www.fedworld.gov
HG.org — Worldwide Legal Directories	hg.org
Library of Congress	loc.gov
National Agricultural Library	nal.usda.gov
Smithsonian Institution	smithsonian.org
THOMAS (Library of Congress)	thomas.loc.gov
Time Service Department	tycho.usno.navy.mil
U.S. Department of Education	ed.gov
United States Department of the Treasury	treas.gov
U.S. Government Printing Office	www.access.gpo.gov
United States National Library of Medicine	nlm.nih.gov
United States Patent and Trademark Office	uspto.gov
USAJOBS	usajobs.opm.gov
The White House	whitehouse.gov

For more information about government Web sites, visit the Microsoft Office and Concepts CourseMate Web site at www.cengagebrain.com and then navigate to the Making Use of the Web Feature resource for this book.

Figure 16 These Web sites offer information about buying U.S.-approved postage online and researching federal agencies.

Government Web Exercises

1. **View the three postage Web sites listed in Figure 16.** Compare and contrast the available services on each one. Consider postage cost, necessary equipment, shipping services, security techniques, and tracking capability. Explain why you would or would not like to use this service.

2. **Visit the HG.org Web site listed in Figure 16.** What are the names, addresses, and phone numbers of your two state senators and your local congressional representative? On what committees do they serve? Who is the chief justice of the Supreme Court, and what has been this justice's opinion on two recently decided cases? Who are the members of the president's cabinet? Then, visit two other Web sites listed in Figure 16. Write a paragraph about each Web site describing its content and features.

Shopping and Auctions

Bargains Galore

Let Your Mouse Do Your Shopping

From groceries to clothing to computers, you can buy just about everything you need with just a few clicks of your mouse. More than one-half of Internet users will make at least one online purchase this year. Books, computer software and hardware, and music are the hottest commodities.

The two categories of Internet shopping Web sites are those with physical counterparts, such as Walmart and Fry's Electronics (Figure 17), and those with only a Web presence, such as Amazon and Buy. Popular Web shopping sites are listed in Figure 18.

Another method of shopping for the items you need, and maybe some you really do not need, is to visit auction Web sites, including those listed in Figure 18. Categories include antiques and collectibles, automotive, computers, electronics, music, sports, sports cards and memorabilia, and toys. Online auction Web sites can offer unusual items, including *Star Wars* memorabilia or a round of golf with Jack Nicklaus. eBay is one of thousands of Internet auction Web sites and is the world's largest personal online trading community. In addition, craigslist is a free online equivalent of classified advertisements.

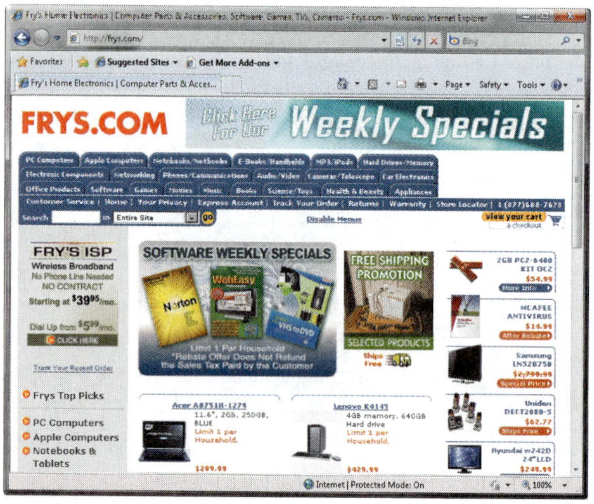

Figure 17 Fry's is a popular electronic retailer that sells a variety of products.

Shopping and Auctions Web Sites

Auctions	Web Address
craigslist	craigslist.org
eBay	ebay.com
Sotheby's	sothebys.com
uBid	ubid.com
U.S. Treasury — Seized Property Auctions	ustreas.gov/auctions
Books and Music	**Web Address**
Amazon	amazon.com
Barnes & Noble	bn.com
BookFinder	bookfinder.com
Computers and Electronics	**Web Address**
BestBuy	bestbuy.com
Buy	buy.com
Fry's Electronics	frys.com
Miscellaneous	**Web Address**
drugstore	drugstore.com
Google Product Search	google.com/products
SmashBuys	smashbuys.com
Walmart	walmart.com

For more information about shopping and auctions Web sites, visit the Microsoft Office and Concepts CourseMate Web site at www.cengagebrain.com and then navigate to the Making Use of the Web Feature resource for this book.

Figure 18 Making online purchases can help ease the burden of driving to and fighting the crowds in local malls.

Shopping and Auctions Web Exercises

1. **Visit two of the computers and electronics and two of the miscellaneous Web sites listed in Figure 18.** Write a paragraph describing the features these Web sites offer compared with the same offerings from stores. In another paragraph, describe any disadvantages of shopping at these Web sites instead of actually visiting a store. Then, describe their policies for returning unwanted merchandise and for handling complaints.

2. **Using one of the auction Web sites listed in Figure 18, search for two objects pertaining to your hobbies.** For example, if you are a sports fan, you can search for a complete set of Upper Deck cards. If you are a car buff, search for your dream car. Describe these two items. How many people have bid on these items? Who are the sellers? What are the opening and current bids?

Weather, Sports, and News

What's News?

Weather, Sports, and News Web Sites Score Big Hits

Rain or sun? Hot or cold? Weather is the leading online news item, with at least 10,000 Web sites devoted to this field. Millions of people view The Weather Channel Web site (Figure 19) each month.

Baseball may be the national pastime, but sports aficionados yearn for everything from auto racing to cricket. The Internet has millions of pages of multimedia sports news, entertainment, and merchandise.

The Internet has emerged as a major source for news, with more than one-third of Americans going online at least once a week and 15 percent going online daily for reports of major news events. Many of these viewers are using RSS (Really Simple Syndication) technology to be notified when new stories about their favorite topics are available on the Internet. Popular weather, sports, and news Web sites are listed in Figure 20.

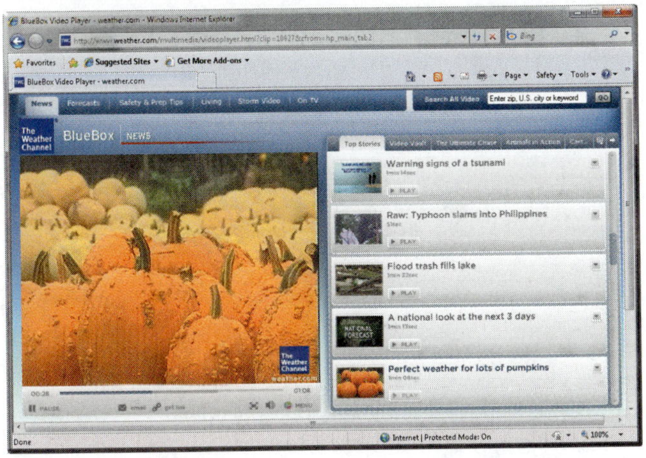

Figure 19 Local, national, and international weather conditions and details about breaking weather stories are available on The Weather Channel Web site.

Weather, Sports, and News Web Sites

Weather	Web Address
AccuWeather	accuweather.com
Infoplease Weather	infoplease.com/weather.html
Intellicast	www.intellicast.com
National Weather Service	www.crh.noaa.gov
The Weather Channel	weather.com
Sports	**Web Address**
CBS Sports	cbssports.com
ESPN	espn.com
NASCAR	nascar.com
International Olympic Committee	www.olympic.org
Sporting News Radio	radio.sportingnews.com
Yahoo! Sports	sports.yahoo.com
News	**Web Address**
FactCheck	factcheck.org
Geek.com	geek.com
Google News	news.google.com
MSNBC	msnbc.com
Onlinenewspapers	onlinenewspapers.com
privacy.org	privacy.org
SiliconValley	siliconvalley.com
starting page	startingpage.com/html/news.html
USA TODAY	usatoday.com
Washington Post	washingtonpost.com

For more information about weather, sports, and news Web sites, visit the Microsoft Office and Concepts CourseMate Web site at www.cengagebrain.com and then navigate to the Making Use of the Web Feature resource for this book.

Figure 20 Keep informed about the latest weather, sports, and news events with these Web sites.

Weather, Sports, and News Web Exercises

1. **Visit two of the sports Web sites in Figure 20** and write a paragraph describing the content these Web sites provide concerning your favorite sport. Visit Google News and then search for stories about this sports team or athlete. Then, create a customized news page with stories about your sports interests. Include RSS feeds to get regularly updated summaries on this subject.

2. **Visit the Onlinenewspapers and starting page Web sites listed in Figure 20** and select two newspapers from each site. Write a paragraph describing the top national news story featured in each of these four Web pages. Then, write another paragraph describing the top international news story displayed at each Web site. In the third paragraph, discuss which of the four Web sites is the most interesting in terms of story selection, photos, and Web page design.

Learning

Yearn to Learn

Discover New Worlds Online

While you may believe your education ends when you finally graduate from college, learning is a lifelong process. You can increase your technological knowledge by visiting several Web sites (Figure 21) with tutorials about building your own Web sites, the latest news about the Internet, and resources for visually impaired users.

Learning Web Sites

Learning How To's	Web Address
Bartleby: Great Books Online	bartleby.com
AT&T Knowledge Network Explorer	www.kn.pacbell.com/wired
BBC Learning	bbc.co.uk/learning
CBT Nuggets	cbtnuggets.com
HowStuffWorks	howstuffworks.com
Internet Public Library	ipl.org
Learn the Net	learnthenet.com
ScienceMaster	sciencemaster.com
Search Engine Watch	searchenginewatch.com
Wiredguide	wiredguide.com
Cooking	**Web Address**
Betty Crocker	bettycrocker.com
Chef2Chef	chef2chef.net
Food Network	foodnetwork.com

For more information about learning Web sites, visit the Microsoft Office and Concepts CourseMate Web site at www.cengagebrain.com and then navigate to the Making Use of the Web Feature resource for this book.

Figure 21 The information gleaned from these Web sites can help you learn about many aspects of our existence.

The HowStuffWorks Web site has won numerous awards for its clear, comprehensive articles that demystify aspects of our everyday life. It includes ratings and reviews of products written by *Consumer Guide* editors.

A consortium of colleges maintains the Internet Public Library, which includes subject collections, reference materials, and a reading room filled with magazines and books. Volunteer librarians will answer your personal questions asked in its Ask an IPL Librarian form.

Enhancing your culinary skills can be a rewarding endeavor. No matter if you are a gourmet chef or a weekend cook, you will be cooking in style with the help of online resources, including those listed in Figure 21.

Have you ever wondered how to make a key lime pie? How about learning how to cook some easy, low-calorie dishes? Are you seeking advice from expert chefs? The Food Network Web site (Figure 22) is filled with information related to cooking, grilling, and healthy eating.

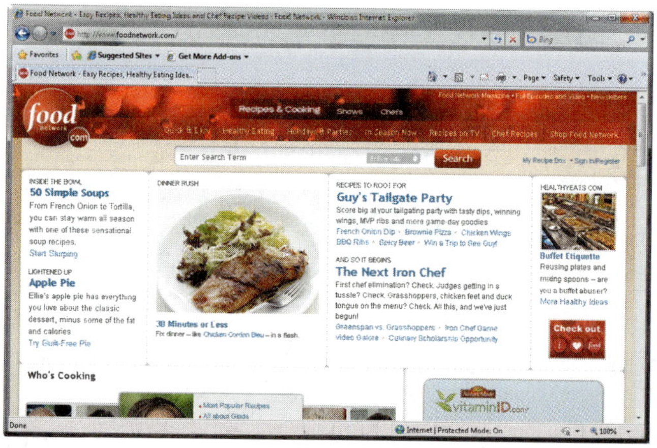

Figure 22 The Food Network Web site provides access to healthy recipes, grilling tips, and cookware.

Learning Web Exercises

1. **Using one of the Learning How To's Web sites listed in Figure 21,** search for information about installing memory in a computer. Write a paragraph about your findings. Then, review the material in the HowStuffWorks Web site listed in Figure 21, and write a paragraph describing articles on this Web site that are pertinent to your major.

2. **Visit one of the cooking Web sites listed in Figure 21** and find two recipes or cooking tips that you can use when preparing your next meal. Write a paragraph about each one, summarizing your discoveries. Which Web sites allow you to create your own online recipe book? What are the advantages and disadvantages of accessing these Web sites on the new appliances and gadgets that might someday be in your kitchen?

Science

$E = mc^2$

Rocket Science on the Web

For some people, space exploration is a hobby. Building and launching model rockets allow these at-home scientists to participate in exploring the great frontier of space. For others, space exploration is their life. Numerous Web sites, including those in Figure 23, provide in-depth information about the universe.

NASA's Web site contains information about rockets, space exploration, the International Space Station, space transportation, and communications. Other science resources explore space-related questions about astronomy, physics, the earth sciences, microgravity, and robotics.

Rockets and space are not the only areas to explore in the world of science. Where can you find the latest pictures taken with the Hubble Space Telescope? Do you know how climate change is affecting the human body? You can find the answers to these questions and many others through the New Scientist Web site (newscientist.com) shown in Figure 24.

The National Science Foundation's Web site features overviews of current topics and an extensive Multimedia Gallery with audio and video files, photos, and paintings.

Science.gov is an outstanding resource for scientific databases and thousands of authoritative science Web sites. The U.S. government science information provided offers 200 million pages of research, with search results ranked by relevance and sorted by topic and year.

Science Web Sites

Periodicals	Web Address
Archaeology Magazine	archaeology.org
Astronomy Magazine	astronomy.com
New Scientist	newscientist.com
OceanLink	oceanlink.info
Science Magazine	sciencemag.org
Scientific American	sciam.com
Resources	**Web Address**
National Science Foundation (NSF)	nsf.gov
Science.gov: USA.gov for Science	science.gov
Thomson Reuters	scientific.thomson.com/free/
Science Community	**Web Address**
American Scientist	amsci.org
Federation of American Scientists	fas.org
NASA	www.nasa.gov
Sigma Xi, The Scientific Research Society	sigmaxi.org

For more information about science Web sites, visit the Microsoft Office and Concepts CourseMate Web site at www.cengagebrain.com and then navigate to the Making Use of the Web Feature resource for this book.

Figure 23 Resources available on the Internet offer a wide range of subjects for enthusiasts who want to delve into familiar and unknown territories in the world of science.

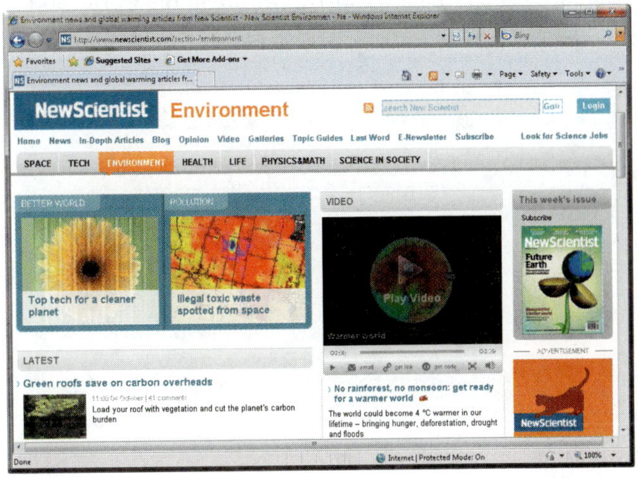

Figure 24 The New Scientist Web site covers news about space exploration, the environment, and technology.

Science Web Exercises

1. **Visit the National Science Foundation Web site listed in the table in Figure 23.** What are the topics of the latest science news and special reports? Which speeches and lectures are featured? What are the titles of image, video, and audio files in the Multimedia Gallery?

2. **Visit the NASA Web site listed in the table in Figure 23.** Click the Missions link and then click the Mission Calendar link. When are the next two launches scheduled? What are the purposes of these missions? Click the Careers @ NASA topic and then write a paragraph describing the internships, cooperative programs, and summer employment opportunities. Then, view two of the science community Web sites listed in Figure 23 and write a paragraph about each of these Web sites describing the information each contains.

Health

No Pain, All Gain

Store Personal Health Records Online

More than 75 million consumers use the Internet yearly to search for health information, so using the Web to store personal medical data is a natural extension of the Internet's capabilities. Internet health services and portals are available to store your personal health history, including prescriptions, lab test results, doctor visits, allergies, and immunizations.

Google Health allows users to create a health profile, import medical records, and locate medical services and doctors. Web sites such as healthfinder.gov (Figure 25) provide free wellness information to consumers. Wise consumers, however, verify the online information they read with their personal physician.

In minutes, you can register with a health Web site by choosing a user name and password. Then, you create a record to enter your medical history. You also can store data for your emergency contacts, primary care physicians, specialists, blood type, cholesterol levels, blood pressure, and insurance plan. No matter where you are in the world, you and medical personnel can obtain records via the Internet or fax machine. Some popular online health databases are shown in Figure 26.

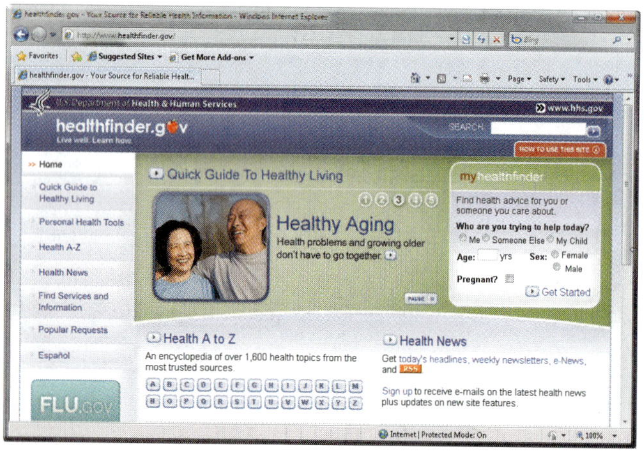

Figure 25 The healthfinder.gov Web site provides advice and tools to prevent illnesses and check drug interactions.

Health Web Sites

Medical History	Web Address
Google Health	google.com/health
Lifestar	mylifestarphr.com
Medem	medem.com
PersonalMD	personalmd.com
Practice Solutions	practicesolutions.ca
Records for Living, Inc — Personal Health and Living Management	recordsforliving.com
WebMD	webmd.com
General Health	**Web Address**
Consumer and Patient Health Information Section (CAPHIS)	caphis.mlanet.org/consumer
Centers for Disease Control and Prevention	cdc.gov
familydoctor	familydoctor.org
healthfinder	healthfinder.gov
KidsHealth	kidshealth.org
LIVESTRONG.COM	livestrong.com
MedlinePlus	medlineplus.gov
PE Central: Health and Nutrition Web Sites	pecentral.org/websites/healthsites.html
Physical Activity Guidelines	health.gov/paguidelines

For more information about health Web sites, visit the Microsoft Office and Concepts CourseMate Web site at www.cengagebrain.com and then navigate to the Making Use of the Web Feature resource for this book.

Figure 26 These health Web sites allow you to organize your medical information and store it in an online database and also obtain information about a variety of medical conditions and treatments.

Health Web Exercises

1. **Access one of the health Web sites listed in Figure 26.** Register yourself or a family member and then enter the full health history. Create an emergency medical card if the Web site provides the card option. Submit this record and emergency card to your instructor. If you feel uncomfortable disclosing medical information for yourself or a family member, you may enter fictitious information.

2. **Visit three of the health Web sites listed in Figure 26.** Describe the features of each. Which of the three is the most user-friendly? Why? Describe the privacy policies of these three Web sites. Submit your analysis of these Web sites to your instructor.

Careers

In Search of the Perfect Job

Web Helps Career Hunt

While your teachers give you valuable training to prepare you for a career, they rarely teach you how to begin that career. You can broaden your horizons by searching the Internet for career information and job openings.

First, examine some of the job search Web sites. These resources list thousands of openings in hundreds of fields, companies, and locations. For example, the USAJOBS Web site, shown in Figure 27, allows you to find information for Federal jobs. This information may include the training and education required, salary data, working conditions, job descriptions, and more. In addition, many companies advertise careers on their Web sites.

When a company contacts you for an interview, learn as much about it and the industry as possible before the interview. Many of the Web sites listed in Figure 28 include detailed company profiles and links to their corporate Web sites.

Figure 27 The USAJOBS Web site is the official location for federal jobs and information for job seekers.

Career Web Sites

Job Search	Web Address
BestJobsUSA	bestjobsusa.com
CareerBuilder	careerbuilder.com
Careerjet	careerjet.com
CareerNET	careernet.com
CAREERXCHANGE	careerxchange.com
CollegeGrad.com	collegegrad.com
EmploymentGuide.com	employmentguide.com
Job.com	job.com
Job Bank USA	jobbankusa.com
JobWeb	jobweb.com
Monster	monster.com
USAJOBS	www.usajobs.gov
VolunteerMatch	volunteermatch.org
Yahoo! HotJobs	hotjobs.yahoo.com
Company/Industry Information	**Web Address**
Careers.org	careers.org
Forbes	forbes.com/leadership/careers
Fortune	fortune.com
Hoover's	hoovers.com
Occupational Outlook Handbook	stats.bls.gov/oco

For more information about career Web sites, visit the Microsoft Office and Concepts CourseMate Web site at www.cengagebrain.com and then navigate to the Making Use of the Web Feature resource for this book.

Figure 28 Career Web sites provide a variety of job openings and information about major companies worldwide.

Careers Web Exercises

1. **Use two of the job search Web sites listed in Figure 28** to find three companies with job openings in your field. Make a table listing the Web site name, position available, description, salary, location, desired education, and desired experience.

2. **It is a good idea to acquire information before graduation about the industry in which you would like to work.** Are you interested in the automotive manufacturing industry, the restaurant service industry, or the financial industry? Use two of the company/industry information Web sites listed in Figure 28 to research a particular career related to your major. Write a paragraph naming the Web sites and the specific information you found, such as the nature of the work, recommended training and qualifications, employment outlook, and earnings. Then, use two other Web sites to profile three companies with positions available in this field. Write a paragraph about each of these companies, describing the headquarters' location, sales and earnings for the previous year, total number of employees, working conditions, benefits, and competitors.

Literature and Arts

Find Some Culture

Get Ready to Read, Paint, and Dance

Brush up your knowledge of Shakespeare, grab a canvas, and put on your dancing shoes. Literature and arts Web sites, including those in Figure 29, are about to sweep you off your cyberfeet.

Literature and Arts Web Sites

Literature	Web Address
Bartleby	bartleby.com
Bibliomania	bibliomania.com
The Complete Review	www.complete-review.com
eNotes	enotes.com
Fantastic Fiction	fantasticfiction.co.uk
Literary History	literaryhistory.com
Nobel Prize in Literature	nobelprize.org/nobel_prizes/literature/laureates/1909/press.html
Project Gutenberg	gutenberg.org
Project MUSE	muse.jhu.edu
Arts	**Web Address**
absolutearts	absolutearts.com
The Children's Museum of Indianapolis	childrensmuseum.org
ARTINFO Gallery Guide	artinfo.com/galleryguide/
The Getty	getty.edu
Louvre Museum	louvre.fr
Montreal Museum of Fine Arts	mmfa.qc.ca
Museumstuff.com	museumstuff.com
The Museum of Online Museums	coudal.com/moom
National Gallery of Art	nga.gov

For more information about literature and arts Web sites, visit the Microsoft Office and Concepts CourseMate Web site at www.cengagebrain.com and then navigate to the Making Use of the Web Feature resource for this book.

Figure 29 Discover culture throughout the world by visiting these literature and arts Web sites.

The full text of hundreds of books is available online from the Bibliomania and Project Gutenberg Web sites. The Complete Review provides summaries, reviews, and Web links about a variety of books and their authors. The Bartleby Web site features biographies, definitions, quotations, dictionaries, and indexes.

When you are ready to absorb more culture, you can turn to various art Web sites. Many museums have images of their collections online. Among them are the Getty Museum in Los Angeles, the Montreal Museum of Fine Arts, and the Louvre Museum in Paris (Figure 30).

The absolutearts Web site focuses on contemporary art and includes video interviews with artists, art history research, and artists' blogs.

The Museum of Online Museums Web site provides links to museum and gallery Web sites, such as the Museum of Modern Art, The Bauhaus Archive, and The Art Institute of Chicago.

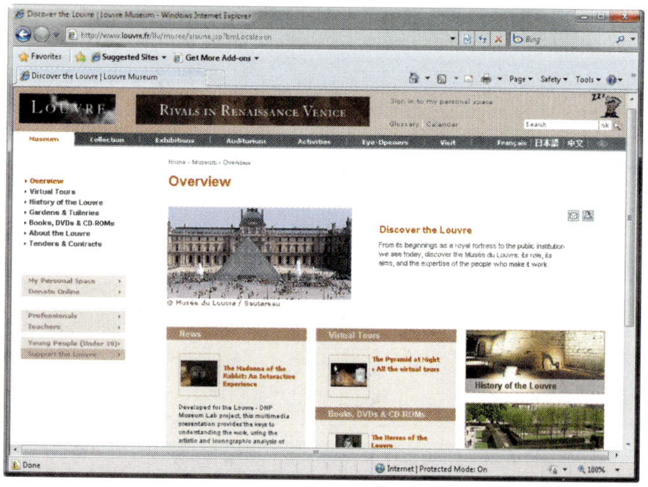

Figure 30 Permanent and temporary exhibitions, educational activities, and a bookstore are featured on the Louvre Museum Web site.

Literature and Arts Web Exercises

1. **Visit the Literary History Web site listed in Figure 29** and view one author in the Twentieth Century Literature, Nineteenth Century Literature, British Poets, and African American Literature sections. Read two literary criticism articles about each of the four authors and write a paragraph describing which of these authors is the most interesting to you. What are the advantages and disadvantages of reading literary criticism electronically?

2. **Using the arts Web sites listed in Figure 29,** search for three temporary exhibitions in galleries throughout the world. Describe the venues, the artists, and the works. Which permanent collections are found in these museums? Some people shop for gifts in the museums' stores. View and describe three items for sale.

Chapter Three

Application Software

Objectives

After completing this chapter, you will be able to:

1. Identify the four categories of application software
2. Describe characteristics of a user interface
3. Identify the key features of widely used business programs: word processing, spreadsheet, database, presentation, note taking, personal information manager, business software for phones, business software suite, project management, accounting, document management, and enterprise computing
4. Identify the key features of widely used graphics and multimedia programs: computer-aided design, professional desktop publishing, professional paint/image editing, professional photo editing, professional video and audio editing, multimedia authoring, and Web page authoring
5. Identify the key features of widely used home, personal, and educational programs: personal finance, legal, tax preparation, personal desktop publishing, personal paint/image editing, personal photo editing and photo management, clip art/image gallery, personal video and audio editing, travel and mapping, reference and educational, and entertainment
6. Discuss Web applications
7. Identify the types of application software used in communications
8. Describe the learning aids available for application software

Application Software

With the proper software, a computer is a valuable tool. Software allows users to create letters, reports, and other documents; develop multimedia presentations; design Web pages and diagrams; draw images; enhance audio and video clips; prepare taxes; play games; compose e-mail messages and instant messages; and much more. To accomplish these and many other tasks, users work with application software. **Application software** consists of programs designed to make users more productive and/or assist them with personal tasks. Application software has a variety of uses:

1. To make business activities more efficient
2. To assist with graphics and multimedia projects
3. To support home, personal, and educational tasks
4. To facilitate communications

The table in Figure 3-1 categorizes popular types of application software by their general use. Although many types of communications software exist, the ones listed in Figure 3-1 are application software oriented.

Application software is available in a variety of forms: packaged, custom, Web application, open source, shareware, freeware, and public domain.

- **Packaged software** is mass-produced, copyrighted retail software that meets the needs of a wide variety of users, not just a single user or company. Packaged software is available in retail stores or on the Web. Figure 3-1 shows some images of packaged software.
- **Custom software** performs functions specific to a business or industry. Sometimes a company cannot find packaged software that meets its unique requirements. In this case, the company may use programmers to develop tailor-made custom software.
- A **Web application** is a Web site that allows users to access and interact with software from any computer or device that is connected to the Internet. Types of Web applications include e-mail, word processing, and game programs.

Four Categories of Application Software

Business	Graphics and Multimedia	Home/Personal/Educational
• Word Processing • Spreadsheet • Database • Presentation • Note Taking • Personal Information Manager (PIM) • Business Software for Phones • Business Software Suite • Project Management • Accounting • Document Management • Enterprise Computing	• Computer-Aided Design (CAD) • Desktop Publishing (for the Professional) • Paint/Image Editing (for the Professional) • Photo Editing (for the Professional) • Video and Audio Editing (for the Professional) • Multimedia Authoring • Web Page Authoring	• Software Suite (for Personal Use) • Personal Finance • Legal • Tax Preparation • Desktop Publishing (for Personal Use) • Paint/Image Editing (for Personal Use) • Photo Editing and Photo Management (for Personal Use) • Clip Art/Image Gallery • Video and Audio Editing (for Personal Use) • Home Design/Landscaping • Travel and Mapping • Reference and Educational • Entertainment

Communications

• Web Browser	• E-Mail	• Instant Messaging	• Chat Room	• Text, Picture, Video Messaging	
• RSS Aggregator	• Blogging	• Newsgroup/Message Board	• FTP	• VoIP	• Video Conferencing

Figure 3-1 The four major categories of popular application software are outlined in this table. Communications software often is bundled with other application or system software.

- **Open source software** is software provided for use, modification, and redistribution. This software has no restrictions from the copyright holder regarding modification of the software's internal instructions and its redistribution. Open source software usually can be downloaded from the Internet, often at no cost.
- **Shareware** is copyrighted software that is distributed at no cost for a trial period. To use a shareware program beyond that period, you send payment to the program developer.
- **Freeware** is copyrighted software provided at no cost to a user by an individual or a company that retains all rights to the software.
- **Public-domain software** has been donated for public use and has no copyright restrictions. Anyone can copy or distribute public-domain software to others at no cost.

Thousands of shareware, freeware, and public-domain programs are available on the Internet for users to download. Examples include communications, graphics, and game programs.

The Role of System Software

System software serves as the interface between the user, the application software, and the computer's hardware (Figure 3-2). To use application software, such as a word processing program, your computer must be running system software — specifically, an operating system. Three popular personal computer operating systems are Windows, Mac OS, and Linux.

Each time you start a computer, the operating system is loaded (copied) from the computer's hard disk into memory. Once the operating system is loaded, it coordinates all the activities of the computer. This includes starting application software and transferring data among input and output devices and memory. While the computer is running, the operating system remains in memory.

Figure 3-2 A user does not communicate directly with the computer hardware. Instead, system software is the interface between the user, the application software, and the hardware. For example, when a user instructs the application software to print a document, the application software sends the print instruction to the system software, which in turn sends the print instruction to the hardware.

Antivirus Programs

For more information, visit the Microsoft Office and Concepts CourseMate Web site at www.cengagebrain.com, navigate to the Chapter 3 Web Link resource for this book, and then click Antivirus Programs.

Utility Programs A utility program is a type of system software that assists users with controlling or maintaining the operation of a computer, its devices, or its software. Utility programs typically offer features that provide an environment conducive to successful use of application software. For example, utility programs protect a computer against malicious software and unauthorized intrusions, manage files and disks, compress files, play media files, and burn optical discs. (To learn more about how to compress files, complete the Learn How To 2 activity on pages 126 and 127.)

One of the more important utility programs protects a computer against malicious software, or **malware**, which is a program that acts without a user's knowledge and deliberately alters the computer's operations. A computer virus is a type of malicious software. Chapter 4 discusses system software and utility programs in more depth.

? FAQ 3-1

How many viruses exist on the Internet?

More than one million viruses exist on the Internet. This statistic stresses the importance of protecting your computer from various threats on the Internet, as well as practicing safe Web browsing habits. Not only is it possible to get a computer virus from downloading and opening an infected file or by opening an infected e-mail message, you also can fall victim to a computer virus simply by visiting a malicious Web site.

For more information, visit the Microsoft Office and Concepts CourseMate Web site at www.cengagebrain.com, navigate to the Chapter 3 FAQ resource for this book, and then click Computer Viruses.

Working with Application Software

To use application software, you must instruct the operating system to start the program. The steps in Figure 3-3 illustrate one way to start and interact with the Paint program, which is included with the Windows operating system. The following paragraphs explain the steps in Figure 3-3.

Personal computer operating systems often use the concept of a desktop to make the computer easier to use. The **desktop** is an on-screen work area that has a graphical user interface. Step 1 of Figure 3-3 shows icons, a button, a pointer, and a menu on the Windows desktop. An **icon** is a small image displayed on the screen that represents a program, a document, or some other object. A **button** is a graphical element that you activate to cause a specific action to occur. One way to activate a button is to click it. To **click** a button on the screen requires moving the pointer to the button and then pressing and releasing a button on the mouse (usually the left mouse button). The **pointer** is a small symbol displayed on the screen that moves as you interact with the mouse or other pointing device. Common pointer shapes are an I-beam (I), a block arrow (), and a pointing hand ().

The Windows desktop contains a Start button on the lower-left corner of the taskbar. When you click the Start button, the Start menu is displayed on the desktop. A **menu** contains a list of commands from which you make selections. A **command** is an instruction that causes a program to perform a specific action.

As illustrated in Steps 1 and 2 of Figure 3-3, when you click the Start button and then click the All Programs command on the Start menu, the All Programs list is displayed on the Start menu. Clicking the Accessories folder in the All Programs list displays the Accessories list.

To start a program, you can click its program name on a menu or in a list. This action instructs the operating system to start the program, which means the program's instructions load from a storage medium (such as a hard disk) into memory. For example, when you click Paint in the Accessories list, Windows loads the Paint program instructions from the computer's hard disk into memory.

Once loaded into memory, the program appears in a window on the desktop (Step 3 of Figure 3-3). A **window** is a rectangular area of the screen that displays data and information. The top of a window has a **title bar**, which is a horizontal space that contains the window's name.

With the program loaded, you can create a new file or open an existing one. A **file** is a named collection of stored data, instructions, or information. A file can contain text, images, audio, and video. To distinguish among various files, each file has a file name. The title bar of the document window usually displays a document's file name. Step 4 of Figure 3-3 shows the contents of the file, Baby Buffalo, displaying in the Paint window.

In some cases, when you instruct a program to perform an activity such as print, the program displays a dialog box. A dialog box is a window that provides information, presents available options, or requests a response. Dialog boxes, such as the one shown in Step 5 of Figure 3-3, often contain option buttons, text boxes, check boxes, and command buttons.

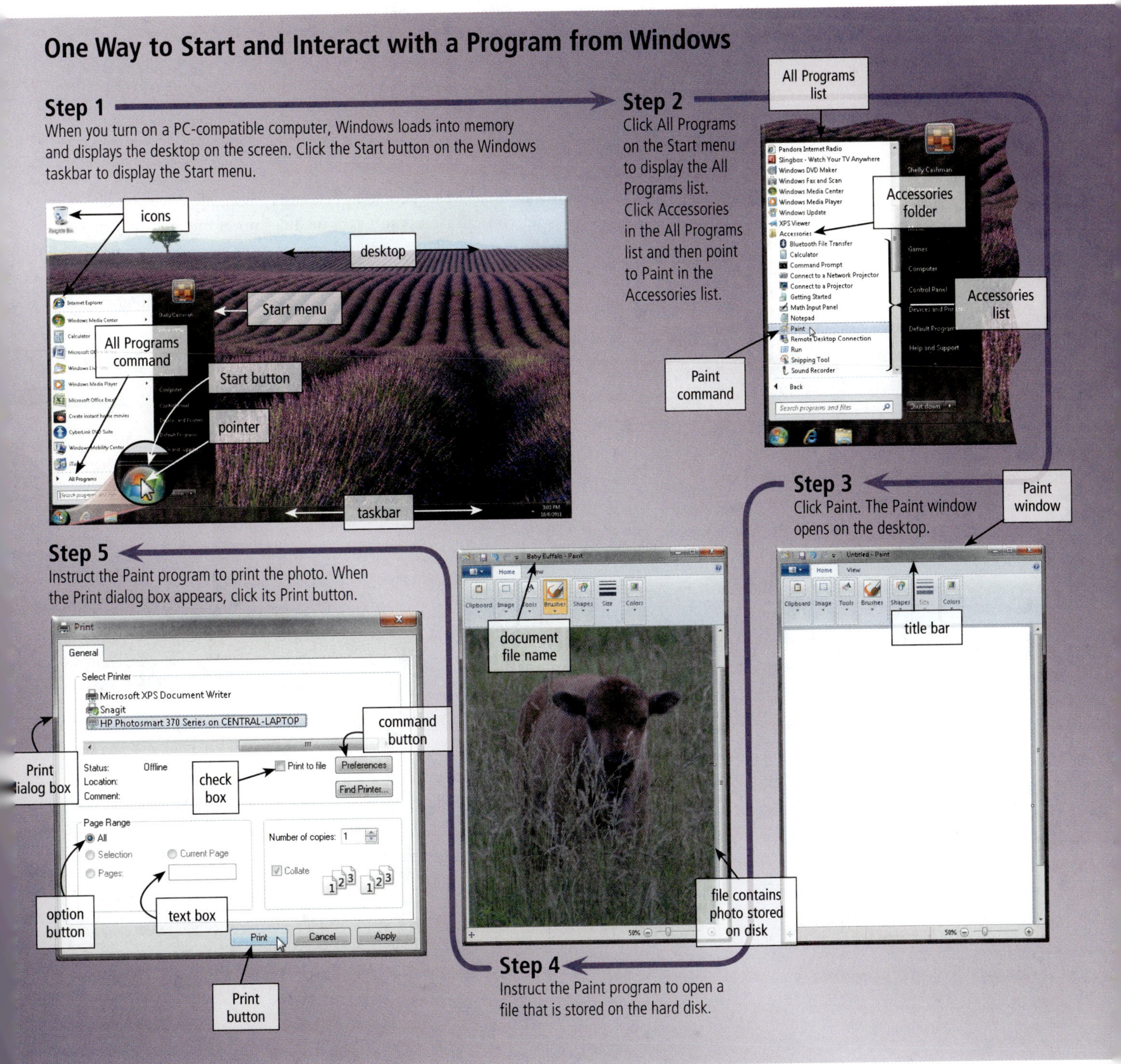

Figure 3-3 This figure shows one way to start and interact with a program from Windows.

✓ QUIZ YOURSELF 3-1

Instructions: Find the true statement below. Then, rewrite the remaining false statements so that they are true.

1. Application software is used to make business activities more efficient; assist with graphics and multimedia projects; support home, personal, and educational tasks; and facilitate communications.
2. Public-domain software is mass-produced, copyrighted retail software that meets the needs of a wide variety of users, not just a single user or company.
3. To use system software, your computer must be running application software.
4. When a program is started, its instructions load from memory into a storage medium.

Quiz Yourself Online: To further check your knowledge of pages 96 through 99, visit the Microsoft Office and Concepts CourseMate Web site at www.cengagebrain.com, navigate to the Chapter 3 Quiz Yourself resource for this book, and then click Objectives 1 – 2.

Business Software

Business software is application software that assists people in becoming more effective and efficient while performing their daily business activities. Business software includes programs such as word processing, spreadsheet, database, presentation, note taking, personal information manager, business software for phones, business software suites, project management, accounting, document management, and enterprise computing software. Figure 3-4 lists popular programs for each of these categories.

Popular Business Programs

Application Software	Manufacturer	Program Name
Word Processing	Microsoft	Word
	Apple	Pages
	Corel	WordPerfect
Spreadsheet	Microsoft	Excel
	Apple	Numbers
	Corel	Quattro Pro
Database	Microsoft	Access
	Corel	Paradox
	Oracle	Oracle Database
	Sun	MySQL
Presentation	Microsoft	PowerPoint
	Apple	Keynote
	Corel	Presentations
Note Taking	Microsoft	OneNote
	Agilix	GoBinder
	Corel	Grafigo
	SnapFiles	KeyNote
Personal Information Manager (PIM)	Microsoft	Outlook
	Google	Calendar
	IBM	Lotus Organizer
	Palm	Desktop
	Mozilla	Thunderbird
Business Software for Phones	CNetX	Pocket SlideShow
	DataViz	Documents To Go
	Microsoft	Word Mobile Excel Mobile PowerPoint Mobile Outlook Mobile
	Mobile Systems	MobiSystems Office Suite
	Ultrasoft	Money

Application Software	Manufacturer	Program Name
Business Software Suite (for the Professional)	Microsoft	Office Office for Mac
	Apple	iWork
	Google	Google Docs
	Sun	OpenOffice.org StarOffice
	Corel	WordPerfect Office
	IBM	Lotus SmartSuite
Project Management	CS Odessa	ConceptDraw PROJECT
	Microsoft	Project
	Oracle	Primavera SureTrak Project Manager
Accounting	Intuit	QuickBooks
	Microsoft	Accounting
	Sage Software	Peachtree
Document Management	Adobe	Acrobat
	Enfocus	PitStop
	Nuance	PDF Converter
Enterprise Computing	Oracle	PeopleSoft Enterprise Human Capital Management
	Sage Software	Sage MAS 500
	MSC Software	MSC.SimManager
	Oracle	Oracle Manufacturing
	SAP	mySAP Customer Relationship Management
	NetSuite	NetERP
	Syntellect	Syntellect Interaction Management Suite

Figure 3-4 Popular business software.

Word Processing Software

Word processing software, sometimes called a word processor, allows users to create and manipulate documents containing mostly text and sometimes graphics (Figure 3-5). Millions of people use word processing software every day to develop documents such as letters, memos, reports, mailing labels, newsletters, and Web pages.

A major advantage of using word processing software is that users easily can change what they have written. Word processing software also has many features to make documents look professional and visually appealing. For example, you can change the shape, size, and color of characters; apply special effects such as three-dimensional shadows; and organize text in newspaper-style columns.

Most word processing software allows users to incorporate graphical images, such as digital photos and clip art, in documents. **Clip art** is a collection of drawings, photos, and other images. In Figure 3-5, a user inserted an image of a baseball player in the document. With word processing software, you easily can modify the appearance of an image after inserting it in the document.

You can use word processing software to define the size of the paper on which to print and specify the margins. A feature, called wordwrap, allows users to type words in a paragraph continually without pressing the ENTER key at the end of each line. As you type more lines of text than can be displayed on the screen, the top portion of the document moves upward, or scrolls, off the screen. Read Ethics & Issues 3-1 for a related discussion.

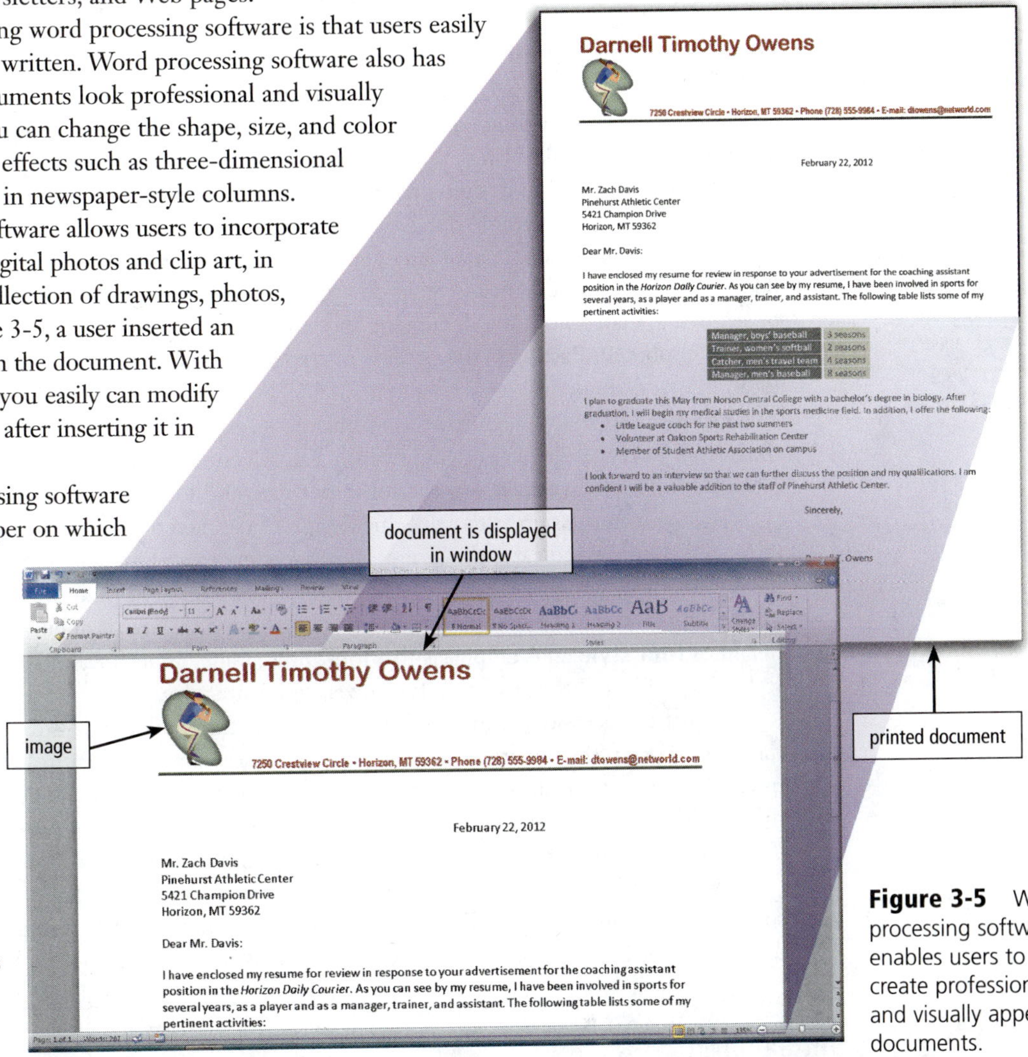

Figure 3-5 Word processing software enables users to create professional and visually appealing documents.

ETHICS & ISSUES 3-1

Are Word Processing Programs Making Students Lazy?

Today, word processing programs fix spelling and grammar mistakes, automatically format documents with templates, help correctly reference works cited in a document, and seem to do everything short of generating an idea for a document. Some educators believe that the proliferation of word processing automation is cheating students of the fundamental ability to perform these tasks on their own. Research shows that as word processing programs became more popular over the past years, the quality of written work done without the aid of this software has dropped dramatically. Opponents of using word processing software for assignments point out the quality of e-mail and instant messages is markedly worse than works written with the aid of modern word processing programs.

Proponents of the use of word processing programs for educational use point out that automation is the way writing should be done now and in the future. The higher quality of works produced using the software is well worth not sacrificing time toward teaching students less modern tactics. Students are more productive and able to focus on the topics at hand, rather than worry about spelling errors.

Are word processing programs making students lazy? Why or why not? Should educators have the ability to turn off time-saving features, such as the AutoCorrect and grammar checker features, in their student's word processing programs? Why? Do students need the ability manually to check spelling and grammar, format a document, and reference cited works in a document, in the same way that students still learn multiplication and long division? Why or why not?

Word Processing Software

For more information, visit the Microsoft Office and Concepts CourseMate Web site at www.cengagebrain.com, navigate to the Chapter 3 Web Link resource for this book, and then click Word Processing Software.

Ethics & Issues

For the complete text of the Ethics & Issues boxes found in this chapter, visit the Microsoft Office and Concepts CourseMate Web site at www.cengagebrain.com and then navigate to the Chapter 3 Ethics & Issues resource for this book.

Word processing software typically includes a spelling checker, which reviews the spelling of individual words, sections of a document, or the entire document. The spelling checker compares the words in the document with an electronic dictionary that is part of the word processing software. Some word processing programs also check for contextual spelling errors, such as a misuse of homophones (words pronounced the same but have different spellings or meanings, such as one and won).

Developing a Document

With application software, such as a word processing program, users create, edit, format, save, and print documents. When you **create** a document, you enter text or numbers, insert images, and perform other tasks using an input device such as a keyboard, mouse, or digital pen. If you are using Microsoft Word to design a flyer, for example, you are creating a document.

To **edit** a document means to make changes to its existing content. Common editing tasks include inserting, deleting, cutting, copying, and pasting. Inserting text involves adding text to a document. Deleting text means that you are removing text or other content. Cutting is the process of removing a portion of the document and storing it in a temporary storage location, sometimes called a clipboard. Pasting is the process of transferring an item from a clipboard to a specific location in a document.

When users **format** a document, they change its appearance. Formatting is important because the overall look of a document significantly can affect its ability to communicate clearly. Examples of formatting tasks are changing the font, font size, and font style.

A **font** is a name assigned to a specific design of characters. Cambria and Calibri are examples of fonts. **Font size** indicates the size of the characters in a particular font. Font size is gauged by a measurement system called points. A single point is about 1/72 of an inch in height. The text you are reading in this book is about 10 point. Thus, each character is about 5/36 (10/72) of an inch in height. A **font style** adds emphasis to a font. Bold, italic, underline, and color are examples of font styles. Figure 3-6 illustrates fonts, font sizes, and font styles.

During the process of creating, editing, and formatting a document, the computer holds it in memory. To keep the document for future use requires that you save it. When you **save** a document, the computer transfers the document from memory to a storage medium such as a USB flash drive or hard disk. Once saved, a document is stored permanently as a file on the storage medium. To learn more about how to save a file, complete the Learn How To 1 activity on page 126.

When you **print** a document, the computer places the contents of the document on paper or some other medium. Instead of printing a document and physically distributing it, some users e-mail the document to others on a network such as the Internet.

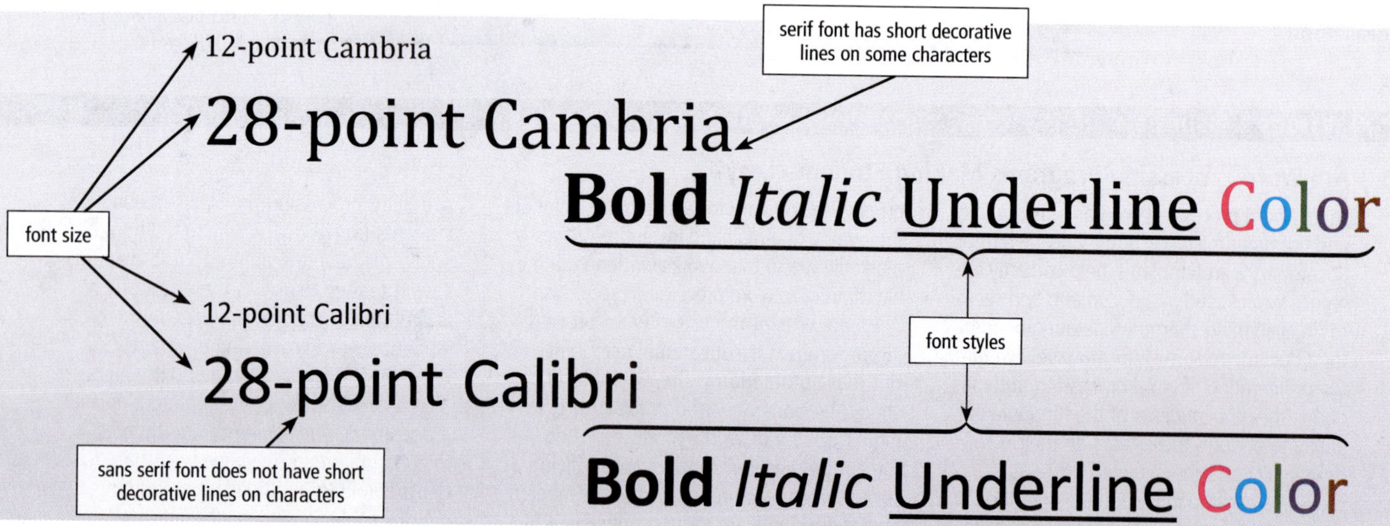

Figure 3-6 The Cambria and Calibri fonts are shown in two font sizes and a variety of font styles.

Spreadsheet Software

Spreadsheet software allows users to organize data in rows and columns and perform calculations on the data. These rows and columns collectively are called a **worksheet** (Figure 3-7). Most spreadsheet software has basic features to help users create, edit, and format worksheets. The following sections describe the features of most spreadsheet programs.

Spreadsheet Organization A spreadsheet file is similar to a notebook that can contain more than 1,000 related individual worksheets. Data is organized vertically in columns and horizontally in rows on each worksheet (Figure 3-7). Each worksheet usually can have more than 16,000 columns and 1 million rows. One or more letters identify each column, and a number identifies each row. Only a small fraction of these columns and rows are visible on the screen at one time. Scrolling through the worksheet displays different parts of it on the screen.

A cell is the intersection of a column and row. The spreadsheet software identifies cells by the column and row in which they are located. For example, the intersection of column B and row 4 is referred to as cell B4. As shown in Figure 3-7, cell B4 contains the number, $3,383,909.82, which represents the sales for January.

Cells may contain three types of data: labels, values, and formulas. The text, or label, entered in a cell identifies the worksheet data and helps organize the worksheet. Using descriptive labels, such as Gross Margin and Total Expenses, helps make a worksheet more meaningful.

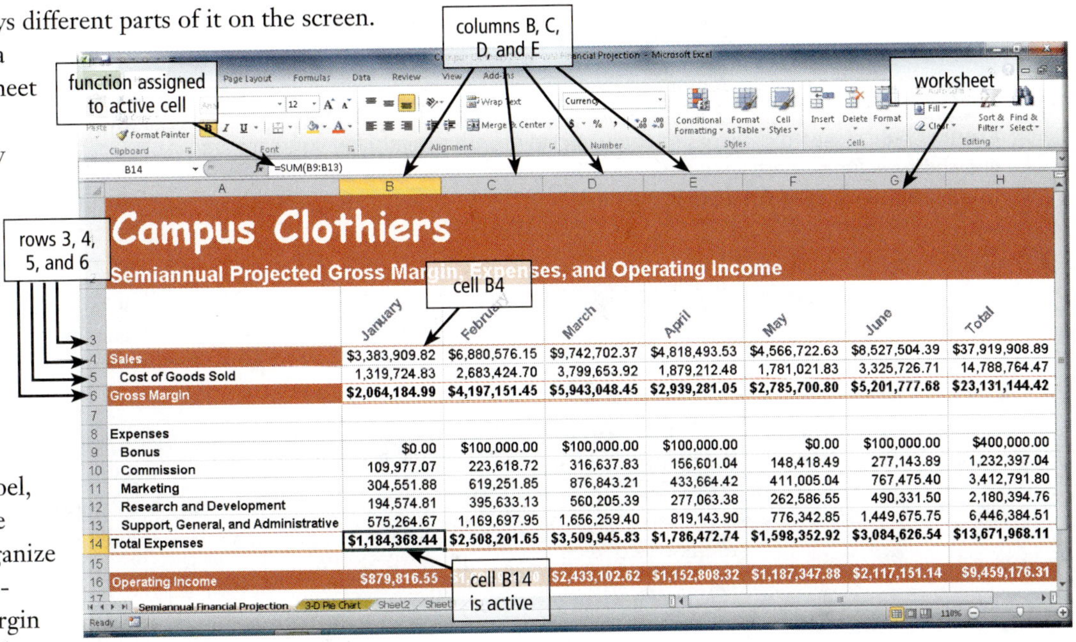

Figure 3-7 With spreadsheet software, you create worksheets that contain data arranged in rows and columns, and you can perform calculations on the data in the worksheets.

Calculations Many of the worksheet cells shown in Figure 3-7 contain a number, called a value, that can be used in a calculation. Other cells, however, contain formulas that generate values. A formula performs calculations on the data in the worksheet and displays the resulting value in a cell, usually the cell containing the formula. When creating a worksheet, you can enter your own formulas. In Figure 3-7, for example, cell B14 could contain the formula B9+B10+B11+B12+B13, which would add together (sum) the contents of cells B9, B10, B11, B12, and B13. That is, this formula calculates the total expenses for January.

A function is a predefined formula that performs common calculations such as adding the values in a group of cells or generating a value such as the time or date. For example, the function =SUM(B9:B13) instructs the spreadsheet program to add all of the numbers in cells B9 through B13.

Recalculation One of the more powerful features of spreadsheet software is its capability of recalculating the rest of the worksheet when data in a worksheet changes. Spreadsheet software's capability of recalculating data also makes it a valuable budgeting, forecasting, and decision making tool.

Spreadsheet Software
For more information, visit the Microsoft Office and Concepts CourseMate Web site at www.cengagebrain.com, navigate to the Chapter 3 Web Link resource for this book, and then click Spreadsheet Software.

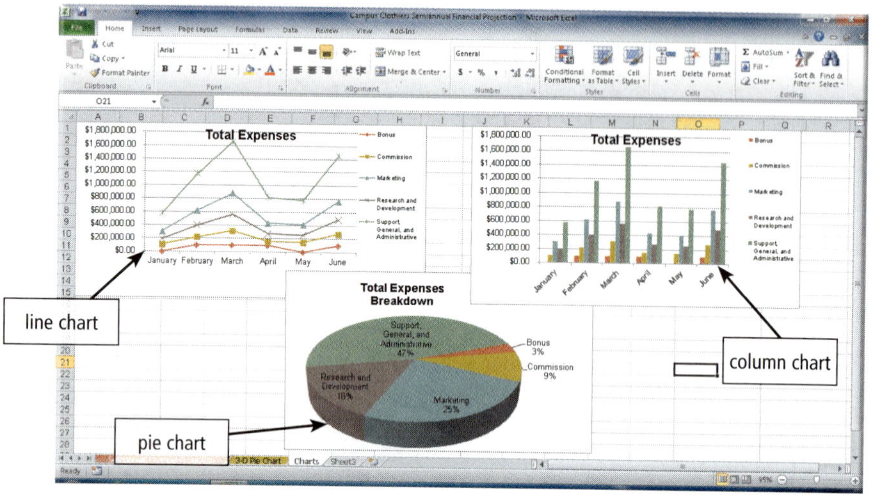

Figure 3-8 Three basic types of charts provided with spreadsheet software are line charts, column charts, and pie charts. The charts shown here were created using the data in the worksheet in Figure 3-7.

Charting Another standard feature of spreadsheet software is charting, which depicts the data in graphical form. A visual representation of data through charts often makes it easier for users to see at a glance the relationship among the numbers. Three popular chart types are line charts, column charts, and pie charts. Figure 3-8 shows examples of these charts that were plotted using the five types of expenses for each of the months shown in the worksheet in Figure 3-7 on the previous page. A line chart shows a trend during a period of time, as indicated by a rising or falling line. A column chart, also called a bar chart, displays bars of various lengths to show the relationship of data. The bars can be horizontal, vertical, or stacked on top of one another. A pie chart, which has the shape of a round pie cut into slices, shows the relationship of parts to a whole.

Database Software

A **database** is a collection of data organized in a manner that allows access, retrieval, and use of that data. In a manual database, you might record data on paper and store it in a filing cabinet. With a computerized database, such as the one shown in Figure 3-9, the computer stores the data in an electronic format on a storage medium such as a hard disk.

Database software is application software that allows users to create, access, and manage a database. Using database software, you can add, change, and delete data in a database; sort and retrieve data from the database; and create forms and reports using the data in the database.

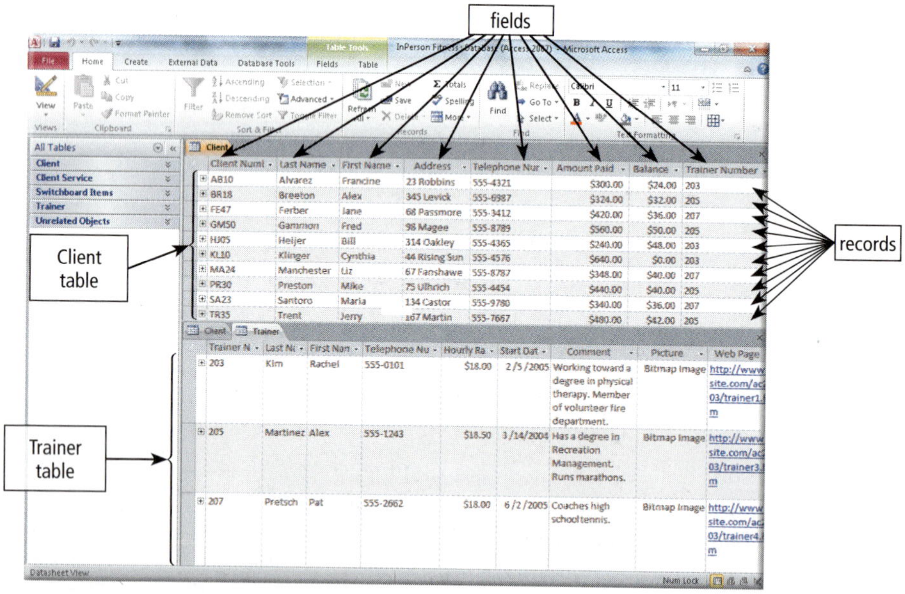

Figure 3-9 This database contains two tables: one for the clients and one for the trainers. The Client table has ten records and eight fields; the Trainer table has three records and eight fields.

With most personal computer database programs, a database consists of a collection of tables, organized in rows and columns. Each row, called a record, contains data about a given person, product, object, or event. Each column, called a field, contains a specific category of data within a record.

The Fitness database shown in Figure 3-9 consists of two tables: a Client table and a Trainer table. The Client table contains ten records (rows), each storing data about one client. The client data is grouped into eight fields (columns): Client Number, Last Name, First Name, Address, Telephone Number, Amount Paid, Balance, and Trainer Number. The Balance field, for instance, contains the balance due from the client. The Client and Trainer tables relate to one another through a common field, Trainer Number.

Users run queries to retrieve data. A query is a request for specific data from the database. For example, a query might request a list of clients whose balance is greater than $45. Database software can take the results of a query and present it in a window on the screen or send it to the printer.

Presentation Software

Presentation software is application software that allows users to create visual aids for presentations to communicate ideas, messages, and other information to a group. The presentations can be viewed as slides, sometimes called a slide show, that are displayed on a large monitor or on a projection screen (Figure 3-10).

Presentation software typically provides a variety of predefined presentation formats that define complementary colors for backgrounds, text, and graphical accents on the slides. This software also provides a variety of layouts for each individual slide such as a title slide, a two-column slide, and a slide with clip art, a chart, a table, or a diagram. In addition, you can enhance any text, charts, and graphical images on a slide with 3-D, animation, and other special effects such as shading, shadows, and textures.

When building a presentation, users can set the slide timing so that the presentation automatically displays the next slide after a preset delay. Presentation software allows you to apply special effects to the transition between slides. One slide, for example, might fade away as the next slide appears.

Presentation software typically includes a clip gallery that provides images, photos, video clips, and audio clips to enhance multimedia presentations. Some audio and video editing programs work with presentation software, providing users with an easy means to record and insert video, music, and audio commentary in a presentation.

You can view or print a finished presentation in a variety of formats, including an outline of text from each slide and audience handouts that show completed slides.

Presentation software incorporates features such as checking spelling, formatting, research, and creating Web pages from existing slide shows.

Figure 3-10
This presentation created with presentation software consists of five slides.

Note Taking Software

Note taking software is application software that enables users to enter typed text, handwritten comments, drawings, or sketches anywhere on a page and then save the page as part of a notebook (Figure 3-11). Users also can include audio recordings as part of their notes. Users find note taking software convenient during meetings, class lectures, conferences, in libraries, and other settings that previously required a pencil and tablet of paper for recording thoughts and discussions.

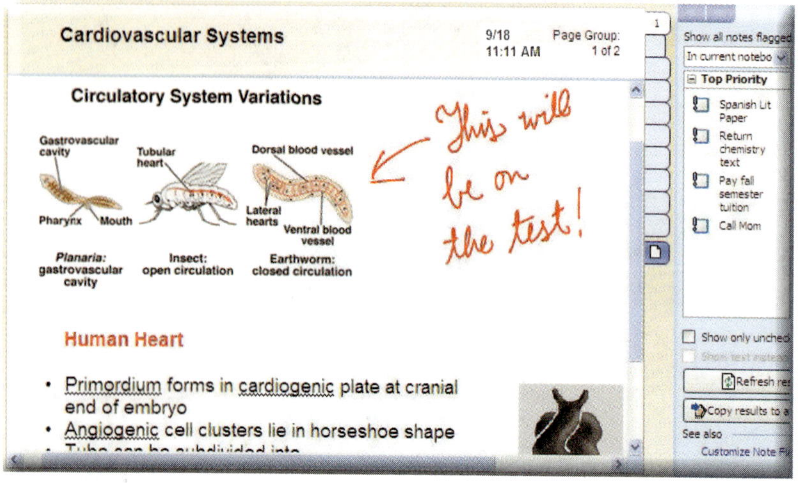

Figure 3-11 With note taking software, mobile users can handwrite notes, draw sketches, and type text.

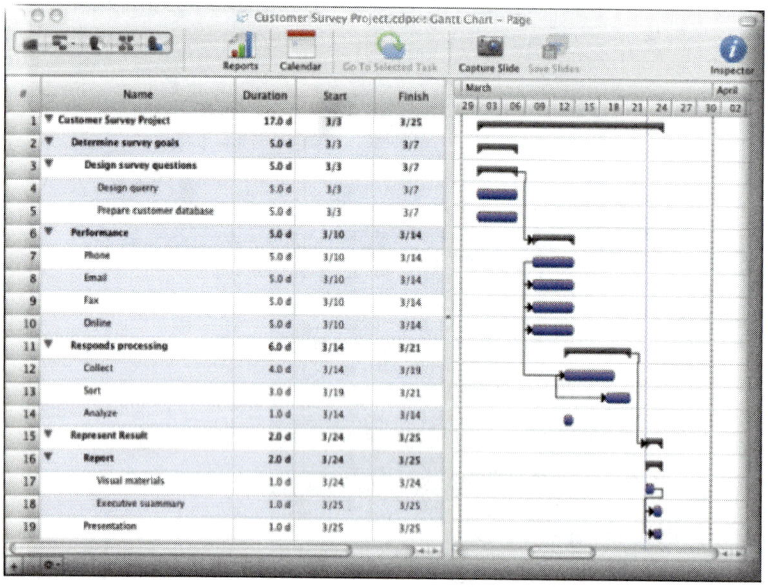

Figure 3-12 With project management software, you plan and schedule a project.

Business Software Suite

A **software suite** is a collection of individual programs available together as a unit. Business software suites typically include, at a minimum, the following programs: word processing, spreadsheet, presentation, and e-mail. Popular software suites are Microsoft Office, Apple iWork, Corel WordPerfect Office, and Google Docs.

Software suites offer two major advantages: lower cost and ease of use. When you purchase a collection of programs as a software suite, the suite usually costs significantly less than purchasing them individually. Software suites provide ease of use because the programs in the suite normally use a similar interface and share features such as clip art and spelling checker.

Project Management Software

Project management software allows a user to plan, schedule, track, and analyze the events, resources, and costs of a project. Project management software helps users manage project variables, allowing them to complete a project on time and within budget. A customer service manager might use project management software to schedule the process of administering customer surveys, evaluating responses, and presenting recommendations (Figure 3-12).

Personal Information Manager Software

A **personal information manager (PIM)** is application software that includes an appointment calendar, address book, notepad, and other features to help users organize personal information.

Mobile devices such as smart phones and PDAs include, among many other features, PIM functionality. You can synchronize, or coordinate, information so that both the mobile device and your personal computer and/or organization's server have the latest version of any updated information.

Business Software for Phones

In addition to PIM software, a huge variety of business and other software is available for phones. Some software is preloaded on the phone, while other programs can be downloaded or accessed on memory cards. Business software for phones enables users to create documents and worksheets, manage databases and lists, create slide shows, take notes, manage budgets and finances, view and edit photos, read electronic books, plan travel routes, compose and read e-mail messages, send instant messages, send text and picture messages, view maps and directions, read the latest news articles, and browse the Web. Many of the programs discussed in this chapter have scaled-down versions that work with smart phones and other mobile devices.

Accounting Software

Accounting software helps companies record and report their financial transactions (Figure 3-13). With accounting software, business users perform accounting activities related to the general ledger, accounts receivable, accounts payable, purchasing, invoicing, and payroll functions. Accounting software also enables business users to write and print checks, track checking account activity, and update and reconcile balances on demand.

Most accounting software supports online credit checks, invoicing, bill payment, direct deposit, and payroll services. Some accounting software offers more complex features such as job costing and estimating, time tracking, multiple company reporting, foreign currency reporting, and forecasting the amount of raw materials needed for products. The cost of accounting software for small businesses ranges from less than one hundred to several thousand dollars. Accounting software for large businesses can cost several hundred thousand dollars.

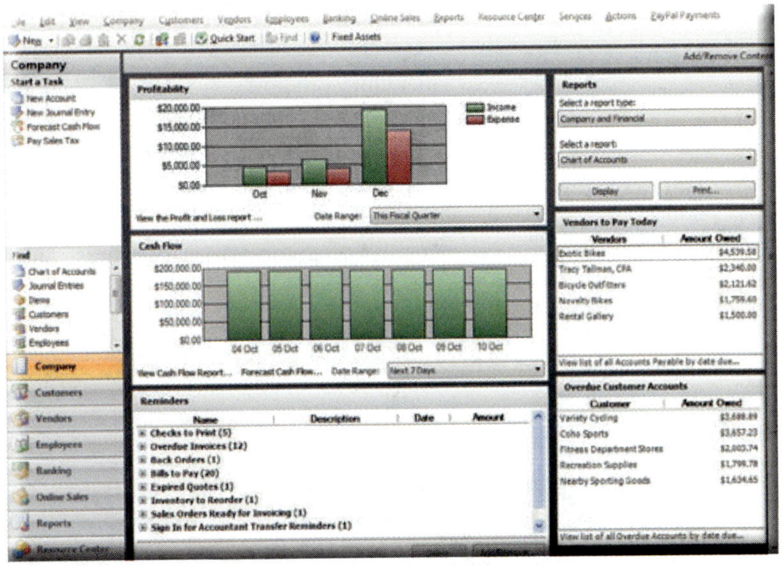

Figure 3-13 Accounting software helps companies record and report their financial transactions.

Document Management Software

Document management software provides a means for sharing, distributing, and searching through documents by converting them into a format that can be viewed by any user. The converted document, which mirrors the original document's appearance, can be viewed and printed without the software that created the original document.

A popular file format that document management software uses to save converted documents is **PDF** (Portable Document Format), developed by Adobe Systems. To view and print a PDF file, you need Acrobat Reader software (Figure 3-14), which can be downloaded free from Adobe's Web site.

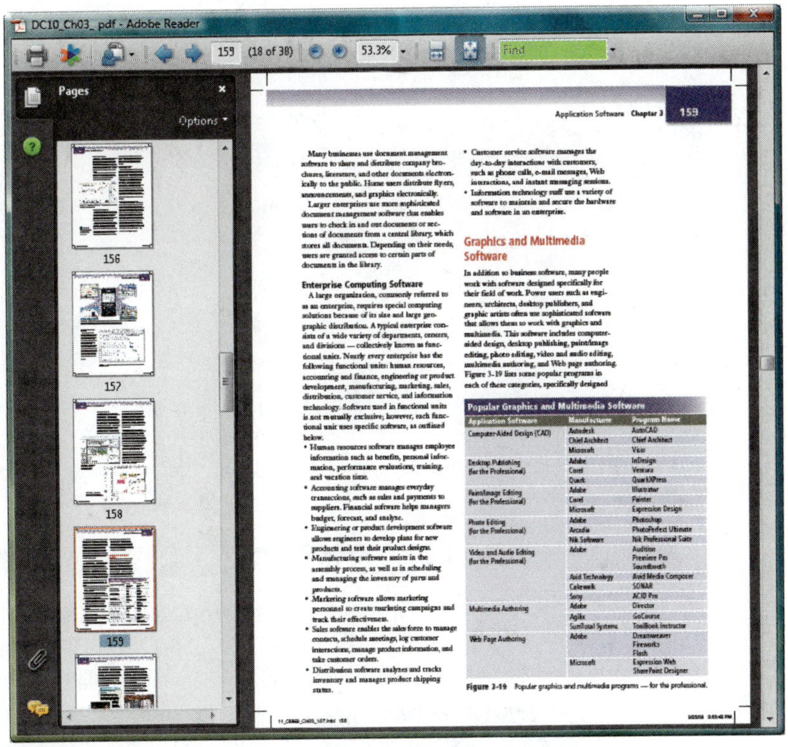

Figure 3-14 With Adobe Reader, you can view any PDF file.

Enterprise Computing Software

A large organization, commonly referred to as an enterprise, requires special computing solutions because of its size and large geographical distribution. A typical enterprise consists of a wide variety of departments, centers, and divisions — collectively known as functional units. Nearly every enterprise has the following functional units: human resources, accounting and finance, engineering or product development, manufacturing, marketing, sales, distribution, customer service, and information technology. Each of these functional units has specialized software requirements.

Graphics and Multimedia Software

In addition to business software, many people work with software designed specifically for their field of work. Power users such as engineers, architects, desktop publishers, and graphic artists often use sophisticated software that allows them to work with graphics and multimedia. This software includes computer-aided design, desktop publishing, paint/image editing, photo editing, video and audio editing, multimedia authoring, and Web page authoring. Figure 3-15 lists the more popular programs for each of these categories, specifically designed for professional or more technically astute users.

Many graphics and multimedia programs incorporate user-friendly interfaces, or scaled-down versions, making it possible for the home and small business users to create documents using these programs. The following sections discuss the features and functions of graphics and multimedia software. Read Innovative Computing 3-1 to find out how fireworks shows can be produced using multimedia software.

Graphics Software

For more information, visit the Microsoft Office and Concepts CourseMate Web site at www.cengagebrain.com, navigate to the Chapter 3 Web Link resource for this book, and then click Graphics Software.

Popular Graphics and Multimedia Software

Application Software	Manufacturer	Program Name
Computer-Aided Design (CAD)	Autodesk	AutoCAD
	Chief Architect	Chief Architect
	Microsoft	Visio
Desktop Publishing (for the Professional)	Adobe	InDesign
	Corel	Ventura
	Quark	QuarkXPress
Paint/Image Editing (for the Professional)	Adobe	Illustrator
	Corel	Painter
	Microsoft	Expression Design
Photo Editing (for the Professional)	Adobe	Photoshop
	Arcadia	PhotoPerfect Ultimate
	Nik Software	Nik Professional Suite
Video and Audio Editing (for the Professional)	Adobe	Audition Premiere Pro Soundbooth
	Avid Technology	Avid Media Composer
	Cakewalk	SONAR
	Sony	ACID Pro
Multimedia Authoring	Adobe	Director
	Agilix	GoCourse
	SumTotal Systems	ToolBook Instructor
Web Page Authoring	Adobe	Dreamweaver Fireworks Flash
	Microsoft	Expression Web SharePoint Designer

Figure 3-15 Popular graphics and multimedia programs — for the professional.

! INNOVATIVE COMPUTING 3-1

Fireworks Software Creates a Real Blast

The "oohs" and "aahs" you hear at a fireworks show may be in response to the music and pyrotechnics synchronized with special multimedia software. Major fireworks productions on Independence Day and at theme parks are choreographed with programs designed to fire each shell, sometimes only one-hundredth of a second apart, at a specific beat of the music.

A 20-minute show can take 4 months to plan. Show choreographers estimate they spend at least four hours planning the firing order for each minute of music, not including testing and setting up the equipment. When the fireworks show operator starts the program, the computer sends a signal to the firing module, which connects to each shell.

The multimedia software can cost from $2,000 to $8,000, while the firing hardware that the computer synchronizes wirelessly or with wires can cost between $30,000 and $50,000.

For more information, visit the Microsoft Office and Concepts CourseMate Web site at www.cengagebrain.com, navigate to the Chapter 3 Innovative Computing resource for this book, and then click Fireworks.

Computer-Aided Design

Computer-aided design (CAD) software is a sophisticated type of application software that assists a professional user in creating engineering, architectural, and scientific designs. For example, engineers create design plans for vehicles and security systems. Architects design building structures and floor plans (Figure 3-16). Scientists design drawings of molecular structures.

Figure 3-16 Architects use CAD software to design building structures.

Desktop Publishing Software (for the Professional)

Desktop publishing (DTP) software enables professional designers to create sophisticated documents that contain text, graphics, and many colors (Figure 3-17). Professional DTP software is ideal for the production of high-quality color documents such as textbooks, corporate newsletters, marketing literature, product catalogs, and annual reports. Designers and graphic artists can print finished publications on a color printer, take them to a professional printer, or post them on the Web in a format that can be viewed by those without DTP software.

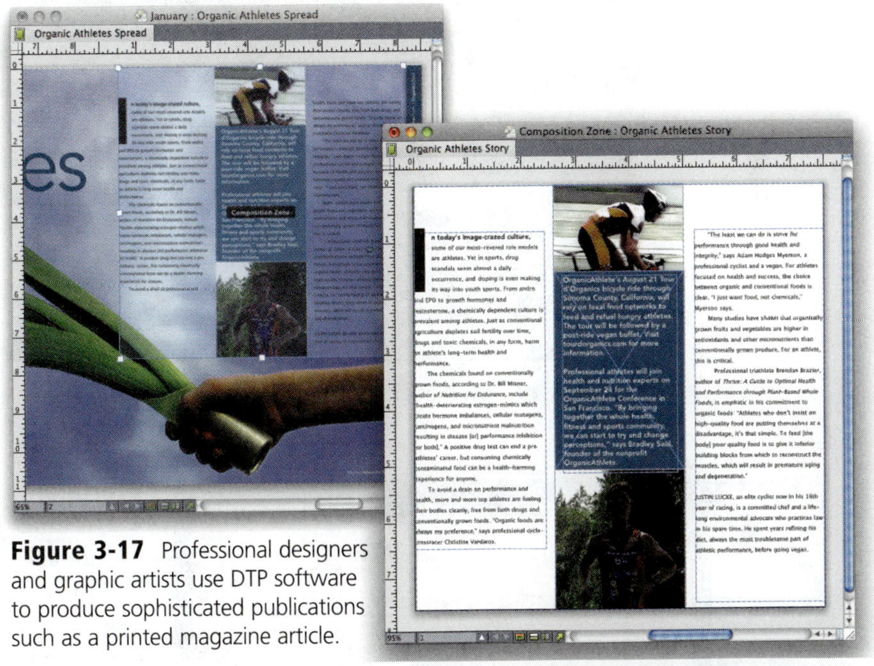

Figure 3-17 Professional designers and graphic artists use DTP software to produce sophisticated publications such as a printed magazine article.

Paint/Image Editing Software (for the Professional)

Graphic artists, multimedia professionals, technical illustrators, and desktop publishers use paint software and image editing software to create and modify graphical images such as those used in DTP documents and Web pages. **Paint software**, also called illustration software, allows users to draw pictures (Figure 3-18), shapes, and other graphical images with various on-screen tools such as a pen, brush, eyedropper, and paint bucket. **Image editing software** provides the capabilities of paint software and also includes the capability to enhance and modify existing pictures and images. Modifications can include adjusting or enhancing image colors, adding special effects such as shadows and glows, creating animations, and image stitching, which is the process of combining multiple images into a larger image.

Figure 3-18 This graphic artist uses paint software to draw characters in a computer game.

Professional photo editing software is a type of image editing software that allows photographers, videographers, engineers, scientists, and other high-volume digital photo users to edit and customize digital photos. With professional photo editing software, users can retouch photos, crop images, remove red-eye, change image shapes, color-correct images, straighten images, remove or rearrange objects in a photo, and apply filters.

Video and Audio Editing Software (for the Professional)

Video editing software allows professionals to modify a segment of a video, called a clip. For example, users can reduce the length of a video clip, reorder a series of clips, or add special effects such as words that move horizontally across the screen. Video editing software typically includes audio editing capabilities. **Audio editing software** lets users modify audio clips, produce studio-quality soundtracks, and add audio to video clips (Figure 3-19). Most television shows and movies are created or enhanced using video and audio editing software.

Figure 3-19 With audio editing software, users modify audio clips.

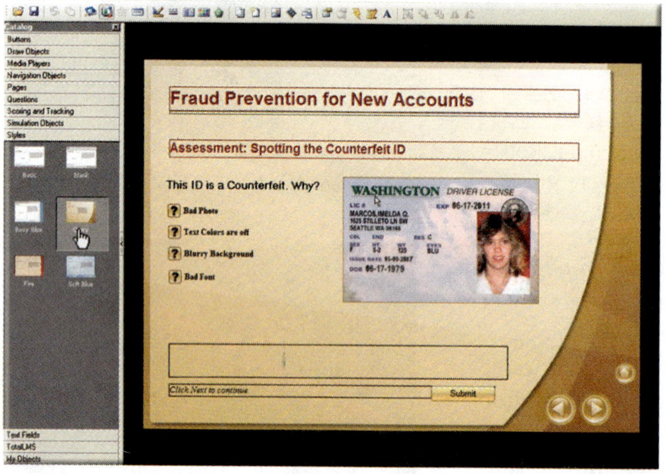

Figure 3-20 Multimedia authoring software allows you to create dynamic presentations that include text, graphics, video, sound, and animation.

Multimedia Authoring Software

Multimedia authoring software allows users to combine text, graphics, audio, video, and animation in an interactive application (Figure 3-20). With this software, users control the placement of text and images and the duration of sounds, video, and animation. Once created, multimedia presentations often take the form of interactive computer-based presentations or Web-based presentations designed to facilitate learning, demonstrate product functionality, and elicit direct-user participation. Training centers, educational institutions, and online magazine publishers all use multimedia authoring software to develop interactive applications. These applications may be available on an optical disc, over a local area network, or via the Internet.

Web Page Authoring Software

Web page authoring software helps users of all skill levels create Web pages that include graphical images, video, audio, animation, and special effects with interactive content. In addition, many Web page authoring programs allow users to organize, manage, and maintain Web sites.

Application software, such as Word and Excel, often includes Web page authoring features. This allows home and small business users to create basic Web pages using application software they already own. For more sophisticated Web pages, users work with Web page authoring software.

QUIZ YOURSELF 3-2

Instructions: Find the true statement below. Then, rewrite the remaining false statements so that they are true.

1. Enterprise computing software provides the capabilities of paint software and also includes the capability to modify existing images.
2. Millions of people use spreadsheet software every day to develop documents such as letters, memos, reports, mailing labels, newsletters, and Web pages.
3. Professional accounting software is ideal for the production of high-quality color documents such as textbooks, corporate newsletters, marketing literature, product catalogs, and annual reports.
4. Database software is application software that allows users to create visual aids for presentations to communicate ideas, messages, and other information to a group.
5. Popular CAD programs include Microsoft Office, Apple iWork, Corel WordPerfect Office, and Google Docs.
6. Web page authoring software helps users of all skill levels create Web pages.

Quiz Yourself Online: To further check your knowledge of pages 100 through 110, visit the Microsoft Office and Concepts CourseMate Web site at www.cengagebrain.com, navigate to the Chapter 3 Quiz Yourself resource for this book, and then click Objectives 3 – 4.

Software for Home, Personal, and Educational Use

A large amount of application software is designed specifically for home, personal, and educational use. Most of the programs in this category are relatively inexpensive, often priced less than $100. Figure 3-21 lists popular programs for many of these categories. The following pages discuss the features and functions of this application software.

Popular Programs for Home/Personal/Educational Use

Application Software	Manufacturer	Program Name
Personal Finance	IGG Software	iBank
	Intuit	Quicken
Legal	Broderbund	Home and Business Lawyer WillWriter
	Cosmi	Perfect Attorney
	Nolo	Quicken Legal Business Quicken WillMaker
Tax Preparation	2nd Story Software	TaxACT
	H&R Block	TaxCut
	Intuit	TurboTax
Desktop Publishing (for Personal Use)	Broderbund	The Print Shop PrintMaster
	Microsoft	Publisher
Paint/Image Editing (for Personal Use)	Corel	CorelDRAW Painter Essentials
	The GIMP Team	The Gimp
Photo Editing and Photo Management (for Personal Use)	Adobe	Photoshop Elements Photoshop Express
	Corel	Paint Shop Pro Photo Ulead PhotoImpact MediaOne Plus
	Yahoo!	Flickr
	Google	Picasa
	Microsoft	Windows Live Photo Gallery
	Roxio	PhotoShow
Clip Art/Image Gallery	Broderbund	ClickArt
	Nova Development	Art Explosion
	CoolArchive	CoolArchive
Video and Audio Editing (for Personal Use)	Corel	VideoStudio
	Microsoft	Windows Live Movie Maker
	Pinnacle Systems	Studio
	Roxio	Buzz
Home Design/ Landscaping	Broderbund	Instant Architect
	Chief Architect	Better Homes and Gardens Home Designer
	IMSI/Design	TurboFLOORPLAN
Travel and Mapping	DeLorme	Street Atlas
	Microsoft	Streets & Trips
	Google	Earth Maps
Reference	Fogware Publishing	Merriam-Webster Collegiate Dictionary & Thesaurus
	Microsoft	MSN Encarta

Figure 3-21 Many popular programs are available for home, personal, and educational use.

Personal Finance Software

Personal finance software is a simplified accounting program that helps home users and small office/home office users balance their checkbooks, pay bills, track personal income and expenses (Figure 3-22), track investments, and evaluate financial plans.

Most personal finance software includes financial planning features, such as analyzing home and personal loans, preparing income taxes, and managing retirement savings. Other features include managing home inventory and setting up budgets. Most of these programs also offer a variety of online services, such as online banking, which require access to the Internet.

? FAQ 3-2

How many people bank online?

The number of people banking online is approximately 50 million, with that number expected to continue growing. The chart to the right depicts the more popular online banking activities.

For more information, visit the Microsoft Office and Concepts CourseMate Web site at www.cengagebrain.com, navigate to the Chapter 3 FAQ resource for this book, and then click Online Banking.

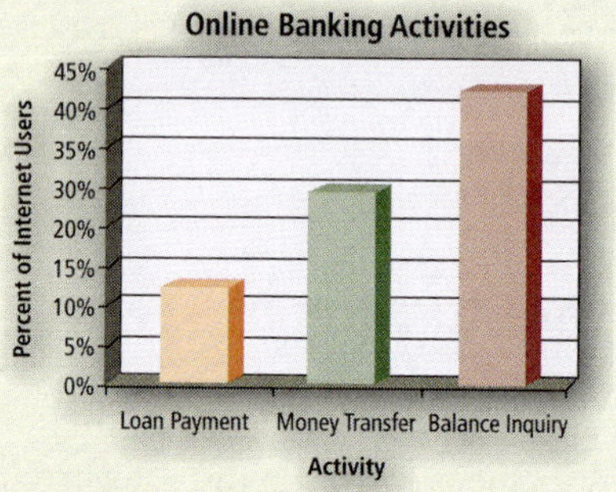

Source: The ClickZ Network

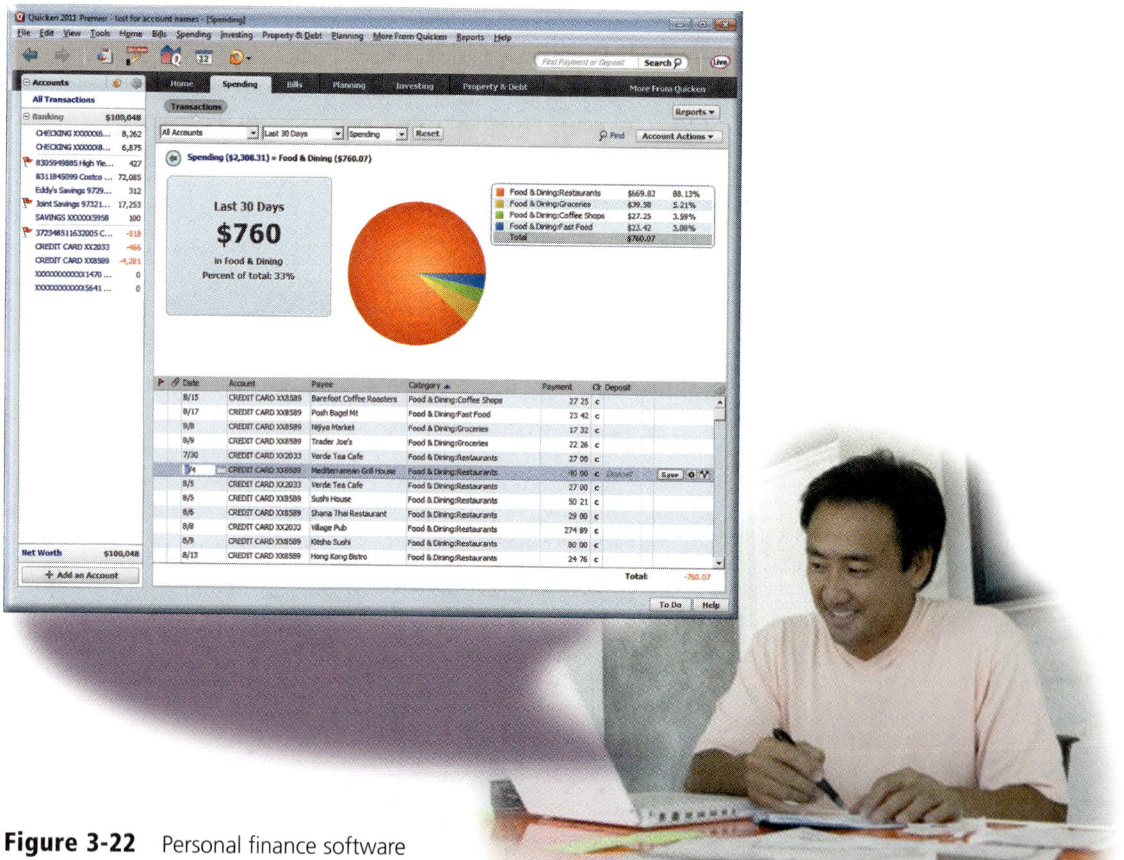

Figure 3-22 Personal finance software assists home users with tracking personal accounts.

Legal Software

Legal software assists in the preparation of legal documents and provides legal information to individuals, families, and small businesses (Figure 3-23). Legal software provides standard contracts and documents associated with buying, selling, and renting property; estate planning; marriage and divorce; and preparing a will or living trust. By answering a series of questions or completing a form, the legal software tailors the legal document to specific needs.

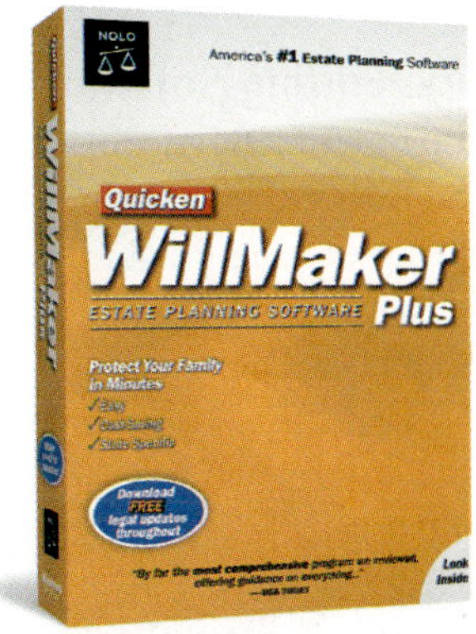

Figure 3-23 Legal software provides legal information and assists in record keeping and the preparation of legal documents.

Tax Preparation Software

Tax preparation software, which is available both as packaged software and Web applications, can guide individuals, families, or small businesses through the process of filing federal taxes (Figure 3-24). These programs forecast tax liability and offer money-saving tax tips, designed to lower your tax bill. After you answer a series of questions and complete basic forms, the software creates and analyzes your tax forms to search for missed potential errors and deduction opportunities.

Once the forms are complete, you can print any necessary paperwork, and then they are ready for filing. Some tax preparation programs also allow you to file your tax forms electronically.

Figure 3-24 Tax preparation software guides individuals, families, or small businesses through the process of filing federal taxes.

Desktop Publishing Software (for Personal Use)

Personal DTP software helps home and small business users create newsletters, brochures, flyers (Figure 3-25), advertisements, postcards, greeting cards, letterhead, business cards, banners, calendars, logos, and Web pages. Although many word processing programs include DTP features, users often prefer to create DTP documents using DTP software because of its enhanced features. For example, personal DTP programs provide hundreds of thousands of graphical images. You also can import (bring in) your own digital photos into the documents. These programs typically guide you through the development of a document by asking a series of questions. Then, you can print a finished publication on a color printer or post it on the Web.

Many personal DTP programs also include paint/image editing software and photo editing and photo management software.

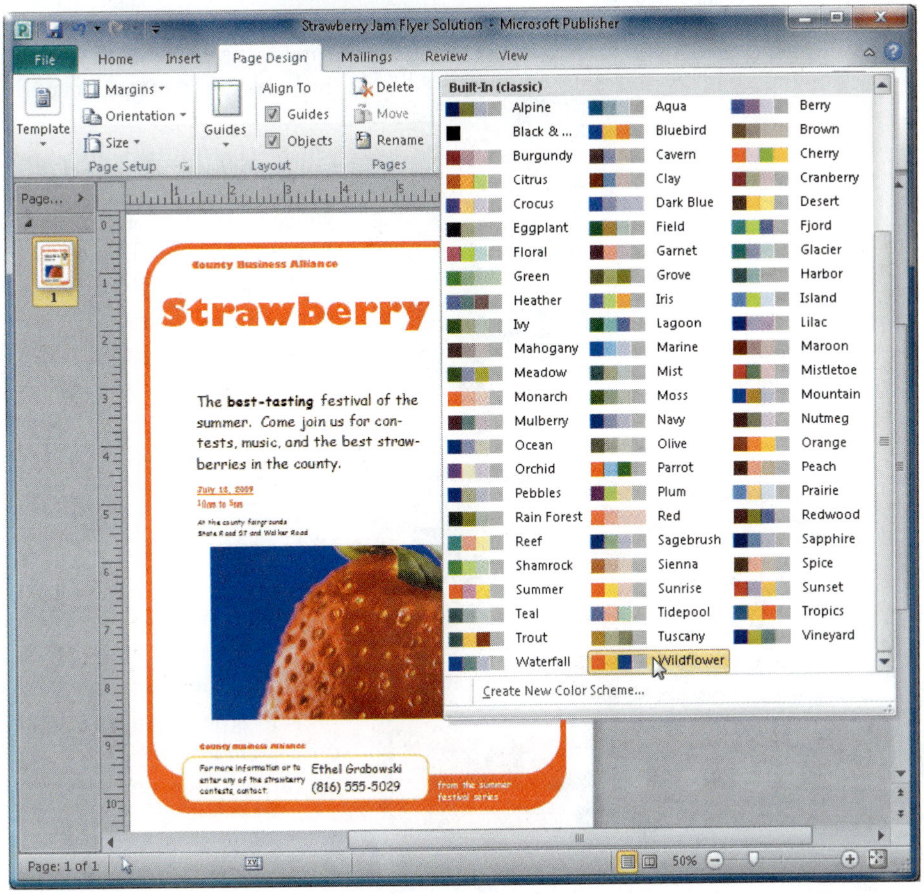

Figure 3-25 With desktop publishing software, home and small business users can create flyers.

Paint/Image Editing Software (for Personal Use)

Personal paint/image editing software provides an easy-to-use interface; includes various simplified tools that allow you to draw pictures, shapes, and other images; and provides the capability of modifying existing graphics and photos. These products also include many templates to assist you in adding images to documents such as greeting cards, banners, calendars, signs, labels, business cards, and letterhead.

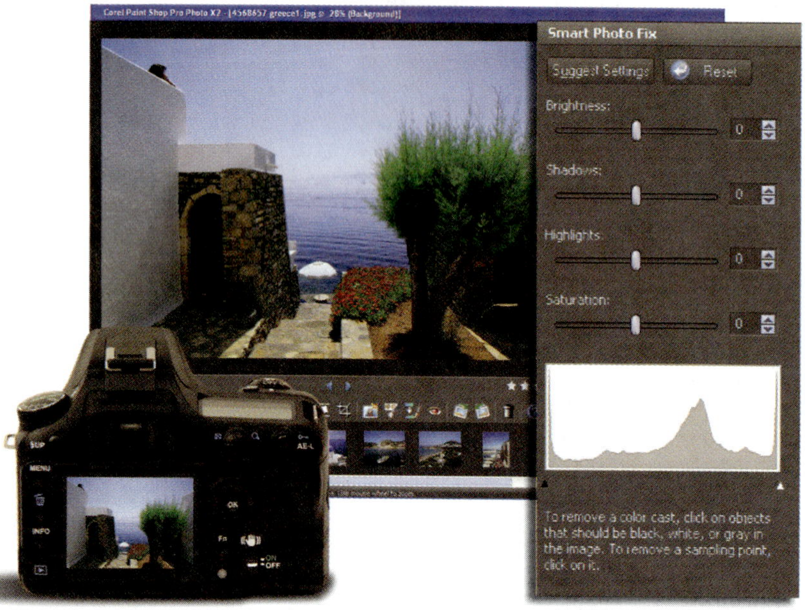

Figure 3-26 As shown here, home users adjust color on their digital photos with personal photo editing software.

Personal photo editing software, a popular type of image editing software available both as packaged software and as Web applications, allows users to edit digital photos by removing red-eye, erasing blemishes, restoring aged photos, adding special effects, enhancing image quality, or creating electronic photo albums. When you purchase a digital camera, it usually includes photo editing software (Figure 3-26). Some digital cameras even have basic photo editing software built in so that you can edit the image directly on the camera. You can print edited photos on labels, calendars, business cards, and banners, or you can post them on the Web.

With **photo management software**, you can view, organize, sort, catalog, print, and share digital photos. Some photo editing software includes photo management functionality.

Figure 3-27 Clip art/image gallery software contains thousands of images.

Clip Art/Image Gallery

Application software often includes a **clip art/image gallery**, which is a collection of clip art and photos. Some programs have links to additional clips available on the Web or are available as Web applications. You also can purchase clip art/image gallery software that contains thousands of images (Figure 3-27).

In addition to clip art, many clip art/image galleries provide fonts, animations, sounds, video clips, and audio clips. You can use the images, fonts, and other items from the clip art/image gallery in all types of documents, including word processing, desktop publishing, spreadsheet, and presentations.

Video and Audio Editing Software (for Personal Use)

Many home users work with easy-to-use video and audio editing software, which is much simpler to use than its professional counterpart, for small-scale movie making projects (Figure 3-28). With these programs, home users can edit home movies, add music or other sounds to the video, and share their movies on the Web. Some operating systems include video editing and audio editing software.

Figure 3-28 With personal video and audio editing software, home users can edit their home movies.

Home Design/Landscaping Software

Homeowners or potential homeowners can use **home design/landscaping software** to assist them with the design, remodeling, or improvement of a home, deck, or landscape (Figure 3-29). This software includes hundreds of predrawn plans that you can customize to meet your needs. These programs show changes to home designs and landscapes, allowing homeowners to preview proposed modifications.

Figure 3-29 Home design/landscaping software can help you design or remodel a home, deck, or landscape.

Travel and Mapping Software

Travel and mapping software enables users to view maps, determine route directions, and locate points of interest (Figure 3-30). Using travel and mapping software, which is available both as packaged software and as Web applications, you can display maps by searching for an address, postal code, telephone number, or point of interest (such as airports, lodging, and historical sites). Most programs also allow you to download construction reports and calculate mileage, time, and expenses. Read Looking Ahead 3-1 for a look at the next generation of navigation software.

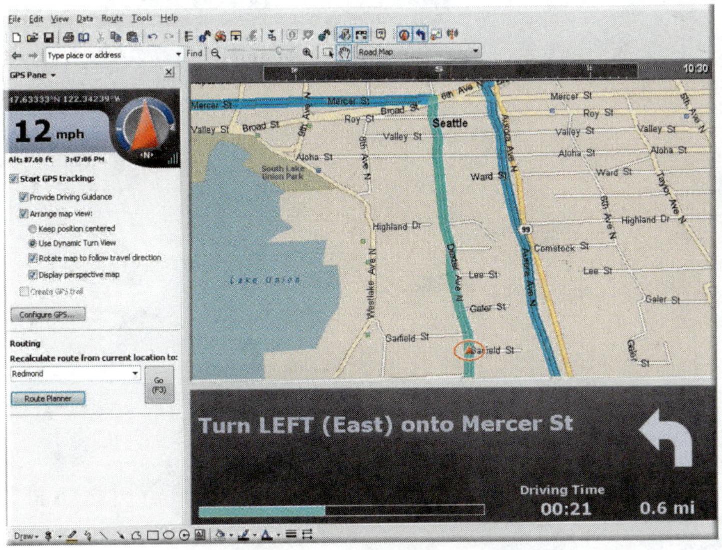

Figure 3-30 This software provides turn-by-turn directions, along with estimated travel times.

LOOKING AHEAD 3-1

Sensors Help Drivers Find Their Way

Navigating through town may become less burdensome with products under development at Microsoft. Current devices are touted as being small enough to fit in a pocket, but this size can be a hindrance for people with large hands. When they attempt to place their fingers on the touch screen to press the commands, their fingers cover information they are trying to see.

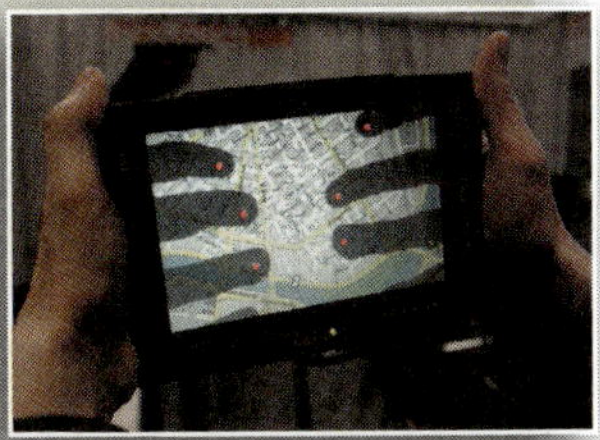

Microsoft's prototype LucidTouch solves this problem by allowing users to place their hands underneath the device, in-between it and a camera attached to the back. The camera captures an image of their hands, and the device overlays a semitransparent shadow of their fingers on the screen.

Microsoft also is developing sensors for a cell phone that collect data as a driver passes through town. These accelerometers sense speed, braking, and even when the driver hits a pothole, and the cell phone's microphone can detect the car's horn. Another potential use of Microsoft's sensors in cell phones is to monitor the behavior and health status of the elderly so that they can lead independent lives.

For more information, visit the Microsoft Office and Concepts CourseMate Web site at www.cengagebrain.com, navigate to the Chapter 3 Looking Ahead resource for this book, and then click Mapping.

Reference and Educational Software

Reference software provides valuable and thorough information for all individuals. Popular reference software includes encyclopedias, dictionaries, and health/medical guides.

Educational software teaches a particular skill. Educational software exists for just about any subject, from learning how to type (Figure 3-31) to learning how to cook to preparing for college entrance exams. Educational software often includes games and other content to make the learning experience more fun. Many educational programs use a computer-based training approach. **Computer-based training (CBT)** is a type of education in which students learn by using and completing exercises with instructional software. CBT typically consists of self-directed, self-paced instruction about a topic.

Figure 3-31 Educational software can teach a skill.

Entertainment Software

Entertainment software for personal computers includes interactive games, videos, and other programs designed to support a hobby or provide amusement and enjoyment. For example, you might use entertainment software to play games individually (Figure 3-32) or with others online, make a family tree, or fly an aircraft. Many games are available as Web applications, allowing you to play individually or with other online players.

Game Software

For more information, visit the Microsoft Office and Concepts CourseMate Web site at www.cengagebrain.com, navigate to the Chapter 3 Web Link resource for this book, and then click Game Software.

? FAQ 3-3

How popular is entertainment software?

The popularity of entertainment software has increased greatly during the past few years. More than 65 percent of American households play computer or video games. Further, more than 36 percent play games on a mobile device such as a smart phone or PDA.

For more information, visit the Microsoft Office and Concepts CourseMate Web site at www.cengagebrain.com, navigate to the Chapter 3 FAQ resource for this book, and then click Entertainment Software.

Figure 3-32 Entertainment software can provide hours of recreation on personal computers, game consoles, and mobile devices.

Web Applications

As previously mentioned, a Web application, or **Web app**, is a Web site that allows users to access and interact with software from any computer or device that is connected to the Internet. Users often interact with Web applications directly at the Web site, referred to as the host, through their Web browser. Some Web sites, however, require you download the software to your local computer or device. Web application hosts often store users' data and information on their servers. Some Web applications provide users with an option of storing data locally on their own personal computer or mobile device. Many of the previously discussed types of application software are available as Web applications (Figure 3-33). Read Ethics & Issues 3-2 for a related discussion.

Popular Web Applications			
Program Name	**Type of Application Software**	**Program Name**	**Type of Application Software**
Britannica.com	Reference	**Office Web Apps**	Productivity Suite
Dictionary.com	Reference	**Photoshop Express**	Photo Editing
Flickr	Photo Editing and Photo Management	**Picnik**	Photo Editing
Gmail	E-Mail	**TaxACT Online**	Tax Preparation
Google Docs	Productivity Suite	**TurboTax Online**	Tax Preparation
Google Earth	Travel and Mapping	**Windows Live Calendar**	Personal Information Manager
Google Maps	Travel and Mapping	**Windows Live Hotmail**	E-Mail
MSN Encarta	Reference	**YouSendIt**	File Transfer and E-Mail

Figure 3-33 Some popular Web applications. For practice using Web applications, complete the last Learn It Online exercise in each chapter.

Many Web application hosts provide free access to their software, such as Google Docs shown in Figure 3-34. Others, such as Google Earth, offer part of their Web application free and charge for access to a more comprehensive program. Some Web applications allow you to use the Web application free and pay a fee when a certain action occurs. For example, you can prepare your tax return free, but if you elect to print it or file it electronically, you pay a minimal fee.

Experts often use the term Web 2.0 to describe Web applications. Recall that Web 2.0 refers to Web sites that provide users with a means to share personal information, allow users to modify Web site content, and/or have application software built into the site for visitors to use.

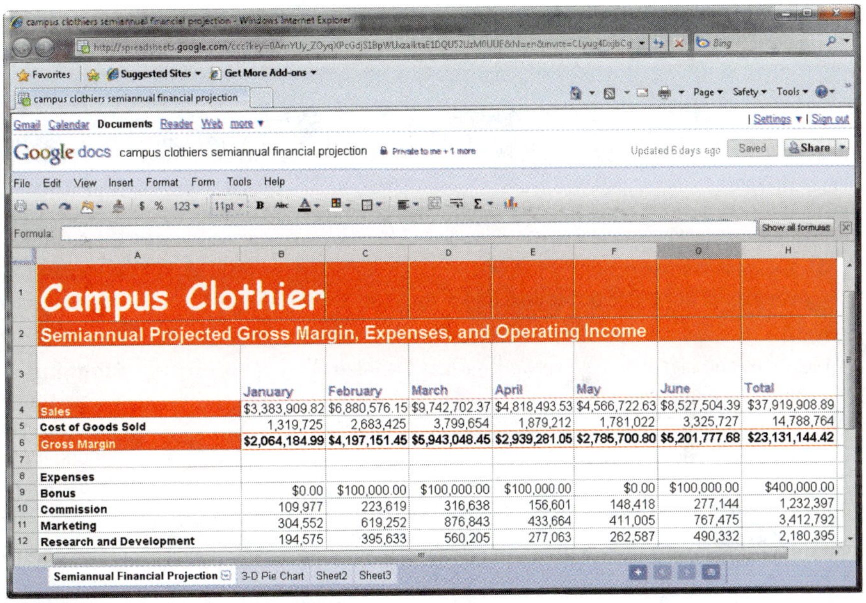

Figure 3-34 The spreadsheet shown here in Google Docs is the same Microsoft Excel spreadsheet that is shown in Figure 3-7 on page 103. Differences between the two figures are due to different features in the two programs.

ETHICS & ISSUES 3-2

Should Online Mapping Services Make You Feel More Secure or More Vulnerable?

Most Internet users find that online maps, such as Google Maps and Bing Maps, provide tremendous convenience and reliability. Instead of searching the house or car for maps or making phone calls for directions, a quick Web search results in a readable map with exact directions. Sometimes, even photos of the route and location are available. Some parents and advocacy groups, however, claim that the services allow predators to locate potential victims quickly. Google Maps, for example, provides photos for neighborhoods of entire cities. The opponents of the services believe that predators may find potential victims in the photos, or find likely locations where a crime may be easier to commit. Opponents of this point of view state that mapping services allow known predators and high-crime areas to be more readily identified. The services, therefore, increase personal security because the location of known predators can be pinpointed before they find victims. The services also provide much more positive value than any potential problems that they create, and, therefore, should thrive.

Do online mapping services make you feel more secure or more vulnerable? Why? Should parents and neighborhood associations have the legal right to have photos and personal information removed from mapping services? Why or why not? Would you feel comfortable if a service such as Google Maps showed a photo of you walking your normal route from home to work or school? Why?

Application Software for Communications

One of the main reasons people use computers is to communicate and share information with others. Some communications software is considered system software because it works with hardware and transmission media. Other communications software performs specific tasks for users, and thus, is considered application software. Chapter 2 presented a variety of application software for communications, which is summarized in the table in Figure 3-35.

? FAQ 3-4

Does text messaging improve typing skills?

Although some individuals are able to send text messages from their phones quickly, the differences in layout between a phone keypad and a standard computer keyboard might not allow for their typing skills to improve at the same rate. Some individuals are able to send text messages more quickly than they can type. In fact, a 20-year-old college student won $50,000 in a text messaging competition when he typed more than 125 characters in 50 seconds with no mistakes.

For more information, visit the Microsoft Office and Concepts CourseMate Web site at www.cengagebrain.com, navigate to the Chapter 3 FAQ resource for this book, and then click Text Messaging.

Application Software for Communications

Web Browser
- Allows users to access and view Web pages on the Internet
- Requires a Web browser program
  - Integrated in some operating systems
  - Available for download on the Web free or for a fee

E-Mail
- Messages and files sent via a network such as the Internet
- Requires an e-mail program
  - Integrated in many software suites and operating systems
  - Available free at portals on the Web
  - Included with paid Internet access service
  - Can be purchased separately from retailers

Instant Messaging
- Real-time exchange of messages, files, audio, and/or video with another online user
- Requires instant messenger software
  - Integrated in some operating systems
  - Available for download on the Web, usually at no cost
  - Included with some paid Internet access services

Chat Room
- Real-time, online typed conversation
- Requires chat client software
  - Integrated in some operating systems, e-mail programs, and Web browsers
  - Available for download on the Web, usually at no cost
  - Included with some paid Internet access services
  - Built into some Web sites

Text, Picture, Video Messaging
- Short text, picture, or video messages sent and received, mainly on mobile devices
- Requires text, picture, video messenger software
  - Integrated in most mobile devices
  - Available for download on the Web, usually at no cost, for personal computers

RSS Aggregator
- Keeps track of changes made to Web sites by checking RSS feeds
- Requires RSS aggregator program
  - Integrated in some e-mail programs and Web browsers
  - Available for download on the Web, usually at no cost

Blogging
- Time-stamped articles, or posts, in a diary or journal format, usually listed in reverse chronological order
- Blogger needs blog software, or blogware, to create/maintain blog
  - Some Web sites do not require installation of blog software

Newsgroup/Message Board
- Online area where users have written discussions
- Newsgroup may require a newsreader program
  - Integrated in some operating systems, e-mail programs, and Web browsers

FTP
- Method of uploading and downloading files with other computers on the Internet
- May require an FTP program
  - Integrated in some operating systems
  - Available for download on the Web for a small fee

VoIP (Internet Telephony)
- Allows users to speak to other users over the Internet
- Requires Internet connection, Internet telephone service, microphone or telephone, and Internet telephone software or telephone adapter

Video Conferencing
- Meeting between geographically separated people who use a network such as the Internet to transmit video/audio
- Requires video conferencing software, a microphone, speakers, and sometimes a video camera attached to your computer

Figure 3-35 A summary of application software for home and business communications.

Learning Tools for Application Software

Learning how to use application software effectively involves time and practice. To assist in the learning process, many programs provide online Help (Figure 3-36) and Web-based Help.

Online Help is the electronic equivalent of a user manual. When working with a program, you can use online Help to ask a question or access the Help topics in subject or alphabetical order. Most online Help also links to Web sites that offer Web-based help, which provides updates and more comprehensive resources to respond to technical issues about software.

Many books are available to help you learn to use the features of personal computer programs. These books typically are available in bookstores and software stores.

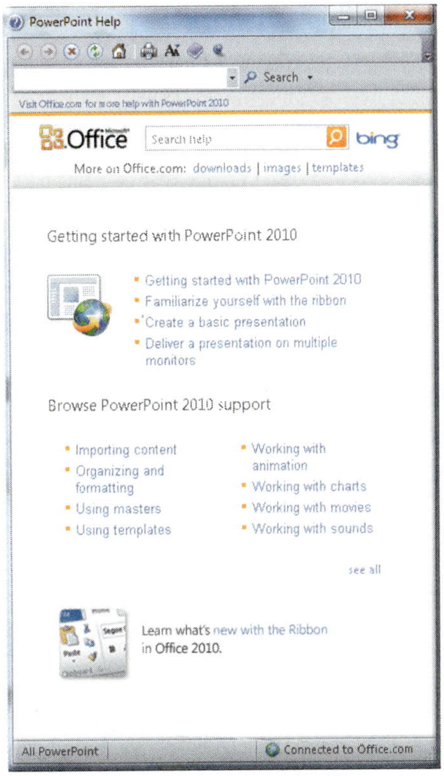

Figure 3-36 Many programs include online Help.

Web-Based Training

Web-based training (WBT) is a type of computer-based training (CBT) that uses Internet technology and consists of application software on the Web. Similar to CBT, WBT typically consists of self-directed, self-paced instruction about a topic. WBT is popular in business, industry, and schools for teaching new skills or enhancing existing skills of employees, teachers, or students.

Many Web sites offer WBT to the general public. Such training covers a wide range of topics, from how to change a flat tire to creating documents in Word. Many of these Web sites are free. Others require registration and payment to take the complete Web-based course.

WBT often is combined with other materials for distance learning and e-learning. **Distance learning** is the delivery of education at one location while the learning takes place at other locations. **E-learning**, short for electronic learning, is the delivery of education via some electronic method such as the Internet, networks, or optical discs. To enhance communications, e-learning systems also may include video conferencing, e-mail, blogs, wikis, newsgroups, chat rooms, and groupware (Figure 3-37).

Figure 3-37 E-learning systems enable instructors to post course materials for their students.

QUIZ YOURSELF 3-3

Instructions: Find the true statement below. Then, rewrite the remaining false statements so that they are true.

1. All Web application hosts provide free access to their software.
2. Computer-based training is a type of Web-based training that uses Internet technology and consists of application software on the Web.
3. E-mail and Web browsers are examples of communications software that are considered application software.
4. Legal software is a simplified accounting program that helps home users and small office/home office users balance their checkbooks, pay bills, track investments, and evaluate financial plans.
5. Personal DTP software is a popular type of image editing software that allows users to edit digital photos.

Quiz Yourself Online: To further check your knowledge of pages 111 through 119, visit the Microsoft Office and Concepts CourseMate Web site at www.cengagebrain.com, navigate to the Chapter 3 Quiz Yourself resource for this book, and then click Objectives 5 – 8.

Chapter Summary

This chapter illustrated how to start and interact with application software. It presented an overview of a variety of business software, graphics and multimedia software, and home/personal/educational software. Finally, Web applications, application software for communications, and learning tools for application software were presented.

Computer Usage @ Work

Construction

Walking the streets, you stop to admire a new skyscraper with the most striking architectural features you ever have seen. You think to yourself that those responsible for designing the building are nothing less than brilliant. While a great deal of work goes into the design and construction of a building, computers and technology also play an important role in the process. In fact, the role of computers not only saves time and provides for more accurate results, it also allows us to preview how a building will look before construction even begins.

As mentioned in the chapter, computer-aided design (CAD) software is a sophisticated type of application software that assists a professional user in creating engineering, architectural, and scientific plans. During the preliminary design process, architects and design firms use CAD software to design the appearance and layout of a new building and can provide clients with a three-dimensional walkthrough of a building so that they can determine whether the proposed design will meet their needs. Later, the program can be used to include the placement of support beams, walls, roof shape, and so on, and also conform to building code.

CAD software allows engineers in various fields, such as mechanical and electrical, to design separate layers in a structure. The CAD software then can superimpose the designs to check for interactions and conflicts, such as if a structural beam in one layer covers a drain in another layer. The CAD software makes it easy to modify and correct the structure before it is built, which can save time and money during the construction process. This software also eliminates most, if not all, of the manual drafting required.

Engineers use computers to determine the type of foundation required to support the building and its occupants; the heating, ventilating, and air conditioning (HVAC); and the electrical requirements, as well as how the building may withstand external threats such as hurricanes and tornadoes.

During construction, contractors and builders are able to use computer software to estimate accurately the amount of materials and time required to complete the job. Without computers, determining materials and time required is a cumbersome and time-consuming task.

The next time you notice a building under construction, stop to think about how computer technology has increased the efficiency of the design and construction process.

For more information, visit the Microsoft Office and Concepts CourseMate Web site at www.cengagebrain.com, navigate to the Chapter 3 Computer Usage @ Work resource for this book, and then click Construction.

Companies on the Cutting Edge

ADOBE SYSTEMS Design Software Leader

Practically all creative professionals involved with art and photography have a copy of Adobe Photoshop on their computer, and the leading computer manufacturers ship their products with a copy of Adobe Reader installed. The worldwide presence of Adobe Systems software attests to the company's success in developing programs that help people communicate effectively.

Charles Geschke and John Warnock founded the company in 1982 and named it after a creek that ran behind Warnock's house in California. Creative Suite contains the fundamental tools that help photographers, designers, and publishers develop and maintain their documents and Web sites, and it includes Dreamweaver, Flash, Fireworks, Contribute, InDesign, Illustrator, and Photoshop.

Recently, Adobe was voted one of the 100 Best Companies to Work For.

MICROSOFT Computer Technology Innovator

Internet users view Microsoft's Web site more than 2.4 million times each day, attesting to the company's presence as the largest software company in the world. Its Office and Internet Explorer programs dominate the computer industry, and it also has assets in the MSNBC cable television network, the Encarta multimedia encyclopedia, SharePoint, and gaming software, including Flight Simulator and Zoo Tycoon. Microsoft also manufactures hardware, such as the Xbox, Zune, mouse devices, keyboards, fingerprint readers, Web cams, and game controllers.

When Microsoft was incorporated in 1975, the company had three programmers, one product, and revenues of $16,000. The company now employs more than 92,000 people and has annual revenues in excess of $58 billion. Windows 7 is the latest version of Microsoft's flagship operating system.

For more information, visit the Microsoft Office and Concepts CourseMate Web site at www.cengagebrain.com and then navigate to the Chapter 3 Companies on the Cutting Edge resource for this book.

Technology Trailblazers

DAN BRICKLIN VisiCalc Developer

Dan Bricklin introduced wikiCalc in 2007 as a free software tool for Web pages that have data in lists and tables. This program is an offshoot of a prototype program he had developed 30 years earlier, named VisiCalc, that performed a series of calculations automatically when numbers were entered.

Bricklin and a friend founded a company, Software Arts, to develop VisiCalc, short for Visible Calculator. They programmed the software using Apple Basic on an Apple II computer. This small program was the first type of application software that provided a reason for businesses to buy Apple computers. It included many features found in today's spreadsheet software.

Bricklin founded a small consulting company, Software Garden, to develop and market software such as wikiCalc. The company also distributes resources to help programmers learn about licensing their products and about open source software.

MASAYOSHI SON Softbank President and CEO

In the 1970s, Masayoshi Son was convinced that the microchip was going to change people's lives. As an economics major at the University of California, Berkeley, each day he attempted to develop one original use for computer technology. One of these ideas made him a millionaire: a multilingual pocket translating device that he sold to Sharp Corporation.

At age 23, Son founded Softbank, which is one of Japan's largest telecommunications and media corporations. He now is one of the richest men in the world with a net worth of $3.7 billion.

Recently, Softbank partnered with Apple to develop a version of the iPhone for the Japanese market. In addition, Son's company collaborated with Tiffany & Co. to manufacture 10 cell phones, each worth more than $910,000, with 400 diamonds weighing more than 20 karats total.

For more information, visit the Microsoft Office and Concepts CourseMate Web site at www.cengagebrain.com and then navigate to the Chapter 3 Technology Trailblazers resource for this book.

Chapter Review

The Chapter Review reinforces the main concepts presented in this chapter.

To listen to an audio version of this Chapter Review, visit the Microsoft Office and Concepts CourseMate Web site at www.cengagebrain.com and then navigate to the Chapter 3 Chapter Review resource for this book.

1. **What Are the Four Categories of Application Software?** **Application software** consists of programs designed to make users more productive and/or assist them with personal tasks. The major categories of application software are business software; graphics and multimedia software; home, personal, and educational software; and communications software.

2. **What Is the User Interface of Application Software?** Personal computer operating systems often use the concept of a **desktop**, which is an on-screen work area that has a graphical user interface. One way to start a program in Windows is to move the **pointer** to the Start **button** on the taskbar and **click** the Start button by pressing and releasing a button on the mouse. Then, click the program name on the menu or in a list. Once loaded in memory, the program is displayed in a **window** on the desktop.

Visit the Microsoft Office and Concepts CourseMate Web site at www.cengagebrain.com, navigate to the Chapter 3 Quiz Yourself resource for this book, and then click Objectives 1 – 2.

3. **What Are the Key Features of Widely Used Business Programs?** **Business software** assists people in becoming more effective and efficient while performing daily business activities. Business software includes the following programs. **Word processing software** allows users to **create** a document by entering text or numbers and inserting graphical images, **edit** the document by making changes to its existing content, and **format** the document by changing its appearance. **Spreadsheet software** allows users to organize data in rows and columns, perform calculations, recalculate when data changes, and chart the data in graphical form. **Database software** allows users to create a **database**, which is a collection of data organized in a manner that allows access, retrieval, and use of that data. **Presentation software** allows users to create slides that are displayed on a monitor or on a projection screen. **Note taking software** enables users to enter typed text, handwritten comments, drawings, and sketches. A **personal information manager (PIM)** includes an appointment calendar, address book, notepad, and other features to help users organize personal information. In addition to PIM software, a huge variety of business and other software is available for phones. A **software suite** is a collection of individual programs available together as a unit. **Project management software** allows users to plan, schedule, track, and analyze the events, resources, and costs of a project. **Accounting software** helps companies record and report their financial transactions. **Document management software** provides a means for sharing, distributing, and searching through documents by converting them into a format that can be viewed by any user.

4. **What Are the Key Features of Widely Used Graphics and Multimedia Programs?** Graphics and multimedia software includes the following. **Computer-aided design (CAD) software** assists a professional user in creating engineering, architectural, and scientific designs. **Desktop publishing (DTP) software** enables professional designers to create sophisticated documents that contain text, graphics, and colors. **Paint software** allows users to draw pictures, shapes, and other graphical images with various on-screen tools. **Image editing software** provides the capabilities of paint software and also includes the capability to modify existing images. **Professional photo editing software** is a type of image editing software that allows photographers, videographers, engineers, scientists, and other high-volume digital photo users to edit and customize digital photos. **Video editing software** allows professionals to modify a segment of a video, called a clip. **Audio editing software** lets users modify audio clips, produce studio-quality soundtracks, and add audio to video clips. **Multimedia authoring software** allows users to combine text, graphics, audio, video, and animation into an interactive application. **Web page authoring software** helps users create Web pages and organize and maintain Web sites.

Visit the Microsoft Office and Concepts CourseMate Web site at www.cengagebrain.com, navigate to the Chapter 3 Quiz Yourself resource for this book, and then click Objectives 3 – 4.

5. **What Are the Key Features of Widely Used Home, Personal, and Educational Programs?** Software for home, personal, and educational use includes the following. **Personal finance software** is a simplified accounting program that helps users balance their checkbooks, pay bills, track personal income and expenses, track investments, and evaluate financial plans. **Legal software** assists in the preparation of legal documents and provides legal information. **Tax preparation software** can guide users through the process of filing federal taxes. **Personal DTP software** helps home and small business users create newsletters, brochures, flyers, advertisements, postcards, greeting cards, letterhead, business cards, banners, calendars, logos, and Web pages. **Personal paint/image editing software** provides an easy-to-use interface and includes various simplified

tools that allow you to draw pictures, shapes, and other images and to modify existing graphics and photos. Application software often includes a **clip art/image gallery**, which is a collection of clip art and photos. **Home design/landscaping software** assists users with the design, remodeling, or improvement of a home, deck, or landscape. **Travel and mapping software** allows users to view maps, determine routes, and locate points of interest. **Reference software** provides valuable and thorough information for all individuals. **Educational software** teaches a particular skill. **Entertainment software** includes interactive games, video, and other programs.

6. **What Are Web Applications?** A **Web application**, or **Web app**, is a Web site that allows users to access and interact with software from any computer or device that is connected to the Internet. Users often interact with Web applications directly at the Web site, referred to as the host, through their Web browser. Some Web sites require you to download the software to your computer or device.

7. **What Are the Types of Application Software Used in Communications?** Application software for communications includes Web browsers to access and view Web pages; e-mail programs to transmit messages via a network; instant messaging software for real-time exchange of messages or files; chat room software to have real-time, online typed conversations; text, picture, and video messaging software; RSS aggregator program to keep track of changes made to Web sites; blog software, or blogware, to create and maintain a blog; newsgroup/message board programs that allow online written discussions; FTP programs to upload and download files on the Internet; VoIP (Internet telephony), which allows users to speak to other users over the Internet; and video conferencing software for meetings on a network.

8. **What Learning Aids Are Available for Application Software?** To assist in the learning process, many programs provide **online Help**, which is the electronic equivalent of a user manual. Most online Help also links to Web-based Help, which provides updates and more comprehensive resources to respond to technical issues about software. Popular in business, industry, and schools, **Web-based training (WBT)** uses Internet technology and consists of application software on the Web.

Visit the Microsoft Office and Concepts CourseMate Web site at www.cengagebrain.com, navigate to the Chapter 3 Quiz Yourself resource for this book, and then click Objectives 5 – 8.

Key Terms

You should know the Key Terms. The list below helps focus your study.

To see an example of and a definition for each term, and to access current and additional information from the Web, visit the Microsoft Office and Concepts CourseMate Web site at www.cengagebrain.com and then navigate to the Chapter 3 Key Terms resource for this book.

accounting software (107)
application software (96)
audio editing software (110)
business software (100)
button (98)
click (98)
clip art (101)
clip art/image gallery (114)
command (98)
computer-aided design (CAD) software (109)
computer-based training (CBT) (115)
create (102)
custom software (96)
database (104)
database software (104)
desktop (98)
desktop publishing (DTP) software (109)
distance learning (119)
document management software (107)
edit (102)
educational software (115)
e-learning (119)
entertainment software (116)
file (98)
font (102)
font size (102)
font style (102)
format (102)
freeware (97)
home design/landscaping software (115)
icon (98)
image editing software (109)
legal software (113)
malware (98)
menu (98)
multimedia authoring software (110)
note taking software (106)
online Help (119)
open source software (97)
packaged software (96)
paint software (109)
PDF (107)
personal DTP software (113)
personal finance software (112)
personal information manager (PIM) (106)
personal paint/image editing software (114)
personal photo editing software (114)
photo management software (114)
pointer (98)
presentation software (105)
print (102)
professional photo editing software (109)
project management software (106)
public-domain software (97)
reference software (115)
save (102)
shareware (97)
software suite (106)
spreadsheet software (103)
system software (97)
tax preparation software (113)
title bar (98)
travel and mapping software (115)
video editing software (110)
Web app (116)
Web application (96)
Web page authoring software (110)
Web-based training (WBT) (119)
window (98)
word processing software (101)
worksheet (103)

STUDENT ASSIGNMENTS

Checkpoint

The Checkpoint exercises test your knowledge of the chapter concepts. The page number containing the answer appears in parentheses after each exercise.

To complete the Checkpoint exercises interactively, visit the Microsoft Office and Concepts CourseMate Web site at www.cengagebrain.com and then navigate to the Chapter 3 Checkpoint resource for this book.

Multiple Choice Select the best answer.

1. _____ is mass-produced, copyrighted retail software that meets the needs of a wide variety of users, not just a single user or company. (96)
   a. Custom software b. Open source software
   c. A Web application d. Packaged software
2. A feature, called _______, allows users of word processing software to type words continually without pressing the ENTER key at the end of each line. (101)
   a. AutoFormat b. clipboard
   c. AutoCorrect d. wordwrap
3. When using spreadsheet software, a function _______. (103)
   a. depicts data in graphical form
   b. changes certain values to reveal the effects of the changes
   c. is a predefined formula that performs common calculations
   d. contains the formatting necessary for a specific worksheet type
4. ______ combines application software such as word processing, spreadsheet, presentation graphics, and e-mail. (106)
   a. Shareware b. A software suite
   c. Packaged software d. Custom software
5. _______ software provides a means for sharing, distributing, and searching through documents by converting them into a format that can be viewed by any user. (107)
   a. Portable Document Format (PDF)
   b. Document management
   c. Database
   d. Word processing
6. With _____, you can view, organize, sort, catalog, print, and share digital photos. (114)
   a. spreadsheet software
   b. photo management software
   c. clip art
   d. desktop publishing software
7. A(n) _______ is an online area where users have written discussions. (118)
   a. FTP program b. text message
   c. newsgroup/message board d. Web browser
8. _______ is the electronic equivalent of a user manual. (119)
   a. Distance learning
   b. Online Help
   c. Web-based training
   d. E-learning

Matching Match the terms with their definitions.

_____ 1. command (98)
_____ 2. format (102)
_____ 3. note taking software (106)
_____ 4. personal finance software (112)
_____ 5. Web app (116)

a. delivers applications to meet a specific business need
b. simplified accounting program that helps home users and small office/home office users balance their checkbooks, pay bills, track personal income and expenses, set up budgets, manage home inventory, track investments, and evaluate financial plans
c. an instruction that causes a program to perform a specific action
d. Web site that allows users to access and interact with software from any computer or device that is connected to the Internet
e. enables users to enter typed text, handwritten comments, drawings, or sketches anywhere on a page
f. change the appearance of a document

Short Answer Write a brief answer to each of the following questions.

1. Describe some types of utility programs. __________ What is malware? __________
2. What are the features of presentation software? __________ What types of media might a person use to enhance a presentation? __________
3. How is video editing software used? _________ How is multimedia authoring software used? __________
4. How is travel and mapping software used? _________ What are some examples of educational software? _________
5. Describe how many Web sites utilize Web-based training. _________ What are some ways that e-learning enhances communications? _________

Problem Solving

The Problem Solving exercises extend your knowledge of the chapter concepts by seeking solutions to practical computer problems that you may encounter at home, school, or work. The Collaboration exercise should be completed with a team.

In the real world, practical problems often can be solved in multiple ways. Provide one solution to each of the following problems using available resources, such as articles on the Web or in print, blogs, podcasts, videos, television, user guides, other individuals, and electronics and computer stores. You may need to use multiple resources to obtain an answer. Present your solutions in the form requested by your instructor (brief report, presentation, discussion, or other means).

@ Home

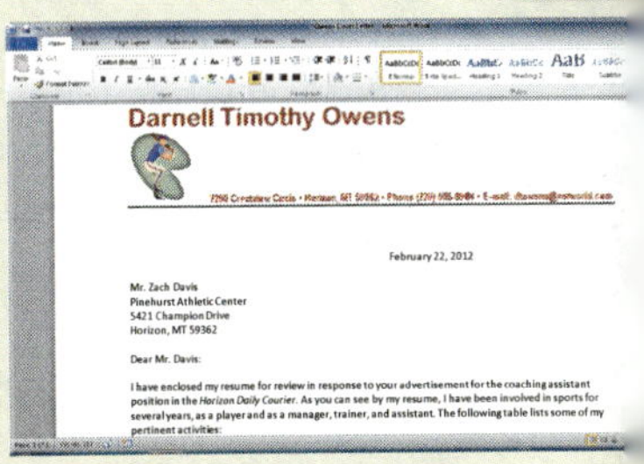

1. **Program Not Responding** While working with a document, Microsoft Word suddenly fails to recognize when you click the mouse or type on the keyboard. The title bar also indicates that the program is not responding. What could be wrong?
2. **Unwanted Page** A local charity in which you are active has asked you to design a one-page brochure. Each time you print the brochure, it prints the first page correctly, but a blank second page also comes out. What steps will you take to eliminate the blank second page?
3. **Audio Not Playing** You are attempting for the first time to transfer video from your video recorder directly to your computer. When you save the file on your computer and play it back, the video quality is acceptable, but there is no audio. What is the first step you will take to troubleshoot this problem?
4. **Unusual File Size** You are using photo editing software to remove red eye from a photo. After successfully removing the red eye, you save the file and notice that the size of the file nearly has doubled. What might be causing this?

@ Work

5. **Missing Font** A coworker has sent you a document that was created in Microsoft Word. She asks you to format the heading of the document with a specific font; however, the font name does not appear in your list of fonts. What steps will you take to retrieve the font?
6. **Insufficient Permission** When reviewing a document in your company's document management system, you attempt to correct a typographical error for the next person who views the file. The document management system prohibits this action and informs you that you do not have the proper permission. What will you do to resolve this problem?
7. **Trial Version Expired** New job responsibilities require that you use Adobe Photoshop to create a new company logo. Your boss has been unable to purchase the latest version of the software for you, and recommends that you download and install the trial version until she is able to purchase the software. The trial period now has expired and you are unable to use the program. How might you be able to continue using the software?
8. **Web-Based Training Difficulties** You have signed up for Web-based training that is designed to teach you how to use your company's new accounting system. During your training, you notice that the Web-based training Web site is not keeping track of your progress. Consequently, you have to start from the beginning each time you log in. What might be causing this?

Collaboration

9. **Computers in Construction** As a student in a drafting class, your instructor has challenged you to design your dream home by using application software wherever possible. Form a team of three people that will determine how to accomplish this objective. One team member should compare and contrast two programs that can be used to create a two-dimensional floor plan, another team member should compare and contrast two computer-aided design programs that can create a more detailed design of the house, and the third team member should compare and contrast two programs that can assist with other aspects of the design process such as landscaping and interior design.

Learn How To

The Learn How To activities step you through fundamental technology skills when using a computer. The Learn How To exercises enable you to become more proficient with these skills.

Premium Activity: To relate this Learn How To activity to your everyday life, see a visual demonstration of the activity, and complete a short assessment, visit the Microsoft Office and Concepts CourseMate Web site at www.cengagebrain.com and then navigate to the Chapter 3 Learn How To resource for this book.

Learn How To 1: Save a File in Application Software

When you use application software, most of the time you either will be creating a new file or modifying an existing file. For example, if you are using a word processor, when you create a new document, the document is a file.

When you create or modify a file, it is contained in RAM. If you turn off your computer or lose electrical power, the file will not be retained. In order to retain the file, you must save it on disk or other permanent storage, such as a USB flash drive.

As you create the file, you should save the file often. To save a new file, you must complete several tasks:

1. Initiate an action indicating you want to save the file, such as selecting Save on the File menu.
2. Designate where the file should be stored. This includes identifying both the device (such as drive C) and the folder or library.
3. Specify the name of the file, using the file name rules as specified by the application or operating system.
4. Click the Save button to save the file.

Tasks 2 through 4 normally can be completed using a dialog box such as the one shown in Figure 3-38.

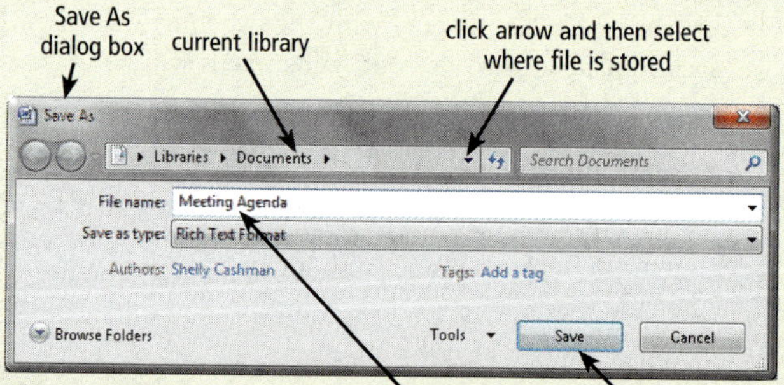

Figure 3-38

If you use application software to create or modify a file and attempt to close the program prior to saving the new or modified file, the program may display a dialog box that asks if you want to save the file. If you click the Yes button, a modified file will be saved using the same file name in the same location from which it was retrieved. Saving a new file requires that you complete tasks 2 through 4.

Exercise

1a. Start the WordPad program from the Accessories list in the All Programs list. Type `Saving a file is the best insurance against losing work.`

1b. Click the Save button on the Quick Access Toolbar. What dialog box is displayed? Where will the file be saved? What is the default file name? If you wanted to save the file on the desktop, what would you do? Click the Cancel button in the dialog box. Submit your answers to your instructor.

1c. Click the Close button in the upper-right corner of the WordPad window. What happened? Click the Yes button in the WordPad dialog box. What happened? Connect a USB flash drive to one of the computer's USB ports. Select the USB flash drive as the location for saving the file. Save the file with the name, Chapter 3 Learn How To 1. What happened when you clicked the Save button? Submit your answers to your instructor.

Learn How To 2: Zip/Compress a File

When you zip or compress one or more files in Windows, it attempts to shrink the file size(s) by reducing the amount of unneeded space. Compressing a file is particularly useful when you attach files to an e-mail message and wish to keep the file size as small as possible. It also is useful when you compress multiple files simultaneously, because Windows compresses the multiple files into a single file. You can compress a file or folder by completing the following steps:

1. Locate the file(s) or folder(s) you want to compress. If the files or folders you wish to compress are located in multiple locations, it might be helpful to first move them so that they are in a single location.
2. Select the file(s) or folder(s) you would like to compress. If you are selecting multiple files or folders, click the first one and then hold down the CTRL key while you select the remaining files and/or folders. Once you are finished making your selections, release the CTRL key.

3. Right-click the selection to display a shortcut menu, point to Send to on the shortcut menu to display the Send to submenu (Figure 3-39), and then click Compressed (zipped) folder to create the compressed folder.
4. If necessary, type a new name for the compressed folder and then press the ENTER key.

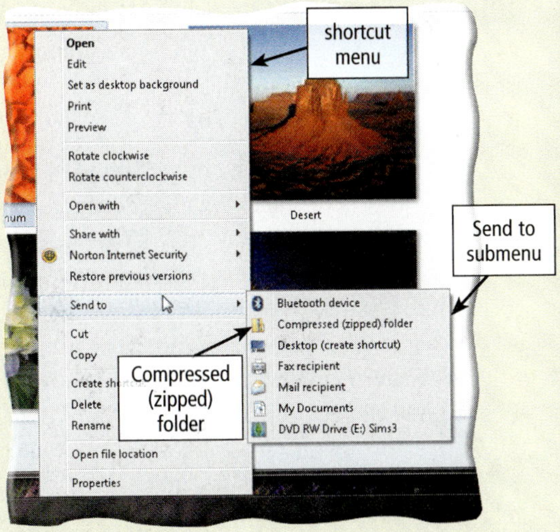

Figure 3-39

Exercise

1. To better organize your hard disk, you decide to compress files you rarely use, but would like to keep as a backup. Click the Start button to display the Start menu, click Pictures to display the Pictures library, and then double-click the Sample Pictures folder to display sample pictures included with Windows 7. Select three pictures and compress them into one compressed folder. Use your first initial and last name as the name of the new compressed folder and then e-mail the folder to your instructor.

Learn It Online

The Learn It Online exercises are interactive Web exercises designed to reinforce and expand your understanding of the chapter concepts. The descriptions below briefly summarize each exercise.

To complete the Learn It Online exercises, visit the Microsoft Office and Concepts CourseMate Web site at www.cengagebrain.com, navigate to the Chapter 3 resources for this book, click the link for the exercise you want to complete, and then read the instructions.

1 At the Movies — MediaCell Video Converter
Watch a movie to learn how to use the MediaCell Video Converter and then answer questions about the movie.

2 Student Edition Labs — Word Processing, Spreadsheets, Databases, and Presentation Software
Enhance your understanding and knowledge about business application software by completing the Word Processing, Spreadsheets, Databases, and Presentation Software Labs.

3 Practice Test
Take a multiple choice test that checks your knowledge of the chapter concepts and review the resulting study guide.

4 Who Wants To Be a Computer Genius²?
Play the Shelly Cashman Series version of this popular game by answering questions to find out if you are a computer genius. Panic buttons are available to provide assistance during game play.

5 Crossword Puzzle Challenge
Complete an interactive crossword puzzle to reinforce concepts presented in this chapter.

6 Windows Exercises
Step through the Windows 7 exercises to learn about working with application programs, creating a word processing document, using WordPad Help, and business software products.

7 Exploring Computer Careers
Read about a career as a help desk specialist, search for related employment advertisements, and then answer related questions.

8 Web Apps — Britannica.com
Learn how to browse world history and search for various encyclopedia articles using Britannica.com.

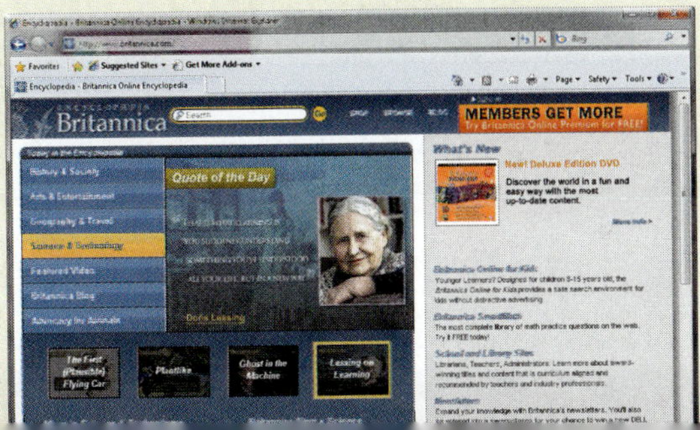

STUDENT ASSIGNMENTS

Web Research

The Web Research exercises broaden your understanding of chapter concepts by presenting questions that require you to search the Web for answers.

1 Search Sleuth

Use one of the search engines listed in Figure 2-8 in Chapter 2 on page 53 or your own favorite search engine to find the answers to the following questions. Copy and paste the Web address from the Web page where you found the answer. Some questions may have more than one answer. If required, submit your answers to your instructor. (1) What company did Bruce Artwick form in 1977, and what game did it license to Microsoft in 1982? (2) In what year did the United States Department of Revenue first provide tax forms and booklets in Adobe PDF format on its Web site? (3) What is the latest security incident listed on the United States Computer Emergency Readiness Team (US-CERT) Web site? (4) What is the name of the sans serif font the German Bauhaus movement developed in 1928? (5) What United States president's speech did Peter Norvig turn into a lighthearted PowerPoint presentation?

2 Green Computing

A typical desktop computer and 17-inch monitor that always are turned on release 750 pounds of carbon dioxide in one year, which is the same amount of carbon dioxide released by a car driven 820 miles. Power management software helps conserve a computer's electricity consumption while maintaining acceptable performance. The programs determine when a computer is inactive and, in turn, power down the computer. Use one of the search engines listed in Figure 2-8 in Chapter 2 on page 53 or your own favorite search engine to find information about power management software. What average return-on-investment do they promise? What features do they have, such as generating reports and exempting critical programs from powering down? What is their cost? Powering down the computer stresses critical components, such as the CPU and memory, so does this practice actually result in more waste because these parts must be replaced? Write a report summarizing your findings, and include a table of links to Web sites that you viewed.

3 Social Networking

Career-minded professionals have turned to LinkedIn as a resource for online networking. The more than 45 million registered users, who represent each of the FORTUNE 500 companies, create public profiles that recruiters scour in search of new talent. Users can link to work contacts who, in turn, give access to their work contacts. Visit the LinkedIn Web site (linkedin.com), click the What is LinkedIn? link at the top of the page, and then read the information about reconnecting with current and former colleagues and classmates, job hunting, and obtaining advice from experts. Click the LinkedIn Jobs link at the bottom of the page, type a keyword describing the type of job you would like to have, and then browse the listings. What tips for finding jobs does LinkedIn provide? Summarize the listings and job information you read.

4 Blogs

Vehicle buyers know that the Internet provides a wealth of information that helps direct them toward the best vehicle for their needs. Those consumers who research blogs can obtain price, safety, performance, and maintenance facts and then employ savvy negotiation techniques that help them make the purchase confidently. Visit several automotive blogs, including those from Popular Mechanics (popularmechanics.com/blogs/automotive_news), Autoblog (autoblog.com), Autoblog Green (autobloggreen.com), Autopia (blog.wired.com/cars), and Ask Patty — Car Advice for Women (caradvice.askpatty.com). What new hybrid, luxury, and high-performance vehicles are profiled? Which are promoted as being environmentally friendly? Write a report summarizing the vehicle information you read.

5 Ethics in Action

A hacker is someone who tries to access a computer or network illegally. Although hacking activity sometimes is a harmless prank, at times it causes extensive damage. Some hackers say their activities allow them to test their skills. Others say their activities are a form of civil disobedience that forces companies to make their products more secure. View online sites such as The Ethical Hacker Network (ethicalhacker.net) that provide information about when hackers provide some benefit to the Internet society. Write a report summarizing your findings and include a table of links to Web sites that provide additional details.

Digital Video Technology

Everywhere you look, people are capturing moments they want to remember. They shoot movies of their vacations, birthday parties, activities, accomplishments, sporting events, weddings, and more. Because of the popularity of digital video cameras and mobile devices with built-in digital cameras, increasingly more people desire to capture their memories digitally, instead of on film. As shown in Figure 1, people have the ability to modify and share the digital videos they create. When you use special hardware and/or software, you can copy, manipulate, and distribute digital videos using your personal computer and the Internet. Amateurs can achieve professional quality results by using more sophisticated hardware and software. This feature describes how to select a video camera, record a video, transfer and manage videos, edit a video, and distribute a video.

Digital recordings deliver significant benefits over film-based movie making. With digital video cameras, recordings reside on storage media such as a hard disk, optical disc, or memory card. Unlike film, storage media can be reused, which reduces costs, saves time, and provides immediate results. Digital technology allows greater control over the creative process, both while recording video and in the editing process. You can check results immediately after capturing a video to determine whether it meets your expectations. If you are dissatisfied with a video, you can erase it and recapture it, again and again. Today, many mobile devices, such as smart phones and PDAs, allow you to capture video.

As shown in Figure 1, digital video cameras, and mobile devices function as input devices when they transmit video to a personal computer. You can transmit video by connecting the video camera or mobile device to your personal computer using a USB or FireWire port, or by placing the storage media used on the camera or mobile device in the computer. Some cameras and devices also can transmit wirelessly to a computer or to the media sharing Web sites.

Figure 1 A variety of input, output, and storage devices are used by home users to process and edit digital video.

When you transmit video that was captured with a digital video camera or mobile device to a computer, you can edit the video using video editing software. If desired, you often can preview the video during the editing process on a television. Finally, you save the finished result to the desired media, such as an optical disc or, perhaps, e-mail the edited video or post it to a media sharing Web site. In this example, an optical disc drive also can be used to input video from an optical disc. Also in the example shown in Figure 1 on the previous page, a mobile device that includes a video camera sends a video directly to a media sharing Web site.

Digital video technology allows you to input, edit, manage, publish, and share your videos using a personal computer. With digital video technology, you can transform home videos into Hollywood-style movies by enhancing the videos with scrolling titles and transitions, cutting out or adding scenes, and adding background music and voice-over narration. The following sections outline the steps involved in the process of using digital video technology.

1 Select a Video Camera

Video cameras record in either analog or digital format. **Analog formats** include 8mm, Hi8, VHS-C, and Super VHS-C. **Digital formats** include Mini-DV, MICROMV, Digital8, DVD, Blu-ray, and HDV (high-definition video format). Some digital video cameras record on an internal hard disk. Others may allow you to record directly on an optical disc drive. Digital video cameras fall into three general categories: high-end consumer, consumer, and webcasting and monitoring (Figure 2). Consumer digital video cameras are by far the most popular type among consumers. High-end consumer models may support the Blu-ray or HDV standards. A video recorded in high-definition can be played back on a high-definition display. Many mobile devices allow you to record video that you later can transmit to your computer or e-mail from the device. Some devices allow you to upload video directly to video sharing Web sites. Digital video cameras provide more features than analog video cameras, such as a higher level of zoom, better sound, or greater control over color and lighting.

2 Record a Video

Most video cameras provide you with a choice of recording programs, which sometimes are called automatic settings. Each recording program includes a different combination of camera settings, so that you can adjust the exposure and other functions to match the recording environment. Usually, several different programs are available, such as point-and-shoot, point-and-shoot with manual adjustment, sports, portrait, spotlit scenes, and low light. You also have the ability to select special digital effects, such as fade, wipe, and black and white. If you are shooting outside on a windy day, then you can enable the windscreen to prevent wind noise. If you are shooting home videos or video meant for a Web site, then the point-and-shoot recording program is sufficient.

3 Transfer and Manage Videos

After recording the video, the next step is to transfer the video to your personal computer or to the Internet. Most video cameras connect directly to a USB or FireWire port on a personal computer (Figure 3). Transferring video with a

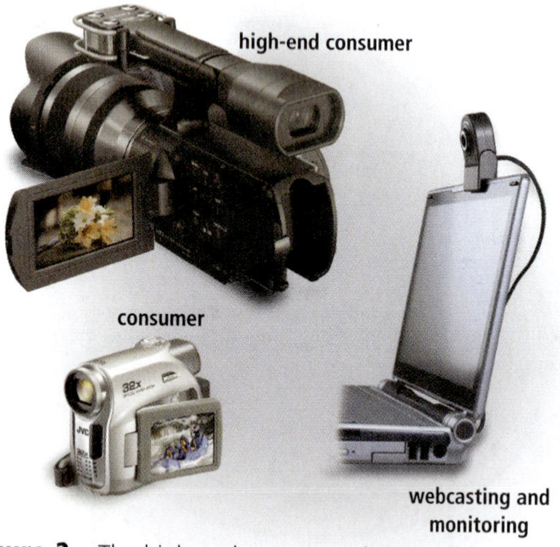

Figure 2 The high-end consumer digital video camera can produce professional-grade results. The consumer digital video camera produces amateur-grade results. The webcasting and monitoring digital video camera is appropriate for webcasting and security monitoring.

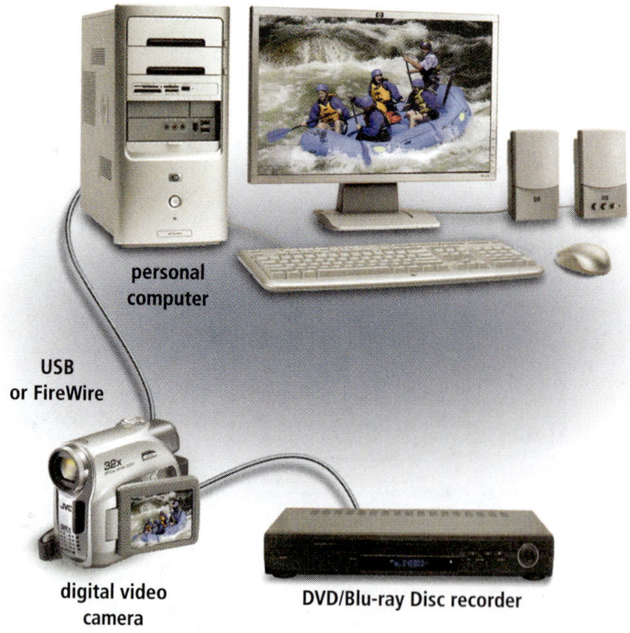

Figure 3 A digital video camera is connected to the personal computer or DVD/Blu-ray Disc recorder via a USB or FireWire port. No additional hardware is needed.

digital camera or mobile device is easy, because the video already is in a digital format that the computer can recognize. Many mobile devices include a special cable used to connect the device to a personal computer or allow you to transfer the videos to a media sharing Web site or your own Web site.

Some people own analog format video tapes that require additional hardware to convert the analog signals to a digital format before the video can be manipulated on a personal computer. The additional hardware includes a special video capture card using a standard RCA video cable or an S-video cable (Figure 4). **S-video** cables provide sharper images and greater overall quality. A personal computer also can record video to an optical disc, or it can be connected to an external DVD/Blu-ray Disc recorder to record videos. Video conversion services often specialize in converting older analog video to a variety of digital formats.

When transferring video, plan to use approximately 15 to 30 GB of hard disk storage per hour of digital video. High-definition formats may require much more storage per hour. A typical video project requires about four times the amount of raw footage as the final product. At the high end, therefore, a video that lasts an hour may require up to 120 GB of storage for the raw footage, editing process, and final video. This storage requirement can vary depending on the software you use to copy the video from the video camera to the hard disk and the format you select to save the video. For example, Microsoft's Windows Live Movie Maker can save 15 hours of standard video in 10 GB when creating video for playback on a computer, but saves only 1 hour of video in 10 GB when creating video for playback on a DVD. A high-definition video file may require more than 10 GB per hour.

The video transfer requires application software on the personal computer (Figure 5). The Windows Live Movie Maker software, available as a free download from Microsoft's Web site, allows you to transfer the video from a video camera. Depending on the length of video and the type of connection used, the video may take a long time to transfer. Make certain that no other programs are running on your personal computer while transferring the video.

Figure 5 Some video editing software allows you to transfer a video from any video source to a hard disk.

The frame rate of a video refers to the number of frames per second (fps) that are captured in the video. The most widely used frame rate is 30 fps. A smaller frame rate results in a smaller file size for the video, but playback of the video will not be as smooth as one recorded with a higher frame rate.

When transferring video, the software may allow you to choose a file format and a codec to store the video. A video **file format** holds the video information in a manner specified by a vendor, such as Apple or Microsoft. Six of the more popular file formats are listed in Figure 6. The 3GP format is widely used on mobile devices.

File formats support codecs to encode the audio and video into the file formats. A **codec** specifies how the audio and video is compressed and stored within the file. A particular file format may be able to store audio and video in a number of

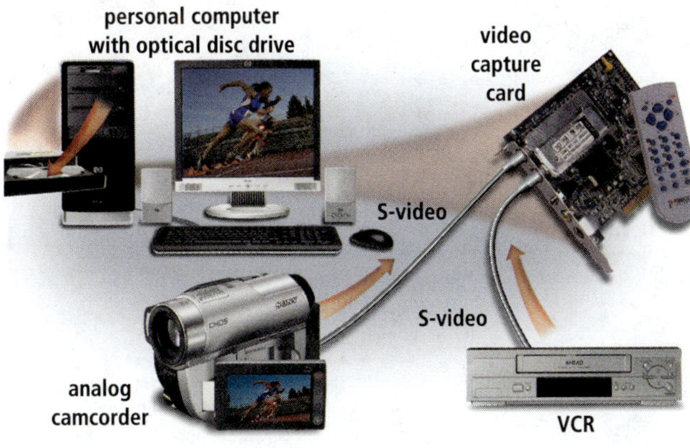

Figure 4 An analog camcorder or VCR is connected to the personal computer via an S-video port on a video capture card.

Popular Video File Formats

File Format	File Extensions
Apple QuickTime	.MOV or .QT
DivX	.DIVX
Microsoft Windows Media Video	.WMV or .ASF
MPEG-4 Part 4	.MP4
Real RealMedia	.RM or .RAM
3GP	.3GP or .3G2

Figure 6 Apple, DivX, Microsoft, and Real offer the more popular video file formats.

different codecs. Figure 7 shows some options available for specifying a file format and video quality settings in a video capture program. The file format and codec you choose often is based on what you plan to do with the movie. For example, if you plan to upload your video to the YouTube video sharing Web site, the best choices are DivX and MPEG-4 file formats. Many users find that they are unable to play their own or others' videos, and the problem often is that the proper codec is not installed on the user's personal computer. Video conversion software often allows the user to convert a video in a less popular format to a better supported format. Many of these programs are available as freeware.

After transferring the video to a personal computer or the Internet, and before manipulating the video, you should store the video files in appropriate folders, named correctly, and backed up. Most video transfer application software helps manage these tasks.

4 Edit a Video

Once the video is stored on your hard disk or the Internet, the next step is to edit, or manipulate, the video. If you used a video capture card to transfer analog video to the computer (Figure 4 on the previous page), the files may require extra initial processing. Some Web sites allow you to perform minor editing and other tasks on the Web site. When you use a video capture card, some of the video frames may be lost in the transfer process. Some video editing programs allow you to fix this problem with **frame rate correction** tools.

The first step in the editing process is to split the video into smaller pieces, or scenes, that you can manipulate more easily. This process is called splitting. Most video software automatically splits the video into scenes, thus sparing you the task. After splitting, you should delete unwanted scenes or portions of scenes. This process is called pruning.

After creating the scenes you want to use in the final production, you edit each individual scene. You can crop, or change the size of, scenes. That is, you may want to delete the top or a side of a scene that is irrelevant. You also can resize the scene. For example, you may be creating a video that will be displayed on a media sharing Web site. Making a smaller video, such as 320 × 200 pixels, instead of 640 × 480 pixels, results in a smaller file that transmits faster over the Internet. Some media sharing Web sites recommend smaller video resolutions, such as 320 × 200 pixels, and some will perform the conversion for you automatically.

Figure 7 Video editing software allows you to specify a combination of file format and video quality settings when saving a video.

If a video has been recorded over a long period, using different cameras or under different lighting conditions, the video may need color correction. Color correction tools analyze your video and match brightness, colors, and other attributes of video clips to ensure a smooth look to the video (Figure 8).

You can add logos, special effects, or titles to scenes. You can place a company logo or personal logo in a video to identify yourself or the company producing the video. Logos often are added on the lower-right corner of a video and remain for the duration of the video. Special effects include warping, changing from color to black and white, morphing, or zoom motion. Morphing is a special effect in which one video image is transformed into another image over the course of several frames of video, creating the illusion of metamorphosis. You usually add titles at the beginning and ending of a video to give the video context. A training video may have titles throughout the video to label a particular scene, or each scene may begin with a title.

The next step in editing a video is to add audio effects, including voice-over narration and background music. Many video editing programs allow you to add additional tracks, or layers, of sound to a video in addition to the sound that was recorded on the video camera or mobile device. You also can add special audio effects.

The final step in editing a video is to combine the scenes into a complete video (Figure 9). This process involves ordering scenes and adding transition effects between scenes. Video editing software allows you to combine scenes and separate each scene with a transition. Transitions include fading, wiping, blurry, bursts, ruptures, erosions, and more.

Figure 8 Color correction tools in video editing software allow a great deal of control over the mood of your video creation.

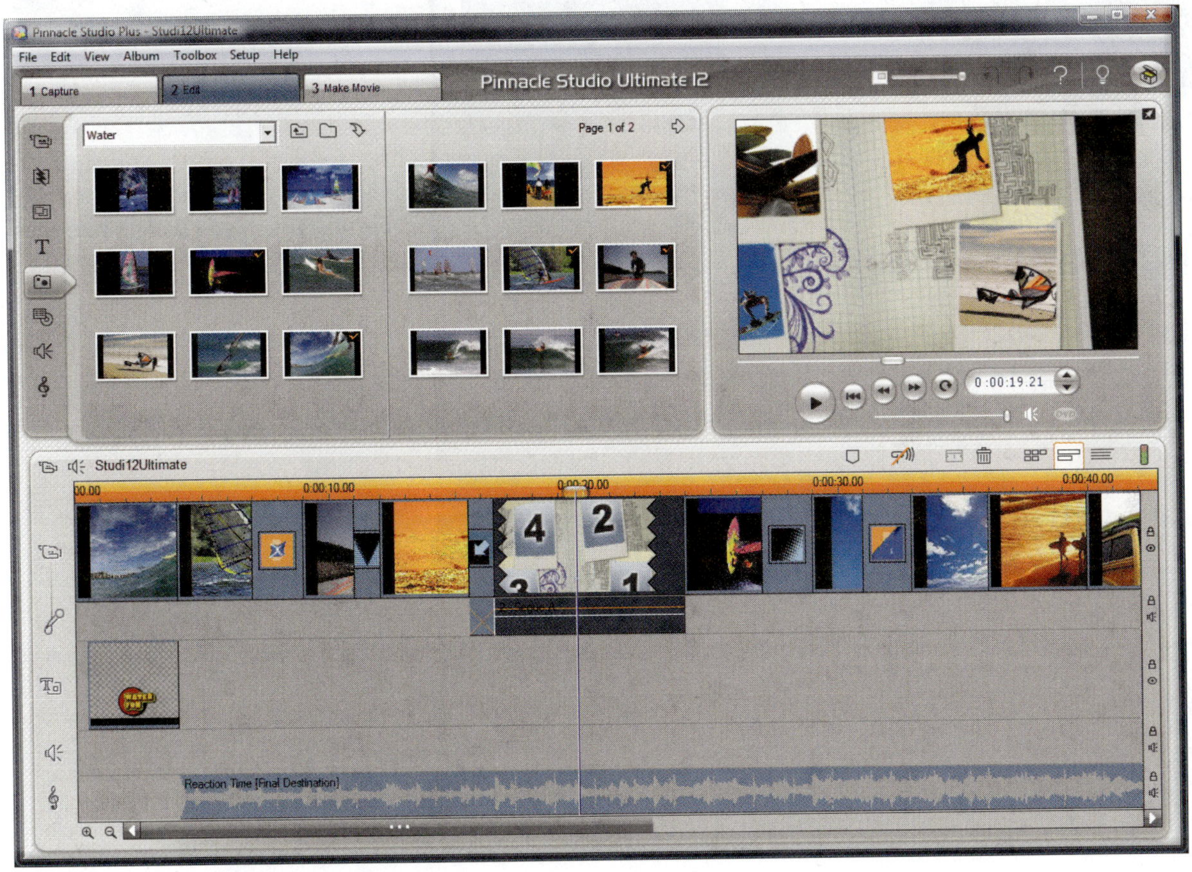

Figure 9 Scenes are combined into a sequence on the bottom of the screen.

5 Distribute the Video

After editing the video, the final step is to distribute it or save it on an appropriate medium. You can save video in a variety of formats. Video recorded on a mobile device often requires conversion to a more widely accepted format.

Video also can be stored in digital formats in any of several optical disc formats or on a media sharing Web site. **Optical disc creation software**, which often is packaged with video editing software, allows you to create, or master, optical discs. You can add interactivity to your optical disc creations. For example, you can allow viewers to jump to certain scenes using a menu.

You also can save your video creation in electronic format for distribution over the Web, via e-mail, or to a mobile device. Some cameras include a button that allows users to upload directly to a media sharing Web site. Popular media sharing Web sites, such as YouTube (Figure 10), have recommendations for the best file format and codecs to use for video that you upload to them (Figure 11). Your video editing software must support the file format and codec you want to use. For example, Apple's iMovie software typically saves files in the QuickTime file format.

Professionals use hardware and software that allow them to create a film version of digital video that can be played in movie theaters. This technology is becoming increasingly popular. The cost of professional video editing software ranges from thousands to hundreds of thousands of dollars. Video editing software for the home user is available for a few hundred dollars or less. Some Hollywood directors believe that eventually all movies will be recorded and edited digitally.

After creating your final video for distribution or for your personal video collection, you should back up the final video file. You can save your scenes for inclusion in other video creations or create new masters using different effects, transitions, and ordering of scenes.

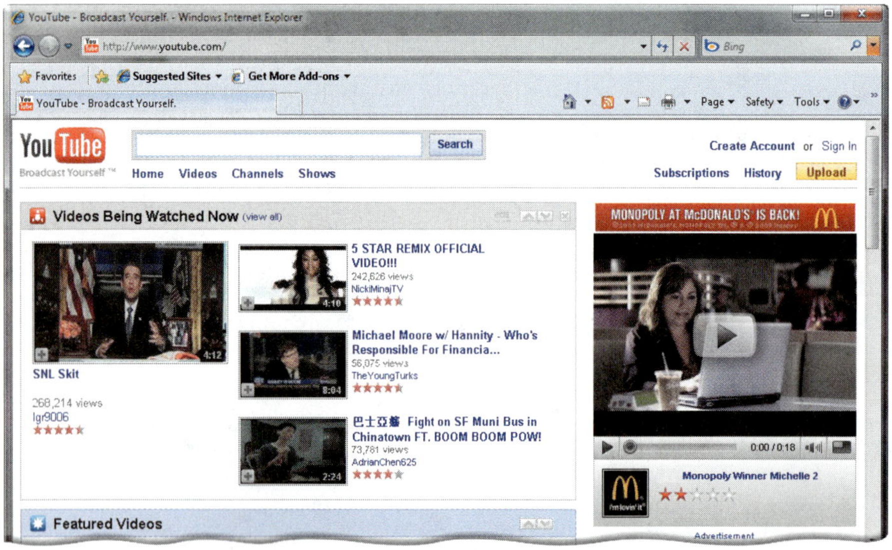

Figure 10 Media sharing Web sites allow you to share your videos with acquaintances or the entire world.

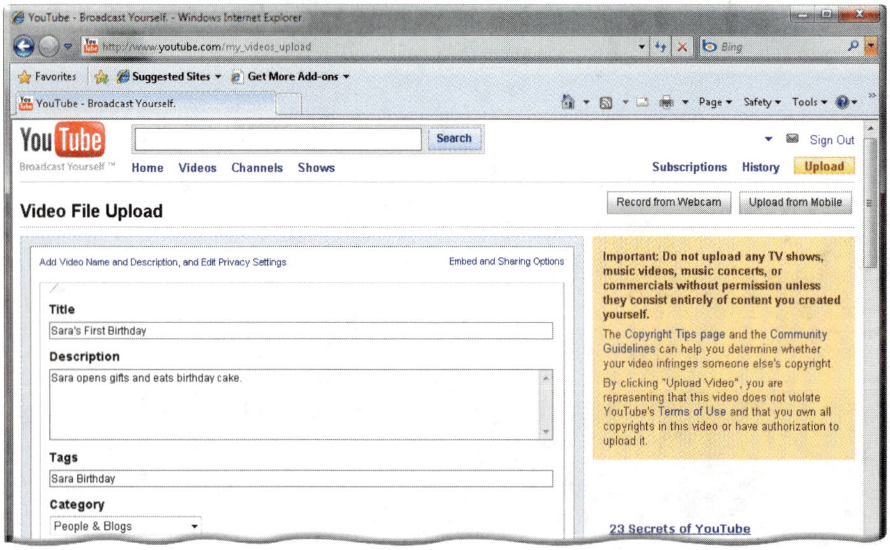

Figure 11 Media sharing Web sites, such as YouTube, provide tools that simplify the process of uploading videos to the site.

Chapter Four

Operating Systems and Utility Programs

Objectives

After completing this chapter, you will be able to:

1. Define system software and identify the two types of system software
2. Describe each of these functions of an operating system: starting and shutting down a computer, providing a user interface, managing memory, coordinating tasks, configuring devices, establishing an Internet connection, monitoring performance, providing file management and other utilities, updating automatically, controlling a network, and administering security
3. Summarize the features of several stand-alone operating systems: Windows, Mac OS, UNIX, and Linux
4. Identify various server operating systems
5. Briefly describe several embedded operating systems: Windows Embedded CE, Windows Phone, Palm OS, iPhone OS, BlackBerry, Google Android, Embedded Linux, and Symbian OS
6. Explain the purpose of several utility programs: file manager, search utility, image viewer, uninstaller, disk cleanup, disk defragmenter, backup and restore utilities, screen saver, personal firewall, antivirus programs, spyware and adware removers, Internet filters, file compression, media player, disc burning, and personal computer maintenance

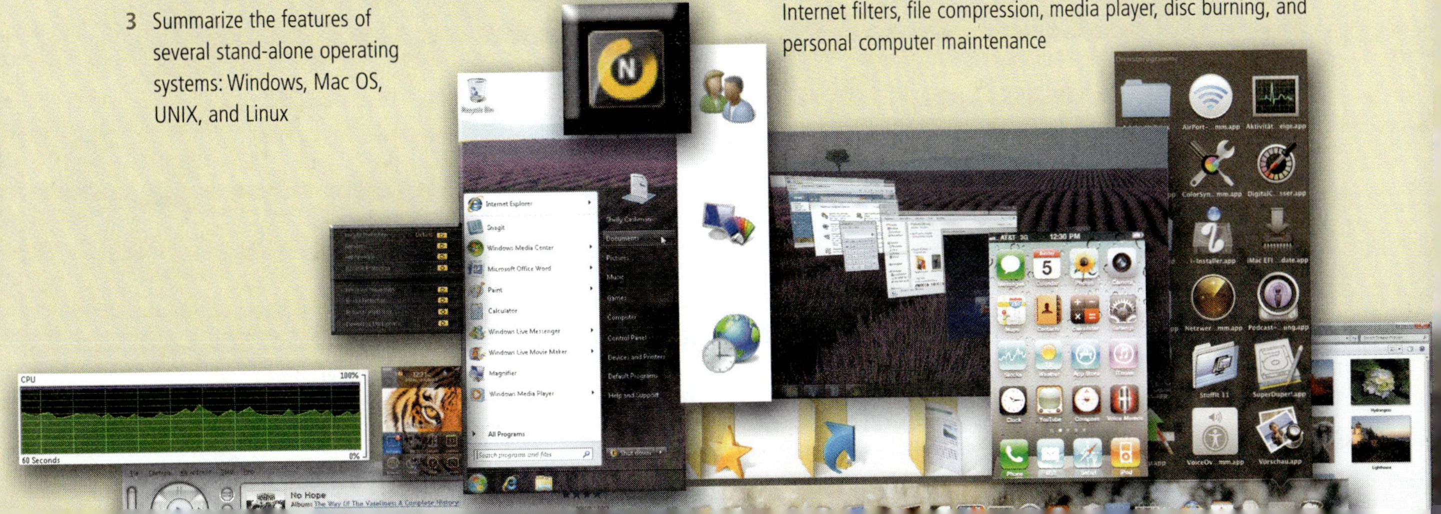

System Software

When you purchase a personal computer, it usually has system software installed on its hard disk. **System software** consists of the programs that control or maintain the operations of the computer and its devices. System software serves as the interface between the user, the application software, and the computer's hardware.

Two types of system software are operating systems and utility programs. This chapter discusses the operating system and its functions, as well as several types of utility programs for personal computers.

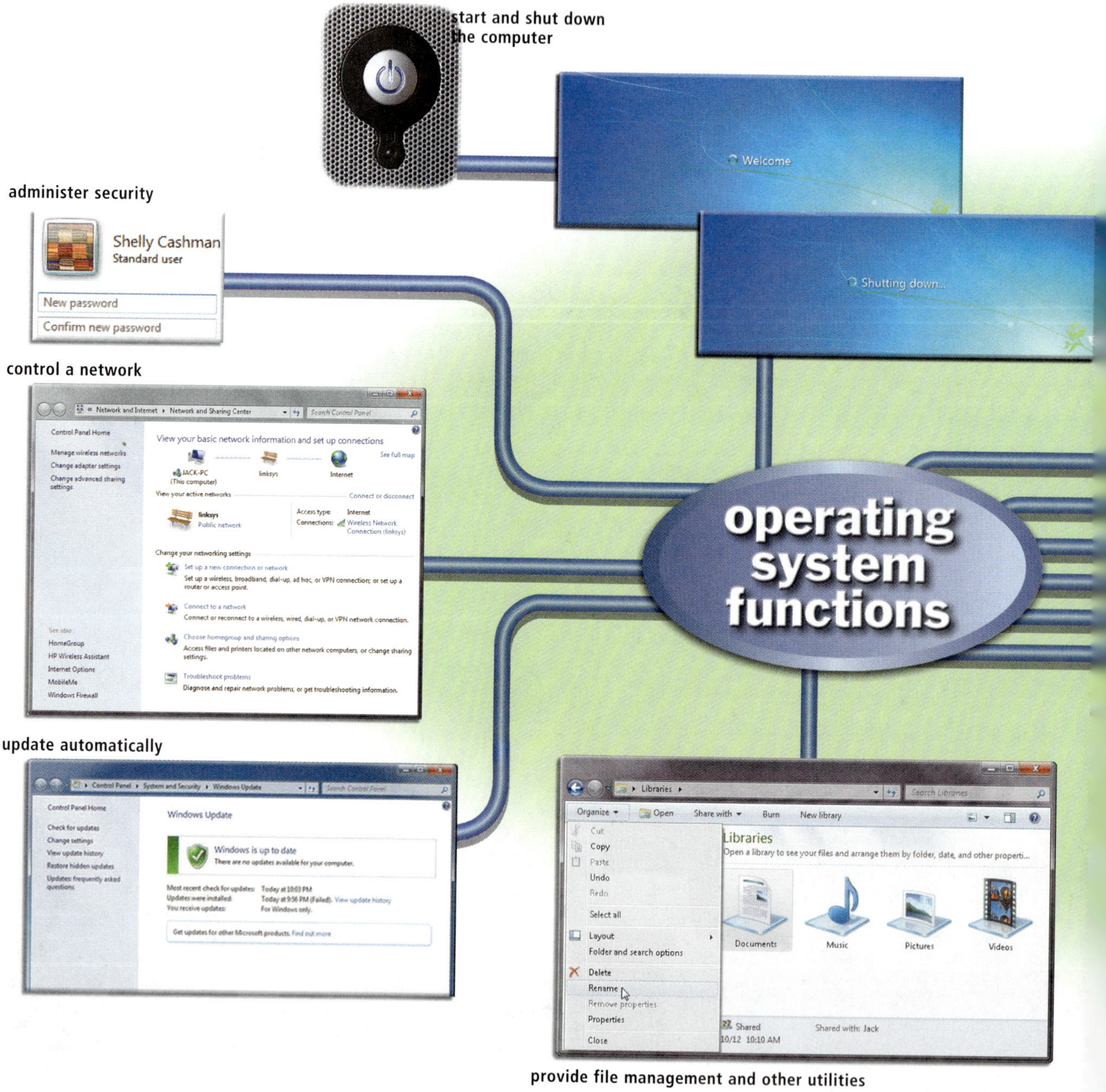

Figure 4-1 Most operating systems perform similar functions, which are illustrated with the latest version of Windows in this figure.

Operating Systems

An **operating system** (**OS**) is a set of programs containing instructions that work together to coordinate all the activities among computer hardware resources. Most operating systems perform similar functions that include starting and shutting down a computer, providing a user interface, managing programs, managing memory, coordinating tasks, configuring devices, establishing an Internet connection, monitoring performance, providing file management and other utilities, and automatically updating itself and certain utility programs. Some operating systems also allow users to control a network and administer security (Figure 4-1).

Although an operating system can run from an optical disc and/or flash memory mobile media, in most cases, the operating system is installed and resides on the computer's hard disk. On handheld computers and many mobile devices, the operating system may reside on a ROM chip.

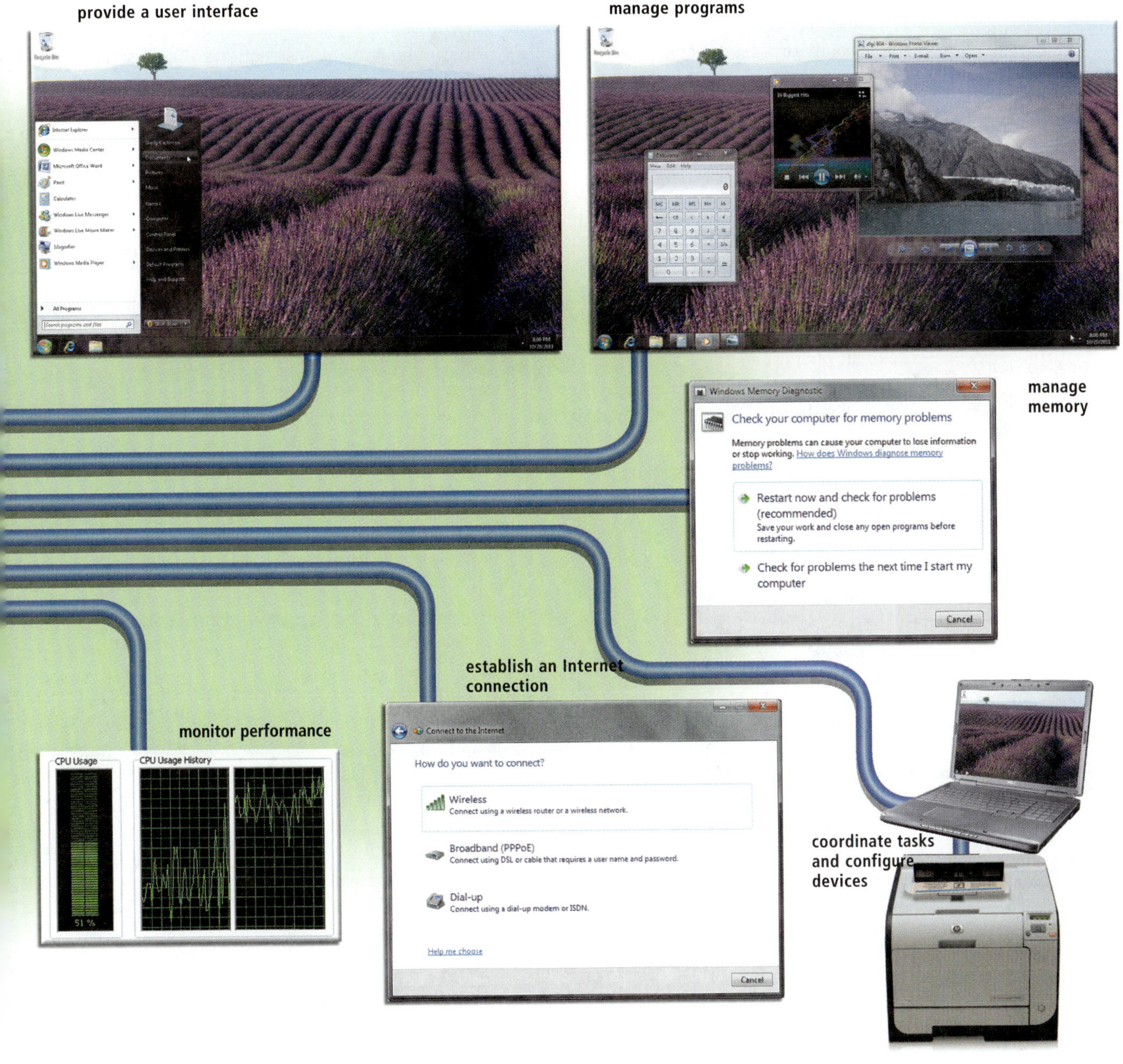

Different sizes of computers typically use different operating systems because operating systems generally are written to run on a specific type of computer. For example, a mainframe computer does not use the same operating system as a personal computer. Even the same types of computers, such as desktop computers, may not use the same operating system. Some, however, can run multiple operating systems. When purchasing application software, you must ensure that it works with the operating system installed on your computer or mobile device.

The operating system that a computer uses sometimes is called the platform. With purchased application software, the package or specifications identify the required platform (operating system). A cross-platform program is one that runs the same on multiple operating systems.

Operating System Functions

Many different operating systems exist; however, most operating systems provide similar functions. The following sections discuss functions common to most operating systems. The operating system handles many of these functions automatically, without requiring any instruction from a user.

Starting and Shutting Down a Computer

Booting is the process of starting or restarting a computer. When turning on a computer that has been powered off completely, you are performing a **cold boot**. A **warm boot**, by contrast, is the process of using the operating system to restart a computer. With Windows, for example, you can perform a warm boot by clicking a menu command (Figure 4-2).

When you install new software or update existing software, often an on-screen prompt instructs you to restart the computer. In this case, a warm boot is appropriate.

Each time you boot a computer, the kernel and other frequently used operating system instructions are loaded, or copied, from storage into the computer's memory (RAM). The kernel is the core of an operating system that manages memory and devices, maintains the computer's clock, starts programs, and assigns the computer's resources, such as devices, programs, data, and information. The kernel is memory resident, which means it remains in memory while the computer is running. Other parts of the operating system are nonresident, that is, these instructions remain on a storage medium until they are needed.

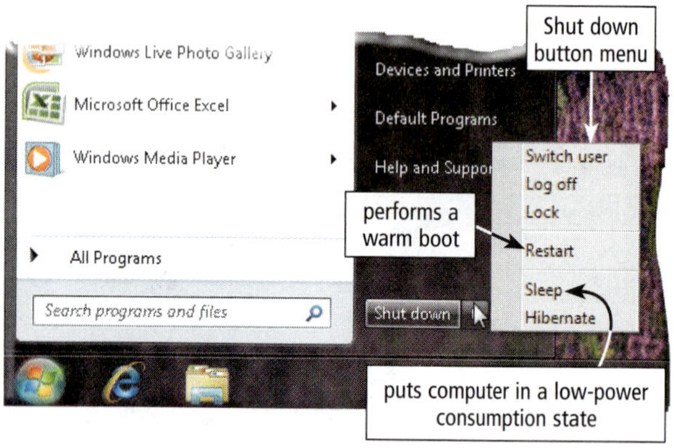

Figure 4-2 To reboot a running computer, click the Shut down button arrow and then click Restart.

When you boot a computer, a series of messages may appear on the screen. The actual information displayed varies depending on the make and type of the computer and the equipment installed. The boot process, however, is similar for large and small computers.

Although some users leave their computers running continually and never turn them off, others choose to shut them down. Shut down options including powering off the computer, placing the computer in sleep mode, and hibernating the computer. Both sleep mode and hibernate are designed to save time when you resume working on the computer. **Sleep mode** saves any open documents and programs to RAM, turns off all unneeded functions, and then places the computer in a low-power state. **Hibernate**, by contrast, saves any open documents and programs to a hard disk before removing power from the computer.

Providing a User Interface

You interact with software through its user interface. That is, a **user interface** controls how you enter data and instructions and how information is displayed on the screen. Two types of user interfaces are graphical and command-line (Figure 4-3). Operating systems sometimes use a combination of these interfaces to define how a user interacts with a computer.

Graphical User Interface Most users today work with a graphical user interface. With a **graphical user interface (GUI)**, you interact with menus and visual images such as buttons and other graphical objects to issue commands (Figure 4-3a). Many current GUI operating systems incorporate features similar to those of a Web browser.

Windows 7 offers two different GUIs, depending on your hardware configuration. Computers with less than 1 GB of RAM work with the Windows 7 Basic interface. Computers with more than 1 GB of RAM that have the required hardware may be able to work with the Windows 7 Aero interface, also known as **Windows Aero**, shown in Figure 4-3a, which provides an enhanced visual look, additional navigation options, and animation.

Command-Line Interface To configure devices, manage system resources, and troubleshoot network connections, network administrators and other advanced users work with a command-line interface. In a **command-line interface**, a user types commands or presses special keys on the keyboard to enter data and instructions (Figure 4-3b). Some people consider command-line interfaces difficult to use because they require exact spelling, grammar, and punctuation.

Figure 4-3a (graphical user interface)

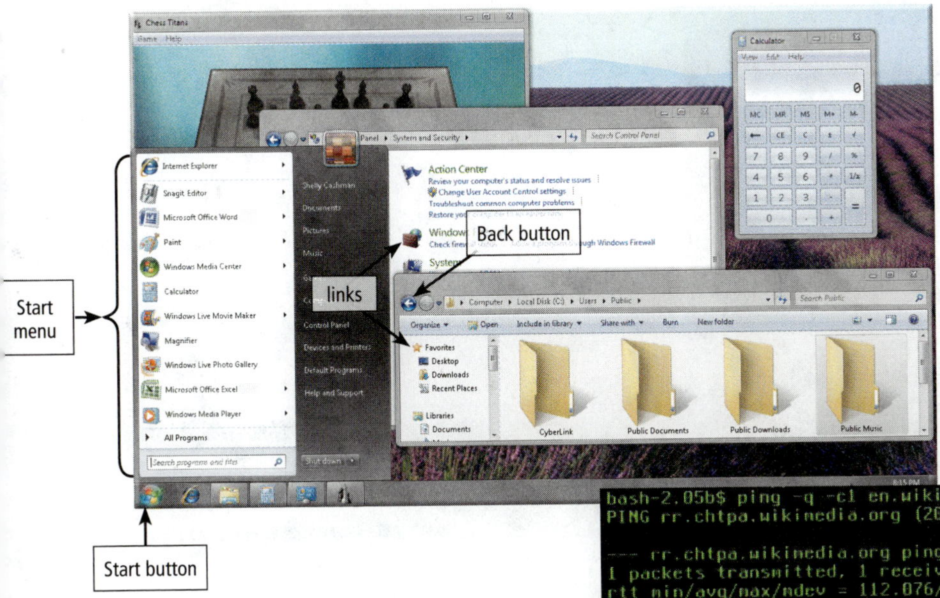

Figure 4-3b (command-line interface)

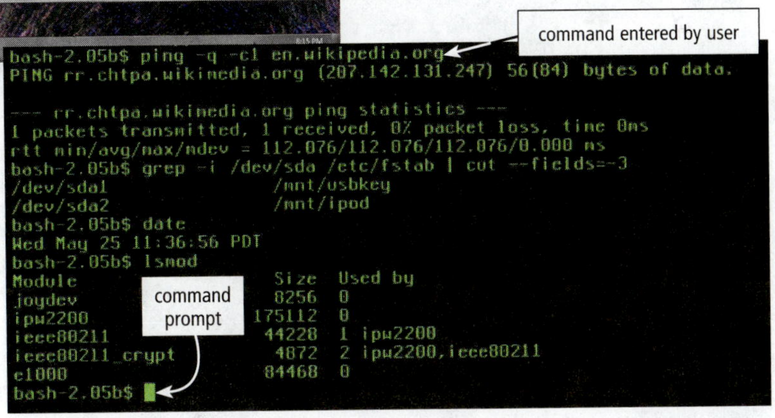

Figure 4-3 Examples of graphical user and command-line interfaces.

Managing Programs

Some operating systems support a single user and only one running program at a time. Others support thousands of users running multiple programs. How an operating system handles programs directly affects your productivity.

A single user/single tasking operating system allows only one user to run one program at a time. Smart phones and other mobile devices often use a single user/single tasking operating system.

A single user/multitasking operating system allows a single user to work on two or more programs that reside in memory at the same time. Users today typically run multiple programs concurrently. It is common to have an e-mail program and Web browser open at all times, while working with application programs such as word processing or graphics.

When a computer is running multiple programs concurrently, one program is in the foreground and the others are in the background. The one in the foreground is the active program, that is, the one you currently are using. The other programs running but not in use are in the background. In Figure 4-4, the Windows Live Movie Maker program is in the foreground, and three other programs are running in the background (Windows Media Player, Microsoft PowerPoint, and Chess Titans).

The foreground program typically is displayed on the desktop but the background programs often are hidden partially or completely behind the foreground program. You easily can switch between foreground and background programs. To make a program active (in the foreground) in Windows, click its program button on the taskbar. This causes the operating system to place all other programs in the background.

Figure 4-4 The foreground program, Windows Live Movie Maker, is displayed on the desktop. The other programs (Windows Media Player, Microsoft PowerPoint, and Chess Titans) are in the background.

A **multiuser** operating system enables two or more users to run programs simultaneously. Networks, servers, mainframes, and supercomputers allow hundreds to thousands of users to connect at the same time, and thus are multiuser.

A **multiprocessing** operating system supports two or more processors running programs at the same time. Multiprocessing involves the coordinated processing of programs by more than one processor. Multiprocessing increases a computer's processing speed.

Managing Memory

The purpose of **memory management** is to optimize the use of random access memory (RAM). RAM consists of one or more chips on the motherboard that hold items such as data and instructions while the processor interprets and executes them. The operating system allocates, or assigns, data and instructions to an area of memory while they are being processed. Then, it carefully monitors the contents of memory. Finally, the operating system releases these items from being monitored in memory when the processor no longer requires them.

Virtual memory is a concept in which the operating system allocates a portion of a storage medium, usually the hard disk, to function as additional RAM. As you interact with a program, part of it may be in physical RAM, while the rest of the program is on the hard disk as virtual memory. Because virtual memory is slower than RAM, users may notice the computer slowing down while it uses virtual memory.

The operating system uses an area of the hard disk for virtual memory, in which it swaps (exchanges) data, information, and instructions between memory and storage. The technique of swapping items between memory and storage is called paging. When an operating system spends much of its time paging, instead of executing application software, it is said to be thrashing. If application software, such as a Web browser, has stopped responding and the hard disk's LED blinks repeatedly, the operating system probably is thrashing.

Instead of using a hard disk as virtual memory, Windows users can increase the size of memory through **Windows ReadyBoost**, which can allocate available storage space on removable flash memory devices as additional memory cache. Users notice better performance with Windows ReadyBoost versus hard disk virtual memory because the operating system accesses a flash memory device, such as a USB flash drive or SD memory card, more quickly than it accesses a hard disk.

Coordinating Tasks

The operating system determines the order in which tasks are processed. A task, or job, is an operation the processor manages. Tasks include receiving data from an input device, processing instructions, sending information to an output device, and transferring items from storage to memory and from memory to storage.

A multiuser operating system does not always process tasks on a first-come, first-served basis. Sometimes, one user may have a higher priority than other users. In this case, the operating system adjusts the schedule of tasks.

Sometimes, a device already may be busy processing one task when it receives a second task. This occurs because the processor operates at a much faster rate of speed than peripheral devices. For example, if the processor sends five documents to a printer, the printer can print only one document at a time and store as many documents as its memory can handle.

While waiting for devices to become idle, the operating system places items in buffers. A **buffer** is a segment of memory or storage in which items are placed while waiting to be transferred from an input device or to an output device.

Spooling
For more information, visit the Microsoft Office and Concepts CourseMate Web site at www.cengagebrain.com, navigate to the Chapter 4 Web Link resource for this book, and then click Spooling.

The operating system commonly uses buffers with printed documents. This process, called **spooling**, sends documents to be printed to a buffer instead of sending them immediately to the printer. If a printer does not have its own internal memory or if its memory is full, the operating system's buffer holds the information waiting to print while the printer prints from the buffer at its own rate of speed. By spooling documents to a buffer, the processor can continue interpreting and executing instructions while the printer prints. This allows users to work on the computer for other tasks while a printer is printing. Multiple print jobs line up in a **queue** (pronounced Q) in the buffer. A program, called a print spooler, intercepts documents to be printed from the operating system and places them in the queue (Figure 4-5).

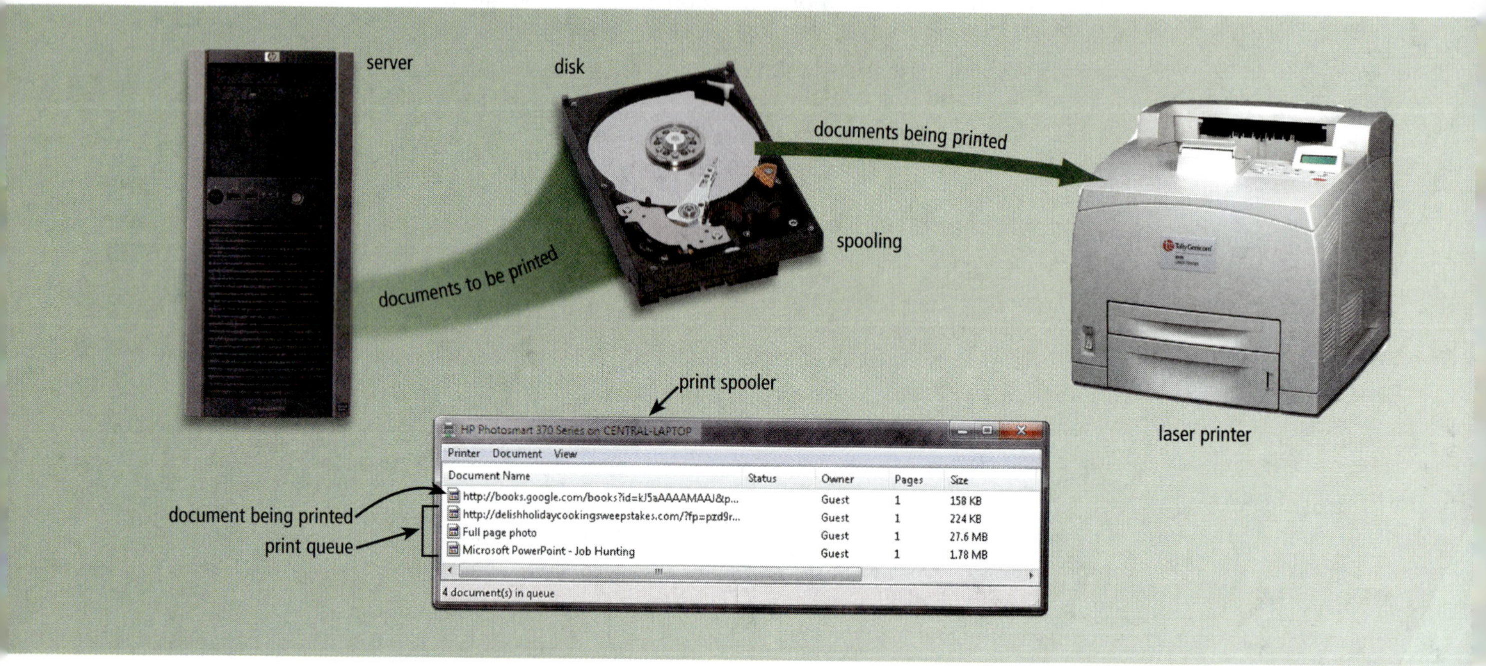

Figure 4-5 Spooling increases both processor and printer efficiency by placing documents to be printed in a buffer on disk before they are printed. This figure illustrates three documents in the queue with one document printing.

Configuring Devices

Plug and Play
For more information, visit the Microsoft Office and Concepts CourseMate Web site at www.cengagebrain.com, navigate to the Chapter 4 Web Link resource for this book, and then click Plug and Play.

A **driver** is a small program that tells the operating system how to communicate with a specific device. Each device on a computer, such as the mouse, keyboard, monitor, printer, and scanner, has its own specialized set of commands and thus requires its own specific driver. When you boot a computer, the operating system loads each device's driver.

If you attach a new device to a computer, such as a printer or scanner, its driver must be installed before you can use the device. Today, most devices and operating systems support Plug and Play. **Plug and Play** means the operating system automatically configures new devices as you install them. With Plug and Play, a user can plug in a device, turn on the computer, and then use the device without having to configure the system manually.

Establishing an Internet Connection

Operating systems typically provide a means to establish Internet connections. For example, Windows includes a Set Up a Connection or Network wizard that guides users through the process of setting up a connection between a computer and an Internet access provider (Figure 4-6).

Some operating systems also include a Web browser and an e-mail program, enabling you to begin using the Web and communicate with others as soon as you set up the Internet connection. Some also include utilities to protect computers from unauthorized intrusions and unwanted software such as viruses and spyware.

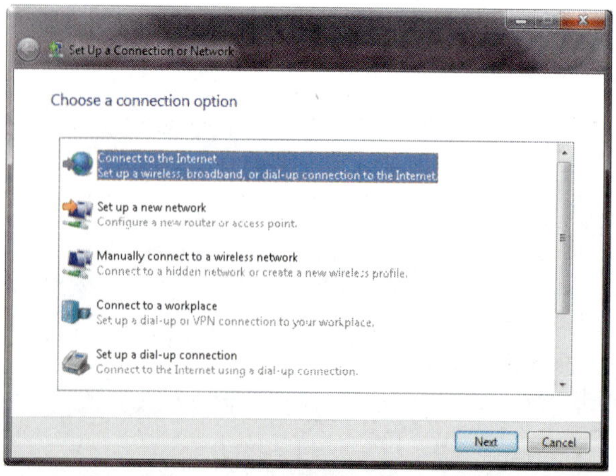

Figure 4-6 To connect to a network using Windows, click the Start button, click Control Panel, click Network and Internet, click Network and Sharing Center, and then click 'Set up a new connection or network' to open the window shown here.

Monitoring Performance

Operating systems typically contain a performance monitor. A **performance monitor** is a program that assesses and reports information about various computer resources and devices (shown in Figure 4-1 on pages 136 and 137).

The information in performance reports helps users and administrators identify a problem with resources so that they can try to resolve any problems. If a computer is running extremely slow, for example, the performance monitor may determine that the computer's memory is being used to its maximum. Thus, you might consider installing additional memory in the computer. Read Looking Ahead 4-1 for a look at a future type of health-based performance monitor.

LOOKING AHEAD 4-1

Contact Lenses Monitor Glaucoma

The future looks good for contact lenses that will help study and treat glaucoma. Biomedical engineers at the University of California – Davis are developing lenses that measure eye pressure and then flow if the readings are abnormal.

Glaucoma occurs when the fluid pressure inside the eye increases. This intraocular pressure can result in total blindness if the optic nerve, which sends messages from the eyes to the brain, is damaged. Doctors can measure the amount of pressure and then perform surgery to correct the blockage in the back of the eye that prevents the fluid from draining. As an alternative to the pressure measurement, the new contact lenses can perform the fluidic resistance evaluation for the drainage network of the eye, which prevents dangerously high levels in the early glaucomatous eyes.

Lasers, too, are expected to become part of a doctor's means of detecting glaucoma. A high-resolution laser can measure 28 million areas of the optic nerve, and then software can create a 3-D view of the eye and assess signs of the disease.

For more information, visit the Microsoft Office and Concepts CourseMate Web site at www.cengagebrain.com, navigate to the Chapter 4 Looking Ahead resource for this book, and then click Contact Lenses.

Providing File Management and Other Utilities

Operating systems often provide users with the capability of managing files, searching for files, viewing images, securing a computer from unauthorized access, uninstalling programs, cleaning up disks, defragmenting disks, diagnosing problems, backing up files and disks, and setting up screen savers. A later section in the chapter discusses these and other utilities in depth.

Updating Software Automatically

Many popular programs, including most operating systems, include an **automatic update** feature that automatically provides updates to the program. With an operating system, these updates can include fixes to program bugs (errors), enhancements to security, modifications to device drivers, access to new or expanded components such as desktop themes or games, and even updates to application software on the computer such as a Web browser or an e-mail program.

Many software makers provide free downloadable updates, sometimes called a **service pack**, to users who have registered and/or activated their software. With operating systems, the automatic update feature automatically alerts users when an update is available; further, it can be configured to download and install the update automatically. Users without an Internet connection usually can order the updates on an optical disc for a minimal shipping fee. To learn about keeping Windows up-to-date, complete the Learn How To 2 exercise on pages 164 and 165.

Controlling a Network

Some operating systems are designed to work with a server on a network. A **server operating system** is an operating system that organizes and coordinates how multiple users access and share resources on a network. Resources include hardware, software, data, and information. For example, a server operating system allows multiple users to share a printer, Internet access, files, and programs.

Some operating systems have network features built into them. In other cases, the server operating system is a set of programs separate from the operating system on the client computers that access the network. When not connected to the network, the client computers use their own operating system. When connected to the network, the server operating system may assume some of the operating system functions.

The network administrator, the person overseeing network operations, uses the server operating system to add and remove users, computers, and other devices to and from the network. The network administrator also uses the server operating system to install software and administer network security.

Administering Security

Computer and network administrators typically have an **administrator account** that enables them to access all files and programs on the computer or network, install programs, and specify settings that affect all users on a computer or network. Settings include creating user accounts and establishing permissions. These permissions define who can access certain resources and when they can access those resources.

For each user, the network administrator establishes a user account, which enables a user to access, or **log on** to, a computer or a network (Figure 4-7). Each user account typically consists of a user name and password. A **user name**, or **user ID**, is a unique combination of characters, such as letters of the alphabet or numbers, that identifies one specific user. Many users select a combination of their first and last names as their user name. A user named Henry Baker might choose H Baker as his user name.

A **password** is a private combination of characters associated with the user name that allows access to certain computer resources. Some operating systems allow the computer or network administrator to assign passwords to files and commands, restricting access to only authorized users.

To prevent unauthorized users from accessing computer resources, keep your password confidential. While users type a password, most computers hide the actual password characters by displaying some other characters, such as asterisks (*) or dots. After entering a user name and password, the operating system compares the user's entry with a list of authorized user names and passwords. If the entry matches the user name and password kept on file, the operating system grants the user access. If the entry does not match, the operating system denies access to the user.

The operating system records successful and unsuccessful logon attempts in a file. This allows the computer or network administrator to review who is using or attempting to use the computer. The administrators also use these files to monitor computer usage.

To protect sensitive data and information as it travels over a network, the operating system may encrypt it. Encryption is the process of encoding data and information into an unreadable form. Administrators can specify that data be encrypted as it travels over a network to prevent unauthorized users from reading the data. When an authorized user attempts to read the data, it automatically is decrypted, or converted back into a readable form.

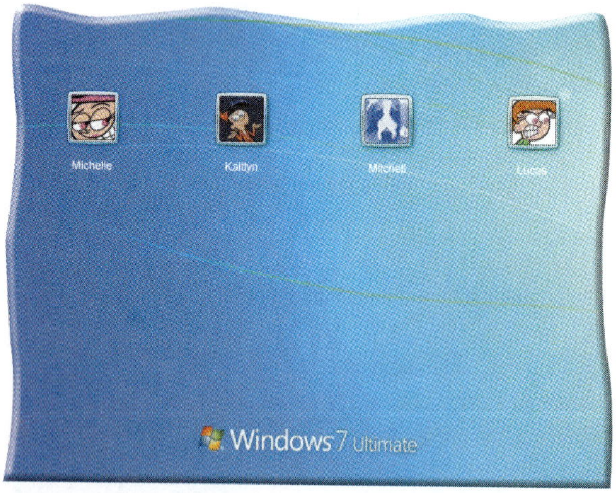

Figure 4-7 Most multiuser operating systems allow each user to log on, which is the process of entering a user name and a password into the computer.

FAQ 4-1

What are the guidelines for selecting a good password?

Choose a password that is easy to remember, and that no one could guess. Do not use any part of your first or last name, your spouse's or child's name, telephone number, street address, license plate number, Social Security number, birthday, and so on. Be sure your password is at least eight characters long, mixed with uppercase and lowercase letters, numbers, and special characters. You also should avoid using single-word passwords that are found in the dictionary. Security experts also recommend using a passphrase, which is similar to a password, but comprised of several words separated by spaces.

For more information, visit the Microsoft Office and Concepts CourseMate Web site at www.cengagebrain.com, navigate to the Chapter 4 FAQ resource for this book, and then click Passwords.

QUIZ YOURSELF 4-1

Instructions: Find the true statement below. Then, rewrite the remaining false statements so that they are true.

1. A buffer is a small program that tells the operating system how to communicate with a specific device.
2. A warm boot is the process of using the operating system to restart a computer.
3. A password is a public combination of characters associated with the user name that allows access to certain computer resources.
4. The program you currently are using is in the background, and the other programs running but not in use are in the foreground.
5. Two types of system software are operating systems and application programs.

Quiz Yourself Online: To further check your knowledge of pages 136 through 144, visit the Microsoft Office and Concepts CourseMate Web site at www.cengagebrain.com, navigate to the Chapter 4 Quiz Yourself resource for this book, and then click Objectives 1 – 2.

Types of Operating Systems

When you purchase a new computer or mobile device, it typically has an operating system preinstalled. As new versions of the operating system are released, users upgrade their existing computers and mobile devices to incorporate features of the new version. Purchasing an operating system upgrade usually costs less than purchasing the entire operating system.

New versions of an operating system usually are backward compatible. That is, they recognize and work with application software written for an earlier version of the operating system (or platform). By contrast, the application software may or may not be upward compatible, meaning it may or may not run on new versions of the operating system.

The three basic categories of operating systems that exist today are stand-alone, server, and embedded. The table in Figure 4-8 lists names of operating systems in each category. The following pages discuss a variety of operating systems.

Categories of Operating Systems

Category	Operating System Name
Stand-alone	• DOS • Early Windows versions (Windows 3.x, Windows 95, Windows NT Workstation, Windows 98, Windows 2000 Professional, Windows Millennium Edition, Windows XP, Windows Vista) • Windows 7 • Mac OS X • UNIX • Linux
Server	• Early Windows Server versions (Windows NT Server, Windows 2000 Server, Windows Server 2003) • Windows Server 2008 • UNIX • Linux • Solaris • NetWare
Embedded	• Windows Embedded CE • Windows Phone 7 • Palm OS • iPhone OS • BlackBerry • Google Android • Embedded Linux • Symbian OS

Figure 4-8 Examples of stand-alone, server, and embedded operating systems. Some stand-alone operating systems include the capability of configuring small home or office networks.

FAQ 4-2

Which operating systems have the most market share?

The Windows operating system family currently dominates the operating system market with more than 93 percent market share. The Mac operating system is in second place with nearly 5 percent market share. The chart to the right illustrates the market share for various operating systems.

For more information, visit the Microsoft Office and Concepts CourseMate Web site at www.cengagebrain.com, navigate to the Chapter 4 FAQ resource for this book, and then click Operating System Market Share.

Operating System Market Share

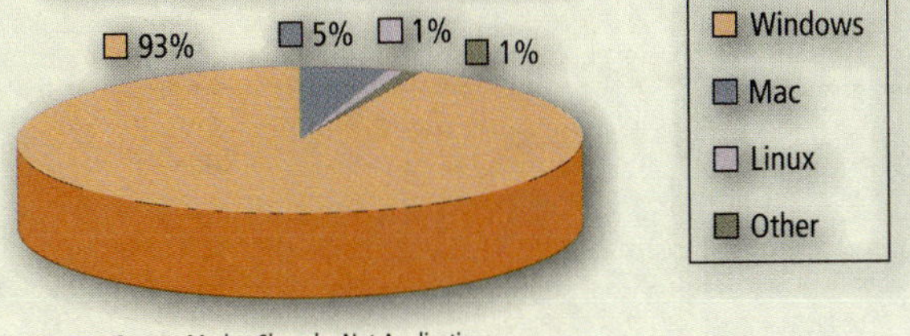

Source: Market Share by Net Applications

Stand-Alone Operating Systems

A **stand-alone operating system** is a complete operating system that works on a desktop computer, notebook computer, or mobile computing device. Some stand-alone operating systems are called client operating systems because they also work in conjunction with a server operating system. Client operating systems can operate with or without a network. Other stand-alone operating systems include networking capabilities, allowing the home and small business user to set up a small network. Examples of currently used stand-alone operating systems are Windows 7, Mac OS X, UNIX, and Linux.

Windows 7

In the mid-1980s, Microsoft developed its first version of Windows, which provided a graphical user interface (GUI). Since then, Microsoft continually has updated its Windows operating system, incorporating innovative features and functions with each new version. **Windows 7** is Microsoft's fastest, most efficient operating system to date, offering quicker program start up, built-in diagnostics, automatic recovery, improved security, enhanced searching and organizing capabilities, and an easy-to-use interface (Figure 4-9).

Most users choose one of these Windows 7 editions: Windows 7 Starter, Windows 7 Home Premium, Windows 7 Ultimate, or Windows 7 Professional.

- Windows 7 Starter, designed for netbooks and other small notebook computers, uses the Windows 7 Basic interface and allows users easily to search for files, connect to printers and devices, browse the Internet, join home networks, and connect to wireless networks. This edition of Windows typically is preinstalled on new computers and not available for purchase in retail stores.
- Windows 7 Home Premium, which includes all the capabilities of Windows 7 Starter, also includes Windows Aero with its Aero Flip 3D feature and provides tools to create and edit high-definition movies, record and watch television shows, connect to a game console, and read from and write on Blu-ray Discs.
- Windows 7 Ultimate, which includes all features of Windows 7 Home Premium, provides additional features designed to keep your files secure and support for 35 languages.
- With Windows 7 Professional, users in all sizes of businesses are provided a secure operating environment that uses Windows Aero where they easily can search for files, protect their computers from unauthorized intruders and unwanted programs, use improved backup technologies, securely connect to Wi-Fi networks, quickly view messages on a powered-off, specially equipped notebook computer, easily share documents and collaborate with other users, and watch and record live television.

Windows 7

For more information, visit the Microsoft Office and Concepts CourseMate Web site at www.cengagebrain.com, navigate to the Chapter 4 Web Link resource for this book, and then click Windows 7.

Windows 7 adapts to the hardware configuration on which it is installed. Thus, two users with the same edition of Windows 7 may experience different functionality and interfaces.

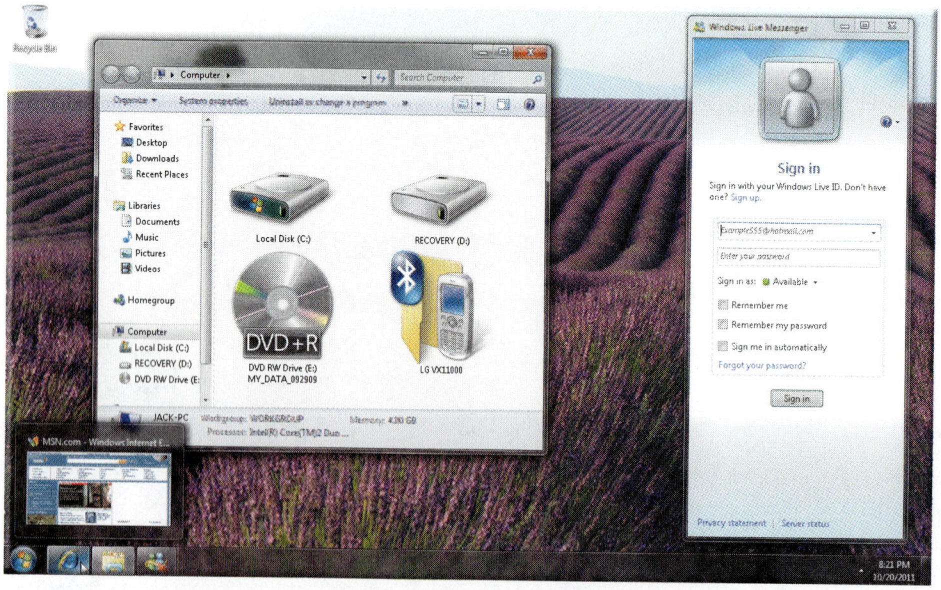

Figure 4-9 Windows 7 has a new interface, easier navigation and searching techniques, and improved security.

Mac OS X

Since it was released with Macintosh computers in 1984, Apple's **Macintosh operating system** has set the standard for operating system ease of use and has been the model for most of the new GUIs developed for non-Macintosh systems. The latest version, **Mac OS X**, is a multitasking operating system available only for computers manufactured by Apple (Figure 4-10).

Mac OS X

For more information, visit the Microsoft Office and Concepts CourseMate Web site at www.cengagebrain.com, navigate to the Chapter 4 Web Link resource for this book, and then click Mac OS X.

Figure 4-10 Mac OS X is the operating system used with Apple Macintosh computers.

UNIX

UNIX (pronounced YOU-nix) is a multitasking operating system. Several versions of this operating system exist, each slightly different. Although some versions of UNIX have a command-line interface, most versions of UNIX offer a graphical user interface (Figure 4-11). Today, a version of UNIX is available for most computers of all sizes. Power users often work with UNIX because of its flexibility and power.

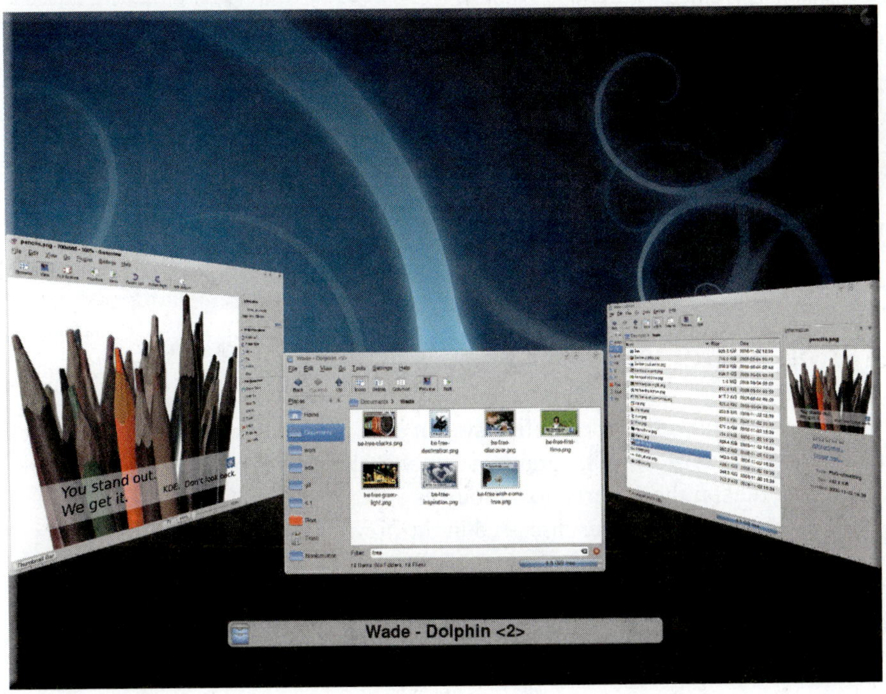

Figure 4-11 Many versions of UNIX have a graphical user interface.

Linux

For more information, visit the Microsoft Office and Concepts CourseMate Web site at www.cengagebrain.com, navigate to the Chapter 4 Web Link resource for this book, and then click Linux.

Linux

Linux is one of the faster growing operating systems. **Linux** (pronounced LINN-uks), introduced in 1991, is a popular, multitasking UNIX-type operating system. In addition to the basic operating system, Linux also includes many free programming languages and utility programs. Linux is not proprietary software like the operating systems discussed thus far. Instead, Linux is open source software, which means its code is available to the public for use, modification, and redistribution. Read Ethics & Issues 4-1 for a related discussion.

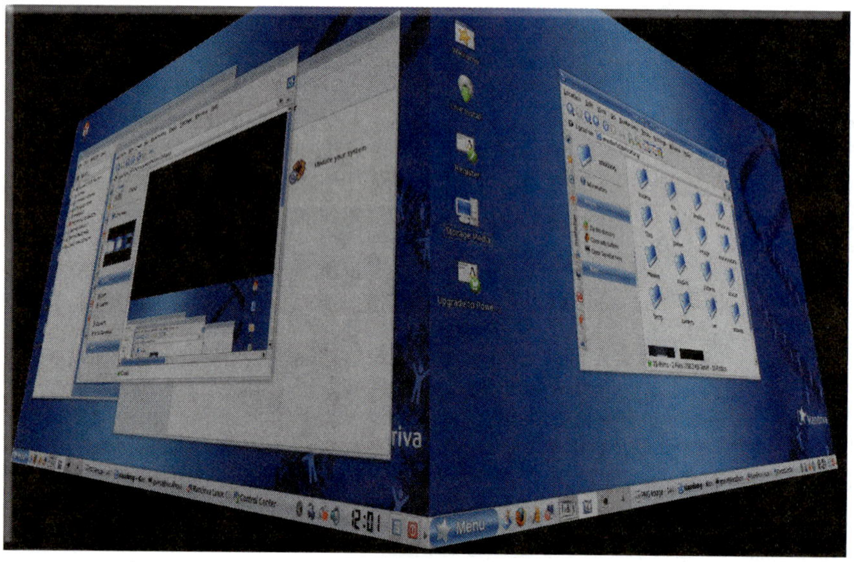

Figure 4-12 This distribution of Linux has a graphical user interface.

Linux is available in a variety of forms, known as distributions. Some distributions of Linux are command-line. Others are GUI (Figure 4-12). Users obtain Linux in a variety of ways. Some people download it free from the Web. Others purchase it from vendors, who bundle their own software with the operating system. Linux optical discs are included in many Linux books and also are available for purchase from vendors. For purchasers of new personal computers, some retailers such as Dell will preinstall Linux on the hard disk on request. If you want to preview the Linux operating system, you can obtain a Live CD or Live USB.

ETHICS & ISSUES 4-1

Closed Source vs. Open Source Operating Systems

One of the features that make Linux different from other operating systems is that Linux is open source and its source code, along with any changes, remains public. Often, when closed source operating system developers refuse to share some or all of the operating system code, third-party software developers become hindered when developing application software for the operating system. Supporters of open source maintain that source code should be open to the public so that it can be scrutinized, corrected, and enhanced. In light of concerns about security and fears of possible virus problems, however, some people are not sure open source software is a good idea. Besides, they argue, companies and programmers should be able to control, and profit from, the operating systems they create. On the other hand, open source software can be scrutinized for errors by a much larger group of people and changes can be made immediately, resulting in better software.

Are open source operating systems a good idea? Why or why not? How can the concerns about open source software be addressed? What are the advantages and disadvantages of open versus closed source operating systems? Does the open source model lead to better software?

Ethics & Issues

For the complete text of the Ethics & Issues boxes found in this chapter, visit the Microsoft Office and Concepts CourseMate Web site at www.cengagebrain.com and then navigate to the Chapter 4 Ethics & Issues resource for this book.

Server Operating Systems

As discussed earlier in this chapter, a server operating system is an operating system that is designed specifically to support a network. A server operating system typically resides on a server. The client computers on the network rely on the server(s) for resources.

Many of the stand-alone operating systems discussed in the previous section function as clients and work in conjunction with a server operating system. Some of these stand-alone operating systems do include networking capability; however, server operating systems are designed specifically to support all sizes of networks, including medium- to large-sized businesses and Web servers.

Following are examples of server operating systems:

- Windows Server 2008 is an upgrade to Windows Server 2003.
- UNIX and Linux often are called multipurpose operating systems because they are both stand-alone and server operating systems.
- Solaris, a version of UNIX developed by Sun Microsystems, is a server operating system designed specifically for e-commerce applications.
- Novell's NetWare is a server operating system designed for client/server networks.

Embedded Operating Systems

The operating system on most mobile devices and many consumer electronics, called an **embedded operating system**, resides on a ROM chip. Popular embedded operating systems include Windows Embedded CE, Windows Phone 7, Palm OS, iPhone OS, BlackBerry, Google Android, embedded Linux, and Symbian OS.

- Windows Embedded CE is a scaled-down Windows operating system designed for use on communications, entertainment, and computing devices with limited functionality. Examples of devices that use Windows Embedded CE include VoIP telephones, digital cameras, point-of-sale terminals, automated teller machines, digital photo frames, fuel pumps, handheld navigation devices, portable media players, ticket machines, and computerized sewing machines.
- Windows Phone 7, which is a successor to Windows Mobile, works on specific types of smart phones. With the Windows Phone 7 operating system and a compatible device, users have access to the basic PIM (personal information manager) functions such as contact lists, schedules, tasks, calendars, and notes. These devices also can check e-mail, browse the Web, listen to music, take pictures or record video, watch a video, send and receive text messages and instant messages, record a voice message, manage finances, view a map, read an e-book, or play a game.
- Palm OS, a competing operating system to Windows Phone 7, runs on smart phones and PDAs. With Palm OS and a compatible device, users manage schedules and contacts, phone messages, notes, tasks and address lists, and appointments. Many Palm OS devices allow users to connect wirelessly to the Internet; browse the Web; send and receive e-mail messages, text messages, and instant messages; listen to music; record voice messages; and view digital photos.
- iPhone OS is an operating system for the iPhone and iPod touch. With finger motions, users can manage contacts and notes, send and receive e-mail and text messages, take pictures, record videos, record voice messages, view a compass, connect to the Internet wirelessly and browse the Web, check stocks, access maps and obtain directions, listen to music, watch movies and videos, and display photos. iPhone OS devices also provide Wi-Fi access to the iTunes Music Store.
- The BlackBerry operating system runs on handheld devices supplied by RIM (Research In Motion), shown in Figure 4-13. BlackBerry devices provide PIM, phone, and wireless capabilities such as sending e-mail messages, text messages, and instant messages; connecting to the Internet and browsing the Web; and accessing Bluetooth devices. Some also allow you to take pictures, play music, and access maps and directions.
- Google Android is an operating system designed by Google for mobile devices. Used on more than 20 different types of mobile devices, Google Android allows programmers to design programs specifically for devices supporting this operating system. Google Android contains features such as access to e-mail accounts, an alarm clock, video capture, access to Google Apps, Wi-Fi access, and easy Web browsing.
- Embedded Linux is a scaled-down Linux operating system designed for smart phones, PDAs, portable media players, Internet telephones, and many other types of devices and computers requiring an embedded operating system. Devices with embedded Linux offer calendar and address book and other PIM functions, touch screens, and handwriting recognition.
- Symbian OS is an open source multitasking operating system designed for smart phones. Users enter data by pressing keys on the keypad or keyboard, touching the screen, and writing on the screen with a stylus.

Figure 4-13 A smart phone that uses the BlackBerry operating system.

QUIZ YOURSELF 4-2

Instructions: Find the true statement below. Then, rewrite the remaining false statements so that they are true.

1. Pocket PCs use Palm OS as their operating system.
2. Examples of embedded operating systems include Windows Server 2008, UNIX, Linux, Solaris, and NetWare.
3. Windows 7 Starter uses Windows Aero.
4. Mac OS X is a multitasking operating system available only for computers manufactured by Apple.
5. Aero Flip 3D is a UNIX-type operating system that is open source software.

Quiz Yourself Online: To further check your knowledge of pages 145 through 149, visit the Microsoft Office and Concepts CourseMate Web site at www.cengagebrain.com, navigate to the Chapter 4 Quiz Yourself resource for this book, and then click Objectives 3 – 5.

Utility Programs

A **utility program**, also called a **utility**, is a type of system software that allows a user to perform maintenance-type tasks, usually related to managing a computer, its devices, or its programs. Most operating systems include several built-in utility programs (Figure 4-14). Users often buy stand-alone utilities, however, because they offer improvements over those included with the operating system.

Functions provided by utility programs include the following: managing files, searching for files, uninstalling programs, viewing images, cleaning up disks, defragmenting disks, backing up files and disks, setting up screen savers, securing a computer from unauthorized access, protecting against viruses, removing spyware and adware, filtering Internet content, compressing files, playing media files, burning optical discs, and maintaining a personal computer. The following sections briefly discuss each of these utilities. Read Innovative Computing 4-1 to find out about utility programs that can help you recover deleted files.

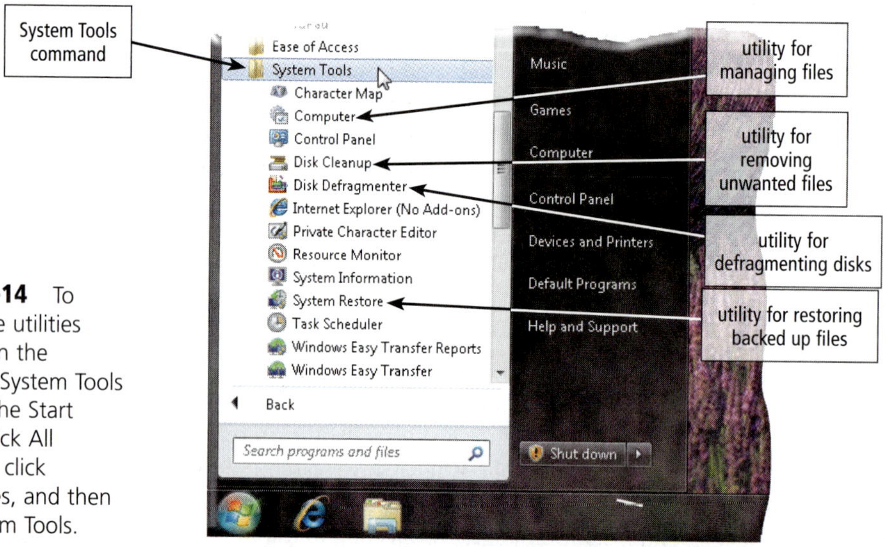

Figure 4-14 To display the utilities available in the Windows System Tools list, click the Start button, click All Programs, click Accessories, and then click System Tools.

INNOVATIVE COMPUTING 4-1

Utility Programs Locate Deleted Files

If you delete a file mistakenly from a USB flash drive, removable flash memory device, or hard disk, you easily can recover that erased file with utility programs. A few of the more popular utility programs have names that explain their purpose: Recuva, Recover My Files, FreeUndelete, FileMakerRecovery, R-Studio, and Recovery Toolbox. Most can be downloaded from the Web, often free of charge.

Data recovery experts offer advice on actions to take immediately when you realize you have erased files, even if you have emptied the Recycle Bin. Although the file name does not appear in the list of files on that storage medium, the file actually remains intact on the storage medium. The computer marks the space on the disk as free so that another file can overwrite the contents of the deleted file. As long as you do not save any file, no matter how small, the utility program generally can locate the marked space and then retrieve the contents of the file.

For more information, visit the Microsoft Office and Concepts CourseMate Web site at www.cengagebrain.com, navigate to the Chapter 4 Innovative Computing resource for this book, and then click Recovering Deleted Files.

File Manager

A **file manager** is a utility that performs functions related to file management. Some of the file management functions that a file manager performs are displaying a list of files on a storage medium (Figure 4-15); organizing files in folders; and copying, renaming, deleting, moving, and sorting files. A **folder** is a specific named location on a storage medium that contains related documents. Operating systems typically include a file manager.

Figure 4-15 Windows includes file managers that allow you to view documents, photos, and music. In this case, thumbnails of photos are displayed.

Search Utility

A **search utility** is a program that attempts to locate a file on your computer based on criteria you specify (Figure 4-16). The criteria could be a word or words contained in a file, date the file was created or modified, size of the file, location of the file, file name, author/artist, and other similar properties. Search utilities can look through documents, photos, music, and other files. Operating systems typically include a built-in search utility.

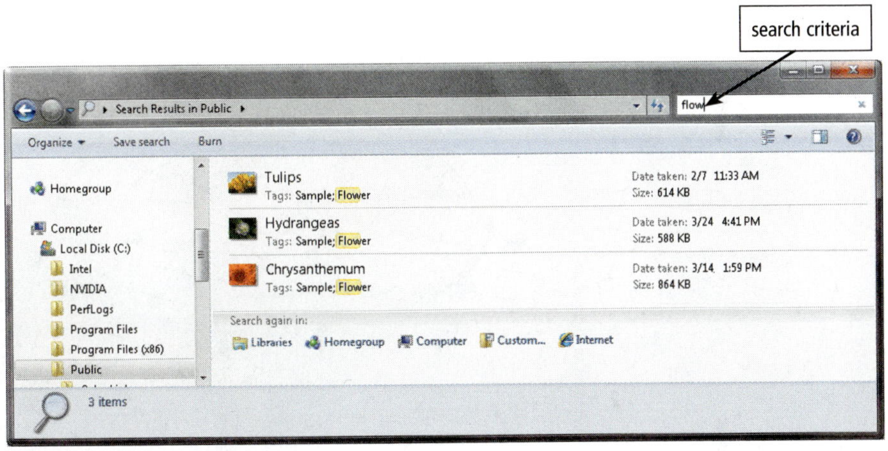

Figure 4-16 This search displays files whose name or contents contain the text, flow.

Uninstaller

An **uninstaller** is a utility that removes a program, as well as any associated entries in the system files. When you install a program, the operating system records the information it uses to run the software in the system files. The uninstaller deletes files and folders from the hard disk, as well as removes program entries from the system files.

Image Viewer

An **image viewer** is a utility that allows users to display, copy, and print the contents of a graphics file. With an image viewer, users can see images without having to open them in a paint or image editing program. Most operating systems include an image viewer. Windows image viewer is called Windows Photo Viewer (Figure 4-17).

Figure 4-17 Windows Photo Viewer allows users to see the contents of a photo file.

Disk Cleanup

A **disk cleanup** utility searches for and removes unnecessary files. Unnecessary files may include downloaded program files, temporary Internet files, deleted files, and unused program files. Operating systems, such as Windows, include a disk scanner utility.

Disk Defragmenter

A **disk defragmenter** is a utility that reorganizes the files and unused space on a computer's hard disk so that the operating system accesses data more quickly and programs run faster. When an operating system stores data on a disk, it places the data in the first available sector on the disk. It attempts to place data in sectors that are contiguous (next to each other), but this is not always possible. When the contents of a file are scattered across two or more noncontiguous sectors, the file is fragmented.

Fragmentation slows down disk access and thus the performance of the entire computer. **Defragmenting** the disk, or reorganizing it so that the files are stored in contiguous sectors, solves this problem (Figure 4-18). Operating systems usually include a disk defragmenter. Windows Disk Defragmenter is available in the System Tools list.

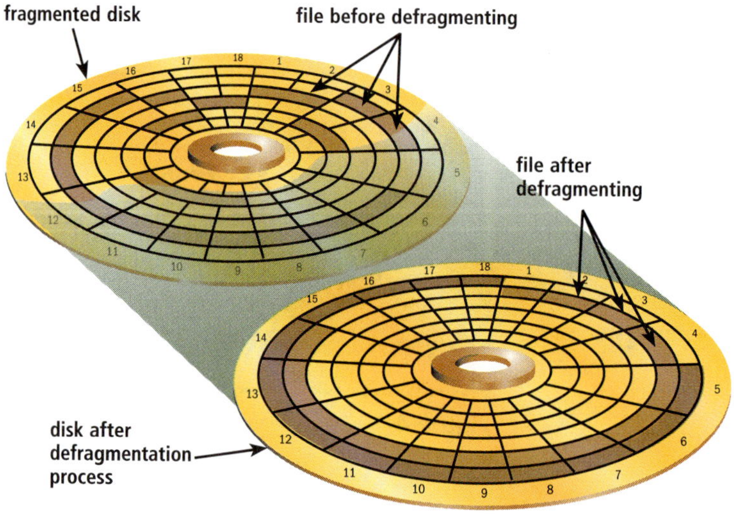

Figure 4-18 A fragmented disk has many files stored in noncontiguous sectors. Defragmenting reorganizes the files so that they are located in contiguous sectors, which speeds access time.

Backup and Restore Utilities

A **backup utility** allows users to copy, or back up, selected files or an entire hard disk to another storage medium such as another hard disk, optical disc, USB flash drive, or tape. During the backup process, the backup utility monitors progress and alerts you if it needs additional media, such as another disc. Many backup programs compress, or shrink the size of, files during the backup process. By compressing the files, the backup program requires less storage space for the backup files than for the original files.

Because they are compressed, you usually cannot use backup files in their backed up form. In the event you need to use a backup file, a **restore utility** reverses the process and returns backed up files to their original form. Backup utilities work with a restore utility.

You should back up files and disks regularly in the event your originals are lost, damaged, or destroyed. Operating systems include backup and restore utilities. Instead of backing up to a local disk storage device, some users opt to use cloud storage to back up their files. Cloud storage is a service on the Web that provides storage to computer users, usually for free or for a minimal monthly fee.

Screen Saver

A **screen saver** is a utility that causes a display device's screen to show a moving image or blank screen if no keyboard or mouse activity occurs for a specified time. When you press a key on the keyboard or move the mouse, the screen saver disappears and the screen returns to the previous state.

Screen savers originally were developed to prevent a problem called ghosting, in which images could be etched permanently on a monitor's screen. Although ghosting is not as severe of a problem with today's displays, manufacturers continue to recommend that users install screen savers for this reason. Screen savers also are popular for security, business, and entertainment purposes. To secure a computer, users configure their screen saver to require a password to deactivate. In addition to those included with the operating system, many screen savers are available for a minimal fee in stores and on the Web.

Personal Firewall

A **personal firewall** is a utility that detects and protects a personal computer from unauthorized intrusions. Personal firewalls constantly monitor all transmissions to and from a computer.

When connected to the Internet, your computer is vulnerable to attacks from a hacker. A hacker is someone who tries to access a computer or network illegally. Users with broadband Internet connections, such as through DSL and cable Internet service, are even more susceptible than those with dial-up access because the Internet connection always is on.

Operating systems often include a personal firewall. Windows automatically enables its built-in personal firewall, called Windows Firewall, upon installation of the operating system. If your operating system does not include a personal firewall or you want additional protection, you can purchase a stand-alone personal firewall utility (Figure 4-19) or a hardware firewall, which is a device such as a router that has a built-in firewall.

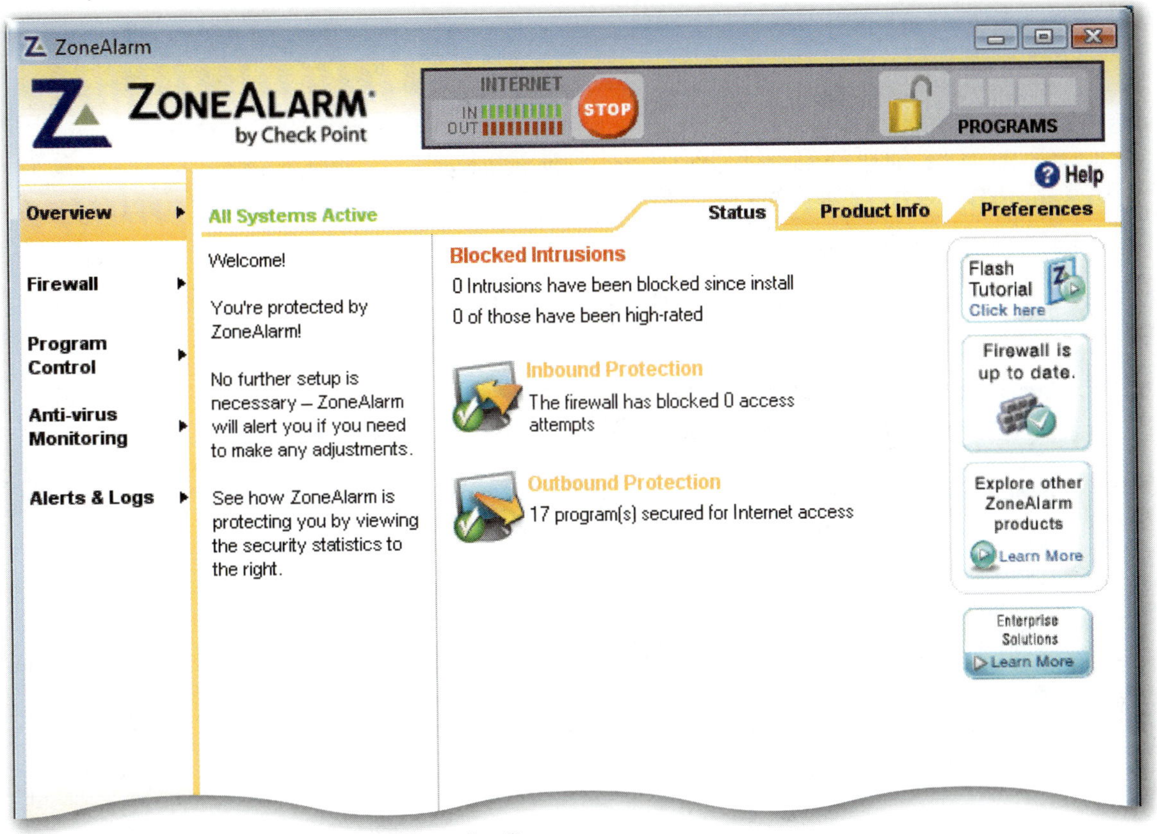

Figure 4-19 A stand-alone personal firewall utility.

Antivirus Programs

The term, computer **virus**, describes a potentially damaging computer program that affects, or infects, a computer negatively by altering the way the computer works without the user's knowledge or permission. Once the virus is in a computer, it can spread throughout and may damage your files and operating system.

Computer viruses do not generate by chance. The programmer of a virus, known as a virus author, intentionally writes a virus program. Some virus authors find writing viruses a challenge. Others write them to cause destruction. Writing a virus program usually requires significant programming skills.

Some viruses are harmless pranks that simply freeze a computer temporarily or display sounds or messages. The Music Bug virus, for example, instructs the computer to play a few chords of music. Other viruses destroy or corrupt data stored on the hard disk of the infected computer. If you notice any unusual changes in your computer's performance, it may be infected with a virus (Figure 4-20).

A **worm** copies itself repeatedly, for example, in memory or over a network, using up system resources and possibly shutting the system down. A **Trojan horse** hides within or looks like a legitimate program such as a screen saver. A certain condition or action usually triggers the Trojan horse. Unlike a virus or worm, a Trojan horse does not replicate itself to other computers. Currently, more than one million known threats to your computer exist.

To protect a computer from virus attacks, users should install an antivirus program and update it frequently. An **antivirus program** protects a computer against viruses by identifying and removing any computer viruses found in memory, on storage media, or on incoming files (Figure 4-21). Most antivirus programs also protect against worms and Trojan horses. When you purchase a new computer, it often includes antivirus software.

Three more popular antivirus programs are McAfee VirusScan, Norton AntiVirus, and Windows Live OneCare, most of which also contains spyware removers, Internet filters, and other utilities. As an alternative to purchasing these products on disc, both McAfee and Norton offer Web-based antivirus programs.

? FAQ 4-3

What steps should I take to prevent virus infections on my computer?

Set up the antivirus program to scan on a regular basis. Never open an e-mail attachment unless you are expecting the attachment and it is from a trusted source. Set macro security in programs such as word processing and spreadsheet so that you can enable or disable macros. Write-protect your recovery disk. Back up files regularly.

For more information, visit the Microsoft Office and Concepts CourseMate Web site at www.cengagebrain.com, navigate to the Chapter 4 FAQ resource for this book, and then click Virus Infections.

Signs of Virus Infection
• An unusual message or image is displayed on the computer screen
• An unusual sound or music plays randomly
• The available memory is less than what should be available
• A program or file suddenly is missing
• An unknown program or file mysteriously appears
• The size of a file changes without explanation
• A file becomes corrupted
• A program or file does not work properly
• System properties change
• The computer operates much slower than usual

Figure 4-20 Viruses attack computers in a variety of ways. This list indicates some of the more common signs of virus infection.

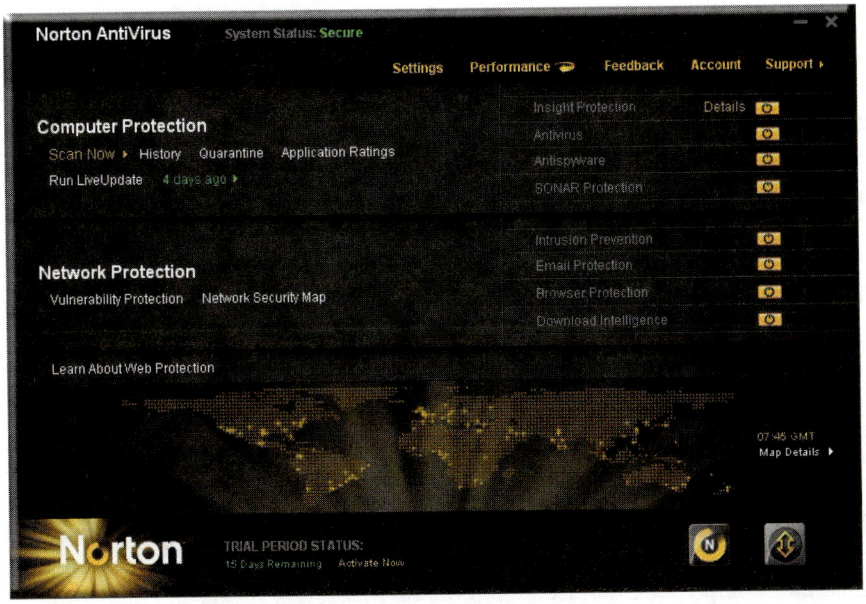

Figure 4-21 An antivirus program scans memory, disks, and incoming e-mail messages and attachments for viruses and attempts to remove any viruses it finds.

Spyware and Adware Removers

Spyware is a program placed on a computer without the user's knowledge that secretly collects information about the user, often related to Web browsing habits. The spyware program communicates information it collects to some outside source while you are online. Adware is a program that displays an online advertisement in a banner or pop-up window on Web pages, e-mail, or other Internet services. Sometimes, spyware is hidden in adware.

A **spyware remover** is a program that detects and deletes spyware, and similar programs. An **adware remover** is a program that detects and deletes adware. Most spyware and adware removers cost less than $50; some are available on the Web at no cost. Some operating systems include spyware and adware removers.

Internet Filters

Filters are programs that remove or block certain items from being displayed. Four widely used Internet filters are anti-spam programs, Web filters, phishing filters, and pop-up blockers.

Anti-Spam Programs **Spam** is an unsolicited e-mail message or newsgroup posting sent to many recipients or newsgroups at once. Spam is Internet junk mail. An **anti-spam program** is a filtering program that attempts to remove spam before it reaches your inbox. Internet access providers often filter spam as a service for their subscribers.

? FAQ 4-4

Where does spam originate?

Research indicates that spam originates from various countries throughout the world. Symantec Corporation found that in a 30-day period, the United States was responsible for more spam than any other country. The chart to the right illustrates the countries responsible for the most spam worldwide.

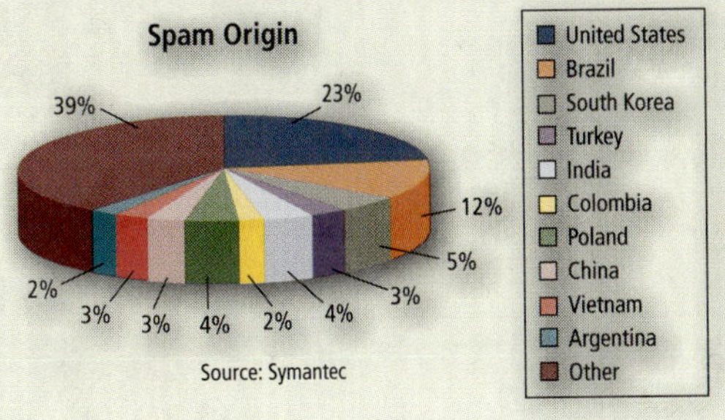

For more information, visit the Microsoft Office and Concepts CourseMate Web site at www.cengagebrain.com, navigate to the Chapter 4 FAQ resource for this book, and then click Spam.

Web Filters **Web filtering software** is a program that restricts access to certain material on the Web. Some restrict access to specific Web sites; others filter sites that use certain words or phrases. Many businesses use Web filtering software to limit employee's Web access. Some schools, libraries, and parents use this software to restrict access to minors. Windows 7 contains parental controls, which allow parents to record and control the types of content their children can access on the Internet.

Phishing Filters **Phishing** is a scam in which a perpetrator attempts to obtain your personal and/or financial information. A **phishing filter** is a program that warns or blocks you from potentially fraudulent or suspicious Web sites. Some Web browsers include phishing filters.

Pop-Up Blockers A pop-up ad is an Internet advertisement that suddenly appears in a new window in the foreground of a Web page displayed in your browser. A **pop-up blocker** is a filtering program that stops pop-up ads from displaying on Web pages. Many Web browsers include a pop-up blocker. You also can download pop-up blockers from the Web at no cost.

File Compression

A **file compression utility** shrinks the size of a file(s). A compressed file takes up less storage space than the original file. Compressing files frees up room on the storage media and improves system performance. Attaching a compressed file to an e-mail message, for example, reduces the time needed for file transmission. Uploading and downloading compressed files to and from the Internet reduces the file transmission time.

WinZip
For more information, visit the Microsoft Office and Concepts CourseMate Web site at www.cengagebrain.com, navigate to the Chapter 4 Web Link resource for this book, and then click WinZip.

Compressed files sometimes are called **zipped files**. When you receive or download a compressed file, you must uncompress it. To **uncompress**, or unzip, a file, you restore it to its original form. Some operating systems such as Windows include file compression and uncompression capabilities. Two popular stand-alone file compression utilities are PKZIP and WinZip.

Media Player

A **media player** is a program that allows you to view images and animation, listen to audio, and watch video files on your computer (Figure 4-22). Media players may also include the capability to organize media files, convert them to different formats, connect to and purchase media from an online media store, download podcasts and vodcasts, burn audio CDs, and transfer media to portable media players. Windows includes Windows Media Player. Three other popular media players are iTunes, RealPlayer, and Rhapsody. Read Ethics & Issues 4-2 for a related discussion.

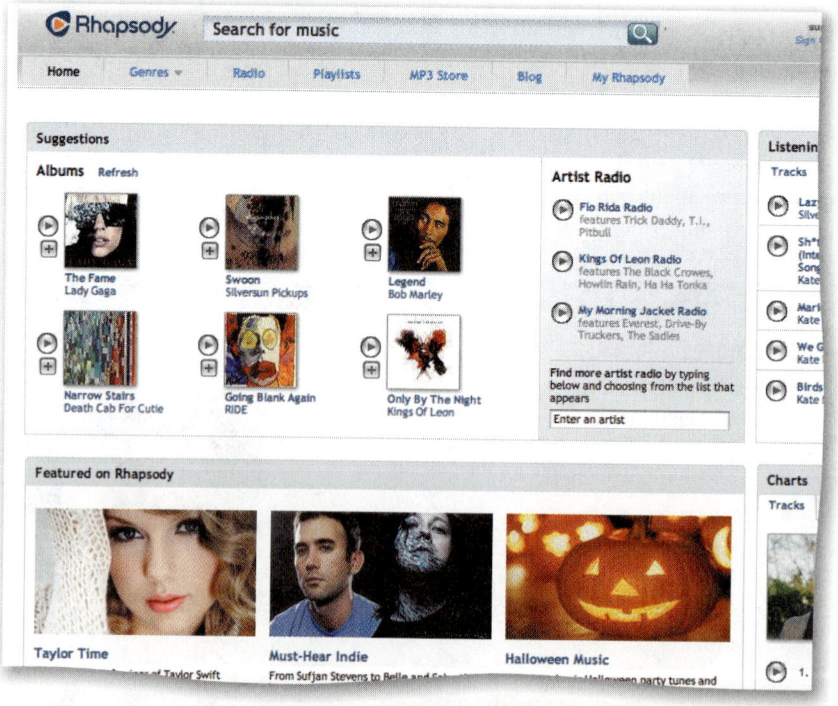

Figure 4-22
A popular media player.

ETHICS & ISSUES 4-2

Should the Government Tax Media Downloads?

When you purchase a DVD or Blu-ray Disc that contains a season or two of your favorite television show, chances are that you also pay a state and/or local sales tax. If you purchase and download the same material online in a digital format, however, chances are that you do not pay a sales tax. Some government taxing bodies seek to change that discrepancy. Two main reasons for the pressure to tax include: state and local governments feeling the pinch of lost revenue to legally downloaded digital content because consumers purchase less taxable, physical media; and pressure from the media industry to recoup lost sales due to illegally downloaded digital content. Some governments go as far as funneling collected taxes directly to the multimedia industry as compensation for illegally downloaded content that occurs in a region. Critics of the new taxes claim that government should not tax the greenest form of media purchases. Digitally downloaded content eliminates packaging, optical discs, trips to the store, and use of delivery vehicles. Critics also claim that governments single out multimedia content due to pressure from the multimedia industry. For example, some governments tax the purchase of newspapers, magazines and books, but often the same content is sold online and is not taxed. Typically, government taxing bodies tax goods, but not food and services.

Should the government tax media downloads, such as music, video, e-books, newspaper articles, and magazine articles? Why or why not? Should digital content delivery be considered a service rather than a good by taxing bodies? Why?

Disc Burning

Disc burning software writes text, graphics, audio, and video files on a recordable or rewritable CD, DVD, or Blu-ray Disc. This software enables the home user easily to back up contents of their hard disk on an optical disc and make duplicates of uncopyrighted music or movies. Disc burning software usually also includes photo editing, audio editing, and video editing capabilities (Figure 4-23). To learn about burning files to a disc, complete the Learn How To 1 exercise on page 164.

When you buy a recordable or rewritable disc, it typically includes burning software. You also can buy disc burning software for a cost of less than $100.

Figure 4-23 You can copy text, graphics, audio, and video files to discs using the digital media suite shown here, provided you have the correct type of drive and media.

Personal Computer Maintenance

Operating systems typically include a diagnostic utility that diagnoses computer problems but does not repair them. A **personal computer maintenance utility** identifies and fixes operating system problems, detects and repairs disk problems, and includes the capability of improving a computer's performance. Additionally, some personal computer maintenance utilities continuously monitor a computer while you use it to identify and repair problems before they occur. Norton SystemWorks is a popular personal computer maintenance utility designed for Windows operating systems (Figure 4-24).

Figure 4-24 A popular maintenance program for Windows users.

QUIZ YOURSELF 4-3

Instructions: Find the true statement below. Then, rewrite the remaining false statements so that they are true.

1. A pop-up blocker shrinks the size of a file(s).
2. An anti-spam program protects a computer against viruses.
3. A personal firewall is a utility that detects and protects a personal computer from unauthorized intrusions.
4. You should uninstall files and disks regularly in the event your originals are lost, damaged, or destroyed.
5. Web filtering software writes text, graphics, audio, and video files to a recordable or rewritable disc.

Quiz Yourself Online: To further check your knowledge of pages 150 through 157, visit the Microsoft Office and Concepts CourseMate Web site at www.cengagebrain.com, navigate to the Chapter 4 Quiz Yourself resource for this book, and then click Objective 6.

Chapter Summary

This chapter defined an operating system and then discussed the functions common to most operating systems. The chapter introduced a variety of stand-alone operating systems, server operating systems, and embedded operating systems. Finally, the chapter described several utility programs. For a consolidated look at various forms of digital communications, read the special feature that follows this chapter.

Computer Usage @ Work

Education

Teachers and students have been using computers in education for many years. Teachers have been taking advantage of advances in computer technology to help provide a better educational experience for their students.

Many grade schools throughout the United States, as well as other countries, enable parents to track their child's performance online. In the past, parents would rely solely on their child bringing home graded assignments and tests to know how he or she was doing. In some cases, parents would be surprised when they saw their child's grades on report cards every two to three months. Teachers now have the opportunity to engage parents in their child's education not only by giving them an up-to-the-minute snapshot of grades, but also by posting lesson plans online so that parents know what their child is learning.

Computers and technology also benefit students in the classroom. Schools now have one or more computers in almost every classroom, enabling students to access the Internet to do research that they otherwise would have had to visit the library to perform. Schools also are able to offer additional technology courses such as Web page design, digital media, and computer programming.

At the college level, many instructors today rely heavily on e-learning systems to provide students with Web-based access to course materials and assessments, discussion forums, chat rooms, and e-mail. Once used mainly in online classes, e-learning systems provide instructors with an easy way to allow students access to the class at any time of the day.

Most instructors go beyond e-learning systems and use additional technologies to enhance their classes. For example, digital media instructors might require students to upload their assignments to a photo sharing community, and an English instructor might save paper by requiring students to upload research papers to Google Docs and share them with the instructor.

Computer use in education not only enhances the teaching experience for instructors and learning experience for students, it also provides students with technological knowledge that will benefit them for the rest of their lives.

For more information, visit the Microsoft Office and Concepts CourseMate Web site at www.cengagebrain.com, navigate to the Chapter 4 Computer Usage @ Work resource for this book, and then click Education.

Companies on the Cutting Edge

VERISIGN Internet Infrastructure Services

Technology users desire immediate access to information and services. Their ability to communicate and conduct commerce securely is aided in large part by VeriSign. More than 30 billion times a day, people interact on the Internet, and their purchases, text messages, downloads, and other transactions are enabled and protected by VeriSign's infrastructure services.

Computer security company Semantic acquired VeriSign's Authentication division business in 2010 to strengthen encryption and identity services and help protect businesses and consumers by protecting information and detecting online fraud. Its domain name services department registers all .com, .net, .cc, and .tv domain names. The VeriSign Secured Seal, which has been issued to more than 100,000 domains in 145 countries, ensures companies and consumers that the Web site is secure.

The California-based company was founded in 1995 and has more than 2,200 employees worldwide.

RESEARCH IN MOTION (RIM) Wireless Mobile Communications Devices Manufacturer

By 2012, 800 million people worldwide are expected to access social networking Web sites on smart phones, up from 82 million in 2007. Research in Motion (RIM) helped fuel this networking frenzy by partnering with MySpace in 2008 to help connect networkers on the go. They can access MySpace Mobile on a BlackBerry smart phone, which is RIM's key product.

The Canadian company was founded in 1984 by Mike Lazaridis, who serves as its president and co-CEO. Lazaridis's vision for wireless technology developed in high school when he was a member of the local amateur radio and television club. He developed RIM's first major product, the Inter@active Pager, which was integrated in the first BlackBerry product in 1998. The BlackBerry gained attention for having the capability to combine a wireless mailbox with a corporate mailbox so that users could assess e-mail continuously.

Recently, Research in Motion launched BlackBerry App World, an application store that allows BlackBerry users to download personal and business programs.

For more information, visit the Microsoft Office and Concepts CourseMate Web site at www.cengagebrain.com and then navigate to the Chapter 4 Companies on the Cutting Edge resource for this book.

Technology Trailblazers

STEVE WOZNIAK Apple Cofounder

Mixing fun with work comes naturally for Steve Wozniak. As Apple's cofounder, he says his computer designing career began and still continues to be a hobby filled with creativity, humor, games, and education. In his opinion, Apple's success evolved because he designed computers that had minimal parts and maximum performance.

Wozniak designed the original Apple computer in 1975 with Apple's current CEO, Steve Jobs, and wrote most of the software. Ten years later he cofounded Pixar, the award winning animation studio. He left Apple in 1985 to spend time with his family, work on community projects, and teach, but he still serves as an advisor to the corporation.

Wozinak was inducted into the Consumer Electronics Hall of Fame and the National Inventors Hall of Fame. One of his current passions is applying artificial intelligence to the area of robotics. He also is a member of the Silicon Valley Aftershocks, a polo team that plays using Segway electric transportation devices.

LINUS TORVALDS Linux Creator

Inductees to the Computer History Museum in Mountain View, CA, are noted for their contribution to computer technology. Linus Torvalds joined the Museum's Hall of Fellows in 2008 for his creation of the open source operating system, Linux.

When he developed an operating system in 1991, he announced his project in an Internet newsgroup. He made the source code available and asked readers for suggestions to enhance the product. Computer users responded by reviewing the system and offering enhancements. Three years later he released a greatly enhanced version he called Linux.

Torvalds developed this innovative operating system when he was a 21-year-old computer science student in Finland. Today, he leads the development of Linux as a fellow at OSDL (Open Source Development Labs), a not-for-profit consortium of companies dedicated to developing and promoting the operating system. Torvalds says his daily involvement with Linux involves coordinating and merging the lines of code submitted by users so that the software runs smoothly.

For more information, visit the Microsoft Office and Concepts CourseMate Web site at www.cengagebrain.com and then navigate to the Chapter 4 Technology Trailblazers resource for this book.

STUDENT ASSIGNMENTS

Chapter Review

The Chapter Review reinforces the main concepts presented in this chapter.

To listen to an audio version of this Chapter Review, visit the Microsoft Office and Concepts CourseMate Web site at www.cengagebrain.com and then navigate to the Chapter 4 Chapter Review resource for this book.

1. **What Is System Software, and What Are the Two Types of System Software?** **System software** consists of the programs that control or maintain the operations of a computer and its devices. Two types of system software are operating systems and utility programs. System software serves as the interface between the user, the application software, and the computer's hardware. An **operating system (OS)** is a set of programs that contains instructions that work together to coordinate all the activities among computer hardware resources. Different sizes of computers typically use different operating systems because operating systems generally are written to run on a specific type of computer. A **utility program,** or **utility,** performs maintenance-type tasks, usually related to managing a computer, its devices, or its programs.

2. **What Are the Functions of an Operating System?** The operating system starts and shuts down a computer, provides a user interface, manages programs, manages memory, coordinates tasks, configures devices, establishes an Internet connection, monitors performance, provides file management and other utilities, updates automatically, controls a network, and administers security. The **user interface** controls how data and instructions are entered and how information is displayed. Two types of user interfaces are a **graphical user interface (GUI)** and a **command-line interface**. Managing programs refers to how many users, and how many programs, an operating system can support at one time. An operating system can be single user/single tasking, single user/multitasking, **multiuser,** or **multiprocessing**. **Memory management** optimizes the use of random access memory (RAM). **Virtual memory** is a concept in which the operating system allocates a portion of a storage medium, usually the hard disk, to function as additional RAM. Coordinating tasks determines the order in which tasks are processed. Configuring devices involves loading each device's driver when a user boots the computer. A **driver** is a small program that tells the operating system how to communicate with a specific device. Establishing an Internet connection sets up a connection between a computer and an Internet access provider. A **performance monitor** is a program that assesses and reports information about computer resources and devices. Operating systems often provide the capability of managing and searching for files, viewing images, securing a computer from unauthorized access, uninstalling programs, and other tasks. Most operating systems include an **automatic update** feature that provides updates to the program. A **server operating system** is an operating system that organizes and coordinates how multiple users access and share network resources. Network administrators typically have an **administrator account** that enables them to access files, install programs, and specify network settings.

Visit the Microsoft Office and Concepts CourseMate Web site at www.cengagebrain.com, navigate to the Chapter 4 Quiz Yourself resource for this book, and then click Objectives 1 – 2.

3. **What Are Features of Windows 7, Mac OS X, UNIX, and Linux Operating Systems?** **Windows 7** is Microsoft's fastest, most efficient operating system to date, offering quicker program start up, built-in diagnostics, automatic recovery, improved security, enhanced searching and organizing capabilities, and an easy-to-use interface. Most users choose between Windows 7 Starter, Windows 7 Home Premium, Windows 7 Ultimate, or Windows 7 Professional editions. **Mac OS X** is a multitasking GUI operating system available only for Apple computers. **UNIX** is a multitasking operating system that is flexible and powerful. **Linux** is a popular, multitasking UNIX-type operating system that is open source software, which means its code is available to the public for use, modification, and redistribution.

4. **What Are the Various Server Operating Systems?** Server operating systems are designed to support all sizes of networks, including medium- to large-sized businesses and Web servers. An example of a server operating system is Windows Server 2008. UNIX and Linux often are called multipurpose operating systems because they are both stand-alone and server operating systems. Solaris is a server operating system designed specifically for e-commerce applications. Novell's NetWare is a server operating system designed for client/server networks.

5. **What Are Several Embedded Operating Systems?** Most mobile devices and many consumer electronics have an **embedded operating system** that resides on a ROM chip. Popular embedded operating systems include the following. Windows Embedded CE is a scaled-down Windows operating system designed for use on communications, entertainment, and computing devices with limited functionality, such as VoIP telephones, digital cameras, point-of-sale terminals, automated teller machines, digital photo frames, handheld navigation devices, and portable media players. Windows Phone 7, which is a successor to Windows Mobile, works on specific types of smart phones. Palm OS is an operating system used on smart

phones and PDAs. iPhone OS is an operating system for iPhone and iPod touch. The BlackBerry operating system runs on handheld devices supplied by RIM. Google Android is an operating system developed by Google for mobile devices. Embedded Linux is a scaled-down Linux operating system for smart phones, PDAs, portable media players, and other devices. Symbian OS is an open source multitasking operating system designed for smart phones.

Visit the Microsoft Office and Concepts CourseMate Web site at www.cengagebrain.com, navigate to the Chapter 4 Quiz Yourself resource for this book, and then click Objectives 3 – 5.

6. **What Is the Purpose of Several Utility Programs?** Most operating systems include several built-in utility programs. A **file manager** performs functions related to file management. A **search utility** attempts to locate a file on your computer based on criteria you specify. An **image viewer** displays, copies, and prints the contents of a graphics file. An **uninstaller** removes a program and any associated entries in the system files. A **disk cleanup** utility searches for and removes unnecessary files. A **disk defragmenter** reorganizes the files and unused space on a computer's hard disk. A **backup utility** is used to copy, or back up, selected files or an entire hard disk to another storage medium. A **restore utility** reverses the backup process and returns backed up files to their original form. A **screen saver** displays a moving image or blank screen if no keyboard or mouse activity occurs for a specified time. A **personal firewall** detects and protects a personal computer from unauthorized intrusions. An **antivirus program** protects computers against a **virus**, or potentially damaging computer program, by identifying and removing any computer viruses. A **spyware remover** detects and deletes spyware and similar programs. An **adware remover** detects and deletes adware. An **anti-spam program** attempts to remove **spam** before it reaches your inbox. **Web filtering software** restricts access to certain material on the Web. A **phishing filter** warns or blocks you from potentially fraudulent or suspicious Web sites. A **pop-up blocker** stops pop-up ads from displaying on Web pages. A **file compression utility** shrinks the size of a file. A **media player** allows you to view images and animation, listen to audio, and watch video files on a computer. **Disc burning software** writes on a recordable or rewritable CD, DVD, or Blu-ray Disc. A **personal computer maintenance utility** identifies and fixes operating system or disk problems and improves a computer's performance.

Visit the Microsoft Office and Concepts CourseMate Web site at www.cengagebrain.com, navigate to the Chapter 4 Quiz Yourself resource for this book, and then click Objective 6.

Key Terms

You should know each key term. The list below helps focus your study.

To see an example of and a definition for each term, and to access current and additional information from the Web, visit the Microsoft Office and Concepts CourseMate Web site at www.cengagebrain.com and then navigate to the Chapter 4 Key Terms resource for this book.

administrator account (144)
adware remover (155)
anti-spam program (155)
antivirus program (154)
automatic update (143)
backup utility (152)
booting (138)
buffer (141)
cold boot (138)
command-line interface (139)
defragmenting (152)
disc burning software (157)
disk cleanup (152)
disk defragmenter (152)
driver (142)
embedded operating system (149)
file compression utility (156)
file manager (151)
folder (151)
graphical user interface (GUI) (139)
hibernate (138)
image viewer (151)
Linux (148)
log on (144)
Mac OS X (147)
Macintosh operating system (147)
media player (156)
memory management (141)
multiprocessing (141)
multiuser (141)
operating system (OS) (137)
password (144)
performance monitor (143)
personal computer maintenance utility (157)
personal firewall (153)
phishing (156)
phishing filter (156)
Plug and Play (142)
pop-up blocker (156)
queue (142)
restore utility (152)
screen saver (153)
search utility (151)
server operating system (143)
service pack (143)
sleep mode (138)
spam (155)
spooling (141)
spyware remover (155)
stand-alone operating system (146)
system software (136)
Trojan horse (154)
uncompress (156)
uninstaller (151)
UNIX (147)
user ID (144)
user interface (138)
user name (144)
utility (150)
utility program (150)
virtual memory (141)
virus (154)
warm boot (138)
Web filtering software (156)
Windows 7 (146)
Windows Aero (139)
Windows ReadyBoost (141)
worm (154)
zipped files (156)

Checkpoint

The Checkpoint exercises test your knowledge of the chapter concepts. The page number containing the answer appears in parentheses after each exercise.

To complete the Checkpoint exercises interactively, visit the Microsoft Office and Concepts CourseMate Web site at www.cengagebrain.com and then navigate to the Chapter 4 Checkpoint resource for this book.

Multiple Choice Select the best answer.

1. In the Windows 7 operating system, _____ provides an enhanced visual look, additional navigation options, and animation. (139)
   a. Windows Aero b. Plug and Play
   c. Mac OS X d. Windows 7 Starter
2. Windows users can increase the size of memory through _____, which can allocate available storage space on removable flash memory devices as additional memory cache. (141)
   a. Windows Aero b. Plug and Play
   c. Windows ReadyBoost d. a disk defragmenter
3. A _____ is a small program that tells the operating system how to communicate with a specific device. (142)
   a. buffer b. driver
   c. performance monitor d. device
4. Computer and network administrators typically have a(n) _____ that enables them to access all files and programs on the computer or network, install programs, and specify settings that affect all users on a computer or network. (144)
   a. file manager
   b. personal computer maintenance utility
   c. administrator account
   d. graphical user interface
5. The operating system on most mobile devices and many consumer electronics, called a(n) _____, resides on a ROM chip. (149)
   a. network operating system
   b. embedded operating system
   c. stand-alone operating system
   d. stand-alone utility program
6. A _____ is a specific named location on a storage medium that contains related documents. (151)
   a. file b. buffer
   c. utility d. folder
7. A(n) _____ is a program that warns or blocks you from potentially fraudulent or suspicious Web sites. (156)
   a. phishing filter
   b. adware remover
   c. Web filter
   d. Trojan horse
8. A(n) _____ is a program that allows you to view images and animation, listen to audio, and watch video files on your computer. (156)
   a. file manager
   b. media player
   c. service pack
   d. image viewer

Matching Match the terms with their definitions.

_____ 1. sleep mode (138)
_____ 2. hibernate (138)
_____ 3. virus (154)
_____ 4. worm (154)
_____ 5. spam (155)

a. a potentially damaging computer program that affects, or infects, a computer negatively by altering the way the computer works without the user's knowledge or permission
b. copies itself repeatedly using up system resources and possibly shutting the system down
c. saves any open documents and programs to a hard disk before removing power from the computer
d. hides within or looks like a legitimate program such as a screen saver
e. saves any open documents and programs to RAM, turns off all unneeded functions, and then places the computer in a low-power state
f. an unsolicited e-mail message or newsgroup posting sent to many recipients or newsgroups at once

Short Answer Write a brief answer to each of the following questions.

1. How is a cold boot different from a warm boot? _______ How is a memory-resident part of an operating system different from a nonresident part of an operating system? _______
2. What is the purpose of an automatic update feature? ______ Why and when might a user receive a service pack? ______
3. How does a file become fragmented? _______ How does a disk defragmenter work? _______
4. What are the differences between Windows 7 Starter and Windows 7 Home Premium? _______ What is the difference between Windows 7 Ultimate and Windows 7 Professional? _______
5. What is a backup utility, and what happens during a backup? _______ What is the purpose of a restore utility? _______

Problem Solving

The Problem Solving exercises extend your knowledge of the chapter concepts by seeking solutions to practical computer problems that you may encounter at home, school, or work. The Collaboration exercise should be completed with a team.

In the real world, practical problems often can be solved in multiple ways. Provide one solution to each of the following problems using available resources, such as articles on the Web or in print, blogs, podcasts, videos, television, user guides, other individuals, and electronics and computer stores. You may need to use multiple resources to obtain an answer. Present your solutions in the form requested by your instructor (brief report, presentation, discussion, or other means).

@ Home

1. **Computer Cannot Boot** You recently purchased a computer from your friend. When you turn on the computer, a message displays that says, "Operating system not found." What steps will you take before calling technical support?

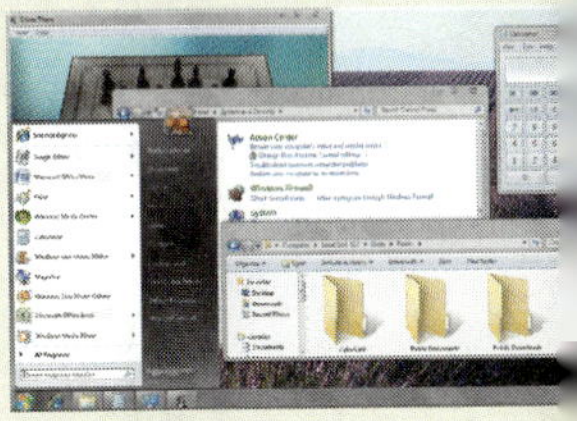

2. **Incorrect Display Settings** You have been using the same display settings since purchasing your computer several months ago. You recently turn on your computer and notice that the screen resolution, desktop background, and color scheme has changed, even though you have not changed the display settings. What might have caused Windows to change your display settings? What are your next steps?

3. **Maximum CPU Usage** Because your computer is performing slowly, you start the Windows Task Manager to investigate. You see that the CPU usage is near 100%. You are not aware of any other programs currently running. What might be causing this?

4. **Unwanted Programs** The new computer that you ordered online arrived today. You anxiously unpack it, connect all the components, and then turn it on. After answering a series of questions to set up the computer, you notice it includes programs that you do not want. How will you remove these unwanted programs?

@ Work

5. **Password Required** After turning on your computer, it prompts you to type a password to continue the boot process; however, you forgot the password. What are your next steps to allow the computer to continue the boot process, start Windows, and access the files on the hard disk?

6. **Automatic Updates** Two or three times per month, your coworker receives a notification on his computer that the computer recently has been updated. You ask your coworker about these messages, and he says that Microsoft periodically installs updates automatically to protect the computer from various threats, as well as to improve performance. You never have seen this message appear on your computer. Does this mean that your computer does not update automatically? How can you configure your computer to update automatically?

7. **Antivirus Schedule** You recently changed your work schedule so that you work until 6:00 p.m. instead of 5:00 p.m. At 5:00 p.m. each day, you notice that the antivirus program on your computer automatically begins scanning all files on your hard disk. This process slows your computer, and the program usually still is scanning when you leave the office. How can you change the configuration so that the antivirus program does not start until after you leave?

8. **Minimum Battery Power** When you use your notebook computer and it is not plugged in, the battery lasts for only one hour, but the documentation states that the computer can last for two hours on battery power. What are some ways that you can increase the battery life?

Collaboration

9. **Computers in Education** A private elementary school in your neighborhood has received a grant to create a computer lab with Internet access so that students can learn about computers and related technologies. Your neighbor, who also is a teacher at the school, asks for advice regarding how they should spend the grant money. Form a team of three people to determine the best configuration for the lab. One team member should research whether a PC or Mac is more beneficial. Another team member should research the application software that should be installed on these computers, and the other team member should determine what, if any, peripheral devices should be attached to the computers in the lab. Compile your findings and submit them to your instructor.

Learn How To

The Learn How To activities step you through fundamental technology skills when using a computer. The Learn How To exercises enable you to become more proficient with these skills.

Premium Activity: To relate this Learn How To activity to your everyday life, see a visual demonstration of the activity, and complete a short assessment, visit the Microsoft Office and Concepts CourseMate Web site at www.cengagebrain.com and then navigate to the Chapter 4 Learn How To resource for this book.

Learn How To 1: Burn Files to an Optical Disc

Many people use USB flash drives to transport files from one location to another. If they wish to share files with someone else, however, they might choose to distribute these files on an optical disc. To learn how to burn files to an optical disc using Windows 7, complete the following steps:

1. Insert a blank optical disc into the optical disc drive.
2. When the AutoPlay dialog box is displayed, click the Burn files to disc using Windows Explorer link.
3. If necessary, change the Disc title, click the 'Like a USB flash drive' option button, and then click the Next button in the Burn a Disc dialog box to prepare the blank disc.
4. Drag the files you wish to burn to the empty window that opens.
5. Click the 'Burn to disk' button.
6. Click the Next button to burn the files to the disc. When the disc has finished burning, remove the disc from the optical disc drive.

Exercise

1. Locate photos on your computer that you are willing to share with others. If you are unable to locate any photos or are using someone else's computer, download at least three photos from the Internet. Insert a blank optical disc into your optical disc drive and then burn the photos to the disc. Once you have finished burning the disc, eject it, write your name on it, and then submit it to your instructor.

Learn How To 2: Keep Windows Up-to-Date

Keeping Windows up-to-date is a critical part of keeping your computer in working order. The updates made available by Microsoft for no charge over the Internet can help to keep errors from occurring on your computer and attempt to ensure that all security safeguards are in place. To update Windows, complete the next steps:

1. Click the Start button on the Windows taskbar, click All Programs, and then click Windows Update in the All Programs list (Figure 4-25) to open the Windows Update window.
2. Click the link indicating that updates are available.
3. If necessary, select those updates you wish to install and then click the OK button. Be aware that some updates might take 20 minutes or more to download and install, based primarily on your Internet access speed.
4. Often, after installation of updates, you must restart your computer to allow those updates to take effect. Be sure to save any open files before restarting your computer.

Figure 4-25

You also can schedule automatic updates for your computer. To do so, complete the following steps:

1. Click the Start button on the Windows taskbar and then click Control Panel on the Start menu.
2. In the Control Panel window, click System and Security to open the System and Security window.
3. In the System and Security window, click 'Turn automatic updating on or off' to open the Change settings window (Figure 4-26).
4. Select the option you want to use for Windows updates. Microsoft, together with all security and operating system experts, strongly recommends you select 'Install updates automatically' so that updates will be installed on your computer automatically. Notice that if you select 'Install updates automatically', you also should select a time when your computer will be on and be connected to the Internet. A secondary choice is to download the suggested updates and then choose when you want to install them, and a third choice allows you to check for updates and then choose when you want to download and install them.
5. When you have made your selection, click the OK button in the Change settings window.

Updating Windows on your computer is vital to maintain security and operational integrity.

Exercises

1. Open the Windows Update window. Make a list of the important updates to Windows on the computer you are using. Add to the list the optional updates that are available. If you are using your own computer, install the updates of your choice on your computer. Submit the list of updates to your instructor.
2. **Optional: If you are not using your own computer, do not complete this exercise.** Open the Control Panel, click System and Security, and then click 'Turn automatic updating on or off'. Select the level of automatic updates you want to use. Write a report justifying your choice of automatic updates and then submit the report to your instructor.

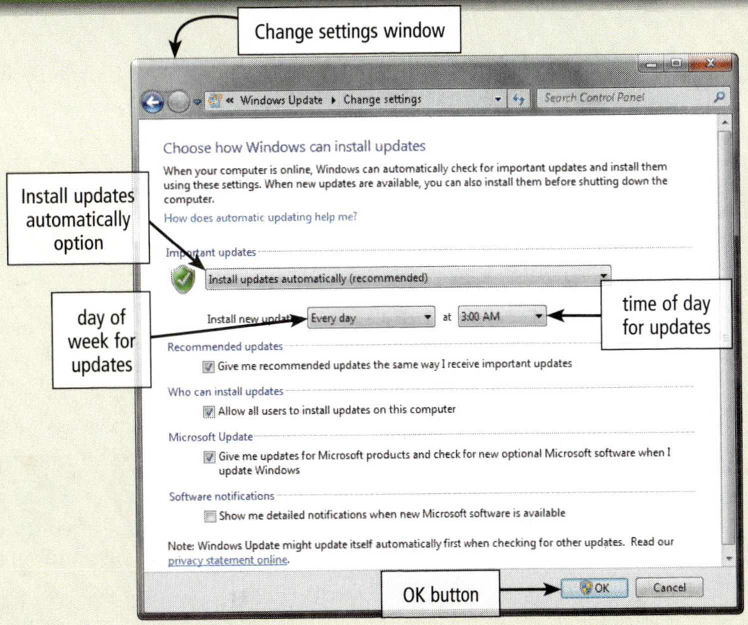

Figure 4-26

Learn It Online

The Learn It Online exercises are interactive Web exercises designed to reinforce and expand your understanding of the chapter concepts. The descriptions below briefly summarize each exercise.

To complete the Learn It Online exercises, visit the Microsoft Office and Concepts CourseMate Web site at www.cengagebrain.com, navigate to the Chapter 4 resources for this book, click the link for the exercise you want to complete, and then read the instructions.

1 At the Movies — Free Online Antivirus

Watch a movie to learn why it is important to run antivirus software on your computer and how to scan your computer for malware online for no cost and then answer questions about the movie.

2 Student Edition Labs — Installing and Uninstalling Software and Keeping Your Computer Virus Free

Enhance your understanding and knowledge about installing and uninstalling software and keeping your computer virus free by completing the Installing and Uninstalling Software and Keeping Your Computer Virus Free Labs.

3 Practice Test

Take a multiple choice test that checks your knowledge of the chapter concepts and review the resulting study guide.

4 Who Wants To Be a Computer Genius^2?

Play the Shelly Cashman Series version of this popular game by answering questions to find out if you are a computer genius. Panic buttons are available to provide assistance during game play.

5 Crossword Puzzle Challenge

Complete an interactive crossword puzzle to reinforce concepts presented in this chapter.

6 Windows Exercises

Step through the Windows 7 exercises to learn about Windows, using a screen saver, changing desktop colors, customizing the desktop for multiple users, and backing up a computer.

7 Exploring Computer Careers

Read about a career as a systems programmer, search for related employment advertisements, and then answer related questions.

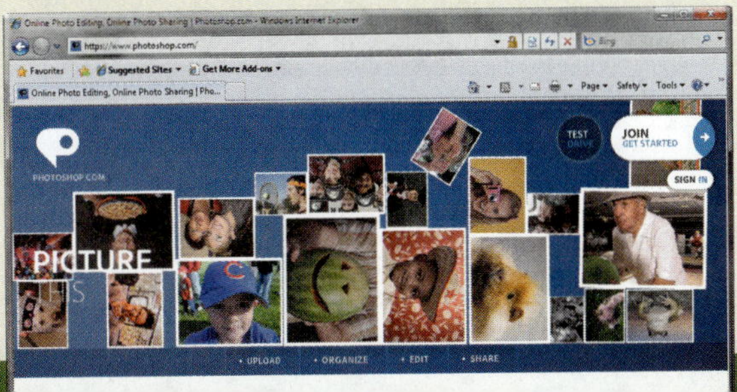

8 Web Apps — Photoshop Express

Learn how to use Photoshop Express to upload new photos as well as photos stored on other photo sharing communities, edit photos, create new pictures, and share them with others.

Web Research

The Web Research exercises broaden your understanding of chapter concepts by presenting questions that require you to search the Web for answers.

1 Search Sleuth

Use one of the search engines listed in Figure 2-8 in Chapter 2 on page 53 or your own favorite search engine to find the answers to the following questions. Copy and paste the Web address from the Web page where you found the answer. Some questions may have more than one answer. If required, submit your answers to your instructor. (1) Who are the "goons" who attend DEFCON? What color shirts do they wear? (2) Which product does IBM propose in its "Reincarnating PCs with Portable SoulPads" paper? (3) Which bird is the mascot for Linux? What is the mascot's name? (4) Why do some computer experts consider the term, spool, a backronym? (5) Who invented the Control-Alt-Delete (CTRL+ALT+DEL) key combination used to reboot a computer? (6) Which virus did the Farooq Alvi brothers invent? (7) Why would a programmer use the EICAR test file? (8) Why are UNIX programmers concerned about the "Year 2038 problem"?

2 Green Computing

Operating systems can help monitor computer energy use and suggest methods of reducing electricity through efficient power management. Experts claim monitoring systems can save each computer user at least $60 per year in electricity costs. Suggestions include not using a screen saver, turning down a monitor's brightness level, maximizing the standby and sleep settings, and using a power saver or high performance power setting that balances processing power with notebook computer battery life. View online Web sites that provide information about power management. Which methods are effective in reducing power consumption, especially for notebook computers? Which sleep state setting gives significant power savings? Which power management settings are recommended for balanced, power saver, and high performance? Write a report summarizing your findings, and include a table of links to Web sites that provide additional details.

3 Social Networking

Social networking Web site advertisers in the United States spent $108 million in 2009, an increase of 119 percent in one year. General Motors and Proctor & Gamble are two of the larger marketers exploring the placement of advertising on social networking Web sites. Millions of registered online social networking users have posted demographic information about themselves, including age, gender, and geographical location. This data helps marketing managers deliver specific advertisements to each user in an attempt to raise revenue to support their Web sites. Adknowledge (adknowledge.com) is one of the primary companies that gathers and studies data regarding online users and then sells targeted ads on social networking, e-mail, and gaming Web sites. Visit the Adknowledge Web site, view the information about targeting social network consumers, and then read articles in the About Us and Press Room sections. How are advertisers using virtual currency? How do traffic networks help advertisers create marketing campaigns? View the posts in the Adverblog Web site (adverblog.com) to read about interactive marketing trends. Summarize the information you read and viewed.

4 Blogs

Search engines help locate Web pages about certain topics based on the search text specified. A number of the search engine Web sites feature blogs describing popular search topics. For example, Ask.com's blog (blog.ask.com) lists its Blogroll, which gives recommended research and search engine Web sites. The Yahoo! Search blog (ysearchblog.com) includes news about consumer search trends (Yahoo! Buzz) and innovations in Web search technology. Google Blog Search (blogsearch.google.com) has search engines to help users find blogs about particular topics, including politics, technology, sports, and business. Visit these sites and read the posts. What topics are discussed? Compose search queries about issues and products discussed in this chapter, such as personal firewalls or antivirus programs, and read a few of the blogs describing these topics. Summarize the information you read and viewed.

5 Ethics in Action

Several automobile insurers, including Progressive Casualty Insurance Company, are promising drivers insurance premium discounts if they install a data recorder in their cars to track their driving and then exercise good driving behavior. Progressive customers voluntarily using the MyRate wireless device hope to decrease their insurance bills by a maximum of 25 percent. Privacy experts predict more insurance companies will offer this monitoring system and that it eventually will become mandatory. These critics fear that negative data will be used against poor drivers and possibly be subpoenaed in litigation. View online sites that provide information about vehicle monitoring devices. Write a report summarizing your findings, and include a table of links to Web sites that provide additional details.

Digital Communications

DIGITAL COMMUNICATIONS, which factor largely in many people's personal and business lives, include any transmission of information from one computer or mobile device to another (Figure 1). This feature covers many forms of digital communications: e-mail; text messaging, instant messaging, and picture/video messaging; digital voice communications; blogs and wikis; online social networks, chat rooms, and Web conferences; and content sharing.

With the Internet, cell phone networks, and other wireless networks increasing in size and speed, digital communications have become more and more prevalent. The most common devices used to communicate digitally are desktop computers, notebook computers, smart phones, and other mobile devices.

Successful use of digital communications involves selecting both the proper communications device and the proper mode of communication for a given situation. Each computer or mobile device and communications method has advantages and disadvantages that you should consider.

The following pages describe how people use different types of digital communications in their personal and business lives to enhance collaboration and increase productivity. The final section of the feature includes an example of how you might use digital communications.

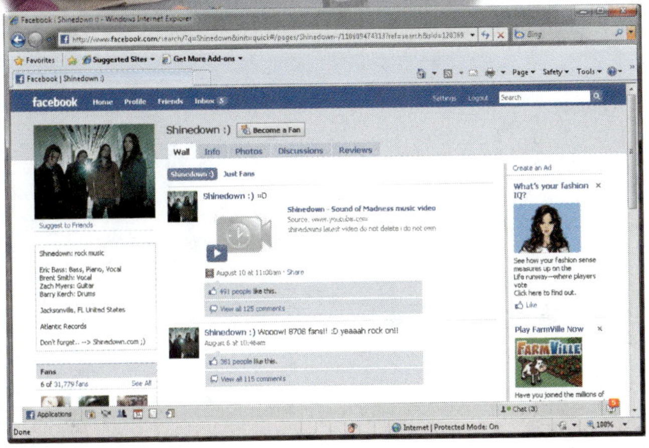

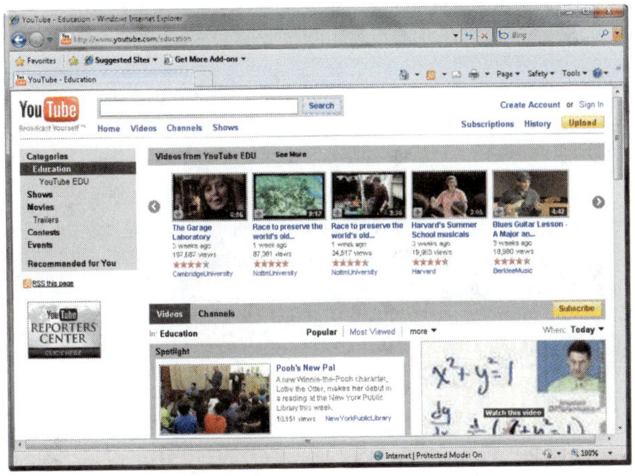

Figure 1 People use a variety of methods in their personal and business lives to engage in digital communications.

E-Mail

E-mail is the transmission of messages and files via a computer network. E-mail quickly has become one of the more widely used forms of digital communications. Although e-mail is primarily a text-based form of digital communications, it also can be used to share photos, videos, and other types of files by attaching files to e-mail messages.

E-Mail: The Personal Perspective

With a computer or mobile device connected to the Internet, you can use e-mail to keep in contact with friends, family, stores, companies, schools, and government agencies. Some people maintain several different e-mail addresses for use in different situations. Figure 2 lists some advantages, disadvantages, and good practices of personal e-mail use. Some e-mail programs are application programs that run on your computer, while others are Web applications (shown in Figure 3).

Personal E-Mail Use

Advantages

- One of the most preferred methods of online communications.
- Available on nearly any computer or mobile device with Internet access.
- Send files, called attachments, via e-mail messages to others.
- Fast, reliable, and proven technology.
- Allows messages to be sent anywhere free of charge or inexpensively.
- Allows communications with more than one person at a time.
- Provides an electronic forum for communications in which the originator has time to consider a thought before it is sent or spoken, unlike face-to-face meetings or telephone conversations.

Disadvantages

- Number of messages received can become overwhelming and unmanageable.
- Spam can overwhelm your e-mail inbox.
- Message tone can be misunderstood.
- Many computer viruses and other malicious programs are transmitted via e-mail messages.

Good practices

- Keep messages as short as possible.
- Check with the recipient before sending attachments, especially large attachments.
- Respond to messages promptly.
- Use a reputable Internet access provider that uses a spam filter, which is a program that detects and removes spam, and use an e-mail program that includes a spam filter.
- Never respond to unsolicited advertisements or spam.
- Informal language and shortcuts are acceptable when communicating with friends and family (e.g., suitable to use HRU? as a shortcut for How are you?).
- Always include a Subject line.
- Always reread your message and edit it before sending it.
- When replying to questions or comments included with a previous message, include the original message.

Figure 2 Personal e-mail remains one of the more popular reasons to use the Internet.

Figure 3 Many home users have e-mail Web applications.

E-Mail: The Business Perspective

Most businesses use e-mail for internal communications among employees and external communications with customers and business partners. E-mail gradually has replaced typed and copied memos, letters, and faxes while increasing the reliability, cost effectiveness, and speed of the communications. Figure 4 indicates some advantages, disadvantages, and good practices of e-mail use in business. Many of the notes listed in Figure 2 also apply to e-mail communications in business. Figure 5 shows an example of the inbox of a business e-mail program user and an example of an appropriate business e-mail message.

E-Mail Use in Business

Advantages

- Easily archive, or store long-term, all e-mail messages sent from or received by the business.
- Generally can guarantee delivery of any e-mail message that is sent within the business.
- A replacement for memos, letters, faxes, and other internal and external business communications when permitted by company policy.
- Communicate with someone who is not available at the time you need to communicate.

Disadvantages

- Volume of e-mail messages often becomes overwhelming.
- Often leads to overcommunication, which can result in important information being lost because it is ignored.
- Sometimes leads to avoidance of personal contact, such as a meeting or telephone call.

Good practices

- Because most companies archive, or save, all e-mail messages, use e-mail when you want a permanent record of a communication.
- Understand your company's e-mail policies. Many companies prohibit sending personal e-mail messages from a business computer.
- Never include any language that would be considered inappropriate in a business environment.
- Check your e-mail inbox regularly.
- Follow your company's or department's guidelines for formatting messages and including contact information and any appropriate disclaimers.
- In most cases, it is appropriate to send larger attachments in business e-mail messages as compared to those permissible in personal messages.
- Avoid sending messages to many people simultaneously or replying to large groups of people. For example, it is almost always inappropriate to send a message to the entire company.
- Avoid using e-mail messages when the content involves sensitive issues, such as a negotiation, legal matter, or employee review.
- When you need to know that the recipient has read your e-mail message, use the return receipt feature of your e-mail program to receive automatic notification as soon as the message is read.

Figure 4 Most businesses provide written policies and guidelines regarding use of e-mail programs.

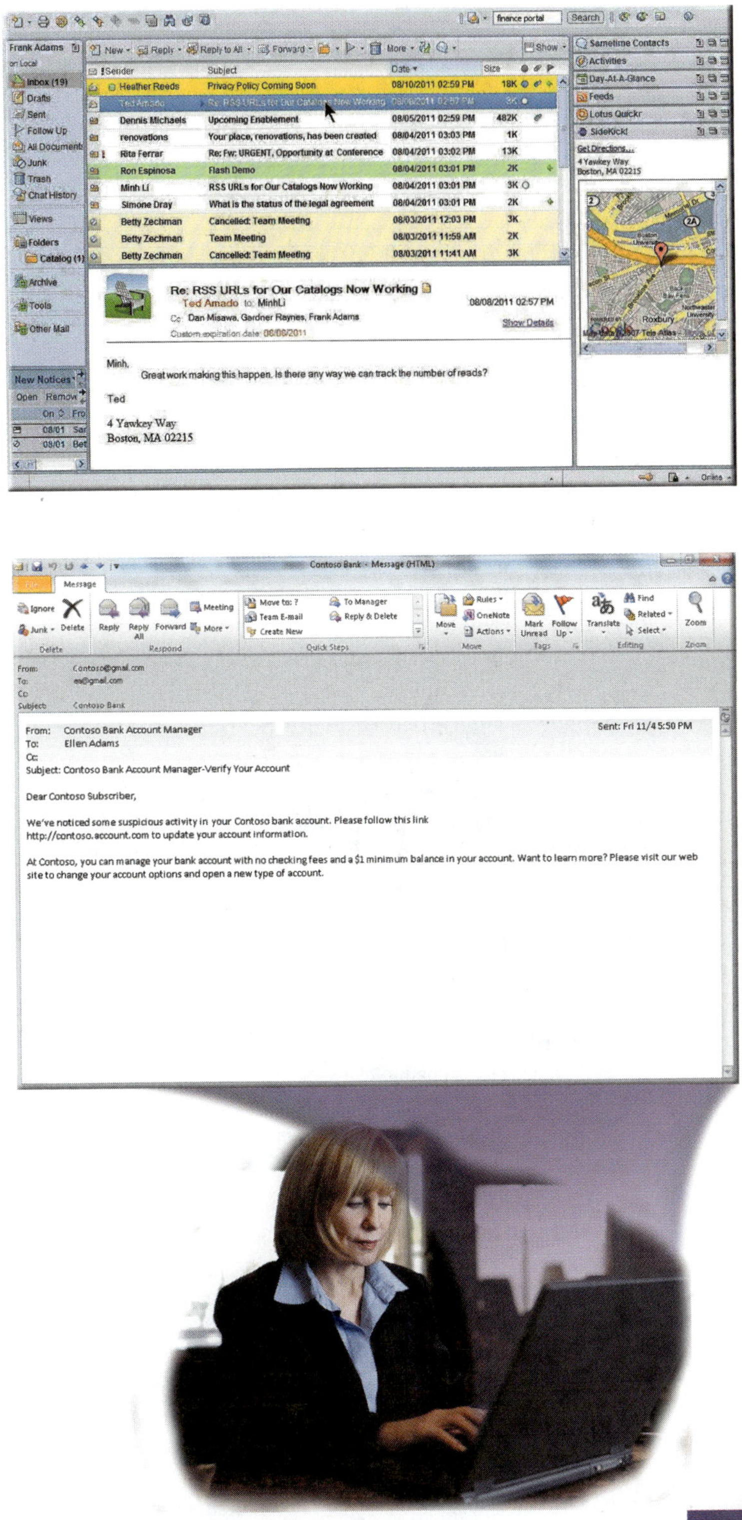

Figure 5 Businesses often use more sophisticated e-mail programs than do home users.

Text Messaging, Instant Messaging, and Picture/Video Messaging

Text messaging, instant messaging, and picture/video messaging allow you to exchange short messages and small multimedia files with other online users. Text messaging is a wireless messaging service that allows users to send and receive short notes on a smart phone or other mobile device. Instant messaging is a real-time Internet communications service that notifies a user when one or more people are online and allows the user to exchange messages or files or join a private chat room with those people. Picture messaging is a wireless messaging service that allows users to send and receive photos and sound files, as well as short text messages, to and from a mobile device, or computer. Video messaging is a wireless messaging service that allows users to send and receive short video clips, usually up to 30 seconds, in addition to all picture messaging services.

Text Messaging, Instant Messaging, and Picture/Video Messaging: The Personal Perspective

Text messaging, instant messaging, and picture/video messaging typically are used on smart phones. Instant messaging often is used on desktop and notebook computers. Virtually instantaneous communication is possible with the various forms of messaging. Figure 6 indicates some advantages, disadvantages, and good practices of using instant messaging, text messaging, and picture/video messaging in your personal life. Figure 7 shows some examples of people using messaging.

Personal Text Messaging, Instant Messaging, and Picture/Video Messaging Use

Advantages

- Virtually instantaneous form of digital communications.
- Fast, reliable, and popular method of digital communications.
- Useful when you prefer an immediate response from the recipient.
- Allows you to carry on several conversations at any time.

Disadvantages

- Can be addictive in nature.
- Receiving a constant stream of messages can be distracting.
- May be very expensive on mobile devices.
- Text messaging: Overuse may result in repetitive stress injuries (RSIs).

Good practices

- Know the person with whom you are exchanging messages.
- Keep in mind that any text, picture, or video you send can be sent to others by the recipient.
- When messaging with a new contact, do not share personal information quickly.
- Always reread your text messages and preview your pictures and videos before you send them.
- Respect the status of others when they indicate they are busy.
- Instant messaging: If the program allows you to indicate your status to others, such as "Busy" or "Do not disturb," use these indicators to let others know when you are unavailable.
- Picture/video messaging: When sending picture/video messages, make sure the content is appropriate.

Figure 6 People use various types of messaging for different reasons. (Where noted, some bullet points apply only to particular technologies.)

Figure 7 Many people interact with messaging software both at home and while away from home or work.

Text Messaging, Instant Messaging, and Picture/Video Messaging: The Business Perspective

Businesses typically use more secure, feature-rich messaging programs that allow all messages to be archived. Archiving of messages often is required by law and allows old messages to be available for future reference. Messaging allows colleagues to collaborate, or work together, online. Figure 8 indicates some advantages, disadvantages, and good practices of text messaging, instant messaging, and picture/video messaging use in business. Many of the notes listed in Figure 6 also apply to the various forms of messaging in business. Figure 9 shows an example of business-level instant messaging software and video messaging at job sites.

Text Messaging, Instant Messaging, and Picture/Video Messaging Use in Business

Advantages

- When used properly, greatly increases collaboration and communications because users have instantaneous access to each other.
- All messages can be archived for retrieval at a later date or for meeting legal requirements.
- Immediate contact with customers when allowed by company policy and agreed to by the customer.
- Collaboration with geographically separated colleagues.
- Instant messaging: Some programs allow conferences of several people at one time, eliminating the need for scheduling meeting rooms or conference calls.
- Picture/video messaging: Provides instant views of remote locations, such as work sites or company assets.

Disadvantages

- Despite policies, business conversations often lead to personal conversations.
- Often leads to over-reliance on simply messaging a colleague for an answer to a question rather than determining the answer on your own.
- Can lead to a significant decline in important face-to-face contact with coworkers, customers, and business partners.
- Instant messaging: Because all messages can be archived, it can lead to difficult situations when inappropriate content is shared.

Good practices

- When beginning a messaging conversation, make your point quickly and keep messages concise.
- Separate your personal messaging habits from your business messaging habits, avoiding use of emoticons and shortcuts, such as "brb" as a shortcut for "Be right back."
- Use proper spelling, grammar, and punctuation, and avoid colloquialisms.
- Be aware of cultural differences that might arise during casual conversations.
- Acknowledge the end of a messaging conversation.
- Follow your company's policies regarding the type of information that can be conveyed in a message and with whom you may engage in messaging.
- Always try to meet or telephone a person to introduce yourself before sending a first message to him or her.
- Review all messages you send to colleagues to make sure that the contents are appropriate for the workplace.

Figure 8 Businesses use a variety of messaging methods to allow employees to collaborate in a timely and secure manner. (Where noted, some bullet points apply only to particular technologies.)

Figure 9 Business users employ instant messaging and video messaging to communicate ideas and multimedia information quickly.

Digital Voice Communications

Digital voice communications includes the use of cell phones, smart phones, and VoIP (Voice over IP). VoIP is a technology that allows users to speak to other users via the Internet. VoIP can be used as a replacement for the traditional telephone at work or in the home.

Digital Voice Communications: The Personal Perspective

With more than 200 million in use in the United States, cell phones are a primary source of digital voice communications. Cell phones can act as a suitable replacement for the traditional, wired, public switched telephone network. Smart phones offer features such as e-mail, text messaging, picture/video messaging, and playing or streaming multimedia.

Figure 10 indicates some advantages, disadvantages, and good practices of digital voice communications in your personal life. Figure 11 shows some examples of digital voice communications, including visual voice mail, which is a service that automatically translates voice mail into text messages or allows you to download voice messages to your smart phone and listen to them at your convenience.

Personal Digital Voice Communications Use

Advantages

- Increase productivity through greater and more timely communications.
- Both cell phones and VoIP offer more choice in providers than the public switched telephone network.
- Cell phones: Widespread coverage of cell phone networks provides voice communications nearly everywhere in the United States.
- Cell phones: Have been instrumental in saving lives in emergency situations.
- VoIP: Often offers free features, such as voice mail, unlimited in-country long distance calling, three-way calling, and call forwarding.
- VoIP: Typically is less expensive for both local and long distance calls than the public switched telephone network.

Disadvantages

- Cell phones: In some situations, such as while driving a car, can contribute to accidents.
- VoIP: Not as strictly regulated as the public switched telephone network, meaning that the quality of service may be lower.
- With many VoIP providers and some cell phone providers, connecting to a local service, such as 911 for emergencies, may be difficult or cumbersome.

Good practices

- Cell phones: Use a headset if you must use a cell phone while driving. Be aware of laws in your area that prohibit or limit cell phone use while driving.
- Cell phones: When using in public, be mindful of and courteous to those around you.
- Cell phones: Be aware of rules or policies at some locations, such as schools, medical facilities, or religious facilities.
- Cell phones: In public locations, use an alternative ring method, such as a vibration setting, to avoid interrupting others.

Figure 10 Cell phones and other forms of digital voice communications have become an essential means of communications throughout the world. (Where noted, some bullet points apply only to particular technologies.)

Figure 11 People use cell phones, VoIP, and visual voice mail in their everyday lives for contact with friends and family.

Digital Voice Communications: The Business Perspective

Businesses embrace digital voice communications because of increased collaboration and productivity, cost savings, and mobility. Figure 12 lists many of the advantages, disadvantages, and good practices of digital voice communications use in business. Many of the notes listed in Figure 10 also apply to the various forms of digital voice communications in business. Figure 13 shows an example of a simple VoIP system.

Digital Voice Communications Use in Business

Advantages

- Increased communications and collaboration can result in increased productivity and cost savings.
- Cell phones: Ability to contact a person almost anywhere at any time.
- VoIP: With some systems, employees can listen to and manage their voice messages on their personal computer.
- VoIP: A computer is not necessary to use a VoIP system.
- VoIP: Allows large companies to consolidate communications between geographically diverse locations.
- VoIP: Implement as an alternative to the public switched telephone network because VoIP allows businesses to use their existing network more efficiently and provides more features than the public switched telephone network.

Disadvantages

- With many VoIP providers and some cell phone providers, connecting to a local service, such as 911 for emergencies, may be difficult or cumbersome.
- The quality of calls may change at times due to excessive network usage.
- Cell phones: Misuse often leads to rude behavior or disruption of meetings.
- Cell phones: Using a cell phone provided by an employer for personal calls may have undesirable tax consequences.
- VoIP: Large companies may find it expensive and difficult to manage.
- VoIP: Unlike a public switched telephone network, many VoIP systems and equipment will not function during a power outage.

Good practices

- Cell phones: Follow company policy regarding the use for business communications. Limit personal calls on your cell phone during business hours.
- Cell phones: Disable the ringer when in meetings or during important discussions.
- Cell phones: Resist the need to answer every call at all times, such as when you are on breaks or when you are not at work.
- Cell phones: Avoid speaking loudly on the phone when walking through others' work areas.
- VoIP: When possible, use a VoIP telephone rather than a cell phone because it generally is less expensive for the company on a per-call basis.

Figure 12 Digital voice communications are used when a more personal form of communications than e-mail or messaging is required in real time. (Where noted, some bullet points apply only to particular technologies.)

Figure 13 VoIP allows businesses to connect their telephone system to their internal network and the Internet for voice telephone calls.

Blogs and Wikis

A **blog** is an informal Web site consisting of time-stamped articles, or posts, in a diary or journal format, usually listed in reverse chronological order. A **wiki** is a collaborative Web site that allows users to create, add to, modify, or delete the Web site content via their Web browser.

Blogs and Wikis: The Personal Perspective

Blog topics often include family life, social life, a personal project, or events during a vacation. You might read and contribute to a wiki regarding classical guitar techniques if your hobbies included playing classical guitar. While blogs can be modified only by the author, a wiki can be authored and edited by any user. Another difference between blogs and wikis is that blog entries typically are not included in search results from search engines, such as Google, while wiki entries are recognized by search engine queries. Figure 14 indicates some advantages, disadvantages, and good practices of using blogs and wikis in your personal life. Figure 15 shows examples of blog and wiki entries.

Personal Blog and Wiki Use

Advantages

- Some blogs and wikis provide secure access so that only a select group of qualified or desired individuals are allowed to read and write entries.
- Blogs: Easy, accessible, and often free method of keeping a group of people informed about events.
- Blogs: Easy way to keep up with an acquaintance or expand your knowledge about political or social points of view.
- Blogs: Often can be read or written using Internet-enabled mobile devices.
- Wikis: Provide free access to concise, almost encyclopedic, information about nearly any topic.

Disadvantages

- Vulnerable to fraudulent or biased entries placed by businesses or special interest groups in an effort to sway public opinion.
- Blogs: Often are biased towards a particular point of view.
- Blogs: Some blogging Web sites are often sources of malicious programs.
- Wikis: Publicly accessible wikis sometimes are vulnerable to vandalism or subject to errors.

Good practices

- Blogs: When writing a blog, be aware that the contents of your blog may be accessible publicly and associated with your identity for a long time.
- Blogs: When reading blogs, be aware of the source of the information and evaluate the credibility of the source.
- Wikis: When performing research using a wiki, check any provided sources and, if possible, check the editorial history of the entries.
- Wikis: If you locate an error, notify the author or editor of the wiki page, or, if possible, edit the page yourself to make the correction.
- Wikis: When possible, contribute your own knowledge to wikis that interest you, being sure to follow the guidelines of the wiki.

Figure 14 While blogs and wikis provide a great deal of information sharing, users and contributors alike should be aware of the risks involved. (Where noted, some bullet points apply only to particular technologies.)

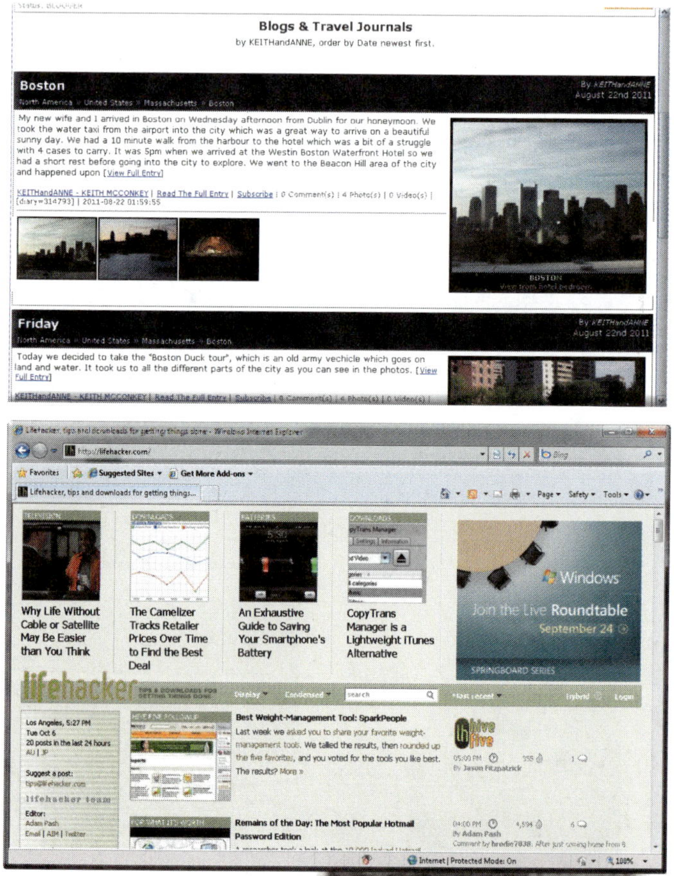

Figure 15 Blogs and wikis allow people to share their knowledge, experience, viewpoints, and personal events on the Internet. People use mobile blogging while away from home or while in interesting locations.

Blogs and Wikis: The Business Perspective

Many businesses use blogs and wikis to share knowledge within the company. One large company claims to maintain more than 300,000 blogs and wikis internally. A key reason that blogs and wikis are so popular in business is that they can be written, read, and searched easily. As the company's resident expert regarding a particular topic, an employee may blog to keep others informed about topics relating to that expertise. A business-oriented wiki may contain a wealth of historical knowledge for a particular department in the company. Figure 16 indicates some advantages, disadvantages, and good practices of using blogs and wikis in business. Many of the notes listed in Figure 14 also apply to using blogs and wikis in business. Figure 17 shows examples of typical business-oriented blog and wiki entries.

Blog and Wiki Use in Business

Advantages

- Provide easy access to gained knowledge and experience.
- Easily can be searched by employees.
- Some may be made available to customers, business partners, or the general public.
- Blogs: Publicly accessible blogs often are used as an effective means to promote products or services.

Disadvantages

- Mistakes, inaccuracies, and inconsistencies in entries can lead to lost productivity and increased costs.
- Internal company blogs and wikis often contain proprietary company information that easily can be leaked to competitors or the press.
- Blogs: When contributing to a blog, some employees become engrossed with capturing every detail of their job.
- Wikis: Information often may become old, or stale, if it is not updated regularly.

Good practices

- Search your company's blogs and wikis for information before telephoning, instant messaging, or e-mailing a colleague with a question.
- If you do not find an answer to a question on your company's blogs or wikis, then contribute to a blog or wiki once you find the answer.
- When contributing to a blog or wiki entry, read your company's policies regarding content, formatting, and style. Some companies employ full-time bloggers and writers who can help you contribute a valuable entry.
- When contributing to a blog or wiki entry, stay on topic and create links within your entry to other related or relevant Web pages, including other blog and wiki entries.
- Blogs: When engaging in personal blogging, do not discredit your employer or potential future employers; many people have lost their jobs as a result of engaging in such behavior.
- Blogs: When engaging in personal blogging, be careful not to divulge proprietary company information.

Figure 16 Business blog and wiki use typically is governed by more guidelines and rules than those for personal blogs and wikis. (Where noted, some bullet points apply only to particular technologies.)

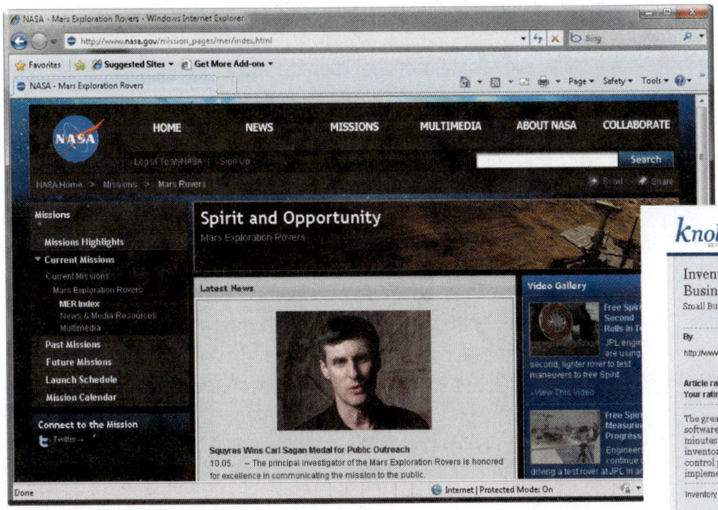

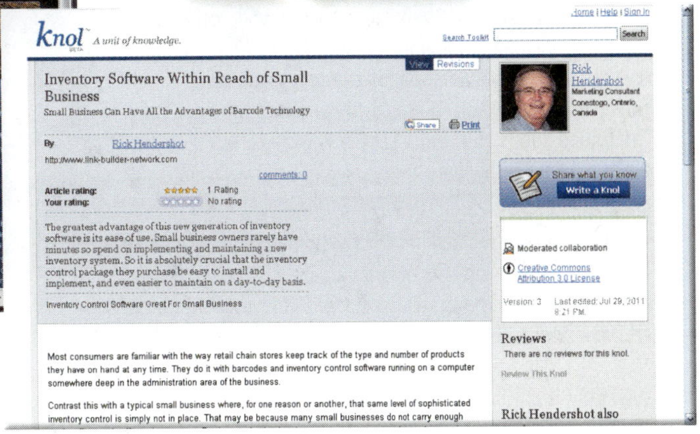

Figure 17 Increasingly more businesses use blogs and wikis to allow employees to share information with each other, customers, and business partners.

Online Social Networks, Chat Rooms, and Web Conferences

An **online social network** is a Web site that encourages members in its online community to share their interest, ideas, stories, photos, music, and videos with other registered users. A **chat room** is a location on the Internet that permits users to chat with one another. A **Web conference** allows two or more people to engage in an online meeting and often allows the attendees to access programs and digital content, such as documents, audio, and video, during the meeting.

Online Social Networks, Chat Rooms, and Web Conferences: The Personal Perspective

The popularity of online social networks such as Facebook continues to skyrocket. Most online social networks allow you to maintain a personal Web site that you can share with other registered users who, after being invited, may view or contribute content to your site. Those invited to your online social network often are known as friends. While chat rooms have decreased in popularity over the years, people often use them for targeted discussions about specific topics. Web conferences often are used by consumers to obtain technical support or assistance from companies and government agencies or in educational settings to engage in online learning. Figure 18 indicates some advantages, disadvantages, and good practices of using online social networks, chat rooms, and Web conferences in your personal life. Figure 19 shows an example of an online social network and a virtual chat room discussion.

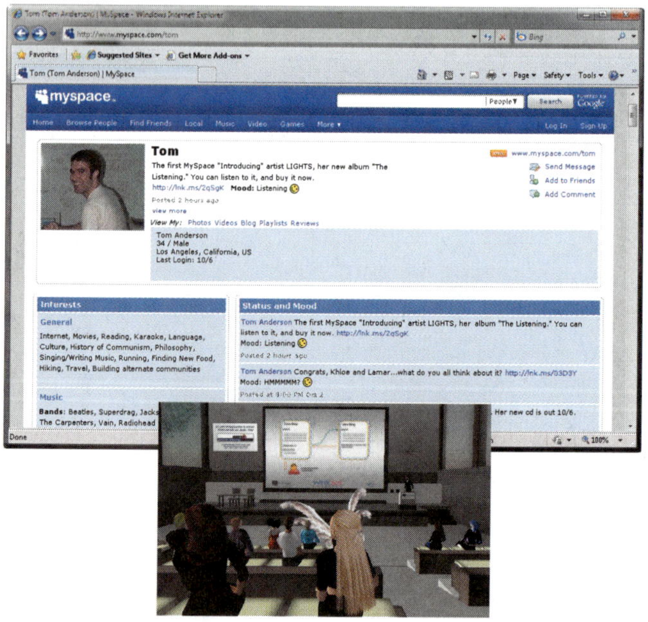

Figure 19 Online social networks and virtual chat rooms allow groups of people with similar interests or lifestyles to enjoy real-time communications.

Personal Use of Online Social Networks, Chat Rooms, and Web Conferences

Advantages
- Online social networks/chat rooms: Easily find friends throughout the world with similar interests or traits.
- Online social networks/chat rooms: Can expand your knowledge about political or social points of view.
- Web conferences: Use Web conferencing when offered by a company for technical support issues because the tenor of the interaction is more personal than a telephone call.
- Web conferences: Often effectively provides the necessary communications to avoid a visit to a store location or a visit from a repair technician.

Disadvantages
- Online social networks/chat rooms: Some people are susceptible to overusing these forms of communications in lieu of real, in-person contacts and relationships. Overuse of these forms of communications may lead to addiction.
- Online social networks/chat rooms: People often hide their real identity to lure others into revealing too much personal information.
- Online social networks/chat rooms: Several high-profile incidents occurred in which people engaged in illegal activity using online social networks and chat rooms.

Good practices
- Online social networks: When submitting information, be aware that the information may be accessible publicly and associated with your identity for a long time.
- Online social networks: While many online social networks encourage the practice, do not try to gather too many friends in your social network. Some experts believe that a functional social network is limited to a maximum of 150 people.
- Chat rooms/Web conferences: Be as polite and courteous as you would be to someone in person.

Figure 18 People use online social networks, chat rooms, and Web conferences as a means of extending their social lives beyond their physical surroundings. (Where noted, some bullet points apply only to particular technologies.)

Online Social Networks, Chat Rooms, and Web Conferences: The Business Perspective

Online social networks, chat rooms, and Web conferences allow business users to interact and collaborate as teams. While online social networks have not been as popular as other forms of digital communications in business, their use is showing promise for many companies and groups who use it for business purposes. One company claims to have signed up more than five million business users for its business-oriented online social network. Chat rooms and Web conferences often serve as forums for online meetings. Figure 20 indicates some advantages, disadvantages, and good practices of using online social networks, chat rooms, and Web conferences in business. Many of the notes listed in Figure 6 on page 170 and Figure 18 also apply to these forms of digital communication in business. Figure 21 shows an example of a business-oriented online social network, chat room, and Web conference.

Online Social Network, Chat Room, and Web Conference Use in Business

Advantages

- Online social networks: Encourage people to collaborate with others with whom they typically would not collaborate.
- Online social networks/chat rooms: Often can be accessed using Internet-enabled mobile devices, providing instant collaboration almost anywhere.
- Online social networks/chat rooms: Provide forums for meeting potential customers, employers, and employees.
- Web conferences: Programs often allow application program sharing, which means that all participants can view the contents of one or more participant's computer screen.
- Online social networks/chat rooms: Some are located internally within a company and allow only employees access to the sites.
- Online social networks/chat rooms: Some are subscription-based and allow people to interact freely with others in related fields or industries.

Disadvantages

- Employees often over-rely on these means of online digital communications and do not interact with others in more personal ways.
- Online social networks: Can be cumbersome and expensive to maintain.

Good practices

- When engaging in online social networks, chat rooms, and Web conferences outside of your company, be careful not to divulge proprietary company information.
- Always maintain a professional demeanor. Often, those who use this technology in their personal lives are quick to behave more casually than is appropriate in a business setting.
- Divulge only that information about yourself that is relevant to the reasons you are participating in an online social network or chat room.

Figure 20 Businesses have embraced online social networks, chat rooms, and Web conferences to drive collaboration among geographically separated teams, employees, and other business contacts. (Where noted, some bullet points apply only to particular technologies.)

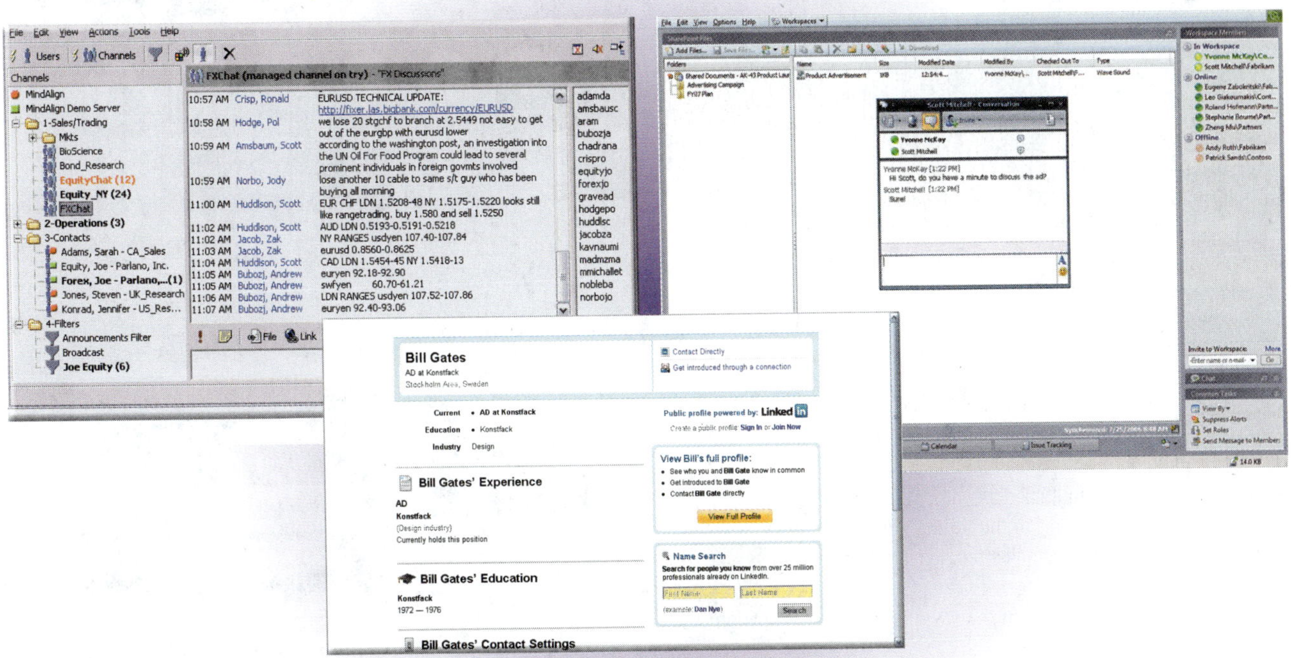

Figure 21 Businesses use online social networks, chat rooms, and Web conferences to allow employees and teams to communicate more effectively.

Content Sharing

Content sharing provides a means by which rich content, such as audio, video, photos, and documents, can be communicated digitally.

Content Sharing: The Personal Perspective

The prolific spread of digital cameras and digital video cameras combined with ever-increasing speeds of home and mobile Internet connections has resulted in the explosive growth of media sharing Web sites, such as YouTube and Flickr. In addition to sharing media, people are sharing documents, spreadsheets, and other content on Web sites. Figure 22 indicates some advantages, disadvantages, and good practices of content sharing in your personal life. Figure 23 shows some examples of a video sharing Web site, a photo sharing group Web site, and a personal photo sharing Web site.

Personal Content Sharing Use

Advantages

- Ability to view broadcasts of events that may not be available through traditional broadcasts in your area.
- Media sharing Web sites provide almost limitless information and entertainment at little or no cost.
- Some services allow you to edit your content or the content of others directly on the site using a Web application.
- View or listen to live broadcasts of sporting events.
- View or listen to news stories.
- Much like online social networks, media sharing Web sites can provide a sense of community to a group of geographically separated individuals.

Disadvantages

- You may find it difficult to locate media and content that interests you.
- When sharing video and photos on a media sharing Web site, you may be giving up some of your rights to the media.
- Many people have been embarrassed by content posted by others to media sharing Web sites.

Good practices

- Before placing your content on a media sharing Web site, make a good effort to edit the content for brevity and clarity. For example, make certain that audio is clear in a video, and use photo editing software to remove red-eye.
- Take advantage of the fact that most media and content sharing Web sites allow you to limit who can access your media and content.
- Before you allow somebody to record video of you or take your picture, remember that the video or photo may end up on a media sharing Web site.
- Before placing your multimedia content on a media sharing Web site, check the terms of the service agreement and make certain you agree to give up certain legal rights to your multimedia content.
- Do not post pictures or videos that are protected by a copyright.

Figure 22 While most people act as consumers of content shared on the Internet, some share their own content.

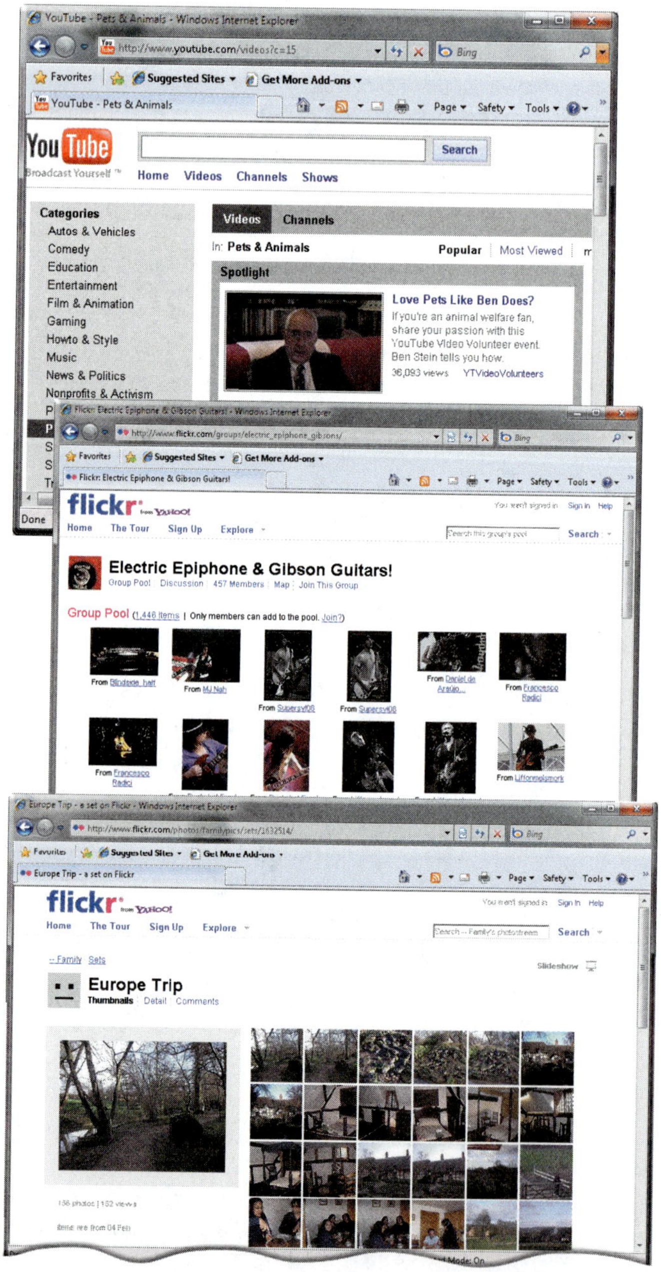

Figure 23 People share and view content on the Internet in a number of ways.

Content Sharing: The Business Perspective

Media sharing Web sites allow business to interact creatively with employees, customers, and prospective customers. Video conferencing is the oldest form of real-time multimedia content sharing in business. Figure 24 outlines some advantages, disadvantages, and good practices of content sharing in business. Many of the notes listed in Figure 22 also apply to content sharing in business. Figure 25 shows examples of content shared in an educational setting and a document management system, which allows for secure storage and management of a company's documents.

Content Sharing Use in Business

Advantages

- Multimedia sharing sites allow companies to archive video conferences, advertisements, employee photos, and other multimedia content.
- Executives and managers create podcasts or vodcasts to spread their vision or message. Vodcasts are podcasts that contain video and usually audio.
- Video conferences allow geographically separate people to transmit audio and video and engage in a meeting remotely.
- Most business-based content sharing software provides for enhanced collaboration by making the content accessible and searchable.
- Multimedia content, such as videos and photos, can be stored in a document management system to archive information about important projects or events.

Disadvantages

- Production and distribution of multimedia content often is more expensive than traditional methods.
- Security on business content sharing systems often frustrates employees who are denied access to information without special approval.

Good practices

- Unless you have permission, do not share company-owned photos and videos on publicly available media sharing Web sites, such as YouTube or Flickr.
- When viewing or sharing photos and videos in the workplace, be certain that the content is appropriate for the workplace. Some businesses have a media department that manages all of the company's multimedia content.

Figure 24 Businesses provide secure content sharing repositories and real-time multimedia.

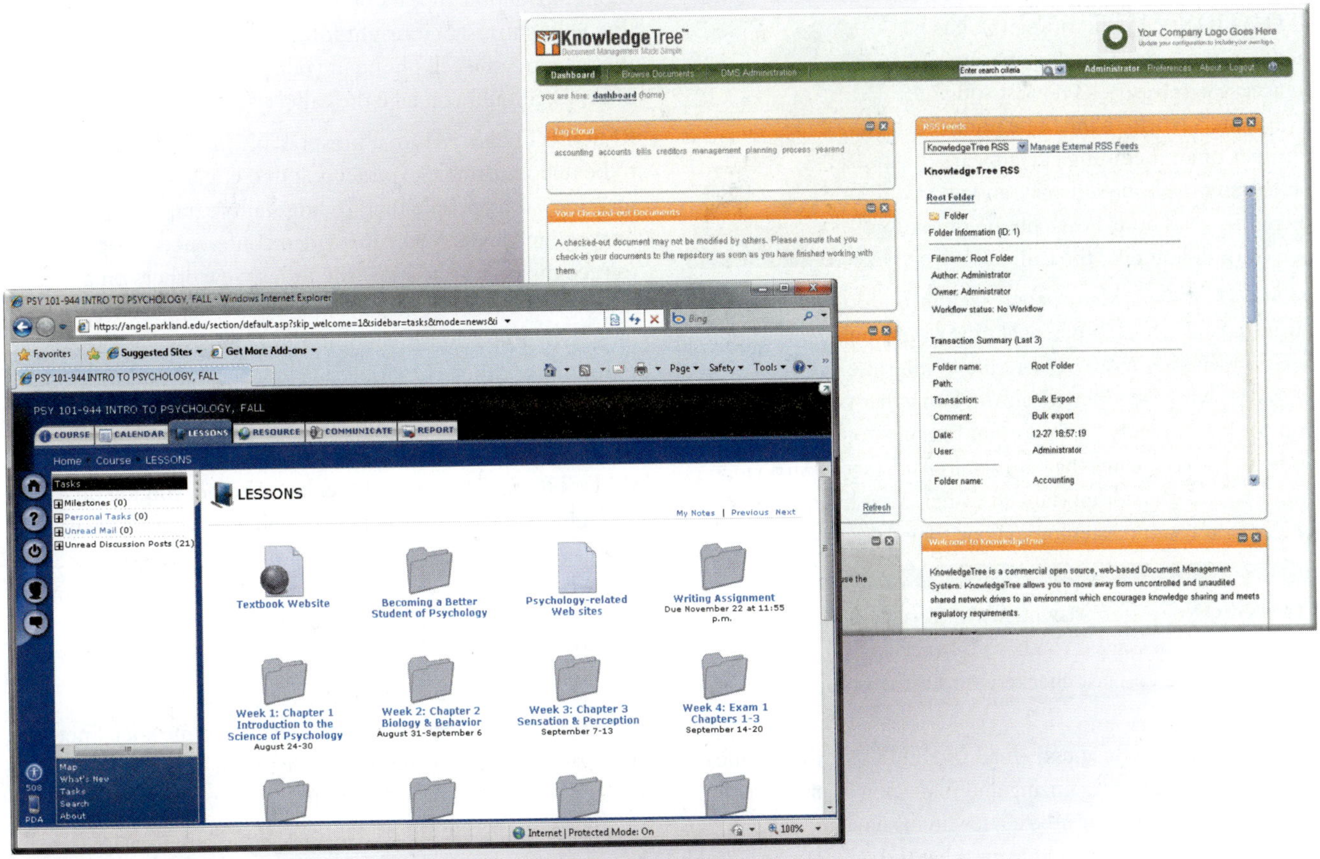

Figure 25 Businesses and other institutions share a variety of digital content in order to facilitate collaboration.

Digital Communications in Your Life

Many people use various forms of digital communications in both their personal and business lives. Imagine you are working in your chosen field and making decisions every day regarding how to communicate best with family, friends, and business contacts. The following scenario presents several situations and decisions regarding digital communications made during a single day.

8:15 a.m.

SITUATION: Before leaving for work, you remember that you are expecting an e-mail confirmation from your travel agent regarding plans for a trip to a friend's birthday party.

RESOLUTION: E-mail is a good tool when instant communication is not necessary. Personal business, such as travel arrangements, is negotiated or confirmed easily via e-mail messages, resulting in a permanent record of the communication.

You receive the e-mail message on your personal computer from your travel agent with the news that your trip is booked.

8:47 a.m.

SITUATION: While riding the bus to work, you use your smart phone to access wirelessly the newest song from your favorite band. The phone number of an incoming call appears on the smart phone's display, and you recognize it as your boss's phone number. Should you take the call?

RESOLUTION: Many people feel uncomfortable answering business calls while on personal time or in a public place. The decision whether to allow work life to interfere with personal life varies with each individual. You know that your boss calls your cell phone only for important reasons. You answer the call and your boss explains that she would like you to join a video conference with an important customer. After hanging up the phone, you resume listening to your song.

9:11 a.m.

SITUATION: After arriving at work, your first task is to check e-mail messages. You have more than 30 new e-mail messages since you last checked your e-mail inbox at 5:00 p.m. yesterday.

RESOLUTION: Business e-mail programs usually include several methods for organizing and managing your e-mail inbox. As you view your inbox, a few items have red exclamation marks next to them, indicating that the sender marked them as urgent. Your e-mail program also allows you to mark e-mail messages in your inbox with colored flags. You quickly flag the urgent items with a red flag, meaning that you will handle these immediately after you flag the remaining messages. You flag messages from customers with a yellow flag. By skimming the subject, you place blue, green, and black flags next to some messages. You use the colors to code messages based on the priority of the messages.

Good practices often suggest you respond by phone to urgent messages or messages from important customers. You put on your headset, and, using your VoIP phone, you begin the process of calling some of the people whose messages you marked with red and yellow flags. When you are finished talking on the phone, you respond to several of the other messages. By 9:45 a.m. your inbox is empty.

10:00 a.m.

SITUATION: By the time you arrive at your office's video conferencing room, five other coworkers already have gathered. After sitting down, you see a large monitor and a camera in front of you. A group of people in another conference room in London appears on the monitor. Your boss whispers that your shirt is a bit bright for the video conference. During the meeting, the cell phone in your pocket buzzes a number of times. Should you take the call?

RESOLUTION: At first, most people find video conferences to be uncomfortable experiences. In comparison to a typical meeting, some people tend to fidget more, tap their fingers, or speak more nervously in a video conference. People tend to recognize those actions when they view others on a monitor in a video conference, so experts suggest keeping these types of actions to a minimum.

You ignore the cell phone calls during the meeting. You plan to check your visual voice mail on your cell phone later.

9:15 p.m.

SITUATION: As you end the day at home, you log on to the online social network that you joined earlier in the year. When you add a friend to your list of contacts, you notice that she currently is logged on. You start your instant messaging program and begin instant messaging with your friend. Your friend reminds you that you still have a home page on another online social network from your days in school.

RESOLUTION: You log on to the old online social network that you used when you were in school. You decide to delete the site. People often forget that once they put content on an online social network, in a blog, or on a wiki that it may remain there forever unless they delete or edit it. Periodically, consider checking how others might perceive you based on content you have placed on the Internet.

Chapter Five

Computer Security and Safety, Ethics, and Privacy

Objectives

After completing this chapter, you will be able to:

1. Describe various types of Internet and network attacks (computer viruses, worms, Trojan horses, rootkits, botnets, denial of service attacks, back doors, and spoofing), and identify ways to safeguard against these attacks, including firewalls and intrusion detection software
2. Discuss techniques to prevent unauthorized computer access and use
3. Identify safeguards against hardware theft and vandalism
4. Explain the ways to protect against software theft and information theft
5. Discuss the types of devices available that protect computers from system failure
6. Identify risks and safeguards associated with wireless communications
7. Discuss ways to prevent health-related disorders and injuries due to computer use
8. Discuss issues surrounding information privacy, including electronic profiles, cookies, spyware and adware, spam, phishing, privacy laws, social engineering, employee monitoring, and content filtering

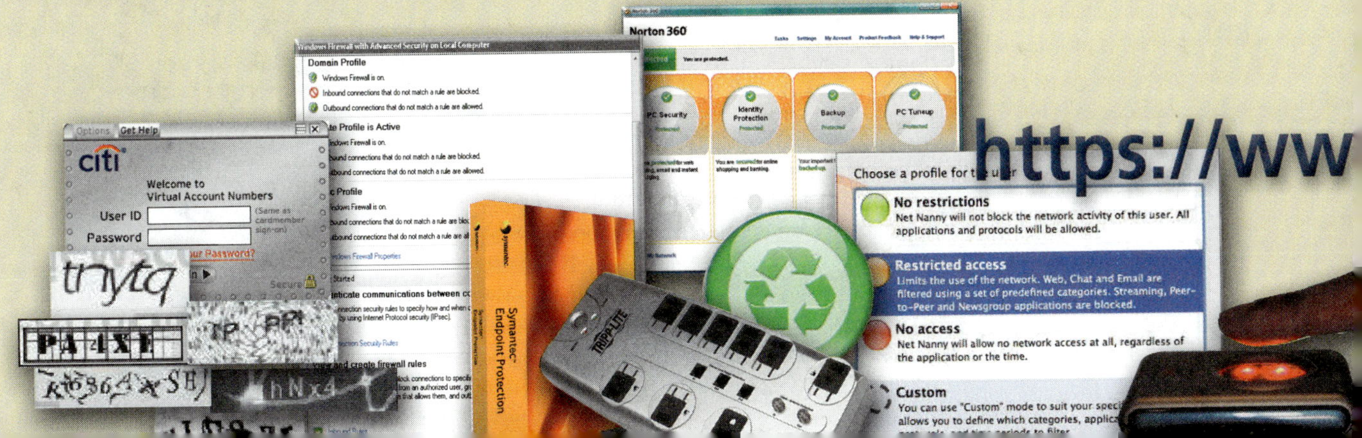

Computer Security Risks

Today, people rely on computers to create, store, and manage critical information. Thus, it is crucial that users take measures to protect their computers and data from loss, damage, and misuse.

A **computer security risk** is any event or action that could cause a loss of or damage to computer hardware, software, data, information, or processing capability. While some breaches to computer security are accidental, many are intentional. Some intruders do no damage; they merely access data, information, or programs on the computer. Other intruders indicate some evidence of their presence either by leaving a message or by deliberately altering or damaging data.

An intentional breach of computer security often involves a deliberate act that is against the law. Any illegal act involving a computer generally is referred to as a **computer crime**. The term **cybercrime** refers to online or Internet-based illegal acts. Today, cybercrime is one of the FBI's top three priorities.

Perpetrators of cybercrime and other intrusions fall into seven basic categories: hacker, cracker, script kiddie, corporate spy, unethical employee, cyberextortionist, and cyberterrorist.

- The term **hacker**, although originally a complimentary word for a computer enthusiast, now has a derogatory meaning and refers to someone who accesses a computer or network illegally. Some hackers claim the intent of their security breaches is to improve security.
- A **cracker** also is someone who accesses a computer or network illegally but has the intent of destroying data, stealing information, or other malicious action. Both hackers and crackers have advanced computer and network skills.
- A **script kiddie** has the same intent as a cracker but does not have the technical skills and knowledge. Script kiddies often use prewritten hacking and cracking programs to break into computers.
- Some corporate spies have excellent computer and networking skills and are hired to break into a specific computer and steal its proprietary data and information. Unscrupulous companies hire corporate spies, a practice known as corporate espionage, to gain a competitive advantage.
- Unethical employees break into their employers' computers for a variety of reasons. Some simply want to exploit a security weakness. Others seek financial gains from selling confidential information. Disgruntled employees may want revenge.
- A **cyberextortionist** is someone who uses e-mail as a vehicle for extortion. These perpetrators send an organization a threatening e-mail message indicating they will expose confidential information, exploit a security flaw, or launch an attack that will compromise the organization's network — if they are not paid a sum of money.

- A **cyberterrorist** is someone who uses the Internet or network to destroy or damage computers for political reasons. The cyberterrorist might target the nation's air traffic control system, electricity-generating companies, or a telecommunications infrastructure. Cyberterrorism usually requires a team of highly skilled individuals, millions of dollars, and several years of planning.

Business and home users must protect, or safeguard, their computers from breaches of security and other computer security risks. Some organizations hire individuals previously convicted of computer crimes to help identify security risks and implement safeguards because these individuals know how criminals attempt to breach security.

The more common computer security risks include Internet and network attacks, unauthorized access and use, hardware theft, software theft, information theft, and system failure (Figure 5-1). The following pages describe these computer security risks and also discuss safeguards users might take to minimize or prevent their consequences.

Figure 5-1 Computers and computer users are exposed to several types of security risks.

Internet and Network Attacks

Information transmitted over networks has a higher degree of security risk than information kept on an organization's premises. In an organization, network administrators usually take measures to protect a network from security risks. On the Internet, where no central administrator is present, the security risk is greater.

Internet and network attacks that jeopardize security include computer viruses, worms, Trojan horses, and rootkits; botnets; denial of service attacks; back doors; and spoofing. The following sections address these computer security risks and suggest measures organizations and individuals can take to protect their computers while on the Internet or connected to a network.

Computer Viruses, Worms, Trojan Horses, and Rootkits

Every unprotected computer is susceptible to the first type of computer security risk — a computer virus, worm, Trojan horse, and/or rootkit.

- A computer **virus** is a potentially damaging computer program that affects, or infects, a computer negatively by altering the way the computer works without the user's knowledge or permission. Once the virus infects the computer, it can spread throughout and may damage files and system software, including the operating system.
- A **worm** is a program that copies itself repeatedly, for example in memory or on a network, using up resources and possibly shutting down the computer or network.
- A **Trojan horse** (named after the Greek myth) is a program that hides within or looks like a legitimate program. A certain condition or action usually triggers the Trojan horse. Unlike a virus or worm, a Trojan horse does not replicate itself to other computers.
- A **rootkit** is a program that hides in a computer and allows someone from a remote location to take full control of the computer. Once the rootkit is installed, the rootkit author can execute programs, change settings, monitor activity, and access files on the remote computer.

Computer viruses, worms, Trojan horses, and rootkits are classified as **malware** (short for malicious software), which are programs that act without a user's knowledge and deliberately alter the computer's operations. Unscrupulous programmers write malware and then test it to ensure it can deliver its payload. The **payload** is the destructive event or prank the program is intended to deliver. A computer infected by a virus, worm, Trojan horse, or rootkit often has one or more of the following symptoms:

- Operating system runs much slower than usual
- Available memory is less than expected
- Files become corrupted
- Screen displays unusual message or image
- Unknown programs or files mysteriously appear
- Music or unusual sound plays randomly
- Existing programs and files disappear
- Programs or files do not work properly
- System properties change
- Operating system does not start up
- Operating system shuts down unexpectedly

Currently, more than 300,000 Web sites can infect your computer with known viruses, worms, Trojan horses, rootkits, and other malware. These malicious programs deliver their payload on a computer in a variety of ways: when a user (1) opens an infected file, (2) runs an infected program, (3) boots the computer with infected removable media inserted in a drive or plugged in a port, (4) connects an unprotected computer to a network, or (5) when a certain condition or event occurs, such as the computer's clock changing to a specific date. A common way computers become infected with viruses and other malware is through users opening infected e-mail attachments (Figure 5-2).

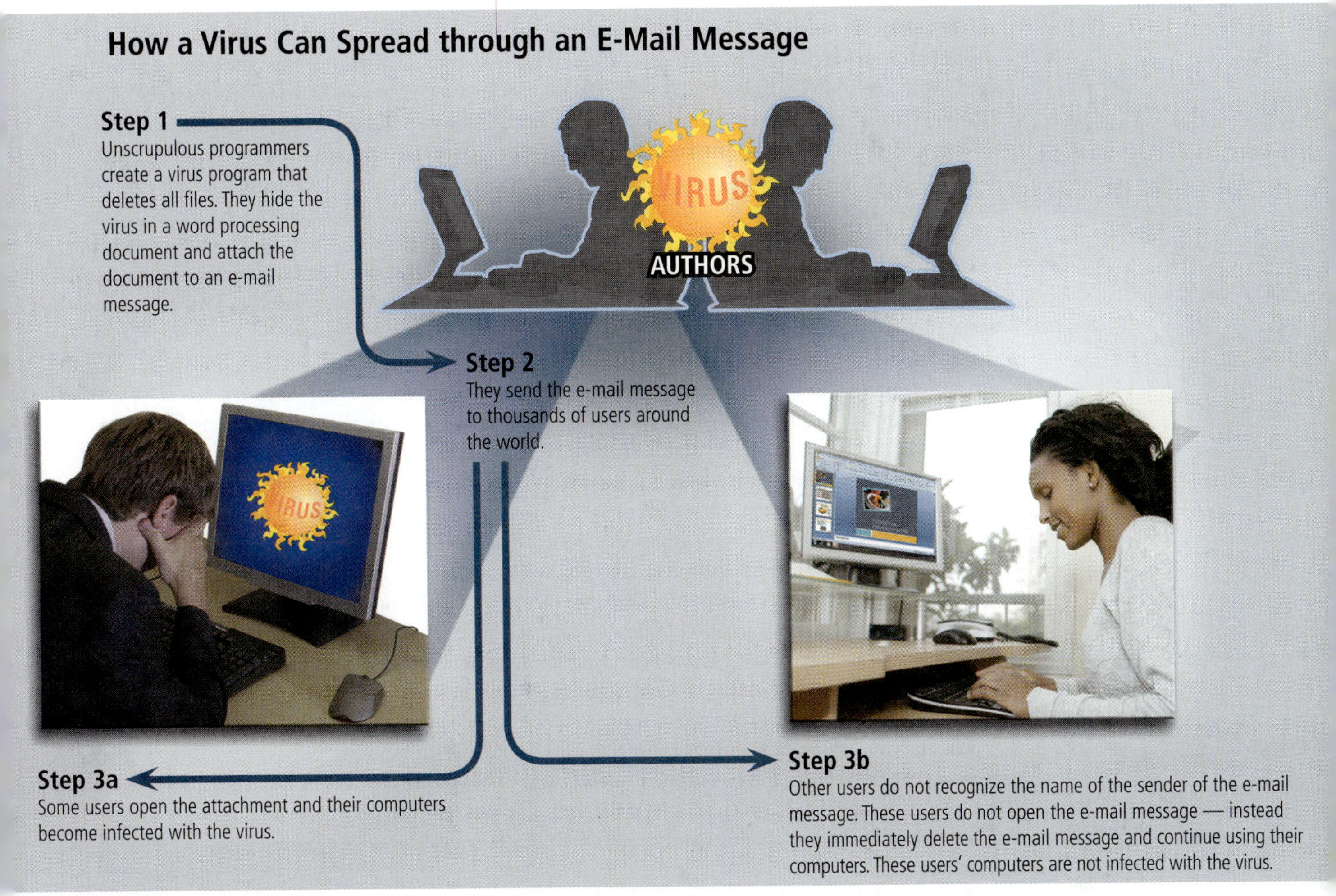

Figure 5-2 This figure shows how a virus can spread through an e-mail message.

FAQ 5-1

Can multimedia files be infected with a virus?

Yes. The increase in popularity of media sharing Web sites provides a great opportunity to distribute malicious programs. During one year, approximately 500,000 people downloaded what they thought was a media file from the Internet. In fact, the file was a Trojan horse that infected many computers with spyware. For this reason, it is important to scan all media files for malware before playing them.

For more information, visit the Microsoft Office and Concepts CourseMate Web site at www.cengagebrain.com, navigate to the Chapter 5 FAQ resource for this book, and then click Infected Media Files.

Safeguards against Computer Viruses and Other Malware

Users can take several precautions to protect their home and work computers and mobile devices from these malicious infections. The following paragraphs discuss these precautionary measures.

Do not start a computer with removable media, such as optical discs and USB flash drives, in the drives or ports — unless you are certain the media are uninfected or from a trusted source. A **trusted source** is an organization or person you believe will not send a virus infected file knowingly. Never open an e-mail attachment unless you are expecting the attachment *and* it is from a trusted source. If the e-mail message is from an unknown source, delete the e-mail message immediately — without opening or executing any attachments. If the e-mail message is from a trusted source, but you were not expecting an attachment, carefully check the spelling of the e-mail address and contents of the message for errors because perpetrators often make typographical errors. If the message is error-free, verify with the source that they intended to send you an attachment — before opening it.

Some viruses are hidden in macros, which are instructions saved in software such as a word processing or spreadsheet program. In programs that allow users to write macros, you should set the macro security level so that the application software warns users that a document they are attempting to open contains a macro. From this warning, a user chooses to disable or enable the macro. If the document is from a trusted source, the user can enable the macro. Otherwise, it should be disabled.

Users should install an antivirus program and update it frequently. An **antivirus program** protects a computer against viruses by identifying and removing any computer viruses found in memory, on storage media, or on incoming files. Most antivirus programs also protect against other malware. When you purchase a new computer, it often includes antivirus software. Many e-mail servers also have antivirus programs installed to check incoming and outgoing e-mail messages for malware.

An antivirus program scans for programs that attempt to modify the boot program, the operating system, and other programs that normally are read from but not modified. In addition, many antivirus programs automatically scan files downloaded from the Web, e-mail attachments, opened files, and all removable media inserted in the computer.

One technique that antivirus programs use to identify a virus is to look for virus signatures. A **virus signature**, also called a **virus definition**, is a known specific pattern of virus code. Computer users should update their antivirus program's signature files regularly (Figure 5-3). This extremely important activity allows the antivirus program to protect against viruses written since the antivirus program was released and/or its last update. Most antivirus programs contain an automatic update feature that regularly prompts users to download the virus signature, usually at least once a week. The vendor usually provides this service to registered users at no cost for a specified time.

If an antivirus program identifies an infected file, it attempts to remove the malware. If the antivirus program cannot remove the infection, it often quarantines the infected file. A **quarantine** is a separate area of a hard disk that holds the infected file until the infection can be removed. This step ensures other files will not become infected. Quarantined files remain on your computer until you delete them or restore them.

Some users also install a personal firewall program to protect a computer and its data from unauthorized intrusions. A section later in this chapter discusses firewalls.

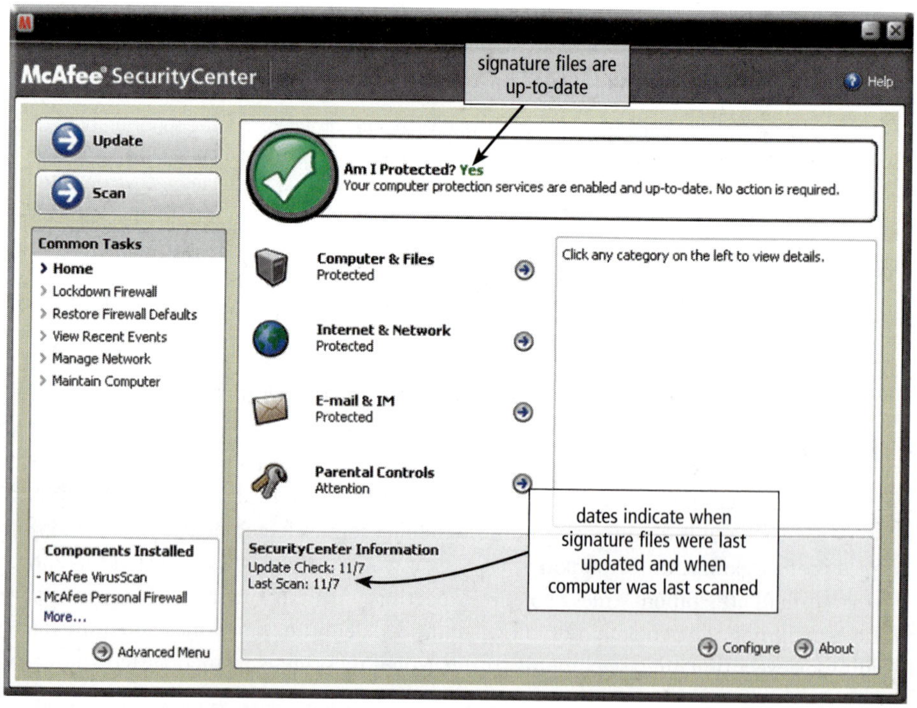

Figure 5-3
This antivirus program, which protects a computer from a variety of malware, regularly checks for the latest virus signatures and other important updates.

Finally, stay informed about new virus alerts and virus hoaxes. A **virus hoax** is an e-mail message that warns users of a nonexistent virus or other malware. Often, these virus hoaxes are in the form of a chain letter that requests the user to send a copy of the e-mail message to as many people as possible. The content of the hoax message, for example, may inform users that an important operating system file on their computer is a virus and encourage them to delete the file, which could make their computer unusable. Instead of forwarding the message, visit a Web site that publishes a list of virus alerts and virus hoaxes.

The list in Figure 5-4 summarizes important tips for protecting your computer from viruses and other malware.

Tips for Preventing Viruses and Other Malware
1. Never start a computer with removable media inserted in the drives or plugged in the ports, unless the media are uninfected.
2. Never open an e-mail attachment unless you are expecting it *and* it is from a trusted source.
3. Set the macro security in programs so that you can enable or disable macros. Enable macros only if the document is from a trusted source and you are expecting it.
4. Install an antivirus program on all of your computers. Update the software and the virus signature files regularly.
5. Scan all downloaded programs for viruses and other malware.
6. If the antivirus program flags an e-mail attachment as infected, delete or quarantine the attachment immediately.
7. Before using any removable media, scan the media for malware. Follow this procedure even for shrink-wrapped software from major developers. Some commercial software has been infected and distributed to unsuspecting users.
8. Install a personal firewall program.
9. Stay informed about new virus alerts and virus hoaxes.

Figure 5-4 With the growing number of new viruses and other malware, it is crucial that users take steps to protect their computers.

Botnets

A **botnet** is a group of compromised computers connected to a network such as the Internet that are used as part of a network that attacks other networks, usually for nefarious purposes. A compromised computer, known as a **zombie**, is one whose owner is unaware the computer is being controlled remotely by an outsider. Cybercriminals use botnets to send spam via e-mail, spread viruses and other malware, or commit a denial of service attack.

? FAQ 5-2

How can I tell if my computer is a zombie or in a botnet?

The number of zombie computers is increasing at a rapid rate. Your computer may be a zombie or part of a botnet if you notice unusually high disk activity, a slower than normal Internet connection, or devices connected to your computer becoming increasingly unresponsive. The chances of your computer becoming a zombie or part of a botnet greatly increase if you do not have an effective firewall.

For more information, visit the Microsoft Office and Concepts CourseMate Web site at www.cengagebrain.com, navigate to the Chapter 5 FAQ resource for this book, and then click Zombies and Botnets.

Denial of Service Attacks

A **denial of service attack**, or **DoS attack**, is an assault whose purpose is to disrupt computer access to an Internet service such as the Web or e-mail. Perpetrators carry out a DoS attack in a variety of ways. For example, they may use an unsuspecting computer to send an influx of confusing data messages or useless traffic to a computer network. The victim computer network slows down considerably and eventually becomes unresponsive or unavailable, blocking legitimate visitors from accessing the network.

Perpetrators have a variety of motives for carrying out a DoS attack. Those who disagree with the beliefs or actions of a particular organization claim political anger motivates their attacks. Some perpetrators use the attack as a vehicle for extortion. Others simply want the recognition, even though it is negative.

DoS Attacks

For more information, visit the Microsoft Office and Concepts CourseMate Web site at www.cengagebrain.com, navigate to the Chapter 5 Web Link resource for this book, and then click DoS Attacks.

Back Doors

A **back door** is a program or set of instructions in a program that allow users to bypass security controls when accessing a program, computer, or network. Once perpetrators gain access to unsecure computers, they often install a back door or modify an existing program to include a back door, which allows them to continue to access the computer remotely without the user's knowledge.

Spoofing

Spoofing is a technique intruders use to make their network or Internet transmission appear legitimate to a victim computer or network. E-mail spoofing occurs when the sender's address or other components of the e-mail header are altered so that it appears the e-mail originated from a different sender. E-mail spoofing commonly is used for virus hoaxes, spam, and phishing scams. IP spoofing occurs when an intruder computer fools a network into believing its IP address is associated with a trusted source. Perpetrators of IP spoofing trick their victims into interacting with a phony Web site.

Safeguards against Botnets, DoS Attacks, Back Doors, and Spoofing

To defend against botnets, DoS attacks, improper use of back doors, and spoofing, users can implement firewall solutions and install intrusion detection software. The following sections discuss these safeguards.

Firewalls

A **firewall** is hardware and/or software that protects a network's resources from intrusion by users on another network such as the Internet (Figure 5-5). All networked and online computer users should implement a firewall solution.

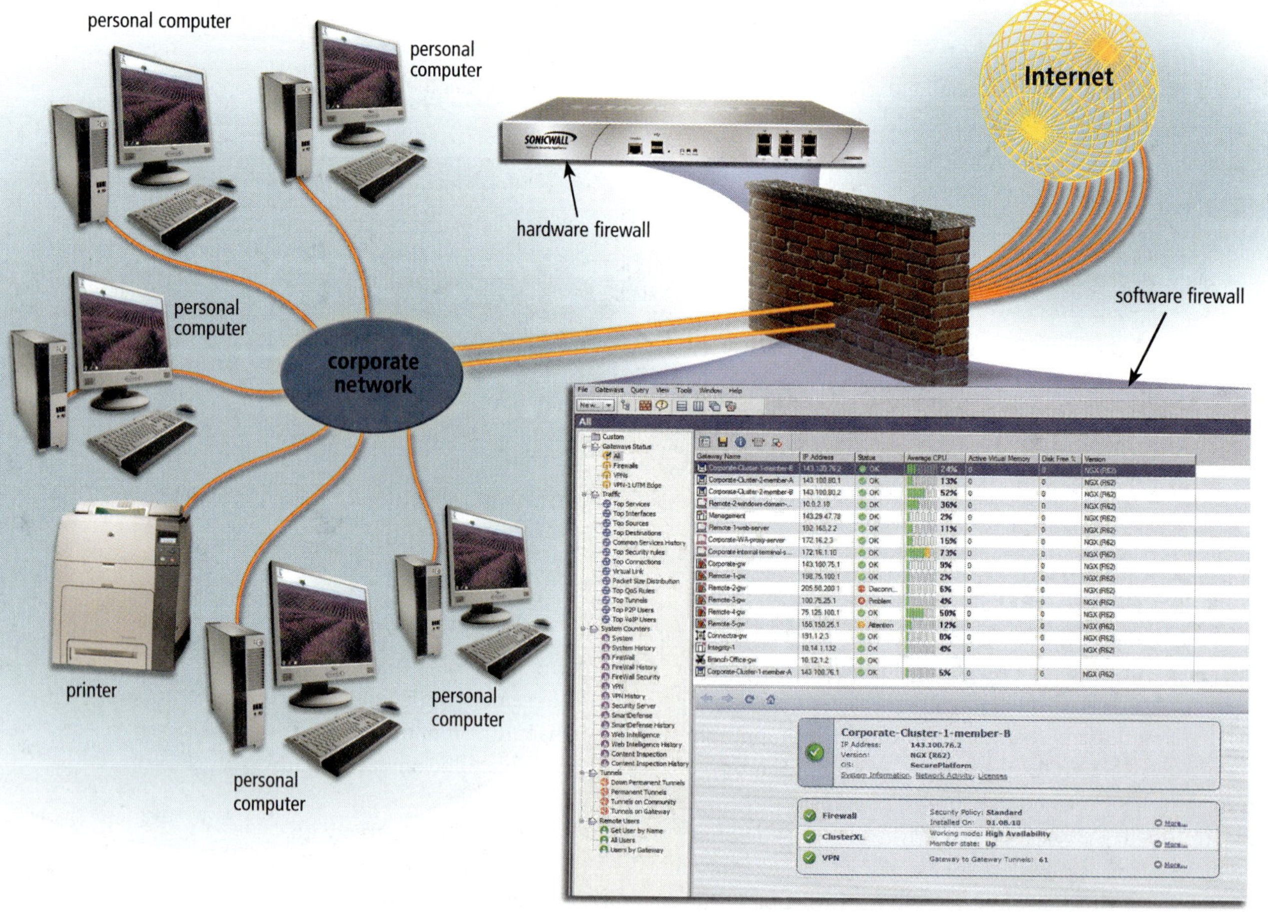

Figure 5-5 A firewall is hardware and/or software that protects a network's resources from intrusion by users on another network such as the Internet.

Organizations use firewalls to protect network resources from outsiders and to restrict employees' access to sensitive data such as payroll or personnel records. They can implement a firewall solution themselves or outsource their needs to a company specializing in providing firewall protection. Large organizations often route all their communications through a proxy server, which is a component of the firewall. A proxy server is a server outside the organization's network that controls which communications pass into the organization's network.

Home and small office/home office users often protect their computers with a personal firewall utility. A **personal firewall** is a utility program that detects and protects a personal computer and its data from unauthorized intrusions. Some operating systems, such as Windows, include personal firewalls.

Some small office/home office users purchase a hardware firewall, such as a router or other device that has a built-in firewall, in addition to or instead of personal firewall software. Hardware firewalls stop intrusions before they attempt to affect your computer maliciously.

Firewalls
For more information, visit the Microsoft Office and Concepts CourseMate Web site at www.cengagebrain.com, navigate to the Chapter 5 Web Link resource for this book, and then click Firewalls.

Intrusion Detection Software

To provide extra protection against hackers and other intruders, large organizations sometimes use intrusion detection software to identify possible security breaches. **Intrusion detection software** automatically analyzes all network traffic, assesses system vulnerabilities, identifies any unauthorized access (intrusions), and notifies network administrators of suspicious behavior patterns or system breaches.

To utilize intrusion detection software requires the expertise of a network administrator because the programs are complex and difficult to use and interpret. These programs also are quite expensive.

Unauthorized Access and Use

Another type of computer security risk is unauthorized access and use. **Unauthorized access** is the use of a computer or network without permission. **Unauthorized use** is the use of a computer or its data for unapproved or possibly illegal activities. Unauthorized use includes a variety of activities: an employee using an organization's computer to send personal e-mail messages, an employee using the organization's word processing software to track his or her child's soccer league scores, or someone gaining access to a bank computer and performing an unauthorized transfer.

Safeguards against Unauthorized Access and Use

Organizations take several measures to help prevent unauthorized access and use. At a minimum, they should have a written acceptable use policy (AUP) that outlines the computer activities for which the computer and network may and may not be used. An organization's AUP should specify the acceptable use of computers by employees for personal reasons. Some organizations prohibit such use entirely. Others allow personal use on the employee's own time such as a lunch hour.

Other measures that safeguard against unauthorized access and use include firewalls and intrusion detection software, which were discussed in the previous section, and identifying and authenticating users.

Identifying and Authenticating Users

Many organizations use access controls to minimize the chance that a perpetrator intentionally may access or an employee accidentally may access confidential information on a computer. An **access control** is a security measure that defines who can access a computer, when they can access it, and what actions they can take while accessing the computer. In addition, the computer should maintain an **audit trail** that records in a file both successful and unsuccessful access attempts. An unsuccessful access attempt could result from a user mistyping his or her password, or it could result from a hacker trying thousands of passwords.

Organizations should investigate unsuccessful access attempts immediately to ensure they are not intentional breaches of security. They also should review successful access for irregularities, such as use of the computer after normal working hours or from remote computers.

Many systems implement access controls using a two-phase process called identification and authentication. Identification verifies that an individual is a valid user. Authentication verifies that the individual is the person he or she claims to be. Three methods of identification and authentication include user names and passwords, possessed objects, and biometric devices. The technique(s) an organization uses should correspond to the degree of risk associated with the unauthorized access.

User Names and Passwords A **user name**, or user ID (identification), is a unique combination of characters, such as letters of the alphabet or numbers, that identifies one specific user. A **password** is a private combination of characters associated with the user name that allows access to certain computer resources.

Most multiuser (networked) operating systems require that users correctly enter a user name and a password before they can access the data, information, and programs stored on a computer or network (Figure 5-6).

Multiuser systems typically require that users select their own passwords. Users typically choose an easy-to-remember word or series of characters for passwords. If your password is too obvious, however, such as your initials or birthday, others can guess it easily. Easy passwords make it simple for hackers and other intruders to break into a system. Hackers use computer automated tools to assist them with guessing passwords. Thus, you should select a password carefully. Longer passwords provide greater security than shorter ones. Each character added to a password significantly increases the number of possible combinations and the length of time it might take for someone or for a hacker's computer to guess the password (Figure 5-7).

In addition to a user name and password, some systems ask users to enter one of several pieces of personal information. Such items can include a spouse's first name, a birth date, a place of birth, or a mother's maiden name. As with a password, if the user's response does not match the information on file, the system denies access.

Some Web sites use a CAPTCHA to further protect a user's password. A **CAPTCHA**, which stands for Completely Automated Public Turing test to tell Computers and Humans Apart, is a program that verifies user input is not computer generated. A CAPTCHA displays a series of distorted characters and requires the user to enter the characters correctly to continue using the Web site. For visually impaired users, the CAPTCHA text can be read aloud. Because unscrupulous individuals attempt to circumvent or decode CAPTCHAs, developers continually are seeking ways to make them more secure or develop alternative authentication techniques.

Figure 5-6 Many Web sites that maintain personal and confidential data require a user to enter a user name and password.

Password Protection

Number of Characters	Possible Combinations	AVERAGE TIME TO DISCOVER Human	Computer
1	36	3 minutes	.000018 second
2	1,300	2 hours	.00065 second
3	47,000	3 days	.02 second
4	1,700,000	3 months	1 second
5	60,000,000	10 years	30 seconds
10	3,700,000,000,000,000	580 million years	59 years

- *Possible characters include the letters A–Z and numbers 0–9*
- *Human discovery assumes 1 try every 10 seconds*
- *Computer discovery assumes 1 million tries per second*
- *Average time assumes the password would be discovered in approximately half the time it would take to try all possible combinations*

Figure 5-7 This table shows the effect of increasing the length of a password that consists of letters and numbers. The longer the password, the more effort required to discover it. Long passwords, however, are more difficult for users to remember.

Possessed Objects A **possessed object** is any item that you must carry to gain access to a computer or computer facility. Examples of possessed objects are badges, cards, smart cards, and keys. The card you use in an automated teller machine (ATM) is a possessed object that allows access to your bank account.

Possessed objects often are used in combination with personal identification numbers. A **personal identification number (PIN)** is a numeric password, either assigned by a company or selected by a user. PINs provide an additional level of security. An ATM card typically requires a four-digit PIN. PINs are passwords. Select them carefully and protect them as you do any other password.

Biometric Devices A **biometric device** authenticates a person's identity by translating a personal characteristic, such as a fingerprint, into a digital code that is compared with a digital code stored in the computer verifying a physical or behavioral characteristic. If the digital code in the computer does not match the personal characteristic code, the computer denies access to the individual.

Biometric devices grant access to programs, computers, or rooms using computer analysis of some biometric identifier. Examples of biometric devices and systems include fingerprint readers (Figure 5-8), hand geometry systems, face recognition systems, voice verification systems, signature verification systems, iris recognition systems, and retinal scanners. Many grocery stores, retail stores, and gas stations now use **biometric payment**, where the customer's fingerprint is read by a fingerprint reader that is linked to a specific payment method such as a checking account or credit card.

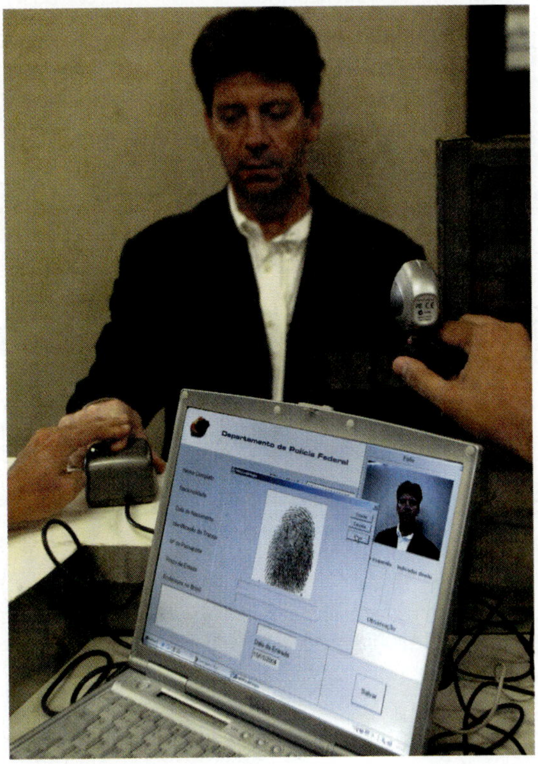

Figure 5-8 A fingerprint reader verifies this traveler's identity.

FAQ 5-3

How many people are victims of identity theft each year?

Studies reveal that identity theft is the fastest growing crime in the United States. In fact, identity theft costs banks, victims, and the government millions of dollars each year, with that amount continually increasing. The chart to the right illustrates the reported number of identity theft cases grouped by age.

For more information, visit the Microsoft Office and Concepts CourseMate Web site at www.cengagebrain.com, navigate to the Chapter 5 FAQ resource for this book, and then click Identity Theft.

Digital Forensics

Digital forensics, also called computer forensics, network forensics, or cyberforensics, is the discovery, collection, and analysis of evidence found on computers and networks. Digital forensics involves the examination of computer media, programs, data and log files on computers, servers, and networks. Many areas use digital forensics, including law enforcement, criminal prosecutors, military intelligence, insurance agencies, and information security departments in the private sector.

A digital forensics examiner must have knowledge of the law, technical experience with many types of hardware and software products, superior communication skills, familiarity with corporate structures and policies, a willingness to learn and update skills, and a knack for problem solving. For a look at the next generation of forensics, read Looking Ahead 5-1.

LOOKING AHEAD 5-1

Brain Waves, Behavior Tracked to Prevent and Solve Crimes

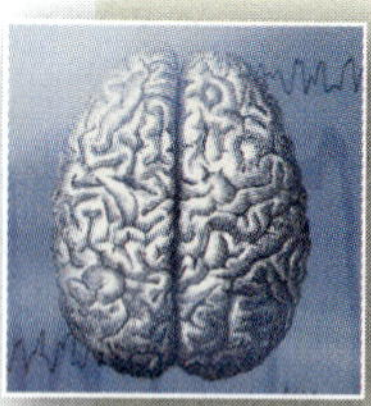

The brain may one day become part of a crime scene investigation. When a person has committed a criminal or fraudulent act, his brain generates unique waves involuntarily when confronted with pictures, sounds, and words related to the crime scene. Computers can capture and analyze this brain fingerprint of distinctive brain waves to determine if a person has stored critical details of a particular felony or misdemeanor situation.

Similarly, behavior detection systems study a person's body language, facial expressions, speech, and emotions to isolate specific patterns that criminals commonly exhibit. The surveillance systems can recognize microexpressions, which are the split-second emotions lasting one-fifteenth of a second, on a person's face.

The U.S. Department of Homeland Security is testing its Future Attribute Screening Technologies (FAST) program, which uses cameras, infrared heat sensors, and lasers to measure pulse and breathing rates. The trial technology is being tested for use at airports and sporting and music events.

For more information, visit the Microsoft Office and Concepts CourseMate Web site at www.cengagebrain.com, navigate to the Chapter 5 Looking Ahead resource for this book, and then click Brain Fingerprinting.

QUIZ YOURSELF 5-1

Instructions: Find the true statement below. Then, rewrite the remaining false statements so that they are true.

1. A back door attack is an assault whose purpose is to disrupt computer access to an Internet service such as the Web or e-mail.
2. All networked and online computer users should implement a firewall solution.
3. Computer viruses, worms, Trojan horses, and rootkits are malware that acts with a user's knowledge.
4. Shorter passwords provide greater security than longer ones.
5. Updating an antivirus program's quarantine protects a computer against viruses written since the antivirus program was released.

Quiz Yourself Online: To further check your knowledge of pages 182 through 192, visit the Microsoft Office and Concepts CourseMate Web site at www.cengagebrain.com, navigate to the Chapter 5 Quiz Yourself resource for this book, and then click Objectives 1 – 2.

Hardware Theft and Vandalism

Hardware theft and vandalism are other types of computer security risks. **Hardware theft** is the act of stealing computer equipment. **Hardware vandalism** is the act of defacing or destroying computer equipment. Hardware vandalism takes many forms, from someone cutting a computer cable to individuals breaking into a business or school computer lab and aimlessly smashing computers.

Companies, schools, and other organizations that house many computers are at risk of hardware theft and vandalism, especially those that have smaller system units that easily can fit in a backpack or briefcase. Mobile users also are susceptible to hardware theft. It is estimated that more than 600,000 notebook computers are stolen each year. The size and weight of these computers, especially netbooks, make them easy to steal.

Safeguards against Hardware Theft and Vandalism

To help reduce the chances of theft, companies and schools use a variety of security measures. Physical access controls, such as locked doors and windows, usually are adequate to protect the equipment. Many businesses, schools, and some homeowners install alarm systems for additional security. School computer labs and other areas with a large number of semifrequent users often attach additional physical security devices such as cables that lock the equipment to a desk (Figure 5-9), cabinet, or floor. Small locking devices also exist that require a key to access a hard disk or optical disc drive.

Some businesses use a **real time location system (RTLS)** to track and identify the location of high-risk or high-value items. One implementation of RTLS places RFID tags in items to be tracked.

RTLS

For more information, visit the Microsoft Office and Concepts CourseMate Web site at www.cengagebrain.com, navigate to the Chapter 5 Web Link resource for this book, and then click RTLS.

Mobile computer users must take special care to protect their equipment. Some users attach a physical device such as a cable to lock a mobile computer temporarily to a stationary object. Other mobile users install a mini-security system in the notebook computer. Some of these security systems shut down the computer and sound an alarm if the computer moves outside a specified distance. Others can be configured to photograph the thieves when they use the computer. Notebook computer security systems and tracking software also can track the location of a stolen notebook computer.

Some notebook computers use passwords, possessed objects, and biometrics as methods of security. When you start these computers, you must enter a password, slide a card in a card reader, or press your finger on a fingerprint reader before the hard disk unlocks. This type of security does not prevent theft, but it renders the computer useless if it is stolen.

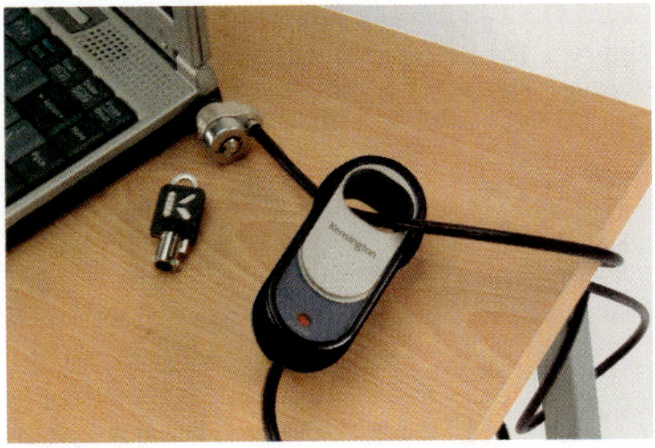

Figure 5-9 Using cables to lock computers can help prevent the theft of computer equipment.

Software Theft

Another type of computer security risk is software theft. **Software theft** occurs when someone steals software media, intentionally erases programs, illegally copies a program, or illegally registers and/or activates a program. One form of software theft involves someone physically stealing the media that contain the software or the hardware that contains the media, as described in the previous section. Another form of software theft occurs when software is stolen from software manufacturers. This type of theft, called piracy, is by far the most common form of software theft. Software **piracy** is the unauthorized and illegal duplication of copyrighted software. A related form of software theft involves users illegally obtaining registration numbers and/or activation codes.

Safeguards against Software Theft

To protect software media from being stolen, owners should keep original software boxes and media in a secure location. All computer users should back up their files and disks regularly, in the event of theft.

To protect themselves from software piracy, software manufacturers issue users license agreements. A **license agreement** is the right to use the software. That is, you do not own the software. The license agreement provides specific conditions for use of the software, which a user must accept before using the software (Figure 5-10). These terms usually are displayed when you install the software.

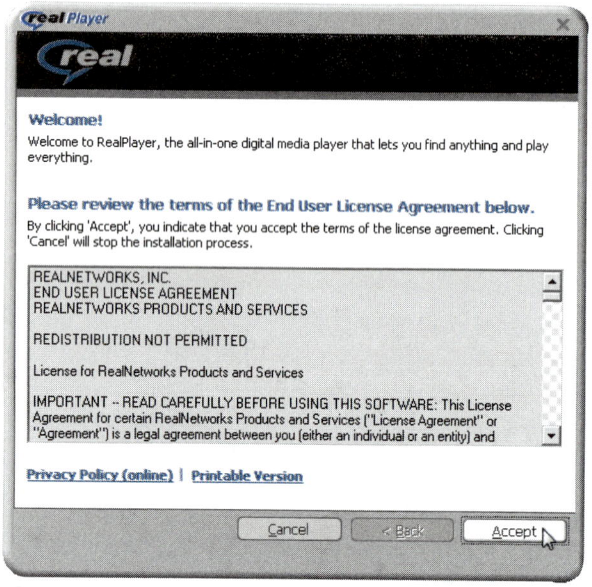

Figure 5-10 A user must accept the terms in the license agreement before using the software.

The most common type of license included with software purchased by individual users is a single-user license agreement, also called an end-user license agreement (EULA). A single-user license agreement typically includes many of the following conditions that specify a user's responsibility upon acceptance of the agreement.

Users are permitted to:

- Install the software on only one computer. (Some license agreements allow users to install the software on one desktop computer and one notebook computer.)
- Make one copy of the software as a backup.
- Give or sell the software to another individual, but only if the software is removed from the user's computer first.

Users are not permitted to:

- Install the software on a network, such as a school computer lab.
- Give copies to friends and colleagues, while continuing to use the software.
- Export the software.
- Rent or lease the software.

Unless otherwise specified by a license agreement, you do not have the right to copy, loan, borrow, rent, or in any way distribute software. Doing so is a violation of copyright law. It also is a federal crime. Despite this, some experts estimate for every authorized copy of software in use, at least one unauthorized copy exists. Read Ethics & Issues 5-1 for a related discussion.

In an attempt to prevent software piracy, Microsoft and other manufacturers have incorporated an activation process into many of its consumer products. During the **product activation**, which is conducted either online or by telephone, users provide the software product's 25-character identification number to receive an installation identification number unique to the computer on which the software is installed.

If you are not completely familiar with your school or employer's policies governing installation of software, check with the information technology department or your school's technology coordinator.

Ethics & Issues

For the complete text of the Ethics & Issues boxes found in this chapter, visit the Microsoft Office and Concepts CourseMate Web site at www.cengagebrain.com and then navigate to the Chapter 5 Ethics & Issues resource for this book.

ETHICS & ISSUES 5-1

Should Online Auctions Be Liable for Pirated Software Sales?

Currently, software companies patrol online auction sites looking for pirated copies of their software that might be for sale. When they find such activity, the software company takes legal action against the seller of the pirated software. With the explosion of online auctions, however, the companies are fighting an uphill battle given the amount of time it takes to discover the sales, find the perpetrators, and then individually bring each perpetrator to justice. Many software companies have joined forces to demand that auction sites, such as eBay, legally be held liable for pirated software sold on their Web sites, and they have offered more than 20 suggestions as to how auction sites could better police their Web sites for pirated software. Online auction Web sites claim that the law clearly states they are not responsible for such sales, but that the software companies legally are responsible for controlling pirated sales. For its part, eBay claims already to enforce more than 13,000 rules to check for suspicious activity on its Web site, and offers trademark holders a special program in which they can enroll and have additional rules enforced.

Should online auctions be liable for pirated software sales on their Web sites? Why or why not? Should new or clearer laws be written to force online auctions to check whether software for sale on their Web sites is pirated? Why? Would you purchase software at an online auction being sold at a substantial discount to prices offered elsewhere? Why or why not?

Information Theft

Information theft is yet another type of computer security risk. **Information theft** occurs when someone steals personal or confidential information. An unethical company executive may steal or buy stolen information to learn about a competitor. A corrupt individual may steal credit card numbers to make fraudulent purchases.

Safeguards against Information Theft

Most companies attempt to prevent information theft by implementing the user identification and authentication controls discussed earlier in this chapter. These controls are best suited for protecting information on computers located on an organization's premises. Information transmitted over networks offers a higher degree of risk because unscrupulous users can intercept it during transmission. To protect information on the Internet and networks, companies and individuals use a variety of encryption techniques.

Encryption

Encryption is the process of converting readable data into unreadable characters to prevent unauthorized access. You treat encrypted data just like any other data. That is, you can store it or send it in an e-mail message. To read the data, the recipient must **decrypt**, or decipher, it into a readable form.

In the encryption process, the unencrypted, readable data is called plaintext. The encrypted (scrambled) data is called ciphertext. An **encryption algorithm** is a set of steps that can convert readable plaintext into unreadable ciphertext. Figure 5-11 shows examples of some simple encryption algorithms. Encryption programs typically use more than one encryption algorithm, along with an encryption key. An **encryption key** is a programmed formula that the originator of the data uses to encrypt the plaintext and the recipient of the data uses to decrypt the ciphertext.

Simple Encryption Algorithms

Name	Algorithm	Plaintext	Ciphertext	Explanation
Transposition	Switch the order of characters	SOFTWARE	OSTFAWER	Adjacent characters swapped
Substitution	Replace characters with other characters	INFORMATION	WLDIMXQUWIL	Each letter replaced with another
Expansion	Insert characters between existing characters	USER	UYSYEYRY	Letter Y inserted after each character
Compaction	Remove characters and store elsewhere	ACTIVATION	ACIVTIN	Every third letter removed (T, A, O)

Figure 5-11 This table shows four simple encryption algorithms. Most encryption keys use a combination of algorithms.

Some operating systems and e-mail programs allow you to encrypt the contents of files and messages that are stored on your computer. You also can purchase an encryption program, such as Pretty Good Privacy (PGP).

A **digital signature** is an encrypted code that a person, Web site, or organization attaches to an electronic message to verify the identity of the message sender. Digital signatures often are used to ensure that an impostor is not participating in an Internet transaction. That is, digital signatures help to prevent e-mail forgery. A digital signature also can verify that the content of a message has not changed.

Many Web browsers and Web sites use encryption. A Web site that uses encryption techniques to secure its data is known as a **secure site** (Figure 5-12). Secure sites often use digital certificates. A **digital certificate** is a notice that guarantees a user or a Web site is legitimate. A **certificate authority** (CA)

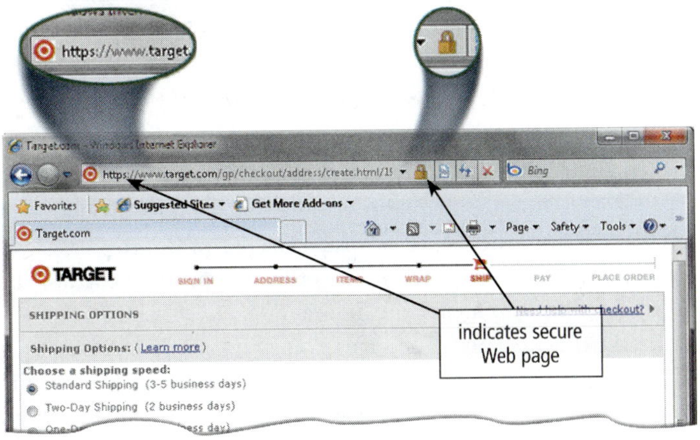

Figure 5-12 Web addresses of secure sites often begin with https instead of http. Browsers also often display a lock symbol in the window.

Digital Certificates
For more information, visit the Microsoft Office and Concepts CourseMate Web site at www.cengagebrain.com, navigate to the Chapter 5 Web Link resource for this book, and then click Digital Certificates.

is an authorized person or a company that issues and verifies digital certificates. Users apply for a digital certificate from a CA. The digital certificate typically contains information such as the user's name, the issuing CA's name and signature, and the serial number of the certificate. The information in a digital certificate is encrypted.

System Failure

System failure is yet another type of computer security risk. A **system failure** is the prolonged malfunction of a computer. System failure can cause loss of hardware, software, data, or information. A variety of causes can lead to system failure. These include aging hardware; natural disasters such as fires, floods, or hurricanes; random events such as electrical power problems; and even errors in computer programs.

One of the more common causes of system failure is an electrical power variation. Electrical power variations can cause loss of data and loss of equipment. If the computer equipment is networked, a single power disturbance can damage multiple systems.

Safeguards against System Failure

Surge Protectors
For more information, visit the Microsoft Office and Concepts CourseMate Web site at www.cengagebrain.com, navigate to the Chapter 5 Web Link resource for this book, and then click Surge Protectors.

To protect against electrical power variations, use a surge protector. A **surge protector** uses special electrical components to provide a stable current flow to the computer and other electronic equipment (Figure 5-13). Sometimes resembling a power strip, the computer and other devices plug in the surge protector, which plugs in the power source.

No surge protectors are 100 percent effective. Typically, the amount of protection offered by a surge protector is proportional to its cost. That is, the more expensive, the more protection the protector offers.

If your computer connects to a network or the Internet, also be sure to have protection for your modem, telephone lines, DSL lines, Internet cable lines, and network lines. Many surge protectors include plug-ins for telephone lines and other cables.

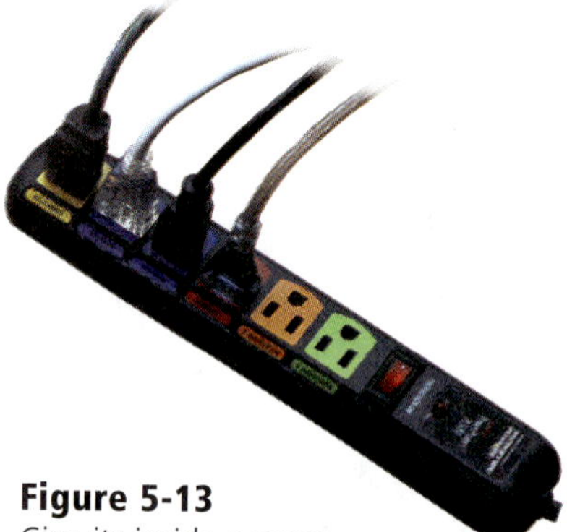

Figure 5-13
Circuits inside a surge protector safeguard against electrical power variations.

Figure 5-14 If power fails, an uninterruptible power supply (UPS) uses batteries to provide electricity for a limited amount of time.

For additional electrical protection, some users connect an uninterruptible power supply to the computer. An **uninterruptible power supply (UPS)** is a device that contains surge protection circuits and one or more batteries that can provide power during a loss of power (Figure 5-14). A UPS connects between your computer and a power source.

As another measure of protection, some companies use duplicate components or computers as a safeguard against system failure.

Backing Up — The Ultimate Safeguard

To protect against data loss caused by a system failure or hardware/software/information theft, computer users should back up files regularly. A **backup** is a duplicate of a file, program, or disk that can be used if the original is lost, damaged, or destroyed. Thus, to **back up** a file means to make a copy of it. In the case of a system failure or the discovery of corrupted files, you **restore** the files by copying the backed up files to their original location on the computer.

You can use just about any media to store backups. A good choice for a home user might be optical discs or external hard disks. Keep backup copies in a fireproof and heatproof safe or vault, or offsite. Offsite means in a location separate from the computer site. A growing trend is to use cloud storage as an offsite location. Recall that cloud storage is an Internet service that provides storage to computer users. To learn more about how to back up files using an Internet service, complete the Learn How To 1 activity on pages 214 and 215.

Most backup programs for the home user provide for a full backup and a selective backup. A full backup copies all of the files in the computer. With a selective backup, users choose which folders and files to include in a backup.

Some users implement a three-generation backup policy to preserve three copies of important files. The grandparent is the oldest copy of the file. The parent is the second oldest copy of the file. The child is the most recent copy of the file. Others use RAID to duplicate the contents of a disk. Instead of multiple backup copies, some users choose continuous backup, where data is backed up whenever a change is made.

Most operating systems include a backup program. Backup devices, such as external disk drives, also include backup programs. Numerous stand-alone backup utilities exist. Many of these can be downloaded from the Web at no cost.

Wireless Security

Wireless technology has made dramatic changes in the way computer users communicate worldwide. Billions of home and business users have notebook computers, smart phones, and other mobile devices to access the Internet, send e-mail and instant messages, chat online, or share network connections — all without wires. Home users set up wireless home networks. Mobile users access wireless networks in hot spots at airports, hotels, shopping malls, bookstores, restaurants, and coffee shops. Schools have wireless networks so that students can access the school network using their mobile computers and devices as they move from building to building.

Although wireless access provides many conveniences to users, it also poses additional security risks. One study showed that about 80 percent of wireless networks have no security protection. Some perpetrators connect to other's wireless networks to gain free Internet access; others may try to access an organization's confidential data.

To access the network, the individual must be in range of the wireless network. Some intruders intercept and monitor communications as they transmit through the air. Others connect to a network through an unsecured wireless access point (WAP). In one technique, called **war driving**, individuals attempt to detect wireless networks via their notebook computer or mobile device while driving a vehicle through areas they suspect have a wireless network.

In addition to using firewalls, some safeguards that improve the security of wireless networks include reconfiguring the wireless access point and ensuring equipment uses one or more wireless security standards such as Wi-Fi Protected Access and 802.11i.

- A wireless access point (WAP) should be configured so that it does not broadcast a network name. The WAP also can be programmed so that only certain devices can access it.
- **Wi-Fi Protected Access** (WPA) is a security standard that improves on older security standards by authenticating network users and providing more advanced encryption techniques.
- An **802.11i** network, sometimes called WPA2, the most recent network security standard, conforms to the government's security standards and uses more sophisticated encryption techniques than WPA.

By implementing these security measures, you can help to prevent unauthorized access to wireless networks.

✔ QUIZ YOURSELF 5-2

Instructions: Find the true statement below. Then, rewrite the remaining false statements so that they are true.

1. An end-user license agreement (EULA) permits users to give copies to friends and colleagues, while continuing to use the software.
2. Encryption is a process of converting ciphertext into plaintext to prevent unauthorized access.
3. Mobile users are not susceptible to hardware theft.
4. Two wireless security standards are Wi-Fi Protected Access and 802.11i.
5. To protect against data loss caused by a system failure, computer users should restore files regularly.

Quiz Yourself Online: To further check your knowledge of pages 193 through 197, visit the Microsoft Office and Concepts CourseMate Web site at www.cengagebrain.com, navigate to the Chapter 5 Quiz Yourself resource for this book, and then click Objectives 3 – 6.

Health Concerns of Computer Use

Users are a key component in any information system. Thus, protecting users is just as important as protecting hardware, software, and data.

The widespread use of computers has led to some important user health concerns. The following sections discuss health risks and preventions, along with measures users can take to keep the environment healthy.

Computers and Health Risks

A **repetitive strain injury (RSI)** is an injury or disorder of the muscles, nerves, tendons, ligaments, and joints. Computer-related RSIs include tendonitis and carpal tunnel syndrome. RSIs are the largest job-related injury and illness problem in the United States today.

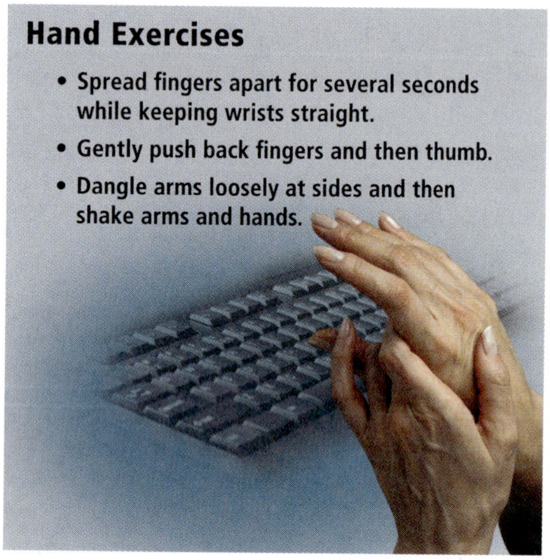

Figure 5-15 To reduce the chance of developing tendonitis or carpal tunnel syndrome, take frequent breaks during computer sessions to exercise your hands and arms.

Tendonitis is inflammation of a tendon due to some repeated motion or stress on that tendon. Carpal tunnel syndrome (CTS) is inflammation of the nerve that connects the forearm to the palm of the wrist. Repeated or forceful bending of the wrist can cause CTS or tendonitis of the wrist. Symptoms of tendonitis of the wrist include extreme pain that extends from the forearm to the hand, along with tingling in the fingers. Symptoms of CTS include burning pain when the nerve is compressed, along with numbness and tingling in the thumb and first two fingers.

Long-term computer work can lead to tendonitis or CTS. Factors that cause these disorders include prolonged typing, prolonged mouse usage, or continual shifting between the mouse and the keyboard. If untreated, these disorders can lead to permanent physical damage.

You can take many precautions to prevent these types of injuries. Take frequent breaks during the computer session to exercise your hands and arms (Figure 5-15). To prevent injury due to typing, place a wrist rest between the keyboard and the edge of your desk. To prevent injury while using a mouse, place the mouse at least six inches from the edge of the desk. In this position, your wrist is flat on the desk. Finally, minimize the number of times you switch between the mouse and the keyboard, and avoid using the heel of your hand as a pivot point while typing or using the mouse.

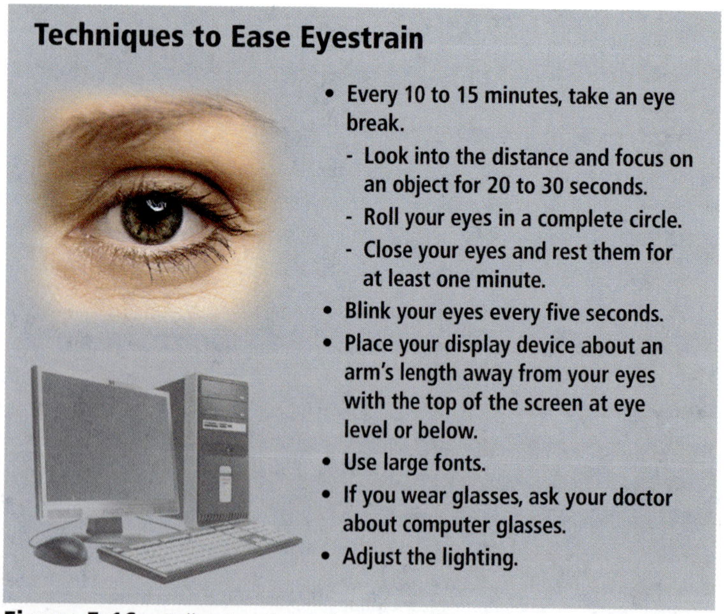

Figure 5-16 Following these tips may help reduce eyestrain while working on a computer.

Another type of health-related condition due to computer usage is **computer vision syndrome** (CVS). You may have CVS if you have sore, tired, burning, itching, or dry eyes; blurred or double vision; distance blurred vision after prolonged staring at a display device; headache or sore neck; difficulty shifting focus between a display device and documents; difficulty focusing on the screen image; color fringes or after-images when you look away from the display device; and increased sensitivity to light. Eyestrain associated with CVS is not thought to have serious or long-term consequences. Figure 5-16 outlines some techniques you can follow to ease eyestrain.

People who spend their workday using the computer sometimes complain of lower back pain, muscle fatigue, and emotional fatigue. Lower back pain sometimes is caused from poor posture. Always sit properly in the chair while you work. To alleviate back pain, muscle fatigue, and emotional fatigue, take a 15- to 30-minute break every 2 hours — stand up, walk around, stretch, and relax. Another way to help prevent these injuries is to be sure your workplace is designed ergonomically.

Ergonomics and Workplace Design

Ergonomics is an applied science devoted to incorporating comfort, efficiency, and safety into the design of items in the workplace. Ergonomic studies have shown that using the correct type and configuration of chair, keyboard, display device, and work surface helps users work comfortably and efficiently and helps protect their health. For the computer work space, experts recommend an area of at least two feet by four feet. Figure 5-17 illustrates additional guidelines for setting up the work area.

Figure 5-17 A well-designed work area should be flexible to allow adjustments to the height and build of different individuals. Good lighting and air quality also are important considerations.

Computer Addiction

Computers can provide entertainment and enjoyment. Some computer users, however, become obsessed with the computer and the Internet. **Computer addiction** occurs when the computer consumes someone's entire social life. Computer addiction is a growing health problem but can be treated through therapy and support groups. Symptoms of a user with computer addiction include the following:

- Craves computer time
- Overjoyed when at the computer
- Neglects family and friends
- Irritable when not at the computer
- Unable to stop computer activity
- Problems at work or school

Ethics and Society

As with any powerful technology, computers can be used for both good and bad intentions. The standards that determine whether an action is good or bad are known as ethics.

Computer ethics are the moral guidelines that govern the use of computers and information systems. Six frequently discussed areas of computer ethics are unauthorized use of computers and networks, software theft (piracy), information accuracy, intellectual property rights, green computing, and information privacy.

Previous sections in this chapter discussed unauthorized use of computers and networks, and software theft (piracy). The following sections discuss issues related to information accuracy, intellectual property rights, green computing, and information privacy. The questionnaire in Figure 5-18 raises issues in each of these areas.

Your Thoughts?

	Ethical	Unethical
1. An organization requires employees to wear badges that track their whereabouts while at work.	☐	☐
2. A supervisor reads an employee's e-mail.	☐	☐
3. An employee uses his computer at work to send e-mail messages to a friend.	☐	☐
4. An employee sends an e-mail message to several coworkers and blind copies his supervisor.	☐	☐
5. An employee forwards an e-mail message to a third party without permission from the sender.	☐	☐
6. An employee uses her computer at work to complete a homework assignment for school.	☐	☐
7. The vice president of your Student Government Association (SGA) downloads a photo from the Web and uses it in a flyer recruiting SGA members.	☐	☐
8. A student copies text from the Web and uses it in a research paper for his English Composition class.	☐	☐
9. An employee sends political campaign material to individuals on her employer's mailing list.	☐	☐
10. As an employee in the registration office, you have access to student grades. You look up grades for your friends, so that they do not have to wait for delivery of grade reports from the postal service.	☐	☐
11. An employee makes a copy of software and installs it on her home computer. No one uses her home computer while she is at work, and she uses her home computer only to finish projects from work.	☐	☐
12. An employee who has been laid off installs a computer virus on his employer's computer.	☐	☐
13. A person designing a Web page finds one on the Web similar to his requirements, copies it, modifies it, and publishes it as his own Web page.	☐	☐
14. A student researches using only the Web to write a report.	☐	☐
15. In a society in which all transactions occur online (a cashless society), the government tracks every transaction you make and automatically deducts taxes from your bank account.	☐	☐
16. Someone copies a well-known novel to the Web and encourages others to read it.	☐	☐
17. A person accesses an organization's network and reports to the organization any vulnerabilities discovered.	☐	☐
18. Your friend uses a neighbor's wireless network to connect to the Internet and check e-mail.	☐	☐
19. A company uses recycled paper to print a 50-page employee benefits manual that is distributed to 425 employees.	☐	☐
20. Your friend donates her old computers and mobile devices to local schools when she purchases newer models.	☐	☐

Figure 5-18 Indicate whether you think the situation described is ethical or unethical. Discuss your answers with your instructor and other students.

Information Accuracy

Information accuracy today is a concern because many users access information maintained by other people or companies, such as on the Internet. Do not assume that because the information is on the Web that it is correct. Users should evaluate the value of a Web page before relying on its content. Be aware that the organization providing access to the information may not be the creator of the information.

In addition to concerns about the accuracy of computer input, some individuals and organizations raise questions about the ethics of using computers to alter output, primarily graphical output such as retouched photos. Using graphics equipment and software, users easily can digitize photos and then add, change, or remove images (Figure 5-19).

One group that completely opposes any manipulation of an image is the National Press Photographers Association. It believes that allowing even the slightest alteration could lead to misrepresentative photos. Others believe that digital photo retouching is acceptable as long as the significant content or meaning of the photo does not change. Digital retouching is an area in which legal precedents so far have not been established.

Figure 5-19 A digitally altered photo shows the movie character Forrest Gump (1994) meeting President John F. Kennedy (who died in 1963).

Intellectual Property Rights

Intellectual property (IP) refers to unique and original works such as ideas, inventions, art, writings, processes, company and product names, and logos. **Intellectual property rights** are the rights to which creators are entitled for their work. Certain issues arise surrounding IP today because many of these works are available digitally.

A **copyright** gives authors and artists exclusive rights to duplicate, publish, and sell their materials. A copyright protects any tangible form of expression.

A common infringement of copyright is piracy. People pirate (illegally copy) software, movies, and music. Many areas are not clear-cut with respect to the law, because copyright law gives the public fair use to copyrighted material. The issues surround the phrase, fair use, which allows use for educational and critical purposes.

This vague definition is subject to widespread interpretation and raises many questions:

- Should individuals be able to download contents of your Web site, modify it, and then put it on the Web again as their own?
- Should a faculty member have the right to print material from the Web and distribute it to all members of the class for teaching purposes only?
- Should someone be able to scan photos or pages from a book, publish them to the Web, and allow others to download them?
- Should students be able to post term papers they have written on the Web, making it tempting for other students to download and submit them as their own work?

These issues with copyright law led to the development of **digital rights management** (DRM), a strategy designed to prevent illegal distribution of movies, music, and other digital content.

Digital Rights Management
For more information, visit the Microsoft Office and Concepts CourseMate Web site at www.cengagebrain.com, navigate to the Chapter 5 Web Link resource for this book, and then click Digital Rights Management.

Green Computing

Green computing involves reducing the electricity and environmental waste while using a computer. People use, and often waste, resources such as electricity and paper while using a computer.

The United States government developed the **ENERGY STAR program** to help reduce the amount of electricity used by computers and related devices. This program encourages manufacturers to create energy-efficient devices that require little power when they are not in use. Computers and devices that meet the ENERGY STAR guidelines display an ENERGY STAR label.

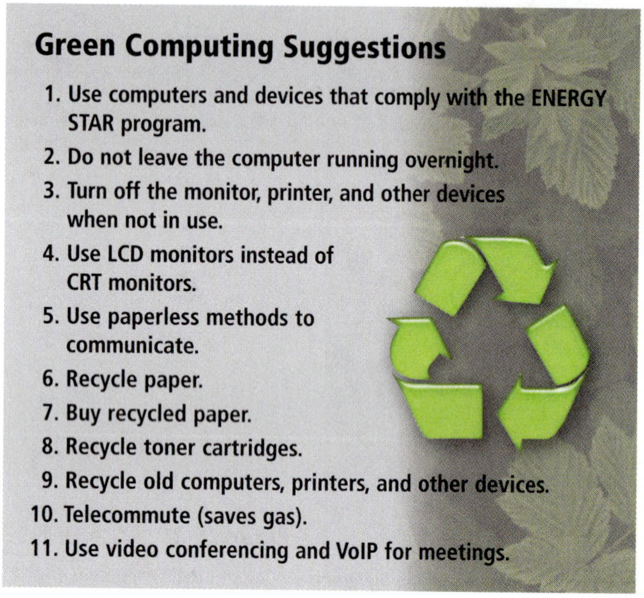

Figure 5-20 A list of suggestions to make computing healthy for the environment.

Users should not store obsolete computers and devices in their basement, storage room, attic, warehouse, or any other location. Computers, monitors, and other equipment contain toxic materials and potentially dangerous elements including lead, mercury, and flame retardants. In a landfill, these materials release into the environment. Recycling and refurbishing old equipment are much safer alternatives for the environment.

Experts estimate that more than 700 million personal computers are obsolete. Because of the huge volumes of electronic waste, the U.S. federal government has proposed a bill that would require computer recycling across the country. Many state and local governments have methods in place to make it easy for consumers to recycle this type of equipment.

To reduce the environmental impact of computing further, users simply can alter a few habits. Figure 5-20 lists the ways you can contribute to green computing. To learn more about green computing, complete the Green Computing exercise on the Web Research pages in this book.

Information Privacy

Information privacy refers to the right of individuals and companies to deny or restrict the collection and use of information about them. In the past, information privacy was easier to maintain because information was kept in separate locations. Each retail store had its own credit files. Each government agency maintained separate records. Doctors had their own patient files.

Today, huge databases store this data online. Much of the data is personal and confidential and should be accessible only to authorized users. Many individuals and organizations, however, question whether this data really is private.

Figure 5-21 lists measures you can take to make your personal data private. The following pages address techniques companies and employers use to collect your personal data. Read Innovative Computing 5-1 to find out how merchants watch shoppers' behaviors.

INNOVATIVE COMPUTING 5-1

Customers' Behavior, Conversations Monitored

Deciding whether to display peanut butter next to jelly on a supermarket shelf is made easier with consumer-monitoring technology. Leading stores, including Best Buy, Walmart, Walgreens, Office Depot, and Abercrombie & Fitch, have installed video cameras and recorders, heat sensors, and sometimes microphones to track customers' movement throughout the store and their buying patterns.

One system, called Smartlane, counts the number of people, known as "hot blobs," entering and exiting the store and records how quickly clerks are completing transactions at cash registers. It alerts management when many hot blobs are waiting in checkout lanes or have entered the store in a short period of time so that additional clerks can be made available to reduce checkout waiting times.

Another system, BehaviorIQ, collects data on where customers walk throughout the store, when and for how long they stop to browse, and what they take from shelves and racks. Some stores claim information gleaned from these monitoring systems has increased sales 300 percent.

Privacy experts warn that consumers might object to being recorded and analyzed. The monitoring companies, however, dispel these concerns by explaining that the data actually resembles audio recordings made when calling customer-service hotlines and when being observed for loss prevention purposes.

For more information, visit the Microsoft Office and Concepts CourseMate Web site at www.cengagebrain.com, navigate to the Chapter 5 Innovative Computing resource for this book, and then click Shopping Behavior.

How to Safeguard Personal Information	
1. Fill in only necessary information on rebate, warranty, and registration forms.	12. Obtain your credit report once a year from each of the three major credit reporting agencies (Equifax, Experian, and TransUnion) and correct any errors.
2. Do not preprint your telephone number or Social Security number on personal checks.	13. Request a free copy of your medical records once a year from the Medical Information Bureau.
3. Have an unlisted or unpublished telephone number.	14. Limit the amount of information you provide to Web sites. Fill in only required information.
4. If Caller ID is available in your area, find out how to block your number from displaying on the receiver's system.	15. Install a cookie manager to filter cookies.
5. Do not write your telephone number on charge or credit receipts.	16. Clear your history file when you are finished browsing.
6. Ask merchants not to write credit card numbers, telephone numbers, Social Security numbers, and driver's license numbers on the back of your personal checks.	17. Set up a free e-mail account. Use this e-mail address for merchant forms.
7. Purchase goods with cash, rather than credit or checks.	18. Turn off file and printer sharing on your Internet connection.
8. Avoid shopping club and buyer cards.	19. Install a personal firewall.
9. If merchants ask personal questions, find out why they want to know before releasing the information.	20. Sign-up for e-mail filtering through your Internet access provider or use an anti-spam program such as Brightmail.
10. Inform merchants that you do not want them to distribute your personal information.	21. Do not reply to spam for any reason.
11. Request, in writing, to be removed from mailing lists.	22. Surf the Web anonymously with a program such as Freedom WebSecure or through an anonymous Web site such as Anonymizer.com.

Figure 5-21 Techniques to keep personal data private.

Electronic Profiles

When you fill out a form such as a magazine subscription, product warranty registration card, or contest entry form, the merchant that receives the form usually enters it into a database. Likewise, every time you click an advertisement on the Web or register software online, your information and preferences enter a database. Merchants then sell the contents of their databases to national marketing firms and Internet advertising firms. By combining this data with information from public sources such as driver's licenses and vehicle registrations, these firms create an electronic profile of individuals.

Critics contend that the information in an electronic profile reveals more about an individual than anyone has a right to know. They also claim that companies should inform people if they plan to provide personal information to others. Many companies today allow people to specify whether they want their personal information distributed.

Cookies

E-commerce and other Web applications often rely on cookies to identify users. A **cookie** is a small text file that a Web server stores on your computer. Cookie files typically contain data about you, such as your user name or viewing preferences.

Many commercial Web sites send a cookie to your browser, and then your computer's hard disk stores the cookie. The next time you visit the Web site, your browser retrieves the cookie from your hard disk and sends the data in the cookie to the Web site.

Web sites use cookies for a variety of purposes:

- Most Web sites that allow for personalization use cookies to track user preferences. On such sites, users may be asked to fill in a form requesting personal information, such as their name, postal code, or site preferences. A news Web site, for example, might allow users to customize their viewing preferences to display certain stock quotes or local weather forecasts. The Web site stores their preferences in a cookie on the users' hard disks.

- Some Web sites use cookies to store users' passwords, so that they do not need to enter it every time they log in to the Web site.
- Online shopping sites generally use a session cookie to keep track of items in a user's shopping cart. This way, users can start an order during one Web session and finish it on another day in another session. Session cookies usually expire after a certain time, such as a week or a month.
- Some Web sites use cookies to track how often users visit a site and the Web pages they visit while at the site.
- Web sites may use cookies to target advertisements. These sites store a user's interests and browsing habits in the cookie.

Cookies
For more information, visit the Microsoft Office and Concepts CourseMate Web site at www.cengagebrain.com, navigate to the Chapter 5 Web Link resource for this book, and then click Cookies.

You can set a browser to accept cookies automatically, prompt you if you want to accept a cookie, or disable cookie use altogether. Keep in mind if you disable cookie use, you will not be able to use many of the e-commerce Web sites. Figure 5-22 illustrates how Web sites work with cookies.

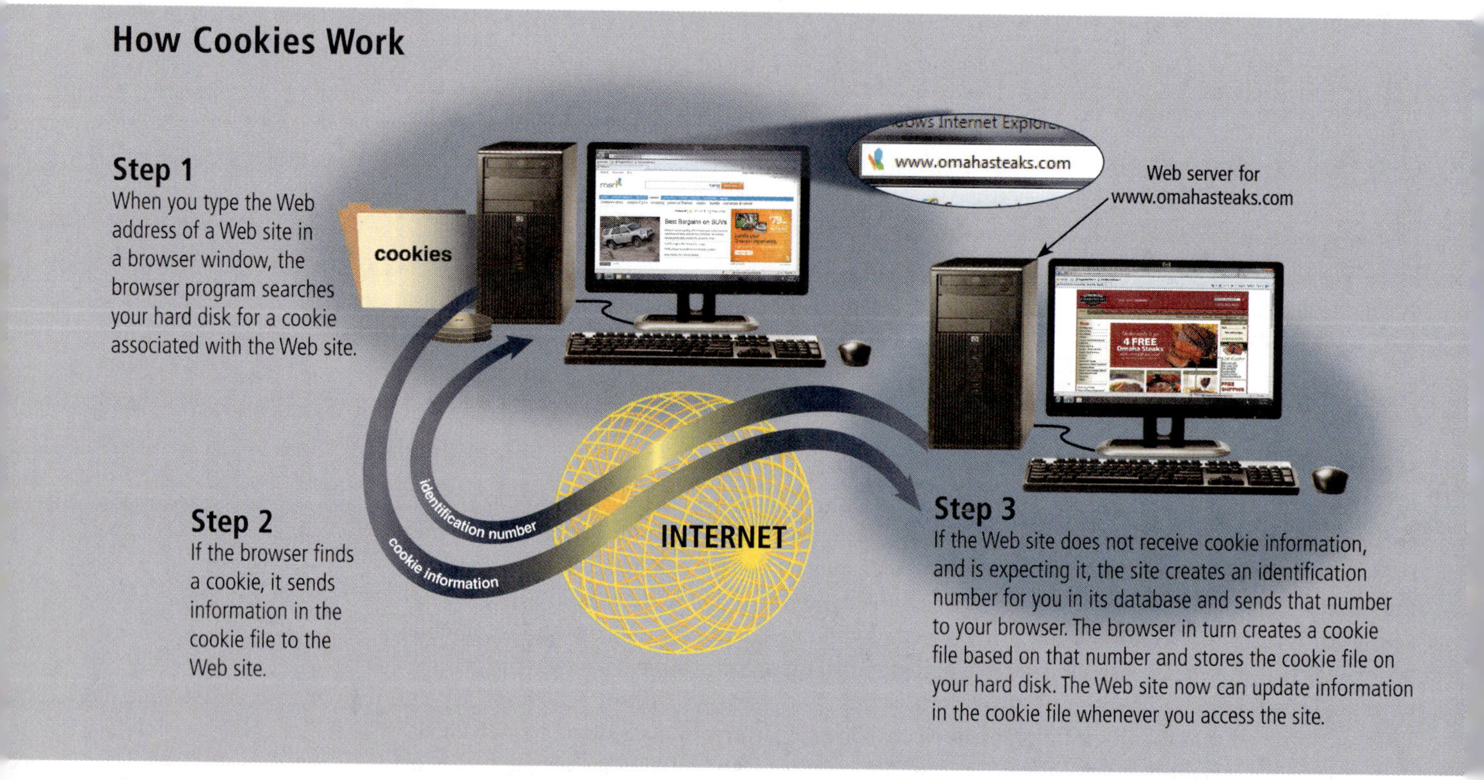

Figure 5-22 This figure shows how cookies work.

Spyware and Adware

Spyware is a program placed on a computer without the user's knowledge that secretly collects information about the user. Some vendors or employers use spyware to collect information about program usage or employees. Internet advertising firms often collect information about users' Web browsing habits by hiding spyware in adware. **Adware** is a program that displays an online advertisement in a banner or pop-up window on Web pages, e-mail messages, or other Internet services. To remove spyware and adware, you can obtain a spyware and adware remover that can detect and delete spyware and adware. Some operating systems and Web browsers include spyware removers.

Spam

Spam is an unsolicited e-mail message or newsgroup posting sent to multiple recipients or newsgroups at once. Spam is Internet junk mail (Figure 5-23). The content of spam ranges from selling a product or service, to promoting a business opportunity, to advertising offensive material. One study indicates more than 92 percent of e-mail is spam.

Users can reduce the amount of spam they receive with a number of techniques. Some e-mail programs have built-in settings that allow users to delete spam automatically. Users also can sign up for e-mail filtering from their Internet access provider. **E-mail filtering** is a service that blocks e-mail messages from designated sources. An alternative to e-mail filtering is to purchase an **anti-spam program** that attempts to remove spam before it reaches your inbox. The disadvantage of e-mail filters and anti-spam programs is that sometimes they remove valid e-mail messages. Thus, users should review the contents of the spam messages periodically to ensure they do not contain valid messages.

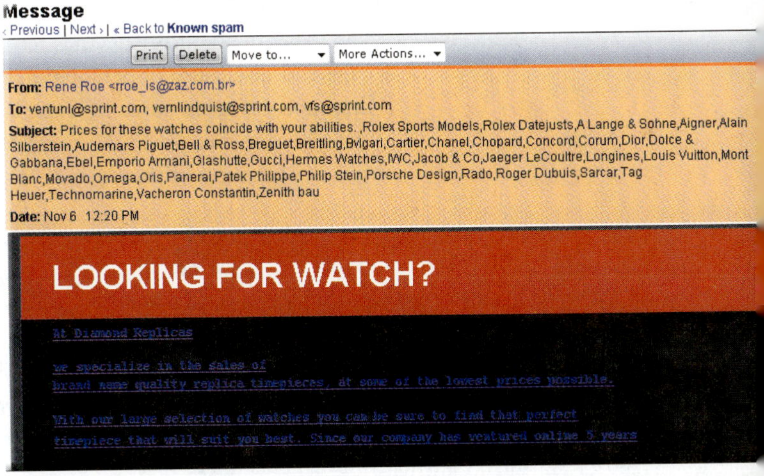

Figure 5-23 An example of spam.

Phishing

Phishing is a scam in which a perpetrator sends an official looking e-mail message that attempts to obtain your personal and financial information (Figure 5-24). Some phishing e-mail messages ask you to reply with your information; others direct you to a phony Web site, or a pop-up window that looks like a Web site, that collects the information.

If you receive an e-mail that looks legitimate and requests you update credit card numbers, Social Security numbers, bank account numbers, passwords, or other private information, the FTC recommends you visit the Web site directly to determine if the request is valid. Never click a link in an e-mail message; instead retype the Web address in your browser.

A **phishing filter** is a program that warns or blocks you from potentially fraudulent or suspicious Web sites. Some Web browsers include phishing filters.

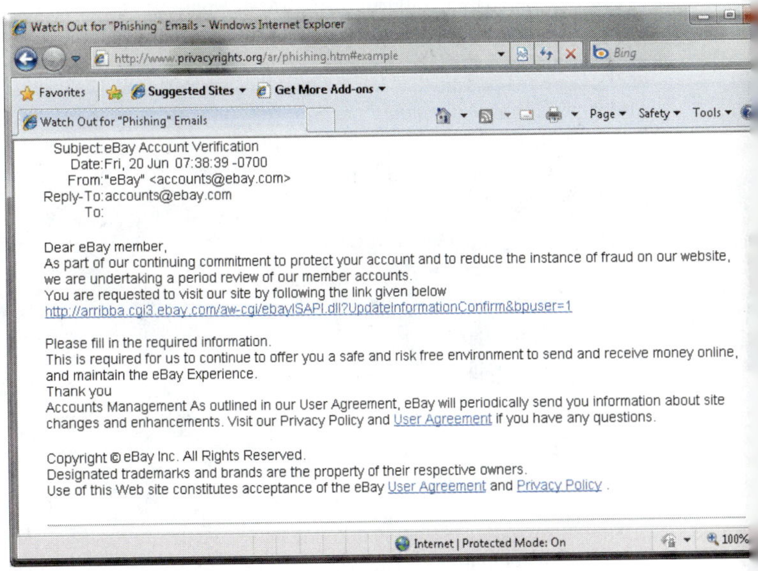

Figure 5-24 An example of a phishing e-mail message.

Pharming is a scam, similar to phishing, where a perpetrator attempts to obtain your personal and financial information, except they do so via spoofing. That is, when you type a Web address in the Web browser, you are redirected to a phony Web site that looks legitimate. The phony Web site requests you enter confidential information.

Clickjacking is yet another similar scam. With **clickjacking**, an object that can be clicked on a Web site, such as a button, image, or link, contains a malicious program. When users click the disguised object, for example, they may be redirected to a phony Web site that requests personal information, or a virus may download to their computer.

Social Engineering

As related to the use of computers, **social engineering** is defined as gaining unauthorized access or obtaining confidential information by taking advantage of the trusting human nature of some victims and the naivety of others. Some social engineers trick their victims into revealing confidential information such as user names and passwords on the telephone, in person, or on the Internet. Techniques they use include pretending to be an administrator or other authoritative figure, feigning an emergency situation, or impersonating an acquaintance. Social engineers also obtain information from users who do not destroy or conceal information properly. These perpetrators sift through company dumpsters, watch or film people dialing telephone numbers or using ATMs, and snoop around computers looking for openly displayed confidential information.

Privacy Laws

The concern about privacy has led to the enactment of federal and state laws regarding the storage and disclosure of personal data (Figure 5-25).

Common points in some of these laws include the following:

1. Information collected and stored about individuals should be limited to what is necessary to carry out the function of the business or government agency collecting the data.

Date	Law	Purpose
2006	Telephone Records and Privacy Protection Act	Makes it illegal to use fraudulent means to obtain someone's telephone records.
2003	CAN-SPAM Act	Gives law enforcement the right to impose penalties on people using the Internet to distribute spam.
2002	Sarbanes-Oxley Act	Requires corporate officers, auditors, and attorneys of publicly-traded companies follow strict financial reporting guidelines.
2001	Children's Internet Protection Act (CIPA)	Protects minors from inappropriate content when accessing the Internet in schools and libraries.
2001	Provide Appropriate Tools Required to Intercept and Obstruct Terrorism (PATRIOT) Act	Gives law enforcement the right to monitor people's activities, including Web and e-mail habits.
1999	Gramm-Leach-Bliley Act (GLBA) or Financial Modernization Act	Protects consumers from disclosure of their personal financial information and requires institutions to alert customers of information disclosure policies.
1998	Children's Online Privacy Protection Act (COPPA)	Requires Web sites protect personal information of children under 13 years of age.
1998	Digital Millennium Copyright Act (DMCA)	Makes it illegal to circumvent antipiracy schemes in commercial software; outlaws sale of devices that copy software illegally.
1997	No Electronic Theft (NET) Act	Closes a narrow loophole in the law that allowed people to give away copyrighted material (such as software) on the Internet without legal repercussions.
1996	Health Insurance Portability and Accountability Act (HIPAA)	Protects individuals against the wrongful disclosure of their health information.
1996	National Information Infrastructure Protection Act	Penalizes theft of information across state lines, threats against networks, and computer system trespassing.
1994	Computer Abuse Amendments Act	Amends 1984 act to outlaw transmission of harmful computer code such as viruses.
1992	Cable Act	Extends the privacy of the Cable Communications Policy Act of 1984 to include cellular and other wireless services.
1991	Telephone Consumer Protection Act	Restricts activities of telemarketers.
1988	Computer Matching and Privacy Protection Act	Regulates the use of government data to determine the eligibility of individuals for federal benefits.
1988	Video Privacy Protection Act	Forbids retailers from releasing or selling video-rental records without customer consent or a court order.
1986	Electronic Communications Privacy Act (ECPA)	Provides the same right of privacy protection for the postal delivery service and telephone companies to the new forms of electronic communications, such as voice mail, e-mail, and cell phones.
1984	Cable Communications Policy Act	Regulates disclosure of cable television subscriber records.
1984	Computer Fraud and Abuse Act	Outlaws unauthorized access of federal government computers.
1978	Right to Financial Privacy Act	Strictly outlines procedures federal agencies must follow when looking at customer records in banks.
1974	Privacy Act	Forbids federal agencies from allowing information to be used for a reason other than that for which it was collected.
1974	Family Educational Rights and Privacy Act	Gives students and parents access to school records and limits disclosure of records to unauthorized parties.
1970	Fair Credit Reporting Act	Prohibits credit reporting agencies from releasing credit information to unauthorized people and allows consumers to review their own credit records.

Figure 5-25 Summary of the major U.S. government laws concerning privacy.

2. Once collected, provisions should be made to restrict access to the data to those employees within the organization who need access to it to perform their job duties.
3. Personal information should be released outside the organization collecting the data only when the person has agreed to its disclosure.
4. When information is collected about an individual, the individual should know that the data is being collected and have the opportunity to determine the accuracy of the data.

Employee Monitoring

Employee monitoring involves the use of computers to observe, record, and review an employee's use of a computer, including communications such as e-mail messages, keyboard activity (used to measure productivity), and Web sites visited. Many programs exist that easily allow employers to monitor employees. Further, it is legal for employers to use these programs.

A frequently debated issue is whether an employer has the right to read employee e-mail messages. Actual policies vary widely. Some companies declare that they will review e-mail messages regularly, and others state that e-mail is private. In some states, if an organization does not have a formal e-mail policy, it can read e-mail messages without employee notification. Several lawsuits have been filed against employers because many believe that such internal communications should be private. Read Ethics & Issues 5-2 for a related discussion.

Another controversial issue relates to the use of cameras to monitor employees, customers, and the public. Many people feel that this use of video cameras is a violation of privacy.

ETHICS & ISSUES 5-2

Should Text Messages Sent by Employees Be Private?

When an employee sends or receives an e-mail message using his or her employer's e-mail server, the company most likely retains a backup of the message, which can be used as evidence against the employee if the employee is suspected of engaging in unscrupulous activity. When an employee sends a text message using a company-issued smart phone for such activity, however, the smart phone provider may store a record of the message. If an employer's workplace policy requires an employee to disclose all text message communications with customers, vendors, and competitors, the employee is required legally to divulge those communications. The U.S. Supreme Court ruled that an employer can read workers' text messages if there is reason to believe the texts violate workplace rules. The Court held that employees can purchase their own cell phones if they need to make personal calls or text messages. Employees may believe they have an expectation of privacy and the right of self-expression when they use an employer's cell phone. Employers argue, however, that because they provide the devices and service to the employee, they should have a right to view the content of the messages.

Should text messages sent by employees be private? Why or why not? How can employers create and enforce policies regarding the content of text messages sent on employer-issued smart phones? Should employers demand that smart phone providers offer the option to send all employee text message communications to the company on a monthly basis? Why or why not?

Content Filtering

One of the more controversial issues that surround the Internet is its widespread availability of objectionable material, such as racist literature, violence, and obscene pictures. Some believe that such materials should be banned. Others believe that the materials should be filtered, that is, restricted. **Content filtering** is the process of restricting access to certain material on the Web. Content filtering opponents argue that banning any materials violates constitutional guarantees of free speech and personal rights.

Many businesses use content filtering to limit employees' Web access. These businesses argue that employees are unproductive when visiting inappropriate or objectionable Web sites. Some schools, libraries, and parents use content filtering to restrict access to minors.

Web filtering software is a program that restricts access to specified Web sites. Some also filter sites that use specific words. Others allow you to filter e-mail messages, chat rooms, and programs. Many Internet security programs include a firewall, antivirus program, and filtering capabilities combined (Figure 5-26).

Figure 5-26 Many Internet security programs include content filtering capabilities, where users can block specified Web sites and applications.

✔ QUIZ YOURSELF 5-3

Instructions: Find the true statement below. Then, rewrite the remaining false statements so that they are true.

1. Factors that cause CVS include prolonged typing, prolonged mouse usage, or continual shifting between the mouse and the keyboard.
2. Phishing is the discovery, collection, and analysis of evidence found on computers and networks.
3. Spam is Internet junk mail.
4. You can assume that information on the Web is correct.

Quiz Yourself Online: To further check your knowledge of pages 198 through 207, visit the Microsoft Office and Concepts CourseMate Web site at www.cengagebrain.com, navigate to the Chapter 5 Quiz Yourself resource for this book, and then click Objectives 7 – 8.

Chapter Summary

This chapter identified some potential computer risks and the safeguards that organizations and individuals can implement to minimize these risks. Wireless security risks and safeguards also were discussed.

The chapter presented computer-related health issues and their preventions. The chapter ended with a discussion about ethical issues surrounding information accuracy, intellectual property rights, green computing, and information privacy.

For detailed personal computer and mobile device purchasing guidelines, read the Buyer's Guide feature that follows this chapter.

Computer Usage @ Work

National and Local Security

Since 2001, the federal government, local governments, businesses, and individuals have been implementing aggressive new security measures because of the increase in terrorist activity. A security threat can exist anywhere, and it is nearly impossible for humans alone to protect the country. As a result, computers now assist governments, law enforcement officials, business owners, and other individuals with monitoring and maintaining security.

Advancements in computer vision enable computers to monitor indoor and outdoor areas that might be subject to a high amount of criminal activity. For example, some cities are installing cameras in problematic areas. A computer program analyzes the output from the camera and can determine whether two or more people in close proximity to one another might be engaged in a physical confrontation. If the computer detects suspicious behavior, it automatically notifies local law enforcement.

Computers also use facial recognition to identify individuals who do not belong in a particular area. For example, one theme park in Florida often takes a picture of individuals they escort out of and ban from the park. As visitors walk from their cars to the park, surveillance cameras positioned in strategic locations scan visitors' faces and compare them to the database containing images of those who are banned from the park. If the computer finds a match, it alerts a security officer who then can investigate the situation. Thousands of people visit theme parks each day, and computers make it easier to perform the otherwise impossible task of identifying those who might be trespassing.

The federal government, particularly the Department of Homeland Security, uses a computerized No Fly List to track individuals who are not authorized to travel on commercial flights within the United States. When an individual makes a reservation, a computer compares his or her name to the names on the No Fly List. If the computer finds a match, the individual must prove that he or she is not the person on the list before being allowed to board an aircraft.

Whether you are walking outside, visiting an attraction, or traveling, the chances are good that computers are, in some way, ensuring your safety.

For more information, visit the Microsoft Office and Concepts CourseMate Web site at www.cengagebrain.com, navigate to the Chapter 5 Computer Usage @ Work resource for this book, and then click National and Local Security.

Companies on the Cutting Edge

MCAFEE Intrusion Prevention Products Developer

The McAfee Initiative to Fight Cybercrime is a global effort to thwart security threats and criminal activity. The world's largest dedicated security technology company has partnered with experts in law enforcement, education, government, and society to investigate, prosecute, and attempt to prevent security breaches.

McAfee products protect more than 60 million consumers, small- and medium-sized businesses, governmental agencies, and large corporations from malware, spam, and unauthorized access. In addition, more than 100 million mobile devices are protected with McAfee software. The corporation takes its name from its founder, John McAfee, who started the company in 1987 from his Santa Clara, California, home.

Recently, McAfee launched a new online backup service with unlimited capacity that allows consumers to back up and encrypt their important files such as documents, photos, music, and e-mail messages.

SYMANTEC Computer Security Solutions Leader

Symantec's programmers analyzed every line of code, rewrote programs, and developed a new security model to create its latest versions of Norton AntiVirus and Norton Internet Security. The results are programs that use less hard disk space, decrease starting and scanning time, and average less than 7 MB of memory. The more than 100 performance improvements offer advanced protection for millions of computer users worldwide.

The California-based company is one of the ten largest software corporations in the world. It was founded in 1982 and has offices in more than 40 countries. Its primary manufacturing facility is located in Dublin, Ireland.

Symantec recently released the latest version of its Norton Internet Security software. A rating service tested the level of protection provided by 10 different security products and gave Norton Internet Security the only perfect score.

For more information, visit the Microsoft Office and Concepts CourseMate Web site at www.cengagebrain.com and then navigate to the Chapter 5 Companies on the Cutting Edge resource for this book

Technology Trailblazers

RICHARD STALLMAN Software Freedom Advocate

The relationship between software and freedom is key to Richard Stallman's philosophy. Since his days as a physics student at Harvard University, he has advocated free software and campaigned against software patents and copyright laws. His pioneering work developed the concept of copyleft, which gives each person who has purchased a software product the ability to copy, adapt, and distribute the program as long as the new software also has the same lack of restrictions.

Stallman began the GNU/Linux Project in 1983 as an effort to develop and use the copyleft concept. Linux is an outgrowth of this project, which continues to be a forum for software development, ethical practices, and political campaigning. He also started the Free Software Foundation (FSF) in 1985 to promote writing free software for the GNU Project. The Free Software Directory catalogs more than 5,300 packages that run on the Linux and GNU operating systems.

GENE SPAFFORD Computer Security Expert

The Morris Worm, also called the MBDF virus, is considered the first computer worm distributed on the Internet, and Gene Spafford gained fame for deconstructing and analyzing this 1988 attack. His work led to the conviction of a Cornell University student, Robert Morris. Today, Spafford, who also is known as Spaf, is recognized as one of the world's foremost experts in the computer security, intelligence, cybercrime, and software engineering fields.

For 30 years, he has advised major corporations, including Microsoft, Intel, and Unisys, the U.S. Air Force, the Federal Bureau of Investigation, and two U.S. presidents. He is noted for several firsts in the computer security field. For example, he defined the terms, software forensics and firewall, wrote the first English-language book on the topics of viruses and malware, and founded the world's first multidisciplinary academic security awareness group: the Center for Education and Research in Information Assurance and Security (CERIAS).

For more information, visit the Microsoft Office and Concepts CourseMate Web site at www.cengagebrain.com and then navigate to the Chapter 5 Technology Trailblazers resource for this book.

Chapter Review

The Chapter Review reinforces the main concepts presented in this chapter.

To listen to an audio version of this Chapter Review, visit the Microsoft Office and Concepts CourseMate Web site at www.cengagebrain.com and then navigate to the Chapter 5 Chapter Review resource for this book.

1. **What Are Various Internet and Network Attacks, and How Can Users Safeguard against These Attacks?** A computer **virus** is a potentially damaging program that infects a computer and negatively affects the way the computer works. A **worm** is a program that copies itself repeatedly, using up resources and possibly shutting down the computer or network. A **Trojan horse** is a program that hides within or looks like a legitimate program. A **rootkit** is a program that hides in a computer and allows someone from a remote location to take full control of the computer. Users can take precautions to guard against this **malware**. Do not start a computer with removable media in the drives or ports unless the media are uninfected. Never open an e-mail attachment unless it is from a **trusted source**. Disable macros in documents that are not from a trusted source. Install an **antivirus program** and a personal firewall program. Stay informed about any new virus alert or **virus hoax**. To defend against a **botnet**, a **denial of service attack**, improper use of a **back door**, and **spoofing**, users can install a **firewall** and install **intrusion detection software**.

2. **What Are Techniques to Prevent Unauthorized Access and Use?** **Unauthorized access** is the use of a computer or network without permission. **Unauthorized use** is the use of a computer or its data for unapproved or illegal activities. A written acceptable use policy (AUP) outlines the activities for which the computer and network may and may not be used. Other measures include firewalls and intrusion detection software. An **access control** defines who can access a computer, when they can access it, and what actions they can take. An **audit trail** records in a file both successful and unsuccessful access attempts. Access controls include a **user name** and **password**, a **possessed object**, and a **biometric device**.

Visit the Microsoft Office and Concepts CourseMate Web site at www.cengagebrain.com, navigate to the Chapter 5 Quiz Yourself resource for this book, and then click Objectives 1 – 2.

3. **What Are Safeguards against Hardware Theft and Vandalism?** **Hardware theft** is the act of stealing computer equipment. **Hardware vandalism** is the act of defacing or destroying computer equipment. Physical devices and practical security measures, passwords, possessed objects, and biometrics can reduce the risk of theft or render a computer useless if it is stolen.

4. **How Do Software Manufacturers Protect against Software Theft and Information Theft?** **Software theft** occurs when someone steals software, intentionally erases programs, illegally copies programs, or illegally registers/activates a program. Software **piracy** is the unauthorized and illegal duplication of copyrighted software. To protect themselves from software piracy, manufacturers issue a **license agreement** that provides specific conditions for use of the software. During **product activation**, users provide the product's identification number to receive an installation identification number unique to their computer. Companies attempt to prevent **information theft** through user identification and authentication controls, **encryption**, a **digital signature**, a **digital certificate**, or a **certificate authority**.

5. **What Types of Devices Are Available to Protect Computers from System Failure?** A **system failure** is the prolonged malfunction of a computer. A common cause of system failure is an electrical power variation. A **surge protector** uses special electrical components to provide a stable current flow to the computer. An **uninterruptible power supply (UPS)** contains surge protection circuits and one or more batteries that can provide power during a power loss.

6. **What Risks and Safeguards Are Associated with Wireless Communications?** Wireless access poses additional security risks. Intruders connect to other wireless networks to gain free Internet access or to access an organization's confidential data. Some individuals intercept and monitor communications as they are transmitted. Others connect to a network through an unsecured wireless access point (WAP). Some safeguards include firewalls, reconfiguring the WAP, and ensuring equipment uses a wireless security standard, such as **Wi-Fi Protected Access** and **802.11i**.

Visit the Microsoft Office and Concepts CourseMate Web site at www.cengagebrain.com, navigate to the Chapter 5 Quiz Yourself resource for this book, and then click Objectives 3 – 6.

7. **How Can Health-Related Disorders and Injuries Due to Computer Use Be Prevented?** A **repetitive strain injury (RSI)** is an injury or disorder of the muscles, nerves, tendons, ligaments, and joints. Computer-related RSIs include tendonitis and carpal tunnel syndrome (CTS). Another health-related condition is eyestrain associated with **computer vision**

syndrome (CVS). To prevent health-related disorders, take frequent breaks, use precautionary exercises and techniques, and incorporate ergonomics when planning the workplace. **Computer addiction** occurs when the computer consumes someone's entire social life.

8. **What Are Issues Surrounding Information Privacy?** **Information privacy** is the right of individuals and companies to restrict the collection and use of information about them. An electronic profile combines data about an individual's Web use with data from public sources. A **cookie** is a file that a Web server stores on a computer to collect data about the user. **Spyware** is a program placed on a computer that secretly collects information about the user. **Adware** is a program that displays an online advertisement in a banner or pop-up window. **Spam** is an unsolicited e-mail message or newsgroup posting sent to many recipients. **Phishing** is a scam in which a perpetrator sends an official looking e-mail message that attempts to obtain a user's personal and financial information. The concern about privacy has led to the enactment of many federal and state laws regarding the storage and disclosure of data. As related to the use of computers, **social engineering** is defined as gaining unauthorized access or obtaining confidential information by taking advantage of the trusting human nature of some victims and the naivety of others. **Employee monitoring** uses computers to observe, record, and review an employee's computer use. **Content filtering** restricts access to certain material on the Web.

Visit the Microsoft Office and Concepts CourseMate Web site at www.cengagebrain.com, navigate to the Chapter 5 Quiz Yourself resource for this book, and then click Objectives 7 – 8.

Key Terms

You should know each key term. The list below helps focus your study.

To see an example of and a definition for each term, and to access current and additional information from the Web, visit the Microsoft Office and Concepts CourseMate Web site at www.cengagebrain.com and then navigate to the Chapter 5 Key Terms resource for this book.

802.11i (197)
access control (189)
adware (204)
anti-spam program (205)
antivirus program (186)
audit trail (189)
back door (188)
back up (196)
backup (196)
biometric device (191)
biometric payment (191)
botnet (187)
CAPTCHA (190)
certificate authority (195)
clickjacking (205)
computer addiction (199)
computer crime (182)
computer ethics (199)
computer security risk (182)
computer vision syndrome (198)
content filtering (207)
cookie (203)
copyright (201)
cracker (182)
cybercrime (182)
cyberextortionist (182)
cyberterrorist (183)
decrypt (195)
denial of service attack (187)
digital certificate (195)
digital forensics (192)
digital rights management (201)
digital signature (195)
DoS attack (187)
e-mail filtering (205)
employee monitoring (207)
encryption (195)
encryption algorithm (195)
encryption key (195)
ENERGY STAR program (201)
firewall (188)
green computing (201)
hacker (182)
hardware theft (193)
hardware vandalism (193)
information privacy (202)
information theft (195)
intellectual property rights (201)
intrusion detection software (189)
license agreement (194)
malware (184)
password (190)
payload (184)
personal firewall (189)
personal identification number (PIN) (191)
pharming (205)
phishing (205)
phishing filter (205)
piracy (193)
possessed object (191)
product activation (194)
quarantine (186)
real time location system (RTLS) (193)
repetitive strain injury (RSI) (198)
restore (196)
rootkit (184)
script kiddie (182)
secure site (195)
social engineering (205)
software theft (193)
spam (204)
spoofing (188)
spyware (204)
surge protector (196)
system failure (196)
Trojan horse (184)
trusted source (185)
unauthorized access (189)
unauthorized use (189)
uninterruptible power supply (UPS) (196)
user name (190)
virus (184)
virus definition (186)
virus hoax (187)
virus signature (186)
war driving (197)
Web filtering software (207)
Wi-Fi Protected Access (197)
worm (184)
zombie (187)

Checkpoint

The Checkpoint exercises test your knowledge of the chapter concepts. The page number containing the answer appears in parentheses after each exercise.

To complete the Checkpoint exercises interactively, visit the Microsoft Office and Concepts CourseMate Web site at www.cengagebrain.com and then navigate to the Chapter 5 Checkpoint resource for this book.

Multiple Choice Select the best answer.

1. A _____ is a program that hides in a computer and allows someone from a remote location to take full control of the computer. (184)
   a. worm b. rootkit
   c. payload d. cookie
2. Malware is a term that can be used to describe _____. (184)
   a. viruses
   b. rootkits
   c. Trojan horses
   d. all of the above
3. The _____ is the destructive event or prank that malware is intended to deliver. (184)
   a. hash
   b. payload
   c. cookie
   d. spam
4. A _____ is an assault whose purpose is to disrupt computer access to an Internet service such as the Web or e-mail. (187)
   a. zombie
   b. denial of service attack
   c. Trojan horse
   d. virus hoax
5. _____ involves the examination of computer media, programs, data and log files on computers, servers, and networks. (192)
   a. Encryption key b. E-mail filtering
   c. Digital forensics d. Trusted source
6. Physical access controls, such as locked doors and windows, usually are adequate to protect against _____. (193)
   a. software piracy b. unauthorized access
   c. hardware theft d. all of the above
7. A(n) _____ is a programmed formula that the originator of the data uses to encrypt the plaintext and the recipient of the data uses to decrypt the ciphertext. (195)
   a. botnet
   b. certificate authority
   c. encryption algorithm
   d. encryption key
8. As related to the use of computers, _____ is defined as gaining unauthorized access or obtaining confidential information by taking advantage of the trusting human nature of some victims and the naivety of others. (205)
   a. phishing b. a virus hoax
   c. social engineering d. pharming

Matching Match the terms with their definitions.

_____ 1. virus (184)
_____ 2. trusted source (185)
_____ 3. spoofing (188)
_____ 4. encryption algorithm (195)
_____ 5. surge protector (196)

a. organization or person you believe will not send a virus infected file knowingly
b. set of steps that can convert readable plaintext into unreadable ciphertext
c. potentially damaging computer program that affects, or infects, a computer negatively by altering the way the computer works without the user's knowledge or permission
d. technique intruders use to make their network or Internet transmission appear legitimate to a victim computer or network
e. uses special electrical components to provide a stable current flow to the computer and other electronic equipment
f. service that blocks e-mail messages from designated sources

Short Answer Write a brief answer to each of the following questions.

1. How do antivirus programs detect and identify a virus? __________ What is a virus hoax? __________
2. Describe the ENERGY STAR program. __________ How should users handle obsolete computers? __________
3. What is information privacy? __________ List five ways to safeguard your personal information. __________
4. What are two methods for avoiding phishing attacks? __________ How does clickjacking work? __________
5. What is content filtering, and who uses it? __________ Why is content filtering controversial? __________

Problem Solving

The Problem Solving exercises extend your knowledge of the chapter concepts by seeking solutions to practical computer problems that you may encounter at home, school, or work. The Collaboration exercise should be completed with a team.

In the real world, practical problems often can be solved in multiple ways. Provide one solution to each of the following problems using available resources, such as articles on the Web or in print, blogs, podcasts, videos, television, user guides, other individuals, and electronics and computer stores. You may need to use multiple resources to obtain an answer. Present your solutions in the form requested by your instructor (brief report, presentation, discussion, or other means).

@ Home

1. **Infected File Detected** A message appears on your computer screen stating that your antivirus program detected an infected file on your computer and is unable to move it to quarantine. What are your next steps?
2. **Product Key in Use** While installing the latest version of Microsoft Office, the installation program prompts you to enter the product key. Once you finish entering the product key, you receive an error message stating that the product key already is in use. What might be causing this?
3. **Questionable Fair Use** A media company's attorney has sent you a letter stating that you are violating their rights by including a short movie clip from one of their movies in one of your videos posted on YouTube. You believe that you are within fair use guidelines by including the movie clip but also feel that you should respond to the attorney's letter. What are your next steps?
4. **Verifying Photo Validity** You are writing a research paper for your history class and have found a photo on the Web that you would like to use. You are cautious about using photos on the Web because of copyright issues and photos that have been altered digitally. How might you verify the validity of a photo on the Web?

@ Work

5. **Password Management** You must remember multiple user names and passwords to access various computer resources within your company. Each time your company introduces a new system, you must remember a new user name and password, some of which you are unable to customize. What steps will you take to manage your passwords?
6. **Problem Reinstalling Software** After recovering from a computer crash, you attempt to reinstall a program that was previously installed. When you insert the installation media, begin the installation, and type the product key, you receive an indication that you are unable to continue installing the software because you have installed it the maximum number of allowable times. What are your next steps?

7. **Missing Security Cable Key** To protect your notebook computer from theft, you use a security cable to secure it to the desk in your cubicle. Your boss assigns you some work to take home and suggests that you take home your notebook computer. You discover, however, that you are unable to locate the key that releases the security cable from the computer. What are your next steps?
8. **Monitored Computer Activities** You receive an e-mail message from the IT department stating that it randomly will monitor employee computers throughout the workday to ensure that they are being used for legitimate purposes. Shortly thereafter, you begin to notice that your computer slows significantly at random times once or twice per week. You suspect the performance decrease is a result of the computer monitoring. How will you address this?

Collaboration

9. **Computers in National and Local Security** National and local security agencies often use computers to protect citizens. For example, computers are used to maintain a list of individuals not cleared to board a commercial aircraft. Form a team of three people to create a list of the various ways computers help to keep us safe. One team member should research how local agencies, such as police departments, use computers to ensure security. Another team member should research ways national security agencies use computers to protect us from threats, and the last team member should research ways that private businesses use computers to guarantee security. Compile these findings into a report and submit it to your instructor.

Learn How To

The Learn How To activities step you through fundamental technology skills when using a computer. The Learn How To exercises enable you to become more proficient with these skills.

Premium Activity: To relate this Learn How To activity to your everyday life, see a visual demonstration of the activity, and complete a short assessment, visit the Microsoft Office and Concepts CourseMate Web site at www.cengagebrain.com and then navigate to the Chapter 5 Learn How To resources for this book.

Learn How To 1: Back Up Files on an Offsite Internet Server

Note: The service described in this exercise allows 15 days of free access. After that time, you may be billed automatically for service unless you cancel your service in the given time frame.

Backing up files stored on your computer on another disk or computer located in a different geographical location is the ultimate safeguard for data on your computer. A good way to back up data is to use one of the services available on the Web. A leading service is found at IBackup.com. To subscribe to the IBackup service, complete the following steps:

1. Start a Web browser, type the Web address `IBackup.com` in the Address bar and then press the ENTER key.
2. When the IBackup Web page is displayed, click Signup on the top horizontal toolbar.
3. Enter your e-mail address in the E-mail Address text box and then click the Continue with Registration button to display a form (Figure 5-27).
4. Fill in the form. Select the plan you want in the Select a Storage Plan list. If you want to try the service for a short period of time before subscribing, select 5 GB 15 day Free Trial Plan.
5. To continue to the next pages, you must enter credit card information. If you select the 15-day trial, your credit card will not be charged at this time, and an automatic billing at the end of 15 days will occur. After entering the required information, click the Continue button at the bottom of the page.
6. A message is displayed that confirms that you have signed up with IBackup and also provides a link for you to download the IBackup for Windows program.
7. Click the DOWNLOAD button to download the IBackup for Windows program and then follow the instructions to install the program on your computer.

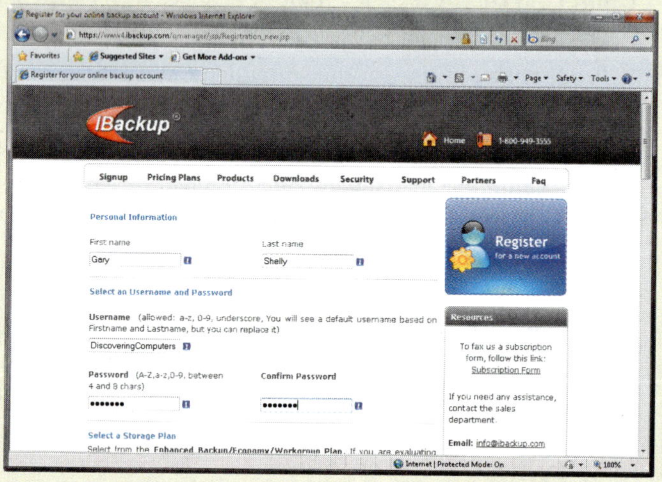

Figure 5-27

After establishing an account, you can use it for the time for which you subscribed. Complete the following steps to use the service:

1. Start the IBackup for Windows program.
2. Enter your user name and password and then click the Connect button to open a window containing your files, as well as the contents of your My IBackup folder (Figure 5-28).
3. To upload a file, locate the file in the left pane of the IBackup window and drag it to the right pane. The Backup Progress dialog box will be displayed while the file is uploading. The file will be placed in the My IBackup folder.

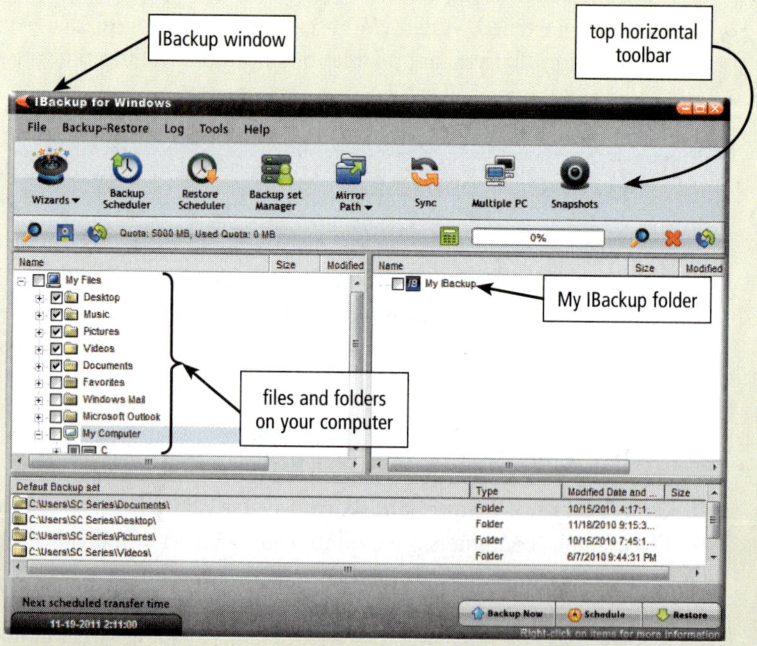

Figure 5-28

4. For further activities you can accomplish in this program for backing up your files, click the buttons on the top horizontal toolbar and experiment.

Exercises

1. Visit the IBackup Web site. Click View Demo and then follow the screen prompts to view all the services offered by IBackup. Which service is most appropriate for your home computer? Which service is most useful for the server that is used in the computer lab at your school? If you had critical data you needed to back up, would you use a service like this? Why or why not? Submit your answers to your instructor.
2. **Optional: Perform this exercise only for your own computer. Do not perform this exercise on a school computer.** Establish an account on IBackup.com. Upload two or more files from your computer. Download the files you uploaded back to your computer. Is this an efficient way to back up your files? Do you think the IBackup service would be useful for businesses? Submit your answers to your instructor.

Learn It Online

The Learn It Online exercises are interactive Web exercises designed to reinforce and expand your understanding of the chapter concepts. The descriptions below briefly summarize each exercise.

To complete the Learn It Online exercises, visit the Microsoft Office and Concepts CourseMate Web site at www.cengagebrain.com, navigate to the Chapter 5 resources for this book, click the link for the exercise you want to complete, and then read the instructions.

1 At the Movies — Attack of the Mobile Viruses

Watch a movie to learn about the recent wave of viruses plaguing mobile device users and then answer questions about the movie.

2 Student Edition Labs — Protecting Your Privacy Online and Computer Ethics

Enhance your understanding and knowledge about online privacy and computer ethics by completing the Protecting Your Privacy Online and Computer Ethics Labs.

3 Practice Test

Take a multiple choice test that checks your knowledge of the chapter concepts and review the resulting study guide.

4 Who Wants To Be a Computer Genius²?

Play the Shelly Cashman Series version of this popular game by answering questions to find out if you are a computer genius. Panic buttons are available to provide assistance during game play.

5 Crossword Puzzle Challenge

Complete an interactive crossword puzzle to reinforce concepts presented in this chapter.

6 Windows Exercises

Step through the Windows 7 exercises to learn about playing audio compact discs, understanding multimedia properties, dragging and dropping Windows objects, and checking for system updates.

7 Exploring Computer Careers

Read about a career as a digital forensics examiner, search for related employment advertisements, and then answer related questions.

8 Web Apps — Dictionary.com

Learn how to use Dictionary.com to search for a dictionary entry, translate a word to other languages, and search for Web pages containing your search term.

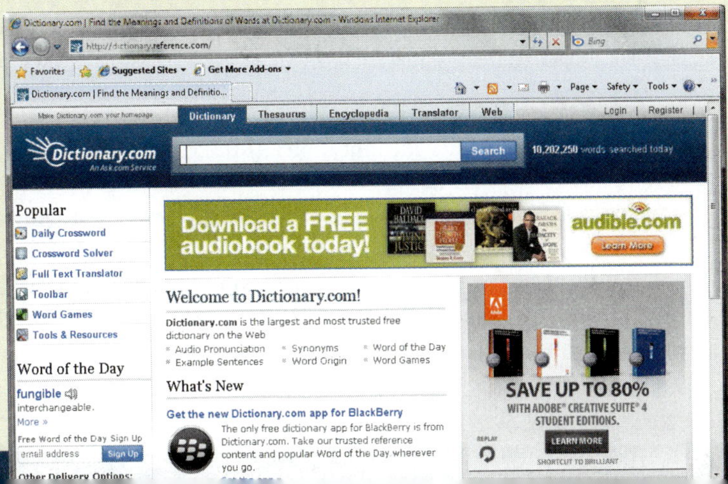

Web Research

The Web Research exercises broaden your understanding of chapter concepts by presenting questions that require you to search the Web for answers.

1 Search Sleuth

Use one of the search engines listed in Figure 2-8 in Chapter 2 on page 53 or your own favorite search engine to find the answers to the following questions. Copy and paste the Web address from the Web page where you found the answer. Some questions may have more than one answer. If required, submit your answers to your instructor. (1) Which five words are among the most commonly used passwords? (2) What do e-mail messages with the subject lines "Sending You All My Love," "Laughing Kitty," and "You've Received a Postcard from a Family Member" have in common? (3) T'ai chi, yoga, and the Alexander technique might offer some relief to computer users suffering from which injury? (4) For which purpose is a gas discharge arrestor used? (5) How many computers in the business world have antivirus software that has been disabled or never was installed properly?

2 Green Computing

The more than 1 billion computers in the world each emit an average of 1,000 pounds of carbon dioxide each year. Many home computer users can help reduce their carbon footprint with the help of devices that monitor energy consumption. Computers are not the only home devices that draw a lot of current; the average home has 27 products that always are turned on, including the television, appliances, and heating and cooling systems. Verdiem's free download, Edison, helps consumers manage their computer power usage. Smart metering devices made by Control4, Colorado vNet, and ZigBee track power usage and give automated tips on how to reduce energy costs. View online Web sites that provide information about reducing home electricity consumption. How do the monitoring devices work? How much do they cost? How do they calculate the money and energy saved per year? Write a report summarizing your findings, and include a table of links to Web sites that provide additional details.

3 Social Networking

People with unique and special talents often desire to share their passions and pastimes with others. Online social networks provide them an opportunity to share their hobbies and creations. In fact, 69 percent of online social networking members say they have a connection with special-interest Web sites. For example, members of the Sports MatchMaker (sportsmatchmaker.com) community can find people who want to play any sport or participate in any hobby at a specific date and time. ShowOffDemo (showoffdemo.com) members spotlight their talents on a virtual stage, and the Instructables community (instructables.com) collaborates to provide instructions for arts, crafts, food, electronics, and games. Visit these Web sites and view the members' products. Which items are popular? Which are unusual? Which photos provide details on documenting the steps necessary to complete a project? How do members share project ideas and requests for information? Summarize the information you read and viewed.

4 Blogs

More than 80,000 blogs are created daily according to Umbria Communications, a service that tracks new Internet media. Many information technology (IT) professionals maintain these blogs to tout companies' products and express personal observations. IT bloggers include Robert Scoble on video (scobleizer.com); Jeff Jaffe, Novell's chief technical officer (novell.com/ctoblog); Ed Brill on IBM (edbrill.com); and Tom Kyte on Oracle (tkyte.blogspot.com). Visit these blogs and read some of the posts. What new products are mentioned? What are the bloggers' backgrounds? What controversial topics are discussed? What personal views do the bloggers express?

5 Ethics in Action

Radio frequency identification (RFID) tags are expected to help merchants in many ways. By placing these tags on such items as prescriptions, computer peripherals, and clothing, retailers hope to reduce theft, track inventory, reduce labor costs, and keep their shelves stocked. Privacy experts, however, claim the tags can store information about consumers' shopping habits and whereabouts. Law enforcement officials, lawyers, marketers, and even thieves could use this detailed electronic data to track people at all times of the day. View Web sites that discuss using RFID tags in stores and the privacy issues that arise from their use. Write a report summarizing your findings, and include a table of links to Web sites that provide additional details.

Buyer's Guide: How to Purchase Computers and Mobile Devices

AT SOME POINT, perhaps while you are taking this course, you may decide to buy a computer or mobile device (Figure 1). The decision is an important one and will require an investment of both time and money. Like many buyers, you may have little experience with technology and find yourself unsure of how to proceed. You can start by talking to your friends, coworkers, and instructors about their computers and mobile devices. What type of computers and mobile devices did they buy? Why? For what purposes do they use their computers and mobile devices?

Figure 1 Computers and mobile devices.

How to Purchase a Desktop Computer

A **desktop computer** sits on or below a desk or table in a stationary location such as a home, office, or dormitory room. Desktop computers are a good option if you work mostly in one place and have plenty of space in a work area. Desktop computers generally provide more performance for your money. Today, manufacturers are placing more emphasis on style by offering bright colors, stylish displays, and theme-based displays so that the computer looks attractive if it is in an area of high visibility. Once you have decided that a desktop computer is most suited to your computing needs, the next step is to determine specific software, hardware, peripheral devices, and services to purchase, as well as where to buy the computer.

1 Determine the specific software to use on your computer.

Before deciding to purchase software, be sure it contains the features necessary for the tasks you want to perform. Rely on the computer users in whom you have confidence to help you decide on the software to use. In addition, consider purchasing software that might help you perform tasks at home that you otherwise would perform at another location, such as at school or at work. The minimum requirements of the software you select may determine the operating system (Microsoft Windows, Mac OS, Linux) you need. If you decide to use a particular operating system that does not support software you want to use, you may be able to purchase similar software from other manufacturers.

Many Web sites and trade magazines provide reviews of software products. These Web sites frequently have articles that rate computers and software on cost, performance, and support.

Your hardware requirements depend on the minimum requirements of the software you will run on your computer. Some software requires more memory and disk space than others, as well as additional input, output, and storage devices. For example, suppose you want to run software that can copy one optical disc's contents directly to another optical disc, without first copying the data to the hard disk. To support that, you should consider a desktop computer or a high-end notebook computer, because the computer will need two optical disc drives: one that reads from an optical disc, and one that writes on an optical disc. If you plan to run software that allows your computer to function as an entertainment system, then you will need an optical disc drive, quality speakers, and an upgraded sound card.

2 Know the system requirements of the operating system.

After determining the software you want to run on your new computer, the next step is to determine the operating system to use. If, however, you purchase a new computer, chances are it will have the latest version of your preferred operating system (Windows, Mac OS, Linux).

3 Look for bundled software.

When you purchase a computer, it may include bundled software. Some sellers even let you choose which software you want. Remember, however, that bundled software has value only if you would have purchased the software even if it had not been included with the computer. At the very least, you probably will want word processing software and an antivirus program. If you need additional programs, such as a spreadsheet, a database, or presentation software, consider purchasing or downloading Microsoft Office, Microsoft Works, OpenOffice.org, or Sun StarOffice, which include several programs at a reduced price or at no cost.

4 Avoid buying the least powerful computer available.

Once you know the application software you want to use, then consider the following important criteria about the computer's components: (1) processor speed, (2) size and types of memory (RAM) and storage, (3) types of input/output devices, (4) types of ports and adapter cards, and (5) types of communications devices. You also should consider if the computer is upgradeable and to what extent you are able to upgrade. For example, all manufacturers limit the amount of memory you can add. The information in Figure 2 on pages 219 and 220 can help you determine which computer components are best for you and outlines considerations for specific hardware components. For a sample Base Components worksheet that lists PC recommendations for each category of user discussed in this

Considerations for Hardware Components

Card Reader/Writer: A card reader/writer is useful for transferring data directly to and from a memory card, such as the type used in a digital camera, smart phone, or portable media player. Make sure the card reader/writer can read from and write on the memory cards that you use.

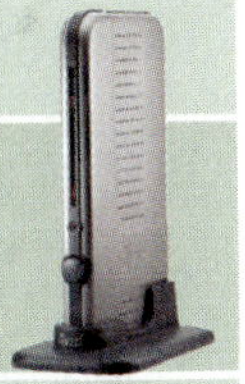

Digital Video Capture Device: A digital video capture device allows you to connect a computer to a video camera or VCR and record, edit, manage, and then write video back on an optical disc or VCR tape. To create quality video (true 30 frames per second, full-sized TV), the digital video capture device should have a USB or FireWire port.

External Hard Disk: An external hard disk can serve many purposes: it can serve as extra storage for your computer, provide a way to store and transport large files or large quantities of files, and provide a convenient way to back up data on other internal and external hard disks. External hard disks can be purchased with the same capacity as any internal disk.

Fingerprint Reader: For added security, you may want to consider purchasing a fingerprint reader. It helps prevent unauthorized access to your computer and also allows you to log onto Web sites quickly via your fingerprint, rather than entering a user name and password each time you access the site. Most use a USB connection and require software installation.

Hard Disk: It is recommended that you buy a computer with at least a 320 GB hard disk if your primary interests are browsing the Web and using e-mail and Office suite-type programs; 1 TB if you also want to edit digital photos or if you plan to edit digital video or manipulate large audio files even occasionally; and 2 TB if you will edit digital video, movies, or photos often; store audio files and music; or consider yourself to be a power user. Internal hard disk controllers are available with the RAID option for added data protection.

Joystick/Wheel: If you use the computer to play games, then you will want to purchase a joystick or a wheel. These devices, especially the more expensive ones, provide for realistic game play with force feedback, programmable buttons, and specialized levers and wheels.

Keyboard: The keyboard is one of the more important devices used to communicate with the computer. For this reason, make sure the keyboard you purchase has 101 to 105 keys, is comfortable and easy to use, and has a USB connection. A wireless keyboard should be considered, especially if you have a small desk area.

Microphone: If you plan to record audio or use speech recognition to enter text and commands, then purchase a close-talk headset with gain adjustment support.

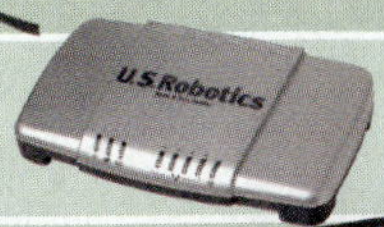

Modem: Most computers include a modem so that you can use a telephone line to access the Internet. Some modems also have fax capabilities. Your modem should be rated at 56 Kbps.

Monitor: The monitor is where you will view documents, read e-mail messages, and view pictures. A minimum of a 19" LCD flat-panel monitor is recommended, but if you plan to use the computer for graphic design or game playing, then you may want to purchase a 22" or 27" monitor. Instead of a single large, widescreen monitor, you may want to consider a side-by-side monitor setup.

Mouse: While working with a desktop computer, you use the mouse constantly. Make sure the mouse has a wheel, which acts as a third button in addition to the top two buttons on the left and right. An ergonomic design also is important because your hand is on the mouse most of the time when you are using the computer. A wireless mouse should be considered to eliminate the cord and allow you to work at short distances from the computer.

Optical Disc Drives: Most computers include a DVD±RW combination drive and/or DVD/Blu-ray Disc drive. A DVD±RW or a Blu-ray Disc drive allows you to read optical discs and to write data on (burn) an optical disc. It also will allow you to store and share video files, digital photos, and other large files with other people who have access to a DVD/Blu-ray Disc drive. A Blu-ray Disc has a capacity of at least 25 GB, and a DVD has a capacity of at least 4.7 GB, versus the 650 MB capacity of a CD.

Figure 2 Hardware guidelines. *(continues)*

Considerations for Hardware Components

Ports: Depending on how you are using the computer, you may need anywhere from 4 to 10 USB ports. USB ports have become the connection of choice in the computer industry. They offer an easy way to connect peripheral devices such as printers, digital cameras, and portable media players. Many computers intended for home or professional audio/video use have built-in FireWire ports. Most personal computers include a minimum of six USB ports, two FireWire ports, and an Ethernet port.

Printer: Your two basic printer choices are ink-jet and laser. Color ink-jet printers cost on average between $50 and $300. Laser printers cost from $200 to $2,000. In general, the less expensive the printer, the lower the resolution and speed, and the more often you are required to change the ink cartridges or toner. Laser printers print faster and with a higher quality than an ink-jet, and their toner on average costs less.

Processor: For a personal computer, an Intel Core i7 processor at 2.93 GHz is more than enough processor power for most home and small office/home office users. Game home, enterprise, and power users should upgrade to faster, more powerful processors.

RAM: RAM plays a vital role in the speed of a computer. Make sure the computer you purchase has at least 2 GB of RAM. If you have extra money to invest in a computer, consider increasing the RAM. The extra money for RAM will be well spent because more RAM typically translates into more speed.

Scanner: The most popular scanner purchased with a computer today is the flatbed scanner. When evaluating a flatbed scanner, check the color depth and resolution. Do not buy anything less than a color depth of 48 bits and a resolution of 1200 x 2400 dpi. The higher the color depth, the more accurate the color. A higher resolution picks up the more subtle gradations of color.

Sound Card: Many computers include a standard sound card that supports Dolby 5.1 surround and are capable of recording and playing digital audio. Make sure they are suitable in the event you decide to use the computer as an entertainment or gaming system.

Speakers: Once you have a good sound card, quality speakers and a separate subwoofer that amplifies the bass frequencies of the speakers can turn the computer into a premium stereo system.

USB Flash Drive: If you work on different computers and need access to the same data and information, then this portable flash memory device is ideal. USB flash drive capacity varies from 1 GB to 16 GB.

USB Hub: If you plan to connect several peripheral devices to the computer at the same time, then you need to be concerned with the number of ports available on the computer. If the computer does not have enough ports, then you should purchase a USB hub. A USB hub plugs into a single USB port and provides several additional ports.

Video Card: Most standard video cards satisfy the monitor display needs of most home and small office users. If you are a game home user or a graphic designer, you will want to upgrade to a higher quality video card. The higher refresh rates will further enhance the display of games, graphics, and movies.

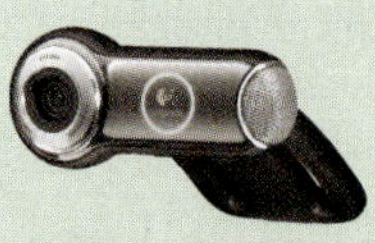

Web Cam: A Web cam is a small digital video camera that can capture and display live video on a Web page. You also can capture, edit, and share video and still photos. Recommended minimum specifications include 640 x 480 resolution, a video with a rate of 30 frames per second, and a USB or FireWire port. Some Web cams are built into computer monitors.

Wireless LAN Access Point: A wireless LAN access point allows you to network several computers, so that multiple users can share files and access the Internet through a single broadband connection. Each device that you connect requires a wireless card. A wireless LAN access point can offer a range of operations up to several hundred feet, so be sure the device has a high-powered antenna.

Figure 2 Hardware guidelines. *(continued)*

book, visit the Microsoft Office and Concepts CourseMate Web site at www.cengagebrain.com and then navigate to the Buyer's Guide Feature resource for this book. In the worksheet, the Home User category is divided into two groups: Application Home User and Game Home User.

Computer technology changes rapidly, meaning a computer that seems powerful enough today may not serve your computing needs in several years. In fact, studies show that many users regret not buying a more powerful computer. To avoid this, plan to buy a computer that will last for at least two to three years. You can help delay obsolescence by purchasing the fastest processor, the most memory, and the largest hard disk you can afford. If you must buy a less powerful computer, be sure you can upgrade it with additional memory, components, and peripheral devices as your computer requirements grow.

5 Consider upgrades to the mouse, keyboard, monitor, printer, microphone, and speakers.

You use these peripheral devices to interact with the computer, so make sure they are up to your standards. Review the peripheral devices listed in Figure 2 and then visit both local computer dealers and large retail stores to test the computers and devices on display. Ask the salesperson which input and output devices would be best for you and whether you should upgrade beyond the standard product. Consider purchasing a wireless keyboard and wireless mouse to eliminate wires on your desktop. A few extra dollars spent on these components when you initially purchase a computer can extend its usefulness by years.

6 Determine whether to use a broadband or dial-up connection to access the Internet.

If your computer has a modem, you can access the Internet using a standard telephone line. Ordinarily, you call a local or toll-free 800 number to connect to an Internet access provider. Using a dial-up Internet connection usually is relatively inexpensive but slow.

Broadband connections provide much faster Internet connections, which are ideal if you want faster file download speeds for software, digital photos, digital video, and music. As you would expect, they can be more expensive than a dial-up connection. If you want to use a broadband connection, your computer should have an Ethernet card installed, unless you are using a wireless broadband connection such as WiMax or 3G. If you will be using a dial-up connection, your computer should have a modem installed.

7 Use a worksheet to compare computers, services, and other considerations.

You can use a separate sheet of paper to take notes about each vendor's computer and then summarize the information on a worksheet. For a sample worksheet that compares prices for a PC or a Mac, visit the Microsoft Office and Concepts CourseMate Web site at www.cengagebrain.com and then navigate to the Buyer's Guide Feature resource for this book. Most companies advertise a price for a base computer that includes components housed in the system unit (processor, RAM, sound card, video card, network card), hard disks, optical disc drives, a keyboard, mouse, monitor, printer, speakers, and modem. Be aware, however, that some advertisements list prices for computers with only some of these components. Monitors and printers, for example, often are not included in a base computer's price. Depending on how you plan to use the computer, you may want to invest in additional or more powerful components. When comparing the prices of computers, make sure you are comparing identical or similar configurations.

8 If you are buying a new computer, you have several purchasing options: buying from a school bookstore, a local computer dealer, a local large retail store, or ordering by mail via telephone or the Web.

Each purchasing option has certain advantages. Many college bookstores, for example, sign exclusive pricing agreements with computer manufacturers and, thus, can offer student discounts. Local dealers and local large retail stores, however, more easily can provide hands-on support. Mail-order companies that sell computers by telephone or online via the Web (Figure 3) often provide the lowest prices, but extend less personal service. Some major mail-order companies, however, have started to provide next-business-day, on-site services. A credit card usually is required to buy from a mail-order company.

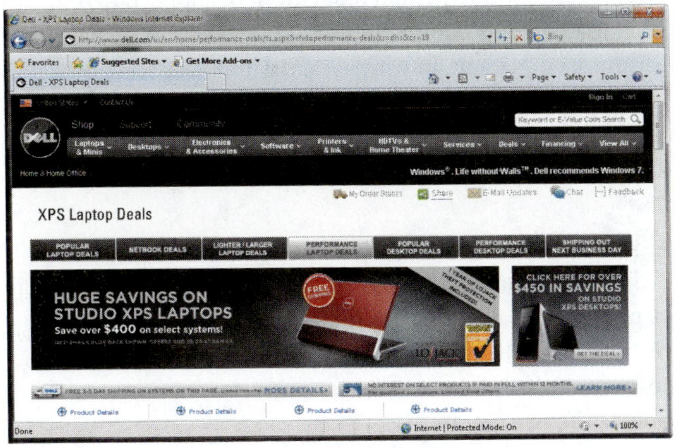

Figure 3 Mail-order companies, such as Dell, sell computers online.

9 If you are buying a used computer, stay with name brands such as Dell, Apple, HP, and Gateway.

Although brand-name equipment can cost more, most brand-name computers have longer, more comprehensive warranties, are better supported, and have more authorized centers for repair services. As with new computers, you can purchase a used computer from local computer dealers, local large retail stores, or mail order via the telephone or the Web. Classified ads and used computer sellers offer additional outlets for purchasing used computers.

10 If you have a computer and are upgrading to a new one, then consider selling or trading in the old one.

If you are a replacement buyer, your older computer still may have value. If you cannot sell the computer through the classified ads, via a Web site, or to a friend, then ask if the computer dealer will buy your old computer.

An increasing number of companies are taking trade-ins, but do not expect too much money for your old computer. Other companies offer to recycle your old computer free or for a fee.

11 Be aware of hidden costs.

Before purchasing, be sure to consider any additional costs associated with buying a computer, such as an additional telephone line, a broadband modem, an uninterruptible power supply (UPS), computer furniture, a USB flash drive, paper, and computer training classes you may want to take. Depending on where you buy the computer, the seller may be willing to include some or all of these in the computer purchase price.

12 Consider more than just price.

The lowest-cost computer may not be the best long-term buy. Consider such intangibles as the vendor's time in business, regard for quality, and reputation for support. If you need to upgrade a computer often, you may want to consider a leasing arrangement, in which you pay monthly lease fees, but can upgrade or add on to your computer as your equipment needs change. No matter what type of buyer you are, insist on a 30-day, no-questions-asked return policy on the computer.

13 Avoid restocking fees.

Some companies charge a restocking fee of 10 to 20 percent as part of their money-back return policy. In some cases, no restocking fee for hardware is applied, but it is applied for software. Ask about the existence and terms of any restocking policies before you buy.

14 Use a credit card to purchase a new computer.

Many credit cards offer purchase protection and extended warranty benefits that cover you in case of loss of or damage to purchased goods. Paying by credit card also gives you time to install and use the computer before you have to pay for it. Finally, if you are dissatisfied with the computer and are unable to reach an agreement with the seller, paying by credit card gives you certain rights regarding withholding payment until the dispute is resolved. Check your credit card terms for specific details.

15 Consider purchasing an extended warranty or service plan.

If you use your computer for business or require fast resolution to major computer problems, consider purchasing an extended warranty or a service plan through a local dealer or third-party company. Most extended warranties cover the repair and replacement of computer components beyond the standard warranty. Most service plans ensure that your technical support calls receive priority response from technicians. You also can purchase an on-site service plan that states that a technician will arrive at your home, work, or school within 24 hours. If your computer includes a warranty and service agreement for a year or less, consider extending the service for two or three years when you buy the computer.

How to Purchase a Notebook Computer

If you need computing capability when you travel or to use in lectures or meetings, you may find a notebook computer to be an appropriate choice. The guidelines mentioned in the previous section also apply to the purchase of a notebook computer. The following are additional considerations unique to notebook computers, including netbooks and Tablet PCs.

1 Determine which computer fits your mobile computing needs.

Before purchasing a notebook computer, you need to determine whether a traditional notebook computer, netbook, or Tablet PC will meet your needs. If you spend most of your time working on spreadsheets, writing and/or editing documents, e-mail, or using the Internet, then a traditional notebook computer will suffice. If your primary use will be to access the Internet while traveling and you are not concerned as much with processing power or hard disk capacity, consider a netbook. If you find yourself in need of a computer in class or that you spend more time in meetings than in your office, then the Tablet PC may be the answer. Before you invest money in a Tablet PC, however, determine which programs you plan to use on it. You should not buy a Tablet PC simply because it is an interesting type of computer.

2 Purchase a notebook computer with a sufficiently large screen.

Active-matrix screens display high-quality color that is viewable from all angles. Less expensive, passive-matrix screens sometimes are difficult to see in low-light conditions and cannot be viewed from an angle.

Notebook computers typically include a 12.1-inch, 13.3-inch, 14.1-inch, 15.4-inch, or 17-inch display. Netbooks have screens as small as 7 inches. For most users, a 14.1-inch display is satisfactory. If you intend to use the notebook computer as a desktop computer replacement, however, you may opt for a 15.4-inch or 17-inch display. The WSXGA+ standard (1680 × 1050) is popular with 17-inch displays, so if you intend to watch HD movies on the computer, take this into consideration. Dell offers a notebook computer with a 20.1-inch display that looks like a briefcase when closed. Some notebook computers with these larger displays weigh more than 10 pounds, however, so if you travel a lot and portability is essential, you might want a lighter computer with a smaller display. The lightest notebook computers, which weigh less than 3 pounds, are equipped with a 12.1-inch display.

Regardless of size, the resolution of the display should be at least 1024 × 768 pixels. To compare the screen size on various notebook computers, including netbooks and Tablet PCs, visit the company Web sites. Tablet PCs use a digitizer below a standard 10.4-inch motion-sensitive LCD display to make the writing experience on the screen feel like writing on paper. To ensure you experience the maximum benefits from the ClearType technology, make sure the LCD display has a resolution of 800 × 600 in landscape mode and a 600 × 800 in portrait mode.

3 Experiment with different keyboards, pointing devices, and digital pens.

Notebook computer keyboards, especially netbook keyboards, are far less standardized than those for desktop computers. Some notebook computers, for example, have wide wrist rests, while others have none, and keyboard layouts on notebook computers often vary. Notebook computers also use a range of pointing devices, including touchpads, pointing sticks, trackballs, and, in the case of Tablet PCs, digital pens.

Before purchasing a notebook computer, try various types of keyboards and pointing devices to determine which is easiest for you to use. Regardless of the device you select, you also may want to purchase a standard mouse to use when you are working at a desk or other large surface. Figure 4 compares the standard point-and-click of a mouse with the gestures made with a digital pen. Other gestures with the digital pen replicate some of the commonly used keys on a keyboard.

Mouse and Digital Pen Operations

Mouse	Digital Pen
Point	Point
Click	Tap
Double-click	Double-tap
Right-click	Tap and hold
Click and drag	Drag

Figure 4 Standard point-and-click of a mouse compared with the gestures made with a digital pen.

4 Make sure the notebook computer you purchase has an optical disc drive.

Most mobile computers include an optical disc drive. Although DVD/Blu-ray Disc drives are slightly more expensive, they allow you to play CDs, DVDs, and Blu-ray Discs using your notebook computer and hear the sound through earbuds. If you decide to purchase a netbook, it might not include an optical disc drive. Instead, you might need to purchase an external optical disc drive.

5 If necessary, upgrade the processor, memory, and disk storage at the time of purchase.

As with a desktop computer, upgrading a notebook computer's memory and disk storage usually is less expensive at the time of initial purchase. Some disk storage is custom designed for notebook computer manufacturers, meaning an upgrade might not be available in the future. If you are purchasing a lightweight notebook computer or Tablet PC, then it should include at least an Intel Core 2 Quad processor, 2 GB RAM, and 250 GB of storage. If you are purchasing a netbook, it should have an Intel Atom processor, at least 1 GB RAM, and 120 GB of storage.

6 The availability of built-in ports and slots and a USB hub on a notebook computer is important.

A notebook computer does not have much room to add adapter cards. If you know the purpose for which you plan to use the notebook computer, then you can determine the ports you will need. Netbooks typically have fewer ports than traditional notebook computers and Tablet PCs. Most notebook computers include common ports, such as a video port, audio port, network port, FireWire port, and multiple USB ports. If you plan to connect the notebook computer to a television, however, then you will need a PC to TV port. To optimize television viewing, you may want to consider DisplayPort, DVI, or HDMI ports. If you want to connect to networks at school or in various offices via a network cable, make sure the notebook computer you purchase has a network port. If the notebook computer does not contain a network port, you will have to purchase an external network card that slides into an expansion slot in your computer, as well as a network cable. You also may want to consider adding a card reader.

7 If you plan to use your notebook computer for note-taking at school or in meetings, consider a convertible Tablet PC.

Some computer manufacturers have developed convertible Tablet PCs that allow the screen to rotate 180 degrees on a central hinge and then fold down to cover the keyboard (Figure 5). You then can use a digital pen to enter text or drawings into the computer by writing on the screen. Some notebook computers have wide screens for better viewing and editing, and some even have a screen on top of the unit in addition to the regular screen. If you spend much of your time attending lectures or meetings, then the slate Tablet PC is ideal. With a slate Tablet PC, users can attach a removable keyboard.

Figure 5
A convertible Tablet PC.

8 If you purchase a Tablet PC, determine whether you require multi-touch technology.

Newer operating systems now support hardware with multi-touch technology. If you choose an operating system that supports this technology, the Tablet PC also must support this technology.

9 Purchase a notebook computer with an integrated Web cam.

If you will be using a notebook computer to connect to the Internet and chat with friends online, consider purchasing one with an integrated Web cam.

10 Check with your wireless carrier to see if it offers netbooks for sale.

Most wireless carriers now offer wireless data plans allowing you to connect to the Internet from almost anywhere with a cell phone signal. Some wireless carriers now are selling netbooks with built-in capability to connect wirelessly to the Internet using a wireless data plan.

11 Purchase a notebook computer with a built-in wireless network connection.

A wireless network connection (Bluetooth, Wi-Fi a/b/g/n, WiMAX, etc.) can be useful when you travel or as part of a home network. Increasingly more airports, hotels, schools, and cafés have wireless networks that allow you to connect to the Internet. Many users today are setting up wireless home networks. With a wireless home network, your notebook computer can access the Internet, as well as other computers in the house, from any location to share files and hardware, such as a printer, and browse the Web. Most home wireless networks allow connections from distances of 150 to 800 feet.

12 If you plan to use your notebook computer for long periods without access to an electrical outlet, purchase a second battery.

The trend among notebook computer users today is power and size over battery life. Many notebook computer users today are willing to give up longer battery life for a larger screen, faster processor, and more storage. In addition, some manufacturers typically sell the notebook computer with the lowest capacity battery. For this reason, be careful in choosing a notebook computer if you plan to use it without access to electrical outlets for long periods, such as an airplane flight. You also might want to purchase a second battery as a backup. If you anticipate running the notebook computer on batteries frequently, choose a computer that uses lithium-ion batteries, which last longer than nickel cadmium or nickel hydride batteries.

13 Purchase a well-padded and well-designed carrying case.

An amply padded carrying case will protect your notebook computer from the bumps it will receive while traveling. A well-designed carrying case will have room for accessories such as spare optical discs, pens, and paperwork (Figure 6). Although a netbook may be small enough to fit in a handbag, make sure that the bag has sufficient padding to protect the computer.

Figure 6
A well-designed notebook computer carrying case.

14 If you plan to connect your notebook computer to a video projector, make sure the notebook computer is compatible with the video projector.

You should check, for example, to be sure that your notebook computer will allow you to display an image on the computer screen and projection device at the same time. Also, ensure that the notebook computer has the ports required to connect to the video projector. You also may consider purchasing a notebook computer with a built-in Web cam for video conferencing purposes.

15 For improved security and convenience, consider a fingerprint reader.

More than half a million notebook computers are stolen or lost each year. If you have critical information stored on your notebook computer, consider purchasing one with a fingerprint reader (Figure 7) to protect the data if your computer is stolen or lost. Fingerprint security offers a level of protection that extends well beyond the standard password protection. If your notebook computer is stolen, the odds of recovering it improve dramatically with anti-theft tracking software. Manufacturers claim recovery rates of 90 percent or more for notebook computers using their product. For convenience, fingerprint readers also allow you to log onto several Web sites in lieu of entering user name and password information.

Figure 7 Fingerprint reader technology offers greater security than passwords.

16 Review the docking capabilities of the Tablet PC.

The Tablet Technology in the Windows operating system supports a grab-and-go form of docking, so that you can pick up and take a docked Tablet PC with you, just as you would pick up a notepad on your way to a meeting (Figure 8).

Figure 8 A Tablet PC docked to create a desktop computer with the Tablet PC as the monitor.

How to Purchase a Smart Phone

You probably will use a smart phone more often than other mobile devices. For this reason, it is important to choose a phone that is available through your preferred wireless carrier, available in your price range, and offers access to the features you will use most frequently. This section lists guidelines you should consider when purchasing a smart phone.

1 Choose a wireless carrier and plan that satisfies your needs and budget.

Multiple wireless carriers exist today, and each one offers a different line of smart phones. For example, the Samsung Alias is available only through Verizon Wireless. Alternatively, some smart phones, such as the BlackBerry line of smart phones, are available from multiple wireless carriers. Before deciding on a smart phone, you first should research the wireless carriers in your area, and be sure to ascertain whether the coverage is acceptable. Additionally, compare the calling plans for the various carriers and determine which one best meets your needs. Once you have determined the wireless carrier to use, you then can choose from one of their available smart phones. Once you purchase a smart phone, most carriers allow you to perform a risk-free evaluation for 30 days. If you are not satisfied with the phone or its performance, you can return the phone and pay only for the service you have used.

2 Decide on the size, style, and weight of the smart phone that will work best for you.

Smart phones are available in various sizes, weights, shapes, and colors. Some people prefer larger, heavier phones because they feel that they are more durable, while others prefer smaller, lightweight phones for easy portability. Some smart phones are flip phones, meaning that you have to open the phone (like a clamshell) to display the screen and keypad, some open by sliding the phone, and others do not need to be opened to use them. Figure 9 shows the various smart phone styles.

Figure 9 Various smart phone styles.

3 Determine whether you prefer a touch screen, keypad, or mini-keyboard.

Modern smart phones provide various ways to enter text. During the past several years, smart phones with touch screens as their primary input device have been penetrating the market. Some smart phone users prefer touch screens because the phone does not require additional space for a keypad or mini-keyboard, but others find it more difficult to type on a touch screen. Most newer smart phones with touch screens also include handwriting recognition. Smart phones with keypads might make it easier to type for some users, but others do not like the unfamiliar feeling of keys arranged in alphabetical order. In addition, you often have to press the keys multiple times before reaching the letter you want to type. Mini-keyboards are available on some smart phones, such as the BlackBerry and Samsung Alias. Mini-keyboards provide a key for each letter, but the keys are significantly smaller than those on a standard keyboard. Most smart phone users type on mini-keyboards using their thumbs.

4 If you will be synchronizing your smart phone with a program on your computer, select a smart phone that is compatible with the program you wish to use.

Programs such as Microsoft Outlook allow you to synchronize your e-mail messages, contacts, and calendar with your smart phone. If you would like this functionality, purchase a smart phone that can synchronize with Microsoft Outlook. Similarly, if your company uses a BlackBerry Enterprise server or Microsoft Exchange server, you should consider purchasing a smart phone that can synchronize, either using wires or wirelessly, with those servers.

5 Compare battery life.

Any smart phone is useful only if it has the power required to run. Talking and using the Internet on your smart phone will shorten battery life more quickly than when the phone is powered on but not in use. If you have a choice, be sure to purchase a battery that will allow the phone to function all day. Pay particular attention to the talk time and standby time. If you plan to talk on the phone more than the advertised talk time, you might consider purchasing a second battery or an extended battery if your phone supports it.

6 Make sure your smart phone has enough memory and storage.

If you are using the smart phone to send and receive picture, video, and e-mail messages, and to store music, purchase a memory card that not only is compatible with your computer and smart phone, but also has adequate storage space for your messages and files. If you purchase a memory card and eventually fill it, you easily can transfer the data to a larger memory card.

7 Check out the accessories.

Determine which accessories you want for the smart phone. Accessories include carrying cases, screen protectors, synchronization cradles and cables, and car chargers.

How to Purchase a Portable Media Player

Portable media players are becoming the preferred device for listening to music and watching videos on the go. When choosing a portable media player, it is important to consider features and characteristics other than the physical size and amount of storage space. This section lists guidelines you should consider when purchasing a portable media player.

1 Choose a device with sufficient storage capacity.

Audio and video files can consume a great deal of storage space, so be sure to purchase a portable media player that has enough capacity to store your audio and video files. You also should consider approximately how many media files you acquire each year, and make sure that your device has enough storage space to accommodate these files for years to come.

2 Determine which file formats your new portable media player should support and how you will add files to your library.

Some portable media players are designed to accept new audio and video files only through a program installed on a computer. For example, it is easiest to add media files to an iPod using the iTunes program. Other portable media players connect to a computer using a cable and are displayed in Windows as a removable disk. You then can add files to the media player by dragging the files to the removable disk icon in Windows. The portable media player must support the file formats you are using. You can determine the file format by looking at the file extension on the media files you wish to transfer to your portable media player. Before purchasing a portable media player, make sure that it can support the file formats you are using.

3 Consider a portable media player that can play video.

Some users prefer to watch videos on their portable media player in addition to playing music. You typically can download videos for portable media players less expensively than purchasing the movie on a DVD/Blu-ray Disc. Although the display on a portable media player is small, many still find entertainment value because they are able to watch videos and stay occupied while waiting for a bus, on an airplane, or at other locations where they otherwise might not have anything to occupy them.

4 Read reviews about the sound quality on the portable media players you are considering.

Sound quality may vary greatly among portable media players. If you are unable to try the portable media player before buying it, read reviews and make sure that those reviewing the devices find the sound quality to be acceptable. You also may consider purchasing higher-quality earbuds or headphones to enhance the sound quality.

5 Select a size and style that works best for you.

Portable media players are available in various shapes and styles. For example, Apple offers the iPod shuffle, iPod nano, iPod classic, and iPod touch (Figure 10). Each type of iPod varies in size and style, and some have capabilities (such as video) that others do not. Choose a size and style that meets your needs and fits your personality.

Figure 10 Portable media players are available in different shapes, styles, and colors.

6 Check out additional memory cards.

Most portable media players have internal storage for your media files. If you wish to increase the available storage, consider purchasing a portable media player that allows you to increase storage capacity by inserting memory cards. Similar to most computers, it is less expensive initially to purchase the largest amount of storage that you can afford, but it is helpful to be able to increase your storage at a later date.

7 Consider rechargeable batteries.

Although most portable media players include rechargeable batteries, some still use traditional alkaline batteries. Portable media players sometimes can last for only a few hours on alkaline batteries, and battery replacement can be costly. Rechargeable batteries often last longer and create less waste. If you are not near a power source, you are unable to recharge the batteries when they die. With alkaline batteries, you simply can insert new ones and continue enjoying your player.

8 Stay within your budget.

As previously mentioned, portable media players are available in a variety of shapes and sizes, and they also are available with various storage capacities. When shopping for a portable media player, be realistic when you consider how you will use the device, as well as how much storage you require. Purchasing the latest and greatest device is not always the best option, and the cost can exceed what you care to spend.

How to Purchase a Digital Camera

Both amateur and professional photographers now are mostly purchasing digital cameras to meet their photography needs. Because digital cameras with new and improved features regularly are introduced to the marketplace, consumers should know how to compare the differences among the multiple cameras that are available. This section lists guidelines you should consider when purchasing a digital camera.

1 Determine the type of digital camera that meets your needs.

Various types of digital cameras exist, including point-and-shoot cameras, field cameras, and studio cameras. Point-and-shoot cameras typically fit in your pocket and meet the needs of most general consumers. Field cameras, which often are used by photojournalists, are portable but flexible. Field cameras allow photographers to change lenses and use other attachments, and also are more customizable than point-and-shoot cameras. Studio cameras are used in photo studios and are stationary. These cameras give you the widest range of lenses and settings.

2 The digital camera with the highest resolution is not always the best.

Many consumers mistakenly believe that the digital camera with the highest resolution is the best camera for their needs. A higher resolution increases quality and clarity of your photos, as well as the size at which you can print the photos before noticing degradation in quality. If you never plan to print photos larger than 8" × 10", for example, you do not need a camera with a resolution greater than 5 megapixels. Many cameras available today advertise higher resolutions, but taking pictures at these high resolutions can use valuable storage space. Just because your camera can take a 10-megapixel photo does not mean that you always should set the resolution to 10 megapixels.

3 Consider size and weight.

Digital cameras are available in various sizes and weights. Some people prefer smaller, lighter cameras because they are easier to transport and take up less space. Others prefer bulkier, heavier cameras because the weight helps steady them to take a clearer picture. Many digital cameras also include an image stabilization feature that reduces the possibility of a blurry picture if you move your hands slightly while taking the picture. Some also believe that heavier cameras are of better quality, although that seldom is true. When choosing a digital camera, practice taking pictures with it and select one that feels comfortable and natural.

4 Different cameras require different memory cards.

When purchasing a digital camera, pay careful attention to the type of memory card the camera uses. Many use SD cards, some use xD Picture cards, and some use CompactFlash memory cards. Some memory cards are more expensive to replace than others, and some have a higher capacity than other cards. If you take a lot of pictures, purchase a camera that supports a memory card with a higher storage capacity so that you can avoid carrying multiple memory cards. You also might consider purchasing a camera that uses a memory card that is compatible with your other mobile devices.

5 Photo editing features can save you time.

Some digital cameras have integrated tools that allow you to edit photos directly from the camera. For instance, you may be able to crop photos, change the brightness, or remove red eye effects. Editing photos directly on the camera after taking them can save you from editing multiple photos at once when you transfer them to a computer. The photo editing capabilities available on digital cameras are limited when compared to photo editing programs, but in many cases they can edit a photo to your satisfaction.

6 Make sure that you can see the LCD screen easily.

LCD screens on digital cameras allow you to configure the settings, frame a shot before taking it, and preview photos after taking them. LCD screens vary by inches, so select a camera with a screen that does not require you to strain your eyes to view. This is especially important if the camera you are considering does not have a viewfinder, because you then will be required to use the display to frame your shots.

7 Determine whether your pictures will require you to zoom.

If you plan to take pictures of people or objects that require you to zoom in, select a digital camera that has a high optical zoom. An optical zoom enlarges the subject by adjusting the camera lens, whereas a digital zoom uses algorithms built into the camera to magnify images. Optical zooms, as opposed to digital zooms, often result in a higher quality photo. While a digital zoom might be capable of magnifying objects that are 100 feet away, the photo will suffer a loss of quality.

8 Price is important.

As with all other devices, locate a digital camera that does not exceed your budget. If you find a great camera that is available for more than you are willing to spend, consider locating a camera with a slightly lower resolution, an alternate brand, or a smaller screen. Digital cameras can last well beyond five years if properly maintained, so consider this a longer-term investment that will create memories lasting you a lifetime.

9 Know your batteries.

Some digital cameras require replaceable alkaline or rechargeable batteries (often AA or AAA), and others have a rechargeable battery. Similar to batteries in portable media players, using disposable batteries in digital cameras can get expensive, and they may not last as long as rechargeable battery packs. Digital camera battery life is not measured in hours (as is the case with smart phones and portable media players); instead, it is measured in how many pictures can be taken on a single charge or set of batteries. Turning off the LCD screen and flash when you take pictures can help to extend battery life.

10 Purchase accessories.

Accessories that are available for digital cameras include carrying cases, extra batteries and battery chargers, and extra memory cards (Figure 11). Carrying cases can help protect your digital camera, especially while traveling, and the extra batteries and chargers can stay inside your carrying case so that they are readily available should you need them. Screen protectors can help protect the LCD screen on your digital camera.

Figure 11 Digital camera accessories include memory cards, cases, batteries, and battery chargers.

Multiple Web sites on the Internet allow you to purchase computers and mobile devices. For a list of Web sites that sell computers and mobile devices, visit the Microsoft Office and Concepts CourseMate Web site at www.cengagebrain.com and then navigate to the Buyer's Guide Feature resource for this book.

Quiz Yourself Answers

Following are possible answers to the Quiz Yourself boxes in Chapters 1 through 5 of this book.

Quiz Yourself 1-1

1. A computer is ~~a motorized~~an electronic device that processes ~~output~~input into ~~input~~output.
2. A storage device records (~~reads~~writes) and/or retrieves (~~writes~~reads) items to and from storage media.
3. An ~~output~~input device is any hardware component that allows you to enter data and instructions in a computer.
4. True Statement
5. Three commonly used ~~input~~output devices are a printer, a monitor, and speakers.

Quiz Yourself 1-2

1. A ~~resource~~network is a collection of computers and devices connected together via communications devices and transmission media.
2. True Statement
3. Popular ~~system~~application software includes Web browsers, word processing software, spreadsheet software, database software, and presentation software.
4. The ~~Internet~~Web is one of the more popular services on the ~~Web~~Internet.
5. Two types of ~~application~~system software are the operating system and utility programs.

Quiz Yourself 1-3

1. A ~~desktop computer~~notebook computer (or laptop computer) is a portable, personal computer designed to fit on your lap.
2. True Statement
3. Each ~~enterprise~~home user spends time on the computer for different reasons that include personal financial management, Web access, communications, and entertainment.
4. A ~~home~~power user requires the capabilities of a workstation or other powerful computer.
5. ~~Mainframes~~Supercomputers are the fastest, most powerful computers — and the most expensive.
6. With ~~embedded computers~~online banking, users access account balances, pay bills, and copy monthly transactions from the bank's computer right into their personal computers.

Quiz Yourself 2-1

1. True Statement
2. ~~A wireless Internet service provider~~An IP address (or Internet Protocol address) is a number that uniquely identifies each computer or device connected to the Internet.
3. ~~An IP address~~A domain name, such as www.google.com, is the text version of ~~a domain name~~ an IP address.
4. ~~Satellite~~Cable Internet service provides high-speed Internet access through the cable television network via a cable modem.

Quiz Yourself 2-2

1. True Statement
2. A ~~Web browser~~subject directory classifies Web pages in an organized set of categories and related subcategories.
3. ~~Business~~Consumer-to-consumer e-commerce occurs when one consumer sells directly to another, such as in an online auction.
4. The more widely used ~~search engines~~Web browsers for personal computers are Internet Explorer, Firefox, Opera, Safari, and Google Chrome.
5. To develop a Web page, you do not have to be a computer programmer.

Quiz Yourself 2-3

1. True Statement
2. An e-mail address is a combination of a user name and ~~an e-mail program~~a domain name that identifies a user so that he or she can receive Internet e-mail.
3. ~~FTP~~Internet telephony uses the Internet (instead of the public switched telephone network) to connect a calling party to one or more called parties.
4. Netiquette is the code of ~~un~~acceptable behaviors while on the Internet.
5. VoIP enables users to ~~subscribe~~speak to other users over the Internet.

Quiz Yourself 3-1

1. True Statement
2. ~~Public-domain~~Packaged software is mass produced, copyrighted retail software that meets the needs of a wide variety of users, not just a single user or company.
3. To use ~~system~~application software, your computer must be running ~~application~~system software.
4. When a program is started, its instructions load from ~~memory~~a storage medium into ~~a storage medium~~memory.

Quiz Yourself 3-2

1. ~~Enterprise computing~~Image editing software provides the capabilities of paint software and also includes the ability to modify existing images.
2. Millions of people use ~~spreadsheet~~word processing software every day to develop documents such as letters, memos, reports, mailing labels, newsletters, and Web pages.
3. Professional ~~accounting~~DTP (or desktop publishing) software is ideal for the production of high-quality color documents such as textbooks, corporate newsletters, marketing literature, product catalogs, and annual reports.
4. ~~Database~~Presentation software is application software that allows users to create visual aids for presentations to communicate ideas, messages, and other information to a group.
5. Popular ~~CAD programs~~software suites include Microsoft Office, Apple iWork, Corel WordPerfect Office, and Google Docs.
6. True Statement

Quiz Yourself 3-3

1. ~~All~~Some Web application hosts provide free access to their software.
2. ~~Computer~~Web-based training is a type of ~~Web~~computer-based training that uses Internet technology and consists of application software on the Web.
3. True Statement
4. ~~Legal~~Personal finance software is a simplified accounting program that helps home users and small office/home office users balance their checkbooks, pay bills, track investments, and evaluate financial plans.
5. ~~Personal DTP~~Photo editing software is a popular type of image editing software that allows users to edit digital photos.

Quiz Yourself 4-1

1. A ~~buffer~~driver is a small program that tells the operating system how to communicate with a specific device.
2. True Statement
3. A password is a ~~public~~private combination of characters associated with the user name that allows access to certain computer resources.
4. The program you currently are using is in the ~~background~~foreground, and the other programs running but not in use are in the ~~foreground~~background.
5. Two types of system software are operating systems and ~~application~~utility programs.

Quiz Yourself 4-2

1. ~~BlackBerry~~Palm OS devices use Palm OS as their operating system.
2. Examples of ~~embedded~~server operating systems include Windows Server 2008, UNIX, Linux, Solaris, and NetWare.
3. Windows 7 Starter uses Windows ~~Aero~~Vista Basic.
4. True Statement
5. ~~Aero Flip 3D~~Linux is a UNIX-type operating system that is open source software.

Quiz Yourself 4-3

1. A ~~pop-up blocker~~file compression utility shrinks the size of a file(s).
2. An ~~anti-spam~~antivirus program protects a computer against viruses.
3. True Statement
4. You should ~~uninstall~~back up files and disks regularly in the event your originals are lost, damaged, or destroyed.
5. ~~Web filtering~~CD/DVD burning software writes text, graphics, audio, and video files to a recordable or rewritable disc.

Quiz Yourself 5-1

1. A ~~back door~~denial of service attack is an assault whose purpose is to disrupt computer access to an Internet service such as the Web or e-mail.
2. True Statement
3. Computer viruses, worms, Trojan horses, and rootkits are malware that acts without a user's knowledge.
4. ~~Shorter~~Longer passwords provide greater security than ~~longer~~shorter ones.
5. Updating an antivirus program's ~~quarantine~~signature file protects a computer against viruses written since the antivirus program was released.

Quiz Yourself 5-2

1. An end-user license agreement (EULA) ~~permits~~does not permit users to give copies to friends and colleagues, while continuing to use the software.
2. Encryption is a process of converting ~~ciphertext~~plaintext into ~~plaintext~~ciphertext to prevent unauthorized access.
3. Mobile users are ~~not~~ susceptible to hardware theft.
4. True Statement
5. To prevent against data loss caused by a system failure, computer users should ~~restore~~back up files regularly.

Quiz Yourself 5-3

1. Factors that cause ~~CVS~~tendonitis and CTS (carpal tunnel syndrome) include prolonged typing, prolonged mouse usage, or continual shifting between the mouse and the keyboard.
2. ~~Phishing~~Digital forensics is the discovery, collection, and analysis of evidence found on computers and networks.
3. True Statement
4. You cannot assume that information on the Web is correct.

Microsoft® Office 2010

Office 2010 and Windows 7: Essential Concepts and Skills

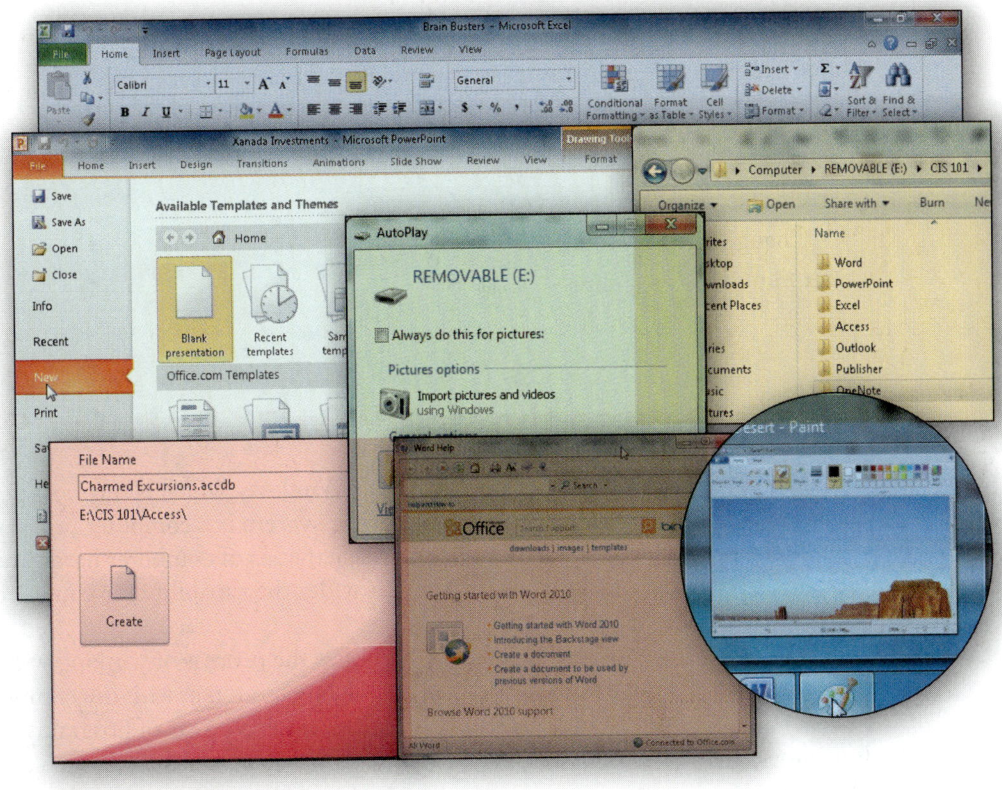

Objectives

You will have mastered the material in this chapter when you can:

- Perform basic mouse operations
- Start Windows and log on to the computer
- Identify the objects on the Windows 7 desktop
- Identify the programs in and versions of Microsoft Office
- Start a program
- Identify the components of the Microsoft Office Ribbon
- Create folders
- Save files
- Change screen resolution
- Perform basic tasks in Microsoft Office programs
- Manage files
- Use Microsoft Office Help and Windows Help

Office 2010 and Windows 7: Essential Concepts and Skills

Office 2010 and Windows 7

This introductory chapter covers features and functions common to Office 2010 programs, as well as the basics of Windows 7.

Overview

As you read this chapter, you will learn how to perform basic tasks in Windows and Office programs by performing these general activities:

- Start programs using Windows.
- Use features common across Office programs.
- Organize files and folders.
- Change screen resolution.
- Quit Office programs.

Introduction to the Windows 7 Operating System

Windows 7 is the newest version of Microsoft Windows, which is the most popular and widely used operating system. An **operating system** is a computer program (set of computer instructions) that coordinates all the activities of computer hardware such as memory, storage devices, and printers, and provides the capability for you to communicate with the computer.

The Windows 7 operating system simplifies the process of working with documents and programs by organizing the manner in which you interact with the computer. Windows 7 is used to run **application software**, which consists of programs designed to make users more productive and/or assist them with personal tasks, such as word processing.

Windows 7 has two interface variations, Windows 7 Basic and Windows 7 Aero. Computers with up to 1 GB of RAM display the Windows 7 Basic interface (Figure 1a). Computers with more than 1 GB of RAM also can display the Windows Aero interface (Figure 1b), which provides an enhanced visual appearance. The Windows 7 Professional, Windows 7 Enterprise, Windows 7 Home Premium, and Windows 7 Ultimate editions have the capability to use Windows Aero.

Using a Mouse

Windows users work with a mouse that has at least two buttons. For a right-handed user, the left button usually is the primary mouse button, and the right mouse button is the secondary mouse button. Left-handed people, however, can reverse the function of these buttons.

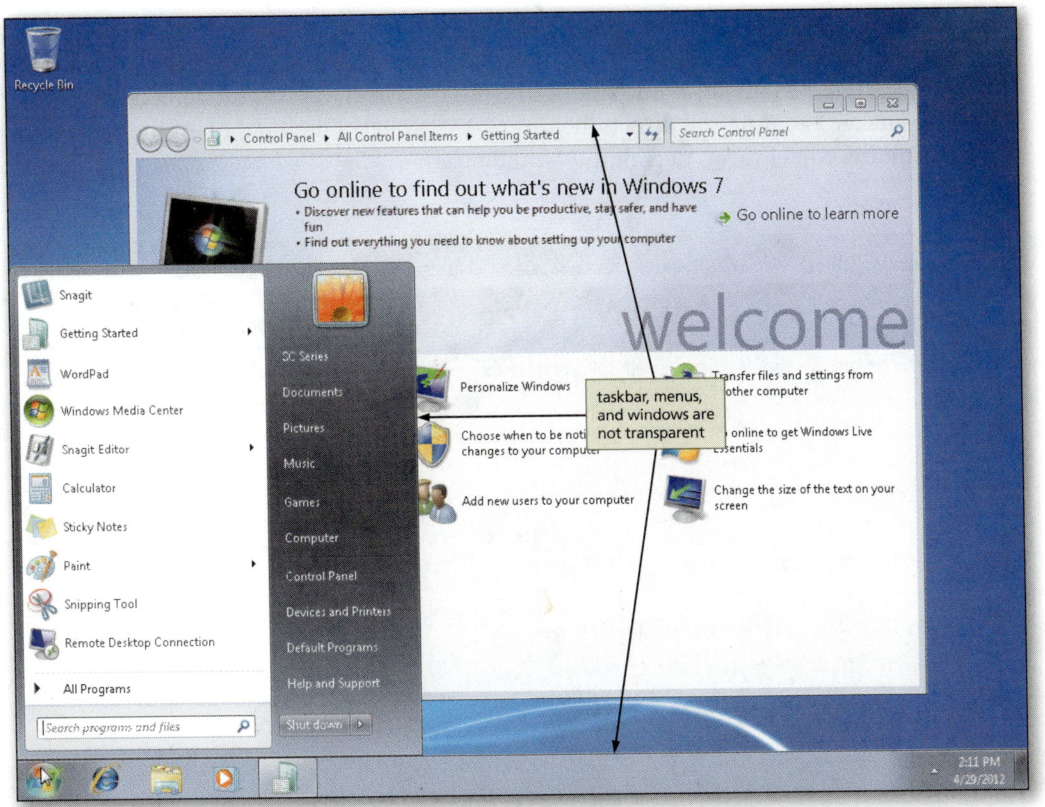

Figure 1 (a) Windows 7 Basic interface

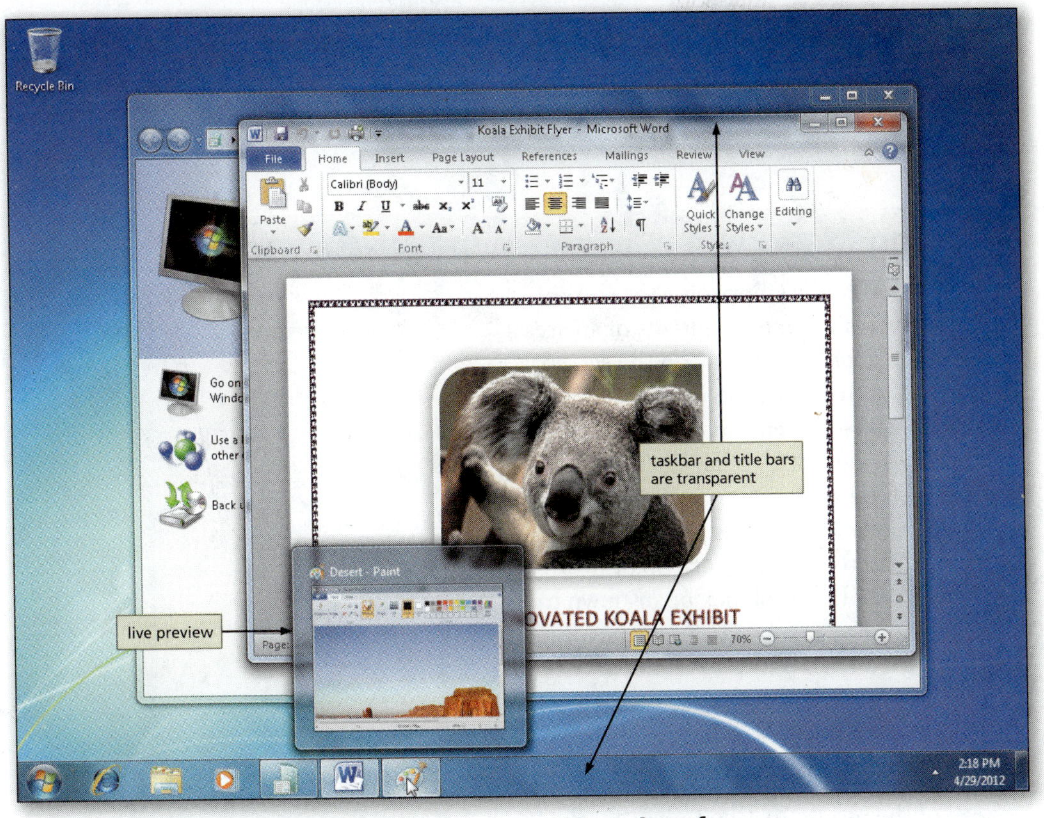

Figure 1 (b) Windows 7 Aero interface

Table 1 explains how to perform a variety of mouse operations. Some programs also use keys in combination with the mouse to perform certain actions. For example, when you hold down the CTRL key while rolling the mouse wheel, text on the screen becomes larger or smaller based on the direction you roll the wheel. The function of the mouse buttons and the wheel varies depending on the program.

Table 1 Mouse Operations

Operation	Mouse Action	Example*
Point	Move the mouse until the pointer on the desktop is positioned on the item of choice.	Position the pointer on the screen.
Click	Press and release the primary mouse button, which usually is the left mouse button.	Select or deselect items on the screen or start a program or program feature.
Right-click	Press and release the secondary mouse button, which usually is the right mouse button.	Display a shortcut menu.
Double-click	Quickly press and release the left mouse button twice without moving the mouse.	Start a program or program feature.
Triple-click	Quickly press and release the left mouse button three times without moving the mouse.	Select a paragraph.
Drag	Point to an item, hold down the left mouse button, move the item to the desired location on the screen, and then release the left mouse button.	Move an object from one location to another or draw pictures.
Right-drag	Point to an item, hold down the right mouse button, move the item to the desired location on the screen, and then release the right mouse button.	Display a shortcut menu after moving an object from one location to another.
Rotate wheel	Roll the wheel forward or backward.	Scroll vertically (up and down).
Free-spin wheel	Whirl the wheel forward or backward so that it spins freely on its own.	Scroll through many pages in seconds.
Press wheel	Press the wheel button while moving the mouse.	Scroll continuously.
Tilt wheel	Press the wheel toward the right or left.	Scroll horizontally (left and right).
Press thumb button	Press the button on the side of the mouse with your thumb.	Move forward or backward through Web pages and/or control media, games, etc.

*Note: the examples presented in this column are discussed as they are demonstrated in this chapter.

Scrolling

BTW
Minimize Wrist Injury
Computer users frequently switch between the keyboard and the mouse during a word processing session; such switching strains the wrist. To help prevent wrist injury, minimize switching. For instance, if your fingers already are on the keyboard, use keyboard keys to scroll. If your hand already is on the mouse, use the mouse to scroll.

A **scroll bar** is a horizontal or vertical bar that appears when the contents of an area may not be visible completely on the screen (Figure 2). A scroll bar contains **scroll arrows** and a **scroll box** that enable you to view areas that currently cannot be seen. Clicking the up and down scroll arrows moves the screen content up or down one line. You also can click above or below the scroll box to move up or down a section, or drag the scroll box up or down to move up or down to move to a specific location.

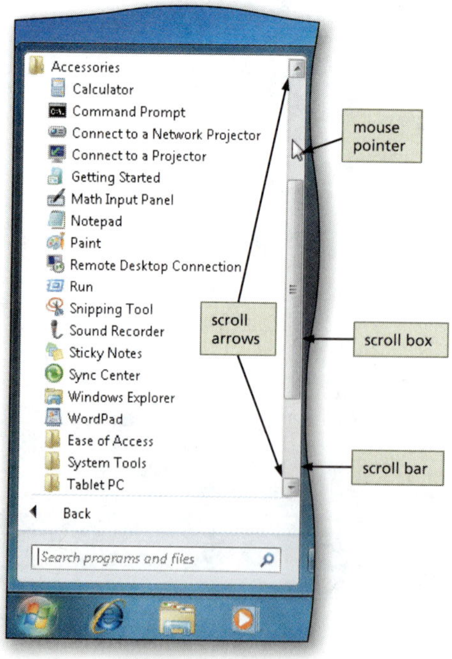

Figure 2

Shortcut Keys

In many cases, you can use the keyboard instead of the mouse to accomplish a task. To perform tasks using the keyboard, you press one or more keyboard keys, sometimes identified as a **shortcut key** or **keyboard shortcut**. Some shortcut keys consist of a single key, such as the F1 key. For example, to obtain help about Windows 7, you can press the F1 key. Other shortcut keys consist of multiple keys, in which case a plus sign separates the key names, such as CTRL+ESC. This notation means to press and hold down the first key listed, press one or more additional keys, and then release all keys. For example, to display the Start menu, press CTRL+ESC, that is, hold down the CTRL key, press the ESC key, and then release both keys.

Starting Windows 7

It is not unusual for multiple people to use the same computer in a work, educational, recreational, or home setting. Windows 7 enables each user to establish a **user account**, which identifies to Windows 7 the resources, such as programs and storage locations, a user can access when working with a computer.

Each user account has a user name and may have a password and an icon, as well. A **user name** is a unique combination of letters or numbers that identifies a specific user to Windows 7. A **password** is a private combination of letters, numbers, and special characters associated with the user name that allows access to a user's account resources. A **user icon** is a picture associated with a user name.

When you turn on a computer, an introductory screen consisting of the Windows logo and copyright messages is displayed. The Windows logo is animated and glows as the Windows 7 operating system is loaded. After the Windows logo appears, depending on your computer's settings, you may or may not be required to log on to the computer. **Logging on** to a computer opens your user account and makes the computer available for use. If you are required to log on to the computer, the **Welcome screen** is displayed, which shows the user names of users on the computer (Figure 3). Clicking the user name or picture begins the process of logging on to the computer.

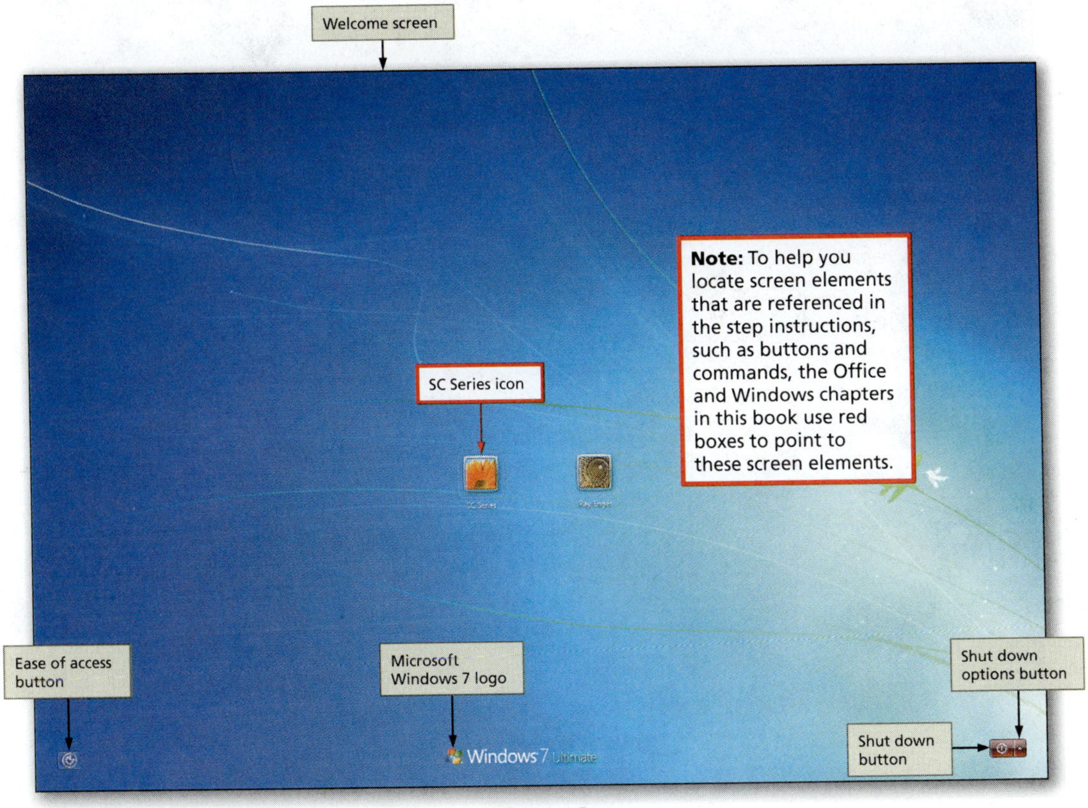

Figure 3

At the bottom of the Welcome screen is the 'Ease of access' button, Windows 7 logo, a Shut down button, and a 'Shut down options' button. The following list identifies the functions of the buttons and commands that typically appear on the Welcome screen:

- Clicking the 'Ease of access' button displays the Ease of Access Center, which provides tools to optimize your computer to accommodate the needs of the mobility, hearing, and vision impaired users.
- Clicking the Shut down button shuts down Windows 7 and the computer.
- Clicking the 'Shut down options' button, located to the right of the Shut down button, provides access to a menu containing commands that perform actions such as restarting the computer, putting the computer in a low-powered state, and shutting down the computer. The commands available on your computer may differ.
  - The **Restart command** closes open programs, shuts down Windows 7, and then restarts Windows 7 and displays the Welcome screen.
  - The **Sleep command** waits for Windows 7 to save your work and then turns off the computer fans and hard disk. To wake the computer from the Sleep state, press the power button or lift a notebook computer's cover, and log on to the computer.
  - The **Shut down command** shuts down and turns off the computer.

To Log On to the Computer

After starting Windows 7, you might need to log on to the computer. The following steps log on to the computer based on a typical installation. You may need to ask your instructor how to log on to your computer. This set of steps uses SC Series as the user name. The list of user names on your computer will be different.

1

- Click the user icon (SC Series, in this case) on the Welcome screen (shown in Figure 3 on the previous page); depending on settings, this either will display a password text box (Figure 4) or will log on to the computer and display the Windows 7 desktop.

Q&A Why do I not see a user icon?

Your computer may require you to type a user name instead of clicking an icon.

Q&A What is a text box?

A text box is a rectangular box in which you type text.

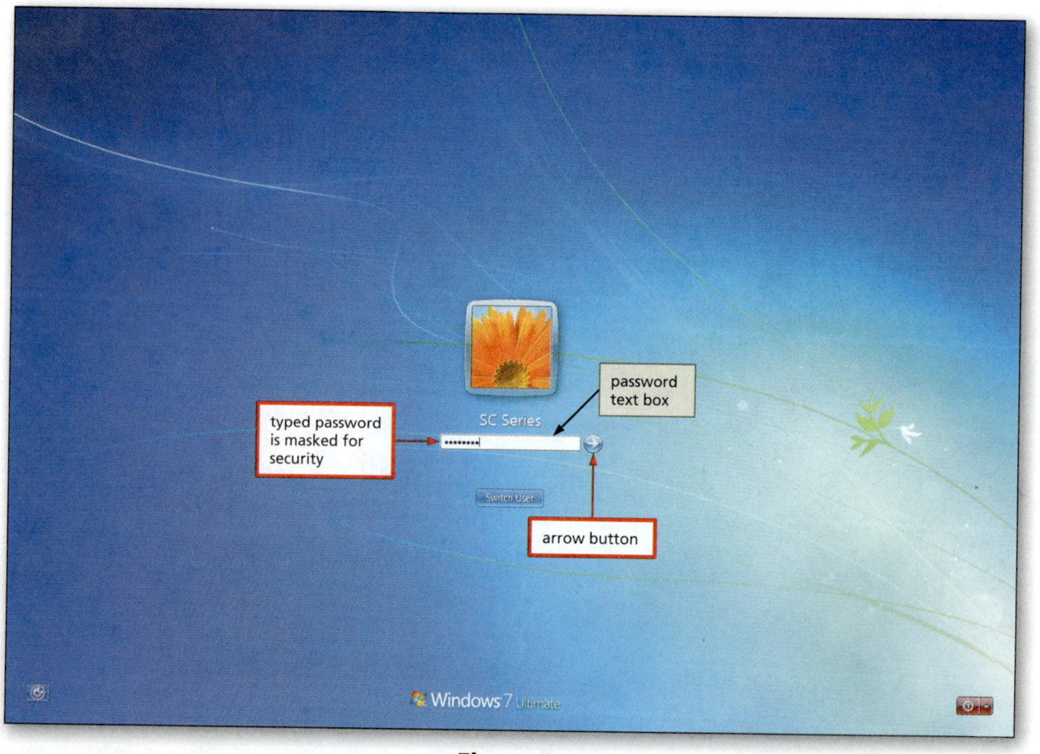

Figure 4

Q&A Why does my screen not show a password text box?

Your account does not require a password.

2

- If Windows 7 displays a password text box, type your password in the text box and then click the arrow button to log on to the computer and display the Windows 7 desktop (Figure 5).

Q&A

Why does my desktop look different from the one in Figure 5?

The Windows 7 desktop is customizable, and your school or employer may have modified the desktop to meet its needs. Also, your screen resolution, which affects the size of the elements on the screen, may differ from the screen resolution used in the Office and Windows chapters in this book. Later in this chapter, you learn how to change screen resolution.

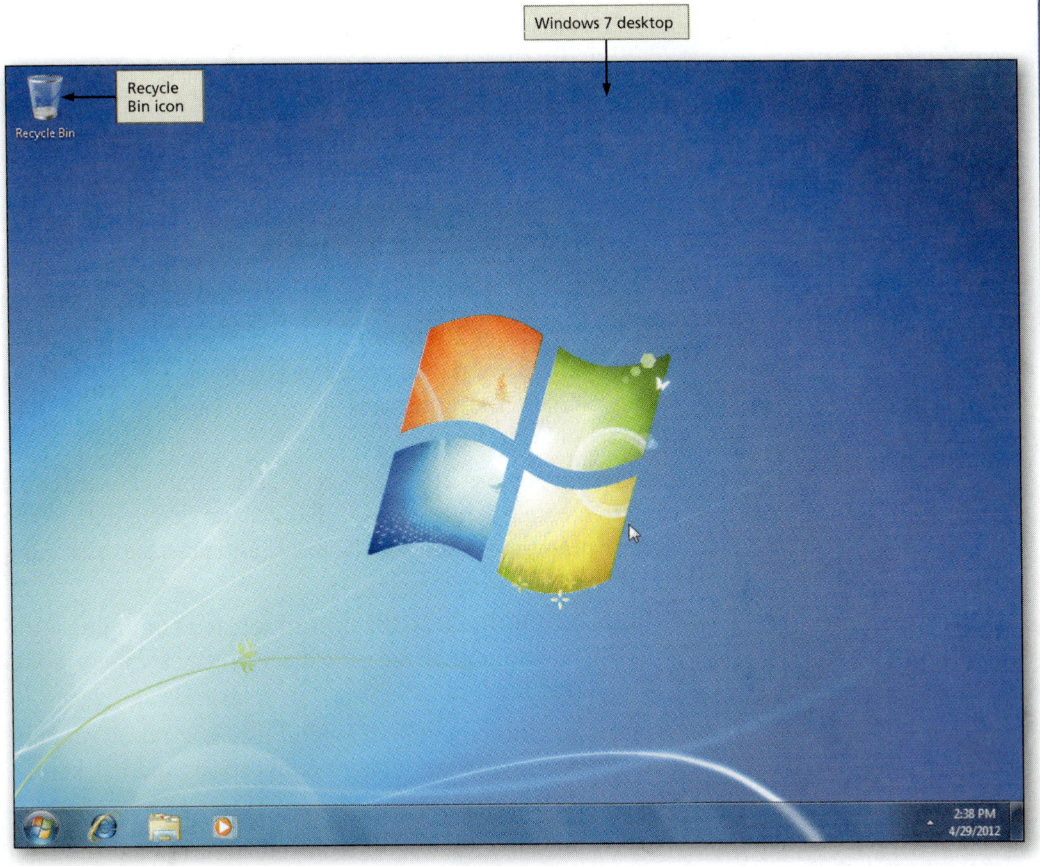

Figure 5

The Windows 7 Desktop

The Windows 7 desktop (Figure 5) and the objects on the desktop emulate a work area in an office. Think of the Windows desktop as an electronic version of the top of your desk. You can perform tasks such as placing objects on the desktop, moving the objects around the desktop, and removing items from the desktop.

When you start a program in Windows 7, it appears on the desktop. Some icons also may be displayed on the desktop. For instance, the icon for the **Recycle Bin**, the location of files that have been deleted, appears on the desktop by default. A **file** is a named unit of storage. Files can contain text, images, audio, and video. You can customize your desktop so that icons representing programs and files you use often appear on your desktop.

Introduction to Microsoft Office 2010

Microsoft Office 2010 is the newest version of Microsoft Office, offering features that provide users with better functionality and easier ways to work with the various files they create. These features include enhanced design tools, such as improved picture formatting tools and new themes, shared notebooks for working in groups, mobile versions of Office programs, broadcast presentation for the Web, and a digital notebook for managing and sharing multimedia information.

Microsoft Office 2010 Programs

Microsoft Office 2010 includes a wide variety of programs such as Word, PowerPoint, Excel, Access, Outlook, Publisher, OneNote, InfoPath, SharePoint Workspace, Communicator, and Web Apps:

- **Microsoft Word 2010**, or Word, is a full-featured word processing program that allows you to create professional-looking documents and revise them easily.
- **Microsoft PowerPoint 2010**, or PowerPoint, is a complete presentation program that allows you to produce professional-looking presentations.
- **Microsoft Excel 2010**, or Excel, is a powerful spreadsheet program that allows you to organize data, complete calculations, make decisions, graph data, develop professional-looking reports, publish organized data to the Web, and access real-time data from Web sites.
- **Microsoft Access 2010**, or Access, is a database management system that allows you to create a database; add, change, and delete data in the database; ask questions concerning the data in the database; and create forms and reports using the data in the database.
- **Microsoft Outlook 2010**, or Outlook, is a communications and scheduling program that allows you to manage e-mail accounts, calendars, contacts, and access to other Internet content.
- **Microsoft Publisher 2010**, or Publisher, is a desktop publishing program that helps you create professional-quality publications and marketing materials that can be shared easily.
- **Microsoft OneNote 2010**, or OneNote, is a note taking program that allows you to store and share information in notebooks with other people.
- **Microsoft InfoPath 2010**, or InfoPath, is a form development program that helps you create forms for use on the Web and gather data from these forms.
- **Microsoft SharePoint Workspace 2010**, or SharePoint, is collaboration software that allows you access and revise files stored on your computer from other locations.
- **Microsoft Communicator** is communications software that allows you to use different modes of communications such as instant messaging, video conferencing, and sharing files and programs.
- **Microsoft Web Apps** is a Web application that allows you to edit and share files on the Web using the familiar Office interface.

Microsoft Office 2010 Suites

A **suite** is a collection of individual programs available together as a unit. Microsoft offers a variety of Office suites. Table 2 lists the Office 2010 suites and their components.

Programs in a suite, such as Microsoft Office, typically use a similar interface and share features. In addition, Microsoft Office programs use **common dialog boxes** for performing actions such as opening and saving files. Once you are comfortable working with these elements and this interface and performing tasks in one program, the similarity can help you apply the knowledge and skills you have learned to another Office program(s). For example, the process for saving a file in Word is the same in PowerPoint, Excel, and the other Office programs. While briefly showing how to use several Office programs, this chapter illustrates some of the common functions across the programs and also identifies the characteristics unique to these programs.

Table 2 Microsoft Office 2010 Suites

	Microsoft Office Professional Plus 2010	Microsoft Office Professional 2010	Microsoft Office Home and Business 2010	Microsoft Office Standard 2010	Microsoft Office Home and Student 2010
Microsoft Word 2010	✔	✔	✔	✔	✔
Microsoft PowerPoint 2010	✔	✔	✔	✔	✔
Microsoft Excel 2010	✔	✔	✔	✔	✔
Microsoft Access 2010	✔	✔	✗	✗	✗
Microsoft Outlook 2010	✔	✔	✔	✔	✗
Microsoft Publisher 2010	✔	✔	✗	✔	✗
Microsoft OneNote 2010	✔	✔	✔	✔	✔
Microsoft InfoPath 2010	✔	✗	✗	✗	✗
Microsoft SharePoint Workspace 2010	✔	✗	✗	✗	✗
Microsoft Communicator	✔	✗	✗	✗	✗

Starting and Using a Program

To use a program, you must instruct the operating system to start the program. Windows 7 provides many different ways to start a program, one of which is presented in this section (other ways to start a program are presented throughout this chapter). After starting a program, you can use it to perform a variety of tasks. The following pages use Word to discuss some elements of the Office interface and to perform tasks that are common to other Office programs.

Word

Word is a full-featured word processing program that allows you to create many types of personal and business documents, including flyers, letters, memos, resumes, reports, fax cover sheets, mailing labels, and newsletters. Word also provides tools that enable you to create Web pages and save these Web pages directly on a Web server. Word has many features designed to simplify the production of documents and add visual appeal. Using Word, you easily can change the shape, size, and color of text. You also can include borders, shading, tables, images, pictures, charts, and Web addresses in documents.

To Start a Program Using the Start Menu

Across the bottom of the Windows 7 desktop is the taskbar. The taskbar contains the **Start button**, which you use to access programs, files, folders, and settings on a computer. A **folder** is a named location on a storage medium that usually contains related documents. The taskbar also displays a button for each program currently running on a computer.

Clicking the Start button displays the Start menu. The **Start menu** allows you to access programs, folders, and files on the computer and contains commands that allow you to start programs, store and search for documents, customize the computer, and obtain help about thousands of topics. A **menu** is a list of related items, including folders, programs, and commands. Each **command** on a menu performs a specific action, such as saving a file or obtaining help.

The following steps, which assume Windows 7 is running, use the Start menu to start an Office program based on a typical installation. You may need to ask your instructor how to start Office programs for your computer. Although the steps illustrate starting the Word program, the steps to start any Office program are similar.

1

- Click the Start button on the Windows 7 taskbar to display the Start menu (Figure 6).

Q&A Why does my Start menu look different?

It may look different depending on your computer's configuration. The Start menu may be customized for several reasons, such as usage requirements or security restrictions.

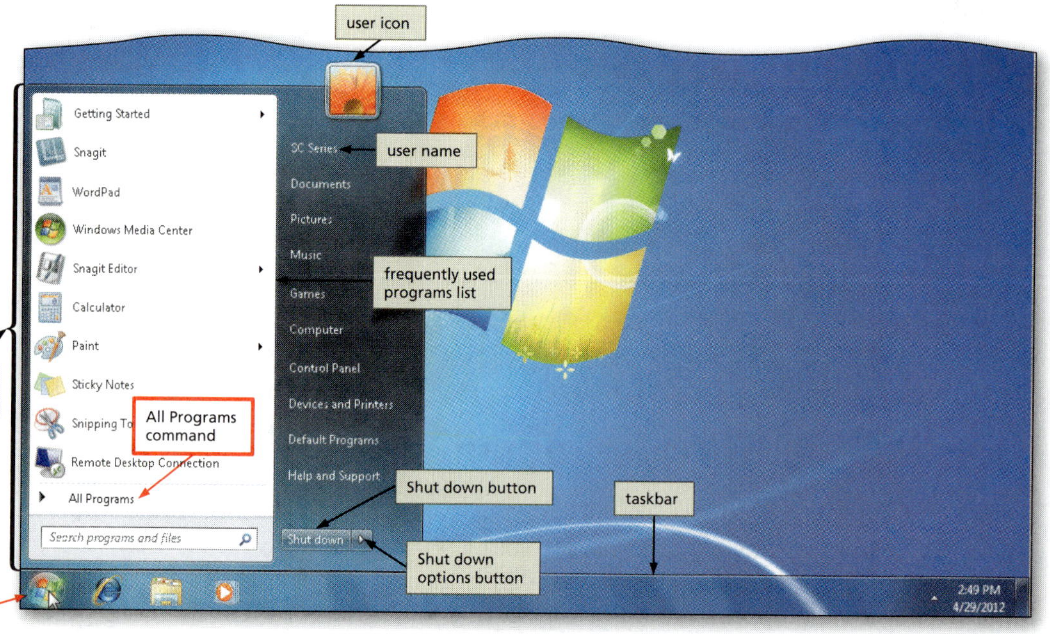

Figure 6

2

- Click All Programs at the bottom of the left pane on the Start menu to display the All Programs list (Figure 7).

Q&A What is a pane?

A **pane** is an area of a window that displays related content. For example, the left pane on the Start menu contains a list of frequently used programs, as well as the All Programs command.

Q&A Why might my All Programs list look different?

Most likely, the programs installed on your computer will differ from those shown in Figure 7. Your All Programs list will show the programs that are installed on your computer.

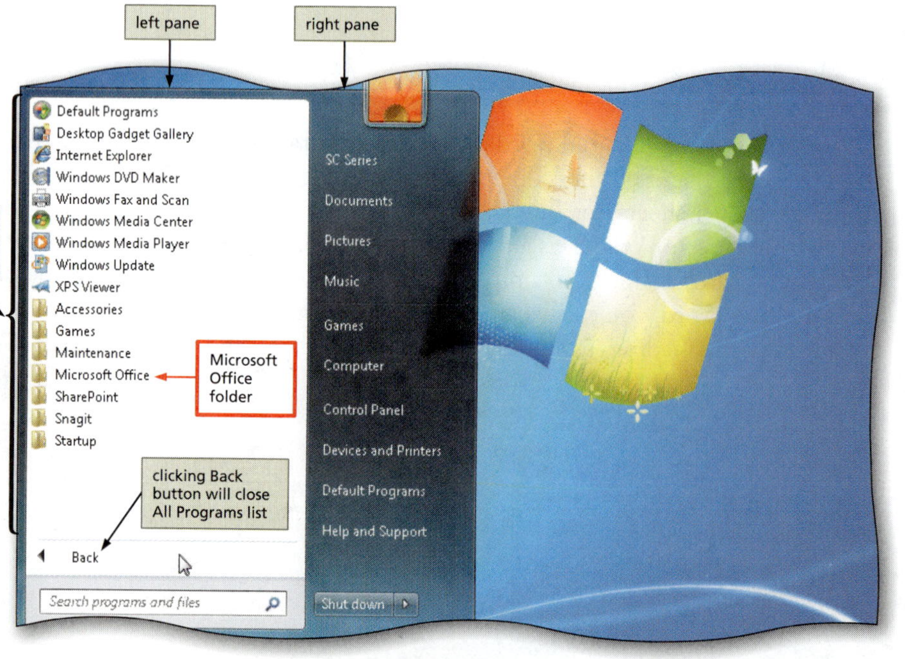

Figure 7

3

- If the program you wish to start is located in a folder, click or scroll to and then click the folder (Microsoft Office, in this case) in the All Programs list to display a list of the folder's contents (Figure 8).

Q&A Why is the Microsoft Office folder on my computer?

During installation of Microsoft Office 2010, the Microsoft Office folder was added to the All Programs list.

Figure 8

4

- Click, or scroll to and then click, the program name (Microsoft Word 2010, in this case) in the list to start the selected program (Figure 9).

Q&A What happens when you start a program?

Many programs initially display a blank document in a program window, as shown in the Word window in Figure 9; others provide a means for you to create a blank document. A **window** is a rectangular area that displays data and information. The top of a window has a **title bar**, which is a horizontal space that contains the window's name.

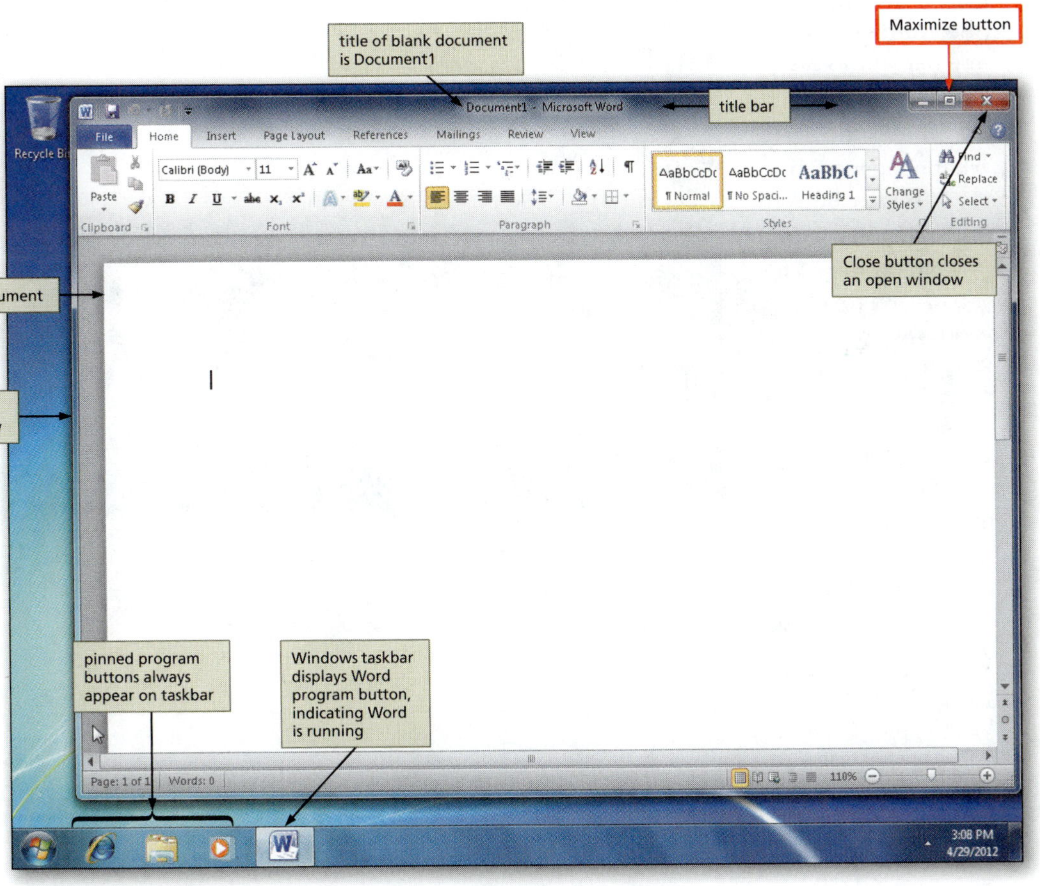

Figure 9

Q&A Why is my program window a different size?

The Word window shown in Figure 9 is not maximized. Your Word window already may be maximized. The next steps maximize a window.

Other Ways	
1. Double-click program icon on desktop, if one is present	3. Display Start menu, type program name in search box, click program name
2. Click program name in left pane of Start menu, if present	4. Double-click file created using program you want to start

To Maximize a Window

Sometimes content is not visible completely in a window. One method of displaying the entire contents of a window is to **maximize** it, or enlarge the window so that it fills the entire screen. The following step maximizes the Word window; however, any Office program's window can be maximized using this step.

1

- If the program window is not maximized already, click the Maximize button (shown in Figure 9 on the previous page) next to the Close button on the window's title bar (the Word window title bar, in this case) to maximize the window (Figure 10).

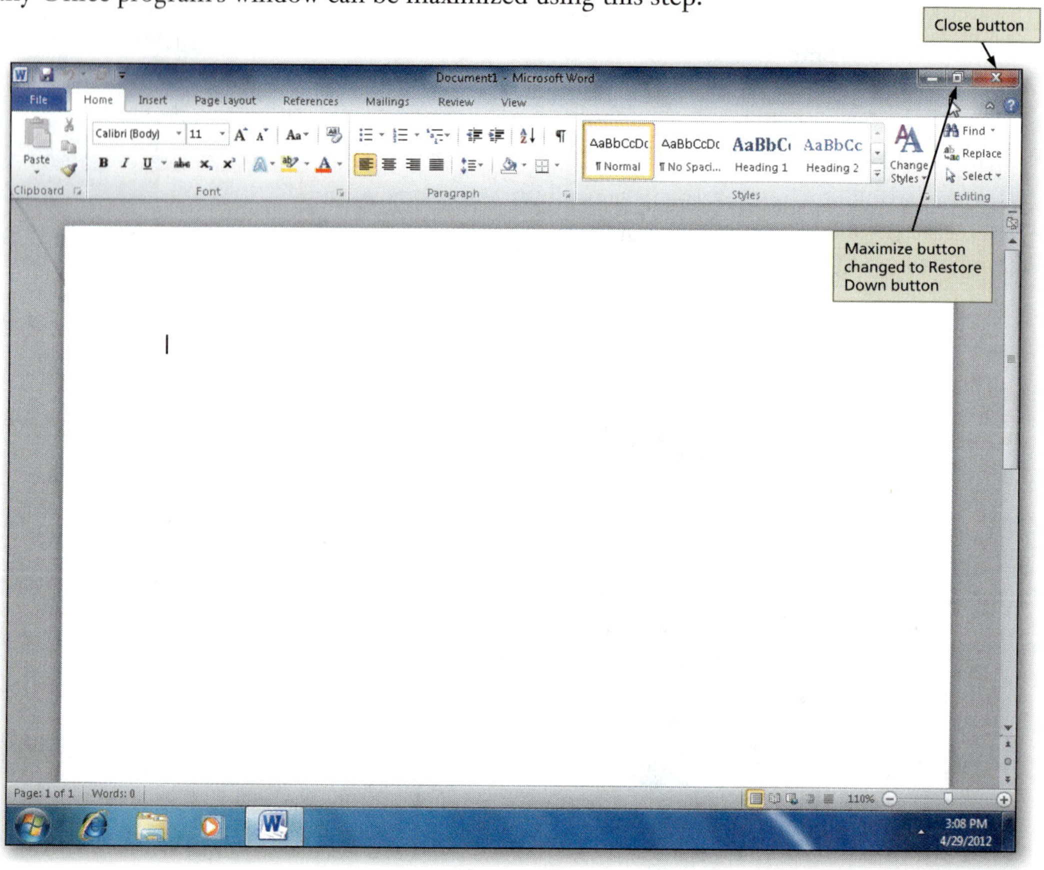

Figure 10

Q&A What happened to the Maximize button?

It changed to a Restore Down button, which you can use to return a window to its size and location before you maximized it.

Q&A How do I know whether a window is maximized?

A window is maximized if it fills the entire display area and the Restore Down button is displayed on the title bar.

Other Ways

1. Double-click title bar
2. Drag title bar to top of screen

The Word Document Window, Ribbon, and Elements Common to Office Programs

The Word window consists of a variety of components to make your work more efficient and documents more professional. These include the document window, Ribbon, Mini toolbar, shortcut menus, and Quick Access Toolbar. Most of these components are common to other Microsoft Office 2010 programs; others are unique to Word.

You view a portion of a document on the screen through a **document window** (Figure 11). The default (preset) view is **Print Layout view**, which shows the document on a mock sheet of paper in the document window.

Scroll Bars You use a scroll bar to display different portions of a document in the document window. At the right edge of the document window is a vertical scroll bar. If a document is too wide to fit in the document window, a horizontal scroll bar also appears at the bottom of the document window. On a scroll bar, the position of the scroll box reflects the location of the portion of the document that is displayed in the document window.

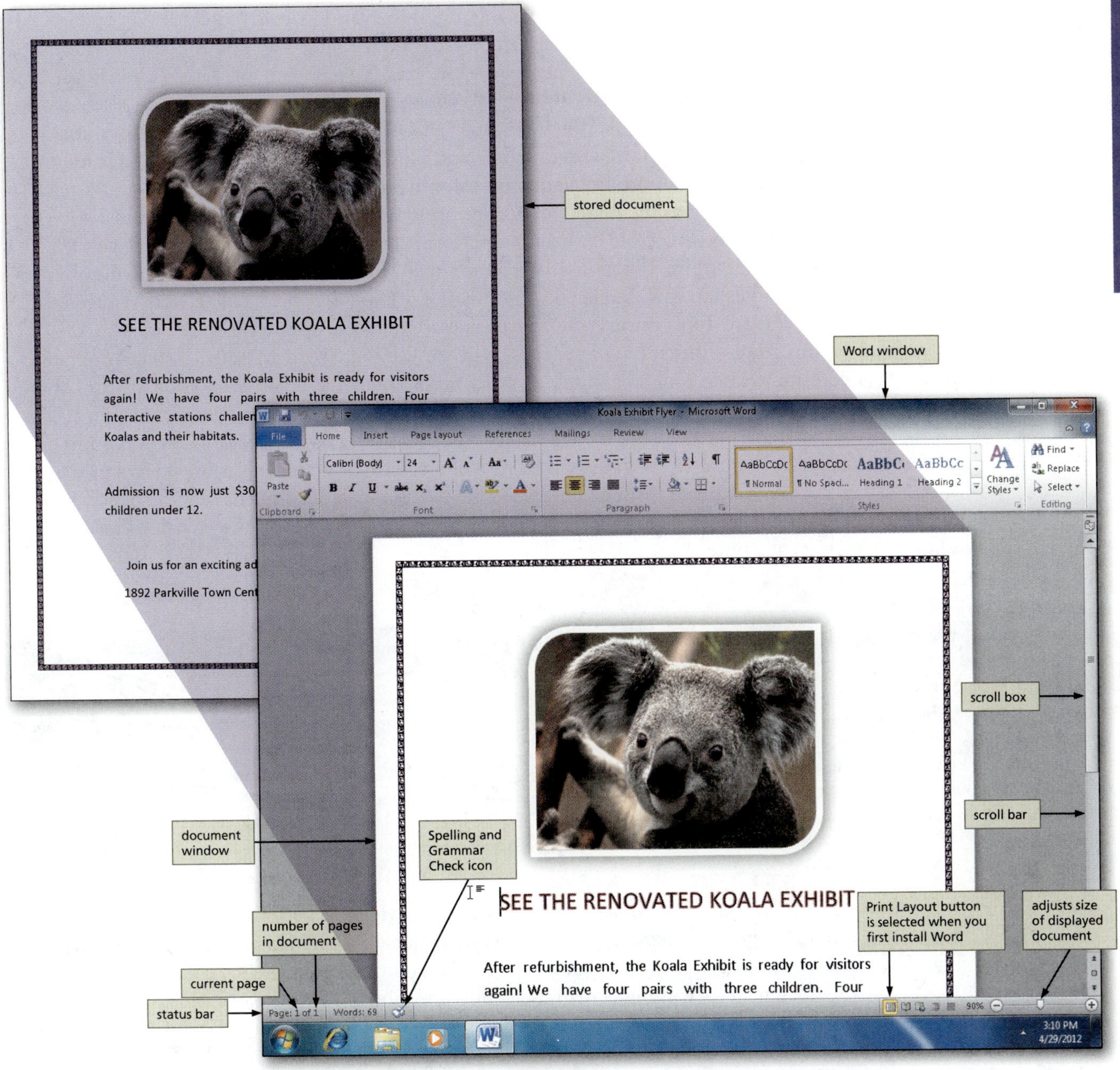

Figure 11

Status Bar The **status bar**, located at the bottom of the document window above the Windows 7 taskbar, presents information about the document, the progress of current tasks, and the status of certain commands and keys; it also provides controls for viewing the document. As you type text or perform certain tasks, various indicators and buttons may appear on the status bar.

The left side of the status bar in Figure 11 shows the current page followed by the total number of pages in the document, the number of words in the document, and an icon to check spelling and grammar. The right side of the status bar includes buttons and controls you can use to change the view of a document and adjust the size of the displayed document.

Ribbon The Ribbon, located near the top of the window below the title bar, is the control center in Word and other Office programs (Figure 12). The Ribbon provides easy, central access to the tasks you perform while creating a document. The Ribbon consists of tabs, groups, and commands. Each **tab** contains a collection of groups, and each **group** contains related functions. When you start an Office program, such as Word, it initially displays several main tabs, also called default tabs. All Office programs have a **Home tab**, which contains the more frequently used commands.

In addition to the main tabs, Office programs display **tool tabs**, also called contextual tabs (Figure 13), when you perform certain tasks or work with objects such as pictures or tables. If you insert a picture in a Word document, for example, the Picture Tools tab and its related subordinate Format tab appear, collectively referred to as the Picture Tools Format tab. When you are finished working with the picture, the Picture Tools Format tab disappears from the Ribbon. Word and other Office programs determine when tool tabs should appear and disappear based on tasks you perform. Some tool tabs, such as the Table Tools tab, have more than one related subordinate tab.

Items on the Ribbon include buttons, boxes (text boxes, check boxes, etc.), and galleries (Figure 12). A **gallery** is a set of choices, often graphical, arranged in a grid or in a list. You can scroll through choices in an in-Ribbon gallery by clicking the gallery's scroll arrows. Or, you can click a gallery's More button to view more gallery options on the screen at a time.

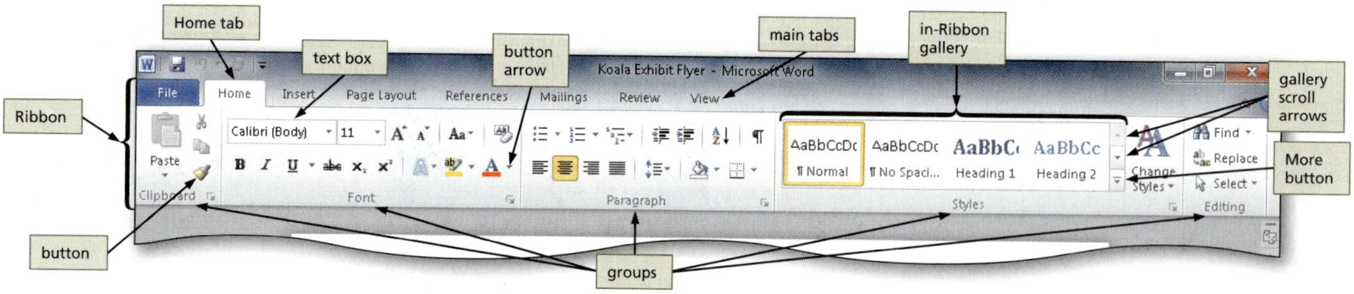

Figure 12

Some buttons and boxes have arrows that, when clicked, also display a gallery; others always cause a gallery to be displayed when clicked. Most galleries support **live preview**, which is a feature that allows you to point to a gallery choice and see its effect in the document — without actually selecting the choice (Figure 13).

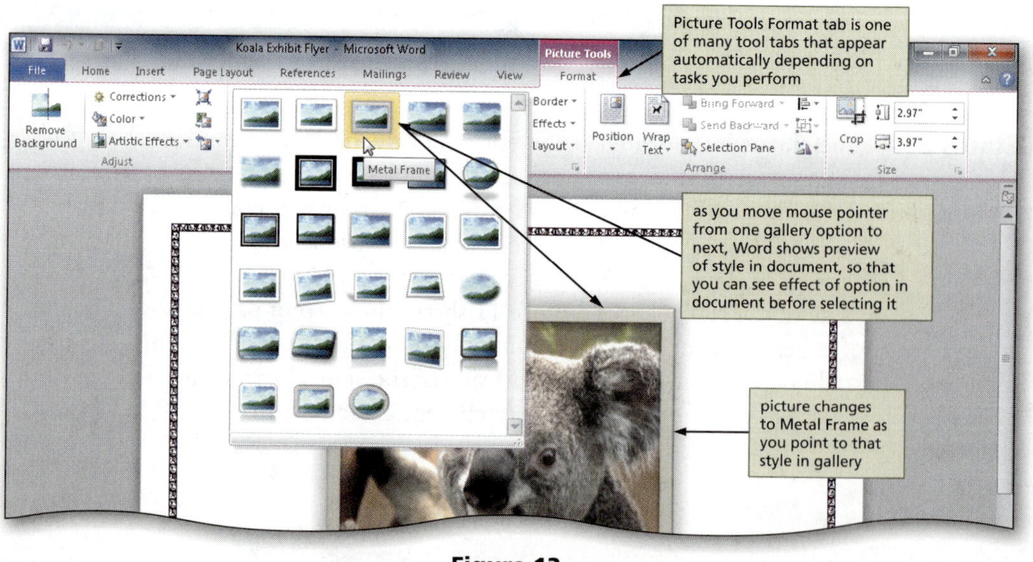

Figure 13

Some commands on the Ribbon display an image to help you remember their function. When you point to a command on the Ribbon, all or part of the command glows in shades of yellow and orange, and an Enhanced ScreenTip appears on the screen. An **Enhanced ScreenTip** is an on-screen note that provides the name of the command, available keyboard shortcut(s), a description of the command, and sometimes instructions for how to obtain help about the command (Figure 14). Enhanced ScreenTips are more detailed than a typical ScreenTip, which usually displays only the name of the command.

Some groups on the Ribbon have a small arrow in the lower-right corner, called a **Dialog Box Launcher**, that when clicked, displays a dialog box or a task pane with additional options for the group (Figure 15). When presented with a dialog box, you make selections and must close the dialog box before returning to the document. A **task pane**, in contrast to a dialog box, is a window that can remain open and visible while you work in the document.

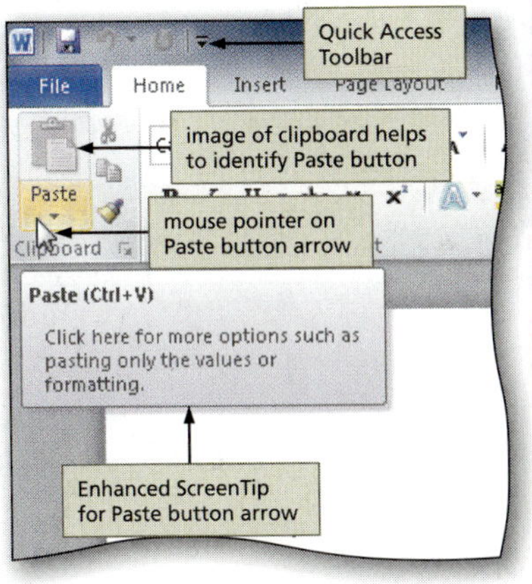

Figure 14

Mini Toolbar The **Mini toolbar**, which appears automatically based on tasks you perform, contains commands related to changing the appearance of text in a document. All commands on the Mini toolbar also exist on the Ribbon. The purpose of the Mini toolbar is to minimize mouse movement.

When the Mini toolbar appears, it initially is transparent (Figure 16a). If you do not use the transparent Mini toolbar, it disappears from the screen. To use the Mini toolbar, move the mouse pointer into the toolbar, which causes the Mini toolbar to change from a transparent to bright appearance (Figure 16b). If you right-click an item in the document window, Word displays both the Mini toolbar and a shortcut menu, which is discussed in a later section in this chapter.

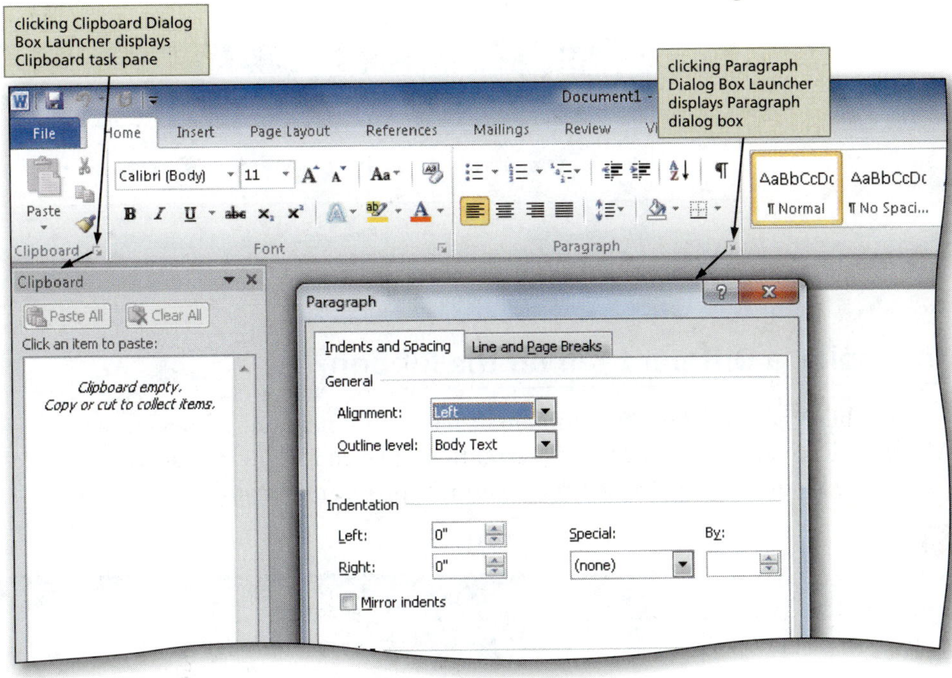

Figure 15

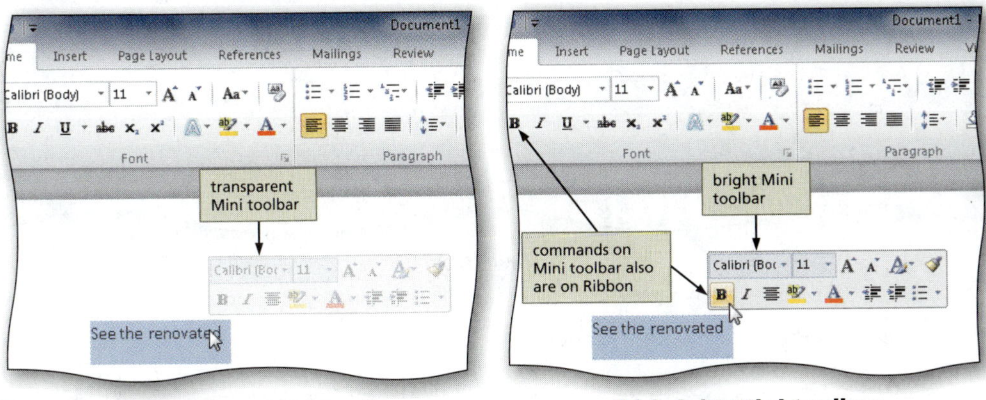

(a) transparent Mini toolbar

(b) bright Mini toolbar

Figure 16

BTW

Turning Off the Mini Toolbar

If you do not want the Mini toolbar to appear, click File on the Ribbon to open the Backstage view, click Options in the Backstage view, click General (Options dialog box), remove the check mark from the Show Mini Toolbar on selection check box, and then click the OK button.

Quick Access Toolbar The **Quick Access Toolbar**, located initially (by default) above the Ribbon at the left edge of the title bar, provides convenient, one-click access to frequently used commands (Figure 14 on the previous page). The commands on the Quick Access Toolbar always are available, regardless of the task you are performing. The Quick Access Toolbar is discussed in more depth later in the chapter.

KeyTips If you prefer using the keyboard instead of the mouse, you can press the ALT key on the keyboard to display **KeyTips**, or keyboard code icons, for certain commands (Figure 17). To select a command using the keyboard, press the letter or number displayed in the KeyTip, which may cause additional KeyTips related to the selected command to appear. To remove KeyTips from the screen, press the ALT key or the ESC key until all KeyTips disappear, or click the mouse anywhere in the program window.

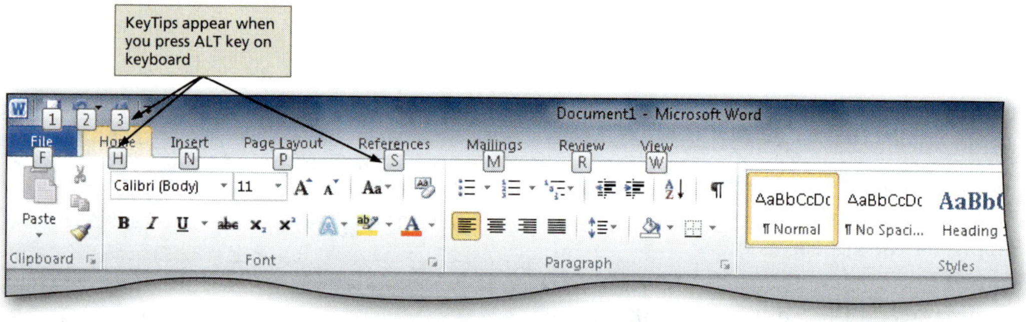

Figure 17

To Display a Different Tab on the Ribbon

When you start Word, the Ribbon displays eight main tabs: File, Home, Insert, Page Layout, References, Mailings, Review, and View. The tab currently displayed is called the **active tab**.

The following step displays the Insert tab, that is, makes it the active tab.

1

- Click Insert on the Ribbon to display the Insert tab (Figure 18).

Experiment

- Click the other tabs on the Ribbon to view their contents. When you are finished, click the Insert tab to redisplay the Insert tab.

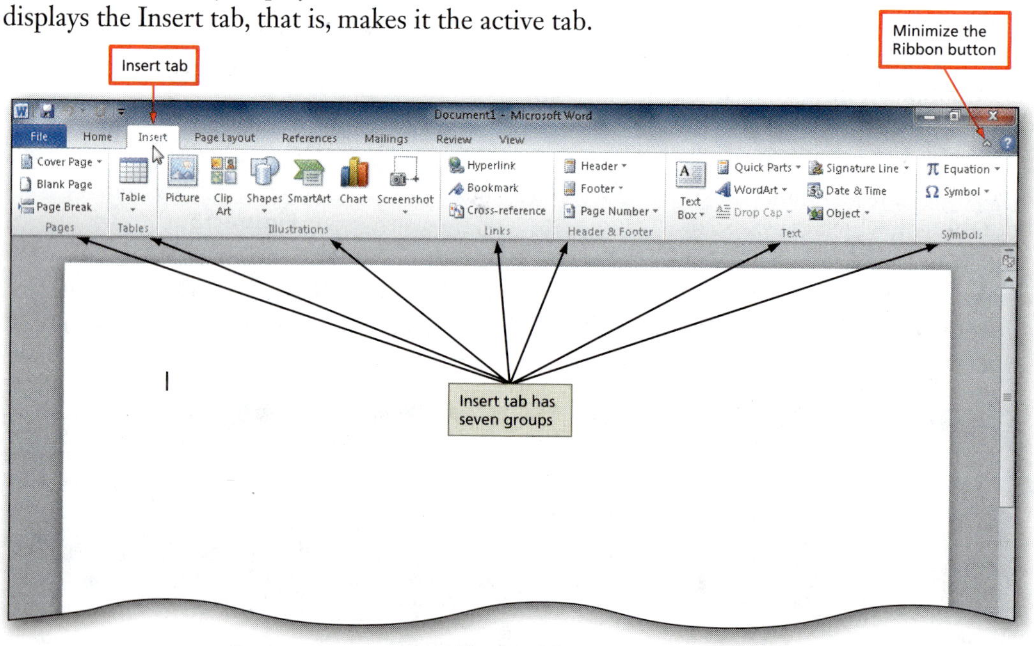

Figure 18

Q&A

If I am working in a different Office program, such as PowerPoint or Access, how do I display a different tab on the Ribbon?

Follow this same procedure; that is, click the desired tab on the Ribbon.

To Minimize, Display, and Restore the Ribbon

To display more of a document or other item in the window of an Office program, some users prefer to minimize the Ribbon, which hides the groups on the Ribbon and displays only the main tabs. Each time you start an Office program, the Ribbon appears the same way it did the last time you used that Office program. The Office and Windows chapters in this book, however, begin with the Ribbon appearing as it did at the initial installation of the software.

The following steps minimize, display, and restore the Ribbon in an Office program.

1

- Click the Minimize the Ribbon button on the Ribbon (shown in Figure 18) to minimize the Ribbon (Figure 19).

Q&A What happened to the groups on the Ribbon?

When you minimize the Ribbon, the groups disappear so that the Ribbon does not take up as much space on the screen.

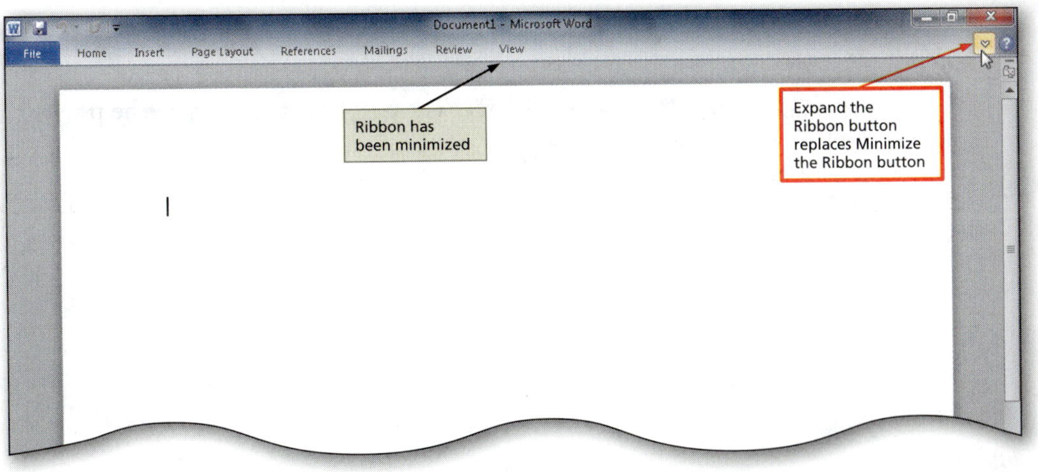

Figure 19

Q&A What happened to the Minimize the Ribbon button?

The Expand the Ribbon button replaces the Minimize the Ribbon button when the Ribbon is minimized.

2

- Click Home on the Ribbon to display the Home tab (Figure 20).

Q&A Why would I click the Home tab?

If you want to use a command on a minimized Ribbon, click the main tab to display the groups for that tab. After you select a command on the Ribbon, the groups will be hidden once again. If you decide not to use a command on the Ribbon, you can hide the groups by clicking the same main tab or clicking in the program window.

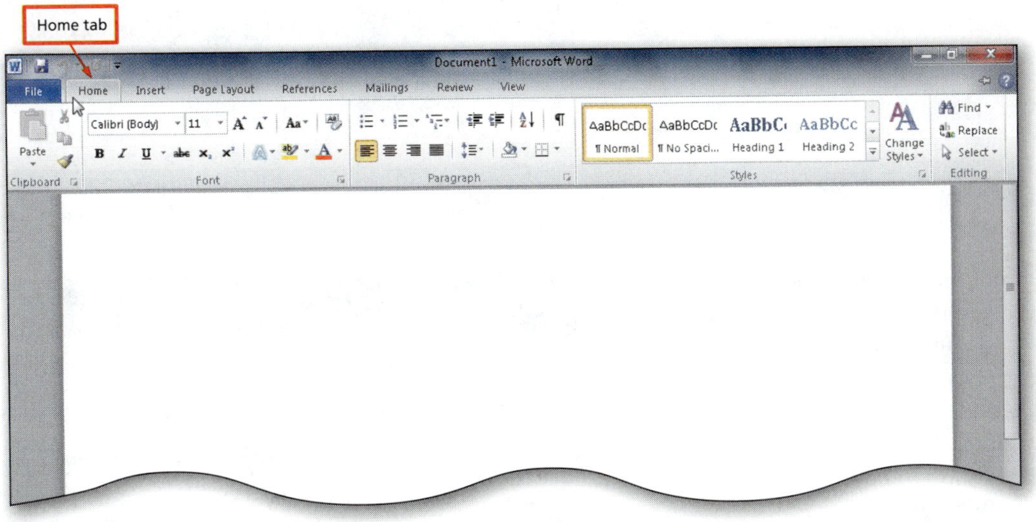

Figure 20

3

- Click Home on the Ribbon to hide the groups again (shown in Figure 19).
- Click the Expand the Ribbon button on the Ribbon (shown in Figure 19) to restore the Ribbon.

Other Ways

1. Double-click Home on the Ribbon
2. Press CTRL+F1

To Display and Use a Shortcut Menu

When you right-click certain areas of the Word and other program windows, a shortcut menu will appear. A **shortcut menu** is a list of frequently used commands that relate to the right-clicked object. When you right-click a scroll bar, for example, a shortcut menu appears with commands related to the scroll bar. When you right-click the Quick Access Toolbar, a shortcut menu appears with commands related to the Quick Access Toolbar. You can use shortcut menus to access common commands quickly. The following steps use a shortcut menu to move the Quick Access Toolbar, which by default is located on the title bar.

1

- Right-click the Quick Access Toolbar to display a shortcut menu that presents a list of commands related to the Quick Access Toolbar (Figure 21).

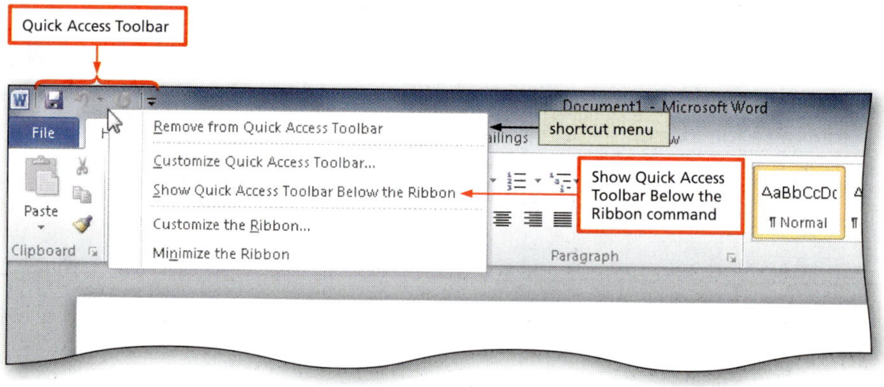

Figure 21

2

- Click Show Quick Access Toolbar Below the Ribbon on the shortcut menu to display the Quick Access Toolbar below the Ribbon (Figure 22).

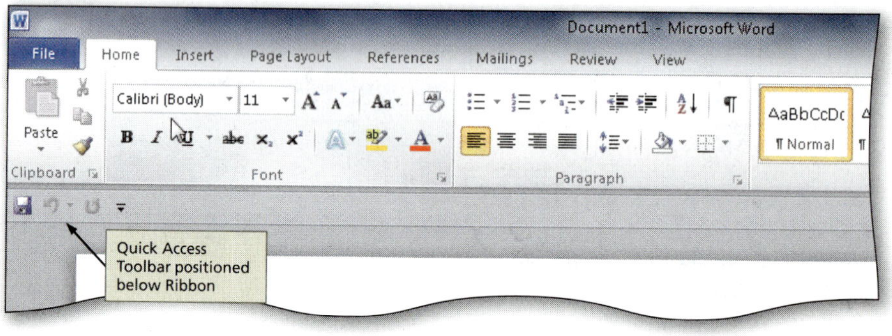

Figure 22

3

- Right-click the Quick Access Toolbar to display a shortcut menu (Figure 23).

4

- Click Show Quick Access Toolbar Above the Ribbon on the shortcut menu to return the Quick Access Toolbar to its original position (shown in Figure 21).

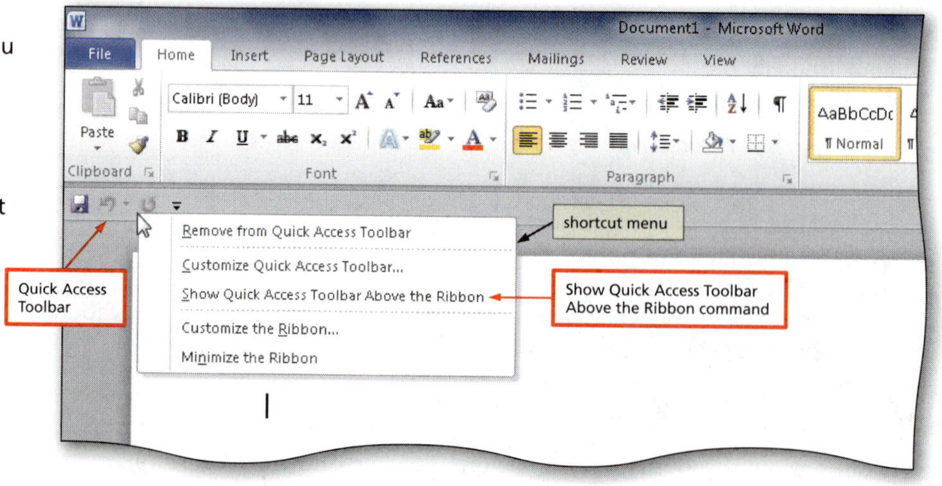

Figure 23

To Customize the Quick Access Toolbar

The Quick Access Toolbar provides easy access to some of the more frequently used commands in Office programs. By default, the Quick Access Toolbar contains buttons for the Save, Undo, and Redo commands. You can customize the Quick Access Toolbar by changing its location in the window, as shown in the previous steps, and by adding more buttons to reflect commands you would like to access easily. The following steps add the Quick Print button to the Quick Access Toolbar.

1

- Click the Customize Quick Access Toolbar button to display the Customize Quick Access Toolbar menu (Figure 24).

Q&A Which commands are listed on the Customize Quick Access Toolbar menu?

It lists commands that commonly are added to the Quick Access Toolbar.

Q&A What do the check marks next to some commands signify?

Check marks appear next to commands that already are on the Quick Access Toolbar. When you add a button to the Quick Access Toolbar, a check mark will be displayed next to its command name.

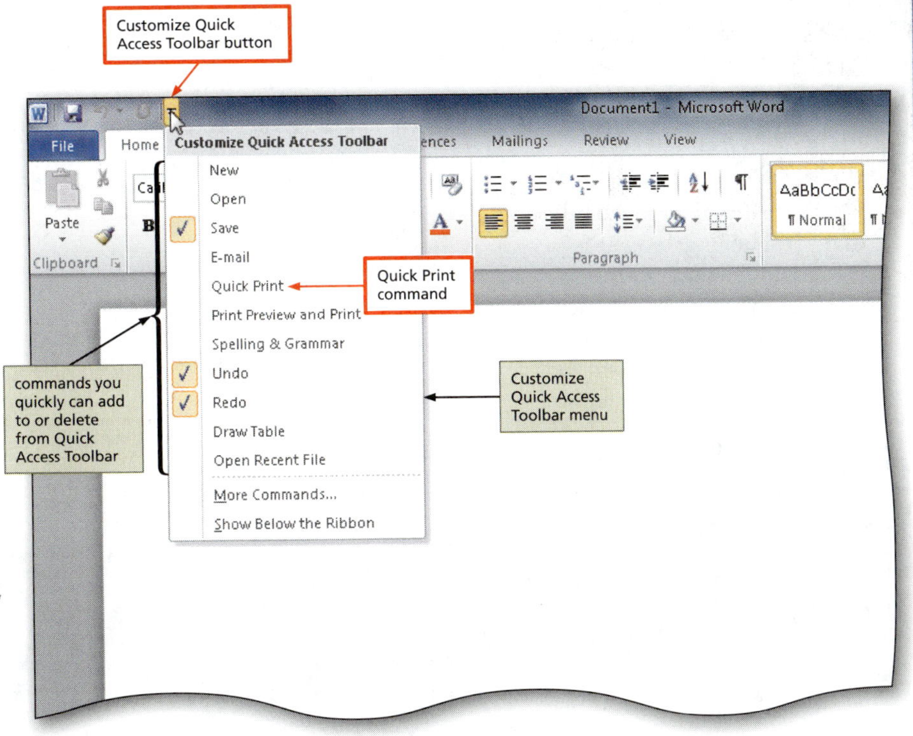

Figure 24

2

- Click Quick Print on the Customize Quick Access Toolbar menu to add the Quick Print button to the Quick Access Toolbar (Figure 25).

Q&A How would I remove a button from the Quick Access Toolbar?

You would right-click the button you wish to remove and then click Remove from Quick Access Toolbar on the shortcut menu.

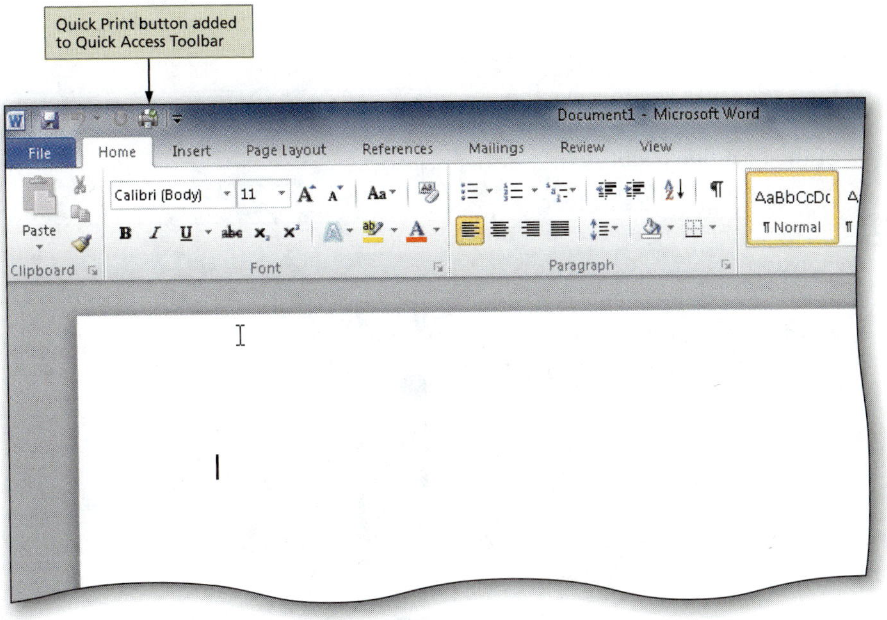

Figure 25

To Enter Text in a Document

The first step in creating a document is to enter its text by typing on the keyboard. By default, Word positions text at the left margin as you type. To begin creating a flyer, for example, you type the headline in the document window. The following steps type this first line of text, a headline, in a document.

1

- Type **SEE THE RENOVATED KOALA EXHIBIT** as the text (Figure 26).

Q&A What is the blinking vertical bar to the right of the text?

The insertion point. It indicates where text, graphics, and other items will be inserted in the document. As you type, the insertion point moves to the right, and when you reach the end of a line, it moves downward to the beginning of the next line.

Q&A What if I make an error while typing?

You can press the BACKSPACE key until you have deleted the text in error and then retype the text correctly.

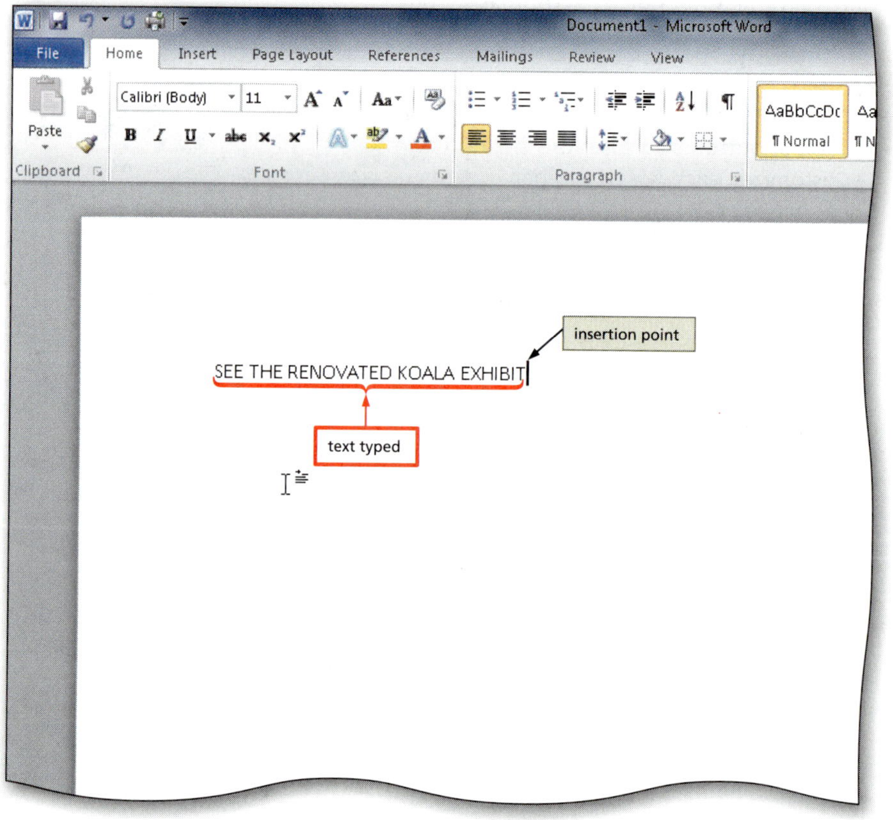

Figure 26

2

- Press the ENTER key to move the insertion point to the beginning of the next line (Figure 27).

Q&A Why did blank space appear between the entered text and the insertion point?

Each time you press the ENTER key, Word creates a new paragraph and inserts blank space between the two paragraphs.

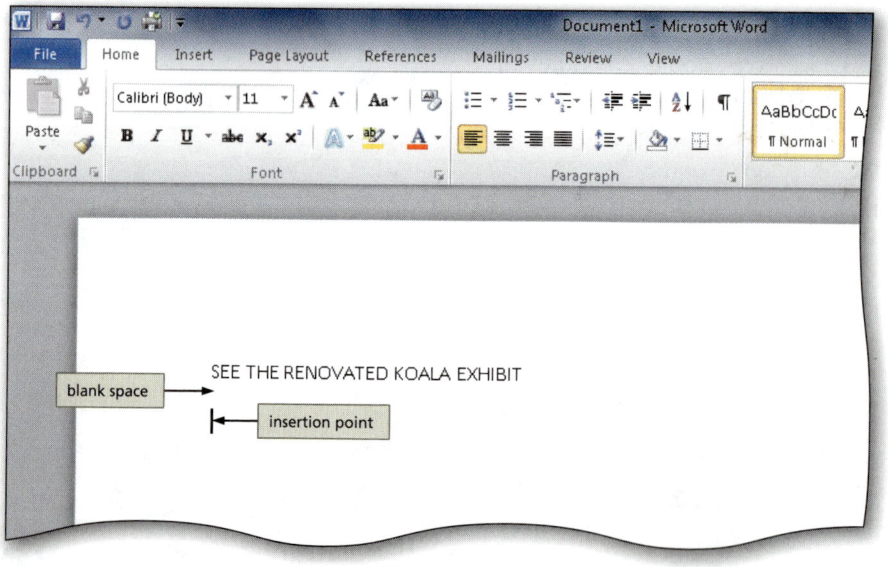

Figure 27

Saving and Organizing Files

While you are creating a document, the computer stores it in memory. When you save a document, the computer places it on a storage medium such as a hard disk, USB flash drive, or optical disc. A saved document is referred to as a file. A **file name** is the name assigned to a file when it is saved. It is important to save a document frequently for the following reasons:

- The document in memory might be lost if the computer is turned off or you lose electrical power while a program is running.
- If you run out of time before completing a project, you may finish it at a future time without starting over.

When saving files, you should organize them so that you easily can find them later. Windows 7 provides tools to help you organize files.

BTW

File Type

Depending on your Windows 7 settings, the file type .docx may be displayed immediately to the right of the file name after you save the file. The file type .docx is a Word 2010 document.

Organizing Files and Folders

A file contains data. This data can range from a research paper to an accounting spreadsheet to an electronic math quiz. You should organize and store these files in folders to avoid misplacing a file and to help you find a file quickly.

If you are a freshman taking an introductory computer class (CIS 101, for example), you may want to design a series of folders for the different subjects covered in the class. To accomplish this, you can arrange the folders in a hierarchy for the class, as shown in Figure 28.

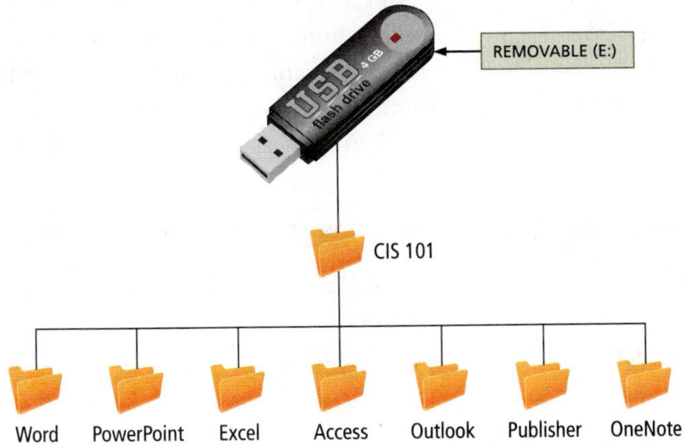

Figure 28

The hierarchy contains three levels. The first level contains the storage device, in this case a USB flash drive. Windows 7 identifies the storage device with a letter, and, in some cases, a name. In Figure 28, the USB flash drive is identified as REMOVABLE (E:). The second level contains the class folder (CIS 101, in this case), and the third level contains seven folders, one each for a different Office program that will be covered in the class (Word, PowerPoint, Excel, Access, Outlook, Publisher, and OneNote).

When the hierarchy in Figure 28 is created, the USB flash drive is said to contain the CIS 101 folder, and the CIS 101 folder is said to contain the separate Office folders (i.e., Word, PowerPoint, Excel, etc.). In addition, this hierarchy easily can be expanded to include folders from other classes taken during additional semesters.

The vertical and horizontal lines in Figure 28 form a pathway that allows you to navigate to a drive or folder on a computer or network. A **path** consists of a drive letter (preceded by a drive name when necessary) and colon, to identify the storage device, and one or more folder names. Each drive or folder in the hierarchy has a corresponding path.

BTW

Saving Online

Instead of saving files on a USB flash drive, some people prefer to save them online so that they can access the files from any computer with an Internet connection. For more information, read Appendix C.

Table 3 shows examples of paths and their corresponding drives and folders.

Table 3 Paths and Corresponding Drives and Folders

Path	Drive and Folder
Computer ▶ REMOVABLE (E:)	Drive E (REMOVABLE (E:))
Computer ▶ REMOVABLE (E:) ▶ CIS 101	CIS 101 folder on drive E
Computer ▶ REMOVABLE (E:) ▶ CIS 101 ▶ Word	Word folder in CIS 101 folder on drive E

The following pages illustrate the steps to organize the folders for this class and save a file in one of those folders:

1. Create the folder identifying your class.
2. Create the Word folder in the folder identifying your class.
3. Create the remaining folders in the folder identifying your class (one each for PowerPoint, Excel, Access, Outlook, Publisher, and OneNote).
4. Save a file in the Word folder.
5. Verify the location of the saved file.

To Create a Folder

When you create a folder, such as the CIS 101 folder shown in Figure 28 on the previous page, you must name the folder. A folder name should describe the folder and its contents. A folder name can contain spaces and any uppercase or lowercase characters, except a backslash (\), slash (/), colon (:), asterisk (*), question mark (?), quotation marks ("), less than symbol (<), greater than symbol (>), or vertical bar (|). Folder names cannot be CON, AUX, COM1, COM2, COM3, COM4, LPT1, LPT2, LPT3, PRN, or NUL. The same rules for naming folders also apply to naming files.

To store files and folders on a USB flash drive, you must connect the USB flash drive to an available USB port on a computer. The following steps create your class folder (CIS 101, in this case) on a USB flash drive.

1

- Connect the USB flash drive to an available USB port on the computer to open the AutoPlay window (Figure 29).

Q&A Why does the AutoPlay window not open?

Some computers are not configured to open an AutoPlay window. Instead, they might display the contents of the USB flash drive automatically, or you might need to access contents of the USB flash drive using the Computer window. To use the Computer window to display the USB flash drive's contents, click the Start button, click Computer on the Start menu, and then click the icon representing the USB flash drive.

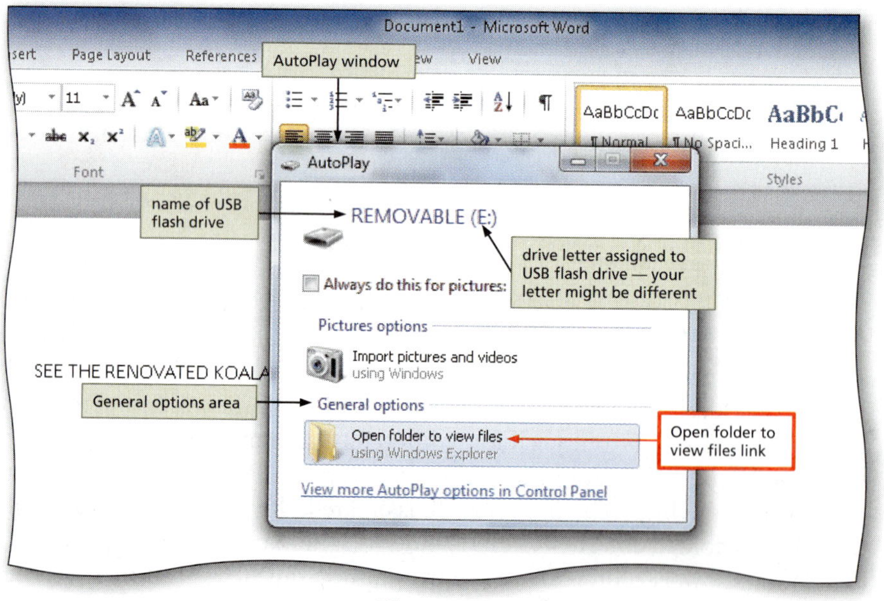

Figure 29

Q&A Why does the AutoPlay window look different from the one in Figure 29?

The AutoPlay window that opens on your computer might display different options. The type of USB flash drive, its contents, and the next available drive letter on your computer all will determine which options are displayed in the AutoPlay window.

2

- Click the 'Open folder to view files' link in the AutoPlay window to open the USB flash drive window (Figure 30).

Q&A Why does Figure 30 show REMOVABLE (E:) for the USB flash drive?

REMOVABLE is the name of the USB flash drive used to illustrate these steps. The (E:) refers to the drive letter assigned by Windows 7 to the USB flash drive. The name and drive letter of your USB flash drive probably will be different.

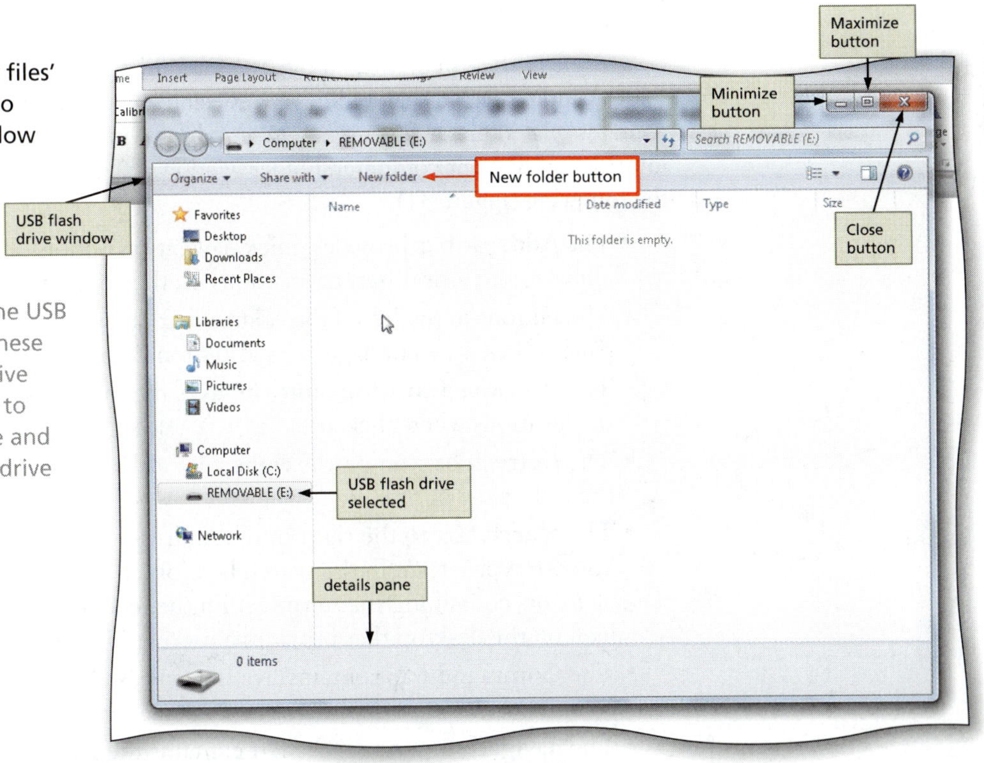

Figure 30

3

- Click the New folder button on the toolbar to display a new folder icon with the name, New folder, selected in a text box.
- Type `CIS 101` (or your class code) in the text box to name the folder.
- Press the ENTER key to create a folder identifying your class on the selected drive (Figure 31). If the CIS 101 folder does not appear in the navigation pane, double-click REMOVABLE (E:) in the navigation pane to display the folder just added.

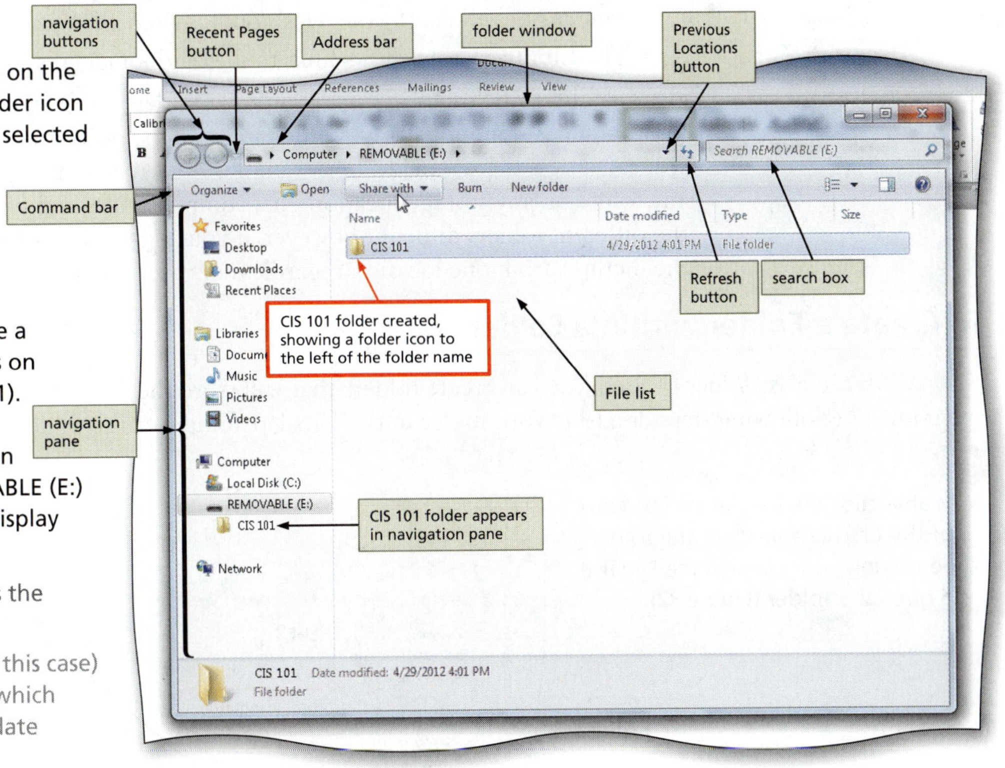

Figure 31

Q&A What happens when I press the ENTER key?

The class folder (CIS 101, in this case) is displayed in the File list, which contains the folder name, date modified, type, and size.

Q&A Why is the folder icon displayed differently on my computer?

Windows might be configured to display contents differently on your computer.

Folder Windows

The USB flash drive window (shown in Figure 31 on the previous page) is called a folder window. Recall that a folder is a specific named location on a storage medium that contains related files. Most users rely on **folder windows** for finding, viewing, and managing information on their computer. Folder windows have common design elements, including the following (Figure 31).

- The **Address bar** provides quick navigation options. The arrows on the Address bar allow you to visit different locations on the computer.
- The buttons to the left of the Address bar allow you to navigate the contents of the left pane and view recent pages. Other buttons allow you to specify the size of the window.
- The **Previous Locations button** saves the locations you have visited and displays the locations when clicked.
- The **Refresh button** on the right side of the Address bar refreshes the contents of the right pane of the folder window.
- The **search box** to the right of the Address bar contains the dimmed word, Search. You can type a term in the search box for a list of files, folders, shortcuts, and elements containing that term within the location you are searching. A **shortcut** is an icon on the desktop that provides a user with immediate access to a program or file.
- The **Command bar** contains five buttons used to accomplish various tasks on the computer related to organizing and managing the contents of the open window.
- The **navigation pane** on the left contains the Favorites area, Libraries area, Computer area, and Network area.
- The **Favorites area** contains links to your favorite locations. By default, this list contains only links to your Desktop, Downloads, and Recent Places.
- The **Libraries area** shows links to files and folders that have been included in a library.

A **library** helps you manage multiple folders and files stored in various locations on a computer. It does not store the files and folders; rather, it displays links to them so that you can access them quickly. For example, you can save pictures from a digital camera in any folder on any storage location on a computer. Normally, this would make organizing the different folders difficult; however, if you add the folders to a library, you can access all the pictures from one location regardless of where they are stored.

To Create a Folder within a Folder

With the class folder created, you can create folders that will store the files you create using each Office program. The following steps create a Word folder in the CIS 101 folder (or the folder identifying your class).

1

- Double-click the icon or folder name for the CIS 101 folder (or the folder identifying your class) in the File list to open the folder (Figure 32).

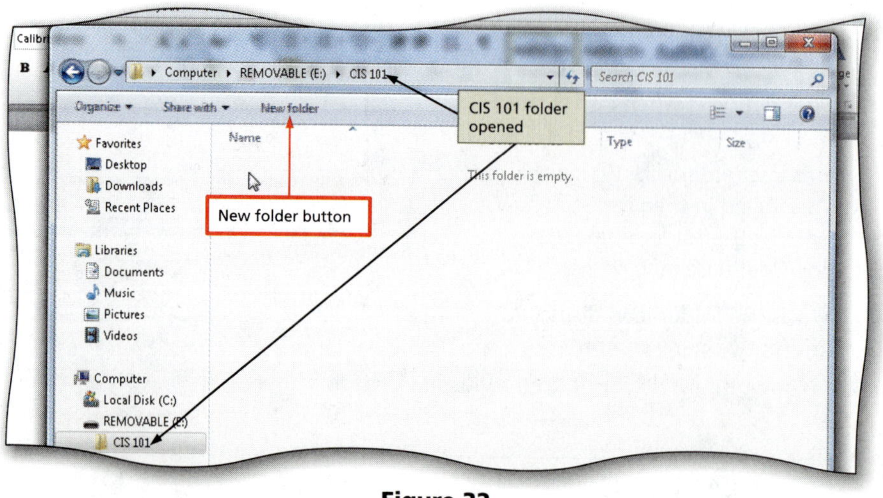

Figure 32

2

- Click the New folder button on the toolbar to display a new folder icon and text box for the folder.
- Type `Word` in the text box to name the folder.
- Press the ENTER key to create the folder (Figure 33).

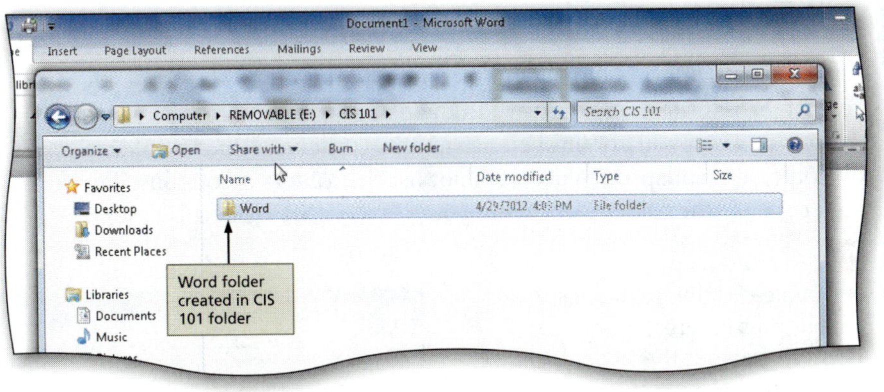

Figure 33

To Create the Remaining Folders

The following steps create the remaining folders in the folder identifying your class (in this case, CIS 101).

1. Click the New folder button on the toolbar to display a new folder icon and text box.
2. Type `PowerPoint` in the text box to name the folder.
3. Repeat Steps 1 and 2 to create each of the remaining folders, using the names Excel, Access, Outlook, Publisher, and OneNote as the folder names (Figure 34).

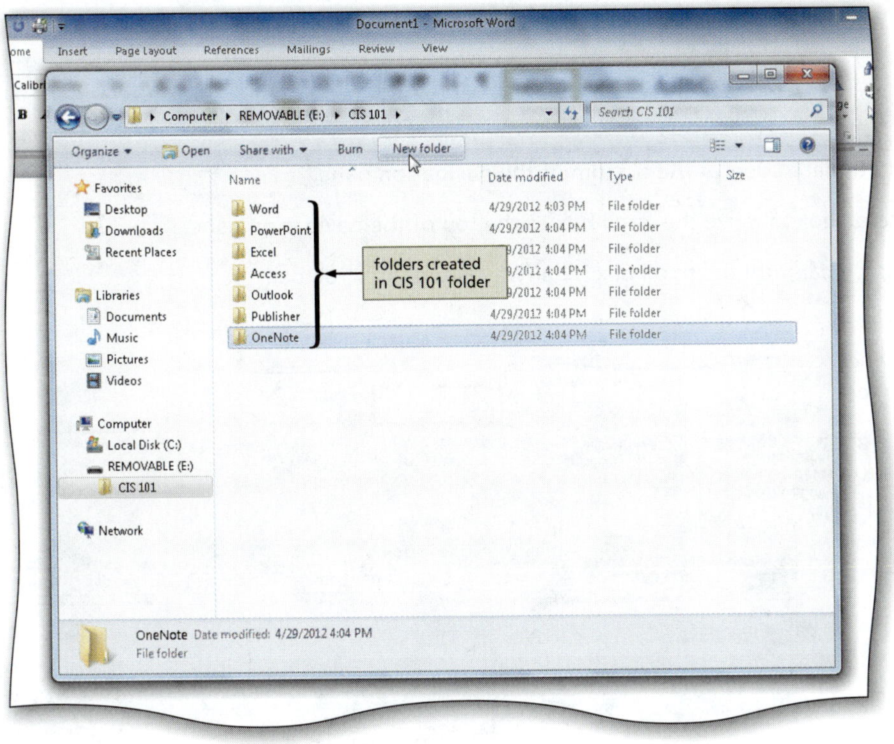

Figure 34

To Expand a Folder, Scroll through Folder Contents, and Collapse a Folder

Folder windows display the hierarchy of items and the contents of drives and folders in the right pane. You might want to expand a drive in the navigation pane to view its contents, scroll through its contents, and collapse it when you are finished viewing its contents. When a folder is expanded, it lists all the folders it contains. By contrast, a collapsed folder does not list the folders it contains. The following steps expand, scroll through, and then collapse the folder identifying your class (CIS 101, in this case).

1

- Double-click the folder identifying your class (CIS 101, in this case), which expands the folder to display its contents and displays a black arrow to the left of the folder icon (Figure 35).

Q&A Why are the subject folders indented below the CIS 101 folder in the navigation pane?

It shows that the folders are contained within the CIS 101 folder.

Q&A Why did a scroll bar appear in the navigation pane?

When all contents cannot fit in a window or pane, a scroll bar appears. As described earlier, you can view areas currently not visible by (1) clicking the scroll arrows, (2) clicking above or below the scroll bar, and (3) dragging the scroll box.

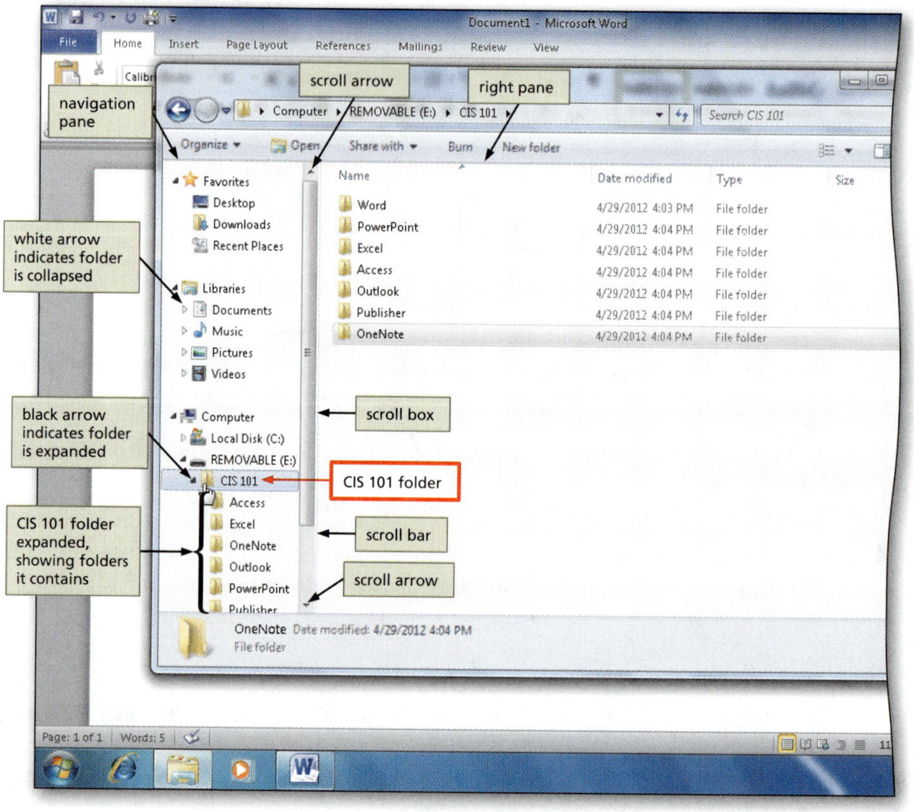

Figure 35

Experiment

- Click the down scroll arrow on the vertical scroll bar to display additional folders at the bottom of the navigation pane.
- Click the scroll bar above the scroll box to move the scroll box to the top of the navigation pane.
- Drag the scroll box down the scroll bar until the scroll box is halfway down the scroll bar.

2

- Double-click the folder identifying your class (CIS 101, in this case) to collapse the folder (Figure 36).

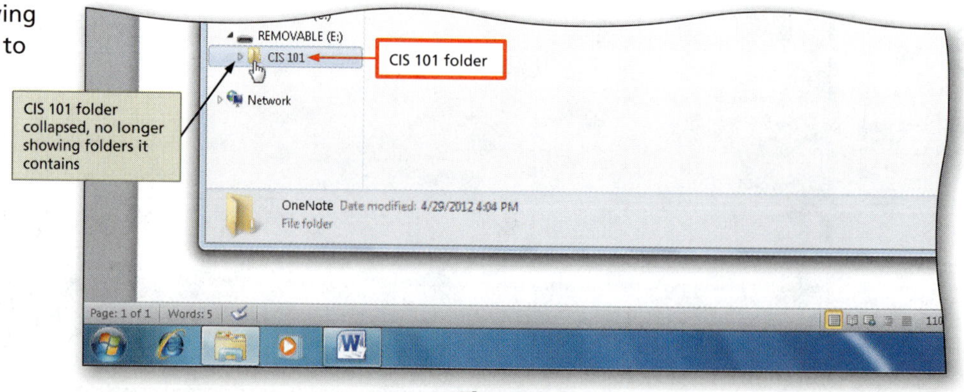

Figure 36

Other Ways

1. Point in navigation pane to display arrows, click white arrow to expand or click black arrow to collapse
2. Select folder to expand or collapse using arrow keys, press RIGHT ARROW to expand; press LEFT ARROW to collapse.

To Switch from One Program to Another

The next step is to save the Word file containing the headline you typed earlier. Word, however, currently is not the active window. You can use the program button on the taskbar and live preview to switch to Word and then save the document in the Word document window.

If Windows Aero is active on your computer, Windows displays a live preview window whenever you move your mouse on a button or click a button on the taskbar. If Aero is not supported or enabled on your computer, you will see a window title instead of a live preview. The steps below use the Word program; however, the steps are the same for any active Office program currently displayed as a program button on the taskbar.

The following steps switch to the Word window.

1

- Point to the Word program button on the taskbar to see a live preview of the open document(s) or the window title(s) of the open document(s), depending on your computer's configuration (Figure 37).

2

- Click the program button or the live preview to make the program associated with the program button the active window (shown in Figure 27 on page OFF 20).

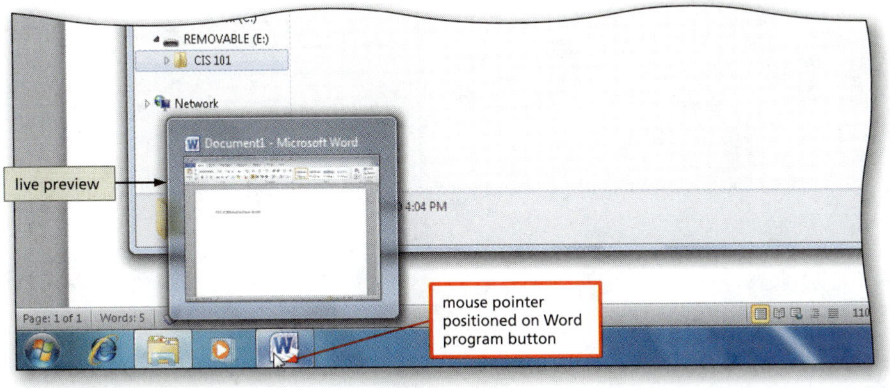

Figure 37

Q&A What if multiple documents are open in a program?

If Aero is enabled on your computer, click the desired live preview. If Aero is not supported or not enabled, click the window title.

To Save a File in a Folder

Now that you have created the folders for storing files, you can save the Word document. The following steps save a file on a USB flash drive in the Word folder contained in your class folder (CIS 101, in this case) using the file name, Koala Exhibit.

1

- With a USB flash drive connected to one of the computer's USB ports, click the Save button on the Quick Access Toolbar to display the Save As dialog box (Figure 38).

Q&A Why does a file name already appear in the File name text box?

Word automatically suggests a file name the first time you save a document. The file name normally consists of the first few words contained in the document. Because the suggested file name is selected, you do not need to delete it; as soon as you begin typing, the new file name replaces the selected text.

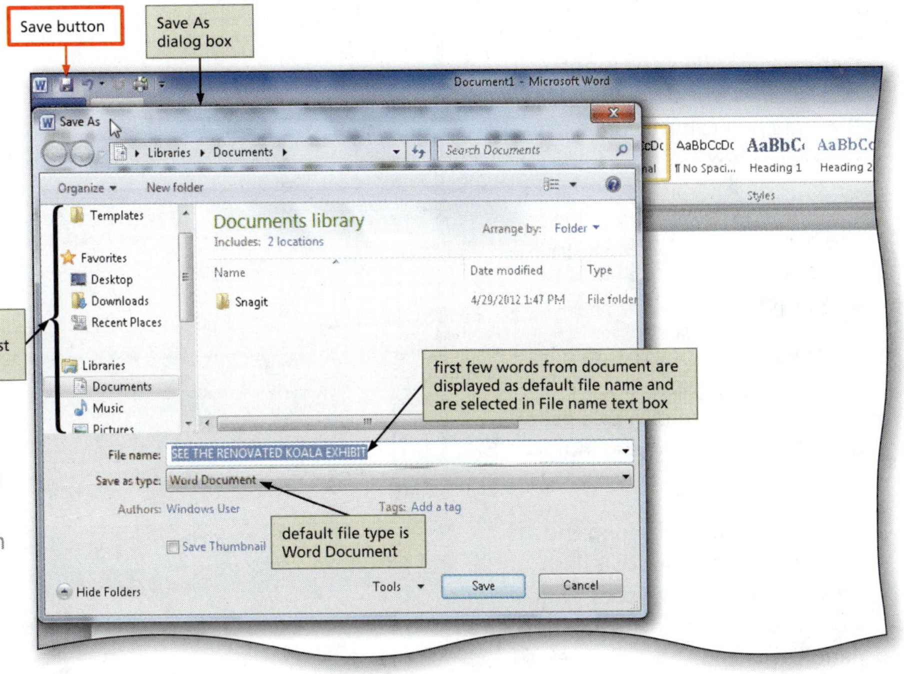

Figure 38

2

- Type `Koala Exhibit` in the File name text box (Save As dialog box) to change the file name. Do not press the ENTER key after typing the file name because you do not want to close the dialog box at this time (Figure 39).

Q&A

What characters can I use in a file name?

The only invalid characters are the backslash (\), slash (/), colon (:), asterisk (*), question mark (?), quotation mark ("), less than symbol (<), greater than symbol (>), and vertical bar (|).

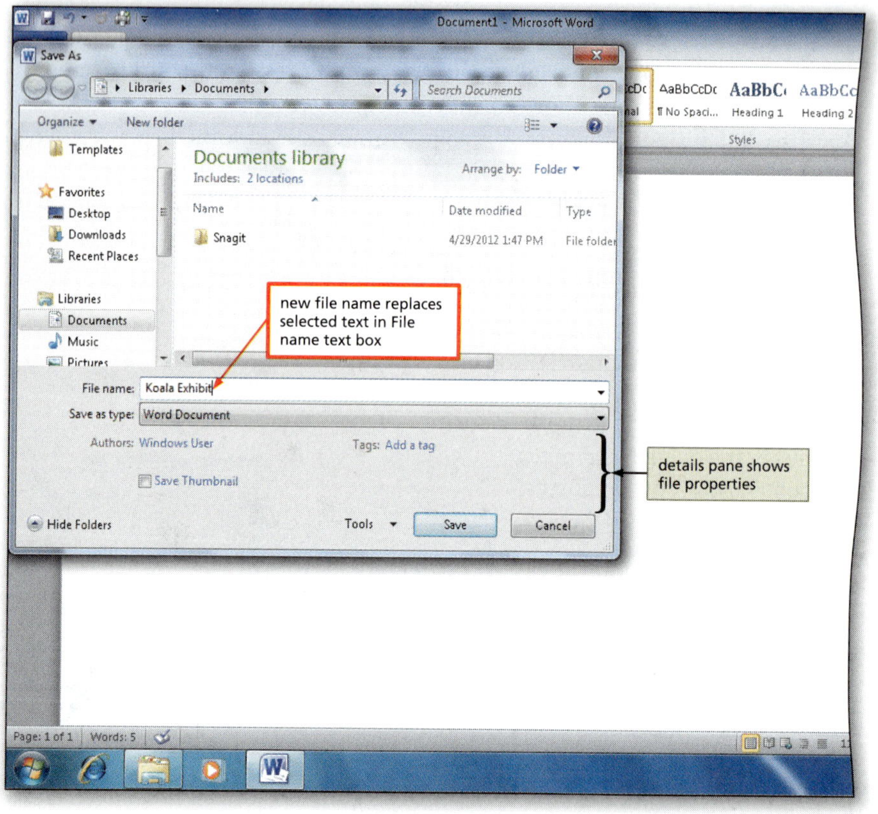

Figure 39

3

- Navigate to the desired save location (in this case, the Word folder in the CIS 101 folder [or your class folder] on the USB flash drive) by performing the tasks in Steps 3a, 3b, and 3c.

3a

- If the navigation pane is not displayed in the dialog box, click the Browse Folders button to expand the dialog box.
- If Computer is not displayed in the navigation pane, drag the navigation pane scroll bar until Computer appears.
- If Computer is not expanded in the navigation pane, double-click Computer to display a list of available storage devices in the navigation pane.
- If necessary, scroll through the dialog box until your USB flash drive appears in the list of available storage devices in the navigation pane (Figure 40).

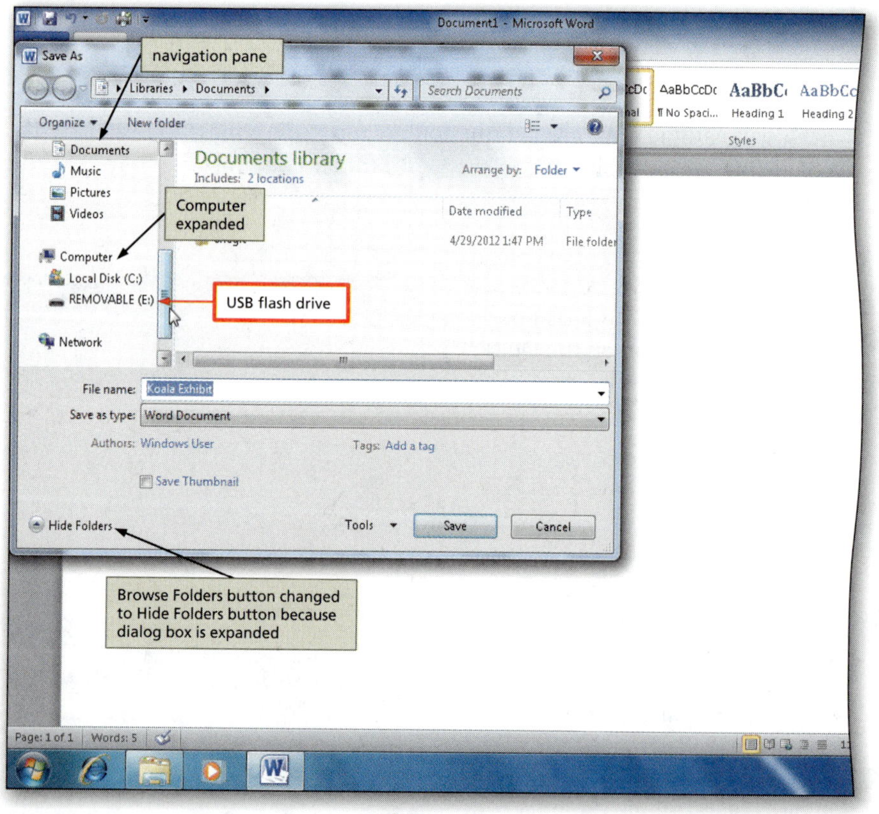

Figure 40

3b

- If your USB flash drive is not expanded, double-click the USB flash drive in the list of available storage devices in the navigation pane to select that drive as the new save location and display its contents in the right pane.

3c

- If your class folder (CIS 101, in this case) is not expanded, double-click the CIS 101 folder to select the folder and display its contents in the right pane.

Q&A What if I do not want to save in a folder?

Although storing files in folders is an effective technique for organizing files, some users prefer not to store files in folders. If you prefer not to save this file in a folder, skip all instructions in Step 3c and proceed to Step 4.

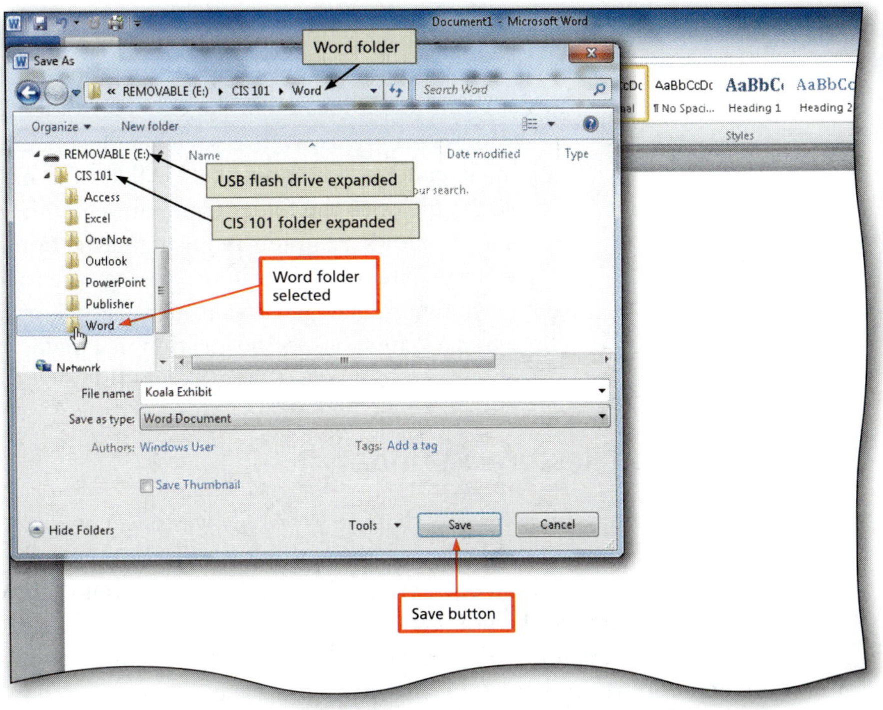

Figure 41

- Click the Word folder to select the folder and display its contents in the right pane (Figure 41).

4

- Click the Save button (Save As dialog box) to save the document in the selected folder on the selected drive with the entered file name (Figure 42).

Q&A How do I know that the file is saved?

While an Office program is saving a file, it briefly displays a message on the status bar indicating the amount of the file saved. In addition, the USB flash drive may have a light that flashes during the save process.

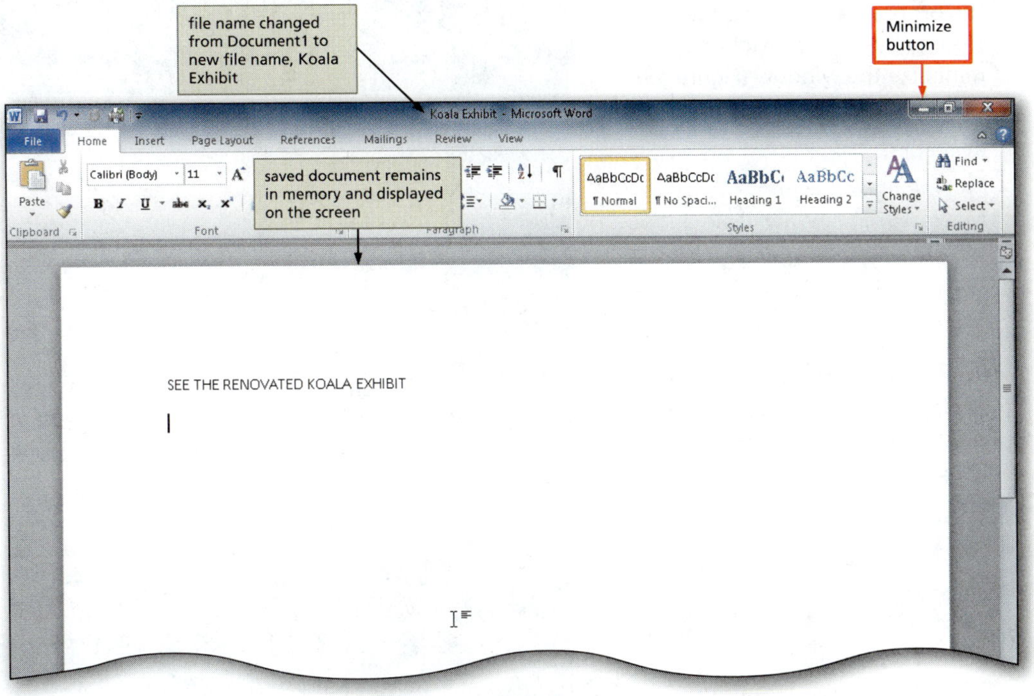

Figure 42

Other Ways

1. Click File on Ribbon, click Save, type file name, navigate to desired save location, click Save button
2. Press CTRL+S or press SHIFT+F12, type file name, navigate to desired save location, click Save button

Navigating in Dialog Boxes

Navigating is the process of finding a location on a storage device. While saving the Koala Exhibit file, for example, Steps 3a – 3c in the previous set of steps navigated to the Word folder located in the CIS 101 folder. When performing certain functions in Windows programs, such as saving a file, opening a file, or inserting a picture in an existing document, you most likely will have to navigate to the location where you want to save the file or to the folder containing the file you want to open or insert. Most dialog boxes in Windows programs requiring navigation follow a similar procedure; that is, the way you navigate to a folder in one dialog box, such as the Save As dialog box, is similar to how you might navigate in another dialog box, such as the Open dialog box. If you chose to navigate to a specific location in a dialog box, you would follow the instructions in Steps 3a – 3c on pages OFF 28 and OFF 29.

To Minimize and Restore a Window

Before continuing, you can verify that the Word file was saved properly. To do this, you will minimize the Word window and then open the USB flash drive window so that you can verify the file is stored on the USB flash drive. A **minimized window** is an open window hidden from view but that can be displayed quickly by clicking the window's program button on the taskbar.

In the following example, Word is used to illustrate minimizing and restoring windows; however, you would follow the same steps regardless of the Office program you are using.

The following steps minimize the Word window, verify that the file is saved, and then restore the minimized window.

1

- Click the Minimize button on the program's title bar (shown in Figure 42 on the previous page) to minimize the window (Figure 43).

Q&A Is the minimized window still available?

The minimized window, Word in this case, remains available but no longer is the active window. It is minimized as a program button on the taskbar.

- If necessary, click the Windows Explorer program button on the taskbar to open the USB flash drive window.

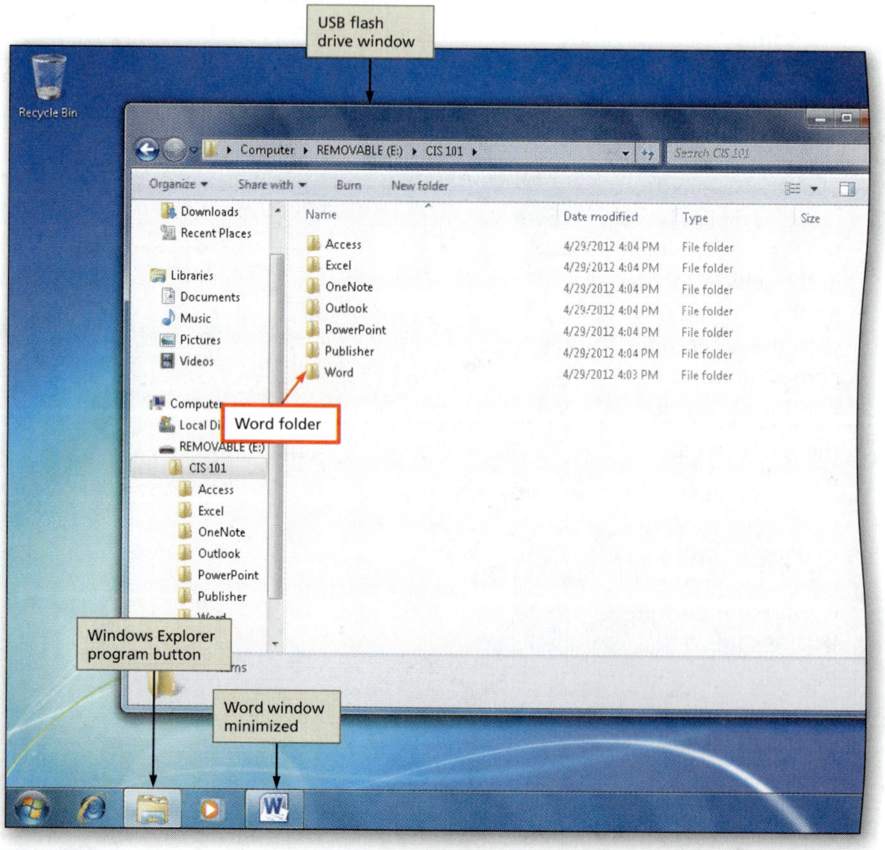

Figure 43

2

- Double-click the Word folder to select the folder and display its contents (Figure 44).

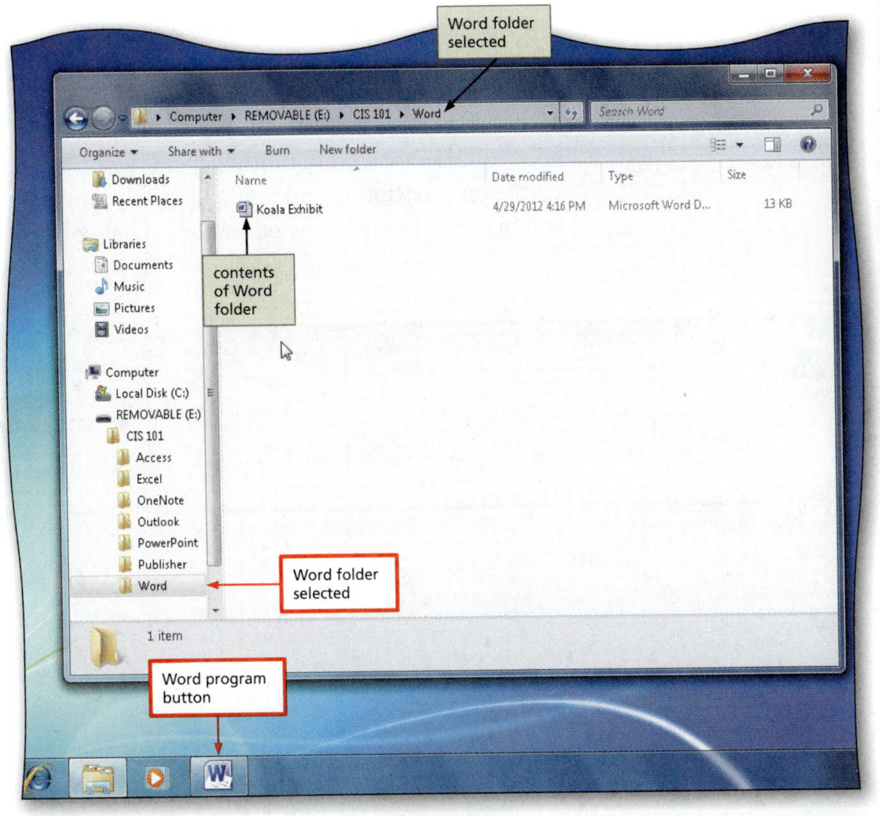

Figure 44

Q&A Why does the Windows Explorer button on the taskbar change?

The button changes to reflect the status of the folder window (in this case, the USB flash drive window). A selected button indicates that the folder window is active on the screen. When the button is not selected, the window is open but not active.

3

- After viewing the contents of the selected folder, click the Word program button on the taskbar to restore the minimized window (as shown in Figure 42 on page OFF 29).

Other Ways

1. Right-click title bar, click Minimize on shortcut menu, click taskbar button in taskbar button area
2. Press WINDOWS+M, press WINDOWS+SHIFT+M

Screen Resolution

Screen resolution indicates the number of pixels (dots) that the computer uses to display the letters, numbers, graphics, and background you see on the screen. When you increase the screen resolution, Windows displays more information on the screen, but the information decreases in size. The reverse also is true: as you decrease the screen resolution, Windows displays less information on the screen, but the information increases in size.

Screen resolution usually is stated as the product of two numbers, such as 1024 × 768 (pronounced "ten twenty-four by seven sixty-eight"). A 1024 × 768 screen resolution results in a display of 1,024 distinct pixels on each of 768 lines, or about

786,432 pixels. Changing the screen resolution affects how the Ribbon appears in Office programs. Figure 45 shows the Word Ribbon at screen resolutions of 1024 × 768 and 1280 × 800. All of the same commands are available regardless of screen resolution. Word, however, makes changes to the groups and the buttons within the groups to accommodate the various screen resolutions. The result is that certain commands may need to be accessed differently depending on the resolution chosen. A command that is visible on the Ribbon and available by clicking a button at one resolution may not be visible and may need to be accessed using its Dialog Box Launcher at a different resolution.

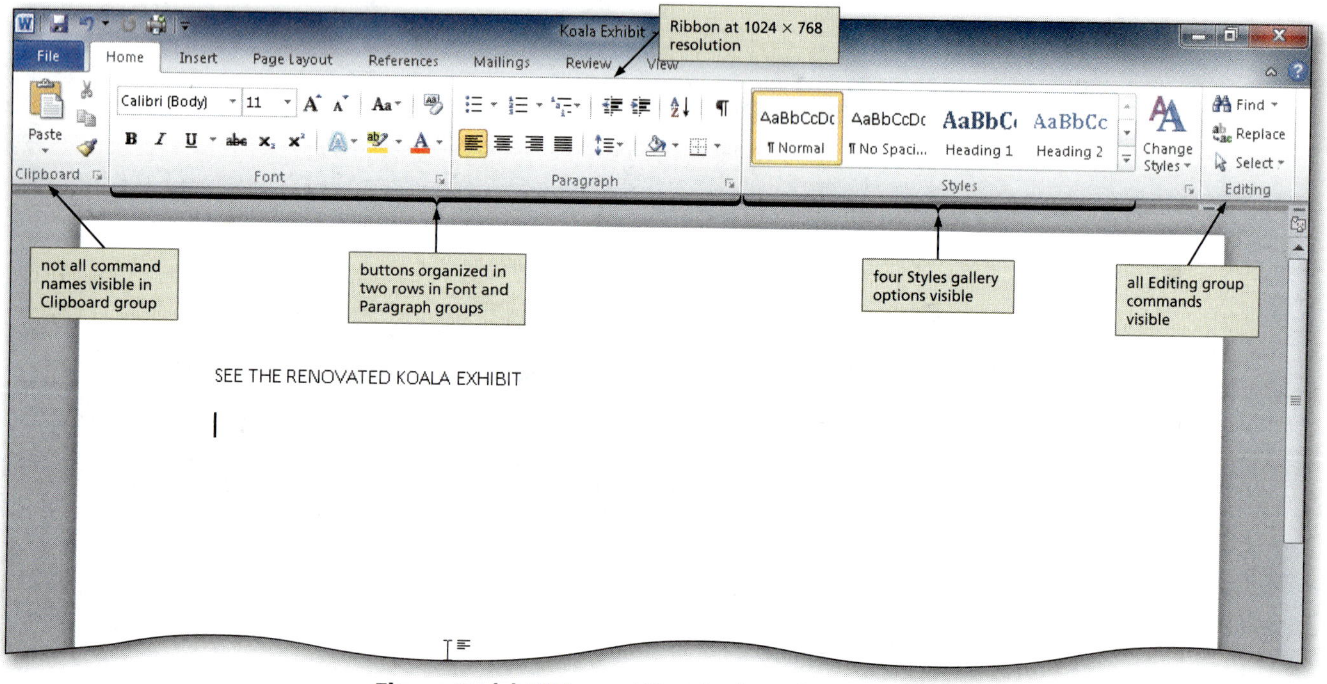

Figure 45 (a) Ribbon at Resolution of 1024 x 768

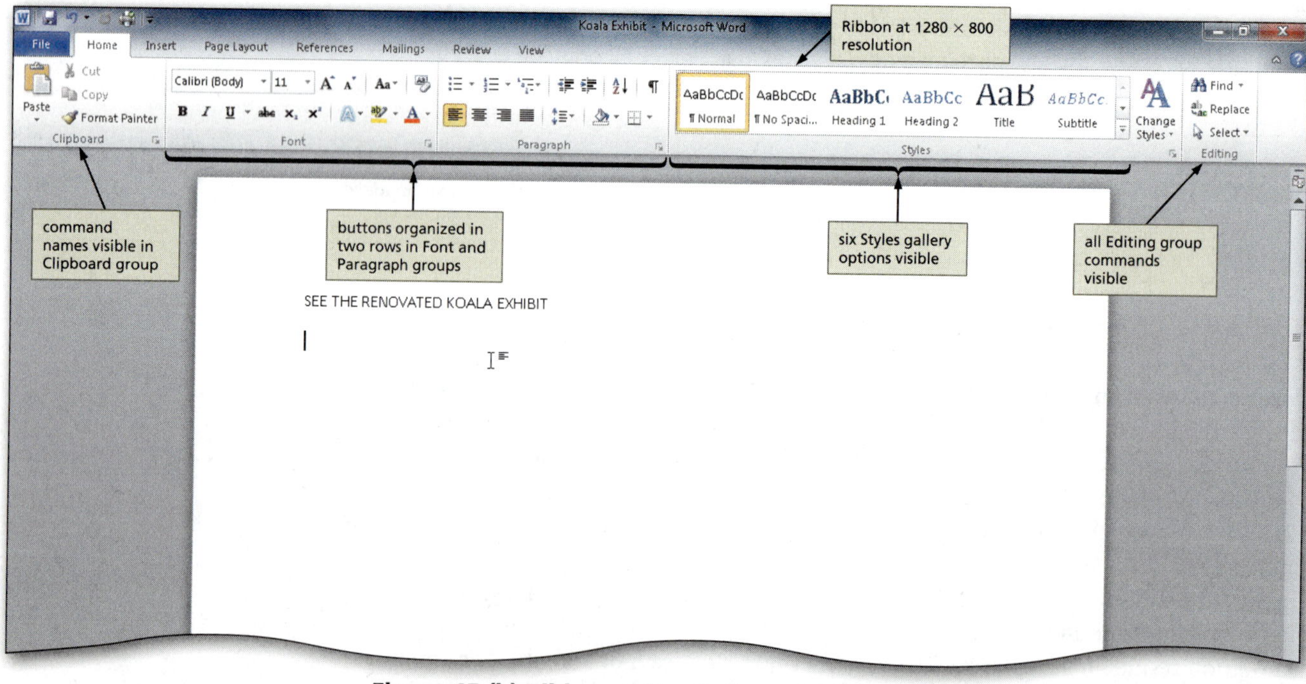

Figure 45 (b) Ribbon at Resolution of 1280 x 800

Comparing the two Ribbons in Figure 45, notice the changes in content and layout of the groups and galleries. In some cases, the content of a group is the same in each resolution, but the layout of the group differs. For example, the same gallery and buttons appear in the Styles groups in the two resolutions, but the layouts differ. In other cases, the content and layout are the same across the resolution, but the level of detail differs with the resolution. In the Clipboard group, when the resolution increases to 1280 × 800, the names of all the buttons in the group appear in addition to the buttons themselves. At the lower resolution, only the buttons appear.

To Change the Screen Resolution

If you are using a computer to step through the Office and Windows chapters in this book and you want your screen to match the figures, you may need to change your screen's resolution. The figures in the Office and Windows chapters in this book use a screen resolution of 1024 × 768. The following steps change the screen resolution to 1024 × 768. Your computer already may be set to 1024 × 768 or some other resolution. Keep in mind that many computer labs prevent users from changing the screen resolution; in that case, read the following steps for illustration purposes.

1

- Click the Show desktop button on the taskbar to display the Windows 7 desktop.
- Right-click an empty area on the Windows 7 desktop to display a shortcut menu that displays a list of commands related to the desktop (Figure 46).

Q&A

Why does my shortcut menu display different commands?

Depending on your computer's hardware and configuration, different commands might appear on the shortcut menu.

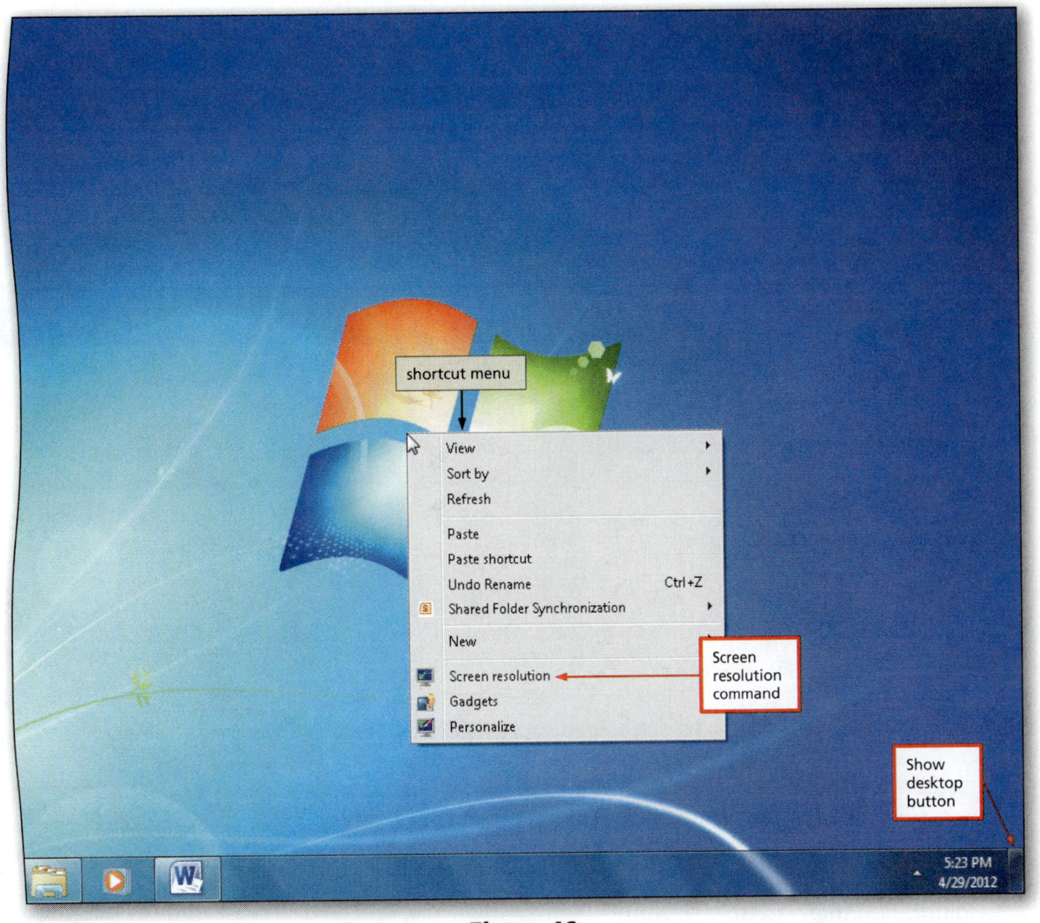

Figure 46

2

- Click Screen resolution on the shortcut menu to open the Screen Resolution window (Figure 47).

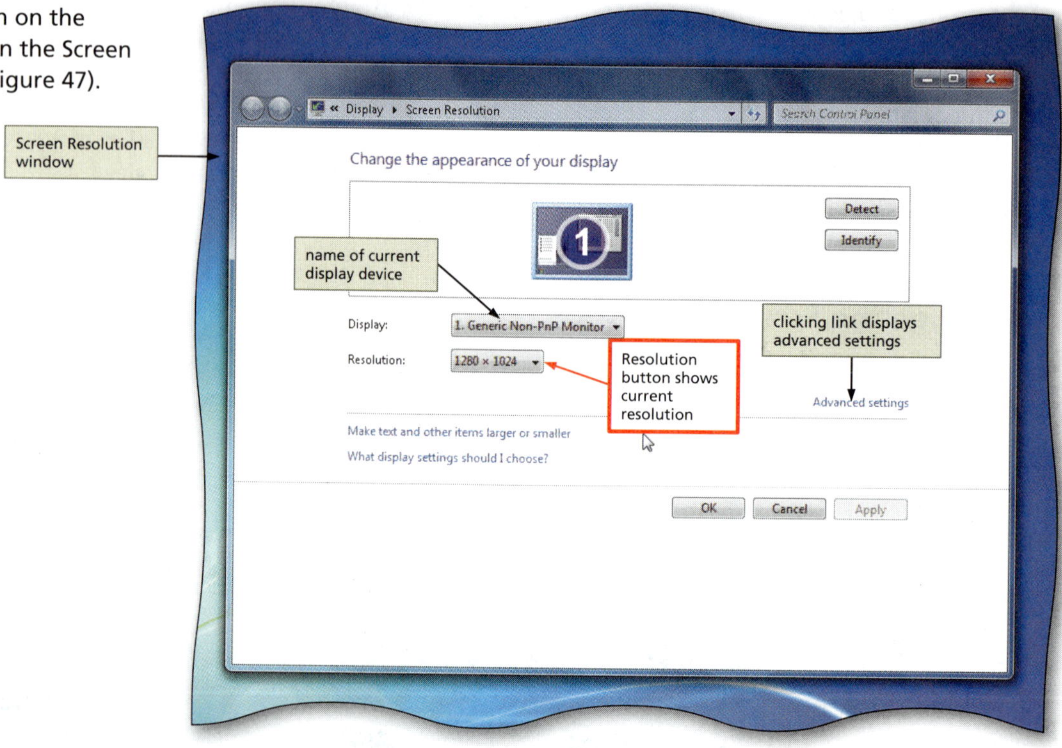

Figure 47

3

- Click the Resolution button in the Screen Resolution window to display the resolution slider.

Q&A

What is a slider?

A **slider** is an object that allows users to choose from multiple predetermined options. In most cases, these options represent some type of numeric value. In most cases, one end of the slider (usually the left or bottom) represents the lowest of available values, and the opposite end (usually the right or top) represents the highest available value.

4

- If necessary, drag the resolution slider until the desired screen resolution (in this case, 1024 × 768) is selected (Figure 48).

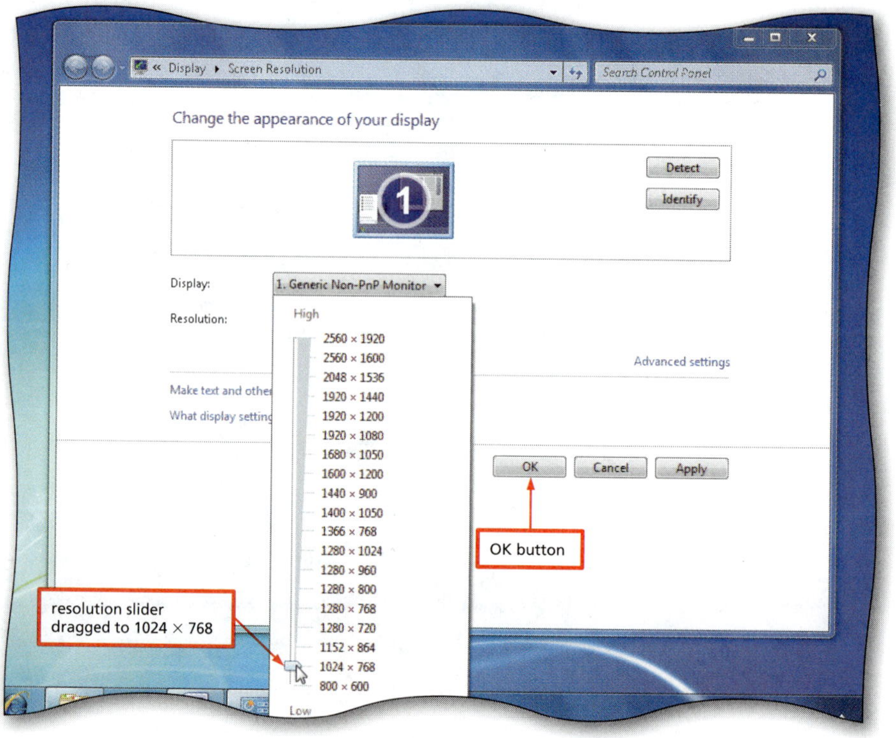

Figure 48

Q&A

What if my computer does not support the 1024 × 768 resolution?

Some computers do not support the 1024 × 768 resolution. In this case, select a resolution that is close to the 1024 × 768 resolution.

5

- Click an empty area of the Screen Resolution window to close the resolution slider.
- Click the OK button to change the screen resolution and display the Display Settings dialog box (Figure 49).
- Click the Keep changes button (Display Settings dialog box) to accept the new screen resolution.

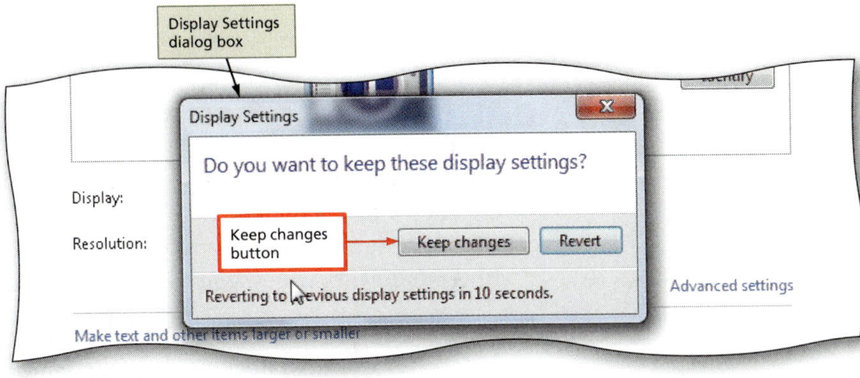

Figure 49

Q&A Why does a message display stating that the image quality can be improved?

Some computer monitors are designed to display contents better at a certain screen resolution, sometimes referred to as an optimal resolution.

To Quit an Office Program with One Document Open

When you quit an Office program, such as Word, if you have made changes to a file since the last time the file was saved, the Office program displays a dialog box asking if you want save the changes you made to the file before it closes the program window. The dialog box contains three buttons with these resulting actions: the Save button saves the changes and then quits the Office program, the Don't Save button quits the Office program without saving changes, and the Cancel button closes the dialog box and redisplays the file without saving the changes.

If no changes have been made to an open document since the last time the file was saved, the Office program will close the window without displaying a dialog box.

The following steps quit an Office program. In the following example, Word is used to illustrate quitting an Office program; however, you would follow the same steps regardless of the Office program you were using.

1

- If necessary, click the Word program button on the taskbar to display the Word window on the desktop.
- Point to the Close button on the right side of the program's title bar, Word in this case (Figure 50).

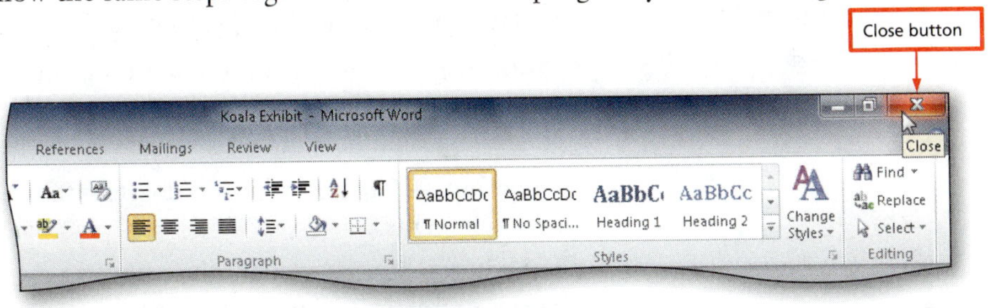

Figure 50

2

- Click the Close button to close the document and quit Word.

Q&A What if I have more than one document open in an Office program?

You would click the Close button for each open document. When you click the last open document's Close button, the Office program also quits. As an alternative, you could click File on the Ribbon to open the Backstage view and then click Exit in the Backstage view to close all open documents and quit the Office program.

Q&A What is the Backstage view?

The **Backstage view** contains a set of commands that enable you to manage documents and data about the documents. The Backstage view is discussed in more depth later in this chapter.

3

- If a Microsoft Word dialog box appears, click the Save button to save any changes made to the document since the last save.

Other Ways

1. Right-click the Office program button on Windows 7 taskbar, click Close window or 'Close all windows' on shortcut menu
2. Press ALT+F4

Break Point: If you wish to take a break, this is a good place to do so. To resume at a later time, continue to follow the steps from this location forward.

Additional Microsoft Office Programs

The previous section used Word to illustrate common features of Office and some basic elements unique to Word. The following sections present elements unique to PowerPoint, Excel, and Access, as well as illustrate additional common features of Office.

In the following pages, you will learn how to do the following:

1. Start an Office program (PowerPoint) using the search box.
2. Create two small documents in the same Office program (PowerPoint).
3. Close one of the documents.
4. Reopen the document just closed.
5. Create a document in a different Office program (Excel).
6. Save the document with a new file name.
7. Create a file in a different Office program (Access).
8. Close the file and then open the file.

PowerPoint

PowerPoint is a complete presentation program that allows you to produce professional-looking presentations (Figure 51). A PowerPoint **presentation** also is called a **slide show**. PowerPoint contains several features to simplify creating a slide show. To make presentations more impressive, you can add diagrams, tables, pictures, video, sound, and animation effects. Additional PowerPoint features include the following:

- **Word processing** — Create bulleted lists, combine words and images, find and replace text, and use multiple fonts and font sizes.
- **Outlining** — Develop a presentation using an outline format. You also can import outlines from Microsoft Word or other word processing programs, including single-level and multilevel lists.
- **Charting** — Create and insert charts into presentations and then add effects and chart elements.
- **Drawing** — Create and modify diagrams using shapes such as arcs, arrows, cubes, rectangles, stars, and triangles. Then, customize and add effects to the diagrams, and arrange these objects by sizing, scaling, and rotating them.
- **Inserting multimedia** — Insert artwork and multimedia effects into a slide show. The Microsoft Clip Organizer, included with Office programs, contains hundreds of media files, including pictures, sounds, and movies.
- **Saving to the Web** — Save presentations or parts of a presentation so that they can be viewed in a Web browser. You can publish your slide show to the Internet or to an intranet.
- **E-mailing** — Send an entire slide show as an attachment to an e-mail message.
- **Collaborating** — Share a presentation with friends and coworkers. Ask them to review the slides and then insert comments that offer suggestions to enhance the presentation.
- **Preparing delivery** — Rehearse integrating PowerPoint slides into your speech by setting timings, using presentation tools, showing only selected slides in a presentation, and packaging the presentation for an optical disc.

Figure 51 (a) Slide 1 (Title)

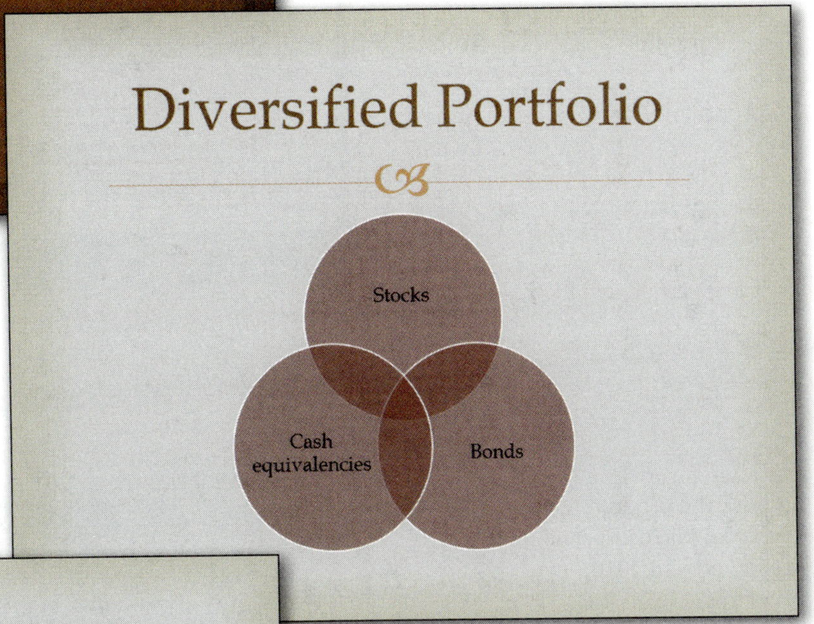

Figure 51 (b) Slide 2 (Text and Diagram)

Figure 51 (c) Slide 3 (Text and Picture)

To Start a Program Using the Search Box

The steps on the next page, which assume Windows 7 is running, use the search box to start the PowerPoint Office program based on a typical installation; however, you would follow similar steps to start any Office program. You may need to ask your instructor how to start programs for your computer.

1

- Click the Start button on the Windows 7 taskbar to display the Start menu.

2

- Type `Microsoft PowerPoint` as the search text in the 'Search programs and files' text box and watch the search results appear on the Start menu (Figure 52).

Q&A

Do I need to type the complete program name or correct capitalization?

No, just enough of it for the program name to appear on the Start menu. For example, you may be able to type PowerPoint or powerpoint, instead of Microsoft PowerPoint.

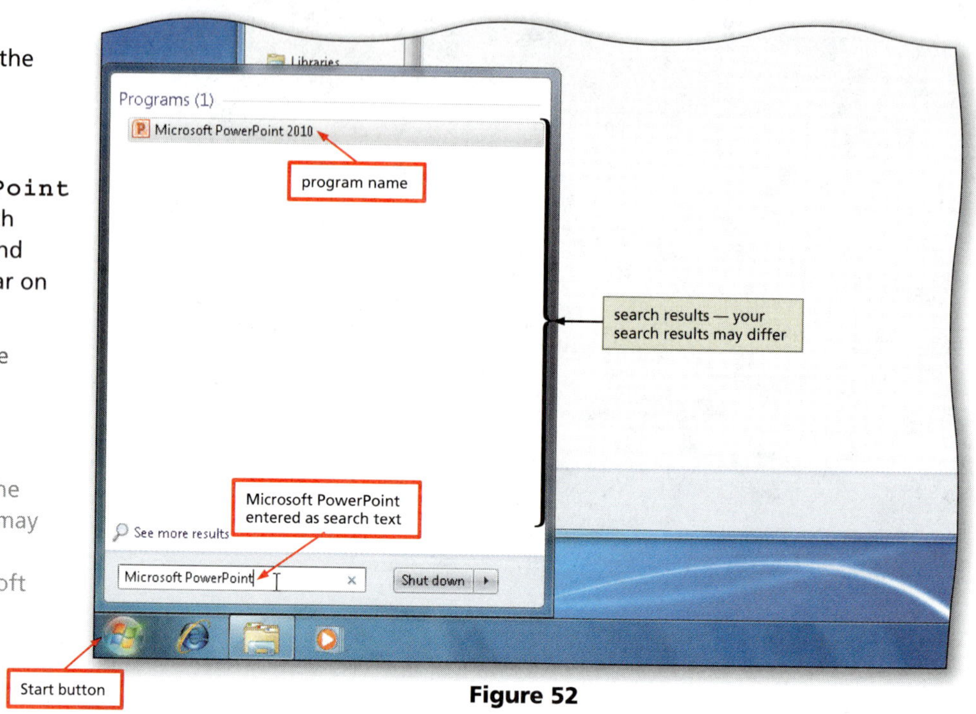

Figure 52

3

- Click the program name, Microsoft PowerPoint 2010 in this case, in the search results on the Start menu to start PowerPoint and display a new blank presentation in the PowerPoint window.
- If the program window is not maximized, click the Maximize button on its title bar to maximize the window (Figure 53).

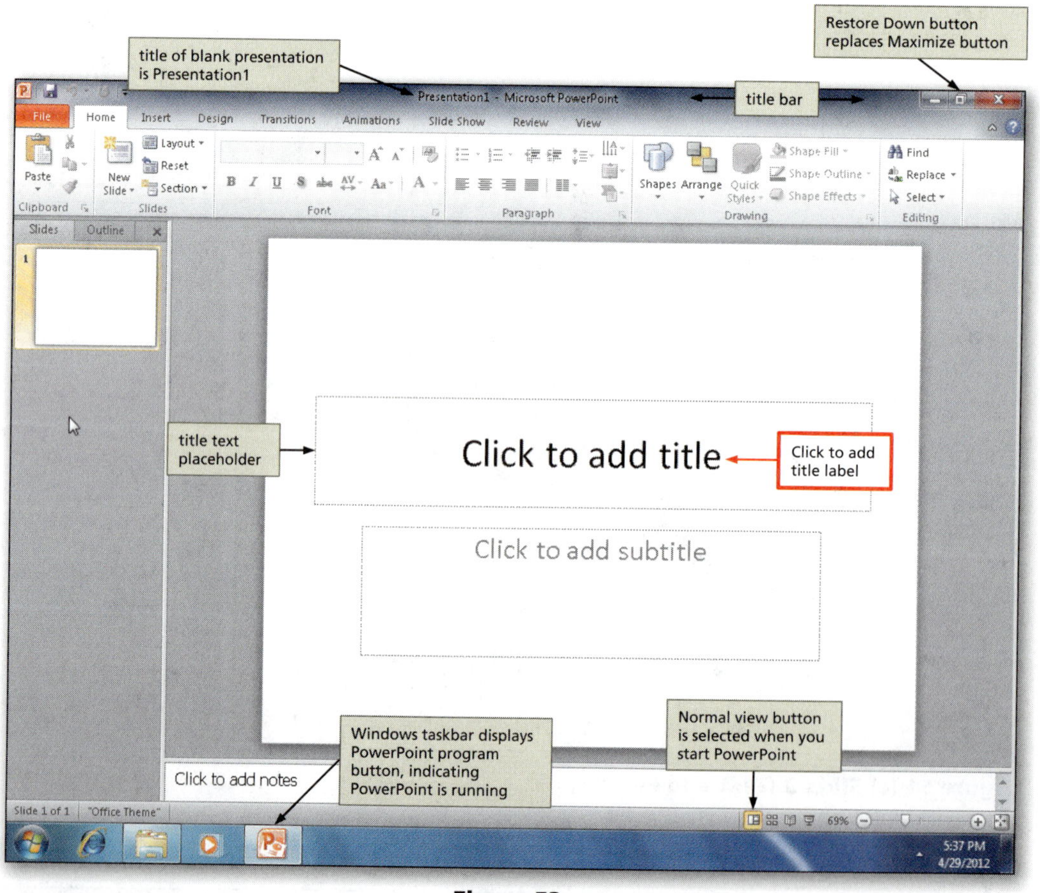

Figure 53

The PowerPoint Window and Ribbon

The PowerPoint window consists of a variety of components to make your work more efficient and documents more professional: the window, Ribbon, Mini toolbar, shortcut menus, and Quick Access Toolbar. Many of these components are common to other Office programs and have been discussed earlier in this chapter. Other components, discussed in the following paragraphs, are unique to PowerPoint.

The basic unit of a PowerPoint presentation is a **slide**. A slide may contain text and objects, such as graphics, tables, charts, and drawings. **Layouts** are used to position this content on the slide. When you create a new presentation, the default **Title Slide** layout appears (Figure 54). The purpose of this layout is to introduce the presentation to the audience. PowerPoint includes eight other built-in standard layouts.

The default slide layouts are set up in **landscape orientation**, where the slide width is greater than its height. In landscape orientation, the slide size is preset to 10 inches wide and 7.5 inches high when printed on a standard sheet of paper measuring 11 inches wide and 8.5 inches high.

BTW

Portrait Orientation
If your slide content is dominantly vertical, such as a skyscraper or a person, consider changing the slide layout to a portrait orientation. To change the orientation to portrait, click the Slide Orientation button (Design tab | Page Setup group) and then click Portrait. You can use both landscape and portrait orientation in the same slide show.

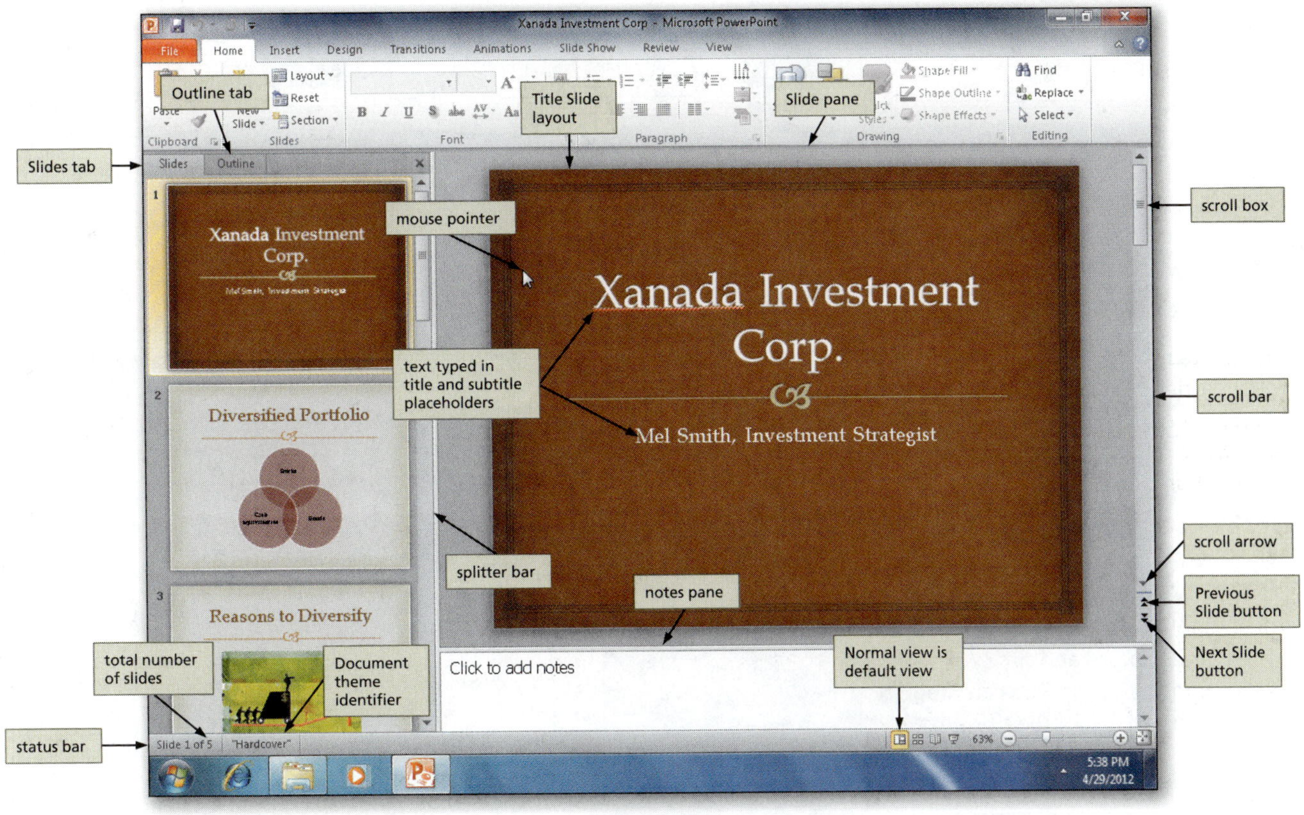

Figure 54

Placeholders **Placeholders** are boxes with dotted or hatch-marked borders that are displayed when you create a new slide. All layouts except the Blank slide layout contain placeholders. Depending on the particular slide layout selected, title and subtitle placeholders are displayed for the slide title and subtitle; a content text placeholder is displayed for text, art, or a table, chart, picture, graphic, or movie. The title slide in Figure 53 has two text placeholders for the main heading, or title, of a new slide and the subtitle.

Ribbon The Ribbon in PowerPoint is similar to the one in Word and the other Microsoft Office programs. When you start PowerPoint, the Ribbon displays nine main tabs: File, Home, Insert, Design, Transitions, Animations, Slide Show, Review, and View.

To Enter Content in a Title Slide

With the exception of a blank slide and a slide with a picture and caption, PowerPoint assumes every new slide has a title. Many of PowerPoint's layouts have both a title text placeholder and at least one content placeholder. To make creating a presentation easier, any text you type after a new slide appears becomes title text in the title text placeholder. As you begin typing text in the title text placeholder, the title text also is displayed in the Slide 1 thumbnail in the Slides tab. The presentation title for this presentation is Xanada Investments. The following steps enter a presentation title on the title slide.

1

- Click the label 'Click to add title' located inside the title text placeholder (shown in Figure 53 on page OFF 38) to select the placeholder (Figure 55).

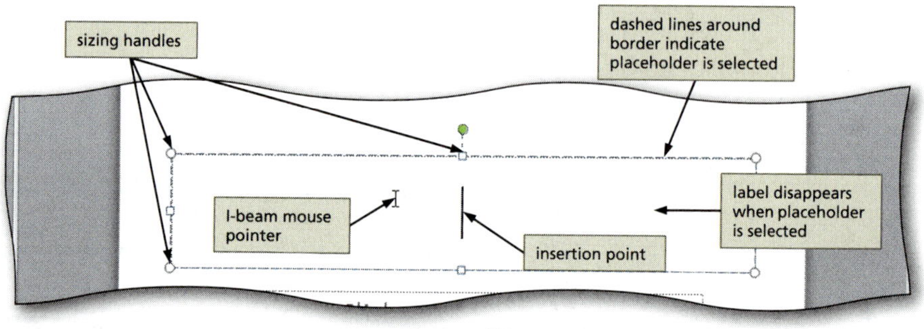

Figure 55

2

- Type **Xanada Investments** in the title text placeholder. Do not press the ENTER key because you do not want to create a new line of text (Figure 56).

Q&A

What are the white squares and circles that appear around the title text placeholder as I type the presentation title?

The white squares and circles are sizing handles, which you can drag to change the size of the title text placeholder. Sizing handles also can be found around other placeholders and objects within a presentation.

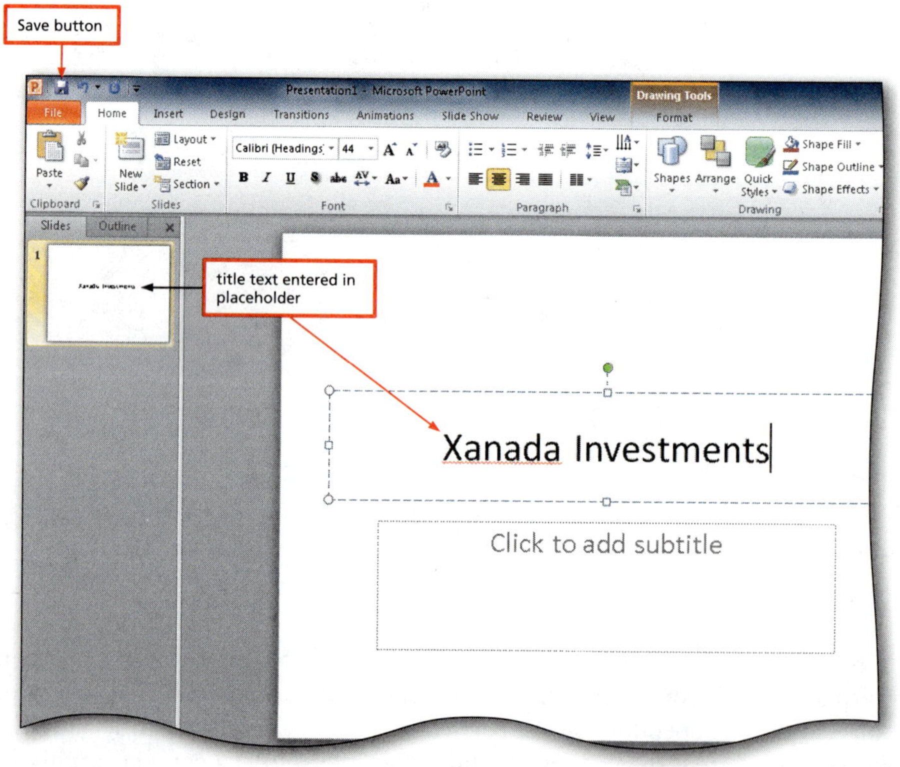

Figure 56

To Save a File in a Folder

The following steps save the presentation in the PowerPoint folder in the class folder (CIS 101, in this case) on a USB flash drive using the file name, Xanada Investments.

1. With a USB flash drive connected to one of the computer's USB ports, click the Save button on the Quick Access Toolbar to display the Save As dialog box.

2. If necessary, type `Xanada Investments` in the File name text box to change the file name. Do not press the ENTER key after typing the file name because you do not want to close the dialog box at this time.

3. Navigate to the desired save location (in this case, the PowerPoint folder in the CIS 101 folder [or your class folder] on the USB flash drive). For specific instructions, perform the tasks in Steps 3a through 3g.

3a. If a navigation pane is not displayed in the Save As dialog box, click the Browse Folders button to expand the dialog box.

3b. If Computer is not displayed in the navigation pane, drag the navigation pane scroll bar (Save As dialog box) until Computer appears.

3c. If Computer is not expanded in the navigation pane, double-click Computer to display a list of available storage devices in the navigation pane.

3d. If necessary, scroll through the Save As dialog box until your USB flash drive appears in the list of available storage devices in the navigation pane.

3e. If your USB flash drive is not expanded, double-click the USB flash drive in the list of available storage devices in the navigation pane to select that drive as the new save location and display its contents in the right pane.

3f. If your class folder (CIS 101, in this case) is not expanded, double-click the CIS 101 folder to select the folder and display its contents.

3g. Click the PowerPoint folder to select it as the new save location and display its contents in the right pane.

4. Click the Save button (Save As dialog box) to save the presentation in the selected folder on the selected drive with the entered file name.

To Create a New Office Document from the Backstage View

As discussed earlier, the Backstage view contains a set of commands that enable you to manage documents and data about the documents. From the Backstage view in PowerPoint, for example, you can create, open, print, and save presentations. You also can share documents, manage versions, set permissions, and modify document properties. In other Office 2010 programs, the Backstage view may contain features specific to those programs. The steps on the following pages create a file, a blank presentation in this case, from the Backstage view.

1

- Click File on the Ribbon to open the Backstage view (Figure 57).

Q&A What is the purpose of the File tab?

The **File** tab is used to display the Backstage view for each Office program.

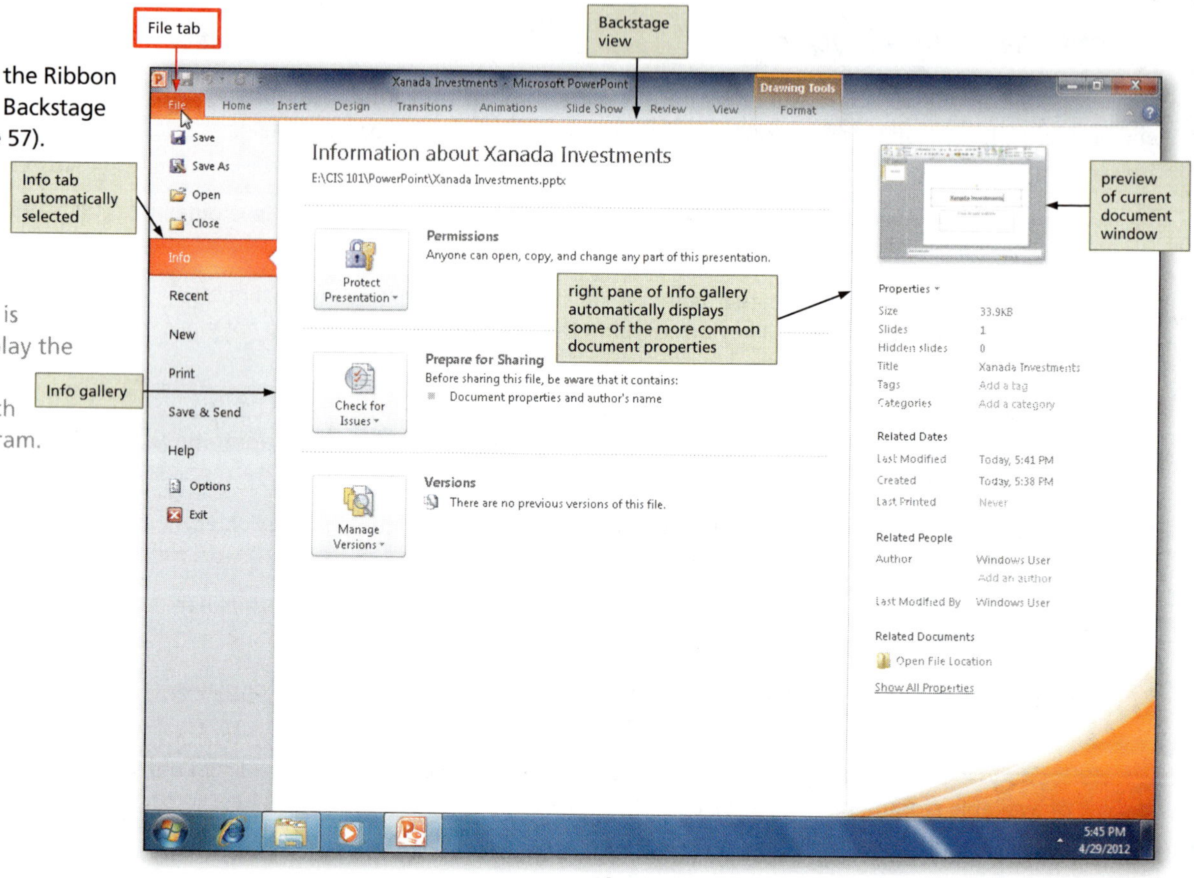

Figure 57

2

- Click the New tab in the Backstage view to display the New gallery (Figure 58).

Q&A Can I create documents through the Backstage view in other Office programs?

Yes. If the Office program has a New tab in the Backstage view, the New gallery displays various options for creating a new file.

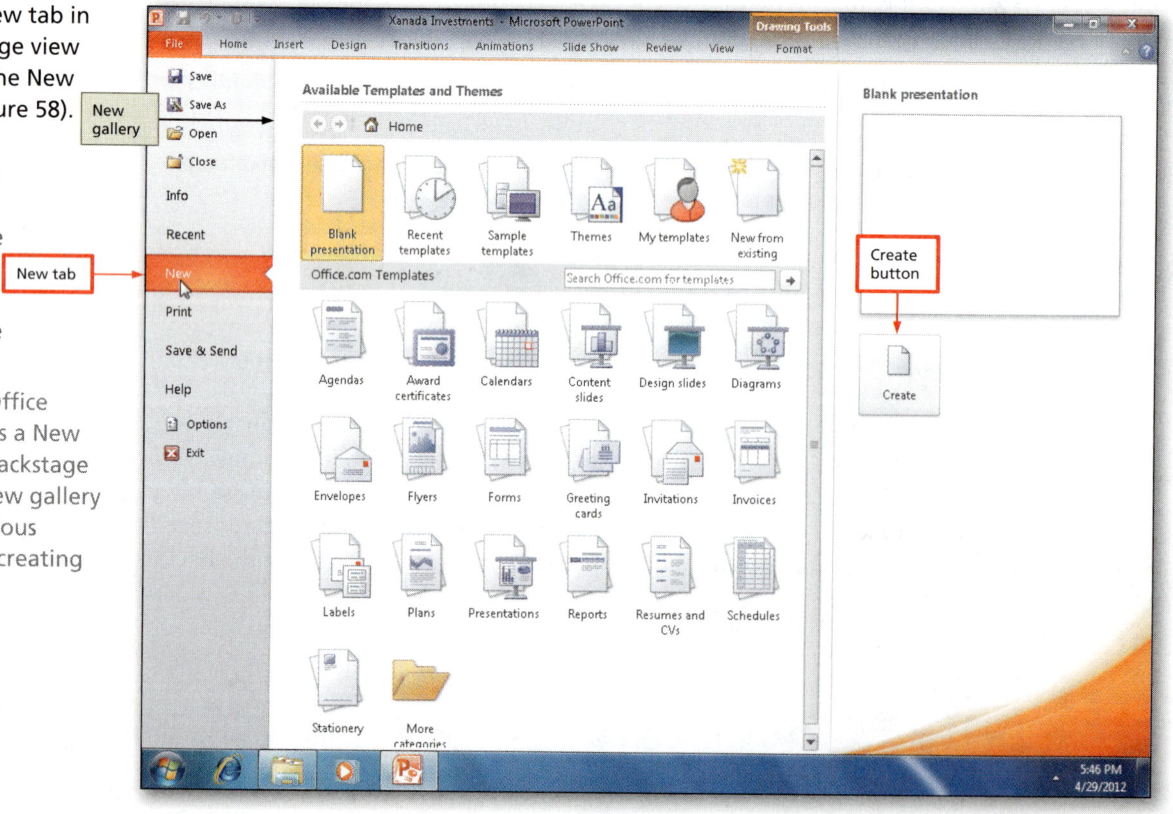

Figure 58

3

- Click the Create button in the New gallery to create a new presentation (Figure 59).

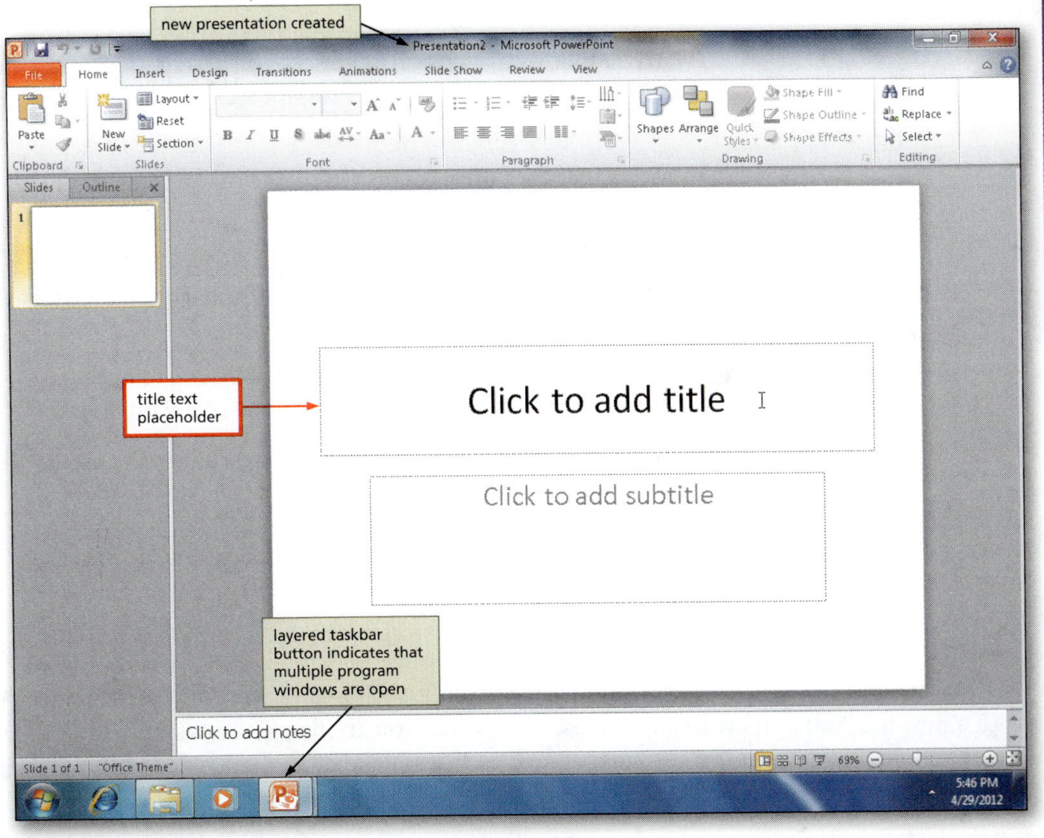

Figure 59

Other Ways
1. Press CTRL+N

To Enter Content in a Title Slide of a Second PowerPoint Presentation

The presentation title for this presentation is Koala Exhibit Gala. The following steps enter a presentation title on the title slide.

1 Click the title text placeholder (shown in Figure 59) to select it.

2 Type `Koala Exhibit Gala` in the title text placeholder. Do not press the ENTER key (Figure 60).

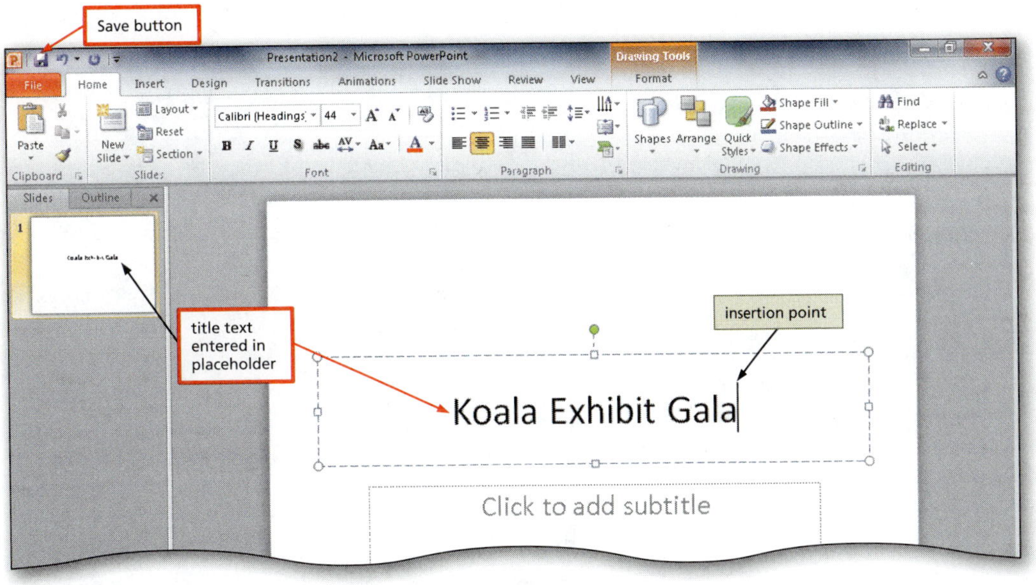

Figure 60

To Save a File in a Folder

The following steps save the second presentation in the PowerPoint folder in the class folder (CIS 101, in this case) on a USB flash drive using the file name, Koala Exhibit Gala.

1. With a USB flash drive connected to one of the computer's USB ports, click the Save button on the Quick Access Toolbar to display the Save As dialog box.
2. If necessary, type **`Koala Exhibit Gala`** in the File name text box to change the file name. Do not press the ENTER key after typing the file name because you do not want to close the dialog box at this time.
3. If necessary, navigate to the desired save location (in this case, the PowerPoint folder in the CIS 101 folder [or your class folder] on the USB flash drive).
4. Click the Save button (Save As dialog box) to save the presentation in the selected folder on the selected drive with the entered file name.

To Close an Office File Using the Backstage View

Sometimes, you may want to close an Office file, such as a PowerPoint presentation, entirely and start over with a new file. You also may want to close a file when you are finished working with it so that you can begin a new file. The following steps close the current active Office file, that is, the Koala Exhibit Gala presentation, without quitting the active program (PowerPoint in this case).

1

- Click File on the Ribbon to open the Backstage view (Figure 61).

2

- Click Close in the Backstage view to close the open file (Koala Exhibit Gala, in this case) without quitting the active program.

Q&A What if the Office program displays a dialog box about saving?

Click the Save button if you want to save the changes, click the Don't Save button if you want to ignore the changes since the last time you saved, and click the Cancel button if you do not want to close the document.

Q&A Can I use the Backstage view to close an open file in other Office programs, such as Word and Excel?

Yes.

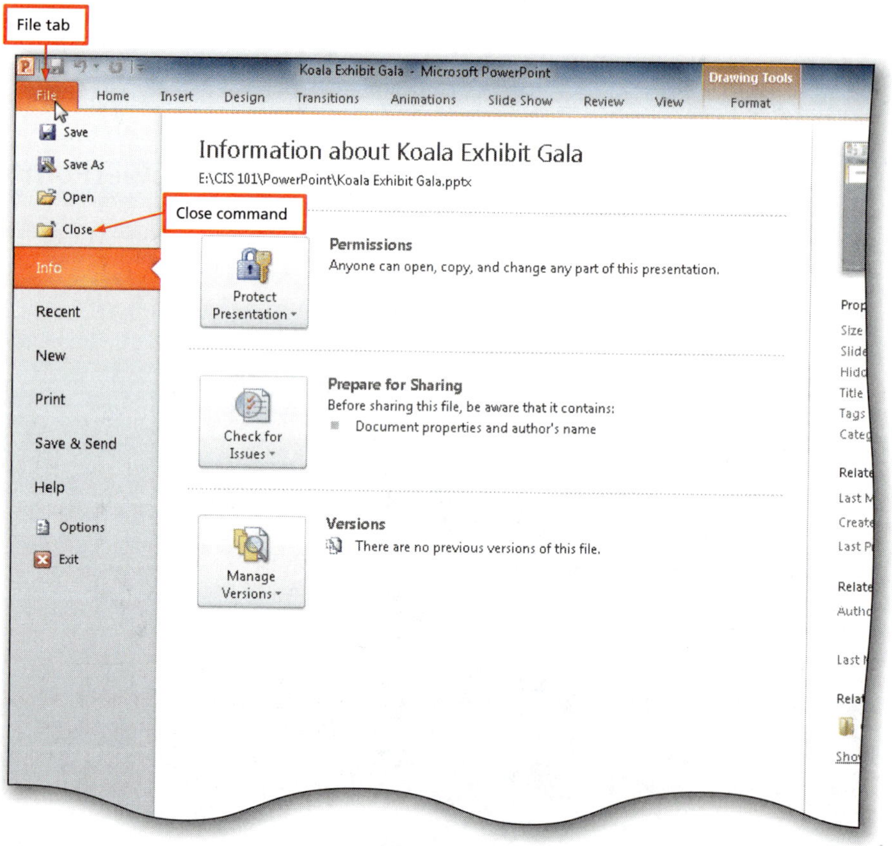

Figure 61

To Open a Recent Office File Using the Backstage View

You sometimes need to open a file that you recently modified. You may have more changes to make such as adding more content or correcting errors. The Backstage view allows you to access recent files easily. The following steps reopen the Koala Exhibit Gala file just closed.

1

- Click File on the Ribbon to open the Backstage view.
- Click the Recent tab in the Backstage view to display the Recent gallery (Figure 62).

2

- Click the desired file name in the Recent gallery, Koala Exhibit Gala in this case, to open the file (shown in Figure 60 on page OFF 43).

Q&A Can I use the Backstage view to open a recent file in other Office programs, such as Word and Excel?

Yes, as long as the file name appears in the list of recent files in the Recent gallery.

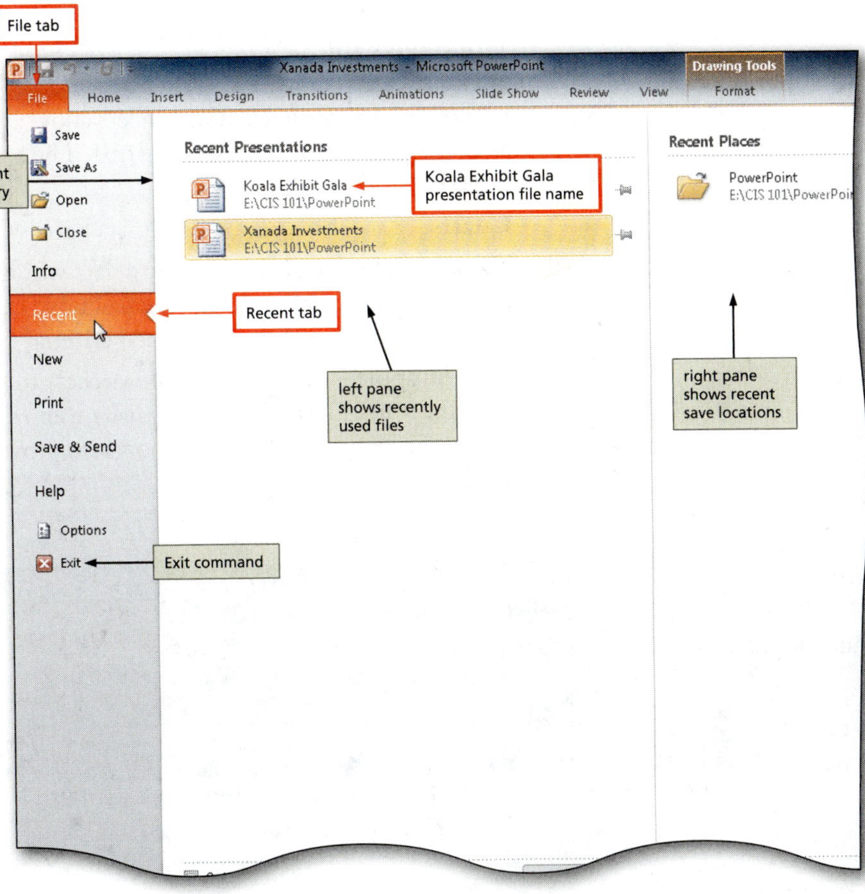

Figure 62

Other Ways

1. Click Start button, point to program name, click file name on submenu
2. Click File on Ribbon, click Open in Backstage view, navigate to file (Open dialog box), click Open button

To Quit an Office Program

You are finished using PowerPoint. Thus, you should quit this Office program. The following steps quit PowerPoint.

1 If you have one Office document open, click the Close button on the right side of the title bar to close the document and quit the Office program; or if you have multiple Office documents open, click File on the Ribbon to open the Backstage view and then click Exit in the Backstage view to close all open documents and quit the Office program.

2 If a dialog box appears, click the Save button to save any changes made to the document since the last save.

Excel

Excel is a powerful spreadsheet program that allows users to organize data, complete calculations, make decisions, graph data, develop professional-looking reports (Figure 63), publish organized data to the Web, and access real-time data from Web sites. The four major parts of Excel are:

- **Workbooks and Worksheets** - A **workbook** is like a notebook. Inside the workbook are sheets, each of which is called a **worksheet**. In other words, a workbook is a collection of worksheets. Worksheets allow users to enter, calculate, manipulate, and analyze data such as numbers and text. The terms worksheet and spreadsheet are interchangeable.
- **Charts** - Excel can draw a variety of charts.
- **Tables** - Tables organize and store data within worksheets. For example, once a user enters data into a worksheet, an Excel table can sort the data, search for specific data, and select data that satisfies defined criteria.
- **Web Support** - Web support allows users to save Excel worksheets or parts of a worksheet in HTML format, so that a user can view and manipulate the worksheet using a browser. Excel Web support also provides access to real-time data, such as stock quotes, using Web queries.

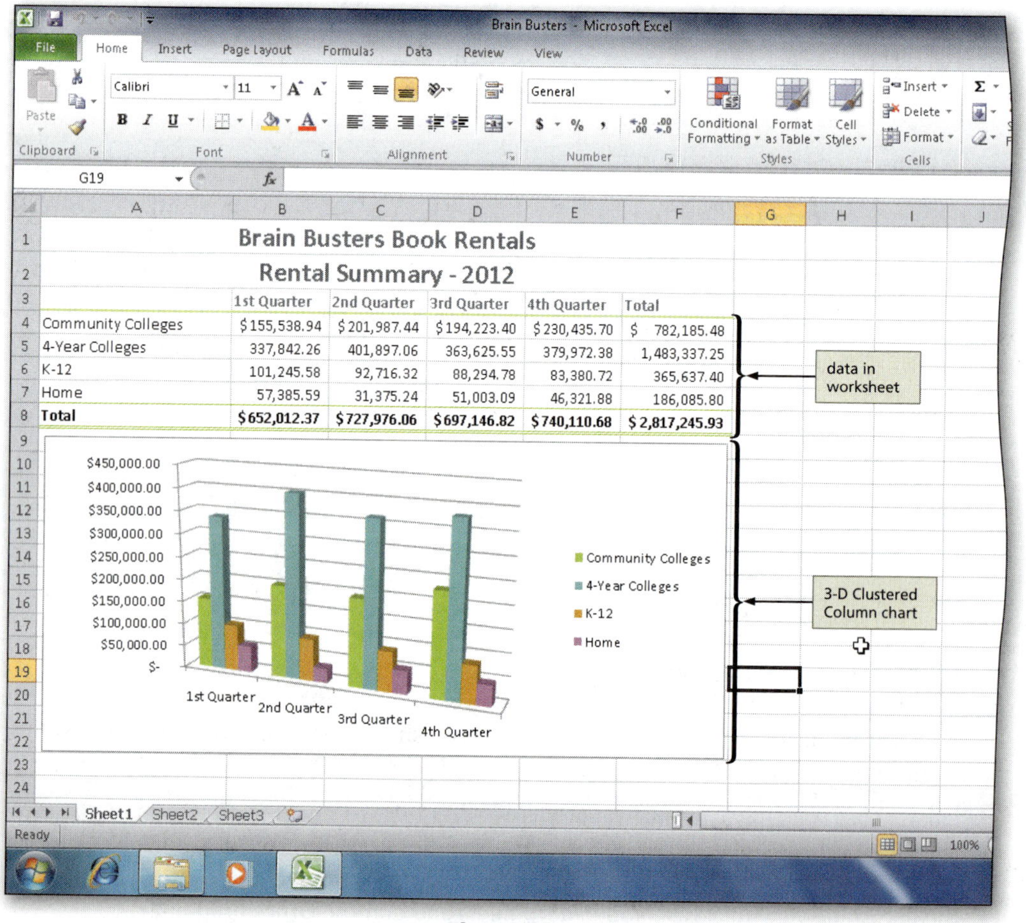

Figure 63

To Create a New Blank Office Document from Windows Explorer

Windows Explorer provides a means to create a blank Office document without ever starting an Office program. The following steps use Windows Explorer to create a blank Excel document.

1

- If necessary, click the Windows Explorer program button on the taskbar to make the folder window the active window in Windows Explorer.
- Double-click your class folder (CIS 101, in this case) in the navigation pane to display the contents of the selected folder.
- Double-click the Excel folder to display its contents in the right pane.
- With the Excel folder selected, right-click an open area in the right pane to display a shortcut menu.
- Point to New on the shortcut menu to display the New submenu (Figure 64).

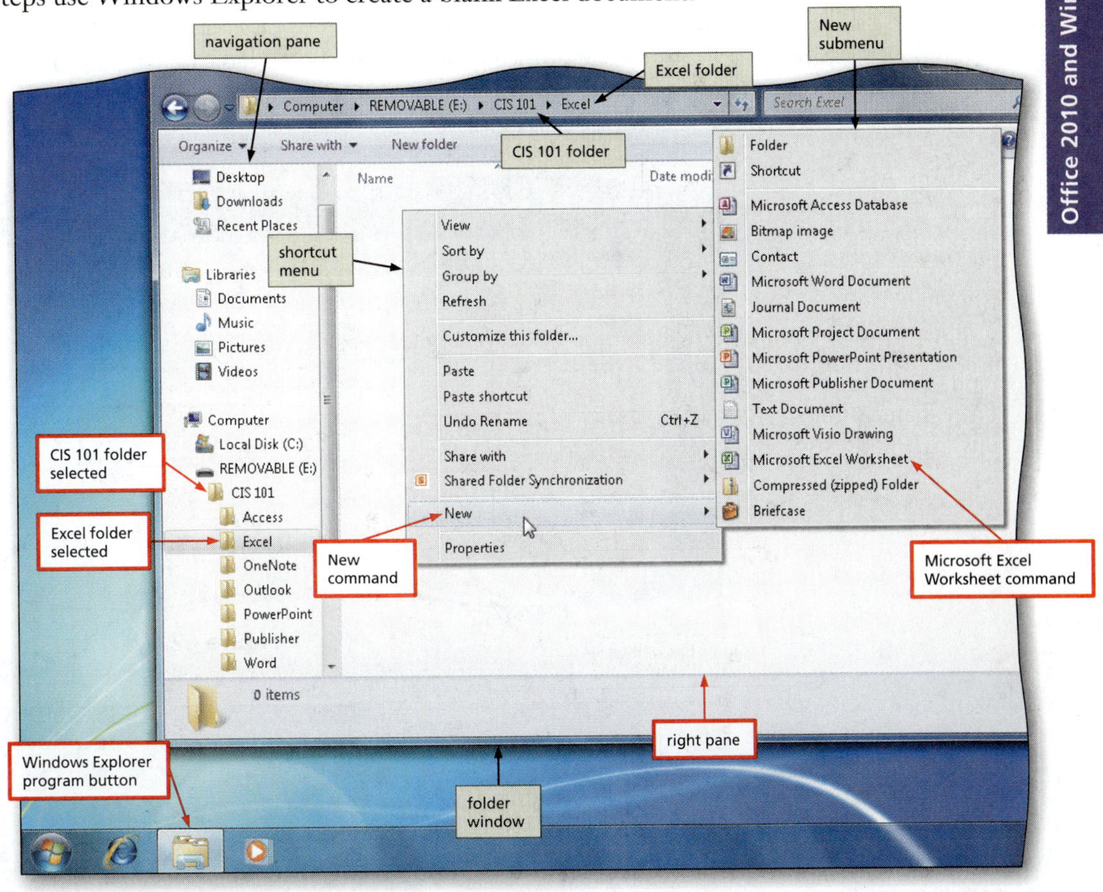

Figure 64

2

- Click Microsoft Excel Worksheet on the New submenu to display an icon and text box for a new file in the current folder window (Figure 65).

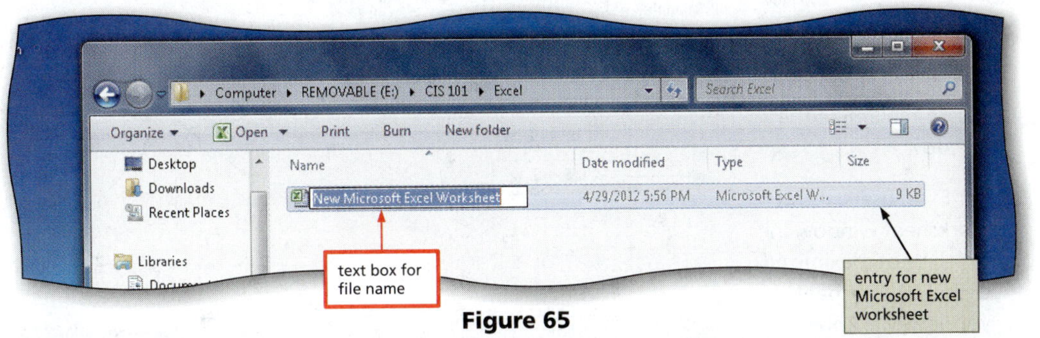

Figure 65

3

- Type `Brain Busters` in the text box and then press the ENTER key to assign a name to the new file in the current folder (Figure 66).

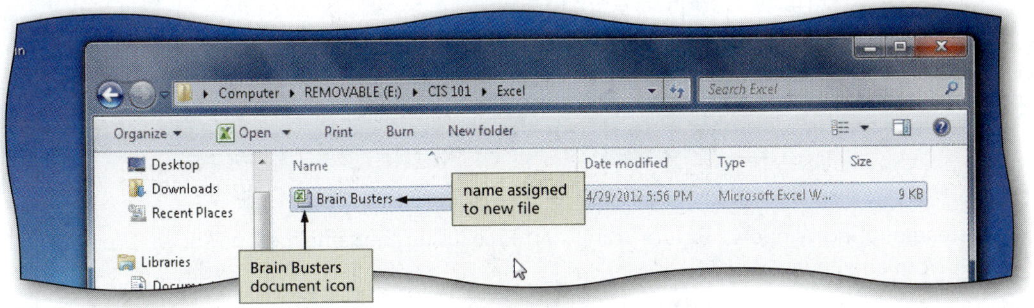

Figure 66

To Start a Program from Windows Explorer and Open a File

Previously, you learned how to start an Office program using the Start menu and the search box. Another way start an Office program is to open an existing file from Windows Explorer, which causes the program in which the file was created to start and then open the selected file. The following steps, which assume Windows 7 is running, use Windows Explorer to start the Excel Office program based on a typical installation. You may need to ask your instructor how to start Office programs for your computer.

1

- If necessary, display the file to open in the folder window in Windows Explorer (shown in Figure 66 on the previous page).
- Right-click the file icon or file name (Brain Busters, in this case) to display a shortcut menu (Figure 67).

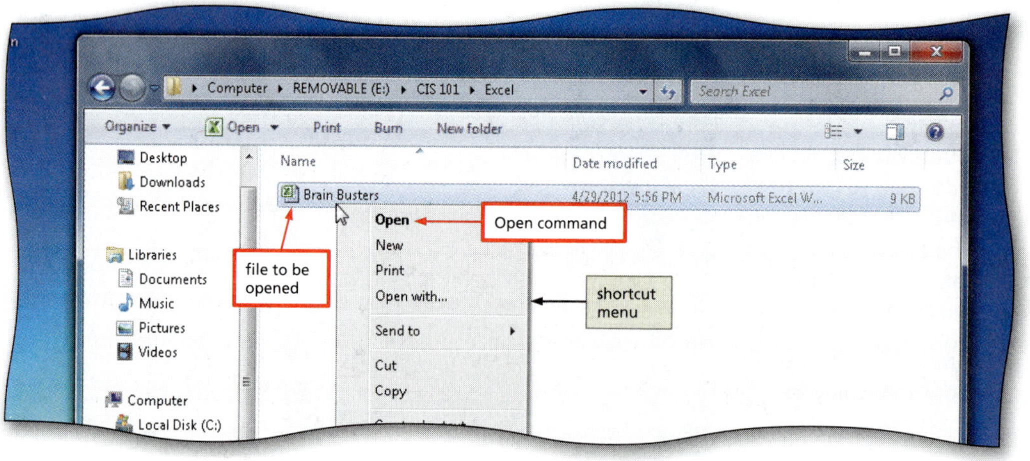

Figure 67

2

- Click Open on the shortcut menu to open the selected file in the program used to create the file, Microsoft Excel in this case (Figure 68).
- If the program window is not maximized, click the Maximize button on the title bar to maximize the window.
- For Excel users, if the worksheet window in Excel is not maximized, click the worksheet window Maximize button to maximize the worksheet window within Excel.

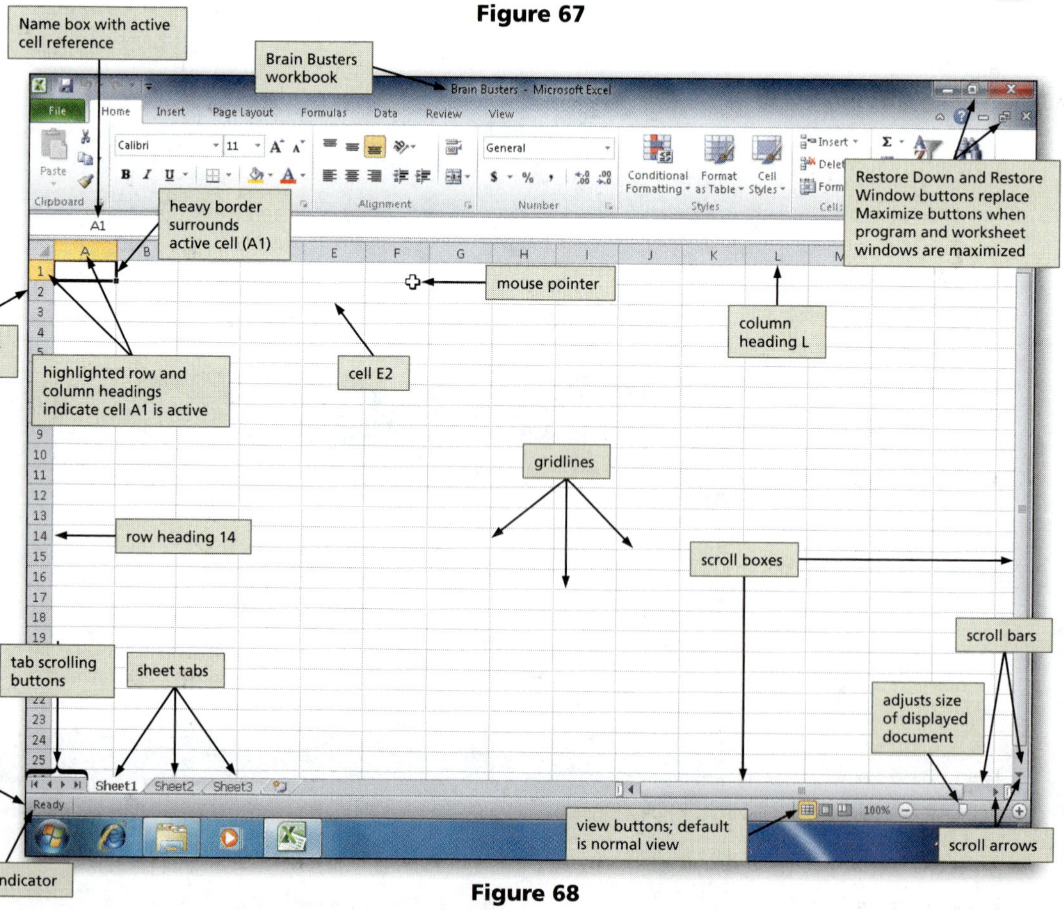

Figure 68

Q&A

Instead of using Windows Explorer, can I start Excel using the same method shown previously for Word and PowerPoint?

Yes, you can use any method of starting an Office program to start Excel.

Unique Features of Excel

The Excel window consists of a variety of components to make your work more efficient and worksheets more professional. These include the document window, Ribbon, Mini toolbar and shortcut menus, Quick Access Toolbar, and the Backstage view. Some of these components are common to other Microsoft Office 2010 programs; others are unique to Excel.

Excel opens a new workbook with three worksheets. If necessary, you can add additional worksheets as long as your computer has enough memory to accommodate them.

Each worksheet has a sheet name that appears on a **sheet tab** at the bottom of the workbook. For example, Sheet1 is the name of the active worksheet displayed in the Brain Busters workbook. If you click the sheet tab labeled Sheet2, Excel displays the Sheet2 worksheet.

The Worksheet The worksheet is organized into a rectangular grid containing vertical columns and horizontal rows. A column letter above the grid, also called the **column heading**, identifies each column. A row number on the left side of the grid, also called the **row heading**, identifies each row. With the screen resolution set to 1024 × 768 and the Excel window maximized, Excel displays 15 columns (A through O) and 25 rows (1 through 25) of the worksheet on the screen, as shown in Figure 68.

The intersection of each column and row is a cell. A **cell** is the basic unit of a worksheet into which you enter data. Each worksheet in a workbook has 16,384 columns and 1,048,576 rows for a total of 17,179,869,180 cells. Only a small fraction of the active worksheet appears on the screen at one time.

A cell is referred to by its unique address, or **cell reference**, which is the coordinates of the intersection of a column and a row. To identify a cell, specify the column letter first, followed by the row number. For example, cell reference E2 refers to the cell located at the intersection of column E and row 2 (Figure 68).

One cell on the worksheet, designated the **active cell**, is the one into which you can enter data. The active cell in Figure 68 is A1. The active cell is identified in three ways. First, a heavy border surrounds the cell; second, the active cell reference shows immediately above column A in the Name box; and third, the column heading A and row heading 1 are highlighted so it is easy to see which cell is active (Figure 68).

The horizontal and vertical lines on the worksheet itself are called **gridlines**. Gridlines make it easier to see and identify each cell in the worksheet. If desired, you can turn the gridlines off so that they do not show on the worksheet, but it is recommended that you leave them on for now.

The mouse pointer in Figure 68 has the shape of a block plus sign. The mouse pointer appears as a block plus sign whenever it is located in a cell on the worksheet. Another common shape of the mouse pointer is the block arrow. The mouse pointer turns into the block arrow when you move it outside the worksheet or when you drag cell contents between rows or columns. The other mouse pointer shapes are described when they appear on the screen.

Ribbon When you start Excel, the Ribbon displays eight main tabs: File, Home, Insert, Page Layout, Formulas, Data, Review, and View. The Formulas and Data tabs are specific to Excel. The Formulas tab allows you to work with Excel formulas, and the Data tab allows you to work with data processing features such as importing and sorting data.

BTW

The Worksheet Size and Window
The 16,384 columns and 1,048,576 rows in Excel make for a huge worksheet that – if you could imagine – takes up the entire side of a building to display in its entirety. Your computer screen, by comparison, is a small window that allows you to view only a minute area of the worksheet at one time. While you cannot see the entire worksheet, you can move the window over the worksheet to view any part of it.

BTW

Customizing the Ribbon
In addition to customizing the Quick Access Toolbar, you can add items to and remove items from the Ribbon. To customize the Ribbon, click File on the Ribbon to open the Backstage view, click Options in the Backstage view, and then click Customize Ribbon in the left pane of the Options dialog box.

Formula Bar The formula bar appears below the Ribbon (Figure 69). As you type, Excel displays the entry in the **formula bar**. You can make the formula bar larger by dragging the sizing handle at the bottom of the formula bar or clicking the expand button to the right of the formula bar. Excel also displays the active cell reference in the **Name box** on the left side of the formula bar.

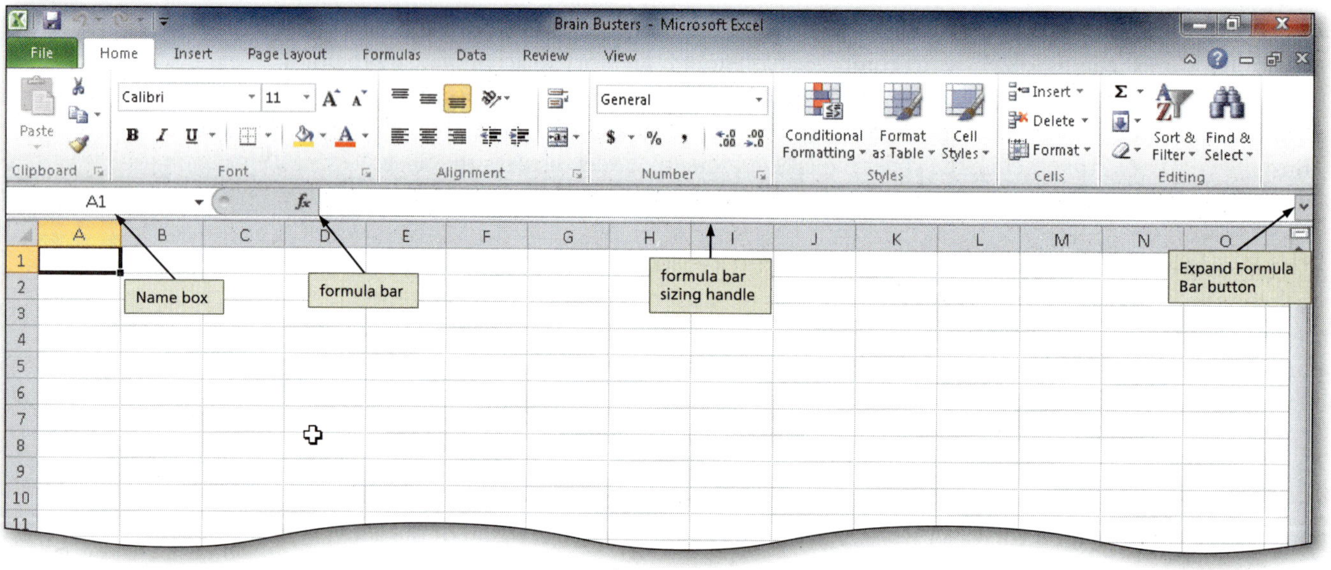

Figure 69

To Enter a Worksheet Title

To enter data into a cell, you first must select it. The easiest way to select a cell (make it active) is to use the mouse to move the block plus sign mouse pointer to the cell and then click. An alternative method is to use the arrow keys that are located just to the right of the typewriter keys on the keyboard. An arrow key selects the cell adjacent to the active cell in the direction of the arrow on the key.

In Excel, any set of characters containing a letter, hyphen (as in a telephone number), or space is considered text. **Text** is used to place titles, such as worksheet titles, column titles, and row titles, on the worksheet. The following steps enter the worksheet title in cell A1.

1

- If it is not already the active cell, click cell A1 to make it the active cell (Figure 70).

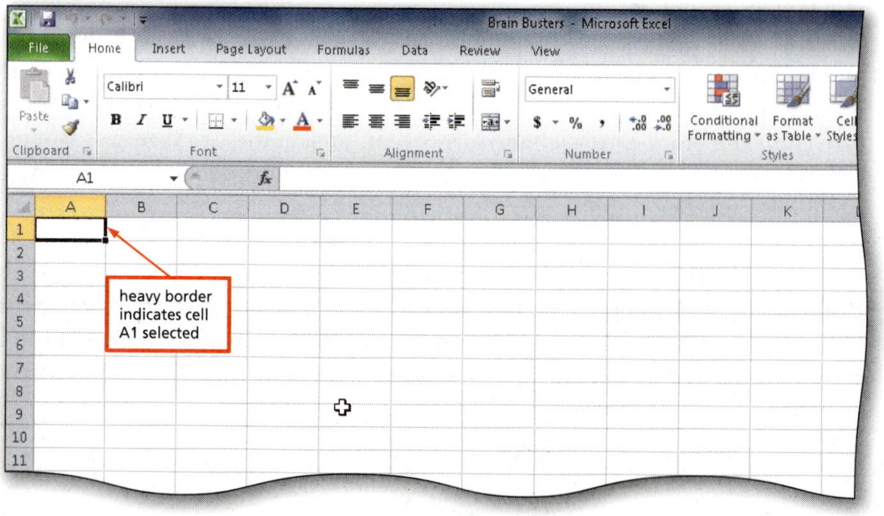

Figure 70

2

- Type **`Brain Buster Book Rentals`** in cell A1 (Figure 71).

Q&A Why did the appearance of the formula bar change?

Excel displays the title in the formula bar and in cell A1. When you begin typing a cell entry, Excel displays two additional boxes in the formula bar: the Cancel box and the Enter box. Clicking the Enter box completes an entry. Clicking the Cancel box cancels an entry.

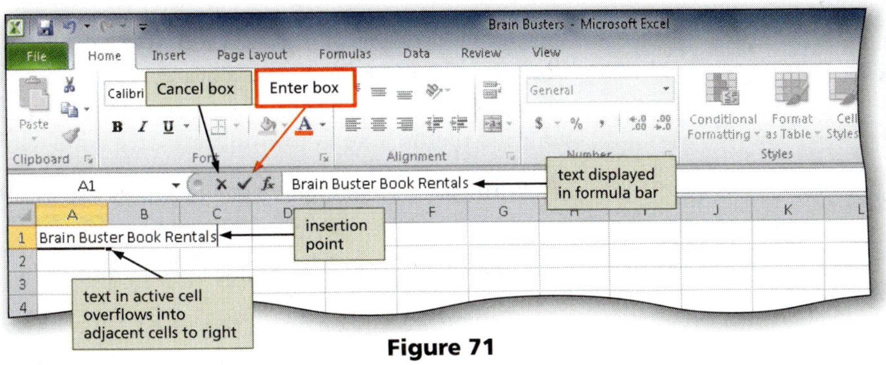

Figure 71

3

- Click the Enter box to complete the entry and enter the worksheet title in cell A1 (Figure 72).

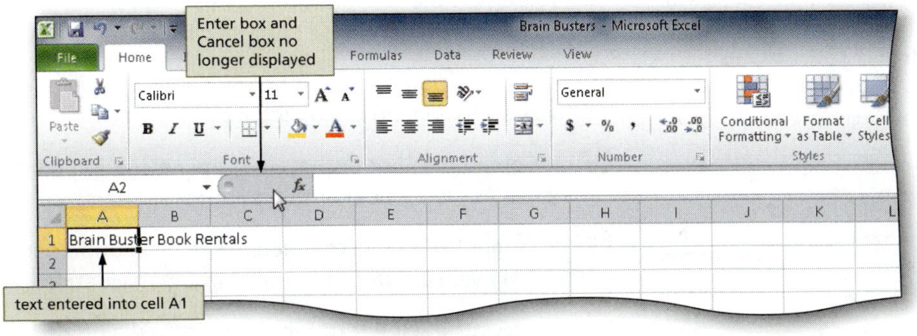

Figure 72

Other Ways

1. To complete entry, click any cell other than active cell
2. To complete entry, press ENTER, HOME, PAGE UP, PAGE DOWN, END, UP, DOWN, LEFT ARROW, or RIGHT ARROW

To Save an Existing Office Document with the Same File Name

Saving frequently cannot be overemphasized. You have made modifications to the file (spreadsheet) since you created it. Thus, you should save again. Similarly, you should continue saving files frequently so that you do not lose your changes since the time you last saved the file. You can use the same file name, such as Brain Busters, to save the changes made to the document. The following step saves a file again.

1

- Click the Save button on the Quick Access Toolbar to overwrite the previously saved file (Brain Busters, in this case) on the USB flash drive (Figure 73).

Q&A Why did the Save As dialog box not appear?

Office programs, including Excel, overwrite the document using the setting specified the first time you saved the document.

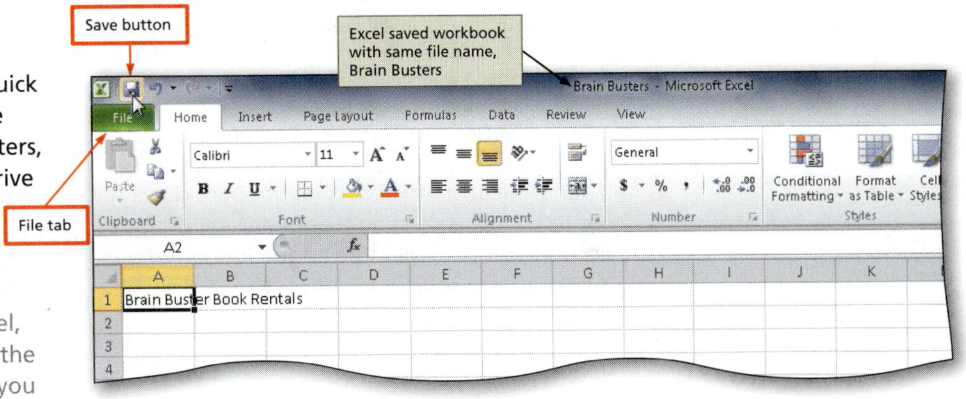

Figure 73

Other Ways

1. Press CTRL+S or press SHIFT+F12

To Use Save As to Change the Name of a File

You might want to save a file with a different name and even to a different location. For example, you might start a homework assignment with a data file and then save it with a final file name for submitting to your instructor, saving it to a location designated by your instructor. The following steps save a file with a different file name.

1. With your USB flash drive connected to one of the computer's USB ports, click File on the Ribbon to open the Backstage view.
2. Click Save As in the Backstage view to display the Save As dialog box.
3. Type `Brain Busters Rental Summary` in the File name text box (Save As dialog box) to change the file name. Do not press the ENTER key after typing the file name because you do not want to close the dialog box at this time.
4. Navigate to the desired save location (the Excel folder in the CIS 101 folder [or your class folder] on the USB flash drive, in this case). For specific instructions, perform the tasks in steps 4a through 4g.

4a. If a navigation pane is not displayed in the Save As dialog box, click the Browse Folders button to expand the dialog box.

4b. If Computer is not displayed in the navigation pane, drag the navigation pane scroll bar (Save As dialog box) until Computer appears.

4c. If Computer is not expanded in the navigation pane, double-click Computer to display a list of available storage devices in the navigation pane.

4d. If necessary, scroll through the Save As dialog box until your USB flash drive appears in the list of available storage devices in the navigation pane.

4e. If your USB flash drive is not expanded, double-click the USB flash drive in the list of available storage devices in the navigation pane to select that drive as the new save location and display its contents in the right pane.

4f. If your class folder (CIS 101, in this case) is not expanded, double-click the CIS 101 folder to select the folder and display its contents.

4g. Double-click the Excel folder to select it and display its contents in the right pane.

5. Click the Save button (Save As dialog box) to save the file in the selected folder on the selected drive with the new file name.

To Quit an Office Program

You are finished using Excel. The following steps quit Excel.

1. If you have one Office document open, click the Close button on the right side of the title bar to close the document and quit the Office program; or if you have multiple Office documents open, click File on the Ribbon to open the Backstage view and then click Exit in the Backstage view to close all open documents and quit the Office program.
2. If a dialog box appears, click the Save button to save any changes made to the file since the last save.

Access

The term **database** describes a collection of data organized in a manner that allows access, retrieval, and use of that data. **Microsoft Access 2010**, usually referred to as simply **Access,** is a database management system. A **database management system** is software that allows you to use a computer to create a database; add, change, and delete data in the database; create queries that allow you to ask questions concerning the data in the database; and create forms and reports using the data in the database.

To Start a Program

The following steps, which assume Windows 7 is running, start the Access program based on a typical installation. You may need to ask your instructor how to start programs for your computer.

1. Click the Start button on the Windows 7 taskbar to display the Start menu.
2. Type the name of the program, `Microsoft Access` in this case, as the search text in the 'Search programs and files' text box and watch the search results appear on the Start menu.
3. Click the name of the program, Microsoft Access 2010 in this case, in the search results on the Start menu to start Access.
4. If the program window is not maximized, click the Maximize button on its title bar to maximize the window (Figure 74).

Q&A Do I have to start Access using these steps?

No. You can use any previously discussed method of starting an Office program to start Access.

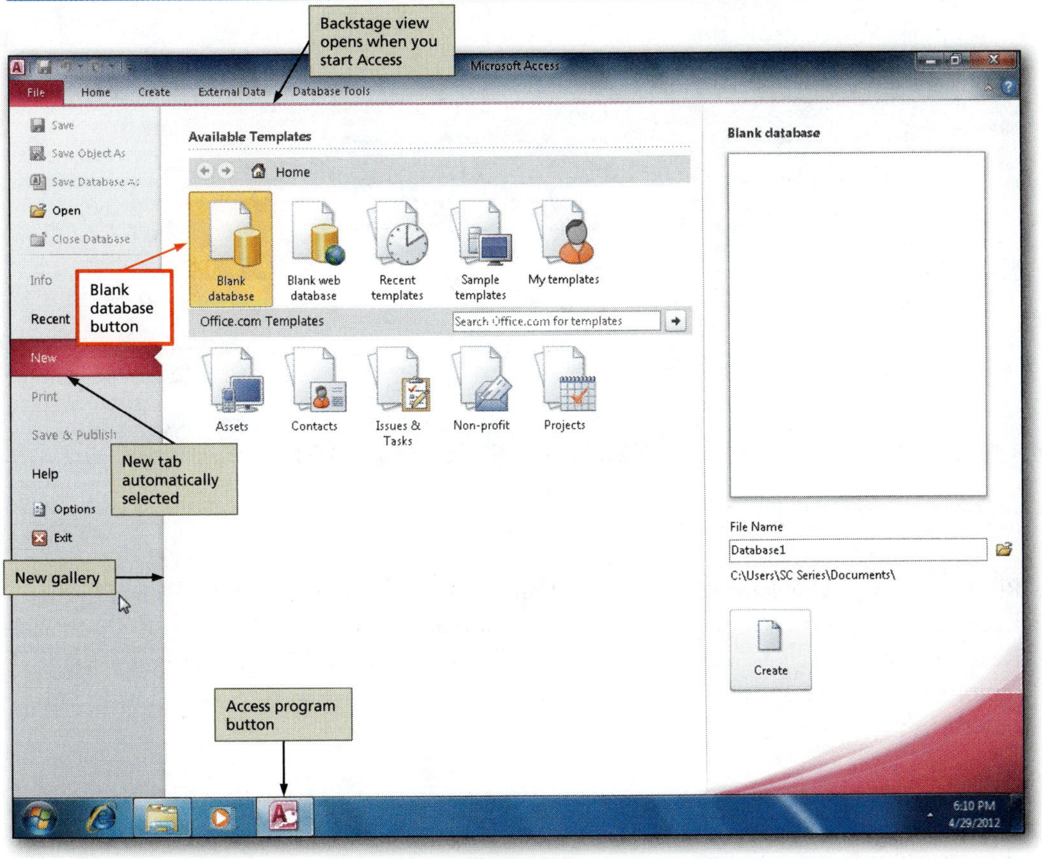

Figure 74

Unique Elements in Access

You work on objects such as tables, forms, and reports in the **Access work area**. In Figure 74, the Access window contains no open objects. Figure 75 shows a work area with multiple objects open. **Object tabs** for the open objects appear at the top of the work area. You select an open object by clicking its tab. In the figure, the Suppliers Split Form is the selected object. To the left of the work area is the Navigation Pane, which contains a list of all the objects in the database. You use this pane to open an object. You also can customize the way objects are displayed in the Navigation Pane.

Because the Navigation Pane can take up space in the window, you may not have as much open space for working as you would with Word or Excel. You can use the Shutter Bar Open/Close button to minimize the Navigation Pane when you are not using it, which allows more space to work with tables, forms, reports, and other database elements.

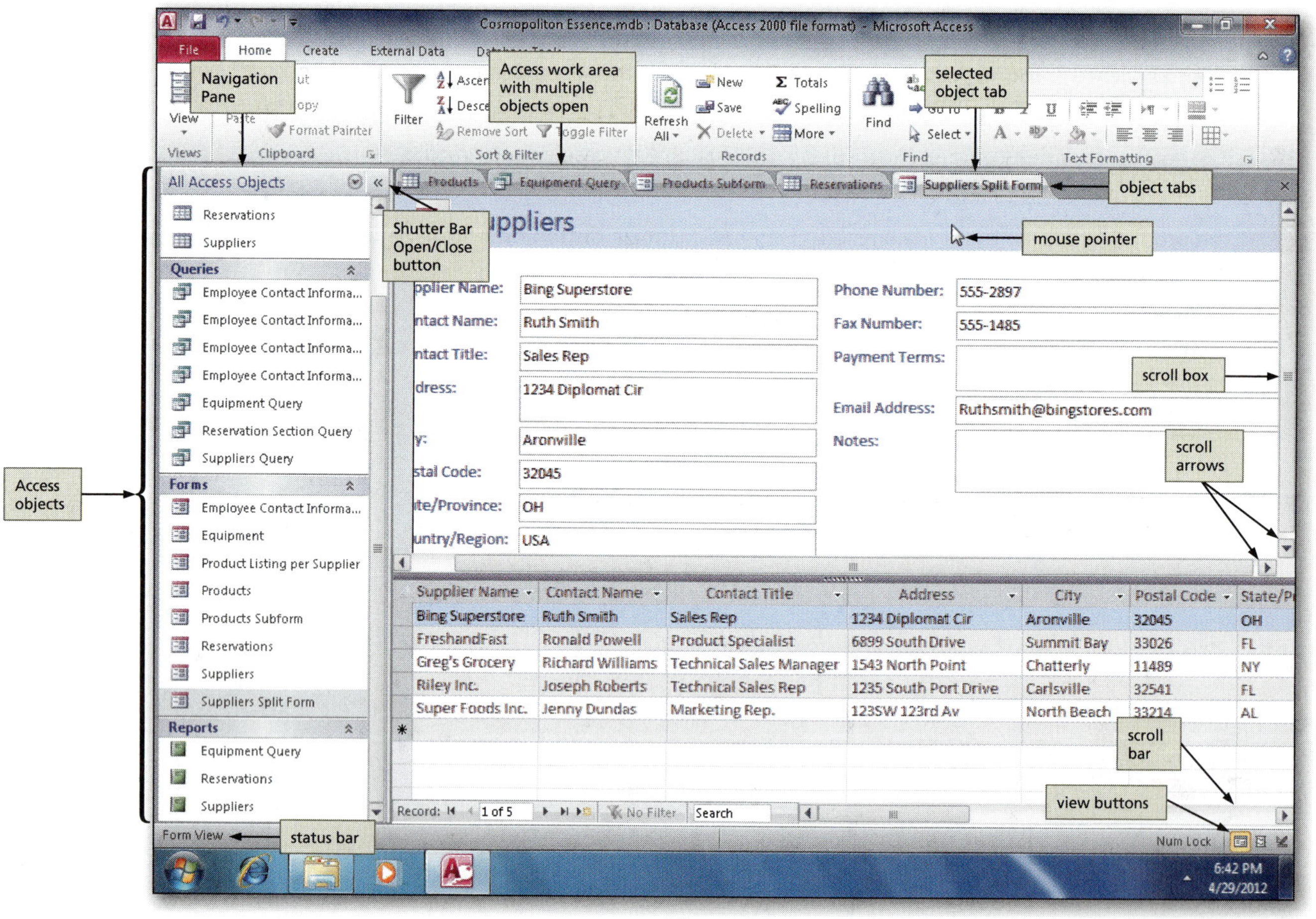

Figure 75

Ribbon When you start Access, the Ribbon displays five main tabs: File, Home, Create, External Data, and Database Tools. Access has unique groupings such as Sort & Filter and Records that are designed specifically for working with databases. Many of the formatting options are reserved for the tool tabs that appear when you are working with forms and reports.

To Create an Access Database

Unlike the other Office programs, Access saves a database when you first create it. When working in Access, you will add data to an Access database. As you add data to a database, Access automatically saves your changes rather than waiting until you manually save the database or quit Access. Recall that in Word and Excel, you entered the data first and then saved it.

Because Access automatically saves the database as you add and change data, you do not have to always click the Save button. In fact, the Save button in Access is used for saving the objects (including tables, queries, forms, reports, and other database objects) a database contains. You can use either the Blank Database option or a template to create a new database. If you already know the organization of your database, you would use the Blank Database option. If not, you can use a template. Templates can guide you by suggesting some commonly used database organizations.

The following steps use the Blank Database option to create a database named Charmed Excursions in the Access folder in the class folder (CIS 101, in this case) on a USB flash drive.

1

- If necessary, click the Blank database button in the New gallery (shown in Figure 74 on page OFF 53) in the Backstage view to select the template type.
- Click the File Name text box to select the default database name.
- Type `Charmed Excursions` in the File Name text box to enter the new file name. Do not press the ENTER key after typing the file name because you do not want to create the database at this time (Figure 76).

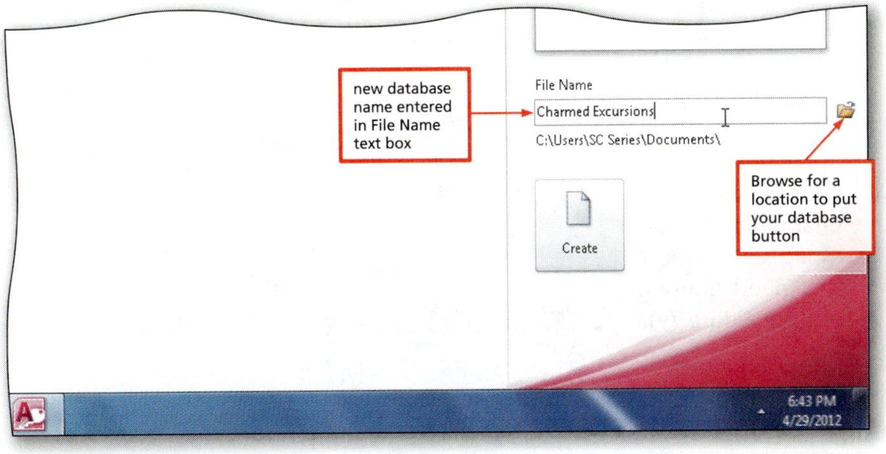

Figure 76

Q&A Why is the Backstage view automatically open when you start Access?

Unlike other Office programs, you first must save a database before adding any data. For this reason, the Backstage view opens automatically when you start Access.

2

- Click the 'Browse for a location to put your database' button to display the File New Database dialog box.
- Navigate to the location for the database, that is, the USB flash drive, then to the folder identifying your class (CIS 101, in this case), and then to the Access folder (Figure 77). For detailed steps about navigating, see Steps 3a – 3c on pages OFF 28 and OFF 29.

Q&A Why does the 'Save as type' box say Microsoft Access 2007 Databases?

Microsoft Access database formats change with some new versions of Microsoft Access. The most recent format is the Microsoft Access 2007 Databases format, which was released with Access 2007.

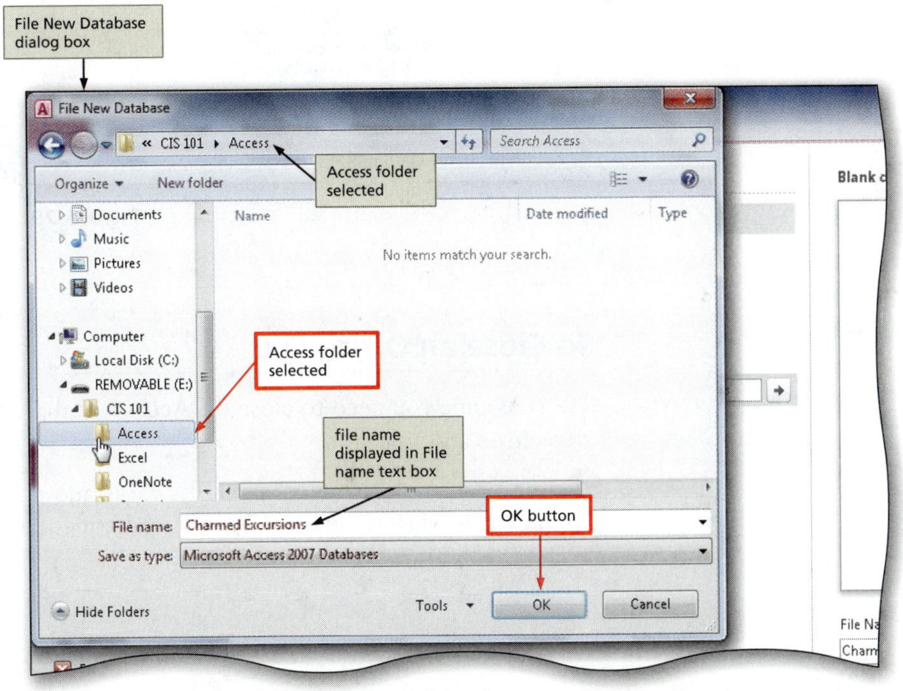

Figure 77

3

- Click the OK button (File New Database dialog box) to select the Access folder as the location for the database and close the dialog box (Figure 78).

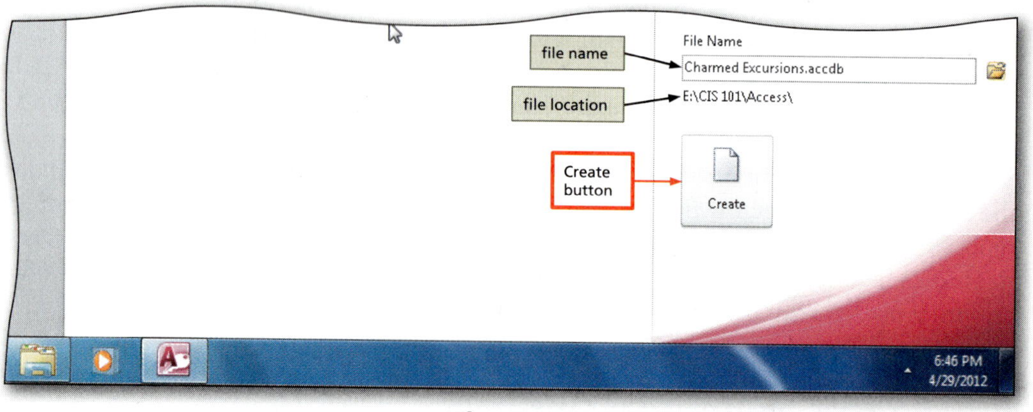

Figure 78

4

- Click the Create button in the Backstage view to create the database on the selected drive in the selected folder with the file name, Charmed Excursions. If necessary, click the Enable Content button (Figure 79).

Q&A How do I know that the Charmed Excursions database is created?

The name of the database appears on the title bar.

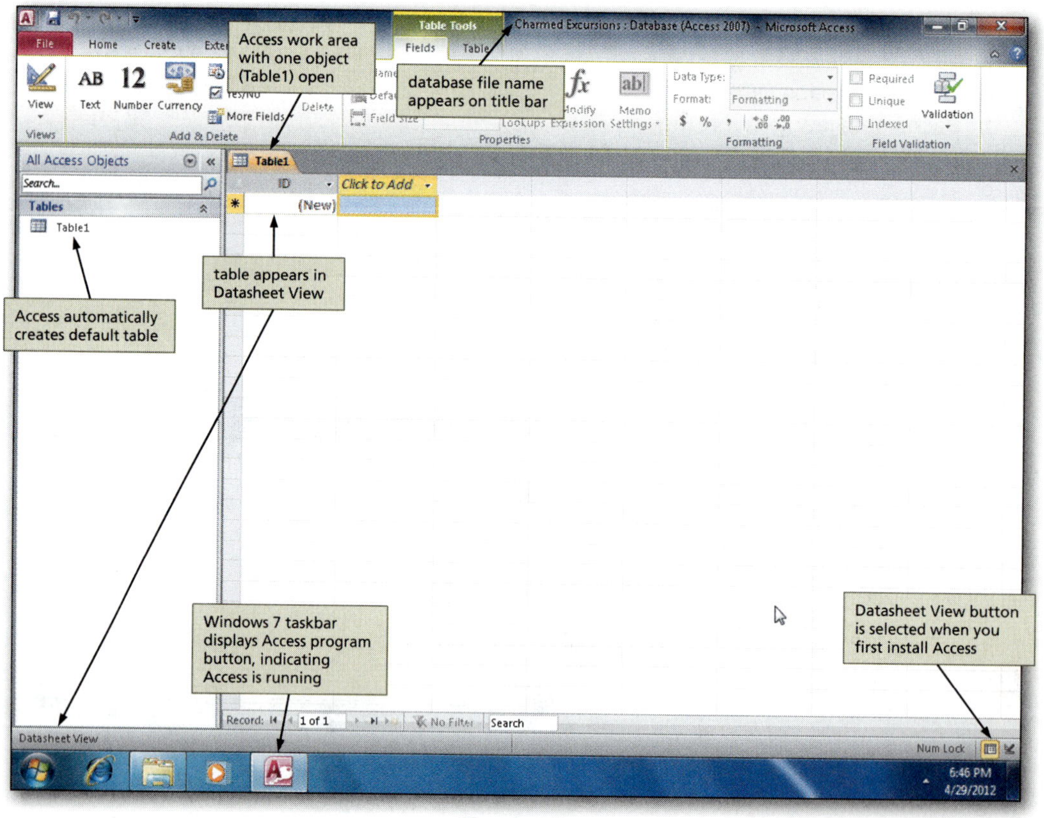

Figure 79

To Close an Office File

Assume you need to close the Access database and return to it later. The following step closes an Office file.

1 Click File on the Ribbon to open the Backstage view and then click Close Database in the Backstage view to close the open file (Charmed Excursions, in this case) without quitting the active program.

Q&A Why is Access still on the screen?

When you close a database, the program remains open.

To Open an Existing Office File

Assume you wish to continue working on an existing file, that is, a file you previously saved. Earlier in this chapter, you learned how to open a recently used file through the Backstage view. The following steps open a database, specifically the Charmed Excursions database, from the USB flash drive.

1

- With your USB flash drive connected to one of the computer's USB ports, if necessary, click File on the Ribbon to open the Backstage view.
- Click Open in the Backstage view to display the Open dialog box (Figure 80).

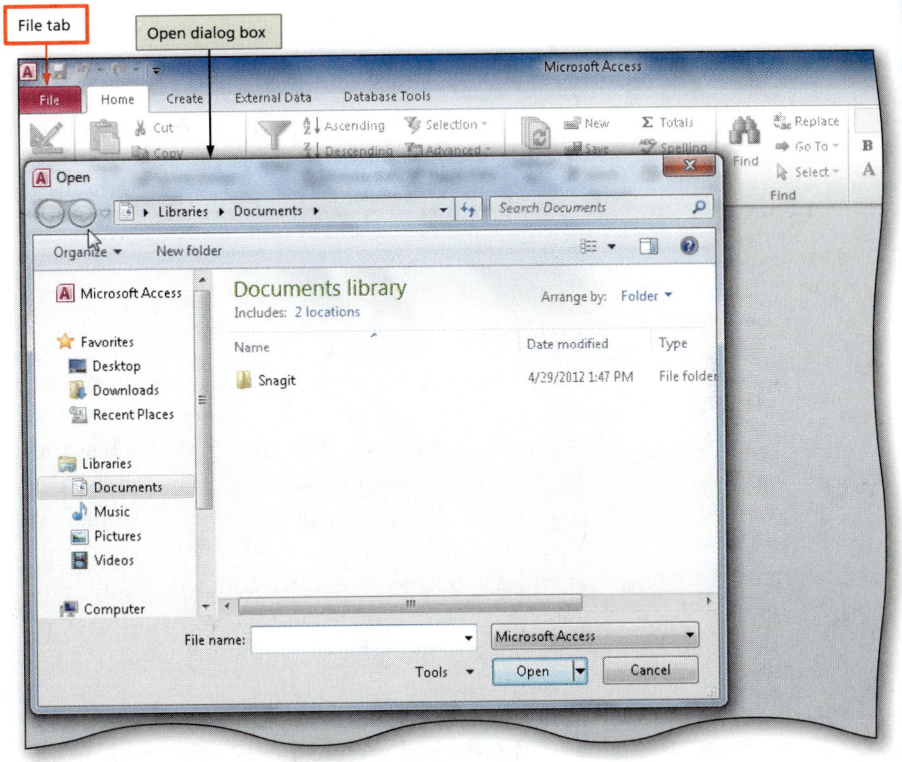

Figure 80

2

- Navigate to the location of the file to be opened (in this case, the USB flash drive, then to the CIS 101 folder [or your class folder], and then to the Access folder). For detailed steps about navigating, see Steps 3a – 3c on pages OFF 28 and OFF 29.

Q&A

What if I did not save my file in a folder?

If you did not save your file in a folder, the file you wish to open should be displayed in the Open dialog box before navigating to any folders.

3

- Click the file to be opened, Charmed Excursions in this case, to select the file (Figure 81).

4

- Click the Open button (Open dialog box) to open the selected file and display the opened file in the current program window (shown in Figure 79).

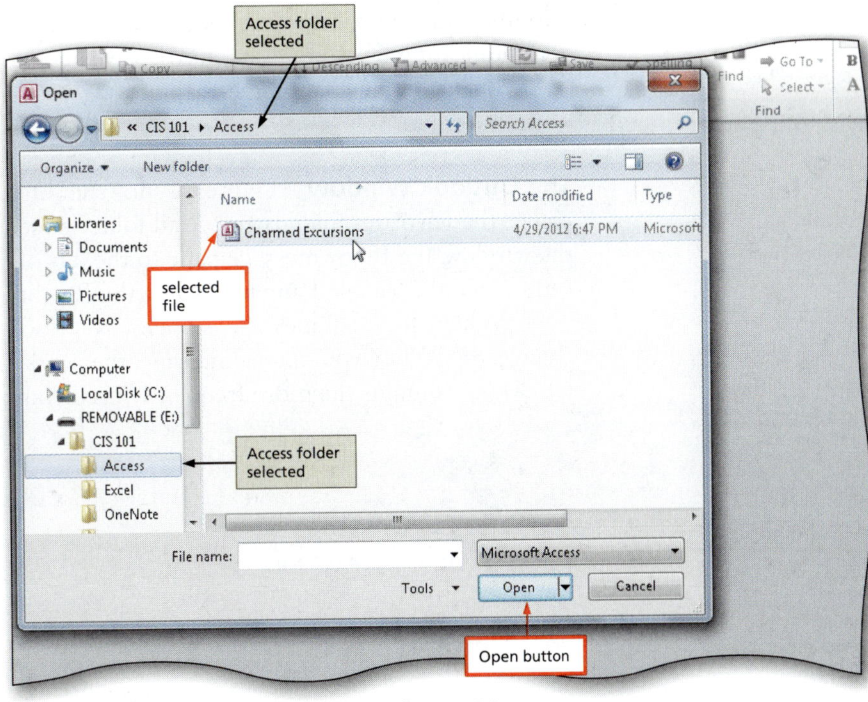

Figure 81

Other Ways

1. Click File on the Ribbon, click Recent in Backstage view, double-click file
2. Press CTRL+O
3. Navigate to file in Windows Explorer, double-click file

To Quit an Office Program

You are finished using Access. The following step quits Access.

1. Click the Close button on the right side of the title bar to close the file and quit the Office program.

Other Office Programs

In addition to the Office programs discussed thus far, three other programs are useful when collaborating and communicating with others: Outlook, Publisher, and OneNote.

Outlook

Outlook is a powerful communications and scheduling program that helps you communicate with others, keep track of contacts, and organize your calendar. Personal information manager (PIM) programs such as Outlook provide a way for individuals and workgroups to organize, find, view, and share information easily. Outlook allows you to send and receive electronic mail (e-mail) and permits you to engage in real-time messaging with family, friends, or coworkers using instant messaging. Outlook also provides a means to organize contacts. Users can track e-mail messages, meetings, and notes related to a particular contact. Outlook's Calendar, Contacts, Tasks, and Notes components aid in this organization. Contact information readily is available from the Outlook Calendar, Mail, Contacts, and Task components by accessing the Find a Contact feature.

Electronic mail (e-mail) is the transmission of messages and files over a computer network. E-mail has become an important means of exchanging information and files between business associates, classmates and instructors, friends, and family. Businesses find that using e-mail to send documents electronically saves both time and money. Parents with students away at college or relatives who live across the country find that communicating by e-mail is an inexpensive and easy way to stay in touch with their family members. Exchanging e-mail messages is one of the more widely used features of the Internet.

The Outlook Window Figure 82 shows an Outlook window, which is divided into six panes: the Favorites folder pane, Mail folder pane, and Navigation Pane on the left side of the window, the Inbox message pane to the left of center, the Reading Pane to the right of center, and the People Pane just below the Reading Pane.

When an e-mail message is open in Outlook, it is displayed in a Message window (Figure 83). When you open a message, the Message window Ribbon displays the Message tab, which contains the more frequently used commands.

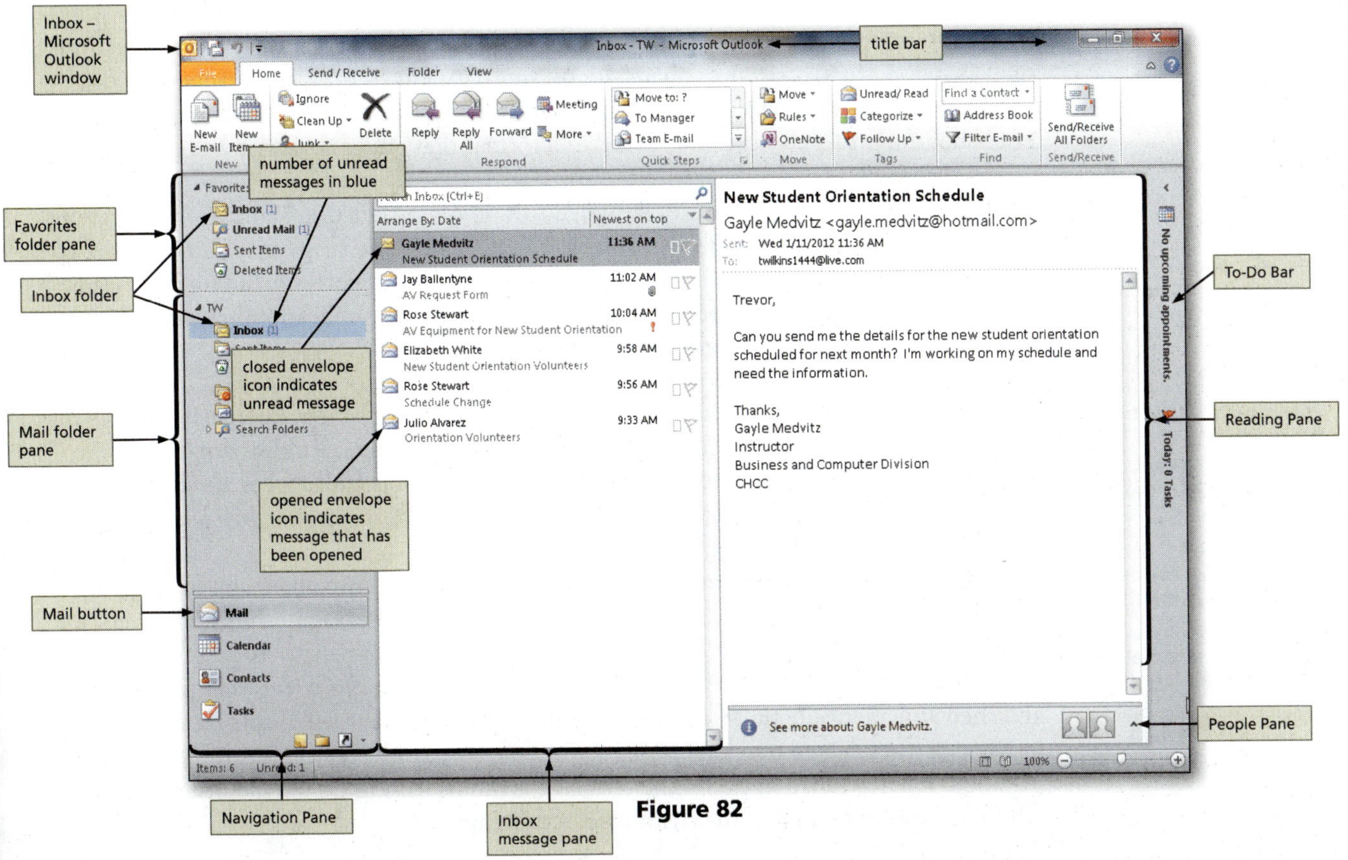

Figure 82

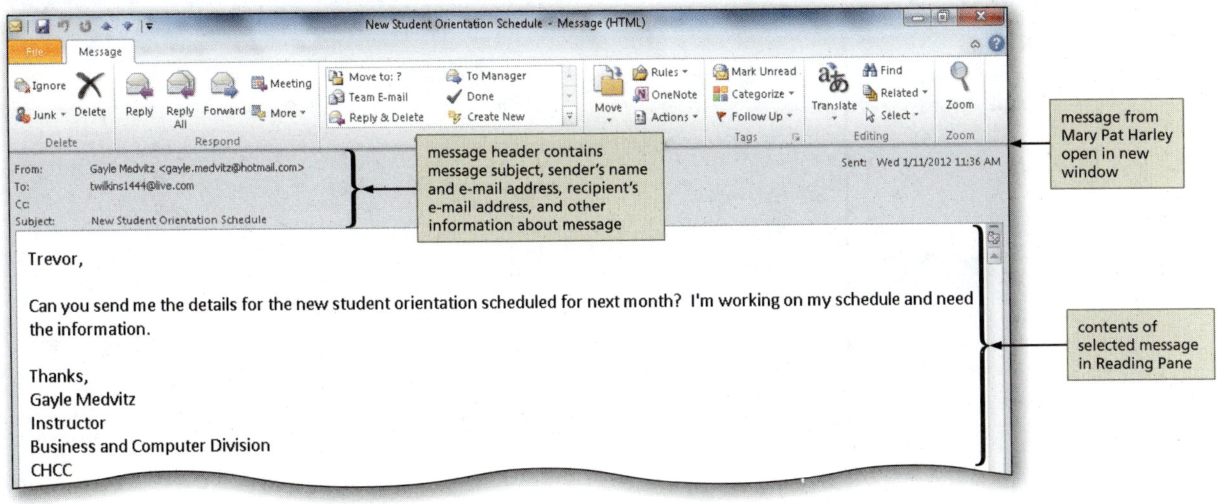

Figure 83

Publisher

Publisher is a powerful desktop publishing (DTP) program that assists you in designing and producing professional-quality documents that combine text, graphics, illustrations, and photos. DTP software provides additional tools beyond those typically found in word processing programs, including design templates, graphic manipulation tools, color schemes or libraries, advanced layout and printing tools, and Web components. For large jobs, businesses use DTP software to design publications that are camera ready, which means the files are suitable for outside commercial printing. In addition, DTP software can be used to create Web pages and interactive Web forms.

Publisher is used by people who regularly produce high-quality color publications, such as newsletters, brochures, flyers, logos, signs, catalogs, cards, and business forms. Saving publications as Web pages or complete Web sites is a powerful component of Publisher. All publications can be saved in a format that easily is viewed and manipulated using a browser.

Publisher has many features designed to simplify production and make publications visually appealing. Using Publisher, you easily can change the shape, size, and color of text and graphics. You can include many kinds of graphical objects, including mastheads, borders, tables, images, pictures, charts, and Web objects in publications, as well as integrate spreadsheets and databases.

BTW

Starting Publisher
When you first start Publisher, the New templates gallery usually is displayed in the Backstage view. If it is not displayed, click File on the Ribbon, click Options in the Backstage view, click General (Options dialog box), and then click Show the New template gallery when starting Publisher to select the check box in the General panel.

The Publisher Window On the right side of the Backstage view, Publisher displays the New template gallery, which includes a list of publication types. **Publication types** are typical publications used by desktop publishers. The more popular types are displayed in the center of the window. Each publication type is a link to display various templates and blank publications from which you may choose.

Once you select a publication type, the window changes to allow you to select a specific template (Figure 84). Some templates are installed with Publisher, and others are available online. Clicking a publication type causes template previews to be displayed in the center of the window. The templates are organized by purpose (for example, Sales) and then alphabetically by design type. On the right, Publisher will display a larger preview of the selected template, along with some customization options if the template is installed or a download option if the template is online. In Figure 84, the installed Arrows template is selected so that the customize options appear.

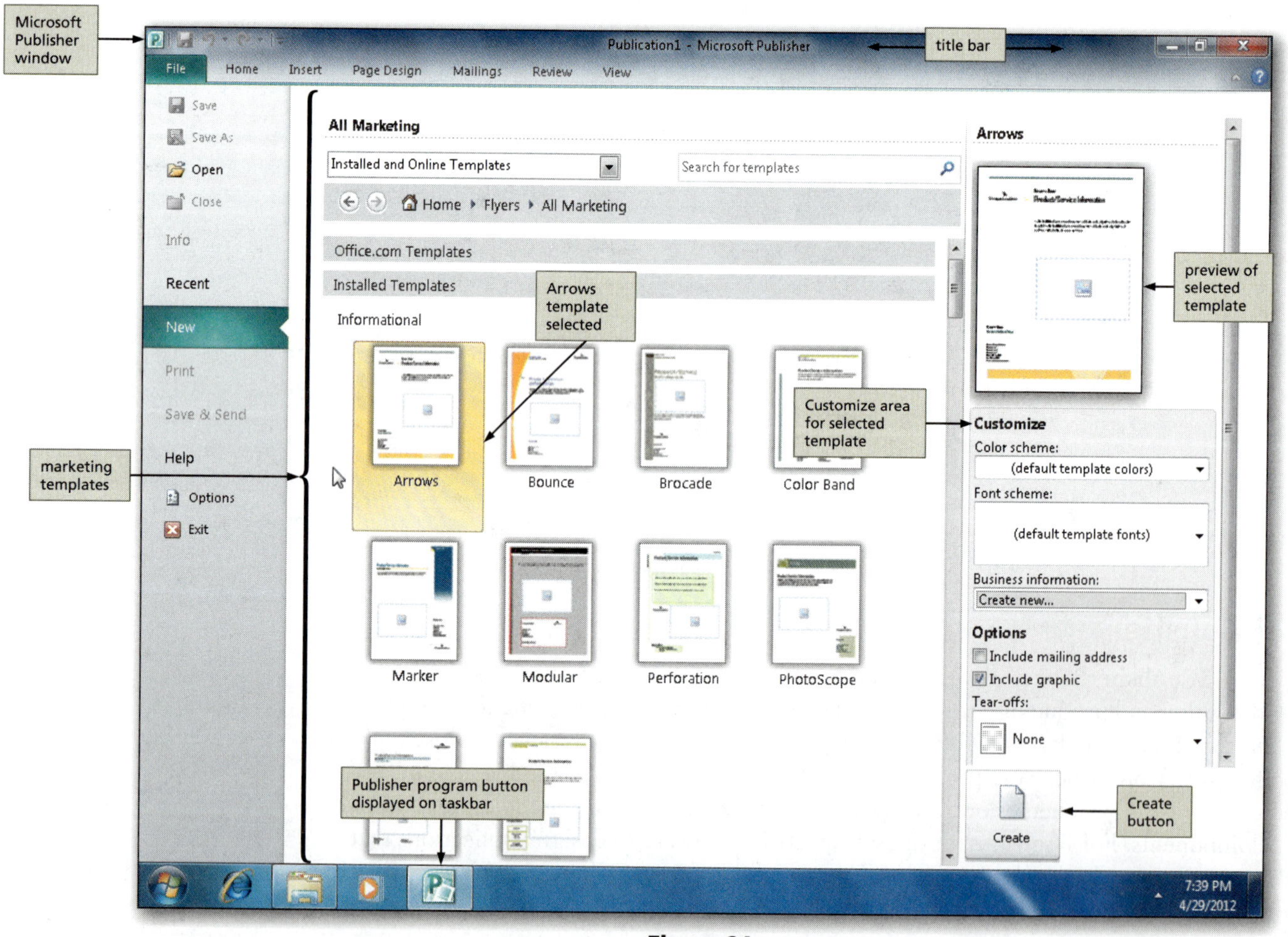

Figure 84

When you click the Create button, Publisher creates the document and sets it up for you to edit. Figure 85 shows the Arrows document that Publisher creates when default options are selected.

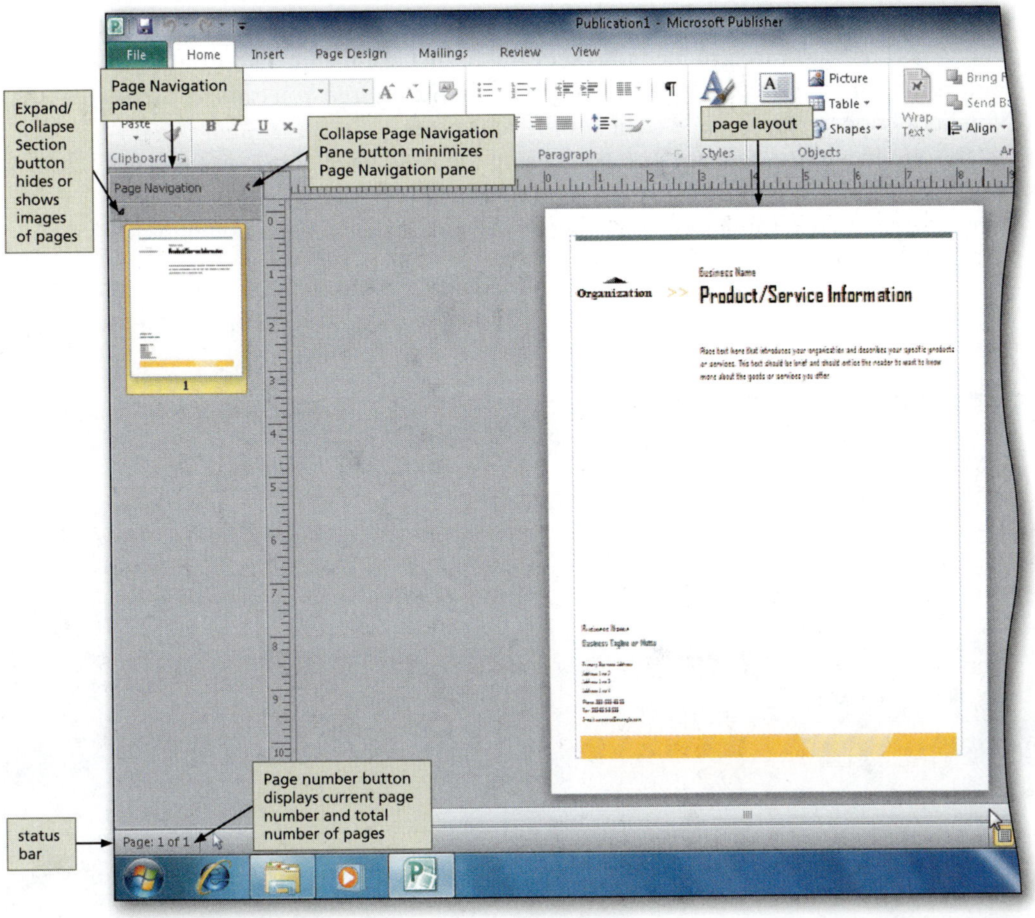

Figure 85

OneNote

OneNote is a note taking program that assists you in entering, saving, organizing, searching, and using notes. It enables you to create pages, which are organized in sections, just as in a physical notebook. In OneNote, you can type notes anywhere on a page and then easily move the notes around on the page. You can create lists and outlines, use handwriting to enter notes, and create drawings. If you use a Tablet PC to add handwritten notes to a document, OneNote can convert the handwriting to text. It also can perform searches on the handwritten entries. Pictures and data from other programs easily are incorporated in your notes.

In addition to typing and handwriting, you can take audio notes. For example, you could record conversations during a meeting or lecture. As you record, you can take additional notes. When you play back the audio notes, you can synchronize the additional notes you took; that is, OneNote will show you during playback the exact points at which you added the notes. A variety of note flags, which are symbols that call your attention to notes on a page, enable you to flag notes as being important. You then can use the Note Flags summary to view the flagged notes, which can be sorted in a variety of ways.

OneNote includes tools to assist you with organizing a notebook and navigating its contents. It also includes a search facility, making it easy to find the specific notes in which you are interested. For short notes that you always want to have available readily, you can use Side Notes, which are used much like the sticky notes that you might use in a physical notebook.

OneNote Window All activity in OneNote takes place in the **notebook** (Figure 86). Like a physical notebook, the OneNote notebook consists of notes that are placed on **pages**. The pages are grouped into **sections**, which can be further grouped into **folders**. (No folders are shown in the notebook in the figure.) You can use the Search All Notebooks box to search for specific text in your notes.

You can add pages to the notebook using the New Page button in the Page Tabs pane. If Page Tabs are displayed, then you can switch to a page by clicking its tab. Figure 86 shows the Top Uses page being displayed for the General notebook.

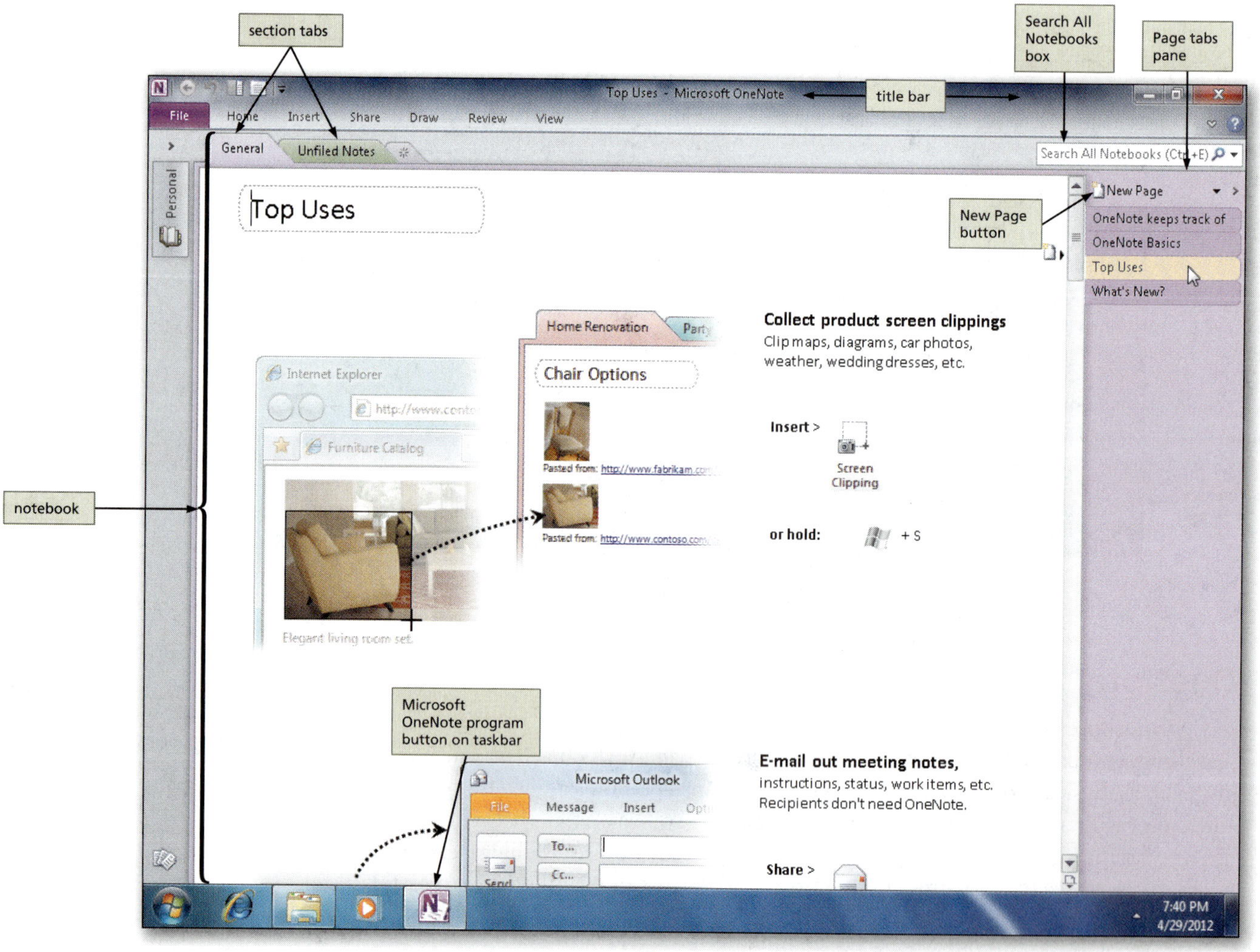

Figure 86

Break Point: If you wish to take a break, this is a good place to do so. To resume at a later time, continue to follow the steps from this location forward.

Moving, Renaming, and Deleting Files

Earlier in this chapter, you learned how to organize files in folders, which is part of a process known as **file management**. The following sections cover additional file management topics including renaming, moving, and deleting files.

To Rename a File

In some circumstances, you may want to change the name of, or rename, a file or a folder. For example, you may want to distinguish a file in one folder or drive from a copy of a similar file, or you may decide to rename a file to better identify its contents. The Word folder shown in Figure 87 contains the Word document, Koala Exhibit. The following steps change the name of the Koala Exhibit file in the Word folder to Koala Exhibit Flyer.

1

- If necessary, click the Windows Explorer program button on the taskbar to display the folder window in Windows Explorer.
- Navigate to the location of the file to be renamed (in this case, the Word folder in the CIS 101 [or your class folder] folder on the USB flash drive) to display the file(s) it contains in the right pane.
- Right-click the Koala Exhibit icon or file name in the right pane to select the Koala Exhibit file and display a shortcut menu that presents a list of commands related to files (Figure 87).

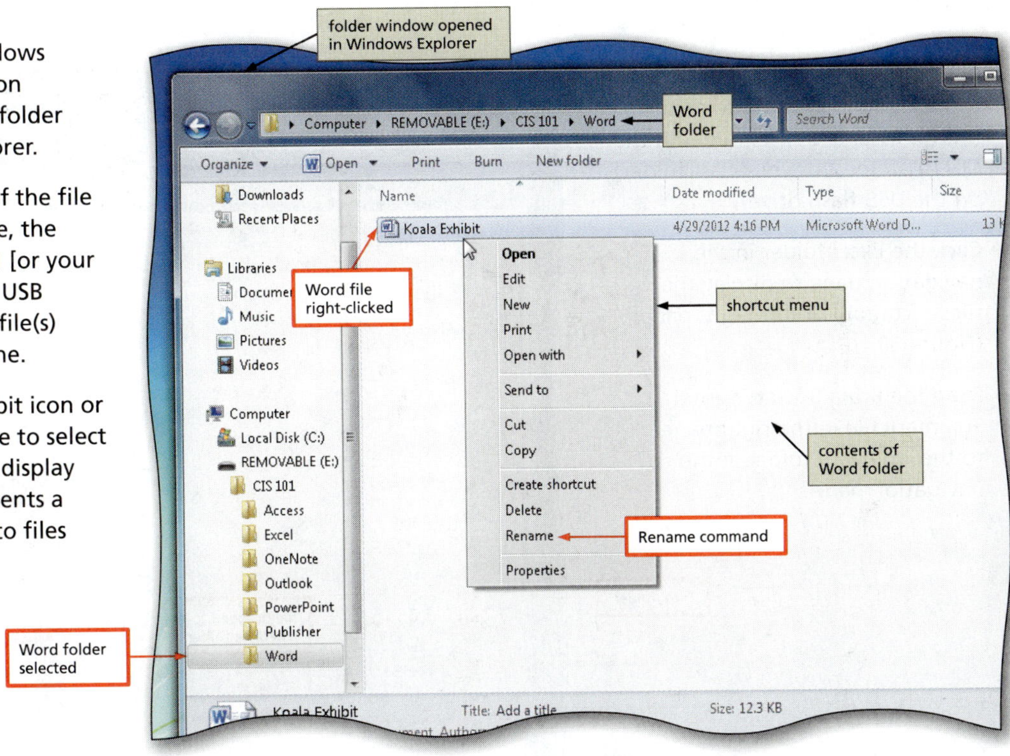

Figure 87

2

- Click Rename on the shortcut menu to place the current file name in a text box.
- Type `Koala Exhibit Flyer` in the text box and then press the ENTER key (Figure 88).

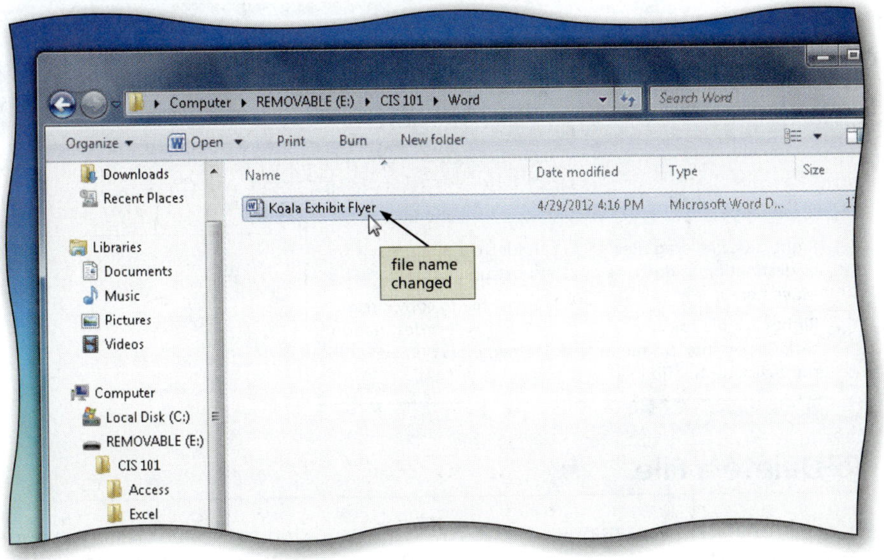

Figure 88

Q&A Are any risks involved in renaming files that are located on a hard disk?

If you inadvertently rename a file that is associated with certain programs, the programs may not be able to find the file and, therefore, may not execute properly. Always use caution when renaming files.

Q&A Can I rename a file when it is open?

No, a file must be closed to change the file name.

Other Ways

1. Select file, press F2, type new file name, press ENTER

To Move a File

At some time, you may want to move a file from one folder, called the source folder, to another, called the destination. When you move a file, it no longer appears in the original folder. If the destination and the source folders are on the same disk drive, you can move a file by dragging it. If the folders are on different disk drives, then you will need to right-drag the file. The following step moves the Brain Busters Rental Summary file from the Excel folder to the OneNote folder.

1

- In Windows Explorer, navigate to the location of the file to be moved (in this case, the Excel folder in the CIS 101 folder [or your class folder] on the USB flash drive).
- Click the Excel folder in the navigation pane to display the files it contains in the right pane (Figure 89).
- Drag the Brain Busters Rental Summary file in the right pane to the OneNote folder in the navigation pane.

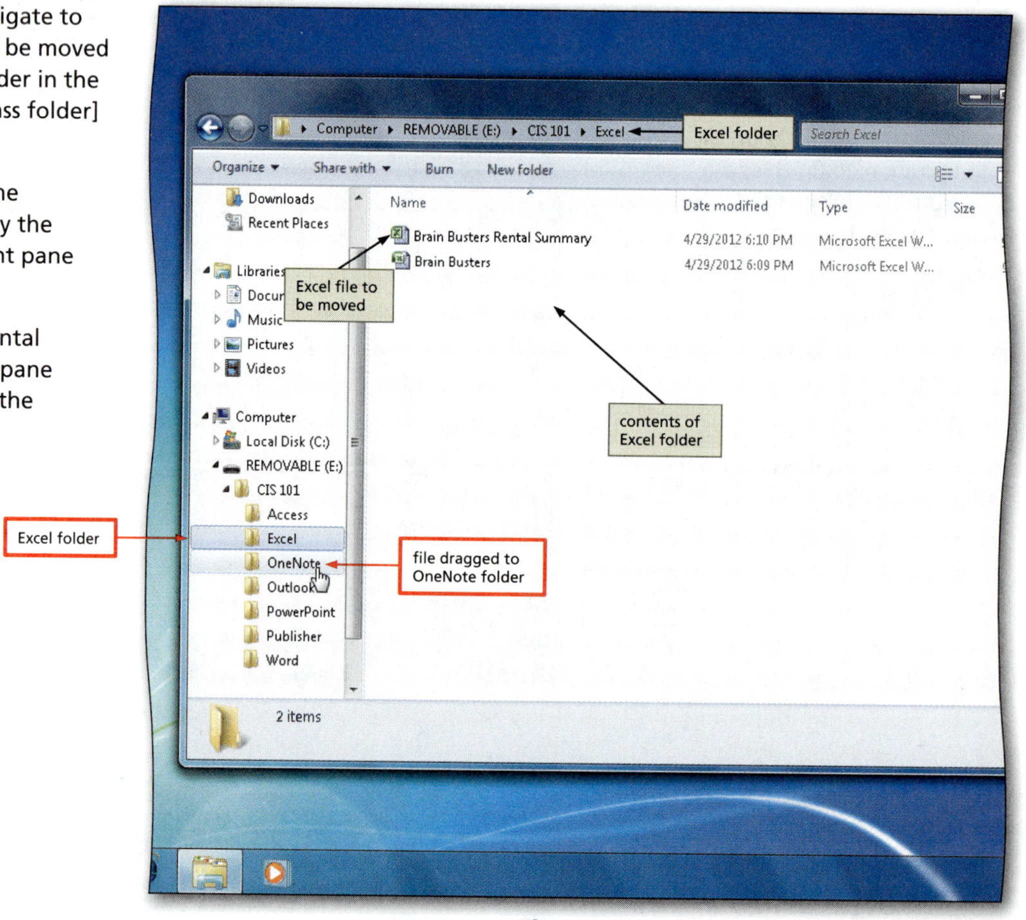

Figure 89

Other Ways

1. Right-click file, drag file to destination folder, click Move here
2. Right-click file to copy, click Cut on shortcut menu, right-click destination folder, click Paste on shortcut menu
3. Select file to copy, press CTRL+X, select destination folder, press CTRL+V

To Delete a File

A final task you may want to perform is to delete a file. Exercise extreme caution when deleting a file or files. When you delete a file from a hard disk, the deleted file is stored in the Recycle Bin where you can recover it until you empty the Recycle Bin. If you delete a file from removable media, such as a USB flash drive, the file is deleted permanently. The next steps delete the Koala Exhibit Gala file from the PowerPoint folder.

1

- In Windows Explorer, navigate to the location of the file to be deleted (in this case, the PowerPoint folder in the CIS 101 folder [or your class folder] on the USB flash drive).
- Click the PowerPoint folder in the navigation pane to display the files it contains in the right pane.
- Right-click the Koala Exhibit Gala icon or file name in the right pane to select the file and display a shortcut menu (Figure 90).

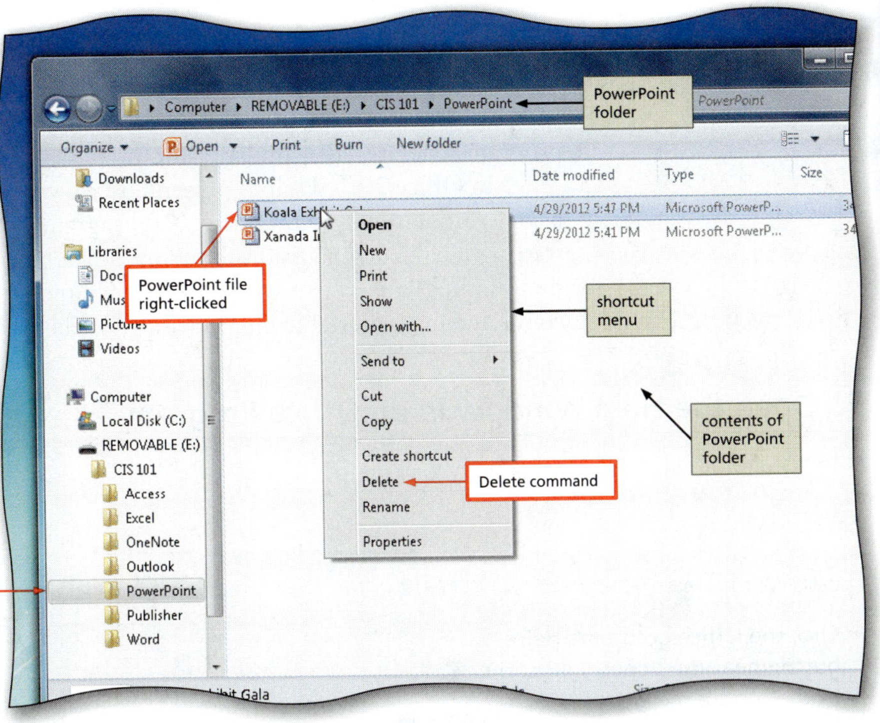

Figure 90

2

- Click Delete on the shortcut menu to display the Delete File dialog box (Figure 91).
- Click the Yes button (Delete File dialog box) to delete the selected file.

Q&A Can I use this same technique to delete a folder?

Yes. Right-click the folder and then click Delete on the shortcut menu. When you delete a folder, all of the files and folders contained in the folder you are deleting, together with any files and folders on lower hierarchical levels, are deleted as well.

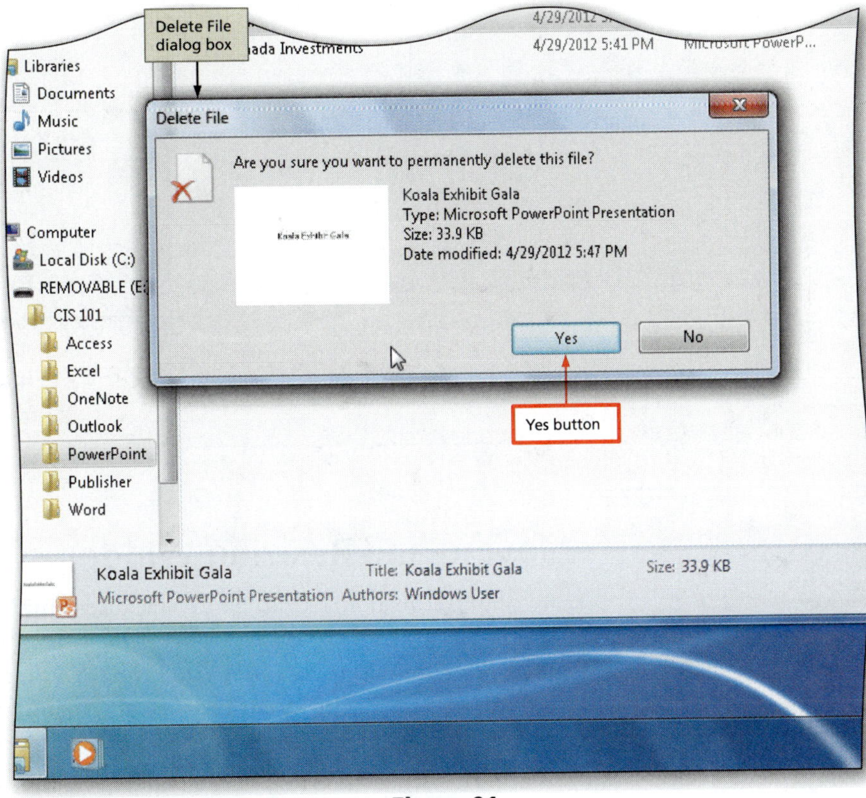

Figure 91

Other Ways

1. Select icon, press DELETE

Microsoft Office and Windows Help

At any time while you are using one of the Microsoft Office 2010 programs, you can use Office Help to display information about all topics associated with the program. To illustrate the use of Office Help, this section uses Word. Help in other Office 2010 programs operates in a similar fashion.

In Office 2010, Help is presented in a window that has Web-browser-style navigation buttons. Each Office 2010 program has its own Help home page, which is the starting Help page that is displayed in the Help window. If your computer is connected to the Internet, the contents of the Help page reflect both the local help files installed on the computer and material from Microsoft's Web site.

To Open the Help Window in an Office Program

The following step opens the Word Help window.

1

- Start an Office program, in this case Word.
- Click the Office program's Help button near the upper-right corner of the program window (the Microsoft Word Help button, in this case) to open the program's Help window (Figure 92).

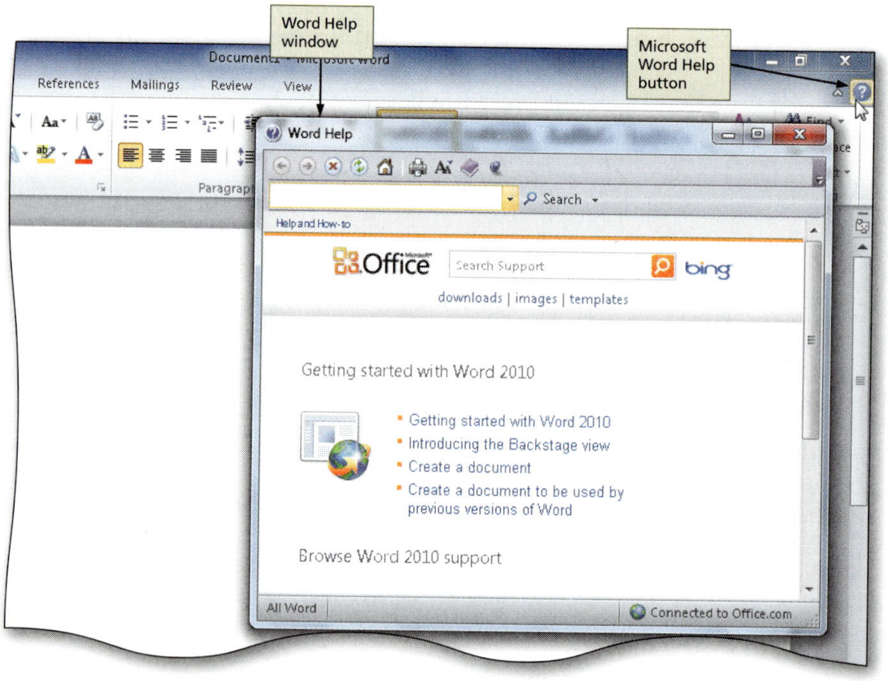

Figure 92

Other Ways

1. Press F1

Moving and Resizing Windows

Up to this point, this chapter has used minimized and maximized windows. At times, however, it is useful, or even necessary, to have more than one window open and visible on the screen at the same time. You can resize and move these open windows so that you can view different areas of and elements in the window. In the case of the Help window, for example, it could be covering document text in the Word window that you need to see.

To Move a Window by Dragging

You can move any open window that is not maximized to another location on the desktop by dragging the title bar of the window. The following step drags the Word Help window to the top left of the desktop.

1

- Drag the window title bar (the Word Help window title bar, in this case) so that the window moves to the top left of the desktop, as shown in Figure 93.

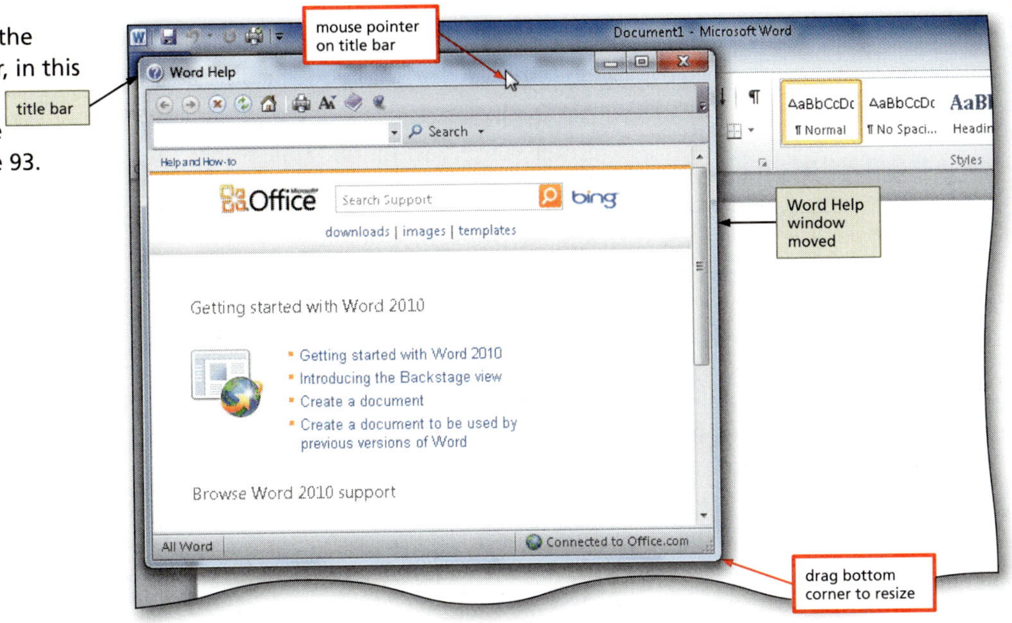

Figure 93

Other Ways

1. Right-click title bar, click Move on shortcut menu, drag window

To Resize a Window by Dragging

Sometimes, information is not visible completely in a window. A method used to change the size of the window is to drag the window borders. The following step changes the size of the Word Help window by dragging its borders.

1

- Point to the lower-right corner of the window (the Word Help window, in this case) until the mouse pointer changes to a two-headed arrow.
- Drag the bottom border downward to display more of the active window (Figure 94).

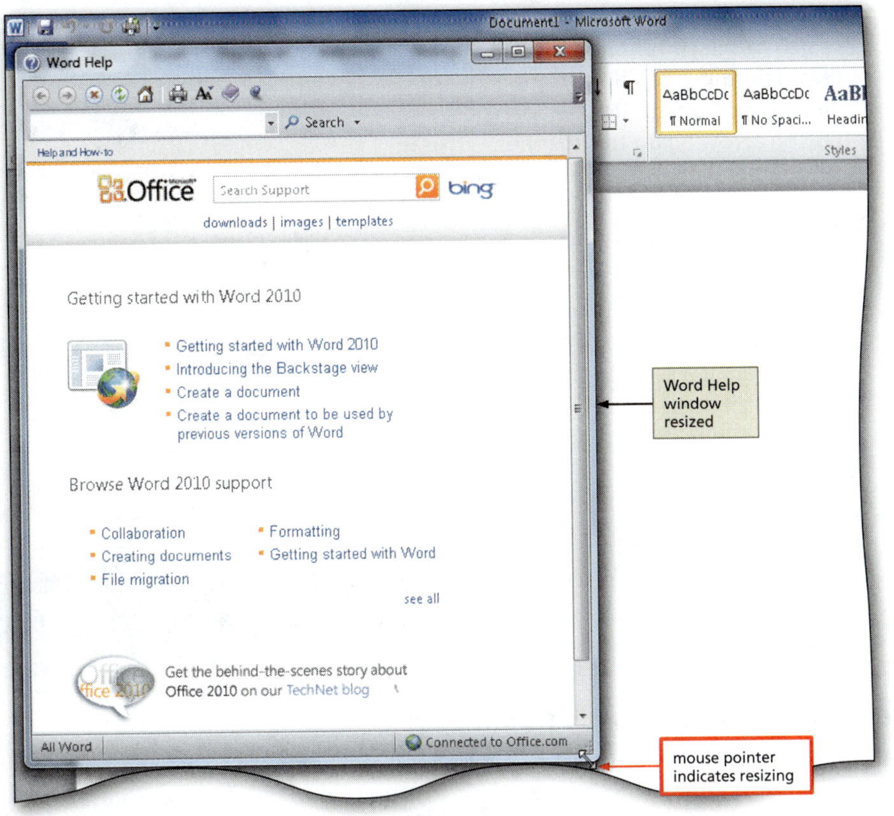

Figure 94

Q&A Can I drag other borders on the window to enlarge or shrink the window?

Yes, you can drag the left, right, and top borders and any window corner to resize a window.

Q&A Will Windows 7 remember the new size of the window after I close it?

Yes. When you reopen the window, Windows 7 will display it at the same size it was when you closed it.

Using Office Help

Once an Office program's Help window is open, several methods exist for navigating Help. You can search for help by using any of the three following methods from the Help window:

1. Enter search text in the 'Type words to search for' text box
2. Click the links in the Help window
3. Use the Table of Contents

To Obtain Help Using the 'Type words to search for' Text Box

Assume for the following example that you want to know more about the Backstage view. The following steps use the 'Type words to search for' text box to obtain useful information about the Backstage view by entering the word, Backstage, as search text.

1

- Type `Backstage` in the 'Type words to search for' text box at the top of the Word Help window to enter the search text.
- Click the Search button arrow to display the Search menu (Figure 95).
- If it is not selected already, click All Word on the Search menu, so that Help performs the most complete search of the current program (Word, in this case). If All Word already is selected, click the Search button arrow again to close the Search menu.

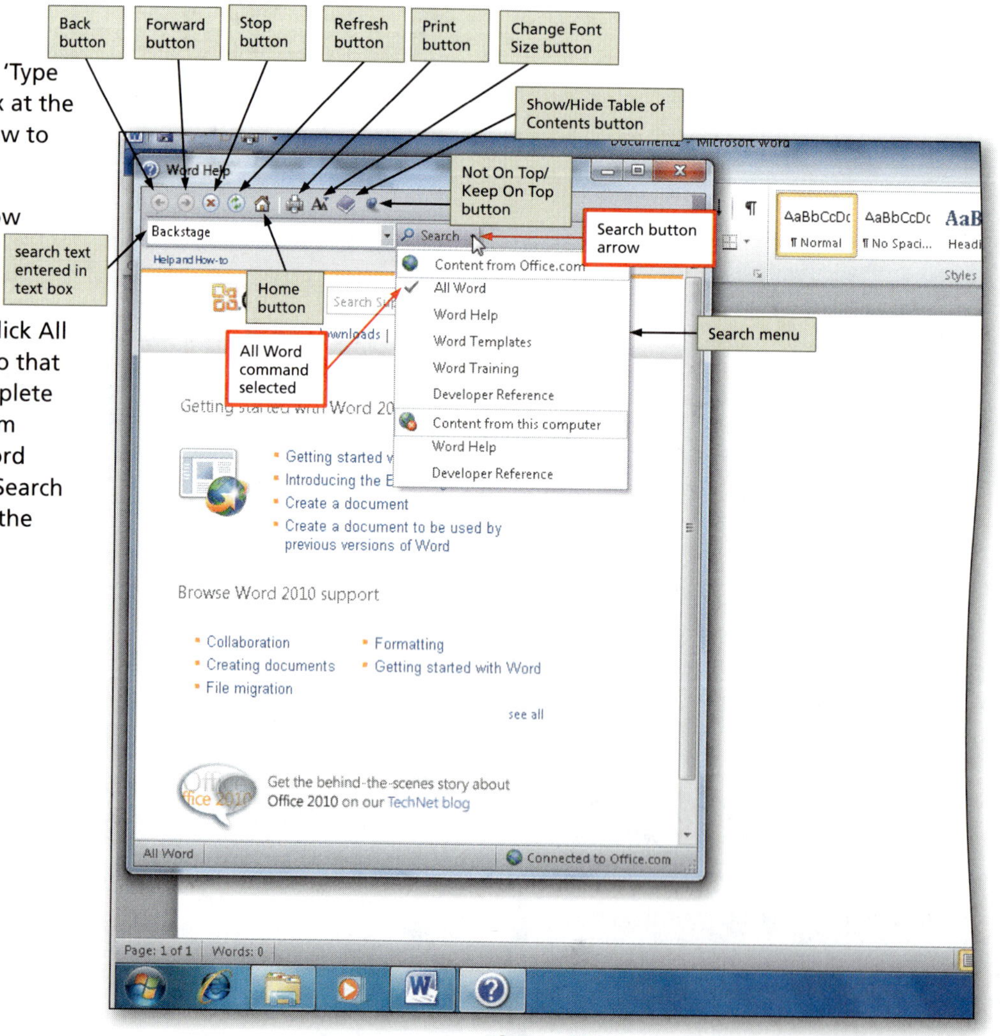

Figure 95

Q&A

Why select All Word on the Search menu?

Selecting All Word on the Search menu ensures that Word Help will search all possible sources for information about your search term. It will produce the most complete search results.

2

- Click the Search button to display the search results (Figure 96).

Q&A

Why do my search results differ?

If you do not have an Internet connection, your results will reflect only the content of the Help files on your computer. When searching for help online, results also can change as material is added, deleted, and updated on the online Help Web pages maintained by Microsoft.

Q&A

Why were my search results not very helpful?

When initiating a search, be sure to check the spelling of the search text; also, keep your search specific, with fewer than seven words, to return the most accurate results.

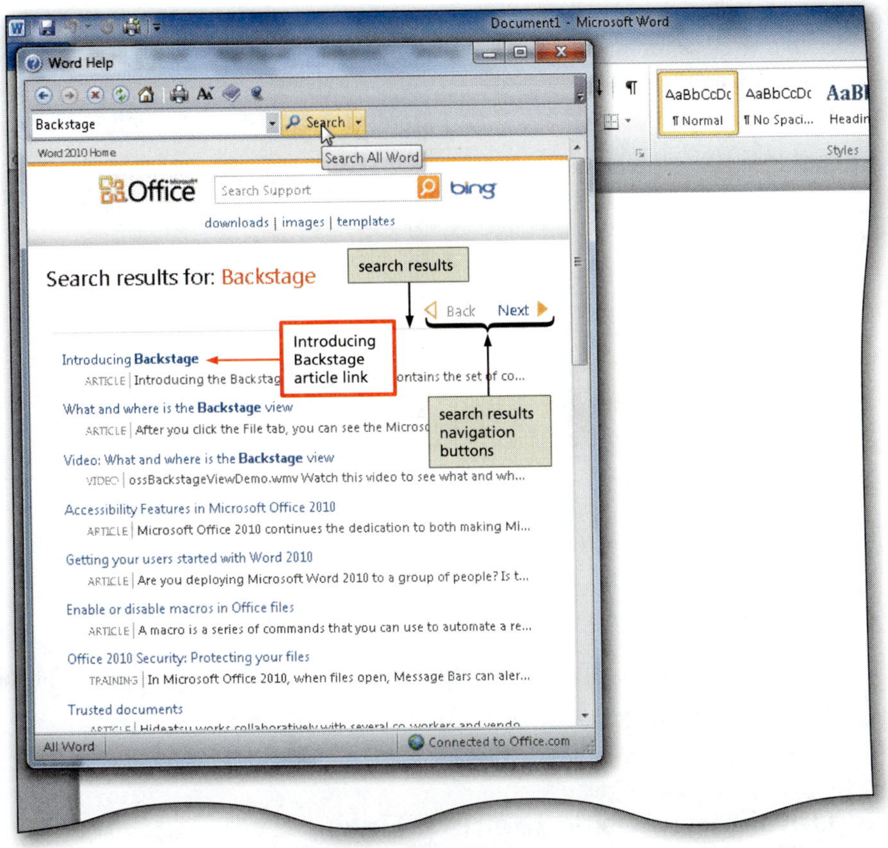

Figure 96

3

- Click the Introducing Backstage link to open the Help document associated with the selected topic (Figure 97).

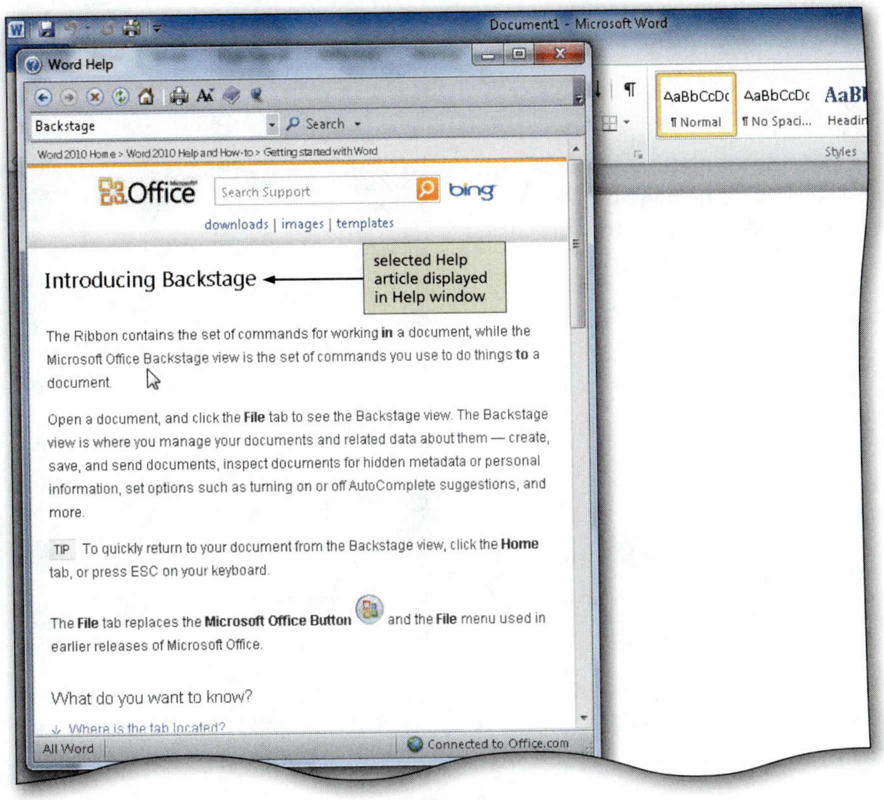

Figure 97

4

- Click the Home button on the toolbar to clear the search results and redisplay the Help home page (Figure 98).

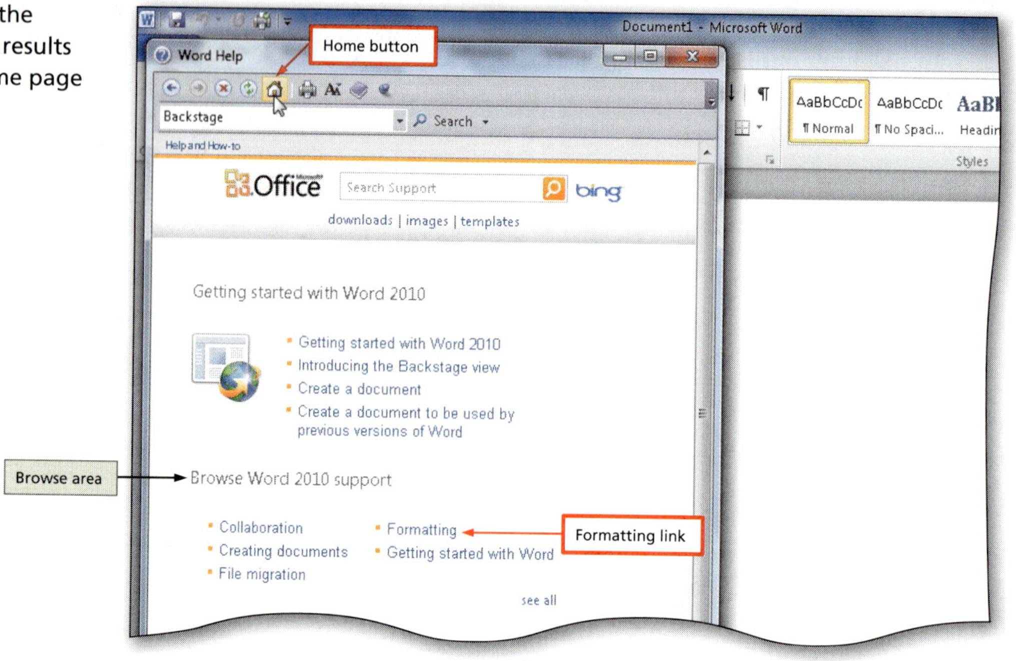

Figure 98

To Obtain Help Using the Help Links

If your topic of interest is listed in the Browse area of the Help window, you can click the link to begin browsing the Help categories instead of entering search text. You browse Help just as you would browse a Web site. If you know which category contains your Help information, you may wish to use these links. The following step finds the Formatting Help information using the category links from the Word Help home page.

1

- Click the Formatting link on the Help home page (shown in Figure 98) to display the Formatting page (Figure 99).

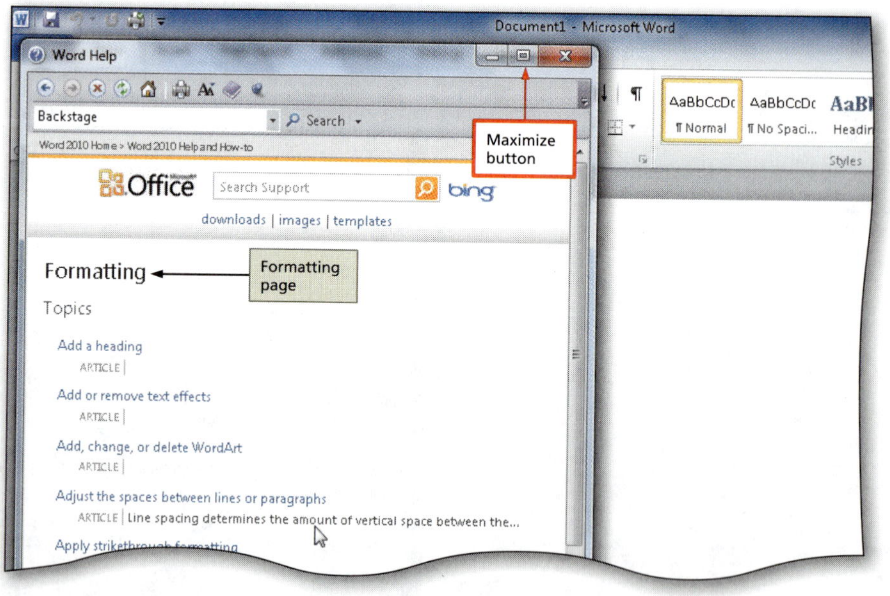

Figure 99

To Obtain Help Using the Help Table of Contents

A third way to find Help in Office programs is through the Help Table of Contents. You can browse through the Table of Contents to display information about a particular topic or to familiarize yourself with an Office program. The following steps access the Help information about themes by browsing through the Table of Contents.

1

- Click the Home button on the toolbar to display the Help home page.
- Click the Show Table of Contents button on the toolbar to display the Table of Contents pane on the left side of the Help window. If necessary, click the Maximize button on the Help title bar to maximize the window (Figure 100).

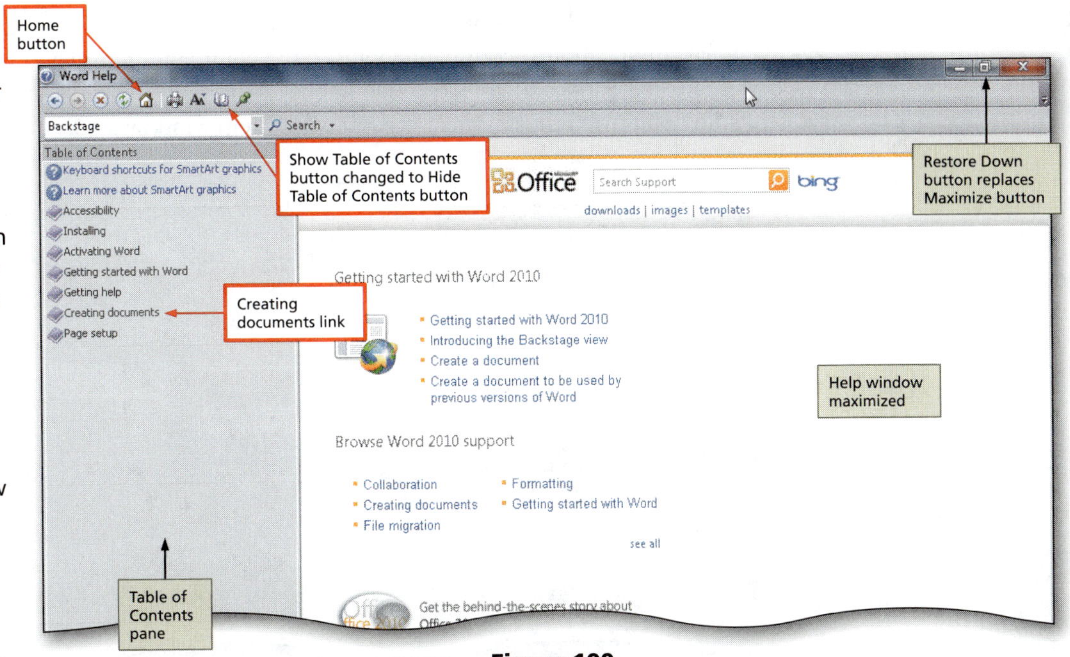

Figure 100

Q&A Why does the appearance of the Show Table of Contents button change?

When the Table of Contents is displayed in the Help window, the Hide Table of Contents button replaces the Show Table of Contents button.

2

- Click the Creating documents link in the Table of Contents pane to view a list of Help subtopics.
- Click the Apply themes to Word documents link in the Table of Contents pane to view the selected Help document in the right pane (Figure 101).
- After reviewing the page, click the Close button to quit Help.

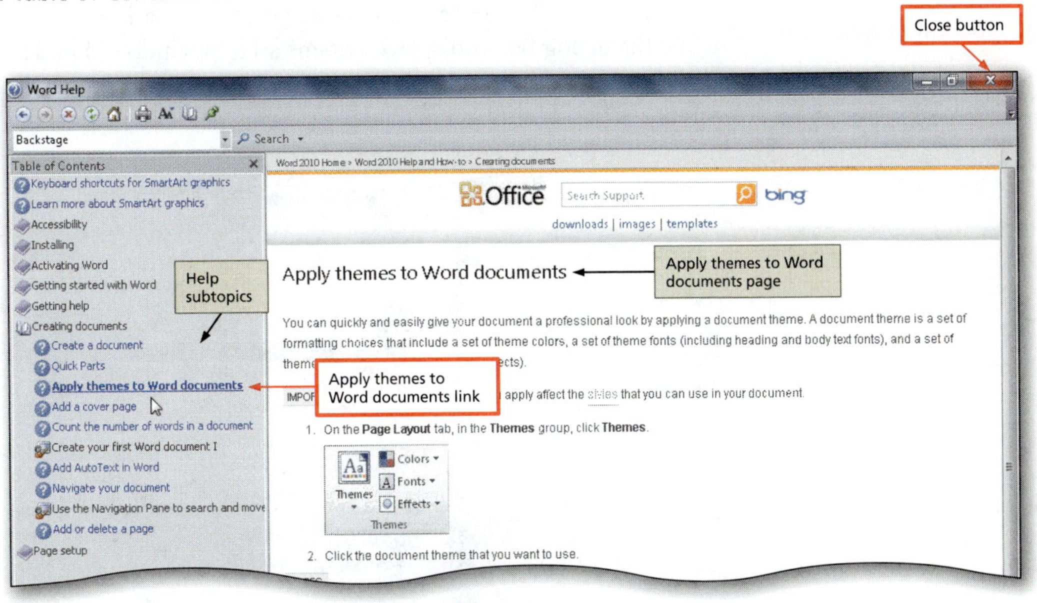

Figure 101

- Click the Office program's Close button (Word, in this case) to quit the Office program.

Q&A How do I remove the Table of Contents pane when I am finished with it?

The Show Table of Contents button acts as a toggle. When the Table of Contents pane is visible, the button changes to Hide Table of Contents. Clicking it hides the Table of Contents pane and changes the button to Show Table of Contents.

Obtaining Help while Working in an Office Program

Help in the Office programs provides you with the ability to obtain help directly, without the need to open the Help window and initiate a search. For example, you may be unsure about how a particular command works, or you may be presented with a dialog box that you are not sure how to use.

Figure 102 shows one option for obtaining help while working in Word. If you want to learn more about a command, point to the command button and wait for the Enhanced ScreenTip to appear. If the Help icon appears in the Enhanced ScreenTip, press the F1 key while pointing to the command to open the Help window associated with that command.

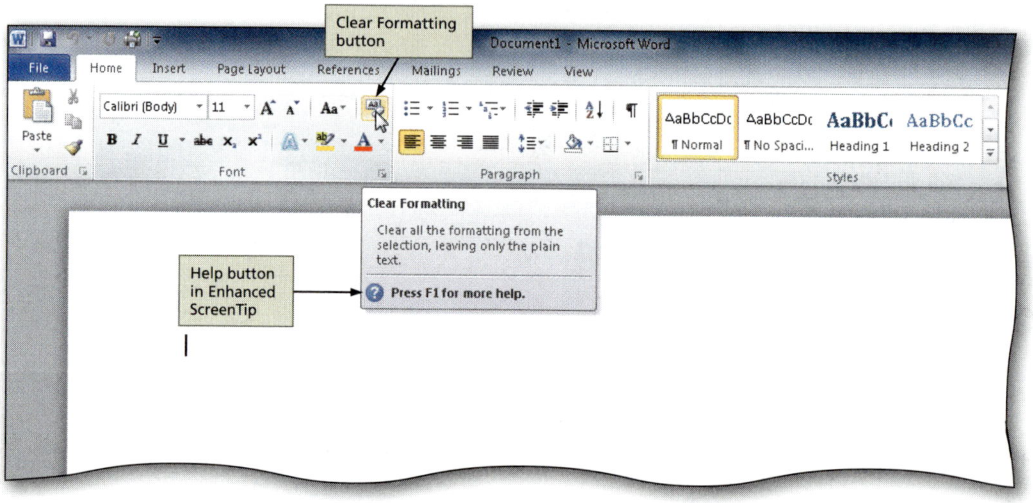

Figure 102

Figure 103 shows a dialog box that contains a Help button. Pressing the F1 key while the dialog box is displayed opens a Help window. The Help window contains help about that dialog box, if available. If no help file is available for that particular dialog box, then the main Help window opens.

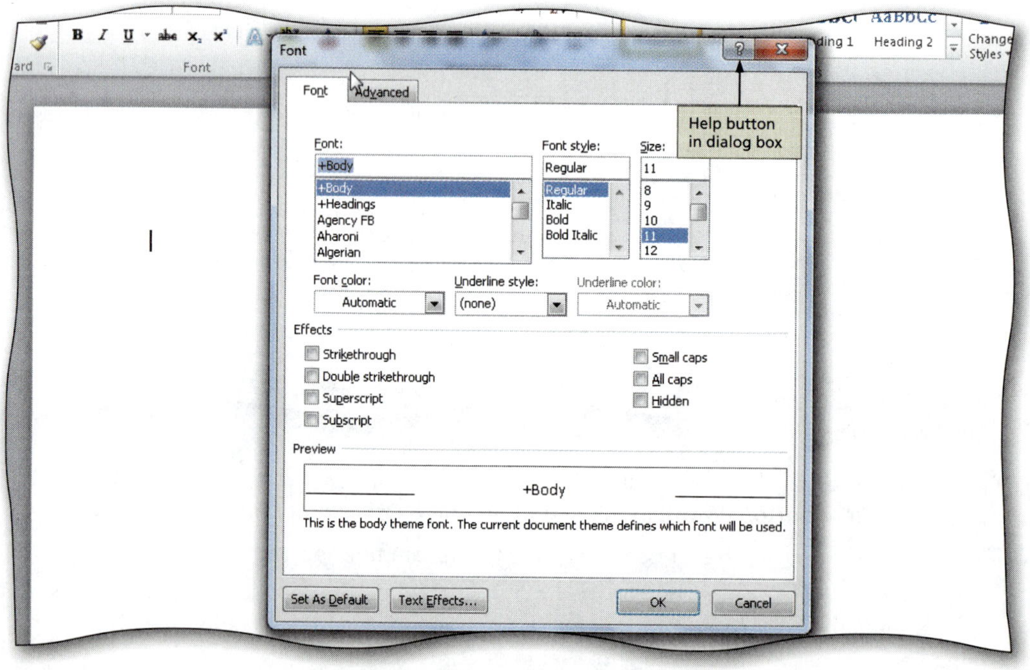

Figure 103

Using Windows Help and Support

One of the more powerful Windows 7 features is Windows Help and Support. **Windows Help and Support** is available when using Windows 7 or when using any Microsoft program running under Windows 7. This feature is designed to assist you in using Windows 7 or the various programs. Table 4 describes the content found in the Help and Support Center. The same methods used for searching Microsoft Office Help can be used in Windows Help and Support. The difference is that Windows Help and Support displays help for Windows 7, instead of for Microsoft Office.

Table 4 Windows Help and Support Center Content Areas

Area	Function
Find an answer quickly	This area contains instructions about how to do a quick search using the search box.
Not sure where to start?	This area displays three topics to help guide a user: How to get started with your computer, Learn about Windows Basics, and Browse Help topics. Clicking one of the options navigates to corresponding Help and Support pages.
More on the Windows Website	This area contains links to online content from the Windows Web site. Clicking the links navigates to the corresponding Web pages on the Web site.

To Start Windows Help and Support

The following steps start Windows Help and Support and display the Windows Help and Support window, containing links to more information about Windows 7.

1

- Click the Start button on the taskbar to display the Start menu (Figure 104).

Q&A Why are the programs that are displayed on the Start menu different?

Windows adds the programs you have used recently to the left pane on the Start menu. You have started several programs while performing the steps in this chapter, so those programs now are displayed on the Start menu.

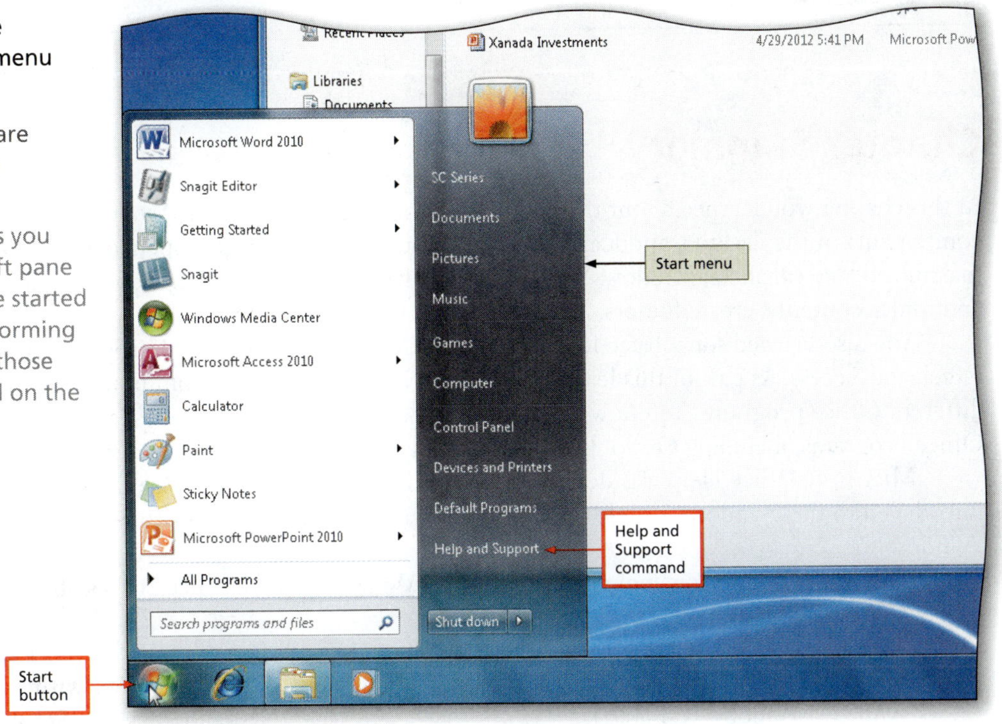

Figure 104

2

- Click Help and Support on the Start menu to open the Windows Help and Support window (Figure 105).
- After reviewing the Windows Help and Support window, click the Close button to quit Windows Help and Support.

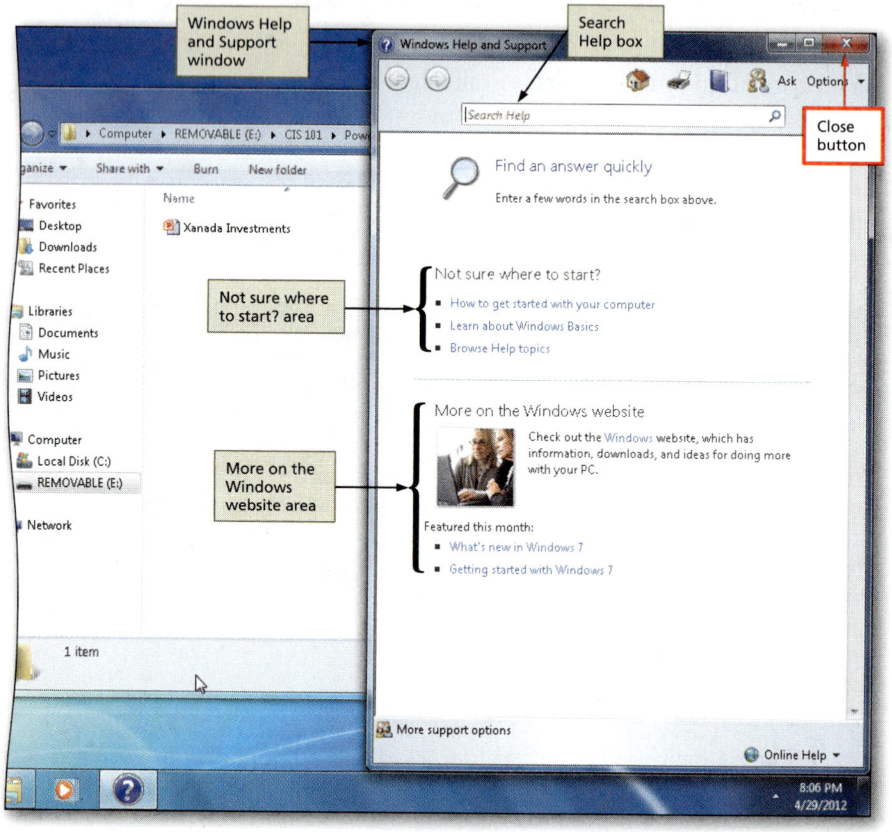

Figure 105

Other Ways

1. Press CTRL+ESC, press RIGHT ARROW, press UP ARROW, press ENTER
2. Press WINDOWS+F1

Chapter Summary

In this chapter, you learned about the Windows 7 interface. You started Windows 7, were introduced to the components of the desktop, and learned several mouse operations. You opened, closed, moved, resized, minimized, maximized, and scrolled a window. You used folder windows to expand and collapse drives and folders, display drive and folder contents, create folders, and rename and then delete a file.

You also learned some basic features of some Microsoft Office 2010 programs, including Word, PowerPoint, Excel, and Access. As part of this learning process, you discovered the common elements that exist among these different Office programs. You now can save basic document, presentation, spreadsheet, and database files. Additional Office programs, including Outlook, Publisher, and OneNote also were discussed.

Microsoft Office Help was demonstrated, and you learned how to use the Office Help window. You were introduced to the Windows 7 Help and Support Center and learned how to use it to obtain more information about Windows 7.

The items listed below include all of the new Windows 7 and Office 2010 skills you have learned in this chapter.

1. Log On to the Computer (OFF 6)
2. Start a Program Using the Start Menu (OFF 10)
3. Maximize a Window (OFF 12)
4. Display a Different Tab on the Ribbon (OFF 16)
5. Minimize, Display, and Restore the Ribbon (OFF 17)
6. Display and Use a Shortcut Menu (OFF 18)
7. Customize the Quick Access Toolbar (OFF 19)
8. Enter Text in a Document (OFF 20)
9. Create a Folder (OFF 22)
10. Create a Folder within a Folder (OFF 24)
11. Expand a Folder, Scroll through Folder Contents, and Collapse a Folder (OFF 26)
12. Switch from One Program to Another (OFF 27)
13. Save a File in a Folder (OFF 27)
14. Minimize and Restore a Window (OFF 30)
15. Change the Screen Resolution (OFF 33)

16. Quit an Office Program with One Document Open (OFF 35)
17. Start a Program Using the Search Box (OFF 37)
18. Enter Content in a Title Slide (OFF 40)
19. Create a New Office Document from the Backstage View (OFF 41)
20. Close an Office File Using the Backstage View (OFF 44)
21. Open a Recent Office File Using the Backstage View (OFF 45)
22. Create a New Blank Office Document from Windows Explorer (OFF 47)
23. Start a Program from Windows Explorer and Open a File (OFF 48)
24. Enter a Worksheet Title (OFF 50)
25. Save an Existing Document with the Same File Name (OFF 51)
26. Create an Access Database (OFF 55)
27. Open an Existing Office File (OFF 57)
28. Rename a File (OFF 63)
29. Move a File (OFF 64)
30. Delete a File (OFF 64)
31. Open the Help Window in an Office Program (OFF 66)
32. Move a Window by Dragging (OFF 66)
33. Resize a Window by Dragging (OFF 67)
34. Obtain Help Using the 'Type words to search for' Text Box (OFF 68)
35. Obtain Help Using the Help Links (OFF 70)
36. Obtain Help Using the Help Table of Contents (OFF 71)
37. Start Windows Help and Support (OFF 73)

> SAM — If you have a SAM 2010 user profile, your instructor may have assigned an autogradable version of this assignment. If so, log into the SAM 2010 Web site at www.cengage.com/sam2010 to download the instruction and start files.

Learn It Online

Test your knowledge of chapter content and key terms.

Instructions: To complete the Learn It Online exercises, visit the Microsoft Office and Concepts CourseMate Web site at www.cengagebrain.com, navigate to the Office 2010 and Windows 7 chapter resources for this book, click the link for the exercise you want to complete, and then read the instructions.

Chapter Reinforcement TF, MC, and SA

A series of true/false, multiple choice, and short answer questions that test your knowledge of the chapter content.

Flash Cards

An interactive learning environment where you identify chapter key terms associated with displayed definitions.

Practice Test

A series of multiple choice questions that test your knowledge of chapter content and key terms.

Who Wants To Be a Computer Genius?

An interactive game that challenges your knowledge of chapter content in the style of a television quiz show.

Wheel of Terms

An interactive game that challenges your knowledge of chapter key terms in the style of the television show *Wheel of Fortune*.

Crossword Puzzle Challenge

A crossword puzzle that challenges your knowledge of key terms presented in the chapter.

Apply Your Knowledge

Reinforce the skills and apply the concepts you learned in this chapter.

Creating a Folder and a Document

Instructions: You will create a Word folder and then create a Word document and save it in the folder.

Perform the following tasks:

1. Connect a USB flash drive to an available USB port and then open the USB flash drive window.
2. Click the New folder button on the toolbar to display a new folder icon and text box for the folder name.
3. Type `Word` in the text box to name the folder. Press the ENTER key to create the folder on the USB flash drive.
4. Start Word.
5. Enter the text shown in Figure 106.
6. Click the Save button on the Quick Access Toolbar. Navigate to the Word folder on the USB flash drive and then save the document using the file name, Apply 1 Class List.
7. If your Quick Access Toolbar does not show the Quick Print button, add the Quick Print button to the Quick Access Toolbar. Print the document using the Quick Print button on the Quick Access Toolbar. When you are finished printing, remove the Quick Print button from the Quick Access Toolbar.
8. Submit the printout to your instructor.
9. Quit Word.

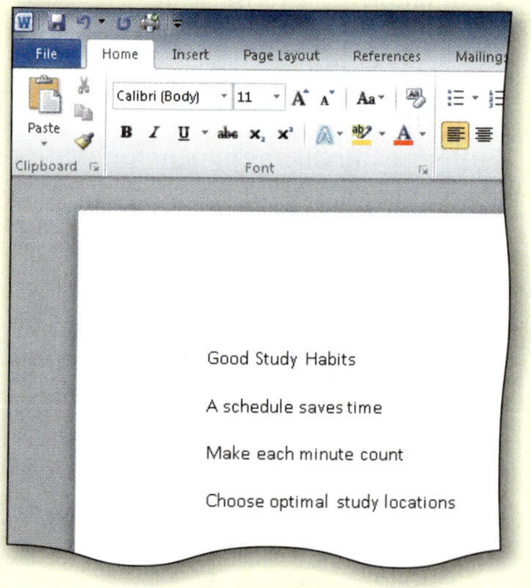

Figure 106

Extend Your Knowledge

Extend the skills you learned in this chapter and experiment with new skills. You will use Help to complete the assignment.

Using Help

Instructions: Use Office Help to perform the following tasks.

Perform the following tasks:

1. Start Word.
2. Click the Microsoft Word Help button to open the Word Help window (Figure 107).
3. Search Word Help to answer the following questions.
   a. What are the steps to add a new group to the Ribbon?
   b. What are Quick Parts?
4. With the Word program still running, start PowerPoint.

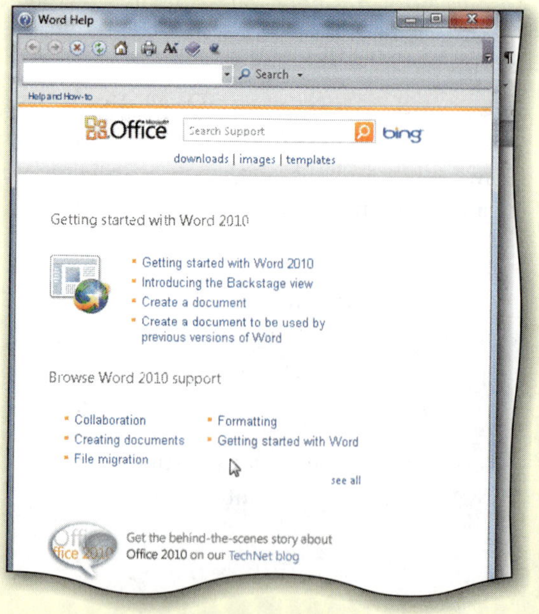

Figure 107

5. Click the Microsoft PowerPoint Help button on the title bar to open the PowerPoint Help window.
6. Search PowerPoint Help to answer the following questions.
   a. What is a slide master?
   b. How do you copy slides from another presentation into the existing presentation?
7. Quit PowerPoint.
8. Start Excel.
9. Click the Microsoft Excel Help button to open the Excel Help window.
10. Search Excel Help to answer the following questions.
    a. What are three different functions available in Excel?
    b. What are sparklines?
11. Quit Excel.
12. Start Access.
13. Click the Microsoft Access Help button to open the Access Help window.
14. Search Access Help to answer the following questions.
    a. What is SQL?
    b. What is a data macro?
15. Quit Access.
16. Type the answers from your searches in the Word document. Save the document with a new file name and then submit it in the format specified by your instructor.
17. Quit Word.

Make It Right

Analyze a file structure and correct all errors and/or improve the design.

Organizing Vacation Photos

Instructions: See the inside back cover of this book for instructions on downloading the Data Files for Students, or contact your instructor for information on accessing the required files.

Traditionally, you have stored photos from past vacations together in one folder. The photos are becoming difficult to manage, and you now want to store them in appropriate folders. You will create the folder structure shown in Figure 108. You then will move the photos to the folders so that they will be organized properly.

1. Connect a USB flash drive to an available USB port to open the USB flash drive window.
2. Using the techniques presented in the chapter, create the hierarchical folder structure shown in Figure 108.
3. Using the techniques presented in the chapter, move the vacation photos to their appropriate folders.
4. Submit your work in the format specified by your instructor.

Figure 108

In the Lab

Use the guidelines, concepts, and skills presented in this chapter to increase your knowledge of Windows 7 and Office 2010. Labs are listed in order of increasing difficulty.

Lab 1: Using Windows Help and Support

Problem: You have a few questions about using Windows 7 and would like to answer these questions using Windows Help and Support.

Instructions: Use Windows Help and Support to perform the following tasks:

1. Display the Start menu and then click Help and Support to start Windows Help and Support.
2. Use the Help and Support Content page to answer the following questions.
   a. How do you reduce computer screen flicker?
   b. Which dialog box do you use to change the appearance of the mouse pointer?
   c. How do you minimize all windows?
   d. What is a VPN?
3. Use the Search Help text box in Windows Help and Support to answer the following questions.
   a. How can you minimize all open windows on the desktop?
   b. How do you start a program using the Run command?
   c. What are the steps to add a toolbar to the taskbar?
   d. What wizard do you use to remove unwanted desktop icons?
4. The tools to solve a problem while using Windows 7 are called **troubleshooters**. Use Windows Help and Support to find the list of troubleshooters (Figure 109), and answer the following questions.
   a. What problems does the HomeGroup troubleshooter allow you to resolve?
   b. List five Windows 7 troubleshooters that are not listed in Figure 109.
5. Use Windows Help and Support to obtain information about software licensing and product activation, and answer the following questions.
   a. What is genuine Windows?
   b. What is activation?
   c. What steps are required to activate Windows?
   d. What steps are required to read the Microsoft Software License Terms?
   e. Can you legally make a second copy of Windows 7 for use at home, work, or on a mobile computer or device?
   f. What is registration?
6. Close the Windows Help and Support window.

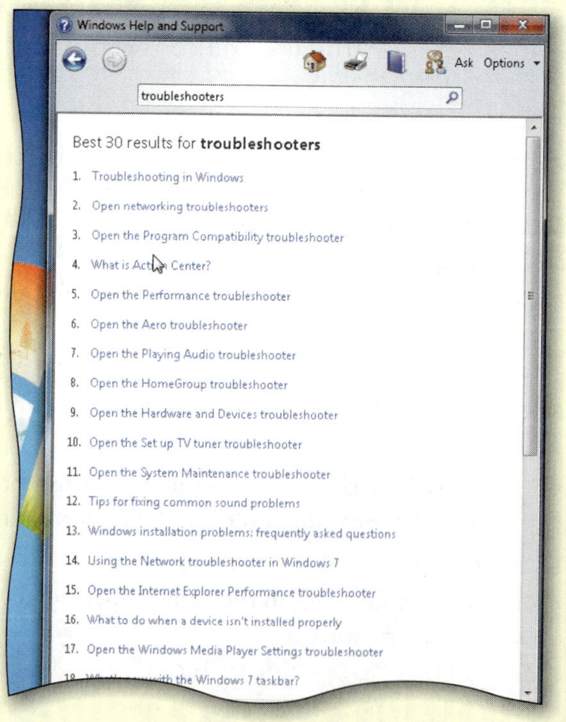

Figure 109

In the Lab

Lab 2: Creating Folders for a Pet Supply Store

Problem: Your friend works for Pete's Pet Supplies. He would like to organize his files in relation to the types of pets available in the store. He has five main categories: dogs, cats, fish, birds, and exotic. You are to create a folder structure similar to Figure 110.

Instructions: Perform the following tasks:

1. Connect a USB flash drive to an available USB port and then open the USB flash drive window.
2. Create the main folder for Pete's Pet Supplies.
3. Navigate to the Pete's Pet Supplies folder.
4. Within the Pete's Pet Supplies folder, create a folder for each of the following: Dogs, Cats, Fish, Birds, and Exotic.
5. Within the Exotic folder, create two additional folders, one for Primates and the second for Reptiles.
6. Submit the assignment in the format specified by your instructor.

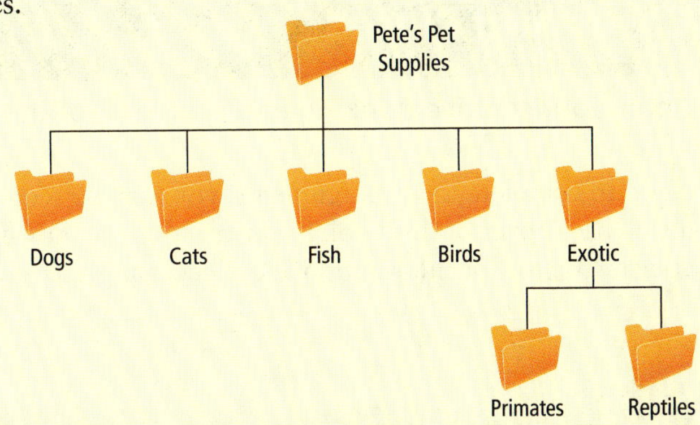

Figure 110

In the Lab

Lab 3: Creating Office Documents

Problem: You are taking a class that requires you to create a Word, PowerPoint, Excel, and Access file. You will save these files to folders named for four different Office programs (Figure 111).

Instructions: Create the folders shown in Figure 111. Then, using the respective Office program, create a small file to save in each folder (i.e., create a Word document to save in the Word folder, a PowerPoint presentation to save in the PowerPoint folder, and so on).

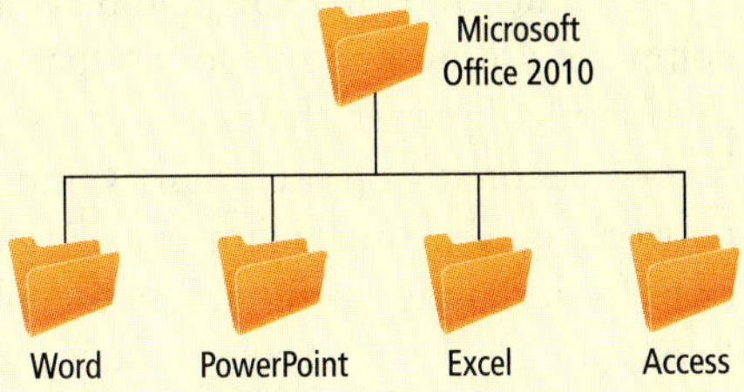

Figure 111

1. Connect a USB flash drive to an available USB port and then open the USB flash drive window.
2. Create the folder structure shown in Figure 111.
3. Navigate to the Word folder.
4. Create a Word document containing the text, My First Word Document, and then save it in the Word folder.
5. Navigate to the PowerPoint folder.
6. Create a PowerPoint presentation containing the title text, My First PowerPoint Presentation, and then save it in the PowerPoint folder.
7. Navigate to the Excel folder.

Continued >

In the Lab *continued*

8. Create an Excel spreadsheet containing the text, My First Excel Spreadsheet, in cell A1 and then save it in the Excel folder.
9. Navigate to the Access folder.
10. Save an Access database named, My First Database, in the Access folder.
11. Close all open Office programs.
12. Submit the assignment in the format specified by your instructor.

Cases and Places

Apply your creative thinking and problem solving skills to design and implement a solution.

Note: To complete these assignments, you may be required to use the Data Files for Students. See the inside back cover of this book for instructions on downloading the Data Files for Students, or contact your instructor for information about accessing the required files.

1: Creating Beginning Files for Classes

Academic

You are taking the following classes: Introduction to Engineering, Beginning Psychology, Introduction to Biology, and Accounting. Create folders for each of the classes. Use the following folder names: Engineering, Psychology, Biology, and Accounting, when creating the folder structure. In the Engineering folder, use Word to create a Word document with the name of the class and the class meeting location and time (MW 10:30 – 11:45, Room 317). In the Psychology folder, use PowerPoint to create your first lab presentation. It should begin with a title slide containing the text, Behavioral Observations. In the Biology folder, save a database named Research in the Biology folder. In the Accounting folder, create an Excel spreadsheet with the text, Tax Information, in cell A1. Use the concepts and techniques presented in this chapter to create the folders and files.

2: Using Help

Personal

Your parents enjoy working and playing games on their home computers. Your mother uses a notebook computer downstairs, and your father uses a desktop computer upstairs. They expressed interest in sharing files between their computers and sharing a single printer, so you offered to research various home networking options. Start Windows Help and Support, and search Help using the keywords, home networking. Use the link for installing a printer on a home network. Start Word and then type the main steps for installing a printer. Use the link for setting up a HomeGroup and then type the main steps for creating a HomeGroup in the Word document. Use the concepts and techniques presented in this chapter to use Help and create the Word document.

3: Creating Folders

Professional

Your boss at the bookstore where you work part-time has asked for help with organizing her files. After looking through the files, you decided upon a file structure for her to use, including the following folders: books, magazines, tapes, DVDs, and general merchandise. Within the books folder, create folders for hardback and paperback books. Within magazines, create folders for special issues and periodicals. In the tapes folder, create folders for celebrity and major release. In the DVDs folder, create a folder for book to DVD. In the general merchandise folder, create folders for novelties, posters, and games. Use the concepts and techniques presented in this chapter to create the folders.

Introduction to Internet Explorer

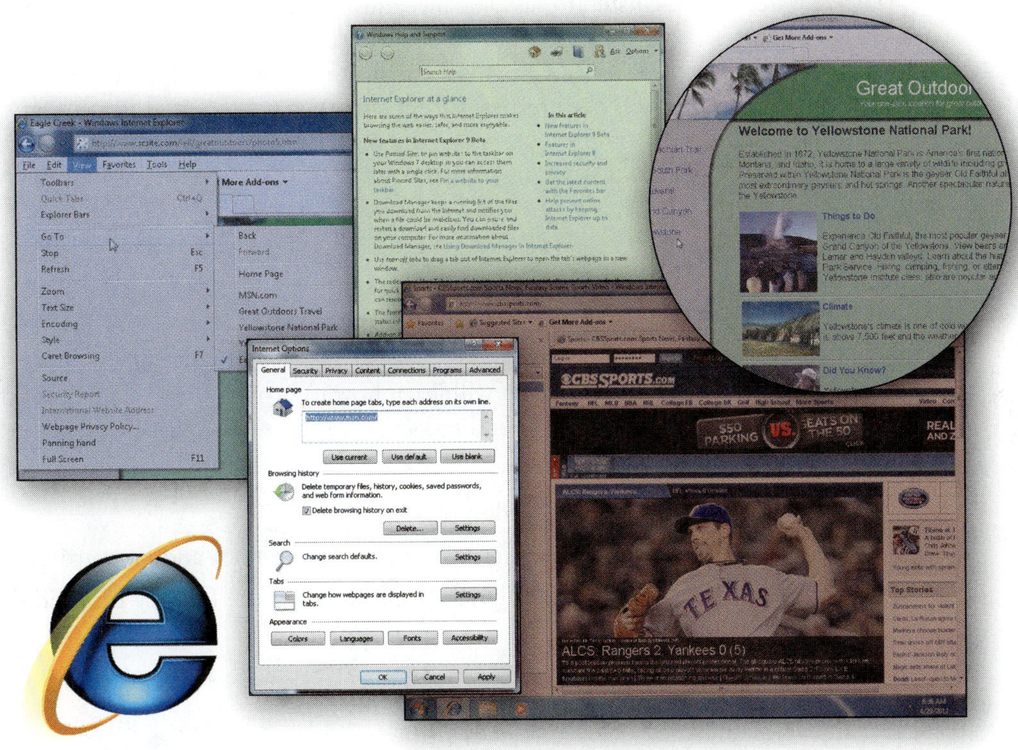

Objectives

You will have mastered the material in this chapter when you can:

- Define the Internet and the World Wide Web
- Discuss security concerns on the Internet
- Explain a link, a Web address, and Hypertext Markup Language (HTML)
- Describe Internet Explorer features
- Enter a Web address
- Use the History List and the Favorites Center
- Use buttons on the toolbar
- Add and remove a favorite
- Save a picture or text from a Web page or an entire Web page
- Copy and paste text or pictures from a Web page into WordPad
- Print a WordPad document and Web page
- Use Internet Explorer Help

Introduction to Internet Explorer

Introduction

The Internet is the most popular and fastest growing area in computing today. Using the Internet, you can do research, send and receive files, obtain a loan, shop for services and merchandise, search for a job, buy and sell stocks, display weather maps, obtain medical advice, watch movies, listen to high-quality music, and converse with people worldwide.

Although a complex system of hardware and software comprises the Internet, it is accessible to the general public because personal computers with user-friendly tools have reduced its complexity. The Internet, with its millions of connected computers, continues to grow with thousands of new users coming online each day. Schools, businesses, newspapers, television stations, and government agencies all can be found on the Internet. All around the world, service providers offer access to the Internet free of charge or for minimal cost.

Overview

As you read this chapter, you will learn how to browse the Web and use Internet Explorer by performing these general tasks:

- Start Internet Explorer
- Enter a Web address in the Address bar
- Browse a Web page by clicking links and using the Back and Forward buttons
- Navigate to previously viewed Web pages by using the History List and the Favorites Center
- Save a Web page
- Print a Web page

Plan Ahead

Internet Usage Guidelines

Internet usage involves navigating to, viewing, and interacting with the various resources on the Internet. Preparations you make before using the Internet will determine the effectiveness of your experience. Before using the Internet, you should follow these general guidelines:

1. **Determine whether your computer has the proper hardware and software necessary to connect to the Internet.** Connecting to the Internet requires your computer to communicate with other computers. Special hardware and software, discussed later in this chapter, are designed to facilitate this communication. If you are unsure of whether your computer is capable of connecting to the Internet, a technician from a company that provides Internet access will be able to help.

(continued)

Plan Ahead

(continued)

2. **Choose an appropriate method to connect to the Internet.** The quality and speed of your Internet connection plays an important role in your overall experience. Various Internet connection options are available, and it is important to choose one that not only allows you to quickly and easily access the information that you desire but also falls within your price range.
3. **Determine whether your computer is protected properly from threats on the Internet.** The Internet can be a breeding ground for software that can do harm to your computer. You should not connect to the Internet unless you have the proper software installed on your computer that will protect you from these various threats.
4. **Determine why you are connecting to the Internet.** Individuals connect to the Internet for many reasons. If you are connecting to the Internet to accomplish a specific task, be clear about what you want to accomplish and identify which resources might prove useful. Many individuals find it easy to become distracted from the task at hand when they are online.
5. **Determine how much time you wish to spend on the Internet.** For some individuals, the Internet can be an extremely addictive environment. In fact, many companies that provide Internet access to their employees have strict policies in place that outline what they consider to be acceptable Internet usage while on the job. The Internet has the potential to significantly lower an employee's productivity, thus costing the employer money. Similarly, parents should be concerned that their children have a safe experience online. Parents can guide children to age-appropriate content and teach their children to keep personal information private.

   Using the Internet not only can be addicting, it also can be costly. Depending upon the method you use to connect to the Internet, the amount that you are charged to connect may directly relate to the number of minutes or hours that you spend connected. Some Internet connection plans allow unlimited usage, while others may only allow you to connect for a certain number of hours before charging an additional fee.

The Internet

The **Internet** is a worldwide collection of networks (Figure 1 on the next page), each of which is composed of a collection of smaller networks. A **network** is composed of several computers connected together to share resources and data. For example, on a college campus, the network in the student computer lab can connect to the faculty computer network, which is connected to the administration network, and they all can connect to the Internet.

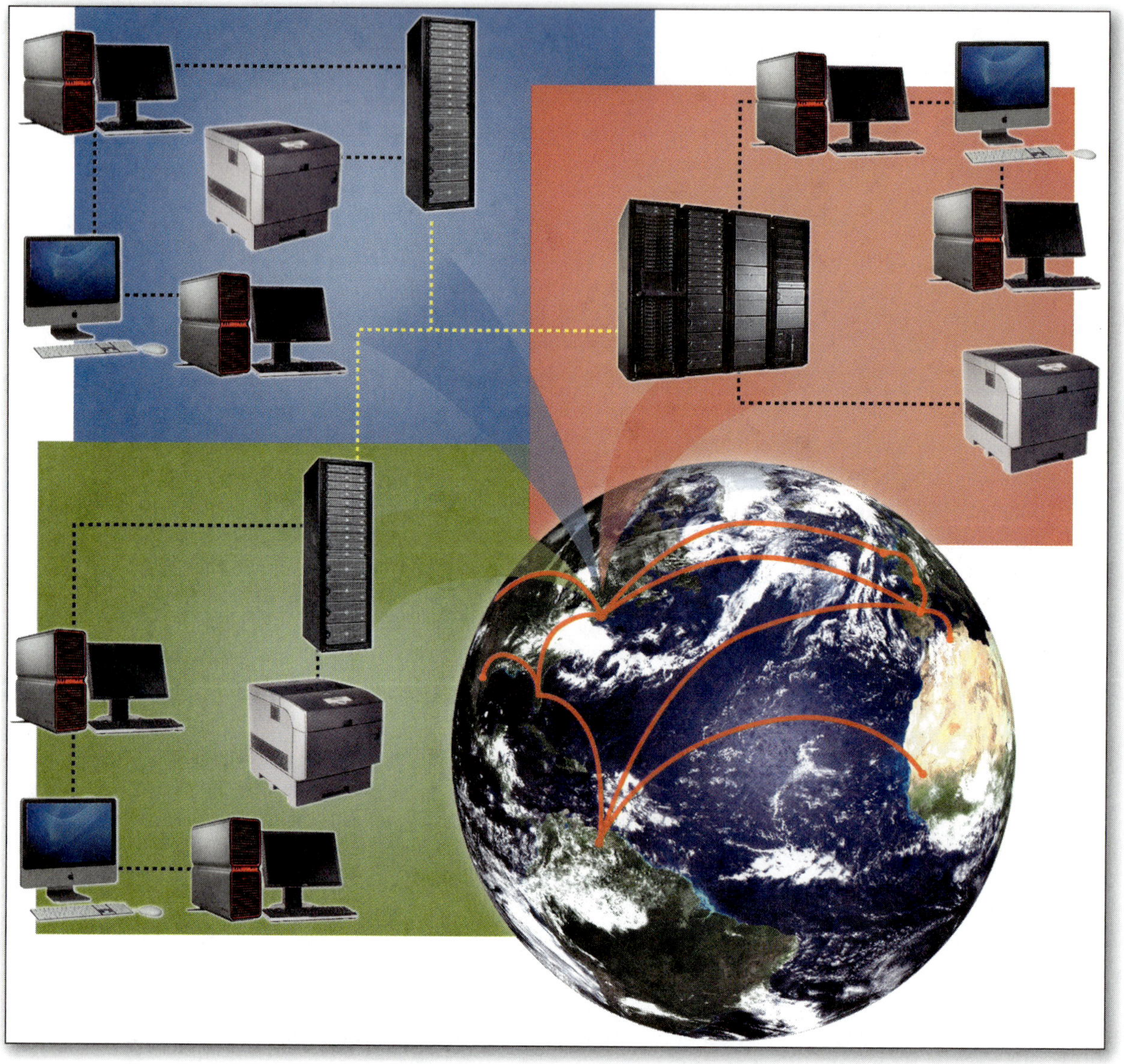

Figure 1

BTW

The Internet
The Internet started as a government experiment for the military. The military wanted the ability to connect to and communicate via different computers running different operating systems. From this experiment, a communication technique originated called Transmission Control Protocol/Internet Protocol, or TCP/IP.

Networks are connected with high-, medium-, and low-speed data lines that allow data to move from one computer to another (Figure 2). The Internet has high-speed data lines that connect major computers located around the world, which form the **Internet backbone**. Other, less powerful computers, such as those used by local ISPs (Internet service providers) often attach to the Internet backbone using medium-speed data lines. Finally, the connection between your computer at home and your local ISP, often called **the last mile**, employs low-speed data lines such as telephone lines, cable television lines, and fiber-optic cable. In some cases today, fixed wireless access is replacing wires over the last mile, which significantly improves access to the Internet.

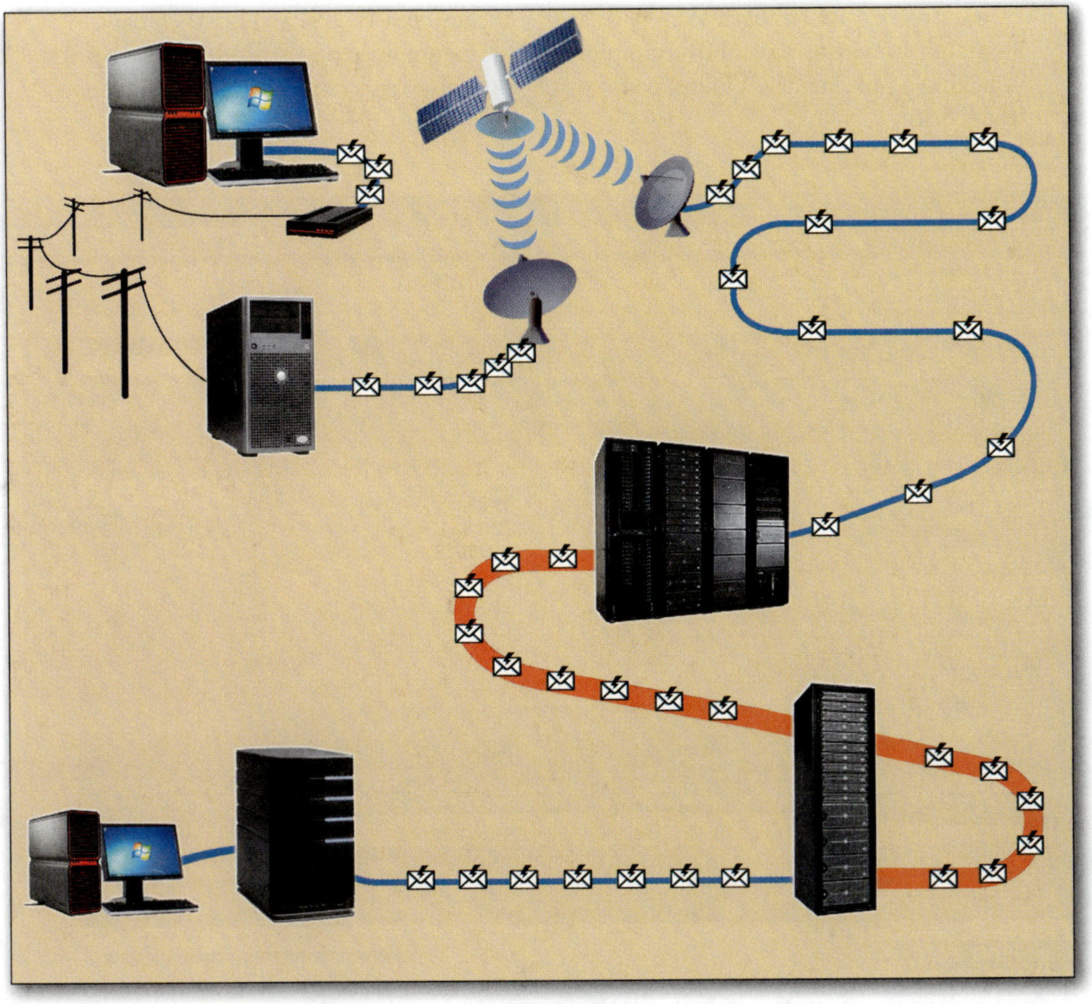

Figure 2

The World Wide Web

Modern computers have the capability of delivering information in a variety of ways, using images, sound, video, animation, virtual reality, and, of course, regular text. On the Internet, this multimedia capability is known as **hypermedia**, which is the combination of text, images, audio, video, and interactivity, delivered over the Internet.

You access hypermedia by clicking a **hyperlink**, or simply a **link**, which points to the location of the computer on which the hypermedia is stored and to the hypermedia itself. A link, which can be in the form of text or an image, can point to hypermedia on any computer connected to the Internet that is configured as a Web server. A **Web server**, which runs Web server software, provides resources such as text, images, files, and links to other computers on the Internet. Thus, clicking a link on a computer in Miami could display hypermedia located in Seattle. All of the resources and links found throughout the Internet create an interconnected network called the **World Wide Web**, which also is referred to as the **Web**, or **WWW**.

Text, images, and other hypermedia available at a Web site are stored in a file called a **Web page**, and a collection of related Web pages make up a **Web site**. When you are viewing hypermedia such as text, images, and video on the World Wide Web, you actually are viewing a Web page.

BTW

Web Sites
An organization can have more than one Web site. Separate departments may have their own Web servers, allowing faster response to requests for Web pages and local control over the Web pages stored at that Web site.

Figure 3 illustrates a Web page at the Disney.com Web site. This Web page contains numerous links. For example, nine of the graphics on the Web page are links. Clicking a link, such as Videos, could display a Web page located on the other side of the world.

Figure 3

Security Concerns on the Internet

> **BTW**
> **Windows Defender**
> Microsoft offers Windows Defender, a program that provides spyware protection, free of charge to Windows users. To download Windows Defender, navigate to Microsoft's Web site (www.microsoft.com) and search for Windows Defender.

Although there are many advantages to accessing and using the Internet, some disadvantages to Internet access also exist that are important to consider. When your computer connects to the Internet, other computers may be able to see your computer and possibly connect to it. Computer-savvy individuals with malicious intentions sometimes take advantage of Internet users who do not take the proper security precautions—by deleting, modifying, or even stealing their data, often without their knowledge. It also is possible for an individual or Web site to install spyware on your computer. **Spyware** is a program that tracks the actions you take on your computer, such as which Web sites you visit, what products you purchase online, and your credit card information, and sends them to a third party. Spyware can decrease your computer's performance, as well as compromise any secure information you have stored on your computer. Another type of malicious software that may be installed on your computer without your knowledge is **adware**. Adware randomly displays advertisements and other messages while you use your computer. Adware and spyware may be installed by someone who connects to an unsecure computer, or by downloading and running a program or file from the Internet. To avoid downloading harmful files and programs, it is important to learn how to tell the difference between legitimate and fraudulent Web sites, files, and programs on the Internet.

In addition to adware and spyware, your computer also may be infected by a **computer virus** if you download an infected file from a Web page or open an infected e-mail attachment. Your computer also can be infected by a virus if someone exploits a security vulnerability, or bug, in a program that is installed on your computer.

Adware, spyware, and viruses are not the only problems that exist on the Internet. **Phishing scams**, or attempts by individuals to obtain confidential information from you, often via the Internet, are growing in popularity. A phishing scam works by falsifying one's identity in an attempt to convince an unsuspecting victim to disclose information such as credit card numbers, bank account information, and Social Security number. A phisher may falsify his or her identity by sending an e-mail that appears to come from someone else, or by creating a Web site that appears to be that of a legitimate company. The worst part about a phishing scam is that the victim often does not know that someone else took advantage of him or her until it is too late. Victims of phishing scams also can be exposed to identity theft and financial loss.

To lower the risk of being victimized by a malicious Web site or a phishing scam, Internet Explorer 8 includes a **SmartScreen Filter**. The SmartScreen Filter is designed to identify malicious and fraudulent Web sites, and will inform you by displaying an appropriate message in the display area and changing the background color of the Address bar to red. While the SmartScreen Filter may not detect all malicious and fraudulent Web sites, it greatly reduces your chances of visiting a malicious Web site or becoming a victim of a phishing scam.

Because these security threats exist, it is important for everyone to practice safe browsing techniques while connected to the Internet. Before connecting your computer to the Internet, you should make sure that you have **antivirus software** installed. Antivirus software immediately will inform you if it detects a virus on your computer. Antivirus software manufacturers also release virus **definition updates** that "teach" the software how to detect newly-created viruses. In addition to installing antivirus software, you also should install a **software firewall** on your computer. A software firewall blocks unauthorized connections to and from your computer. When using your computer on the Internet, it is important to regularly scan your computer for adware and spyware. Some adware and spyware scanners are available online free or for a fee, and some are available in retail stores that sell computer software.

To combat security vulnerabilities that are present in programs installed on your computer, software manufactures may release updates, also known as **patches** or **service packs**, which correct these vulnerabilities. It is good practice to install these updates as soon as they become available. The **Automatic Update feature** in Windows, for example, can be configured to automatically download and install security updates as they become available. Finally, be selective with the Web sites you visit. Millions of Web sites exist on the Internet today, and it is easy to arrive inadvertently at a site other than the one you intended to visit. In addition, you should take extra precaution while visiting Web sites that are hosted by unknown individuals or obscure companies. Avoid downloading anything from these sites or entering any personal information. If you are unsure of whether a Web site is legitimate, it is better to be cautious and simply navigate to another site.

BTW

Online Security
Because of the importance of protecting yourself and your computer while you are connected to the Internet, some Web sites have been developed that offer advice and guidelines for ensuring a safe online experience. For more information, visit onguardonline.gov or staysafeonline.org.

BTW

Children and the Internet
The Internet can be a great source of entertainment and education for children, but there also is the potential for children to encounter inappropriate content or behavior. While there are many ongoing efforts to make the Internet safer for children, children still should be properly supervised and educated about Internet threats. For more information, visit enough.org.

Web Address

Each Web page has a unique address, called a **Web address**, sometimes referred to as a Uniform Resource Locator (URL), which distinguishes it from all other pages on the Internet. The Web address in Figure 3 is http://disney.go.com/index.

A Web address is composed of multiple parts (Figure 4). The first part is the protocol. A **protocol** is a set of rules. Most Web pages use the Hypertext Transfer Protocol. **Hypertext Transfer Protocol (HTTP)** describes the rules used to transmit Web pages electronically over the Internet. You enter the protocol in lowercase as http followed by a colon and two forward slashes (http://). If you do not begin a Web address with a protocol, Internet Explorer will assume it is http, and automatically will append http:// to the front of the Web address.

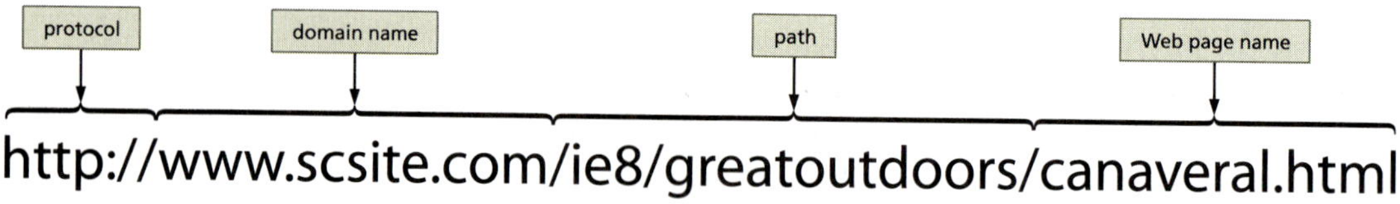

Figure 4

BTW

HTTPS

You may notice that when browsing the Web, some Web sites use the *https* protocol, instead of *http*. The https protocol is a more secure version of the http protocol. The https protocol is designed to make it difficult for others to see the data being transferred between your computer and the Web server.

The second part of a Web address is the domain name. The **domain name** is the Internet address of the computer where the Web page is located. Each computer on the Internet has a unique address, called an **Internet Protocol address**, or **IP address**. The domain name identifies where to forward a request for the Web page referenced by the Web address. The domain name in the Web address in Figure 4 is www.scsite.com. The last part of the domain name (com in Figure 4) is called an **extension** and indicates the type of organization that owns the Web site. For example, the extension .com indicates a commercial organization, usually a business or corporation. Countries throughout the world also have their own domain name extensions. For example, Germany's domain name extension is .de, and China's domain name extension is .cn. Table 1 shows some types of organizations and their extensions.

Table 1 Organizations and Their Domain Name Extensions

Types of Organizations	Original Domain Name Extensions
Commercial organizations, businesses, and companies	.com
Educational institutions	.edu
Government agencies	.gov
Military organizations	.mil
Network providers	.net
Nonprofit organizations	.org
Types of Organizations	**Additional Domain Name Extensions**
Accredited museums	.museum
Aviation community members	.aero
Business cooperatives such as credit unions and rural electric co-ops	.coop
Businesses of all sizes	.biz
Businesses, organizations, or individuals providing general information	.info
Certified professionals such as doctors, lawyers, and accountants	.pro
Individuals or families	.name
Web sites offering media and other broadband content	.tv

The optional third part of a Web address is the file specification of the Web page. The **file specification** includes the file name and possibly a directory or folder name. This information is called the **path**. If no file specification of a Web page is specified in the Web address, a default Web page appears. This means you can display a Web page even though you do not know its file specification.

You can find Web addresses that identify Web sites in magazines or newspapers, on television, from friends, or even from just browsing the Web. Web addresses of well-known companies and organizations usually contain the company's name and institution's name. For example, ibm.com is the Web address for IBM (International Business Machines Corp.), and ucf.edu is the University of Central Florida.

Hypertext Markup Language

Web page authors use a special language called **Hypertext Markup Language (HTML)** to create Web pages. Behind all the formatted text and eye-catching graphics is plain text. Special HTML formatting codes and functions that control attributes of a page, such as font size, colors, and text alignment, surround the text and picture references. Figure 5 shows part of the Hypertext Markup Language used to create the Web page shown in Figure 3 on page IE 6.

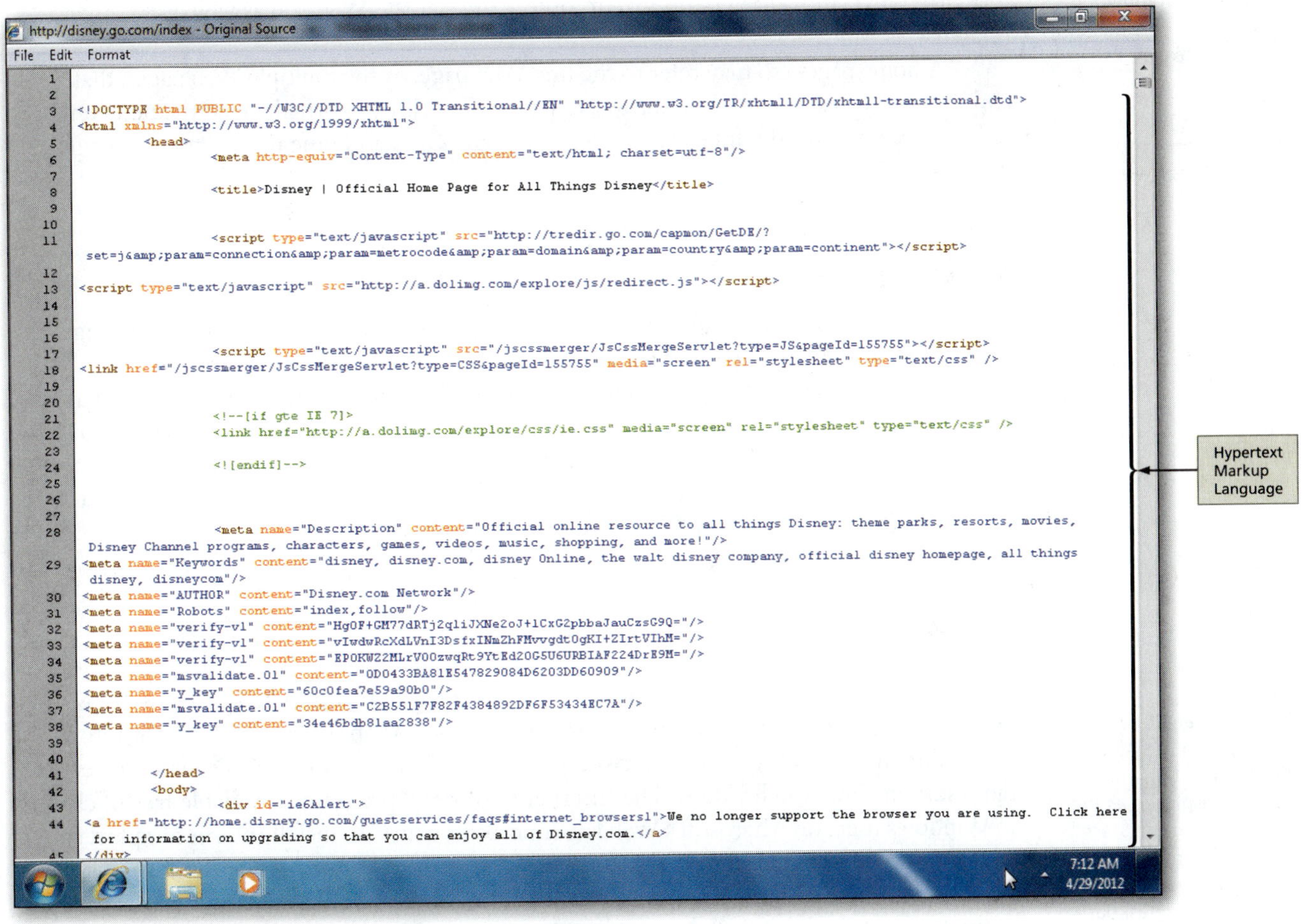

Figure 5

BTW **Web Page Authoring**
Many Web page authoring programs make it easy to create Web pages without learning HTML syntax. Editing programs include Expression Web, Adobe Dreamweaver, CoffeeCup, WebExpress, and Cool Page.

HTML is considered a markup language. A **markup language** contains text, as well as information about the text. This information can include how the text is formatted and positioned on a page. Using HTML, you can create your own Web pages and place them on the Web for others to see. If you want to create Web pages without learning HTML, many easy-to-use Web page authoring programs are available, such as Microsoft Expression Web or Adobe Dreamweaver. New versions of HTML are released periodically to allow Web developers to take advantage of new and exciting technologies that can be delivered over the World Wide Web. As new versions of HTML are released, software on your computer must be updated to support new and updated features.

Home Pages

BTW **Customize Your Home Page**
You can change the home page by clicking Tools on the Command bar, clicking the Internet Options command, and in the General sheet clicking the Use current, Use default, or Use blank button, or typing your desired Web address in the text box.

No main menus or particular starting points exist in the World Wide Web, but most people start a visit to the Web via specially designated Web pages called home pages. A **home page** is the introductory page for a Web site. All other Web pages for that site usually are accessible from the home page via links. When you enter a domain name with no file specification, such as disneyland.com or nbc.com, the home page is the page that is displayed.

Because it is the starting point for most Web sites, Web designers try to make a good first impression. These pages often display attractive, eye-catching images, specially formatted text, and a variety of links to other pages at the Web site as well as to other related Web sites.

A home page also may refer to the first Web page, or the multiple Web pages, that appear when you start your Web browser. For example, if you normally read the news online when you connect to the Internet, you may set your browser's home page to your favorite news Web site.

Web Browsers

Graphical user interfaces (GUIs) such as Microsoft Windows simplify working with a computer by using a point-and-click method. Similarly, a browser such as Internet Explorer makes using the World Wide Web easier by removing the complexity of having to remember the syntax, or rules, of commands used to reference Web pages at Web sites. A **Web browser** takes the Web address associated with a link or the Web address entered by a user, locates the computer containing the associated Web page, and then reads the returned HTML to display a Web page.

BTW **The Internet Explorer Icon**
When you install Internet Explorer 8, the Internet Explorer icon and name are displayed in the All Programs list and also may be displayed as the first entry on the Start menu. The Internet Explorer icon also may appear on the taskbar.

What Is Internet Explorer 8?

Microsoft Windows Internet Explorer 8, also known as **Internet Explorer** or **IE,** is Web browsing software that allows you to search for and view Web pages, save links for future use, maintain a list of the pages you visit, obtain information from various sources, listen to radio stations, and watch videos. The Internet Explorer 8 program is available free of charge to Windows users on Microsoft's Web site (microsoft.com). To install Internet Explorer 8, you must be using one of the following operating systems: Windows XP, Windows Vista, Windows 7, Windows Server 2003, or Windows Server 2008. This chapter illustrates the use of the Internet Explorer 8 Web browser.

Starting Internet Explorer

If you are stepping through this chapter on a computer and want your screen to match the figures in the Office and Windows chapters in this book, your monitor's resolution should be set to 1024 × 768. For more information about how to change the resolution on your computer, read the Office 2010 and Windows 7 chapter in this book.

To Start Internet Explorer

The following steps, which assume Windows is running, start Internet Explorer based on a typical installation. You may need to ask your instructor how to start Internet Explorer on your computer.

1

- Click the Start button on the Windows taskbar to display the Start menu.
- Point to All Programs on the Start menu to display the All Programs list, and then point to Internet Explorer in the All Programs list (Figure 6).

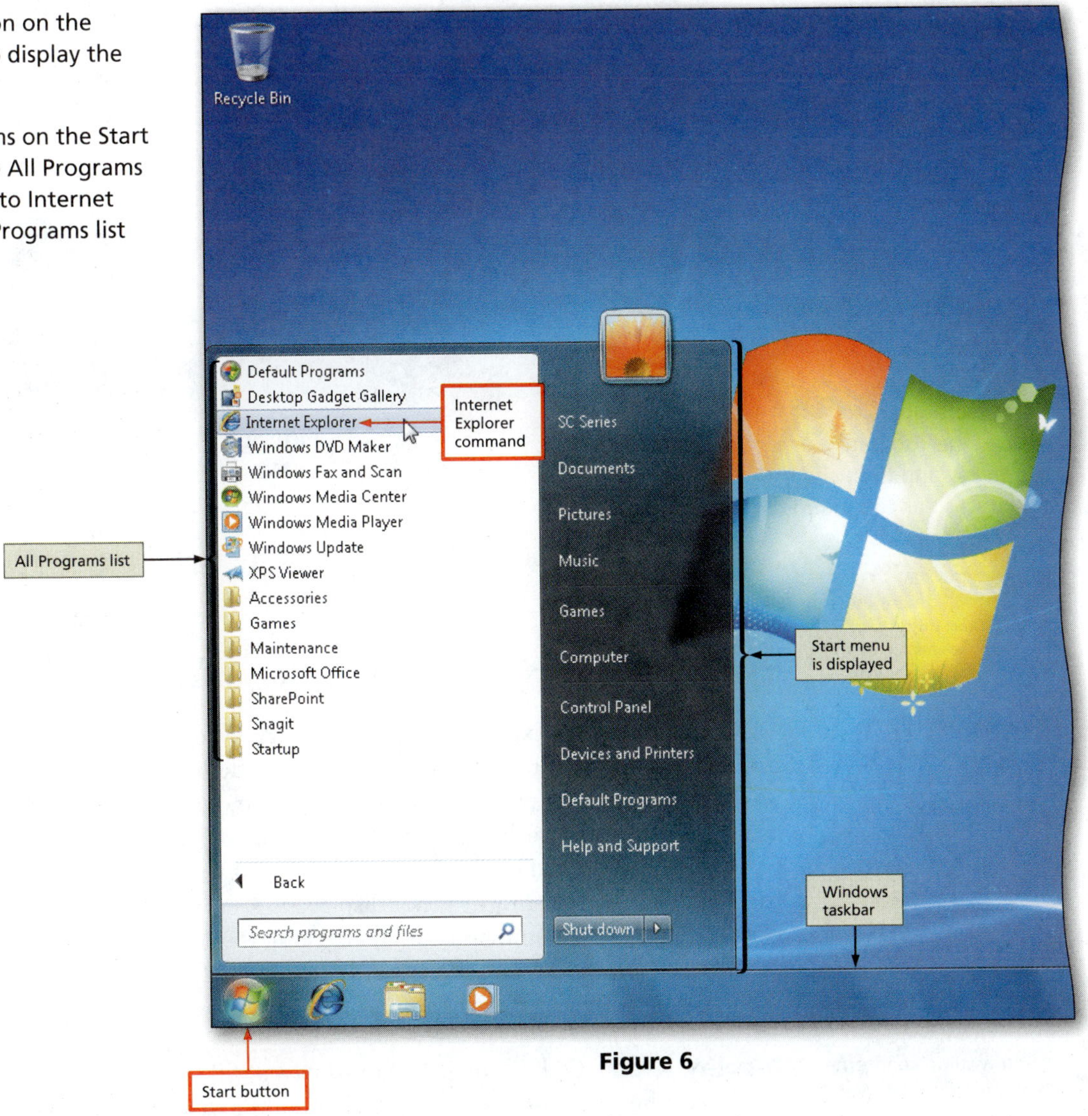

Figure 6

2

- Click Internet Explorer to start Internet Explorer and open the MSN.com - Windows Internet Explorer window (Figure 7). Depending on your computer's configuration, a different home page may be displayed.
- If the Internet Explorer window is not maximized, double-click its title bar to maximize it.
- Press the ALT key to display the menu bar, click View to display the View menu, point to Toolbars to display the Toolbars submenu, and then click the Status Bar command to hide the status bar.

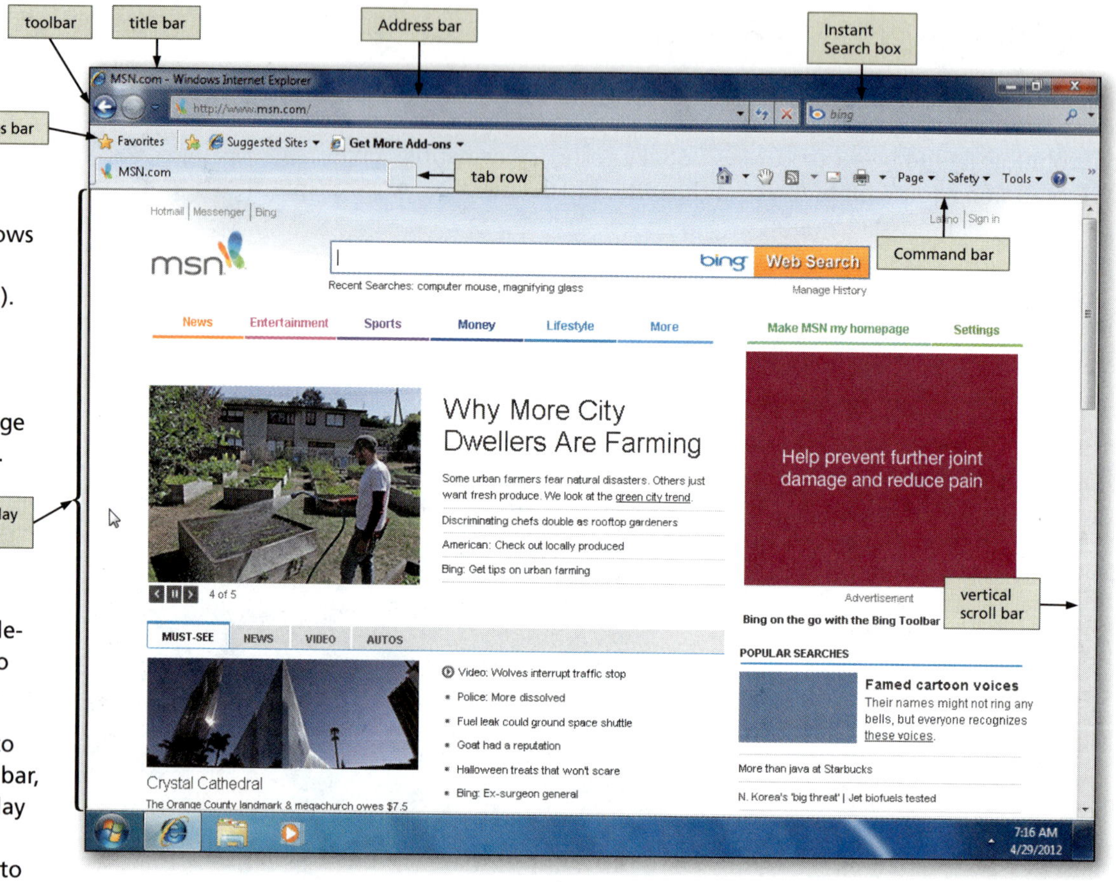

Figure 7

Other Ways

1. Click Start button on Windows taskbar, click Internet Explorer icon on Start menu
2. Double-click Internet Explorer icon on desktop
3. Press CTRL+ESC, press I, press ENTER

The Internet Explorer Window

The **Internet Explorer window** (Figure 7) consists of a range of features that make browsing the Internet easy. It contains a title bar, the menu bar, the Instant Search box, an Address bar, a tab row, the Command bar, Favorites bar, scroll bars, and a display area where pages from the Web appear. The menu bar, Favorites bar, Address bar, Instant Search box, Command bar, and tab row appear at the top of the screen just below the title bar. By default, the menu bar is not displayed. You can display the menu bar by right-clicking on the the Command bar and clicking the Menu Bar command, or by pressing the ALT key. The status bar appears at the bottom of the screen. Some users choose to hide the status bar so that it does not take space away from the display area.

BTW

Full Screen Mode

If you would like Internet Explorer to display Web pages in full screen mode (without the title bar, toolbars, or other components of the window), you can either press the F11 key on the keyboard or select the Full Screen command on the View menu.

Display Area Only a portion of most pages will be visible on the screen. You view the portion of the page displayed on the screen in the **display area** (Figure 7). To the right of the display area is a scroll bar, scroll arrows, and a scroll box, which you can use to move the text in the display area up and down and reveal other parts of the page. Occasionally a Web page may be wider than the display area can show, and a horizontal scroll bar will appear at the bottom of the display area.

Notice the links on the Internet Explorer home page shown in Figure 7. When you position the mouse pointer on one of these links, the mouse pointer changes to a pointing hand. This change in the shape of the mouse pointer identifies these elements as links. Clicking a link retrieves the Web page associated with the link and displays it in the display area.

Title Bar The title bar appears at the top of the Internet Explorer window. As shown at the top of Figure 7, the **title bar** includes the Internet Explorer menu icon on the left, the title of the active Web page, and the Minimize, Restore (or Maximize), and Close buttons on the right. Clicking the **Internet Explorer menu icon** on the title bar will display the System menu, which contains commands to carry out the actions associated with the Internet Explorer window. Double-click the Internet Explorer menu icon or click the Close button to close the window and quit Internet Explorer.

Click the **Minimize button** to minimize the Internet Explorer window. When you minimize the window, it still is open but it no longer appears on the desktop and the Internet Explorer button on the taskbar becomes inactive (a lighter color). After minimizing, clicking the button with the Internet Explorer icon on the Windows taskbar displays the Internet Explorer window in the previous position it occupied on the desktop and changes the button to an active state (a darker color).

Click the **Maximize button** to maximize the Internet Explorer window so that it expands to fill the entire desktop. When the window is maximized, the Restore button replaces the Maximize button on the title bar. Click the **Restore button** to return the window to the size and position it occupied before being maximized. The Restore button changes to the Maximize button when the Internet Explorer window is in a restored state.

You also can double-click the title bar to restore and maximize the Internet Explorer window. If the window is in a restored state, you can drag the title bar to move the window around the desktop.

Menu Bar The **menu bar** is located below the title bar. Because the most common Internet Explorer commands are accessible via the Favorites bar and the Command bar, by default Internet Explorer hides the menu bar. Each **menu name** on the menu bar represents a menu of commands you can use to perform actions such as saving Web pages, copying and pasting, using the Find on this page command, sending a page as an e-mail message, setting Internet Explorer options, quitting Internet Explorer, and so on. To display a menu when the menu bar is displayed, click the menu name on the menu bar. To select a command on a menu, click the command name or press the **keyboard shortcut** shown to the right of some commands on the menu.

Navigation Buttons The **navigation buttons** (Figure 7) in Internet Explorer include the **Back button** and the **Forward button**. Clicking the Back button retrieves the previous page. To go more than one page back, click the Recent Pages list arrow, and then click a Web page title in the list. The Forward button retrieves the next page. To navigate more than one page forward, click the Recent Pages list arrow, and then click a Web page title in the list. The Forward button only is available after you have clicked the Back button one or more times to return to a previous page.

Favorites Bar The **Favorites bar** (Figure 7) contains buttons that allow you to display the Favorites Center and add a Web site to your Favorites bar. As you add to your favorites (discussed later in this chapter), more buttons may appear on this bar.

BTW

The Address Bar
To move the insertion point to the Address bar when the box is empty, or to highlight the Web address in the Address bar, press ALT+D.

Address Bar The **Address bar** (Figure 7 on page IE 12) contains the Web address for the page currently shown in the display area. The Address bar also can be used to search for information on the World Wide Web.

The Web address updates automatically as you browse from page to page. If you know the Web address of a Web page you want to visit, click the Web address in the Address bar to highlight it, type the new Web address, and then press the ENTER key to display the corresponding page. As you type a Web address in the Address bar, Internet Explorer will display a list of suggestions, including AutoComplete suggestions and previously visited Web pages, files, and feeds. In addition, you can click the **Address bar arrow** at the right end of the Address bar to display a list of previously displayed Web pages. Clicking a Web address in the Address list displays the corresponding Web page.

New to Internet Explorer 8, the Address bar now includes a security feature known as domain highlighting. **Domain highlighting** displays the top-level domain in a black font, while the remainder of the Web address is displayed in a gray font (Figure 8). This helps to protect the user from phishing scams by allowing the user easily to identify whether the Web site currently displayed in the window is the Web site he or she intended to visit.

Figure 8

You also can access information on your computer by typing a program name in the Address bar and pressing the ENTER key to start the corresponding program, typing a folder name and pressing the ENTER key to open a folder window, typing a document name and pressing the ENTER key to start a program and display the document in the program window, or typing a keyword or phrase (search inquiry) and pressing the ENTER key to display Web pages containing the keyword or phrase.

Command Bar

The **Command bar** provides quick and easy access to most Internet Explorer functions. The buttons on the Command bar allow you to change your home page options, access your e-mail account, print the current Web page and access printing options, access Web page options, access safety options, access Internet Explorer tools, and more. You can customize the tools that appear on the Command bar by right-clicking the Command bar, pointing to Customize on the shortcut menu, and then clicking Add or Remove Commands. Depending on the size of the Command bar in your Internet Explorer window, not all commands may be displayed. If a small double caret appears to the right of the Command bar, it indicates additional Command bar options are available. The options on your Command bar may be different, depending on the software installed on your computer and your computer's configuration. Table 2 identifies the default commands on the Command bar and briefly describes the function of each command.

Table 2 Commands on the Command Bar

Commands	Function
	Displays the home page, and includes options to add, change, or remove the home page
	When active, these buttons allow you to view the RSS feeds or Web Slices on the current Web page
	Starts your default e-mail program
	Prints the current Web page, or displays a menu providing access to various printing options
Page ▾	Displays a menu containing selected popular commands from the menu bar's File, Edit, and View menus
Safety ▾	Displays a menu containing commands that allow you to configure safety and security options
Tools ▾	Displays commonly used commands that are also accessible on the View and Tools menus on the menu bar
	Displays the Help menu, which is also accessible via the menu bar

Instant Search Box The **Instant Search box** is located to the right of the Address bar and allows you to perform a search on the World Wide Web by entering your search criteria and pressing the ENTER key. By default, the Instant Search box will perform your search using Bing, but other searching options are available by customizing the Instant Search box.

Tab Row The **tab row** is located adjacent to the Command bar. The tab row enables you to keep multiple Web pages open simultaneously in one browser window. After clicking the New Tab button in the tab row, you can type the Web address of the Web page in the Address bar and it will be displayed in the new tab. The tab row also allows you to switch between tabs, reorder tabs, close single tabs, and view the Web pages you currently have open in tabs. Older versions of Web browsers, including versions of Internet Explorer prior to version 7, did not support tabbed browsing, and it was necessary to open a new browser window each time you wanted to display additional Web pages. Opening multiple browser windows consumes additional system resources, which can decrease your computer's performance. Even though you are able to open multiple Internet Explorer windows simultaneously, it is recommended that you open new Web pages in tabs. While a Web page loads in the display area, the Internet Explorer icon in the corresponding tab changes to an animated circle. When the Web page finishes loading, the Internet Explorer icon is displayed on the tab.

BTW **The Command Bar**
If the text label is not displayed on the buttons on the Command bar, right-click the Command bar, point to Customize on the shortcut menu, and then click Show All Text Labels. You also can change the size of the icons on the Command bar by using the Use Large Icons command on the shortcut menu. When a check mark appears next to the Use Large Icons command, the icons on the Command bar are displayed in their largest size. When a check mark does not appear, small icons are displayed on the Command bar.

Browsing the World Wide Web

The most common way to browse the World Wide Web is to obtain the Web address of a Web page you want to visit and then enter it into the Address bar. By visiting various Web sites, you can begin to understand the enormous appeal of the Web. The following steps show how to visit the Web page titled Great Outdoors Travel, which contains information and photographs of five popular outdoor destinations in the United States. The Web address for The Great Outdoors Web site is www.scsite.com/ie8/greatoutdoors.

BTW **The Great Outdoors Travel Web Site**
Notice that the Web address you enter for The Great Outdoors page contains a domain name (scsite.com) that belongs to the publishing company. The Great Outdoors Travel Web site has been developed exclusively for use with this chapter.

To Browse the Web by Entering a Web Address

To navigate to the home page for the Great Outdoors Travel Web site, you will need to enter the Web address in the Address bar.

1

- Click the Address bar to highlight the Web address (Figure 9).

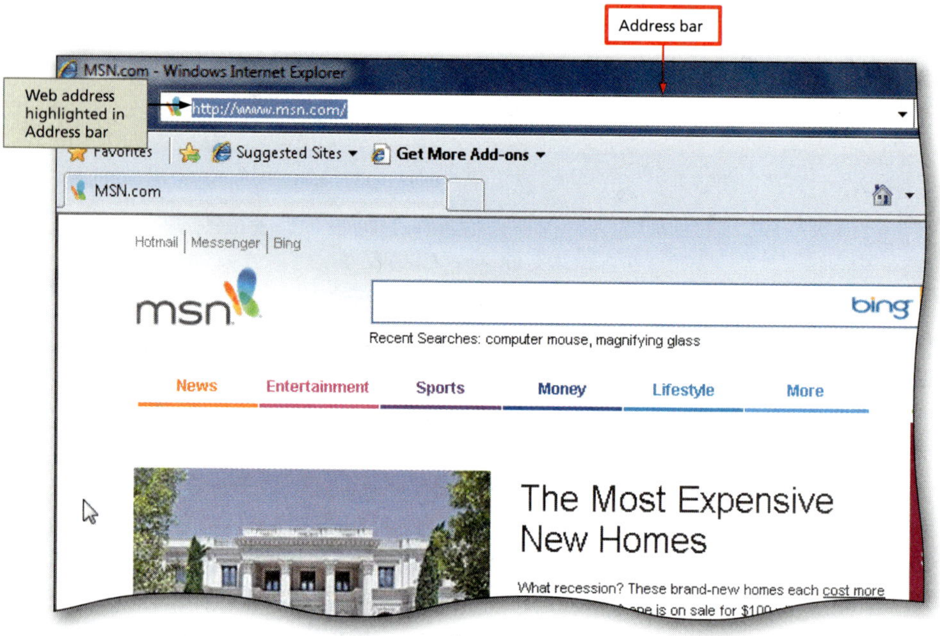

Figure 9

2

- Type **scsite.com/ie8/greatoutdoors** in the Address bar to enter the new Web address (Figure 10).

Q&A Why is it unnecessary to type http:// or www. at the beginning of each Web address?

Depending on how the Web server is configured, it may not require you to type http:// or www. at the beginning of the Web address. In the case of this Web site, you can type `scsite.com/ie8/greatoutdoors` or `www.scsite.com/ie8/greatoutdoors` as the Web address.

Q&A What happens if a Web page is not displayed correctly?

Internet Explorer 8 follows a more strict interpretation of HTML, and as a result some Web pages may not be displayed as expected. If you encounter a Web page that is not displayed correctly, you may be able to correct the problem by displaying the Web page in Compatibility View. To display a Web page in Compatibility View, click the Compatibility View button on the Address bar.

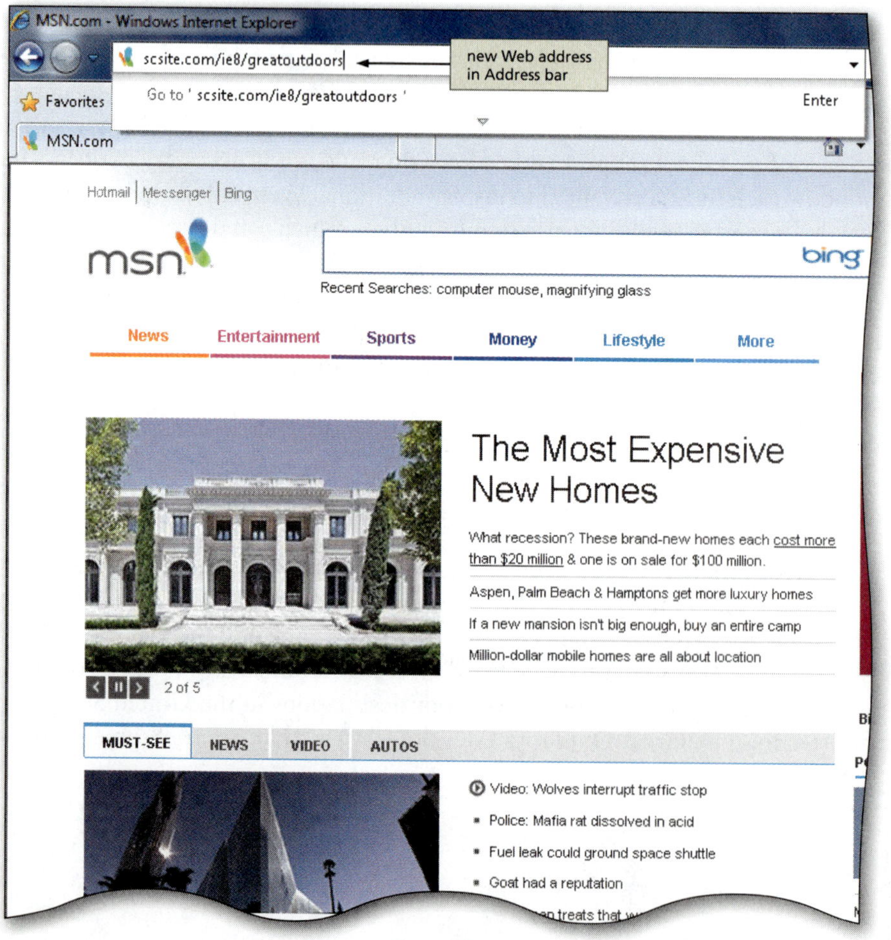

Figure 10

3

- Press the ENTER key to load the Great Outdoors Travel Web page (Figure 11).

Q&A

What if I typed the wrong Web address?

If you type the wrong letter and notice the error before pressing the ENTER key, use the BACKSPACE key to erase all the characters back to and including the one that is wrong. If the error is easier to retype than correct, click the Web address in the Address bar and retype it correctly.

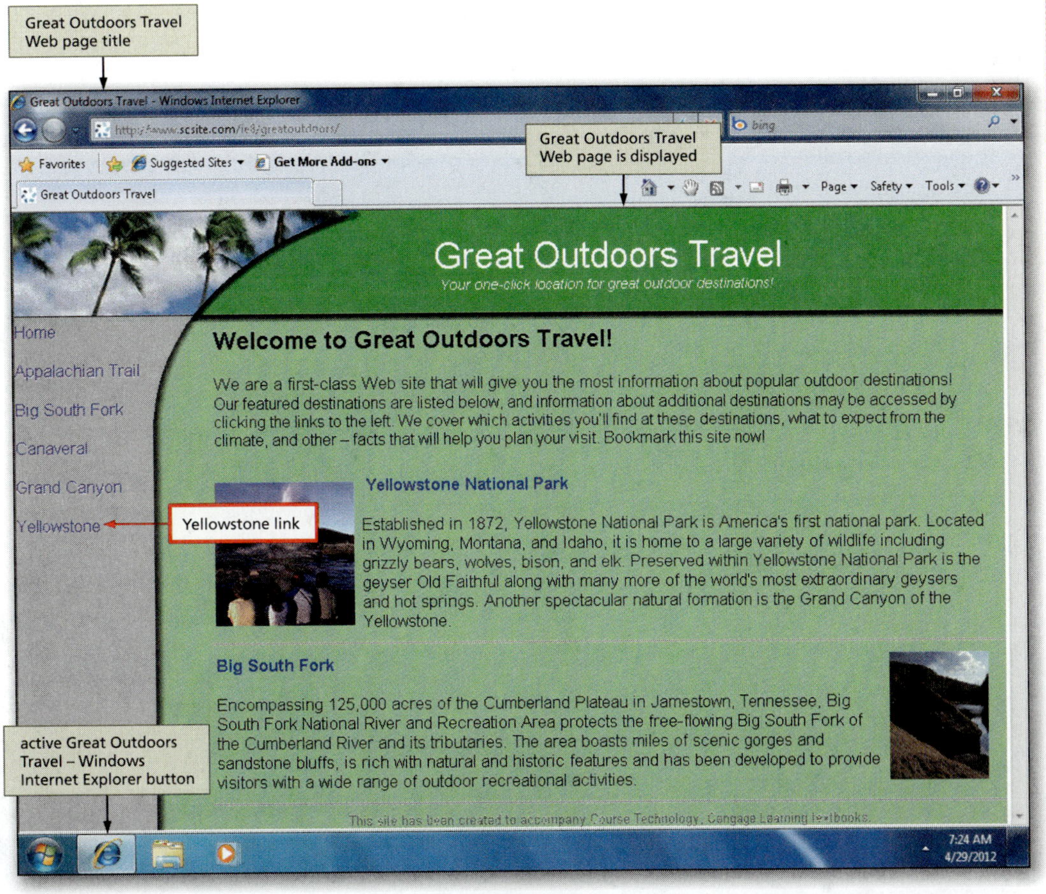

Figure 11

4

- Click the Yellowstone link to display the Yellowstone National Park Web page (Figure 12).

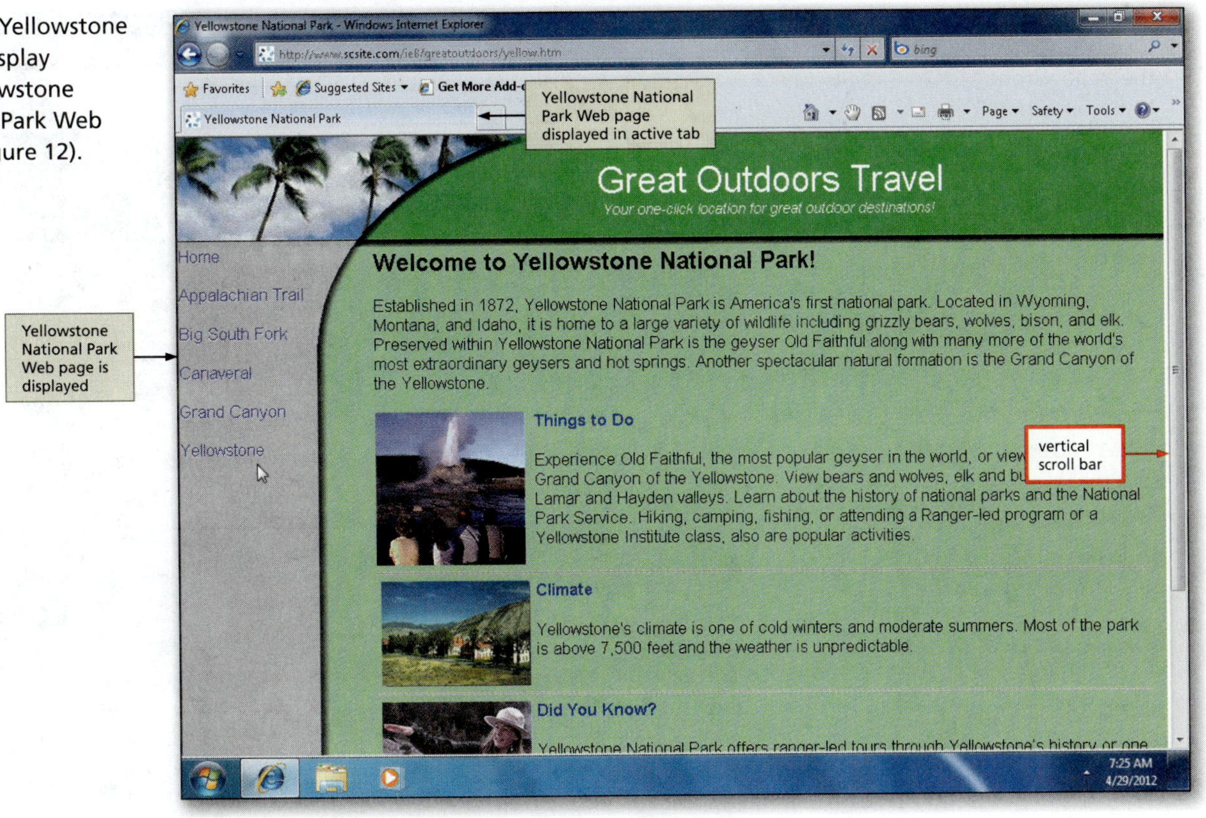

Figure 12

5

- Scroll through the display area using the vertical scroll bar to display the photo gallery link (Figure 13).

Q&A

Why is the text, photo gallery, underlined?

Links to other Web pages and Web sites usually are underlined. Individuals who create Web pages typically do not underline text unless the text will act as a hyperlink.

Figure 13

6

- Click the photo gallery link to display the Yellowstone National Park Photo Gallery Web page (Figure 14).

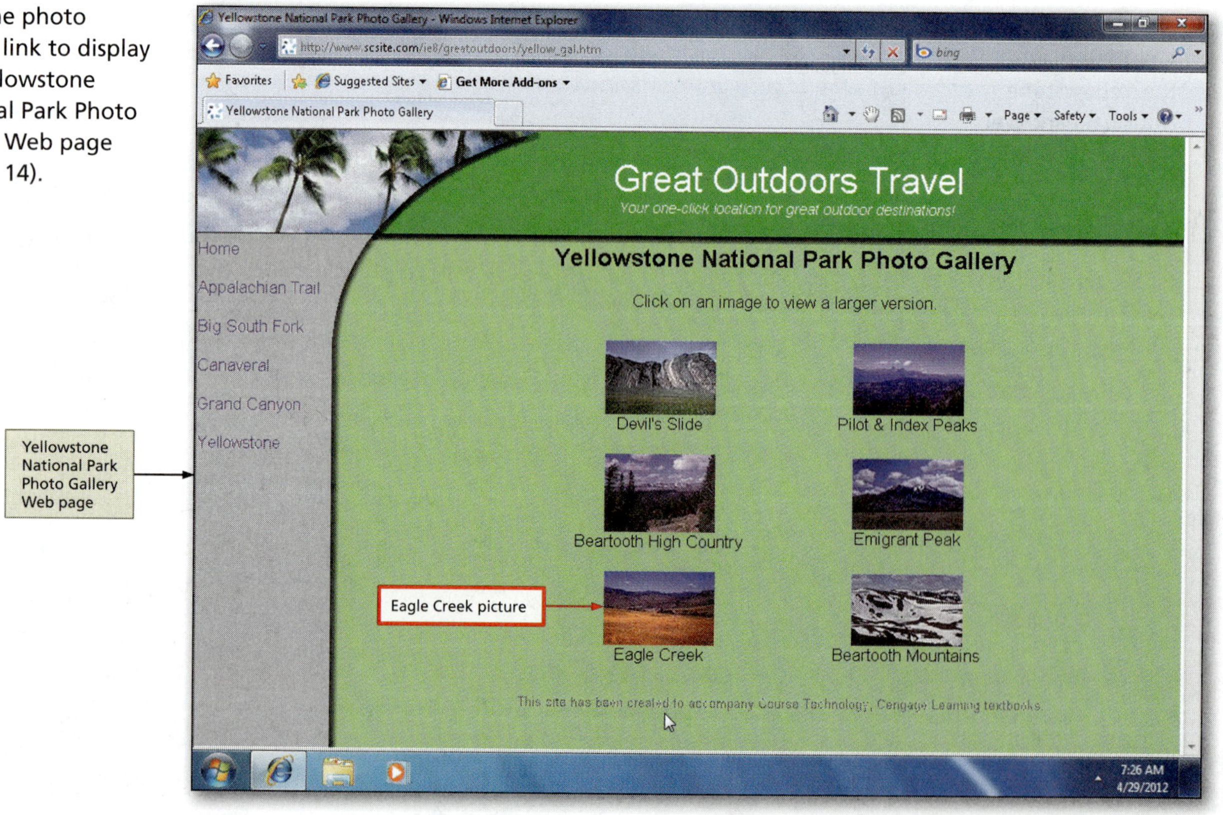

Figure 14

7

- If necessary, scroll through the display area to view the six pictures.
- Click the Eagle Creek picture to display the Eagle Creek Web page, which contains a larger version of the Eagle Creek picture (Figure 15).

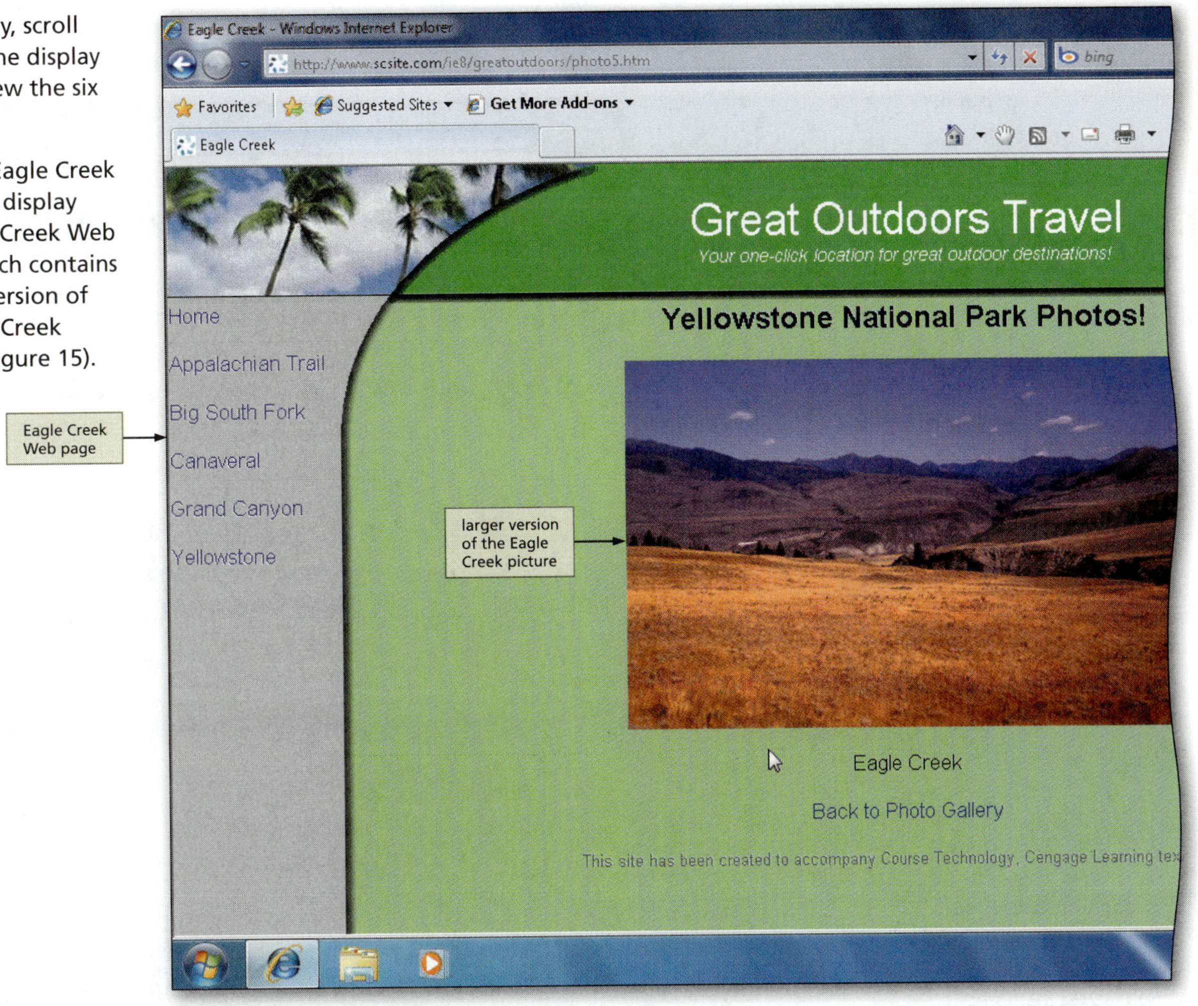

Figure 15

Other Ways
1. On File menu click Open, type Web address in Open box, click OK button
2. Press CTRL+O, type Web address in Open box, click OK button
3. Press ALT+F, press O, type Web address in Open box, click OK button

The preceding steps illustrate how simple it is to browse the World Wide Web. Displaying a Web page associated with a link is as easy as clicking a text or picture link.

Pointing to an image on a Web page may display **alternate text** in a small pop-up box (Figure 16 on the next page). Alternate text is text that is displayed in place of the image if a user configures his or her Web browser not to display images. In addition, visually impaired users typically have special software installed on their computer that reads the contents of their screen through the computer's speakers. Because this software cannot read an image, it reads the alternate text instead. Web page authors typically write alternate text that briefly describes the image it represents. Poorly written alternate text can make it difficult for visually impaired users to understand what is on the Web page.

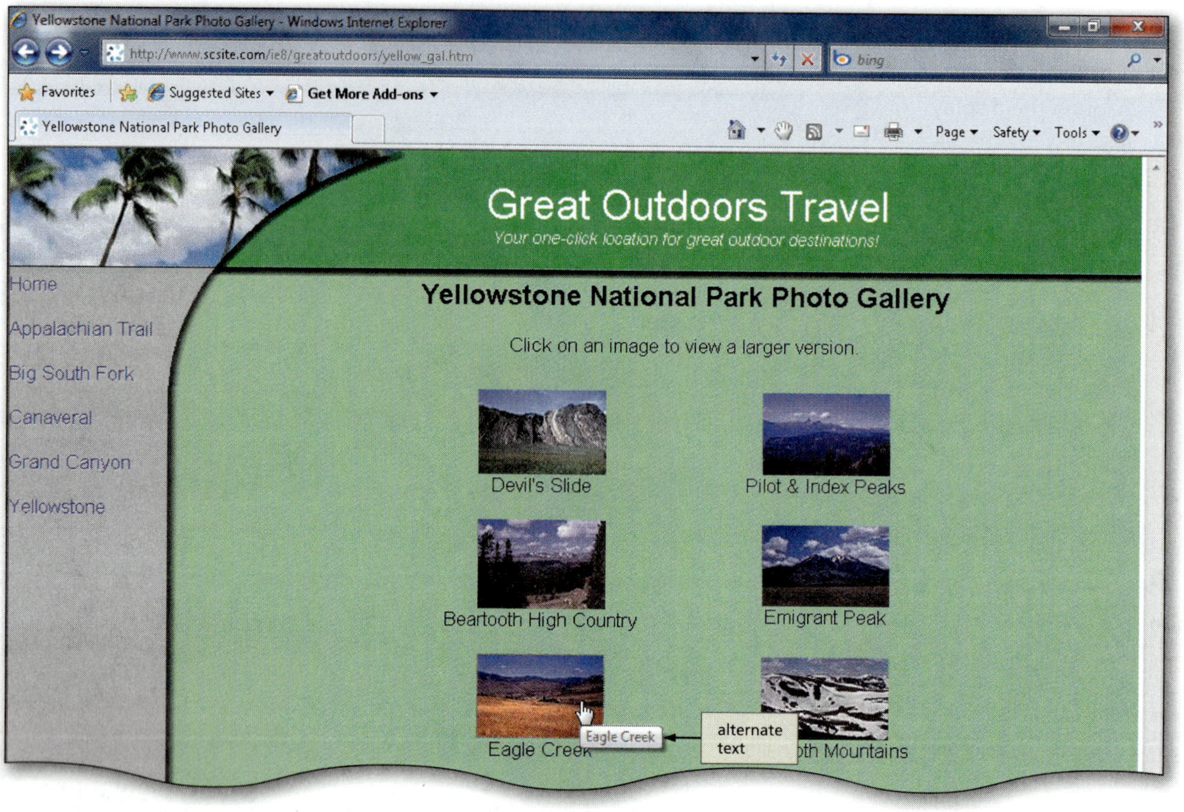

Figure 16

BTW

Stopping the Transfer of a Web Page
In addition to clicking the Stop button on the toolbar to stop the transfer of a Web page, you also can click the Stop command on the View menu, press the ESC key, or press ALT+V and then press the P key.

Stopping the Transfer of a Page

If a Web page you are trying to view is taking too long to transfer or if you have clicked the wrong link, you may decide not to wait for the page to finish transferring. The Stop button on the toolbar (Figure 17) allows you to stop the transfer of a page while the transfer is in progress. You will know that the transfer still is in progress if the icon on the current tab is in motion. Stopping the transfer of a Web page will leave a partially transferred Web page in the display area. Pictures or text displayed before the Stop button is clicked remain visible in the display area and any links can be clicked to display the associated Web pages. Because high-speed Internet connections are increasingly common, Web pages load quickly and the need for the Stop button is decreasing. Individuals who connect to the Internet with a slower Internet connection, such as dial-up access, however, may have a greater need to use the Stop button.

Refreshing a Web Page

One of the great features of the Internet is how quickly content on Web pages can be updated or changed. As you display different Web pages, Internet Explorer keeps track of the pages you visit, so that you can find those pages quickly in the future. Internet Explorer stores the Web pages you visit in a folder on the hard disk. When you display a previously viewed Web page, the page is displayed quickly because Internet Explorer is able to retrieve the page from the folder on the hard disk instead of from a Web server on the Internet. For this reason, the Web page you are viewing may not be the most up-to-date version. Web pages containing stock quotes, weather, and news are updated frequently to reflect the most current information. If you are unsure of whether the content you are viewing on a Web page is current, you should refresh the Web page. You also should refresh a Web page if you think the Web page has loaded incorrectly. You can refresh the Web page by using the **Refresh button** on the toolbar (Figure 17).

To Refresh a Web Page

The following steps refresh the contents of the Web page to ensure that you are viewing the most recent version of the page.

1

- Click the Refresh button on the toolbar to cause Internet Explorer to initiate a new transfer of the Web page from the Web server to your computer (Figure 17).

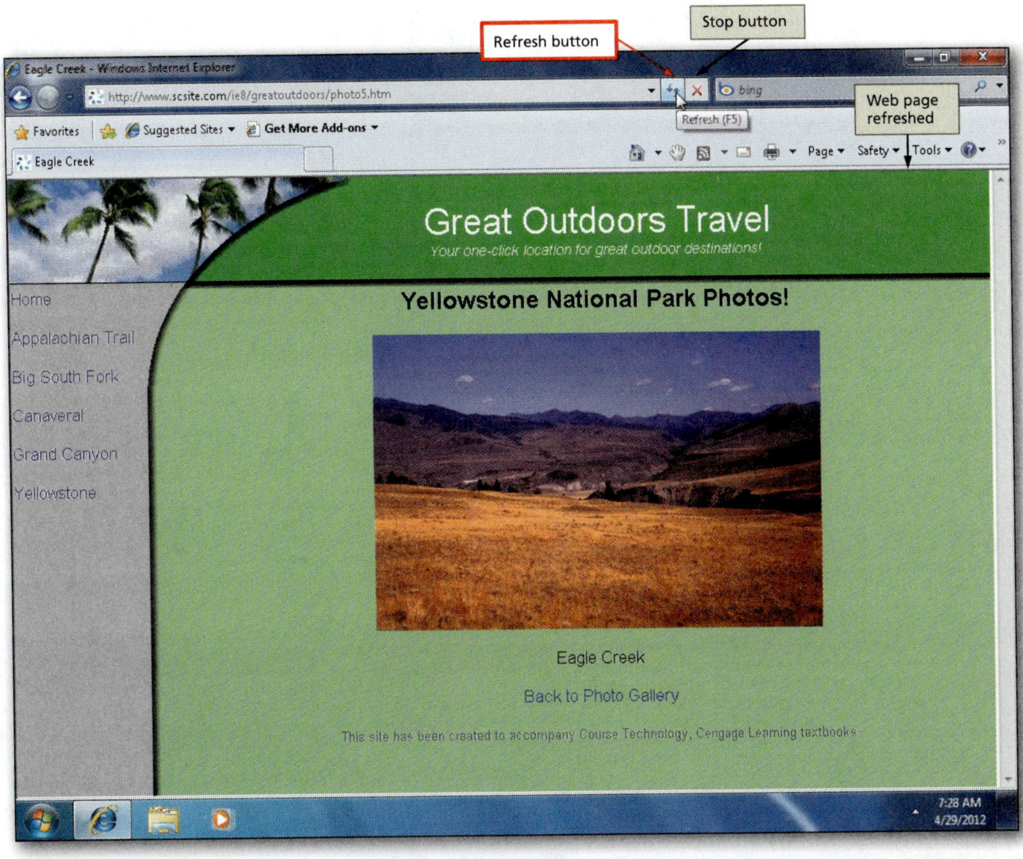

Figure 17

Other Ways

1. Click Web address in Address bar, press ENTER key
2. On View menu click Refresh
3. Press ALT+V, press R
4. Press F5

Finding a Previously Displayed Web Page

One method to find a previously displayed Web page is to use the Back button and the Recent Pages list (Figure 18a on the next page). Each time a Web page appears in the display area, the title of the Web page is added to the **Recent Pages list**. You can redisplay a previously viewed page by clicking the Recent Pages list arrow and selecting the desired Web page from the Recent Pages list (Figure 18a). The Forward button activates only after you click the Back button to return to a recent page. Each time you end an Internet session by quitting Internet Explorer, the entries on the Recent Pages list are cleared.

Another method for retrieving previously viewed pages is the **Go To list**, which contains the titles of all Web pages in the order they were displayed during the current session (Figure 18b). A check mark preceding a name in the list identifies the page currently displayed. To view the Go To list, press the ALT key to display the menu bar, click View on the menu bar, and then point to Go To on the View menu. Clicking a title in the Go To list displays the associated Web page in the display area.

A third method uses the Address bar arrow to display previously viewed Web pages. Clicking the Address bar arrow displays the **Address bar list**, which also contains a list of previously visited Web addresses (Figure 18c).

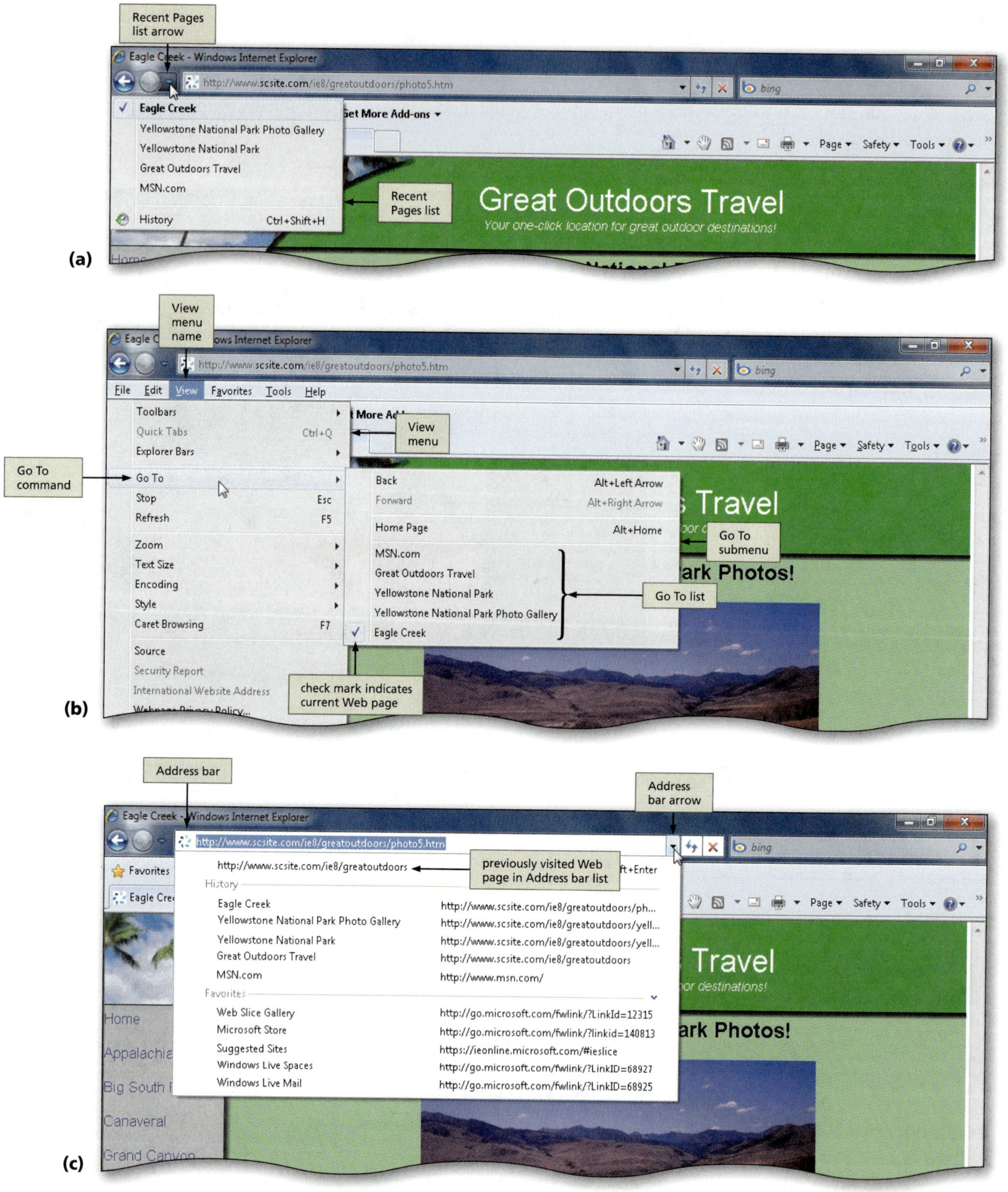

Figure 18

Finding a Recently Displayed Web Page Using the Navigation Buttons

When you visit the first Web page after starting Internet Explorer, the Back button is available for use. Pointing to the button changes the color of the button, indicating the button is active.

To Use the Navigation Buttons to Find Recently Displayed Web Pages

The Back and Forward buttons often are used when you wish to revisit a Web page you recently have visited since you last opened Internet Explorer. The following steps use the Back and Forward buttons.

1

- Click the Back button on the toolbar to display the Yellowstone National Park Photo Gallery Web page (Figure 19).

Back button

active Forward button

Yellowstone National Park Photo Gallery Web page

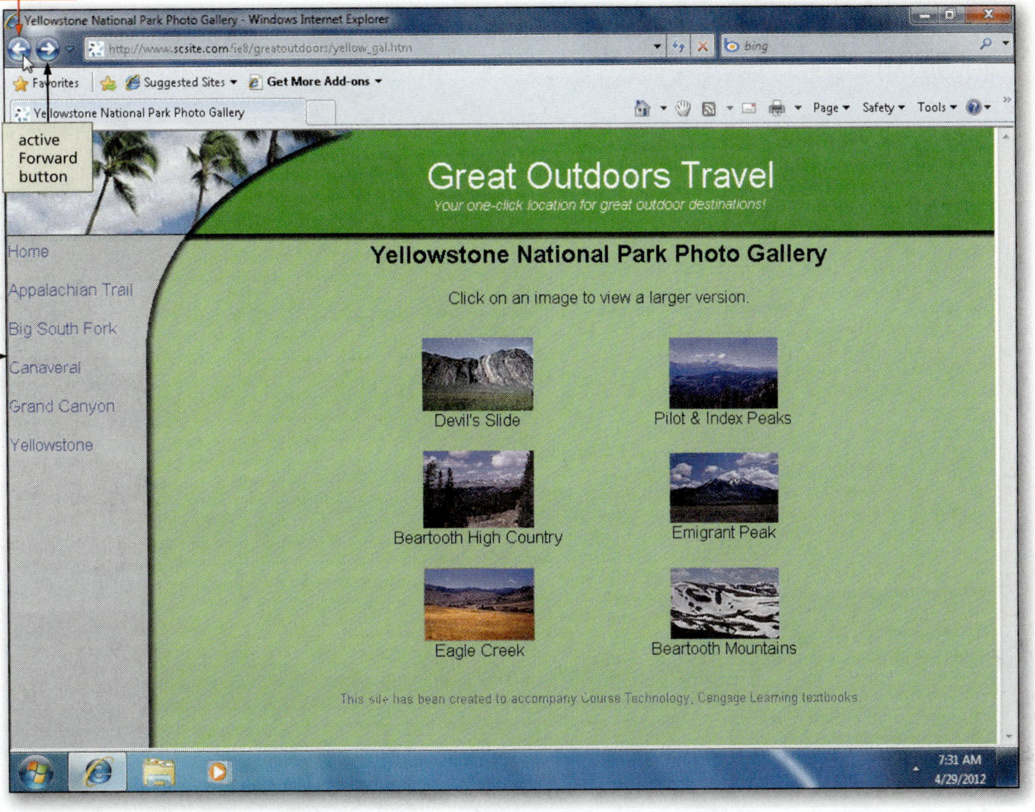

Figure 19

2

- Click the Back button again to display the Yellowstone National Park Web page (Figure 20).

Back button

Yellowstone National Park Web page

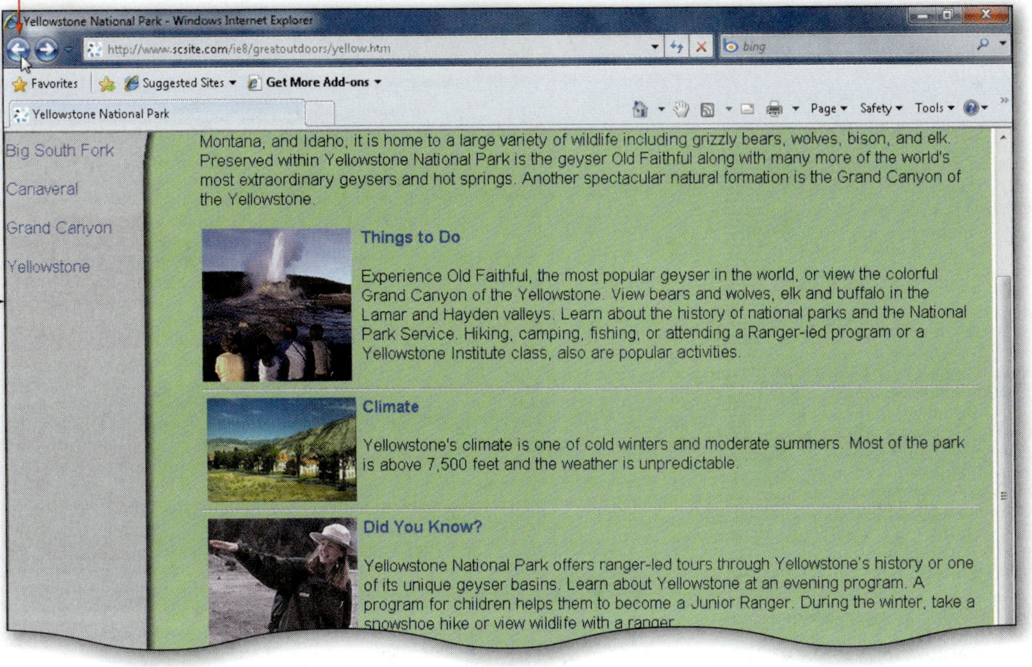

Figure 20

3

- Click the Forward button on the toolbar to display the Yellowstone National Park Photo Gallery Web page (Figure 21).

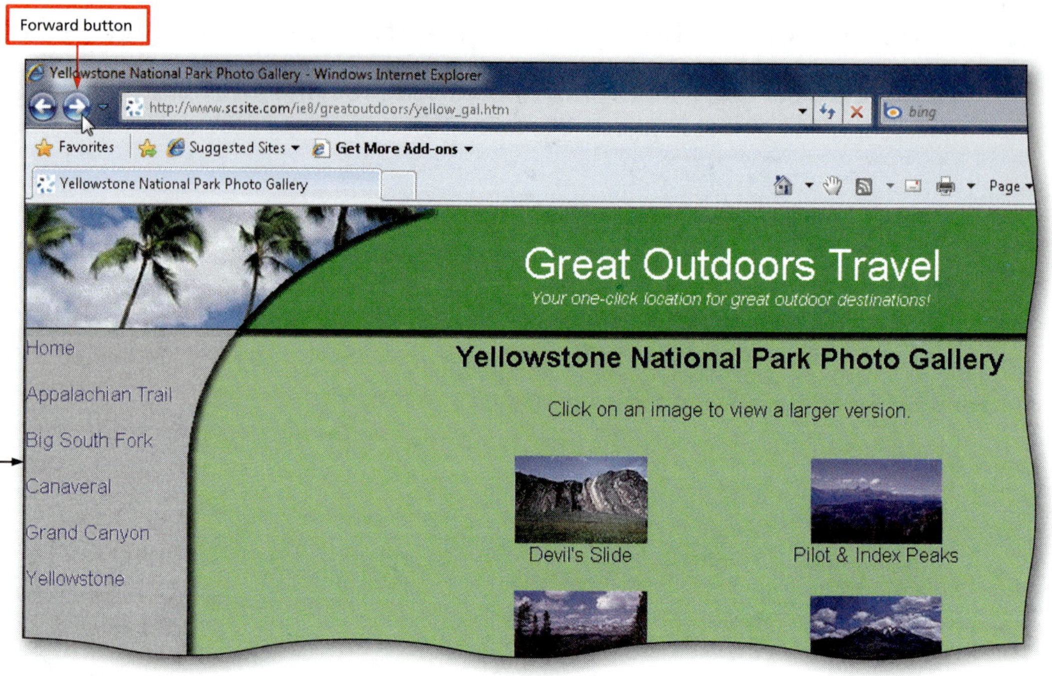

Figure 21

4

- Click the Forward button again to display the Eagle Creek Web page (Figure 22).

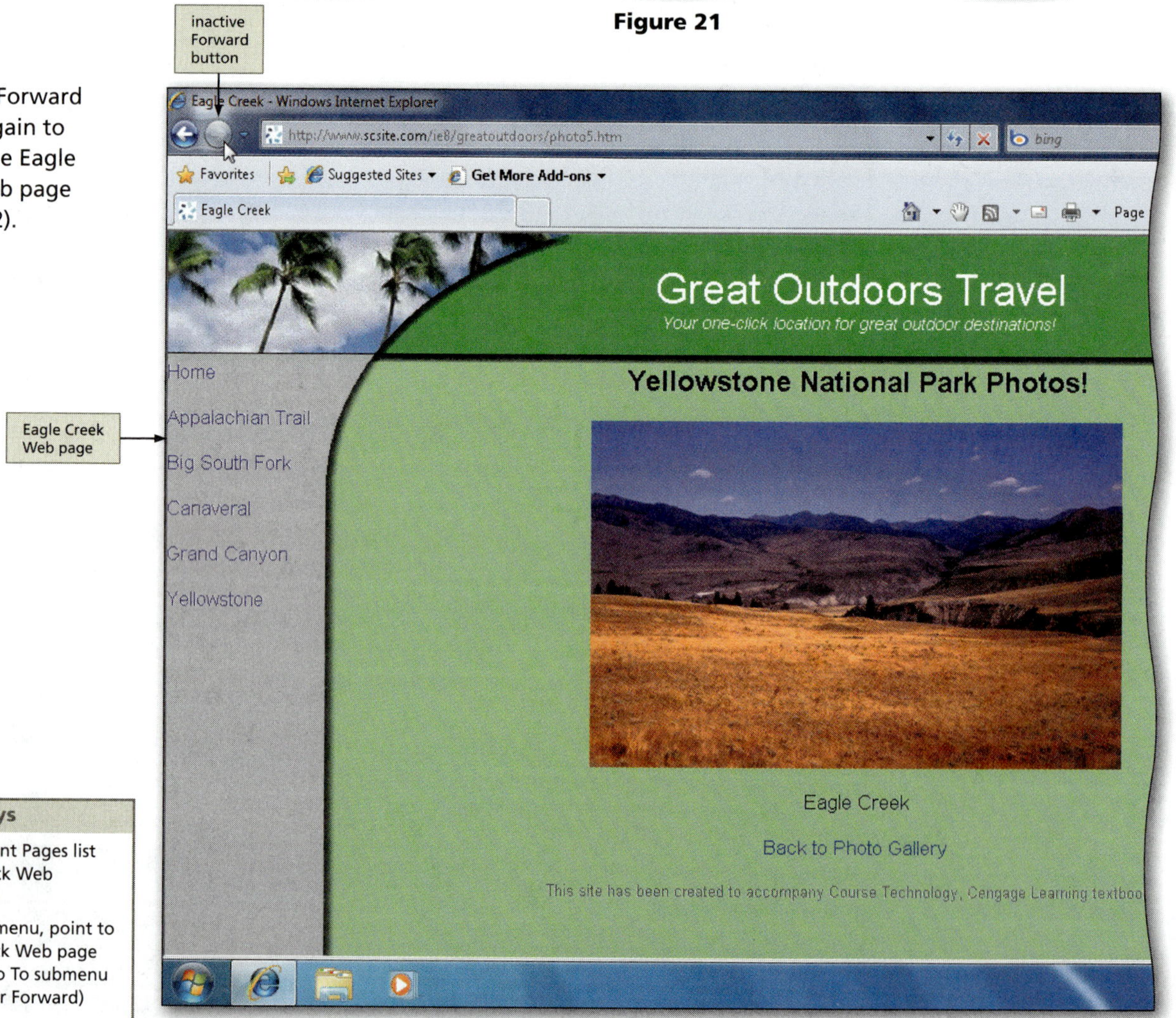

Figure 22

Other Ways

1. Click Recent Pages list arrow, click Web page title
2. On View menu, point to Go To, click Web page title on Go To submenu (or Back or Forward)
3. Back: press ALT+LEFT ARROW; forward: press ALT+RIGHT ARROW

You can continue to page backward until you reach the beginning of the Recent Pages list. At that time, the Back button becomes inactive, which indicates that the list contains no additional pages to which you can move back. You can move forward, however, by clicking the Forward button.

You can see that traversing the list of pages is easy using the Back and Forward buttons. This method can be time consuming, however, if you must navigate through many pages before you reach the one you want to view.

To Display a Web Page Using the Recent Pages List

It is possible to jump to any previously visited page by clicking its title in the Recent Pages list. In this way, you can find a recently visited page without displaying an intermediate page. The following steps illustrate how to navigate quickly and easily to a recently visited page without having to click the Back button multiple times to reach the page.

1

- Click the Recent Pages list arrow on the toolbar to display the Recent Pages list (Figure 23).

Q&A Why does my Recent Pages list look different?

If Internet Explorer was running before beginning this chapter, your Recent Pages list may contain additional pages.

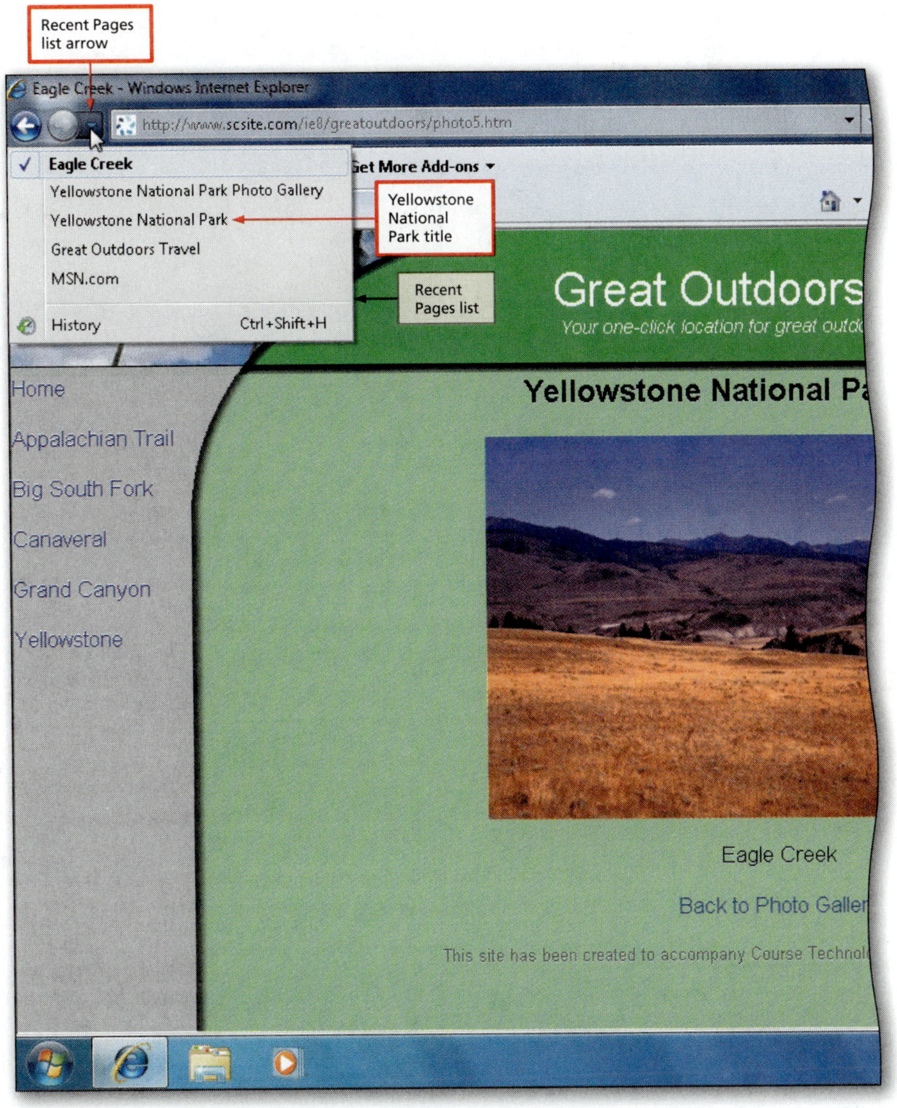

Figure 23

2

- Click Yellowstone National Park on the Recent Pages list to display the Yellowstone National Park Web page (Figure 24).

Q&A Why are some Web page titles displayed only partially in the Recent Pages list?

Some Web page titles are too long to display fully in the Recent Pages list. For this reason, the end of the Web page names might not be displayed.

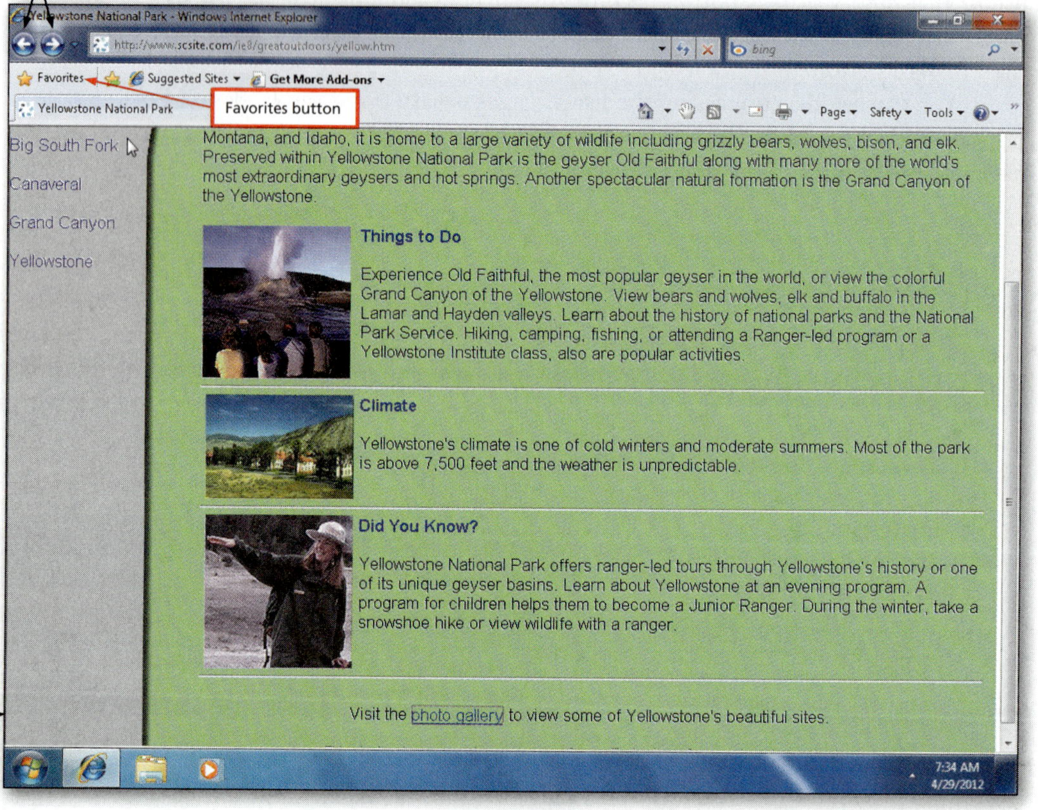

Figure 24

Other Ways

1. On View menu point to Go To, click Back on Go To submenu
2. Press ALT+LEFT ARROW

If you have a small list of pages you have visited, or the Web page you wish to view is only one or two pages away, using the Back and Forward buttons to traverse the lists will likely be faster than displaying the Recent Pages list and selecting the correct title. If you have visited a large number of pages, however, you will need to step forward or back through many pages, and it may be easier to use the Recent Pages list to select the exact page.

BTW **Clearing the History List**
If the list of Web sites you have visited has become too large to be meaningful, you may want to clear the History List. You can clear the History List by clicking Safety on the Command bar, clicking Delete Browsing History, verifying that a check mark appears in the History check box, and then clicking the Delete button (Delete Browsing History dialog box). Clearing the History List also clears the Address bar list.

Using the History List to Display Web Pages

Internet Explorer maintains another list of previously visited Web pages in the History List. The **History List** is a list of Web pages visited over a period of days or weeks (over many sessions). You can use this list to display Web pages you may have accessed during that time. Clicking the Favorites button on the Favorites bar, clicking the History tab, and then clicking Today displays the History List.

When the Explorer bar is visible, the display area contains two panes. The left pane contains the Explorer bar and the right pane contains the current Web page. The Explorer bar will remain on the screen until you close it. To find a recently visited Web page using the History List, first display the entire History List, select the order in which you want to view the history, and then click the desired Web page title. The Web page titles can be categorized by date, site, most visited, or order visited today. You also are able to search this History List for a particular Web site.

If you are browsing the World Wide Web from a public or shared computer, you might not want Internet Explorer to save any information about the Web sites you have visited. **InPrivate Browsing** is a new feature in Internet Explorer 8 that allows you to visit Web pages without the Web browser recording any information. For example, if you visit your bank's Web site using InPrivate Browsing, Internet Explorer will not save the site in your History List, nor will it save any cookies or other temporary Internet files from the Web site. To enable InPrivate Browsing, click the Safety button on the Command bar, and then click InPrivate Browsing on the Safety menu. Internet Explorer will open a new window with an InPrivate icon in the Address bar. When you wish to exit InPrivate Browsing mode, simply close the window.

To Display a Web Page Using the History List

To display a recently visited Web page without having to click the Back button multiple times, perform the following steps to display the Web page using the History List.

1

- Click the Favorites button on the Favorites bar to display the Favorites Center.
- Click the Pin the Favorites Center button to pin the Favorites Center to the Internet Explorer window (Figure 25).

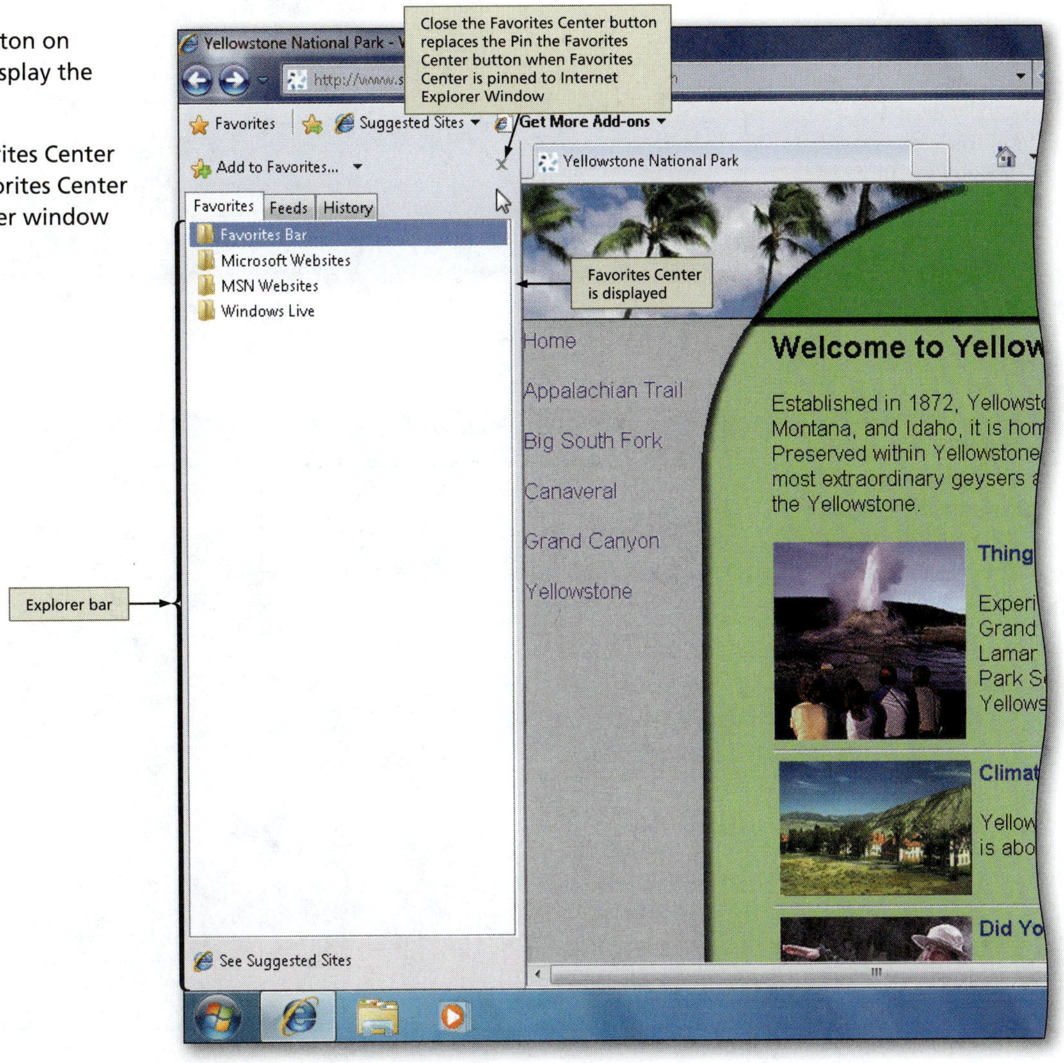

Figure 25

2

- Click the History tab on the Explorer bar to display the History List on the Explorer bar in the left pane of the Internet Explorer display area (Figure 26).

Q&A Why is the Explorer bar often hidden from the Internet Explorer window?

Internet Explorer reserves as much space as possible to display the Web pages in the display area. Continuously displaying the Explorer bar consumes space on the Web page, possibly resulting in visitors needing to scroll the page horizontally to view all content.

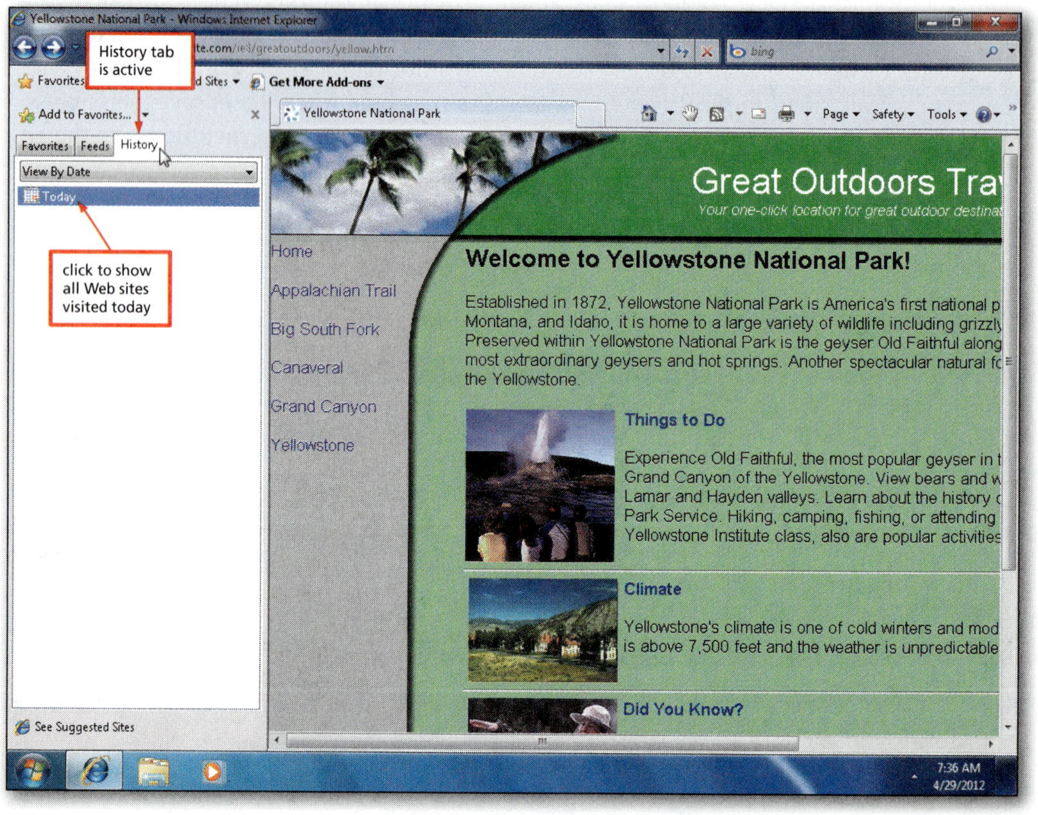

Figure 26

3

- Click Today in the History List to display a list of Web sites that have been accessed today (Figure 27). Your History List might differ.

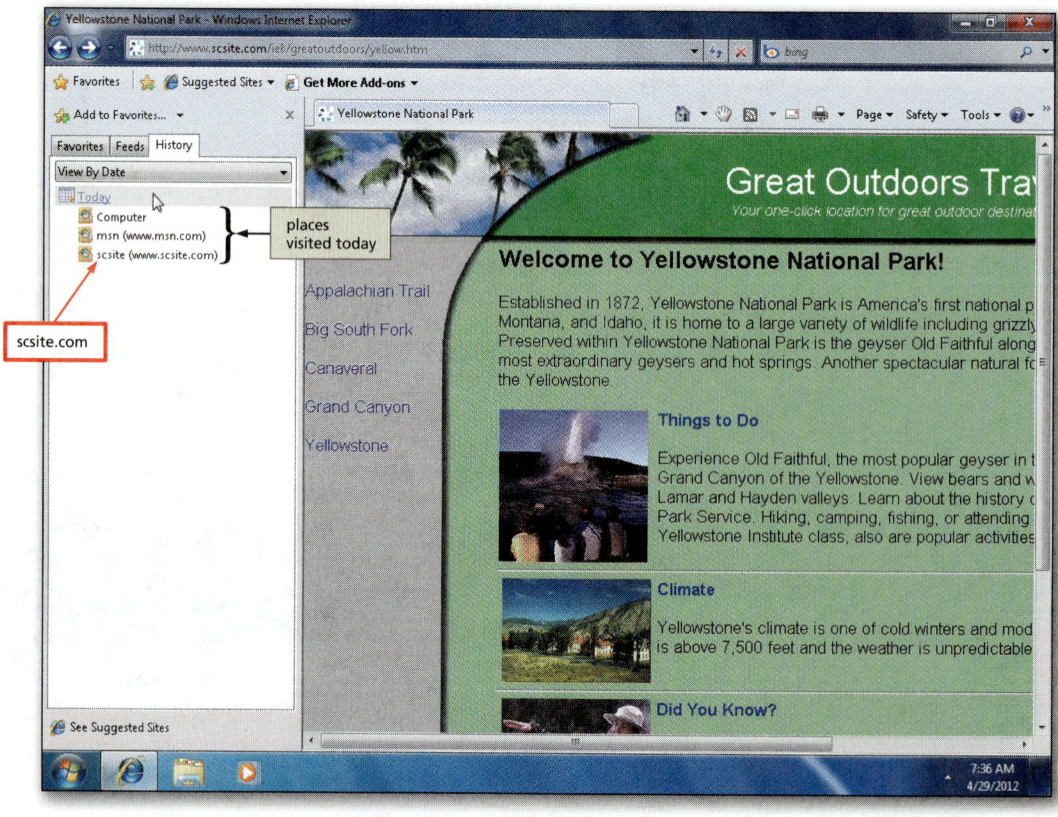

Figure 27

4

- Click scsite (www.scsite.com) to display the list of Web pages that were accessed from scsite.com.
- Click Great Outdoors Travel to display the Great Outdoors Travel Web page (Figure 28).

Figure 28

5

- Click the Close button on the Explorer bar to close the Explorer bar (Figure 29).

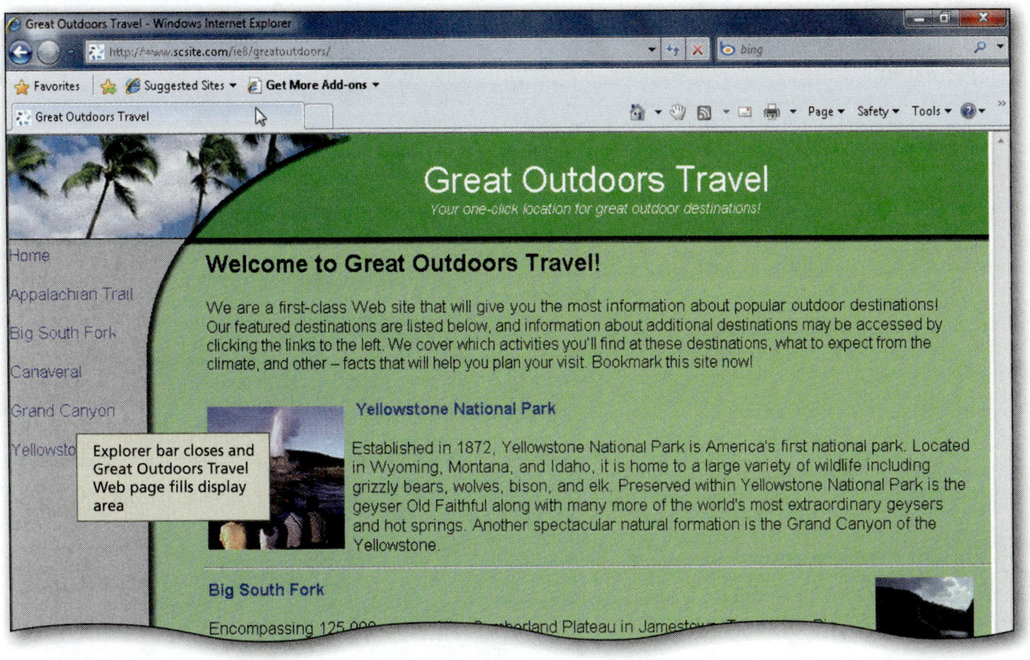

Figure 29

Other Ways

1. Click Tools on the Command bar, point to Explorer Bars, click History
2. Press CTRL+SHIFT+H

The History List is useful for returning to a Web page you have visited recently. You can set the number of days Internet Explorer keeps the Web addresses in the History List by using the Internet Options command on the Tools menu. Because the History List does not keep a permanent list of Web pages you have visited, you should not use the History List to store the Web addresses of favorite or frequently visited pages.

BTW

Suggested Sites
The new Suggested Sites feature in Internet Explorer keeps a record of Web pages you frequently visit. It then uses this information to suggest other Web sites that might be of interest to you. To turn on Suggested Sites, click the Favorites button on the Favorites bar, and then click Turn on Suggested Sites.

Keeping Track of Favorite Web Pages

You can see from the previous figures that Web addresses can be long and cryptic. It is easy to make a mistake while entering complex Web addresses. Fortunately, Internet Explorer can keep track of favorite Web pages. You can store the Web addresses of favorite Web pages permanently in an area appropriately called the Favorites list.

A **favorite** consists of the title of the Web page and the Web address of that page. The title of the Web page is added to the Favorites Center. Your favorites appear in both the Favorites menu and the Favorites Center.

To Add a Web Page to the Favorites Center

The following steps add a Web page to the Favorites Center, so that you easily can access the Web page in the future.

1

- Click the Favorites button on the Favorites bar to display the Explorer bar.
- If necessary, click the Favorites tab to display the Favorites Center (Figure 30).

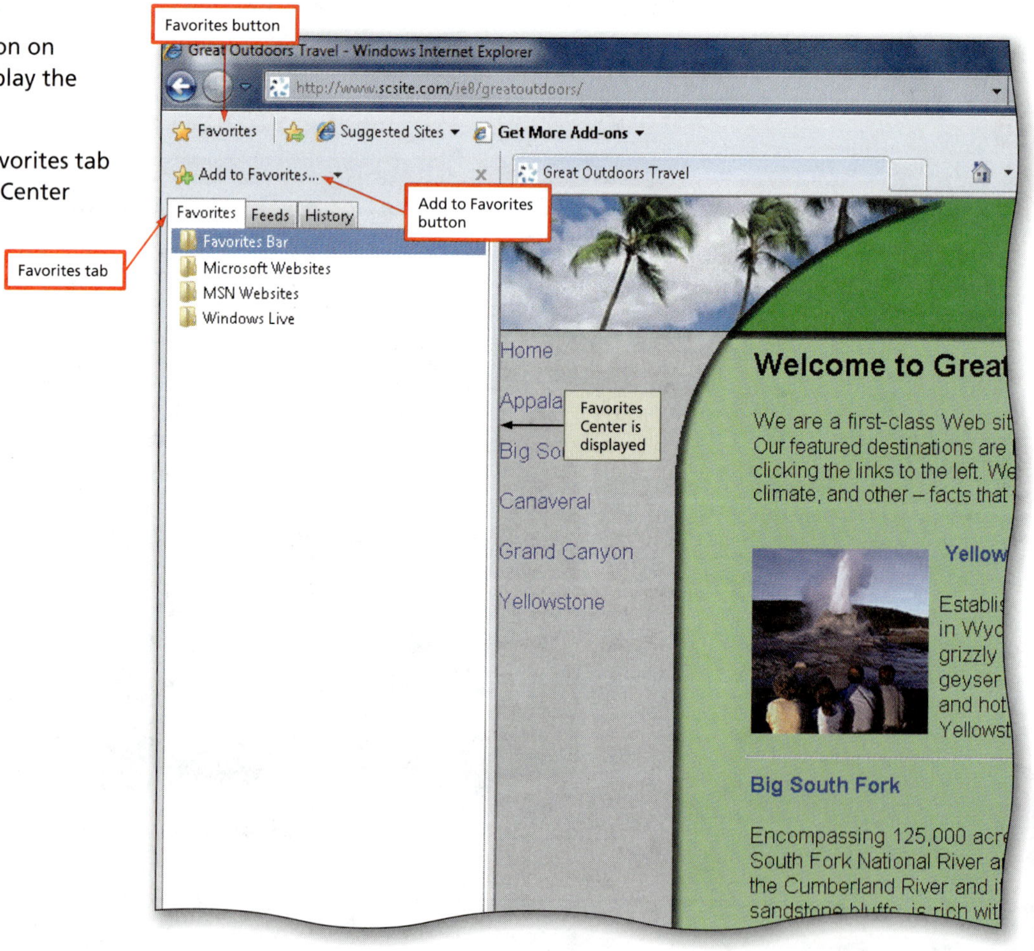

Figure 30

2

- Click the Add to Favorites button in the Favorites Center to display the Add a Favorite dialog box (Figure 31).

3

- Click the Add button (Add a Favorite dialog box) to add the Great Outdoors Travel Web page to the Favorites Center.

Q&A What if I want to add a Web site to my Favorites bar?

To add a Web site to your Favorites bar, simply click the Add to Favorites bar button on the Favorites bar.

Experiment

- After you add the favorite, check the Favorites menu to verify that your new favorite appears in the list. Press the ALT key to display the menu bar, click the Favorites menu, verify that the favorite appears, and then press the ESC key twice to close the Favorites menu and hide the menu bar.

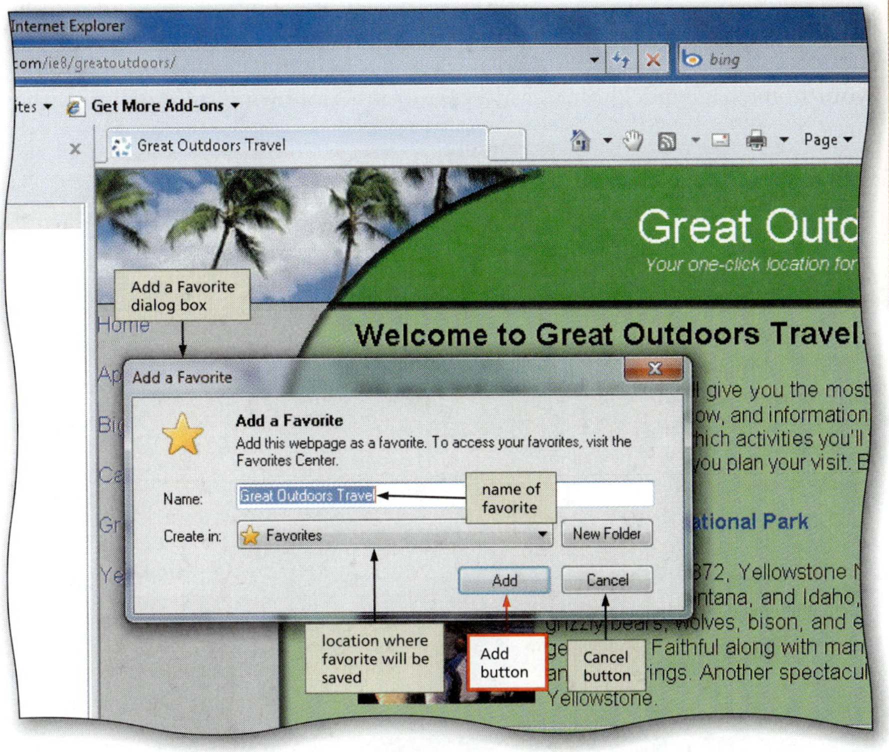

Figure 31

Other Ways

1. Press the ALT key, click Favorites on the menu bar, and then click Add to Favorites
2. Press CTRL+D
3. Press ALT+A, press A, press ENTER

In Figure 30, clicking the Add to Favorites button arrow and then clicking the Organize Favorites command displays the Organize Favorites dialog box, which allows you to move, rename, organize, and delete your favorites.

If you plan to store many favorites on your computer, you might choose to give your favorite Web sites meaningful names by renaming them and storing them in folders. In Figure 31, clicking the New Folder button adds a new folder to the Favorites list. Immediately after adding a new folder to the Favorites list, you can name the folder by typing an appropriate name and then pressing the ENTER key. After renaming the folder, you can drag an existing favorite to the folder to store the favorite in that folder. You also can change the name of a folder or favorite by clicking a folder or favorite, clicking the Rename button, typing the new name, and then pressing the ENTER key. For example, if you frequently visit many Web sites to read the news, you might choose to store the Web addresses of these sites as favorites in a News folder. A student, for example, may store school-related Web sites in an Academics folder.

BTW

Importing and Exporting Favorites

If you already have favorite Web sites set up on another computer or Web browser, or wish to transfer your favorite Web sites to another computer, you can use Internet Explorer's Import/Export Wizard to preserve your favorites. Click the Favorites button on the Favorites bar, click the Add to Favorites list arrow in the Favorites Center, and then click Import and Export to start the Import/Export Wizard. Follow the steps in the wizard to import or export your favorites.

To Display the Home Page Using the Home Button

In many cases, individuals designate the Web page they most frequently visit as their home page. The Home button on the Command bar provides a quick way to navigate to your home page. If you want to navigate back to your home page quickly and easily, perform the following step to display the home page in Internet Explorer's display area.

1

- Click the Home button on the toolbar to display the MSN.com home page in the Internet Explorer window (Figure 32). Your computer may display a different home page.

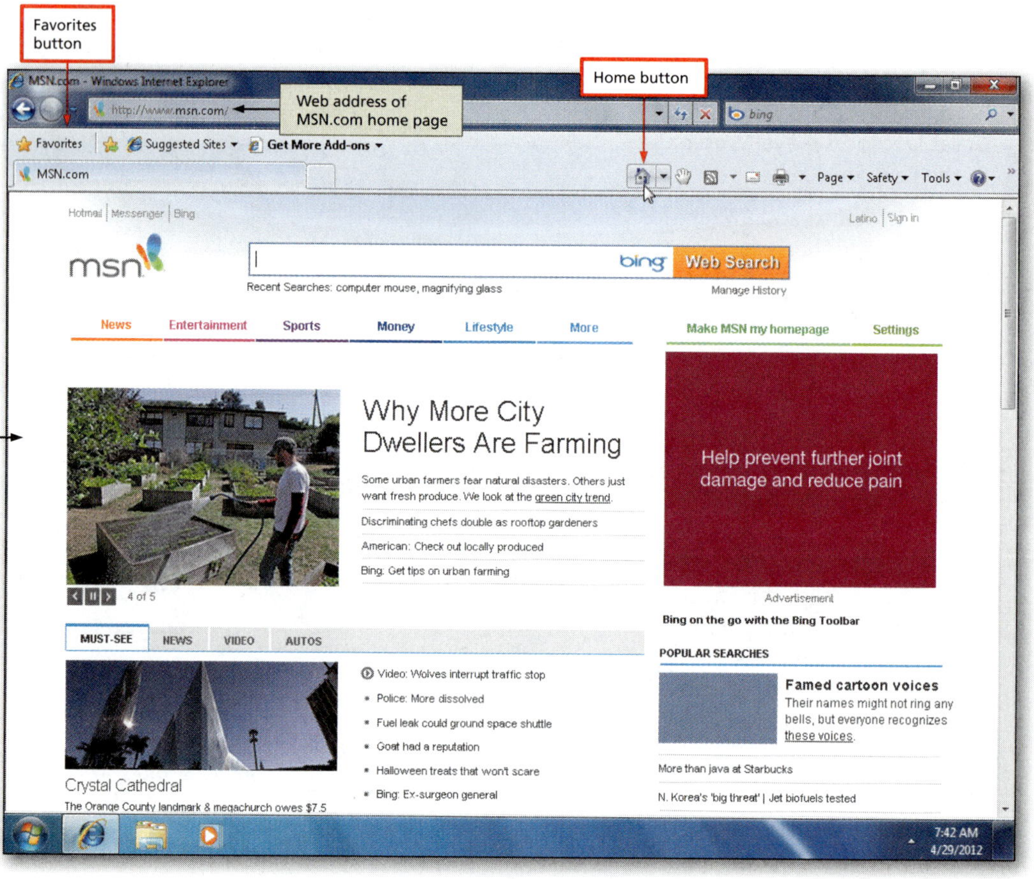

Figure 32

Q&A

Can I have more than one home page?

Yes. If you designate more than one Web page as your home page, Internet Explorer will open each home page in a separate tab when you start Internet Explorer or when you click the Home button on the Command bar. To create multiple home pages, click Tools on the Command bar, click the Internet Options command, type the Web address for each Web page on its own line in the Home page box, and then click the OK button. You also can click the Home button list arrow, click the Add or Change Home Page command, and then click the 'Add this webpage to your home page tabs' option button to add the current page to your current home pages.

Other Ways

1. Click Home button list arrow on Command bar, click home page title
2. On View menu point to Go To, click Home Page on Go To submenu
3. Press ALT+V, press G, press H
4. Press ALT+HOME

To Display a Web Page Using the Favorites Center

The Favorites Center is used to display your list of favorite Web pages quickly, without having to navigate through several unwanted pages. Using a favorite to display a Web page is similar to using the History List to display a Web page. While you are browsing the Internet, you may want to access one of your favorites. The following steps display the Great Outdoors Travel home page by using the Favorites Center.

1

- Click the Favorites button on the Favorites bar to display the Explorer bar.
- If necessary, click the Favorites tab on the Explorer bar to display the Favorites Center (Figure 33).

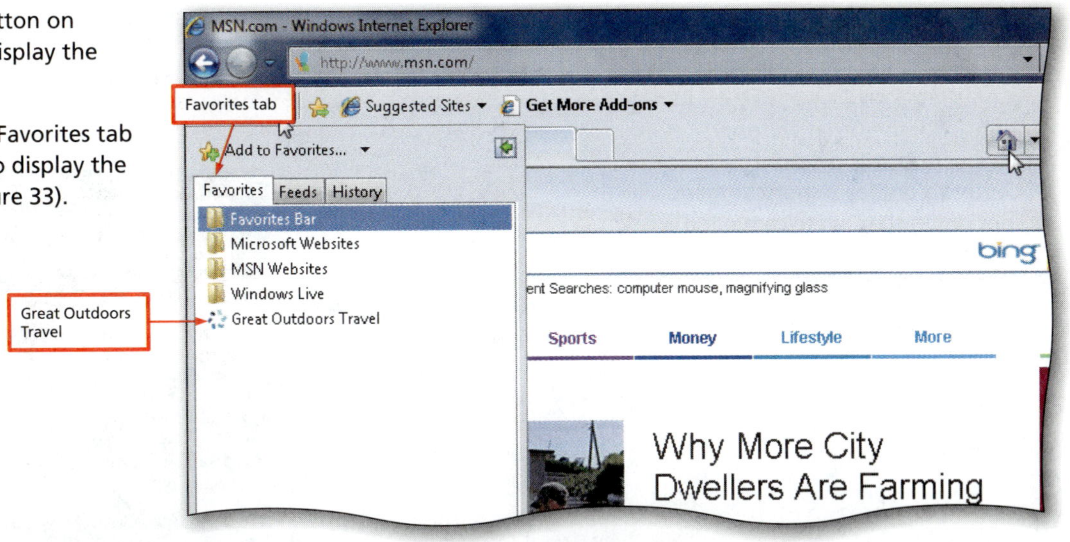

Figure 33

2

- Click the Great Outdoors Travel command on the Explorer bar to display the Great Outdoors Travel Web page in the display area (Figure 34).

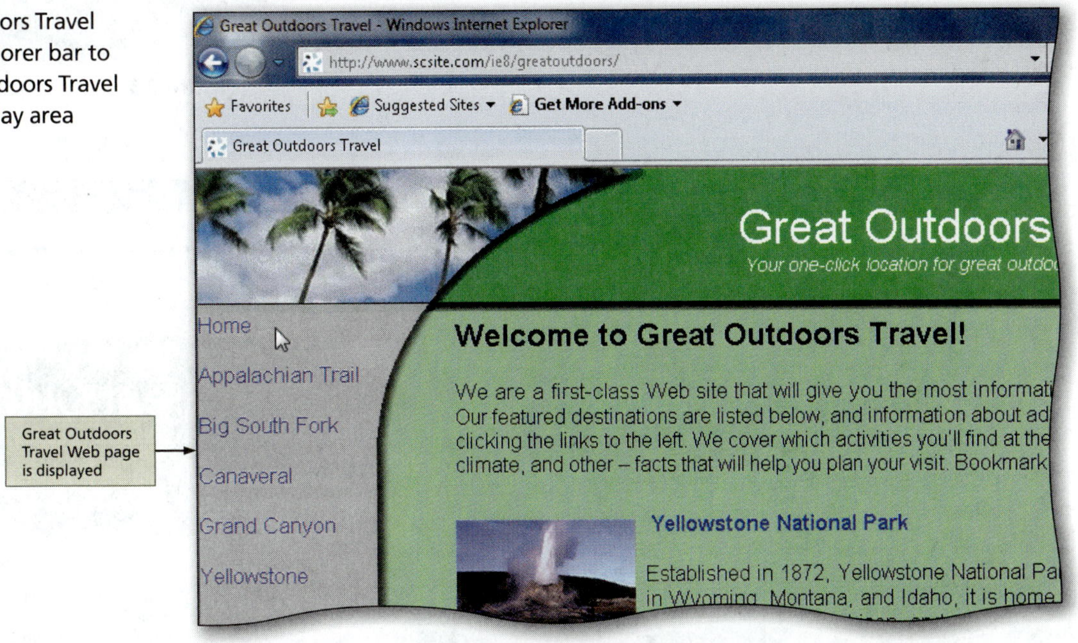

Figure 34

Other Ways

1. On Favorites menu click favorite
2. Press ALT+A, click favorite
3. Press CTRL+I, click favorite

Additional favorites are displayed in the Favorites Center shown in Figure 33. Folders included in the favorites list include the Favorites Bar folder, the Microsoft Websites folder, the MSN Websites folder, and the Windows Live folder. Other folders and favorites may be displayed in the Favorites Center on your computer.

To Remove a Web Page from the Favorites Center

You may have a variety of reasons for wanting to remove a favorite. With the Web changing every day, the Web address that worked today may not work tomorrow, or perhaps the Web site is no longer of use to you, or your favorites list is getting too big to be meaningful. Once you decide that you no longer need a favorite, the following steps delete the favorite.

1

- Click the Favorites button on the Favorites bar to display a list of your favorites on the Explorer bar.
- Right-click the Great Outdoors Travel entry in the Favorites Center to display a shortcut menu containing the Delete command (Figure 35).

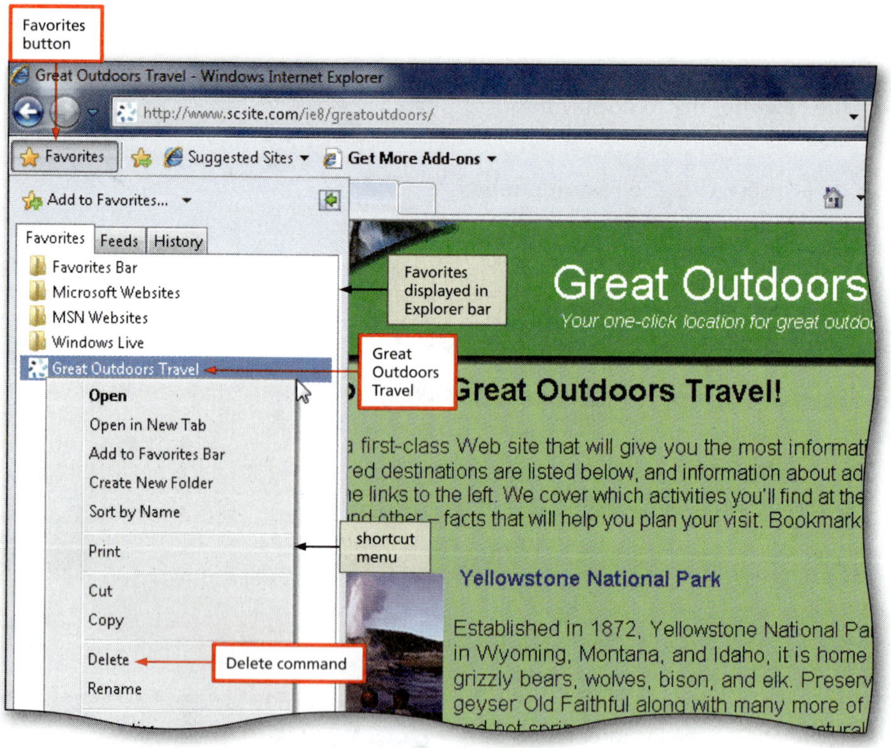

Figure 35

2

- Click Delete on the shortcut menu to display the Delete Shortcut dialog box (Figure 36).

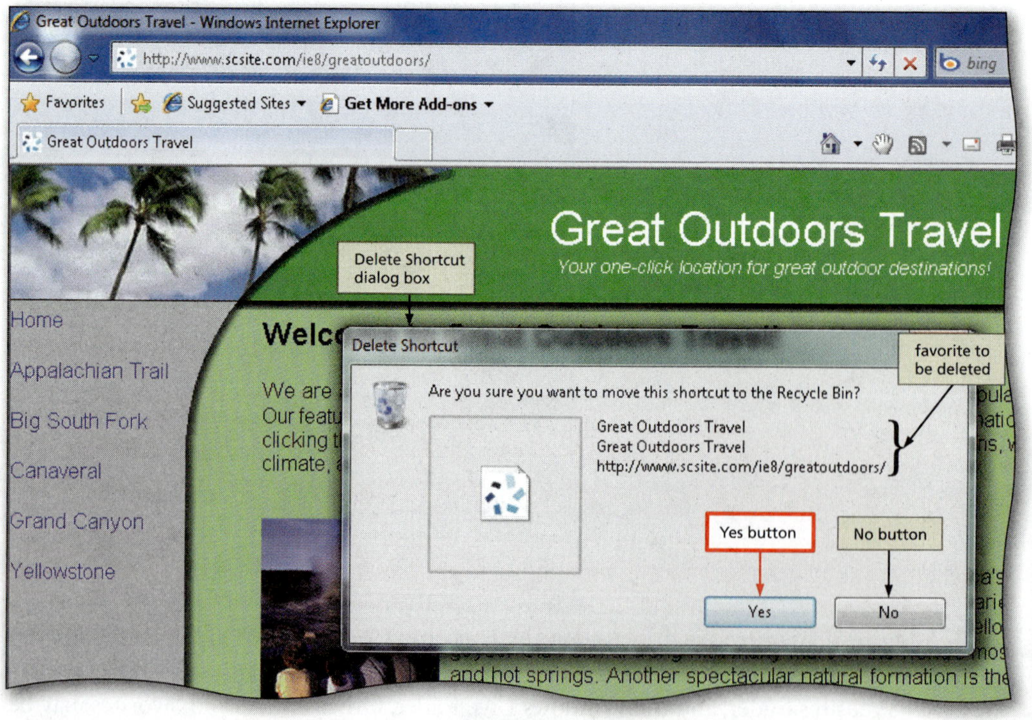

Figure 36

3

- Click the Yes button (Delete Shortcut dialog box) to move the Great Outdoors Travel Web page Favorite to the Recycle Bin.
- Click the Favorites button to display the Explorer bar (Figure 37).

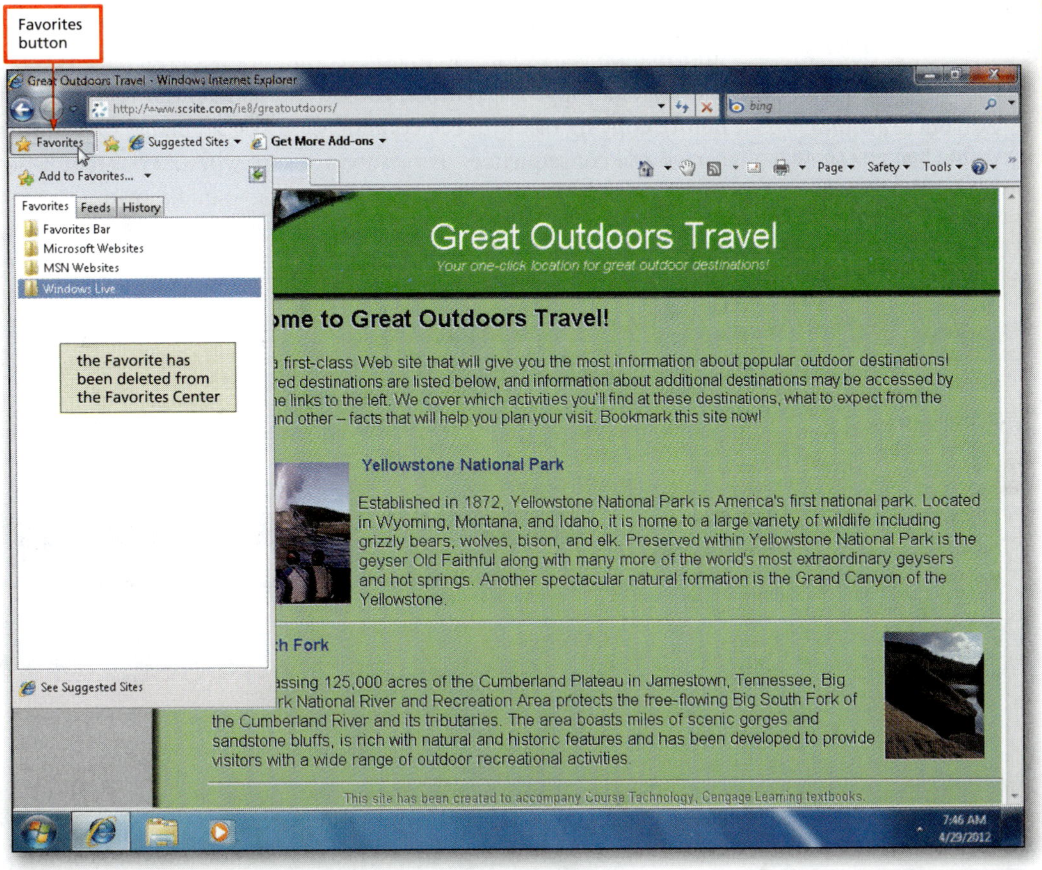

Figure 37

Other Ways

1. On Favorites menu click Organize Favorites, click favorite, click Delete button, click Yes button

The steps required to delete a folder in the favorites list are the same as those required to delete a favorite. If you delete a folder, however, Internet Explorer also will delete all favorites stored in that folder. Because favorites are stored as files on your computer, deleting a folder or favorite will move it to the Recycle Bin. The Recycle Bin stores files marked for deletion before they are permanently deleted. While a file or folder is in the Recycle Bin, it can be restored by double-clicking the Recycle Bin icon on the desktop, clicking the item you wish to restore, and then clicking the 'Restore this item' button. Because not all operating systems are configured to handle deleted items in the same manner, you should not delete a favorite or a folder unless you are sure that you no longer want it.

Saving Information Obtained with Internet Explorer

Many different types of Web pages are accessible on the World Wide Web. Because these pages can help you gather information about areas of interest, you may wish to save the information you discover for future reference. The different types of Web pages and the various uses you have for the information require different methods of saving. Internet Explorer allows you to save an entire Web page, individual pictures, or selected pieces of text. Before

BTW

Citing Web Sites
Whenever you use content from a Web site, you should cite the Web site as a source. Word Chapter 2 contains additional information about citing Internet sources.

saving a Web page or information from a Web page, you first should determine whether the information is free for you to use. If content on a Web page is protected by a copyright, or if it displays a copyright symbol, you should contact the Web page author to obtain permission before copying or using the content. Copying an image that is protected by a copyright could carry legal consequences. If you are not sure whether content is protected by a copyright, you should seek permission before duplicating it. The following pages illustrate how to save an entire Web page, how to save a single picture, and how to save text.

To Save a Web Page

One method of saving information on a Web page is to save the entire page. The following steps save the Great Outdoors Travel home page on your computer so that you can access it even when you are not connected to the Internet.

1

- Click the Page button on the Command bar to display the Page menu (Figure 38).

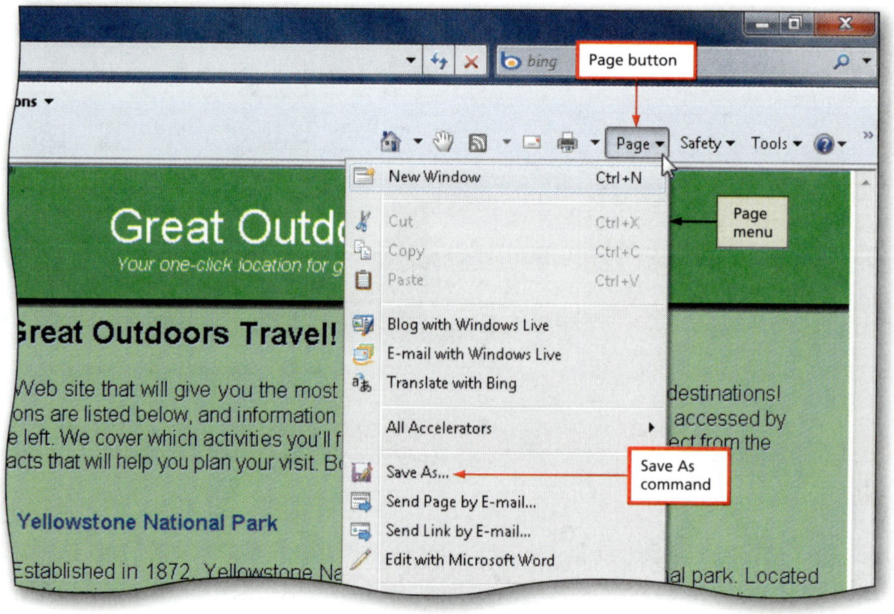

Figure 38

2

- Click Save As on the Page menu to display the Save Webpage dialog box. If the Save Webpage dialog box is not expanded, click the Browse Folders button to expand it.
- Click the Documents link below Libraries in the navigation pane to select the location for the saved Web page and then click the Hide Folders button to collapse the dialog box (Figure 39).
- Click the Save button (Save Webpage dialog box) to save the Web page to the Documents library on your computer.

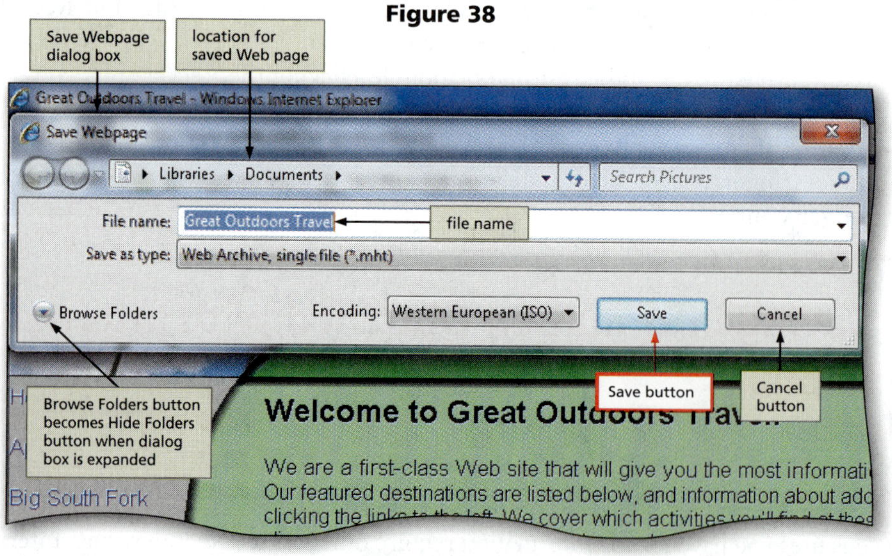

Figure 39

Other Ways
1. Press ALT+F, press A

Internet Explorer saves the instructions to display the saved Web page in the Great Outdoors Travel.mht file in the Documents library on your computer. You can view the saved Web page in the Internet Explorer window by double-clicking the Great Outdoors Travel.mht file in your Documents library. An .mht file is a Web archive file, capable of storing the text and images for a Web page in a single file.

To Save a Picture on a Web Page

In some cases, you may want to save only an image located on a Web page. The following steps save the Yellowstone National Park picture in the Pictures library on your computer in the **Joint Photographic Experts Group** (**JPEG**) file format using the file name yellowstone.jpg. The JPEG file format is a method of encoding pictures that then can be displayed by a variety of programs.

1

- Right-click the Yellowstone National Park picture on the Great Outdoors Travel Web page to display a shortcut menu containing the Save Picture As command (Figure 40).

Q&A What else will Internet Explorer allow me to do with a picture?

The shortcut menu that is displayed after right-clicking a picture also allows you to e-mail the picture, print the picture, navigate to your Pictures folder, or set the picture as your desktop background.

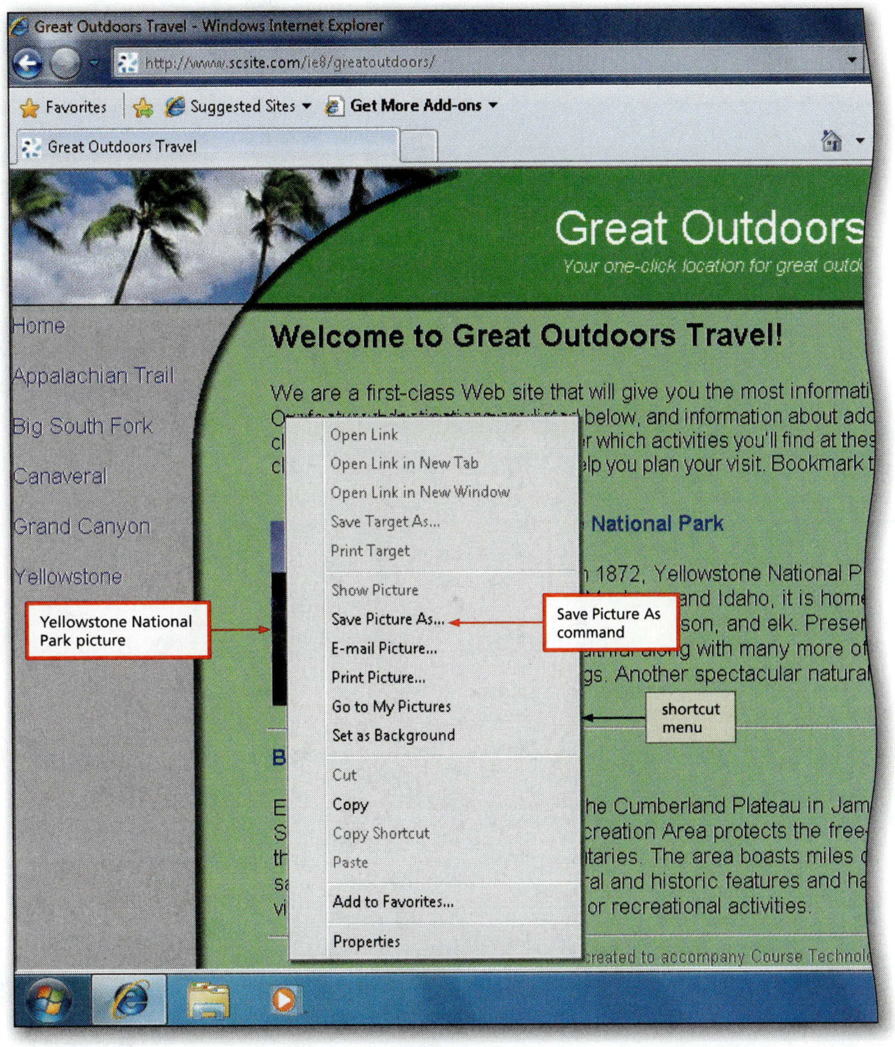

Figure 40

2

- Click Save Picture As on the shortcut menu to display the Save Picture dialog box (Figure 41).

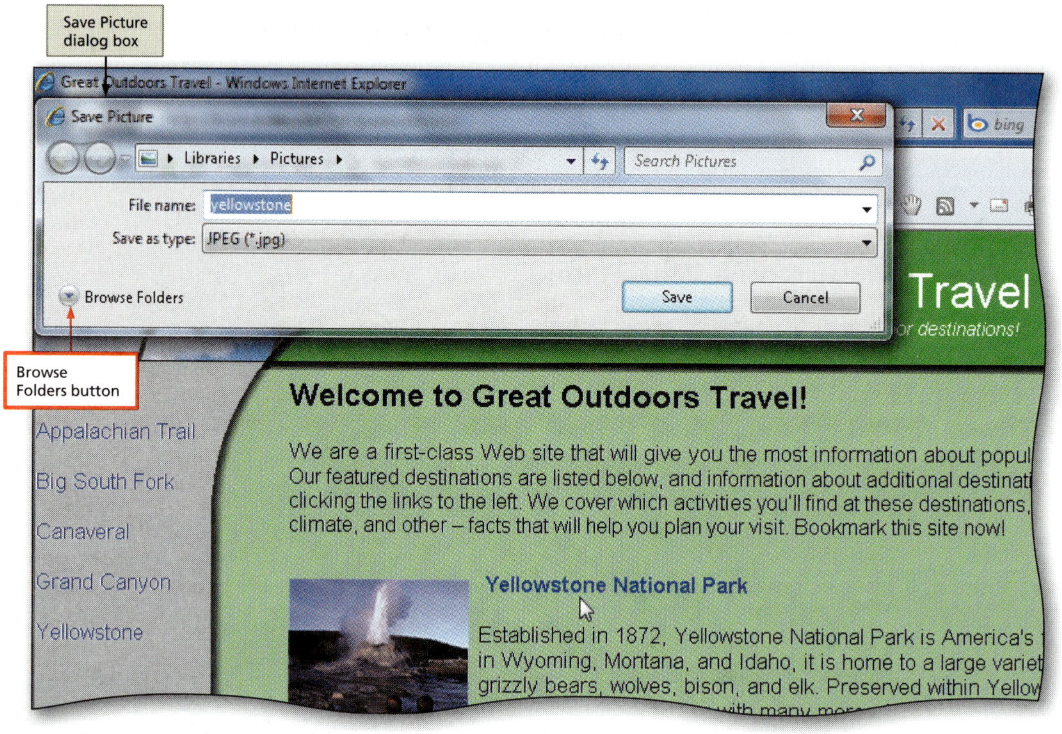

Figure 41

3

- If necessary, click the Browse Folders button to expand the Save Picture dialog box.
- If necessary, click the Pictures link (Save Picture dialog box) (Figure 42).

4

- Click the Save button (Save Picture dialog box) to save the picture in the Pictures library on your computer and to close the Save Picture dialog box.

Figure 42

Q&A

Should I store all my pictures in the Pictures library?

Yes. Windows provides a Pictures library to help you organize your pictures and make backing up the pictures in the Pictures library to another storage device for safekeeping easy. Three other libraries (Documents, Music, and Videos) are available to store document, music, and video files.

Copying and Pasting Using the Clipboard

A third method of saving information, called the **copy and paste method**, allows you to copy an entire Web page, or portions of a page, and insert the information into any Windows document. The **Clipboard** is a storage area in main memory that temporarily holds the information being copied. The portion of the Web page you select is **copied** from the page to the Clipboard and then **pasted** from the Clipboard into the document. Information you copy to the Clipboard remains there until you add more information or clear it.

The following pages demonstrate how to copy text and pictures from the Yellowstone National Park Web page into a WordPad document using the Clipboard. **WordPad** is a word processing program that is supplied with Microsoft Windows.

BTW

Copy and Paste Web Addresses

You can use the copy and paste operation to insert a Web address that appears in the Address bar into a document or e-mail message. You also can copy a Web address that appears in an e-mail message into the Address bar.

To Start WordPad

Before copying information from the Web page in Internet Explorer to the Clipboard, you first should start WordPad. The following steps start WordPad.

1

- Click the Start button on the Windows taskbar to display the Start menu.
- Click All Programs on the Start menu to display the All Programs list.
- Click Accessories on the All Programs list to display the Accessories list (Figure 43).

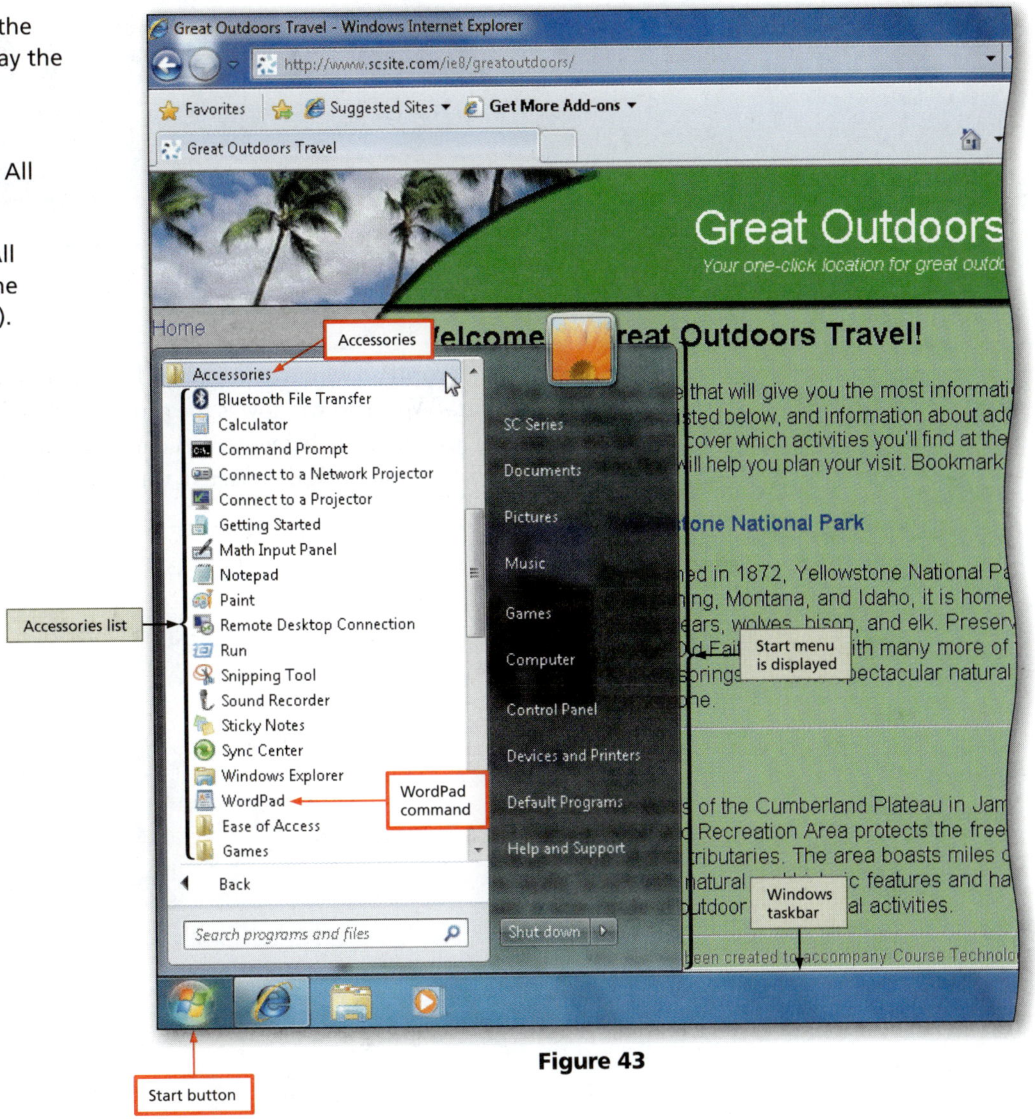

Figure 43

2

- Click WordPad to start WordPad (Figure 44).

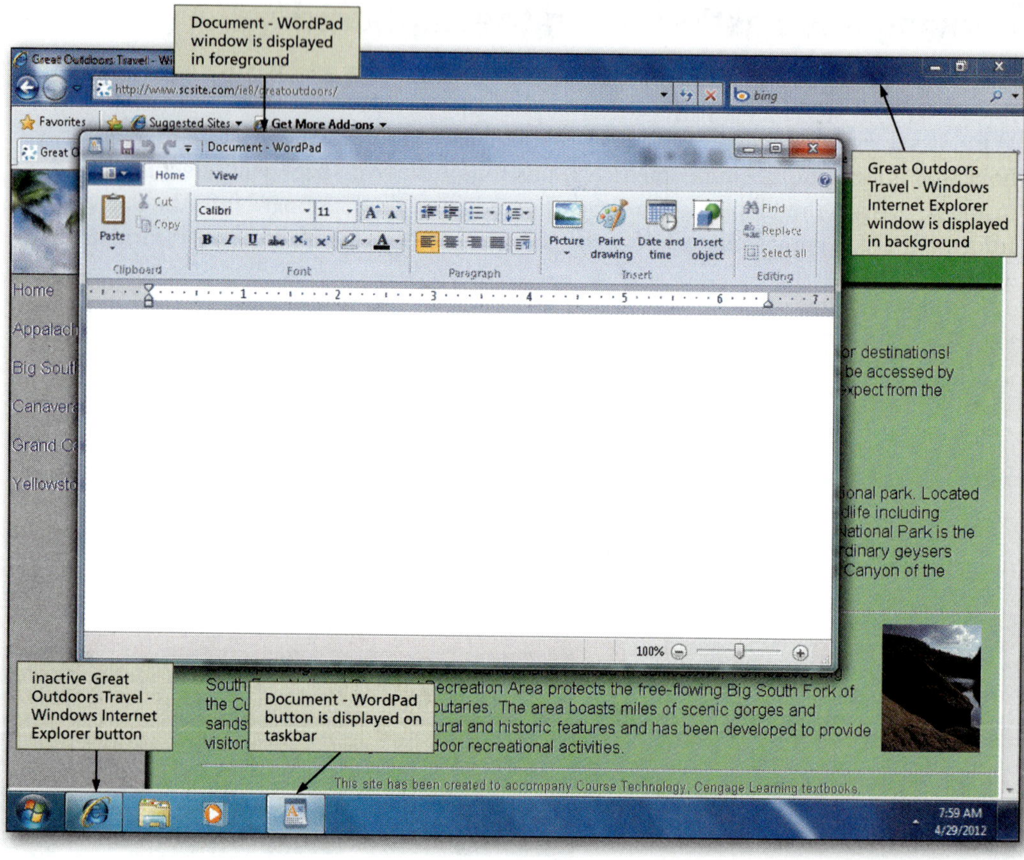

Figure 44

Other Ways

1. Click Start button, click All Programs, click Accessories, click Run, type **wordpad**, click OK button

The Document - WordPad window is displayed on top of the Great Outdoors Travel window. The Document - WordPad window is the active window. Being the **active window** means that it is the window currently being used. A dark title bar identifies the active window. The Great Outdoors Travel window is the inactive window. A light title bar identifies the **inactive window**.

To Display the Yellowstone National Park Web Page

Currently, the active Document - WordPad window is displayed on top of the inactive Great Outdoors Travel window. After starting WordPad and before copying text from a Web page to the Clipboard, make the Great Outdoors Travel window active and then display the Yellowstone National Park Web page. The following steps display the Yellowstone National Park Web page.

1

- Click the Great Outdoors Travel - Windows Internet Explorer button on the taskbar to make the Great Outdoors Travel window the active window (Figure 45).

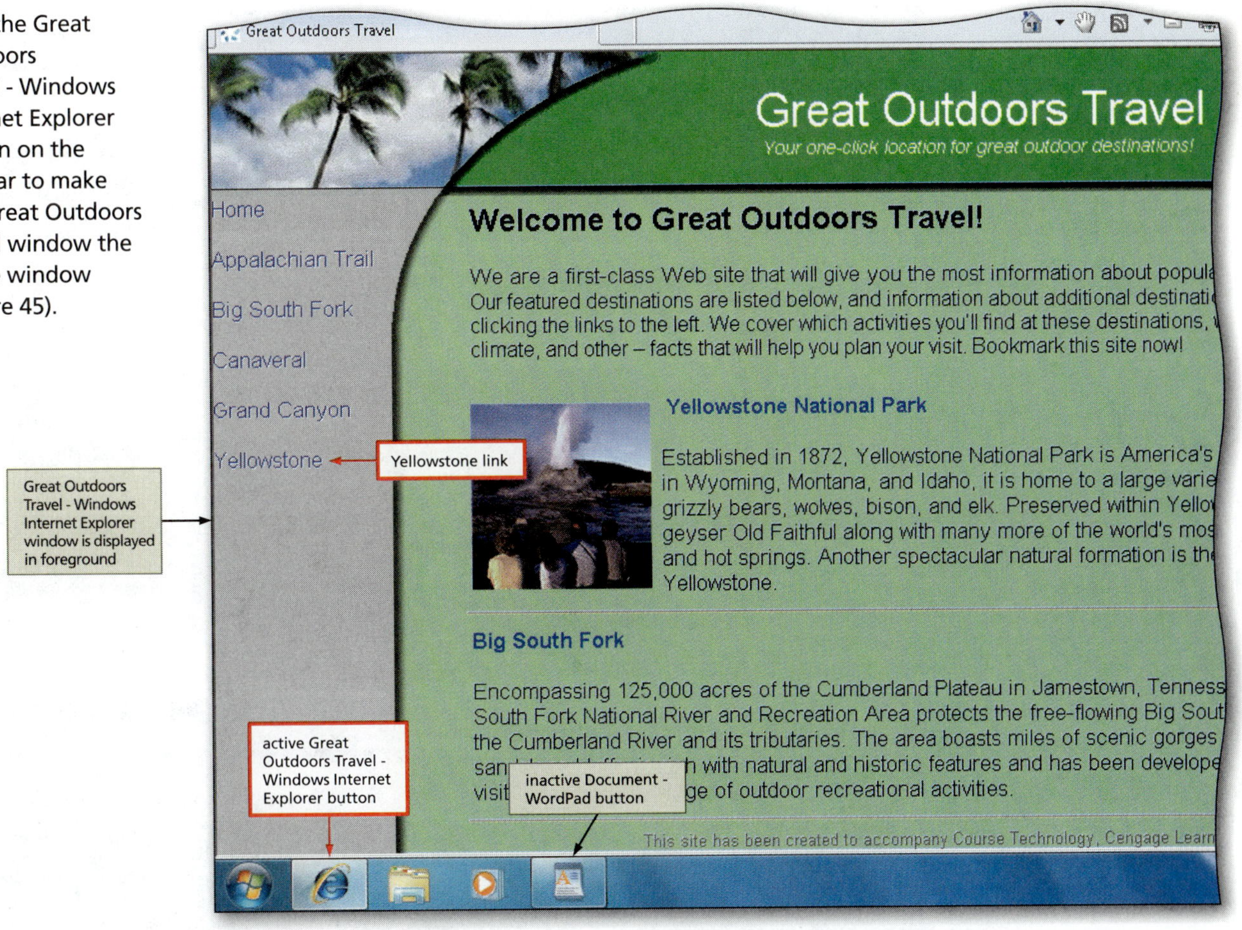

Figure 45

2

- Click the Yellowstone link on the Great Outdoors Travel Web page to display the Yellowstone National Park Web page (Figure 46).

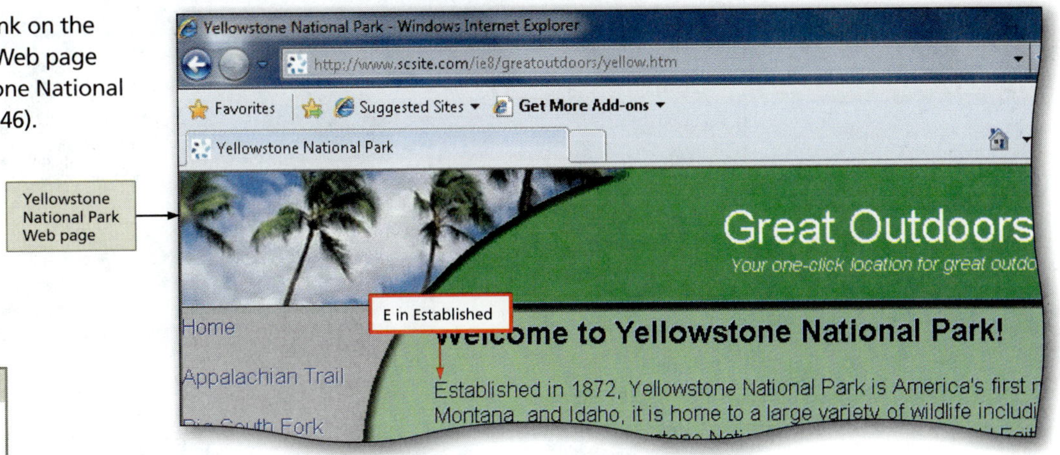

Figure 46

Other Ways

1. Press ALT+TAB, hold down ALT, press TAB to select
2. If visible, click window title bar

To Copy and Paste Text from a Web Page into a WordPad Document

With the Document - WordPad window open and the text you wish to copy contained on the Yellowstone National Park Web page, the next steps are to copy the text from the Yellowstone National Park Web page to the Clipboard, and then paste the text into the WordPad document. The following steps copy the text about Yellowstone National Park into the WordPad document.

1

- Position the mouse pointer (I-beam) to the left of the E in Established to prepare to select the text to be copied (Figure 47).

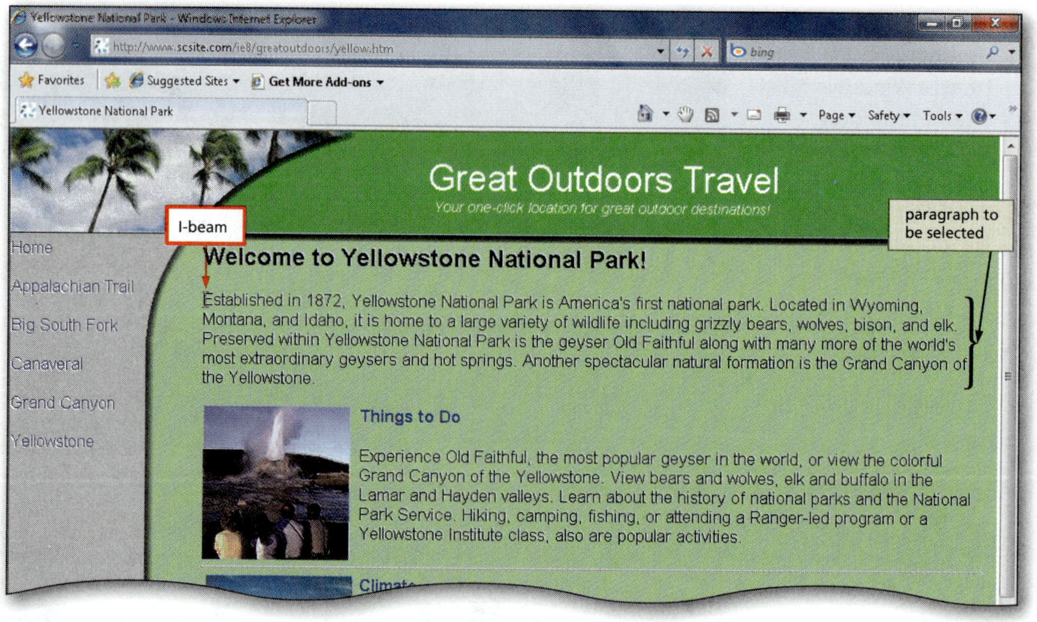

Figure 47

2

- Drag to select the text in the entire paragraph.
- Right-click the selected text to display a shortcut menu (Figure 48).

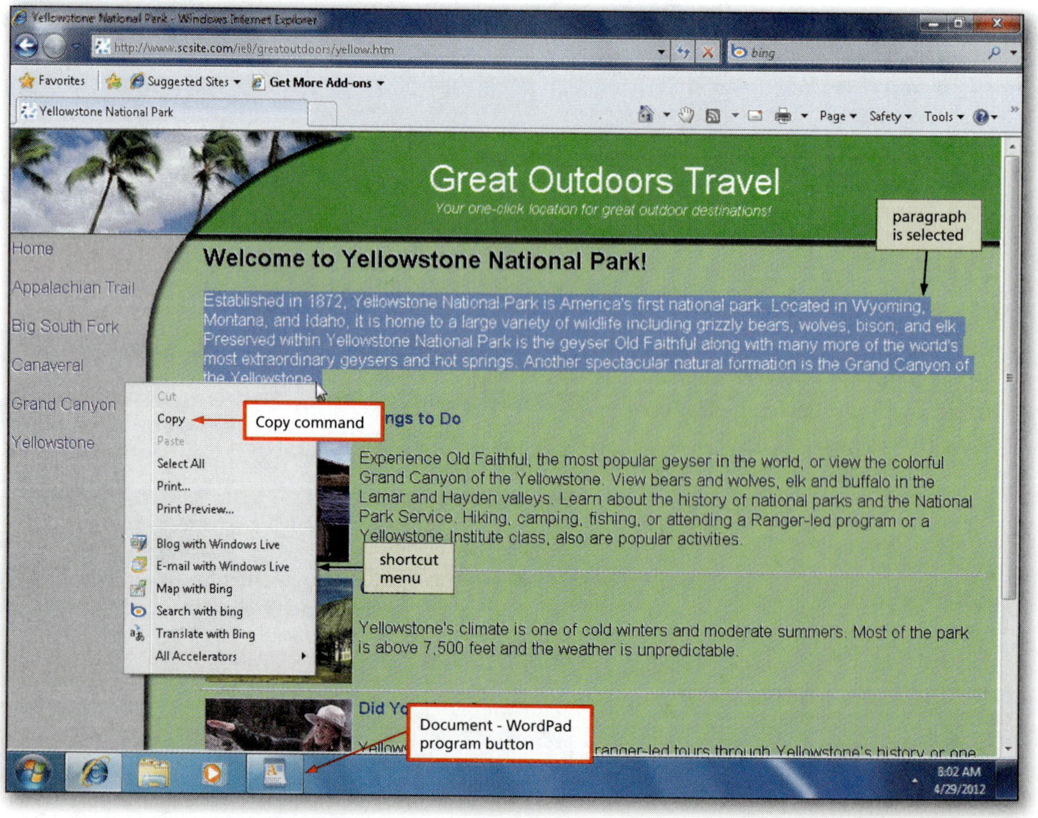

Figure 48

3

- Click the Save button (Save As dialog box) to save the WordPad document.
- Click the Close button on the Yellowstone National Park - WordPad title bar to quit WordPad (Figure 56).

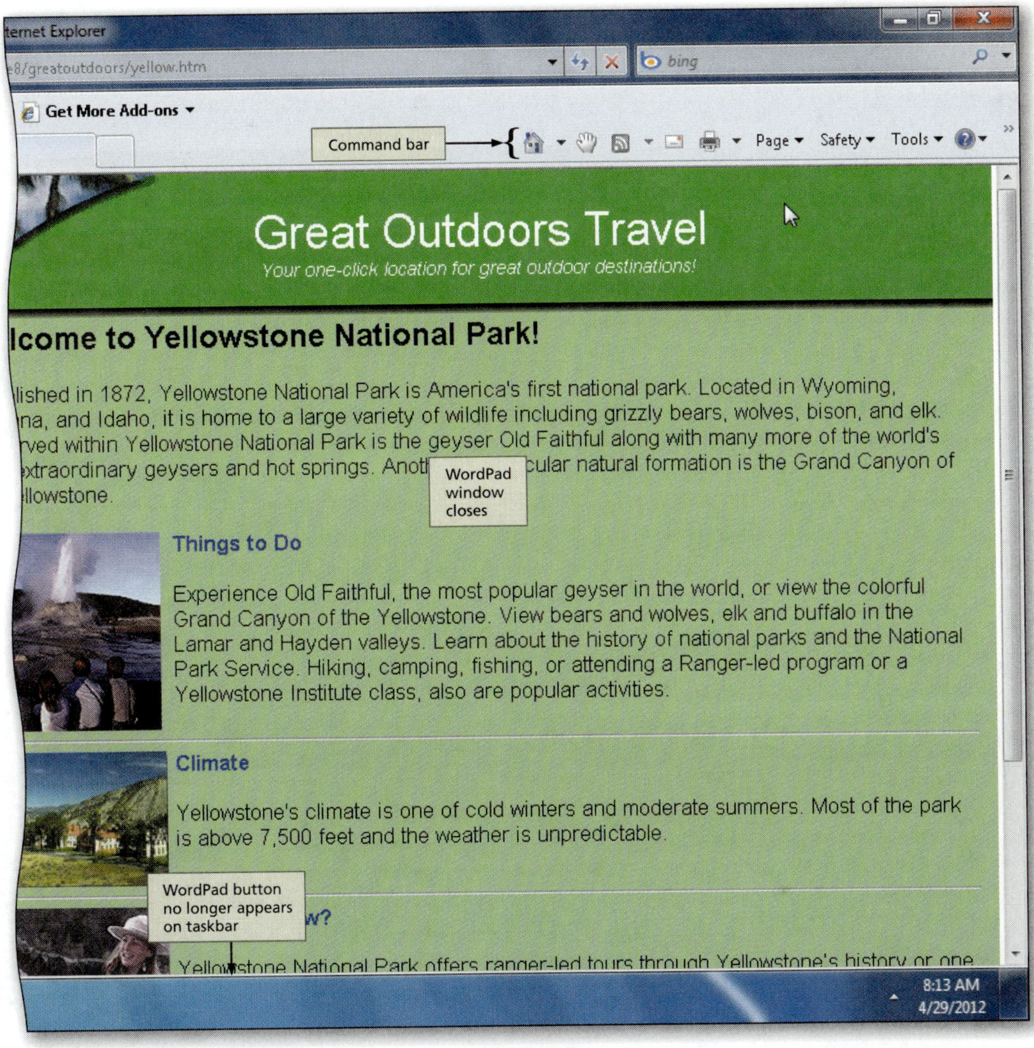

Figure 56

Other Ways

1. Press ALT+F, press A, type file name, press ENTER
2. Press CTRL+S, type file name, press ENTER

Printing a Web Page in Internet Explorer

As you browse the Web, you may want to print some of the pages you view. You may need to print driving directions, your airline ticket, or a record of your tax documents, if you submitted your taxes online. A printed version of a Web page is called a **hard copy** or **printout**.

You can suppress the title and Web address of a Web page that are displayed at the top of a printout using the Page Setup dialog box. You can display the Page Setup dialog box by clicking the Print button arrow on the Command bar and then selecting the Page Setup command. The Header and Footer buttons allow you to specify the information that is displayed in the header and footer areas of the printout.

To Print a Web Page

Internet Explorer allows you to print both the text and picture portions of a Web page. The following steps print the Yellowstone National Park Web page.

1

- Ready the printer according to the printer instructions.
- Point to the Print button on the Command bar (Figure 57).

Figure 57

2

- Click the Print button on the Command bar to begin printing the Web page.
- When the printer stops printing the document, retrieve the printout, which should look like Figure 58.

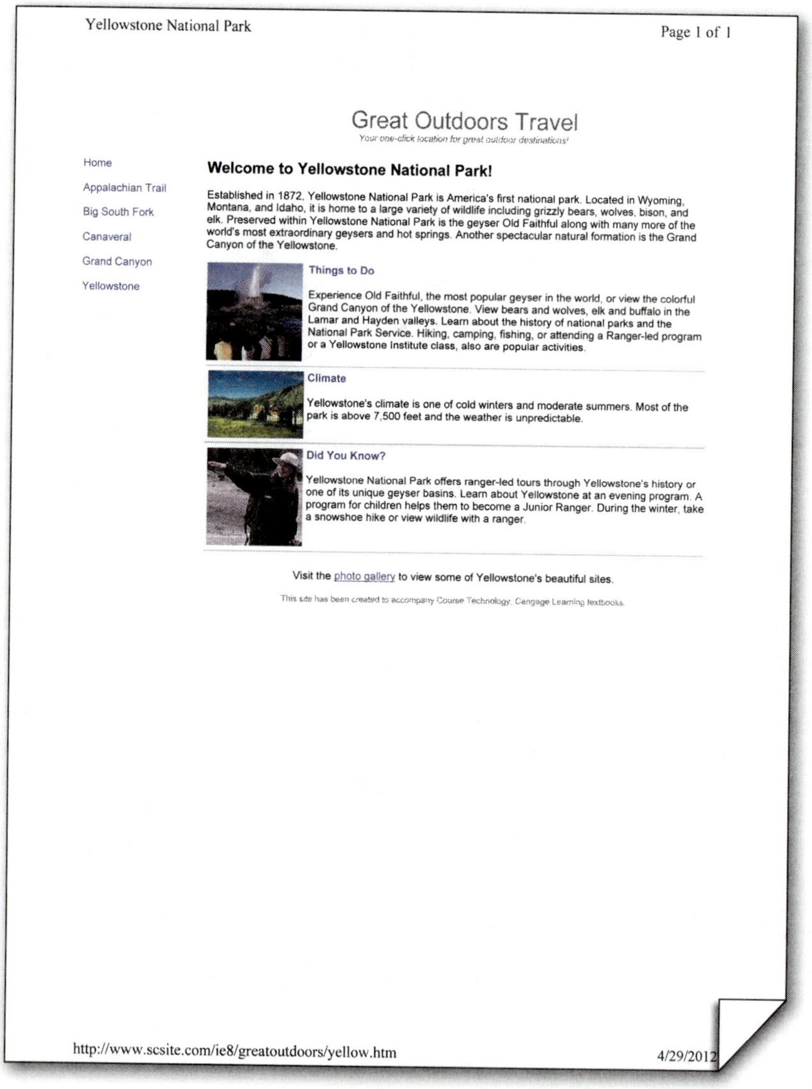

Yellowstone National Park

Page 1 of 1

Great Outdoors Travel

Your one-click location for great outdoor destinations!

Home
Appalachian Trail
Big South Fork
Canaveral
Grand Canyon
Yellowstone

Welcome to Yellowstone National Park!

Established in 1872, Yellowstone National Park is America's first national park. Located in Wyoming, Montana, and Idaho, it is home to a large variety of wildlife including grizzly bears, wolves, bison, and elk. Preserved within Yellowstone National Park is the geyser Old Faithful along with many more of the world's most extraordinary geysers and hot springs. Another spectacular natural formation is the Grand Canyon of the Yellowstone.

Things to Do

Experience Old Faithful, the most popular geyser in the world, or view the colorful Grand Canyon of the Yellowstone. View bears and wolves, elk and buffalo in the Lamar and Hayden valleys. Learn about the history of national parks and the National Park Service. Hiking, camping, fishing, or attending a Ranger-led program or a Yellowstone Institute class, also are popular activities.

Climate

Yellowstone's climate is one of cold winters and moderate summers. Most of the park is above 7,500 feet and the weather is unpredictable.

Did You Know?

Yellowstone National Park offers ranger-led tours through Yellowstone's history or one of its unique geyser basins. Learn about Yellowstone at an evening program. A program for children helps them to become a Junior Ranger. During the winter, take a snowshoe hike or view wildlife with a ranger.

Visit the photo gallery to view some of Yellowstone's beautiful sites.

This site has been created to accompany Course Technology, Cengage Learning textbooks.

http://www.scsite.com/ie8/greatoutdoors/yellow.htm 4/29/2012

Figure 58

Other Ways

1. On File menu click Print, click Print button
2. Press CTRL+P, click Print button

Using the Print button arrow provides access to the Print Preview and Page Setup commands. The printing options available in the Print dialog box allow you to print the entire document, print selected pages of a document, print to a file, print multiple copies, change the printer properties, and cancel the print request.

BTW

Print Options
You can choose to print a table containing a list of all links on the Web page you are printing, or you can choose to print all documents with links on the Web page. Click the Options tab in the Print dialog box and then click the 'Print all linked documents' check box or 'Print table of links' check box to print the documents or table.

Internet Explorer Help

Internet Explorer offers users many features and options. Although you will master some features and options quickly, it is not necessary for you to remember everything about all of them. Reference materials and other forms of assistance are available within **Internet Explorer Help**.

To Access Internet Explorer Help

The following steps use Internet Explorer Help to find more information about favorites.

1

- Click the Help button on the Command bar to display the Help menu (Figure 59).

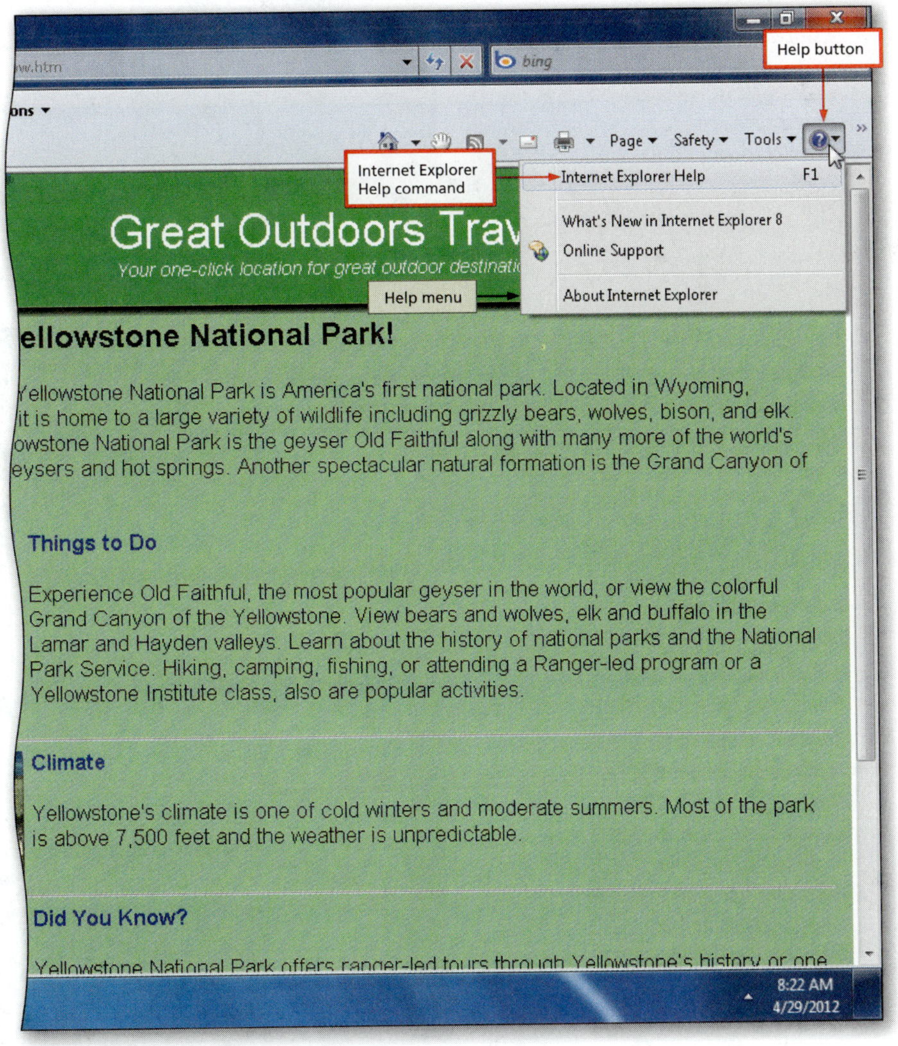

Figure 59

2

- Click Internet Explorer Help on the Help menu to open the Windows Help and Support window (Figure 60).

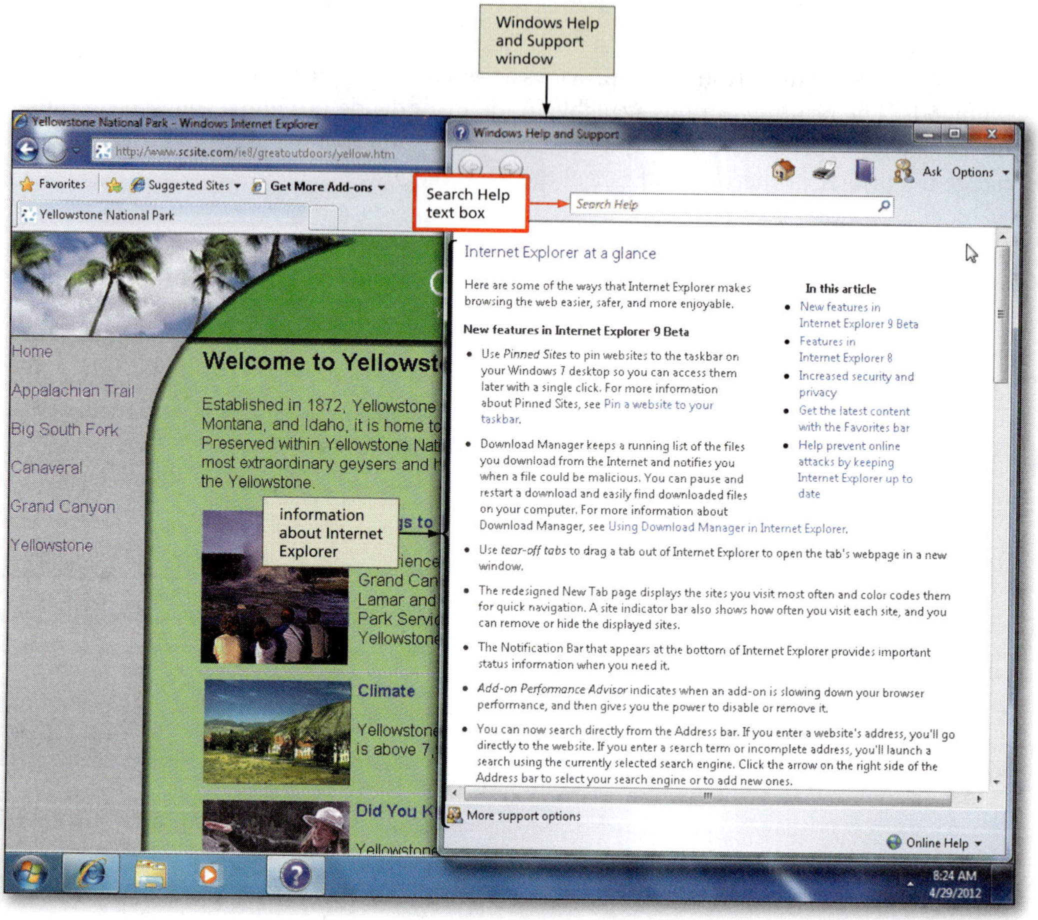

Figure 60

3

- Type **favorites** in the Search Help text box, and then press the ENTER key to display the search results matching your search text (Figure 61).

Q&A

Why do my search results differ?

When you search for help using Windows Help and Support, your search results also include online resources that match your search criteria. Microsoft regularly updates these online resources to provide you with an effective and up-to-date Help system.

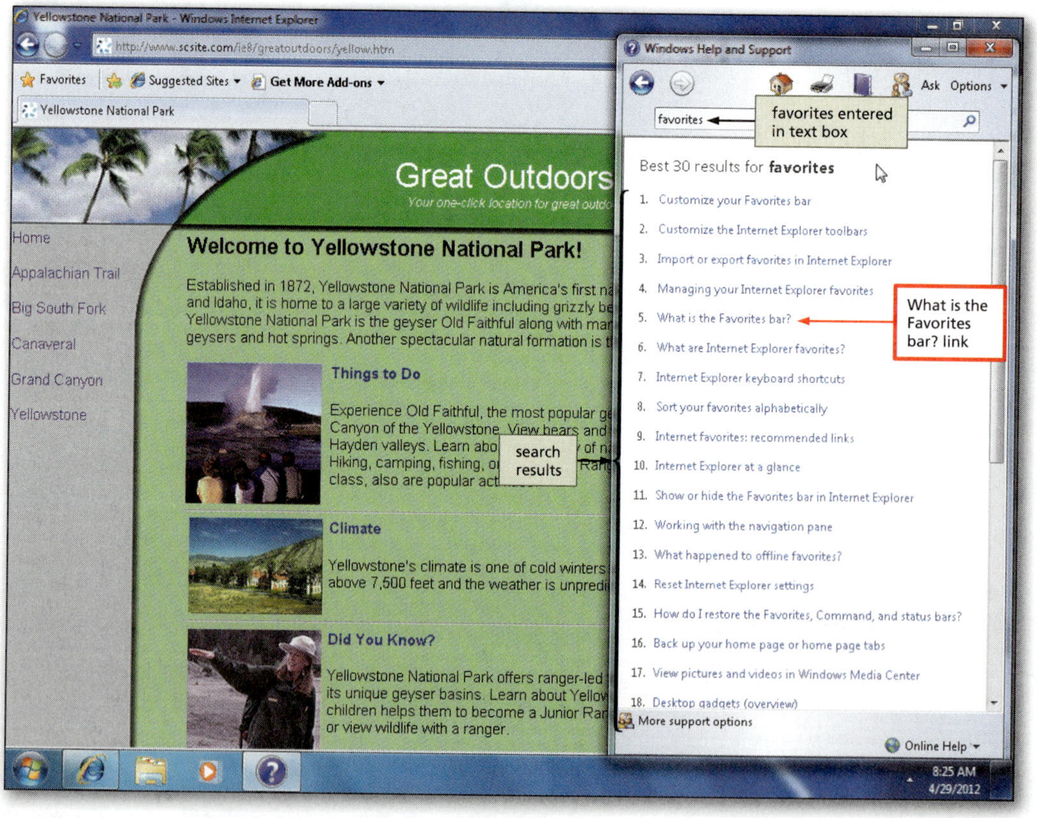

Figure 61

4

- Click the What is the Favorites bar? link in the list of Help topics to display information about favorites (Figure 62).
- When you are finished viewing the information, click the Close button on the right side of the title bar to close the Windows Help and Support window.

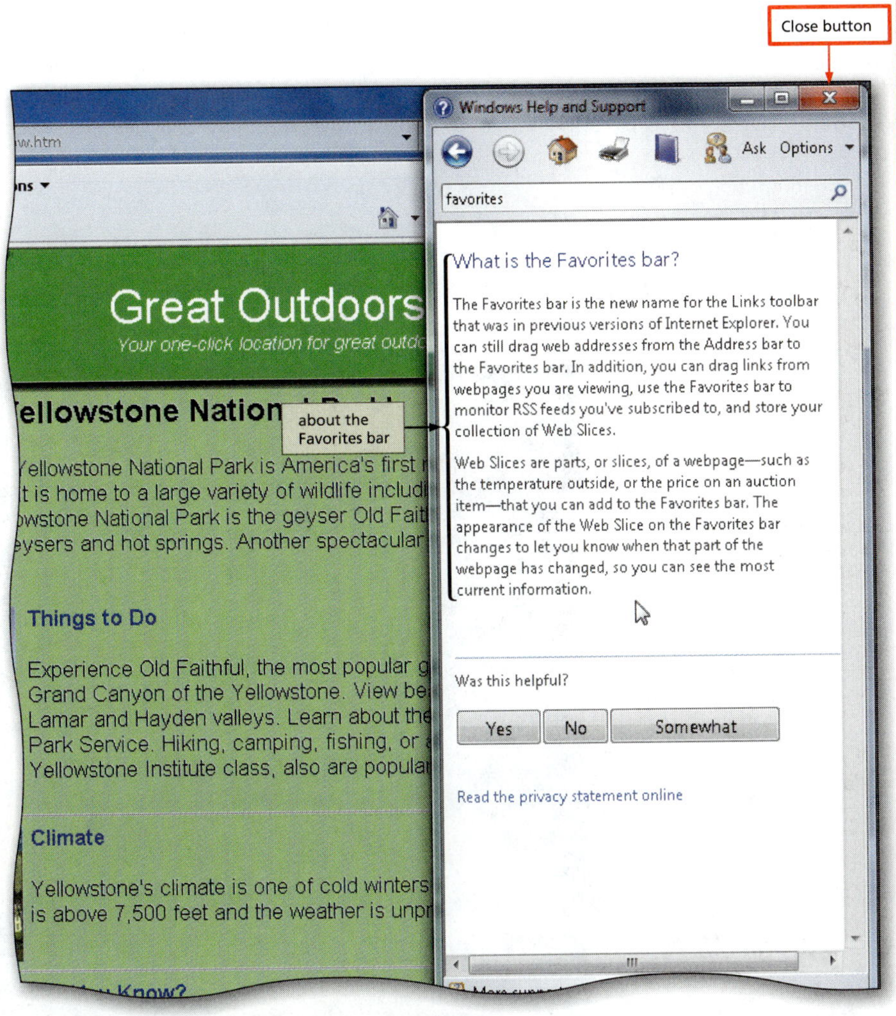

Figure 62

Other Ways

1. Press ALT+H, press I
2. Press F1

In Figure 60, buttons on the Help toolbar in the Windows Help and Support window allow you to perform activities such as going back to the most recent help topic, going forward to a help page you have visited prior to clicking the Back button, displaying the Windows Help and Support Center home page, printing the current page, requesting additional help, and changing Internet options.

The Help menu in Figure 59 on page IE 49 contains several other commands, which are summarized in Table 3.

Table 3 Commands on the Help Menu

Menu Command	Function
Internet Explorer Help	Displays the Windows Help and Support window
What's New in Internet Explorer 8	Displays a Web page highlighting new features in Internet Explorer 8
Online Support	Displays Microsoft Help and Support Web site
About Internet Explorer	Displays version, cipher strength, product ID, license information, and copyright information about Internet Explorer

Quitting Internet Explorer

After browsing the Web and learning how to navigate Web sites, add favorites, copy and paste content, and print Web pages, this chapter is complete.

To Quit Internet Explorer

The following step quits Internet Explorer.

1

- Click the Close button in the upper-right corner of the Internet Explorer window to close the window (Figure 63).

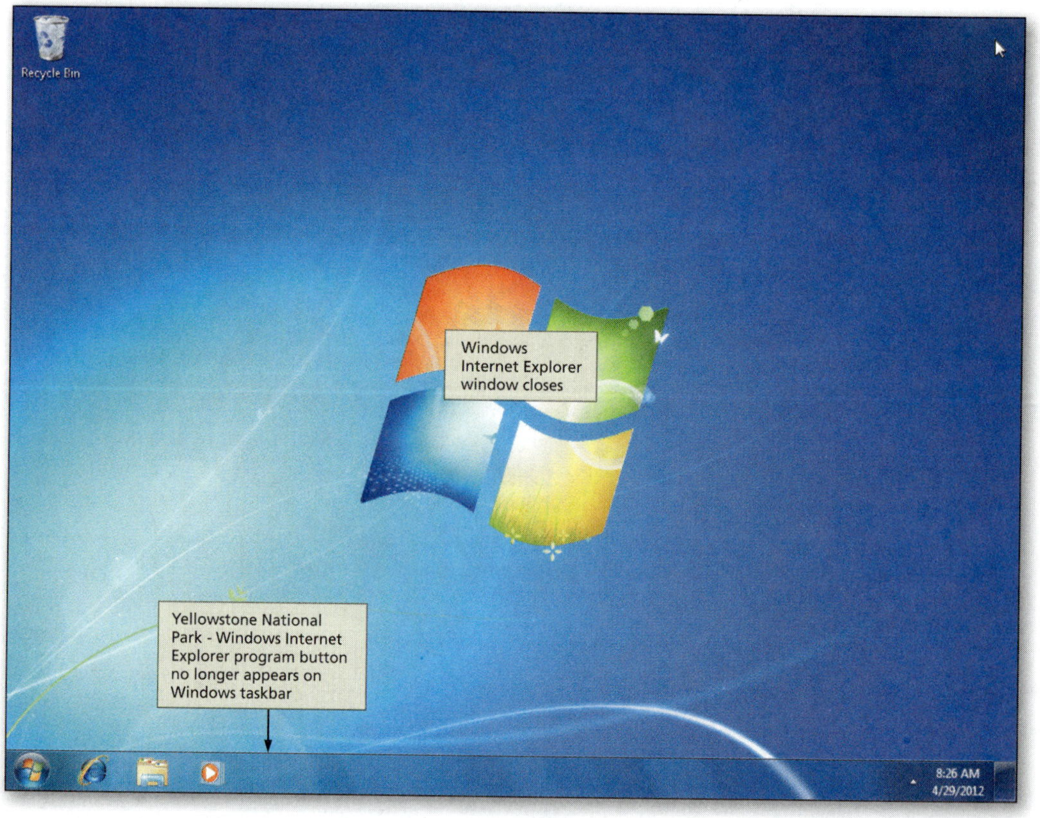

Figure 63

Other Ways

1. Double-click Internet Explorer menu icon at left end of title bar
2. On File menu click Exit
3. Press ALT+F, press X

Chapter Summary

This chapter introduced you to the Internet and World Wide Web. You learned how to start Internet Explorer; use the Address bar, Command bar, Favorites bar, History List, and the navigation buttons on the toolbar; and enter a Web address to browse the Web. You learned how to add and remove favorites; copy and paste text from a Web page into a WordPad document; print a Web page; and save text, a picture, and an entire Web page to the hard disk. In addition, you learned how to use Help to obtain help about Internet Explorer. The items listed below include all the new Internet Explorer skills you have learned in this chapter.

1. Start Internet Explorer (IE 11)
2. Browse the Web by Entering a Web Address (IE 16)
3. Refresh a Web Page (IE 21)
4. Use the Navigation Buttons to Find Recently Displayed Web Pages (IE 23)
5. Display a Web Page Using the Recent Pages List (IE 25)
6. Display a Web Page Using the History List (IE 27)
7. Add a Web Page to the Favorites Center (IE 30)
8. Display the Home Page Using the Home Button (IE 32)
9. Display a Web Page Using the Favorites Center (IE 33)
10. Remove a Web Page from the Favorites Center (IE 34)
11. Save a Web Page (IE 36)
12. Save a Picture on a Web Page (IE 37)
13. Start WordPad (IE 39)
14. Display the Yellowstone National Park Web Page (IE 41)
15. Copy and Paste Text from a Web Page into a WordPad Document (IE 42)
16. Copy and Paste a Picture from a Web Page into a WordPad Document (IE 44)
17. Save the WordPad Document and Quit WordPad (IE 46)
18. Print a Web Page (IE 48)
19. Access Internet Explorer Help (IE 49)
20. Quit Internet Explorer (IE 52)

Learn It Online

Test your knowledge of chapter content and key terms.

Instructions: To complete the Learn It Online exercises, visit the Microsoft Office and Concepts CourseMate Web site at www.cengagebrain.com, navigate to the Internet Explorer chapter resources for this book, click the link for the exercise you want to complete, and then read the instructions.

Chapter Reinforcement TF, MC, and SA

A series of true/false, multiple choice, and short answer questions that test your knowledge of the chapter content.

Flash Cards

An interactive learning environment where you identify key terms from the chapter associated with displayed definitions.

Practice Test

A series of multiple-choice questions that test your knowledge of chapter content and key terms.

Who Wants To Be a Computer Genius?

An interactive game that challenges your knowledge of chapter content in the style of the television quiz show.

Wheel of Terms

An interactive game that challenges your knowledge of key terms from the chapter in the style of the television show *Wheel of Fortune*.

Crossword Puzzle Challenge

A crossword puzzle that challenges your knowledge of key terms presented in the chapter.

Apply Your Knowledge

Reinforce the skills and apply the concepts you learned in this chapter.

Browsing the World Wide Web Using Web Addresses and Links

Problem: You work part-time for CNN, one of the nation's leading sources of news. Your editor has asked you to search for information on several informational Web sites and print the first page of each Web site.

Instructions: Perform the following tasks.

Part 1: Using the Address Bar to Find Web Pages

1. If necessary, connect to the Internet and start Internet Explorer.

2. Click the Address bar, type **`www.fbi.gov`** in the box, and then press the ENTER key to display the Federal Bureau of Investigation's home page (Figure 64).

Figure 64

3. Point to the ABOUT US link and then click the Quick Facts link to display the Web page that contains facts about the FBI.
4. Click the Print button on the Command bar toolbar to print the Web page.
5. Use the Back button on the toolbar to display the FBI home page.
6. Click the Print button on the Command bar to print the Web page.
7. Click the Address bar, type **`www.nbc.com`** to enter the Web address, and then press the ENTER key to display the NBC home page (Figure 65 on the next page).

Continued >

Apply Your Knowledge *continued*

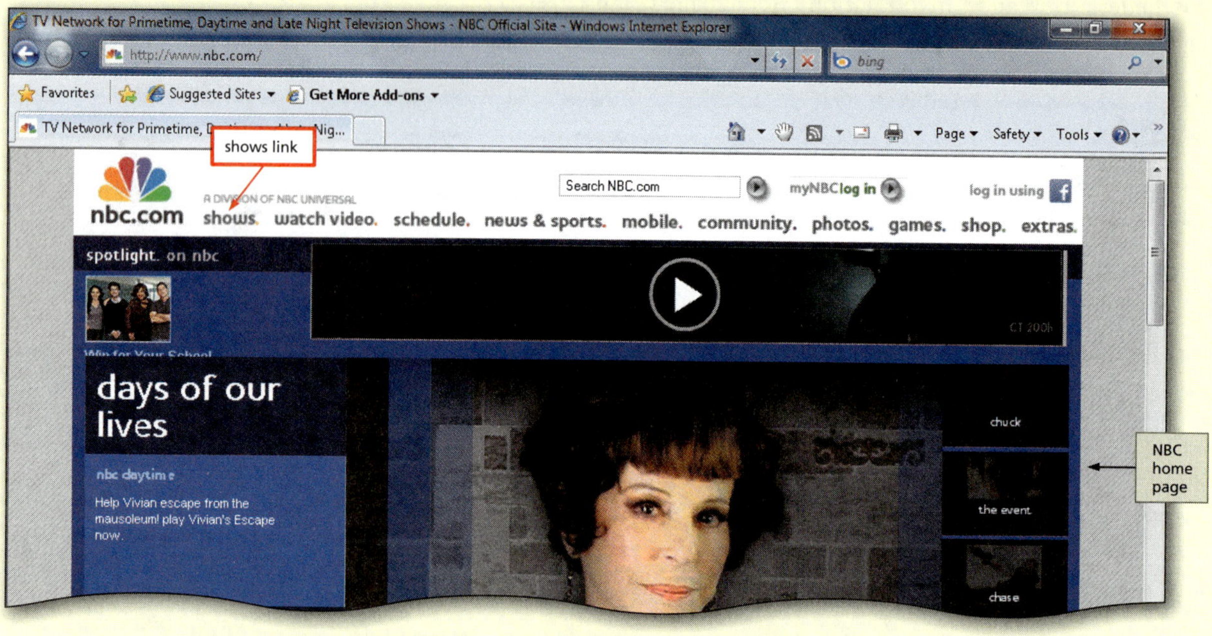

Figure 65

8. Click the shows link, and then click the The Office link in the NBC Web site to display the Web page about the show, *The Office*.
9. Click the Print button on the Command bar to print the Web page.
10. Click the Address bar, type **`www.weather.com`** in the box, and then press the ENTER key to display the weather.com home page (Figure 66).

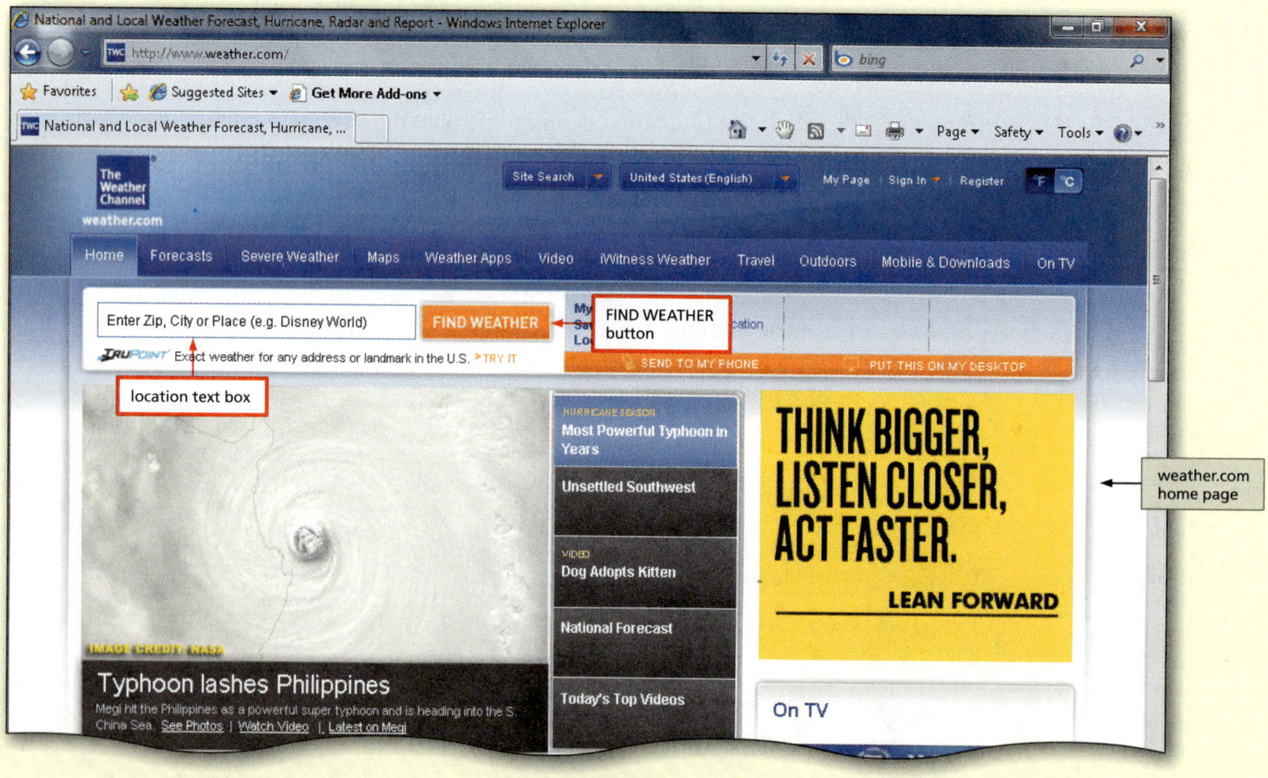

Figure 66

11. Type your ZIP code in the location text box, and then click the FIND WEATHER button to display the Web page containing the weather report for your area.
12. Click the Print button on the Command bar to print the Web page.
13. Click the Address bar, type **`www.abc.com`** to enter the Web address, and then press the ENTER key to display the ABC home page (Figure 67).

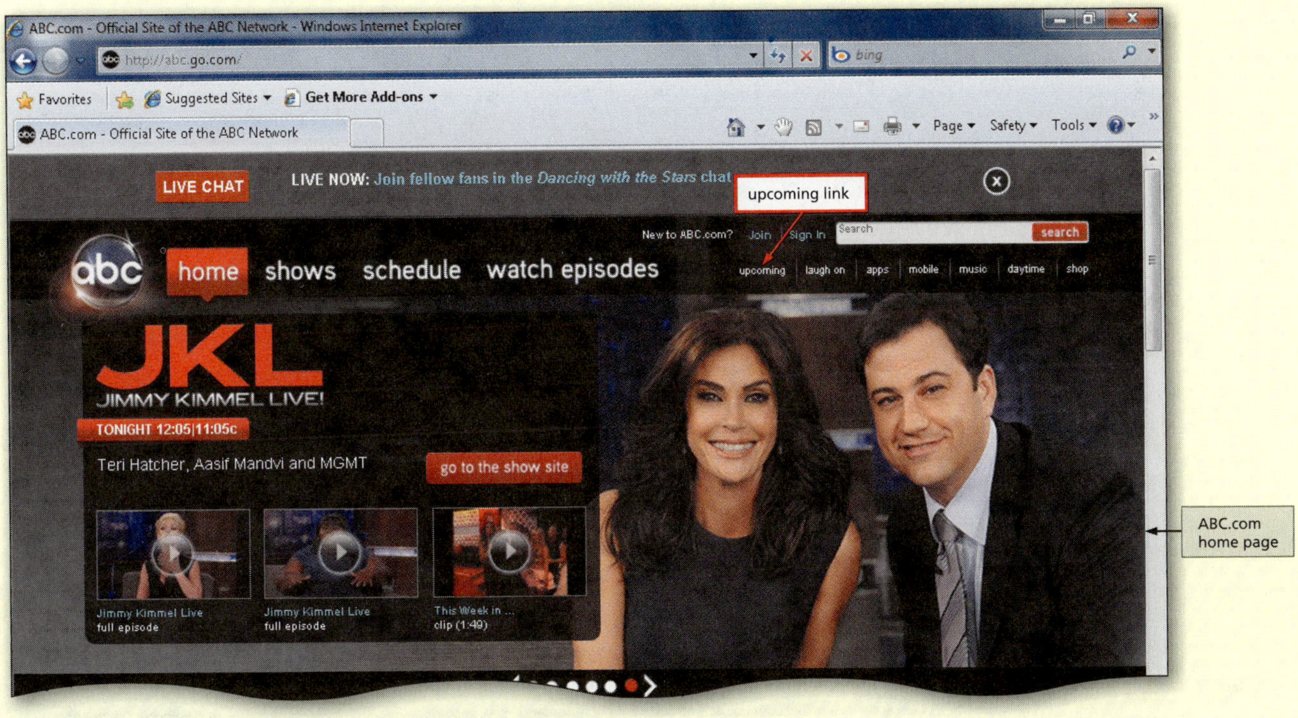

Figure 67

14. Click the upcoming link to display the Web page containing information about upcoming shows.
15. Click the Print button on the Command bar to print the Web page.

Part 2: Using the History List to Find a Web Page

1. Click the Home button on the Command bar to display your default home page.
2. Click the Favorites button on the Favorites bar, click the History tab to display the History List, click Today, click nbc (www.nbc.com) folder name in the History List, and then click the TV Network for Primetime, Daytime and Late Night Television Shows - NBC Official Site link to display the NBC home page.
3. Click the Print button on the Command bar to print the Web page.
4. If necessary, click the Close button on the Explorer bar.

Part 3: Using the Back Button Arrow to Find a Web Page

1. Click the Recent Pages list arrow and then click the ABC.com - Official Site of the ABC Network entry on the menu to display the ABC home page.
2. Click the Print button on the Command bar to print the Web page.

Continued >

Apply Your Knowledge *continued*

Part 4: Using the Address Bar List Arrow to Find a Web Page

1. Click the Address bar list arrow and then click http://www.weather.com in the Address list to display the weather.com home page.
2. Click the Print button on the Command bar to print the Web page.
3. Click the Close button in the Internet Explorer window.
4. Submit the printed pages to your instructor.

Extend Your Knowledge

Extend the skills you learned in this chapter and experiment with new skills. You may need to use Help to complete the assignment.

Browsing the World Wide Web Using the Instant Search Box and Links

Problem: Concerned about keeping your personal information and your computer safe when you access the Internet, you decide to visit the Web site of a leading computer security company.

Instructions: Perform the following tasks.

1. Use the Instant Search box to locate the official McAfee Web site. What keywords did you type to locate this page?
2. Navigate to the McAfee home page (Figure 68).

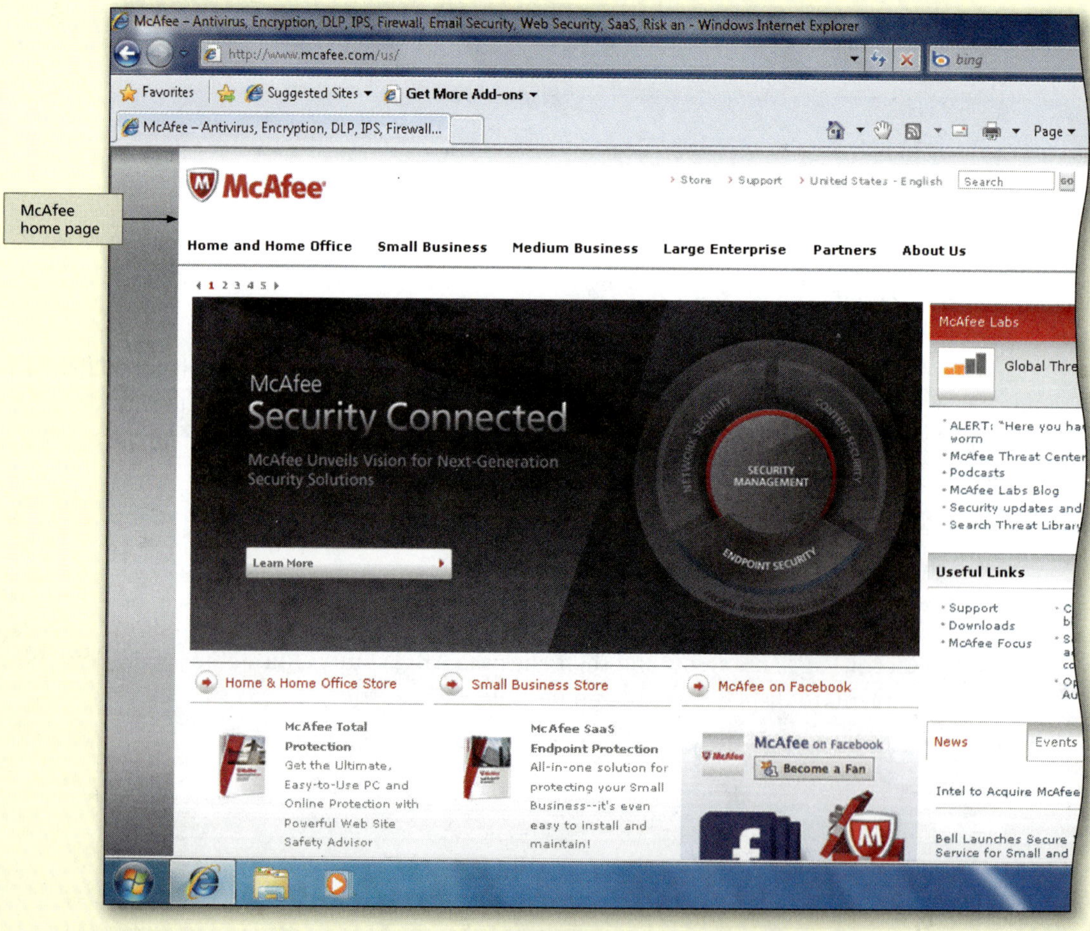

Figure 68

3. View the Web page in Print Preview. What buttons appear at the top of the Print Preview window? How many pages will it take to print this Web page?
4. Print the McAfee home page from the Print Preview window, and then close the Print Preview window.
5. Use the links on the McAfee home page to answer the following questions:
   a. What are five latest computer vulnerabilities?
   b. On what date was the latest vulnerability made public?
   c. How does McAfee measure the severity of threats?
   d. What must you do to protect your computer from threats? What programs does McAfee offer to help you protect your computer?
   e. What is the current Global Threat Condition?
   f. If your computer already has been infected by a threat, such as a virus or spyware, what should you do?
6. Use the History List to navigate back to the McAfee home page.
7. Browse McAfee's Web site for a page that discusses an example of current malware. Print the Web page.
8. Add the Web page to your Favorites Center.
9. Remove the Web page from your Favorites Center.
10. Organize your printed Web pages and submit them, along with the answers to the questions in this exercise, to your instructor.

In the Lab

Use Internet Explorer to navigate the World Wide Web by using the guidelines, concepts, and skills presented in this chapter. Labs are listed in order of increasing difficulty.

Lab 1: Using the History List to Locate Previously Viewed Pages

Problem: Your instructor would like you to practice browsing the Internet for Web sites and using the History List. As proof of completing this assignment, you should print the first page of each Web site you visit.

Instructions: Perform the following tasks.

Part 1: Clearing the History List

1. Click Tools on the Command bar and then click Internet Options to display the Internet Options dialog box (Figure 69 on the next page).

Continued >

In the Lab *continued*

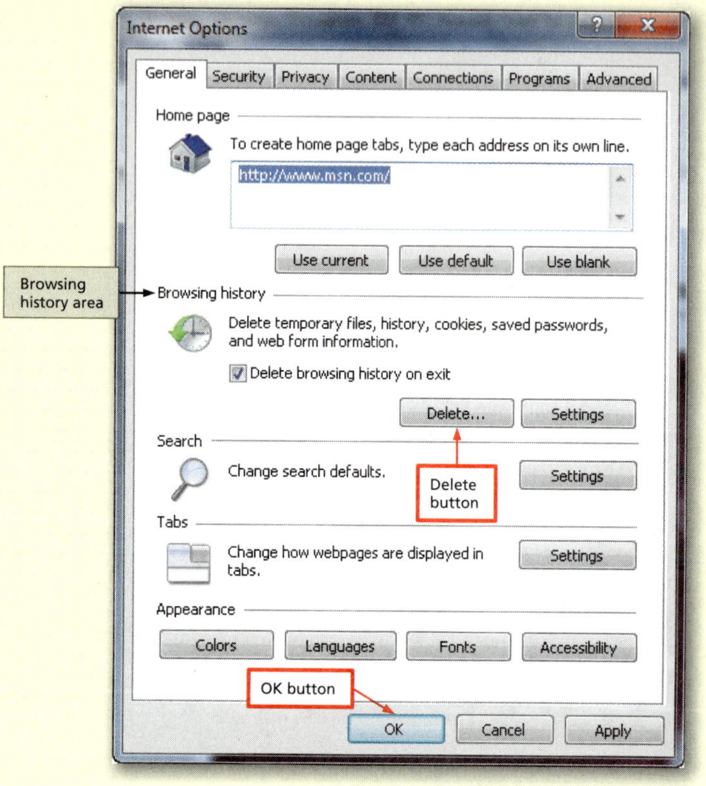

Figure 69

2. Click the Delete button in the Browsing history area and then click the Delete button in the Delete Browsing History dialog box.
3. Click the OK button in the Internet Options dialog box.

Part 2: Browsing the World Wide Web

1. Click the Address bar, type **`www.youtube.com`** to enter the Web address, and then press the ENTER key to display the YouTube home page.
2. Click the Address bar, type **`www.ucf.edu`** to enter the Web address, and then press the ENTER key to display the University of Central Florida home page.
3. Click the Address bar, type **`www.geocaching.com`** to enter the Web address, and then press the ENTER key to display the Geocaching home page.
4. Click the Address bar, type **`www.cbssports.com`** to enter the Web address, and then press the ENTER key to display the CBSSports home page.

Part 3: Using the History List to Print a Web Page

1. Click the Favorites button on the Favorites bar, click the History tab (Figure 70), and then click Today to display the current History List. Click the Pin the Favorites Center button to pin the Favorites Center.

Figure 70

2. Click the ucf (www.ucf.edu) folder in the History List and then click the University of Central Florida link. Print the Web page.
3. Click the youtube (www.youtube.com) folder in the History List and then click the YouTube - Broadcast Yourself link. Print the Web page.
4. Click the cbssports (www.cbssports.com) folder in the History List and then click the CBSSports.com link. Print the Web page.
5. Delete the geocaching (www.geocaching.com) folder by right-clicking the folder, clicking Delete on the shortcut menu, and then clicking the Yes button in the WARNING dialog box.
6. If necessary, click the Close the Favorites Center button.

Part 4: Clearing the History List

1. Click Safety on the Command bar and then click Delete Browsing History to display the Delete Browsing History dialog box.
2. If necessary, click the History check box so that it contains a check mark, and then click the Delete button.
3. Submit the printed Web pages to your instructor.

In the Lab

Lab 2: Adding, Viewing, Printing, and Removing Your Favorites

Problem: Your instructor would like you to practice browsing the Internet for Web sites and adding them to the Favorites Center. As proof of completing this assignment, print out the first page of each Web site you visit.

Instructions: Perform the following tasks.

Part 1: Creating a Folder in the Favorites Center

1. Click the Favorites button on the Favorites bar, click the Add to Favorites list arrow, and then click Organize Favorites to display the Organize Favorites dialog box (Figure 71 on the next page).

Continued >

In the Lab *continued*

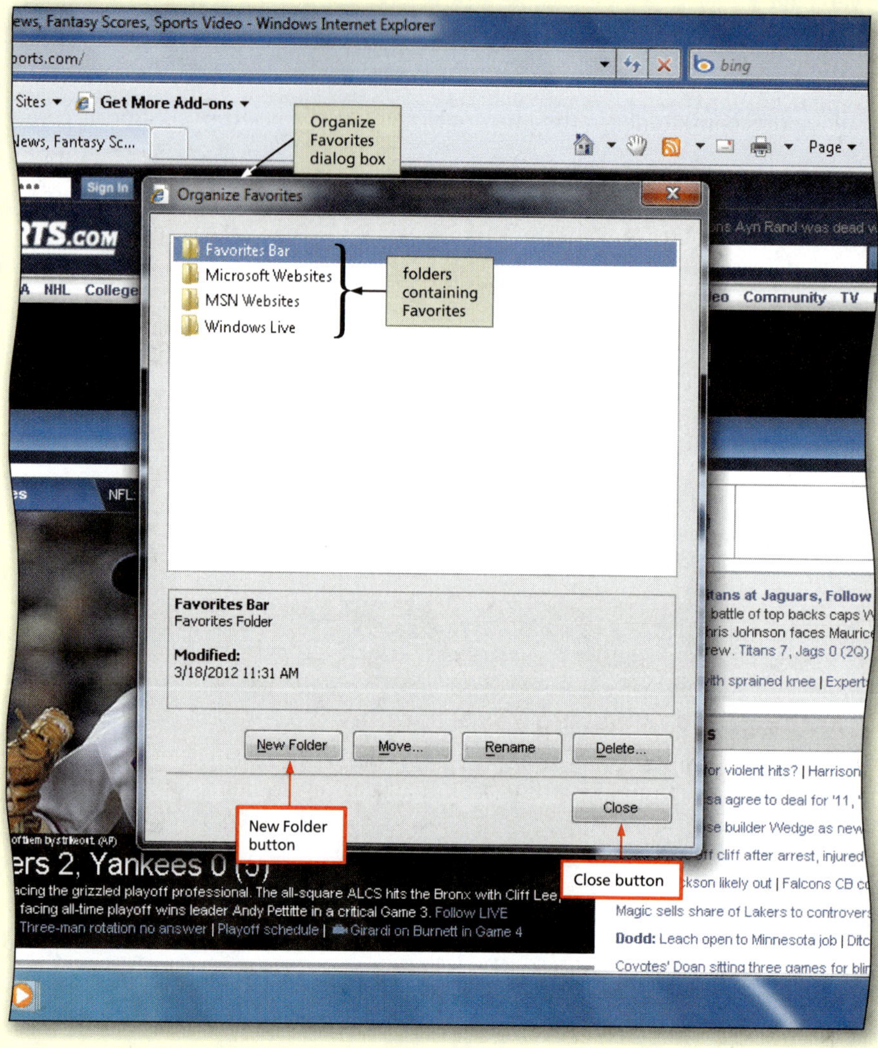

Figure 71

2. Click the New Folder button in the Organize Favorites dialog box to create a folder titled New Folder, type your first and last name as the folder name, and then press the ENTER key.
3. Click the Close button to close the Organize Favorites dialog box.

Part 2: Adding Favorites to Your Folder

1. Click the Address bar, type **`www.pentagon.gov`** to enter the Web address, and then press the ENTER key to display The Official Home of the Department of Defense home page.
2. Add The Official Home of the Department of Defense favorite to the folder identified by your name by clicking the Favorites button on the Favorites bar, and then clicking the Add to Favorites button (Figure 72). Click the Create in drop-down list button to display the Create in list.

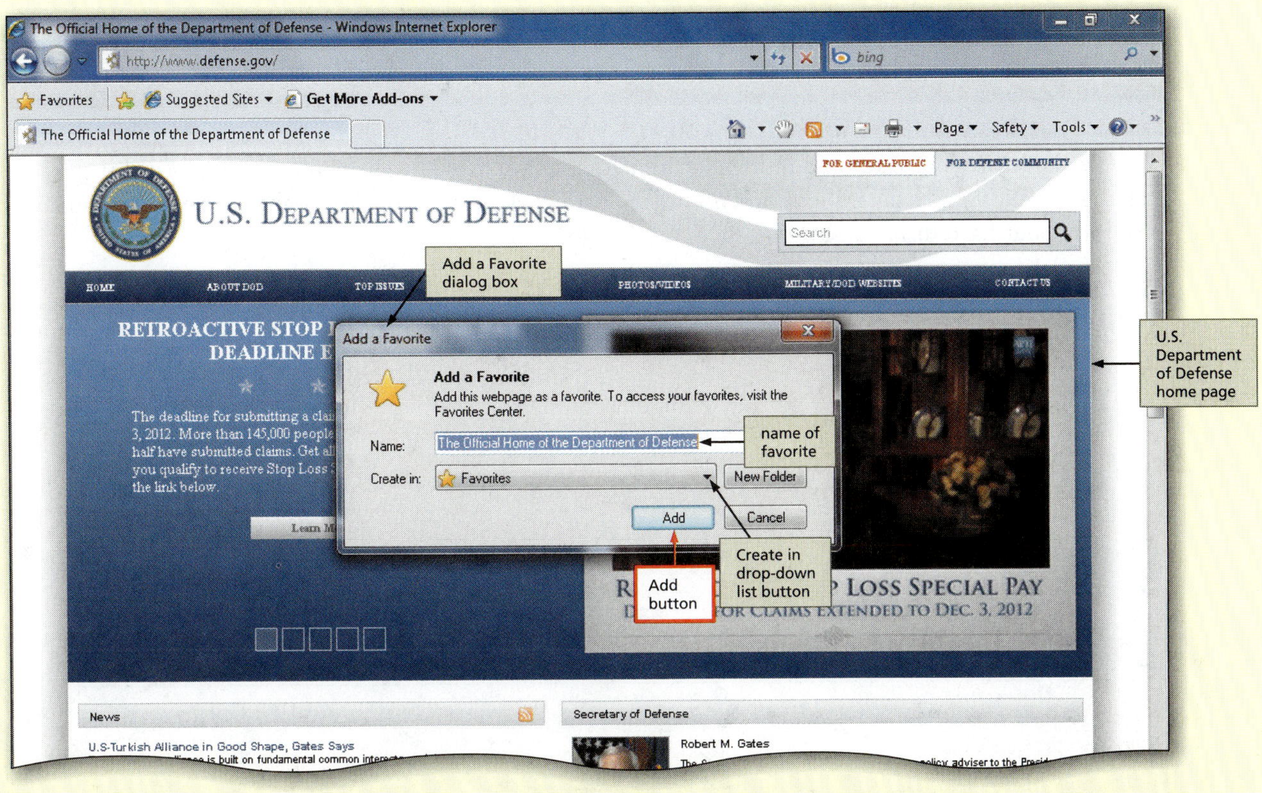

Figure 72

3. Click your folder in the Create in list and then click the Add button.
4. Click the Address bar, type **`www.orbitz.com`** to enter the Web address, and then press the ENTER key to display the Orbitz home page.
5. Add this Web page as a favorite, change the name of the favorite to Orbitz, and then create the favorite in your folder.
6. Click the Home button on the Command bar to display your default home page.

Part 3: Displaying and Printing a Favorite from Your Folder

1. Click the Favorites button on the Favorites bar to display the Favorites Center. If necessary, click the Favorites tab.
2. Click your folder in the Favorites Center and then click The Official Home of the Department of Defense.
3. Print the Web page.
4. If necessary, click the Favorites button on the Favorites bar to display the Favorites Center.
5. Click Orbitz in the Favorites Center.
6. Print the Web page.

Part 4: Deleting a Folder in the Favorites Center

1. If necessary, display the Favorites Center.
2. Right-click your folder name, click the Delete command on the shortcut menu, and then click the Yes button in the Delete Folder dialog box.
3. If necessary, close the Favorites Center.
4. Verify that you have deleted your folder.
5. Submit the printed pages to your instructor.

In the Lab

Lab 3: Printing and Saving the Current U.S. Weather Map

Problem: You are interested in finding a current United States weather map to use on a road trip starting in San Diego, California, and ending in Boston, Massachusetts. You want to print the map and save it on your hard disk.

Instructions: Perform the following tasks.

1. Type **`www.weather.com`** in the Address bar and then press the ENTER key to display the weather.com home page.
2. Point to Maps and then click the US Current Temperatures link to display an enlarged weather map for the United States. If necessary scroll down to view the weather map (Figure 73). The map that is displayed on your computer might differ from Figure 73.

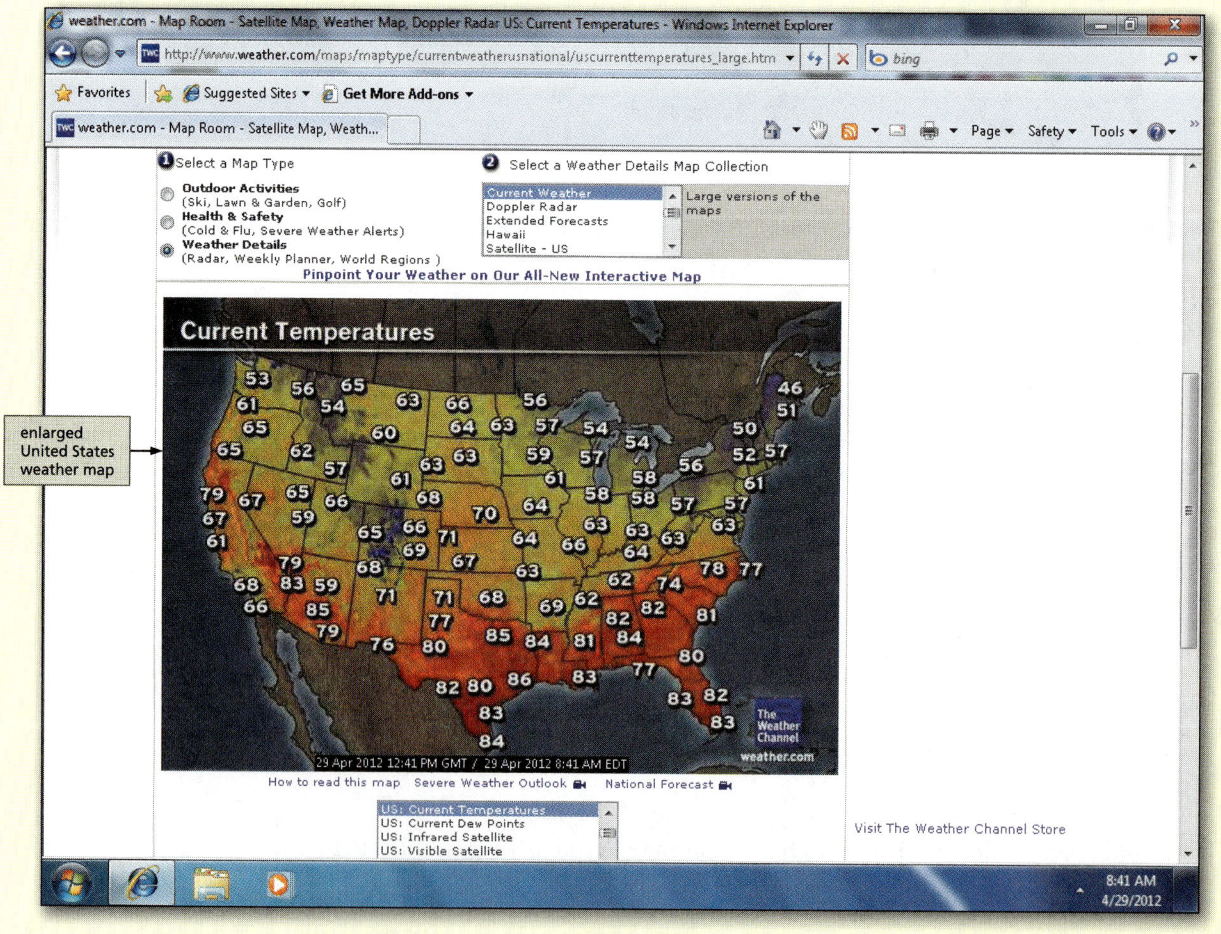

Figure 73

3. Right-click the weather map, click Print Picture on the shortcut menu, and then click the Print button in the Print dialog box to print the weather map.

4. Right-click the weather map and click Save Picture As on the shortcut menu to display the Save Picture dialog box. Click the Documents library in the left pane of the Save Picture dialog box, click the File name text box, type **`U.S. Weather map`** as the file name, and then click the Save button (Save Picture dialog box) to save the picture on your hard disk.
5. Submit the printed weather map to your instructor.

In the Lab

Lab 4: Collecting Biographical Information

Problem: To complete an assignment in history class, you must locate the Biography.com Web site and select an individual whose biography is on the Web site. When you find the biography of your chosen individual, copy his or her picture and the text of the biography into WordPad, and then print the WordPad document.

Instructions: Perform the following tasks.

Part 1: Retrieving a Web Page

1. Type **`www.biography.com`** in the Address bar and then press the ENTER key to display the Biography.com home page (Figure 74).

Figure 74

Continued >

In the Lab *continued*

2. Using the links on the Web site, search for the biography of an individual in whom you are interested. (Suggestions: Thomas Edison, Mia Hamm, Martin Luther King, George Lucas, Oprah Winfrey, Elvis Presley, Eleanor Roosevelt, Jack Nicklaus)

Part 2: Copying a Picture and Text to Microsoft WordPad

1. If a picture of the individual is available, copy the picture to the Clipboard.
2. Start Microsoft WordPad.
3. Paste the picture from the Clipboard into the WordPad document, click anywhere off the picture, and then press the ENTER key.
4. Switch back to the Internet Explorer window.
5. If necessary, click the link that contains the biography.
6. Copy the biography text to the Clipboard.
7. Switch to the WordPad window.
8. Paste the text on the Clipboard into the WordPad document.
9. Save the WordPad document on your hard disk using the file name, Biography Assignment.
10. Print the WordPad document.
11. Quit WordPad.
12. Submit the WordPad document to your instructor.

In the Lab

Lab 5: Searching the Web for a Job in Computer Programming

Problem: You are job hunting for a position that uses your expertise in computer programming. Instead of using the newspaper to find a job, you decide to search for jobs on the Internet. You decide to visit three Web sites in hopes of finding the perfect job.

Instructions: Perform the following tasks.

1. Click the Address bar, type **`www.computerjobs.com`** to enter the Web address, and then press the ENTER key to display the ComputerJobs.com home page (Figure 75).

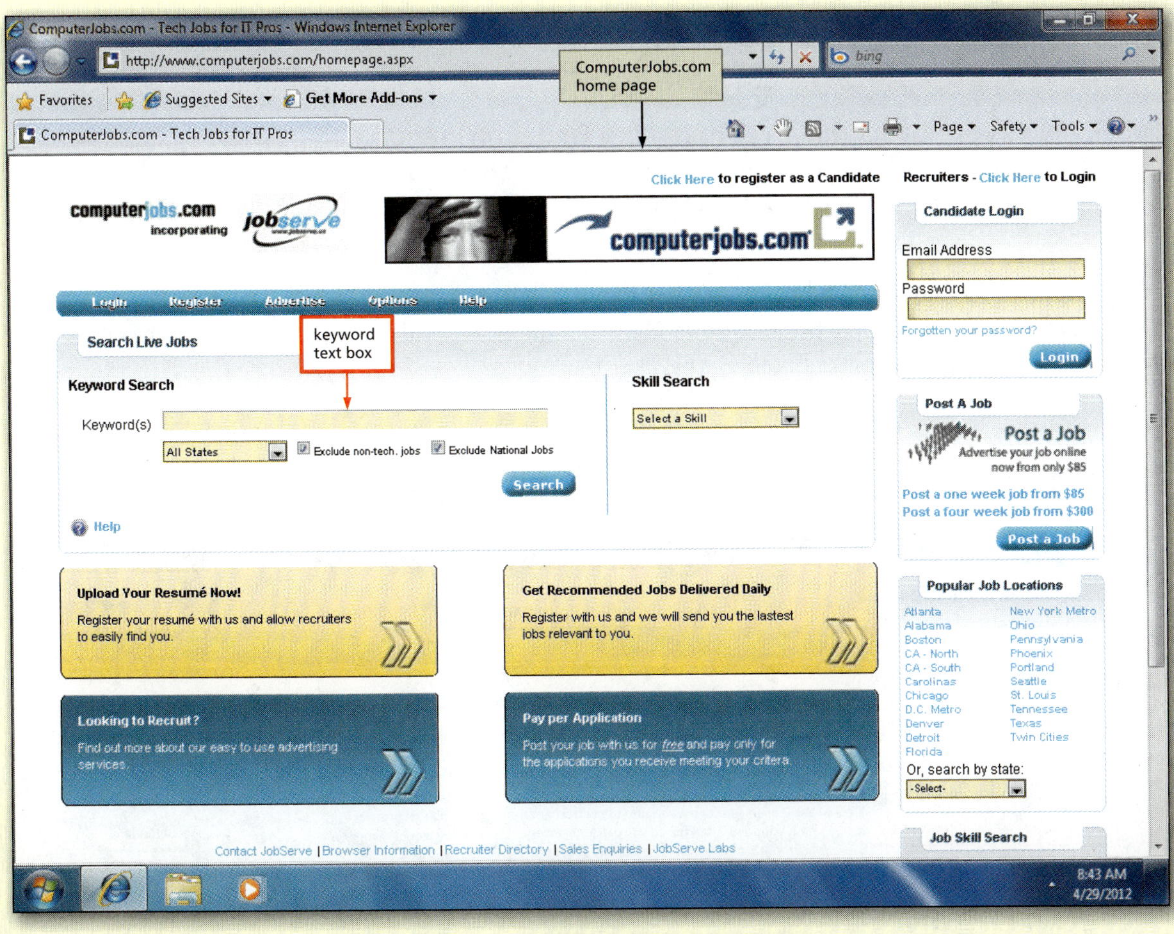

Figure 75

2. When the ComputerJobs.com home page displays, type `computer programming` in the Keyword(s) text box and then press the ENTER key. When the first page of the computer programming listings is displayed, print it.
3. Type `www.monster.com` in the Address bar and then press the ENTER key.
4. When the Monster home page appears, type `computer programming` in the Skills/Keywords text box and then click the Search button. When the first page of the computer programming listings is displayed, print it.
5. Type `www.careerbuilder.com` in the Address bar and then press the ENTER key.
6. When the careerbuilder.com page displays, type `computer programming` in the Keywords text box, and then click the Find Jobs button. When the first page of the computer programming listings is displayed, print it.
7. Submit the printouts to your instructor.

In the Lab

Lab 6: Using Windows Help and Support to Find Information about Internet Explorer

Problem: Because you do not know much about Windows Help and Support, you decide to learn more by using it to search for the following topics: cookies, AutoComplete, certificates, content advisor, and shortcut keys.

Instructions: Use Windows Help and Support to perform the following tasks.

1. Press the F1 key to display the Windows Help and Support window, which contains general information about Internet Explorer (Figure 76).

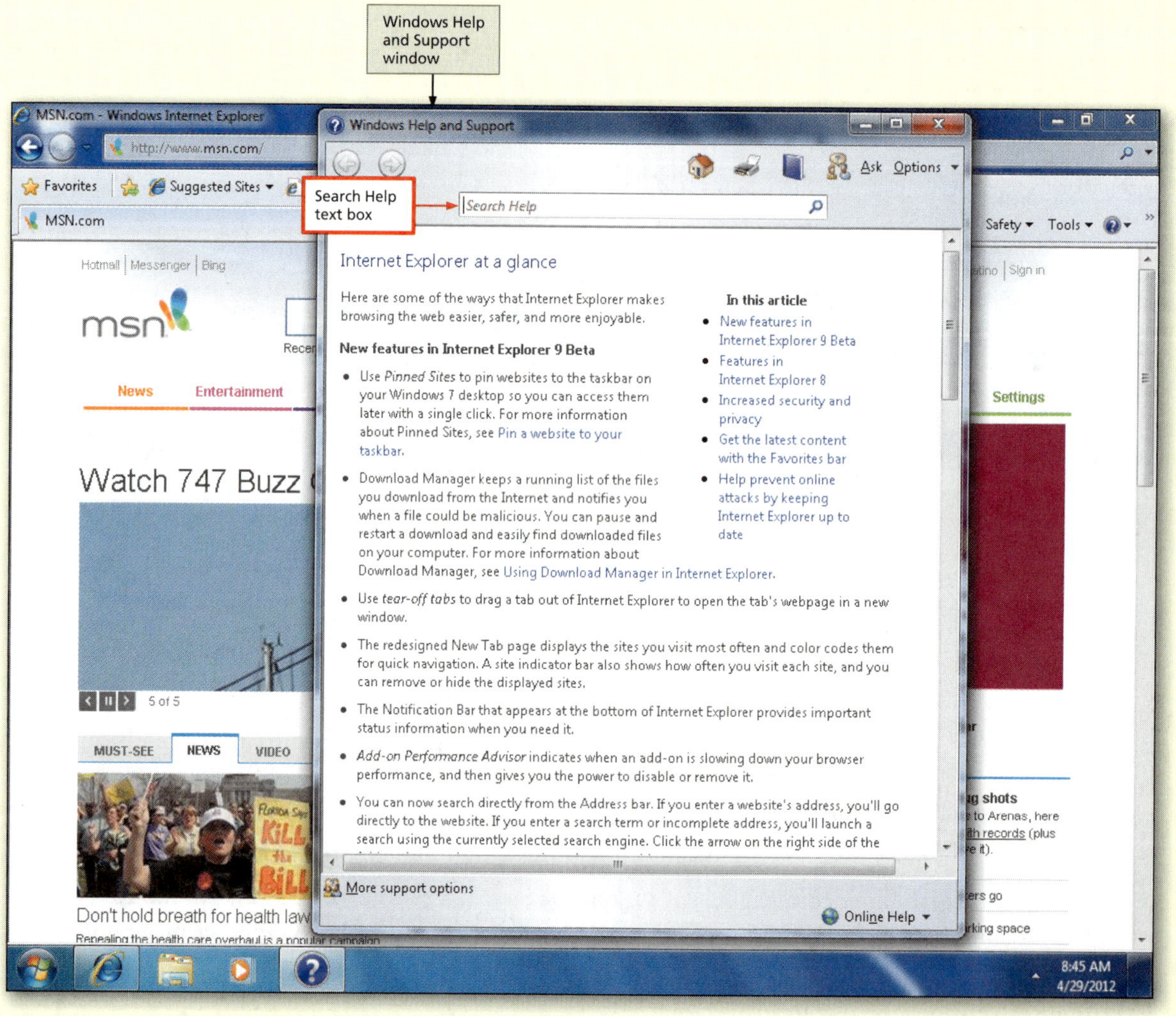

Figure 76

2. Type `cookies` in the Search Help text box, press the ENTER key, and browse the topics necessary to answer the following questions.
   a. What is a cookie?
   b. What does a cookie contain?

3. Select the text in the text box, type `autocomplete` in the box, press the ENTER key, and browse the search results to answer the following questions.
   a. What does the AutoComplete feature save?
   b. What does AutoComplete do?
4. Select the text in the text box, type `certificates` in the box, press the ENTER key, and browse the search results to answer the following questions.
   a. List two types of certificates.
   b. What is EFS?
5. Select the text in the text box, type `content advisor` in the box, press the ENTER key, and browse the search results to answer the following question.
   a. What is the purpose of Content Advisor?
6. Select the text in the text box, type `shortcut keys` in the box, press the ENTER key, and browse the search results to answer the following questions.
   a. What is the shortcut key to go to the next Web page?
   b. What is the shortcut key to refresh the current Web page?
   c. What is the shortcut key to stop downloading a Web page?
7. Close the Windows Help and Support window.
8. Close the Internet Explorer window.
9. Submit the answers to the questions to your instructor.

Cases and Places

Apply your creative thinking and problem solving skills to browse for information.

Note: To complete these assignments, you may be required to use the Data Files for Students. See the inside back cover of this book for instructions on downloading the Data Files for Students, or contact your instructor for information about accessing the required files.

1: Browsing the Web for Stock Information

Academic

Your assignment in your finance class is to find fundamental stock information about three companies of your choice (for example, Microsoft Corporation (MSFT), Google Inc. (GOOG), or TiVo Inc. (TIVO)). Use the Yahoo! Finance Web site (finance.yahoo.com) to obtain today's stock price, dividend rate, daily volume, 52-week range, and the P/E (price earnings ratio). To display this information, enter the stock symbol and click the Get Quotes button to display the information. Print the detailed results for each stock. In addition, when the stock information for Google displays, click the first Headline and print the page.

Continued >

Cases and Places *continued*

2: Browsing the Web for a New Car

Personal

Your old car broke down and you are in the market for a new one. Type `autotrader.com` in the Address bar of your browser to display the AutoTrader home page. Select your favorite make, type your ZIP code, and then click the Next button to search for a new car. Select two competitors of the car you chose. Print the information on your favorite car and its two competitors.

3: Browsing the Web for Travel Specials

Professional

You are planning a business trip to Hong Kong. You want to leave exactly one month from today and plan to stay seven days, including the travel days. Check with at least two different travel Web sites such as orbitz.com and expedia.com for travel specials to Hong Kong. Print any Web pages containing flight information and then summarize the information you find in a brief report.

1 Creating, Formatting, and Editing a Word Document with Pictures

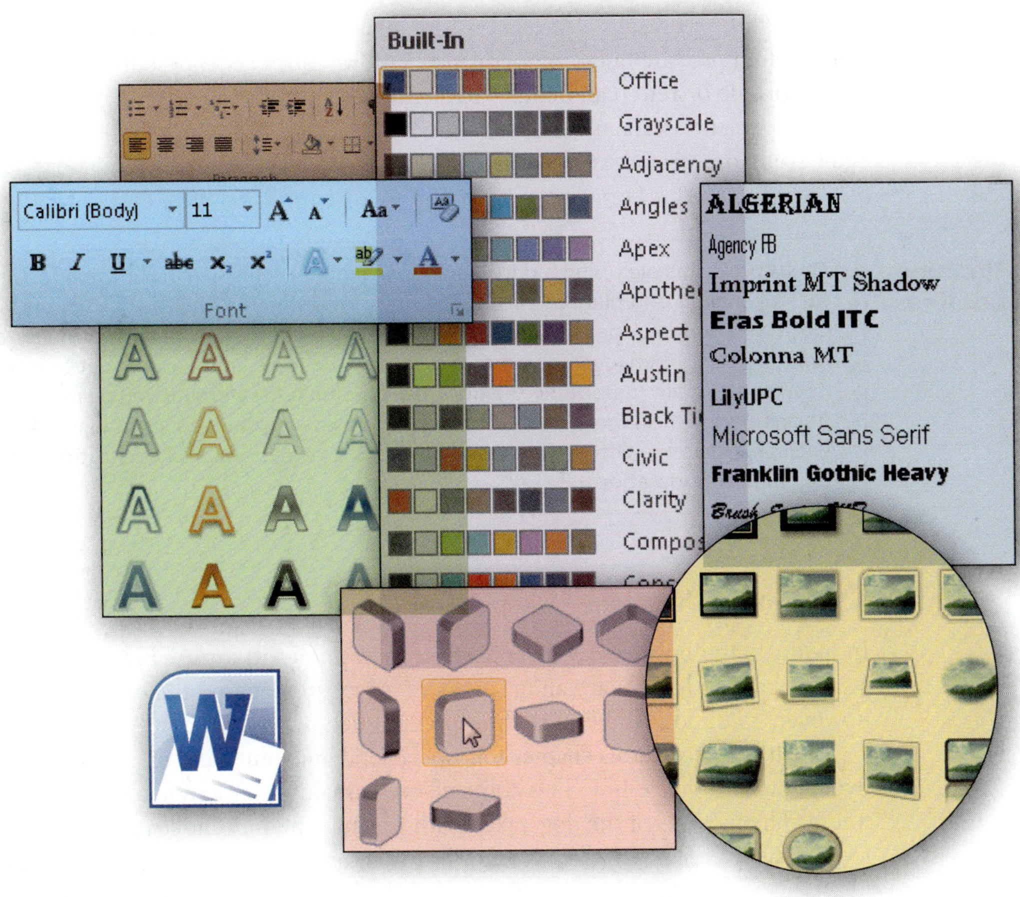

Objectives

You will have mastered the material in this chapter when you can:

- Enter text in a Word document
- Check spelling as you type
- Format paragraphs
- Format text
- Undo and redo commands or actions
- Change theme colors
- Insert digital pictures in a Word document
- Format pictures
- Add a page border
- Correct errors and revise a document
- Change document properties
- Print a document

1 Creating, Formatting, and Editing a Word Document with Pictures

Introduction

To advertise a sale, promote a business, publicize an event, or convey a message to the community, you may want to create a flyer and hand it out in person or post it in a public location. Libraries, schools, religious organizations, grocery stores, coffee shops, and other places often provide bulletin boards or windows for flyers. These flyers announce personal items for sale or rent (car, boat, apartment); garage or block sales; services being offered (animal care, housecleaning, lessons); membership, sponsorship, or donation requests (club, religious organization, charity); and other messages such as a lost or found pet.

Project Planning Guidelines

The process of developing a document that communicates specific information requires careful analysis and planning. As a starting point, establish why the document is needed. Once the purpose is determined, analyze the intended readers of the document and their unique needs. Then, gather information about the topic and decide what to include in the document. Finally, determine the document design and style that will be most successful at delivering the message. Details of these guidelines are provided in Appendix A. In addition, each project in the Office chapters in this book provides practical applications of these planning considerations.

Project — Flyer with Pictures

Individuals and businesses create flyers to gain public attention. Flyers, which usually are a single page in length, are an inexpensive means of reaching the community. Many flyers, however, go unnoticed because they are designed poorly.

The project in this chapter follows general guidelines and uses Word to create the flyer shown in Figure 1–1. This colorful, eye-catching flyer announces that a dog has been found. The pictures of the dog, taken with a camera phone, entice passersby to stop and look at the flyer. The headline on the flyer is large and colorful to draw attention into the text. The body copy below the pictures briefly describes where and when the dog was found, along with a bulleted list that concisely highlights important identifying information. The signature line of the flyer calls attention to the contact phone number. The dog's name, Bailey, and signature line are in a different color so that they stand apart from the rest of the text on the flyer. Finally, the graphical page border nicely frames and complements the contents of the flyer.

FOUND DOG
headline
page border
digital photos of dog
Adorable, loving, friendly, well-behaved dog found early Friday morning, June 1, wandering on the bike trail at Filcher Park in Hampton Township.
• Male, adult cocker spaniel
• Tan color with patches of white on his chest
• Green and silver collar with the name, Bailey, on the tag
body copy
bulleted list
If this is your lost dog, call 555-1029.
signature line

Figure 1–1

Overview

As you read this chapter, you will learn how to create the flyer shown in Figure 1–1 on the previous page by performing these general tasks:

- Enter text in the document.
- Format the text in the document.
- Insert the pictures in the document.
- Format the pictures in the document.
- Enhance the page with a border and additional spacing.
- Correct errors and revise the document.
- Print the document.

Plan Ahead

General Project Guidelines

When creating a Word document, the actions you perform and decisions you make will affect the appearance and characteristics of the finished document. As you create a flyer, such as the project shown in Figure 1–1, you should follow these general guidelines:

1. **Choose the words for the text.** Follow the *less is more* principle. The less text, the more likely the flyer will be read. Use as few words as possible to make a point.
2. **Identify how to format various elements of the text.** The overall appearance of a document significantly affects its ability to communicate clearly. Examples of how you can modify the appearance, or **format**, of text include changing its shape, size, color, and position on the page.
3. **Find the appropriate graphical image(s).** An eye-catching graphical image should convey the flyer's overall message. It could show a product, service, result, or benefit, or visually convey a message that is not expressed easily with words.
4. **Establish where to position and how to format the graphical image(s).** The position and format of the graphical image(s) should grab the attention of passersby and draw them into reading the flyer.
5. **Determine whether the page needs enhancements such as a border or spacing adjustments.** A graphical, color-coordinated page border can further draw attention to a flyer and nicely frame its contents. Increasing or decreasing spacing between elements on a flyer can improve its readability and overall appearance.
6. **Correct errors and revise the document as necessary.** Post the flyer on a wall and make sure all text and images are legible from a distance. Ask someone else to read the flyer and give you suggestions for improvements.
7. **Determine the best method for distributing the document.** Documents can be distributed on paper or electronically. A flyer should be printed on paper so that it can be posted.

When necessary, more specific details concerning the above guidelines are presented at appropriate points in the chapter. The chapter also will identify the actions performed and decisions made regarding these guidelines during the creation of the flyer shown in Figure 1–1.

For an introduction to Windows 7 and instruction about how to perform basic Windows 7 tasks, read the Office 2010 and Windows 7 chapter in this book, where you can learn how to resize windows, change screen resolution, create folders, move and rename files, use Windows Help, and much more.

To Start Word

If you are using a computer to step through the project in this chapter and you want your screens to match the figures in the Office and Windows chapters in this book, you should change your screen's resolution to 1024 × 768. For information about how to change a computer's resolution, refer to the Office 2010 and Windows 7 chapter in this book.

The following steps, which assume Windows 7 is running, start Word based on a typical installation. You may need to ask your instructor how to start Word for your computer. For a detailed example of the procedure summarized below, refer to the Office 2010 and Windows 7 chapter.

For an introduction to Office 2010 and instruction about how to perform basic tasks in Office 2010 programs, read the Office 2010 and Windows 7 chapter in this book, where you can learn how to start a program, use the Ribbon, save a file, open a file, quit a program, use Help, and much more.

1. Click the Start button on the Windows 7 taskbar to display the Start menu.
2. Type `Microsoft Word` as the search text in the 'Search programs and files' text box and watch the search results appear on the Start menu.
3. Click Microsoft Word 2010 in the search results on the Start menu to start Word and display a new blank document in the Word window.
4. If the Word window is not maximized, click the Maximize button next to the Close button on its title bar to maximize the window.
5. If the Print Layout button on the status bar is not selected (shown in Figure 1–2 on the next page), click it so that your screen is in Print Layout view.

Q&A What is Print Layout view?

The default (preset) view in Word is **Print Layout view**, which shows the document on a mock sheet of paper in the document window.

6. If Normal (Home tab | Styles group) is not selected in the Quick Style gallery (shown in Figure 1–2), click it so that your document uses the Normal style.

Q&A What is the Normal style?

When you create a document, Word formats the text using a particular style. The default style in Word is called the **Normal style**, which is discussed in the next chapter.

Q&A What if rulers appear on my screen?

Click the View Ruler button above the vertical scroll bar to hide the rulers, or click View on the Ribbon to display the View tab and then place a check mark in the Ruler check box.

BTW **The Word Window**
The Word chapters in this book begin with the Word window appearing as it did at the initial installation of the software. Your Word window may look different depending on your screen resolution and other Word settings.

Entering Text

The first step in creating a document is to enter its text. With the projects in the Word chapters in this book, you enter text by typing on the keyboard. By default, Word positions text you type at the left margin. In a later section of this chapter, you will learn how to format, or change the appearance of, the entered text.

Plan Ahead

Choose the words for the text.
The text in a flyer is organized into three areas: headline, body copy, and signature line.

- The **headline** is the first line of text on the flyer. It conveys the product or service being offered, such as a car for sale or personal lessons, or the benefit that will be gained, such as a convenience, better performance, greater security, higher earnings, or more comfort; or it can contain a message such as a lost or found pet.
- The **body copy** consists of all text between the headline and the signature line. This text highlights the key points of the message in as few words as possible. It should be easy to read and follow. While emphasizing the positive, the body copy must be realistic, truthful, and believable.
- The **signature line**, which is the last line of text on the flyer, contains contact information or identifies a call to action.

BTW **Zooming**
If text is too small for you to read on the screen, you can zoom the document by dragging the Zoom slider on the status bar or clicking the Zoom Out or Zoom In buttons on the status bar. Changing the zoom has no effect on the printed document.

To Type Text

To begin creating the flyer in this chapter, type the headline in the document window. The following steps type this first line of text in the document.

1

- Type **Found Dog** as the headline (Figure 1–2).

Q&A What if I make an error while typing?

You can press the BACKSPACE key until you have deleted the text in error and then retype the text correctly.

Q&A Why did the Spelling and Grammar Check icon appear on the status bar?

When you begin typing text, the **Spelling and Grammar Check icon** appears on the status bar with an animated pencil writing on paper to indicate that Word is checking for spelling and grammar errors. When you stop typing, the pencil changes to a blue check mark (no errors) or a red X (potential errors found). Word flags potential errors in the document with a red, green, or blue wavy underline. Later in this chapter, you will learn how to fix flagged errors.

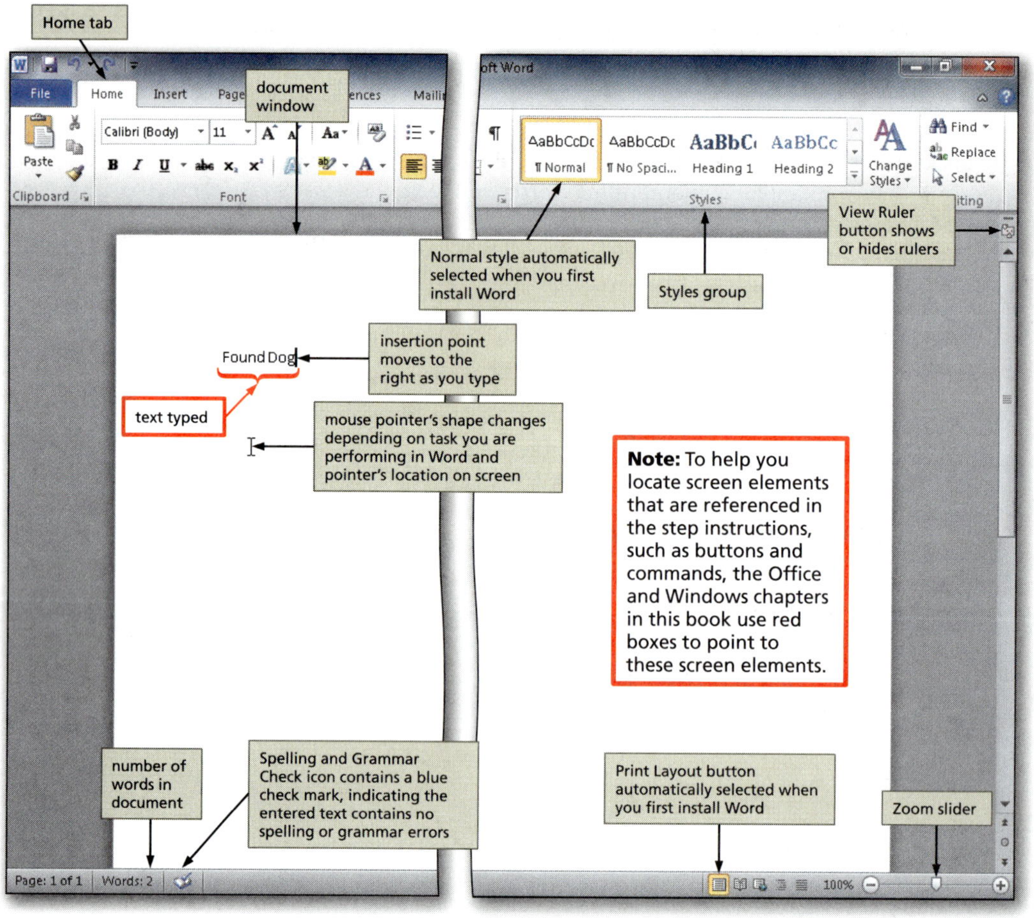

Figure 1–2

2

- Press the ENTER key to move the insertion point to the beginning of the next line (Figure 1–3).

Q&A Why did blank space appear between the headline and the insertion point?

Each time you press the ENTER key, Word creates a new paragraph and inserts blank space between the two paragraphs. Later in this chapter, you will learn how to adjust the spacing between paragraphs.

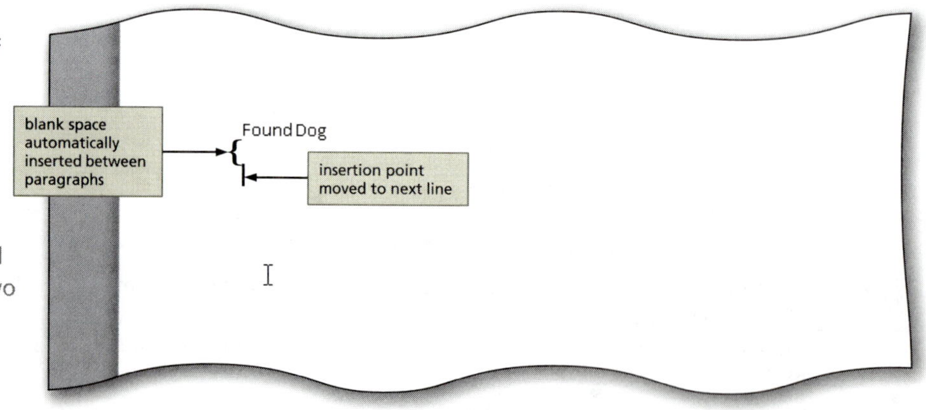

Figure 1–3

To Display Formatting Marks

To indicate where in a document you press the ENTER key or SPACEBAR, you may find it helpful to display formatting marks. A **formatting mark**, sometimes called a **nonprinting character**, is a character that Word displays on the screen but is not visible on a printed document. For example, the paragraph mark (¶) is a formatting mark that indicates where you press the ENTER key. A raised dot (·) shows where you press the SPACEBAR. Other formatting marks are discussed as they appear on the screen.

Depending on settings made during previous Word sessions, your Word screen already may display formatting marks (Figure 1–4). The following step displays formatting marks, if they do not show already on the screen.

1

- If the Home tab is not the active tab, click Home on the Ribbon to display the Home tab.
- If it is not selected already, click the Show/Hide ¶ button (Home tab | Paragraph group) to display formatting marks on the screen (Figure 1–4).

Q&A What if I do not want formatting marks to show on the screen?

You can hide them by clicking the Show/Hide ¶ button (Home tab | Paragraph group) again. It is recommended that you display formatting marks so that you visually can identify when you press the ENTER key, SPACEBAR, and other keys associated with nonprinting characters; therefore, most of the document windows presented in the Word chapters in this book show formatting marks.

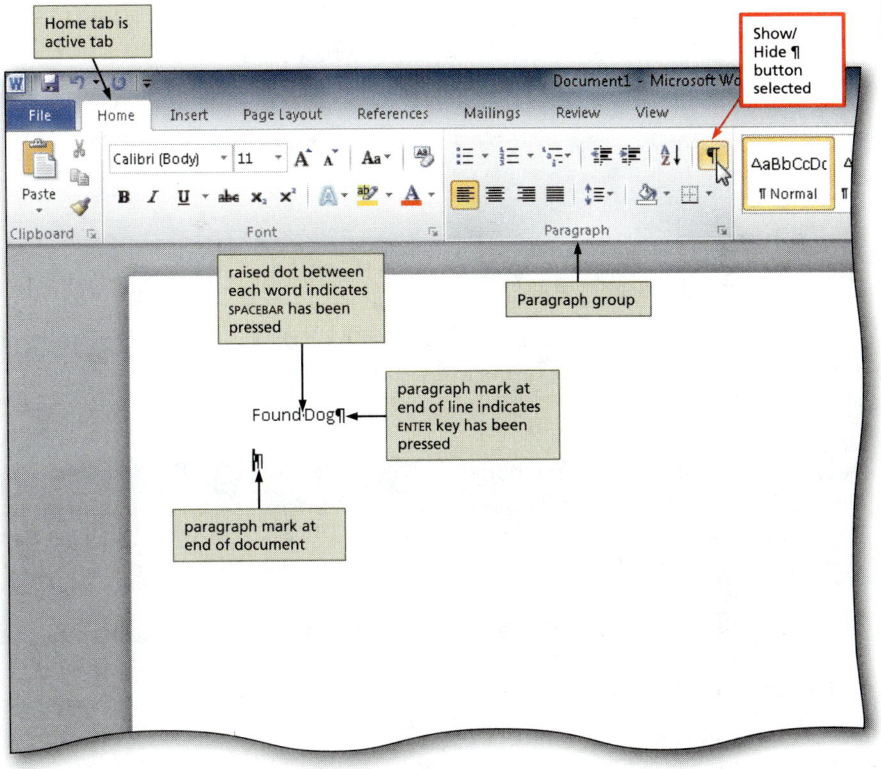

Figure 1–4

Other Ways
1. Press CTRL+SHIFT+*

To Insert a Blank Line

In the flyer, the digital pictures of the dog appear between the headline and body copy. You will not insert these pictures, however, until after you enter and format all text. Thus, you leave a blank line in the document as a placeholder for the pictures. To enter a blank line in a document, press the ENTER key without typing any text on the line. The following step inserts one blank line below the headline.

1

- Press the ENTER key to insert a blank line in the document (Figure 1–5).

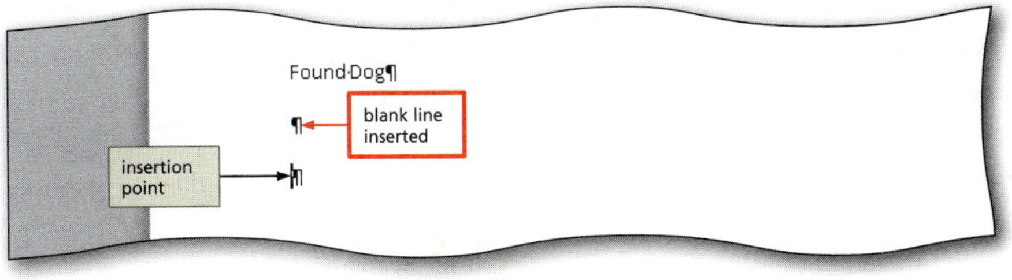

Figure 1–5

Wordwrap

BTW

The Ribbon and Screen Resolution
Word may change how the groups and buttons within the groups appear on the Ribbon, depending on the computer's screen resolution. Thus, your Ribbon may look different from the ones in the Word chapters in this book if you are using a screen resolution other than 1024 × 768.

Wordwrap allows you to type words in a paragraph continually without pressing the ENTER key at the end of each line. As you type, if a word extends beyond the right margin, Word also automatically positions that word on the next line along with the insertion point.

Word creates a new paragraph each time you press the ENTER key. Thus, as you type text in the document window, do not press the ENTER key when the insertion point reaches the right margin. Instead, press the ENTER key only in these circumstances:

1. To insert a blank line(s) in a document (as shown in the steps on the previous page)
2. To begin a new paragraph
3. To terminate a short line of text and advance to the next line
4. To respond to questions or prompts in Word dialog boxes, task panes, and other on-screen objects

To Wordwrap Text as You Type

The next step in creating the flyer is to type the body copy. The following step illustrates how the body copy text wordwraps as you enter it in the document.

1

- Type the first sentence of the body copy: **Adorable, loving, friendly, well-behaved dog found early Friday morning, June 1, wandering on the bike trail at Filcher Park in Hampton Township.**

Q&A

Why does my document wrap on different words?

The printer connected to a computer is one factor that can control where wordwrap occurs for each line in a document. Thus, it is possible that the same document could wordwrap differently if printed on different printers.

- Press the ENTER key to position the insertion point on the next line in the document (Figure 1–6).

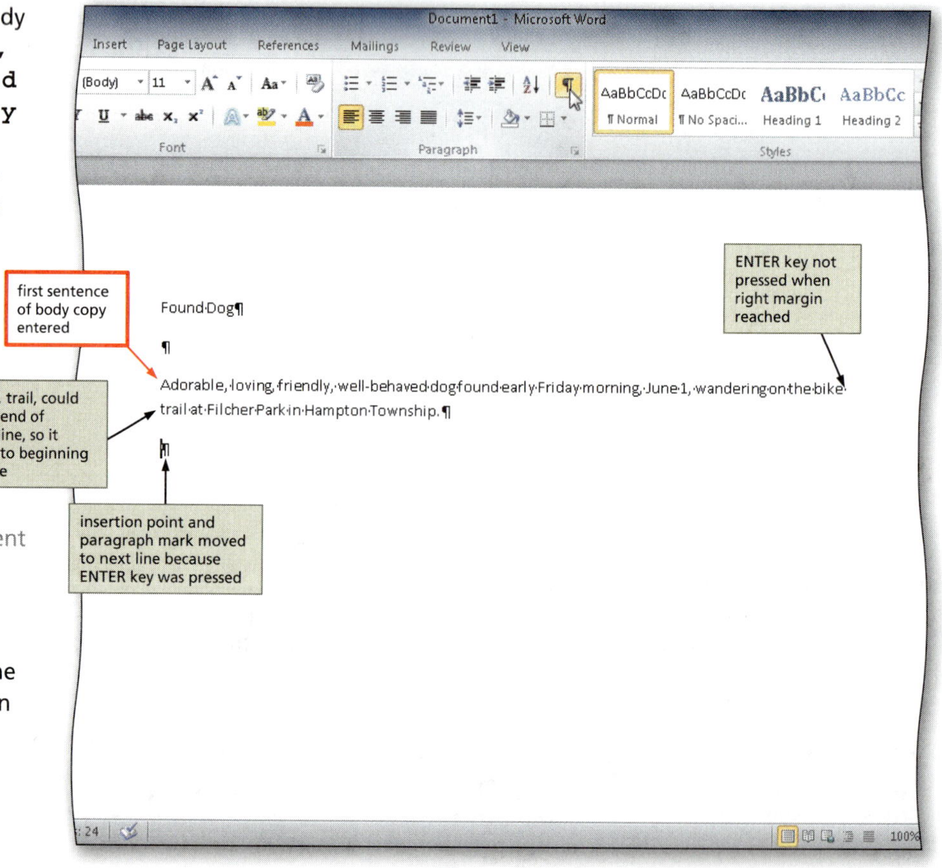

Figure 1–6

Spelling and Grammar Check

As you type text in a document, Word checks your typing for possible spelling and grammar errors. If all of the words you have typed are in Word's dictionary and your grammar is correct, as mentioned earlier, the Spelling and Grammar Check icon on the status bar displays a blue check mark. Otherwise, the icon shows a red X. In this case, Word flags the potential error in the document window with a red, green, or blue wavy underline. A red wavy underline means the flagged text is not in Word's dictionary (because it is a proper name or misspelled). A green wavy underline indicates the text may be incorrect grammatically. A blue wavy underline indicates the text may contain a contextual spelling error such as the misuse of homophones (words that are pronounced the same but that have different spellings or meanings, such as one and won). Although you can check the entire document for spelling and grammar errors at once, you also can check flagged errors as they appear on the screen.

A flagged word is not necessarily misspelled. For example, many names, abbreviations, and specialized terms are not in Word's main dictionary. In these cases, you can instruct Word to ignore the flagged word. As you type, Word also detects duplicate words while checking for spelling errors. For example, if your document contains the phrase, to the the store, Word places a red wavy underline below the second occurrence of the word, the.

BTW

Automatic Spelling Correction

As you type, Word automatically corrects some misspelled words. For example, if you type recieve, Word automatically corrects the misspelling and displays the word, receive, when you press the SPACEBAR or type a punctuation mark. To see a complete list of automatically corrected words, click File on the Ribbon to open the Backstage view, click Options in the Backstage view, click Proofing in the left pane (Word Options dialog box), click the AutoCorrect Options button, and then scroll through the list near the bottom of the dialog box.

To Check Spelling and Grammar as You Type

In the following steps, the word, patches, has been misspelled intentionally as paches to illustrate Word's check spelling as you type feature. If you are doing this project on a computer, your flyer may contain different misspelled words, depending on the accuracy of your typing.

1

- Type `Tan color with paches` and then press the SPACEBAR so that a red wavy line appears below the misspelled word (Figure 1–7).

Q&A What if Word does not flag my spelling and grammar errors with wavy underlines?

To verify that the check spelling and grammar as you type features are enabled, click File on the Ribbon to open the Backstage view and then click Options in the Backstage view. When the Word Options dialog box is displayed, click Proofing in the left pane, and then ensure the 'Check spelling as you type' and 'Mark grammar errors as you type' check boxes contain check marks. Also ensure the 'Hide spelling errors in this document only' and 'Hide grammar errors in this document only' check boxes do not have check marks. Click the OK button.

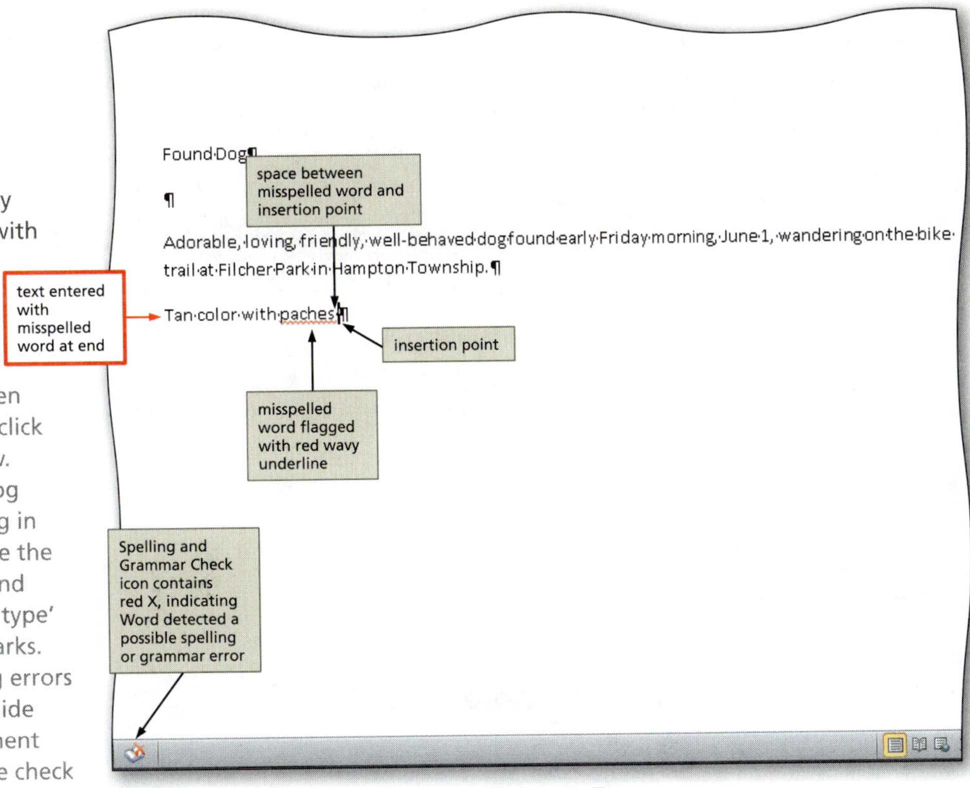

Figure 1–7

2

- Right-click the flagged word (paches, in this case) to display a shortcut menu that presents a list of suggested spelling corrections for the flagged word (Figure 1–8).

Q&A What if, when I right-click the misspelled word, my desired correction is not in the list on the shortcut menu?

You can click outside the shortcut menu to close the shortcut menu and then retype the correct word, or you can click Spelling on the shortcut menu to display the Spelling dialog box. Chapter 2 discusses the Spelling dialog box.

Q&A What if a flagged word actually is, for example, a proper name and spelled correctly?

Right-click it and then click Ignore All on the shortcut menu to instruct Word not to flag future occurrences of the same word in this document.

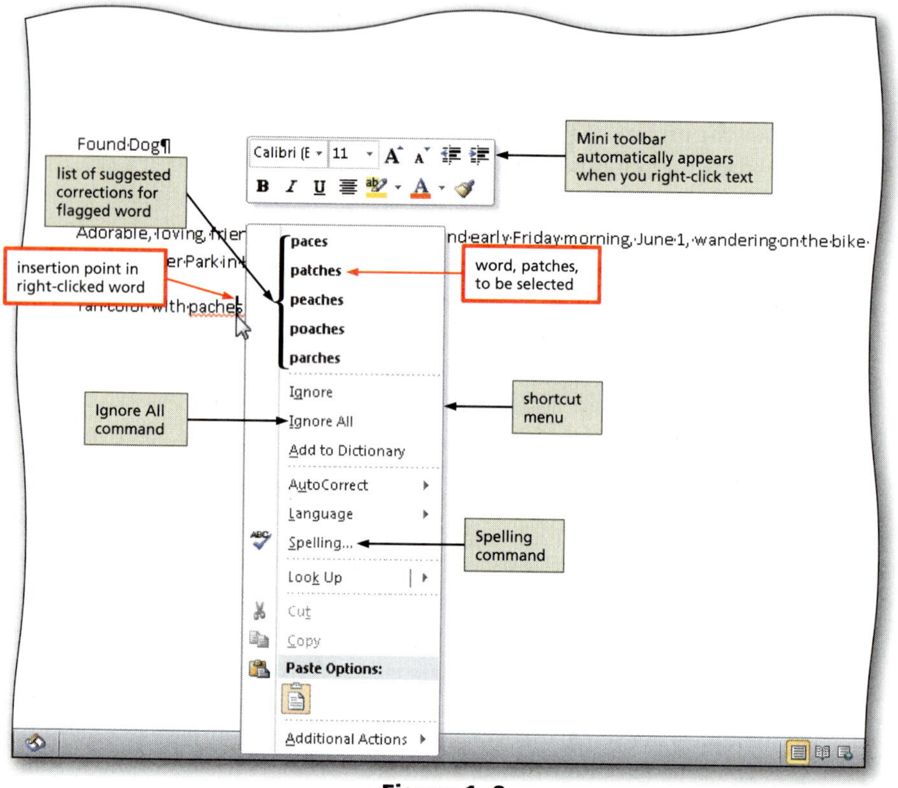

Figure 1–8

3

- Click patches on the shortcut menu to replace the misspelled word in the document with a correctly spelled word (Figure 1–9).

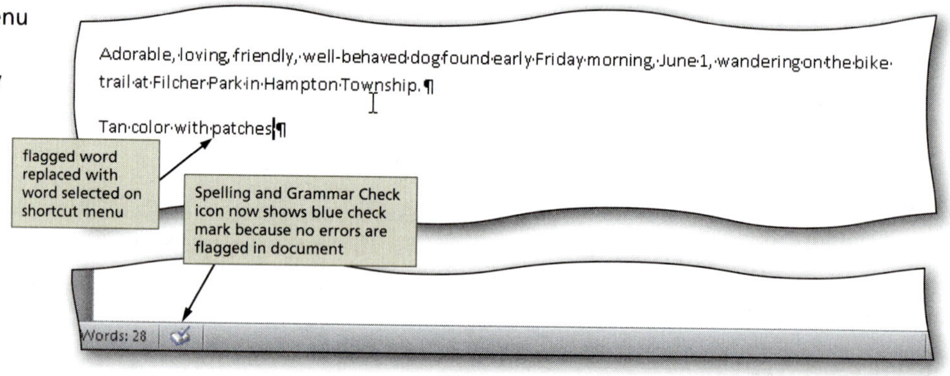

Figure 1–9

Other Ways

1. Click Spelling and Grammar Check icon on status bar, click desired word on shortcut menu

BTW

Character Widths

Many word processing documents use variable character fonts, where some characters are wider than others; for example, the letter w is wider than the letter i.

To Enter More Text

In the flyer, the text yet to be entered includes the remainder of the body copy, which will be formatted as a bulleted list, and the signature line. The next steps enter the remainder of text in the flyer.

1. Press the END key to move the insertion point to the end of the current line.
2. Type `of white on his chest` and then press the ENTER key.
3. Type `Male, adult cocker spaniel` and then press the ENTER key.
4. Type `Green and silver collar with the name, Bailey, on the tag` and then press the ENTER key.
5. Type the signature line in the flyer (Figure 1–10): `If this is your lost dog, call 555-1029.`

Figure 1–10

Navigating a Document

You view only a portion of a document on the screen through the document window. At some point when you type text or insert graphics, Word probably will **scroll** the top or bottom portion of the document off the screen. Although you cannot see the text and graphics once they scroll off the screen, they remain in the document.

You can use either the keyboard or the mouse to scroll to a different location in a document and/or move the insertion point around a document. When you use the keyboard, the insertion point automatically moves when you press the desired keys. For example, the previous steps used the END key to move the insertion point to the end of the current line. Table 1–1 outlines various techniques to navigate a document using the keyboard.

With the mouse, you can use the scroll arrows or the scroll box on the scroll bar to display a different portion of the document in the document window and then click the mouse to move the insertion point to that location. Table 1–2 explains various techniques for using the scroll bar to scroll vertically with the mouse.

BTW

Minimize Wrist Injury
Computer users frequently switch between the keyboard and the mouse during a word processing session; such switching strains the wrist. To help prevent wrist injury, minimize switching. For instance, if your fingers already are on the keyboard, use keyboard keys to scroll. If your hand already is on the mouse, use the mouse to scroll.

Table 1–1 Moving the Insertion Point with the Keyboard

Insertion Point Direction	Key(s) to Press	Insertion Point Direction	Key(s) to Press
Left one character	LEFT ARROW	Up one paragraph	CTRL+UP ARROW
Right one character	RIGHT ARROW	Down one paragraph	CTRL+DOWN ARROW
Left one word	CTRL+LEFT ARROW	Up one screen	PAGE UP
Right one word	CTRL+RIGHT ARROW	Down one screen	PAGE DOWN
Up one line	UP ARROW	To top of document window	ALT+CTRL+PAGE UP
Down one line	DOWN ARROW	To bottom of document window	ALT+CTRL+PAGE DOWN
To end of line	END	To beginning of document	CTRL+HOME
To beginning of line	HOME	To end of document	CTRL+END

Table 1–2 Using the Scroll Bar to Scroll Vertically with the Mouse

Scroll Direction	Mouse Action	Scroll Direction	Mouse Action
Up	Drag the scroll box upward.	Down one screen	Click anywhere below the scroll box on the vertical scroll bar.
Down	Drag the scroll box downward.	Up one line	Click the scroll arrow at the top of the vertical scroll bar.
Up one screen	Click anywhere above the scroll box on the vertical scroll bar.	Down one line	Click the scroll arrow at the bottom of the vertical scroll bar.

BTW

Organizing Files and Folders

You should organize and store files in folders so that you easily can find the files later. For example, if you are taking an introductory computer class called CIS 101, a good practice would be to save all Word files in a Word folder in a CIS 101 folder. For a discussion of folders and detailed examples of creating folders, refer to the Office 2010 and Windows 7 chapter in this book.

To Save a Document

You have performed many tasks while creating this flyer and do not want to risk losing work completed thus far. Accordingly, you should save the document.

The following steps assume you already have created folders for storing your files, for example, a CIS 101 folder (for your class) that contains a Word folder (for your assignments). Thus, these steps save the document in the Word folder in the CIS 101 folder on a USB flash drive using the file name, Found Dog Flyer. For a detailed example of the procedure summarized below, refer to the Office 2010 and Windows 7 chapter in this book.

1. With a USB flash drive connected to one of the computer's USB ports, click the Save button on the Quick Access Toolbar to display the Save As dialog box.
2. Type `Found Dog Flyer` in the File name text box to change the file name. Do not press the ENTER key after typing the file name because you do not want to close the dialog box at this time.
3. Navigate to the desired save location (in this case, the Word folder in the CIS 101 folder [or your class folder] on the USB flash drive).
4. Click the Save button (Save As dialog box) to save the document in the selected folder on the selected drive with the entered file name.

Formatting Paragraphs and Characters

With the text for the flyer entered, the next step is to **format**, or change the appearance of, its text. A paragraph encompasses the text from the first character in the paragraph up to and including its paragraph mark (¶). **Paragraph formatting** is the process of changing the appearance of a paragraph. For example, you can center or add bullets to a paragraph. Characters include letters, numbers, punctuation marks, and symbols. **Character formatting** is the process of changing the way characters appear on the screen and in print. You use character formatting to emphasize certain words and improve readability of a document. For example, you can color or underline characters. Often, you apply both paragraph and character formatting to the same text. For example, you may center a paragraph (paragraph formatting) and underline some of the characters in the same paragraph (character formatting).

Although you can format paragraphs and characters before you type, many Word users enter text first and then format the existing text. Figure 1–11a shows the flyer in this chapter before formatting its paragraphs and characters. Figure 1–11b shows the flyer after formatting. As you can see from the two figures, a document that is formatted is easier to read and looks more professional. The following pages discuss how to format the flyer so that it looks like Figure 1–11b.

Characters that appear on the screen are a specific shape and size. The **font**, or typeface, defines the appearance and shape of the letters, numbers, and special characters. In Word, the default font usually is Calibri (shown in Figure 1–12 on page WD 14). You can leave characters in the default font or change them to a different font. **Font size** specifies the size of the characters and is determined by a measurement system called points. A single **point** is about 1/72 of one inch in height. The default font size in Word typically is 11 (Figure 1–12). Thus, a character with a font size of 11 is about 11/72 or a little less than 1/6 of one inch in height. You can increase or decrease the font size of characters in a document.

A document **theme** is a set of unified formats for fonts, colors, and graphics. Word includes a variety of document themes to assist you with coordinating these visual elements in a document. The default theme fonts are Cambria for headings and Calibri for body text. By changing the document theme, you quickly can give your document a new look. You also can define your own document themes.

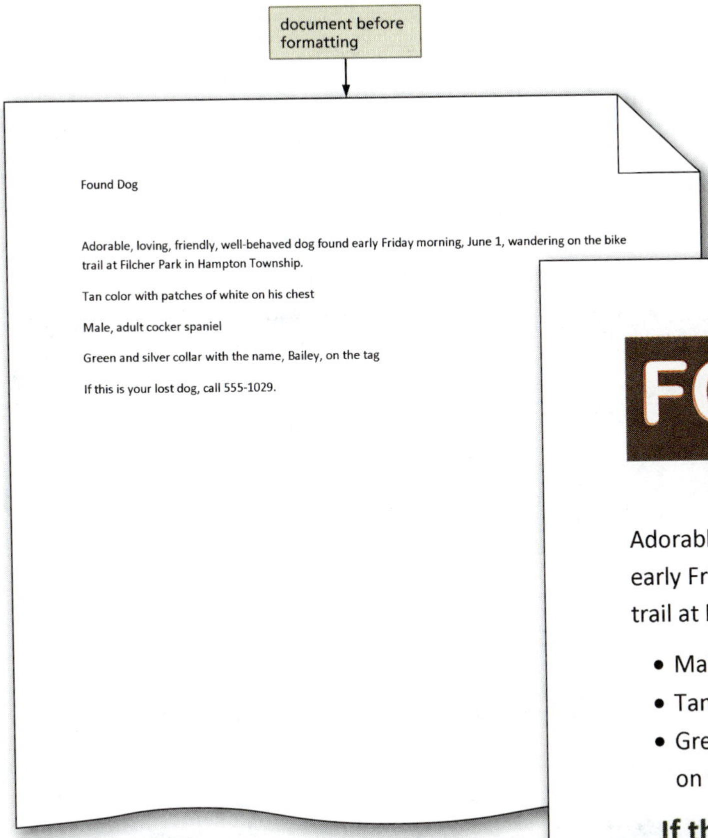

Found Dog

Adorable, loving, friendly, well-behaved dog found early Friday morning, June 1, wandering on the bike trail at Filcher Park in Hampton Township.

Tan color with patches of white on his chest

Male, adult cocker spaniel

Green and silver collar with the name, Bailey, on the tag

If this is your lost dog, call 555-1029.

Figure 1-11 (a) Unformatted Document

FOUND DOG

Adorable, loving, friendly, well-behaved dog found early Friday morning, June 1, wandering on the bike trail at Filcher Park in Hampton Township.

- Male, adult cocker spaniel
- Tan color with patches of white on his chest
- Green and silver collar with the name, *Bailey*, on the tag

If this is your lost dog, call 555-1029.

Figure 1-11 (b) Formatted Document

Plan Ahead

Identify how to format various elements of the text.
By formatting the characters and paragraphs in a document, you can improve its overall appearance. In a flyer, consider the following formatting suggestions.

- **Increase the font size of characters.** Flyers usually are posted on a bulletin board or in a window. Thus, the font size should be as large as possible so that passersby easily can read the flyer. To give the headline more impact, its font size should be larger than the font size of the text in the body copy. If possible, make the font size of the signature line larger than the body copy but smaller than the headline.
- **Change the font of characters.** Use fonts that are easy to read. Try to use only two different fonts in a flyer, for example, one for the headline and the other for all other text. Too many fonts can make the flyer visually confusing.
- **Change paragraph alignment.** The default alignment for paragraphs in a document is **left-aligned**, that is, flush at the left margin of the document with uneven right edges. Consider changing the alignment of some of the paragraphs to add interest and variety to the flyer.
- **Highlight key paragraphs with bullets.** A bulleted paragraph is a paragraph that begins with a dot or other symbol. Use bulleted paragraphs to highlight important points in a flyer.
- **Emphasize important words.** To call attention to certain words or lines, you can underline them, italicize them, or bold them. Use these formats sparingly, however, because overuse will minimize their effect and make the flyer look too busy.
- **Use color.** Use colors that complement each other and convey the meaning of the flyer. Vary colors in terms of hue and brightness. Headline colors, for example, can be bold and bright. Signature lines should stand out more than body copy but less than headlines. Keep in mind that too many colors can detract from the flyer and make it difficult to read.

To Center a Paragraph

The headline in the flyer currently is left-aligned (Figure 1–12). You want the headline to be **centered**, that is, positioned horizontally between the left and right margins on the page. Recall that Word considers a single short line of text, such as the two-word headline, a paragraph. Thus, you will center the paragraph containing the headline. The following steps center a paragraph.

1

- Click somewhere in the paragraph to be centered (in this case, the headline) to position the insertion point in the paragraph to be formatted (Figure 1–12).

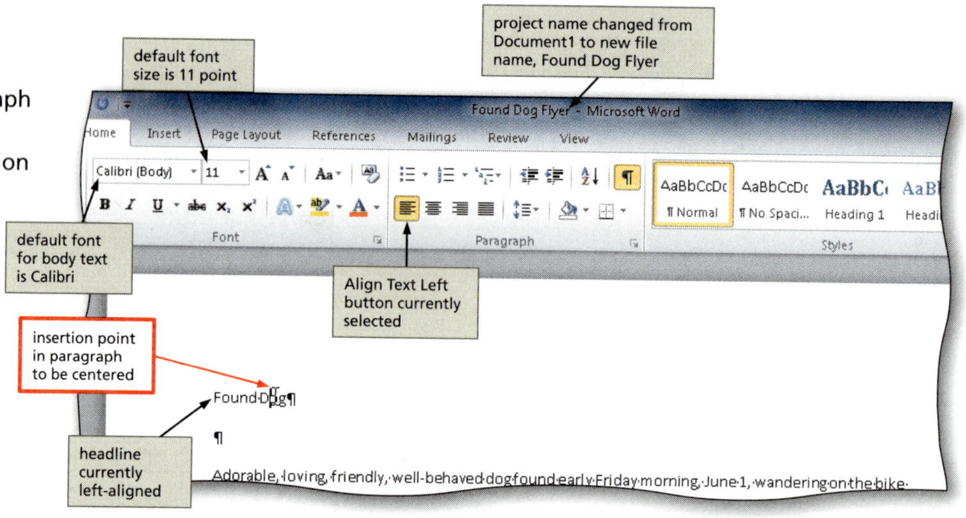

Figure 1–12

2

- Click the Center button (Home tab | Paragraph group) to center the paragraph containing the insertion point (Figure 1–13).

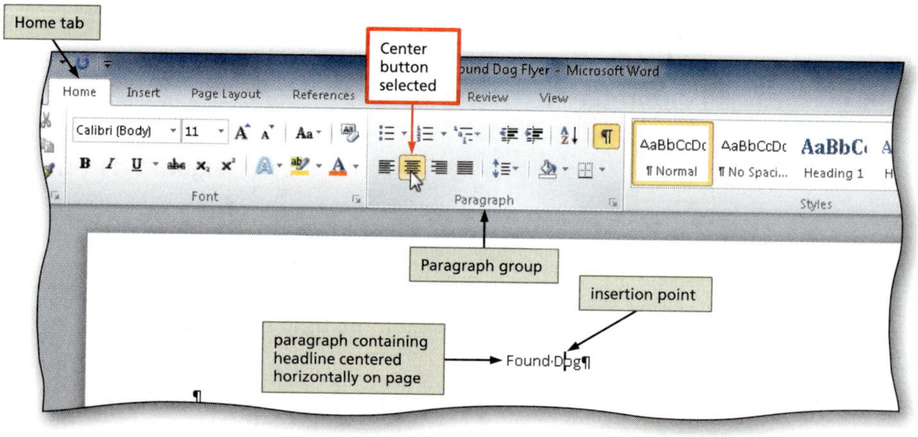

Figure 1–13

Q&A

What if I want to return the paragraph to left-aligned?

You would click the Center button again or click the Align Text Left button (Home tab | Paragraph group).

Other Ways

1. Right-click paragraph, click Center button on Mini toolbar
2. Right-click paragraph, click Paragraph on shortcut menu, click Indents and Spacing tab (Paragraph dialog box), click Alignment box arrow, click Centered, click OK button
3. Click Paragraph Dialog Box Launcher (Home tab or Page Layout tab | Paragraph group), click Indents and Spacing tab (Paragraph dialog box), click Alignment box arrow, click Centered, click OK button
4. Press CTRL+E

BTW

File Type
Depending on your Windows settings, the file type .docx may be displayed on the title bar immediately to the right of the file name after you save the file. The file type .docx is a Word 2010 document.

To Center Another Paragraph

In the flyer, the signature line is to be centered to match the paragraph alignment of the headline. The following steps center the signature line.

1 Click somewhere in the paragraph to be centered (in this case, the signature line) to position the insertion point in the paragraph to be formatted.

2 Click the Center button (Home tab | Paragraph group) to center the paragraph containing the insertion point (shown in Figure 1–14).

Formatting Single versus Multiple Paragraphs and Characters

As shown on the previous pages, to format a single paragraph, simply move the insertion point in the paragraph, to make it the current paragraph, and then format the paragraph. Similarly, to format a single word, position the insertion point in the word, to make it the current word, and then format the word.

To format multiple paragraphs or words, however, you first must select the paragraphs or words you want to format and then format the selection. If your screen normally displays dark letters on a light background, which is the default setting in Word, then selected text displays light letters on a dark background.

BTW

Selecting Nonadjacent Items

In Word, you can select nonadjacent items, that is, items not next to each other. This is helpful when you are applying the same formatting to multiple items. To select nonadjacent items (text or graphics), select the first item, such as a word or paragraph, as usual; then, press and hold down the CTRL key. While holding down the CTRL key, select additional items.

To Select a Line

The default font size of 11 point is too small for a headline in a flyer. To increase the font size of the characters in the headline, you first must select the line of text containing the headline. The following steps select a line.

1

- Move the mouse pointer to the left of the line to be selected (in this case, the headline) until the mouse pointer changes to a right-pointing block arrow (Figure 1–14).

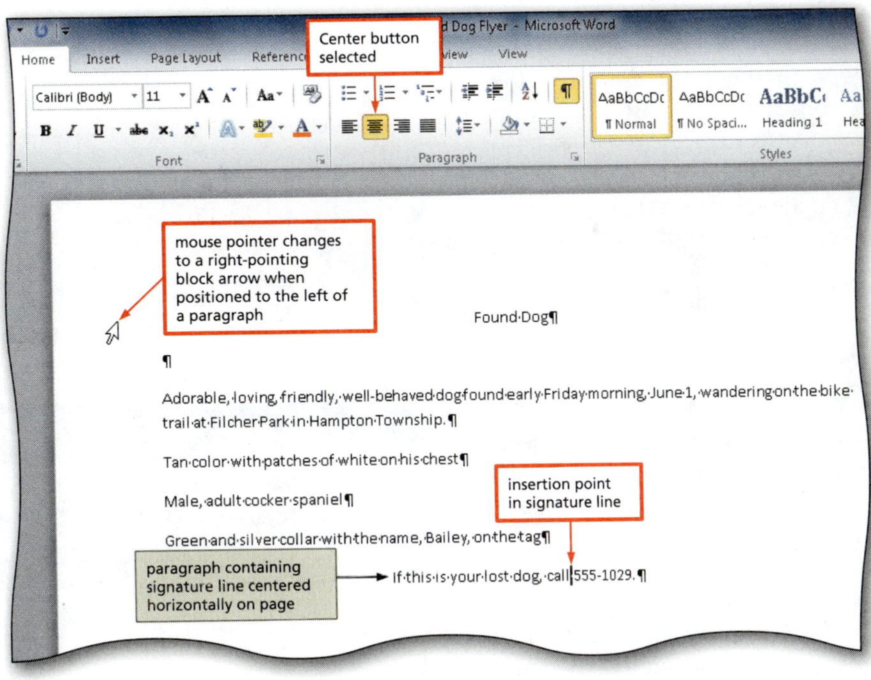

Figure 1–14

2

- While the mouse pointer is a right-pointing block arrow, click the mouse to select the entire line to the right of the mouse pointer (Figure 1–15).

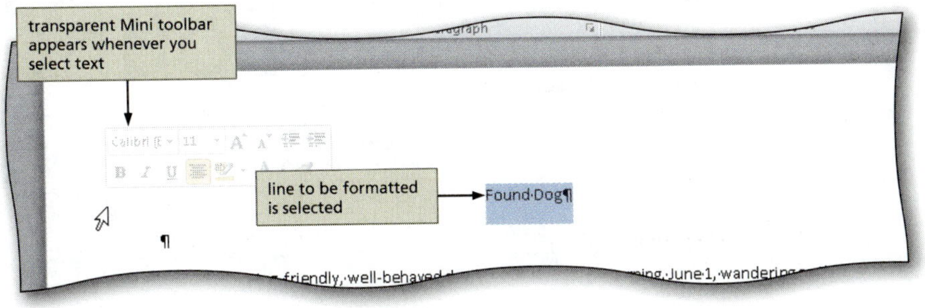

Figure 1–15

Other Ways

1. Drag mouse through line
2. With insertion point at beginning of desired line, press SHIFT+DOWN ARROW

To Change the Font Size of Selected Text

The next step is to increase the font size of the characters in the selected headline. You would like the headline to be as large as possible and still fit on a single line, which in this case is 72 point. The following steps increase the font size of the headline from 11 to 72 point.

1

- With the text selected, click the Font Size box arrow (Home tab | Font group) to display the Font Size gallery (Figure 1–16).

Q&A Why are the font sizes in my Font Size gallery different from those in Figure 1–16?

Font sizes may vary depending on the current font and your printer driver.

Q&A What happened to the Mini toolbar?

The Mini toolbar disappears if you do not use it. These steps use the Font Size box arrow on the Home tab instead of the Font Size box arrow on the Mini toolbar.

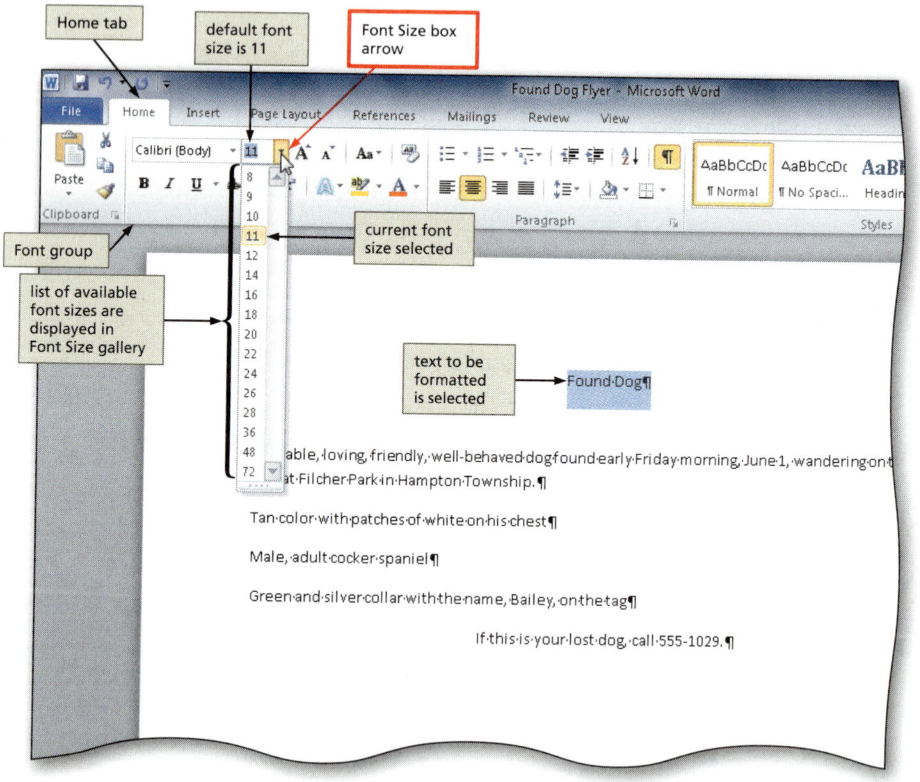

Figure 1–16

2

- Point to 72 in the Font Size gallery to display a live preview of the selected text at the selected point size (Figure 1–17).

Experiment

- Point to various font sizes in the Font Size gallery and watch the font size of the selected text change in the document window.

3

- Click 72 in the Font Size gallery to increase the font size of the selected text.

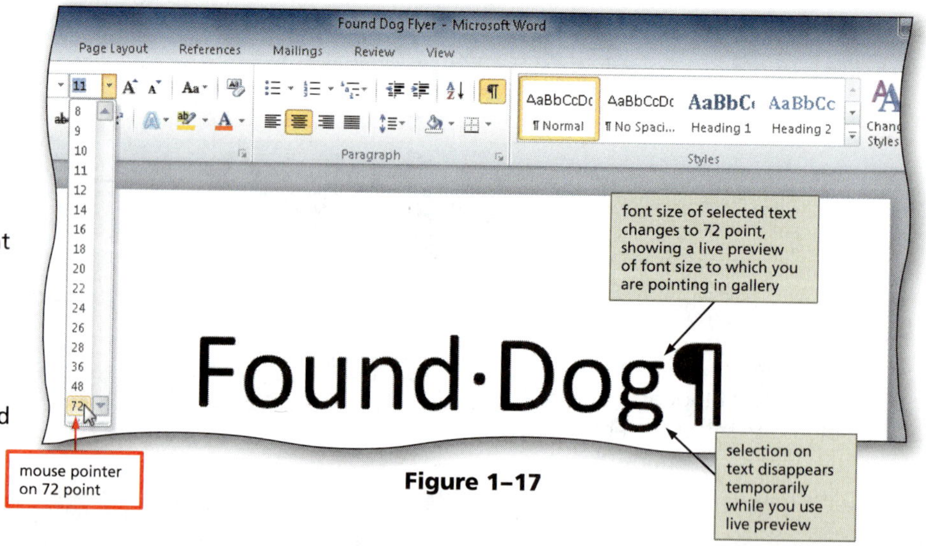

Figure 1–17

Other Ways

1. Click Font Size box arrow on Mini toolbar, click desired font size in Font Size gallery
2. Right-click selected text, click Font on shortcut menu, click Font tab (Font dialog box), select desired font size in Size list, click OK button
3. Click Font Dialog Box Launcher, click Font tab (Font dialog box), select desired font size in Size list, click OK button
4. Press CTRL+D, click Font tab (Font dialog box), select desired font size in Size list, click OK button

To Change the Font of Selected Text

The default theme font for headings is Cambria and for all other text, called body text in Word, is Calibri. Many other fonts are available, however, so that you can add variety to documents.

To draw more attention to the headline, you change its font so that it differs from the font of other text in the flyer. The following steps change the font of the headline from Calibri to Arial Rounded MT Bold.

1

- With the text selected, click the Font box arrow (Home tab | Font group) to display the Font gallery (Figure 1–18).

Q&A Will the fonts in my Font gallery be the same as those in Figure 1–18?

Your list of available fonts may differ, depending on the type of printer you are using and other settings.

Q&A What if the text is no longer selected?

Follow the steps on page WD 15 to select a line.

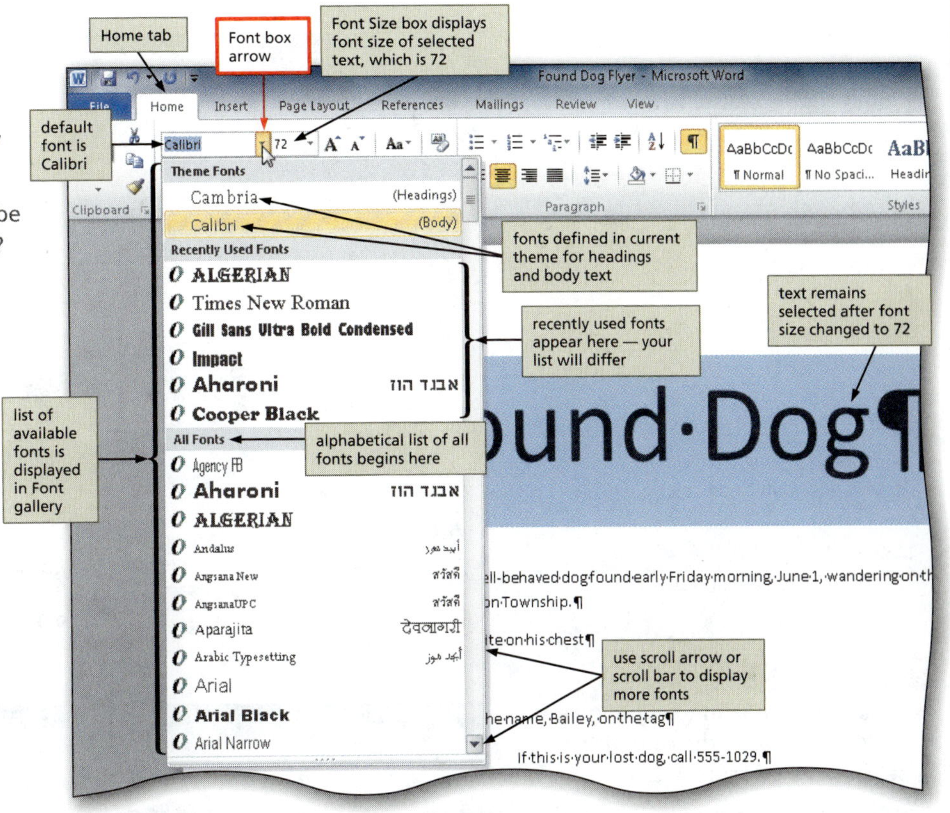

Figure 1–18

2

- Scroll through the Font gallery, if necessary, and then point to Arial Rounded MT Bold (or a similar font) to display a live preview of the selected text in the selected font (Figure 1–19).

Experiment

- Point to various fonts in the Font gallery and watch the font of the selected text change in the document window.

3

- Click Arial Rounded MT Bold (or a similar font) to change the font of the selected text.

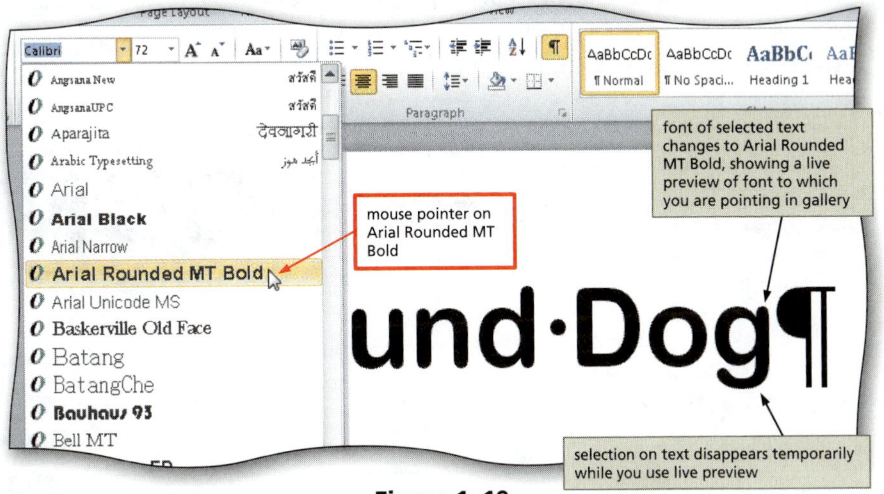

Figure 1–19

Other Ways

1. Click Font box arrow on Mini toolbar, click desired font in Font gallery
2. Right-click selected text, click Font on shortcut menu, click Font tab (Font dialog box), select desired font in Font list, click OK button
3. Click Font Dialog Box Launcher (Home tab | Font group), click Font tab (Font dialog box), select desired font in Font list, click OK button
4. Press CTRL+D, click Font tab (Font dialog box), select desired font in the Font list, click OK button

To Change the Case of Selected Text

The headline currently shows the first letter in each word capitalized, which sometimes is referred to as initial cap. To draw more attention to the headline, you would like the entire line of text to be capitalized, or in uppercase letters. The following steps change the headline to uppercase.

1

- With the text selected, click the Change Case button (Home tab | Font group) to display the Change Case gallery (Figure 1–20).

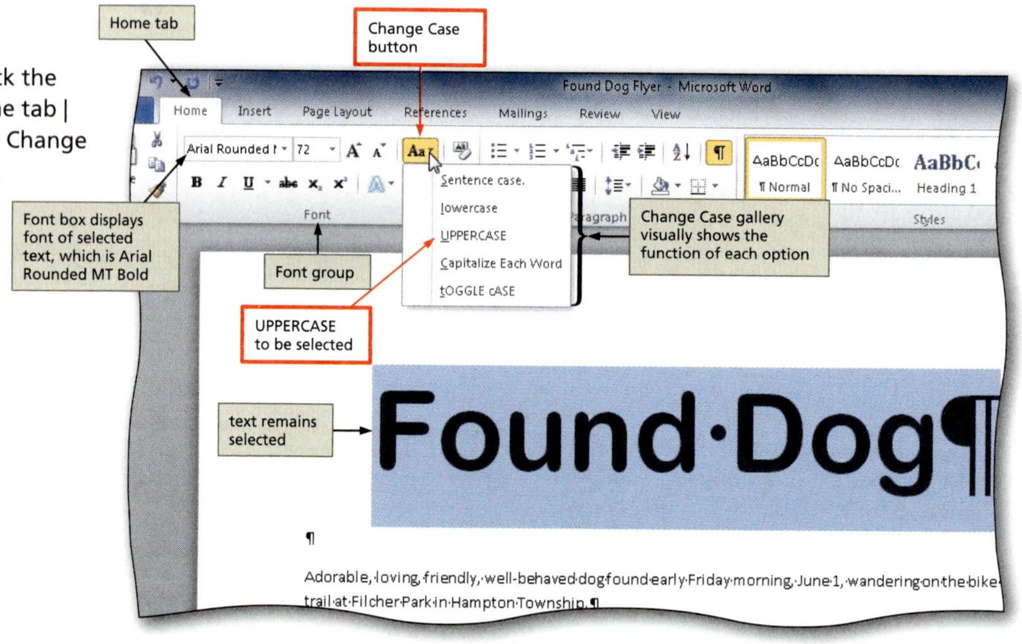

Figure 1–20

2

- Click UPPERCASE in the Change Case gallery to change the case of the selected text (Figure 1–21).

Q&A

What if a ruler appears on the screen or the mouse pointer shape changes?

Depending on the position of your mouse pointer and locations you click on the screen, a ruler may automatically appear or the mouse pointer shape may change. Simply move the mouse and the ruler should disappear and/or the mouse pointer shape will change.

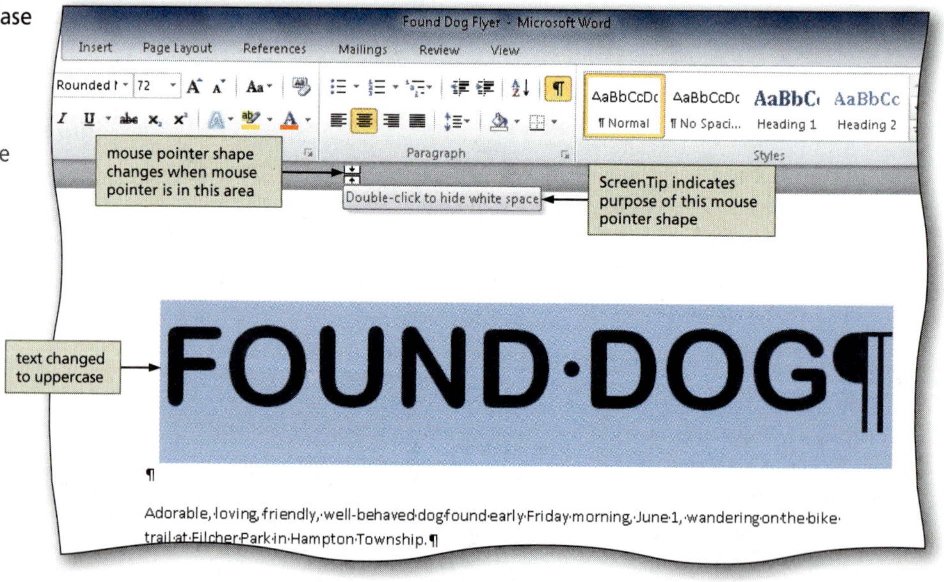

Figure 1–21

Other Ways

1. Right-click selected text, click Font on shortcut menu, click Font tab (Font dialog box), select All caps in Effects area, click OK button
2. Click Font Dialog Box Launcher (Home tab | Font group), click Font tab (Font dialog box), select All caps in Effects area, click OK button
3. Press SHIFT+F3 repeatedly until text is desired case

To Apply a Text Effect to Selected Text

You would like the text in the headline to be even more noticeable. Word provides many text effects to add interest and variety to text. The following steps apply a text effect to the headline.

1

- With the text selected, click the Text Effects button (Home tab | Font group) to display the Text Effects gallery (Figure 1–22).

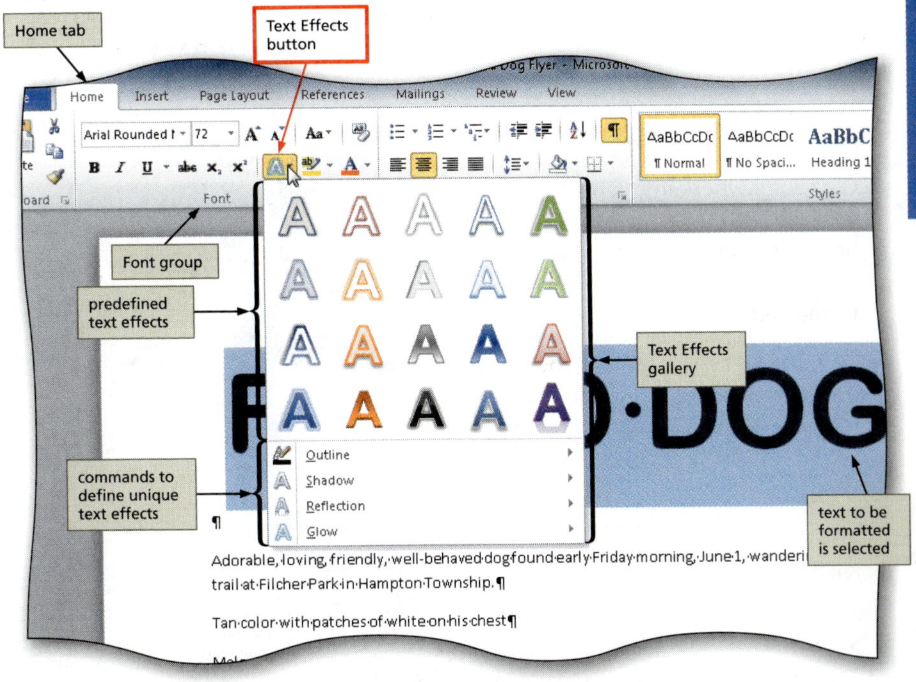

Figure 1–22

2

- Point to Fill – White, Gradient Outline – Accent 1 (first text effect in third row) to display a live preview of the selected text in the selected text effect (Figure 1–23).

Experiment

- Point to various text effects in the Text Effects gallery and watch the text effects of the selected text change in the document window.

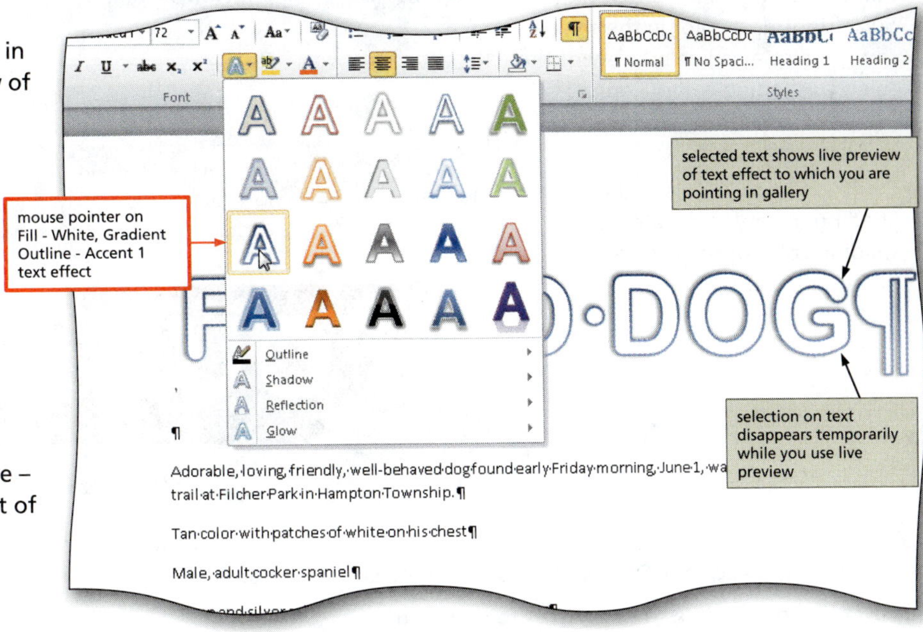

Figure 1–23

3

- Click Fill – White, Gradient Outline – Accent 1 to change the text effect of the selected text.

4

- Click anywhere in the document window to remove the selection from the selected text.

Other Ways
1. Right-click selected text, click Font on shortcut menu, click Font tab (Font dialog box), click Text Effects button, select desired text effects (Format Text Effects dialog box), click Close button, click OK button 2. Click Font Dialog Box Launcher (Home tab | Font group), click Font tab (Font dialog box), click Text Effects button, select desired text effects (Format Text Effects dialog box), click Close button, click OK button

To Shade a Paragraph

To make the headline of the flyer more eye-catching, you would like to shade it. When you **shade** text, Word colors the rectangular area behind any text or graphics. If the text to shade is a paragraph, Word shades the area from the left margin to the right margin of the current paragraph. To shade a paragraph, place the insertion point in the paragraph. To shade any other text, you must first select the text to be shaded. This flyer uses brown as the shading color for the headline. The following steps shade a paragraph.

1

- Click somewhere in the paragraph to be shaded (in this case, the headline) to position the insertion point in the paragraph to be formatted.
- Click the Shading button arrow (Home tab | Paragraph group) to display the Shading gallery (Figure 1–24).

Q&A What if I click the Shading button by mistake?

Click the Shading button arrow and proceed with Step 2.

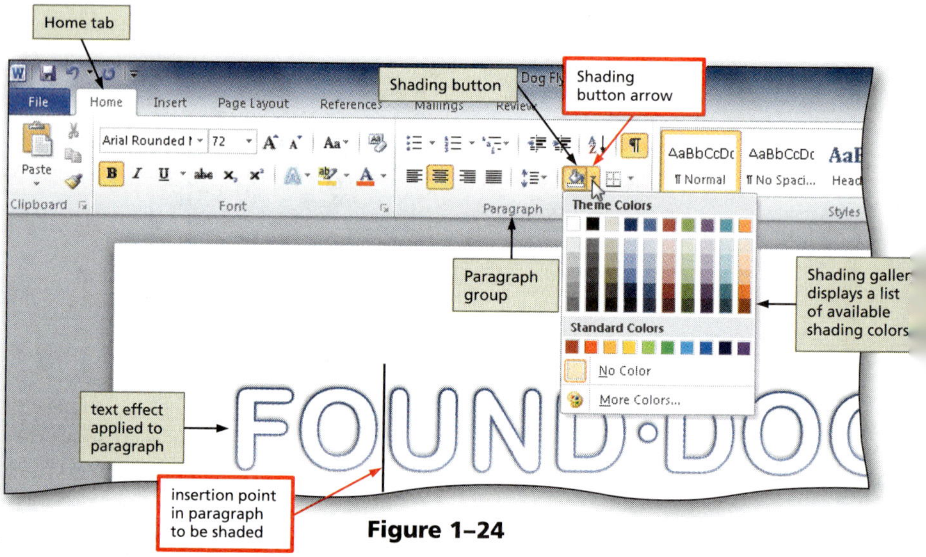

Figure 1–24

2

- Point to Orange, Accent 6, Darker 50% (rightmost color in the sixth row) to display a live preview of the selected shading color (Figure 1–25).

Experiment

- Point to various colors in the Shading gallery and watch the shading color of the current paragraph change.

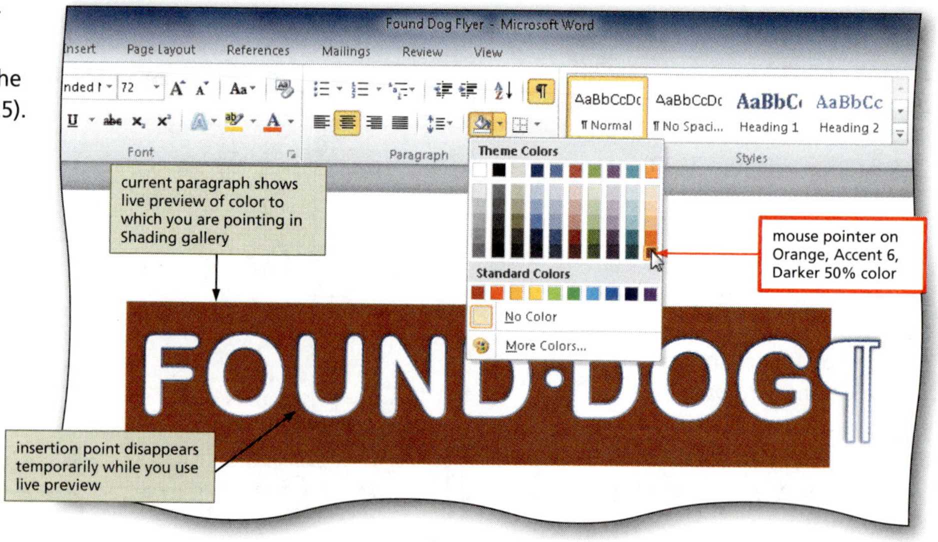

Figure 1–25

3

- Click Orange, Accent 6, Darker 50% to shade the current paragraph.

Q&A What if I apply a dark shading color to dark text?

When the font color of text is Automatic, it usually is black. If you select a dark shading color, Word automatically may change the text color to white so that the shaded text is easier to read.

Other Ways

1. Click Border button arrow (Home tab | Paragraph group), click Borders and Shading, click Shading tab (Borders and Shading dialog box), click Fill box arrow, select desired color, click OK button

To Select Multiple Lines

The next formatting step for the flyer is to increase the font size of the characters between the headline and the signature line so that they are easier to read from a distance. To change the font size of the characters in multiple lines, you first must select all the lines to be formatted. The following steps select multiple lines.

1

- Move the mouse pointer to the left of the first paragraph to be selected until the mouse pointer changes to a right-pointing block arrow (Figure 1–26).

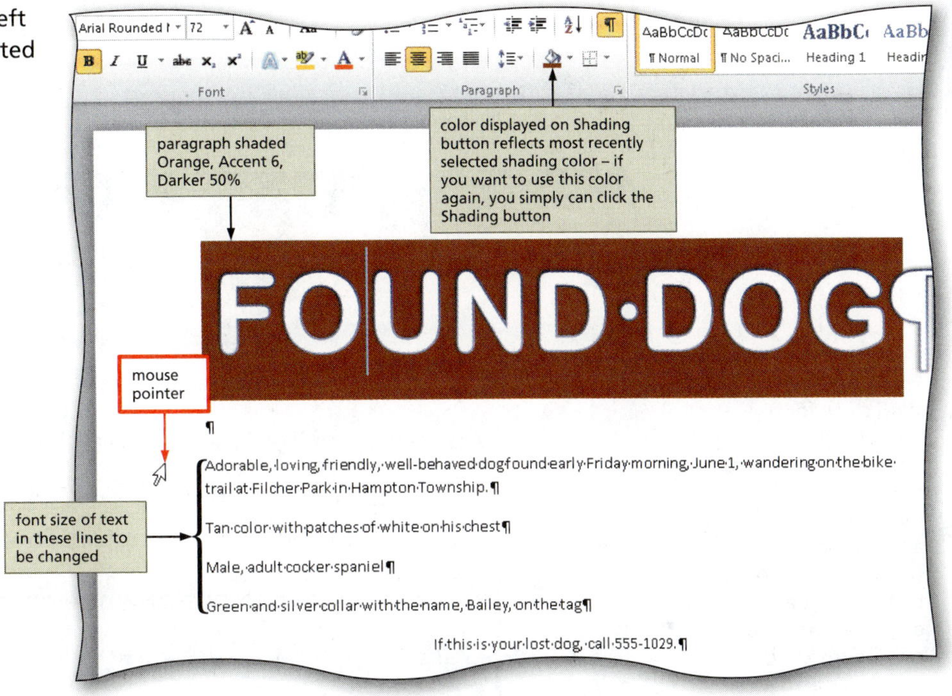

Figure 1–26

2

- Drag downward to select all lines that will be formatted (Figure 1–27).

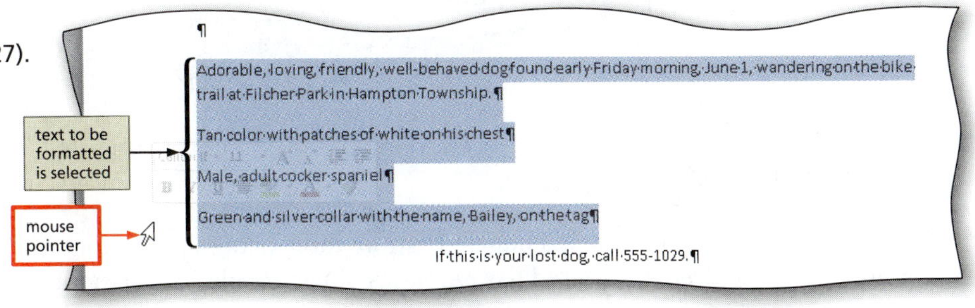

Figure 1–27

Other Ways

1. With insertion point at beginning of desired line, press SHIFT+DOWN ARROW repeatedly until all lines are selected

To Change the Font Size of Selected Text

The characters between the headline and the signature line in the flyer currently are 11 point. To make them easier to read from a distance, this flyer uses 22 point for these characters. The steps on the next page change the font size of the selected text.

1. With the text selected, click the Font Size box arrow (Home tab | Font group) to display the Font Size gallery.
2. Click 22 in the Font Size gallery to increase the font size of the selected text.
3. Click anywhere in the document window to remove the selection from the text.
4. If necessary, scroll so that you can see all the text on the screen (Figure 1–28).

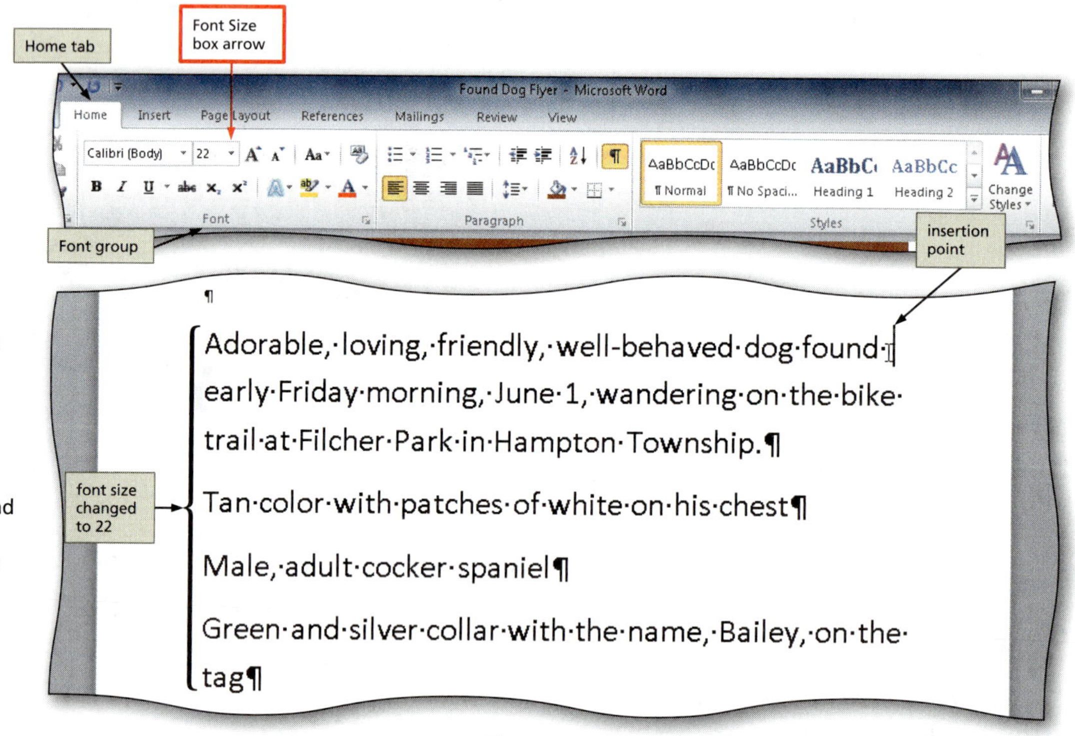

Figure 1–28

BTW

Formatting Marks
With some fonts, formatting marks do not display properly on the screen. For example, the raised dot that signifies a blank space between words may be displayed behind a character instead of in the blank space, causing the characters to look incorrect.

To Bullet a List of Paragraphs

The next step is to format as a bulleted list the three paragraphs of identifying information that are above the signature line in the flyer. A **bulleted list** is a series of paragraphs, each beginning with a bullet character.

To format a list of paragraphs with bullets, you first must select all the lines in the paragraphs. The following steps bullet a list of paragraphs.

1.
- Move the mouse pointer to the left of the first paragraph to be selected until the mouse pointer changes to a right-pointing block arrow.
- Drag downward until all paragraphs that will be formatted with a bullet character are selected (Figure 1–29).

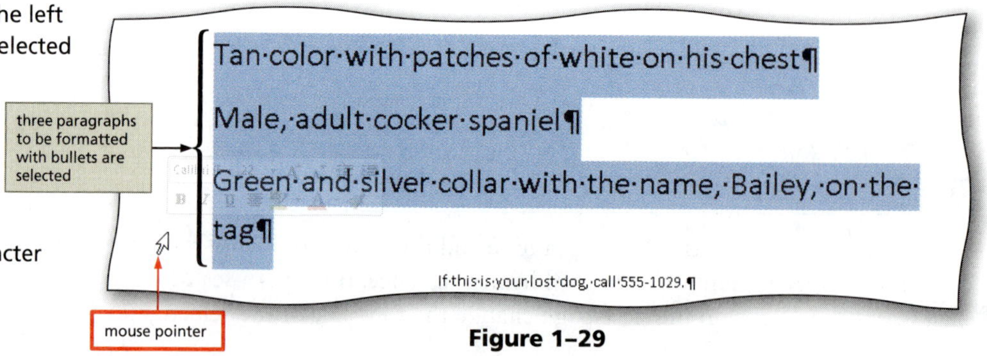

Figure 1–29

2

- Click the Bullets button (Home tab | Paragraph group) to place a bullet character at the beginning of each selected paragraph (Figure 1–30).

Q&A How do I remove bullets from a list or paragraph?

Select the list or paragraph and then click the Bullets button again.

Q&A What if I accidentally click the Bullets button arrow?

Press the ESCAPE key to remove the Bullets gallery from the screen and then repeat Step 2.

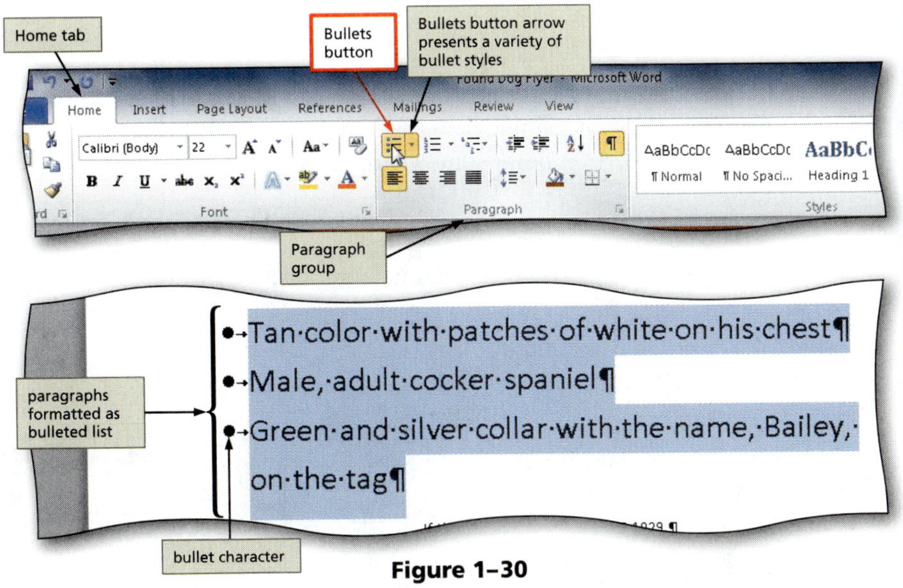

Figure 1–30

Other Ways

1. Right-click selected paragraphs, point to Bullets on shortcut menu, click desired bullet style

To Undo and Redo an Action

Word provides a means of canceling your recent command(s) or action(s). For example, if you format text incorrectly, you can undo the format and try it again. When you point to the Undo button, Word displays the action you can undo as part of a ScreenTip.

If, after you undo an action, you decide you did not want to perform the undo, you can redo the undone action. Word does not allow you to undo or redo some actions, such as saving or printing a document. The next steps undo the bullet format just applied and then redo the bullet format.

1

- Click the Undo button on the Quick Access Toolbar to reverse your most recent action (in this case, remove the bullets from the paragraphs) (Figure 1–31).

2

- Click the Redo button on the Quick Access Toolbar to reverse your most recent undo (in this case, place a bullet character on the paragraphs again) (shown in Figure 1–30).

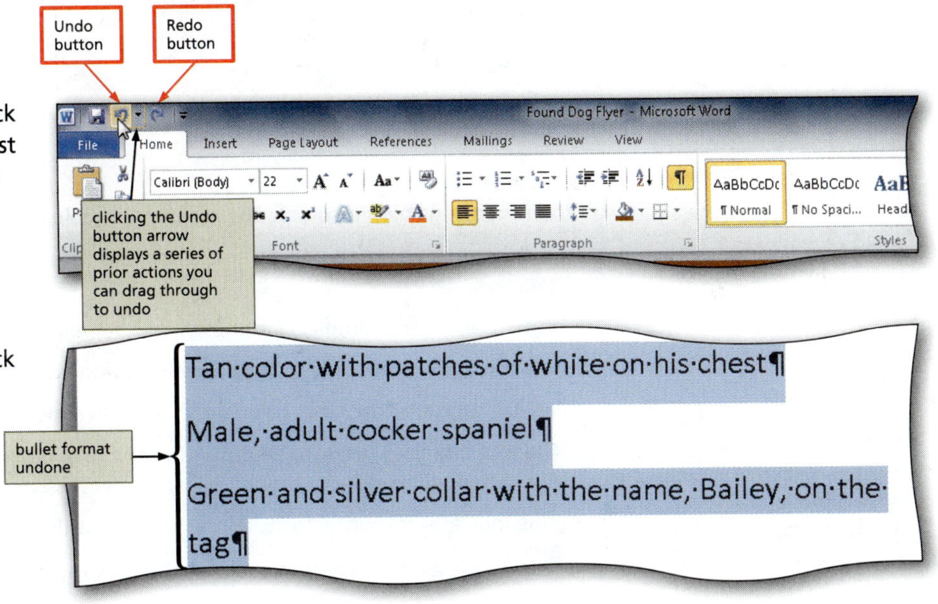

Figure 1–31

Other Ways

1. Press CTRL+Z to undo; press CTRL+Y to redo

To Italicize Text

The next step is to italicize the dog's name, Bailey, in the flyer to further emphasize it. **Italicized** text has a slanted appearance. As with a single paragraph, if you want to format a single word, you do not need to select it. Simply position the insertion point somewhere in the word and apply the desired format. The following step formats a word in italics.

1

- Click somewhere in the word to be italicized (Bailey, in this case) to position the insertion point in the word to be formatted.
- Click the Italic button (Home tab | Font group) to italicize the word containing the insertion point (Figure 1–32).

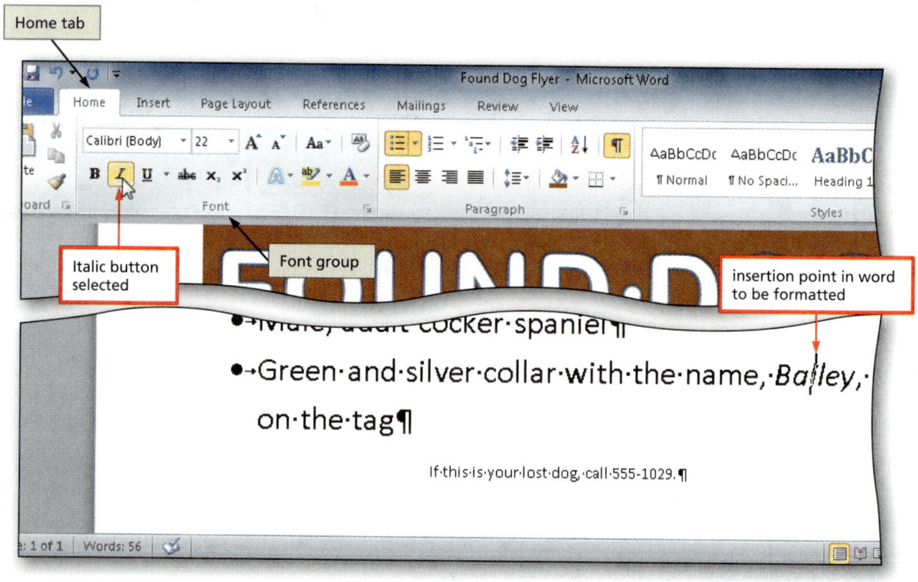

Figure 1–32

Q&A How would I remove an italic format?

You would click the Italic button a second time, or you immediately could click the Undo button on the Quick Access Toolbar or press CTRL+Z.

Q&A How can I tell what formatting has been applied to text?

The selected buttons and boxes on the Home tab show formatting characteristics of the location of the insertion point. With the insertion point in the word, Bailey, the Home tab shows these formats: 22-point Calibri italic font, bulleted paragraph.

Other Ways

1. Click Italic button on Mini toolbar
2. Right-click selected text, click Font on shortcut menu, click Font tab (Font dialog box), click Italic in Font style list, click OK button
3. Click Font Dialog Box Launcher (Home tab | Font group), click Font tab (Font dialog box), click Italic in Font style list, click OK button
4. Press CTRL+I

Plan Ahead

Use color.

When choosing color, associate the meaning of color to your message:

- Red expresses danger, power, or energy, and often is associated with sports or physical exertion.
- Brown represents simplicity, honesty, and dependability.
- Orange denotes success, victory, creativity, and enthusiasm.
- Yellow suggests sunshine, happiness, hope, liveliness, and intelligence.
- Green symbolizes growth, healthiness, harmony, blooming, and healing, and often is associated with safety or money.
- Blue indicates integrity, trust, importance, confidence, and stability.
- Purple represents wealth, power, comfort, extravagance, magic, mystery, and spirituality.
- White stands for purity, goodness, cleanliness, precision, and perfection.
- Black suggests authority, strength, elegance, power, and prestige.
- Gray conveys neutrality and thus often is found in backgrounds and other effects.

BTW

Q&As

For a complete list of the Q&As found in many of the step-by-step sequences in the Office and Windows chapters in this book, visit the Microsoft Office and Concepts CourseMate Web site at www.cengagebrain.com and then navigate to the Q&A resource for this book.

To Color Text

To emphasize the dog's name even more, its color is changed to a shade of blue. The following steps change the color of the word, Bailey.

1

- With the insertion point in the word to format, click the Font Color button arrow (Home tab | Font group) to display the Font Color gallery (Figure 1–33).

Q&A What if I click the Font Color button by mistake?

Click the Font Color button arrow and then proceed with Step 2.

2

- Point to Blue, Accent 1, Darker 25% (fifth color in the fifth row) to display a live preview of the selected font color.

Experiment

- Point to various colors in the Font Color gallery and watch the color of the current word change.

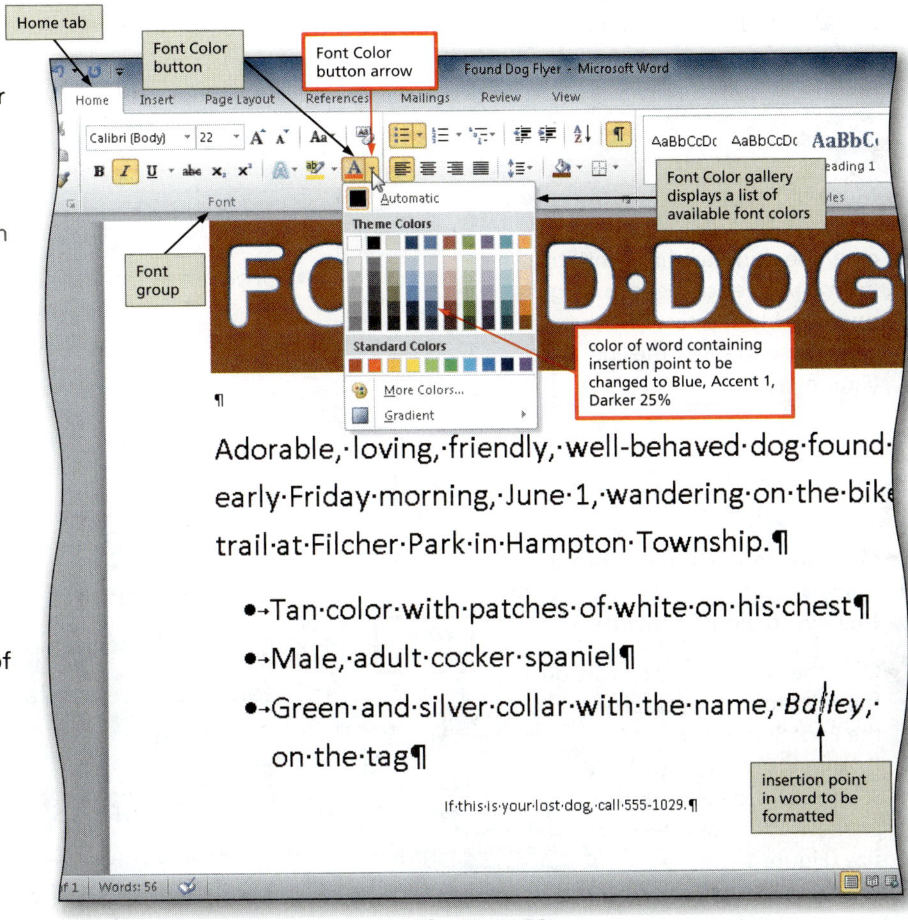

Figure 1–33

3

- Click Blue, Accent 1, Darker 25% to change the color of the text (Figure 1–34).

Q&A How would I change the text color back to black?

You would position the insertion point in the word or select the text, click the Font Color button arrow (Home tab | Font group) again, and then click Automatic in the Font Color gallery.

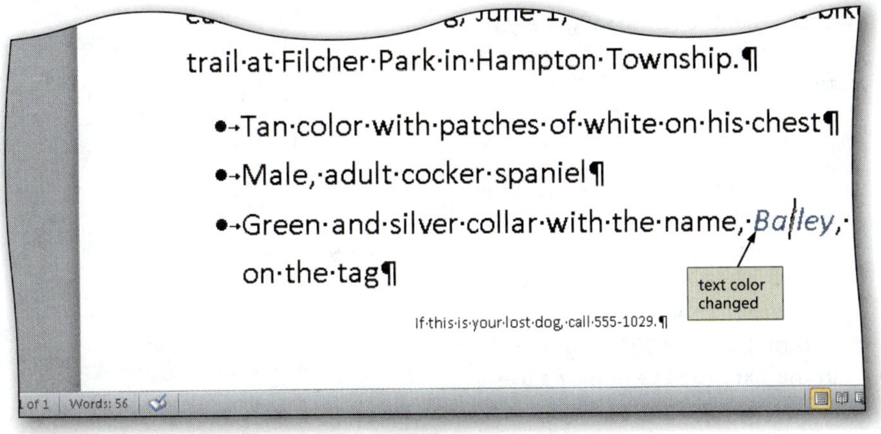

Figure 1–34

Other Ways

1. Click Font Color button arrow on Mini toolbar, click desired color
2. Right-click selected text, click Font on shortcut menu, click Font tab (Font dialog box), click Font color box arrow, click desired color, click OK button
3. Click Font Dialog Box Launcher (Home tab | Font group), click Font tab (Font dialog box), click Font color box arrow, click desired color, click OK button

To Use the Mini Toolbar to Format Text

Recall from the Office 2010 and Windows 7 chapter in this book that the Mini toolbar, which automatically appears based on certain tasks you perform, contains commands related to changing the appearance of text in a document. All commands on the Mini toolbar also exist on the Ribbon.

When the Mini toolbar appears, it initially is transparent. If you do not use the transparent Mini toolbar, it disappears from the screen. The following steps use the Mini toolbar to change the color and font size of text in the signature line of the flyer.

1

- Move the mouse pointer to the left of the line to be selected (in this case, the signature line) until the mouse pointer changes to a right-pointing block arrow and then click the mouse to select the line (Figure 1–35).

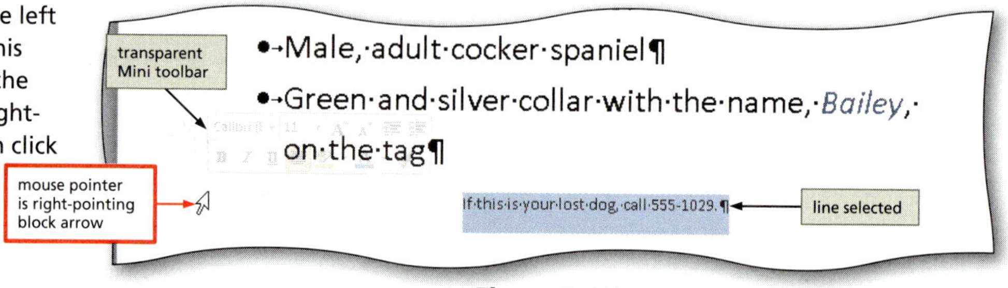

Figure 1–35

2

- Move the mouse pointer into the transparent Mini toolbar, so that it changes to a bright toolbar.
- Click the Font Size box arrow on the Mini toolbar to display the Font Size gallery and then point to 28 in the Font Size gallery to display a live preview of the selected font size (Figure 1–36).

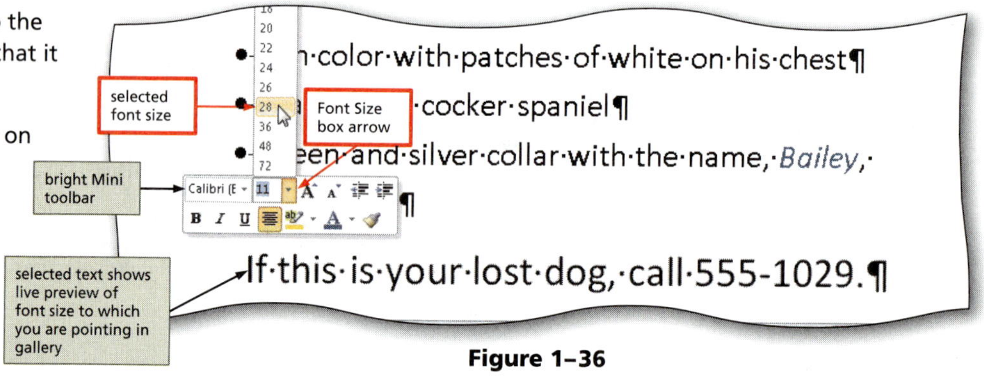

Figure 1–36

3

- Click 28 in the Font Size gallery to increase the font size of the selected text.

4

- With the text still selected and the Mini toolbar still displayed, click the Font Color button arrow on the Mini toolbar to display the Font Color gallery and then point to Purple, Accent 4, Darker 50% (eighth color in the sixth row) to display a live preview of the selected font color (Figure 1–37).

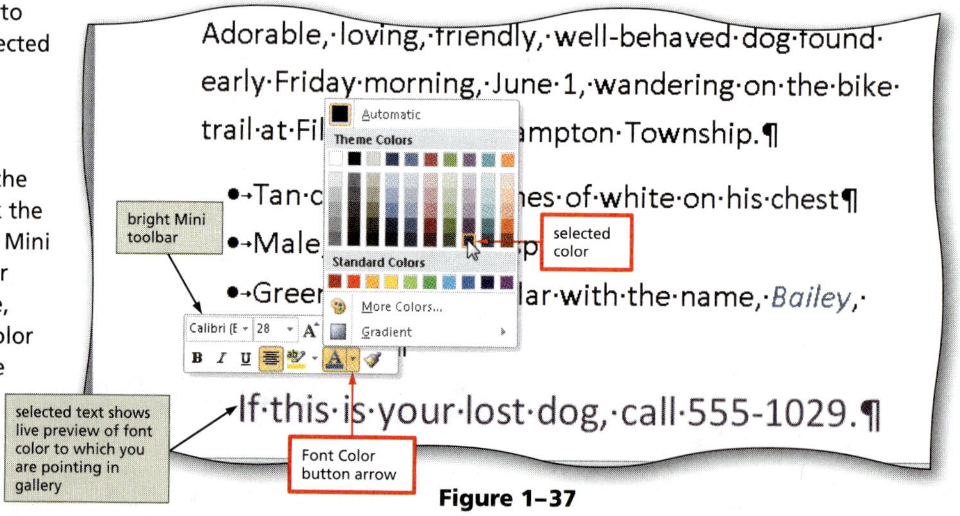

Figure 1–37

5

- Click Purple, Accent 4, Darker 50% to change the color of the text.
- Click anywhere in the document window to remove the selection from the text.

To Select a Group of Words

To emphasize the contact information (call 555-1029), these words are underlined in the flyer. To format a group of words, you first must select them. The following steps select a group of words.

1

- Position the mouse pointer immediately to the left of the first character of the text to be selected, in this case, the c in call (Figure 1–38).

Q&A Why did the shape of the mouse pointer change?

The mouse pointer's shape is an I-beam when positioned in unselected text in the document window.

Figure 1–38

2

- Drag the mouse pointer through the last character of the text to be selected, in this case, the 9 in the phone number (Figure 1–39).

Q&A Why did the mouse pointer shape change again?

When the mouse pointer is positioned in selected text, its shape is a left-pointing block arrow.

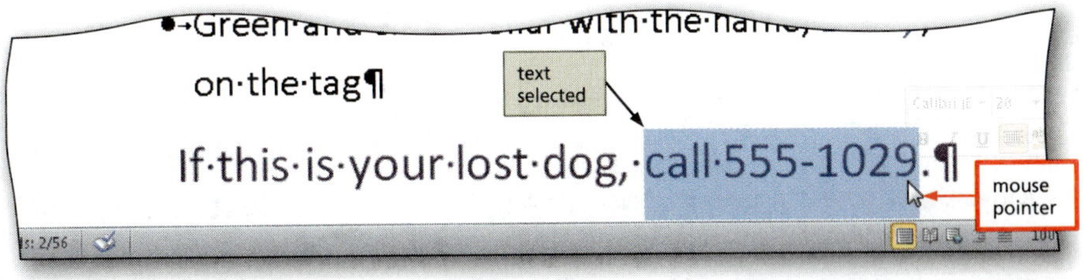

Figure 1–39

Other Ways

1. With insertion point at beginning of first word in group, press CTRL+SHIFT+RIGHT ARROW repeatedly until all words are selected

To Underline Text

Underlines are used to emphasize or draw attention to specific text. **Underlined** text prints with an underscore (_) below each character. In the flyer, the contact information, call 555-1029, in the signature line is emphasized with an underline. The following step formats selected text with an underline.

1

- With the text selected, click the Underline button (Home tab | Font group) to underline the selected text (Figure 1–40).

Q&A How would I remove an underline?

You would click the Underline button a second time, or you immediately could click the Undo button on the Quick Access Toolbar.

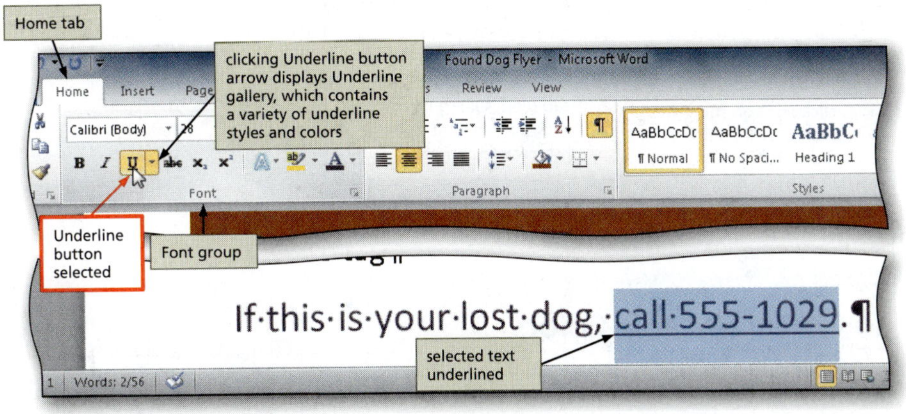

Figure 1–40

Other Ways

1. Right-click text, click Font on shortcut menu, click Font tab (Font dialog box), click Underline style box arrow, click desired underline style, click OK button
2. Click Font Dialog Box Launcher (Home tab | Font group), click Font tab (Font dialog box), click Underline style box arrow, click desired underline style, click OK button
3. Press CTRL+U

To Bold Text

Bold characters appear somewhat thicker and darker than those that are not bold. To further emphasize the signature line, it is bold in the flyer. To format the line, as you have learned previously, you select the line first. The following steps format the signature line bold.

1

- Move the mouse pointer to the left of the line to be selected (in this case, the signature line) until the mouse pointer changes to a right-pointing block arrow and then click the mouse to select the text to be formatted.
- With the text selected, click the Bold button (Home tab | Font group) to bold the selected text (Figure 1–41).

Q&A How would I remove a bold format?

You would click the Bold button a second time, or you immediately could click the Undo button on the Quick Access Toolbar.

2

- Click anywhere in the document window to remove the selection from the screen.

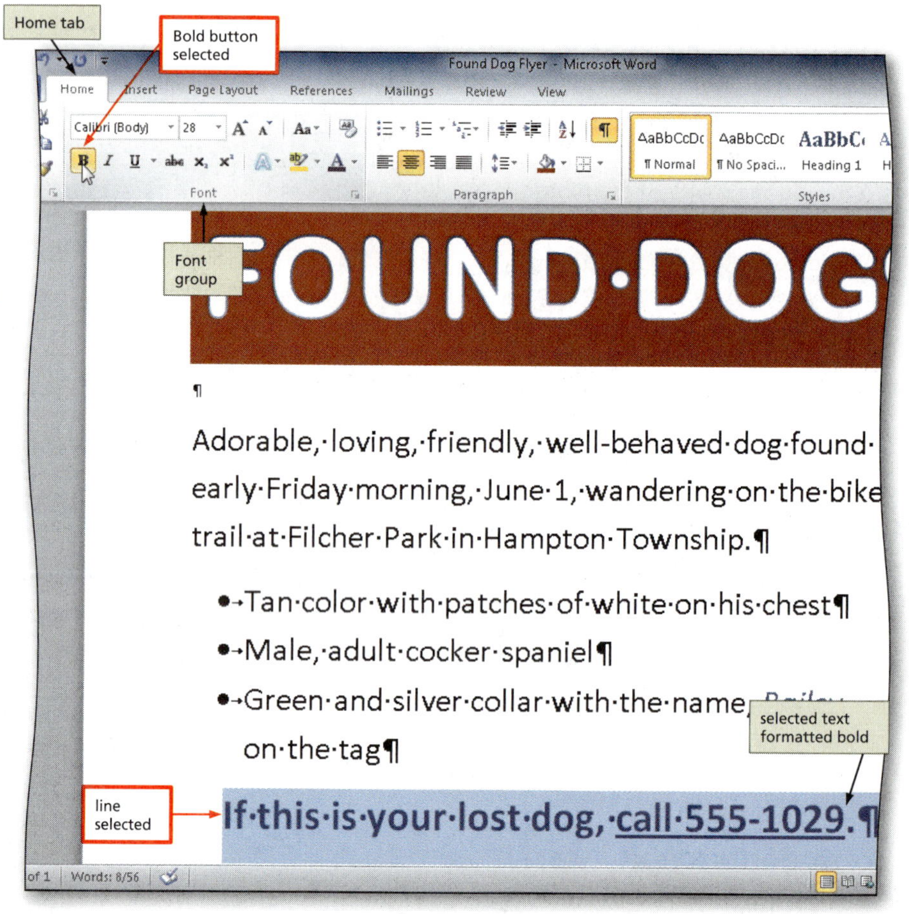

Figure 1–41

Other Ways

1. Click Bold button on Mini toolbar
2. Right-click selected text, click Font on shortcut menu, click Font tab (Font dialog box), click Bold in Font style list, click OK button
3. Click Font Dialog Box Launcher (Home tab | Font group), click Font tab (Font dialog box), click Bold in Font style list, click OK button
4. Press CTRL+B

To Change Theme Colors

A **color scheme** in Word is a document theme that identifies 12 complementary colors for text, background, accents, and links in a document. With more than 20 predefined color schemes, Word provides a simple way to select colors that work well together.

In the flyer, you want all the colors to convey honesty, dependability, and healing, that is, shades of browns and greens. In Word, the Aspect color scheme uses these colors. Thus, you will change the color scheme from the default, Office, to Aspect. The next steps change theme colors.

1

- Click the Change Styles button (Home tab | Styles group) to display the Change Styles menu.
- Point to Colors on the Change Styles menu to display the Colors gallery (Figure 1–42).

Experiment

- Point to various color schemes in the Colors gallery and watch the colors change in the document window.

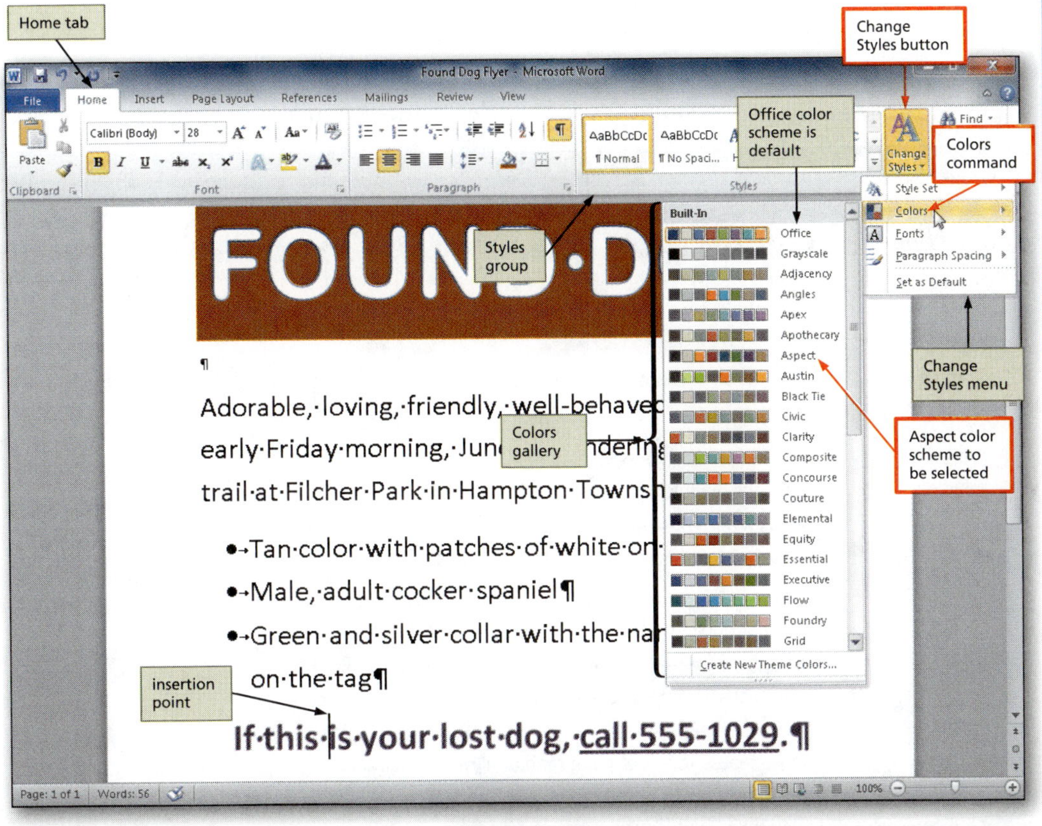

Figure 1–42

2

- Click Aspect in the Colors gallery to change the document theme colors (Figure 1–43).

Q&A

What if I want to return to the original color scheme?

You would click the Change Styles button again, click Colors on the Change Styles menu, and then click Office in the Colors gallery.

Figure 1–43

Other Ways

1. Click Theme Colors button (Page Layout tab | Themes group), select desired color scheme

Selecting Text

In many of the previous steps, you have selected text. Table 1–3 summarizes the techniques used to select various items.

Table 1–3 Techniques for Selecting Text

Item to Select	Mouse	Keyboard (where applicable)
Block of text	Click at beginning of selection, scroll to end of selection, position mouse pointer at end of selection, hold down SHIFT key and then click; or drag through the text.	
Character(s)	Drag through character(s).	SHIFT+RIGHT ARROW or SHIFT+LEFT ARROW
Document	Move mouse to left of text until mouse pointer changes to a right-pointing block arrow and then triple-click.	CTRL+A
Graphic	Click the graphic.	
Line	Move mouse to left of line until mouse pointer changes to a right-pointing block arrow and then click.	HOME, then SHIFT+END or END, then SHIFT+HOME
Lines	Move mouse to left of first line until mouse pointer changes to a right-pointing block arrow and then drag up or down.	HOME, then SHIFT+DOWN ARROW or END, then SHIFT+UP AROW
Paragraph	Triple-click paragraph; or move mouse to left of paragraph until mouse pointer changes to a right-pointing block arrow and then double-click.	CTRL+SHIFT+DOWN ARROW or CTRL+SHIFT+UP ARROW
Paragraphs	Move mouse to left of paragraph until mouse pointer changes to a right-pointing block arrow, double-click, and then drag up or down.	CTRL+SHIFT+DOWN ARROW or CTRL+SHIFT+UP ARROW repeatedly
Sentence	Press and hold down CTRL key and then click sentence.	
Word	Double-click the word.	CTRL+SHIFT+RIGHT ARROW or CTRL+SHIFT+LEFT ARROW
Words	Drag through words.	CTRL+SHIFT+RIGHT ARROW or CTRL+SHIFT+LEFT ARROW repeatedly

To Save an Existing Document with the Same File Name

You have made several modifications to the document since you last saved it. Thus, you should save it again. The following step saves the document again. For an example of the step listed below, refer to the Office 2010 and Windows 7 chapter in this book.

1. Click the Save button on the Quick Access Toolbar to overwrite the previously saved file.

Break Point: If you wish to take a break, this is a good place to do so. You can quit Word now (refer to page WD 44 for instructions). To resume at a later time, start Word (refer to pages WD 4 and WD 5 for instructions), open the file called Found Dog Flyer (refer to page WD 45 for instructions), and continue following the steps from this location forward.

Inserting and Formatting Pictures in a Word Document

With the text formatted in the flyer, the next step is to insert digital pictures in the flyer and format the pictures. Flyers usually contain graphical images, such as a picture, to attract the attention of passersby. In the following pages, you will perform these tasks:

1. Insert the first digital picture into the flyer and then reduce its size.
2. Insert the second digital picture into the flyer and then reduce its size.
3. Change the look of the first picture and then the second picture.

Plan Ahead

Find the appropriate graphical image.
To use a graphical image, also called a graphic, in a Word document, the image must be stored digitally in a file. Files containing graphical images are available from a variety of sources:

- Word includes a collection of predefined graphical images that you can insert in a document.
- Microsoft has free digital images on the Web for use in a document. Other Web sites also have images available, some of which are free, while others require a fee.
- You can take a picture with a digital camera or camera phone and **download** it, which is the process of copying the digital picture from the camera or phone to your computer.
- With a scanner, you can convert a printed picture, drawing, or diagram to a digital file.

If you receive a picture from a source other than yourself, do not use the file until you are certain it does not contain a virus. A **virus** is a computer program that can damage files and programs on your computer. Use an antivirus program to verify that any files you use are virus free.

Plan Ahead

Establish where to position and how to format the graphical image.
The content, size, shape, position, and format of a graphic should capture the interest of passersby, enticing them to stop and read the flyer. Often, the graphic is the center of attraction and visually the largest element on a flyer. If you use colors in the graphical image, be sure they are part of the document's color scheme.

To Insert a Picture

The next step in creating the flyer is to insert one of the digital pictures of the dog so that it is centered on the blank line below the headline. The picture, which was taken with a camera phone, is available on the Data Files for Students. See the inside back cover of this book for instructions on downloading the Data Files for Students, or contact your instructor for information about accessing the required files.

The following steps insert a centered picture, which, in this example, is located in the Chapter 01 folder in the Word folder in the Data Files for Students folder on a USB flash drive.

1

- Position the insertion point on the blank line below the headline, which is the location where you want to insert the picture.
- Click the Center button (Home tab | Paragraph group) to center the paragraph that will contain the picture.
- Click Insert on the Ribbon to display the Insert tab (Figure 1–44).

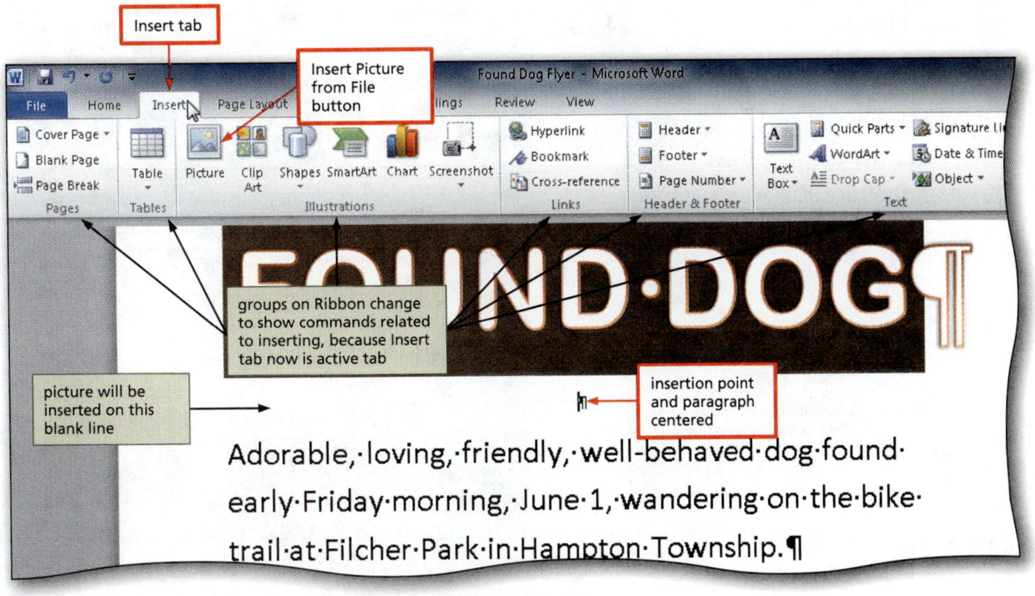

Figure 1–44

2

- With your USB flash drive connected to one of the computer's USB ports, click the Insert Picture from File button (Insert tab | Illustrations group) (shown in Figure 1-44) to display the Insert Picture dialog box (shown in Figure 1-45 on the next page).

3

- Navigate to the picture location (in this case, the Chapter 01 folder in the Word folder in the Data Files for Students folder on a USB flash drive). For a detailed example of this procedure, refer to Steps 3a – 3c in the To Save a File in a Folder section in the Office 2010 and Windows 7 chapter in this book.
- Click Dog Picture 1 to select the file (Figure 1–45).

Q&A What if the picture is not on a USB flash drive?

Use the same process, but select the storage location containing the picture.

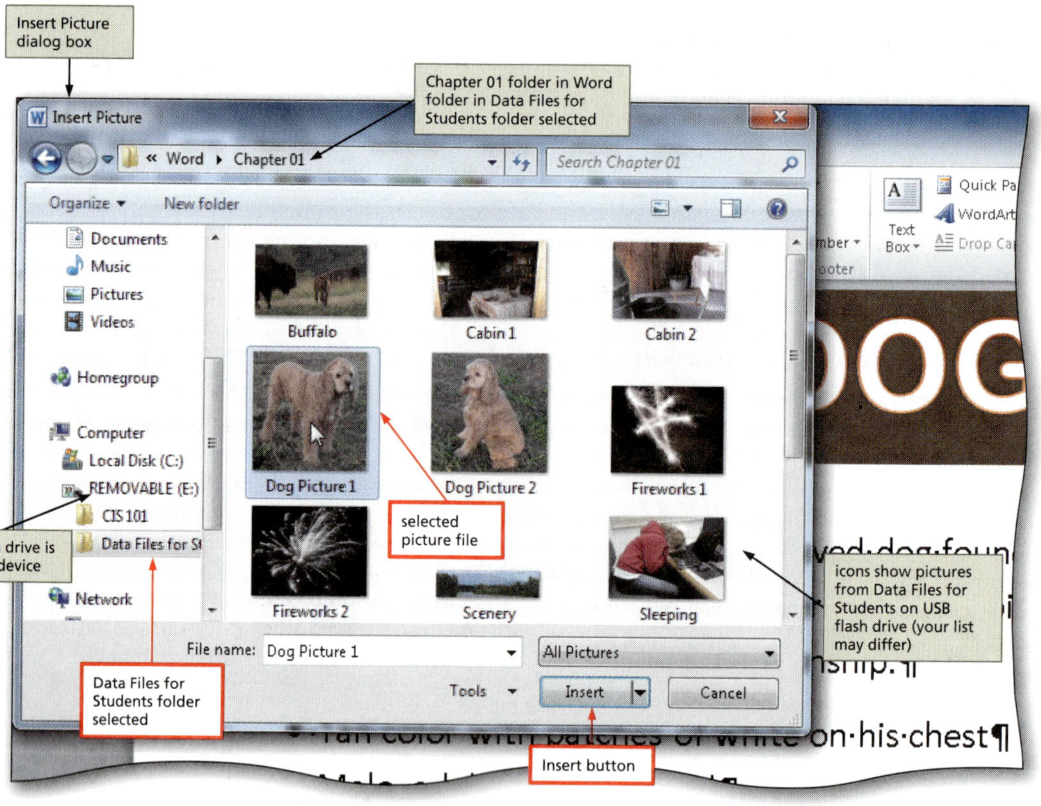

Figure 1–45

4

- Click the Insert button (Insert Picture dialog box) to insert the picture at the location of the insertion point in the document (Figure 1–46).

Q&A What are the symbols around the picture?

A selected graphic appears surrounded by a **selection rectangle**, which has small squares and circles, called **sizing handles**, at each corner and middle location.

Figure 1–46

To Zoom the Document

The next step is to reduce the size of the picture so that both pictures will fit side-by-side on the same line. With the current picture size, the flyer now has expanded to two pages. The final flyer, however, should fit on a single page. In Word, you can change the zoom so that you can see the entire document (that is, both pages) on the screen at once. Seeing the entire document at once helps you determine the appropriate size for the picture. The following step zooms the document.

1

Experiment

- Repeatedly click the Zoom Out and Zoom In buttons on the status bar and watch the size of the document change in the document window.

- Click the Zoom Out or Zoom In button as many times as necessary until the Zoom button on the status bar displays 50% on its face (Figure 1–47).

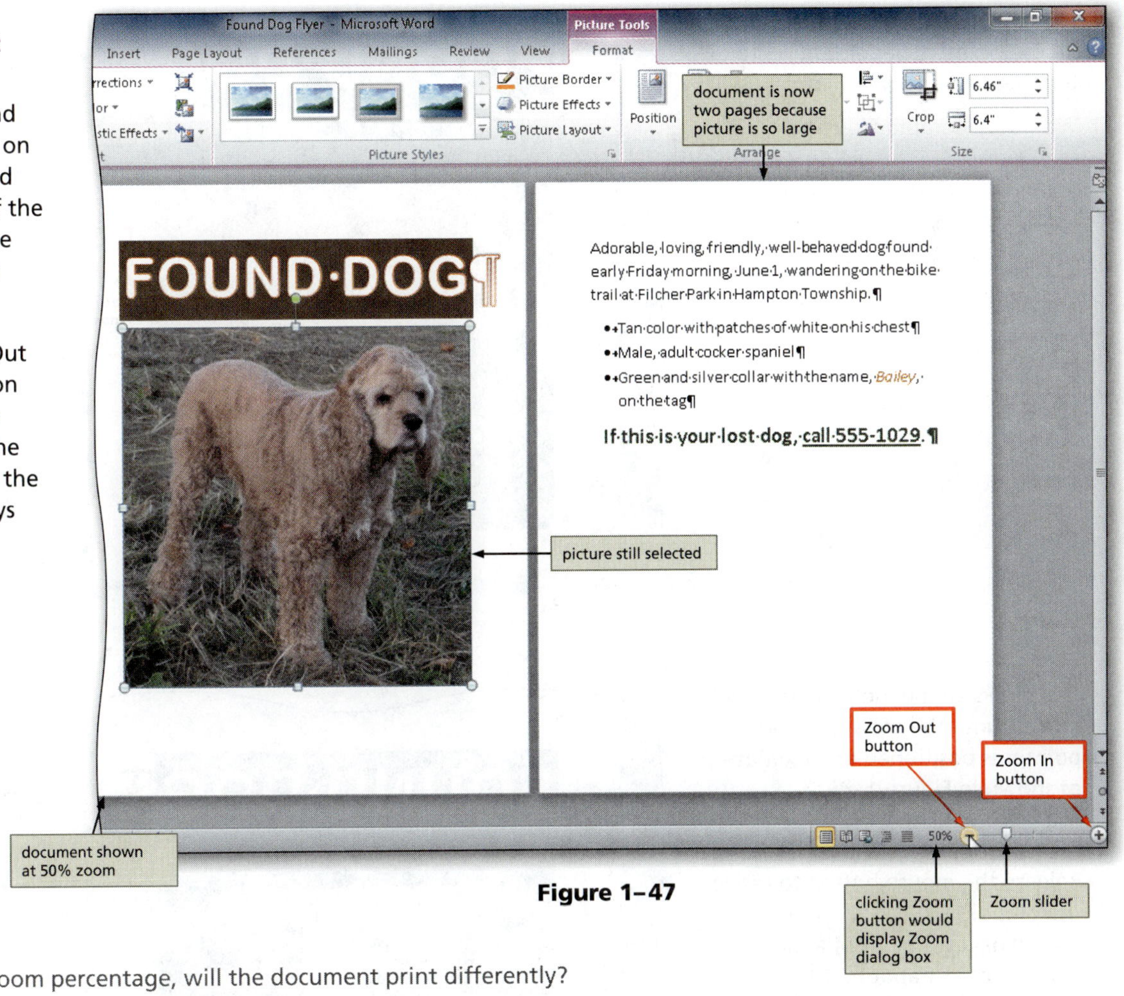

Figure 1–47

Q&A If I change the zoom percentage, will the document print differently?

Changing the zoom has no effect on the printed document.

Q&A Are there predefined zoom options?

Yes. Through the View tab | Zoom group or the Zoom dialog box, you can zoom to one page, two pages, many pages, page width, text width, and a variety of set percentages. Page width zoom places the edges of the page at the edges of the Word window, whereas Text width zoom places the contents of the page at the edges of the Word window.

Other Ways

1. Drag Zoom slider on status bar
2. Click Zoom button on status bar, select desired zoom percent or type (Zoom dialog box), click OK button
3. Click Zoom button (View tab | Zoom group), select desired zoom percent or type (Zoom dialog box), click OK button

To Resize a Graphic

The next step is to resize the picture so that both pictures will fit side-by-side on the same line below the headline. **Resizing** includes both enlarging and reducing the size of a graphic. In this flyer, you will reduce the size of the picture. With the entire document displayed in the document window, you will be able to see how the resized graphic will look on the entire page. The following steps resize a selected graphic.

1

- With the graphic still selected, point to the upper-right corner sizing handle on the picture so that the mouse pointer shape changes to a two-headed arrow (Figure 1–48).

Q&A What if my graphic (picture) is not selected?

To select a graphic, click it.

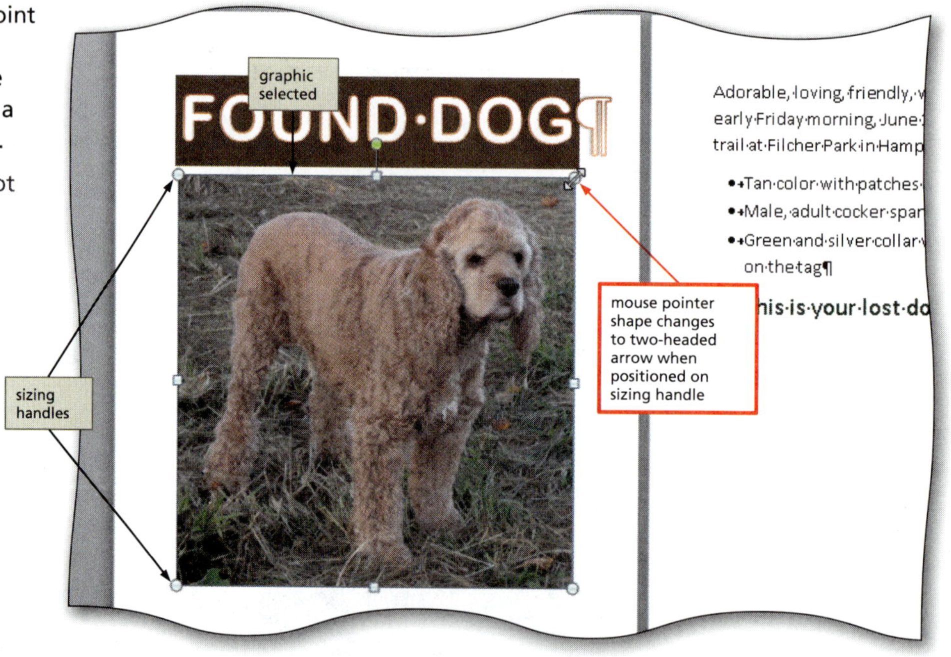

Figure 1–48

2

- Drag the sizing handle diagonally inward until the crosshair mouse pointer is positioned approximately as shown in Figure 1–49.

3

- Release the mouse button to resize the graphic, which in this case should have a height of about 2.74" and a width of about 2.73".

Q&A How can I see the height and width measurements?

Look in the Size group on the Picture Tools Format tab to see the height and width measurements of the currently selected graphic (shown in Figure 1–46 on page WD 32).

Q&A What if the graphic is the wrong size?

Repeat Steps 1, 2, and 3; or enter the desired height and width values in the Shape Height and Shape Width boxes (Picture Tools Format tab | Size group).

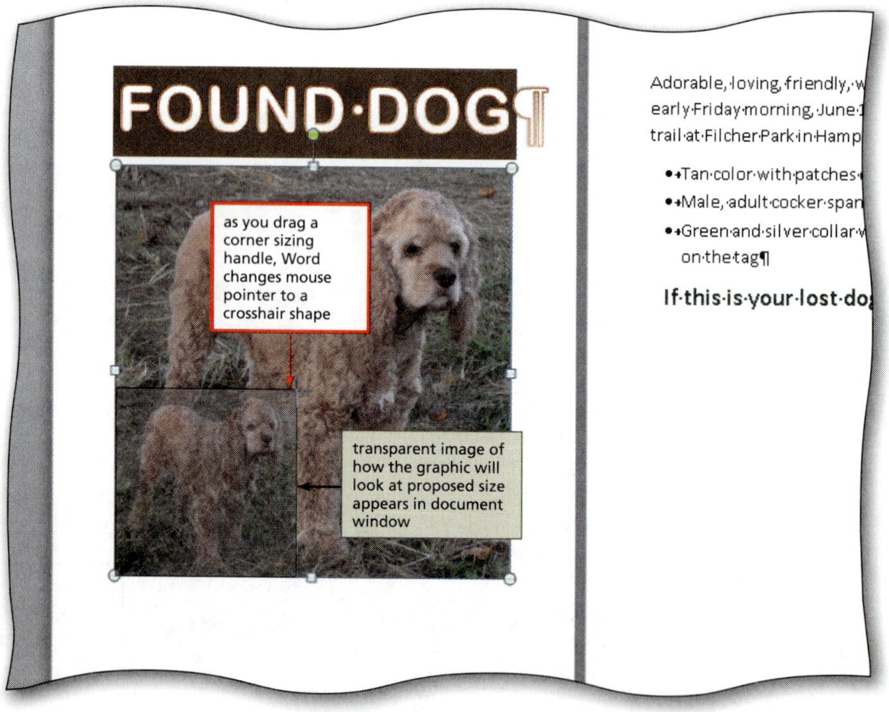

Figure 1–49

4

- Click to the right of the graphic to deselect it (Figure 1–50).

Q&A What happened to the Picture Tools Format tab?

When you click outside of a graphic or press a key to scroll through a document, Word deselects the graphic and removes the Picture Tools Format tab from the screen.

Q&A What if I want to return a graphic to its original size and start again?

With the graphic selected, click the Size Dialog Box Launcher (Picture Tools Format tab | Size group), click the Size tab (Layout dialog box), click the Reset button, and then click the OK button.

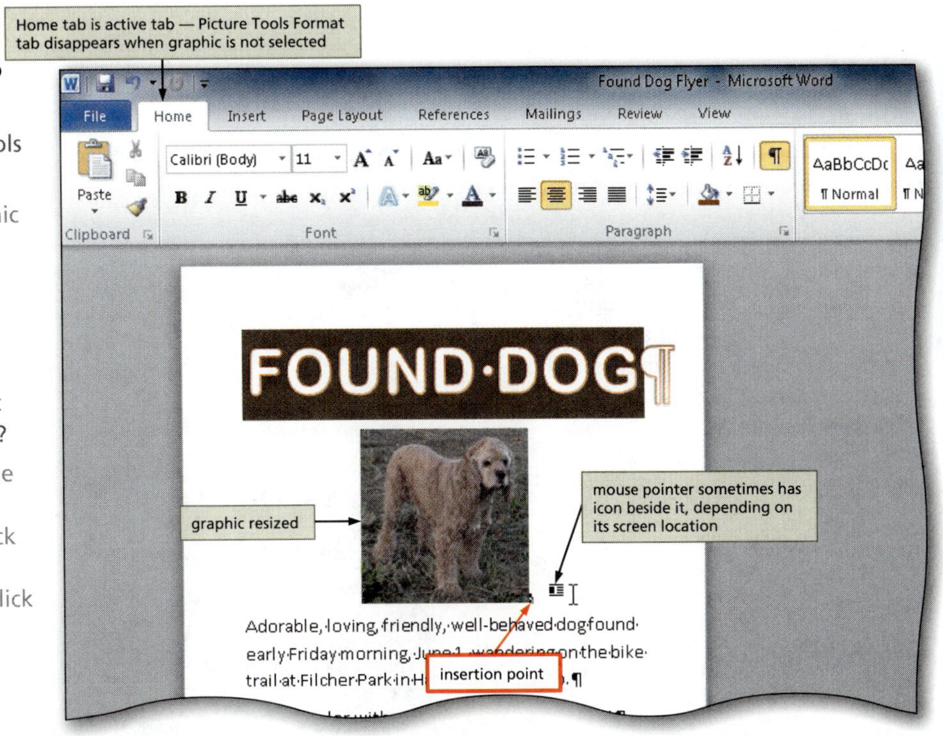

Figure 1–50

Other Ways

1. Enter height and width of graphic in Shape Height and Shape Width boxes (Picture Tools Format tab | Size group)
2. Click Size Dialog Box Launcher (Picture Tools Format tab | Size group), click Size tab (Layout dialog box), enter desired height and width values in boxes, click OK button

To Insert Another Picture

The next step is to insert the other digital picture of the dog immediately to the right of the current picture. This second picture also is available on the Data Files for Students. See the inside back cover of this book for instructions on downloading the Data Files for Students, or contact your instructor for information about accessing the required files.

The following steps insert another picture immediately to the right of the current picture.

1. With the insertion point positioned as shown in Figure 1–50, click Insert on the Ribbon to display the Insert tab.
2. With your USB flash drive connected to one of the computer's USB ports, click the Insert Picture from File button (Insert tab | Illustrations group) to display the Insert Picture dialog box.
3. If necessary, navigate to the picture location (in this case, the Word folder in the CIS 101 folder [or your class folder] on the USB flash drive). For a detailed example of this procedure, refer to Steps 3a – 3c in the To Save a File in a Folder section in the Office 2010 and Windows 7 chapter in this book.
4. Click Dog Picture 2 to select the file.
5. Click the Insert button (Insert Picture dialog box) to insert the picture at the location of the insertion point in the document.

BTW **Word Help**

At any time while using Word, you can find answers to questions and display information about various topics through Word Help. Used properly, this form of assistance can increase your productivity and reduce your frustrations by minimizing the time you spend learning how to use Word. For instruction about Word Help and exercises that will help you gain confidence in using it, read the Office 2010 and Windows 7 in this book.

To Resize a Graphic by Entering Exact Measurements

The next step is to resize the second picture so that it is the exact same size as the first picture. The height and width measurements of the first graphic are approximately 2.74" and 2.73", respectively. When a graphic is selected, its height and width measurements show in the Size group of the Picture Tools Format tab. The following steps resize a selected graphic by entering its desired exact measurements.

1

- With the second graphic still selected, click the Shape Height box (Picture Tools Format tab | Size group) to select the contents in the box and then type `2.74` as the height.

Q&A What if the Picture Tools Format tab no longer is displayed on my Ribbon?

Double-click the picture to display the Picture Tools Format tab.

Q&A What if the contents of the Shape Height box are not selected?

Triple-click the Shape Height box.

2

- Click the Shape Width box to select the contents in the box, type `2.73` as the width, and then click the picture to apply the settings.
- If necessary, scroll up to display the entire document in the window (Figure 1–51).

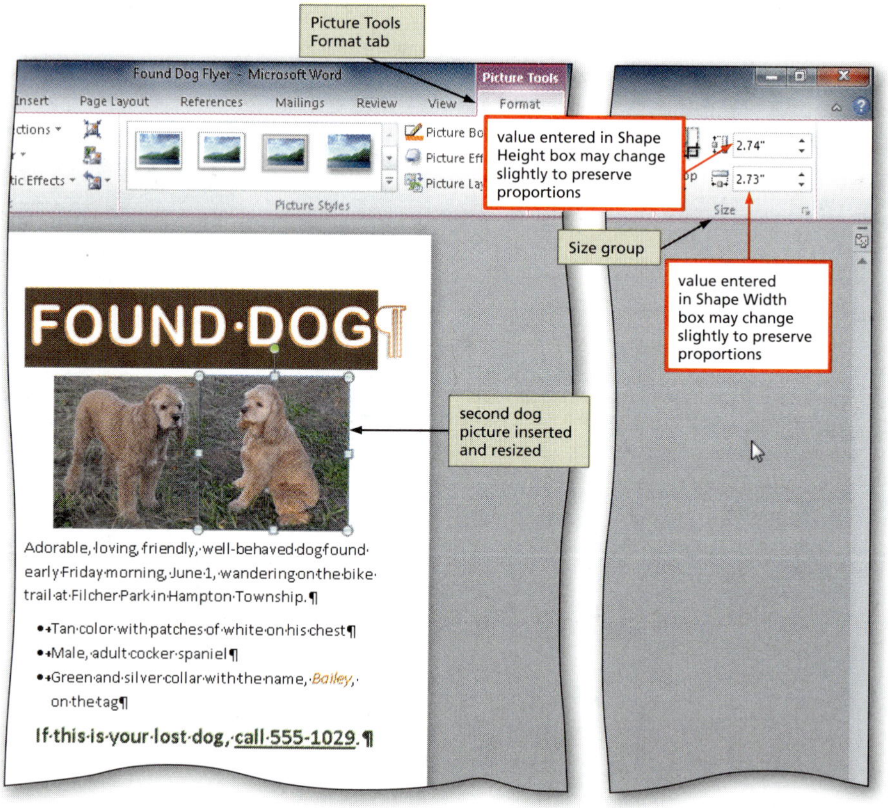

Figure 1–51

Q&A Why did my measurements change slightly?

Depending on relative measurements, the height and width values entered may change slightly.

Other Ways		
1. Right-click picture, enter shape height and width values in boxes on shortcut menu	2. Right-click picture, click Size and Position on shortcut menu, click Size tab (Layout dialog box),	enter shape height and width values in boxes, click OK button

To Zoom the Document

You are finished resizing the graphics and no longer need to view the entire page in the document window. Thus, the following step changes the zoom back to 100 percent.

1 Click the Zoom In button on the status bar as many times as necessary until the Zoom button displays 100% on its face (shown in Figure 1–52).

To Apply a Picture Style

A **style** is a named group of formatting characteristics. Word provides more than 25 picture styles that enable you easily to change a picture's look to a more visually appealing style, including a variety of shapes, angles, borders, and reflections. The flyer in this chapter uses a style that applies soft edges to the picture. The following steps apply a picture style to a picture.

1

- Click the leftmost dog picture to select it (Figure 1–52).

Q&A What is the green circle attached to the selected graphic?

It is called a rotate handle. When you drag a graphic's rotate handle, the graphic moves in either a clockwise or counterclockwise direction.

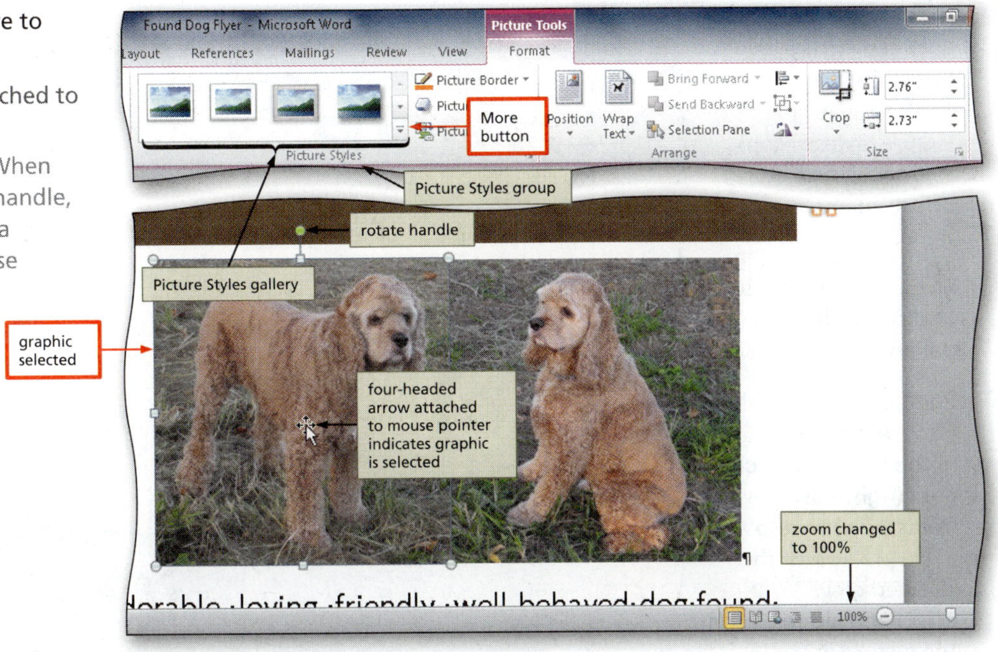

Figure 1–52

2

- Click the More button in the Picture Styles gallery (Picture Tools Format tab | Picture Styles group) (shown in Figure 1–52) to expand the gallery.
- Point to Soft Edge Rectangle in the Picture Styles gallery to display a live preview of that style applied to the picture in the document (Figure 1–53).

Experiment

- Point to various picture styles in the Picture Styles gallery and watch the style of the picture change in the document window.

3

- Click Soft Edge Rectangle in the Picture Styles gallery to apply the style to the selected picture.

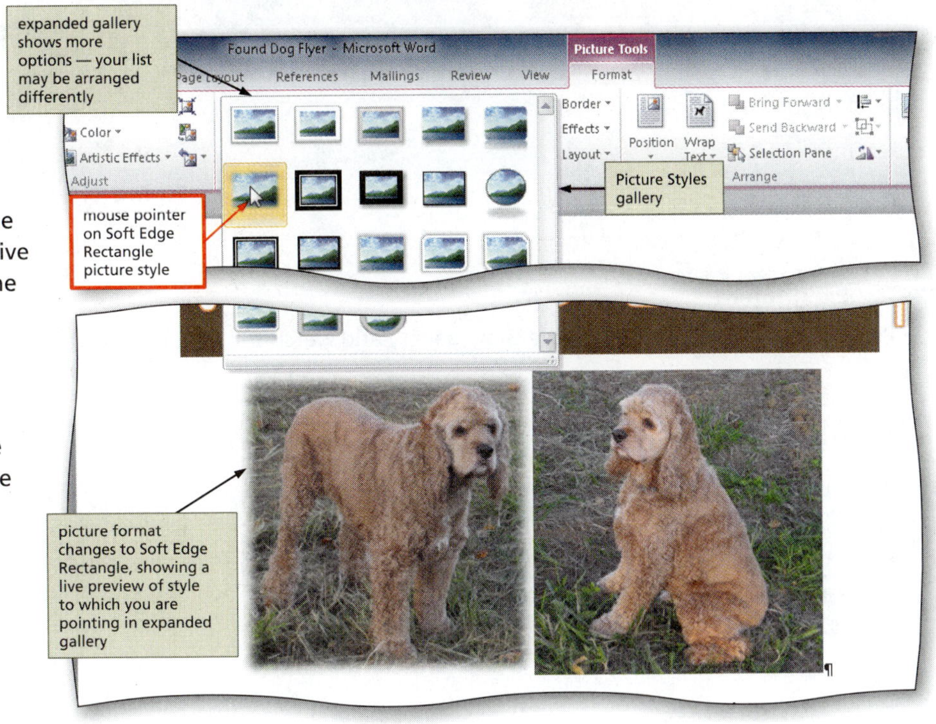

Figure 1–53

To Apply Picture Effects

Word provides a variety of picture effects so that you can further customize a picture. Effects include shadows, reflections, glow, soft edges, bevel, and 3-D rotation. The difference between the effects and the styles is that each effect has several options, providing you with more control over the exact look of the image.

In this flyer, the leftmost dog picture has a slight tan glow effect and is turned inward toward the center of the page. The following steps apply picture effects to the selected picture.

1

- Click the Picture Effects button (Picture Tools Format tab | Picture Styles group) to display the Picture Effects menu.
- Point to Glow on the Picture Effects menu to display the Glow gallery.
- Point to Tan, 5 pt glow, Accent color 6 in the Glow Variations area (rightmost glow in first row) to display a live preview of the selected glow effect applied to the picture in the document window (Figure 1–54).

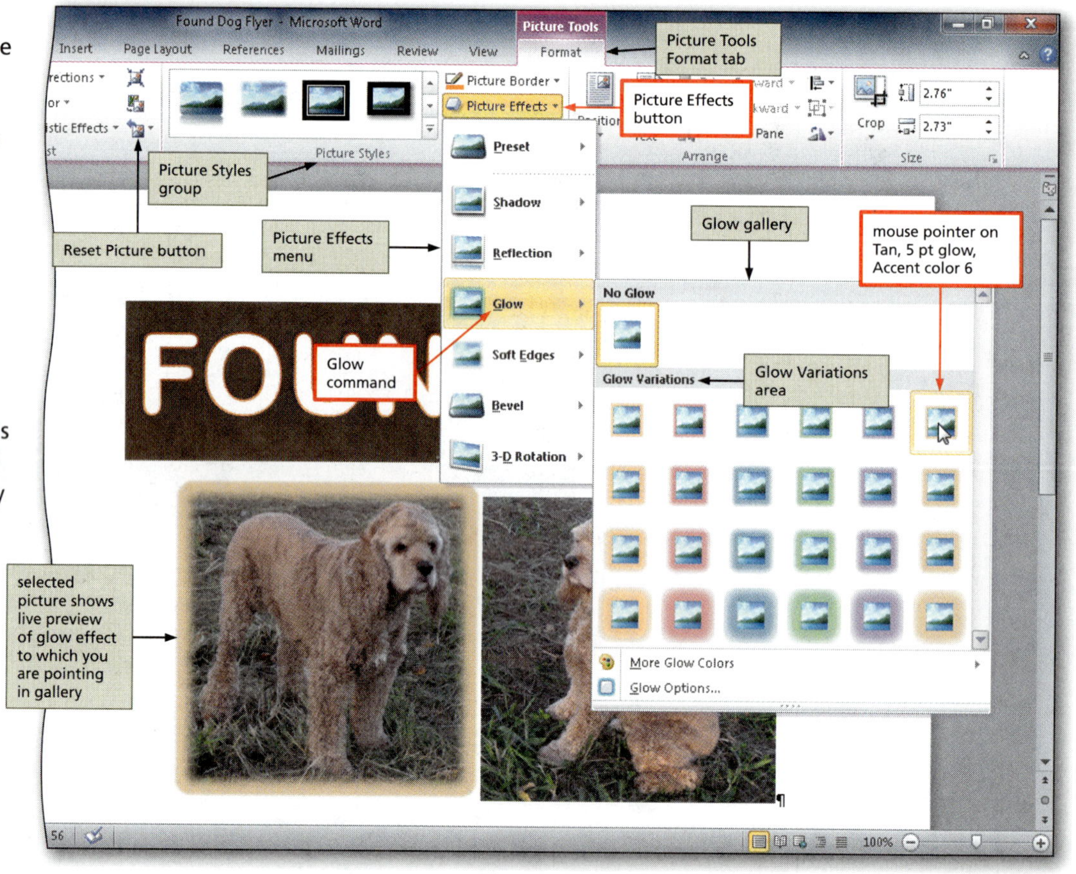

Figure 1–54

Experiment

- Point to various glow effects in the Glow gallery and watch the picture change in the document window.

2

- Click Tan, 5 pt glow, Accent color 6 in the Glow gallery to apply the selected picture effect.

Q&A

What if I wanted to discard formatting applied to a picture?

You would click the Reset Picture button (Picture Tools Format tab | Adjust group). To reset formatting and size, you would click the Reset Picture button arrow (Picture Tools Format tab | Adjust group) and then click Reset Picture & Size on the Reset Picture menu.

3

- Click the Picture Effects button (Picture Tools Format tab | Picture Styles group) to display the Picture Effects menu again.
- Point to 3-D Rotation on the Picture Effects menu to display the 3-D Rotation gallery.
- Point to Off Axis 1 Right in the Parallel area (second rotation in second row) to display a live preview of the selected 3-D effect applied to the picture in the document window (Figure 1–55).

Experiment

- Point to various 3-D rotation effects in the 3-D Rotation gallery and watch the picture change in the document window.

4

- Click Off Axis 1 Right in the 3-D Rotation gallery to apply the selected picture effect.

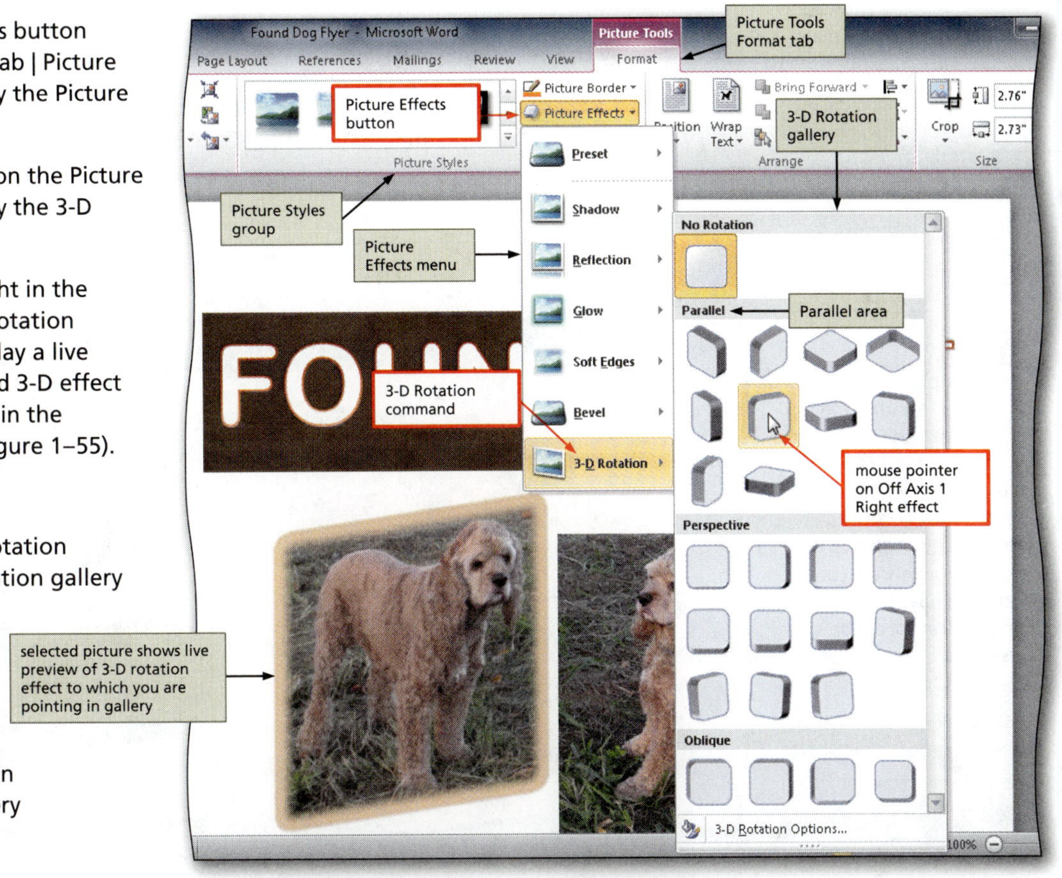

Figure 1–55

Other Ways

1. Right-click picture, click Format Picture on shortcut menu, select desired options (Format Picture dialog box), click Close button
2. Click Format Shape Dialog Box Launcher (Picture Tools Format tab | Picture Styles group), select desired options (Format Picture dialog box), click Close button

To Apply a Picture Style and Effects to Another Picture

In this flyer, the rightmost dog picture also uses the soft edge picture style, has a slight tan glow effect, and is turned inward toward the center of the page. The following steps apply the picture style and picture effects to the picture.

1. Click the rightmost dog picture to select it.
2. Click the More button in the Picture Styles gallery (Picture Tools Format tab | Picture Styles group) to expand the gallery and then click Soft Edge Rectangle in the Picture Styles gallery to apply the selected style to the picture.
3. Click the Picture Effects button (Picture Tools Format tab | Picture Styles group) to display the Picture Effects menu and then point to Glow on the Picture Effects menu to display the Glow gallery.
4. Click Tan, 5 pt glow, Accent color 6 (rightmost glow in first row) in the Glow gallery to apply the picture effect to the picture.

5. Click the Picture Effects button (Picture Tools Format tab | Picture Styles group) to display the Picture Effects menu again and then point to 3-D Rotation on the Picture Effects menu to display the 3-D Rotation gallery.

6. Click Off Axis 2 Left (rightmost rotation in second row) in the Parallel area in the 3-D Rotation gallery to apply the picture effect to the selected picture.

7. Click to the right of the picture to deselect it (Figure 1–56).

BTW **BTWs**
For a complete list of the BTWs found in the margins of the Office and Windows chapters in this book, visit the Microsoft Office and Concepts CourseMate Web site at www.cengagebrain.com and then navigate to the BTW resource for this book.

Figure 1–56

Enhancing the Page

BTW **Centering Page Contents Vertically**
You can center page contents vertically between the top and bottom margins. To do this, click the Page Setup Dialog Box Launcher (Page Layout tab | Page Setup group), click the Layout tab (Page Setup dialog box), click the Vertical alignment box arrow, click Center in the list, and then click the OK button.

With the text and graphics entered and formatted, the next step is to look at the page as a whole and determine if it looks finished in its current state. As you review the page, answer these questions:

- Does it need a page border to frame its contents, or would a page border make it look too busy?
- Is the spacing between paragraphs and graphics on the page adequate? Do any sections of text or graphics look as if they are positioned too closely to the items above or below them?

You determine that a graphical, color-coordinated border would enhance the flyer. You also notice that the flyer would look more proportionate if it had a little more space above and below the pictures. The following pages make these enhancements to the flyer.

To View One Page

Earlier in this chapter, you changed the zoom using the Zoom Out and Zoom In buttons on the status bar. If you want to display an entire page as large as possible in the document window, Word can compute the correct zoom percentage for you. The next steps display a single page in its entirety in the document window as large as possible.

1

- Click View on the Ribbon to display the View tab.

2

- Click the One Page button (View tab | Zoom group) to display the entire page in the document window as large as possible (Figure 1–57).

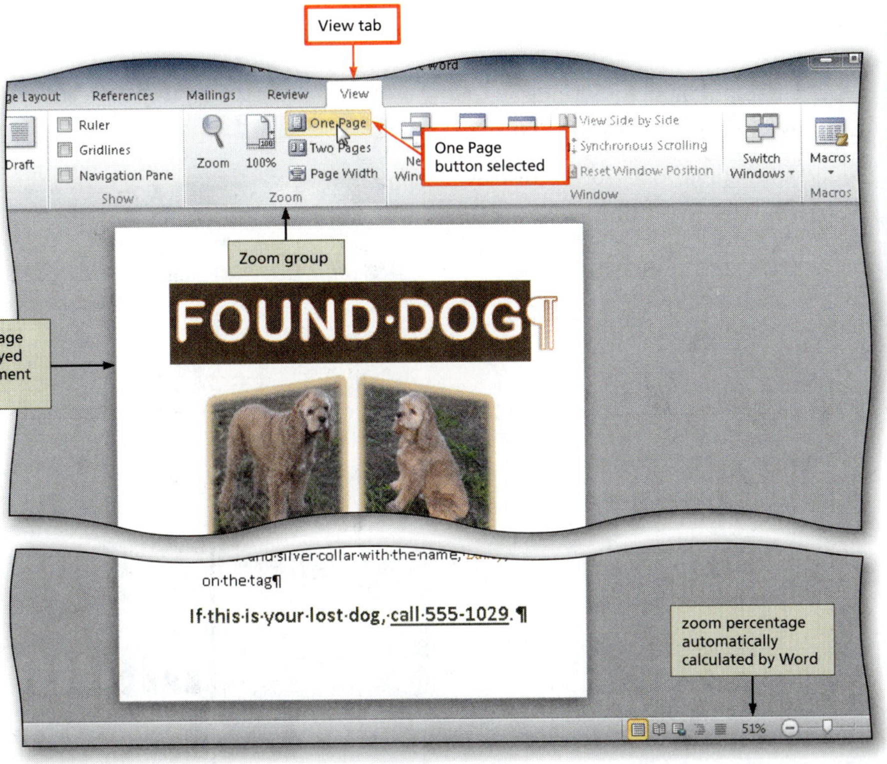

Figure 1–57

To Add a Page Border

In Word, you can add a border around the perimeter of an entire page. The flyer in this chapter has a light green dashed border. The following steps add a page border.

1

- Click Page Layout on the Ribbon to display the Page Layout tab.
- Click the Page Borders button (Page Layout tab | Page Background group) to display the Borders and Shading dialog box (Figure 1–58).

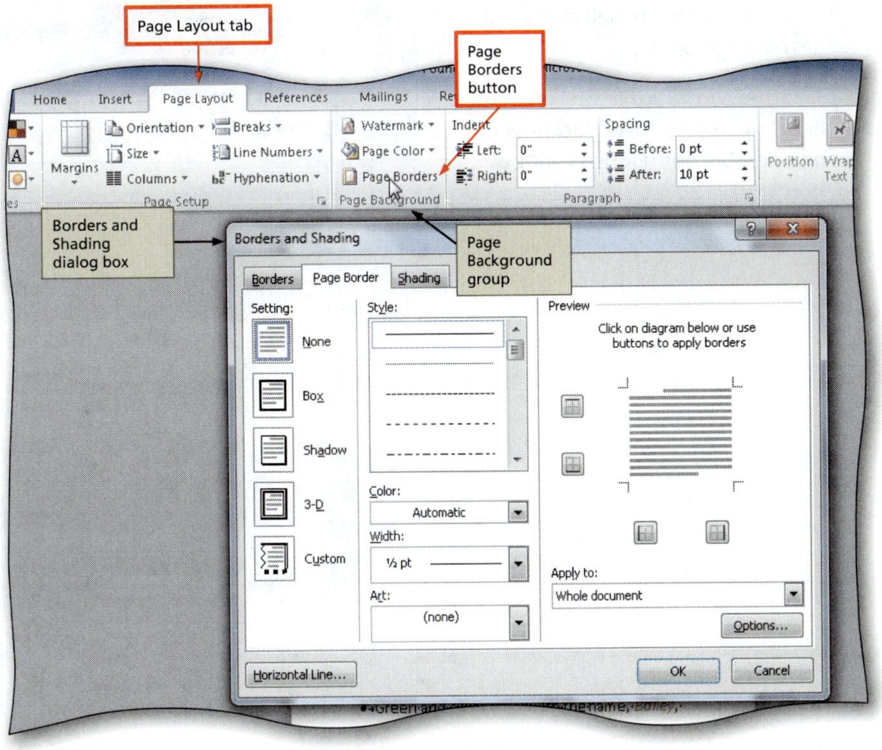

Figure 1–58

2

- Scroll through the Style list (Borders and Shading dialog box) and select the style shown in Figure 1–59.
- Click the Color box arrow to display a Color palette (Figure 1–59).

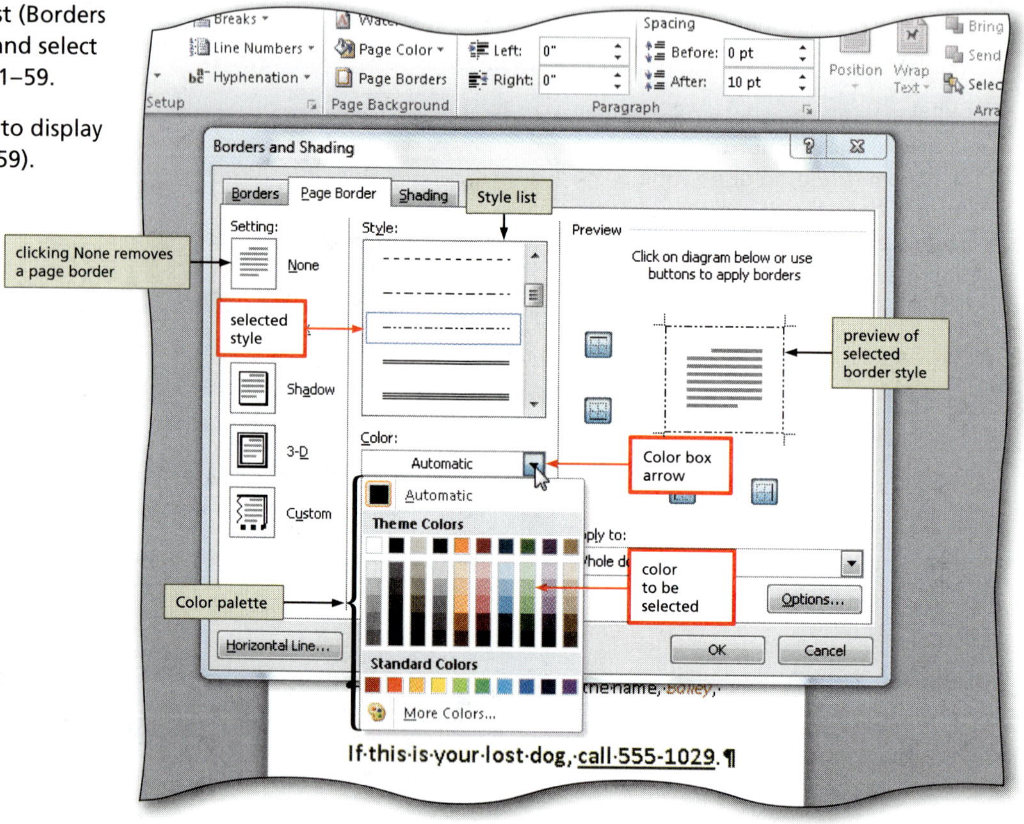

Figure 1–59

3

- Click Dark Green, Accent 4, Lighter 60% (eighth color in third row) in the Color palette to select the color for the page border.
- Click the Width box arrow and then click 3 pt to select the thickness of the page border (Figure 1–60).

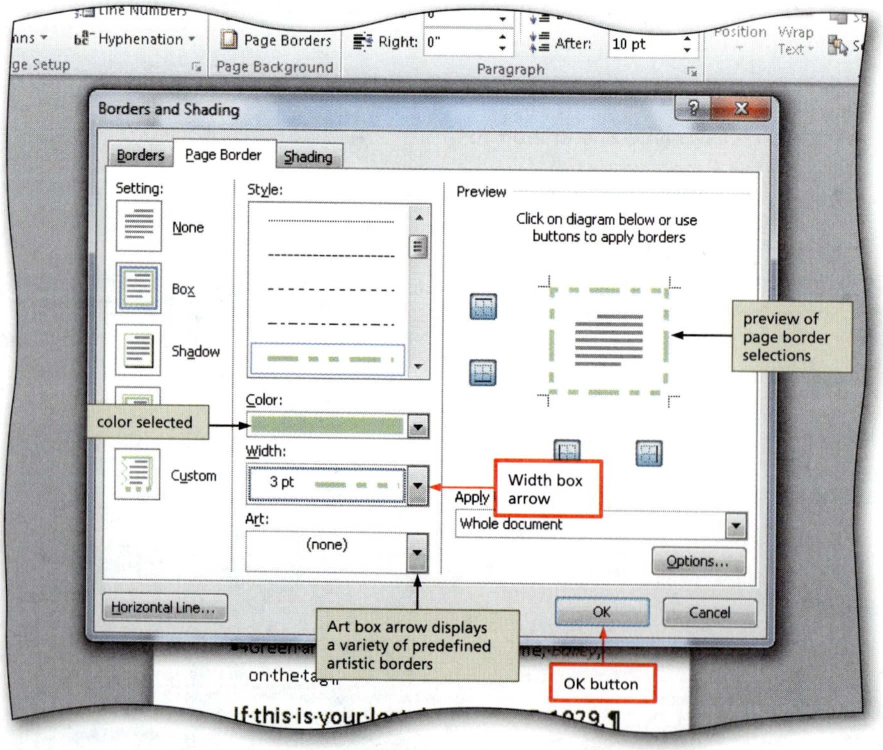

Figure 1–60

4

- Click the OK button to add the border to the page (Figure 1–61).

Q&A What if I wanted to remove the border?

You would click None in the Setting list in the Borders and Shading dialog box.

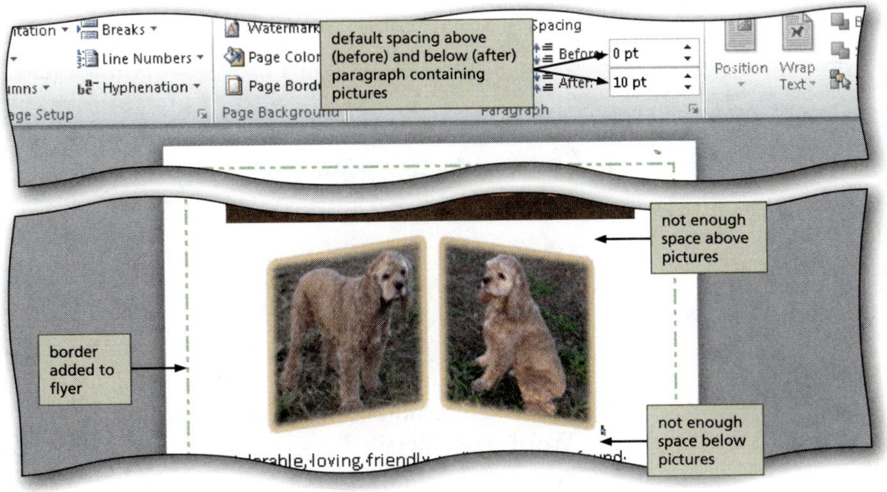

Figure 1–61

To Change Spacing before and after a Paragraph

The default spacing above (before) a paragraph in Word is 0 points and below (after) is 10 points. In the flyer, you want to increase the spacing above and below the paragraph containing the pictures. The following steps change the spacing above and below a paragraph.

1

- Position the insertion point in the paragraph to be adjusted, in this case, the paragraph containing the pictures.
- Click the Spacing Before box up arrow (Page Layout tab | Paragraph group) as many times as necessary until 24 pt is displayed in the Spacing Before box to increase the space above the current paragraph.

2

- Click the Spacing After box up arrow (Page Layout tab | Paragraph group) so that 12 pt is displayed in the Spacing After box to increase the space below the current paragraph (Figure 1–62).
- If the text flows to two pages, reduce the spacing above and below paragraphs as necessary.

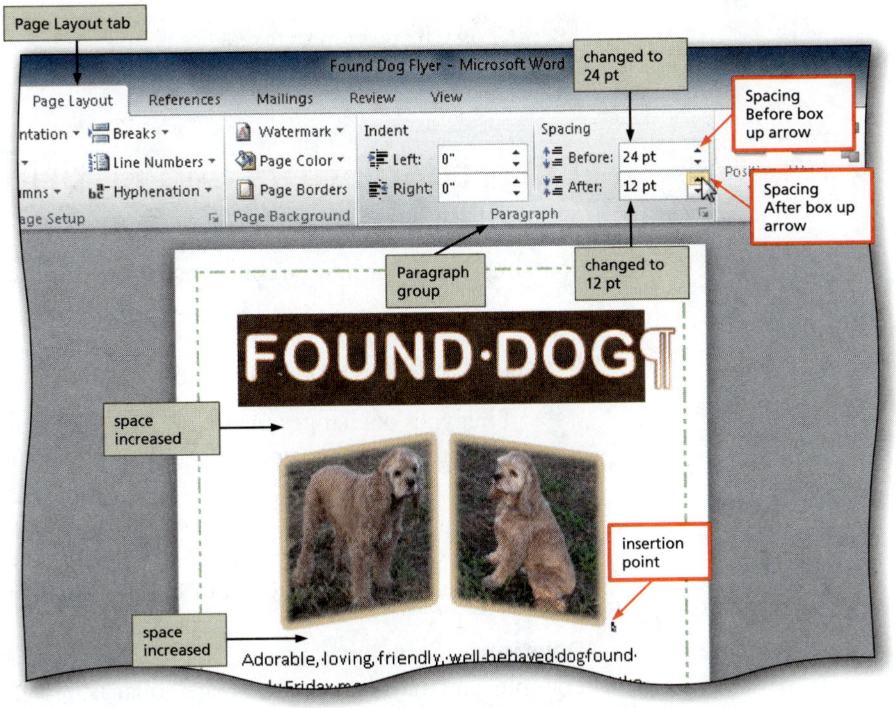

Figure 1–62

Other Ways

1. Right-click paragraph, click Paragraph on shortcut menu, click Indents and Spacing tab (Paragraph dialog box), enter spacing before and after values, click OK button
2. Click Paragraph Dialog Box Launcher (Home tab or Page Layout tab | Paragraph group), click Indents and Spacing tab (Paragraph dialog box), enter spacing before and after values, click OK button

To Save an Existing Document with the Same File Name

You have made several modifications to the document since you last saved it. Thus, you should save it again. The following step saves the document again. For an example of the step listed below, refer to the Office 2010 and Windows 7 chapter in this book.

1. Click the Save button on the Quick Access Toolbar to overwrite the previously saved file.

To Quit Word

Although you still need to make some edits to this document, you want to quit Word and resume working on the project at a later time. Thus, the following steps quit Word. For a detailed example of the procedure summarized below, refer to the Office 2010 and Windows 7 chapter in this book.

1. If you have one Word document open, click the Close button on the right side of the title bar to close the document and quit Word; or if you have multiple Word documents open, click File on the Ribbon to open the Backstage view and then click Exit in the Backstage view to close all open documents and quit Word.
2. If a Microsoft Word dialog box appears, click the Save button to save any changes made to the document since the last save.

Break Point: If you wish to take a break, this is a good place to do so. To resume at a later time, continue following the steps from this location forward.

Correcting Errors and Revising a Document

After creating a document, you may need to change it. For example, the document may contain an error, or new circumstances may require you to add text to the document.

Types of Changes Made to Documents

The types of changes made to documents normally fall into one of the three following categories: additions, deletions, or modifications.

Additions Additional words, sentences, or paragraphs may be required in a document. Additions occur when you omit text from a document and want to insert it later. For example, you may want to add your e-mail address to the flyer.

Deletions Sometimes, text in a document is incorrect or is no longer needed. For example, you may discover the dog's collar is just green. In this case, you would delete the words, and silver, from the flyer.

Modifications If an error is made in a document or changes take place that affect the document, you might have to revise a word(s) in the text. For example, the dog may have been found in Hampton Village instead of Hampton Township.

To Start Word

Once you have created and saved a document, you may need to retrieve it from your storage medium. For example, you might want to revise the document or print it. The following steps, which assume Windows 7 is running, start Word so that you can open and modify the flyer. You may need to ask your instructor how to start Word for your computer. For a detailed example of the procedure summarized below, refer to the Office 2010 and Windows 7 chapter in this book.

1. Click the Start button on the Windows 7 taskbar to display the Start menu.
2. Type `Microsoft Word` as the search text in the 'Search programs and files' text box and watch the search results appear on the Start menu.
3. Click Microsoft Word 2010 in the search results on the Start menu to start Word and display a new blank document in the Word window.
4. If the Word window is not maximized, click the Maximize button next to the Close button on its title bar to maximize the window.

To Open a Document from Word

Earlier in this chapter, you saved your project on a USB flash drive using the file name, Found Dog Flyer. The following steps open the Found Dog Flyer file from the Word folder in the CIS 101 folder on the USB flash drive. For a detailed example of the procedure summarized below, refer to the Office 2010 and Windows 7 chapter in this book.

1. With your USB flash drive connected to one of the computer's USB ports, click File on the Ribbon to open the Backstage view.
2. Click Open in the Backstage view to display the Open dialog box.
3. Navigate to the location of the file to be opened (in this case, the Word folder in the CIS 101 folder [or your class folder] on the USB flash drive). For a detailed example of this procedure, refer to Steps 3a – 3c in the To Save a File in a Folder section in the Office 2010 and Windows 7 chapter in this book.
4. Click Found Dog Flyer to select the file to be opened.
5. Click the Open button (Open dialog box) to open the selected file and display the opened document in the Word window.

Q&A Could I have clicked the Recent tab to open the file?

Yes. Because the file was recently closed, it should appear in the Recent Documents list.

To Zoom the Document

While modifying the document, you prefer the document at 100 percent so that it is easier to read. Thus, the following step changes the zoom back to 100 percent.

1. If necessary, click the Zoom In button on the status bar as many times as necessary until the Zoom button displays 100% on its face (shown in Figure 1–63 on the next page).

To Insert Text in an Existing Document

Word inserts text to the left of the insertion point. The text to the right of the insertion point moves to the right and downward to fit the new text. The following steps insert the word, very, to the left of the word, early, in the flyer.

1

- Scroll through the document and then click to the left of the location of text to be inserted (in this case, the e in early) to position the insertion point where text should be inserted (Figure 1–63).

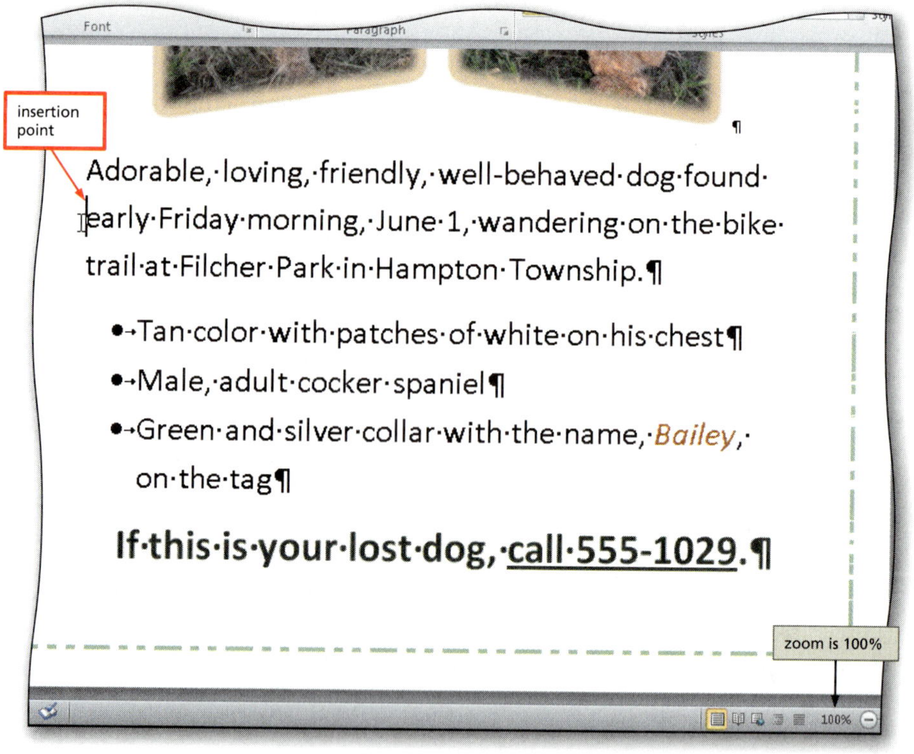

Figure 1–63

2

- Type **very** and then press the SPACEBAR to insert the word to the left of the insertion point (Figure 1–64).

Q&A

Why did the text move to the right as I typed?

In Word, the default typing mode is **insert mode**, which means as you type a character, Word moves all the characters to the right of the typed character one position to the right.

Figure 1–64

Deleting Text from a Document

It is not unusual to type incorrect characters or words in a document. As discussed earlier in this chapter, you can click the Undo button on the Quick Access Toolbar to undo a command or action immediately — this includes typing. Word also provides other methods of correcting typing errors.

To delete an incorrect character in a document, simply click next to the incorrect character and then press the BACKSPACE key to erase to the left of the insertion point, or press the DELETE key to erase to the right of the insertion point.

To Delete Text

To delete a word or phrase, you first must select the word or phrase. The following steps select the word, very, that was just added in the previous steps and then delete the selection.

1

- Position the mouse pointer somewhere in the word to be selected (in this case, very) and then double-click to select the word (Figure 1–65).

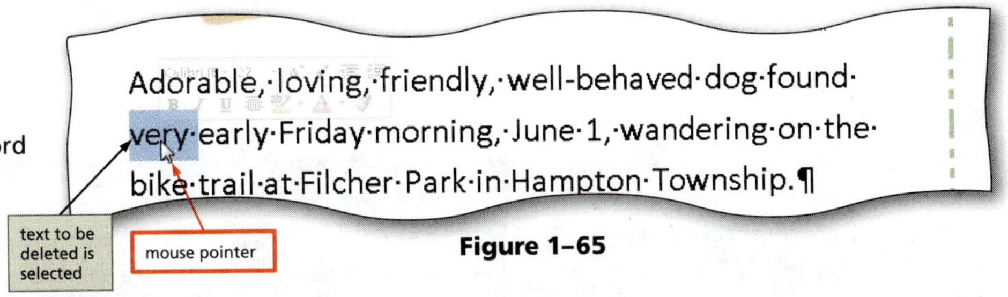

Figure 1–65

2

- With the text selected, press the DELETE key to delete the selected text (shown in Figure 1–63).

To Move Text

While proofreading the flyer, you realize that the body copy would read better if the first two bulleted paragraphs were reversed. An efficient way to move text a short distance, such as reversing two paragraphs, is drag-and-drop editing. With **drag-and-drop editing**, you select the text to be moved and then drag the selected item to the new location and then *drop*, or insert, it there. Another technique for moving text is the cut-and-paste technique, which is discussed in the next chapter. The following steps use drag-and-drop editing to move text.

1

- Position the mouse pointer in the paragraph to be moved (in this case, the second bulleted item) and then triple-click to select the paragraph.
- With the mouse pointer in the selected text, press and hold down the mouse button, which displays a dotted insertion point and a small dotted box with the mouse pointer (Figure 1–66).

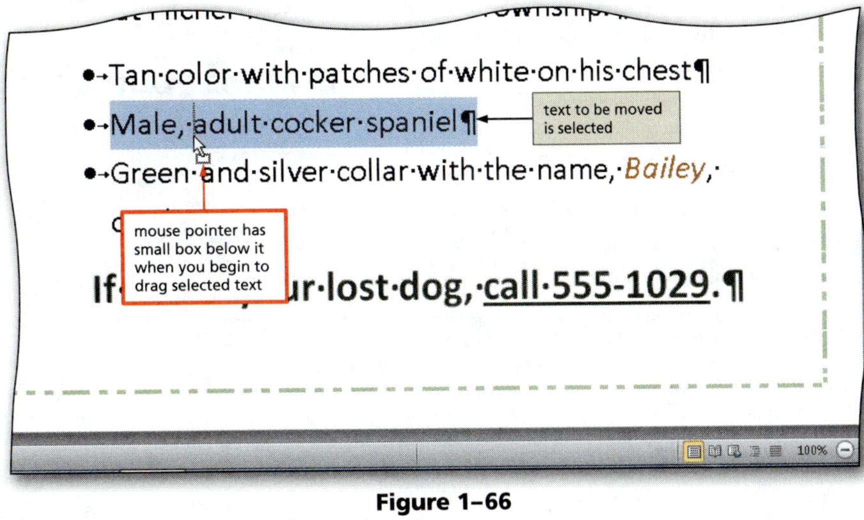

Figure 1–66

2

- Drag the dotted insertion point to the location where the selected text is to be moved, as shown in Figure 1–67.

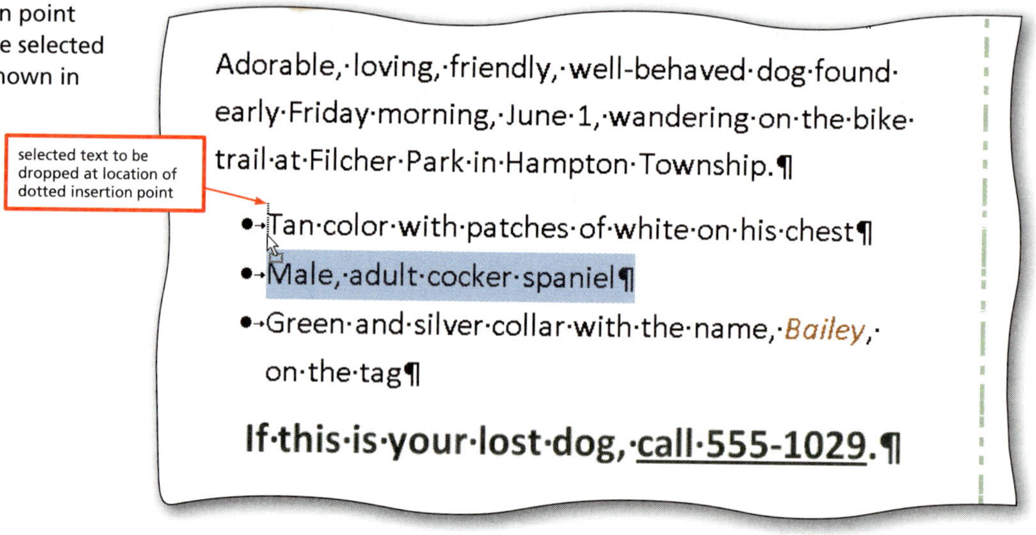

Figure 1–67

3

- Release the mouse button to move the selected text to the location of the dotted insertion point (Figure 1–68).

Q&A What if I accidentally drag text to the wrong location?

Click the Undo button on the Quick Access Toolbar and try again.

Q&A Can I use drag-and-drop editing to move any selected item?

Yes, you can select words, sentences, phrases, and graphics and then use drag-and-drop editing to move them.

Q&A What is the purpose of the Paste Options button?

If you click the Paste Options button, a menu appears that allows you to change the format of the item that was moved. The next chapter discusses the Paste Options menu.

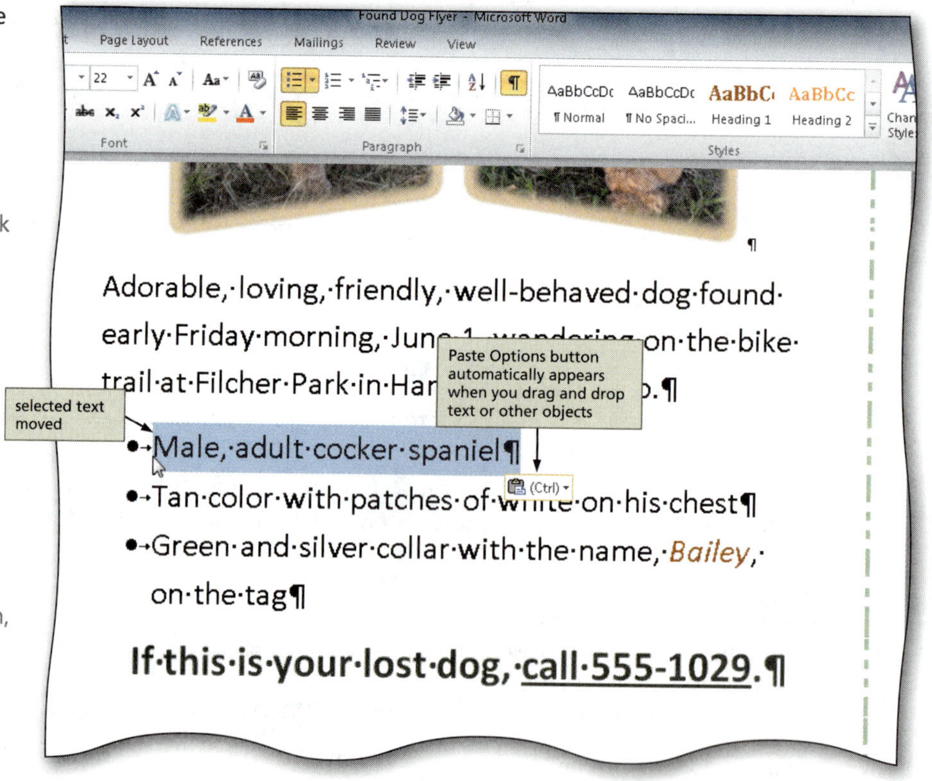

Figure 1–68

- Click anywhere in the document window to remove the selection from the bulleted item.

Other Ways

1. Click Cut button (Home tab | Clipboard group), click where text or object is to be pasted, click Paste button (Home tab | Clipboard group)
2. Right-click selected text, click Cut on shortcut menu, right-click where text or object is to be pasted, click Keep Source Formatting on shortcut menu
3. Press CTRL+X, position insertion point where text or object is to be pasted, press CTRL+V

Changing Document Properties

Word helps you organize and identify your files by using **document properties**, which are the details about a file. Document properties, also known as **metadata**, can include information such as the project author, title, subject, and keywords. A **keyword** is a word or phrase that further describes the document. For example, a class name or document topic can describe the file's purpose or content.

Document properties are valuable for a variety of reasons:

- Users can save time locating a particular file because they can view a document's properties without opening the document.
- By creating consistent properties for files having similar content, users can better organize their documents.
- Some organizations require Word users to add document properties so that other employees can view details about these files.

Five different types of document properties exist, but the more common ones used in the Word chapters in this book are standard and automatically updated properties. **Standard properties** are associated with all Microsoft Office documents and include author, title, and subject. **Automatically updated properties** include file system properties, such as the date you create or change a file, and statistics, such as the file size.

BTW
Printing Document Properties
To print document properties, click File on the Ribbon to open the Backstage view, click the Print tab in the Backstage view to display the Print gallery, click the first button in the Settings area to display a list of options specifying what you can print, click Document Properties in the list to specify you want to print the document properties instead of the actual document, and then click the Print button in the Print gallery to print the document properties on the currently selected printer.

To Change Document Properties

The **Document Information Panel** contains areas where you can view and enter document properties. You can view and change information in this panel at any time while you are creating a document. Before saving the flyer again, you want to add your name and course information as document properties. The following steps use the Document Information Panel to change document properties.

1

- Click File on the Ribbon to open the Backstage view.
- If necessary, click the Info tab to display the Info gallery (Figure 1–69).

Q&A
How do I close the Backstage view?
Click File on the Ribbon or click the preview of the document in the Info gallery to return to the Word document window.

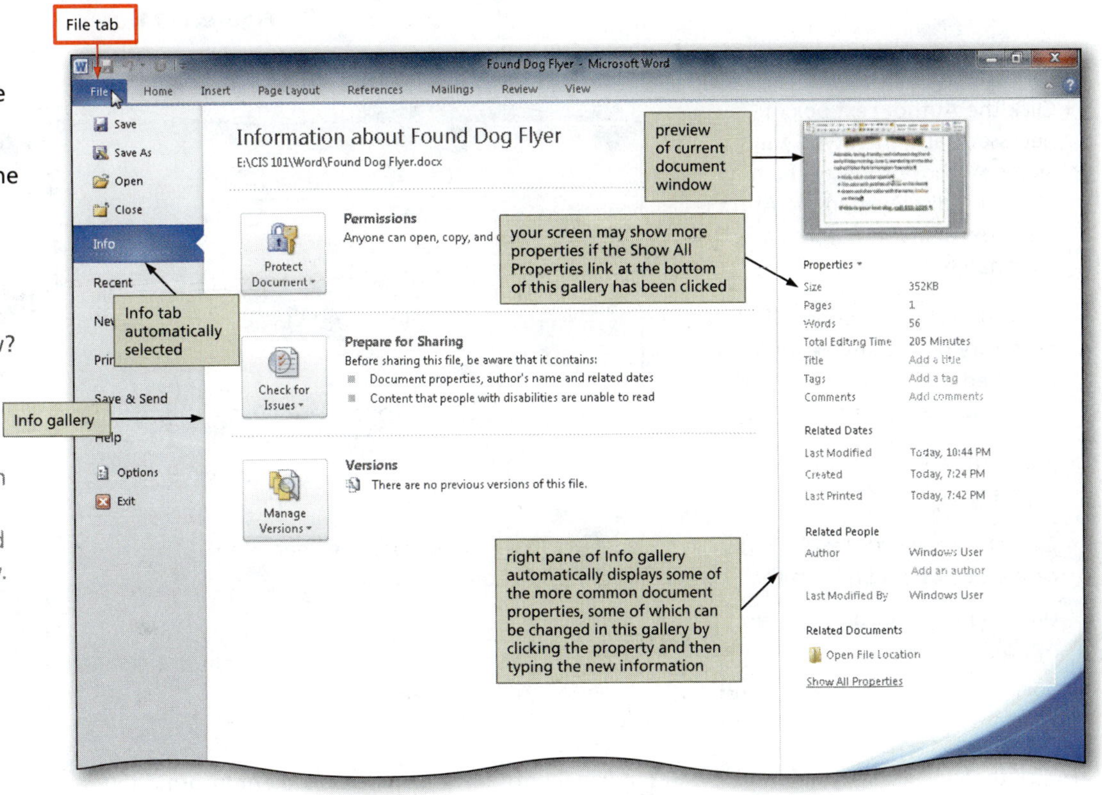

Figure 1–69

2

- Click the Properties button in the right pane of the Info gallery to display the Properties menu (Figure 1–70).

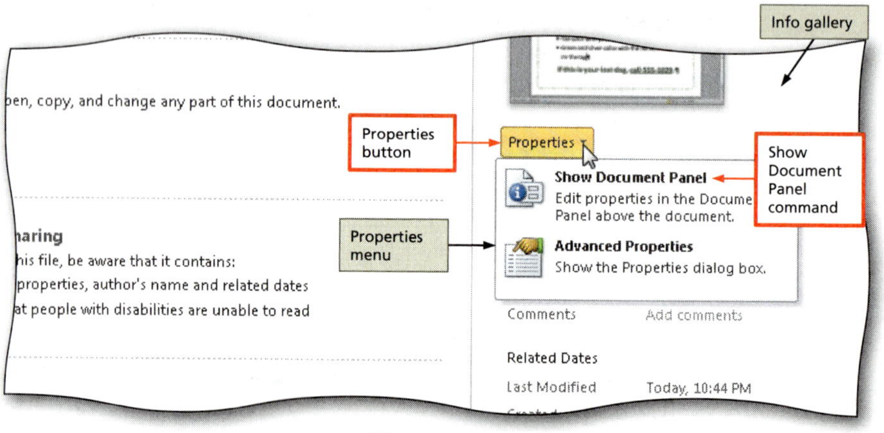

Figure 1–70

3

- Click Show Document Panel on the Properties menu to close the Backstage view and display the Document Information Panel in the Word document window (Figure 1–71).

Q&A Why are some of the document properties in my Document Information Panel already filled in?

The person who installed Microsoft Office 2010 on your computer or network may have set or customized the properties.

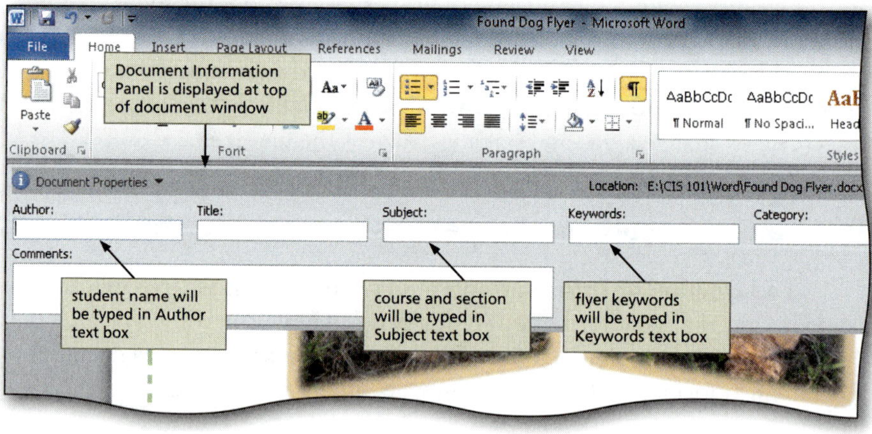

Figure 1–71

4

- Click the Author text box, if necessary, and then type your name as the Author property. If a name already is displayed in the Author text box, delete it before typing your name.
- Click the Subject text box, if necessary delete any existing text, and then type your course and section as the Subject property.
- If an AutoComplete dialog box appears, click its Yes button.

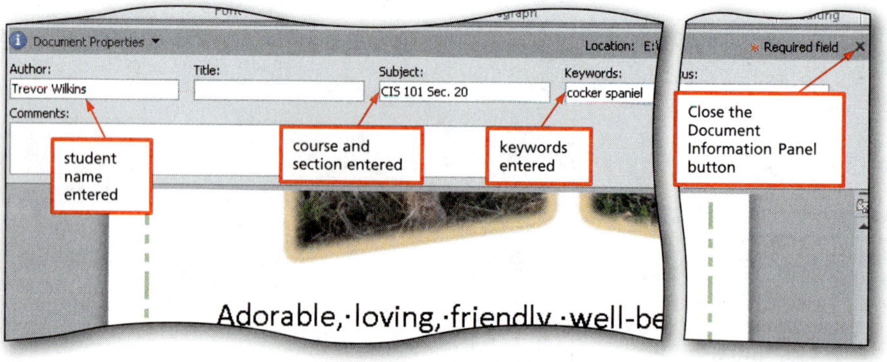

Figure 1–72

- Click the Keywords text box, if necessary delete any existing text, and then type `cocker spaniel` as the Keywords property (Figure 1–72).

Q&A What types of document properties does Word collect automatically?

Word records details such as time spent editing a document, the number of times a document has been revised, and the fonts and themes used in a document.

5

- Click the Close the Document Information Panel button so that the Document Information Panel no longer is displayed.

Other Ways

1. Click File on Ribbon, click Info in Backstage view, if necessary click Show All Properties link in Info gallery, click property to change and then type new information, close Backstage view

To Save an Existing Document with the Same File Name

You are finished editing the flyer. Thus, you should save it again. The following step saves the document again. For an example of the step listed below, refer to the Office 2010 and Windows 7 chapter in this book.

1. Click the Save button on the Quick Access Toolbar to overwrite the previously saved file.

Printing a Document

After creating a document, you may want to print it. Printing a document enables you to distribute the document to others in a form that can be read or viewed but typically not edited. It is a good practice to save a document before printing it, in the event you experience difficulties printing.

Plan Ahead

Determine the best method for distributing the document.

The traditional method of distributing a document uses a printer to produce a hard copy. A **hardcopy** or **printout** is information that exists on a physical medium such as paper. For users that can receive fax documents, you can elect to print a hard copy on a remote fax machine. Hard copies can be useful for the following reasons:

- Many people prefer proofreading a hard copy of a document rather than viewing it on the screen to check for errors and readability.
- Hard copies can serve as reference material if your storage medium is lost or becomes corrupted and you need to recreate the document.

Instead of distributing a hard copy of a document, users can choose to distribute the document as an electronic image that mirrors the original document's appearance. The electronic image of the document can be e-mailed, posted on a Web site, or copied to a portable storage medium such as a USB flash drive. Two popular electronic image formats, sometimes called fixed formats, are PDF by Adobe Systems and XPS by Microsoft. In Word, you can create electronic image files through the Print tab in the Backstage view, the Send & Save tab in the Backstage view, and the Save As dialog box. Electronic images of documents, such as PDF and XPS, can be useful for the following reasons:

- Users can view electronic images of documents without the software that created the original document (e.g., Word). Specifically, to view a PDF file, you use a program called Acrobat Reader, which can be downloaded free from Adobe's Web site. Similarly, to view an XPS file, you use a program called an XPS Viewer, which is included in the latest versions of Windows and Internet Explorer.
- Sending electronic documents saves paper and printer supplies. Society encourages users to contribute to **green computing**, which involves reducing the environmental waste generated when using a computer.

BTW

Conserving Ink and Toner

If you want to conserve ink or toner, you can instruct Word to print draft quality documents by clicking File on the Ribbon to open the Backstage view, clicking Options in the Backstage view to display the Word Options dialog box, clicking Advanced in the left pane (Word Options dialog box), scrolling to the Print area in the right pane, placing a check mark in the 'Use draft quality' check box, and then clicking the OK button. Then, use the Backstage view to print the document as usual.

To Print a Document

With the completed document saved, you may want to print it. Because this flyer is being posted, you will print a hard copy on a printer. The steps on the next page print a hard copy of the contents of the saved Found Dog Flyer document.

1

- Click File on the Ribbon to open the Backstage view.
- Click the Print tab in the Backstage view to display the Print gallery (Figure 1–73).

Q&A How can I print multiple copies of my document?

Increase the number in the Copies box in the Print gallery.

Q&A What if I decide not to print the document at this time?

Click File on the Ribbon to close the Backstage view and return to the Word document window.

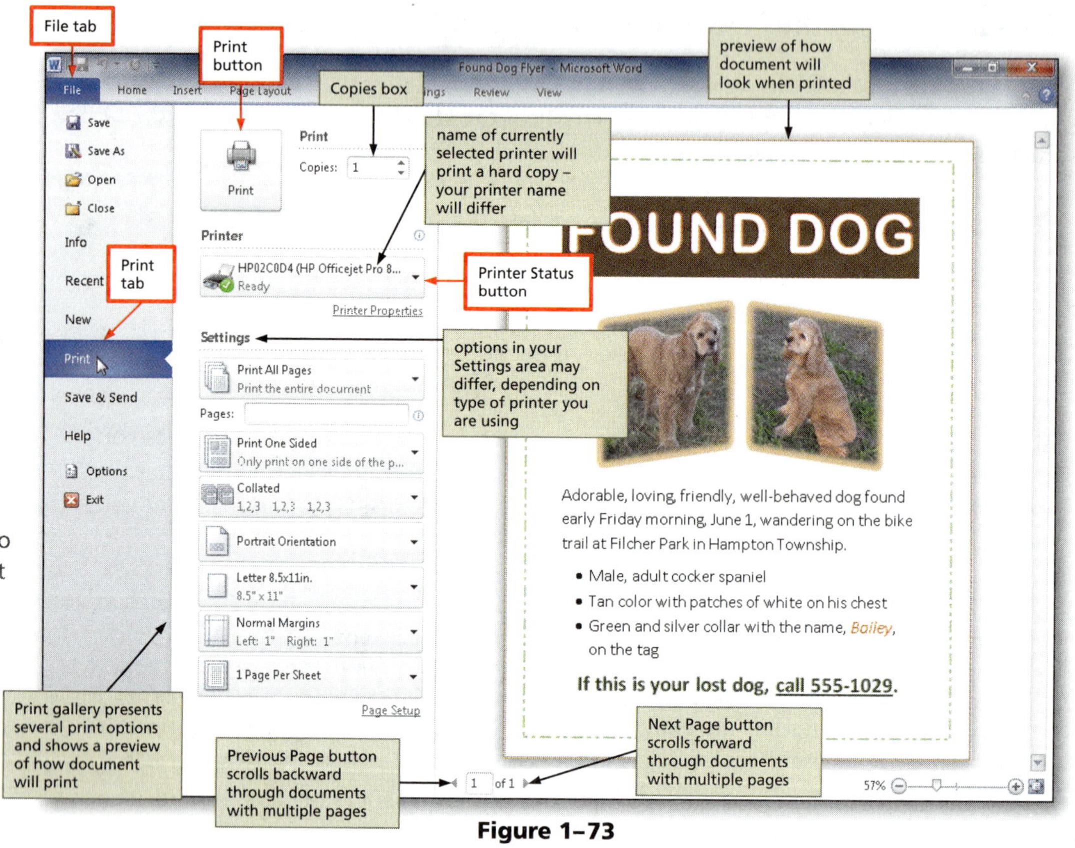

Figure 1–73

2

- Verify the printer name that appears on the Printer Status button will print a hard copy of the document. If necessary, click the Printer Status button to display a list of available printer options and then click the desired printer to change the currently selected printer.

3

- Click the Print button in the Print gallery to print the document on the currently selected printer.
- When the printer stops, retrieve the hard copy (Figure 1–74).

Q&A Do I have to wait until my document is complete to print it?

No, you can follow these steps to print a document at any time while you are creating it.

Q&A What if I want to print an electronic image of a document instead of a hard copy?

You would click the Printer Status button in the Print gallery and then select the desired electronic image option such as a Microsoft XPS Document Writer, which would create an XPS file.

Figure 1–74

Other Ways
1. Press CTRL+P, press ENTER

To Quit Word

The project now is complete. Thus, the following steps quit Word. For an example of the step listed below, refer to the Office 2010 and Windows 7 chapter in this book.

1. If you have one Word document open, click the Close button on the right side of the title bar to close the document and quit Word; or if you have multiple Word documents open, click File on the Ribbon to open the Backstage view and then click Exit in the Backstage view to close all open documents and quit Word.

2. If a Microsoft Word dialog box appears, click the Save button to save any changes made to the document since the last save.

BTW

Printed Borders
If one or more of your borders do not print, click the Page Borders button (Page Layout tab | Page Background group), click the Options button (Borders and Shading dialog box), click the Measure from box arrow and click Text, change the four text boxes to 15 pt, and then click the OK button in each dialog box. Try printing the document again. If the borders still do not print, adjust the text boxes in the dialog box to a number smaller than 15 point.

Chapter Summary

In this chapter, you have learned how to enter text in a document, format text, insert a picture, format a picture, add a page border, and print a document. The items listed below include all the new Word skills you have learned in this chapter.

1. Start Word (WD 4)
2. Type Text (WD 6)
3. Display Formatting Marks (WD 7)
4. Insert a Blank Line (WD 7)
5. Wordwrap Text as You Type (WD 8)
6. Check Spelling and Grammar as You Type (WD 9)
7. Save a Document (WD 12)
8. Center a Paragraph (WD 14)
9. Select a Line (WD 15)
10. Change the Font Size of Selected Text (WD 16)
11. Change the Font of Selected Text (WD 17)
12. Change the Case of Selected Text (WD 18)
13. Apply a Text Effect to Selected Text (WD 19)
14. Shade a Paragraph (WD 20)
15. Select Multiple Lines (WD 21)
16. Bullet a List of Paragraphs (WD 22)
17. Undo and Redo an Action (WD 23)
18. Italicize Text (WD 24)
19. Color Text (WD 25)
20. Use the Mini Toolbar to Format Text (WD 26)
21. Select a Group of Words (WD 27)
22. Underline Text (WD 27)
23. Bold Text (WD 28)
24. Change Theme Colors (WD 28)
25. Save an Existing Document with the Same File Name (WD 30)
26. Insert a Picture (WD 31)
27. Zoom the Document (WD 33)
28. Resize a Graphic (WD 34)
29. Resize a Graphic by Entering Exact Measurements (WD 36)
30. Apply a Picture Style (WD 37)
31. Apply Picture Effects (WD 38)
32. View One Page (WD 40)
33. Add a Page Border (WD 41)
34. Change Spacing before and after a Paragraph (WD 44)
35. Quit Word (WD 44)
36. Open a Document from Word (WD 45)
37. Insert Text in an Existing Document (WD 46)
38. Delete Text (WD 47)
39. Move Text (WD 47)
40. Change Document Properties (WD 49)
41. Print a Document (WD 51)

SAM

If you have a SAM 2010 user profile, your instructor may have assigned an autogradable version of this assignment. If so, log into the SAM 2010 Web site at www.cengage.com/sam2010 to download the instruction and start files.

BTW

Quick Reference
For a table that lists how to complete the tasks covered in the Office chapters in this book using the mouse, Ribbon, shortcut menu, and keyboard, see the Quick Reference Summary at the back of this book, or visit the Microsoft Office and Concepts CourseMate Web site at www.cengagebrain.com and then navigate to the Quick Reference resource for this book.

Learn It Online

Test your knowledge of chapter content and key terms.

Instructions: To complete the Learn It Online exercises, start your browser, visit the Microsoft Office and Concepts CourseMate Web site at www.cengagebrain.com, navigate to the Word Chapter 1 resources for this book, click the link for the exercise you want to complete, and then read the instructions.

Chapter Reinforcement TF, MC, and SA

A series of true/false, multiple choice, and short answer questions that test your knowledge of the chapter content.

Flash Cards

An interactive learning environment where you identify chapter key terms associated with displayed definitions.

Practice Test

A series of multiple choice questions that test your knowledge of chapter content and key terms.

Who Wants To Be a Computer Genius?

An interactive game that challenges your knowledge of chapter content in the style of a television quiz show.

Wheel of Terms

An interactive game that challenges your knowledge of chapter key terms in the style of the television show *Wheel of Fortune.*

Crossword Puzzle Challenge

A crossword puzzle that challenges your knowledge of key terms presented in the chapter.

Apply Your Knowledge

Reinforce the skills and apply the concepts you learned in this chapter.

Modifying Text and Formatting a Document

Note: To complete this assignment, you will be required to use the Data Files for Students. See the inside back cover of this book for instructions on downloading the Data Files for Students, or contact your instructor for information about accessing the required files.

Instructions: Start Word. Open the document, Apply 1-1 Buffalo Photo Shoot Flyer Unformatted, from the Data Files for Students. The document you open is an unformatted flyer. You are to modify text, format paragraphs and characters, and insert a picture in the flyer.

Perform the following tasks:

1. Delete the word, single, in the sentence of body copy below the headline.
2. Insert the word, Creeks, between the words, Twin Buffalo, in the sentence of body copy below the headline.
3. At the end of the signature line, change the period to an exclamation point.
4. Center the headline and the signature line.
5. Change the theme colors to the Aspect color scheme.
6. Change the font and font size of the headline to 48-point Impact, or a similar font. Change the case of the headline text to all capital letters. Apply the text effect called Gradient Fill – Orange, Accent 1, Outline – White to the headline.
7. Change the font size of body copy between the headline and the signature line to 20 point.
8. Use the Mini toolbar to change the font size of the signature line to 26 point.
9. Select the words, hundreds of buffalo, in the paragraph below the headline and underline them.

10. Italicize the word, every, in the paragraph below the headline. Undo this change and then redo the change.
11. Select the three lines (paragraphs) of text above the signature line and add bullets to the selected paragraphs.
12. Switch the last two bulleted paragraphs. That is, select the Questions bullet and move it so that it is the last bulleted paragraph.
13. Bold the first word of each bulleted paragraph. Change the font color of these same three words to Dark Green, Accent 4, Darker 50%.
14. Bold the text in the signature line. Shade the signature line Dark Green, Accent 4, Darker 50%. If the font color does not automatically change to a lighter color, change it to a shade of white.
15. Change the zoom so that the entire page is visible in the document window.
16. Insert the picture of the buffalo centered on the blank line below the headline. The picture is called Buffalo and is available on the Data Files for Students. Apply the Snip Diagonal Corner, White picture style to the inserted picture. Apply the glow called Dark Green, 5 pt glow, Accent color 4 to the picture.
17. Change the spacing after the headline paragraph to 6 point.
18. The entire flyer now should fit on a single page. If it flows to two pages, resize the picture or decrease spacing before and after paragraphs until the entire flyer text fits on a single page.
19. Change the zoom to text width, then page width, then 100% and notice the differences.
20. Enter the text, Twin Creeks, as the keywords in the document properties. Change the other document properties, as specified by your instructor.
21. Click File on the Ribbon and then click Save As. Save the document using the file name, Apply 1-1 Buffalo Photo Shoot Flyer Formatted.
22. Print the document. Submit the revised document, shown in Figure 1–75, in the format specified by your instructor.
23. Quit Word.

Figure 1–75

Extend Your Knowledge

Extend the skills you learned in this chapter and experiment with new skills. You may need to use Help to complete the assignment.

Modifying Text and Picture Formats and Adding Page Borders

Note: To complete this assignment, you will be required to use the Data Files for Students. See the inside back cover of this book for instructions on downloading the Data Files for Students, or contact your instructor for information about accessing the required files.

Instructions: Start Word. Open the document, Extend 1-1 TVC Cruises Flyer, from the Data Files for Students. You will enhance the look of the flyer shown in Figure 1–76. *Hint:* Remember, if you make a mistake while formatting the picture, you can reset it by clicking the Reset Picture button or Reset Picture button arrow (Picture Tools Format tab | Adjust group).

Perform the following tasks:

1. Use Help to learn about the following formats: remove bullets, grow font, shrink font, art page borders, decorative underline(s), picture bullets, picture border shading, shadow picture effects, and color saturation and tone.
2. Remove the bullet from the paragraph below the picture.
3. Select the text, 10 percent, and use the Grow Font button to increase its font size.
4. Add an art page border to the flyer. If the border is not in color, add color to it.
5. Change the solid underline below the word, cruises, to a decorative underline. Change the color of the underline.
6. Change the style of the bullets to picture bullet(s).
7. Change the color of the picture border. Add a shadow picture effect to the picture.
8. Change the color saturation and color tone of the picture.
9. Change the document properties, including keywords, as specified by your instructor. Save the revised document with a new file name and then submit it in the format specified by your instructor.

Figure 1–76

Make It Right

Analyze a document and correct all errors and/or improve the design.

Correcting Spelling and Grammar Errors

Note: To complete this assignment, you will be required to use the Data Files for Students. See the inside back cover of this book for instructions on downloading the Data Files for Students, or contact your instructor for information about accessing the required files.

Instructions: Start Word. Open the document, Make It Right 1-1 Karate Academy Flyer Unchecked, from the Data Files for Students. The document is a flyer that contains spelling and grammar errors, as shown in Figure 1–77. You are to correct each spelling (red wavy underline) and grammar error (green and blue wavy underlines) by right-clicking the flagged text and then clicking the appropriate correction on the shortcut menu.

If your screen does not display the wavy underlines, click File on the Ribbon and then click Options in the Backstage view. When the Word Options dialog box is displayed, click Proofing in the left pane, be sure the 'Hide spelling errors in this document only' and 'Hide grammar errors in this document only' check boxes do not contain check marks, and then click the OK button. If your screen still does not display the wavy underlines, redisplay the Word Options dialog box, click Proofing, and then click the Recheck Document button.

Change the document properties, including keywords, as specified by your instructor. Save the revised document with the name, Make It Right 1-1 Karate Academy Flyer, and then submit it in the format specified by your instructor.

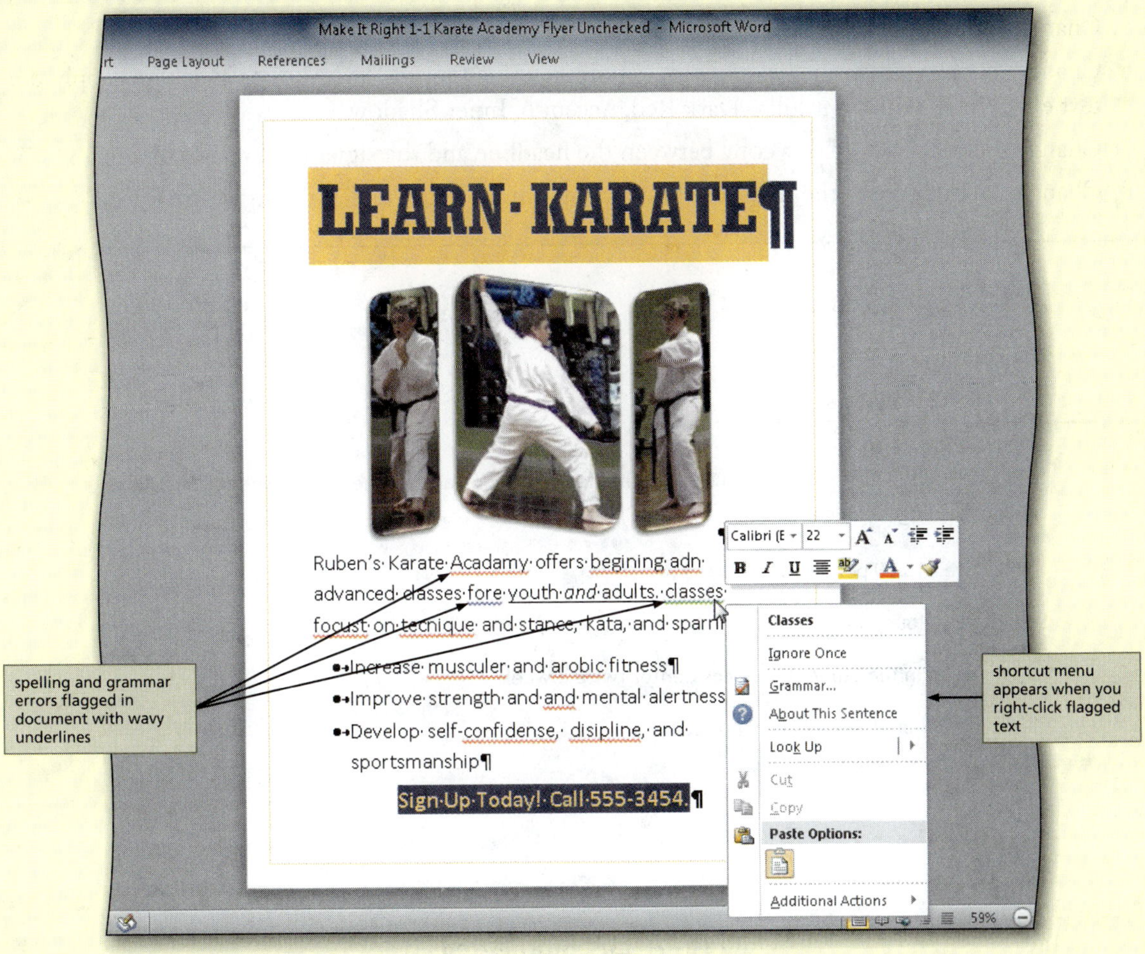

Figure 1–77

In the Lab

Design and/or create a document using the guidelines, concepts, and skills presented in this chapter. Labs are listed in order of increasing difficulty.

Lab 1: Creating a Flyer with a Picture

Problem: As a part-time employee in the Student Services Center at school, you have been asked to prepare a flyer that advertises study habits classes. First, you prepare the unformatted flyer shown in Figure 1–78a, and then you format it so that it looks like Figure 1–78b. *Hint:* Remember, if you make a mistake while formatting the flyer, you can click the Undo button on the Quick Access Toolbar to undo your last action.

Note: To complete this assignment, you will be required to use the Data Files for Students. See the inside back cover of this book for instructions on downloading the Data Files for Students, or contact your instructor for information about accessing the required files.

Instructions: Perform the following tasks:

1. Start Word. Display formatting marks on the screen.
2. Type the flyer text, unformatted, as shown in Figure 1–78a, inserting a blank line between the headline and the body copy. If Word flags any misspelled words as you type, check their spelling and correct them.
3. Save the document using the file name, Lab 1-1 Study Habits Flyer.
4. Center the headline and the signature line.
5. Change the theme colors to Concourse.
6. Change the font size of the headline to 36 point and the font to Ravie, or a similar font. Apply the text effect called Gradient Fill – Dark Red, Accent 6, Inner Shadow.
7. Change the font size of body copy between the headline and the signature line to 20 point.
8. Change the font size of the signature line to 22 point. Bold the text in the signature line.

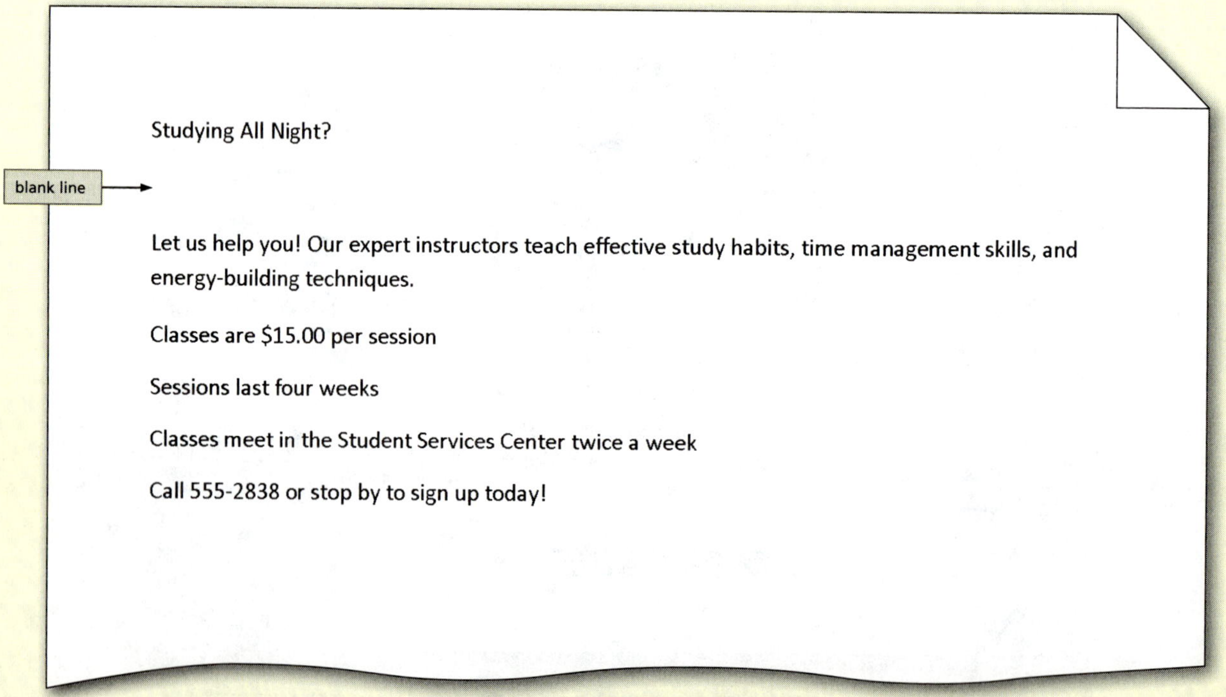
Studying All Night?

blank line

Let us help you! Our expert instructors teach effective study habits, time management skills, and energy-building techniques.

Classes are $15.00 per session

Sessions last four weeks

Classes meet in the Student Services Center twice a week

Call 555-2838 or stop by to sign up today!

Figure 1–78 (a) Unformatted Flyer

9. Change the font of the body copy and signature line to Rockwell, and change the color of the signature line to Dark Red, Accent 6.
10. Bullet the three lines (paragraphs) of text above the signature line.
11. Bold and capitalize the text, Let us help you!, and change its color to Dark Red, Accent 6.
12. Italicize the word, or, in the signature line.
13. Underline the text, Student Services Center, in the third bulleted paragraph.
14. Change the zoom so that the entire page is visible in the document window.

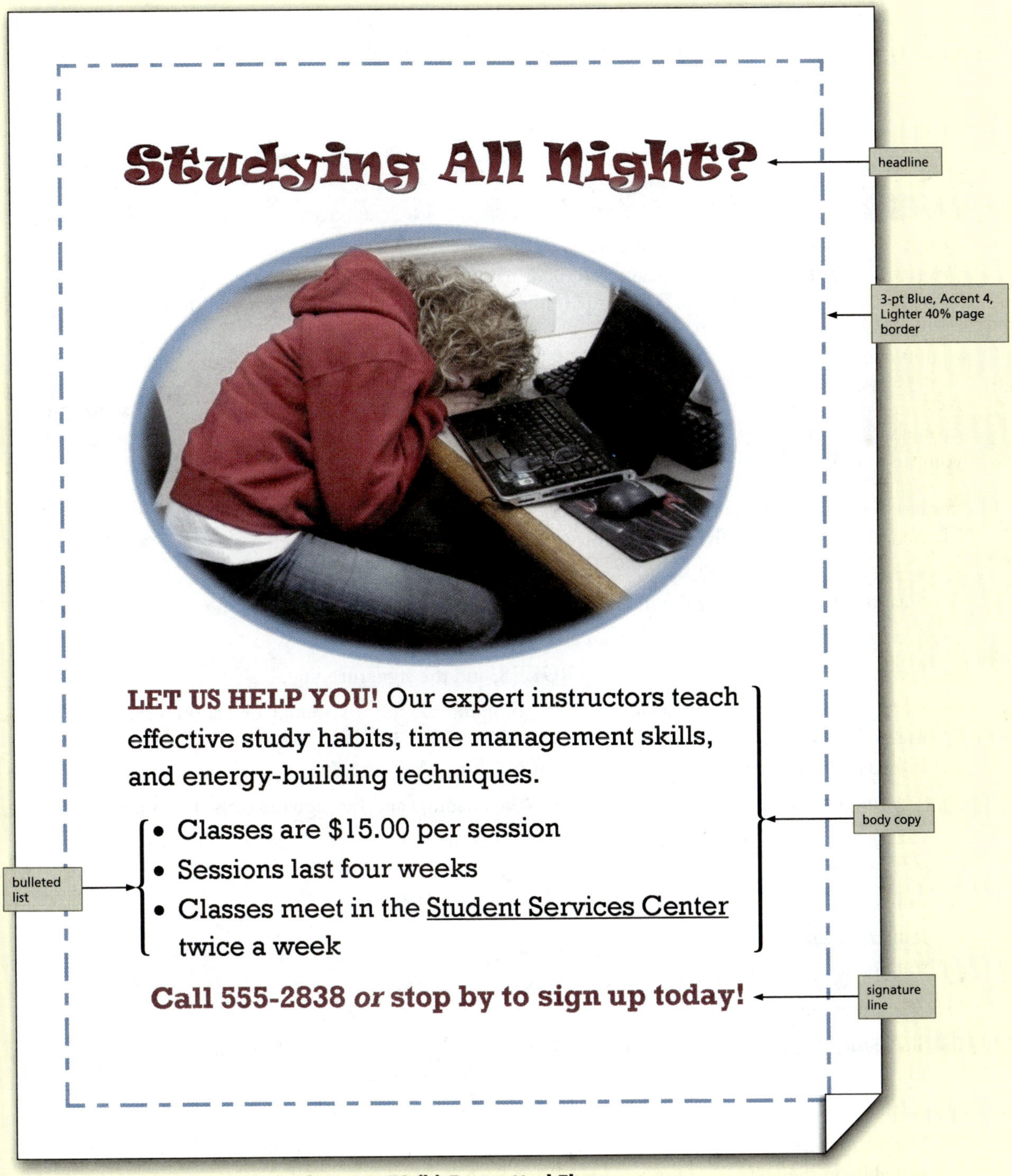

Figure 1–78 (b) Formatted Flyer

Continued >

In the Lab *continued*

15. Insert the picture centered on a blank line below the headline. The picture is called Sleeping and is available on the Data Files for Students.
16. Apply the Soft Edge Oval picture style to the inserted picture. Apply the glow effect called Blue, 5 pt glow, Accent color 4 to the picture.
17. The entire flyer should fit on a single page. If it flows to two pages, resize the picture or decrease spacing before and after paragraphs until the entire flyer text fits on a single page.
18. Add the page border shown in Figure 1–78b on the previous page.
19. Change the document properties, including keywords, as specified by your instructor. Save the flyer again with the same file name. Submit the document, shown in Figure 1–78b, in the format specified by your instructor.

In the Lab

Lab 2: Creating a Flyer with a Resized Picture

Problem: Your boss at Granger Camera House has asked you to prepare a flyer that announces the upcoming photography contest. You prepare the flyer shown in Figure 1–79. *Hint:* Remember, if you make a mistake while formatting the flyer, you can click the Undo button on the Quick Access Toolbar to undo your last action.

Note: To complete this assignment, you will be required to use the Data Files for Students. See the inside back cover of this book for instructions on downloading the Data Files for Students, or contact your instructor for information about accessing the required files.

Instructions: Perform the following tasks:

1. Start Word. Type the flyer text, unformatted. If Word flags any misspelled words as you type, check their spelling and correct them.
2. Save the document using the file name, Lab 1-2 Photography Contest Flyer.
3. Change the theme colors to the Apex color scheme.
4. Center the headline, the line that says RULES, and the signature line.
5. Change the font size of the headline to 36 point and the font to Stencil, or a similar font. Shade the headline paragraph Lavender, Background 2, Darker 50%. Apply the text effect called Fill – Lavender, Accent 6, Outline – Accent 6, Glow – Accent 6.
6. Change the font size of body copy between the headline and the signature line to 18 point.
7. Change the font size of the signature line to 24 point and the font to Stencil. Bold the text in the signature line. Change the font color of the text in the signature line to Gray-50%, Text 2.
8. Bullet the three paragraphs of text above the signature line.
9. Italicize the word, not.
10. Bold the word, landscape.
11. Underline the text, August 31.
12. Shade the line that says RULES to the Gray-50%, Text 2 color. If the font color does not automatically change to a lighter color, change it to White, Background 1.
13. Change the zoom so that the entire page is visible in the document window.
14. Insert the picture on a blank line below the headline. The picture is called Wind Power and is available on the Data Files for Students.

15. Resize the picture so that it is approximately 3.5" × 5.25". Apply the Rotated, White picture style to the inserted picture. Apply the glow effect called Lavender, 5 pt glow, Accent color 6 to the picture.
16. The entire flyer should fit on a single page. If it flows to two pages, resize the picture or decrease spacing before and after paragraphs until the entire flyer text fits on a single page.
17. Add the page border shown in Figure 1–79.
18. Change the document properties, including keywords, as specified by your instructor. Save the flyer again with the same file name. Submit the document, shown in Figure 1–79, in the format specified by your instructor.

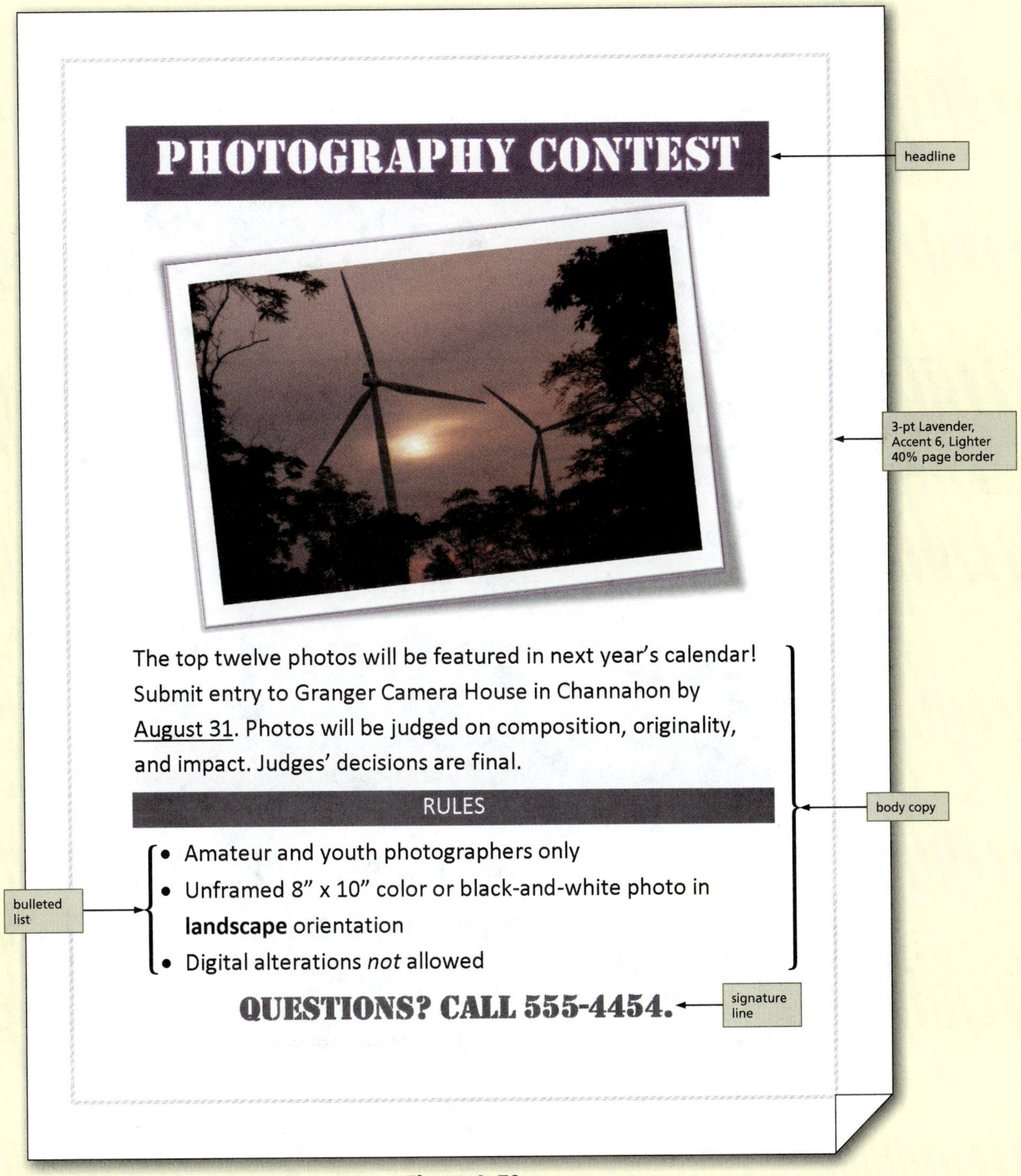

Figure 1–79

In the Lab

Lab 3: Creating a Flyer with Pictures

Problem: Your boss at Warner Depot has asked you to prepare a flyer that advertises its scenic train ride. You prepare the flyer shown in Figure 1–80.

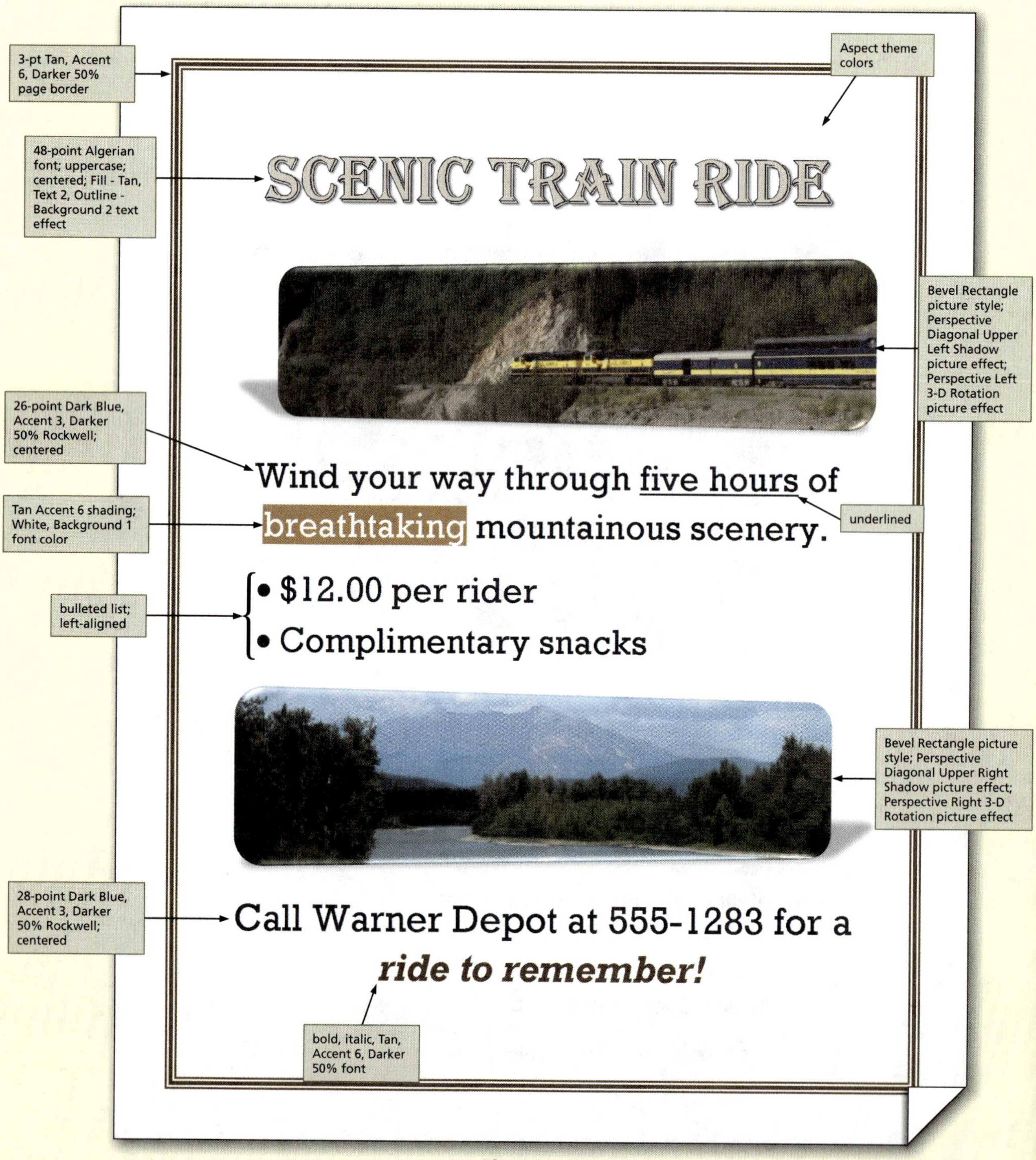

Figure 1–80

Note: To complete this assignment, you will be required to use the Data Files for Students. See the inside back cover of this book for instructions on downloading the Data Files for Students, or contact your instructor for information about accessing the required files.

Instructions: Start Word. Enter the text in the flyer, checking spelling as you type, and then format it as shown in Figure 1–80. The pictures to be inserted are called Train and Scenery and are available on the Data Files for Students. Adjust spacing before and after paragraphs and resize pictures as necessary so that the flyer fits on a single page.

Change the document properties, including keywords, as specified by your instructor. Save the document using the file name, Lab 1-3 Train Ride Flyer. Submit the document, shown in Figure 1–80, in the format specified by your instructor.

Cases and Places

Apply your creative thinking and problem solving skills to design and implement a solution.

Note: To complete these assignments, you may be required to use the Data Files for Students. See the inside back cover of this book for instructions on downloading the Data Files for Students, or contact your instructor for information about accessing the required files.

1: Design and Create a Spring Break Flyer

Academic

As secretary of your school's Student Government Association, you are responsible for creating and distributing flyers for spring break group outings. This year, you have planned a trip to Settlers Resort. The flyer should contain two digital pictures appropriately resized; the Data Files for Students contains two pictures called Cabin 1 and Cabin 2, or you can use your own digital pictures if they are appropriate for the topic of the flyer. The flyer should contain the headline, Feeling Adventurous?, and this signature line: Call Lyn at 555-9901 to sign up. The body copy consists of the following, in any order: Spring Break – Blast to the Past. Settlers Resort is like a page right out of a history textbook! Spend five days living in the 1800s. The bulleted list in the body copy is as follows: One-room cabins with potbelly stoves, Campfire dining with authentic meals, and Horseback riding and much more.

Use the concepts and techniques presented in this chapter to create and format this flyer. Be sure to check spelling and grammar. Submit your assignment in the format specified by your instructor.

2: Design and Create a Yard Sale Flyer

Personal

You are planning a yard sale and would like to create and post flyers around town advertising the upcoming sale. The flyer should contain two digital pictures appropriately resized; the Data Files for Students contains two pictures called Yard Sale 1 and Yard Sale 2, or you can use your own digital pictures if they are appropriate for the topic of the flyer. The flyer should contain the headline, Yard Sale!, and this signature line: Questions? Call 555-9820. The body copy consists of the following, in any order: Hundreds of items for sale. After 20 years, we are moving to a smaller house and are selling anything that won't fit. Everything for sale must go! The bulleted list in the body copy is as follows: When: August 7, 8, 9 from 9:00 a.m. to 7:00 p.m.; Where: 139 Ravel Boulevard; and What: something for everyone – from clothing to collectibles.

Use the concepts and techniques presented in this chapter to create and format this flyer. Be sure to check spelling and grammar. Submit your assignment in the format specified by your instructor.

Continued >

Cases and Places *continued*

3: Design and Create a Village Fireworks Flyer

Professional

As a part-time employee at the Village of Crestwood, your boss has asked you to create and distribute flyers for the upcoming fireworks extravaganza. The flyer should contain two digital pictures appropriately resized; the Data Files for Students contains two pictures called Fireworks 1 and Fireworks 2, or you can use your own digital pictures if they are appropriate for the topic of the flyer. The flyer should contain the headline, Light Up The Sky, and this signature line: Call 555-2983 with questions. The body copy consists of the following, in any order: Join Us! The Village of Crestwood will present its tenth annual Light Up The Sky fireworks extravaganza on August 8 at 9:00 p.m. during the end of summer celebration in Douglas Park. The bulleted list in the body copy is as follows: Pork chop dinners will be sold for $3.00 beginning at 6:00 p.m., Bring chairs and blankets, and Admission is free.

Use the concepts and techniques presented in this chapter to create and format this flyer. Be sure to check spelling and grammar. Submit your assignment in the format specified by your instructor.

2 Creating a Research Paper with Citations and References

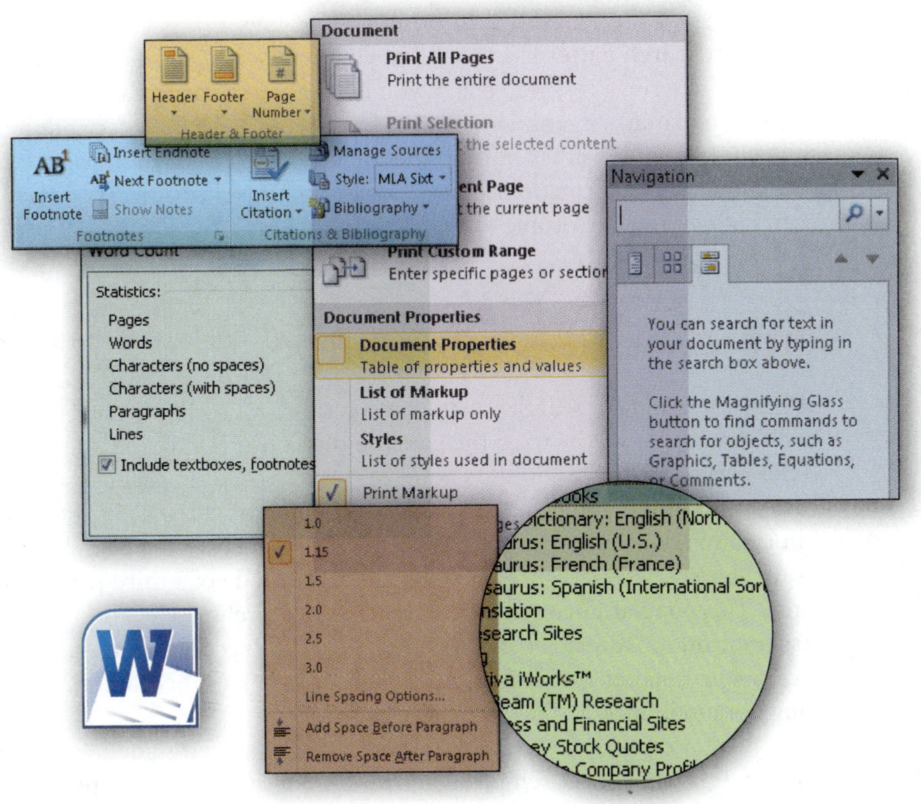

Objectives

You will have mastered the material in this chapter when you can:

- Describe the MLA documentation style for research papers
- Change line and paragraph spacing in a document
- Modify a style
- Use a header to number pages of a document
- Apply formatting using shortcut keys
- Modify paragraph indentation
- Insert and edit citations and their sources
- Add a footnote to a document
- Insert a manual page break
- Create a bibliographical list of sources
- Cut, copy, and paste text
- Find text and replace text
- Find a synonym
- Use the Research task pane to look up information

2 Creating a Research Paper with Citations and References

Introduction

In both academic and business environments, you will be asked to write reports. Business reports range from proposals to cost justifications to five-year plans to research findings. Academic reports focus mostly on research findings.

A **research paper** is a document you can use to communicate the results of research findings. To write a research paper, you learn about a particular topic from a variety of sources (research), organize your ideas from the research results, and then present relevant facts and/or opinions that support the topic. Your final research paper combines properly credited outside information along with personal insights. Thus, no two research papers — even if about the same topic — will or should be the same.

Project — Research Paper

When preparing a research paper, you should follow a standard documentation style that defines the rules for creating the paper and crediting sources. A variety of documentation styles exists, depending on the nature of the research paper. Each style requires the same basic information; the differences in styles relate to requirements for presenting the information. For example, one documentation style uses the term bibliography for the list of sources, whereas another uses references, and yet a third prefers the title works cited. Two popular documentation styles for research papers are the **Modern Language Association of America** (**MLA**) and **American Psychological Association** (**APA**) styles. This chapter uses the MLA documentation style because it is used in a wide range of disciplines.

The project in this chapter follows research paper guidelines and uses Word to create the short research paper shown in Figure 2–1. This paper, which discusses triangulation, follows the MLA documentation style. Each page contains a page number. The first two pages present the name and course information (student name, instructor name, course name, and paper due date), paper title, an introduction with a thesis statement, details that support the thesis, and a conclusion. This section of the paper also includes references to research sources and a footnote. The third page contains a detailed, alphabetical list of the sources referenced in the research paper. All pages include a header at the upper-right edge of the page.

BTW

APA Appendix
If your version of this book includes the Word APA Appendix and you are required to create a research paper using the APA documentation style instead of the MLA documentation style, the appendix shows the steps required to create the research paper in this chapter using the APA guidelines. If your version of this book does not include the Word APA Appendix, see print publications or search the Web for the APA guidelines.

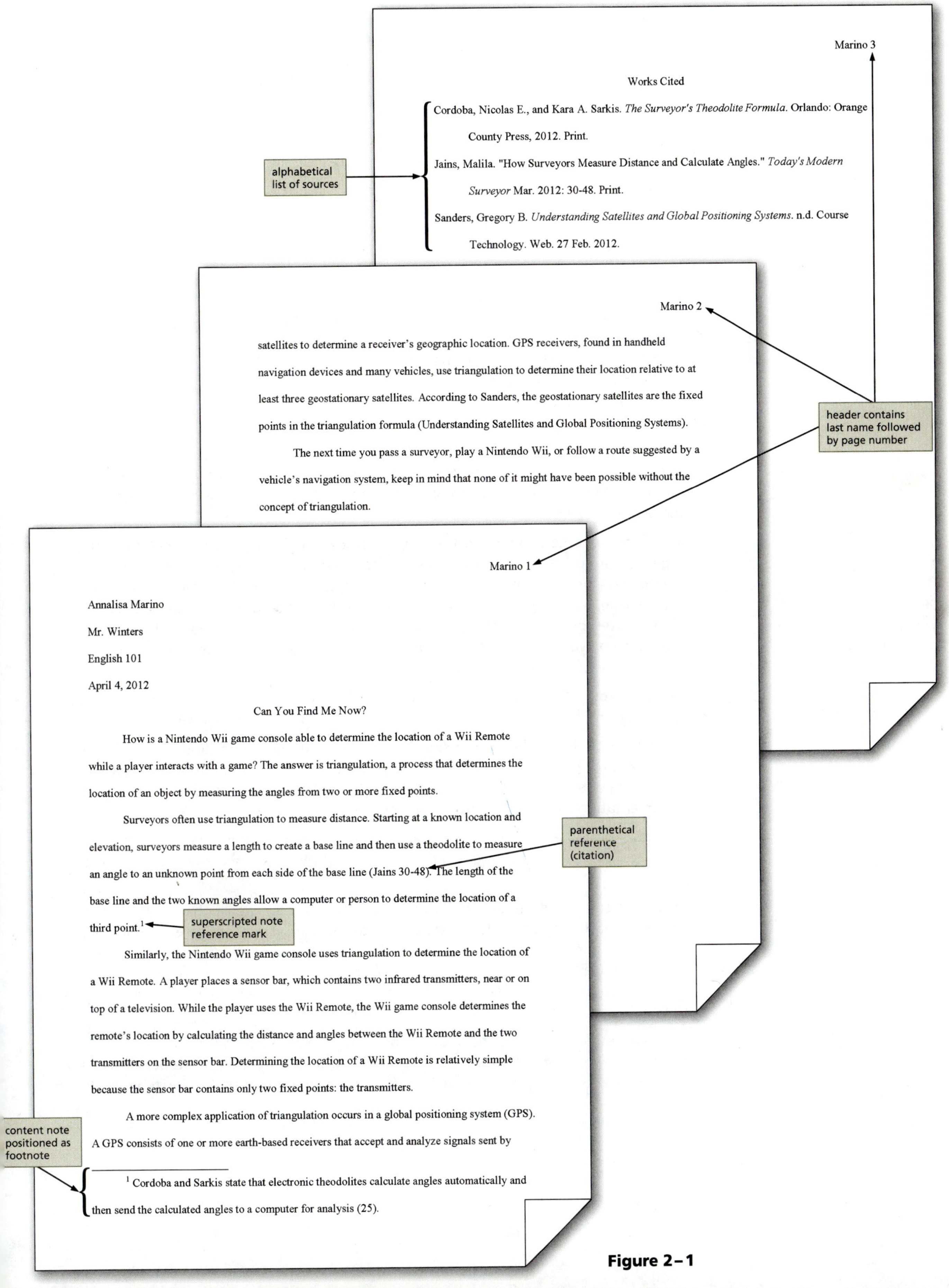

Marino 1

Annalisa Marino

Mr. Winters

English 101

April 4, 2012

Can You Find Me Now?

How is a Nintendo Wii game console able to determine the location of a Wii Remote while a player interacts with a game? The answer is triangulation, a process that determines the location of an object by measuring the angles from two or more fixed points.

Surveyors often use triangulation to measure distance. Starting at a known location and elevation, surveyors measure a length to create a base line and then use a theodolite to measure an angle to an unknown point from each side of the base line (Jains 30-48). The length of the base line and the two known angles allow a computer or person to determine the location of a third point.[1]

Similarly, the Nintendo Wii game console uses triangulation to determine the location of a Wii Remote. A player places a sensor bar, which contains two infrared transmitters, near or on top of a television. While the player uses the Wii Remote, the Wii game console determines the remote's location by calculating the distance and angles between the Wii Remote and the two transmitters on the sensor bar. Determining the location of a Wii Remote is relatively simple because the sensor bar contains only two fixed points: the transmitters.

A more complex application of triangulation occurs in a global positioning system (GPS). A GPS consists of one or more earth-based receivers that accept and analyze signals sent by

[1] Cordoba and Sarkis state that electronic theodolites calculate angles automatically and then send the calculated angles to a computer for analysis (25).

Marino 2

satellites to determine a receiver's geographic location. GPS receivers, found in handheld navigation devices and many vehicles, use triangulation to determine their location relative to at least three geostationary satellites. According to Sanders, the geostationary satellites are the fixed points in the triangulation formula (Understanding Satellites and Global Positioning Systems).

The next time you pass a surveyor, play a Nintendo Wii, or follow a route suggested by a vehicle's navigation system, keep in mind that none of it might have been possible without the concept of triangulation.

Marino 3

Works Cited

Cordoba, Nicolas E., and Kara A. Sarkis. *The Surveyor's Theodolite Formula.* Orlando: Orange County Press, 2012. Print.

Jains, Malila. "How Surveyors Measure Distance and Calculate Angles." *Today's Modern Surveyor* Mar. 2012: 30-48. Print.

Sanders, Gregory B. *Understanding Satellites and Global Positioning Systems.* n.d. Course Technology. Web. 27 Feb. 2012.

Figure 2–1

Overview

As you read through this chapter, you will learn how to create the research paper shown in Figure 2–1 on the previous page by performing these general tasks:

- Change the document settings.
- Type the research paper.
- Save the research paper.
- Create an alphabetical list of sources.
- Proof and revise the research paper.
- Print the research paper.

Plan Ahead

General Project Guidelines

When creating a Word document, the actions you perform and decisions you make will affect the appearance and characteristics of the finished document. As you create a research paper, such as the project shown in Figure 2–1, you should follow these general guidelines:

1. **Select a topic.** Spend time brainstorming ideas for a topic. Choose one you find interesting. For shorter papers, narrow the scope of the topic; for longer papers, broaden the scope. Identify a tentative thesis statement, which is a sentence describing the paper's subject matter.
2. **Research the topic and take notes.** Gather credible, relevant information about the topic that supports the thesis statement. Sources of research include books, magazines, newspapers, and the Internet. As you record facts and ideas, list details about the source: title, author, place of publication, publisher, date of publication, etc. When taking notes, be careful not to **plagiarize**. That is, do not use someone else's work and claim it to be your own. If you copy information directly, place it in quotation marks and identify its source.
3. **Organize your ideas.** Classify your notes into related concepts. Make an outline from the categories of notes. In the outline, identify all main ideas and supporting details.
4. **Write the first draft, referencing sources.** From the outline, compose the paper. Every research paper should include an introduction containing the thesis statement, supporting details, and a conclusion. Follow the guidelines identified in the required documentation style. Reference all sources of information.
5. **Create the list of sources.** Using the formats specified in the required documentation style, completely list all sources referenced in the body of the research paper in alphabetical order.
6. **Proofread and revise the paper.** If possible, proofread the paper with a fresh set of eyes, that is, at least one to two days after completing the first draft. Proofreading involves reading the paper with the intent of identifying errors (spelling, grammar, etc.) and looking for ways to improve the paper (wording, transitions, flow, etc.). Try reading the paper out loud, which helps to identify unclear or awkward wording. Ask someone else to proofread the paper and give you suggestions for improvements.

When necessary, more specific details concerning the above guidelines are presented at appropriate points in the chapter. The chapter also will identify the actions performed and decisions made regarding these guidelines during the creation of the research paper shown in Figure 2–1.

MLA Documentation Style

The research paper in this project follows the guidelines presented by the MLA. To follow the MLA documentation style, use 12-point Times New Roman, or a similar, font. Double-space text on all pages of the paper using one-inch top, bottom, left, and right margins. Indent the first word of each paragraph one-half inch from the left margin. At the right margin of each page, place a page number one-half inch from the top margin. On each page, precede the page number by your last name.

The MLA documentation style does not require a title page. Instead, place your name and course information in a block at the left margin beginning one inch from the top of the page. Center the title one double-spaced line below your name and course information.

In the text of the paper, place author references in parentheses with the page number(s) of the referenced information. The MLA documentation style uses in-text **parenthetical references** instead of noting each source at the bottom of the page or at the end of the paper. In the MLA documentation style, notes are used only for optional content or bibliographic notes.

If used, content notes elaborate on points discussed in the paper, and bibliographic notes direct the reader to evaluations of statements in a source or provide a means for identifying multiple sources. Use a superscript (raised number) both to signal that a note exists and to sequence the notes (shown in Figure 2-1 on page WD 67). Position notes at the bottom of the page as footnotes or at the end of the paper as endnotes. Indent the first line of each note one-half inch from the left margin. Place one space following the superscripted number before beginning the note text. Double-space the note text (shown in Figure 2–1).

The MLA documentation style uses the term **works cited** to refer to the bibliographic list of sources at the end of the paper. The works cited page alphabetically lists sources that are referenced directly in the paper. Place the list of sources on a separate numbered page. Center the title, Works Cited, one inch from the top margin. Double-space all lines. Begin the first line of each source at the left margin, indenting subsequent lines of the same source one-half inch from the left margin. List each source by the author's last name, or, if the author's name is not available, by the title of the source.

BTW

APA Documentation Style

In the APA documentation style, a separate title page is required instead of placing name and course information on the paper's first page. Double-space all pages of the paper with one-inch top, bottom, left, and right margins. Indent the first word of each paragraph one-half inch from the left margin. In the upper-right margin of each page, including the title page, place a running head that consists of the page number preceded by a brief summary of the paper title.

Changing Document Settings

The MLA documentation style defines some global formats that apply to the entire research paper. Some of these formats are the default in Word. For example, the default left, right, top, and bottom margin settings in Word are one inch, which meets the MLA documentation style. You will modify, however, the font, font size, line and paragraph spacing, and header formats as required by the MLA documentation style.

To Start Word

If you are using a computer to step through the project in this chapter and you want your screens to match the figures in the Office and Windows chapters in this book, you should change your screen's resolution to 1024 × 768. For information about how to change a computer's resolution, refer to the Office 2010 and Windows 7 chapter in this book.

For an introduction to Windows 7 and instruction about how to perform basic Windows 7 tasks, read the Office 2010 and Windows 7 chapter in this book, where you can learn how to resize windows, change screen resolution, create folders, move and rename files, use Windows Help, and much more.

BTW

New Document Window

If you wanted to open a new blank document window, you could press CTRL+N or click File on the Ribbon to open the Backstage view, click the New tab to display the New gallery, click the Blank document button, and then click the Create button.

The following steps, which assume Windows 7 is running, start Word based on a typical installation. You may need to ask your instructor how to start Word for your computer. For a detailed example of the procedure summarized below, refer to the Office 2010 and Windows 7 chapter.

1. Click the Start button on the Windows 7 taskbar to display the Start menu.
2. Type `Microsoft Word` as the search text in the 'Search programs and files' text box and watch the search results appear on the Start menu.
3. Click Microsoft Word 2010 in the search results on the Start menu to start Word and display a new blank document in the Word window.
4. If the Word window is not maximized, click the Maximize button next to the Close button on its title bar to maximize the window.
5. If the Print Layout button on the status bar is not selected (shown in Figure 2–2), click it so that your screen is in Print Layout view.
6. If Normal (Home tab | Styles group) is not selected in the Quick Style gallery (shown in Figure 2–2), click it so that your document uses the Normal style.
7. If your zoom percent is not 100, click the Zoom Out or Zoom In button as many times as necessary until the Zoom button displays 100% on its face (shown in Figure 2–2).

BTW

Style Formats

To see the formats assigned to a particular style in a document, click the Styles Dialog Box Launcher (Home tab | Styles group) and then click the Style Inspector button in the Styles task pane. Position the insertion point in the style in the document and then point to the Paragraph formatting or Text level formatting areas in the Style Inspector task pane to display an Enhanced ScreenTip describing formats assigned to the location of the insertion point. You also can click the Reveal Formatting button in the Style Inspector task pane to display the Reveal Formatting task pane.

To Display Formatting Marks

As discussed in Chapter 1, it is helpful to display formatting marks that indicate where in the document you press the ENTER key, SPACEBAR, and other keys. The following steps display formatting marks.

1. If the Home tab is not the active tab, click Home on the Ribbon to display the Home tab.
2. If the Show/Hide ¶ button (Home tab | Paragraph group) is not selected already, click it to display formatting marks on the screen.

Styles

When you create a document, Word formats the text using a particular style. A **style** is a named group of formatting characteristics, including font and font size. The default style in Word is called the **Normal style**, which most likely uses 11-point Calibri font. If you do not specify a style for text you type, Word applies the Normal style to the text. In addition to the Normal style, Word has many other built-in, or predefined, styles that you can use to format text. Styles make it easy to apply many formats at once to text. You can modify existing styles and create your own styles. Styles are discussed as they are used in the Word chapters in this book.

To Modify a Style

The MLA documentation style requires that all text in the research paper use 12-point Times New Roman, or a similar, font. If you change the font and font size using buttons on the Ribbon, you will need to make the change many times during the course of creating the paper because Word formats different areas of a document using the Normal style, which uses 11-point Calibri font. For example, body text, headers, and bibliographies all display text based on the Normal style. Thus, instead of changing the font and font size for each of these document elements, a more efficient technique would be to change the Normal style for this document to 12-point Times New Roman. By changing the Normal style, you ensure that all text in the document will use the format required by the MLA. The next steps change the Normal style.

1

- Right-click Normal in the Quick Style gallery (Home tab | Styles group) to display a shortcut menu related to styles (Figure 2–2).

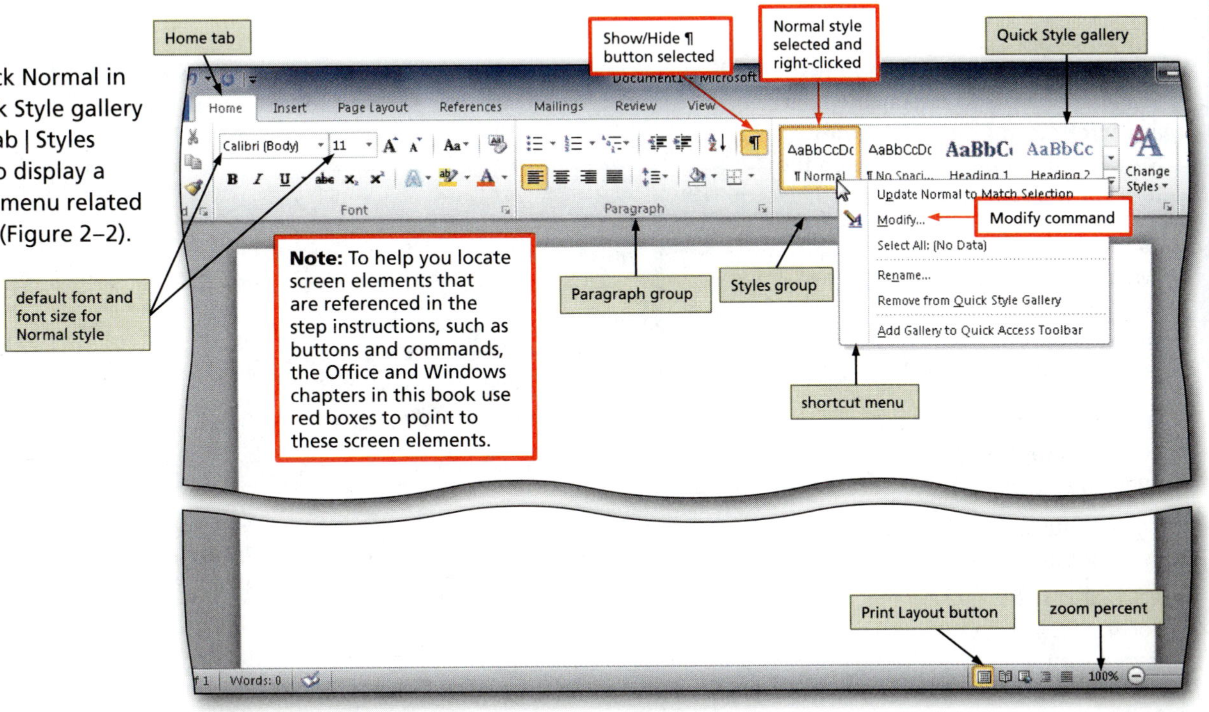

Figure 2–2

2

- Click Modify on the shortcut menu to display the Modify Style dialog box (Figure 2–3).

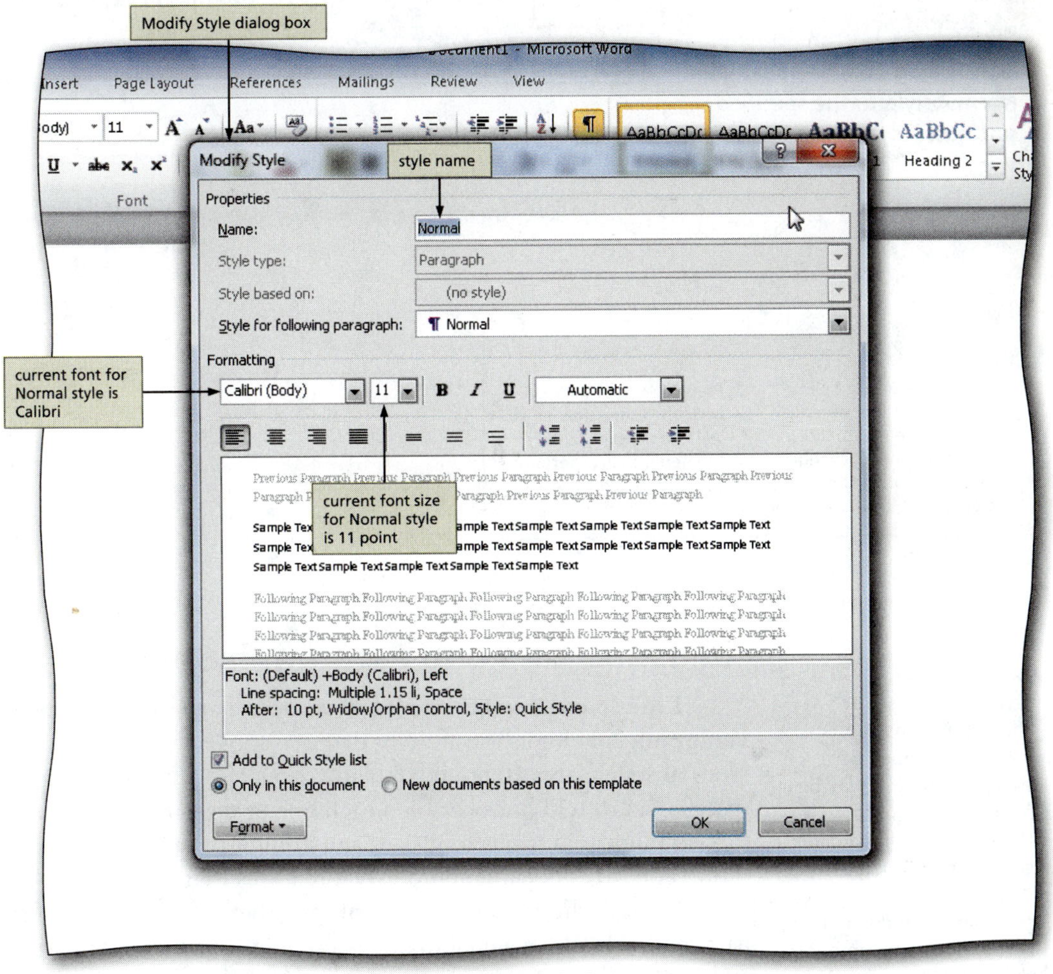

Figure 2–3

3

- Click the Font box arrow (Modify Style dialog box) to display the Font list. Scroll to and then click Times New Roman in the list to change the font for the style being modified.
- Click the Font Size box arrow (Modify Style dialog box) and then click 12 in the Font Size list to change the font size for the style being modified.
- Ensure that the 'Only in this document' option button is selected (Figure 2–4).

Q&A Will all future documents use the new font and font size?

No, because the 'Only in this document' option button is selected. If you want all future documents to use a new setting, you would select the 'New documents based on this template' option button.

4

- Click the OK button (Modify Style dialog box) to update the Normal style to the specified settings.

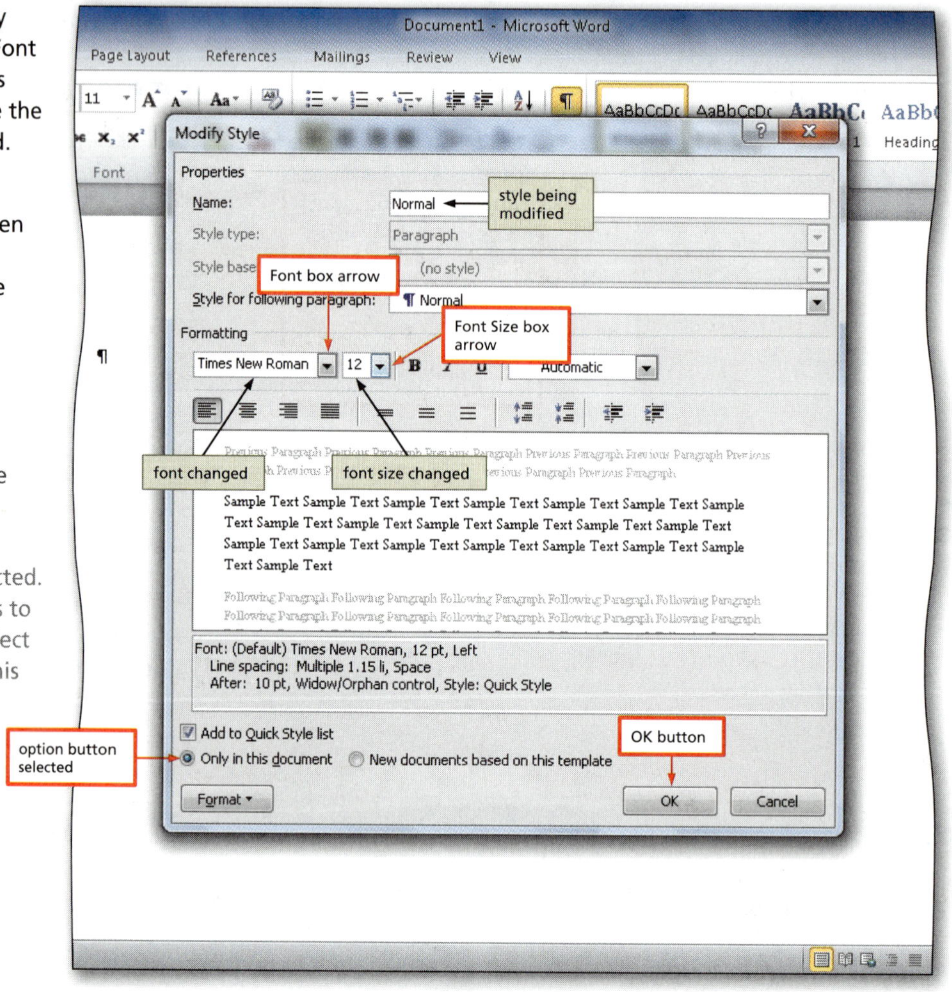

Figure 2–4

Other Ways	
1. Click Styles Dialog Box Launcher, click box arrow next to style name, click Modify on menu, change settings (Modify Style dialog box), click OK button	2. Press ALT+CTRL+SHIFT+S, click box arrow next to style name, click Modify on menu, change settings (Modify Style dialog box), click OK button

BTW **Line Spacing**
If the top of a set of characters or a graphical image is chopped off, then line spacing may be set to Exactly. To remedy the problem, change line spacing to 1.0, 1.15, 1.5, 2.0, 2.5, 3.0, or At least (in the Paragraph dialog box), all of which accommodate the largest font or image.

Adjusting Line and Paragraph Spacing

Line spacing is the amount of vertical space between lines of text in a paragraph. **Paragraph spacing** is the amount of space above and below a paragraph. By default, the Normal style places 10 points of blank space after each paragraph and inserts a vertical space equal to 1.15 lines between each line of text. It also automatically adjusts line height to accommodate various font sizes and graphics.

The MLA documentation style requires that you **double-space** the entire research paper. That is, the amount of vertical space between each line of text and above and below paragraphs should be equal to one blank line. The next sets of steps adjust line spacing and paragraph spacing according to the MLA documentation style.

To Change Line Spacing

The lines of the research paper should be double-spaced, according to the MLA documentation style. In Word, you change the line spacing to 2.0 to double-space lines in a paragraph. The following steps change the line spacing to double.

1

- Click the Line and Paragraph Spacing button (Home tab | Paragraph group) to display the Line and Paragraph Spacing gallery (Figure 2–5).

Q&A What do the numbers in the Line and Paragraph Spacing gallery represent?

The default line spacing is 1.15 lines. The options 1.0, 2.0, and 3.0 set line spacing to single, double, and triple, respectively. Similarly, the 1.5 and 2.5 options set line spacing to 1.5 and 2.5 lines. All these options adjust line spacing automatically to accommodate the largest font or graphic on a line.

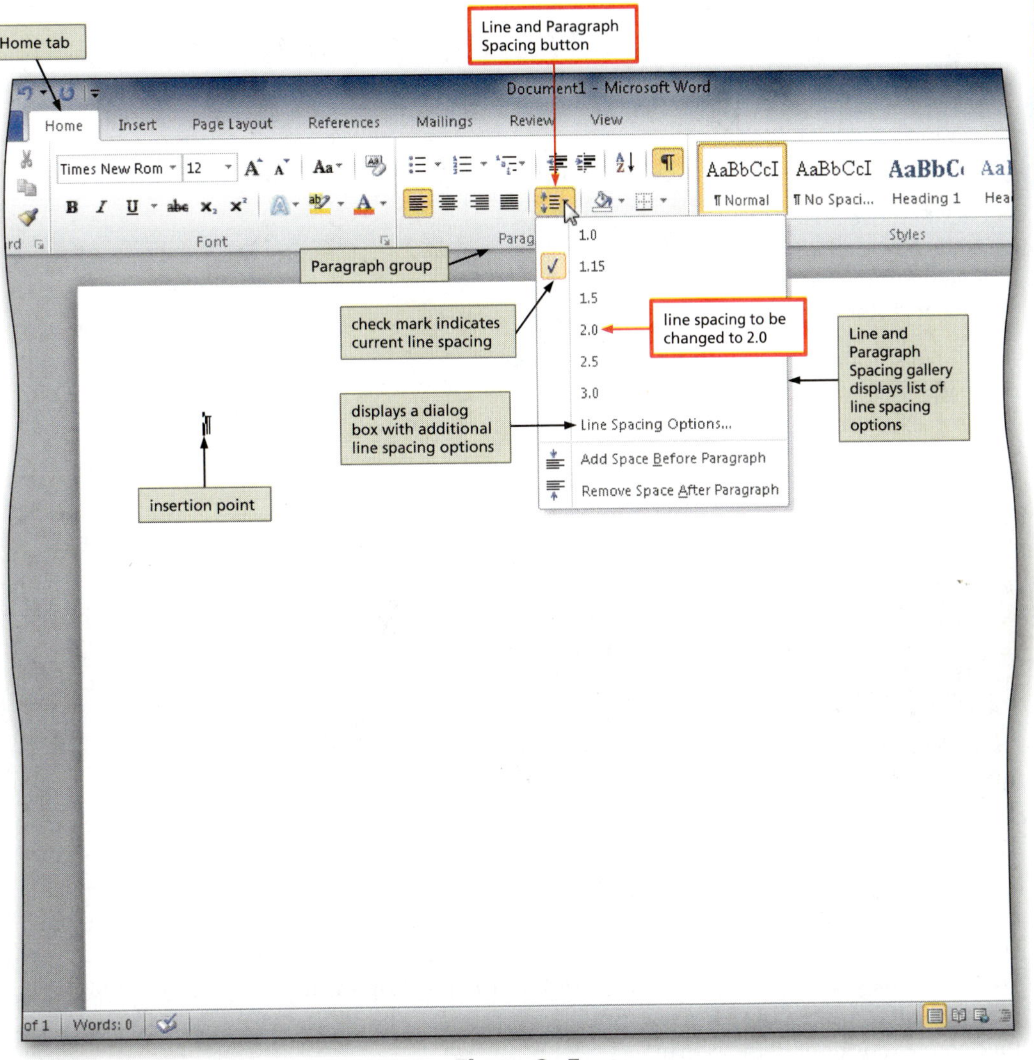

Figure 2–5

2

- Click 2.0 in the Line and Paragraph Spacing gallery to change the line spacing at the location of the insertion point.

Q&A Can I change the line spacing of existing text?

Yes. Select the text first and then change the line spacing as described in these steps.

Other Ways

1. Right-click paragraph, click Paragraph on shortcut menu, click Indents and Spacing tab (Paragraph dialog box), click Line spacing box arrow, click desired spacing, click OK button
2. Click Paragraph Dialog Box Launcher (Home tab or Page Layout tab | Paragraph group), click Indents and Spacing tab (Paragraph dialog box), click Line spacing box arrow, click desired spacing, click OK button
3. Press CTRL+2 for double-spacing

To Remove Space after a Paragraph

The research paper should not have additional blank space after each paragraph. The following steps remove space after a paragraph.

1

- Click the Line and Paragraph Spacing button (Home tab | Paragraph group) to display the Line and Paragraph Spacing gallery (Figure 2–6).

2

- Click Remove Space After Paragraph in the Line and Paragraph Spacing gallery so that no blank space appears after paragraphs.

Q&A Can I remove space after existing paragraphs?

Yes. Select the paragraphs first and then remove the space as described in these steps.

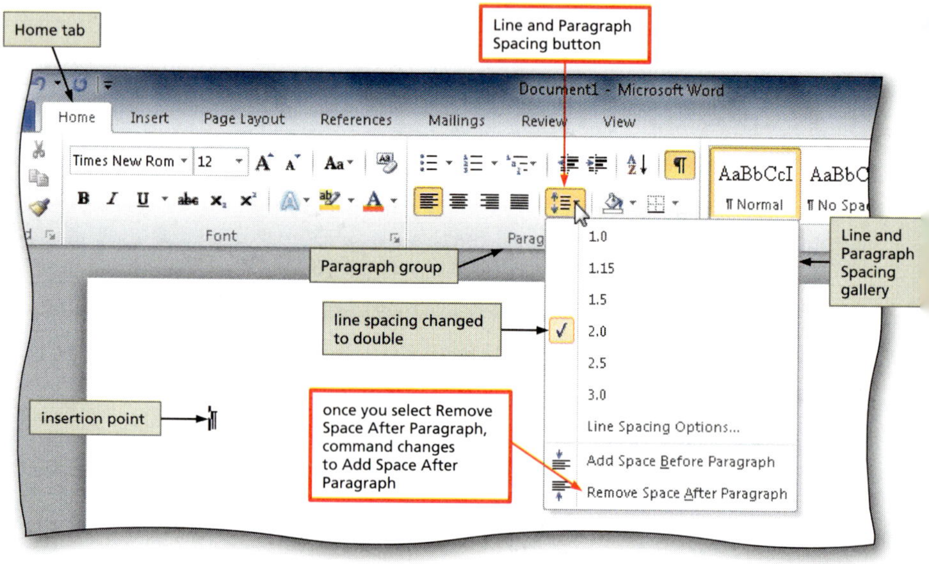

Figure 2–6

Other Ways

1. Click Spacing After box arrows (Page Layout tab | Paragraph group) until 0 pt is displayed
2. Right-click paragraph, click Paragraph on shortcut menu, click Indents and Spacing tab (Paragraph dialog box), click After box arrows until 0 pt is displayed, click OK button
3. Click Paragraph Dialog Box Launcher (Home tab or Page Layout tab | Paragraph group), click Indents and Spacing tab (Paragraph dialog box), click After box arrows until 0 pt is displayed, click OK button

To Update a Style to Match a Selection

To ensure that all paragraphs in the paper will be double-spaced and do not have space after the paragraphs, you want the Normal style to include the line and paragraph spacing changes made in the previous two sets of steps. You can update a style to reflect the settings of the location of the insertion point or selected text. Because no text has yet been typed in the research paper, you do not need to select text prior to updating the Normal style. The following steps update the Normal style.

1

- Right-click Normal in the Quick Style gallery (Home tab | Styles group) to display a shortcut menu (Figure 2–7).

2

- Click Update Normal to Match Selection on the shortcut menu to update the selected (or current) style to reflect the settings at the location of the insertion point.

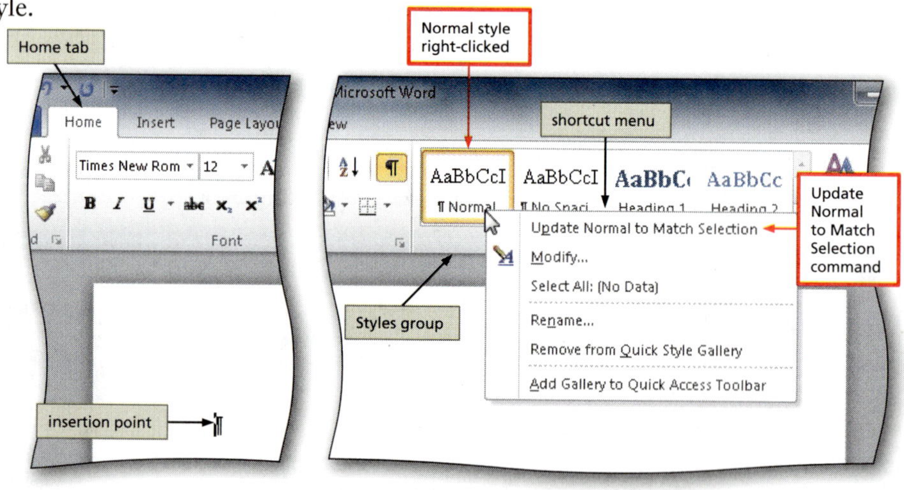

Figure 2–7

Other Ways

1. Right-click text, point to Styles on shortcut menu, click Update [style name] to Match Selection on submenu

Headers and Footers

A **header** is text and graphics that print at the top of each page in a document. Similarly, a **footer** is text and graphics that print at the bottom of every page. In Word, headers print in the top margin one-half inch from the top of every page, and footers print in the bottom margin one-half inch from the bottom of each page, which meets the MLA documentation style. In addition to text and graphics, headers and footers can include document information such as the page number, current date, current time, and author's name.

In this research paper, you are to precede the page number with your last name placed one-half inch from the upper-right edge of each page. The procedures on the following pages enter your name and the page number in the header, as specified by the MLA documentation style.

BTW

The Ribbon and Screen Resolution

Word may change how the groups and buttons within the groups appear on the Ribbon, depending on the computer's screen resolution. Thus, your Ribbon may look different from the ones in the Office and Windows chapters in this book if you are using a screen resolution other than 1024 x 768.

To Switch to the Header

To enter text in the header, you instruct Word to edit the header. The following steps switch from editing the document text to editing the header.

1

- Click Insert on the Ribbon to display the Insert tab.
- Click the Header button (Insert tab | Header & Footer group) to display the Header gallery (Figure 2–8).

Q&A

Can I use a built-in header for this research paper?

None of the built-in headers adheres to the MLA documentation style. Thus, you enter your own header content, instead of using a built-in header, for this research paper.

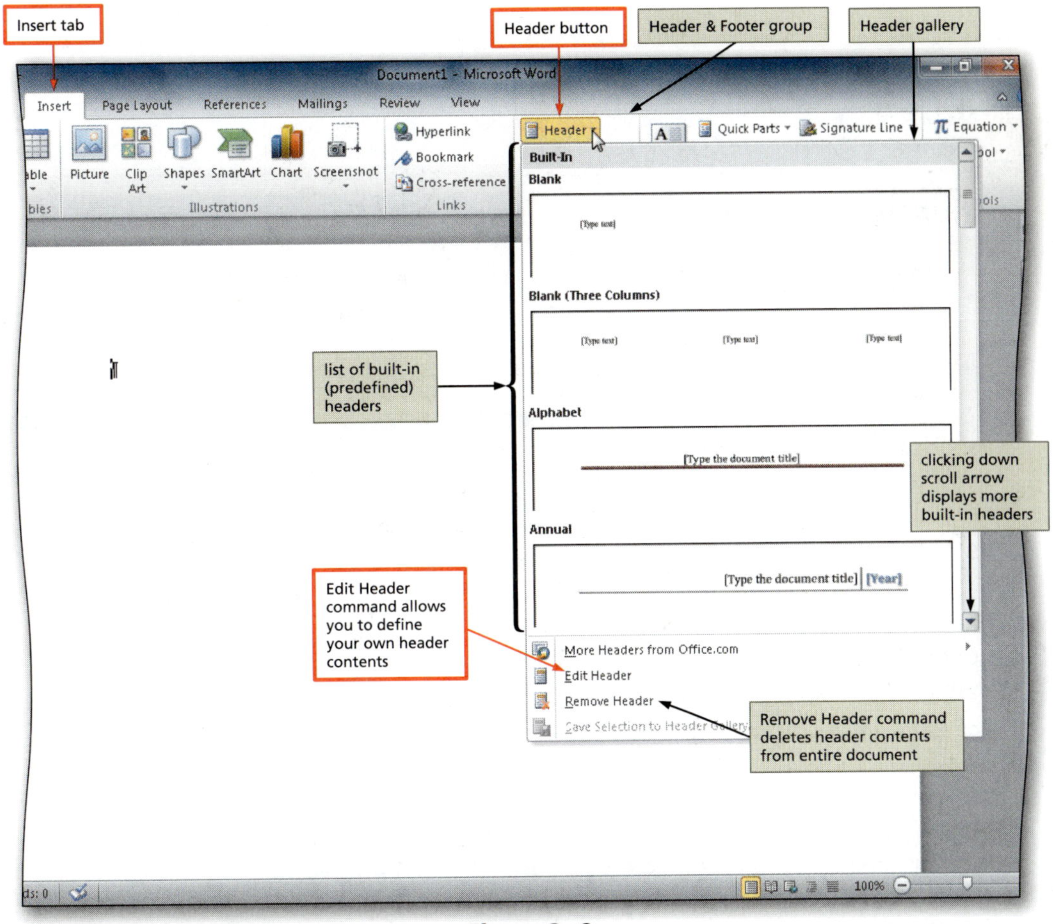

Figure 2–8

Q&A

How would I remove a header from a document?

You would click Remove Header in the Header gallery (shown in Figure 2–8). Similarly, to remove a footer, you would click Remove Footer in the Footer gallery.

Experiment

- Click the down scroll arrow in the Header gallery to see the available built-in headers.

2

- Click Edit Header in the Header gallery to switch from the document text to the header, which allows you to edit the contents of the header (Figure 2–9).

Q&A

How do I remove the Header & Footer Tools Design tab from the Ribbon?

When you are finished editing the header, you will close it, which removes the Header & Footer Tools Design tab.

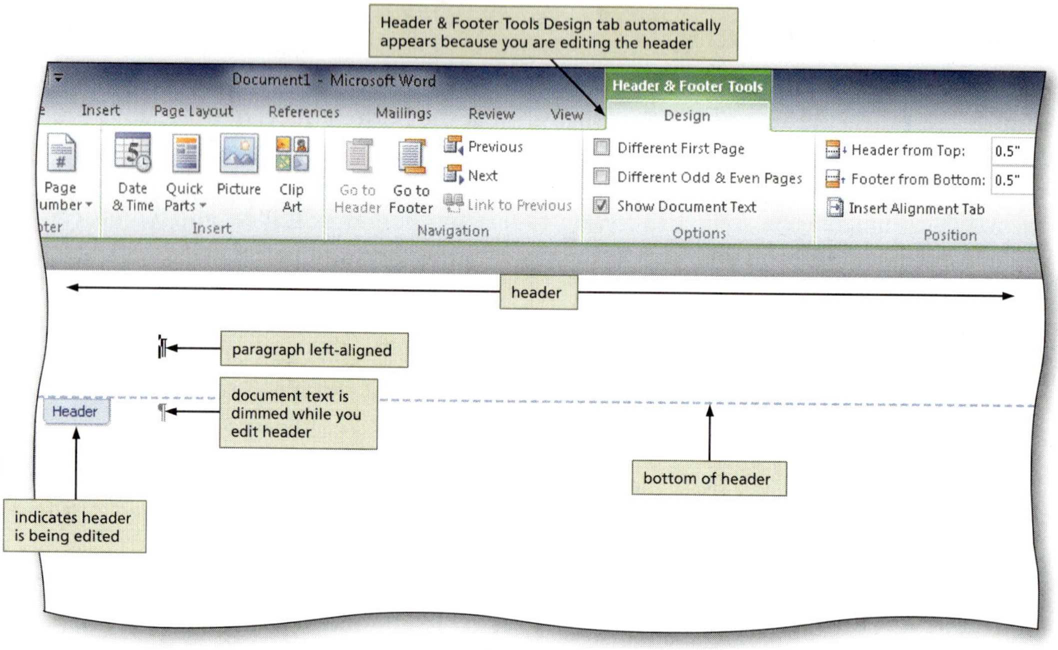

Figure 2–9

Other Ways

1. Double-click dimmed header
2. Right-click header in document, click Edit Header button that appears

To Right-Align a Paragraph

The paragraph in the header currently is left-aligned (Figure 2–9). Your last name and the page number should print **right-aligned**, that is, at the right margin. The following step right-aligns a paragraph.

1

- Click Home on the Ribbon to display the Home tab.
- Click the Align Text Right button (Home tab | Paragraph group) to right-align the current paragraph (Figure 2–10).

Q&A

What if I wanted to return the paragraph to left-aligned?

Click the Align Text Right button again, or click the Align Text Left button.

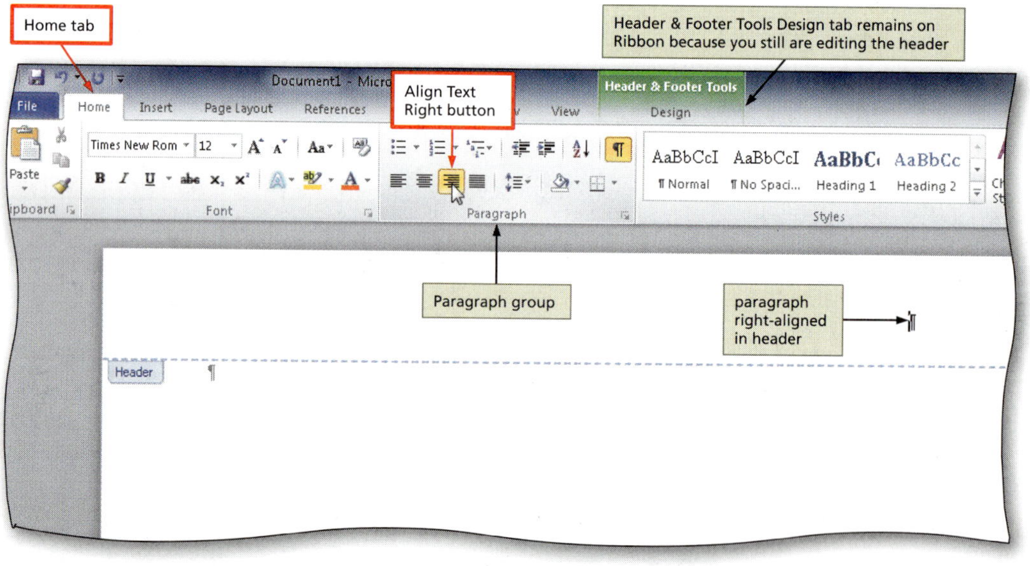

Figure 2–10

Other Ways

1. Right-click paragraph, click Paragraph on shortcut menu, click Indents and Spacing tab (Paragraph dialog box), click Alignment box arrow, click Right, click OK button
2. Click Paragraph Dialog Box Launcher (Home tab or Page Layout tab | Paragraph group), click Indents and Spacing tab (Paragraph dialog box), click Alignment box arrow, click Right, click OK button
3. Press CTRL+R

To Enter Text

The following steps enter your last name right-aligned in the header area.

1. Click Design on the Ribbon to display the Header & Footer Tools Design tab.
2. Type **Marino** and then press the SPACEBAR to enter the last name in the header.

BTW

Footers

If you wanted to create a footer, you would click the Footer button (Insert tab | Header & Footer group) and then select the desired built-in footer or click Edit Footer to create a customized footer; you also could double-click the dimmed footer, or right-click the footer and then click the Edit Footer button that appears.

To Insert a Page Number

The next task is to insert the current page number in the header. The following steps insert a page number at the location of the insertion point.

1

- Click the Insert Page Number button (Header & Footer Tools Design tab | Header & Footer group) to display the Insert Page Number menu.
- Point to Current Position on the Insert Page Number menu to display the Current Position gallery (Figure 2–11).

Experiment

- Click the down scroll arrow in the Current Position gallery to see the available page number formats.

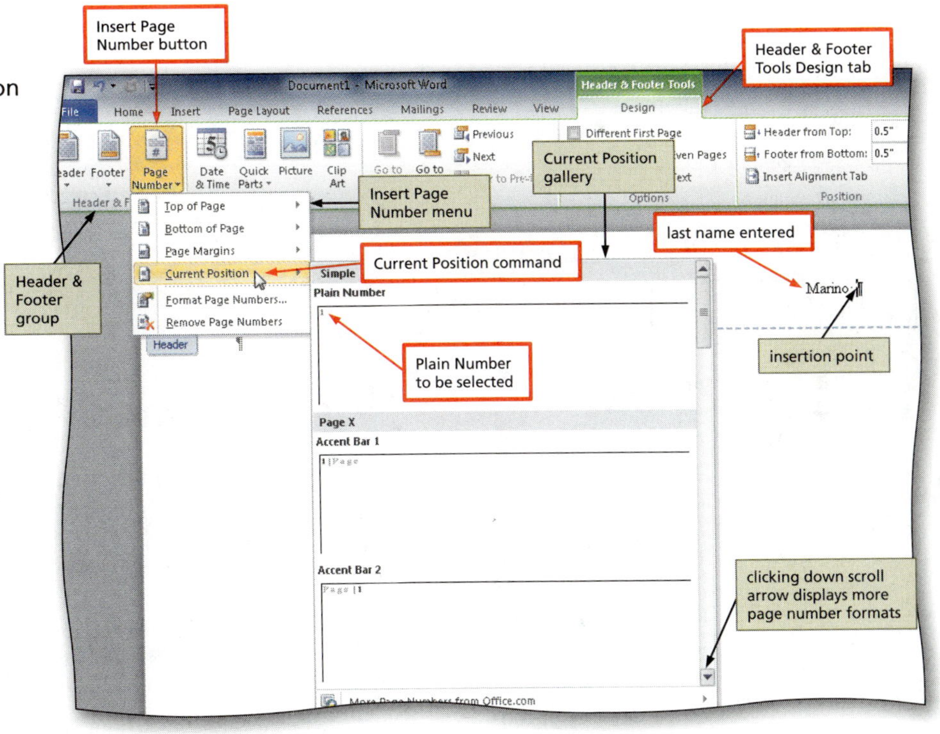

Figure 2–11

2

- If necessary, scroll to the top of the Current Position gallery. Click Plain Number in the Current Position gallery to insert an unformatted page number at the location of the insertion point (Figure 2–12).

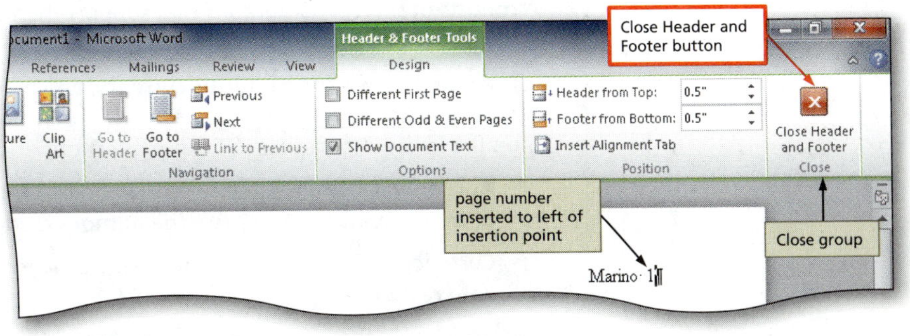

Figure 2–12

Other Ways

1. Click Insert Page Number button (Insert tab | Header & Footer group)
2. Click Quick Parts button (Insert tab | Text group or Header & Footer Tools Design tab | Insert group), click Field on Quick Parts menu, select Page in Field names list (Field dialog box), click OK button

To Close the Header

You are finished entering text in the header. Thus, the next task is to switch back to the document text. The following step closes the header.

1

- Click the Close Header and Footer button (Header & Footer Tools Design tab | Close group) (shown in Figure 2–12 on the previous page) to close the header and switch back to the document text (Figure 2–13).

Q&A How do I make changes to existing header text?

Switch to the header using the steps described on pages WD 75 and WD 76, edit the header as you would edit text in the document window, and then switch back to the document text.

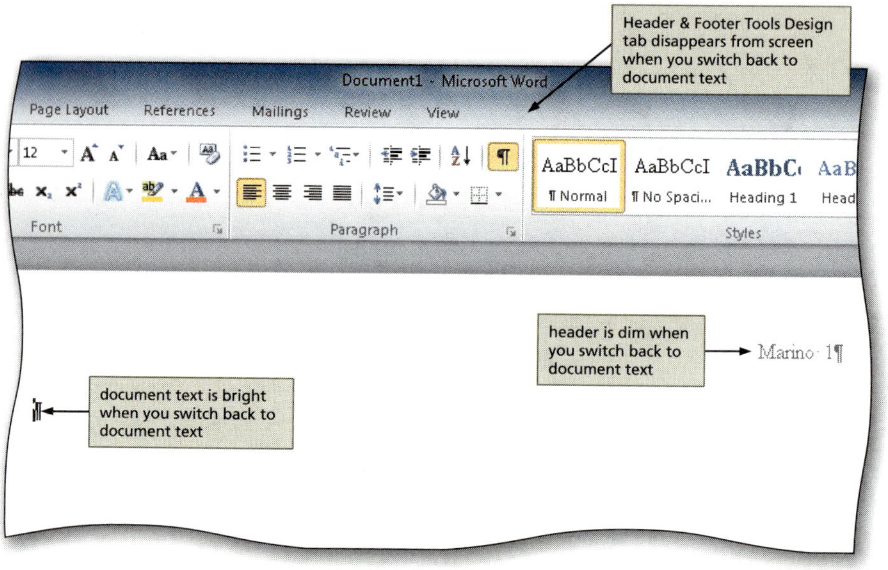

Figure 2–13

Other Ways

1. Double-click dimmed document text

Typing the Research Paper Text

The text of the research paper in this chapter encompasses the first two pages of the paper. You will type the text of the research paper and then modify it later in the chapter, so that it matches Figure 2–1 on page WD 67.

Plan Ahead

Write the first draft, referencing sources.

As you write the first draft of a research paper, be sure it includes the proper components, uses credible sources, and does not contain any plagiarized material.

- **Include an introduction, body, and conclusion.** The first paragraph of the paper introduces the topic and captures the reader's attention. The body, which follows the introduction, consists of several paragraphs that support the topic. The conclusion summarizes the main points in the body and restates the topic.
- **Evaluate sources for authority, currency, and accuracy.** Be especially wary of information obtained from the Web. Any person, company, or organization can publish a Web page on the Internet. Ask yourself these questions about the source:
  - Authority: Does a reputable institution or group support the source? Is the information presented without bias? Are the author's credentials listed and verifiable?
  - Currency: Is the information up to date? Are dates of sources listed? What is the last date revised or updated?
  - Accuracy: Is the information free of errors? Is it verifiable? Are the sources clearly identified?

(continued)

(continued)

- **Acknowledge all sources of information; do not plagiarize.** Not only is plagiarism unethical, but it is considered an academic crime that can have severe punishments such as failing a course or being expelled from school.

When you summarize, paraphrase (rewrite information in your own words), present facts, give statistics, quote exact words, or show a map, chart, or other graphical image, you must acknowledge the source. Information that commonly is known or accessible to the audience constitutes common knowledge and does not need to be acknowledged. If, however, you question whether certain information is common knowledge, you should document it — just to be safe.

Plan Ahead

To Enter Name and Course Information

As discussed earlier in this chapter, the MLA documentation style does not require a separate title page for research papers. Instead, place your name and course information in a block at the top of the page, below the header, at the left margin. The following steps enter the name and course information in the research paper.

1. Type `Annalisa Marino` as the student name and then press the ENTER key.
2. Type `Mr. Winters` as the instructor name and then press the ENTER key.
3. Type `English 101` as the course name and then press the ENTER key.
4. Type `April 4, 2012` as the paper due date and then press the ENTER key (Figure 2–14).

BTW

Date Formats
The MLA documentation style prefers the day-month-year (4 April 2012) or month-day-year (April 4, 2012) format.

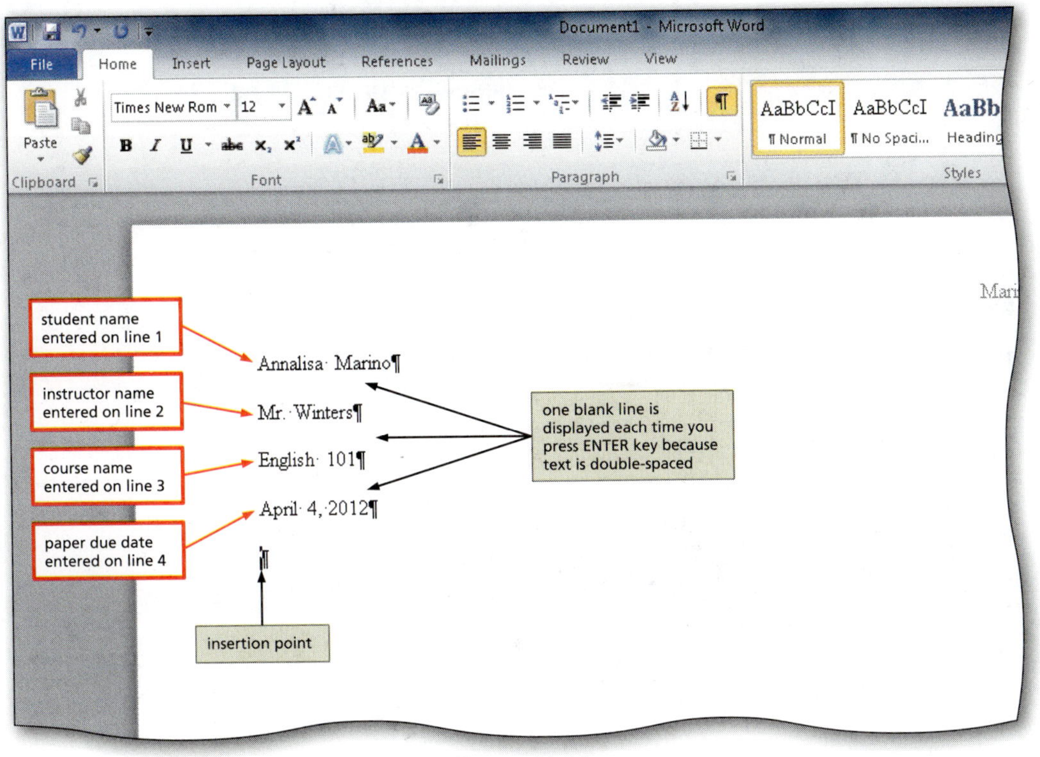

Figure 2–14

To Click and Type

The next step is to enter the title of the research paper centered between the page margins. In Word Chapter 1, you used the Center button (Home tab | Paragraph group) to center text and graphics. As an alternative, you can use Word's **Click and Type** feature to format and enter text, graphics, and other items. To use Click and Type, you double-click a blank area of the document window. Word automatically formats the item you type or insert according to the location where you double-clicked. The following steps use Click and Type to center and then type the title of the research paper.

1

Experiment

- Move the mouse pointer around the document below the entered name and course information and observe the various icons that appear with the I-beam.

- Position the mouse pointer in the center of the document at the approximate location for the research paper title until a center icon appears below the I-beam (Figure 2–15).

Q&A What are the other icons that appear in the Click and Type pointer?

A left-align icon appears to the right of the I-beam when the Click and Type pointer is in certain locations on the left side of the document window. A right-align icon appears to the left of the I-beam when the Click and Type pointer is in certain locations on the right side of the document window.

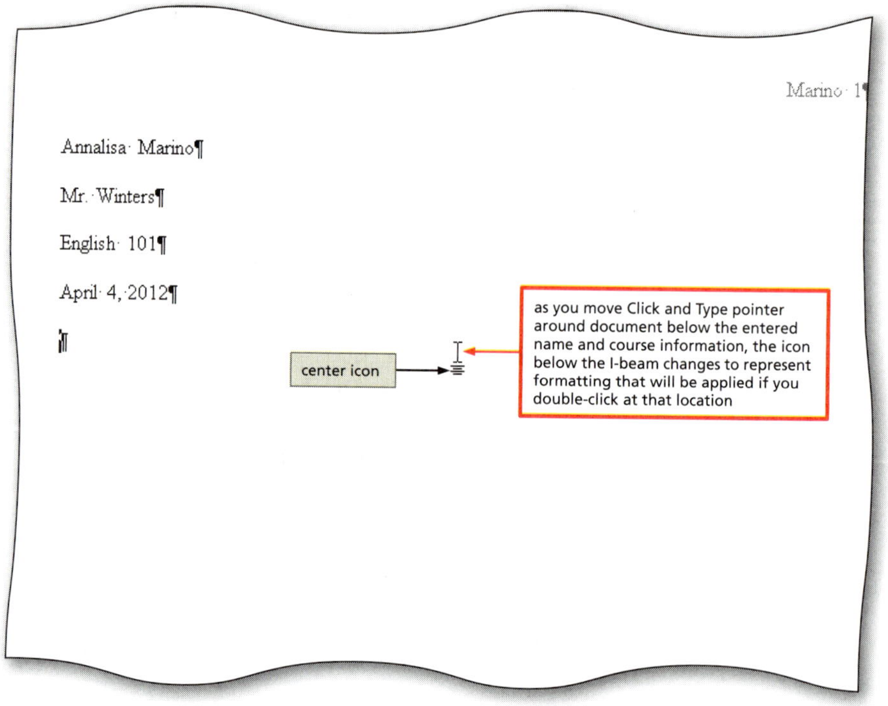

Figure 2–15

2

- Double-click to center the paragraph mark and insertion point between the left and right margins.

- Type `Can You Find Me Now?` as the paper title and then press the ENTER key to position the insertion point on the next line (Figure 2–16).

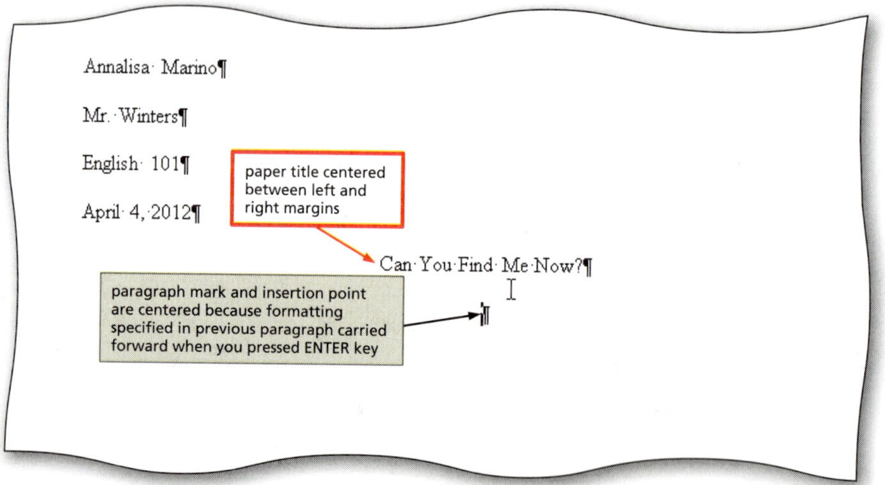

Figure 2–16

Shortcut Keys

Word has many **shortcut keys**, or keyboard key combinations, for your convenience while typing. Table 2–1 lists the common shortcut keys for formatting characters. Table 2–2 lists common shortcut keys for formatting paragraphs.

Table 2–1 Shortcut Keys for Formatting Characters

Character Formatting Task	Shortcut Keys	Character Formatting Task	Shortcut Keys
All capital letters	CTRL+SHIFT+A	Italic	CTRL+I
Bold	CTRL+B	Remove character formatting (plain text)	CTRL+SPACEBAR
Case of letters	SHIFT+F3	Small uppercase letters	CTRL+SHIFT+K
Decrease font size	CTRL+SHIFT+<	Subscript	CTRL+EQUAL SIGN
Decrease font size 1 point	CTRL+[	Superscript	CTRL+SHIFT+PLUS SIGN
Double-underline	CTRL+SHIFT+D	Underline	CTRL+U
Increase font size	CTRL+SHIFT+>	Underline words, not spaces	CTRL+SHIFT+W
Increase font size 1 point	CTRL+]		

Table 2–2 Shortcut Keys for Formatting Paragraphs

Paragraph Formatting	Shortcut Keys	Paragraph Formatting	Shortcut Keys
1.5 line spacing	CTRL+5	Justify paragraph	CTRL+J
Add/remove one line above paragraph	CTRL+0 (zero)	Left-align paragraph	CTRL+L
Center paragraph	CTRL+E	Remove hanging indent	CTRL+SHIFT+T
Decrease paragraph indent	CTRL+SHIFT+M	Remove paragraph formatting	CTRL+Q
Double-space lines	CTRL+2	Right-align paragraph	CTRL+R
Hanging indent	CTRL+T	Single-space lines	CTRL+1
Increase paragraph indent	CTRL+M		

To Format Text Using Shortcut Keys

The paragraphs below the paper title should be left-aligned, instead of centered. Thus, the next step is to left-align the paragraph below the paper title. When your fingers are already on the keyboard, you may prefer using shortcut keys to format text as you type it. The following step left-aligns a paragraph using the shortcut keys CTRL+L. (Recall from Word Chapter 1 that a notation such as CTRL+L means to press the letter L on the keyboard while holding down the CTRL key.)

1. Press CTRL+L to left-align the current paragraph, that is, the paragraph containing the insertion point (shown in Figure 2–17 on the next page).

Q&A Why would I use a keyboard shortcut instead of the Ribbon to format text?

Switching between the mouse and the keyboard takes time. If your hands are already on the keyboard, use a shortcut key. If your hand is on the mouse, use the Ribbon.

BTW

Shortcut Keys
To print a complete list of shortcut keys in Word, click the Microsoft Word Help button near the upper-right corner of the Word window, type `shortcut keys` in the 'Type words to search for' text box at the top of the Word Help window, press the ENTER key, click the Keyboard shortcuts for Microsoft Word link, click the Show All link in the upper-right corner of the Help window, click the Print button in the Help window, and then click the Print button in the Print dialog box.

For an introduction to Office 2010 and instruction about how to perform basic tasks in Office 2010 programs, read the Office 2010 and Windows 7 chapter in this book, where you can learn how to start a program, use the Ribbon, save a file, open a file, quit a program, use Help, and much more.

To Save a Document

You have performed many tasks while creating this research paper and do not want to risk losing work completed thus far. Accordingly, you should save the document. The following steps assume you already have created folders for storing your files, for example, a CIS 101 folder (for your class) that contains a Word folder (for your assignments). Thus, these steps save the document in the Word folder in the CIS 101 folder on a USB flash drive using the file name, Triangulation Paper.

1. With a USB flash drive connected to one of the computer's USB ports, click the Save button on the Quick Access Toolbar to display the Save As dialog box.
2. Type `Triangulation Paper` in the File name text box to change the file name. Do not press the ENTER key after typing the file name because you do not want to close the dialog box at this time.
3. Navigate to the desired save location (in this case, the Word folder in the CIS 101 folder [or your class folder] on the USB flash drive).
4. Click the Save button (Save As dialog box) to save the document in the selected folder on the selected drive with the entered file name.

To Display the Rulers

According to the MLA documentation style, the first line of each paragraph in the research paper is to be indented one-half inch from the left margin. Although you can use a dialog box to indent paragraphs, Word provides a quicker way through the **horizontal ruler**. This ruler is displayed at the top edge of the document window just below the Ribbon. Word also provides a **vertical ruler** that is displayed along the left edge of the Word window. The following step displays the rulers because you want to use the ruler to indent paragraphs.

1

Experiment

- Repeatedly click the View Ruler button on the vertical scroll bar to see the how this button is used to both show and hide the rulers.
- If the rulers are not displayed, click the View Ruler button on the vertical scroll bar to display the horizontal and vertical rulers on the screen (Figure 2–17).

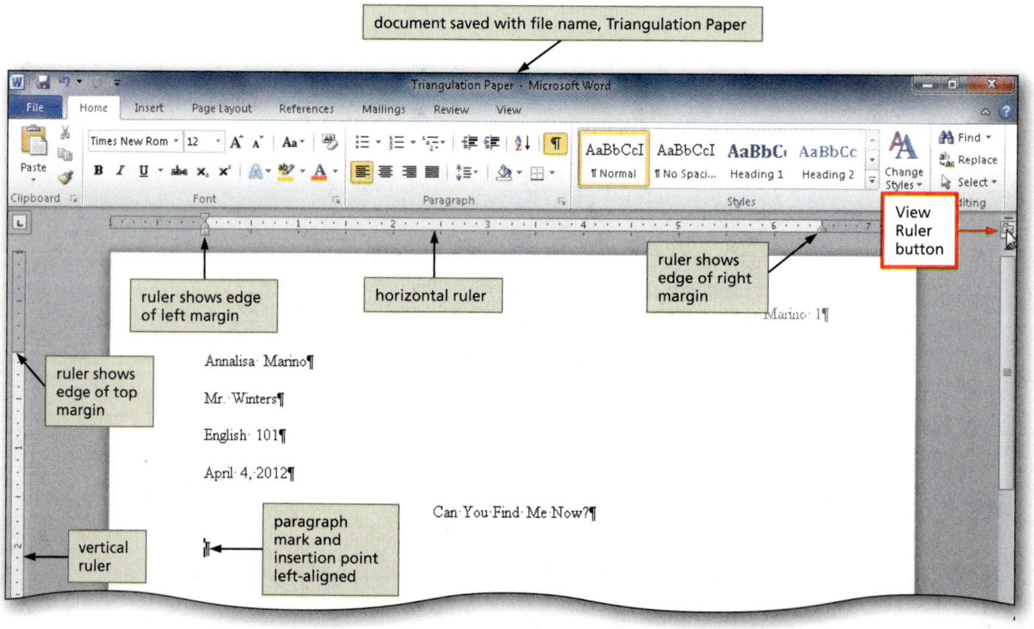

Figure 2–17

Q&A

For what tasks would I use the rulers?

You can use the rulers to indent paragraphs, set tab stops, change page margins, and adjust column widths.

Other Ways

1. Click View Ruler check box (View tab | Show group)

To First-Line Indent Paragraphs

The first line of each paragraph in the research paper is to be indented one-half inch from the left margin. You can use the horizontal ruler, usually simply called the **ruler**, to indent just the first line of a paragraph, which is called a **first-line indent**.

The left margin on the ruler contains two triangles above a square. The **First Line Indent marker** is the top triangle at the 0" mark on the ruler (Figure 2–18). The bottom triangle is discussed later in this chapter. The small square at the 0" mark is the Left Indent marker. The **Left Indent marker** allows you to change the entire left margin, whereas the First Line Indent marker indents only the first line of the paragraph. The following steps first-line indent paragraphs in the research paper.

1

- With the insertion point on the paragraph mark below the research paper title, point to the First Line Indent marker on the ruler (Figure 2–18).

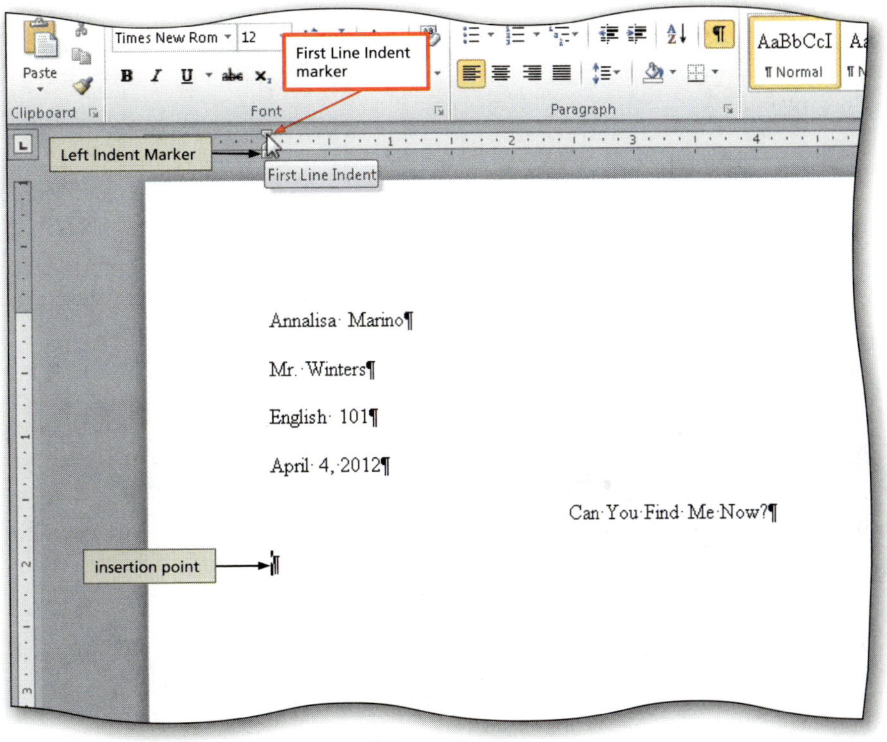

Figure 2–18

2

- Drag the First Line Indent marker to the .5" mark on the ruler to display a vertical dotted line in the document window, which indicates the proposed location of the first line of the paragraph (Figure 2–19).

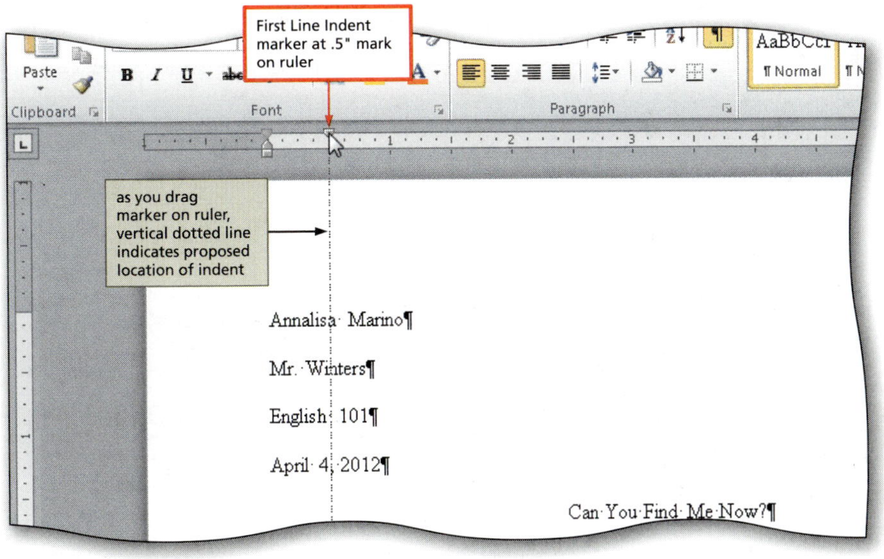

Figure 2–19

3

- Release the mouse button to place the First Line Indent marker at the .5" mark on the ruler, or one-half inch from the left margin (Figure 2–20).

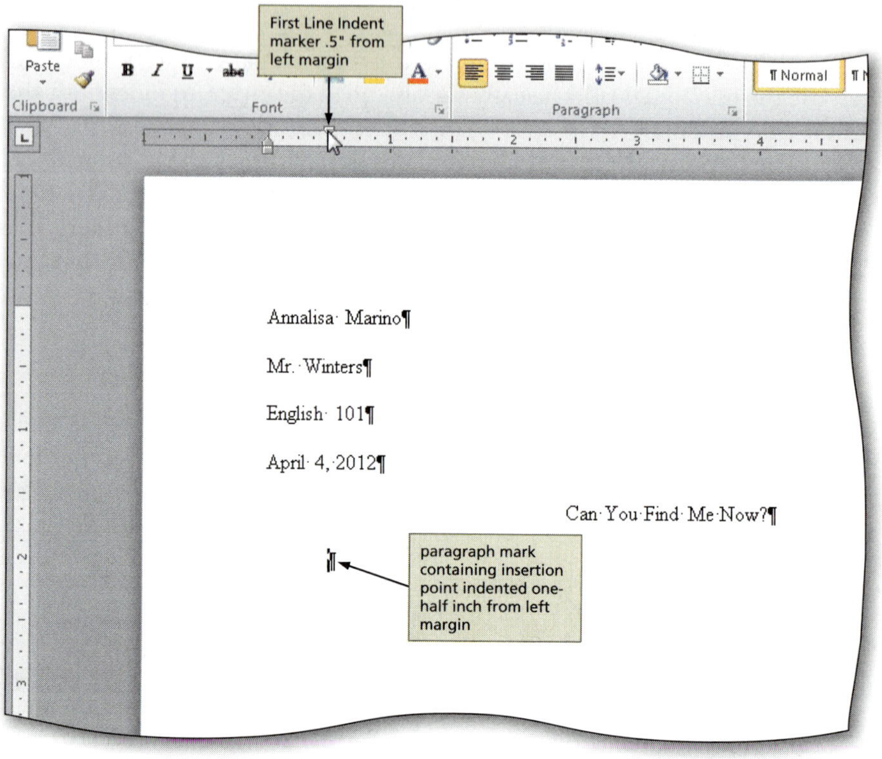

Figure 2–20

4

- Type **`How is a Nintendo Wii console able to determine the location of a Wii Remote while a player interacts with a game?`** and notice that Word automatically indented the first line of the paragraph by one-half inch (Figure 2–21).

Q&A

Will I have to set a first-line indent for each paragraph in the paper?

No. Each time you press the ENTER key, paragraph formatting in the previous paragraph carries forward to the next paragraph. Thus, once you set the first-line indent, its format carries forward automatically to each subsequent paragraph you type.

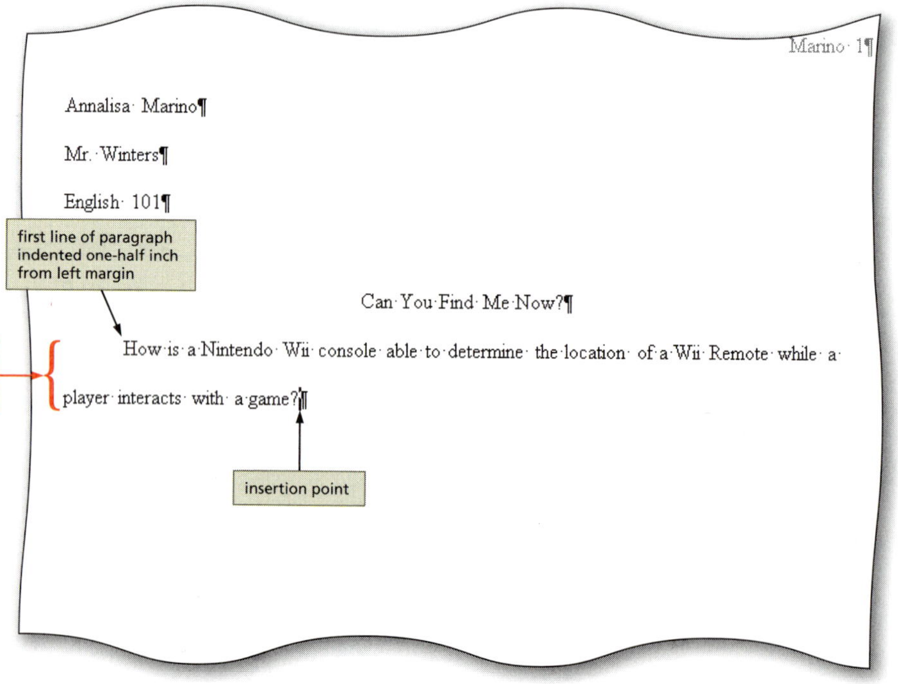

Figure 2–21

Other Ways

1. Right-click paragraph, click Paragraph on shortcut menu, click Indents and Spacing tab (Paragraph dialog box), click Special box arrow, click First line, click OK button
2. Click Paragraph Dialog Box Launcher (Home tab or Page Layout tab | Paragraph group), click Indents and Spacing tab (Paragraph dialog box), click Special box arrow, click First line, click OK button
3. Press TAB key at beginning of paragraph

To AutoCorrect as You Type

As you type, you may make typing, spelling, capitalization, or grammar errors. For this reason, Word provides an **AutoCorrect** feature that automatically corrects these kinds of errors as you type them in the document. For example, if you type ahve, Word automatically changes it to the correct spelling, have, when you press the SPACEBAR or a punctuation mark key such as a period or comma.

Word has predefined many commonly misspelled words, which it automatically corrects for you. The following steps intentionally misspell the word, the, as teh to illustrate the AutoCorrect feature.

1

- Press the SPACEBAR.
- Type the beginning of the next sentence, misspelling the word, the, as follows: **`The answer is triangulation, a process that determines teh`** (Figure 2–22).

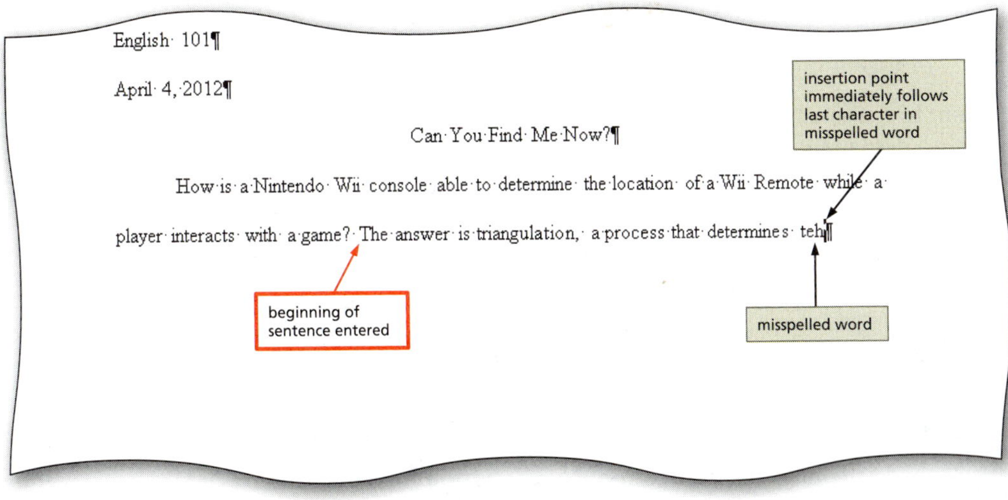

Figure 2–22

2

- Press the SPACEBAR and watch Word automatically correct the misspelled word.
- Type the rest of the sentence (Figure 2–23): **`location of an object by measuring the angles from two or more fixed points.`**

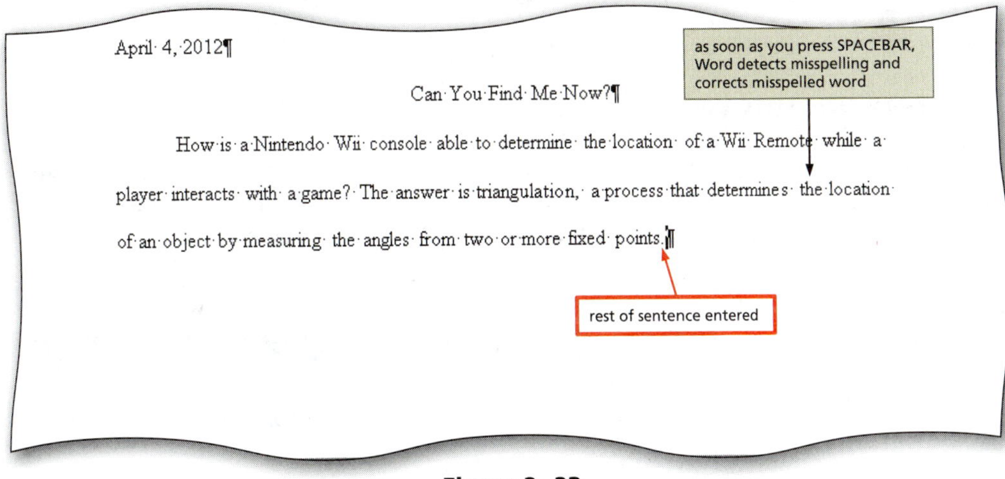

Figure 2–23

To Use the AutoCorrect Options Button

When you position the mouse pointer on text that Word automatically corrected, a small blue box appears below the text. If you point to the small blue box, Word displays the AutoCorrect Options button. When you click the **AutoCorrect Options button**, Word displays a menu that allows you to undo a correction or change how Word handles future automatic corrections of this type. The steps on the next page illustrate the AutoCorrect Options button and menu.

1

- Position the mouse pointer in the text automatically corrected by Word (the word, the, in this case) to display a small blue box below the automatically corrected word (Figure 2–24).

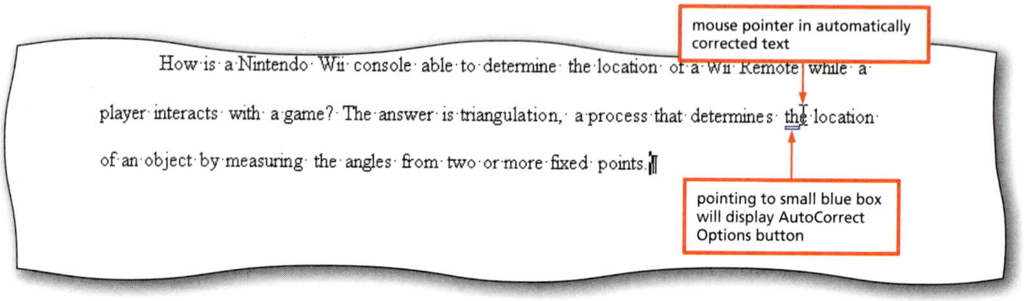

Figure 2–24

2

- Point to the small blue box to display the AutoCorrect Options button.
- Click the AutoCorrect Options button to display the AutoCorrect Options menu (Figure 2–25).

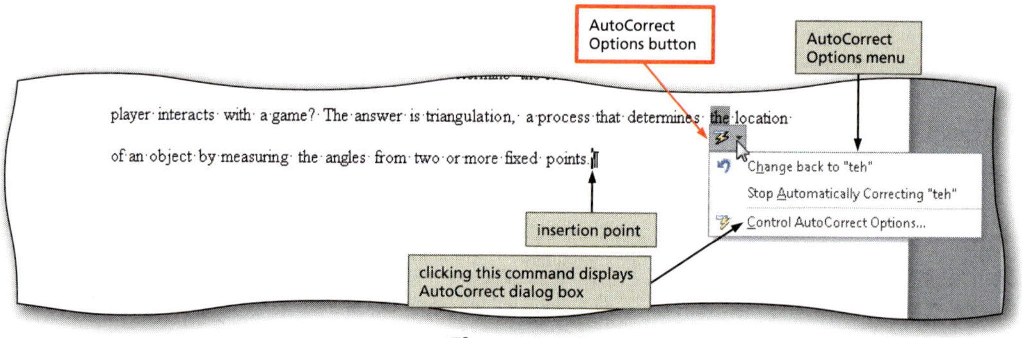

Figure 2–25

- Press the ESCAPE key to remove the AutoCorrect Options menu from the screen.

Q&A Do I need to remove the AutoCorrect Options button from the screen?

No. When you move the mouse pointer, the AutoCorrect Options button will disappear from the screen. If, for some reason, you wanted to remove the AutoCorrect Options button from the screen, you could press the ESCAPE key a second time.

To Create an AutoCorrect Entry

In addition to the predefined list of AutoCorrect spelling, capitalization, and grammar errors, you can create your own AutoCorrect entries to add to the list. For example, if you tend to mistype the word sensor as senser, you should create an AutoCorrect entry for it. The following steps create an AutoCorrect entry.

1

- Click File on the Ribbon to open the Backstage view (Figure 2–26).

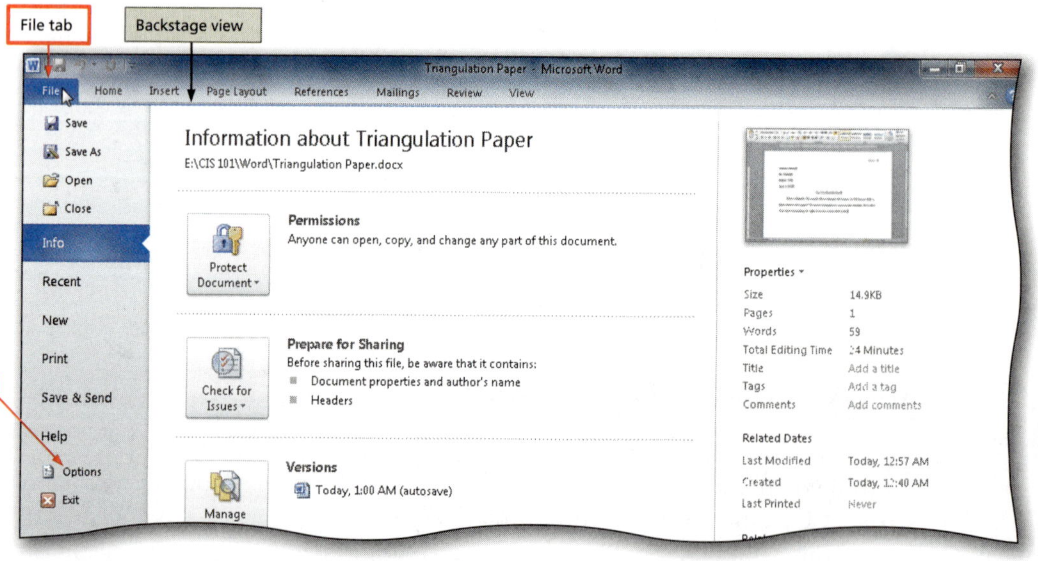

Figure 2–26

2

- Click Options in the Backstage view to display the Word Options dialog box.
- Click Proofing in the left pane (Word Options dialog box) to display proofing options in the right pane.
- Click the AutoCorrect Options button in the right pane to display the AutoCorrect dialog box.
- When Word displays the AutoCorrect dialog box, type **senser** in the Replace text box.
- Press the TAB key and then type **sensor** in the With text box (Figure 2–27).

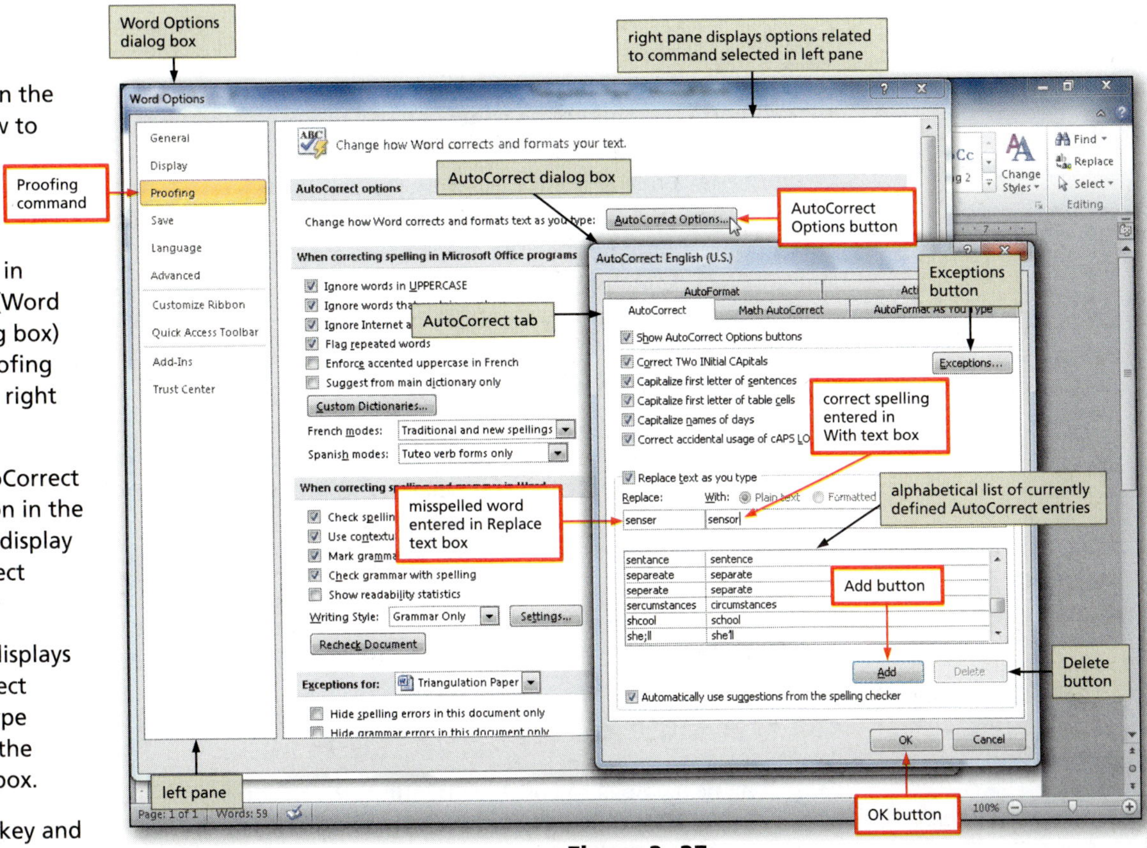

Figure 2–27

Q&A

How would I delete an existing AutoCorrect entry?

You would select the entry to be deleted in the list of defined entries in the AutoCorrect dialog box and then click the Delete button.

3

- Click the Add button (AutoCorrect dialog box) to add the entry alphabetically to the list of words to correct automatically as you type. (If your dialog box displays a Replace button instead, click it and then click the Yes button in the Microsoft Word dialog box to replace the previously defined entry.)
- Click the OK button (AutoCorrect dialog box) to close the dialog box.
- Click the OK button (Word Options dialog box) to close the dialog box.

The AutoCorrect Dialog Box

In addition to creating AutoCorrect entries for words you commonly misspell or mistype, you can create entries for abbreviations, codes, and so on. For example, you could create an AutoCorrect entry for asap, indicating that Word should replace this text with the phrase, as soon as possible.

If, for some reason, you do not want Word to correct automatically as you type, you can turn off the 'Replace text as you type' feature by clicking Options in the Backstage view, clicking Proofing in the left pane (Word Options dialog box), clicking the AutoCorrect Options button in the right pane (Figure 2–27), removing the check mark from the 'Replace text as you type' check box, and then clicking the OK button in each open dialog box.

The AutoCorrect sheet in the AutoCorrect dialog box (Figure 2–27) contains other check boxes that correct capitalization errors if the check boxes are selected. If you

BTW

Automatic Corrections

If you do not want to keep a change automatically made by Word and you immediately notice the automatic correction, you can undo the change by clicking the Undo button on the Quick Access Toolbar or pressing CTRL+Z. You also can undo a correction through the AutoCorrect Options button, which was shown above.

type two capital letters in a row, such as TH, Word makes the second letter lowercase, Th. If you begin a sentence with a lowercase letter, Word capitalizes the first letter of the sentence. If you type the name of a day in lowercase letters, such as tuesday, Word capitalizes the first letter in the name of the day, Tuesday. If you leave the CAPS LOCK key on and begin a new sentence, such as aFTER, Word corrects the typing, After, and turns off the CAPS LOCK key. If you do not want Word to automatically perform any of these corrections, simply remove the check mark from the appropriate check box in the AutoCorrect dialog box.

Sometimes you do not want Word to AutoCorrect a particular word or phrase. For example, you may use the code WD. in your documents. Because Word automatically capitalizes the first letter of a sentence, the character you enter following the period will be capitalized (in the previous sentence, it would capitalize the letter i in the word, in). To allow the code WD. to be entered into a document and still leave the AutoCorrect feature turned on, you would set an exception. To set an exception to an AutoCorrect rule, click Options in the Backstage view, click Proofing in the left pane (Word Options dialog box), click the AutoCorrect Options button in the right pane, click the Exceptions button (Figure 2–27 on the previous page), click the appropriate tab in the AutoCorrect Exceptions dialog box, type the exception entry in the text box, click the Add button, click the Close button (AutoCorrect Exceptions dialog box), and then click the OK button in each of the remaining dialog boxes.

To Enter More Text

BTW

Spacing after Punctuation

Because word processing documents use variable character fonts, it often is difficult to determine in a printed document how many times someone has pressed the SPACEBAR between sentences. Thus, the rule is to press the SPACEBAR only once after periods, colons, and other punctuation marks.

The next step is to continue typing text in the research paper up to the location of the in-text parenthetical reference. The following steps enter this text.

1. With the insertion point positioned at the end of the first paragraph in the paper, as shown in Figure 2–25 on page WD 86, press the ENTER key, so that you can begin typing the text in the second paragraph.
2. Type `Surveyors often use triangulation to measure distance. Starting at a known location and elevation, surveyors measure a length to create a base line and then use a theodolite to measure an angle to an unknown point from each side of the base line` and then press the SPACEBAR.

Citations

Both the MLA and APA guidelines suggest the use of in-text parenthetical references (placed at the end of a sentence), instead of footnoting each source of material in a paper. These parenthetical references, called citations in Word, guide the reader to the end of the paper for complete information about the source.

Plan Ahead

Reference all sources.

During your research, be sure to record essential publication information about each of your sources. Following is a sample list of types of required information for the MLA documentation style.

- Book: full name of author(s), complete title of book, edition (if available), volume (if available), publication city, publisher name, publication year, publication medium
- Magazine: full name of author(s), complete title of article, magazine title, issue number (if available), date of magazine, page numbers of article, publication medium
- Web site: full name of author(s), title of Web site, Web site publisher or sponsor (if none, write N.p.), publication date (if none, write n.d.), publication medium, date viewed

Word provides tools to assist you with inserting citations in a paper and later generating a list of sources from the citations. With a documentation style selected, Word automatically formats the citations and list of sources according to that style. The process for adding citations in Word is as follows:

1. Modify the documentation style, if necessary.
2. Insert a citation placeholder.
3. Enter the source information for the citation.

You can combine Steps 2 and 3, where you insert the citation placeholder and enter the source information at once. Or, you can insert the citation placeholder as you write and then enter the source information for the citation at a later time. While creating the research paper in this chapter, you will use both methods.

To Change the Bibliography Style

The first step in inserting a citation is to be sure the citations and sources will be formatted using the correct documentation style, called the bibliography style in Word. The following steps change the specified documentation style.

1

- Click References on the Ribbon to display the References tab.
- Click the Bibliography Style box arrow (References tab | Citations & Bibliography group) to display a gallery of predefined documentation styles (Figure 2–28).

2

- Click MLA Sixth Edition in the Bibliography Style gallery to change the documentation style to MLA.

Q&A What if I am using a different edition of a documentation style shown in the Bibliography Style gallery?

Select the closest one and then, if necessary, perform necessary edits before submitting the paper.

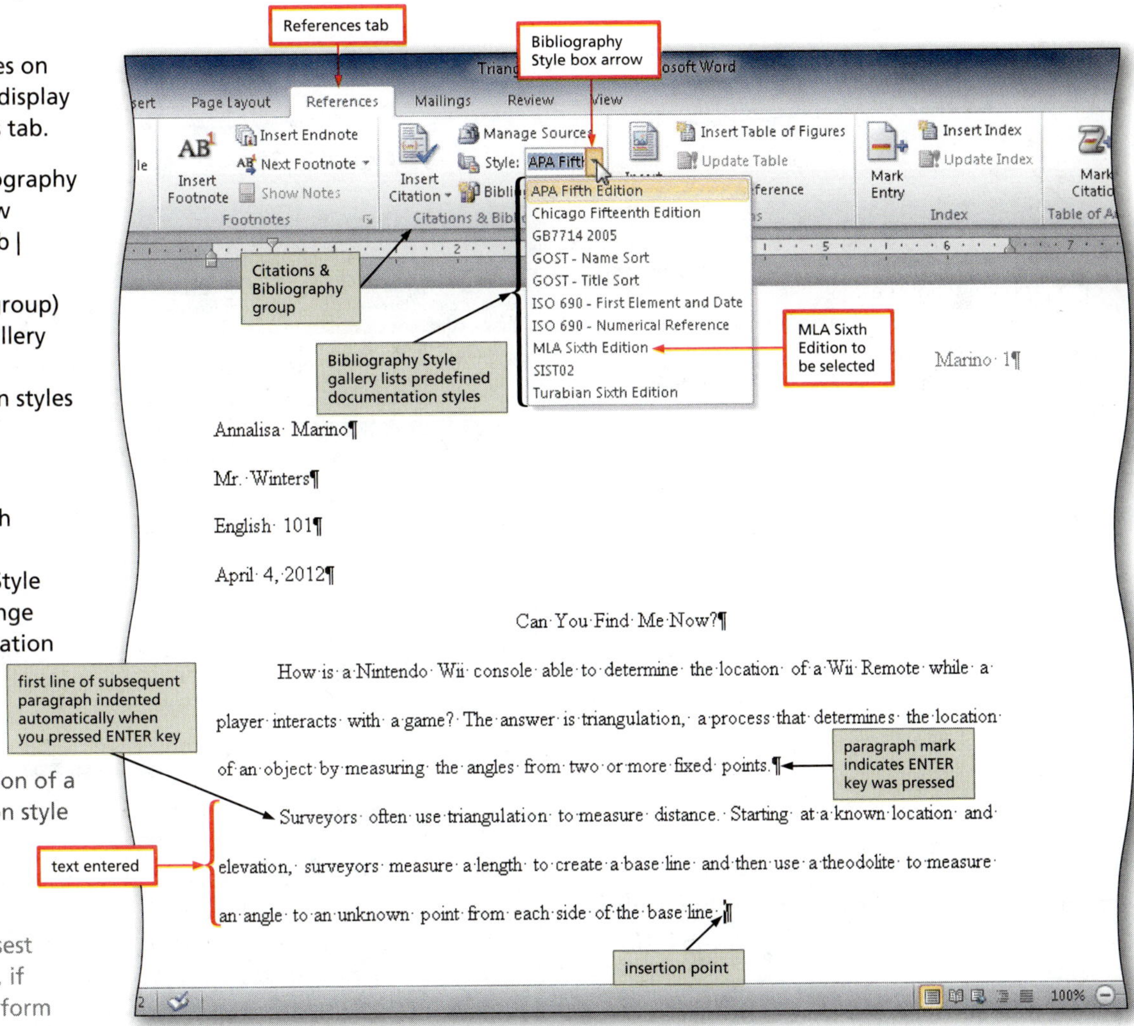

Figure 2–28

To Insert a Citation and Create Its Source

With the documentation style selected, the next task is to insert a citation placeholder and enter the source information for the citation. You can accomplish these steps at once by instructing Word to add a new source. The following steps add a new source for a magazine (periodical) article.

1

- Click the Insert Citation button (References tab | Citations & Bibliography group) to display the Insert Citation menu (Figure 2–29).

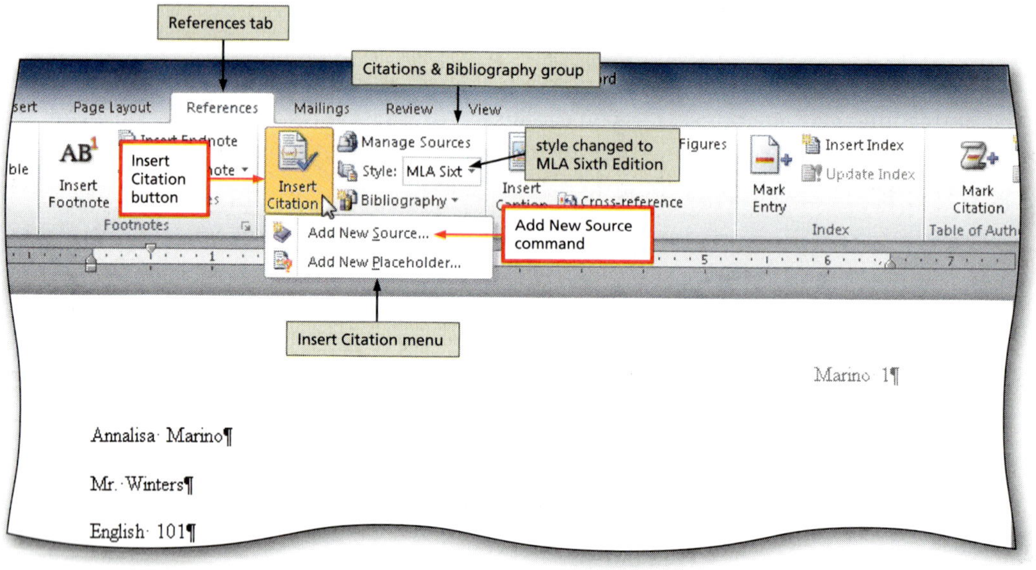

Figure 2–29

2

- Click Add New Source on the Insert Citation menu to display the Create Source dialog box (Figure 2–30).

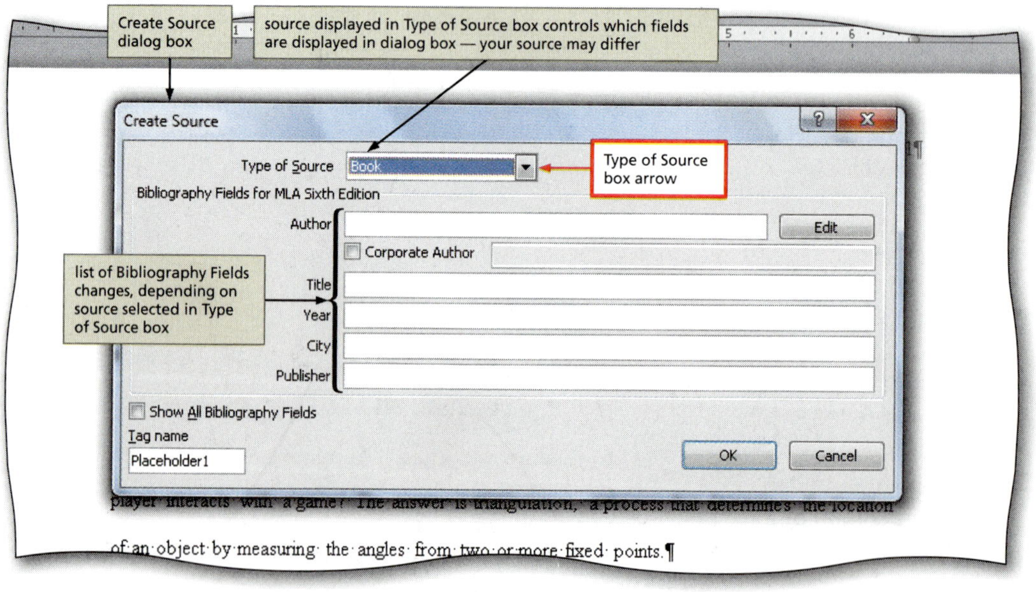

Figure 2–30

Q&A What are the Bibliography Fields in the Create Source dialog box?

A **field** is a placeholder for data whose contents can change. You enter data in some fields; Word supplies data for others. In this case, you enter the contents of the fields for a particular source, for example, the author name in the Author field.

Experiment

- Click the Type of Source box arrow and then click one of the source types in the list, so that you can see how the list of fields changes to reflect the type of source you selected.

3

- If necessary, click the Type of Source box arrow (Create Source dialog box) and then click Article in a Periodical, so that the list shows fields required for a magazine (periodical).
- Click the Author text box. Type **Jains, Malila** as the author.
- Click the Title text box. Type **How Surveyors Measure and Calculate Angles** as the article title.
- Press the TAB key and then type **Today's Modern Surveyor** as the periodical title.
- Press the TAB key and then type **2012** as the year.
- Press the TAB key and then type **Mar.** as the month.
- Press the TAB key twice and then type **30-48** as the pages (Figure 2–31).

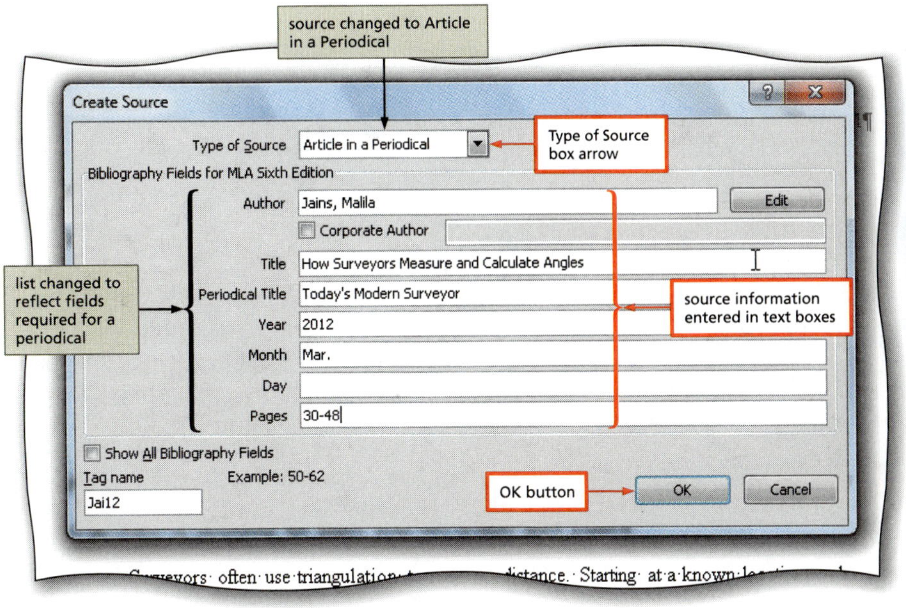

Figure 2–31

4

- Click the OK button to close the dialog box, create the source, and insert the citation in the document at the location of the insertion point (Figure 2–32).

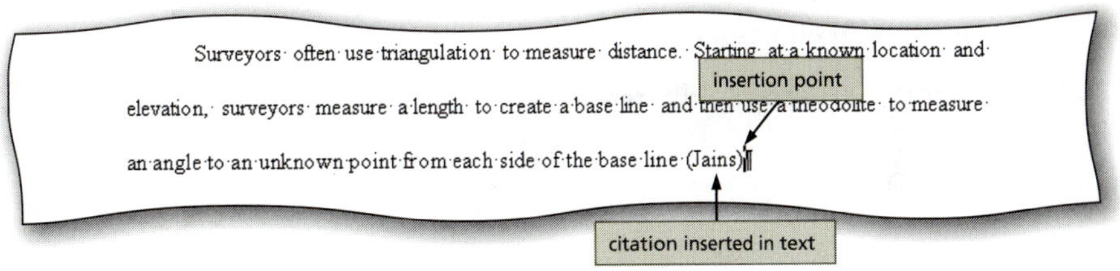

Figure 2–32

To Edit a Citation

In the MLA documentation style, if a source has page numbers, you should include them in the citation. Thus, Word provides a means to enter the page numbers to be displayed in the citation. The following steps edit a citation, so that the page numbers appear in it.

1

- Click somewhere in the citation to be edited, in this case somewhere in (Jains), which selects the citation and displays the Citation Options box arrow.
- Click the Citation Options box arrow to display the Citation Options menu (Figure 2–33).

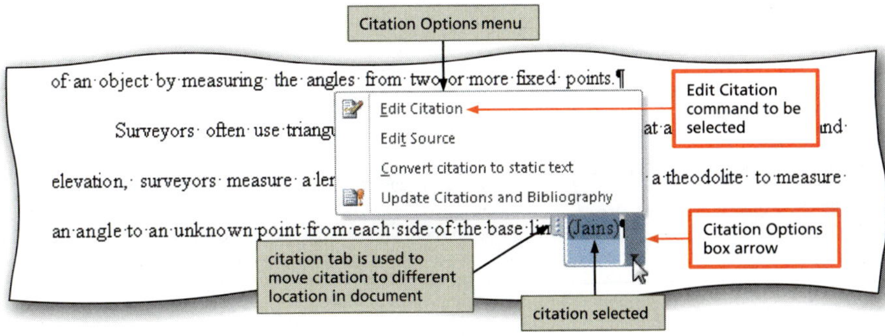

Figure 2–33

Q&A What is the purpose of the tab to the left of the selected citation?

If, for some reason, you wanted to move a citation to a different location in the document, you would select the citation and then drag the citation tab to the desired location.

2

- Click Edit Citation on the Citation Options menu to display the Edit Citation dialog box.
- Type **30-48** in the Pages text box (Edit Citations dialog box) (Figure 2–34).

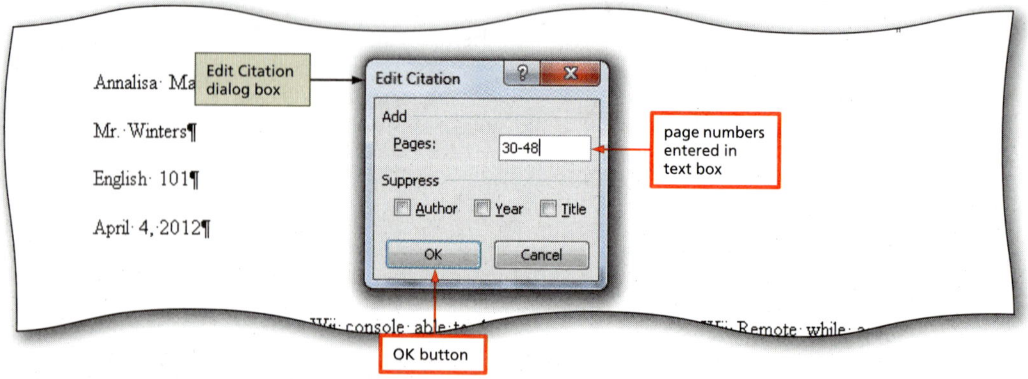

Figure 2–34

3

- Click the OK button to close the dialog box and add the page numbers to the citation in the document (Figure 2–35).

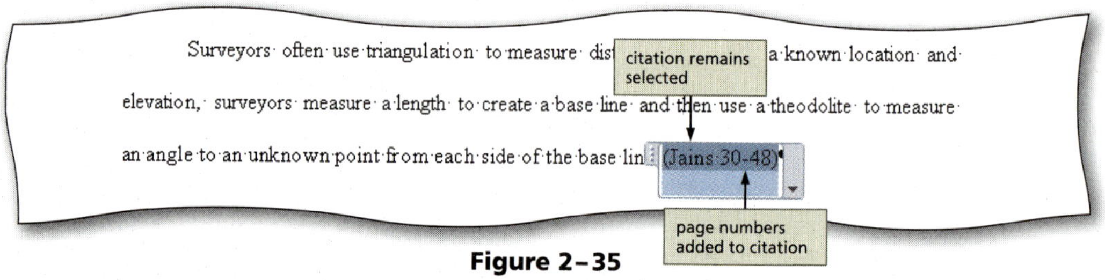

Figure 2–35

4

- Press the END key to move the insertion point to the end of the line, which also deselects the citation.
- Press the PERIOD key to end the sentence.

BTW

Edit a Source
To edit a source, click somewhere in the citation, click the Citation Options box arrow, and then click Edit Source on the Citation Options menu to display the Edit Source dialog box (which resembles the Create Source dialog box). Make necessary changes and then click the OK button.

To Enter More Text

The next step is to continue typing text in the research paper up to the location of the footnote. The following steps enter this text.

1. Press the SPACEBAR.
2. Type the next sentence (Figure 2–36): **The length of the base line and the two known angles allow a computer or person to determine the location of a third point.**

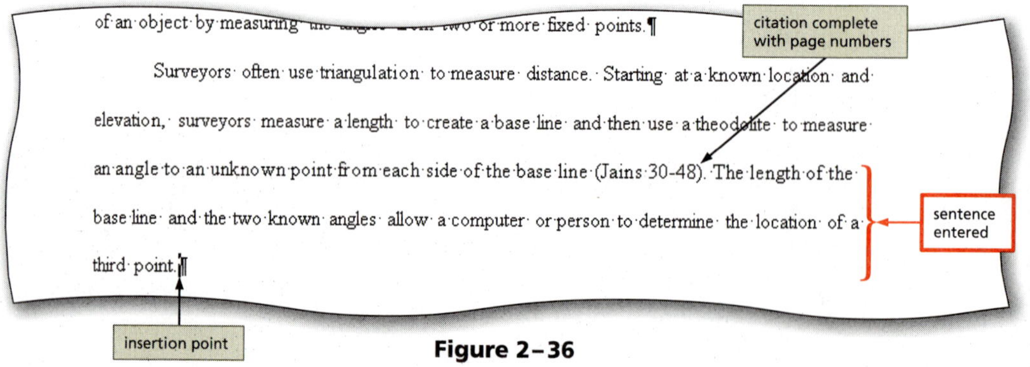

Figure 2–36

To Save an Existing Document with the Same File Name

You have made several modifications to the document since you last saved it. Thus, you should save it again. The following step saves the document again.

1. Click the Save button on the Quick Access Toolbar to overwrite the previously saved file.

Footnotes

As discussed earlier in this chapter, notes are optional in the MLA documentation style. If used, content notes elaborate on points discussed in the paper, and bibliographic notes direct the reader to evaluations of statements in a source or provide a means for identifying multiple sources. The MLA documentation style specifies that a superscript (raised number) be used for a **note reference mark** to signal that a note exists either at the bottom of the page as a **footnote** or at the end of the document as an **endnote**.

In Word, **note text** can be any length and format. Word automatically numbers notes sequentially by placing a note reference mark both in the body of the document and to the left of the note text. If you insert, rearrange, or remove notes, Word renumbers any subsequent note reference marks according to their new sequence in the document.

To Insert a Footnote Reference Mark

The following step inserts a footnote reference mark in the document at the location of the insertion point and at the location where the footnote text will be typed.

1.
- With the insertion point positioned as shown in Figure 2–36, click the Insert Footnote button (References tab | Footnotes group) to display a note reference mark (a superscripted 1) in two places: (1) in the document window at the location of the insertion point and (2) at the bottom of the page where the footnote will be positioned, just below a separator line (Figure 2–37).

Q&A What if I wanted notes to be positioned as endnotes instead of as footnotes?

You would click the Insert Endnote button (References tab | Footnotes group), which places the separator line and the endnote text at the end of the document, instead of the bottom of the page containing the reference.

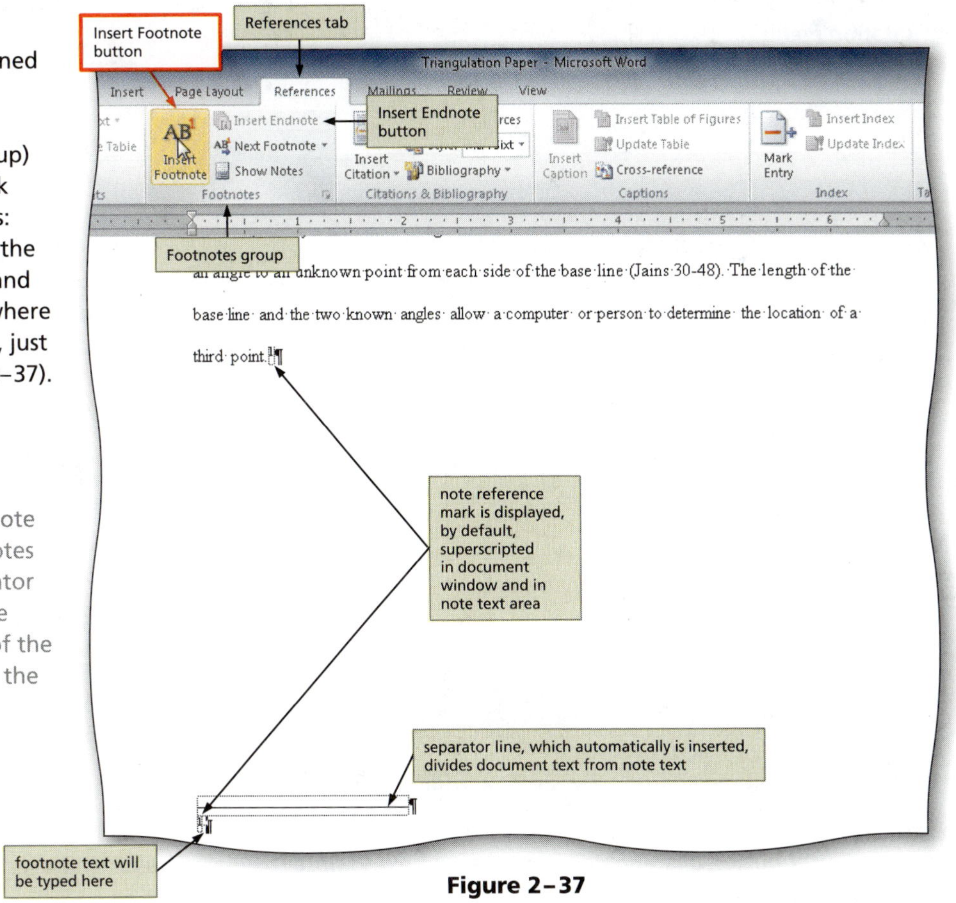

Figure 2–37

Other Ways

1. Press CTRL+ALT+F

To Enter Footnote Text

The following step types the footnote text to the right of the note reference mark below the separator line.

1 Type the footnote text up to the citation: `Cordoba and Sarkis state that electronic theodolites calculate angles automatically and then send the calculated angles to a computer for analysis` and then press the SPACEBAR.

To Insert a Citation Placeholder

Earlier in this chapter, you inserted a citation and its source at once. Sometimes, you may not have the source information readily available and would prefer entering it at a later time.

In the footnote, you will insert a placeholder for the citation and enter the source information later. The following steps insert a citation placeholder.

1

- With the insertion point positioned as shown in Figure 2–38, click the Insert Citation button (References tab | Citations & Bibliography group) to display the Insert Citation menu (Figure 2–38).

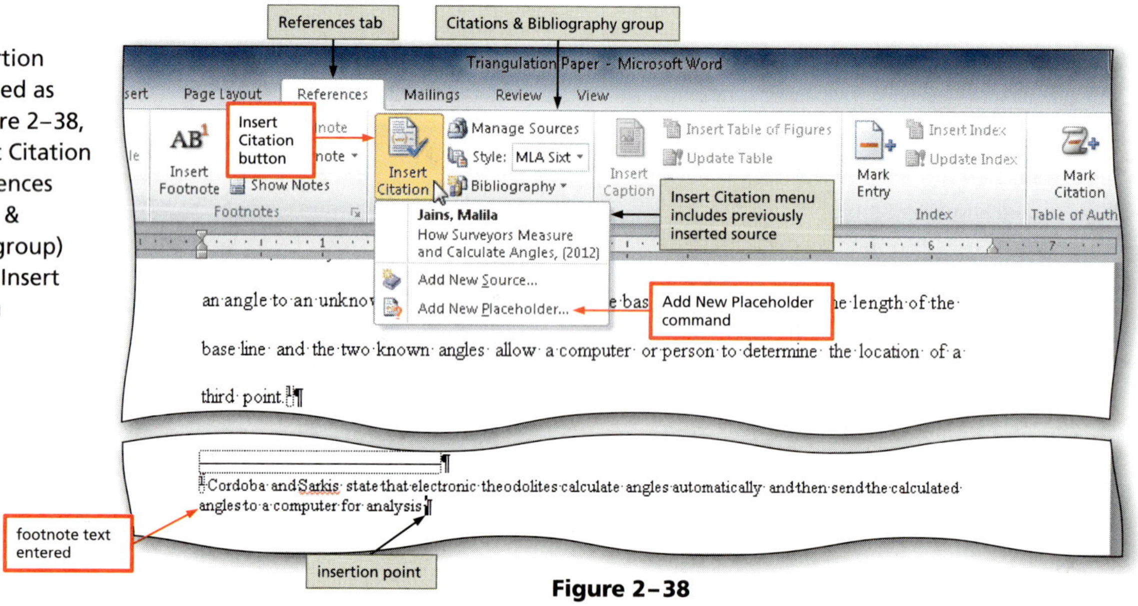

Figure 2–38

2

- Click Add New Placeholder on the Insert Citation menu to display the Placeholder Name dialog box.
- Type `Cordoba` as the tag name for the source (Figure 2–39).

Figure 2–39

Q&A

What is a tag name?

A tag name is an identifier that links a citation to a source. Word automatically creates a tag name when you enter a source. When you create a citation placeholder, enter a meaningful tag name, which will appear in the citation placeholder until you edit the source.

3

- Click the OK button (Placeholder Name dialog box) to close the dialog box and insert the entered tag name in the citation placeholder in the document.
- Press the PERIOD key to end the sentence.

Footnote Text Style

When you insert a footnote, Word formats it using the Footnote Text style, which does not adhere to the MLA documentation style. For example, notice in Figure 2–38 that the footnote text is single-spaced, left-aligned, and a smaller font size than the text in the research paper. According to the MLA documentation style, notes should be formatted like all other paragraphs in the paper.

You could change the paragraph formatting of the footnote text to first-line indent and double-spacing and then change the font size from 10 to 12 point. If you use this technique, however, you will need to change the format of the footnote text for each footnote you enter into the document.

A more efficient technique is to modify the format of the Footnote Text style so that every footnote you enter in the document will use the formats defined in this style.

To Modify a Style Using a Shortcut Menu

The Footnote Text style specifies left-aligned single-spaced paragraphs with a 10-point font size for text. To meet MLA documentation style, the footnotes should be double-spaced with a first line indent and a 12-point font size for text. The following steps modify the Footnote Text style.

1

- Right-click the note text in the footnote to display a shortcut menu related to footnotes (Figure 2–40).

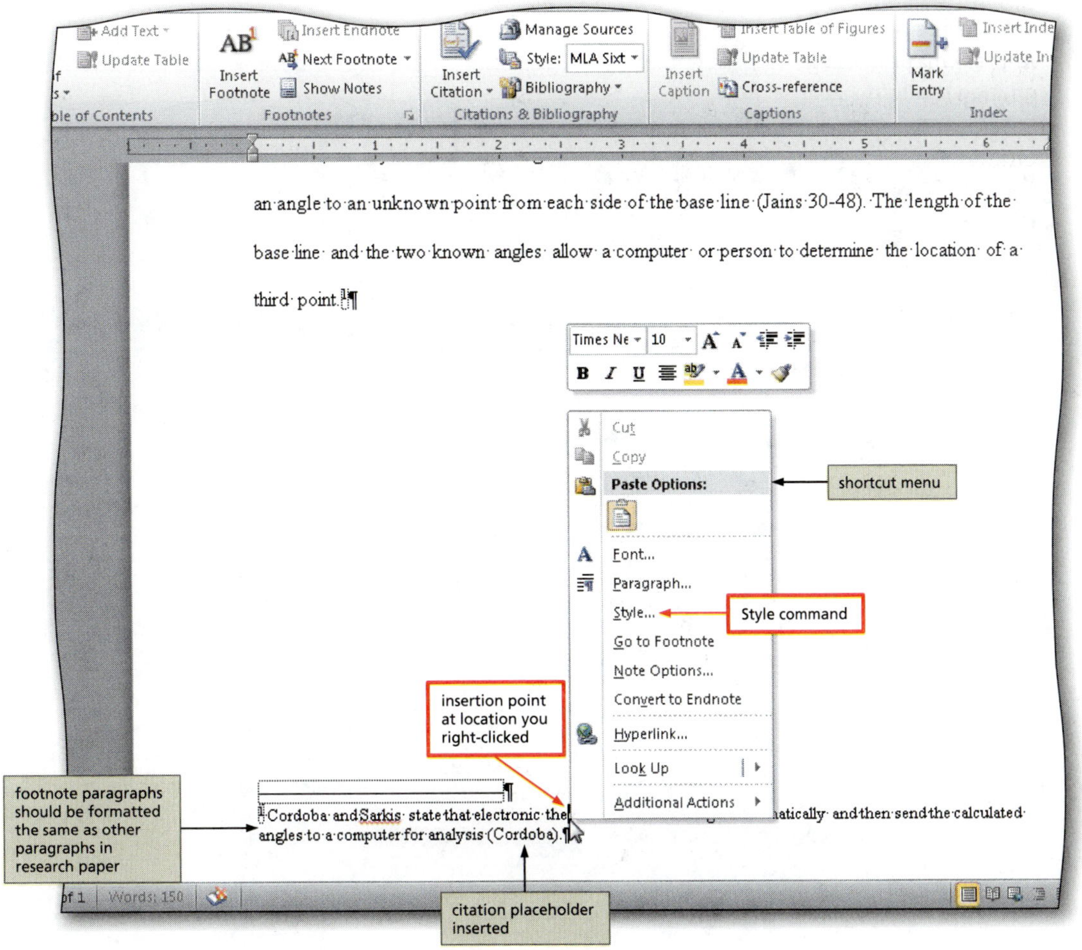

Figure 2–40

2

- Click Style on the shortcut menu to display the Style dialog box. If necessary, click the Category box arrow, click All styles in the Cagetory list, and then click Footnote Text in the Styles list.
- Click the Modify button (Style dialog box) to display the Modify Style dialog box.
- Click the Font Size box arrow (Modify Style dialog box) to display the Font Size list and then click 12 in the Font Size list to change the font size.
- Click the Double Space button to change the line spacing.
- Click the Format button to display the Format menu (Figure 2–41).

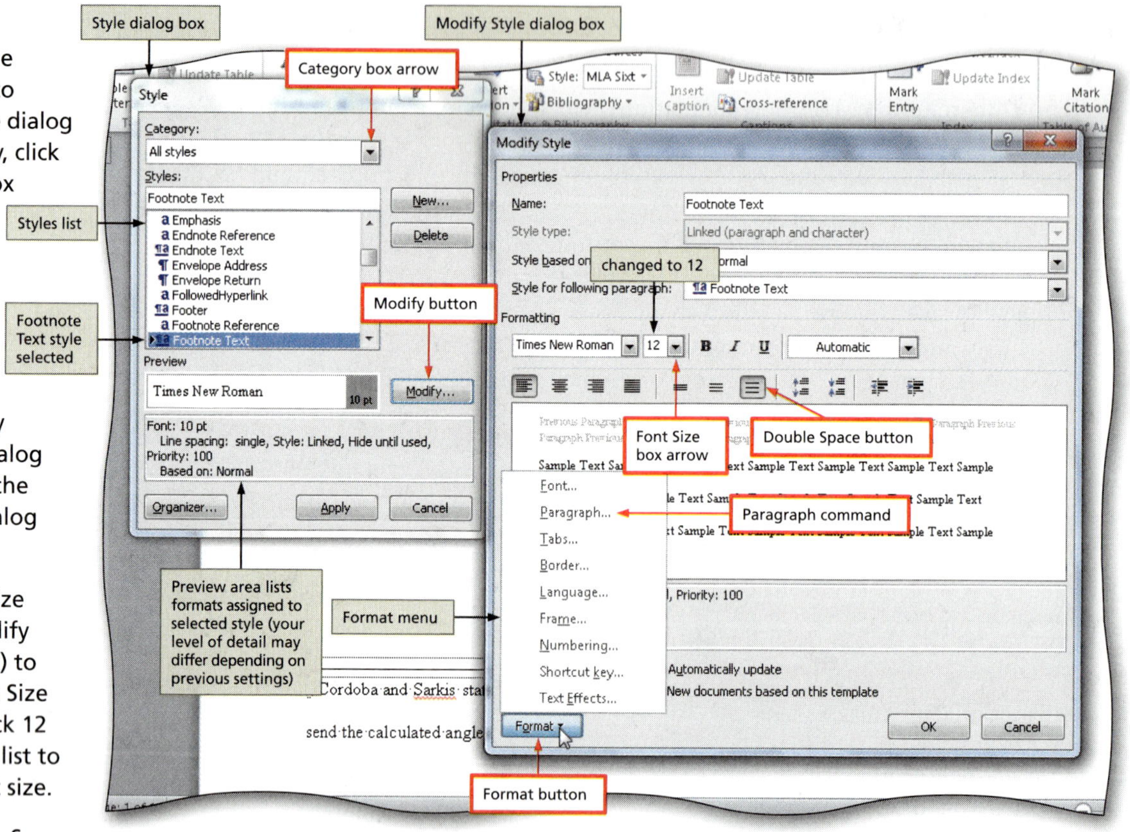

Figure 2–41

3

- Click Paragraph on the Format menu (Modify Style dialog box) to display the Paragraph dialog box.
- Click the Special box arrow (Paragraph dialog box) and then click First line (Figure 2–42).

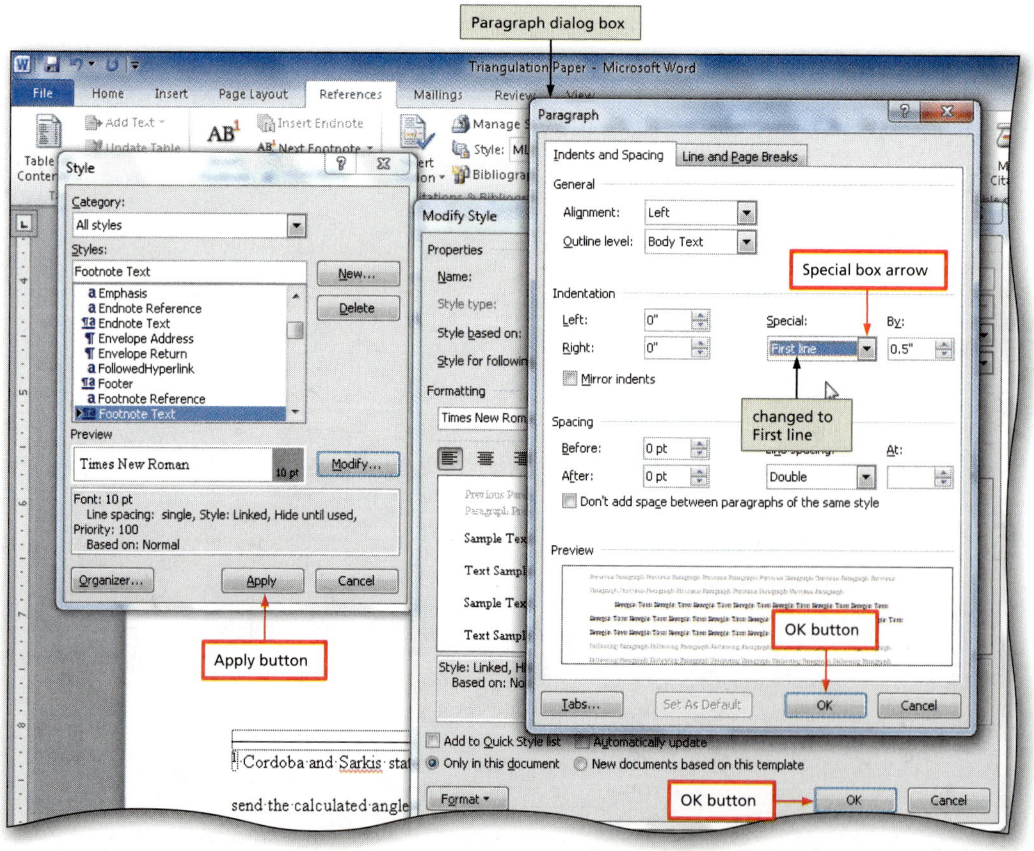

Figure 2–42

4

- Click the OK button (Paragraph dialog box) to close the dialog box.
- Click the OK button (Modify Style dialog box) to close the dialog box.
- Click the Apply button (Style dialog box) to apply the style changes to the footnote text (Figure 2–43).

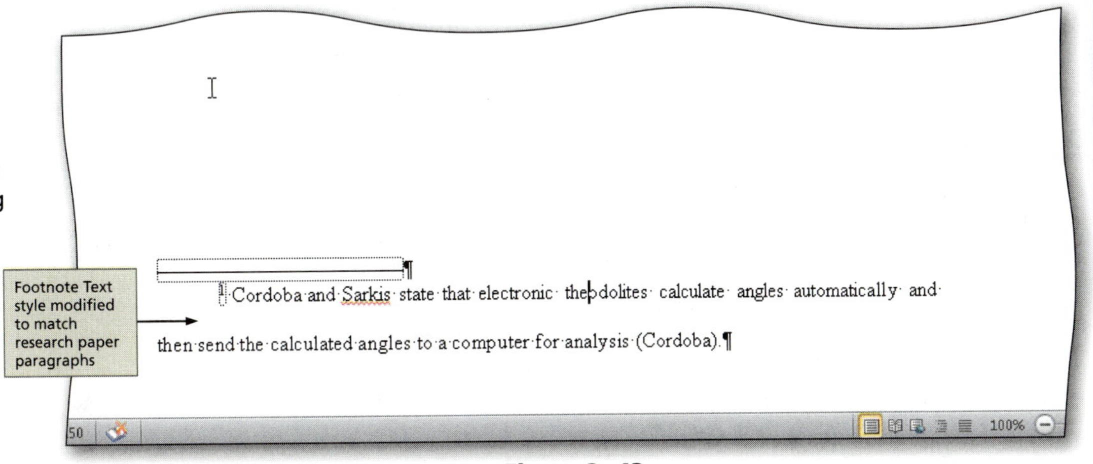

Figure 2–43

Q&A

Will all footnotes use this modified style?

Yes. Any future footnotes entered in the document will use a 12-point font with the paragraphs first-line indented and double-spaced.

Other Ways

1. Click Styles Dialog Box Launcher (Home tab | Styles group), point to style name in list, click style name box arrow, click Modify, change settings (Modify Style dialog box), click OK button
2. Click Styles Dialog Box Launcher (Home tab | Styles group), click Manage Styles button in task pane, select style name in list, click Modify button, change settings (Modify Style dialog box), click OK button in each dialog box

To Edit a Source

When you typed the footnote text for this research paper, you inserted a citation placeholder for the source. Assume you now have the source information and are ready to enter it. The following steps edit a source.

1

- Click somewhere in the citation placeholder to be edited, in this case (Cordoba), to select the citation placeholder.
- Click the Citation Options box arrow to display the Citation Options menu (Figure 2–44).

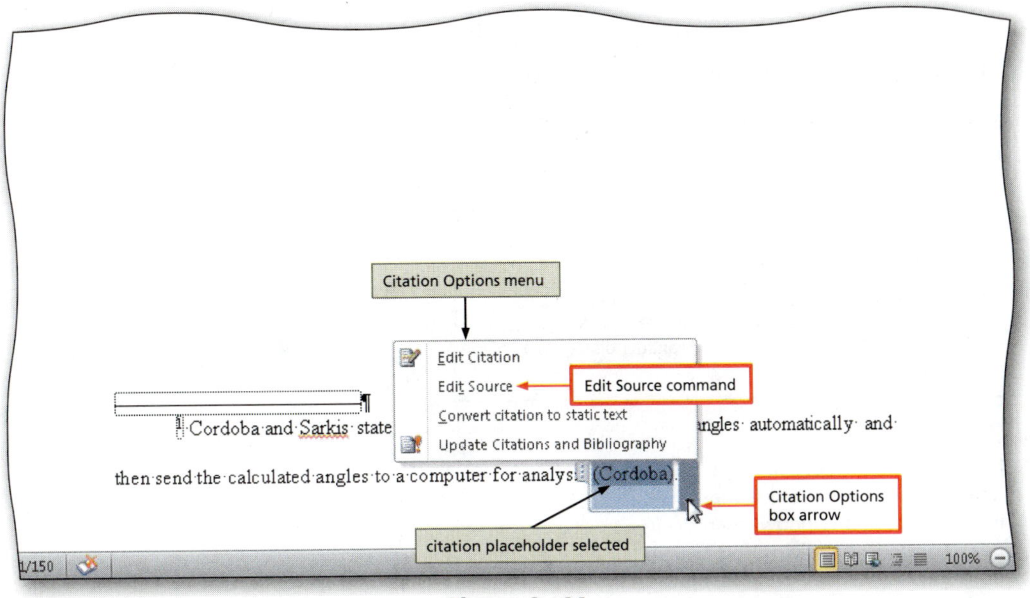

Figure 2–44

2

- Click Edit Source on the Citation Options menu to display the Edit Source dialog box.
- If necessary, click the Type of Source box arrow (Edit Source dialog box) and then click Book, so that the list shows fields required for a book.
- Click the Author text box. Type **`Cordoba, Nicolas E.,; Sarkis, Kara A.`** as the author.

Q&A

What if I do not know how to punctuate the author entry so that Word formats it properly?

Click the Edit button (Edit Source dialog box) to the right of the Author entry for assistance. For example, you should separate multiple author names with a semicolon as shown in this figure.

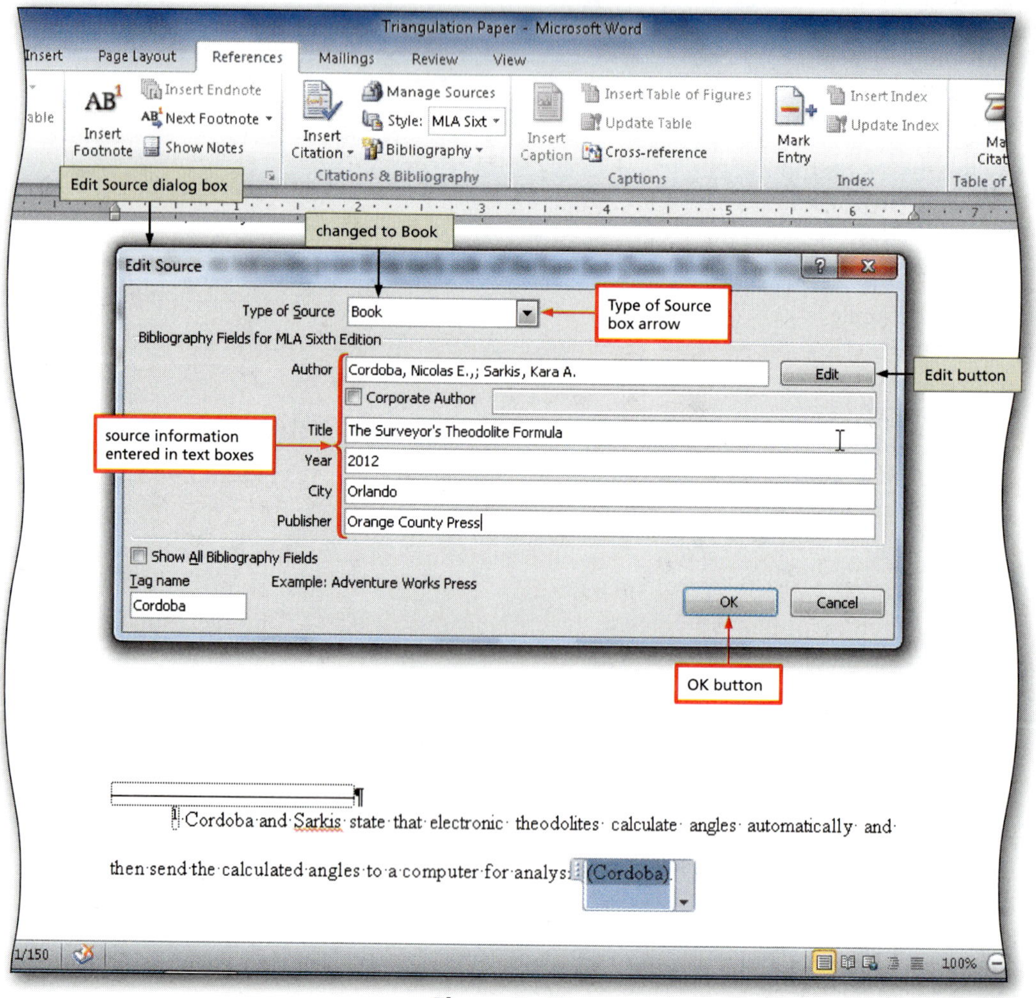

Figure 2–45

- Click the Title text box. Type **`The Surveyor's Theodolite Formula`** as the book title.
- Press the TAB key and then type **`2012`** as the year.
- Press the TAB key and then type **`Orlando`** as the city.
- Press the TAB key and then type **`Orange County Press`** as the publisher (Figure 2–45).

3

- Click the OK button to close the dialog box and create the source.

Other Ways

1. Click Manage Sources button (References tab | Citations & Bibliography group), click placeholder source in Current List, click Edit button (Source Manager dialog box)

BTW

Q&As

For a complete list of the Q&As found in many of the step-by-step sequences in the Office and Windows chapters in this book, visit the Microsoft Office and Concepts CourseMate Web site at www.cengagebrain.com and then navigate to the Q&A resource for this book.

To Edit a Citation

In the MLA documentation style, if you reference the author's name in the text, you should not list it again in the parenthetical citation. Instead, just list the page number in the citation. To do this, you instruct Word to suppress author and title. The following steps edit the citation, suppressing the author and title but displaying the page numbers.

1. If necessary, click somewhere in the citation to be edited, in this case (Cordoba), to select the citation and display the Citation Options box arrow.
2. Click the Citation Options box arrow to display the Citation Options menu.
3. Click Edit Citation on the Citation Options menu to display the Edit Citation dialog box.
4. Type **25** in the Pages text box (Edit Citation dialog box).
5. Click the Author check box to place a check mark in it.
6. Click the Title check box to place a check mark in it (Figure 2–46).
7. Click the OK button to close the dialog box, remove the author name from the citation in the footnote, suppress the title from showing, and add a page number to the citation (shown in Figure 2-47 on page WD 101).

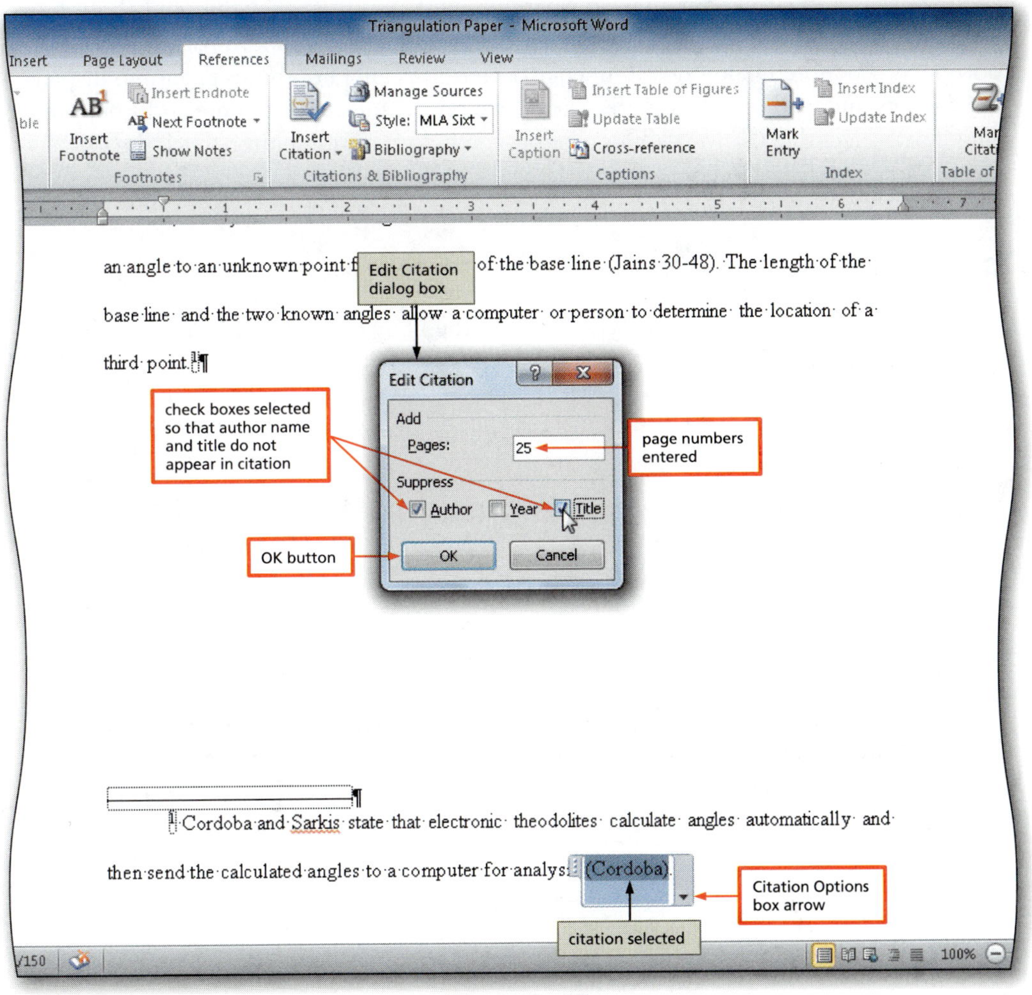

Figure 2–46

Working with Footnotes and Endnotes

You edit footnote text just as you edit any other text in the document. To delete or move a note reference mark, however, the insertion point must be in the document text (not in the footnote text).

To delete a note, select the note reference mark in the document text (not in the footnote text) by dragging through the note reference mark and then click the Cut button (Home tab | Clipboard group). Or, click immediately to the right of the note reference mark in the document text and then press the BACKSPACE key twice, or click immediately to the left of the note reference mark in the document text and then press the DELETE key twice.

To move a note to a different location in a document, select the note reference mark in the document text (not in the footnote text), click the Cut button (Home tab | Clipboard group), click the location where you want to move the note, and then click the Paste button (Home tab | Clipboard group). When you move or delete notes, Word automatically renumbers any remaining notes in the correct sequence.

If you position the mouse pointer on the note reference mark in the document text, the note text is displayed above the note reference mark as a ScreenTip. To remove the ScreenTip, move the mouse pointer.

If, for some reason, you wanted to change the format of note reference marks in footnotes or endnotes (i.e., from 1, 2, 3, to A, B, C), you would click the Footnote & Endnote Dialog Box Launcher (References tab | Footnotes group) to display the Footnote and Endnote dialog box, click the Number format box arrow (Footnote and Endnote dialog box), click the desired number format in the list, and then click the Apply button.

If, for some reason, you wanted to convert footnotes to endnotes, you would click the Footnote & Endnote Dialog Box Launcher (References tab | Footnotes group) to display the Footnote and Endnote dialog box, click the Convert button (Footnote and Endnote dialog box), select the 'Convert all footnotes to endnotes' option button, click the OK button, and then click the Close button (Footnote and Endnote dialog box).

BTW

Footnote and Endnote Location

You can change the location of footnotes from the bottom of the page to the end of the text by clicking the Footnotes and Endnote Dialog Box Launcher (References tab | Footnotes group), clicking the Footnotes box arrow (Footnote and Endnote dialog box), and then clicking Below text. Similarly, clicking the Endnotes box arrow (Footnote and Endnote dialog box) enables you to change the location of endnotes from the end of the document to the end of a section.

To Enter More Text

The next step is to continue typing text in the body of the research paper. The following steps enter this text.

1. Position the insertion point after the note reference mark in the document and then press the ENTER key.

2. Type the third paragraph of the research paper (Figure 2–47): `Similarly, the Nintendo Wii console uses triangulation to determine the location of a Wii Remote. A player places a sensor bar, which contains two infrared transmitters, near or on top of a television. While the player uses the Wii Remote, the Wii console determines the remote's location by calculating the distance and angles between the Wii Remote and the two transmitters on the sensor bar. Determining the location of a Wii Remote is relatively simple because the sensor bar contains only two fixed points: the transmitters.`

To Count Words

Often when you write papers, you are required to compose the papers with a minimum number of words. The minimum requirement for the research paper in this chapter is 325 words. You can look on the status bar and see the total number of words thus far in a document. For example, Figure 2–47 shows the research paper has 236 words, but you are not sure if that count includes the words in your footnote. The following steps display the Word Count dialog box, so that you can verify the footnote text is included in the count.

1

- Click the Word Count indicator on the status bar to display the Word Count dialog box.
- If necessary, place a check mark in the 'Include textboxes, footnotes and endnotes' check box (Word Count dialog box) (Figure 2–47).

Q&A Why do the statistics in my Word Count dialog box differ from Figure 2–47?

Depending on the accuracy of your typing, your statistics may differ.

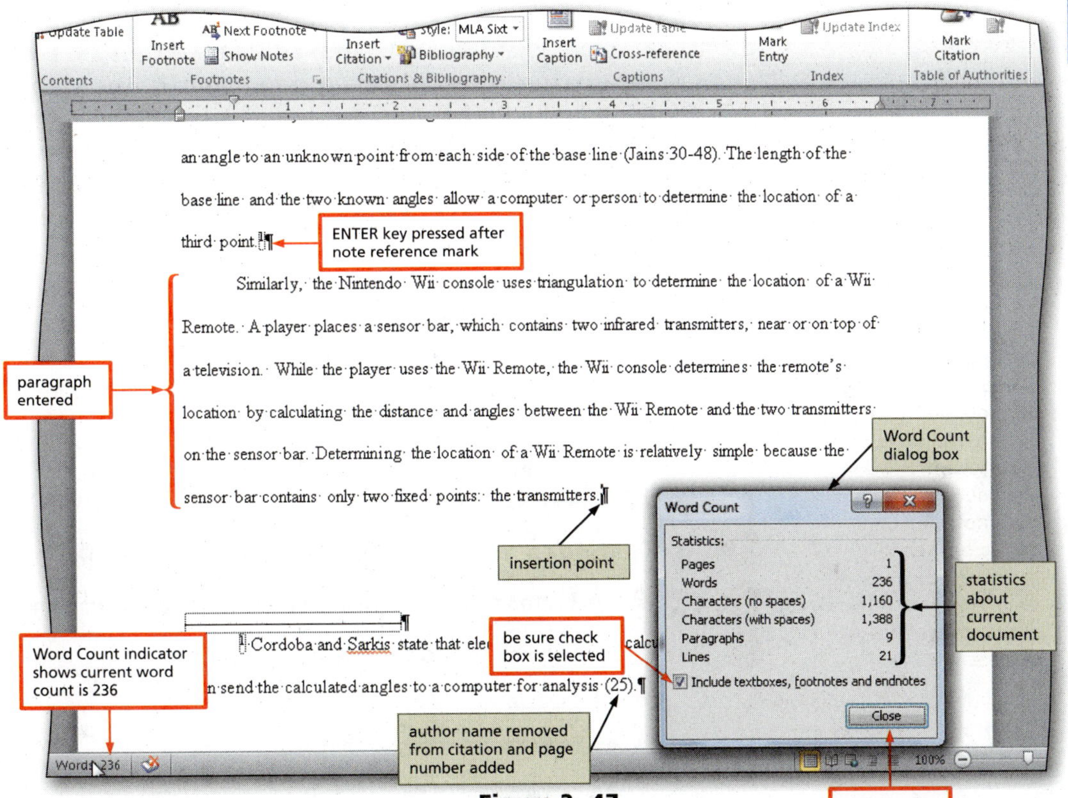

Figure 2–47

2

- Click the Close button to close the dialog box.

Q&A Can I display statistics for just a section of the document?

Yes. Select the section and then click the Word Count indicator on the status bar to display statistics about the selected text.

Other Ways

1. Click Word Count button (Review tab | Proofing group)
2. Press CTRL+SHIFT+G

Automatic Page Breaks

As you type documents that exceed one page, Word automatically inserts page breaks, called **automatic page breaks** or **soft page breaks**, when it determines the text has filled one page according to paper size, margin settings, line spacing, and other settings. If you add text, delete text, or modify text on a page, Word recomputes the location of automatic page breaks and adjusts them accordingly.

Word performs page recomputation between the keystrokes, that is, in between the pauses in your typing. Thus, Word refers to the automatic page break task as **background repagination**. The steps on the next page illustrate Word's automatic page break feature.

To Enter More Text and Insert a Citation Placeholder

The next task is to type the fourth paragraph in the body of the research paper. The following steps enter this text and a placeholder.

1. With the insertion point positioned at the end of the third paragraph as shown in Figure 2–47 on the previous page, press the ENTER key.

2. Type the fourth paragraph of the research paper (Figure 2–48): **A more complex application of triangulation occurs in a global positioning system (GPS). A GPS consists of one or more earth-based receivers that accept and analyze signals sent by satellites to determine a receiver's geographic location. GPS receivers, found in handheld navigation devices and many vehicles, use triangulation to determine their location relative to at least three geostationary satellites. According to Sanders, the satellites are the fixed points in the triangulation formula** and then press the SPACEBAR.

Q&A Why does the text move from the second page to the first page as I am typing?

Word, by default, will not allow the first line of a paragraph to be by itself at the bottom of a page (an orphan) or the last line of a paragraph to be by itself at the top of a page (a widow). As you type, Word adjusts the placement of the paragraph to avoid orphans and widows.

BTW **Page Break Locations**
As you type, your page break may occur at different locations depending on Word settings and the type of printer connected to the computer.

3. Click the Insert Citation button (References tab | Citations & Bibliography group) to display the Insert Citation menu. Click Add New Placeholder on the Insert Citation menu to display the Placeholder Name dialog box.

4. Type **Sanders** as the tag name for the source.

5. Click the OK button to close the dialog box and insert the tag name in the citation placeholder.

6. Press the PERIOD key to end the sentence.

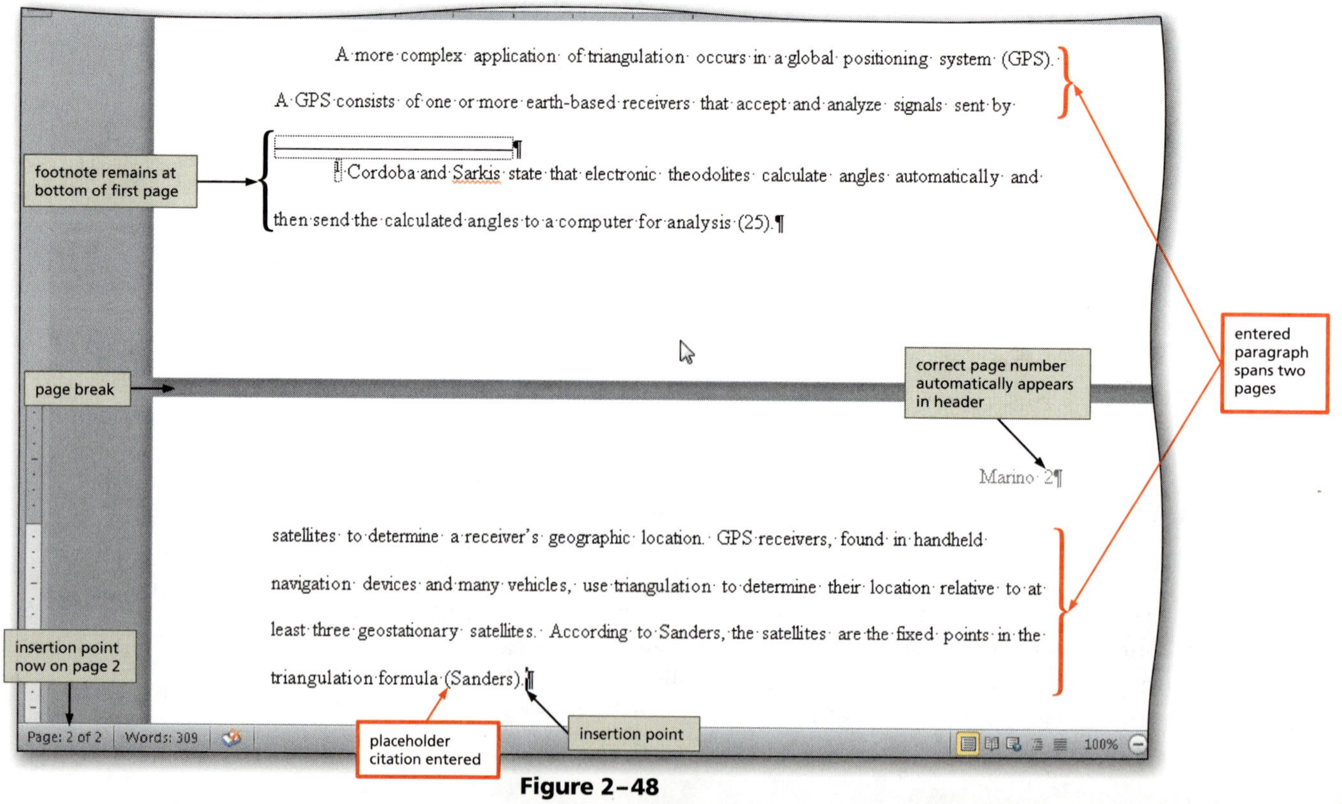

Figure 2–48

To Edit a Source

When you typed the fourth paragraph of the research paper, you inserted a citation placeholder, Sanders, for the source. You now have the source information, which is for a Web site, and are ready to enter it. The following steps edit the source for the Sanders citation placeholder.

1. Click somewhere in the citation placeholder to be edited, in this case (Sanders), to select the citation placeholder.
2. Click the Citation Options box arrow to display the Citation Options menu.
3. Click Edit Source on the Citation Options menu to display the Edit Source dialog box.
4. If necessary, click the Type of Source box arrow (Edit Source dialog box); scroll to and then click Web site, so that the list shows fields required for a Web site.
5. Place a check mark in the Show All Bibliography Fields check box to display more fields related to Web sites.
6. Click the Author text box. Type **`Sanders, Gregory B.`** as the author.
7. Click the Name of Web Page text box. Type **`Understanding Satellites and Global Positioning Systems`** as the Web page name.
8. Click the Production Company text box. Type **`Course Technology`** as the production company.
9. Click the Year Accessed text box. Type **`2012`** as the year accessed.
10. Press the TAB key and then type **`Feb.`** as the month accessed.

Q&A What if some of the text boxes disappear as I enter the Web site fields?

With the Show All Bibliography Fields check box selected, the dialog box may not be able to display all Web site fields at the same time. In this case, some may scroll up.

11. Press the TAB key and then type **`27`** as the day accessed (Figure 2–49).

Q&A Do I need to enter a Web address (URL)?

The latest MLA documentation style update does not require the Web address in the source.

12. Click the OK button to close the dialog box and create the source.

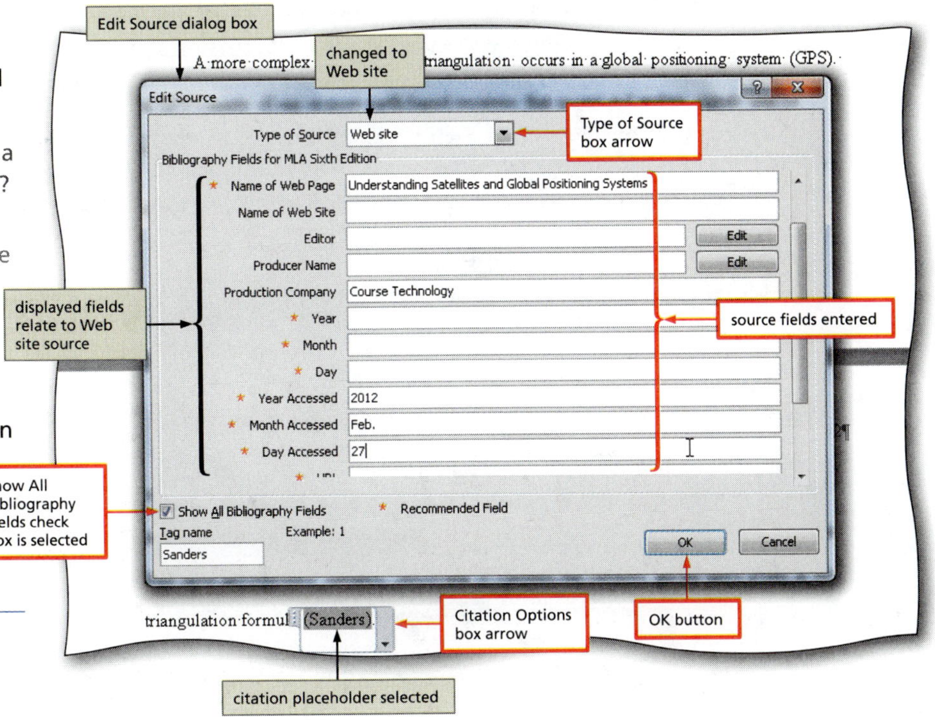

Figure 2–49

To Edit a Citation

As mentioned earlier, if you reference the author's name in the text, you should not list it again in the parenthetical citation. For Web site citations, when you suppress the author's name, the citation shows the Web site name because page numbers do not apply. The following steps edit the citation, suppressing the author and displaying the name of the Web site instead.

1. If necessary, click somewhere in the citation to be edited, in this case (Sanders), to select the citation and display the Citation Options box arrow.
2. Click the Citation Options box arrow and then click Edit Citation on the Citation Options menu to display the Edit Citation dialog box.
3. Click the Author check box (Edit Citation dialog box) to place a check mark in it (Figure 2–50).
4. Click the OK button to close the dialog box, remove the author name from the citation, and show the name of the Web site in the citation (shown in Figure 2–51).

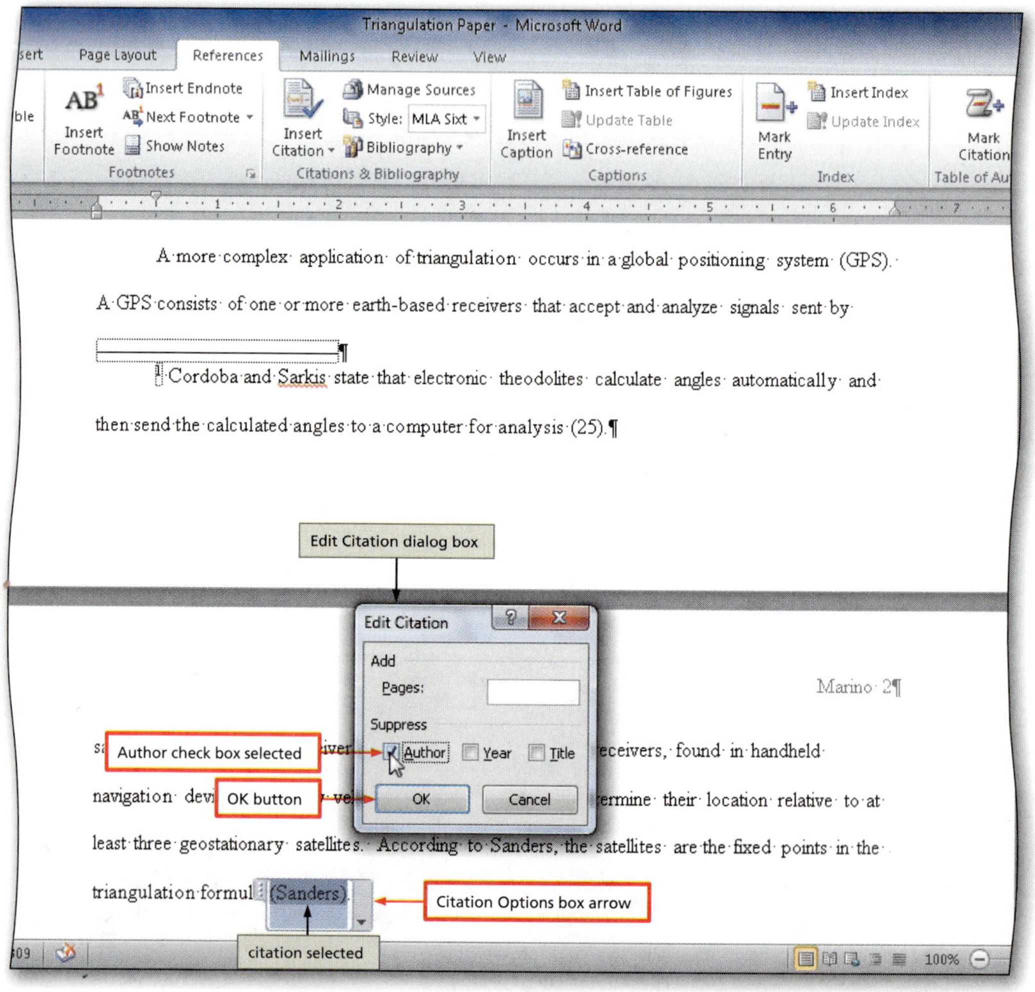

Figure 2–50

To Enter More Text

The next step is to type the last paragraph of text in the research paper. The following steps enter this text.

1. Press the END key to position the insertion point at the end of the fourth paragraph and then press the ENTER key.

2. Type the last paragraph of the research paper (Figure 2–51): **The next time you pass a surveyor, play a Nintendo Wii, or follow a route prescribed by a vehicle's navigation system, keep in mind that none of it might have been possible without the concept of triangulation.**

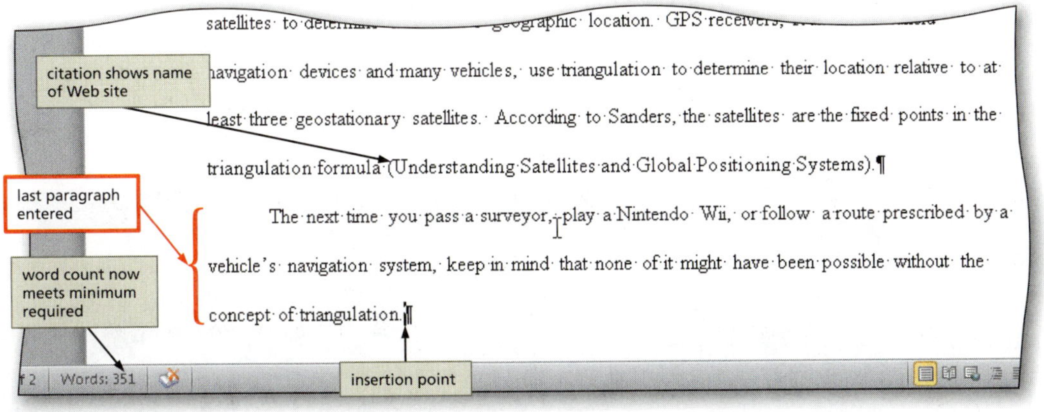

Figure 2–51

To Save an Existing Document with the Same File Name

You have made several modifications to the document since you last saved it. Thus, you should save it again. The following step saves the document again.

1. Click the Save button on the Quick Access Toolbar to overwrite the previously saved file.

Break Point: If you wish to take a break, this is a good place to do so. You can quit Word now (refer to page WD 125 for instructions). To resume at a later time, start Word (refer to page WD 70 for instructions), open the file called Triangulation Paper (refer to page WD 45 for instructions), and continue following the steps from this location forward.

Creating an Alphabetical Works Cited Page

According to the MLA documentation style, the **works cited page** is a list of sources that are referenced directly in a research paper. You place the list on a separate numbered page with the title, Works Cited, centered one inch from the top margin. The works are to be alphabetized by the author's last name or, if the work has no author, by the work's title. The first line of each entry begins at the left margin. Indent subsequent lines of the same entry one-half inch from the left margin.

Plan Ahead

Create the list of sources.
A **bibliography** is an alphabetical list of sources referenced in a paper. Whereas the text of the research paper contains brief references to the source (the citations), the bibliography lists all publication information about the source. Documentation styles differ significantly in their guidelines for preparing a bibliography. Each style identifies formats for various sources, including books, magazines, pamphlets, newspapers, Web sites, television programs, paintings, maps, advertisements, letters, memos, and much more. You can find information about various styles and their guidelines in printed style guides and on the Web.

To Page Break Manually

The works cited are to be displayed on a separate numbered page. Thus, you must insert a manual page break following the body of the research paper so that the list of sources is displayed on a separate page. A **manual page break**, or **hard page break**, is one that you force into the document at a specific location.

Word never moves or adjusts manual page breaks. Word, however, does adjust any automatic page breaks that follow a manual page break. Word inserts manual page breaks immediately above or to the left of the location of the insertion point. The following step inserts a manual page break after the text of the research paper.

1

- Verify that the insertion point is positioned at the end of the text of the research paper, as shown in Figure 2–51 on the previous page.
- Click Insert on the Ribbon to display the Insert tab.
- Click the Page Break button (Insert tab | Pages group) to insert a manual page break immediately to the left of the insertion point and position the insertion point immediately below the manual page break (Figure 2–52).

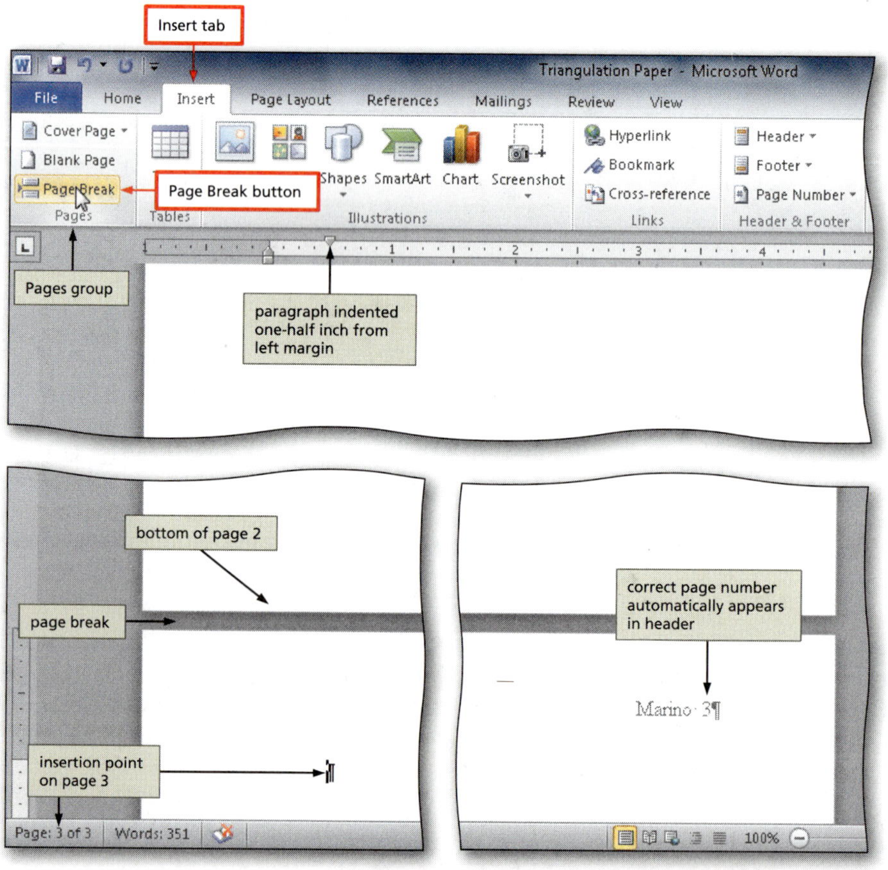

Figure 2–52

Other Ways
1. Press CTRL+ENTER

To Apply a Style

The works cited title is to be centered between the margins of the paper. If you simply issue the Center command, the title will not be centered properly. Instead, it will be one-half inch to the right of the center point because earlier you set the first-line indent for paragraphs to one-half inch.

To properly center the title of the works cited page, you could drag the First Line Indent marker back to the left margin before centering the paragraph, or you could apply the Normal style to the location of the insertion point. Recall that you modified the Normal style for this document to 12-point Times New Roman with double-spaced, left-aligned paragraphs that have no space after the paragraphs.

To apply a style to a paragraph, first position the insertion point in the paragraph and then apply the style. The following step applies the modified Normal style to the location of the insertion point.

1

- Click Home on the Ribbon to display the Home tab.
- With the insertion point on the paragraph mark at the top of page 3 (as shown in Figure 2–52) even if Normal is selected, click Normal in the Quick Style gallery (Home tab | Styles group) to apply the Normal style to the paragraph containing the insertion point (Figure 2–53).

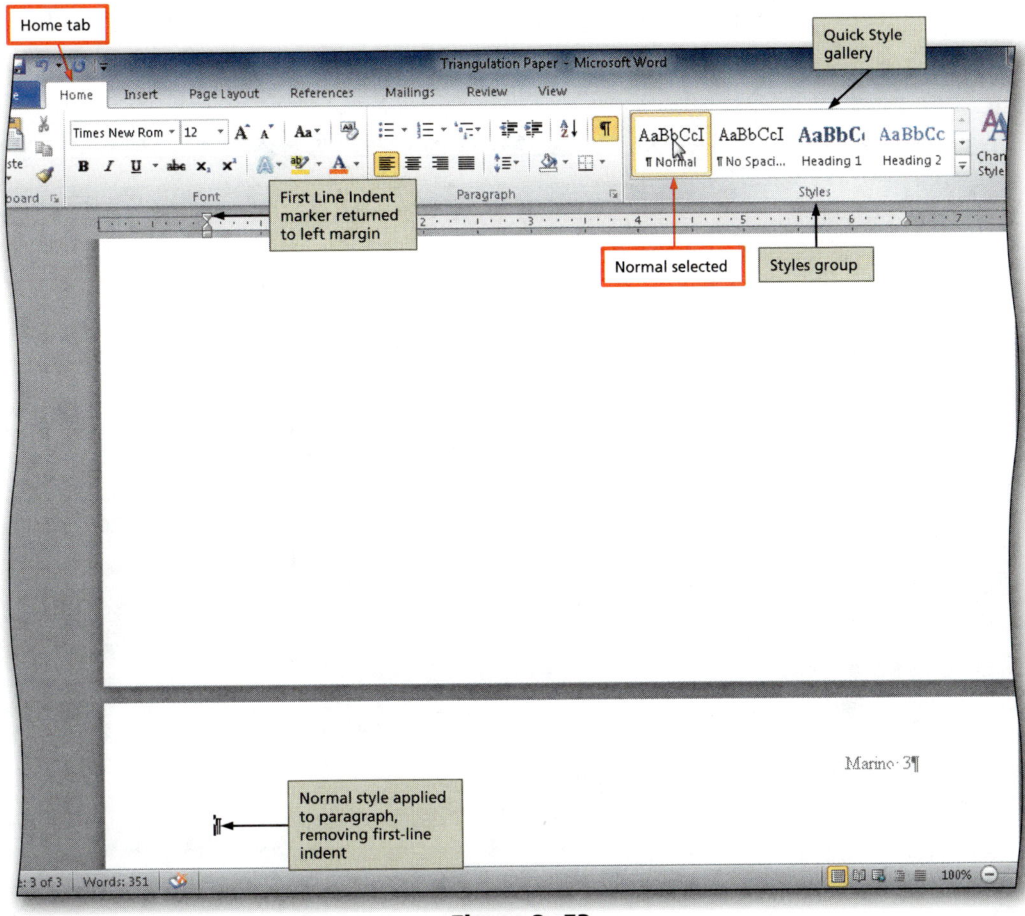

Figure 2–53

Other Ways

1. Click Styles Dialog Box Launcher (Home tab | Styles group), click desired style in Styles task pane
2. Press CTRL+SHIFT+S, click Style Name box arrow in Apply Styles task pane, click desired style in list

To Center Text

The next step is to enter the title, Works Cited, centered between the margins of the paper. The following steps use shortcut keys to format the title.

1. Press CTRL+E to center the paragraph mark.
2. Type `Works Cited` as the title.
3. Press the ENTER key.
4. Press CTRL+L to left-align the paragraph mark (shown in Figure 2–54 on the next page).

BTW

BTWs
For a complete list of the BTWs found in the margins of the Office and Windows chapters in this book, visit the Microsoft Office and Concepts CourseMate Web site at www.cengagebrain.com and then navigate to the BTW resource for this book.

To Create the Bibliographical List

While typing the research paper, you created several citations and their sources. Word can format the list of sources and alphabetize them in a **bibliographical list**, saving you time looking up style guidelines. That is, Word will create a bibliographical list with each element of the source placed in its correct position with proper punctuation, according to the specified style. For example, in this research paper, the book source will list, in this order, the author name(s), book title, publisher city, publishing company name, and publication year with the correct punctuation between each element according to the MLA documentation style. The following steps create an MLA-styled bibliographical list from the sources previously entered.

1

- Click References on the Ribbon to display the References tab.
- With the insertion point positioned as shown in Figure 2–54, click the Bibliography button (References tab | Citations & Bibliography group) to display the Bibliography gallery (Figure 2–54).

Q&A Will I select the Works Cited option from the Bibliography gallery?

No. The title it inserts is not formatted according to the MLA documentation style. Thus, you will use the Insert Bibliography command instead.

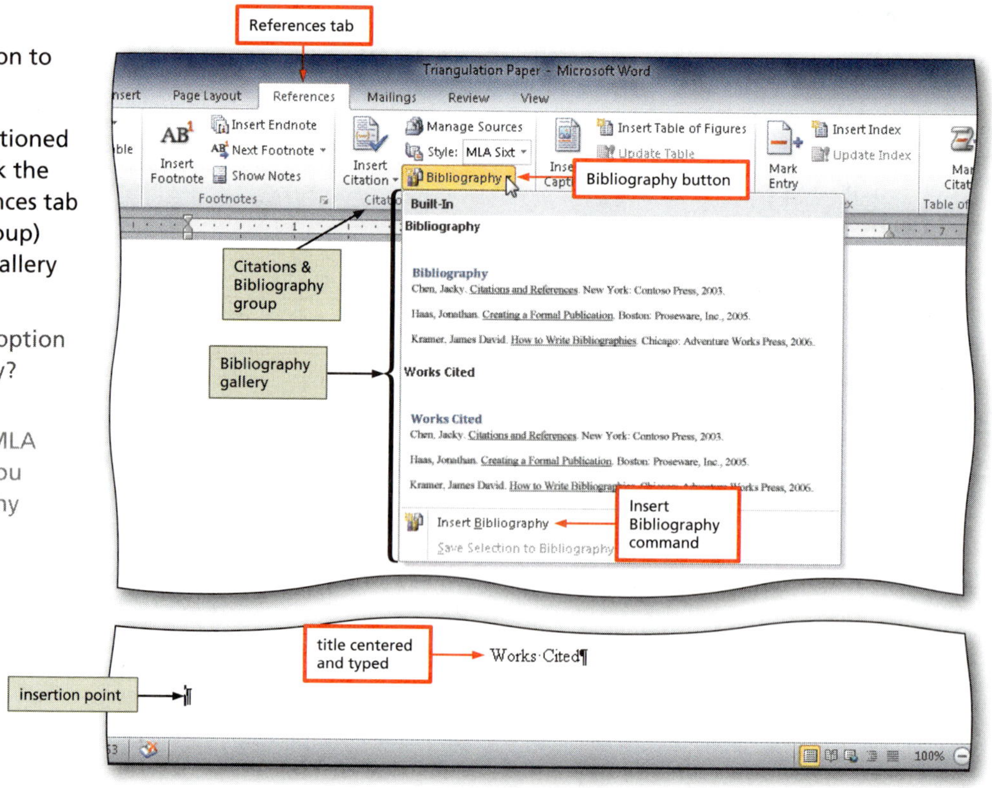

Figure 2–54

2

- Click Insert Bibliography in the Bibliography gallery to insert a list of sources at the location of the insertion point.
- If necessary, scroll to display the entire list of sources in the document window (Figure 2–55).

Q&A What is the n.d. in the last work?

The MLA documentation style uses the abbreviation n.d. for no date, for example, no date on the Web page.

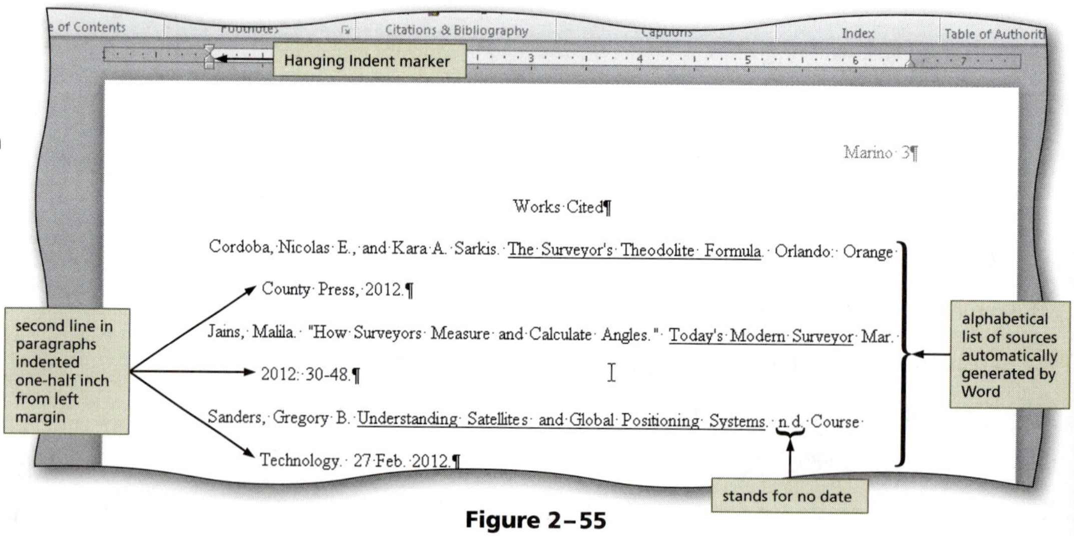

Figure 2–55

To Format Paragraphs with a Hanging Indent

Notice in Figure 2–55 that the first line of each source entry begins at the left margin, and subsequent lines in the same paragraph are indented one-half inch from the left margin. In essence, the first line hangs to the left of the rest of the paragraph; thus, this type of paragraph formatting is called a **hanging indent**. The Bibliography style in Word automatically formats the works cited paragraphs with a hanging indent.

If you wanted to format paragraphs with a hanging indent, you would use one of the following techniques.

- With the insertion point in the paragraph to format, drag the **Hanging Indent marker** (the bottom triangle) on the ruler to the desired mark on the ruler (i.e., .5") to set the hanging indent at that location from the left margin.

or

- Right-click the paragraph to format, click Paragraph on shortcut menu, click Indents and Spacing tab (Paragraph dialog box), click Special box arrow, click Hanging, and then click the OK button.

or

- Click the Paragraph Dialog Box Launcher (Home tab or Page Layout tab | Paragraph group), click Indents and Spacing tab (Paragraph dialog box), click Special box arrow, click Hanging, and then click the OK button.

or

- With the insertion point in the paragraph to format, press CTRL+T.

To Modify a Source and Update the Bibliographical List

If you modify the contents of any source, the list of sources automatically updates because the list is a field. The following steps modify the title of the magazine article.

1

- Click the Manage Sources button (References tab | Citations & Bibliography group) to display the Source Manager dialog box.
- Click the source you wish to edit in the Current List, in this case the article by Jains, to select the source.
- Click the Edit button (Source Manager dialog box) to display the Edit Source dialog box.
- In the Title text box, insert the word, Distance, between the words, Measure and, in the title (Figure 2–56).

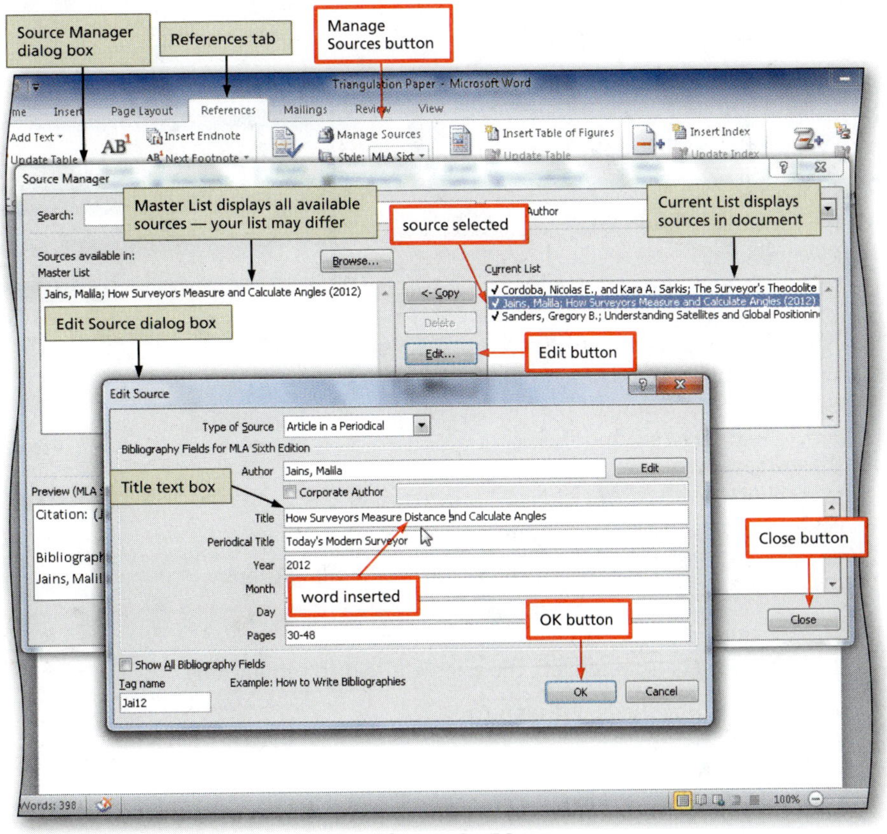

Figure 2–56

2

- Click the OK button (Edit Source dialog box) to close the dialog box.
- If a Microsoft Word dialog box appears, click its Yes button to update all occurrences of the source.
- Click the Close button (Source Manager dialog box) to update the list of sources in the document and close the dialog box (Figure 2–57).

Q&A What if the list of sources in the document is not updated automatically?

Click in the list of sources and then press the F9 key, which is the shortcut key to update a field.

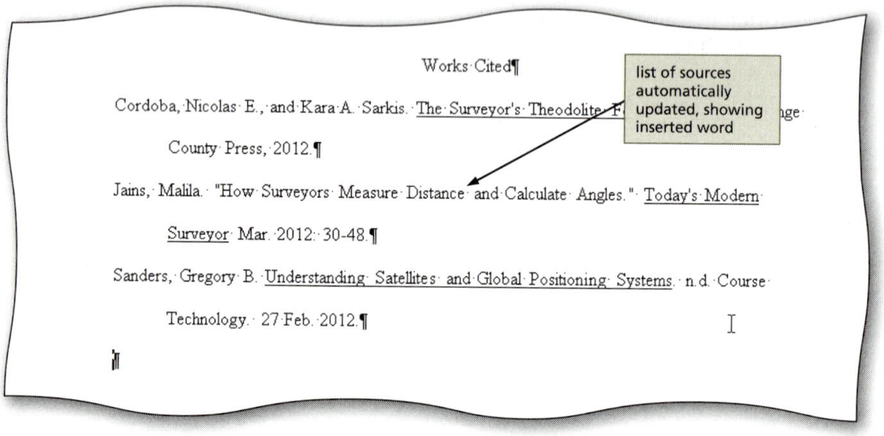

Figure 2–57

To Convert a Field to Regular Text

Word may use an earlier version of the MLA documentation style to format the bibliography. The latest guidelines for the MLA documentation style, for example, state that titles should be italicized instead of underlined, and each work should identify the source's publication medium (e.g., Print for printed media, Web for online media, etc.). If you format or add text to the bibliography, Word automatically will change it back to the Bibliography style's predetermined formats when the bibliography field is updated. To preserve modifications you make to the format of the bibliography, you can convert the bibliography field to regular text. Keep in mind, though, once you convert the field to regular text, it no longer is a field that can be updated. The following step converts a field to regular text.

1

- Click somewhere in the field to select it, in this case, somewhere in the bibliography (Figure 2–58).

Q&A What if the bibliography field is not shaded gray?

Click File on the Ribbon to open the Backstage view, click Options in the Backstage view, click Advanced in the left pane (Word Options dialog box), scroll to the 'Show document content' area, click the Field shading box arrow, click When selected, and then click the OK button.

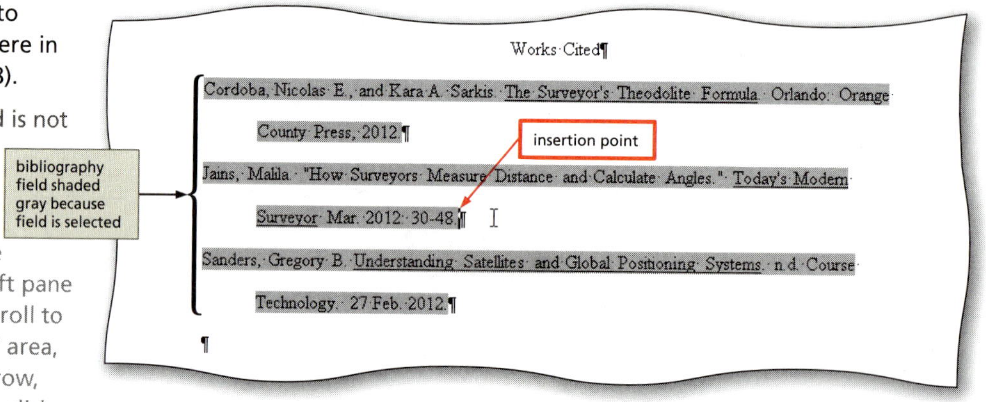

Figure 2–58

Q&A Why are all the words in the bibliography shaded?

The bibliography field consists of all text in the bibliography.

2

- Press CTRL+SHIFT+F9 to convert the selected field to regular text.

Q&A Why did the gray shading disappear?

The bibliography no longer is a field, so it is not shaded gray.

- Click anywhere in the document to remove the selection from the text.

To Format the Works Cited to the Latest MLA Documentation Style

As mentioned earlier, the latest the MLA documentation style guidelines state that titles should be italicized instead of underlined, and each work should identify the source's publication medium (e.g., Print, Web, Radio, Television, CD, DVD, Film, etc.). The following steps format and modify the Works Cited as specified by the latest MLA guidelines, if yours are not already formatted this way.

1. Drag through the book title, The Surveyor's Theodolite Formula, to select it.
2. Click Home on the Ribbon to display the Home tab. Click the Underline button (Home tab | Font group) to remove the underline from the selected text and then click the Italic button (Home tab | Font group) to italicize the selected text.
3. Select the magazine title, Today's Modern Surveyor. Remove the underline from the selected title and then italicize the selected title.
4. Select the Web page title, Understanding Satellites and Global Positioning Systems. Remove the underline from the selected title and then italicize the selected title.
5. After the period following the year in the first work, press the SPACEBAR and then type **`Print.`**
6. After the period following the page range in the second work, press the SPACEBAR and then type **`Print.`**
7. Before the date in the third work, type **`Web.`** and then press the SPACEBAR (Figure 2–59).

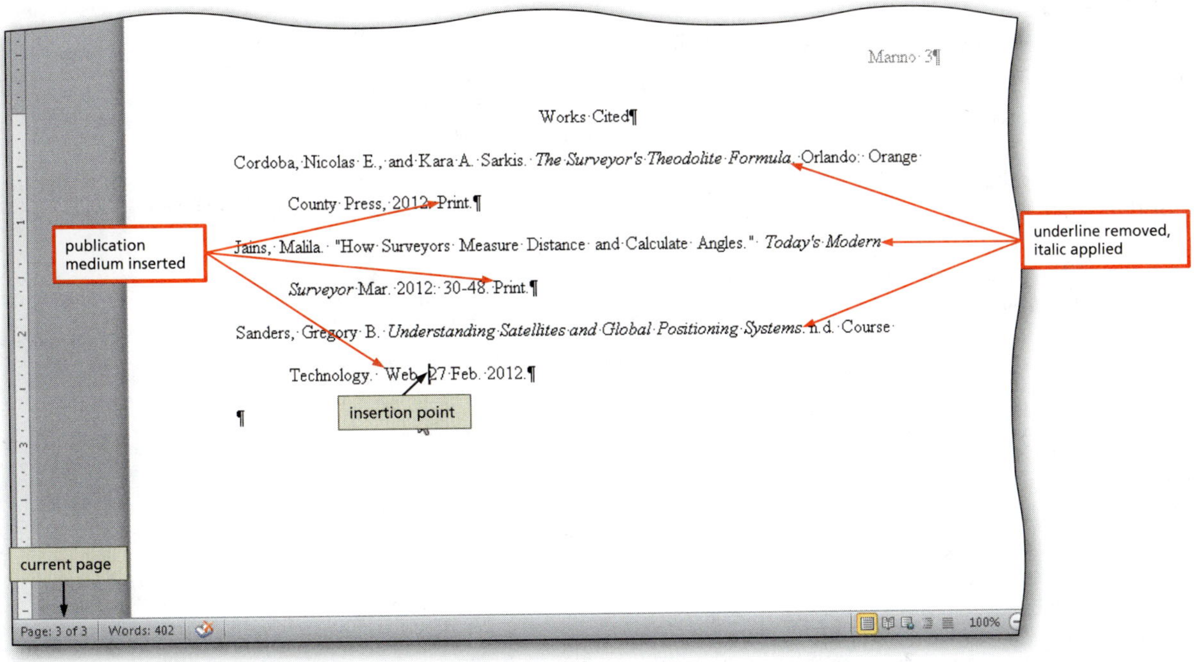

Figure 2–59

To Save an Existing Document with the Same File Name

You have made several modifications to the document since you last saved it. Thus, you should save it again. The following step saves the document again.

1. Click the Save button on the Quick Access Toolbar to overwrite the previously saved file.

Proofing and Revising the Research Paper

As discussed in Word Chapter 1, once you complete a document, you might find it necessary to make changes to it. Before submitting a paper to be graded, you should proofread it. While **proofreading**, look for grammatical errors and spelling errors. You also should ensure the transitions between sentences flow smoothly and the sentences themselves make sense.

Plan Ahead

Proofread and revise the paper.

As you proofread the paper, look for ways to improve it. Check all grammar, spelling, and punctuation. Be sure the text is logical and transitions are smooth. Where necessary, add text, delete text, reword text, and move text to different locations. Ask yourself these questions:

- Does the title suggest the topic?
- Is the thesis clear?
- Is the purpose of the paper clear?
- Does the paper have an introduction, body, and conclusion?
- Does each paragraph in the body relate to the thesis?
- Is the conclusion effective?
- Are all sources acknowledged?

To assist you with the proofreading effort, Word provides several tools. You can browse through pages, copy text, find text, replace text, insert a synonym, check spelling and grammar, and look up information. The following pages discuss these tools.

To Scroll Page by Page through a Document

The next step is to modify text on the second page of the paper. Currently, the third page is the active page (Figure 2–59 on the previous page). The following step scrolls up one page in the document.

1

- With the insertion point on the third page of the paper, click the Previous Page button on the vertical scroll bar to position the insertion point at the top of the previous page (Figure 2–60).

Q&A The button on my screen shows a ScreenTip different from Previous Page. Why?

By default, the functions of the buttons above and below the Select Browse Object button are Previous Page and Next Page, respectively. You can change the commands associated with these buttons by clicking the Select Browse Object button and then clicking the desired browse object. The Browse by Page command on the Select Browse Object menu, for example, changes the buttons back to Previous Page and Next Page.

Q&A How do I display the next page?

Click the Next Page button on the vertical scroll bar.

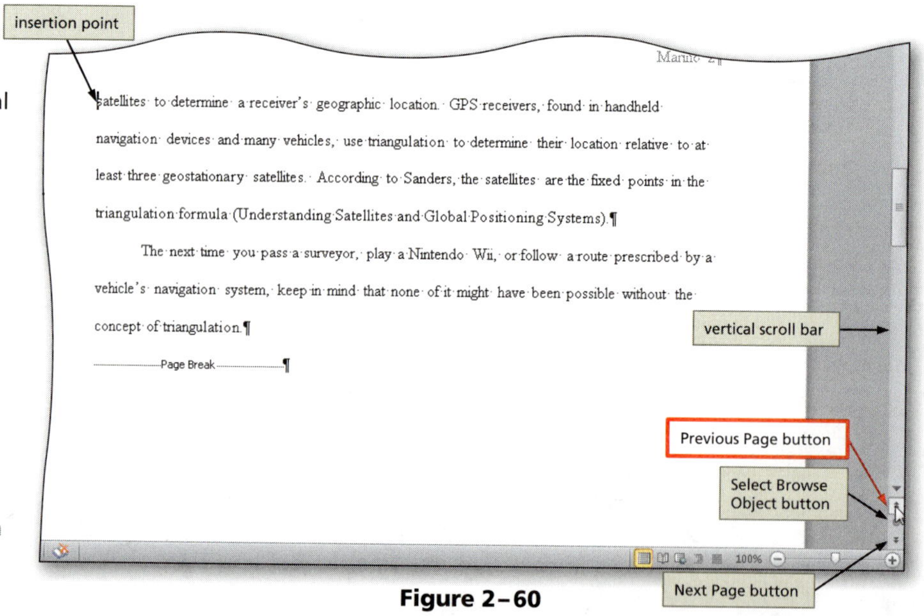

Figure 2–60

Other Ways

1. Click Page Number indicator on status bar, click Page in 'Go to what' list (Find and Replace dialog box), type desired page number in 'Enter page number' text box, click Go To button
2. Press CTRL+PAGE UP or CTRL+PAGE DOWN

Copying, Cutting, and Pasting

While proofreading the research paper, you decide it would read better if the word, geostationary, appeared in front of the word, satellites, in the last sentence of the fourth paragraph. You could type the word at the desired location, but because this is a difficult word to spell, you decide to use the Office Clipboard. The **Office Clipboard** is a temporary storage area that holds up to 24 items (text or graphics) copied from any Office program.

Copying is the process of placing items on the Office Clipboard, leaving the item in the document. **Cutting**, by contrast, removes the item from the document before placing it on the Office Clipboard. **Pasting** is the process of copying an item from the Office Clipboard into the document at the location of the insertion point.

To Copy and Paste

In the research paper, you copy a word from one sentence to another. The following steps copy and paste a word.

1

- Select the item to be copied (the word, geostationary, in this case).
- Click the Copy button (Home tab | Clipboard group) to copy the selected item in the document to the Office Clipboard (Figure 2–61).

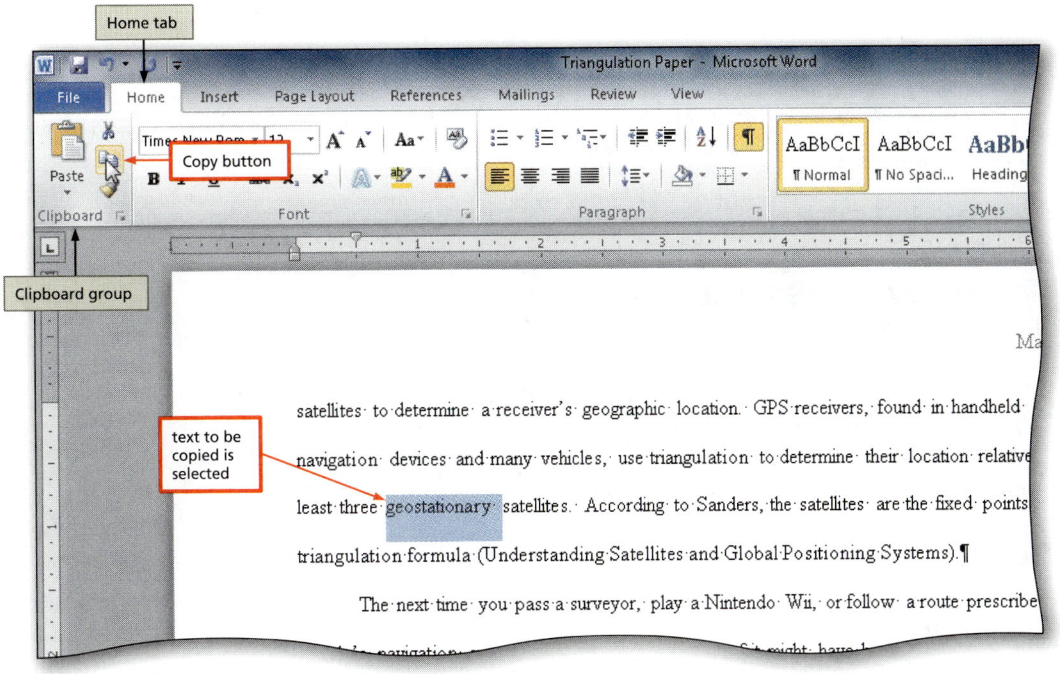

Figure 2–61

2

- Position the insertion point at the location where the item should be pasted (immediately to the left of the word, satellites, in this case) (Figure 2–62).

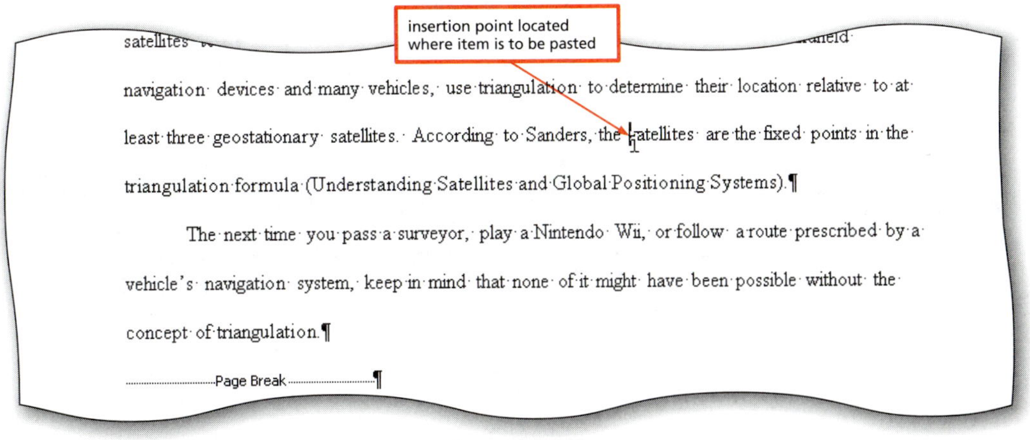

Figure 2–62

3

- Click the Paste button (Home tab | Clipboard group) to paste the copied item in the document at the location of the insertion point (Figure 2–63).

Q&A What if I click the Paste button arrow by mistake?

Click the Paste button arrow again to remove the Paste menu.

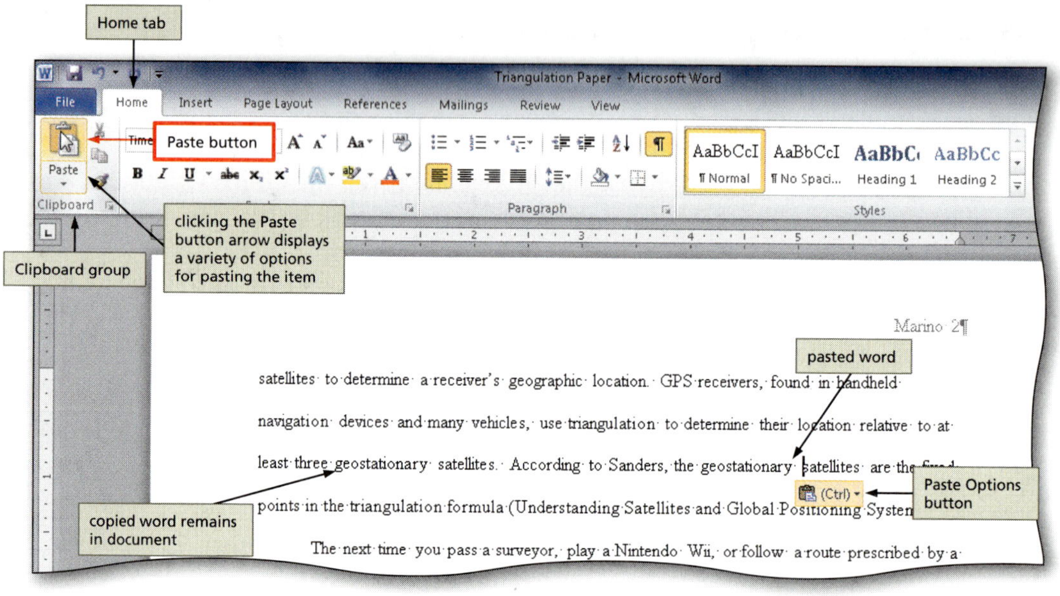

Figure 2–63

Other Ways

1. Right-click selected item, click Copy on shortcut menu, right-click where item is to be pasted, click Keep Source Formatting in Paste Options area on shortcut menu
2. Select item, press CTRL+C, position insertion point at paste location, press CTRL+V

To Display the Paste Options Menu

When you paste an item or move an item using drag-and-drop editing, which was discussed in the previous chapter, Word automatically displays a Paste Options button near the pasted or moved text (Figure 2–63). The Paste Options button allows you to change the format of a pasted item. For example, you can instruct Word to format the pasted item the same way as where it was copied, or format it the same way as where it is being pasted. The following steps display the Paste Options menu.

1

- Click the Paste Options button to display the Paste Options menu (Figure 2–64).

Q&A What are the functions of the buttons on the Paste Options menu?

In general, the left button indicates the pasted item should look the same as it did in its original location. The second button formats the pasted text to match the rest of the item where it was pasted. The third button removes all formatting from the pasted item. The Set Default Paste command displays the Word Options dialog box. Keep in mind that the buttons shown on a Paste Options menu will vary, depending on the item being pasted.

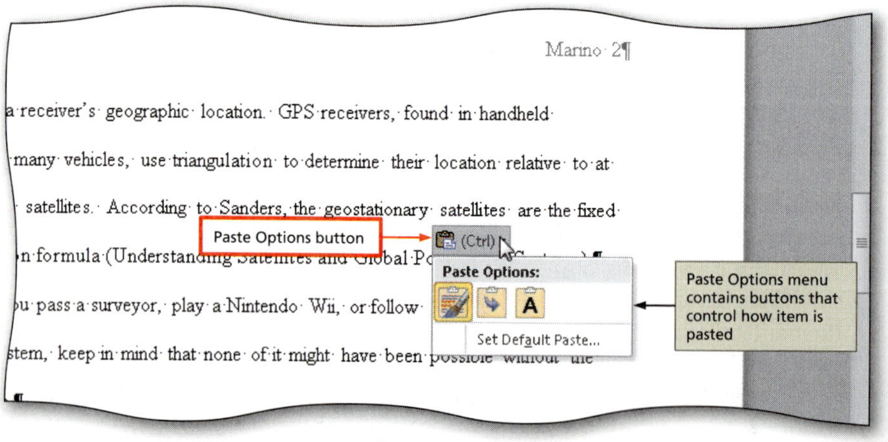

Figure 2–64

2

- Press the ESCAPE key to remove the Paste Options menu from the window.

To Find Text

While proofreading the paper, you would like to locate all occurrences of Wii console because you are contemplating changing this text to Wii game console. The following steps find all occurrences of specific text in a document.

1

- Click the Find button (Home tab | Editing group) to display the Navigation Pane (Figure 2–65).

Q&A What is the Navigation Pane?

The **Navigation Pane** is a window that enables you to search for text in a document, browse through pages in a document, or browse through headings in a document.

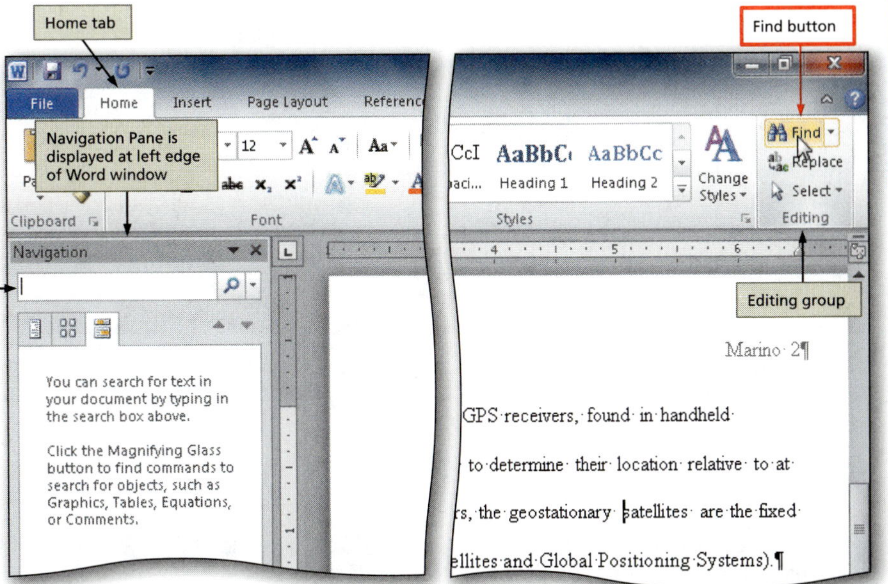

Figure 2–65

2

- Type `Wii console` in the Navigation Pane text box to display all occurrences of the typed text, called the search text, in the Navigation Pane and to highlight the occurrences of the search text in the document window (Figure 2–66).

3

Experiment

- Type various search text in the Navigation Pane text box, and watch Word both list matches in the Navigation Pane and highlight matches in the document window. When you are finished experimenting, repeat Step 2.

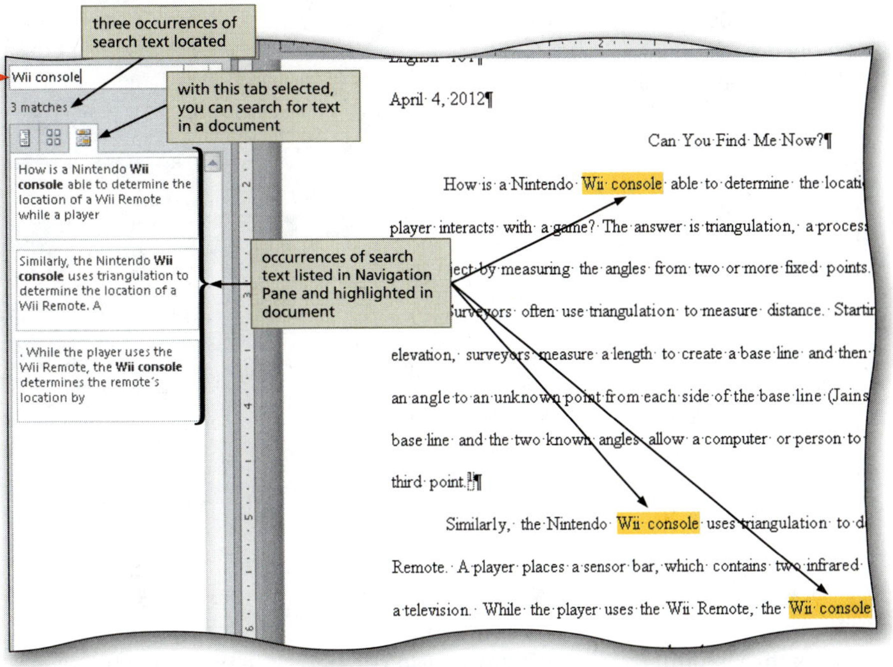

Figure 2–66

Other Ways

1. Click Find button arrow (Home tab | Editing group), click Find on Find menu, enter search text in Navigation Pane
2. Click Select Browse Object button on vertical scroll bar, click Find icon on Select Browse Object menu, enter search text (Find and Replace dialog box), click Find Next button
3. Click Page Number indicator on status bar, click Find tab (Find and Replace dialog box), enter search text, click Find Next button
4. Press CTRL+F

To Replace Text

You decide to change all occurrences of Wii console to Wii game console. To do this, you can use Word's find and replace feature, which automatically locates each occurrence of a word or phrase and then replaces it with specified text. The following steps replace all occurrences of Wii console with Wii game console.

1

- Click the Replace button (Home tab | Editing group) to display the Replace sheet in the Find and Replace dialog box.
- If necessary, type `Wii console` in the Find what text box (Find and Replace dialog box).
- Press the TAB key. Type `Wii game console` in the Replace with text box (Figure 2–67).

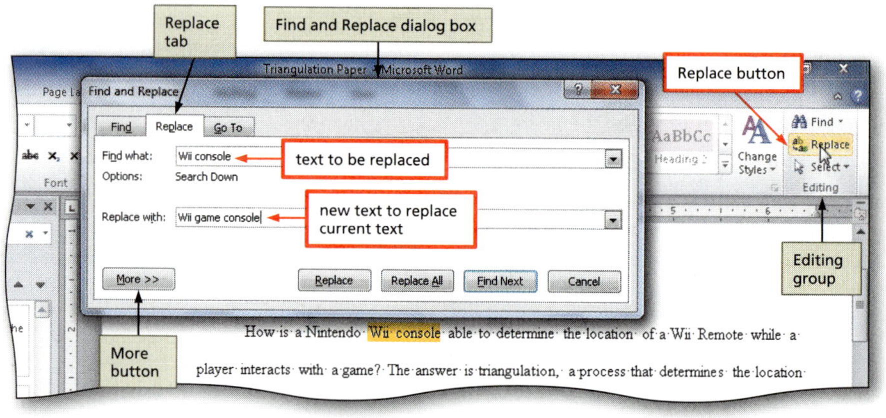

Figure 2–67

2

- Click the Replace All button to instruct Word to replace all occurrences of the Find what text with the Replace with text (Figure 2–68). If Word displays a dialog box asking if you want to continue searching from the beginning of the document, click the Yes button.

Q&A Does Word search the entire document?

If the insertion point is at the beginning of the document, Word searches the entire document; otherwise, Word searches from the location of the insertion point to the end of the document and then displays a dialog box asking if you want to continue searching from the beginning. You also can search a section of text by selecting the text before clicking the Replace button.

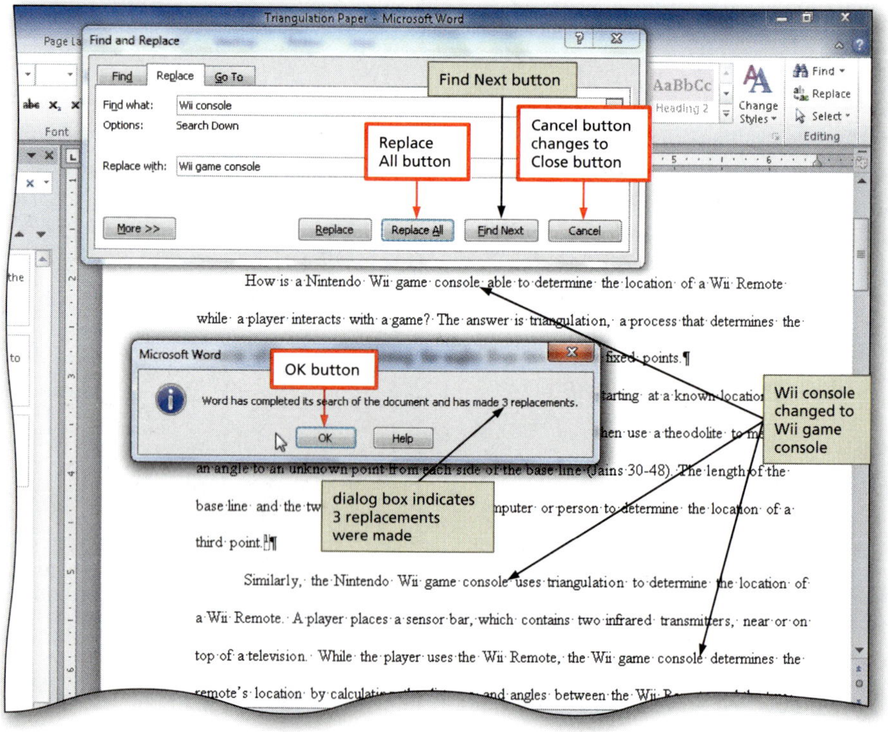

Figure 2–68

3

- Click the OK button (Microsoft Word dialog box) to close the dialog box.
- Click the Close button (Find and Replace dialog box) to close the dialog box.

Other Ways

1. Click Select Browse Object button on vertical scroll bar, click Find icon on Select Browse Object menu, click Replace tab
2. Click Page Number indicator on status bar, click Replace tab (Find and Replace dialog box)
3. Press CTRL+H

Find and Replace Dialog Box

The Replace All button (Find and Replace dialog box) replaces all occurrences of the Find what text with the Replace with text. In some cases, you may want to replace only certain occurrences of a word or phrase, not all of them. To instruct Word to confirm each change, click the Find Next button (Find and Replace dialog box) (Figure 2–68), instead of the Replace All button. When Word locates an occurrence of the text, it pauses and waits for you to click either the Replace button or the Find Next button. Clicking the Replace button changes the text; clicking the Find Next button instructs Word to disregard the replacement and look for the next occurrence of the Find what text.

If you accidentally replace the wrong text, you can undo a replacement by clicking the Undo button on the Quick Access Toolbar. If you used the Replace All button, Word undoes all replacements. If you used the Replace button, Word undoes only the most recent replacement.

BTW

Finding Formatting
To search for formatting or a special character, click the More button (shown in Figure 2–67) to expand the Find dialog box. To find formatting, use the Format button in the expanded Find dialog box. To find a special character, use the Special button.

To Go to a Page

The next step in revising the paper is to change a word on the second page of the document. You could scroll to the location in the document, or as mentioned earlier, you can use the Navigation Pane to browse through pages in a document. The following steps display the top of the second page in the document window and position the insertion point at the beginning of that page.

1

- Click the 'Browse the pages in your document' tab in the Navigation Pane to display thumbnail images of the pages in the document (Figure 2–69).

Q&A

What if the Navigation Pane is not on the screen anymore?

Click View on the Ribbon to display the View tab and then click Navigation Pane (View tab | Show group) to select the check box.

2

- Click the thumbnail of the second page, even if the second page already is selected, to display the top of the selected page in the top of the document window (shown in Figure 2–70 on the next page).

3

- Click the Close button in the Navigation Pane to close the pane.

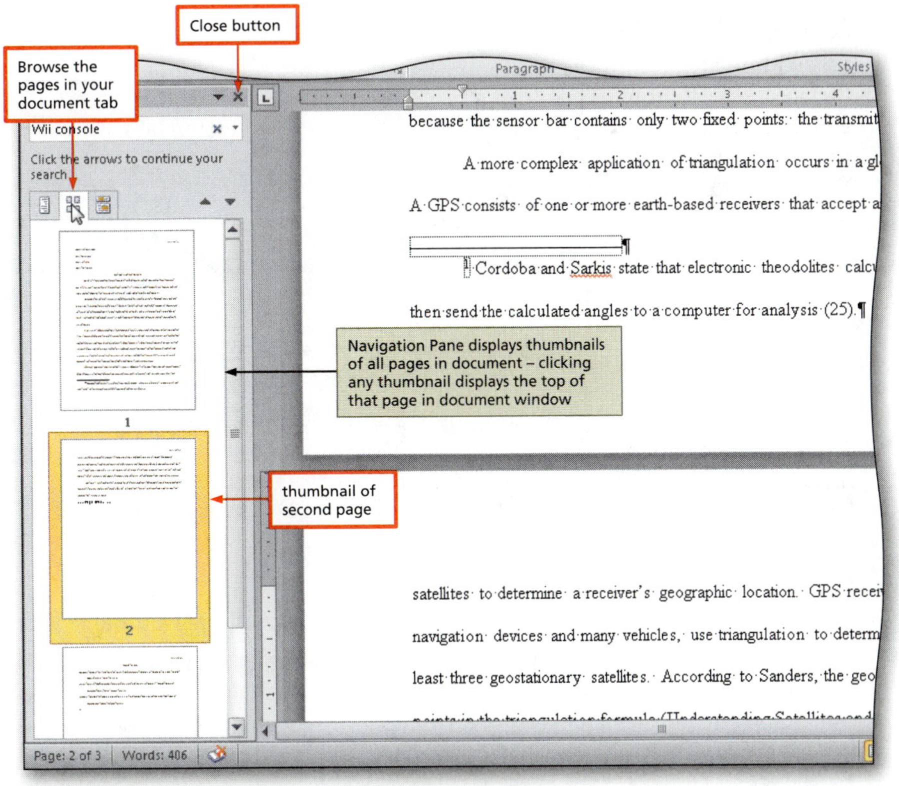

Figure 2–69

Other Ways

1. Click Find button arrow (Home tab | Editing group), click Go To on Find menu, click Go To tab (Find and Replace dialog box), enter page number, click Go To button
2. Click Select Browse Object button on vertical scroll bar, click Go To icon on Select Browse Object menu, enter page number (Find and Replace dialog box), click Go To button
3. Click Page Number indicator on status bar, click Go To tab (Find and Replace dialog box), enter page number, click Go To button
4. Press CTRL+G

To Find and Insert a Synonym

When writing, you may discover that you used the same word in multiple locations or that a word you used was not quite appropriate. In these instances, you will want to look up a **synonym**, or a word similar in meaning, to the duplicate or inappropriate word. A **thesaurus** is a book of synonyms. Word provides synonyms and a thesaurus for your convenience.

In this project, you would like a synonym for the word, prescribed, in the fourth paragraph of the research paper. The following steps find a suitable synonym.

1

- Locate and then right-click the word for which you want to find a synonym (in this case, prescribed) to display a shortcut menu related to the word you right-clicked.
- Point to Synonyms on the shortcut menu to display a list of synonyms for the word you right-clicked (Figure 2–70).

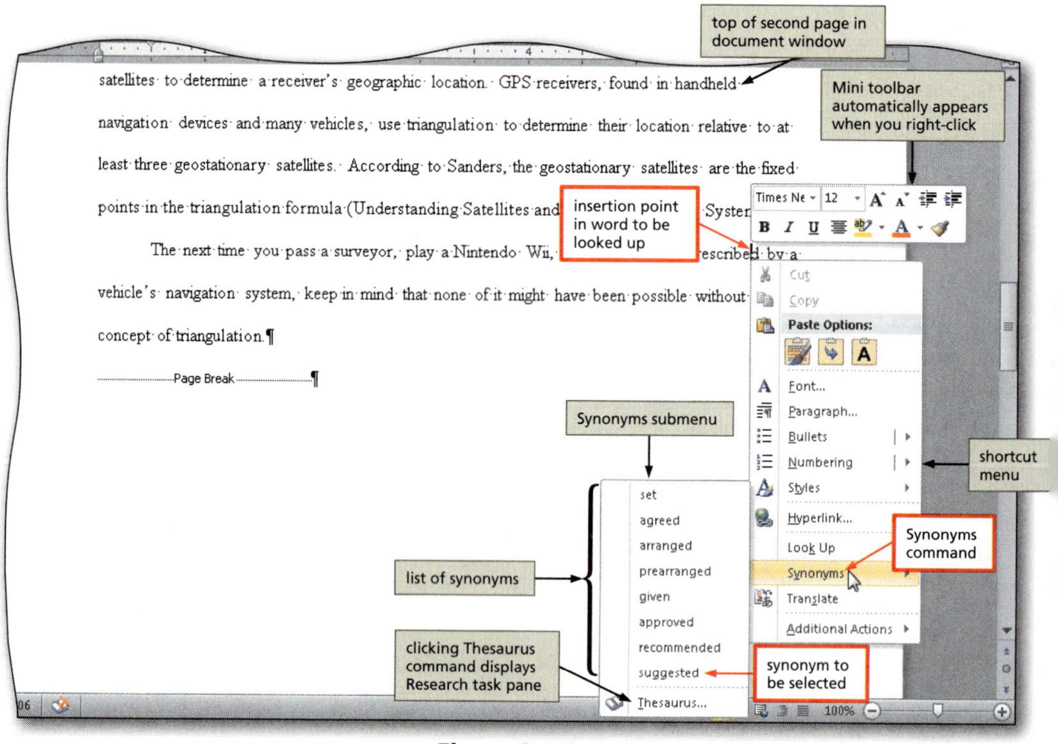

Figure 2–70

2

- Click the synonym you want (in this case, suggested) on the Synonyms submenu to replace the selected word in the document with the selected synonym (Figure 2–71).

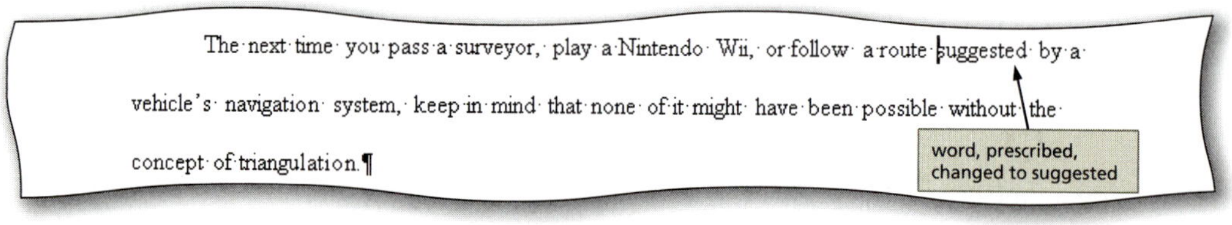

Figure 2–71

Q&A

What if the synonyms list on the shortcut menu does not display a suitable word?

You can display the thesaurus in the Research task pane by clicking Thesaurus on the Synonyms submenu. The Research task pane displays a complete thesaurus, in which you can look up synonyms for various meanings of a word. You also can look up an **antonym,** or word with an opposite meaning. The Research task pane is discussed later in this chapter.

Other Ways

1. Click Thesaurus (Review tab | Proofing group)
2. Press SHIFT+F7

To Check Spelling and Grammar at Once

As discussed in Word Chapter 1, Word checks spelling and grammar as you type and places a wavy underline below possible spelling or grammar errors. Word Chapter 1 illustrated how to check these flagged words immediately. As an alternative, you can wait and check the entire document for spelling and grammar errors at once. The next steps check spelling and grammar at once.

Note: In the following steps, the word, theodolite, has been misspelled intentionally as theadalight to illustrate the use of Word's check spelling and grammar at once feature. If you are completing this project on a personal computer, your research paper may contain different misspelled words, depending on the accuracy of your typing.

1

- Press CTRL+HOME because you want the spelling and grammar check to begin from the top of the document.
- Click Review on the Ribbon to display the Review tab.
- Click the Spelling & Grammar button (Review tab | Proofing group) to begin the spelling and grammar check at the location of the insertion point, which in this case, is at the beginning of the document.
- Click the desired spelling in the Suggestions list (theodolite, in this case) (Figure 2–72).

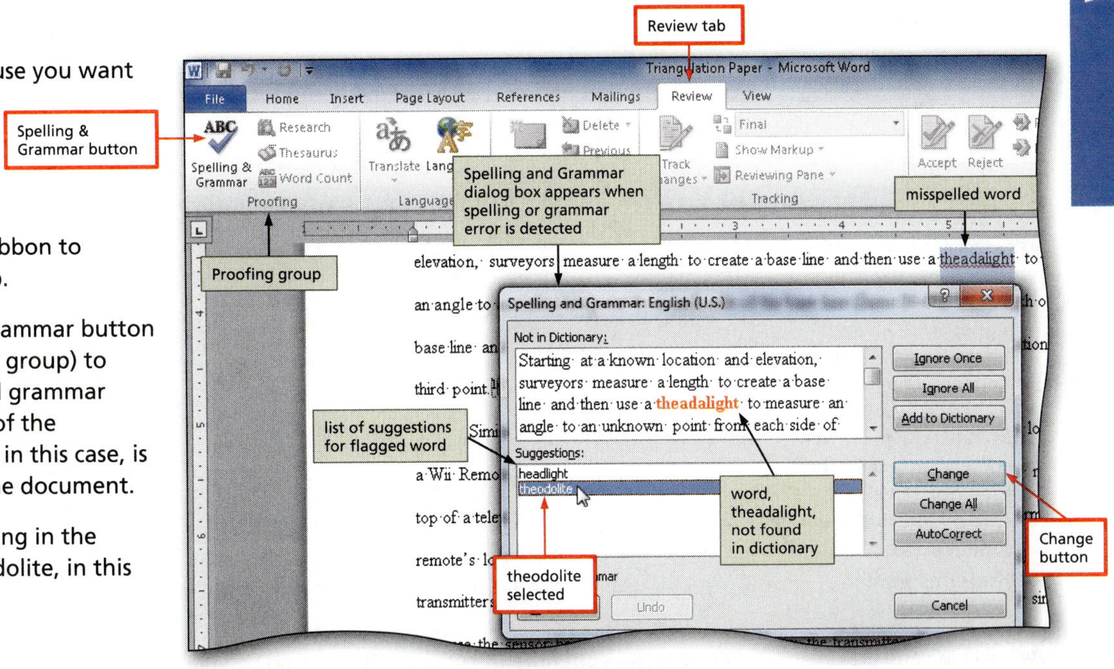

Figure 2–72

2

- With the word, theodolite, selected in the Suggestions list, click the Change button (Spelling and Grammar dialog box) to change the flagged word to the selected suggestion and then continue the spelling and grammar check until the next error is identified or the end of the document is reached (Figure 2–73).

3

- Click the Ignore All button (Spelling and Grammar dialog box) to ignore this and future occurrences of the flagged proper noun and then continue the spelling and grammar check until the next error is identified or the end of the document is reached.

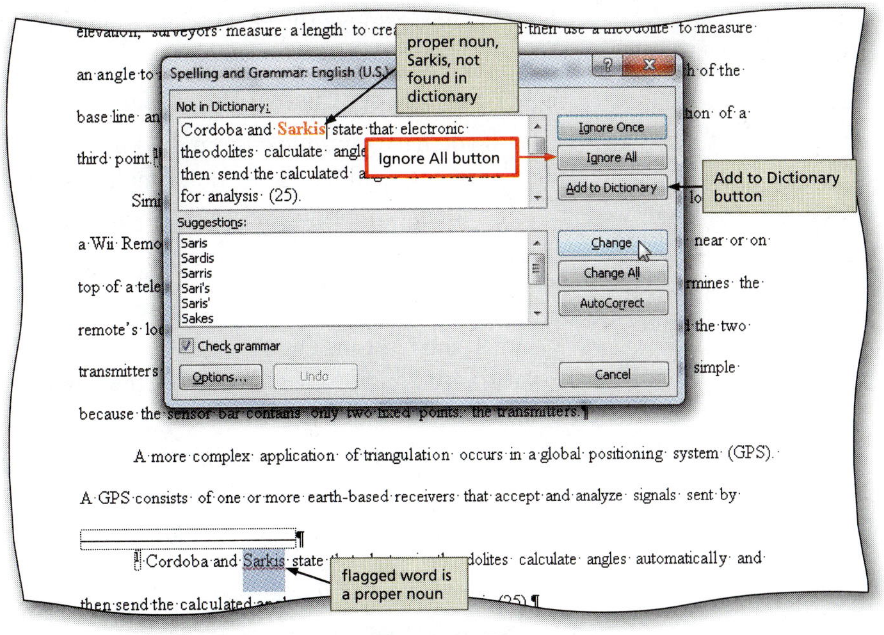

Figure 2–73

4

- When the spelling and grammar check is finished and Word displays a dialog box, click its OK button.

Q&A

Can I check spelling of just a section of a document?

Yes, select the text before starting the spelling and grammar check.

Other Ways

1. Click Spelling and Grammar Check icon on status bar, click Spelling on shortcut menu
2. Right-click flagged word, click Spelling on shortcut menu
3. Press F7

BTW

Readability Statistics
You can instruct Word to display readability statistics when it has finished a spelling and grammar check on a document. Three readability statistics presented are the percent of passive sentences, the Flesch Reading Ease score, and the Flesch-Kincaid Grade Level score. The Flesch Reading Ease score uses a 100-point scale to rate the ease with which a reader can understand the text in a document. A higher score means the document is easier to understand. The Flesch-Kincaid Grade Level score rates the text in a document on a U.S. school grade level. For example, a score of 10.0 indicates a student in the tenth grade can understand the material. To show readability statistics when the spelling and grammar check is complete, open the Backstage view, click Options in the Backstage view, click Proofing in the left pane (Word Options dialog box), place a check mark in the 'Show readability statistics' check box, and then click the OK button. Readability statistics will be displayed the next time you check spelling and grammar at once in the document.

The Main and Custom Dictionaries

As shown in the steps on the previous page, Word may flag a proper noun as an error because the proper noun is not in its main dictionary. To prevent Word from flagging proper nouns as errors, you can add the proper nouns to the custom dictionary. To add a correctly spelled word to the custom dictionary, click the Add to Dictionary button (Spelling and Grammar dialog box) or right-click the flagged word and then click Add to Dictionary on the shortcut menu. Once you have added a word to the custom dictionary, Word no longer will flag it as an error.

To View or Modify Entries in a Custom Dictionary

To view or modify the list of words in a custom dictionary, you would follow these steps.

1. Click File on the Ribbon and then click Options in the Backstage view.
2. Click Proofing in the left pane (Word Options dialog box).
3. Click the Custom Dictionaries button.
4. When Word displays the Custom Dictionaries dialog box, place a check mark next to the dictionary name to view or modify. Click the Edit Word List button (Custom Dictionaries dialog box). (In this dialog box, you can add or delete entries to and from the selected custom dictionary.)
5. When finished viewing and/or modifying the list, click the OK button in the dialog box.
6. Click the OK button (Custom Dictionaries dialog box).
7. If the 'Suggest from main dictionary only' check box is selected in the Word Options dialog box, remove the check mark. Click the OK button (Word Options dialog box).

To Set the Default Custom Dictionary

If you have multiple custom dictionaries, you can specify which one Word should use when checking spelling. To set the default custom dictionary, you would follow these steps.

1. Click File on the Ribbon and then click Options in the Backstage view.
2. Click Proofing in the left pane (Word Options dialog box).
3. Click the Custom Dictionaries button.
4. When the Custom Dictionaries dialog box is displayed, place a check mark next to the desired dictionary name. Click the Change Default button (Custom Dictionaries dialog box).
5. Click the OK button (Custom Dictionaries dialog box).
6. If the 'Suggest from main dictionary only' check box is selected in the Word Options dialog box, remove the check mark. Click the OK button (Word Options dialog box).

To Use the Research Task Pane to Look Up Information

From within Word, you can search through various forms of reference information. Earlier, this chapter discussed the Research task pane with respect to looking up a synonym in a thesaurus. Other services available in the Research task pane include a dictionary and, if you are connected to the Web, a search engine and other Web sites that provide information such as stock quotes, news articles, and company profiles.

Assume you want to know more about the word, geostationary. The following steps use the Research task pane to look up a definition of a word.

1

- Locate the word you want to look up.
- While holding down the ALT key, click the word you want to look up (in this case, geostationary) to open the Research task pane and display a dictionary entry for the ALT+clicked word. Release the ALT key.

2

- Click the Search for box arrow in the Research task pane to display a list of search locations (Figure 2–74).

Q&A Why does my Research task pane look different?

Depending on your settings and Microsoft's Web site search settings, your Research task pane may appear different from the figures shown here.

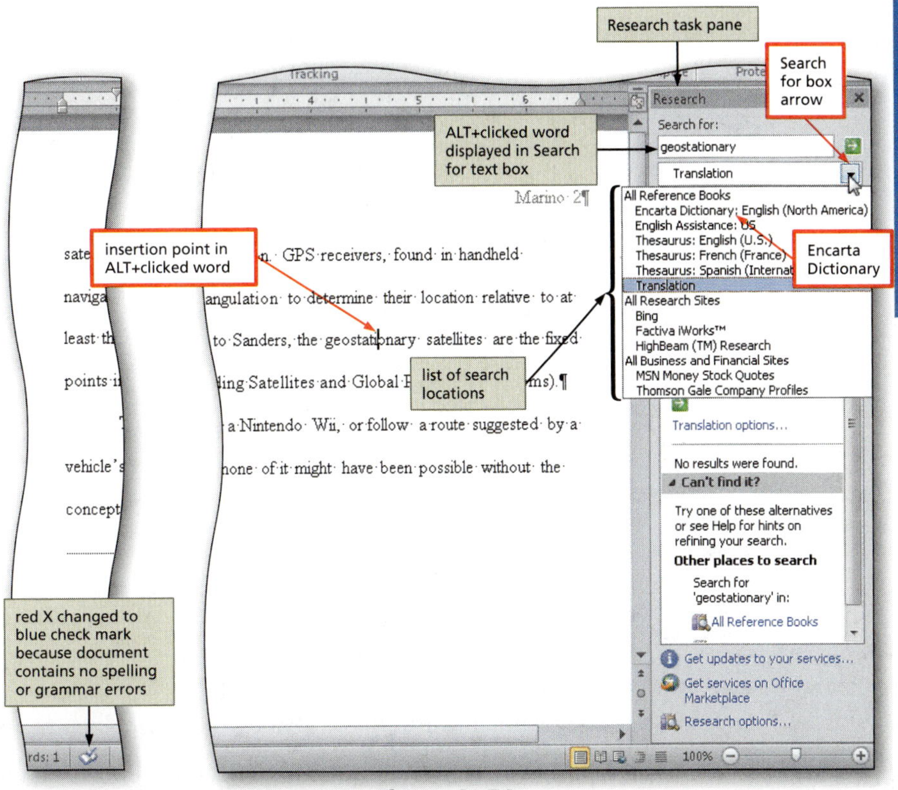

Figure 2–74

- Click Encarta Dictionary in the list to display a definition for the ALT+clicked word (Figure 2–75).

Q&A Can I copy information from the Research task pane into my document?

Yes, you can use the Copy and Paste commands. When using Word to insert material from the Research task pane or any other online reference, however, be careful not to plagiarize.

3

- Click the Close button in the Research task pane.

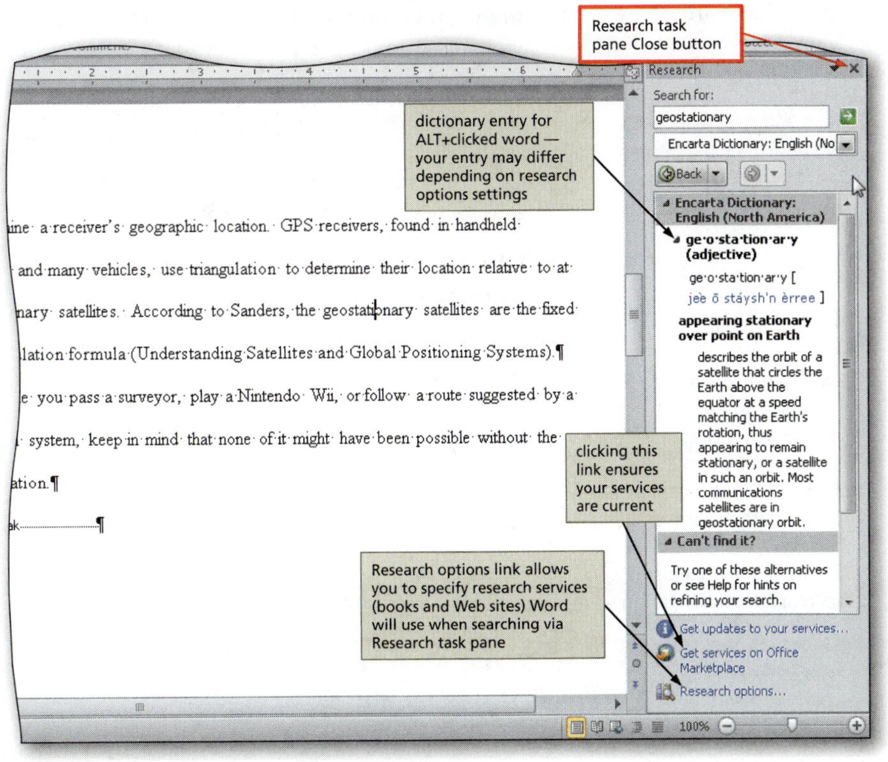

Figure 2–75

Other Ways

1. Click Research button (Review tab | Proofing group)

Research Task Pane Options

When you install Word, it selects a series of services (reference books and Web sites) that it searches through when you use the Research task pane. You can view, modify, and update the list of services at any time.

Clicking the Research options link at the bottom of the Research task pane (shown in Figure 2–75 on the previous page) displays the Research Options dialog box, where you can view or modify the list of installed services. You can view information about any installed service by clicking the service in the list and then clicking the Properties button. To activate an installed service, click the check box to its left; likewise, to deactivate a service, remove the check mark. To add a particular Web site to the list, click the Add Services button, enter the Web address in the Address text box, and then click the Add button (Add Services dialog box). To update or remove services, click the Update/Remove button, select the service in the list, click the Update (or Remove) button (Update or Remove Services dialog box), and then click the Close button. You also can install parental controls through the Parental Control button (Research Options dialog box), for example, if you want to prevent minor children who use Word from accessing the Web.

To Change Document Properties

Before saving the research paper again, you want to add your name, course information, and some keywords as document properties. The following steps use the Document Information Panel to change document properties.

1. Click File on the Ribbon to open the Backstage view and, if necessary, select the Info tab.
2. Click the Properties button in the right pane of the Info gallery to display the Properties menu and then click Show Document Panel on the Properties menu to close the Backstage view and display the Document Information Panel in the Word document window.
3. Click the Author text box, if necessary, and then type your name as the Author property. If a name already is displayed in the Author text box, delete it before typing your name.
4. Click the Subject text box, if necessary delete any existing text, and then type your course and section as the Subject property.
5. Click the Keywords text box, if necessary delete any existing text, and then type `surveyor, Wii, GPS` as the Keywords property.
6. Click the Close the Document Information Panel button so that the Document Information Panel no longer is displayed.

BTW

Conserving Ink and Toner
If you want to conserve ink or toner, you can instruct Word to print draft quality documents by clicking File on the Ribbon to open the Backstage view, clicking Options in the Backstage view to display the Word Options dialog box, clicking Advanced in the left pane (Word Options dialog box), scrolling to the Print area in the right pane, placing a check mark in the 'Use draft quality' check box, and then clicking the OK button. Then, use the Backstage view to print the document as usual.

To Save an Existing Document with the Same File Name

You have made several modifications to the document since you last saved it. Thus, you should save it again. The following step saves the document again.

1. Click the Save button on the Quick Access Toolbar to overwrite the previously saved file.

To Print Document Properties

With the document properties entered and the completed document saved, you may want to print the document properties along with the document. The following steps print the document properties for the Triangulation Paper.

1

- Click File on the Ribbon to open the Backstage view and then click the Print tab in the Backstage view to display the Print gallery.
- Verify the printer name that appears on the Printer Status button will print a hard copy of the document. If necessary, click the Printer Status button to display a list of available printer options and then click the desired printer to change the currently selected printer.
- Click the first button in the Settings area to display a list of options specifying what you can print (Figure 2–76).

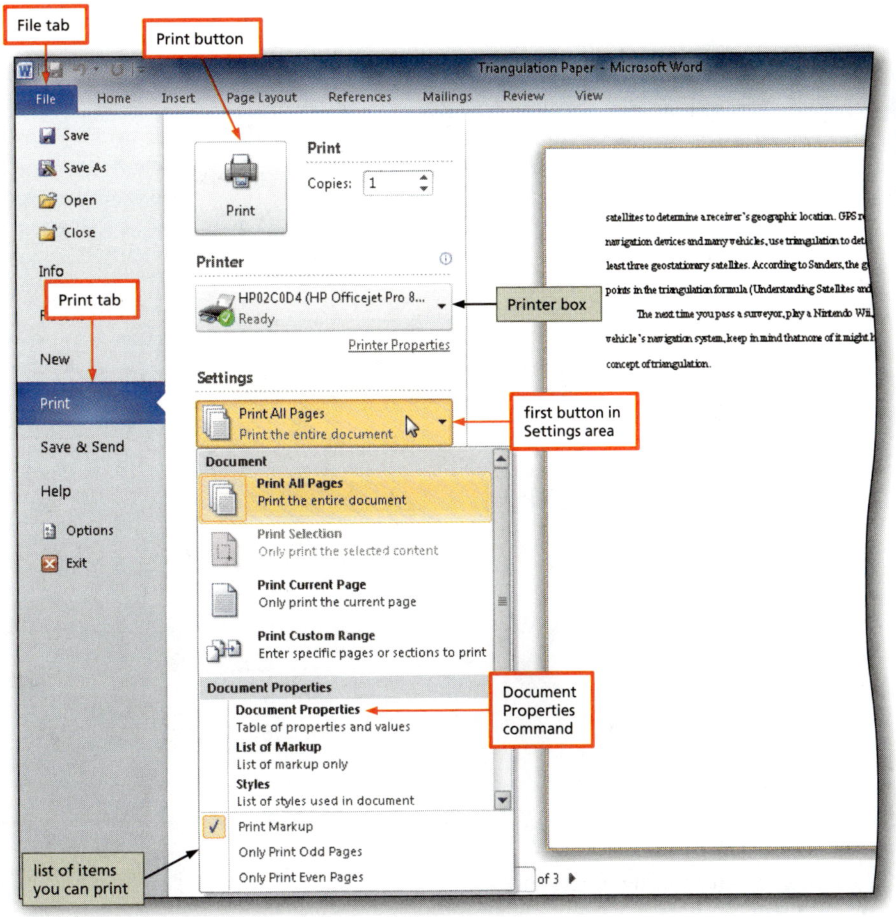

Figure 2–76

2

- Click Document Properties in the list to specify you want to print the document properties instead of the actual document.
- Click the Print button in the Print gallery to print the document properties on the currently selected printer (Figure 2–77).

Q&A What if the currently updated document properties do not print on the hard copy?

Try closing the document, reopening the document, and then repeating these steps.

printed document properties — your properties may differ, depending on settings

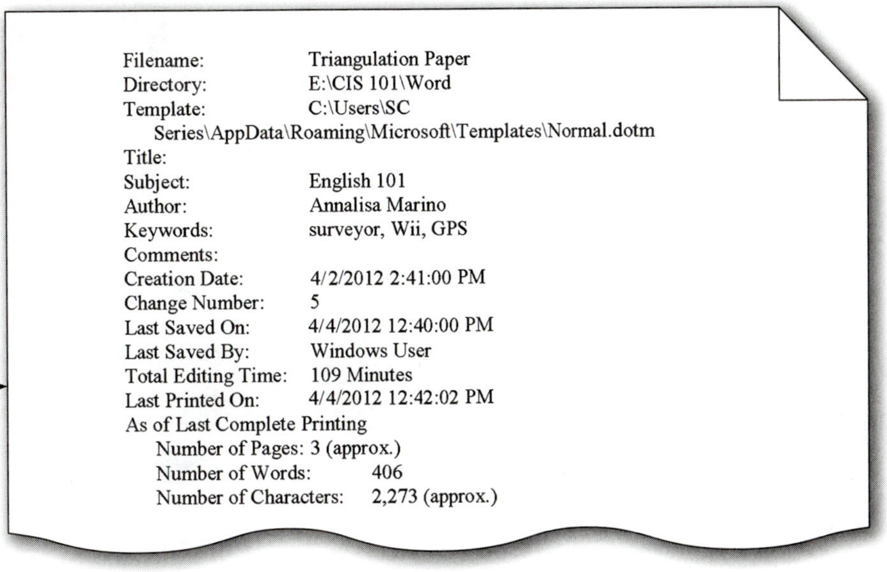

Filename: Triangulation Paper
Directory: E:\CIS 101\Word
Template: C:\Users\SC Series\AppData\Roaming\Microsoft\Templates\Normal.dotm
Title:
Subject: English 101
Author: Annalisa Marino
Keywords: surveyor, Wii, GPS
Comments:
Creation Date: 4/2/2012 2:41:00 PM
Change Number: 5
Last Saved On: 4/4/2012 12:40:00 PM
Last Saved By: Windows User
Total Editing Time: 109 Minutes
Last Printed On: 4/4/2012 12:42:02 PM
As of Last Complete Printing
Number of Pages: 3 (approx.)
Number of Words: 406
Number of Characters: 2,273 (approx.)

Figure 2–77

Other Ways

1. Press CTRL+P, press ENTER

To Preview the Document and Then Print It

Before printing the research paper, you want to verify the page layouts. The following steps change the print option to print the document (instead of the document properties), preview the printed pages in the research paper, and then print the document.

1

- Position the insertion point at the top of the document because you want initially to view the first page in the document.
- Click File on the Ribbon to open the Backstage view and then click the Print tab in the Backstage view to display the Print gallery.
- Verify the printer name that appears on the Printer Status button will print a hard copy of the document. If necessary, select a different printer.
- Click the first button in the Settings area to display a list of options specifying what you can print (Figure 2–78).

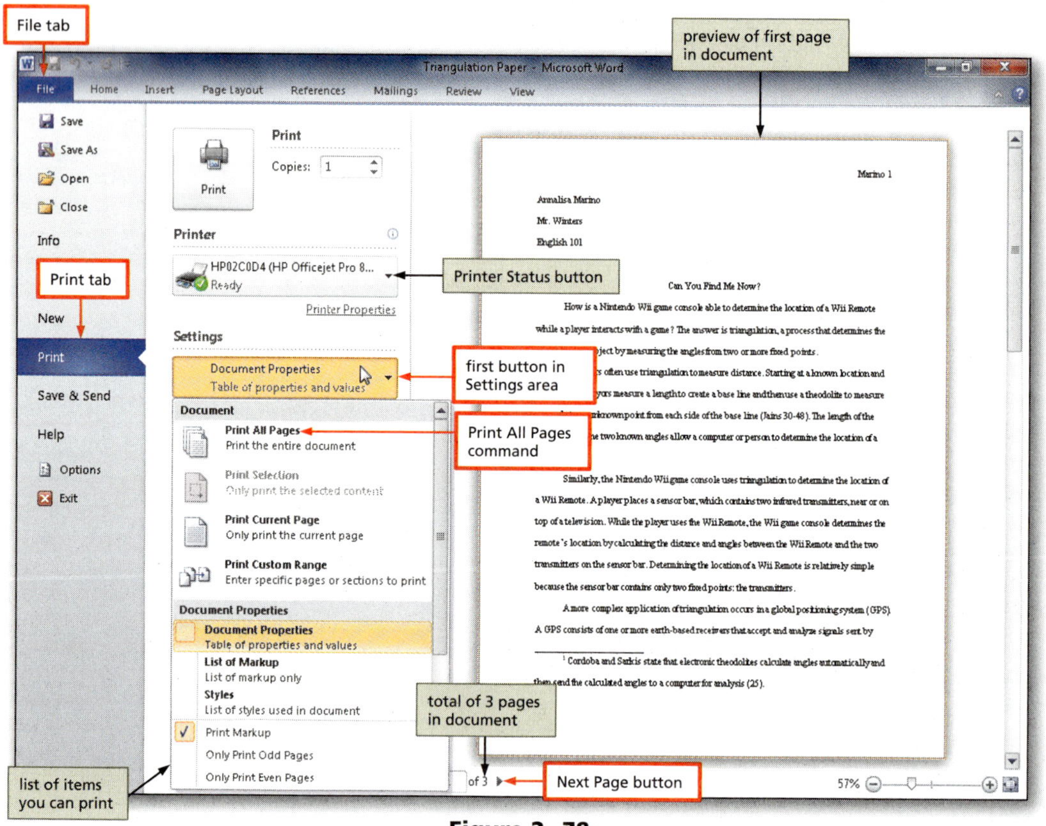

Figure 2–78

2

- Click Print All Pages in the list to specify you want to print all pages in the actual document.

3

- Click the Next Page button in the Print gallery to preview the second page of the research paper in the Print gallery.
- Click the Next Page button again to preview the third page of the research paper in the Print gallery (Figure 2–79).

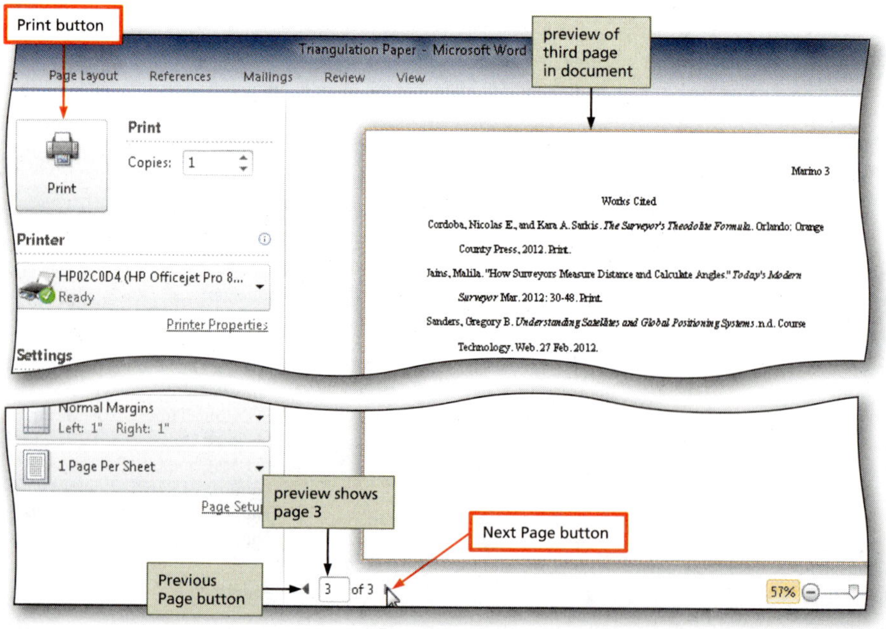

Figure 2–79

4

- Click the Print button in the Print gallery to print the research paper on the currently selected printer (shown in Figure 2–1 on page WD 67).

Other Ways

1. Press CTRL+P, press ENTER

To Quit Word

This project now is complete. The following steps quit Word. For a detailed example of the procedure summarized below, refer to the Office 2010 and Windows 7 chapter in this book.

1. If you have one Word document open, click the Close button on the right side of the title bar to close the document and quit Word; or if you have multiple Word documents open, click File on the Ribbon to open the Backstage view and then click Exit in the Backstage view to close all open documents and quit Word.

2. If a Microsoft Word dialog box appears, click the Save button to save any changes made to the document since the last save.

BTW

Quick Reference
For a table that lists how to complete the tasks covered in the Office chapters in this book using the mouse, Ribbon, shortcut menu, and keyboard, see the Quick Reference Summary at the back of this book, or visit the Microsoft Office and Concepts CourseMate Web site at www.cengagebrain.com and then navigate to the Quick Reference resource for this book.

Chapter Summary

In this chapter, you have learned how to change document settings, use headers to number pages, modify a style, insert and edit citations and their sources, add footnotes, create a bibliographical list of sources, and use the Research task pane. The items listed below include all the new Word skills you have learned in this chapter.

1. Modify a Style (WD 70)
2. Change Line Spacing (WD 73)
3. Remove Space after a Paragraph (WD 74)
4. Update a Style to Match a Selection (WD 74)
5. Switch to the Header (WD 75)
6. Right-Align a Paragraph (WD 76)
7. Insert a Page Number (WD 77)
8. Close the Header (WD 78)
9. Click and Type (WD 80)
10. Display the Rulers (WD 82)
11. First-Line Indent Paragraphs (WD 83)
12. AutoCorrect as You Type (WD 85)
13. Use the AutoCorrect Options Button (WD 85)
14. Create an AutoCorrect Entry (WD 86)
15. Change the Bibliography Style (WD 89)
16. Insert a Citation and Create Its Source (WD 90)
17. Edit a Citation (WD 91)
18. Insert a Footnote Reference Mark (WD 93)
19. Insert a Citation Placeholder (WD 94)
20. Modify a Style Using a Shortcut Menu (WD 95)
21. Edit a Source (WD 97)
22. Count Words (WD 101)
23. Page Break Manually (WD 106)
24. Apply a Style (WD 106)
25. Create the Bibliographical List (WD 108)
26. Format Paragraphs with a Hanging Indent (WD 109)
27. Modify a Source and Update the Bibliographical List (WD 109)
28. Convert a Field to Regular Text (WD 110)
29. Scroll Page by Page through a Document (WD 112)
30. Copy and Paste (WD 113)
31. Display the Paste Options Menu (WD 114)
32. Find Text (WD 115)
33. Replace Text (WD 116)
34. Go to a Page (WD 117)
35. Find and Insert a Synonym (WD 118)
36. Check Spelling and Grammar at Once (WD 118)
37. View or Modify Entries in a Custom Dictionary (WD 120)
38. Set the Default Custom Dictionary (WD 120)
39. Use the Research Task Pane to Look Up Information (WD 120)
40. Print Document Properties (WD 123)
41. Preview the Document and Then Print It (WD 124)

SAM

If you have a SAM 2010 user profile, your instructor may have assigned an autogradable version of this assignment. If so, log into the SAM 2010 Web site at www.cengage.com/sam2010 to download the instruction and start files.

Learn It Online

Test your knowledge of chapter content and key terms.

Instructions: To complete the Learn It Online exercises, start your browser, visit the Microsoft Office and Concepts CourseMate Web site at www.cengagebrain.com, navigate to the Word Chapter 2 resources for this book, click the link for the exercise you want to complete, and then read the instructions.

Chapter Reinforcement TF, MC, and SA
A series of true/false, multiple choice, and short answer questions that test your knowledge of the chapter content.

Flash Cards
An interactive learning environment where you identify chapter key terms associated with displayed definitions.

Practice Test
A series of multiple choice questions that test your knowledge of chapter content and key terms.

Who Wants To Be a Computer Genius?
An interactive game that challenges your knowledge of chapter content in the style of a television quiz show.

Wheel of Terms
An interactive game that challenges your knowledge of chapter key terms in the style of the television show *Wheel of Fortune*.

Crossword Puzzle Challenge
A crossword puzzle that challenges your knowledge of key terms presented in the chapter.

Apply Your Knowledge

Reinforce the skills and apply the concepts you learned in this chapter.

Revising Text and Paragraphs in a Document
Note: To complete this assignment, you will be required to use the Data Files for Students. See the inside back cover of this book for instructions on downloading the Data Files for Students, or contact your instructor for information about accessing the required files.

Instructions: Start Word. Open the document, Apply 2-1 Space Paragraph Draft, from the Data Files for Students. The document you open contains a paragraph of text. You are to revise the document as follows: move a word, move another word and change the format of the moved word, change paragraph indentation, change line spacing, find all occurrences of a word, replace all occurrences of a word with another word, locate a synonym, and edit the header.

Perform the following tasks:

1. Copy the word, exploration, from the first sentence and paste it in the last sentence after the word, space, so that it is the eighth word in the sentence.
2. Select the underlined word, safe, in the paragraph. Use drag-and-drop editing to move the selected word, safe, so that it is before the word, mission, in the same sentence. Click the Paste Options button that displays to the right of the moved word, safe. Remove the underline format from the moved sentence by clicking Keep Text Only on the Paste Options menu.
3. Display the ruler, if necessary. Use the ruler to indent the first line of the paragraph one-half inch.
4. Change the line spacing of the paragraph to double.
5. Use the Navigation Pane to find all occurrences of the word, sensors. How many are there?
6. Use the Find and Replace dialog box to replace all occurrences of the word, issues, with the word, problems. How many replacements were made?

7. Use Word to find the word, height. Use Word's thesaurus to change the word, height, to the word, altitude.
8. Switch to the header so that you can edit it. In the first line of the header, change the word, Draft, to the word, Modified, so that it reads: Space Paragraph Modified.
9. In the second line of the header, insert the page number (with no formatting) one space after the word, Page.
10. Change the alignment of both lines of text in the header from left-aligned to right-aligned. Switch back to the document text.
11. Change the document properties, as specified by your instructor.
12. Click File on the Ribbon and then click Save As. Save the document using the file name, Apply 2-1 Space Paragraph Modified.
13. Print the document properties and then print the revised document, shown in Figure 2–80.
14. Use the Research task pane to look up the definition of the word, NASA, in the paragraph. Handwrite the definition of the word on your printout, as well as your response to the question in #6.
15. Change the Search for box to All Research Sites. Print an article from one of the sites.
16. Display the Research Options dialog box and, on your printout, handwrite the currently active Reference Books, Research Sites, and Business and Financial Sites. If your instructor approves, activate one of the services.

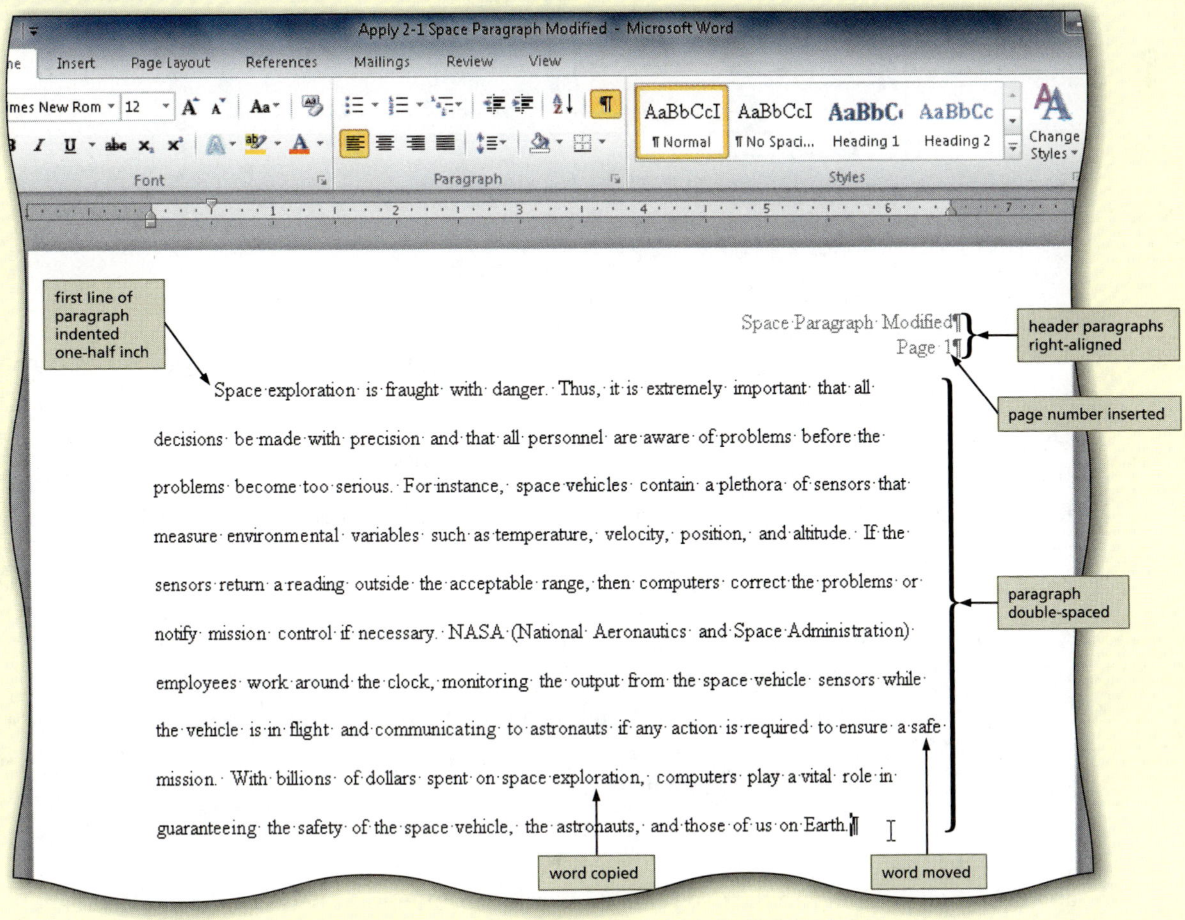

Figure 2–80

Extend Your Knowledge

Extend the skills you learned in this chapter and experiment with new skills. You may need to use Help to complete the assignment.

Working with References and Proofing Tools

Note: To complete this assignment, you will be required to use the Data Files for Students. See the inside back cover of this book for instructions on downloading the Data Files for Students, or contact your instructor for information about accessing the required files.

Instructions: Start Word. Open the document, Extend 2-1 Digital Camera Paper Draft, from the Data Files for Students. You will add another footnote to the paper, use the thesaurus, convert the document from MLA to APA documentation style, convert the footnotes to endnotes, modify the Endnote Text style, change the format of the note reference marks, and translate the document to another language (Figure 2–81).

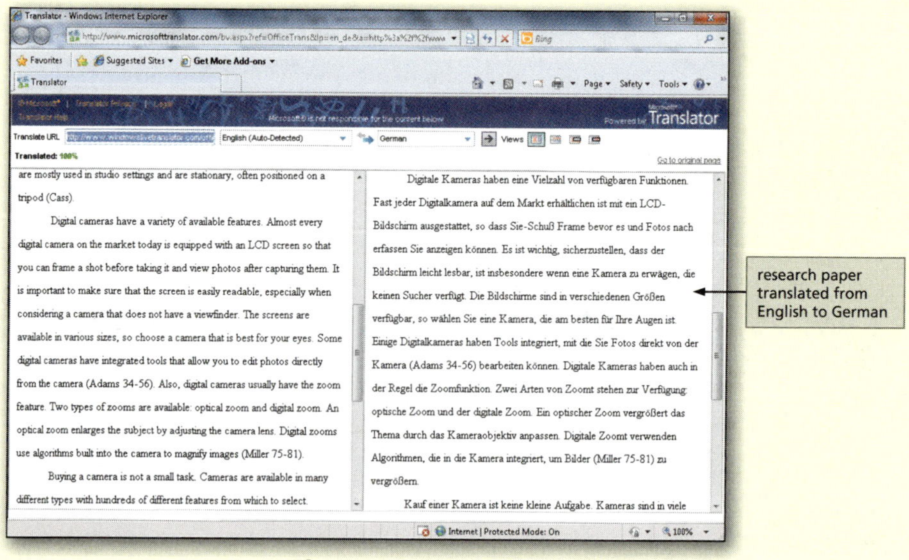

Figure 2–81

Perform the following tasks:

1. Use Help to learn more about footers, footnotes and endnotes, bibliography styles, AutoCorrect, and the Mini Translator.
2. Delete the footer from the document.
3. Insert a second footnote at an appropriate place in the research paper. Use the following footnote text: For instance, Adams states that you may be able to crop photos, change the brightness, or remove red eye effects.
4. Change the location of the footnotes from bottom of page to below text.
5. Use the Find and Replace dialog box to find the word, small, in the document and then replace it with a word of your choice.
6. Save the document with a new file name and then print it. On the printout, write the number of words, characters without spaces, characters with spaces, paragraphs, and lines in the document. Be sure to include footnote text in the statistics.
7. Select the entire document and then change the documentation style of the citations and bibliography from MLA to APA. Save the APA version of the document with a new file name and then print it. Compare the two versions. Circle the differences between the two documents.
8. Convert the footnotes to endnotes.

9. Modify the Endnote Text style to 12-point Times New Roman font, double-spaced text with a hanging-line indent.
10. Change the format of the note reference marks to capital letters (A, B, etc.).
11. Add an AutoCorrect entry that replaces the word, camora, with the word, camera. Add this sentence, A field camora usually is more than sufficient for most users., to the end of the second paragraph, misspelling the word camera to test the AutoCorrect entry. Delete the AutoCorrect entry that replaces camora with the word, camera.
12. Display readability statistics. What are the Flesch-Kincaid Grade Level, the Flesch Reading Ease score, and the percent of passive sentences?
13. Save the revised document with endnotes with a new file name and then print it. On the printout, write your response to the question in #12.
14. If you have an Internet connection, translate the research paper into a language of your choice using the Translate button (Review tab | Language group). Submit the translated document in the format specified by your instructor. Use the Mini Translator to hear how to pronounce three words in your paper.

Make It Right

Analyze a document and correct all errors and/or improve the design.

Inserting Missing Elements in an MLA-Styled Research Paper

Note: To complete this assignment, you will be required to use the Data Files for Students. See the inside back cover of this book for instructions on downloading the Data Files for Students, or contact your instructor for information about accessing the required files.

Instructions: Start Word. Open the document, Make It Right 2-1 Biometrics Paper Draft, from the Data Files for Students. The document is a research paper that is missing several elements. You are to insert these missing elements, all formatted according to the MLA documentation style: header with a page number, name and course information, paper title, footnote, and source information for a citation.

Perform the following tasks:

1. Insert a header with a page number (use your own last name), name and course information (your name, your instructor name, your course name, and today's date), and an appropriate paper title, all formatted according to the MLA documentation style.
2. The Jenkins citation placeholder is missing its source information (Figure 2–82). Use the following source information to edit the source: magazine article titled "Fingerprint Readers" written by Arthur D. Jenkins and Marissa K. Weavers, magazine name is *Security Today*, publication date is February 2012, article is on pages 55–60. Edit the citation so that it displays the author name and the page numbers of 55–56 for this reference.

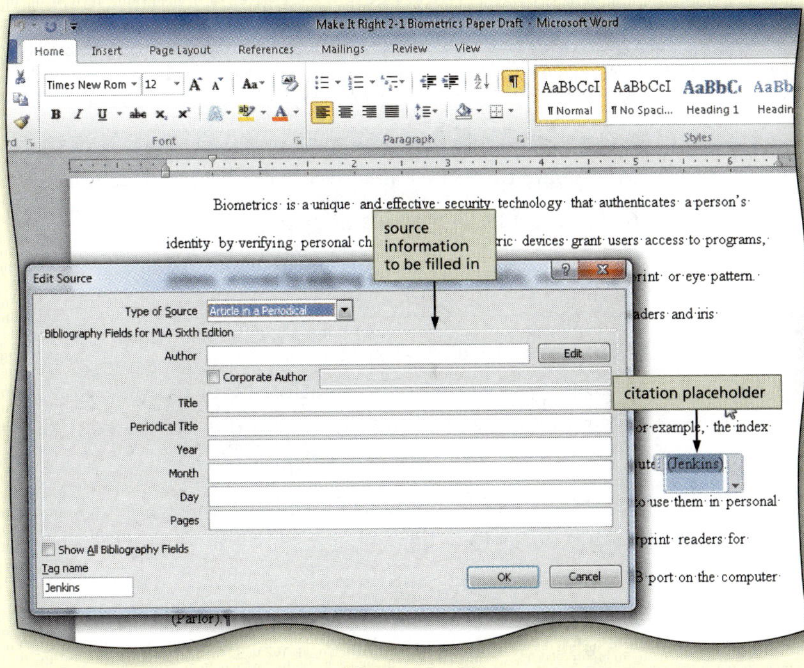

Figure 2–82

Continued >

Make It Right *continued*

3. Modify the source of the book authored by Carolina Doe, so that the publisher city is Chicago instead of Dallas.
4. Change the Footnote Text style to 12-point Times New Roman, double-spaced paragraphs with a first-line indent.
5. Insert the following footnote with the note reference at an appropriate place in the paper, formatted according to the MLA documentation style: Parlor states that one use of fingerprint readers is for users to log on to programs and Web sites via their fingerprint instead of entering a user name and password.
6. Use the Navigation Pane to display page 3. Use Word to insert the bibliographical list (bibliography). Convert the works cited to regular text. Change the underline format on the titles of the works to the italic format, and insert the correct publication medium for each work.
7. Change the document properties, as specified by your instructor. Save the revised document with the file name, Make It Right 2-1 Biometrics Paper Modified, and then submit it in the format specified by your instructor.

In the Lab

Design and/or create a document using the guidelines, concepts, and skills presented in this chapter. Labs are listed in order of increasing difficulty.

Lab 1: Preparing a Short Research Paper

Problem: You are a college student currently enrolled in an introductory business class. Your assignment is to prepare a short research paper (275–300 words) about video or computer games. The requirements are that the paper be presented according to the MLA documentation style and have three references. One of the three references must be from the Web. You prepare the paper shown in Figure 2–83 on pages WD 131 and WD 132, which discusses game controllers.

Instructions: Perform the following tasks:

1. Start Word. If necessary, display formatting marks on the screen.
2. Modify the Normal style to 12-point Times New Roman font.
3. Adjust line spacing to double.
4. Remove space below (after) paragraphs.
5. Update the Normal style to reflect the adjusted line and paragraph spacing.
6. Create a header to number pages.
7. Type the name and course information at the left margin. Center and type the title.
8. Set a first-line indent to one-half inch for paragraphs in the body of the research paper.
9. Type the research paper as shown in Figures 2–83a and 2–83b. Change the bibliography style to MLA. As you insert citations, enter their source information (shown in Figure 2–83c). The first citation is a book; the second is an article in a periodical; and the third is a Web site. Edit the citations so that they are displayed according to Figures 2–83a and 2–83b.
10. At the end of the research paper text, press the ENTER key and then insert a manual page break so that the Works Cited page begins on a new page. Enter and format the works cited title (Figure 2–83c). Use Word to insert the bibliographical list (bibliography). Convert the bibliography field to text. Change the underline format on the titles of the works to the italic format and insert the correct publication medium for each work (shown in Figure 2–83c).

(b) Page 2

Kimble 2

Game controllers are used primarily to direct movement and actions of on-screen objects. Two popular types are gamepads and motion-sensing game controllers. Games become more enjoyable every day with the use of new and exciting game controllers. What will be next?

(a) Page 1

Kimble 1

Harley Kimble

Ms. Longherst

English 101

April 30, 2012

From One Controller to Another

Video games and computer games use a game controller as the input device that directs movements and actions of on-screen objects. Two commonly used game controllers are gamepads and motion-sensing game controllers (Joyce). Game controllers not only enrich the gaming experience but also aid in the movements and actions of players.

A gamepad is held by the player with both hands, allowing the player to control the movement or actions of the objects in the video or computer games. Players press buttons on the gamepad, often with their thumbs, to carry out actions. Some gamepads have swiveling sticks that also can trigger events during game play (Cortez 20-24). Some gamepads include wireless capabilities; others connect via a cable directly to the game console or a personal computer.

Motion-sensing game controllers allow the user to guide on-screen elements or trigger events by moving a handheld input device in predetermined directions through the air. These controllers communicate with a game console or personal computer via wired or wireless technology. A variety of games, from sports to simulations, use motion-sensing game controllers. Some of these controllers, such as baseball bats and golf clubs, are designed for only one specific kind of game; others are general purpose. A popular, general-purpose, motion-sensing game controller is Nintendo's Wii Remote. Shaped like a television remote control and operated with one hand, the Wii Remote uses Bluetooth wireless technology to communicate with the Wii game console (Bloom 56-59).

Figure 2–83

Continued >

In the Lab *continued*

(c) Page 3

Kimble 3

Works Cited

Bloom, June. *The Gaming Experience*. New York: Buffalo Works Press, 2012. Print.

Cortez, Domiciano Isachar. "Today's Game Controllers." *Gaming, Gaming, Gaming* Jan. 2012: 12-34. Print.

Joyce, Andrea D. *What Gamers Want*. 15 Feb. 2012. Web. 28 Mar. 2012.

11. Check the spelling and grammar of the paper at once.
12. Change the document properties, as specified by your instructor. Save the document using Lab 2-1 Game Controllers Paper as the file name.
13. Print the research paper. Handwrite the number of words, paragraphs, and characters in the research paper above the title of your printed research paper.

In the Lab

Lab 2: Preparing a Research Report with a Footnote

Problem: You are a college student enrolled in an introductory English class. Your assignment is to prepare a short research paper in any area of interest to you. The requirements are that the paper be presented according to the MLA documentation style, contain at least one note positioned as a footnote, and have three references. One of the three references must be from the Internet. You prepare a paper about trends in agriculture (Figure 2–84).

Instructions: Perform the following tasks:

1. Start Word. Modify the Normal style to 12-point Times New Roman font. Adjust line spacing to double and remove space below (after) paragraphs. Update the Normal style to include the adjusted line and paragraph spacing. Create a header to number pages. Type the name and course information at the left margin. Center and type the title. Set a first-line indent for paragraphs in the body of the research paper.
2. Type the research paper as shown in Figures 2–84a and 2–84b. Insert the footnote as shown in Figure 2–84a. Change the Footnote Text style to the format specified in the MLA documentation style. Change the bibliography style to MLA. As you insert citations, use the source information listed below and on page WD 134:
   a. Type of Source: Article in a Periodical
   Author: Barton, Blake
   Title: Computers in Agriculture
   Periodical Title: Agriculture Today and Tomorrow
   Year: 2012
   Month: Feb.
   Pages 53–86
   Publication Medium: Print

(b) Page 2

Gander 2

Brewster, the discovery of pests might trigger a pesticide to discharge in the affected area automatically (Agriculture: Expanding and Growing).

Many farmers use technology on a daily basis to regulate soil moisture and to keep their crops pest free. With technology, farming can be much more convenient and efficient.

(a) Page 1

Gander 1

Samuel Gander

Mr. Dunham

English 102

April 25, 2012

Farming on a Whole New Level

Although people have worked in agriculture for more than 10,000 years, advances in technology assist with maintaining and protecting land, crops, and animals. The demand to keep food prices affordable encourages those working in the agriculture industry to operate as efficiently as possible (Newman and Ruiz 33-47).

Almost all people and companies in this industry have many acres of land they must maintain, and it is not always feasible for farmers to take frequent trips around the property to perform basic tasks such as watering soil in the absence of rain. The number of people-hours required to water soil manually on several thousand acres of land might result in businesses spending thousands of dollars in labor and utility costs. If the irrigation process is automated, sensors detect how much rain has fallen recently, as well as whether the soil is in need of watering. The sensors then send this data to a computer that processes it and decides when and how much to water.[1]

In addition to keeping the soil moist and reducing maintenance costs, computers also can utilize sensors to analyze the condition of crops in the field and determine whether pests or diseases are affecting the crops. If sensors detect pests and/or diseases, computers send a notification to the appropriate individual to take corrective action. In some cases, according to

[1] Barton states that many automated home irrigation systems also are programmable and use rain sensors (67-73).

Figure 2–84

Continued >

In the Lab *continued*

b. Type of Source: Book
Author: Newman, Albert D., and Carmen W. Ruiz
Title: The Agricultural Industry Today
Year: 2012
City: New York
Publisher: Alabama Press
Publication Medium: Print

c. Type of Source: Web site
Author: Brewster, Letty
Name of Web page: Agriculture: Expanding and Growing
Year: 2012
Month: Jan.
Day: 3
Publication Medium: Web
Year Accessed: 2012
Month Accessed: Feb.
Day Accessed: 9

3. At the end of the research paper text, press the ENTER key once and insert a manual page break so that the Works Cited page begins on a new page. Enter and format the works cited title. Use Word to insert the bibliographical list. Convert the bibliography field to text. Change the underline format on the titles of the works to the italic format, and insert the correct publication medium for each work.
4. Check the spelling and grammar of the paper.
5. Save the document using Lab 2-2 Agriculture Paper as the file name.
6. Print the research paper. Handwrite the number of words, including the footnotes, in the research paper above the title of your printed research paper.

In the Lab

Lab 3: Composing a Research Paper from Notes

Problem: You have drafted the notes shown in Figure 2–85. Your assignment is to prepare a short research paper from these notes.

Instructions: Perform the following tasks:

1. Start Word. Review the notes in Figure 2–85 and then rearrange and reword them. Embellish the paper as you deem necessary. Present the paper according to the MLA documentation style.

   Create an AutoCorrect entry that automatically corrects the spelling of the misspelled word, digtal, to the correct spelling, digital. Set an AutoCorrect exception for CD., so that Word does not lowercase the next typed letter.

   Insert a footnote that refers the reader to the Web for more information. Enter citations and their sources as shown.

   Create the works cited page (bibliography) from the listed sources. Convert the bibliography field to text. Change the underline format on the titles of the works to the italic format, and insert the correct publication medium for each work.
2. If necessary, set the default dictionary. Add the word, Flickr, to the dictionary. Check the spelling and grammar of the paper.

3. Use the Research task pane to look up a definition of a word in the paper. Copy and insert the definition into the document as a footnote. Be sure to quote the definition and cite the source. *Hint:* Use a Web site as the type of source.

4. Save the document using Lab 2-3 Cloud Storage Paper as the file name. Print the research paper. Handwrite the number of words, including the footnotes, in the research paper above the title of the printed research paper.

Cloud Storage:

- When storing data using cloud storage, the user must locate the appropriate Web site. Some sites support only certain file types. Other sites provide more than just storage.
- Cloud storage is one of the many different features available on the Internet.
- Cloud storage allows users to store files on Web sites.
- Computer users may use this type of storage if they do not want to store their data locally on a hard disk or other type of media.

Different Web sites provide different types of cloud storage. Three are Google's Gmail, YouTube, and Windows Live SkyDrive (source: "Cloud Storage and the Internet," an article on pages 23-37 in March 2012 issue of *Internet Usage and Trends* by Leona Carter).

- Google's e-mail program, Gmail, is cloud storage that stores e-mail messages.
- YouTube is different from Gmail, however, because it stores only digital videos (source: pages 22-24 in a book called *Working with the Internet: Cloud Storage* by Robert M. Gaff, published at Jane Lewis Press in New York in 2012).
- Windows Live SkyDrive is a cloud storage provider that accepts any type of file. This type of Web site is used mainly for backup or additional storage space.

Some cloud storage Web sites also provide other services (source: a Web site titled *The Internet: Cloud Storage* by Rebecca A. Ford and Harry I. Garland of Course Technology dated January 2, 2012, viewed on March 7, 2012).

- Flickr provides cloud storage for digital photos and also enables users to manage their photos and share them with others.
- Facebook provides cloud storage for a number of different file types including digital photos, digital videos, messages, and personal information. Facebook also provides a means of social networking.
- Google Docs not only stores documents, spreadsheets, and presentations in its cloud, it also enables its users to create these documents.

Figure 2–85

Cases and Places

Apply your creative thinking and problem solving skills to design and implement a solution.

Note: To complete these assignments, you may be required to use the Data Files for Students. See the inside back cover of this book for instructions on downloading the Data Files for Students, or contact your instructor for information about accessing the required files.

1: Create a Research Paper about Preparing for a Career in the Computer Industry

Academic

As a student in an introductory computer class, your instructor has assigned a research paper that discusses educational options available for students pursuing a career in the computer industry. The source for the text in your research paper is in a file called Preparing for a Career in the Computer Industry, which is located on the Data Files for Students. In addition to this source, if your instructor requests, use the Research task pane to obtain information from another source. Include a note positioned as a footnote. Add an AutoCorrect entry to correct a word you commonly mistype.

Using the concepts and techniques presented in this chapter, along with the text in the file on the Data Files for Students, create and format this research paper according to the MLA documentation style. Be sure to check spelling and grammar of the finished paper. Submit your assignment in the format specified by your instructor.

2: Create a Research Paper about Computer Viruses

Personal

The computer you recently purchased included an antivirus program. Because you need practice writing research papers and you want to learn more about computer viruses, you decide to write a paper about computer viruses. The source for the text in your research paper is in a file called Computer Viruses, which is located on the Data Files for Students. In addition to this source, if your instructor requests, use the Research task pane to obtain information from another source. Include a note positioned as a footnote. Add an AutoCorrect entry to correct a word you commonly mistype.

Using the concepts and techniques presented in this chapter, along with the text in the file on the Data Files for Students, create and format this research paper according to the MLA documentation style. Be sure to check spelling and grammar of the finished paper. Submit your assignment in the format specified by your instructor.

3: Create a Research Paper about a Disaster Recovery Plan

Professional

Your boss has asked you to research the components of a disaster recovery plan. Because you learned in college how to write research papers, you decide to present your findings in a research paper. The source for the text in your research paper is in a file called Disaster Recovery Plan, which is located on the Data Files for Students. In addition to this source, if your instructor requests, use the Research task pane to obtain information from another source. Include a note positioned as a footnote. Add an AutoCorrect entry to correct a word you commonly mistype.

Using the concepts and techniques presented in this chapter, along with the text in the file on the Data Files for Students, create and format this research paper according to the MLA documentation style. Be sure to check spelling and grammar of the finished paper. Submit your assignment in the format specified by your instructor.

3 Creating a Business Letter with a Letterhead and Table

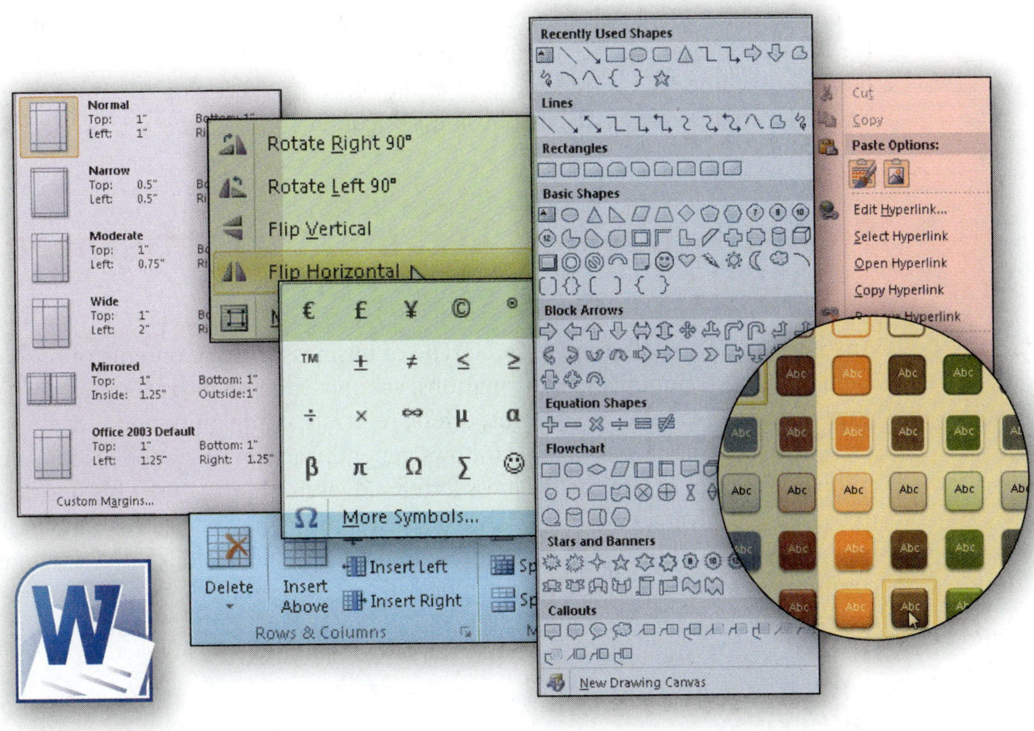

Objectives

You will have mastered the material in this chapter when you can:

- Change margins
- Insert and format a shape
- Change text wrapping
- Insert and format a clip art image
- Insert a symbol
- Add a border to a paragraph
- Clear formatting
- Convert a hyperlink to regular text
- Create a file from an existing file
- Apply a Quick Style
- Set and use tab stops
- Insert the current date
- Create, insert, and modify a building block
- Insert a Word table, enter data in the table, and format the table
- Address and print an envelope

3 Creating a Business Letter with a Letterhead and Table

Introduction

In a business environment, people use documents to communicate with others. Business documents can include letters, memos, newsletters, proposals, and resumes. An effective business document clearly and concisely conveys its message and has a professional, organized appearance. You can use your own creative skills to design and compose business documents. Using Word, for example, you can develop the content and decide on the location of each item in a business document.

Project — Business Letter with a Letterhead and Table

At some time, you will prepare some type of business letter. Contents of business letters include requests, inquiries, confirmations, acknowledgements, recommendations, notifications, responses, invitations, offers, referrals, complaints, and more.

The project in this chapter follows generally accepted guidelines for writing letters and uses Word to create the business letter shown in Figure 3–1. This business letter to a potential advertiser (Wilcox Tractor Restorations) includes a custom letterhead, as well as all essential business letter components: date line, inside address, salutation, body, complimentary close, and signature block. To easily present the advertisement rates, this information appears in a table, and the discounts are in a bulleted list.

Overview

As you read through this chapter, you will learn how to create the business letter in Figure 3–1 by performing these general tasks:

- Design and create a letterhead.
- Compose a business letter.
- Print the business letter.
- Address and print an envelope.

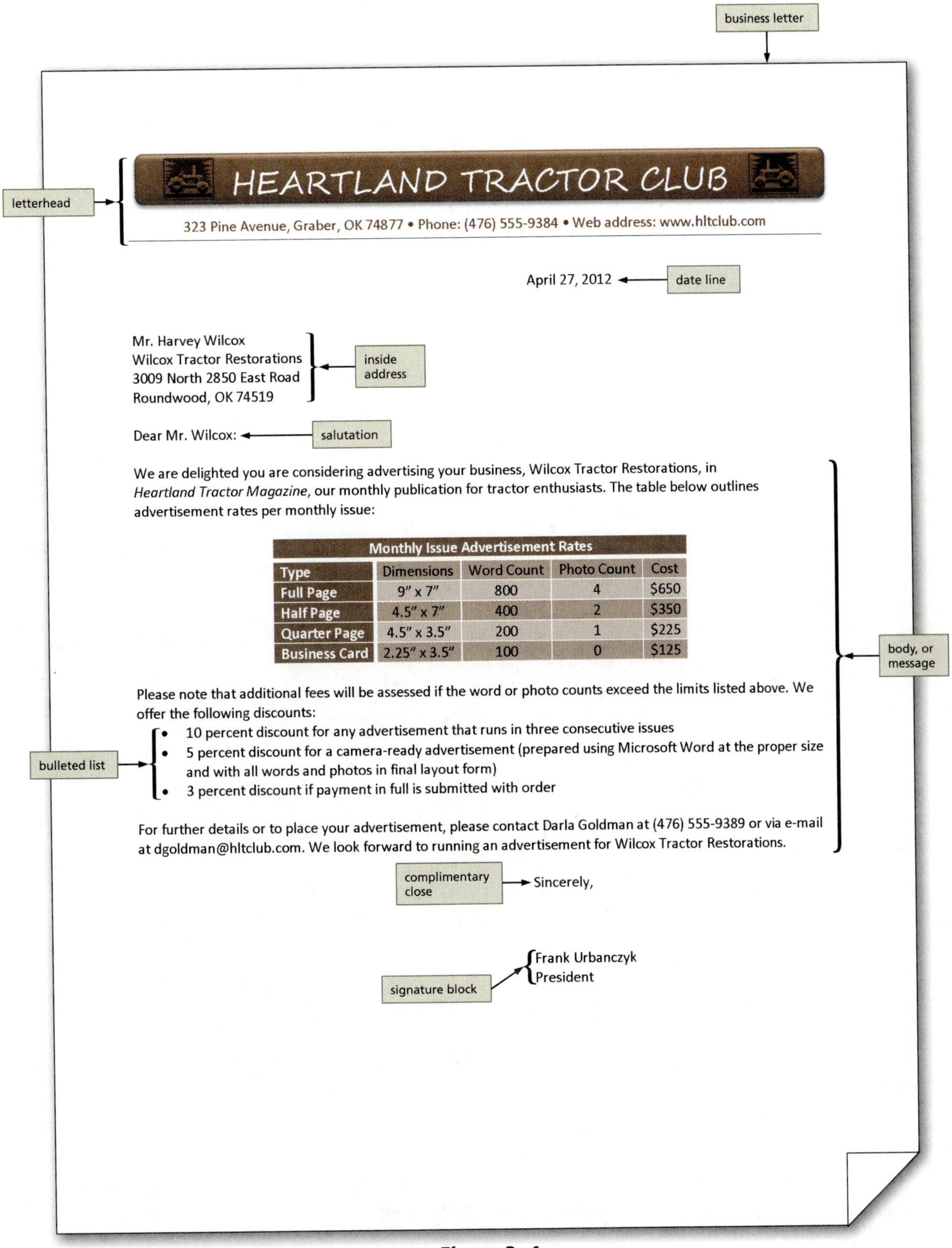

HEARTLAND TRACTOR CLUB

323 Pine Avenue, Graber, OK 74877 • Phone: (476) 555-9384 • Web address: www.hltclub.com

April 27, 2012

Mr. Harvey Wilcox
Wilcox Tractor Restorations
3009 North 2850 East Road
Roundwood, OK 74519

Dear Mr. Wilcox:

We are delighted you are considering advertising your business, Wilcox Tractor Restorations, in *Heartland Tractor Magazine*, our monthly publication for tractor enthusiasts. The table below outlines advertisement rates per monthly issue:

Monthly Issue Advertisement Rates				
Type	Dimensions	Word Count	Photo Count	Cost
Full Page	9" x 7"	800	4	$650
Half Page	4.5" x 7"	400	2	$350
Quarter Page	4.5" x 3.5"	200	1	$225
Business Card	2.25" x 3.5"	100	0	$125

Please note that additional fees will be assessed if the word or photo counts exceed the limits listed above. We offer the following discounts:

- 10 percent discount for any advertisement that runs in three consecutive issues
- 5 percent discount for a camera-ready advertisement (prepared using Microsoft Word at the proper size and with all words and photos in final layout form)
- 3 percent discount if payment in full is submitted with order

For further details or to place your advertisement, please contact Darla Goldman at (476) 555-9389 or via e-mail at dgoldman@hltclub.com. We look forward to running an advertisement for Wilcox Tractor Restorations.

Sincerely,

Frank Urbanczyk
President

Figure 3–1

Plan Ahead

General Project Guidelines

When creating a Word document, the actions you perform and decisions you make will affect the appearance and characteristics of the finished document. As you create a business letter, such as the project shown in Figure 3–1 on the previous page, you should follow these general guidelines:

1. **Determine how to create a letterhead.** A **letterhead** is the section of a letter that identifies an organization or individual. Often, the letterhead appears at the top of a letter. Although you can design and print a letterhead yourself, many businesses pay an outside firm to design and print their letterhead, usually on higher-quality paper. They then use the professionally preprinted paper for external business communications.
2. **If you do not have preprinted letterhead paper, design a creative letterhead.** Use text, graphics, formats, and colors that reflect the organization or individual. Include the organization's or individual's name, postal mailing address, and telephone number. If the organization or individual has an e-mail address and Web address, you may include those as well.
3. **Compose an effective business letter.** A finished business letter should look like a symmetrically framed picture with evenly spaced margins, all balanced below an attractive letterhead. The letter should be well-written, properly formatted, logically organized, and use visuals where appropriate. The content of a letter should contain proper grammar, correct spelling, logically constructed sentences, flowing paragraphs, and sound ideas. If possible, keep the length of a business letter to one page. Be sure to proofread the finished letter carefully.

When necessary, more specific details concerning the above guidelines are presented at appropriate points in the chapter. The chapter also will identify the actions performed and decisions made regarding these guidelines during the creation of the business letter shown in Figure 3–1.

For an introduction to Windows 7 and instruction about how to perform basic Windows 7 tasks, read the Office 2010 and Windows 7 chapter in this book, where you can learn how to resize windows, change screen resolution, create folders, move and rename files, use Windows Help, and much more.

To Start Word and Display Formatting Marks

If you are using a computer to step through the project in this chapter and you want your screens to match the figures in the Office and Windows chapters in this book, you should change your screen's resolution to 1024 × 768. For information about how to change a computer's resolution, refer to the Office 2010 and Windows 7 chapter in this book.

The following steps start Word and display formatting marks.

1. Start Word. If necessary, maximize the Word window.
2. If the Print Layout button on the status bar is not selected (shown in Figure 3–2), click it so that your screen is in Print Layout view.
3. Change your zoom to 110% (or a percent where the document is large enough for you easily to see its contents).
4. If the Show/Hide ¶ button (Home tab | Paragraph group) is not selected already, click it to display formatting marks on the screen.

For an introduction to Office 2010 and instruction about how to perform basic tasks in Office 2010 programs, read the Office 2010 and Windows 7 chapter in this book, where you can learn how to start a program, use the Ribbon, save a file, open a file, quit a program, use Help, and much more.

To Change Theme Colors

Recall that Word provides document themes that contain a variety of color schemes to assist you in selecting complementary colors in a document. In a letter, select a color scheme that adequately reflects the organization or person. The letter in this chapter uses the Executive color scheme. The following steps change theme colors.

1. Click the Change Styles button (Home tab | Styles group) to display the Change Styles menu and then point to Colors on the Change Styles menu to display the Colors gallery.

2. Click Executive in the Colors gallery to change the document theme colors to the selected color scheme.

BTW

The Ribbon and Screen Resolution

Word may change how the groups and buttons within the groups appear on the Ribbon, depending on the computer's screen resolution. Thus, your Ribbon may look different from the ones in the Office and Windows chapters in this book if you are using a screen resolution other than 1024 × 768.

To Change Margin Settings

Word is preset to use standard 8.5-by-11-inch paper, with 1-inch top, bottom, left, and right margins. If you change the default (preset) margin settings, the new margin settings affect every page in the document. If you wanted the margins to affect just a portion of the document, you would divide the document into sections, which enables you to specify different margin settings for each section.

The business letter in this chapter uses .75-inch left and right margins and 1-inch top and bottom margins, so that more text can fit from left to right on the page. The following steps change margin settings.

1

- Display the Page Layout tab.
- Click the Margins button (Page Layout tab | Page Setup group) to display the Margins gallery (Figure 3–2).

2

- Click Moderate in the Margins gallery to change the margins to the specified settings.

Q&A

What if the margin settings I want are not in the Margins gallery?

You can click Custom Margins in the Margins gallery and then enter your desired margin values in the top, bottom, left, and right text boxes in the dialog box.

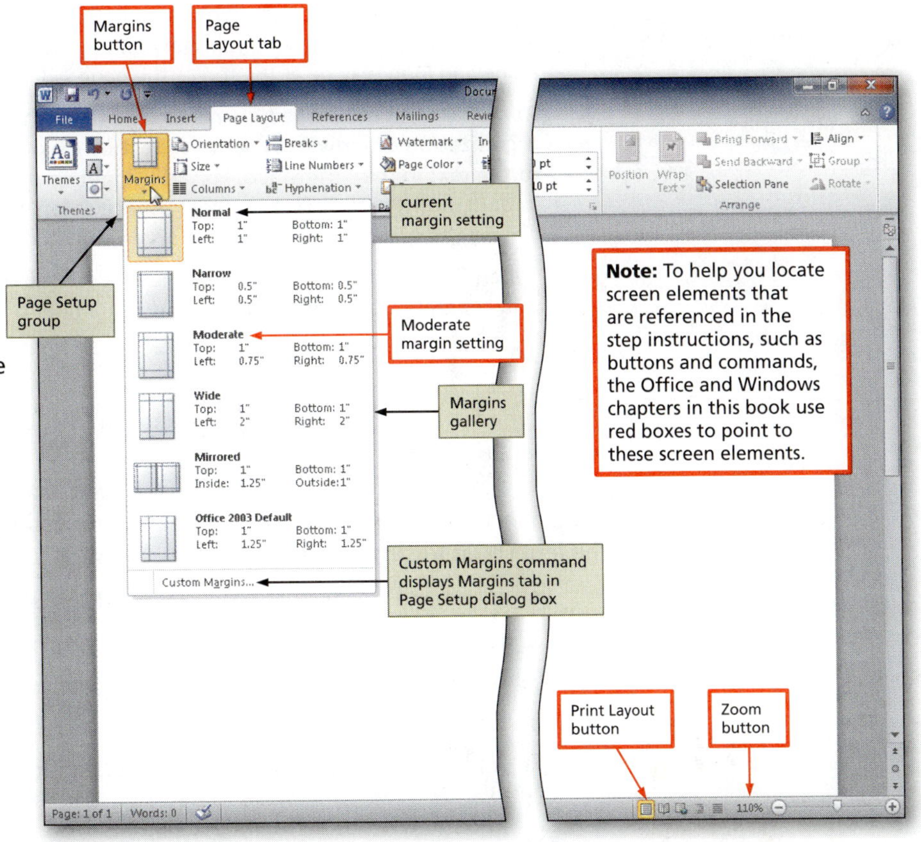

Figure 3–2

Other Ways

1. Position mouse pointer on margin boundary on ruler; when mouse pointer changes to two-headed arrow, drag margin boundary on ruler

Creating a Letterhead

The cost of preprinted letterhead can be high. Thus, an alternative is to create your own letterhead and save it in a file. When you want to create a letter at a later time using the letterhead, simply create a new document from the letterhead file. In this chapter, you create a letterhead and then save it in a file for future use.

Plan Ahead

Design a creative letterhead.

A letterhead often is the first section a reader notices on a letter. Thus, it is important the letterhead appropriately reflect the essence of the business or individual (i.e., formal, technical, creative, etc.). The letterhead should leave ample room for the contents of the letter. When designing a letterhead, consider its contents, placement, and appearance.

- **Contents of letterhead.** A letterhead should contain these elements:
  - Complete legal name of the individual, group, or company
  - Complete mailing address: street address including building, room, suite number, or post office box, along with city, state, and postal code
  - Telephone number(s) and fax number, if one exists

  Many letterheads also include a Web address, an e-mail address, and a logo or other image. If you use an image, select one that expresses your personality or goals.
- **Placement of elements in the letterhead.** Many letterheads center their elements across the top of the page. Others align some or all of the elements with the left or right margins. Sometimes, the elements are split between the top and bottom of the page. For example, a name and logo may be at the top of the page with the address at the bottom of the page.
- **Appearance of letterhead elements.** Use fonts that are easy to read. Give the organization or individual name impact by making its font size larger than the rest of the text in the letterhead. For additional emphasis, consider formatting the name in bold, italic, or a different color. Choose colors that complement each other and convey the goals of the organization or individual.

When finished designing the letterhead, determine if a divider line would help to visually separate the letterhead from the remainder of the letter.

The letterhead for the business letter in this chapter consists of the organization name, appropriate graphics, postal address, telephone number, and Web address. The name and graphics are enclosed in a rectangular shape (Figure 3–1 on page WD 139), and the contact information is below the shape. You will follow these general steps to create the letterhead for the business letter:

1. Insert and format a shape.
2. Enter and format the organization name in the shape.
3. Insert, format, and position the images in the shape.
4. Enter the contact information below the shape.
5. Add a border below the contact information.

To Insert a Shape

The first step is in creating the letterhead in this chapter is to draw a rectangular shape. Word has a variety of predefined shapes, which are a type of drawing object, that you can insert in documents. A **drawing object** is a graphic that you create using Word. Examples of shape drawing objects include rectangles, circles, triangles, arrows, flowcharting symbols, stars, banners, and callouts. The next steps insert a rounded rectangle shape.

1

- Display the Insert tab.
- Click the Shapes button (Insert tab | Illustrations group) to display the Shapes gallery (Figure 3–3).

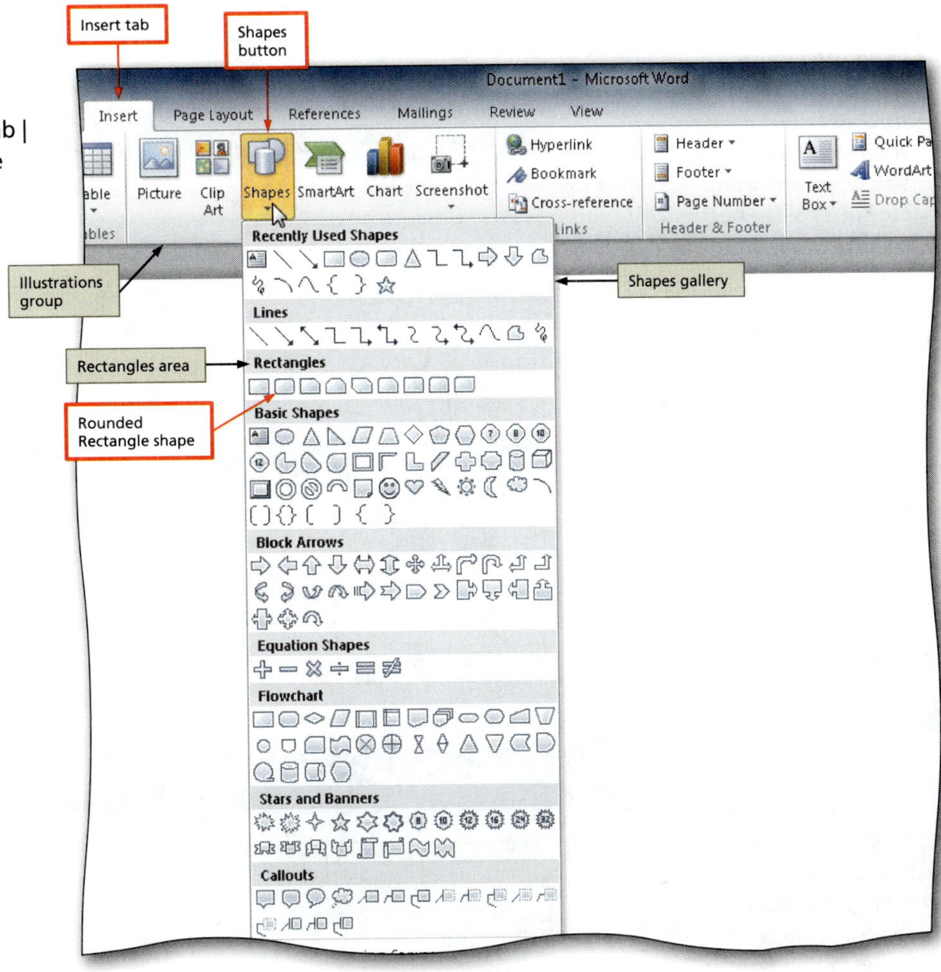

Figure 3–3

2

- Click the Rounded Rectangle shape in the Rectangles area of the Shapes gallery, which removes the gallery and changes the mouse pointer to the shape of a crosshair.
- Position the mouse pointer (a crosshair) by the insertion point in the document window, as shown in Figure 3–4, which is the location for the upper-left corner of the desired shape.

Q&A What is the purpose of the crosshair mouse pointer?

In the document window, you will drag the crosshair mouse pointer from the upper-left corner to the lower-right corner to form the desired location and size of the shape.

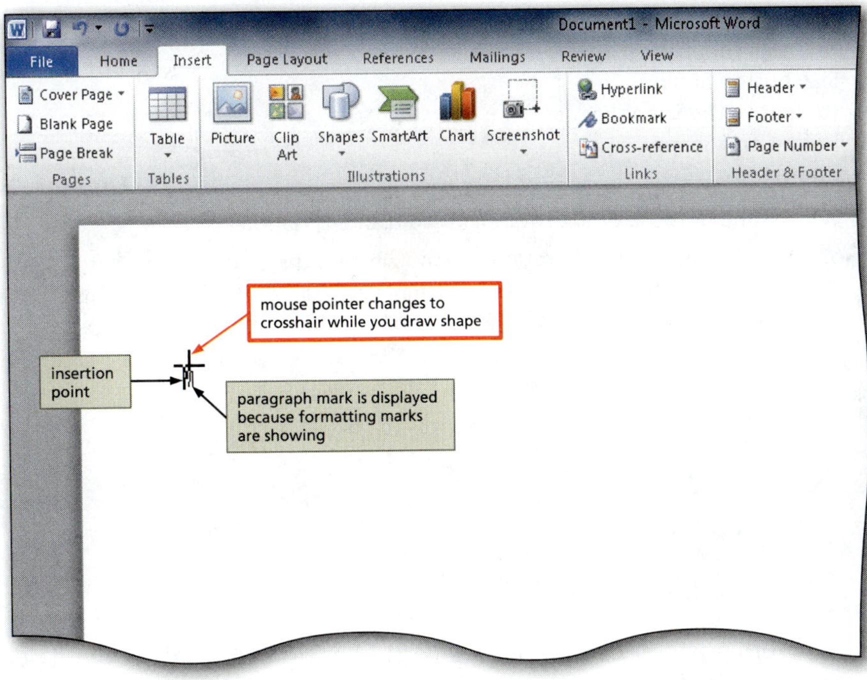

Figure 3–4

3

- Drag the mouse to the right and downward to form the boundaries of the shape, as shown in Figure 3–5. Do not release the mouse button.

Figure 3–5

4

- Release the mouse button so that Word draws the shape according to your drawing in the document window.
- Verify your shape is the same approximate height and width as the one in this project by clicking the Size button (Drawing Tools Format tab | Size group) and then, if necessary, changing the values in the Shape Height box and Shape Width boxes to 0.5"and 7", respectively (Figure 3–6). When finished, click the Size button again to remove the Shape Height and Shape Width boxes.

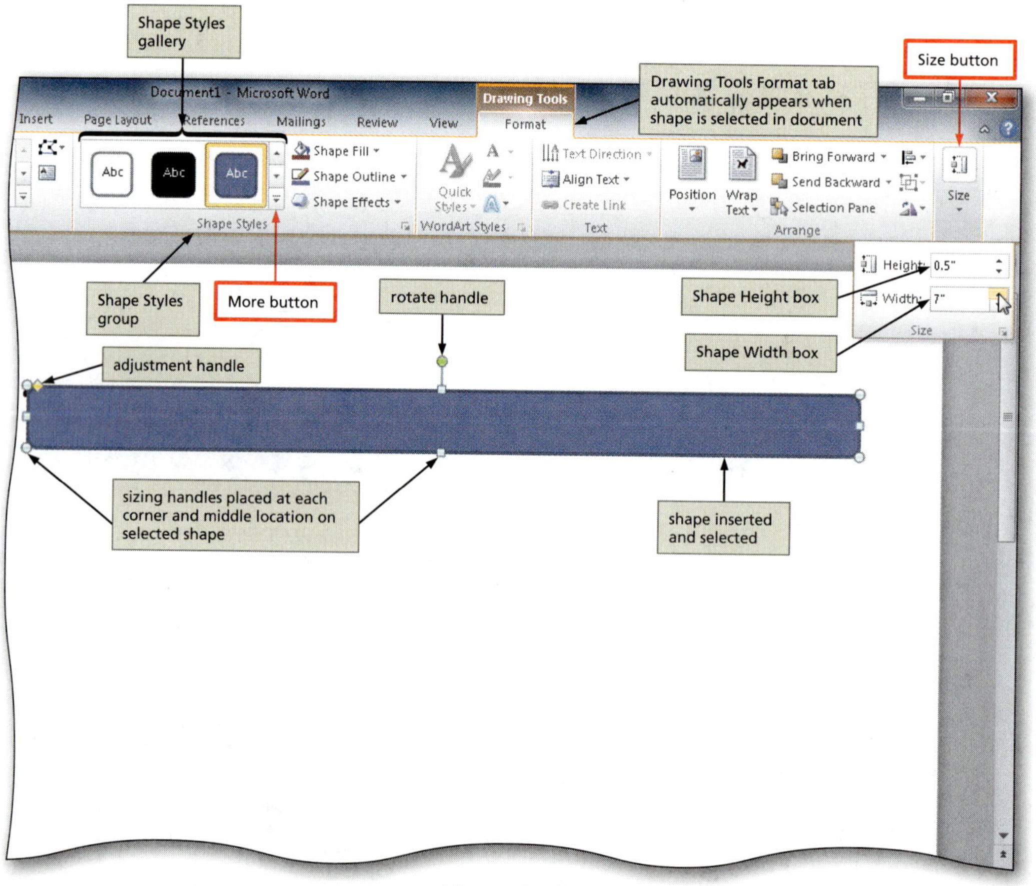

Figure 3–6

Q&A What is the purpose of the rotate and adjustment handles?

When you drag an object's **rotate handle**, which is the green circle, Word rotates the object in the direction you drag the mouse. When you drag an object's **adjustment handle**, which is the yellow diamond, Word changes the object's shape.

Q&A What if I wanted to delete a shape and start over?

With the shape selected, you would press the DELETE key.

To Apply a Shape Style

Word provides a Shape Styles gallery, allowing you to change the appearance of the shape. Because the organization in this project, Heartland Tractor Club, supports many different tractor manufacturers, its letterhead should use a color that is not commonly associated with a particular tractor manufacturer. The next steps apply a shape style that uses a shade of brown.

1

- With the shape still selected, click the More button (shown in Figure 3–6) in the Shape Styles gallery (Drawing Tools Format tab | Shape Styles group) to expand the gallery.

Q&A What if my shape is no longer selected?

Click the shape to select it.

- Point to Intense Effect - Brown, Accent 4 in the Shape Styles gallery to display a live preview of that style applied to the shape in the document (Figure 3–7).

Experiment

- Point to various styles in the Shape Styles gallery and watch the style of the shape change in the document.

2

- Click Intense Effect - Brown, Accent 4 in the Shape Styles gallery to apply the selected style to the shape.

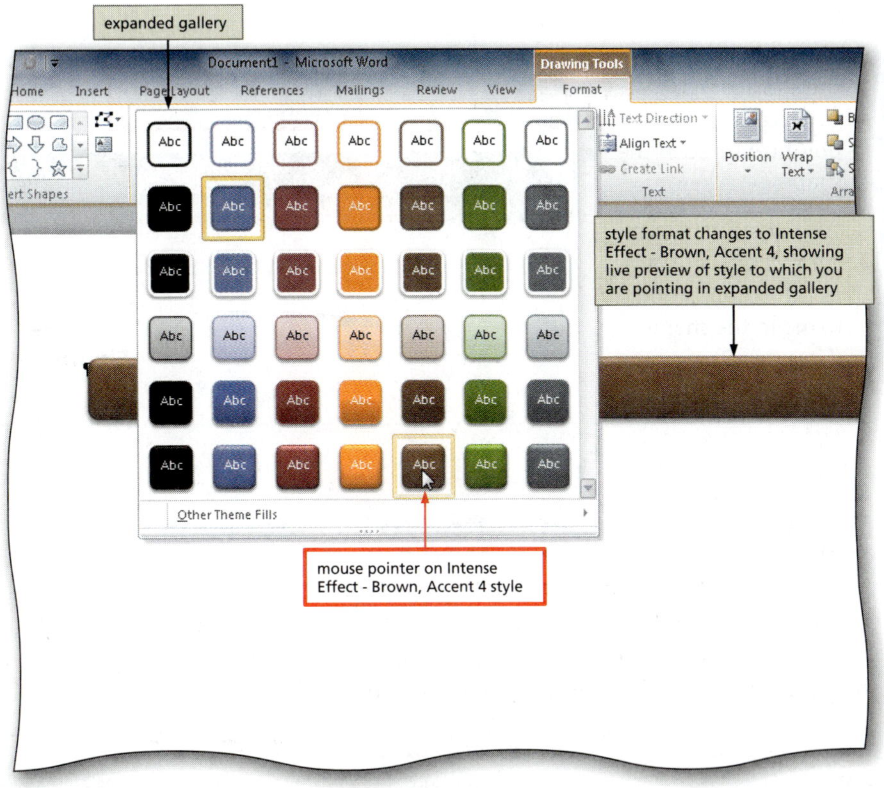

Figure 3–7

Other Ways

1. Click Format Shape Dialog Box Launcher (Drawing Tools Format tab | Shape Styles group), click Picture Color in left pane (Format Shape dialog box), select desired colors, click Close button
2. Right-click shape, click Format Shape on shortcut menu, click Picture Color in left pane (Format Shape dialog box), select desired colors, click Close button

To Add Text to a Shape

The next step is to add the organization name to the shape. The following steps add text to a shape.

1

- Right-click the shape to display a shortcut menu and the Mini toolbar (Figure 3–8).

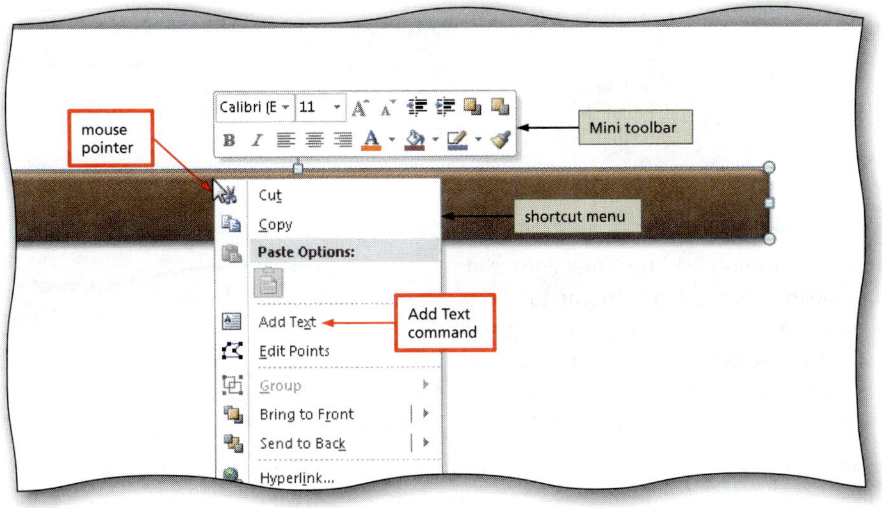

Figure 3–8

2

- Click Add Text on the shortcut menu to place an insertion point centered in the shape.
- Type **HEARTLAND TRACTOR CLUB** as the organization name in the shape (Figure 3–9).

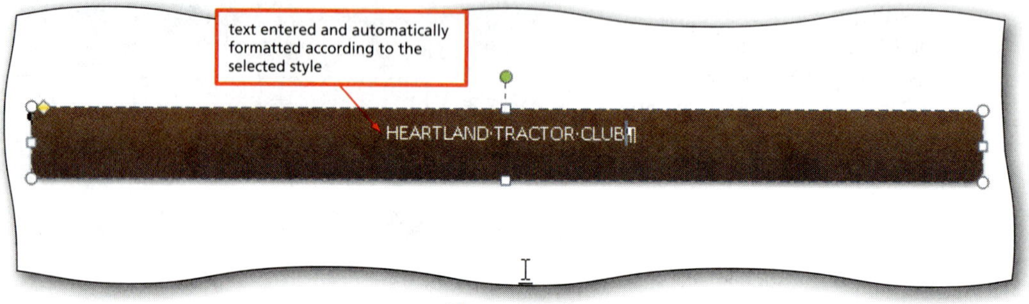

Figure 3–9

To Use the Grow Font Button to Increase Font Size

You want the font size of the organization name to be much larger in the shape. In previous Word chapters, you used the Font Size box arrow (Home tab | Font group) to change the font size of text. Word also provides a Grow Font button (Home tab | Font group), which increases the font size of selected text each time you click the button. The following steps use the Grow Font button to increase the font size of the organization name to 22 point.

1

- Drag through the organization name in the shape to select the text to be formatted.

2

- Display the Home tab.
- Repeatedly click the Grow Font button (Home tab | Font group) until the Font Size box displays 22 to increase the font size of the selected text (Figure 3–10).

Q&A What if I click the Grow Font button (Home tab | Font group) too many times, causing the font size to be too big?

Click the Shrink Font button (Home tab | Font group) until the desired font size is displayed.

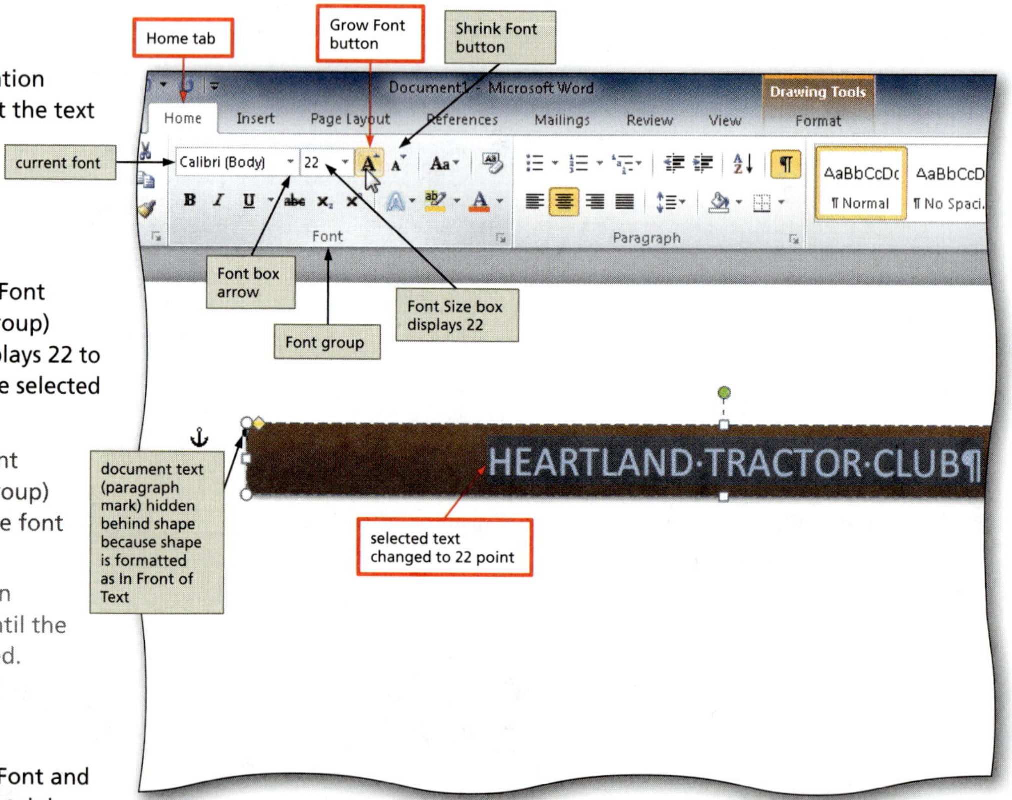

Figure 3–10

Experiment

- Repeatedly click the Grow Font and Shrink Font buttons (Home tab | Font group) and watch the font size of the selected name change in the document window. When you are finished experimenting with these two buttons, set the font size to 22.

Other Ways

1. Press CTRL+SHIFT+>

To Change the Font of Selected Text

The font of the organization name currently is Calibri. To make the organization name stand out even more, change the font of the name in the letterhead to a font different from the rest of the letter. The following steps change the font of the selected text.

1. With the text selected, click the Font box arrow (Home tab | Font group) to display the Font gallery.
2. Scroll to and then click Segoe Script in the Font gallery to change the font of the selected text (shown in Figure 3–11 on the next page).
3. Click anywhere in the text in the shape to remove the selection and place the insertion point in the shape.

Floating versus Inline Objects

When you insert an object, such as a shape, in a document, Word inserts it as either an inline object or a floating object. An **inline object** is an object that is part of a paragraph. With inline objects, you change the location of the object by setting paragraph options, such as centered, right-aligned, and so on. A **floating object** is an object that can be positioned at a specific location in a document or in a layer over or behind text in a document. You have more flexibility with floating objects because you can position a floating object anywhere on the page.

In addition to changing an object from inline to floating and vice versa, Word provides several floating options. All of these options affect how text wraps with the object. Table 3–1 lists the various text wrapping options and explains the function of each one.

Table 3–1 Text Wrapping Options

Text Wrapping Option	Object Type	How It Works
In Line with Text	Inline	Object positioned according to paragraph formatting; for example, if paragraph is centered, object will be centered with any text in the paragraph.
Square	Floating	Text wraps around object, with text forming a box around the object.
Tight	Floating	Text wraps around object, with text forming to shape of the object.
Through	Floating	Object appears at beginning, middle, or end of text. Moving object changes location of text.
Top and Bottom	Floating	Object appears above or below text. Moving object changes location of text.
Behind Text	Floating	Object appears behind text.
In Front of Text	Floating	Object appears in front of text and may cover the text.

BTW

Positioning Objects
If you want to use the Square text wrapping option, you can specify where the object should be positioned on the page. To specify the position, select the object, click the Object Position button (Picture Tools Format tab | Arrange group), and then click the desired location in the Object Position gallery.

To Change an Object's Text Wrapping

When you insert a shape in a Word document, the default text wrapping is In Front of Text, which means the object will cover any text behind it. Because you want the letterhead above the contents of the letter, instead of covering the contents of the letter, you change the text wrapping for the shape to Top and Bottom. The following steps change a shape's text wrapping.

1

- Click the edge of the shape to select the shape.
- Display the Drawing Tools Format tab.
- Click the Wrap Text button (Drawing Tools Format tab | Arrange group) to display the Wrap Text gallery (Figure 3–11).

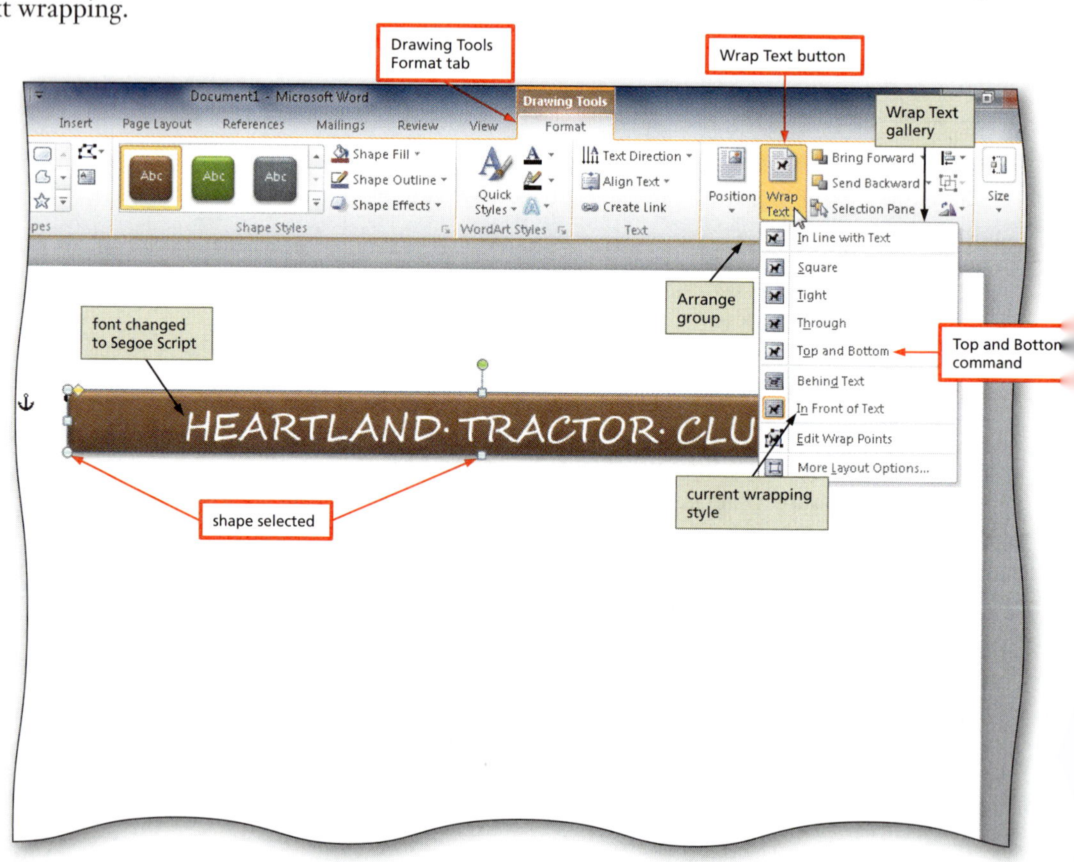

Figure 3–11

2

Experiment

- Point to various text wrapping options in the Wrap Text gallery and watch the shape configure to the selected wrapping option, which in this case, moves the paragraph mark to different locations in the document.
- Click Top and Bottom in the Wrap Text gallery so that the object does not cover the document text.

Other Ways
1. Right-click object, point to Wrap Text on shortcut menu, click desired wrapping style

To Insert Clip Art

Files containing graphical images, or graphics, are available from a variety of sources. In the Word Chapter 1 document, you inserted a digital picture taken with a camera phone. In this project, you insert **clip art**, which is a predefined graphic. In Microsoft Office programs, clip art is located in the **Clip Organizer**, which contains a collection of clip art, photos, animations, sounds, and videos.

The letterhead in this project contains clip art of a tractor (Figure 3–1 on page WD 139). Thus, the next steps insert a clip art image on the line below the shape in the document.

1

- Click the paragraph mark below the shape to position the insertion point where you want to insert the clip art image.
- Display the Insert tab.
- Click the Clip Art button (Insert tab | Illustrations group) to display the Clip Art pane (Figure 3–12).

Q&A What is a pane?

Recall from the Office 2010 and Windows 7 chapter in this book that a pane, or task pane, is a separate window that enables you to carry out some Word tasks more efficiently.

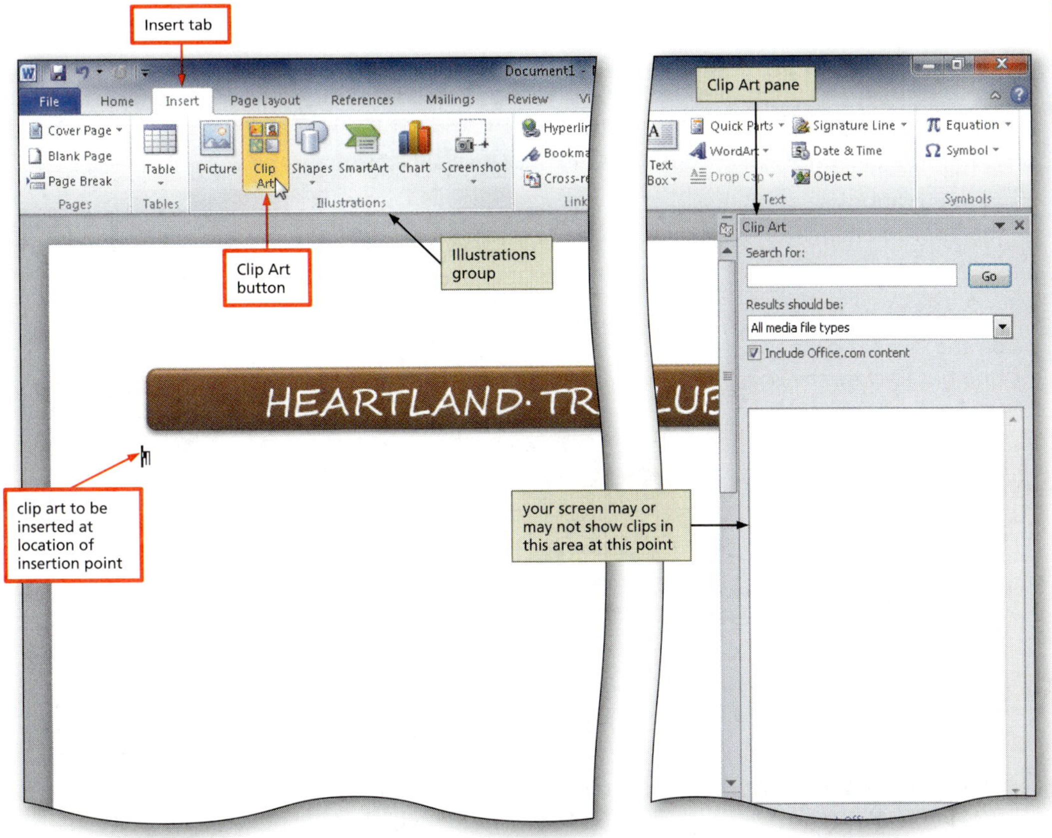

Figure 3–12

2

- If the Search for text box displays text, drag through the text to select it.
- Type `tractor` in the Search for text box to specify the search text, which in this case indicates the type of image you wish to locate.
- Click the Go button to display a list of clips that match the entered search text (Figure 3–13).

Q&A Why is my list of clips different from Figure 3–13?

If your Include Office.com content check box is selected and you are connected to the Internet, the Clip Art pane displays clips from the Web as well as those installed on your hard disk.

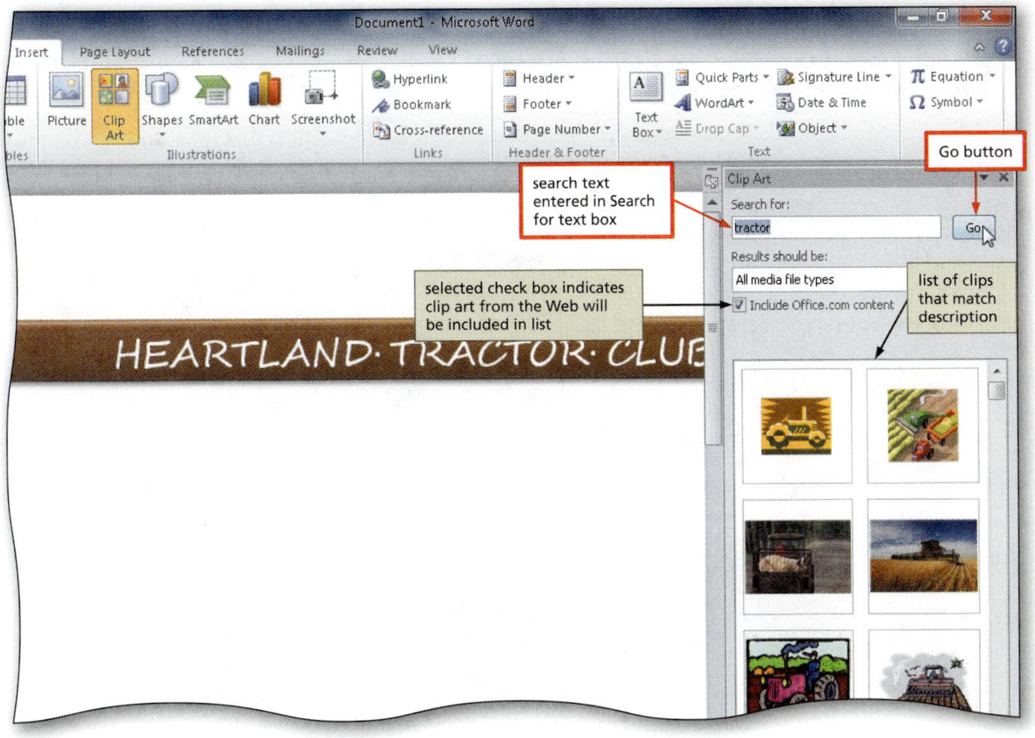

Figure 3–13

3

- Click the clip art of the yellow tractor to insert this clip art image in the document at the location of the insertion point (Figure 3–14).
- Click the Close button on the Clip Art pane title bar to close the task pane.

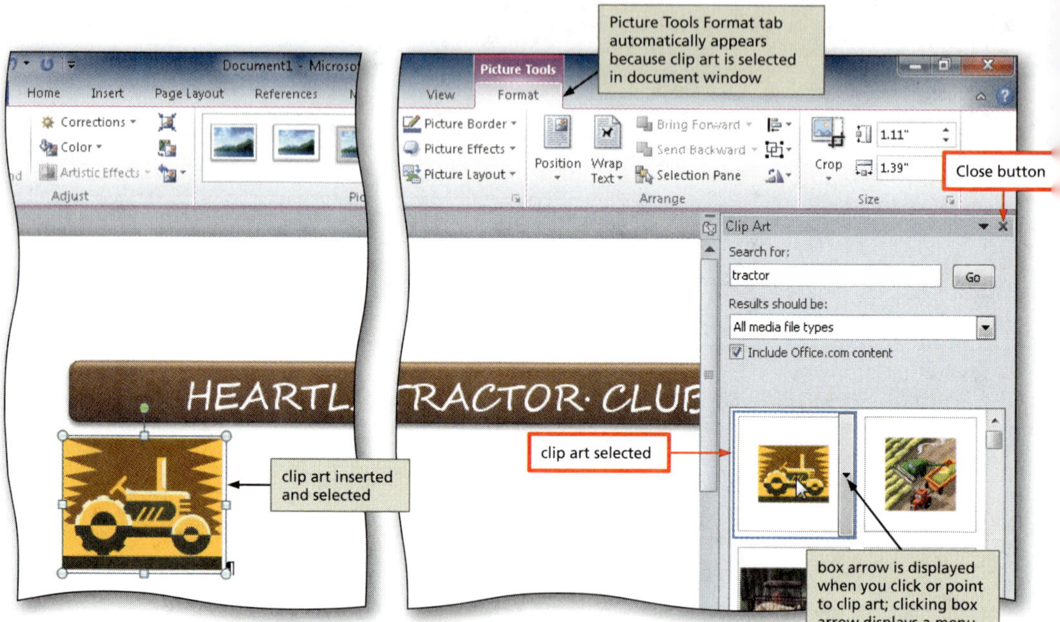

Figure 3–14

To Resize a Graphic to a Percent of the Original

In this project, the graphic is 35 percent of its original size. Instead of dragging a sizing handle to change the graphic's size, as you learned in Word Chapter 1, you can set exact size percentages. The following steps resize a graphic to a percent of the original.

1

- With the graphic still selected, click the Advanced Layout: Size Dialog Box Launcher (Picture Tools Format tab | Size group) to display the Layout dialog box.

Q&A What if the graphic is not selected or the Picture Tools Format tab is not on the Ribbon?

Click the graphic to select it or double-click the graphic to make the Picture Tools Format tab the active tab.

2

- In the Scale area (Layout dialog box), double-click the current value in the Height box to select it.
- Type **35** in the Height box and then press the TAB key to display the same percent value in the Width box (Figure 3–15).

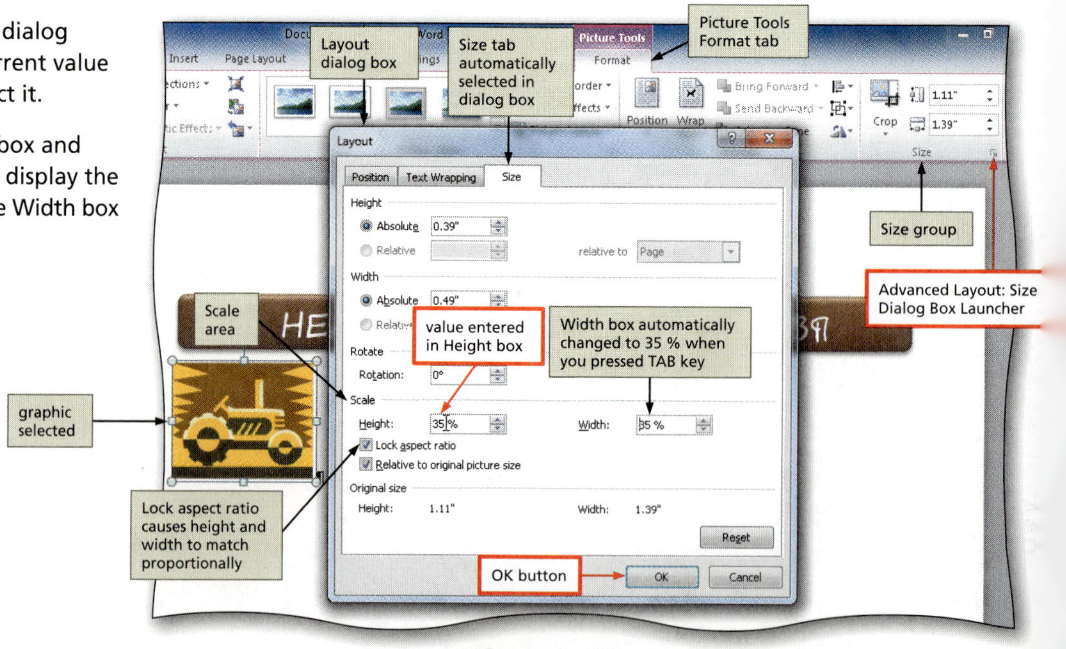

Figure 3–15

Q&A Why did Word automatically fill in the value in the Width box?

When the 'Lock aspect ratio' check box (Layout dialog box) is selected, Word automatically maintains the size proportions of the graphic.

Q&A How do I know to use 35 percent for the resized graphic?

The larger graphic consumed too much room on the page. Try various percentages to determine the size that works best in the letterhead design.

3

- Click the OK button to close the dialog box and resize the selected graphic (Figure 3–16).

Figure 3–16

Other Ways

1. Right-click graphic, click Size and Position on shortcut menu, enter values (Layout dialog box), click OK button

To Change the Color of a Graphic

In Word, you can change the color of a graphic. The clip art currently consists of shades of yellow and brown. Because the clip art in this project will be placed in a rectangle shape, you prefer to use colors that blend better with the current color scheme. The following steps change the color of the graphic to a shade in the current color scheme that matches the color of the shape.

1

- With the graphic still selected (shown in Figure 3–16), click the Color button (Picture Tools Format tab | Adjust group) to display the Color gallery.
- Point to Orange, Accent color 3 Dark in the Color gallery (fourth color in second row) to display a live preview of that color applied to the selected graphic in the document (Figure 3–17).

Experiment

- Point to various colors in the Color gallery and watch the color of the graphic change in the document.

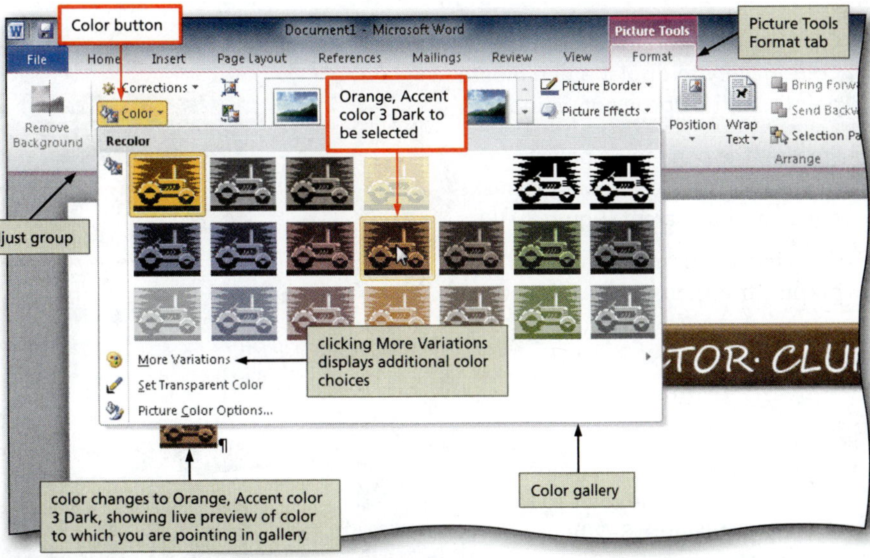

Figure 3–17

2

- Click Orange, Accent color 3 Dark in the Color gallery to change the color of the selected graphic.

Q&A How would I change a graphic back to its original colors?

With the graphic selected, you would click No Recolor in the Color gallery (upper-left color).

Other Ways

1. Right-click graphic, click Format Picture on shortcut menu, click Picture Color button in left pane (Format Picture dialog box), select color, click Close button

To Set a Transparent Color in a Graphic

In Word, you can make one color in a graphic transparent, that is, remove the color. You would make a color transparent if you wanted to remove part of a graphic or see text or colors behind a graphic. In this project, you will remove the lighter brown from the edges of the tractor graphic so that when you move the graphic on the rectangular shape, the color of the shape can be seen in the transparent locations. The following steps set a transparent color in a graphic.

1

- With the graphic still selected, click the Color button (Picture Tools Format tab | Adjust group) to display the Color gallery (Figure 3–18).

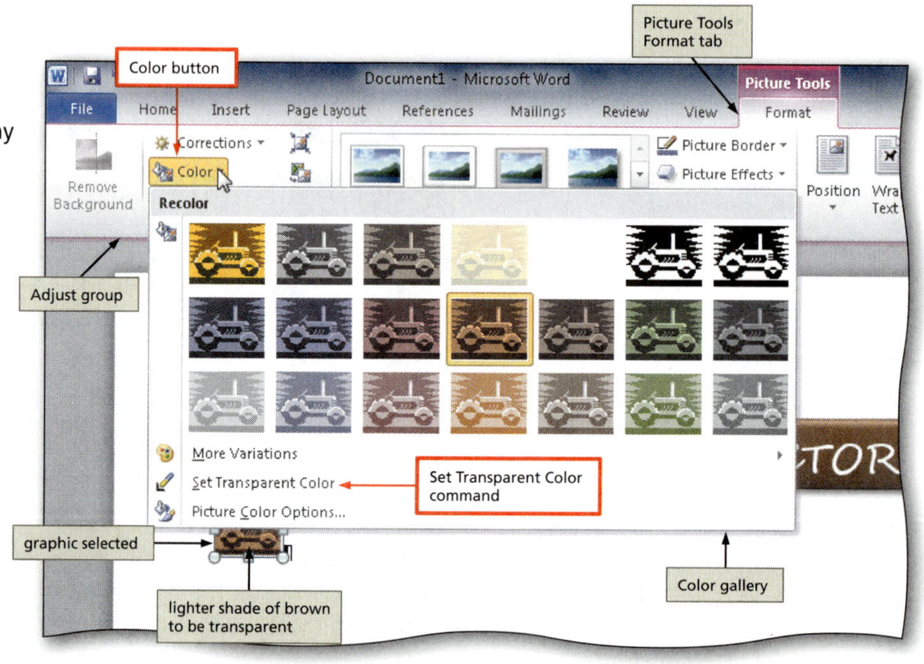

Figure 3–18

2

- Click Set Transparent Color in the Color gallery to display a pen mouse pointer in the document window.
- Position the pen mouse pointer in the graphic where you want to make the color transparent (Figure 3–19).

Q&A Can I make multiple colors in a graphic transparent?

No, you can make only one color transparent.

Figure 3–19

3

- Click the location in the graphic where you want the color to be transparent (Figure 3–20).

Q&A What if I make the wrong color transparent?

Click the Undo button on the Quick Access Toolbar, or press CTRL+Z, and then repeat these steps.

Figure 3–20

To Adjust the Brightness and Contrast of a Graphic

In Word, you can adjust the lightness (brightness) of a graphic and also contrast, which is the difference between the lightest and darkest areas of the graphic. The following steps decrease the brightness and contrast of the tractor graphic, each by 20%.

1

- With the graphic still selected (shown in Figure 3–20), click the Corrections button (Picture Tools Format tab | Adjust group) to display the Corrections gallery (Figure 3–21).

Q&A Does live preview work in this gallery?

Yes, but the graphic is covered by the gallery in this case. To see the live preview, you would need to position the graphic so that you can see it while the gallery is displayed.

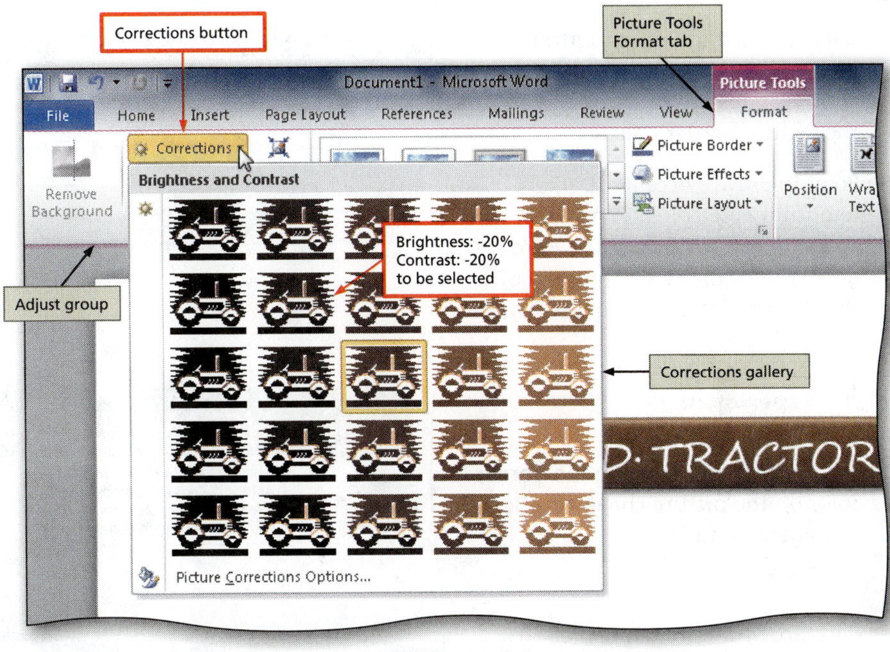

Figure 3–21

2

- Click Brightness: −20% Contrast: −20% in the Corrections gallery (second image in second row) to change the brightness and contrast of the selected graphic (Figure 3–22).

Q&A Can I remove all formatting applied to a graphic and start over?

Yes. With the graphic selected, you would click the Reset Picture button (Picture Tools Format tab | Adjust group).

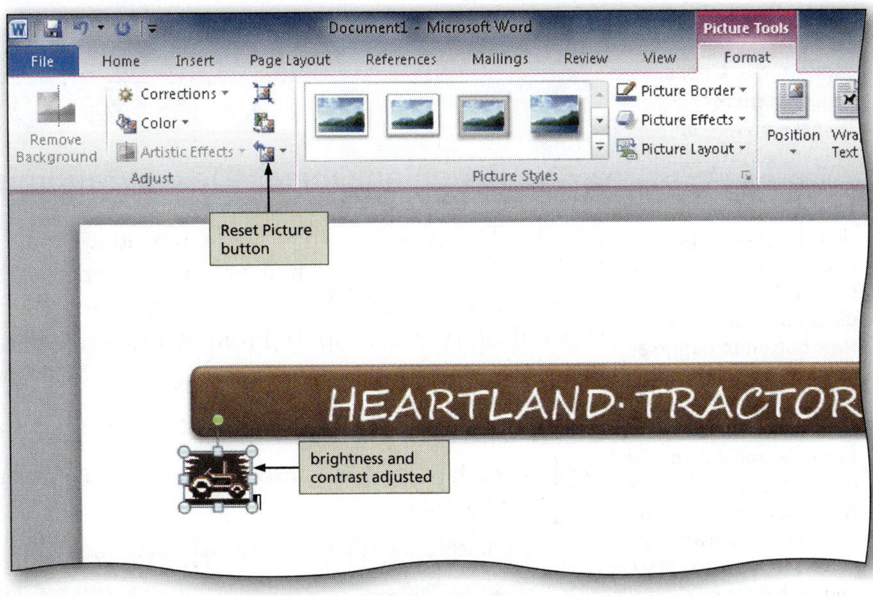

Figure 3–22

Other Ways

1. Right-click graphic, click Format Picture on shortcut menu, click Picture Corrections button in left pane (Format Picture dialog box), adjust settings, click Close button

To Change the Border Color on a Graphic

The tractor graphic currently has no border (outline). You would like the graphic to have a brown border. The following steps change the border color on a graphic.

1

- Click the Picture Border button arrow (Picture Tools Format tab | Picture Styles group) to display the Picture Border gallery.
- Point to Brown, Accent 4, Darker 50% (eighth theme color from left in the sixth row) in the Picture Border gallery to display a live preview of that border color around the picture (Figure 3–23).

Experiment

- Point to various colors in the Picture Border gallery and watch the border color on the picture change in the document window.

2

- Click Brown, Accent 4, Darker 50% in the Picture Border gallery to change the picture border color.

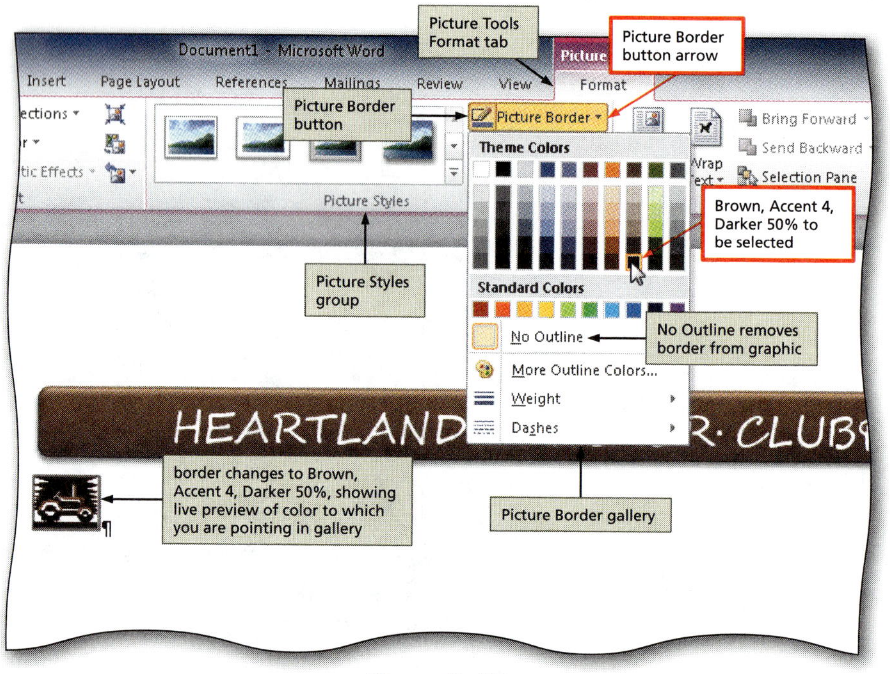

Figure 3–23

Q&A How would I remove a border from a graphic?

With the graphic selected, you would click the No Outline in the Picture Border gallery.

BTW **Clip Organizer**
To make a Web clip available on your hard disk, point to the clip in the Clip Art pane, click its box arrow, click Make Available Offline, select the collection to store the clip (Copy to Collection dialog box) or click the New button to define a new collection, and then click the OK button. You can use the Clip Organizer to create, rename, or delete collections; add clips to a collection from the Web, a camera, or a scanner; delete, move, and copy clips; and search for existing clips. Start the Clip Organizer by clicking the Start button on the taskbar, clicking All Programs on the Start menu, clicking the Microsoft Office folder to its contents, clicking the Microsoft Office 2010 Tools folder to display its contents, and then clicking Microsoft Clip Organizer.

To Change an Object's Text Wrapping

The tractor graphic is to be positioned to the left of the organization name in the shape. Clip art, by default, is formatted as an inline graphic, which cannot be moved into a shape. To move the graphic in the shape so that it not covered by any text, you format it as a floating object with In Front of Text wrapping. The following steps change a graphic's text wrapping.

1. If necessary, click the graphic to select it. If necessary, display the Picture Tools Format tab.
2. Click the Wrap Text button (Picture Tools Format tab | Arrange group) to display the Wrap Text gallery.

Q&A Do both the Picture Tools Format and Drawing Tools Format tabs have a Wrap Text button?

Yes. You can specify how to wrap text with both pictures and drawings.

3. Click In Front of Text in the Wrap Text gallery so that you can position the object on top of any item in the document, in this case, on top of the rectangular shape.

To Move a Graphic

The next step is to move the tractor graphic up so that it is positioned to the left of the text on the rectangle shape. The following steps move a graphic.

1

- Position the mouse pointer in the graphic so that the mouse pointer has a four-headed arrow attached to it (Figure 3–24).

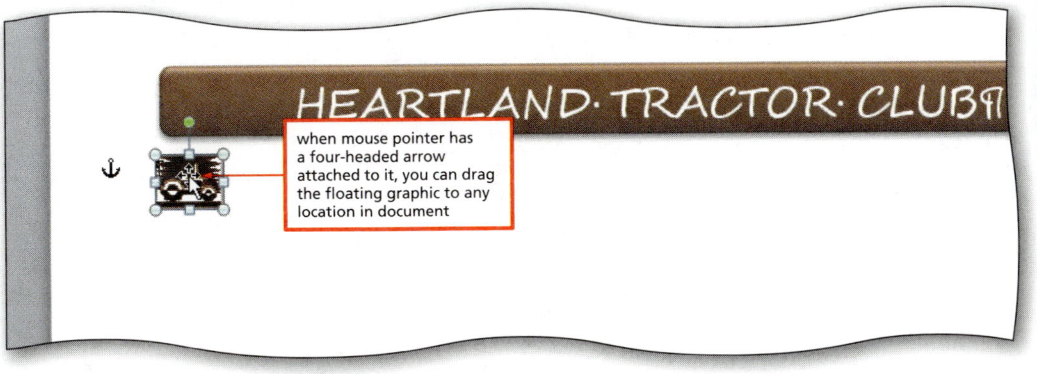

Figure 3–24

2

- Drag the graphic to the location shown in Figure 3–25.

Q&A What if I moved the graphic to the wrong location?

Repeat these steps. You can drag a floating graphic to any location in a document.

Figure 3–25

To Copy a Graphic

In this project, the same tractor graphic is to be placed to the right of the organization name in the shape. Instead of performing the same steps to insert and format another tractor graphic, you can copy the graphic to the Office Clipboard, paste the graphic from the Office Clipboard, and then move the graphic to the desired location.

You use the same steps to copy a graphic as you used in Word Chapter 2 to copy text. The following steps copy a graphic.

1. If necessary, click the graphic to select it.
2. Display the Home tab.
3. Click the Copy button, shown in Figure 3–26 on the next page, (Home tab | Clipboard group) to copy the selected item to the Office Clipboard.

To Use Paste Options

The next step is to paste the copied graphic in the document. The following steps paste a graphic using the Paste Options gallery.

1

- Click the Paste button arrow (Home tab | Clipboard group) to display the Paste gallery.

Q&A What if I accidentally click the Paste button?

Click the Paste Options button below the graphic pasted in the document to display a Paste Options gallery.

- Point to the Keep Source Formatting button in the Paste gallery to display a live preview of that paste option (Figure 3–26).

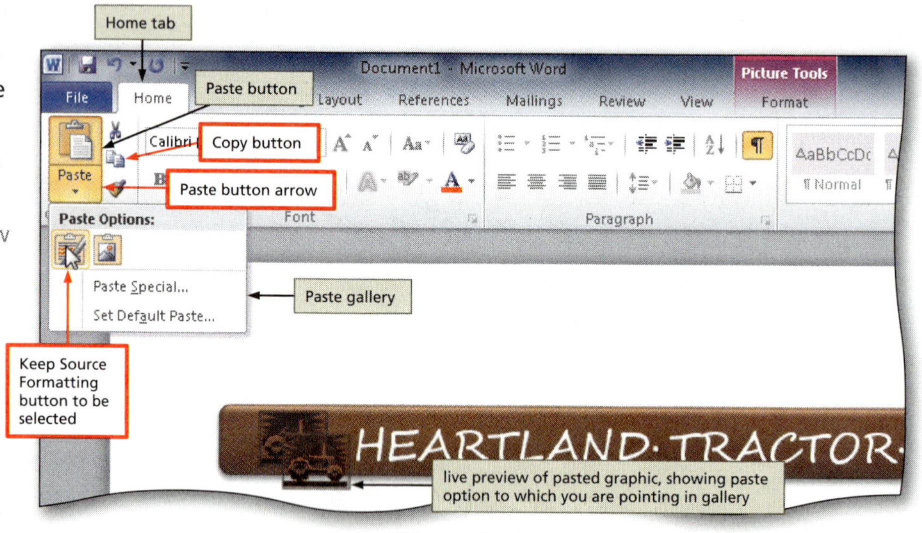

Figure 3–26

Experiment

- Point to the two buttons in the Paste gallery and watch the appearance of the pasted graphic change.

Q&A What do the buttons in the Paste gallery mean?

The Keep Source Formatting button indicates the pasted graphic should have the same formats as it did in its original location. The second button removes all formatting from the graphic.

Q&A Why are these paste buttons different from the ones in Word Chapter 2?

The buttons that appear in the Paste gallery differ depending on the item you are pasting. Use live preview to see how the pasted object will look in the document.

2

- Click the Keep Source Formatting button in the Paste gallery to paste the object using the same formatting as the original.

To Move a Graphic

The next step is to move the second tractor graphic so that it is positioned to the right of the text in the rectangle shape. The following step moves a graphic.

1 Position the mouse pointer in the graphic so that the mouse pointer has a four-headed arrow attached to it and then drag the graphic to the location shown in Figure 3–27.

Q&A Why does my graphic not look like it is positioned the same as the graphic on the left?

The paragraph mark at the end of the organization name may be obstructing your view. To determine if the graphic is positioned properly, you can temporarily turn off formatting marks by clicking the Show/Hide ¶ button (Home tab | Paragraph group).

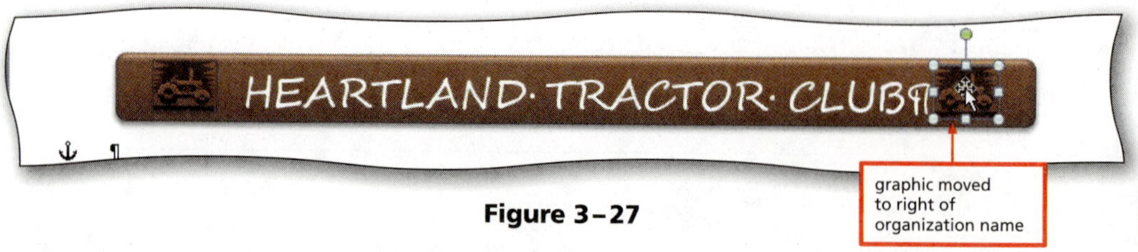

Figure 3–27

To Flip a Graphic

The next step is to flip the clip art image on the right so that the tractor is facing the opposite direction. The following steps flip a graphic horizontally.

1

- If necessary, display the Picture Tools Format tab.
- With the graphic still selected, click the Rotate button (Picture Tools Format tab | Arrange group) to display the Rotate gallery.
- Point to Flip Horizontal in the Rotate gallery to display a live preview of the selected rotate option applied to the selected graphic (Figure 3–28).

Experiment

- Point to the rotate options in the Rotate gallery and watch the picture rotate in the document window.

2

- Click Flip Horizontal in the Rotate gallery, so that Word flips the graphic to display its mirror image.

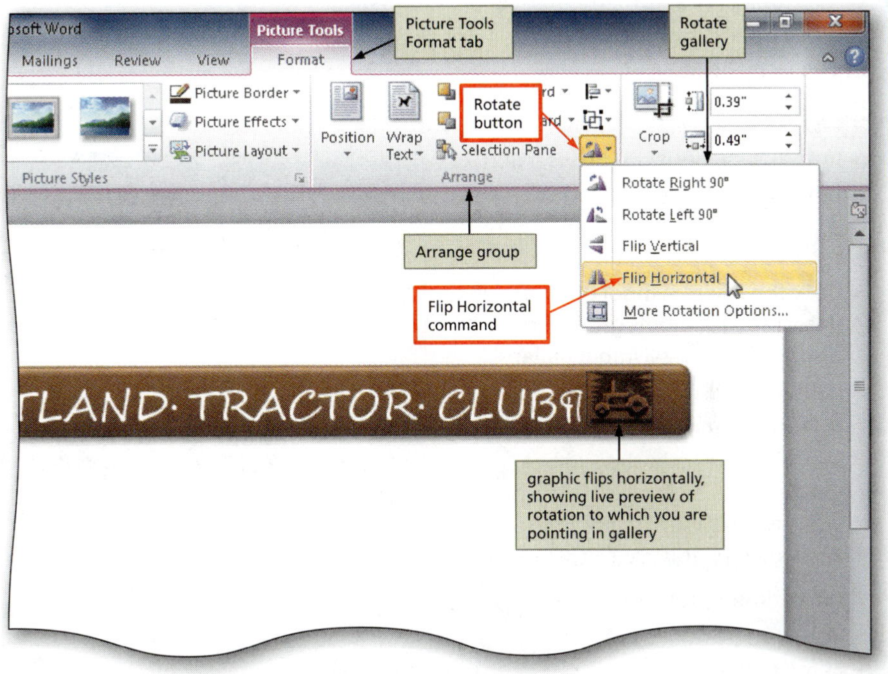

Figure 3–28

Q&A

Can I flip a graphic vertically?

Yes, you would click Flip Vertical in the Rotate gallery. You also can rotate a graphic clockwise or counterclockwise by clicking the Rotate Right 90° and Rotate Left 90° commands, respectively, in the Rotate gallery.

To Specify Formatting before Typing and Then Enter Text

The contact information for the organization in this project is located on the line below the organization name. The following steps format and then enter the postal address in the letterhead.

1. Position the insertion point on the line below the shape containing the organization name.
2. If necessary, display the Home tab. Click the Center button (Home tab | Paragraph group) to center the paragraph.
3. Click the Font Color button arrow (Home tab | Font group) to display the Font Color gallery and then click Orange, Accent 3, Darker 50% (seventh color in sixth row) in the Font Color gallery to change the font color.
4. Type `323 Pine Avenue, Graber, OK 74877` and then press the SPACEBAR (shown in Figure 3–29 on the next page).

BTW

Q&As

For a complete list of the Q&As found in many of the step-by-step sequences in the Office and Windows chapters in this book, visit the Microsoft Office and Concepts CourseMate Web site at www.cengagebrain.com and then navigate to the Q&A resource for this book.

To Insert a Symbol from the Symbol Dialog Box

In the letterhead in this chapter, a small round dot separates the postal address and phone number, and the same type of dot separates the phone number and Web address information. This special symbol (the round dot) is not on the keyboard. Thus, Word provides a method of inserting dots and other symbols, such as letters in the Greek alphabet and mathematical characters.

The following steps insert a dot symbol, called a bullet symbol, between the postal address and phone number in the letterhead.

1

- If necessary, position the insertion point as shown in Figure 3–29.
- Display the Insert tab.
- Click the Insert Symbol button (Insert tab | Symbols group) to display the Insert Symbol gallery (Figure 3–29).

Q&A What if the symbol I want to insert already appears in the Symbol gallery?

You can click any symbol shown in the Symbol gallery to insert it in the document.

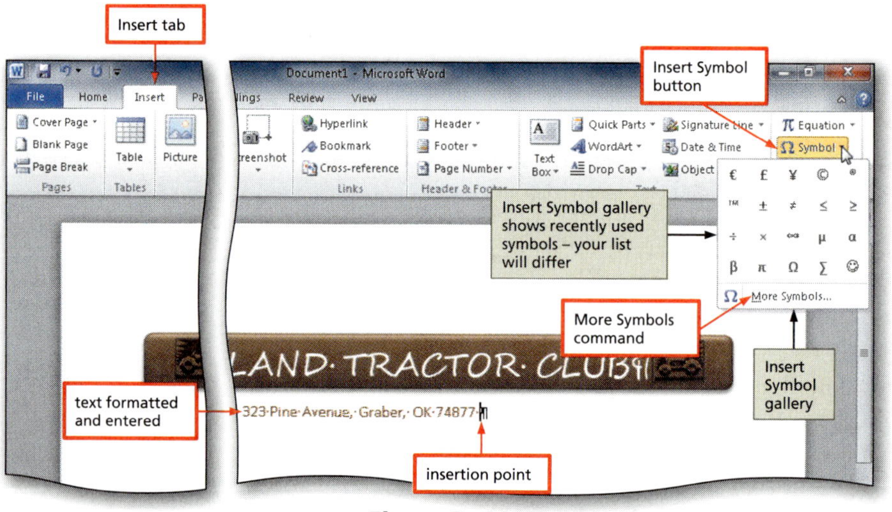

Figure 3–29

2

- Click More Symbols in the Insert Symbol gallery to display the Symbol dialog box.
- If the font in the Font box is not (normal text), click the Font box arrow (Symbol dialog box) and then scroll to (normal text) and click it to select this font.
- If the subset in the Subset box is not General Punctuation, click the Subset box arrow and then scroll to General Punctuation and click it to select this subset.
- In the list of symbols, if necessary, scroll to the bullet symbol shown in Figure 3–30 and then click the symbol to select it.

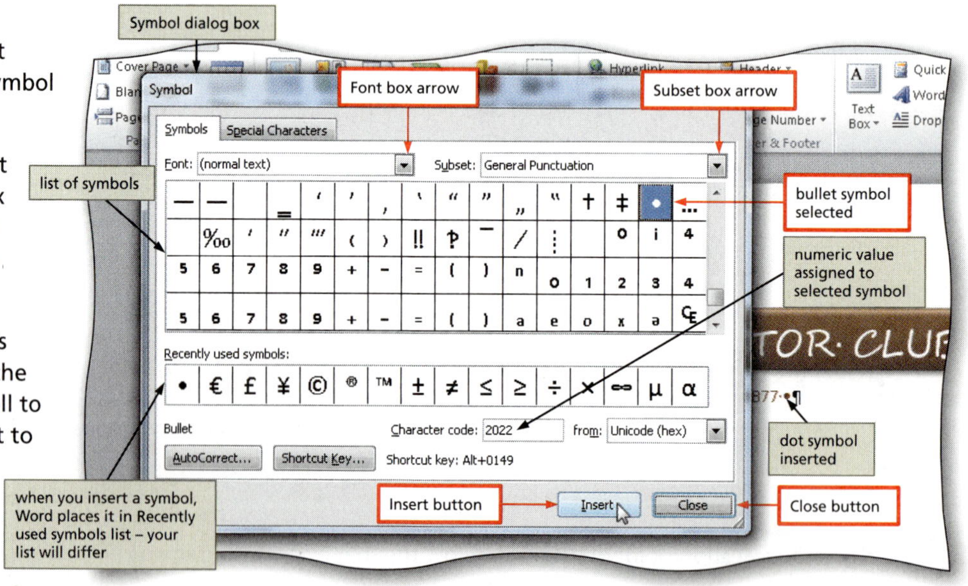

Figure 3–30

- Click the Insert button (Symbol dialog box) to place the selected symbol in the document to the left of the insertion point (Figure 3–30).

Q&A Why is the Symbol dialog box still open?

The Symbol dialog box remains open, allowing you to insert additional symbols.

3

- Click the Close button (Symbol dialog box) to close the dialog box.

To Insert a Symbol from the Symbol Gallery

In the letterhead, another bullet symbol separates the phone number from the Web address information. Once you insert a symbol using the Symbol dialog box, Word adds that symbol to the Symbol gallery so that it is more readily available. The following steps use the Symbol gallery to insert a bullet symbol between the phone number and Web address.

1

- Press the SPACEBAR, type **`Phone: (476) 555-9384`** and then press the SPACEBAR.

2

- Click the Insert Symbol button (Insert tab | Symbols group) to display the Insert Symbol gallery (Figure 3–31).

Q&A

Why is the bullet symbol now in the Insert Symbol gallery?

When you insert a symbol from the Symbol dialog box, Word automatically adds the symbol to the Insert Symbol gallery.

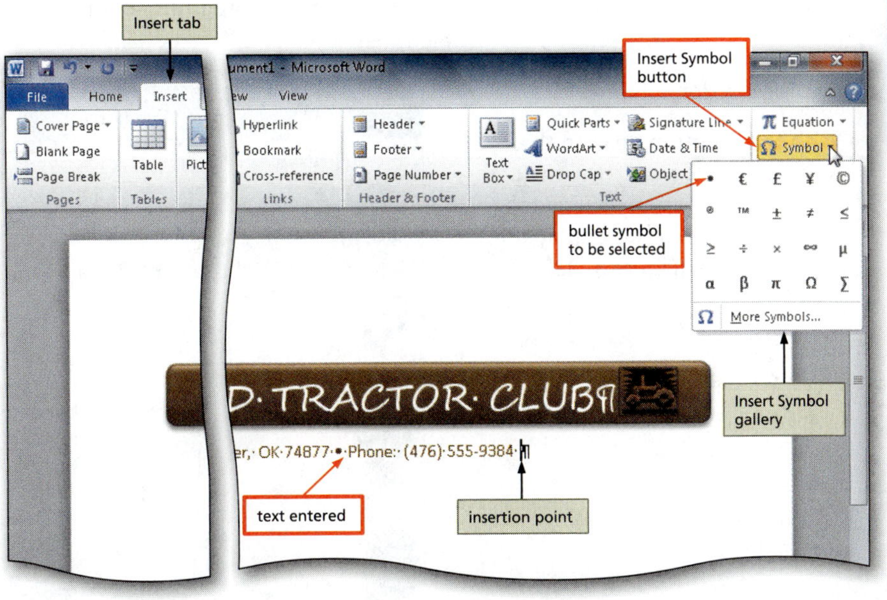

Figure 3–31

3

- Click the bullet symbol in the Insert Symbol gallery to insert the symbol at the location of the insertion point (shown in Figure 3–32).

To Enter Text

The following steps enter the Web address in the letterhead.

1 Press the SPACEBAR.

2 Type **`Web Address: www.hltclub.com`** to finish the text in the letterhead (Figure 3–32).

BTW

Inserting Special Characters

In addition to symbols, you can insert a variety of special characters including dashes, hyphens, spaces, apostrophes, and quotation marks. Click the Special Characters tab in the Symbols dialog box (Figure 3–30), click the desired character in the Character list, click the Insert button, and then click the Close button.

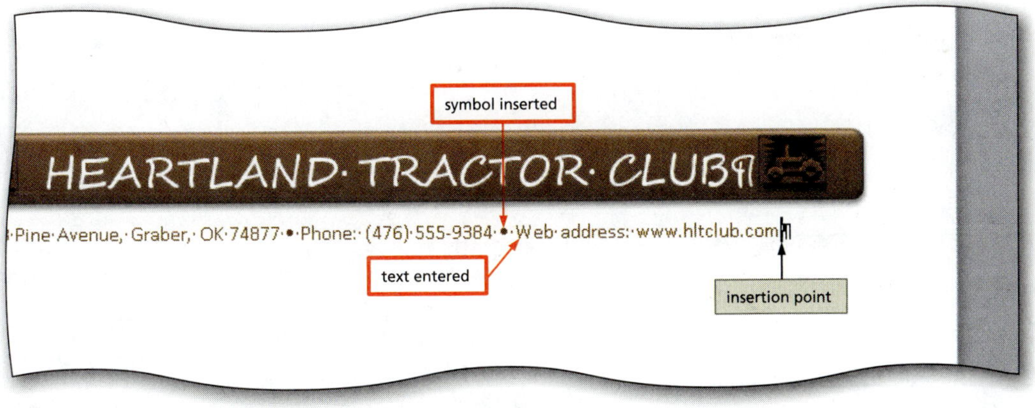

Figure 3–32

To Bottom Border a Paragraph

The letterhead in this project has a horizontal line that extends from the left margin to the right margin immediately below the address, phone, and Web address information, which separates the letterhead from the rest of the letter. In Word, you can draw a solid line, called a **border**, at any edge of a paragraph. That is, borders may be added above or below a paragraph, to the left or right of a paragraph, or in any combination of these sides. The following steps add a bottom border to the paragraph containing address, phone, and Web information.

1

- Display the Home tab.
- With the insertion point in the paragraph to border, click the Border button arrow (Home tab | Paragraph group) to display the Border gallery (Figure 3–33).

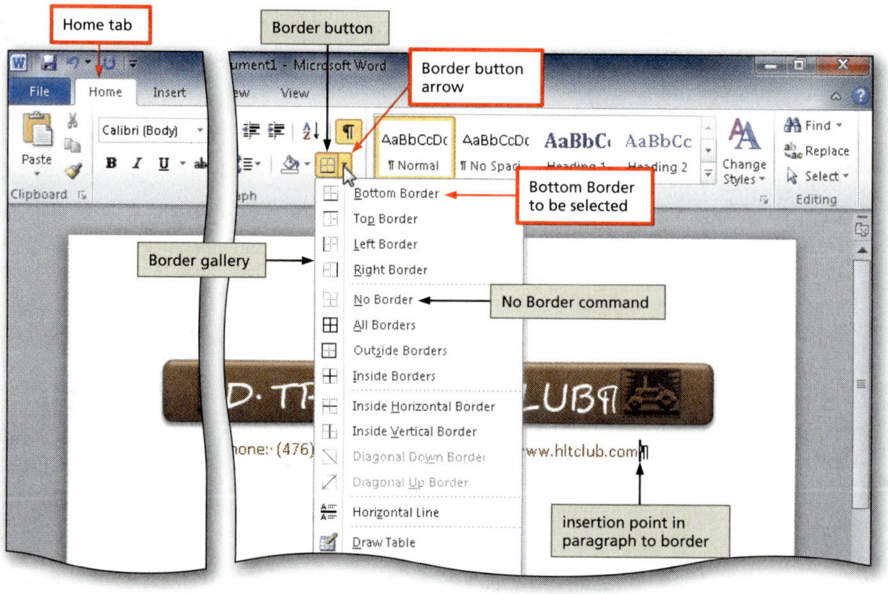

Figure 3–33

2

- Click Bottom Border in the Border gallery to place a border below the paragraph containing the insertion point (Figure 3–34).

Q&A If the face of the Border button displays the border icon I want to use, can I click the Border button instead of using the Border button arrow?

Yes.

Q&A How would I remove an existing border from a paragraph?

If, for some reason, you wanted to remove a border from a paragraph, you would position the insertion point in the paragraph, click the Border button arrow (Home tab | Paragraph group), and then click No Border in the Border gallery.

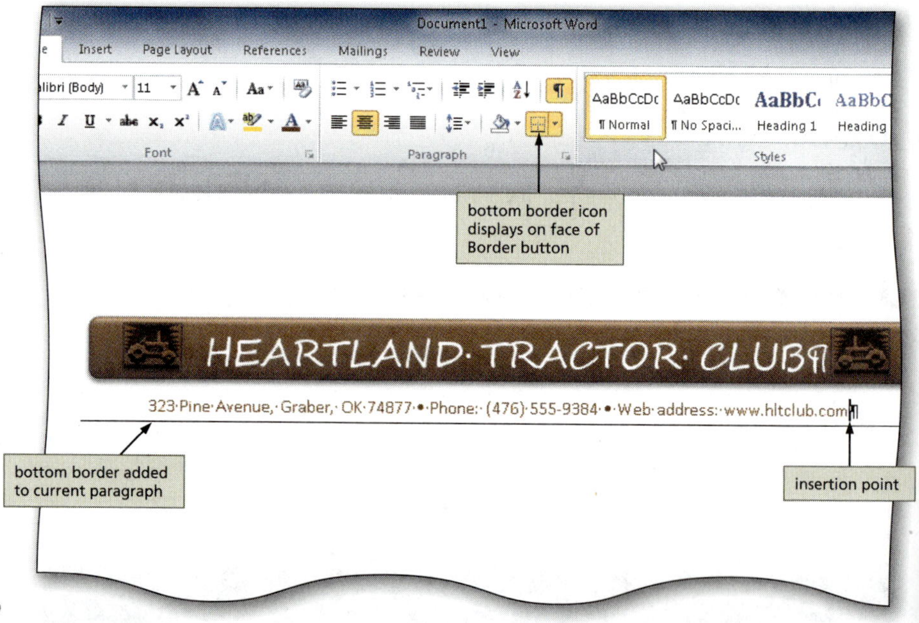

Figure 3–34

Other Ways

1. Click Page Borders button (Page Layout tab | Page Background group), click Borders tab (Borders and Shading dialog box), select desired border options, click OK button

To Clear Formatting

The next step is to position the insertion point below the letterhead, so that you can type the contents of the letter. When you press the ENTER key at the end of a paragraph containing a border, Word moves the border forward to the next paragraph. The paragraph also retains all current settings, such as the center format. Instead, you want the paragraph and characters on the new line to use the Normal style: black font with no border.

In Word, the term, **clear formatting**, refers to returning the formatting to the Normal style. The following steps clear formatting at the location of the insertion point.

1

- With the insertion point between the Web address and paragraph mark at the end of the line (as shown in Figure 3–34), press the ENTER key to move the insertion point and paragraph to the next line (Figure 3–35).

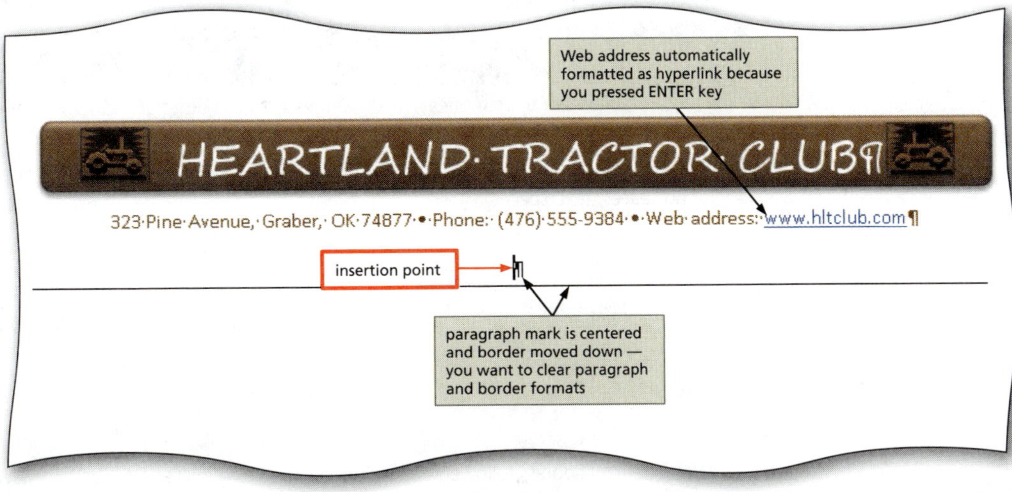

Figure 3–35

2

- Click the Clear Formatting button (Home tab | Font group) to apply the Normal style to the location of the insertion point (Figure 3–36).

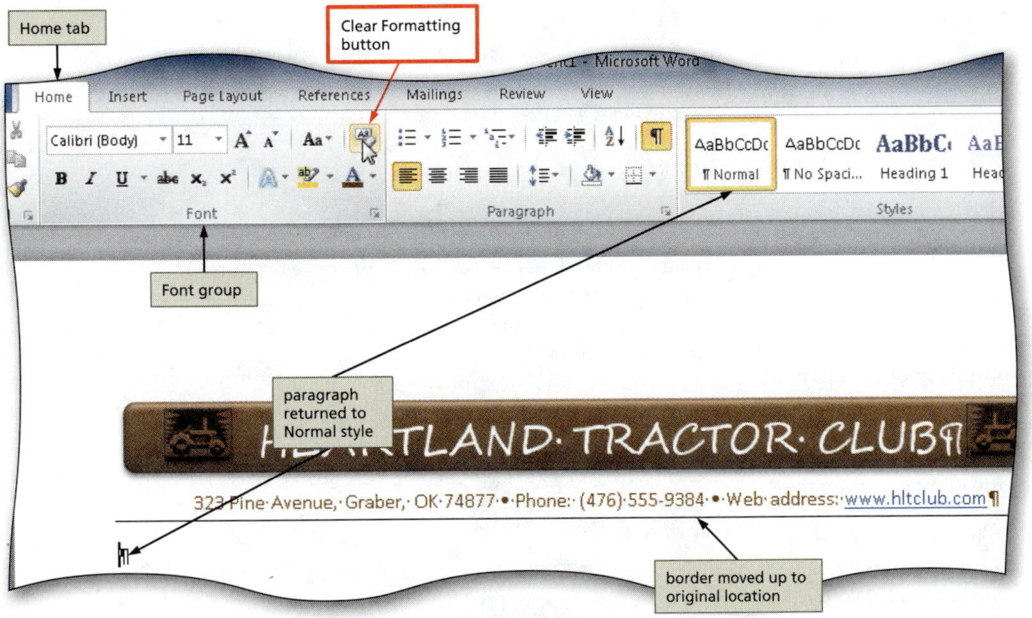

Figure 3–36

Other Ways

1. Click More button in Styles gallery (Home tab | Styles group), click Clear Formatting
2. Click Styles Dialog Box Launcher (Home tab | Styles group), click Clear All in Styles task pane
3. Select text, press CTRL+SPACEBAR, press CTRL+Q

AutoFormat as You Type

As you type text in a document, Word automatically formats some of it for you. For example, when you press the ENTER key or SPACEBAR after typing an e-mail address or Web address, Word automatically formats the address as a hyperlink, that is, colored blue and underlined. In Figure 3–35 on the previous page, for example, Word formatted the Web address as a hyperlink because you pressed the ENTER key at the end of the line. Table 3–2 outlines commonly used AutoFormat As You Type options and their results.

Table 3–2 Commonly Used AutoFormat As You Type Options

Typed Text	AutoFormat Feature	Example
Quotation marks or apostrophes	Changes straight quotation marks or apostrophes to curly ones	"the" becomes “the”
Text, a space, one hyphen, one or no spaces, text, space	Changes the hyphen to an en dash	ages 20 - 45 becomes ages 20 – 45
Text, two hyphens, text, space	Changes the two hyphens to an em dash	Two types--yellow and red becomes Two types—yellow and red
Web or e-mail address followed by SPACEBAR or ENTER key	Formats Web or e-mail address as a hyperlink	www.cengagebrain.com becomes www.cengagebrain.com
Three hyphens, underscores, equal signs, asterisks, tildes, or number signs and then ENTER key	Places a border above a paragraph	--- This line becomes ______________ This line
Number followed by a period, hyphen, right parenthesis, or greater than sign and then a space or tab followed by text	Creates a numbered list	1. Word 2. PowerPoint becomes 1. Word 2. PowerPoint
Asterisk, hyphen, or greater than sign and then a space or tab followed by text	Creates a bulleted list	* Home tab * Insert tab becomes • Home tab • Insert tab
Fraction and then a space or hyphen	Condenses the fraction entry so that it consumes one space instead of three	1/2 becomes ½
Ordinal and then a space or hyphen	Makes part of the ordinal a superscript	3rd becomes 3rd

BTW

AutoFormat Settings
Before you can use them, AutoFormat options must be enabled. To check if an AutoFormat option is enabled, click File on the Ribbon to open the Backstage view, click Options in the Backstage view, click Proofing in the left pane (Word Options dialog box), click the AutoCorrect Options button, click the AutoFormat As You Type tab, select the appropriate check boxes, and then click the OK button in each open dialog box.

To Convert a Hyperlink to Regular Text

The Web address in the letterhead should be formatted as regular text; that is, it should not be blue or underlined. Thus, the following steps remove the hyperlink format from the Web address in the letterhead.

1

- Right-click the hyperlink (in this case, the Web address) to display the Mini toolbar and a shortcut menu (Figure 3–37).

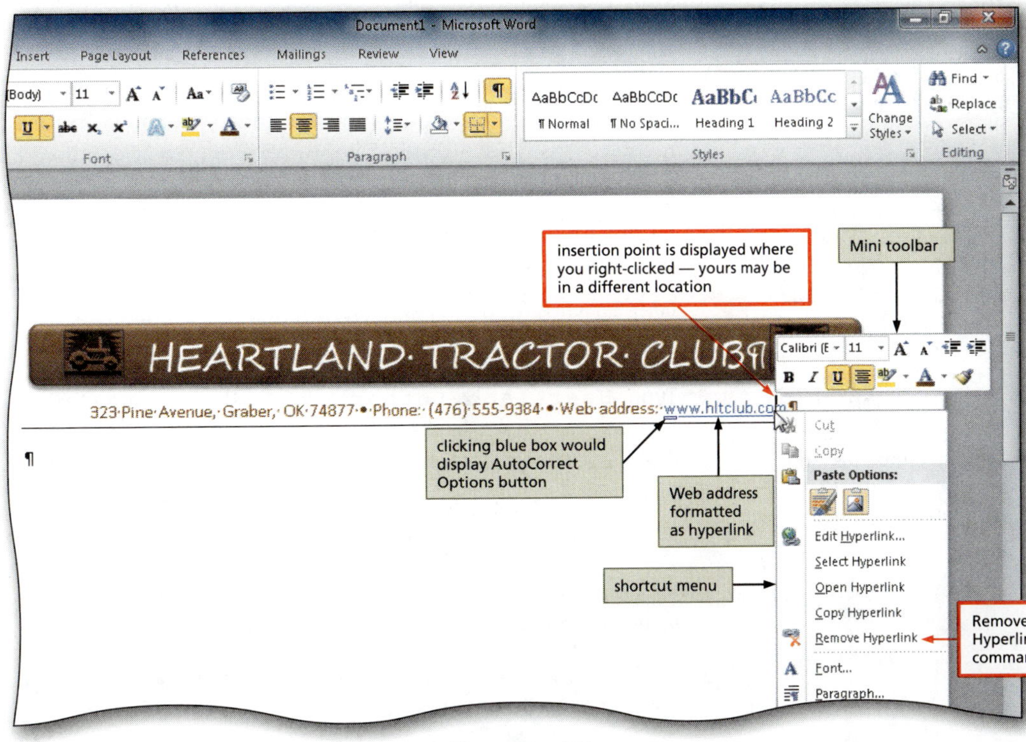

Figure 3–37

2

- Click Remove Hyperlink on the shortcut menu to remove the hyperlink format from the text.
- Position the insertion point on the paragraph mark below the border because you are finished with the letterhead (Figure 3–38).

Figure 3–38

Q&A

Could I have used the AutoCorrect Options button instead of the Remove Hyperlink command?

Yes. Alternatively, you could have pointed to the small blue box at the beginning of the hyperlink, clicked the AutoCorrect Options button, and then clicked Undo Hyperlink on the AutoCorrect Options menu.

Other Ways

1. With insertion point in hyperlink, click Hyperlink button (Insert tab | Links group), click Remove Link button

BTW

Saving a Template
As an alternative to saving the letterhead as a Word document, you could save it as a template. To do so, click File on the Ribbon to open the Backstage view, click the Save & Send tab to display the Save & Send gallery, click Change File Type, click Template in the right pane, click the Save As button, enter the template name (Save As dialog box), if necessary select the Templates folder, and then click the Save button in the dialog box. To use the template, click File on the Ribbon to open the Backstage view, click the New tab to display the New gallery, click My templates, and then double-click the template icon or name.

To Change Document Properties, Then Save and Close a File

The letterhead now is complete. Thus, you should save it in a file. The following steps assume you already have created folders for storing your files, for example, a CIS 101 folder (for your class) that contains a Word folder (for your assignments). Thus, these steps change document properties, save the file in the Word folder in the CIS 101 folder on a USB flash drive using the file name, Heartland Letterhead, and then close the file.

1. Click File on the Ribbon to open the Backstage view and then, if necessary, select the Info tab. Display the Properties menu and then click Show Document Panel on the Properties menu to close the Backstage view and display the Document Information Panel in the Word document window.
2. Enter your name in the Author property, and enter your course and section in the Subject property. Close the Document Information Panel.
3. With a USB flash drive connected to one of the computer's USB ports, click the Save button on the Quick Access Toolbar to display the Save As dialog box.
4. Type `Heartland Letterhead` in the File name text box to change the file name. Do not press the ENTER key after typing the file name because you do not want to close the dialog box at this time.
5. Navigate to the desired save location (in this case, the Word folder in the CIS 101 folder [or your class folder] on the USB flash drive).
6. Click the Save button (Save As dialog box) to save the file in the selected folder on the selected drive with the entered file name.
7. Click File on the Ribbon to open the Backstage view and then click Close in the Backstage view to close the document.

Break Point: If you wish to take a break, this is a good place to do so. To resume at a later time, start Word and continue following the steps from this location forward.

Creating a Business Letter

You have created a letterhead for the business letter. The next step is to compose the rest of the content in the business letter. The following pages use Word to create a business letter that contains a table and a bulleted list.

Plan Ahead

Compose an effective business letter.
When composing a business letter, you need to be sure to include all essential elements and to decide which letter style to use.

- **Include all essential letter elements, properly spaced and sized.** All business letters contain the same basic elements, including the date line, inside address, message, and signature block (shown in Figure 3–1 on page WD 139). If a business letter does not use a letterhead, then the top of the letter should include return address information in a heading.
- **Use proper spacing and formats for the contents of the letter below the letterhead.** Use a font that is easy to read, in a size between 8 and 12 point. Add emphasis with bold, italic, and bullets where appropriate, and use tables to present numeric information. Paragraphs should be single-spaced, with double-spacing between paragraphs.
- **Determine which letter style to use.** You can follow many different styles when creating business letters. A letter style specifies guidelines for the alignment and spacing of elements in the business letter.

To Create a New File from an Existing File

The top of the business letter in this chapter contains the letterhead, which you saved in a separate file. You could open the letterhead file and then save it with a new name, so that the letterhead file remains intact for future use. A more efficient technique is to create a new file from the letterhead file. Doing this enables you to save the document the first time using the Save button on the Quick Access Toolbar instead of requiring you to use the Save As command in the Backstage view. The following steps create a new file from an existing file.

1

- Click File on the Ribbon to open the Backstage view.
- Click the New tab in the Backstage view to display the New gallery (Figure 3–39).

Q&A What are the templates in the New gallery?

A template is a document that includes prewritten text and/or formatting common to documents of the specified type. Word provides many templates to simplify the task of creating documents.

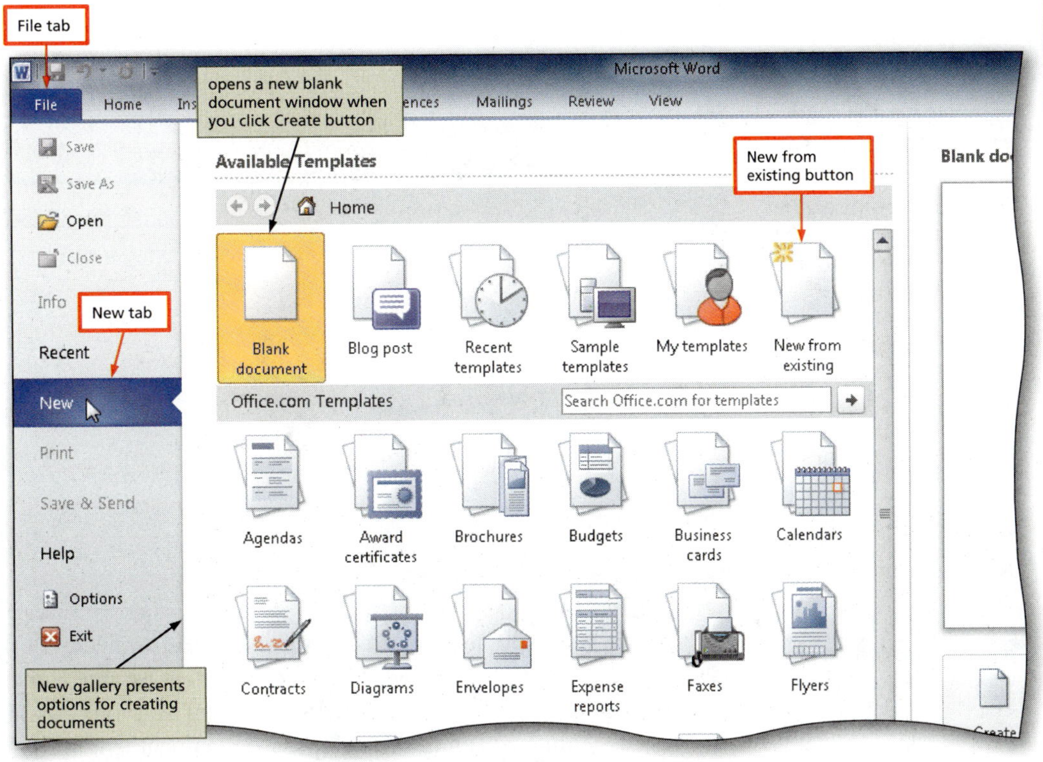

Figure 3–39

2

- Click the 'New from existing' button in the New gallery to display the New from Existing Document dialog box.
- If necessary, navigate to the location of the saved Heartland Letterhead file (in this case, the Word folder in the CIS 101 folder on the USB flash drive).
- Click Heartland Letterhead to select the file (Figure 3–40).

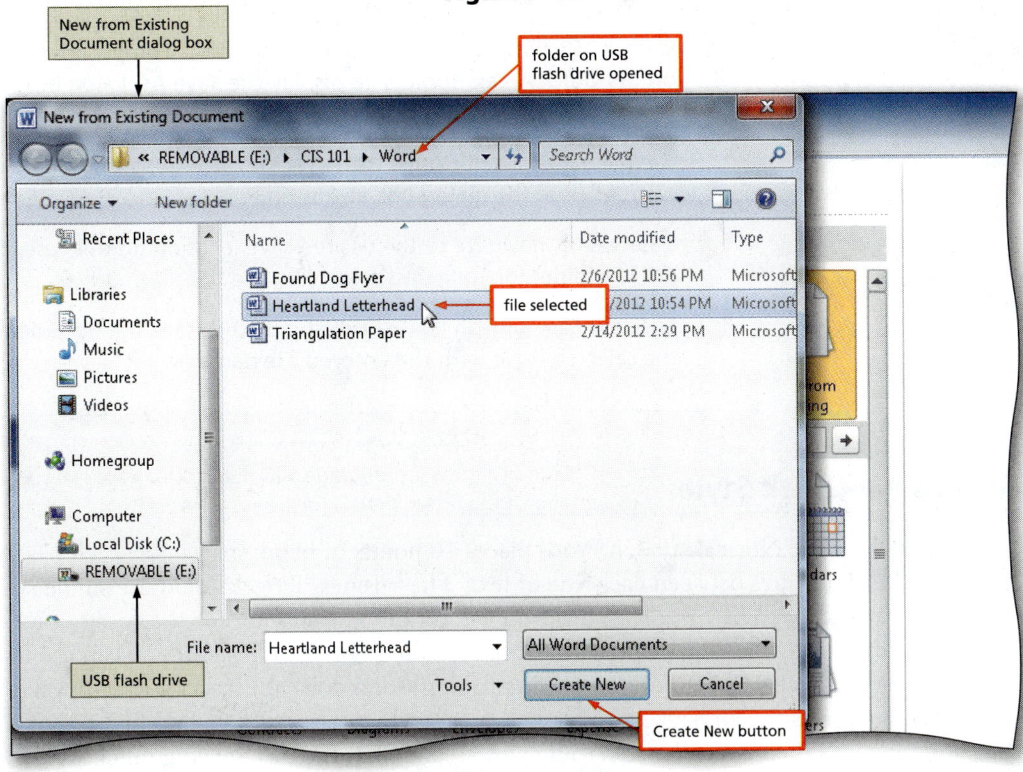

Figure 3–40

3

- Click the Create New button (New from Existing Document dialog box) to open a new document window that contains the contents of the selected file.
- If necessary, click the paragraph mark below the letterhead to position the insertion point at that location (Figure 3–41).

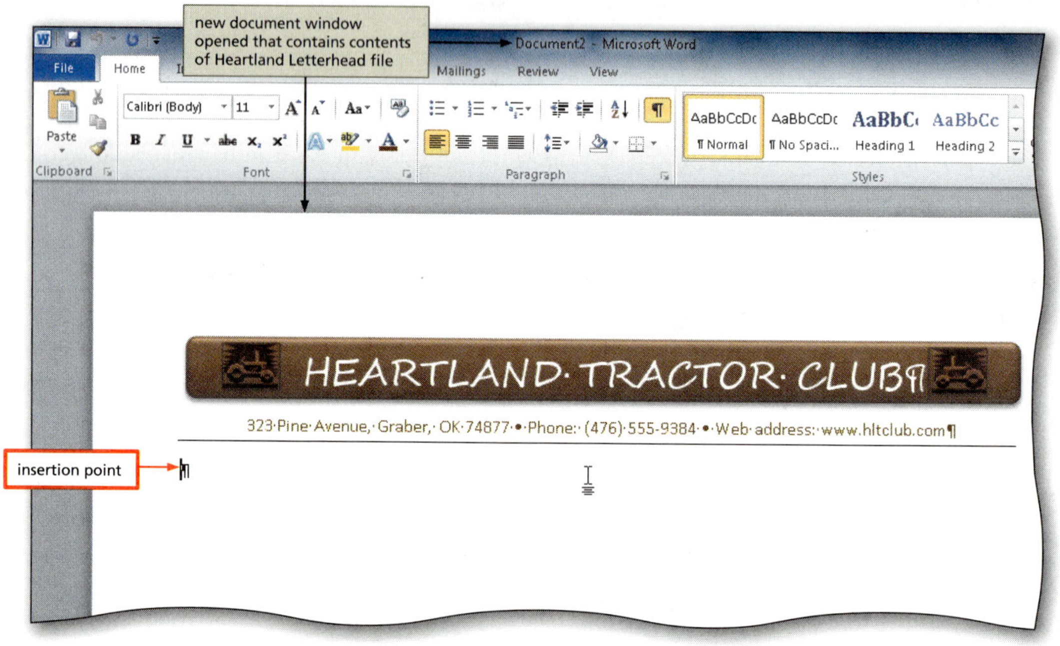

Figure 3–41

BTW

New Document Window
If you wanted to open a new blank document window, you could press CTRL+N or click File on the Ribbon to open the Backstage view, click the New tab to display the New gallery, click the Blank document button, and then click the Create button.

To Save a Document

Because you do not want to lose the letterhead at the top of this document, you should save the letter before continuing. The following steps assume you already have created folders for storing your files, for example, a CIS 101 folder (for your class) that contains a Word folder (for your assignments). Thus, these steps save the document in the Word folder in the CIS 101 folder on a USB flash drive using the file name, Heartland Advertisement Letter.

1. With a USB flash drive connected to one of the computer's USB ports, click the Save button on the Quick Access Toolbar to display the Save As dialog box.
2. Type `Heartland Advertisement Letter` in the File name text box to change the file name. Do not press the ENTER key after typing the file name because you do not want to close the dialog box at this time.
3. If necessary, navigate to the desired save location (in this case, the Word folder in the CIS 101 folder [or your class folder] on the USB flash drive).
4. Click the Save button (Save As dialog box) to save the document in the selected folder on the selected drive with the entered file name.

To Apply a Quick Style

Recall that the Normal style in Word places 10 points of blank space after each paragraph and inserts a vertical space equal to 1.15 lines between each line of text. The business letter should use single spacing for paragraphs and double spacing between paragraphs. Thus, you will modify the spacing for the paragraphs.

Word has many built-in, or predefined, styles called Quick Styles that you can use to format text. The No Spacing style, for example, defines line spacing to single and does not insert any additional blank space between lines when you press the ENTER key. To apply a quick style to a paragraph, you first position the insertion point in the paragraph and then apply the style. The next step applies the No Spacing quick style to a paragraph.

1

- With the insertion point positioned in the paragraph to be formatted, click No Spacing in the Quick Style gallery (Home tab | Styles group) to apply the selected style to the current paragraph (Figure 3–42).

Q&A Will this style be used in the rest of the document?

Yes. The paragraph formatting, which includes the style, will carry forward to subsequent paragraphs each time you press the ENTER key.

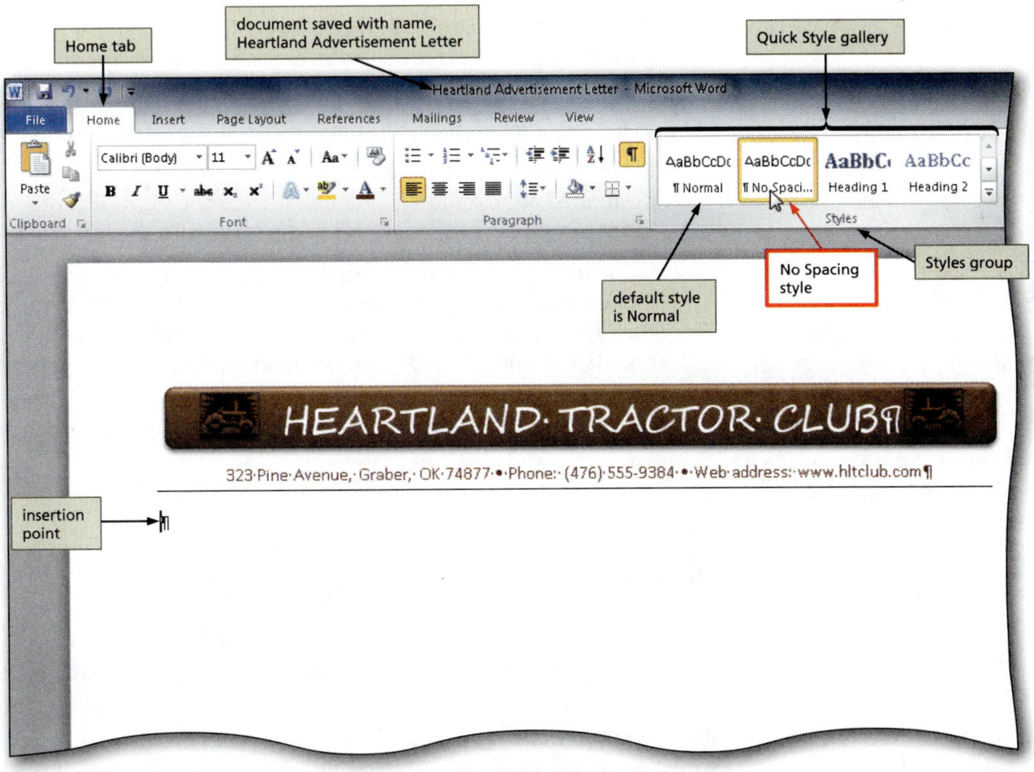

Figure 3–42

Other Ways	
1. Click Styles Dialog Box Launcher (Home tab | Styles group), click desired style in Styles task pane	2. Press CTRL+SHIFT+S, click Style Name box arrow in Apply Styles task pane, click desired style in list

Plan Ahead

Include all essential letter elements.

Be sure to include all essential business letter elements, properly spaced, in your letter.

- The **date line**, which consists of the month, day, and year, is positioned two to six lines below the letterhead.
- The **inside address**, placed three to eight lines below the date line, usually contains the addressee's courtesy title plus full name, job title, business affiliation, and full geographical address.
- The **salutation**, if present, begins two lines below the last line of the inside address. If you do not know the recipient's name, avoid using the salutation "To whom it may concern" — it is impersonal. Instead, use the recipient's title in the salutation, e.g., Dear Personnel Director. In a business letter, use a colon (:) at the end of the salutation; in a personal letter, use a comma.
- The body of the letter, the **message**, begins two lines below the salutation. Within the message, paragraphs are single-spaced with one blank line between paragraphs.
- Two lines below the last line of the message, the **complimentary close** is displayed. Capitalize only the first word in a complimentary close.
- Type the **signature block** at least four blank lines below the complimentary close, allowing room for the author to sign his or her name.

Plan Ahead

Determine which letter style to use.
Three common business letter styles are the block, the modified block, and the modified semi-block. Each style specifies different alignments and indentations.

- In the block letter style, all components of the letter begin flush with the left margin.
- In the modified block letter style, the date, complimentary close, and signature block are positioned approximately one-half inch to the right of center or at the right margin. All other components of the letter begin flush with the left margin.
- In the modified semi-block letter style, the date, complimentary close, and signature block are centered, positioned approximately one-half inch to the right of center or at the right margin. The first line of each paragraph in the body of the letter is indented one-half to one inch from the left margin. All other components of the letter begin flush with the left margin.

The business letter in this project follows the modified block style.

Using Tab Stops to Align Text

A **tab stop** is a location on the horizontal ruler that tells Word where to position the insertion point when you press the TAB key on the keyboard. Word, by default, places a tab stop at every one-half inch mark on the ruler. These default tab stops are indicated at the bottom of the horizontal ruler by small vertical tick marks (shown in Figure 3–43). You also can set your own custom tab stops. Tab settings are a paragraph format. Thus, each time you press the ENTER key, any custom tab stops are carried forward to the next paragraph.

To move the insertion point from one tab stop to another, press the TAB key on the keyboard. When you press the TAB key, a **tab character** formatting mark appears in the empty space between the tab stops.

When you set a custom tab stop, you specify how the text will align at a tab stop. The tab marker on the ruler reflects the alignment of the characters at the location of the tab stop. Table 3–3 shows types of tab stop alignments in Word and their corresponding tab markers.

Table 3–3 Types of Tab Stop Alignments

Tab Stop Alignment	Tab Marker	Result of Pressing TAB Key	Example
Left Tab		Left-aligns text at the location of the tab stop	toolbar ruler
Center Tab		Centers text at the location of the tab stop	toolbar ruler
Right Tab		Right-aligns text at the location of the tab stop	toolbar ruler
Decimal Tab		Aligns text on decimal point at the location of the tab stop	45.72 223.75
Bar Tab		Aligns text at a bar character at the location of the tab stop	| toolbar | ruler

BTW

Tabs Dialog Box
You can use the Tabs dialog box to set, change the alignment of, and remove custom tab stops. To display the Tabs dialog box, click the Paragraph Dialog Box Launcher (Home tab or Page Layout tab | Paragraph group) and then click the Tabs button (Paragraph dialog box), or double-click a tab marker on the ruler. To set a custom tab stop, enter the desired position (Tabs dialog box) and then click the Set button. To change the alignment of a custom tab stop, click the tab stop position to be changed, click the new alignment, and then click the Set button. To remove an existing tab stop, click the tab stop position to be removed and then click the Clear button. To remove all tab stops, click the Clear All button in the Tabs dialog box.

To Display the Ruler

One way to set custom tab stops is by using the horizontal ruler. Thus, the following step displays the ruler in the document window.

1 If the rulers are not displayed already, click the View Ruler button on the vertical scroll bar (shown in Figure 3–43).

Q&A What if the View Ruler button is not visible on the vertical scroll bar?

Display the View tab and then place a check mark in the Ruler check box.

To Set Custom Tab Stops

The first required element of the business letter is the date line, which in this letter is positioned two lines below the letterhead. The date line contains the month, day, and year, and begins four inches from the left margin, which is approximately one-half inch to the right of center. Thus, you should set a custom tab stop at the 4" mark on the ruler. The following steps set a left-aligned tab stop.

1

- With the insertion point on the paragraph mark below the border (shown in Figure 3–42 on page WD 167), press the ENTER key so that a blank line appears above the insertion point.
- If necessary, click the tab selector at the left edge of the horizontal ruler until it displays the type of tab you wish to use, which is the Left Tab icon in this case.
- Position the mouse pointer on the 4" mark on the ruler, which is the location of the desired custom tab stop (Figure 3–43).

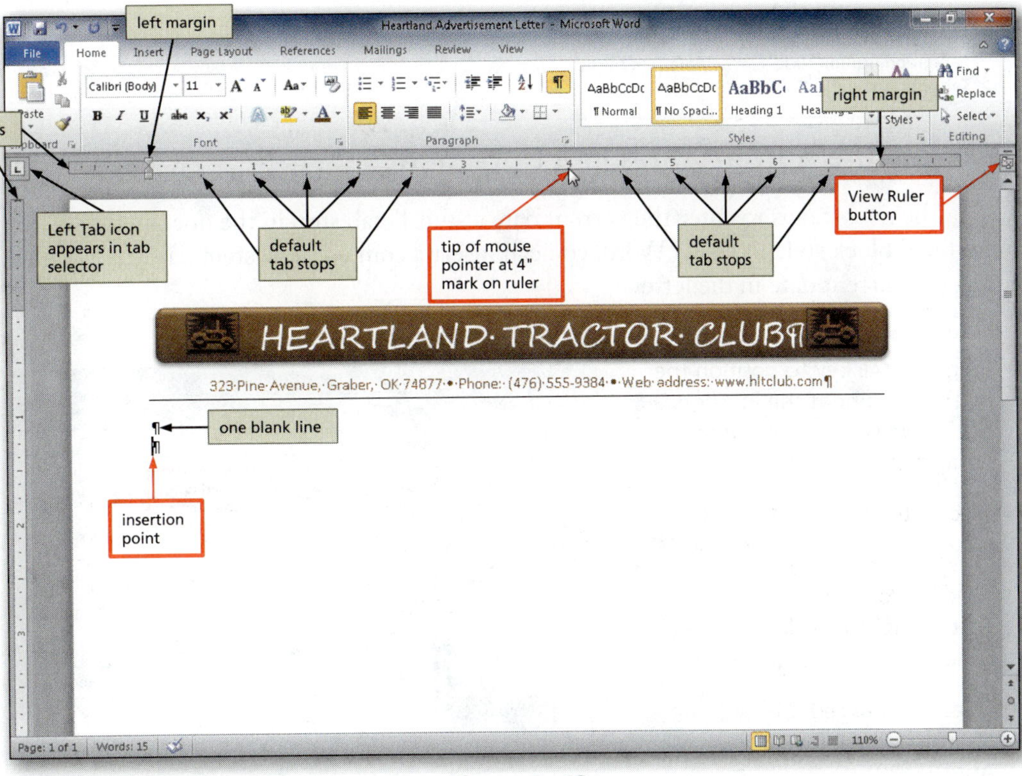

Figure 3–43

Q&A What is the purpose of the tab selector?

Before using the ruler to set a tab stop, ensure the correct tab stop icon appears in the tab selector. Each time you click the tab selector, its icon changes. The Left Tab icon is the default. For a list of the types of tab stops, see Table 3–3.

2

- Click the 4" mark on the ruler to place a tab marker at that location (Figure 3–44).

Q&A What if I click the wrong location on the ruler?

You can move a custom tab stop by dragging the tab marker to the desired location on the ruler. Or, you can remove an existing custom tab stop by pointing to the tab marker on the ruler and then dragging the tab marker down and out of the ruler.

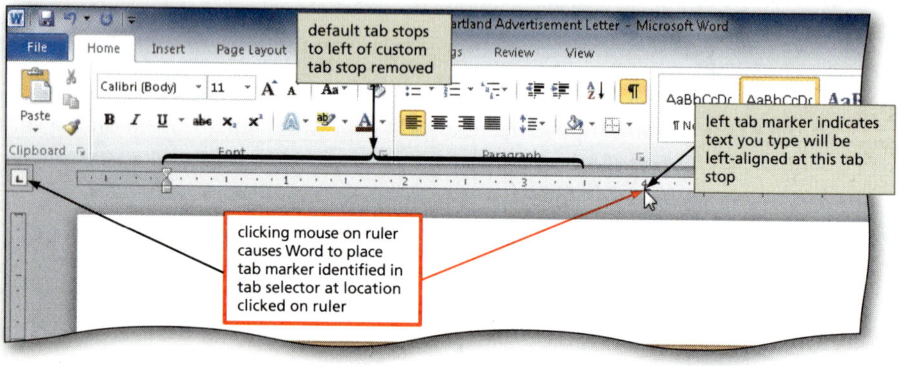

Figure 3–44

Q&A What happened to all the default tab stops on the ruler?

When you set a custom tab stop, Word clears all default tab stops to the left of the newly set custom tab stop on the ruler.

Other Ways

1. Click Paragraph Dialog Box Launcher (Home tab or Page Layout tab | Paragraph group), click Tabs button (Paragraph dialog box), type tab stop position (Tabs dialog box), click Set button, click OK button

To Insert the Current Date in a Document

The next step is to enter the current date at the 4" tab stop in the document, as specified in the guidelines for a modified block style letter. In Word, you can insert a computer's system date in a document. The following steps insert the current date in the letter.

1

- Press the TAB key to position the insertion point at the location of the tab stop in the current paragraph.
- Display the Insert tab.
- Click the Insert Date and Time button (Insert tab | Text group) to display the Date and Time dialog box.
- Select the desired format (Date and Time dialog box), in this case April 27, 2012.
- If the Update automatically check box is selected, click the check box to remove the check mark (Figure 3–45).

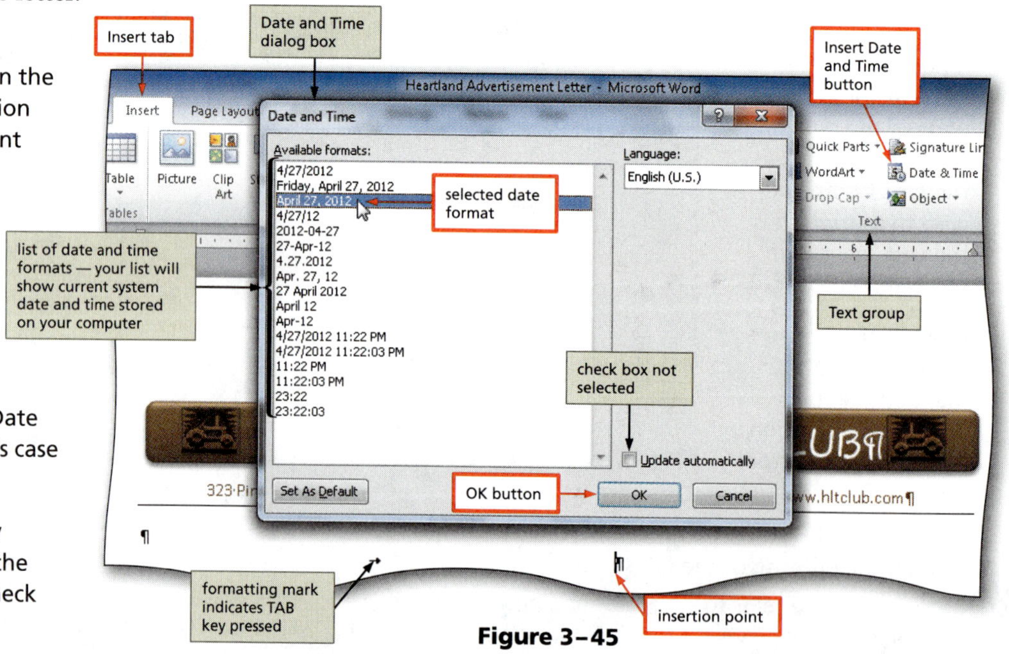

Figure 3–45

Q&A Why should the Update automatically check box not be selected?

In this project, the date at the top of the letter always should show today's date (for example, April 27, 2012). If, however, you wanted the date always to change to reflect the current computer date (for example, showing the date you open or print the letter), then you would place a check mark in this check box.

2

- Click the OK button to insert the current date at the location of the insertion point (Figure 3–46).

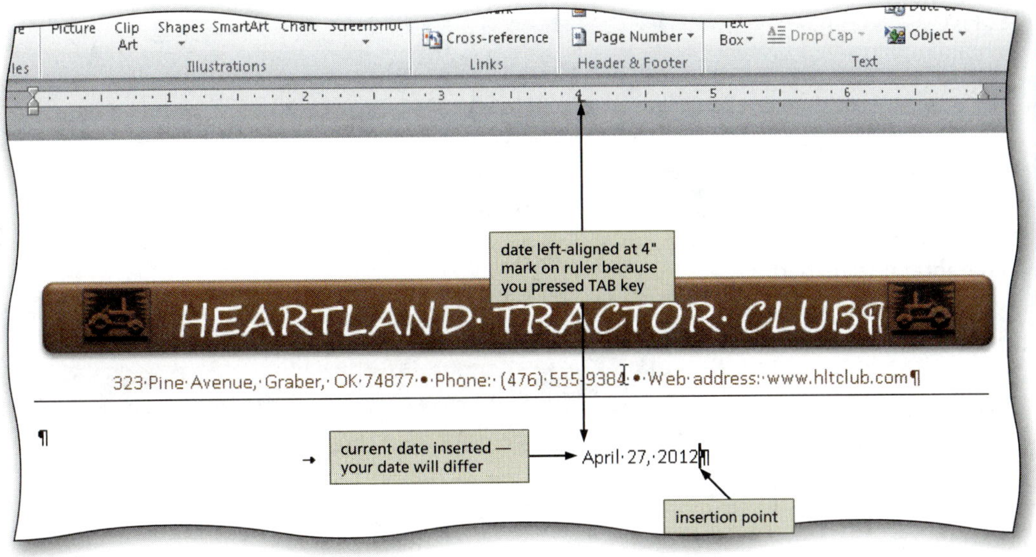

Figure 3–46

To Enter the Inside Address and Salutation

The next step in composing the business letter is to type the inside address and salutation. The following steps enter this text.

1. With the insertion point at the end of the date (shown in Figure 3–46), press the ENTER key three times.
2. Type `Mr. Harvey Wilcox` and then press the ENTER key.
3. Type `Wilcox Tractor Restorations` and then press the ENTER key.
4. Type `3009 North 2850 East Road` and then press the ENTER key.
5. Type `Roundwood, OK 74519` and then press the ENTER key twice.
6. Type `Dear Mr. Wilcox:` to complete the inside address and salutation entries (Figure 3–47).

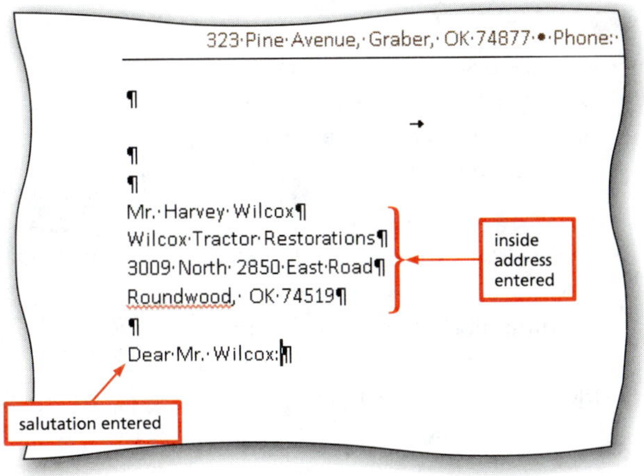

Figure 3–47

To Create a Building Block

If you use the same text or graphic frequently, you can store the text or graphic as a **building block** and then insert the stored building block entry in the open document, as well as in future documents. That is, you can create the entry once as a building block and then insert the building block when you need it. In this way, you avoid entering the text or graphics inconsistently or incorrectly in different locations throughout the same or multiple documents.

The steps on the next page create a building block for the prospective advertiser's name, Wilcox Tractor Restorations. Later, you will insert the building block in the document instead of typing the advertiser's name.

1

- Select the text to be a building block, in this case Wilcox Tractor Restorations. Do not select the paragraph mark at the end of the text because you do not want the paragraph to be part of the building block.

Q&A Why is the paragraph mark not part of the building block?

Select the paragraph mark only if you want to store paragraph formatting, such as indentation and line spacing, as part of the building block.

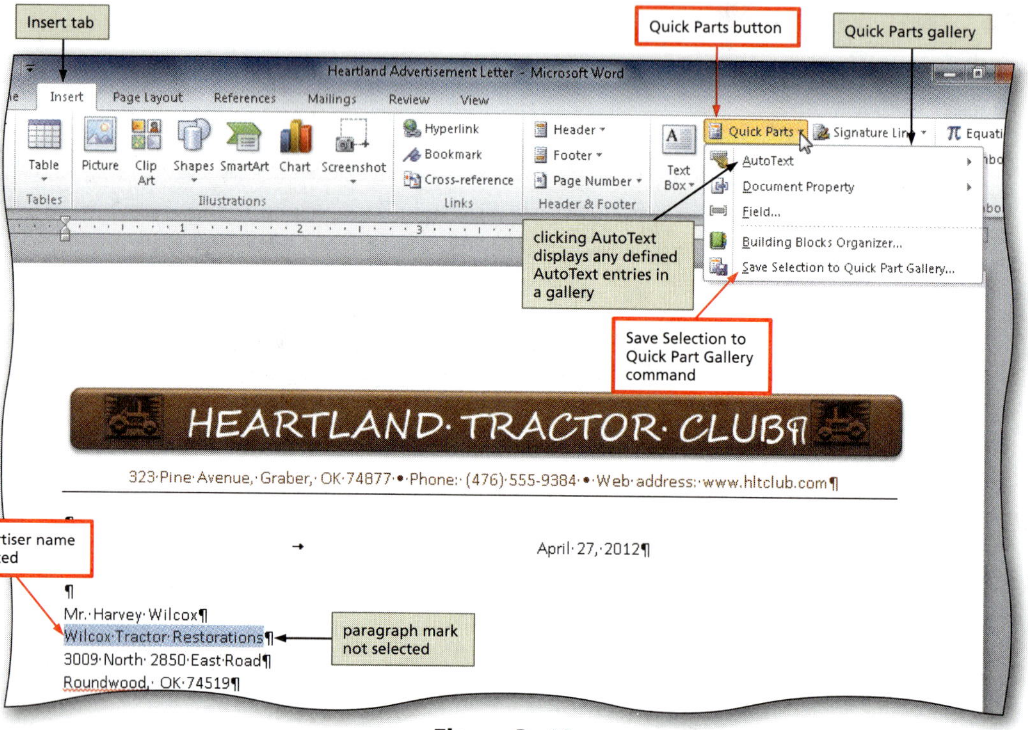

Figure 3–48

- Click the Quick Parts button (Insert tab | Text group) to display the Quick Parts gallery (Figure 3–48).

2

- Click Save Selection to Quick Part Gallery in the Quick Parts gallery to display the Create New Building Block dialog box.
- Type `wtr` in the Name text box (Create New Building Block dialog box) to replace the proposed building block name (Wilcox Tractor, in this case) with a shorter building block name (Figure 3–49).

3

- Click the OK button to store the building block entry and close the dialog box.

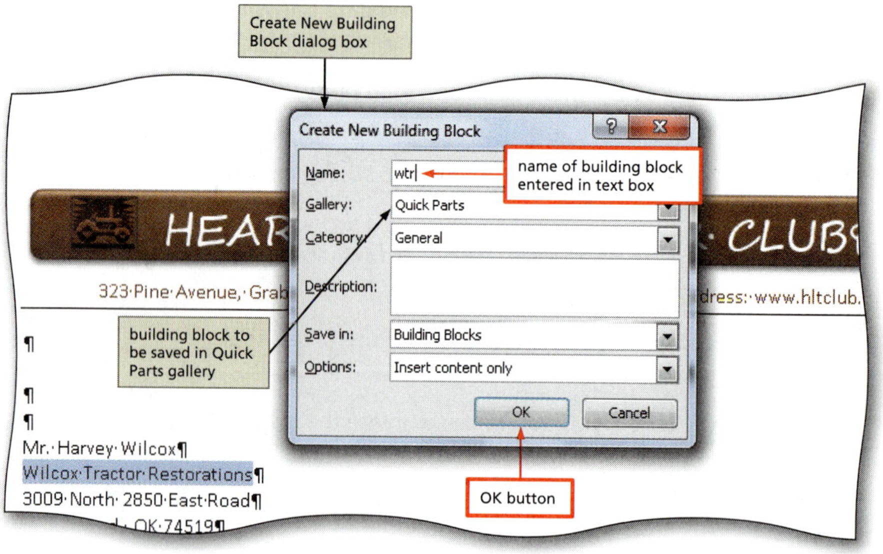

Figure 3–49

- If Word displays another dialog box, click the Yes button, to save changes to the building blocks.

Q&A Will this building block be available in future documents?

When you quit Word, a dialog box may appear asking if you want to save changes to the "Building Blocks". Click the Save button if you want to use the new building block in future documents.

Other Ways

1. Select text, press ALT+F3

To Modify a Building Block

When you save a building block in the Quick Parts gallery, it is displayed at the top of the Quick Parts gallery. If the building block is a text entry, you can place it in the AutoText gallery instead, which also is accessible through the Quick Parts gallery.

When you point to the building block in the Quick Parts gallery, a ScreenTip displays the building block name. If you want to display more information when the user points to the building block, you can include a description as an Enhanced ScreenTip. The following steps modify a building block to include a description and change its category to AutoText.

1

- Click the Quick Parts button (Insert tab | Text group) to display the Quick Parts gallery.
- Right-click the Wilcox Tractor Restorations building block to display a shortcut menu (Figure 3–50).

Figure 3–50

2

- Click Edit Properties on the shortcut menu to display the Modify Building Block dialog box, filled in with information related to the selected building block.
- Click the Gallery box arrow (Modify Building Block dialog box) and then click AutoText to change the gallery in which the building block will be displayed.
- Type `Potential Advertiser` in the Description text box (Figure 3–51).

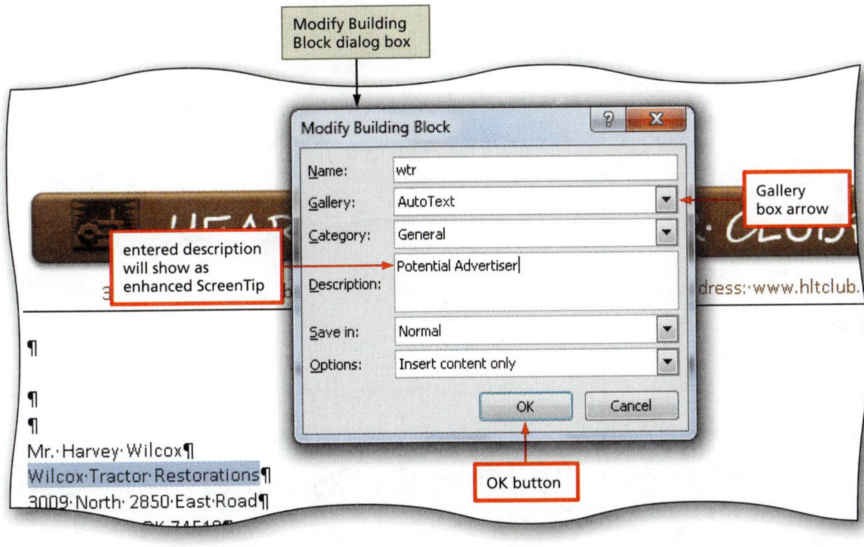

Figure 3–51

3

- Click the OK button to store the building block entry and close the dialog box.
- Click the Yes button when asked if you want to redefine the building block entry.

To Insert a Building Block

In the first sentence in the body of the letter, you want the prospective advertiser name, Wilcox Tractor Restorations, to be displayed. Recall that you stored a building block name of wtr for Wilcox Tractor Restorations. Thus, you will type the building block name and then instruct Word to replace a building block name with the stored building block entry. The following steps insert a building block.

1

- Click to the right of the colon in the salutation and then press the ENTER key twice to position the insertion point one blank line below the salutation.
- Type the beginning of the first sentence as follows, entering the building block name as shown: **`We are delighted you are considering advertising your business, wtr`** (Figure 3–52).

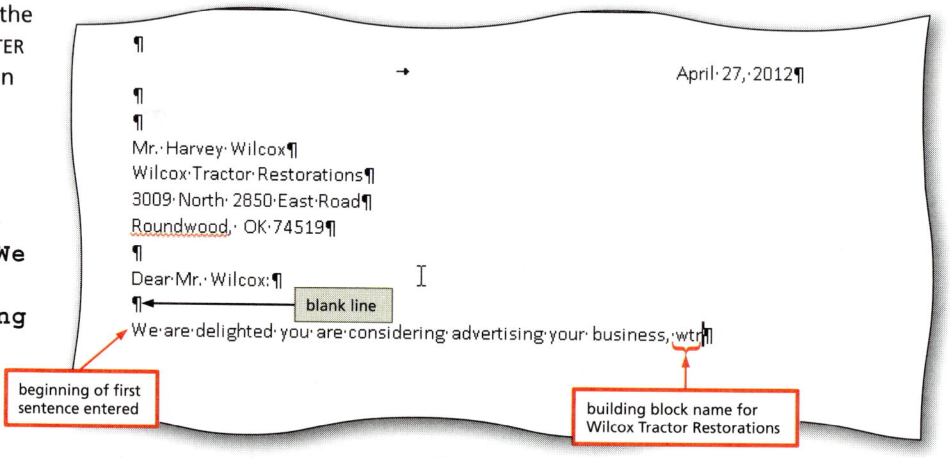

Figure 3–52

2

- Press the F3 key to instruct Word to replace the building block name (wtr) with the stored building block entry (Wilcox Tractor Restorations) (Figure 3–53).

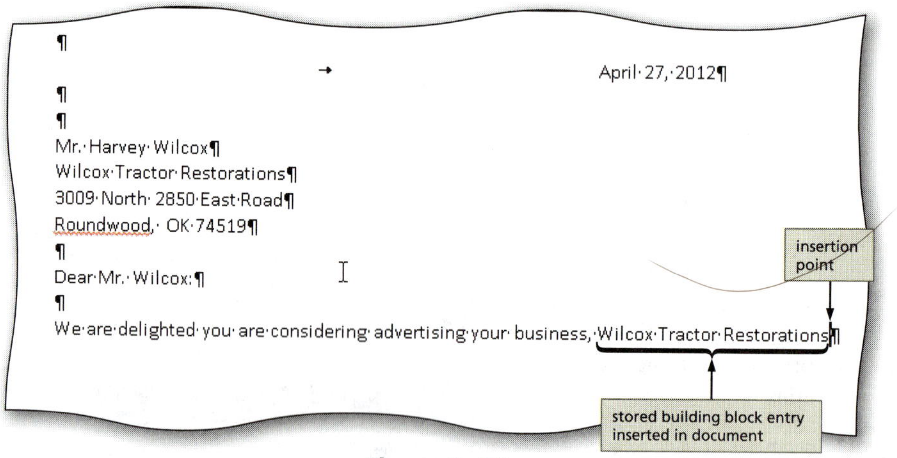

Figure 3–53

Other Ways

1. Click Quick Parts button (Insert tab | Text group), if necessary point to AutoText, click desired building block

Building Blocks versus AutoCorrect

In Word Chapter 2, you learned how to use the AutoCorrect feature, which enables you to insert and create AutoCorrect entries, similarly to how you created and inserted building blocks in this chapter. The difference between an AutoCorrect entry and a building block entry is that the AutoCorrect feature makes corrections for you automatically as soon as you press the SPACEBAR or type a punctuation mark, whereas you must instruct Word to insert a building block. That is, you enter the building block name and then press the F3 key, or click the Quick Parts button and select the building block from one of the galleries.

To Insert a Nonbreaking Space

Some compound words, such as proper nouns, dates, units of time and measure, abbreviations, and geographic destinations, should not be divided at the end of a line. These words either should fit as a unit at the end of a line or be wrapped together to the next line.

Word provides two special characters to assist with this task: the nonbreaking space and the nonbreaking hyphen. A **nonbreaking space** is a special space character that prevents two words from splitting if the first word falls at the end of a line. Similarly, a **nonbreaking hyphen** is a special type of hyphen that prevents two words separated by a hyphen from splitting at the end of a line.

The following steps insert a nonbreaking space between the words in the magazine name.

1

- With the insertion point at the end of the building block entry in the document (as shown in Figure 3–53), press the COMMA key and then press the SPACEBAR.
- Type `in` and then press the SPACEBAR. Press CTRL+I to turn on italics because magazine names should be italicized.
- Type `Heartland` as the first word in the magazine name and then press CTRL+SHIFT+SPACEBAR to insert a nonbreaking space after the entered word (Figure 3–54).

Figure 3–54

2

- Type `Tractor` and then press CTRL+SHIFT+SPACEBAR to insert another nonbreaking space after the entered word.
- Type `Magazine` and then press CTRL+I to turn off italics (Figure 3–55).

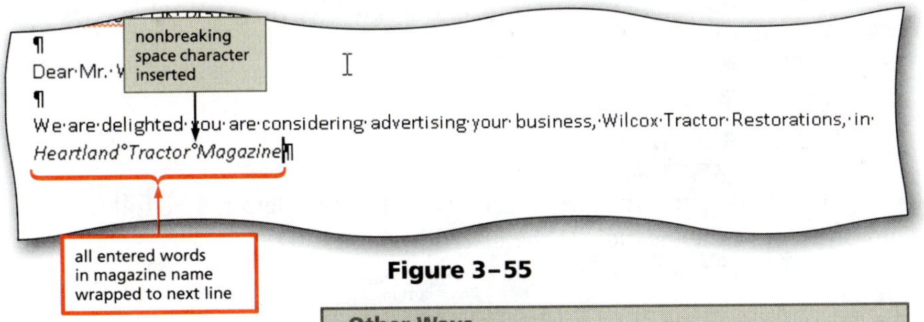

Figure 3–55

Other Ways

1. Click Symbol button (Insert tab | Symbols group), click More Symbols, click Special Characters tab (Symbol dialog box), click Nonbreaking Space in Character list, click Insert button, click Close button

To Enter Text

The next step in creating the letter is to enter the rest of the text in the first paragraph. The following steps enter this text.

1. Press the COMMA key and then press the SPACEBAR.
2. Type this text: `our monthly publication for tractor enthusiasts. The table below outlines advertisement rates per monthly issue:`
3. Press the ENTER key twice to place a blank line between paragraphs (shown in Figure 3–56 on the next page).

Q&A Why does my document wrap on different words?

Differences in wordwrap may relate to the printer connected to your computer. Thus, it is possible that the same document could wordwrap differently if associated with a different printer.

BTW **Nonbreaking Hyphen**
If you wanted to insert a nonbreaking hyphen, you would press CTRL+SHIFT+HYPHEN.

To Save an Existing Document with the Same File Name

You have made several modifications to the document since you last saved it. Thus, you should save it again. The following step saves the document again.

1. Click the Save button on the Quick Access Toolbar to overwrite the previously saved file.

Break Point: If you wish to take a break, this is a good place to do so. You can quit Word now. To resume at a later time, start Word, open the file called Heartland Advertisement Letter, and continue following the steps from this location forward.

Tables

The next step in composing the business letter is to place a table listing the rates for various types of advertisements (shown in Figure 3–1 on page WD 139). A Word **table** is a collection of rows and columns. The intersection of a row and a column is called a **cell**, and cells are filled with data.

The first step in creating a table is to insert an empty table in the document. When inserting a table, you must specify the total number of rows and columns required, which is called the **dimension** of the table. The table in this project has five columns. You often do not know the total number of rows in a table. Thus, many Word users create one row initially and then add more rows as needed. In Word, the first number in a dimension is the number of columns, and the second is the number of rows. For example, in Word, a 5 × 1 (pronounced "five by one") table consists of five columns and one row.

To Insert an Empty Table

The next step is to insert an empty table in the letter. The following steps insert a table with five columns and one row at the location of the insertion point.

1

- Scroll the document up so that you will be able to see the table in the document window.
- With the insertion point positioned as shown in Figure 3–56, click the Table button (Insert tab | Tables group) to display the Table gallery (Figure 3–56).

Experiment

- Point to various cells on the grid to see a preview of various table dimensions in the document window.

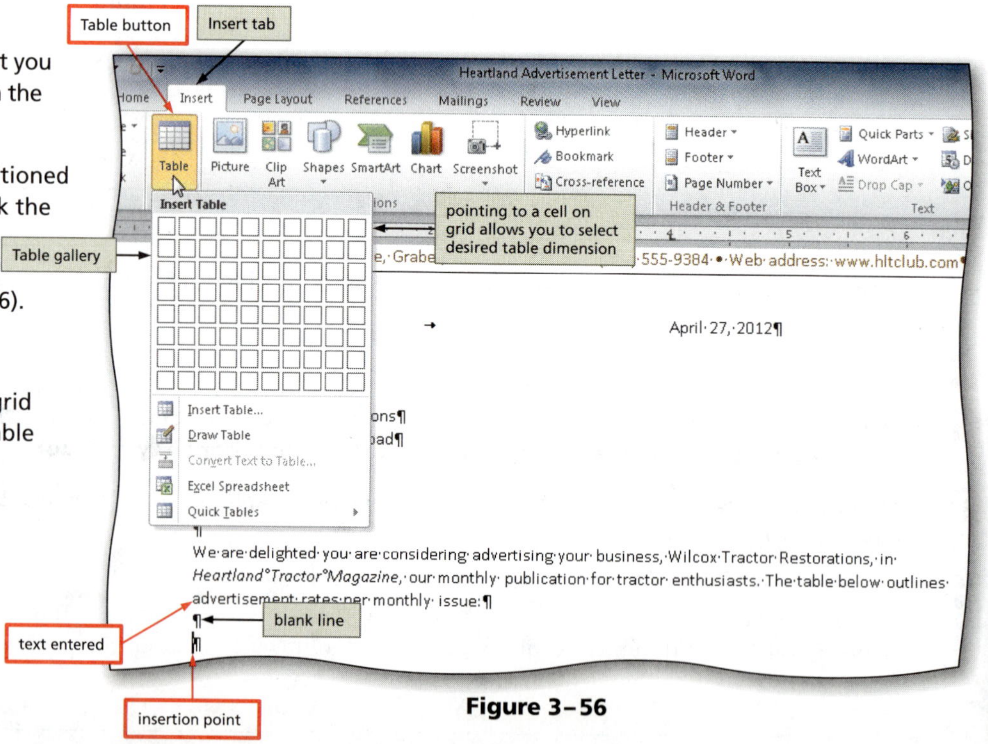

Figure 3–56

2

- Position the mouse pointer on the cell in the first row and fifth column of the grid to preview the desired table dimension (Figure 3–57).

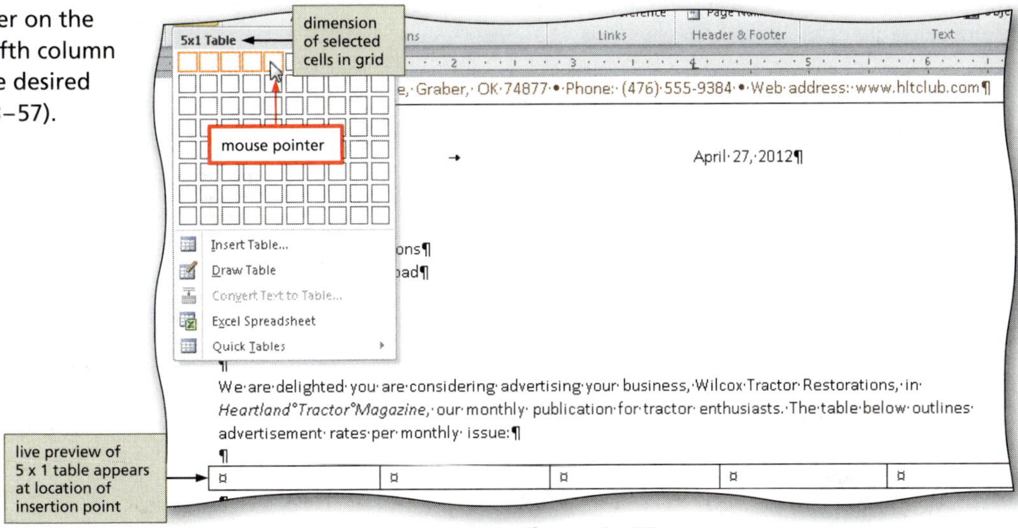

Figure 3–57

3

- Click the cell in the first row and fifth column of the grid to insert an empty table with one row and five columns in the document.
- If necessary, scroll the table up in the document window (Figure 3–58).

Q&A What are the small circles in the table cells?

Each table cell has an **end-of-cell mark**, which is a formatting mark that assists you with selecting and formatting cells. Similarly, each row has an **end-of-row mark**, which you can use to add columns to the right of a table. Recall that formatting marks do not print on a hard copy. The end-of-cell marks currently are left-aligned, that is, positioned at the left edge of each cell.

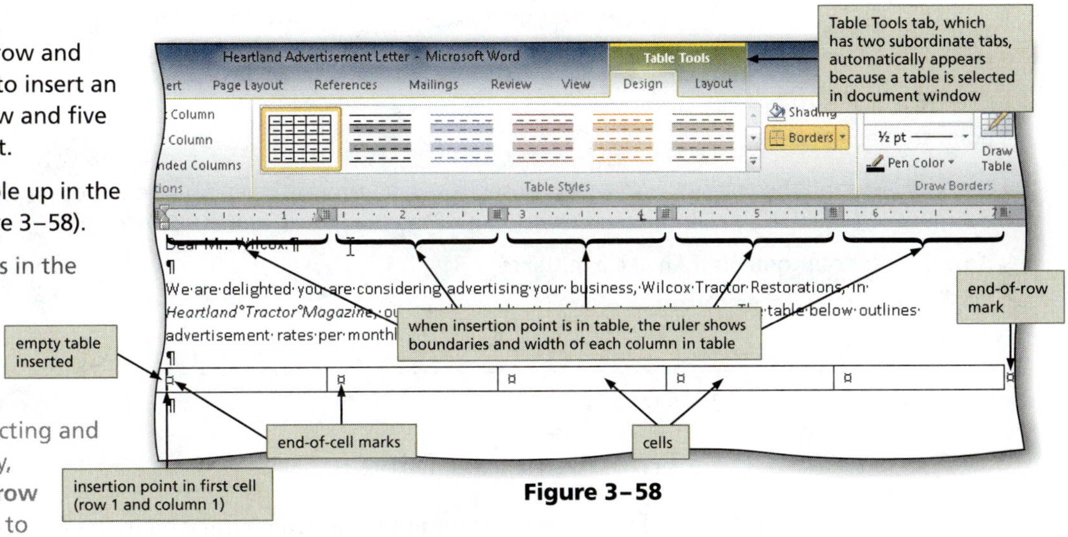

Figure 3–58

Other Ways
1. Click Table (Insert tab | Tables group), click Insert Table in Table gallery, enter number of columns and rows (Insert Table dialog box), click OK button

To Enter Data in a Table

The next step is to enter data in the cells of the empty table. The data you enter in a cell wordwraps just as text wordwraps between the margins of a document. To place data in a cell, you click the cell and then type.

To advance rightward from one cell to the next, press the TAB key. When you are at the rightmost cell in a row, press the TAB key to move to the first cell in the next row; do not press the ENTER key. The ENTER key is used to begin a new paragraph within a cell. One way to add new rows to a table is to press the TAB key when the insertion point is positioned in the bottom-right corner cell of the table. The step on the next page enters data in the first row of the table and then inserts a blank second row.

1

- With the insertion point in the left cell of the table, type `Type` and then press the TAB key to advance the insertion point to the next cell.
- Type `Dimensions` and then press the TAB key to advance the insertion point to the next cell.
- Type `Word Count` and then press the TAB key to advance the insertion point to the next cell.
- Type `Photo Count` and then press the TAB key to advance the insertion point to the next cell.

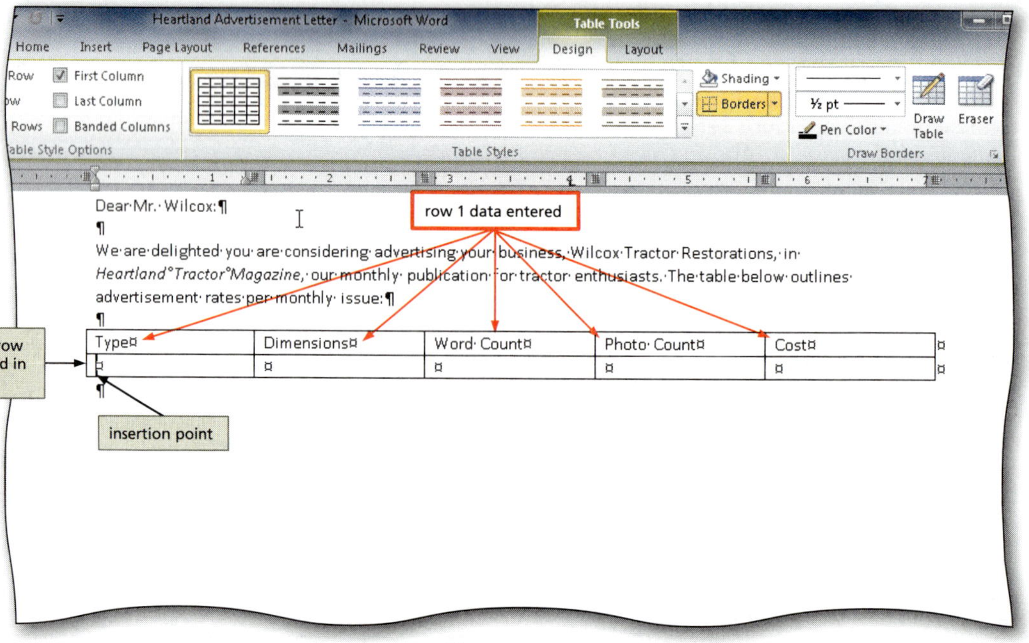

Figure 3–59

- Type `Cost` and then press the TAB key to insert a second row at the end of the table and position the insertion point in the first column of the new row (Figure 3–59).

Q&A How do I edit cell contents if I make a mistake?

Click in the cell and then correct the entry.

BTW **Tables**
For simple tables, such as the one just created, Word users often select the table dimension in the Table gallery to create the table. For a more complex table, such as one with a varying number of columns per row, Word has a Draw Table feature that allows users to draw a table in the document using a pencil pointer. To use this feature, click the Table button (Insert tab | Tables group) and then click Draw Table.

To Enter Data in a Table

The following steps enter the remaining data in the table.

1. Type `Full Page` and then press the TAB key to advance the insertion point to the next cell. Type `9" x 7"` and then press the TAB key to advance the insertion point to the next cell. Type `800` and then press the TAB key to advance the insertion point to the next cell. Type `4` and then press the TAB key to advance the insertion point to the next cell. Type `$650` and then press the TAB key to insert a row at the end of the table and position the insertion point in the first column of the new row.
2. In the third row, type `Half Page` in the first column, `4.5" x 7"` as the dimensions, `400` as the word count, `2` as the photo count, and `$350` as the cost. Press the TAB key to position the insertion point in the first column of a new row.
3. In the fourth row, type `Quarter Page` in the first column, `4.5" x 3.5"` as the dimensions, `200` as the word count, `1` as the photo count, and `$225` as the cost. Press the TAB key.
4. In the fifth row, type `Business Card` in the first column, `2.25" x 3.5"` as the dimensions, `100` as the word count, `0` as the photo count, and `$125` as the cost (Figure 3–60).

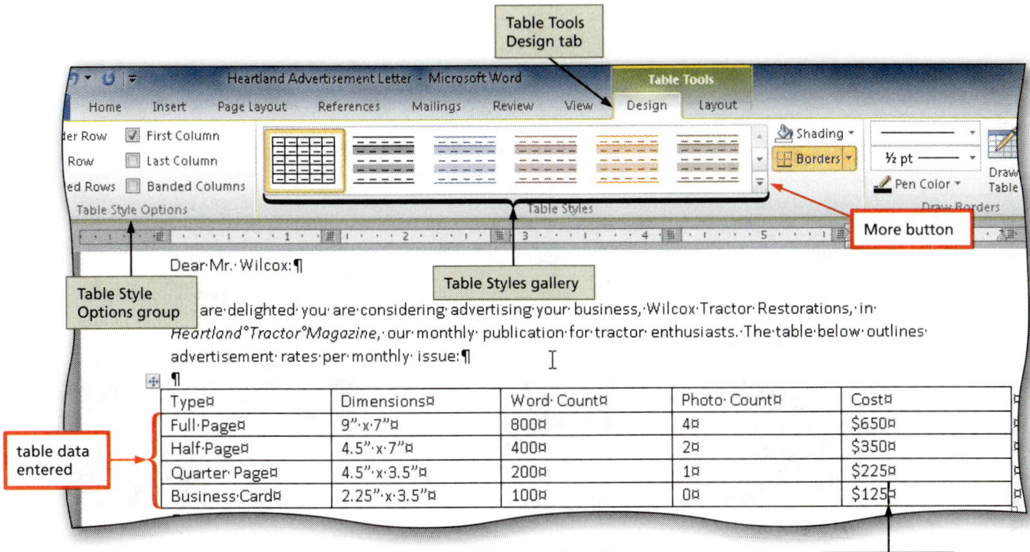

Figure 3–60

To Apply a Table Style

The next step is to apply a table style to the table. Word provides a Table Styles gallery, allowing you to change the basic table format to a more visually appealing style. Word provides a gallery of more than 90 table styles, which include a variety of colors and shading. The following steps apply a table style to the table in the letter.

1

- With the insertion point in the table, be sure the check marks match those in the Table Style Options group (Table Tools Design tab) as shown in Figure 3–60.

Q&A What if the Table Tools Design tab no longer is the active tab?

Click in the table and then display the Table Tools Design tab.

Q&A What do the options in the Table Style Options group mean?

When you apply table styles, if you want the top row of the table (header row), a row containing totals (total row), first column, or last column to be formatted differently, select those check boxes. If you want the rows or columns to alternate with colors, select Banded Rows or Banded Columns, respectively.

2

- Click the More button in the Table Styles gallery (shown in Figure 3–60) (Table Tools Design tab | Table Styles group) to expand the gallery.
- Scroll and then point to Medium Grid 3 - Accent 4 in the Table Styles gallery to display a live preview of that style applied to the table in the document (Figure 3–61).

Experiment

- Point to various table styles in the Table Styles gallery and watch the format of the table change in the document window.

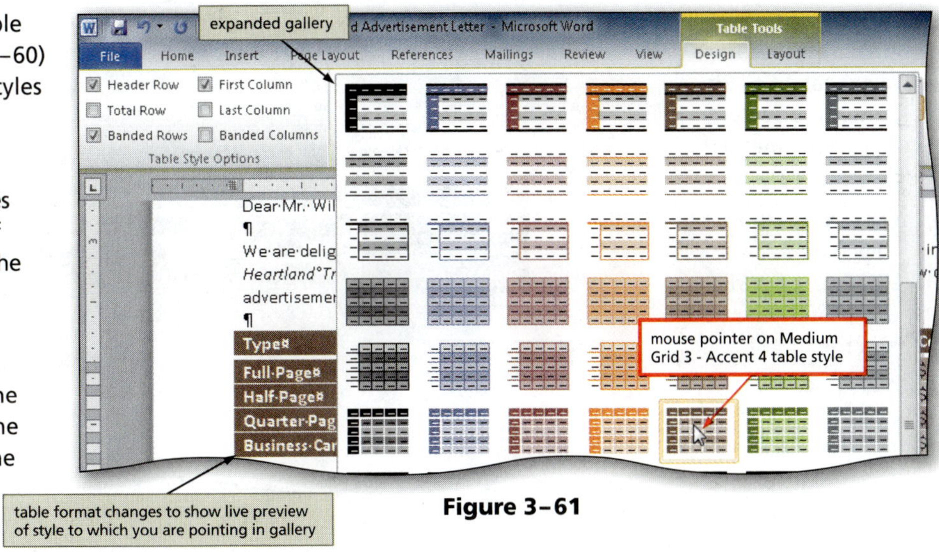

Figure 3–61

3

- Click Medium Grid 3 - Accent 4 in the Table Styles gallery to apply the selected style to the table (Figure 3–62).

Experiment

- Select and remove check marks from various check boxes in the Table Style Options group and watch the format of the table change in the document window. When finished experimenting, be sure the check marks match those shown in Figure 3–62.

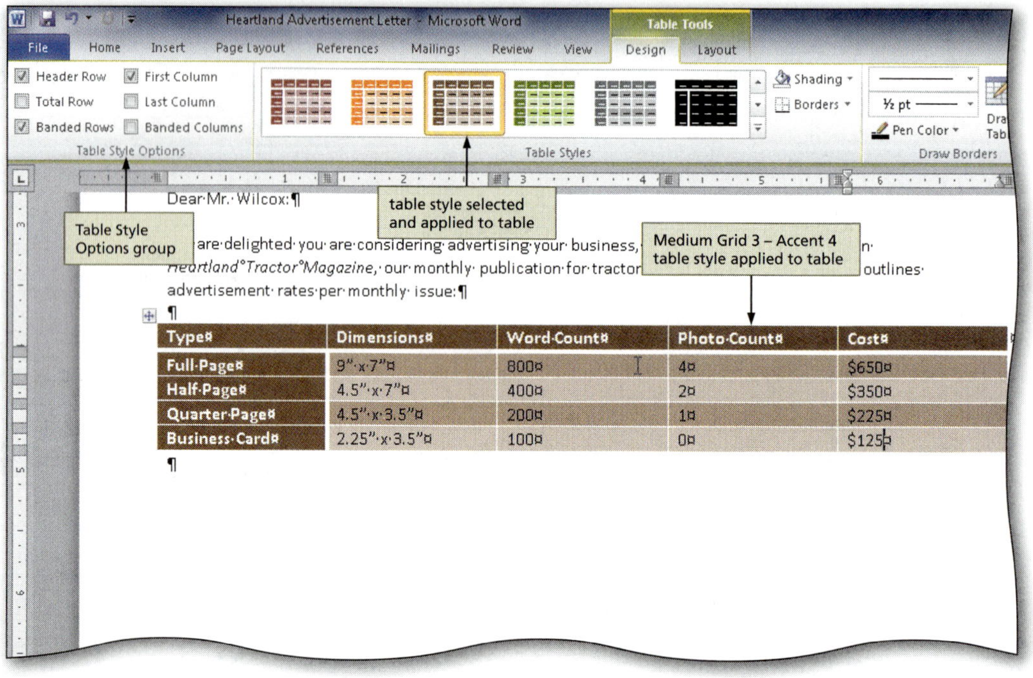

Figure 3–62

To Resize Table Columns to Fit Table Contents

The table in this project currently extends from the left margin to the right margin of the document. You want each column to be only as wide as the longest entry in the table. That is, the first column must be wide enough to accommodate the words, Business Card, and the second column should be only as wide as the title, Dimensions, and so on. The following steps instruct Word to fit the width of the columns to the contents of the table automatically.

1

- With the insertion point in the table, display the Table Tools Layout tab.
- Click the AutoFit button (Table Tools Layout tab | Cell Size group) to display the AutoFit menu (Figure 3–63).

Q&A What causes the table move handle and table resize handle to appear and disappear from the table?

They appear whenever you position the mouse pointer in the table.

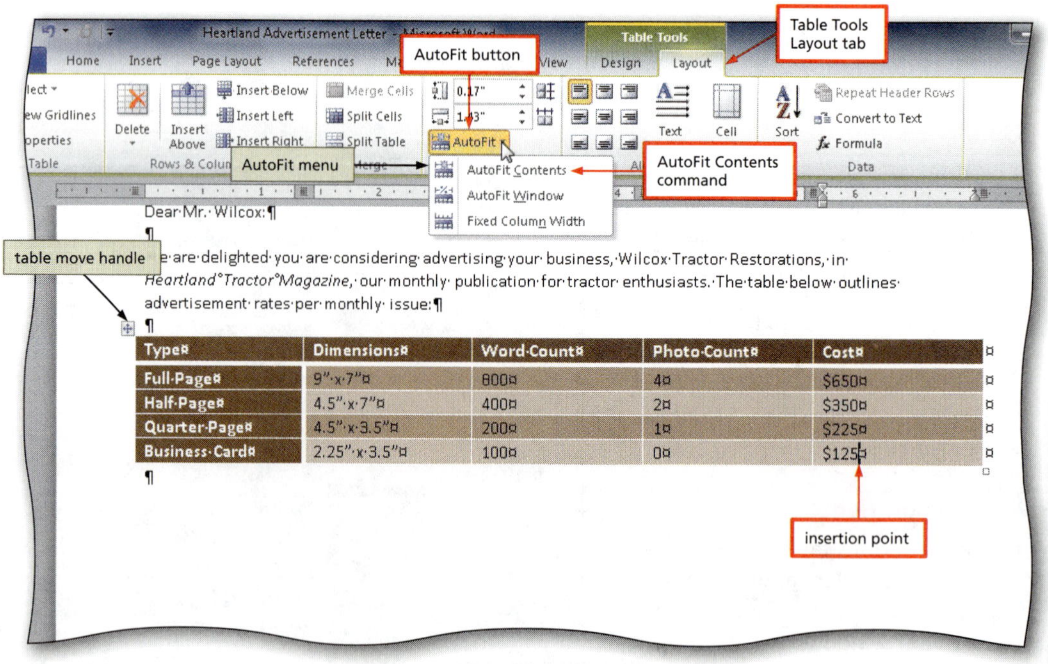

Figure 3–63

2

- Click AutoFit Contents on the AutoFit menu, so that Word automatically adjusts the widths of the columns based on the text in the table (Figure 3–64).

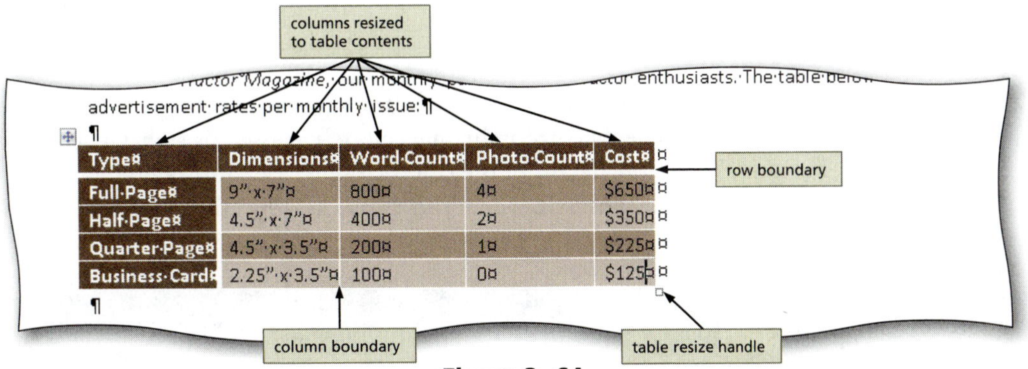

Figure 3–64

Q&A

Can I resize columns manually?

Yes, you can drag a **column boundary**, the border to the right of a column, until the column is the desired width. Similarly, you can resize a row by dragging the **row boundary**, the border at the bottom of a row, until the row is the desired height. You also can resize the entire table by dragging the **table resize handle**, which is a small square that appears when you point to a corner of the table (shown in Figure 3–63).

Other Ways

1. Right-click table, point to AutoFit on shortcut menu, click AutoFit to Contents
2. Double-click column boundary

Selecting Table Contents

When working with tables, you may need to select the contents of cells, rows, columns, or the entire table. Table 3–4 identifies ways to select various items in a table.

Table 3–4 Selecting Items in a Table

Item to Select	Action
Cell	Point to left edge of cell and click when the mouse pointer changes to a small solid upward angled pointing arrow. Or, position insertion point in cell, click Select button (Table Tools Layout tab | Table group), and then click Select Cell on the Select menu.
Column	Point to border at top of column and click when the mouse pointer changes to a small solid downward-pointing arrow. Or, position insertion point in column, click Select button (Table Tools Layout tab | Table group), and then click Select Column on the Select menu.
Row	Point to the left of the row and click when mouse pointer changes to a right-pointing block arrow. Or, position insertion point in row, click Select button (Table Tools Layout tab | Table group), and then click Select Row on the Select menu.
Multiple cells, rows, or columns adjacent to one another	Drag through cells, rows, or columns.
Multiple cells, rows, or columns not adjacent to one another	Select first cell, row, or column (as described above) and then hold down CTRL key while selecting next cell, row, or column.
Next cell	Press TAB key.
Previous cell	Press SHIFT+TAB.
Table	Point somewhere in table and then click table move handle that appears in upper-left corner of table. Or, position insertion point in table, click Select button (Table Tools Layout tab | Table group), and then click Select Table on the Select menu.

BTW

Resizing Table Columns and Rows

To change the width of a column or height of a row to an exact measurement, hold down the ALT key while dragging markers on the ruler. Or, enter values in the Table Column Width or Table Row Height text boxes (Table Tools Layout tab | Cell Size group).

BTW

Tab Character in Tables

In a table, the TAB key advances the insertion point from one cell to the next. To insert a tab character in a cell, you must press CTRL+TAB.

To Align Data in Cells

The next step is to change the alignment of the data in cells in the second, third, fourth, and fifth columns of the table. In addition to aligning text horizontally in a cell (left, center, or right), you can align it vertically within a cell (top, center, bottom). When the height of the cell is close to the same height as the text, however, differences in vertical alignment are not readily apparent, which is the case for this table. The following steps center data in cells.

1

- Select the cells in the second, third, fourth, and fifth columns using one of the techniques described in Table 3–4 on the previous page (Figure 3–65).

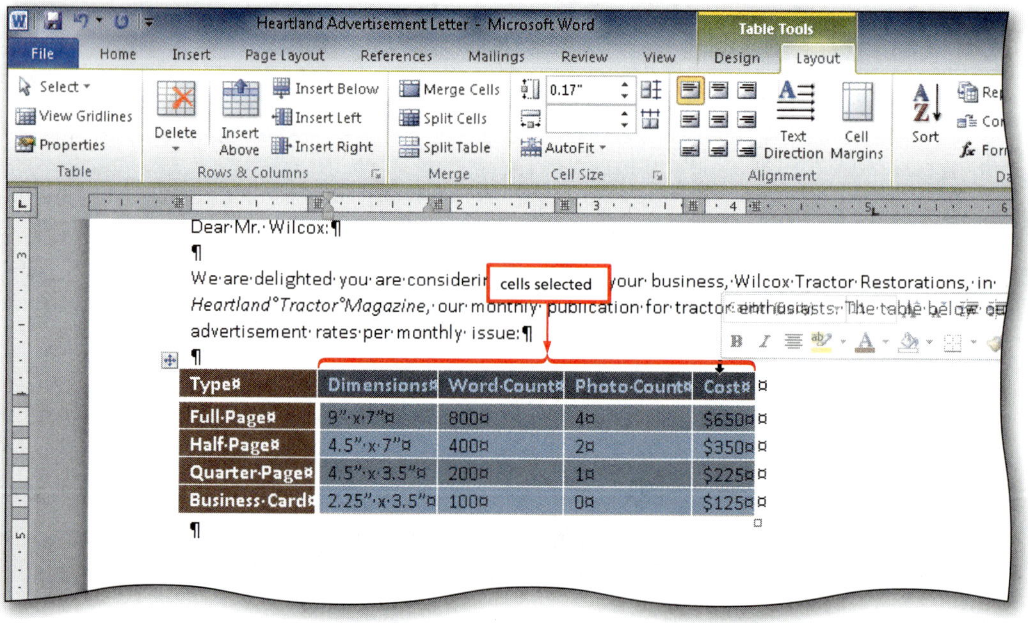

Figure 3–65

2

- Click the Align Top Center button (Table Tools Layout tab | Alignment group) to center the contents of the selected cells.
- Click in the table to remove the selection (Figure 3–66).

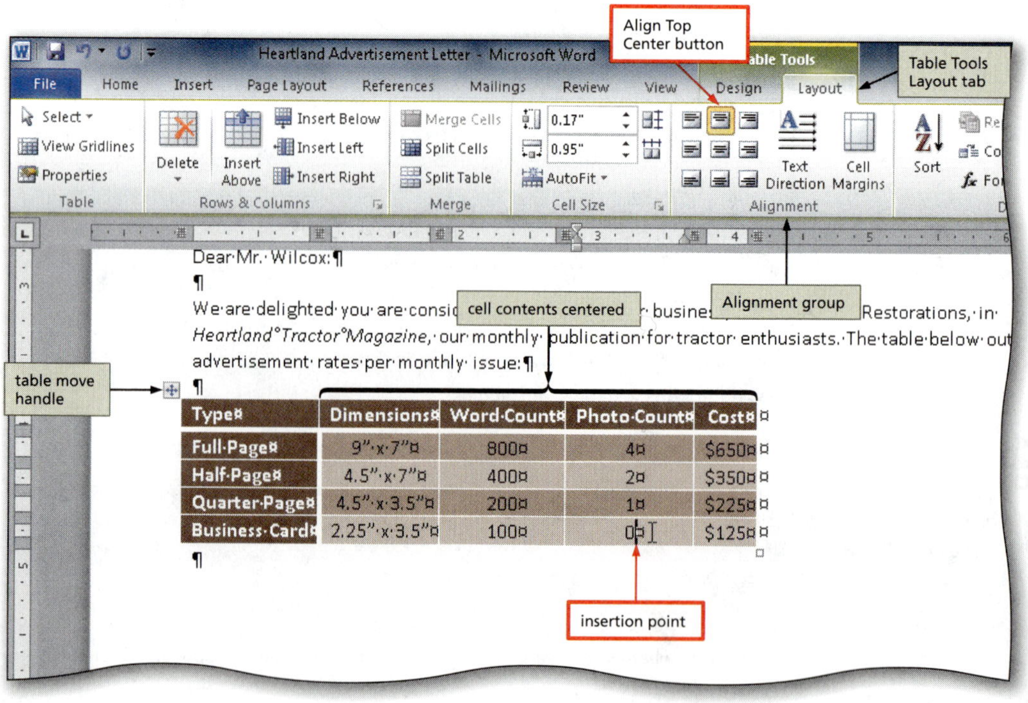

Figure 3–66

To Center a Table

When you first create a table, it is left-aligned, that is, flush with the left margin. In this letter, the table should be centered between the margins. To center a table, you first select the entire table. The following steps select and center a table using the Mini toolbar.

1

- Position the mouse pointer in the table so that the table move handle appears (shown in Figure 3–66).

Q&A What if the table move handle does not appear?

You also can select a table by clicking the Select button (Table Tools Layout tab | Table group) and then clicking Select Table on the menu.

2

- Click the table move handle to select the entire table (Figure 3–67).

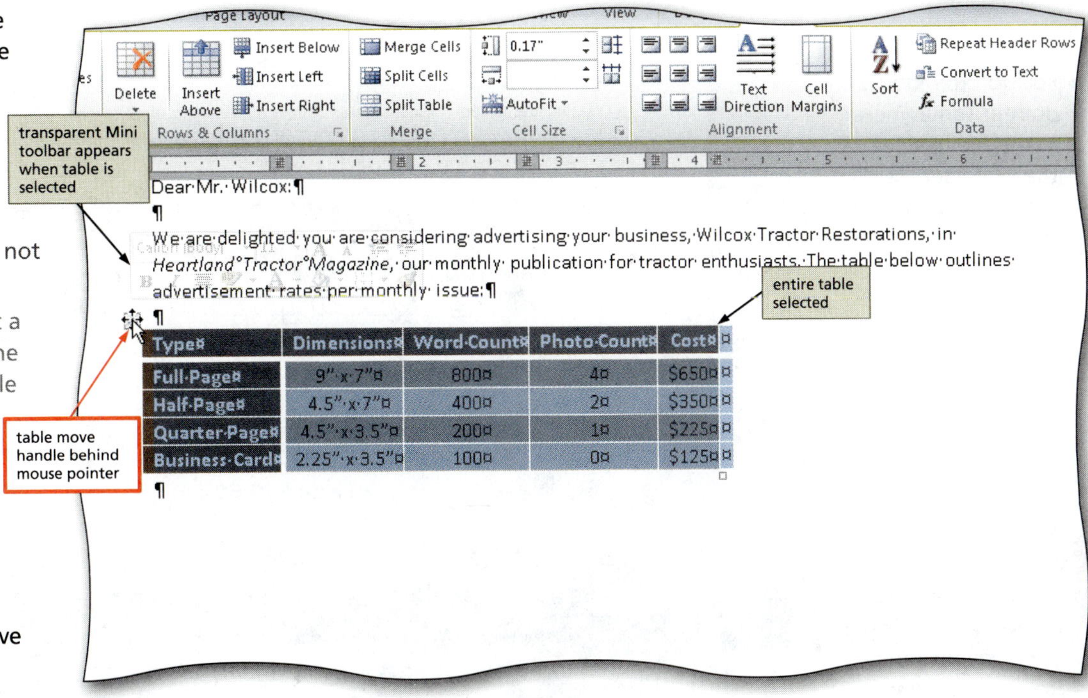

Figure 3–67

3

- Move the mouse pointer into the Mini toolbar, so that the toolbar changes to a bright toolbar. Click the Center button on the Mini toolbar to center the selected table between the left and right margins (Figure 3–68).

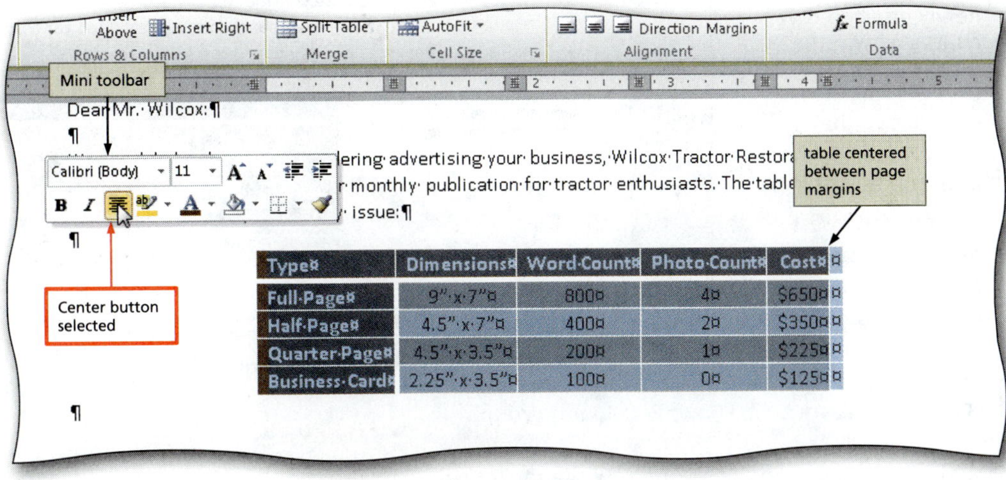

Figure 3–68

Q&A Could I have clicked the Center button on the Home tab?

Yes. If the command you want to use is not on the currently displayed tab on the Ribbon and it is available on the Mini toolbar, use the Mini toolbar instead of switching to a different tab. This technique minimizes mouse movement.

To Insert a Row in a Table

The next step is to insert a row at the top of the table because you want to place a title on the table. As discussed earlier, you can insert a row at the end of a table by positioning the insertion point in the bottom-right corner cell and then pressing the TAB key. You cannot use the TAB key to insert a row at the beginning or middle of a table. Instead, you use the Insert Rows Above or Insert Rows Below command. The following steps insert a row in a table.

1

- Position the mouse pointer somewhere in the first row of the table because you want to insert a row above this row (Figure 3–69).

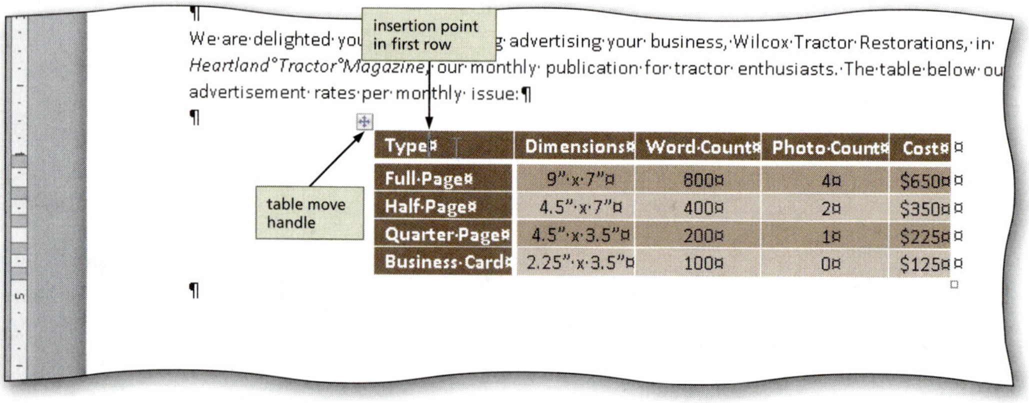

Figure 3–69

2

- Click the Insert Rows Above button (Table Tools Layout tab | Rows & Columns group) to insert a row above the row containing the insertion point and then select the newly inserted row (Figure 3–70).

Q&A Do I have to insert rows above the row containing the insertion point?

No. You can insert below the row containing the insertion point by clicking the Insert Rows Below button (Table Tools Layout tab | Rows & Columns group).

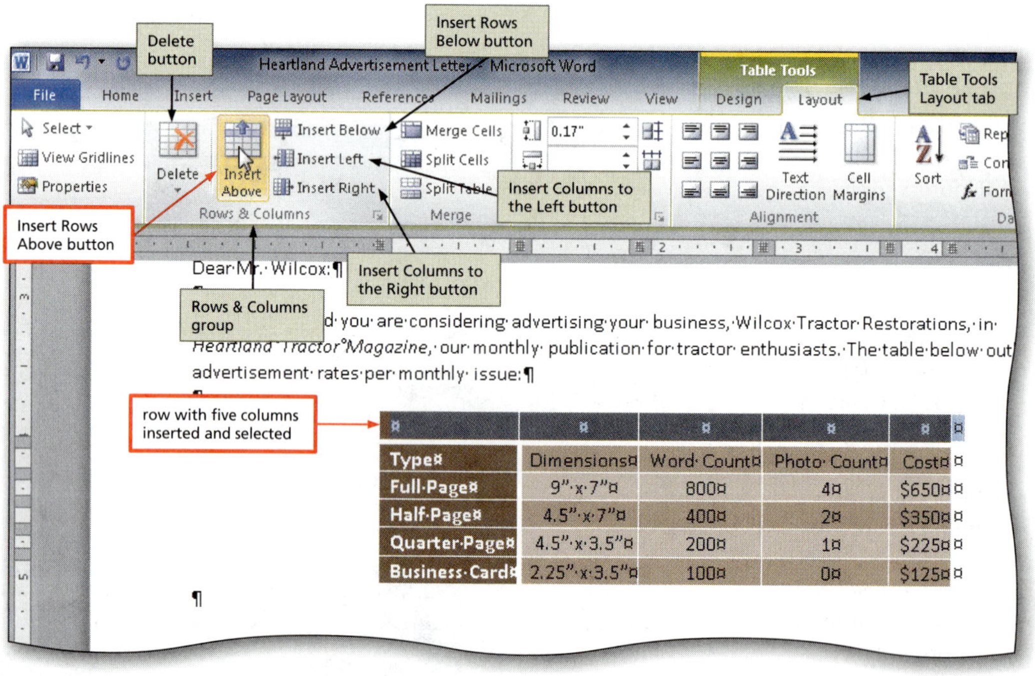

Figure 3–70

Q&A Why did the colors in the second row change?

The table style specifies to format the Header row differently, which is the first row.

Other Ways

1. Right-click row, point to Insert on shortcut menu, click desired command on Insert submenu

To Insert a Column in a Table

If, instead of inserting rows, you wanted to insert a column in a table, you would perform the following steps.

1. Position the insertion point in the column to the left or right of where you want to insert the column.
2. Click the Insert Columns to the Left button (Table Tools Layout tab | Rows & Columns group) to insert a column to the left of the current column, or click the Insert Columns to the Right button (Table Tools Layout tab | Rows & Columns group) to insert a column to the right of the current column. Or you could right-click the table, point to Insert on the shortcut menu, and click Insert Columns to the Left or Insert Columns to the Right on the Insert submenu.

BTW

Moving Tables
If you wanted to move a table to a new location, you would point to the upper-left corner of the table until the table move handle appears (shown in Figure 3–69), point to the table move handle, and the drag it to move the entire table to a new location.

Deleting Table Data

If you want to delete row(s) or delete column(s) from a table, position the insertion point in the row(s) or column(s) to delete, click the Delete button (Table Tools Layout tab | Rows & Columns group), and then click Delete Rows or Delete Columns on the Delete menu. Or, select the row or column to delete, right-click the selection, and then click Delete Rows or Delete Columns on the shortcut menu.

To delete the contents of a cell, select the cell contents and then press the DELETE or BACKSPACE key. You also can drag and drop or cut and paste the contents of cells. To delete an entire table, select the table, click the Delete button (Table Tools Layout tab | Rows & Columns group), and then click Delete Table on the Delete menu. To delete the contents of a table and leave an empty table, you would select the table and then press the DELETE key.

To Merge Cells

The top row of the table is to contain the table title, which should be centered above the columns of the table. The row just inserted has one cell for each column, in this case, five cells (shown in Figure 3–70). The title of the table, however, should be in a single cell that spans all rows. Thus, the following steps merge the five cells into a single cell.

1

- With the cells to merge selected (as shown in Figure 3–70), click the Merge Cells button (Table Tools Layout tab | Merge group) to merge the five cells into one cell (Figure 3–71).

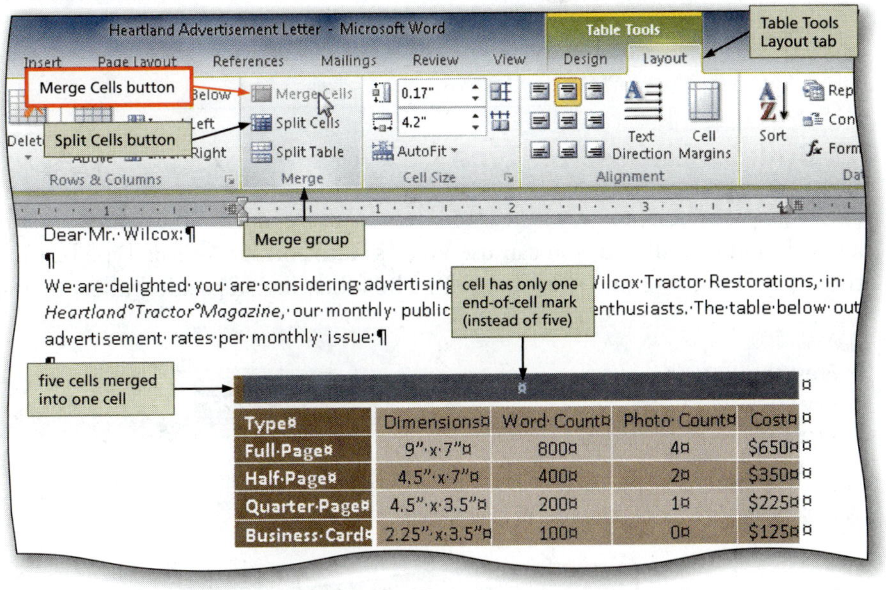

Figure 3–71

2

- Position the insertion point in the first row and then type **`Monthly Issue Advertisement Rates`** as the table title (Figure 3–72).

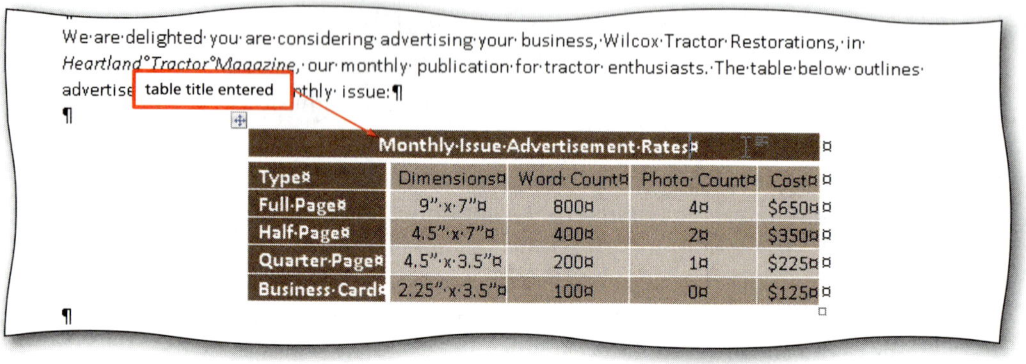

Figure 3–72

Other Ways

1. Right-click selected cells to merge, click Merge Cells on shortcut menu

To Split Table Cells

Instead of merging multiple cells into a single cell, sometimes you want to split a single cell into multiple cells. If you wanted to split cells, you would perform the following steps.

1. Position the insertion point in the cell to split.
2. Click the Split Cells button (Table Tools Layout tab | Merge group), or right-click the cell and then click Split Cells on the shortcut menu, to display the Split Cells dialog box.
3. Enter the number of columns and rows into which you want the cell split (Split Cells dialog box).
4. Click the OK button.

To Add More Text

The table now is complete. The next step is to enter text below the table. The following steps enter text.

1 Position the insertion point on the paragraph mark below the table and then press the ENTER key.

2 Type **`Please note that additional fees will be assessed if the word or photo counts exceed the limits listed above. We offer the following discounts:`** and then press the ENTER key (shown in Figure 3–73).

To Bullet a List as You Type

In Word Chapter 1, you learned how to apply bullets to existing paragraphs. If you know before you type that a list should be bulleted, you can use Word's AutoFormat As You Type feature to bullet the paragraphs as you type them (see Table 3–2 on page WD 162). The following steps add bullets to a list as you type.

1

- Press the ASTERISK key (*) as the first character on the line (Figure 3–73).

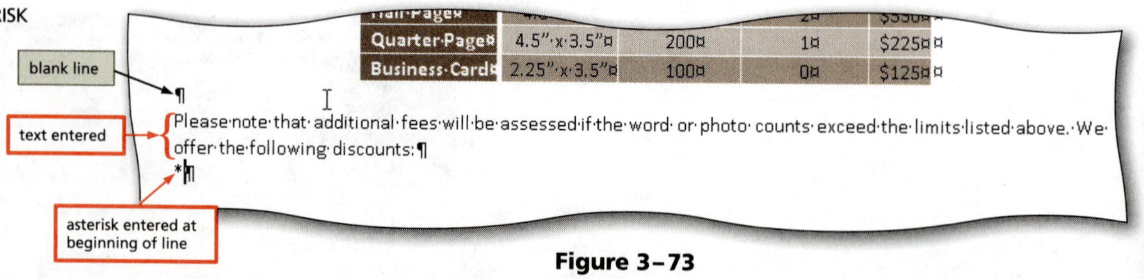

Figure 3–73

2

- Press the SPACEBAR to convert the asterisk to a bullet character.

Q&A

What if I did not want the asterisk converted to a bullet character?

You could undo the AutoFormat by clicking the Undo button, pressing CTRL+Z, clicking the AutoCorrect Options button that appears to the left of the bullet character as soon as you press the SPACEBAR, and then clicking Undo Automatic Bullets on the AutoCorrect Options menu, or by clicking the Bullets button (Home tab | Paragraph group).

- Type `10 percent discount for any advertisement that runs in three consecutive issues` as the first bulleted item.
- Press the ENTER key to place another bullet character at the beginning of the next line (Figure 3–74).

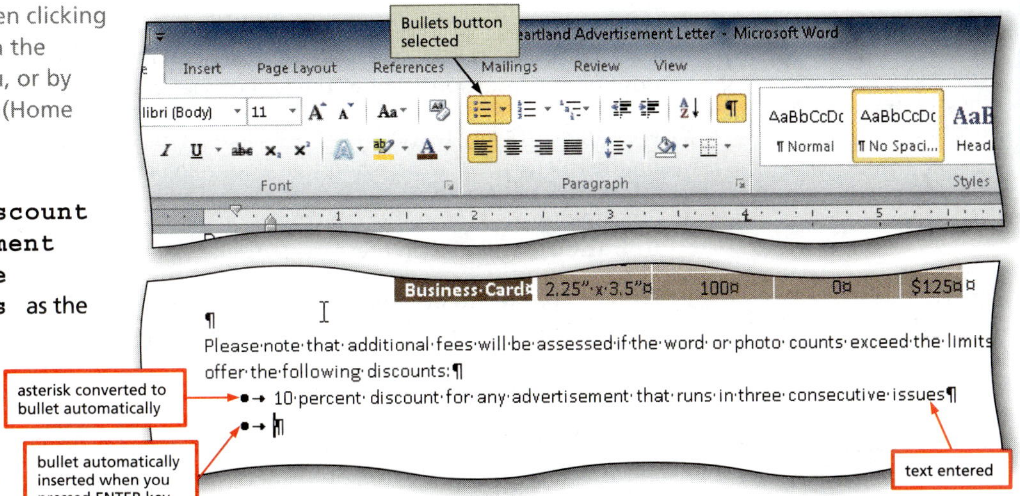

Figure 3–74

3

- Type `5 percent discount for a camera-ready advertisement (prepared using Microsoft Word at the proper size and with all words and photos in final layout form)` and then press the ENTER key.
- Type `3 percent discount if payment in full is submitted with order` and then press the ENTER key.
- Press the ENTER key to turn off automatic bullets as you type (Figure 3–75).

Q&A

Why did automatic bullets stop?

When you press the ENTER key without entering any text after the automatic bullet character, Word turns off the automatic bullets feature.

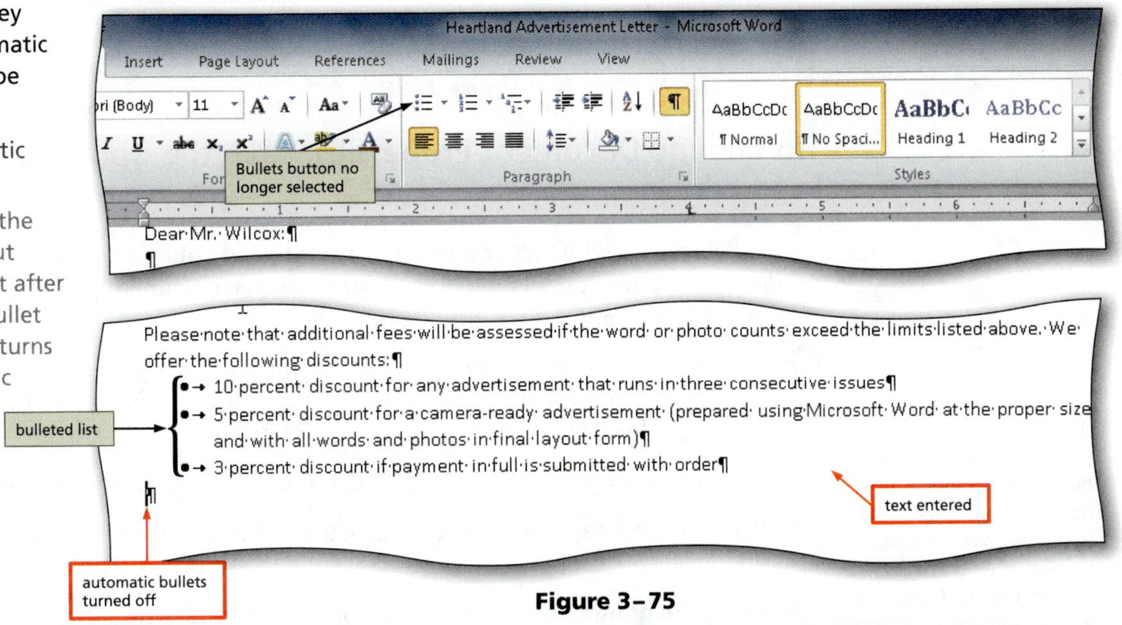

Figure 3–75

Other Ways	
1. Click Bullets button (Home tab | Paragraph group)	2. Right-click paragraph to be bulleted, point to Bullets on shortcut menu, click desired bullet style

BTW

BTWs
For a complete list of the BTWs found in the margins of the Office and Windows chapters in this book, visit the Microsoft Office and Concepts CouseMate Web site at www.cengagebrain.com and then nevigate to the BTW resource for this book.

To Enter More Text

The following steps enter the remainder of text in the letter.

1. Press the ENTER key and then type the paragraph shown in Figure 3–76, making certain you use the building block name, wtr, to insert the advertiser name.

2. If necessary, remove the hyperlink from the e-mail address by right-clicking the e-mail address and then clicking Remove Hyperlink on the shortcut menu. Press the END key to position the insertion point at the end of the line.

3. Press the ENTER key twice. Press the TAB key to position the insertion point at the 4" mark on the ruler. Type `Sincerely,` and then press the ENTER key four times.

4. Press the TAB key to position the insertion point at the 4" mark on the ruler. Type `Frank Urbanczyk` and then press the ENTER key.

5. Press the TAB key to position the insertion point at the 4" mark on the ruler. Type `President` as the final text in the business letter (Figure 3–76).

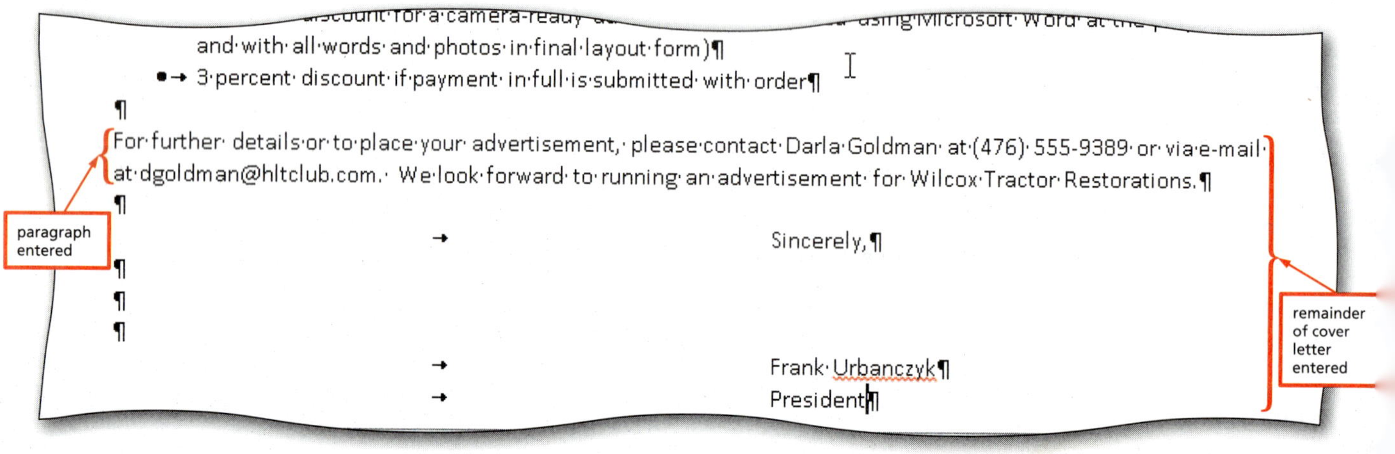

Figure 3–76

To Change Document Properties, Save the Document Again, and Print It

BTW

Conserving Ink and Toner
If you want to conserve ink or toner, you can instruct Word to print draft quality documents by clicking File on the Ribbon to open the Backstage view, clicking Options in the Backstage view to display the Word Options dialog box, clicking Advanced in the left pane (Word Options dialog box), scrolling to the Print area in the right pane, placing a check mark in the 'Use draft quality' check box, and then clicking the OK button. Then, use the Backstage view to print the document as usual.

Before saving the letter again, you want to add your name and course and section as document properties. The following steps change document properties, save the document again, and then print the document.

1. Display the Document Information Panel in the Word document window. If necessary, enter your name in the Author property, and enter your course and section in the Subject property. Close the Document Information Panel.

2. Click the Save button on the Quick Access Toolbar to overwrite the previously saved file.

3. Open the Backstage view and then click the Print tab in the Backstage view to display the Print gallery.

4. Verify the printer name that appears on the Printer Status button will print a hard copy of the document. If necessary, click the Printer Status button to display a list of available printer options and then click the desired printer to change the currently selected printer.

5. Click the Print button in the Print gallery to print the letter on the currently selected printer (shown in Figure 3–1 on page WD 139).

Addressing and Printing Envelopes and Mailing Labels

With Word, you can print address information on an envelope or on a mailing label. Computer-printed addresses look more professional than handwritten ones.

To Address and Print an Envelope

The following steps address and print an envelope. If you are in a lab environment, check with your instructor before performing these steps.

1

- Scroll through the letter to display the inside address in the document window.
- Drag through the inside address to select it (Figure 3–77).

Figure 3–77

2

- Display the Mailings tab.
- Click the Create Envelopes button (Mailings tab | Create group) to display the Envelopes and Labels dialog box.
- If necessary, click the Envelopes tab (Envelopes and Labels dialog box) (Figure 3–78).

3

- Insert an envelope in your printer, as shown in the Feed area of the dialog box (your Feed area may be different depending on your printer).

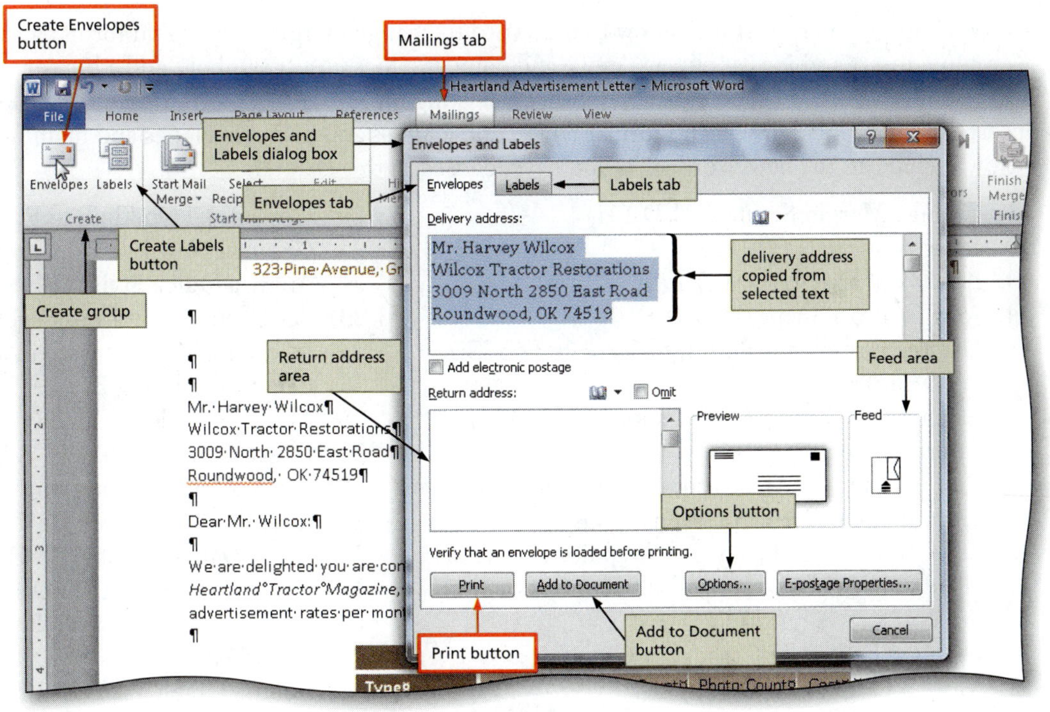

Figure 3–78

- Click the Print button (Envelopes and Labels dialog box) to print the envelope.

Envelopes and Labels

Instead of printing the envelope immediately, you can add it to the document by clicking the Add to Document button (Envelopes and Labels dialog box). To specify a different envelope or label type (identified by a number on the box of envelopes or labels), click the Options button (Envelopes and Labels dialog box).

Instead of printing an envelope, you can print a mailing label. To do this, click the Create Labels button (Mailings tab | Create group) (shown in Figure 3–78 on the previous page). Type the delivery address in the Delivery address box. To print the same address on all labels on the page, click 'Full page of the same label' in the Print area. Click the Print button (Envelopes and Labels dialog box) to print the label(s).

BTW **Quick Reference**
For a table that lists how to complete the tasks covered in the Office chapters in this book using the mouse, Ribbon, shortcut menu, and keyboard, see the Quick Reference Summary at the back of this book, or visit the Microsoft Office and Concepts CourseMate Web site at www.cengagebrain.com and then navigate to the Quick Reference resource for this book.

To Quit Word

This project now is complete. The following steps quit Word.

1. If you have one Word document open, click the Close button on the right side of the title bar to close the document and quit Word; or if you have multiple Word documents open, click File on the Ribbon to open the Backstage view and then click Exit in the Backstage view to close all open documents and quit Word.
2. If a Microsoft Word dialog box appears, click the Save button to save any changes made to the document since the last save.
3. If Word displays a dialog box asking if you want to save modified "Building Blocks", click the Save button.

Chapter Summary

In this chapter, you have learned how to use Word to change margins, insert and format a shape, change text wrapping, insert and format clip art, move and copy graphics, insert symbols, add a border, clear formatting, convert a hyperlink to regular text, create a file from an existing file, set and use tab stops, insert the current date, create and insert building blocks, insert and format tables, and address and print envelopes and mailing labels. The items listed below include all the new Word skills you have learned in this chapter.

1. Change Margin Settings (WD 141)
2. Insert a Shape (WD 142)
3. Apply a Shape Style (WD 144)
4. Add Text to a Shape (WD 145)
5. Use the Grow Font Button to Increase Font Size (WD 146)
6. Change an Object's Text Wrapping (WD 148)
7. Insert Clip Art (WD 148)
8. Resize a Graphic to a Percent of the Original (WD 150)
9. Change the Color of a Graphic (WD 151)
10. Set a Transparent Color in a Graphic (WD 152)
11. Adjust the Brightness and Contrast of a Graphic (WD 153)
12. Change the Border Color on a Graphic (WD 154)
13. Move a Graphic (WD 155)
14. Use Paste Options (WD 156)
15. Flip a Graphic (WD 157)
16. Insert a Symbol from the Symbol Dialog Box (WD 158)
17. Insert a Symbol from the Symbol Gallery (WD 159)
18. Bottom Border a Paragraph (WD 160)
19. Clear Formatting (WD 161)
20. Convert a Hyperlink to Regular Text (WD 163)
21. Create a New File from an Existing File (WD 165)
22. Apply a Quick Style (WD 166)
23. Set Custom Tab Stops (WD 169)
24. Insert the Current Date in a Document (WD 170)
25. Create a Building Block (WD 171)
26. Modify a Building Block (WD 173)
27. Insert a Building Block (WD 174)
28. Insert a Nonbreaking Space (WD 175)
29. Insert an Empty Table (WD 176)
30. Enter Data in a Table (WD 177)
31. Apply a Table Style (WD 179)
32. Resize Table Columns to Fit Table Contents (WD 180)
33. Align Data in Cells (WD 182)
34. Center a Table (WD 183)
35. Insert a Row in a Table (WD 184)
36. Insert a Column in a Table (WD 185)
37. Merge Cells (WD 185)
38. Split Table Cells (WD 186)
39. Bullet a List as You Type (WD 186)
40. Address and Print an Envelope (WD 189)

SAM If you have a SAM 2010 user profile, your instructor may have assigned an autogradable version of this assignment. If so, log into the SAM 2010 Web site at www.cengage.com/sam2010 to download the instruction and start files.

Learn It Online

Test your knowledge of chapter content and key terms.

Instructions: To complete the Learn It Online exercises, start your browser, visit the Microsoft Office and Concepts CourseMate Web site at www.cengagebrain.com, navigate to the Word Chapter 3 resources for this book, click the link for the exercise you want to complete, and then read the instructions.

Chapter Reinforcement TF, MC, and SA

A series of true/false, multiple choice, and short answer questions that test your knowledge of the chapter content.

Flash Cards

An interactive learning environment where you identify chapter key terms associated with displayed definitions.

Practice Test

A series of multiple choice questions that test your knowledge of chapter content and key terms.

Who Wants To Be a Computer Genius?

An interactive game that challenges your knowledge of chapter content in the style of a television quiz show.

Wheel of Terms

An interactive game that challenges your knowledge of chapter key terms in the style of the television show *Wheel of Fortune.*

Crossword Puzzle Challenge

A crossword puzzle that challenges your knowledge of key terms presented in the chapter.

Apply Your Knowledge

Reinforce the skills and apply the concepts you learned in this chapter.

Working with Tabs and a Table

Note: To complete this assignment, you will be required to use the Data Files for Students. See the inside back cover of this book for instructions on downloading the Data Files for Students, or contact your instructor for information about accessing the required files.

Instructions: Start Word. Create a new document from the file called Apply 3-1 Projected College Expenses Draft, located on the Data Files for Students. The document is a Word table that you are to edit and format. The revised table is shown in Figure 3–79.

Projected College Expenses

	Freshman	Sophomore	Junior	Senior
Room & Board	3390.00	3627.30	3881.21	4152.90
Tuition & Books	4850.50	5189.50	5552.72	5941.46
Entertainment	635.00	679.45	727.01	777.90
Cell Phone	359.88	365.78	372.81	385.95
Miscellaneous	325.00	347.75	372.09	398.14
Clothing	540.25	577.80	618.29	661.52
Total	$10,100.63	$10,787.58	$11,524.13	$12,317.87

Figure 3–79

Continued >

Apply Your Knowledge *continued*

Perform the following tasks:

1. In the line containing the table title, Projected College Expenses, remove the tab stop at the 1" mark on the ruler.
2. Set a centered tab at the 3" mark on the ruler.
3. Bold the characters in the title. Use the Grow Font button to increase their font size to 14. Change their color to Dark Blue, Text 2, Darker 25%.
4. In the table, delete the row containing the Food expenses.
5. Insert a new row at the bottom of the table. In the first cell of the new row, enter Total in the cell. Enter these values in the next three cells: Freshman – $10,100.63; Sophomore – $10,787.58; Senior – $12,317.87.
6. Insert a column between the Sophomore and Senior columns. Fill in the column as follows: Column Title – Junior; Room & Board – 3881.21; Tuition & Books – 5552.72; Entertainment – 727.01; Cell Phone – 372.81; Miscellaneous – 372.09; Clothing – 618.29; Total – $11,524.13.
7. In the Table Style Options group (Table Tools Design tab), these check boxes should have check marks: Header Row, Total Row, Banded Rows, and First Column. The Last Column and Banded Columns check boxes should not be selected.
8. Apply the Medium Grid 3 - Accent 2 style to the table.
9. Make all columns as wide as their contents (AutoFit Contents).
10. Center the cells containing the column headings.
11. Right-align all cells containing numbers in the table.
12. Center the table between the left and right margins of the page.
13. Change the document properties, as specified by your instructor.
14. Save the document using the file name, Apply 3-1 Projected College Expenses Modified and submit it in the format specified by your instructor.

Extend Your Knowledge

Extend the skills you learned in this chapter and experiment with new skills. You may need to use Help to complete the assignment.

Working with Formulas, Clip Art, Sorting, Picture Bullets, Tabs, and Mailing Labels

Note: To complete this assignment, you will be required to use the Data Files for Students. See the inside back cover of this book for instructions on downloading the Data Files for Students, or contact your instructor for information about accessing the required files.

Instructions: Start Word. Create a new document from the file called Extend 3-1 Herbals Letter Draft, located on the Data Files for Students. You will enter formulas in the table, change the clip art to Web clip art, change the table style, sort paragraphs, use picture bullets, move tabs, print mailing labels, and work with the Clip Organizer.

Perform the following tasks:

1. Use Help to learn about entering formulas, clip art from the Web, sorting, picture bullets, and printing mailing labels.
2. Use the Formula dialog box (Figure 3–80) to add formulas to the last column in the table so that the total due displays for each item; be sure to enter a number format so that the products are

displayed with dollar signs. Then, add formulas to the last row in the table so that the total quantity and total due are displayed, also with dollar signs. Write down the formulas that Word uses to find the product of values in the rows and to sum the values in a column.

3. Delete the current clip art images in the letterhead. Use the Clip Art pane to locate appropriate clip art from the Web, make the clip available offline, and insert an image on each side of the business name in the letterhead.
4. Change the table style. One at a time, select and deselect each check box in the Table Style Options group. Write down the function of each check box: Header Row, Total Row, Banded Rows, First Column, Last Column, and Banded Columns. Select the check boxes you prefer for the table.
5. Sort the paragraphs in the bulleted list.
6. Change the bullets in the bulleted list to picture bullets.
7. Move the tab stops in the date line, complimentary close, and signature block from the 3.5" mark to the 4" mark on the ruler.
8. Change the document properties, as specified by your instructor. Save the revised document and then submit it in the format specified by your instructor.
9. Print a single mailing label for the letter.
10. Print a full page of mailing labels, each containing the address shown in Figure 3–80.
11. If your instructor approves, start the Clip Organizer. How many collections appear? Expand the Office Collections. Copy one of the Academic clips to the Favorites folder in the My Collections folder. Locate the clip you made available offline in Step 3 and then preview it. What are five of its properties? Add a keyword to the clip. Delete the clip you made available offline.

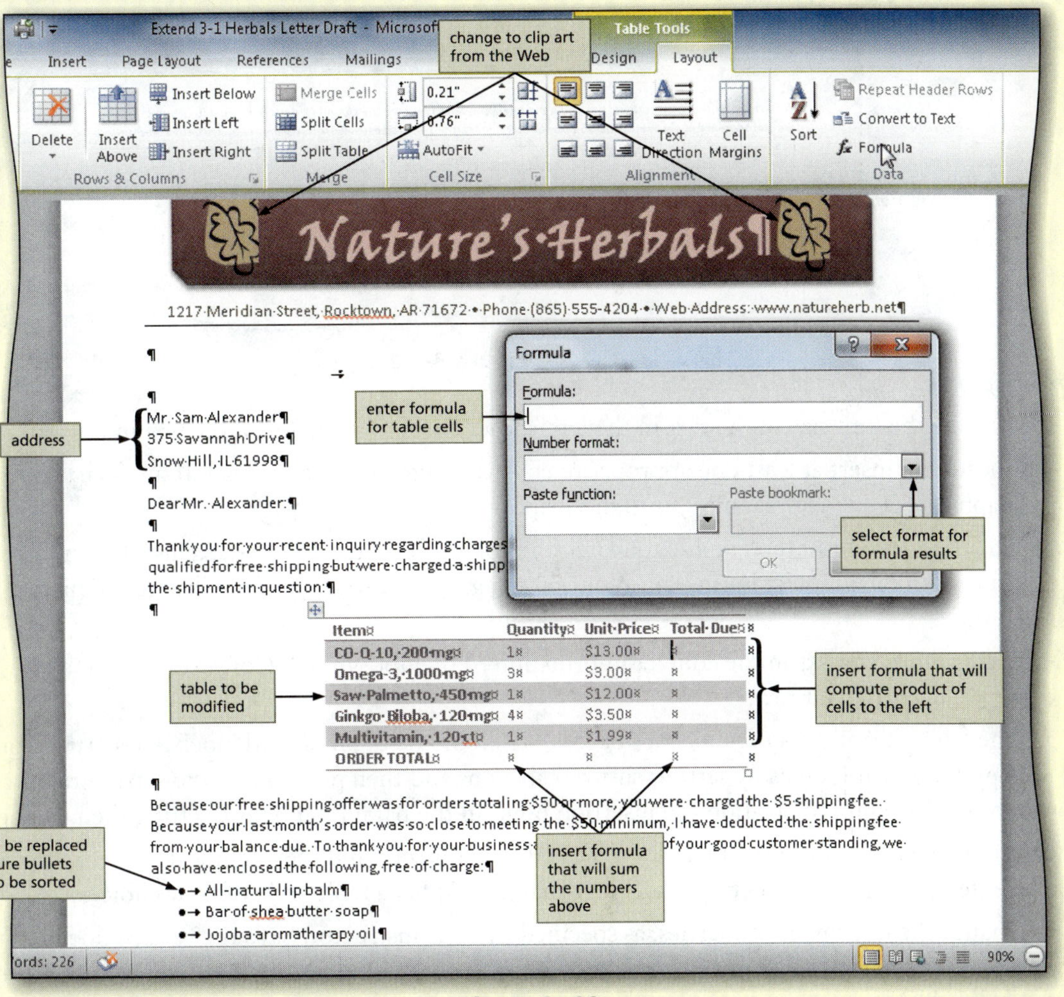

Figure 3–80

Make It Right

Analyze a document and correct all errors and/or improve the design.

Formatting a Business Letter

Note: To complete this assignment, you will be required to use the Data Files for Students. See the inside back cover of this book for instructions on downloading the Data Files for Students, or contact your instructor for information about accessing the required files.

Instructions: Start Word. Create a new document from the file called Make It Right 3-1 Scholarship Letter Draft, located on the Data Files for Students. The document is a business letter that is missing elements and is formatted poorly or incorrectly (Figure 3–81). You are to insert and format clip art in the letterhead, change the color of the text and graphic(s), insert symbols, remove a hyperlink, change the letter style from block to modified block, and format the table.

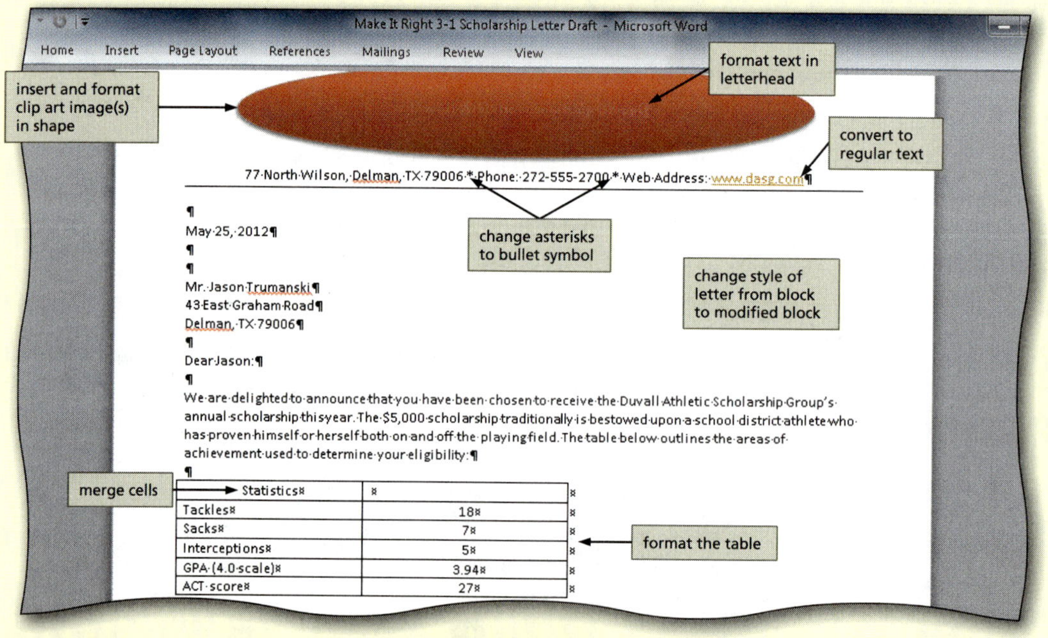

Figure 3–81

Perform the following tasks:

1. Increase the font size of the text in the letterhead. Change the color of the text in the letterhead.
2. Locate and insert at least one appropriate clip art image in the letterhead. If necessary, resize the graphic(s). Move the graphic(s) into the shape.
3. Change the color of the graphic to match the color of the text or shape. Adjust the brightness and contrast of the graphic. Format one color in the graphic as transparent. Change the picture border color.
4. Change the asterisks in the contact information to the dot symbol. Convert the Web address hyperlink to regular text.
5. The letter currently is the block letter style. It should be the modified block letter style. Format the appropriate paragraphs by setting custom tab stops and then positioning those paragraphs at the tab stops. Be sure to position the insertion point in the paragraph before setting the tab stop.
6. Merge the two cells in the first row of the table to one cell and then center the title in the cell. Center the entire table between the page margins. Apply a table style of your choice.
7. Change the document properties, as specified by your instructor. Save the revised document using the file name, Make It Right 3-1 Scholarship Letter Modified, and then submit it in the format specified by your instructor.

In the Lab

Design and/or create a document using the guidelines, concepts, and skills presented in this chapter. Labs are listed in order of increasing difficulty.

Lab 1: Creating a Letter with a Letterhead

Problem: As a consultant for DataLock Storage, you respond to queries from potential customers. One letter you prepare is shown in Figure 3–82.

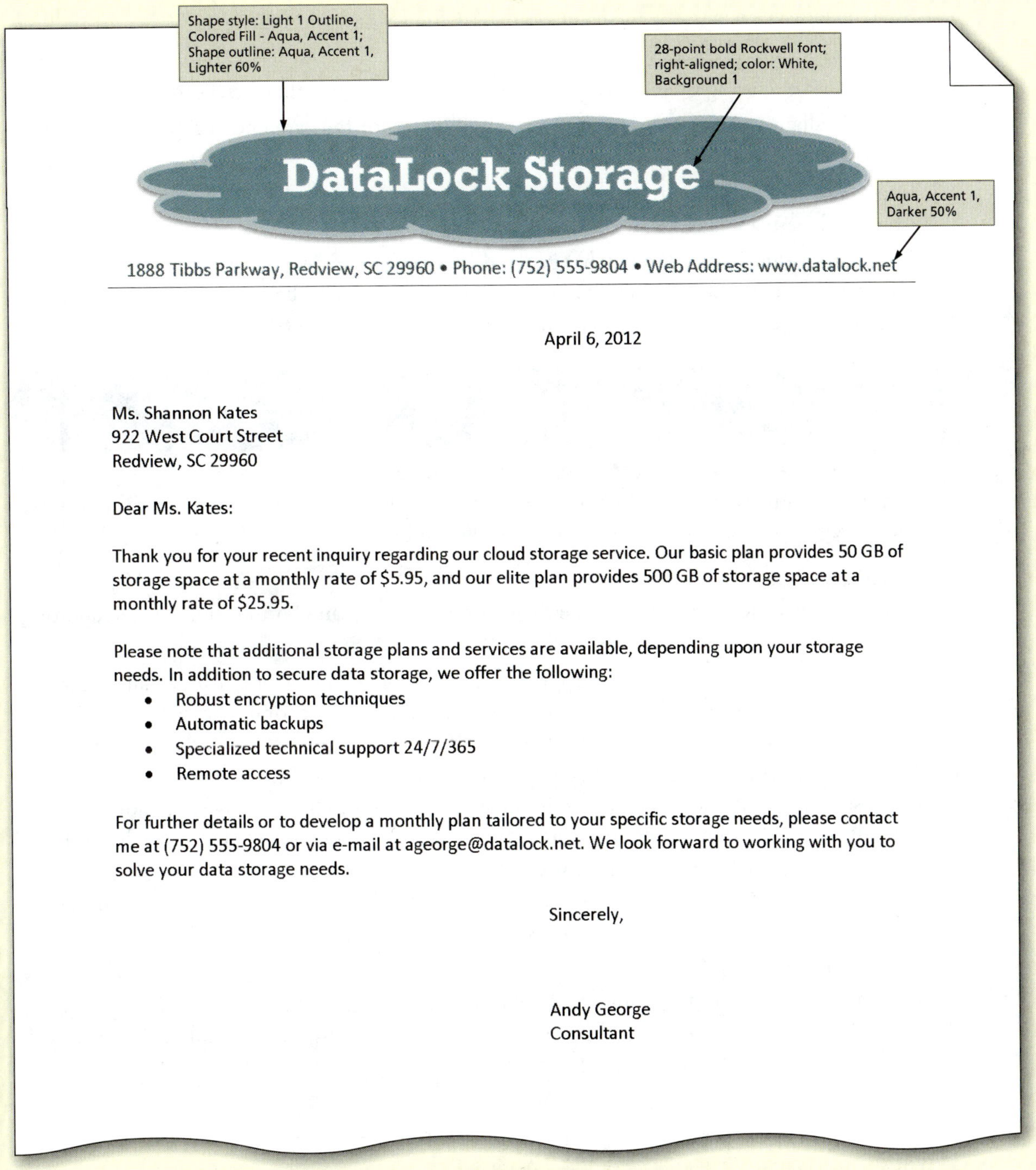

DataLock Storage

1888 Tibbs Parkway, Redview, SC 29960 • Phone: (752) 555-9804 • Web Address: www.datalock.net

April 6, 2012

Ms. Shannon Kates
922 West Court Street
Redview, SC 29960

Dear Ms. Kates:

Thank you for your recent inquiry regarding our cloud storage service. Our basic plan provides 50 GB of storage space at a monthly rate of $5.95, and our elite plan provides 500 GB of storage space at a monthly rate of $25.95.

Please note that additional storage plans and services are available, depending upon your storage needs. In addition to secure data storage, we offer the following:

- Robust encryption techniques
- Automatic backups
- Specialized technical support 24/7/365
- Remote access

For further details or to develop a monthly plan tailored to your specific storage needs, please contact me at (752) 555-9804 or via e-mail at ageorge@datalock.net. We look forward to working with you to solve your data storage needs.

Sincerely,

Andy George
Consultant

Figure 3–82

Continued >

STUDENT ASSIGNMENTS

In the Lab *continued*

Perform the following tasks:

1. Change the theme colors to Technic.
2. Create the letterhead shown at the top of Figure 3–82 on the previous page, following these guidelines:
   a. Insert the cloud shape at an approximate height of 0.95" and width of 5.85". Change text wrapping for the shape to Top and Bottom. Add the company name, DataLock Storage, to the shape. Format the shape and its text as indicated in the figure.
   b. Insert the bullet symbols as shown in the contact information. Remove the hyperlink format from the Web address. If necessary, clear formatting after entering the bottom border.
   c. Save the letterhead with the file name, Lab 3-1 Cloud Storage Letterhead.
3. Create the letter shown in Figure 3–82 using the modified block letter style, following these guidelines:
   a. Apply the No Spacing Quick Style to the document text (below the letterhead).
   b. Set a left-aligned tab stop at the 3.5" mark on the ruler for the date line, complimentary close, and signature block. Insert the current date.
   c. Bullet the list as you type it.
   d. Convert the e-mail address to regular text.
   e. Check the spelling of the letter. Change the document properties, as specified by your instructor. Save the letter with Lab 3-1 Cloud Storage Letter as the file name.
4. If your instructor permits, address and print an envelope or a mailing label for the letter.

In the Lab

Lab 2: Creating a Letter with a Letterhead and Table

Problem: As head librarian at Jonner Public Library, you are responsible for sending confirmation letters for class registrations. You prepare the letter shown in Figure 3–83.

Perform the following tasks:

1. Change the theme colors to Trek. Change the margins to 1" top and bottom and .75" left and right.
2. Create the letterhead shown at the top of Figure 3–83, following these guidelines:
   a. Insert the down ribbon shape at an approximate height of 1" and width of 7". Change text wrapping for the shape to Top and Bottom. Add the library name to the shape. Format the shape and its text as indicated in the figure.
   b. Insert the clip art image, resize it, change text wrapping to Top and Bottom, move it to the left of the shape, and format it as indicated in the figure. Copy the clip art image and move the copy of the image to the right of the shape, as shown in the figure. Flip the copied image horizontally.
   c. Insert the black small square symbols as shown in the contact information. Remove the hyperlink format from the Web address. If necessary, clear formatting after entering the bottom border.
   d. Save the letterhead with the file name, Lab 3-2 Library Letterhead.
3. Create the letter shown in Figure 3–83, following these guidelines:
   a. Apply the No Spacing Quick Style to the document text (below the letterhead).
   b. Set a left-aligned tab stop at the 4" mark on the ruler for the date line, complimentary close, and signature block. Insert the current date.
   c. Insert and center the table. Format the table as specified in the figure.
   d. Bullet the list as you type it. Convert the e-mail address to regular text.
   e. Check the spelling of the letter. Change the document properties, as specified by your instructor. Save the letter with Lab 3-2 Library Letter as the file name.
4. If your instructor permits, address and print an envelope or a mailing label for the letter.

Shape style: Colored Fill - Orange, Accent 1

24-point bold Harrington font, centered

Clip art search text: information; Clip art color: Orange, Accent color 6 Light

Orange, Accent 1, Darker 50%

Jonner Public Library

4992 Surrey Court, Jonner, MA 02198 ▪ 291-555-9454 ▪ Web Address: www.jpl.net

March 10, 2012

Mr. Brent Jackson
5153 Anlyn Drive
Jonner, MA 02198

Dear Mr. Jackson:

Thank you for registering online for our spring classes. As a library patron, you are aware that we offer a great deal more than books and magazines. The table below outlines the classes for which you have registered, along with the dates and locations:

Table style: Medium Grid 3 - Accent 1; Table style options: Header Row and Banded Columns

Class	Date	Location
Intro to Windows 7	April 10	Room 10B
eBay Basics	April 18	Room 24C
Genealogy Searches	April 24	Room 10B
Overview of Office 2010	April 28	Room 22A

Note that all classes, regardless of date, begin at 10:00 a.m. and last four hours. Although no materials or textbooks are required for the classes, you are strongly encouraged to bring the following items:

- Pens, pencils, or other writing implements
- Blank CD or DVD to store documents and notes created during class
- Notebook or loose-leaf binder for handwritten notes
- Your valid library card to verify enrollment eligibility

Please note that no food or drinks are allowed in any of our computer facilities. If you have any questions or would like to register for additional courses, please contact me at (291) 555-9454 or via e-mail at mtlawrence@jpl.net.

Again, thank you for your interest in and continued patronage of Jonner Public Library. We look forward to seeing you when your first class begins.

Sincerely,

Marcia Lawrence
Head Librarian

Figure 3–83

In the Lab

Lab 3: Creating a Letter with a Letterhead and Table

Problem: As president of the County Education Board, you communicate with schools in your district. One of the schools has just been awarded a four-star rating.

Instructions: Prepare the letter shown in Figure 3–84. Change the theme colors to Pushpin. Change the margins to 1" top and bottom and .75" left and right. Follow the guidelines in the modified semi-block letter style. Use proper spacing between elements of the letter. After entering the inside address,

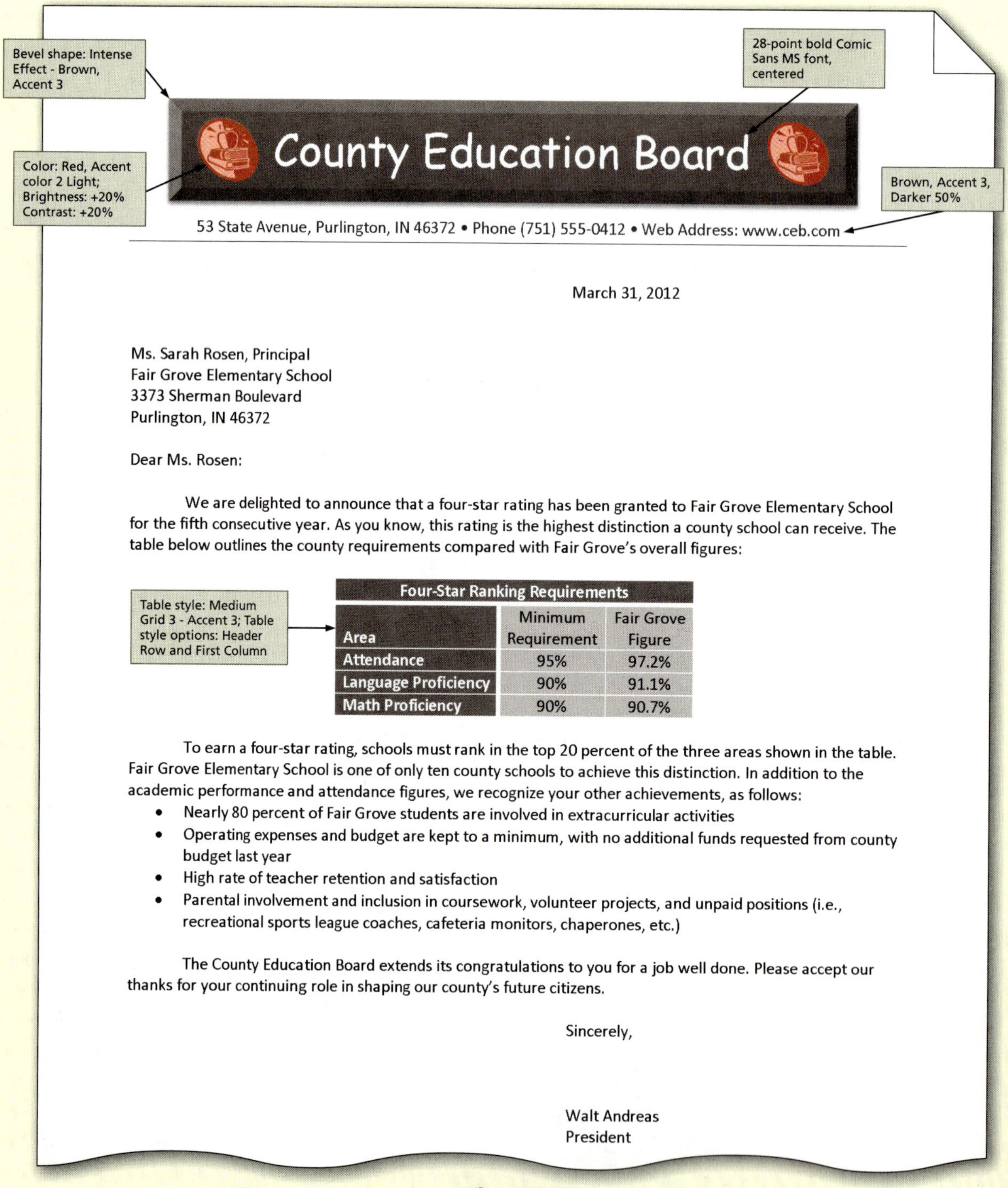

County Education Board

53 State Avenue, Purlington, IN 46372 • Phone (751) 555-0412 • Web Address: www.ceb.com

March 31, 2012

Ms. Sarah Rosen, Principal
Fair Grove Elementary School
3373 Sherman Boulevard
Purlington, IN 46372

Dear Ms. Rosen:

We are delighted to announce that a four-star rating has been granted to Fair Grove Elementary School for the fifth consecutive year. As you know, this rating is the highest distinction a county school can receive. The table below outlines the county requirements compared with Fair Grove's overall figures:

Four-Star Ranking Requirements		
Area	Minimum Requirement	Fair Grove Figure
Attendance	95%	97.2%
Language Proficiency	90%	91.1%
Math Proficiency	90%	90.7%

To earn a four-star rating, schools must rank in the top 20 percent of the three areas shown in the table. Fair Grove Elementary School is one of only ten county schools to achieve this distinction. In addition to the academic performance and attendance figures, we recognize your other achievements, as follows:

- Nearly 80 percent of Fair Grove students are involved in extracurricular activities
- Operating expenses and budget are kept to a minimum, with no additional funds requested from county budget last year
- High rate of teacher retention and satisfaction
- Parental involvement and inclusion in coursework, volunteer projects, and unpaid positions (i.e., recreational sports league coaches, cafeteria monitors, chaperones, etc.)

The County Education Board extends its congratulations to you for a job well done. Please accept our thanks for your continuing role in shaping our county's future citizens.

Sincerely,

Walt Andreas
President

Figure 3–84

create a building block for Fair Grove Elementary School and insert the building block whenever you have to enter the school name. Resize table columns to fit contents. Check the spelling of the letter. Change the document properties, as specified by your instructor. Save the letter with Lab 3-3 Education Board Letter as the file name.

Cases and Places

Apply your creative thinking and problem solving skills to design and implement a solution.

Note: To complete these assignments, you may be required to use the Data Files for Students. See the inside back cover of this book for instructions on downloading the Data Files for Students, or contact your instructor for information about accessing the required files.

1: Create a Letter to a Potential Employer

Academic

As a student about to graduate, you are actively seeking employment in your field and have located an advertisement for a job in which you are interested. You decide to write a letter to the potential employer: Ms. Janice Tremont at Home Health Associates, 554 Mountain View Lane, Blue Dust, MO 64319.

The draft wording for the letter is as follows: I am responding to your advertisement for the nursing position in the *Blue Dust Press*. I have tailored my activities and education for a career in geriatric medicine. This month, I will graduate with concentrations in Geriatric Medicine (24 hours), Osteopathic Medicine (12 hours), and Holistic Nursing (9 hours). In addition to receiving my bachelor degree in nursing, I have enhanced my education by participating in the following activities: volunteered at Blue Dust's free health care clinic; attended several continuing education and career-specific seminars, including An Aging Populace, Care of the Homebound, and Special Needs of the Elderly; completed one-semester internship at Blue Dust Community Hospital in spring semester of 2012; completed Certified Nursing Assistant (CNA) program at Blue Dust Community College; and worked as nurse's aide for two years during college. I look forward to an interview so that we can discuss the position you offer and my qualifications. With my background and education, I am confident that I will make a positive contribution to Home Health Associates.

The letter should contain a letterhead that uses a shape and clip art, a table (use a table to present the areas of concentration), and a bulleted list (use a bulleted list to present the activities). Insert nonbreaking spaces in the newspaper name. Use the concepts and techniques presented in this chapter to create and format a letter according to the modified block style, creating appropriate paragraph breaks and rewording the draft as necessary. Use your personal information for contact information in the letter. Be sure to check the spelling and grammar of the finished letter. Submit your assignment in the format specified by your instructor.

2: Create a Letter Requesting Donations

Personal

As an alumnus of your historic high school, you are concerned that the building is being considered for demolition. You decide to write a letter to another graduate: Mr. Jim Lemon, 87 Travis Parkway, Vigil, CT 06802.

The draft wording for the letter is as follows: As a member of the class of 1988, you, like many others, probably have many fond memories of our alma mater, Vigil East High School. I recently learned that the building is being considered for demolition because of its age and structural integrity.

Continued >

Cases and Places *continued*

As a result, I have decided to call upon the many graduating classes of the school to band together and save the historic building from demolition. According to the documents I have reviewed and information from meetings I have attended, a minimum of $214,000 is necessary to save the school and bring it up to code. Once the repairs are made, I plan to start the process of having it declared an historic landmark. You can help by donating your time, skills, or money. We need skilled tradesmen, including carpenters, roofers, plumbers, and electricians, as well as laborers. In addition, we are asking for monetary donations, as follows, although donations in any amount will be accepted gladly: a donation of $100 categorizes you as a Save Our School Friend, $250 a Patron, and $500 a Benefactor. Once our monetary goal has been reached, the necessary repairs and replacements will be made as follows: Phase I: roof and exterior, Phase II: electrical and plumbing, and Phase III: interior walls, trim, flooring, and fixtures. I hope you will join our conservation efforts so that Vigil East High School will continue to stand proudly for many more years. If you have questions, please contact me at the phone number or e-mail address above. I hope to hear from you soon.

The letter should contain a letterhead that uses a shape and clip art, a table (use a table to present the Save Our School donor categories), and a bulleted list (use a bulleted list to present the phases). Use the concepts and techniques presented in this chapter to create and format a letter according to the modified block style, creating appropriate paragraph breaks and rewording the draft as necessary. Use your personal information for contact information in the letter and Save Our School as the text in the letterhead. Be sure to check spelling and grammar of the finished letter. Submit your assignment in the format specified by your instructor.

3: Create a Confirmation Letter

Professional

As coordinator for Condor Parks and Recreation, you send letters to confirm registration for activities. You write a confirmation letter to this registrant: Ms. Tracey Li, 52 West 15th Street, Harpville, KY 42194. Condor Parks and Recreation is located at 2245 Community Place, Harpville, KY 42194; phone number is (842) 555-0444; and Web address is www.condorparks.com.

The draft wording for the letter is as follows: Thank you for your interest in our new spring activities recently listed in the *Condor Daily Press*. The courses for which you have enrolled, along with their dates and times are Introductory Golf Clinic on May 5 – 6 from 4:00 – 6:00 p.m. at a cost of $25, Recreational League Volleyball on April 30 – May 28 from 7:30 – 9:00 p.m. at a cost of $130, Pilates on May 30 – June 27 from 8:00 – 9:00 p.m. at a cost of $75, and Intermediate Golf Clinic on June 9 – 10 from 12:00 – 2:00 p.m. at a cost of $30. By paying your annual $25 parks and recreation fee, you also are entitled to the following benefits: free access to racquetball and tennis courts, on a first-come-first-served basis; attendance at any park-sponsored events, including plays, musical performances, and festivals; and free parking at any parks and recreation facility. Please confirm your registration by calling me at [enter your phone number here] or via e-mail at [enter your e-mail address here]. Thank you for your interest in Condor Parks and Recreation offerings. We look forward to seeing you at upcoming events.

The letter should contain a letterhead that uses a shape and clip art, a table (use a table to present the courses enrolled), and a bulleted list (use a bulleted list to present the benefits). Insert nonbreaking spaces in the newspaper name. Use the concepts and techniques presented in this chapter to create and format a letter according to the modified block style, creating appropriate paragraph breaks and rewording the draft as necessary. Be sure to check spelling and grammar of the finished letter. Submit your assignment in the format specified by your instructor.

1 Creating and Editing a Presentation with Clip Art

Objectives

You will have mastered the material in this chapter when you can:

- Select a document theme
- Create a title slide and a text slide with a multi-level bulleted list
- Add new slides and change slide layouts
- Insert clips and pictures into a slide with and without a content placeholder
- Move and size clip art
- Change font size and color
- Bold and italicize text
- Duplicate a slide
- Arrange slides
- Select slide transitions
- View a presentation in Slide Show view
- Print a presentation

1 Creating and Editing a Presentation with Clip Art

Introduction

A PowerPoint **presentation,** also called a **slide show**, can help you deliver a dynamic, professional-looking message to an audience. PowerPoint allows you to produce slides to use in an academic, business, or other environment. One of the more common uses of these slides is to enhance an oral presentation. A speaker may desire to convey information, such as urging students to volunteer at a fund-raising event, explaining changes in employee compensation packages, or describing a new laboratory procedure. The PowerPoint slides should reinforce the speaker's message and help the audience retain the information presented. Custom slides can fit your specific needs and contain diagrams, charts, tables, pictures, shapes, video, sound, and animation effects to make your presentation more effective. An accompanying handout gives audience members reference notes and review material for your presentation.

Project Planning Guidelines

The process of developing a presentation that communicates specific information requires careful analysis and planning. As a starting point, establish why the presentation is needed. Next, analyze the intended audience for the presentation and its unique needs. Then, gather information about the topic and decide what to include in the presentation. Finally, determine the presentation design and style that will be most successful at delivering the message. Details of these guidelines are provided in Appendix A. In addition, each project in the Office chapters in this book provides practical applications of these planning considerations.

Project — Presentation with Bulleted Lists and Clip Art

In this chapter's project, you will follow proper design guidelines and learn to use PowerPoint to create, save, and print the slides shown in Figures 1–1a through 1–1e. The objective is to produce a presentation, called It Is Easy Being Green, to help consumers understand basic steps they can take to save energy in their homes. This slide show has a variety of clip art and visual elements to add interest and illustrate energy-cutting measures. Some of the text has formatting and color enhancements. Transitions help one slide flow gracefully into the next during a slide show. In addition, you will print a handout of your slides to distribute to audience members.

BTW

Energy-Saving Information

The U.S. Department of Energy's Web site has myriad information available on the topics of energy efficiency and renewable energy. These features can provide news and product research that you can share with audiences with the help of a PowerPoint presentation.

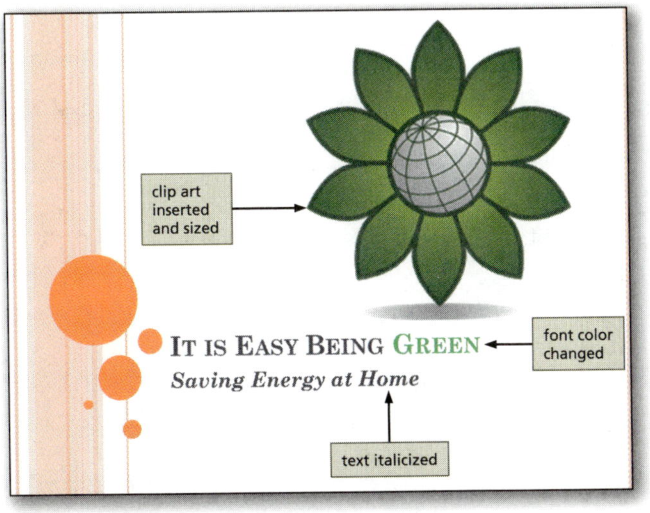

(a) Slide 1 (Title Slide with Clip Art)

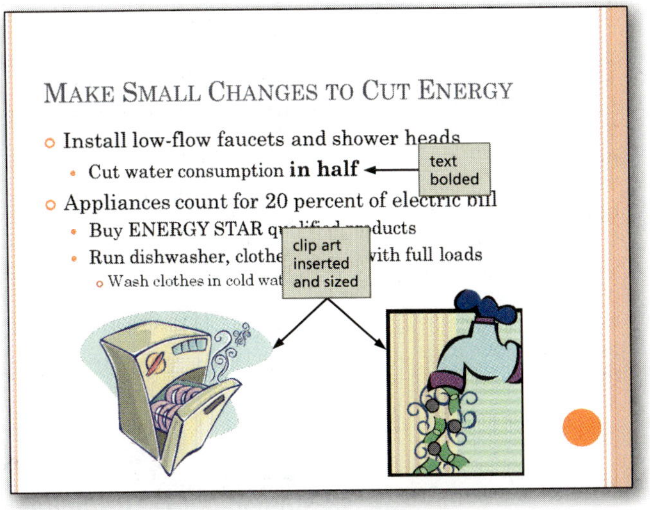

(b) Slide 2 (Multi-Level Bulleted List with Clip Art)

(c) Slide 3 (Title and Photograph)

(d) Slide 4 (Comparison Layout and Clip Art)

(e) Slide 5 (Closing Slide)

Figure 1–1

Overview

BTW

BTWs
For a complete list of the BTWs found in the margins of the Office and Windows chapters in this book, visit the Microsoft Office and Concepts CourseMate Web site at www.cengagebrain.com and then navigate to the BTW resource for this book.

As you read this chapter, you will learn how to create the presentation shown in Figure 1–1 on the previous page by performing these general tasks:

- Select an appropriate document theme.
- Enter titles and text on slides.
- Change the size, color, and style of text.
- Insert clips and a photograph.
- Add a transition to each slide.
- View the presentation on your computer.
- Print your slides.

Plan Ahead

General Project Guidelines
When creating a PowerPoint document, the actions you perform and decisions you make will affect the appearance and characteristics of the finished document. As you create a presentation such as the project shown in Figure 1–1, you should follow these general guidelines:

1. **Find the appropriate theme.** The overall appearance of a presentation significantly affects its capability to communicate information clearly. The slides' graphical appearance should support the presentation's overall message. Colors, fonts, and layouts affect how audience members perceive and react to the slide content.
2. **Choose words for each slide.** Use the less is more principle. The less text, the more likely the slides will enhance your speech. Use the fewest words possible to make a point.
3. **Format specific elements of the text.** Examples of how you can modify the appearance, or **format**, of text include changing its shape, size, color, and position on the slide.
4. **Determine where to save the presentation.** You can store a document permanently, or **save** it, on a variety of storage media, including a hard disk, USB flash drive, or CD. You also can indicate a specific location on the storage media for saving the document.
5. **Determine the best method for distributing the presentation.** Presentations can be distributed on paper or electronically. You can print a hard copy of the presentation slides for proofing or reference, or you can distribute an electronic image in various formats.

When necessary, more specific details concerning the above guidelines are presented at appropriate points in the chapter. The chapter also will identify the actions performed and decisions made regarding these guidelines during the creation of the slides shown in Figure 1–1.

To Start PowerPoint

For an introduction to Windows 7 and instruction about how to perform basic Windows 7 tasks, read the Office 2010 and Windows 7 chapter in this book, where you can learn how to resize windows, change screen resolution, create folders, move and rename files, use Windows Help, and much more.

If you are using a computer to step through the project in this chapter and you want your screens to match the figures in the Office and Windows chapters in this book, you should change your screen's resolution to 1024 × 768. For information about how to change a computer's resolution, refer to the Office 2010 and Windows 7 chapter in this book.

The following steps, which assume Windows 7 is running, start PowerPoint based on a typical installation. You may need to ask your instructor how to start PowerPoint for your computer. For a detailed example of the procedure summarized below, refer to the Office 2010 and Windows 7 chapter.

1. Click the Start button on the Windows 7 taskbar to display the Start menu.
2. Type `Microsoft PowerPoint` as the search text in the 'Search programs and files' text box and watch the search results appear on the Start menu.

3 Click Microsoft PowerPoint 2010 in the search results on the Start menu to start PowerPoint and display a new blank document in the PowerPoint window.

4 If the PowerPoint window is not maximized, click the Maximize button next to the Close button on its title bar to maximize the window.

Choosing a Document Theme

You can give a presentation a professional and integrated appearance easily by using a document theme. A **document theme** provides consistency in design and color throughout the entire presentation by setting the color scheme, font set, and layout of a presentation. This collection of formatting choices includes a set of colors (the Theme Colors group), a set of heading and content text fonts (the Theme Fonts group), and a set of lines and fill effects (the Theme Effects group). These groups allow you to choose and change the appearance of all the slides or individual slides in your presentation. The left edge of the status bar in Figure 1–2 shows the current slide number followed by the total number of slides in the document and a document theme identifier.

Plan Ahead

Find the appropriate theme.
In the initial steps of this project, you will select a document theme by locating a particular built-in theme in the Themes group. You could, however, apply a theme at any time while creating the presentation. Some PowerPoint slide show designers create presentations using the default Office Theme. This blank design allows them to concentrate on the words being used to convey the message and does not distract them with colors and various text attributes. Once the text is entered, the designers then select an appropriate document theme.

To Choose a Document Theme

The document theme identifier shows the theme currently used in the slide show. PowerPoint initially uses the **Office Theme** until you select a different theme. The following steps change the theme for this presentation from the Office Theme to the Oriel document theme.

1
- Click Design on the Ribbon to display the Design tab (Figure 1–2).

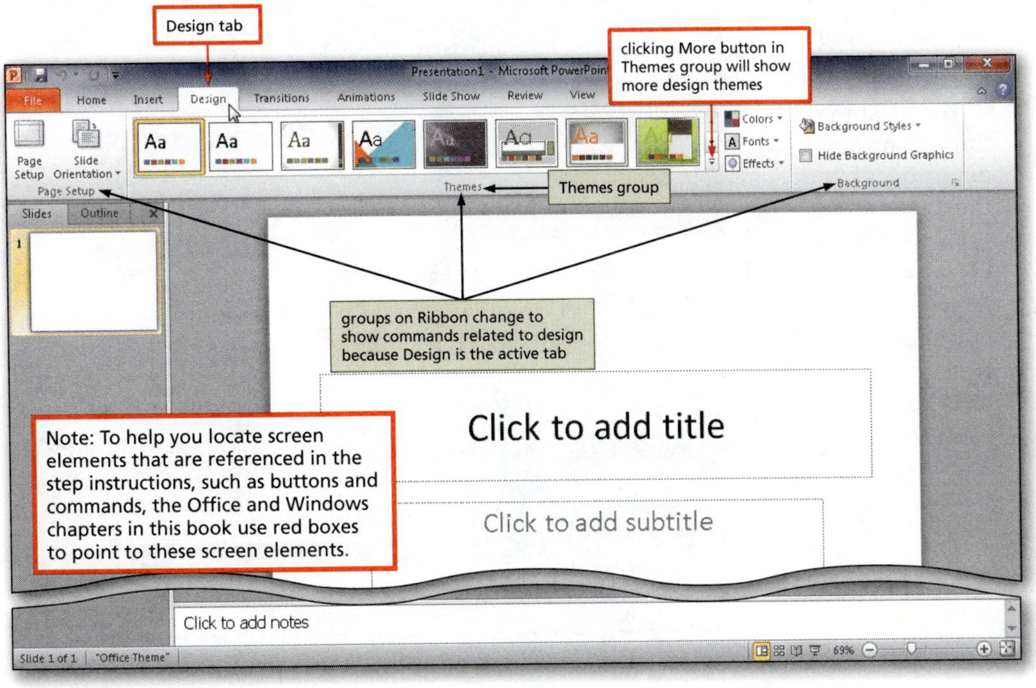

Figure 1–2

2

- Click the More button (Design tab | Themes group) to expand the gallery, which shows more Built-In theme gallery options (Figure 1–3).

Experiment

- Point to various document themes in the Themes gallery and watch the colors and fonts change on the title slide.

Q&A Are the themes displayed in a specific order?

Yes. They are arranged in alphabetical order running from left to right. If you point to a theme, a ScreenTip with the theme's name appears on the screen.

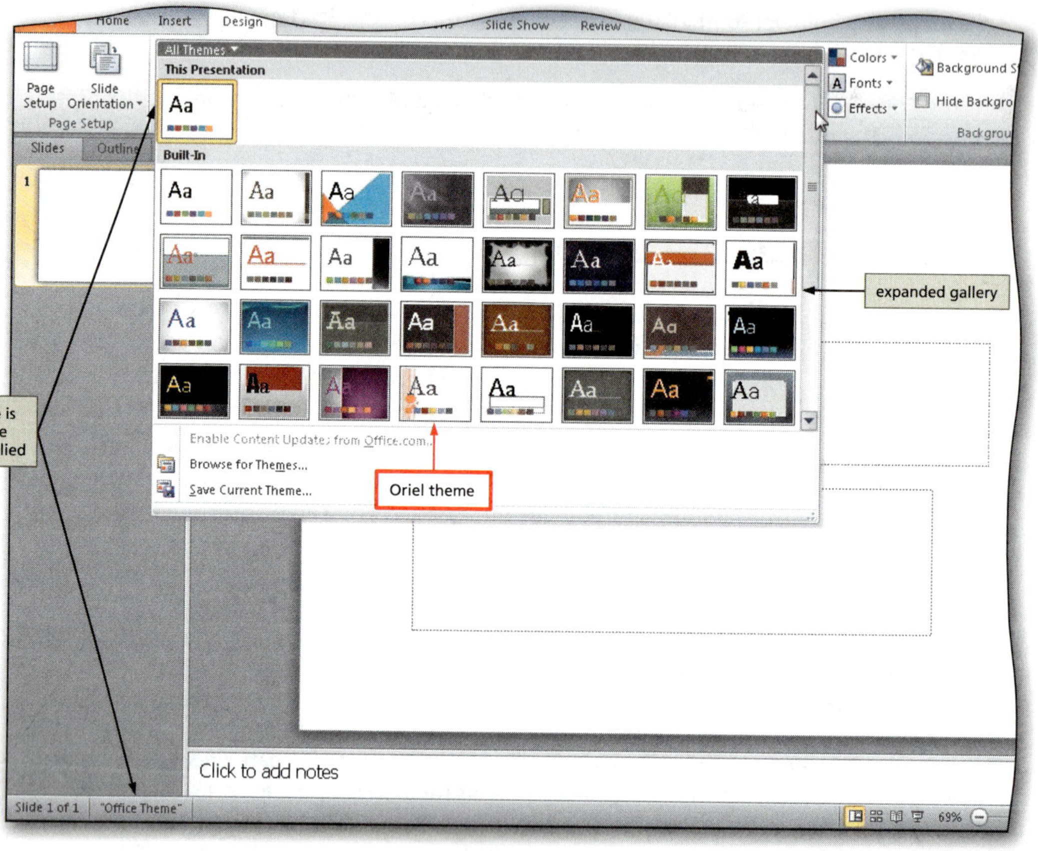

Figure 1–3

Q&A What if I change my mind and do not want to select a new theme?

Click anywhere outside the All Themes gallery to close the gallery.

3

- Click the Oriel theme to apply this theme to Slide 1 (Figure 1–4).

Q&A If I decide at some future time that this design does not fit the theme of my presentation, can I apply a different design?

Yes. You can repeat these steps at any time while creating your presentation.

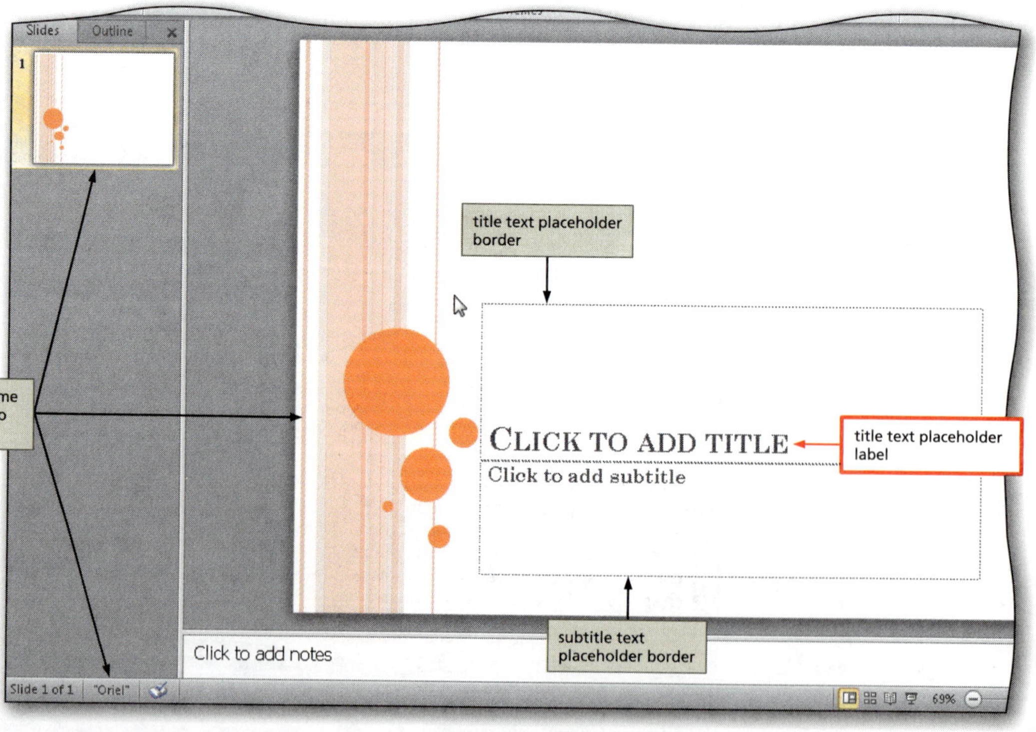

Figure 1–4

Creating a Title Slide

When you open a new presentation, the default **Title Slide** layout appears. The purpose of this layout is to introduce the presentation to the audience. PowerPoint includes eight other built-in standard layouts. The default (preset) slide layouts are set up in **landscape orientation**, where the slide width is greater than its height. In landscape orientation, the slide size is preset to 10 inches wide and 7.5 inches high when printed on a standard sheet of paper measuring 11 inches wide and 8.5 inches high.

Placeholders are boxes with dotted or hatch-marked borders that are displayed when you create a new slide. Most layouts have both a title text placeholder and at least one content placeholder. Depending on the particular slide layout selected, title and subtitle placeholders are displayed for the slide title and subtitle; a content text placeholder is displayed for text, art, or a table, chart, picture, graphic, or movie. The title slide has two text placeholders where you can type the main heading, or title, of a new slide and the subtitle.

With the exception of a blank slide, PowerPoint assumes every new slide has a title. To make creating a presentation easier, any text you type after a new slide appears becomes title text in the title text placeholder. The following steps create the title slide for this presentation.

Plan Ahead

Choose the words for the slide.
No doubt you have heard the phrase, "You get only one chance to make a first impression." The same philosophy holds true for a PowerPoint presentation. The title slide gives your audience an initial sense of what they are about to see and hear. It is, therefore, extremely important to choose the text for this slide carefully. Avoid stating the obvious in the title. Instead, create interest and curiosity using key ideas from the presentation.

Some PowerPoint users create the title slide as their last step in the design process so that it reflects the tone of the presentation. They begin by planning the final slide in the presentation so that they know where and how they want to end the slide show. All the slides in the presentation should work toward meeting this final slide.

To Enter the Presentation Title

The presentation title for Project 1 is It Is Easy Being Green. This title creates interest by introducing the concept of simple energy conservation tasks. The following step creates the slide show's title.

1

- Click the label, Click to add title, located inside the title text placeholder to select the placeholder (Figure 1–5).

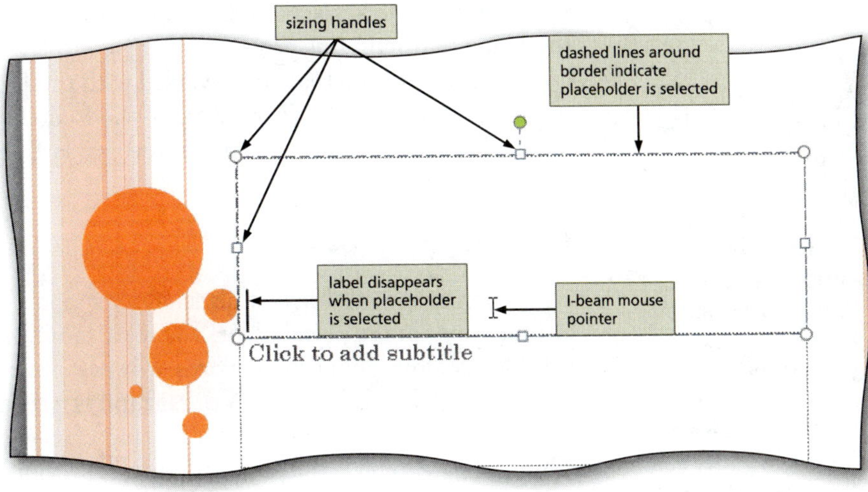

Figure 1–5

2

- Type `It Is Easy Being Green` in the title text placeholder. Do not press the ENTER key (Figure 1–6).

Q&A Why does the text display with capital letters despite the fact I am typing uppercase and lowercase letters?

The Oriel theme uses the Small Caps effect for the title text. This effect converts lowercase letters to uppercase and reduces their size.

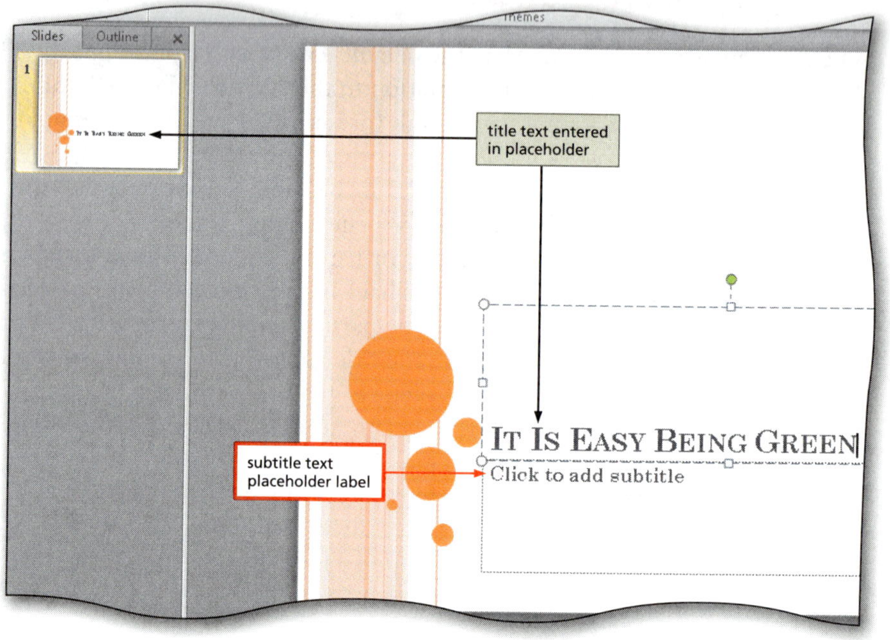

Figure 1–6

Correcting a Mistake When Typing

If you type the wrong letter, press the BACKSPACE key to erase all the characters back to and including the one that is incorrect. If you mistakenly press the ENTER key after typing the title and the insertion point is on the new line, simply press the BACKSPACE key to return the insertion point to the right of the letter n in the word, Green.

When you install PowerPoint, the default setting allows you to reverse up to the last 20 changes by clicking the Undo button on the Quick Access Toolbar. The ScreenTip that appears when you point to the Undo button changes to indicate the type of change just made. For example, if you type text in the title text placeholder and then point to the Undo button, the ScreenTip that appears is Undo Typing. For clarity, when referencing the Undo button in this project, the name displaying in the ScreenTip is referenced. You can reapply a change that you reversed with the Undo button by clicking the Redo button on the Quick Access Toolbar. Clicking the Redo button reverses the last undo action. The ScreenTip name reflects the type of reversal last performed.

For an introduction to Office 2010 and instruction about how to perform basic tasks in Office 2010 programs, read the Office 2010 and Windows 7 chapter in this book, where you can learn how to start a program, use the Ribbon, save a file, open a file, quit a program, use Help, and much more.

Paragraphs

Text in the subtitle text placeholder supports the title text. It can appear on one or more lines in the placeholder. To create more than one subtitle line, you press the ENTER key after typing some words. PowerPoint creates a new line, which is the second paragraph in the placeholder. A **paragraph** is a segment of text with the same format that begins when you press the ENTER key and ends when you press the ENTER key again. This new paragraph is the same level as the previous paragraph. A **level** is a position within a structure, such as an outline, that indicates the magnitude of importance. PowerPoint allows for five paragraph levels.

To Enter the Presentation Subtitle Paragraph

The first subtitle paragraph links to the title by giving further detail that the presentation will focus on energy-saving measures at home. The following steps enter the presentation subtitle.

1

- Click the label, Click to add subtitle, located inside the subtitle text placeholder to select the placeholder (Figure 1–7).

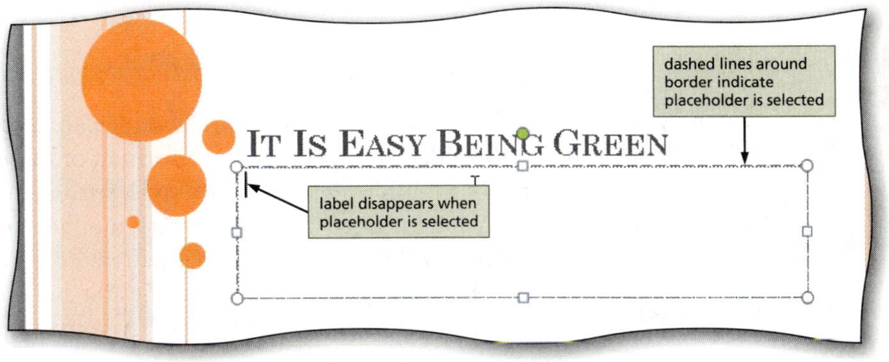

Figure 1–7

2

- Type **`Saving Energy at Home`** but do not press the ENTER key (Figure 1–8).

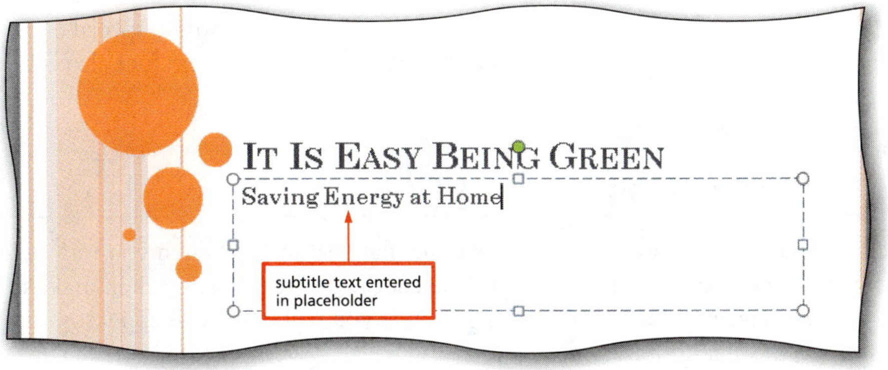

Figure 1–8

Plan Ahead

Identify how to format specific elements of the text.
Most of the time, you use the document theme's text attributes, color scheme, and layout. Occasionally, you may want to change the way a presentation looks, however, and still keep a particular document theme. PowerPoint gives you that flexibility.

Graphic designers use several rules when formatting text.

- Avoid all capital letters, if possible. Audiences have difficulty comprehending sentences typed in all capital letters, especially when the lines exceed seven words. All capital letters leaves no room for emphasis or inflection, so readers get confused about what material deserves particular attention. Some document themes, however, have a default title text style of all capital letters.
- Avoid text with a font size less than 30 point. Audience members generally will sit a maximum of 50 feet from a screen, and at this distance 30-point type is the smallest size text they can read comfortably without straining.
- Make careful color choices. Color evokes emotions, and a careless color choice may elicit the incorrect psychological response. PowerPoint provides a color gallery with hundreds of colors. The built-in document themes use complementary colors that work well together. If you stray from these themes and add your own color choices, without a good reason to make the changes, your presentation is apt to become ineffective.

Formatting Characters in a Presentation

Recall that each document theme determines the color scheme, font set, and layout of a presentation. You can use a specific document theme and then change the characters' formats any time before, during, or after you type the text.

BTW

Q&As
For a complete list of the Q&As found in many of the step-by-step sequences in the Office and Windows chapters in this book, visit the Microsoft Office and Concepts CourseMate Web site at www.cengagebrain.com and then navigate to the Q&A resource for this book.

Fonts and Font Styles

Characters that appear on the screen are a specific shape and size. Examples of how you can modify the appearance, or **format**, of these typed characters on the screen and in print include changing the font, style, size, and color. The **font**, or typeface, defines the appearance and shape of the letters, numbers, punctuation marks, and symbols. **Style** indicates how the characters are formatted. PowerPoint's text font styles include regular, italic, bold, and bold italic. **Size** specifies the height of the characters and is gauged by a measurement system that uses points. A **point** is 1/72 of an inch in height. Thus, a character with a font size of 36 is 36/72 (or 1/2) of an inch in height. **Color** defines the hue of the characters.

This presentation uses the Oriel document theme, which uses particular font styles and font sizes. The Oriel document theme default title text font is named Century Schoolbook. It has a bold style with no special effects, and its size is 30 point. The Oriel document theme default subtitle text font also is Century Schoolbook with a font size of 18 point.

To Select a Paragraph

You can use many techniques to format characters. When you want to apply the same formats to multiple words or paragraphs, it is efficient to select the desired text and then make the desired changes to all the characters simultaneously. The first formatting change you will make will apply to the title slide subtitle. The following step selects this paragraph.

1

- Triple-click the paragraph, Saving Energy at Home, in the subtitle text placeholder to select the paragraph (Figure 1–9).

Q&A

Can I select the paragraph using a technique other than triple-clicking?

Yes. You can move your mouse pointer to the left of the first paragraph and then drag to the end of the line.

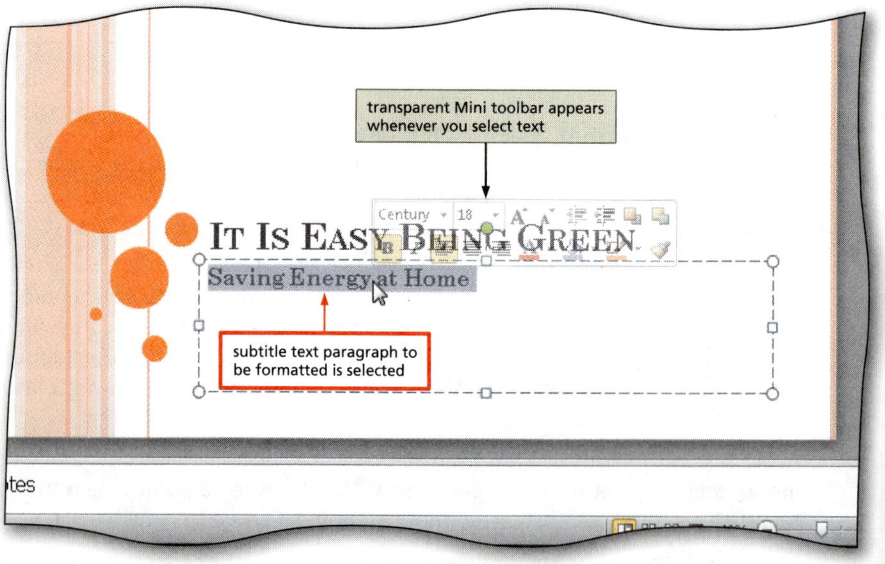

Figure 1–9

To Italicize Text

Different font styles often are used on slides to make them more appealing to the reader and to emphasize particular text. **Italicized** text has a slanted appearance. Used sparingly, it draws the readers' eyes to these characters. The following step adds emphasis to the second line of the subtitle text by changing regular text to italic text.

1

- With the subtitle text still selected, click the Italic button on the Mini toolbar to italicize that text on the slide (Figure 1–10).

Q&A If I change my mind and decide not to italicize the text, how can I remove this style?

Click the Italic button a second time or immediately click the Undo button on the Quick Access Toolbar or press CTRL+Z.

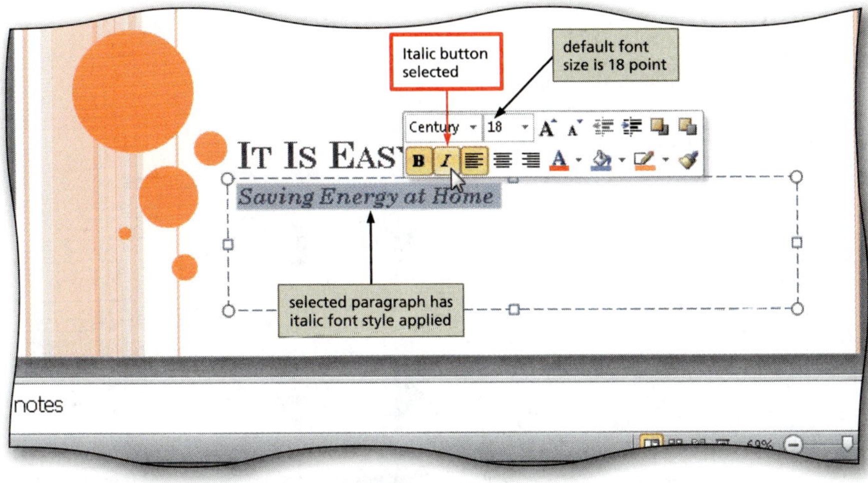

Figure 1–10

Other Ways

1. Right-click selected text, click Font on shortcut menu, click Font tab (Font dialog box), click Italic in Font style list, click OK button
2. Select text, click Italic button (Home tab | Font group)
3. Click Font Dialog Box Launcher (Home tab | Font group), click Font tab (Font dialog box), click Italic in Font style list, click OK button
4. Select text, press CTRL+I

To Increase Font Size

To add emphasis, you increase the font size for the subtitle text. The Increase Font Size button on the Mini toolbar increases the font size in preset increments. The following step uses this button to increase the font size.

1

- Click the Increase Font Size button on the Mini toolbar twice to increase the font size of the selected text from 18 to 24 point (Figure 1–11).

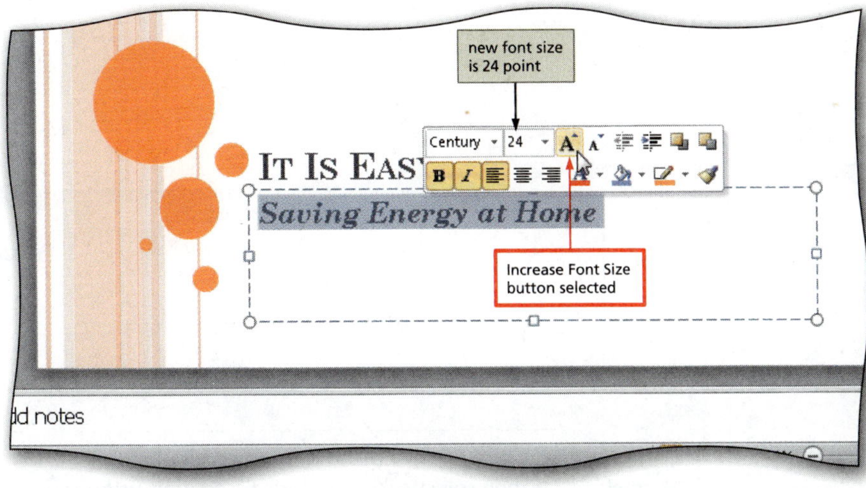

Figure 1–11

Other Ways

1. Click Font Size box arrow on Mini toolbar, click desired font size in Font Size gallery
2. Click Increase Font Size button (Home tab | Font group)
3. Click Font Size box arrow (Home tab | Font group), click desired font size in Font size gallery
4. Press CTRL+SHIFT+>

To Select a Word

PowerPoint designers use many techniques to emphasize words and characters on a slide. To add emphasis to the energy-saving concept of your slide show, you want to increase the font size and change the font color to green for the word, Green, in the title text. You could perform these actions separately, but it is more efficient to select the word and then change the font attributes. The following steps select a word.

1

- Position the mouse pointer somewhere in the word to be selected (in this case, in the word, Green) (Figure 1–12).

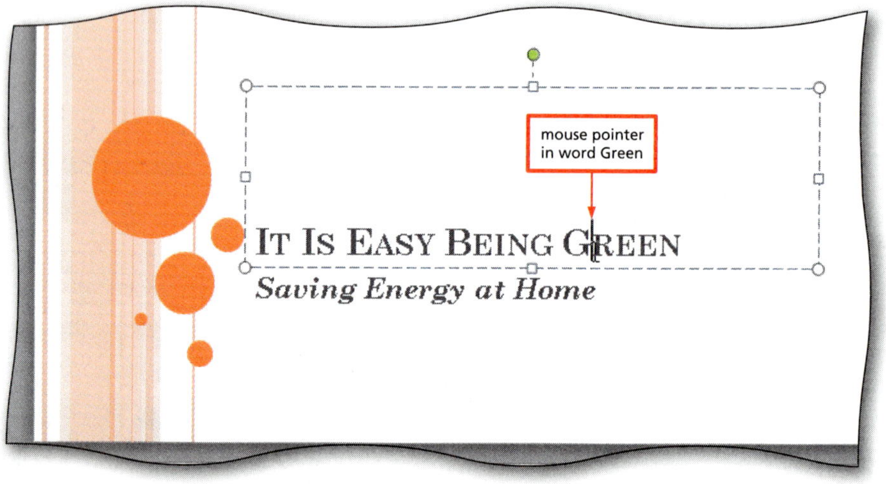

Figure 1–12

2

- Double-click the word to select it (Figure 1–13).

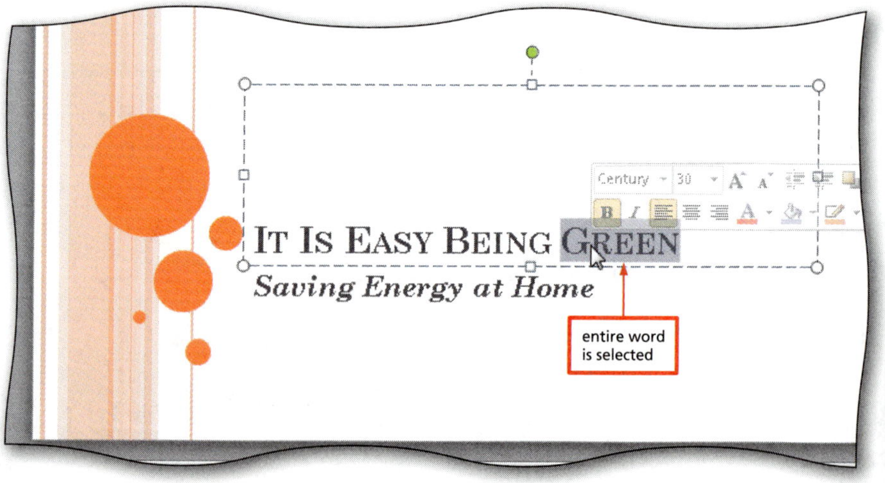

Figure 1–13

Other Ways

1. Position mouse pointer before first character, press CTRL+SHIFT+RIGHT ARROW

Plan Ahead

Format text colors.
When selecting text colors, try to limit using red. This color often is associated with dangerous or alarming situations. In addition, at least 15 percent of men have difficulty distinguishing varying shades of green or red. They also often see the color purple as blue and the color brown as green. This problem is more pronounced when the colors appear in small areas, such as slide paragraphs or line chart bars.

To Change the Text Color

PowerPoint allows you to use one or more text colors in a presentation. To add more emphasis to the word, Green, in the title slide text, you decide to change the color. The following steps add emphasis to this word by changing the font color from black to green.

1

- With the word, Green, selected, click the Font Color arrow on the Mini toolbar to display the gallery of Theme Colors and Standard Colors (Figure 1–14).

Q&A If the Mini toolbar disappears from the screen, how can I display it once again?

Right-click the text, and the Mini toolbar should appear.

Experiment

- Point to various colors in the gallery and watch the word's font color change.

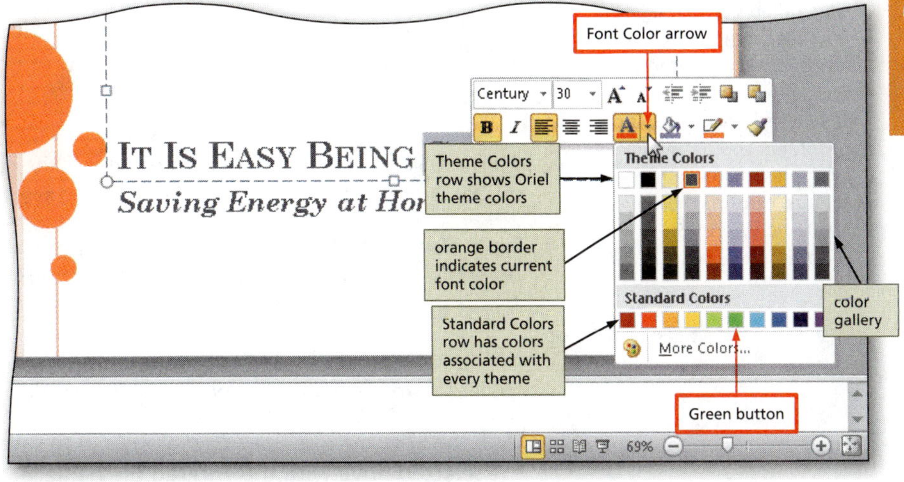

Figure 1–14

2

- Click the Green button in the Standard Colors row on the Mini toolbar (sixth color) to change the font color to green (Figure 1–15).

Q&A Why did I select the color Green?

Green is one of the 10 standard colors associated with every document theme, and it is a universal color to represent respecting natural resources. The color will emphasize the fact that the presentation focuses on green conservation measures.

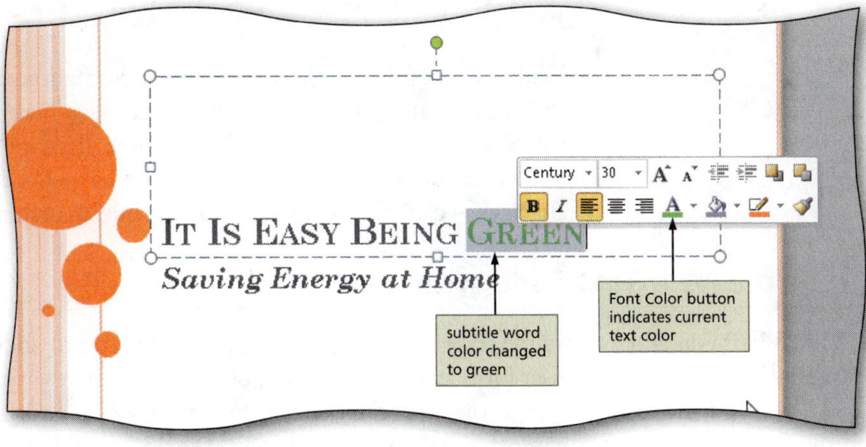

Figure 1–15

Q&A What is the difference between the colors shown in the Theme Colors area and the Standard Colors?

The 10 colors in the top row of the Theme Colors area are two text, two background, and six accent colors in the Oriel theme; the five colors in each column under the top row display different transparencies. These colors are available in every document theme.

3

- Click outside the selected area to deselect the word.

Other Ways

1. Right-click selected text, click Font on shortcut menu, click Font Color button, click Green in Standard Colors row
2. Click Font Color arrow (Home tab | Font group), click Green in Standard Colors row

BTW

Organizing Files and Folders

You should organize and store files in folders so that you easily can find the files later. For example, if you are taking an introductory computer class called CIS 101, a good practice would be to save all PowerPoint files in a PowerPoint folder in a CIS 101 folder. For a discussion of folders and detailed examples of creating folders, refer to the Office 2010 and Windows 7 chapter in this book.

To Save a Presentation

You have performed many tasks while creating this slide and do not want to risk losing work completed thus far. Accordingly, you should save the document.

The following steps assume you already have created folders for storing your files, for example, a CIS 101 folder (for your class) that contains a PowerPoint folder (for your assignments). Thus, these steps save the document in the PowerPoint folder in the CIS 101 folder on a USB flash drive using the file name, Saving Energy. For a detailed example of the procedure summarized below, refer to the Office 2010 and Windows 7 chapter in this book.

1. With a USB flash drive connected to one of the computer's USB ports, click the Save button on the Quick Access Toolbar to display the Save As dialog box.
2. Type `Saving Energy` in the File name text box to change the file name. Do not press the ENTER key after typing the file name because you do not want to close the dialog box at this time.
3. Navigate to the desired save location (in this case, the PowerPoint folder in the CIS 101 folder [or your class folder] on the USB flash drive).
4. Click the Save button (Save As dialog box) to save the document in the selected folder on the selected drive with the entered file name.

Adding a New Slide to a Presentation

With the text for the title slide for the presentation created, the next step is to add the first text slide immediately after the title slide. Usually, when you create a presentation, you add slides with text, clip art, graphics, or charts. Some placeholders allow you to double-click the placeholder and then access other objects, such as media clips, charts, diagrams, and organization charts. You can change the layout for a slide at any time during the creation of a presentation.

To Add a New Text Slide with a Bulleted List

When you add a new slide, PowerPoint uses the Title and Content slide layout. This layout provides a title placeholder and a content area for text, art, charts, and other graphics. A vertical scroll bar appears in the Slide pane when you add the second slide so that you can move from slide to slide easily. A thumbnail of this slide also appears in the Slides tab. The following steps add a new slide with the Title and Content slide layout.

1

- Click Home on the Ribbon to display the Home tab (Figure 1–16).

Figure 1–16

2

- Click the New Slide button (Home tab | Slides group) to insert a new slide with the Title and Content layout (Figure 1–17).

Q&A Why does the bullet character display an orange circle?

The Oriel document theme determines the bullet characters. Each paragraph level has an associated bullet character.

Q&A I clicked the New Slide arrow instead of the New Slide button. What should I do?

Click the Title and Content slide thumbnail in the layout gallery.

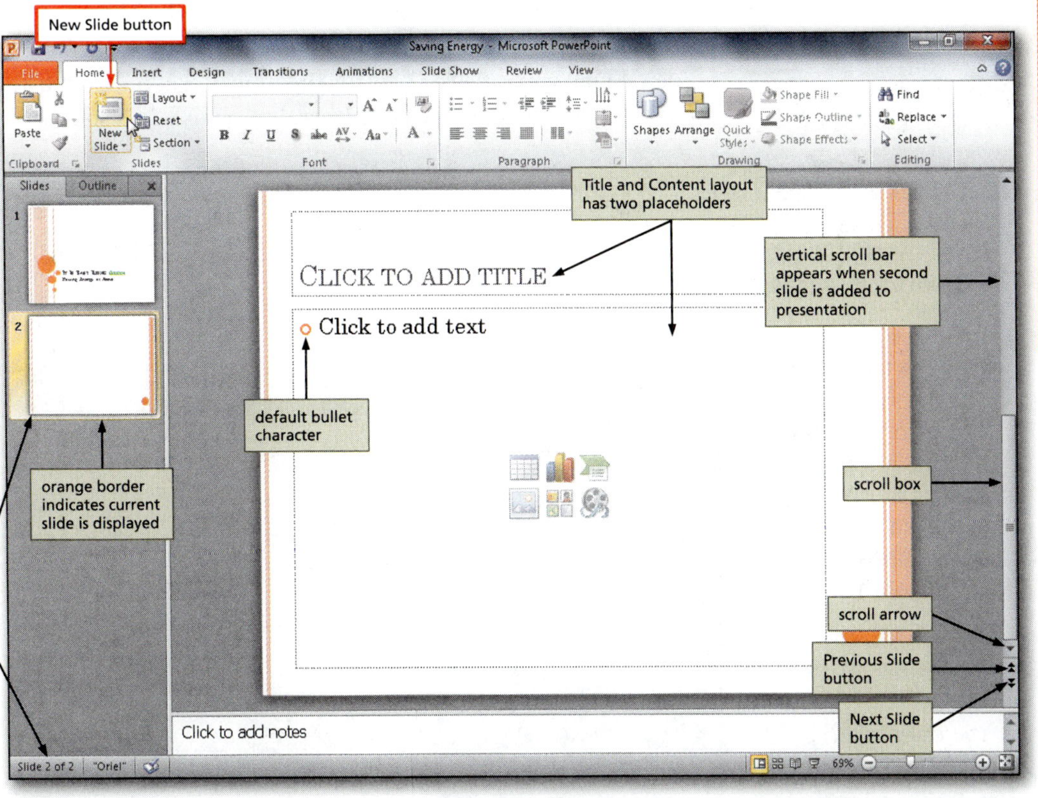

Figure 1–17

Other Ways

1. Press CTRL+M

Plan Ahead

Choose the words for the slide.

All presentations should follow the 7 × 7 rule, which states that each slide should have a maximum of seven lines, and each line should have a maximum of seven words. PowerPoint designers must choose their words carefully and, in turn, help viewers read the slides easily.

Avoid line wraps. Your audience's eyes want to stop at the end of a line. Thus, you must plan your words carefully or adjust the font size so that each point displays on only one line.

Creating a Text Slide with a Multi-Level Bulleted List

The information in the Slide 2 text placeholder is presented in a bulleted list with three levels. A **bulleted list** is a list of paragraphs, each of which is preceded by a bullet. A slide that consists of more than one level of bulleted text is called a **multi-level bulleted list slide**. In a multi-level bulleted list, a lower-level paragraph is a subset of a higher-level paragraph. It usually contains information that supports the topic in the paragraph immediately above it.

Two of the Slide 2 bullets appear at the same paragraph level, called the first level: Install low-flow faucets and shower heads, and Appliances count for 20 percent of electric bill. Beginning with the second level, each paragraph indents to the right of the preceding level and is pushed down to a lower level. For example, if you increase the indent of a first-level paragraph, it becomes a second-level paragraph. The second, fourth, and fifth paragraphs on Slide 2 are second-level paragraphs. The last paragraph, Wash clothes in cold water, is a third-level paragraph.

BTW

The Ribbon and Screen Resolution

PowerPoint may change how the groups and buttons within the groups appear on the Ribbon, depending on the computer's screen resolution. Thus, your Ribbon may look different from the ones in the Office and Windows chapters in this book if you are using a screen resolution other than 1024 x 768.

Creating a text slide with a multi-level bulleted list requires several steps. Initially, you enter a slide title in the title text placeholder. Next, you select the content text placeholder. Then, you type the text for the multi-level bulleted list, increasing and decreasing the indents as needed. The next several sections add a slide with a multi-level bulleted list.

To Enter a Slide Title

PowerPoint assumes every new slide has a title. The title for Slide 2 is Make Small Changes to Cut Energy. The following step enters this title.

1

- Click the label, Click to add title, to select it and then type **Make Small Changes to Cut Energy** in the placeholder. Do not press the ENTER key (Figure 1–18).

Q&A What are those six icons grouped in the middle of the slide?

You can click one of the icons to insert a specific type of content: table, chart, SmartArt graphic, picture, clip art, or media clip.

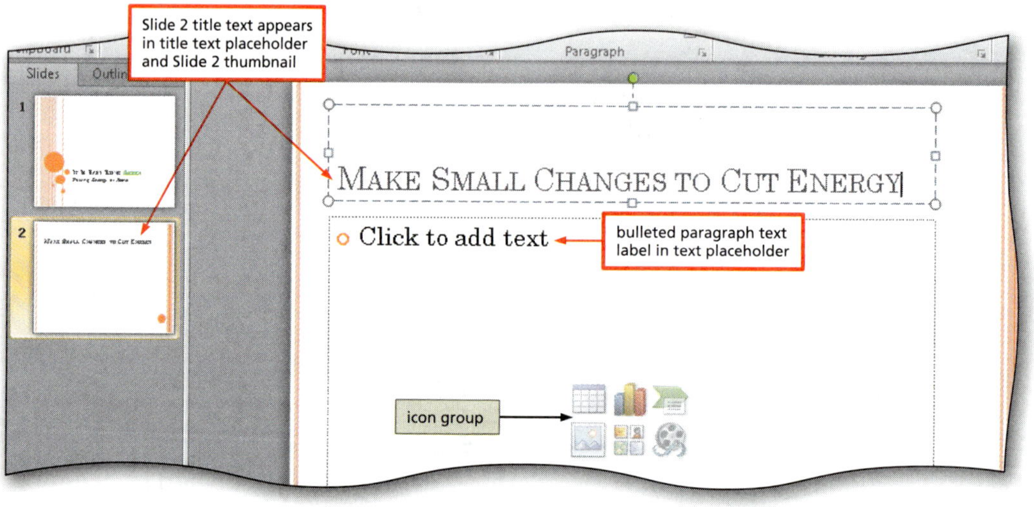

Figure 1–18

To Select a Text Placeholder

Before you can type text into the text placeholder, you first must select it. The following step selects the text placeholder on Slide 2.

1

- Click the label, Click to add text, to select the text placeholder (Figure 1–19).

Q&A Why does my mouse pointer have a different shape?

If you move the mouse pointer away from the bullet, it will change shape.

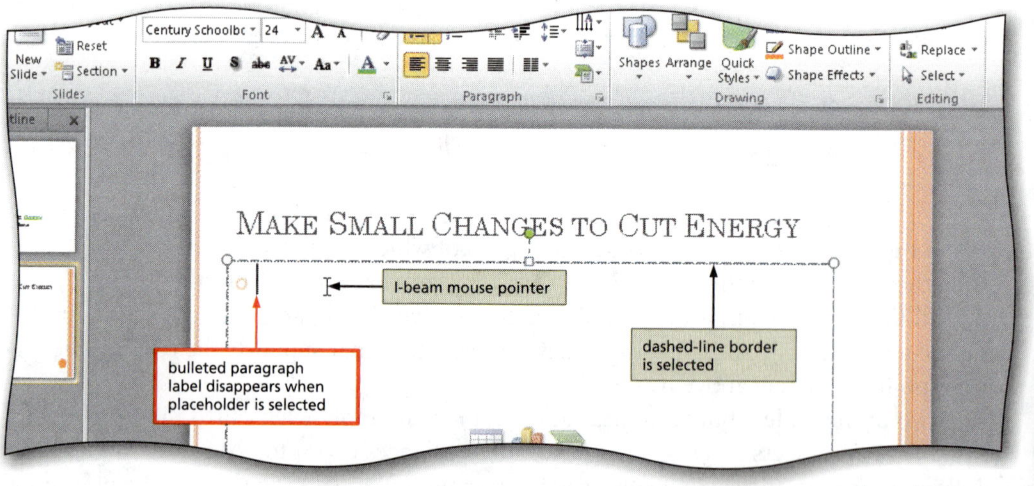

Figure 1–19

Other Ways

1. Press CTRL+ENTER

To Type a Multi-Level Bulleted List

The content placeholder provides an area for the text characters. When you click inside a placeholder, you then can type or paste text. As discussed previously, a bulleted list is a list of paragraphs, each of which is preceded by a bullet. A paragraph is a segment of text ended by pressing the ENTER key.

The content text placeholder is selected, so the next step is to type the multi-level bulleted list that consists of six paragraphs, as shown in Figure 1–1b on page PPT 3. Creating a lower-level paragraph is called **demoting** text; creating a higher-level paragraph is called **promoting** text. The following steps create a multi-level bulleted list consisting of three levels.

1

- Type `Install low-flow faucets and shower heads` and then press the ENTER key (Figure 1–20).

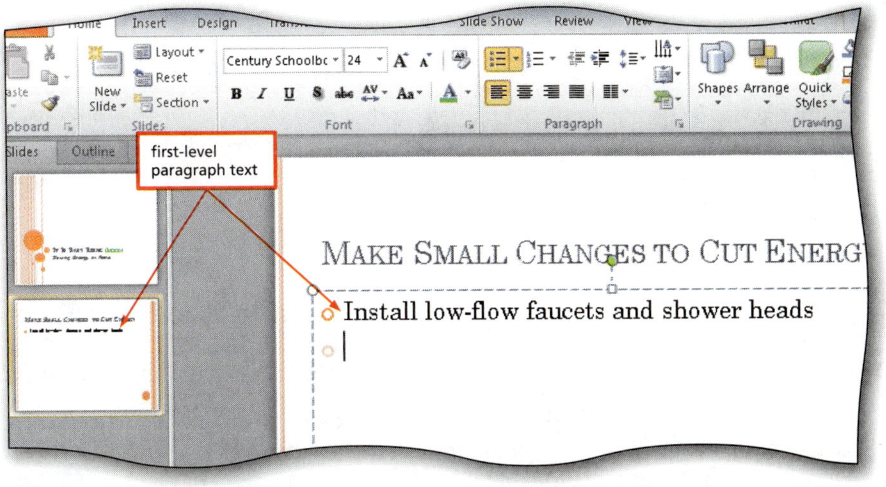

Figure 1–20

2

- Click the Increase List Level button (Home tab | Paragraph group) to indent the second paragraph below the first and create a second-level paragraph (Figure 1–21).

Q&A Why does the bullet for this paragraph have a different size and color?

A different bullet is assigned to each paragraph level.

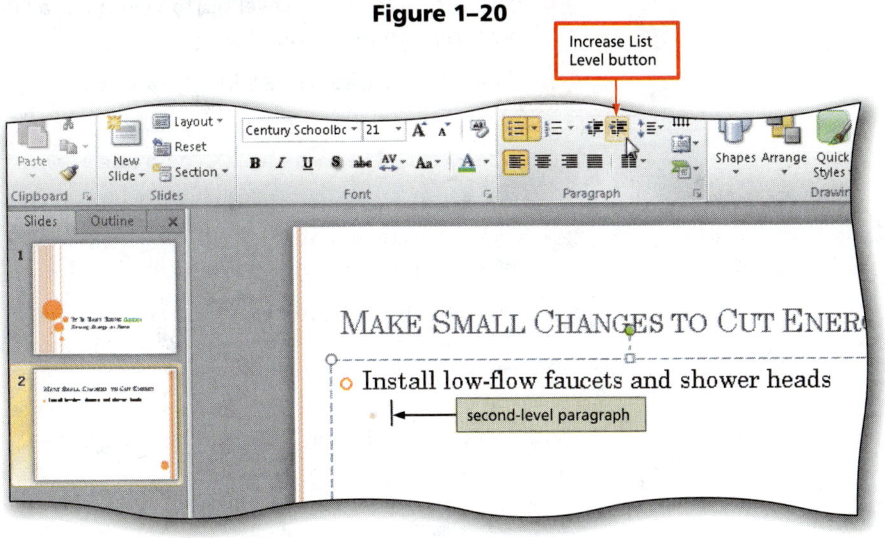

Figure 1–21

3

- Type `Cut water consumption in half` and then press the ENTER key (Figure 1–22).

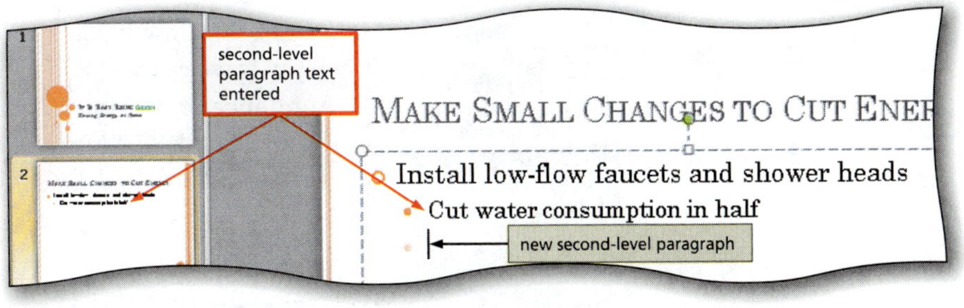

Figure 1–22

4

- Click the Decrease List Level button (Home tab | Paragraph group) so that the second-level paragraph becomes a first-level paragraph (Figure 1–23).

Q&A Can I delete bullets on a slide?

Yes. If you do not want bullets to display in a particular paragraph, click the Bullets button (Home tab | Paragraph group) or right-click the paragraph and then click the Bullets button on the shortcut menu.

Other Ways

1. Press TAB to promote paragraph; press SHIFT+TAB to demote paragraph

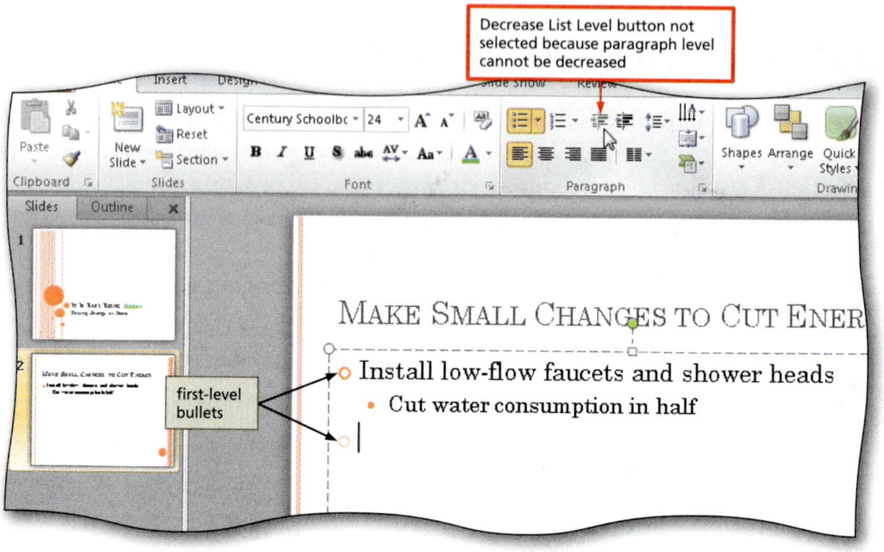

Figure 1–23

To Type the Remaining Text for Slide 2

The following steps complete the text for Slide 2.

1. Type **Appliances count for 20 percent of electric bill** and then press the ENTER key.
2. Click the Increase List Level button (Home tab | Paragraph group) to demote the paragraph to the second level.
3. Type **Buy ENERGY STAR qualified products** and then press the ENTER key to add a new paragraph at the same level as the previous paragraph.
4. Type **Run dishwasher, clothes washer with full loads** and then press the ENTER key.
5. Click the Increase List Level button (Home tab | Paragraph group) to demote the paragraph to the third level.
6. Type **Wash clothes in cold water** but do not press the ENTER key (Figure 1–24).

Q&A I pressed the ENTER key in error, and now a new bullet appears after the last entry on this slide. How can I remove this extra bullet?

Press the BACKSPACE key twice.

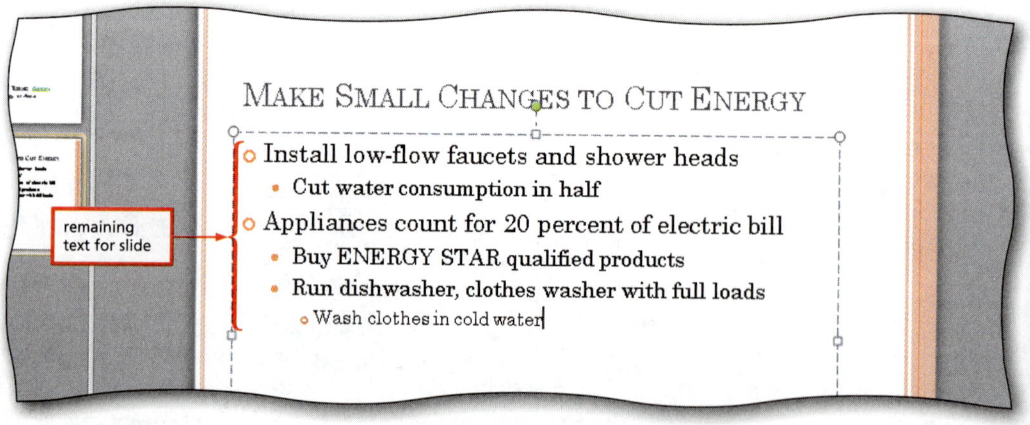

Figure 1–24

To Select a Group of Words

PowerPoint designers use many techniques to emphasize words and characters on a slide. To add emphasis to your slide show's concept of saving natural resources, you want to bold and increase the font size of the words, in half, in the body text. You could perform these actions separately, but it is more efficient to select the words and then change the font attributes. The following steps select two words.

1

- Position the mouse pointer immediately to the left of the first character of the text to be selected (in this case, the i in the word, in) (Figure 1–25).

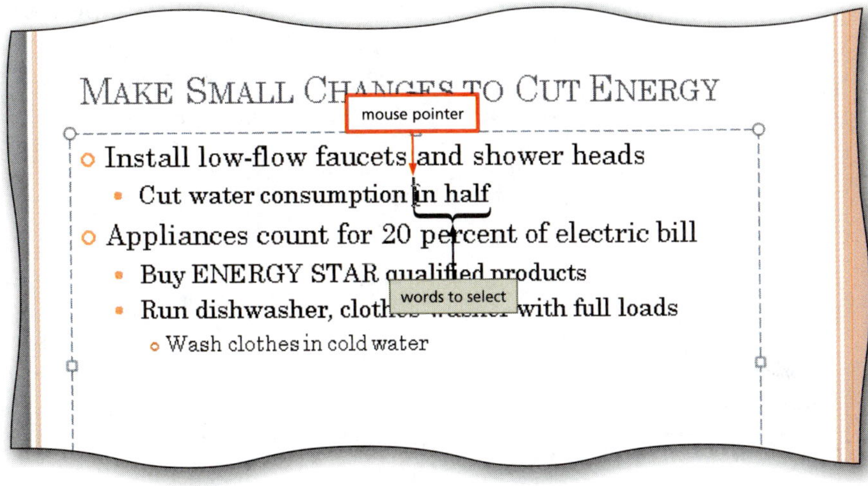

Figure 1–25

2

- Drag the mouse pointer through the last character of the text to be selected (in this case, the f in half) (Figure 1–26).

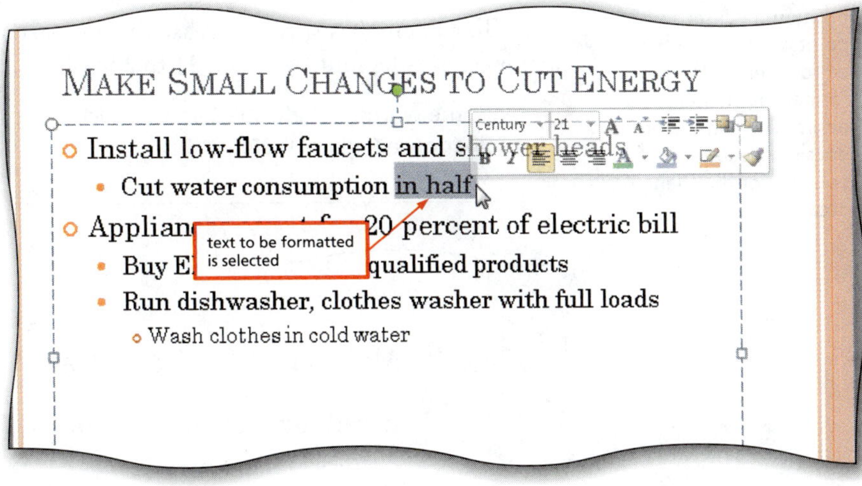

Figure 1–26

Other Ways
1. Press CTRL+SHIFT+RIGHT ARROW

To Bold Text

Bold characters display somewhat thicker and darker than those that display in a regular font style. Clicking the Bold button on the Mini toolbar is an efficient method of bolding text. To add more emphasis to the amount of water savings that can occur by installing low-flow faucets and shower heads, you want to bold the words, in half. The step on the next page bolds this text.

1

- With the words, in half, selected, click the Bold button on the Mini toolbar to bold the two words (Figure 1–27).

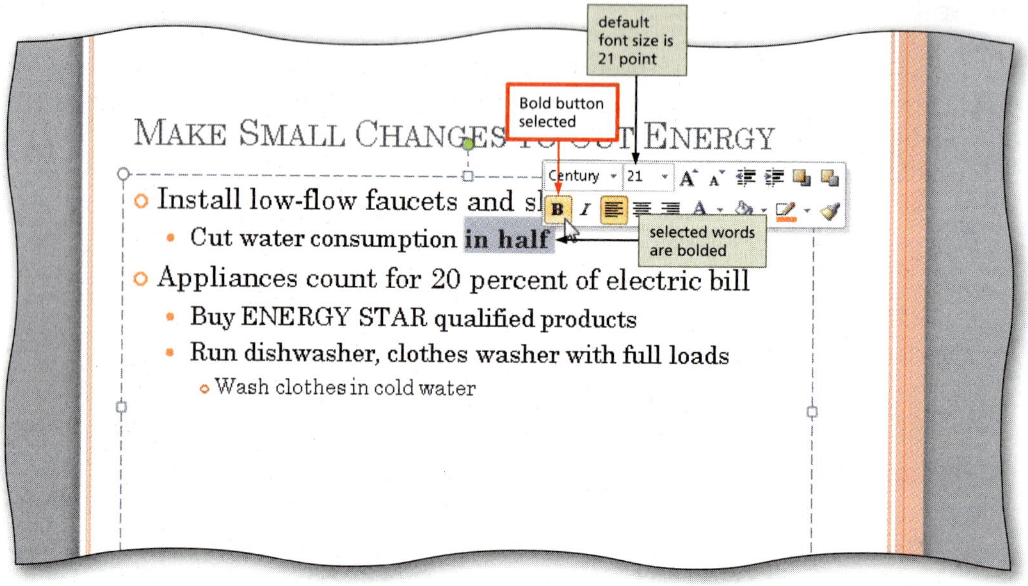

Figure 1–27

Other Ways

1. Click Bold button (Home tab | Font group)
2. Press CTRL+B

BTW

Formatting Words
To format one word, position the insertion point anywhere in the word. Then make the formatting changes you desire. The entire word does not need to be selected for the change to occur.

To Increase Font Size

To add emphasis, you increase the font size for the words, in half. The following step increases the font size from 21 to 24 point.

1 With the words, in half, still selected, click the Increase Font Size button on the Mini toolbar once (Figure 1–28).

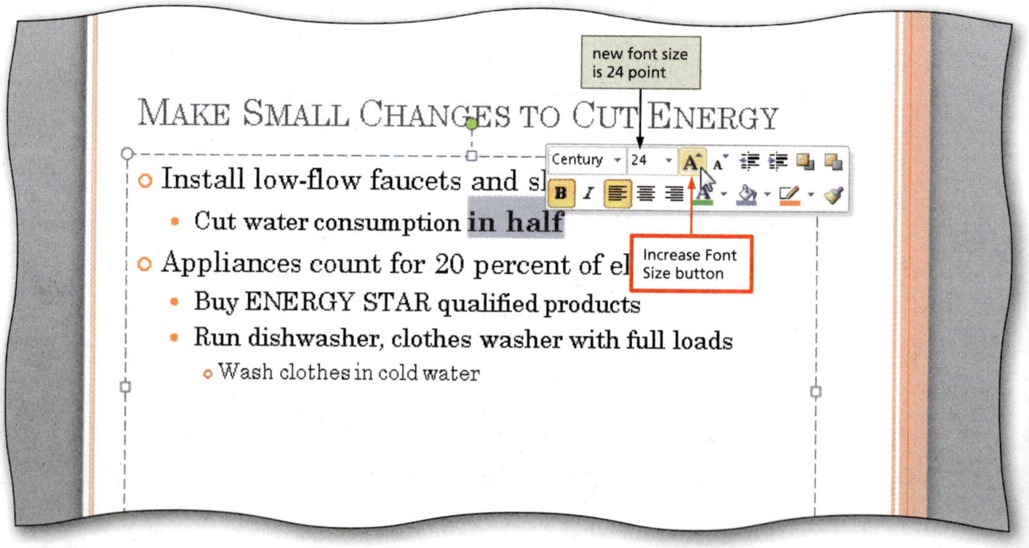

Figure 1–28

Adding New Slides and Changing the Slide Layouts

Slide 3 in Figure 1–1c on page PPT 3 contains a photograph and does not contain a bulleted list. When you add a new slide, PowerPoint applies the Title and Content layout. This layout along with the Title Slide layout for Slide 1 are the default styles. A **layout** specifies the arrangement of placeholders on a slide. These placeholders are arranged in various configurations and can contain text, such as the slide title or a bulleted list, or they can contain content, such as SmartArt graphics, pictures, charts, tables, shapes, and clip art. The placement of the text, in relationship to content, depends on the slide layout. You can specify a particular slide layout when you add a new slide to a presentation or after you have created the slide.

Using the **Layout gallery**, you can choose a slide layout. The nine layouts in this gallery have a variety of placeholders to define text and content positioning and formatting. Three layouts are for text: Title Slide, Section Header, and Title Only. Five are for text and content: Title and Content, Two Content, Comparison, Content with Caption, and Picture with Caption. The Blank layout has no placeholders. If none of these standard layouts meets your design needs, you can create a **custom layout**. A custom layout specifies the number, size, and location of placeholders, background content, and optional slide and placeholder-level properties.

When you change the layout of a slide, PowerPoint retains the text and objects and repositions them into the appropriate placeholders. Using slide layouts eliminates the need to resize objects and the font size because PowerPoint automatically sizes the objects and text to fit the placeholders.

BTW

Experimenting with Normal View

As you learn to use PowerPoint's features, experiment with using the Outline tab and with closing the Tabs pane to maximize the slide area. To close the Tabs pane, click the x to the right of the Outline tab. To redisplay the Tabs pane, click the View tab on the Ribbon and then click Normal in the Presentation Views group.

To Add a Slide with the Title Only Layout

The following steps add Slide 3 to the presentation with the Title Only slide layout style.

1

- If necessary, click Home on the Ribbon to display the Home tab.
- Click the New Slide arrow (Home tab | Slides group) to display the Layout gallery (Figure 1–29).

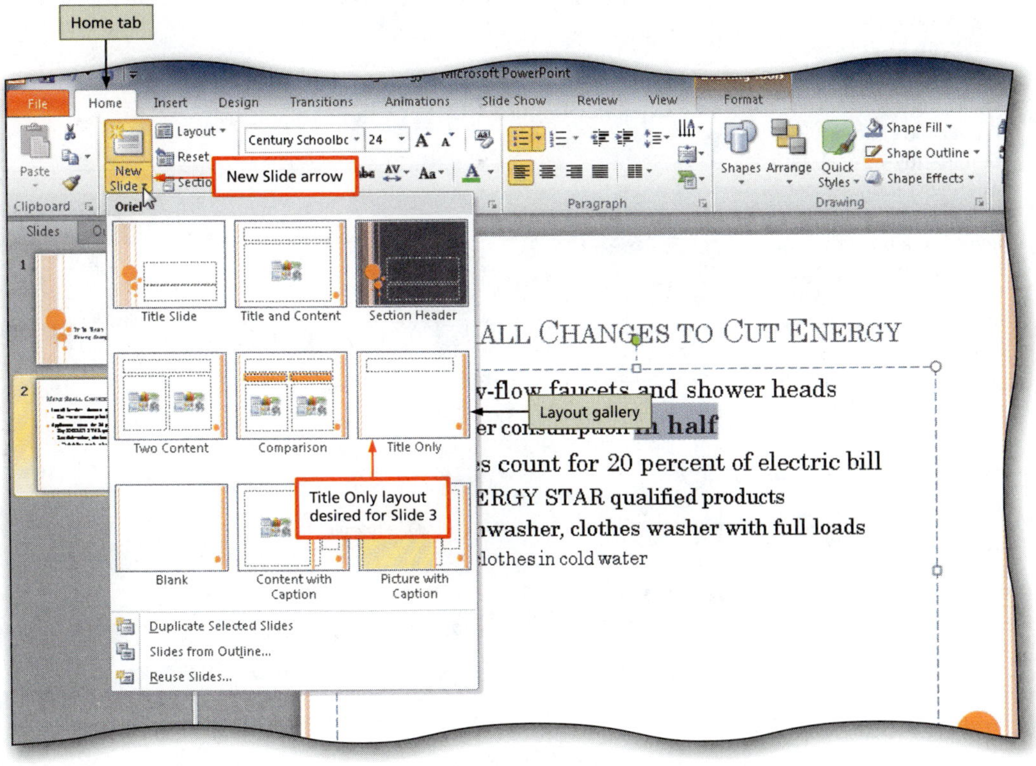

Figure 1–29

2

- Click Title Only to add a new slide and apply that layout to Slide 3 (Figure 1–30).

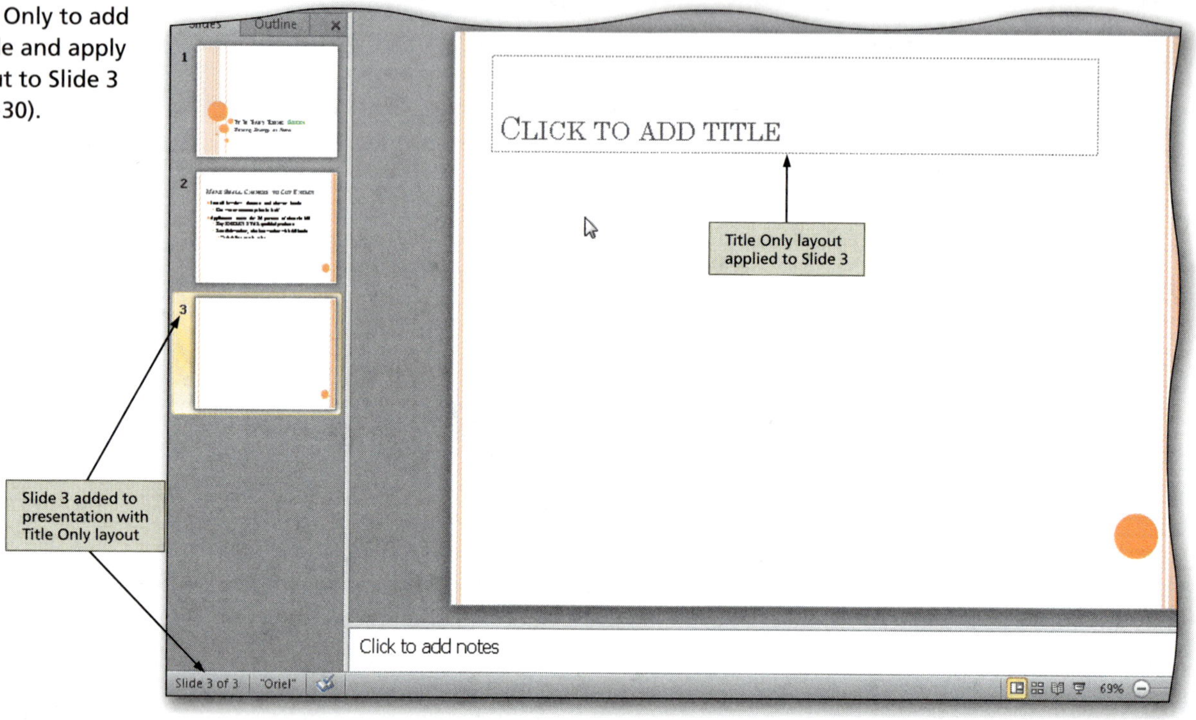

Figure 1–30

Other Ways

1. Press CTRL+M

To Enter a Slide Title

The only text on Slide 3 is the title. The following step enters the title text for this slide.

1 Type `Use Energy Efficient Lighting` as the title text but do not press the ENTER key (Figure 1–31).

BTW

Portrait Page Orientation

If your slide content is dominantly vertical, such as a skyscraper or a person, consider changing the slide layout to a portrait page orientation. To change the orientation, click the Slide Orientation button (Design tab | Page Setup group) and then click the desired orientation.

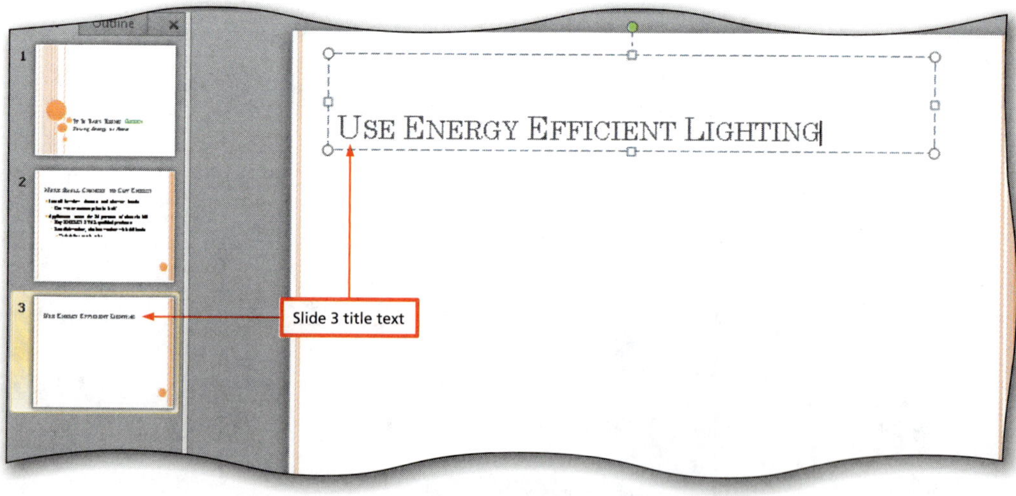

Figure 1–31

To Add a New Slide and Enter a Slide Title and Headings

The text on Slide 4 in Figure 1–1d on page PPT 3 consists of a title and two headings. The appropriate layout for this slide is named Comparison. The following steps add Slide 4 to the presentation with the Comparison layout and then enter the title and heading text for this slide.

1

- Click the New Slide arrow in the Slides group to display the Layout gallery (Figure 1–32).

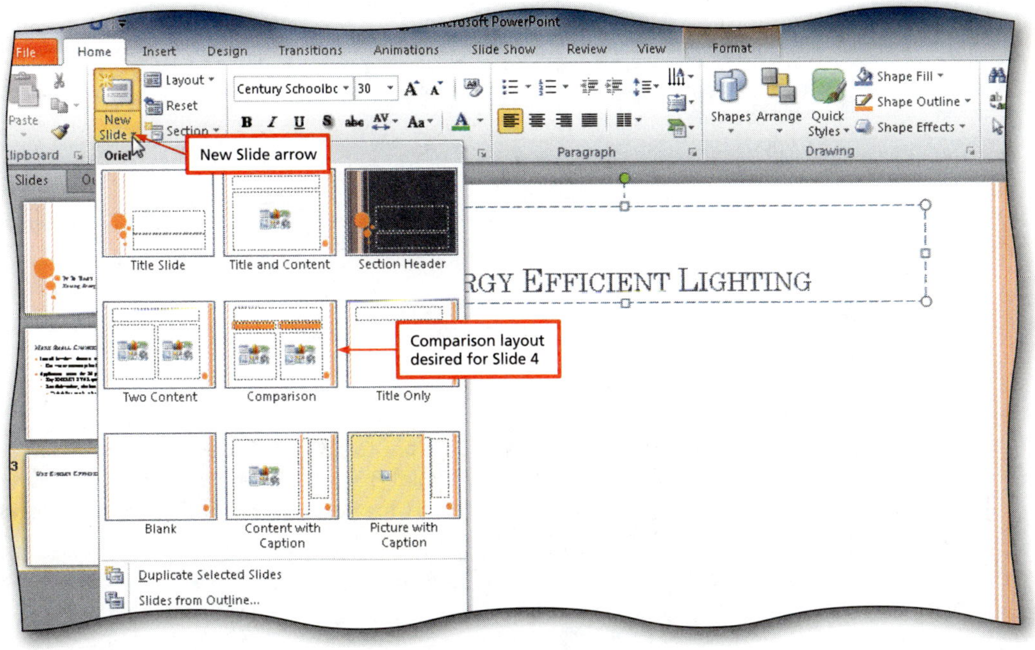

Figure 1–32

2

- Click Comparison to add Slide 4 and apply that layout.
- Type **Adjust Your Thermostats** in the title text placeholder but do not press the ENTER key.
- Click the left orange heading placeholder with the label, Click to add text, to select this placeholder (Figure 1–33).

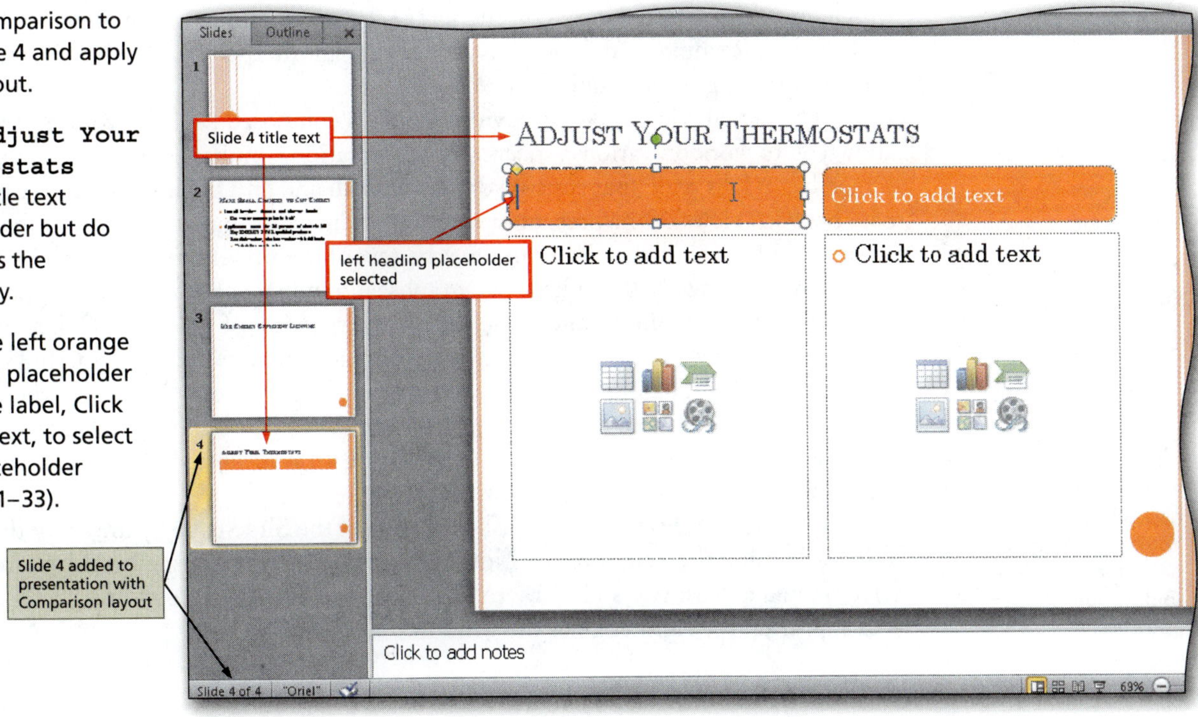

Figure 1–33

3

- Type **Furnace: 68 degrees** but do not press the ENTER key.
- Click the right orange heading placeholder and then type **Water heater: 120 degrees** but do not press the ENTER key (Figure 1–34).

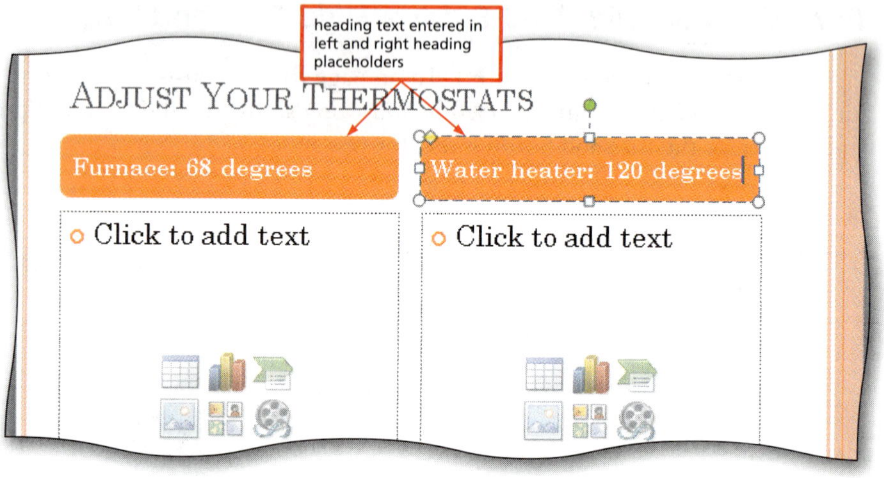

Figure 1–34

Break Point: If you wish to take a break, this is a good place to do so. You can quit PowerPoint now (refer to page PPT 50 for instructions). To resume at a later time, start PowerPoint (refer to pages PPT 4 and PPT 5 for instructions), open the file called Saving Energy (refer to pages PPT 50 and PPT 51 for instructions), and continue following the steps from this location forward.

PowerPoint Views

The PowerPoint window display varies depending on the view. A **view** is the mode in which the presentation appears on the screen. PowerPoint has four main views: Normal, Slide Sorter, Reading, and Slide Show. It also has another view, called Notes Page view, used for entering information about a slide.

The default view is **Normal view**, which is composed of three working areas that allow you to work on various aspects of a presentation simultaneously. The left side of the screen has a Tabs pane that consists of a **Slides tab** and an **Outline tab**. These tabs alternate between views of the presentation in a thumbnail, or miniature, view of the slides and an outline of the slide text. You can type the text of the presentation on the Outline tab and easily rearrange bulleted lists, paragraphs, and individual slides. As you type, you can view this text in the **Slide pane**, which shows a large view of the current slide on the right side of the window. You also can enter text, graphics, animations, and hyperlinks directly in the Slide pane. The **Notes pane** at the bottom of the window is an area where you can type notes and additional information. This text can consist of notes to yourself or remarks to share with your audience. If you want to work with your notes in full page format, you can display them in **Notes Page view**.

In Normal view, you can adjust the width of the Slide pane by dragging the **splitter bar** and the height of the Notes pane by dragging the pane borders. After you have created at least two slides, a scroll bar containing **scroll arrows** and **scroll boxes** will appear on the right edge of the window.

BTW

Using the Notes Pane
As you create your presentation, type comments to yourself in the Notes pane. This material can be used as part of the spoken information you will share with your audience as you give your presentation. You can print these notes for yourself or to distribute to your audience.

To Move to Another Slide in Normal View

When creating or editing a presentation in Normal view (the view you are currently using), you often want to display a slide other than the current one. Before continuing with developing this project, you want to display the title slide by dragging the scroll box on the vertical scroll bar. When you drag the scroll box, the **slide indicator** shows the number and title of the slide you are about to display. Releasing the mouse button shows the slide. The following steps move from Slide 4 to Slide 1 using the scroll box on the Slide pane.

1

- Position the mouse pointer on the scroll box.
- Press and hold down the mouse button so that Slide: 4 of 4 Adjust Your Thermostats appears in the slide indicator (Figure 1–35).

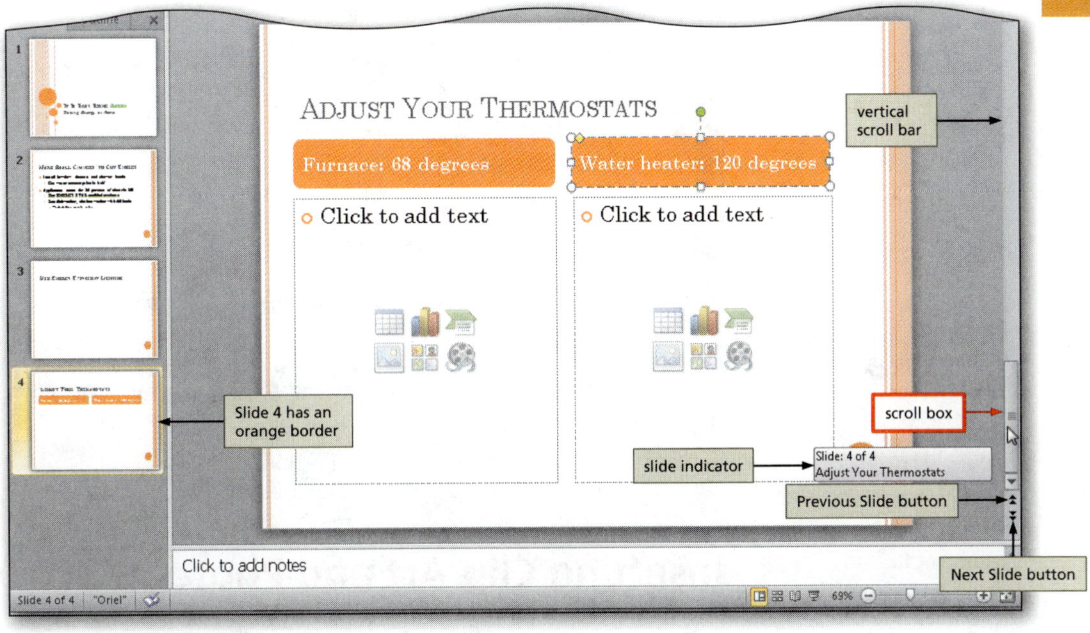

Figure 1–35

2

- Drag the scroll box up the vertical scroll bar until Slide: 1 of 4 It Is Easy Being Green appears in the slide indicator (Figure 1–36).

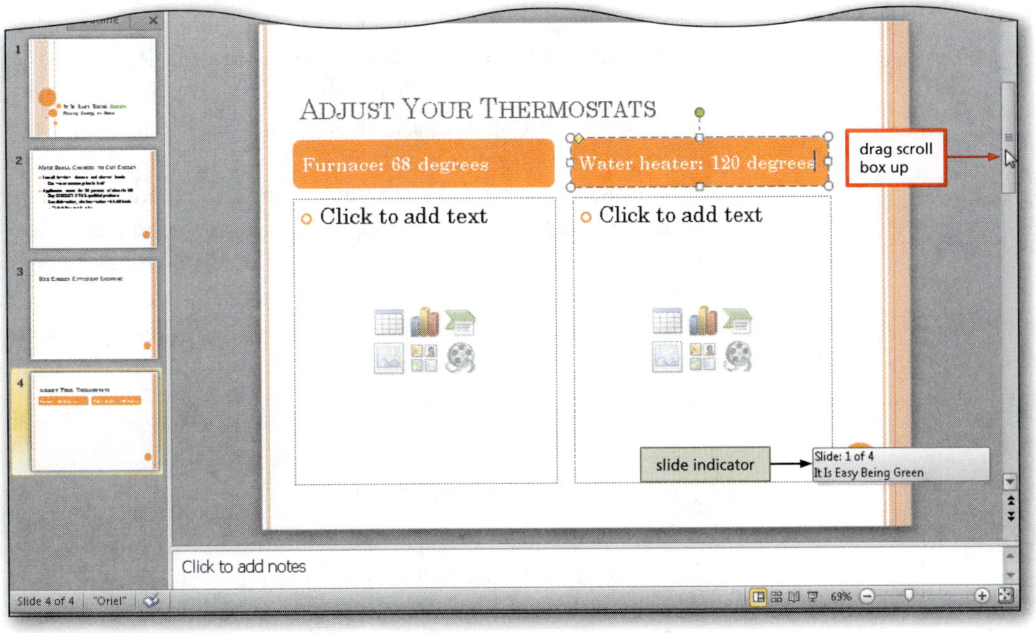

Figure 1–36

3

- Release the mouse button so that Slide 1 appears in the Slide pane and the Slide 1 thumbnail has an orange border in the Slides tab (Figure 1–37).

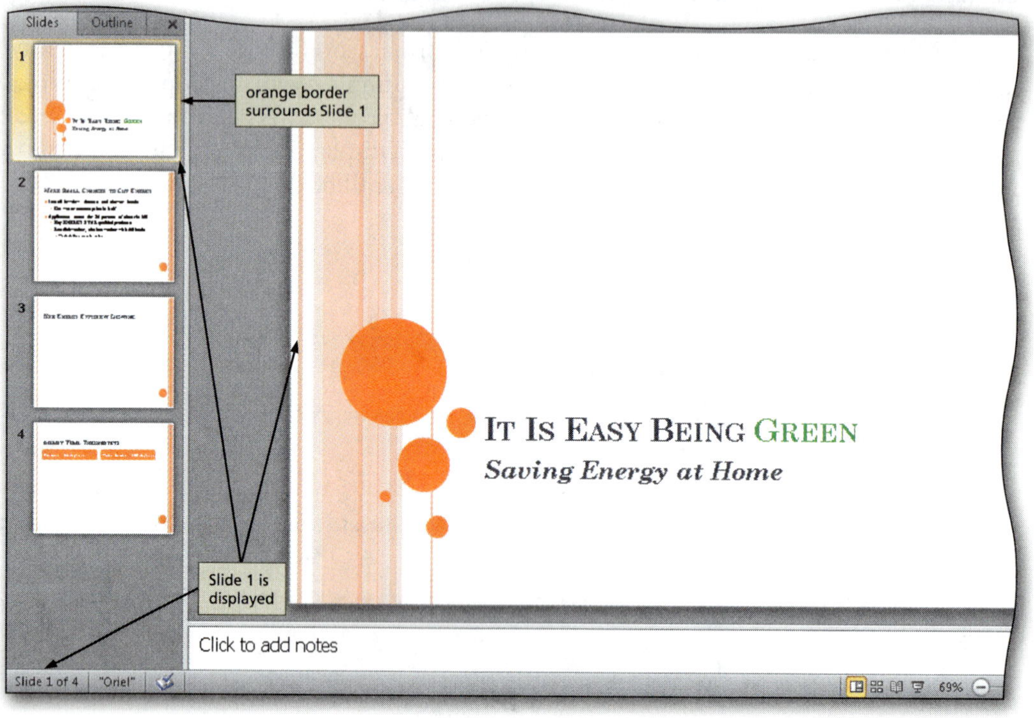

Figure 1–37

Other Ways

1. Click Next Slide button or Previous Slide button to move forward or back one slide
2. Click slide thumbnail on Slides tab
3. Press PAGE DOWN or PAGE UP to move forward or back one slide

BTW

Today's Clip
Each day, Microsoft features "today's clip," which reflects events or themes specific to this time. For example, the pictures, illustrations, and clip art have back-to-school images, winter scenes, and holiday characters.

Inserting Clip Art and Photographs into Slides

A **clip** is a single media file that can include art, sound, animation, or movies. Adding a clip can help increase the visual appeal of many slides and can offer a quick way to add professional-looking graphic images and sounds to a presentation without creating these files yourself. This art is contained in the **Microsoft Clip Organizer**, a collection of drawings, photographs, sounds, videos, and other media files shared among Microsoft Office applications. The **Office Collections** contains all these media files included with Microsoft Office.

You also can add your own clips to slides. You can insert these files directly from a storage medium, such as a USB flash drive. In addition, you can add them to the other files in the Clip Organizer so that you can search for and reuse these images, sounds, animations, and movies. When you create these media files, they are stored on your hard disk in **My Collections**. The Clip Organizer will find these files and create a new collection with these files. Two other locations for clips are Shared Collections and Web Collections. Files in the **Shared Collections** typically reside on a shared network file server and are accessible to multiple users. The **Web Collections** clips reside on the Microsoft Clip Art and Media Home page on the Microsoft Office Online Web site. They are available only if you have an active Internet connection.

The Clip Art Task Pane

You can add clips to your presentation in two ways. One way is by selecting one of the slide layouts that includes a content placeholder with a Clip Art button. A second method is by clicking the Clip Art button in the Images area on the Insert tab. Clicking the Clip Art button opens the Clip Art task pane. The **Clip Art task pane** allows you to search for clips by using descriptive keywords, file names, media file formats, and clip collections. Specific file formats could be for clip art, photographs, movies, and sounds.

Clips are organized in hierarchical **clip collections** that combine topic-related clips into categories, such as Academic, Business, and Technology.

Clips have one or more keywords associated with various entities, activities, labels, and emotions. In most instances, the keywords give the name of the clip and related categories. For example, an image of a cow in the Animals category has the keywords animals, cattle, cows, dairies, farms, and Holsteins. You can enter these keywords in the Search for text box to find clips when you know one of the words associated with the image. Otherwise, you might find it necessary to scroll through several categories to find an appropriate clip.

Depending on the installation of the Microsoft Clip Organizer on your computer, you might not have the clip art used in this chapter. Contact your instructor if you are missing clips used in the following steps. If you have an active connection to the Internet, clips from the Microsoft Office Online Web site will display automatically as the result of your search results.

Plan Ahead

Adhere to copyright regulations.
You have permission to use the clips from the Microsoft Clip Organizer. If you want to use a clip from another source, be certain you have the legal right to insert this file in your presentation. Read the copyright notices that may accompany the clip and may be posted on the Web site where you obtained the clip. The owners of these images and files often ask you to give them credit for using their work, which may be satisfied by stating where you obtained the images.

To Insert a Clip from the Clip Organizer into the Title Slide

Slide 1 uses the Title Slide layout, which has two placeholders for text but none for graphical content. You desire to place a graphic on Slide 1, so you will locate a clip art image of a green globe and flower and then insert it in this slide. Later in this chapter, you will size and position it in an appropriate location. The following steps add a clip to Slide 1.

1

- Click Insert on the Ribbon to display the Insert tab.
- Click the Clip Art button (Insert tab | Images group) to display the Clip Art task pane.
- Click the Search for text box in the Clip Art task pane, if necessary delete any letters that are present, and then type `green globe` in the Search for text box.
- If necessary, click the 'Include Office.com content' check box to select it (Figure 1–38).

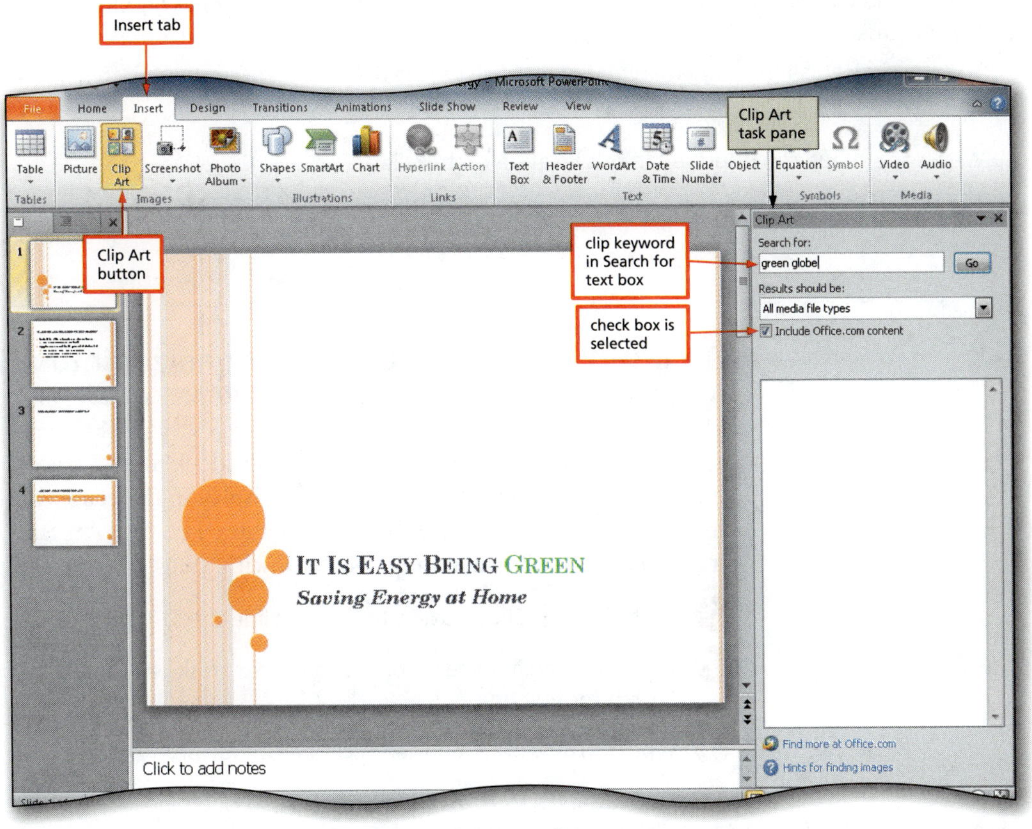

Figure 1–38

2

- Click the Go button so that the Microsoft Clip Organizer will search for and display all clips having the keywords, green globe.
- If necessary, click the Yes button if a Microsoft Clip Organizer dialog box appears asking if you want to include additional clip art images from Office.com.
- If necessary, scroll down the list to display the globe clip shown in Figure 1–39.
- Click the clip to insert it into the slide (Figure 1–39).

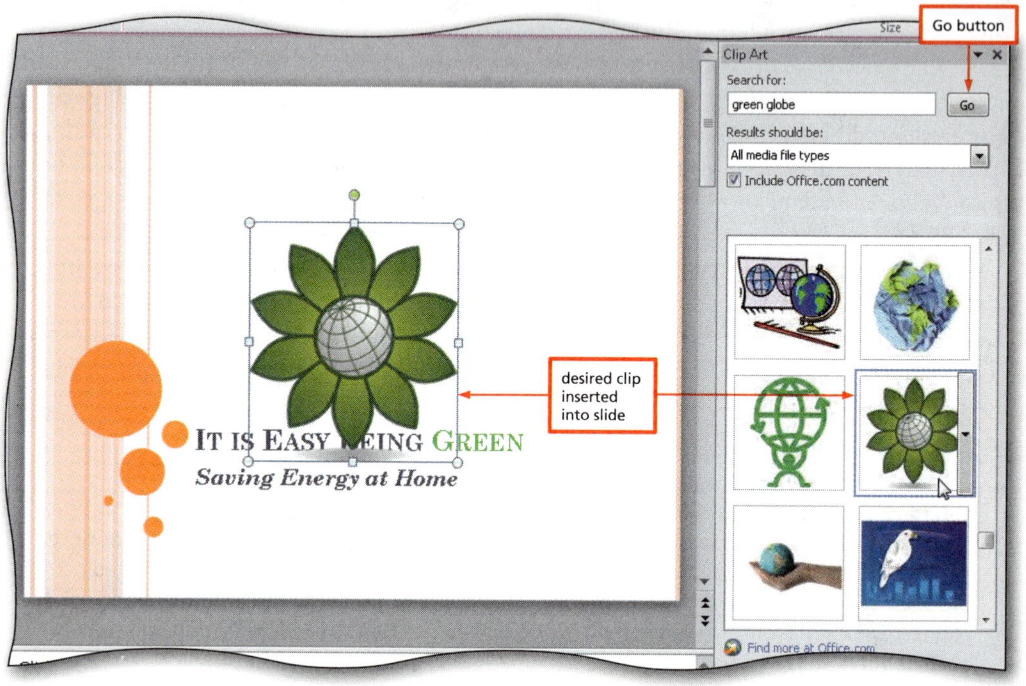

Figure 1–39

Q&A What if the globe image displayed in Figure 1–39 is not shown in my Clip Art task pane?
Select a similar clip. Your clips may be different depending on the clips installed on your computer and if you have an active connection to the Internet.

Q&A What is the yellow star image that displays in the lower-right corner of some clips in the Clip Art task pane?
The star indicates the image is animated and will move when the slide containing this clip is displayed during a slide show.

Q&A Why is this globe clip displayed in this location on the slide?
The slide layout does not have a content placeholder, so PowerPoint inserts the clip in the center of the slide.

To Insert a Clip from the Clip Organizer into a Slide without a Content Placeholder

The next step is to add two clips to Slide 2. Slide 2 has a bulleted list in the text placeholder, so the icon group does not display in the center of the placeholder. Later in this chapter, you will resize the inserted clips. The Clip Art task pane is displayed and will remain open until you close it. The following steps add one clip to Slide 2.

1. Click the Next Slide button to display Slide 2.
2. Click the Search for text box in the Clip Art task pane and then delete the letters in the Search for text box.
3. Type `faucets` and then click the Go button.
4. If necessary, scroll down the list to display the faucet clip shown in Figure 1–40 and then click the clip to insert it into Slide 2 (Figure 1–40).

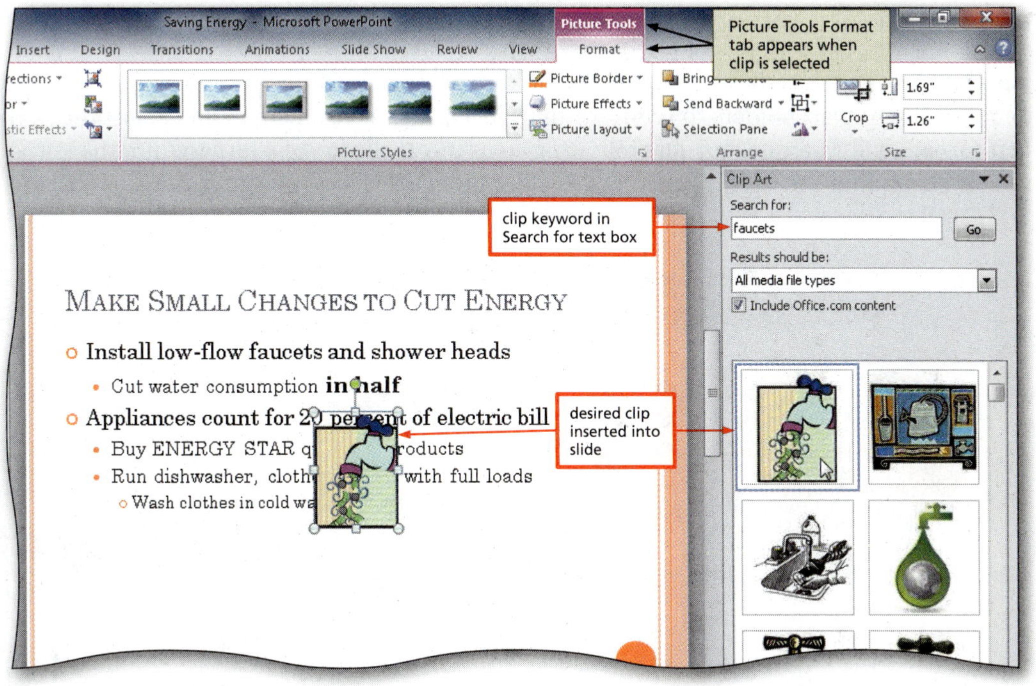

Figure 1–40

To Insert a Second Clip from the Clip Organizer into a Slide without a Content Placeholder

The following steps add a second clip to Slide 2. PowerPoint inserts this clip on top of the faucet clip in the center of the slide. Both clips will be moved and resized later in this chapter.

1. Click the Search for text box in the Clip Art task pane and then delete the letters in the text box.

2. Type **dishwasher**, click the Go button, locate the clip shown in Figure 1–41, and then click the clip to insert it into Slide 2 (Figure 1–41).

BTW

Clip Properties
Each clip has properties that identify its characteristics. When you right-click a clip in the Microsoft Clip Organizer, you will see details of the clip's name, file type, size, dimensions, keywords, and creation date. You also can preview the clip and edit its assigned keywords.

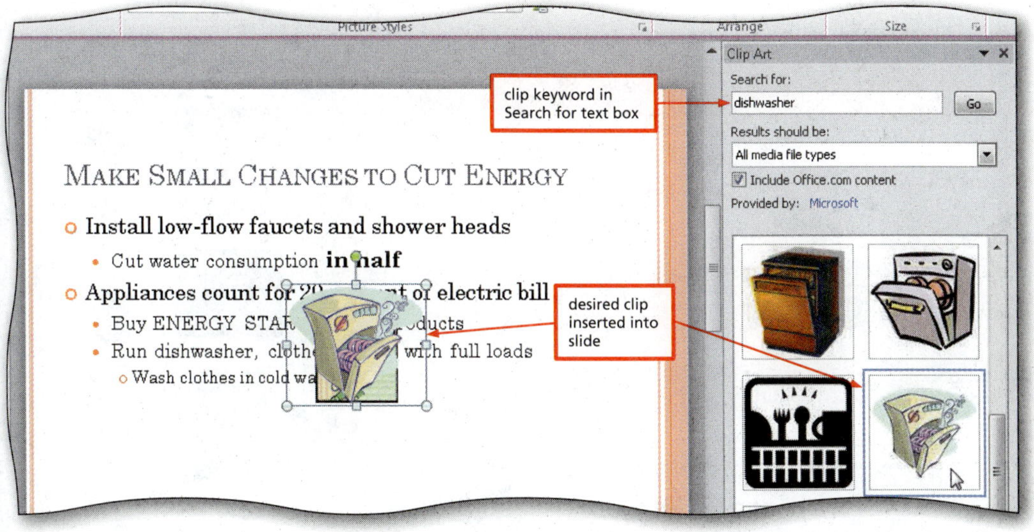

Figure 1–41

To Insert a Clip from the Clip Organizer into a Content Placeholder

Slide 4 uses the Comparison layout, which has a content placeholder below each of the two headings. You desire to insert clip art into both content placeholders to reinforce the concept that consumers should adjust the heating temperatures of their furnace and water heater. The following steps insert clip art of a furnace into the left content placeholder and a water heater into the right content placeholder on Slide 4.

1

- Click the Close button in the Clip Art task pane so that it no longer is displayed.
- Click the Next Slide button twice to display Slide 4.
- Click the Clip Art icon in the left content placeholder to select that placeholder and to open the Clip Art task pane (Figure 1–42).

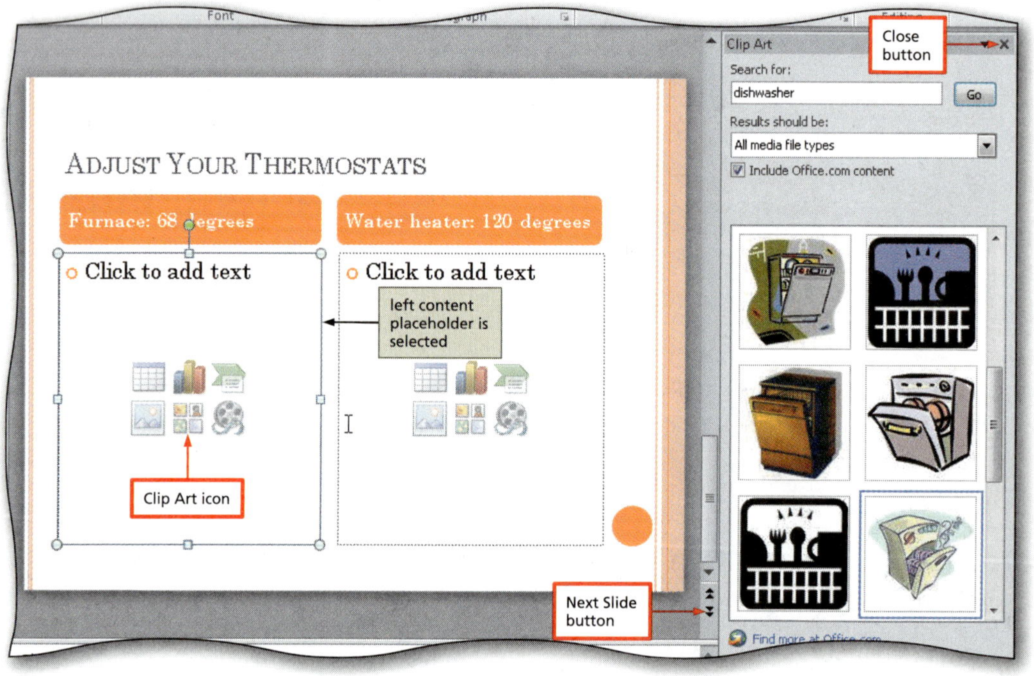

Figure 1–42

Q&A Do I need to close the Clip Art task pane when I am finished inserting the two clips into Slide 2?

No. You can leave the Clip Art task pane open and then display Slide 4. It is often more convenient, however, to open this pane when you are working with a layout that has a content placeholder so that the clip is inserted in the desired location.

2

- Click the Search for text box in the Clip Art task pane, delete any letters that are present, type **furnace** in the Search for text box, and then click the Go button to search for and display all pictures having the keyword, furnace.
- If necessary, scroll down the list to display the furnace clip shown in Figure 1–43.
- Click the clip to insert it into the left content placeholder (Figure 1–43).

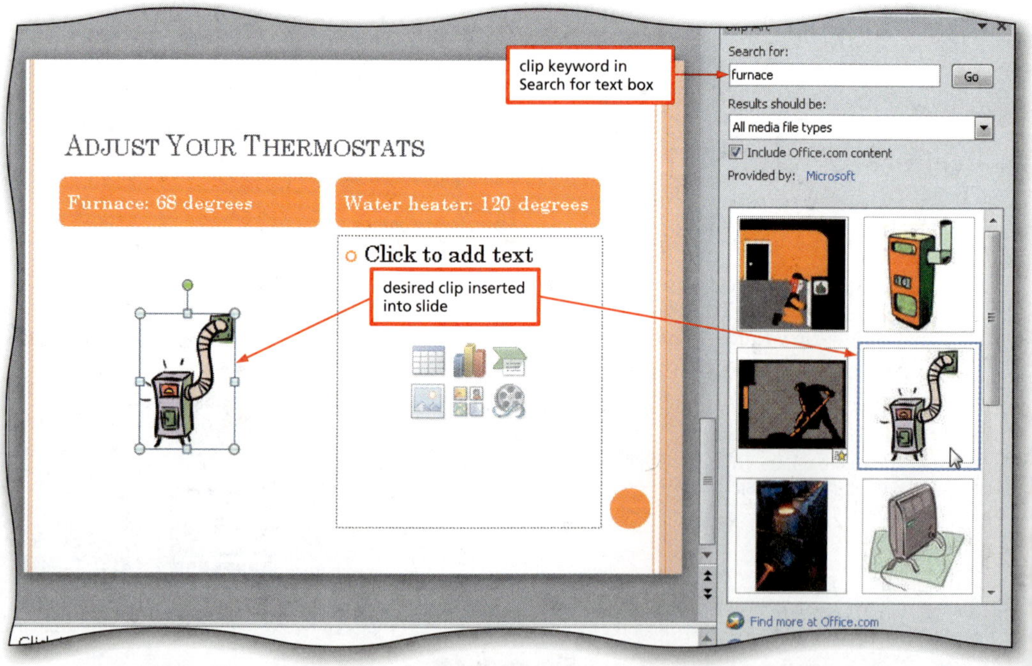

Figure 1–43

3

- Click anywhere in the right placeholder except one of the six icons to select the placeholder.

Q&A I clicked the Clip Art icon by mistake, which closed the Clip Art task pane. How do I open it?

Click the Clip Art icon.

4

- Click the Search for text box in the Clip Art task pane, delete any letters that are present, type `water heater` in the Search for text box, and then click the Go button.
- If necessary, scroll down the list to display the water heater clip shown in Figure 1–44 and then click the clip to insert it into the right content placeholder (Figure 1–44).

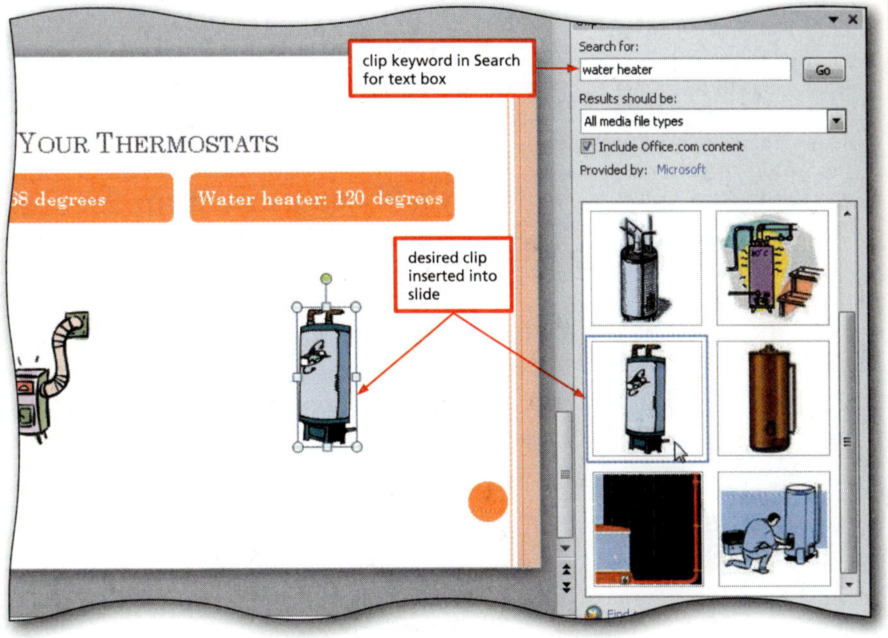

Figure 1–44

Photographs and the Clip Organizer

In addition to clip art, you can insert pictures into a presentation. These may include scanned photographs, line art, and artwork from storage media, such as USB flash drives, hard disks, optical discs, and memory cards. To insert a picture into a presentation, the picture must be saved in a format that PowerPoint can recognize. Table 1–1 identifies some of the formats PowerPoint recognizes.

Table 1–1 Primary File Formats PowerPoint Recognizes

Format	File Extension
Computer Graphics Metafile	.cgm
CorelDRAW	.cdr, .cdt, .cmx, and .pat
Encapsulated PostScript	.eps
Enhanced Metafile	.emf
FlashPix	.fpx
Graphics Interchange Format	.gif
Hanako	.jsh, .jah, and .jbh
Joint Photographic Experts Group (JPEG)	.jpg
Kodak PhotoCD	.pcd
Macintosh PICT	.pct
PC Paintbrush	.pcx
Portable Network Graphics	.png
Tagged Image File Format	.tif
Windows Bitmap	.bmp, .rle, .dib
Microsoft Windows Metafile	.wmf
WordPerfect Graphics	.wpg

BTW

Compressing File Size
When you add a picture to a presentation, PowerPoint automatically compresses this image. Even with this compression applied, a presentation that contains pictures usually has a large file size. To reduce this size, you can compress a picture further without affecting the quality of how it displays on the slide. To compress a picture, select the picture and then click the Compress Pictures button (Picture Tools Format tab | Adjust group). You can restore the picture's original settings by clicking the Reset Picture button (Picture Tools Format tab | Adjust group).

BTW

Wrapping Text around a Picture
PowerPoint 2010 does not allow you to wrap text around a picture or other graphics, such as tables, shapes, charts, or graphics. This feature, however, is available in Word 2010.

You can import files saved with the .emf, .gif, .jpg, .png, .bmp, .rle, .dib, and .wmf formats directly into PowerPoint presentations. All other file formats require separate filters that are shipped with the PowerPoint installation software and must be installed separately. You can download additional filters from the Microsoft Office Online Web site.

To Insert a Photograph from the Clip Organizer into a Slide without a Content Placeholder

Next, you will add a photograph to Slide 3. You will not insert this picture into a content placeholder, so it will display in the center of the slide. Later in this chapter, you will resize this picture. To start the process of locating this photograph, you do not need to click the Clip Art button icon in the content placeholder because the Clip Art task pane already is displayed. The following steps add a photograph to Slide 3.

1. Click the Previous Slide button to display Slide 3.
2. Click the Search for text box in the Clip Art task pane, delete the letters in the text box, type **CFL**, and then click the Go button.
3. If necessary, scroll down the list to display the picture of a light bulb shown in Figure 1–45, and then click the photograph to insert it into Slide 2 (Figure 1–45).

Q&A

Why is my photograph a different size from the one shown in Figure 1–1c on page PPT 3?

The photograph was inserted into the slide and not into a content placeholder. You will resize the picture later in this chapter.

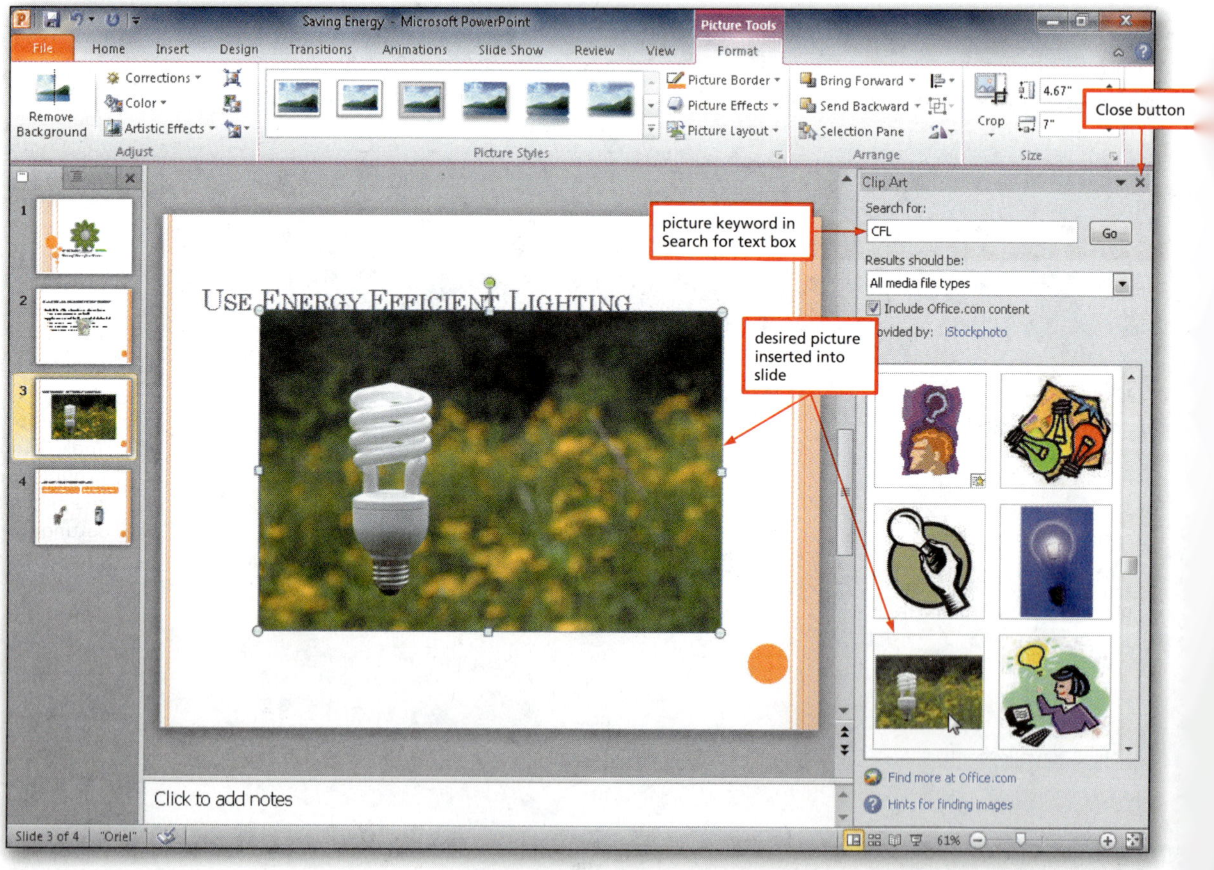

Figure 1–45

Break Point: If you wish to take a break, this is a good place to do so. You can quit PowerPoint now (refer to page PPT 50 for instructions). To resume at a later time, start PowerPoint (refer to pages PPT 4 and PPT 5 for instructions), open the file called Saving Energy (refer to pages PPT 50 and PPT 51 for instructions), and continue following the steps from this location forward.

Resizing Clip Art and Photographs

Sometimes it is necessary to change the size of clip art. **Resizing** includes enlarging or reducing the size of a clip art graphic. You can resize clip art using a variety of techniques. One method involves changing the size of a clip by specifying exact dimensions in a dialog box. Another method involves dragging one of the graphic's sizing handles to the desired location. A selected graphic appears surrounded by a **selection rectangle**, which has small squares and circles, called **sizing handles** or move handles, at each corner and middle location.

To Resize Clip Art

On Slides 1, 2, and 4, much space appears around the clips, so you can increase their sizes. Likewise, the photograph on Slide 3 can be enlarged to fill more of the space below the slide title. To change the size, drag the corner sizing handles to view how the clip will look on the slide. Using these corner handles maintains the graphic's original proportions. Dragging the square sizing handles alters the proportions so that the graphic's height and width become larger or smaller. The following steps increase the size of the Slide 1 clip using a corner sizing handle.

1

- Click the Close button in the Clip Art task pane so that it no longer is displayed.
- Click the Previous Slide button two times to display Slide 1.
- Click the globe clip to select it and display the selection rectangle.
- Point to the lower-left corner sizing handle on the clip so that the mouse pointer changes to a two-headed arrow (Figure 1–46).

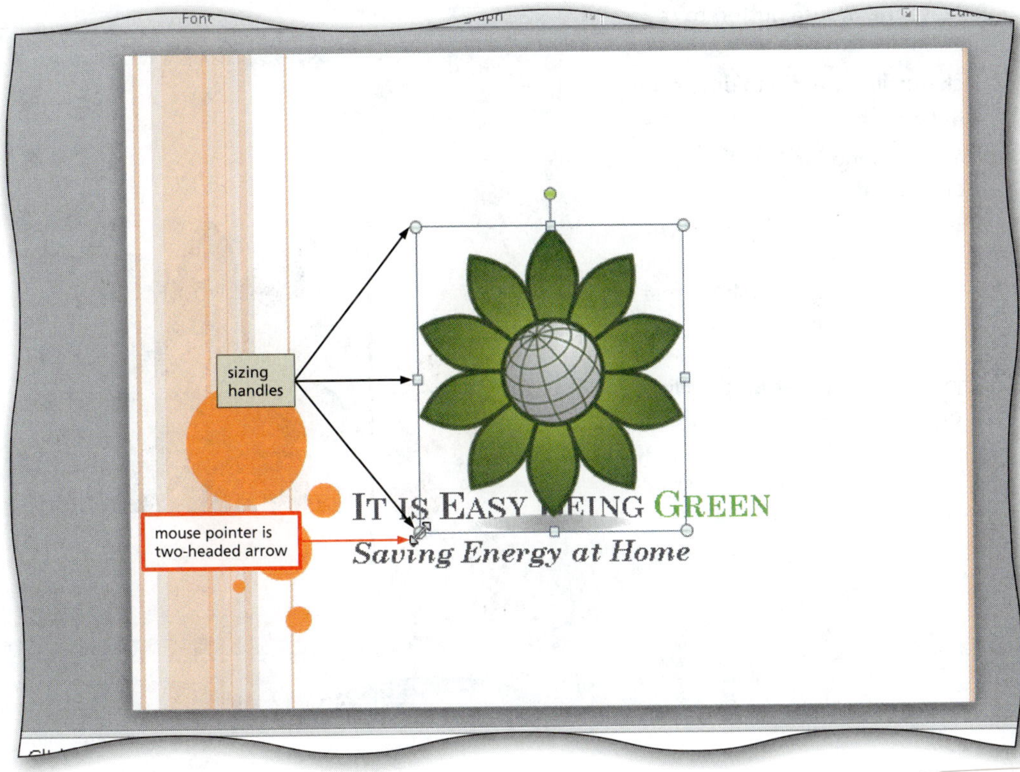

Figure 1–46

2

- Drag the sizing handle diagonally toward the lower-left corner of the slide until the mouse pointer is positioned approximately as shown in Figure 1–47.

Q&A What if the clip is not the same size as the one shown in Figure 1–47?

Repeat Steps 1 and 2.

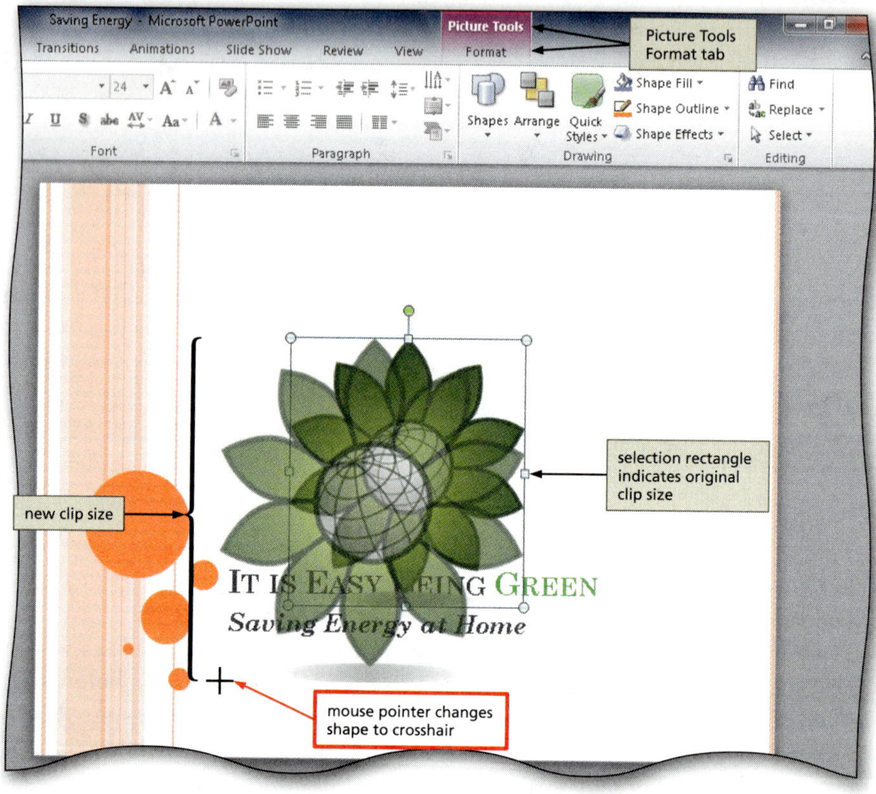

Figure 1–47

3

- Release the mouse button to resize the clip.
- Click outside the clip to deselect it (Figure 1–48).

Q&A What happened to the Picture Tools Format tab?

When you click outside the clip, PowerPoint deselects the clip and removes the Picture Tools Format tab from the screen.

Q&A What if I want to return the clip to its original size and start again?

With the graphic selected, click the Reset Picture button (Picture Tools Format tab | Adjust group).

Figure 1–48

To Resize Clips on Slide 4

The two clip art images on Slide 4 also can be enlarged to fill much of the white space below the headings. You will reposition the clips in a later step. The following steps resize these clips using a sizing handle.

1. Click the Next Slide button three times to display Slide 4.
2. Click the furnace clip to select it.
3. Drag the lower-left corner sizing handle on the clip diagonally outward until the clip is resized approximately as shown in Figure 1–49.
4. Click the water heater clip to select it.
5. Drag the lower-right corner sizing handle on the clip diagonally outward until the clip is resized approximately as shown in Figure 1–49.

Figure 1–49

BTW

Minimalist Design
Resist the urge to fill your slides with clips from the Microsoft Clip Organizer. Minimalist style reduces clutter and allows the slide content to display prominently. This simple, yet effective design helps audience members with short attention spans to focus on the message.

To Resize a Photograph

The light bulb picture in Slide 3 can be enlarged slightly to fill much of the space below the slide title. You resize a photograph in the same manner that you resize clip art. The following steps resize this photograph using a sizing handle.

1. Click the Previous Slide button to display Slide 3.
2. Click the light bulb photograph to select it.

3 Drag the lower-left corner sizing handle on the photograph diagonally outward until the photograph is resized approximately as shown in Figure 1–50.

Figure 1–50

To Move Clips

After you insert clip art or a photograph on a slide, you might want to reposition it. The light bulb photograph on Slide 3 could be centered in the space between the slide title and the left and right edges of the slide. The clip on Slide 1 could be positioned in the upper-right corner of the slide. On Slide 4, the furnace and water heater clips could be centered under each heading. The following steps move these graphics.

1

- If necessary, click the light bulb photograph on Slide 3 to select it.
- Press and hold down the mouse button and then drag the photograph diagonally downward below the title text (Figure 1–51).
- If necessary, select the photograph and then use the ARROW keys to position it precisely as shown in Figure 1–51.

Q&A The photograph still is not located exactly where I want it to display. What can I do to align the photograph?

Press the CTRL key while you press the ARROW keys. This key combination moves the clip in smaller increments than when you press only an ARROW key.

Figure 1–51

2

- Click the Next Slide button to display Slide 4.
- Click the furnace clip to select it, press and hold down the mouse button, and then drag the clip to center it under the furnace heading.
- Click the water heater clip and then drag the clip to center it under the water heater heading (Figure 1–52).

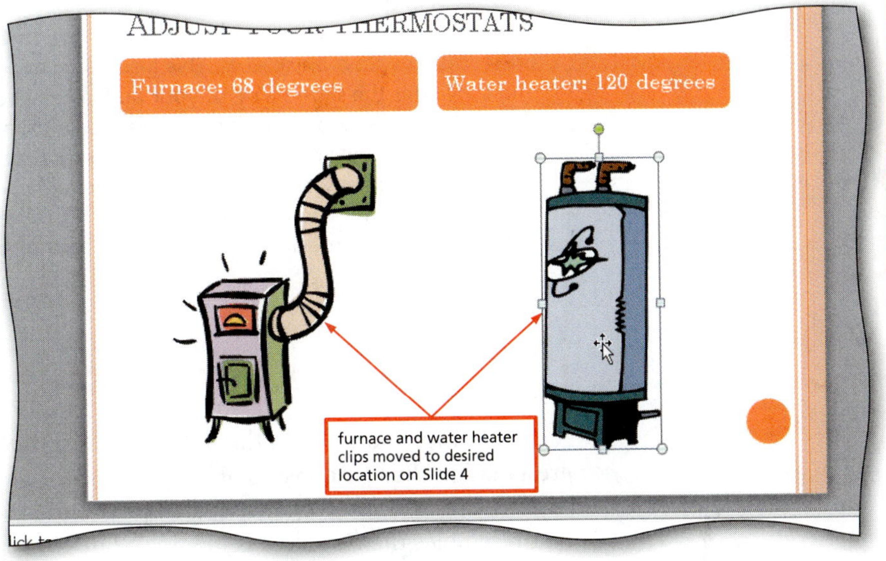

Figure 1–52

3

- Click the Previous Slide button twice to display Slide 2.
- Click the dishwasher clip, which is on top of the faucet clip, and then drag the clip to center it under the last bulleted paragraph, Wash clothes in cold water.
- Click the faucet clip and then drag the clip so that the faucet handle is centered under the words, full loads.
- Drag a corner sizing handle on the faucet clip diagonally outward until the clip is resized approximately as shown in Figure 1–53. You may need to drag the clip to position it in the desired location.
- Select the dishwasher clip and then resize and move it so that the clip displays approximately as shown in Figure 1–53.

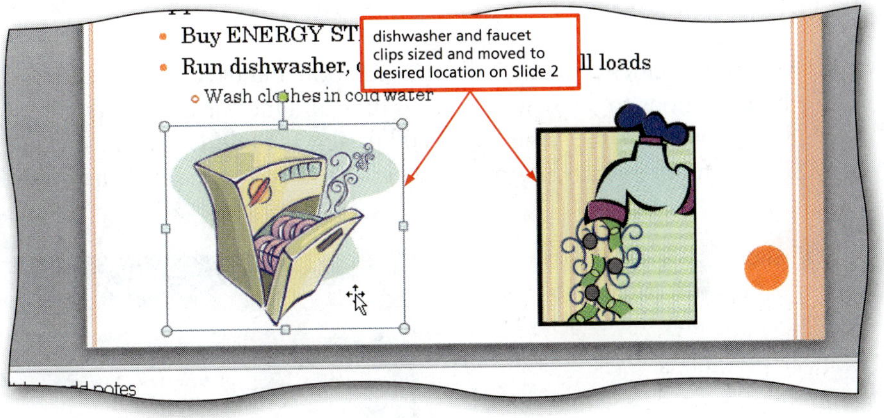

Figure 1–53

4

- Click the Previous Slide button to display Slide 1.
- Click the globe clip and then drag it to the upper-right corner of the slide. You may want to adjust its size by selecting it and then dragging the corner sizing handles.
- Click outside the clip to deselect it (Figure 1–54).

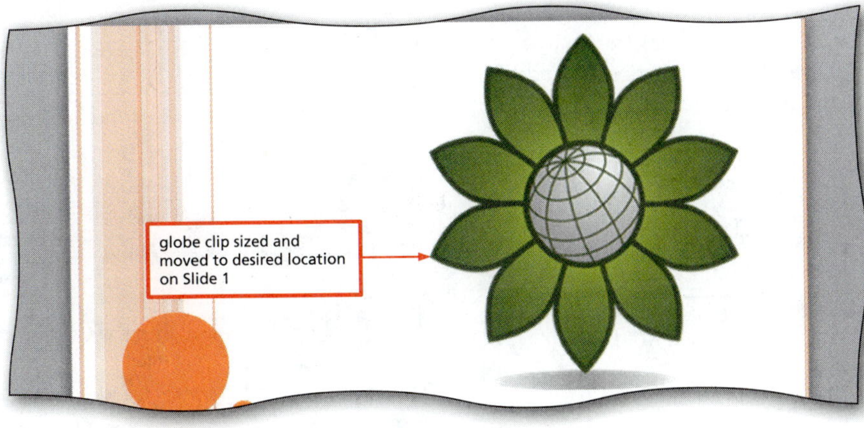

Figure 1–54

Plan Ahead

Choose a closing slide.
After the last slide appears during a slide show, the default PowerPoint setting is to end the presentation with a **black slide.** This black slide appears only when the slide show is running and concludes the slide show, so your audience never sees the PowerPoint window. It is a good idea, however, to end the presentation with a final closing slide to display at the end of the presentation. This slide ends the presentation gracefully and should be an exact copy, or a very similar copy, of your title slide. The audience will recognize that the presentation is drawing to a close when this slide appears. It can remain on the screen when the audience asks questions, approaches the speaker for further information, or exits the room.

Ending a Slide Show with a Closing Slide

All the text for the slides in the Saving Energy slide show has been entered. This presentation thus far consists of a title slide, one text slide with a multi-level bulleted list, a third slide for a photograph, and a fourth slide with a Comparison layout. A closing slide that resembles the title slide is the final slide to create.

To Duplicate a Slide

When two slides contain similar information and have the same format, duplicating one slide and then making minor modifications to the new slide saves time and increases consistency.

Slide 5 will have the same layout and design as Slide 1. The most expedient method of creating this slide is to copy Slide 1 and then make minor modifications to the new slide. The following steps duplicate the title slide.

1

- With Slide 1 selected, click the New Slide arrow (Home tab | Slides group) to display the Oriel layout gallery (Figure 1–55).

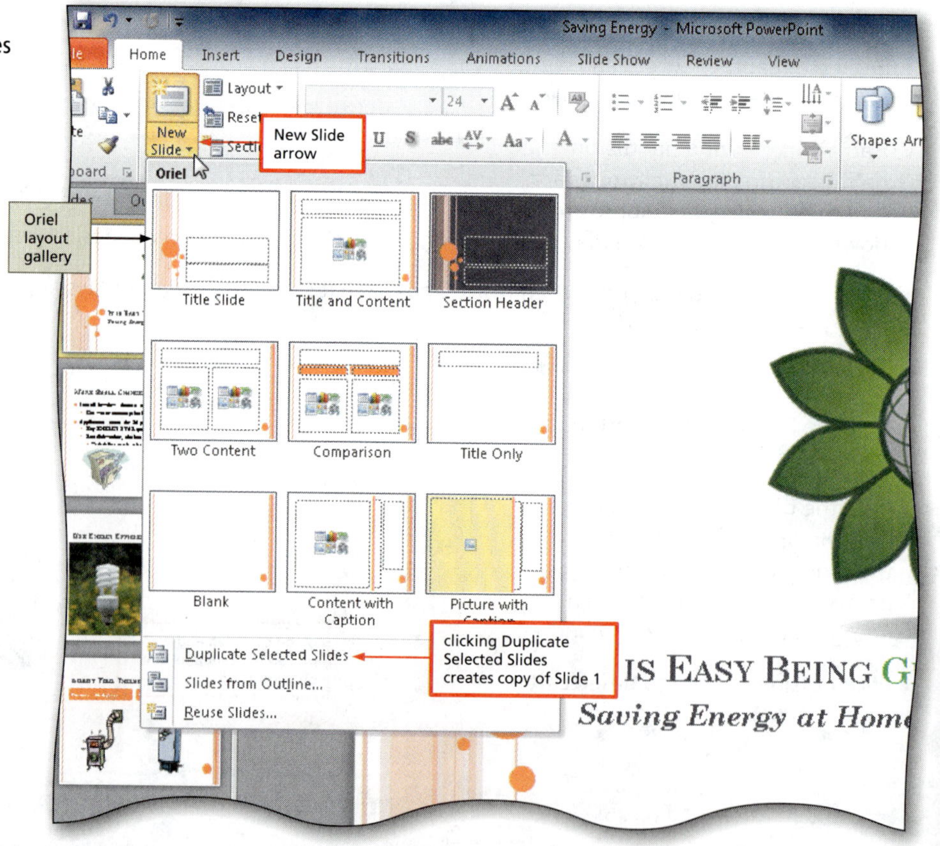

Figure 1–55

2

- Click Duplicate Selected Slides in the Oriel layout gallery to create a new Slide 2, which is a duplicate of Slide 1 (Figure 1–56).

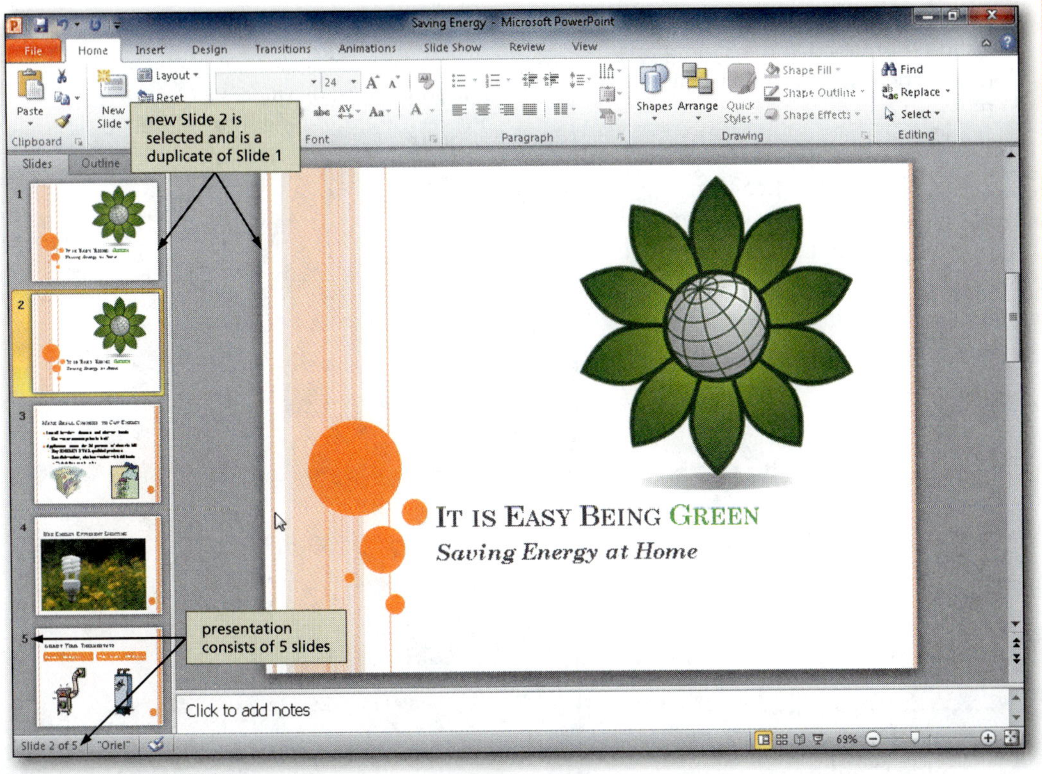

Figure 1–56

Break Point: If you wish to take a break, this is a good place to do so. You can quit PowerPoint now (refer to page PPT 50 for instructions). To resume at a later time, start PowerPoint (refer to pages PPT 4 and PPT 5 for instructions), open the file called Saving Energy (refer to pages PPT 50 and PPT 51 for instructions), and continue following the steps from this location forward.

To Arrange a Slide

The new Slide 2 was inserted directly below Slide 1 because Slide 1 was the selected slide. This duplicate slide needs to display at the end of the presentation directly after the final title and content slide.

Changing slide order is an easy process and is best performed in the Slides pane. When you click the slide thumbnail and begin to drag it to a new location, a line indicates the new location of the selected slide. When you release the mouse button, the slide drops into the desired location. Hence, this process of dragging and then dropping the thumbnail in a new location is called **drag and drop**. You can use the drag-and-drop method to move any selected item, including text and graphics. The step on the next page moves the new Slide 2 to the end of the presentation so that it becomes a closing slide.

1

- With Slide 2 selected, drag the Slide 2 slide thumbnail in the Slides pane below the last slide thumbnail (Figure 1–57).

Q&A

The Slide 2 thumbnail is not visible in the Slides pane when I am dragging the thumbnail downward. How do I know it will be positioned in the desired location?

A blue horizontal bar indicates where the slide will move.

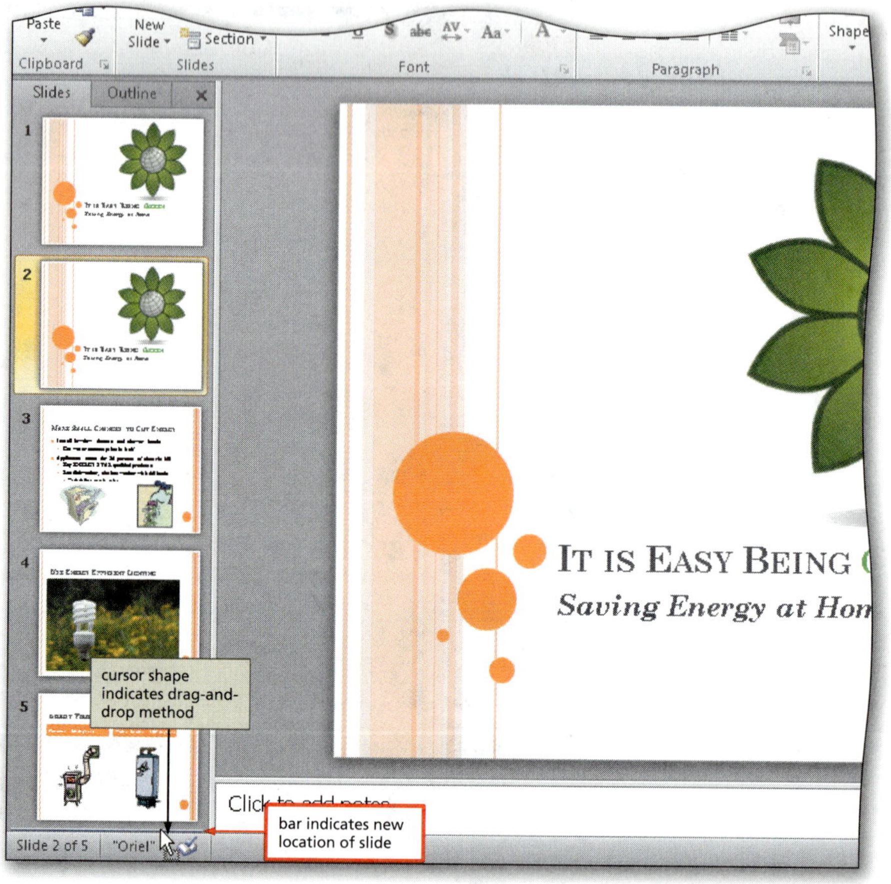

Figure 1–57

Other Ways

1. Click slide icon on Outline tab, drag icon to new location
2. Click Slide Sorter (View tab | Presentation Views group), click slide thumbnail, drag thumbnail to new location

Making Changes to Slide Text Content

After creating slides in a presentation, you may find that you want to make changes to the text. Changes may be required because a slide contains an error, the scope of the presentation shifts, or the style is inconsistent. This section explains the types of changes that commonly occur when creating a presentation.

You generally make three types of changes to text in a presentation: additions, replacements, and deletions.

- Additions are necessary when you omit text from a slide and need to add it later. You may need to insert text in the form of a sentence, word, or single character. For example, you may want to add the presenter's middle name on the title slide.
- Replacements are needed when you want to revise the text in a presentation. For example, you may want to substitute the word *their* for the word *there*.
- Deletions are required when text on a slide is incorrect or no longer is relevant to the presentation. For example, a slide may look cluttered. Therefore, you may want to remove one of the bulleted paragraphs to add more space.

Editing text in PowerPoint basically is the same as editing text in a word processing program. The following sections illustrate the most common changes made to text in a presentation.

BTW

Checking Spelling
As you review your slides, you should examine the text for spelling errors. In PowerPoint Chapter 3, you will learn to use PowerPoint's built-in spelling checker to help you perform this task.

Replacing Text in an Existing Slide

When you need to correct a word or phrase, you can replace the text by selecting the text to be replaced and then typing the new text. As soon as you press any key on the keyboard, the selected text is deleted and the new text is displayed.

PowerPoint inserts text to the left of the insertion point. The text to the right of the insertion point moves to the right (and shifts downward if necessary) to accommodate the added text.

Deleting Text

You can delete text using one of three methods. One is to use the BACKSPACE key to remove text just typed. The second is to position the insertion point to the left of the text you want to delete and then press the DELETE key. The third method is to drag through the text you want to delete and then press the DELETE or BACKSPACE key. Use the third method when deleting large sections of text.

To Delete Text in a Placeholder

To keep the ending slide clean and simple, you want to delete a few words in the slide show title and subtitle text. The following steps change It Is Easy Being Green to Be Green and then change Saving Energy at Home to Save Energy.

1

- With Slide 5 selected, position the mouse pointer immediately to the left of the first character of the text to be selected (in this case, the I in the word, It).
- Drag the mouse pointer through the last character of the text to be selected (in this case, the space after the y in Easy) (Figure 1–58).

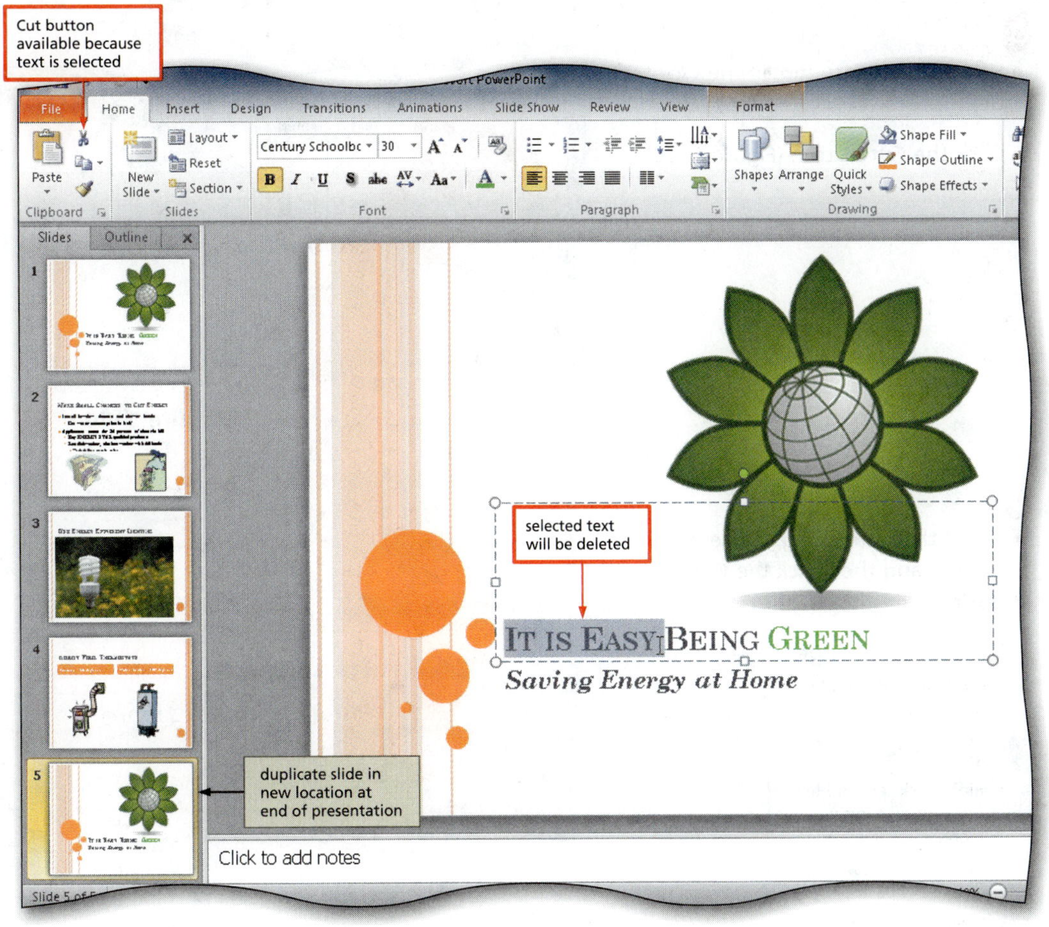

Figure 1–58

2

- Click the Cut button (Home tab | Clipboard group) to delete all the selected text (Figure 1–59).

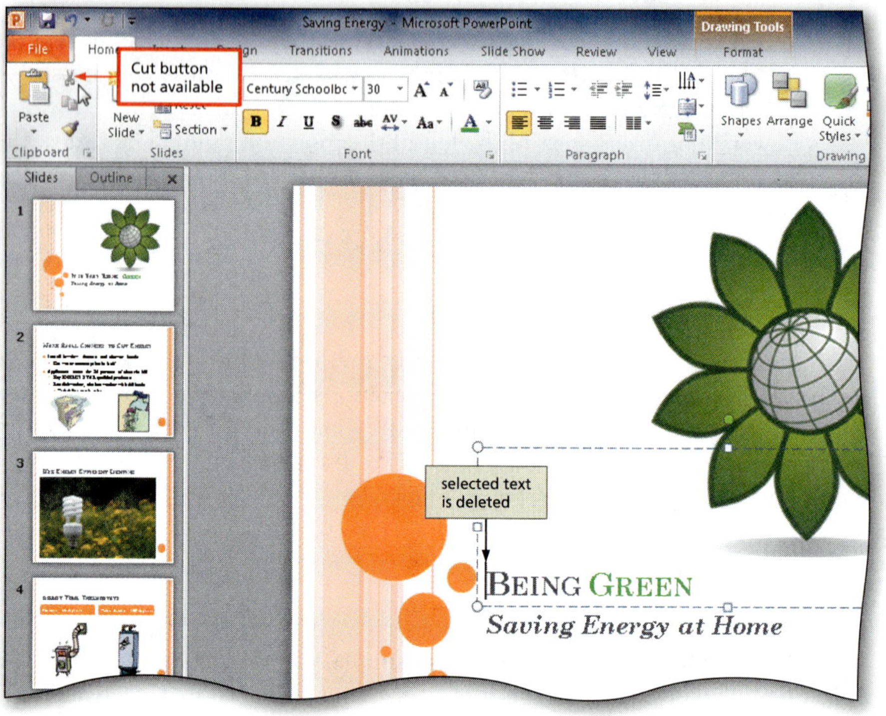

Figure 1–59

3

- Select the letters, ing, in the word, Being.
- Click the Cut button (Figure 1–60).

Figure 1–60

4

- Select the letters, ing, in the word, Saving, and then click the Cut button.
- Type e to change the word to Save (Figure 1–61).

Figure 1–61

Other Ways

1. Right-click selected text, click Cut on shortcut menu
2. Select text, press DELETE or BACKSPACE key
3. Select text, press CTRL+X

Adding a Transition

PowerPoint provides many animation effects to add interest and make a slide show presentation look professional. **Animation** includes special visual and sound effects applied to text or content. A **slide transition** is a special animation effect used to progress from one slide to the next in a slide show. You can control the speed of the transition effect and add a sound.

PowerPoint provides a variety of transitions arranged into three categories that describe the types of effects: Subtle, Exciting, and Dynamic Content.

To Add a Transition between Slides

In this presentation, you apply the Doors transition in the Exciting category to all slides and change the transition speed from 1.40 seconds to 2 seconds. The following steps apply this transition to the presentation.

1

- Click the Transitions tab on the Ribbon and then point to the More button (Transitions tab | Transition to This Slide group) (Figure 1–62).

Q&A Is a transition applied now?

No. The first slide icon in the Transitions group has an orange border, which indicates no transition has been applied.

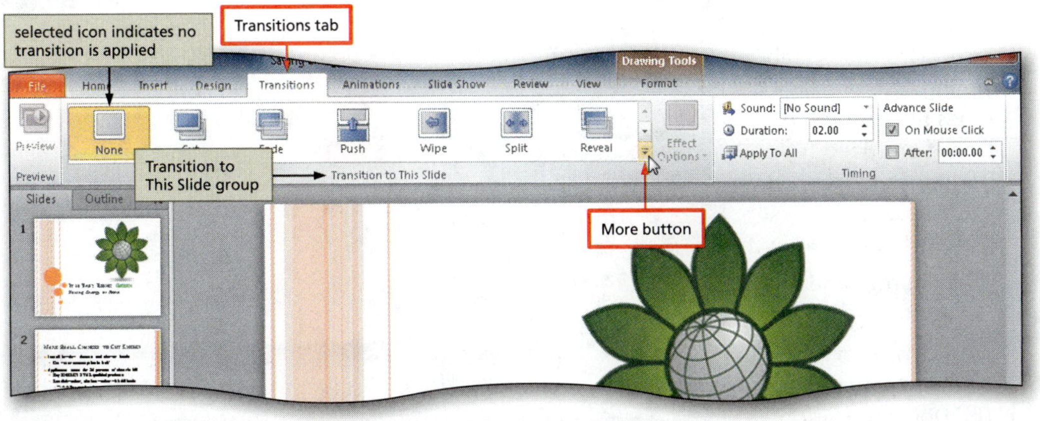

Figure 1–62

2

- Click the More button to expand the Transitions gallery.
- Point to the Doors transition in the Exciting category in the Transitions gallery (Figure 1–63).

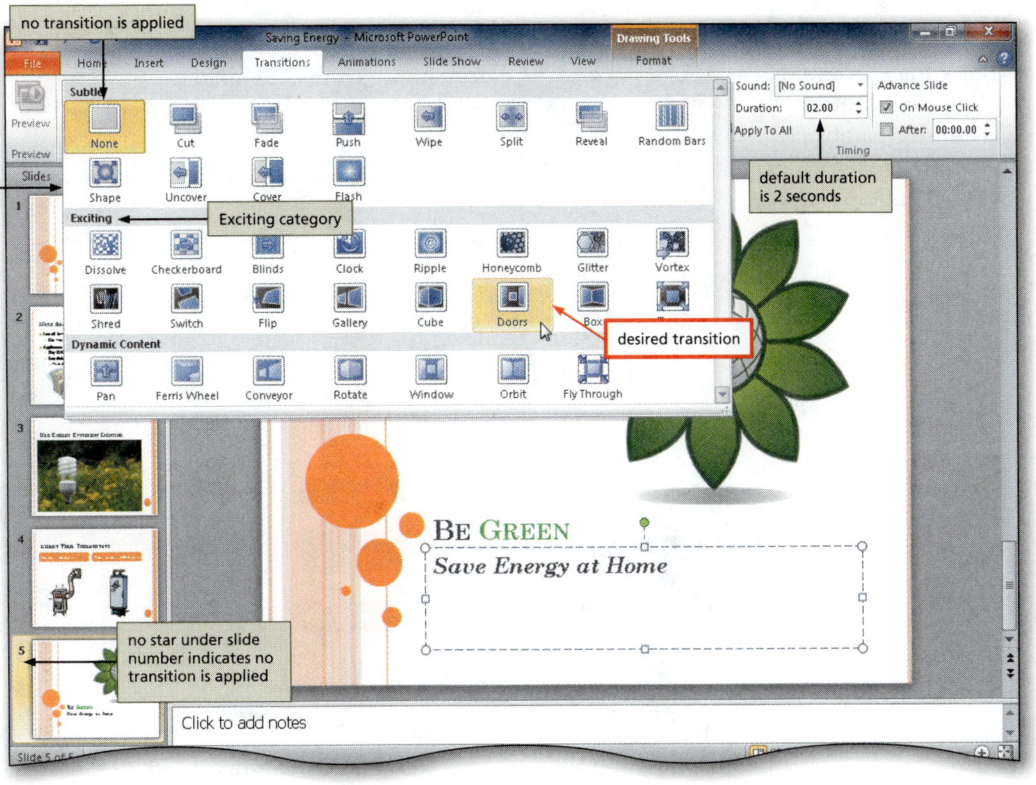

Figure 1–63

3

- Click Doors in the Exciting category in the Transitions gallery to apply this transition to the closing slide.

Q&A Why does a star appear next to Slide 5 in the Slides tab?

The star indicates that a transition animation effect is applied to that slide.

- Click the Duration up arrow (Transitions tab | Timing group) three times to change the transition speed from 01.40 seconds to 02.00 seconds (Figure 1–64).

Q&A Why did the time change?

Each transition has a default duration time. The Doors transition time is 1:40 seconds.

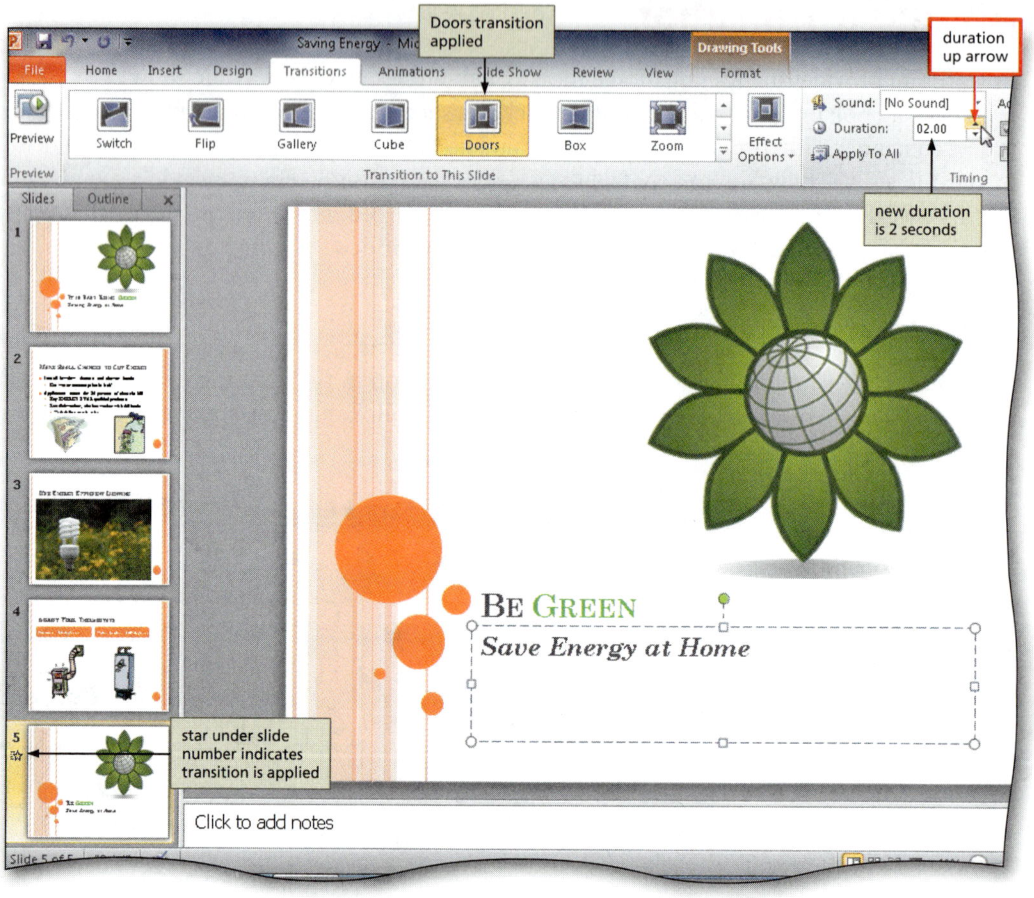

Figure 1–64

4

- Click the Preview Transitions button (Transitions tab | Preview area) to view the transition and the new transition time (Figure 1–65).

Q&A Can I adjust the duration time I just set?

Yes. Click the Duration up or down arrows or type a speed in the Duration text box and preview the transition until you find the time that best fits your presentation.

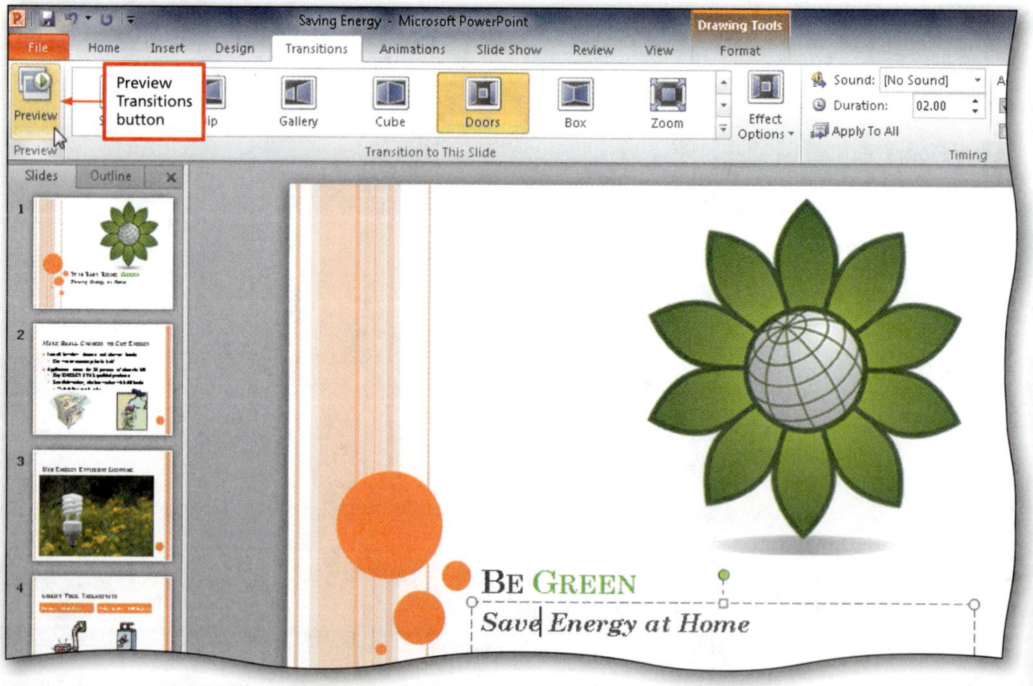

Figure 1–65

5

- Click the Apply To All button (Transitions tab | Timing group) to apply the Doors transition and the increased transition time to Slides 1 through 4 in the presentation (Figure 1–66).

Q&A

What if I want to apply a different transition and duration to each slide in the presentation?

Repeat Steps 2 and 3 for each slide individually.

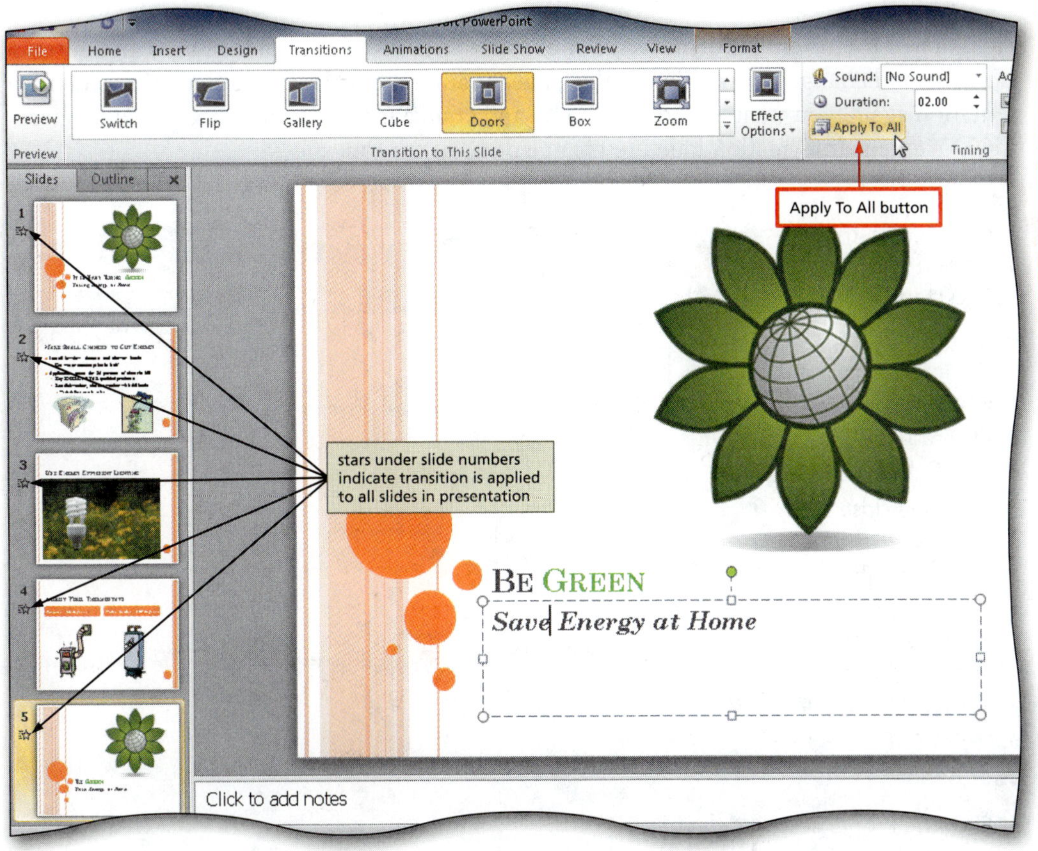

Figure 1–66

Changing Document Properties

PowerPoint helps you organize and identify your files by using **document properties**, which are the details about a file. Document properties, also known as **metadata**, can include information such as the project author, title, subject, and keywords. A **keyword** is a word or phrase that further describes the document. For example, a class name or document topic can describe the file's purpose or content.

Document properties are valuable for a variety of reasons:

- Users can save time locating a particular file because they can view a document's properties without opening the document.
- By creating consistent properties for files having similar content, users can better organize their documents.
- Some organizations require PowerPoint users to add document properties so that other employees can view details about these files.

Five different types of document properties exist, but the more common ones used in the Office and Windows chapters in this book are standard and automatically updated properties. **Standard properties** are associated with all Microsoft Office documents and include author, title, and subject. **Automatically updated properties** include file system properties, such as the date you create or change a file, and statistics, such as the file size.

BTW

PowerPoint Help
At any time while using PowerPoint, you can find answers to questions and display information about various topics through PowerPoint Help. Used properly, this form of assistance can increase your productivity and reduce your frustrations by minimizing the time you spend learning how to use PowerPoint. For instruction about PowerPoint Help and exercises that will help you gain confidence in using it, read the Office 2010 and Windows 7 chapter in this book.

To Change Document Properties

The **Document Information Panel** contains areas where you can view and enter document properties. You can view and change information in this panel at any time while you are creating a document. Before saving the presentation again, you want to add your name and course information as document properties. The following steps use the Document Information Panel to change document properties.

1

- Click File on the Ribbon to open the Backstage view.
- If necessary, click the Info tab in the Backstage view to display the Info gallery (Figure 1–67).

Q&A How do I close the Backstage view?

Click File on the Ribbon or click the preview of the document in the Info gallery to return to the PowerPoint document window.

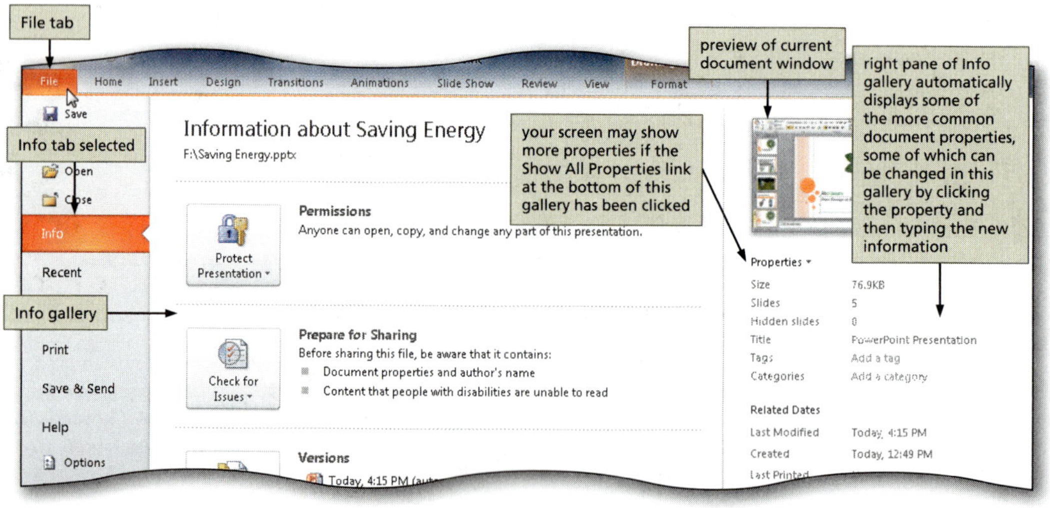

Figure 1–67

2

- Click the Properties button in the right pane of the Info gallery to display the Properties menu (Figure 1–68).

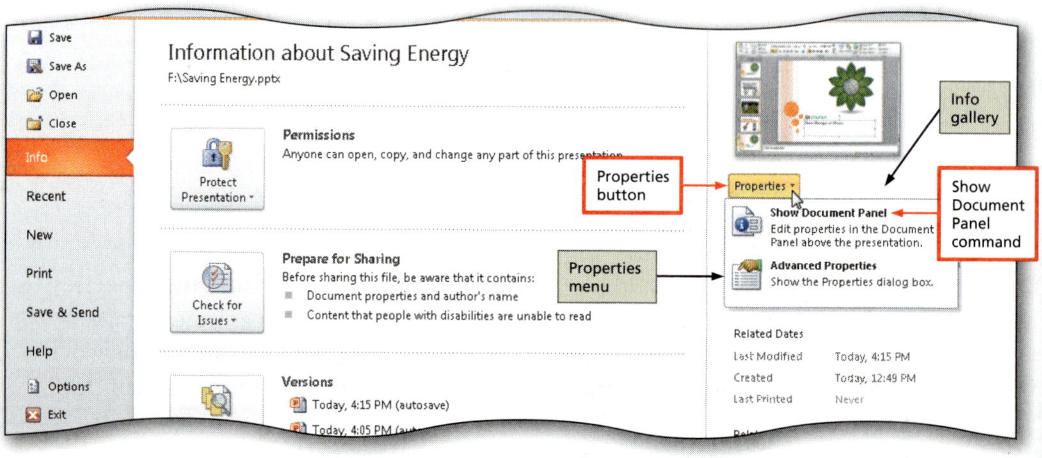

Figure 1–68

3

- Click Show Document Panel on the Properties menu to close the Backstage view and display the Document Information Panel in the PowerPoint document window (Figure 1–69).

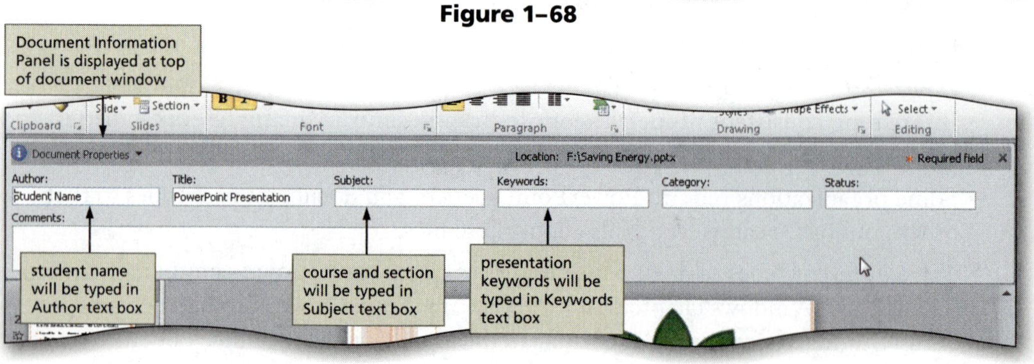

Figure 1–69

Q&A Why are some of the document properties in my Document Information Panel already filled in?

The person who installed Microsoft Office 2010 on your computer or network may have set or customized the properties.

4

- Click the Author text box, if necessary, and then type your name as the Author property. If a name already is displayed in the Author text box, delete it before typing your name.
- Click the Subject text box, if necessary delete any existing text, and then type your course and section as the Subject property.
- If an AutoComplete dialog box appears, click its Yes button.
- Click the Keywords text box, if necessary delete any existing text, and then type **energy savings** as the Keywords property (Figure 1–70).

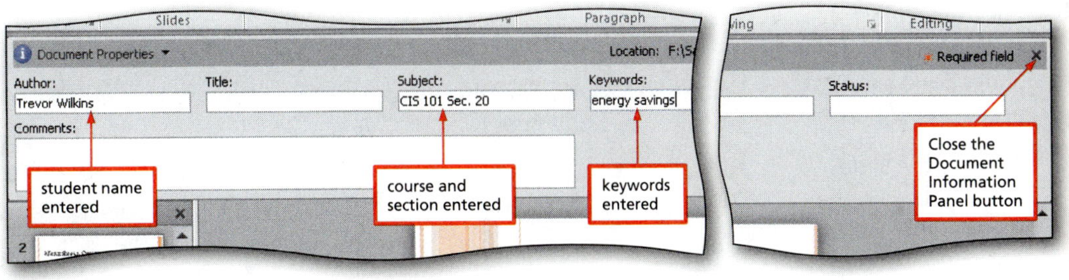

Figure 1–70

Q&A What types of document properties does PowerPoint collect automatically?

PowerPoint records details such as time spent editing a document, the number of times a document has been revised, and the fonts and themes used in a document.

5

- Click the Close the Document Information Panel button so that the Document Information Panel no longer is displayed.

Other Ways

1. Click File on Ribbon, click Info in Backstage view, if necessary click Show All Properties link in Info gallery, click property to change and type new information, close Backstage view

To Save an Existing Presentation with the Same File Name

You have made several modifications to the presentation since you last saved it. Thus, you should save it again. The following step saves the document again. For an example of the step listed below, refer to the Office 2010 and Windows 7 chapter in this book.

1 Click the Save button on the Quick Access Toolbar to overwrite the previously saved file.

BTW **Saving in a Previous PowerPoint Format**
To ensure that your presentation will open in PowerPoint 2003 or older versions of this software, you must save your file in PowerPoint 97-2003 format. These files will have the .ppt extension.

Viewing the Presentation in Slide Show View

The Slide Show button, located in the lower-right corner of the PowerPoint window above the status bar, allows you to show a presentation using a computer. The computer acts like a slide projector, displaying each slide on a full screen. The full-screen slide hides the toolbars, menus, and other PowerPoint window elements.

To Start Slide Show View

When making a presentation, you use **Slide Show view**. You can start Slide Show view from Normal view or Slide Sorter view. Slide Show view begins when you click the Slide Show button in the lower-right corner of the PowerPoint window above the status bar. PowerPoint then shows the current slide on the full screen without any of the PowerPoint window objects, such as the menu bar or toolbars. The steps on the next page start Slide Show view.

1

- Click the Slide 1 thumbnail in the Slides pane to select and display Slide 1.
- Point to the Slide Show button in the lower-right corner of the PowerPoint window on the status bar (Figure 1–71).

Q&A Why did I need to select Slide 1?

When you run a slide show, PowerPoint begins the show with the currently displayed slide. If you had not selected Slide 1, then only Slide 5 would have displayed in the slide show.

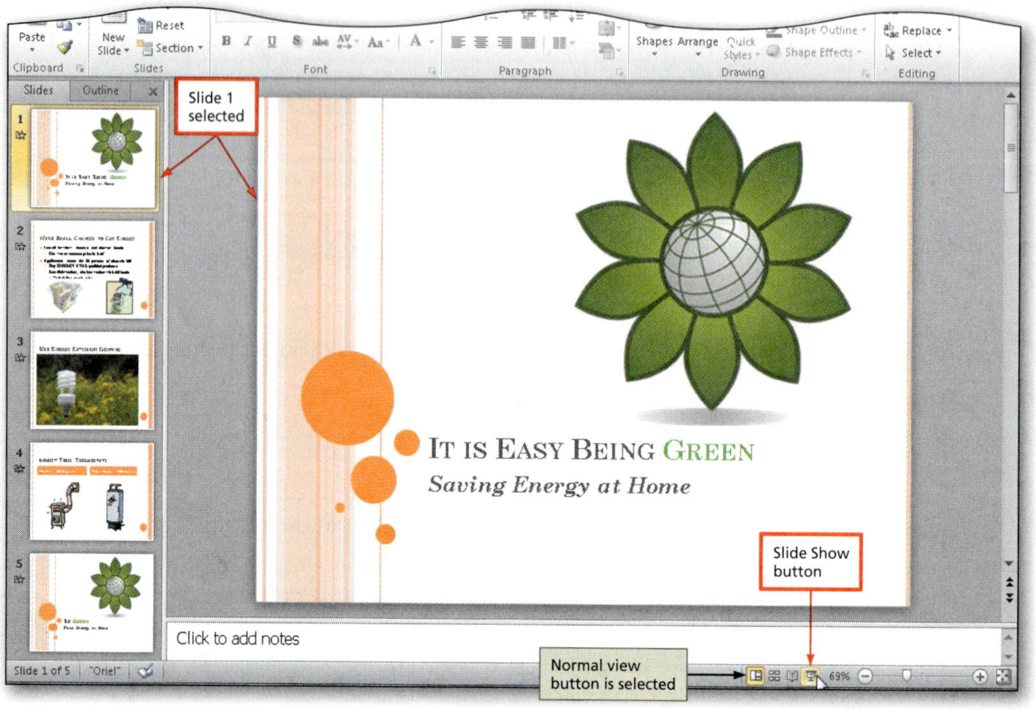

Figure 1–71

2

- Click the Slide Show button to display the title slide (Figure 1–72).

Q&A Where is the PowerPoint window?

When you run a slide show, the PowerPoint window is hidden. It will reappear once you end your slide show.

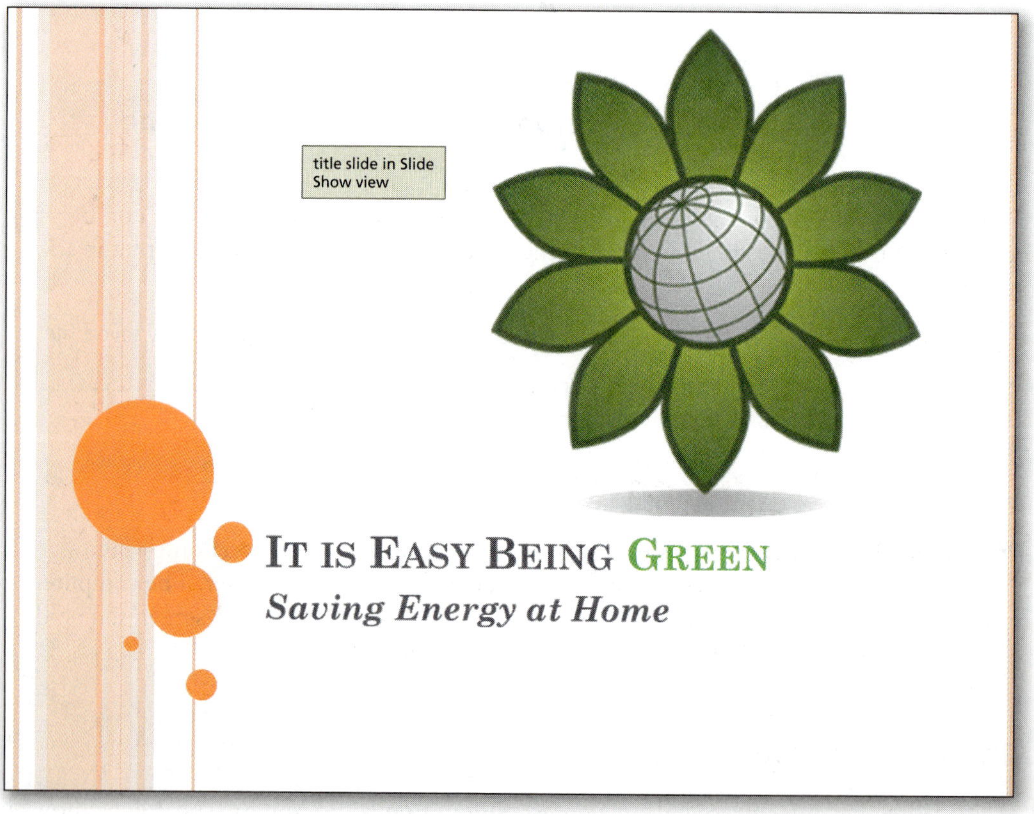

Figure 1–72

Other Ways

1. Click Slide Show From Beginning button (Slide Show tab | Start Slide Show group)
2. Press F5

To Move Manually through Slides in a Slide Show

After you begin Slide Show view, you can move forward or backward through the slides. PowerPoint allows you to advance through the slides manually or automatically. During a slide show, each slide in the presentation shows on the screen, one slide at a time. Each time you click the mouse button, the next slide appears. The following steps move manually through the slides.

1

- Click each slide until Slide 5 (Be Green) is displayed (Figure 1–73).

Q&A I see a small toolbar in the lower-left corner of my slide. What is this toolbar?

The Slide Show toolbar appears when you begin running a slide show and then move the mouse pointer. The buttons on this toolbar allow you to navigate to the next slide, the previous slide, to mark up the current slide, or to change the current display.

Figure 1–73

2

- Click Slide 5 so that the black slide appears with a message announcing the end of the slide show (Figure 1–74).

Q&A How can I end the presentation at this point?

Click the black slide to return to Normal view in the PowerPoint window or press the ESC key.

Figure 1–74

Other Ways

1. Press PAGE DOWN to advance one slide at a time, or press PAGE UP to go back one slide at a time
2. Press RIGHT ARROW or DOWN ARROW to advance one slide at a time, or press LEFT ARROW or UP ARROW to go back one slide at a time
3. If Slide Show toolbar is displayed, click Next Slide or Previous Slide button on toolbar

To Quit PowerPoint

This project now is complete. The following steps quit PowerPoint. For a detailed example of the procedure summarized below, refer to the Office 2010 and Windows 7 chapter in this book.

1. If you have one PowerPoint presentation open, click the Close button on the right side of the title bar to close the document and quit PowerPoint; or if you have multiple PowerPoint presentations open, click File on the Ribbon to open the Backstage view and then click Exit in the Backstage view to close all open documents and quit PowerPoint.
2. If a Microsoft PowerPoint dialog box appears, click the Save button to save any changes made to the document since the last save.

To Start PowerPoint

Once you have created and saved a document, you may need to retrieve it from your storage medium. For example, you might want to revise the presentation or print it. The following steps, which assume Windows 7 is running, start PowerPoint so that you can open and modify the presentation. You may need to ask your instructor how to start PowerPoint for your computer. For a detailed example of the procedure summarized below, refer to the Office 2010 and Windows 7 chapter in this book.

1. Click the Start button on the Windows 7 taskbar to display the Start menu.
2. Type **`Microsoft PowerPoint`** as the search text in the 'Search programs and files' text box and watch the search results appear on the Start menu.
3. Click Microsoft PowerPoint 2010 in the search results on the Start menu to start PowerPoint and display a new blank document in the PowerPoint window.
4. If the PowerPoint window is not maximized, click the Maximize button next to the Close button on its title bar to maximize the window.

To Open a Document from PowerPoint

Earlier in this chapter you saved your project on a USB flash drive using the file name, Saving Energy. The following steps open the Saving Energy file from the PowerPoint folder in the CIS 101 folder on the USB flash drive. For a detailed example of the procedure summarized below, refer to the Office 2010 and Windows 7 chapter in this book.

1. With your USB flash drive connected to one of the computer's USB ports, click File on the Ribbon to open the Backstage view.
2. Click Open in the Backstage view to display the Open dialog box.
3. Navigate to the location of the file to be opened (in this case, the USB flash drive, then to the CIS 101 folder [or your class folder], and then to the PowerPoint folder).

4. Click Saving Energy to select the file to be opened.
5. Click the Open button (Open dialog box) to open the selected file and display the opened document in the PowerPoint window.

Printing a Presentation

After creating a presentation, you may want to print the slides. Printing a presentation enables you to distribute the document to others in a form that can be read or viewed but typically not edited. It is a good practice to save a presentation before printing it, in the event you experience difficulties printing.

Plan Ahead

Determine the best method for distributing the presentation.

The traditional method of distributing a presentation uses a printer to produce a hard copy. A **hardcopy** or **printout** is information that exists on a physical medium such as paper. For users who can receive fax documents, you can elect to print a hard copy on a remote fax machine. Hard copies can be useful for the following reasons:

- Many people prefer proofreading a hard copy of a document rather than viewing it on the screen to check for errors and readability.
- Hard copies can serve as reference material if your storage medium is lost or becomes corrupted and you need to recreate the document.

Instead of distributing a hard copy of a presentation slides, users can choose to distribute the presentation as an electronic image that mirrors the original document's appearance. The electronic image of the document can be e-mailed, posted on a Web site, or copied to a portable storage medium such as a USB flash drive. Two popular electronic image formats, sometimes called fixed formats, are PDF by Adobe Systems and XPS by Microsoft. In PowerPoint, you can create electronic image files through the Print tab in the Backstage view, the Save & Send tab in the Backstage view, and the Save As dialog box. Electronic images of documents, such as PDF and XPS, can be useful for the following reasons.

- Users can view electronic images of documents without the software that created the original document (e.g., PowerPoint). Specifically, to view a PDF file, you use a program called Acrobat Reader, which can be downloaded free from Adobe's Web site. Similarly, to view an XPS file, you use a program called an XPS Viewer, which is included in the latest versions of Windows and Internet Explorer.
- Sending electronic documents saves paper and printer supplies. Society encourages users to contribute to **green computing**, which involves reducing the environmental waste generated when using a computer.

To Print a Presentation

With the completed presentation saved, you may want to print it. If copies of the presentation are being distributed to audience members, you will print a hard copy of each individual slide on a printer. The steps on the next page print a hard copy of the contents of the saved Saving Energy presentation.

1

- Click File on the Ribbon to open the Backstage view.
- Click the Print tab in the Backstage view to display the Print gallery (Figure 1–75).

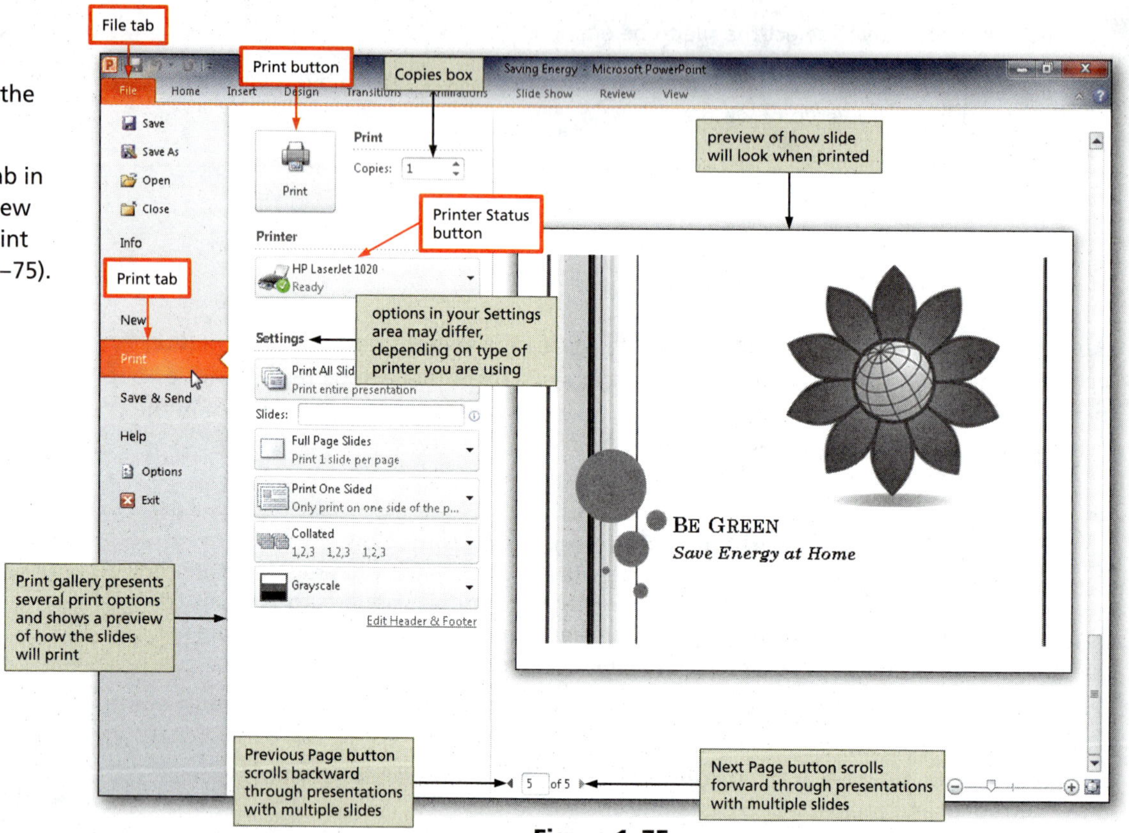

Figure 1–75

Q&A How do I preview Slides 2 through 5?

Click the Next Page button in the Print gallery to scroll forward through pages in the document; similarly, click the Previous Page button to scroll backward through pages.

Q&A How can I print multiple copies of my slides?

Increase the number in the Copies box in the Print gallery.

Q&A What if I decide not to print the document at this time?

Click File on the Ribbon to close the Backstage view and return to the PowerPoint document window.

2

- Verify the printer name that appears on the Printer box Status button will print a hard copy of the document. If necessary, click the Printer Status button to display a list of available printer options and then click the desired printer to change the currently selected printer.

BTW

Quick Reference

For a table that lists how to complete the tasks covered in the Office chapters in this book using the mouse, Ribbon, shortcut menu, and keyboard, see the Quick Reference Summary at the back of this book, or visit the Microsoft Office and Concepts CourseMate Web site at www.cengagebrain.com and then navigate to the Quick Reference resource for this book.

3

- Click the Print button in the Print gallery to print the document on the currently selected printer.
- When the printer stops, retrieve the hard copy (Figure 1–76).

Q&A Do I have to wait until my document is complete to print it?

No, you can follow these steps to print a document at any time while you are creating it.

Q&A What if I want to print an electronic image of a document instead of a hard copy?

You would click the Printer Status button in the Print gallery and then select the desired electronic image option such as a Microsoft XPS Document Writer, which would create an XPS file.

(a) Slide 1

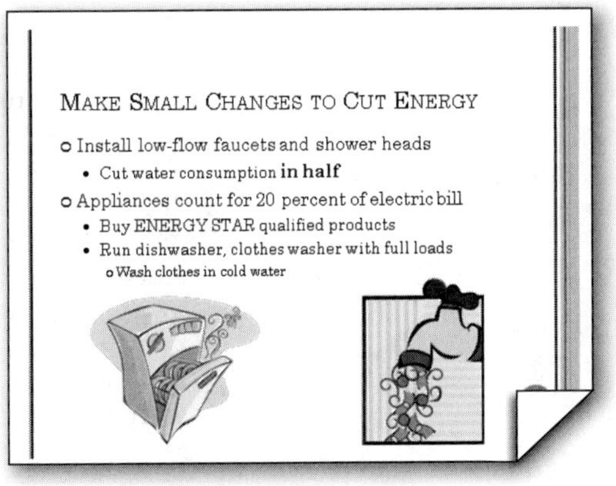

(b) Slide 2

(c) Slide 3

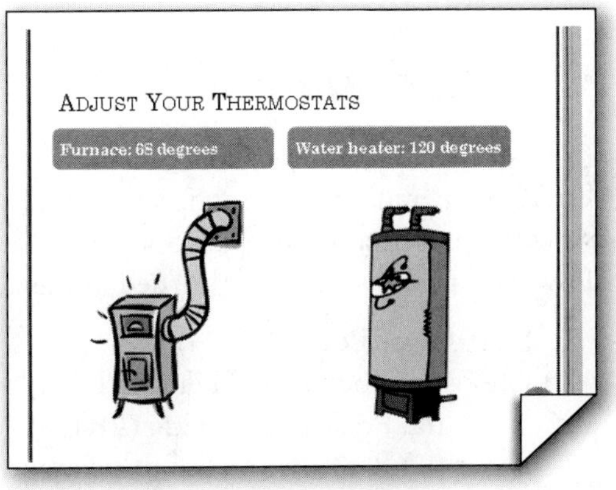

(d) Slide 4

(e) Slide 5

Figure 1–76

Other Ways
1. Press CTRL+P, press ENTER

To Quit PowerPoint

The project now is complete. The following steps quit PowerPoint. For a detailed example of the procedure summarized below, refer to the Office 2010 and Windows 7 chapter in this book.

1. If you have one PowerPoint document open, click the Close button on the right side of the title bar to close the document and quit PowerPoint; or if you have multiple PowerPoint documents open, click File on the Ribbon to open the Backstage view and then click Exit in the Backstage view to close all open documents and quit PowerPoint.
2. If a Microsoft Office PowerPoint dialog box appears, click the Save button to save any changes made to the document since the last save.

Chapter Summary

In this chapter you have learned how to apply a document theme, create a title slide and text slides with a bulleted list, clip art, and a photograph, size and move clip art and a photograph, format and edit text, add a slide transition, view the presentation in Slide Show view, and print slides as handouts. The items listed below include all the new PowerPoint skills you have learned in this chapter.

1. Start PowerPoint (PPT 4)
2. Choose a Document Theme (PPT 5)
3. Enter the Presentation Title (PPT 7)
4. Enter the Presentation Subtitle Paragraph (PPT 9)
5. Select a Paragraph (PPT 10)
6. Italicize Text (PPT 11)
7. Increase Font Size (PPT 11)
8. Select a Word (PPT 12)
9. Change the Text Color (PPT 13)
10. Save a Presentation (PPT 14)
11 Add a New Text Slide with a Bulleted List (PPT 14)
12. Enter a Slide Title (PPT 16)
13. Select a Text Placeholder (PPT 16)
14. Type a Multi-Level Bulleted List (PPT 17)
15. Select a Group of Words (PPT 19)
16. Bold Text (PPT 19)
17. Add a Slide with the Title Only Layout (PPT 21)
18. Add a New Slide and Enter a Slide Title and Headings (PPT 23)
19. Move to Another Slide in Normal View (PPT 25)
20. Insert a Clip from the Clip Organizer into the Title Slide (PPT 27)
21. Insert a Clip from the Clip Organizer into a Content Placeholder (PPT 30)
22. Insert a Photograph from the Clip Organizer into a Slide without a Content Placeholder (PPT 32)
23. Resize Clip Art (PPT 33)
24. Move Clips (PPT 36)
25. Duplicate a Slide (PPT 38)
26. Arrange a Slide (PPT 39)
27. Delete Text in a Placeholder (PPT 41)
28. Add a Transition between Slides (PPT 43)
29. Change Document Properties (PPT 46)
30. Save an Existing Presentation with the Same File Name (PPT 47)
31. Start Slide Show View (PPT 47)
32. Move Manually through Slides in a Slide Show (PPT 49)
33. Quit PowerPoint (PPT 50)
34. Open a Document from PowerPoint (PPT 50)
35. Print a Presentation (PPT 51)

SAM

If you have a SAM 2010 user profile, your instructor may have assigned an autogradable version of this assignment. If so, log into the SAM 2010 Web site at www.cengage.com/sam2010 to download the instruction and start files.

Learn It Online

Test your knowledge of chapter content and key terms.

Instructions: To complete the Learn It Online exercises, visit the Microsoft Office and Concepts CourseMate Web site at www.cengagebrain.com, navigate to the PowerPoint Chapter 1 resources for this book, click the link for the exercise you want to complete, and then read the instructions.

Chapter Reinforcement TF, MC, and SA

A series of true/false, multiple choice, and short answer questions that test your knowledge of the chapter content.

Flash Cards

An interactive learning environment where you identify chapter key terms associated with displayed definitions.

Practice Test

A series of multiple choice questions that test your knowledge of chapter content and key terms.

Who Wants To Be a Computer Genius?

An interactive game that challenges your knowledge of chapter content in the style of a television quiz show.

Wheel of Terms

An interactive game that challenges your knowledge of chapter key terms in the style of the television show *Wheel of Fortune*.

Crossword Puzzle Challenge

A crossword puzzle that challenges your knowledge of key terms presented in the chapter.

Apply Your Knowledge

Reinforce the skills and apply the concepts you learned in this chapter.

Modifying Character Formats and Paragraph Levels and Moving a Clip

Note: To complete this assignment, you will be required to use the Data Files for Students. See the inside back cover of this book for instructions on downloading the Data Files for Students, or contact your instructor for information about accessing the required files.

Instructions: Start PowerPoint. Open the presentation, Apply 1-1 Flu Season, from the Data Files for Students.

The two slides in the presentation discuss ways to avoid getting or spreading the flu. The document you open is an unformatted presentation. You are to modify the document theme, indent the paragraphs, resize and move the clip art, and format the text so the slides look like Figure 1–77 on the next page.

Continued >

Apply Your Knowledge *continued*

Perform the following tasks:

1. Change the document theme to Urban. On the title slide, use your name in place of Student Name and bold and italicize your name. Increase the title text font size to 60 point. Resize and position the clip as shown in Figure 1–77a.
2. On Slide 2, increase the indent of the second, third, and fifth paragraphs (Cover mouth and nose with a tissue; No tissue? Use your elbow or sleeve; Use soap, warm water for 20 seconds) to second-level paragraphs. Then combine paragraphs six and seven (Drink fluids; Get plenty of rest) to read, Drink fluids and get plenty of rest, as shown in Figure 1–77b.
3. Change the document properties, as specified by your instructor. Save the presentation using the file name, Apply 1-1 Avoid the Flu. Submit the revised document in the format specified by your instructor.

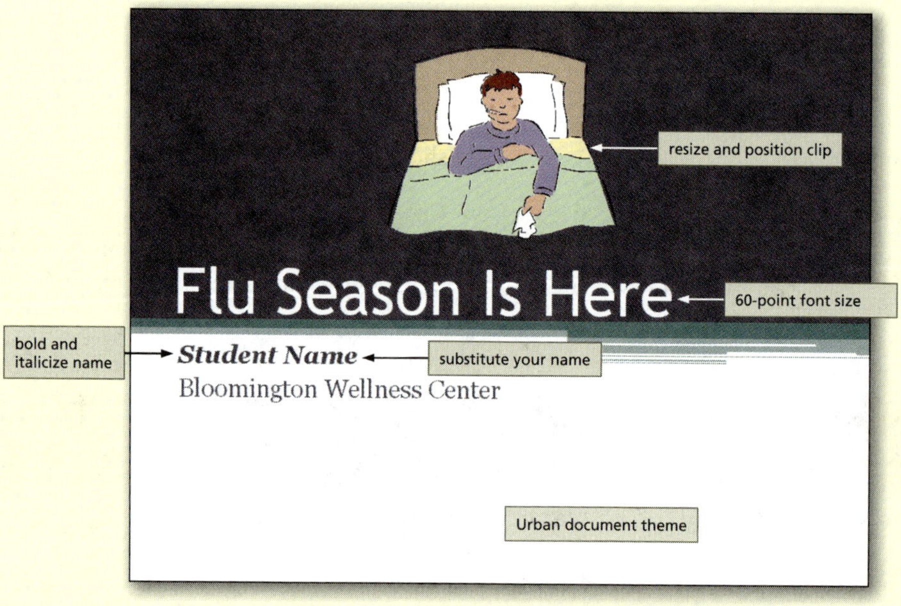

(a) Slide 1 (Title Slide with Clip Art)

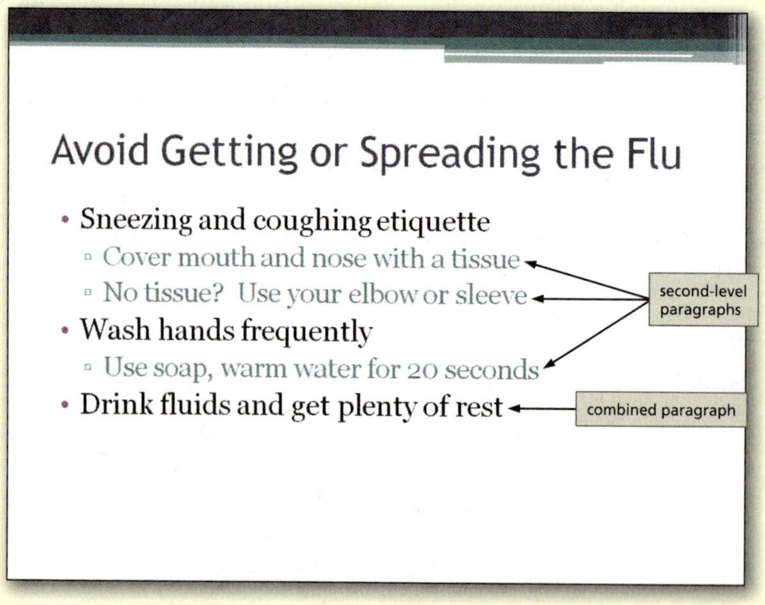

(b) Slide 2 (Multi-Level Bulleted List)

Figure 1–77

Extend Your Knowledge

Extend the skills you learned in this chapter and experiment with new skills. You may need to use Help to complete the assignment.

Changing Slide Theme, Layout, and Text

Note: To complete this assignment, you will be required to use the Data Files for Students. See the inside back cover of this book for instructions on downloading the Data Files for Students, or contact your instructor for information about accessing the required files.

Instructions: Start PowerPoint. Open the presentation that you are going to prepare for your dental hygiene class, Extend 1–1 Winning Smile, from the Data Files for Students.

You will choose a theme, format slides, and create a closing slide.

Perform the following tasks:

1. Apply an appropriate document theme.
2. On Slide 1, use your name in place of Student Name. Format the text on this slide using techniques you learned in this chapter, such as changing the font size and color and also bolding and italicizing words.
3. On Slide 2, change the slide layout and adjust the paragraph levels so that the lines of text are arranged under two headings: Discount Dental and Dental Insurance (Figure 1–78).
4. On Slide 3, create paragraphs and adjust the paragraph levels to create a bulleted list. Edit the text so that the slide meets the 7 × 7 rule, which states that each line should have a maximum of seven words, and each slide should have a maximum of seven lines.
5. Create an appropriate closing slide using the title slide as a guide.
6. The slides contain a variety of clips downloaded from the Microsoft Clip Organizer. Size and move them when necessary.
7. Apply an appropriate transition to all slides.
8. Change the document properties, as specified by your instructor. Save the presentation using the file name, Extend 1–1 Dental Plans.
9. Submit the revised document in the format specified by your instructor.

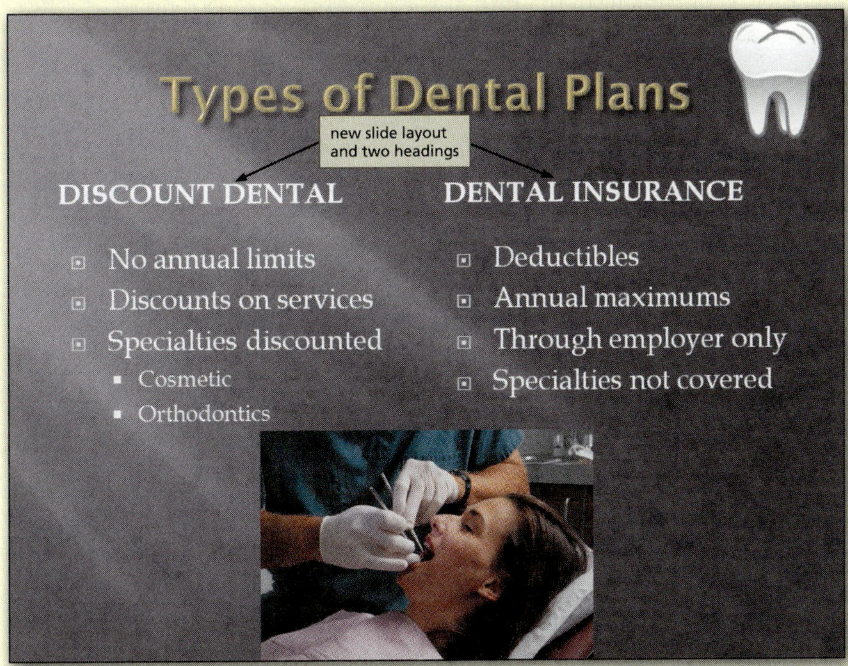

Figure 1–78

Make It Right

Analyze a presentation and correct all errors and/or improve the design.

Correcting Formatting and List Levels

Note: To complete this assignment, you will be required to use the Data Files for Students. See the inside back cover of this book for instructions on downloading the Data Files for Students, or contact your instructor for information about accessing the required files.

Instructions: Start PowerPoint. Open the presentation, Make It Right 1–1 Air Ducts, from the Data Files for Students.

Members of your homeowners' association are having their semiannual meeting, and each member of the board is required to give a short presentation on the subject of energy savings. You have decided to discuss the energy-saving benefits of maintaining the air ducts in your home. Correct the formatting problems and errors in the presentation while keeping in mind the guidelines presented in this chapter.

Perform the following tasks:

1. Change the document theme from Origin, shown in Figure 1–79, to Module.
2. On Slide 1, replace the words, Student Name, with your name. Format your name so that it displays prominently on the slide.
3. Increase the size of the clip on Slide 1 and move it to the upper-right corner.
4. Move Slide 2 to the end of the presentation so that it becomes the new Slide 3.
5. On Slide 2, correct the spelling errors and then increase the font size of the Slide 2 title text, Check Hidden Air Ducts, to 54 point. Increase the size of the clip and move it up to fill the white space on the right of the bulleted list.
6. On Slide 3, correct the spelling errors and then change the font size of the title text, Energy Savings, to 54 point. Increase the indent levels for paragraphs 2 and 4. Increase the size of the clips. Center the furnace clip at the bottom of the slide.
7. Change the document properties, as specified by your instructor. Save the presentation using the file name, Make It Right 1–1 Ducts Presentation.
8. Apply the same transition and duration to all slides.
9. Submit the revised document in the format specified by your instructor.

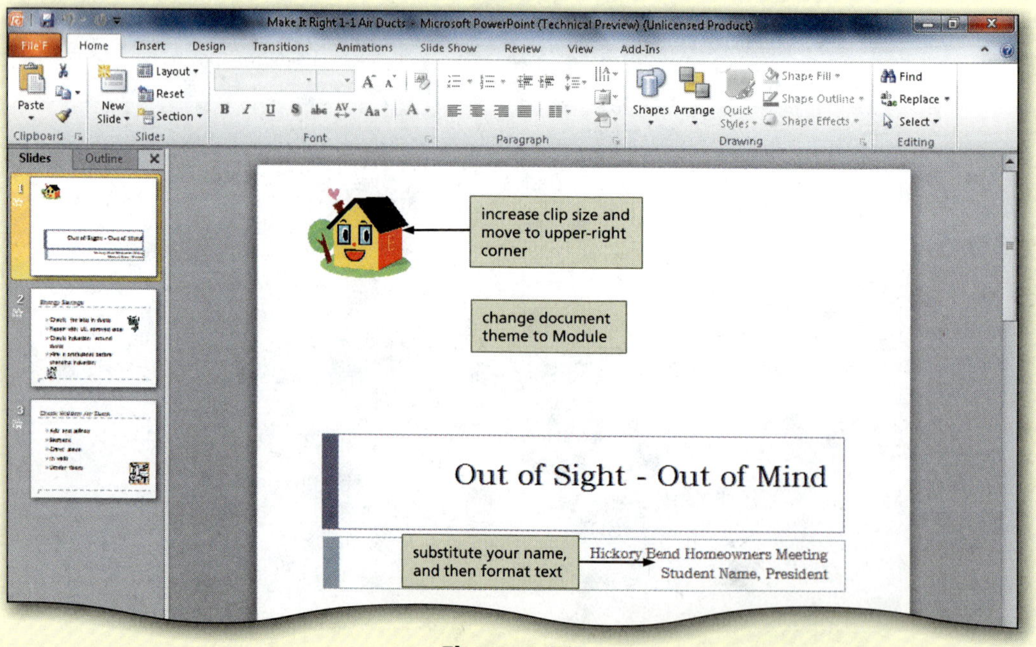

Figure 1–79

In the Lab

Design and/or create a presentation using the guidelines, concepts, and skills presented in this chapter. Labs 1, 2, and 3 are listed in order of increasing difficulty.

Lab1: Creating a Presentation with Bulleted Lists, a Closing Slide, and Clips

Problem: You are working with upper-level students to host a freshmen orientation seminar. When you attended this seminar, you received some helpful tips on studying for exams. Your contribution to this year's seminar is to prepare a short presentation on study skills. You develop the outline shown in Figure 1–80 and then prepare the PowerPoint presentation shown in Figures 1–81a through 1–81d.

Studying for an Exam
Freshmen Orientation Seminar
Sarah Jones

Prepare in Advance
- Location
    - Quiet, well-lit
- Timing
    - 15-minute breaks every hour
- Material
    - Quiz yourself

Exam Time
- Day of Exam
    - Rest properly
    - Eat a good meal
    - Wear comfy clothes
    - Be early
    - Be confident

Figure 1–80

Perform the following tasks:

1. Create a new presentation using the Aspect document theme.
2. Using the typed notes illustrated in Figure 1–80, create the title slide shown in Figure 1–81a, using your name in place of Sarah Jones. Italicize your name and increase the font size to 24 point. Increase the font size of the title text paragraph, Hit the Books, to 48 point. Increase the font size of the first paragraph of the subtitle text, Studying for an Exam, to 28 point.

(a) Slide 1 (Title Slide)

Figure 1–81

Continued >

In the Lab *continued*

3. Using the typed notes in Figure 1–80, create the two text slides with bulleted lists and find and insert clips from the Microsoft Clip Organizer, as shown in Figures 1–81b and 1–81c.
4. Create a closing slide by duplicating Slide 1, deleting your name, replacing the photograph with the photograph shown in Figure 1–81d, and moving the slide to the end of the presentation.
5. On Slide 3, change the font color of the words, Be confident, to Yellow (fourth color in the Standard Colors row).
6. Apply the Uncover transition in the Subtle category to all slides. Change the duration to 1.25 seconds.
7. Drag the scroll box to display Slide 1. Click the Slide Show button to start Slide Show view. Then click to display each slide.
8. Change the document properties, as specified by your instructor. Save the presentation using the file name, Lab 1–1 Study Skills.
9. Submit the document in the format specified by your instructor.

(b) Slide 2

(c) Slide 3

(d) Slide 4 (Closing Slide)

Figure 1–81 (continued)

In the Lab

Lab 2: Creating a Presentation with Bulleted Lists and Clips

Problem: Your health class instructor has assigned every student a different vitamin to research. She hands you the outline shown in Figure 1–82 and asks you to create the presentation about Vitamin D shown in Figures 1–83a through 1–83d on pages PPT 62 and PPT 63.

Vitamin D

The Sunshine Vitamin
Are You D-ficient?
Presented by Jim Warner

Why Is Vitamin D Important?

- We need Vitamin D
  - Vital to our bodies
    - Promotes absorption of calcium and magnesium
      - For healthy teeth and bones
    - Maintains calcium and phosphorus in blood
- Daily Requirements
  - How much do we need?
    - Child: 5 mcg (200 IU)
    - Adult: 10-20 mcg (400-600 IU)

Vitamin D Sources

- Sunshine
  - Is our primary source
    - Vitamin manufactured by our body after exposure
      - Three times a week
      - For 10-15 minutes
- Foods and Supplements
  - Contained in few foods
    - Some fish liver oils
    - Flesh of fatty fish
  - Fortified products
    - Milk and cereals
  - Available as supplement

Vitamin D History

- Research began in 1924
  - Found to prevent rickets
- United States and Canada
  - Instituted policy of fortifying foods with Vitamin D
    - Milk – food of choice
- Other countries
  - Fortified cereal, bread, margarine

Figure 1–82

Continued >

STUDENT ASSIGNMENTS

In the Lab *continued*

Perform the following tasks:

1. Create a new presentation using the Solstice document theme.
2. Using the typed notes illustrated in Figure 1–82, create the title slide shown in Figure 1–83a, using your name in place of Jim Warner. Italicize the title, The Sunshine Vitamin, and increase the font size to 48 point. Change the font size of the first line of the subtitle text, Are You D-ficient?, to 36 point. Change the font color of the title text to Orange (third color in the Standard Colors row) and both lines of the subtitle text to Light Blue (seventh color in the Standard Colors row).
3. Using the typed notes in Figure 1–82, create the three text slides with bulleted lists shown in Figures 1–83b through 1–83d. Change the color of the title text on all slides and the text above the bulleted lists on Slides 2 and 3 to Orange.
4. Add the photographs and clip art shown in Figures 1–83a through 1–83d from the Microsoft Clip Organizer. Adjust the clip sizes when necessary.
5. Apply the Ripple transition in the Exciting category to all slides. Change the duration to 2.00 seconds.
6. Drag the scroll box to display Slide 1. Click the Slide Show button to start Slide Show view. Then click to display each slide.

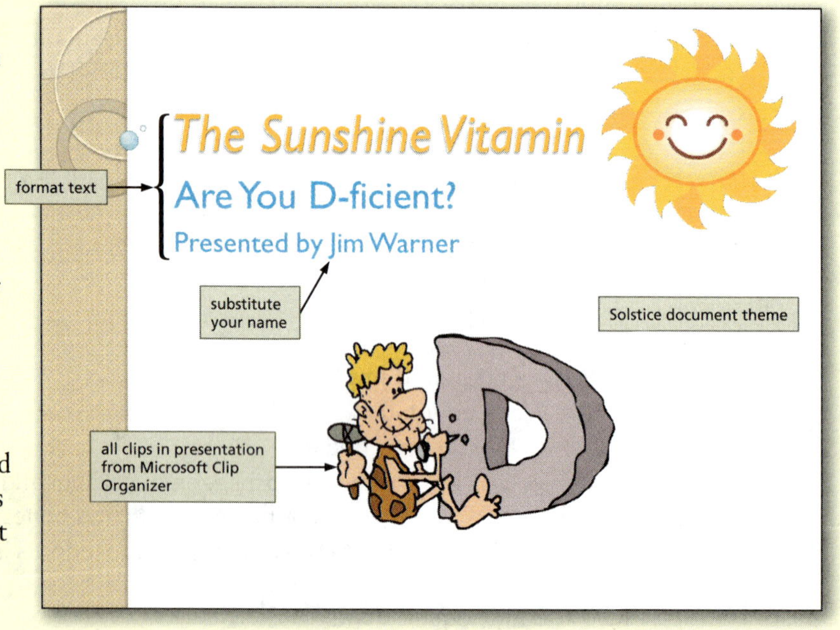

(a) Slide 1 (Title Slide)

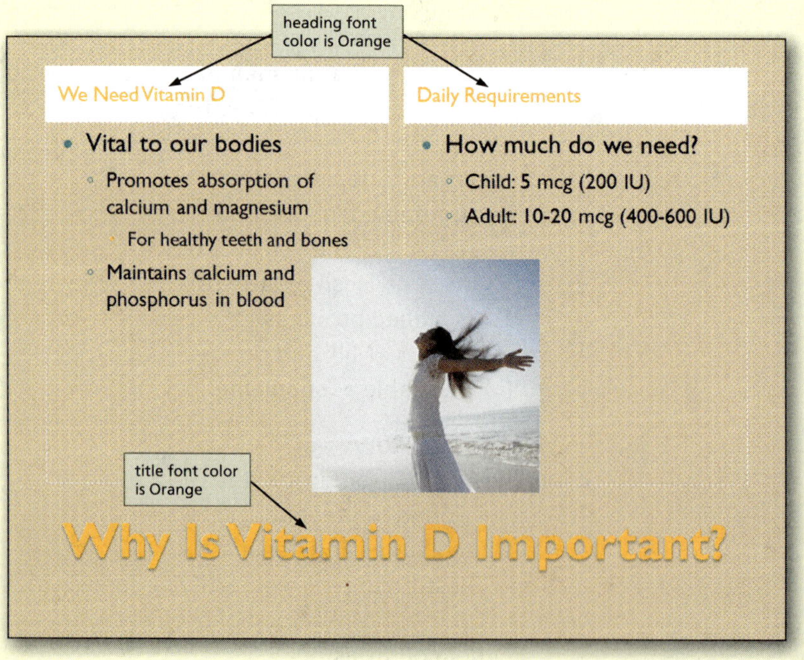

(b) Slide 2

Figure 1–83

7. Change the document properties, as specified by your instructor. Save the presentation using the file name, Lab 1–2 Vitamin D.
8. Submit the revised document in the format specified by your instructor.

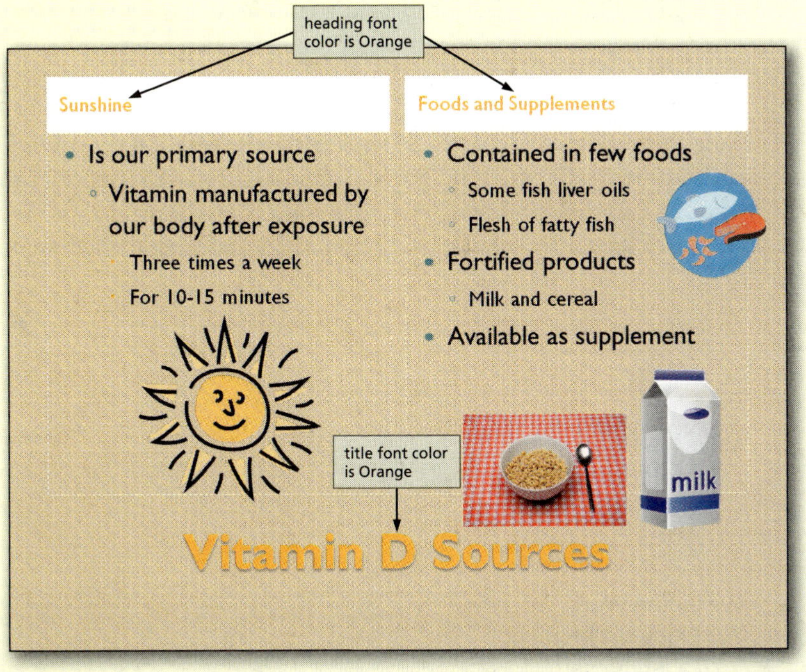

(c) Slide 3

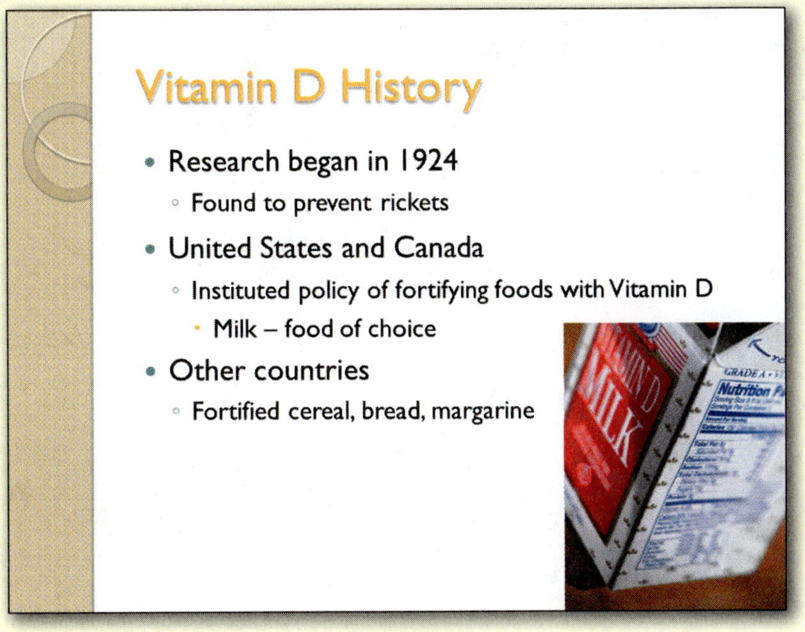

(d) Slide 4

Figure 1–83 (continued)

In the Lab

Lab 3: Creating and Updating Presentations with Clip Art

Problem: You are employed part time at your health club, and the Child Care Center director has asked you to put together a presentation for her to use at the next open house. The club has a large playroom that is perfect for children's parties.

Instructions Part 1: Using the outline in Figure 1–84, create the presentation shown in Figure 1–85. Use the Office Theme document theme. On the title slide shown in Figure 1–85a, increase the font size of the title paragraph, Make It a Party!, to 48, change the font color to Red, and change the text font style to italic. Decrease the font size of the entire subtitle paragraph to 28, and change the font color to Blue.

Make It a Party!
- Host Your Child's
- Next Birthday Party
- At The Oaks Health Club

We Do the Work
You Enjoy the Moment
- Two-hour party
- Two chaperones
- Lunch & cake provided
- Game or craft activity available
- Decorations

Two Party Packages
- Package No. 1 - $8/child
  - Lunch
    - Hot Dogs
    - Pizza
- Package No. 2 - $12/child
  - Lunch including beverage
    - Hot Dogs
    - Pizza
  - Game
  - Craft (age appropriate)

Reserve Your Party Date
- Reserve 2 weeks in advance
- Deposit required
- Party room can hold 20 children
- Sign up in the Child Care Center

Figure 1–84

Create the three text slides with multi-level bulleted lists, photographs, and clip art shown in Figures 1–85b through 1–85d on the next page. Adjust the clip sizes when necessary. Apply the Vortex transition in the Exciting category to all slides and decrease the duration to 3.00 seconds. Change the document properties, as specified by your instructor. Save the presentation using the file name, Lab 1–3 Part One Child Party.

(a) Slide 1 (Title Slide)

(b) Slide 2

Figure 1–85

Continued >

In the Lab *continued*

(c) Slide 3

(d) Slide 4

Figure 1–85 (continued)

Instructions Part 2: The children's parties have proved to be a great perk for members of the health club. A large group of older adults work out at the club and also meet socially once a month. These members have asked about renting the playroom to hold a retirement party for some of their friends. You decide to modify the children's party presentation to promote retirement parties. Use the outline in Figure 1–86 to modify the presentation created in Part 1 to create the presentation shown in Figure 1–87 on the next page. Required changes are indicated by a yellow highlight.

To begin, save the current presentation with the new file name, Lab 1–3 Part Two Retirement Party. Change the document theme to Flow. On Slide 3, change the pianist's name from Ms. Winn to your name. Apply the Fade transition in the Subtle category to all slides and change the duration speed to 2.25 seconds. View the slide show. Change the document properties, as specified by your instructor. Submit both Part One and Part Two documents in the format specified by your instructor.

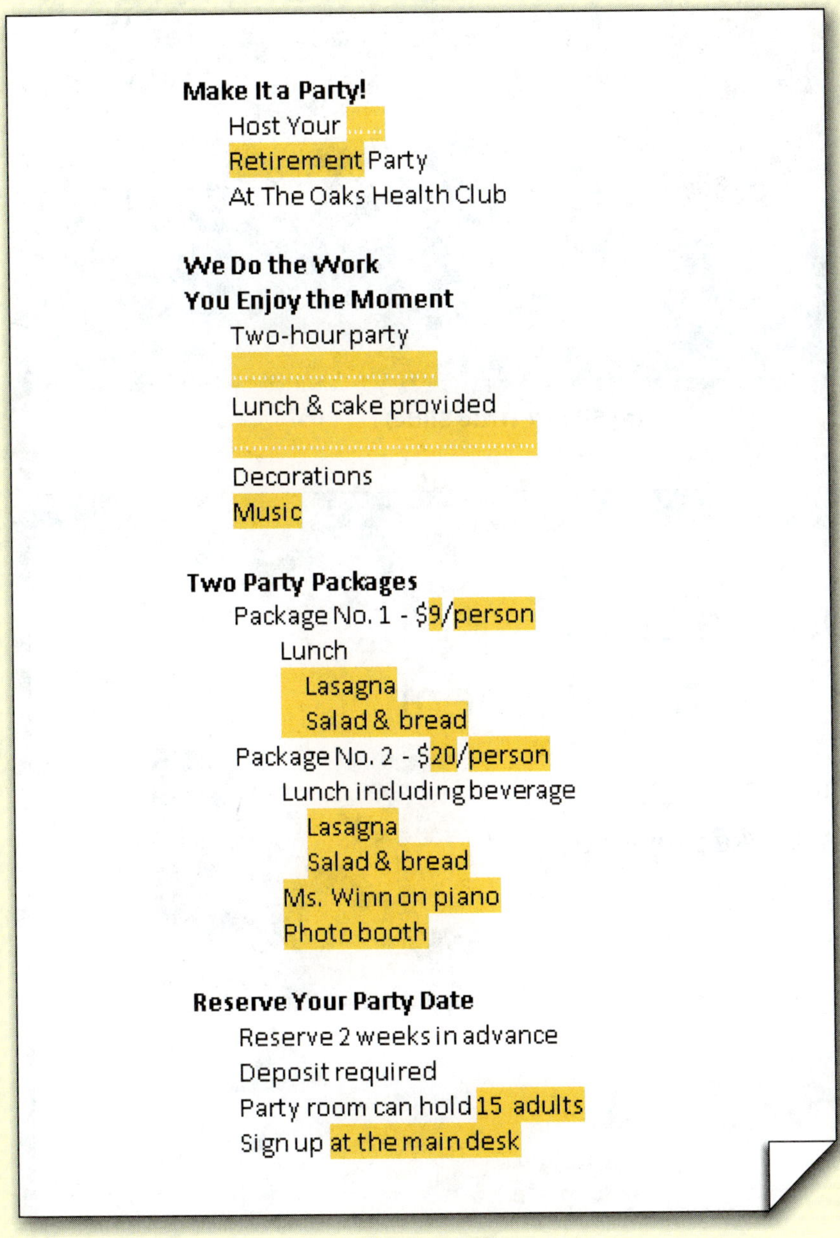

Make It a Party!
Host Your ......
Retirement Party
At The Oaks Health Club

We Do the Work
You Enjoy the Moment
Two-hour party
....
Lunch & cake provided
....
Decorations
Music

Two Party Packages
Package No. 1 - $9/person
Lunch
Lasagna
Salad & bread
Package No. 2 - $20/person
Lunch including beverage
Lasagna
Salad & bread
Ms. Winn on piano
Photo booth

Reserve Your Party Date
Reserve 2 weeks in advance
Deposit required
Party room can hold 15 adults
Sign up at the main desk

Figure 1–86

Continued >

In the Lab *continued*

(a) Slide 1 (Title Slide)

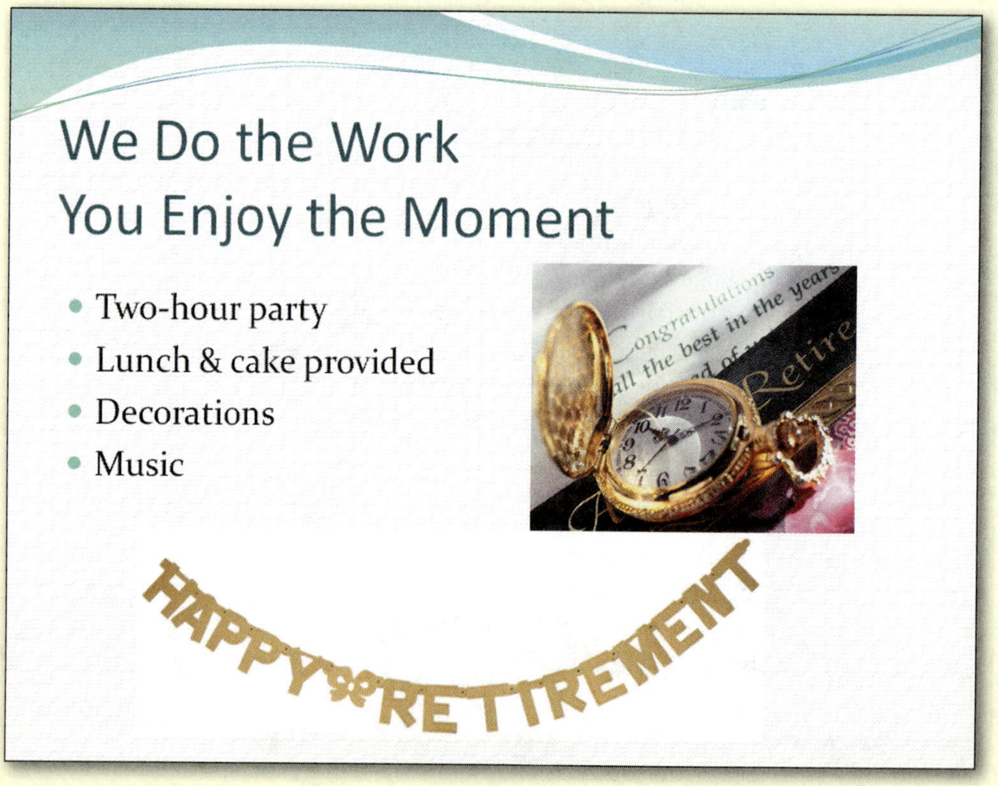

(b) Slide 2

Figure 1–87

(c) Slide 3

(d) Slide 4

Figure 1–87 (continued)

Cases and Places

Apply your creative thinking and problem-solving skills to design and implement a solution.

Note: To complete these assignments, you may be required to use the Data Files for Students. See the inside back cover of this book for instructions on downloading the Data Files for Students, or contact your instructor for information about accessing the required files.

As you design the presentations, remember to use the 7 × 7 rule: a maximum of seven words on a line and a maximum of seven lines on one slide.

1: Design and Create a Presentation about Galileo

Academic

Italian-born Galileo is said to be the father of modern science. After the invention of the telescope by a Dutch eyeglass maker named Hans Lippershey, Galileo made his own telescope and made many discoveries. You decide to prepare a PowerPoint presentation to accompany a speech that is required in your Astronomy class. You create the outline shown in Figure 1–88 about Galileo. Use this outline, along with the concepts and techniques presented in this chapter, to develop and format a slide show with a title slide and three text slides with bulleted lists. Add photographs and clip art from the Microsoft Clip Organizer and apply a transition. Submit your assignment in the format specified by your instructor.

Galileo Galilei
- Father of Modern Science
- Astronomy 201
- Sandy Wendt

Major Role in Scientific Revolution

February 15, 1564 - January 8, 1642
- Physicist
- Mathematician
- Astronomer
- Philosopher

Galileo's Research Years
- 1581 - Studied medicine
- 1589-1592 - Studied math and physics
- 1592-1607 - Padua University
  - Developed Law of Inertia
- 1609 - Built telescope
  - Earth's moon
  - Jupiter's moons

Galileo's Later Years
- Dialogue - Two Chief World Systems
  - Controversy develops
- 1633 - Rome
  - Heresy trial
  - Imprisoned
- 1642 - Dies

Figure 1–88

2: Design and Create a Presentation Promoting Hiking for Family Fitness

Personal

A great way for the entire family to get exercise is by participating in a hiking adventure. Employees at the local forest preserve district near your home have remodeled the nature center, and you have volunteered to give a presentation at the open house to help families plan their hikes. Use the outline shown in Figure 1–89 and then create an accompanying PowerPoint presentation. Use the concepts and techniques presented in this chapter to develop and format this slide show with a title slide, three text slides with bulleted lists, and clip art. Add photographs and clip art from the Microsoft Clip Organizer and apply a transition. Submit your assignment in the format specified by your instructor.

Take a Hike
- An Adventure with Kids
- Presented by Joshua Lind
- Pines Nature Center

Planning the Adventure
- Trail length – varies by child's age
  - Ages 2 to 4: 1 to 2 miles
  - Ages 5 to 7: 3 to 4 miles
  - Ages 8 to 12: 5 to 7 miles
- Backpack – limit to 20 percent of child's weight

Packing Supplies
- Snacks and Drinks
  - Child's favorite healthy foods
    - Fruit and nuts
  - Water
- Miscellaneous
  - Sunscreen
  - Insect repellent
  - First-aid kit

Wearing the Right Clothes
- Dress in layers
  - Children get cold quicker than adults
- Wear long pants and long-sleeved shirt
  - Protect against insects and cuts
- Wear a hat and comfortable shoes
  - Keep body warm

Figure 1–89

Continued >

Cases and Places *continued*

3: Design and Create a Landscaping Service Presentation

Professional

The home and garden center where you work is hosting weekend clinics for customers. The owner asks you to give a presentation about the center's new landscaping division and hands you the outline shown in Figure 1–90. Use the concepts and techniques presented in this chapter to develop and format a PowerPoint presentation with a title slide, three text slides with bulleted lists, and clip art. Add photographs and clip art from the Microsoft Clip Organizer and apply a transition. Submit your assignment in the format specified by your instructor.

Barry's Landscaping Service
Bensenville, Indiana

Full-Service Landscaping
- Initial design
- Installation
- Maintenance

Scope of Services
- Landscape design
- Irrigation
- Lighting
- Lawn-care programs
- Tree/shrub maintenance
- Masonry, carpentry
- Water features

Our Promise to You
- Deliver on-time service
- Provide highest level of workmanship
- Give maximum value for your dollar
- Install high-quality plants and materials
- Respond quickly to your needs

Figure 1–90

2 Enhancing a Presentation with Pictures, Shapes, and WordArt

Objectives

You will have mastered the material in this chapter when you can:

- Change theme colors
- Insert a picture to create a background
- Format slide backgrounds
- Insert and size a shape
- Add text to a shape
- Apply effects to a shape
- Change the font and add a shadow
- Format pictures
- Apply a WordArt style
- Format WordArt
- Format text using the Format Painter

2 Enhancing a Presentation with Pictures, Shapes, and WordArt

Introduction

In our visually oriented culture, audience members enjoy viewing effective graphics. Whether reading a document or viewing a PowerPoint presentation, people increasingly want to see photographs, artwork, graphics, and a variety of typefaces. Researchers have known for decades that documents with visual elements are more effective than those that consist of only text because the illustrations motivate audiences to study the material. People remember at least one-third more information when the document they are seeing or reading contains visual elements. These graphics help clarify and emphasize details, so they appeal to audience members with differing backgrounds, reading levels, attention spans, and motivations.

Project — Presentation with Pictures, Shapes, and WordArt

BTW **Yoga's Origins**
The term, yoga, is derived from the Sanskrit word yuj, meaning to join or unite. Yogis have been practicing this system of exercises and philosophy of mental control for more than 26,000 years.

The project in this chapter follows graphical guidelines and uses PowerPoint to create the presentation shown in Figure 2–1. This slide show, which discusses yoga and meditation, has a variety of illustrations and visual elements. For example, pictures have particular shapes and effects. The enhanced type has a style that blends well with the background and illustrations. Pictures and type are formatted using Quick Styles and WordArt, which give your presentation a professional look.

Overview

As you read through this chapter, you will learn how to create the presentation shown in Figure 2–1 by performing these general tasks:

- Format slide backgrounds.
- Insert and format pictures by applying styles and effects.
- Insert and format shapes.
- Format text using WordArt.
- Print a handout of your slides.

(a) Slide 1 (Title Slide with Picture Background and Shapes)

(b) Slide 2 (Formatted Picture)

(c) Slide 3 (Formatted Picture)

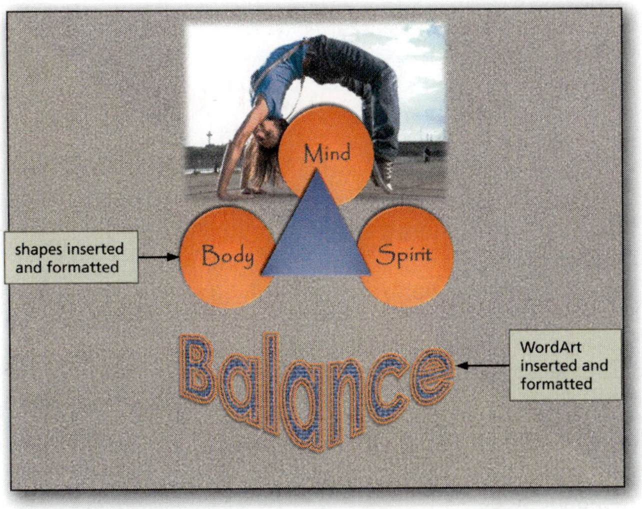

(d) Slide 4 (Inserted and Formatted Shapes)

Figure 2–1

Plan Ahead

General Project Guidelines

When creating a PowerPoint presentation, the actions you perform and decisions you make will affect the appearance and characteristics of the finished document. As you create a presentation with illustrations, such as the project shown in Figure 2–1, you should follow these general guidelines:

1. **Focus on slide text content.** Give some careful thought to the words you choose. Some graphic designers advise starting with a blank screen so that the document theme does not distract from or influence the words.
2. **Apply style guidelines.** Many organizations and publishers establish guidelines for writing styles. These rules apply to capitalization, punctuation, word usage, and document formats. Ask your instructor or manager for a copy of these guidelines or use popular writing guides, such as the *The Chicago Manual of Style*, *The Associated Press Stylebook*, and *The Elements of Style*.
3. **Use color effectively.** Your audience's eyes are drawn to color on a slide. Used appropriately, color can create interest by emphasizing material and promoting understanding. Be aware of symbolic meanings attached to colors, such as red generally representing danger, electricity, and heat.
4. **Adhere to copyright regulations.** Copyright laws apply to printed and electronic materials. You can copy an existing photograph or artwork if it is in the public domain, if your company owns the graphic, or if you have obtained permission to use it. Be certain you have the legal right to use a desired graphic in your presentation.
5. **Consider graphics for multicultural audiences.** In today's intercultural society, your presentation might be viewed by people whose first language is different from yours. Some graphics have meanings specific to a culture, so be certain to learn about your intended audience and their views.
6. **Use WordArt in moderation.** Used correctly, the graphical nature of WordArt can add interest and set a tone. Format text with a WordArt style only when needed for special emphasis.

When necessary, more specific details concerning the above guidelines are presented at appropriate points in the chapter. The chapter also will identify the actions you perform and decisions made regarding these guidelines during the creation of the presentation shown in Figure 2–1.

Starting PowerPoint

PowerPoint Chapter 1 introduced you to starting PowerPoint, selecting a document theme, creating slides with clip art and a bulleted list, and printing a presentation. The following steps, which assume Windows 7 is running, start PowerPoint. You may need to ask your instructor how to start PowerPoint for your computer. For a detailed example of the procedure summarized on the next page, refer to the Office 2010 and Windows 7 chapter.

For an introduction to Windows 7 and instruction about how to perform basic Windows 7 tasks, read the Office 2010 and Windows 7 chapter in this book, where you can learn how to resize windows, change screen resolution, create folders, move and rename files, use Windows Help, and much more.

To Start PowerPoint and Apply a Document Theme

1. Click the Start button on the Windows 7 taskbar to display the Start menu.
2. Type `Microsoft PowerPoint` as the search text in the 'Search programs and files' text box.
3. Click Microsoft PowerPoint 2010 in the search results on the Start menu to start PowerPoint and display a new blank document.
4. If the PowerPoint window is not maximized, click the Maximize button.
5. Apply the Verve document theme.

Plan Ahead

Focus on slide text content.
Once you have researched your presentation topic, many methods exist to begin developing slide content.

- Select a document theme and then enter text, illustration, and tables.
- Open an existing presentation and modify the slides and theme.
- Import an outline created in Microsoft Word.
- Start with a blank presentation that uses the default Office Theme. Consider this practice similar to an artist who begins creating a painting with a blank, white canvas.

Experiment using different methods of developing the initial content for slides. Experienced PowerPoint users sometimes find one technique works better than another to stimulate creativity or help them organize their ideas in a particular circumstance.

For an introduction to Office 2010 and instruction about how to perform basic tasks in Office 2010 programs, read the Office 2010 and Windows 7 chapter in this book, where you can learn how to start a program, use the Ribbon, save a file, open a file, quit a program, use Help, and much more.

Creating Slides and Changing Font Colors and Background Style

In PowerPoint Chapter 1, you selected a document theme and then typed the content for the title and text slides. In this chapter, you will type the slide content for the title and text slides, select a background, insert and format pictures and shapes, and then insert and format WordArt. To begin creating the four slides in this presentation, you will enter text in four different layouts, change the theme colors, and then change the background style.

Plan Ahead

Apply style guidelines.
A good stylebook is useful to decide when to use numerals or words to represent numbers, as in the sentence, More than 25 students are waiting for the bus to arrive. Stylebooks also offer rules on forming possessives, capitalizing titles, and using commas. Once you decide on a style to use in your presentation, apply it consistently throughout your presentation.

To Create a Title Slide

Recall from PowerPoint Chapter 1 that the title slide introduces the presentation to the audience. In addition to introducing the presentation, this project uses the title slide to capture the audience's attention by using title text and a background picture. The steps on the next page create the slide show's title slide.

1. Type **Yoga and Meditation** in the title text placeholder.
2. Type **Unify Your Mind,** in the subtitle text placeholder.
3. Press the ENTER key and then type **Body,** as the second line in the subtitle text placeholder.
4. Press the ENTER key and then type **and Spirit** as the third line in the subtitle text placeholder. Change the capital letter 'A' in the word, And, at the beginning of this line to a lowercase 'a' (Figure 2–2).

Q&A

Some stylebooks recommend using lowercase letters when using coordinating conjunctions (for, and, nor, but, or, yet, so) and also when using articles (a, an, the). Why is the case of the word, and, changed in the subtitle text?

By default, PowerPoint capitalizes the first word of each paragraph. For consistency, you can decide to lowercase this word to apply a particular style rule so that the word, and, is lowercase in both the title and subtitle text.

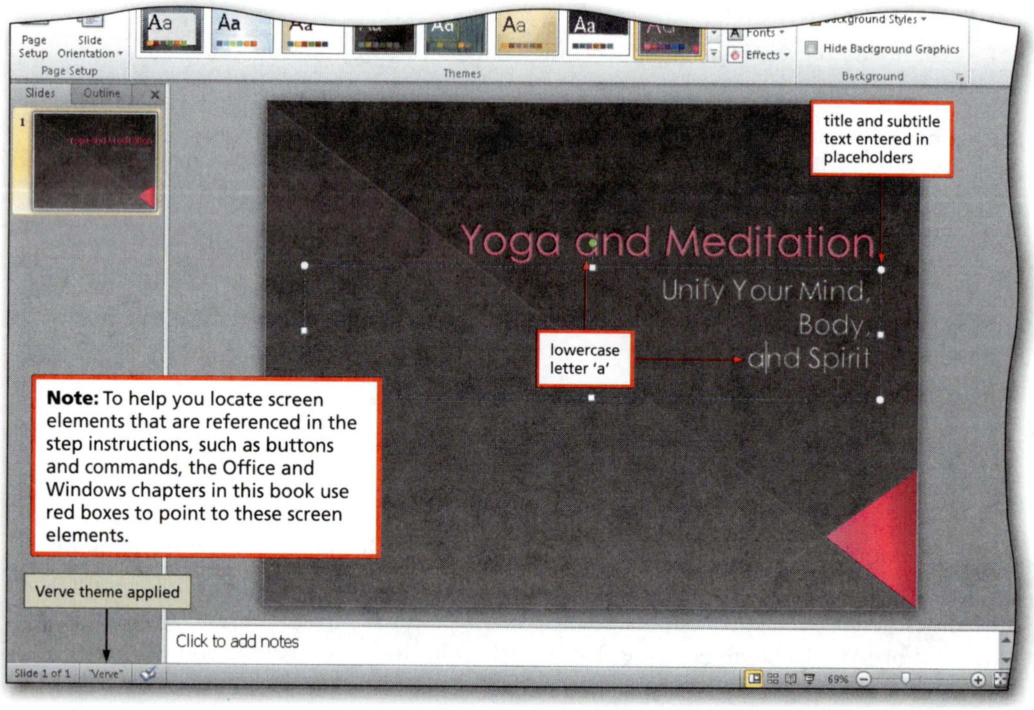

Figure 2–2

BTW

Q&As

For a complete list of the Q&As found in many of the step-by-step sequences in the Office and Windows chapters in this book, visit the Microsoft Office and Concepts CourseMate Web site at www.cengagebrain.com and then navigate to the Q&A resource for this book.

To Create the First Text Slide

The first text slide you create in this chapter emphasizes the relaxation and restoration benefits derived from practicing yoga and meditation. The following steps add a new slide (Slide 2) and then create a text slide using the Picture with Caption layout.

1. Click Home on the Ribbon to display the Home tab, click the New Slide button arrow, and then click Picture with Caption in the Layout gallery to add a new slide with this layout.
2. Type **Relax and Restore** in the title text placeholder.
3. Press CTRL+ENTER to move to the caption placeholder and then type **Calm the mind and boost oxygen levels in the brain.** in this placeholder (Figure 2–3).

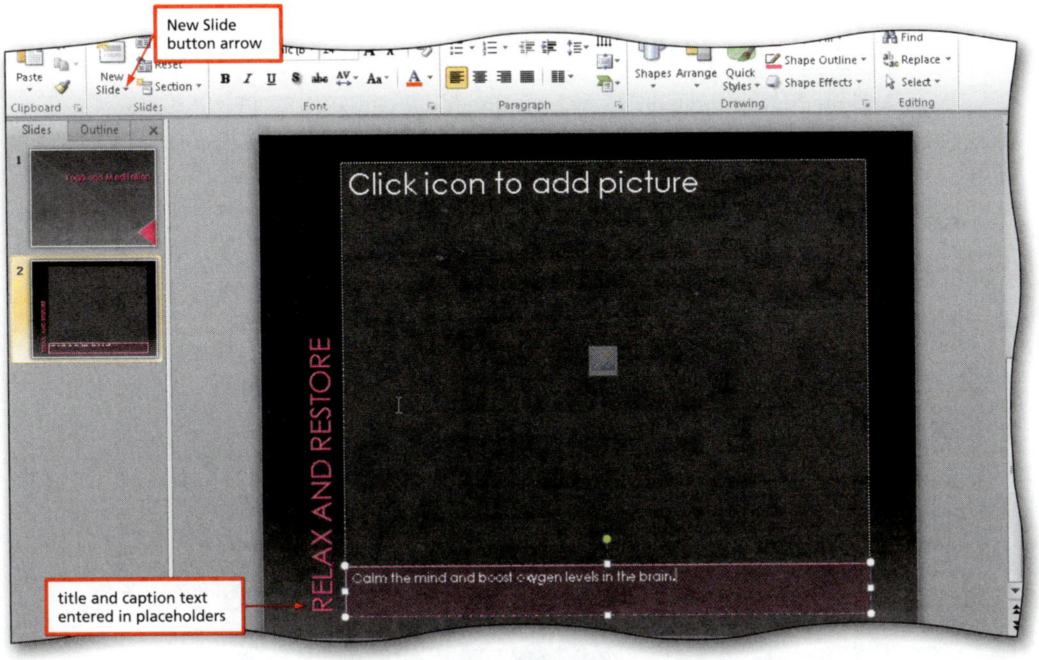

Figure 2–3

To Create the Second Text Slide

The second text slide you create stresses the fact that yoga and meditation strengthen the body in multiple ways. The following steps add a new text slide (Slide 3) that uses the Content with Caption layout.

1. Click the New Slide button arrow and then click Content with Caption in the Layout gallery to add a new slide with this layout.
2. Type `Strengthen Body` in the title text placeholder.
3. Press CTRL+ENTER and then type `Increase flexibility and tone muscles.` in the caption placeholder (Figure 2–4).

Q&A

Why does the text display with capital letters despite the fact I am typing uppercase and lowercase letters?

The Verve theme uses the All Caps effect for the title text. This effect converts lowercase letters to uppercase.

BTW

BTWs

For a complete list of the BTWs found in the margins of the Office and Windows chapters in this book, visit the Microsoft Office and Concepts CourseMate Web site at www.cengagebrain.com and then navigate to the BTW resource for this book.

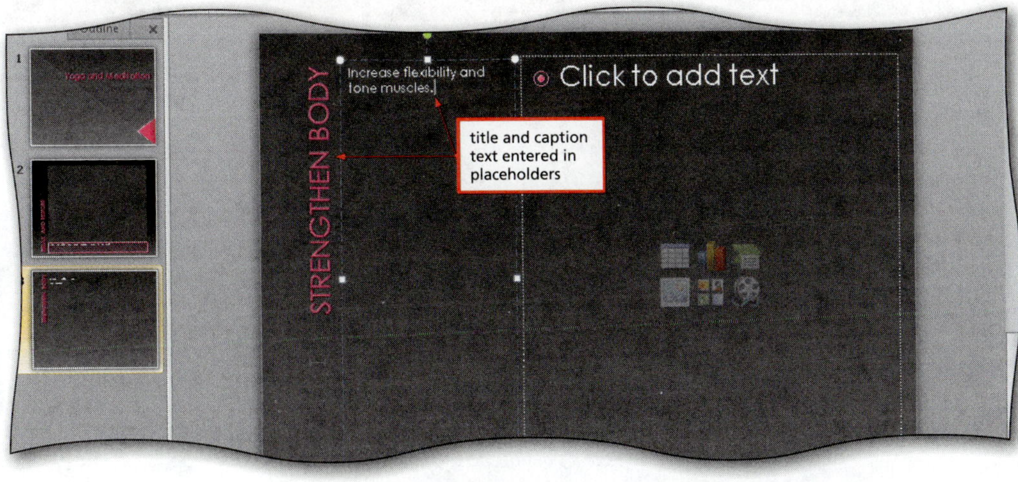

Figure 2–4

To Create the Third Text Slide

Yoga and meditation help create balance in an individual's life. The last slide you create uses graphics to depict the connection among the mind, body, and spirit. You will insert symbols later in this chapter to create this visual element. For now, you want to create the basic slide. The following step adds a new text slide (Slide 4) that uses the Blank layout.

1. Click the New Slide button arrow and then click Blank in the Layout gallery. (Figure 2–5).

Figure 2–5

BTW **The Ribbon and Screen Resolution**
PowerPoint may change how the groups and buttons within the groups appear on the Ribbon, depending on the computer's screen resolution. Thus, your Ribbon may look different from the ones in the Office and Windows chapters in this book if you are using a screen resolution other than 1024 × 768.

Presentation Template Color Scheme

Each presentation template has 12 complementary colors, which collectively are called the **color scheme**. You can apply these colors to all slides, an individual slide, notes pages, or audience handouts. A color scheme consists of four colors for a background and text, six accent colors, and two hyperlink colors. The Theme Colors button on the Design tab contains a square with four colors; the top two colors indicate the primary text and background colors, and the bottom two colors indicate the accent colors. You also can customize the theme colors to create your own set and give them a unique name. Table 2–1 explains the components of a color scheme.

Table 2–1 Color Scheme Components

Component	Description
Background color	The background color is the fundamental color of a PowerPoint slide. For example, if the background color is black, you can place any other color on top of it, but the fundamental color remains black. The black background shows everywhere you do not add color or other objects.
Text color	The text color contrasts with the background color of the slide. As a default, the text border color is the same as the text color. Together with the background color, the text and border colors set the tone for a presentation. For example, a gray background with black text and border sets a dramatic tone. In contrast, a red background with yellow text and border sets a vibrant tone.
Accent colors	Accent colors are designed as colors for secondary features on a slide. They often are used as fill colors on graphs and as shadows.
Hyperlink colors	The default hyperlink color is set when you type the text. When you click the hyperlink text during a presentation, the color changes to the Followed Hyperlink color.

To Change the Presentation Theme Colors

The first modification to make is to change the color scheme throughout the presentation. The following steps change the color scheme for the template from a gray title slide background with pink text and accents to a blue background with pink and orange accents.

1

- Click Design on the Ribbon and then click the Theme Colors button (Design tab | Themes group) to display the Theme Colors gallery.
- Scroll down and then point to the Oriel built-in theme to display a live preview of this color scheme (Figure 2–6).

Experiment

- Point to various themes in the Theme Colors gallery and watch the colors change on Slide 4.

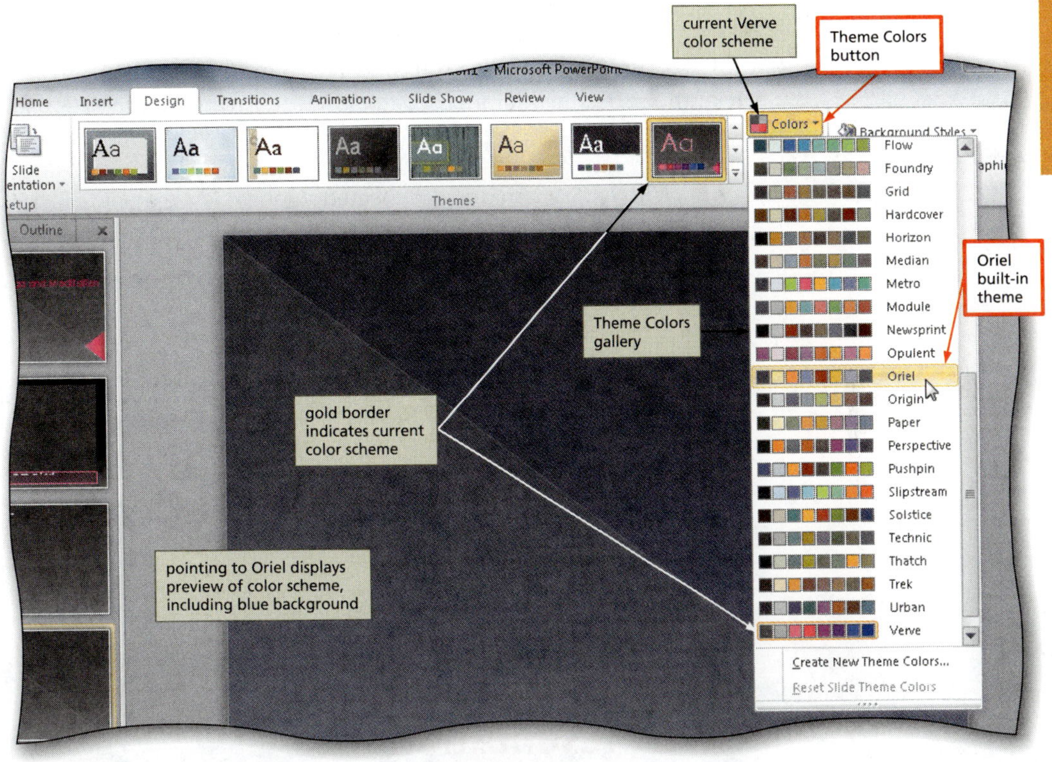

Figure 2–6

Q&A Why does a gold line surround the Verve color scheme in the Theme Colors gallery?

It shows the Verve document theme is applied, and those eight colors are associated with that theme.

2

- Click Oriel in the Theme Colors gallery to change the presentation theme colors to Oriel (Figure 2–7).

Q&A What if I want to return to the original theme color?

You would click the Theme Colors button and then click Verve in the Theme Colors gallery.

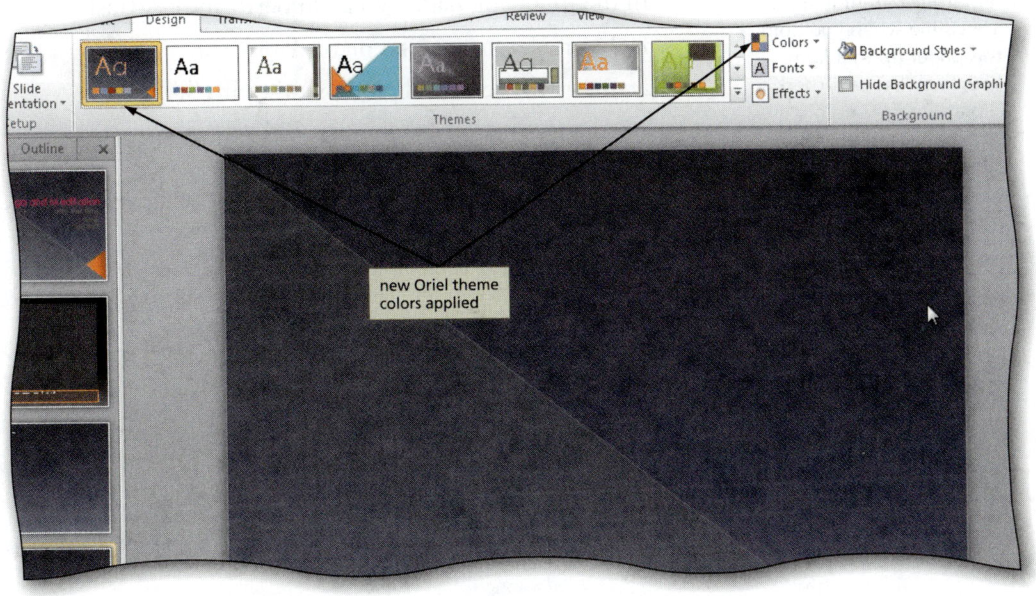

Figure 2–7

To Save a Presentation

You have performed many tasks while creating this slide and do not want to risk losing work completed thus far. Accordingly, you should save the document.

The following steps assume you already have created folders for storing your files, for example, a CIS 101 folder (for your class) that contains a PowerPoint folder (for your assignments). Thus, these steps save the document in the PowerPoint folder in the CIS 101 folder on a USB flash drive using the file name, Yoga. For a detailed example of the procedure summarized below, refer to the Office 2010 and Windows 7 chapter in this book.

1. With a USB flash drive connected to one of the computer's USB ports, click the Save button on the Quick Access Toolbar to display the Save As dialog box.
2. Type `Yoga` in the File name text box to change the file name. Do not press the ENTER key after typing the file name because you do not want to close the dialog box at this time.
3. Navigate to the desired save location (in this case, the PowerPoint folder in the CIS 101 folder [or your class folder] on the USB flash drive).
4. Click the Save button (Save As dialog box) to save the document in the selected folder on the selected drive with the entered file name.

Inserting and Formatting Pictures in a Presentation

With the text entered and background formatted in the presentation, the next step is to insert digital pictures into the placeholders on Slides 2 and 3 and then format the pictures. These graphical images draw the viewers' eyes to the slides and help them retain the information presented.

In the following pages, you will perform these tasks:

1. Insert the first digital picture into Slide 3.
2. Insert the second digital picture into Slide 2.
3. Change the look of the first picture.
4. Change the look of the second picture.
5. Resize the second picture.
6. Insert a digital picture into the Slide 1 background.
7. Format slide backgrounds.

BTW

Inserting Watermarks
Checks, currency, business cards, and legal documents use watermarks to verify their authenticity. These semi-transparent images are visible when you hold this paper up to a light. You, likewise, can insert a clip art image or a picture as a watermark behind all or part of your slide to identify your unique PowerPoint presentation.

Plan Ahead

Adhere to copyright regulations.
You have permission to use the clips from the Microsoft Clip Organizer. If you want to use a clip from another source, be certain you have the legal right to insert this file in your presentation. Read the copyright notices that accompany the clip and are posted on the Web site. The owners of these images and files often ask you to give them credit for using their work, which may be satisfied by stating where you obtained the images.

To Insert a Picture

The next step in creating the presentation is to insert one of the digital yoga pictures in the picture placeholder in Slide 3. The picture is available on the Data Files for Students. See the inside back cover of this book for instructions on downloading the Data Files for Students, or contact your instructor for information about accessing the required files.

The following steps insert a picture, which, in this example, is located in the PowerPoint Chapter 02 folder on the same USB flash drive that contains the saved presentation, into Slide 3.

1

- With your USB flash drive connected to one of the computer's USB ports, click the Previous Slide button to display Slide 3.
- Click the Insert Picture from File icon in the content placeholder to display the Insert Picture dialog box.

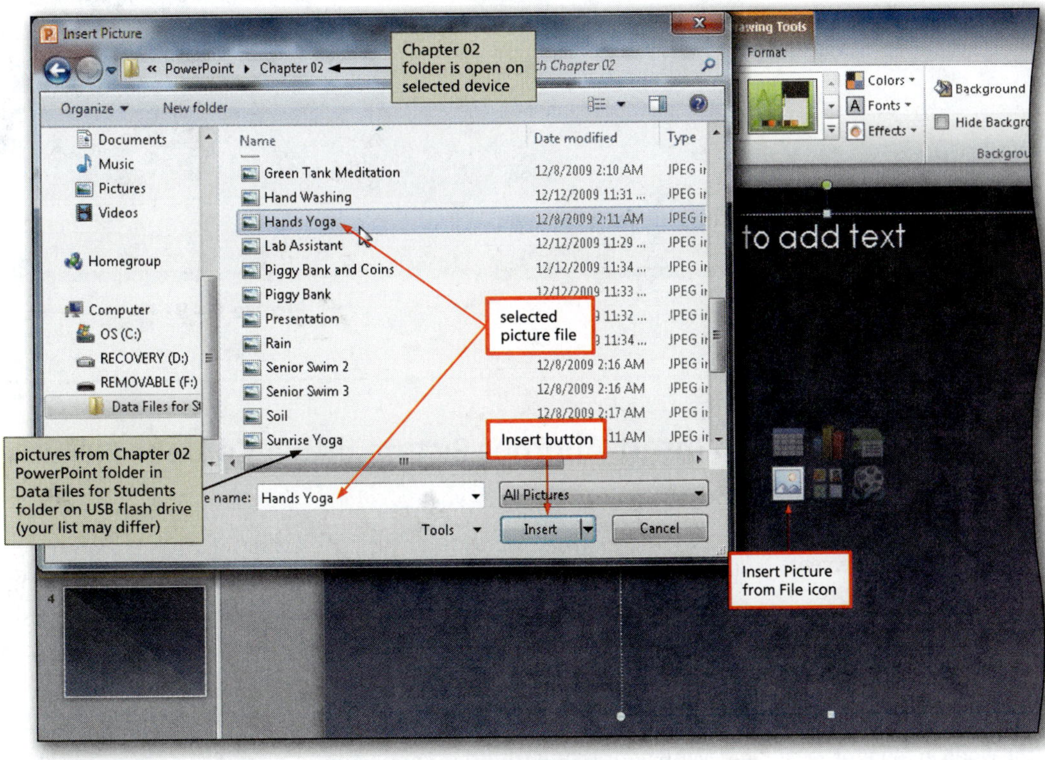

Figure 2–8

2

- If Computer is not displayed in the navigation pane, drag the navigation pane scroll bar (Insert Picture dialog box) until Computer appears.
- Click Computer in the navigation pane to display a list of available storage devices in the Insert Picture dialog box. If necessary, scroll through the dialog box until your USB flash drive appears in the list of available storage devices.
- Double-click your USB flash drive in the list of available storage devices to display a list of files and folders on the selected USB flash drive. Double-click the Data Files for Students folder, double-click the PowerPoint folder, and then double-click the Chapter 02 folder to display a list of files in that folder.
- Scroll down and then click Hands Yoga to select the file name (Figure 2–8).

Q&A What if the picture is not on a USB flash drive?

Use the same process, but select the drive containing the picture.

3

- Click the Insert button (Insert Picture dialog box) to insert the picture into the content placeholder in Slide 3 (Figure 2–9).

Q&A

What are the symbols around the picture?

A selected graphic appears surrounded by a **selection rectangle**, which has small squares and circles, called **sizing handles**, at each corner and middle location.

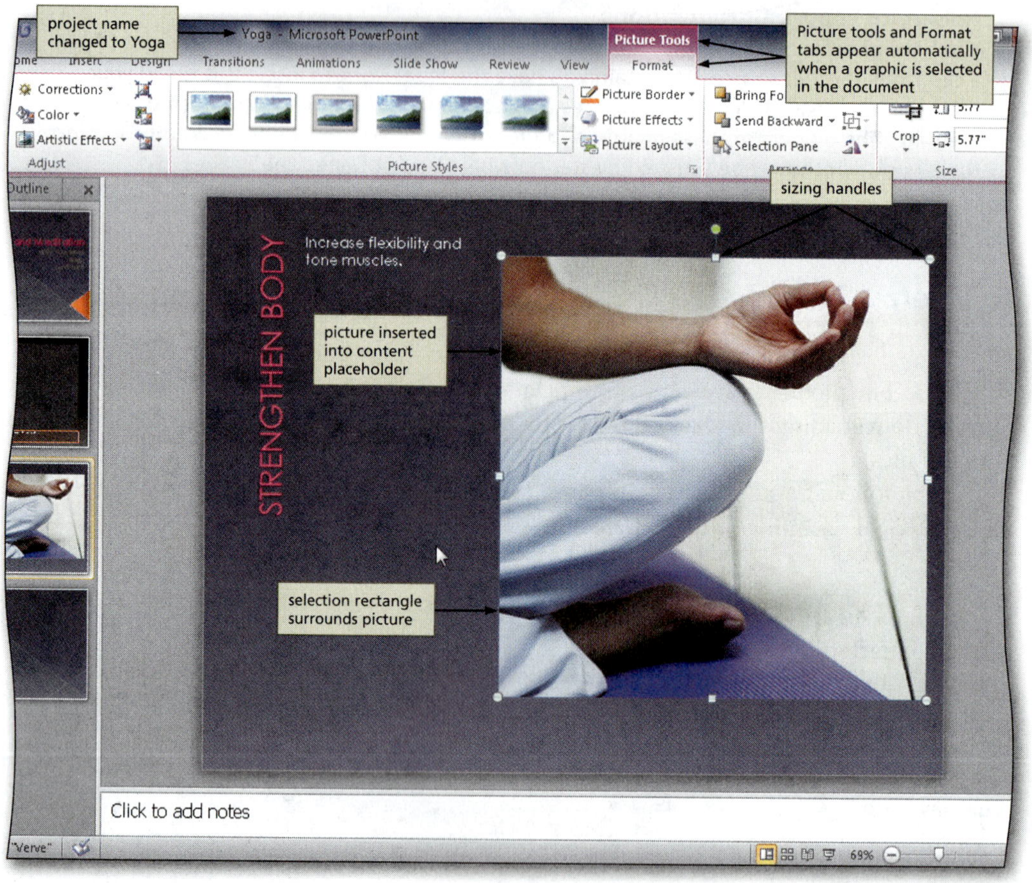

Figure 2–9

To Insert Another Picture into a Content Placeholder

BTW

Modernism's Effect on Graphic Design

The modernist movement of the late nineteenth and twentieth centuries influenced the design principles in use today. Artists and architects of that era simplified the world in terms of legible fonts, abstract shapes, and balanced layouts. Modernists sought to create works independent of language so their message could reach people throughout the world.

The next step is to insert another digital yoga picture into the Slide 2 content placeholder. This second picture also is available on the Data Files for Students. See the inside back cover of this book for instructions on downloading the Data Files for Students, or contact your instructor for information about accessing the required files.

The following steps insert a picture into Slide 2.

1. Click the Previous Slide button to display Slide 2.
2. With your USB flash drive connected to one of the computer's USB ports, click the Insert Picture from File icon in the content placeholder to display the Insert Picture dialog box.
3. If the list of files and folders on the selected USB flash drive are not displayed in the Insert Picture dialog box, double-click your USB flash drive to display them and then navigate to the PowerPoint Chapter 02 folder.
4. Scroll down and then click Green Tank Meditation to select the file name.
5. Click the Insert button (Insert Picture dialog box) to insert the picture into the Slide 2 content placeholder (Figure 2–10).

Figure 2–10

To Insert a Picture into a Slide without a Content Placeholder

In PowerPoint Chapter 1, you inserted a clip into a slide without a content placeholder. You also can insert a picture into a slide that does not have a content placeholder. The picture for Slide 4 is available on the Data Files for Students. See the inside back cover of this book for instructions on downloading the Data Files for Students, or contact your instructor for information about accessing the required files. The following steps insert a picture into Slide 4.

1

- Click the Next Slide button two times to display Slide 4.
- With your USB flash drive connected to one of the computer's USB ports, click Insert on the Ribbon (Figure 2–11).

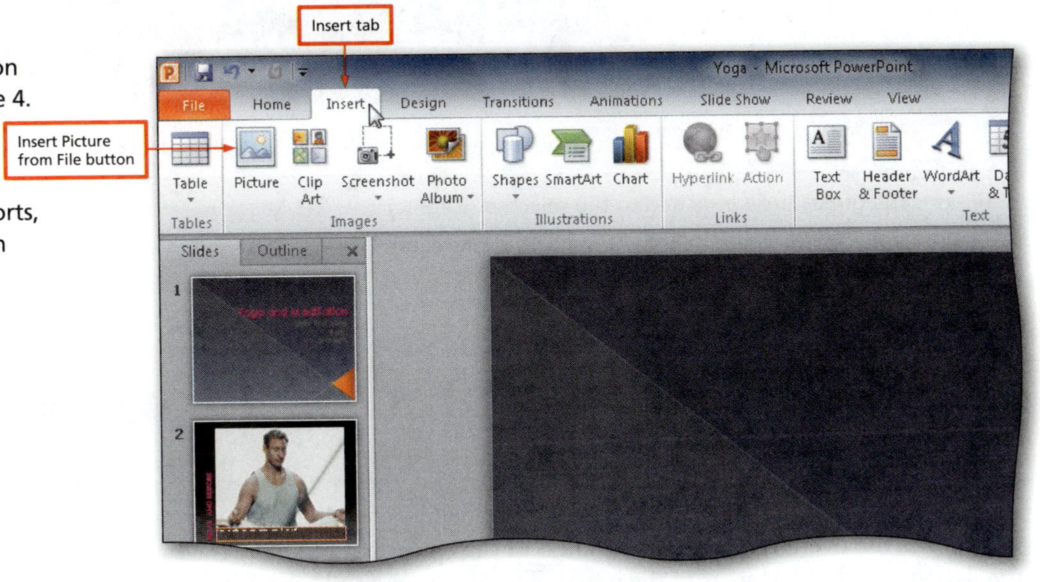

Figure 2–11

2

- Click Insert Picture from File (Insert tab | Images group) to display the Insert Picture dialog box. If the list of files and folders on the selected USB flash drive are not displayed in the Insert Picture dialog box, double-click your USB flash drive to display them and then navigate to the PowerPoint Chapter 02 folder.
- Click Arch Yoga to select the file name (Figure 2–12).

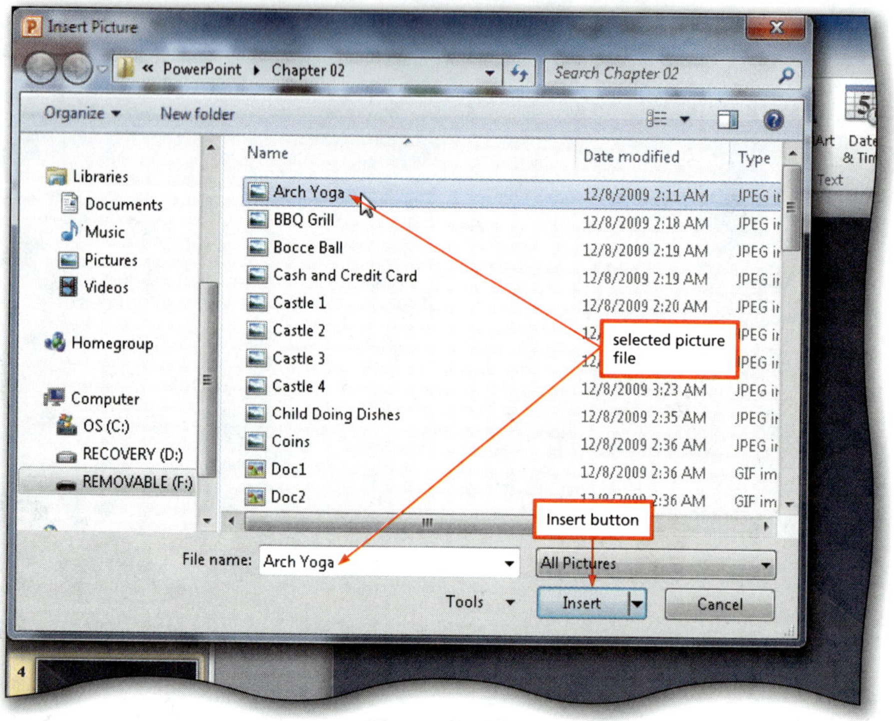

Figure 2–12

3

- Click the Insert button (Insert Picture dialog box) to insert the picture into the Slide 4 content placeholder.
- Move the picture so that it displays approximately as shown in Figure 2–13.

Figure 2–13

Q&A

What is the green circle attached to the selected graphic?

The green circle is a rotate handle. When you drag a graphic's rotate handle, the graphic moves in either a clockwise or counter clockwise direction.

To Correct a Picture

A photograph's color intensity can be modified by changing the brightness and contrast. **Brightness** determines the overall lightness or darkness of the entire image, whereas **contrast** is the difference between the darkest and lightest areas of the image. The brightness and contrast are changed in predefined percentage increments. The following step increases the brightness and decreases the contrast to intensify the picture colors.

1

- With the Arch Yoga picture on Slide 4 still selected, click the Corrections button (Picture Tools Format tab | Adjust group) to display the Corrections gallery.
- Point to Brightness: +20% Contrast: −40% (fourth picture in first row of Brightness and Contrast area) to display a live preview of these corrections on the picture (Figure 2–14).

Experiment

- Point to various pictures in the Brightness and Contrast area and watch the brightness and contrast change on the picture in Slide 4.

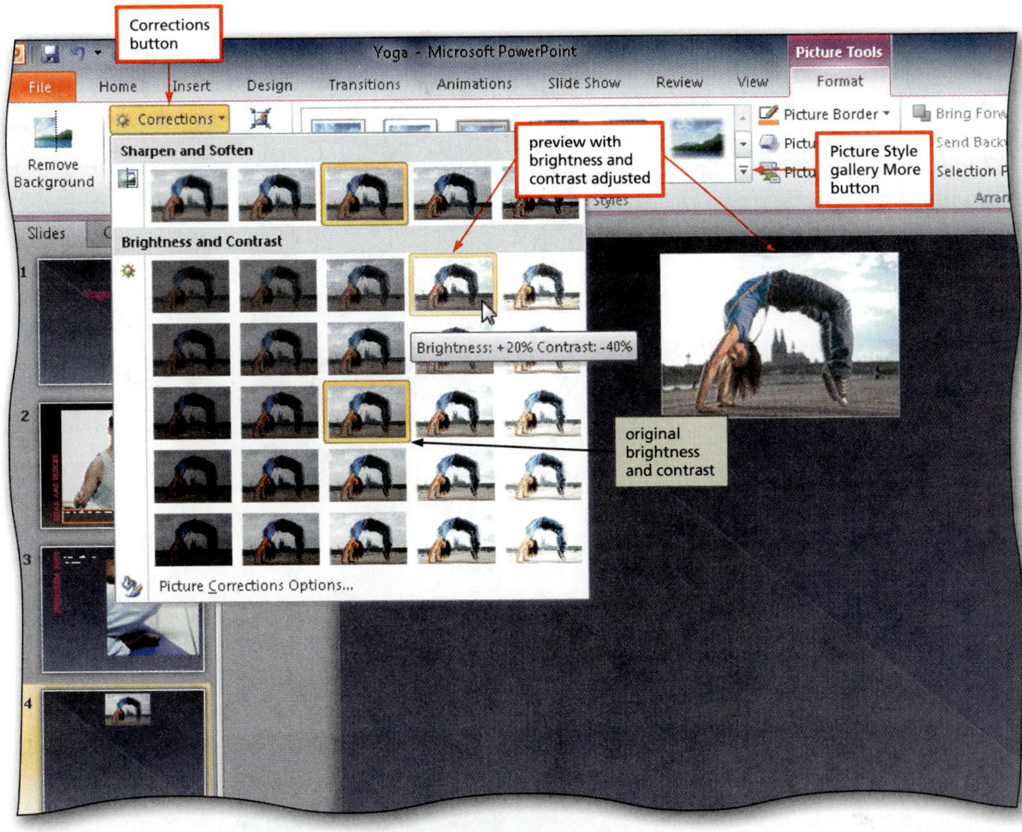

Figure 2–14

Q&A Why is a yellow border surrounding the picture in the center of the gallery?

The image on Slide 4 currently has normal brightness and contrast (0%), which is represented by this center image in the gallery.

- Click Brightness: +20% Contrast: −40% to apply this correction to the yoga picture.

Q&A How can I remove all effects from the picture?

Click the Reset Picture button (Picture Tools Format tab | Adjust group).

Other Ways

1. Click Picture Corrections Options, move Brightness or Contrast sliders or enter number in box next to slider (Format Picture dialog box)

To Apply a Picture Style

The pictures on Slides 2, 3, and 4 grasp the audience's attention, but you can increase their visual appeal by applying a style. A **style** is a named group of formatting characteristics. PowerPoint provides more than 25 picture styles that enable you easily to change a picture's look to a more visually appealing style, including a variety of shapes, angles, borders, and reflections. The photos in Slides 2, 3, and 4 in this chapter use styles that apply soft edges, reflections, or angled perspectives to the pictures. The steps on the next page apply a picture style to the Slide 4 picture.

1

- With the Slide 4 picture selected, click the Picture Tools Format tab and then click the More button in the Picture Styles gallery (Picture Tools Format tab | Picture Styles group) (shown in Figure 2–14 on the previous page) to expand the gallery.
- Point to Soft Edge Rectangle in the Picture Styles gallery to display a live preview of that style applied to the picture in the document (Figure 2–15).

Experiment

- Point to various picture styles in the Picture Styles gallery and watch the style of the picture change in the document window.

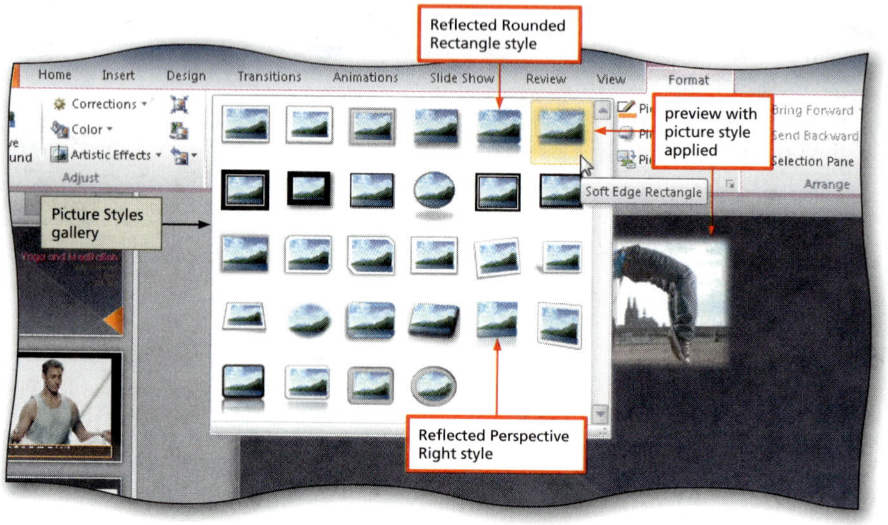

Figure 2–15

2

- Click Soft Edge Rectangle in the Picture Styles gallery to apply the style to the selected picture (Figure 2–16).

Figure 2–16

To Apply Other Picture Styles

The next step is to apply picture styles to the yoga pictures in Slides 3 and 2. To provide continuity, both of these styles will have a reflection. The following steps apply other picture styles to the Slide 3 and Slide 2 pictures.

1. Click the Previous Slide button to display Slide 3.
2. Click the Slide 3 picture to select it, click the Picture Tools Format tab, and then click the More button in the Picture Styles gallery to expand the gallery.
3. Click Reflected Perspective Right in the Picture Styles gallery to apply this style to the picture in Slide 3.
4. Click the Previous Slide button to display Slide 2.
5. Click the Slide 2 picture to select it, click the Picture Tools Format tab, and then click the More button in the Picture Styles gallery to expand the gallery.
6. Click Reflected Rounded Rectangle in the Picture Styles gallery to apply this style to the picture in Slide 2 (Figure 2–17).

Figure 2–17

To Apply Picture Effects

PowerPoint provides a variety of picture effects so that you can further customize a picture. Effects include shadows, reflections, glow, soft edges, bevel, and 3-D rotation. The difference between the effects and the styles is that each effect has several options, providing you with more control over the exact look of the image.

In this presentation, the photos on Slides 2 and 3 have an orange glow effect and have a bevel applied to their edges. The following steps apply picture effects to the selected picture.

1

- With the Slide 2 picture selected, click the Picture Effects button (Picture Tools Format tab | Picture Styles group) to display the Picture Effects menu.

Q&A What if the Picture Tools Format tab no longer is displayed on my Ribbon?

Double-click the picture to display the Picture Tools and Format tabs.

- Point to Glow on the Picture Effects menu to display the Glow gallery.

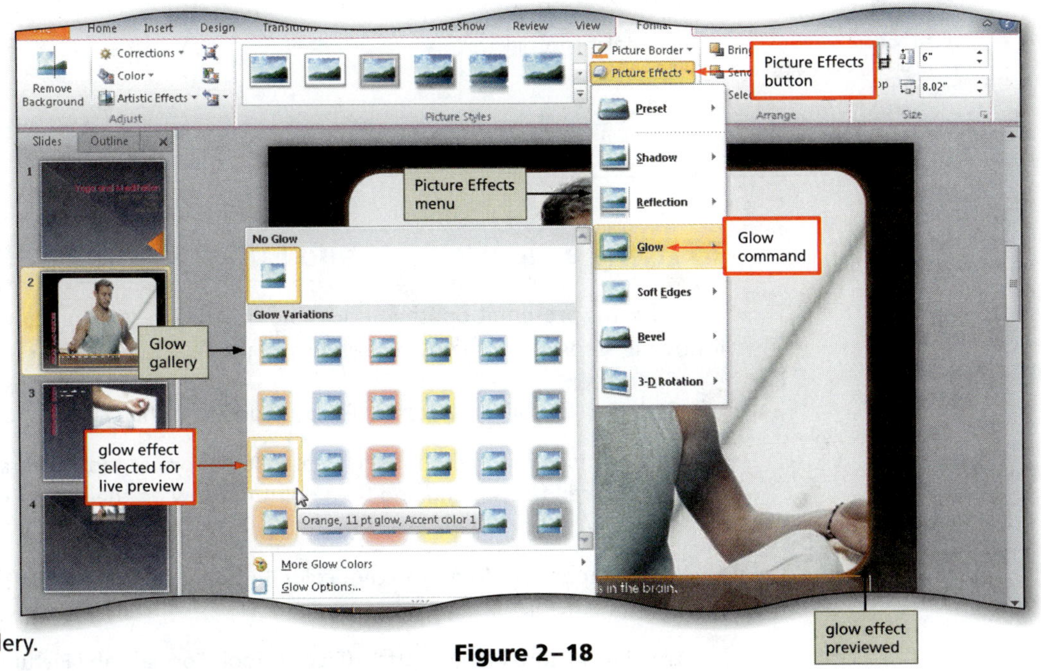

Figure 2–18

- Point to Orange, 11 pt glow, Accent color 1 in the Glow Variations area (leftmost glow in third row) to display a live preview of the selected glow effect applied to the picture in the document window (Figure 2–18).

Experiment

- Point to various glow effects in the Glow gallery and watch the picture change in the document window.

2

- Click Orange, 11 pt glow, Accent color 1 in the Glow gallery to apply the selected picture effect.

3

- Click the Picture Effects button (Picture Tools Format tab | Picture Styles group) to display the Picture Effects menu again.
- Point to Bevel on the Picture Effects menu to display the Bevel gallery.
- Point to Angle (leftmost bevel in second row) to display a live preview of the selected bevel effect applied to the Slide 2 picture (Figure 2–19).

Experiment

- Point to various bevel effects in the Bevel gallery and watch the picture change in the slide.

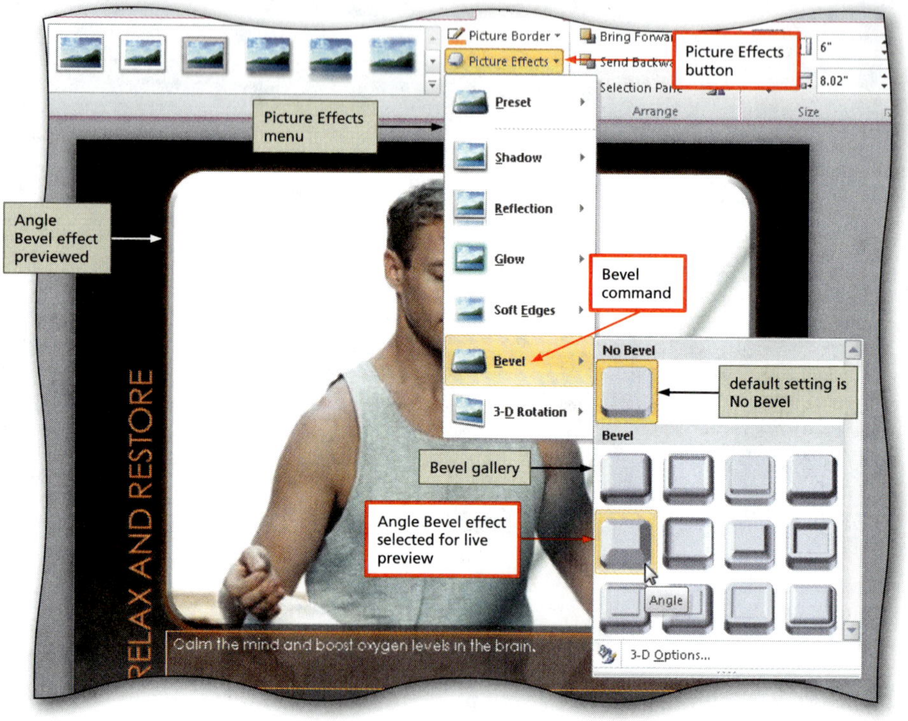

Figure 2–19

4

- Click Angle in the Bevel gallery to apply the selected picture effect.

Other Ways

1. Right-click picture, click Format Picture on shortcut menu, select desired options (Format Picture dialog box), click Close button
2. Click Format Shape dialog box launcher (Picture Tools Format tab | Picture Styles group), select desired options (Format Picture dialog box), click Close button

To Apply a Picture Style and Effect to Another Picture

In this presentation, the Slide 3 picture also has orange glow and bevel effects. The following steps apply the picture style and picture effects to the picture.

1. Click the Next Slide button to display Slide 3 and then click the picture to select it.
2. Click the Picture Effects button (Picture Tools Format tab | Picture Styles group) to display the Picture Effects menu and then point to Glow on the Picture Effects menu to display the Glow gallery.
3. Click Orange, 11 pt glow, Accent color 1 (leftmost glow in third row) in the Glow gallery to apply the picture effect to the picture.
4. Click the Picture Effects button (Picture Tools Format tab | Picture Styles group) to display the Picture Effects menu again and then point to Bevel on the Picture Effects menu to display the Bevel gallery.
5. Click Convex (third bevel in second row) in the Bevel area to apply the picture effect to the selected picture (Figure 2–20).

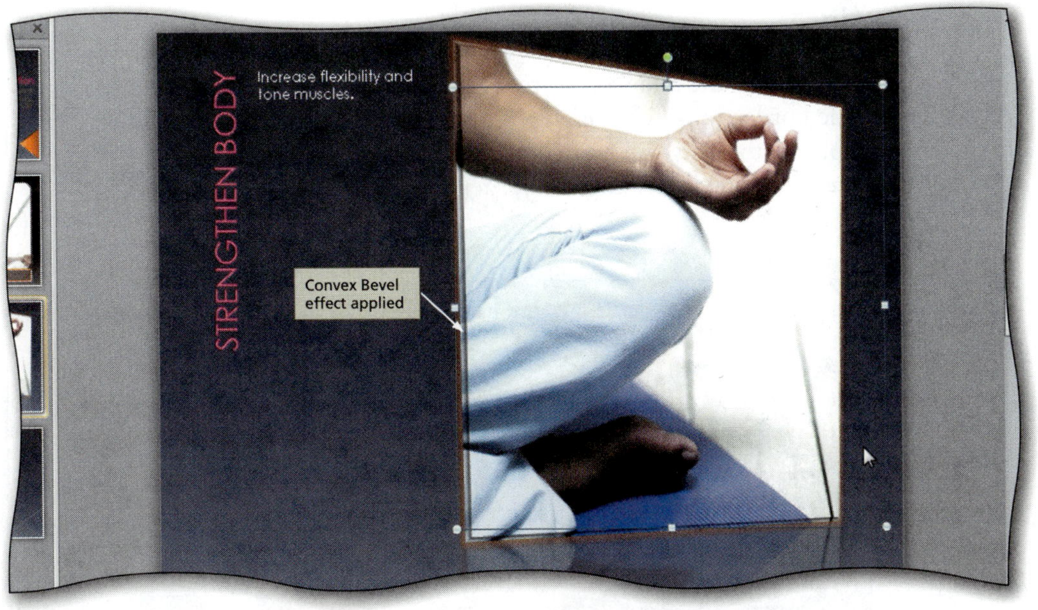

Figure 2–20

To Add a Picture Border

The next step is to add a small border to the Slide 3 picture. Some picture styles provide a border, but the Reflected Rounded Rectangle style you applied to this picture does not. The following steps add a border to the Slide 3 picture.

1

- With the Slide 3 picture still selected, click the Picture Border button (Picture Tools Format tab | Picture Styles group) to display the Picture Border gallery.

Q&A What if the Picture Tools Format tab no longer is displayed on my Ribbon?
Double-click the picture to display the Picture Tools and Format tabs.

2

- Point to Weight on the Picture Border gallery to display the Weight list.
- Point to 1½ pt to display a live preview of this line weight on the picture (Figure 2–21).

Experiment

- Point to various line weights in the Weight list and watch the line thickness change.

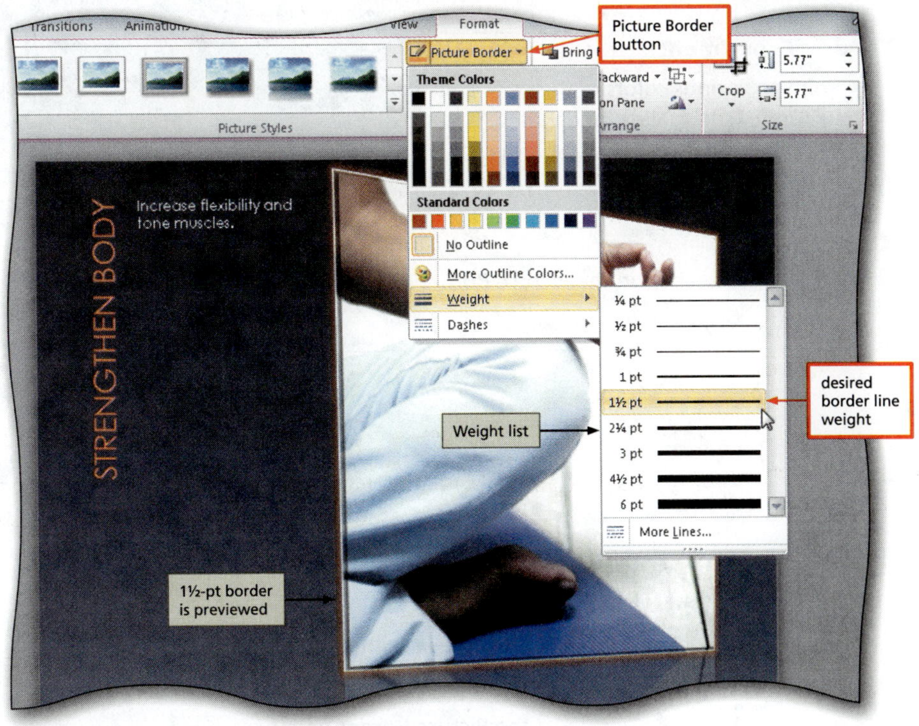

Figure 2–21

Q&A Can I make the line width more than 6 pt?
Yes. Click More Lines and then increase the amount in the Width box.

3

- Click 1½ pt to add this line weight to the picture.

To Change a Picture Border Color

The default color for the border you added to the Slide 3 picture is White. Earlier in this chapter, you changed the color scheme to Oriel. To coordinate the border color with the title text color and other elements of this theme, you will use a shade of red in the Oriel color scheme. Any color galleries you display show colors defined in this current color scheme. The following steps change the Slide 3 picture border color.

1

- With the Slide 3 photo still selected, click the Picture Border button (Picture Tools Format tab | Picture Styles group) to display the Picture Border gallery.

Q&A What if the Picture Tools Format tab no longer is displayed on my Ribbon?

Double-click the picture to display the Picture Tools and Format tabs.

2

- Point to Red, Accent 3 (seventh theme color from left in first row) in the Picture Border gallery to display a live preview of that border color on the picture (Figure 2–22).

Experiment

- Point to various colors in the Picture Border gallery and watch the border on the picture change in the slide.

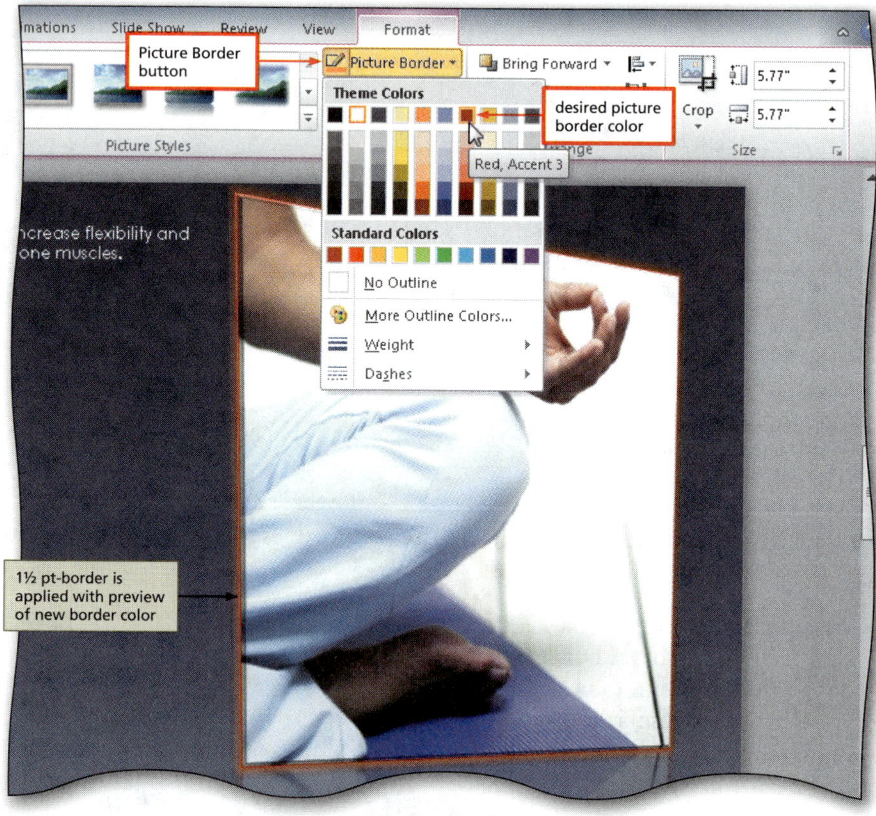

Figure 2–22

3

- Click Red, Accent 3 in the Picture Border gallery to change the picture border color.

To Add a Picture Border and Color to Another Picture

In this presentation, the Slide 2 picture does not have a border as part of the Reflected Perspective Right picture style. The following steps add a border to Slide 2 and change the color.

1. Click the Previous Slide button to display Slide 2 and then click the picture to select it.
2. Click the Picture Border button (Picture Tools Format tab | Picture Styles group) to display the Picture Border gallery.
3. Point to Weight on the Picture Border gallery to display the Weight list and then point to 1½ pt to display a live preview of this line weight on the picture.
4. Click 1½ pt to add this line weight to the picture.

5 Click the Picture Border button (Picture Tools Format tab | Picture Styles group) to display the Picture Border gallery again and then click Red, Accent 3 in the Picture Border gallery to change the picture border color (Figure 2–23).

Figure 2–23

To Resize a Graphic by Entering Exact Measurements

The next step is to resize the Slide 3 picture so that it fills much of the empty space in the slide. In PowerPoint Chapter 1, you resized clips by dragging the sizing handles. This technique also applies to changing the size of photos. You also can resize graphics by specifying exact height and width measurements. The yoga picture can be enlarged so that its height and width measurements are 6.0". When a graphic is selected, its height and width measurements show in the Size group of the Picture Tools Format tab. The following steps resize the Slide 3 picture by entering its desired exact measurements.

1

- Click the Next Slide button to display Slide 3 and then select the picture. Click the Shape Height text box (Picture Tools Format tab | Size group) to select the contents in the text box and then type 6 as the height (Figure 2–24).

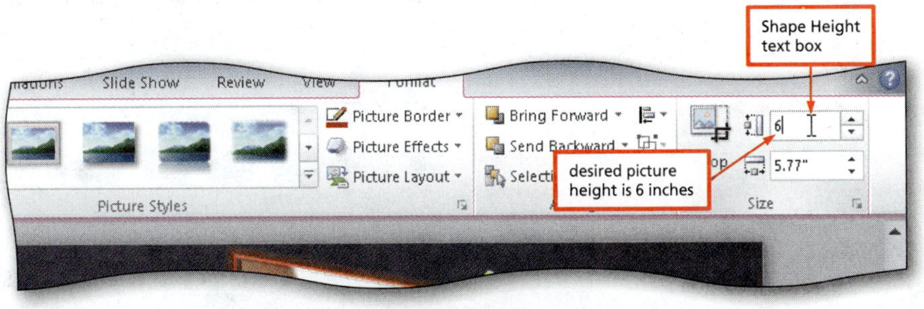

Figure 2–24

Q&A What if the contents of the Shape Height text box are not selected?
Triple-click the Shape Height text box.

Q&A Why did the width size also change?
PowerPoint kept the photo in proportion so that the width changed the same amount as the height changed.

2

- Click the Shape Width text box (Picture Tools Format tab | Size group) to select the contents in the text box and then type 6 as the width if this number does not display automatically.
- If necessary, move the photo to the location shown in Figure 2–25.

Q&A What if I want to return a graphic to its original size and start again?

With the graphic selected, click the Size and Position dialog box launcher (Picture Tools Format tab | Size group), if necessary click the Size tab (Format Picture dialog box), click the Reset button, and then click the Close button.

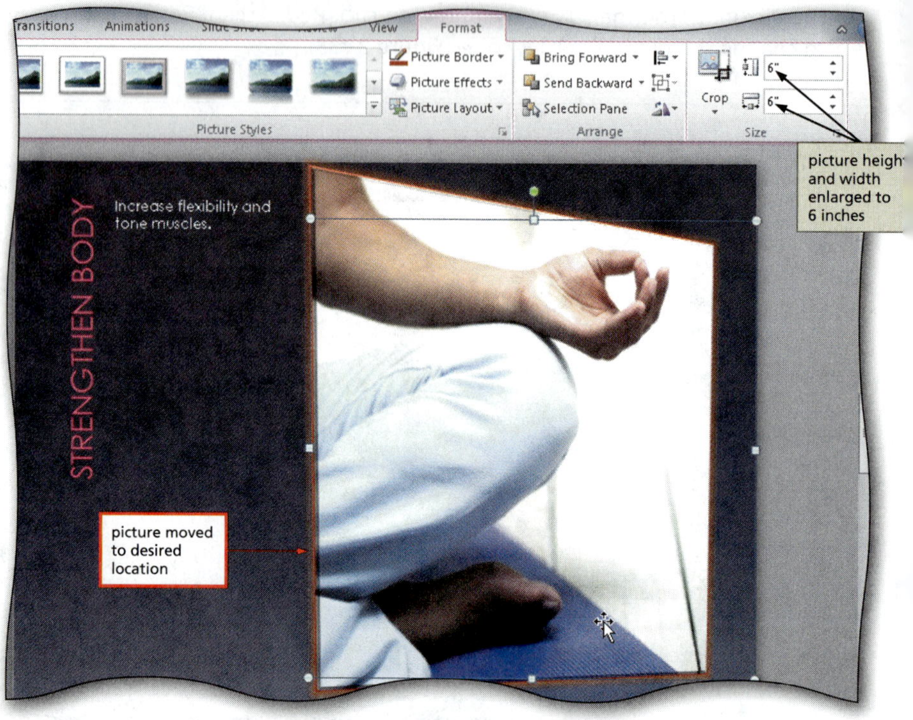

Figure 2–25

Other Ways

1. Right-click picture, enter shape height and width values in text boxes on shortcut menu
2. Right-click picture, click Format Picture on shortcut menu, click Size (Format Picture dialog box), enter shape height and width values in text boxes, click Close button

To Resize Another Graphic Using Exact Measurements

The Arch Yoga picture on Slide 4 also can be enlarged to fill space at the top of the slide. The yoga picture can be enlarged so that its height and width measurements are 3" and 4.48", respectively. The following steps resize the Slide 4 picture.

1. Click the Next Slide button to display Slide 4 and then select the picture. Click the Shape Height text box (Picture Tools Format tab | Size group) to select the contents in the text box and type 3 as the height.

2. Move the photo to the location shown in Figure 2–26.

Figure 2–26

To Save an Existing Document with the Same File Name

You have made several modifications to the document since you last saved it. Thus, you should save it again. The following step saves the document again. For an example of the step listed below, refer to the Office 2010 and Windows 7 chapter in this book.

1 Click the Save button on the Quick Access Toolbar to overwrite the previously saved file.

Break Point: If you wish to take a break, this is a good place to do so. You can quit PowerPoint now. To resume at a later time, start PowerPoint, open the file called Yoga, and continue following the steps from this location forward.

Formatting Slide Backgrounds

A slide's background is an integral part of a presentation because it can generate audience interest. Every slide can have the same background, or different backgrounds can be used in a presentation. This background is considered **fill**, which is the content that makes up the interior of a shape, line, or character. Three fills are available: solid, gradient, and picture or texture. **Solid fill** is one color used throughout the entire slide. **Gradient fill** is one color shade gradually progressing to another shade of the same color or one color progressing to another color. **Picture or texture fill** uses a specific file or an image that simulates a material, such as cork, granite, marble, or canvas.

Once you add a fill, you can adjust its appearance. For example, you can adjust its **transparency**, which allows you to see through the background, so that any text on the slide is visible. You also can select a color that is part of the theme or a custom color. You can use **offsets**, another background feature, to move the background from the slide borders in varying distances by percentage. **Tiling options** repeat the background image many times vertically and horizontally on the slide; the smaller the tiling percentage, the greater the number of times the image is repeated.

BTW

Resetting Backgrounds
If you have made many changes to the background and want to start the process over, click the Reset Background button in the Format Background dialog box.

To Insert a Texture Fill

A wide variety of texture fills are available to give your presentation a unique look. The 24 pictures in the Textures gallery give the appearance of a physical object, such as water drops, sand, tissue paper, and a paper bag. You also can use your own texture pictures for custom backgrounds. When you insert a fill, PowerPoint assumes you want this custom background on only the current slide displayed. To make this background appear on all slides in the presentation, click the Apply to All button in the Format Background dialog box. The following steps insert the Sand fill on Slide 4 in the presentation.

1

- Right-click anywhere on the Slide 4 blue background to display the shortcut menu (Figure 2–27).

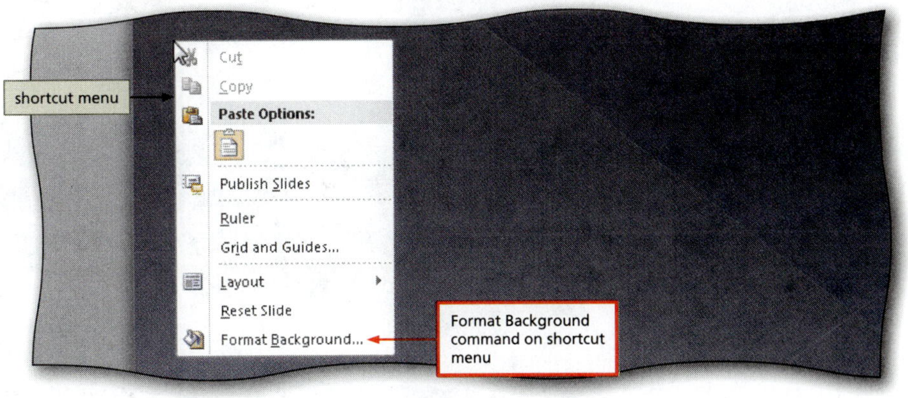

Figure 2–27

2

- Click Format Background on the shortcut menu to display the Format Background dialog box.
- With the Fill pane displaying, click 'Picture or texture fill' to expand the fill options (Figure 2–28).

Q&A Why did the background change to a yellow texture?

This texture is the Papyrus background, which is the default texture fill.

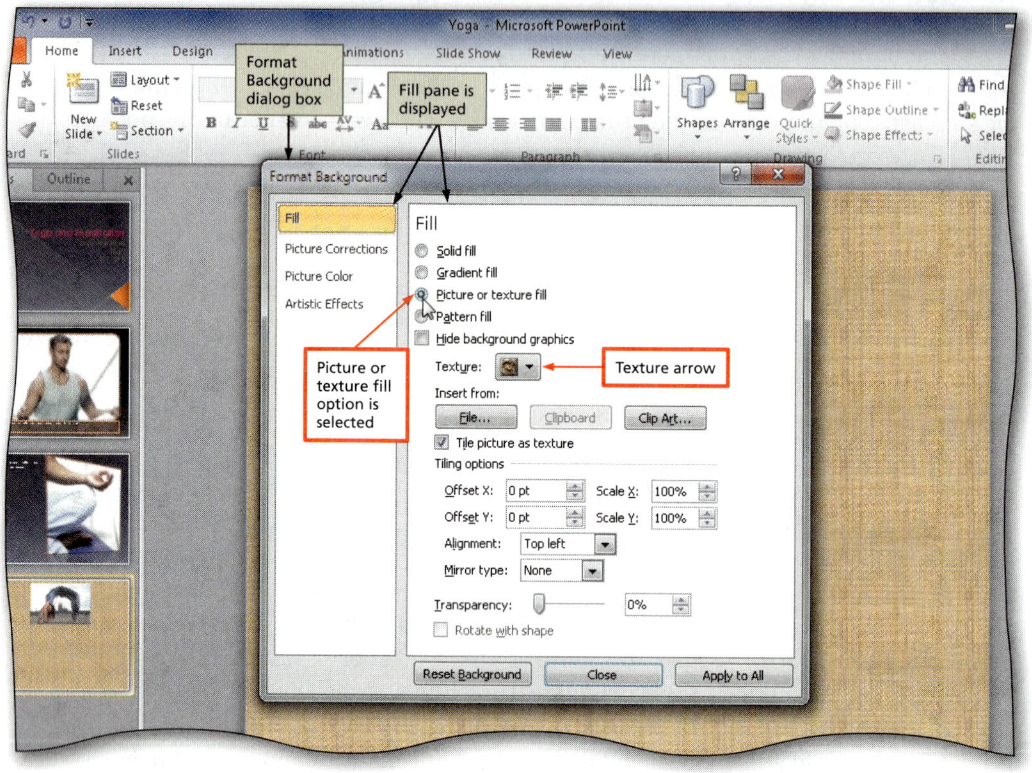

Figure 2–28

3

- Click the Texture arrow to display the Texture gallery (Figure 2–29).

Q&A Is a live preview available to see the various textures on this slide?

No. Live preview is not an option with the background textures and fills.

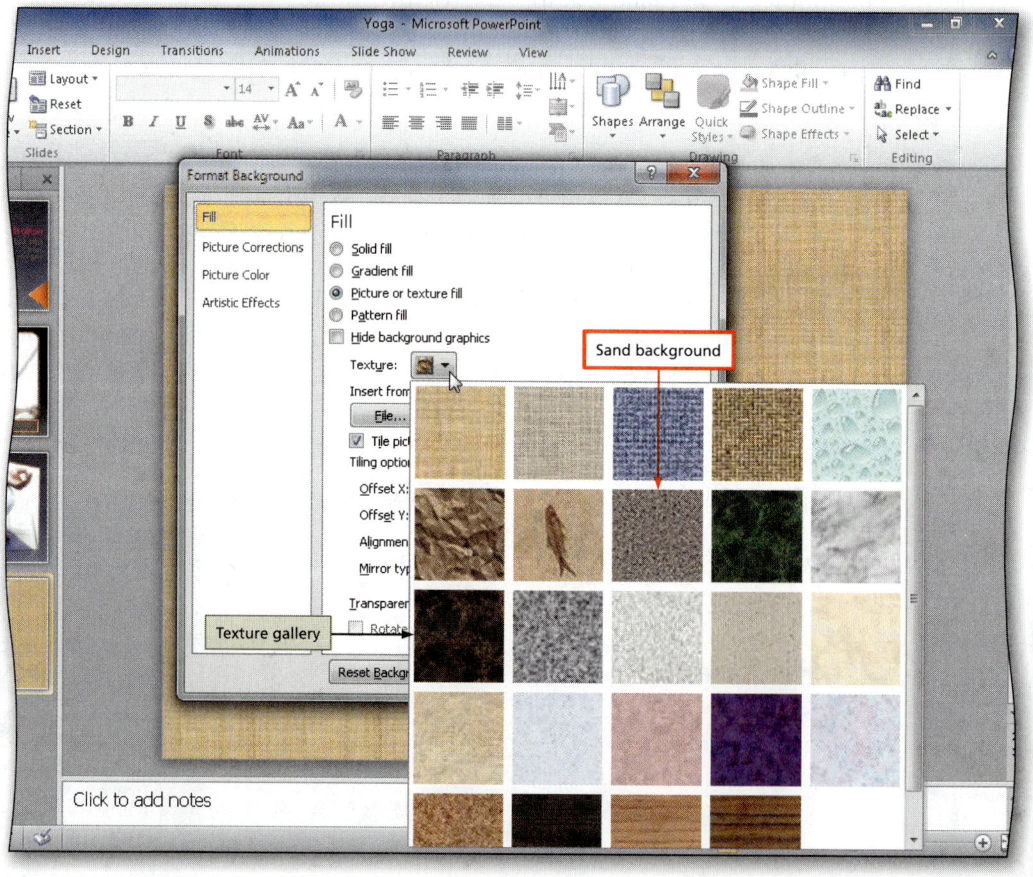

Figure 2–29

4

- Click the Sand background (third texture in second row) to insert this background on Slide 4 (Figure 2–30).

Q&A The Format Background dialog box is covering part of the slide. Can I move this box?

Yes. Click the dialog box title and drag it to a different location so that you can view the slide.

Q&A Could I insert this background on all four slides simultaneously?

Yes. You would click the Apply to All button to insert the Sand background on all slides.

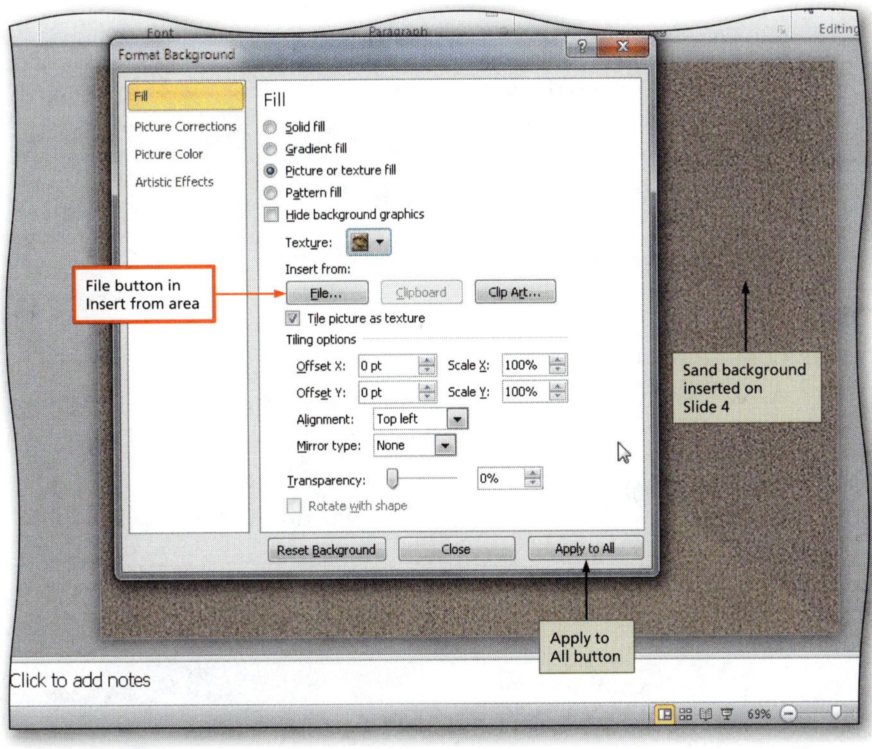

Figure 2–30

Other Ways

1. Click Design tab, Background Styles, click Format Background (Design tab | Background group)

To Insert a Picture to Create a Background

For variety and interest, you want to use another yoga picture as the Slide 1 background. This picture is stored on the Data Files for Students. PowerPoint will stretch the height and width of this picture to fill the slide area. The following steps insert the picture, Sunrise Yoga, on only Slide 1.

1

- Click the Previous Slide button three times to display Slide 1.
- With the Fill pane displaying (Format Background dialog box), click 'Picture or texture fill'.
- Click the File button in the Insert from area (shown in Figure 2–30) to display the Insert Picture dialog box.
- If necessary, double-click your USB flash drive in the list of available storage devices to display a list of files and folders on the selected USB flash drive and then navigate to the PowerPoint Chapter 02 folder.
- Scroll down and then click Sunrise Yoga to select the file name (Figure 2–31).

Q&A What if the picture is not on a USB flash drive?

Use the same process, but select the drive containing the picture.

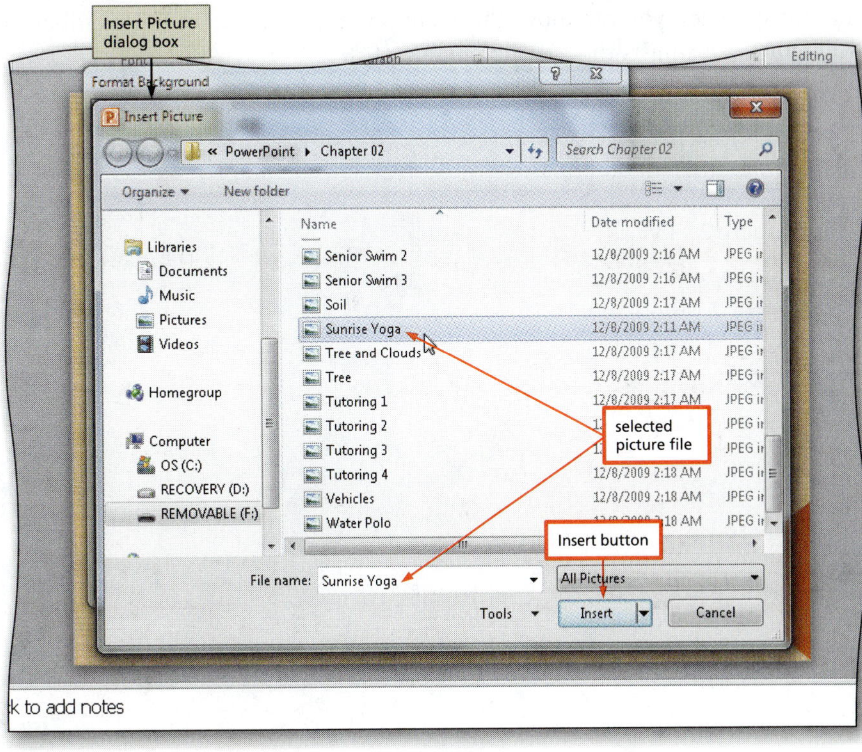

Figure 2–31

2

- Click the Insert button (Insert Picture dialog box) to insert the Sunrise Yoga picture as the Slide 1 background (Figure 2–32).

Q&A What if I do not want to use this picture?

Click the Undo button on the Quick Access Toolbar.

Q&A Why do the Left and Right offsets in the Stretch options area show a −6% value?

PowerPoint automatically reduced the photograph slightly so that it fills the entire slide.

Q&A Can I move the Format Background dialog box to the left so that I can see more of the subtitle text?

Yes. Click the dialog box title and then drag the box to the desired location on the slide.

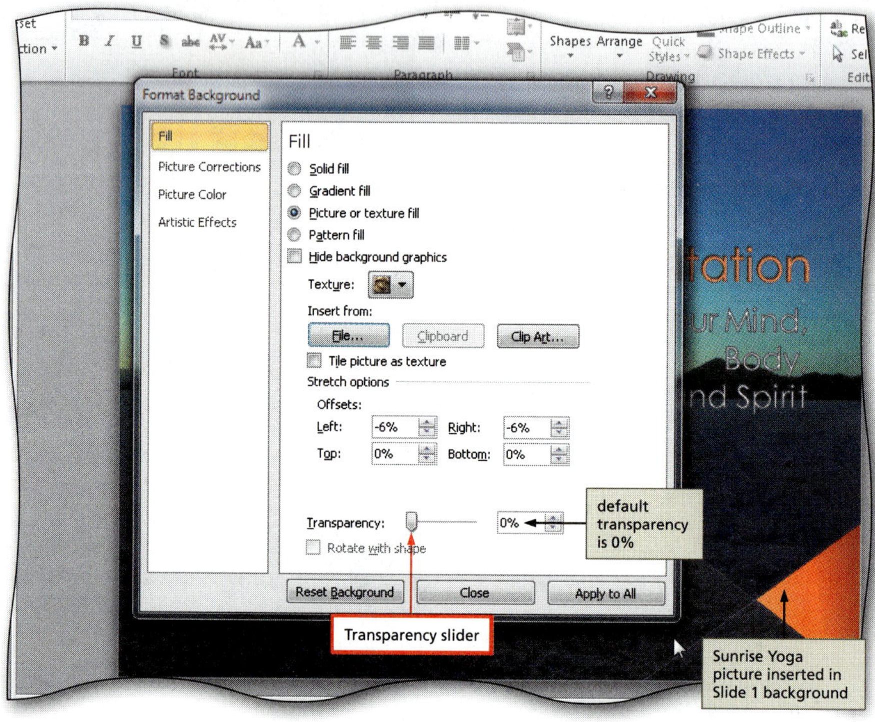

Figure 2–32

To Format the Background Picture Fill Transparency

The Sunrise Yoga picture on Slide 1 is a rich color and conflicts with the title and subtitle text. One method of reducing this richness is to change the transparency. The **Transparency slider** indicates the amount of opaqueness. The default setting is 0, which is fully opaque. The opposite extreme is 100%, which is fully transparent. To change the transparency, you can move the Transparency slider or enter a number in the text box next to the slider. The following step adjusts the transparency to 10%.

1

- Click the Transparency slider and drag it to the right until 10% is displayed in the Transparency text box (Figure 2–33).

Q&A Can I move the slider in small increments so that I can get a precise percentage easily?

Yes. Press the RIGHT ARROW or LEFT ARROW key to move the slider in one-percent increments.

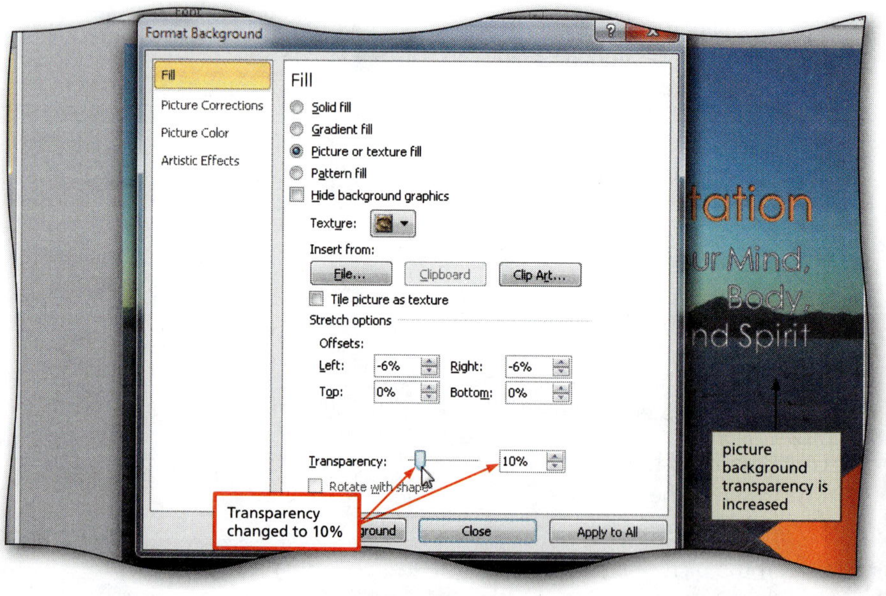

Figure 2–33

To Format the Background Texture Fill Transparency

The Sand texture on Slide 4 is dark and may not offer sufficient contrast with the symbols and text you are going to insert on this slide. You can adjust the transparency of slide texture in the same manner that you change a picture transparency. The following steps adjust the texture transparency to 50%.

1

- Click the Next Slide button three times to display Slide 4.
- Click the Transparency slider and drag it to the right until 50% is displayed in the Transparency text box (Figure 2–34).

2

- Click the Close button (Format Background dialog box).

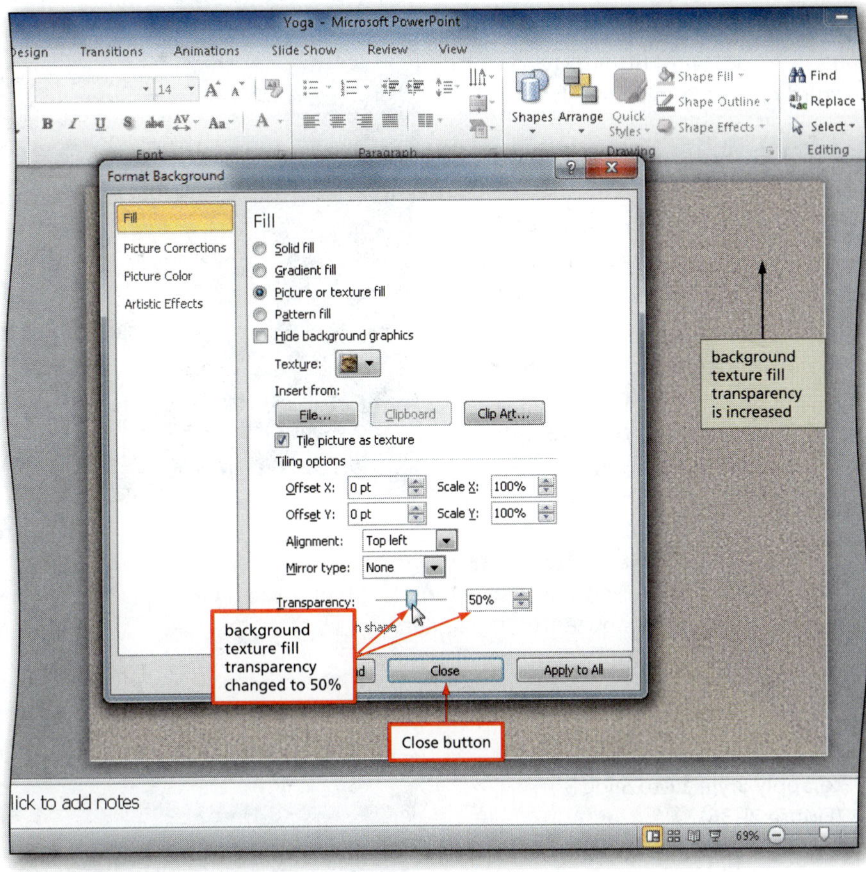

Figure 2–34

To Choose a Background Style

Now that the backgrounds for Slides 1 and 4 are set, and the title and text paragraphs for the presentation have been entered, you need to make design decisions for Slides 2 and 3. In this project, you will choose a background for these slides. For each theme, PowerPoint provides 12 **background styles** with designs that may include color, shading, patterns, and textures. **Fill effects** add pattern and texture to a background, which add depth to a slide. The steps on the next page add a background style to Slides 2 and 3 in the presentation.

1

- Click the Previous Slide button once to display Slide 3 and then click the Design tab on the Ribbon.
- Click the Background Styles button (Design tab | Background group) to display the Background Styles gallery.
- Right-click Style 11 (third style in third row) to display the shortcut menu (Figure 2–35).

Experiment

- Point to various styles themes in the Background Styles gallery and watch the backgrounds change on the slide.

Q&A Are the backgrounds displayed in a specific order?

Yes. They are arranged in order from light to dark running from left to right. The first row has solid backgrounds; the middle row has darker fills at the top and bottom; the bottom row has fill patterns. If you point to a background, a ScreenTip with the background's name appears on the screen.

Figure 2–35

2

- Click Apply to Selected Slides to apply Style 11 to Slide 3 (Figure 2–36).

Q&A If I decide later that this background style does not fit the theme of my presentation, can I apply a different background?

Yes. You can repeat these steps at any time while creating your presentation.

Q&A What if I want to apply this background style to all slides in the presentation?

Click the desired style or click Apply to All Slides in the shortcut menu.

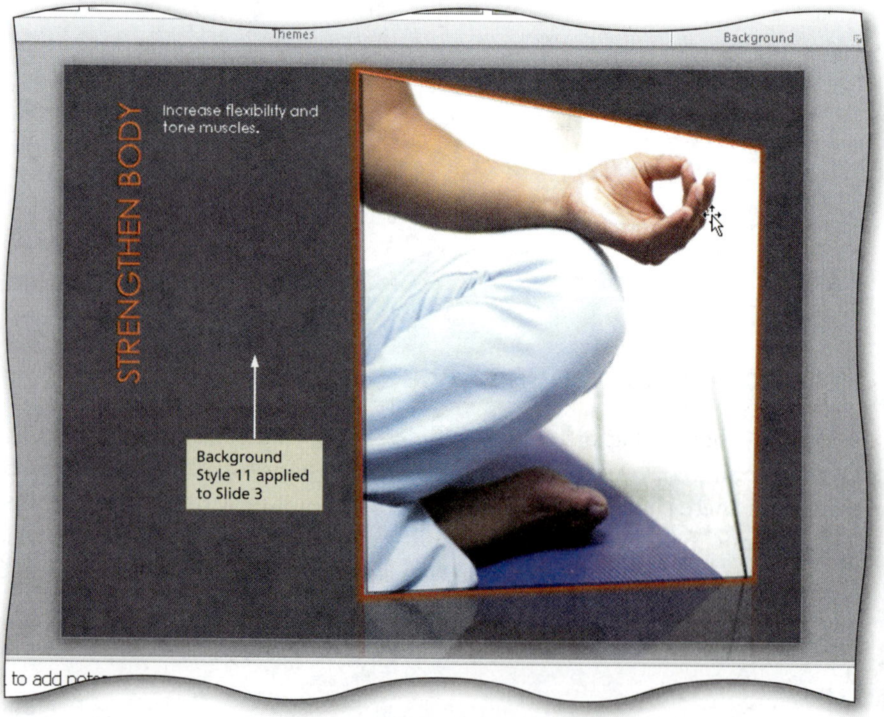

Figure 2–36

Other Ways

1. Click Background Styles, right-click desired background, press S

To Choose Another Background Style

In this presentation, the Slide 2 background can have a coordinating background to complement the yoga picture. The following steps add a background to Slide 2.

1. Click the Previous Slide button to display Slide 2. Click the Background Styles button (Design tab | Background group) and then right-click Style 10 (second style in third row) to display the shortcut menu.
2. Click Apply to Selected Slides to apply this background style to Slide 2 (Figure 2–37).

Figure 2–37

Formatting Title and Content Text

Choosing well-coordinated colors and styles for text and objects in a presentation is possible. Once you select a particular Quick Style and make any other font changes, you then can copy these changes to other text using the **Format Painter**. The Format Painter allows you to copy all formatting changes from one object to another.

BTW
Introducing the Presentation
Before your audience enters the room, start the presentation and then display Slide 1. This slide should be visually appealing and provide general interest in the presentation. An effective title slide gives a good first impression.

To Change the Subtitle and Caption Font

The default Verve theme heading, subtitle, and caption text font is Century Gothic. To draw more attention to subtitle and caption text and to help differentiate these slide elements from the title text, you want to change the font from Century Gothic to Papyrus. To change the font, you must select the letters you want to format. In PowerPoint Chapter 1, you selected a paragraph and then formatted the characters. To format the text in multiple paragraphs quickly and simultaneously, you can select all the paragraphs to be formatted and then apply formatting changes. The steps on the next page change the subtitle and caption font.

1

- Click the Previous Slide button to display Slide 1. Move the mouse pointer to the left of the first subtitle paragraph, Unify Your Mind, until the mouse pointer changes to an I-beam (Figure 2–38).

Figure 2–38

2

- Drag downward to select all three subtitle lines that will be formatted (Figure 2–39).

Figure 2–39

3

- With the text selected, click Home on the Ribbon and then click the Font box arrow (Home tab | Font group) to display the Font gallery (Figure 2–40).

Q&A

Will the fonts in my Font gallery be the same as those shown in Figure 2–40?

Your list of available fonts may differ, depending on what fonts you have installed and the type of printer you are using.

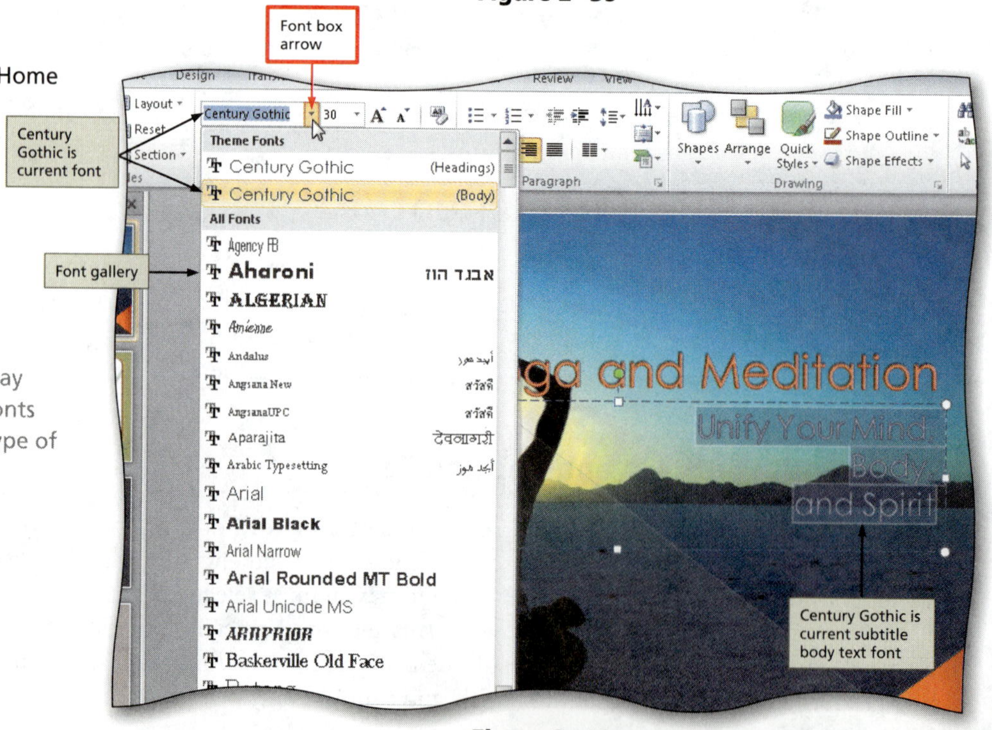

Figure 2–40

4

- Scroll through the Font gallery and then point to Papyrus (or a similar font) to display a live preview of the title text in the Papyrus font (Figure 2–41).

Experiment

- Point to various fonts in the Font gallery and watch the subtitle text font change in the slide.

- Click Papyrus (or a similar font) to change the font of the selected text to Papyrus.

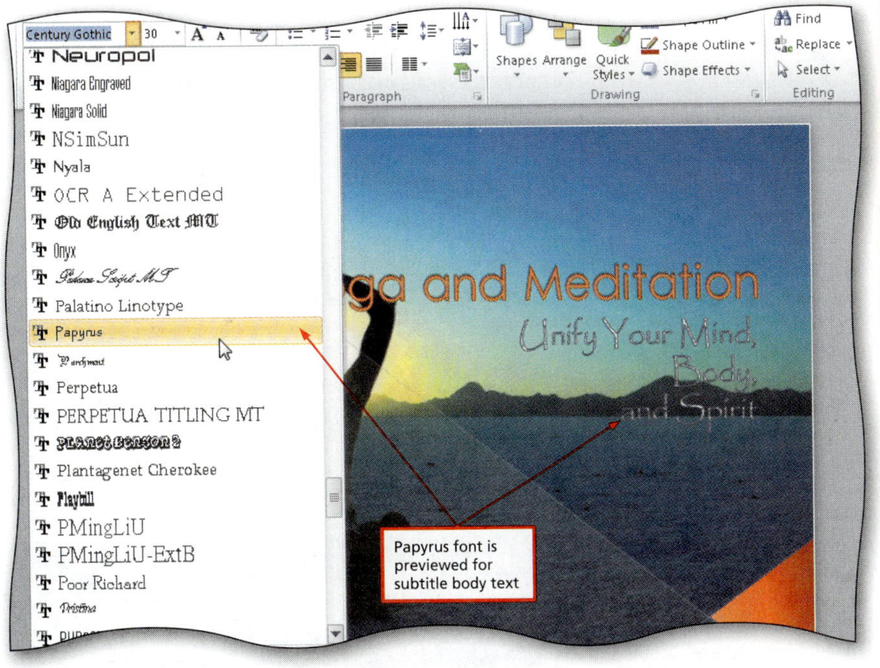

Figure 2–41

Other Ways

1. Click Font box arrow on Mini toolbar, click desired font in Font gallery
2. Right-click selected text, click Font on shortcut menu (Font dialog box), click Font tab, select desired font in Font list, click OK button
3. Click Font dialog box launcher (Home tab | Font group), click Font tab (Font dialog box), select desired font in Font list, click OK button
4. Press CTRL+SHIFT+F, click Font tab (Font dialog box), select desired font in the Font list, click OK button

To Shadow Text

A **shadow** helps letters display prominently by adding a shadow behind the text. The following step adds a shadow to the selected subtitle text, Unify Your Mind, Body, and Spirit.

1

- With the subtitle text selected, click the Text Shadow button (Home tab | Font group) to add a shadow to the selected text (Figure 2–42).

Q&A

How would I remove a shadow?

You would click the Shadow button a second time, or you immediately could click the Undo button on the Quick Access Toolbar.

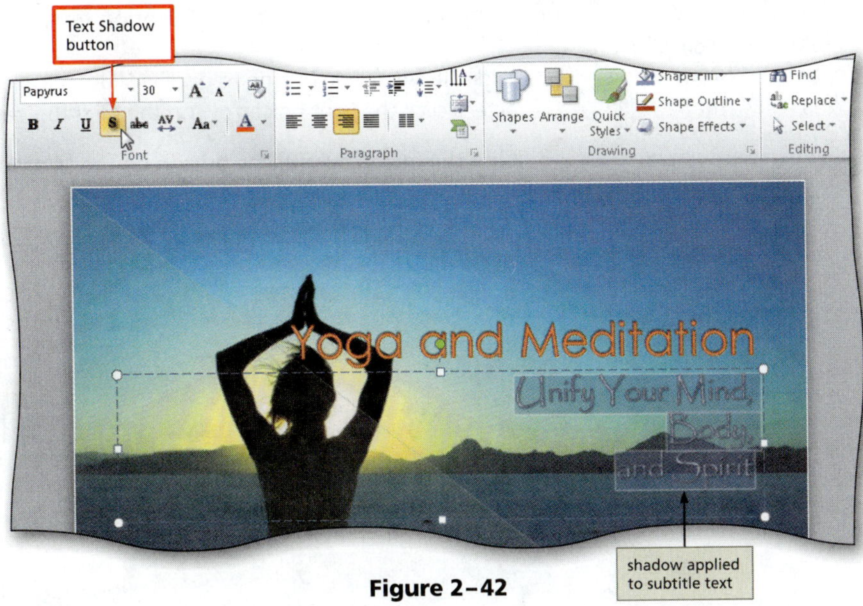

Figure 2–42

To Format the Subtitle Text

To increase readability, you can format the Slide 1 subtitle text by bolding the characters and changing the font color to yellow. The following steps format the Slide 1 subtitle text.

1. With the subtitle text selected, click the Bold button (Home tab | Font group) to bold the text.
2. Click the Font Color arrow and change the color to Light Yellow, Text 2 (fourth color in first row) (Figure 2–43).

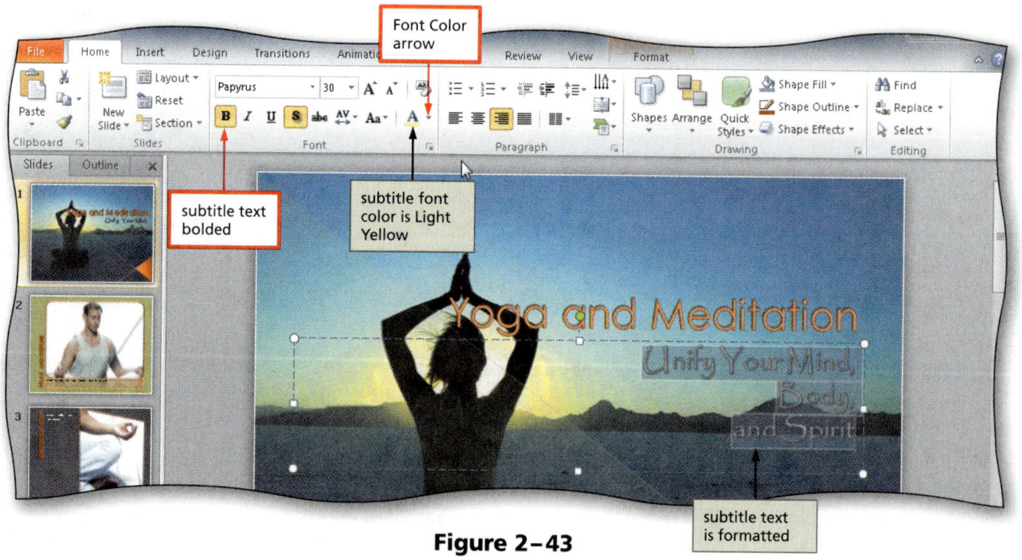

Figure 2–43

BTW

Decreasing Font Size
The Increase Font Size buttons on the Mini toolbar and in the Font group (Home tab) enlarge the selected characters in predetermined amounts. The Decrease Font Size buttons, which appear to the right of the Increase Font Size buttons, reduce the characters' size in the same predetermined point sizes.

To Format the Slide 2 Caption

The caption on a slide should be large enough for audience members to read easily and should coordinate with the font styles in other parts of the presentation. The caption on Slide 2 can be enhanced by changing the font, the font color, and the font size. The following steps format the Slide 2 caption text.

1. Click the Next Slide button to display Slide 2. Triple-click the caption text to select all the characters, click the Font box arrow on the Mini toolbar, and then scroll down and click Papyrus.
2. Click the Increase Font Size button on the Mini toolbar three times to increase the font size to 20 point.
3. Click the Bold button on the Mini toolbar to bold the text (Figure 2–44).

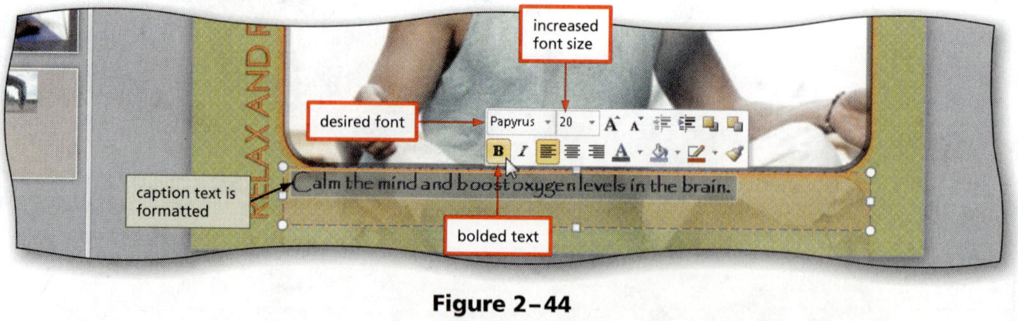

Figure 2–44

Format Painter

To save time and avoid formatting errors, you can use the Format Painter to apply custom formatting to other places in your presentation quickly and easily. You can use this feature in three ways:

- To copy only character attributes, such as font and font effects, select text that has these qualities.
- To copy both paragraph attributes, such as alignment and indentation and character attributes, select the entire paragraph.
- To apply the same formatting to multiple words, phrases, or paragraphs, double-click the Format Painter button and then select each item you want to format. You then can press the ESC key or click the Format Painter button to turn off this feature.

To Format Text Using the Format Painter

To save time and duplicated effort, you quickly can use the Format Painter to copy formatting attributes from the Slide 2 caption text and apply them to Slide 3. The following steps use the Format Painter to copy formatting features.

1

- With the Slide 2 caption text still selected, double-click the Format Painter button (Home tab | Clipboard group).
- Move the mouse pointer off the Ribbon (Figure 2–45).

Q&A Why did my mouse pointer change shape?

The mouse pointer changed shape by adding a paintbrush to indicate that the Format Painter function is active.

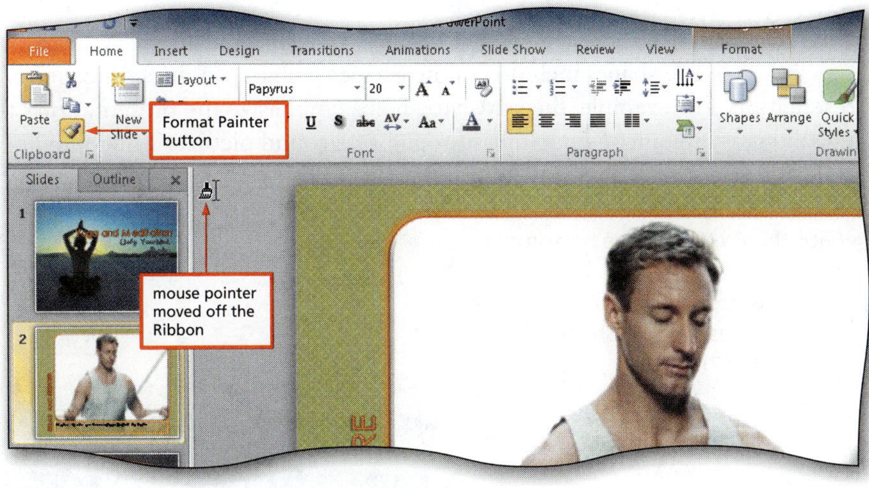

Figure 2–45

2

- Click the Next Slide button to display Slide 3. Triple-click the caption placeholder to apply the format to all the caption text (Figure 2–46).
- Press the ESC key to turn off the Format Painter feature.

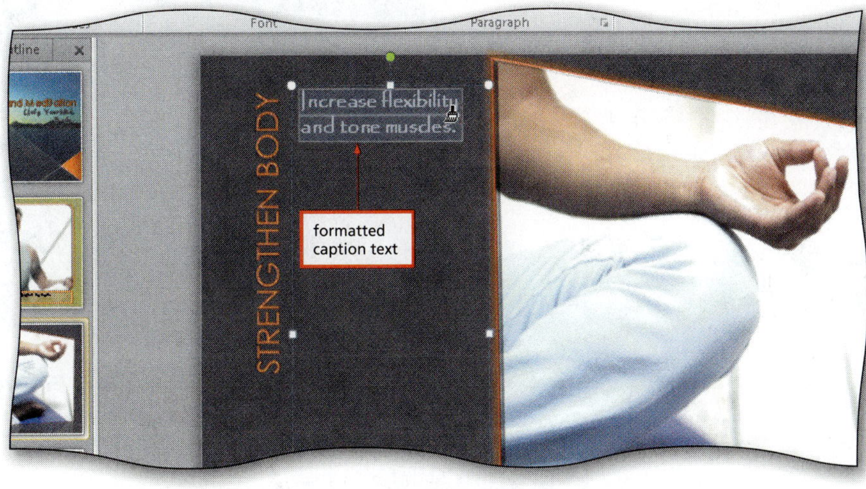

Figure 2–46

Other Ways

1. Click Format Painter button on Mini toolbar

Break Point: If you wish to take a break, this is a good place to do so. Be sure to save the Yoga file again and then you can quit PowerPoint. To resume at a later time, start PowerPoint, open the file called Yoga, and continue following the steps from this location forward.

BTW

Sizing Shapes
PowerPoint's Shapes gallery provides a wide variety of symbols that can help emphasize your major points on each slide. As you select the shapes and then size them, keep in mind that your audience will focus on the largest shapes first. The most important information, therefore, should be placed in or near the shapes with the most visual size.

Adding and Formatting a Shape

One method of getting the audience's attention and reinforcing the major concepts being presented is to have graphical elements on the title slide. PowerPoint provides a wide variety of predefined shapes that can add visual interest to a slide. Shape elements include lines, basic geometrical shapes, arrows, equation shapes, flowchart symbols, stars, banners, and callouts. After adding a shape to a slide, you can change its default characteristics by adding text, bullets, numbers, and styles. You also can combine multiple shapes to create a more complex graphic.

Slides 1 and 4 in this presentation are enhanced in a variety of ways. First, a sun shape is added to the Slide 1 title text in place of the letter o. Then a circle shape is inserted on Slide 4 and copied twice, and text is added to each circle and then formatted. Finally, a triangle is inserted on top of the three circle shapes on Slide 4.

To Add a Shape

Many of the shapes included in the Shapes gallery can direct the viewer to important aspects of the presentation. For example, the sun shape helps emphasize the presentation's theme of practicing yoga and meditation, and it complements the Sunrise Yoga background picture. The following steps add the Sun shape to Slide 1.

1

- Click the Previous Slide button two times to display Slide 1. Click the Shapes button (Home tab | Drawing group) to display the Shapes gallery (Figure 2–47).

Figure 2–47

Q&A

I do not see a Shapes button in the Drawing group. Instead, I have three rows of the shapes I have used recently in presentations. Why?

Monitor dimensions and resolution affect how buttons display on the Ribbon. Click the Shapes More button to display the entire Shapes gallery.

2

- Click the Sun shape in the Basic Shapes area of the Shapes gallery.

Q&A Why did my pointer change shape?
The pointer changed to a plus shape to indicate the Sun shape has been added to the Clipboard.

- Position the mouse pointer (a crosshair) above the person's hands in the picture, as shown in Figure 2–48.

Figure 2–48

3

- Click Slide 1 to insert the Sun shape (Figure 2–49).

Figure 2–49

Other Ways

1. Click More button (Drawing Tools Format tab | Insert Shapes group)

To Resize a Shape

The next step is to resize the Sun shape. The shape should be reduced so that it is approximately the same size as the letter o in the words Yoga and Meditation. The following steps resize the selected Sun shape.

1

- With the mouse pointer appearing as two-headed arrow, drag a corner sizing handle on the picture diagonally inward until the Sun shape is resized approximately as shown in Figure 2–50.

Q&A What if my shape is not selected?
To select a shape, click it.

Q&A What if the shape is the wrong size?
Repeat Steps 1 and 2.

Figure 2–50

2

- Release the mouse button to resize the shape.
- Drag the Sun shape on top of the letter o in the word, Yoga (Figure 2–51).

Q&A What if I want to move the shape to a precise location on the slide?

With the shape selected, press the ARROW keys or the CTRL+ARROW keys to move the shape to the desired location.

Figure 2–51

Other Ways

1. Enter shape height and width in Height and Width text boxes (Drawing Tools Format tab | Size group)
2. Click Size and Position dialog box launcher (Drawing Tools Format tab | Size group), click Size tab, enter desired height and width values in text boxes, click Close button

To Copy and Paste a Shape

The next step is to copy the Sun shape. The duplicate shape will be placed over the letter, o, in the word, Meditation. The following steps copy and move the identical second Sun shape.

1

- With the Sun shape still selected, click the Copy button (Home tab | Clipboard group) (Figure 2–52).

Q&A What if my shape is not selected?

To select a shape, click it.

Figure 2–52

2

- Click the Paste button on the Home tab to insert a duplicate Sun shape on Slide 1.
- Drag the Sun shape on top of the letter o in the word, Meditation, and release the mouse button when a dashed line connects this Sun shape to the Sun shape that is displaying in the word, Yoga (Figure 2–53).

Figure 2–53

Q&A What does the dashed line represent?

PowerPoint displays this Smart Guide when two shapes are aligned precisely. In this case, the two Sun shapes are centered horizontally.

Other Ways

1. Right-click selected shape, click Copy on shortcut menu, right-click, click Paste on shortcut menu
2. Select shape, press CTRL+C, press CTRL+V

To Add Other Shapes

Circles, squares, and triangles are among the geometric shapes included in the Shapes gallery. These shapes can be combined to show relationships among the elements, and they can help illustrate the basic concepts presented in your slide show. The following steps add the Oval and Isosceles Triangle shapes to Slide 4.

1

- Click the Next Slide button three times to display Slide 4 and then click the Shapes button (Home tab | Drawing group) to display the Shapes gallery (Figure 2–54).

Figure 2–54

2

- Click the Oval shape in the Basic Shapes area of the Shapes gallery.
- Position the mouse pointer in the center of Slide 4 and then click to insert the Oval shape.

3

- Press and hold down the SHIFT key and then drag a corner sizing handle until the Oval shape forms a circle and is the size shown in Figure 2–55.

Q&A Why did I need to press the SHIFT key while enlarging the shape?

Holding down the SHIFT key while dragging draws a perfect circle.

- Move the shape so it is positioned approximately as shown in the figure.

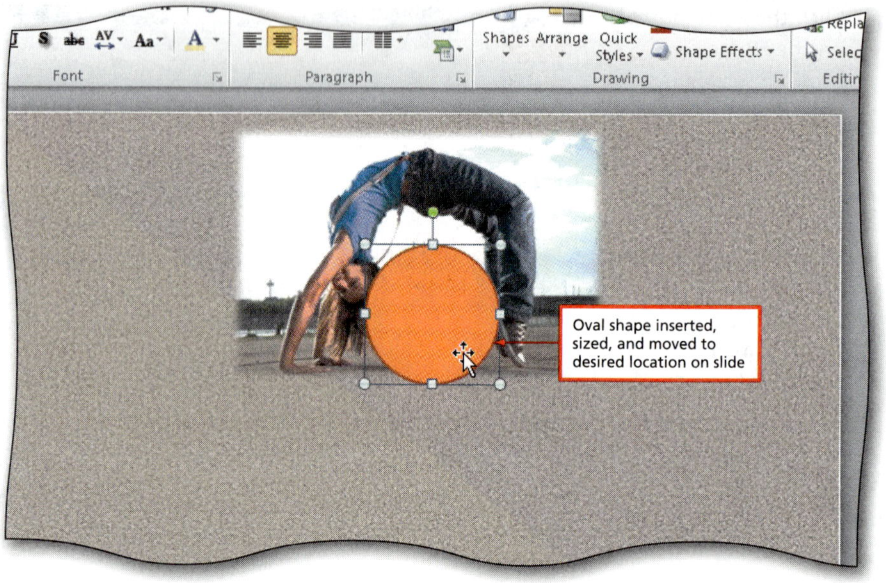

Figure 2–55

4

- Click the Shapes button (Home tab | Drawing group) and then click the Isosceles Triangle shape in the Basic Shapes area of the Shapes gallery.
- Position the mouse pointer in the right side of Slide 4 and then click to insert the Isosceles Triangle shape.

5

- Resize the shape so that it displays approximately as shown in Figure 2–56.

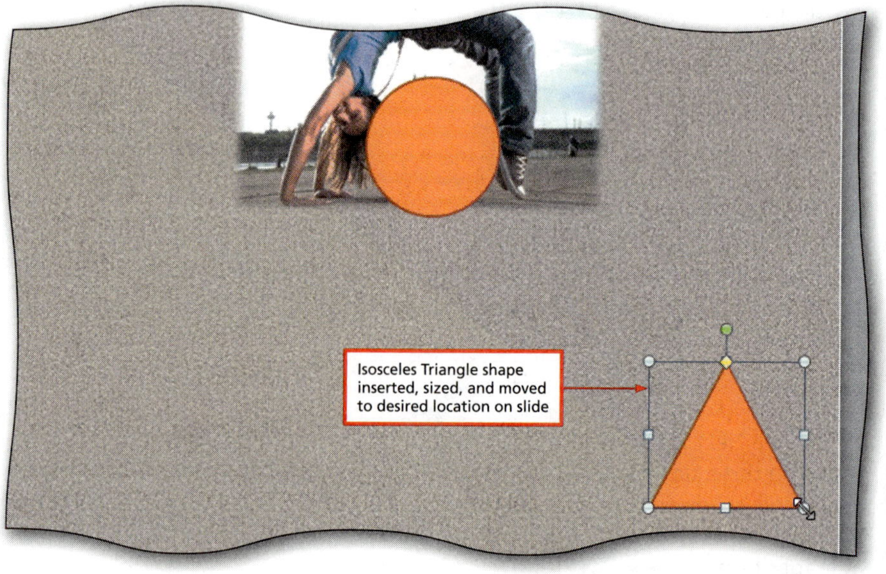

Figure 2–56

To Apply a Shape Style

Formatting text in a shape follows the same techniques as formatting text in a placeholder. You can change font, font color and size, and alignment. The next step is to apply a shape style to the oval so that it appears to have depth. The Shape Styles gallery has a variety of styles that change depending upon the theme applied to the presentation. The following steps apply a style to the Oval shape.

1

- Click the Oval shape to select it and then display the Drawing Tools Format tab (Figure 2–57).

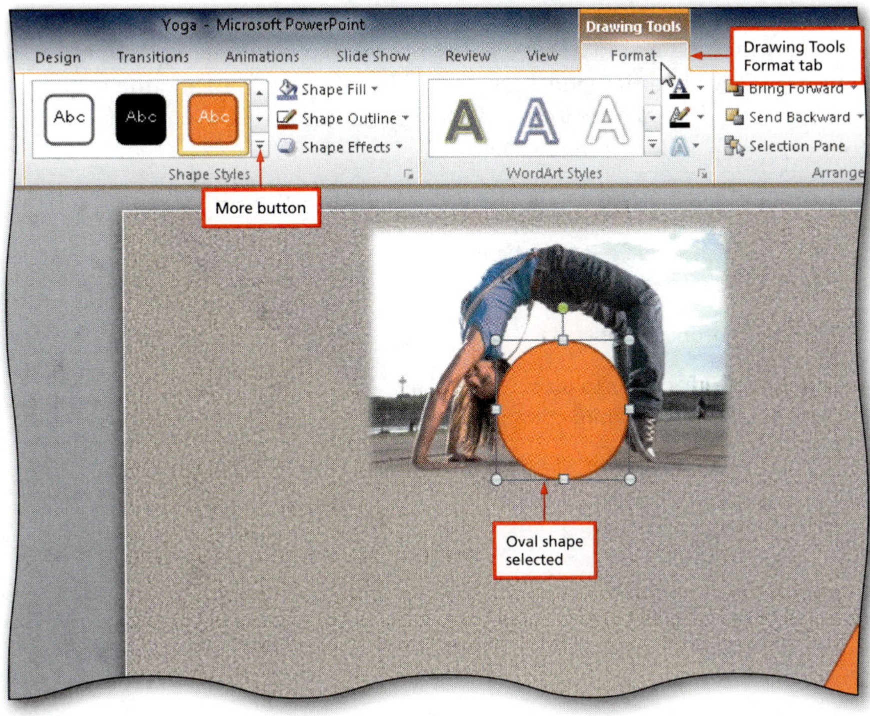

Figure 2–57

2

- Click the More button in the Shape Styles gallery (Drawing Tools Format tab | Shape Styles group) to expand the Shape Styles gallery.
- Point to Intense Effect – Orange, Accent 1 in the Shape Styles gallery (second shape in last row) to display a live preview of that style applied to the shape in the slide (Figure 2–58).

Experiment

- Point to various styles in the Shape Styles gallery and watch the style of the shape change.

3

- Click Intense Effect – Orange, Accent 1 in the Shape Styles gallery to apply the selected style to the Oval shape.

Figure 2–58

Other Ways

1. Click Format Shape dialog box launcher (Drawing Tools Format tab | Shape Styles group), select desired colors (Format Shape dialog box), click Close button
2. Right-click shape, click Format Shape on shortcut menu, select desired colors (Format Shape dialog box), click Close button

To Add Formatted Text to a Shape

Formatting text in a shape follows the same techniques as formatting text in a placeholder. You can change font, font color and size, and alignment. The next step is to add the word, Mind, to the shape, change the font to Papyrus and the font color to Blue-Gray, center and bold the text, and increase the font size to 24 point. The following step adds text to the Oval shape.

1

- With the Oval shape selected, type **`Mind`** in the shape.
- Change the font to Papyrus.
- Change the font color to Blue-Gray, Background 2 (third color in first Theme Colors row).
- Change the font size to 24 point and bold the text (Figure 2–59).

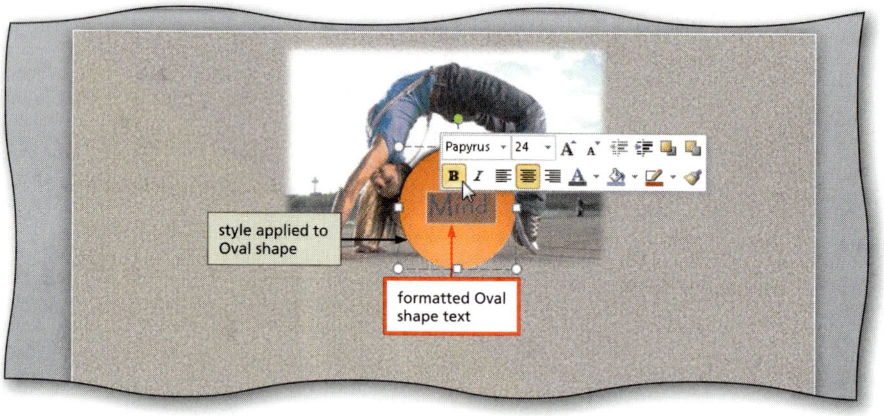

Figure 2–59

BTW **Drawing a Square**
Holding down the SHIFT key while dragging a Rectangle shape draws a square.

To Copy a Shape

Your presentation emphasizes that mind, body, and spirit are equal components in finding balance in life. Each of these elements can be represented by an oval. The following steps copy the Oval shape.

1. Click Home on the Ribbon. Click the edge of the Oval shape so that it is a solid line.
2. Click the Copy button (Home tab | Clipboard group).
3. Click the Paste button (Home tab | Clipboard group) two times to insert two duplicate Oval shapes on Slide 4.
4. Move the Oval shapes so they appear approximately as shown in Figure 2–60.
5. In the left oval, select the word, Mind, and then type the word, **`Body`**, in the oval.
6. In the right oval, select the word, Mind, and then type the word, **`Spirit`**, in the oval (Figure 2–60). You may need to enlarge the size of the oval shapes slightly so that each word is displayed on one line.

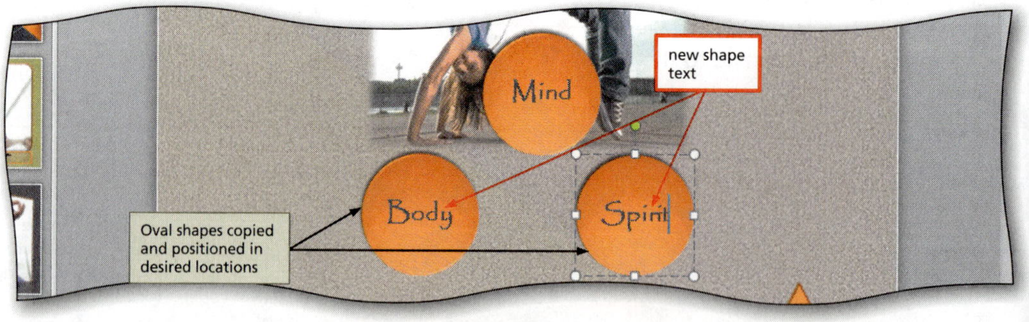

Figure 2–60

To Apply Another Style

The triangle shape helps show the unity among body, mind, and spirit. You can apply a coordinating shape style to the isosceles triangle and then place it on top of the three ovals. The following steps apply a style to the Isosceles Triangle shape.

1. Display the Drawing Tools Format tab. Click the Isosceles Triangle shape on Slide 4 to select it.
2. Click the More button in the Shape Styles gallery (Drawing Tools Format tab | Shape Styles group) to expand the Shape Styles gallery and then click Intense Effect – Blue, Accent 2 (third style in last row) to apply that style to the triangle.
3. Move the triangle shape to the center of the Ovals.
4. Click the Bring Forward button twice (Drawing Tools Format tab | Arrange group) to display the triangle on top of the ovals. Resize the triangle if necessary so that it displays as shown in Figure 2–61.

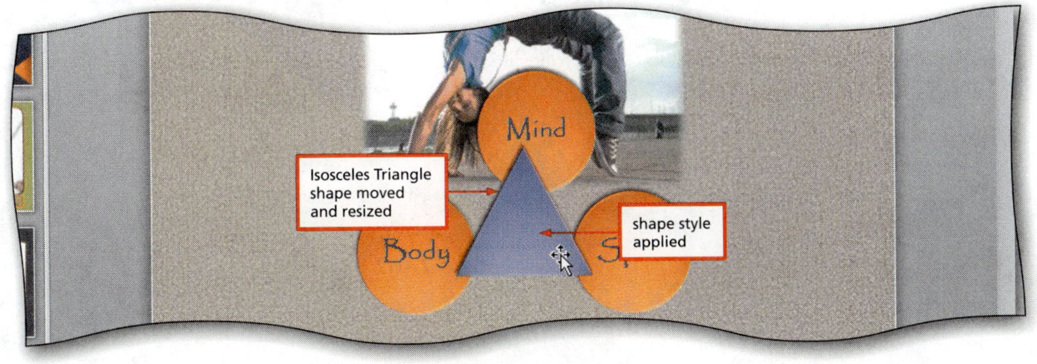

Figure 2–61

Break Point: If you wish to take a break, this is a good place to do so. Be sure to save the Yoga file again and then you can quit PowerPoint. To resume at a later time, start PowerPoint, open the file called Yoga, and continue following the steps from this location forward.

Using WordArt

One method of adding appealing visual elements to a presentation is by using **WordArt** styles. This feature is found in other Microsoft Office applications, including Word and Excel. This gallery of decorative effects allows you to type new text or convert existing text to WordArt. You then can add elements such as fills, outlines, and effects.

As with slide backgrounds, WordArt fill in the interior of a letter can consist of a solid color, texture, picture, or gradient. The WordArt **outline** is the exterior border surrounding each letter or symbol. PowerPoint allows you to change the outline color, weight, and style. You also can add an **effect**, which helps add emphasis or depth to the characters. Some effects are shadows, reflections, glows, bevels, and 3-D rotations.

BTW

Creating Logos
Many companies without graphic arts departments create their logos using WordArt. The bevels, glows, and shadows allow corporate designers to develop unique images with 3-D effects that give depth to their companies' emblems.

Plan Ahead

Use WordArt in moderation.
Some WordArt styles are bold and detailed, and they can detract from the message you are trying to present if not used carefully. Select a WordArt style when needed for special emphasis, such as a title slide that audience members will see when they enter the room. WordArt can have a powerful effect, so do not overuse it.

To Insert WordArt

Yoga and meditation can help individuals find balance among the mind, body, and spirit. The symbols on Slide 4 emphasize this relationship, and you want to call attention to the concept. You quickly can add a visual element to the slide by selecting a WordArt style from the WordArt Styles gallery and then applying it to a word. The following steps insert WordArt.

1

- With Slide 4 displaying, click Insert on the Ribbon.
- Click the WordArt button (Insert tab | Text group) to display the WordArt gallery (Figure 2–62).

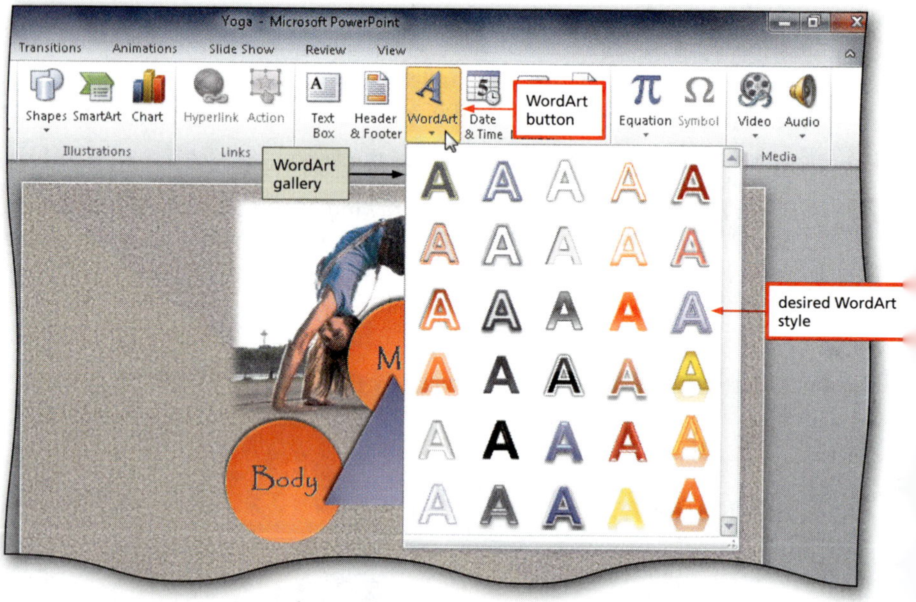

Figure 2–62

2

- Click Fill – Blue, Accent 2, Double Outline – Accent 2 (last letter A in third row) to display the WordArt text box (Figure 2–63).

Q&A What is a matte bevel style that is part of some of the styles in the gallery?

A matte finish gives a dull and rough effect. A bevel edge is angled or sloped and gives the effect of a three-dimensional object.

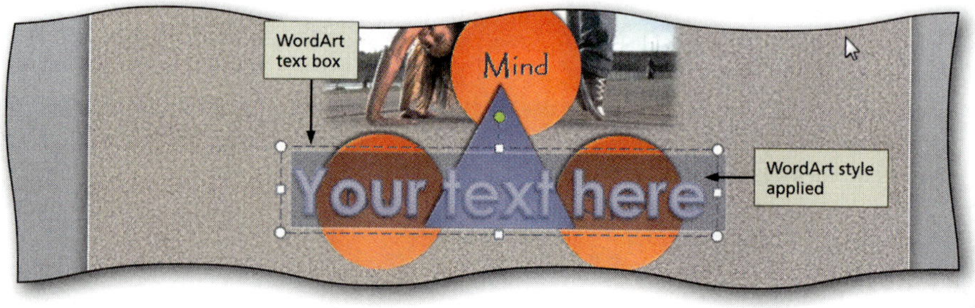

Figure 2–63

3

- Type **Balance** in the text box, as the WordArt text (Figure 2–64).

Q&A Why did the Format tab appear automatically in the Ribbon?

It appears when you select text to which you could add a WordArt style or other effect.

Figure 2–64

To Change the WordArt Shape

The WordArt text is useful to emphasize the harmony among the mind, body, and spirit. You can further emphasize this word by changing its shape. PowerPoint provides a variety of graphical shapes that add interest to text. The following steps change the WordArt to Triangle Down shape.

1

- With the Slide 4 text still selected, click the Text Effects button (Drawing Tools Format tab | WordArt Styles group) to display the Text Effects menu (Figure 2–65).

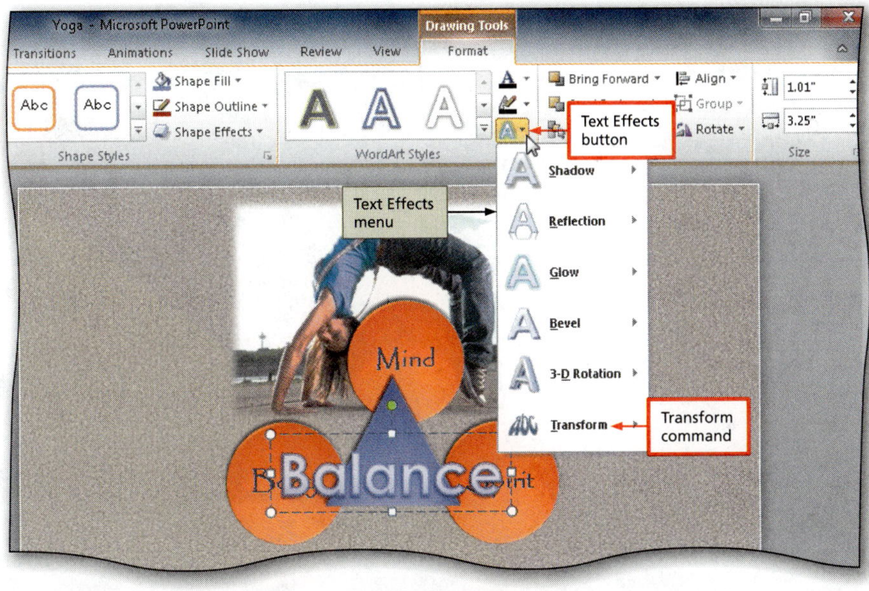

Figure 2–65

2

- Point to Transform in the Text Effects menu to display the WordArt Transform gallery (Figure 2–66).

Experiment

- Point to various styles in the Transform gallery and watch the format of the text and borders change.

Q&A

How can I see the preview of a Transform effect if the gallery is overlaying the WordArt letters?

Move the WordArt text box to the left or right side of the slide and then repeat Steps 1 and 2.

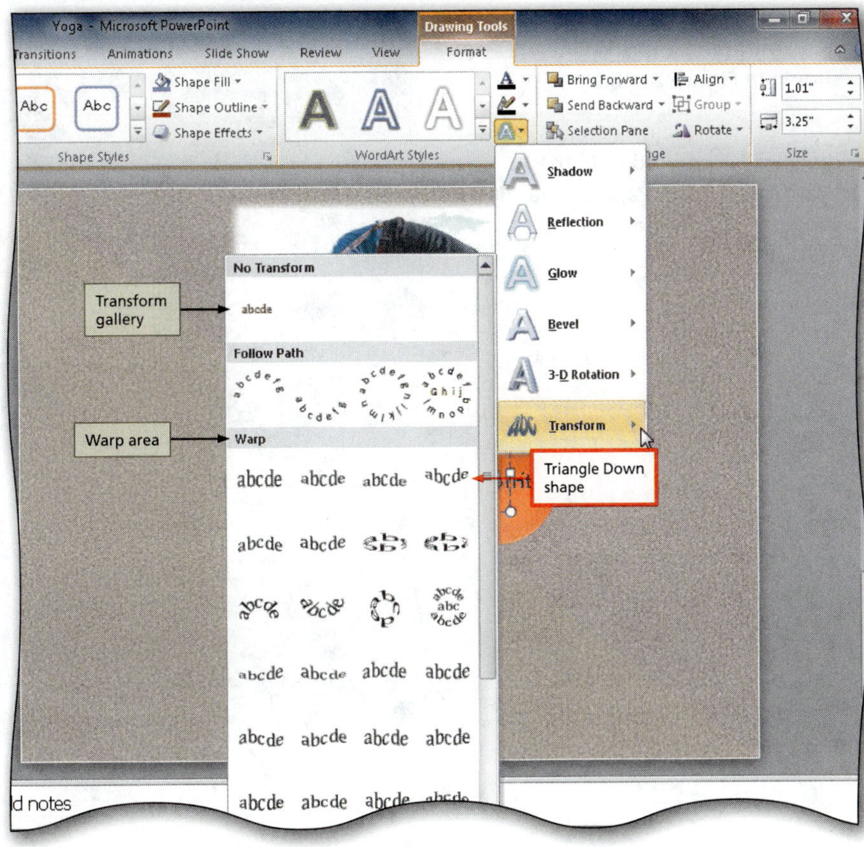

Figure 2–66

3

- Click the Triangle Down shape in the Warp area to apply the Triangle Down shape to the WordArt text (Figure 2–67).

Q&A Can I change the shape I applied to the WordArt?

Yes. Position the insertion point in the text box and then repeat Steps 1 and 2.

Figure 2–67

4

- Drag the WordArt downward until it is positioned approximately as shown in Figure 2–68.
- Drag a corner sizing handle diagonally outward until the WordArt is resized approximately as shown in the figure.

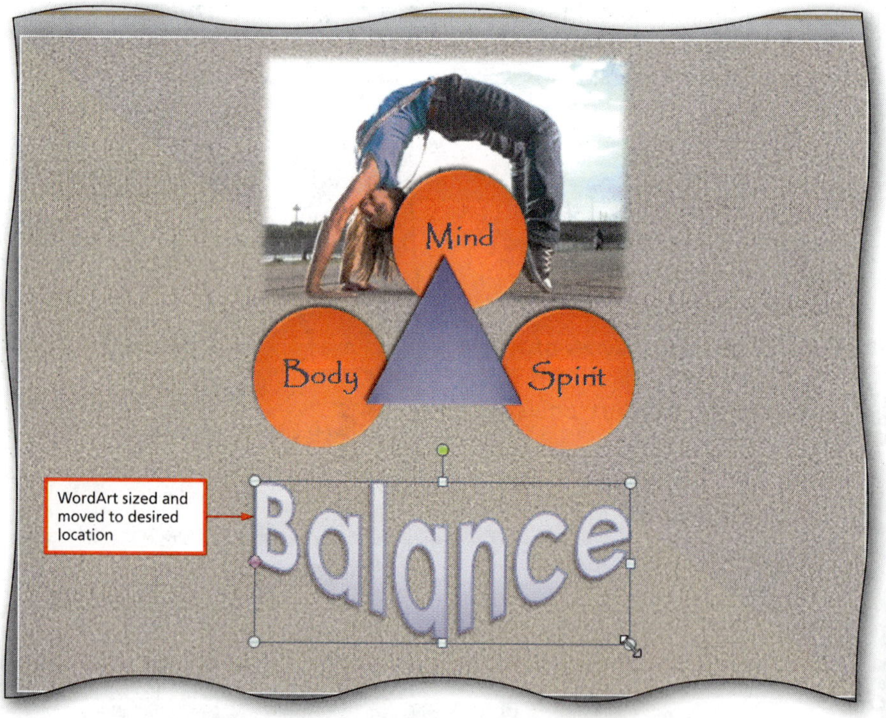

Figure 2–68

To Apply a WordArt Text Fill

The Slide 4 background has a Sand texture for the background, and you want to coordinate the WordArt fill with a similar texture. The following steps add the Denim texture as a fill for the WordArt characters.

1

- With the WordArt text selected, click the Text Fill button arrow (Drawing Tools Format tab | WordArt Styles group) to display the Text Fill gallery.

Q&A The Text Fill gallery did not display. Why not?

Be sure you click the Text Fill button arrow, which is to the right of the Text Fill button. If you mistakenly click the Text Fill button, PowerPoint places the default fill in the WordArt instead of displaying the Text Fill gallery.

- Point to Texture in the Text Fill gallery to display the Texture gallery (Figure 2–69).

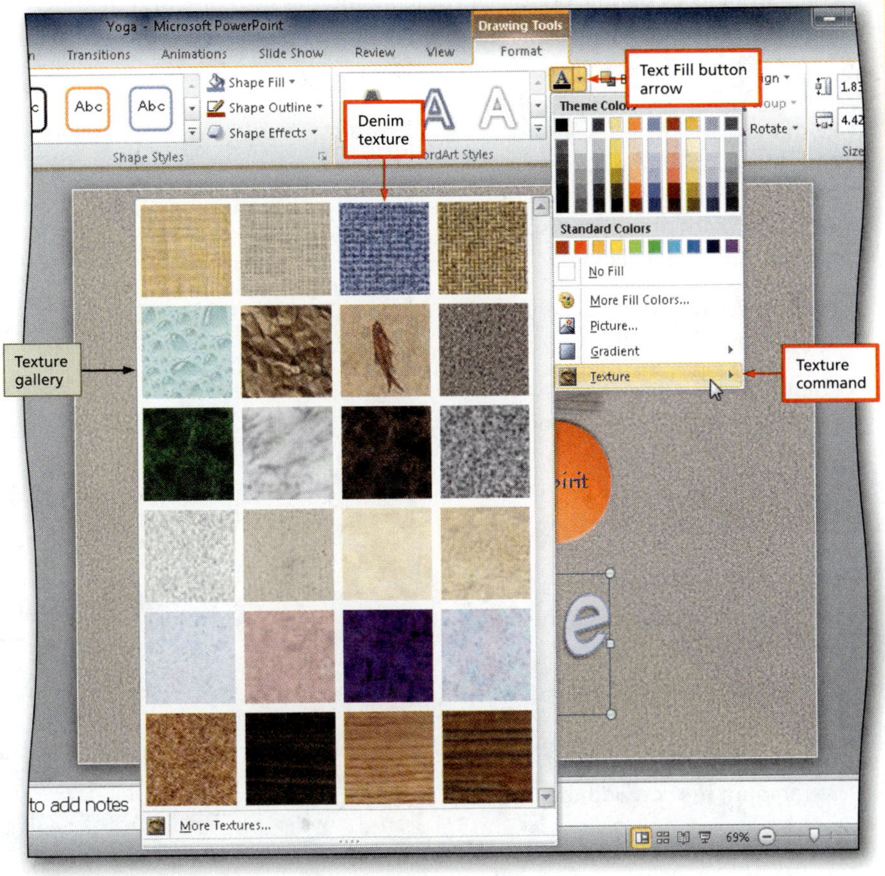

Figure 2–69

Experiment

- Point to various styles in the Text Fill gallery and watch the fill change.

Q&A How can I see the preview of a fill if the gallery is overlaying the WordArt letters?

Move the WordArt text box to the left or right side of the slide and then repeat Step 1.

2

- Click the Denim texture (third texture in first row) to apply this texture as the fill for the WordArt.

Q&A Can I apply this texture simultaneously to text that appears in more than one place on my slide?

Yes. Select one area of text, press and then hold the CTRL key while you select the other text, and then apply the texture.

To Change the Weight of the WordArt Outline

The letters in the WordArt style applied have a double outline around the edges. To emphasize this characteristic, you can increase the width of the lines. As with font size, lines also are measured in point size, and PowerPoint gives you the option to change the line **weight**, or thickness, starting with ¼ point (pt) and increasing in one-fourth–point increments. Other outline options include modifying the color and the line style, such as changing to dots or dashes or a combination of dots and dashes. The following steps change the WordArt outline weight to 6 pt.

1

- With the WordArt still selected, click the Text Outline button arrow (Drawing Tools Format tab | WordArt Styles group) to display the Text Outline gallery.
- Point to Weight in the gallery to display the Weight list.
- Point to 6 pt to display a live preview of this line weight on the WordArt text outline (Figure 2–70).

Experiment

- Point to various line weights in the Weight list and watch the line thickness change.

Q&A Can I make the line width more than 6 pt?

Yes. Click More Lines and increase the amount in the Width box.

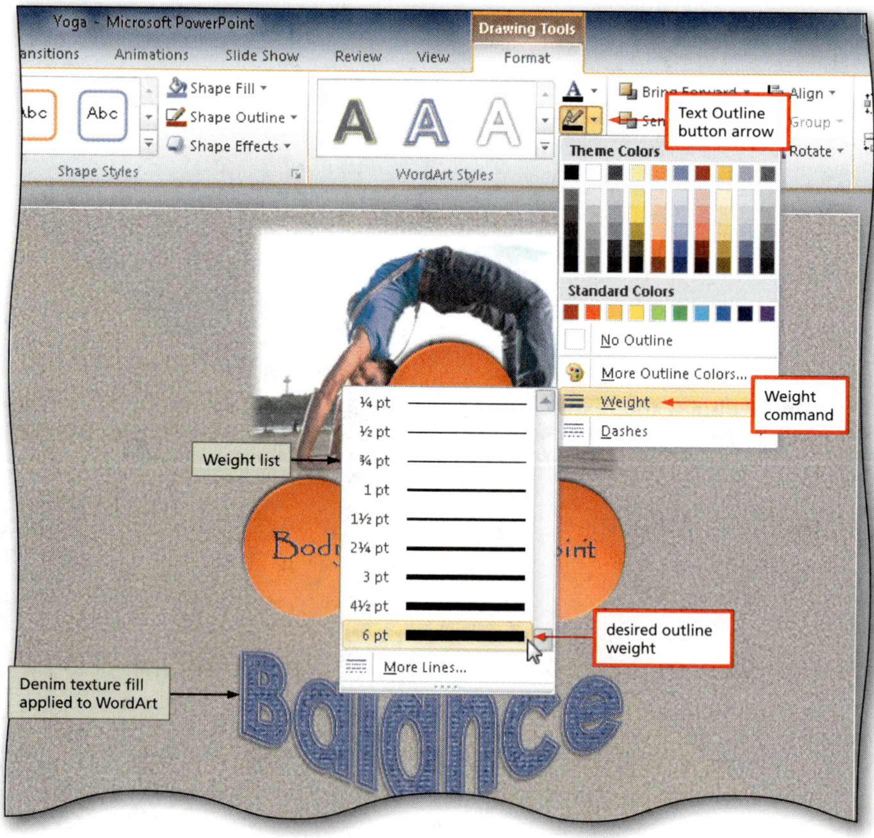

Figure 2–70

2

- Click 6 pt to apply this line weight to the title text outline.

Q&A Must my text have an outline?

No. To delete the outline, click No Outline in the Text Outline gallery.

To Change the Color of the WordArt Outline

The WordArt outline color is similar to the Denim fill color. To add variety, you can change the outline color. The following steps change the WordArt outline color.

1

- With the WordArt still selected, click the Text Outline button arrow (Drawing Tools Format tab | WordArt Styles group) to display the Text Outline gallery.
- Point to Orange, Accent 1 (fifth color in first row) to display a live preview of this outline color (Figure 2–71).

Experiment

- Point to various colors in the gallery and watch the outline colors change.

2

- Click Orange, Accent 1 to apply this color to the WordArt outline.

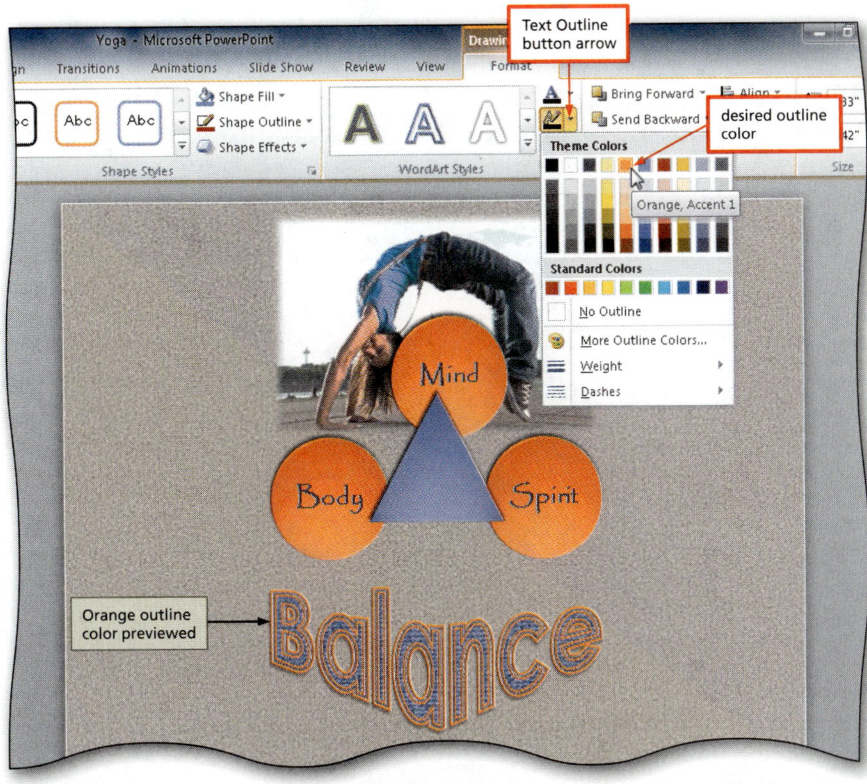

Figure 2–71

To Add a Transition between Slides

A final enhancement you will make in this presentation is to apply the Rotate transition in the Dynamic Content category to all slides and change the transition speed to Slow. The following steps apply this transition to the presentation.

1. Click Transitions on the Ribbon. Click the More button (Transitions tab | Transition to This Slide group) to expand the Transitions gallery.
2. Click the Rotate transition in the Dynamic Content category to apply this transition to Slide 4.
3. Click the Duration up arrow in the Timing group four times to change the transition speed from 02.00 to 03.00.
4. Click the Preview Transitions button (Transitions tab | Preview area) to view the new transition time.
5. Click the Apply To All button (Transitions tab | Timing group) to apply this transition and speed to all four slides in the presentation (Figure 2–72 on the next page).

BTW

Selecting Effect Options

Many PowerPoint transitions have options that you can customize to give your presentation a unique look. When you click the Effect Options button (Transitions tab | Transition to This Slide group), you can, for example, select the option to have a slide appear on the screen from the left or the right, or the screen can fade to black before the next slide is displayed.

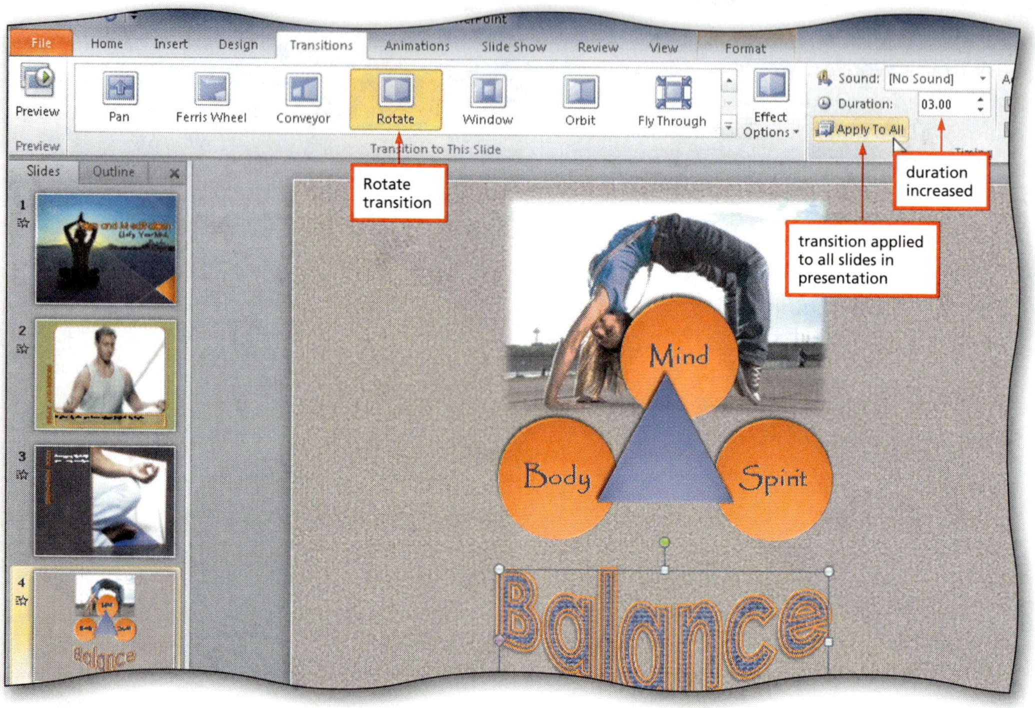

Figure 2–72

To Change Document Properties

Before saving the presentation again, you want to add your name, class name, and some keywords as document properties. The following steps use the Document Information Panel to change document properties.

1. Click File on the Ribbon to open the Backstage view. If necessary, click the Info tab.
2. Click the Properties button in the right pane of the Info gallery.
3. Click Show Document Panel on the Properties menu to close the Backstage view and display the Document Information Panel.
4. Click the Author box, if necessary, and then type your name as the Author property.
5. Click the Subject text box and then type your course and section as the Subject property.
6. Click the Keywords text box and then type `yoga, meditation` as the Keywords property.
7. Click the Close the Document Information Panel button so that the Document Information Panel no longer is displayed.

To Print a Presentation

With the completed presentation saved, you may want to print it. If copies of the presentation are being distributed to audience members, you will print a hard copy of each individual slide on a printer. The following steps print a hard copy of the contents of the saved Yoga presentation.

1. Click File on the Ribbon to open the Backstage view. Click the Print tab in the Backstage view to display the Print gallery.
2. Verify the printer name in the Printer box will print a hard copy of the document. If necessary, click the Printer box arrow to display a list of available Printer options and then click the desired printer to change the currently selected printer.
3. Click the Print button in the Print gallery to print the document on the currently selected printer. When the printer stops, retrieve the hard copy (Figure 2–73).

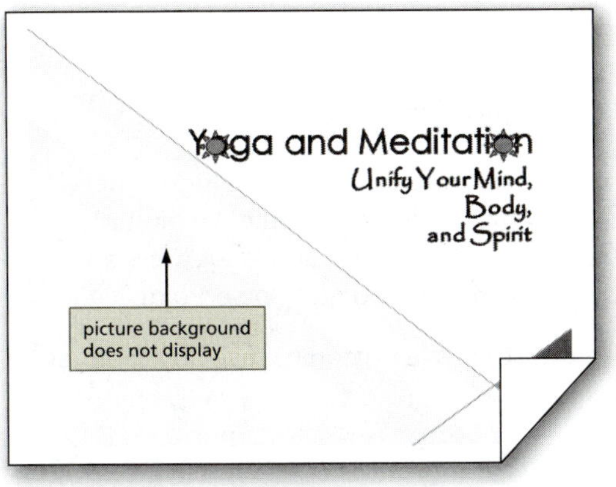

(a) Slide 1

(b) Slide 2

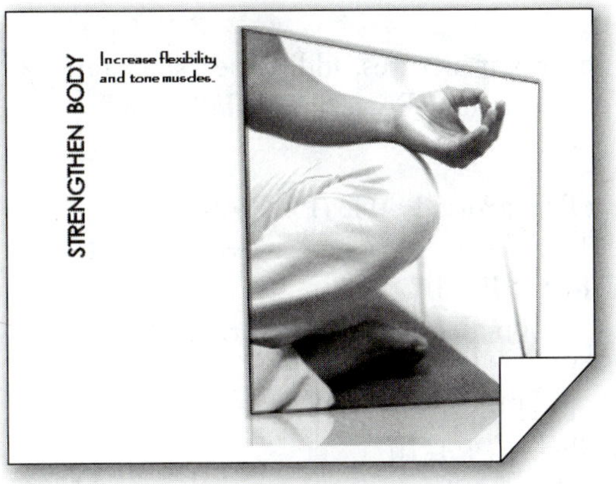

(c) Slide 3

(d) Slide 4

Figure 2–73 (Handouts printed using a black-and-white printer)

BTW

Quick Reference
For a table that lists how to complete the tasks covered in the Office chapters in this book using the mouse, Ribbon, shortcut menu, and keyboard, see the Quick Reference Summary at the back of this book, or visit the Microsoft Office and Concepts CourseMate Web site at www.cengagebrain.com and then navigate to the Quick Reference resource for this book.

To Save an Existing Presentation with the Same File Name

You have made several changes to the presentation since you last saved it. Thus, you should save it again. The following step saves the document again.

1. Click the Save button on the Quick Access Toolbar to overwrite the previously saved file.

To Run an Animated Slide Show

All changes are complete, and the presentation is saved. You now can view the Yoga presentation. The following steps start Slide Show view.

1. Click the Slide 1 thumbnail in the Slides tab to select and display Slide 1.
2. Click the Slide Show button to display the title slide and then click each slide to view the transition effect and slides.

To Quit PowerPoint

This project is complete. The following steps quit PowerPoint.

1. If you have one PowerPoint document open, click the Close Button on the right side of the title bar to close the document and then quit PowerPoint; or if you have multiple PowerPoint documents open, click File on the Ribbon to open the Backstage view and then click Exit in the Backstage view to close all open documents and quit PowerPoint.
2. If a Microsoft PowerPoint dialog box appears, click the Save button to save any changes made to the presentation since the last save.

Chapter Summary

In this chapter you have learned how to add a background style, insert and format pictures, add shapes, size graphic elements, apply styles, and insert WordArt. The items listed below include all the new PowerPoint skills you have learned in this chapter.

1. Change the Presentation Theme Colors (PPT 81)
2. Insert a Picture (PPT 83)
3. Insert a Picture into a Slide without a Content Placeholder (PPT 85)
4. Correct a Picture (PPT 86)
5. Apply a Picture Style (PPT 87)
6. Apply Picture Effects (PPT 89)
7. Add a Picture Border (PPT 91)
8. Change a Picture Border Color (PPT 92)
9. Resize a Graphic by Entering Exact Measurements (PPT 93)
10. Insert a Texture Fill (PPT 95)
11. Insert a Picture to Create a Background (PPT 97)
12. Format the Background Picture Fill Transparency (PPT 98)
13. Format the Background Texture Fill Transparency (PPT 99)
14. Choose a Background Style (PPT 99)
15. Change the Subtitle and Caption Font (PPT 101)
16. Shadow Text (PPT 103)
17. Format Caption Text Using the Format Painter (PPT 105)
18. Add a Shape (PPT 106)
19. Resize a Shape (PPT 107)
20. Copy and Paste a Shape (PPT 108)
21. Add Other Shapes (PPT 109)
22. Apply a Shape Style (PPT 110)
23. Add Formatted Text to a Shape (PPT 112)
24. Insert WordArt (PPT 114)
25. Change the WordArt Shape (PPT 115)
26. Apply a WordArt Text Fill (PPT 117)
27. Change the Weight of the WordArt Outline (PPT 118)
28. Change the Color of the WordArt Outline (PPT 118)

SAM If you have a SAM 2010 user profile, your instructor may have assigned an autogradable version of this assignment. If so, log into the SAM 2010 Web site at www.cengage.com/sam2010 to download the instruction and start files.

Learn It Online

Test your knowledge of chapter content and key terms.

Instructions: To complete the Learn It Online exercises, start your browser, visit the Microsoft Office and Concepts CourseMate Web site at www.cengagebrain.com, navigate to the PowerPoint Chapter 2 resources for this book, click the link for the exercise you want to complete, and then read the instructions.

Chapter Reinforcement TF, MC, and SA

A series of true/false, multiple choice, and short answer questions that test your knowledge of the chapter content.

Flash Cards

An interactive learning environment where you identify chapter key terms associated with displayed definitions.

Practice Test

A series of multiple choice questions that test your knowledge of chapter content and key terms.

Who Wants To Be a Computer Genius?

An interactive game that challenges your knowledge of chapter content in the style of a television quiz show.

Wheel of Terms

An interactive game that challenges your knowledge of chapter key terms in the style of the television show *Wheel of Fortune*.

Crossword Puzzle Challenge

A crossword puzzle that challenges your knowledge of key terms presented in the chapter.

Apply Your Knowledge

Reinforce the skills and apply the concepts you learned in this chapter.

Changing the Background and Adding Photographs, WordArt, and a Shape Quick Style

Note: To complete this assignment, you will be required to use the Data Files for Students. See the inside back cover of this book for instructions on downloading the Data Files for Students, or contact your instructor for information about accessing the required files.

Instructions: Start PowerPoint. Open the presentation, Apply 2-1 Lab Procedures, from the Data Files for Students.

The four slides in the presentation present laboratory safety procedures for your chemistry class. The document you open is an unformatted presentation. You are to add pictures, which are available on the Data Files for Students. You also will change the background style, change slide layouts, apply a transition, and use the Format Painter so the slides look like Figure 2–74 on the next page.

Perform the following tasks:

1. Change the background style to Style 5 (row 2, column 1).
2. On the title slide (Figure 2–74a), create a background by inserting the picture called Lab Assistant. Change the transparency to 30%.
3. Apply the WordArt style, Fill – Red, Accent 2, Matte Bevel (row 6, column 3) to the title text and increase the font size to 54 point. Also, apply the WordArt Transform text effect, Chevron Up (row 2, column 1 in the Warp area) to this text.
4. In the Slide 1 subtitle area, replace the words, Student Name, with your name. Bold and italicize your name and the words, Presented by, and then apply the WordArt style, Fill – Red, Accent 2, Warm Matte Bevel (row 5, column 3). Position this subtitle text and the title text as shown in Figure 2–74a.

Continued >

Apply Your Knowledge *continued*

5. On Slide 2, change the layout to Two Content and insert the pictures shown in Figure 2–74b called Female in Lab Coat and Female with Goggles. In the left placeholder, apply the Rotated, White picture style to the inserted picture. In the right placeholder, apply the Reflected Bevel, Black picture style to the inserted picture and then change the picture border color to Purple.
6. On Slide 3, change the layout to Two Content and insert the Fire Extinguisher picture shown in Figure 2–74c. Apply the Soft Edge Oval picture style and change the picture brightness to +20% (row 3, column 4 in the Brightness and Contrast area).
7. On Slide 4, change the layout to Picture with Caption and then insert the picture, Hand Washing shown in Figure 2–74d. Increase the subtitle text font size to 18 point. Change the title text font size to 28 point, add a shadow, change font to Algerian, and change the font color to Purple.
8. Use the Format Painter to format the title text on Slides 2 and 3 with the same features as the title text on Slide 4.
9. Apply the Wipe transition in the Subtle category to all slides. Change the duration to 2.00 seconds.

(a) Slide 1

(b) Slide 2

Figure 2 – 74

10. Change the document properties, as specified by your instructor. Save the presentation using the file name, Apply 2-1 Chemistry Lab Safety. Submit the revised document in the format specified by your instructor.

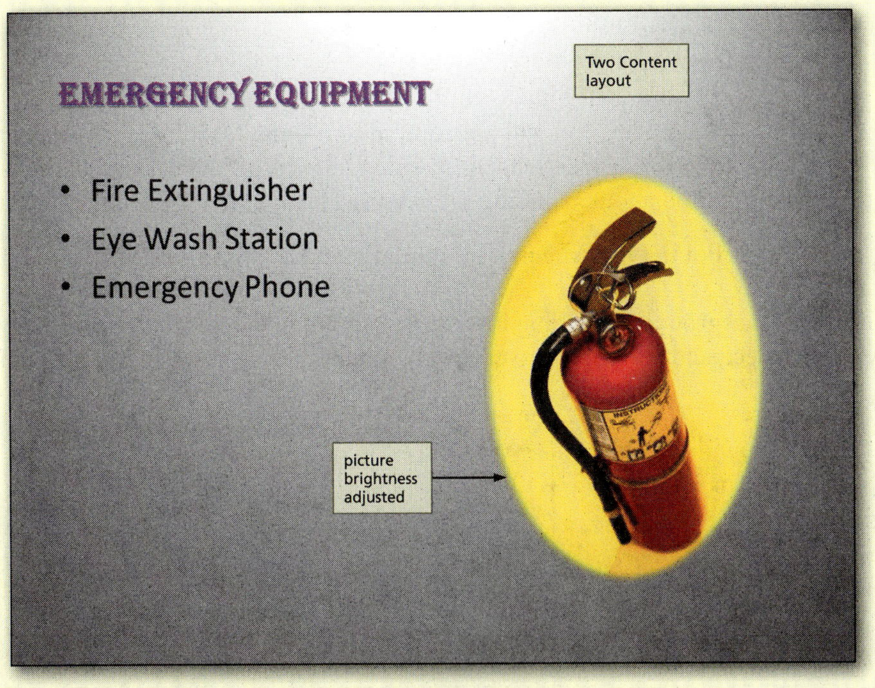

(c) Slide 3

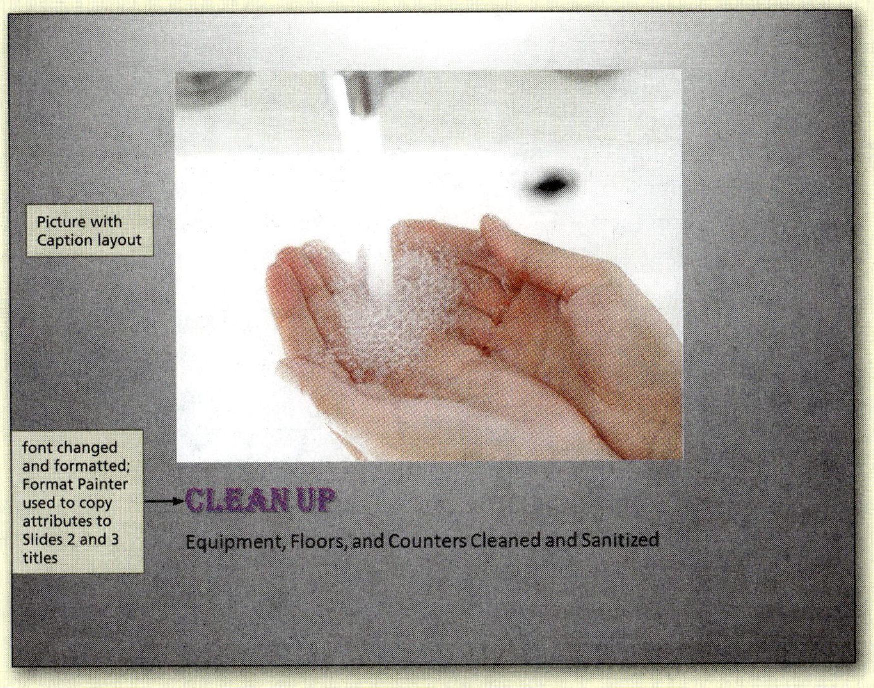

(d) Slide 4

Figure 2 – 74 (Continued)

STUDENT ASSIGNMENTS

Extend Your Knowledge

Extend the skills you learned in this chapter and experiment with new skills. You may need to use Help to complete the assignment.

Changing Slide Backgrounds and Picture Contrast, and Inserting Shapes and WordArt

Note: To complete this assignment, you will be required to use the Data Files for Students. See the inside back cover of this book for instructions on downloading the Data Files for Students, or contact your instructor for information about accessing the required files.

Instructions: Start PowerPoint. Open the presentation, Extend 2-1 Smith Family Reunion, from the Data Files for Students.

You will create backgrounds including inserting a picture to create a background, apply a WordArt Style and Effect, and add shapes to create the presentation shown in Figure 2–75.

Perform the following tasks:

1. Change the background style to Denim (row 1, column 3) and change the transparency to 48%. On Slides 2 through 5, change the title text to bold.
2. On the title slide (Figure 2–75a), create a background by inserting the picture called Tree, which is available on the Data Files for Students. Change the transparency to 40%.
3. Apply the WordArt style, Gradient Fill – Blue, Accent 1, to the title text and increase the font size to 66 point. Also, apply the WordArt Transform text effect, Arch Up (row 1, column 1 in the Follow Path area), to this text.
4. In the Slide 1 subtitle area, insert the Wave shape in the Stars and Banners area. Also, apply the Shape Style, Subtle Effect – Orange, Accent 6 to the Wave shape. Type **`Highlights From Our Last Reunion`** and increase the font size to 40 point, change the text to bold italic and change the color to Green. Position the shape as shown in Figure 2–75a.

(a) Slide 1

(b) Slide 2

Figure 2 – 75

5. On Slide 2, change the layout to Two Content and insert the pictures shown in Figure 2–75b. The pictures to be inserted are called Bocce Ball and Frisbee Catcher and are available on the Data Files for Students. In the left placeholder, apply the Rotated White picture style to the inserted picture and change the picture border to Light Green. In the right placeholder, apply the Beveled Oval Black picture style to the inserted picture.
6. Insert the Plaque shape in the Basic Shapes area. Also, apply the Shape Style, Subtle Effect, Olive Green, Accent 3 and apply the Shape Effect, 3-D Rotation, Parallel, Off Axis 1 Right. Type `Cousin Tom & His Frisbee Moves` and increase the font size to 28 point. Move the shape as shown in Figure 2–75b.

(c) Slide 3

7. On Slide 3, change the layout to Picture with Caption and insert the picture shown in Figure 2–75c. The picture to be inserted is called BBQ Grill. Increase the title font size to 44 point. Also, increase the subtitle font size to 32 point, and then bold and italicize this text.
8. On Slide 4, change the layout to Two Content and insert the pictures shown in Figure 2–75d. The pictures to be inserted are called Reunion Boys and Reunion Toddler. In the left placeholder, apply the Rotated, White picture effect to the picture. In the right placeholder, apply the Bevel Perspective picture effect. Move the pictures as shown in Figure 2–75d.

(d) Slide 4

Figure 2 – 75 (Continued)

Continued >

Extend Your Knowledge *continued*

9. On Slide 5, change the layout to Title and Content and insert the picture shown in Figure 2–75e. The picture to be inserted is called Reunion. Enlarge the picture as shown.
10. Insert the Oval Callout and Cloud Callout shapes in the Callouts area. In the Oval Callout shape, type **I hope Grandma makes cookies!** and change the font size to 24 point bold italic. Also add a Shape Style, Moderate Effect – Olive Green Accent 3 to this shape. In the Cloud Callout shape, type **I'm looking forward to our next reunion!** and change the font size to 24 point and the style to bold italic. Move the shapes as shown in Figure 2–75e. Use the adjustment handles (the yellow diamond below each shape) to move the callout arrows as shown in Figure 2–75e. You may need to use Help to learn how to move these arrows.
11. On Slide 6, change the layout to Picture with Caption and insert the picture shown in Figure 2–75f and change the picture contrast to +20. The picture to be inserted is called Reunion Tree.
12. Insert the Up Ribbon shape in the Stars and Banners area and type the words **Announcing Our Next Reunion**. Change the font color to Green, the font size to 32 point, and the style to bold italic. Also, apply the Shape Style, Subtle Effect – Orange Accent 6. In the title placeholder, type **Save the date – June 20, 2012** and change the font size to 28 point. Bold this text.
13. Add the Orbit transition under the Dynamic Content section to Slide 6 only. You may need to use Help to learn how to apply the transition to only one slide. Change the duration to 2.00 seconds.
14. Change the document properties, as specified by your instructor. Save the presentation using the file name, Extend 2-1 Smith Reunion.
15. Submit the revised document in the format specified by your instructor.

(e) Slide 5

(f) Slide 6

Figure 2–75 (Continued)

Make It Right

Analyze a presentation and correct all errors and/or improve the design.

Changing a Theme and Background Style

Note: To complete this assignment, you will be required to use the Data Files for Students. See the inside back cover of this book for instructions on downloading the Data Files for Students, or contact your instructor for information about accessing the required files.

Instructions: Start PowerPoint. Open the presentation, Make It Right 2-1 New Aerobics Classes, from the Data Files for Students.

Correct the formatting problems and errors in the presentation while keeping in mind the guidelines presented in this chapter.

Perform the following tasks:

1. Change the document theme from Flow, shown in Figure 2–76, to Waveform. Apply the Background Style 10 (row 3, column 2) to Slide 5 only.
2. On the title slide, change the title from New Aerobics Classes to New Pool Programs. Type your name in place of Northlake Fitness Center and change the font to bold italic.
3. Move Slide 2 to the end of the presentation so that it becomes the new Slide 5.
4. Adjust the picture sizes, font sizes, and shapes so they do not overlap text and are the appropriate dimensions for the slide content.
5. Apply the Ripple transition to all slides. Change the duration to 02.00.
6. Change the document properties, as specified by your instructor. Save the presentation using the file name, Make It Right 2-1 New Pool Programs.
7. Submit the revised document in the format specified by your instructor.

Figure 2–76

SAM

In the Lab

Design and/or create a presentation using the guidelines, concepts, and skills presented in this chapter. Labs 1, 2, and 3 are listed in order of increasing difficulty.

Lab 1: Creating a Presentation Inserting Pictures and Applying Picture Styles

Problem: You are studying German operas in your Music Appreciation class. Wilhelm Richard Wagner (pronounced 'va:gner') lived from 1813 to 1883 and was a composer, conductor, theatre director, and essayist known for his operas. Wagner wrote and composed many operas, and King Ludwig II of Bavaria was one of his biggest supporters. Because you recently visited southern Germany and toured King Ludwig's castles, you decide to create a PowerPoint presentation with some of your photos to accompany your class presentation. These pictures are available on the Data Files for Students. Create the slides shown in Figure 2–77 from a blank presentation using the Office Theme document theme.

Note: To complete this assignment, you will be required to use the Data Files for Students. See the inside back cover of this book for instructions on downloading the Data Files for Students, or contact your instructor for information about accessing the required files.

Instructions: Perform the following tasks:

1. On Slide 1, create a background by inserting the picture called Castle 1, which is available on the Data Files for Students.
2. Type **`Fairy Tale Trip to Germany`** as the Slide 1 title text. Apply the WordArt style, Fill – Tan, Text 2, Outline – Background 2, and increase the font size to 60 point. Change the text fill to the Papyrus texture, and then change the text outline weight to 1½ pt. Also, apply the Transform text effect, Arch Up (in the Follow Path area), to this text. Position this WordArt as shown in Figure 2–77a.
3. Type the title and content for the four text slides shown in Figure 2–77. Apply the Two Content layout to Slides 2 and 3 and the Picture with Caption layout to Slides 4 and 5.
4. On Slide 2, insert the picture called Castle 2 from the Data Files for Students in the right placeholder. Apply the Bevel Perspective picture style. Resize the picture so that it is approximately 4.5" × 6", change the border color to Purple, change the border weight to 6 pt, and then move the picture, as shown in Figure 2–77b.
5. On Slide 3, insert the picture called Castle 3 from the Data Files for Students. Apply the Reflected Bevel, Black picture style and then change the border color to Green. Do not change the border weight.
6. On Slide 4, insert the picture called Castle 4 from the Data Files for Students. Apply the Beveled Oval, Black picture style, change the border color to Blue, and then change the border weight to 6 pt.
7. On Slide 5, insert the picture called Castle 5 from the Data Files for Students. Apply the Moderate Frame, Black picture style, change the border color to Purple, and then change the border weight to 6 pt.
8. For both Slides 4 and 5, increase the title text size to 28 point and the caption text size to 24 point.
9. On Slide 2, change the title text font to Algerian, change the color to purple, and bold this text. Use the Format Painter to apply these formatting changes to the Slide 3 title text. In Slide 3, insert the Vertical Scroll shape located in the Stars and Banners area, apply the Subtle Effect – Purple, Accent 4 shape style, and change the shape outline weight to 3 pt. Type the text, **`Inspiration for Disney's Sleeping Beauty Castle`**, and then change the font to Curlz MT, or a similar font. Bold this text, change the color to Dark Blue, and then change the size to 28 point. Increase the scroll shape size, as shown in Figure 2–77c.
10. On Slides 2, 3, 4, and 5, change the background style to the White marble fill texture (row 2, column 5) and change the transparency to 35%. Apply the Glitter transition to all slides. Change the duration to 04.50.

11. Change the document properties, as specified by your instructor. Save the presentation using the file name, Lab 2-1 Trip to Germany.
12. Submit the revised document in the format specified by your instructor.

(a) Slide 1

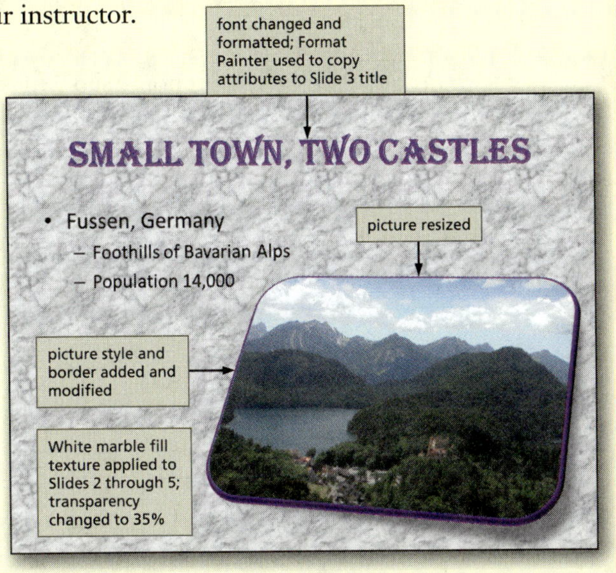

(b) Slide 2

(c) Slide 3

(d) Slide 4

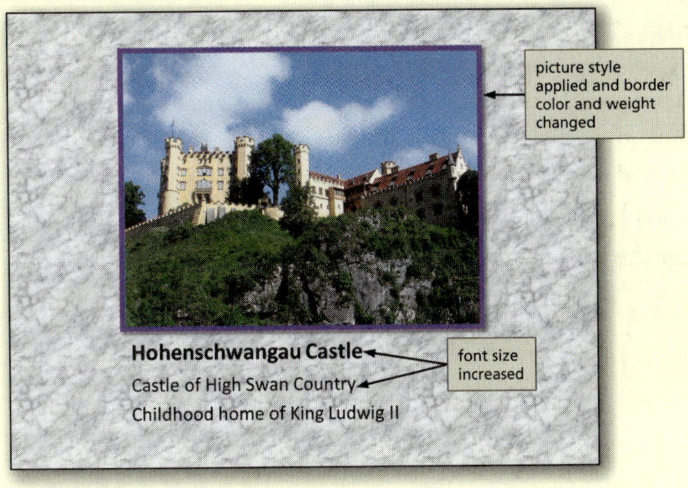

(e) Slide 5

Figure 2 – 77

In the Lab

Lab 2: Creating a Presentation with a Shape and with WordArt

Problem: With the economy showing some improvement, many small businesses are approaching lending institutions for loans to expand their businesses. You work part-time for Loans Are Us, and your manager asked you to prepare a PowerPoint presentation for the upcoming Small Business Fair in your community. The pictures for this presentation are available on the Data Files for Students.

Note: To complete this assignment, you will be required to use the Data Files for Students. See the inside back cover of this book for instructions on downloading the Data Files for Students, or contact your instructor for information about accessing the required files.

Instructions: Perform the following tasks:

1. Create a new presentation using the Austin document theme.
2. Type the title and content for the title slide and the three text slides shown in Figure 2–78a–d. Apply the Title Only layout to Slide 2, the Two Content layout to Slide 3, and the Picture with Caption layout to Slide 4.
3. On both Slides 2 and 4, create a background by inserting the picture called Money. Change the transparency to 35%.
4. On Slide 1, insert the picture called Meeting. Apply the Reflected Bevel, White picture style. Resize the picture so that it is approximately 3.76" × 4.7", change the border color to Dark Blue, change the border weight to 3 pt, and then move the picture, as shown in Figure 2–78a. Increase the title text font size to 60 point, and then apply the WordArt style, Fill – Orange, Accent 6, Warm Matte Bevel.
5. Increase the subtitle text, Loans Are Us, font size to 28 point and then bold and italicize this text. Apply the WordArt style, Fill – Green, Accent 1, Metal Bevel, Reflection.
6. On Slide 2, bold the title text. Insert the pictures called Doc1, Doc2, and Doc3. Resize these pictures so they are approximately 3" x 2.7" and then move them to the locations shown in Figure 2–78b. Insert the Flowchart: Decision shape located in the Flowchart area, apply the Subtle Effect – Orange, Accent 6 shape style, and then resize the shape so that it is approximately 1.5" × 5.83". Change the shape outline weight to 6 pt. Type **`Assets, Liabilities & Sales Reports`** as the shape text, change the font to Aharoni, or a similar font, change the color to Dark Blue, and then change the size to 24 point.
7. On Slide 3, bold the title text. Insert the picture called Presentation into the right placeholder, apply the Beveled Oval, Black shape picture style, resize the picture so that it is approximately 3.5" × 5.25", and then sharpen the picture 50%.
8. On Slide 4, insert the picture called Cash and Credit Card. Change the title text font size to 36 point and bold this text. Change the subtitle text font size to 24 point and then bold and italicize these words.
9. Apply the Shape transition to all slides. Change the duration to 01.25.
10. Change the document properties, as specified by your instructor. Save the presentation using the file name, Lab 2-2 Small Business Loans.
11. Submit the document in the format specified by your instructor.

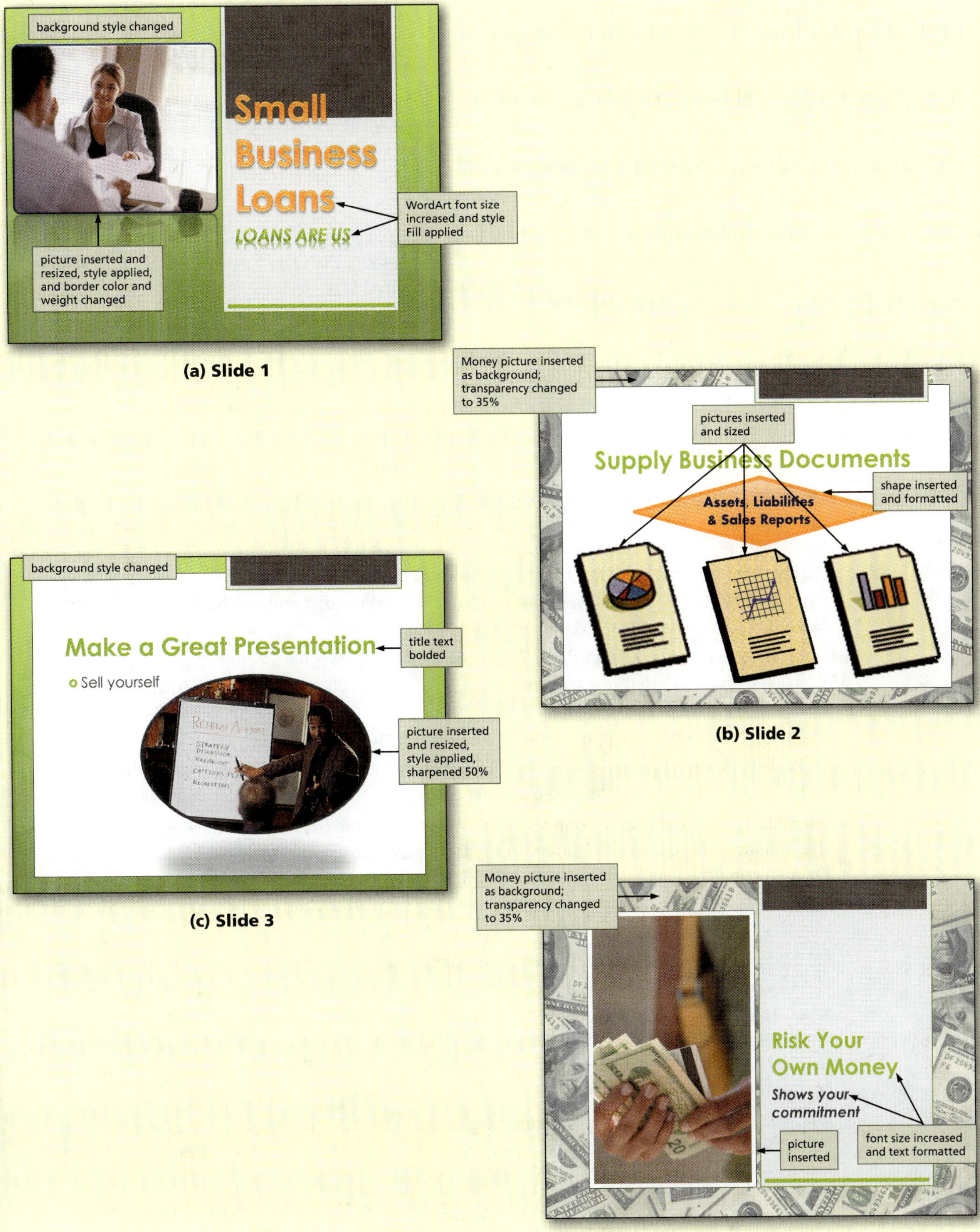

(a) Slide 1

(b) Slide 2

(c) Slide 3

(d) Slide 4

Figure 2–78

In the Lab

Lab 3: Creating a Presentation with Pictures and Shapes

Problem: One of your assignments in your child development class is to give a speech about teaching children the value of money, so you decide to create a PowerPoint presentation to add a little interest to your speech. Prepare the slides shown in Figures 2–79a through 2–79e. The pictures for this presentation are available on the Data Files for Students.

Note: To complete this assignment, you will be required to use the Data Files for Students. See the inside back cover of this book for instructions on downloading the Data Files for Students, or contact your instructor for information about accessing the required files.

Instructions: Perform the following tasks:

1. Create a new presentation using the Median document theme, and then change the presentation theme colors to Flow. This presentation should have five slides; apply the Title Slide layout to Slide 1, the Picture with Caption layout to Slides 2 and 5, the Comparison layout to Slide 3, and the Blank layout to Slide 4.
2. Type the title and content text for the title slide and the four text slides shown in Figure 2–79a–d.
3. On Slide 1, change the title text font size to 54 point. To make the letter 's' appear smaller than the other letters in the first word of the title slide title text placeholder, change the font size of this letter to 44 point. Insert the Oval shape, resize it so that it is approximately 0.5" × 0.5", and change the shape fill to white, which is the second color in the first row of the Theme Colors gallery. Type **$**, increase the font size to 48 point, change the color to green, and bold this dollar sign. Cover the letter 'o' in the word, Do, with this shape.
4. Insert the picture called Piggy Bank. Apply the Rounded Diagonal Corner, White picture style. Resize the picture so that it is approximately 4.4" × 5.03", change the border color to Light Blue, change the border weight to 3 pt, and then move the picture, as shown in Figure 2–79a. Change the subtitle font size to 32 point and then bold this text.
5. On Slide 2, insert the picture called Child Doing Dishes and then decrease the picture's contrast to –20%. Change the title text size to 36 point and bold this text. Change the caption text size to 32 point.
6. On Slide 3, change the background style to Style 6. Bold the title text. Change the heading title text size in both placeholders to 32 point. In the right placeholder, insert the picture called Father and Daughter and then apply the Reflected Bevel, White picture style. Resize the picture so that it is approximately 3" × 4", change the border color to Light Blue, and then change the border weight to 3 pt, as shown in Figure 2–79c.
7. On Slide 4, create a background by inserting the picture called Piggy Bank and Coins. Insert the Cloud shape located in the Basic Shapes area and then increase the cloud shape size so that it is approximately 3" × 5.6". Change the shape outline color to Yellow and then change the shape outline weight to 3 pt. Type **`Teach your children to save for a big purchase.`** as the shape text, and then change the font to Comic Sans MS. Bold and italicize this text and then change the font size to 32 point.
8. On Slide 5, create a background by inserting the picture called Coins. Insert the picture called Father and Child Shopping and then decrease the picture's brightness to −20%. Change the title text font size to 36 point and bold this text.
9. Apply the Box transition to all slides. Change the duration to 02.00. Check the spelling and correct any errors.
10. Change the document properties, as specified by your instructor. Save the presentation using the file name, Lab 2-3 ABCs of Money.
11. Submit the revised document in the format specified by your instructor.

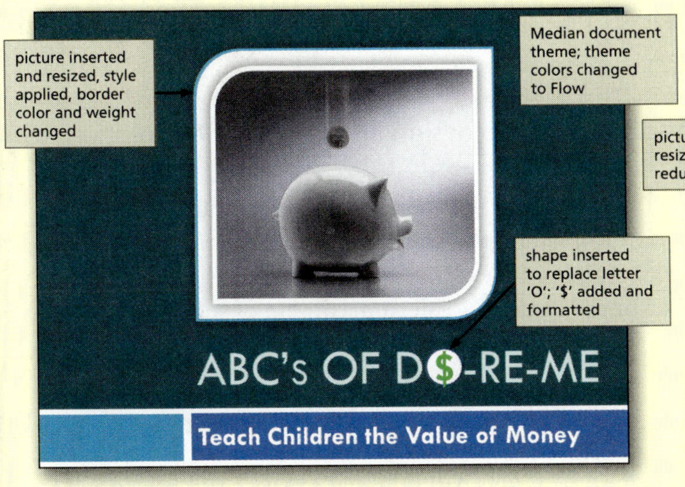

(a) Slide 1

(b) Slide 2

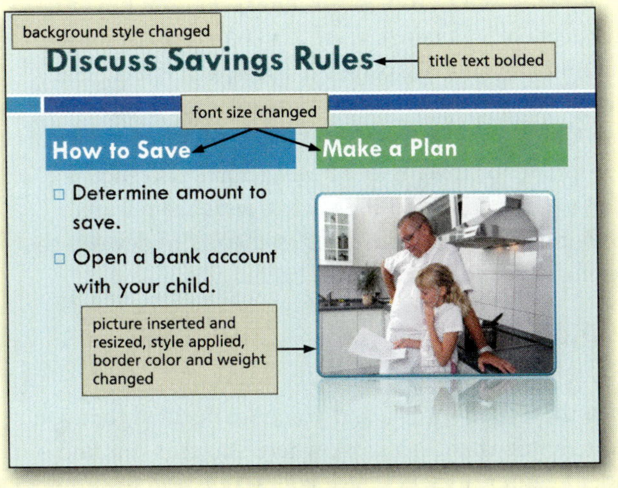

(c) Slide 3

(d) Slide 4

(e) Slide 5

Figure 2–79

Cases and Places

Apply your creative thinking and problem-solving skills to design and implement a solution.

Note: To complete these assignments, you may be required to use the Data Files for Students. See the inside back cover of this book for instructions on downloading the Data Files for Students, or contact your instructor for information about accessing the required files.

As you design the presentations, remember to use the 7 × 7 rule: a maximum of seven words on a line and a maximum of seven lines on one slide.

1: Design and Create a Presentation about Acid Rain

Academic

Nature depends on the correct pH balance. Although some rain is naturally acidic with a pH level of around 5.0, human activities have increased the amount of acid in this water. Burning fossil fuels, including coal, oil, and natural gas, produces sulfur dioxide. Exhaust from vehicles releases nitrogen oxides. Both of these gases, when released into the atmosphere, mix with water droplets, forming acid rain. In your science class, you are studying about the causes and effects of acid rain. Create a presentation to show what causes acid rain and what effects it can have on humans, animals, plant life, lakes, and rivers. The presentation should contain at least three pictures appropriately resized. The Data Files for Students contains five pictures called Factory, Rain, Soil, Tree and Clouds, and Vehicles; you can use your own digital pictures or pictures from Office.com if they are appropriate for this topic. These pictures also should have appropriate styles and border colors. Use shapes such as arrows to show what gases are released into the atmosphere. Apply at least three objectives found at the beginning of this chapter to develop the presentation. Add a title slide with a shape and a closing slide. Be sure to check spelling.

2: Design and Create a Presentation about Tutoring

Personal

You have been helping some of your classmates with their schoolwork, and you have decided that you should start a small tutoring business. In the student center, there is a kiosk where students can find out about programs and activities on campus. The student center manager gave you permission to submit a short PowerPoint presentation promoting your tutoring business; this presentation will be added to the kiosk. The presentation should contain pictures appropriately resized. The Data Files for Students contains four pictures called Tutoring 1, Tutoring 2, Tutoring 3, and Tutoring 4, or you can use your own digital pictures or pictures from Office.com if they are appropriate for this topic. Change the contrast and brightness for at least one picture. Insert shapes and WordArt to enhance your presentation. Apply a transition in the Subtle area to all slides and increase the duration. Be sure to check spelling.

3: Design and Create a Presentation on Setting Up Children's Fish Tanks

Professional

Fish make great pets for young children, but there is a lot to learn before they can set up a fish tank properly. The owner of the pet store where you work has asked you to create a presentation for the store to give parents an idea of what they need to purchase and consider when setting up a fish tank. He would like you to cover the main points such as the appropriate size bowl or tank, setup procedures, filtration, water quality, types of fish, care, and feeding. The presentation should contain pictures appropriately resized. The Data Files for Students contains five pictures called Fish 1, Fish 2, Fish 3, Fish 4, and Fish 5, or you can use your own digital pictures or pictures from Office.com if they are appropriate for this topic. Add a title slide and closing slide to complete your presentation. Format the title slide with a shape and change the theme color scheme. Change the title text font on the title slide. Format the background with at least one picture and apply a background texture to at least one slide. This presentation is geared to parents of young children, so keep it colorful, simple, and fun.

3 Reusing a Presentation and Adding Media

Objectives

You will have mastered the material in this chapter when you can:

- Color a picture
- Add an artistic effect to a picture
- Delete and move placeholders
- Align paragraph text
- Copy a slide element from one slide to another
- Ungroup, change the color, and regroup a clip
- Insert and edit a video clip
- Insert audio
- Control audio and video clips
- Check for spelling errors
- Print a presentation as a handout

3 Reusing a Presentation and Adding Media

Introduction

At times, you will need to revise a PowerPoint presentation. Changes may include inserting and adding effects to pictures, altering the colors of clips and pictures, and updating visual elements displayed on a slide. Applying a different theme, changing fonts, and substituting graphical elements can give a slide show an entirely new look. Adding media, including sounds, video, and music, can enhance a presentation and help audience members retain the information being presented.

Project — Presentation with Video, Audio, and Pictures with Effects

BTW

PowerPoint 2010 Video Enhancements
New video tools in PowerPoint 2010 enable you to develop a presentation filled with professional-quality features. You now can embed and edit videos from within PowerPoint instead of needing to use a separate program to customize your media files. You can add fades and effects to captivate your audience, and you can trim specific pieces of the video file to show the exact scenes needed to make a point. Video and audio files now are embedded in your PowerPoint file, so they become part of the entire presentation. These enhanced features help make your media fit the message you are sending to your audience.

The project in this chapter follows graphical guidelines and uses PowerPoint to create the presentation shown in Figure 3–1. The slides in this revised presentation, which discusses Bird Migration, have a variety of audio and visual elements. For example, the pictures have artistic effects applied that soften the pictures and help the audience focus on other elements on the slides. The bird clip has colors that blend well with the background. The video has been edited to play only the portion with Bird Migration and has effects to add audience interest. Bird calls integrate with the visual elements. Overall, the slides have myriad media elements and effects that are exciting for your audience to watch and hear.

Overview

As you read through this chapter, you will learn how to create the presentation shown in Figure 3–1 by performing these general tasks:

- Format pictures by recoloring and adding artistic effects.
- Insert and format video and audio clips.
- Modify clip art.
- Vary paragraph alignment.
- Check a presentation for spelling errors.
- Print a handout of your slides.

(a) Slide 1 (Title Slide with Picture Background, Modified Clip, and Animated Clip)

(b) Slide 2 (Bulleted List)

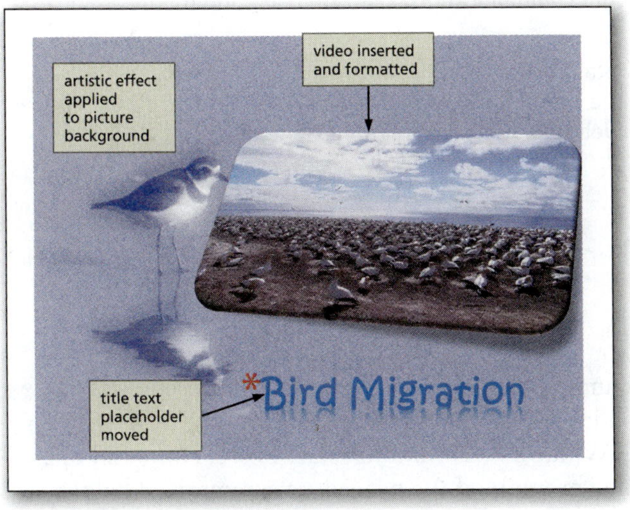

(c) Slide 3 (Picture Background and Video Clip)

(d) Slide 4 (Video Playing Full Screen)

Figure 3–1

Plan Ahead

General Project Guidelines

When creating a PowerPoint presentation, the actions you perform and the decisions you make will affect the appearance and characteristics of the finished document. As you create a presentation with illustrations, such as the project shown in Figure 3–1, you should follow these general guidelines:

1. **Use the color wheel to determine color choices.** Warm colors and cool colors evoke opposite effects on audience members. As you make decisions to color pictures, consider the emotions you want to generate and choose colors that match these sentiments.
2. **Vary paragraph alignment.** Different effects are achieved when text alignment shifts in a presentation. Themes dictate whether paragraph text is aligned left, center, or right in a placeholder, but you can modify these design decisions when necessary.
3. **Use multimedia selectively.** Video, music, and sound files can add interest to your presentation. Use these files only when necessary, however, because they draw the audience's attention away from the presenter and toward the slides. Using too many multimedia files can be overwhelming.
4. **Use handouts to organize your speech.** Effective speakers take much time to prepare their verbal message that will accompany each slide. They practice their speeches and decide how to integrate the material displayed. Viewing the thumbnails, or miniature versions of the slides, will help you associate the slide image with the script. These thumbnails also can be cut out and arranged when organizing the presentation.
5. **Evaluate your presentation.** As soon as you finish your presentation, critique your performance. You will improve your communication skills by eliminating the flaws and accentuating the positives.

When necessary, more specific details concerning the above guidelines are presented at appropriate points in the chapter. The chapter also will identify the actions performed and decisions made regarding these guidelines during the creation of the presentation shown in Figure 3–1.

For an introduction to Windows 7 and instruction about how to perform basic Windows 7 tasks, read the Office 2010 and Windows 7 chapter in this book, where you can learn how to resize windows, change screen resolution, create folders, move and rename files, use Windows Help, and much more.

Starting PowerPoint

PowerPoint Chapter 1 introduced you to starting PowerPoint, selecting a document theme, creating slides with clip art and a bulleted list, and printing a presentation. PowerPoint Chapter 2 enhanced slides by adding pictures, shapes, and WordArt. The following steps, which assume Windows 7 is running, start PowerPoint and open the Birds presentation. For a detailed example of the procedure summarized below, refer to the Office 2010 and Windows 7 chapter in this book.

BTW

The Ribbon and Screen Resolution

PowerPoint may change how the groups and buttons within the groups appear on the Ribbon, depending on the computer's screen resolution. Thus, your Ribbon may look different from the ones in the Office and Windows chapters in this book if you are using a screen resolution other than 1024 × 768.

To Start PowerPoint and Open and Save a Presentation

1. Click the Start button on the Windows 7 taskbar to display the Start menu, type `Microsoft PowerPoint` as the search text in the 'Search programs and files' text box, and then click Microsoft PowerPoint 2010 in the search results on the Start menu to start PowerPoint and display a new blank document.
2. If the PowerPoint window is not maximized, click the Maximize button.
3. Open the presentation, Birds, from the Data Files for Students. See the inside back cover of this book for instructions on downloading the Data Files for Students, or contact your instructor for more information on accessing the required files.
4. Save the presentation using the file name, Bird Migration.

Inserting Pictures and Adding Effects

The Bird Migration presentation consists of four slides that have some text, a clip art image, a formatted background, and a transition applied to all slides. You will insert pictures into two slides and then modify them by adding artistic effects and recoloring. You also will copy the clip art from Slide 2 to Slide 1 and modify the objects in this clip. In PowerPoint Chapter 2, you inserted pictures, made corrections, and added styles and effects; the new effects you apply in this chapter will add to your repertoire of picture enhancements that increase interest in your presentation.

In the following pages, you will perform these tasks:

1. Insert the first digital picture into Slide 1.
2. Insert the second digital picture into Slide 3.
3. Recolor the Slide 3 picture.
4. Recolor and add an artistic effect to the Slide 1 picture.
5. Add an artistic effect to the Slide 3 picture.
6. Send the Slide 3 picture back behind all other slide objects.
7. Send the Slide 1 picture back behind all other slide objects.

For an introduction to Office 2010 and instruction about how to perform basic tasks in Office 2010 programs, read the Office 2010 and Windows 7 chapter in this book, where you can learn how to start a program, use the Ribbon, save a file, open a file, quit a program, use Help, and much more.

To Insert and Resize Pictures into Slides without Content Placeholders

The next step is to insert digital pictures into Slides 1 and 3. These pictures are available on the Data Files for Students. See the inside back cover of this book for instructions on downloading the Data Files for Students, or contact your instructor for information about accessing the required files.

The following steps insert pictures into Slides 1 and 3.

1. With Slide 1 displaying and your USB flash drive connected to one of the computer's USB ports, click Insert on the Ribbon to display the Insert tab and then click the Picture button (Insert tab | Images group) to display the Insert Picture dialog box.
2. If necessary, navigate to the picture location (in this case, the PowerPoint folder in the CIS 101 folder [or your class folder] on the USB flash drive). For a detailed example of this procedure, refer to Steps 3a–3c in the To Save a File in a Folder section in the Office 2010 and Windows 7 chapter in this book.
3. Click Birds in Sky to select the file.
4. Click the Insert button (Insert Picture dialog box) to insert the picture into Slide 1.
5. Resize the picture so that it covers the entire slide (approximately 7.5" × 10").
6. Display Slide 3, display the Insert tab, click the Picture button to display the Insert Picture dialog box, and then insert the Bird Reflect picture into Slide 3.
7. Resize the picture so that it covers the entire slide (approximately 7.5" × 10") (Figure 3–2).

Q&A

How do I resize the picture so that it maintains its proportions?

Press and hold the SHIFT key while dragging a sizing handle away from or toward the center of the picture. To maintain the picture's proportions and keep its center in the same location, press and hold down both the CTRL and SHIFT keys while you drag a sizing handle.

BTW

Inserting Text Boxes

If you want to add text in an area of the slide where a content placeholder is not located, you can insert a text box. This object allows you to emphasize or set off text that you consider important for your audience to read. To create a text box, click the Text Box button (Insert tab | Text group), click the slide, and then drag this object to the desired location on the slide. Click inside the text box to add or paste text. You also can change the look and style of the text box characters by using formatting features (Home tab | Font group).

Figure 3–2

Plan Ahead

Use the color wheel to determine color choices.

The color wheel is one of designers' basic tools. Twelve colors on the wheel are arranged in a specific order, with the three primary colors — red, yellow, and blue — forming a triangle. Between the primary colors are the secondary colors that are formed when the primary colors are mixed. For example, red and yellow mixed together form orange; red and blue form purple; and yellow and blue form green. The six other colors on the wheel are formed when the primary colors are mixed with the secondary colors.

Red, orange, and yellow are considered warm colors, and they display adjacent to each other on one side of the wheel. They are bold and lively, so you should use them when your message is intended to invigorate an audience and create a pleasing effect. Opposite the warm colors are the cool colors: green, blue, and purple. They generate a relaxing, calming atmosphere.

If you put a primary and secondary color together, such as red and purple, your slide will make a very bold and vivid statement. Be certain that effect is one you intend when planning your message.

Adjusting Picture Colors

BTW **Q&As**
For a complete list of the Q&As found in many of the step-by-step sequences in the Office and Windows chapters in this book, visit the Microsoft Office and Concepts CourseMate Web site at www.cengagebrain.com and then navigate to the Q&A resource for this book.

PowerPoint allows you to adjust colors to match or add contrast to slide elements by coloring pictures. The Color Picture gallery has a wide variety of preset formatting combinations. The thumbnails in the gallery display the more common color saturation, color tone, and recolor adjustments. **Color saturation** changes the intensity of colors. High saturation produces vivid colors; low saturation produces gray tones. **Color tone** affects the coolness, called blue, or the warmness, called orange, of pictures. When a digital camera does not measure the tone correctly, a **color cast** occurs, and, as a result, one color dominates the picture. **Recolor** effects convert the picture into a wide variety of hues. The more common are **grayscale**, which changes the color picture into black, white, and shades of gray, and **sepia**, which changes the picture colors into brown, gold, and yellow, reminiscent of a faded photo. You also can fine-tune the color adjustments by clicking Picture Color Options and More Variations commands in the Color gallery.

To Color a Picture

The Slipstream theme and text on Slides 1 and 3 have many shades of blue. The inserted pictures, in addition, have blue backgrounds. The following steps recolor the Slide 3 picture to coordinate with the blue colors on the slide.

1

- With Slide 3 displaying and the Bird Reflect picture selected, click the Color button (Picture Tools Format tab | Adjust group) to display the Color gallery (Figure 3–3).

Q&A Why does the Adjust group look different on my screen?

Your monitor is set to a different resolution. See the Office 2010 and Windows 7 chapter in this book for an explanation of screen resolution and the appearance of the Ribbon.

Q&A Why are yellow borders surrounding the thumbnails in the Color Saturation and Color Tone areas in the gallery?

The image on Slide 3 currently has normal color saturation and a normal color tone.

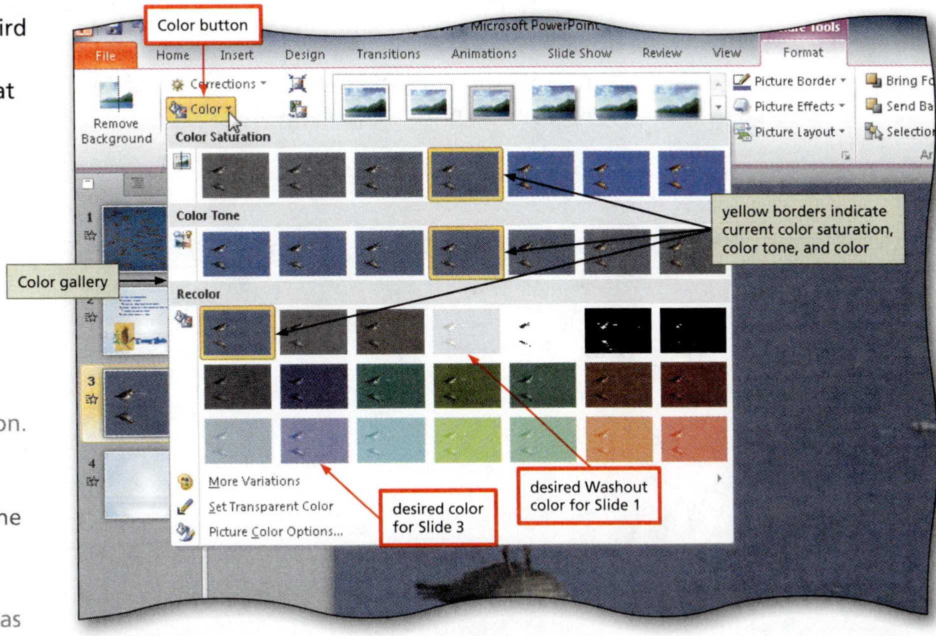

Figure 3–3

2

- Point to Blue, Accent color 1 Light (second picture in last row of Recolor area) to display a live preview of this adjustment on the picture.

Experiment

- Point to various thumbnails in the Recolor area and watch the hues change on the picture in Slide 3.
- Click Blue, Accent color 1 Light to apply this correction to the Bird Reflect picture (Figure 3–4).

Q&A Could I have applied this correction to the picture if it had been a background instead of a file inserted into the slide?

No. Artistic effects cannot be applied to backgrounds.

Figure 3–4

To Color a Second Picture

The Slide 1 picture has rich hues and is very prominent on the slide. To soften its appearance and to provide continuity with the Slide 3 picture, you can color this picture. The following steps color the picture on the title slide.

1. Display Slide 1 and then click the picture to select it. Click the Color button (Picture Tools Format tab | Adjust group) to display the Color gallery.

2. Click Washout (fourth picture in first row of Recolor area) to apply this correction to the Bird Reflect picture (Figure 3–5).

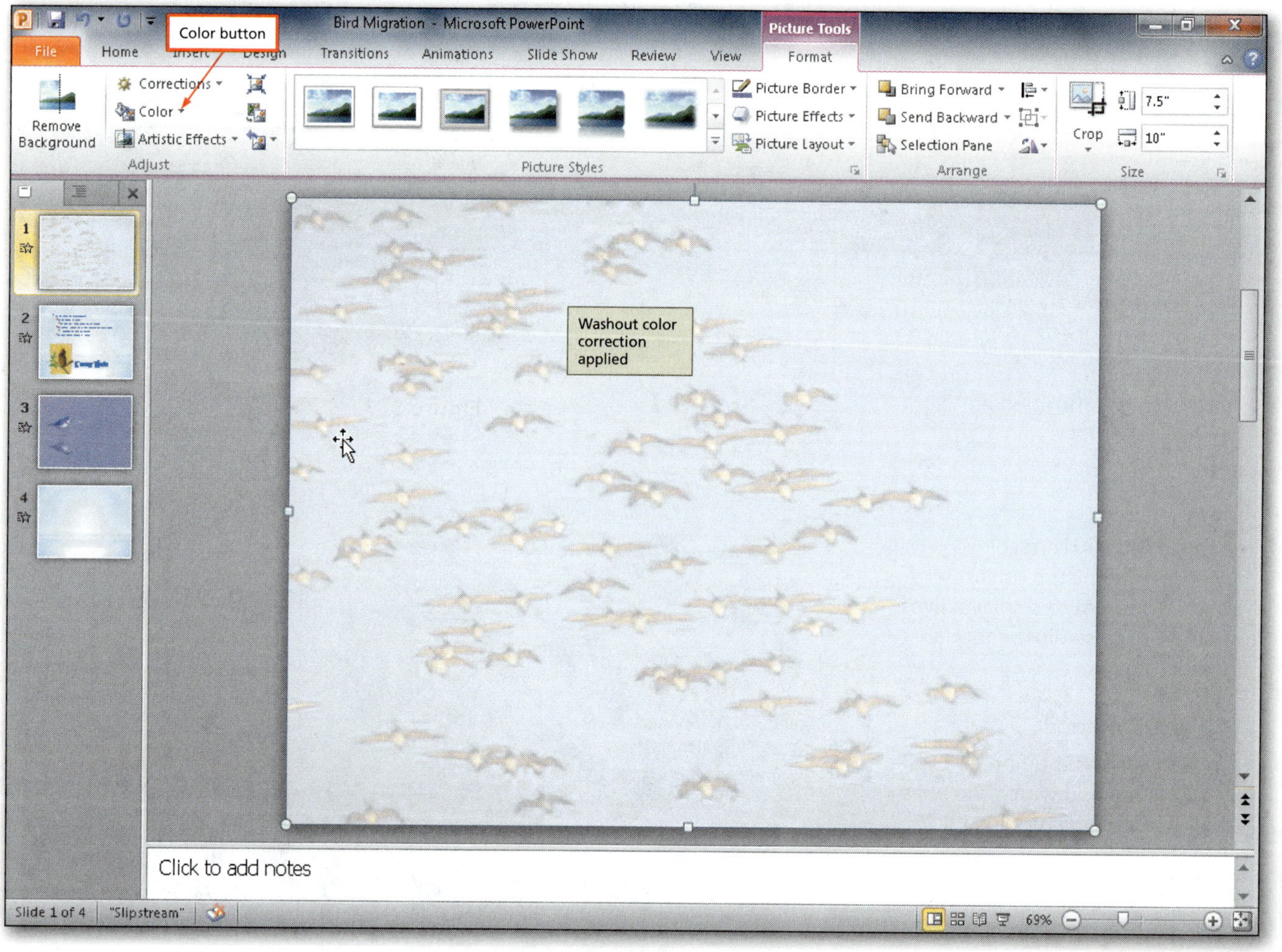

Figure 3–5

To Add an Artistic Effect to a Picture

Artists use a variety of techniques to create effects in their paintings. For example, they can vary the amount of paint on their brushstroke, use fine bristles to add details, mix colors to increase or decrease intensity, and smooth their paints together to blend the colors. You, likewise, can add similar effects to your pictures using PowerPoint's built-in artistic effects. The following steps add an artistic effect to the Slide 3 picture.

1

- With the Birds in Sky picture selected in Slide 1, click the Artistic Effects button (Picture Tools Format tab | Adjust group) to display the Artistic Effects gallery (Figure 3–6).

Q&A Why does the Adjust group look different on my screen?

Your monitor is set to a different resolution. See the Office 2010 and Windows 7 chapter in this book for an explanation of screen resolution and the appearance of the Ribbon.

Q&A Why is a yellow border surrounding the first thumbnail in the gallery?

The first thumbnail shows a preview of the image on Slide 1 with no artistic effect applied.

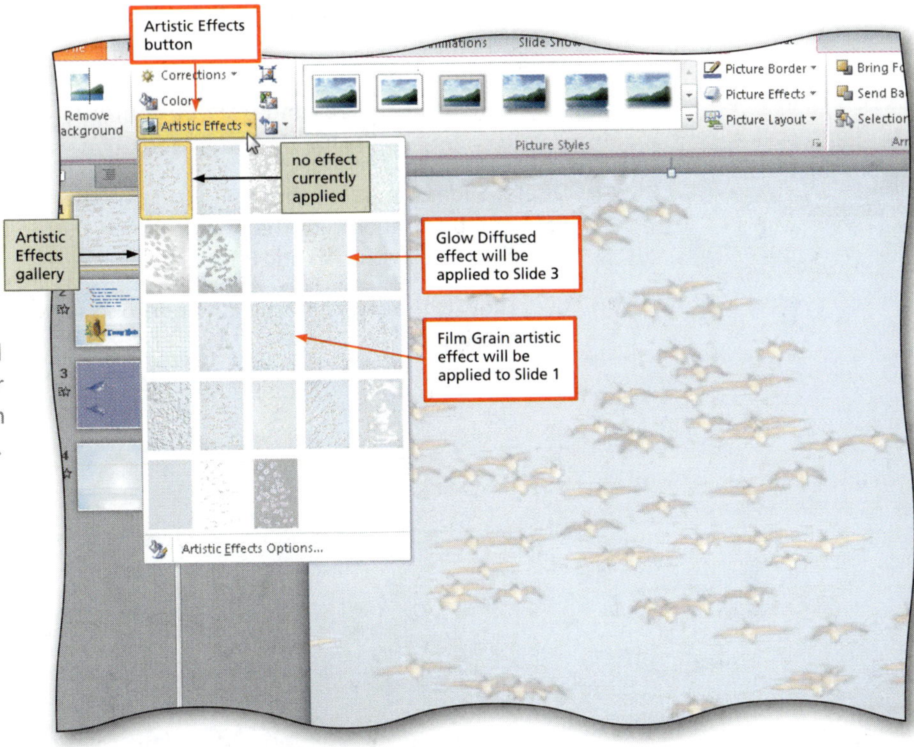

Figure 3–6

2

- Point to Film Grain (third picture in third row) to display a live preview of this adjustment on the picture.

Experiment

- Point to various thumbnails and watch the hues change on the picture in Slide 1.

- Click Film Grain to apply this correction to the Birds in Sky picture (Figure 3–7).

Q&A Must I adjust a picture by recoloring and applying an artistic effect?

No. You can apply either a color or an effect. You may prefer at times to mix these adjustments to create a unique image.

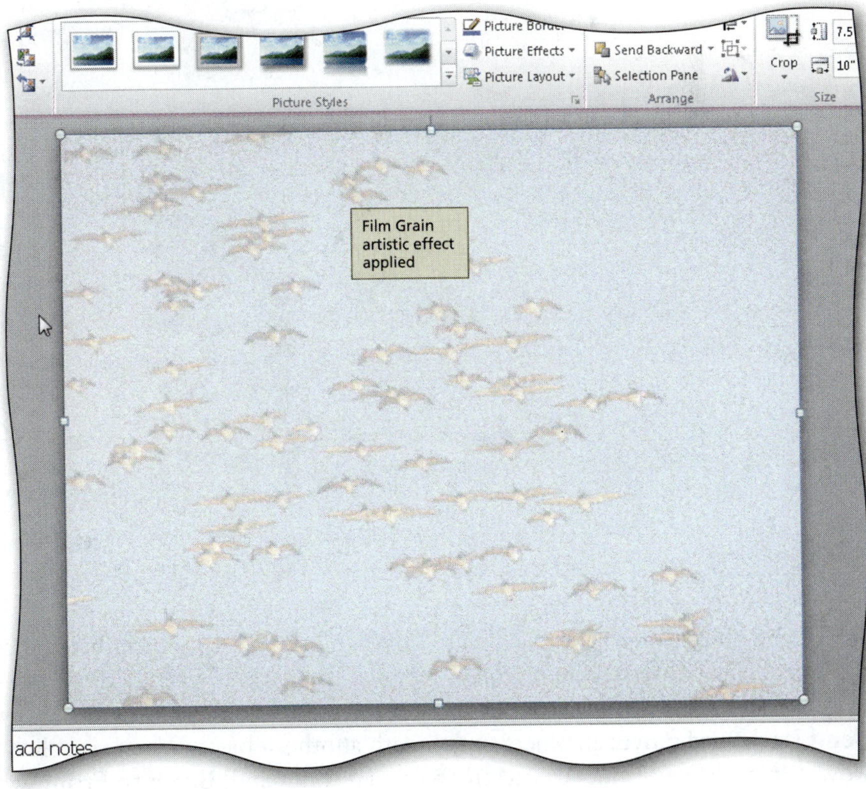

Figure 3–7

To Add an Artistic Effect to a Second Picture

The Slide 3 picture was softened when you applied a blue accent color. You can further change the images and provide continuity with the Slide 1 picture by applying an artistic effect. The following steps add an artistic effect to the Slide 3 picture.

1. Display Slide 3 and then click the picture to select it. If necessary, click the Picture Tools Format tab and then click the Artistic Effects button (Picture Tools Format tab | Adjust group) to display the Artistic Effects gallery.

2. Click Glow Diffused (fourth picture in second row) to apply this effect to the Bird Reflect picture (Figure 3–8).

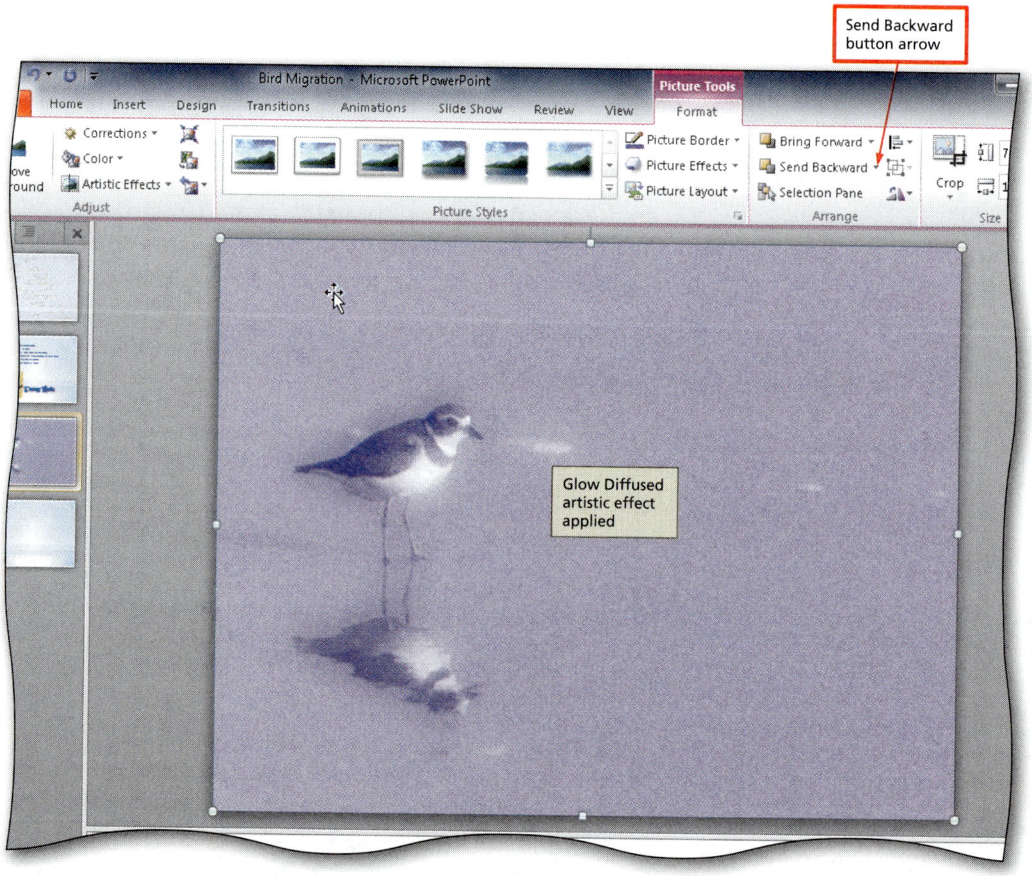

Figure 3–8

To Change the Stacking Order

The objects on a slide stack on top of each other, much like individual cards in a deck. On Slides 1 and 3, the pictures you inserted are on top of text placeholders. To change the order of these objects, you use the Bring Forward and Send Backward commands. **Bring Forward** moves an object toward the top of the stack, and **Send Backward** moves an object underneath another object. When you click the Bring Forward button arrow, PowerPoint displays a menu with an additional command, **Bring to Front**, which moves a selected object to the top of the stack. Likewise, when you click the Send Backward button arrow, the **Send to Back** button moves the selected object underneath all objects on the slide. The following steps arrange the Slide 3 and Slide 1 pictures by sending them to the bottom of the stack on each slide.

1

- With the Bird Reflect picture selected in Slide 3, click the Send Backward button arrow (Picture Tools Format tab | Arrange group) to display the Send Backward menu (Figure 3–9).

Q&A How can I see objects that are not on the top of the stack?

Press TAB or SHIFT+TAB to display each slide object.

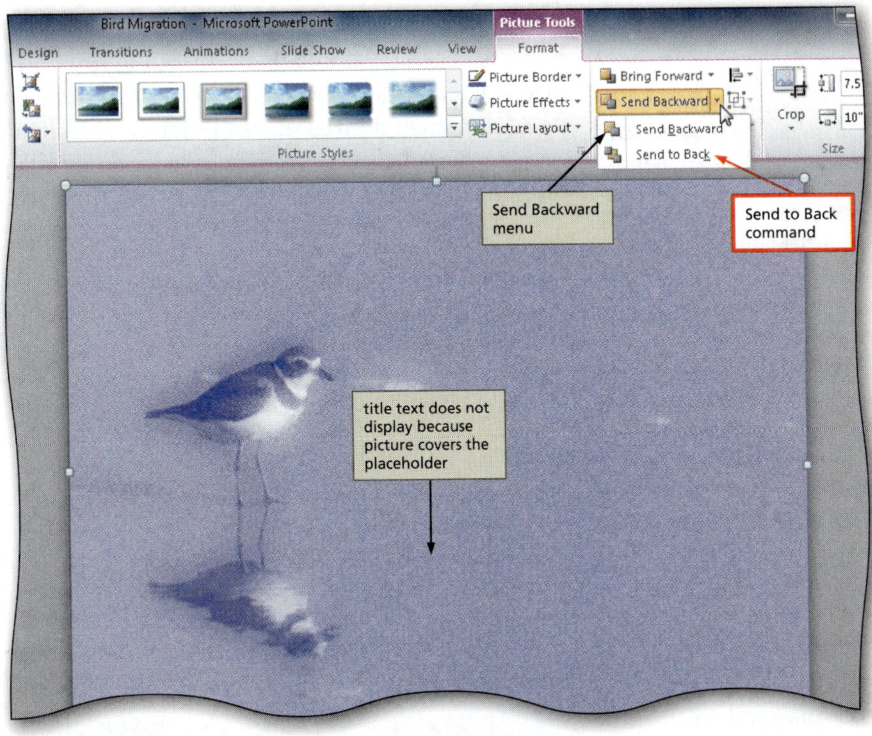

Figure 3–9

2

- Click Send to Back to move the picture underneath all slide objects (Figure 3–10).

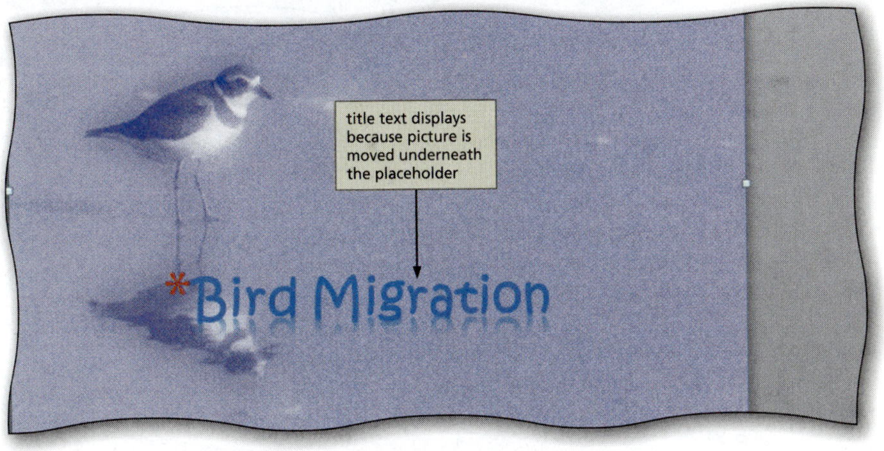

Figure 3–10

3

- Display Slide 1, select the Birds in Sky picture, and then click the Send Backward button arrow (Picture Tools Format tab | Arrange group).
- Click Send to Back to move the picture underneath all slide objects (Figure 3–11).

Figure 3–11

Other Ways

1. Click Send to Back (Picture Tools Format tab | Arrange group), press K
2. Point to Send to Back on shortcut menu, click Send to Back

Modifying Placeholders and Deleting a Slide

BTW

BTWs
For a complete list of the BTWs found in the margins of the Office and Windows chapters in this book, visit the Microsoft Office and Concepts CourseMate Web site at www.cengagebrain.com and then navigate to the BTW resource for this book.

You have become familiar with inserting text and graphical content in the three types of placeholders: title, subtitle, and content. These placeholders can be moved, resized, and deleted to meet desired design requirements. In addition, placeholders can be added to a slide when needed. After you have modified the placeholder locations, you can view thumbnails of all your slides simultaneously by changing views.

In the following pages, you will perform these tasks:

1. Resize and move the Slide 1 title text placeholder.
2. Delete the Slide 1 subtitle text placeholder.
3. Align the Slide 1 and Slide 3 paragraph text.
4. Delete Slide 4.
5. Change views.

To Resize a Placeholder

The AutoFit button displays on the left side of the Slide 1 title text placeholder because the two lines of text exceed the placeholder's borders. PowerPoint attempts to reduce the font size when the text does not fit, and you can click this button to resize the existing text in the placeholder so the spillover text will fit within the borders. You also can resize the placeholder so that the letters fit within the rectangle. The following step increases the Slide 1 title text placeholder.

1

- With Slide 1 displaying, click somewhere in the title text paragraph to position the insertion point in the paragraph. Click the border of the title text placeholder to select it. Point to the bottom-middle sizing handle so that the mouse pointer changes to a two-headed arrow.
- Drag the bottom border downward to enlarge the text placeholder (Figure 3–12).

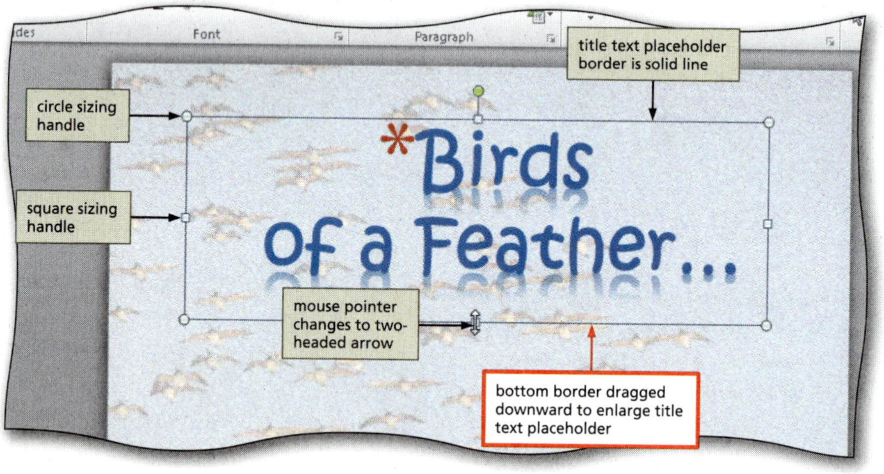

Figure 3–12

Q&A

Can I drag other sizing handles to enlarge or shrink the placeholder?

Yes, you also can drag the left, right, top, and corner sizing handles to resize a placeholder.

Q&A

How do the square sizing handles differ from circle sizing handles?

Dragging a square handle alters the shape of the text box so that it is wider or taller. Dragging a circle handle keeps the box in the same proportion and simply enlarges the overall shape.

To Move a Placeholder

The theme layouts determine where the text and content placeholders display on the slide. If you desire to have a placeholder appear in a different area of the slide, you can move it to a new location. The Slide 1 title text placeholder currently displays in the upper third of the slide, but the text in this placeholder would be more aesthetically pleasing if it were moved toward the center of the slide. The following step moves the Slide 1 title text placeholder.

1

- With the Slide 1 title text placeholder border displaying as a solid line, point to an area of the bottom border between two sizing handles so that the mouse pointer changes to a four-headed arrow.

Q&A What if the placeholder border displays as a dotted line?

Click the border to change the line from dotted to solid.

Q&A Can I click any part of the border, or do I need to click the bottom edge?

You can click any of the four border lines.

- Drag the placeholder downward so that it overlaps part of the subtitle text placeholder (Figure 3–13).
- Click to set the placeholder in its new location.

Figure 3–13

To Delete a Placeholder

When you run a slide show, empty placeholders do not display. You may desire to delete unused placeholders from a slide so that they are not a distraction when you are designing slide content. The subtitle text placeholder on Slide 1 is not required for this presentation, so you can remove it. The following steps remove the Slide 1 subtitle text placeholder.

1 Click a border of the subtitle text placeholder so that it displays as a solid line or fine dots (Figure 3–14).

Q&A What if the placeholder border is displaying as a dotted line?

Click the border to change the line from dotted to solid or fine dots.

2 Press the DELETE key to remove the placeholder.

Q&A Can I click the Cut button (Home tab | Clipboard group) to delete the placeholder?

Yes. Clicking the Cut button deletes the placeholder if it does not contain any text.

Figure 3–14

BTW **Reusing Placeholders**

If you need to show the same formatted placeholder on multiple slides, you may want to customize a slide master and insert a placeholder into a slide layout. Using a slide master saves you time because you do not need to type the same information in more than one slide. The slide master is useful when you have extremely long presentations. Every document theme has several slide masters that indicate the size and position of text and object placeholders. Any change you make to a slide master results in changing that component in every slide of the presentation.

Plan Ahead

Vary paragraph alignment.
Designers use alignment within paragraphs to aid readability and to indicate relationships among slide elements. English language readers are accustomed to seeing paragraphs that are aligned left. When paragraphs are aligned right, the viewer's eyes are drawn to this unexpected text design. If your paragraph is short, consider centering or right-aligning the text for emphasis.

To Align Paragraph Text

The presentation theme determines the formatting characteristics of fonts and colors. It also establishes paragraph formatting, including the alignment of text. Some themes center the text paragraphs between the left and right placeholder borders, while others **left-align** the paragraph so that the first character of a text line is near the left border or **right-align** the paragraph so that the last character of a text line is near the right border. The paragraph also can be **justified** so that the text is aligned to both the left and right borders. When PowerPoint justifies text, it adds extras spaces between the words to fill the entire line.

The words, Birds of a Feather, are centered in the Slide 1 title text placeholder. Later, you will add clip art above the word, Feather, so you desire to left-align the paragraph to make room for this art. In addition, the words in the Slide 3 title text placeholder, Bird Migration, are covering the bird in the picture. You can right-align these words to uncover the bird in the lower-left corner. The following steps change the alignment of the Slide 1 and Slide 3 title placeholders.

1

- With the Home tab displayed, click somewhere in the title text paragraph of Slide 1 to position the insertion point in the paragraph to be formatted (Figure 3–15).

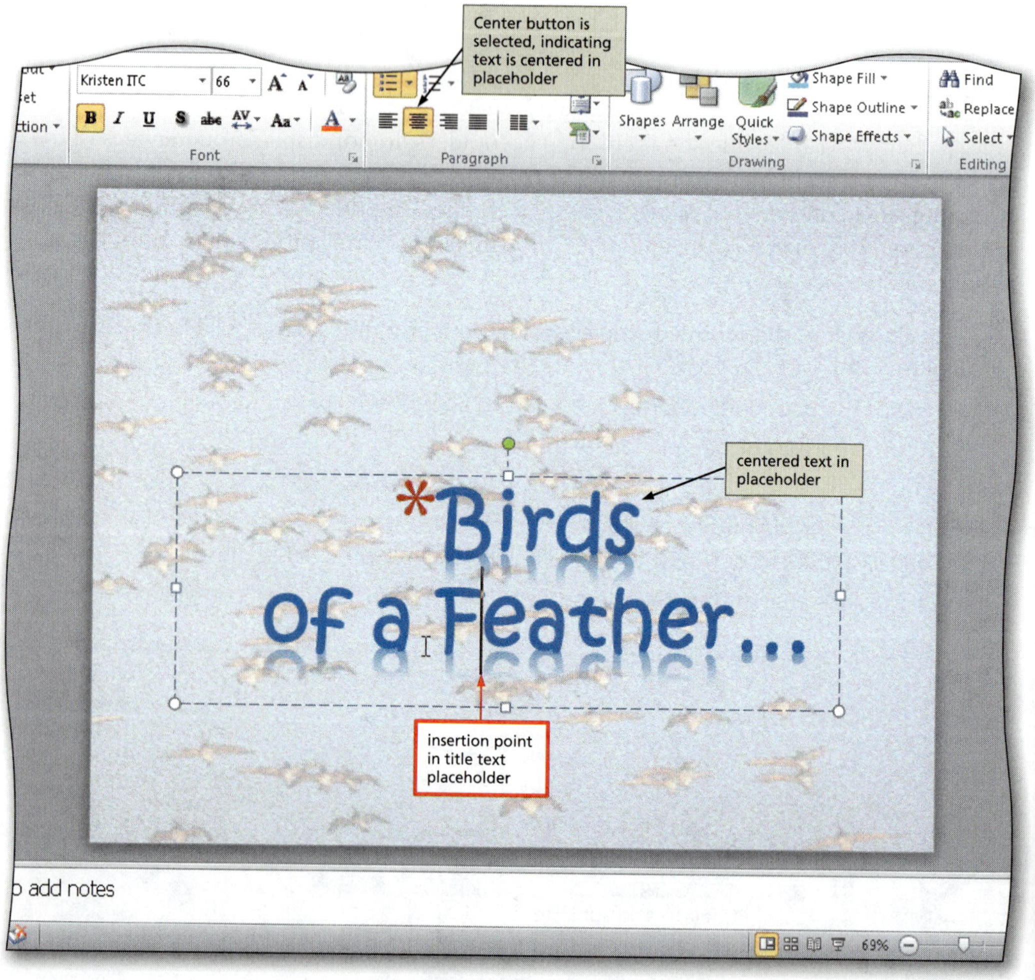

Figure 3–15

2

- Click the Align Text Left button (Home tab | Paragraph group) to left-align the paragraph (Figure 3–16).

Q&A What if I want to return the paragraph to center alignment?

Click the Center button (Home tab | Paragraph group).

3

- Display Slide 3. Click somewhere in the title text paragraph to position the insertion point in the paragraph to be formatted.

4

- Click the Align Text Right button (Home tab | Paragraph group) to right-align the paragraph.

Figure 3–16

5

- Move the Slide 3 title text placeholder downward so that it displays approximately as shown in Figure 3–17.

Figure 3–17

Other Ways

1. Right-click paragraph, click Align Text Right button on Mini toolbar
2. Right-click paragraph, click Paragraph on shortcut menu, click Indents and Spacing tab (Paragraph dialog box), click Alignment box arrow, click Right, click OK button
3. Click Paragraph Dialog Box Launcher (Home tab | Paragraph group), click Indents and Spacing tab (Paragraph dialog box), click Alignment box arrow, click Right, click OK button
4. Press CTRL+R

To Delete a Slide

The Bird Migration presentation has a blank slide at the end. You decide that you will not use this slide, so you need to remove it from the file. The following steps delete Slide 4 from the presentation.

1

- Right-click the Slide 4 thumbnail in the Slides tab to display the shortcut menu (Figure 3–18).

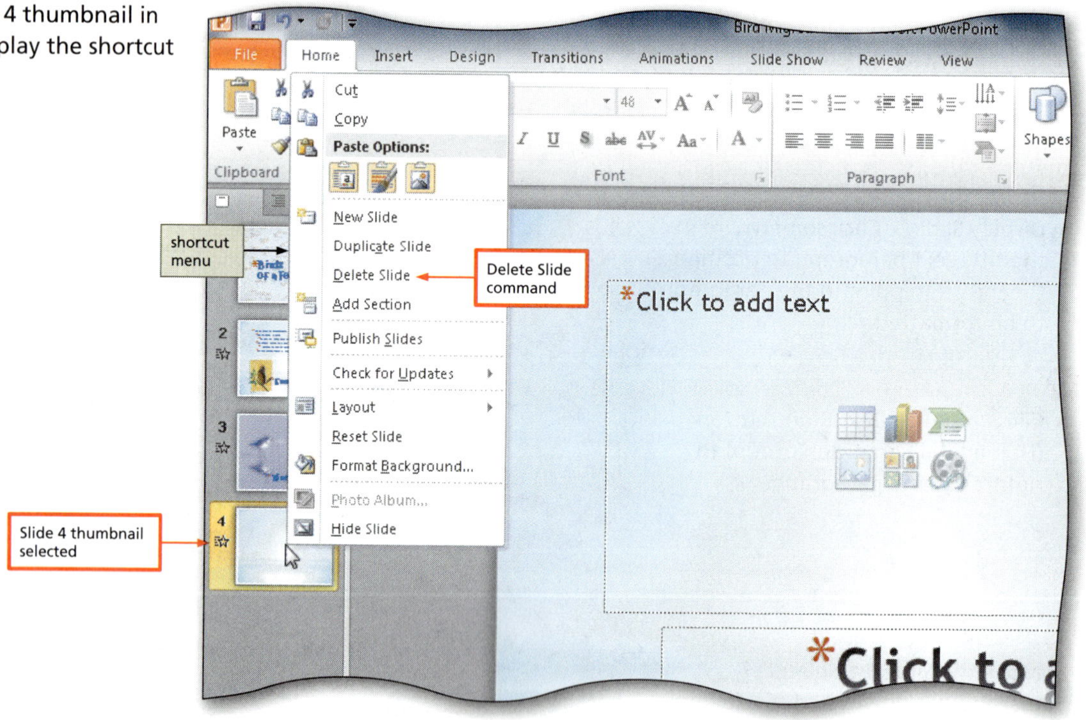

Figure 3–18

2

- Click Delete Slide to delete Slide 4 from the presentation (Figure 3–19).

Figure 3–19

Q&A

Can I delete multiple slides simultaneously?

Yes. If the slides are sequential, click the first slide you want to delete, press and hold the SHIFT key, click the last slide that you want to delete, right-click any selected slide, and then click Delete Slide on the shortcut menu. If the slides are not sequential, press and hold the CTRL key while you click each slide that you want to delete, right-click any selected slide, and then click Delete Slide on the shortcut menu.

Changing Views

You have been using Normal view to create and edit your slides. Once you completed your slides, you reviewed the final products by displaying each slide in Slide Show view, which occupies the full computer screen. You were able to view how the transitions, graphics, and effects will display in an actual presentation before an audience.

PowerPoint has other views to help review a presentation for content, organization, and overall appearance. Slide Sorter view allows you to look at several slides at one time. Reading view is similar to Slide Show view because each slide displays individually, but the slides do not fill the entire screen. Using this view, you easily can control the progression through the slides forward or backward with simple controls at the bottom of the window. Switching between Slide Sorter view, Reading view, and Normal view helps you review your presentation, assess whether the slides have an attractive design and adequate content, and make sure they are organized for the most impact. After reviewing the slides, you can change the view to Normal so that you may continue working on the presentation.

To Change Views

You have made several modifications to the slides, so you should check for balance and consistency. The following steps change the view from Normal view to Slide Sorter view, then Reading view, and back to Normal view.

1

- Click the Slide Sorter view button in the lower right of the PowerPoint window to display the presentation in Slide Sorter view (Figure 3–20).

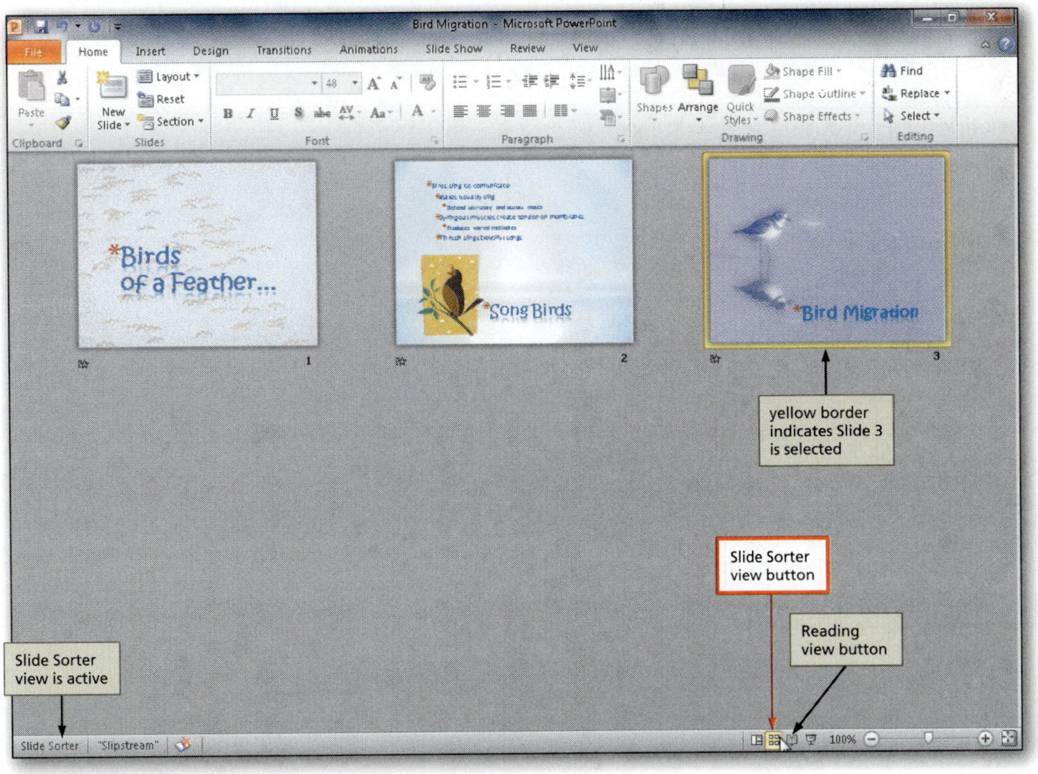

Figure 3–20

Q&A

Why is Slide 3 selected?

It is the current slide in the Slide pane.

2

- Click the Reading view button in the lower right of the PowerPoint window to display Slide 3 of the presentation in Reading view (Figure 3–21).

Figure 3–21

3

- Click the Previous button two times to display Slide 2 and then Slide 1.
- Click the Next button two times to advance through the presentation.
- Click the Menu button to display a menu of commonly used commands (Figure 3–22).

4

- Click End Show to return to Slide Sorter view, which is the view you were using before Reading view.
- Click the Normal view button to display the presentation in Normal view.

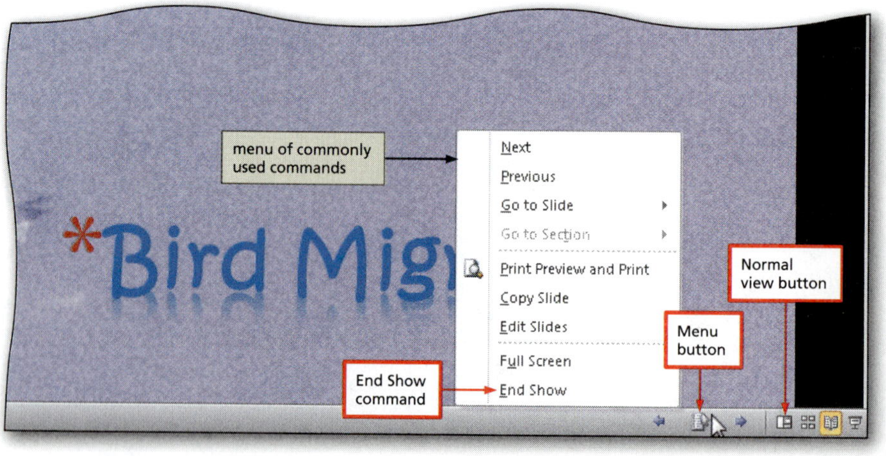

Figure 3–22

Copying and Modifying a Clip

Slide 1 (shown in Figure 3–1a on PPT 139) contains a modified version of a songbird. You may want to modify a clip art picture for various reasons. Many times, you cannot find a clip art picture that precisely illustrates your topic. For example, you want a picture of a red sports car, but the only available clip art picture is painted black.

Occasionally, you may want to remove or change a portion of a clip art picture or you might want to combine two or more clip art pictures. For example, you can use one clip art picture for the background and another picture as the foreground. Other times, you may want to combine a clip art picture with another type of object. In this presentation, the bird picture has a yellow background that is not required to display on the slide, so you will ungroup the clip art picture and remove the background.

Modifying the clip on Slide 1 requires several steps. You first must copy it using the Office Clipboard and then paste it in the desired location. The **Office Clipboard** is a temporary storage location that can hold a maximum of 24 text or graphics items copied from any Office program. The same procedure of copying and pasting objects works for copying and pasting text from one placeholder to another. In the following pages, you will perform these tasks:

1. Copy the clip from Slide 2 to Slide 1.
2. Zoom Slide 1 to examine the clip.
3. Ungroup the clip.
4. Edit and change the clip colors.
5. Delete a clip object.
6. Regroup the clip.

To Copy a Clip from One Slide to Another

The bird clip on Slide 2 also can display in a modified form on the title slide. The following steps copy this slide element from Slide 2 to Slide 1.

1

- Display Slide 2. With the Home tab displayed, click the bird clip to select it and then click the Copy button (Home tab | Clipboard group) (Figure 3–23).

Q&A Why are some words on Slide 2 underlined with red wavy lines?

Those words are not in PowerPoint's main or custom dictionaries, so PowerPoint indicates that they may be misspelled. For example, the word, Syringeal, is spelled correctly, but is not in PowerPoint's dictionaries.

2

- Display Slide 1 and then click the Paste button (Home tab | Clipboard group) to insert the bird clip into the title slide.

Q&A Is the clip deleted from the Office Clipboard when I paste it into the slide?

No.

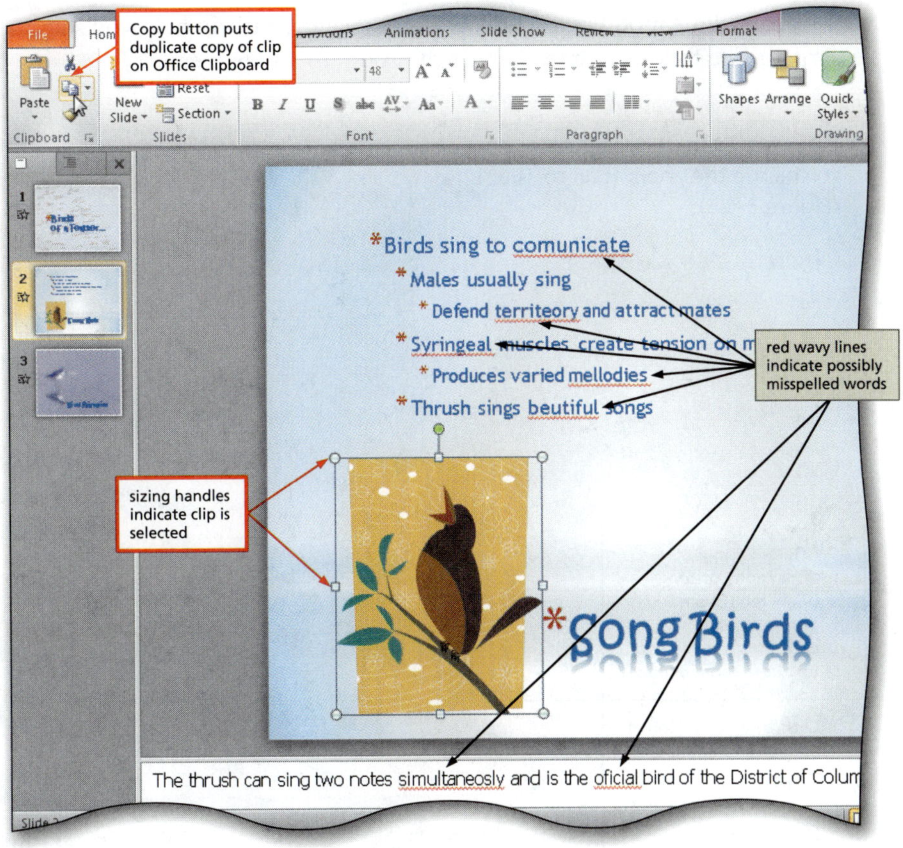

Figure 3–23

3

- Decrease the clip size by dragging one of the corner sizing handles inward until the clip is the size shown in Figure 3–24. Drag the clip to the location shown in this figure.

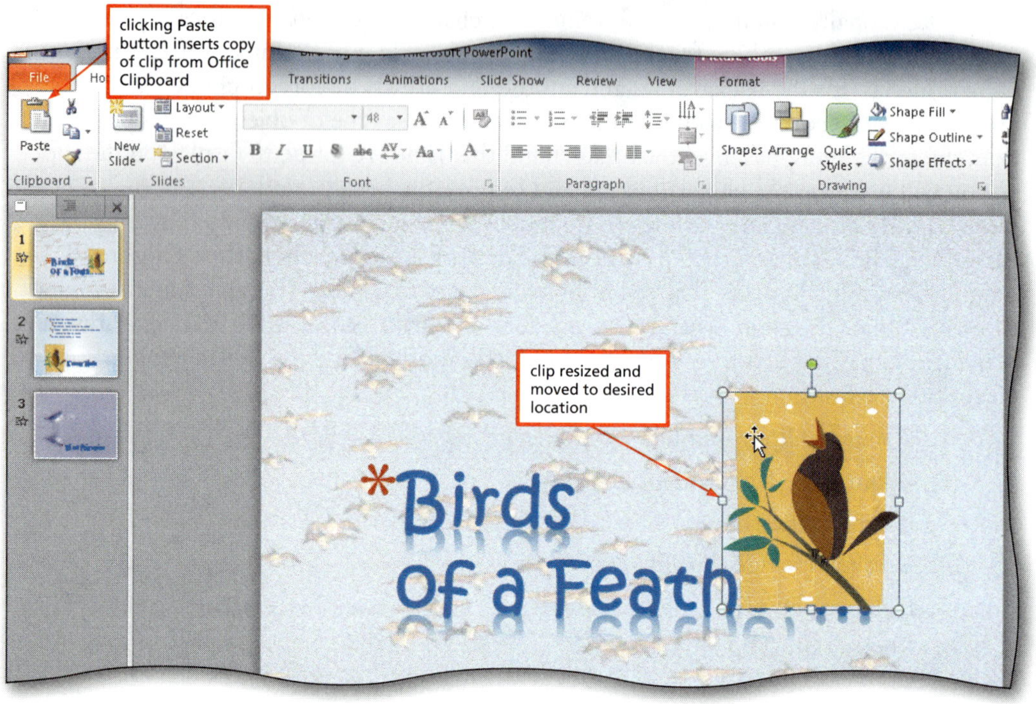

Figure 3–24

To Zoom a Slide

You will be modifying small areas of the clip, so it will help you select the relevant pieces if the graphic is enlarged. The following step changes the zoom to 150 percent.

1

- Drag the Zoom slider to the right to change the zoom level to 150% (Figure 3–25).

Figure 3–25

Other Ways

1. Click Zoom button (View tab | Zoom group), change percentage in Percent text box (Zoom dialog box), click OK button
2. Click Zoom In button at end of slider
3. Click Zoom level on left side of slider, change percentage in Percent text box (Zoom dialog box), click OK button

To Ungroup a Clip

The next step is to ungroup the bird clip on Slide 1. When you **ungroup** a clip art picture, PowerPoint breaks it into its component objects. A clip may be composed of a few individual objects or several complex groups of objects. These groups can be ungrouped repeatedly until they decompose into individual objects. Because a clip art picture is a collection of complex groups of objects, you may need to ungroup a complex object into less complex objects before being able to modify a specific object. When you ungroup a clip and click the Yes button in the Microsoft PowerPoint dialog box, PowerPoint converts the clip to a PowerPoint object. The following steps ungroup a clip.

1

- With the bird clip selected, click Format on the Ribbon to display the Picture Tools Format tab.
- Click the Group button (Picture Tools Format tab | Arrange group) to display the Group menu (Figure 3–26).

Q&A Why does the Group button look different on my screen?

Your monitor is set to a different resolution. See the Office 2010 and Windows 7 chapter in this book for an explanation of screen resolution and the appearance of the Ribbon.

Figure 3–26

2

- Click Ungroup on the Group menu to display the Microsoft PowerPoint dialog box (Figure 3–27).

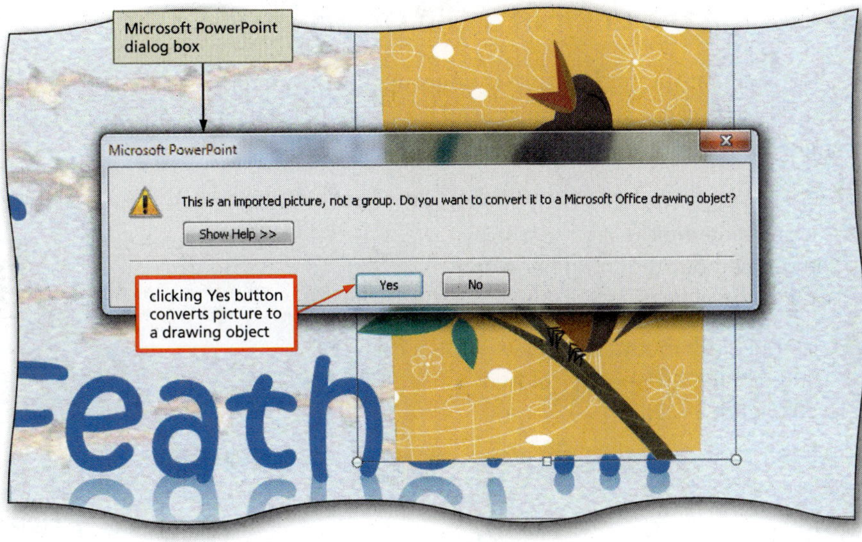

Figure 3–27

3

- Click the Yes button (Microsoft PowerPoint dialog box) to convert the clip to a Microsoft Office drawing.

Q&A What happens if I click the No button?

The clip will remain displayed on the slide as a clip art picture and will not ungroup.

- Click Format on the Ribbon to display the Drawing Tools Format tab. Click the Group button (Drawing Tools Format tab | Arrange group) and then click Ungroup again.

Q&A Why does the Drawing Tools Format tab show different options this time?

The clip has become a drawing object, so tools related to drawing now display.

- With the Drawing Tools Format tab displayed, click the Group button (Drawing Tools Format tab | Arrange group), and then click Ungroup a third time to display the objects that constitute the bird clip (Figure 3–28).

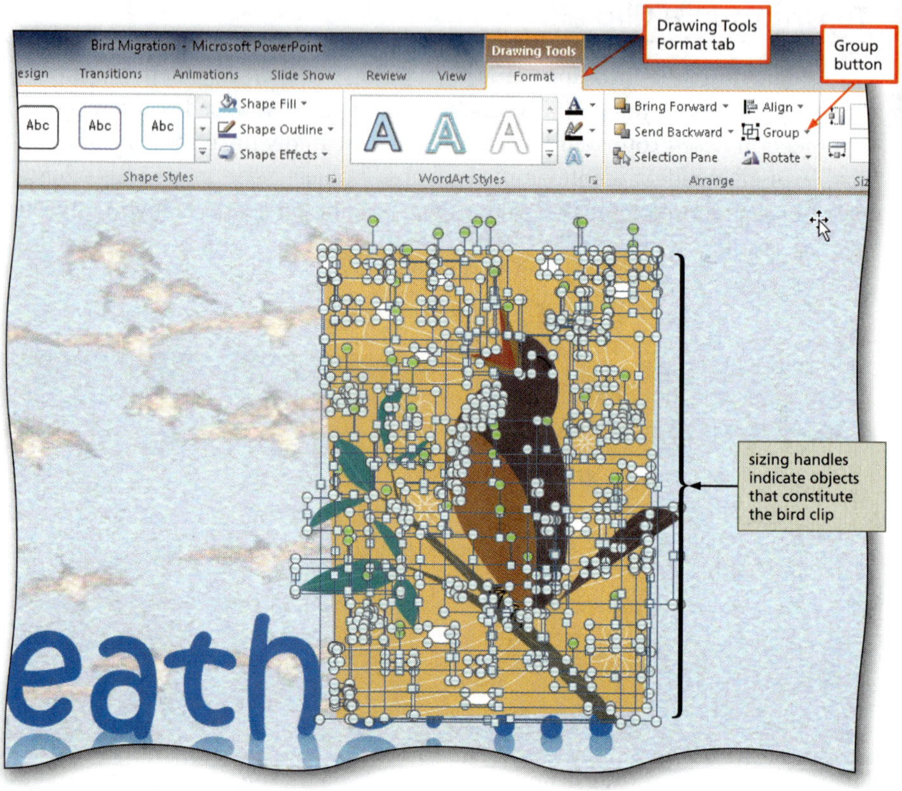

Figure 3–28

Q&A Why do all those circles and squares display in the clip?

The circles and squares are sizing handles for each of the clip's objects, which resemble pieces of a jigsaw puzzle.

Other Ways
1. Right-click clip, point to Group on shortcut menu, click Ungroup
2. Press SHIFT+CTRL+G

To Change the Color of a Clip Object

Now that the bird picture is ungrouped, you can change the color of the objects. The clip is composed of hundreds of objects, so you must exercise care when selecting the correct object to modify. The following steps change the color of the bird's mouth and the leaves.

1

- Click outside the clip area to display the clip without the sizing handles around the objects.
- Click the bird's mouth to display sizing handles around the colored area (Figure 3–29).

Q&A What if I selected a different area by mistake?

Click outside the clip and retry.

Figure 3–29

2

- Click the Shape Fill button arrow (Drawing Tools Format tab | Shape Styles group) to display the Shape Fill gallery.
- Point to Yellow in the Standard Colors area (fourth color) to display a live preview of the mouth color (Figure 3–30).

Experiment

- Point to various colors and watch the bird's mouth color change.

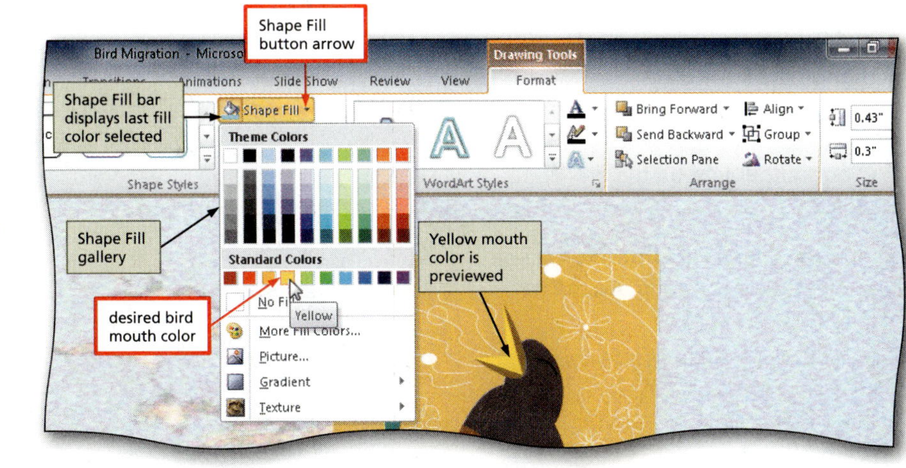

Figure 3–30

3

- Click the color Yellow to change the bird's mouth color.

Q&A

Why is the bar under the Shape Fill button now yellow?

The button displays the last fill color selected.

- Click a leaf on the branch to display the sizing handles around the colored area (Figure 3–31).

Figure 3–31

4

- Click the Shape Fill button arrow (Drawing Tools Format tab | Shape Styles group) and then point to Green, Accent 3 in the Theme Colors area (seventh color in first row) to display a live preview of the color of the selected leaf in the graphic (Figure 3–32).

Experiment

- Point to various colors and watch the leaf color change.

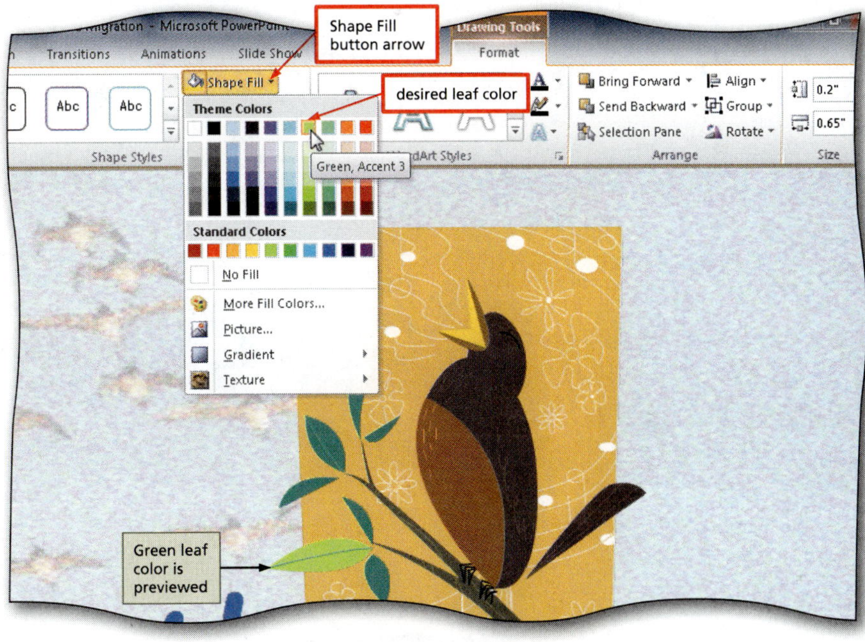

Figure 3–32

5

- Click the Green, Accent 3 color to change the leaf color.

6

- Click another leaf on the branch to select it.
- Click the Shape Fill button to change the leaf color to Green, Accent 3 (Figure 3–33).

Q&A Why did I not need to click the Shape Fill button arrow to select this color?

PowerPoint uses the last fill color selected. This color displays in the bar under the bucket icon on the button.

Figure 3–33

7

- Repeat Step 6 until all the leaves have been recolored (Figure 3–34).

Q&A Can I open the Microsoft Clip Organizer when I am not using PowerPoint?

Yes. On the Start menu, point to All Programs, point to Microsoft Office, point to Microsoft Office 2010 Tools, and then click Microsoft Clip Organizer.

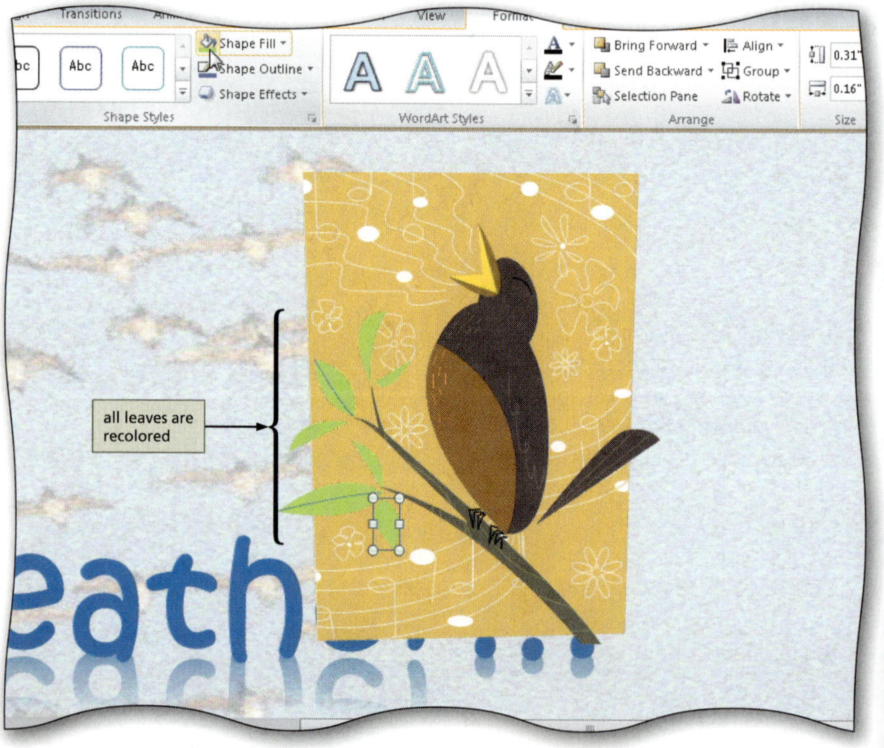

Figure 3–34

Other Ways

1. Right-click object, click Format Shape on shortcut menu, click Color button

To Delete a Clip Object

With the bird mouth and leaf colors changed, you want to delete the gold background object. The following steps delete this object.

1

- Click the background in any area where the gold color displays to select this object (Figure 3–35).

Q&A Can I select multiple objects so I can delete them simultaneously?

Yes. While pressing the SHIFT key, click the unwanted elements to select them.

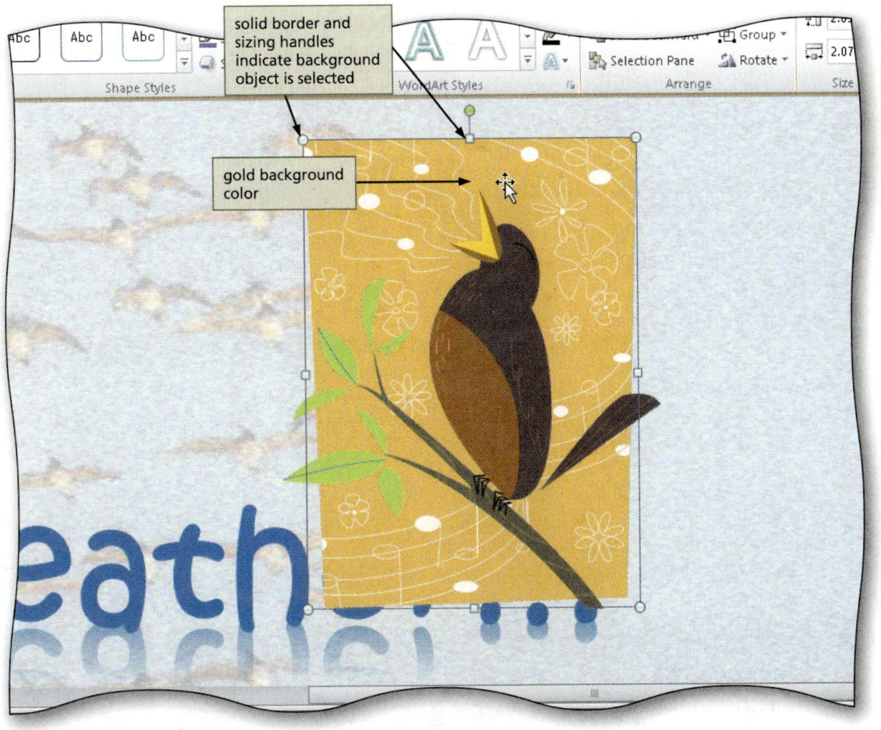

Figure 3–35

2

- Press the DELETE key to delete this object (Figure 3–36).

Q&A Should the white musical staff display on the slide?

Yes. It is part of the bird clip.

Figure 3–36

To Regroup Objects

When you ungrouped the bird clip, you eliminated the embedding data or linking information that tied all the individual pieces together. If you attempt to move or size this clip now, you might encounter difficulties because it consists of hundreds of objects and is no longer one unified piece. Dragging or sizing affects only a selected object, not the entire collection of objects, so you must use caution when objects are not completely regrouped. All of the ungrouped objects in the bird clip must be regrouped so they are not accidentally moved or manipulated. The following steps regroup these objects into one object.

1

- With the clip selected, click the Drawing Tools Format tab and then click the Group button (Drawing Tools Format tab | Arrange group) to display the Group menu (Figure 3–37).

2

- Click Regroup to combine all the objects.

3

- Use the Zoom slider to change the zoom level to 69%.

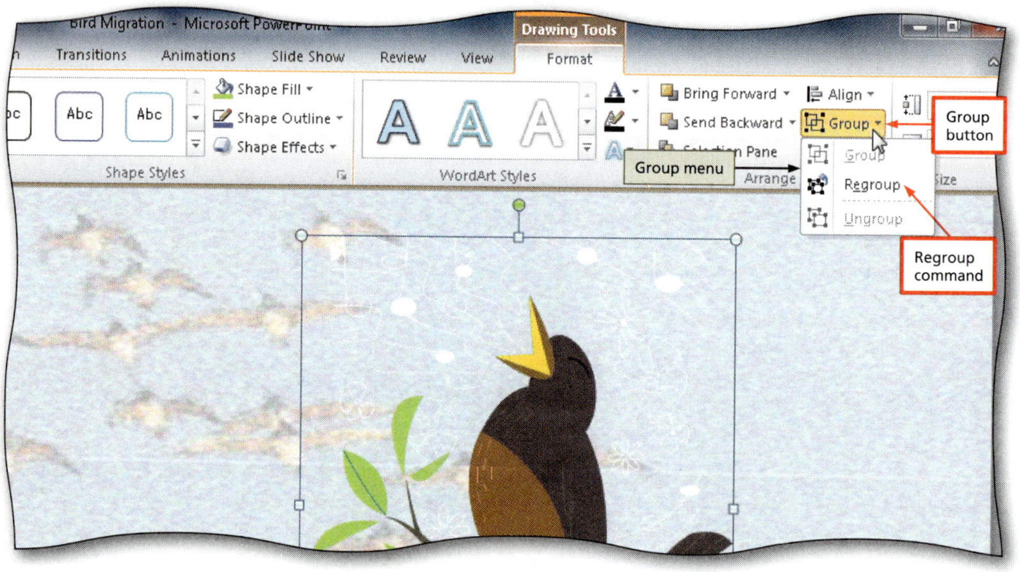

Figure 3–37

Other Ways

1. Right-click clip, point to Group on shortcut menu, click Regroup
2. Press CTRL+G

Plan Ahead

Use multimedia selectively.

PowerPoint makes it easy to insert multimedia into a presentation. Well-produced video clips add value when they help explain a procedure or show movement that cannot be captured in a photograph. Music can help calm or energize an audience, when appropriate. A sound, such as applause when a correct answer is given, can emphasize an action. Before you insert these files on a slide, however, consider whether they really add any value to your overall slide show. If you are inserting them just because you can, you might want to reconsider your decision. Audiences quickly tire of extraneous sounds and movement on slides, and they will find these media clips annoying. Keep in mind that the audience's attention should focus primarily on the presenter; extraneous or inappropriate media files may divert their attention and, in turn, decrease the quality of the presentation.

Break Point: If you wish to take a break, this is a good place to do so. Be sure to save the Bird Migration file again and then you can quit PowerPoint. To resume at a later time, start PowerPoint, open the file called Bird Migration, and continue following the steps from this location forward.

Adding Media to Slides

Media files can enrich a presentation if they are used correctly. Movies files can have two formats: digital video produced with a camera and editing software or animated GIF (Graphics Interchange Format) files composed of multiple images combined into a single file. Sound files can be from the Microsoft Clip Organizer, files stored on your computer, or an audio track on a CD. To hear the sounds, you need a sound card and speakers on your system.

In the following pages, you will perform these tasks:

1. Insert a video file into Slide 3.
2. Trim the video file so only the final few seconds play.
3. Add video options that determine the clip's appearance and playback.
4. Insert audio files.
5. Add audio options that determine the clips' appearance and playback.
6. Add a video style to the Slide 3 clip.
7. Resize the video.
8. Insert a movie clip into Slide 1.

To Insert a Video File

Slide 3 has the title, Bird Migration, and you have a video clip that is composed of many scenes featuring various animals and birds. A short segment of this clip shows a flock of birds on a beach, and you want to use only this part of the clip in your presentation. PowerPoint allows you to insert this clip into your slide and then trim the file so that just a portion will play when you preview the clip or run the slide show. This clip is available on the Data Files for Students. See the inside back cover of this book for instructions on downloading the Data Files for Students, or contact your instructor for more information about accessing the required file. The following steps insert this video clip into Slide 3.

1

- Display Slide 3 and then display the Insert tab. With your USB flash drive connected to one of the computer's USB ports, click the Insert Video button (Insert tab | Media group) to display the Insert Video dialog box.
- If the list of files and folders on the selected USB flash drive are not displayed in the Insert Video dialog box, double-click your USB flash drive to display them.
- Click Wildlife to select the file (Figure 3–38).

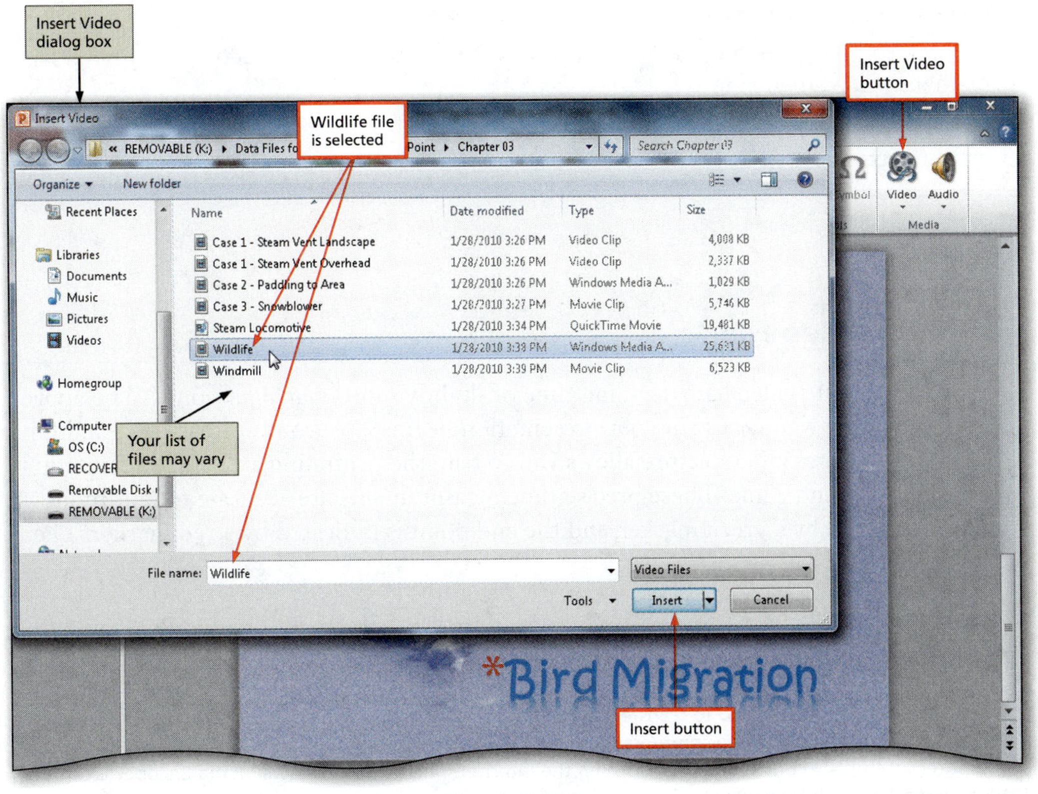

Figure 3–38

2

- Click the Insert button (Insert Video dialog box) to insert the movie clip into Slide 3 (Figure 3–39).

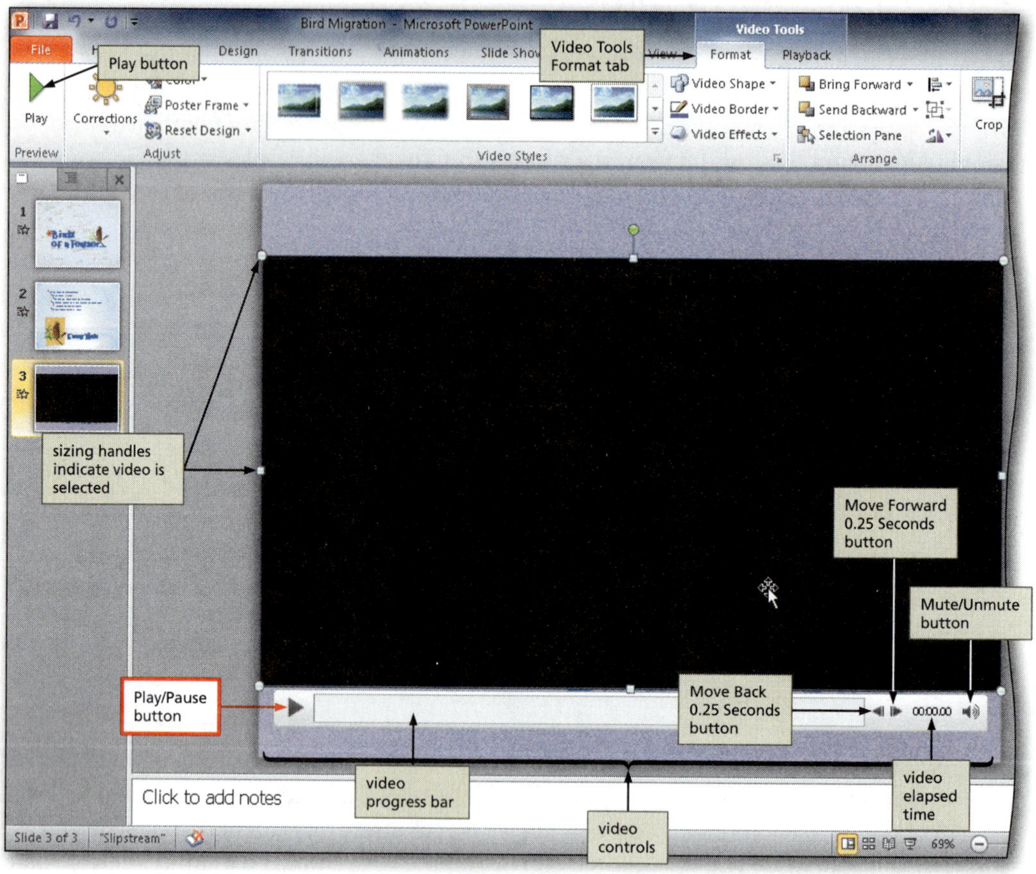

Figure 3–39

Q&A

Can I adjust the color of a video clip?

Yes. You correct the brightness and contrast, and you also recolor a video clip using the same methods you learned in this chapter to color a picture.

To Trim a Video File

The Wildlife video has a running time of slightly more than 30 seconds. The approximately six-second segment that you want to use in your presentation begins 24 seconds into the file and finishes at the end of the clip. PowerPoint's **Trim Video** feature allows you to trim the beginning and end of your clip by designating your desired Start Time and End Time. These precise time measurements are accurate to one-thousandth of a second. The start point is indicated by a green marker, and the end point is indicated by a red marker. The following steps trim the Wildlife video clip.

BTW

Using Codecs

Digital media file sizes often are quite large, so video and audio content developers use a codec (**co**mpressor/**dec**ompressor) to reduce the required storage space and to transfer the files across the Internet quickly and smoothly. Your computer can play any compressed file if the specific codec used to compress the file is available on your computer. If the codec is not installed or is not recognized, your computer attempts to download this file from the Internet. Microsoft Windows Media Encoder is a free program that makes some media files compatible with PowerPoint.

1

- With the video clip selected on Slide 3, click the Play/Pause button to play the entire video.

Q&A Can I play the video by clicking the Play button in the Preview group?

Yes. This Play button plays the entire clip. You may prefer to click the Play/Pause button displayed in the Video Controls to stop the video and examine one of the frames.

- Click Playback on the Ribbon to display the Video Tools Playback tab. Click the Trim Video button (Editing group) to display the Trim Video dialog box (Figure 3–40).

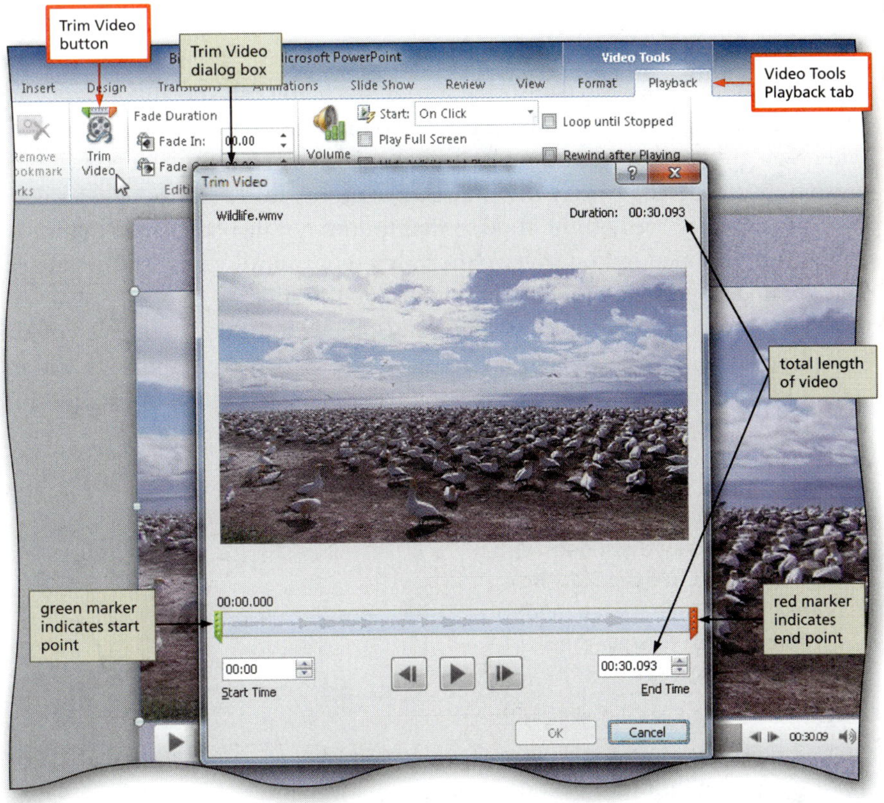

Figure 3–40

2

- Point to the start point, which is indicated by the green marker on the left side, so that the mouse pointer changes to a two-headed arrow.
- Drag the green marker to the right until the Start Time is 00:24:634 (Figure 3–41).

Q&A Can I specify the start or end times without dragging the markers?

Yes. You can enter the time in the Start Time or End Time boxes, or you can click the Start Time or End Time box arrows. You also can click the Next Frame and Previous Frame buttons (Trim Video dialog box).

Q&A How would I indicate an end point if I want the clip to end at a time other than at the end of the clip?

You would drag the red marker to the left until the desired end time displays.

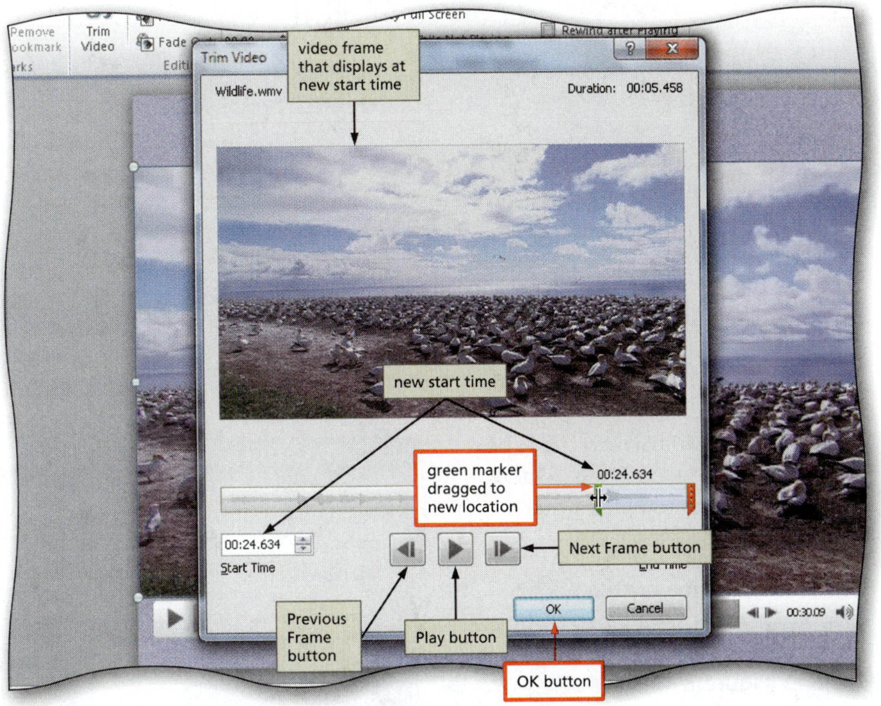

Figure 3–41

3

- Click the Play button (Trim Video dialog box) to review the shortened video clip.
- Click the OK button to set the Start Time and End Time and to close the Trim Video dialog box.

Other Ways

1. Right-click clip, click Trim Video on shortcut menu

To Add Video Options

Once the video clip is inserted into Slide 3, you can specify options that affect how the file is displayed and played. For example, you can have the video play automatically when the slide is displayed, or you can click the slide when you are ready to start the playback. You also can have the video fill the entire slide, which is referred to as **full screen**. If you decide to play the slide show automatically and have it display full screen, you can drag the video frame to the gray area off the slide so that it does not display briefly before going to full screen. You can select the Loop until Stopped option to have the video repeat until you click the next slide, or you can choose to not have the video frame display on the slide until you click the slide.

If your video clip has recorded sounds, the volume controls give you the option to set how loudly this audio will play. They also allow you to mute the sound so that your audience will hear no background noise or music.

The following steps add the options of playing the video full screen automatically when Slide 3 is displayed and also mutes the background music recorded on the video clip.

1

- If necessary, click Playback on the Ribbon to display the Video Tools Playback tab. Click the Start box (Video Tools Playback tab | Video Options group) to view the Start menu (Figure 3–42).

Q&A What does the On Click option do?

The video clip would begin playing when a presenter clicks the slide during the slide show.

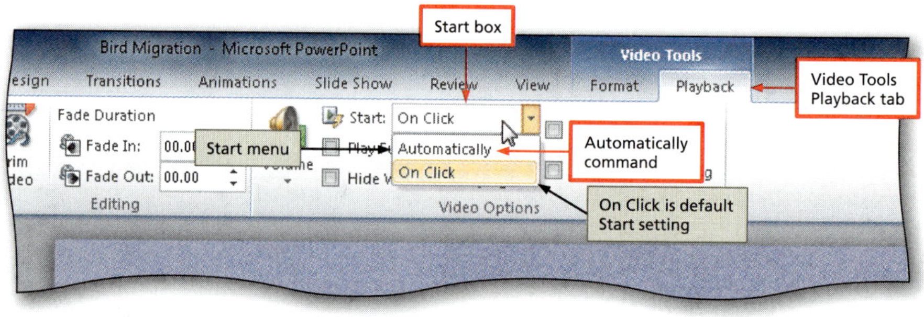

Figure 3–42

2

- Click Automatically in the Start menu (Figure 3–43).

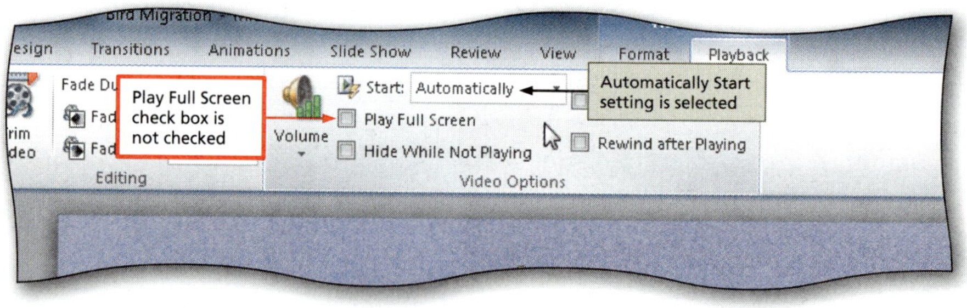

Figure 3–43

3

- Click the Play Full Screen check box (Video Tools Playback tab | Video Options group) to place a check mark in it.
- Click the Volume button (Video Tools Playback tab | Video Options group) to display the Volume menu (Figure 3–44).

4

- Click Mute in the Volume menu.

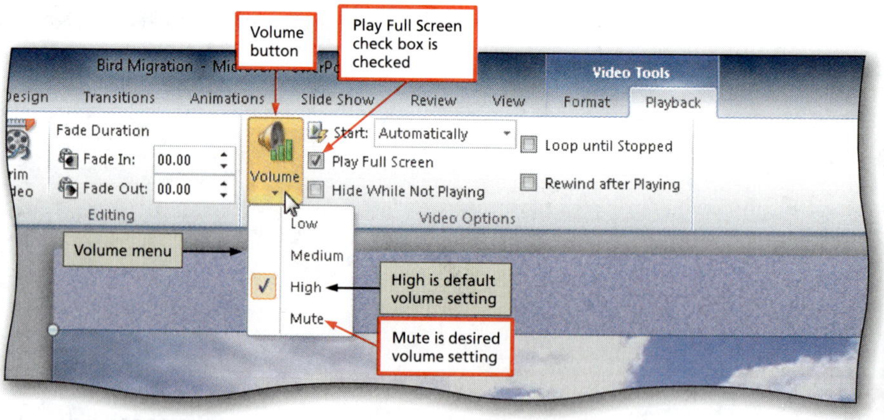

Figure 3–44

To Insert an Audio File

Avid bird watchers listen to the songs and calls birds make to each other. The Microsoft Clip Organizer and Office.com have several of these sounds in audio files that you can download and insert into your presentation. Once these audio files are inserted into a slide, you can add options that specify how long and how loudly the clip will play; these options are similar to the video options you just selected for the Wildlife video clip. The following steps insert an audio clip into Slide 3.

1

- With Slide 3 displaying, click Insert on the Ribbon to display the Insert tab and then click the Insert Audio button arrow (Insert tab | Media group) to display the Insert Audio menu (Figure 3–45).

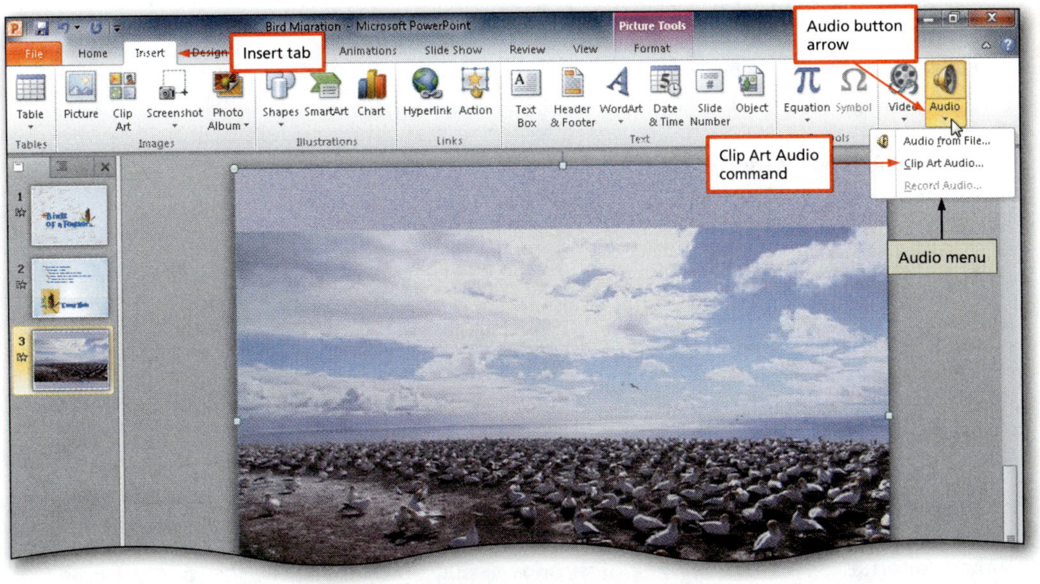

Figure 3–45

2

- Click Clip Art Audio in the Insert Audio menu to open the Clip Art task pane.
- Click the 'Results should be' box arrow and then click the 'All media types' check box to remove the check mark from each of the four types of media files.
- Click the Audio check box to place a check mark in it (Figure 3–46).

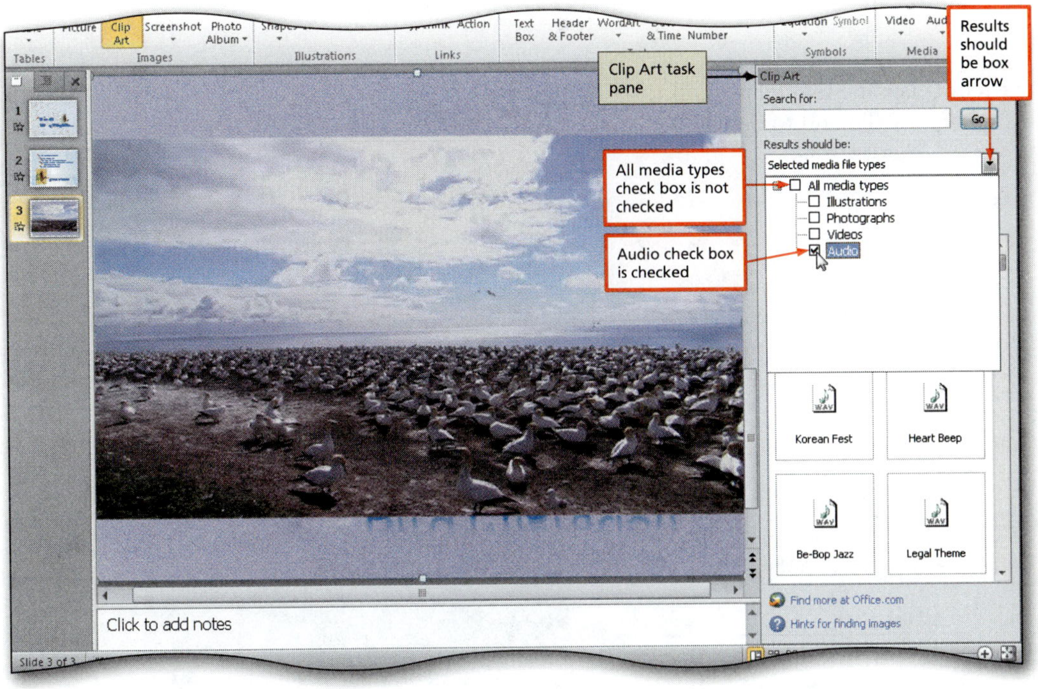

Figure 3–46

Q&A

Can I use this technique to search solely for videos, photographs, or illustrations?

Yes. You also can search for a combination of these file types, such as both video and audio files.

3

- If necessary, delete any letters that are present in the Search for text box and then type `Glade Birds` in the Search for text box. If necessary, click the 'Include Office.com content' check box to select it.
- Click the Go button so that the Microsoft Clip Organizer will search for and display all clips having the keyword or title, Glade Birds.

4

- Point to the Glade Birds clip to display the properties of this file (Figure 3–47).

Q&A What if the Glade Birds audio clip is not shown in my Clip Art task pane?

Select a similar clip. Your clips may be different depending on the clips installed on your computer and if you have an active Internet connection.

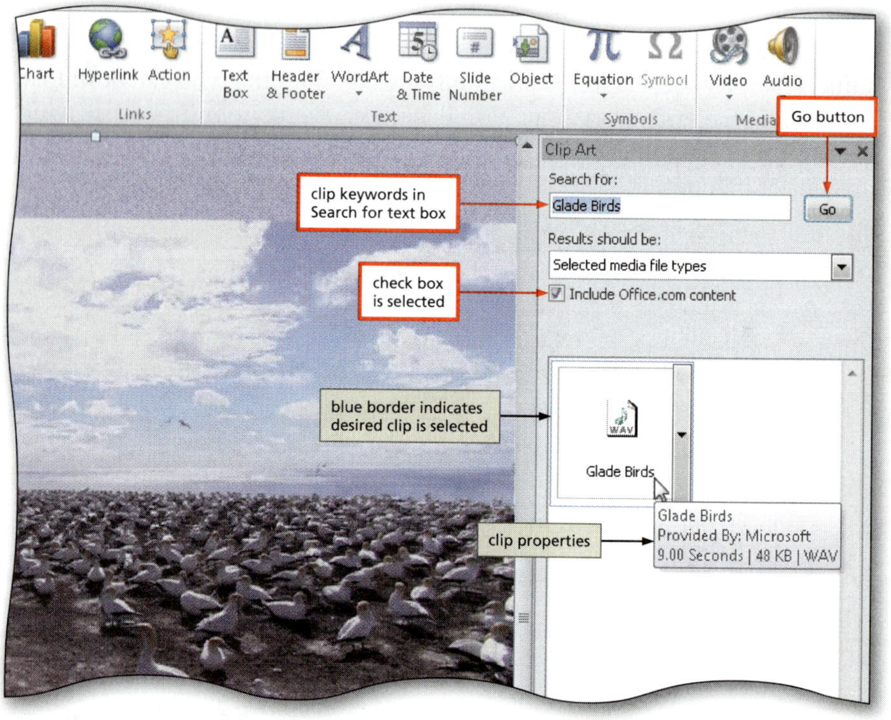

Figure 3–47

Q&A What are the properties associated with this clip?

The properties include the number of seconds of playing time, the file size, and the type of audio file. This file is a **Windows waveform (.wav)** file, which uses a standard format to encode and communicate music and sound between computers, music synthesizers, and instruments.

5

- Right-click the Glade Birds clip to select the clip and to display the Edit menu (Figure 3–48).

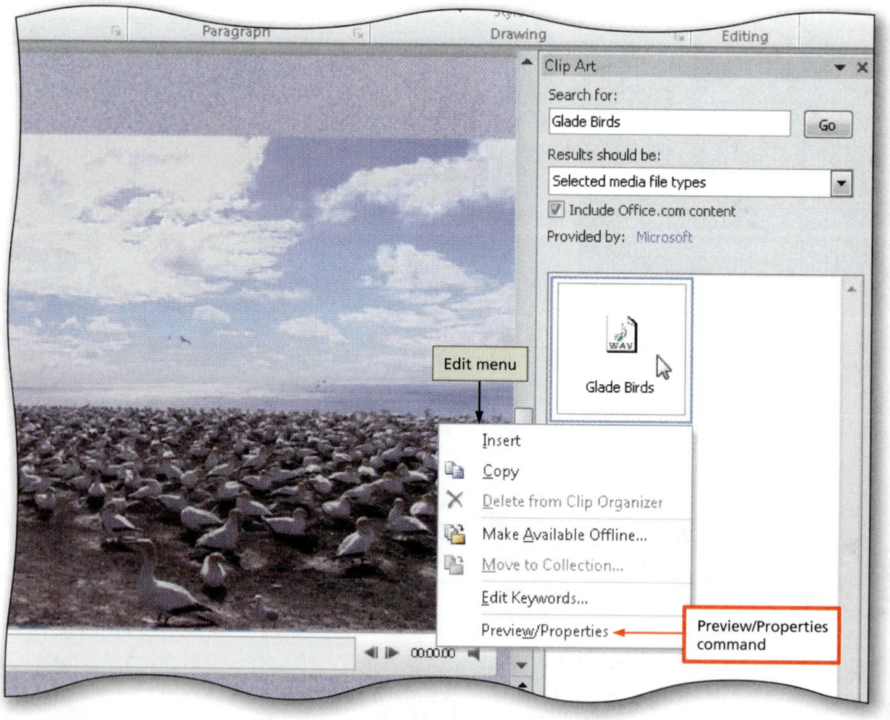

Figure 3–48

6

- Click Preview/ Properties to display the Preview/Properties dialog box and to hear the clip (Figure 3–49).

Q&A What are the words listed in the Keywords box?

Those words are the search terms associated with the file. If you enter any of those words in the Search for text box, this audio file would display in the results list.

Q&A Can I preview the clip again?

Yes. Click the Play button in the Preview/ Properties dialog box.

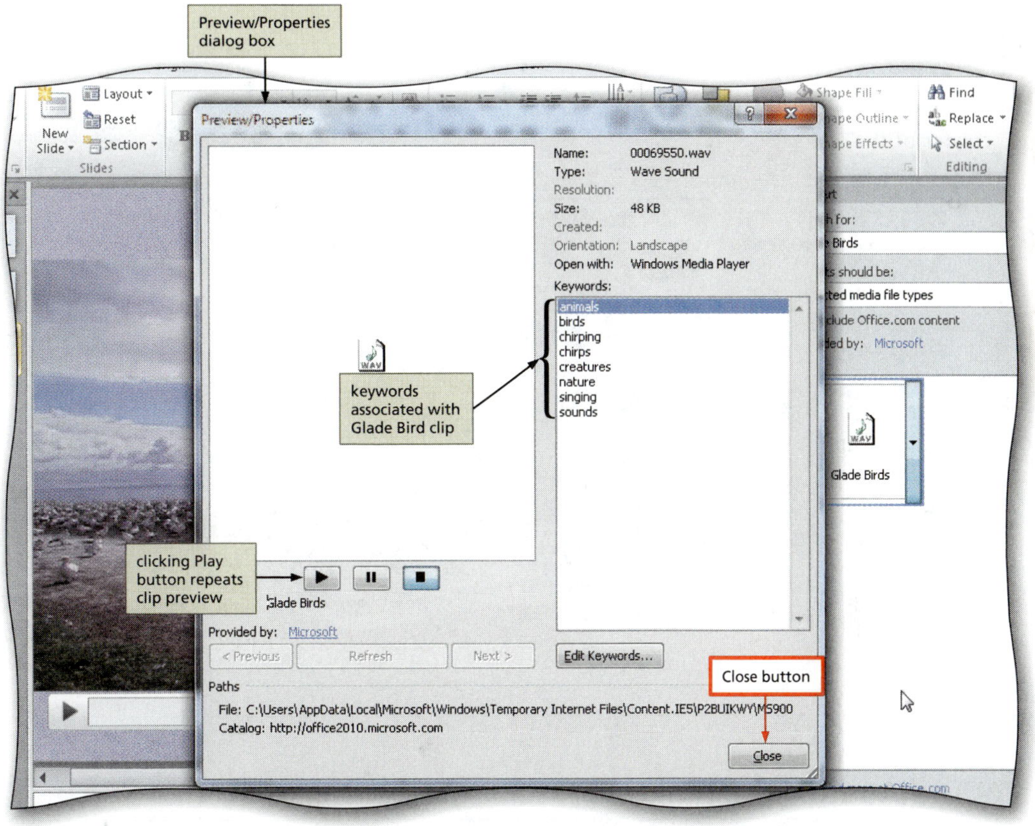

Figure 3–49

7

- Click the Close button (Preview/Properties dialog box) to close the dialog box.
- Click Glade Birds in the results list (Clip Art task pane) to insert that file into Slide 3 (Figure 3–50).

Q&A Why does a sound icon display in the video?

The icon indicates an audio file is inserted.

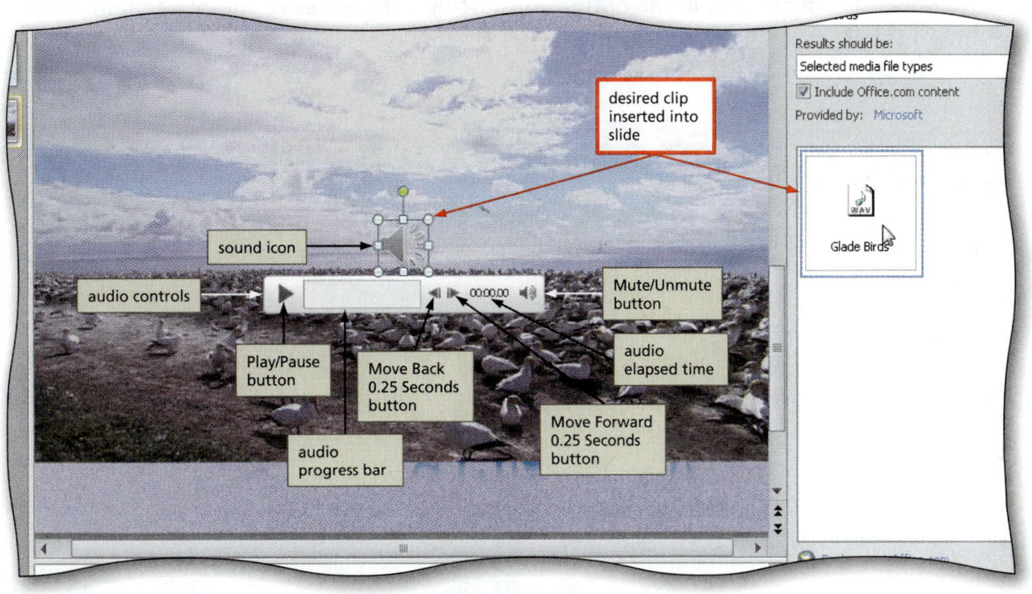

Figure 3–50

Q&A Do the Audio Controls buttons have the same functions as the Video Controls buttons that displayed when I inserted the Wildlife clip?

Yes. The controls include playing and pausing the sound, moving back or forward 0.25 seconds, audio progress, elapsed time, and muting or unmuting the sound.

8

- Drag the sound icon to the upper-left corner of the slide (Figure 3–51).

Q&A Must I move the icon on the slide?

No. Although your audience will not see the icon when you run the slide show, it is easier for you to see the media elements when they are separated on the slide rather than stacked on top of each other.

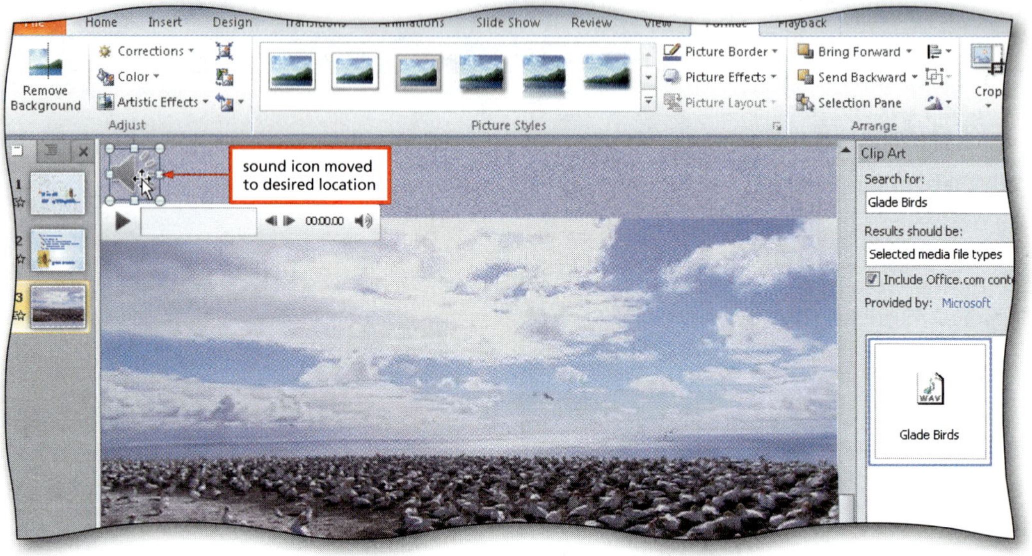

Figure 3–51

To Add Audio Options

Once an audio clip is inserted into a slide, you can specify options that control playback and appearance. As with the video options you applied to the Wildlife clip, the audio clip can play either automatically or when clicked, it can repeat the clip while a particular slide is displayed, and you can drag the sound icon off the slide and set the volume.

The following steps add the options of starting automatically and playing until the slide no longer is displayed, hiding the sound icon on the slide, and increasing the volume.

1

- Click Playback on the Ribbon to display the Audio Tools Playback tab. Click the Start box (Audio Tools Playback tab | Audio Options group) to display the Start box menu (Figure 3–52).

2

- Click Automatically in the Start menu.

Q&A Does the On Click option function the same way for an audio clip as On Click does for a video clip?

Yes. If you were to select On Click, the sound would begin playing only after the presenter clicks Slide 1 during a presentation.

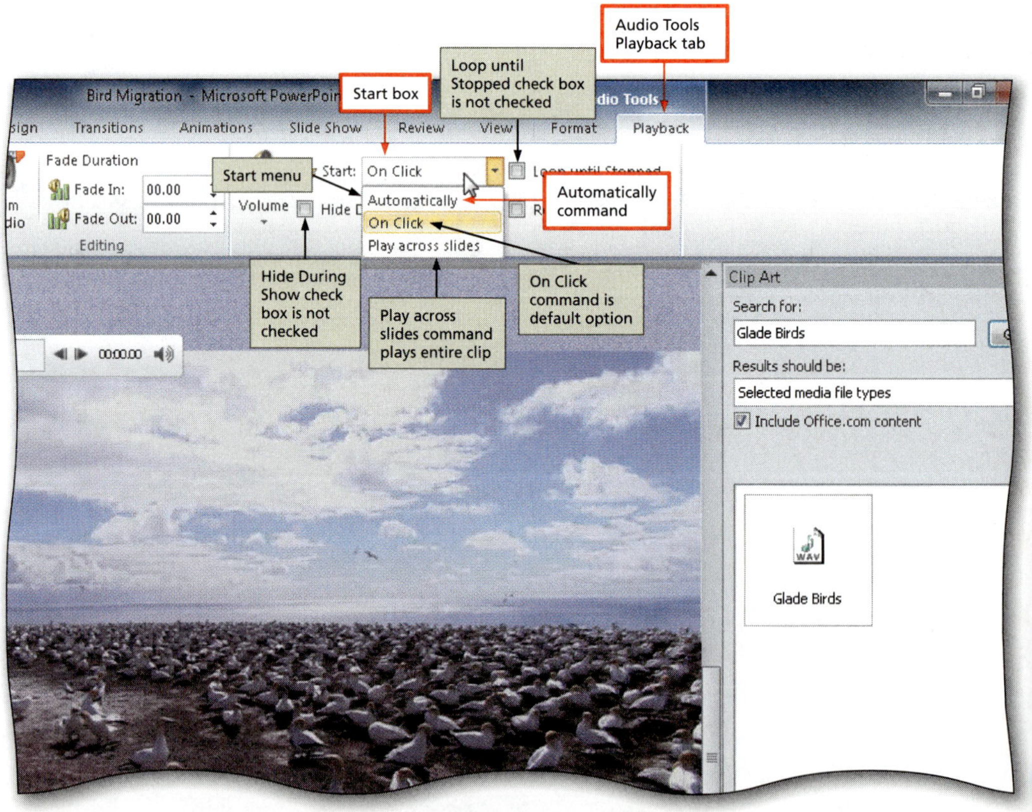

Figure 3–52

3

- Click the Loop until Stopped check box (Audio Tools Playback tab | Audio Options group) to place a check mark in it.

Q&A What is the difference between the Loop until Stopped option and the Play across slides option?

The audio clip in the Loop until Stopped option repeats for as long as one slide is displayed. In contrast, the Play across slides option clip would play only once, but it would continue to play while other slides in the presentation are displayed. Once the end of the clip is reached, the sound would end and not repeat.

4

- Click the Hide During Show check box (Video Tools Playback tab | Audio Options group) to place a check mark in it (Figure 3–53).

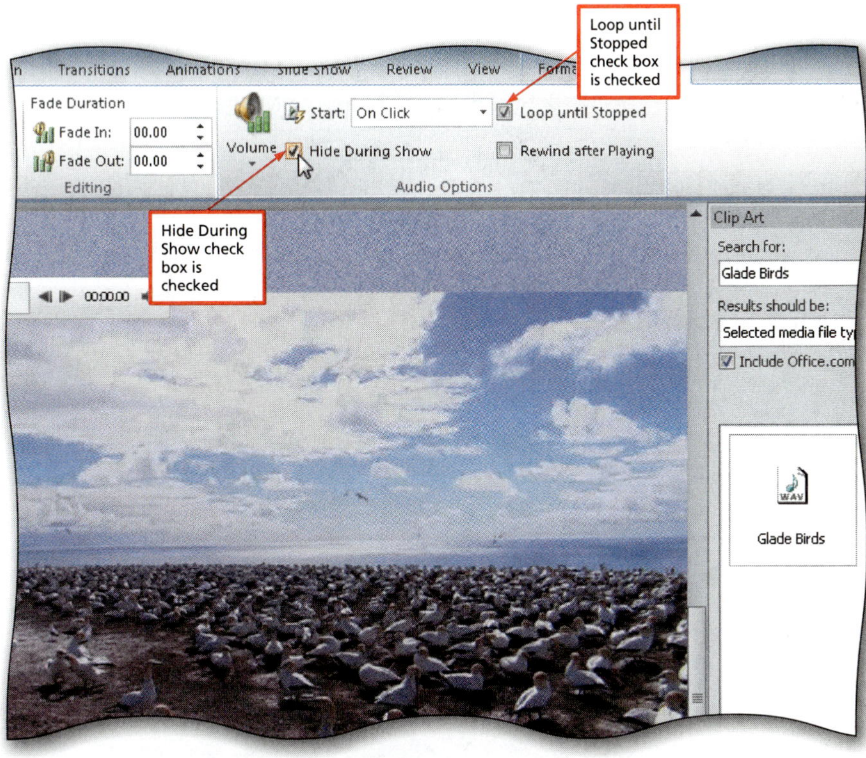

Figure 3–53

Q&A Why would I want the icon to display during the show?

If you had selected the On Click start option, you would need to find this icon on the slide and click it to start playing the clip.

To Insert an Additional Audio File and Set Options

Having an audio clip play when Slide 1 is displayed would add interest and help set the tone of the presentation. Only one bird appears on that slide, and it appears to be singing heartily. A single bird singing would coordinate nicely with this clip art image. The following steps insert a songbird audio clip into Slide 1 and set playback options.

1. Display Slide 1, delete any letters that are present in the Search for text box, and then type `Birds at dawn` in the Search for text box (Clip Art task pane), and search for this audio clip.
2. Insert the Birds at dawn clip into Slide 1 and then drag the sound icon to the lower-left corner of the slide.
3. Close the Clip Art task pane.
4. Display the Audio Tools Playback tab. Click the Start box (Audio Tools Playback tab | Audio Options group) and then click Automatically in the Start menu.
5. Click the Loop until Stopped check box (Audio Tools Playback tab | Audio Options group) to place a check mark in it.

BTW

Playing Audio Continuously

You can play one audio file throughout an entire presentation instead of only when one individual slide is displayed. When you select the 'Play across slides' option in the Start box (Audio Tools Playback tab | Audio Options group), the audio clip will play continuously as you advance through the slides in your presentation. If you select this option, be certain the length of the clip exceeds the total time you will display all slides in your slide show.

6. Click the Hide During Show check box (Audio Tools Playback tab | Audio Options group).

7. Click the Volume button (Audio Tools Playback tab | Audio Options group) and then change the volume to Medium (Figure 3–54).

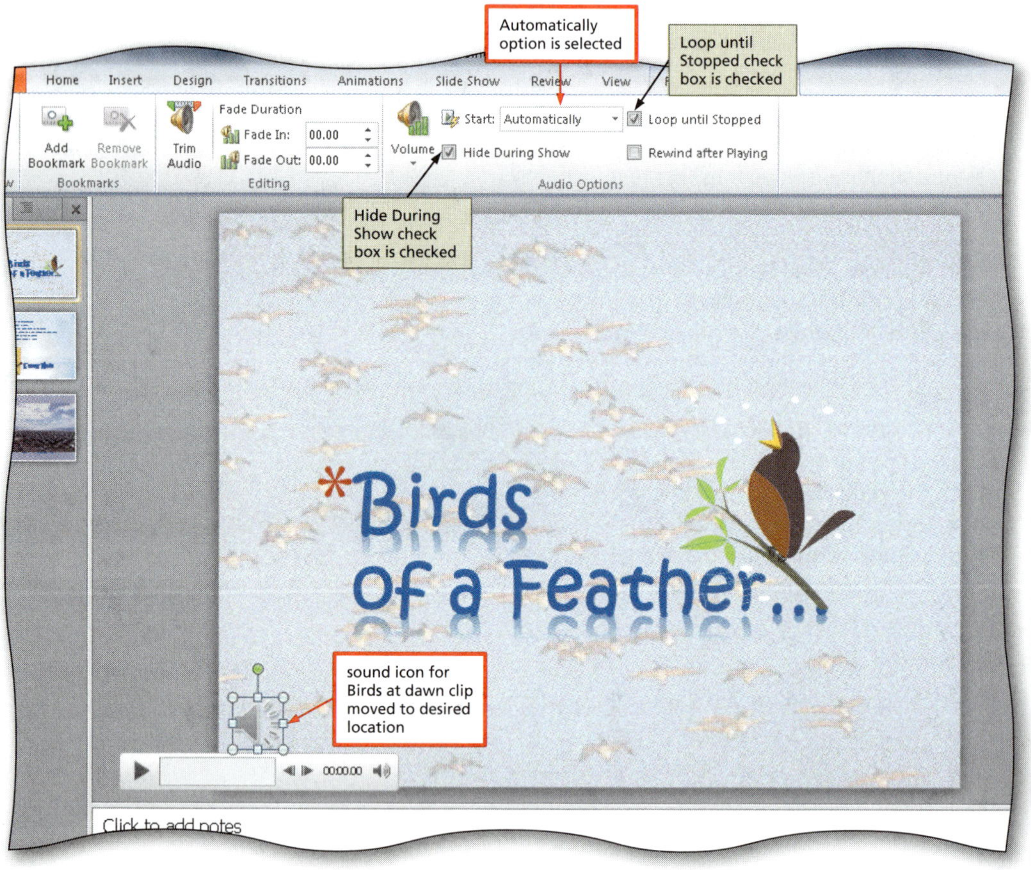

Figure 3–54

To Add a Video Style

The Wildlife video clip on Slide 3 displays full screen when it is playing, but you can increase the visual appeal of the clip when it is not playing by applying a video style. The video styles are similar to the picture styles you applied in PowerPoint Chapter 2 and include various shapes, angles, borders, and reflections. The following steps apply a video style to the Wildlife clip on Slide 3.

1

- Display Slide 3 and select the video. Click Format on the Ribbon to display the Video Tools Format tab (Figure 3–55).

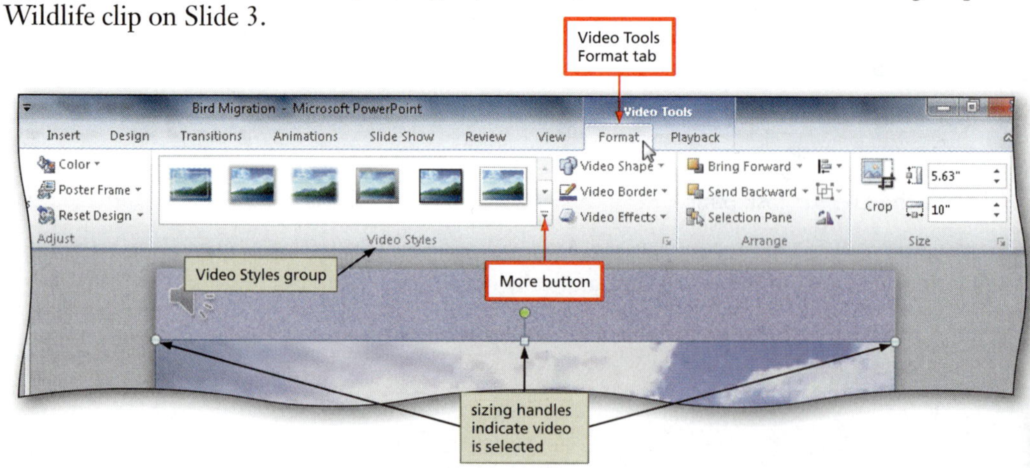

Figure 3–55

2

- With the video selected, click the More button in the Video Styles gallery (Video Tools Format tab | Video Styles group) (shown in Figure 3–55) to expand the gallery.
- Point to Bevel Perspective in the Intense area of the Video Styles gallery to display a live preview of that style applied to the video on the slide (Figure 3–56).

Experiment

- Point to various picture styles in the Video Styles gallery and watch the style of the video frame change in the document window.

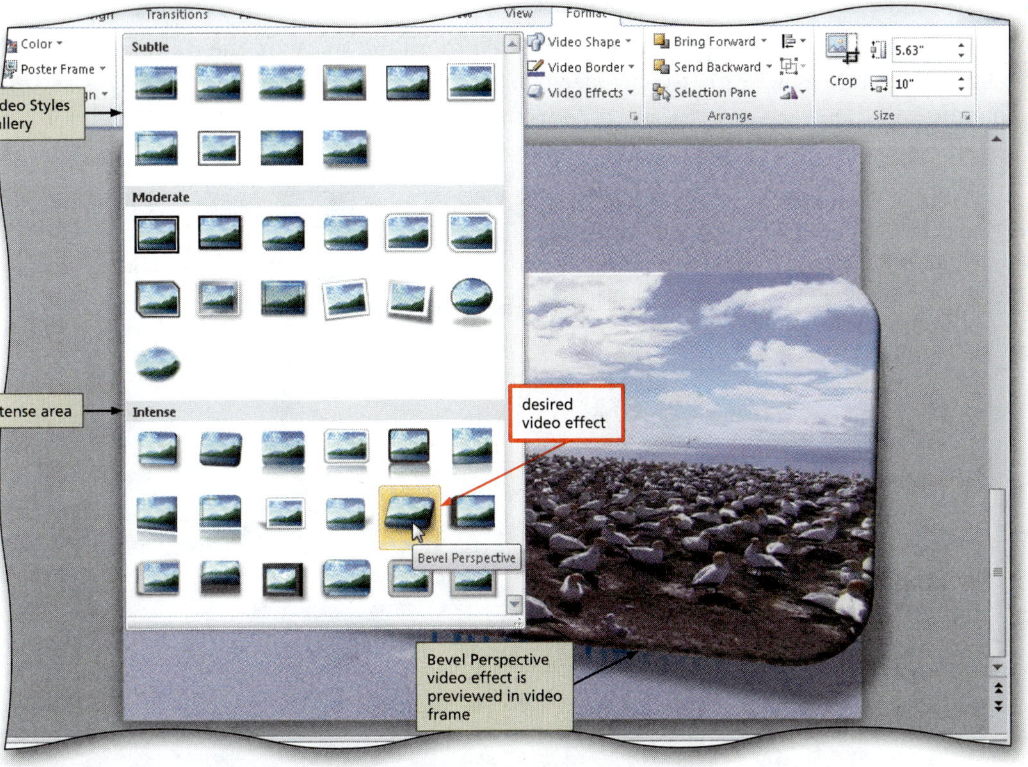

Figure 3–56

3

- Click Bevel Perspective in the Video Styles gallery to apply the style to the selected video (Figure 3–57).

Q&A Can I preview the movie clip?

Yes. Point to the clip and then click the Play/Pause button on the Video Controls below the video.

Q&A Can I add a border to a video style?

Yes. You add a border using the same method you learned in PowerPoint Chapter 2 to add a border to a picture. Click the Video Border button (Video Tools Format tab | Video Styles gallery) and then select a border line weight and color.

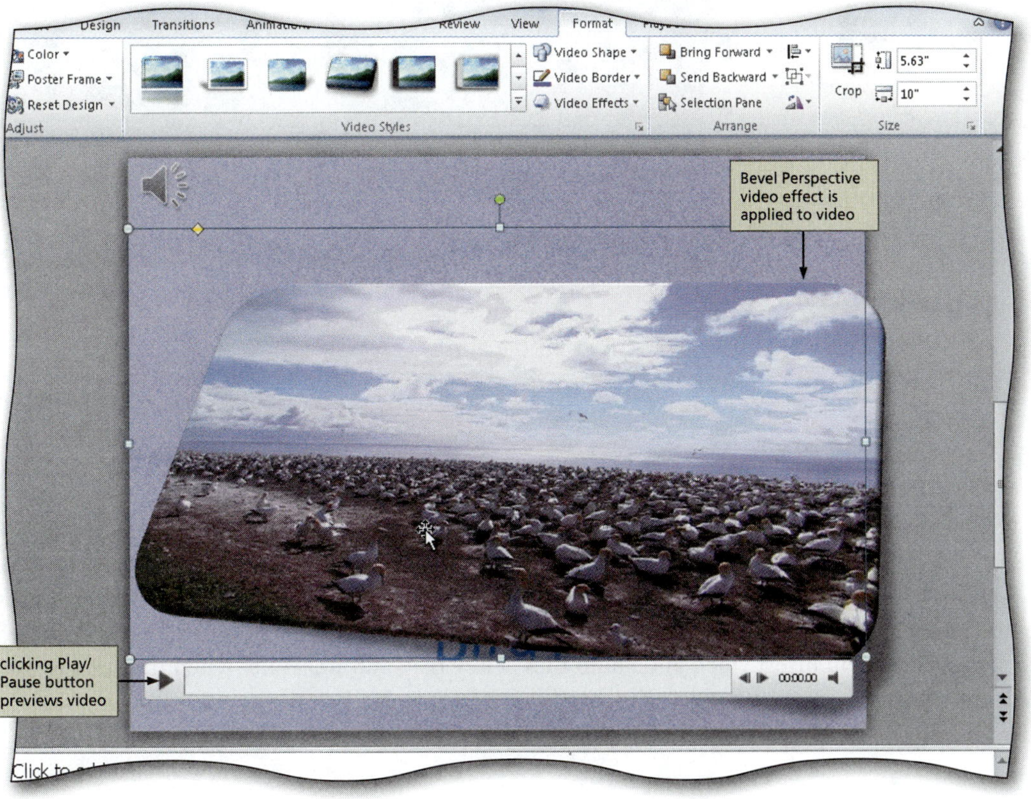

Figure 3–57

To Resize a Video

The Wildlife video size can be decreased to fill the space on the right side of the slide. You resize a video clip in the same manner that you resize clip art and pictures. The following steps resize this video using a sizing handle.

1

- With the video clip selected, drag the lower-left corner sizing handle on the photograph diagonally inward until the photograph is resized to approximately 3.9" × 6.93".

2

- Drag the clip to the location shown in Figure 3–58.

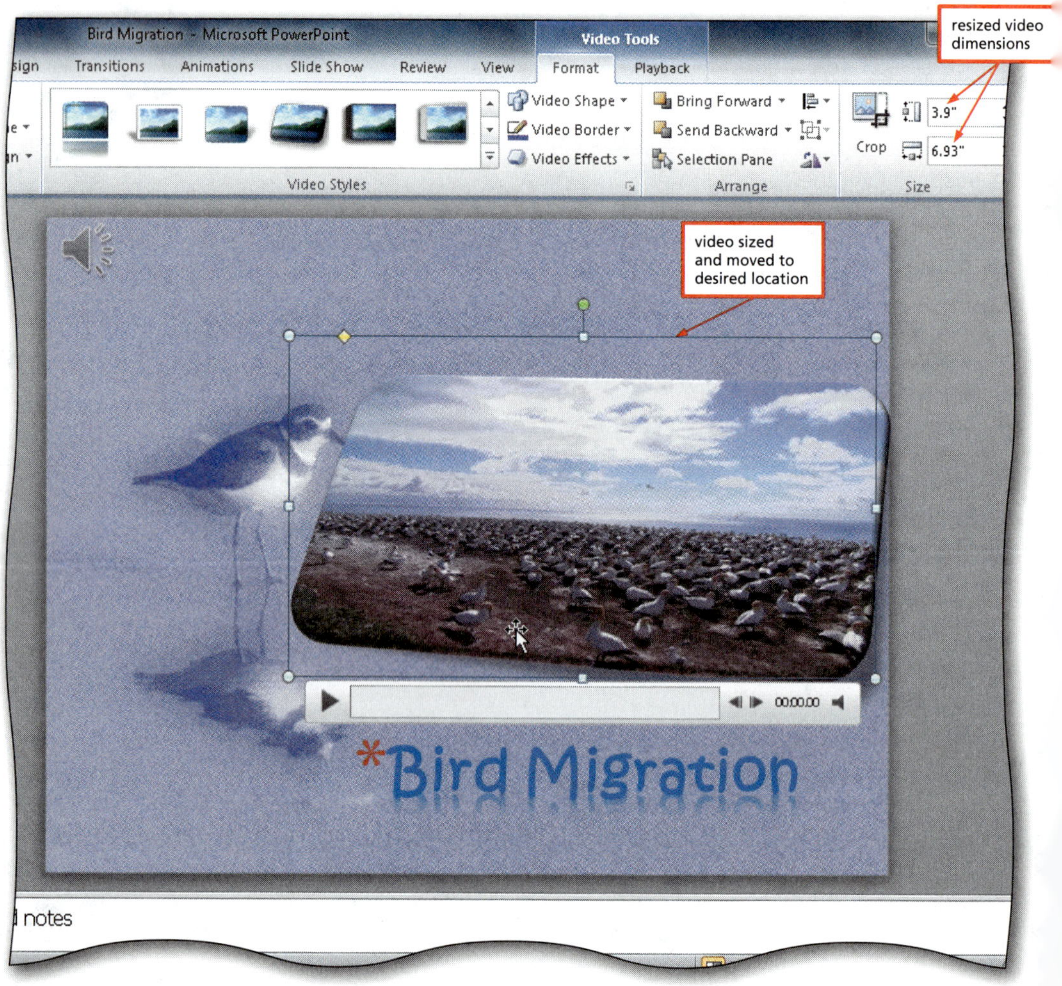

Figure 3–58

To Insert a Movie Clip

PowerPoint classifies animated GIF files as a type of video or movie because the clips have movement or action. These files are commonplace on Web sites. They also are found in PowerPoint presentations when you want to call attention to material on a particular slide. You can insert them into a PowerPoint presentation in the same manner that you insert video and audio files. They play automatically when the slide is displayed. The following steps insert a music notes video clip into Slide 1.

1

- Display Slide 1 and then display the Insert tab.
- Click the Picture button (Insert tab | Images group) to display the Insert Picture dialog box.
- If necessary, navigate to the Chapter 03 files on your USB drive.
- Click Music Notes to select the file (Figure 3–59).

Q&A Why does my list of files look different?

The list of picture files can vary depending upon the contents of your USB drive and the organization of those files into folders for each chapter.

Q&A Can I search for animated GIF files in the Microsoft Clip Organizer?

Yes. Click the Video button arrow (Insert tab | Media group), click Clip Art Video, click the Videos check box (Clip Art task pane), type the search text, and then click the Go button.

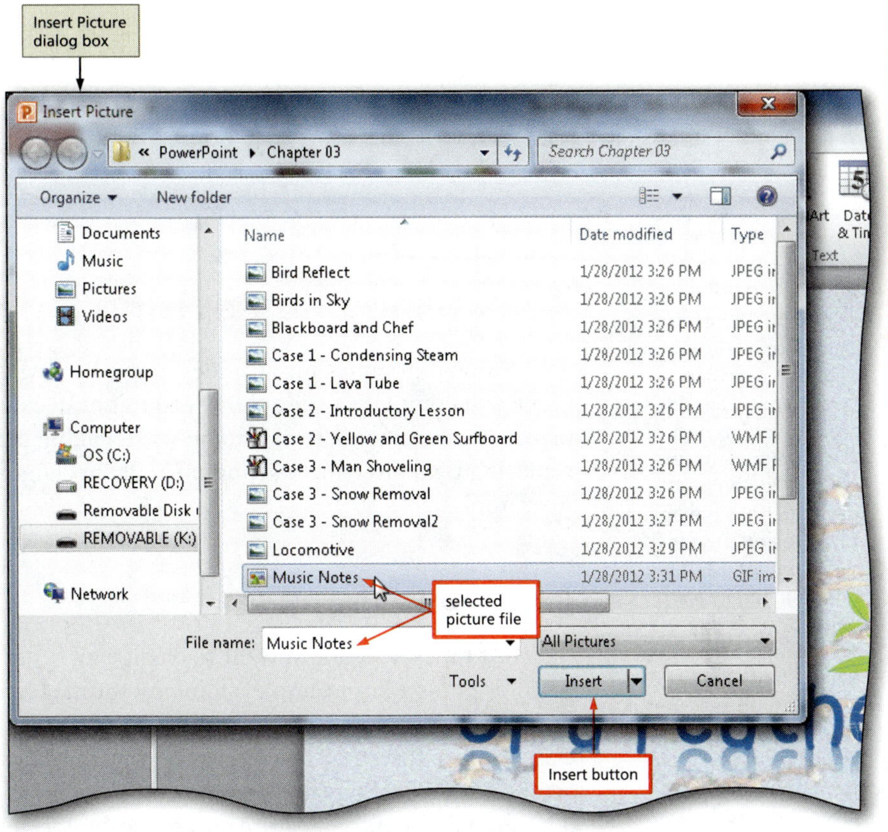

Figure 3–59

2

- Click the Insert button (Insert Picture dialog box) to insert the Music Notes animated GIF clip into Slide 1.
- Resize the clip so that it is approximately 1" × 1.47".
- Drag the clip to the location shown in Figure 3–60.

Q&A Why is the animation not showing?

Animated GIF files move only in Slide Show view and Reading view.

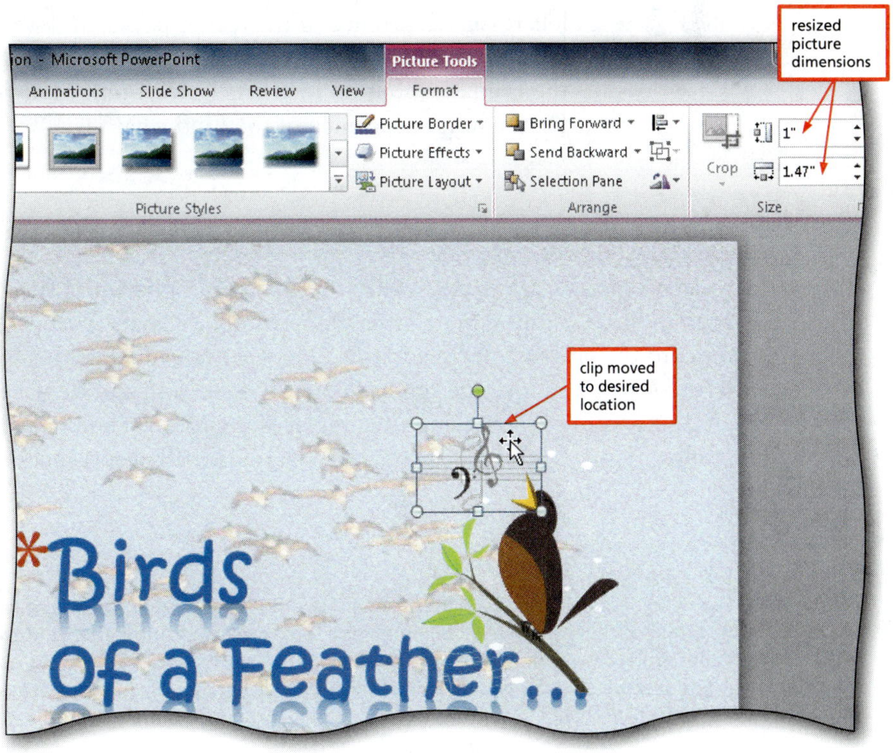

Figure 3–60

Break Point: If you wish to take a break, this is a good place to do so. Be sure to save the Bird Migration file again and then you can quit PowerPoint. To resume at a later time, start PowerPoint, open the file called Bird Migration, and continue following the steps from this location forward.

BTW

Revising Your Text

Generating ideas, revising slides, editing graphics and text, and then proofreading all slide text are required as part of the development process. A good PowerPoint developer has the ability to write and then revise slide content. Multiple drafts generally are needed to complete a successful presentation. PowerPoint's Find and Replace feature is useful if you need to change all instances of a word throughout a large presentation when you are revising slides.

Reviewing and Revising Individual Slides

The text and graphics for all slides in the Bird Migration presentation have been entered. Once you complete a slide show, you might decide to change elements. PowerPoint provides several tools to assist you with making changes. They include finding and replacing text, inserting a synonym, and checking spelling. The following pages discuss these tools.

Replace Dialog Box

At times, you might want to change all occurrences of a word or phrase to another word or phrase. For example, an instructor may have one slide show to accompany a lecture for several introductory classes, and he wants to update slides with the particular class name and section that appear on several slides. He manually could change the characters, but PowerPoint includes an efficient method of replacing one word with another. The Find and Replace feature automatically locates specific text and then replaces it with desired text.

In some cases, you may want to replace only certain occurrences of a word or phrase, not all of them. To instruct PowerPoint to confirm each change, click the Find Next button in the Replace dialog box instead of the Replace All button. When PowerPoint locates an occurrence of the text, it pauses and waits for you to click either the Replace button or the Find Next button. Clicking the Replace button changes the text; clicking the Find Next button instructs PowerPoint to disregard that particular instance and look for the next occurrence of the Find what text.

To Find and Replace Text

While reviewing your slides, you realize that you could give more specific information regarding the type of thrush discussed in Slide 2. The Wood Thrush's songs especially are melodic and beautiful, so you decide to add the word, Wood, to the bird's name. In addition, you want to capitalize the word, Thrush, because it is a specific type of thrush. To perform this action, you can use PowerPoint's Find and Replace feature, which automatically locates each occurrence of a word or phrase and then replaces it with specified text. The word, thrush, displays twice on Slide 2. The following steps use Find and Replace to replace all occurrences of the word, thrush, with the words, Wood Thrush.

BTW

Matching Case and Finding Whole Words

Two options in the Replace dialog box are useful when revising slides. Match case maintains the upper- or lowercase letters within a word, such as a capitalized word at the beginning of a sentence. In addition, the 'Find whole words only' option specifies that PowerPoint makes replacements only when the word typed in the Find what box is a complete word and is not embedded within another word. For example, if you want to change the word 'diction' to 'pronunciation,' clicking the 'Find whole words only' option prevents PowerPoint from changing the word, dictionary, to 'pronunciationary.'

1

- Display the Home tab and then display Slide 2. Click the Replace button (Home tab | Editing group) to display the Replace dialog box.
- Type `thrush` in the Find what text box (Replace dialog box).
- Press the TAB key. Type `Wood Thrush` in the Replace with text box (Figure 3–61).

Q&A

Do I need to display the slide that contains the words for which I want to search?

No. But to allow you to see the results of this search and replace action, you can display the slide where the changes will occur.

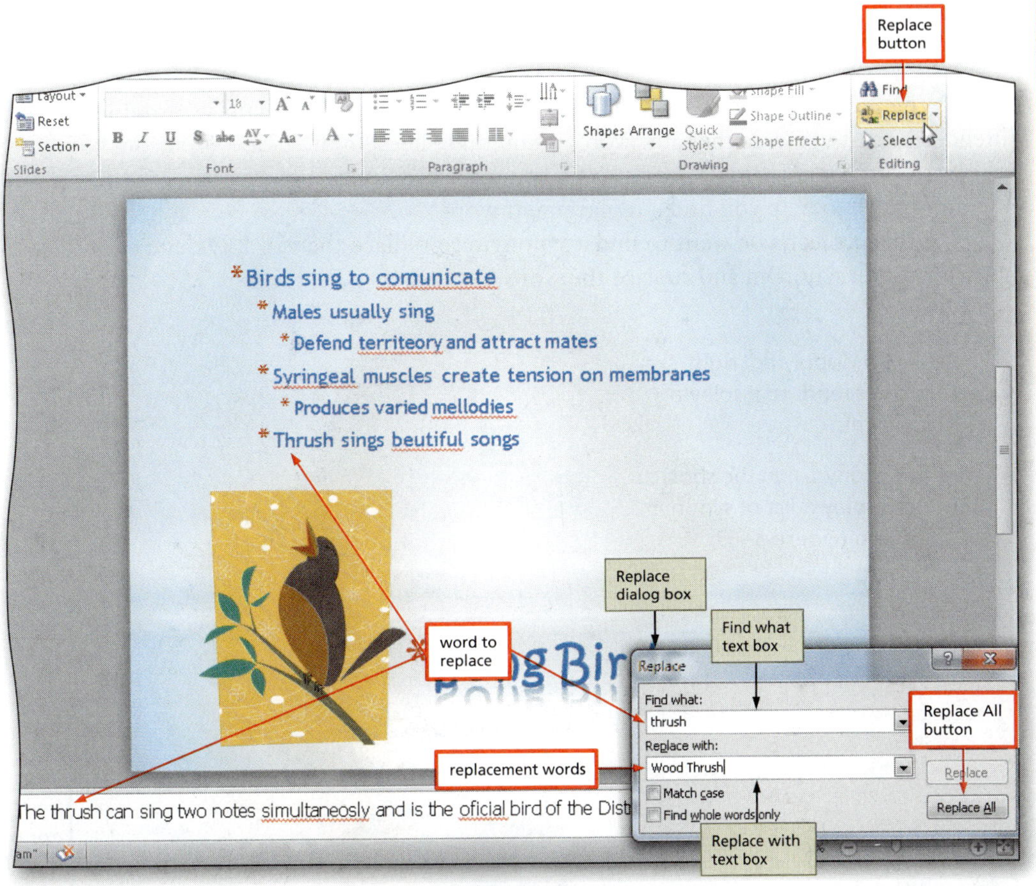

Figure 3–61

2

- Click the Replace All button (Replace dialog box) to instruct PowerPoint to replace all occurrences of the Find what word, thrush, with the Replace with words, Wood Thrush (Figure 3–62).

Q&A

If I accidentally replaced the wrong text, can I undo this replacement?

Yes. Click the Undo button on the Quick Access Toolbar to undo all replacements. If you had clicked the Replace button instead of the Replace All button, PowerPoint would undo only the most recent replacement.

Figure 3–62

3

- Click the OK button (Microsoft PowerPoint dialog box).
- Click the Close button (Replace dialog box).

Other Ways
1. Press CTRL+H

To Find and Insert a Synonym

When reviewing your slide show, you may decide that a particular word does not express the exact usage you intended or that you used the same word on multiple slides. In these cases, you could find a **synonym**, or word similar in meaning, to replace the inappropriate or duplicate word. PowerPoint provides a **thesaurus**, which is a list of synonyms and antonyms, to help you find a replacement word.

In this project, you want to find a synonym to replace the word, Defend, on Slide 2. The following steps locate an appropriate synonym and replace the word.

1

- With Slide 2 displaying, right-click the word, Defend, to display a shortcut menu.
- Point to Synonyms on the shortcut menu to display a list of synonyms for this word (Figure 3–63).

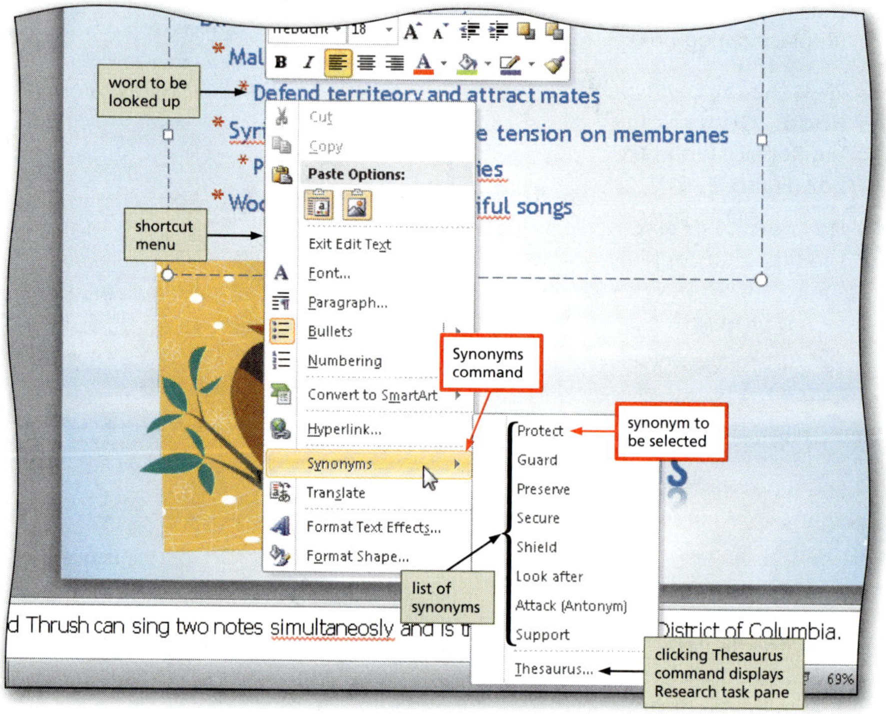

Figure 3–63

2

- Click the synonym you want (Protect) on the Synonyms submenu to replace the word, Defend, in the presentation with the word, Protect (Figure 3–64).

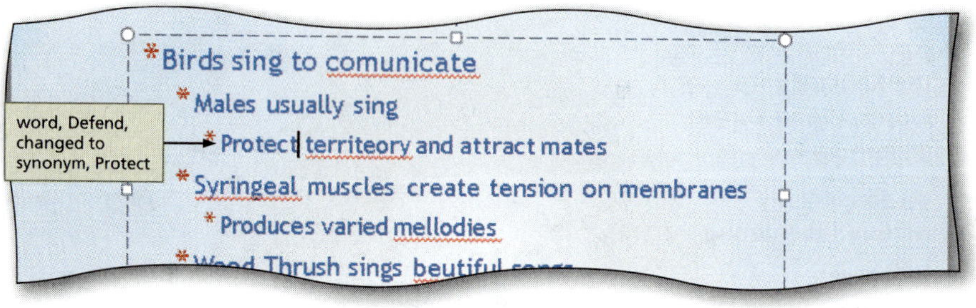

Figure 3–64

Q&A What if a suitable word does not display in the Synonyms submenu?

You can display the thesaurus in the Research task pane by clicking Thesaurus on the Synonyms submenu. A complete thesaurus with synonyms displays in the Research task pane along with an **antonym**, which is a word with an opposite meaning.

Other Ways

1. Click Thesaurus (Review tab | Proofing group)
2. Press SHIFT+F7

BTW

Foreign Language Synonyms

The thesaurus contains synonyms for languages other than English. To look up words in the thesaurus of another language, click the Thesaurus button (Review tab | Proofing group), click Research options (Research task pane), select the desired languages in the Reference Books area, and then click the OK button.

To Add Notes

As you create slides, you may find material you want to state verbally and do not want to include on the slide. You can type and format notes in the **Notes pane** as you work in Normal view and then print this information as **notes pages**. After adding comments, you can print a set of speaker notes. These notes will print below a small image of the slide. Charts, tables, and pictures added to the Notes pane also print on these pages. In this project, comments were included on Slide 2 when you opened that file. The following steps add text to the Notes pane on Slides 1 and 3.

1

- Display Slide 1, click the Notes pane, and then type `More than 10,000 species of birds exist in the world. The largest bird is the ostrich, and the smallest is the hummingbird. They generally live in small groups, but some form huge flocks with thousands of members and a variety of species. Flocks help keep the birds safe while they search for food.` (Figure 3–65).

Figure 3–65

Q&A

What if I cannot see all the lines I typed?

You can drag the splitter bar up to enlarge the Notes pane. Clicking the Notes pane scroll arrows allows you to view the entire text.

2

- Display Slide 3, click the Notes pane, and then type `Birds migrate to benefit from warm weather. Some can fly more than 6,000 miles without stopping. We can help bird migration by providing food, shelters, nest sites, and water.` (Figure 3–66).

Figure 3–66

BTW

Using AutoCorrect Features

Microsoft Office programs use the AutoCorrect feature to correct typing mistakes and commonly misspelled words. When you install Microsoft Office, a default list of typical misspellings is created. You can modify the AutoCorrect list with words you are apt to misspell. The first column of this list contains the word that you often mistype, and the second column contains the replacement text. The AutoCorrect feature also inserts symbols, such as replacing (c) with the copyright symbol, ©.

Checking Spelling

After you create a presentation, you should check it visually for spelling errors and style consistency. In addition, you use PowerPoint's Spelling tool to identify possible misspellings on the slides and in the notes. Do not rely on the spelling checker to catch all your mistakes. Although PowerPoint's spelling checker is a valuable tool, it is not infallible. You should proofread your presentation carefully by pointing to each word and saying it aloud as you point to it. Be mindful of commonly misused words such as its and it's, through and though, and to and too.

PowerPoint checks the entire presentation for spelling mistakes using a standard dictionary contained in the Microsoft Office group. This dictionary is shared with the other Microsoft Office applications such as Word and Excel. A **custom dictionary** is available if you want to add special words such as proper names, cities, and acronyms. When checking a presentation for spelling errors, PowerPoint opens the standard dictionary and the custom dictionary file, if one exists. When a word appears in the Spelling dialog box, you can perform one of several actions, as described in Table 3–1.

Table 3–1 Spelling Dialog Box Buttons and Actions

Button Name	When To Use	Action
Ignore	Word is spelled correctly but not found in dictionaries	PowerPoint continues checking rest of the presentation but will flag that word again if it appears later in document.
Ignore All	Word is spelled correctly but not found in dictionaries	PowerPoint ignores all occurrences of the word and continues checking rest of presentation.
Change	Word is misspelled	Click proper spelling of the word in Suggestions list. PowerPoint corrects word, continues checking rest of presentation, but will flag that word again if it appears later in document.
Change All	Word is misspelled	Click proper spelling of word in Suggestions list. PowerPoint changes all occurrences of misspelled word and continues checking rest of presentation.
Add	Add word to custom dictionary	PowerPoint opens custom dictionary, adds word, and continues checking rest of presentation.
Suggest	Correct spelling is uncertain	Lists alternative spellings. Click the correct word from the Suggestions box or type the proper spelling. Corrects the word and continues checking the rest of the presentation.
AutoCorrect	Add spelling error to AutoCorrect list	PowerPoint adds spelling error and its correction to AutoCorrect list. Any future misspelling of word is corrected automatically as you type.
Close	Stop spelling checker	PowerPoint closes spelling checker and returns to PowerPoint window.

The standard dictionary contains commonly used English words. It does not, however, contain many proper names, abbreviations, technical terms, poetic contractions, or antiquated terms. PowerPoint treats words not found in the dictionaries as misspellings.

To Check Spelling

The following steps check the spelling on all slides in the Bird Migration presentation.

1

- Click Review on the Ribbon to display the Review tab.
- Click the Spelling button (Review Tab | Proofing group) to start the spelling checker and display the Spelling dialog box (Figure 3–67).

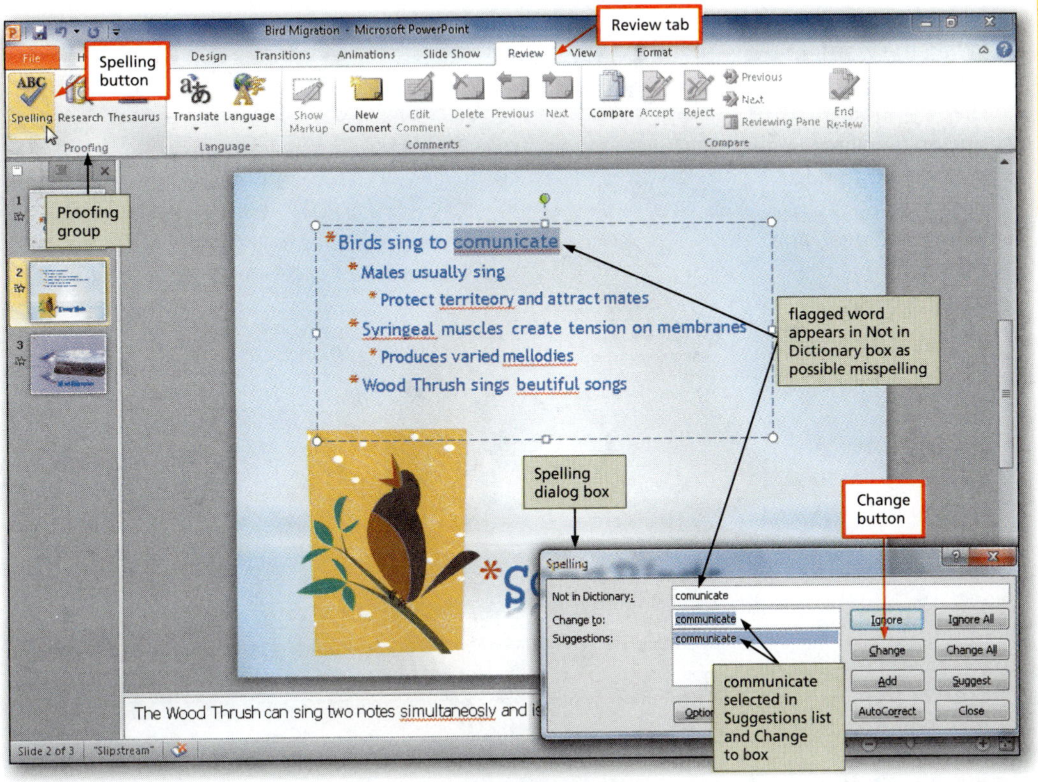

Figure 3–67

2

- With the word, communicate, selected in the Suggestions list, click the Change button (Spelling dialog box) to replace the misspelled flagged word, comunicate, with the selected correctly spelled word, communicate, and then continue the spelling check (Figure 3–68).

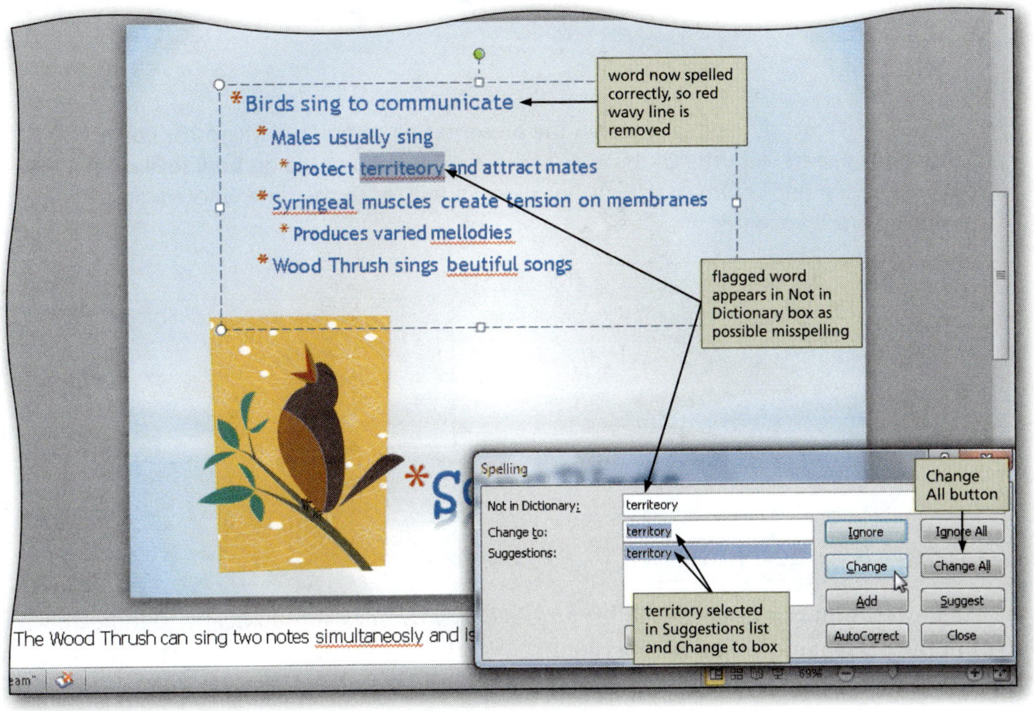

Figure 3–68

Q&A

Could I have clicked the Change All button instead of the Change button?

Yes. When you click the Change All button, you change the current and future occurrences of the misspelled word. The misspelled word, comunicate, appears only once in the presentation, so clicking the Change or the Change All button in this instance produces identical results.

3

- Replace the misspelled word, territeory, with the word, territory (Figure 3–69).
- When the word, Syringeal, is flagged, click the Ignore button (Spelling dialog box) to skip the correctly spelled word, Syringeal, and then continue the spelling check.

Q&A Syringeal is flagged as a possible misspelled word. Why?

Your custom dictionary does not contain the word, so it is recognized as spelled incorrectly. You can add this word to a custom dictionary to prevent the spelling checker from flagging it as a mistake.

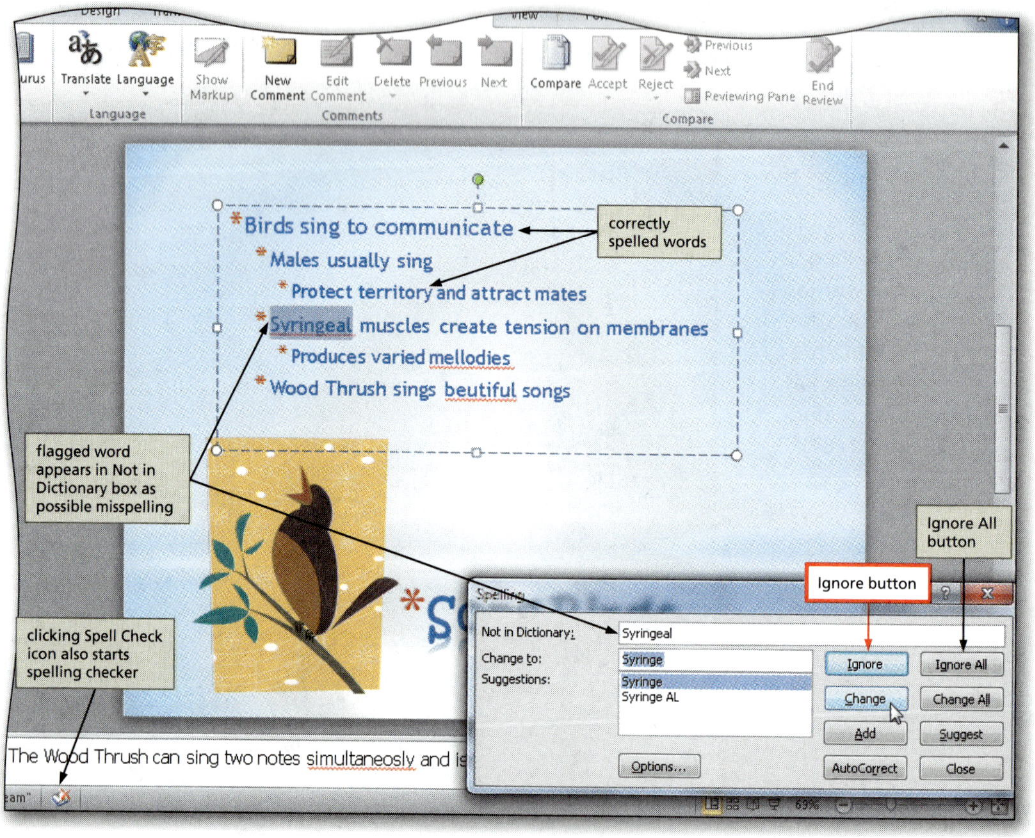

Figure 3–69

Q&A Could I have clicked the Ignore All button instead of the Ignore button?

Yes. When you click the Ignore All button, you ignore the current and future occurrences of the word.

4

- Continue checking all flagged words in the presentation. When the Microsoft PowerPoint dialog box appears, click the OK button (Microsoft PowerPoint dialog box) to close the spelling checker and return to the current slide, Slide 2, or to the slide where a possible misspelled word appeared.

Other Ways

1. Click Spell Check icon on status bar, click Spelling on shortcut menu
2. Right-click flagged word, click correct word or click Spelling on shortcut menu
3. Press F7

To Insert a Slide Number

PowerPoint can insert the slide number on your slides automatically to indicate where the slide is positioned within the presentation. The number location on the slide is determined by the presentation theme. You have the option to not display this slide number on the title slide. The following steps insert the slide number on all slides except the title slide.

1

- If a word in the Notes pane is selected, click the Slide 2 Slide pane. Display the Insert tab and then click the Insert Slide Number button (Insert tab | Text group) to display the Header and Footer dialog box (Figure 3–70).

Q&A Why did I need to click the Slide pane?

The page number would have been inserted in the Notes pane instead of on the slide.

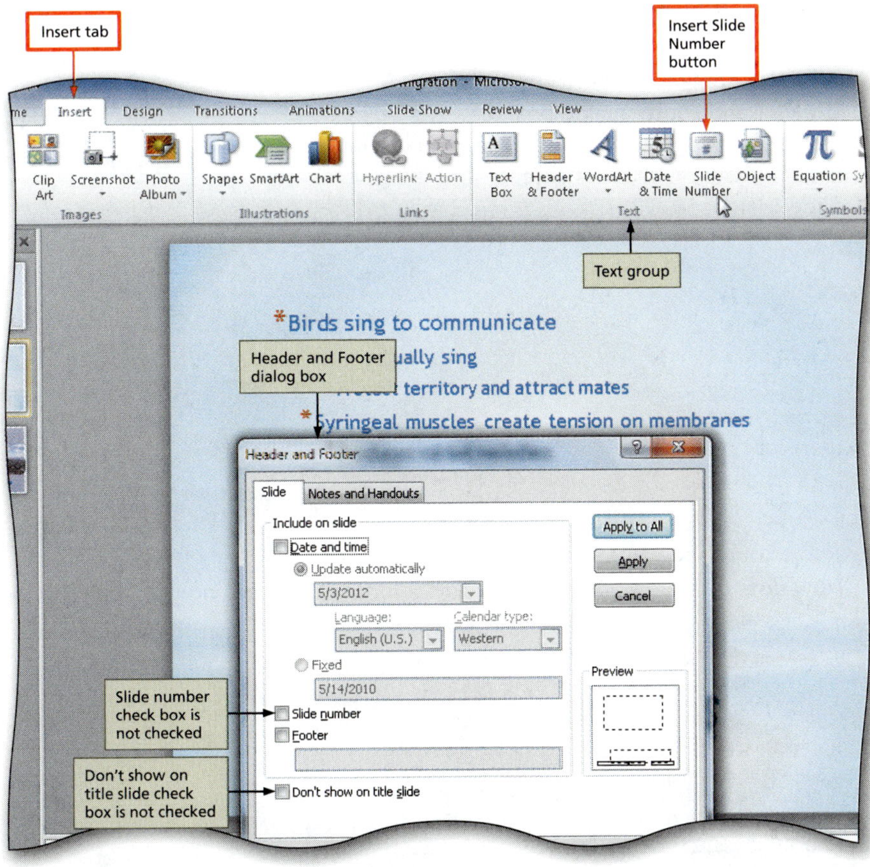

Figure 3–70

2

- Click the Slide number check box (Header and Footer dialog box) to place a check mark in it.
- Click the 'Don't show on title slide' check box (Header and Footer dialog box) to place a check mark in it (Figure 3–71).

Q&A Where does the slide number display on the slide?

Each theme determines where the slide number is displayed in the footer. In the Slipstream theme, the slide number location is the center of the footer, as indicated by the black box at the bottom of the Preview area.

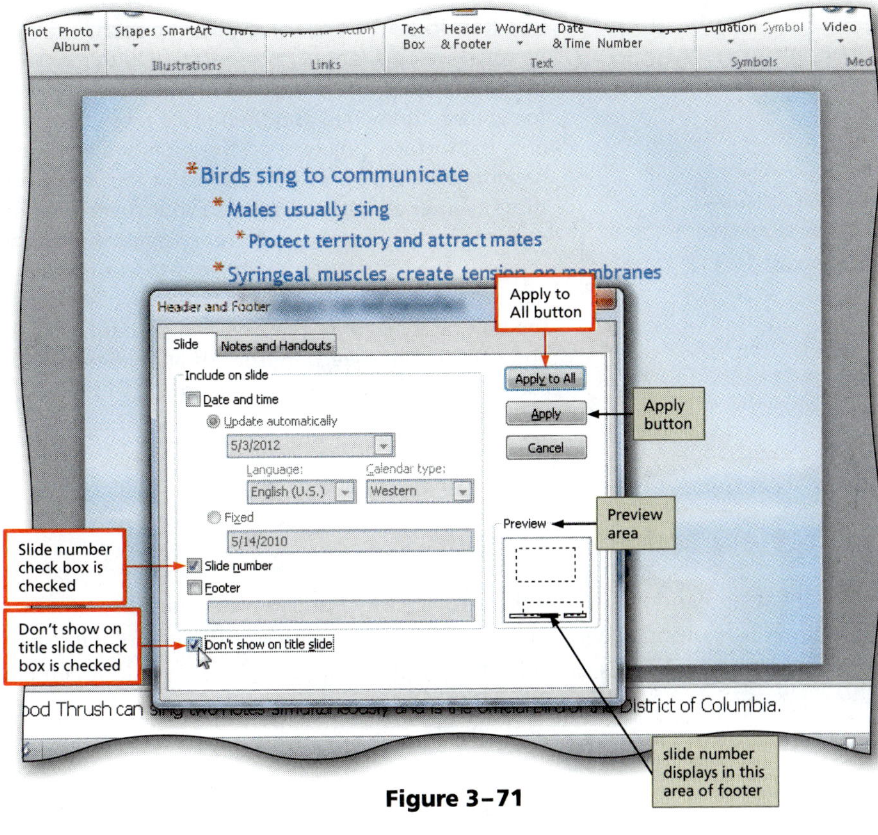

Figure 3–71

3

- Click the Apply to All button (Header and Footer dialog box) to close the dialog box and insert the slide number on all slides except Slide 1 (Figure 3–72).

Figure 3–72

Q&A

How does clicking the Apply to All button differ from clicking the Apply button?

The Apply button inserts the slide number only on the currently displayed slide whereas the Apply to All button inserts the slide number on every slide.

Other Ways

1. Click Header & Footer button (Insert tab | Text group), click Slide Number box (Header and Footer dialog box), click 'Slide number' and 'Don't show on title slide' boxes, click Apply to All button

Plan Ahead

Use handouts to organize your speech.

As you develop a lengthy presentation with many visuals, handouts may help you organize your material. Print handouts with the maximum number of slides per page. Use scissors to cut each thumbnail and then place these miniature slide images adjacent to each other on a flat surface. Any type on the thumbnails will be too small to read, so the images will need to work with only the support of the verbal message you provide. You can rearrange these thumbnails as you organize your speech. When you return to your computer, you can rearrange the slides on your screen to match the order of your thumbnail printouts. Begin speaking the actual words you want to incorporate in the body of the talk. This process of glancing at the thumbnails and hearing yourself say the key ideas of the speech is one of the best methods of organizing and preparing for the actual presentation. Ultimately, when you deliver your speech in front of an audience, the images on the slides or on your note cards should be sufficient to remind you of the accompanying verbal message.

To Preview and Print a Handout

Printing handouts is useful for reviewing a presentation because you can analyze several slides displayed simultaneously on one page. Additionally, many businesses distribute handouts of the slide show before or after a presentation so attendees can refer to a copy. Each page of the handout can contain reduced images of one, two, three, four, six, or nine slides. The three-slides-per-page handout includes lines beside each slide so that your audience can write notes conveniently. The following steps preview and print a presentation handout.

1

- Click File on the Ribbon to open the Backstage view and then click the Print tab to display Slide 2 in the Print gallery.
- Click Full Page Slides in the Settings area to display the Full Page Slides gallery (Figure 3–73).

Q&A Why does the preview of my slide appear in color?

Your printer determines how the preview appears. If your printer is not capable of printing color images, the preview will not appear in color.

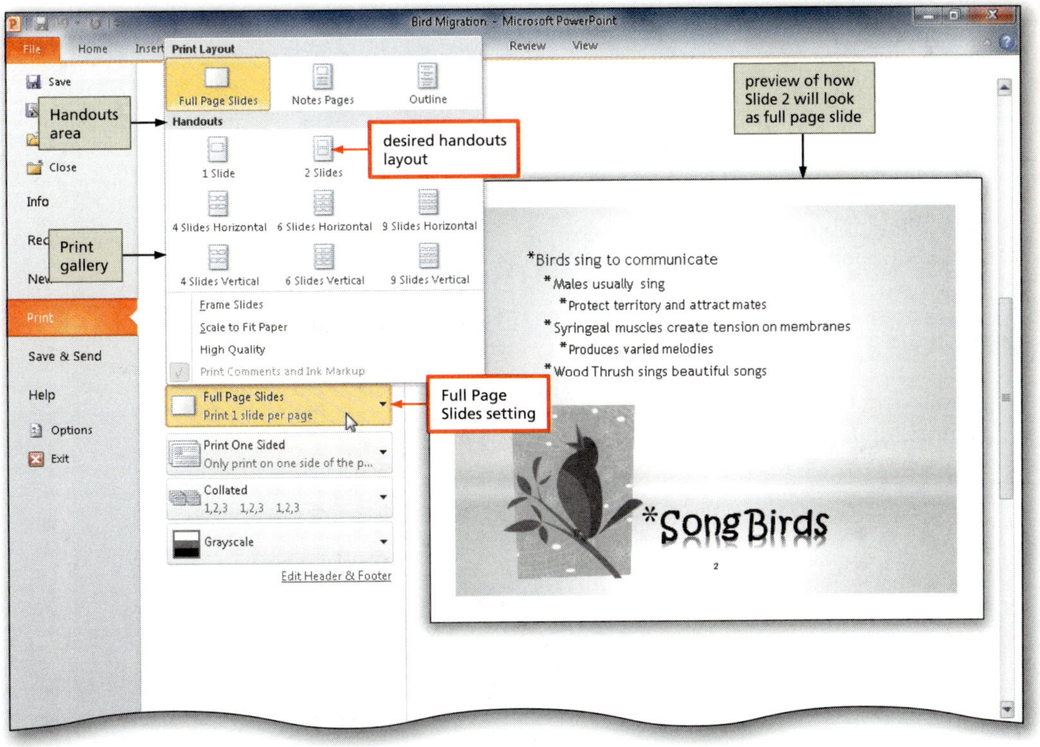

Figure 3–73

2

- Click 2 Slides in the Handouts area to select this option and display a preview of the handout (Figure 3–74).

Q&A The current date displays in the upper-right corner of the handout, and the page number displays in the lower-right corner of the footer. Can I change their location or add other information to the header and footer?

Yes. Click the Edit Header & Footer link at the bottom of the Print gallery, click the Notes and Handouts tab (Header and Footer dialog box), and then decide what content to include on the handout page.

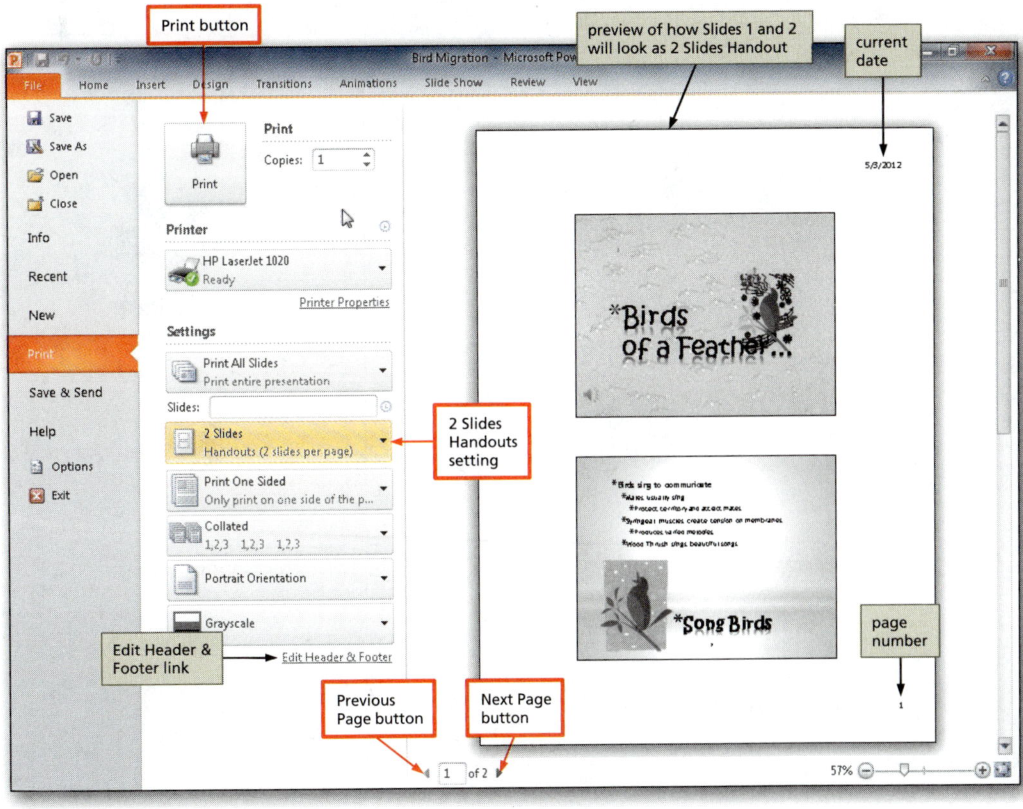

Figure 3–74

3

- Click the Next Page and Previous Page buttons to display previews of the two pages in the presentation.
- Click the Print button in the Print gallery to print the handout.
- When the printer stops, retrieve the printed handout (Figure 3–75).

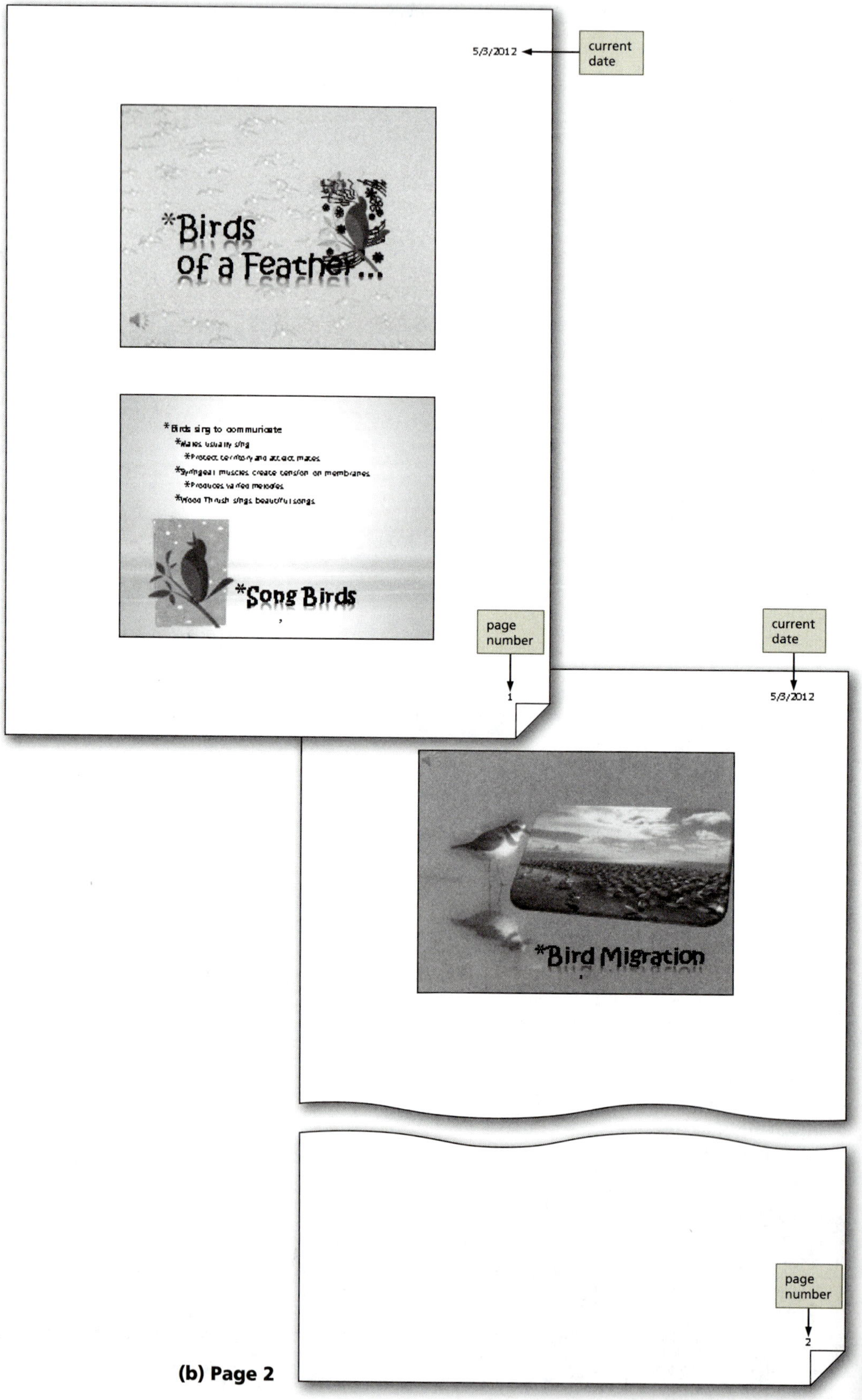

(a) Page 1

(b) Page 2

Figure 3–75

To Print Speaker Notes

Comments added to slides in the Notes pane give the speaker information that supplements the text on the slide. They will print with a small image at the top and the comments below the slide. The following steps print the speaker notes.

1

- Click the Print tab in the Backstage view and then click 2 Slides in the Settings area to display the gallery (Figure 3–76).

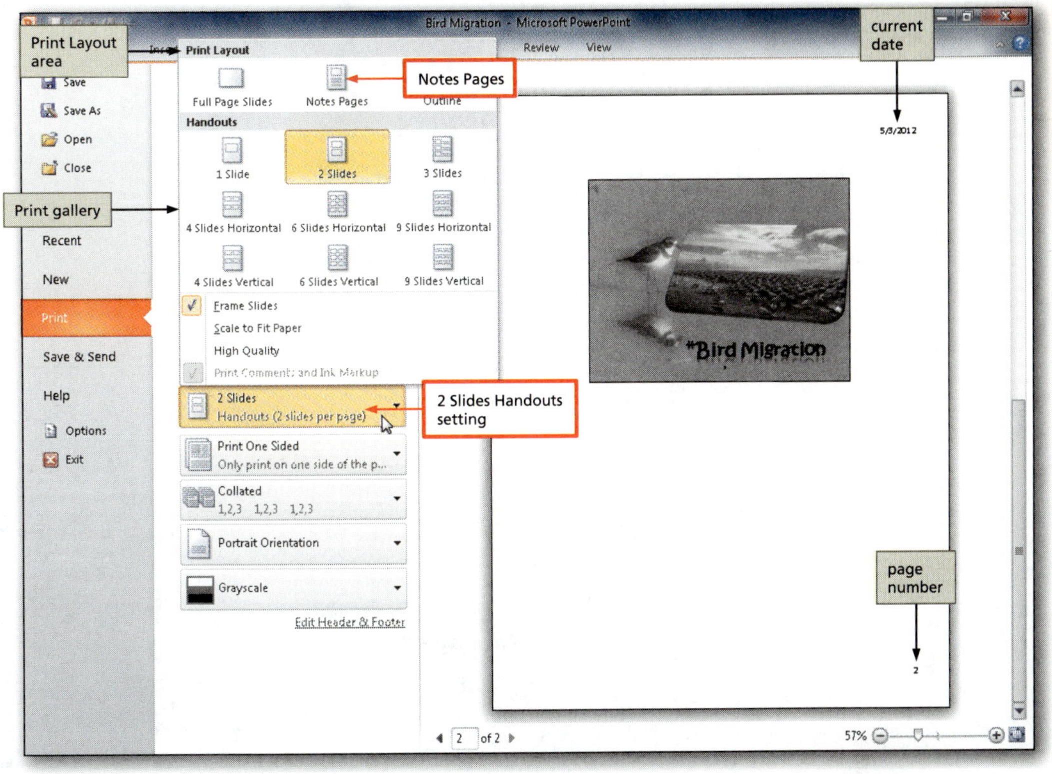

Figure 3–76

2

- Click Notes Pages in the Print Layout area to select this option and display a preview of the current page (Figure 3–77).
- Click the Previous Page and Next Page buttons to display previews of other pages in the presentation.

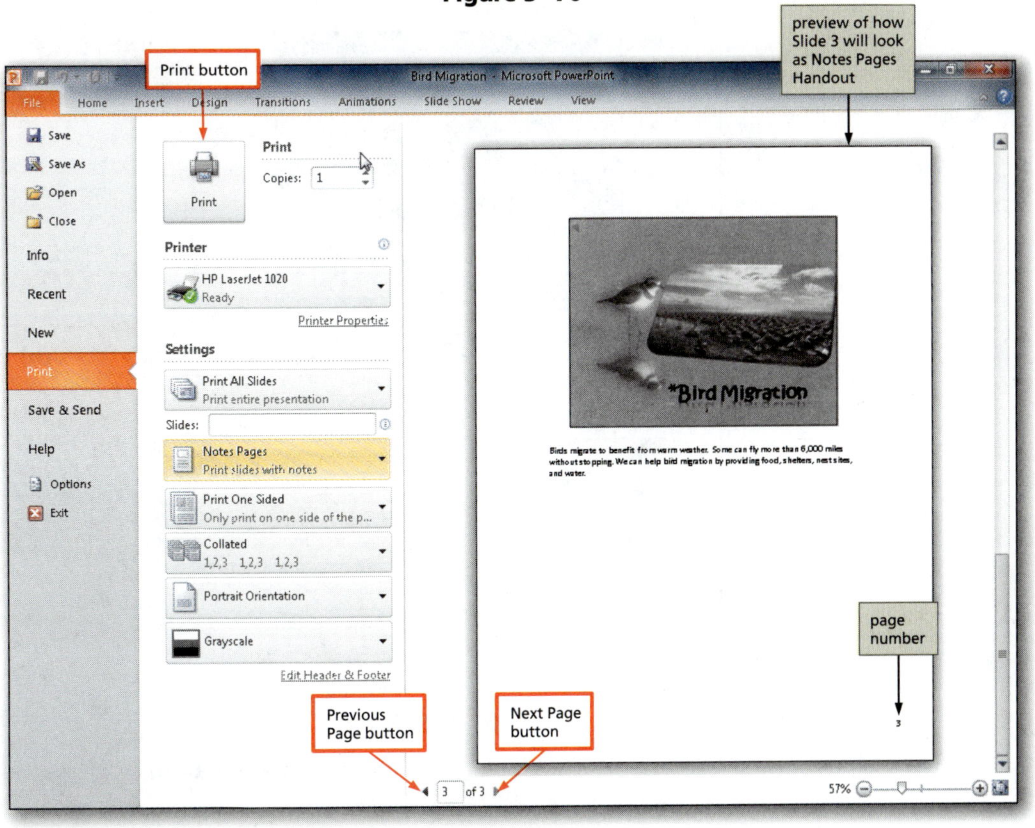

Figure 3–77

3

- Click the Print button in the Print gallery to print the notes.
- When the printer stops, retrieve the printed pages (Figure 3–78).

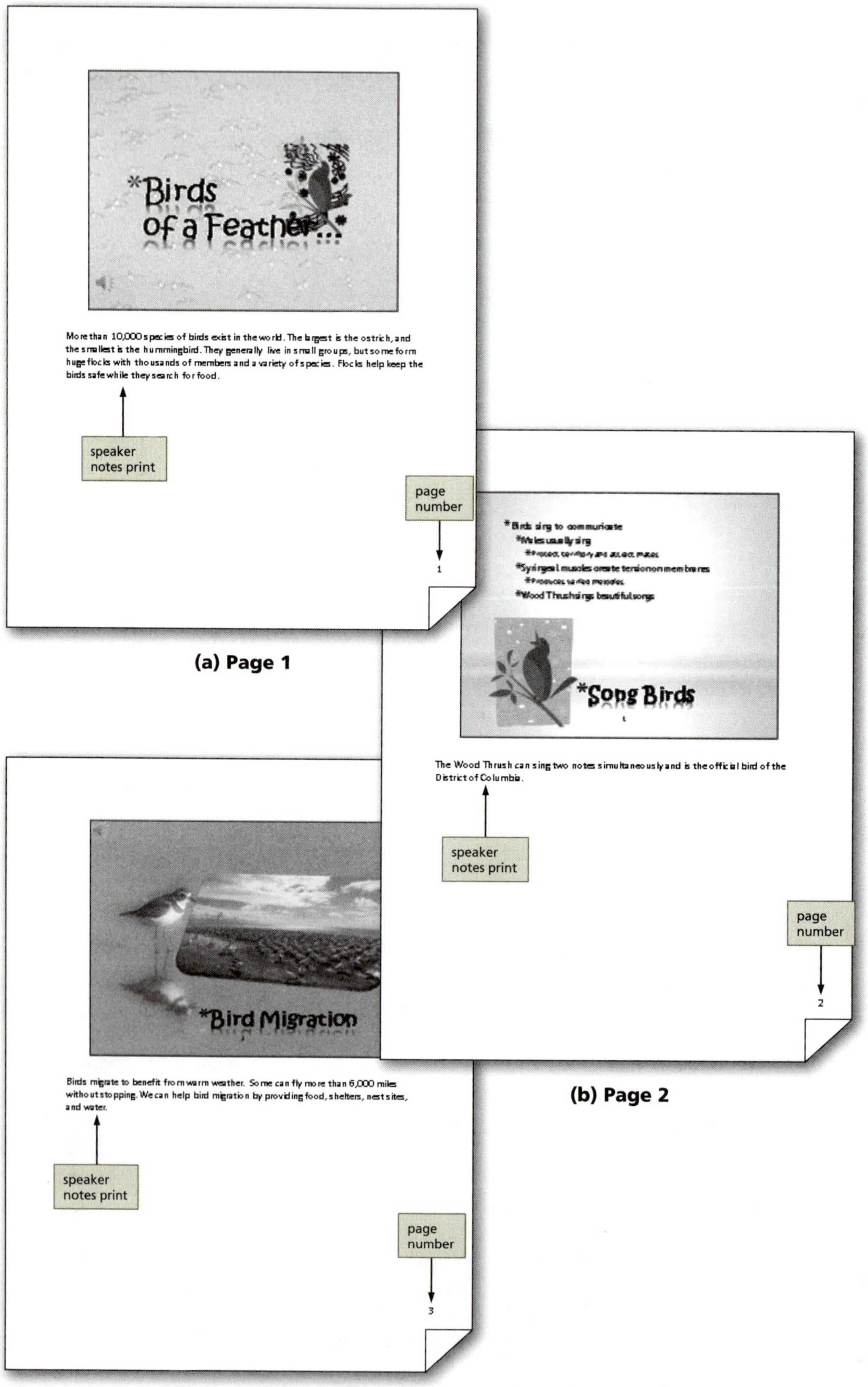

(a) Page 1

(b) Page 2

(c) Page 3

Figure 3–78

Evaluate your presentation.
One of the best methods of improving your communication skills is to focus on what you learned from the experience. Respond to these questions:

- How successfully do you feel you fulfilled your assignment?
- What strategies did you use to develop your slides and the accompanying oral presentation?
- What revisions did you make?
- If you could go back to the speaking engagement and change one thing, what would it be?
- What feedback did you receive from your instructor or audience?

Plan Ahead

To Change Document Properties

Before saving the presentation again, you want to add your name, class name, and some keywords as document properties. The following steps use the Document Information Panel to change document properties.

1. In the Backstage view, click the Properties button in the right pane of the Info gallery, and then click Show Document Panel on the Properties menu to close the Backstage view and display the Document Information Panel.
2. Enter your name in the Author text box. Enter your course and section in the Subject text box. Enter the text, `bird, migration, singing` in the Keywords text box.
3. Close the Document Information Panel.
4. Click the Save button on the Quick Access Toolbar to overwrite the previous Bird Migration file on the USB flash drive.

BTW

Quick Reference
For a table that lists how to complete the tasks covered in the Office chapters in this book using the mouse, Ribbon, shortcut menu, and keyboard, see the Quick Reference Summary at the back of this book, or visit the Microsoft Office and Concepts CourseMate Web site at www.cengagebrain.com and then navigate to the Quick Reference resource for this book.

To Run a Slide Show with Media

All changes are complete, and the presentation is saved. You now can view the Bird Migration presentation. The following steps start Slide Show view.

1. Click the Slide 1 thumbnail in the Slide pane to select and display Slide 1.
2. Click the Slide Show button to display the title slide, watch the animations, and listen to the bird calls. Allow the audio clip to repeat several times.
3. Press the SPACEBAR to display Slide 2.
4. Press the SPACEBAR to display Slide 3. Listen to the audio clip, watch the video clip, and then allow the audio clip to repeat several times.
5. Press the SPACEBAR to end the slide show and click to exit the slide show.

To Quit PowerPoint

This project is complete. The following steps quit PowerPoint.

1. Click the Close button on the right side of the title bar to close the document and then quit PowerPoint.
2. If a Microsoft PowerPoint dialog box appears, click the Save button to save any changes made to the presentation since the last save.

Chapter Summary

In this chapter you have learned how to enhance an existing presentation by adding video, audio, and pictures with effects. You also learned to modify placeholders, align text, and review a presentation by checking spelling and creating handouts. The items listed below include all the new PowerPoint skills you have learned in this chapter.

1. Color a Picture (PPT 143)
2. Add an Artistic Effect to a Picture (144)
3. Change the Stacking Order (PPT 146)
4. Resize a Placeholder (PPT 148)
5. Move a Placeholder (PPT 148)
6. Delete a Placeholder (PPT 149)
7. Align Paragraph Text (PPT 150)
8. Delete a Slide (PPT 152)
9. Change Views (PPT 153)
10. Copy a Clip from One Slide to Another (PPT 155)
11. Zoom a Slide (PPT 156)
12. Ungroup a Clip (PPT 157)
13. Change the Color of a Clip Object (PPT 158)
14. Delete a Clip Object (PPT 161)
15. Regroup Objects (PPT 162)
16. Insert a Video File (PPT 163)
17. Trim a Video File (PPT 164)
18. Add Video Options (PPT 166)
19. Insert an Audio File (PPT 167)
20. Add Audio Options (PPT 170)
21. Add a Video Style (PPT 172)
22. Resize a Video (PPT 174)
23. Insert a Movie Clip (PPT 174)
24. Find and Replace Text (PPT 176)
25. Find and Insert a Synonym (PPT 178)
26. Add Notes (PPT 179)
27. Check Spelling (PPT 181)
28. Insert a Slide Number (PPT 182)
29. Preview and Print a Handout (PPT 184)
30. Print Speaker Notes (PPT 187)

SAM If you have a SAM 2010 user profile, your instructor may have assigned an autogradable version of this assignment. If so, log into the SAM 2010 Web site at www.cengage.com/sam2010 to download the instruction and start files.

Learn It Online

Test your knowledge of chapter content and key terms.

Instructions: To complete the Learn It Online exercises, visit the Microsoft Office and Concepts CourseMate Web site at www.cengagebrain.com, navigate to the PowerPoint Chapter 3 resources for this book, click the link for the exercise you want to complete, and then read the instructions.

Chapter Reinforcement TF, MC, and SA

A series of true/false, multiple choice, and short answer questions that test your knowledge of the chapter content.

Flash Cards

An interactive learning environment where you identify chapter key terms associated with displayed definitions.

Practice Test

A series of multiple choice questions that test your knowledge of chapter content and key terms.

Who Wants To Be a Computer Genius?

An interactive game that challenges your knowledge of chapter content in the style of a television quiz show.

Wheel of Terms

An interactive game that challenges your knowledge of chapter key terms in the style of the television show *Wheel of Fortune*.

Crossword Puzzle Challenge

A crossword puzzle that challenges your knowledge of key terms presented in the chapter.

Apply Your Knowledge

Reinforce the skills and apply the concepts you learned in this chapter.

Adding Artistic Effects to Pictures, Moving a Placeholder, and Inserting and Controlling Audio Clips

Note: To complete this assignment, you will be required to use the Data Files for Students. See the inside back cover of this book for instructions on downloading the Data Files for Students, or contact your instructor for information about accessing the required files.

Instructions: Start PowerPoint. Open the presentation, Apply 3-1 SAD, from the Data Files for Students.

The five slides in the presentation, shown in Figure 3–79, present information about Seasonal Affective Disorder, also known as SAD, which is a mood disorder that occurs generally during the winter months. The document you open is composed of slides containing pictures and clip art, and you will apply artistic effects or modify some of these graphic elements. You also will insert audio clips from Office.com. In addition, you will move the placeholder on the final slide.

Perform the following tasks:

1. Insert the audio clip, Sad Piano Music, into Slide 1 (Figure 3–79a). Change the volume to Medium, start the clip automatically, and hide the sound icon during the slide show. Then copy this audio clip to Slides 2, 3, and 4 with the same options. Insert the audio clip, Variety Hour, into Slide 5, change the volume to Medium, start the clip automatically, and hide the sound icon during the slide show.
2. On Slide 2, color the picture by selecting Yellow, Accent color 2 Dark from the Recolor area, as shown in Figure 3–79b.
3. On Slide 3, apply the Watercolor Sponge artistic effect to the picture, as shown in Figure 3–79c.
4. On Slide 4, select the lamp clip and then change the Zoom level to 120%. Ungroup the lamp clip and then recolor the arms to Dark Teal, Text 2, Lighter 10% (last color in fourth Theme Colors column), as shown in Figure 3–79d. Regroup the clip. Change the Zoom level to 69%.
5. On Slide 5, move the WordArt placeholder above the bird in the picture, as shown in Figure 3–79e.
6. On Slide 1, type **`Up to 9 percent of U.S. adults may suffer from SAD.`** in the Notes pane.
7. Check the slides for spelling errors and then run the revised presentation.
8. Change the document properties, as specified by your instructor. Save the presentation using the file name, Apply 3-1 Seasonal Affective Disorder.
9. Submit the revised document in the format specified by your instructor.

(a) Slide 1

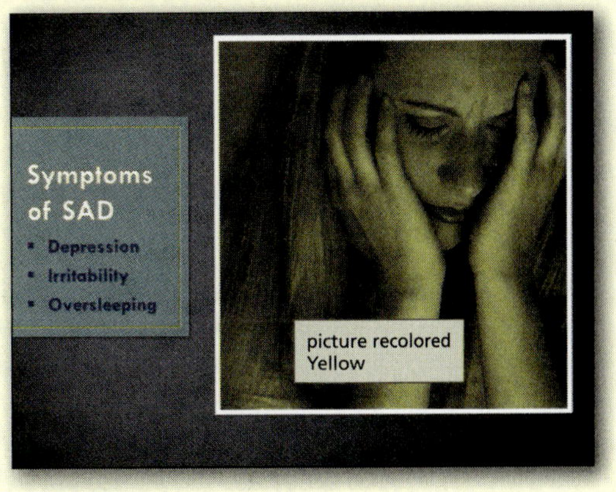

(b) Slide 2

Figure 3–79

Continued >

Apply Your Knowledge *continued*

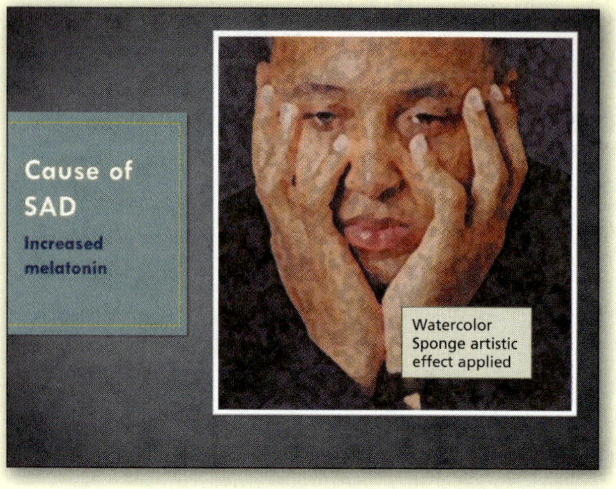

(c) Slide 3

(d) Slide 4

(e) Slide 5

Figure 3–79 (Continued)

Extend Your Knowledge

Extend the skills you learned in this chapter and experiment with new skills. You may need to use Help to complete the assignment.

Formatting a Video Border, Deleting Audio, Adding a Font Effect, and Pausing and Resuming Video Playback

Note: To complete this assignment, you will be required to use the Data Files for Students. See the inside back cover of this book for instructions on downloading the Data Files for Students, or contact your instructor for information about accessing the required files.

Instructions: Start PowerPoint. Open the presentation, Extend 3-1 Nature, from the Data Files for Students.

You will add the Small Caps font effect to the title text on the title slide, delete an audio clip, and format a video border, as shown in Figure 3–80a. While the slide show is running, you will adjust the video playback to pause and then resume playing the clip.

Perform the following tasks:

1. On Slide 1, move the title text placeholder up so that it is positioned in the upper-right corner of the slide, as shown in Figure 3–80a. Right-align the title text and then add the Small Caps font effect to these letters. *Hint:* Font effects are located in the Font dialog box (Home tab | Font group).
2. On the title slide, delete the audio clip positioned in the upper-left corner of the slide. The three audio clips on the right side of the slide will remain.
3. Change the video style from Soft Edge Oval to Beveled Oval, Black (in the Moderate area). Then change the video border color to Gold, Accent 2 and change the border weight to 10 pt. *Hint:* Click More Lines in the Video Border Weight gallery and then change the Border Style Width.
4. On Slide 2, add a border to each of the six pictures that surround the center deer video frame, and then change the border colors and the border weights. Use Figure 3–80b as a guide. Add the Compound Frame, Black video style (in the Moderate area) to the bird feeder clip.
5. Change the document properties, as specified by your instructor. Save the presentation using the file name, Extend 3-1 Observing Nature.
6. Start the slide show. When a few seconds of the video have elapsed, pause the video and then move your mouse pointer to an area other than the video and listen to the bird audio clips. Then move the mouse pointer over the video clip to display the Video Controls. Resume the video playback.
7. Submit the revised document in the format specified by your instructor.

(a) Slide 1

(b) Slide 2

Figure 3–80

Make It Right

Analyze a presentation and correct all errors and/or improve the design.

Editing Clips, Finding and Replacing Text, and Correcting Spelling

Note: To complete this assignment, you will be required to use the Data Files for Students. See the inside back cover of this book for instructions on downloading the Data Files for Students, or contact your instructor for information about accessing the required files.

Instructions: Start PowerPoint. Open the presentation, Make It Right 3-1 Flamingos, from the Data Files for Students.

Correct the formatting problems and errors in the presentation while keeping in mind the guidelines presented in this chapter.

Perform the following tasks:

1. On Slide 1 (Figure 3–81), change the audio clip volume to High and hide the sound icon during the show. Loop this clip for the duration of the slide show.
2. On Slide 2, add the Reflection video effect located in the Reflection Variations area, Tight Reflection 4 pt offset (first reflection in second row) to the video.
3. Trim the Slide 2 video so that the Start Time is 00:21.087 and the End Time is 01:44.273. The duration should be 01:23.186 minutes.
4. Copy the flamingo clip from Slide 4 to Slide 3 and then delete Slide 4. Place this clip on the left side of the picture frame and then adjust the picture frame size so it is the appropriate dimension for the slide content. Ungroup the flamingo clip and then recolor the flamingo to match the color of its legs, the palm tree leaves to a shade of green, and the bird to a shade of blue. Regroup the clip.
5. Find the word, Antarctica, in the Slide 1 Notes pane, and then replace it with the words, South America. Then find the number, 14, and replace it with the number, 4.
6. Check the slides for spelling errors and then run the revised presentation.
7. Change the document properties, as specified by your instructor. Save the presentation using the file name, Make It Right 3-1 Chilean Flamingos.
8. Submit the revised document in the format specified by your instructor.

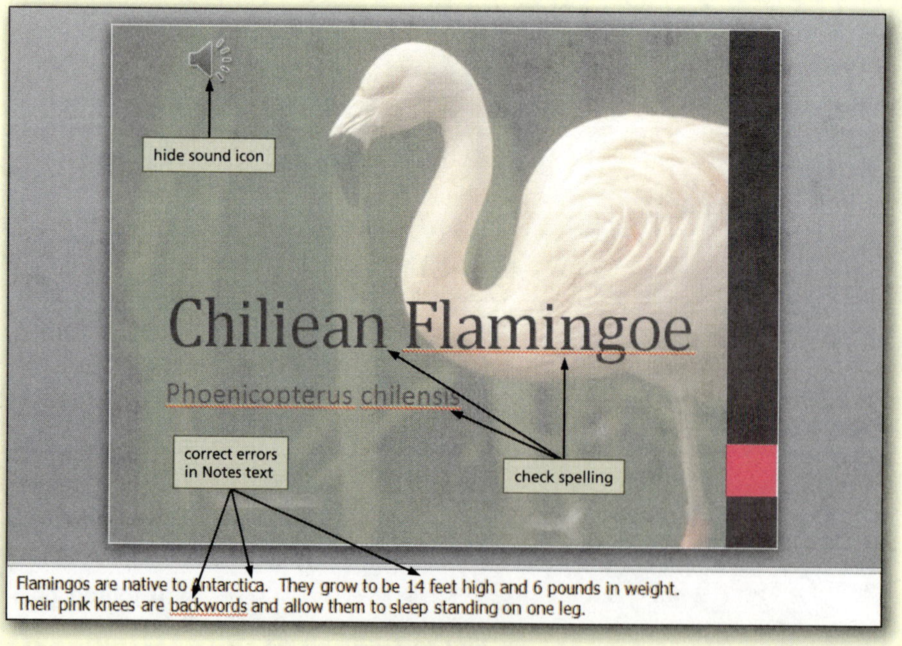

Figure 3–81

In the Lab

Design and/or create a presentation using the guidelines, concepts, and skills presented in this chapter. Labs 1, 2, and 3 are listed in order of increasing difficulty.

Lab 1: Inserting Audio Clips, Coloring a Picture, and Applying Artistic Effects to Pictures

Note: To complete this assignment, you will be required to use the Data Files for Students. See the inside back cover of this book for instructions on downloading the Data Files for Students, or contact your instructor for information about accessing the required files.

Problem: Start PowerPoint. Open the presentation, Lab 3-1 Cooking, from the Data Files for Students.

Your college has an outstanding culinary program, and you are preparing a PowerPoint presentation to promote an upcoming seafood cooking class. The slides will feature audio clips and graphics with applied effects. Create the slides shown in Figure 3–82.

Instructions: Perform the following tasks.

1. On Slide 1, insert the Mr. Light music audio clip from Office.com. Change the volume to Low, play across slides, and hide the sound icon during the show. Move the subtitle text placeholder downward to the location shown in Figure 3–82a and center both paragraphs.
2. On Slide 2, insert the picture called Blackboard and Chef, which is available on the Data Files for Students. Change the color of the picture to Gold, Accent color 3 Dark (Recolor area). Add a border to this picture using Dark Red, Accent 5, and then change the border weight to 6 pt., as shown in Figure 3–82b.

(a) Slide 1

(b) Slide 2

Figure 3–82

Continued >

In the Lab *continued*

3. On Slide 3, right-align all the text. Insert the Chef video clip from Office.com and resize this clip so that it is approximately 4.08" × 3.99", as shown in Figure 3–82c. Insert the Pepper Grinder video clip from Office.com and resize this clip so that it is approximately 3.81" × 2.25". Move the Pepper Grinder video clip to the lower-left corner of the slide. Insert the audio clips, Pepper Grinder and Cartoon Crash, from Office.com. Start these clips automatically, hide the sound icons during the show, and loop until stopped.
4. On Slide 4, apply the Watercolor Sponge artistic effect to the lobster picture in the left content placeholder and the Plastic Wrap artistic effect to the paella picture in the right content placeholder, as shown in Figure 3–82d.
5. On Slide 5, insert the Bottle Open audio clip from Office.com. Move the sound icon to the lower-right corner of the slide. Start this clip on click. Center the text in the caption placeholder and then move this placeholder downward to the location shown in Figure 3–82e.
6. Review the slides in Slide Sorter view to check for consistency, and then change the view to Normal.
7. Drag the scroll box to display Slide 1. Start Slide Show view and display each slide.
8. Change the document properties, as specified by your instructor. Save the presentation using the file name, Lab 3-1 Cooking Classes.
9. Submit the revised document in the format specified by your instructor.

(c) Slide 3

(d) Slide 4

(e) Slide 5

Figure 3–82 (Continued)

In the Lab

Lab 2: Adding Slide Numbers, Applying Artistic Effects to Pictures, and Recoloring a Video

Note: To complete this assignment, you will be required to use the Data Files for Students. See the inside back cover of this book for instructions on downloading the Data Files for Students, or contact your instructor for information about accessing the required files.

Problem: The Dutch tradition is continuing with Klompen dancers, who take their name from their traditional wooden clog shoes. You attended an annual festival this past spring and captured some video clips of teenagers dancing a traditional dance. In addition, you have some video of a hand-built windmill. In your speech class, you desire to inform your classmates of a few aspects of Dutch life, so you prepare the presentation shown in Figure 3–83.

Instructions: Perform the following tasks.

1. Start PowerPoint. Open the presentation, Lab 3-2 Dancers, from the Data Files for Students. On Slide 1, apply the Mosaic Bubbles artistic effect to the tulips picture, as shown in Figure 3–83a. Insert the audio clip, Spring Music, from Office.com. Start this clip automatically, hide the sound icon during the show, and change the volume to Medium.
2. On Slide 2, apply the Marker artistic effect to the wooden shoe picture, as shown in Figure 3–83b. Change the Start option for the video clip from On Click to Automatically. Apply the Rotated, Gradient video style (Moderate area) to the video clip, change the video border color to Tan, Accent 6, and then change the border width to 18 pt.
3. On Slide 2, type `Many dancers wear traditional, hand-sewn Dutch costumes. Dancers wear thick socks to make the wooden shoes comfortable during this annual event.` in the Notes pane.

(a) Slide 1

(b) Slide 2

Figure 3–83

Continued >

In the Lab *continued*

4. On Slide 3, insert the video clip called Windmill from the Data Files for Students. Apply the Reflected Bevel, White video style (Intense area). Change the color of the video to Dark Blue, Accent color 3 Dark (Recolor area). Start this clip automatically and loop until stopped. Center the text in the title placeholder, as shown in Figure 3–83c.
5. Use the thesaurus to change the word, Custom, to Tradition. Check the slides for spelling errors.
6. Add the slide number to all slides except the title slide.
7. Review the slides in Slide Sorter view to check for consistency. Then click the Reading view button to display the current slide and click the Next and Previous buttons to display each slide. Change the view to Normal.
8. Change the document properties, as specified by your instructor. Save the presentation using the file name, Lab 3-2 Klompen Dancers.
9. Submit the revised document in the format specified by your instructor.

(c) Slide 3

Figure 3–83 (Continued)

In the Lab

Lab 3: Applying Artistic Effects to and Recoloring Pictures, Inserting Audio, and Trimming Video

Note: To complete this assignment, you will be required to use the Data Files for Students. See the inside back cover of this book for instructions on downloading the Data Files for Students, or contact your instructor for information about accessing the required files.

Problem: Your Uncle Barney is an avid railroad buff, and he especially is interested in viewing steam locomotives. He has a collection of video clips and photographs of historic steam engines, and he asks you to create a presentation for the next Hessville Train Club meeting he is planning to attend. Start PowerPoint and then open the presentation, Lab 3-3 Locomotives, from the Data Files for Students. Prepare the slides shown in Figures 3–84a through 3–84c.

Instructions: Perform the following tasks.

1. Delete the subtitle text placeholder on Slide 1. Then insert the picture, Steamer 624, from the Data Files for Students and apply the Glow Diffused artistic effect. Position the picture as shown in Figure 3–84a. Center the title text. Insert the audio clip, Train Whistle By, from Office.com. Start this clip automatically, hide the sound icon during the show, and loop until stopped.

2. On Slide 2, insert the picture, Locomotive, from the Data Files for Students and resize it so that it fills the entire slide height and width (approximately 7.5" × 10"). Change the color of the picture to Tan, Accent color 1 Light (Recolor area), as shown in Figure 3–84b.
3. Insert the video clip, Steam Locomotive, from the Data Files for Students. Resize this clip to approximately 4.54" × 8.07" and move the clip to the location shown in Figure 3–84b. Apply the Metal Rounded Rectangle video style (Intense area). Change the color of the border to Olive Green, Accent 2. Trim the Slide 2 video so that the Start Time is 00:06.186 and the End Time is 00:23.432. The duration should be 00:17.246 seconds. Start this clip automatically and loop until stopped.
4. On Slide 3, insert the picture, Railroad Track Border, and the video clip, Red Locomotive, from the Data Files for Students. Resize the Red Locomotive clip to approximately 2.78" × 5.36" and move it to the location shown in Figure 3–84c. Also, insert the audio clip, Steam Train Pass, from Office.com, and move this sound icon to the lower-left corner of the slide. Copy the audio clip, Train Whistle By, from Slide 1 and then move the sound icon to the upper-right corner of the slide. Start both audio clips automatically, hide the sound icons during the show, and loop until stopped.
5. Review the slides in Slide Sorter view. Then click the Reading view button to display the current slide and click the Next and Previous buttons to display each slide. Change the view to Normal.
6. Change the document properties, as specified by your instructor. Save the presentation using the file name, Lab 3-3 Steam Locomotives.
7. Submit the revised document in the format specified by your instructor.

(a) Slide 1

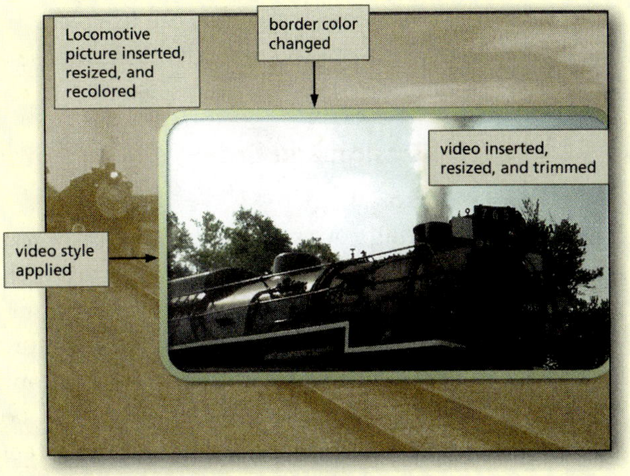

(b) Slide 2

(c) Slide 3

Figure 3–84

Cases and Places

Apply your creative thinking and problem-solving skills to design and implement a solution.

Note: To complete these assignments, you will be required to use the Data Files for Students. See the inside back cover of this book for instructions on downloading the Data Files for Students, or contact your instructor for information about accessing the required files.

As you design the presentations, remember to use the 7 × 7 rule: a maximum of seven words on a line and a maximum of seven lines on one slide.

1: Design and Create a Presentation about Kilauea Volcano

Academic

Most of the volcanic eruptions in Hawaii have occurred within Hawaii Volcanoes National Park. One of these volcanoes, Kilauea, has been erupting since 1983, and visitors to the National Park can drive on two roads to see lava tubes, steam vents, and plants returning to the barren landscape. Rainwater drains through cracks in the ground, is heated, and then is released through fissures and condenses in the cool air. Lava flows in underground tubes, and vents release volcanic gases that consist mainly of carbon dioxide, steam, and sulfur dioxide. During your recent trip to Hawaii Volcanoes National Park, you drove on these roads and captured these geological wonders with your video and digital cameras. You want to share your experience with your Geology 101 classmates. Create a presentation to show the pictures and video clips, which are located in the Data Files for Students and begin with the file name, Case 1. You also can use pictures from Office.com if they are appropriate for this topic. Apply appropriate styles and effects, and use at least three objectives found at the beginning of this chapter to develop the presentation. Be sure to check spelling.

2: Design and Create a Presentation about Surfing

Personal

During your summer vacation, you took surfing lessons and enjoyed the experience immensely. You now want to share your adventure with friends, so you decide to create a short PowerPoint presentation with video clips of the surf and of your paddling on your surfboard to the instruction area in the ocean. You also have pictures of your introductory lesson on shore and of your first successful run catching a wave. The Data Files for Students contains these media files that begin with the file name, Case 2. You also can use your own digital pictures or pictures from Office.com if they are appropriate for this topic. Use the clip, Case 2 - Yellow and Green Surfboard, on one slide, but ungroup this clip and then change the surfboard's colors to your school's team colors. Trim the video clips and apply appropriate styles and effects. Use at least three objectives found at the beginning of this chapter to develop the presentation. Be sure to check spelling.

3: Design and Create a Presentation to Promote Your Snow Removal Business

Professional

Record snowfalls have wreaked havoc in your neighborhood, so you have decided to earn tuition money by starting a snow removal business. You are willing to clear sidewalks and driveways when snowfall exceeds three inches. To promote your business, you desire to create a PowerPoint presentation to run behind the counter at the local hardware store. The Data Files for Students contains pictures and a video clip that begin with the file name, Case 3. You also can use your own digital pictures or pictures from Office.com if they are appropriate for this topic. Use the clip, Case 3 - Man Shoveling, on one slide, but ungroup this clip and then zoom in and delete the white area of the clip depicting the man's breath. Also, recolor at least one picture and apply an artistic effect. Be sure to check spelling.

1 Creating a Worksheet and an Embedded Chart

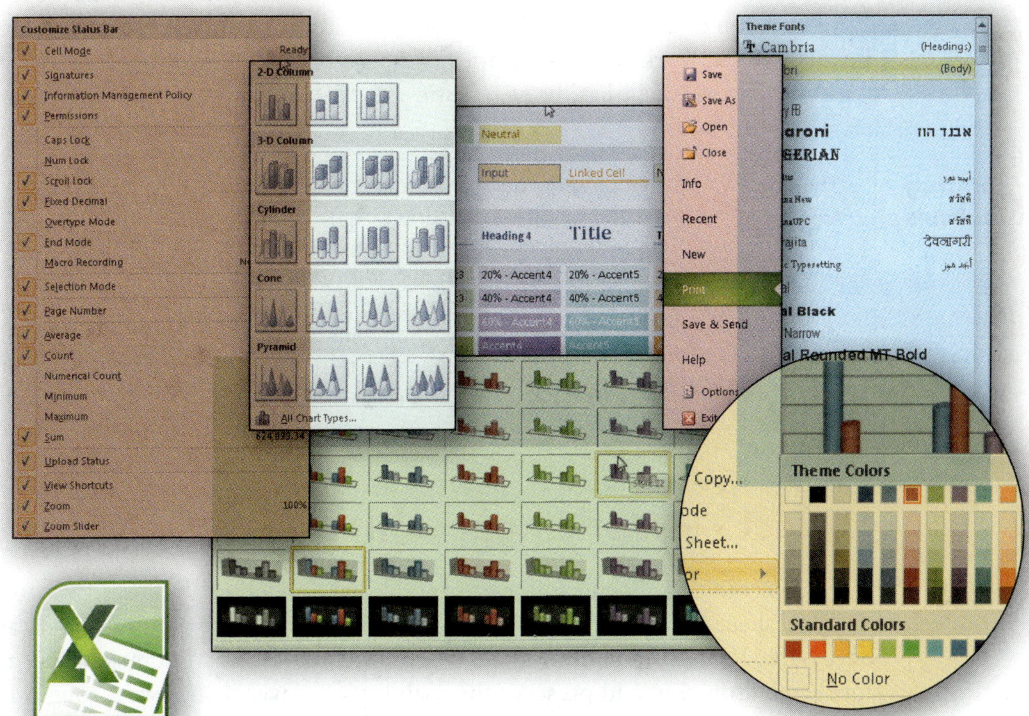

Objectives

You will have mastered the material in this chapter when you can:

- Describe the Excel worksheet
- Enter text and numbers
- Use the Sum button to sum a range of cells
- Copy the contents of a cell to a range of cells using the fill handle
- Apply cell styles
- Format cells in a worksheet
- Create a Clustered Cylinder chart
- Change a worksheet name and worksheet tab color
- Change document properties
- Preview and print a worksheet
- Use the AutoCalculate area to display statistics
- Correct errors on a worksheet

1 Creating a Worksheet and an Embedded Chart

Introduction

Almost any organization collects vast amounts of data. Often, data is consolidated into a summary so that people in the organization better understand the meaning of the data. An Excel worksheet allows data easily to be summarized and charted. A chart conveys a visual representation of data. In this chapter, you will create a worksheet that includes a chart. The data in the worksheet and chart includes data for donations made to a not-for-profit organization that operates in several cities.

Project Planning Guidelines

The process of developing a worksheet that communicates specific information requires careful analysis and planning. As a starting point, establish why the worksheet is needed. Once the purpose is determined, analyze the intended users of the worksheet and their unique needs. Then, gather information about the topic and decide what to include in the worksheet. Finally, determine the worksheet design and style that will be most successful at delivering the message. Details of these guidelines are provided in Appendix A. In addition, each project developed in the Office chapters in this book provides practical applications of these planning considerations.

Project — Worksheet with an Embedded Chart

The project in this chapter follows proper design guidelines and uses Excel to create the worksheet shown in Figure 1–1. The worksheet contains fundraising data for the Save Sable River Foundation. The Save Sable River Foundation raises funds to care for the environment and preserve the usability of a river that flows through six cities. The foundation raises funds by using five different fundraising activities. Through a concentrated marketing campaign and providing visible results to the communities, the Save Sable River Foundation quickly became a popular local institution. After several years of successful fundraising, senior management requested an easy-to-read worksheet that shows lifetime fundraising amounts for each fundraising technique by city. In addition, they asked for a chart showing lifetime fundraising amounts because the president of the foundation likes to have a graphical representation that allows him quickly to identify stronger and weaker fundraising activities by city.

Selecting a Cell

To enter data into a cell, you first must select it. The easiest way **to select a cell** (make it active) is to use the mouse to move the block plus sign mouse pointer to the cell and then click.

An alternative method is to use the arrow keys that are located just to the right of the alphanumeric keys on a standard keyboard. An arrow key selects the cell adjacent to the active cell in the direction of the arrow on the key.

You know a cell is selected, or active, when a heavy border surrounds the cell and the active cell reference appears in the Name box on the left side of the formula bar. Excel also changes the active cell's column heading and row heading to a gold color.

BTW

Selecting a Cell
You can select any cell by entering its cell reference, such as B4, in the Name box on the left side of the formula bar.

For an introduction to Office 2010 and instruction about how to perform basic tasks in Office 2010 programs, read the Office 2010 and Windows 7 chapter in this book, where you can learn how to start a program, use the Ribbon, save a file, open a file, quit a program, use Help, and much more.

Entering Text

In Excel, any set of characters containing a letter, hyphen (as in a telephone number), or space is considered text. **Text** is used to place titles, such as worksheet titles, column titles, and row titles, on the worksheet.

Plan Ahead

Select titles and subtitles for the worksheet.
Worksheet titles and subtitles should be as brief and meaningful as possible. A worksheet title could include the name of the organization, department, or a description of the content of the worksheet. A worksheet subtitle, if included, could include a more detailed description of the content of the worksheet. Examples of worksheet titles are December 2010 Payroll and Year 2011 Projected Budget, and examples of subtitles are Marketing Department and Rent and Utilities, respectively.

Plan Ahead

Determine the contents of rows and columns.
As shown in Figure 1–4, data in a worksheet often is identified by row and column titles so that the user of a worksheet easily can identify the meaning of the data. Rows typically contain information that is similar to items in a list. Columns typically contain descriptive information about items in rows or contain information that helps to group the data in the worksheet. Examples of row titles are Product and Total, and examples of column titles are Name and Address.

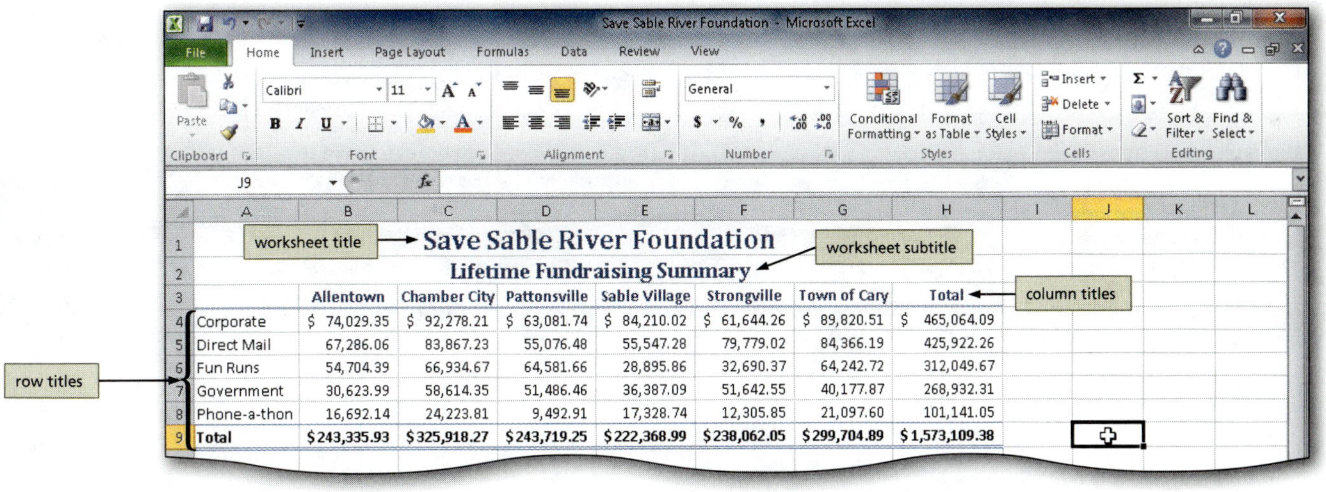

Figure 1–4

To Enter the Worksheet Titles

As shown in Figure 1–4 on the previous page, the worksheet title, Save Sable River Foundation, identifies the organization for which the worksheet is being created in Excel Chapter 1. The worksheet subtitle, Lifetime Fundraising Summary, identifies the type of report.

The following steps enter the worksheet titles in cells A1 and A2. Later in this chapter, the worksheet titles will be formatted so they appear as shown in Figure 1–4.

1

- If necessary, click cell A1 to make cell A1 the active cell (Figure 1–5).

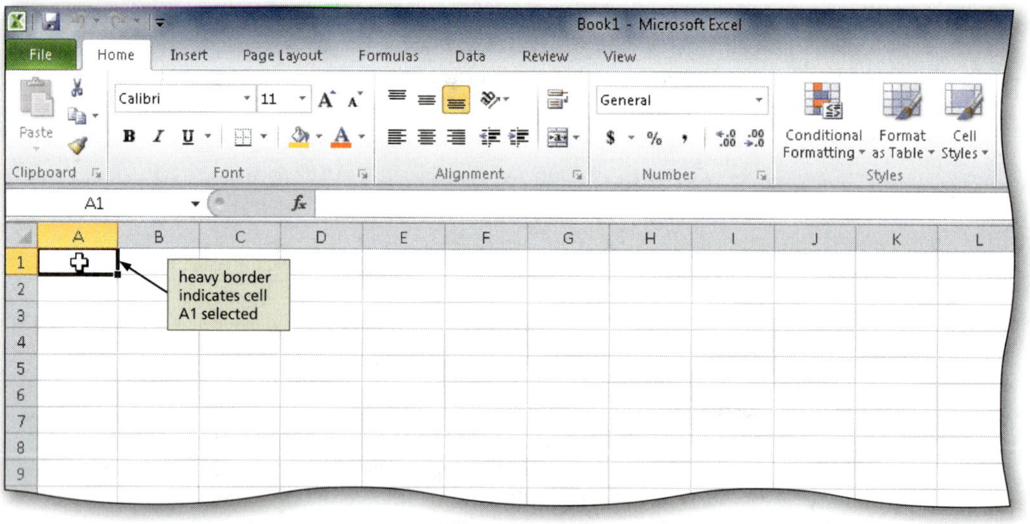

Figure 1–5

Q&A What if I make a mistake while typing?

If you type the wrong letter and notice the error before clicking the Enter box or pressing the ENTER key, use the BACKSPACE key to delete all the characters back to and including the incorrect letter. To cancel the entire entry before entering it into the cell, click the Cancel box in the formula bar or press the ESC key. If you see an error in a cell after entering the text, select the cell and retype the entry.

2

- Type **Save Sable River Foundation** in cell A1 and then point to the Enter box in the formula bar to prepare to enter text in the active cell (Figure 1–6).

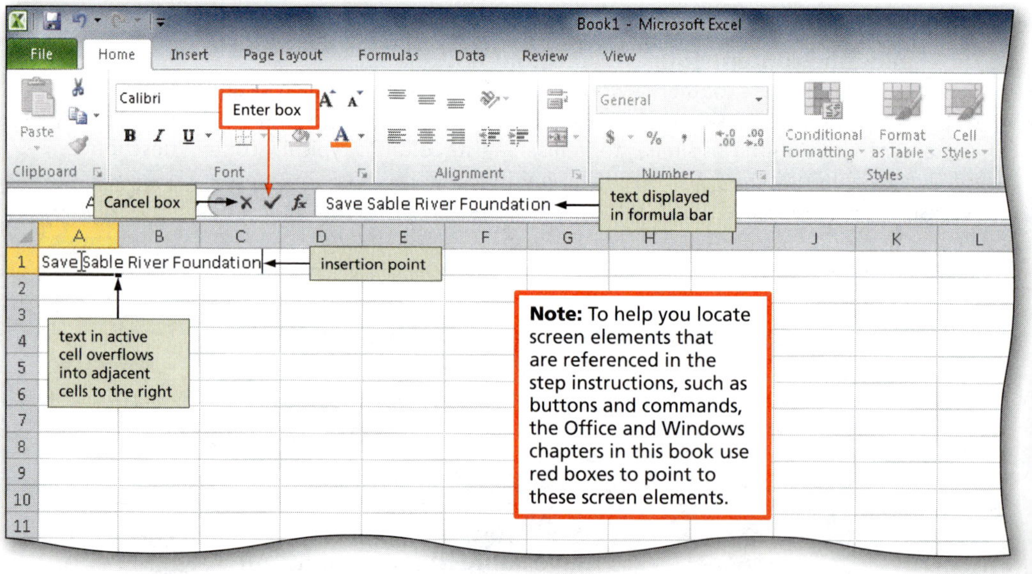

Figure 1–6

Q&A Why did the appearance of the formula bar change?

Excel displays the title in the formula bar and in cell A1. When you begin typing a cell entry, Excel displays two additional boxes in the formula bar: the Cancel box and the Enter box. Clicking the **Enter box** completes an entry. Clicking the **Cancel box** cancels an entry.

Q&A What is the vertical line in cell A1?

The text in cell A1 is followed by the insertion point. The **insertion point** is a blinking vertical line that indicates where the next typed character will appear.

3

- Click the Enter box to complete the entry and enter a worksheet title (Figure 1–7).

Q&A Why does the entered text appear in three cells?

When the text is longer than the width of a column, Excel displays the overflow characters in adjacent cells to the right as long as those adjacent cells contain no data. If the adjacent cells contain data, Excel would hide the overflow characters. Excel displays the overflow characters in the formula bar whenever that cell is the active cell.

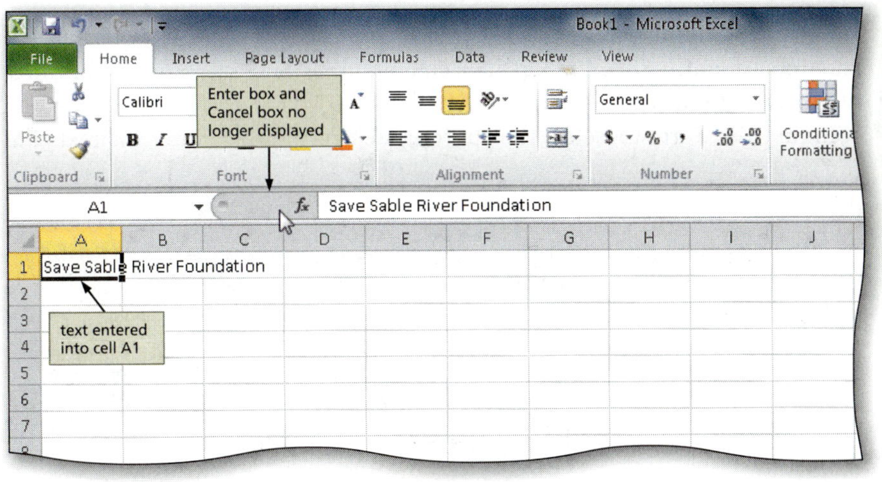

Figure 1–7

4

- Click cell A2 to select it.
- Type `Lifetime Fundraising Summary` as the cell entry.
- Click the Enter box to complete the entry and enter a worksheet subtitle (Figure 1–8).

Q&A What happens when I click the Enter box?

When you complete an entry by clicking the Enter box, the insertion point disappears and the cell in which the text is entered remains the active cell.

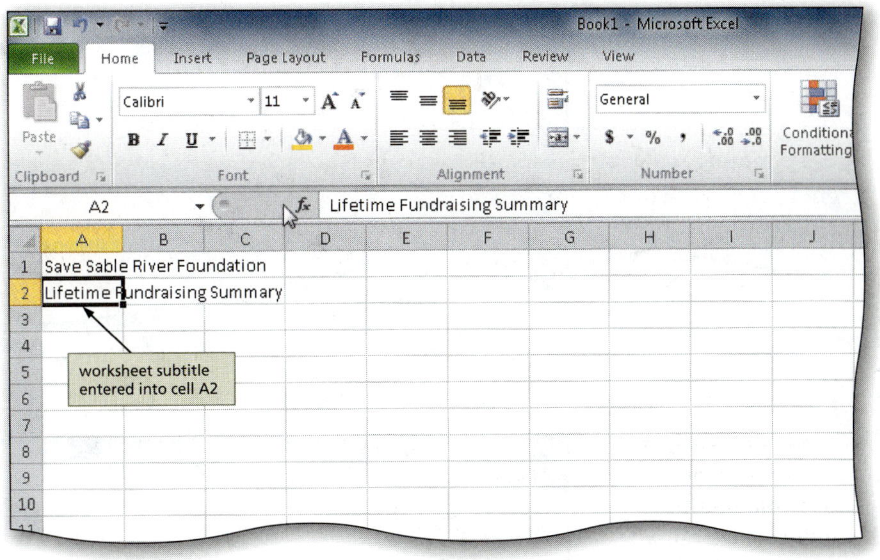

Figure 1–8

Other Ways

1. To complete entry, click any cell other than active cell
2. To complete entry, press ENTER
3. To complete entry, press HOME, PAGE UP, PAGE DOWN, or END
4. To complete entry, press UP ARROW, DOWN ARROW, LEFT ARROW, or RIGHT ARROW.

AutoCorrect

The **AutoCorrect feature** of Excel works behind the scenes, correcting common mistakes when you complete a text entry in a cell. AutoCorrect makes three types of corrections for you:

1. Corrects two initial capital letters by changing the second letter to lowercase.
2. Capitalizes the first letter in the names of days.
3. Replaces commonly misspelled words with their correct spelling. For example, it will change the misspelled word *recieve* to *receive* when you complete the entry. AutoCorrect will correct the spelling of hundreds of commonly misspelled words automatically.

BTW **Q&As**
For a complete list of the Q&As found in many of the step-by-step sequences in the Office and Windows chapters in this book, visit the Microsoft Office and Concepts CourseMate Web site at www.cengagebrain.com and then navigate to the Q&A resource for this book.

To Enter Column Titles

The column titles in row 3 (Allentown, Chamber City, Pattonsville, Sable Village, Strongville, Town of Cary, and Total) identify the numbers in each column. In the case of the Save the Sable River Foundation data, the cities identify the funds raised using each fundraising type. The cities, therefore, are placed in columns. To enter the column titles in row 3, select the appropriate cell and then enter the text. The following steps enter the column titles in row 3.

1

- Click cell B3 to make it the active cell (Figure 1–9).

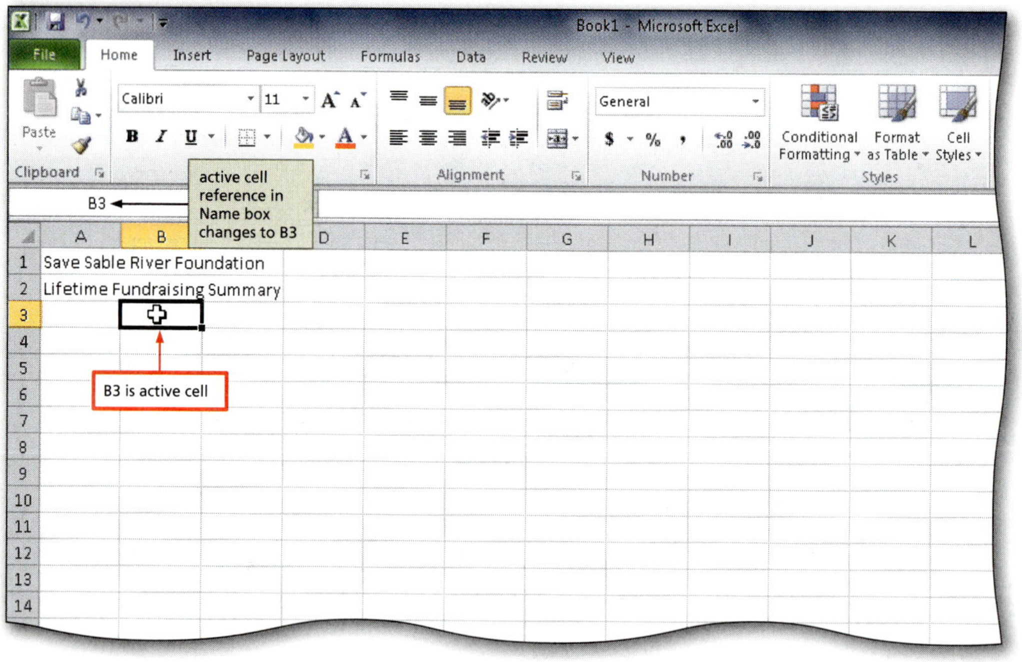

Figure 1–9

2

- Type **Allentown** to begin entry of a column title in the active cell (Figure 1–10).

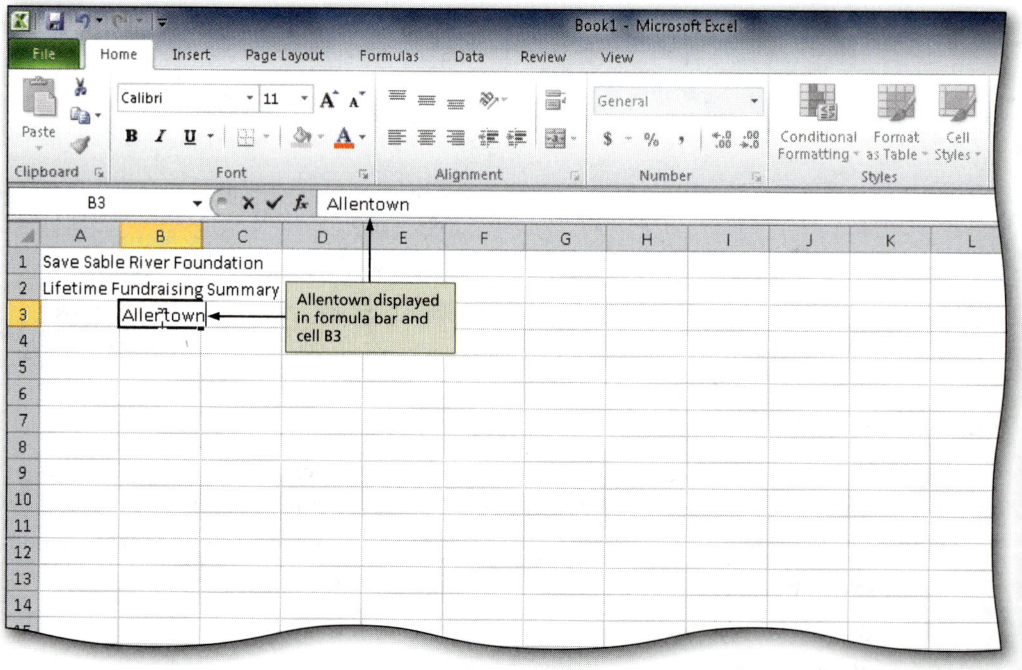

Figure 1–10

3

- Press the RIGHT ARROW key to enter a column title and make the cell to the right the active cell (Figure 1–11).

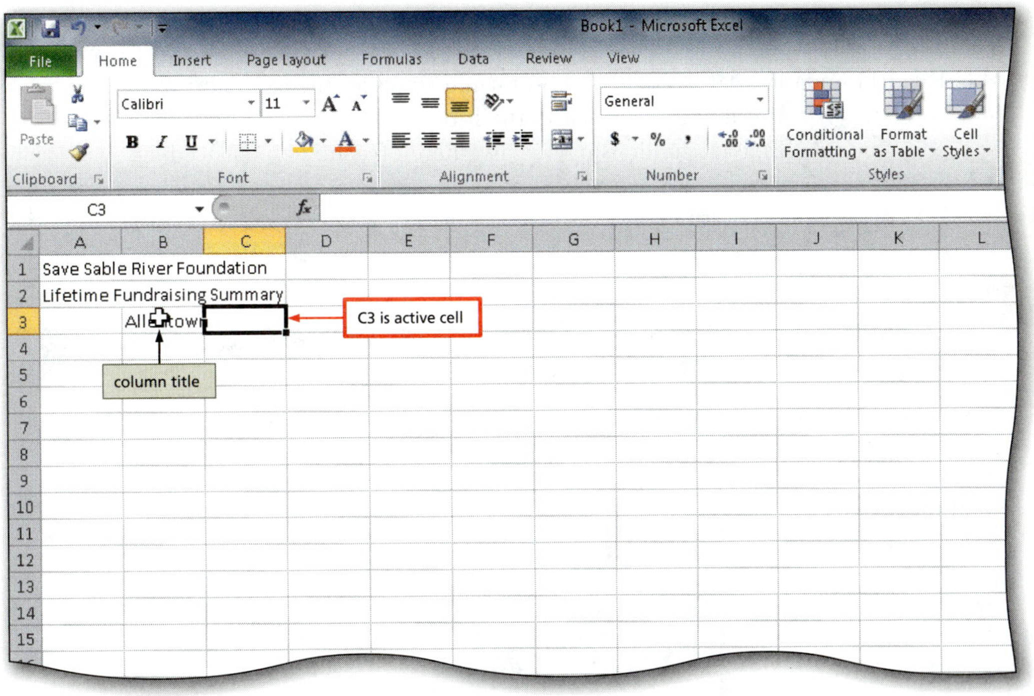

Figure 1–11

Q&A

Why is the RIGHT ARROW key used to complete the entry in the cell?

If the next entry you want to enter is in an adjacent cell, use the arrow keys to complete the entry in a cell. When you press an arrow key to complete an entry, the adjacent cell in the direction of the arrow (up, down, left, or right) becomes the active cell. If the next entry is in a nonadjacent cell, complete the current entry by clicking the next cell in which you plan to enter data. You also can click the Enter box or press the ENTER key and then click the appropriate cell for the next entry.

4

- Repeat Steps 2 and 3 to enter the remaining column titles; that is, enter **`Chamber City`** in cell C3, **`Pattonsville`** in cell D3, **`Sable Village`** in cell E3, **`Strongville`** in cell F3, **`Town of Cary`** in cell G3, and **`Total`** in cell H3 (complete the last entry in cell H3 by clicking the Enter box in the formula bar) (Figure 1–12).

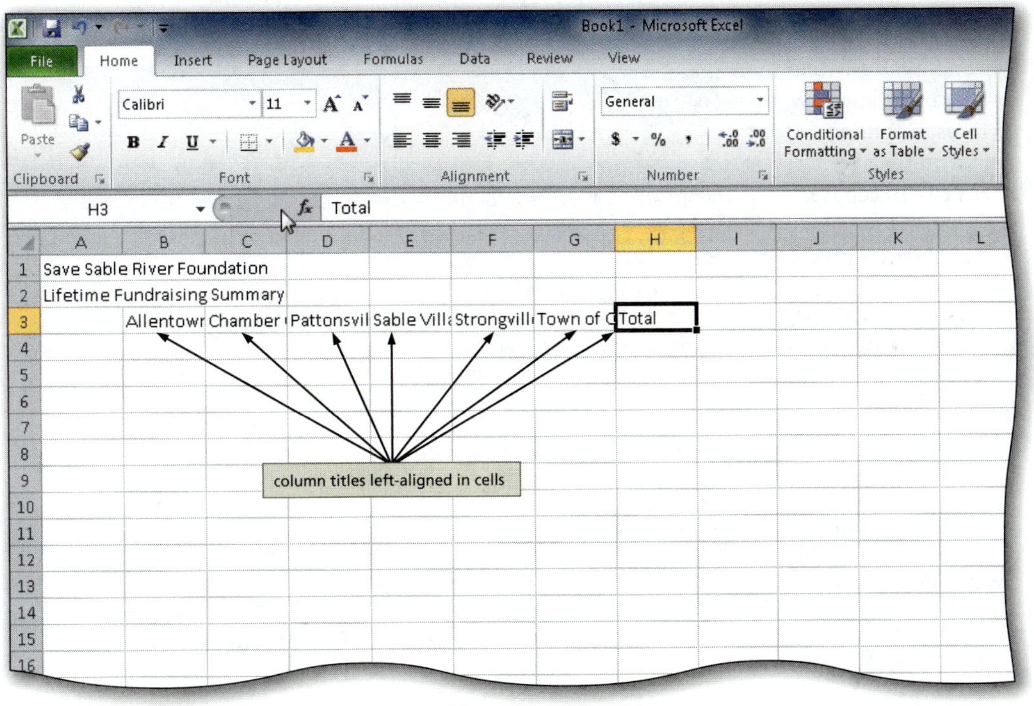

Figure 1–12

To Enter Row Titles

The next step in developing the worksheet for this project is to enter the row titles in column A. For the Save Sable River Foundation data, the list of fundraising activities meets the criterion that information that identifies columns be in a list. It is more likely that in the future, the organization will add more fundraising activities as opposed to more cities. Each fundraising activity, therefore, should be placed in its own row. The row titles in column A (Corporate, Direct Mail, Fun Runs, Government, Phone-a-thon, and Total) identify the numbers in each row.

This process for entering row titles is similar to the process for entering column titles. The following steps enter the row titles in the worksheet.

1

- Click cell A4 to select it.
- Type `Corporate` and then press the DOWN ARROW key to enter a row title and to make the cell below the current cell the active cell (Figure 1–13).

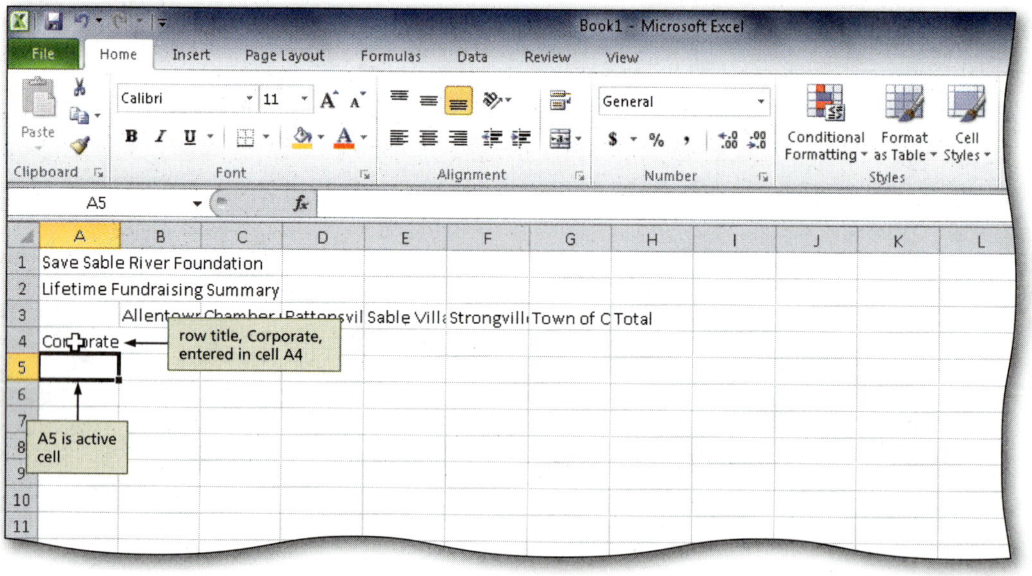

Figure 1–13

2

- Repeat Step 1 to enter the remaining row titles in column A; that is, enter `Direct Mail` in cell A5, `Fun Runs` in cell A6, `Government` in cell A7, `Phone-a-thon` in cell A8, and `Total` in cell A9 (Figure 1–14).

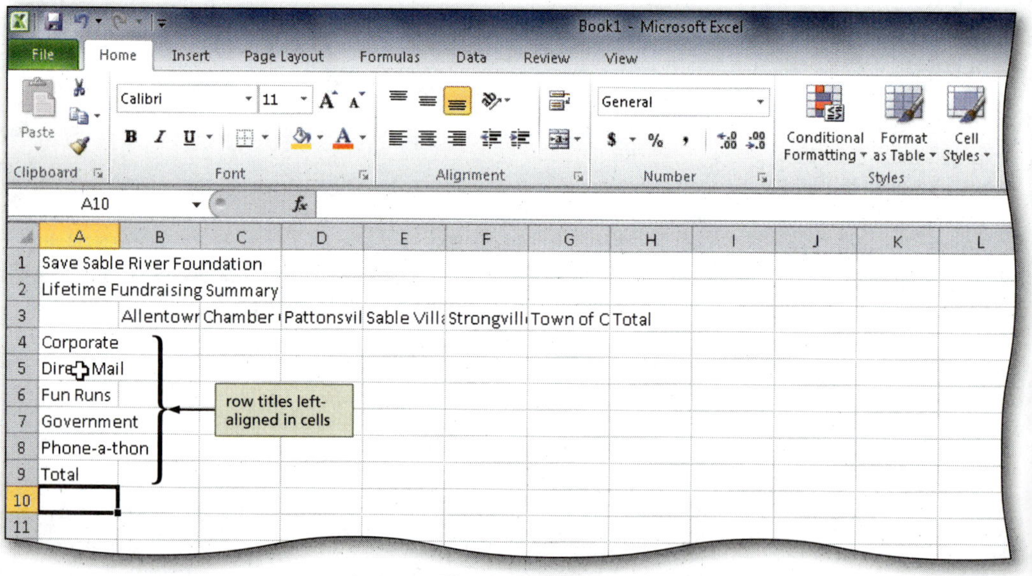

Figure 1–14

Q&A

Why is the text left-aligned in the cells?

When you enter text, Excel automatically left-aligns the text in the cell. Excel treats any combination of numbers, spaces, and nonnumeric characters as text. For example, Excel recognizes the following entries as text:

401AX21, 921–231, 619 321, 883XTY

You can change the text alignment in a cell by realigning it. Other alignment techniques are discussed later in this chapter.

Entering Numbers

In Excel, you can enter numbers into cells to represent amounts. A **number** can contain only the following characters:

0 1 2 3 4 5 6 7 8 9 + - ( ) , / . $ % E e

If a cell entry contains any other keyboard character (including spaces), Excel interprets the entry as text and treats it accordingly. The use of the special characters is explained when they are used.

BTW

Numeric Limitations

In Excel, a number can be between approximately -1×308^{10} and 1×308^{10}. This means it can be between a negative 1 followed by 308 zeros and a positive 1 followed by 308 zeros. To enter a number such as 6,000,000,000,000,000, you can type 6,000,000,000,000,000, or you can type 6E15, which translates to 6 × 1015.

To Enter Numbers

The Save Sable River Foundation Lifetime Fundraising Summary numbers used in Excel Chapter 1 are summarized in Table 1–1. These numbers, which represent lifetime fundraising amounts for each of the fundraising activities and cities, must be entered in rows 4, 5, 6, 7, and 8.

Table 1–1 Save Sable River Foundation Lifetime Fundraising Summary

	Allentown	Chamber City	Pattonsville	Sable Village	Strongville	Town of Cary
Corporate	74029.35	92278.21	63081.74	84210.02	61644.26	89820.51
Direct Mail	67286.06	83867.23	55076.48	55547.28	79779.02	84366.19
Fun Runs	54704.39	66934.67	64581.66	28895.86	32690.37	64242.72
Government	30623.99	58614.35	51486.46	36387.09	51642.55	40177.87
Phone-a-thon	16692.14	24223.81	9492.91	17328.74	12305.85	21097.60

The following steps enter the numbers in Table 1–1 one row at a time.

1

- Click cell B4 to select it.
- Type `74029.35` and then press the RIGHT ARROW key to enter the data in the selected cell and make the cell to the right the active cell (Figure 1–15).

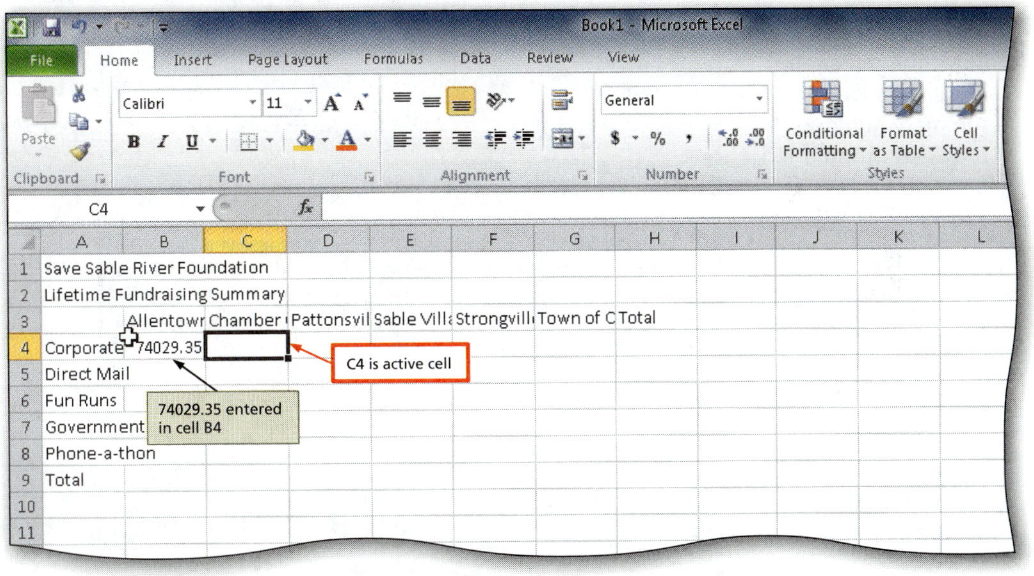

Figure 1–15

Q&A

Do I need to enter dollar signs, commas, or trailing zeros for the fundraising summary amounts?

You are not required to type dollar signs, commas, or trailing zeros. When you enter a dollar value that has cents, however, you must add the decimal point and the numbers representing the cents. Later in this chapter, the numbers will be formatted to use dollar signs, commas, and trailing zeros to improve the appearance and readability of the numbers.

2

- Enter `92278.21` in cell C4, `63081.74` in cell D4, `84210.02` in cell E4, `61644.26` in cell F4, and `89820.51` in cell G4 to complete the first row of numbers in the worksheet (Figure 1–16).

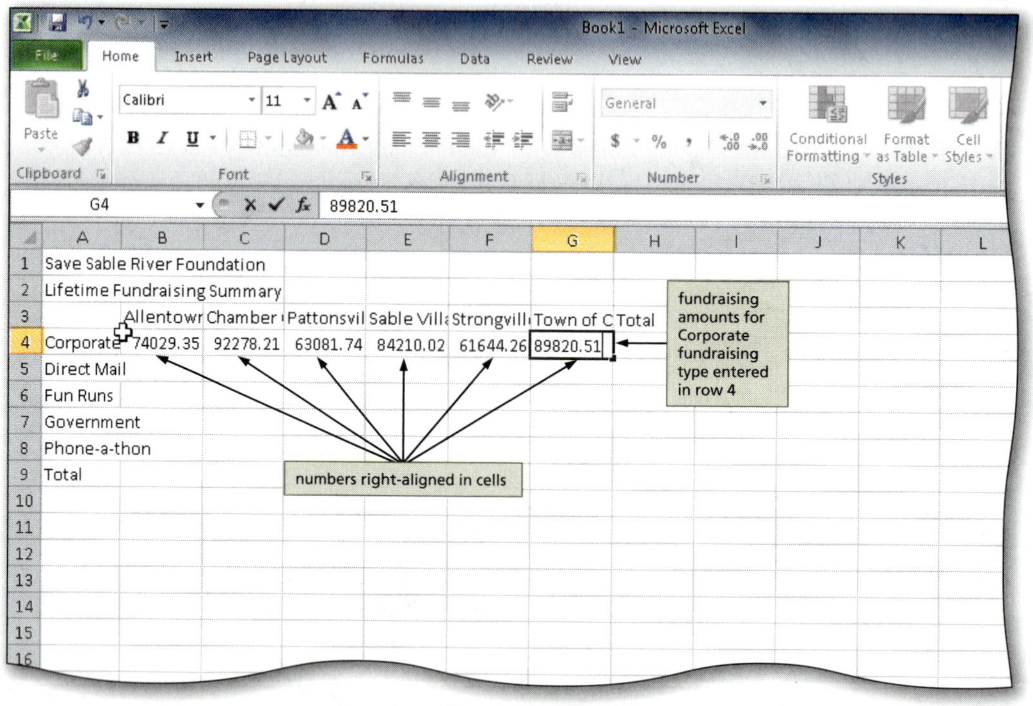

Figure 1–16

Q&A Why are the numbers right-aligned?

When you enter numeric data in a cell, Excel recognizes the values as numbers and right-aligns the values in order to properly vertically align decimal and integer values. For example, values entered below those entered in this step automatically will be right-aligned as well so that the decimals of the values properly align.

3

- Click cell B5 to select it and complete the entry in the previously selected cell.
- Enter the remaining lifetime fundraising summary numbers provided in Table 1–1 on page EX 13 for each of the four remaining fundraising activities in rows 5, 6, 7, and 8 to finish entering numbers in the worksheet (Figure 1–17).

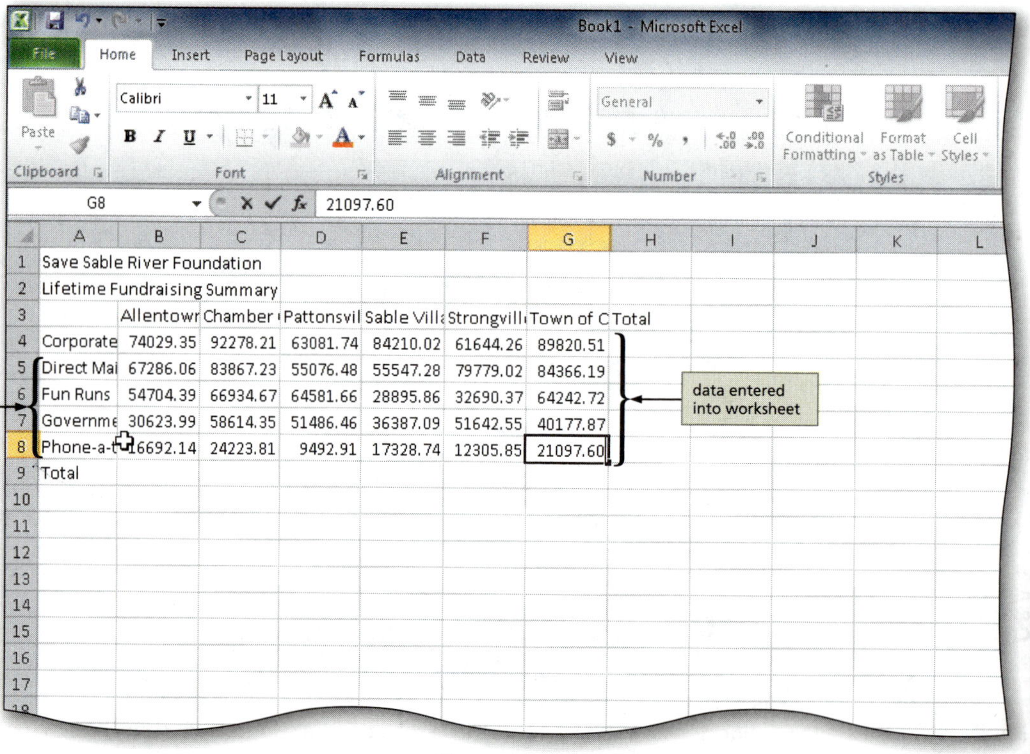

Figure 1–17

Q&A Why did clicking cell B5 complete the entry in cell G4?

Selecting another cell completes the entry in the previously selected cell in the same way as pressing the ENTER key, pressing an arrow key, or clicking the Enter box on the formula bar. In the next set of steps, the entry of the number in cell G4 will be completed by selecting another cell.

Calculating a Sum

The next step in creating the worksheet is to perform any necessary calculations, such as calculating the column and row totals.

To Sum a Column of Numbers

As stated in the requirements document in Figure 1–2 on page EX 4, totals are required for each city, each fundraising activity, and the organization. The first calculation is to determine the fundraising total for the fundraising activities in the city of Allentown in column B. To calculate this value in cell B9, Excel must add, or sum, the numbers in cells B4, B5, B6, B7, and B8. Excel's **SUM function**, which adds all of the numbers in a range of cells, provides a convenient means to accomplish this task.

A **range** is a series of two or more adjacent cells in a column or row or a rectangular group of cells. For example, the group of adjacent cells B4, B5, B6, B7, and B8 is called a range. Many Excel operations, such as summing numbers, take place on a range of cells.

After the total lifetime fundraising amount for the fundraising activities in the city of Allentown in column B is determined, the totals for the remaining cities and totals for each fundraising activity will be determined. The following steps sum the numbers in column B.

1

- Click cell B9 to make it the active cell and complete the entry in the previously selected cell.
- Click the Sum button (Home tab | Editing group) to display a formula in the formula bar and in the active cell (Figure 1–18).

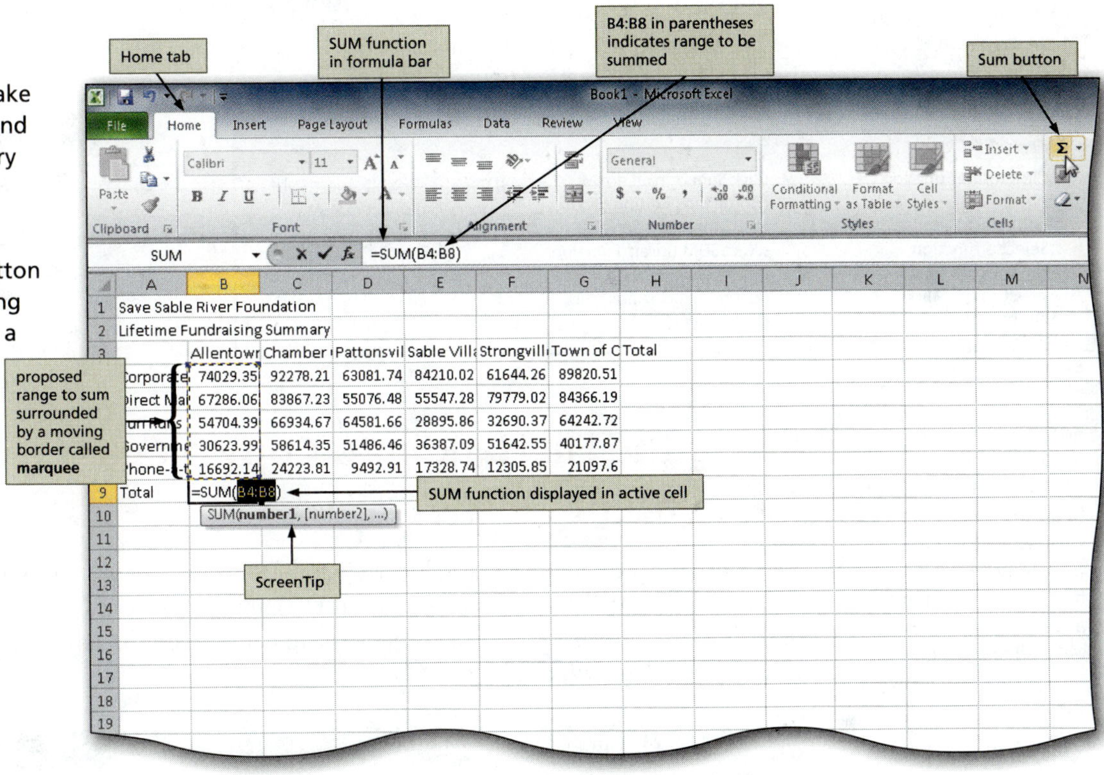

Figure 1–18

Q&A How does Excel know which cells to sum?

When you enter the SUM function using the Sum button, Excel automatically selects what it considers to be your choice of the range to sum. When proposing the range to sum, Excel first looks for a range of cells with numbers above the active cell and then to the left. If Excel proposes the wrong range, you can correct it by dragging through the correct range before pressing the ENTER key. You also can enter the correct range by typing the beginning cell reference, a colon (:), and the ending cell reference.

BTW **Calculating Sums**

Excel calculates sums for a variety of data types. For example, Boolean values, such as TRUE and FALSE, can be summed. Excel treats the value of TRUE as 1 and the value of FALSE as 0. Times also can be summed. For example, Excel treats the sum of 1:15 and 2:45 as 4:00.

2

- Click the Enter box in the formula bar to enter a sum in the active cell (Figure 1–19).

Q&A What is the purpose of the Sum button arrow?

If you click the Sum button arrow on the right side of the Sum button (Home tab | Editing group) (Figure 1–19), Excel displays a list of often used functions from which you can choose. The list includes functions that allow you to determine the average, the number of items in the selected range, the maximum value, or the minimum value of a range of numbers.

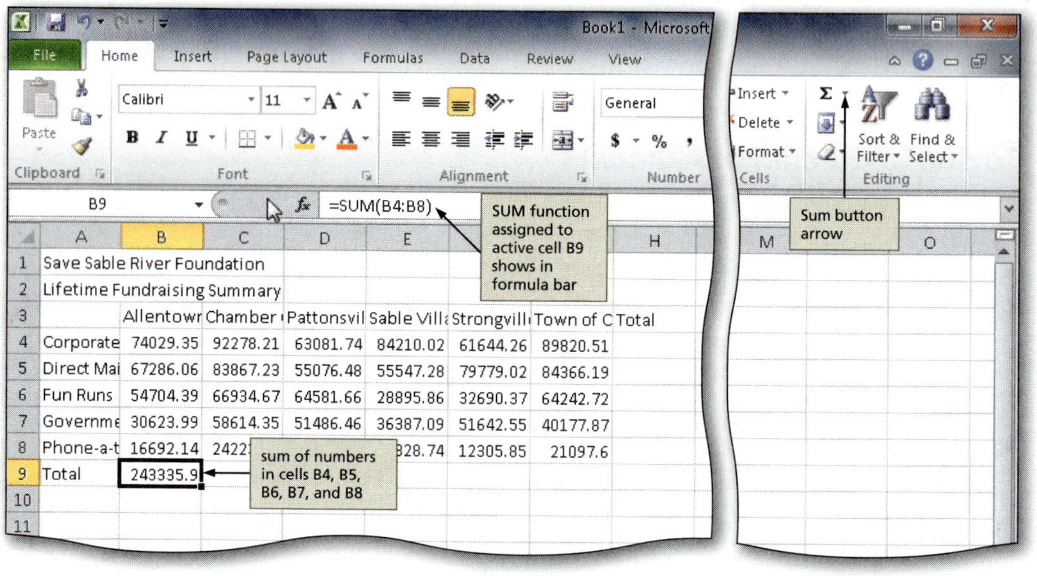

Figure 1–19

Other Ways

1. Click Insert Function button in the formula bar, select SUM in Select a function list, click OK button, select range, click OK button
2. Click Sum button arrow (Home tab | Editing group), click More Functions, select SUM (Insert Function dialog box), click OK button, select range, click OK button
3. Type = S in cell, select SUM from list, select range
4. Press ALT + EQUAL SIGN (=) twice

BTW

Entering Numbers as Text

Sometimes, you will want Excel to treat numbers, such as postal codes and telephone numbers, as text. To enter a number as text, start the entry with an apostrophe (').

Using the Fill Handle to Copy a Cell to Adjacent Cells

Excel also must calculate the totals for Chamber City in cell C9, Pattonsville in cell D9, Sable Village in cell E9, Strongville in cell F9, and the Town of Cary in cell G9. Table 1–2 illustrates the similarities between the entry in cell B9 and the entries required to sum the totals in cells C9, D9, E9, F9 and G9.

Table 1–2 Sum Function Entries in Row 9

Cell	Sum Function Entries	Remark
B9	=SUM(B4:B8)	Sums cells B4, B5, B6, B7, and B8
C9	=SUM(C4:C8)	Sums cells C4, C5, C6, C7, and C8
D9	=SUM(D4:D8)	Sums cells D4, D5, D6, D7, and D8
E9	=SUM(E4:E8)	Sums cells E4, E5, E6, E7, and E8
F9	=SUM(F4:F8)	Sums cells F4, F5, F6, F7, and F8
G9	=SUM(G4:G8)	Sums cells G4, G5, G6, G7, and G8

To place the SUM functions in cells C9, D9, E9, F9, and G9, you could follow the same steps shown previously in Figures 1–18 on page EX 15 and 1–19. A second, more efficient method, however, is to copy the SUM function from cell B9 to the range C9:G9. The cell being copied is called the **source area** or **copy area**. The range of cells receiving the copy is called the **destination area** or **paste area**.

Although the SUM function entries in Table 1–2 are similar, they are not exact copies. The range in each SUM function entry uses cell references that are one column to the right of the previous column. When you copy formulas that include cell references, Excel automatically adjusts them for each new position, resulting in the SUM function entries illustrated in Table 1–2. Each adjusted cell reference is called a **relative reference**.

To Copy a Cell to Adjacent Cells in a Row

The easiest way to copy the SUM formula from cell B9 to cells C9, D9, E9, F9, and G9 is to use the fill handle. The **fill handle** is the small black square located in the lower-right corner of the heavy border around the active cell. The following steps use the fill handle to copy cell B9 to the adjacent cells C9:G9.

1

- With cell B9 active, point to the fill handle to activate it (Figure 1–20).

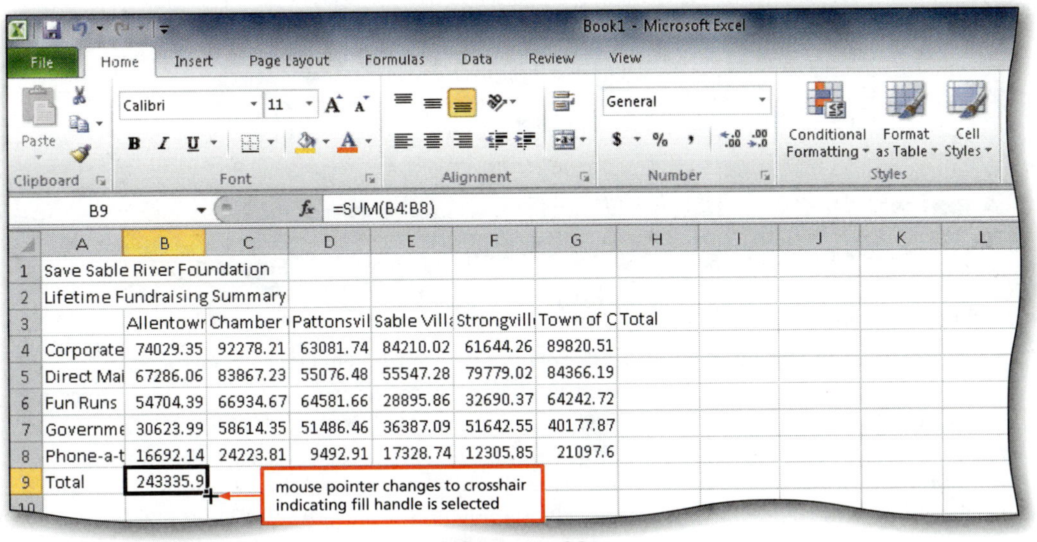

Figure 1–20

2

- Drag the fill handle to select the destination area, range C9:G9, to display a shaded border around the source area and the destination area (Figure 1–21). Do not release the mouse button.

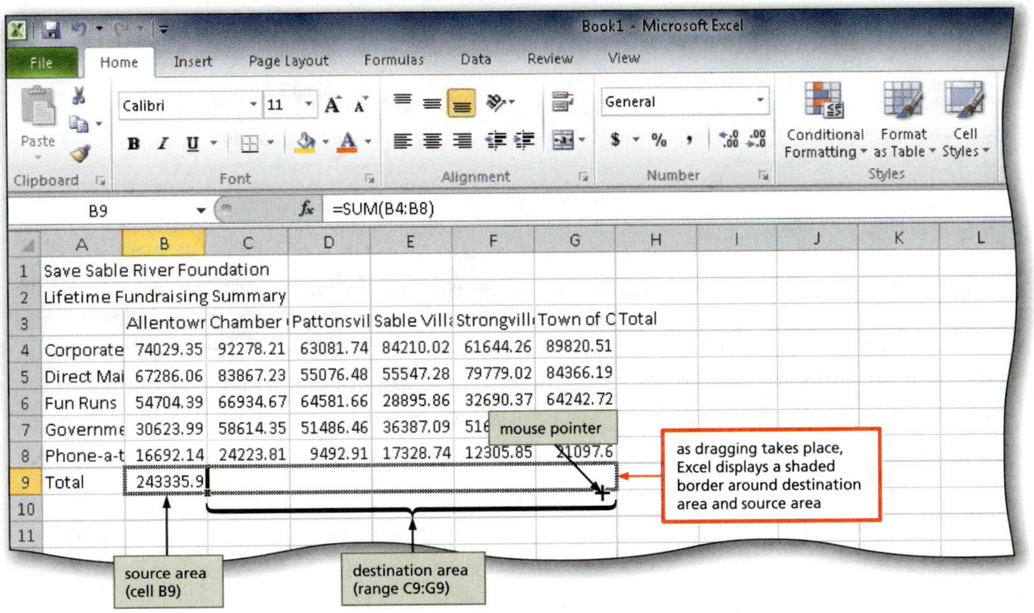

Figure 1–21

3

- Release the mouse button to copy the SUM function from the active cell to the destination area and calculate the sums (Figure 1–22).

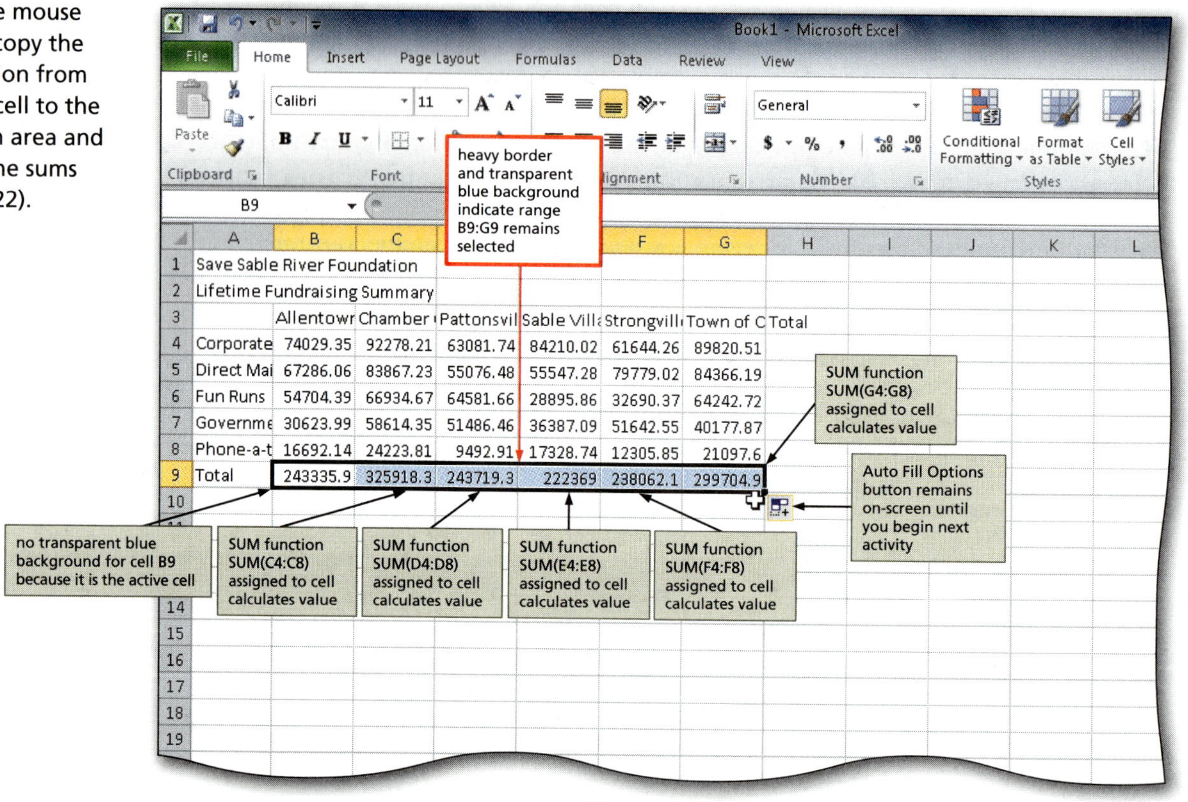

Figure 1–22

Q&A

What is the purpose of the Auto Fill Options button?

When you copy one range to another, Excel displays an Auto Fill Options button (Figure 1–22). The Auto Fill Options button allows you to choose whether you want to copy the values from the source area to the destination area with formatting, do so without formatting, or copy only the format. To view the available fill options, click the Auto Fill Options button. The Auto Fill Options button disappears when you begin another activity in Excel, such as typing data in another cell or applying formatting to a cell or range of cells.

Other Ways

1. Select source area, click Copy button (Home tab | Clipboard group), select destination area, click Paste button (Home tab | Clipboard group)
2. Right-click source area, click Copy on shortcut menu, right-click destination area, click Paste on shortcut menu
3. Select source area and then point to border of range; while holding down CTRL, drag source area to destination area

To Determine Multiple Totals at the Same Time

The next step in building the worksheet is to determine the lifetime fundraising totals for each fundraising activity and total lifetime fundraising for the organization in column H. To calculate these totals, you can use the SUM function much as it was used to total the lifetime fundraising amounts by city in row 9. In this example, however, Excel will determine totals for all of the rows at the same time. The following steps sum multiple totals at once.

1

- Click cell H4 to make it the active cell (Figure 1–23).

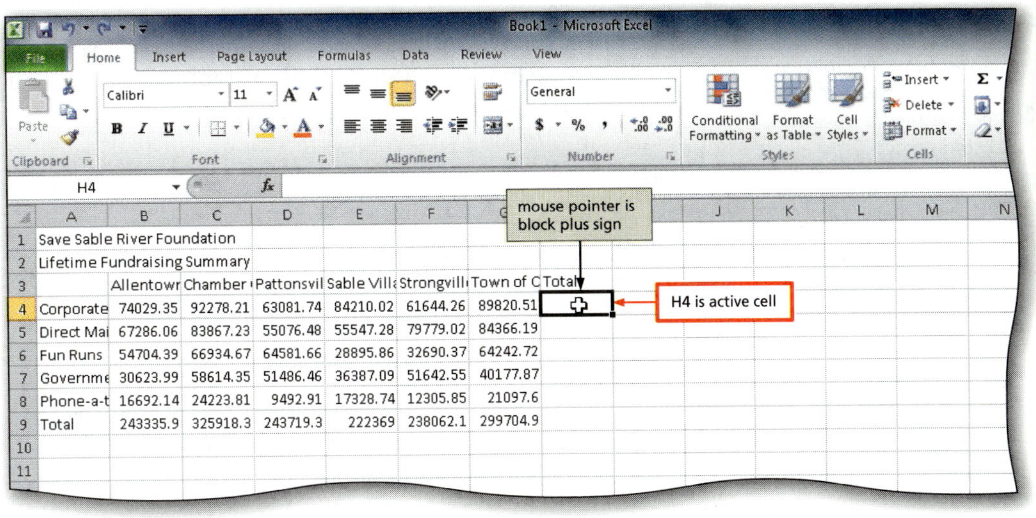

Figure 1–23

2

- With the mouse pointer in cell H4 and in the shape of a block plus sign, drag the mouse pointer down to cell H9 to highlight the range with a transparent view (Figure 1–24).

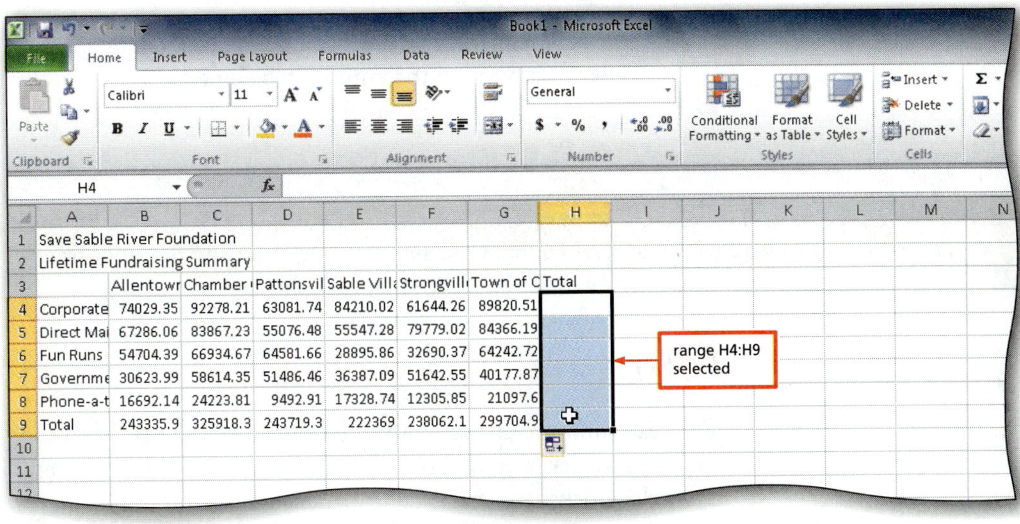

Figure 1–24

3

- Click the Sum button (Home tab | Editing group) to calculate and display the sums of the corresponding rows (Figure 1–25).
- Select cell A10 to deselect the selected range.

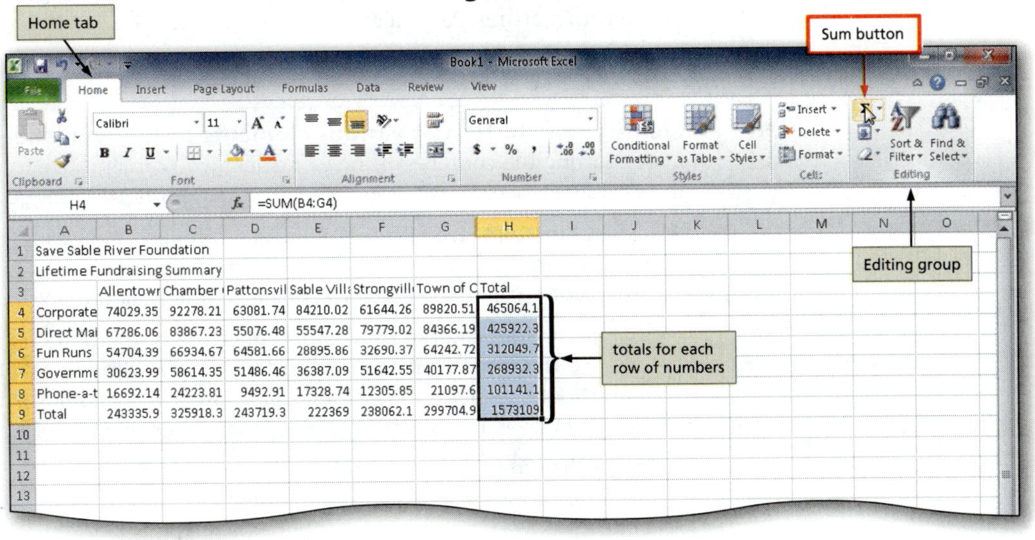

Figure 1–25

Q&A

How does Excel create unique totals for each row?

If each cell in a selected range is next to a row of numbers, Excel assigns the SUM function to each cell when you click the Sum button.

BTW

Organizing Files and Folders
You should organize and store files in folders so that you easily can find the files later. For example, if you are taking an introductory computer class called CIS 101, a good practice would be to save all Excel files in an Excel folder in a CIS 101 folder. For a discussion of folders and detailed examples of creating folders, refer to the Office 2010 and Windows 7 chapter in this book.

To Save a Workbook

You have performed many tasks while creating this workbook and do not want to risk losing work completed thus far. Accordingly, you should save the workbook.

The following steps assume you already have created folders for storing your files, for example, a CIS 101 folder (for your class) that contains an Excel folder (for your assignments). Thus, these steps save the workbook in the Excel folder in the CIS 101 folder on a USB flash drive using the file name, Save Sable River Foundation. For a detailed example of the procedure summarized below, refer to the Office 2010 and Windows 7 chapter in this book.

1. With a USB flash drive connected to one of the computer's USB ports, click the Save button on the Quick Access Toolbar to display the Save As dialog box.
2. Type `Save Sable River Foundation` in the File name text box to change the file name. Do not press the ENTER key after typing the file name because you do not want to close the dialog box at this time.
3. Navigate to the desired save location (in this case, the Excel folder in the CIS 101 folder [or your class folder] on the USB flash drive).
4. Click the Save button (Save As dialog box) to save the document in the selected folder on the selected drive with the entered file name.

Break Point: If you wish to take a break, this is a good place to do so. You can quit Excel. To resume at a later time, start Excel, open the file called Save Sable River Foundation, and continue following the steps from this location forward.

Formatting the Worksheet

The text, numeric entries, and functions for the worksheet now are complete. The next step is to format the worksheet. You **format** a worksheet to emphasize certain entries and make the worksheet easier to read and understand.

Figure 1–26a shows the worksheet before formatting. Figure 1–26b shows the worksheet after formatting. As you can see from the two figures, a worksheet that is formatted not only is easier to read but also looks more professional.

Plan Ahead

Identify how to format various elements of the worksheet.
By formatting the contents of the worksheet, you can improve its overall appearance. When formatting a worksheet, consider the following formatting suggestions:

- **Increase the font size of cells.** An increased font size gives more impact to the text in a cell. In order to indicate their relative importance, worksheet titles should have the largest font size, followed by worksheet subtitles, and then column and row headings.
- **Change the font color of cells.** Different cell colors help the reader of a worksheet quickly differentiate between the sections of a worksheet. Worksheet titles and subtitles easily should be identifiable from column and row headings. The overuse of too many colors, however, may be distracting to the reader of a worksheet.
- **Center the worksheet titles, subtitles, and column headings.** Centering text in worksheet titles and subtitles over the portion of the worksheet that they represent helps the reader of a worksheet quickly to identify the information that is of interest to them.

(continued)

Plan Ahead

(continued)

- **Modify column widths to best fit text in cells.** Make certain that text in a cell does not overflow into another cell. A column's width should be adjusted to accommodate the largest amount of text used in a cell in the column. Columns that contain data that is similar in nature to other columns should share the same column width.
- **Change the font style of cells.** Use a bold font style to make worksheet titles, worksheet subtitles, column headings, row heading, and totals stand out. Use italics and underline font styles judiciously, as specific rules of grammar apply to their use.

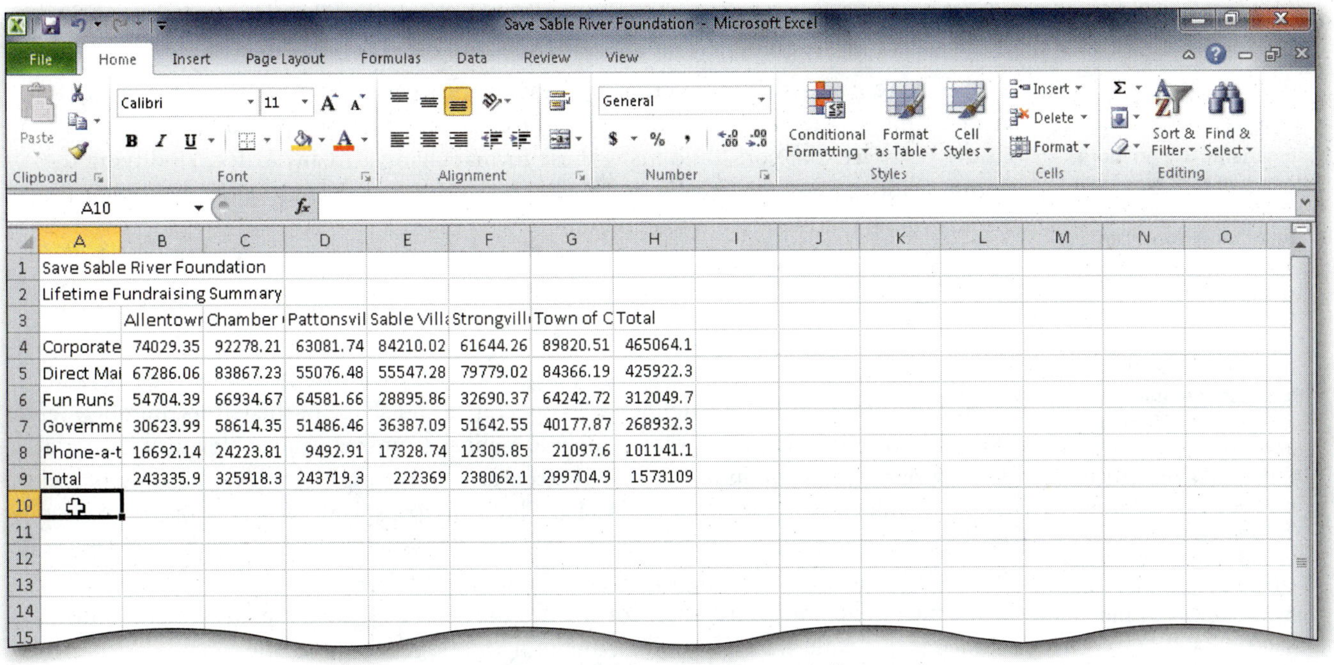

Figure 1–26 (a) Before Formatting

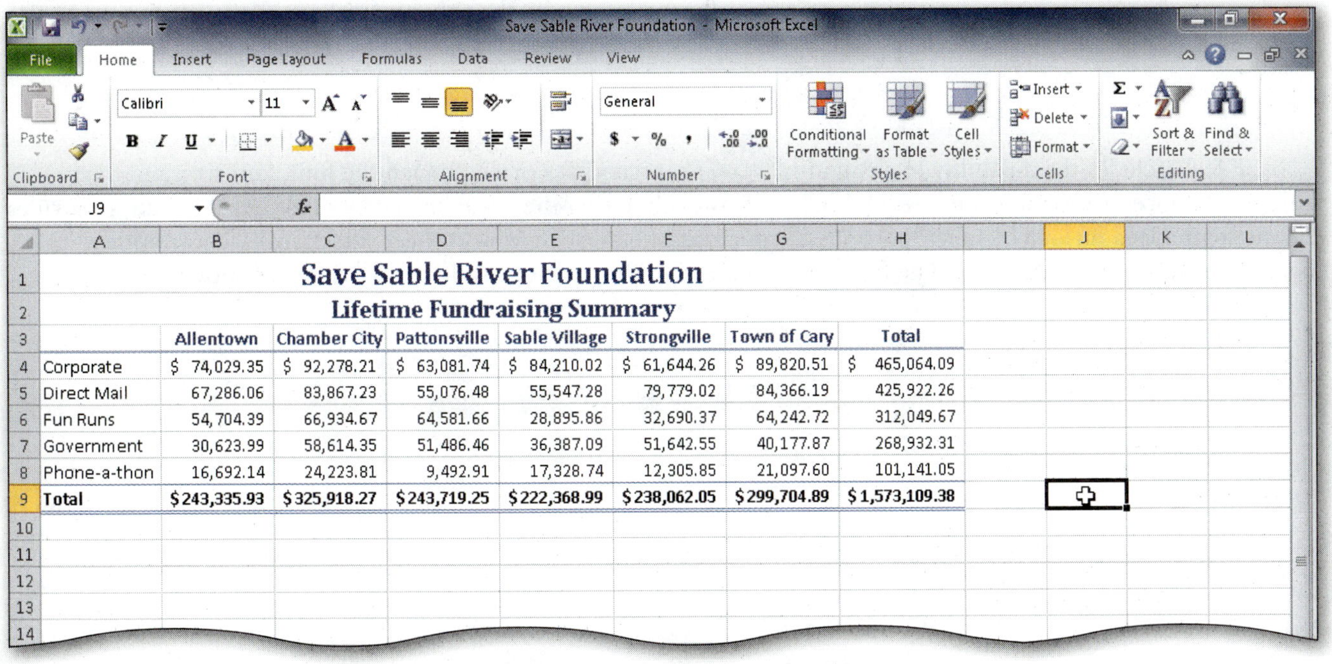

Figure 1–26 (b) After Formatting

To change the unformatted worksheet in Figure 1–26a on the previous page to the formatted worksheet in Figure 1–26b on the previous page, the following tasks must be completed:

1. Change the font, change the font style to bold, increase the font size, and change the font color of the worksheet titles in cells A1 and A2.
2. Center the worksheet titles in cells A1 and A2 across columns A through H.
3. Format the body of the worksheet. The body of the worksheet, range A3:H9, includes the column titles, row titles, and numbers. Formatting the body of the worksheet changes the numbers to use a dollars-and-cents format, with dollar signs in the first row (row 4) and the total row (row 9); adds underlining that emphasizes portions of the worksheet; and modifies the column widths to fit the text in the columns and make the text and numbers readable.

The remainder of this section explains the process required to format the worksheet. Although the formatting procedures are explained in the order described above, you should be aware that you could make these format changes in any order. Modifying the column widths, however, usually is done last because other formatting changes may affect the size of data in the cells in the column.

BTW **Fonts**
In general, use no more than two font types in a worksheet because the use of more fonts can make a worksheet difficult to read.

Font, Style, Size, and Color

BTW **Fonts and Themes**
Excel uses default recommended fonts based on the workbook's theme. A theme is a collection of fonts and color schemes. The default theme is named Office, and the two default fonts for the Office theme are Calibri and Cambria. Excel, however, allows you to apply any font to a cell or range as long as the font is installed on your computer.

The characters that Excel displays on the screen are a specific font, style, size, and color. The **font**, or font face, defines the appearance and shape of the letters, numbers, and special characters. Examples of fonts include Calibri, Cambria, Times New Roman, Arial, and Courier. **Font style** indicates how the characters are emphasized. Common font styles include regular, bold, underline, and italic. The **font size** specifies the size of the characters on the screen. Font size is gauged by a measurement system called points. A single point is about 1/72 of one inch in height. Thus, a character with a **point size** of 10 is about 10/72 of one inch in height. The **font color** defines the color of the characters. Excel can display characters in a wide variety of colors, including black, red, orange, and blue.

When Excel begins, the preset font for the entire workbook is Calibri, with a font size, font style, and font color of 11–point regular black. Excel allows you to change the font characteristics in a single cell, a range of cells, the entire worksheet, or the entire workbook.

To Change a Cell Style

Excel includes the capability of changing several characteristics of a cell, such the font, font size, and font color, all at once by assigning a predefined cell style to a cell. Using the predefined styles that Excel includes provides a consistent appearance to common portions of your worksheets, such as worksheet titles, worksheet subtitles, column headings, and total rows. The following steps assign the Title cell style to the worksheet title in cell A1.

1

- Click cell A1 to make cell A1 the active cell.
- Click the Cell Styles button (Home tab | Styles group) to display the Cell Styles gallery (Figure 1–27).

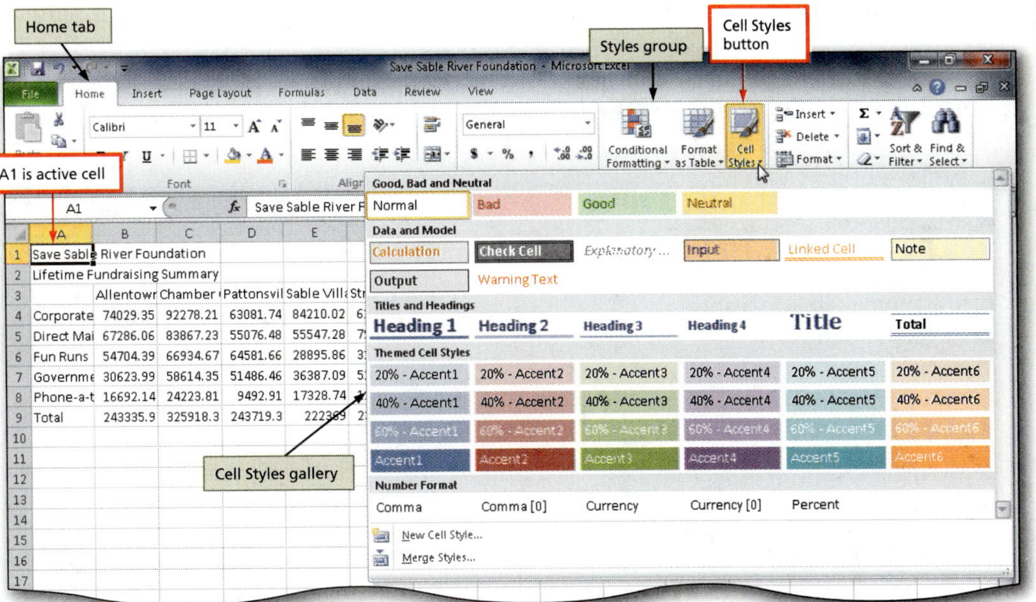

Figure 1–27

2

- Point to the Title cell style in the Titles and Headings area of the Cell Styles gallery to see a live preview of the cell style in the active cell (Figure 1–28).

Experiment

- Point to several other cell styles in the Cell Styles gallery to see a live preview of other cell styles in cell A1.

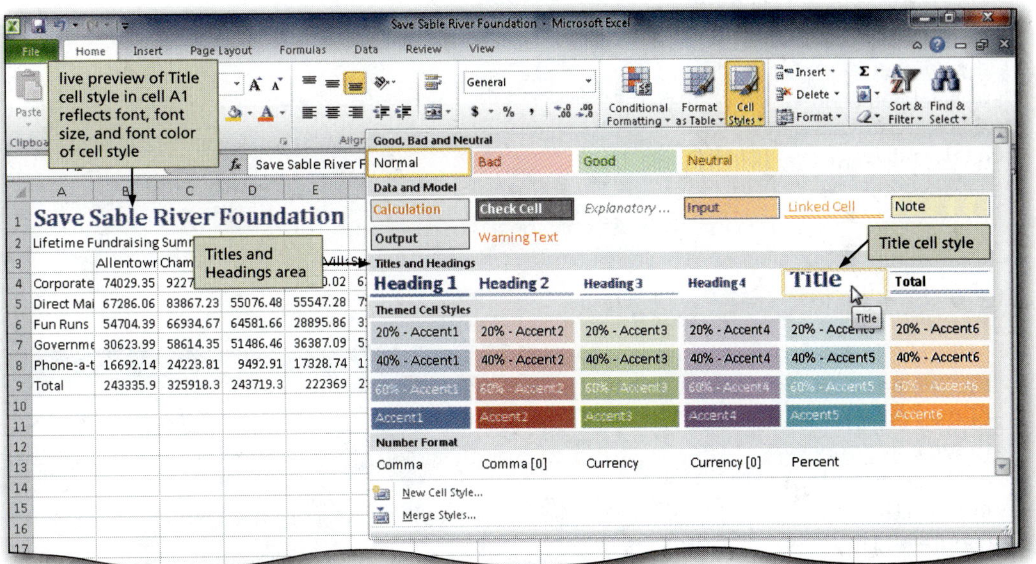

Figure 1–28

3

- Click the Title cell style to apply the cell style to the active cell (Figure 1–29).

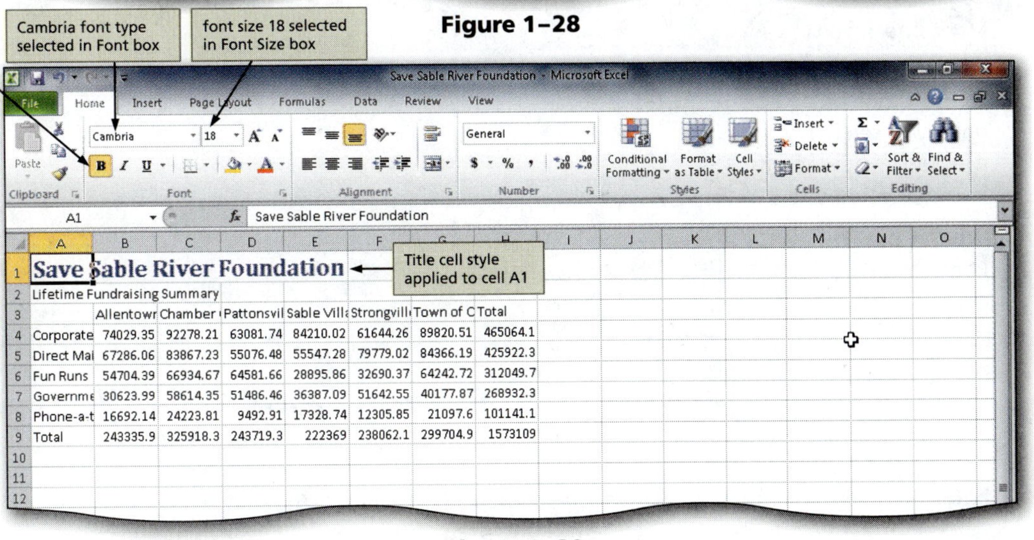

Figure 1–29

Q&A

Why do several items in the Font group on the Ribbon change?

The changes to the Font box, Bold button, and Font Size box indicate the font changes applied to the active cell, cell A1, as a result of applying the Title cell style.

To Change the Font

Different fonts often are used in a worksheet to make it more appealing to the reader and to relate or distinguish data in the worksheet. The following steps change the worksheet subtitle's fonts from Calibri to Cambria.

1

- Click cell A2 to make it the active cell.
- Click the Font box arrow (Home tab | Font group) to display the Font gallery (Figure 1–30).

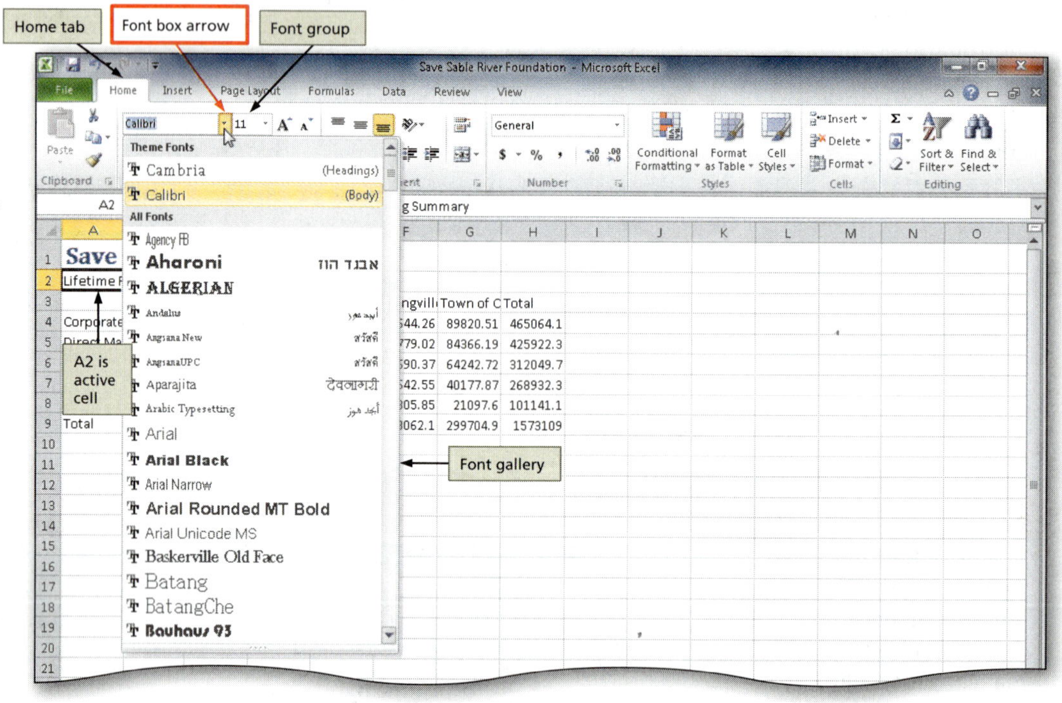

Figure 1–30

Q&A Which fonts are displayed in the Font gallery?

Because many programs supply additional fonts beyond what comes with the Windows 7 operating system, the number of fonts available on your computer will depend on the programs installed. The Office and Windows chapters in this book use only fonts that come with the Windows 7 operating system and Microsoft Office 2010.

2

- Point to Cambria in the Theme Fonts area of the Font gallery to see a live preview of the selected font in the active cell (Figure 1–31).

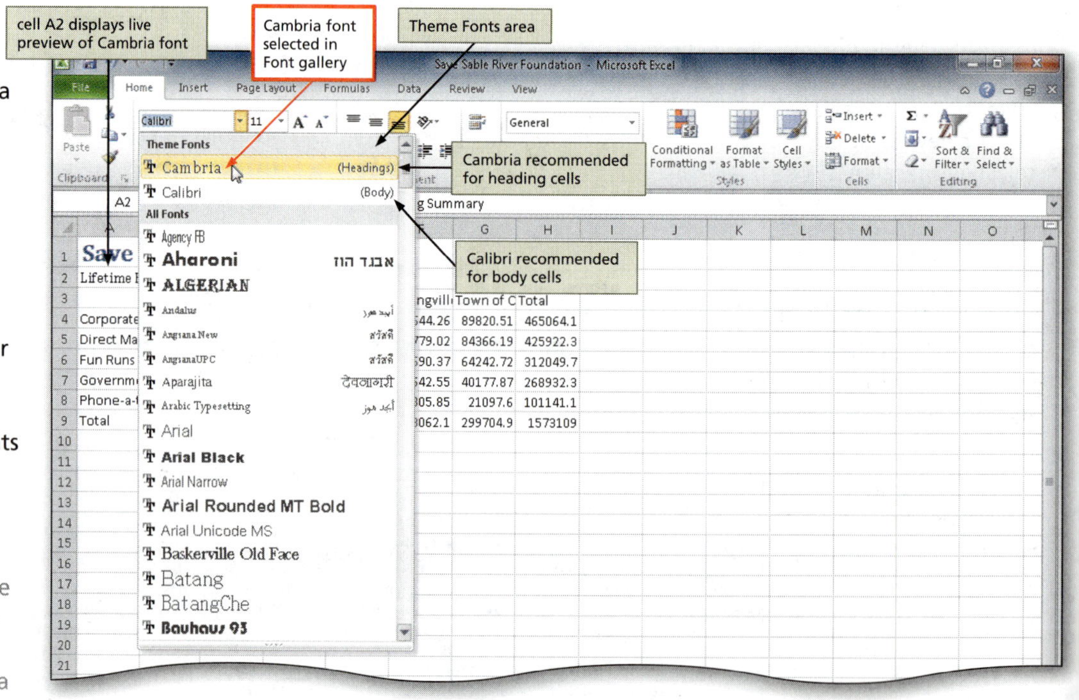

Figure 1–31

Experiment

- Point to several other fonts in the Font gallery to see a live preview of other fonts in the selected cell.

Q&A What is the Theme Fonts area?

Excel applies the same default theme to any new workbook that you start. A **theme** is a collection of cell styles and other styles that have common characteristics, such as a color scheme and font. The default theme for an Excel workbook is the Office theme. The Theme Fonts area of the Font gallery includes the fonts included in the default Office theme. Cambria is recommended for headings and Calibri is recommended by Microsoft for cells in the body of the worksheet (Figure 1–31).

3

- Click Cambria in the Theme Fonts area to change the font of the worksheet subtitle to Cambria (Figure 1–32).

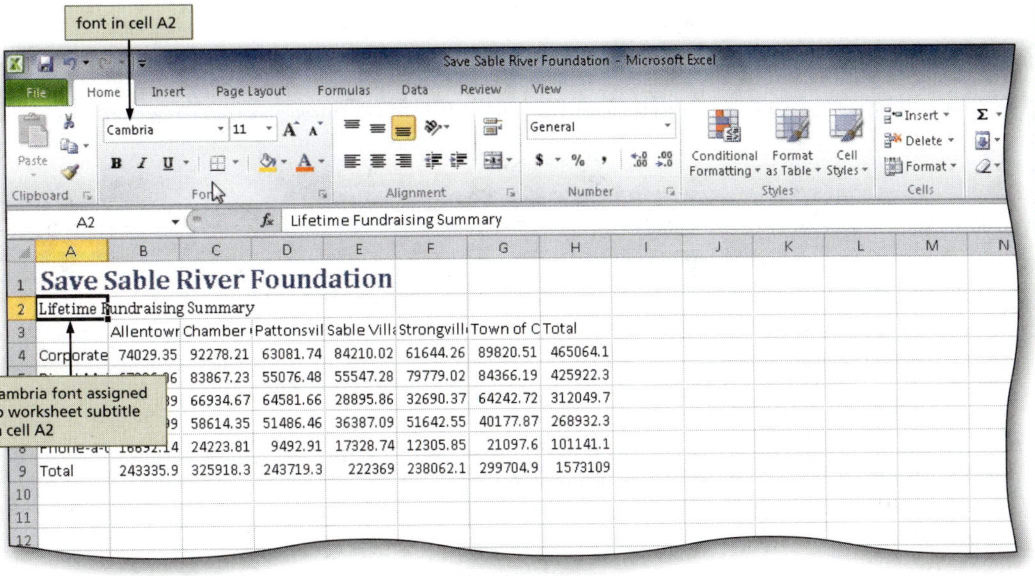

Figure 1–32

Other Ways

1. Click Font box arrow on Mini toolbar, click desired font in Font gallery
2. Right-click cell, click Format Cells on shortcut menu, click Font tab (Format Cells dialog box), click desired font, click OK button

To Bold a Cell

You **bold** an entry in a cell to emphasize it or make it stand out from the rest of the worksheet. The following step bolds the worksheet subtitle in cell A2.

1

- With cell A2 active, click the Bold button (Home tab | Font group) to change the font style of the active cell to bold (Figure 1–33).

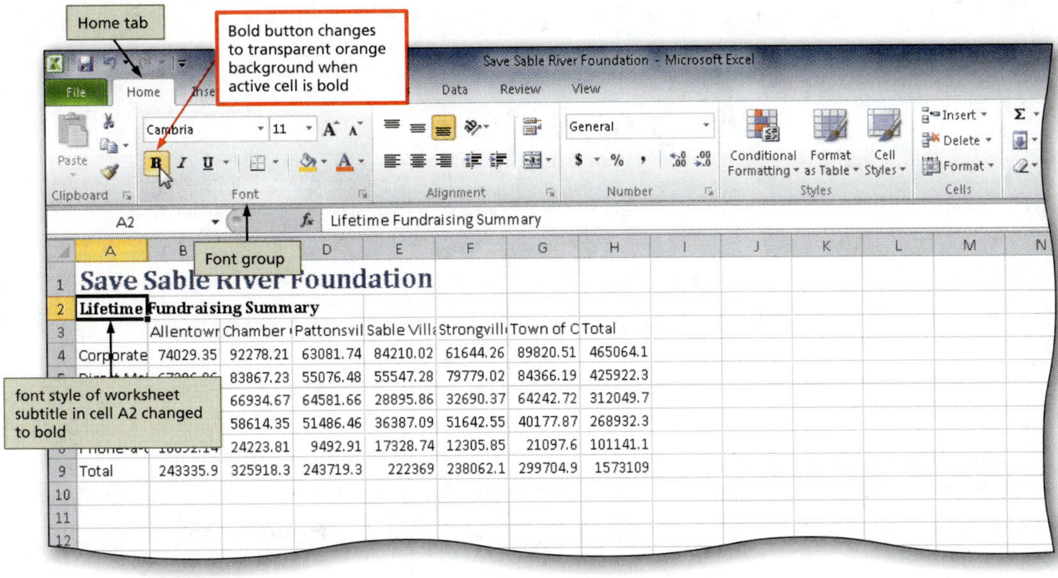

Figure 1–33

Q&A What if a cell already includes a bold style?

If the active cell is already bold, then Excel displays the Bold button with a transparent orange background.

Q&A How do I remove the bold style from a cell?

Clicking the Bold button (Home tab | Font group) a second time removes the bold font style.

Other Ways

1. Click Bold button on Mini toolbar
2. Right-click cell, click Format Cells on shortcut menu, click Font tab (Format Cells dialog box), click Bold, click OK button
3. Press CTRL+B

To Increase the Font Size of a Cell Entry

Increasing the font size is the next step in formatting the worksheet subtitle. You increase the font size of a cell so that the entry stands out and is easier to read. The following steps increase the font size of the worksheet subtitle in cell A2.

1

- With cell A2 selected, click the Font Size box arrow (Home tab | Font group) to display the Font Size list.
- Point to 14 in the Font Size list to see a live preview of the active cell with the selected font size (Figure 1–34).

Experiment

- Point to several other font sizes in the Font Size list to see a live preview of other font sizes in the selected cell.

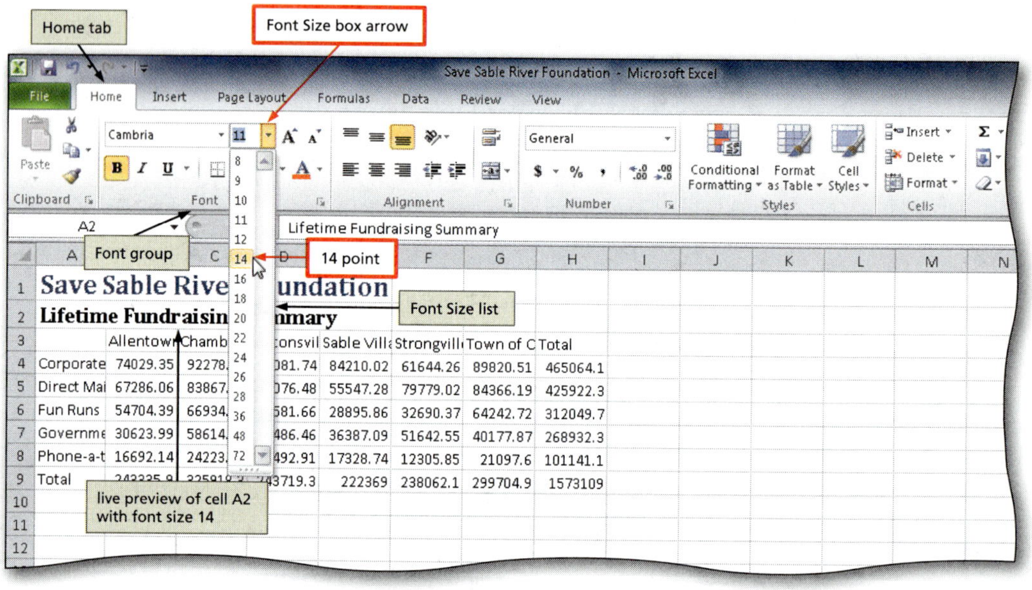

Figure 1–34

2

- Click 14 in the Font Size list to change the font size in the active cell (Figure 1–35).

Q&A

Can I assign a font size that is not in the Font Size list?

Yes. An alternative to clicking a font size in the Font Size list is to click the Font Size box (Home tab | Font group), type the font size, and then press the ENTER key. This procedure allows you to assign a font size not available in the Font Size list to a selected cell entry.

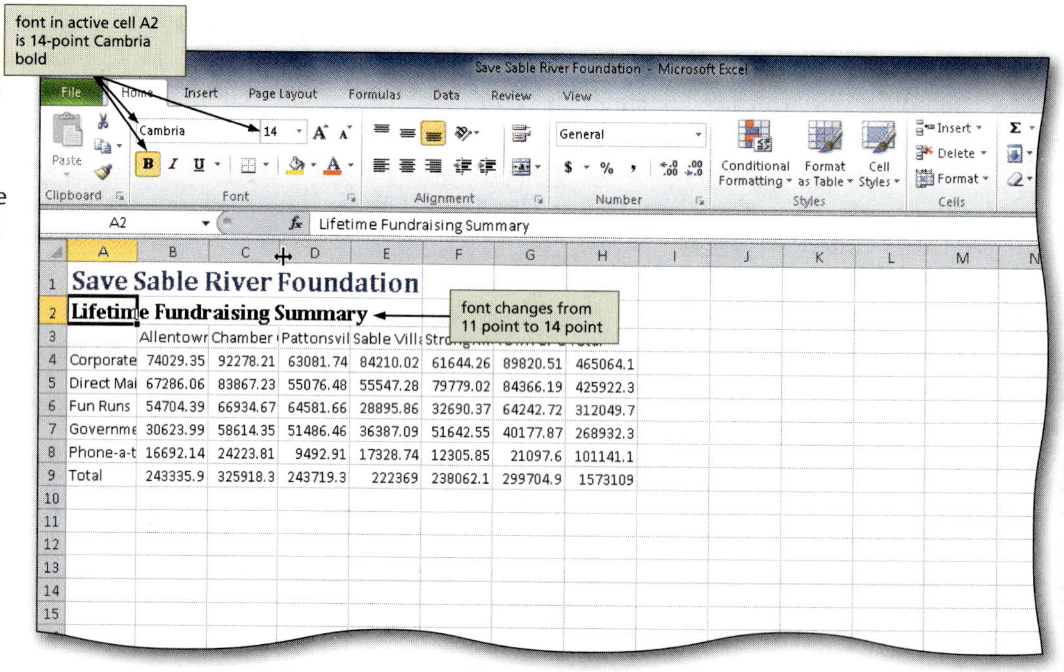

Figure 1–35

Other Ways

1. Click Increase Font Size button (Home tab | Font group) or Decrease Font Size button (Home tab | Font group)
2. Click Font Size box arrow on Mini toolbar, click desired font size in Font Size gallery
3. Right-click cell, click Format Cells on shortcut menu, click Font tab (Format Cells dialog box), select font size in Size box, click OK button

To Change the Font Color of a Cell Entry

The next step is to change the color of the font in cell A2 from black to dark blue. The following steps change the font color of a cell entry.

1

- With cell A2 selected, click the Font Color button arrow (Home tab | Font group) to display the Font Color gallery.
- Point to Dark Blue, Text 2 (dark blue color in column 4, row 1) in the Theme Colors area of the Font Color gallery to see a live preview of the font color in the active cell (Figure 1–36).

Experiment

- Point to several other colors in the Font Color gallery to see a live preview of other font colors in the active cell.

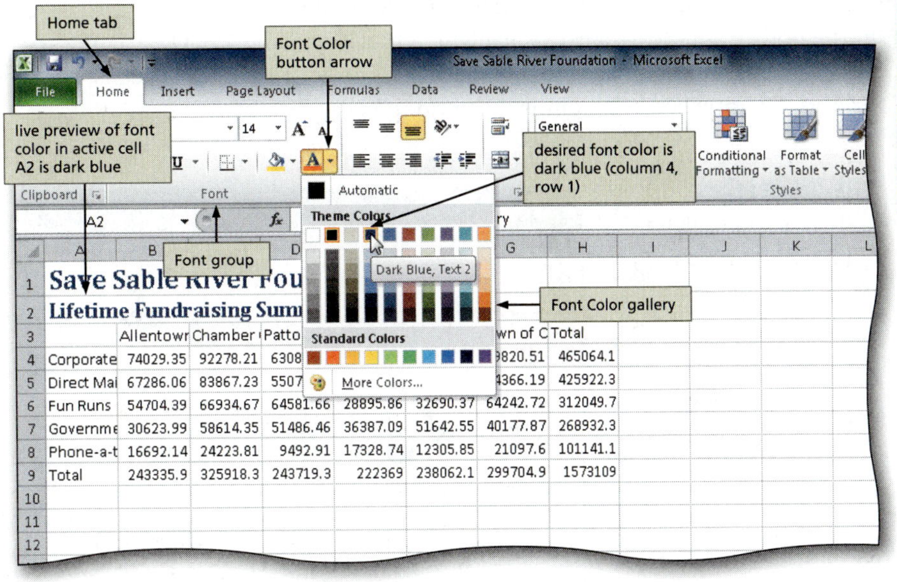

Figure 1–36

Q&A

Which colors does Excel make available on the Font Color gallery?

You can choose from more than 60 different font colors on the Font Color gallery (Figure 1–36). Your Font Color gallery may have more or fewer colors, depending on color settings of your operating system. The Theme Colors area includes colors that are included in the current workbook's theme.

2

- Click Dark Blue, Text 2 (column 4, row 1) on the Font Color gallery to change the font of the worksheet subtitle in the active cell (Figure 1–37).

Q&A

Why does the Font Color button change after I select the new font color?

When you choose a color on the Font Color gallery, Excel changes the Font Color button (Home tab | Font group) to the chosen color. Thus, to change the font color of the cell entry in another cell to the same color, you need only to select the cell and then click the Font Color button (Home tab | Font group).

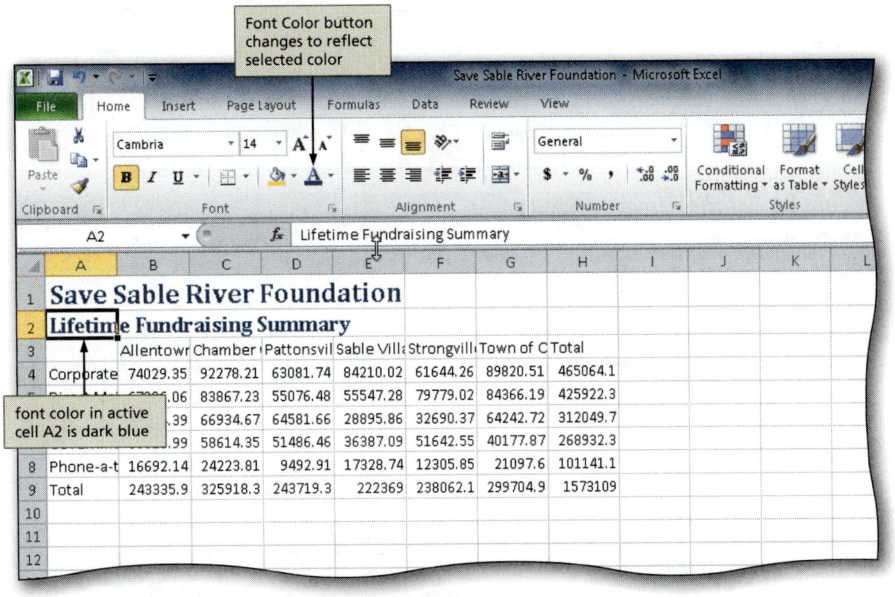

Figure 1–37

Other Ways

1. Click Font Color box arrow on Mini toolbar, click desired font color in the Font Color gallery
2. Right-click cell, click Format Cells on shortcut menu, click Font tab (Format Cells dialog box), select color in Font Color gallery, click OK button

To Center Cell Entries across Columns by Merging Cells

The final step in formatting the worksheet title and subtitle is to center them across columns A through H. Centering a title across the columns used in the body of the worksheet improves the worksheet's appearance. To do this, the eight cells in the range A1:H1 are combined, or merged, into a single cell that is the width of the columns in the body of the worksheet. The eight cells in the range A2:H2 are merged in a similar manner. **Merging cells** involves creating a single cell by combining two or more selected cells. The following steps center the worksheet title and subtitle across columns by merging cells.

1

- Select cell A1 and then drag to cell H1 to highlight the range to be merged and centered (Figure 1–38).

Q&A What if a cell in the range B1:H1 contains data?

For the Merge & Center button (Home tab | Alignment group) to work properly, all the cells except the leftmost cell in the selected range must be empty.

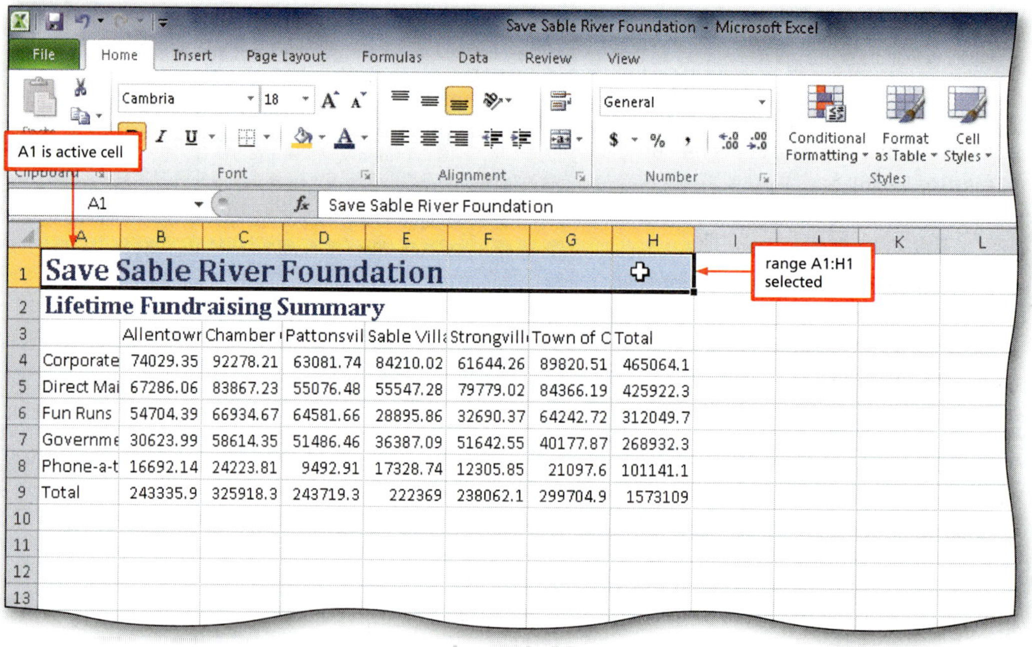

Figure 1–38

2

- Click the Merge & Center button (Home tab | Alignment group) to merge cells A1 through H1 and center the contents of the leftmost cell across the selected columns (Figure 1–39).

Q&A What happened to cells B1 through H1?

After the merge, cells B1 through H1 no longer exist. The new cell A1 now extends across columns A through H.

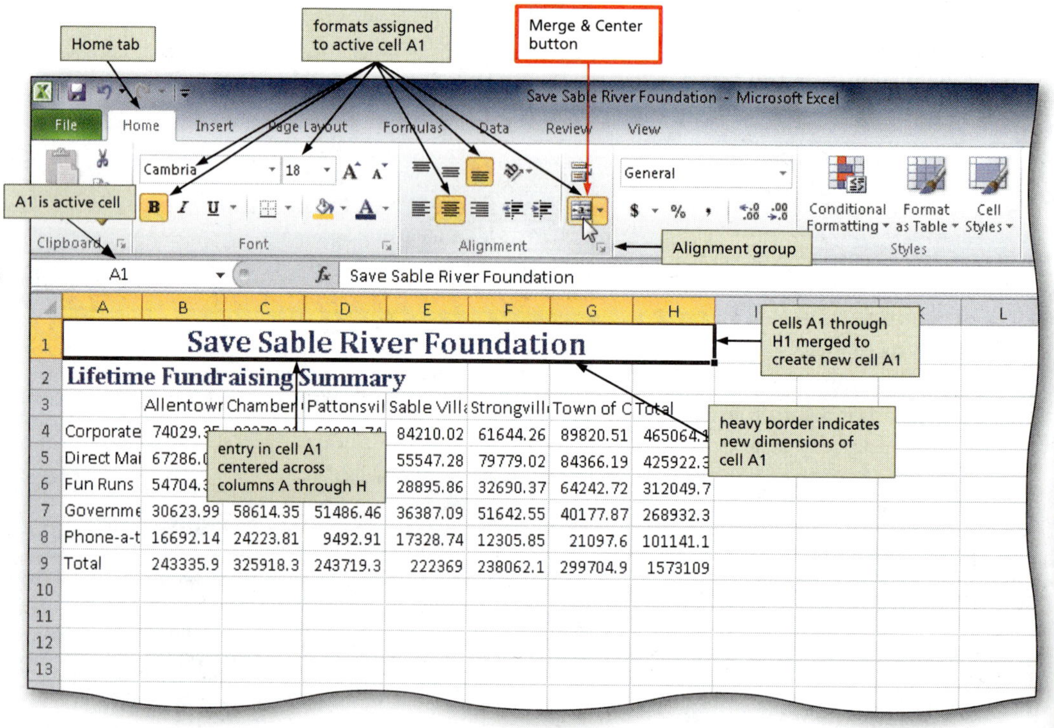

Figure 1–39

3

- Repeat Steps 1 and 2 to merge and center the worksheet subtitle across cells A2 through H2 (Figure 1–40).

Q&A Are cells B1 through H1 and B2 through H2 lost forever?

No. The opposite of merging cells is **splitting a merged cell**. After you have merged multiple cells to create one merged cell, you can unmerge, or split, the merged cell to display the original cells on the worksheet. You split a merged cell by selecting it and clicking the Merge & Center button. For example, if you click the Merge & Center button a second time in Step 2, it will split the merged cell A1 into cells A1, B1, C1, D1, E1, F1, G1, and H1.

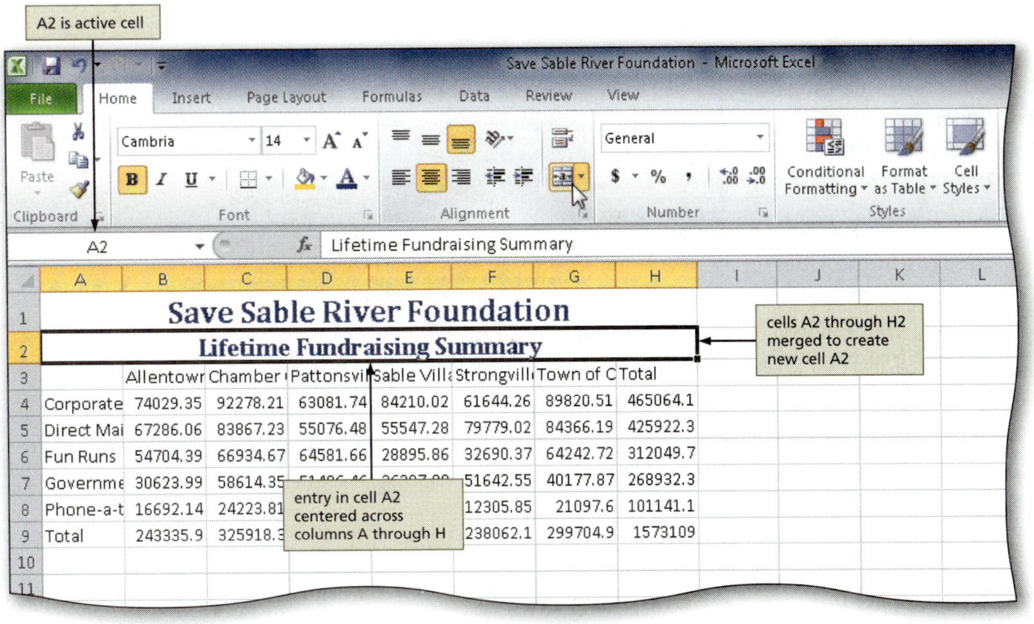

Figure 1–40

Other Ways

1. Right-click selection, click Merge & Center button on Mini toolbar
2. Right-click selection, click Format Cells on shortcut menu, click Alignment tab (Format Cells dialog box), select Center Across Selection in Horizontal list, click OK button

To Format Column Titles and the Total Row

The next step to format the worksheet is to format the column titles in row 3 and the total values in row 9. Column titles and the total row should be formatted so anyone who views the worksheet quickly can distinguish the column titles and total row from the data in the body of the worksheet. The following steps format the column titles and total row using cell styles in the default worksheet theme.

1

- Click cell A3 and then drag the mouse pointer to cell H3 to select a range (Figure 1–41).

Q&A Why is cell A3 selected in the range for the column headings?

The style to be applied to the column headings includes an underline that will help to distinguish the column headings from the rest of the worksheet. Including cell A3 in the range ensures that the cell will include the underline, which is visually appealing and further helps to separate the data in the worksheet.

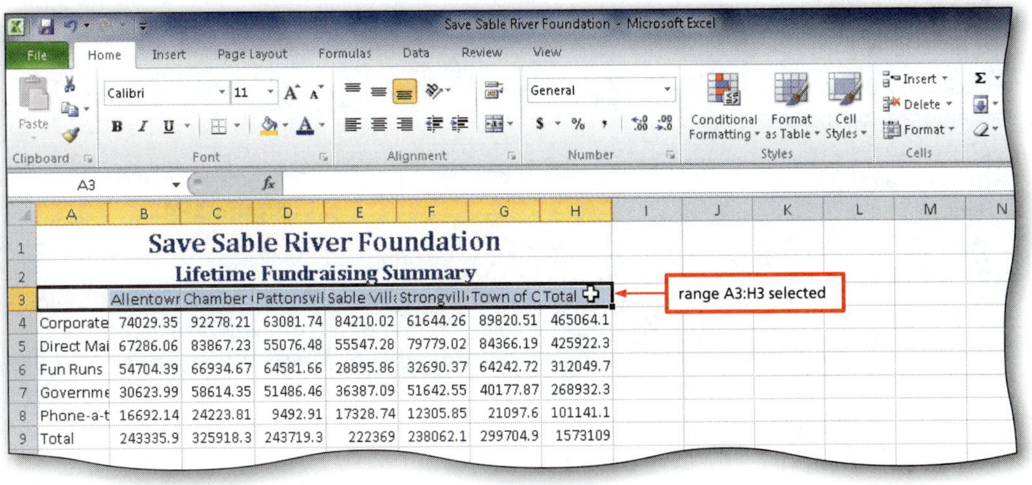

Figure 1–41

2

- Click the Cell Styles button (Home tab | Styles group) to display the Cell Styles gallery.
- Point to the Heading 3 cell style in the Titles and Headings area of the Cell Styles gallery to see a live preview of the cell style in the selected range (Figure 1–42).

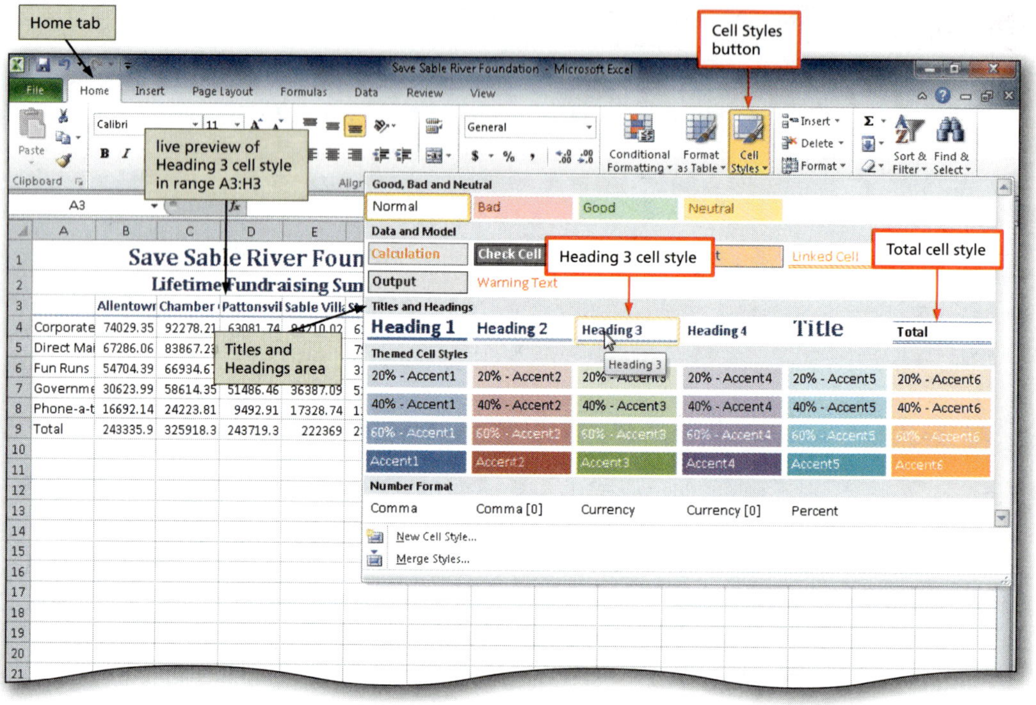

Figure 1–42

Experiment

- Point to other cell styles in the Titles and Headings area of the Cell Styles gallery to see a live preview of other cell styles in the selected range, A3:H3.

3

- Click the Heading 3 cell style to apply the cell style to the selected range.
- Click the Center button (Home tab | Alignment group) to center the column headings in the selected range.
- Click cell A9 and then drag the mouse pointer to cell H9 to select a range (Figure 1–43).

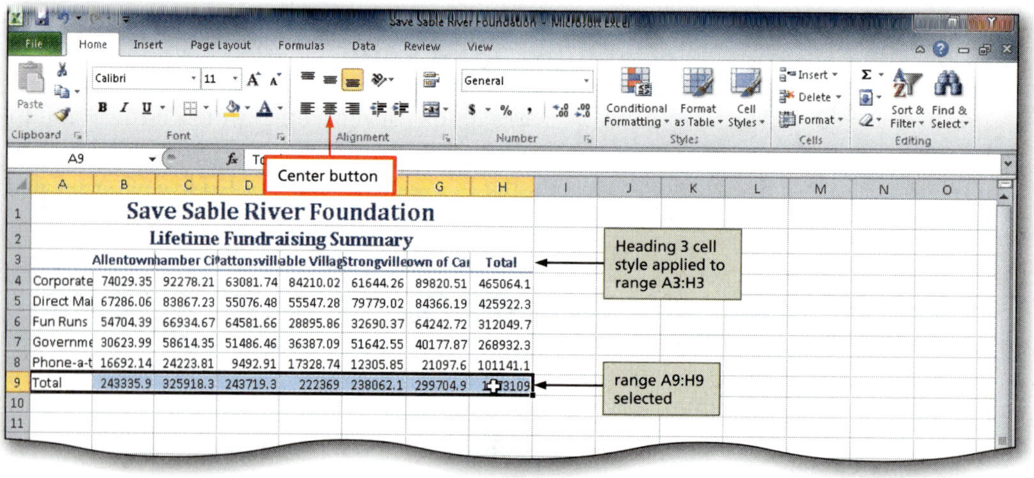

Figure 1–43

Q&A

Why should I choose Heading 3 instead of another heading cell style?

Excel includes many types of headings, such as Heading 1 and Heading 2, because worksheets often include many levels of headings above columns. In the case of the worksheet created for this project, the Heading 3 title includes formatting that makes the column titles' font size smaller than the title and subtitle and makes the column titles stand out from the data in the body of the worksheet.

4

- Click the Cell Styles button (Home tab | Styles group) to display the Cell Styles gallery and then click the Total cell style in the Titles and Headings area to apply the selected cell style to the cells in the selected range.
- Click cell A11 to select it (Figure 1–44).

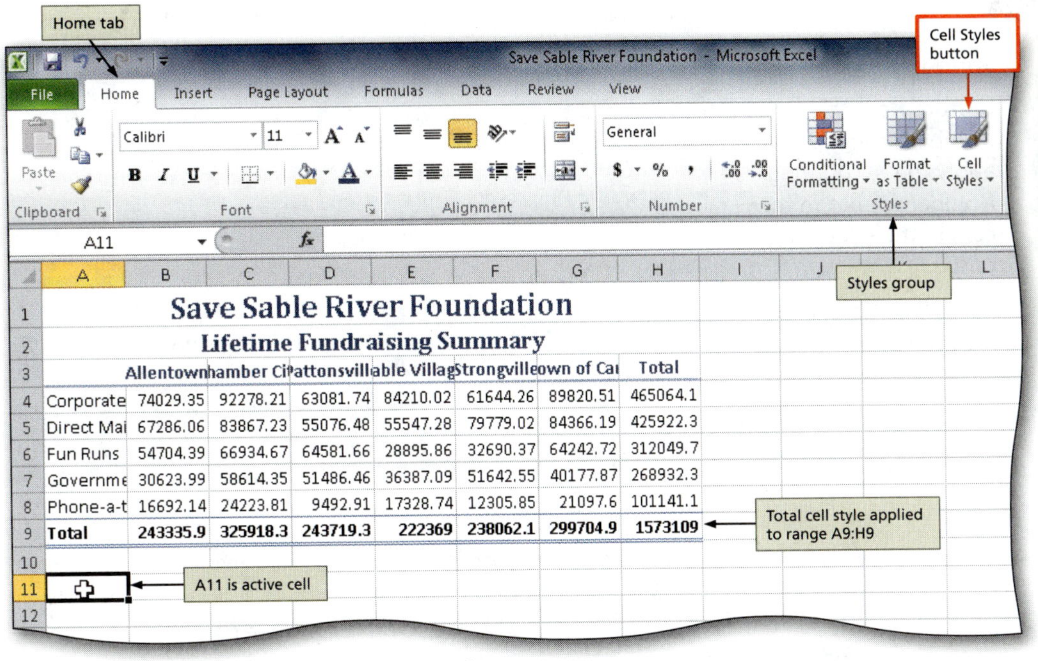

Figure 1–44

To Format Numbers in the Worksheet

As previously noted, the numbers in the worksheet should be formatted to use a dollar-and-cents format, with dollar signs in the first row (row 4) and the total row (row 9). Excel allows you to format numbers in a variety of ways. The following steps use buttons on the Ribbon to format the numbers in the worksheet.

1

- Select cell B4 and drag the mouse pointer to cell H4 to select a range (Figure 1–45).

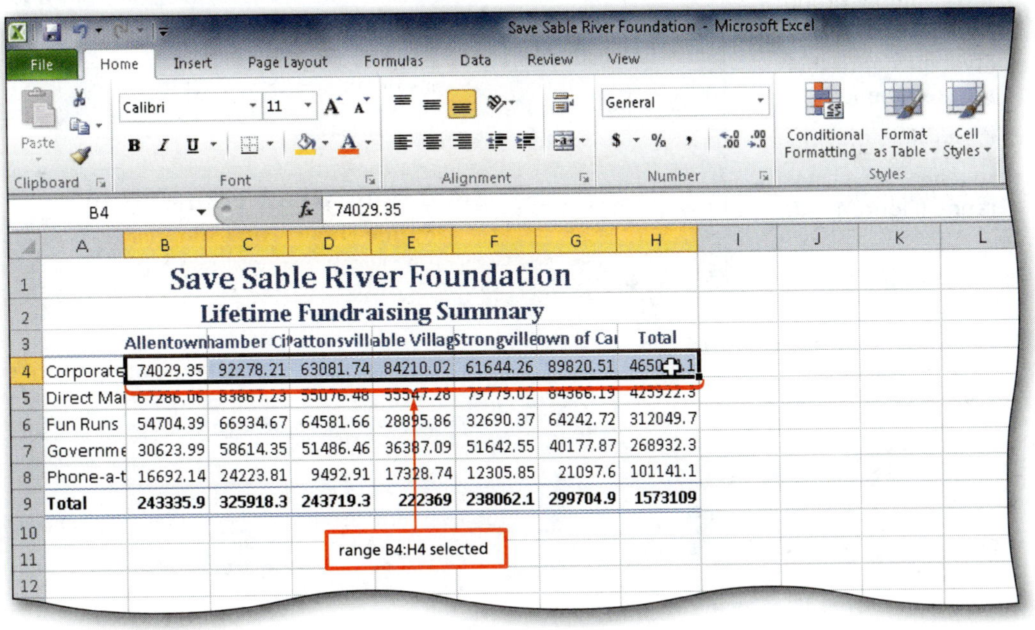

Figure 1–45

2

- Click the Accounting Number Format button (Home tab | Number group) to apply the Accounting Number format to the cells in the selected range.
- Select the range B5:H8 (Figure 1–46).

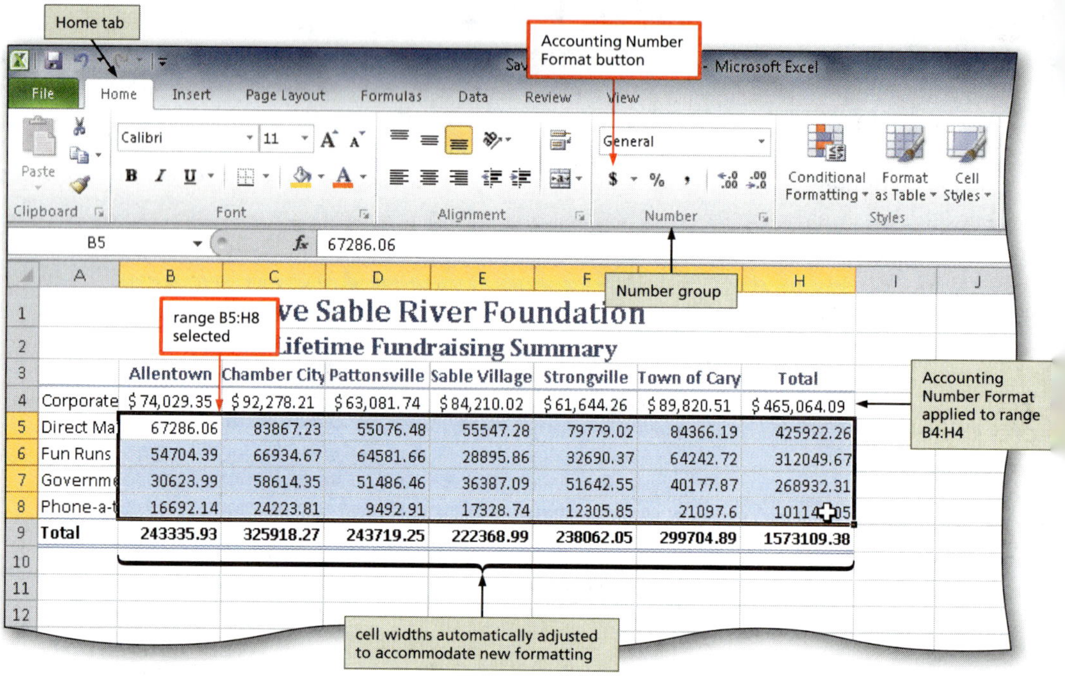

Figure 1–46

Q&A

What effect does the Accounting Number format have on the selected cells?

The Accounting Number format causes the cells to be displayed with two decimal places so that decimal places in cells below the selected cells align vertically. Cell widths are adjusted automatically to accommodate the new formatting.

3

- Click the Comma Style button (Home tab | Number group) to apply the Comma Style format to the selected range.
- Select the range B9:H9 to make it the active range (Figure 1–47).

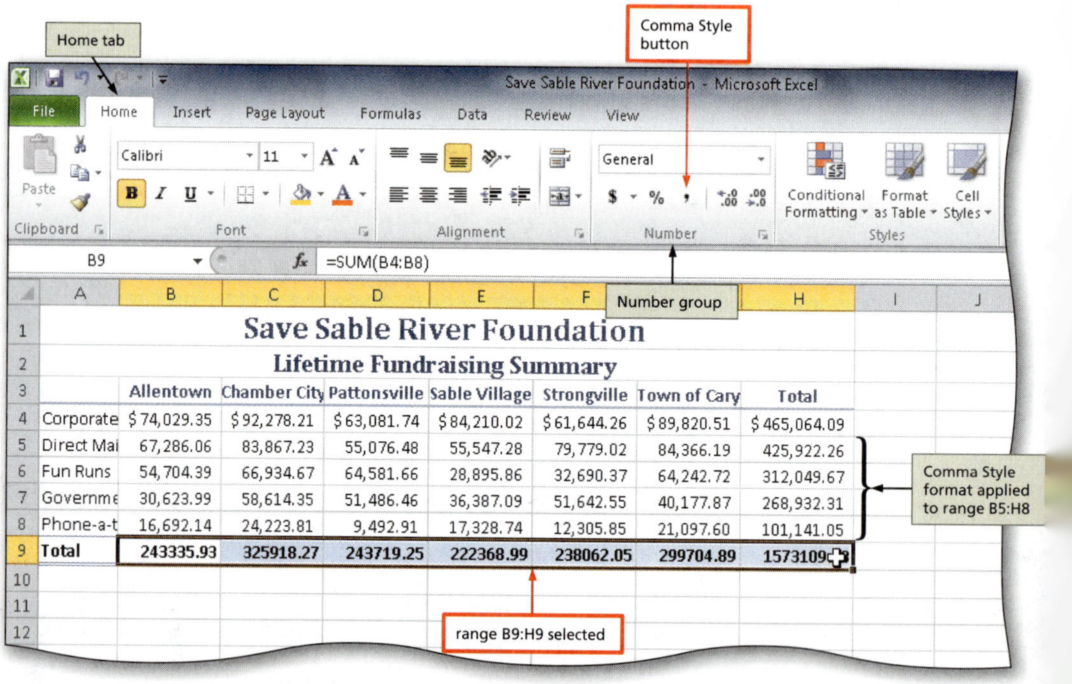

Figure 1–47

Q&A

What effect does the Comma Style format have on the selected cells?

The Comma Style format causes the cells to be displayed with two decimal places and commas as thousands separators.

4

- Click the Accounting Number Format button (Home tab | Number group) to apply the Accounting Number format to the cells in the selected range.
- Select cell A11 (Figure 1–48).

Q&A Why did the column widths automatically adjust again?

Because the total row contains larger numbers, the Accounting Number format again causes the cell widths automatically to adjust to accommodate the new formatting just as occurred in Step 2.

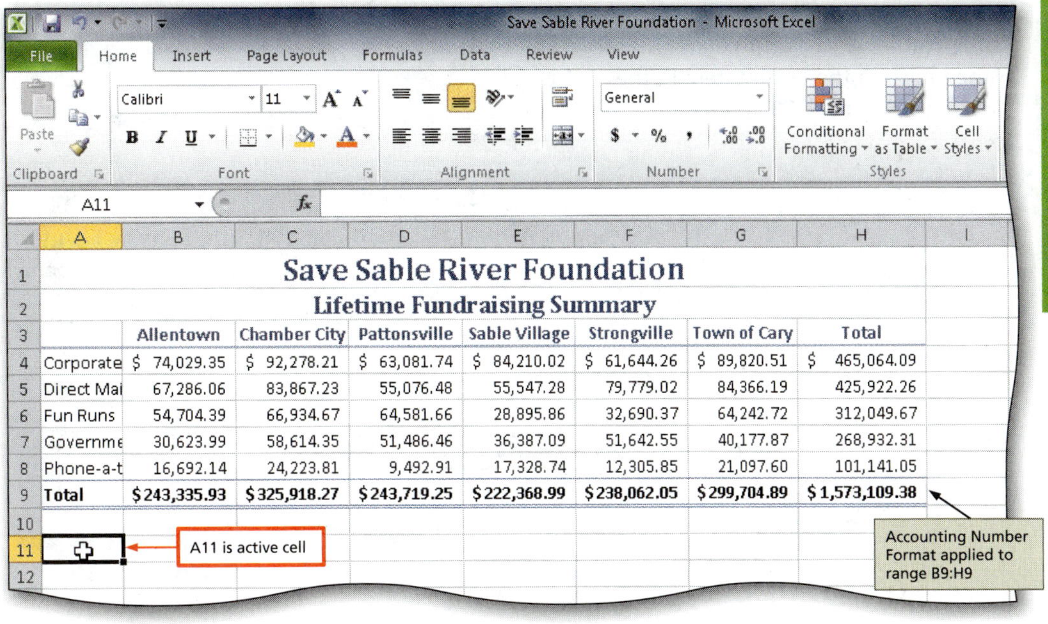

Figure 1–48

Other Ways
1. Click Accounting Number Format or Comma Style button on Mini toolbar 2. Right-click selection, click Format Cells on the shortcut menu, click Number tab (Format Cells dialog box), select Accounting in Category list or select Number and click Use 1000 Separator, click OK button

To Adjust the Column Width

The last step in formatting the worksheet is to adjust the width of column A so that the word Phone-a-thon in cell A8 is shown in its entirety in the cell. Excel includes several methods for adjusting cell widths and row heights. The following steps adjust the width of column A so that the contents of cell A8 are displayed in the cell.

1

- Point to the boundary on the right side of the column A heading above row 1 to change the mouse pointer to a split double arrow (Figure 1–49).

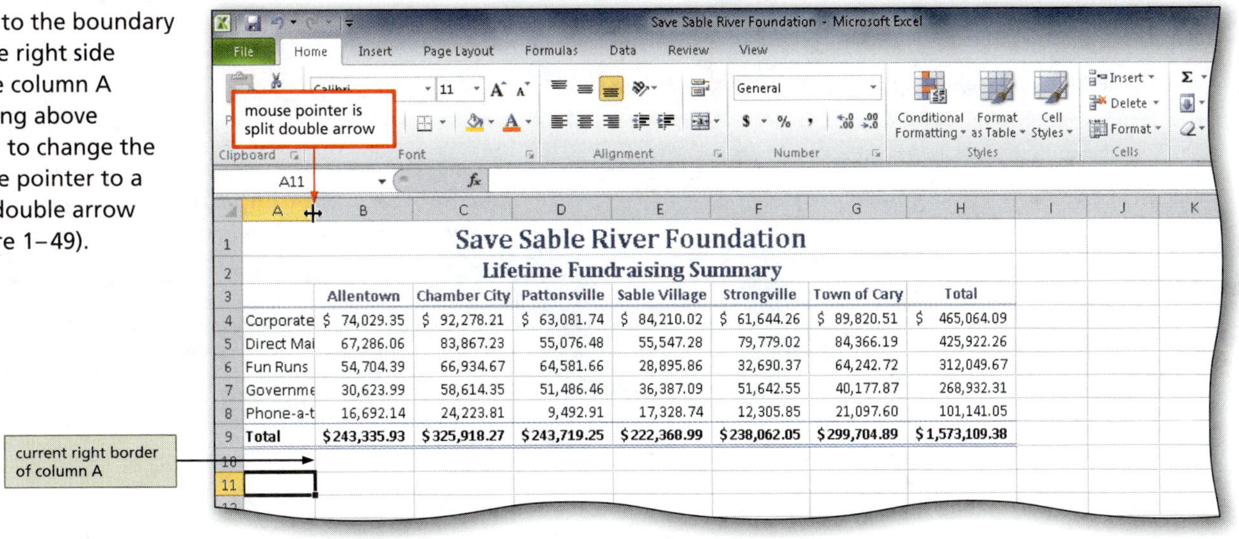

Figure 1–49

2

- Double-click on the boundary to adjust the width of the column to the width of the largest item in the column (Figure 1–50).

Q&A What if none of the items in column A extends through the entire width of the column?

If all of the items in column A were shorter in length than the width of the column when you double-click the right side of the column A heading, then Excel still would adjust the column width to the largest item in the column. That is, Excel would reduce the width of the column to the largest item.

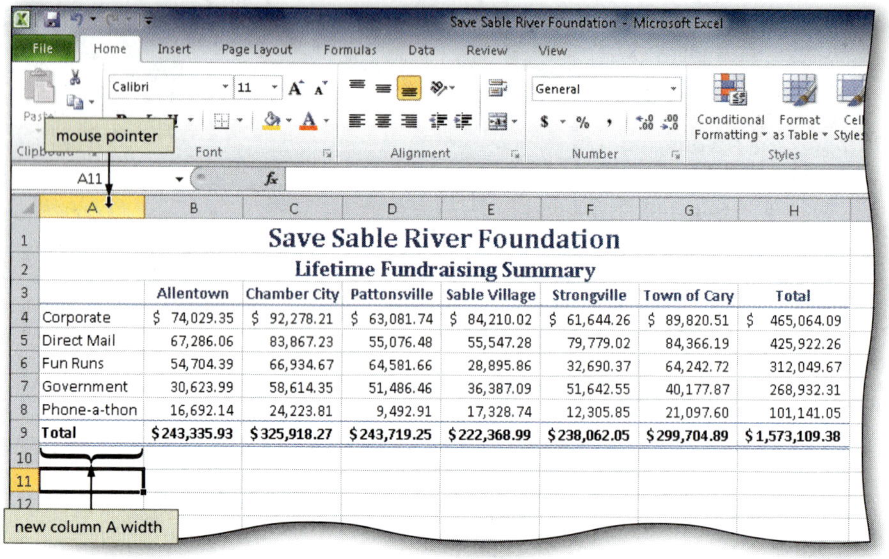

Figure 1–50

Using the Name Box to Select a Cell

The next step is to chart the lifetime fundraising amounts for the five fundraising activities used by the organization. To create the chart, you first must select the cell in the upper-left corner of the range to chart (cell A3). Rather than clicking cell A3 to select it, the next section describes how to use the Name box to select the cell.

To Use the Name Box to Select a Cell

The Name box is located on the left side of the formula bar. To select any cell, click the Name box and enter the cell reference of the cell you want to select. The following steps select cell A3 using the Name box.

1

- Click the Name box in the formula bar and then type **a3** as the cell you wish to select (Figure 1–51).

Q&A Why is cell A11 still selected?

Even though cell A11 is the active cell, Excel displays the typed cell reference a3 in the Name box until you press the ENTER key.

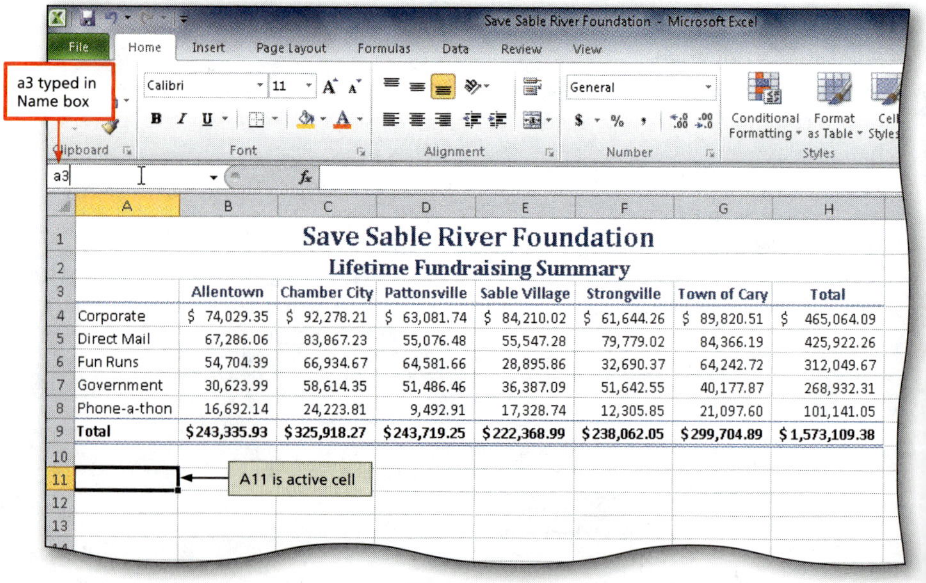

Figure 1–51

2

- Press the ENTER key to change the active cell in the Name box (Figure 1–52).

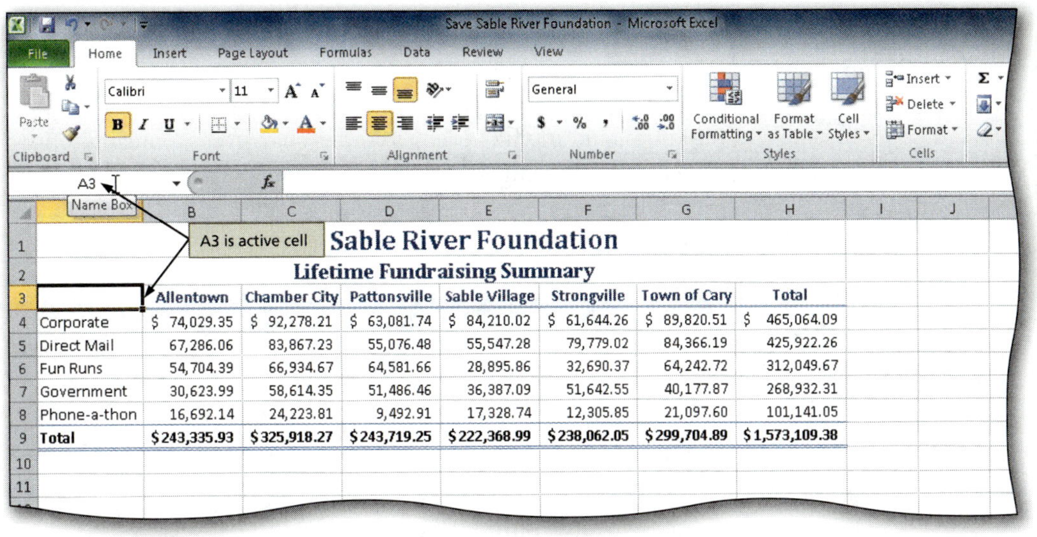

Figure 1–52

Other Ways to Select Cells

In addition to using the Name box to select any cell in a worksheet, you also can use it to assign names to a cell or range of cells. Excel supports several additional ways to select a cell, as summarized in Table 1–3.

Table 1–3 Selecting Cells in Excel

Key, Box, or Command	Function
ALT+PAGE DOWN	Selects the cell one worksheet window to the right and moves the worksheet window accordingly.
ALT+PAGE UP	Selects the cell one worksheet window to the left and moves the worksheet window accordingly.
ARROW	Selects the adjacent cell in the direction of the arrow on the key.
CTRL+ARROW	Selects the border cell of the worksheet in combination with the arrow keys and moves the worksheet window accordingly. For example, to select the rightmost cell in the row that contains the active cell, press CTRL+RIGHT ARROW. You also can press the END key, release it, and then press the appropriate arrow key to accomplish the same task.
CTRL+HOME	Selects cell A1 or the cell one column and one row below and to the right of frozen titles and moves the worksheet window accordingly.
Find command on Find and Select menu or SHIFT+F5	Finds and selects a cell that contains specific contents that you enter in the Find and Replace dialog box. If necessary, Excel moves the worksheet window to display the cell. You also can press CTRL+F to display the Find dialog box.
Go To command on Find and Select menu or F5	Selects the cell that corresponds to the cell reference you enter in the Go To dialog box and moves the worksheet window accordingly. You also can press CTRL+G to display the Go To dialog box.
HOME	Selects the cell at the beginning of the row that contains the active cell and moves the worksheet window accordingly.
Name box	Selects the cell in the workbook that corresponds to the cell reference you enter in the Name box.
PAGE DOWN	Selects the cell down one worksheet window from the active cell and moves the worksheet window accordingly.
PAGE UP	Selects the cell up one worksheet window from the active cell and moves the worksheet window accordingly.

Break Point: If you wish to take a break, this is a good place to do so. Be sure to save the Save Sable River Foundation file again and then you can quit Excel. To resume at a later time, start Excel, open the file called Save Sable River Foundation, and continue following the steps from this location forward.

Adding a Clustered Cylinder Chart to the Worksheet

As outlined in the requirements document in Figure 1–2 on page EX 4, the worksheet should include a Clustered Cylinder chart to graphically represent the lifetime fundraising for each fundraising activity in which the organization engages. The Clustered Cylinder chart shown in Figure 1–53 is called an **embedded chart** because it is drawn on the same worksheet as the data.

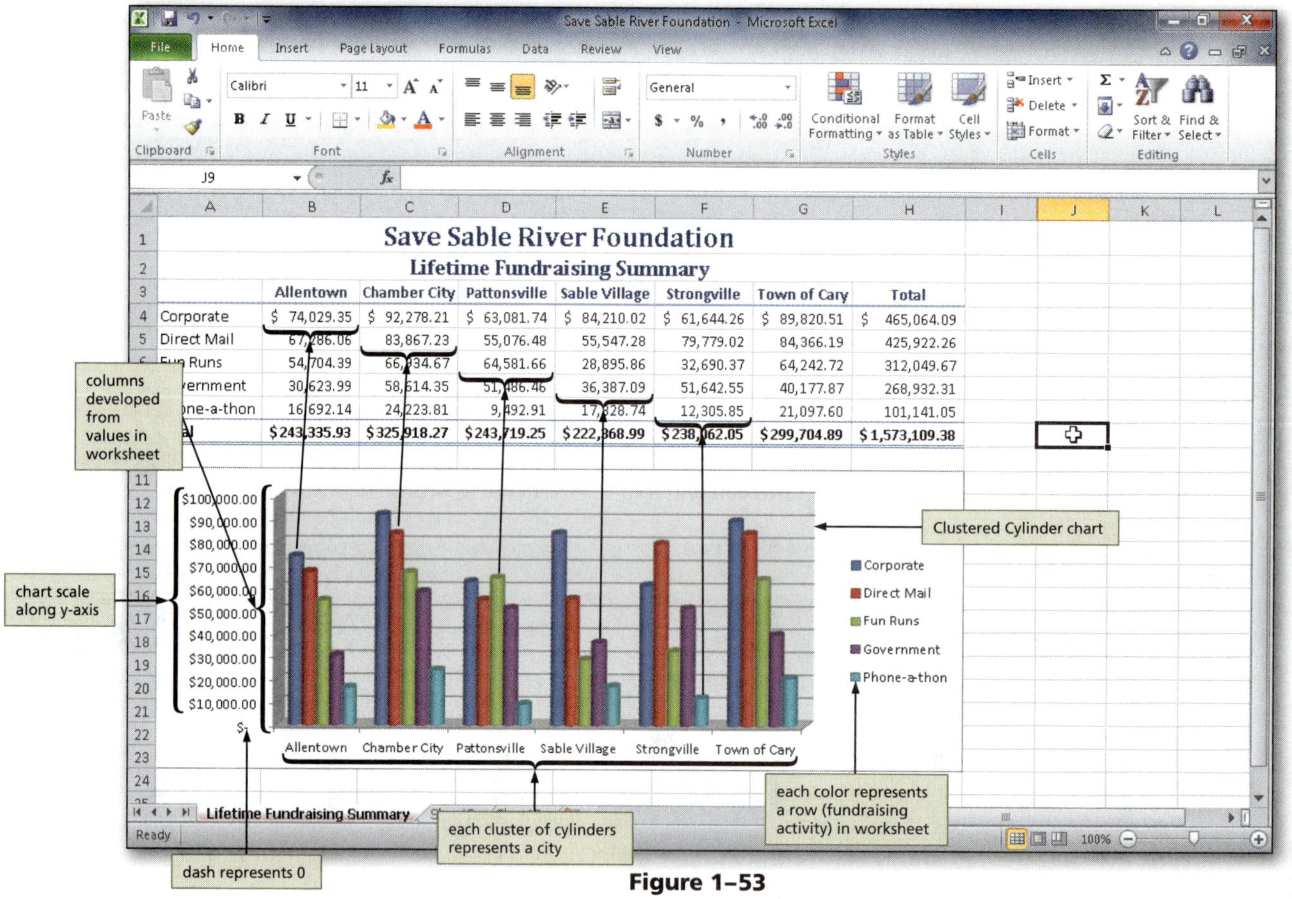

Figure 1–53

Plan Ahead

Decide on the type of chart needed.

Excel includes 11 chart types from which you can choose, including column, line, pie, bar, area, X Y (scatter), stock, surface, doughnut, bubble, and radar. The type of chart you choose depends on the type of data that you have, how much data you have, and the message you want to convey.

A line chart often is used to illustrate changes in data over time. Pie charts show the contribution of each piece of data to the whole, or total, of the data. Area charts, like line charts, illustrate changes over time, but often are used to compare more than one set of data and the area under the lines is filled in with a different color for each set of data. An X Y (scatter) chart is used much line a line chart, but each piece of data is represented by a dot and is not connected with a line. A stock chart provides a number of methods commonly

(continued)

Plan Ahead

(continued)

used in the financial industry to show stock market data. A surface chart compares data from three columns and/or rows in a three-dimensional manner. A doughnut chart is much like a pie chart, but a doughnut chart allows for comparing more than one set of data, resulting in a chart that looks like a doughnut, with each subsquent set of data surrounding the previous set. A bubble chart is much like an X Y (scatter) chart, but a third set of data results indicates how large each individual dot, or bubble, is on the chart. A radar chart can compare several sets of data in a manner that resembles a radar screen, with each set of data represented by a different color. A column or cylinder chart is a good way to compare values side by side. A Clustered Cylinder chart can go even further in comparing values across categories.

Establish where to position and how to format the chart.

- When possible, try to position charts so that both the data and chart appear on the screen on the worksheet together and so that the data and chart can be printed in the most readable manner possible.
- When choosing/selecting colors for a chart, consider the color scheme of the rest of the worksheet. The chart should not present colors that are in stark contrast to the rest of the worksheet. If the chart will be printed in color, minimize the amount of dark colors on the chart so that the chart both prints quickly and conserves ink.

BTW

Cell Values and Charting

When you change a cell value on which a chart is dependent, Excel redraws the chart instantaneously, unless automatic recalculation is disabled. If automatic recalculation is disabled, then you must press the F9 key to redraw the chart. To enable or disable automatic recalculation, click the Calculations Options button (Formulas tab | Calculation group).

In the case of the Save Sable River Foundation Lifetime Fundraising Summary, comparisons of fundraising activities within each city can be made side by side with a Clustered Cylinder chart. The chart uses differently colored cylinders to represent amounts raised for different fundraising activities. Each city uses the same color scheme for identifying fundraising activities, which allows for easy identification and comparison.

- For the city of Allentown, for example, the dark blue cylinder representing Corporate donations shows lifetime donations of $74,029.35
- For Chamber City, the maroon cylinder representing Direct Mail donations shows lifetime donations of $83,867.23
- For the city of Pattonsville, the lime green cylinder representing donations for Fun Runs shows lifetime donations of $64,581.66
- For Sable Village, the purple cylinder representing Government donations shows lifetime donations of $36,387.09
- For the city of Strongville, the light blue cylinder representing Phone-a-thon donations shows lifetime donations of $12,305.85

Because the same color scheme is used in each city to represent the five fundraising activities, you easily can compare funds raised by each fundraising activity among the cities. The totals from the worksheet are not represented, because the totals are not in the range specified for charting.

Excel derives the chart scale based on the values in the worksheet and then displays the scale along the vertical axis (also called the **y-axis** or **value axis**) of the chart. For example, no value in the range B4:G8 is less than 0 or greater than $100,000.00, so the scale ranges from 0 to $100,000.00. Excel also determines the $10,000.00 increments of the scale automatically. For the numbers along the y-axis, Excel uses a format that includes representing the 0 value with a dash (Figure 1–53).

To Add a Clustered Cylinder Chart to the Worksheet

The area on the worksheet where the chart appears is called the chart location. As shown in Figure 1–53 on page EX 36, the chart location in this worksheet is the range A11:G23; this range is immediately below the worksheet data. Placing the chart below the data on the Save Sable River Foundation Lifetime Fundraising Summary worksheet makes it easier to read the chart along with the data, and the chart and data easily can be printed on one sheet of paper.

The following steps draw a Clustered Cylinder chart that compares the funds raised by fundraising activity for the six cities.

1

- Click cell A3 and then drag the mouse pointer to cell G8 to select the range to be charted (Figure 1–54).

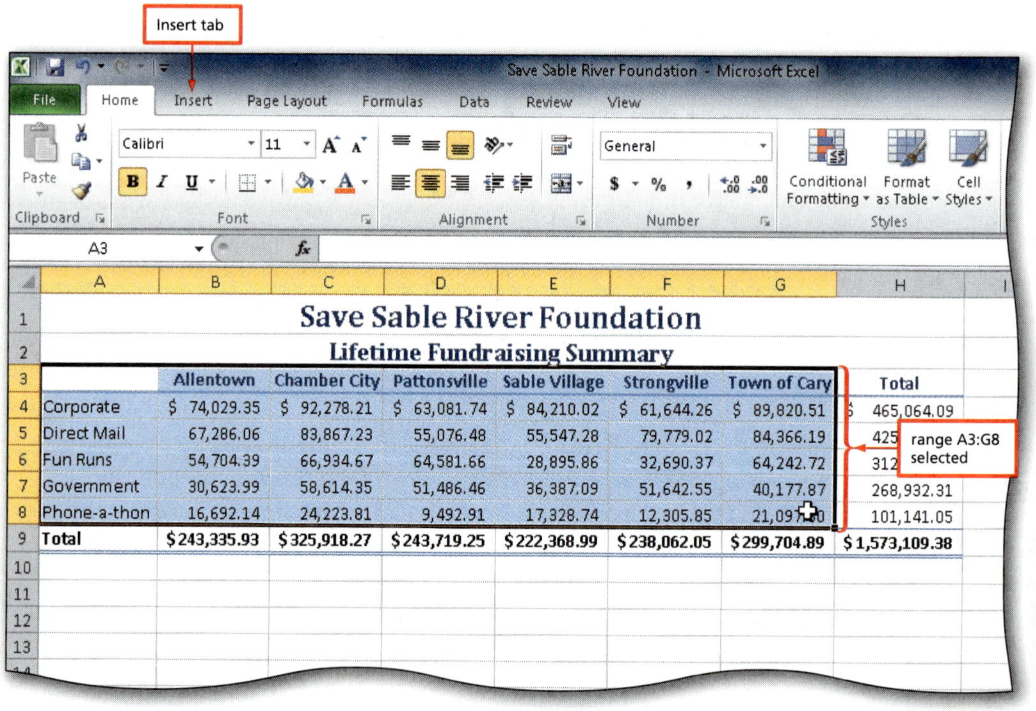

Figure 1–54

2

- Click Insert on the Ribbon to display the Insert tab (Figure 1–55).

Q&A What tasks can I perform with the Insert tab?

The Insert tab includes commands that allow you to insert various objects, such as shapes, tables, illustrations, and charts, into a worksheet.

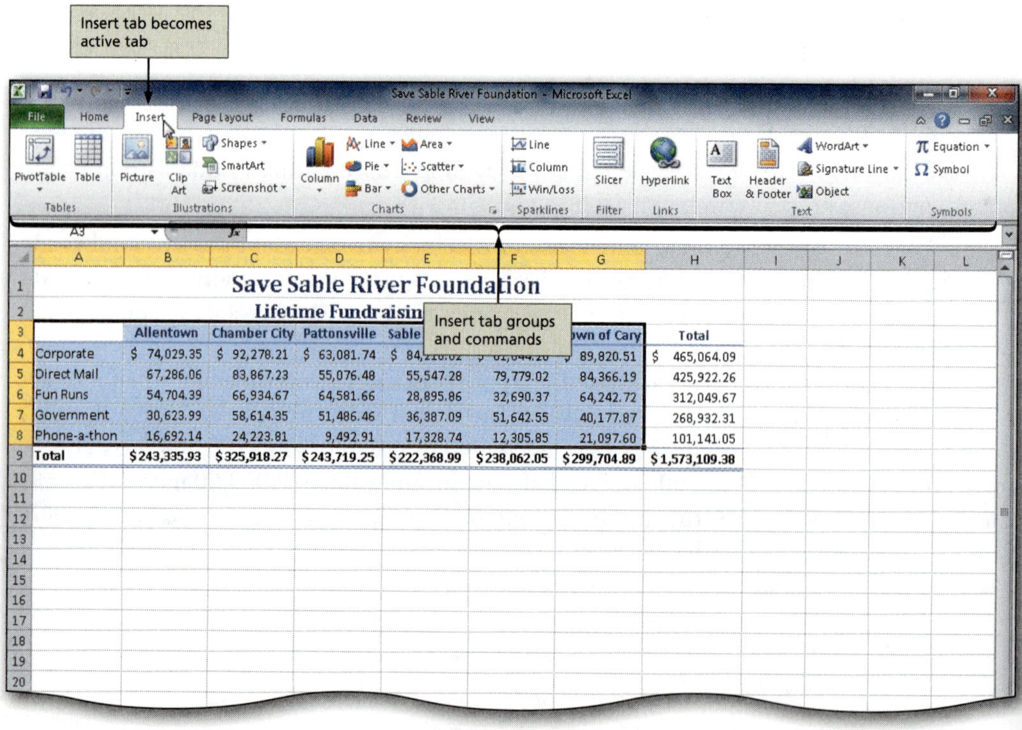

Figure 1–55

3

- Click the Column button (Insert tab | Charts group) to display the Column gallery (Figure 1–56).

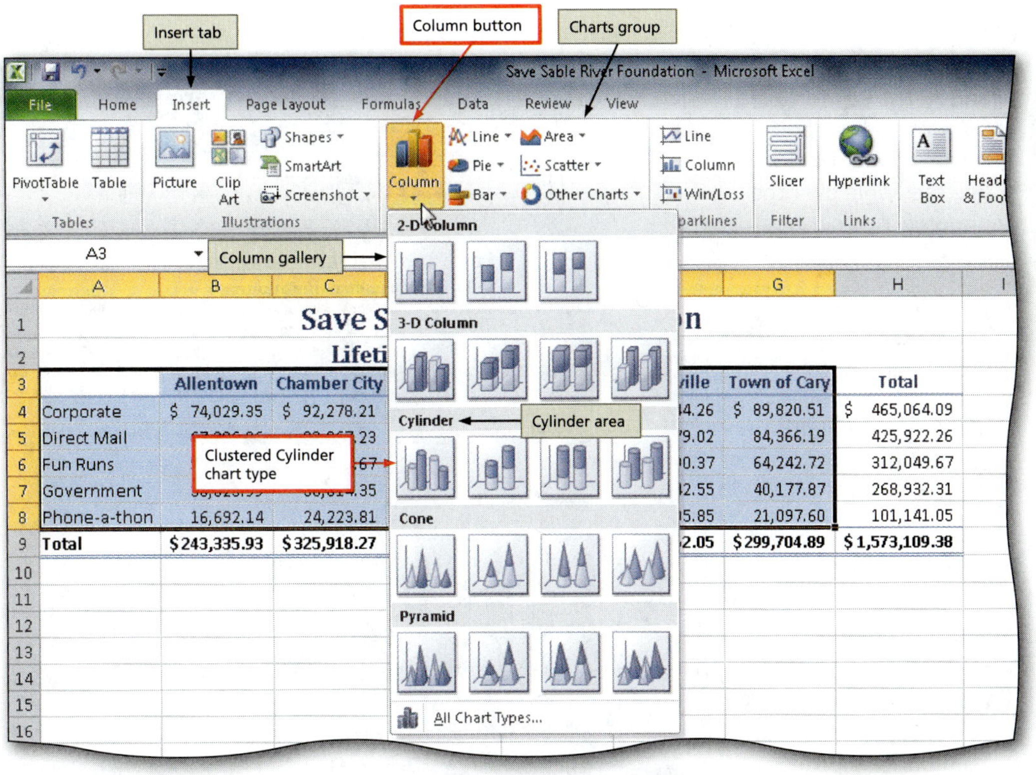

Figure 1–56

4

- Click the Clustered Cylinder chart type in the Cylinder area of the Column gallery to add the selected chart type to the middle of the worksheet in a selection rectangle.
- Press and hold down the mouse button while pointing to the upper-right edge of the selection rectangle to change the mouse pointer to a double two-headed arrow (Figure 1–57).

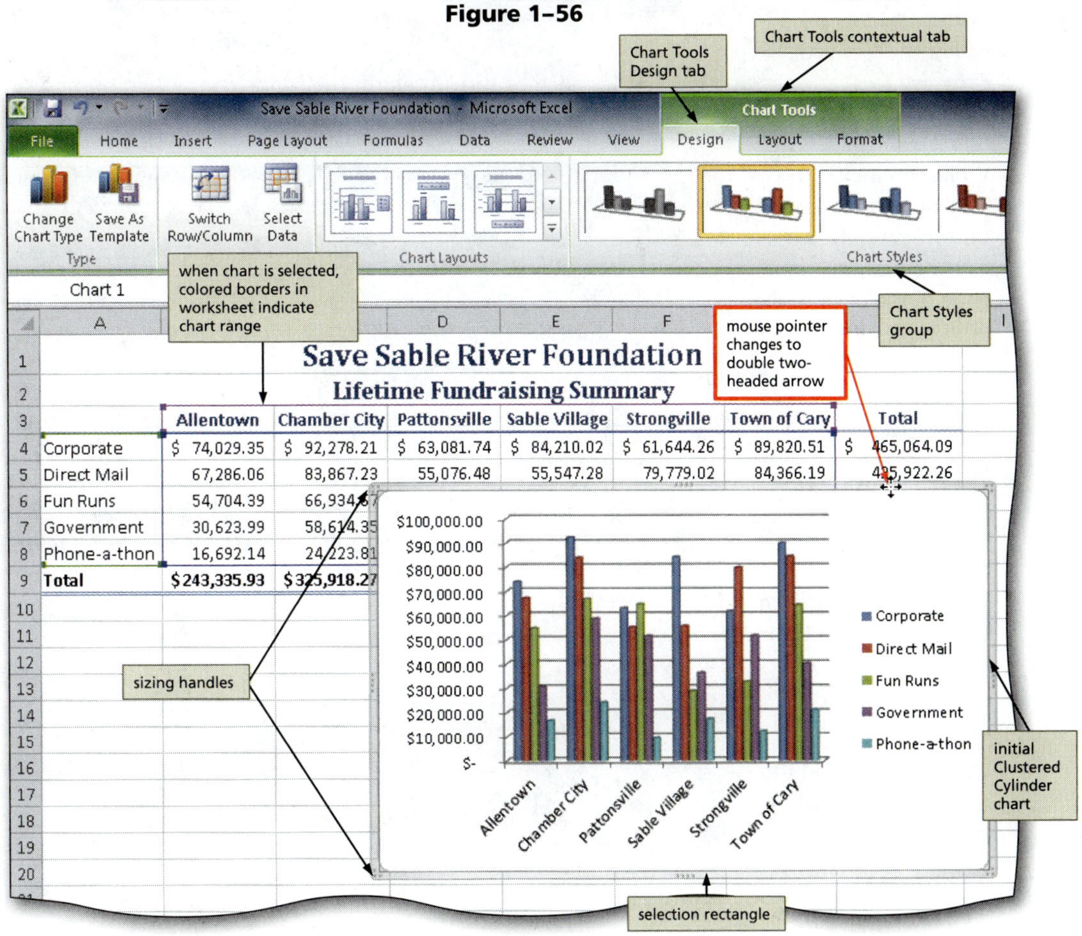

Figure 1–57

Q&A

Why is a new tab displayed on the Ribbon?

When you select objects such as shapes or charts, Excel displays contextual tabs that include special commands that are used to work with the type of object selected. Because a chart is selected, Excel displays the Chart Tools contextual tab. The three tabs below the Chart Tools contextual tab, Design, Layout, and Format, are tabs that include commands to work with charts.

5

- Drag the chart down and to the left to position the upper-left corner of the dotted line rectangle over the upper-left corner of cell A11.
- Press and hold down the mouse button while pointing to the middle sizing handle on the right edge of the chart (Figure 1–58).

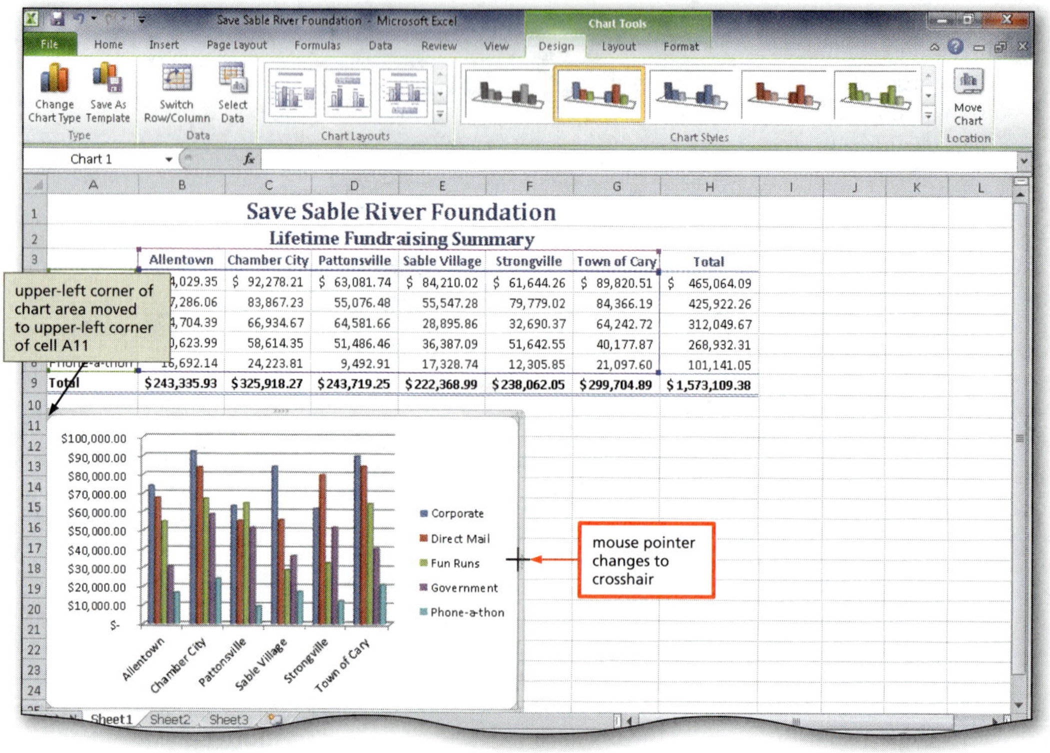

Figure 1–58

Q&A How does Excel know which data to use to create the chart?

Excel automatically selects the entries in the topmost row of the chart range (row 3) as the titles for the horizontal axis (also called the **x-axis** or **category axis**) and draws a column for each of the 30 cells in the range containing numbers.

6

- While continuing to hold down the mouse button, press the ALT key and drag the right edge of the chart to the right edge of column H and then release the mouse button to resize the chart.
- Press and hold down the mouse button while pointing to the middle sizing handle on the bottom edge of the selection rectangle and do not release the mouse button (Figure 1–59).

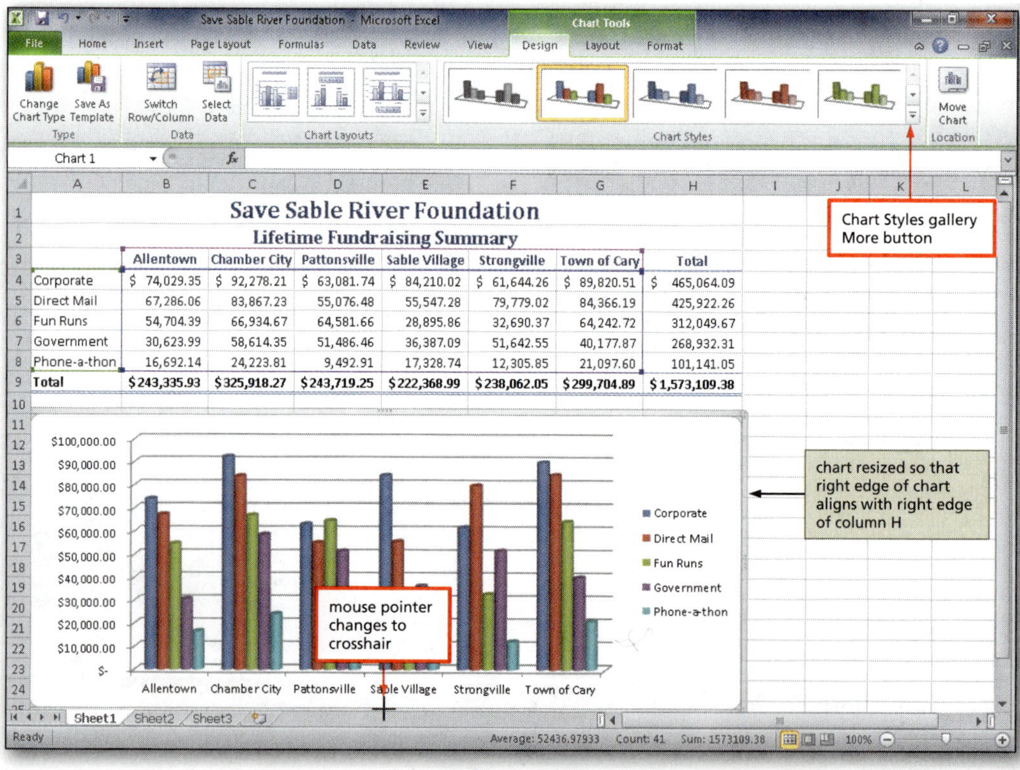

Figure 1–59

Q&A Why should I hold the ALT key down while I resize a chart?

Holding down the ALT key while you drag a chart **snaps** (aligns) the edge of the chart area to the worksheet gridlines. If you do not hold down the ALT key, then you can place an edge of a chart in the middle of a column or row.

7

- While continuing to hold down the mouse button, press the ALT key and drag the bottom edge of the chart up to the bottom edge of row 23 and then release the mouse button to resize the chart.
- If necessary, scroll the worksheet so that row 1 displays at the top of the worksheet.
- Click the More button in the Chart Styles gallery (Chart Tools Design tab | Chart Styles group) to expand the gallery (Figure 1–60).

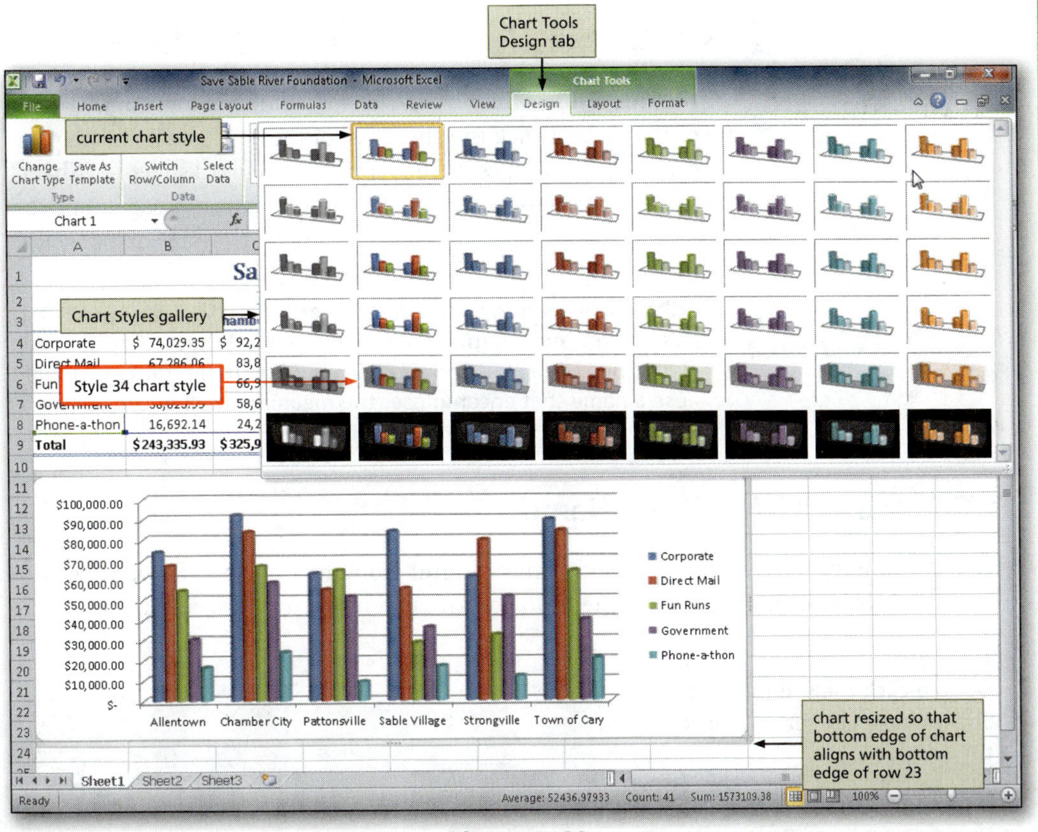

Figure 1–60

8

- Click Style 34 in the Chart Styles gallery (column 2, row 5) to apply the chart style to the chart.
- Click cell J9 to deselect the chart and complete the worksheet (Figure 1–61).

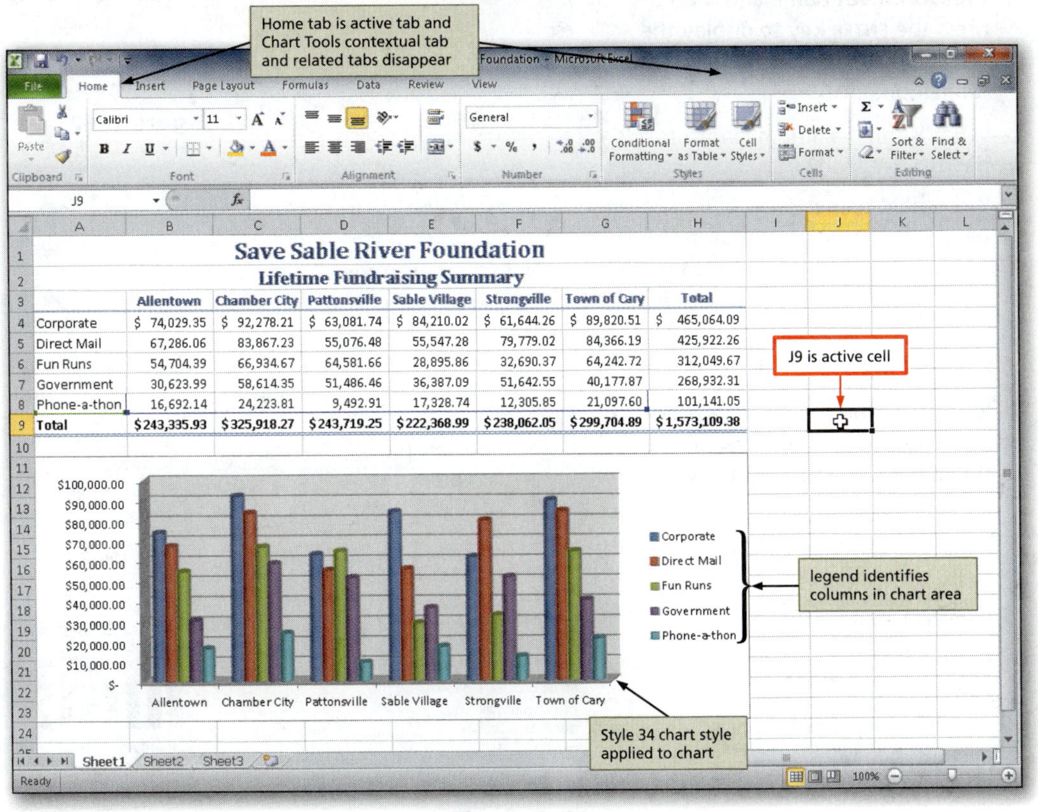

Figure 1–61

Q&A

What is the purpose of the items on the right side of the chart?

The items to the right of the column chart in Figure 1–61 are the **legend**, which identifies the colors assigned to each bar in the chart. Excel automatically selects the entries in the leftmost column of the chart range (column A) as titles within the legend.

Changing the Worksheet Names

The sheet tabs at the bottom of the window allow you to view any worksheet in the workbook. You click the sheet tab of the worksheet you want to view in the Excel window. By default, Excel presets the names of the worksheets to Sheet1, Sheet2, and so on. The worksheet names become increasingly important as you move toward more sophisticated workbooks, especially workbooks in which you reference cells between worksheets.

Plan Ahead

Choose a name for the worksheet.
Use simple, meaningful names for each worksheet. Worksheet names often match the worksheet title. If a worksheet includes multiple titles in multiple sections of the worksheet, use a name that encompasses the meaning of all of the sections.

To Change the Worksheet Names

Lifetime Fundraising Summary is a meaningful name for the Save Sable River Foundation Lifetime Fundraising Summary worksheet. The following steps rename worksheets by double-clicking the sheet tabs.

1

- Double-click the sheet tab labeled Sheet1 in the lower-left corner of the window.
- Type `Lifetime Fundraising Summary` as the worksheet name and then press the ENTER key to display the new worksheet name on the sheet tab (Figure 1–62).

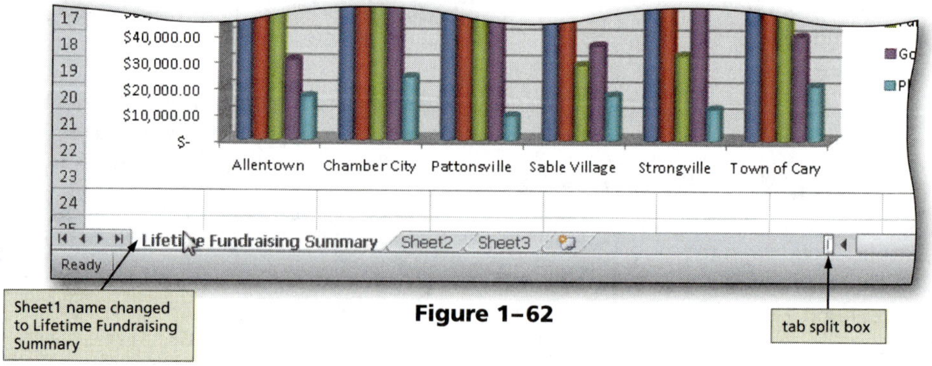

Figure 1–62

Q&A

What is the maximum length for a worksheet tab?

Worksheet names can be up to 31 characters (including spaces) in length. Longer worksheet names, however, mean that fewer sheet tabs will show. To view more sheet tabs, you can drag the tab split box (Figure 1–62) to the right. This will reduce the size of the scroll bar at the bottom of the screen. Double-click the tab split box to reset it to its normal position.

2

- Right-click the sheet tab labeled Lifetime Fundraising Summary in the lower-left corner of the window to display a shortcut menu.
- Point to Tab Color on the shortcut menu to display the color gallery (Figure 1–63).

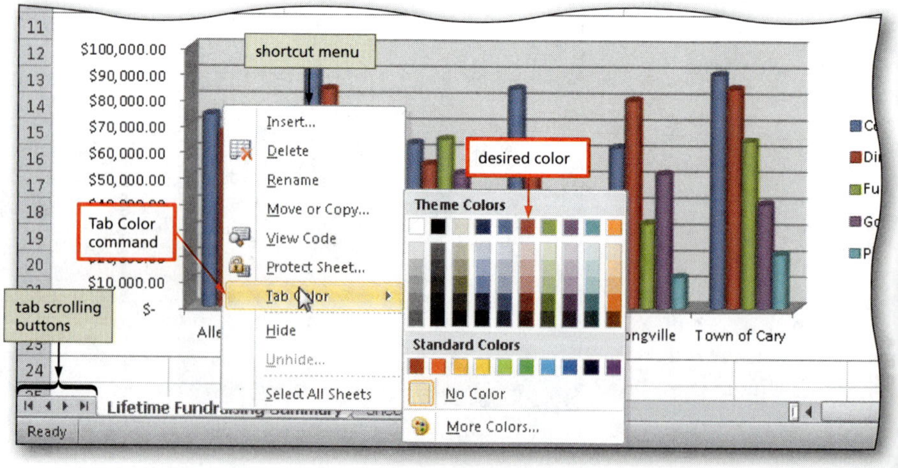

Figure 1–63

Q&A

How can I quickly move between worksheet tabs?

You can use the tab scrolling buttons to the left of the sheet tabs (Figure 1–63) to move between worksheets. The leftmost and rightmost scroll buttons move to the first or last worksheet in the workbook. The two middle scroll buttons move one worksheet to the left or right.

3

- Click Red, Accent 2 (column 6, row 1) in the Theme Colors area to change the color of the tab (Figure 1–64)

4

- If necessary, click Home on the Ribbon to display the Home tab.

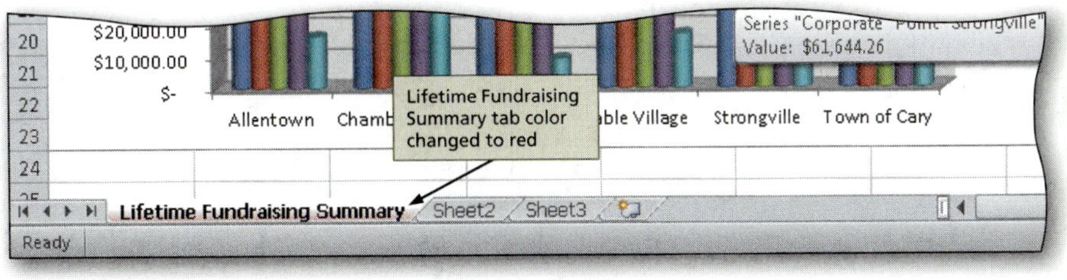

Figure 1–64

Changing Document Properties

Excel helps you organize and identify your files by using **document properties**, which are the details about a file. Document properties, also known as **metadata**, can include information such as the project author, title, subject, and keywords. A **keyword** is a word or phrase that further describes the document. For example, a class name or document topic can describe the file's purpose or content.

Document properties are valuable for a variety of reasons:

- Users can save time locating a particular file because they can view a document's properties without opening the document.
- By creating consistent properties for files having similar content, users can better organize their documents.
- Some organizations require Excel users to add document properties so that other employees can view details about these files.

Five different types of document properties exist, but the more common ones used in the Excel chapters in this book are standard and automatically updated properties. **Standard properties** are associated with all Microsoft Office documents and include author, title, and subject. **Automatically updated properties** include file system properties, such as the date you create or change a file, and statistics, such as the file size.

To Change Document Properties

The **Document Information Panel** contains areas where you can view and enter document properties. You can view and change information in this panel at any time while you are creating a workbook. Before saving the workbook again, you want to add your name and course information as document properties. The following steps use the Document Information Panel to change document properties.

1

- Click File on the Ribbon to open the Backstage view. If necessary, click the Info tab in the Backstage view to display the Info gallery (Figure 1–65).

Q&A

How do I close the Backstage view?

Click File on the Ribbon or click the preview of the document in the Info gallery to return to the Excel document window.

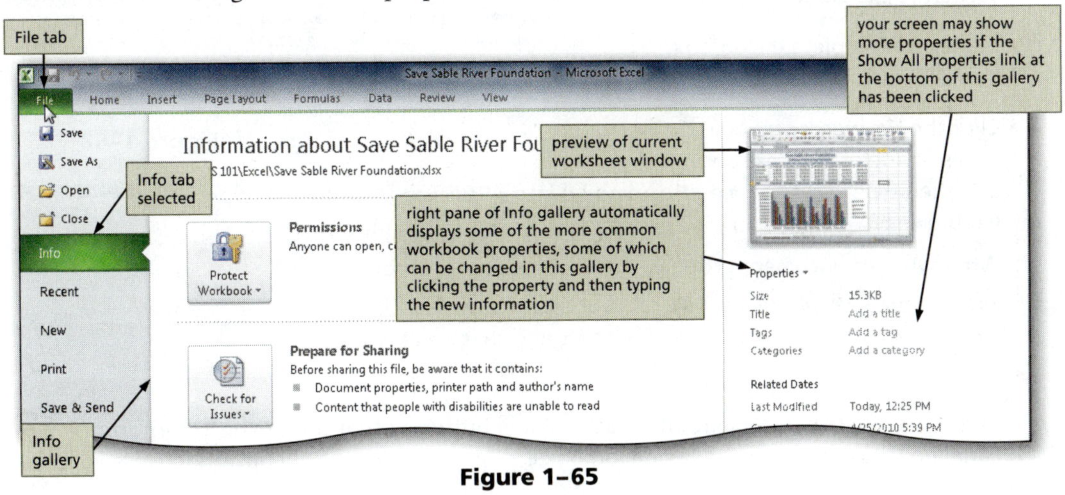

Figure 1–65

2

- Click the Properties button in the right pane of the Info gallery to display the Properties menu (Figure 1–66).

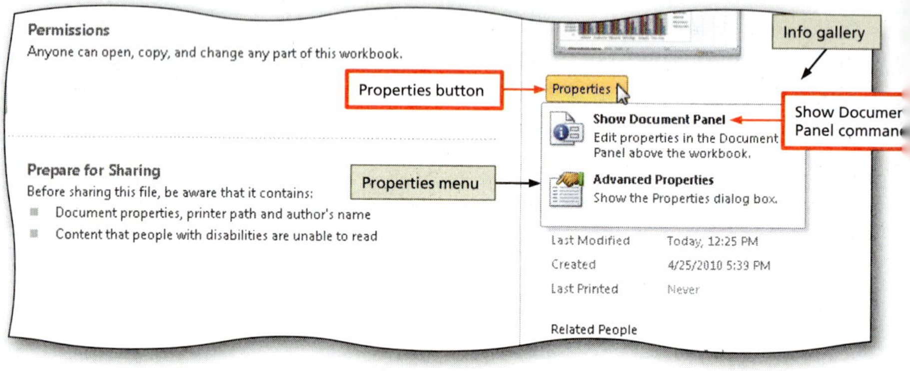

Figure 1–66

3

- Click Show Document Panel on the Properties menu to close the Backstage view and display the Document Information Panel in the Excel workbook window (Figure 1–67).

Q&A Why are some of the document properties in my Document Information Panel already filled in?

The person who installed Microsoft Office 2010 on your computer or network may have set or customized the properties.

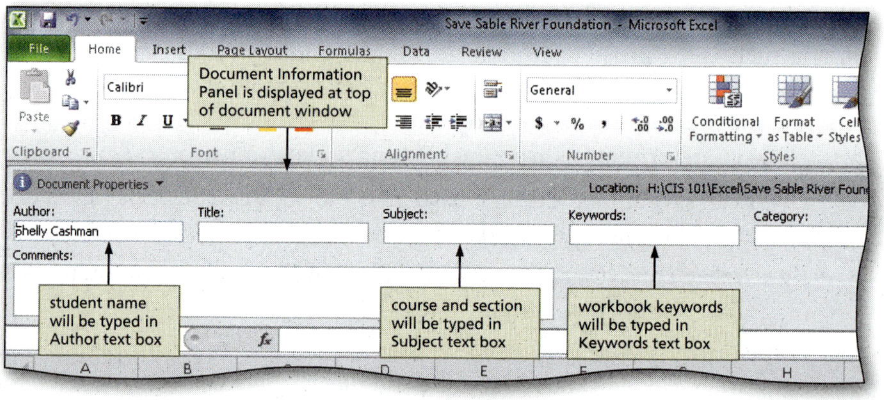

Figure 1–67

4

- Click the Author text box, if necessary, and then type your name as the Author property. If a name already is displayed in the Author text box, delete it before typing your name.
- Click the Subject text box, if necessary delete any existing text, and then type your course and section as the Subject property.
- If an AutoComplete dialog box appears, click its Yes button.

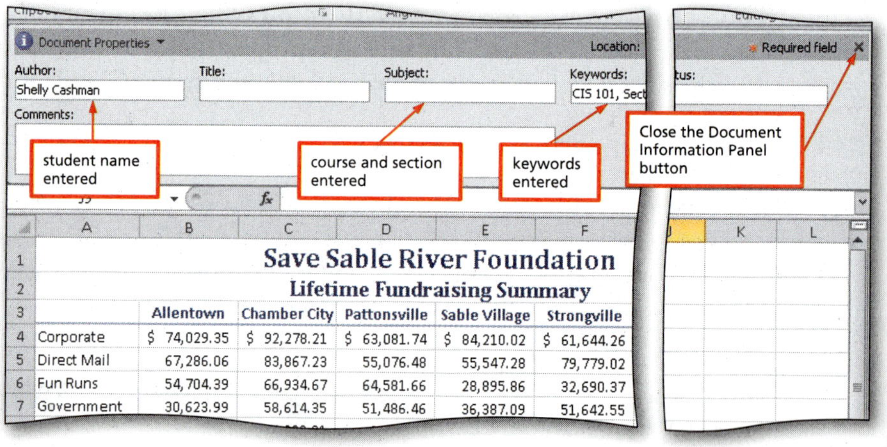

Figure 1–68

- Click the Keywords text box, if necessary delete any existing text, and then type `Lifetime Fundraising Summary` as the Keywords property (Figure 1–68).

Q&A What types of document properties does Excel collect automatically?

Excel records details such as time spent editing a workbook, the number of times a workbook has been revised, and the fonts and themes used in a workbook.

5

- Click the Close the Document Information Panel button so that the Document Information Panel no longer is displayed. If a dialog box is displayed, click the No button to close it.

Other Ways

1. Click File on Ribbon, click Info in the Backstage view, if necessary click Show All Properties link in Info gallery, click property to change and type new information, close the Backstage view

To Save an Existing Workbook with the Same File Name

You have made several modifications to the workbook since you last saved it. Thus, you should save it again. The following step saves the workbook again. For an example of the step listed below, refer to the Introduction to Office 2010 and Windows 7 chapter in this book.

1. Click the Save button on the Quick Access Toolbar to overwrite the previously saved file.

BTW

Printing Document Properties

To print document properties, click File on the Ribbon to open the Backstage view, click the Print tab in the Backstage view to display the Print gallery, click the first button in the Settings area to display a list of options specifying what you can print, click Document Properties in the list to specify you want to print the document properties instead of the actual document, and then click the Print button in the Print gallery to print the document properties on the currently selected printer.

Previewing and Printing a Worksheet

After creating a worksheet, you may want to print it. Printing a worksheet enables you to distribute the worksheet to others in a form that can be read or viewed but typically not edited. It is a good practice to save a workbook before printing a worksheet, in the event you experience difficulties printing.

Plan Ahead

Determine the best method for distributing the worksheet.

The traditional method of distributing a worksheet uses a printer to produce a hard copy. A **hardcopy or printout** is information that exists on a physical medium such as paper. For users that can receive fax documents, you can elect to print a hard copy on a remote fax machine. Hard copies can be useful for the following reasons:

- Many people prefer proofreading a hard copy of a worksheet rather than viewing it on the screen to check for errors and readability.
- Hard copies can serve as reference material if your storage medium is lost or becomes corrupted and you need to re-create the worksheet.

Instead of distributing a hard copy of a worksheet, users can choose to distribute the worksheet as an electronic image that mirrors the original worksheet's appearance. The electronic image of the worksheet can be e-mailed, posted on a Web site, or copied to a portable storage medium such as a USB flash drive. Two popular electronic image formats, sometimes called fixed formats, are PDF by Adobe Systems and XPS by Microsoft. In Excel, you can create electronic image files through the Print tab in the Backstage view, the Save & Send tab in the Backstage view, and the Save As dialog box. Electronic images of worksheets, such as PDF and XPS, can be useful for the following reasons:

- Users can view electronic images of worksheets without the software that created the original worksheet (e.g., Excel). Specifically, to view a PDF file, you use a program called Acrobat Reader, which can be downloaded free from Adobe's Web site. Similarly, to view an XPS file, you use a program called an XPS Viewer, which is included in the latest versions of Windows and Internet Explorer.
- Sending electronic documents saves paper and printer supplies. Society encourages users to contribute to **green computing**, which involves reducing the environmental waste generated when using a computer.

BTW

Conserving Ink and Toner

If you want to conserve ink or toner, you can instruct Excel to print draft quality documents by clicking File on the Ribbon to open the Backstage view, clicking Options in the Backstage view to display the Excel Options dialog box, clicking Advanced in the left pane (Excel Options dialog box), scrolling to the Print area in the right pane, placing a check mark in the 'Use draft quality' check box, and then clicking the OK button. Then, use the Backstage view to print the document as usual.

To Preview and Print a Worksheet in Landscape Orientation

With the completed workbook saved, you may want to print it. Because the worksheet is included in a report, you will print a hard copy on a printer. The following steps print a hard copy of the contents of the Save Sable River Foundation Lifetime Fundraising Summary worksheet.

1

- Click File on the Ribbon to open the Backstage view.
- Click the Print tab in the Backstage view to display the Print gallery (Figure 1–69).

Q&A How can I print multiple copies of my worksheet?

Increase the number in the Copies box in the Print gallery.

Q&A What if I decide not to print the worksheet at this time?

Click File on the Ribbon to close the Backstage view and return to the Excel workbook window.

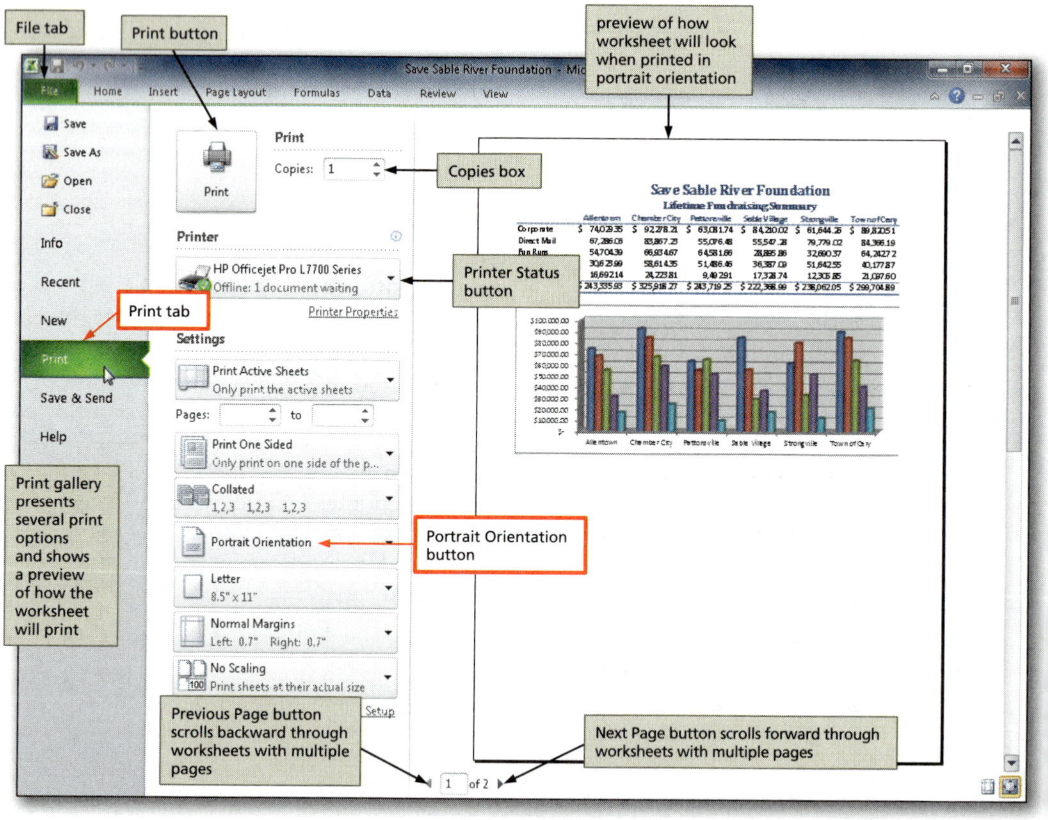

Figure 1–69

2

- Verify the printer name that appears on the Printer Status button will print a hard copy of the document. If necessary, click the Printer Status button to display a list of available printer options and then click the desired printer to change the currently selected printer.

3

- Click the Portrait Orientation button in the Settings area and then select Landscape Orientation to change the orientation of the page to landscape and view the entire worksheet on one page (Figure 1–70).

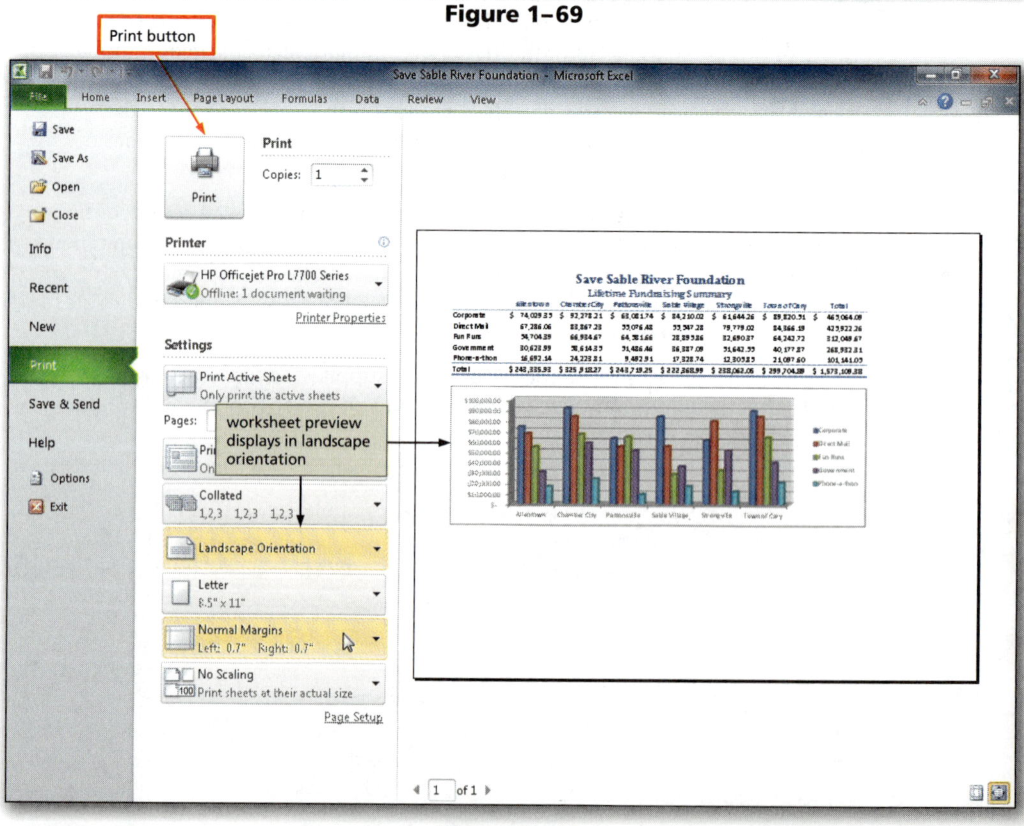

Figure 1–70

4

- Click the Print button in the Print gallery to print the worksheet in landscape orientation on the currently selected printer.
- When the printer stops, retrieve the hard copy (Figure 1–71).

Q&A Do I have to wait until my worksheet is complete to print it?

No, you can follow these steps to print a document at any time while you are creating it.

Q&A What if I want to print an electronic image of a worksheet instead of a hard copy?

You would click the Printer Status button in the Print gallery and then select the desired electronic image option such as a Microsoft XPS Document Writer, which would create an XPS file.

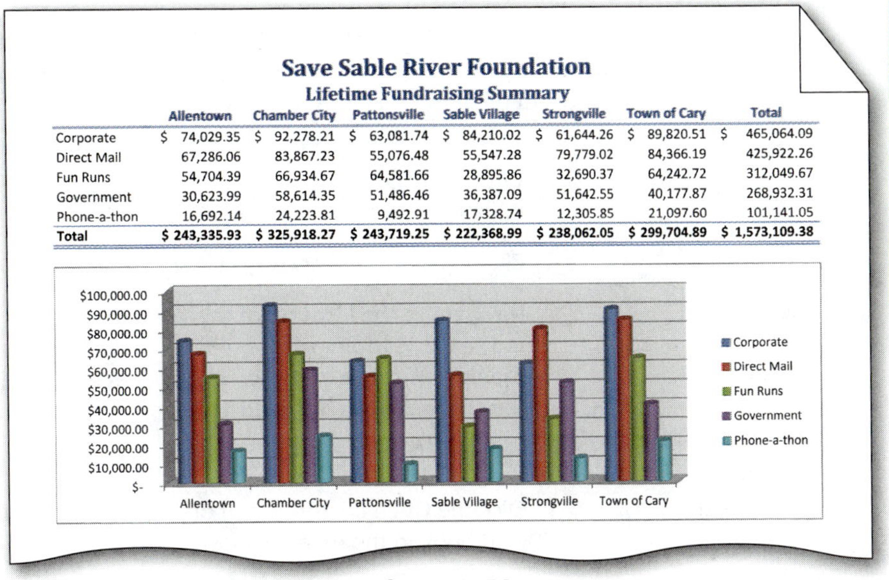
Save Sable River Foundation

Lifetime Fundraising Summary

	Allentown	Chamber City	Pattonsville	Sable Village	Strongville	Town of Cary	Total
Corporate	$ 74,029.35	$ 92,278.21	$ 63,081.74	$ 84,210.02	$ 61,644.26	$ 89,820.51	$ 465,064.09
Direct Mail	67,286.06	83,867.23	55,076.48	55,547.28	79,779.02	84,366.19	425,922.26
Fun Runs	54,704.39	66,934.67	64,581.66	28,895.86	32,690.37	64,242.72	312,049.67
Government	30,623.99	58,614.35	51,486.46	36,387.09	51,642.55	40,177.87	268,932.31
Phone-a-thon	16,692.14	24,223.81	9,492.91	17,328.74	12,305.85	21,097.60	101,141.05
Total	**$ 243,335.93**	**$ 325,918.27**	**$ 243,719.25**	**$ 222,368.99**	**$ 238,062.05**	**$ 299,704.89**	**$ 1,573,109.38**

Figure 1–71

Other Ways

1. Press CTRL+P, press ENTER

To Quit Excel

This Save Sable River Foundation workbook now is complete. The following steps quit Excel if only one workbook is open. For a detailed example of the procedure summarized below, refer to the Office 2010 and Windows 7 chapter in this book.

1. If you have one Excel workbook open, click the Close button on the right side of the title bar to close the document and quit Excel; or if you have multiple Excel workbooks open, click File on the Ribbon to open the Backstage view and then click the Exit button to close all open workbooks and quit Excel.
2. If a Microsoft Office Excel dialog box appears, click the Save button to save any changes made to the workbook since the last save.

Starting Excel and Opening a Workbook

Once you have created and saved a workbook, you may need to retrieve it from your storage medium. For example, you might want to revise a worksheet or reprint it. Opening a workbook requires that Excel is running on your computer.

To Start Excel

1. Click the Start button on the Windows 7 taskbar to display the Start menu.
2. Type `Microsoft Excel` as the search text in the 'Search programs and files' text box and watch the search results appear on the Start menu.
3. Click Microsoft Excel 2010 in the search results on the Start menu to start Excel and display a new blank workbook in the Excel window.
4. If the Excel window is not maximized, click the Maximize button next to the Close button on its title bar to maximize the window.

To Open a Workbook from Excel

Earlier in this chapter you saved your project on a USB flash drive using the file name, Save Sable River Foundation. The following steps open the Save Sable River Foundation file from the Excel folder in the CIS 101 folder on the USB flash drive. For a detailed example of the procedure summarized below, refer to the Office 2010 and Windows 7 chapter in this book.

1. With your USB flash drive connected to one of the computer's USB ports, click File on the Ribbon to open the Backstage view.
2. Click Open in the Backstage view to display the Open dialog box.
3. Navigate to the location of the file to be opened (in this case, the USB flash drive, then to the CIS 101 folder [or your class folder], and then to the Excel folder). For a detailed example of this procedure, refer to Steps 3a – 3c in the To Save a File in a Folder section in the Office 2010 and Windows 7 chapter in this book.
4. Click Save Sable River Foundation to select the file to be opened.
5. Click the Open button (Open dialog box) to open the selected file and display the opened workbook in the Excel window.

AutoCalculate

You easily can obtain a total, an average, or other information about the numbers in a range by using the **AutoCalculate area** on the status bar. First, select the range of cells containing the numbers you want to check. Next, right-click the AutoCalculate area to display the Status Bar Configuration shortcut menu (Figure 1–72). The check mark to the left of the active functions (Average, Count, and Sum) indicates that the sum, count, and average of the selected range are displayed in the AutoCalculate area on the status bar. The functions of the AutoCalculate commands on the Status Bar Configuration shortcut menu are described in Table 1–4.

BTW

AutoCalculate
Use the AutoCalculate area on the status bar to check your work as you enter data in a worksheet. If you enter large amounts of data, you select a range of data and then check the AutoCalculate area to provide insight into statistics about the data you entered. Often, you will have an intuitive feel for whether the numbers are accurate or if you may have made a mistake while entering the data.

Table 1–4 AutoCalculate Shortcut Menu Commands

Command	Function
Average	AutoCalculate area displays the average of the numbers in the selected range
Count	AutoCalculate area displays the number of nonblank cells in the selected range
Numerical Count	AutoCalculate area displays the number of cells containing numbers in the selected range
Minimum	AutoCalculate area displays the lowest value in the selected range
Maximum	AutoCalculate area displays the highest value in the selected range
Sum	AutoCalculate area displays the sum of the numbers in the selected range

To Use the AutoCalculate Area to Determine a Maximum

The following steps display the largest amounts of funds raised for any city for the Fun Runs fundraising activity.

1

- Select the range B6:G6 and then right-click the AutoCalculate area on the status bar to display the Customize Status Bar shortcut menu (Figure 1–72).

Q&A

What is displayed on the Customize Status Bar shortcut menu?

This shortcut menu includes several commands that allow you to control the items displayed on the Customize Status Bar shortcut menu. The AutoCalculate area includes six commands as well as the result of the associated calculation on the right side of the menu.

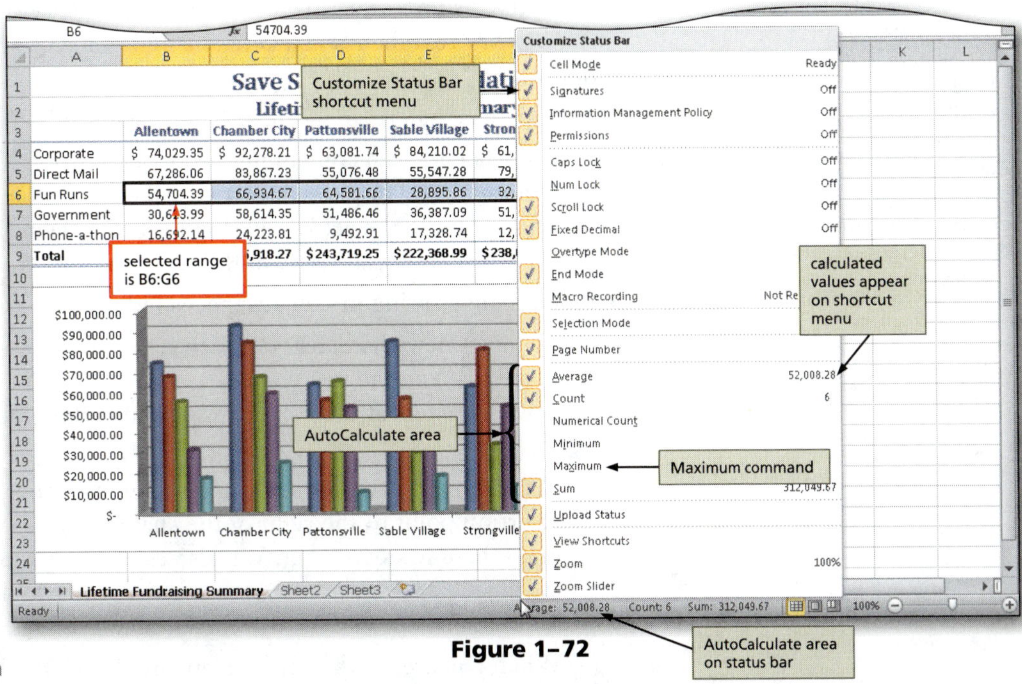

Figure 1–72

2

- Click Maximum on the shortcut menu to display the Maximum value in the range B6:G6 in the AutoCalculate area of the status bar.

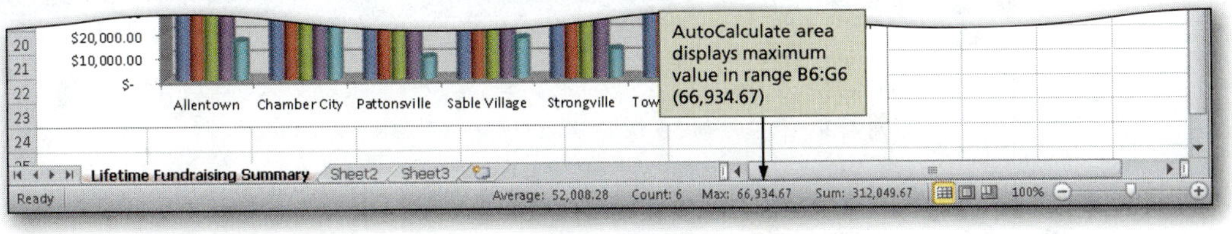

Figure 1–73

- Click anywhere on the worksheet to cause the shortcut menu to disappear (Figure 1–73).

3

- Right-click the AutoCalculate area and then click Maximum on the shortcut menu to cause the Maximum value to no longer appear in the AutoCalculate area.
- Click anywhere on the worksheet to cause the shortcut menu to disappear.

Correcting Errors

You can correct errors on a worksheet using one of several methods. The method you choose will depend on the extent of the error and whether you notice it while typing the data or after you have entered the incorrect data into the cell.

Correcting Errors While You Are Typing Data into a Cell

If you notice an error while you are typing data into a cell, press the BACKSPACE key to erase the incorrect characters and then type the correct characters. If the error is a major one, click the Cancel box in the formula bar or press the ESC key to erase the entire entry and then reenter the data from the beginning.

BTW

Quick Reference

For a table that lists how to complete the tasks covered in the Office chapters in this book using the mouse, Ribbon, shortcut menu, and keyboard, see the Quick Reference Summary at the back of this book, or visit the Microsoft Office and Concepts CourseMate Web site at www.cengagebrain.com and then navigate to the Quick Reference resource for this book.

BTW

In-Cell Editing

An alternative to double-clicking the cell to edit it is to select the cell and then press the F2 key.

Correcting Errors After Entering Data into a Cell

If you find an error in the worksheet after entering the data, you can correct the error in one of two ways:

1. If the entry is short, select the cell, retype the entry correctly, and then click the Enter box or press the ENTER key. The new entry will replace the old entry.
2. If the entry in the cell is long and the errors are minor, using Edit mode may be a better choice than retyping the cell entry. Use the Edit mode as described below.
   a. Double-click the cell containing the error to switch Excel to Edit mode. In **Edit mode**, Excel displays the active cell entry in the formula bar and a flashing insertion point in the active cell (Figure 1–74). With Excel in Edit mode, you can edit the contents directly in the cell — a procedure called **in-cell editing**.
   b. Make changes using in-cell editing, as indicated below.
      (1) To insert new characters between two characters, place the insertion point between the two characters and begin typing. Excel inserts the new characters at the location of the insertion point.
      (2) To delete a character in the cell, move the insertion point to the left of the character you want to delete and then press the DELETE key or place the insertion point to the right of the character you want to delete and then press the BACKSPACE key. You also can use the mouse to drag through the character or adjacent characters you want to delete and then press the DELETE key or click the Cut button (Home tab | Clipboard group).
      (3) When you are finished editing an entry, click the Enter box or press the ENTER key.

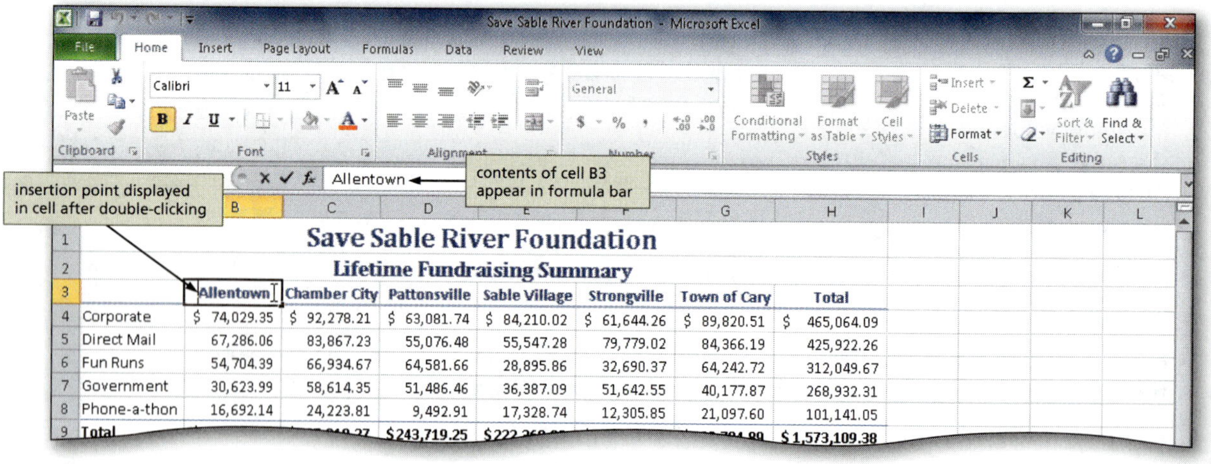

Figure 1–74

BTW

Editing the Contents of a Cell

Rather than using in-cell editing, you can select the cell and then click the formula bar to edit the contents.

When Excel enters the Edit mode, the keyboard usually is in Insert mode. In **Insert mode**, as you type a character, Excel inserts the character and moves all characters to the right of the typed character one position to the right. You can change to Overtype mode by pressing the INSERT key. In **Overtype mode**, Excel overtypes, or replaces, the character to the right of the insertion point. The INSERT key toggles the keyboard between Insert mode and Overtype mode.

While in Edit mode, you may have reason to move the insertion point to various points in the cell, select portions of the data in the cell, or switch from inserting characters to overtyping characters. Table 1–5 summarizes the more common tasks performed during in-cell editing.

Table 1–5 Summary of In-Cell Editing Tasks

	Task	Mouse	Keyboard
1	Move the insertion point to the beginning of data in a cell.	Point to the left of the first character and click.	Press HOME
2	Move the insertion point to the end of data in a cell.	Point to the right of the last character and click.	Press END
3	Move the insertion point anywhere in a cell.	Point to the appropriate position and click the character.	Press RIGHT ARROW or LEFT ARROW
4	Highlight one or more adjacent characters.	Drag the mouse pointer through adjacent characters.	Press SHIFT+RIGHT ARROW or SHIFT+LEFT ARROW
5	Select all data in a cell.	Double-click the cell with the insertion point in the cell if there are no spaces in the data in the cell.	
6	Delete selected characters.	Click the Cut button (Home tab | Clipboard group)	Press DELETE
7	Delete characters to the left of the insertion point.		Press BACKSPACE
8	Delete characters to the right of the insertion point.		Press DELETE
9	Toggle between Insert and Overtype modes.		Press INSERT

BTW

Excel Help
At any time while using Excel, you can find answers to questions and display information about various topics through Excel Help. Used properly, this form of assistance can increase your productivity and reduce your frustrations by minimizing the time you spend learning how to use Excel. For instruction about Excel Help and exercises that will help you gain confidence in using it, read the Office 2010 and Windows 7 chapter in this book.

Undoing the Last Cell Entry

Excel provides the Undo command on the Quick Access Toolbar (Figure 1–75), which allows you to erase recent cell entries. Thus, if you enter incorrect data in a cell and notice it immediately, click the Undo button and Excel changes the cell entry to what it was prior to the incorrect data entry.

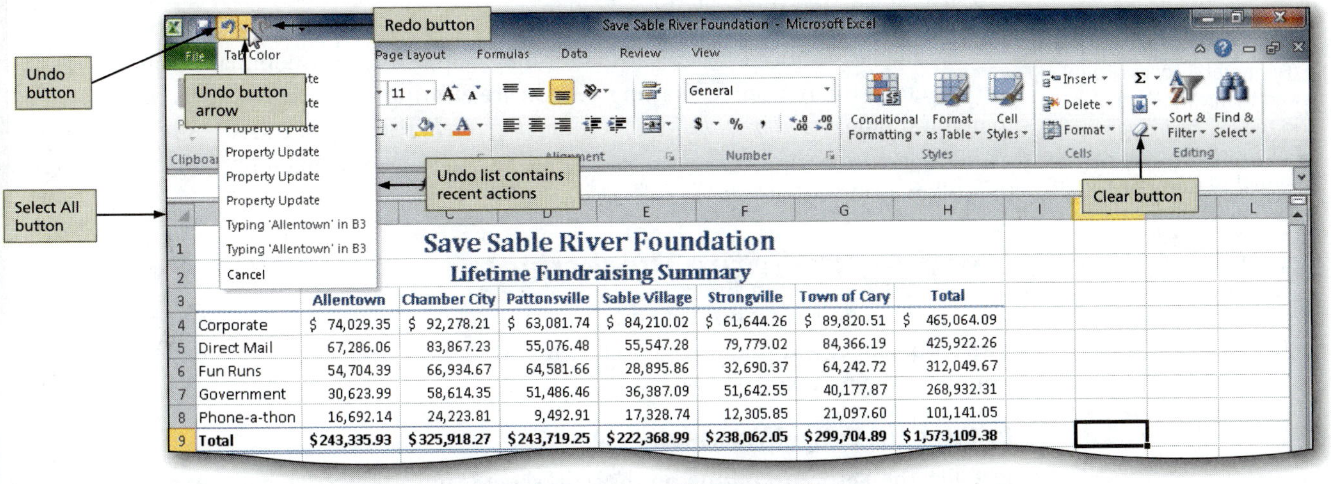

Figure 1–75

Excel remembers the last 100 actions you have completed. Thus, you can undo up to 100 previous actions by clicking the Undo button arrow to display the Undo list and then clicking the action to be undone (Figure 1–75). You can drag through several actions in the Undo list to undo all of them at once. If no actions are available for Excel to undo, then the Undo button is dimmed and inoperative.

The Redo button, next to the Undo button on the Quick Access Toolbar, allows you to repeat previous actions.

Clearing a Cell or Range of Cells

If you enter data into the wrong cell or range of cells, you can erase, or clear, the data using one of the first four methods listed below. The fifth method clears the formatting from the selected cells.

To Clear Cell Entries Using the Fill Handle

1. Select the cell or range of cells and then point to the fill handle so the mouse pointer changes to a crosshair.
2. Drag the fill handle back into the selected cell or range until a shadow covers the cell or cells you want to erase. Release the mouse button.

To Clear Cell Entries Using the Shortcut Menu

1. Select the cell or range of cells to be cleared.
2. Right-click the selection.
3. Click Clear Contents on the shortcut menu.

To Clear Cell Entries Using the DELETE Key

1. Select the cell or range of cells to be cleared.
2. Press the DELETE key.

To Clear Cell Entries and Formatting Using the Clear Button

1. Select the cell or range of cells to be cleared.
2. Click the Clear button (Home tab | Editing group) (Figure 1–75 on the previous page).
3. Click Clear Contents on the menu.

To Clear Formatting Using the Cell Styles Button

1. Select the cell or range of cells from which you want to remove the formatting.
2. Click the Cell Styles button (Home tab | Styles group) and point to Normal.
3. Click Normal in the Cell Styles Gallery.

BTW

Getting Back to Normal
If you accidentally assign unwanted formats to a range of cells, you can use the Normal cell style selection in the Cell Styles gallery. Click Cell Styles (Home tab | Styles group) and then click Normal in the Cell Styles gallery. Doing so changes the format to Normal style. To view the characteristics of the Normal style, right-click the style in the Cell Styles gallery and then click Modify or press ALT+APOSTROPHE (').

The Clear button (Home tab | Editing group) is the only command that clears both the cell entry and the cell formatting. As you are clearing cell entries, always remember that you should *never press the* SPACEBAR *to clear a cell.* Pressing the SPACEBAR enters a blank character. A blank character is text and is different from an empty cell, even though the cell may appear empty.

Clearing the Entire Worksheet

If the required worksheet edits are extremely extensive, you may want to clear the entire worksheet and start over. To clear the worksheet or delete an embedded chart, you would use the following steps.

To Clear the Entire Worksheet

1. Click the Select All button on the worksheet (Figure 1–75).
2. Click the Clear button (Home tab | Editing group) and then click Clear All on the Clear menu to delete both the entries and formats.

The Select All button selects the entire worksheet. Instead of clicking the Select All button, you can press CTRL+A. To clear an unsaved workbook, click the workbook's Close Window button or click the Close button in the Backstage view. Click the No button if the Microsoft Excel dialog box asks if you want to save changes. To start a new, blank workbook, click the New button in the Backstage view.

To delete an embedded chart, you would complete the following steps.

TO DELETE AN EMBEDDED CHART

1. Click the chart to select it.
2. Press the DELETE key.

> **BTW**
> **Quitting Excel**
> Do not forget to remove your USB flash drive from the USB port after quitting Excel, especially if you are working in a laboratory environment. Nothing can be more frustrating than leaving all of your hard work behind on a USB flash drive for the next user.

To Quit Excel

The project now is complete. The following steps quit Excel. For a detailed example of the procedure summarized below, refer to the Office 2010 and Windows 7 chapter in this book.

1. If you have one Excel workbook open, click the Close button on the right side of the title bar to close the document and quit Excel; or if you have multiple Excel workbooks open, click File on the Ribbon to open the Backstage view and then click Exit in the Backstage view to close all open workbooks and quit Excel.

2. If a Microsoft Office Excel dialog box appears, click the Save button to save any changes made to the document since the last save.

Chapter Summary

In this chapter you have learned how to enter text and numbers to create a worksheet, how to select a range, how to use the Sum button, format cells, insert a chart, and preview and print a worksheet. The items listed below include all the new Excel skills you have learned in this chapter.

1. To Start Excel (EX 6)
2. Enter the Worksheet Titles (EX 8)
3. Enter Column Titles (EX 10)
4. Enter Row Titles (EX 12)
5. Enter Numbers (EX 13)
6. Sum a Column of Numbers (EX 15)
7. Copy a Cell to Adjacent Cells in a Row (EX 17)
8. Determine Multiple Totals at the Same Time (EX 18)
9. Save a Workbook (EX 20)
10. Change a Cell Style (EX 22)
11. Change the Font (EX 24)
12. Bold a Cell (EX 25)
13. Increase the Font Size of a Cell Entry (EX 26)
14. Change the Font Color of a Cell Entry (EX 27)
15. Center Cell Entries Across Columns by Merging Cells (EX 28)
16. Format Column Titles and the Total Row (EX 29)
17. Format Numbers in the Worksheet (EX 31)
18. Adjust the Column Width (EX 33)
19. Use the Name Box to Select a Cell (EX 34)
20. Add a Clustered Cylinder Chart to the Worksheet (EX 38)
21. Change the Worksheet Names (EX 42)
22. Change Document Properties (EX 43)
23. Save an Existing Workbook with the Same File Name (EX 45)
24. Preview and Print a Worksheet in Landscape Orientation (EX 46)
25. Quit Excel (EX 47)
26 Start Excel (EX 47)
27. Open a Workbook from Excel (EX 48)
28. Use the AutoCalculate Area to Determine a Maximum (EX 49)
29. Clear Cell Entries Using the Fill Handle (EX 52)
30. Clear Cell Entries Using the Shortcut Menu (EX 52)
31. Clear Cell Entries Using the DELETE Key (EX 52)
32. Clear Cell Entries and Formatting Using the Clear Button (EX 52)
33. Clear Formatting Using the Cell Styles Button (EX 52)
34. Clear the Entire Worksheet (EX 52)
35. Delete an Embedded Chart (EX 53)

> SAM
> If you have a SAM 2010 user profile, your instructor may have assigned an autogradable version of this assignment. If so, log into the SAM 2010 Web site at www.cengage.com/sam2010 to download the instruction and start files.

STUDENT ASSIGNMENTS

Learn It Online

Test your knowledge of chapter content and key terms.

Instructions: To complete the Learn It Online exercises, visit the Microsoft Office and Concepts CourseMate Web site at www.cengagebrain.com, navigate to the Excel Chapter 1 resources for this book, click the link for the exercise you want to complete, and then read the instructions.

Chapter Reinforcement TF, MC, and SA

A series of true/false, multiple choice, and short answer questions that test your knowledge of the chapter content.

Flash Cards

An interactive learning environment where you identify chapter key terms associated with displayed definitions.

Practice Test

A series of multiple choice questions that test your knowledge of chapter content and key terms.

Who Wants To Be a Computer Genius?

An interactive game that challenges your knowledge of chapter content in the style of a television quiz show.

Wheel of Terms

An interactive game that challenges your knowledge of chapter key terms in the style of the television show *Wheel of Fortune*.

Crossword Puzzle Challenge

A crossword puzzle that challenges your knowledge of key terms presented in the chapter.

Apply Your Knowledge

Reinforce the skills and apply the concepts you learned in this chapter.

Changing the Values in a Worksheet

Instructions: Start Excel. Open the workbook Apply 1–1 Clothes Campus Third Quarter Expenses (Figure 1–76a). See the inside back cover of this book for instructions for downloading the Data Files for Students, or see your instructor for information on accessing the files required in this book.

1. Make the changes to the worksheet described in Table 1–6 so that the worksheet appears as shown in Figure 1–76b. As you edit the values in the cells containing numeric data, watch the totals in row 7, the totals in column F, and the chart change.
2. Change the worksheet title in cell A1 to the Title cell style and then merge and center it across columns A through F. Use buttons in the Font group on the Home tab on the Ribbon to change the worksheet subtitle in cell A2 to 16-point Cambria red, bold font and then center it across columns A through F. Use the Red, Accent 2 theme color (column 6, row 1 on the Font gallery) for the red font color.
3. Apply the worksheet name, Third Quarter Expenses, to the sheet tab and apply the Red, Accent 2 theme color to the sheet tab.
4. Change the document properties as specified by your instructor. Save the workbook using the file name, Apply 1–1 Clothed for Campus Third Quarter Expenses. Submit the revised workbook as specified by your instructor.

Table 1–6 New Worksheet Data

Cell	Change Cell Contents To
A1	Clothed for Campus
B4	7829.50
C4	19057.83
D5	24217.92
E5	25859.62
E6	35140.84

(a) Before

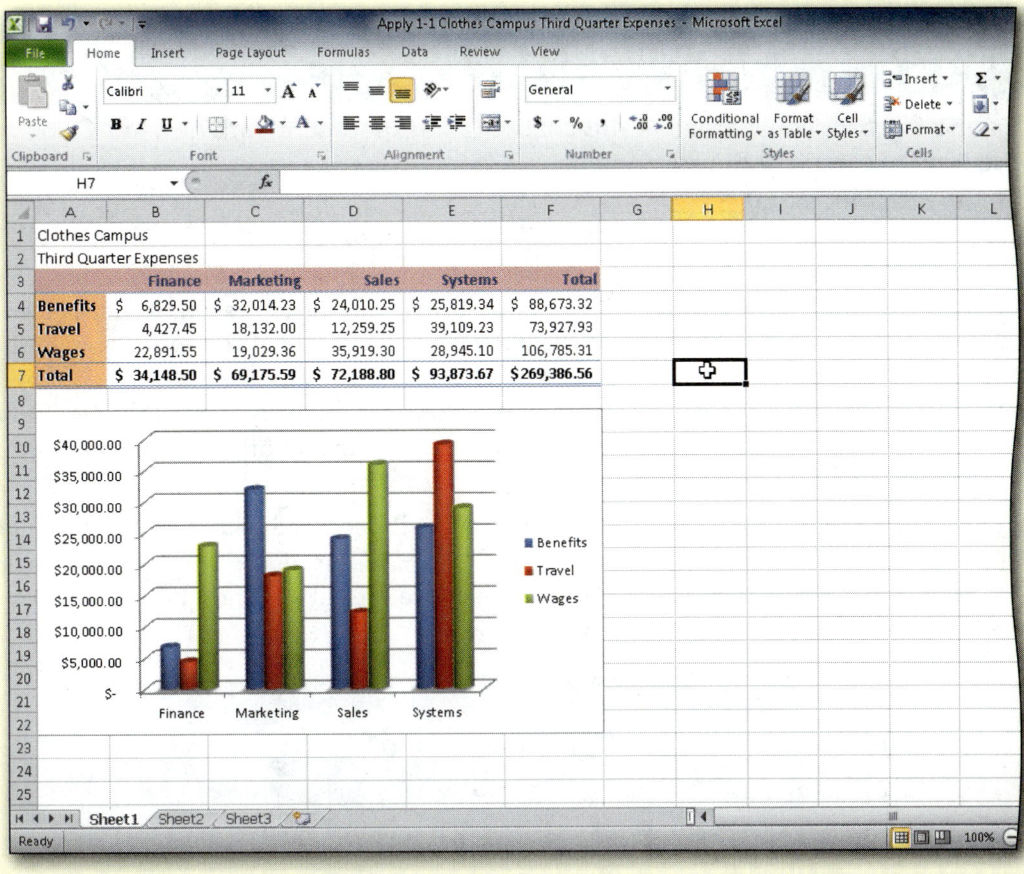

(b) After

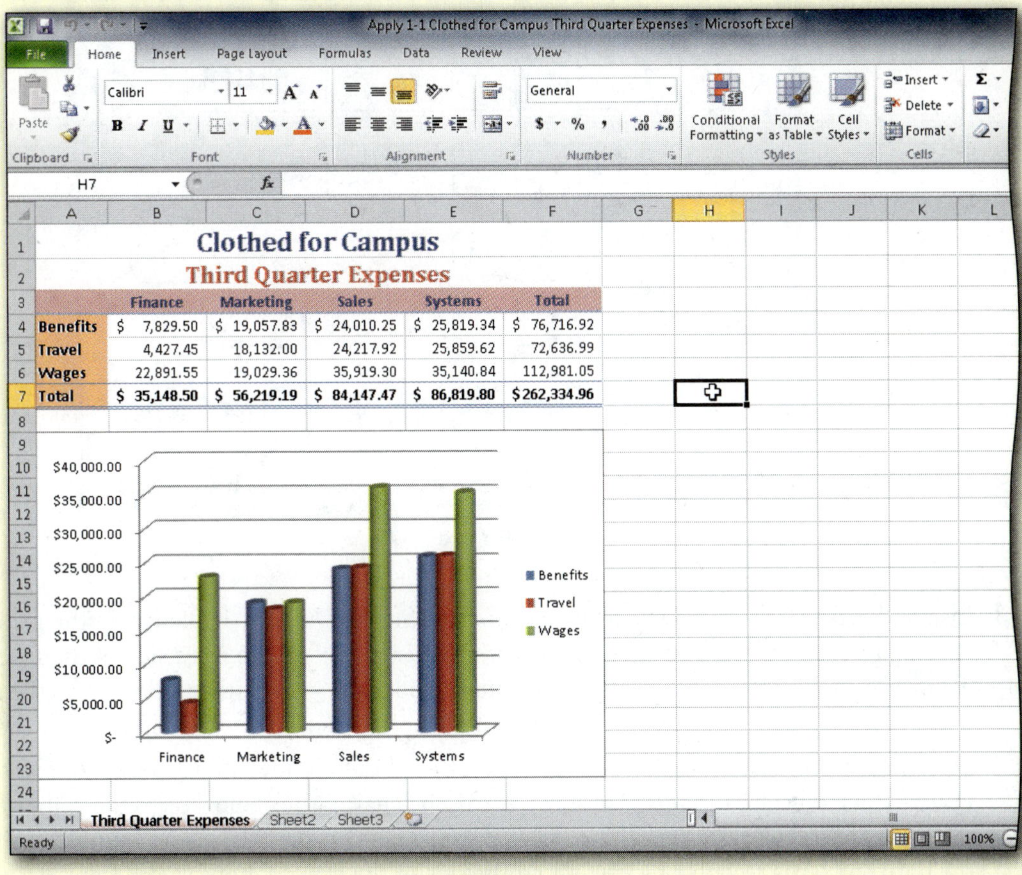

Figure 1–76

Extend Your Knowledge

Extend the skills you learned in this chapter and experiment with new skills. You may need to use Help to complete the assignment.

Formatting a Worksheet and Adding Additional Charts

Instructions: Start Excel. Open the workbook Extend 1–1 Pack Right Moving Supplies. See the inside back cover of this book for instructions for downloading the Data Files for Students, or see your instructor for information on accessing the files required in this book. Perform the following tasks to format cells in the worksheet and to add two charts to the worksheet.

1. Use the commands in the Font group on the Home tab on the Ribbon to change the font of the title in cell A1 to 22-point Arial Black, green, bold, and the subtitle of the worksheet to 14-point Arial, red, bold.
2. Select the range A3:G8, click the Insert tab on the Ribbon, and then click the Dialog Box Launcher in the Charts group on the Ribbon to open the Insert Chart dialog box. If necessary, drag the lower-right corner of the Insert Chart dialog box to expand it (Figure 1–77).

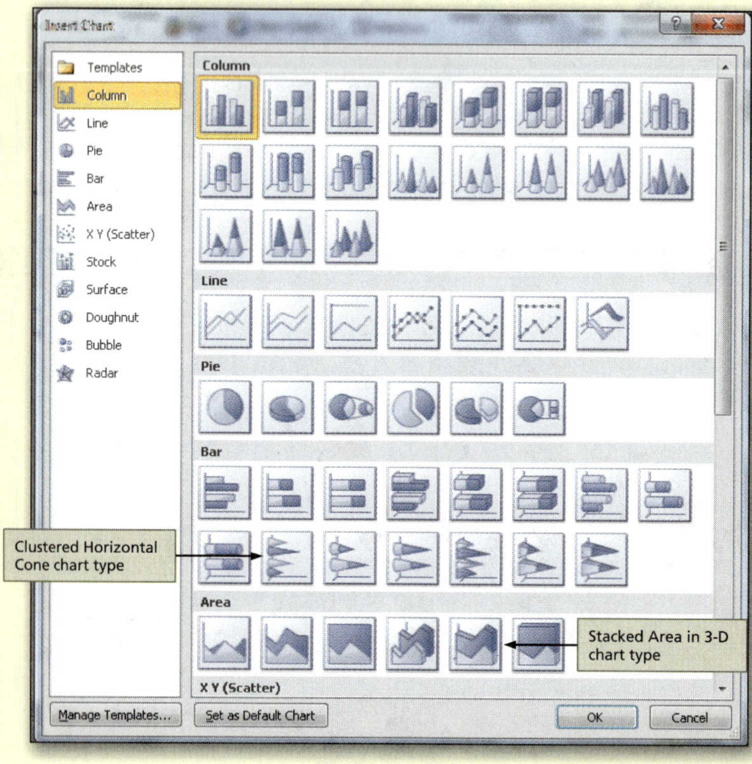

Figure 1–77

3. Insert a Stacked Area in 3-D chart by clicking the Stacked Area in 3-D chart in the gallery and then clicking the OK button. You may need to use the scroll box on the right side of the Insert Chart dialog box to view the Area charts in the gallery. Move the chart either below or to the right of the data in the worksheet. Click the Design tab and apply a chart style of your choice to the chart.
4. Deselect the chart and reselect the range A3:G8, and then follow Step 3 above to insert a Clustered Horizontal Cone chart in the worksheet. Move the chart either below or to the right of the data so that each chart does not overlap the Stacked Area in 3-D chart. Make sure to make the values on the horizontal axis readable by expanding the size of the chart. Choose a different chart style for this chart than the one you selected for the Stacked Area in 3-D chart.

5. Resize each chart so that each snaps to the worksheet gridlines. You may need to scroll the worksheet to resize and view the charts. Preview the worksheet.
6. Apply a worksheet name to the sheet tab and apply a color of your choice to the sheet tab.
7. Change the document properties as specified by your instructor. Save the workbook using the file name, Extend 1–1 Pack Right Moving Supplies Charts. Submit the revised workbook as specified by your instructor.

Make It Right

Analyze a workbook and correct all errors and/or improve the design.

Fixing Formatting Problems and Data Errors in a Worksheet

Instructions: Start Excel. Open the workbook Make It Right 1–1 Pets. See the inside back cover of this book for instructions for downloading the Data Files for Students, or see your instructor for information on accessing the files required for this book. Correct the following formatting problems and data errors (Figure 1–78) in the worksheet, while keeping in mind the guidelines presented in this chapter.

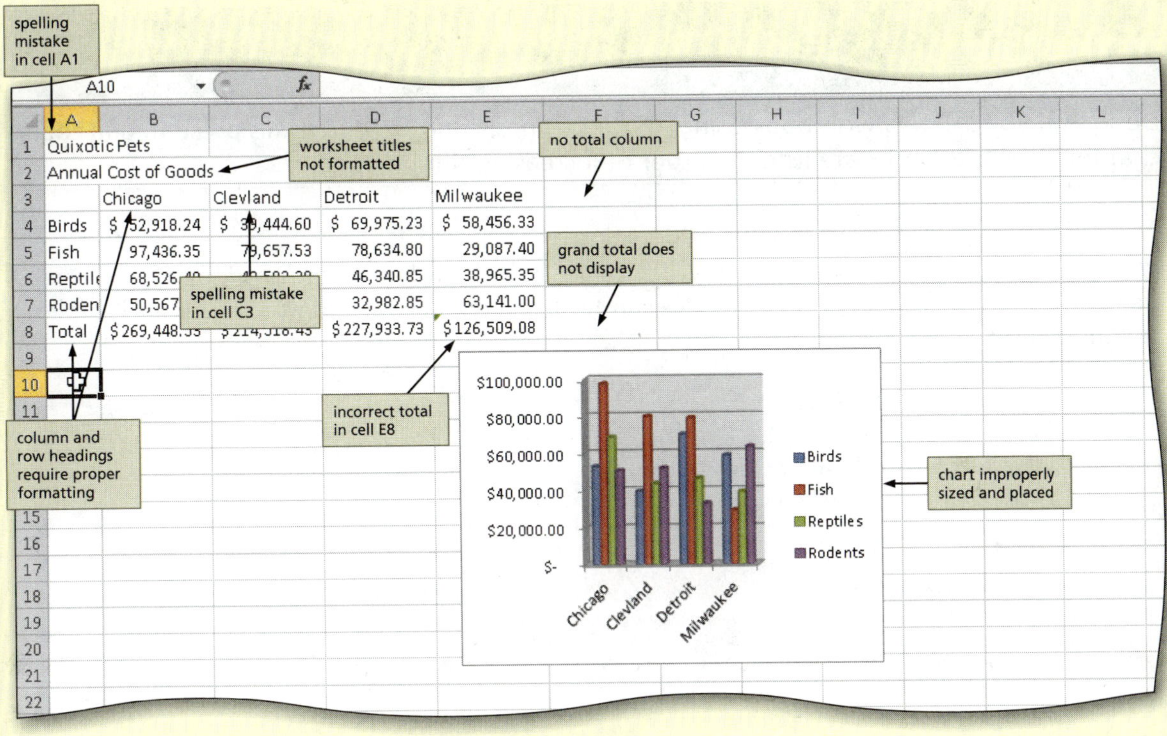

Figure 1–78

1. Merge and center the worksheet title and subtitle appropriately.
2. Format the worksheet title with a cell style appropriate for a worksheet title.
3. Format the subtitle using commands in the Font group on the Home tab on the Ribbon and apply the Red, Accent 2 color to the subtitle.
4. Correct the spelling mistake in cell A1 by changing Quixotic to Exotic. Correct the spelling mistake in cell C3 by changing Clevland to Cleveland.

Continued >

STUDENT ASSIGNMENTS

Make It Right *continued*

5. Add a column header for totals in column F and create the necessary totals in row 8.
6. Apply proper formatting to the column headers and total row, including centering the column headers.
7. Adjust the column sizes so that all data in each column is visible.
8. Create the grand total for the annual cost of goods.
9. The SUM function in cell E8 does not sum all of the numbers in the column. Correct this error by editing the range for the SUM function in the cell.
10. Resize and move the chart so that it is below the worksheet data and does not extend past the right edge of the worksheet data. Be certain to snap the chart to the worksheet gridlines by holding down the ALT key as you resize the chart to the right edge of column F and the bottom of row 22.
11. Apply a worksheet name to the sheet tab and apply the Aqua, Accent 5 color to the sheet tab.
12. Change the document properties as specified by your instructor. Save the workbook using the file name, Make It Right 1–1 Exotic Pets Annual Cost of Goods. Submit the revised workbook as specified by your instructor.

SAM

In the Lab

Design and/or create a workbook using the guidelines, concepts, and skills presented in this chapter. Labs 1, 2, and 3 are listed in order of increasing difficulty.

Lab 1: Annual Revenue Analysis Worksheet

Problem: You work as a spreadsheet specialist for A Healthy Body Shop, a high-end total fitness center franchise. Your manager has asked you to develop an annual revenue analysis worksheet similar to the one shown in Figure 1–79.

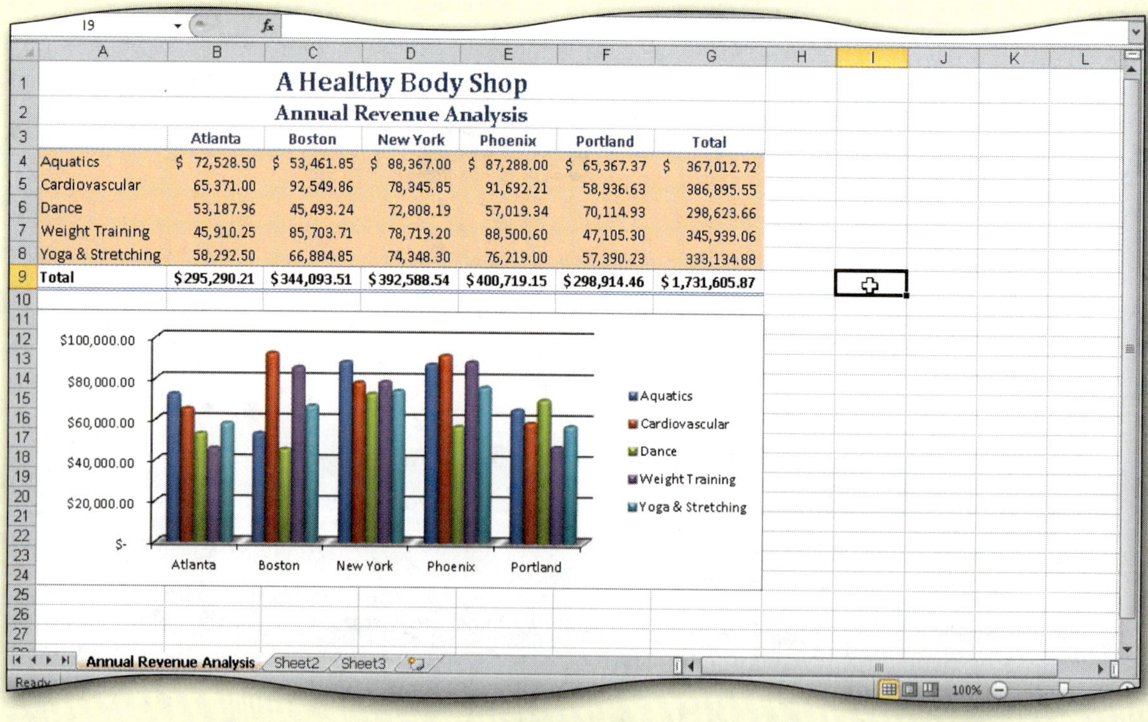

Figure 1–79

Instructions: Perform the following tasks.

1. Start Excel. Enter the worksheet title, A Healthy Body Shop, in cell A1 and the worksheet subtitle, Annual Revenue Analysis, in cell A2. Beginning in row 3, enter the franchise locations, fitness activities, and annual revenues shown in Table 1–7.

Table 1–7 A Healthy Body Shop Annual Revenues

	Atlanta	Boston	New York	Phoenix	Portland
Aquatics	72528.50	53461.85	88367.00	87288.00	65367.37
Cardiovascular	65371.00	92549.86	78345.85	91692.21	58936.63
Dance	53187.96	45493.24	72808.19	57019.34	70114.93
Weight Training	45910.25	85703.71	78719.20	88500.60	47105.30
Yoga & Stretching	58292.50	66884.85	74348.30	76219.00	57390.23

2. Create totals for each franchise location, fitness activity, and company grand total.
3. Format the worksheet title with the Title cell style. Center the title across columns A through G. Do not be concerned if the edges of the worksheet title are not displayed.
4. Format the worksheet subtitle to 14-point Constantia dark blue, bold font, and center it across columns A through G.
5. Use Cell Styles to format the range A3:G3 with the Heading 3 cell style, the range A4:G8 with the 40% - Accent 6 cell style, and the range A9:G9 with the Total cell style. Center the column headers in row 3. Apply the Accounting Number format to the range B4:G4 and the range B9:G9. Apply the Comma Style to the range B5:G8. Adjust any column widths to the widest text entry in each column.
6. Select the range A3:F8 and then insert a Clustered Cylinder chart. Apply the Style 26 chart style to the chart. Move and resize the chart so that it appears in the range A11:G24. If the labels along the horizontal axis (x-axis) do not appear as shown in Figure 1–79, then drag the right side of the chart so that it is displayed in the range A11:G24.
7. Apply the worksheet name, Annual Revenue Analysis, to the sheet tab and apply the Orange, Accent 6, Darker 25% color to the sheet tab. Change the document properties, as specified by your instructor.
8. Save the workbook using the file name Lab 1-1 A Healthy Body Shop Annual Revenue Analysis.
9. Preview and print the worksheet in landscape orientation.
10. Make the following two corrections to the sales amounts: 62,675.45 for New York Weight Training (cell D7), 67,238.56 for Portland Cardiovascular (cell F5). After you enter the corrections, the company totals in cell G8 should equal $1,723,864.05.
11. Preview and print the revised worksheet in landscape orientation. Close the workbook without saving the changes.
12. Submit the assignment as specified by your instructor.

In the Lab

Lab 2: Semiannual Sales Analysis Worksheet

Problem: As the chief accountant for Play 'em Again, a reseller of cell phones, DVDs, electronic games, MP3 players, and accessories, you have been asked by the vice president to create a worksheet to analyze the semiannual sales for the company by products across sales channels (Figure 1–80 on the following page). The sales channels and corresponding revenue by product for the year are shown in Table 1–8.

Continued >

In the Lab *continued*

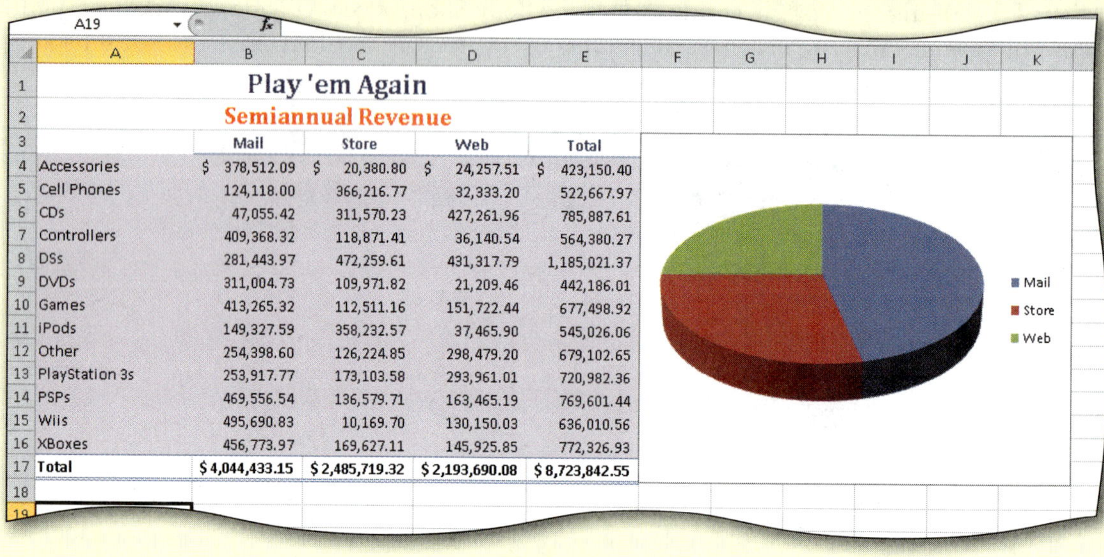

Figure 1–80

Instructions: Perform the following tasks.

1. Create the worksheet shown in Figure 1–80 using the data in Table 1–8.
2. Use the SUM function to determine total revenue for the three sales channels, the totals for each product, and the company total. Add column and row headings for the totals row and totals column, as appropriate.

Table 1–8 Play 'em Again Semiannual Revenue

	Mail	Store	Web
Accessories	378512.09	20380.80	24257.51
Cell Phones	124118.00	366216.77	32333.20
CDs	47055.42	311570.23	427261.96
Controllers	409368.32	118871.41	36140.54
DSs	281443.97	472259.61	431317.79
DVDs	311004.73	109971.82	21209.46
Games	413265.32	112511.16	151722.44
iPods	149327.59	358232.57	37465.90
Other	254398.60	126224.85	298479.20
PlayStation 3s	253917.77	173103.58	293961.01
PSPs	469556.54	136579.71	163465.19
Wiis	495690.83	10169.70	130150.03
XBoxes	456773.97	169627.11	145925.85

3. Format the worksheet title with the Title cell style and center it across columns A through E. Use the Font group on the Ribbon to format the worksheet subtitle to 16-point Cambria red, bold font. Center the title across columns A through E.
4. Format the range B3:E3 with the Heading 3 cell style and center the text in the cells. Format the range A4:E16 with the 20% - Accent 4 cell style, and the range B9:E9 with the Total cell style. Format cells B4:E4 and B17:E17 with the Accounting Number Format and cells B5:E16 with the Comma Style numeric format.

5. Create a pie chart that shows the revenue contributions of each sales channel. Chart the sales channel names (B3:D3) and corresponding totals (B17:D17). That is, select the range B3:D3, and then while holding down the CTRL key, select the range B17:D17. Insert the Pie in 3-D chart, as shown in Figure 1–80, by using the Pie button (Insert tab | Charts group). Use the chart location F3: K17.
6. Apply the worksheet name, Semiannual Revenue, to the sheet tab and apply the Purple, Accent 4, Lighter 80% color to the sheet tab. Change the document properties, as specified by your instructor.
7. Save the workbook using the file name, Lab 1-2 Play 'em Again Semiannual Revenue. Print the worksheet in landscape orientation.
8. Two corrections to the figures were sent in from the accounting department. The correct revenue is $118,124.45 for Cell Phones sold through the mail (cell B5) and $43,573.67 for iPods sold over the Web (cell D11). After you enter the two corrections, the company total in cell E17 should equal $8,723,956.77. Print the revised worksheet in landscape orientation.
9. Use the Undo button to change the worksheet back to the original numbers in Table 1–8. Use the Redo button to change the worksheet back to the revised state.
10. Close Excel without saving the latest changes. Start Excel and open the workbook saved in Step 7. Double-click cell E6 and use in-cell editing to change the PSPs revenue (cell C14) to $128,857.32. Write the company total in cell E17 at the top of the first printout. Click the Undo button.
11. Click cell A1 and then click the Merge & Center button on the Home tab on the Ribbon to split cell A1 into cells A1, B1, C1, D1, and E1. To merge the cells into one again, select the range A1:E1 and then click the Merge & Center button.
12. Close the workbook without saving the changes. Submit the assignment as specified by your instructor.

In the Lab

Lab 3: Projected College Cash Flow Analysis Worksheet

Problem: Attending college is an expensive proposition and your resources are limited. To plan for your four-year college career, you have decided to organize your anticipated resources and expenses in a worksheet. The data required to prepare your worksheet is shown in Table 1–9.

Table 1–9 College Cost and Resources

Resources	Freshman	Sophomore	Junior	Senior
529 Plans	2700.00	2889.00	3091.23	3307.62
Financial Aid	5250.00	5617.50	6010.73	6431.48
Job	3100.00	3317.00	3549.19	3797.63
Parents	3700.00	3959.00	4236.13	4532.66
Savings	4250.00	4547.50	4865.83	5206.43
Other	1100.00	1177.00	1259.39	1347.55
Expenses	**Freshman**	**Sophomore**	**Junior**	**Senior**
Activities Fee	500.00	535.00	572.45	612.52
Books	650.00	695.50	744.19	796.28
Clothes	750.00	802.50	858.68	918.78
Entertainment	1650.00	1765.50	1889.09	2021.32
Room & Board	7200.00	7704.00	8243.28	8820.31
Tuition	8250.00	8827.50	9445.43	10106.60
Miscellaneous	1100.00	1177.00	1259.39	1347.55

Continued >

In the Lab *continued*

Instructions Part 1: Using the numbers in Table 1–9, create the worksheet shown in columns A through F in Figure 1–81. Format the worksheet title as Calibri 24-point bold purple. Merge and center the worksheet title in cell A1 across columns A through F. Format the worksheet subtitles in cells A2 and A11 as Calibri 16-point bold red. Format the ranges A3:F3 and A12:F12 with the Heading 2 cell style and center the text in the cells. Format the ranges A4:F9 and A13:F19 with the 20% - Accent 2 cell style, and the ranges A10:F10 and A20:F20 with the Total cell style.

Change the name of the sheet tab and apply the Purple color from the Standard Colors area to the sheet tab. Update the document properties, including the addition of at least one keyword to the properties, and save the workbook using the file name, Lab 1-3 Part 1 College Resources and Expenses. Print the worksheet. Submit the assignment as specified by your instructor.

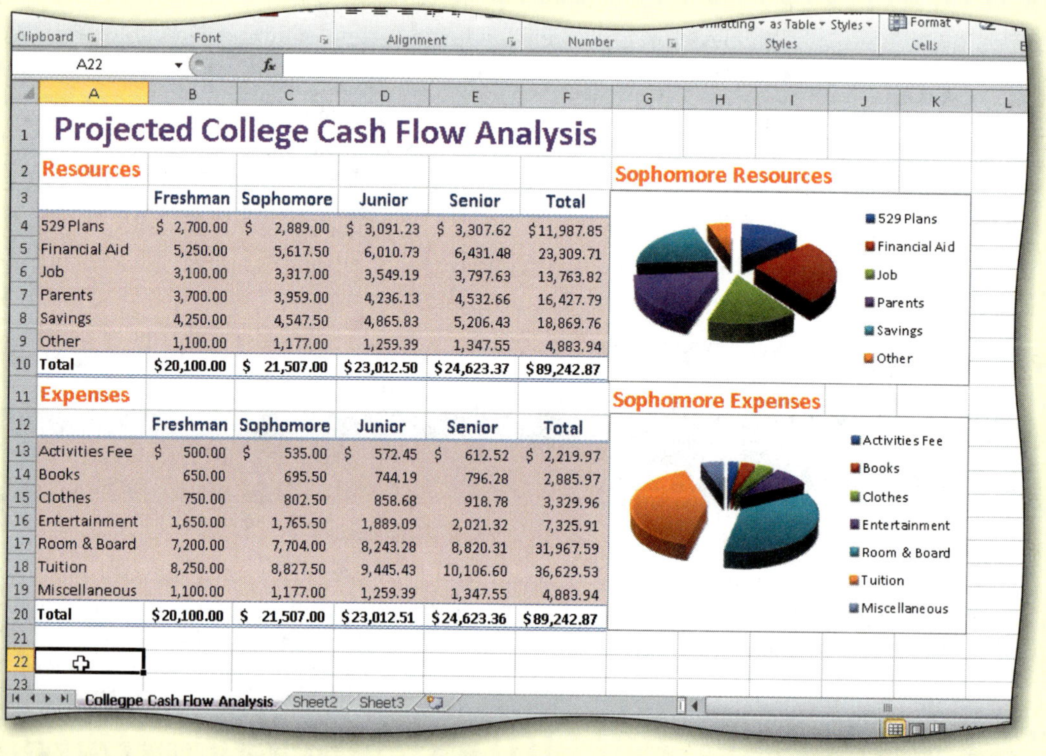

Figure 1–81

After reviewing the numbers, you realize you need to increase manually each of the Sophomore-year expenses in column C by $400, except for the Activities Fee. Change the Sophomore-year expenses to reflect this change. Manually change the Parents resources for the Sophomore year by the amount required to cover the increase in costs. The totals in cells F10 and F20 should equal $91,642.87. Print the worksheet. Close the workbook without saving changes.

Instructions Part 2: Open the workbook Lab 1-3 Part 1 College Resources and Expenses and then save the workbook using the file name, Lab 1-3 Part 2 College Resources and Expenses. Insert an Exploded pie in 3-D chart in the range G3:K10 to show the contribution of each category of resources for the Freshman year. Chart the range A4:B9 and apply the Style 26 chart style to the chart. Add the Pie chart title as shown in cell G2 in Figure 1–81. Insert an Exploded pie in 3-D chart in the range G12:K20 to show the contribution of each category of expenses for the Freshman year. Chart the range A13:B19 and apply the Style 26 chart style to the chart. Add the Pie chart title shown in cell G11 in Figure 1–81. Save the workbook. Print the worksheet in landscape orientation. Submit the assignment as specified by your instructor.

Instructions Part 3: Open the workbook Lab 1-3 Part 2 College Resources and Expenses and then save the workbook using the file name, Lab 1-3 Part 3 College Resources and Expenses. A close inspection of Table 1–9 shows that both cost and financial support figures increase 7% each year. Use Excel Help to learn how to enter the data for the last three years using a formula and the Copy and Paste buttons (Home tab | Clipboard group). For example, the formula to enter in cell C4 is =B4*1.07. Enter formulas to replace all the numbers in the range C4:E9 and C13:E19. If necessary, reformat the tables, as described in Part 1. The worksheet should appear as shown in Figure 1–81, except that some of the totals will be off by approximately 0.01 due to rounding errors. Save the workbook. Submit the assignment as specified by your instructor. Close the workbook without saving changes.

Cases and Places

Apply your creative thinking and problem solving skills to design and implement a solution.

1: Analyzing Quarterly Expenses

Academic

To estimate the funds needed by your school's Travel Club to make it through the upcoming quarter, you decide to create a report for the club itemizing the expected quarterly expenses. The anticipated expenses are listed in Table 1–10. Use the concepts and techniques presented in this chapter to create the worksheet and an embedded Clustered Cylinder chart. Be sure to use an appropriate chart style that compares the quarterly cost of each expense. Total each expense item and each quarter. Include a grand total for all of the expenses. Use the AutoCalculate area to determine the average amount spent per quarter on each expense. Manually insert the averages with appropriate titles in an appropriate area on the worksheet.

Table 1–10 Travel Club Quarterly Expenses

	1st Quarter	2nd Quarter	3rd Quarter	4th Quarter
Copies and Supplies	75	50	80	150
Meeting Room Rent	400	425	400	425
Miscellaneous	150	100	175	70
Refreshments	130	155	150	225
Speaker Fees	200	200	400	500
Travel	450	375	500	375

2: Create an Exploded Pie in 3-D Chart to Summarize Property Values

Personal

Your wealthy Aunt Nicole owns several properties of varying value. She would like to see the values of the properties in a worksheet and chart that helps her to better understand her investments. She has asked you to develop a worksheet totaling the values of the properties and also to include other relevant statistics. The property values are: Property 1, $56,671.99; Property 2, $82,276.58; Property 3, $60,135.45; Property 4, $107,373.39; and Property 5, $87,512.82. Create an Exploded pie in 3-D chart to illustrate the relative property values. Use the AutoCalculate area to find the average, maximum, and minimum property values and manually enter them and their corresponding identifiers in an appropriate area of the worksheet. Use the Sum button to total the property values.

Continued >

Cases and Places *continued*

3: Analyzing Historical Yearly Sales

Business

You are working part-time for Noble's Mobile Services. Your manager has asked you to prepare a worksheet to help her analyze historical yearly sales by type of product (Table 1–11). Use the concepts and techniques presented in this chapter to create the worksheet and an embedded 3-D Clustered Column chart that includes proper numerical formatting, totaling, and formatting of the worksheet.

Table 1–11 Noble's Mobile Services Historical Yearly Sales

	2008	2009	2010	2011
Camera Phones	92598	10487	136791	176785
Headsets	9035	8909	4886	6512
Music Phones	57942	44923	54590	67696
Other Accessories	27604	38793	24483	33095
Satellite Radios	17161	19293	30763	44367
Standard Mobile Phones	8549	9264	7600	6048
Wireless PDAs	57963	68059	103025	87367

2 Formulas, Functions, and Formatting

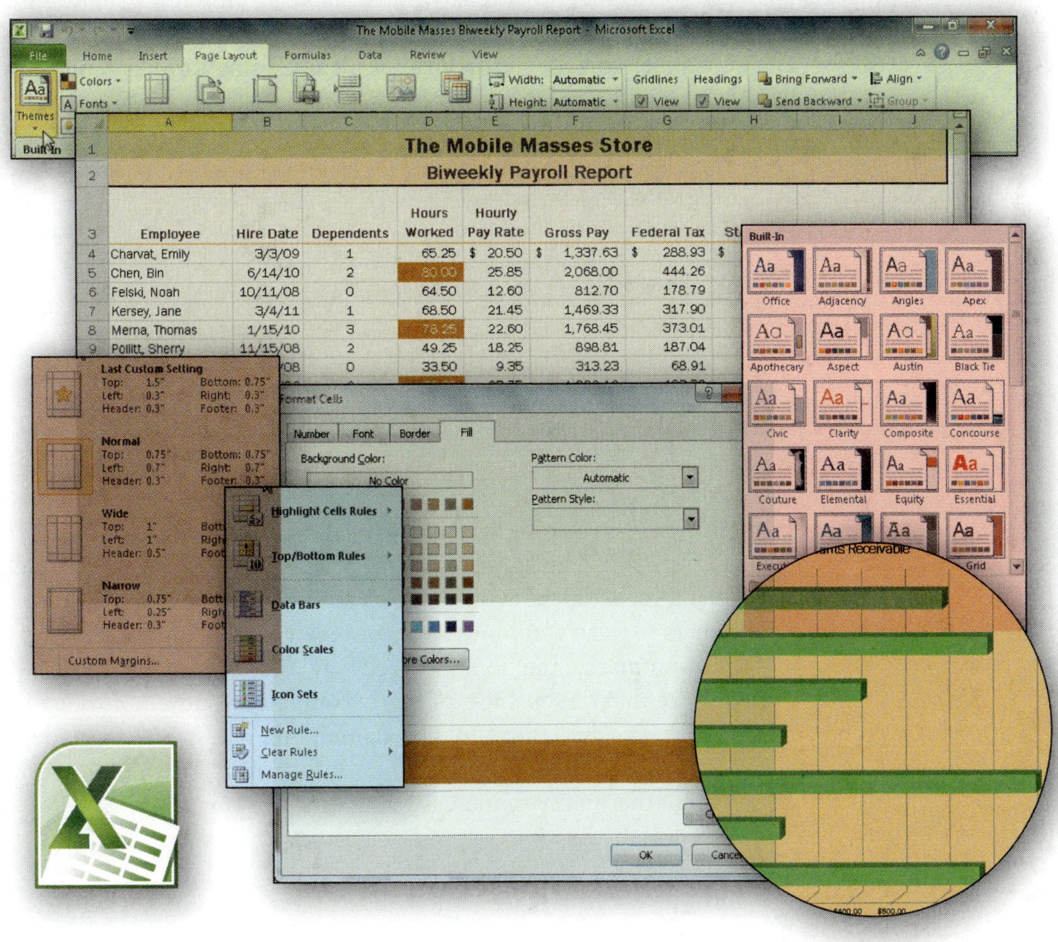

Objectives

You will have mastered the material in this chapter when you can:

- Enter formulas using the keyboard
- Enter formulas using Point mode
- Apply the AVERAGE, MAX, and MIN functions
- Verify a formula using Range Finder
- Apply a theme to a workbook
- Apply a date format to a cell or range
- Add conditional formatting to cells
- Change column width and row height
- Check the spelling in a worksheet
- Set margins, headers, and footers in Page Layout view
- Preview and print versions of a worksheet

2 Formulas, Functions, and Formatting

Introduction

In Excel Chapter 1, you learned how to enter data, sum values, format a worksheet to make it easier to read, and draw a chart. This chapter continues to highlight these topics and presents some new ones.

The new topics covered in this chapter include using formulas and functions to create a worksheet. A **function** is a prewritten formula that is built into Excel. Other new topics include option buttons, verifying formulas, applying a theme to a worksheet, adding borders, formatting numbers and text, using conditional formatting, changing the widths of columns and heights of rows, spell checking, using alternative types of worksheet displays and printouts, and adding page headers and footers to a worksheet. One alternative worksheet display and printout shows the formulas in the worksheet instead of the values. When you display the formulas in the worksheet, you see exactly what text, data, formulas, and functions you have entered into it.

Project — Worksheet with Formulas and Functions

The project in this chapter follows proper design guidelines and uses Excel to create the worksheet shown in Figure 2–1. The Mobile Masses Store opened its doors when consumer demand for mobile devices, such as mobile phones and PDAs, had just begun. The store's owners pay each employee on a biweekly basis. Before the owners pay the employees, they summarize the hours worked, pay rate, and tax information for each employee to ensure that the business properly compensates its employees. This summary includes information such as the employee names, hire dates, number of dependents, hours worked, hourly pay rate, net pay, and tax information. As the complexity of the task of creating the summary increases, the owners want to use Excel to create a biweekly payroll report.

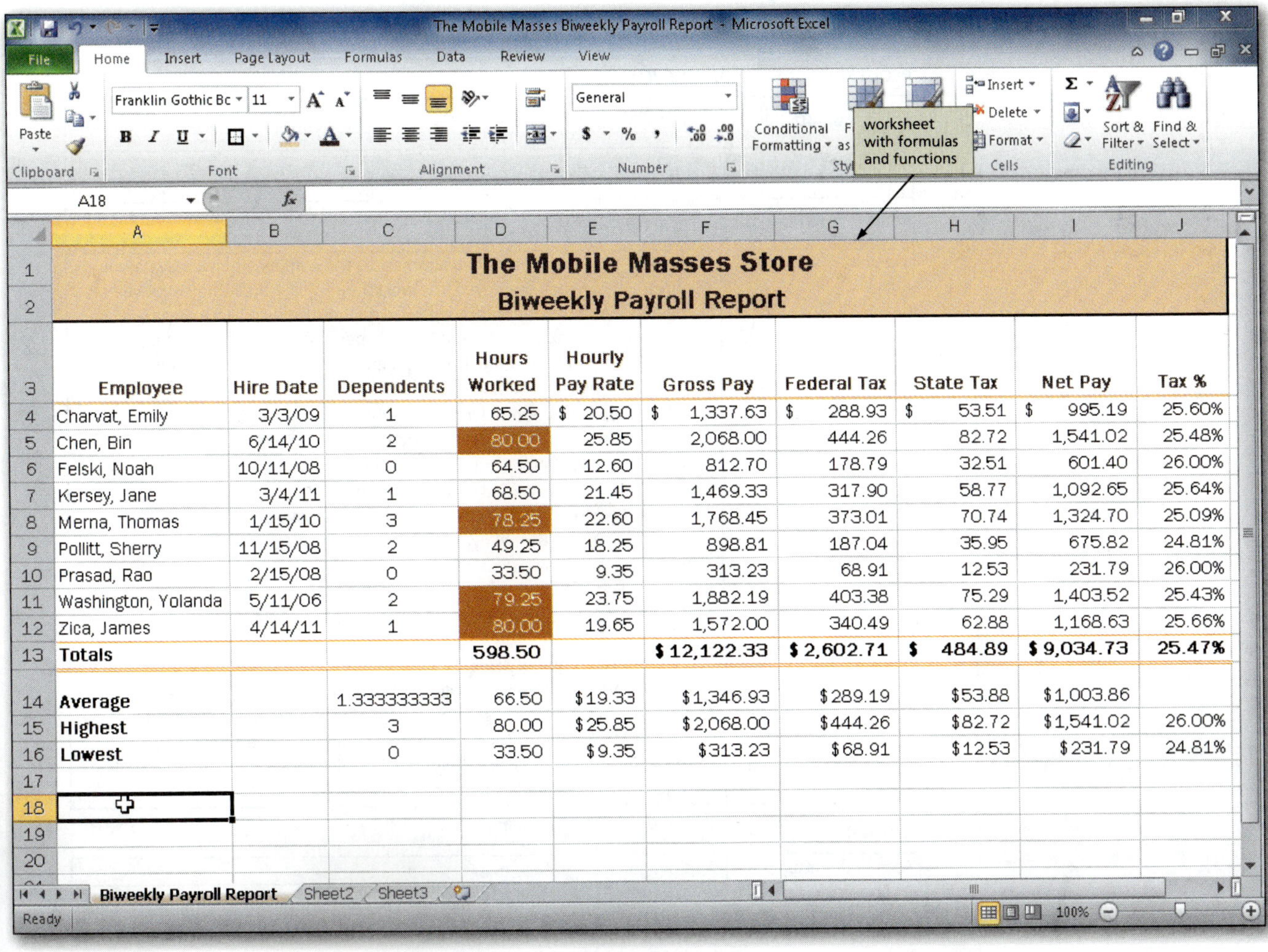

Figure 2–1

Recall that the first step in creating an effective worksheet is to make sure you understand what is required. The people who will use the worksheet usually provide the requirements. The requirements document for The Mobile Masses Store Biweekly Payroll Report worksheet includes the following needs: source of data, summary of calculations, and other facts about its development (Figure 2–2 on the following page).

REQUEST FOR NEW WORKSHEET

Date Submitted:	April 16, 2012
Submitted By:	Samuel Snyder
Worksheet Title:	The Mobile Masses Store Biweekly Payroll Report
Needs:	An easy-to-read worksheet that summarizes the company's biweekly payroll (Figure 2-3). For each employee, the worksheet is to include the employee's name, hire date, dependents, hours worked, hourly pay rate, gross pay, federal tax, state tax, net pay, and total tax percent. The worksheet also should include totals and the average, highest value, and lowest value for column of numbers specified below.
Source of Data:	The data supplied by Samuel includes the employee names, hire dates, hours worked, and hourly pay rates. This data is shown in Table 2-1 on page EX 72.
Calculations:	The following calculations must be made for each of the employees: 1. Gross Pay = Hours Worked × Hourly Pay Rate 2. Federal Tax = 0.22 × (Gross Pay – Dependents * 24.32) 3. State Tax = 0.04 × Gross Pay 4. Net Pay = Gross Pay – (Federal Tax + State Tax) 5. Tax % = (Federal Tax + State Tax) / Gross Pay 6. Compute the totals for hours worked, gross pay, federal tax, state tax, and net pay. 7. Compute the total tax percent. 8. Use the AVERAGE function to determine the average for dependents, hours worked, hourly pay rate, gross pay, federal tax, state tax, and net pay. 9. Use the MAX and MIN functions to determine the highest and lowest values for dependents, hours worked, hourly pay rate, gross pay, federal tax, state tax, net pay, and total tax percent.

Approvals

Approval Status:	X	Approved
		Rejected
Approved By:	Julie Adams	
Date:	April 23, 2012	
Assigned To:	J. Quasney, Spreadsheet Specialist	

Figure 2–2

Overview

As you read this chapter, you will learn how to create the worksheet shown in Figure 2–1 by performing these general tasks:

- Enter formulas and apply functions in the worksheet
- Add conditional formatting to the worksheet
- Apply a theme to the worksheet
- Set margins, and add headers and footers to a worksheet
- Work with the worksheet in Page Layout view
- Change margins on the worksheet
- Print a section of the worksheet

Plan Ahead

General Project Decisions

While creating an Excel worksheet, you need to make several decisions that will determine the appearance and characteristics of the finished worksheet. As you create the worksheet necessary to meet the requirements shown in Figure 2–2, you should follow these general guidelines:

1. **Plan the layout of the worksheet.** Rows typically contain items analogous to items in a list. A name could serve as an item in a list, and, therefore, each name could be placed in a row. As a list grows, such as a list of employees, the number of rows in the worksheet will increase. Information about each item in the list and associated calculations should appear in columns.
2. **Determine the necessary formulas and functions needed.** Calculations result from known values. Formulas for such calculations should be known in advance of creating a worksheet. Values such as the average, highest, and lowest values can be calculated using Excel functions as opposed to relying on complex formulas.
3. **Identify how to format various elements of the worksheet.** The appearance of the worksheet affects its ability to express information clearly. Numeric data should be formatted in generally accepted formats, such as using commas as thousands separators and parentheses for negative values.
4. **Establish rules for conditional formatting.** Conditional formatting allows you to format a cell based on the contents of the cell. Decide under which circumstances you would like a cell to stand out from related cells and determine in what way the cell will stand out.
5. **Specify how the hard copy of a worksheet should appear.** When it is possible that a person will want to create a hard copy of a worksheet, care should be taken in the development of the worksheet to ensure that the contents can be presented in a readable manner. Excel prints worksheets in landscape or portrait orientation, and margins can be adjusted to fit more or less data on each page. Headers and footers add an additional level of customization to the printed page.

When necessary, more specific details concerning the above guidelines are presented at appropriate points in the chapter. The chapter also will identify the actions performed and decisions made regarding these guidelines during the creation of the worksheet shown in Figure 2–1 on page EX 67.

In addition, using a sketch of the worksheet can help you visualize its design. The sketch for The Mobile Masses Store Biweekly Payroll Report worksheet includes a title, a subtitle, column and row headings, and the location of data values (Figure 2–3 on the following page). It also uses specific characters to define the desired formatting for the worksheet, as follows:

1. The row of Xs below the leftmost column defines the cell entries as text, such as employee names.
2. The rows of Zs and 9s with slashes, dollar signs, decimal points, commas, and percent signs in the remaining columns define the cell entries as numbers. The Zs indicate that the selected format should instruct Excel to suppress leading 0s. The 9s indicate that the selected format should instruct Excel to display any digits, including 0s.
3. The decimal point means that a decimal point should appear in the cell entry and indicates the number of decimal places to use.
4. The slashes in the second column identify the cell entry as a date.
5. The dollar signs that are not adjacent to the Zs in the first row below the column headings and in the total row signify a fixed dollar sign. The dollar signs that are adjacent to the Zs below the total row signify a floating dollar sign, or one that appears next to the first significant digit.

BTW

Aesthetics versus Function

The function, or purpose, of a worksheet is to provide a user with direct ways to accomplish tasks. In designing a worksheet, functional considerations should come before visual aesthetics. Avoid the temptation to use flashy or confusing visual elements within the worksheet. One exception to this guideline occurs when you may need to draw the user's attention to an area of a worksheet that will help the user more easily complete a task.

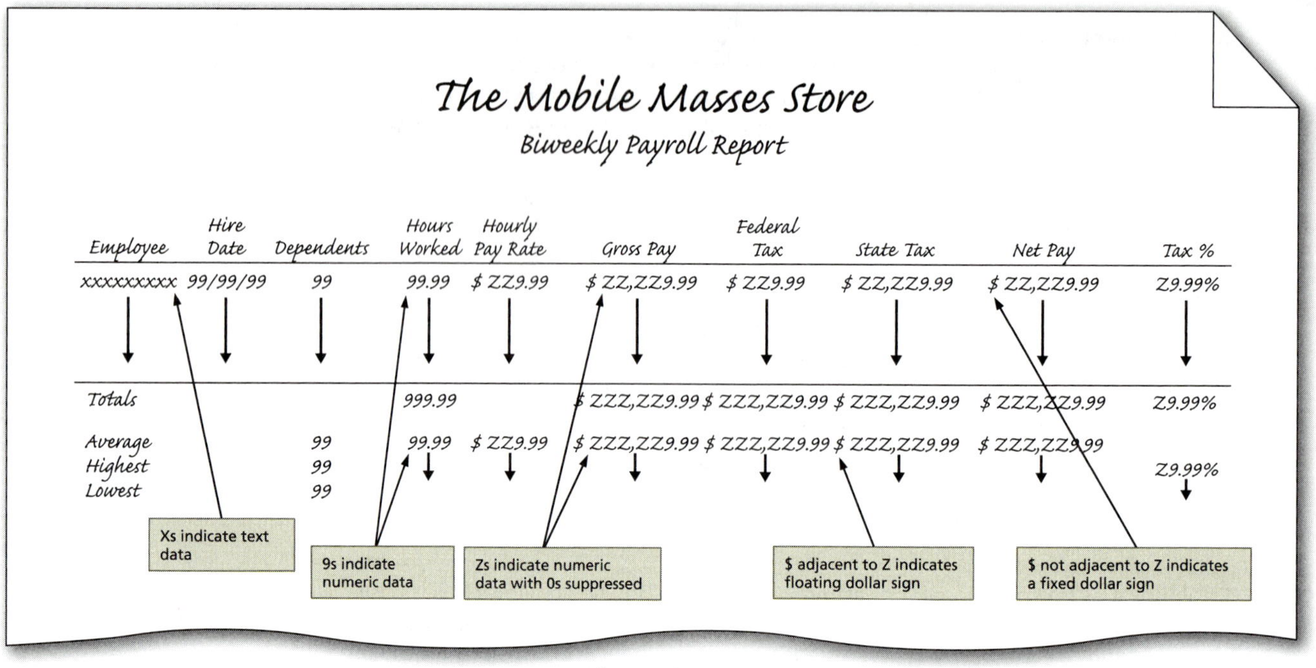

Figure 2–3

6. The commas indicate that the selected format should instruct Excel to display a comma separator only if the number has enough digits to the left of the decimal point.
7. The percent sign (%) in the far-right column indicates a percent sign should appear after the number.

With a good comprehension of the requirements document, an understanding of the necessary decisions, and a sketch of the worksheet, the next step is to use Excel to create the worksheet.

For an introduction to Windows 7 and instruction about how to perform basic Windows 7 tasks, read the Office 2010 and Windows 7 chapter in this book, where you can learn how to resize windows, change screen resolution, create folders, move and rename files, use Windows Help, and much more.

To Start Excel

If you are using a computer to step through the project in this chapter and you want your screens to match the figures in the Office and Windows chapters in this book, you should change your screen's resolution to 1024 × 768. For information about how to change a computer's resolution, refer to the Office 2010 and Windows 7 chapter in this book.

The following steps, which assume Windows 7 is running, start Excel based on a typical installation. You may need to ask your instructor how to start Excel for your computer. For a detailed example of the procedure summarized below, refer to the Office 2010 and Windows 7 chapter.

1. Click the Start button on the Windows 7 taskbar to display the Start menu.
2. Type `Microsoft Excel` as the search text in the 'Search programs and files' text box, and watch the search results appear on the Start menu.
3. Click Microsoft Excel 2010 in the search results on the Start menu to start Excel and display a new blank workbook in the Excel window.
4. If the Excel window is not maximized, click the Maximize button next to the Close button on its title bar to maximize the window.

Entering the Titles and Numbers into the Worksheet

The first step in creating the worksheet is to enter the titles and numbers into the worksheet. The following sets of steps enter the worksheet title and subtitle and then the biweekly payroll report data shown in Table 2–1.

For an introduction to Office 2010 and instruction about how to perform basic tasks in Office 2010 programs, read the Office 2010 and Windows 7 chapter in this book, where you can learn how to start a program, use the Ribbon, save a file, open a file, quit a program, use Help, and much more.

To Enter the Worksheet Title and Subtitle

The following steps enter the worksheet title and subtitle into cells A1 and A2.

1. If necessary, select cell A1. Type `The Mobile Masses Store` in the selected cell and then press the DOWN ARROW key to enter the worksheet title.
2. Type `Biweekly Payroll Report` in cell A2 and then press the DOWN ARROW key to enter the worksheet subtitle (Figure 2–4 on page 73).

The employee names and the row titles Totals, Average, Highest, and Lowest in the leftmost column begin in cell A4 and continue down to cell A16. The employee data is entered into rows 4 through 12 of the worksheet. The remainder of this section explains the steps required to enter the column titles, payroll data, and row titles, as shown in Figure 2–4, and then save the workbook.

To Enter the Column Titles

The column titles in row 3 begin in cell A3 and extend through cell J3. Some of the column titles in Figure 2–3 include multiple lines of text, such as Hours Worked in cell D3. To start a new line in a cell, press ALT+ENTER after each line, except for the last line, which is completed by clicking the Enter box, pressing the ENTER key, or pressing one of the arrow keys. When you see ALT+ENTER in a step, press the ENTER key while holding down the ALT key and then release both keys. The following steps enter the column titles.

1. With cell A3 selected, type `Employee` and then press the RIGHT ARROW key to enter the column heading.
2. Type `Hire Date` in cell B3 and then press the RIGHT ARROW key to enter the column heading.
3. Type `Dependents` and then press the RIGHT ARROW key to enter the column heading.
4. In cell D3, type `Hours` and then press ALT+ENTER to enter the first line of the column heading. Type `Worked` and then press the RIGHT ARROW key to enter the column heading.
5. Type `Hourly` and then press ALT+ENTER to begin a new line in the cell. Type `Pay Rate` and then press the RIGHT ARROW key to enter the column heading.
6. Type `Gross Pay` in cell F3 and then press the RIGHT ARROW key to enter the column heading.
7. Type `Federal Tax` in cell G3 and then press the RIGHT ARROW key to enter the column heading.
8. Type `State Tax` in cell H3 and then press the RIGHT ARROW key to enter the column heading.
9. Type `Net Pay` in cell I3 and then press the RIGHT ARROW key to enter the column heading.
10. Type `Tax %` in cell J3 to enter the column heading.

BTW

The Ribbon and Screen Resolution

Excel may change how the groups and buttons within the groups appear on the Ribbon, depending on the computer's screen resolution. Thus, your Ribbon may look different from the ones in the Office and Windows chapters in this book if you are using a screen resolution other than 1024 × 768.

BTW

BTWs

For a complete list of the BTWs found in the margins of the Office and Windows chapters in this book, visit the Microsoft Office and Concepts CourseMate Web site at www.cengagebrain.com and then navigate to the BTW resource for this book.

To Enter the Biweekly Payroll Data

The biweekly payroll data in Table 2–1 includes a hire date for each employee. Excel considers a date to be a number and, therefore, it displays the date right-aligned in the cell. The following steps enter the data for each employee: name, hire date, dependents, hours worked, and hourly pay rate.

1. Select cell A4, type `Charvat, Emily`, and then press the RIGHT ARROW key to enter the employee name.
2. Type `3/3/09` in cell B4 and then press the RIGHT ARROW key to enter a date in the selected cell.
3. Type `1` in cell C4 and then press the RIGHT ARROW key to enter a number in the selected cell.
4. Type `65.25` in cell D4 and then press the RIGHT ARROW key to enter a number in the selected cell.
5. Type `20.50` in cell E4 and then click cell A5 to enter a number in the selected cell.
6. Enter the payroll data in Table 2–1 for the eight remaining employees in rows 5 through 12 (Figure 2–4).

Q&A In step 2, why did the date that was entered change from 3/3/09 to 3/3/2009?

When Excel recognizes that you entered a date in mm/dd/yy format, it automatically formats the date as mm/dd/yyyy for you. Most professionals prefer to view dates in mm/dd/yyyy format as opposed to mm/dd/yy format because the latter can cause confusion regarding the intended year. For example, a date displayed as 3/3/50 could imply a date of 3/3/1950 or 3/3/2050. The use of a four-digit year eliminates this confusion.

BTW Q&As
For a complete list of the Q&As found in many of the step-by-step sequences in the Office and Windows chapters in this book, visit the Microsoft Office and Concepts CourseMate Web site at www.cengagebrain.com and then navigate to the Q&A resource for this book.

BTW Two-Digit Years
When you enter a two-digit year value (xx) that is less than 30, Excel changes that value to 20xx; when you enter a value that is 30 or greater (zz), Excel changes the value to 19zz. Use four-digit years, if necessary, to ensure that Excel interprets year values the way you intend.

Table 2–1 The Mobile Masses Store Biweekly Payroll Report Data

Employee	Hire Date	Dependents	Hours Worked	Hourly Pay Rate
Charvat, Emily	3/3/09	1	65.25	20.50
Chen, Bin	6/14/10	2	80.00	25.85
Felski, Noah	10/11/08	0	64.50	12.60
Kersey, Jane	3/4/11	1	68.50	21.45
Merna, Thomas	1/15/10	3	78.25	22.60
Pollitt, Sherry	11/15/08	2	49.25	18.25
Prasad, Rao	2/15/08	0	33.50	9.35
Washington, Yolanda	5/11/06	2	79.25	23.75
Zica, James	4/14/11	1	80.00	19.65

To Enter the Row Titles

The following steps add row titles for the rows that will contain the totals, average, highest, and lowest amounts.

1. Select cell A13. Type `Totals` and then press the DOWN ARROW key to enter a row header.
2. Type `Average` in cell A14 and then press the DOWN ARROW key to enter a row header.
3. Type `Highest` in cell A15 and then press the DOWN ARROW key to enter a row header.
4. Type `Lowest` in cell A16 and then press the ENTER key to enter a row header. Select cell F4 to prepare to enter a formula in the cell (Figure 2–4).

BTW Wrapping Text
If you have a long text entry, such as a paragraph, you can instruct Excel to wrap the text in a cell. This method is easier than your pressing ALT+ENTER to end each line of text within the paragraph. To wrap text, right-click in the cell, click Format Cells on a shortcut menu, click the Alignment tab, and then click Wrap text. Excel will increase the height of the cell automatically so that the additional lines will fit. If you want to control where each line ends in the cell, rather than letting Excel wrap the text based on the cell width, you must end each line with ALT+ENTER.

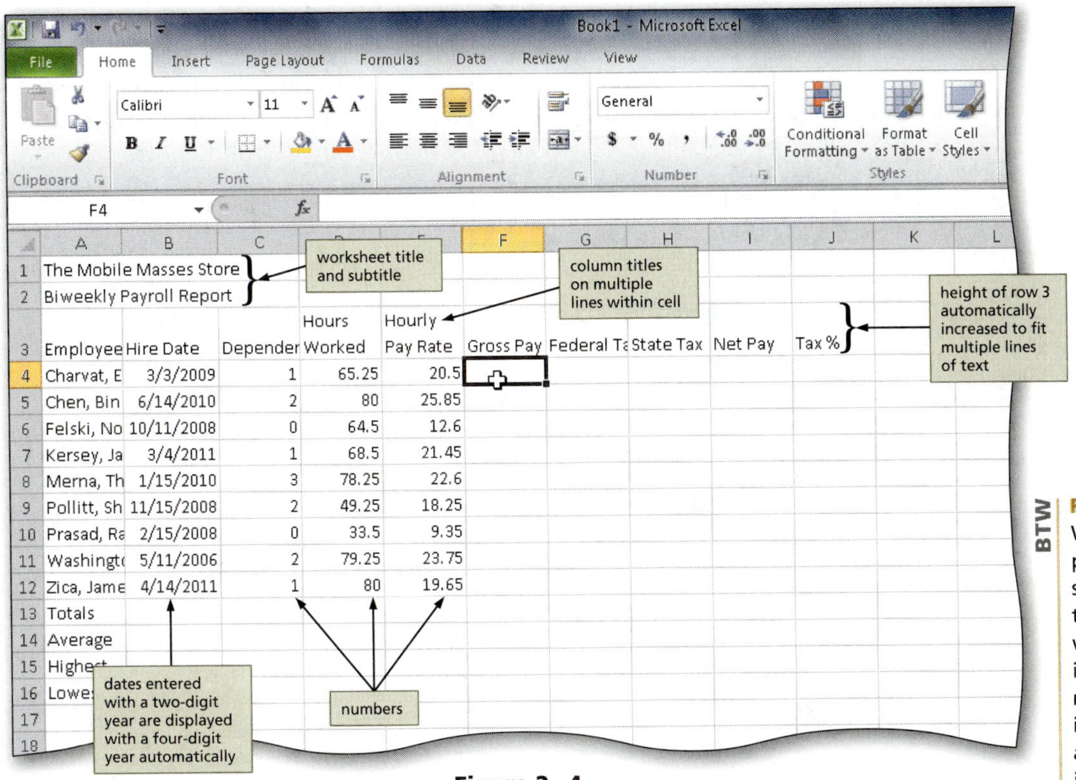

Figure 2–4

BTW

Formatting Worksheets
With early worksheet programs, users often skipped rows to improve the appearance of the worksheet. With Excel it is not necessary to skip rows because you can increase row heights to add white space between information.

To Change Document Properties

As discussed in Excel Chapter 1, the first time you save a workbook, you should change the document properties. The following steps change the document properties.

1. Click File on the Ribbon to open the Backstage view. If necessary, click the Info tab in the Backstage view to display the Info gallery.
2. Click the Properties button in the right pane of the Info gallery to display the Properties menu.
3. Click Show Document Panel on the Properties menu to close the Backstage view and display the Document Information Panel in the Excel workbook window.
4. Click the Author text box, if necessary, and then type your name as the Author property. If a name already is displayed in the Author text box, delete it before typing your name.
5. Click the Subject text box, if necessary delete any existing text, and then type your course and section as the Subject property.
6. If an AutoComplete dialog box appears, click its Yes button.
7. Click the Keywords text box, if necessary delete any existing text, and then type `Biweekly Payroll Report` as the Keywords property.
8. If an AutoComplete dialog box appears, click its Yes button.
9. Click the Close the Document Information Panel button so that the Document Information Panel no longer is displayed.

To Change the Sheet Name and Save the Workbook

The following steps change the sheet name to Biweekly Payroll Report, change the sheet tab color, and save the workbook on a USB flash drive in the Excel folder (for your assignments) using the file name, The Mobile Masses Biweekly Payroll Report.

1. Double-click the Sheet1 tab and then enter **`Biweekly Payroll Report`** as the sheet name and then press the ENTER key.

2. Right-click the tab to display the shortcut menu and then click Tab Color on the shortcut menu to display the Color gallery. Click Blue, Accent 1, Darker 25% (column 5, row 5) in the Theme Colors area to apply a new color to the sheet tab.

3. With a USB flash drive connected to one of the computer's USB ports, click the Save button on the Quick Access Toolbar to display the Save As dialog box.

4. Type **`The Mobile Masses Biweekly Payroll Report`** in the File name text box to change the file name. Do not press the ENTER key after typing the file name because you do not want to close the dialog box at this time.

5. Navigate to the desired save location (in this case, the Excel folder in the CIS 101 folder [or your class folder] on the USB flash drive).

6. Click the Save button (Save As dialog box) to save the document in the selected folder on the selected drive with the entered file name.

BTW

Entering Numbers in a Range

An efficient way to enter data into a range of cells is to select a range and then enter the first number in the upper-left cell of the range. Excel responds by accepting the value and moving the active cell selection down one cell. When you enter the last value in the first column, Excel moves the active cell selection to the top of the next column.

Entering Formulas

One of the reasons Excel is such a valuable tool is that you can assign a **formula** to a cell, and Excel will calculate the result. Consider, for example, what would happen if you had to multiply 65.25 by 20.5 and then manually enter the product for Gross Pay, 1,337.625, in cell F4. Every time the values in cells D4 or E4 changed, you would have to recalculate the product and enter the new value in cell F4. By contrast, if you enter a formula in cell F4 to multiply the values in cells D4 and E4, Excel recalculates the product whenever new values are entered into those cells and displays the result in cell F4.

Plan Ahead

Determine the formulas and functions needed.

As you have learned, formulas and functions simplify the creation and maintenance of worksheets because Excel performs calculations for you. When formulas and functions are used together properly, the amount of data that a user manually must enter in a worksheet greatly can be diminished:

- **Utilize proper algebraic notation.** Most Excel formulas are the result of algebraic calculations. A solid understanding of algebraic operators and the order of operations is important to writing sound formulas.
- **Utilize the fill handle and copy and paste operations to copy formulas.** The fill handle and the Excel copy and paste functionality help to minimize errors caused by retyping formulas. When possible, if a similar formula will be used repeatedly in a worksheet, avoid retyping the formula and instead use the fill handle.
- **Be careful about using invalid and circular cell references.** An invalid reference occurs when Excel does not understand a cell reference used in a formula, resulting in Excel displaying a #REF! error message in the cell.

(continued)

(*continued*)

A formula in a cell that contains a reference back to itself is called a **circular reference**. Excel often warns you when you create a circular reference. In almost all cases, circular references are the result of an incorrect formula. A circular reference can be direct or indirect. For example, placing the formula =A1 in cell A1 results in a direct circular reference. An indirect circular reference occurs when a formula in a cell refers to another cell or cells that include a formula that refers back to the original cell.

- **Employ the Excel built-in functions whenever possible.** Excel includes prewritten formulas called **functions** to help you compute a range of values and statistics. A function takes a value or values, performs an operation, and returns a result to the cell. The values that you use with a function are called **arguments**. All functions begin with an equal sign and include the arguments in parentheses after the function name. For example, in the function =AVERAGE(C4:C12), the function name is AVERAGE, and the argument is the range C4:C12. Become familiar with the extensive number of built-in functions. When you have the choice, always use built-in functions instead of writing and typing a formula version of your mathematical expression. Such a practice reduces the possibility of errors and simplifies the formula used in a cell, resulting in improved readability.

Plan Ahead

BTW **Automatic Recalculation**
Every time you enter a value into a cell in the worksheet, Excel automatically recalculates all formulas. You can change to manual recalculation by clicking the Calculation Options button (Formulas tab | Calculation group) and then clicking Manual. In manual calculation mode, pressing the F9 key instructs Excel to recalculate all formulas.

To Enter a Formula Using the Keyboard

The formulas needed in the worksheet are noted in the requirements document as follows:

1. Gross Pay (column F) = Hours Worked × Hourly Pay Rate
2. Federal Tax (column G) = 0.22 × (Gross Pay – Dependents × 24.32)
3. State Tax (column H) = 0.04 × Gross Pay
4. Net Pay (column I) = Gross Pay – (Federal Tax + State Tax)
5. Tax% (column J) = (Federal Tax + State Tax) / Gross Pay

The gross pay for each employee, which appears in column F, is equal to hours worked in column D times hourly pay rate in column E. Thus, the gross pay for Emily Charvat in cell F4 is obtained by multiplying 65.25 (cell D4) by 20.50 (cell E4) or =D4*E4. The following steps enter the initial gross pay formula in cell F4 using the keyboard.

1

- With cell F4 selected, type **=d4*e4** in the cell to display the formula in the formula bar and in the current cell and to display colored borders around the cells referenced in the formula (Figure 2–5).

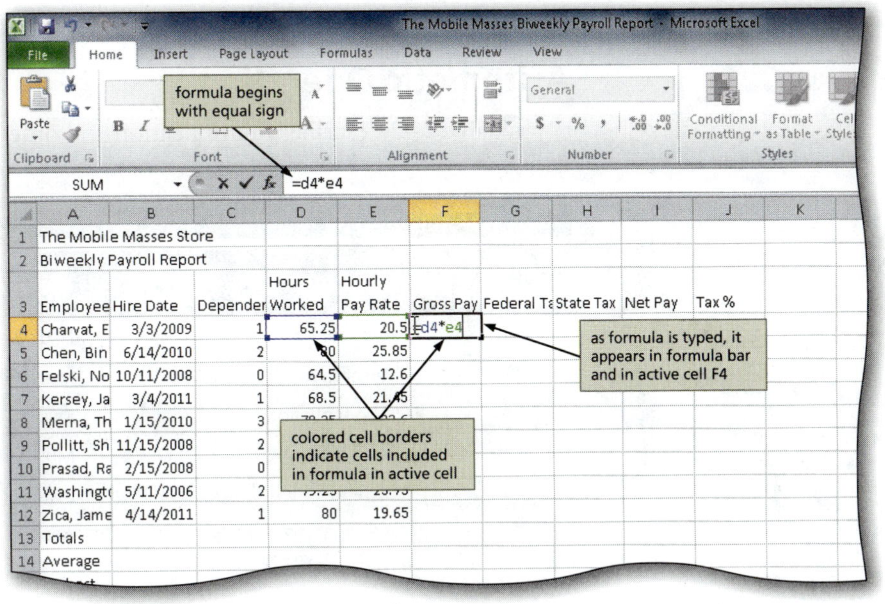

Figure 2–5

Q&A What occurs on the worksheet as I enter the formula?

The **equal sign** (=) preceding d4*e4 alerts Excel that you are entering a formula or function and not text. Because the most common error when entering a formula is to reference the wrong cell in a formula mistakenly, Excel colors the borders of the cells referenced in the formula. The coloring helps in the reviewing process to ensure the cell references are correct. The **asterisk** (*) following d4 is the arithmetic operator that directs Excel to perform the multiplication operation.

2

- Press the RIGHT ARROW key to complete the arithmetic operation indicated by the formula, to display the result in the worksheet, and to select the cell to the right (Figure 2–6). The number of decimal places shown in cell F4 may be different, but these values will be adjusted later in this chapter.

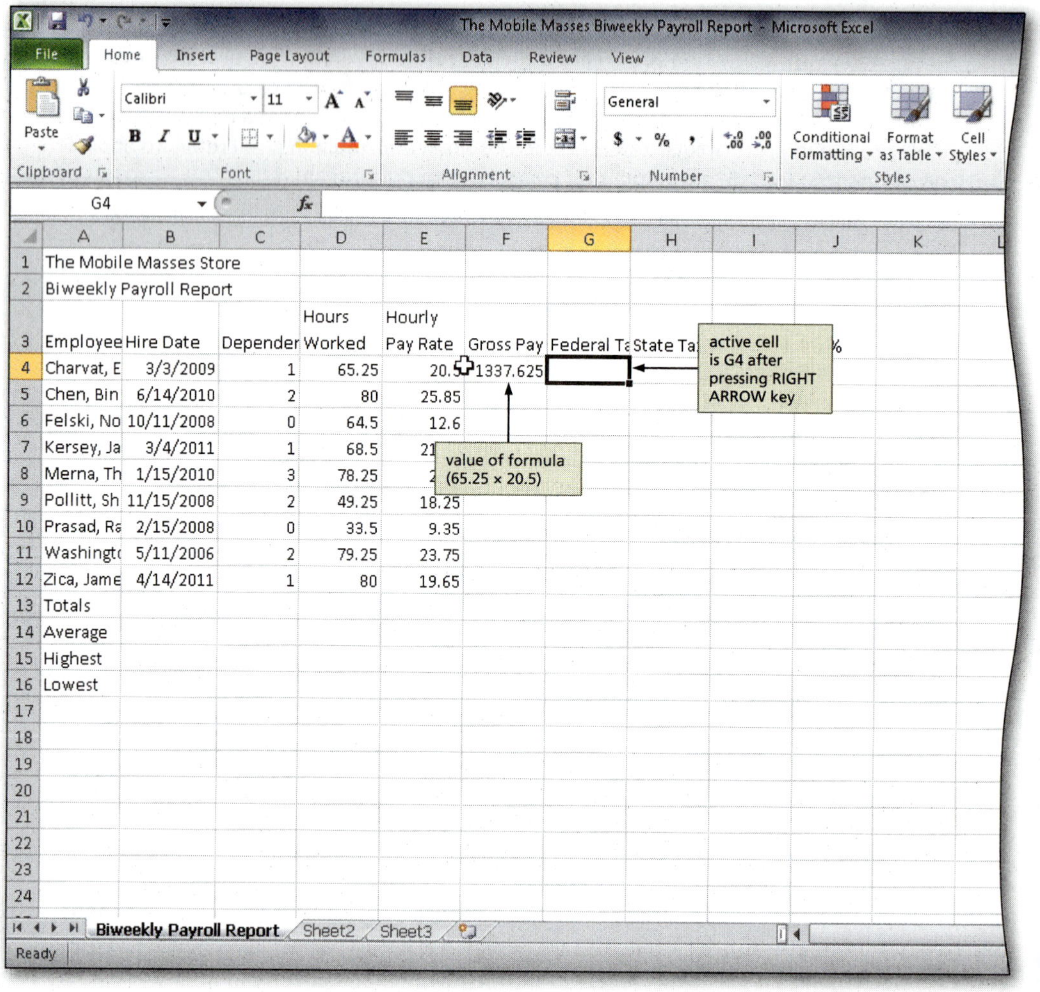

Figure 2–6

Arithmetic Operations

Table 2–2 describes multiplication and other valid Excel arithmetic operators.

Table 2–2 Summary of Arithmetic Operators

Arithmetic Operator	Meaning	Example of Usage	Meaning
–	Negation	–78	Negative 78
%	Percentage	=23%	Multiplies 23 by 0.01
^	Exponentiation	=3 ^ 4	Raises 3 to the fourth power
*	Multiplication	=61.5 * C5	Multiplies the contents of cell C5 by 61.5
/	Division	=H3 / H11	Divides the contents of cell H3 by the contents of cell H11
+	Addition	=11 + 9	Adds 11 and 9
–	Subtraction	=22 – F15	Subtracts the contents of cell F15 from 22

Order of Operations

When more than one arithmetic operator is involved in a formula, Excel follows the same basic order of operations that you use in algebra. Moving from left to right in a formula, the **order of operations** is as follows: first negation (–), then all percentages (%), then all exponentiations (^), then all multiplications (*) and divisions (/), and finally, all additions (+) and subtractions (–).

As in algebra, you can use parentheses to override the order of operations. For example, if Excel follows the order of operations, 8 * 3 + 2 equals 26. If you use parentheses, however, to change the formula to 8 * (3 + 2), the result is 40, because the parentheses instruct Excel to add 3 and 2 before multiplying by 8. Table 2–3 illustrates several examples of valid Excel formulas and explains the order of operations.

BTW

Troubling Formulas
If Excel does not accept a formula, remove the equal sign from the left side and complete the entry as text. Later, after you have entered additional data in the cells reliant on the formula or determined the error, reinsert the equal sign to change the text back to a formula and edit the formula as needed.

Table 2–3 Examples of Excel Formulas

Formula	Meaning
=G15	Assigns the value in cell G15 to the active cell.
=2^4 + 7	Assigns the sum of 16 + 7 (or 23) to the active cell.
=100 + D2 or =D2 +100 or =(100 + D2)	Assigns 100 plus the contents of cell D2 to the active cell.
=25% * 40	Assigns the product of 0.25 times 40 (or 10) to the active cell.
– (K15 * X45)	Assigns the negative value of the product of the values contained in cells K15 and X45 to the active cell. You do not need to type an equal sign before an expression that begins with minus signs, which indicates a negation.
=(U8 – B8) * 6	Assigns the product of the difference between the values contained in cells U8 and B8 times 6 to the active cell.
=J7 / A5 + G9 * M6 – Z2 ^ L7	Completes the following operations, from left to right: exponentiation (Z2 ^ L7), then division (J7 / A5), then multiplication (G9 * M6), then addition (J7 / A5) + (G9 * M6), and finally subtraction (J7 / A5 + G9 * M6) – (Z2 ^ L7). If cells A5 = 6, G9 = 2, J7 = 6, L7 = 4, M6 = 5, and Z2 = 2, then Excel assigns the active cell the value –5; that is, 6 / 6 + 2 * 5 – 2 ^ 4 = –5.

To Enter Formulas Using Point Mode

The sketch of the worksheet in Figure 2–3 on page EX 70 calls for the federal tax, state tax, net pay, and tax % for each employee to appear in columns G, H, I, and J, respectively. All four of these values are calculated using formulas in row 4:

Federal Tax (cell G4) = 0.22 × (Gross Pay – Dependents × 24.32) or =0.22*(F4–C4*24.32)
State Tax (cell H4) = 0.04 × Gross Pay or = 0.04* F4
Net Pay (cell I4) = Gross Pay – (Federal Tax + State Tax) or =F4-(G4+H4)
Tax % (cell J4) = (Federal Tax + State Tax) / Gross Pay or =(G4+H4)/F4

An alternative to entering the formulas in cells G4, H4, I4, and J4 using the keyboard is to enter the formulas using the mouse and Point mode. **Point mode** allows you to select cells for use in a formula by using the mouse. The steps on the following pages enter formulas using Point mode.

1

- With cell G4 selected type **=0.22*(** to begin the formula and then click cell F4 to add a cell reference in the formula (Figure 2–7).

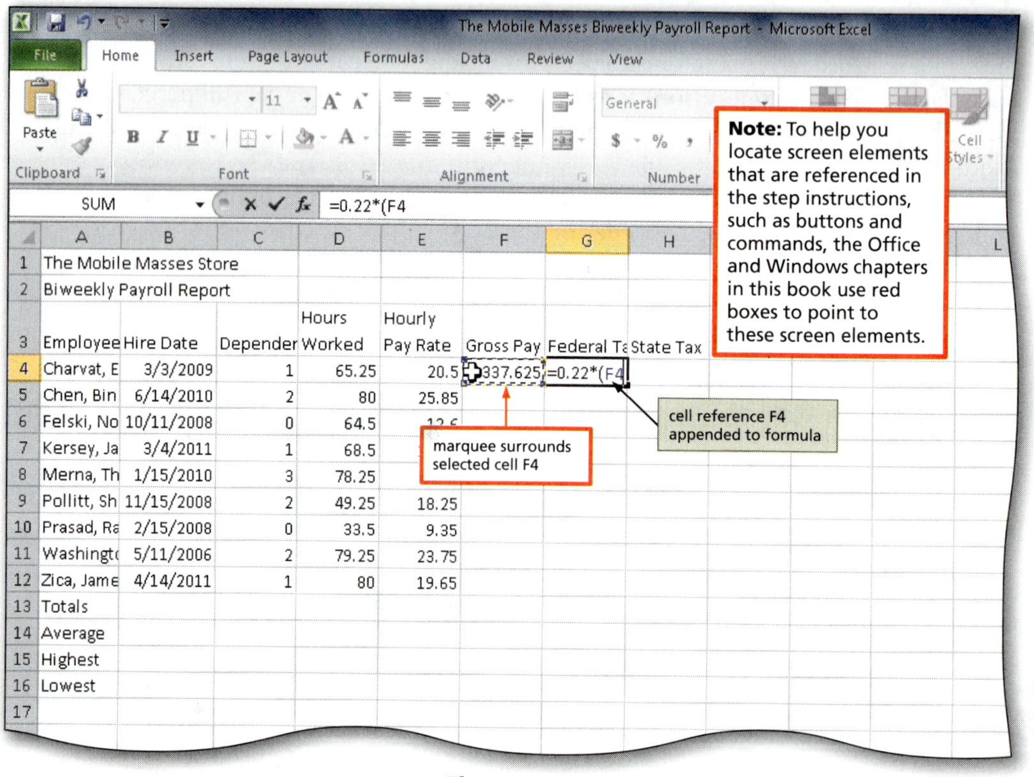

Figure 2–7

2

- Type **–** (minus sign) and then click cell C4 to add a subtraction operator and a reference to another cell to the formula.
- Type ***24.32)** to complete the formula (Figure 2–8).

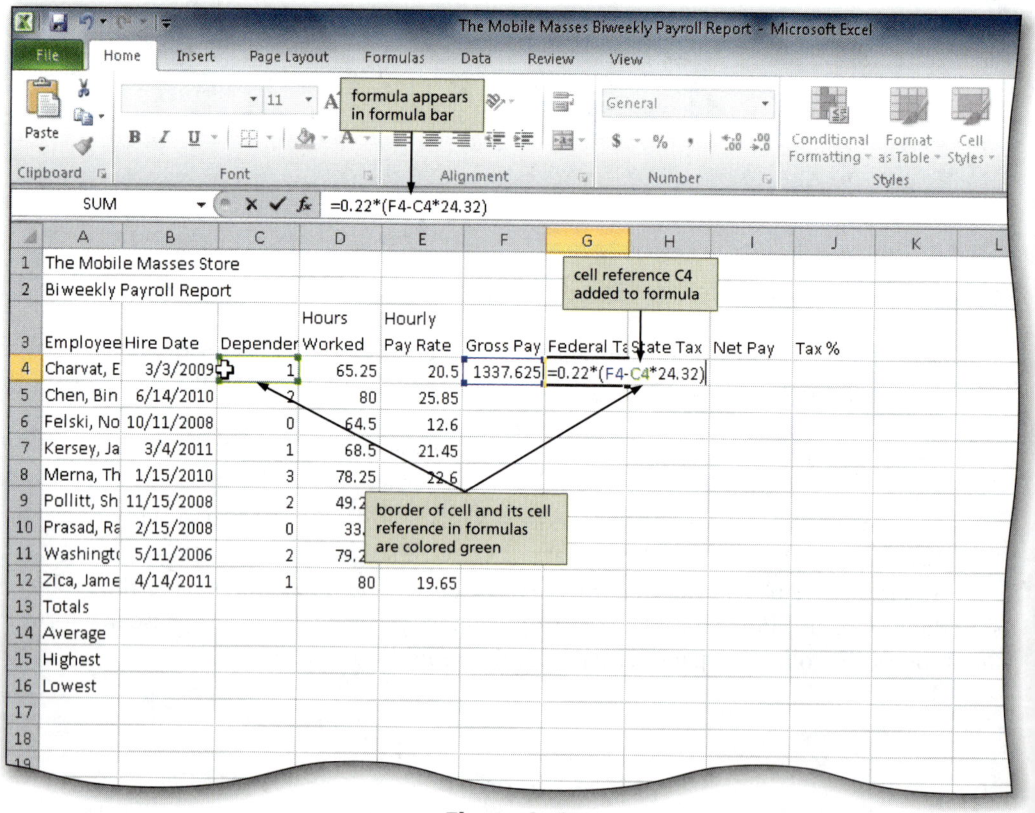

Figure 2–8

3

- Click the Enter box in the formula bar and then select cell H4 to prepare to enter the next formula.
- Type =0.04* and then click cell F4 to add a cell reference to the formula (Figure 2–9).

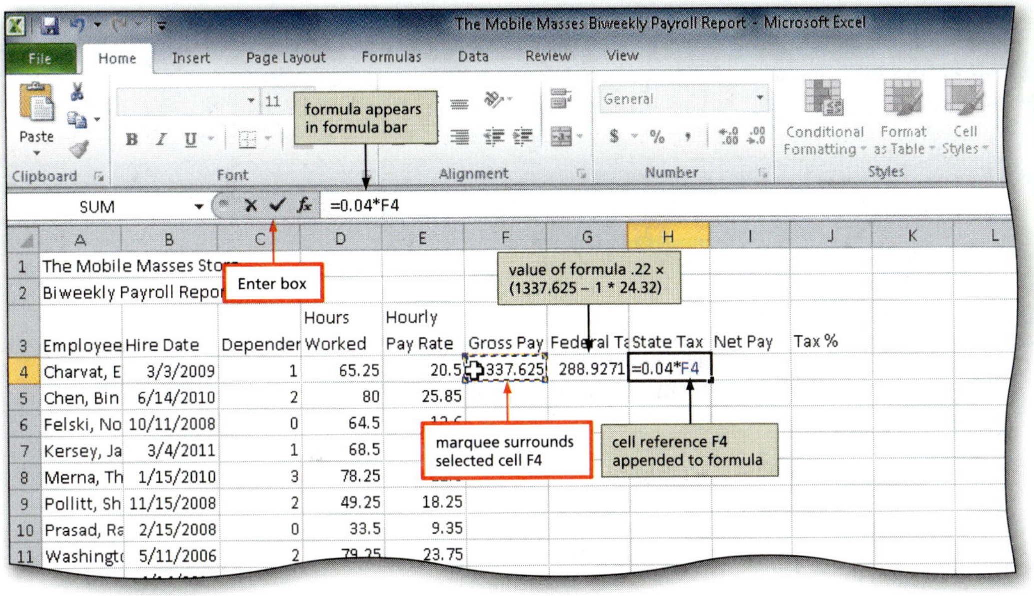

Figure 2–9

Q&A

Why should I use Point mode to enter formulas?

Using Point mode to enter formulas often is faster and more accurate than using the keyboard to type the entire formula when the cell you want to select does not require you to scroll. In many instances, as in these steps, you may want to use both the keyboard and mouse when entering a formula in a cell. You can use the keyboard to begin the formula, for example, and then use the mouse to select a range of cells.

4

- Click the Enter box in the formula bar and then select cell I4 to prepare to enter the next formula.
- Type = (equal sign) and then click cell F4 to begin the formula and add a cell reference to the formula.
- Type –((minus sign followed by an open parenthesis) and then click cell G4 to add a subtraction operator, open parenthesis, and cell reference to the formula.

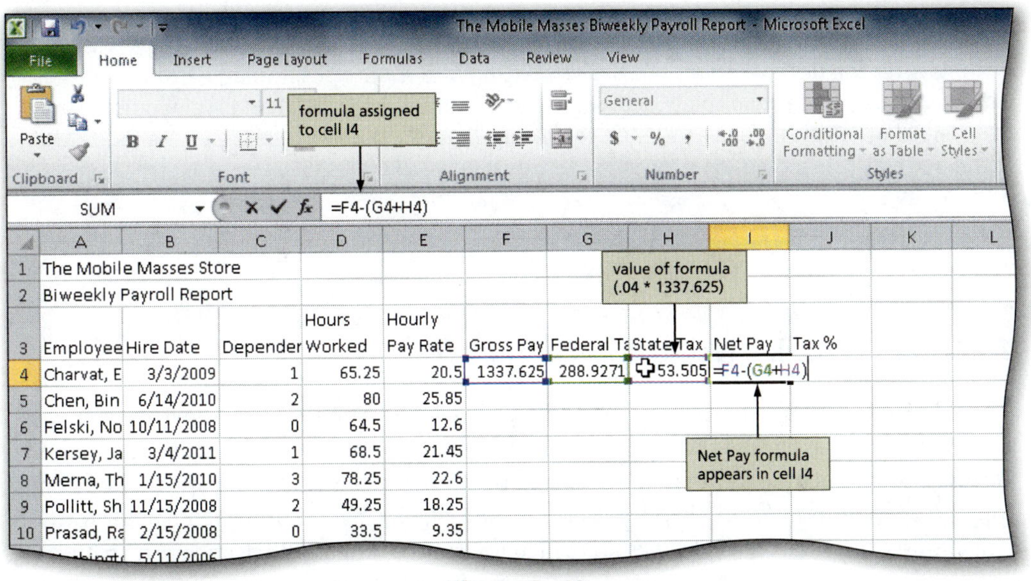

Figure 2–10

- Type + (plus sign) and then click cell H4 to add an addition operator and cell reference to the formula.
- Type) (close parenthesis) to complete the formula (Figure 2–10).

5

- Click the Enter box in the formula bar to enter the formula in cell I4.
- Select cell J4. Type = ((equal sign followed by an open parenthesis) and then click cell G4 to add a reference to the formula.
- Type + (plus sign) and then click cell H4 to add a cell reference to the formula.
- Type) / (close parenthesis followed by a forward slash), and then click cell F4 to add a cell reference to the formula.
- Click the Enter box in the formula bar to enter the formula in cell J4 (Figure 2–11).

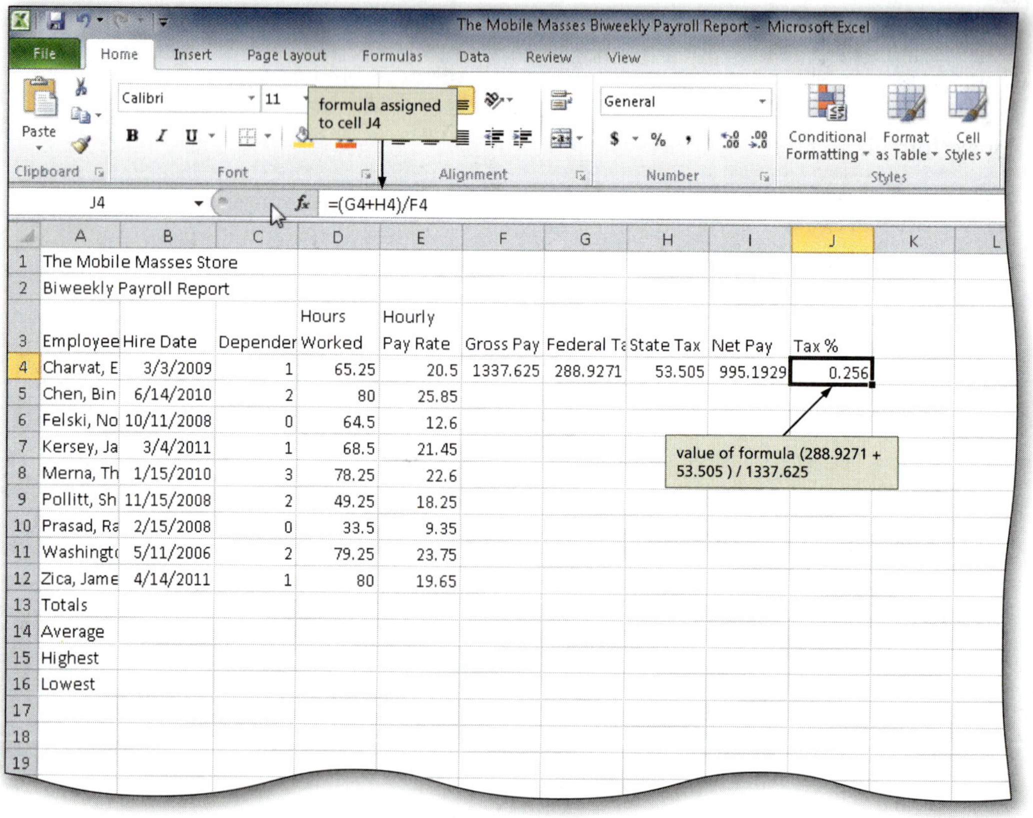

Figure 2–11

Q&A

Why do three decimal places show in cell J4?

The actual value assigned by Excel to cell J4 from the division operation in step 5 is 0.256000075. While not all the decimal places appear in Figure 2–11, Excel maintains all of them for computational purposes. Thus, if referencing cell J4 in a formula, the value used for computational purposes is 0.256000075, not 0.256. The cell formatting is set to display six digits after the decimal point, but the formatting also suppresses trailing zeroes. If the cell formatting were set to display six digits and show trailing zeroes, then Excel would display 0.256000 in cell J4. If you change the cell formatting of column J to display nine digits after the decimal point, then Excel displays the true value 0.256000075.

To Copy Formulas Using the Fill Handle

The five formulas for Emily Charvat in cells F4, G4, H4, I4, and J4 now are complete. You could enter the same five formulas one at a time for the eight remaining employees. A much easier method of entering the formulas, however, is to select the formulas in row 4 and then use the fill handle to copy them through row 12. When performing copying operations in Excel, the source area is the cell, or range, from which data or formulas are being copied. When a range is used as a source, sometimes it is called the source range. The destination area is the cell, or range, to which data or formulas are being copied. When a range is used as a destination, sometimes it is called the destination range. Recall from Excel Chapter 1 that the fill handle is a small rectangle in the lower-right corner of the active cell or active range. The following steps copy the formulas using the fill handle.

1

- Select the source range, F4:J4 in this case, and then point to the fill handle.
- Drag the fill handle down through cell J12 and continue to hold the mouse button to select the destination range (Figure 2–12).

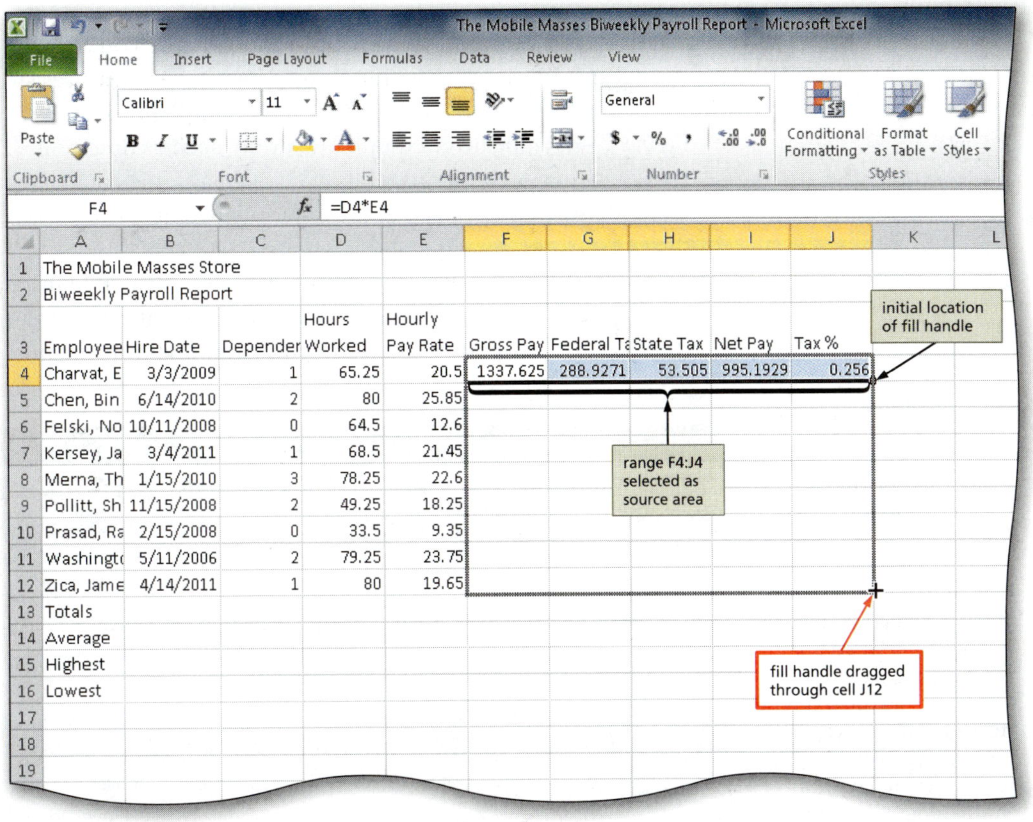

Figure 2–12

2

- Release the mouse button to copy the formulas to the destination range (Figure 2–13).

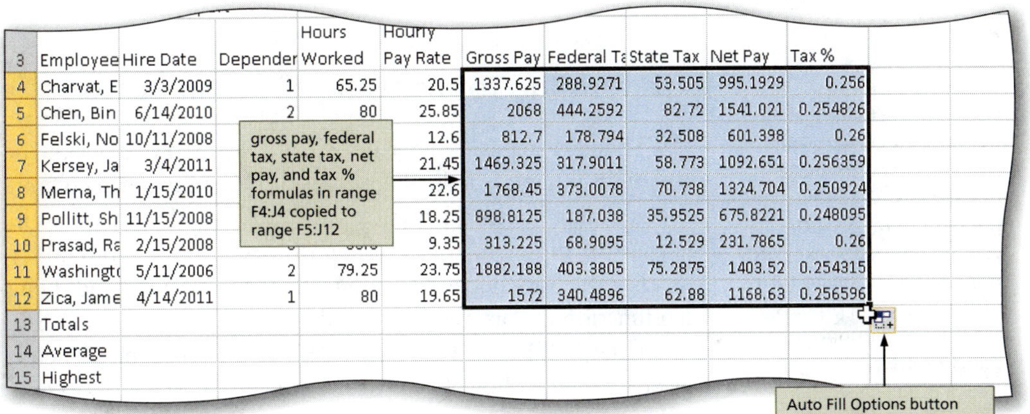

Figure 2–13

Q&A

How does Excel adjust the cell references in the formulas in the destination area?

Recall that when you copy a formula, Excel adjusts the cell references so that the new formulas contain references corresponding to the new location and perform calculations using the appropriate values. Thus, if you copy downward, Excel adjusts the row portion of cell references. If you copy across, then Excel adjusts the column portion of cell references. These cell references are called **relative cell references**.

Other Ways

1. Select source area, click Copy button (Home tab | Clipboard group), select destination area, click Paste button (Home tab | Clipboard group)
2. Right-click source area, click Copy on shortcut menu, right-click destination area, click Paste icon on shortcut menu
3. Select source area and then point to border of range; while holding down CTRL, drag source area to destination area

Option Buttons

Excel displays Option buttons in a workbook while you are working on it to indicate that you can complete an operation using automatic features such as AutoCorrect, Auto Fill, error checking, and others. For example, the Auto Fill Options button shown in Figure 2–13 appears after a fill operation, such as dragging the fill handle. When an error occurs in a formula in a cell, Excel displays the Trace Error button next to the cell and identifies the cell with the error by placing a green triangle in the upper left of the cell.

Table 2–4 summarizes the Option buttons available in Excel. When one of these buttons appears on your worksheet, click the button arrow to produce the list of options for modifying the operation or to obtain additional information.

BTW

The Paste Options Button
The Paste Options button provides powerful functionality. When performing copy and paste operations, the button allows you great freedom in specifying what it is you want to paste. For example, you could choose to paste an exact copy of what you copied, including the cell contents and formatting. You also could copy just formulas, just formatting, just the cell values, a combination of these options, or a picture of what you copied.

Table 2–4 Options Buttons in Excel

Button	Name	Menu Function
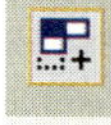	Auto Fill Options	Gives options for how to fill cells following a fill operation, such as dragging the fill handle.
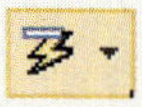	AutoCorrect Options	Undoes an automatic correction, stops future automatic corrections of this type, or causes Excel to display the AutoCorrect Options dialog box.
	Insert Options	Lists formatting options following an insertion of cells, rows, or columns.
	Paste Options	Specifies how moved or pasted items should appear (for example, with original formatting, without formatting, or with different formatting).
	Trace Error	Lists error-checking options following the assignment of an invalid formula to a cell.

BTW

Selecting a Range
You can select a range using the keyboard. Press the F8 key and then use the arrow keys to select the desired range. After you are finished, make sure to press the F8 key to turn off the selection process or you will continue to select ranges.

To Determine Totals Using the Sum Button

The next step is to determine the totals in row 13 for the hours worked in column D, gross pay in column F, federal tax in column G, state tax in column H, and net pay in column I. To determine the total hours worked in column D, the values in the range D4 through D12 must be summed. To do so, enter the function =sum(d4:d12) in cell D13 or select cell D13, click the Sum button (Home tab | Editing group), and then press the ENTER key. Recall that a function is a prewritten formula that is built into Excel. Similar SUM functions can be used in cells F13, G13, H13, and I13 to total gross pay, federal tax, state tax, and net pay, respectively. The following steps determine totals in cell D13 and the range F13:I13.

1. Select cell to contain the sum, cell D13 in this case. Click the Sum button (Home tab | Editing group) to sum the contents of the range D4:D12 in cell D13 and then click the Enter box to display a total in the selected cell.

2. Select the range to contain the sums, range F13:I13 in this case. Click the Sum button (Home tab | Editing group) to display totals in the selected range (Figure 2–14).

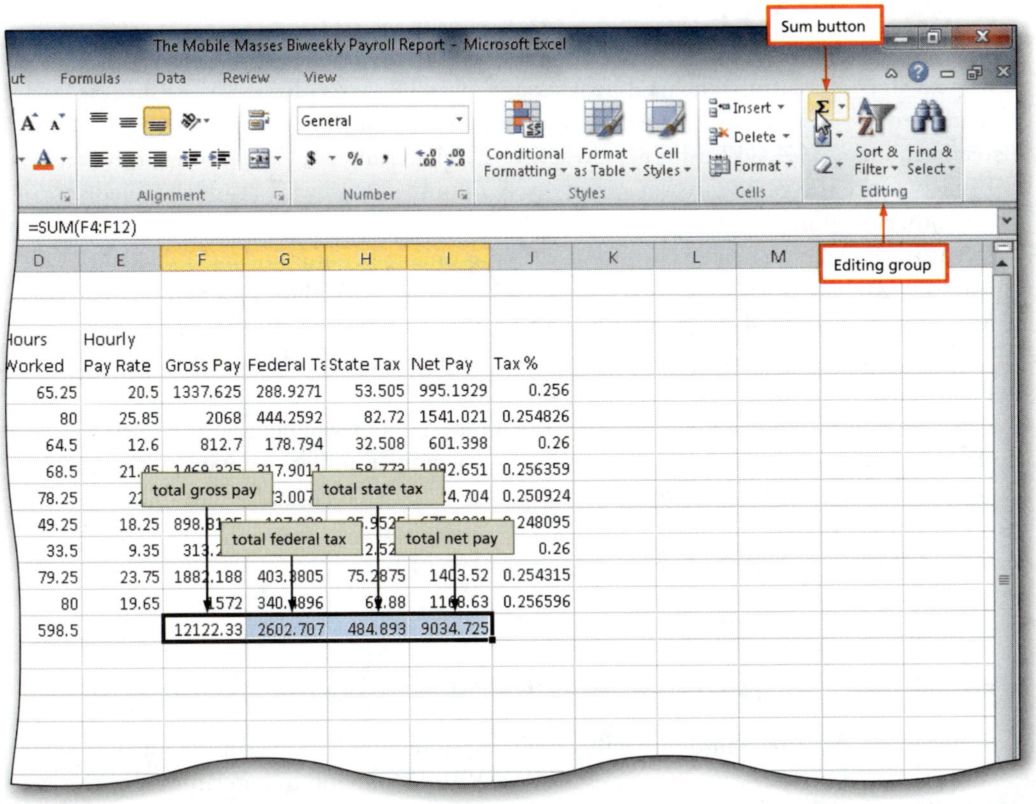

Figure 2–14

To Determine the Total Tax %

With the totals in row 13 determined, the next step is to copy the tax % formula in cell J12 to cell J13 as performed in the following steps.

1. Select the cell to be copied, J12 in this case, and then point to the fill handle.
2. Drag the fill handle down through cell J13 to copy the formula (Figure 2–15).

Q&A

Why was the formula I13/F13 not copied to cell J13 earlier?

The formula, I13/F13, was not copied to cell J13 when cell J4 was copied to the range J5:J12 because both cells involved in the computation (I13 and F13) were blank, or zero, at the time. A **blank cell** in Excel has a numerical value of zero, which would have resulted in an error message in cell J13. Once the totals were determined, both cells I13 and F13 (especially F13, because it is the divisor) had nonzero numerical values.

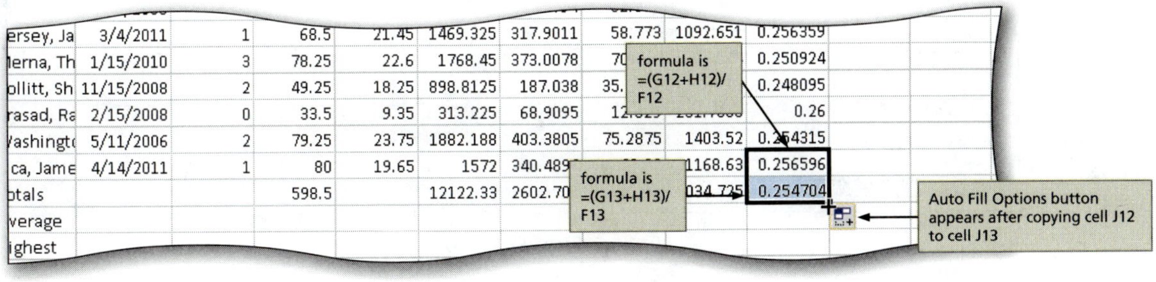

Figure 2–15

Using the AVERAGE, MAX, and MIN Functions

The next step in creating The Mobile Masses Biweekly Payroll Report worksheet is to compute the average, highest value, and lowest value for the number of dependents listed in the range C4:C12 using the AVERAGE, MAX, and MIN functions in the range C14:C16. Once the values are determined for column C, the entries can be copied across to the other columns.

With Excel, you can enter functions using one of five methods: (1) the keyboard or mouse, (2) the Insert Function box in the formula bar, (3) the Sum menu, (4) the Sum command (Formulas tab | Function Library group), and (5) the Name box area in the formula bar (Figure 2–16). The method you choose will depend on your typing skills and whether you can recall the function name and required arguments.

In the following pages, each of the first three methods will be used. The keyboard and mouse method will be used to determine the average number of dependents (cell C14). The Insert Function button in the formula bar method will be used to determine the highest number of dependents (cell C15). The Sum menu method will be used to determine the lowest number of dependents (cell C16).

BTW

Statistical Functions
Excel usually considers a blank cell to be equal to 0. The statistical functions, however, ignore blank cells. Excel thus calculates the average of three cells with values of 10, blank, and 8 to be 9 [(10 + 8) / 2] and not 6 [(10 + 0 + 8) / 3].

To Determine the Average of a Range of Numbers Using the Keyboard and Mouse

The **AVERAGE function** sums the numbers in the specified range and then divides the sum by the number of cells with numeric values in the range. The following steps use the AVERAGE function to determine the average of the numbers in the range C4:C12.

1

- Select the cell to contain the average, cell C14 in this case.
- Type `=av` in the cell to display the Formula AutoComplete list. Press the DOWN ARROW key to highlight the required formula (Figure 2–16).

Q&A

What is happening as I type?

As you type the equal sign followed by the characters in the name of a function, Excel displays the Formula AutoComplete list. This list contains those functions that alphabetically match the letters you have typed. Because you typed =av, Excel displays all the functions that begin with the letters av.

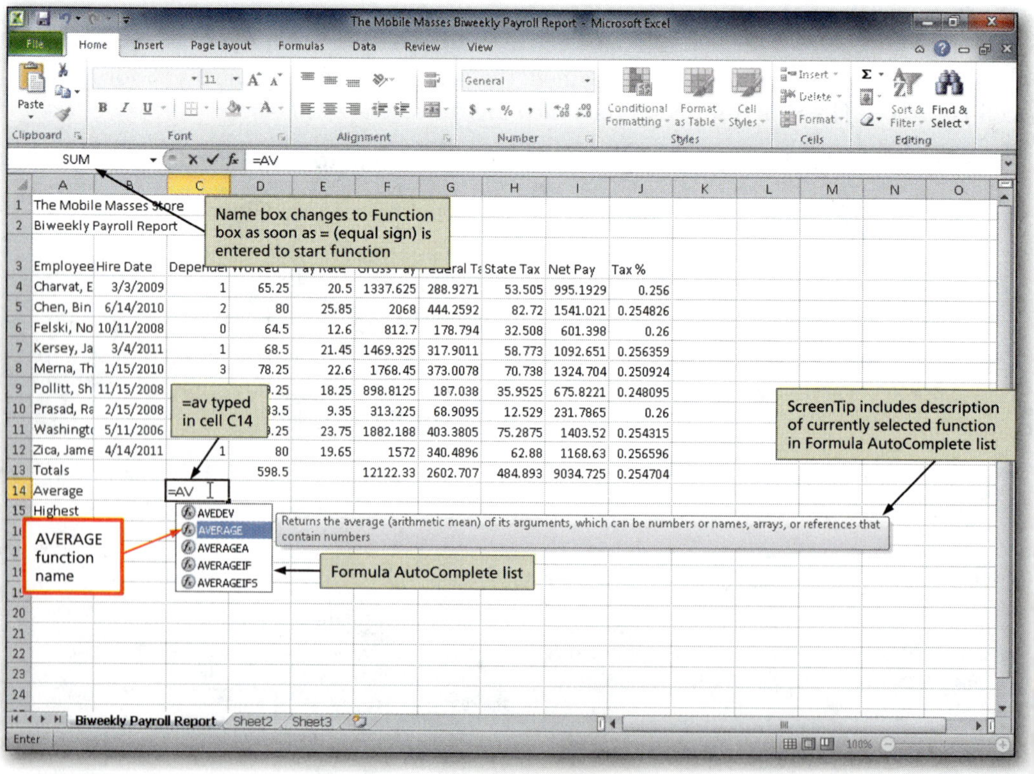

Figure 2–16

2

- Double-click AVERAGE in the Formula AutoComplete list to select the function.
- Select the range to be averaged, C4:C12 in this case, to insert the range as the argument to the function (Figure 2–17).

Q&A As I drag, why does the function in cell C14 change?

When you click cell C4, Excel appends cell C4 to the left parenthesis in the formula bar and surrounds cell C4 with a marquee. When you begin dragging, Excel appends to the argument a colon (:) and the cell reference of the cell where the mouse pointer is located.

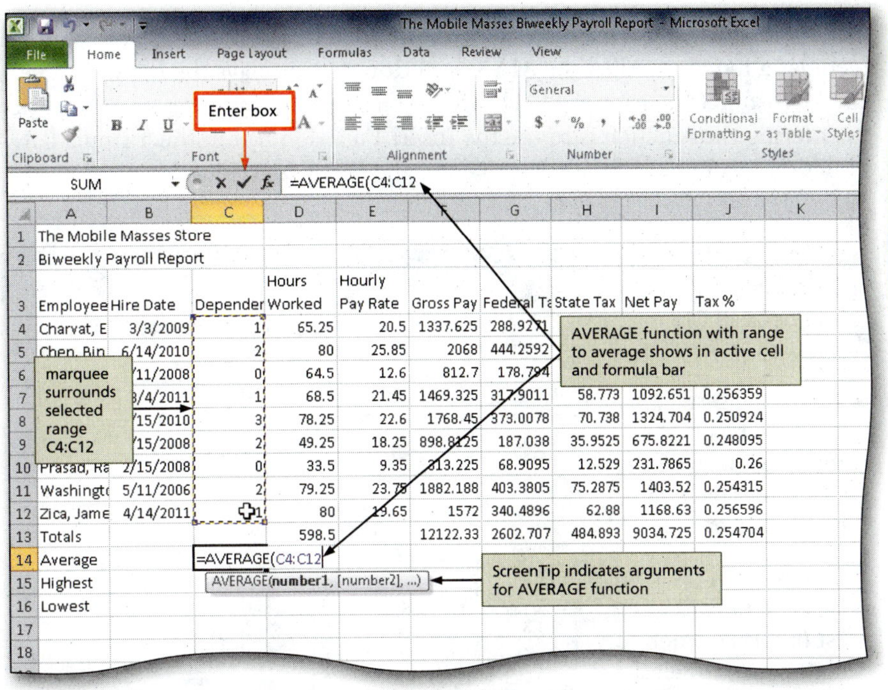

Figure 2–17

3

- Click the Enter box to compute the average of the numbers in the selected range and display the result in the selected cell (Figure 2–18).

Q&A Can I use the arrow keys to complete the entry instead?

No. When you use Point mode you cannot use the arrow keys to complete the entry. While in Point mode, the arrow keys change the selected cell reference in the range you are selecting.

Q&A What is the purpose of the parentheses in the function?

The AVERAGE function requires that the argument (in this case, the range C4:C12) be included within parentheses following the function name. Excel automatically appends the right parenthesis to complete the AVERAGE function when you click the Enter box or press the ENTER key.

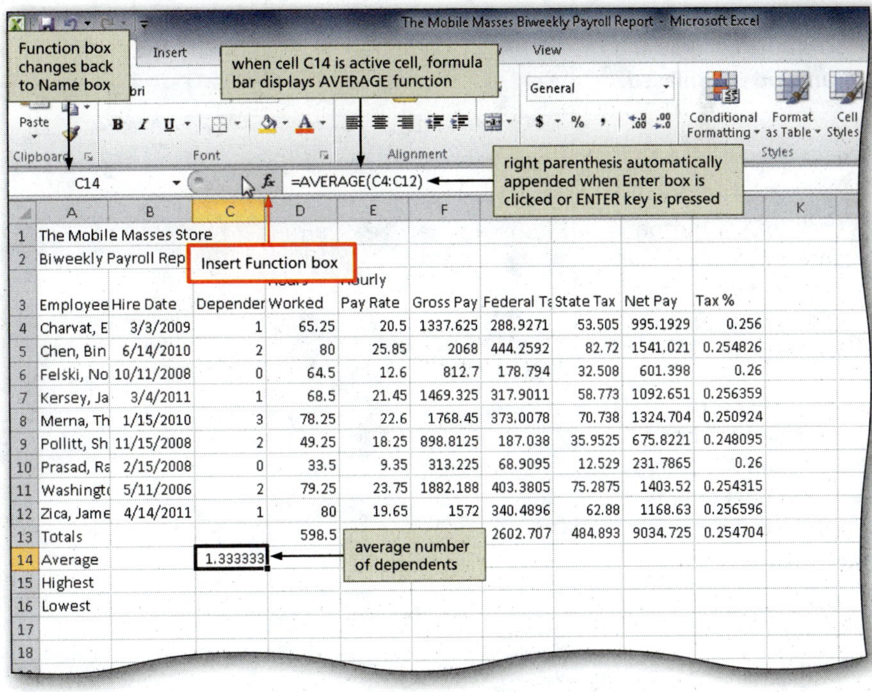

Figure 2–18

Other Ways

1. Click Insert Function box in the formula bar, click AVERAGE
2. Click Sum button arrow (Home tab | Editing group), click Average
3. Click Sum button arrow (Formulas tab | Function Library group), click Average

To Determine the Highest Number in a Range of Numbers Using the Insert Function Box

The next step is to select cell C15 and determine the highest (maximum) number in the range C4:C12. Excel includes a function called the **MAX function** that displays the highest value in a range. Although you could enter the MAX function using the keyboard and Point mode as described in the previous steps, an alternative method to entering the function is to use the Insert Function box in the formula bar. The following steps use the Insert Function box in the formula bar to enter the MAX function.

1

- Select the cell to contain the maximum number, cell C15 in this case.
- Click the Insert Function box in the formula bar to display the Insert Function dialog box.
- Click MAX in the 'Select a function' list (Insert Function dialog box) to select it (Figure 2–19). If the MAX function is not displayed in the 'Select a function' list, scroll the list until the function is displayed.

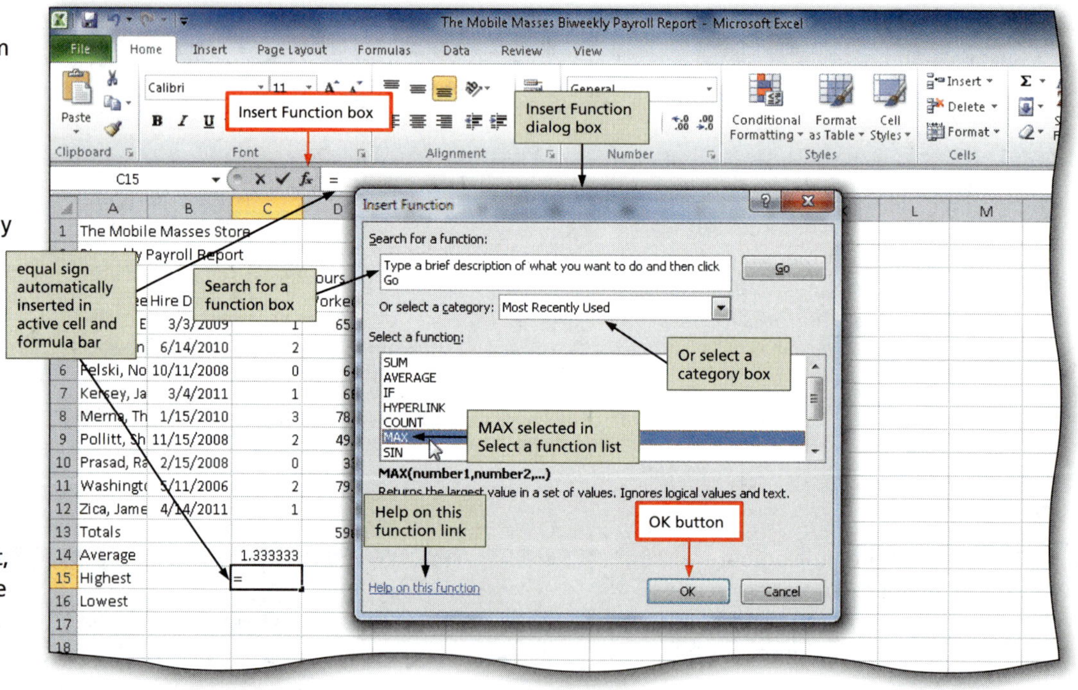

Figure 2–19

2

- Click the OK button (Insert Function dialog box) to display the Function Arguments dialog box.
- Type `c4:c12` in the Number1 box (Function Arguments dialog box) to enter the first argument of the function (Figure 2–20).

Q&A Why did numbers appear in the Function Arguments dialog box?

As shown in Figure 2–20, Excel displays the value the MAX function will return to cell C15 in the Function Arguments dialog box. It also lists the first few numbers in the selected range, next to the Number1 box.

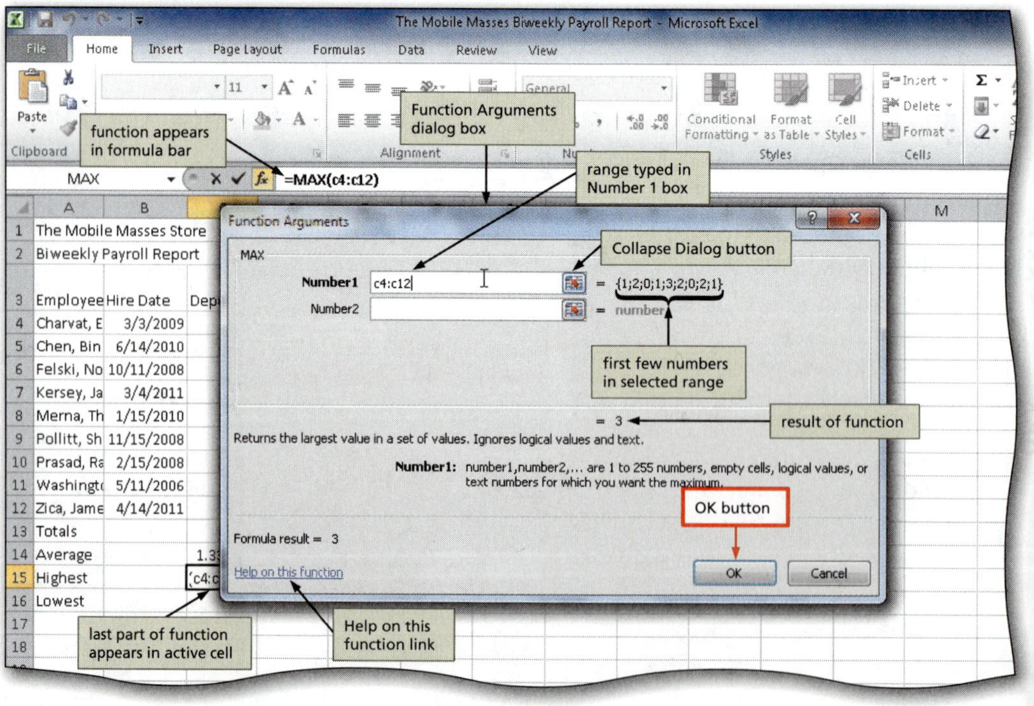

Figure 2–20

3

- Click the OK button (Function Arguments dialog box) to display the highest value in the chosen range in the selected cell (Figure 2–21).

Q&A Why should I not just enter the highest value that I see in the range C4:C12 in cell C15?

In this example, rather than entering the MAX function, you visually could scan the range C4:C12, determine that the highest number of dependents is 3, and manually enter the number 3 as a constant in cell C15. Excel would display the number the same as in Figure 2–21. Because it contains a constant, however, Excel will continue to display 3 in cell C15, even if the values in the range C4:C12 change. If you use the MAX function, Excel will recalculate the highest value in the range C4:C12 each time a new value is entered into the worksheet.

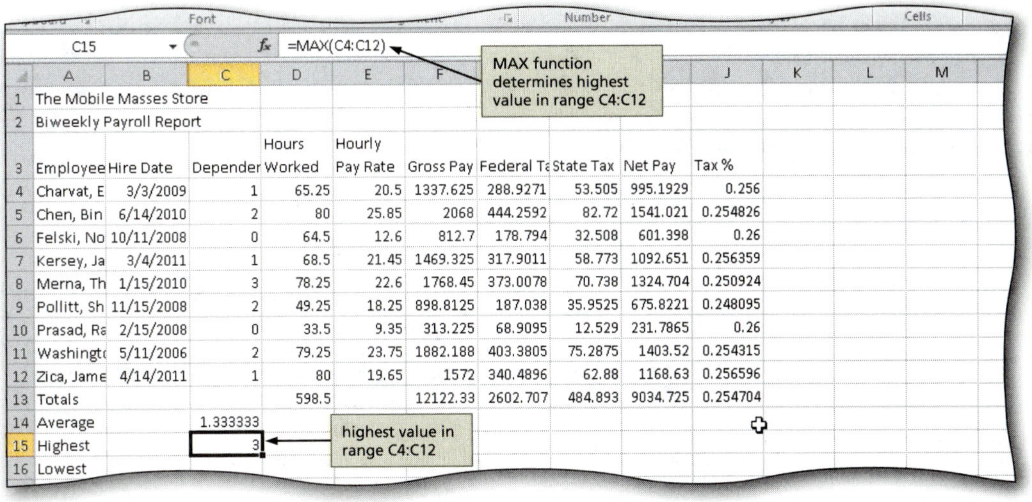

Figure 2–21

Other Ways		
1. Click Sum button arrow (Home tab | Editing group), click Max	2. Click Sum button arrow (Formulas tab | Function Library group), click Max	3. Type **=MAX** in cell

To Determine the Lowest Number in a Range of Numbers Using the Sum Menu

The next step is to enter the **MIN function** in cell C16 to determine the lowest (minimum) number in the range C4:C12. Although you can enter the MIN function using either of the methods used to enter the AVERAGE and MAX functions, the following steps perform an alternative using the Sum button (Home tab | Editing group).

1

- Select cell C16 to prepare to enter the next function.
- Click the Sum button arrow (Home tab | Editing group) to display the Sum button menu (Figure 2–22).

Q&A Why should I use the Sum button menu?

Using the Sum button menu allows you to enter one of five often-used functions easily into a cell, without having to memorize its name or the required arguments.

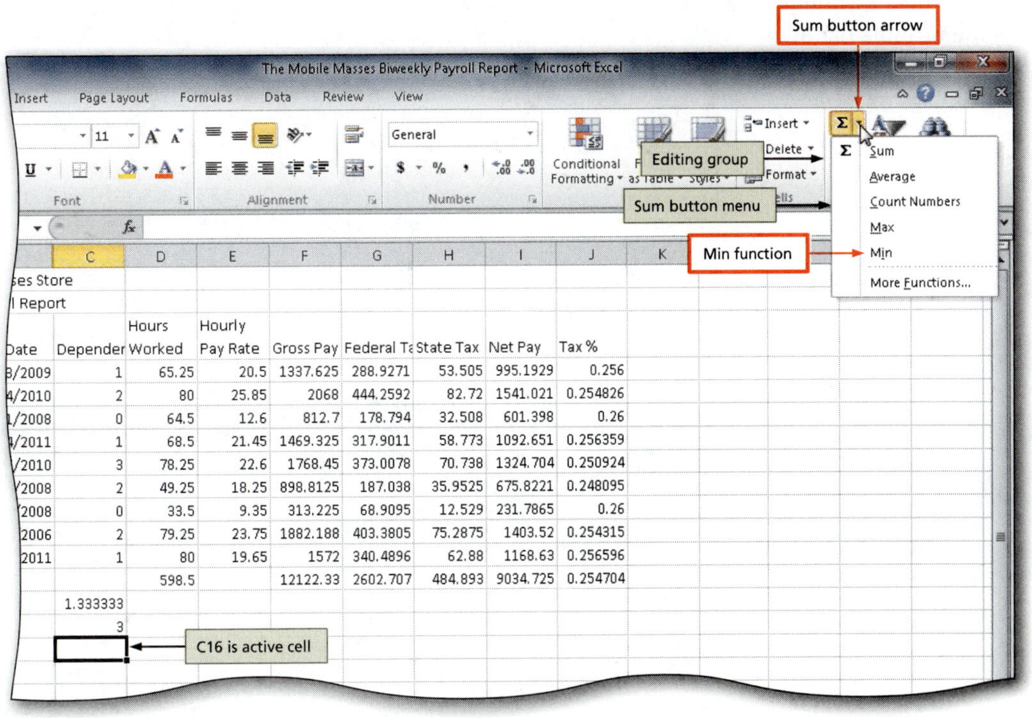

Figure 2–22

2

- Click Min to display the MIN function in the formula bar and in the active cell (Figure 2–23).

Q&A

Why does Excel select the range C14:C15?

The range C14:C15 automatically selected by Excel is not correct. Excel attempts to guess which cells you want to include in the function by looking for ranges that are adjacent to the selected cell and that contain numeric data.

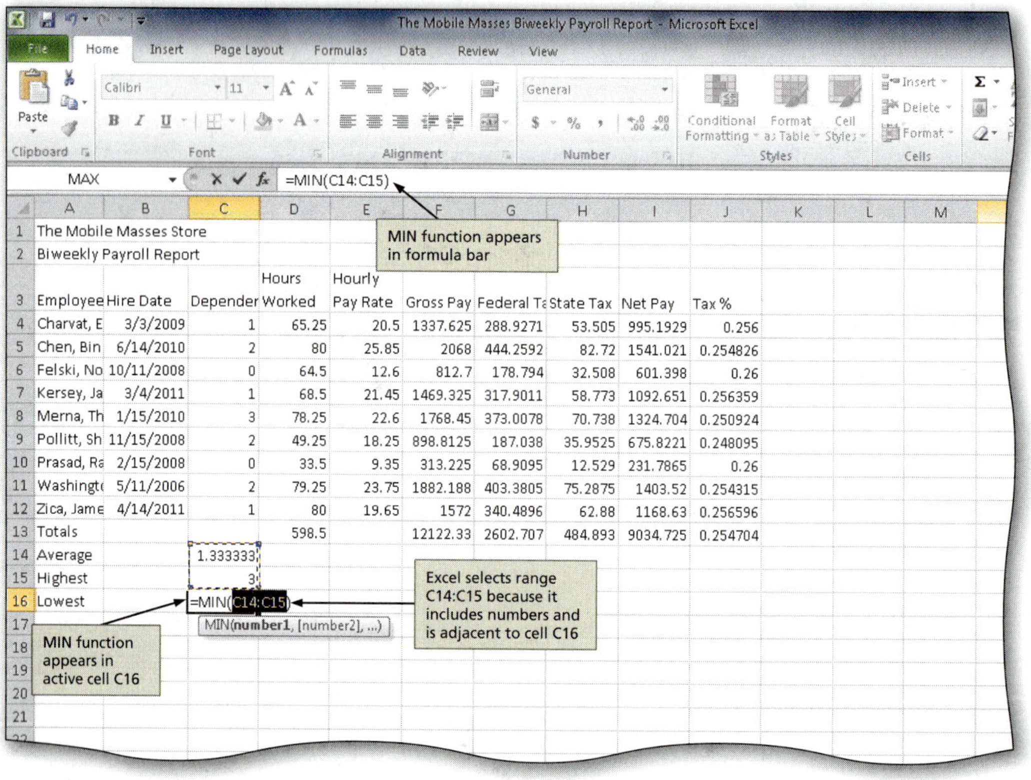

Figure 2–23

3

- Click cell C4 and then drag through cell C12 to display the function with the new range in the formula bar and in the selected cell (Figure 2–24).

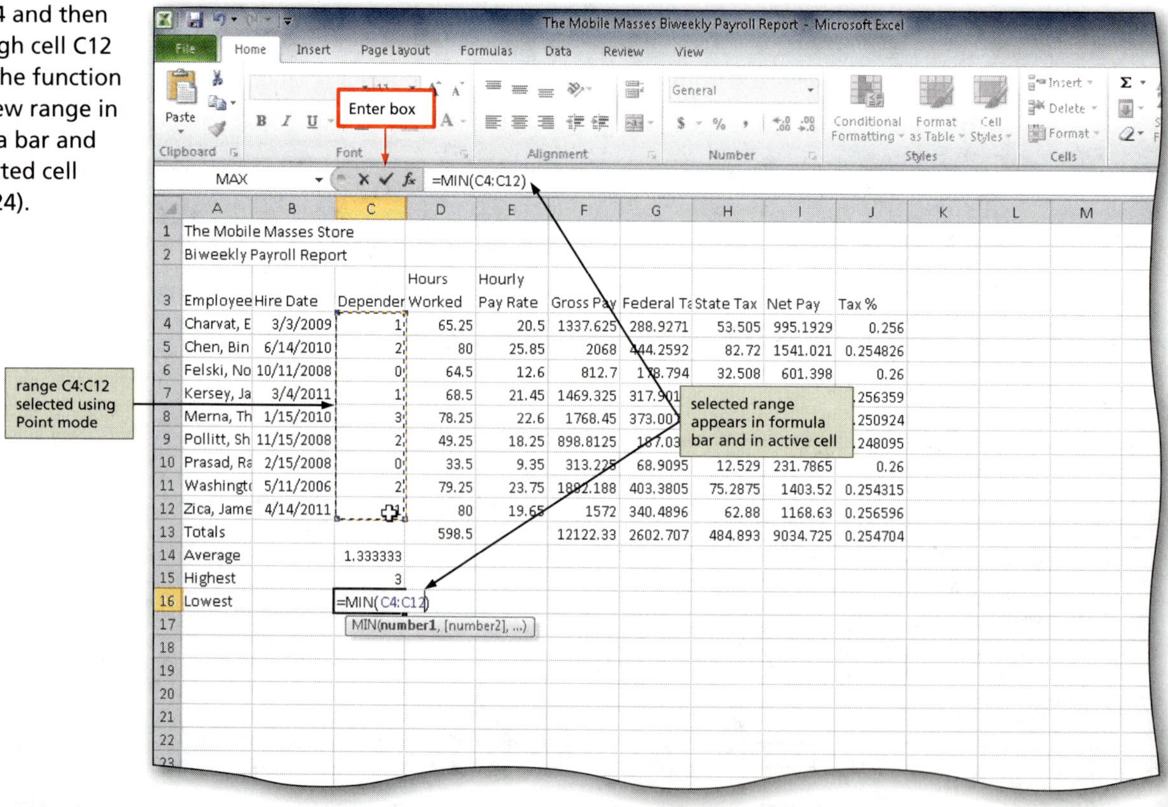

Figure 2–24

4

- Click the Enter box to determine the lowest value in the range C4:C12 and display the result in the formula bar and in the selected cell (Figure 2–25).

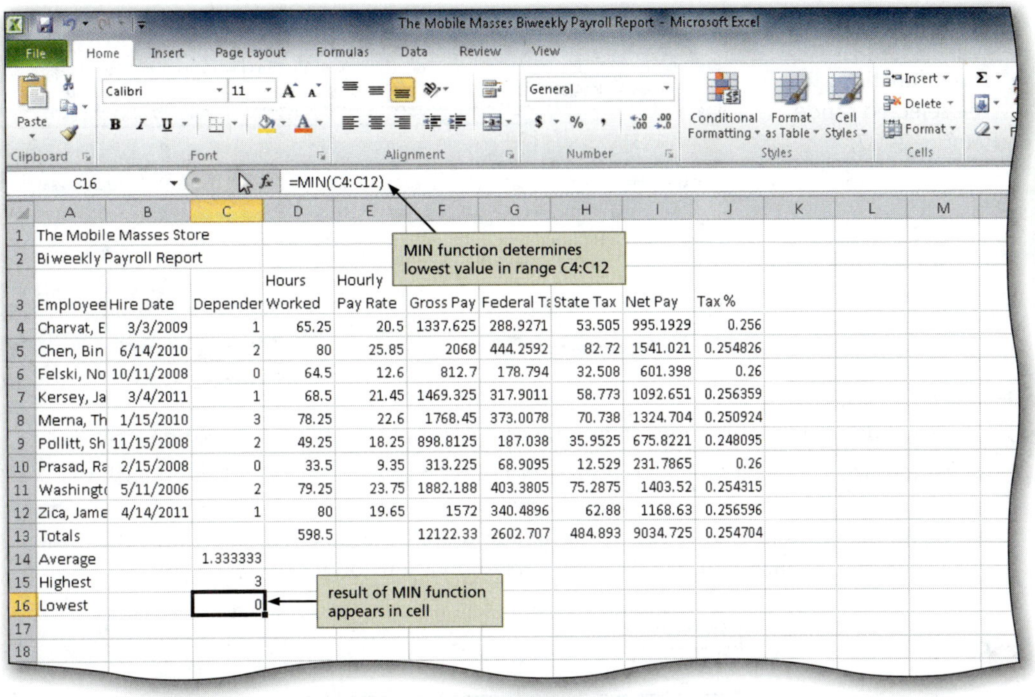

Figure 2–25

Q&A

How can I learn about other functions?

Excel has more than 400 additional functions that perform just about every type of calculation you can imagine. These functions are categorized in the Insert Function dialog box shown in Figure 2–19 on page EX 86. To view the categories, click the 'Or select a category' box arrow. To obtain a description of a selected function, select its name in the Insert Function dialog box. Excel displays the description of the function below the Select a function list in the dialog box.

Other Ways

1. Click Insert Function box in the formula bar (if necessary, select Statistical category), click MIN
2. Click Sum button arrow (Formulas tab | Function Library group), click Min
3. Type =MIN in cell

To Copy a Range of Cells Across Columns to an Adjacent Range Using the Fill Handle

The next step is to copy the AVERAGE, MAX, and MIN functions in the range C14:C16 to the adjacent range D14:J16. The following steps use the fill handle to copy the functions.

1

- Select the source range from which to copy the functions, in this case C14:C16.
- Drag the fill handle in the lower-right corner of the selected range through cell J16 and continue to hold down the mouse button to begin a fill operation (Figure 2–26).

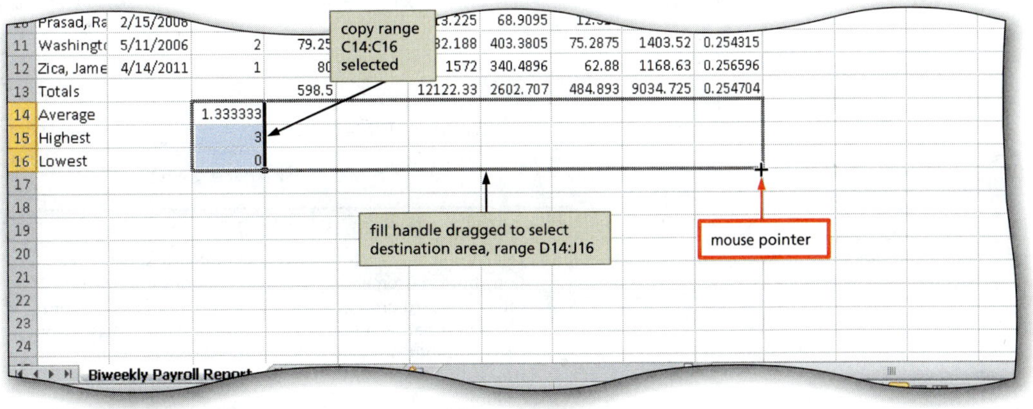

Figure 2–26

2

- Release the mouse button to copy the three functions to the selected range (Figure 2–27).

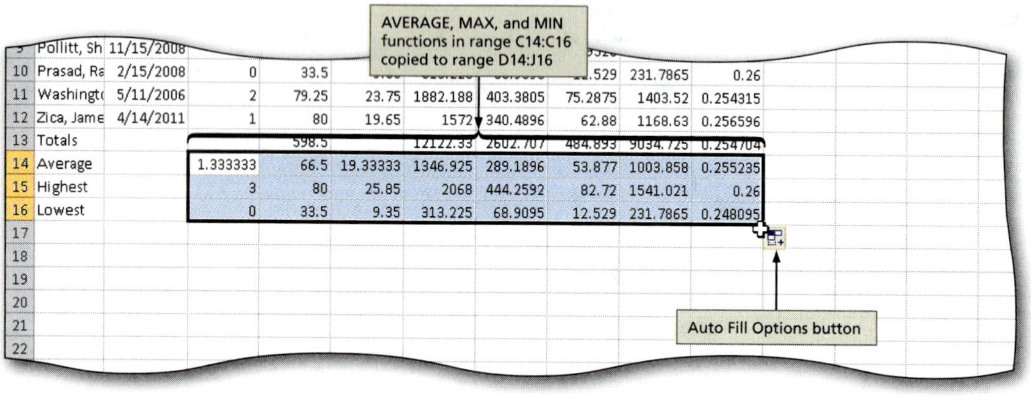

Figure 2–27

Q&A How can I be sure that the function arguments are proper for the cells in range D14:J16?

Remember that Excel adjusts the cell references in the copied functions so that each function refers to the range of numbers above it in the same column. Review the numbers in rows 14 through 16 in Figure 2–27. You should see that the functions in each column return the appropriate values, based on the numbers in rows 4 through 12 of that column.

3

- Select cell J14 and then press the DELETE key to delete the average of the tax % (Figure 2–28).

Q&A Why is the formula in cell J14 deleted?

The average of the tax % in cell J14 is deleted because an average of percentages of this type is mathematically invalid.

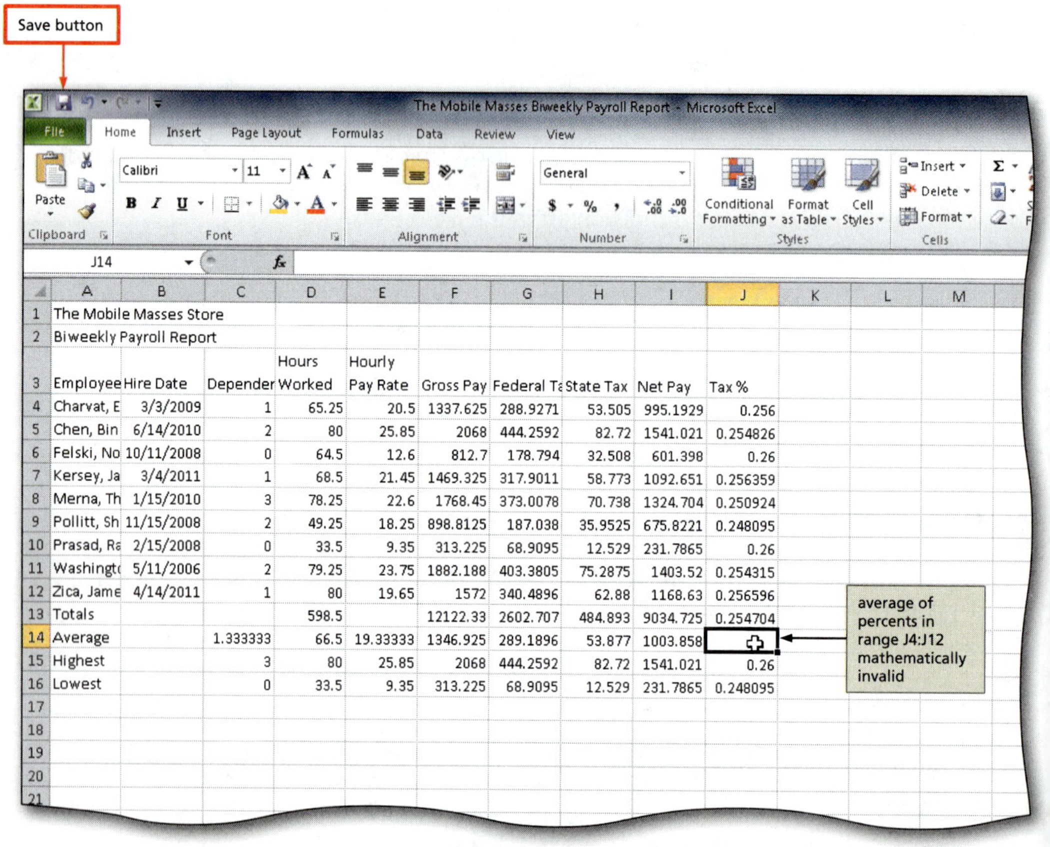

Figure 2–28

Other Ways

1. Select source area, click Copy button (Home tab | Clipboard group), select destination area, click Paste button (Home tab | Clipboard group)
2. Right-click source area, click Copy on shortcut menu, right-click destination area, click Paste icon on shortcut menu
3. Select source area and then point to border of range; while holding down CTRL, drag source area to destination area
4. Select source area, press CTRL+C, select destination area, press CTRL+V

To Save a Workbook Using the Same File Name

Earlier in this project, an intermediate version of the workbook was saved using the file name, The Mobile Masses Biweekly Payroll Report. The following step saves the workbook a second time, using the same file name.

1. Click the Save button on the Quick Access Toolbar to overwrite the previously saved file.

Break Point: If you wish to take a break, this is a good place to do so. You can quit Excel now. To resume at a later time, start Excel, open the file called Mobile Masses Biweekly Payroll Report, and continue following the steps from this location forward.

Verifying Formulas Using Range Finder

One of the more common mistakes made with Excel is to include a wrong cell reference in a formula. An easy way to verify that a formula references the cells you want it to reference is to use the Excel Range Finder. Use **Range Finder** to check which cells are referenced in the formula assigned to the active cell. Range Finder allows you to make immediate changes to the cells referenced in a formula.

To use Range Finder to verify that a formula contains the intended cell references, double-click the cell with the formula you want to check. Excel responds by highlighting the cells referenced in the formula so that you can check that the cell references are correct.

BTW

Entering Functions

You can drag the Function Arguments dialog box (Figure 2–20 on page EX 86) out of the way in order to select a range. You also can click the Collapse Dialog button to the right of the Number 1 box to hide the Function Arguments dialog box. The dialog box then collapses and the Collapse Dialog button becomes an Expand Dialog box button. After selecting the range, click the Expand Dialog to expand the dialog box.

To Verify a Formula Using Range Finder

The following steps use Range Finder to check the formula in cell J4.

1.
   - Double-click cell J4 to activate Range Finder (Figure 2–29).

2.
   - Press the ESC key to quit Range Finder and then click anywhere in the worksheet, such as cell A18, to deselect the current cell.

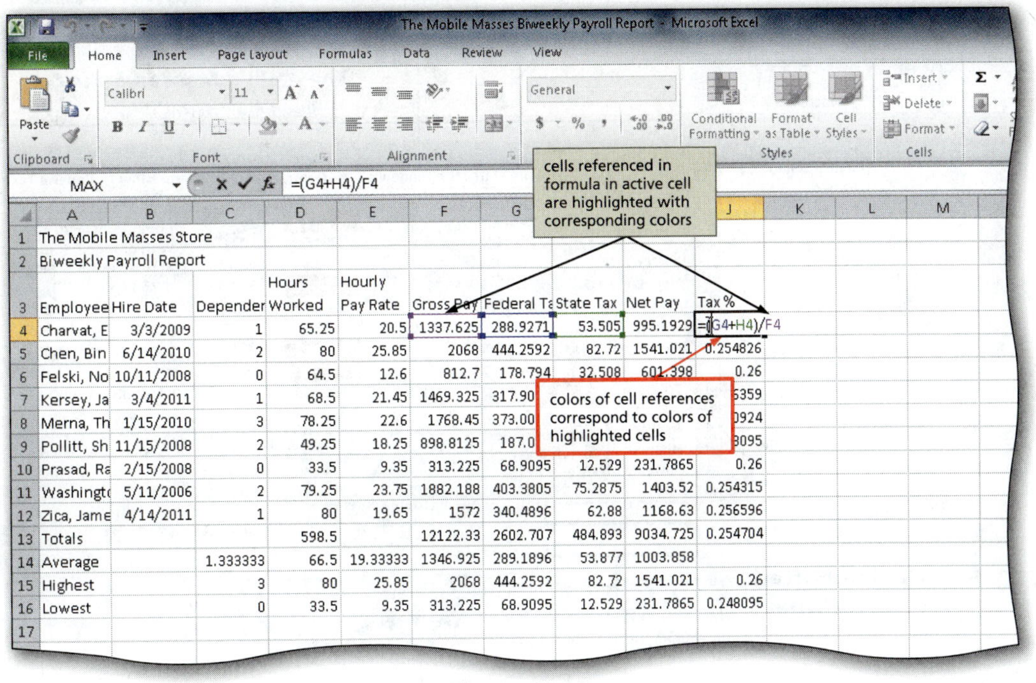

Figure 2–29

Formatting the Worksheet

Although the worksheet contains the appropriate data, formulas, and functions, the text and numbers need to be formatted to improve their appearance and readability.

In Excel Chapter 1, cell styles were used to format much of the worksheet. This section describes how to change the unformatted worksheet in Figure 2–30a to the formatted worksheet in Figure 2–30b using a theme and other commands on the Ribbon. The colors and fonts that are used in the worksheet shown in Figure 2–30b are those that are associated with the Trek theme.

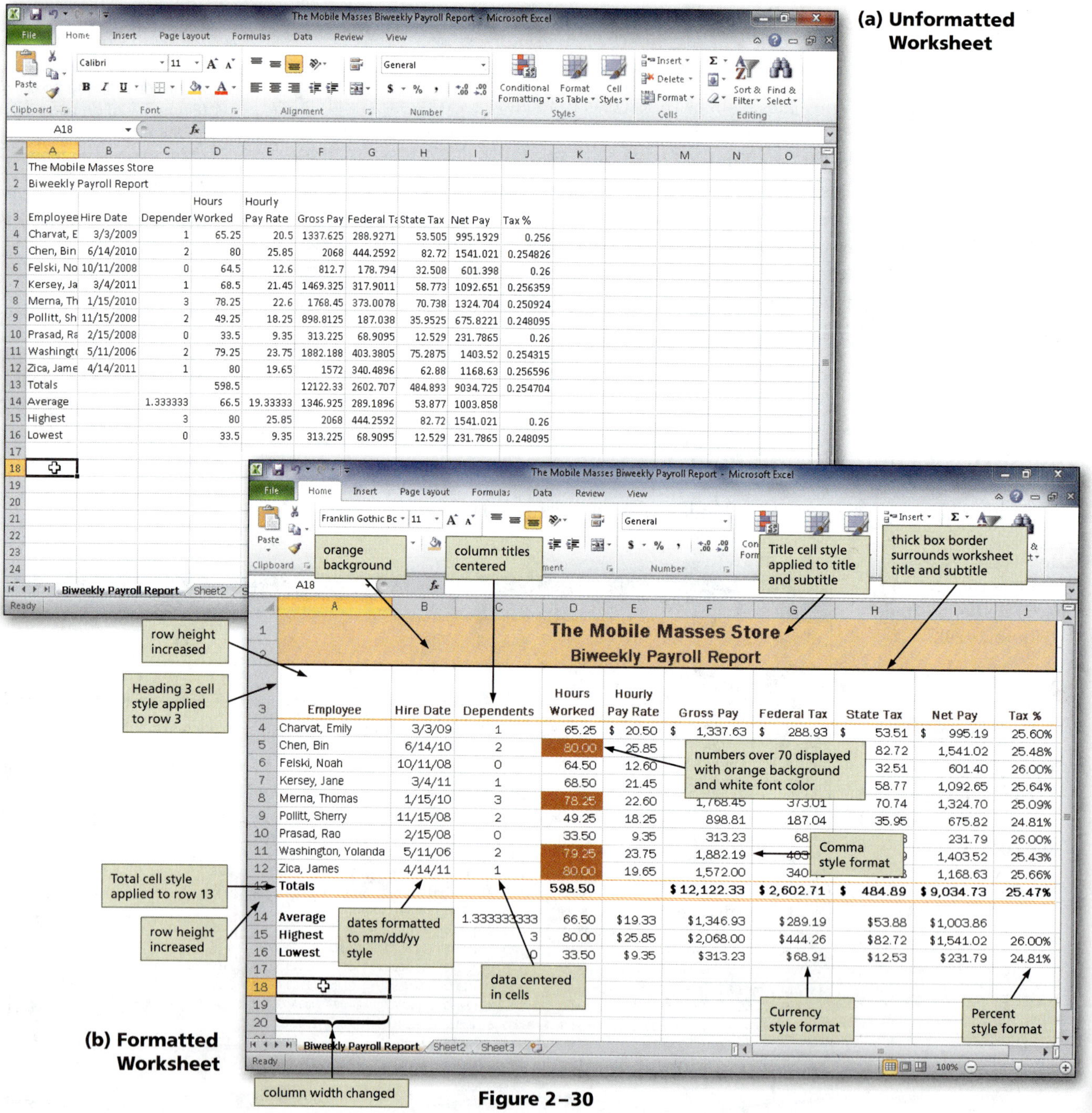

Figure 2–30

Plan Ahead

Identify how to format various elements of the worksheet.

As you have learned, applying proper formatting to a worksheet improves its appeal and readability. The following list includes additional worksheet formatting considerations.

- **Consider using cell borders and fill colors for various portions of the worksheet.** Cell borders, or box borders, draw a border around a cell or range of cells to set the cell or range off from other portions of the worksheet. For example, worksheet titles often include cell borders. Similarly, the use of a fill color in a cell or range of cells sets off the cell or range from other portions of the worksheet and provides visual impact to draw the user's eye toward the cell or range.
- **Use good judgment when centering values in columns.** If a cell entry is short, such as the dependents in column C, centering the entries within their respective columns improves the appearance of the worksheet.
- **Consider the use of a different theme.** A **theme** is a predefined set of colors, fonts, chart styles, cell styles, and fill effects that can be applied to an entire workbook. Every new workbook that you create is assigned a default theme named Office. Excel, however, includes a variety of other themes that provide a range of visual effects for your workbooks.
- **Apply proper formatting for cells that include dates.** Excel provides a number of date formats so that date values can be formatted to meet your needs. How you decide to format a date depends on a number of factors. For example, dates that include years both before and after the year 2000 should be formatted with a four-digit year. Your organization or department may insist on the use of certain standard date formats. Industry standards also may indicate how you should format date values.

The following outlines the formatting suggested in the sketch of the worksheet in Figure 2–3 on page EX 70.

1. Workbook theme — Trek
2. Worksheet title and subtitle
   a. Alignment — center across columns A through J
   b. Cell style — Title
   c. Font size — title 18; subtitle 16
   d. Background color (range A1:J2) — Orange Accent 1, Lighter 60%
   e. Border — thick box border around range A1:J2
3. Column titles
   a. Cell style — Heading 3
   b. Alignment — center
4. Data
   a. Dates in column B — mm/dd/yy format
   b. Alignment — center data in range C4:C12
   c. Numbers in column D — Comma style and two decimal places; if a cell in range D4:D12 is greater than 70, then cell appears with background color of orange and a font color of white
   d. Numbers in top row (range E4:I4) — Accounting number format
   e. Numbers below top row (range E5:I12) — Comma style and decimal places
5. Total line
   a. Cell style — Total
   b. Numbers — Accounting number format

6. Average, highest, and lowest rows
   a. Font style of row titles in range A14:A16 — bold
   b. Numbers — Currency style with floating dollar sign in the range E14:I16
7. Percentages in column J
   a. Numbers — Percentage style with two decimal places
8. Column widths
   a. Columns A, B, and C — best fit
   b. Column H — 10.22 characters
   c. Column D, E, and J — 7.56 characters
9. Row heights
   a. Row 3 — 48.00 points
   b. Row 14 — 27.00 points
   c. Remaining rows — default

To Change the Workbook Theme

The Trek theme includes fonts and colors that provide the worksheet a professional and subtly colored appearance. The following steps change the workbook theme to the Trek theme.

1

- Display the Page Layout tab.
- Click the Themes button (Page Layout tab | Themes group) to display the Themes gallery.
- Scroll to the bottom of the gallery (Figure 2–31).

Experiment

- Point to several themes in the Themes gallery to see a live preview of the themes.

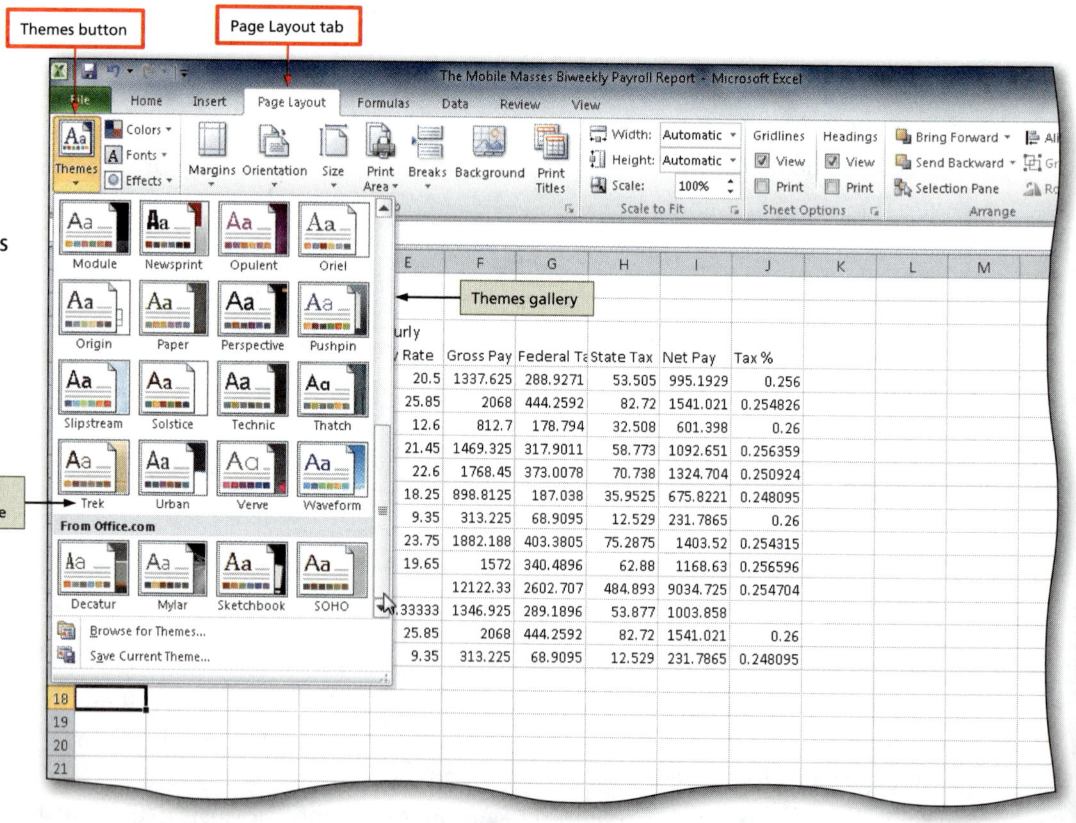

Figure 2–31

Q&A

Why should I change the theme of a workbook?

A company or department may standardize on a specific theme so that all of their documents have a similar appearance. Similarly, an individual may want to have a theme that sets his or her work apart from the work of others. Other Office programs, such as Word and PowerPoint, include the same themes included with Excel, meaning that all of your Microsoft Office documents can share a common theme.

2

- Click Trek in the Themes gallery to change the workbook theme (Figure 2–32).

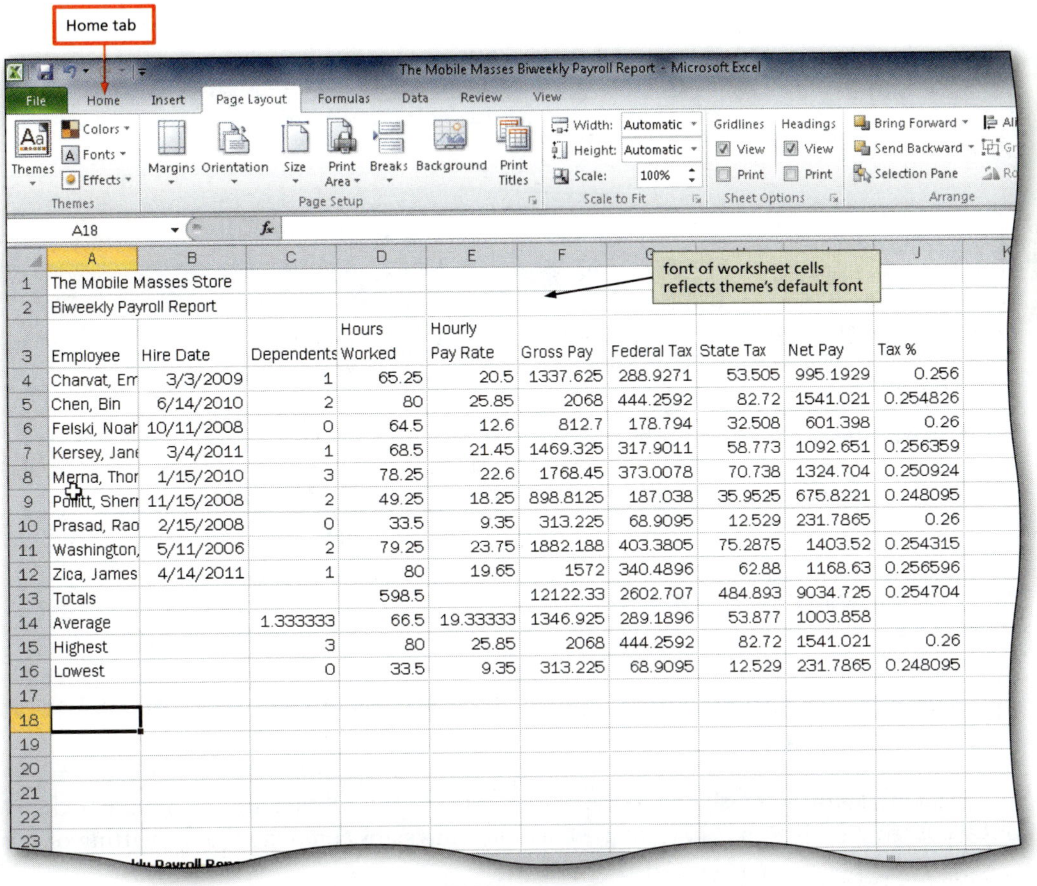

Figure 2–32

Q&A

Why did the cells in the worksheet change?

The cells in the worksheet originally were formatted with the default font for the default Office theme. The default font for the Trek theme is different from that of the default font for the Office theme and, therefore, changed on the worksheet when you changed the theme. If you had modified the font for any of the cells, those cells would not receive the default font for the Trek theme.

To Format the Worksheet Titles

The following steps merge and center the worksheet titles, apply the Title cells style to the worksheet titles, and decrease the font of the worksheet subtitle.

1. Display the Home tab.
2. Select the range to be merged, A1:J1 in this case, and then click the Merge & Center button (Home tab | Alignment group) to merge and center the text in the selected range.
3. Select the range A2:J2 and then click the Merge & Center button (Home tab | Alignment group) to merge and center the text in the selected range.
4. Select the range to contain the Title cell style, in this case A1:A2, click the Cell Styles button (Home tab | Styles group) to display the cell styles gallery, and then click the Title cell style in the Cell Styles gallery to apply the Title cell style to the selected range.
5. Select cell A2 and then click the Decrease Font Size button (Home tab | Font group) to decrease the font size of the selected cell to the next lowest font size (Figure 2–33 on the following page).

Q&A

What is the effect of clicking the Decrease Font Size button?

When you click the Decrease Font Size button, Excel assigns the next lowest font size in the Font Size gallery to the selected range. The Increase Font Size button works in a similar manner but causes Excel to assign the next highest font size in the Font Size gallery to the selected range.

BTW

Color Selection
Knowing how people perceive colors helps you emphasize parts of your worksheet. Warmer colors (red and orange) tend to reach toward the reader. Cooler colors (blue, green, and violet) tend to pull away from the reader. Bright colors jump out of a dark background and are easiest to see. White or yellow text on a dark blue, green, purple, or black background is ideal.

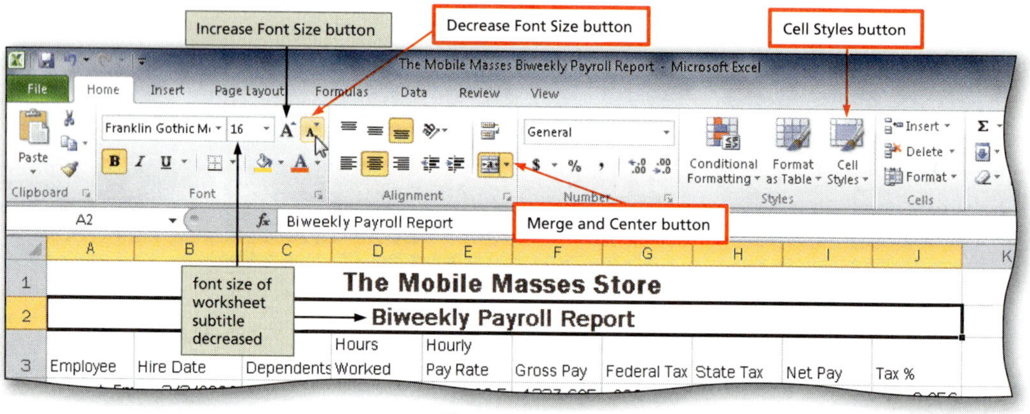

Figure 2–33

To Change the Background Color and Apply a Box Border to the Worksheet Title and Subtitle

The final formats assigned to the worksheet title and subtitle are the orange background color and thick box border (Figure 2–30b on page EX 92). The following steps complete the formatting of the worksheet titles.

1

- Select the range A1:A2 and then click the Fill Color button arrow (Home tab | Font group) to display the Fill Color gallery (Figure 2–34).

Experiment

- Point to a number of colors in the Fill Color gallery to display a live preview of the color in the range A1:A2.

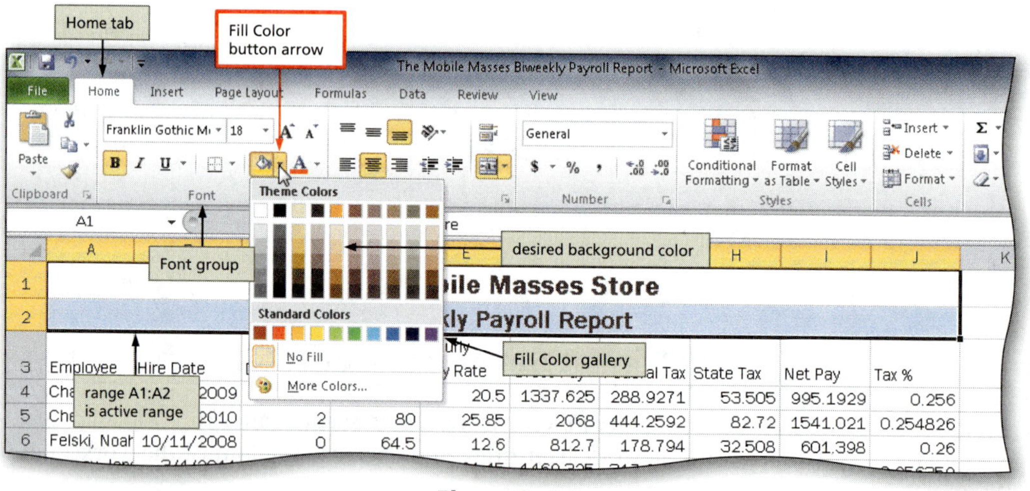

Figure 2–34

2

- Click Orange, Accent 1, Lighter 60% (column 5, row 3) in the Fill Color gallery to change the background color of the range of cells (Figure 2–35).

Figure 2–35

3

- Click the Borders button arrow (Home tab | Font group) to display the Borders list (Figure 2–36).

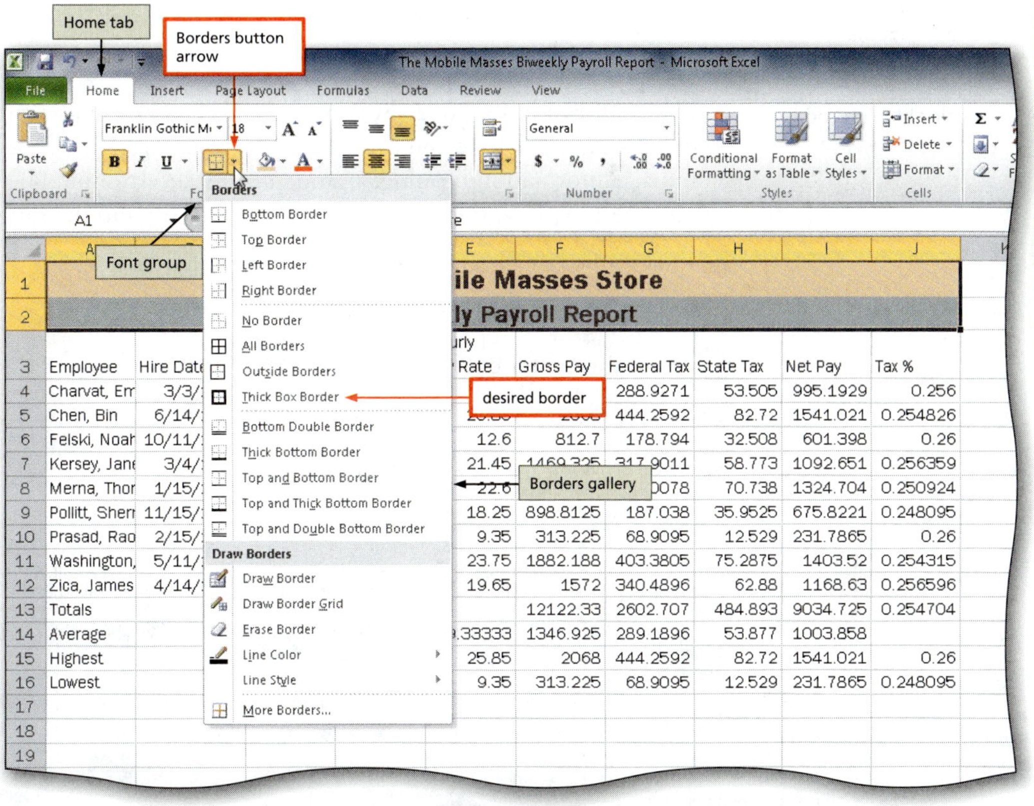

Figure 2–36

4

- Click Thick Box Border in the Borders list to display a thick box border around the selected range.
- Click anywhere in the worksheet, such as cell A18, to deselect the current range (Figure 2–37).

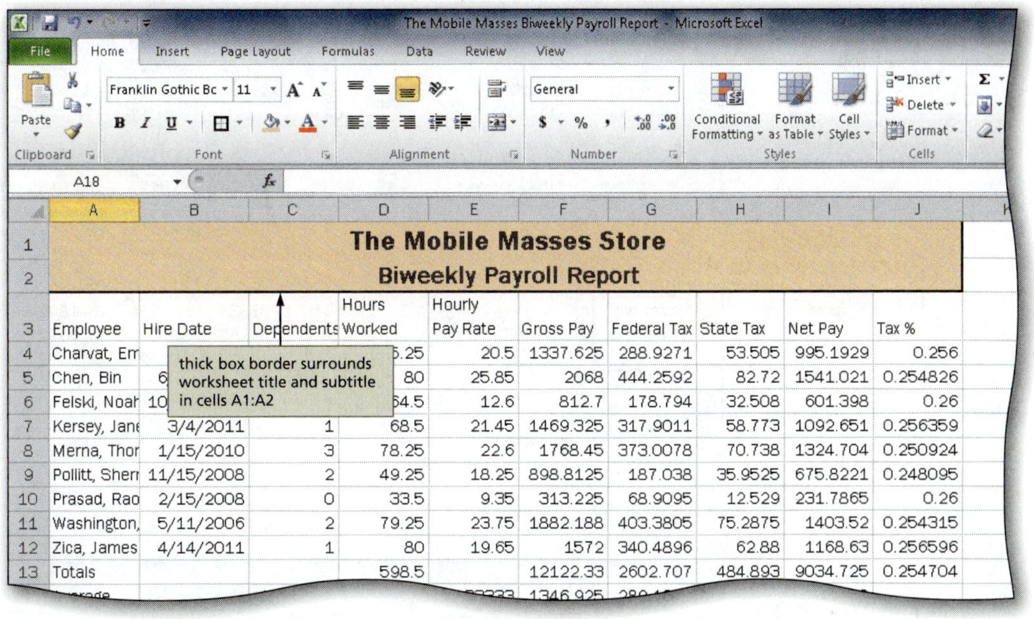

Figure 2–37

Other Ways

1. Click Format Cells Dialog Box Launcher (Home tab | Font group), click appropriate tab (Format Cells dialog box), click desired format, click OK button
2. Right-click range, click Format Cells on shortcut menu, click appropriate tab (Format Cells dialog box), click desired format, click OK button
3. Press CTRL+1, click appropriate tab (Format Cells dialog box), click desired format, click OK button

BTW

Background Colors
The most popular background color is blue. Research shows that the color blue is used most often because this color connotes serenity, reflection, and proficiency.

To Apply a Cell Style to the Column Headings and Format the Total Rows

As shown in Figure 2–30b on page EX 92, the column titles (row 3) should have the Heading 3 cell style and the totals row (row 13) should have the Total cell style. The summary information headings in the range A14:A16 should be bold. The following steps assign these styles and formats to row 3 and row 13 and the range A14:A16.

1. Select the range to be formatted, cells A3:J3 in this case.
2. Apply the Heading 3 cell style to the range A3:J3.
3. Click the Center button (Home tab | Alignment group) to center the column headings.
4. Apply the Total cell style to the range A13:J13.
5. Bold the range A14:A16 (Figure 2–38).

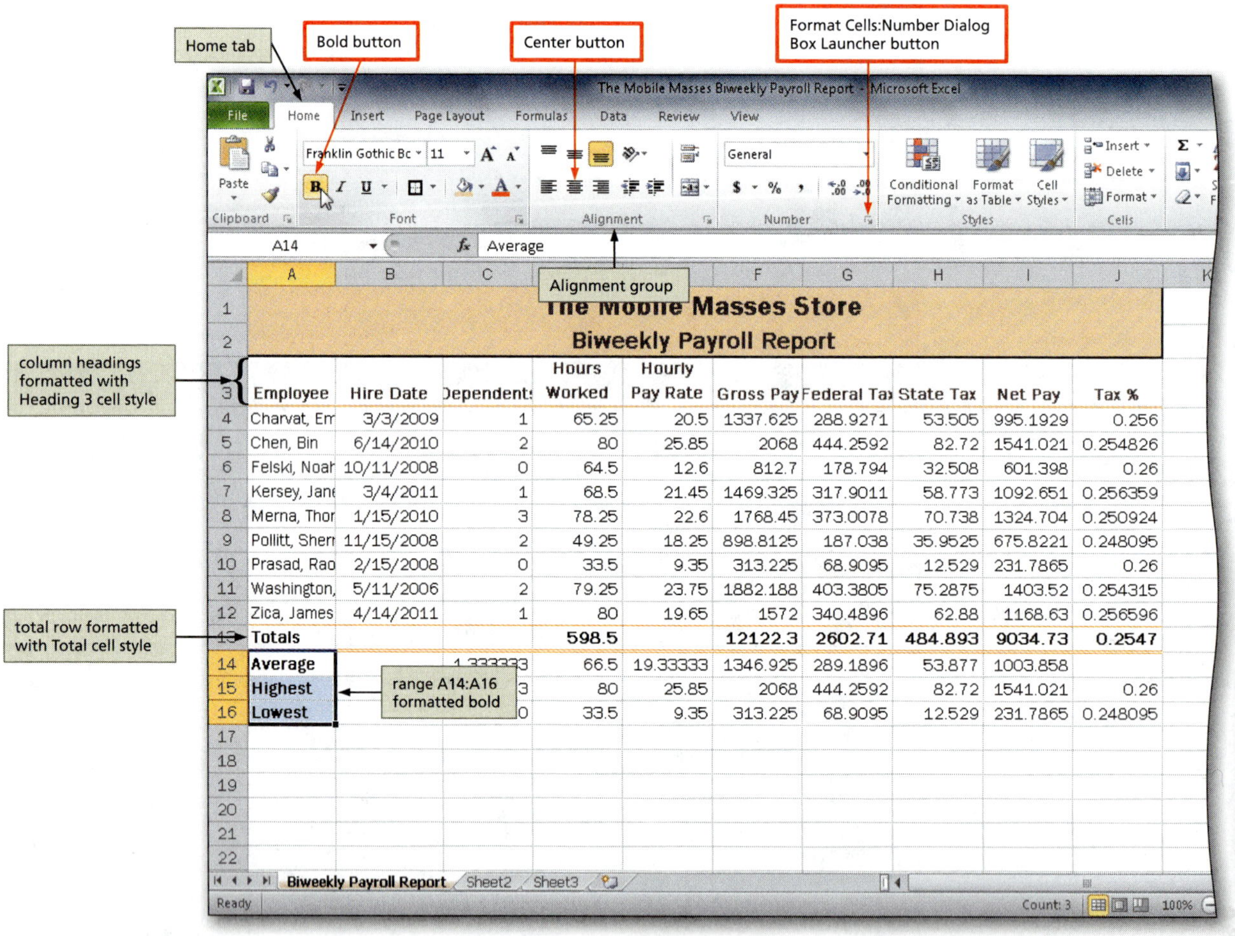

Figure 2–38

To Format Dates and Center Data in Cells

With the column titles and total rows formatted, the next step is to format the dates in column B and center the dependents in column C. The following steps format the dates in the range B4:B12 and center the data in the range C4:C12.

1

- Select the range to contain the new date format, cells B4:B12 in this case.
- Click the Format Cells: Number Dialog Box Launcher (Home tab | Number group) to display the Format Cells dialog box.
- If necessary, click the Number tab (Format Cells dialog box), click Date in the Category list, and then click 3/14/01 in the Type list to choose the format for the selected range (Figure 2–39).

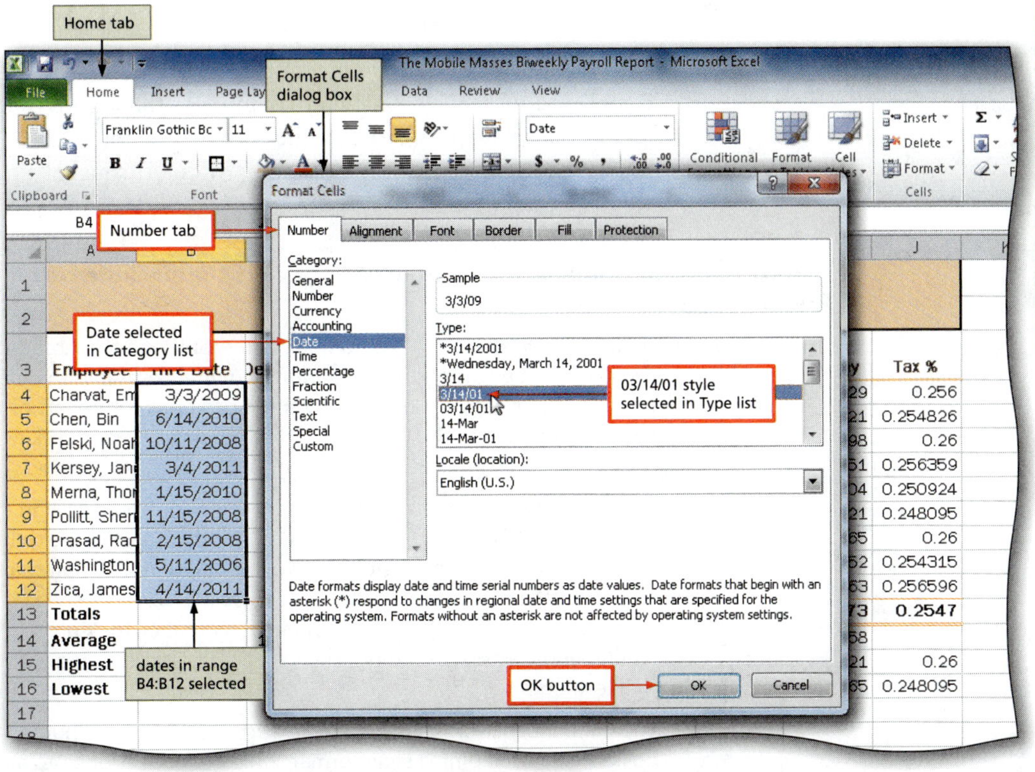

Figure 2–39

2

- Click the OK button (Format Cells dialog box) to format the dates in the current column using the selected date format style.

3

- Select the range C4:C12 and then click the Center button (Home tab | Alignment group) to center the data in the selected range.
- Select cell E4 to deselect the selected range (Figure 2–40).

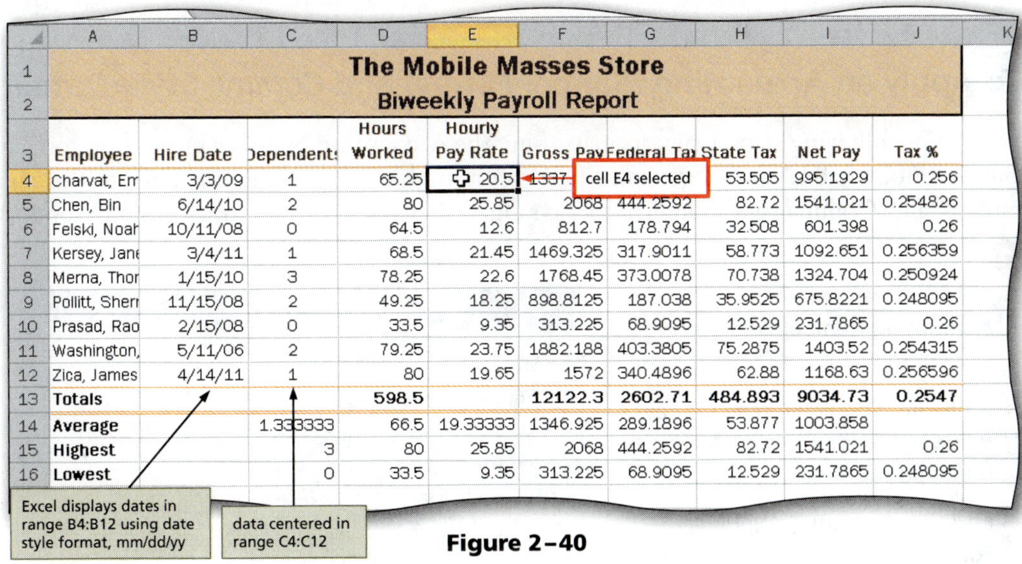

Figure 2–40

Q&A

Can I format an entire column at once?

Yes. Rather than selecting the range B4:B12 in Step 1, you could have clicked the column B heading immediately above cell B1, and then clicked the Center button (Home tab | Alignment group). In this case, all cells in column B down to the last cell in the worksheet would have been formatted to use center alignment. This same procedure could have been used to format the dates in column C.

Other Ways

1. Right-click range, click Format Cells on shortcut menu, click appropriate tab (Format Cells dialog box), click desired format, click OK button
2. Press CTRL+1, click appropriate tab (Format Cells dialog box), click desired format, click OK button

Formatting Numbers Using the Ribbon

As shown in Figure 2–30b on page EX 92, the worksheet is formatted to resemble an accounting report. For example, in columns E through I, the numbers in the first row (row 4), the totals row (row 13), and the rows below the totals (rows 14 through 16) have dollar signs, while the remaining numbers (rows 5 through 12) in column E through column I do not.

Plan Ahead

Determine proper formatting for cells that include currency and other numeric amounts.

- To append a dollar sign to a number, you should use the Accounting number format. Excel displays numbers using the **Accounting number format** with a dollar sign to the left of the number, inserts a comma every three positions to the left of the decimal point, and displays numbers to the nearest cent (hundredths place). Clicking the Accounting Number Format button (Home tab | Number group) assigns the desired Accounting number format.
- When you use the Accounting Number Format button to assign the Accounting number format, Excel displays a **fixed dollar sign** to the far left in the cell, often with spaces between it and the first digit. To assign a **floating dollar sign** that appears immediately to the left of the first digit with no spaces, use the Currency style (Format Cells dialog box). Whether you use the Accounting number format or the Currency style format depends on a number of factors, including the preference of your organization, industry standards, and the aesthetics of the worksheet.
- The Comma style format is used to instruct Excel to display numbers with commas and no dollar signs. The **Comma style format**, which can be assigned to a range of cells by clicking the Comma Style button (Home tab | Number group), inserts a comma every three positions to the left of the decimal point and causes numbers to be displayed to the nearest hundredths.

To Apply an Accounting Number Format and Comma Style Format Using the Ribbon

The following steps assign formats using the Accounting Number Format button and the Comma Style button (Home tab | Number group). The Accounting Number format is applied to the currency amounts in rows 4 and 13. The Comma style is applied to the range E4:I12 and to column D (Hours Worked).

1

- Select the range to contain the Accounting Number Format, cells E4:I4 in this case.
- While holding down the CTRL key, select the range F13:I13 to select the nonadjacent range.
- Click the Accounting Number Format button (Home tab | Number group) to apply the Accounting number format with fixed dollar signs to the selected nonadjacent ranges (Figure 2–41).

Q&A What is the effect of applying the Accounting number format?

The Accounting Number Format button assigns a fixed dollar sign to the numbers in the ranges E4:I4 and F13:I13. In each cell in these ranges, Excel displays the dollar sign to the far left with spaces between it and the first digit in the cell.

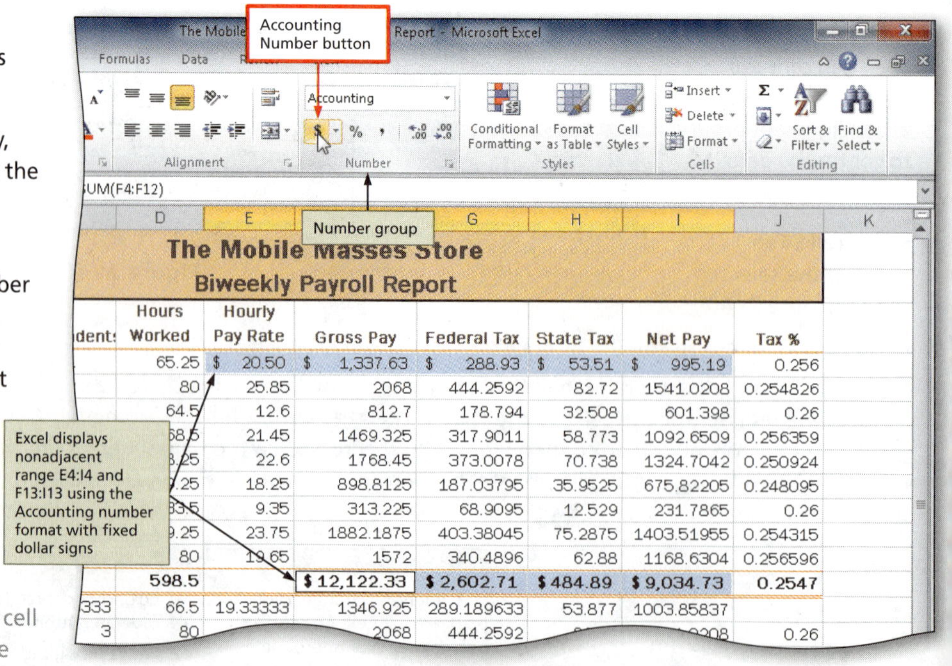

Figure 2–41

2

- Select the range to contain the Comma style format, cells E5:I12 in this case.
- Click the Comma Style button (Home tab | Number group) to assign the Comma style format to the selected range (Figure 2–42).

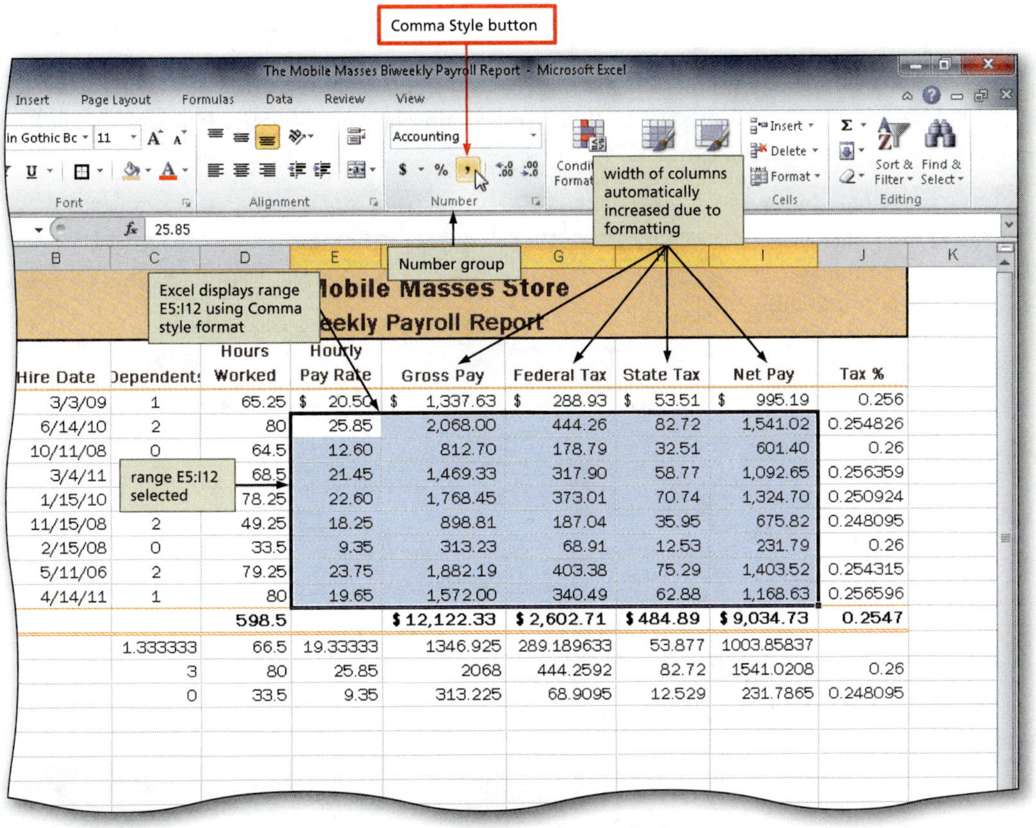

Figure 2–42

3

- Select the range to contain the Comma style format, cells D4:D16 in this case.
- Click the Comma Style button (Home tab | Number group) to assign the Comma style format to the selected range (Figure 2–43).

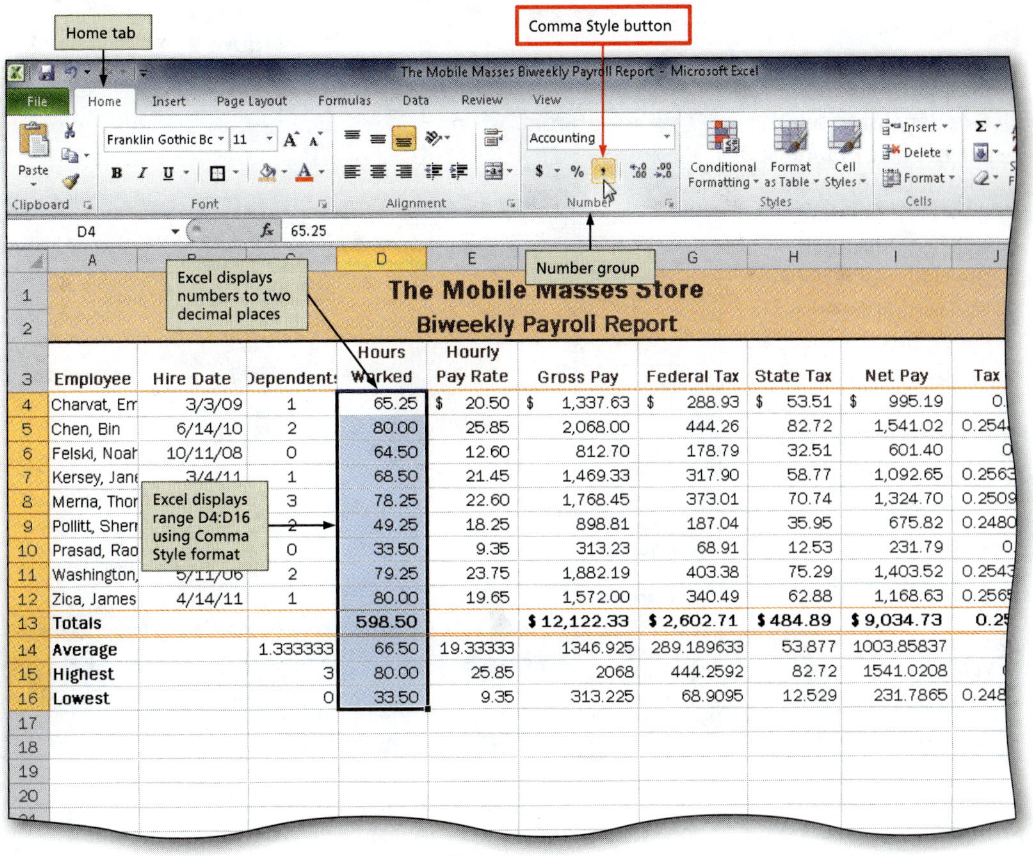

Figure 2–43

To Apply a Currency Style Format with a Floating Dollar Sign Using the Format Cells Dialog Box

The following steps use the Format Cells dialog box to apply the Currency style format with a floating dollar sign to the numbers in the range E14:I16.

1

- Select the range E14:I16 and then click the Format Cells: Number Dialog Box Launcher (Home tab | Number group) to display the Format Cells dialog box.
- If necessary, click the Number tab (Format Cells dialog box) to display the Number tab (Format Cells dialog box) (Figure 2–44).

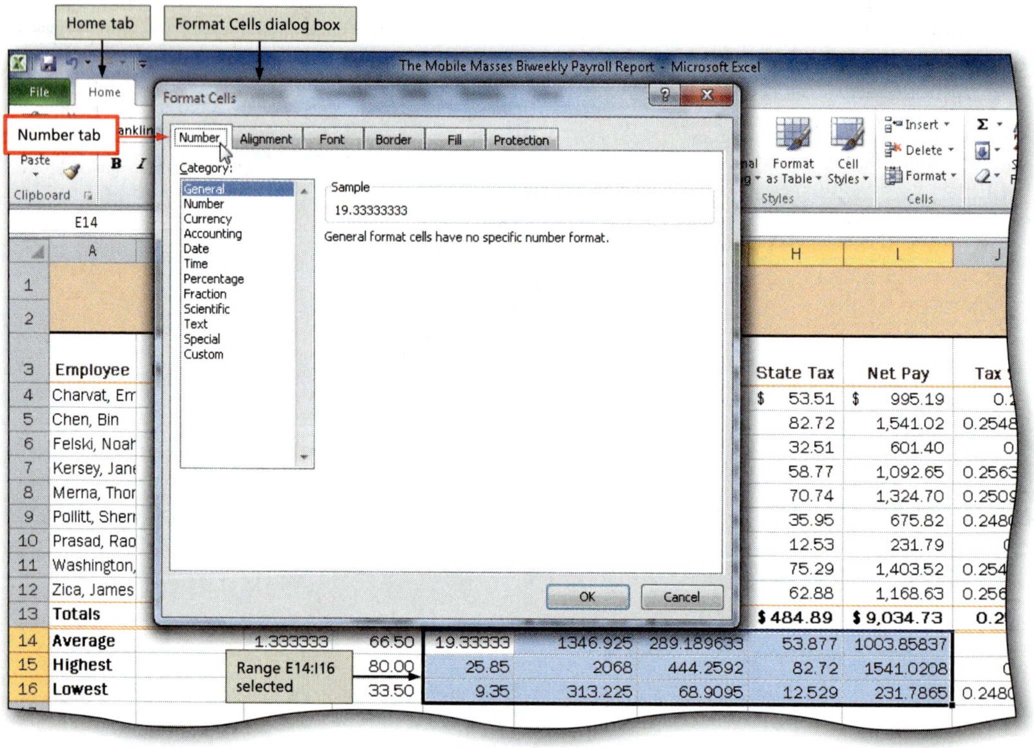

Figure 2–44

2

- Click Currency in the Category list to select the necessary number format category, and then click the third style ($1,234.10) in the Negative numbers list (Format Cells dialog box) to select the desired currency format for negative numbers (Figure 2–45).

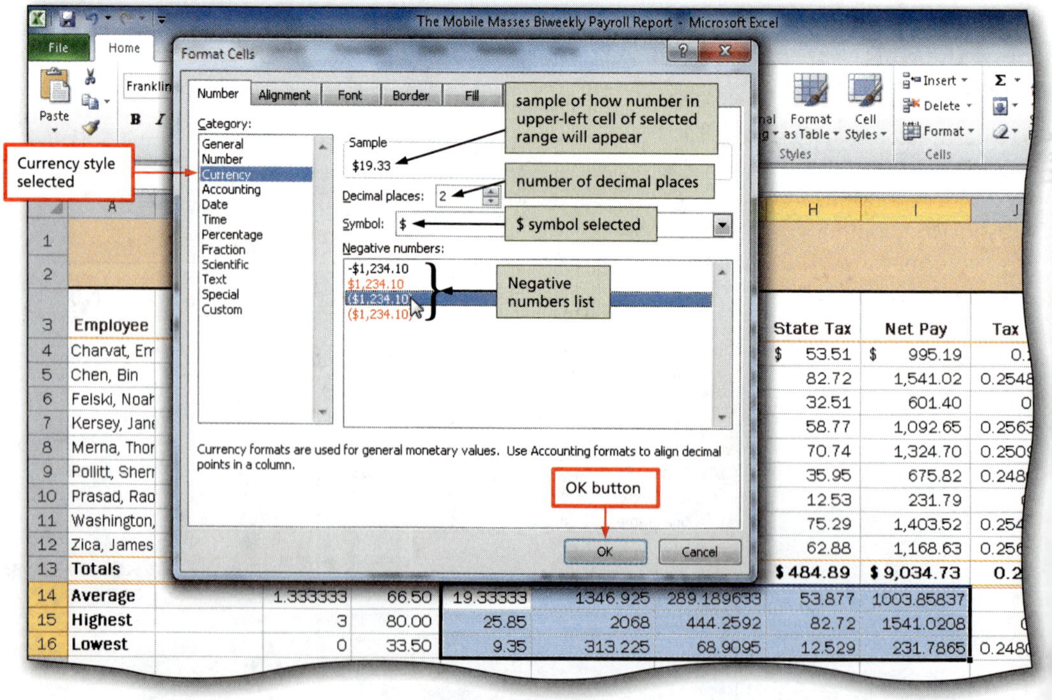

Figure 2–45

Q&A How do I select the proper format?

You can choose from 12 categories of formats. Once you select a category, you can select the number of decimal places, whether or not a dollar sign should be displayed, and how negative numbers should appear. Selecting the appropriate negative numbers format is important, because doing so adds a space to the right of the number in order to align the numbers in the worksheet on the decimal points. Some of the available negative number formats do not align the numbers in the worksheet on the decimal points.

3

- Click the OK button (Format Cells dialog box) to assign the Currency style format with a floating dollar sign to the selected range (Figure 2–46).

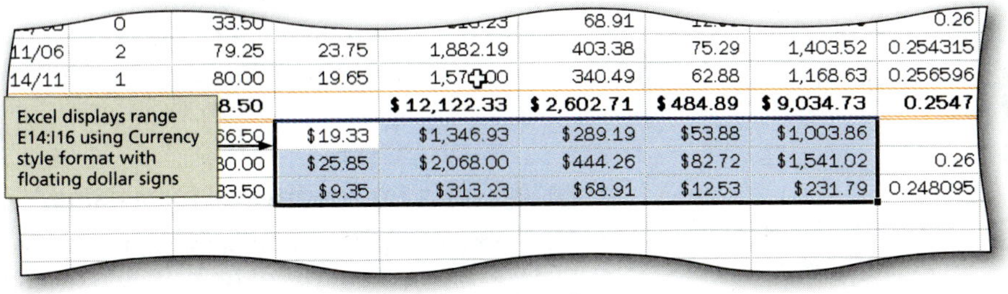

Figure 2–46

Q&A What is the difference between using the Accounting Number style and Currency style?

When using the Accounting Number Style button, recall that a floating dollar sign always appears immediately to the left of the first digit, and the fixed dollar sign always appears on the left side of the cell. Cell E4, for example, has a fixed dollar sign, while cell E14 has a floating dollar sign. The Currency style was assigned to cell E14 using the Format Cells dialog box and the result is a floating dollar sign.

Other Ways

1. Press CTRL+1, click Number tab (Format Cells dialog box), click Currency in Category list, select format, click OK button
2. Press CTRL+SHIFT+DOLLAR SIGN ($)

To Apply a Percent Style Format and Use the Increase Decimal Button

The next step is to format the tax % in column J. Currently, Excel displays the numbers in column J as a decimal fraction (for example, 0.256 in cell J4). The following steps format the range J4:J16 to the Percent style format with two decimal places.

1

- Select the range to format, cell J4:J16 in this case.
- Click the Percent Style button (Home tab | Number group) to display the numbers in the selected range as a rounded whole percent.

Q&A What is the result of clicking the Percent Style button?

The Percent Style button instructs Excel to display a value as a percentage, determined by multiplying the cell entry by 100, rounding the result to the nearest percent, and adding a percent sign. For example, when cell J4 is formatted using the Percent Style buttons, Excel displays the actual value 0.256 as 26%.

2

- Click the Increase Decimal button (Home tab | Number group) two times to display the numbers in the selected range with two decimal places (Figure 2–47).

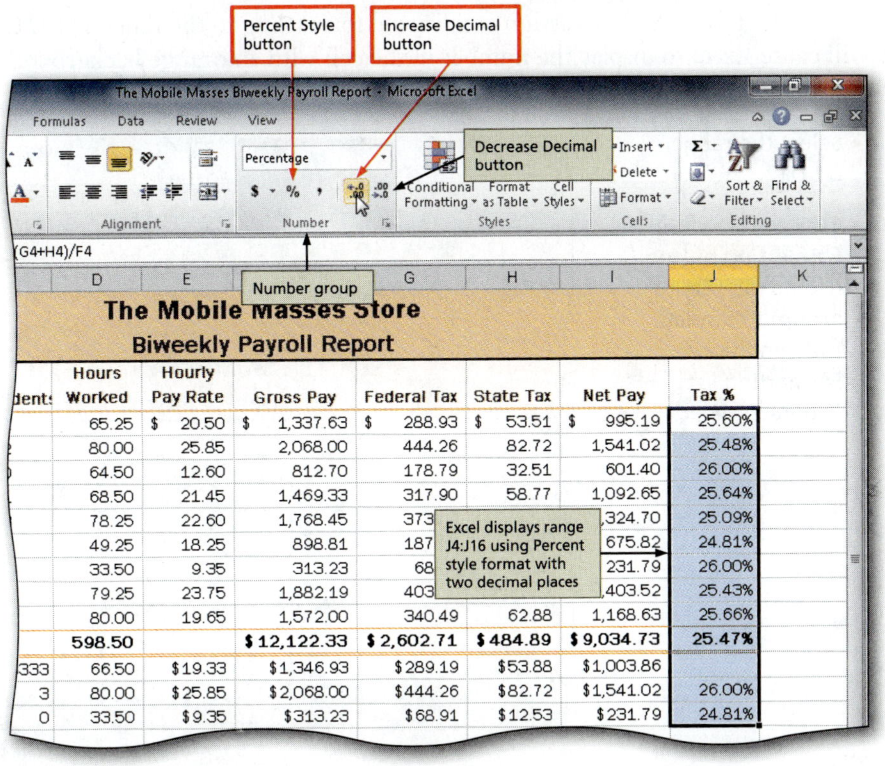

Figure 2–47

Other Ways

1. Right-click range, click Format Cells on shortcut menu, click Number tab (Format Cells dialog box), click Percentage in Category list, select format, click OK button
2. Press CTRL+1, click Number tab (Format Cells dialog box), click Percentage in Category list, select format, click OK button
3. Press CTRL+SHIFT+ percent sign (%)

Conditional Formatting

The next step is to emphasize the values greater than 70 in column D by formatting them to appear with an orange background and white font color (Figure 2–48).

Plan Ahead

Establish rules for conditional formatting.

- Excel lets you apply formatting that appears only when the value in a cell meets conditions that you specify. This type of formatting is called **conditional formatting**. You can apply conditional formatting to a cell, a range of cells, the entire worksheet, or the entire workbook. Usually, you apply conditional formatting to a range of cells that contains values you want to highlight, if conditions warrant.
- A **condition**, which is made up of two values and a relational operator, is true or false for each cell in the range. If the condition is true, then Excel applies the formatting. If the condition is false, then Excel suppresses the formatting. What makes conditional formatting so powerful is that the cell's appearance can change as you enter new values in the worksheet.
- As with worksheet formatting, follow the less-is-more rule when considering conditional formatting. Use conditional formatting to make cells and ranges stand out and raise attention. Too much conditional formatting can result in confusion for the reader of the worksheet.

BTW

Conditional Formatting
You can assign any format to a cell, a range of cells, a worksheet, or an entire workbook conditionally. If the value of the cell changes and no longer meets the specified condition, Excel suppresses the conditional formatting.

To Apply Conditional Formatting

The following steps assign conditional formatting to the range D4:D12, so that any cell value greater than 70 will cause Excel to display the number in the cell with an orange background and a white font color.

1

- Select the range D4:D12.
- Click the Conditional Formatting button (Home tab | Styles group) to display the Conditional Formatting list (Figure 2–48).

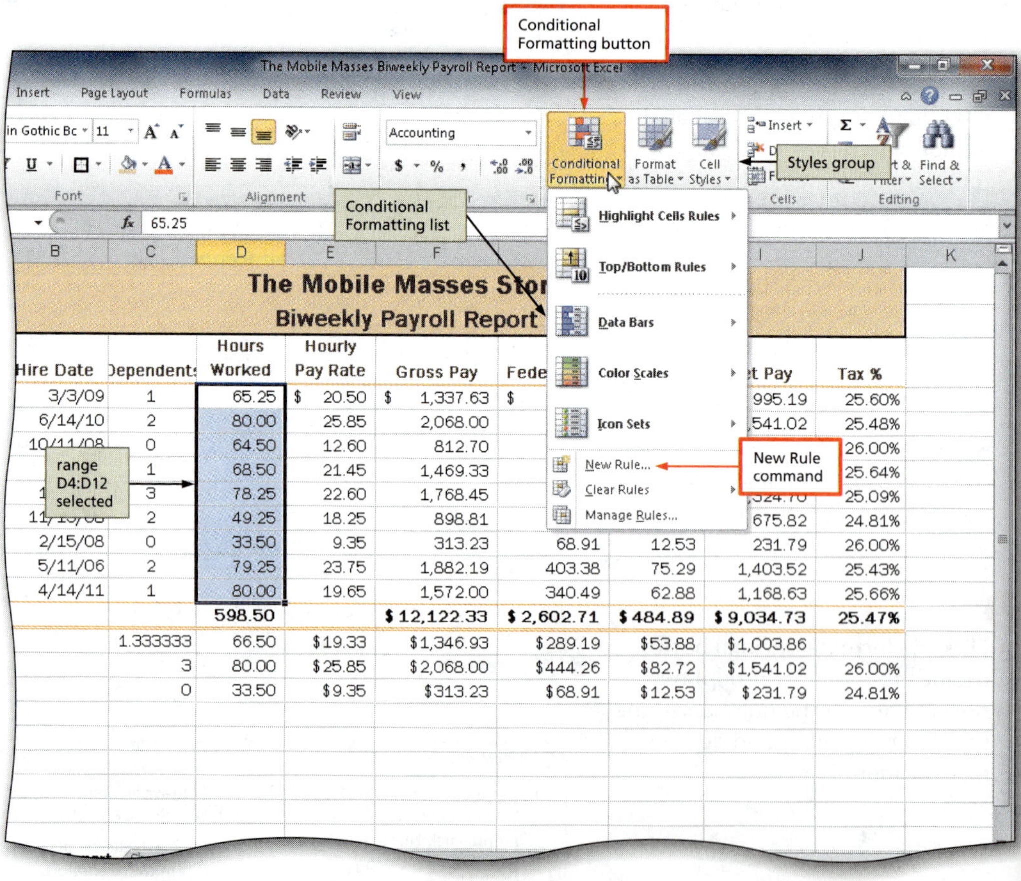

Figure 2–48

2

- Click New Rule in the Conditional Formatting list to display the New Formatting Rule dialog box.
- Click 'Format only cells that contain' in the Select a Rule Type area (New Formatting Rule dialog box) to change the 'Edit the Rule Description' area.
- In the 'Edit the Rule Description' area, click the box arrow in the relational operator box (second text box) to display a list of relational operators, and then select greater than to select the desired operator.

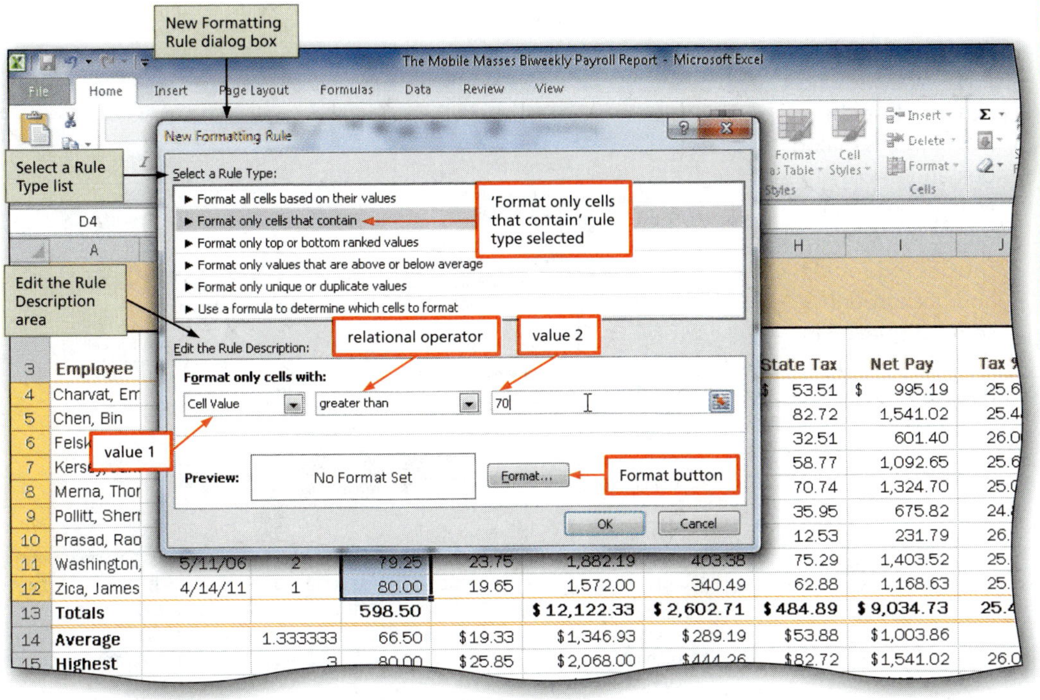

Figure 2–49

- Select the rightmost box, and then type 70 in the box in the 'Edit the Rule Description' area to enter the second value of the rule description (Figure 2–49).

Q&A What do the changes in the 'Edit the Rule Description' indicate?

The 'Edit the Rule Description' area allows you to view and edit the rules for the conditional format. In this case, reading the area indicates that Excel should conditionally format only cells with cell values greater than 70.

3

- Click the Format button (New Formatting Rule dialog box) to display the Format Cells dialog box.
- If necessary, click the Font tab. Click the Color box arrow (Format Cells dialog box) to display the Color gallery and then click White, Background 1 (column 1, row 1) in the Color gallery to select the font color.
- Click the Fill tab (Format Cells dialog box) to display the Fill sheet and then click the orange color in column 5, row 5 to select the background color (Figure 2–50).

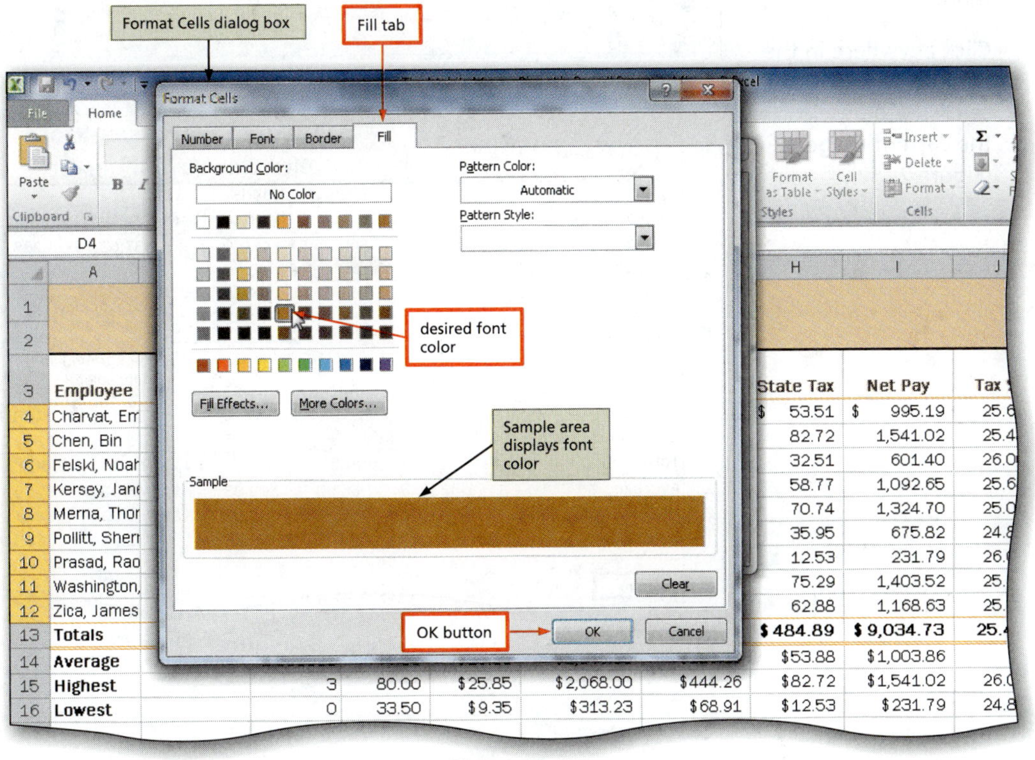

Figure 2–50

4

- Click the OK button (Format Cells dialog box) to close the Format Cells dialog box and display the New Formatting Rule dialog box with the desired font and background colors displayed in the Preview box (Figure 2–51).

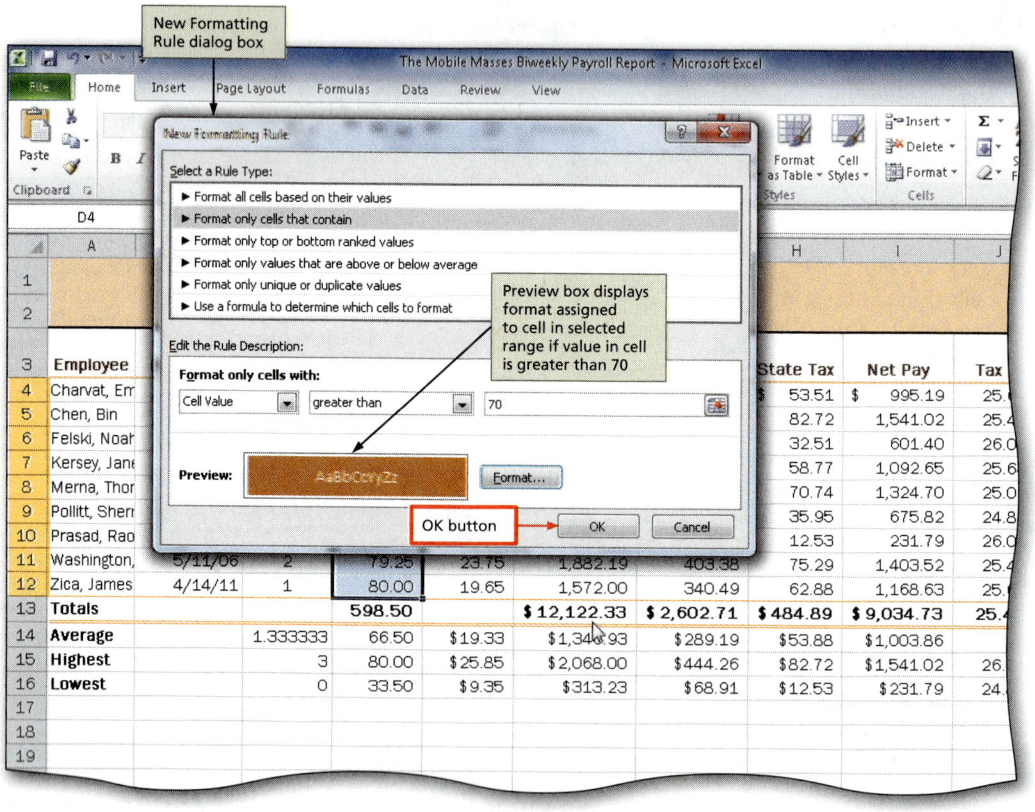

Figure 2–51

5

- Click the OK button to assign the conditional format to the selected range.
- Click anywhere in the worksheet, such as cell A18, to deselect the current range (Figure 2–52).

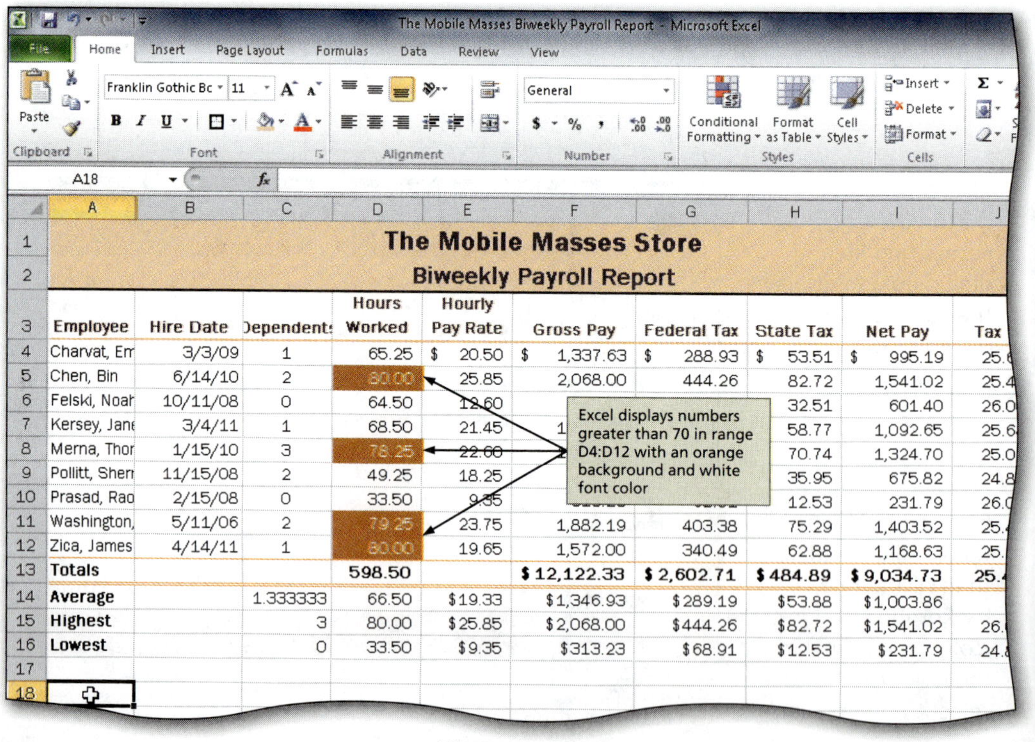

Figure 2–52

Conditional Formatting Operators

As shown in Figure 2–49 on page EX 105, the second text box in the New Formatting Rule dialog box allows you to select a relational operator, such as less than, to use in the condition. The eight different relational operators from which you can choose for conditional formatting in the New Formatting Rule dialog box are summarized in Table 2–5.

Table 2–5 Summary of Conditional Formatting Relational Operators

Relational Operator	Description
between	Cell value is between two numbers.
not between	Cell value is not between two numbers.
equal to	Cell value is equal to a number.
not equal to	Cell value is not equal to a number.
greater than	Cell value is greater than a number.
less than	Cell value is less than a number.
greater than or equal to	Cell value is greater than or equal to a number.
less than or equal to	Cell value is less than or equal to a number.

Changing the Widths of Columns and Heights of Rows

When Excel starts and displays a blank worksheet on the screen, all of the columns have a default width of 8.43 characters, or 64 pixels. These values may change depending on the theme applied to the workbook. For example, in this chapter, the Trek theme was applied to the workbook, resulting in columns having a default width of 8.11 characters. A character is defined as a letter, number, symbol, or punctuation mark in 11-point Calibri font, the default font used by Excel. An average of 8.43 characters in 11-point Calibri font will fit in a cell.

Another measure of the height and width of cells is pixels, which is short for picture element. A **pixel** is a dot on the screen that contains a color. The size of the dot is based on your screen's resolution. At the resolution of 1024 × 768 used in the Office and Windows chapters in this book, 1024 pixels appear across the screen and 768 pixels appear down the screen for a total of 786,432 pixels. It is these 786,432 pixels that form the font and other items you see on the screen.

The default row height in a blank worksheet is 15 points (or 20 pixels). Recall from Excel Chapter 1 that a point is equal to 1/72 of an inch. Thus, 15 points is equal to about 1/5 of an inch. You can change the width of the columns or height of the rows at any time to make the worksheet easier to read or to ensure that Excel displays an entry properly in a cell.

BTW

Hidden Rows and Columns

For some people, trying to unhide a range of columns using the mouse can be frustrating. An alternative is to use the keyboard: select the columns to the right and left of the hidden columns and then press CTRL+SHIFT+) (RIGHT PARENTHESIS). To use the keyboard to hide a range of columns, press CTRL+0 (ZERO). You also can use the keyboard to unhide a range of rows by selecting the rows immediately above and below the hidden rows and then pressing CTRL+SHIFT+((LEFT PARENTHESIS). To use the keyboard to hide a range of rows, press CTRL+9.

To Change the Widths of Columns

When changing the column width, you can set the width manually or you can instruct Excel to size the column to best fit. **Best fit** means that the width of the column will be increased or decreased so that the widest entry will fit in the column. Sometimes, you may prefer more or less white space in a column than best fit provides. To change the white space, Excel allows you to change column widths manually.

When the format you assign to a cell causes the entry to exceed the width of a column, Excel autor[illegible] changes the column width to best fit. If you do not assign a format to a cell or cells in a column, th[illegible] will remain 8.43 characters. To set a column width to best fit, double-click the right bound[illegible] above row 1.

The steps on the following pages change the column widths: column A [illegible] 10.22 characters; and columns D, E, and J to 7.56 characters.

1

- Drag through column headings A, B, and C above row 1 to select the columns.
- Point to the boundary on the right side of column heading C to cause the mouse pointer to become a split double arrow (Figure 2–53).

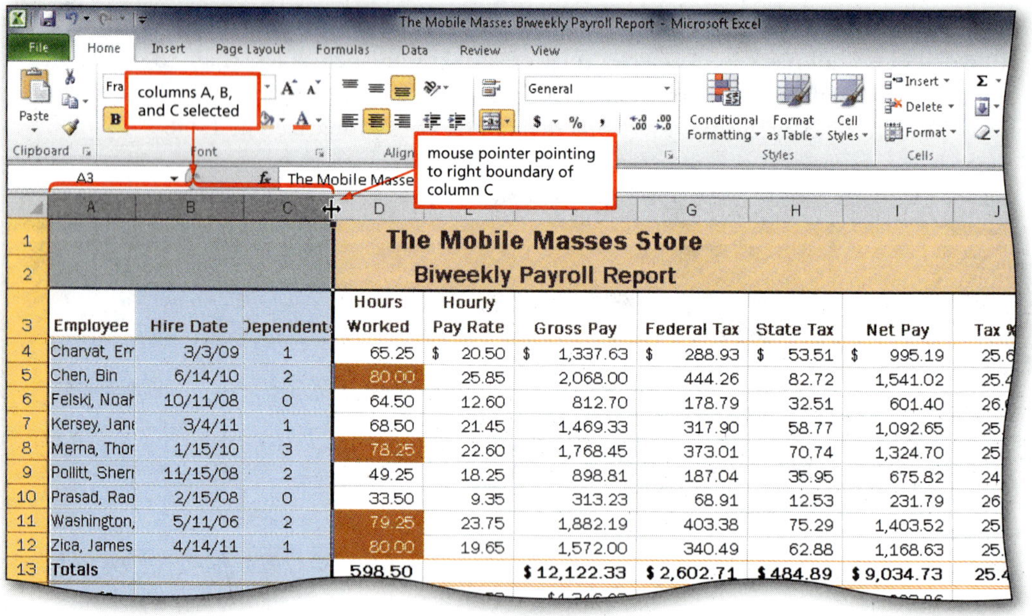

Figure 2–53

Q&A What if I want to make a large change to the column width?

If you want to increase or decrease column width significantly, you can right-click a column heading and then use the Column Width command on the shortcut menu to change the column's width. To use this command, however, you must select one or more entire columns.

2

- Double-click the right boundary of column heading C to change the width of the selected columns to best fit.
- Point to the boundary on the right side of the column H heading above row 1.
- When the mouse pointer changes to a split double arrow, drag until the ScreenTip indicates Width: 10.22 (99 pixels). Do not release the mouse button (Figure 2–54).

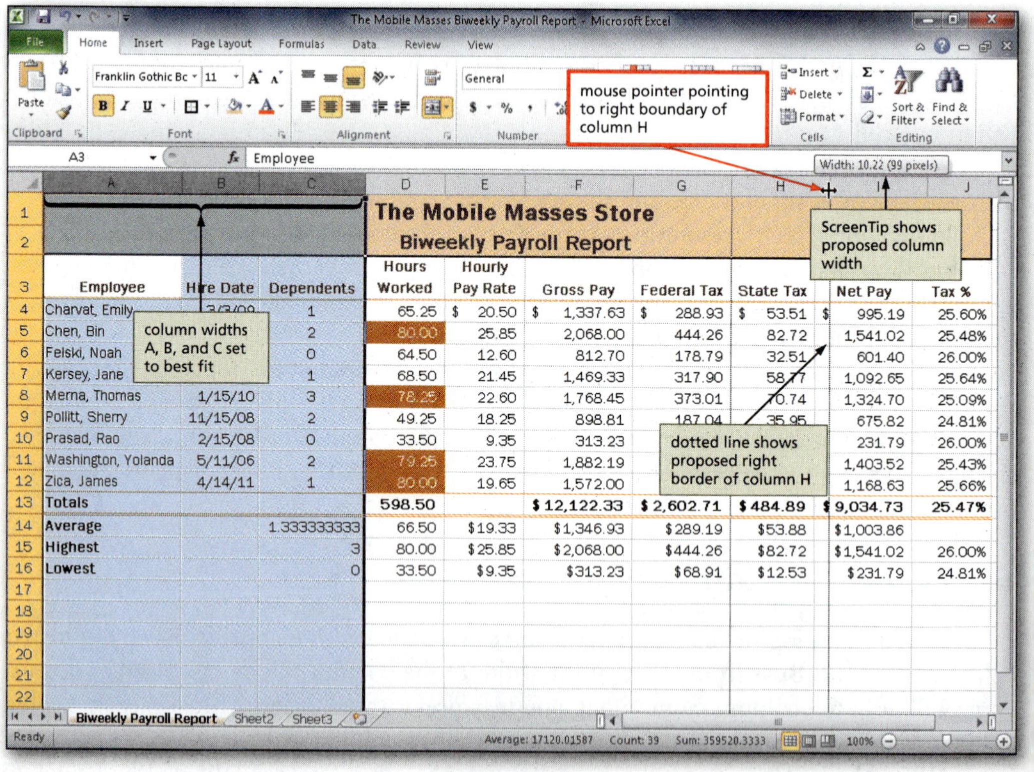

Figure 2–54

Q&A What happens if I change the column width to zero (0)?

f you … column w… the column is … be relevant to a p… instruct Excel to display… column heading boundary …nique you can use to hide data that might not …a that you do not want others to see. To …he mouse pointer to the right of the … located and then drag to the right.

3

- Release the mouse button to change the column width.
- Click the column D heading above row 1 to select the column.
- While holding down the CTRL key, click the column E heading and then the column J heading above row 1 so that nonadjacent columns are selected (Figure 2–55).

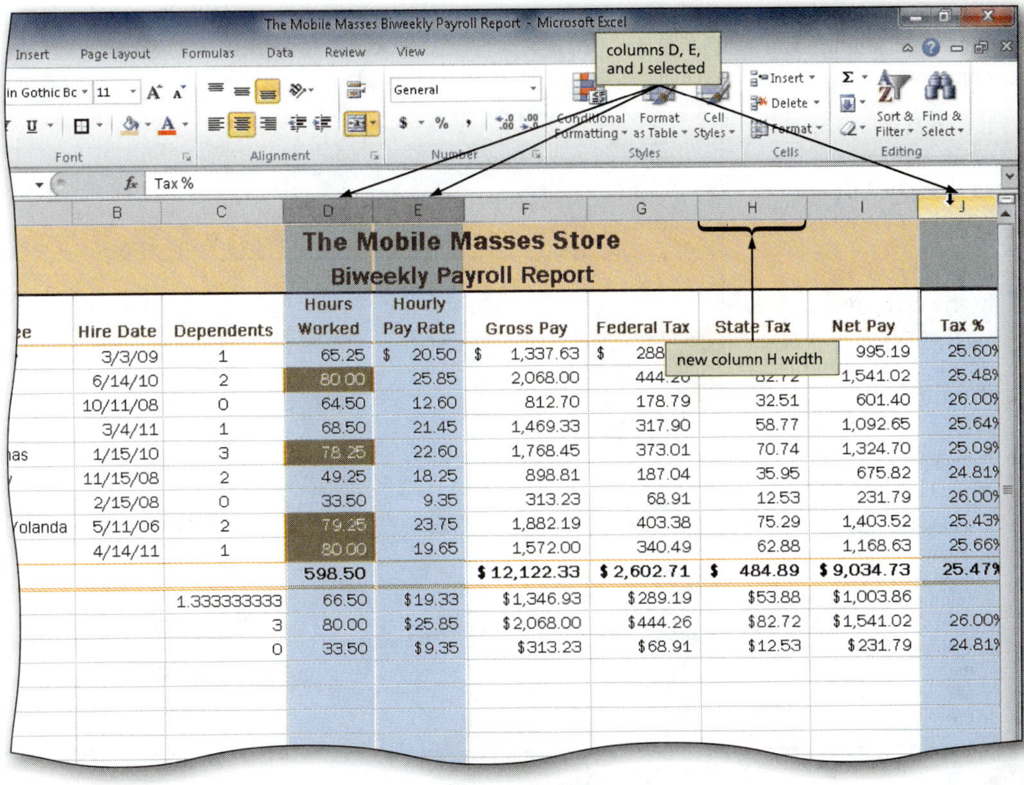

Figure 2–55

4

- If necessary, scroll the worksheet to the right so that the right border of column J is visible. Point to the boundary on the right side of the column J heading above row 1.
- Drag until the ScreenTip indicates Width: 7.56 (75 pixels). Do not release the mouse button (Figure 2–56).

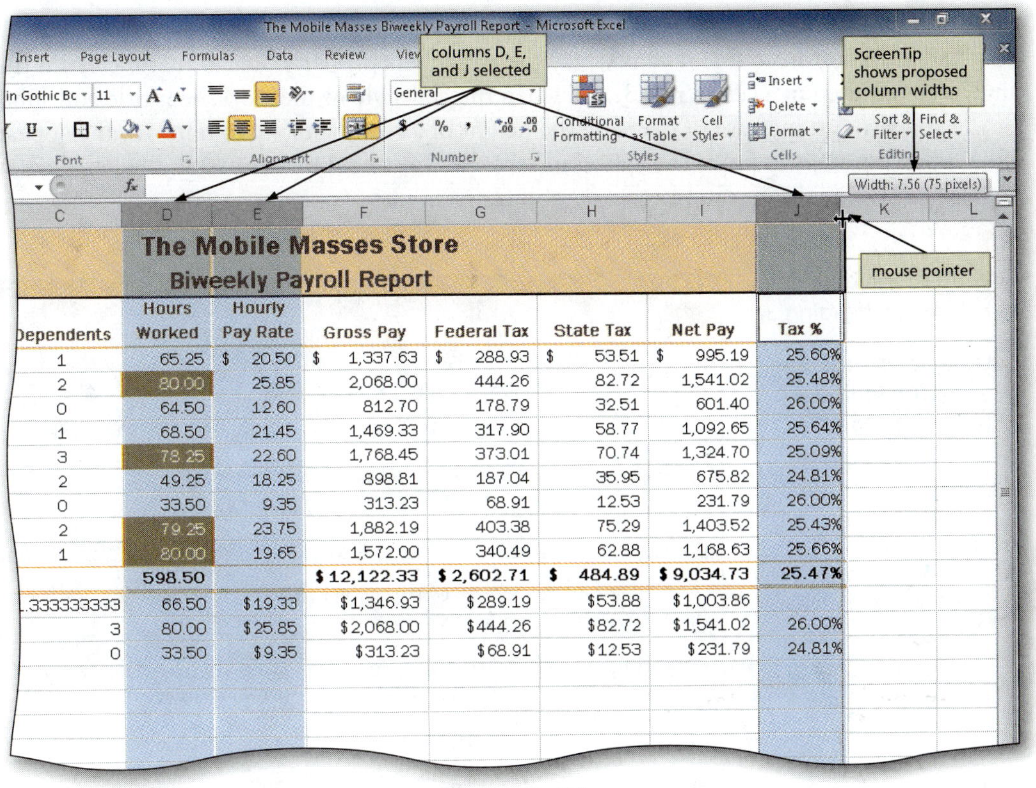

Figure 2–56

5

- Release the mouse button to change the column widths.
- If necessary, scroll the worksheet to the left so that the left border of column A is visible.
- Click anywhere in the worksheet, such as cell A18, to deselect the columns (Figure 2–57).

Other Ways

1. Right-click column heading or drag through multiple column headings and right-click, click Column Width on shortcut menu, enter desired column width, click OK button

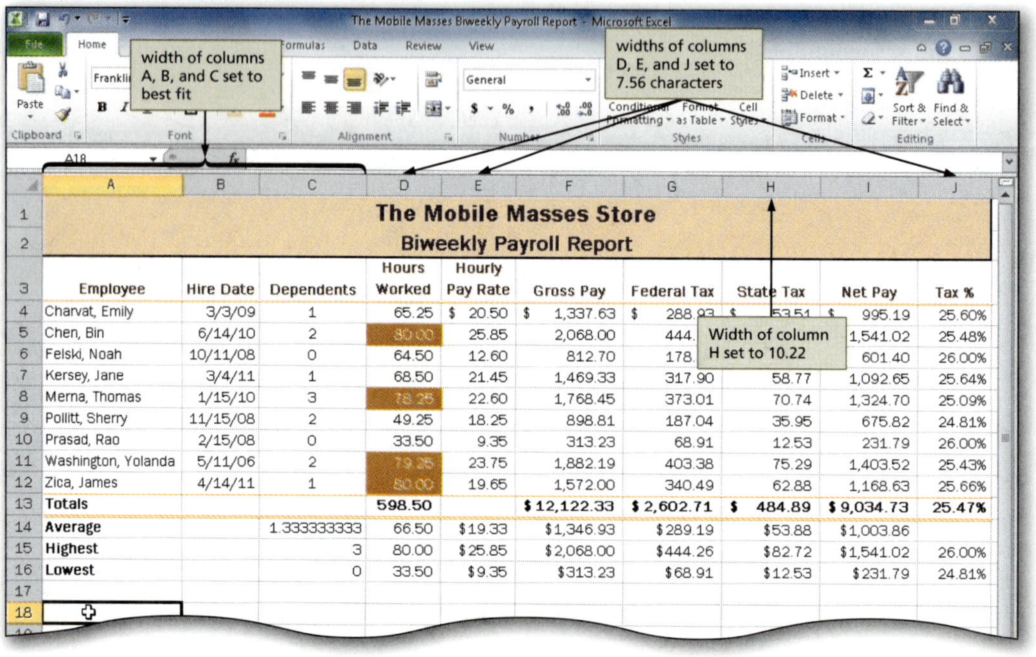

Figure 2–57

To Change the Heights of Rows

When you increase the font size of a cell entry, such as the title in cell A1, Excel automatically increases the row height to best fit so that it can display the characters properly. Recall that Excel did this earlier when multiple lines were entered in a cell in row 3, and when the cell style of the worksheet title and subtitle was changed.

You also can increase or decrease the height of a row manually to improve the appearance of the worksheet. The following steps improve the appearance of the worksheet by increasing the height of row 3 to 48.00 points and increasing the height of row 14 to 27.00 points.

1

- Point to the boundary below row heading 3.
- Drag down until the ScreenTip indicates Height: 48.00 (64 pixels). Do not release the mouse button (Figure 2–58).

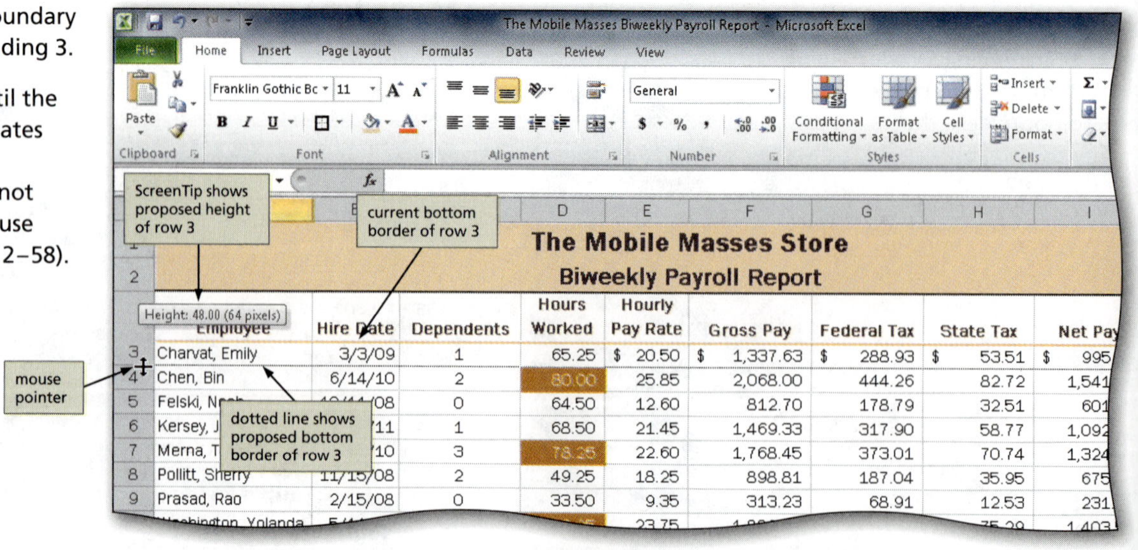

Figure 2–58

2

- Release the mouse button to change the row height.
- Point to the boundary below row heading 14.
- Drag down until the ScreenTip indicates Height: 27.00 (36 pixels). Do not release the mouse button (Figure 2–59).

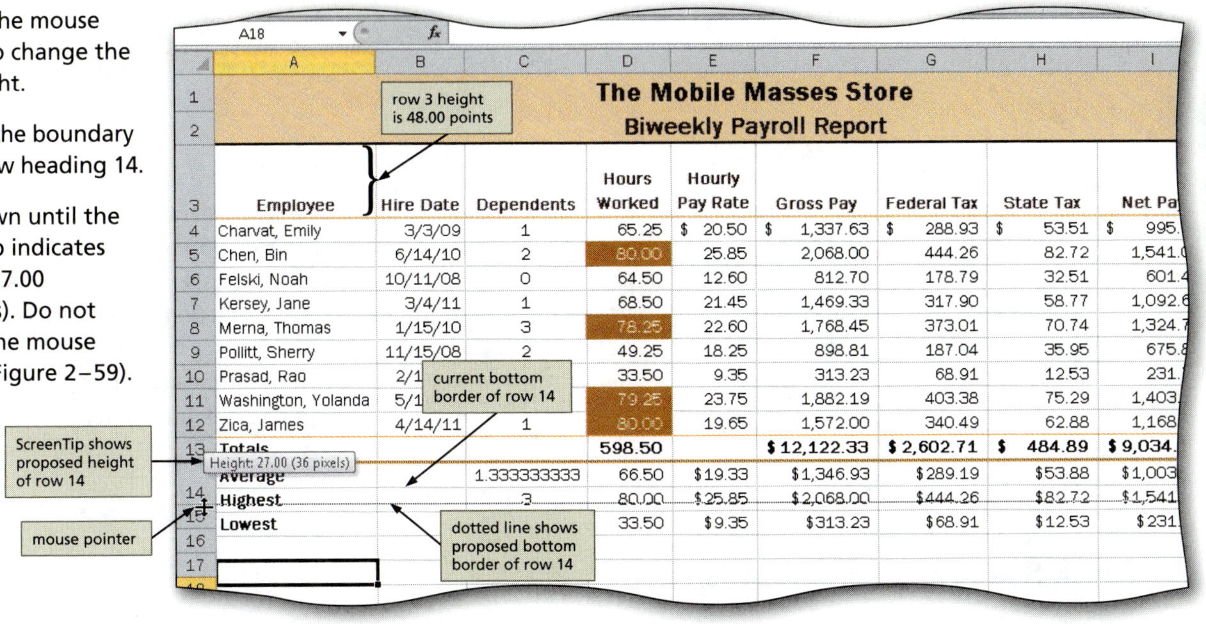

Figure 2–59

3

- Release the mouse button to change the row height.
- Click anywhere in the worksheet, such as cell A18, to deselect the current cell (Figure 2–60).

Q&A Can I hide a row?

Yes. As with column widths, when you decrease the row height to 0, the row is hidden. To instruct Excel to display a hidden row, position the mouse pointer just below the row heading boundary where the row is hidden and then drag down. To set a row height to best fit, double-click the bottom boundary of the row heading.

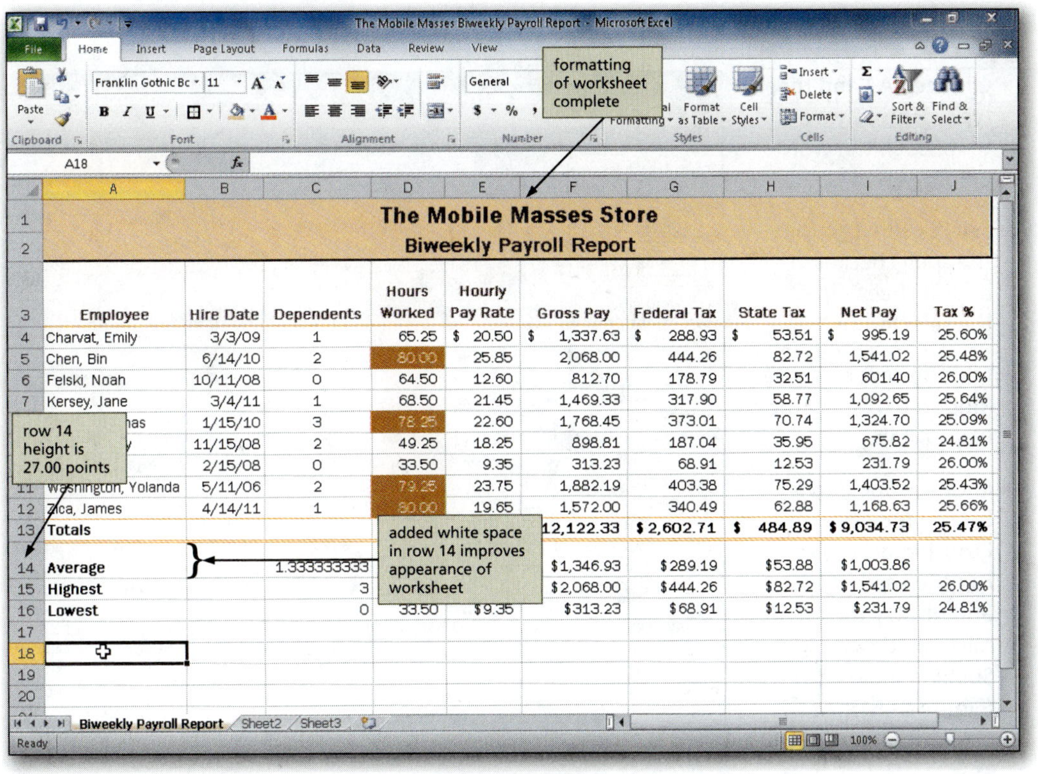

Figure 2–60

Other Ways

1. Right-click row heading or drag through multiple row headings and right-click, click Row Height on shortcut menu, enter desired row height, click OK button

Break Point: If you wish to take a break, this is a good place to do so. Be sure to save the The Mobile Masses Biweekly Payroll Report file again and then you can quit Excel. To resume at a later time, start Excel, open the file called The Mobile Masses Biweekly Payroll Report and continue following the steps from this location forward.

BTW

Spell Checking

While Excel's spell checker is a valuable tool, it is not infallible. You should proofread your workbook carefully by pointing to each word and saying it aloud as you point to it. Be mindful of misused words such as its and it's, through and though, and to and too. Nothing undermines a good impression more than a professional looking report with misspelled words.

Checking Spelling

Excel includes a **spell checker** you can use to check a worksheet for spelling errors. The spell checker looks for spelling errors by comparing words on the worksheet against words contained in its standard dictionary. If you often use specialized terms that are not in the standard dictionary, you may want to add them to a custom dictionary using the Spelling dialog box.

When the spell checker finds a word that is not in either dictionary, it displays the word in the Spelling dialog box. You then can correct it if it is misspelled.

To Check Spelling on the Worksheet

To illustrate how Excel responds to a misspelled word, the following steps misspell purposely the word, Employee, in cell A3 as the word, Empolyee, as shown in Figure 2–61.

1

- Click cell A3 and then type `Empolyee` to misspell the word Employee.
- Select cell A1 so that the spell checker begins checking at the selected cell.
- Click Review on the Ribbon to display the Review tab.
- Click the Spelling button (Review tab | Proofing group) to run the spell checker and display the misspelled word in the Spelling dialog box (Figure 2–61).

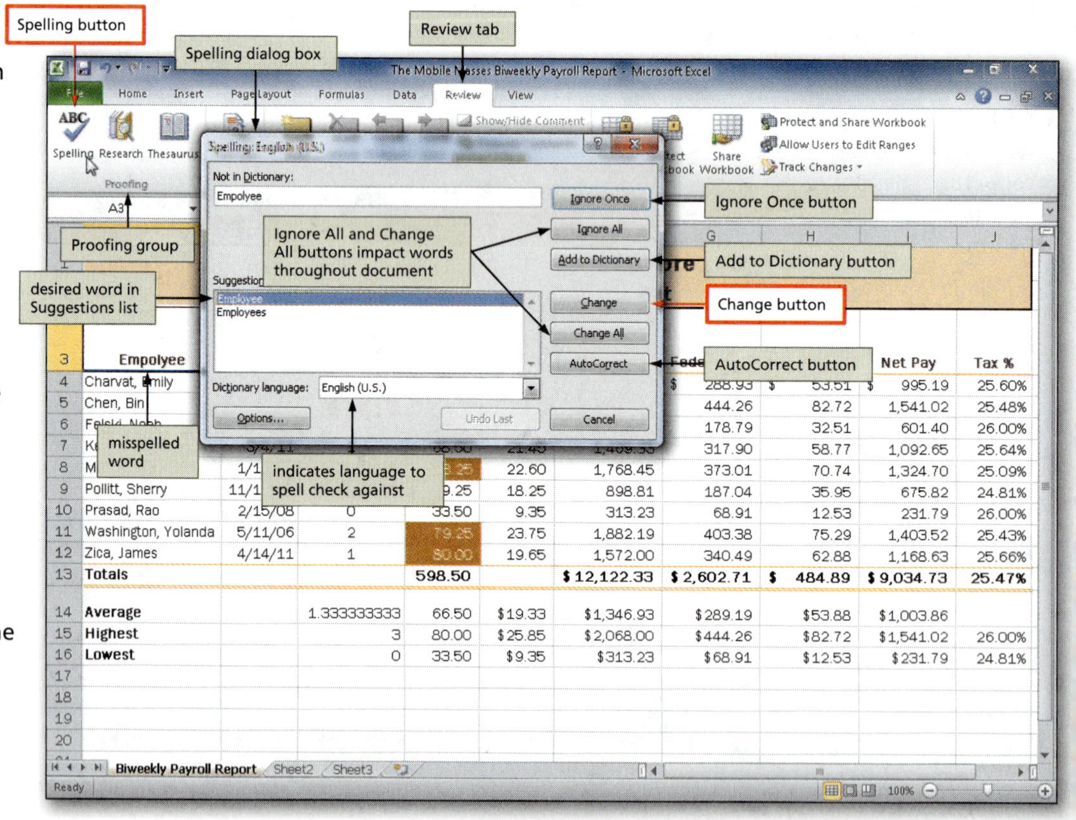

Figure 2–61

Q&A

What happens when the spell checker finds a misspelled word?

When the spell checker identifies that a cell contains a word not in its standard or custom dictionary, it selects that cell as the active cell and displays the Spelling dialog box. The Spelling dialog box lists the word not found in the dictionary and a list of suggested corrections (Figure 2–61).

2

- Click the Change button (Spelling dialog box) to change the misspelled word to the correct word (Figure 2–62).
- Click the Close button (Spelling dialog box) to close the Spelling dialog box.
- If the Microsoft Excel dialog box is displayed, click the OK button.

3

- Click anywhere in the worksheet, such as cell A18, to deselect the current cell.
- Display the Home tab.
- Click the Save button on the Quick Access Toolbar to save the workbook.

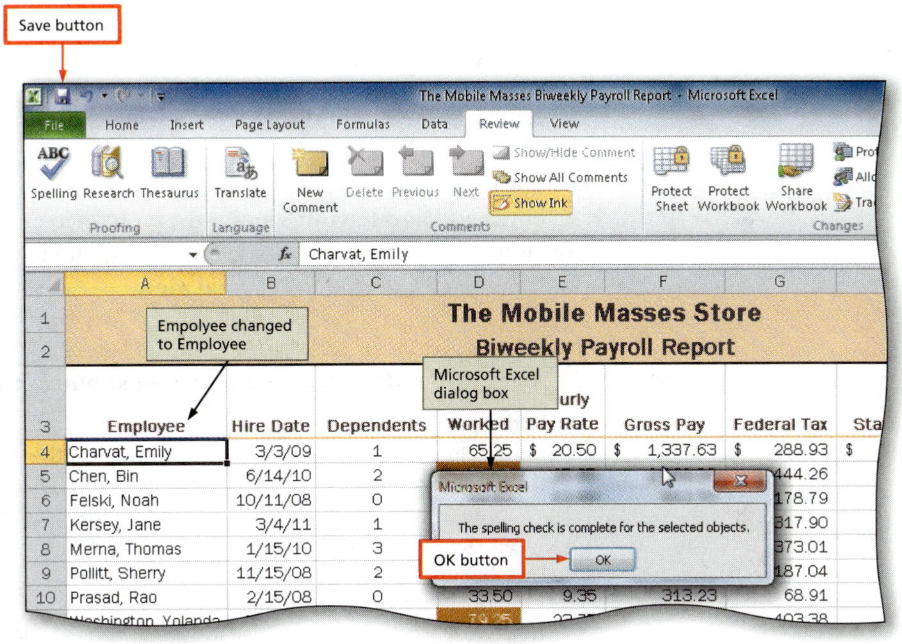

Figure 2–62

Q&A

What other actions can I take in the Spelling dialog box?

If one of the words in the Suggestions list is correct, click it and then click the Change button. If none of the suggestions is correct, type the correct word in the Not in Dictionary text box and then click the Change button. To change the word throughout the worksheet, click the Change All button instead of the Change button. To skip correcting the word, click the Ignore Once button. To have Excel ignore the word for the remainder of the worksheet, click the Ignore All button.

Other Ways

1. Press F7

Additional Spell Checker Considerations

Consider these additional guidelines when using the spell checker:

- To check the spelling of the text in a single cell, double-click the cell to make the formula bar active and then click the Spelling button (Review tab | Proofing group).
- If you select a single cell so that the formula bar is not active and then start the spell checker, Excel checks the remainder of the worksheet, including notes and embedded charts.
- If you select a cell other than cell A1 before you start the spell checker, Excel will display a dialog box when the spell checker reaches the end of the worksheet, asking if you want to continue checking at the beginning.
- If you select a range of cells before starting the spell checker, Excel checks the spelling of the words only in the selected range.
- To check the spelling of all the sheets in a workbook, right-click any sheet tab, click Select All Sheets on the sheet tab shortcut menu, and then start the spell checker.
- To add words to the dictionary such as your last name, click the Add to Dictionary button in the Spelling dialog box (Figure 2–61) when Excel identifies the word as not in the dictionary.
- Click the AutoCorrect button (Spelling dialog box) to add the misspelled word and the correct version of the word to the AutoCorrect list. For example, suppose that you misspell the word, do, as the word, dox. When the spell checker displays the Spelling dialog box with the correct word, do, in the Change to box, click the AutoCorrect button. Then, anytime in the future that you type the word dox, Excel automatically will change it to the word, do.

BTW

Error Checking

Always take the time to check the formulas of a worksheet before submitting it to your supervisor. You can check formulas by clicking the Error Checking button (Formulas tab | Formula Auditing group). You also should test the formulas by employing data that tests the limits of formulas. Experienced spreadsheet specialists spend as much time testing a workbook as they do creating it, and they do so before placing the workbook into production.

Preparing to Print the Worksheet

Excel allows for a great deal of customization in how a worksheet appears when printed. For example, the margins on the page can be adjusted. A header or footer can be added to each printed page as well. Excel also has the capability to work on the worksheet in Page Layout view. **Page Layout view** allows you to create or modify a worksheet while viewing how it will look in printed format. The default view that you have worked in up until this point in the book is called **Normal view**.

Plan Ahead

Specify how the printed worksheet should appear.

Before printing a worksheet, you should consider how the worksheet will appear when printed. In order to fit as much information on the printed page as possible, the margins of the worksheet should be set to a reasonably small width and height. While the current version of a worksheet may print on one page, you may add more data in the future that causes the worksheet to extend to multiple pages. It is, therefore, a good idea to add a page header to the worksheet that prints in the top margin of each page. A **header** is common content that prints on every page of a worksheet. Landscape orientation is a good choice for large worksheets because the printed worksheet's width is greater than its length.

To Change the Worksheet's Margins, Header, and Orientation in Page Layout View

The following steps change to Page Layout view, narrow the margins of the worksheet, change the header of the worksheet, and set the orientation of the worksheet to landscape. Often, you may want to reduce margins so that the printed worksheet better fits the page. **Margins** are those portions of a printed page outside the main body of the printed document and always are blank when printed. Recall that in Excel Chapter 1, the worksheet was printed in landscape orientation. The current worksheet also is too wide for a single page and requires landscape orientation to fit on one page in a readable manner.

1

- Click the Page Layout button on the status bar to view the worksheet in Page Layout view (Figure 2–63).

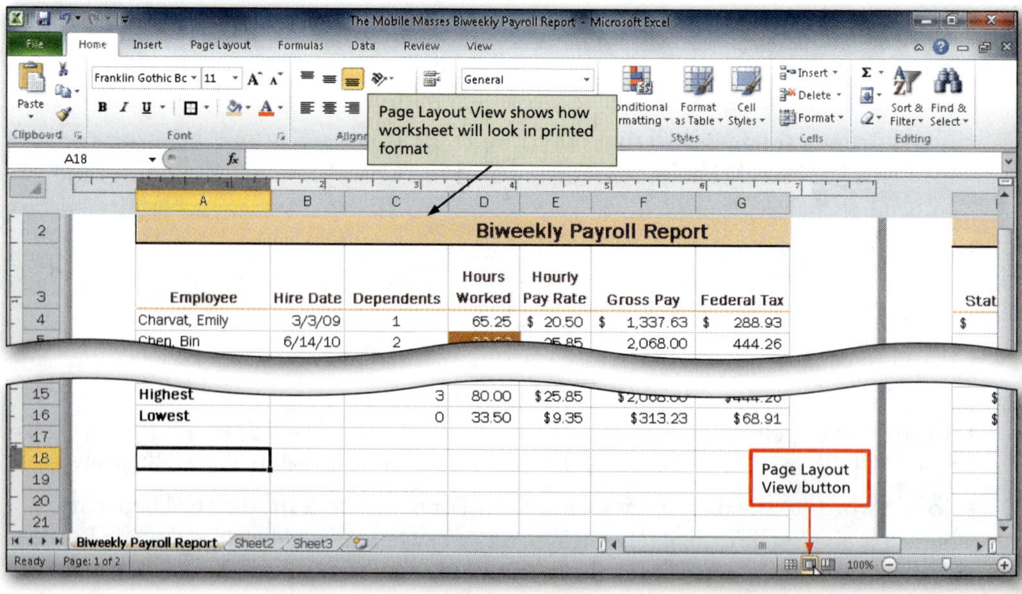

Figure 2–63

Q&A What are some key features of Page Layout view?

Page Layout view shows the worksheet divided into pages. A gray background separates each page. The white areas surrounding each page indicate the print margins. The top of each page includes a Header area, and the bottom of each page includes a Footer area. Page Layout view also includes a ruler at the top of the page that assists you in placing objects on the page, such as charts and pictures.

2

- Display the Page Layout tab.
- Click the Margins button (Page Layout tab | Page Setup group) to display the Margins gallery (Figure 2–64).

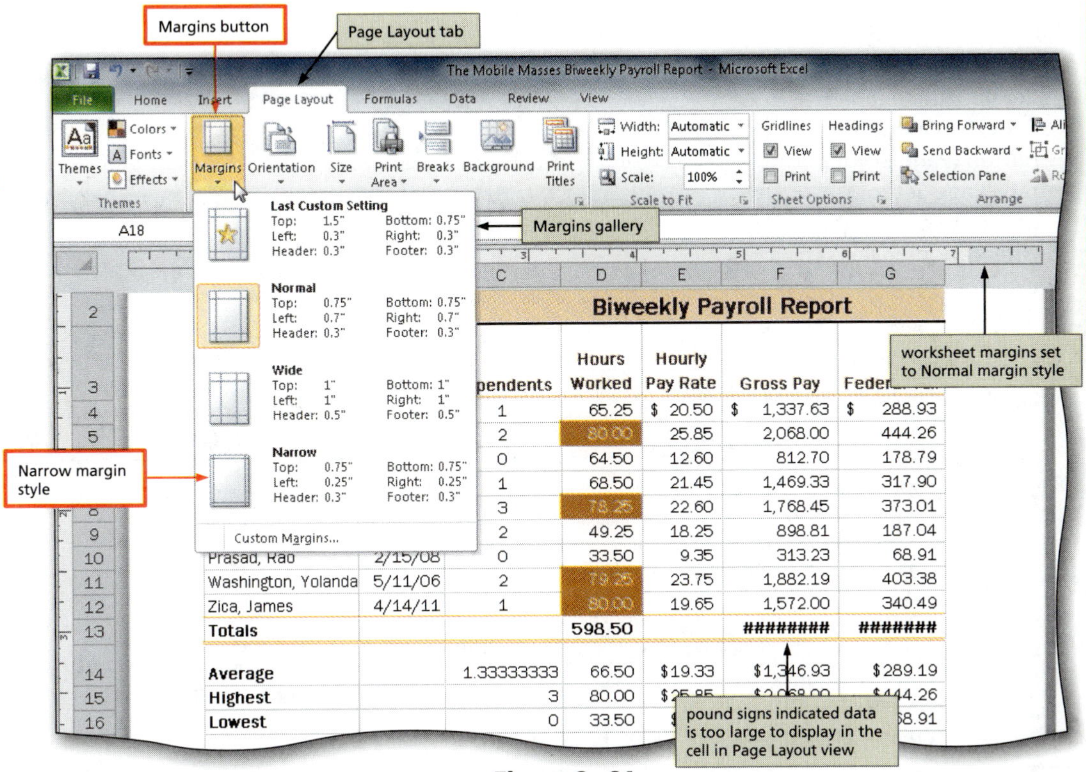

Figure 2–64

3

- Click Narrow in the Margins gallery to change the worksheet margins to the Narrow margin style.
- Drag the scroll bar on the right side of the worksheet to the top so that row 1 of the worksheet is displayed.
- Click above the worksheet title in cell A1 in the center area of the Header area.
- Type `Samuel Snyder` and then press the ENTER key. Type `Chief Financial Officer` to complete the worksheet header (Figure 2–65).

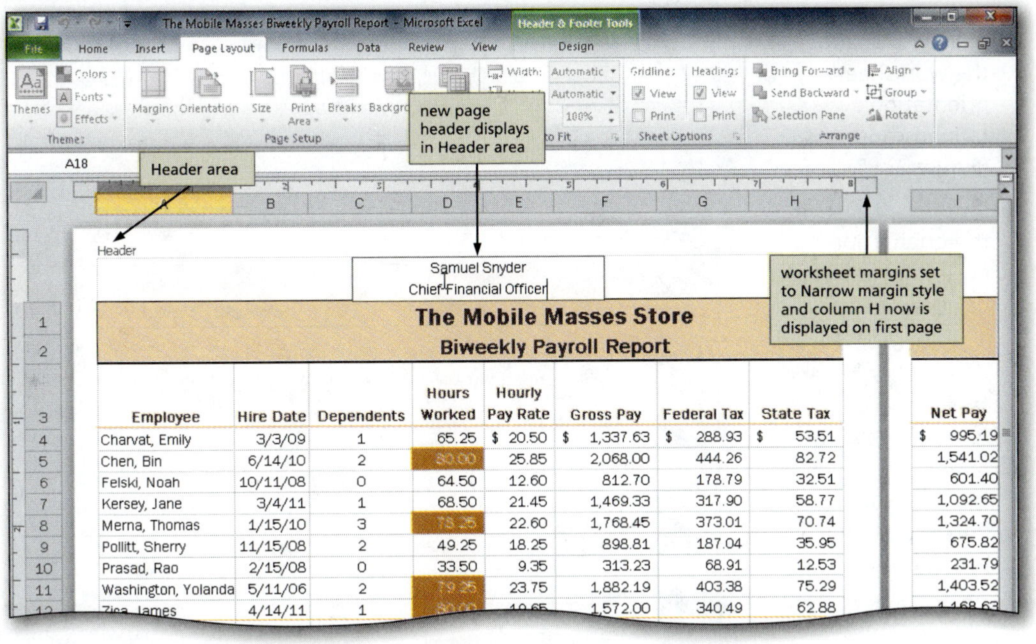

Figure 2–65

Q&A

What else can I place in a header?

You can add text, page number information, date and time information, the file path of the workbook, the file name of the workbook, the sheet name of the workbook, and pictures to a header.

4

- Select cell B16 to deselect the header. Click the Orientation button (Page Layout tab | Page Setup group) to display the Orientation gallery (Figure 2–66).

Q&A

Why do I need to deselect the header?

Excel disables almost all of the buttons on the Ribbon as you edit a header or footer. In addition to the commands on the Design tab (Figure 2–65 on the previous page), only a few commands remain available on the Home tab on the Ribbon. To continue working in Excel, therefore, you should select a cell in the worksheet so that all of the commands on the Ribbon are available for your use.

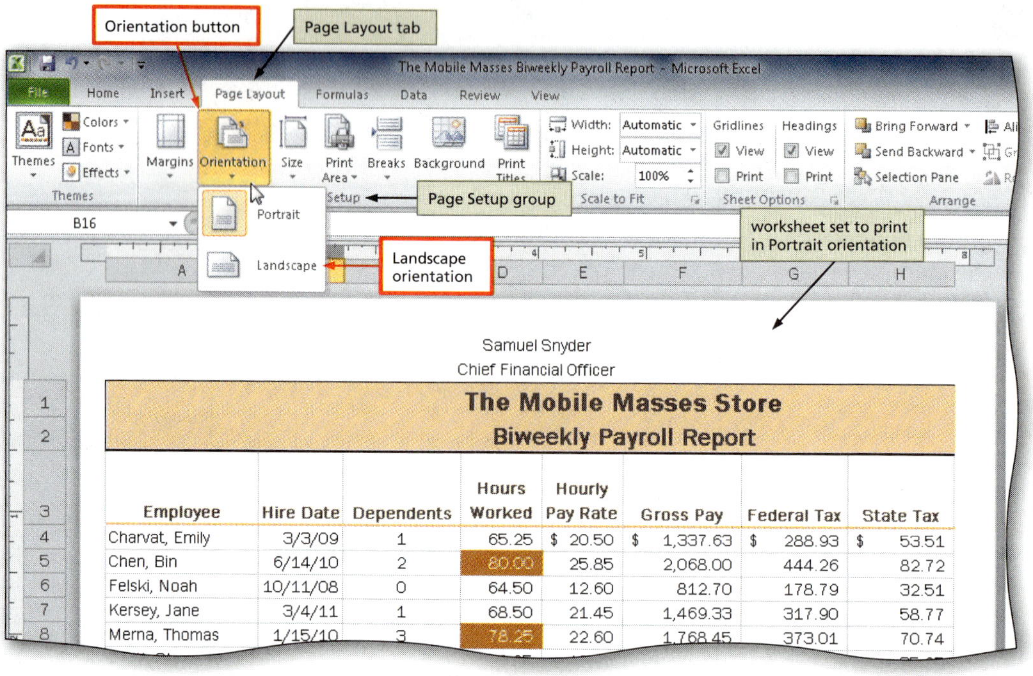

Figure 2–66

5

- Click Landscape in the Orientation gallery to change the worksheet's orientation to landscape (Figure 2–67).

Q&A

Do I need to change the orientation every time I want to print the worksheet?

No. Once you change the orientation and save the workbook, Excel will save the orientation setting for that workbook until you change it. When you open a new workbook, Excel sets the orientation to portrait.

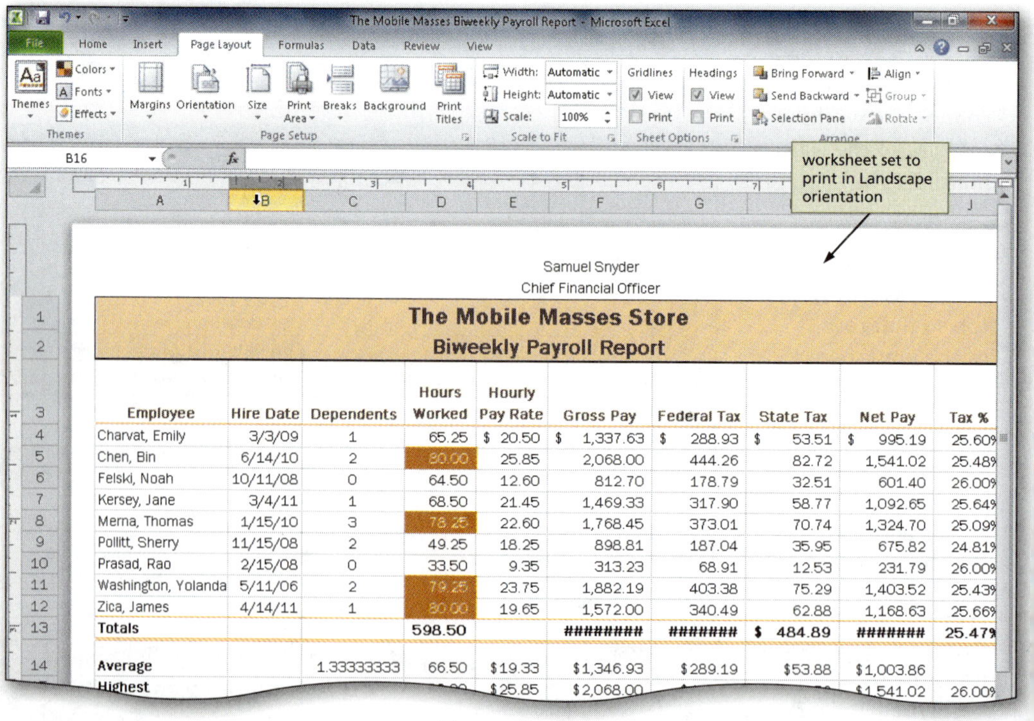

Figure 2–67

Other Ways

1. Click Page Setup Dialog Box Launcher (Page Layout tab | Page Setup group), click Page tab (Page Setup dialog box), click Portrait or Landscape, click OK button

Printing the Worksheet

Excel provides other options for printing a worksheet. The following sections print the worksheet and print a section of the worksheet.

To Print a Worksheet

The following steps print the worksheet.

1. Click File on the Ribbon to open the Backstage view.
2. Click the Print tab in the Backstage view to display the Print gallery.
3. If necessary, click the Printer Status button in the Print gallery to display a list of available Printer options and then click the desired printer to change the currently selected printer.
4. Click the Print button in the Print gallery to print the worksheet in landscape orientation on the currently selected printer.
5. When the printer stops, retrieve the hard copy (Figure 2–68).

BTW

Conserving Ink and Toner

If you want to conserve ink or toner, you can instruct Excel to print draft quality documents by clicking File on the Ribbon to open the Backstage view, clicking Options in the Backstage view to display the Excel Options dialog box, clicking Advanced in the left pane (Excel Options dialog box), scrolling to the Print area in the right pane, placing a check mark in the 'Use draft quality' check box, and then clicking the OK button. Then, use the Backstage view to print the document as usual.

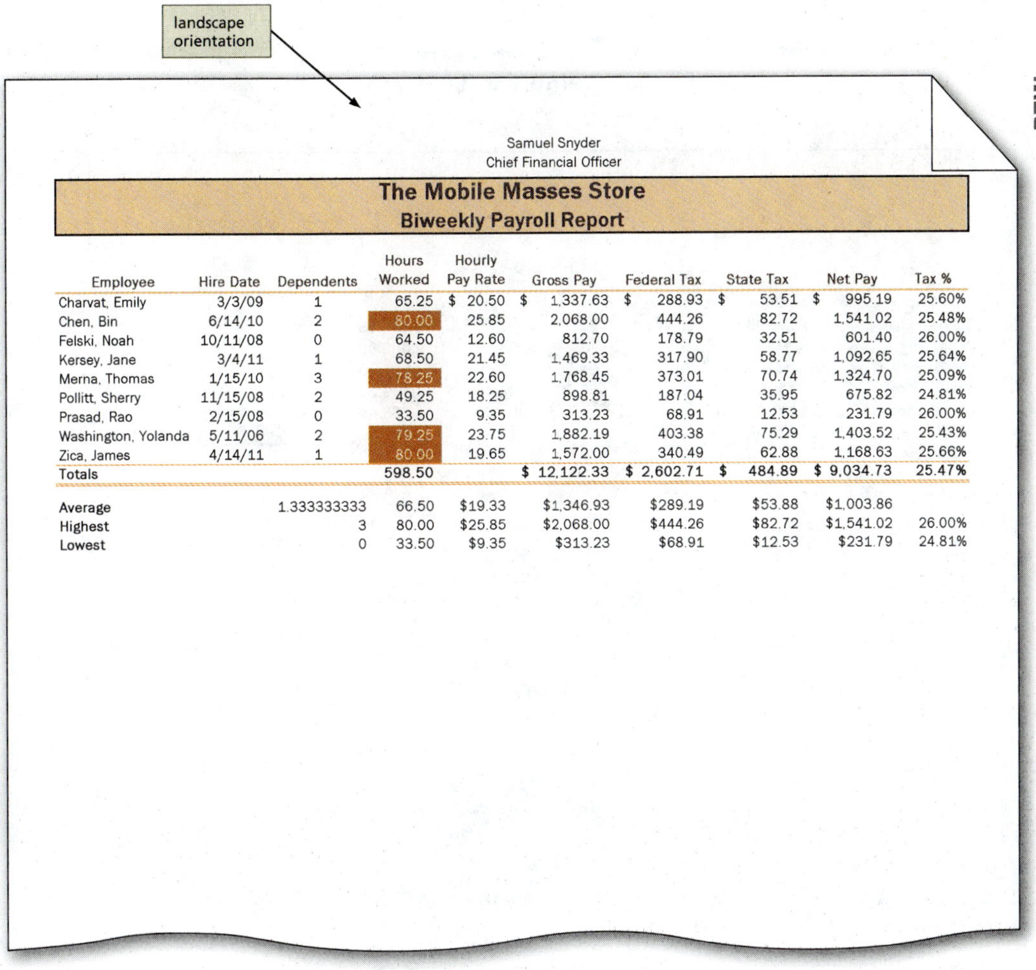

Samuel Snyder
Chief Financial Officer

The Mobile Masses Store
Biweekly Payroll Report

Employee	Hire Date	Dependents	Hours Worked	Hourly Pay Rate	Gross Pay	Federal Tax	State Tax	Net Pay	Tax %
Charvat, Emily	3/3/09	1	65.25	$ 20.50	$ 1,337.63	$ 288.93	$ 53.51	$ 995.19	25.60%
Chen, Bin	6/14/10	2	80.00	25.85	2,068.00	444.26	82.72	1,541.02	25.48%
Felski, Noah	10/11/08	0	64.50	12.60	812.70	178.79	32.51	601.40	26.00%
Kersey, Jane	3/4/11	1	68.50	21.45	1,469.33	317.90	58.77	1,092.65	25.64%
Merna, Thomas	1/15/10	3	78.25	22.60	1,768.45	373.01	70.74	1,324.70	25.09%
Pollitt, Sherry	11/15/08	2	49.25	18.25	898.81	187.04	35.95	675.82	24.81%
Prasad, Rao	2/15/08	0	33.50	9.35	313.23	68.91	12.53	231.79	26.00%
Washington, Yolanda	5/11/06	2	79.25	23.75	1,882.19	403.38	75.29	1,403.52	25.43%
Zica, James	4/14/11	1	80.00	19.65	1,572.00	340.49	62.88	1,168.63	25.66%
Totals			598.50		$ 12,122.33	$ 2,602.71	$ 484.89	$ 9,034.73	25.47%
Average		1.333333333	66.50	$19.33	$1,346.93	$289.19	$53.88	$1,003.86	
Highest		3	80.00	$25.85	$2,068.00	$444.26	$82.72	$1,541.02	26.00%
Lowest		0	33.50	$9.35	$313.23	$68.91	$12.53	$231.79	24.81%

Figure 2–68

BTW

Printing Document Properties

To print document properties, click File on the Ribbon to open the Backstage view, click the Print tab in the Backstage view to display the Print gallery, click the first button in the Settings area to display a list of options specifying what you can print, click Document Properties in the list to specify you want to print the document properties instead of the actual document, and then click the Print button in the Print gallery to print the document properties on the currently selected printer.

To Print a Section of the Worksheet

You might not always want to print the entire worksheet. You can print portions of the worksheet by selecting the range of cells to print and then clicking the Selection option button in the Print what area in the Print dialog box. The following steps print the range A3:F16.

1

- Select the range to print, cells A3:F16 in this case.
- Click File on the Ribbon to open the Backstage view.
- Click the Print tab to display the Print gallery.
- Click Print Active Sheets in the Settings area (Print tab | Print gallery) to display a list of options that determine what Excel should print (Figure 2–69).

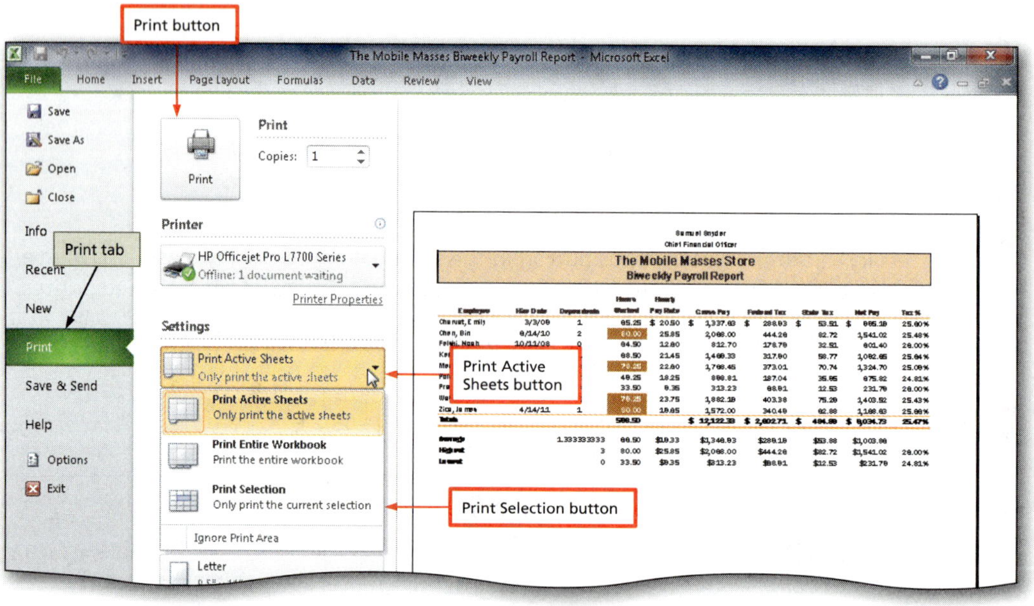

Figure 2–69

2

- Click Print Selection to instruct Excel to print only the selected range.
- Click the Print button in the Print gallery to print the selected range of the worksheet on the currently selected printer (Figure 2–70).
- Click the Normal button on the status bar to return to Normal view.
- Click cell A18 to deselect the range A3:F16.

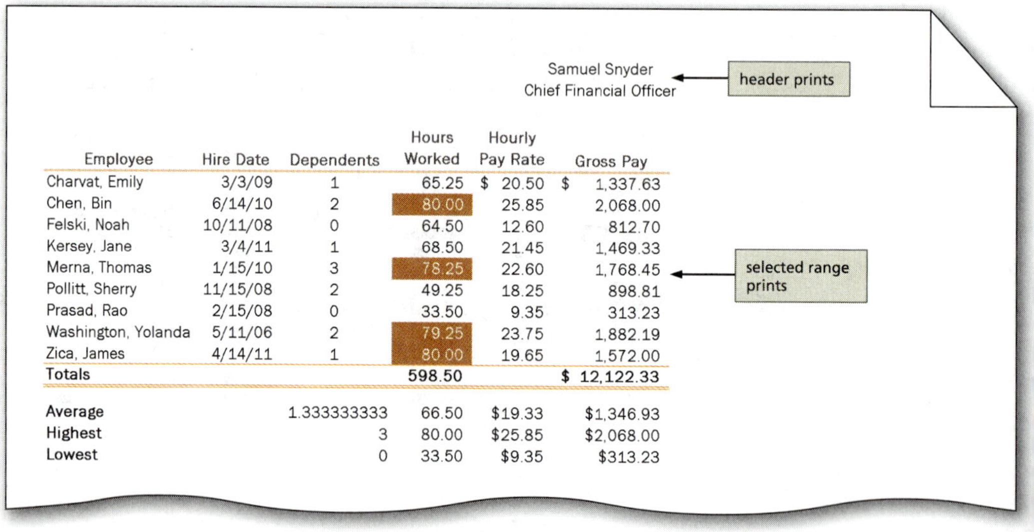

Samuel Snyder
Chief Financial Officer

Employee	Hire Date	Dependents	Hours Worked	Hourly Pay Rate	Gross Pay
Charvat, Emily	3/3/09	1	65.25	$ 20.50	$ 1,337.63
Chen, Bin	6/14/10	2	80.00	25.85	2,068.00
Felski, Noah	10/11/08	0	64.50	12.60	812.70
Kersey, Jane	3/4/11	1	68.50	21.45	1,469.33
Merna, Thomas	1/15/10	3	78.25	22.60	1,768.45
Pollitt, Sherry	11/15/08	2	49.25	18.25	898.81
Prasad, Rao	2/15/08	0	33.50	9.35	313.23
Washington, Yolanda	5/11/06	2	79.25	23.75	1,882.19
Zica, James	4/14/11	1	80.00	19.65	1,572.00
Totals			598.50		$ 12,122.33
Average		1.333333333	66.50	$19.33	$1,346.93
Highest		3	80.00	$25.85	$2,068.00
Lowest		0	33.50	$9.35	$313.23

Figure 2–70

Q&A

What are my options for telling Excel what to print?

Excel includes three options to allow you to determine what should be printed (Figure 2–69). As shown in the previous steps, the Print Selection button instructs Excel to print the selected range. The Print Active Sheets button instructs Excel to print the active worksheet (the worksheet currently on the screen) or the selected worksheets. Finally, the Print Entire Workbook button instructs Excel to print all of the worksheets in the workbook.

Other Ways

1. Select range, click Print Area button (Page Layout tab | Page Setup group), click Set Print Area, click Quick Print button on Quick Access Toolbar, click Print Area, click Clear Print Area
2. Select range, click Print Area button (Page Layout tab | Page Setup group), click Set Print Area, click File tab to open Backstage view, click Print tab, click Print button

Displaying and Printing the Formulas Version of the Worksheet

Thus far, you have been working with the **values version** of the worksheet, which shows the results of the formulas you have entered, rather than the actual formulas. Excel also can display and print the **formulas version** of the worksheet, which shows the actual formulas you have entered, rather than the resulting values.

The formulas version is useful for debugging a worksheet. **Debugging** is the process of finding and correcting errors in the worksheet. Viewing and printing the formulas version instead of the values version makes it easier to see any mistakes in the formulas.

When you change from the values version to the formulas version, Excel increases the width of the columns so that the formulas and text do not overflow into adjacent cells on the right. The formulas version of the worksheet, thus, usually is significantly wider than the values version. To fit the wide printout on one page, you can use landscape orientation, which has already been selected for the workbook, and the Fit to option in the Page sheet in the Page Setup dialog box.

BTW

Values versus Formulas
When completing class assignments, do not enter numbers in cells that require formulas. Most instructors will check both the values version and formulas version of your worksheets. The formulas version verifies that you entered formulas, rather than numbers, in formula-based cells.

To Display the Formulas in the Worksheet and Fit the Printout on One Page

The following steps change the view of the worksheet from the values version to the formulas version of the worksheet and then print the formulas version on one page.

1

- Press CTRL+ACCENT MARK (`) to display the worksheet with formulas.
- Click the right horizontal scroll arrow until column J appears (Figure 2–71).

2

- Click the Page Setup Dialog Box Launcher (Page Layout tab | Page Setup group) to display the Page Setup dialog box.

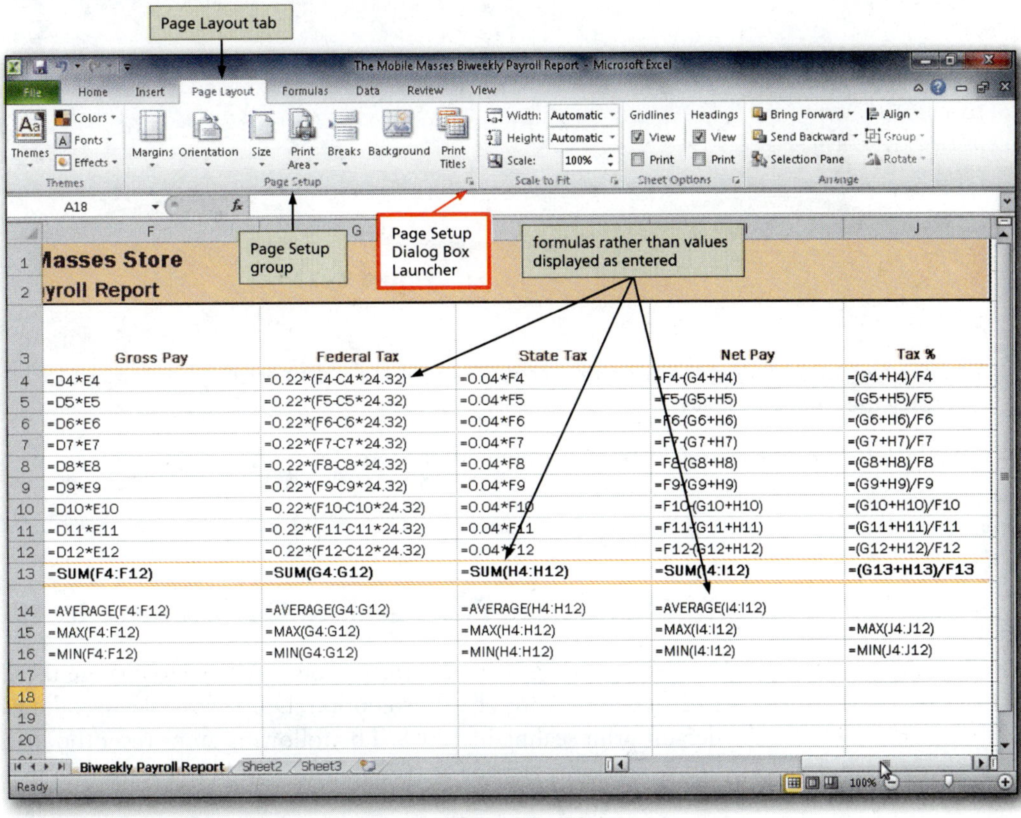

Figure 2–71

3

- If necessary, click Landscape in the Orientation area to select it.
- If necessary, click Fit to in the Scaling area to select it.

4

- Click the Print button (Page Setup dialog box) to print the formulas in the worksheet on one page in landscape orientation (Figure 2–72). If necessary, in the Backstage view, select the Print Active Sheets option in the Settings area of the Print gallery.
- When Excel displays the Backstage view, click the Print button to print the worksheet.

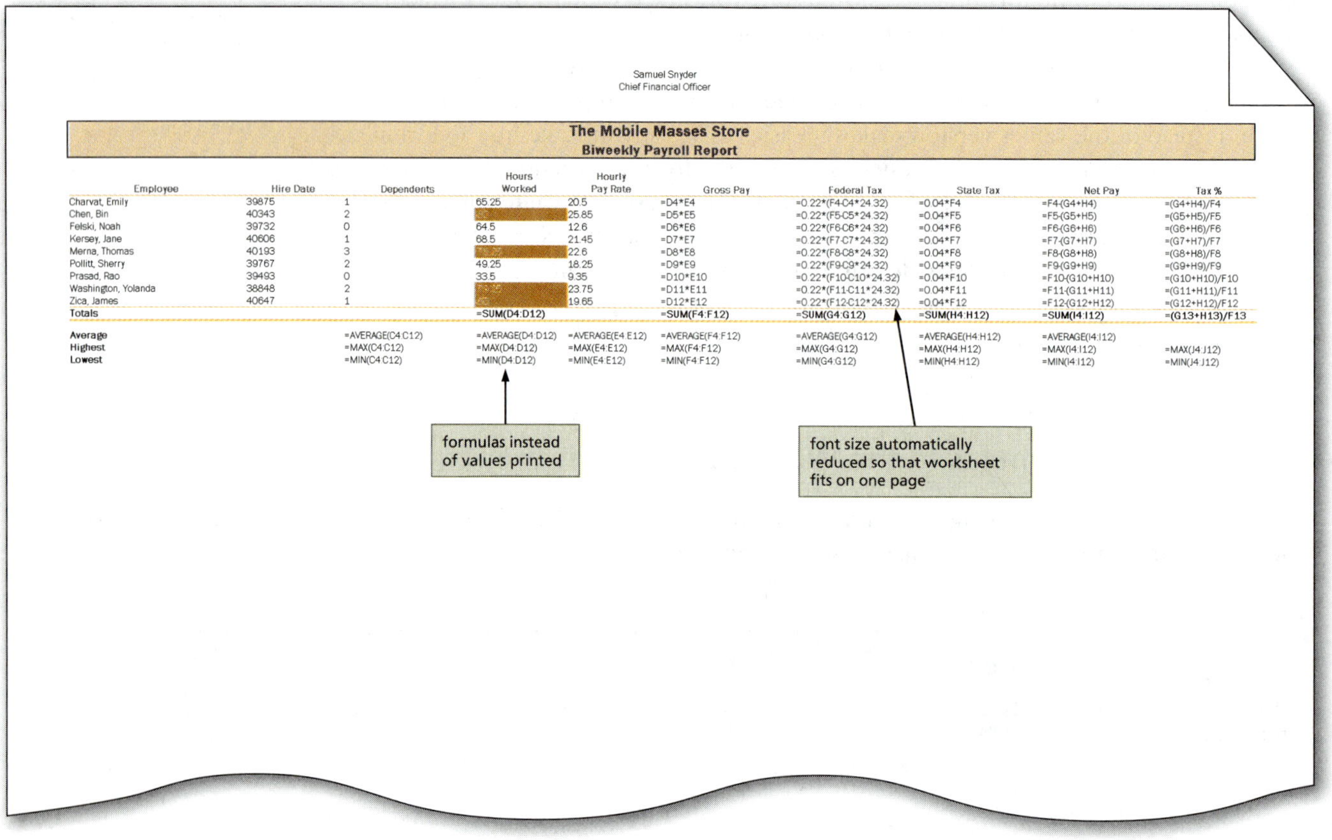
Samuel Snyder
Chief Financial Officer

The Mobile Masses Store
Biweekly Payroll Report

Employee	Hire Date	Dependents	Hours Worked	Hourly Pay Rate	Gross Pay	Federal Tax	State Tax	Net Pay	Tax %
Charvat, Emily	39875	1	65.25	20.5	=D4*E4	=0.22*(F4-C4*24.32)	=0.04*F4	=F4-(G4+H4)	=(G4+H4)/F4
Chen, Bin	40343	2	[illegible]	25.85	=D5*E5	=0.22*(F5-C5*24.32)	=0.04*F5	=F5-(G5+H5)	=(G5+H5)/F5
Felski, Noah	39732	0	64.5	12.6	=D6*E6	=0.22*(F6-C6*24.32)	=0.04*F6	=F6-(G6+H6)	=(G6+H6)/F6
Kersey, Jane	40606	1	68.5	21.45	=D7*E7	=0.22*(F7-C7*24.32)	=0.04*F7	=F7-(G7+H7)	=(G7+H7)/F7
Merna, Thomas	40193	3	[illegible]	22.6	=D8*E8	=0.22*(F8-C8*24.32)	=0.04*F8	=F8-(G8+H8)	=(G8+H8)/F8
Pollitt, Sherry	39767	2	49.25	18.25	=D9*E9	=0.22*(F9-C9*24.32)	=0.04*F9	=F9-(G9+H9)	=(G9+H9)/F9
Prasad, Rao	39493	0	33.5	9.35	=D10*E10	=0.22*(F10-C10*24.32)	=0.04*F10	=F10-(G10+H10)	=(G10+H10)/F10
Washington, Yolanda	38848	2	[illegible]	23.75	=D11*E11	=0.22*(F11-C11*24.32)	=0.04*F11	=F11-(G11+H11)	=(G11+H11)/F11
Zica, James	40647	1	[illegible]	19.65	=D12*E12	=0.22*(F12-C12*24.32)	=0.04*F12	=F12-(G12+H12)	=(G12+H12)/F12
Totals			**=SUM(D4:D12)**		**=SUM(F4:F12)**	**=SUM(G4:G12)**	**=SUM(H4:H12)**	**=SUM(I4:I12)**	**=(G13+H13)/F13**
Average		=AVERAGE(C4:C12)	=AVERAGE(D4:D12)	=AVERAGE(E4:E12)	=AVERAGE(F4:F12)	=AVERAGE(G4:G12)	=AVERAGE(H4:H12)	=AVERAGE(I4:I12)	
Highest		=MAX(C4:C12)	=MAX(D4:D12)	=MAX(E4:E12)	=MAX(F4:F12)	=MAX(G4:G12)	=MAX(H4:H12)	=MAX(I4:I12)	=MAX(J4:J12)
Lowest		=MIN(C4:C12)	=MIN(D4:D12)	=MIN(E4:E12)	=MIN(F4:F12)	=MIN(G4:G12)	=MIN(H4:H12)	=MIN(I4:I12)	=MIN(J4:J12)

Figure 2–72

5

- After viewing and printing the formulas version, press CTRL+ACCENT MARK (`) to instruct Excel to display the values version.
- Click the left horizontal scroll arrow until column A appears.

To Change the Print Scaling Option Back to 100%

Depending on your printer, you may have to change the Print Scaling option back to 100% after using the Fit to option. Doing so will cause the worksheet to print at the default print scaling of 100%. The following steps reset the Print Scaling option so that future worksheets print at 100%, instead of being resized to print on one page.

1. If necessary, display the Page Layout tab and then click the Page Setup Dialog Box Launcher (Page Layout tab | Page Setup group) to display the Page Setup dialog box.
2. Click Adjust to in the Scaling area to select the Adjust to setting.
3. If necessary, type `100` in the Adjust to box to adjust the print scaling to a new percentage.

4. Click the OK button (Page Setup dialog box) to set the print scaling to normal.
5. Display the Home tab.

Q&A

What is the purpose of the Adjust to box in the Page Setup dialog box?

The Adjust to box allows you to specify the percentage of reduction or enlargement in the printout of a worksheet. The default percentage is 100%. When you click the Fit to option, this percentage automatically changes to the percentage required to fit the printout on one page.

BTW

Quick Reference

For a table that lists how to complete the tasks covered in the Office chapters in this book using the mouse, Ribbon, shortcut menu, and keyboard, see the Quick Reference Summary at the back of this book, or visit the Microsoft Office and Concepts CourseMate Web site at www.cengagebrain.com and then navigate to the Quick Reference resource for this book.

To Save the Workbook and Quit Excel

With the workbook complete, the following steps save the workbook and quit Excel.

1. Click the Save button on the Quick Access Toolbar.
2. Click the Close button on the upper-right corner of the title bar.

Chapter Summary

In this chapter you have learned how to enter formulas, calculate an average, find the highest and lowest numbers in a range, verify formulas using Range Finder, added borders, align text, format numbers, change column widths and row heights, and add conditional formatting to a range of numbers. In addition, you learned to spell check a worksheet, print a section of a worksheet, and display and print the formulas version of the worksheet using the Fit to option. The items listed below include all the new Excel skills you have learned in this chapter.

1. Enter a Formula Using the Keyboard (EX 75)
2. Enter Formulas Using Point Mode (EX 77)
3. Copy Formulas Using the Fill Handle (EX 80)
4. Determine the Average of a Range of Numbers Using the Keyboard and Mouse (EX 84)
5. Determine the Highest Number in a Range of Numbers Using the Insert Function Box (EX 86)
6. Determine the Lowest Number in a Range of Numbers Using the Sum Menu (EX 87)
7. Copy a Range of Cells Across Columns to an Adjacent Range Using the Fill Handle (EX 89)
8. Verify a Formula Using Range Finder (EX 91)
9. Change the Workbook Theme (EX 94)
10. Change the Background Color and Apply a Box Border to the Worksheet Title and Subtitle (EX 96)
11. Format Dates and Center Data in Cells (EX 98)
12. Apply an Accounting Number Format and Comma Style Format Using the Ribbon (EX 100)
13. Apply a Currency Style Format with a Floating Dollar Sign Using the Format Cells Dialog Box (EX 102)
14. Apply a Percent Style Format and Use the Increase Decimal Button (EX 103)
15. Apply Conditional Formatting (EX 104)
16. Change the Widths of Columns (EX 107)
17. Change the Heights of Rows (EX 110)
18. Check Spelling on the Worksheet (EX 112)
19. Change the Worksheet's Margins, Header, and Orientation in Page Layout View (EX 114)
20. Print a Section of the Worksheet (EX 118)
21. Display the Formulas in the Worksheet and Fit the Printout on One Page (EX 119)

SAM

If you have a SAM 2010 user profile, your instructor may have assigned an autogradable version of this assignment. If so, log into the SAM 2010 Web site at www.cengage.com/sam2010 to download the instruction and start files.

Learn It Online

Test your knowledge of chapter content and key terms.

Instructions: To complete the Learn It Online exercises, visit the Microsoft Office and Concepts CourseMate Web site at www.cengagebrain.com, navigate to the Excel Chapter 2 resources for this book, click the link for the exercise you want to complete, and then read the instructions.

Chapter Reinforcement TF, MC, and SA

A series of true/false, multiple choice, and short answer questions that test your knowledge of the chapter content.

Flash Cards

An interactive learning environment where you identify chapter key terms associated with displayed definitions.

Practice Test

A series of multiple choice questions that test your knowledge of chapter content and key terms.

Who Wants To Be a Computer Genius?

An interactive game that challenges your knowledge of chapter content in the style of a television quiz show.

Wheel of Terms

An interactive game that challenges your knowledge of chapter key terms in the style of the television show *Wheel of Fortune*.

Crossword Puzzle Challenge

A crossword puzzle that challenges your knowledge of key terms presented in the chapter.

Apply Your Knowledge

Reinforce the skills and apply the concepts you learned in this chapter.

Profit Analysis Worksheet

Instructions: The purpose of this exercise is to open a partially completed workbook, enter formulas and functions, copy the formulas and functions, and then format the worksheet titles and numbers. As shown in Figure 2–73, the completed worksheet analyzes the costs associated with a police department's fleet of vehicles.

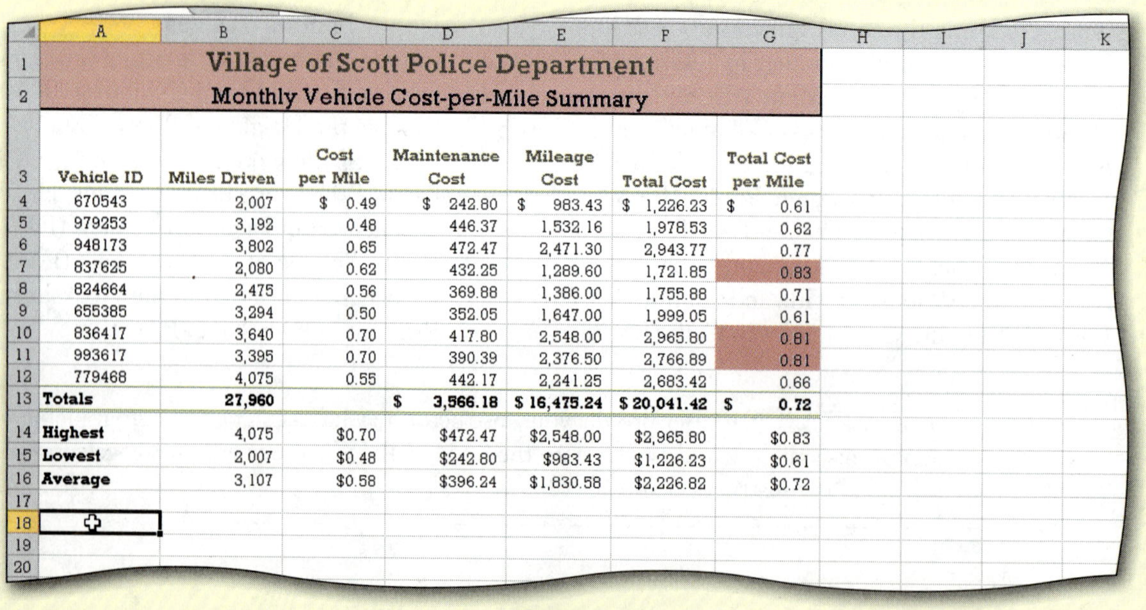

	A	B	C	D	E	F	G
1	Village of Scott Police Department						
2	Monthly Vehicle Cost-per-Mile Summary						
3	Vehicle ID	Miles Driven	Cost per Mile	Maintenance Cost	Mileage Cost	Total Cost	Total Cost per Mile
4	670543	2,007	$ 0.49	$ 242.80	$ 983.43	$ 1,226.23	$ 0.61
5	979253	3,192	0.48	446.37	1,532.16	1,978.53	0.62
6	948173	3,802	0.65	472.47	2,471.30	2,943.77	0.77
7	837625	2,080	0.62	432.25	1,289.60	1,721.85	0.83
8	824664	2,475	0.56	369.88	1,386.00	1,755.88	0.71
9	655385	3,294	0.50	352.05	1,647.00	1,999.05	0.61
10	836417	3,640	0.70	417.80	2,548.00	2,965.80	0.81
11	993617	3,395	0.70	390.39	2,376.50	2,766.89	0.81
12	779468	4,075	0.55	442.17	2,241.25	2,683.42	0.66
13	Totals	27,960		$ 3,566.18	$ 16,475.24	$ 20,041.42	$ 0.72
14	Highest	4,075	$0.70	$472.47	$2,548.00	$2,965.80	$0.83
15	Lowest	2,007	$0.48	$242.80	$983.43	$1,226.23	$0.61
16	Average	3,107	$0.58	$396.24	$1,830.58	$2,226.82	$0.72

Figure 2–73

1. Start Excel. Open the workbook Apply 2-1 Village of Scott Police Department. See the inside back cover of this book for instructions for downloading the Data Files for Students or see your instructor for information on accessing the files required in this book.
2. Use the following formulas in cells E4, F4, and G4:

   Mileage Cost (cell E4) = Miles Driven * Cost per Mile or = B4 * C4

   Total Cost (cell F4) = Maintenance Cost + Mileage Cost or = D4 + E4

   Total Cost per Mile (cell G4) = Total Cost / Miles Driven or = F4 / B4

   Use the fill handle to copy the three formulas in the range E4:G4 to the range E5:G12.
3. Determine totals for the miles driven, maintenance cost, mileage cost, and total cost in row 13. Copy the formula in cell G12 to G13 to assign the formula in cell G12 to G13 in the total line. If necessary, reapply the Total cell style to cell G13.
4. In the range B14:B16, determine the highest value, lowest value, and average value, respectively, for the values in the range B4:B12. Use the fill handle to copy the three functions to the range C14:G16.
5. Format the worksheet as follows:
   a. change the workbook theme to Foundry by using the Themes button (Page Layout tab | Themes group)
   b. cell A1 — change to Title cell style
   c. cell A2 — change to a font size of 16
   d. cells A1:A2 — Rose background color and a thick box border
   e. cells C4:G4 and D13:G13 — Accounting number format with two decimal places and fixed dollar signs by using the Accounting Number Format button (Home tab | Number group)
   f. cells C5:G12 — Comma style format with two decimal places by using the Comma Style button (Home tab | Number group)
   g. cells B4:B16 — Comma style format with no decimal places
   h. cells C14:G16 — Currency style format with floating dollar signs by using the Format Cells: Number Dialog Box Launcher (Home tab | Number group)
   i. cells G4:G12 — apply conditional formatting so that cells with a value greater than 0.80 appear with a rose background color
6. Switch to Page Layout View and delete any current text in the Header area. Enter your name, course, laboratory assignment number, and any other information, as specified by your instructor, in the Header area. Preview and print the worksheet in landscape orientation. Change the document properties, as specified by your instructor. Save the workbook using the file name, Apply 2-1 Village of Scott Police Department Complete.
7. Use Range Finder to verify the formula in cell G13.

Continued >

Apply Your Knowledge *continued*

8. Print the range A3:D16. Press CTRL+ACCENT MARK (`) to change the display from the values version of the worksheet to the formulas version. Print the formulas version in landscape orientation on one page (Figure 2–74) by using the Fit to option in the Page sheet in the Page Setup dialog box. Press CTRL+ACCENT MARK (`) to change the display of the worksheet back to the values version. Close the workbook without saving it.
9. Submit the workbook and results as specified by your instructor.

Jeff Quasney
Apply 2-1 Village of Scott Police Department

Village of Scott Police Department
Monthly Vehicle Cost-per-Mile Summary

Vehicle ID	Miles Driven	Cost per Mile	Maintenance Cost	Mileage Cost	Total Cost	Total Cost per Mile
670543	2007	0.49	242.8	=B4*C4	=D4+E4	=F4/B4
979253	3192	0.48	446.37	=B5*C5	=D5+E5	=F5/B5
948173	3802	0.65	472.47	=B6*C6	=D6+E6	=F6/B6
837625	2080	0.62	432.25	=B7*C7	=D7+E7	=F7/B7
824664	2475	0.56	369.88	=B8*C8	=D8+E8	=F8/B8
655385	3294	0.5	352.05	=B9*C9	=D9+E9	=F9/B9
836417	3640	0.7	417.8	=B10*C10	=D10+E10	=F10/B10
993617	3395	0.7	390.39	=B11*C11	=D11+E11	=F11/B11
779468	4075	0.55	442.17	=B12*C12	=D12+E12	=F12/B12
Totals	**=SUM(B4:B12)**		**=SUM(D4:D12)**	**=SUM(E4:E12)**	**=SUM(F4:F12)**	**=F13/B13**
Highest	=MAX(B4:B12)	=MAX(C4:C12)	=MAX(D4:D12)	=MAX(E4:E12)	=MAX(F4:F12)	=MAX(G4:G12)
Lowest	=MIN(B4:B12)	=MIN(C4:C12)	=MIN(D4:D12)	=MIN(E4:E12)	=MIN(F4:F12)	=MIN(G4:G12)
Average	=AVERAGE(B4:B12)	=AVERAGE(C4:C12)	=AVERAGE(D4:D12)	=AVERAGE(E4:E12)	=AVERAGE(F4:F12)	=AVERAGE(G4:G12)

Figure 2–74

Extend Your Knowledge

Extend the skills you learned in this chapter and experiment with new skills. You may need to use Help to complete the assignment.

Applying Conditional Formatting to Cells

Instructions: Start Excel. Open the workbook Extend 2-1 State Wildlife Department Employee Ratings. See the inside back cover of this book for instructions for downloading the Data Files for Students, or see your instructor for information on accessing the files required in this book. Perform the following tasks to apply three types of conditional formatting to cells in a worksheet:

1. Select the range C4:C18. Click the Conditional Formatting button (Home tab | Styles group) and then click New Rule in the Conditional Formatting list. Select 'Format only top or bottom ranked values' in the Select a Rule Type area (Conditional Formatting Rules Manager dialog box), as shown in Figure 2–75. Enter any value between 10 and 25 in the text box in the Edit the Rule Description (New Formatting Rule dialog box) area, and click the '% of the selected range' check box to select it. Click the Format button, and choose a blue background to assign this conditional format. Click the OK button in each dialog box and view the worksheet.
2. With range C4:C18 selected, apply a conditional format to the range that uses a green background color to highlight cells with scores that are below average.

3. With range D4:D18 selected, apply a conditional format to the range that uses an orange background to highlight cells that contain Exemplary or Exceeds Requirements.
4. With range B4:B18 selected, apply a conditional format to the range that uses a red background color to highlight cells with duplicate student names.
5. Change the document properties as specified by your instructor. Save the workbook using the file name, Extend 2-1 State Wildlife Department Employee Ratings Complete. Submit the revised workbook as specified by your instructor.

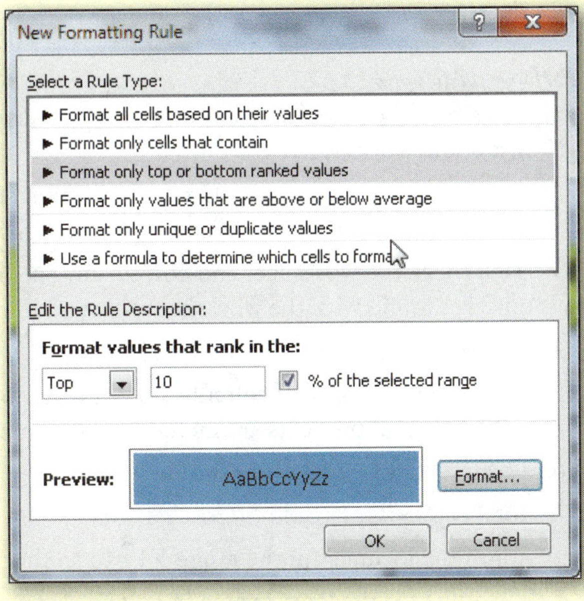

Figure 2–75

Make It Right

Analyze a workbook and correct all errors and/or improve the design.

Correcting Formatting, Functions, and Formulas in a Worksheet

Instructions: Start Excel. Open the workbook Make It Right 2-1 Dion Designwear Profit Analysis. See the inside back cover of this book for instructions for downloading the Data Files for Students, or see your instructor for information on accessing the files required for this book.

In this exercise you will learn how to correct formatting, functions, and formula problems in a worksheet (Figure 2–76).

	A	B	C	D	E	F	G	H
1	Dion Designwear							
2	Profit Anaylsis							
3	Product	Desciption	Cost	Profit	Units Sold	Total Sales	Total Profit	% Profit
4	4835	Coat	$247.63	$144.83	95,159	$37,346,101.14	$13,781,877.97	36.903%
5	7563	Custom	210.08	142.18	75,762	26,687,922.12	10,771,841.16	40.362%
6	8191	Dress	186.53	99.48	69,297	19,819,634.97	6,893,665.56	34.782%
7	8409	Hat	146.82	59.97	39,164	8,098,723.56	2,348,665.08	29.000%
8	5677	Jacket	140.68	85.63	38,261	8,658,846.91	3,276,289.43	37.837%
9	8985	Shirt	68.38	8.15	42,420	3,246,402.60	345,723.00	10.649%
10	5871	Slacks	144.54	30.44	68,536	11,992,429.28	2,086,235.84	17.396%
11	7796	Sleepwear	93.74	11.80	77,413	8,170,168.02	913,473.40	11.181%
12	7777	Suit	305.91	126.00	19,999	8,637,768.09	2,519,874.00	29.173%
13	8178	Sweater	112.21	9.24	61,257	7,439,662.65	566,014.68	7.608%
14	Totals				587,268	$140,097,659.34	$43,503,660.12	31.052%
15	Lowest		$68.38	$8.15	19,999	$3,246,402.60	$345,723.00	7.608%
16	Highest		$305.91	$144.83	95,159	$37,346,101.14	$13,781,877.97	40.362%
17	Average		$156.54	$71.77	54,679	$14,009,765.93	$3,302,420.24	25.489%
18								
19								

Figure 2–76

Continued >

Make It Right *continued*

Perform the following tasks:

1. Add a thick box border around the title and subtitle so that they appear more separated from the rest of the worksheet.
2. Adjust the width of column D to 8.11 pixels so that the word in the column header does not wrap. Adjust the column widths of columns F and G to best fit.
3. Spell check the worksheet and correct any spelling mistakes that are found, but ignore any spelling mistakes found with the worksheet title and the product descriptions.
4. Center the values in the Product column.
5. The averages in several columns do not include the product in row 4. Adjust the functions in these cells so that all products are included in the calculation.
6. The total sales calculations should be:

   Total Sales = Units Sold * (Cost + Profit)

   Adjust the formulas in the range F4:F13 so that the correct formula is used.
7. The value for the lowest value in column E was entered as a number rather than as a function. Replace the value with the appropriate function.
8. The currency values in rows 4 and 14 should be formatted with the Accounting Number Format button (Home tab | Number group). They are currently formatted with the Currency format (floating dollar sign). The Accounting number format displays a fixed dollar sign.
9. Delete the function in the cell containing the average of % Profit because it is mathematically invalid.
10. Change the document properties as specified by your instructor. Save the workbook using the file name, Make It Right 2–1 Dion Designwear Profit Analysis Corrected. Submit the revised workbook as specified by your instructor.

SAM

In the Lab

Design and/or create a workbook using the guidelines, concepts, and skills presented in this chapter. Labs 1, 2, and 3 are listed in order of increasing difficulty.

Lab 1: Accounts Receivable Balance Worksheet

Problem: You are a part-time assistant in the accounting department at Aficionado Guitar Parts, a Chicago-based supplier of custom guitar parts. You have been asked to use Excel to generate a report that summarizes the monthly accounts receivable balance (Figure 2–77). A chart of the balances also is desired. The customer data in Table 2–6 is available for test purposes.

Table 2–6 Aficionado Guitar Parts Accounts Receivable Data

Customer	Beginning Balance	Credits	Payments	Purchases
Cervantes, Katriel	803.01	56.92	277.02	207.94
Cummings, Trenton	285.05	87.41	182.11	218.22
Danielsson, Oliver	411.45	79.33	180.09	364.02
Kalinowski, Jadwiga	438.37	60.90	331.10	190.39
Lanctot, Royce	378.81	48.55	126.15	211.38
Raglow, Dora	710.99	55.62	231.37	274.71
Tuan, Lin	318.86	85.01	129.67	332.89

Instructions Part 1: Create a worksheet similar to the one shown in Figure 2–77. Include the five columns of customer data in Table 2–6 in the report, plus two additional columns to compute a service charge and a new balance for each customer. Assume no negative unpaid monthly balances.

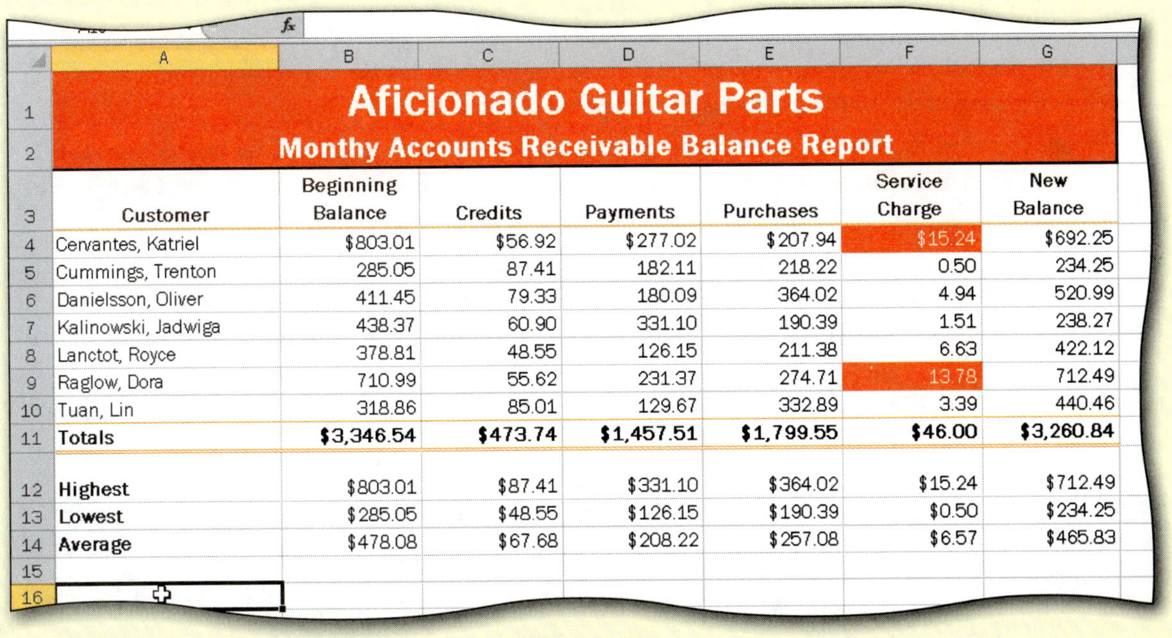

	A	B	C	D	E	F	G
1	Aficionado Guitar Parts						
2	Monthy Accounts Receivable Balance Report						
3	Customer	Beginning Balance	Credits	Payments	Purchases	Service Charge	New Balance
4	Cervantes, Katriel	$803.01	$56.92	$277.02	$207.94	$15.24	$692.25
5	Cummings, Trenton	285.05	87.41	182.11	218.22	0.50	234.25
6	Danielsson, Oliver	411.45	79.33	180.09	364.02	4.94	520.99
7	Kalinowski, Jadwiga	438.37	60.90	331.10	190.39	1.51	238.27
8	Lanctot, Royce	378.81	48.55	126.15	211.38	6.63	422.12
9	Raglow, Dora	710.99	55.62	231.37	274.71	13.78	712.49
10	Tuan, Lin	318.86	85.01	129.67	332.89	3.39	440.46
11	**Totals**	**$3,346.54**	**$473.74**	**$1,457.51**	**$1,799.55**	**$46.00**	**$3,260.84**
12	**Highest**	$803.01	$87.41	$331.10	$364.02	$15.24	$712.49
13	**Lowest**	$285.05	$48.55	$126.15	$190.39	$0.50	$234.25
14	**Average**	$478.08	$67.68	$208.22	$257.08	$6.57	$465.83
15							
16							

Figure 2–77

Perform the following tasks:

1. Enter and format the worksheet title **Aficionado Guitar Parts** and worksheet subtitle **Monthly Accounts Receivable Balance Report** in cells A1 and A2. Change the theme of the worksheet to the Trek theme. Apply the Title cell style to cells A1 and A2. Change the font size in cell A1 to 28 points. Merge and center the worksheet title and subtitle across columns A through G. Change the background color of cells A1 and A2 to the Red standard color. Change the font color of cells A1 and A2 to the White theme color. Draw a thick box border around the range A1:A2.
2. Change the width of column A to 20.00 points. Change the widths of columns B through G to 12.00 points. Change the heights of row 3 to 36.00 points and row 12 to 30.00 points.
3. Enter the column titles in row 3 and row titles in the range A11:A14, as shown in Figure 2–77. Center the column titles in the range A3:G3. Apply the Heading 3 cell style to the range A3:G3. Apply the Total cell style to the range A11:G11. Bold the titles in the range A12:A14. Change the font size in the range A3:G14 to 12 points.
4. Enter the data in Table 2–6 in the range A4:E10.
5. Use the following formulas to determine the service charge in column F and the new balance in column G for the first customer. Copy the two formulas down through the remaining customers.

   a. Service Charge (cell F4) = 3.25% * (Beginning Balance – Payments – Credits)

   b. New Balance (G4) = Beginning Balance + Purchases – Credits – Payments + Service Charge
6. Determine the totals in row 11.
7. Determine the maximum, minimum, and average values in cells B12:B14 for the range B4:B10, and then copy the range B12:B14 to C12:G14.

Continued >

In the Lab *continued*

8. Format the numbers as follows: (a) assign the Currency style with a floating dollar sign to the cells containing numeric data in the ranges B4:G4 and B11:G14, and (b) assign a number style with two decimal places and a thousand's separator (currency with no dollar sign) to the range B5:G10.
9. Use conditional formatting to change the formatting to white font on a red background in any cell in the range F4:F10 that contains a value greater than 10.
10. Change the worksheet name from Sheet1 to Accounts Receivable and the sheet tab color to the Red standard color. Change the document properties, as specified by your instructor. Change the worksheet header with your name, course number, and other information as specified by your instructor.
11. Spell check the worksheet. Preview and then print the worksheet in landscape orientation. Save the workbook using the file name, Lab 2-1 Part 1 Aficionado Guitar Parts Accounts Receivable Balance Report.
12. Print the range A3:D14. Print the formulas version on another page. Close the workbook without saving the changes. Submit the assignment as specified by your instructor.

Instructions Part 2: In this part of the exercise, you will create a 3-D Bar chart on a new worksheet in the workbook (Figure 2–78). If necessary, use Excel Help to obtain information on inserting a chart on a separate sheet in the workbook.

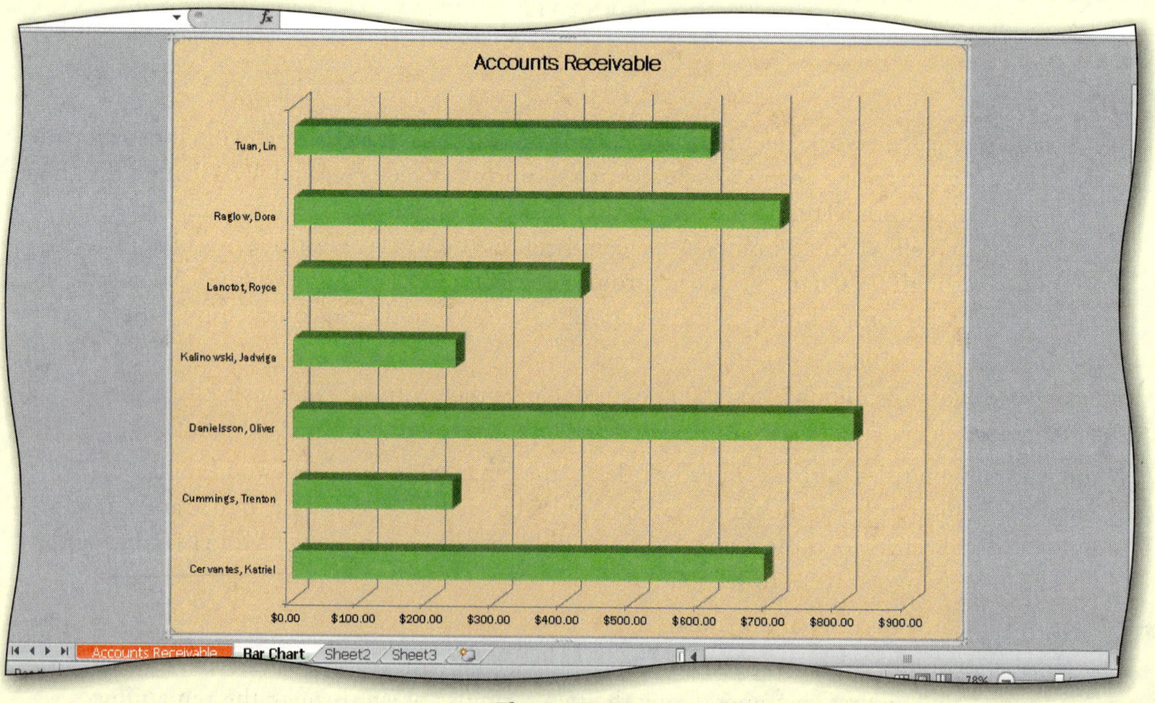

Figure 2–78

1. Open the workbook Lab 2-1 Part 1 Aficionado Guitar Parts Accounts Receivable Balance Report workbook created in Part 1. Save the workbook using the file name, Lab 2-1 Part 2 Aficionado Guitar Parts Accounts Receivable Balance Report.

2. Use the CTRL key and mouse to select the nonadjacent chart ranges A4:A10 and G4:G10. That is, select the range A4:A10 and while holding down the CTRL key, select the range G4:G10.
3. Click the Bar button (Insert tab | Charts group) and then select Clustered Bar in 3-D in the 3-D Bar area. When the chart is displayed on the worksheet, click the Move Chart button (Chart Tools Design tab | Location group). When the Move Chart dialog box appears, click New sheet and then type Bar Chart for the sheet name. Click the OK button (Move Chart dialog box). Change the sheet tab color to the Green standard color.
4. When the chart is displayed on the new worksheet, click the Series 1 series label and then press the DELETE key to delete it. Click the chart area, which is a blank area near the edge of the chart, click the Shape Fill button (Chart Tools Format tab | Shape Styles group), and then select Orange, Accent 1, Lighter 60% in the gallery (column 5, row 3). Click one of the bars in the chart. Click the Shape Fill button (Chart Tools Format tab | Shape Styles group) and then select the Green standard color. Click the Chart Title button (Chart Tools Layout tab | Labels group) and then select Above Chart in the Chart Title gallery. If necessary, use the scroll bar on the right side of the worksheet to scroll to the top of the chart. Click the edge of the chart title to select it and then type `Accounts Receivable` as the chart title.
5. Drag the Accounts Receivable tab at the bottom of the worksheet to the left of the Bar Chart tab to reorder the sheets in the workbook. Preview and print the chart.
6. Click the Accounts Receivable sheet tab. Change the following beginning balances: customer Oliver Danielsson to $702.13 and customer Lin Tuan to $482.74. The company also decided to change the service charge from 3.25% to 2.75% for all customers. After copying the adjusted formula in cell F4 to the range F5:F10, click the Auto Fill Options button and then click Fill without Formatting to maintain the original formatting in the range F5:F10. The total new balance in cell G11 should equal $3,720.82.
7. Select both sheets by holding down the SHIFT key and then clicking the Bar Chart tab. Preview and print the selected sheets. Save the workbook. Submit the assignment as specified by your instructor.

In the Lab

Lab 2: Sales Summary Worksheet

Problem: You have been asked to build a worksheet for a start-up company, Electry Auto, that analyzes the financing needs for the company's first six months in business. The company plans to begin operations in January with an initial investment of $500,000.00. The expected revenue and costs for the company's first six months are shown in Table 2–7. The desired worksheet is shown in Figure 2–79 on the following page. The initial investment is shown at the starting balance for January (cell B4). The amount of financing required by the company is shown as the lowest ending balance (cell F12).

Table 2–7 Electry Auto Start-Up Financing Needs Data

Month	Revenue	Costs
January	105000	220000
February	82000	260000
March	200000	255000
April	250000	320000
May	325000	420000
June	510000	540000

Continued >

In the Lab *continued*

Instructions Part 1: Perform the following tasks to build the worksheet shown in Figure 2–79.

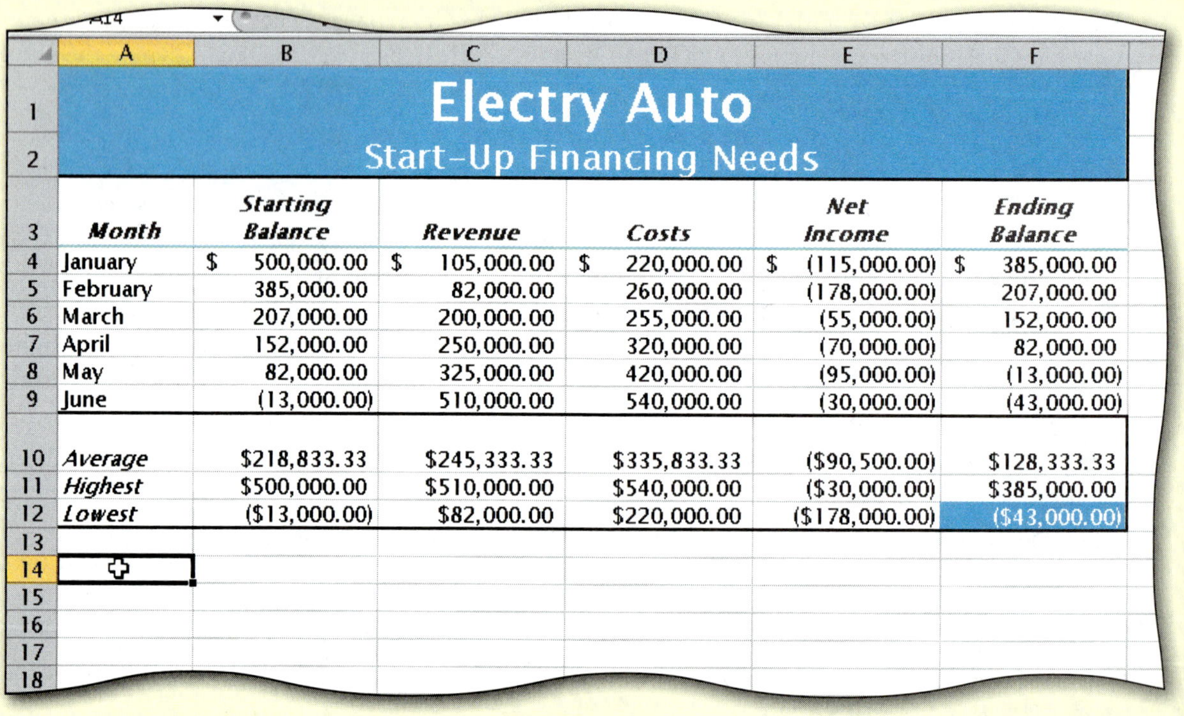

	A	B	C	D	E	F
1	Electry Auto					
2	Start-Up Financing Needs					
3	*Month*	*Starting Balance*	*Revenue*	*Costs*	*Net Income*	*Ending Balance*
4	January	$ 500,000.00	$ 105,000.00	$ 220,000.00	$ (115,000.00)	$ 385,000.00
5	February	385,000.00	82,000.00	260,000.00	(178,000.00)	207,000.00
6	March	207,000.00	200,000.00	255,000.00	(55,000.00)	152,000.00
7	April	152,000.00	250,000.00	320,000.00	(70,000.00)	82,000.00
8	May	82,000.00	325,000.00	420,000.00	(95,000.00)	(13,000.00)
9	June	(13,000.00)	510,000.00	540,000.00	(30,000.00)	(43,000.00)
10	*Average*	$218,833.33	$245,333.33	$335,833.33	($90,500.00)	$128,333.33
11	*Highest*	$500,000.00	$510,000.00	$540,000.00	($30,000.00)	$385,000.00
12	*Lowest*	($13,000.00)	$82,000.00	$220,000.00	($178,000.00)	($43,000.00)

Figure 2–79

1. Start Excel. Apply the Concourse theme to a new workbook.
2. Increase the width of column A to 10.00 and the width of columns B through F to 14.00.
3. Enter the worksheet title **Electry Auto** in cell A1 and the worksheet subtitle **Start-Up Financing Needs** in cell A2. Enter the column titles in row 3, as shown in Figure 2–79. In row 3, use ALT+ENTER to start a new line in a cell.
4. Enter the start-up financing needs data described in Table 2–7 in columns A, C, and D in rows 4 through 9. Enter the initial starting balance (cell B4) of 500000.00. Enter the row titles in the range A10:A12, as shown in Figure 2–79.
5. For the months of February through March, the starting balance is equal to the previous month's ending balance. Obtain the starting balance for February by setting the starting balance of February to the ending balance of January. Use a cell reference rather than typing in the data. Copy the formula for February to the remaining months.
6. Obtain the net income amounts in column E by subtracting the costs in column D from the revenues in column C. Enter the formula in cell E4 and copy it to the range E5:E9. Obtain the ending balance amounts in column F by adding the starting balance in column B to the net income in column F. Enter the formula in cell F4 and copy it to the range F5:F9.
7. In the range B10:B12, use the AVERAGE, MAX, and MIN functions to determine the average value, highest value, and lowest value in the range B4:B9. Copy the range B10:B12 to the range C10:F12.

8. One at a time, merge and center the worksheet title and subtitle across columns A through F. Select cells A1 and A2 and change the background color to light blue (column 7 in the Standard Colors area in the Fill Color gallery). Apply the Title cell style to cells A1 and A2. Change the worksheet title in cell A1 to 28-point white (column 1, row 1 on the Font Color gallery). Change the worksheet subtitle to the same color. Assign a thick box border to the range A1:A2.
9. Center the titles in row 3, columns A through F. Apply the Heading 3 cell style to the range A3:F3. Use the Italic button (Home tab | Font group) to italicize the column titles in row 3 and the row titles in the range A10:A12.
10. Assign a thick box border to the range A10:F12. Change the background and font color for cell F12 to the same colors applied to the worksheet title in Step 8.
11. Change the row heights of row 3 to 36.00 points and row 10 to 30.00 points.
12. Assign the Accounting number format to the range B4:F4. Assign the Comma style format to the range B5:F9. Assign a Currency format with a floating dollar sign to the range B10:F12.
13. Rename the sheet tab as Start-Up Financing Needs. Apply the Light Blue color to the sheet tab. Change the document properties, as specified by your instructor. Change the worksheet header with your name, course number, and other information as specified by your instructor. Save the workbook using the file name Lab 2-1 Part 1 Electry Auto Start-Up Financing Needs. Print the entire worksheet in landscape orientation. Next, print only the range A3:B9.
14. Display the formulas version by pressing CTRL+ACCENT MARK (`). Print the formulas version using the Fit to option button in the Scaling area on the Page tab in the Page Setup dialog box. After printing the worksheet, reset the Scaling option by selecting the Adjust to option button on the Page tab in the Page Setup dialog box and changing the percent value to 100%. Change the display from the formulas version to the values version by pressing CTRL+ACCENT MARK (`). Do not save the workbook.
15. Submit the revised workbook as requested by your instructor.

Instructions Part 2: In this part of the exercise, you will change the revenue amounts until the lowest ending balance is greater than zero, indicating that the company does not require financing in its first six months of operation. Open the workbook created in Part 1 and save the workbook as Lab 2-1 Part 2 Electry Auto Start-Up Financing Needs. Manually increment each of the six values in the revenue column by $1,000.00 until the lowest ending balance in cell F12 is greater than zero. The value of cell F12 should equal $5,000.00 All six values in column C must be incremented the same number of times. Update the worksheet header and save the workbook. Print the worksheet. Submit the assignment as specified by your instructor.

Instructions Part 3: In this part of the exercise, you will change the monthly costs until the lowest ending balance is greater than zero, indicating that the company does not require financing in its first six months of operation. Open the workbook created in Part 1 and then save the workbook as Lab 2–1 Part 3 Electry Auto Start-Up Financing Needs. Manually decrement each of the six values in the costs column by $1,000.00 until the lowest ending balance in cell F12 is greater than zero. Decrement all six values in column C the same number of times. Your worksheet is correct when the lowest ending balance in cell F12 is $5,000.00. Update the worksheet header and save the workbook. Print the worksheet. Submit the assignment as specified by your instructor.

In the Lab

Lab 3: Stock Club Investment Analysis

Problem: Several years ago, you and a large group of friends started a stock club. Each year every member invests more money per month. You have decided to create a portfolio worksheet (Figure 2–80) that summarizes the club's current stock holdings so that you can share the information with your group of friends. The club's portfolio is summarized in Table 2–8. Table 2–8 also shows the general layout of the worksheet to be created.

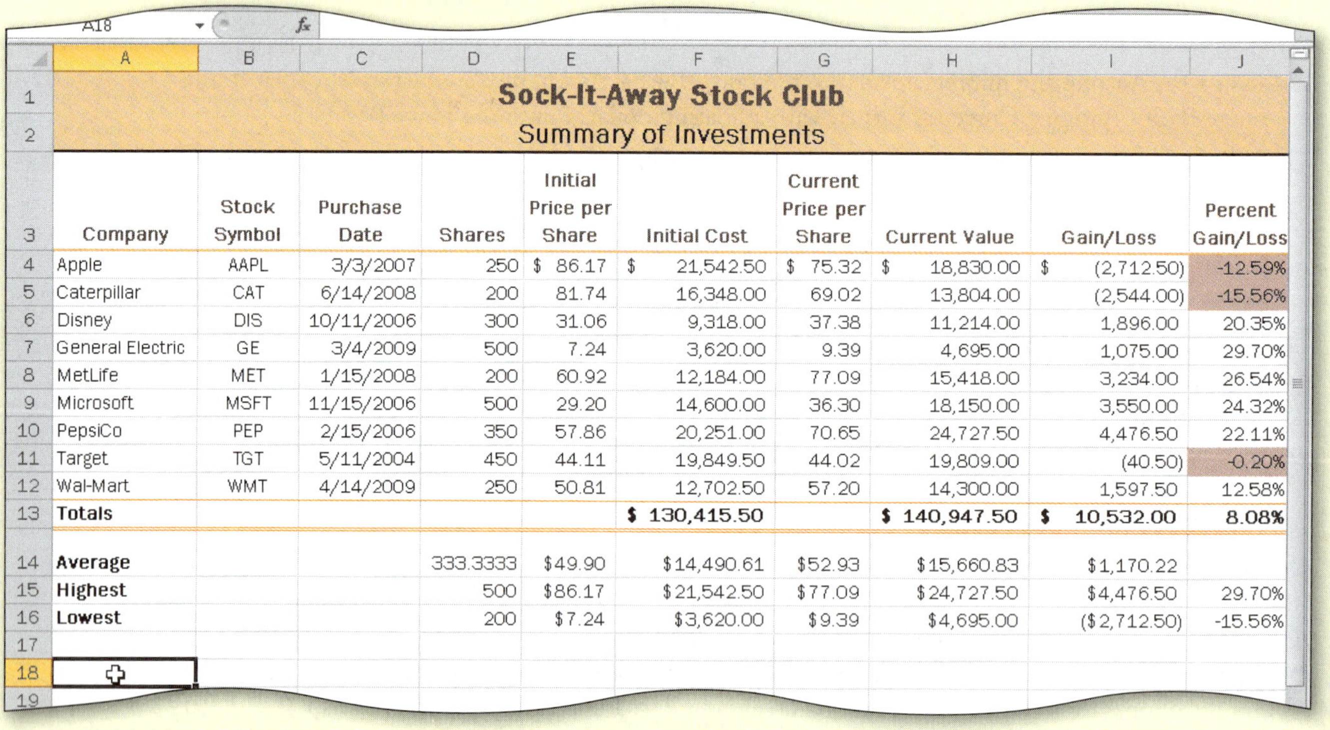

Sock-It-Away Stock Club

Summary of Investments

Company	Stock Symbol	Purchase Date	Shares	Initial Price per Share	Initial Cost	Current Price per Share	Current Value	Gain/Loss	Percent Gain/Loss
Apple	AAPL	3/3/2007	250	$ 86.17	$ 21,542.50	$ 75.32	$ 18,830.00	$ (2,712.50)	-12.59%
Caterpillar	CAT	6/14/2008	200	81.74	16,348.00	69.02	13,804.00	(2,544.00)	-15.56%
Disney	DIS	10/11/2006	300	31.06	9,318.00	37.38	11,214.00	1,896.00	20.35%
General Electric	GE	3/4/2009	500	7.24	3,620.00	9.39	4,695.00	1,075.00	29.70%
MetLife	MET	1/15/2008	200	60.92	12,184.00	77.09	15,418.00	3,234.00	26.54%
Microsoft	MSFT	11/15/2006	500	29.20	14,600.00	36.30	18,150.00	3,550.00	24.32%
PepsiCo	PEP	2/15/2006	350	57.86	20,251.00	70.65	24,727.50	4,476.50	22.11%
Target	TGT	5/11/2004	450	44.11	19,849.50	44.02	19,809.00	(40.50)	-0.20%
Wal-Mart	WMT	4/14/2009	250	50.81	12,702.50	57.20	14,300.00	1,597.50	12.58%
Totals					**$ 130,415.50**		**$ 140,947.50**	**$ 10,532.00**	**8.08%**
Average			333.3333	$49.90	$14,490.61	$52.93	$15,660.83	$1,170.22	
Highest			500	$86.17	$21,542.50	$77.09	$24,727.50	$4,476.50	29.70%
Lowest			200	$7.24	$3,620.00	$9.39	$4,695.00	($2,712.50)	-15.56%

Figure 2–80

Table 2–8 Sock-It-Away Stock Club

Company	Stock Symbol	Purchase Date	Shares	Initial Price per Share	Initial Cost	Current Price per Share	Current Value	Gain/ Loss	Percent Gain/ Loss
Apple	AAPL	3/3/2007	250	86.17	Formula A	75.32	Formula B	Formula C	Formula D
Caterpillar	CAT	6/14/2008	200	81.74	↓	69.02	↓	↓	↓
Disney	DIS	10/11/2006	300	31.06	↓	37.38	↓	↓	↓
General Electric	GE	3/4/2009	500	7.24	↓	9.39	↓	↓	↓
MetLife	MET	1/15/2008	200	60.92	↓	77.09	↓	↓	↓
Microsoft	MSFT	11/15/2006	500	29.20	↓	36.30	↓	↓	↓
PepsiCo	PEP	2/15/2006	350	57.86	↓	70.65	↓	↓	↓
Target	TGT	5/11/2004	450	44.11	↓	44.02	↓	↓	↓
Wal-Mart	WMT	4/14/2009	250	50.81	↓	57.20	↓	↓	↓
Totals			Formula E →						
Average			Formula F →						
Highest			Formula G →						
Lowest			Formula H →						

Instructions: Perform the following tasks:

1. Start Excel. Enter the worksheet titles Sock-It-Away Stock Club in cell A1 and Summary of Investments in cell A2.
2. Enter the column titles and data in Table 2–8 beginning in row 3.
3. Change the column widths and row heights as follows: column A — 11.78; column C — 10.00; columns E and G — 7.44; columns F, H, and I — 13.00; column J — 8.22; row 3 — 56.25 points; row 14 — 27.00 points.
4. Enter the following formulas in row 4 and then copy them down through row 12:
   a. Enter Formula A in cell F4: Initial Cost = Shares × Initial Price per Share
   b. Enter Formula B in cell H4: Current Value = Shares × Current Price Per Share
   c. Enter Formula C in cell I4: Gain/Loss = Current Value – Initial Cost
   d. Enter Formula D in cell J4: Percent Gain/Loss = Gain/Loss / Initial Cost
5. Compute the totals for initial cost, current value, gain/loss, and percent gain loss. For the percent gain/loss in cell J13, copy cell J12 to J13 using the fill handle.
6. In cells D14, D15, and D16, enter Formulas E, F, and G using the AVERAGE, MAX, and MIN functions. Copy the three functions across through the range J14: J16. Delete the invalid formula in cell J14.
7. Format the worksheet as follows:
   a. Apply the Trek theme to the worksheet.
   b. Format the worksheet title with Title cell style. Merge and center across columns A through J.
   c. Format the worksheet subtitle with Franklin Gothic Book font, 16 point font size, Black, Text 1 theme font color. Merge and Center across columns A through J.
   d. Format the worksheet title and subtitle background with Orange, Accent 1, Lighter 60% theme color and a thick box border.
   e. Format row 3 with the Heading 3 cell style and row 13 with the Total cell style.
   f. Format the data in rows 4 through 12: center data in column B; format dates in column C to the mm/dd/yy date format; range E4:I4 — Accounting number format style with fixed dollar sign; range E5:I12 — Comma style; range J4:J13 — Percent style with two decimal places; cells F13, H13, and I13 — Accounting Number format with fixed dollar sign.
   g. Format E14:I16 — Currency format with floating decimal places; J15:J16 — Percent style with two decimal places.
   h. Format J4:J12 — apply conditional formatting so that if a cell in range is less than 0, then cell appears with a pink background color.
8. Spell check the worksheet. Change the name of the sheet tab to Summary of Investments and apply the Orange, Accent 1, Darker 25% theme color to the sheet tab. Update the document properties, and save the workbook using the file name, Lab 2-3 Sock-It-Away Stock Club Summary of Investments. Print the worksheet in landscape orientation. Print the formulas version on one page. Close the workbook without saving changes. Submit the assignment as specified by your instructor.

Cases and Places

Apply your creative thinking and problem-solving skills to design and implement a solution.

1: Analyzing Emergency Student Loans

Academic

The Student Assistance office at your school provides emergency loans at simple interest. The data obtained from six types of loans and the desired report format are shown in Table 2–9. The required formulas are shown in Table 2–10. Use the concepts and techniques presented in this chapter to create and format the worksheet. Include total, average, maximum, and minimum values for Principal, Interest, and Amount Due.

Table 2–9 Emergency Student Loan Data and Worksheet Layout

Loan Type	Principal	Rate	Time in Years
Academic Supplies	$40,000	7.5%	.4
Medical Emergency	$25,500	12%	.33
Personal Emergency	$12,750	8.25%	.5
Room and Board	$27,000	6.5%	1
Travel Expenses	$4,550	12%	.5
Tuition Reimbursement	$107,000	6%	1

Table 2–10 Emergency Student Loan Formulas

Interest = Principal × Rate × Time
Amount Due = Principal + Interest
Average = AVERAGE function
Minimum = MIN function
Maximum = MAX function

2: Analyzing Energy Consumption

Personal

Your parents believe that your late night studying sessions and household appliance usage contribute to excessive electricity bills. You have decided to try to prove them wrong by analyzing your daily and monthly electricity consumption. You research the energy consumption of your personal items and appliance usage to obtain consumption costs per hour for each item. Table 2–11 contains the data and format for the report you want to create.

Use the concepts and techniques presented in this project to create and format the worksheet. Include an embedded 3-D Pie chart that shows the cost per month. Use Microsoft Excel Help to create a professional looking 3-D Pie chart with title and data labels.

Table 2–11 Appliance Electricity Usage Costs

Appliance	Cost per Hour	Hours Used Daily	Total Cost Per Day	Total Cost per Month (30 Days)
Clothes dryer	$0.325	1		
Computer	$0.02	6		
DVD player	$0.035	1		
Light bulbs	$0.043	8		
Refrigerator	$0.035	24		
Stereo	$0.02	5		
Television	$0.04	4		
Washing machine	$0.03	2	↓	↓

3: Analyzing Profit Potential

Professional

You work for HumiCorp, an online retailer of home humidifiers. Your manager wants to know the profit potential of their inventory based on the items in inventory listed in Table 2–12. Table 2–12 contains the format of the desired report. The required formulas are shown in Table 2–13. Use the concepts and techniques developed in this chapter to create and format the worksheet. The company just received 67 additional desk-sized humidifiers and shipped out 48 room-sized humidifiers. Update the appropriate cells to reflect the change in inventory.

Table 2–12 HumiCorp Inventory Profit Potential Data and Worksheet Layout

Item	Units on Hand	Unit Cost	Total Cost	Unit Price	Total Value	Potential Profit
Desk	187	27.58	Formula A	Formula B	Formula C	Formula D
Filtered home-sized	42	324.14				
Filtered room-sized	118	86.55				
Home-sized	103	253.91				
Room-sized	97	53.69	↓	↓	↓	↓
Total	—	—	—	—	—	—
Average	Formula E →					
Lowest	Formula F →					
Highest	Formula G →					

Table 2–13 HumiCorp Inventory Profit Potential Formulas

Formula A = Units on Hand × Unit Cost
Formula B = Unit Cost × (1 / (1 – .66))
Formula C = Units on Hand × Unit Price
Formula D = Total Value – Total Cost
Formula E = AVERAGE function
Formula F = MIN function
Formula G = MAX function

3 What-If Analysis, Charting, and Working with Large Worksheets

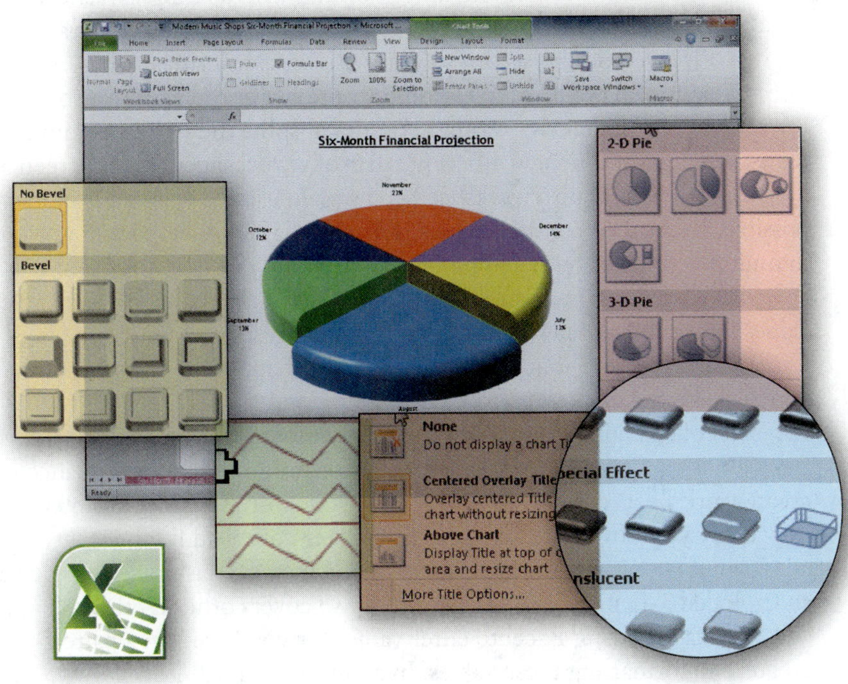

Objectives

You will have mastered the material in this chapter when you can:

- Rotate text in a cell
- Create a series of month names
- Copy, paste, insert, and delete cells
- Format numbers using format symbols
- Freeze and unfreeze rows and columns
- Show and format the system date
- Use absolute and mixed cell references in a formula
- Use the IF function to perform a logical test
- Create Sparkline charts
- Use the Format Painter button to format cells
- Create a 3-D Pie chart on a separate chart sheet
- Rearrange worksheet tabs
- Change the worksheet view
- Answer what-if questions
- Goal seek to answer what-if questions

3 What-If Analysis, Charting, and Working with Large Worksheets

Introduction

Worksheets normally are much larger than those created in the previous Excel chapters, often extending beyond the size of the Excel window. Because you cannot see the entire worksheet on the screen at one time, working with a large worksheet sometimes can be frustrating. This chapter introduces several Excel commands that allow you to control what is displayed on the screen so that you can view critical parts of a large worksheet at one time. One command allows you to freeze rows and columns so that Excel always displays them on the screen. Another command splits the worksheet into separate windowpanes so that you can view different parts of a worksheet on the screen at one time.

When you set up a worksheet, you should use cell references in formulas whenever possible, rather than constant values. The use of a cell reference allows you to change a value in multiple formulas by changing the value in a single cell. The cell references in a formula are called assumptions. Assumptions are values in cells that you can change to determine new values for formulas. This chapter emphasizes the use of assumptions and shows how to use Excel to answer what-if questions, such as what happens to the six-month operating income if you decrease the marketing expenses assumption by 3 percent? Being able to analyze quickly the effect of changing values in a worksheet is an important skill in making business decisions.

This chapter also introduces you to techniques that will enhance your ability to create worksheets and draw charts. From your work in Excel Chapter 1, you are aware of how easily you can create charts. This chapter covers additional charting techniques that allow you to convey a message in a dramatic pictorial fashion, such as Sparkline charts and an exploded 3-D pie chart. This chapter also covers other methods for entering values in cells, such as allowing Excel to enter values for you based on a pattern of values that you create, and formatting these values. In addition, you will learn how to use absolute cell references and how to use the IF function to assign a value to a cell based on a logical test.

Project — Financial Projection Worksheet with What-If Analysis and Chart

The project in the chapter follows proper design guidelines and uses Excel to create the worksheet and pie chart shown in Figures 3–1a and 3–1b. Modern Music Shops operates several stores that sell and service musical instruments. Each June and December, the director of finance and accounting submits a plan to the management team to show projected monthly sales revenues, costs of goods sold, gross margin, expenses, and operating income for the next six months. The director requires an easy-to-read worksheet that shows financial projections for the next six months. The worksheet should allow for quick analysis if projections for certain numbers change, such as the percentage of expenses allocated to marketing. In addition, a 3-D pie chart is required that shows the projected operating income contribution for each of the six months.

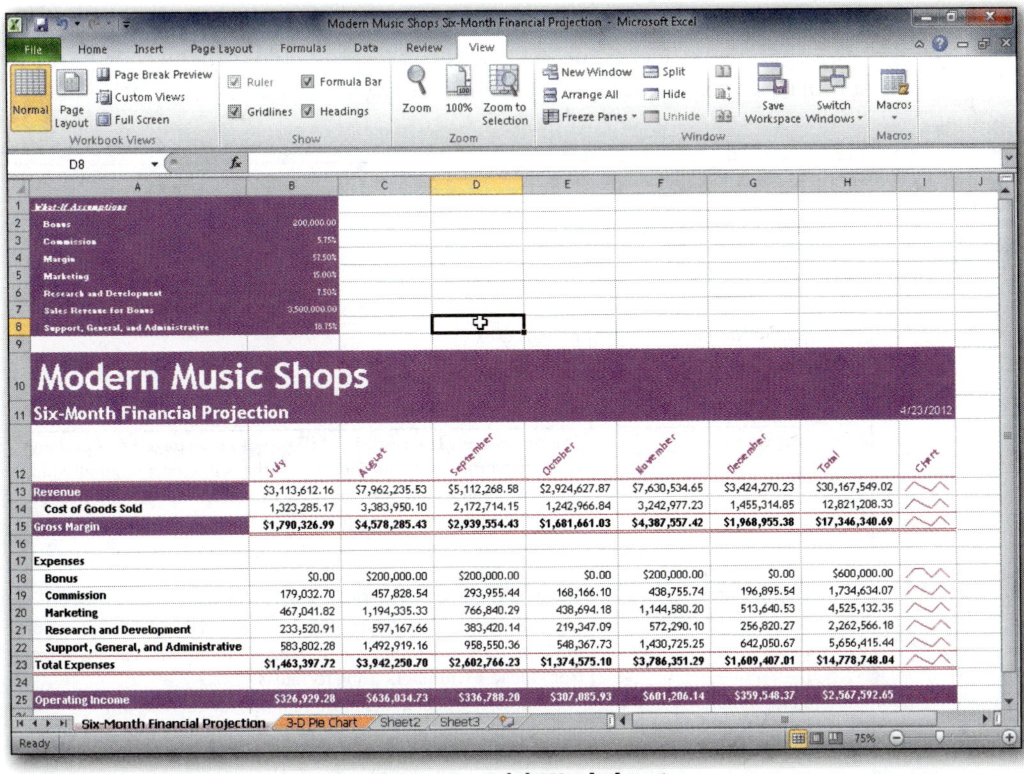

Figure 3–1 (a) Worksheet

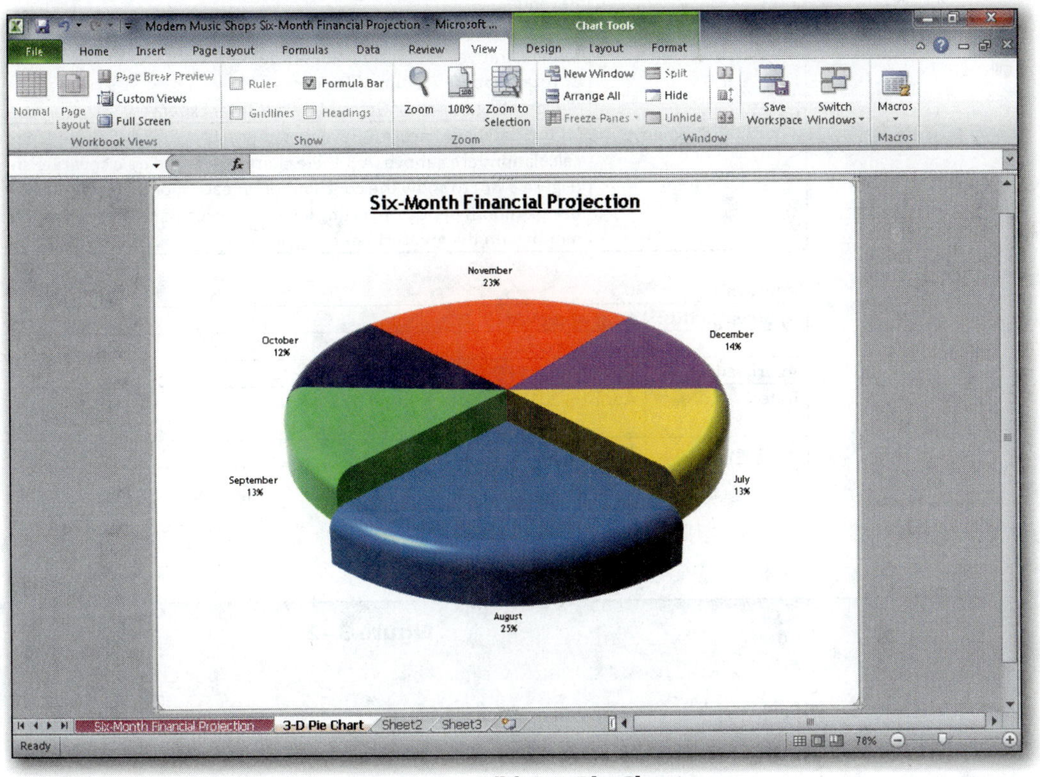

Figure 3–1 (b) 3-D Pie Chart

BTW

Correctness
Studies have shown that more than 25 percent of all business worksheets have errors. You can ensure correctness in your formulas by carefully checking them using Range Finder. The Formula Auditing group on the Formulas tab on the Ribbon also can be helpful when verifying formulas.

The requirements document for the Modern Music Shops Six-Month Financial Projection worksheet is shown in Figure 3–2. It includes the needs, source of data, summary of calculations, chart requirements, and other facts about its development.

REQUEST FOR NEW WORKBOOK

Date Submitted:	April 9, 2012
Submitted By:	Marcus Olek
Worksheet Title:	Modern Music Shops' Six-Month Financial Projection
Needs:	The needs are: (1) a worksheet (Figure 3-3a on page EX 142) that shows Modern Music Shops' projected monthly sales, cost of goods sold, gross margin, expenses, and operating income for a six-month period; and (2) a 3-D Pie chart (Figure 3-3b on page EX 142) that shows the projected contribution of each month's operating income to the six-month period operating income.
Source of Data:	The data supplied by the Finance department includes projections of the monthly sales and expenses (Table 3-1 on page EX 143) that are based on prior years. All the remaining numbers in the worksheet are determined from these 13 numbers using formulas.
Calculations:	The following calculations must be made for each month: 1. Cost of Goods Sold = Revenue – Revenue × Margin 2. Gross Margin = Revenue – Cost of Goods Sold 3. Bonus Expense = $200,000.00 if the Revenue exceeds the Revenue for Bonus; otherwise Bonus Expense = 0 4. Commission Expense = Commission Assumption × Revenue 5. Marketing Expense = Marketing Assumption × Revenue 6. Research and Development = Research and Development Assumption × Revenue 7. Support, General, and Administrative Expense = Support, General, and Administrative Assumption × Revenue 8. Total Expenses = Sum of Expenses 9. Operating Income = Gross Margin – Total Expenses
Chart Requirements:	Show Sparkline charts for Revenue and each of the items noted in the calculations area above. A 3-D Pie chart is required on a separate sheet (Figure 3-3b) to show the contribution of each month's operating income to the six-month period operating income. The chart should also emphasize the month with the greatest operating income.

Approvals

Approval Status:	X	Approved
		Rejected
Approved By:	Farah Qadir, CFO	
Date:	April 16, 2012	
Assigned To:	J. Quasney, Spreadsheet Specialist	

Figure 3–2

Overview

As you read this chapter, you will learn how to create the worksheet shown in Figure 3–1 by performing these general tasks:

- Create a series of month names
- Use absolute cell references in a formula
- Use the IF function to perform a logical test
- Create Sparkline charts in a range of cells
- Use the Format Painter button to format cells
- Create a 3-D pie chart on a separate chart sheet
- Answer what-if questions
- Manipulate large worksheets

BTW

Excel's Usefulness

Just a short time ago, a what-if question of any complexity could be answered only by using a large, expensive computer programmed by highly paid computer professionals, and generating a result could take days. Excel gives the noncomputer professional the ability to get complex business-related questions answered instantaneously and economically.

Plan Ahead

General Project Decisions

While creating an Excel worksheet, you need to make several decisions that will determine the appearance and characteristics of the finished worksheet. As you create the worksheet required to meet the requirements shown in Figure 3–2, you should follow these general guidelines:

1. **Plan the layout of the worksheet.** Worksheets that include financial data associated with time frames typically include dates, such as months, quarters, or years, as column headers. What-if assumptions should not clutter the worksheet, but placing them in an easily located portion of the worksheet allows for quicker creation of new projections.

2. **Determine the necessary formulas and functions needed.** Often, financial calculations rely on strict definitions and commonly accepted formulas for performing the calculations. Look for such situations and always use the accepted formulas. When using a what-if section on a worksheet, make certain to create formulas that use the what-if criteria. When a requirement necessitates a calculation only under a certain condition, a function can check for the condition and make the calculation when necessary.

3. **Specify how to best utilize Sparkline charts.** Sparkline charts allow worksheet users quickly to visualize information in a small chart within a cell. The use of multiple Sparkline charts in the worksheet will provide the user with a visual comparison of the various data items for each month. The user, therefore, can see trends for each line item over time and also compare relationships among various line items.

4. **Identify how to format various elements of the worksheet.** Format separate parts of a worksheet, such as what-if assumptions, in a manner that indicates that they are separate from the main area of the worksheet. Other financial items, such as sales revenue and expenses, are distinct categories of financial data and should be separated visually. Totals and subtotals should stand out to draw the reader's attention.

5. **Specify how charts should convey necessary information.** As you have learned, different chart types convey different messages and are appropriate in different situations. For example, a 3-D pie chart is a good way to compare visually a small set of numbers. Often one or two slices of a pie chart displays as exploded, meaning that the slice appears pulled away from the cart, in order to emphasize the slice to the user. Format chart data points so that the worksheet user's eye is drawn to important information.

6. **Perform what-if analysis and goal seeking using the best techniques.** What-if analysis allows you quickly to answer questions regarding various predictions. A what-if area of a worksheet allows users of the worksheet efficiently to ask questions. Goal seeking allows you automatically to modify values in a what-if area of a worksheet based on a goal that you have for another cell in the worksheet.

When necessary, more specific details concerning the above guidelines are presented at appropriate points in the chapter. The chapter also will identify the actions you perform and decisions made regarding these guidelines during the creation of the worksheet shown in Figure 3–1 on page EX 139.

Using a sketch of the worksheet can help you visualize its design. The sketch of the worksheet consists of titles, column and row headings, location of data values, calculations, and a rough idea of the desired formatting (Figure 3–3a). The sketch of the 3-D pie chart shows the expected contribution of each month's operating income to the six-month operating income (Figure 3–3b). The assumptions will be entered at the top of the worksheet (Figure 3–3a). The projected monthly sales revenue will be entered in row 13 of the worksheet. The projected monthly sales revenue and the assumptions shown in Table 3–1 will be used to calculate the remaining numbers in the worksheet.

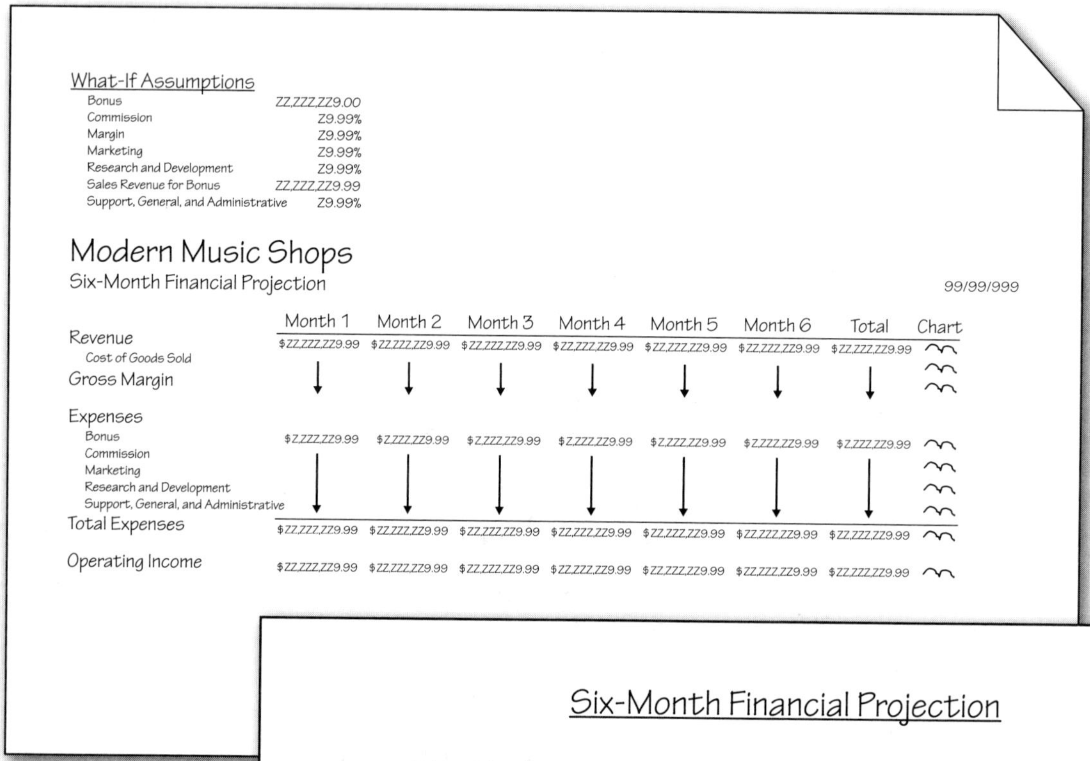

Figure 3–3 (a) Worksheet Sketch

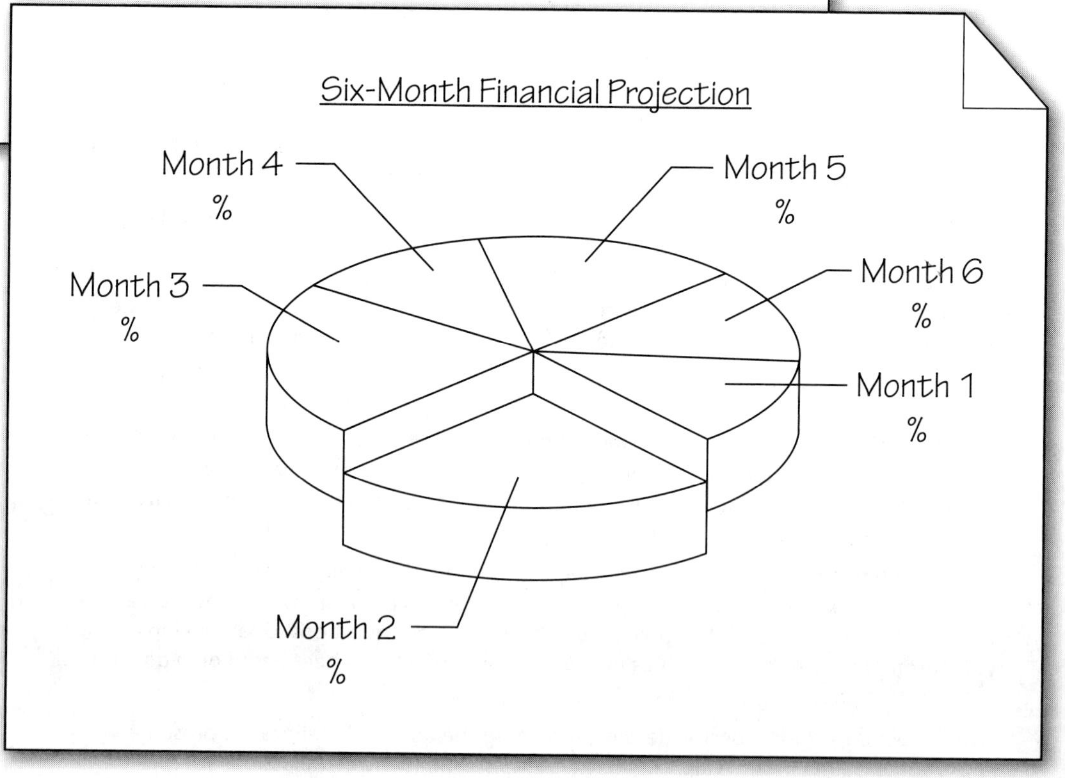

Figure 3–3 (b) 3-D Pie Chart Sketch

With a solid understanding of the requirements document, an understanding of the necessary decisions, and a sketch of the worksheet, the next step is to use Excel to create the worksheet.

Table 3–1 Modern Music Shops Six-Month Financial Projections Data and What-If Assumptions

Projected Monthly Total Sales Revenues	
July	$3,113,612.16
August	7,962,235.53
September	5,112,268.58
October	2,924,627.87
November	7,630,534.65
December	3,424,270.23
What-If Assumptions	
Bonus	$200,000.00
Commission	5.75%
Margin	57.50%
Marketing	15.00%
Research and Development	7.50%
Sales Revenue for Bonus	$3,500,000.00
Support, General, and Administrative	18.75%

To Start Excel

If you are using a computer to step through the project in this chapter and you want your screens to match the figures in the Office and Windows chapters in this book, you should change your screen's resolution to 1024 × 768. For information about how to change a computer's resolution, refer to the Introduction to Office 2010 and Windows 7 chapter in this book.

The following steps, which assume Windows 7 is running, start Excel based on a typical installation. You may need to ask your instructor how to start Excel for your computer. For a detailed example of the procedure summarized below, refer to the Office 2010 and Windows 7 chapter in this book.

1. Click the Start button on the Windows 7 taskbar to display the Start menu.
2. Type `Microsoft Excel` as the search text in the 'Search programs and files' text box, and watch the search results appear on the Start menu.
3. Click Microsoft Excel 2010 in the search results on the Start menu to start Excel and display a new blank workbook in the Excel window.
4. If the Excel window is not maximized, click the Maximize button next to the Close button on its title bar to maximize the window.

For an introduction to Windows 7 and instruction about how to perform basic Windows 7 tasks, read the Office 2010 and Windows 7 chapter in this book, where you can learn how to resize windows, change screen resolution, create folders, move and rename files, use Windows Help, and much more.

For an introduction to Office 2010 and instruction about how to perform basic tasks in Office 2010 programs, read the Office 2010 and Windows 7 chapter in this book, where you can learn how to start a program, use the Ribbon, save a file, open a file, quit a program, use Help, and much more.

To Enter the Worksheet Titles, Change Document Properties, Apply a Theme, and Save the Workbook

The worksheet contains two titles, initially in cells A8 and A9. In the previous Excel chapters, titles were centered across the worksheet. With large worksheets that extend beyond the size of a window, it is best to enter titles left-aligned as shown in the sketch of the worksheet in Figure 3–3a because the worksheet prints with the title on the first page if the worksheet requires multiple pages, and the user more easily finds the worksheet title when necessary. The following steps enter the worksheet titles, change the workbook theme to Opulent, change document properties, and then save the workbook.

1. Select cell A8 and then type `Modern Music Shops` as the worksheet title.
2. Select cell A9 and then type `Six-Month Financial Projection` as the worksheet subtitle and then press the ENTER key to enter the worksheet subtitle.
3. Change the document properties as specified by your instructor.
4. Apply the Opulent theme to the workbook.
5. With a USB flash drive connected to one of the computer's USB ports, click the Save button on the Quick Access Toolbar to display the Save As dialog box.
6. Type `Modern Music Shops Six-Month Financial Projection` in the File name text box to change the file name. Do not press the ENTER key after typing the file name because you do not want to close the dialog box at this time.
7. Navigate to the desired save location (in this case, the Excel folder in the CIS 101 folder [or your class folder] on the USB flash drive).
8. Click the Save button (Save As dialog box) to save the document in the selected folder on the selected drive with the entered file name.

BTW

The Ribbon and Screen Resolution

Excel may change how the groups and buttons within the groups appear on the Ribbon, depending on the computer's screen resolution. Thus, your Ribbon may look different from the ones in the Office and Windows chapters in this book if you are using a screen resolution other than 1024 x 768.

Rotating Text and Using the Fill Handle to Create a Series

The data on the worksheet, including month names and the What-If Assumptions section, now can be added to the worksheet.

Plan Ahead

Plan the layout of the worksheet.

Excel allows you to rotate text in a cell. Rotated text often provides a strong visual appeal. Rotated text also allows you to fit more text into a smaller column width. Excel Chapters 1 and 2 used the fill handle to copy a cell or a range of cells to adjacent cells. The fill handle also allows creation of a series of numbers, dates, or month names automatically. Using the fill handle in this way eliminates the need to type in such data, saving time and eliminating typographical errors.

BTW

BTWs

For a complete list of the BTWs found in the margins of the Office and Windows chapters in this book, visit the Microsoft Office and Concepts CourseMate Web site at www.cengagebrain.com and then navigate to the BTW resource for this book.

To Rotate Text and Use the Fill Handle to Create a Series of Month Names

The design of the worksheet calls specifically for only six months of data. Because there always will be only six months of data in the worksheet, the months should be placed across the top of the worksheet as column headings rather than as row headings. The data for the worksheet includes more data items regarding each month than there are months, and, possibly, more expense categories could be added in the future. A proper layout, therefore, includes placing each month as column headings.

When you first enter text, its angle is zero degrees (0°), and it reads from left to right in a cell. Excel allows you to rotate text in a cell counterclockwise by entering a number between 1° and 90°.

The following steps enter the month name, July, in cell B10; format cell B10 (including rotating the text); and then use the fill handle to enter the remaining month names in the range C10:G10.

1

- If necessary, select the Home tab and then select cell B10 because this cell will include the first month name in the series of month names.
- Type **July** as the cell entry and then click the Enter box.
- Click the Format Cells: Alignment Dialog Box Launcher (Home tab | Alignment group) to display the Format Cells dialog box (Figure 3–4).

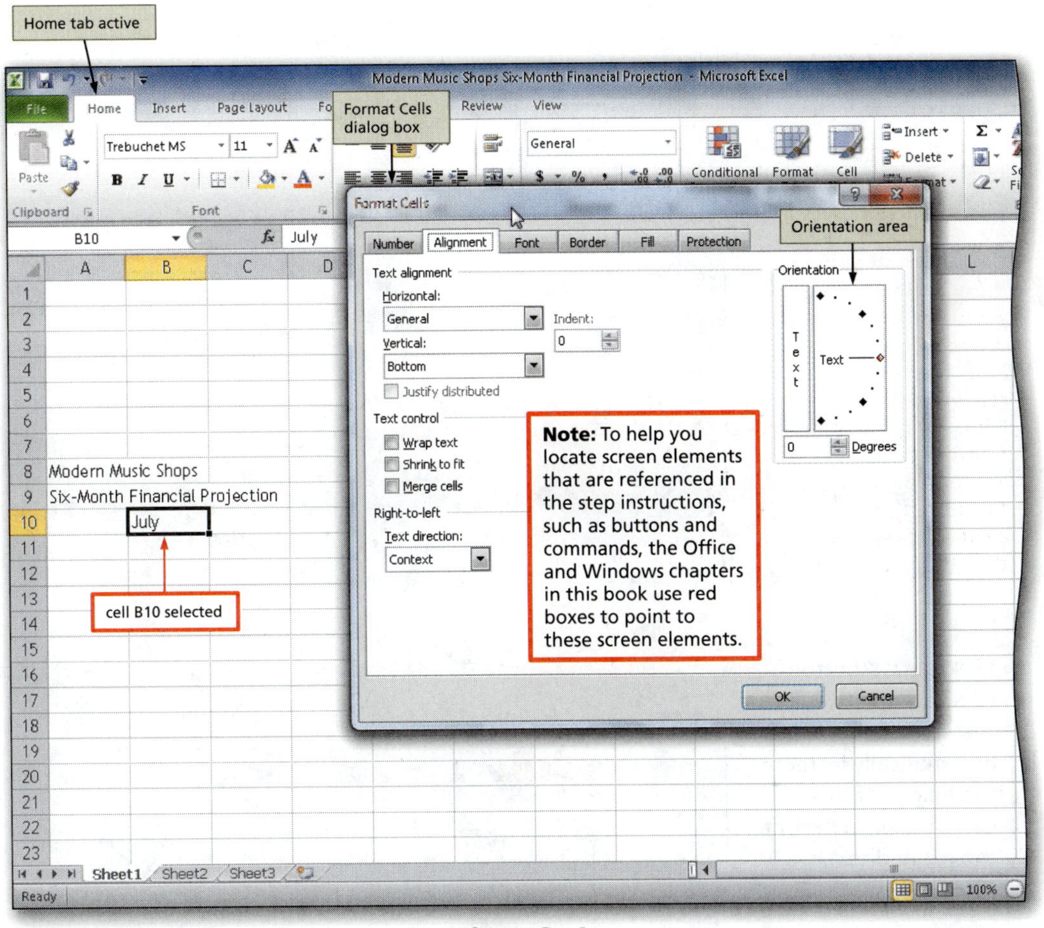

Figure 3–4

2

- Click the 45° point in the Orientation area (Format Cells dialog box) to move the Text hand in the Orientation area to the 45° point and to display a new orientation in the Degrees box (Figure 3–5).

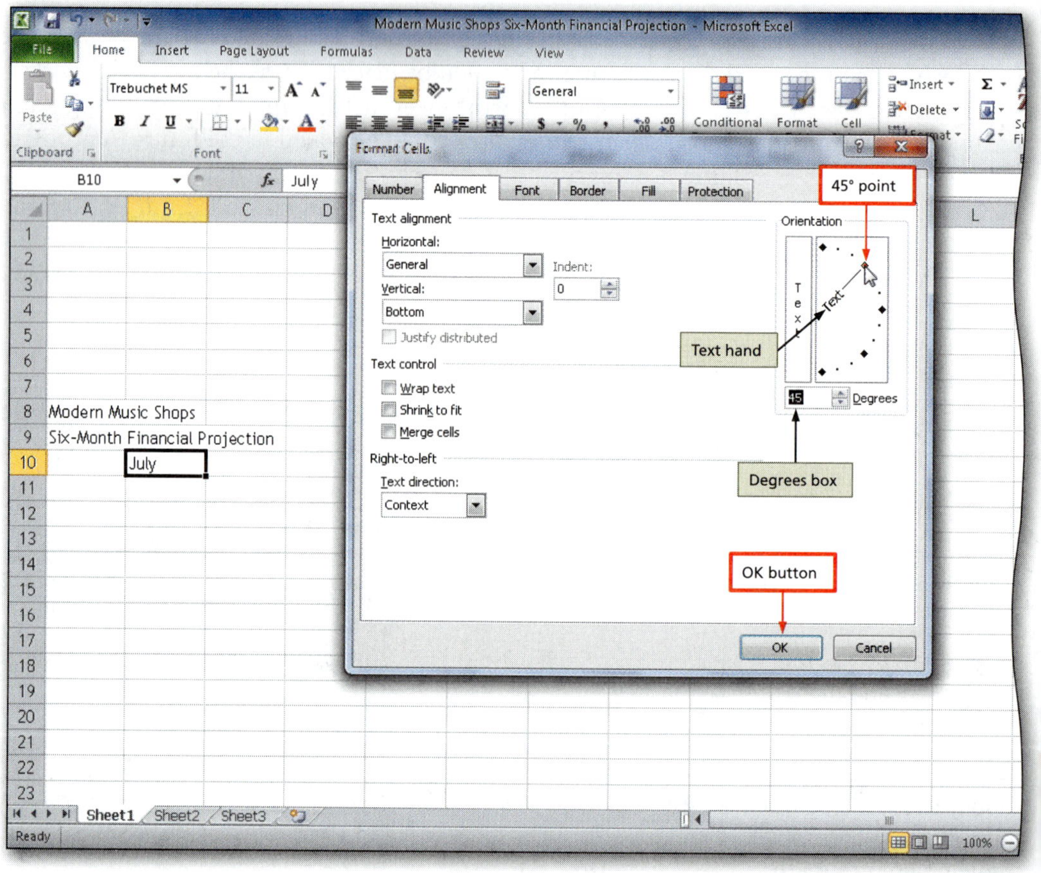

Figure 3–5

3

- Click the OK button to rotate the text in the active cell and automatically increase the height of the current row to best fit the rotated text.
- Point to the fill handle on the lower-right corner of cell B10 to display the crosshair mouse pointer in preparation of filling the month series (Figure 3–6).

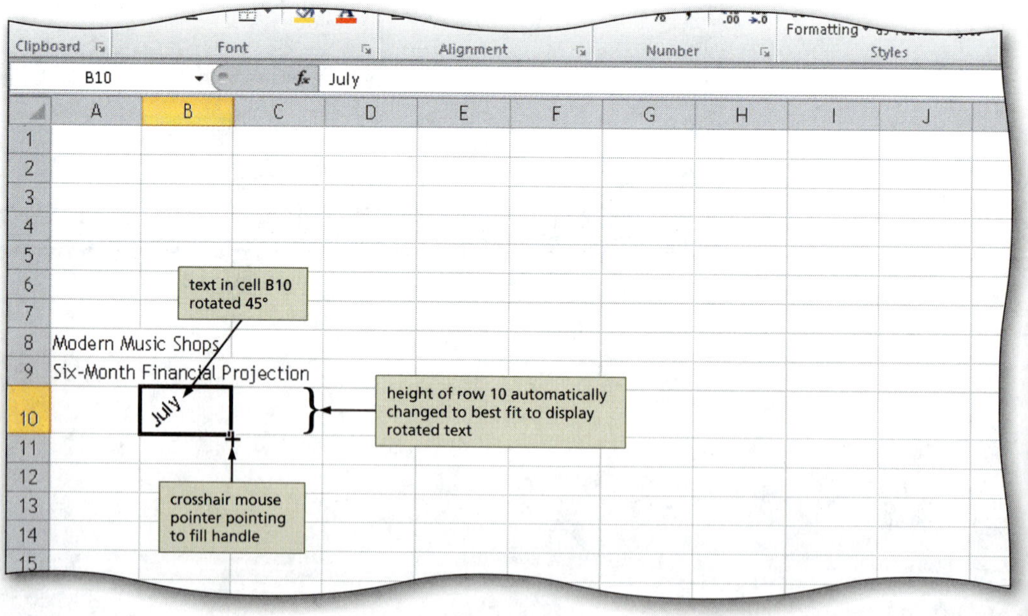

Figure 3–6

4

- Drag the fill handle to the right to select the range to fill, C10:G10 in this case. Do not release the mouse button (Figure 3–7).

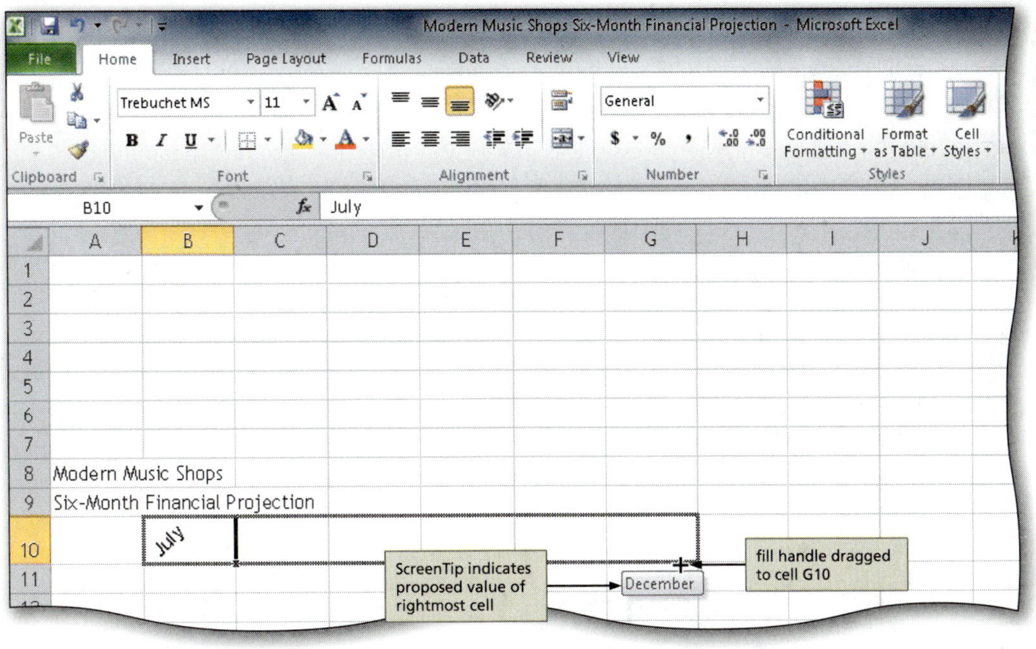

Figure 3–7

5

- Release the mouse button to create a month name series in the selected range and copy the format of the selected cell to the selected range.
- Click the Auto Fill Options button below the lower-right corner of the fill area to display the Auto Fill Options menu (Figure 3–8).

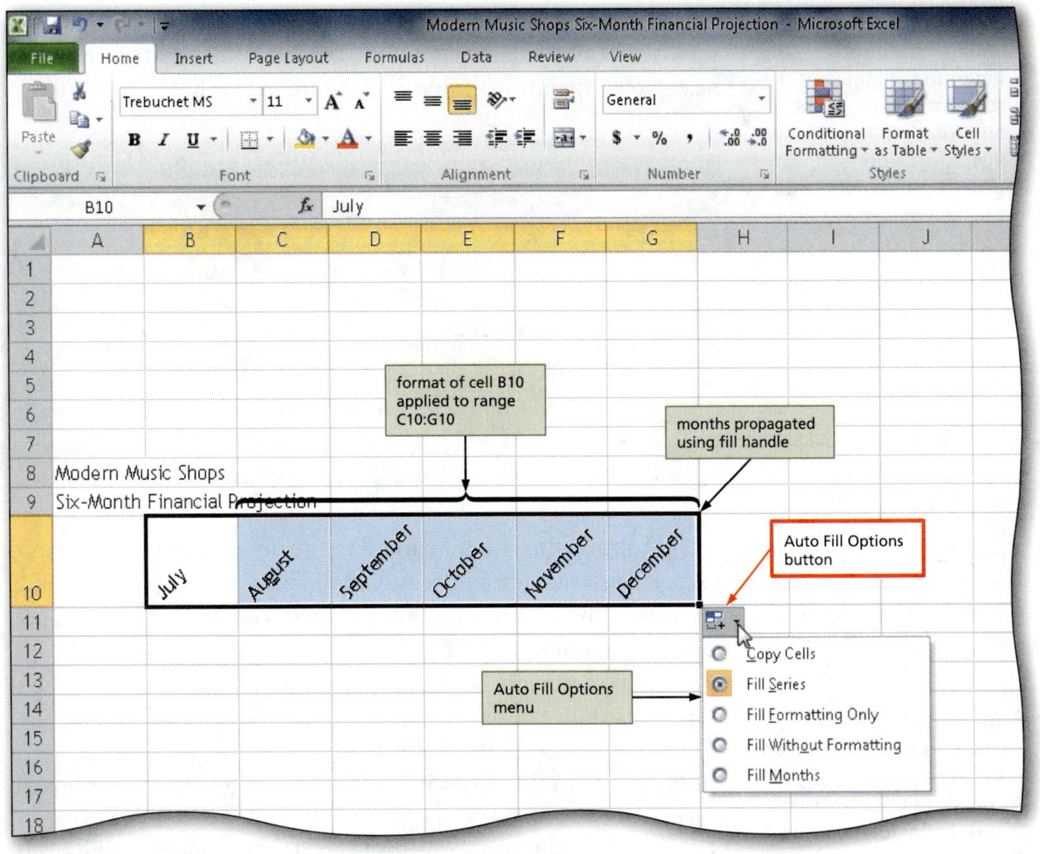

Figure 3–8

Q&A

What if I do not want to copy the format of cell B10 during the auto fill operation?

In addition to creating a series of values, dragging the fill handle instructs Excel to copy the format of cell B10 to the range C10:G10. With some fill operations, you may not want to copy the formats of the source cell or range to the destination cell or range. If this is the case, click the Auto Fill Options button after the range fills and then select the option you desire on the Auto Fill Options menu (Figure 3–8).

6

- Click the Auto Fill Options button to hide the Auto Fill Options menu.
- Select cell H10, type `Total,` and then press the RIGHT ARROW key to enter a column heading.
- Type Chart in cell I10 and then press the RIGHT ARROW key to enter a column heading.

Q&A Why is the word Total automatically formatted with a 45° rotation?

Excel tries to save you time by automatically recognizing the adjacent cell format in cell G10 and applying it to cell H10. Such behavior also occurs when typing the column heading in cell I10.

Other Ways

1. Enter start month in cell, apply formatting, right-drag fill handle in direction to fill, click Fill Months on shortcut menu
2. Enter start month in cell, apply formatting, select range, click Fill button (Home tab | Editing group), click Series, click AutoFill

BTW

Rotating Text in a Cell

In Excel, you use the Alignment sheet of the Format Cells dialog box, as shown in Figure 3–5 on page 146, to position data in a cell by centering, left-aligning, or right-aligning; indenting; aligning at the top, bottom, or center; and rotating. If you enter 90 in the Degrees box in the Orientation area, the text will appear vertically and read from bottom to top in the cell.

Using the Auto Fill Options Menu

As shown in Figure 3–8 on the previous page, Fill Series is the default option that Excel uses to fill an area, which means it fills the destination area with a series, using the same formatting as the source area. If you choose another option on the Auto Fill Options menu, then Excel immediately changes the contents of the destination range. Following the use of the fill handle, the Auto Fill Options button remains active until you begin the next Excel operation. Table 3–2 summarizes the options on the Auto Fill Options menu.

Table 3–2 Options Available on the Auto Fill Options Menu

Auto Fill Option	Description
Copy Cells	Fill destination area with contents using format of source area. Do not create a series.
Fill Series	Fill destination area with series using format of source area. This option is the default.
Fill Formatting Only	Fill destination area using format of source area. No content is copied unless fill is series.
Fill Without Formatting	Fill destination area with contents, without the formatting of source area.
Fill Months	Fill destination area with series of months using format of source area. Same as Fill Series and shows as an option only if source area contains a month.

BTW

The Mighty Fill Handle

If you drag the fill handle to the left or up, Excel will decrement the series rather than increment the series. To copy a word, such as January or Monday, which Excel might interpret as the start of a series, hold down the CTRL key while you drag the fill handle to a destination area. If you drag the fill handle back into the middle of a cell, Excel erases the contents of the cell.

You can use the fill handle to create a series longer than the one shown in Figure 3–8. If you drag the fill handle past cell G10 in Step 4, Excel continues to increment the months and logically will repeat July, August, and so on, if you extend the range far enough to the right.

You can create several different types of series using the fill handle. Table 3–3 illustrates several examples. Notice in examples 4 through 7, 9, and 11 that, if you use the fill handle to create a series of numbers or nonsequential months, you must enter the first item in the series in one cell and the second item in the series in an adjacent cell. Excel still creates the series, however, if the first two items are in a range and the cells between the items are empty. Next, select both cells and drag the fill handle through the destination area.

Table 3–3 Examples of Series Using the Fill Handle

Example	Contents of Cell(s) Copied Using the Fill Handle	Next Three Values of Extended Series
1	4:00	5:00, 6:00, 7:00
2	Qtr2	Qtr3, Qtr4, Qtr1
3	Quarter 1	Quarter 2, Quarter 3, Quarter 4
4	22-Jul, 22-Sep	22-Nov, 22-Jan, 22-Mar
5	2012, 2013	2014, 2015, 2016
6	1, 2	3, 4, 5
7	625, 600	575, 550, 525
8	Mon	Tue, Wed, Thu
9	Sunday, Tuesday	Thursday, Saturday, Monday
10	4th Section	5th Section, 6th Section, 7th Section
11	−205, −208	−211, −214, −217

BTW

Custom Fill Sequences
You can create your own custom lists for use with the fill handle. For example, if you often type in the same list of products or names into Excel, you can create a custom fill sequence. You then can type the first product or name and then use the fill handle automatically to fill in the remaining products or names. To create a custom fill sequence, open the Excel Options dialog box by clicking the Options button in the Backstage view. Click the Advanced tab (Excel Options dialog box) and then click the Edit Custom Lists button (Excel Options dialog box).

To Increase Column Widths

In Excel Chapter 2, you increased column widths after the values were entered into the worksheet. Sometimes, you may want to increase the column widths before you enter the values and, if necessary, adjust them later. The following steps increase the column widths.

1

- Move the mouse pointer to the boundary between column heading A and column heading B so that the mouse pointer changes to a split double arrow in preparation of adjusting the column widths.
- Drag the mouse pointer to the right until the ScreenTip displays the desired column width, Width: 36.00 (293 pixels) in this case. Do not release the mouse button (Figure 3–9).

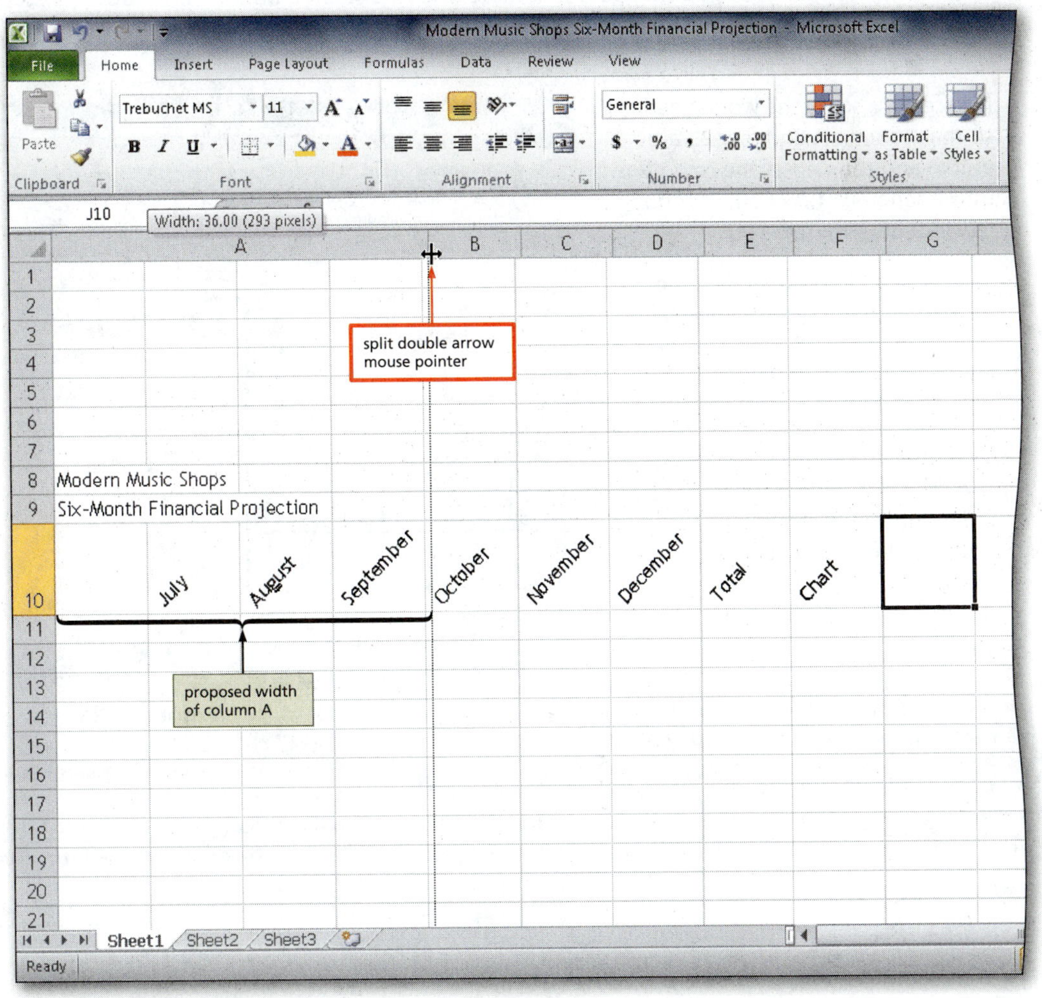

Figure 3–9

2

- Release the mouse button to change the width of the column.
- Click column heading B to select the column and then drag through column heading G to select the range in which to change the widths.
- Move the mouse pointer to the boundary between column headings B and C in preparation of resizing column B, and then drag the mouse to the right until the ScreenTip displays the desired width, Width: 14.88 (124 pixels) in this case. Do not release the mouse button (Figure 3–10).

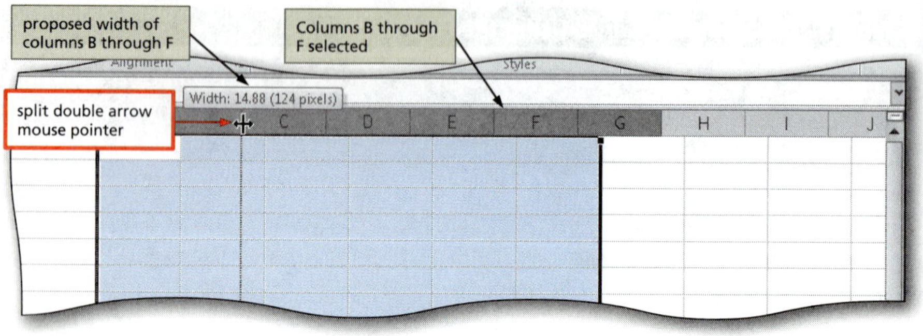

Figure 3–10

3

- Release the mouse button to change the width of the selected columns.
- If necessary, scroll the worksheet so that column H is visible and then use the technique described in Step 1 to increase the width of column H to 16.00.

To Enter Row Titles

Excel allows you to indent text in cells. Often, indentation sets off titles, such as row titles, from other titles to create a hierarchy, such as you may find in a table of contents in a book. The following steps enter the row titles in column A and indent several of the row titles.

1

- If necessary, scroll the worksheet so that column A and row 23 are visible and then enter the row titles in the range A11:A23 but without the indents (Figure 3–11).
- Select cell A12 and then click the Increase Indent button (Home tab | Alignment group) to increase the indentation of the text in the selected cell.
- Select the range A16:A20 and then click the Increase Indent button (Home tab | Alignment group) to increase the indentation of the text in the selected range (Figure 3–11).

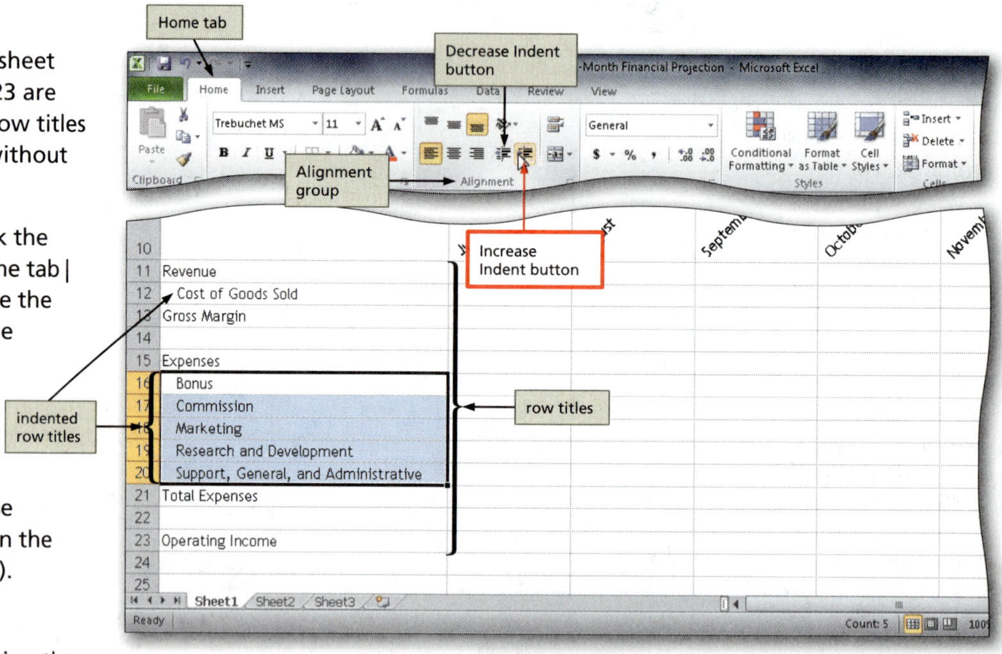

Figure 3–11

2

- Select cell A1 to finish entering the row titles and deselect the current cell.

Q&A What happens when I click the Increase Indent button?

The Increase Indent button (Home tab | Alignment group) indents the contents of a cell to the right by three spaces each time you click it. The Decrease Indent button decreases the indent by three spaces each time you click it.

Other Ways

1. To indent, right-click range, click Format Cells on shortcut menu, click Alignment tab (Format Cells dialog box), click Left (Indent) in Horizontal list, type number of spaces to indent in Indent text box, click OK button (Format Cells dialog box)

Copying a Range of Cells to a Nonadjacent Destination Area

The What-If Assumptions section should be placed in an area of the worksheet that is accessible easily yet does not impair the view of the main section of the worksheet. As shown in Figure 3–3a on page EX 142, the What-If Assumptions should be placed above the calculations in the worksheet. Additionally, the row titles in the Expenses area are the same as the row titles in the What-If Assumptions table, with the exception of the two additional entries in cells A4 (Margin) and A7 (Sales Revenue for Bonus). Hence, the What-If Assumptions table row titles can be created by copying the range A16:A20 to the range A2:A6 and then inserting two rows for the additional entries in cells A4 and A7. The source area (range A16:A20) is not adjacent to the destination area (range A2:A6). The first two Excel chapters used the fill handle to copy a source area to an adjacent destination area. To copy a source area to a nonadjacent destination area, however, you cannot use the fill handle.

A more versatile method of copying a source area is to use the Copy button and Paste button (Home tab | Clipboard group). You can use these two buttons to copy a source area to an adjacent or nonadjacent destination area.

BTW

Fitting Entries in a Cell
An alternative to increasing column widths or row heights is to shrink the characters in a cell to fit the current width of the column. To shrink to fit, click Format Cells: Alignment Dialog Box Button Launcher (Home tab | Alignment group), and click Shrink to fit in the Text control area. After shrinking entries to fit in cells, consider using the Zoom slider on the status bar to make the entries more readable.

To Copy a Range of Cells to a Nonadjacent Destination Area

The Copy button copies the contents and format of the source area to the **Office Clipboard**, a reserved place in the computer's memory that allows you to collect text and graphics from an Office document and then paste them into almost any other type of document. The Paste button copies the item from the Office Clipboard to the destination area.

The following steps enter the what-if area row heading and use the Copy and Paste buttons to copy the range A16:A20 to the nonadjacent range A2:A6.

1

- With cell A1 selected, type `What-If Assumptions` as the new row title.
- Select the range A16:A20 and then click the Copy button (Home tab | Clipboard group) to copy the values and formats of the selected range, A16:A20 in this case, to the Office Clipboard.
- Select cell A2, the top cell in the destination area (Figure 3–12).

Q&A

Why do I not need to select the entire destination area?

You are not required to select the entire destination area (range A2:A6) before clicking the Paste button (Home tab | Clipboard group). Excel needs to know only the upper-left cell of the destination area. In the case of a single column range, such as A2:A6, the top cell of the destination area (cell A2) also is the upper-left cell of the destination area.

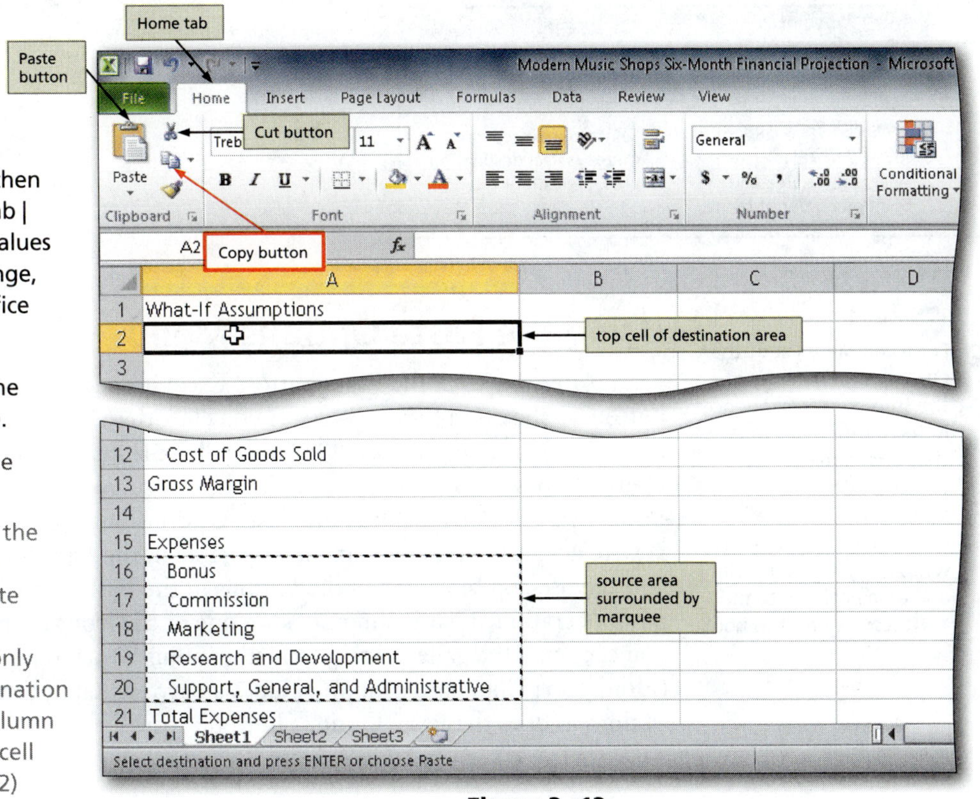

Figure 3–12

2

- Click the Paste button (Home tab | Clipboard group) to copy the values and formats of the last item placed on the Office Clipboard, range A16:A20 in this case, to the destination area, A2:A6 in this case (Figure 3–13).

Q&A

What if data already existed in the destination area?

When you complete a copy, the values and formats in the destination area are replaced with the values and formats of the source area. Any data contained in the destination area prior to the copy and paste is lost. If you accidentally delete valuable data, immediately click the Undo button on the Quick Access Toolbar.

3

- Press the ESC key to remove the marquee from the source area and disable the Paste button (Home tab | Clipboard group).

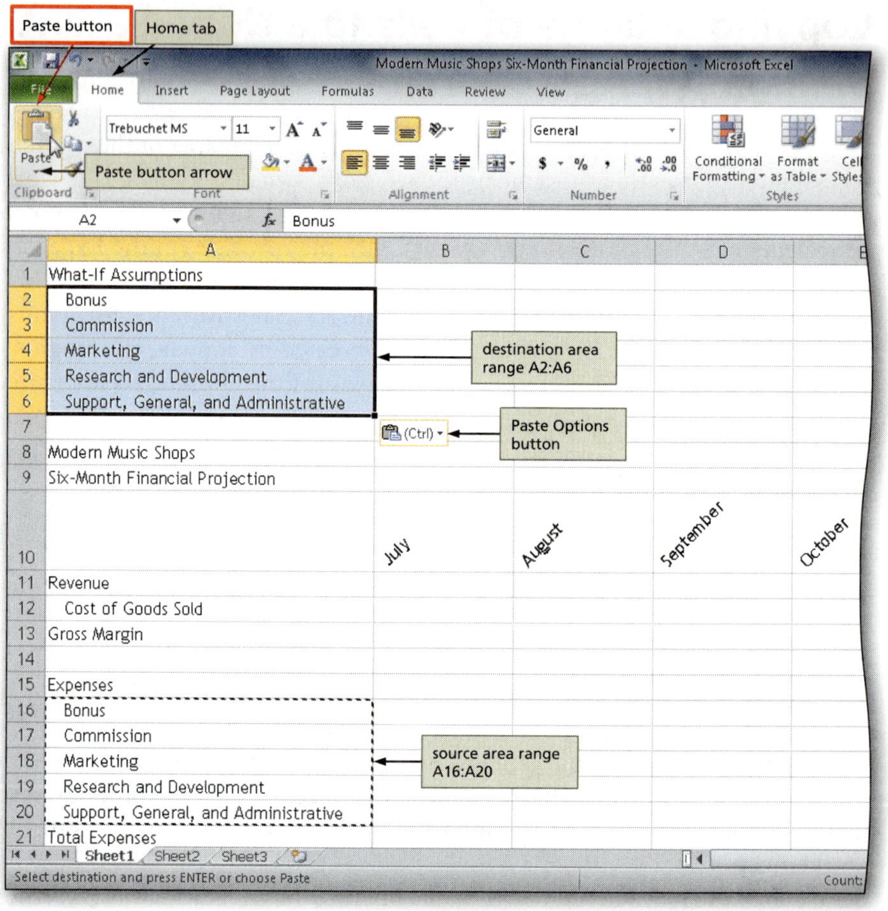

Figure 3–13

Other Ways

1. Right-click source area, click Copy on shortcut menu, right-click destination area, click Paste icon on shortcut menu
2. Select source area and point on border of range; while holding down CTRL key, drag source area to destination area
3. Select source area, press CTRL+C, select destination area, press CTRL+V

BTW

Q&As

For a complete list of the Q&As found in many of the step-by-step sequences in the Office and Windows chapters in this book, visit the Microsoft Office and Concepts CourseMate Web site at www.cengagebrain.com and then navigate to the Q&A resource for this book.

Using the Paste Options Menu

After you click the Paste button, Excel immediately displays the Paste Options button, as shown in Figure 3–13. If you click the Paste Options button arrow and select an option on the Paste Options gallery, Excel modifies the most recent paste operation based on your selection. Table 3–4 summarizes the options available on the Paste Options gallery. When the Paste Options button is visible, you can use shortcut keys to access the paste commands available in the Paste Options gallery. Additionally, you can use combinations of the options in the Paste Options gallery to customize your paste operation. That is, after clicking one of the icons in the Paste Options gallery, you can open the gallery again to further adjust your paste operation. The Paste button (Home tab | Clipboard group) includes an arrow that, when clicked, displays the same options as does the Paste Options button arrow.

Table 3–4 Options Available in the Paste Options Gallery

Paste Option Icon	Paste Option	Shortcut Key	Description
	Paste	CTRL+P	Copy contents and format of source area. This option is the default.
	Formulas	CTRL+F	Copy formulas from the source area, but not the contents and format.
	Formulas & Number Formatting	CTRL+O	Copy formulas and format for numbers and formulas of source area, but not the contents.
	Keep Source Formatting	CTRL+K	Copy contents, format, and styles of source area.
	No Borders	CTRL+B	Copy contents and format of source area, but not any borders.
	Keep Source Column Widths	CTRL+W	Copy contents and format of source area. Change destination column widths to source column widths.
	Transpose	CTRL+T	Copy the contents and format of the source area, but transpose, or swap, the rows and columns.
	Values	CTRL+V	Copy contents of source area, but not the formatting for formulas.
	Values & Number Formatting	CTRL+A	Copy contents and format of source area for numbers or formulas, but use format of destination area for text.
	Values & Source Formatting	CTRL+E	Copy contents and formatting of source area, but not the formula.
	Formatting	CTRL+R	Copy format of source area, but not the contents.
	Paste Link	CTRL+N	Copy contents and format and link cells so that a change to the cells in source area updates the corresponding cells in destination area.
	Picture	CTRL+U	Copy an image of the source area as a picture.
	Linked Pictures	CTRL+I	Copy an image of the source area as a picture so that a change to the cells in source area updates the picture in destination area.

BTW

Copying and Pasting from Other Programs
If you have data you need in Excel, but the data is stored in another program, copying and pasting likely will help you. You might need to experiment before you are successful because Excel might attempt to copy formatting or other information that you did not intend to paste from the other program. Using the various Paste buttons likely will solve most of such problems.

An alternative to clicking the Paste button is to press the ENTER key. The ENTER key completes the paste operation, removes the marquee from the source area, and disables the Paste button so that you cannot paste the copied source area to other destination areas. The ENTER key was not used in the previous set of steps so that the capabilities of the Paste Options button could be discussed. The Paste Options button does not appear on the screen when you use the ENTER key to complete the paste operation.

Using Drag and Drop to Move or Copy Cells

You also can use the mouse to move or copy cells. First, you select the source area and point to the border of the cell or range. You know you are pointing to the border of the cell or range when the mouse pointer changes to a block arrow. To move the selected cell or cells, drag the selection to the destination area. To copy a selection, hold down the CTRL key while dragging the selection to the destination area. You know Excel is in copy mode when a small plus sign appears next to the block arrow mouse pointer. Be sure to release the mouse button before you release the CTRL key. Using the mouse to move or copy cells is called **drag and drop**.

BTW

Move It or Copy It
Contrary to popular belief, move and copy operations are not the same. When you move a cell, the data in the original location is cleared and the format of the cell is reset to the default. When you copy a cell, the data and format of the copy area remains intact. In short, you should copy cells to duplicate entries and move cells to rearrange entries.

BTW

Cutting
When you cut a cell or range of cells using the Cut command on a shortcut menu or Cut button (Home tab | Clipboard group), Excel copies the cells to the Office Clipboard, but does not remove the cells from the source area until you paste the cells in the destination area by either clicking the Paste button (Home tab | Clipboard group) or pressing the ENTER key. When you complete the paste, Excel clears the cell's or range of cell's entries and their formats from the source area.

Using Cut and Paste to Move Cells

Another way to move cells is to select them, click the Cut button (Home tab | Clipboard group) (Figure 3–12 on page EX 151) to remove them from the worksheet and copy them to the Office Clipboard, select the destination area, and then click the Paste button (Home tab | Clipboard group) or press the ENTER key. You also can use the Cut command on the shortcut menu, instead of the Cut button.

Inserting and Deleting Cells in a Worksheet

At any time while the worksheet is on the screen, you can insert cells to enter new data or delete cells to remove unwanted data. You can insert or delete individual cells; a range of cells, rows, columns; or entire worksheets.

To Insert a Row

According to the sketch of the worksheet in Figure 3–3a on page EX 142, two rows must be inserted in the What-If Assumptions table, one between Commission and Marketing for the Margin assumption and another between Research and Development and Support, General, and Administrative for the Sales Revenue for Bonus assumption. The following steps insert the new rows into the worksheet.

1

- Right-click row heading 4, the row below where you want to insert a row, to display the shortcut menu and the Mini toolbar (Figure 3–14).

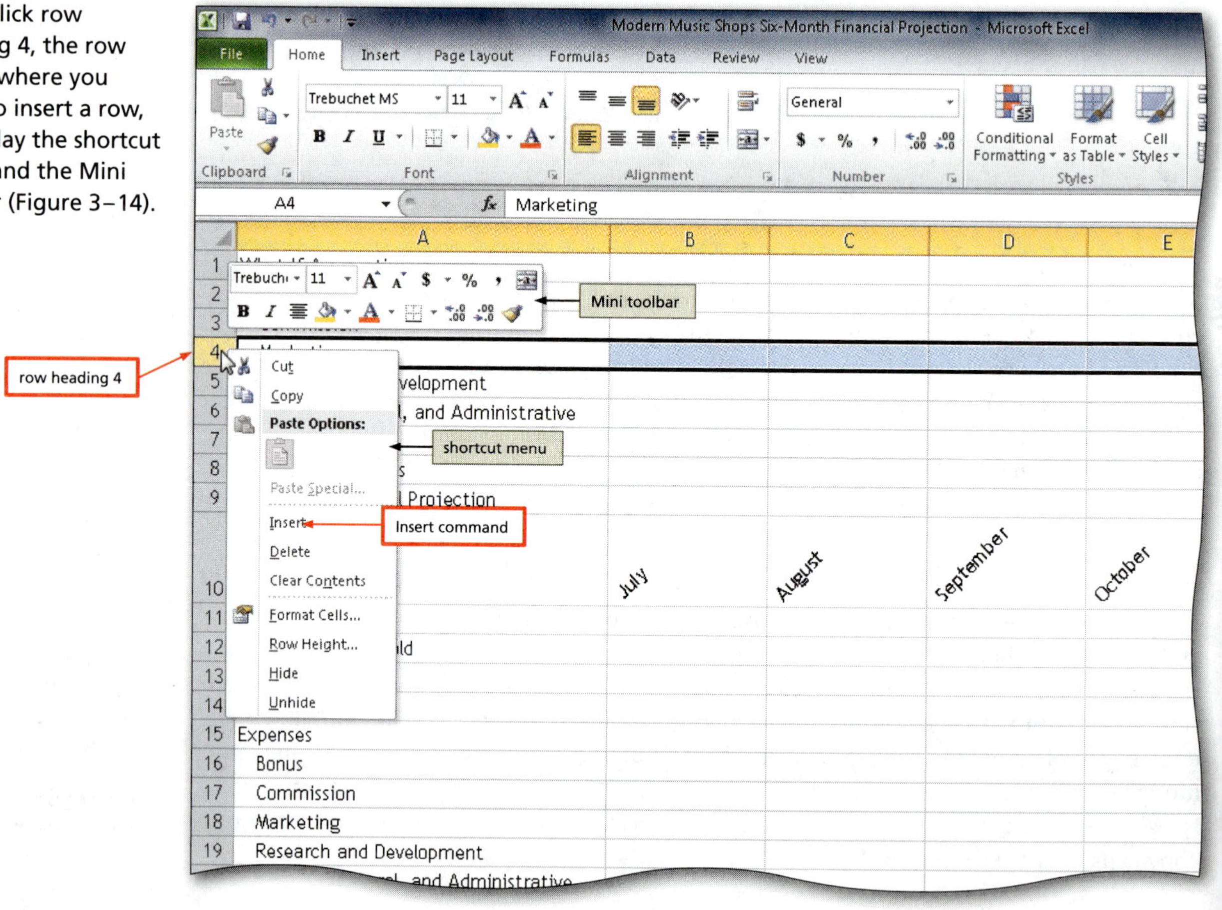

Figure 3–14

2

- Click Insert on the shortcut menu to insert a new row in the worksheet by shifting the selected row and all rows below it down one row.
- Select cell A4 in the new row and then enter `Margin` to enter a new row title (Figure 3–15).

Q&A What is the resulting format of the new row?

The cells in the new row inherit the formats of the cells in the row above them. You can change this behavior by clicking the Insert Options button that appears immediately below the inserted row. Following the insertion of a row, the Insert Options button allows you to select from the following options: (1) 'Format Same As Above'; (2) 'Format Same As Below'; and (3) Clear Formatting. The 'Format Same as Above' option is the default. The Insert Options button remains active until you begin the next Excel operation. Excel does not display the Insert Options button if the initial row does not contain any formatted data.

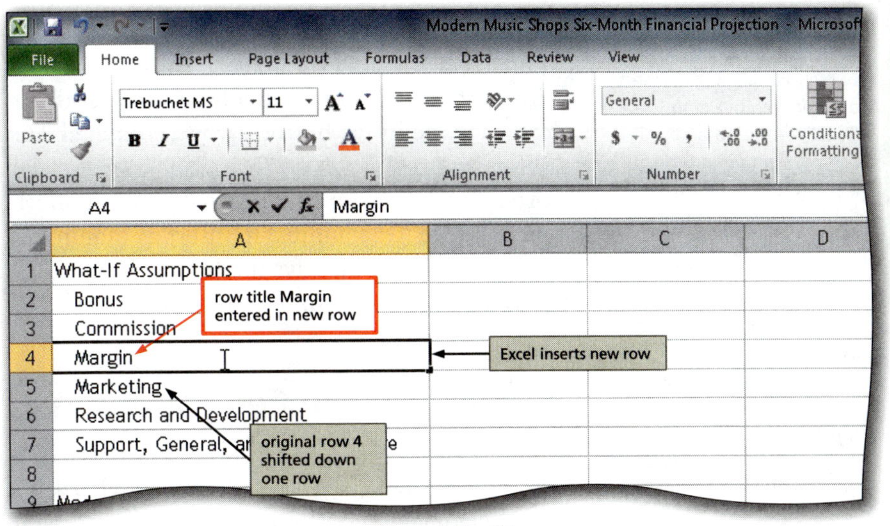

Figure 3–15

3

- Right-click row heading 7 to display a shortcut menu and then click Insert on the shortcut menu to insert a new row in the worksheet.
- Select cell A7 in the new row and then enter `Sales Revenue for Bonus` to enter a new row title (Figure 3–16).

Q&A What would happen if cells in the shifted rows were included in formulas?

If the rows that shift down include cell references in formulas located in the worksheet, Excel automatically would adjust the cell references in the formulas to their new locations. Thus, in Step 2, if a formula in the worksheet references a cell in row 7 before the insert, then Excel adjusts the cell reference in the formula to row 8 after the insert.

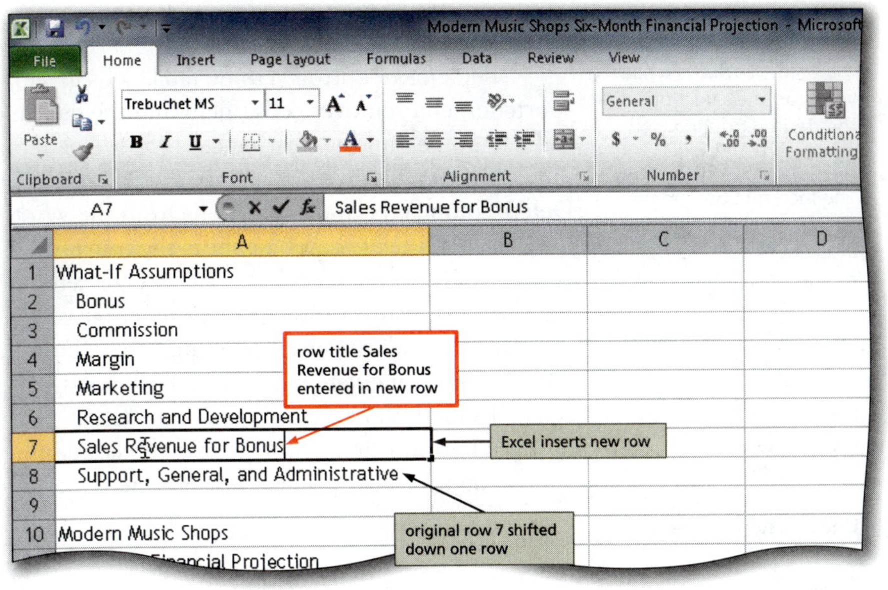

Figure 3–16

Other Ways

1. Insert (Home tab | Cells group), click Insert Sheet Rows
2. Press CTRL+SHIFT+PLUS SIGN, click Entire row, click OK button

BTW

Inserting Multiple Rows
If you want to insert multiple rows, you have two choices. You can insert a single row by using the Insert command on the shortcut menu and then repeatedly press F4 to continue inserting rows. Alternatively, you can select any number of existing rows to choose the number of rows that you want to insert. For instance, if you want to insert five rows, select five existing rows in the worksheet, right-click the rows, and then click Insert on the shortcut menu.

BTW

Dragging Ranges
You can move and insert a selected cell or range between existing cells by holding down the SHIFT key while you drag the selection to the gridline where you want to insert the selected cell or range. You also can copy and insert by holding down the CTRL+SHIFT keys while you drag the selection to the desired gridline.

BTW

Ranges and Undo
The incorrect use of copying, deleting, inserting, and moving ranges of cells have the potential to render a worksheet useless. Carefully review the results of these actions before continuing on to the next task. If you are not sure the result of the action is correct, click the Undo button on the Quick Access Toolbar.

Inserting Columns

You insert columns into a worksheet in the same way you insert rows. To insert columns, select one or more columns immediately to the right of where you want Excel to insert the new column or columns. Select the number of columns you want to insert. Next, click the Insert button arrow (Home tab | Cells group) and then click Insert Sheet Columns in the Insert list or right-click the selected column(s), then click Insert on the shortcut menu. The Insert command on the shortcut menu requires that you select an entire column (or columns) to insert a column (or columns). Following the insertion of a column, Excel displays the Insert Options button, which allows you to modify the insertion in a fashion similar to that discussed earlier when inserting rows.

Inserting Single Cells or a Range of Cells

The Insert command on the shortcut menu or the Insert Cells command on the Insert list of the Insert button (Home tab | Cells group) allows you to insert a single cell or a range of cells. You should be aware that if you shift a single cell or a range of cells, however, it no longer lines up with its associated cells. To ensure that the values in the worksheet do not get out of order, spreadsheet experts recommend that you insert only entire rows or entire columns. When you insert a single cell or a range of cells, Excel displays the Insert Options button so that you can change the format of the inserted cell, using options similar to those for inserting rows and columns.

Deleting Columns and Rows

The Delete button (Home tab | Cells group) or the Delete command on the shortcut menu removes cells (including the data and format) from the worksheet. Deleting cells is not the same as clearing cells. The Clear command, described in Excel Chapter 1 on page EX 52, clears the data from the cells, but the cells remain in the worksheet. The Delete command removes the cells from the worksheet and shifts the remaining rows up (when you delete rows) or shifts the remaining columns to the left (when you delete columns). If formulas located in other cells reference cells in the deleted row or column, Excel does not adjust these cell references. Excel displays the error message **#REF!** in those cells to indicate a cell reference error. For example, if cell A7 contains the formula =A4+A5 and you delete row 5, Excel assigns the formula =A4+#REF! to cell A6 (originally cell A7) and displays the error message #REF! in cell A6. Excel also displays an Error Options button when you select the cell containing the error message #REF!, which allows you to select options to determine the nature of the problem.

To Enter Numbers with Format Symbols

The next step in creating the Six-Month Financial Projection worksheet is to enter the what-if assumptions values in the range B2:B8. The numbers in the table can be entered and then formatted as in Excel Chapters 1 and 2, or each one can be entered with format symbols. When a number is entered with a **format symbol**, Excel immediately displays it with the assigned format. Valid format symbols include the dollar sign ($), comma (,), and percent sign (%).

If you enter a whole number, it appears without any decimal places. If you enter a number with one or more decimal places and a format symbol, Excel displays the number with two decimal places. Table 3–5 illustrates several examples of numbers entered with format symbols. The number in parentheses in column 4 indicates the number of decimal places.

Table 3–5 Numbers Entered with Format Symbols

Format Symbol	Typed in Formula Bar	Displays in Cell	Comparable Format
,	374, 149	374, 149	Comma(0)
	5,833.6	5,833.60	Comma(2)
$	$58917	$58,917	Currency(0)
	$842.51	$842.51	Currency(2)
	$63,574.9	$63,574.90	Currency(2)
%	85%	85%	Percent(0)
	12.80%	12.80%	Percent(2)
	68.4222%	68.2242%	Percent(4)

The following step enters the numbers in the What-If Assumptions table with format symbols.

1

- Enter `200,000.00` in cell B2, `5.75%` in cell B3, `57.50%` in cell B4, `15.00%` in cell B5, `7.50%` in cell B6, `3,500,000.00` in cell B7, and `18.75%` in cell B8 to display the entries using formats based on the format symbols entered with the numbers (Figure 3–17).

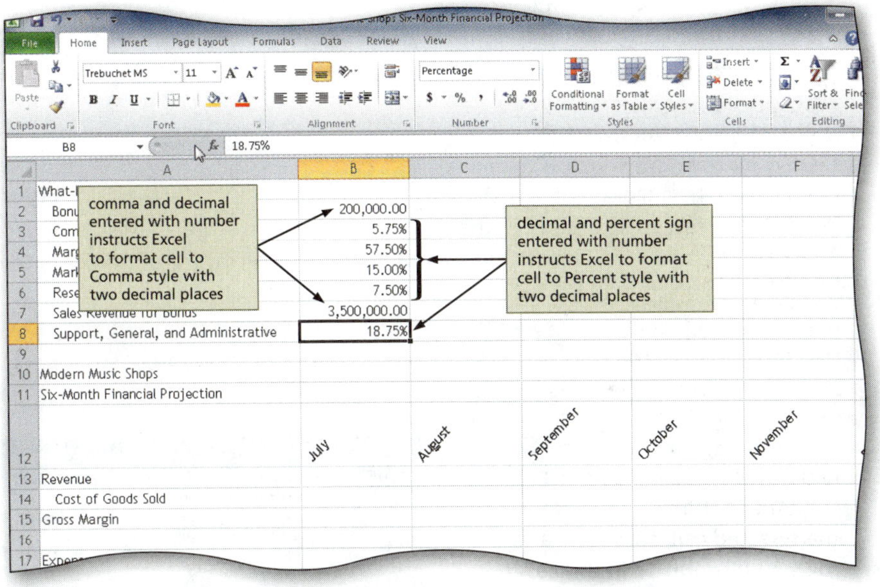

Figure 3–17

Other Ways

1. Right-click range, click Format Cells on shortcut menu, click Number tab (Format Cells dialog box), click category in Category list, [select desired format], click OK button (Format Cells dialog box)
2. Press CTRL+1, click Number tab (Format Cells dialog box), click category in Category list, [select desired format], click OK button (Format Cells dialog box)

To Freeze Column and Row Titles

Freezing worksheet titles is a useful technique for viewing large worksheets that extend beyond the window. Normally, when you scroll down or to the right, the column titles in row 12 and the row titles in column A that define the numbers no longer appear on the screen. This makes it difficult to remember what the numbers in these rows and columns represent. To alleviate this problem, Excel allows you to **freeze the titles**, so that Excel displays the titles on the screen, no matter how far down or to the right you scroll.

The steps on the following page use the Freeze Panes button (View tab | Window group) to freeze the worksheet title and column titles in rows 10, 11, and 12, and the row titles in column A.

1

- Scroll the worksheet to ensure that Excel displays row 10 as the first row and column A on the screen.
- Select cell B13 to select the cell on which to freeze panes.
- Display the View tab and then click the Freeze Panes button (View tab | Window group) to display the Freeze Panes gallery (Figure 3–18).

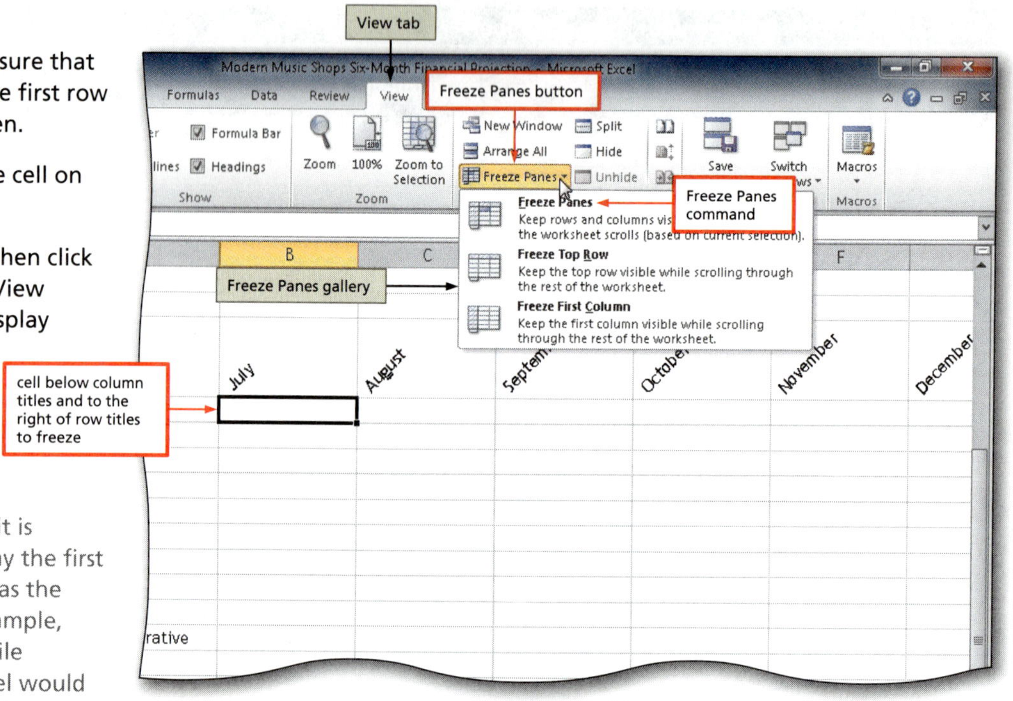

Figure 3–18

Q&A

Why should I ensure that row 10 is the first row displayed?

Before freezing the titles, it is important that Excel display the first row that you want frozen as the first row displayed. For example, if cell B13 was selected while displaying row 1, then Excel would freeze the what-if assumptions and only show a few rows of data in the Six-Month Financial Project area of the worksheet. To ensure that you can view as much data as possible, always scroll to a row that maximizes the view of your important data before freezing panes.

2

- Click Freeze Panes in the Freeze Panes gallery to freeze rows and columns to the left and above the selected cell, column A and rows 10 through 12 in this case (Figure 3–19).

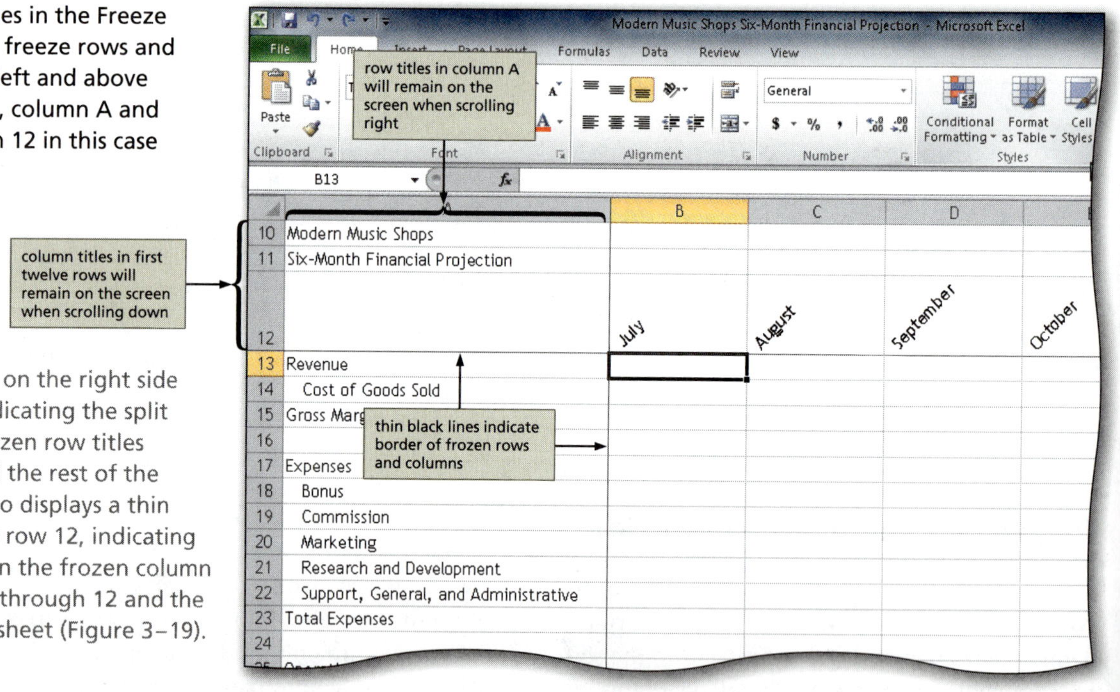

Figure 3–19

Q&A

What happens after I click the Freeze Panes command?

Excel displays a thin black line on the right side of column A, indicating the split between the frozen row titles in column A and the rest of the worksheet. It also displays a thin black line below row 12, indicating the split between the frozen column titles in rows 10 through 12 and the rest of the worksheet (Figure 3–19).

To Enter the Projected Monthly Sales

The following steps enter the projected revenue, listed earlier in Table 3–1 on page EX 143, in row 13 and compute the projected six-month revenue in cell H13.

1. If necessary, display the Home tab.
2. Enter `3113612.16` in cell B13, `7962235.53` in cell C13, `5112268.58` in cell D13, `2924627.87` in cell E13, `7630534.65` in cell F13, and `3424270.23` in cell G13.
3. Select cell H13 and then click the Sum button (Home tab | Editing group) twice to create a sum in the selected cell (Figure 3–20).

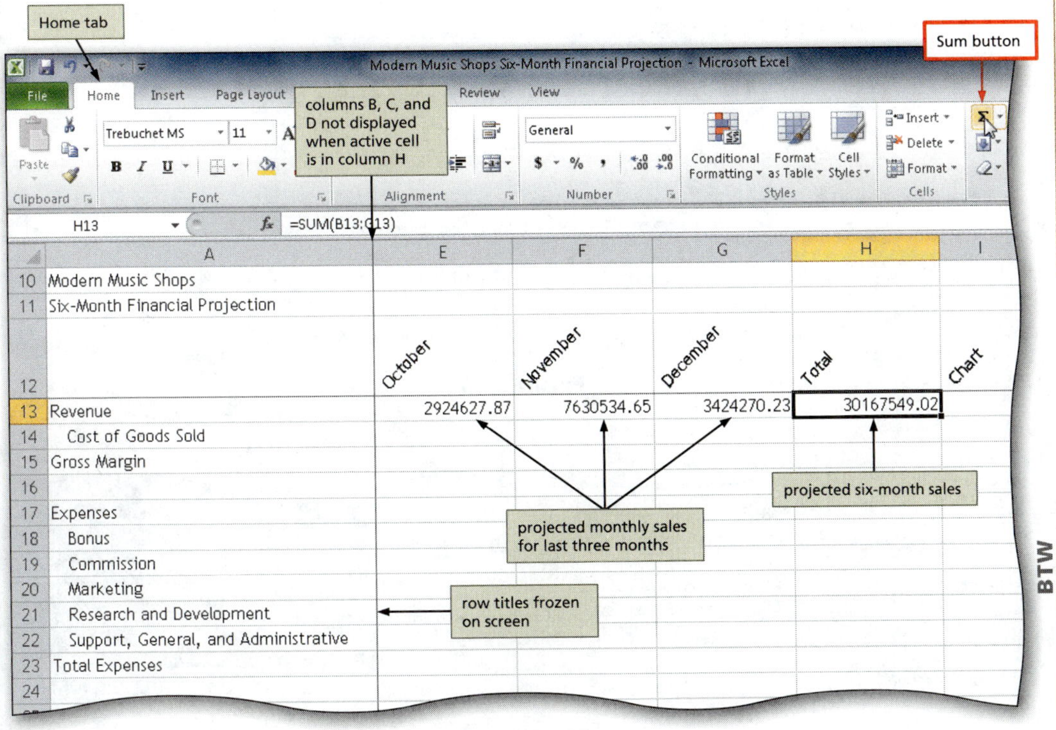

Figure 3–20

BTW

Freezing Titles
If you want to freeze only column headings, select the appropriate cell in column A before you click the Freeze Panes button (View tab | Window group). If you want to freeze only row titles, select the appropriate cell in row 1 before you click the Freeze Panes button (View tab | Window group). To freeze both column headings and row titles, select the cell that is the intersection of the column and row titles before you click the Freeze Panes button (View tab | Window group).

BTW

The Insert Options Button
When you insert columns or rows, Excel displays the Insert Options button only if formats are assigned to the leftmost column or top row of the selection.

To Enter and Format the System Date

The sketch of the worksheet in Figure 3–3a on page EX 142 includes a date stamp on the right side of the heading section. A **date stamp** shows the date a workbook, report, or other document was created or the period it represents. In business, a report often is meaningless without a date stamp. For example, if a printout of the worksheet in this chapter were distributed to the company's analysts, the date stamp would show when the six-month projections were made, as well as what period the report represents.

A simple way to create a date stamp is to use the NOW function to enter the system date tracked by your computer in a cell in the worksheet. The **NOW function** is one of 22 date and time functions available in Excel. When assigned to a cell, the NOW function returns a number that corresponds to the system date and time beginning with December 31, 1899. For example, January 1, 1900 equals 1, January 2, 1900 equals 2, and so on. Noon equals .5. Thus, noon on January 1, 1900 equals 1.5 and 6 P.M. on January 1, 1900 equals 1.75. If the computer's system date is set to the current date, which normally it is, then the date stamp is equivalent to the current date.

The steps on the following pages enter the NOW function and then change the format from mm/dd/yyyy hh:mm to mm/dd/yyyy.

1

- Select cell I11 and then click the Insert Function box in the formula bar to display the Insert Function dialog box.
- Click the 'Or select a category' box arrow (Insert Function dialog box) and then select Date & Time in the list to populate the 'Select a function' list with data and time functions.
- Scroll down in the 'Select a function list' and then click NOW to select the required function (Figure 3–21).

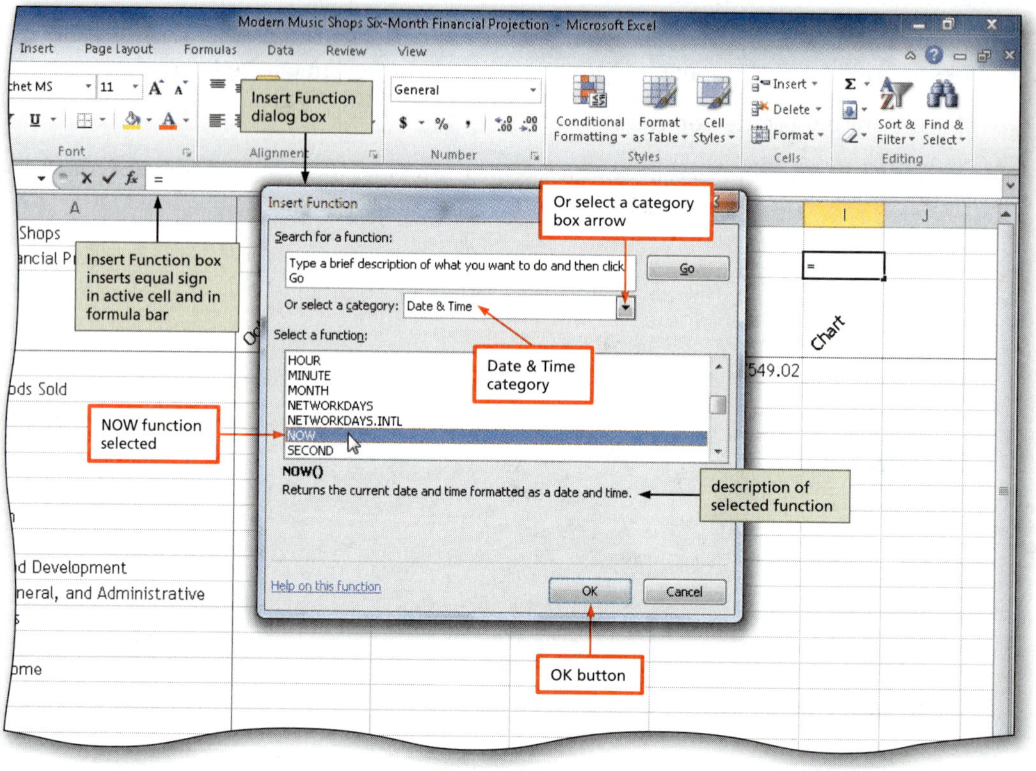

Figure 3–21

2

- Click the OK button (Insert Function dialog box) to close the Insert Function dialog box and display the Function Arguments dialog box.
- Click the OK button (Function Arguments dialog box) to display the system date and time in the selected cell, using the default date and time format mm/dd/yyyy hh:mm.
- Right-click cell I11 to display a shortcut menu and Mini toolbar (Figure 3–22).

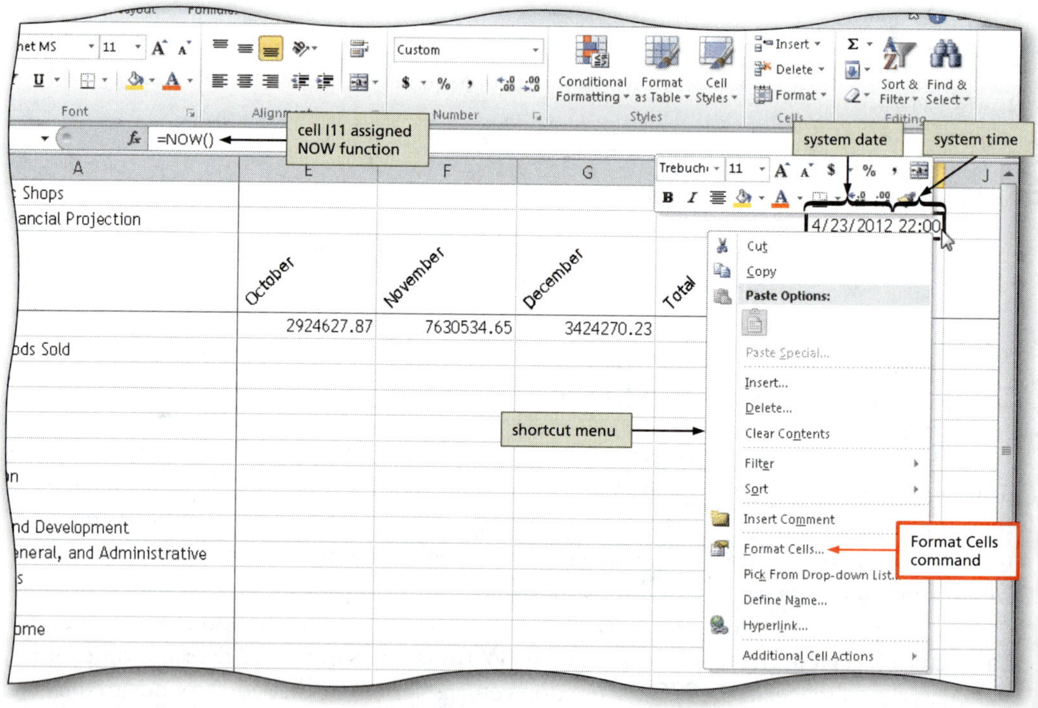

Figure 3–22

Q&A Why does the date appear with the mm/dd/yyyy hh:mm format?

Excel automatically formats the result of the NOW function as a date, using the date and time format, mm/dd/yyyy hh:mm, where the first mm is the month, dd is the day of the month, yyyy is the year, hh is the hour of the day, and mm is the minutes past the hour.

3

- Click Format Cells on the shortcut menu to display the Format Cells dialog box.
- If necessary, click the Number tab (Format Cells dialog box) to display the Number sheet.
- Click Date in the Category list (Format Cells dialog box) to display the types of date formats in the Type list. Scroll down in the Type list and then click 3/14/2001 to display a sample of the data in the active cell, I11 in this case, using the selected format in the Sample area (Figure 3–23).

Q&A Why do the dates in the Type box show March 14, 2001 instead of the current date?

The date March 14, 2001 is used as a sample date in the Format cells dialog box.

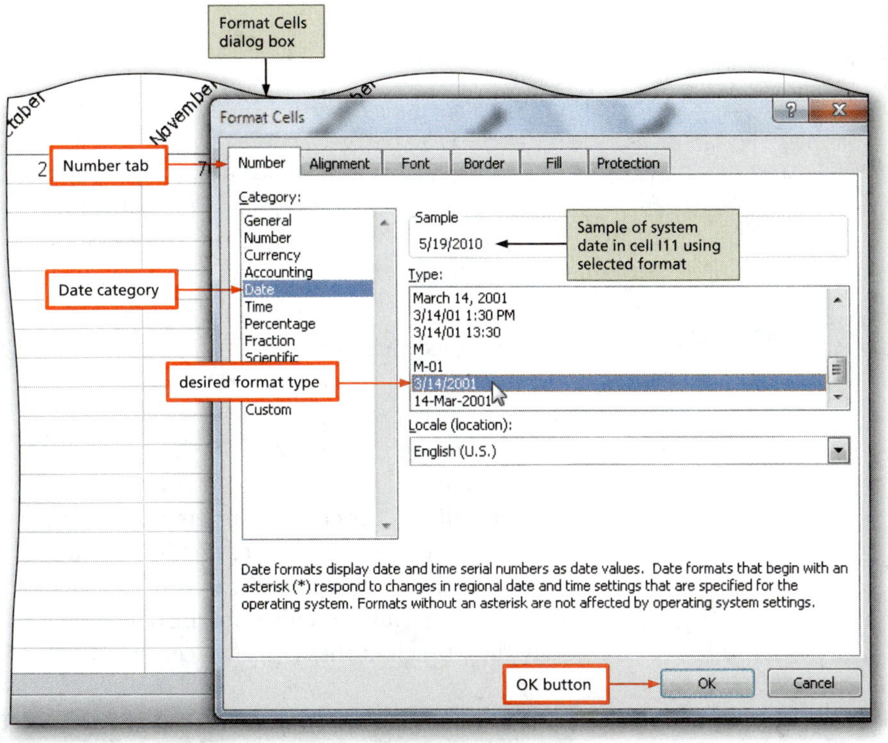

Figure 3–23

4

- Click the OK button (Format Cells dialog box) to display the system date in the format mm/dd/yyyy.
- Double-click the border between columns I and J to change the width of the column to best fit (Figure 3–24).

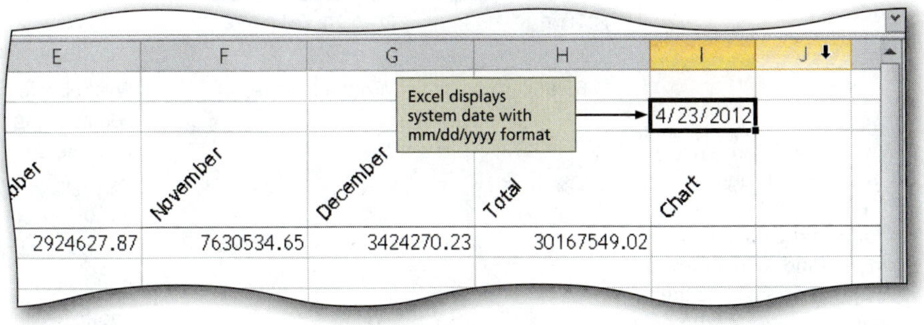

Figure 3–24

Q&A How does Excel format a date?

In Figure 3–24, the date is displayed right-aligned in the cell because Excel treats a date as a number formatted to display as a date. If you assign the General format (Excel's default format for numbers) to a date in a cell, the date is displayed as a number with two decimal places. For example, if the system time and date is 9:00 AM on November 13, 2012 and the cell containing the NOW function is assigned the General format, then Excel displays the following number in the cell:

41226.375

Number of days since December 31, 1899 — Time of day is 9:00 AM (Portion of day complete)

The whole number portion of the number (41226) represents the number of days since December 31, 1899. The decimal portion of the number (.375) represents 9:00 AM as the time of day, at which point 37.5% of the day is complete. To assign the General format to a cell, click General in the Category list in the Format Cells dialog box (Figure 3–23).

Other Ways

1. Click Date & Time (Formulas tab | Function Library group), click now
2. Press CTRL+SEMICOLON (not a volatile date)
3. Press CTRL+SHIFT+# to format date to day-month-year

Break Point: If you wish to stop working through the chapter at this point, you can quit Excel now and then resume the project at a later point in time by starting Excel, opening the file called Modern Music Shops Six-Month Financial Projection, and continuing to follow the steps from this location forward.

BTW

Your Age in Days
How many days have you been alive? Enter today's date (e.g., 12/5/2012) in cell A1. Next, enter your birth date (e.g., 6/22/1996) in cell A2. Select cell A3 and enter the formula = A1−A2. Format cell A3 to the General style using the Format Cells dialog box, and cell A3 will display your age in days.

Absolute versus Relative Addressing

The next sections describe the formulas and functions needed to complete the calculations in the worksheet.

As you learned in Excel Chapters 1 and 2, Excel modifies cell references when copying formulas. While copying formulas, however, sometimes you do not want Excel to change cell references. To keep a cell reference constant when copying a formula or function, Excel uses a technique called absolute cell referencing. To specify an absolute cell reference in a formula, enter a dollar sign ($) before any column letters or row numbers you want to keep constant in formulas you plan to copy. For example, $B$4 is an absolute cell reference, whereas B4 is a relative cell reference. Both reference the same cell. The difference becomes apparent when they are copied to a destination area. A formula using the **absolute cell reference** $B$4 instructs Excel to keep the cell reference B4 constant (absolute) in the formula as it copies it to the destination area. A formula using the **relative cell reference** B4 instructs Excel to adjust the cell reference as it copies it to the destination area. A cell reference with only one dollar sign before either the column or the row is called a **mixed cell reference**. When planning formulas, be aware of when you need to use absolute, relative, and mixed cell references. Table 3–6 gives some additional examples of each of these types of cell references.

Table 3–6 Examples of Absolute, Relative, and Mixed Cell References

Cell Reference	Type of Reference	Meaning
$B$4	Absolute cell reference	Both column and row references remain the same when you copy this cell, because the cell references are absolute.
B$4	Mixed reference	This cell reference is mixed. The column reference changes when you copy this cell to another column because it is relative. The row reference does not change because it is absolute.
$B4	Mixed reference	This cell reference is mixed. The column reference does not change because it is absolute. The row reference changes when you copy this cell reference to another row because it is relative.
B4	Relative cell reference	Both column and row references are relative. When copied to another cell, both the column and row in the cell reference are adjusted to reflect the new location.

BTW

Absolute Referencing
Absolute referencing is one of the more difficult worksheet concepts to understand. One point to keep in mind is that the paste operation is the only operation affected by an absolute cell reference. An absolute cell reference instructs the paste operation to keep the same cell reference as it copies a formula from one cell to another.

The next step is to enter the formulas that calculate the following values for July: cost of goods sold (cell B14), gross margin (cell B15), expenses (range B18:B22), total expenses (cell B23), and the operating income (cell B25). The formulas are based on the projected monthly revenue in cell B13 and the assumptions in the range B2:B8.

To Enter a Formula Containing Absolute Cell References

The formulas for each column (month) are the same, except for the reference to the projected monthly revenue in row 13, which varies according to the month (B13 for July, C13 for August, and so on). Thus, the formulas for July can be entered in column B and then copied to columns C through G. Table 3–7 shows the formulas for determining the July cost of goods sold, gross margin, expenses, total expenses, and operating income in column B.

Table 3–7 Formulas for Determining Cost of Goods Sold, Margin, Expenses, Total Expenses, and Operating Income for July

Cell	Row Title	Formula	Comment
B14	Cost of Goods Sold	=B13 * (1 – B4)	Revenue times (1 minus Margin %)
B15	Gross Margin	= B13 – B14	Revenue minus Cost of Goods Sold
B18	Bonus	=IF(B13 >= B7, B2, 0)	Bonus equals value in B2 or 0
B19	Commission	=B13 * B3	Revenue times Commission %
B20	Marketing	=B13 * B5	Revenue times Marketing %
B21	Research and Development	=B13 * B6	Revenue times Research and Development %
B22	Support, General, and Administrative	=B13 * B8	Revenue times Support, General, and Administrative %
B23	Total Expenses	=SUM(B18:B22)	Sum of July Expenses
B25	Operating Income	=B15 – B23	Gross Margin minus Total Expenses

As the formulas are entered as shown in Table 3–7 in column B for July and then copied to columns C through G (August through December) in the worksheet, Excel will adjust the cell references for each column automatically. Thus, after the copy, the August Commission expense in cell C19 would be =C13 * C3. While the cell reference C13 (February Revenue) is correct, the cell reference C3 references an empty cell. The formula for cell C7 should read =C13 * B3, rather than =C13 * C3, because B3 references the Commission % value in the What-If Assumptions table. In this instance, a way is needed to keep a cell reference in a formula the same, or constant, when it is copied.

The following steps enter the cost of goods formula = B13*(1 – $B$4) in cell B14 using Point mode. To enter an absolute cell reference, you can type the dollar sign ($) as part of the cell reference or enter it by pressing F4 with the insertion point in or to the right of the cell reference to change it to absolute.

1

- Press CTRL+HOME to select cell B13 and then click cell B14 to show cell B13 and to select the cell in which to enter the first formula.
- Type **=** (equal sign), select cell B13, type **`*(1-b4`** to continue entering the formula, and then press F4 to change the most recently typed cell reference, in this case cell b4, from a relative cell reference to an absolute cell reference. Type **)** to complete the formula (Figure 3–25).

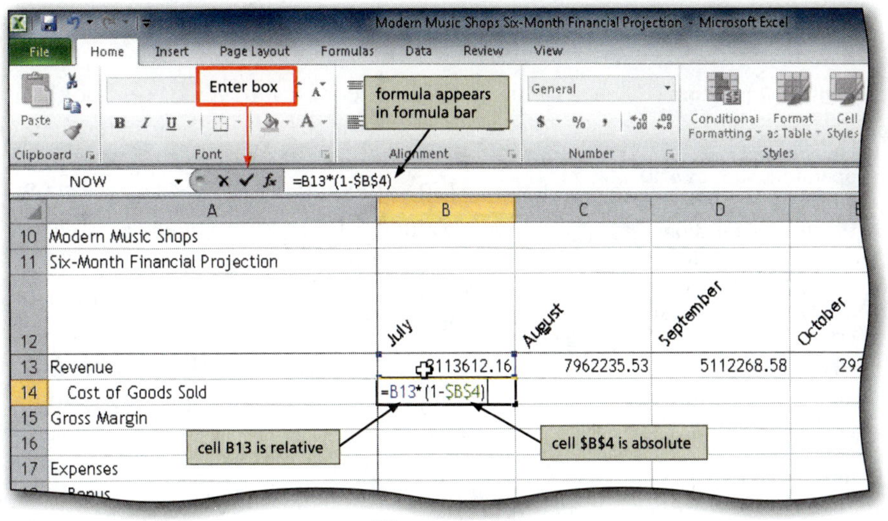

Figure 3–25

Q&A

Is an absolute reference required in this formula?

No, because a mixed cell reference could have been used. The formula in cell B14 will be copied across columns, rather than down rows. So, the formula entered in cell B14 in Step 1 could have been entered as =B13*(1–$B4), rather than =B13*(1–$B$4). That is, the formula could have included the mixed cell reference $B4, rather than the absolute cell reference $B$4. When you copy a formula across columns, the row does not change anyway. The key is to ensure that column B remains constant as you copy the formula across columns. To change the absolute cell reference to a mixed cell reference, continue to press the F4 key until you achieve the desired cell reference.

2

- Click the Enter box in the formula bar to display the result, 1323285.168, instead of the formula in B14 (Figure 3–26).

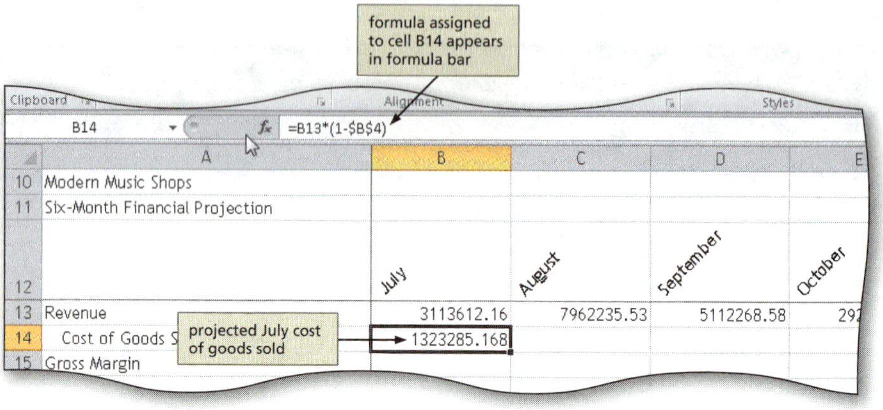

Figure 3–26

3

- Click cell B15 to select the cell in which to enter the next formula, type = (equal sign), click cell B13, type – (minus sign), and then click cell B14 to add a reference to the cell to the formula.
- Click the Enter box in the formula bar to display the result in the selected cell, in this case gross margin for July, 1790326.992, in cell B15 (Figure 3–27).

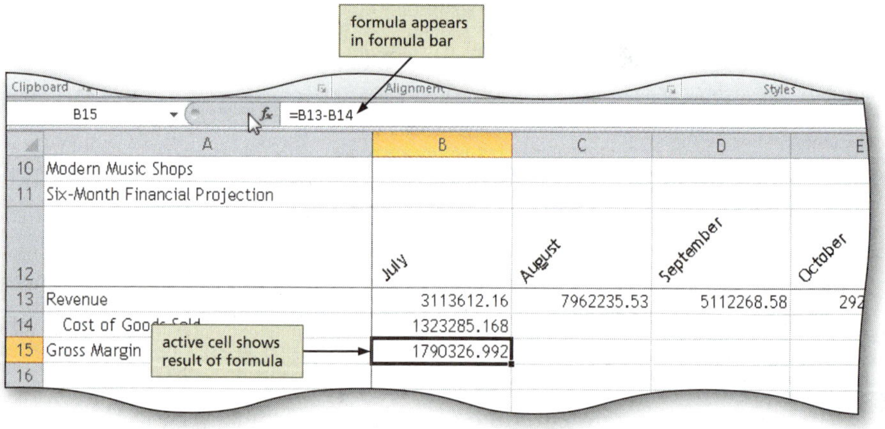

Figure 3–27

Making Decisions — The IF Function

BTW

Logical Operators in IF Functions

IF functions can use logical operators, such as AND, OR, and NOT. For example, the three IF functions =IF(AND(A1>C1, B1<C2), "OK", "Not OK") and =IF(OR(K5>J5, C3<K6), "OK", "Not OK") and =IF(NOT(B10<C10), "OK", "Not OK") use logical operators. In the first example, both logical tests must be true for the value_if_true OK to be assigned to the cell. In the second example, one or the other logical tests must be true for the value_if_true OK to be assigned to the cell. In the third example, the logical test B10<C10 must be false for the value_if_true OK to be assigned to the cell.

According to the Request for New Workbook in Figure 3–2 on page EX 140, if the projected July revenue in cell B13 is greater than or equal to the sales revenue for bonus in cell B7 (3,500,000.00), then the July bonus value in cell B18 is equal to the bonus value in cell B2 (200,000.00); otherwise, cell B18 is equal to 0. One way to assign the July bonus value in cell B18 is to check to see if the revenue in cell B13 equals or exceeds the sales revenue for the bonus amount in cell B7 and, if so, then to enter 200,000.00 in cell B18. You can use this manual process for all six months by checking the values for the corresponding months.

Because the data in the worksheet changes each time a report is prepared or the figures are adjusted, however, it is preferable to have Excel assign the monthly bonus to the entries in the appropriate cells automatically. To do so, cell B18 must include a formula or function that displays 200,000.00 or 0.00 (zero), depending on whether the projected July revenue in cell B13 is greater than, equal to, or less than the sales revenue for bonus value in cell B7.

The **IF function** is useful when you want to assign a value to a cell based on a logical test. For example, using the IF function, cell B18 can be assigned the following IF function:

=IF(B13>=$B$7, $B$2, 0)

logical_test value_if_true value_if_false

The IF function instructs Excel that, if the projected July revenue in cell B13 is greater than or equal to the sales revenue for bonus value in cell B7, then Excel should display the value 200000 in cell B2, in cell B18. If the projected July revenue in cell B13 is less than the sales revenue for bonus value in cell B7, then Excel displays a 0 (zero) in cell B18.

The general form of the IF function is:

=IF(logical_test, value_if_true, value_if_false)

The argument, logical_test, is made up of two expressions and a comparison operator. Each expression can be a cell reference, a number, text, a function, or a formula. Valid comparison operators, their meaning, and examples of their use in IF functions are shown in Table 3–8. The argument, value_if_true, is the value you want Excel to display in the cell when the logical test is true. The argument, value_if_false, is the value you want Excel to display in the cell when the logical test is false.

Table 3–8 Comparison Operators

Comparison Operator	Meaning	Example
=	Equal to	=IF(B12 = 200, F3 * H4, E10 + F3)
<	Less than	=IF(G56 * Q56 < D12, $M$10, B9 ^ 5)
>	Greater than	=IF(MIN(A12:A52) > 75, 0, 1)
>=	Greater than or equal to	=IF($T$9 >= B7, P3 - H12, 1000)
<=	Less than or equal to	=IF(C9 * G2 <= 99, $T35, 350 * C9)
<>	Not equal to	=IF(G15 <> 1, "No", "Yes")

To Enter an IF Function

The following steps assign the IF function =IF(B13>=$B$7,$B$2,0) to cell B18. This IF function determines whether or not the worksheet assigns a bonus for July.

1

- Click cell B18 to select the cell for the next formula.
- Click the Insert Function box in the formula bar to display the Insert Function dialog box.
- Click the 'Or select a category' box arrow (Insert Function dialog box) and then select Logical in the list to populate the 'Select a function' list with logic functions.
- Click IF in the 'Select a function list' to select the required function (Figure 3–28).

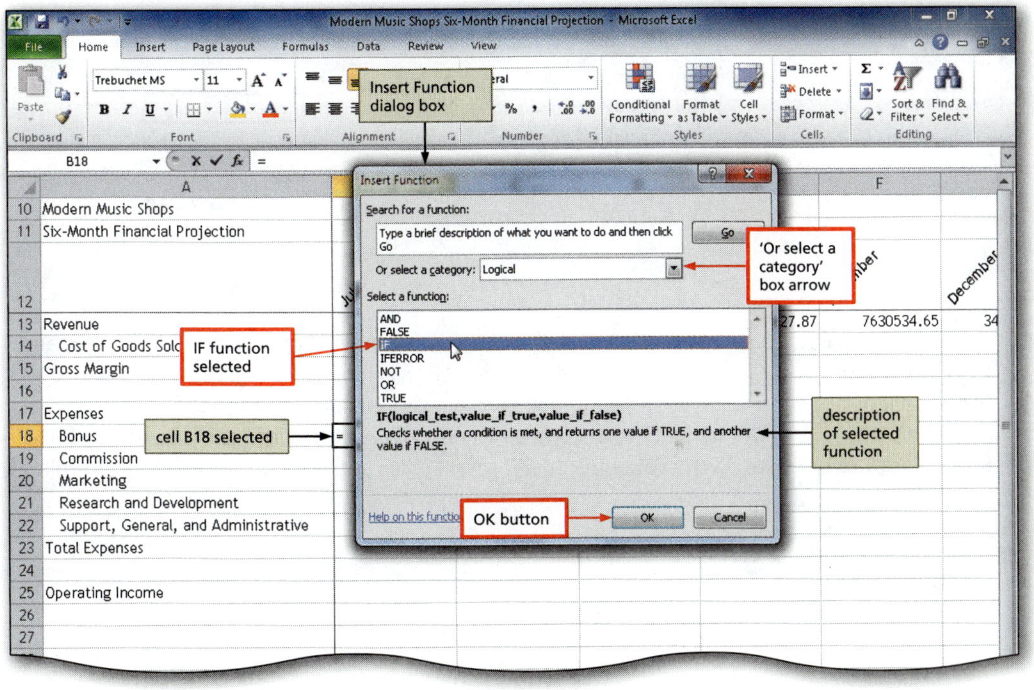

Figure 3–28

2

- Click the OK button (Insert Function dialog box) to display the Function Arguments dialog box.
- Type **b13>=b7** in the Logical test box to enter a logical test for the IF function.
- Type **b2** in the Value_if_true box to enter the result of the IF function if the logical test is true.
- Type **0** in the Value_if_false box to enter the result of the IF function if the logical test is false (Figure 3–29).

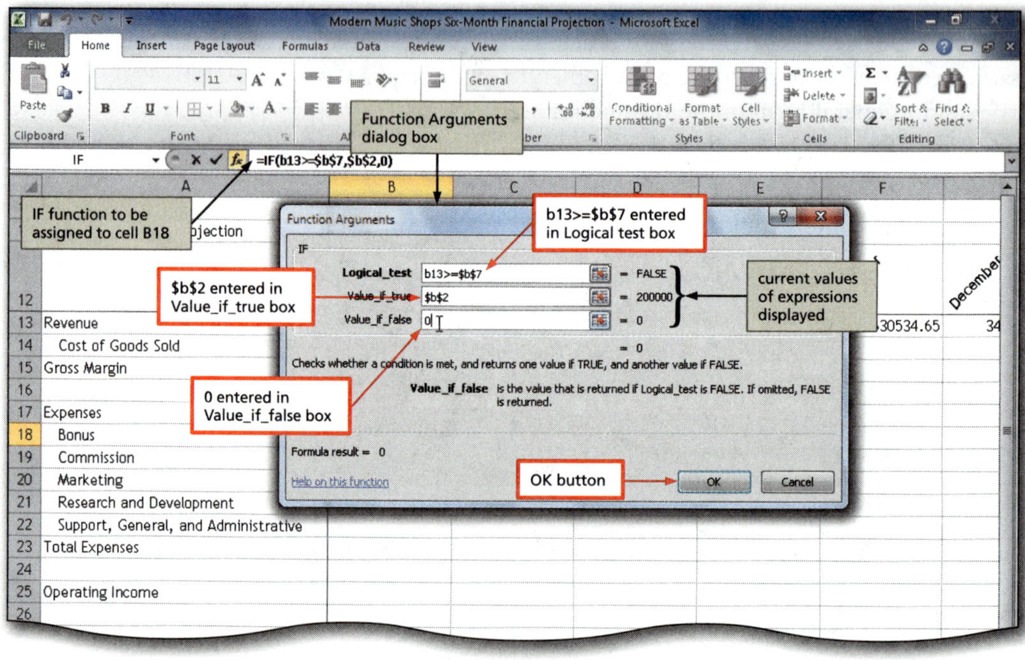

Figure 3–29

3

- Click the OK button (Function Arguments dialog box) to insert the IF function in the selected cell (Figure 3–30).

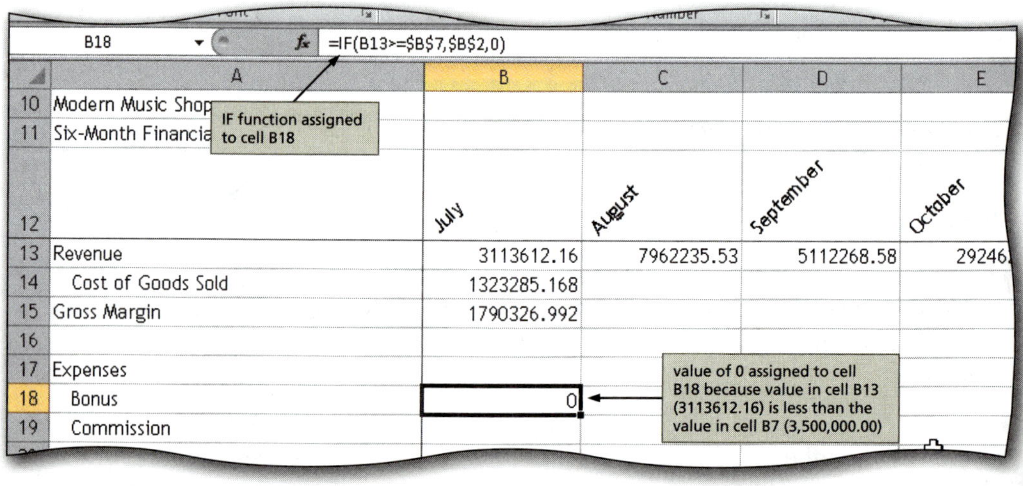

Figure 3–30

Q&A

Why is the value 0 displayed in cell B18?

The value that Excel displays in cell B18 depends on the values assigned to cells B13, B2, and B7. For example, if the value for July revenue in cell B13 is increased above 3,500,000.00, then the IF function in cell B18 will cause Excel to display 200,000.00. If you change the sales revenue for bonus in cell B7 from 3,500,000.00 to another number and the value in cell B13 is greater than or equal to the value in cell B7, it will change the results in cell B18 as well.

Other Ways

1. Click Logical button (Formulas tab | Function Library group), click IF

To Enter the Remaining July Formulas

The July commission expense in cell B19 is equal to the revenue in cell B13 times the commission assumption in cell B3 (5.75%). The July marketing expense in cell B20 is equal to the projected July revenue in cell B13 times the marketing assumption in cell B5 (15.00%). Similar formulas determine the remaining July expenses in cells B21 and B22.

The total expenses value in cell B23 is equal to the sum of the expenses in the range B18:B22. The operating income in cell B25 is equal to the gross margin in cell B15 minus the total expenses in cell B23. The formulas are short, and therefore, they are typed in the following steps, rather than entered using Point mode.

1. Select cell B19. Type **=b13*b3** and then press the DOWN ARROW key to enter the formula in the selected cell. Type **=b13*b5** and then press the DOWN ARROW key to enter the formula in the selected cell. Type **=b13*b6** and then press the DOWN ARROW key to enter the formula in the selected cell. Type **=b13*b8** and then press the DOWN ARROW key to enter the formula in the selected cell.

2. With cell B23 selected, click the Sum button (Home tab | Editing group) twice to insert a SUM function in the selected cell. Select cell B25 to prepare to enter the next formula. Type **=b15-b23** and then press the ENTER key to enter the formula in the selected cell.

3. Press CTRL+ACCENT MARK (`) to display the formulas version of the worksheet (Figure 3–31).

4. When you are finished viewing the formulas version, press CTRL+ACCENT MARK (`) to display the values version of the worksheet.

Q&A

Why should I view the formulas version of the worksheet?

Viewing the formulas version (Figure 3–31) of the worksheet allows you to check the formulas assigned to the range B14:B25. Recall that formulas were entered in lowercase. You can see that Excel converts all the formulas from lowercase to uppercase.

BTW

Replacing a Formula with a Constant

By doing the following, you can replace a formula with its result so that the cell value remains constant: (1) click the cell with the formula; (2) press F2 or click in the formula bar; (3) press F9 to display the value in the formula bar; and (4) press the ENTER key.

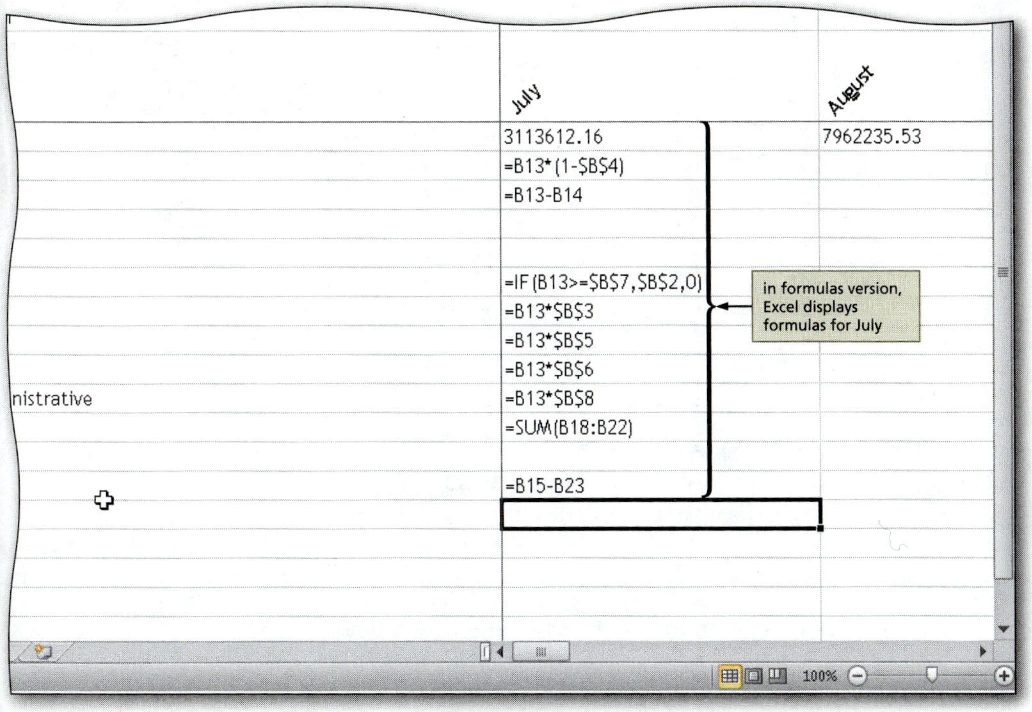

Figure 3–31

To Copy Formulas with Absolute Cell References Using the Fill Handle

The following steps use the fill handle to copy the July formulas in column B to the other five months in columns C through G.

1

- Select the range B14:B25 and then point to the fill handle in the lower-right corner of the selected cell, B25 in this case, to display the crosshair mouse pointer (Figure 3–32).

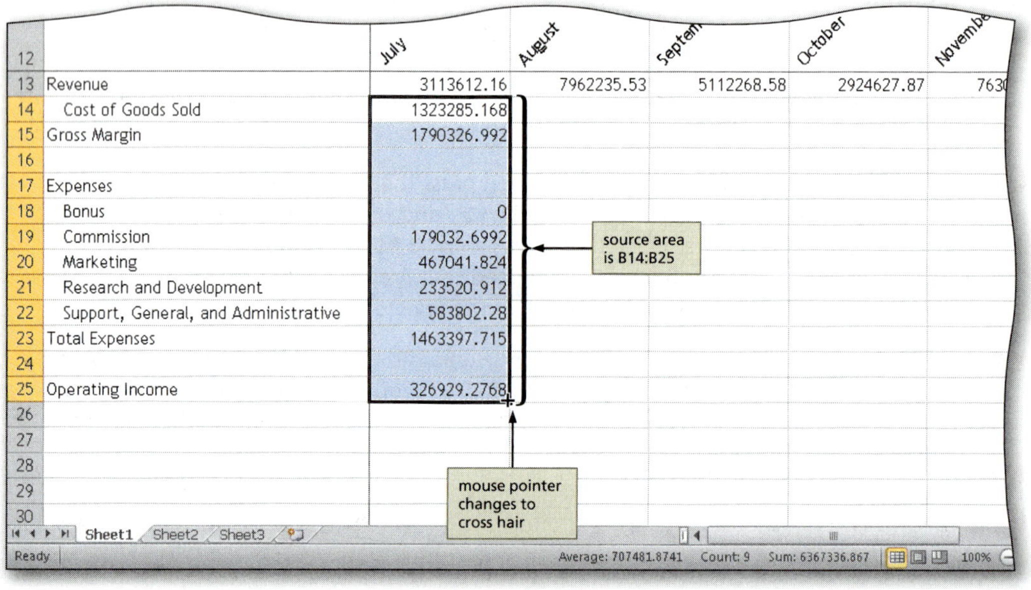

Figure 3–32

2

- Drag the fill handle to the right to copy the formulas from the source area, B14:B25 in this case, to the destination area, C14:G25 in this case, and display the calculated amounts and Auto Fill Options button (Figure 3–33).

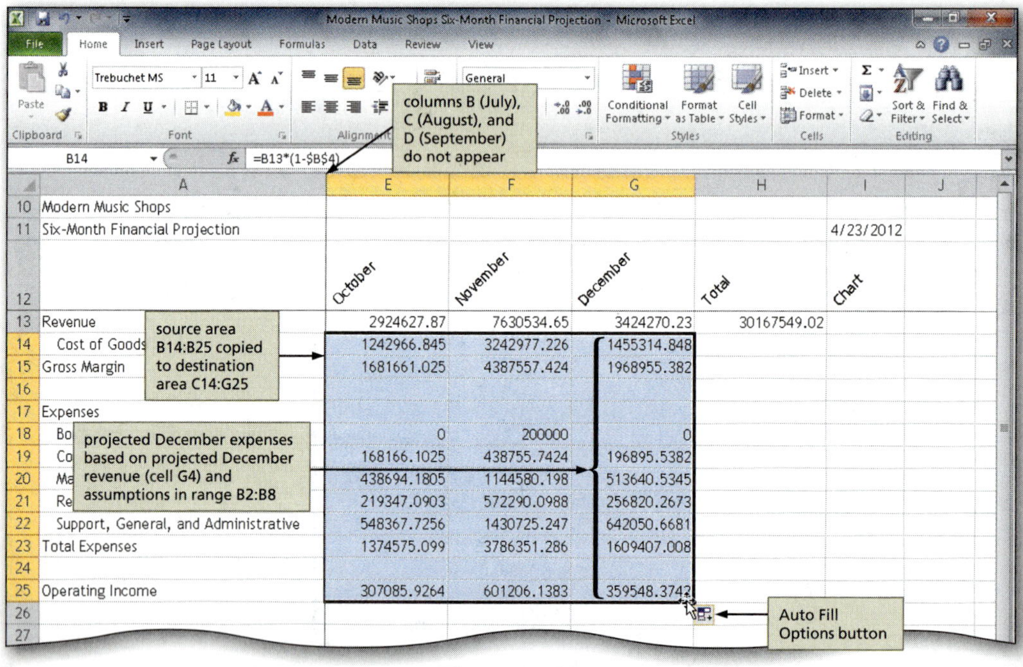

Figure 3–33

Q&A What happens to the formulas after performing the copy operation?

Because the formulas in the range B14:B25 use absolute cell references, the formulas still refer to the current values in the Assumptions table when the formulas are copied to the range C14:G25.

Q&A What happened to columns B, C, and D?

As shown in Figure 3–33, as the fill handle is dragged to the right, columns B, C, and D no longer appear on the screen because column A now acts just as the row numbers do in that columns scrolled off of the visible portion of the worksheet disappear behind column A. Column A, however, remains on the screen, because the row titles were frozen earlier in this chapter.

To Determine Row Totals in Nonadjacent Cells

The following steps determine the row totals in column H. To determine the row totals using the Sum button, select only the cells in column H containing numbers in adjacent cells to the left. If, for example, you select the range H14:H25, Excel will display 0s as the sum of empty rows in cells H16, H17, and H24.

1. Select the range H14:H15. While holding down the CTRL key, select the range H18:H23 and cell H25, as shown in Figure 3–34.
2. Click the Sum button (Home tab | Editing group) to display the row totals in the selected ranges (Figure 3–34).

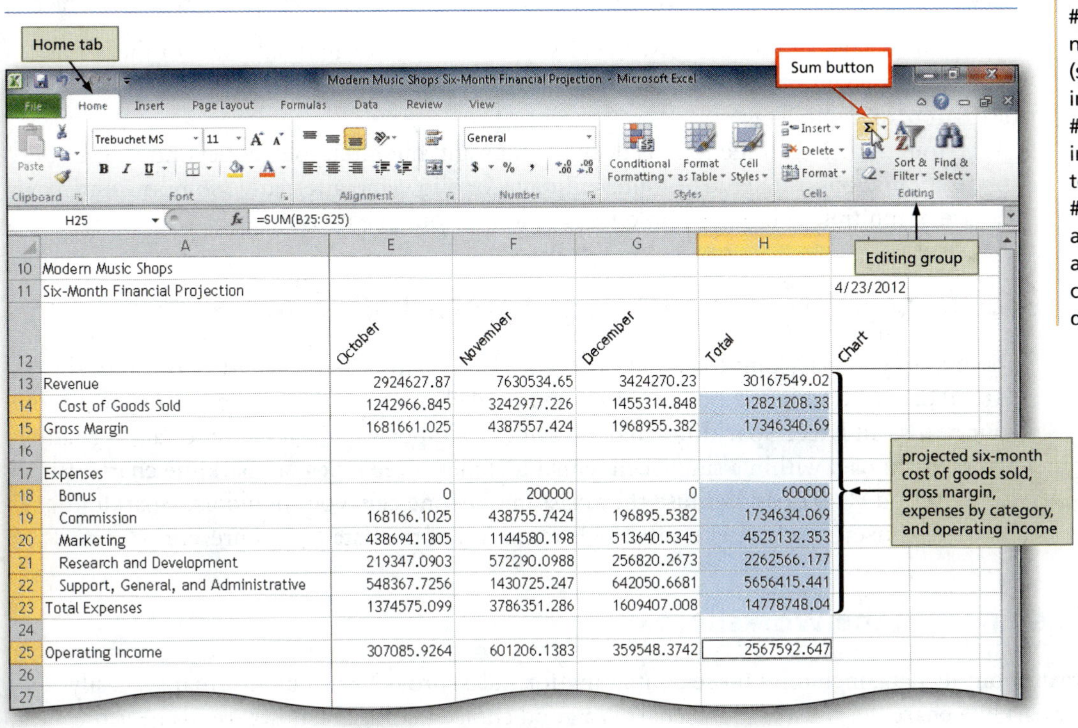

Figure 3–34

BTW

Error Messages

When Excel cannot calculate a formula, it displays an error message in a cell. These error messages always begin with a number sign (#). The more commonly occurring error messages are as follows: #DIV/0! (tries to divide by zero); #NAME? (uses a name Excel does not recognize); #N/A (refers to a value not available); #NULL! (specifies an invalid intersection of two areas); #NUM! (uses a number incorrectly); #REF (refers to a cell that is not valid); #VALUE! (uses an incorrect argument or operand); and ##### (refers to cells not wide enough to display entire entry).

To Unfreeze the Worksheet Titles and Save the Workbook

All the text, data, and formulas have been entered into the worksheet. The following steps unfreeze the titles to allow you to work with the worksheet without frozen rows and columns, and save the workbook using its current file name, Modern Music Shops Six-Month Financial Projection.

1. Press CTRL+HOME to select cell B13 and view the upper-left corner of the screen.
2. Display the View tab and then click the Freeze Panes button (View tab | Window group) to display the Freeze Panes gallery.
3. Click Unfreeze Panes in the Freeze Panes gallery to unfreeze the frozen columns and rows.
4. Display the Home tab and then click the Save button on the Quick Access Toolbar to save the workbook.

Q&A

Why does pressing CTRL+HOME select cell B13?

When the titles are frozen and you press CTRL+HOME, Excel selects the upper-left cell of the unfrozen section of the worksheet. For example, in Step 1 of the previous steps, Excel selected cell B13. When the titles are unfrozen, pressing CTRL+HOME selects cell A1.

Nested Forms of the IF Function

A **nested IF function** is one in which the action to be taken for the true or false case includes yet another IF function. The second IF function is considered to be nested, or layered, within the first. Study the nested IF function below, which determines the eligibility of a student to go on a field trip. The school permits the student to attend the field trip if the student's age is at least 14 and the student has provided a signed permission form. Assume the following in this example: (1) the nested IF function is assigned to cell L9, which instructs Excel to display one of three messages in the cell; (2) cell L7 contains a student's age; and (3) cell L8 contains a Y or N, based on whether the person provided a signed permission form.

=IF(L7>=14, IF(L8="Y","Allowed","Can Travel, but No Permission"),"Too Young to Travel")

The nested IF function instructs Excel to display one, and only one, of the following three messages in cell L9: (1) Allowed; or (2) Can Travel, but No Permission; or (3) Too Young to Travel.

You can nest IF functions as deep as you want, but after you get beyond a nest of three IF functions, the logic becomes difficult to follow and alternative solutions, such as the use of multiple cells and simple IF functions, should be considered.

BTW
Using IFERROR
Similar to the IF function, the IFERROR function checks a formula for correctness. For example, =IFERROR(formula, "Error Message") examines the formula argument. If an error appears (such as #N/A), Excel displays the Error Message text in the cell instead of the Excel #N/A error.

Adding and Formatting Sparkline Charts

Sometimes you may want to condense a range of data into a small chart in order to show a trend or variation in the range. Excel's standard charts may be too large or extensive for your needs. An Excel **Sparkline chart** provides a simple way to show trends and variations in a range of data within a single cell. Excel includes three types of Sparkline charts: Line, Column, and Win/Loss. Because they exist in only one cell, you should use Sparkline charts to convey succinct, eye-catching summaries of the data they represent.

To Add a Sparkline Chart to the Worksheet

Each of the rows of monthly data, including those containing formulas, provides useful information easily summarized by a Line Sparkline chart. A Line Sparkline chart is a good choice because it shows trends over the six-month period for each row of data.

The following steps add a Line Sparkline chart to cell I13 and then use the fill handle to create Line Sparkline charts in the range I14:I25 that represent the monthly data in rows 13 through 25.

1

- Scroll the worksheet so that both columns B and I are displayed on the screen.
- Select cell I13 to prepare to insert a Sparkline chart in the cell.
- Display the Insert tab and then click Line (Insert tab | Sparklines group) to display the Create Sparklines dialog box (Figure 3–35).

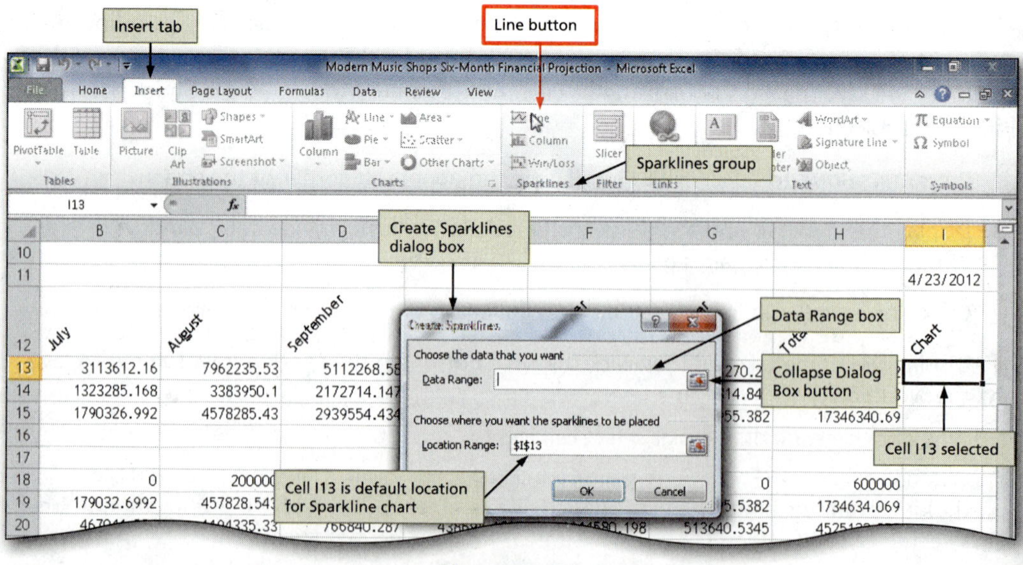

Figure 3–35

2

- Drag through the range B13:G13 to select the range. Do not release the mouse (Figure 3–36).

Q&A

What happened to the Create Sparklines dialog box?

When a dialog box includes a Collapse Dialog Box button (Figure 3–35), selecting cells or a range collapses the dialog box so that only the current text box is displayed. Once the selection is made, the dialog box expands back to its original size. You also can click the Collapse Dialog Box button to make your selection and then click the Expand Dialog Box button (Figure 3–36) to expand the dialog box.

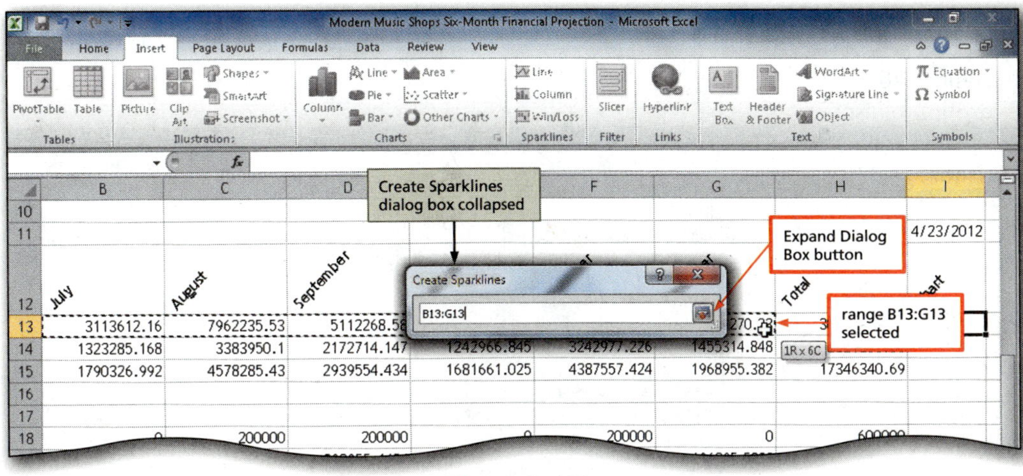

Figure 3–36

3

- Release the mouse button to insert the selected range, B13:G13 in this case, in the Data Range text box.
- Click the OK button (Create Sparklines dialog box) to insert a Line Sparkline chart in the selected cell and display the Sparkline Tools contextual tab (Figure 3–37).

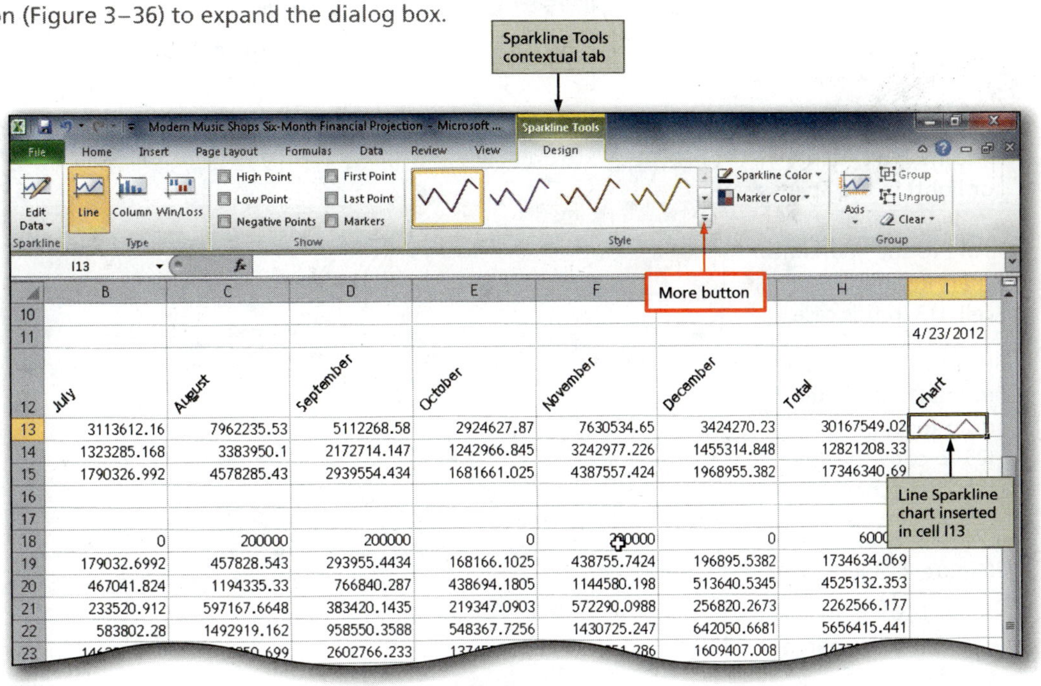

Figure 3–37

To Format and Copy the Sparkline Chart

Just as with standard charts, Excel provides formatting options for Sparkline charts. Sparkline chart formatting is restricted greatly as compared to standard charts. As shown in Figure 3–37, the Show group (Sparkline Tools Design tab) allows you to highlight various points in the chart. Markers provide a point on the chart for each cell represented in the chart. The Style group (Sparkline Tools Design tab) allows you to specify the style and color for the parts of a Sparkline chart.

The steps on the following page format the Sparkline chart in cell I13 using the Style 13 Sparkline chart style.

1

- Click the More button (Sparkline Tools Design tab | Style group) to display the Style gallery (Figure 3–38).

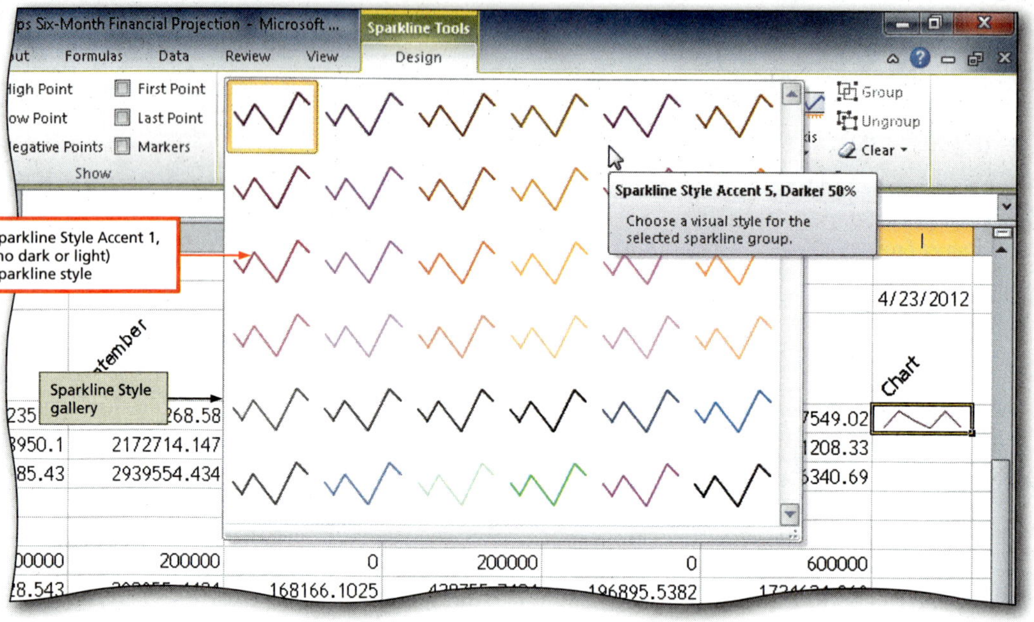

Figure 3–38

2

- Click Sparkline Style Accent 1, (no dark or light) in the Styles gallery to apply the style to the Sparkline chart in the selected cell, I13 in this case.
- Point to the fill handle in cell I13 and then drag through cell I25 to copy the Line Sparkline chart.
- Select cell I27 (Figure 3–39).

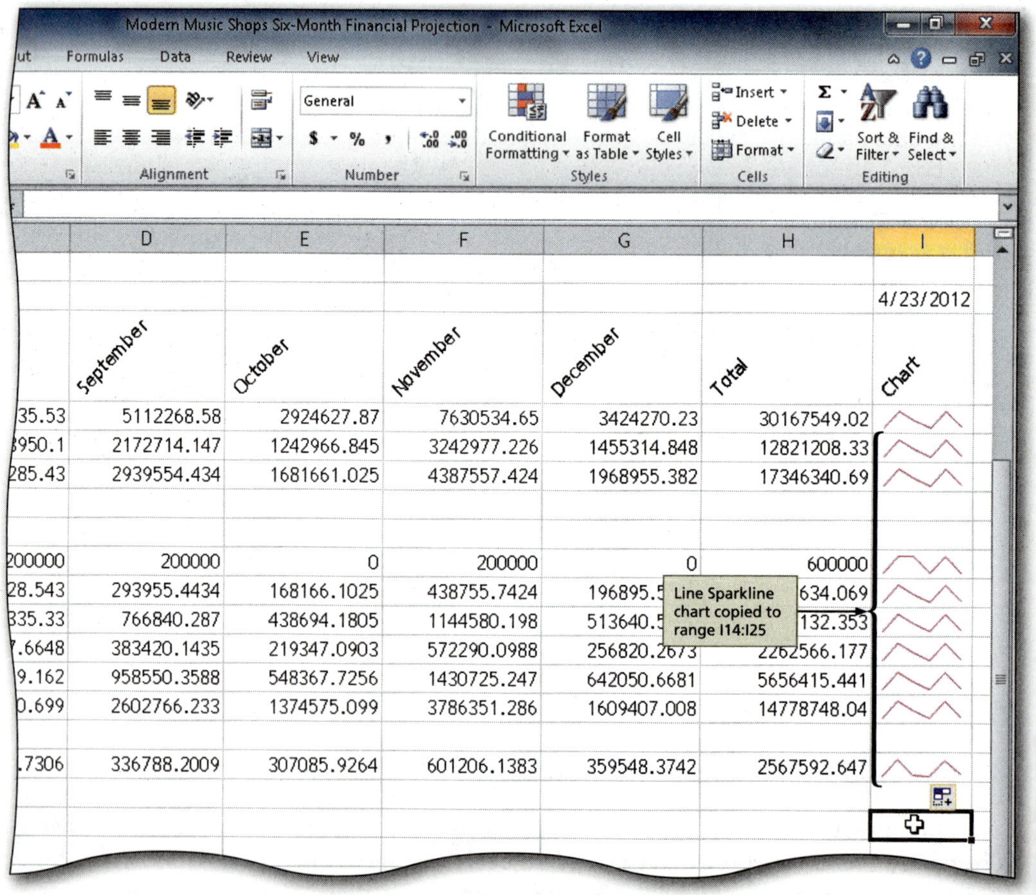

Figure 3–39

Q&A

Why do Sparkline charts not appear in cells I16, I17, and I24?

Excel does not draw Sparkline charts if the range for the Sparkline chart contains no data. In this case the ranges B16:G16, B17:G17, and B24:G24 do not contain data, so Excel draws no Sparkline chart. If you add data to cells in those ranges, then Excel automatically would draw Line Sparkline charts for the rows to which you added data because the Sparkline charts were defined for cells I16, I17, and I24 by the drag operation.

Formatting the Worksheet

The worksheet created thus far shows the financial projections for the six-month period, from July to December. Its appearance is uninteresting, however, even though some minimal formatting (formatting assumptions numbers, changing the column widths, formatting the date, and formatting the Sparkline chart) was performed earlier. This section will complete the formatting of the worksheet to make the numbers easier to read and to emphasize the titles, assumptions, categories, and totals as shown in Figure 3–40.

Plan Ahead

Identify how to format various elements of the worksheet.

A worksheet, such as the one presented in this chapter, should be formatted in the following manner: (1) format the numbers; (2) format the worksheet title, column titles, row titles, and total rows; and (3) format an assumptions table. Numbers in heading rows and total rows should be formatted with a currency symbol. Other dollar amounts should be formatted with a Comma style. An assumptions table should be diminished in its formatting so that it does not distract from the main calculations and data in the worksheet. Assigning the data in an assumptions table a smaller font size would set it apart from other data formatted with a larger font size.

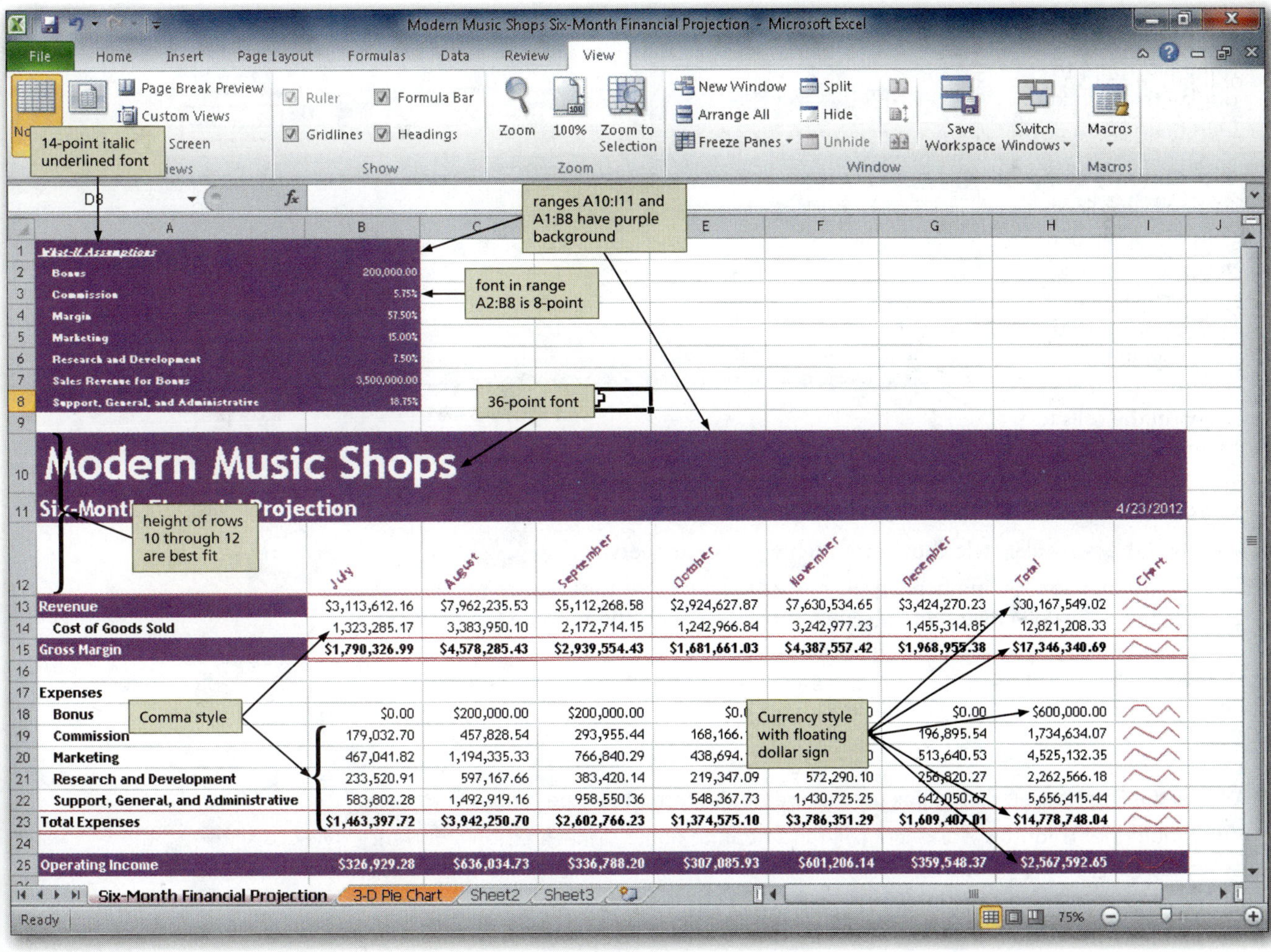

Figure 3–40

To Assign Formats to Nonadjacent Ranges

The numbers in the range B13:H25 are to be formatted as follows:

1. Assign the Currency style with a floating dollar sign to rows 13, 15, 18, 23, and 25.
2. Assign a Comma style to rows 14 and 19 through 22.

The following steps assign formats to the numbers in rows 13 through 25.

1

- Select the range B13:H13 as the first range to format.
- While holding down the CTRL key, select the nonadjacent ranges B15:H15, B18:H18, B23:H23, and B25:H25, and then release the CTRL key to select nonadjacent ranges.
- Click the Format Cells: Number Dialog Box Launcher (Home tab | Number group) to display the Format Cells dialog box.
- Click Currency in the Category list (Format Cells dialog box), if necessary select 2 in the Decimal places box, if necessary click $ in the Symbol list to ensure a dollar sign shows in the cells to be formatted, and click the black font color ($1,234.10) in the Negative numbers list to prepare the desired Currency style for the selected ranges (Figure 3–41).

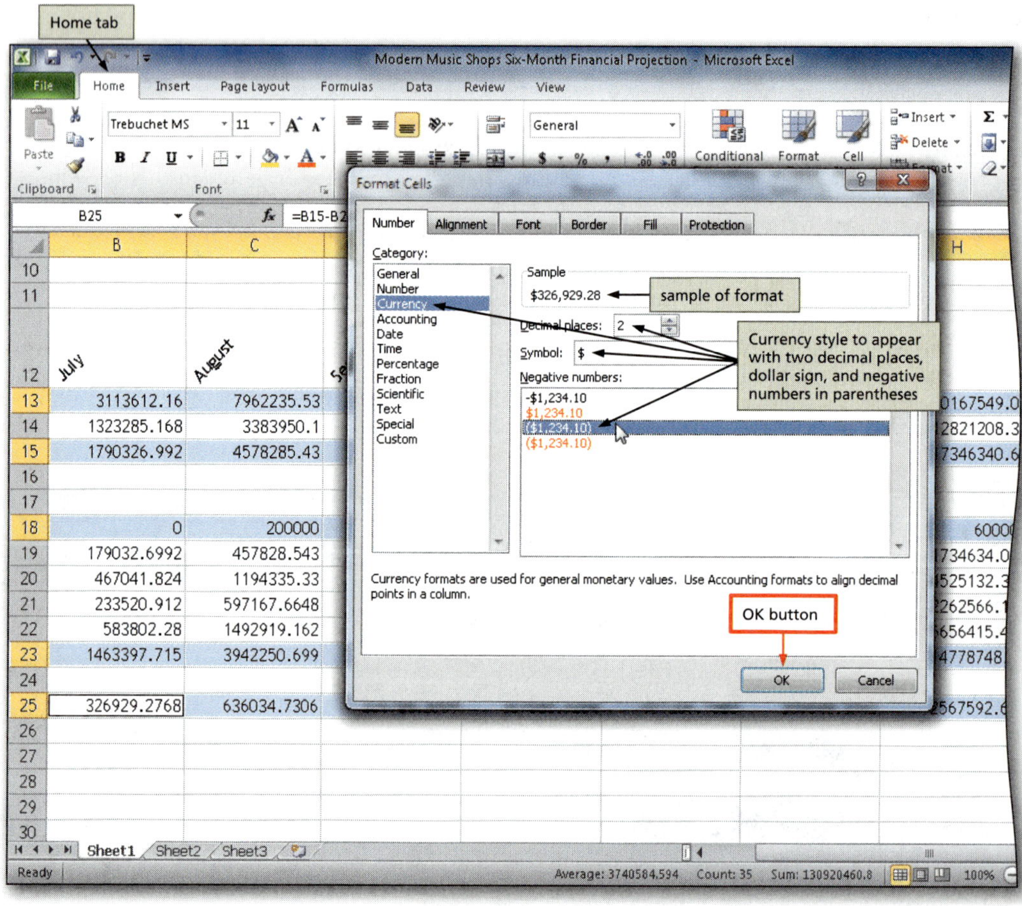

Figure 3–41

Q&A Why was the particular style chosen for the negative numbers?

In accounting, negative numbers often are shown with parentheses surrounding the value rather than with a negative sign preceding the value. Thus, the format (1,234.10) in the Negative numbers list was clicked. The data being used in this chapter contains no negative numbers. You must select a format for negative numbers, however, and you must be consistent if you are choosing different formats in a column; otherwise, the decimal points may not line up.

Q&A Why is the Format Cells dialog box used to create the format for the ranges in this step?

The requirements for this worksheet call for a floating dollar sign. To assign a Currency style with a floating dollar sign, use the Format Cells dialog box rather than the Accounting Style button (Home tab | Number group), which assigns a fixed dollar sign.

2

- Click the OK button (Format Cells dialog box) to close the Format Cells dialog box and apply the desired format to the selected ranges.
- Select the range B14:H14 as the next range to format.
- While holding down the CTRL key, select the range B19:H22, and then release the CTRL key to select nonadjacent ranges.
- Click the Format Cells: Number Dialog Box Launcher (Home tab | Number group) to display the Format Cells dialog box.

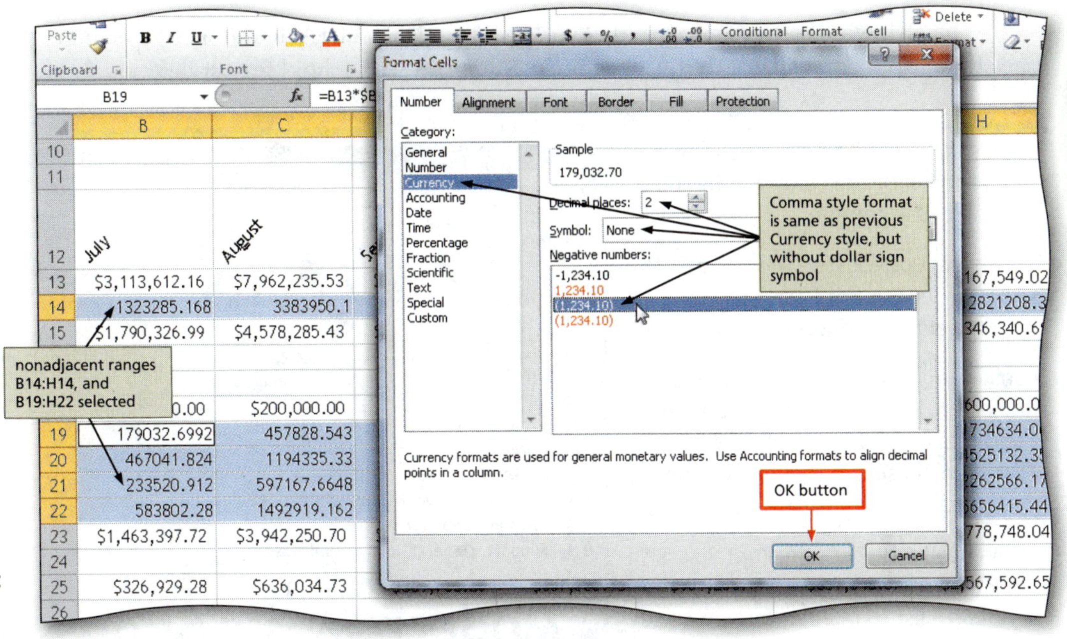

Figure 3–42

- Click Currency in the Category list (Format Cells dialog box), if necessary select 2 in the Decimal places box, click None in the Symbol list so a dollar sign does not show in the cells to be formatted, and click the black font color (1,234.10) in the Negative numbers list (Figure 3–42).

3

- Click the OK button (Format Cells dialog box) to close the Format Cells dialog box and apply the desired format to the selected ranges.
- Select cell B27 to select an empty cell and display the formatted numbers as shown in Figure 3–43.

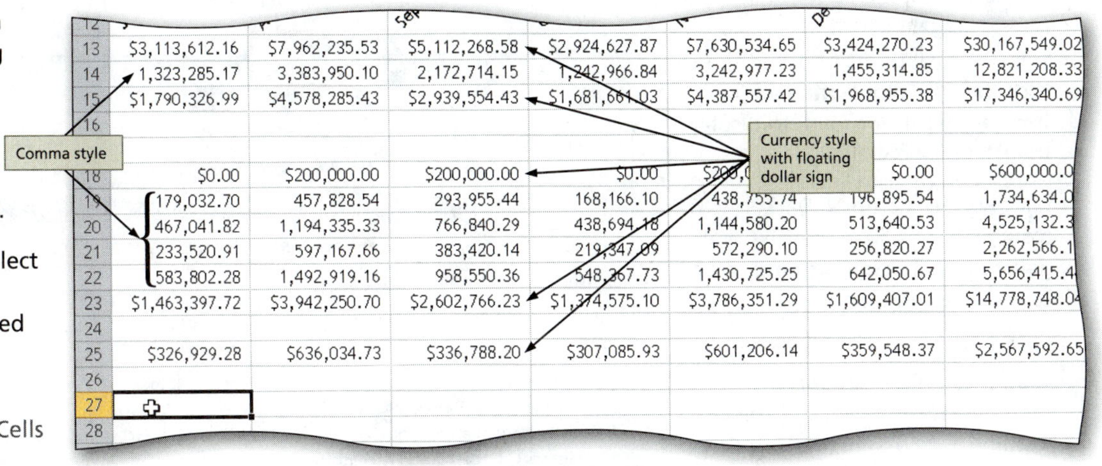

Figure 3–43

Q&A

Why is the Format Cells dialog box used to create the style for the ranges in Steps 2 and 3?

The Format Cells dialog box is used to assign the Comma style, because the Comma Style button (Home tab | Number group) assigns a format that displays a dash (–) when a cell has a value of 0. The specifications for this worksheet call for displaying a value of 0 as 0.00 (see cell B18 in Figure 3–40) rather than as a dash. To create a Comma style using the Format Cells dialog box, you can assign a Currency style with no dollar sign.

Other Ways

1. Right-click range, click Format Cells on shortcut menu, click Number tab (Format Cells dialog box), click category in Category list, select format, click OK button (Format Cells dialog box)
2. Press CTRL+1, click Number tab (Format Cells dialog box), click category in Category list, select format, click OK button (Format Cells dialog box)

To Format the Worksheet Titles

The following steps emphasize the worksheet titles in cells A10 and A11 by changing the font, size, and color. The steps also format all of the row headers in column A with a bold font style.

1

- Press CTRL+HOME to select cell A1 and then click the column A heading to select the column.
- Click the Bold button (Home tab | Font group) to bold all of the data in the selected column.
- Select cell A10, click the Font Size box arrow (Home tab | Font group), and then click 36 in the Font Size list to increase the font size of the selected cell.
- Select cell A11, click the Font Size box arrow, and then click 18 in the Font Size list to increase the font size of the selected cell (Figure 3–44).

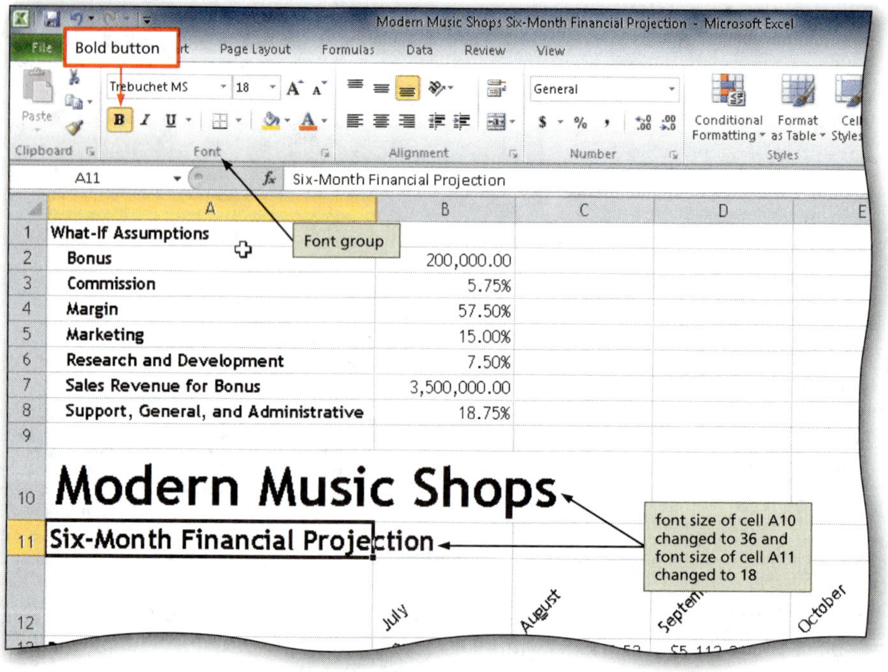

Figure 3–44

2

- Select the range A10:I11 and then click the Fill Color button arrow (Home tab | Font group) to display the Fill Color gallery.
- Click Purple, Accent 2, Darker 25% (column 6, row 5) in the Fill Color gallery to add a background color to the selected range.
- Click the Font Color button arrow (Home tab | Font group) and then select White, Background 1 (column 1, row 1) in the Font Color gallery to change the font color of the selected range (Figure 3–45).

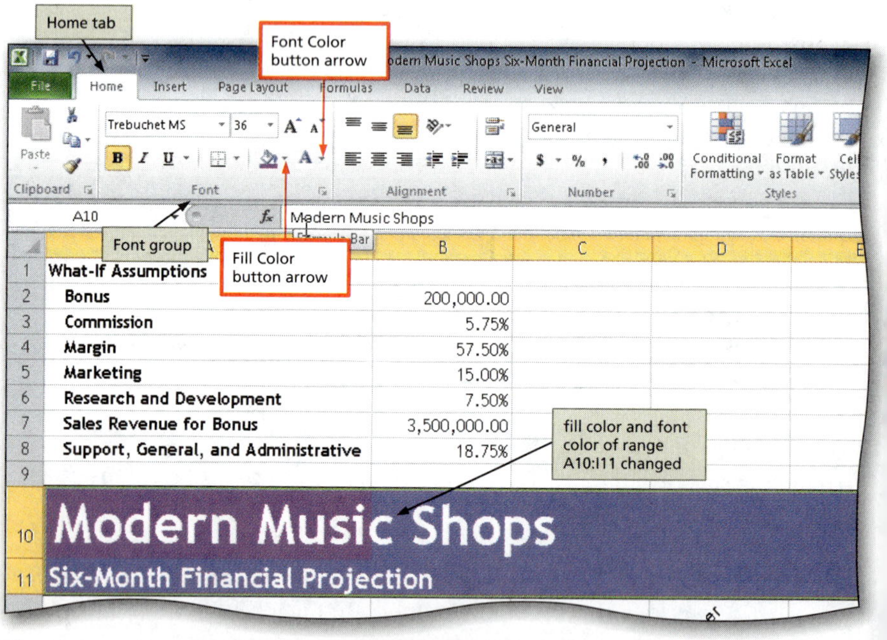

Figure 3–45

Other Ways

1. Right-click range, click Format Cells on shortcut menu, click Fill tab (Format Cells dialog box) to color background (or click Font tab to color font), click OK button
2. Press CTRL+1, click Fill tab (Format Cells dialog box) to color background (or click Font tab to color font), click OK button

To Assign Cell Styles to Nonadjacent Rows and Colors to a Cell

The next step to improving the appearance of the worksheet is to format the heading in row 12 and the totals in rows 15, 23, and 25. The following steps format the heading in row 13 with the Heading 3 cell style and the totals in rows 15, 23, and 25 with the Total cell style. Cell A13 also is formatted with a background color and font color.

1. Select the range A12:I12 and apply the Heading 3 cell style.
2. Select the range A15:I15 and while holding down the CTRL key, select the ranges A23:I23 and A25:I25.
3. Apply the Total cell style to the selected nonadjacent ranges.
4. Select cell A13, click the Fill Color button arrow (Home tab | Font group), and then click the Purple, Accent 2, Darker 25% color (column 6, row 5) in the Fill Color gallery.
5. Click the Font Color button arrow (Home tab | Font group) and then click the White, Background 1 color (column 1, row 1) in the Font Color gallery (Figure 3–46).

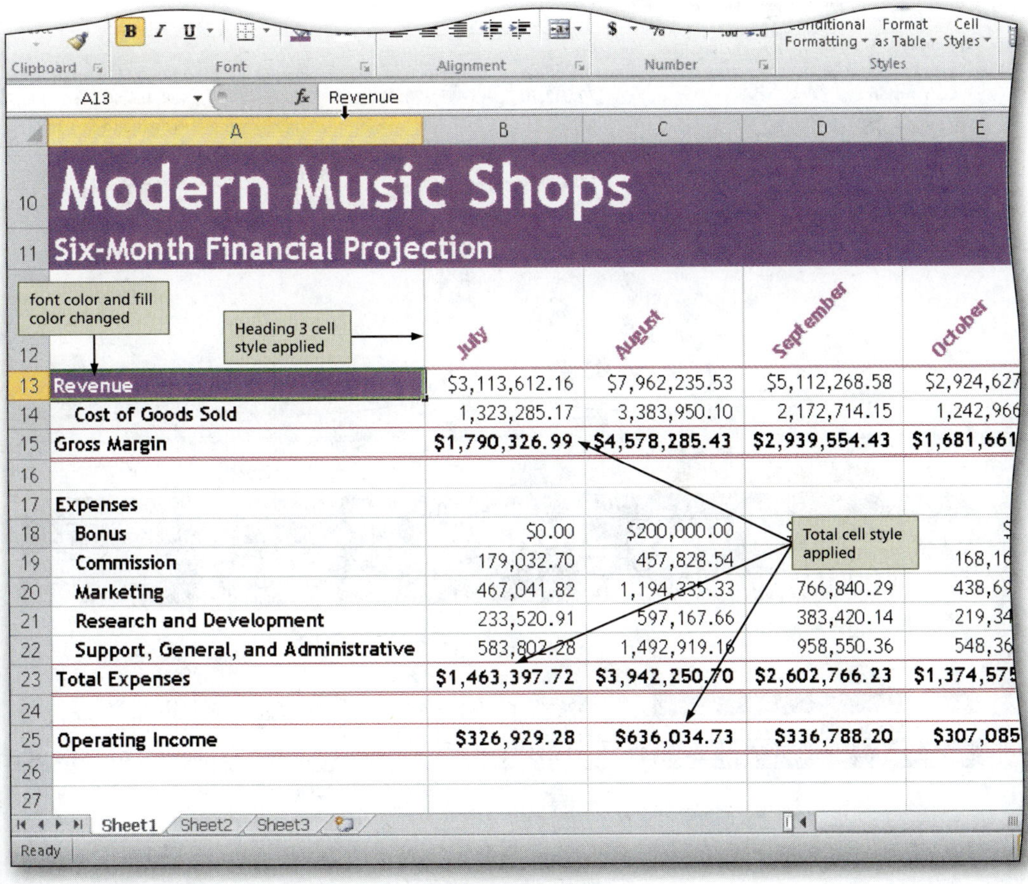

Figure 3–46

BTW

Toggle Commands
Many of the commands on the Ribbon, on the galleries, and the shortcut keys function as toggles. For example, if you click the Freeze Panes command on the Freeze Panes gallery, the command changes to Unfreeze Panes the next time you view the gallery. These types of commands work like on-off switches or toggles.

BTW

Work Days
Assume that you have two dates, one in cell A1 and the other in cell A2. Assume further that the date in cell A1 is your starting date and the date in cell A2 is the ending date. To calculate the work days between the two dates (excluding weekends), use the following formula: =NETWORKDAYS(A1, A2). For this function to work, make sure the Analysis ToolPak add-in is installed. You can install it on the Add-Ins page of the Excel Options dialog box.

BTW

The Fill and Font Color Buttons
You may have noticed that the color bar at the bottom of the Fill Color and Font Color buttons (Home tab | Font group) (Figure 3–45) changes to the most recently selected color. To apply this same color to a cell background or text, select a cell and then click the Fill Color button to use the color as a background or click the Font Color button to use the color as a font color.

To Copy a Cell's Format Using the Format Painter Button

Using the Format Painter, you can format a cell quickly by copying a cell's format to another cell or a range of cells. The following steps format cells A15 and the range A25:I25 using the Format Painter.

1

- If necessary, click cell A13 to select a source cell for the format to paint.
- Double-click the Format Painter button (Home tab | Clipboard group) and then move the mouse pointer onto the worksheet to cause the mouse pointer to change to a block plus sign with a paintbrush (Figure 3–47).

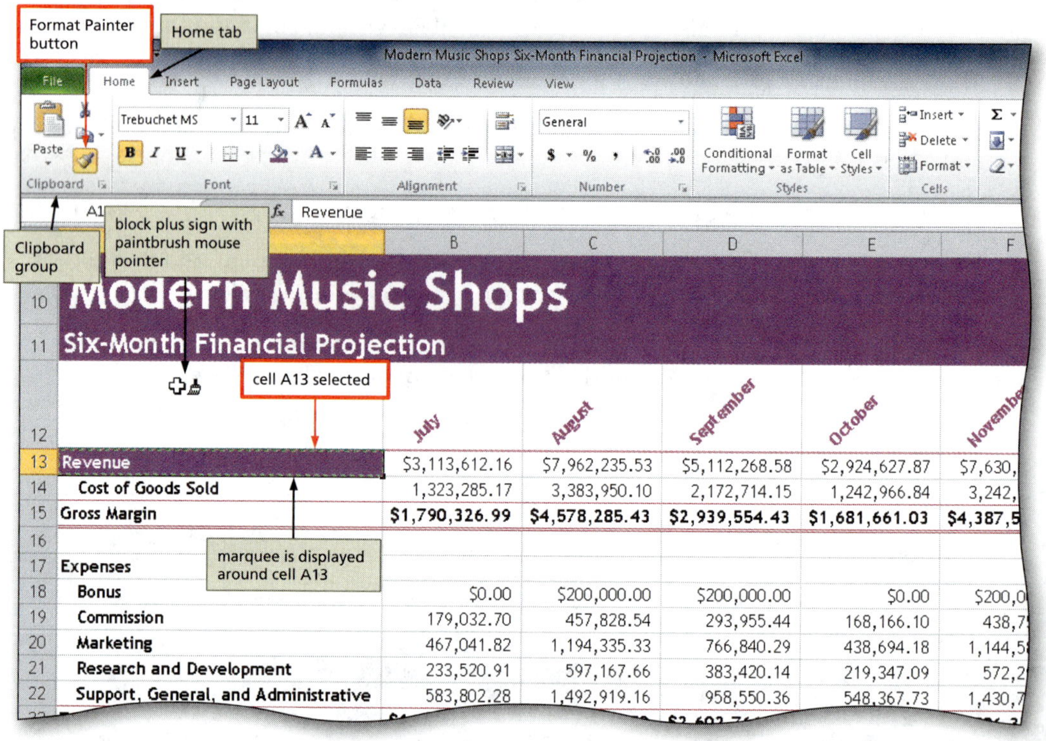

Figure 3–47

2

- Click cell A15 to assign the format of the source cell, A13 in this case, to the destination cell, A15 in this case (Figure 3–48).

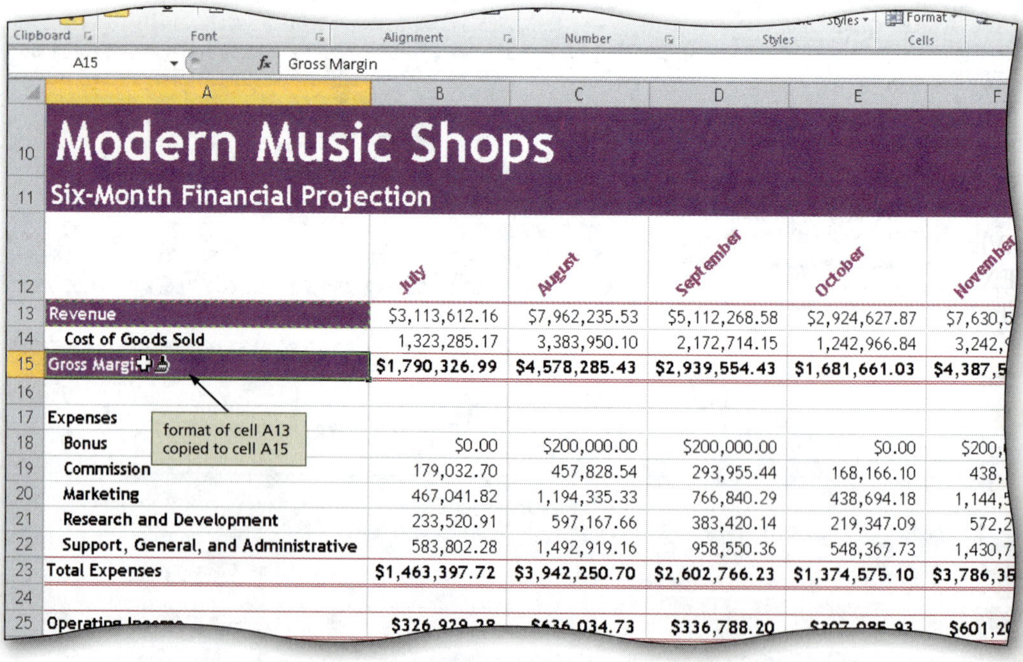

Figure 3–48

3

- With the mouse pointer still a block plus sign with a paintbrush, drag through the range A25:I25 to assign the format of the source cell, A13 in this case, to the destination range, A25:I25 in this case.
- Press the ESC key to stop the format painter.
- Apply the Currency style to the range B25:H25 to cause the cells in the range to appear with a floating dollar sign and two decimal places and then scroll the worksheet so that column A is displayed (Figure 3–49).

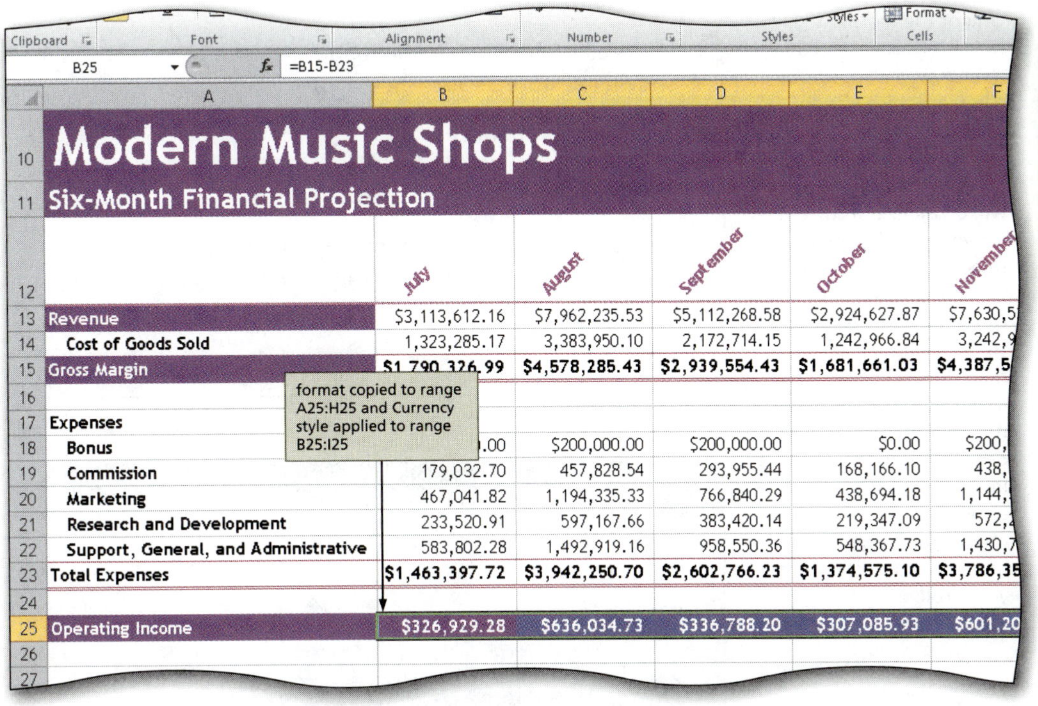

Figure 3–49

Q&A Why does the Currency style need to be reapplied to the range B25:H25?

Sometimes, the use of the format painter results in unintended outcomes. In this case, the changing of the background fill color and font color for the range B25:H25 resulted in the loss of the Currency style because the format being copied did not included the Currency style. Reapplying the Currency style to the range results in the proper number style, fill color, and font color.

Other Ways

1. Click Copy button (Home tab | Clipboard group), select cell, click Paste button arrow (Home tab | Clipboard group), click Formatting icon on Paste gallery
2. Right-click cell, click Copy, right-click cell, click Formatting icon on shortcut menu

To Format the What-If Assumptions Table and Save the Workbook

The last step to improving the appearance of the worksheet is to format the What-If Assumptions table in the range A1:B8. The specifications in Figure 3–40 on page EX 173 require an 8-point italic underlined font for the title in cell A1 and 8-point font in the range A2:B8. The following steps format the What-If Assumptions table.

BTW **Painting a Format to Nonadjacent Ranges**
Double-click the Format Painter button (Home tab | Clipboard group) and then drag through the nonadjacent ranges to paint the formats to the ranges. Click the Format Painter button (Home tab | Clipboard group) to deactivate it.

1. Press CTRL+HOME to select cell A1.
2. Click the Font Size button arrow (Home tab | Font group) and then click 8 in the Font Size list to decrease the font size of the selected cell.
3. Click the Italic button (Home tab | Font Group) and then click the Underline button (Home tab | Font group) to italicize and underline the text in the selected cell.
4. Select the range A2:B8, click the Font Size button arrow (Home tab | Font group) and then click 8 in the Font Size list to apply a smaller font size to the selected range.
5. Select the range A1:B8 and then click the Fill Color button (Home tab | Font group) to apply the most recently used background color to the selected range.

BTW

Selecting Nonadjacent Ranges
One of the more difficult tasks to learn is selecting nonadjacent ranges. To complete this task, do not hold down the CTRL key when you select the first range because Excel will consider the current active cell to be the first selection, and you may not want the current active cell in the selection. Once the first range is selected, hold down the CTRL key and drag through the nonadjacent ranges. If a desired range is not visible in the window, use the scroll arrows to view the range. You need not hold down the CTRL key while you scroll.

6. Click the Font Color button (Home tab | Font group) to apply the most recently used font color to the selected range.

7. Click cell D8 to deselect the range A2:B8 and display the What-If Assumptions table, as shown in Figure 3–50.

8. Save the workbook.

Q&A

What happens when I click the Italic and Underline buttons?

Recall that when you assign the italic font style to a cell, Excel slants the characters slightly to the right, as shown in cell A1 in Figure 3–50. The **underline** format underlines only the characters in the cell, rather than the entire cell, as is the case when you assign a cell a bottom border.

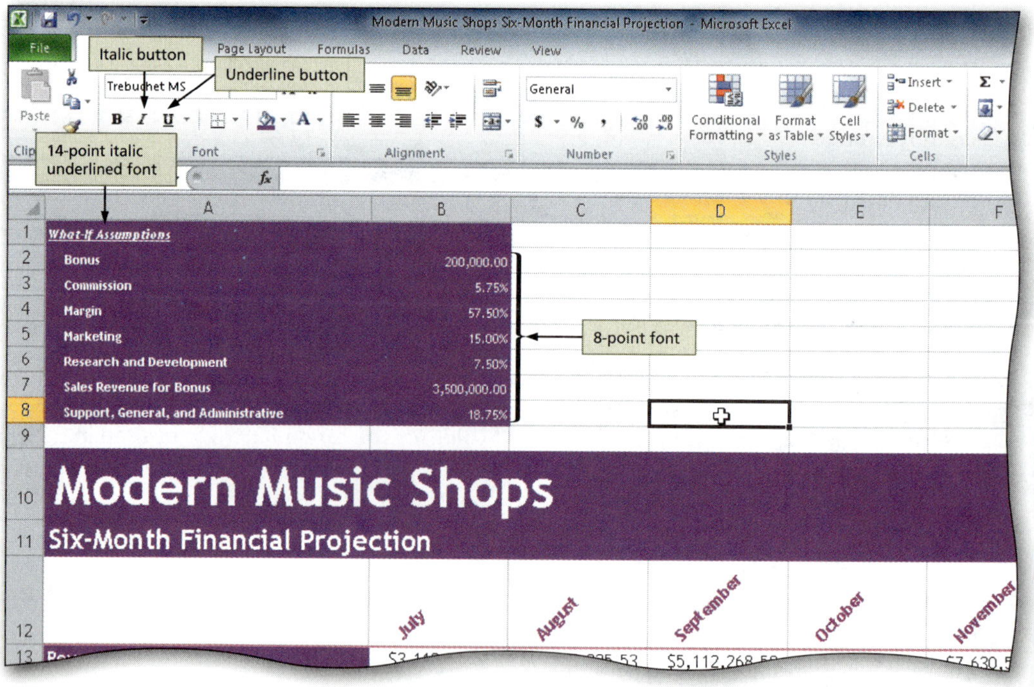

Figure 3–50

Break Point: If you wish to stop working through the chapter at this point, you can quit Excel now and then resume the project at a later point in time by starting Excel, opening the file called Modern Music Shops Six-Month Financial Projection, and continuing to follow the steps from this location forward.

BTW

Charts
When you change a value on which a chart is dependent, Excel immediately redraws the chart based on the new value. With bar charts, you can drag the bar in the chart in one direction or another to change the corresponding value in the worksheet.

Adding a 3-D Pie Chart to the Workbook

The next step in the chapter is to draw the 3-D Pie chart on a separate sheet in the workbook, as shown in Figure 3–51. Use a **pie chart** to show the relationship or proportion of parts to a whole. Each slice (or wedge) of the pie shows what percent that slice contributes to the total (100%).

The 3-D Pie chart in Figure 3–51 shows the contribution of each month's projected operating income to the six-month projected operating income. The 3-D Pie chart makes it easy to evaluate the contribution of one month in comparison to the other months.

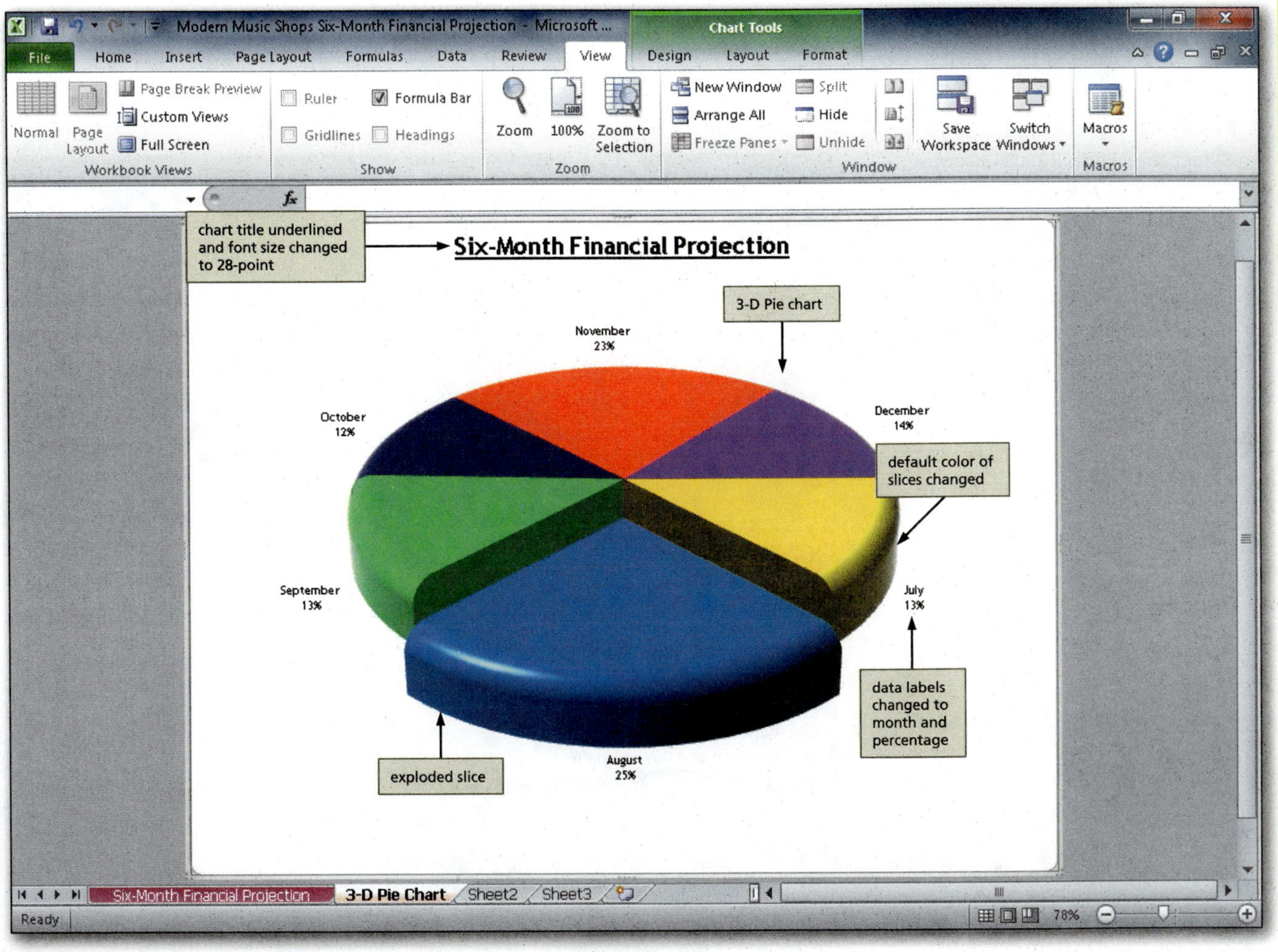

Figure 3–51

Unlike the 3-D Column chart created in Excel Chapter 1, the 3-D Pie chart shown in Figure 3–51 is not embedded in the worksheet. Instead, the Pie chart resides on a separate sheet, called a **chart sheet**, which contains only the chart.

In this worksheet, the ranges to chart are the nonadjacent ranges B12:G12 (month names) and B25:G25 (monthly operating incomes). The month names in the range B12:G12 will identify the slices of the Pie chart; these entries are called **category names**. The range B25:G25 contains the data that determines the size of the slices in the pie; these entries are called the **data series**. Because six months are being charted, the 3-D Pie chart contains six slices.

The sketch of the 3-D Pie chart in Figure 3–3b on page EX 142 also calls for emphasizing the month of August by offsetting its slice from the main portion. A Pie chart with one or more slices offset is called an **exploded Pie chart**.

As shown in Figure 3–51, the default 3-D Pie chart also has been enhanced by rotating it, changing the colors of the slices, adding a bevel, and modifying the chart title and labels that identify the slices.

BTW

Chart Items
When you rest the mouse pointer over a chart item, such as a legend, bar, or axis, Excel displays a chart tip containing the name of the item.

To Draw a 3-D Pie Chart on a Separate Chart Sheet

The following steps draw the 3-D Pie chart on a separate chart sheet.

1

- Select the range B12:G12 to identify the range of the category name of the 3-D Pie Chart.
- If necessary, scroll the worksheet so that row 25 is displayed, and while holding down the CTRL key, select the range B25:G25.
- Display the Insert tab.
- Click the Pie button (Insert tab | Charts group) to display the Pie gallery (Figure 3–52).

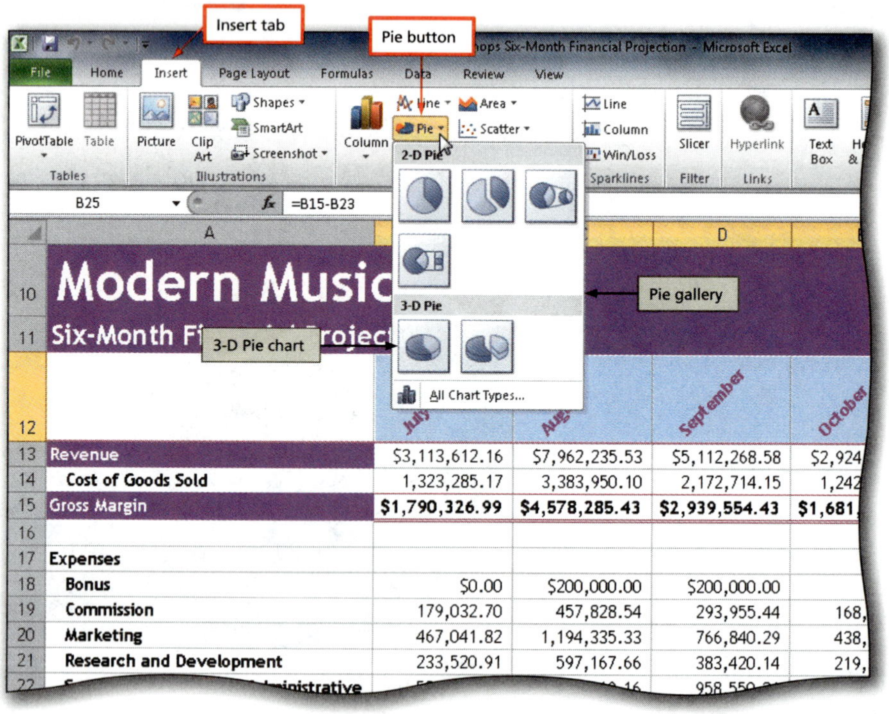

Figure 3–52

2

- Click Pie in 3-D chart in the Pie gallery to select the desired chart type.
- When Excel draws the chart, click the Move Chart button (Chart Tools Design tab | Location group) to display the Move Chart dialog box (Figure 3–53).

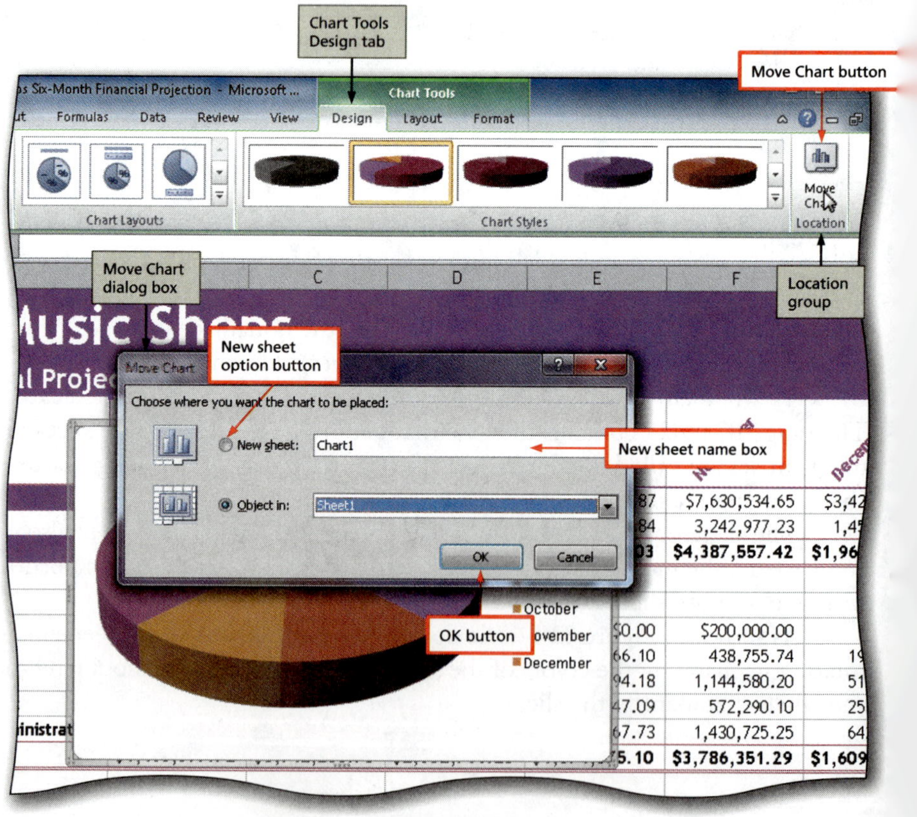

Figure 3–53

3

- Click New sheet (Move Chart dialog box) and then type `3-D Pie Chart` in the 'New sheet name' text box to enter a sheet tab name for the chart sheet.
- Click the OK button (Move Chart dialog box) to move the chart to a new chart sheet with a new sheet name, 3-D Pie Chart in this case (Figure 3–54).

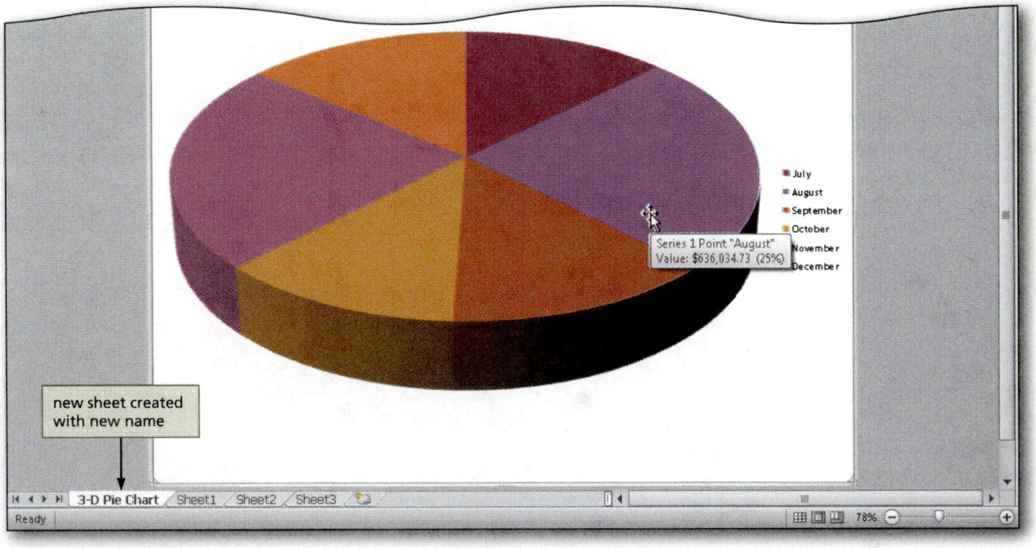

Figure 3–54

Other Ways
1. Select range to chart, press F11

To Insert a Chart Title and Data Labels

The next step is to insert a chart title and labels that identify the slices. Before you can format a chart item, such as the chart title or data labels, you must select it. The following steps insert a chart title, remove the legend, and add data labels.

1

- Click anywhere in the chart area outside the chart to select the chart.
- Display the Chart Tools Layout tab and then click the Chart Title button (Chart Tools Layout tab | Labels group) to display the Chart Title gallery.
- Click the Centered Overlay Title command in the Chart Title gallery to add a chart title centered on top of the chart.
- Select the text in the chart title and then type `Six-Month Financial Projection` to add a new chart title (Figure 3–55).

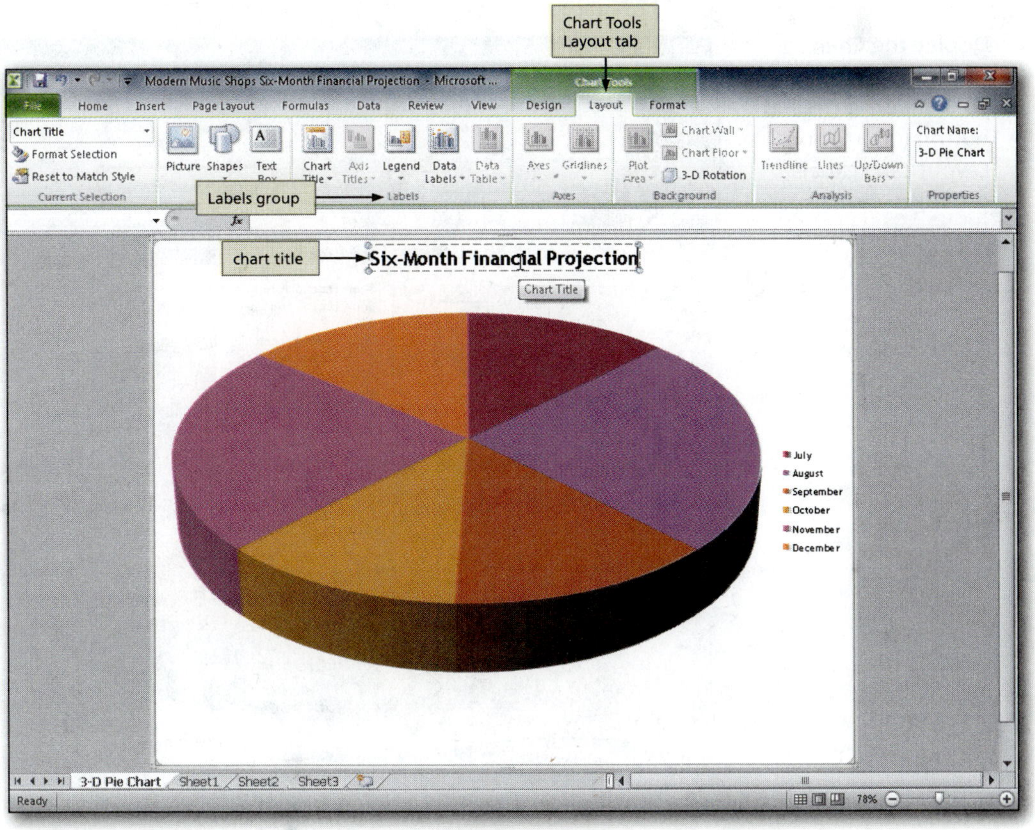

Figure 3–55

2

- Select the text in the new title and then display the Home tab.
- Click the Underline button (Home tab | Font group) to assign an underline font style to the chart title (Figure 3–56).

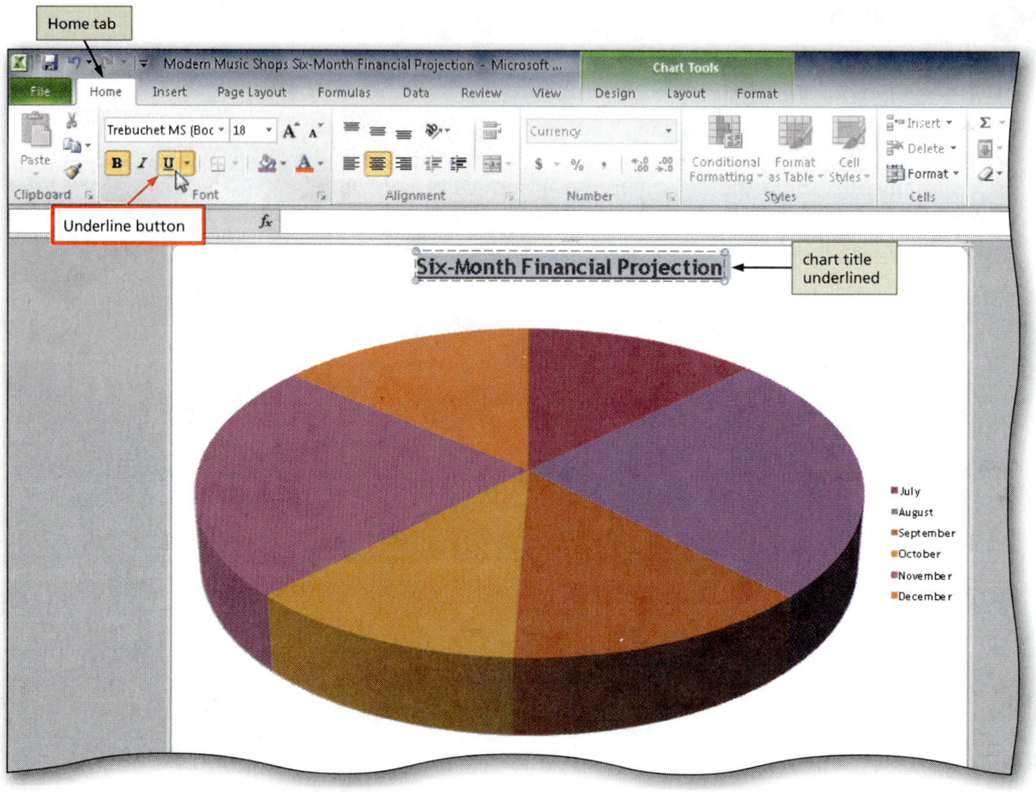

Figure 3–56

3

- Display the Chart Tools Layout tab and then click the Legend button (Chart Tools Layout tab | Labels group) to display the Legend gallery (Figure 3–57).

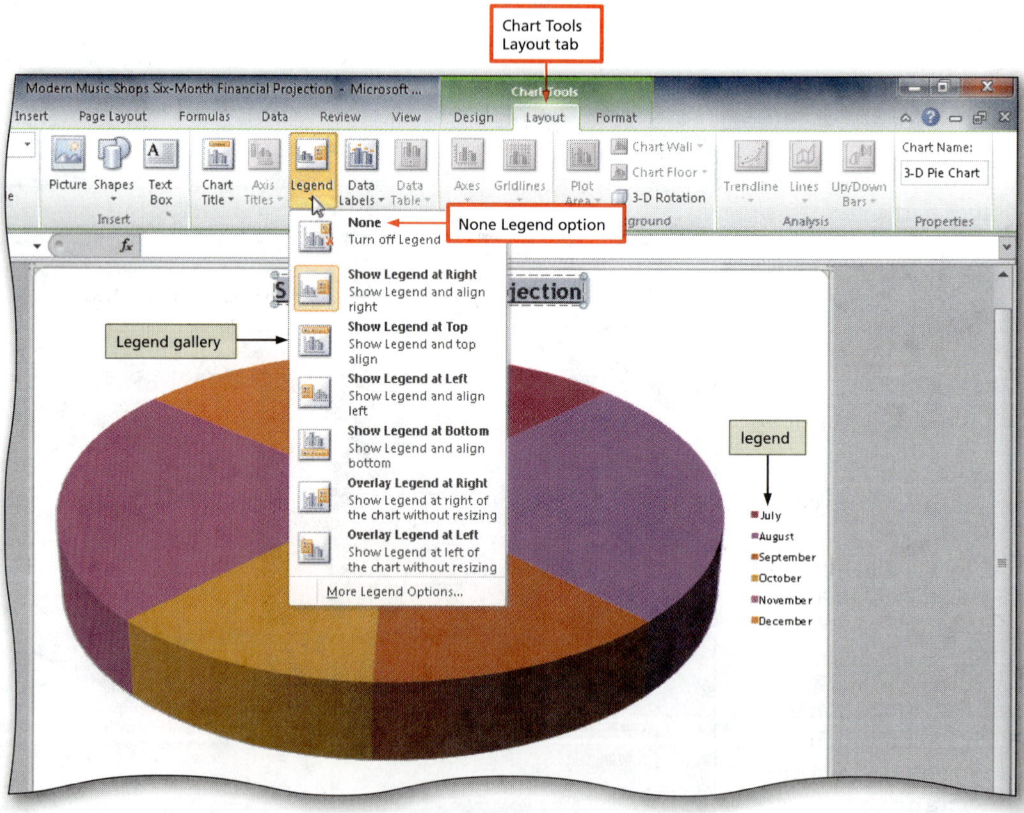

Figure 3–57

4

- Click the None Legend option in the Legend gallery to turn off the legend on the chart.
- Click the Data Labels button (Layout tab | Labels group) and then click Outside End in the Data Labels gallery to display data labels outside the chart at the end of each slice (Figure 3–58).

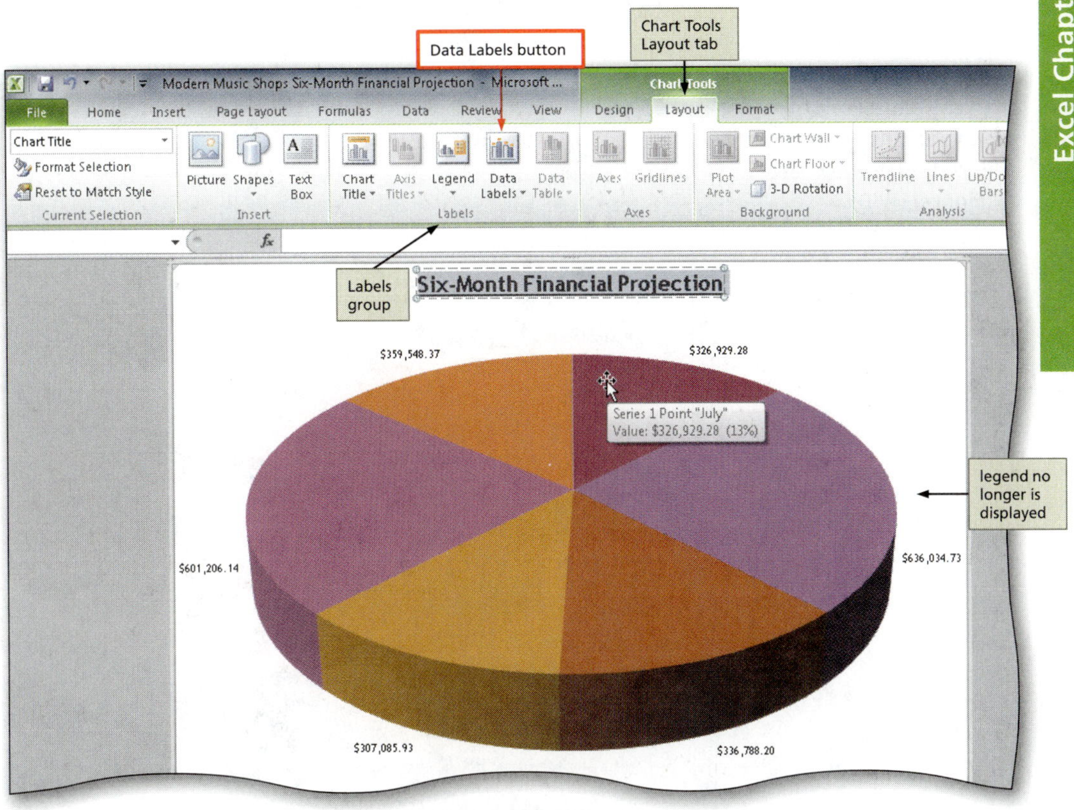

Figure 3–58

5

- If necessary, right-click any data label to select all of the data labels on the chart and to display a shortcut menu.
- Click the Format Data Labels command on the shortcut menu to display the Format Data Labels dialog box.
- If necessary, click the Series Name, Value, and Show Leader Lines check boxes to deselect them (Format Data Labels dialog box) and then click the Category Name and Percentage check boxes to cause the data labels to be displayed with category names and percent values, rather than currency values (Figure 3–59).

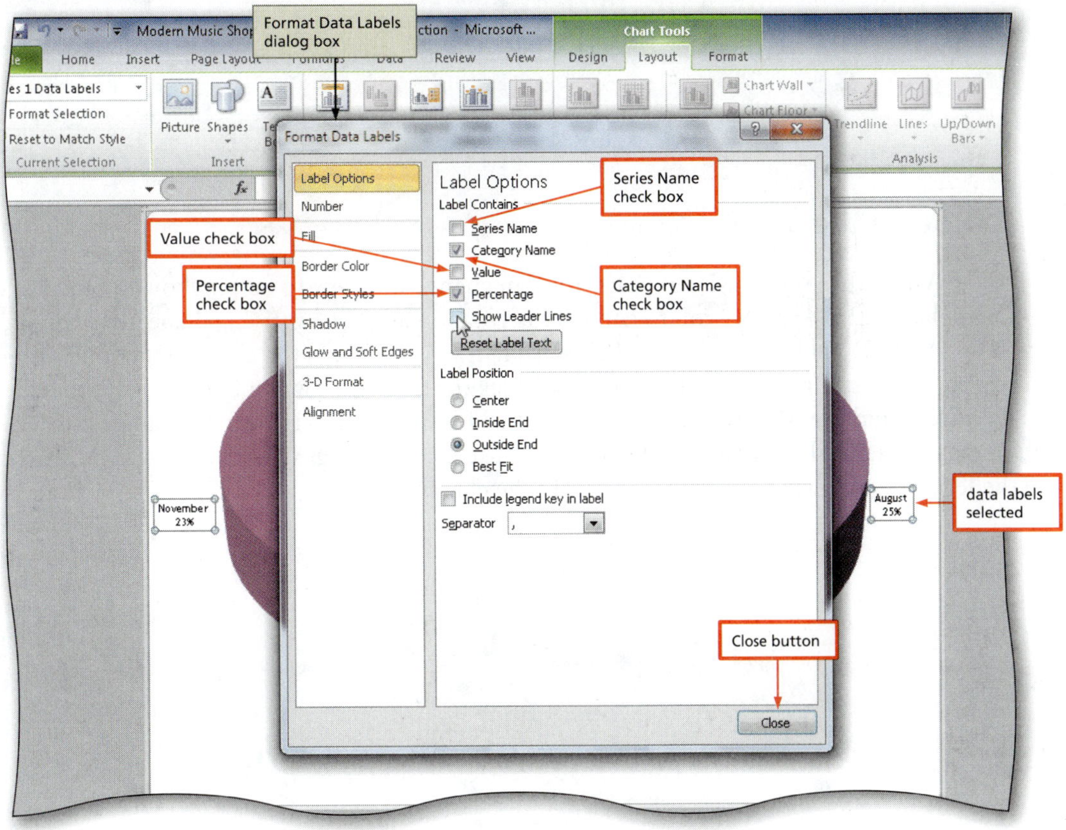

Figure 3–59

6

- Click the Close button to close the Format Data Labels dialog box and display the chart (Figure 3–60).

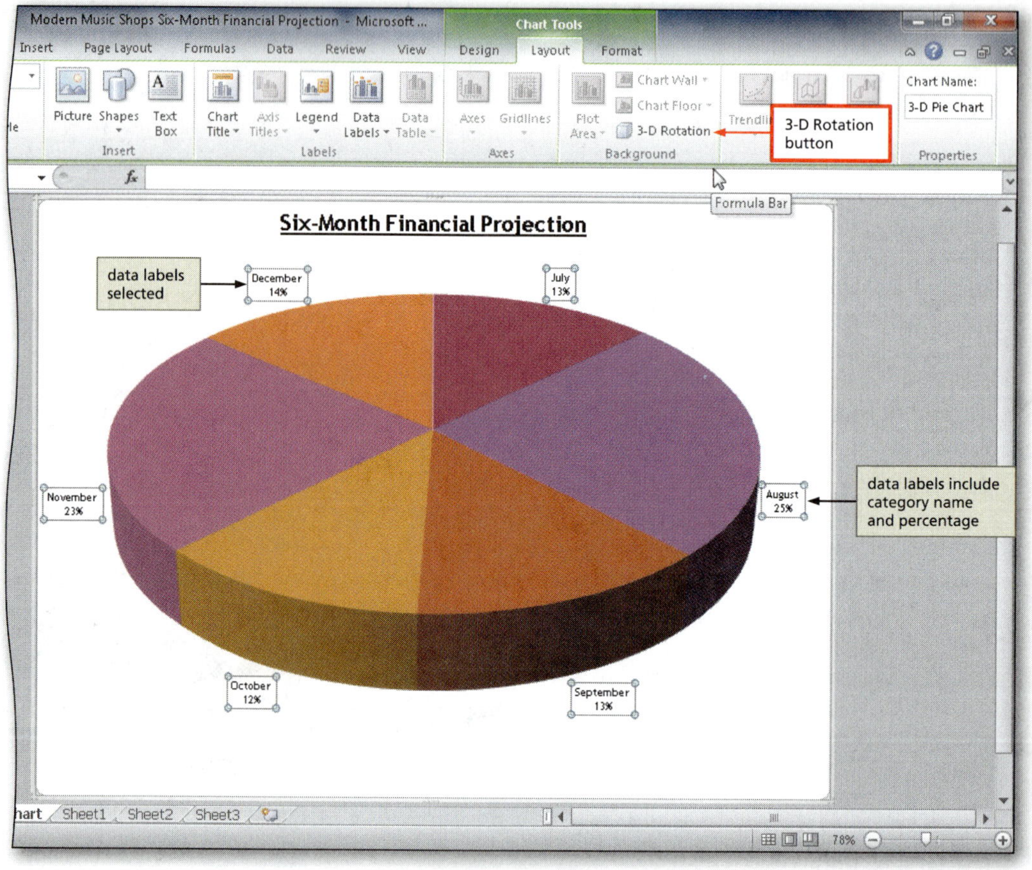

Figure 3–60

To Rotate the 3-D Pie Chart

With a three-dimensional chart, you can change the view to better show the section of the chart you are trying to emphasize. Excel allows you to control the rotation angle, elevation, perspective, height, and angle of the axes.

When Excel initially draws a Pie chart, it always positions the chart so that one of the dividing lines between two slices is a straight line pointing to 12 o'clock (or 0°). As shown in Figure 3–60, the line that divides the December and July slices currently is set to 0°. This line defines the rotation angle of the 3-D Pie chart.

To obtain a better view of the offset August slice, the largest slice, the 3-D Pie chart can be rotated 90° to the left. The following steps rotate the 3-D Pie chart.

1

- Click the 3-D Rotation button (Chart Tools Layout tab | Background group) to display the Format Chart Area dialog box.
- Click the Increase X Rotation button in the Rotation area of the Format Chart Area dialog box until the X rotation is at 90° to rotate the chart (Figure 3–61).

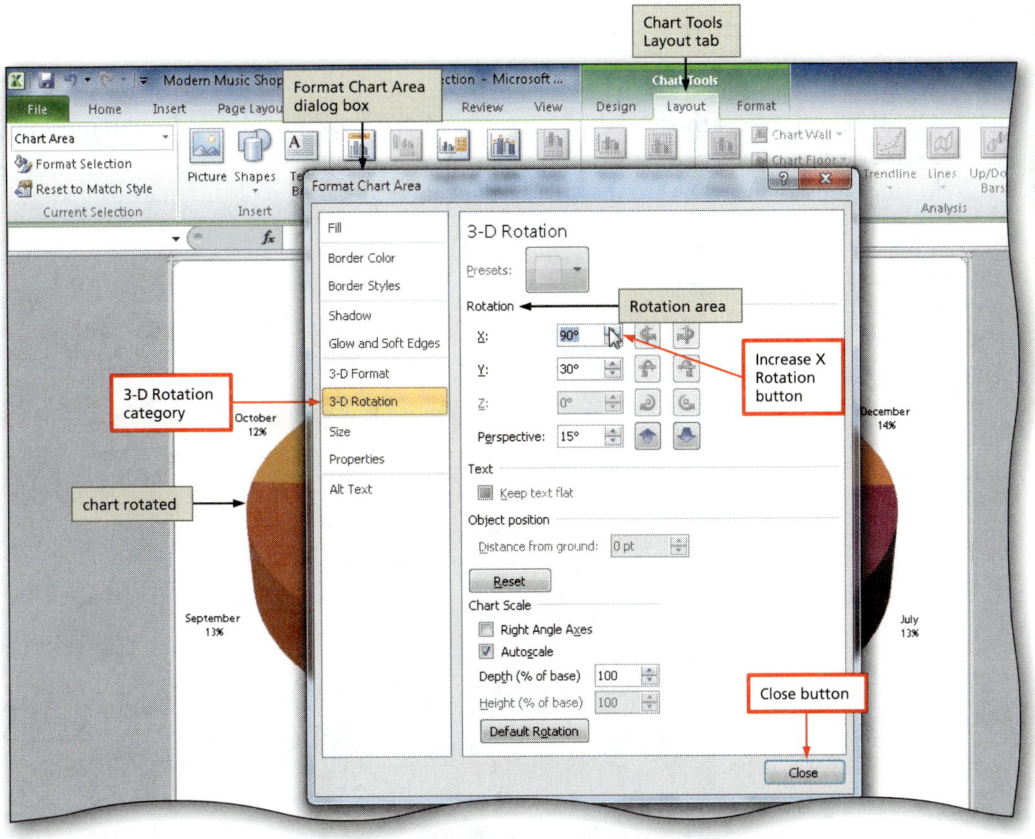

Figure 3–61

Q&A What happens as I click the Increase X Rotation button?

Excel rotates the chart 10° in a clockwise direction each time you click the Increase X Rotation button. The Y box in the Rotation area allows you to control the tilt, or elevation, of the chart. You can tilt the chart towards or away from your view in order to enhance the view of the chart.

2

- Click the Close button (Format Chart Area dialog box) to close the dialog box and display the rotated chart (Figure 3–62).

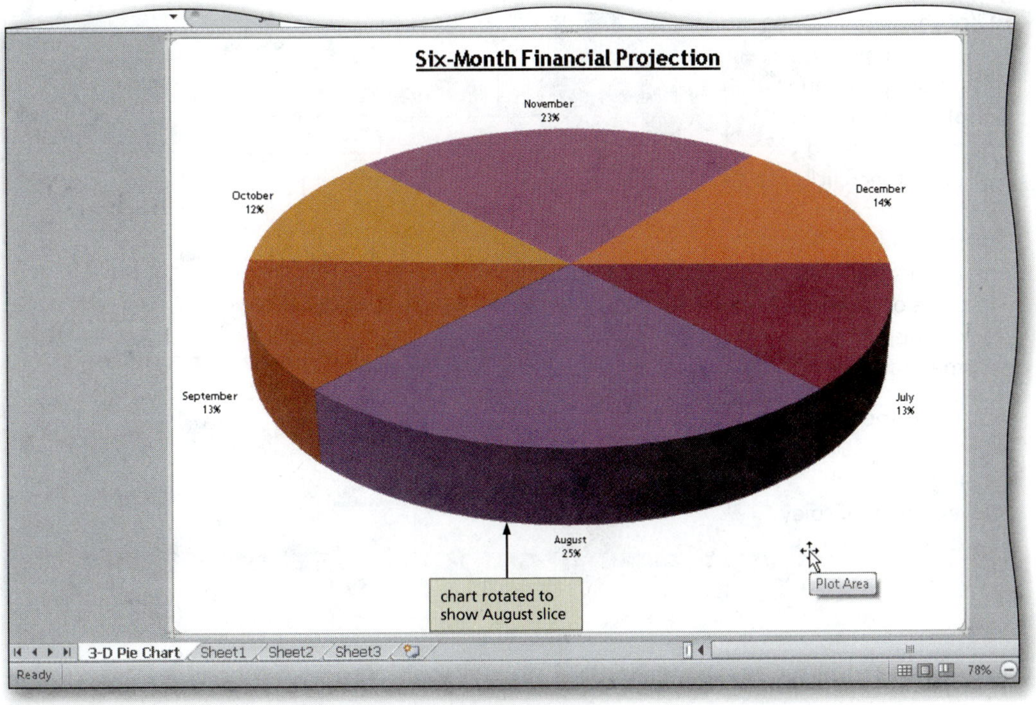

Figure 3–62

To Apply a 3-D Format to the Pie Chart

Excel allows you to apply dramatic 3-D visual effects to charts. The chart shown in Figure 3–62 could be enhanced with a bevel along the top edge. A bevel is a curve that is applied to soften the appearance of a straight edge. Excel also allows you to change the appearance of the material from which the surface of the chart appears to be constructed. The following steps apply a bevel to the chart and change the surface of the chart to a softer-looking material.

1

- Right-click the chart to display a shortcut menu and Mini toolbar (Figure 3–63).

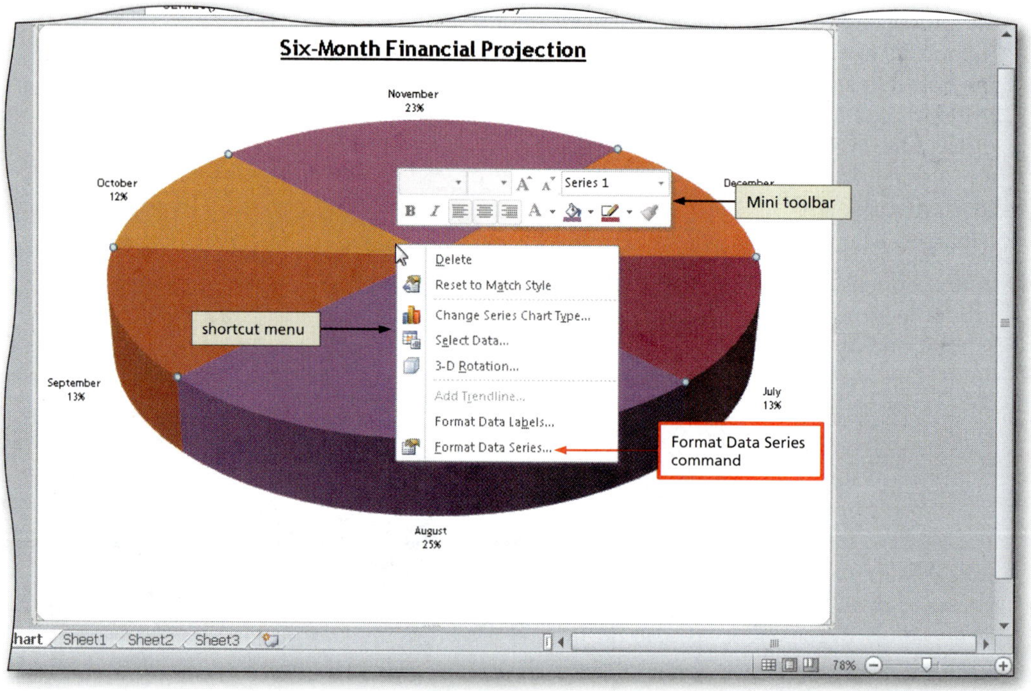

Figure 3–63

2

- Click the Format Data Series command on the shortcut menu to display the Format Data Series dialog box and then click the 3-D Format category (Format Data Series dialog box) on the left side of the dialog box to display the 3-D Format panel.
- Click the Top button (Format Data Series dialog box) in the Bevel area to display the Bevel gallery (Figure 3–64).

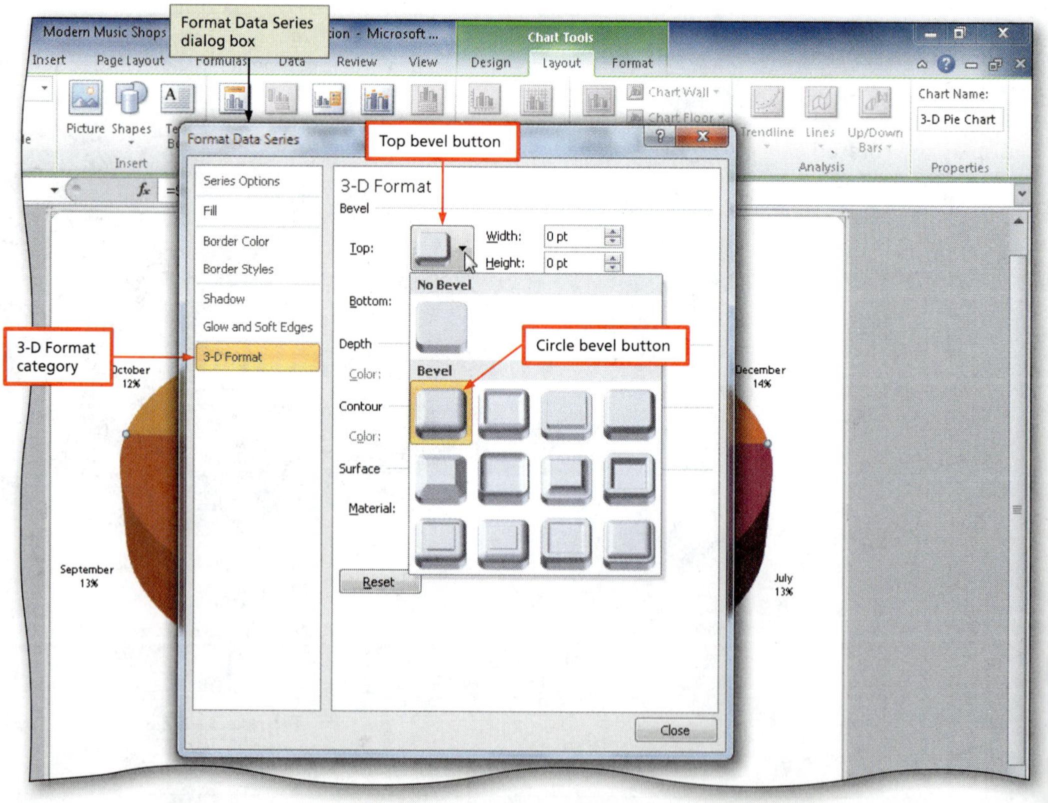

Figure 3–64

3

- Click the Circle bevel button (column 1, row 1) in the Bevel gallery (Format Data Series dialog box) to add a bevel to the chart.
- Type `50 pt` in the uppermost Width box in the Bevel area (Format Data Series dialog box) and then type `50 pt` in the uppermost Height box in the Bevel area of the dialog box to increase the width and height of the bevel on the chart (Figure 3–65).

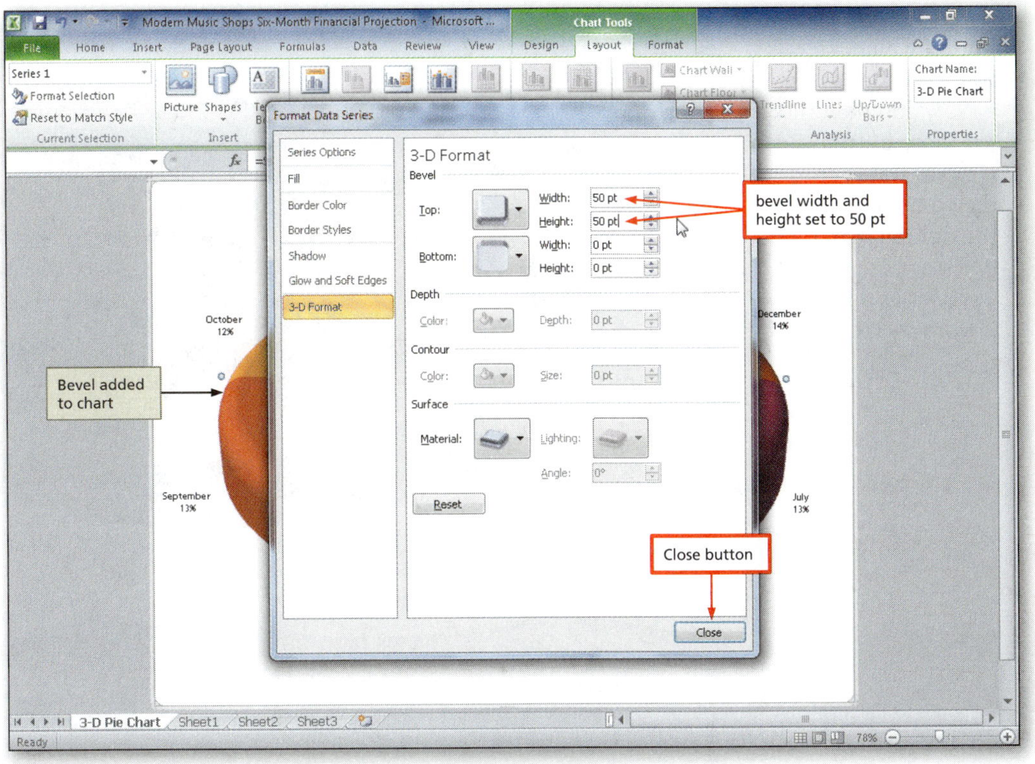

Figure 3–65

4

- Click the Material button in the Surface area (Format Data Series dialog box) to display the Material gallery (Figure 3–66).

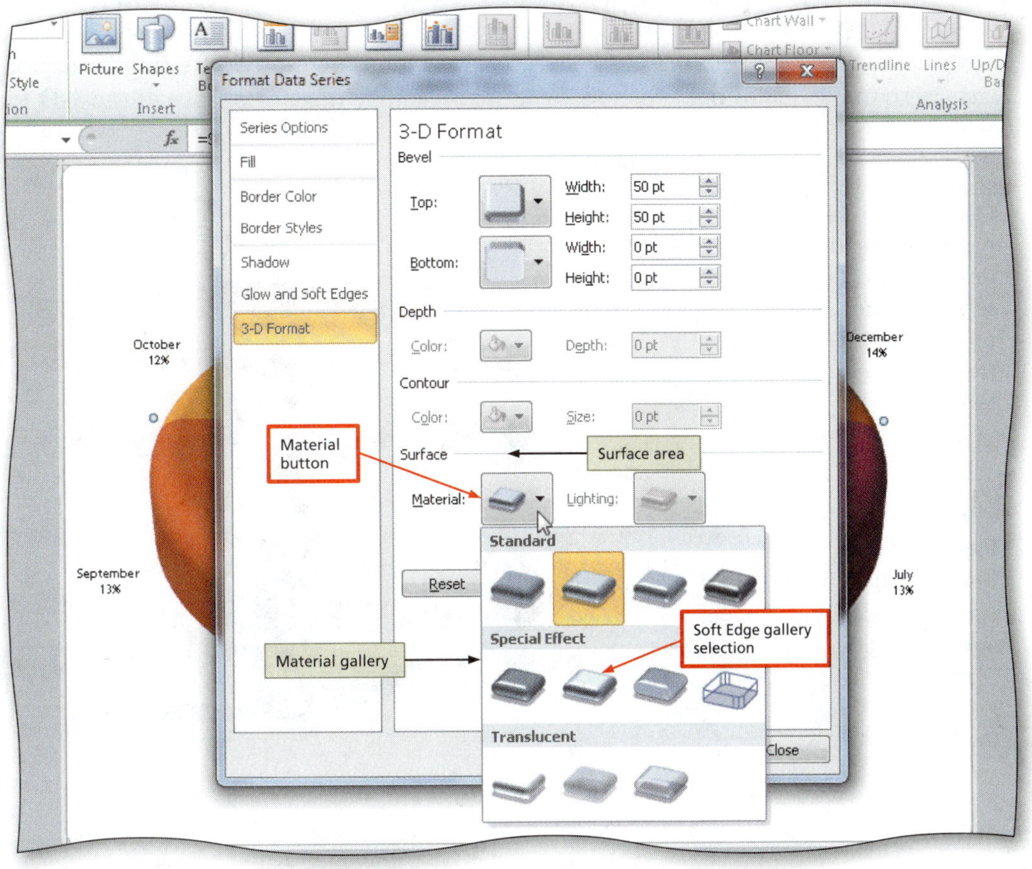

Figure 3–66

5

- Click the Soft Edge button (column 2, row 2) in the Material gallery and then click the Close button (Format Data Series dialog box) to apply the desired material and close the Format Data Series dialog box (Figure 3–67).

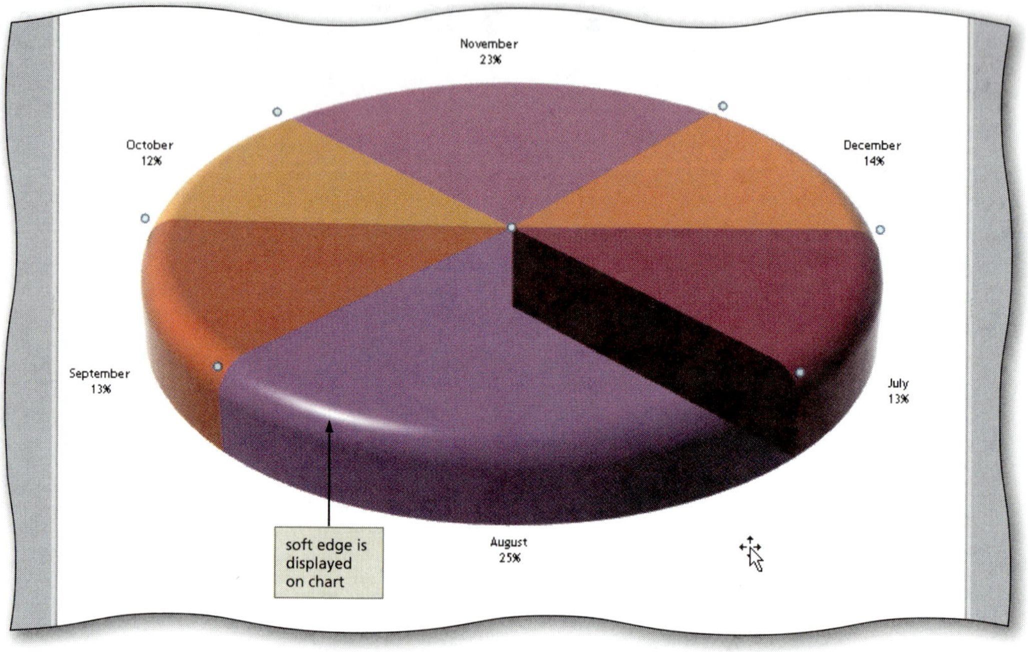

Figure 3–67

To Explode the 3-D Pie Chart and Change the Color of a Slice

The next step is to emphasize the slice representing August by offsetting, or exploding, it from the rest of the slices so that it stands out. The following steps explode the largest slice of the 3-D Pie chart and then change its color.

1

- Click the slice labeled August twice (do not double-click) to select only one slice of the 3-D Pie chart, the August slice in this case.
- Right-click the slice labeled August to display a shortcut menu and Mini toolbar (Figure 3–68).

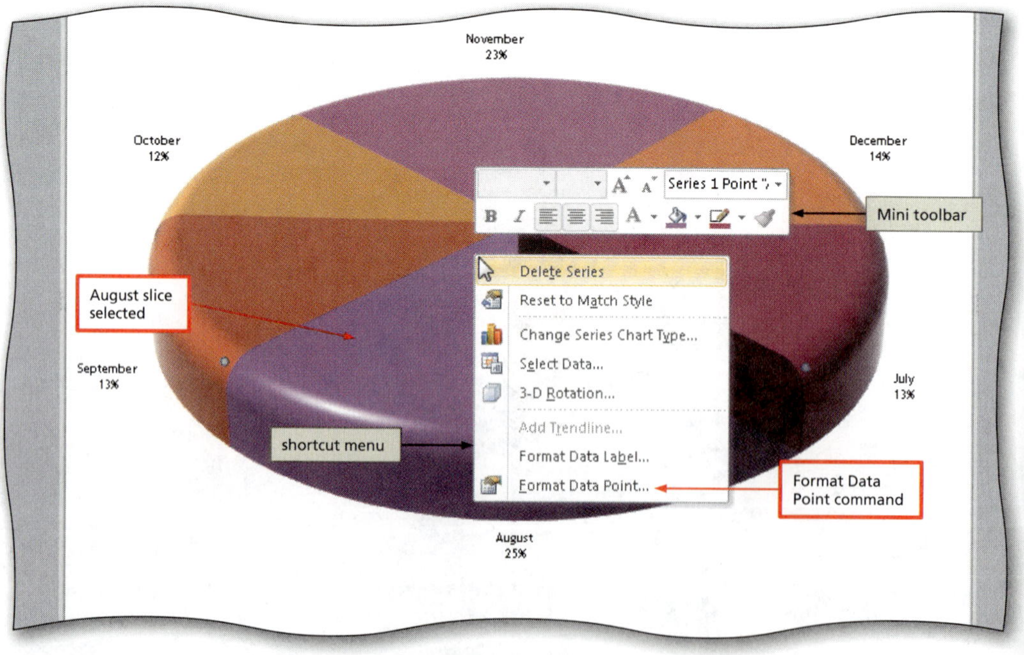

Figure 3–68

2

- Click Format Data Point on the shortcut menu to display the Format Data Point dialog box.
- Drag the Point Explosion slider (Format Data Point dialog box) to the right until the Point Explosion box reads 28% to set how far the slice in the 3-D Pie chart should be offset from the rest of the chart (Figure 3–69).

Q&A Should I offset more slices?

You can offset as many slices as you want, but remember that the reason for offsetting a slice is to emphasize it. Offsetting multiple slices tends to reduce the impact on the reader and reduces the overall size of the Pie chart.

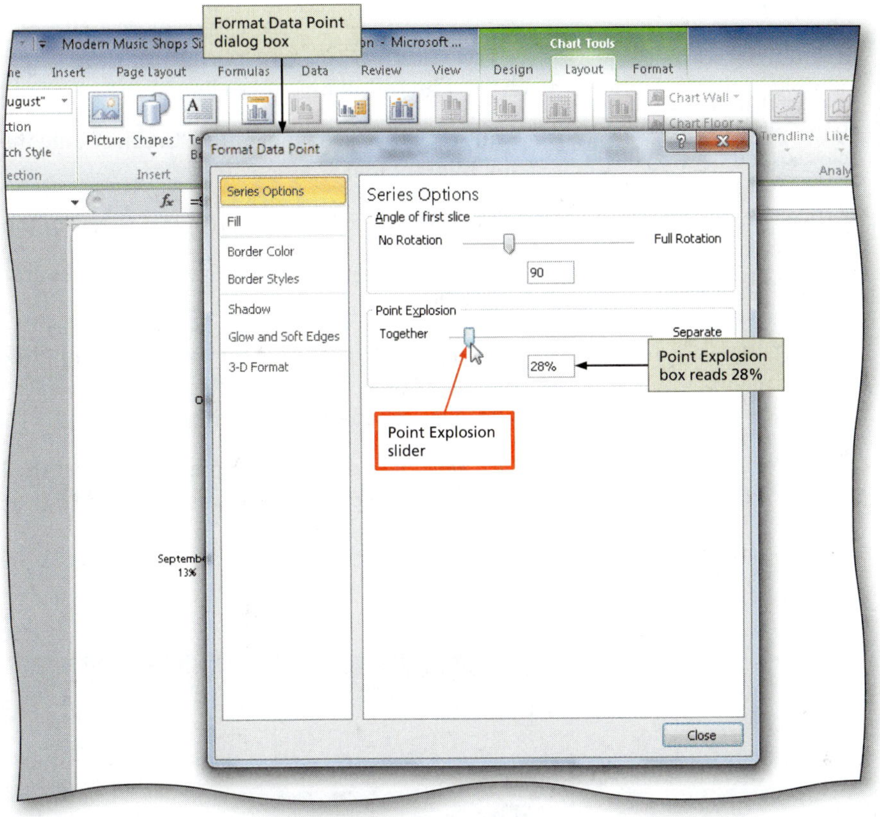

Figure 3–69

3

- Click the Fill category (Format Data Point dialog box) on the left side of the dialog box to display the Fill panel.
- Click Solid fill to display the Fill Color area and then click the Color button to display the Color gallery.
- Click the Blue color in the Standard Colors area of the color gallery and then click the Close button (Format Data Point dialog box) to change the color of the selected slice and close the dialog box (Figure 3–70).

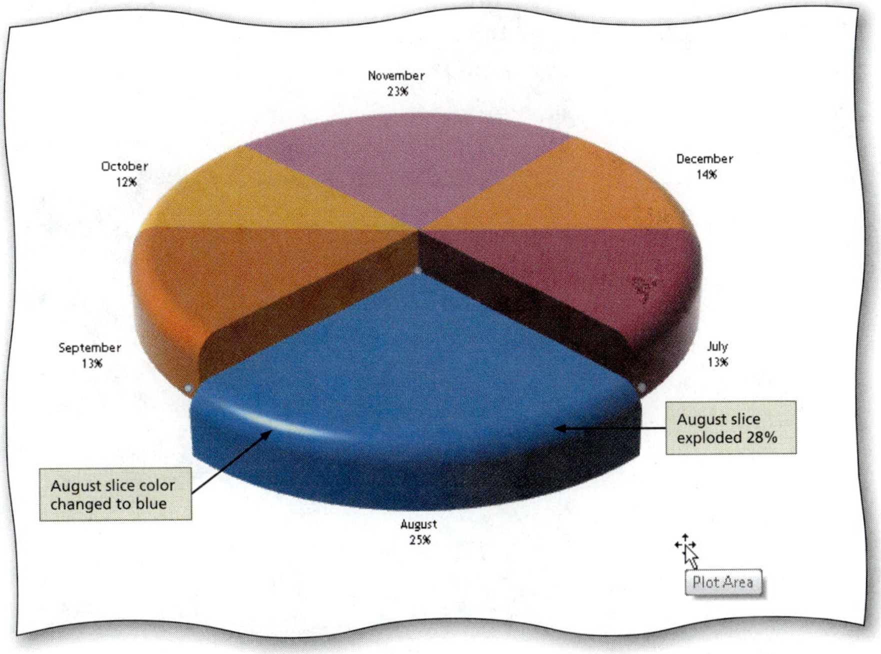

Figure 3–70

Other Ways

1. Right-click slice, click Shape Fill Color button arrow on Mini toolbar, select color

To Change the Colors of the Remaining Slices

BTW

Exploding a 3-D Pie Chart

If you click a 3-D Pie chart so that all of the slices are selected, you can drag one of the slices to explode all of the slices.

The colors of the remaining slices also can be changed to enhance the appeal of the chart. The following steps change the color of the remaining five chart slices.

1. Right-click the slice labeled July to select only the July slice, and display a shortcut menu and Mini toolbar.
2. Click the Shape Fill button arrow on the Mini toolbar to display the Color gallery.
3. Click the Yellow color in the Standard Colors area in the Color gallery to change the color of the slice.
4. Repeat Steps 1 through 3 for the remaining four slices. Assign the following colors in the Standard Colors area in the color gallery to each slice: September – Green; October – Dark Blue; November – Red; December – Purple.
5. Click anywhere outside the chart to deselect the December slice (Figure 3–71). The completed chart appears as shown in Figure 3–71.

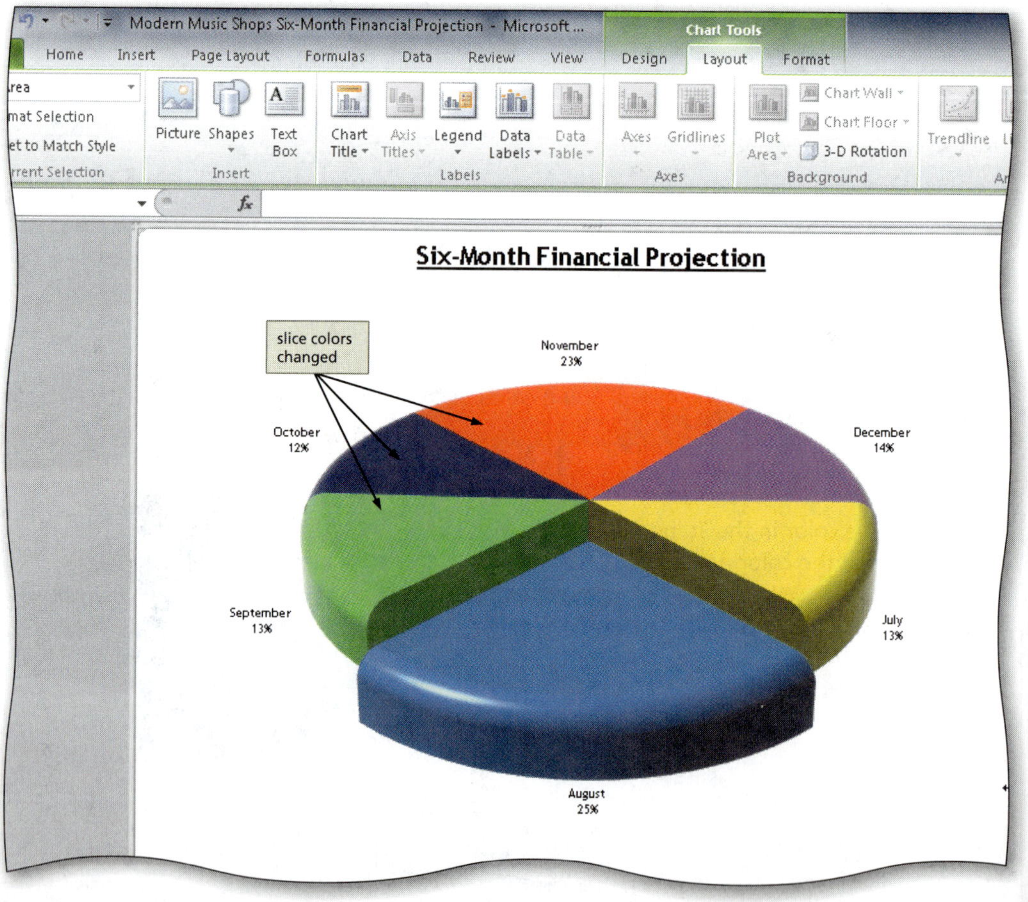

Figure 3–71

Renaming and Reordering the Sheets and Coloring their Tabs

The final step in creating the workbook is to reorder the sheets and modify the tabs at the bottom of the screen.

To Rename the Sheets and Color Their Tabs

The following steps rename the sheets and color the sheet tabs.

1. Change the sheet tab color of the 3-D Pie Chart sheet to Orange, Accent 6 (column 10, row 1).
2. Double-click the tab labeled Sheet1 at the bottom of the screen.
3. Type `Six-Month Financial Projection` as the new sheet name and then press the ENTER key.
4. Change the sheet tab color of the Six-Month Financial Projection sheet to Pink, Accent 1 (column 5, row 1) and then select cell D8 (Figure 3–72).

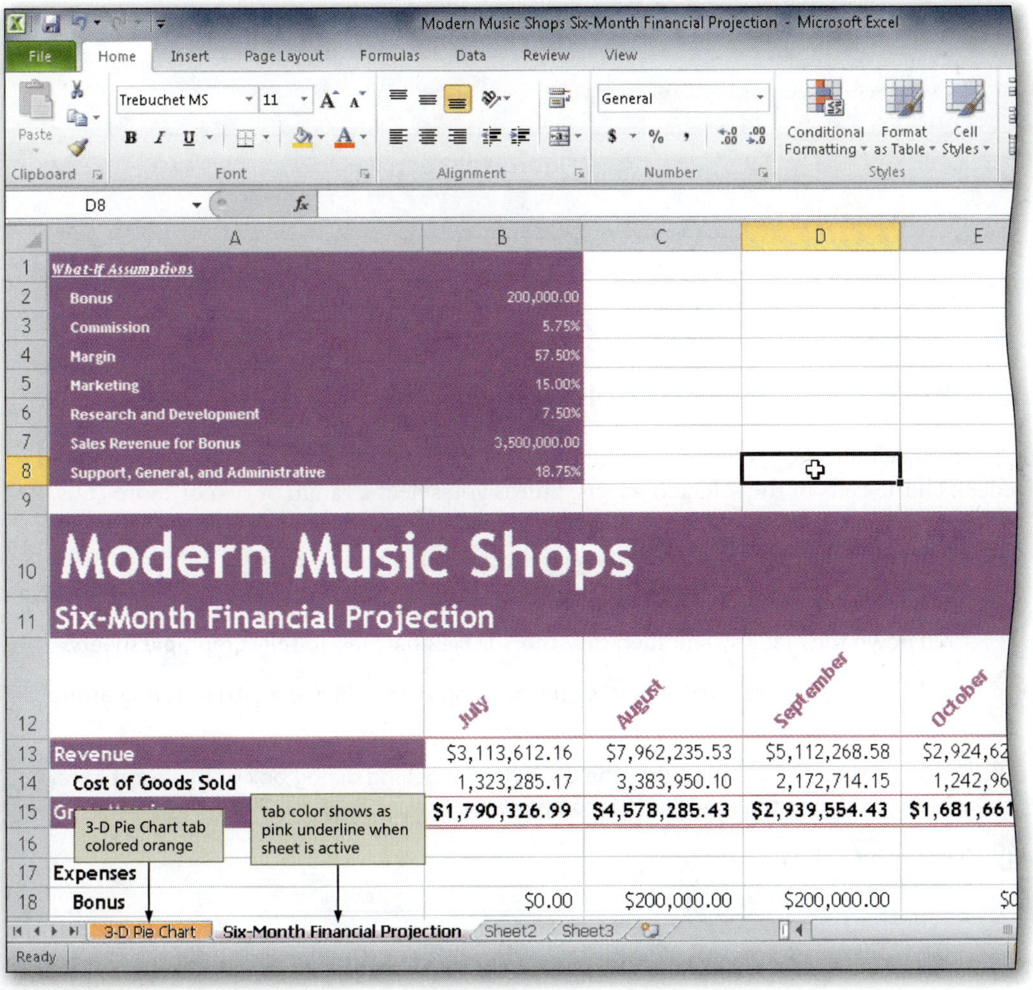

Figure 3–72

To Reorder the Sheet Tabs

Change the order sheets in a workbook so that they appear with the most important worksheets first. The following steps reorder the sheets so that the worksheet precedes the chart sheet in the workbook.

1

- Drag the Six-Month Financial Projection tab to the left in front of the 3-D Pie Chart tab to rearrange the sequence of the sheets (Figure 3–73).

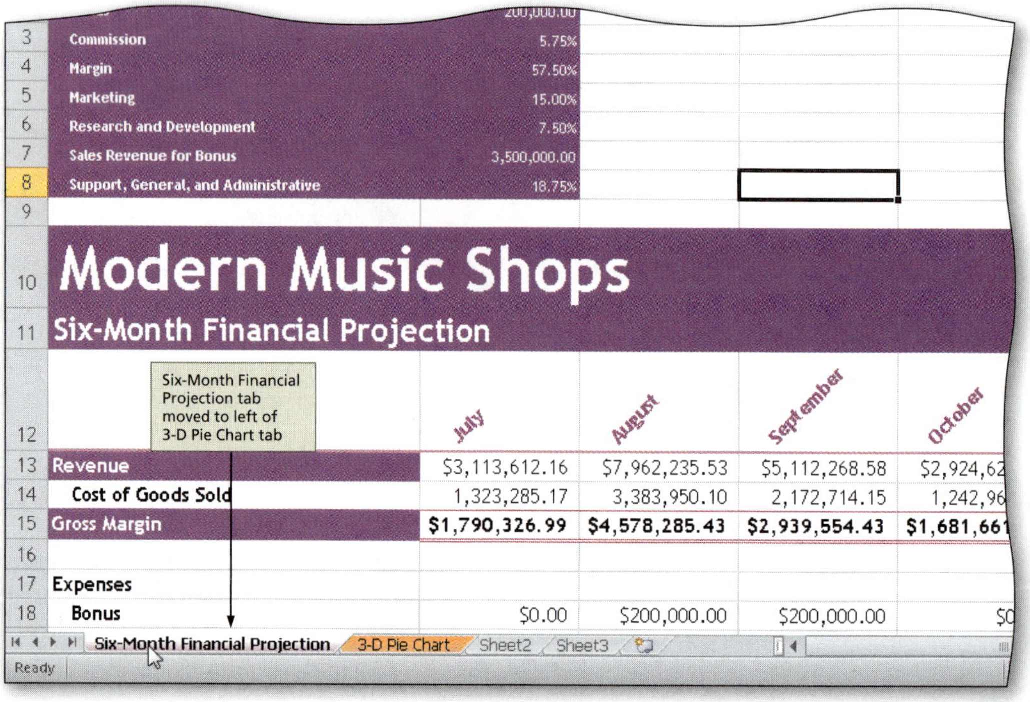

Figure 3–73

Other Ways

1. To move sheet, right-click sheet tab, click Move or Copy on shortcut menu

To Check Spelling in Multiple Sheets

By default, the spell checker checks the spelling only in the selected sheets. It will check all the cells in the selected sheets, unless you select a range of two or more cells. Before checking the spelling, the following steps select both sheets in the workbook so that both worksheets in the workbook are checked for spelling errors.

1. With the Six-Month Financial Projection sheet active, press CTRL+HOME to select cell A1. Hold down the CTRL key and then click the 3-D Pie Chart tab to select multiple sheets.
2. Display the Review tab and then click the Spelling button (Review tab | Proofing group) to check spelling in the selected sheets.
3. Correct any errors and then click the OK button (Spelling dialog box or Microsoft Excel dialog box) when the spell check is complete.
4. Save the workbook.

BTW

Checking Spelling
Unless you first select a range of cells or an object before starting the spell checker, Excel checks the entire selected worksheet, including all cell values, cell comments, embedded charts, text boxes, buttons, and headers and footers.

To Preview and Print the Workbook

After checking the spelling, the next step is to preview and print the sheets. As with spelling, Excel previews and prints only the selected sheets. In addition, because the worksheet is too wide to print in portrait orientation, the orientation must be changed to landscape. The following steps adjust the orientation and scale, preview the workbook, and then print the workbook.

1. Ready the printer. If both sheets are not selected, hold down the CTRL key and then click the tab of the inactive sheet.
2. Click File on the Ribbon to open the Backstage view.
3. Click the Print tab in the Backstage view to display the Print gallery.
4. If necessary, click the Portrait Orientation button in the Settings area and then select Landscape Orientation to select the desired orientation.
5. If necessary, click the No Scaling button in the Settings area and then select 'Fit Sheet on One Page' to cause the workbook to print on one page.
6. If necessary, click the Printer Status button to display a list of available Printer options and then click the desired printer to change the currently selected printer.
7. Click the Print button in the Print gallery to print the worksheet in landscape orientation on the currently selected printer.
8. When the printer stops, retrieve the printed worksheet (Figure 3–74a and Figure 3–74b on the following page).
9. Right-click the Six-Month Financial Projection tab. Click Ungroup Sheets on the shortcut menu to deselect the 3-D Pie Chart tab.
10. Save the workbook.

BTW

Conserving Ink and Toner

If you want to conserve ink or toner, you can instruct Excel to print draft quality documents by clicking File on the Ribbon to open the Backstage view, clicking Options in the Backstage view to display the Excel Options dialog box, clicking Advanced in the left pane (Excel Options dialog box), scrolling to the Print area in the right pane, placing a check mark in the 'Use draft quality' check box, and then clicking the OK button. Then, use the Backstage view to print the document as usual.

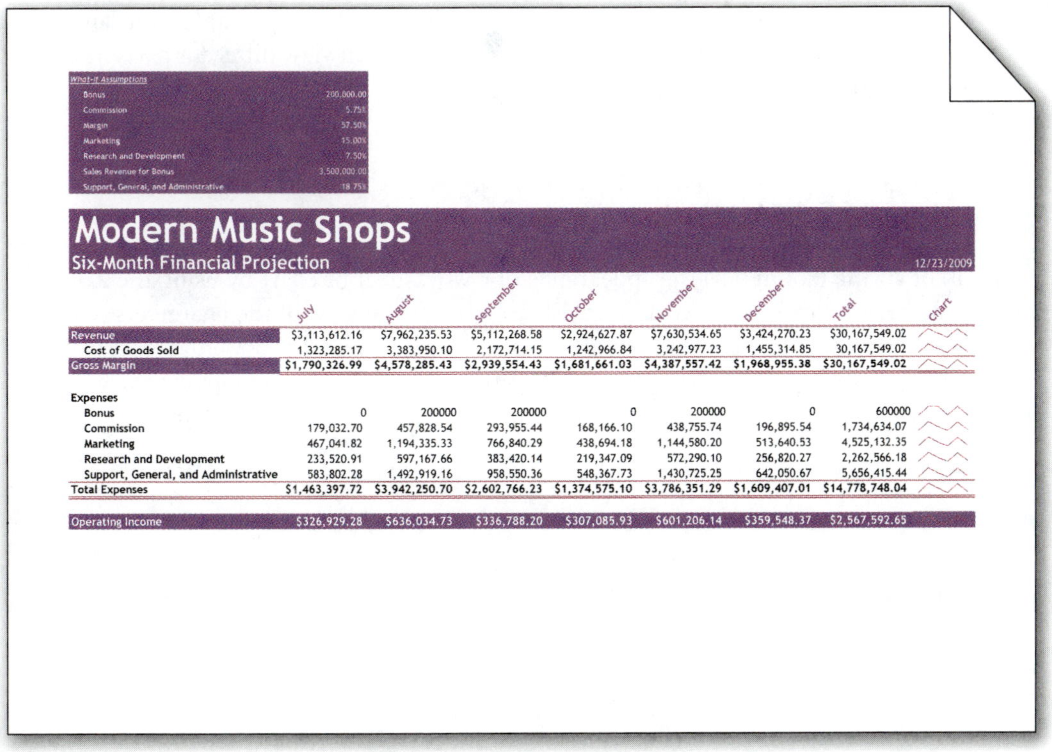

What-If Assumptions	
Bonus	200,000.00
Commission	5.75%
Margin	57.50%
Marketing	15.00%
Research and Development	7.50%
Sales Revenue for Bonus	3,500,000.00
Support, General, and Administrative	18.75%

Modern Music Shops

Six-Month Financial Projection 12/23/2009

	July	August	September	October	November	December	Total	Chart
Revenue	$3,113,612.16	$7,962,235.53	$5,112,268.58	$2,924,627.87	$7,630,534.65	$3,424,270.23	$30,167,549.02	
Cost of Goods Sold	1,323,285.17	3,383,950.10	2,172,714.15	1,242,966.84	3,242,977.23	1,455,314.85	30,167,549.02	
Gross Margin	$1,790,326.99	$4,578,285.43	$2,939,554.43	$1,681,661.03	$4,387,557.42	$1,968,955.38	$30,167,549.02	
Expenses								
Bonus	0	200000	200000	0	200000	0	600000	
Commission	179,032.70	457,828.54	293,955.44	168,166.10	438,755.74	196,895.54	1,734,634.07	
Marketing	467,041.82	1,194,335.33	766,840.29	438,694.18	1,144,580.20	513,640.53	4,525,132.35	
Research and Development	233,520.91	597,167.66	383,420.14	219,347.09	572,290.10	256,820.27	2,262,566.18	
Support, General, and Administrative	583,802.28	1,492,919.16	958,550.36	548,367.73	1,430,725.25	642,050.67	5,656,415.44	
Total Expenses	$1,463,397.72	$3,942,250.70	$2,602,766.23	$1,374,575.10	$3,786,351.29	$1,609,407.01	$14,778,748.04	
Operating Income	$326,929.28	$636,034.73	$336,788.20	$307,085.93	$601,206.14	$359,548.37	$2,567,592.65	

Figure 3–74 (a) Worksheet

BTW

Printing Document Properties

To print document properties, click the File on the Ribbon to open the Backstage view, click the Print tab in the Backstage view to display the Print gallery, click the first button in the Settings area to display a list of options specifying what you can print, click Document Properties in the list to specify you want to print the document properties instead of the actual document, and then click the Print button in the Print gallery to print the document properties on the currently selected printer.

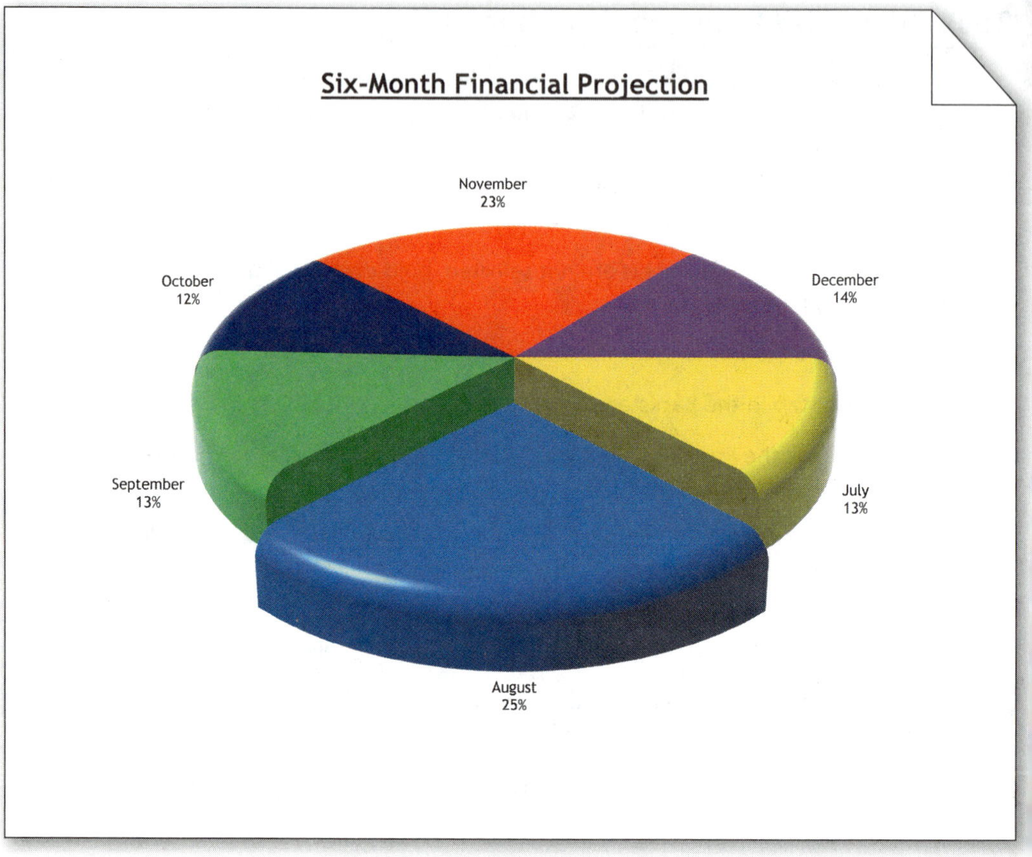

Figure 3–74 (b) 3-D Pie Chart

Changing the View of the Worksheet

With Excel, you easily can change the view of the worksheet. For example, you can magnify or shrink the worksheet on the screen. You also can view different parts of the worksheet through windowpanes.

To Shrink and Magnify the View of a Worksheet or Chart

You can magnify (zoom in) or shrink (zoom out) the appearance of a worksheet or chart by using the Zoom button (View tab | Zoom group). When you magnify a worksheet, Excel enlarges the view of the characters on the screen, but displays fewer columns and rows. Alternatively, when you shrink a worksheet, Excel is able to display more columns and rows. Magnifying or shrinking a worksheet affects only the view; it does not change the window size or printout of the worksheet or chart. The following steps shrink and magnify the view of the worksheet.

1

- If cell A1 is not active, press CTRL+HOME.
- Display the View tab and then click the Zoom button (View tab | Zoom group) to display a list of magnifications in the Zoom dialog box (Figure 3–75).

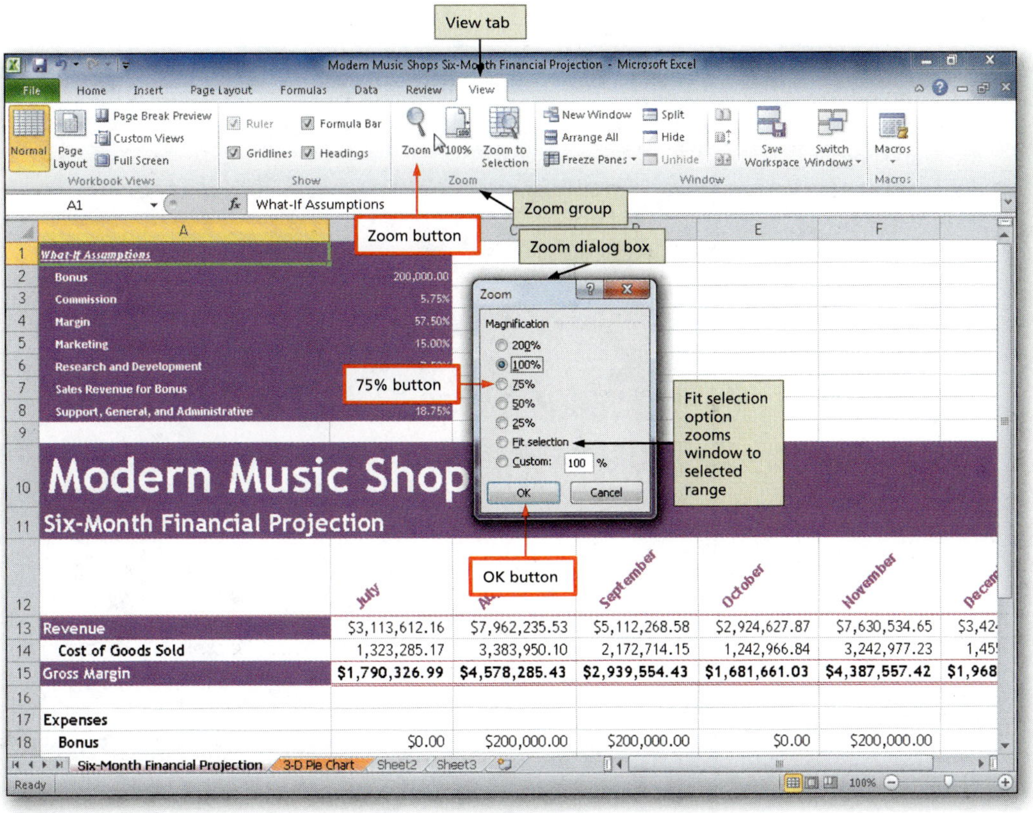

Figure 3–75

2

- Click 75% and then click the OK button (Zoom dialog box) to shrink the display of the worksheet (Figure 3–76).

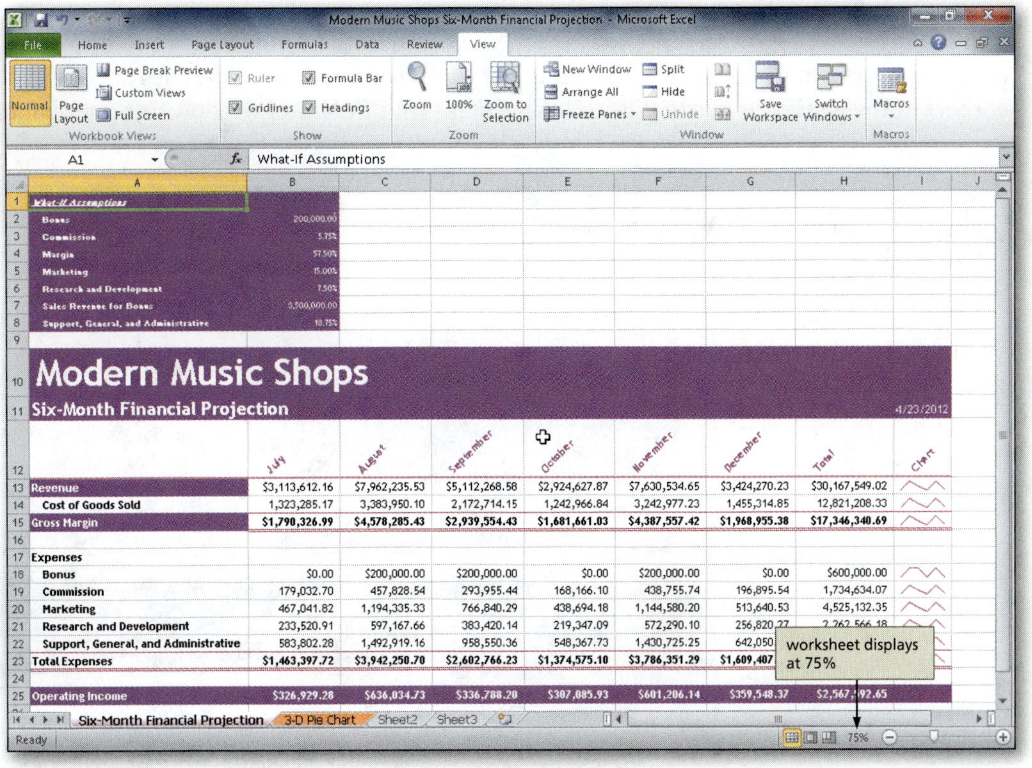

Figure 3–76

3

- Click the Zoom In button on the status bar until the worksheet is displayed at 100% (Figure 3–77).

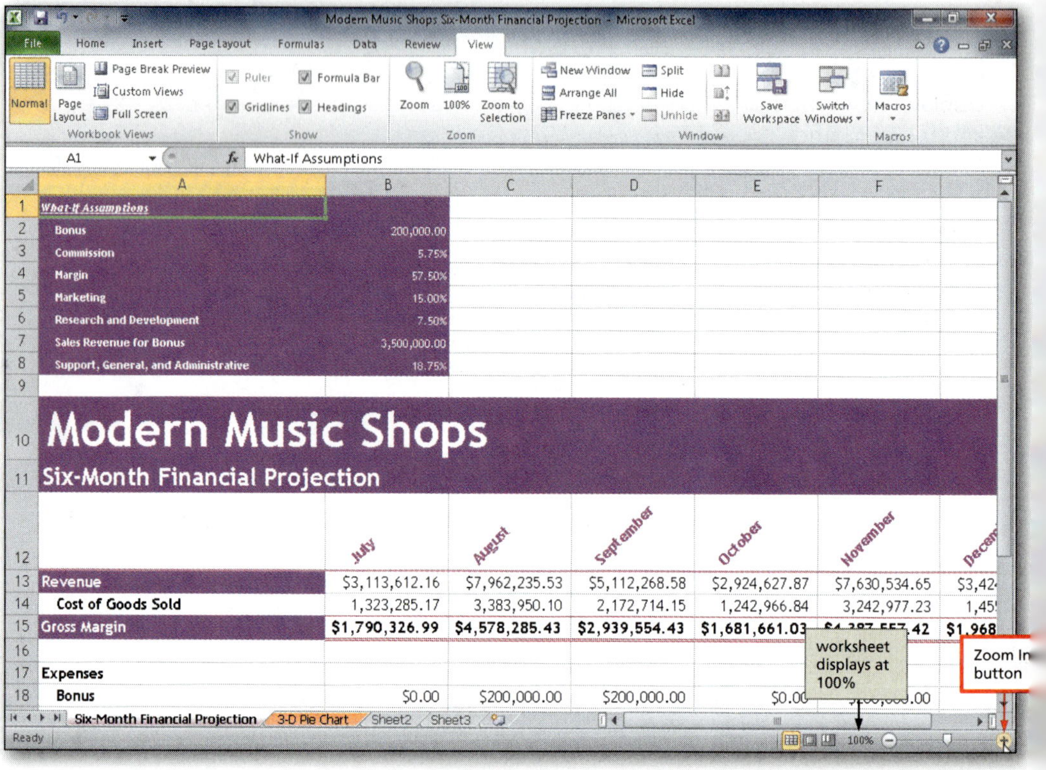

Figure 3–77

To Split a Window into Panes

When working with a large worksheet, you can split the window into two or four panes to view different parts of the worksheet at the same time. Splitting the Excel window into four panes at cell D13 allows you to view all four corners of the worksheet easily. The following steps split the Excel window into four panes.

1

- Select cell D13, the intersection of the four proposed panes, to select the cell at which to split the window.
- If necessary, display the View tab (Figure 3–78).

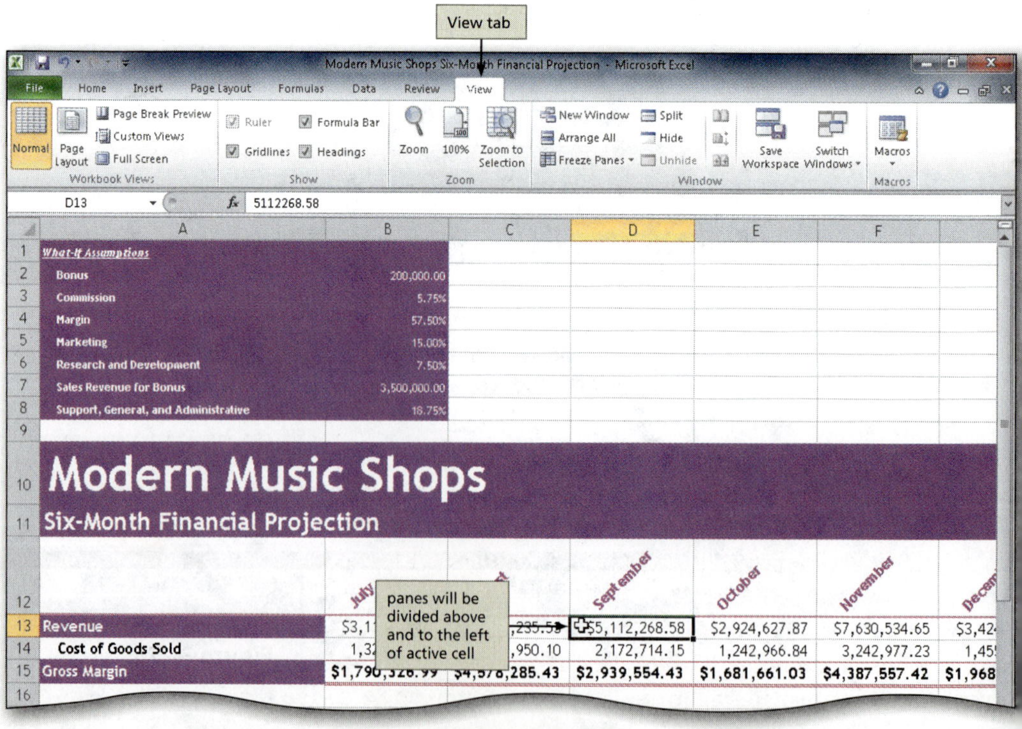

Figure 3–78

2

- Click the Split button (View tab | Window group) to divide the window into four panes.
- Use the scroll arrows to show the four corners of the worksheet at the same time (Figure 3–79).

Q&A What is shown in the four panes?

The four panes in Figure 3–79 are used to show the following: (1) range A1:C12 in the upper-left pane; (2) range G1:I12 in the upper-right pane; (3) range A19:C24 in the lower-left pane; and (4) range G19:I24 in the lower-right pane. The vertical split bar is the vertical bar going up and down the middle of the window. The horizontal split bar is the horizontal bar going across the middle of the window. If you use the scroll bars below the window and to the right of the window to scroll the window, you will see that the panes split by the horizontal split bar scroll together vertically. The panes split by the vertical split bar scroll together horizontally. To resize the panes, drag either split bar to the desired location in the window.

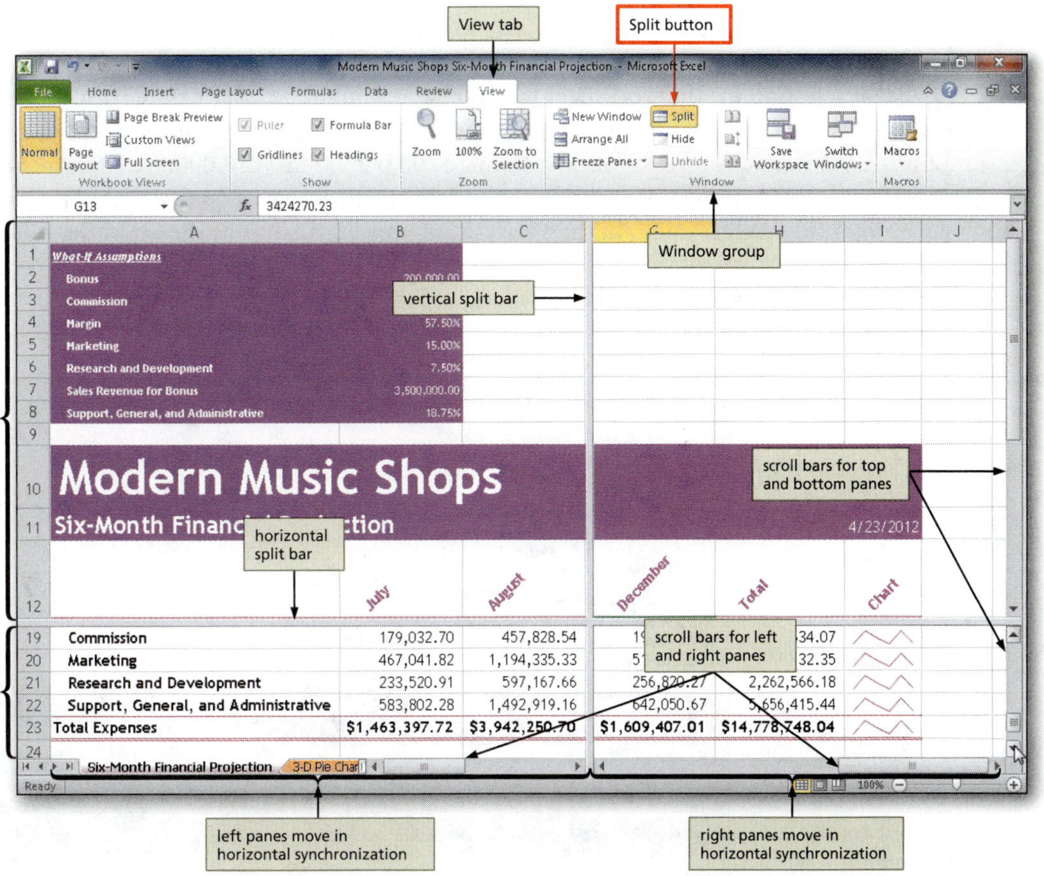

Figure 3–79

Other Ways

1. Drag horizontal split box and vertical split box to desired locations

To Remove the Panes from the Window

1. Position the mouse pointer at the intersection of the horizontal and vertical split bars.
2. When the mouse pointer changes to a four-headed arrow, double-click to remove the four panes from the window.

What-If Analysis

The automatic recalculation feature of Excel is a powerful tool that can be used to analyze worksheet data. Using Excel to scrutinize the impact of changing values in cells that are referenced by a formula in another cell is called what-if analysis or **sensitivity analysis**. When new data is entered, Excel not only recalculates all formulas in a worksheet but also redraws any associated charts.

In the workbook created in this chapter, many of the formulas are dependent on the assumptions in the range B2:B8. Thus, if you change any of the assumption values, Excel immediately recalculates all formulas. Excel redraws the 3-D Pie chart as well, because it is based on these numbers.

BTW

Zooming

You can use the Zoom in and Zoom out buttons on the status bar to zoom from 10% to 400% to reduce or enlarge the display of a worksheet.

To Analyze Data in a Worksheet by Changing Values

A what-if question for the worksheet in this chapter might be *what* would happen to the six-month operating income in cell H25 *if* the Bonus, Commission, Support, General, and Administrative assumptions in the What-If Assumptions table were changed as follows: Bonus $200,000.00 to $150,000.00; Commission 5.75% to 4.00%; Support, General, and Administrative 18.75% to 15.75%? To answer a question like this, you need to change only the first, second, and seventh values in the What-If Assumptions table, as shown in the following steps. The steps also divide the window into two vertical panes. Excel instantaneously recalculates the formulas in the worksheet and redraws the 3-D Pie chart to answer the question.

1

- Press CTRL+HOME to select cell A1.
- Drag the vertical split box from the lower-right corner of the screen to the left so that the vertical split bar is positioned as shown in Figure 3–80 to split the screen vertically.
- Drag the horizontal split box from the upper-right corner of the screen down so that the horizontal split bar is positioned as shown in Figure 3–80 to split the screen horizontally.
- Use the scroll arrows in the lower-right pane to view the total operating income in column H in the lower-right pane.

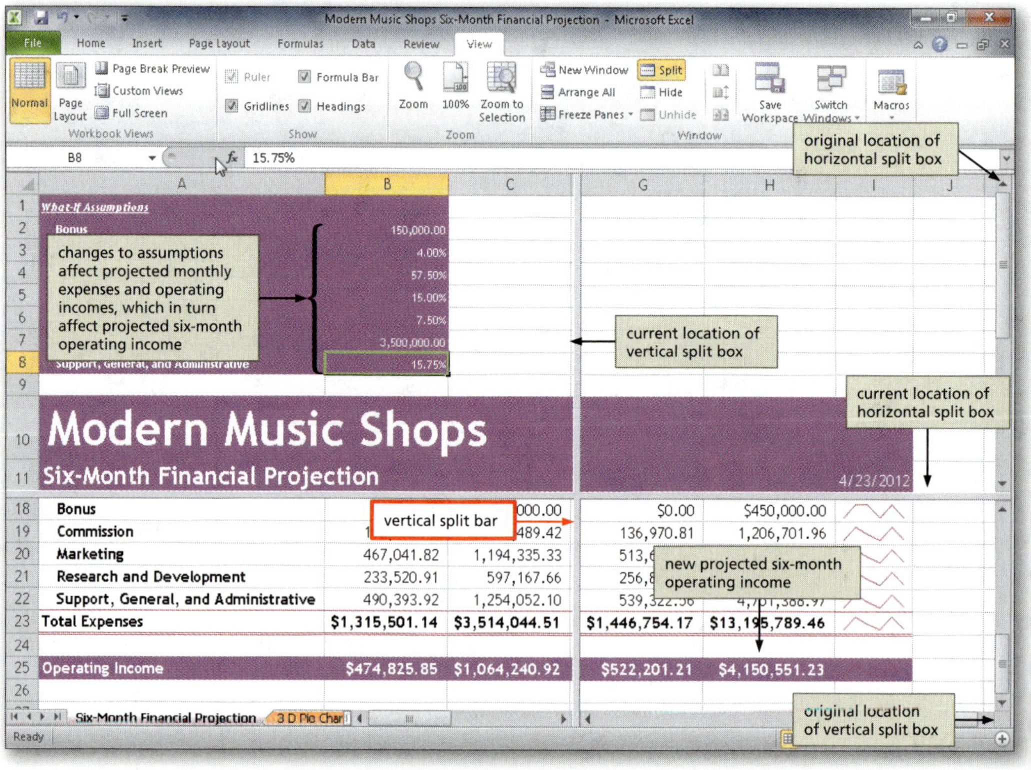

Figure 3–80

- Enter `150000` in cell B2, `4%` in cell B3, and `15.75%` in cell B8 (Figure 3–80), which causes the six-month operating income in cell H25 to increase from $2,567,592.65 to $4,150,551.23.

To Goal Seek

If you know the result you want a formula to produce, you can use **goal seeking** to determine the value of a cell on which the formula depends. The following steps close and reopen the Modern Music Shops Six-Month Financial Projection workbook. They then use the Goal Seek command (Data tab | Data Tools group) to determine the Support, General, and Administrative percentage in cell B8 that will yield a six-month operating income of $3,000,000.00 in cell H25, rather than the original $2,567,592.65.

1

- Close the workbook without saving the changes and then reopen it.
- Drag the vertical split box from the lower-right corner of the screen to the left so that the vertical split bar is positioned as shown in Figure 3–81 to split the screen vertically.
- Drag the horizontal split box from the upper-right corner of the screen down so that the horizontal split bar is positioned as shown in Figure 3–81 to split the screen horizontally.
- Use the scroll arrows in the lower-right pane to view the total operating income in column H in the lower-right pane.
- Select cell H25, the cell that contains the six-month operating income.
- Display the Data tab and then click the What-If Analysis button (Data tab | Data Tools group) to display the What-If Analysis menu (Figure 3–81).

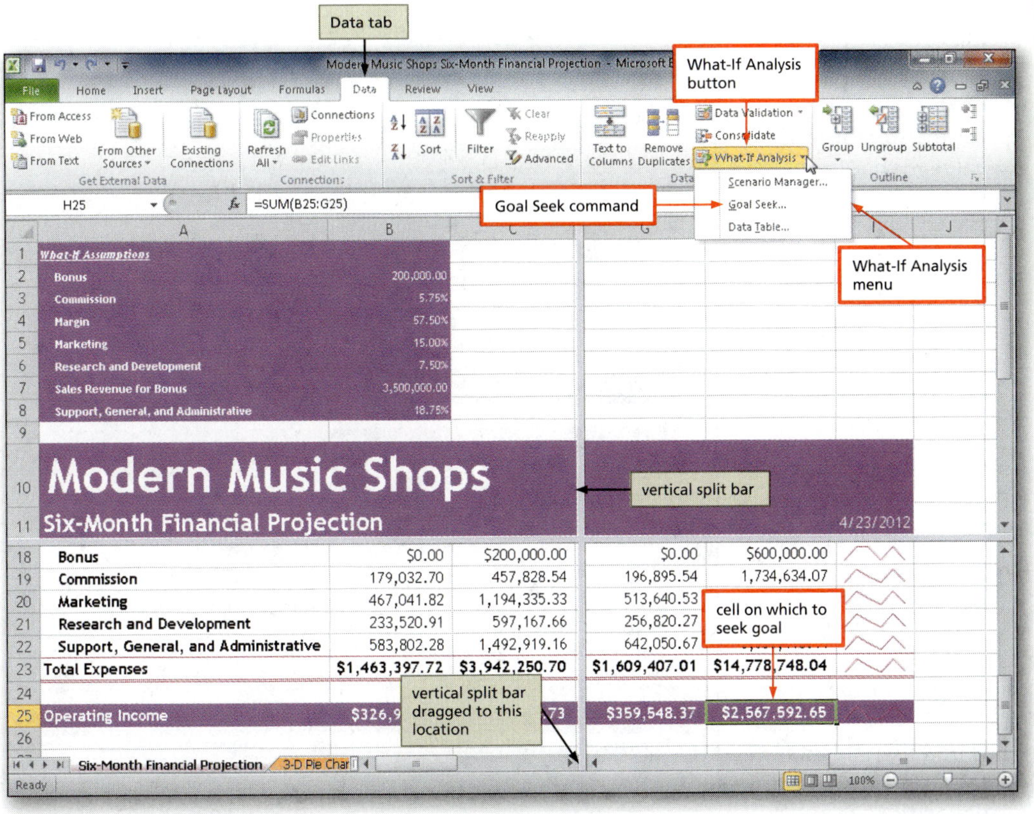

Figure 3–81

2

- Click Goal Seek to display the Goal Seek dialog box with the Set cell box set to the selected cell, H25 in this case.
- When Excel displays the Goal Seek dialog box, click the To value text box, type **3,000,000** and then click the 'By changing cell' box to select the 'By changing cell' box.
- Click cell B8 on the worksheet to assign the current cell, B8 in this case, to the 'By changing cell' box (Figure 3–82).

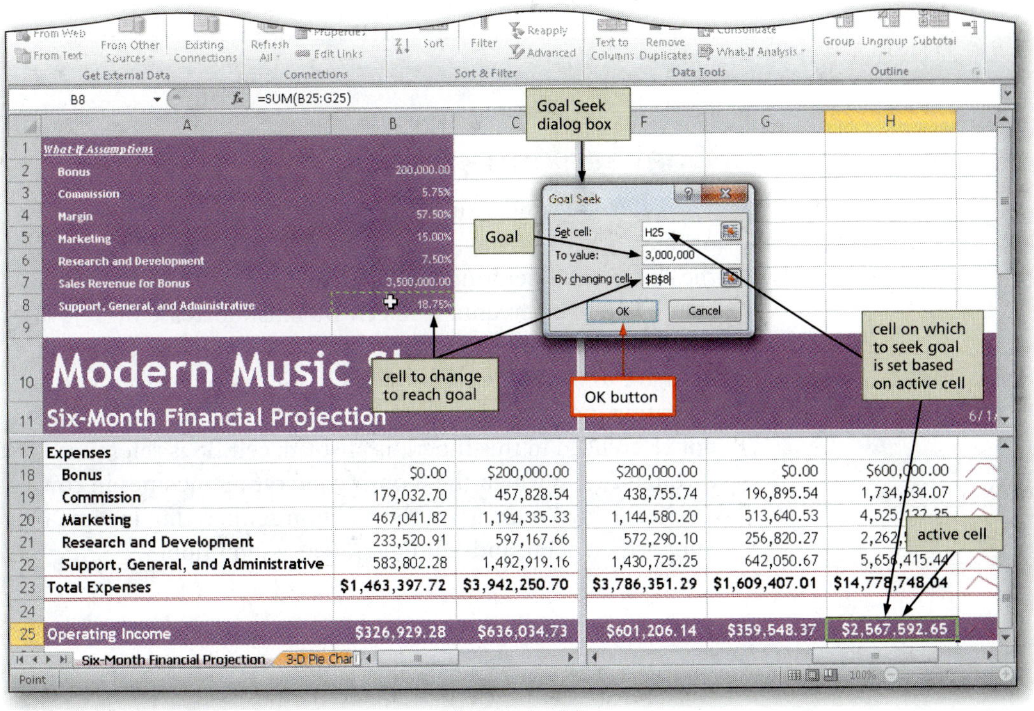

Figure 3–82

3

- Click the OK button (Goal Seek dialog box) to goal seek for the sought-after value in the 'To value' box, $3,000,000.00 in cell H25 in this case (Figure 3–83).

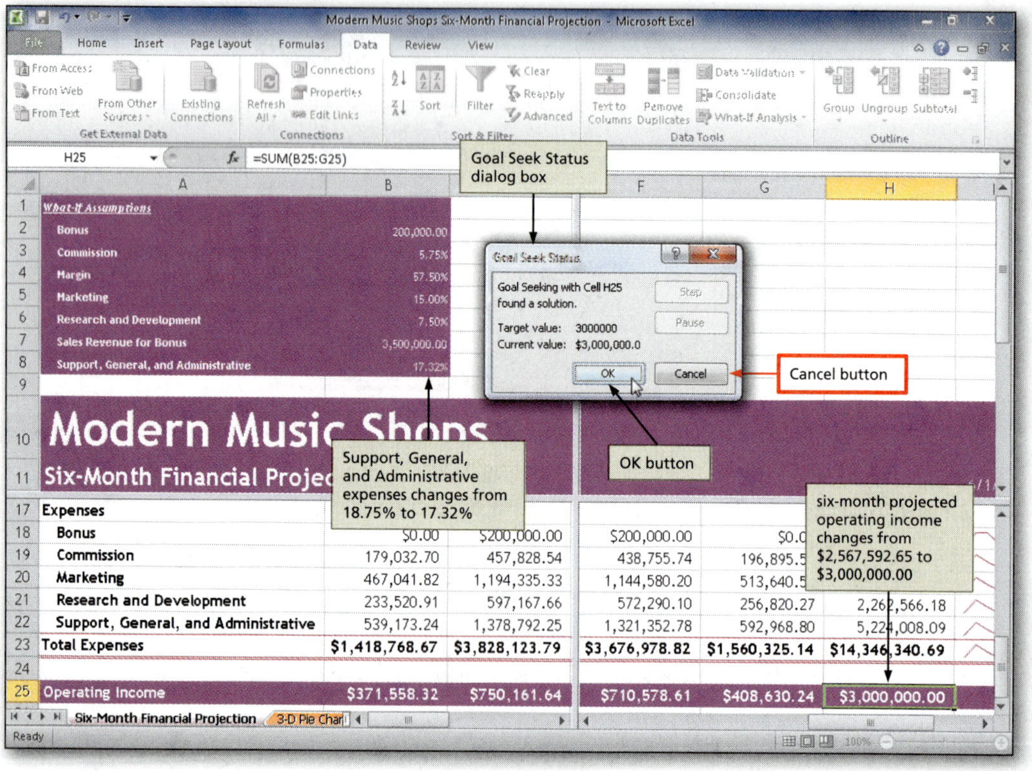

Figure 3–83

Q&A

What happens when I click the OK button?

Excel immediately changes cell H25 from $2,567,592.65 to the desired value of $3,000,000.00. More importantly, Excel changes the Support, General, and Administrative assumption in cell B8 from 18.75% to 17.32% (Figure 3–83). Excel also displays the Goal Seek Status dialog box. If you click the OK button, Excel keeps the new values in the worksheet. If you click the Cancel button, Excel redisplays the original values.

4

- Click the Cancel button in the Goal Seek Status dialog box to redisplay the original values in the worksheet.

Goal Seeking

Goal seeking assumes you can change the value of only one cell referenced directly or indirectly to reach a specific goal for a value in another cell. In this example, to change the six-month operating income in cell H25 to $3,000,000.00, the Support, General, and Administrative percentage in cell B8 must decrease by 1.43% from 18.75% to 17.32%.

You can see from this goal seeking example that the cell to change (cell B8) does not have to be referenced directly in the formula or function. For example, the six-month operating income in cell H25 is calculated by the function =SUM(B25:G25). Cell B8 is not referenced in this function. Instead, cell B8 is referenced in the formulas in rows 18 through 22, on which the monthly operating incomes in row 25 are based. Excel thus is capable of goal seeking on the six-month operating income by varying the value for the Support, General, and Administrative assumption.

To Quit Excel

With the workbook complete, the following steps quit Excel.

1. Click the Close button on the upper-right corner of the title bar.
2. If the Microsoft Excel dialog box is displayed, click the Don't Save button.

BTW

Quick Reference
For a table that lists how to complete the tasks covered in the Office chapters in this book using the mouse, Ribbon, shortcut menu, and keyboard, see the Quick Reference Summary at the back of this book, or visit the Microsoft Office and Concepts CourseMate Web site at www.cengagebrain.com and then navigate to the Quick Reference resource for this book.

Chapter Summary

In this chapter you learned how to work with large worksheets that extend beyond the window, how to use the fill handle to create a series, new formatting techniques, about the difference between absolute cell references and relative cell references, how to use the IF function, and how to rotate text in a cell, freeze titles, add Sparkline charts, change the magnification of the worksheet, show different parts of the worksheet at the same time through multiple panes, create a 3-D Pie chart, and improve the appearance of a 3-D Pie chart. This chapter also introduced you to using Excel to do what-if analysis by changing values in cells and goal seeking. The items listed below include all the new Excel skills you have learned in this chapter.

1. Rotate Text and Use the Fill Handle to Create a Series of Month Names (EX 145)
2. Increase Column Widths (EX 149)
3. Enter Row Titles (EX 150)
4. Copy a Range of Cells to a Nonadjacent Destination Area (EX 151)
5. Insert a Row (EX 154)
6. Enter Numbers with Format Symbols (EX 156)
7. Freeze Column and Row Titles (EX 157)
8. Enter and Format the System Date (EX 159)
9. Enter a Formula Containing Absolute Cell References (EX 162)
10. Enter an IF Function (EX 165)
11. Copy Formulas with Absolute Cell References Using the Fill Handle (EX 168)
12. Unfreeze the Worksheet Titles and Save the Workbook (EX 169)
13. Add a Sparkline Chart to the Worksheet (EX 170)
14. Format and Copy the Sparkline Chart (EX 171)
15. Assign Formats to Nonadjacent Ranges (EX 174)
16. Format the Worksheet Titles (EX 176)
17. Copy a Cell's Format Using the Format Painter Button (EX 178)
18. Draw a 3-D Pie Chart on a Separate Chart Sheet (EX 182)
19. Insert a Chart Title and Data Labels (EX 183)
20. Rotate the 3-D Pie Chart (EX 186)
21. Apply a 3-D Format to the Pie Chart (EX 188)
22. Explode the 3-D Pie Chart and Change the Color of a Slice (EX 190)
23. Reorder the Sheet Tabs (EX 194)
24. Check Spelling in Multiple Sheets (EX 194)
25. Shrink and Magnify the View of a Worksheet or Chart (EX 196)
26. Split a Window into Panes (EX 198)
27. Analyze Data in a Worksheet by Changing Values (EX 200)
28. Goal Seek (EX 200)

SAM

If you have a SAM 2010 user profile, your instructor may have assigned an autogradable version of this assignment. If so, log into the SAM 2010 Web site at www.cengage.com/sam2010 to download the instruction and start files.

Learn It Online

Test your knowledge of chapter content and key terms.

Instructions: To complete the Learn It Online exercises, visit the Microsoft Office and Concepts CourseMate Web site at www.cengagebrain.com, navigate to the Excel Chapter 3 resources for this book, click the link for the exercise you want to complete, and then read the instructions.

Chapter Reinforcement TF, MC, and SA

A series of true/false, multiple choice, and short answer questions that test your knowledge of the chapter content.

Flash Cards

An interactive learning environment where you identify chapter key terms associated with displayed definitions.

Practice Test

A series of multiple choice questions that test your knowledge of chapter content and key terms.

Who Wants To Be a Computer Genius?

An interactive game that challenges your knowledge of chapter content in the style of a television quiz show.

Wheel of Terms

An interactive game that challenges your knowledge of chapter key terms in the style of the television show *Wheel of Fortune*.

Crossword Puzzle Challenge

A crossword puzzle that challenges your knowledge of key terms presented in the chapter.

Apply Your Knowledge

Reinforce the skills and apply the concepts you learned in this chapter.

Understanding Logical Tests and Absolute Cell Referencing

Instructions Part 1: Determine the truth value (true or false) of the following logical tests, given the following cell values: B4 = 30; W3 = 100; H5 = 32; L2 = 25; and M8 = 15. Enter true or false.

a. M8 > B4 Truth value: ____________________

b. W3 = L2 Truth value: ____________________

c. L2 + 15 * B4 / 10 <> W3 Truth value: ____________________

d. H5 – L2 < B4 / M8 Truth value: ____________________

e. (M8 + B4) * 2 <> W3 – (M8 / 3) * 2 Truth value: ____________________

f. M8 + 300 > B4 * H5 + 10 Truth value: ____________________

g. H5 * L2 >= 2 * (W3 + 25) Truth value: ____________________

h. B4 = 10 * (M8 / 5) Truth value: ____________________

Instructions Part 2: Write cell J49 as a relative reference, absolute reference, mixed reference with the column varying, and mixed reference with the row varying.

____________ ____________ ____________ ____________

Instructions Part 3: Start Excel. Open the workbook Apply 3-1 Absolute Cell References. See the inside back cover of this book for instructions for downloading the Data Files for Students, or see your instructor for information on accessing the files required in this book. You will re-create the numerical grid pictured in Figure 3–84.

Perform the following tasks:

1. Enter a formula in cell C7 that multiplies the sum of cells C3 through C6 times cell C2. Write the formula so that when you copy it to cells D7 and E7, Excel adjusts all the cell references according to the destination cells. Verify your formula by checking it with the values found in cells C7, D7, and E7 in Figure 3–84.
2. Enter a formula in cell F3 that multiplies cell B3 times the sum of cells C3 through E3. Write the formula so that when you copy the formula to cells F4, F5, and F6, Excel adjusts all the cell references according to the destination cells. Verify your formula by checking it with the values found in cells F3, F4, F5, and F6 in Figure 3–84.
3. Enter a formula in cell C8 that multiplies the sum of cells C3 through C6 times cell C2. Write the formula so that when you copy the formula to cells D8 and E8, cell C2 remains absolute. Verify your formula by checking it with the values found in cells C8, D8, and E8 in Figure 3–84.
4. Enter a formula in cell G3 that multiplies the sum of cells C3, D3, and E3 times cell B3. Write the formula so that when you copy the formula to cells G4, G5, and G6, cell B3 remains absolute. Verify your formula by checking it with the values found in cells G3, G4, G5, and G6 in Figure 3–84.
5. Apply the worksheet name, Cell References, to the sheet tab and apply the Red, Accent 2 theme color to the sheet tab.
6. Change the document properties, as specified by your instructor. Change the worksheet header with your name, course number, and other information as specified by your instructor. Save the workbook using the file name, Apply 3-1 Absolute Cell References Complete, and submit the workbook as requested by your instructor.

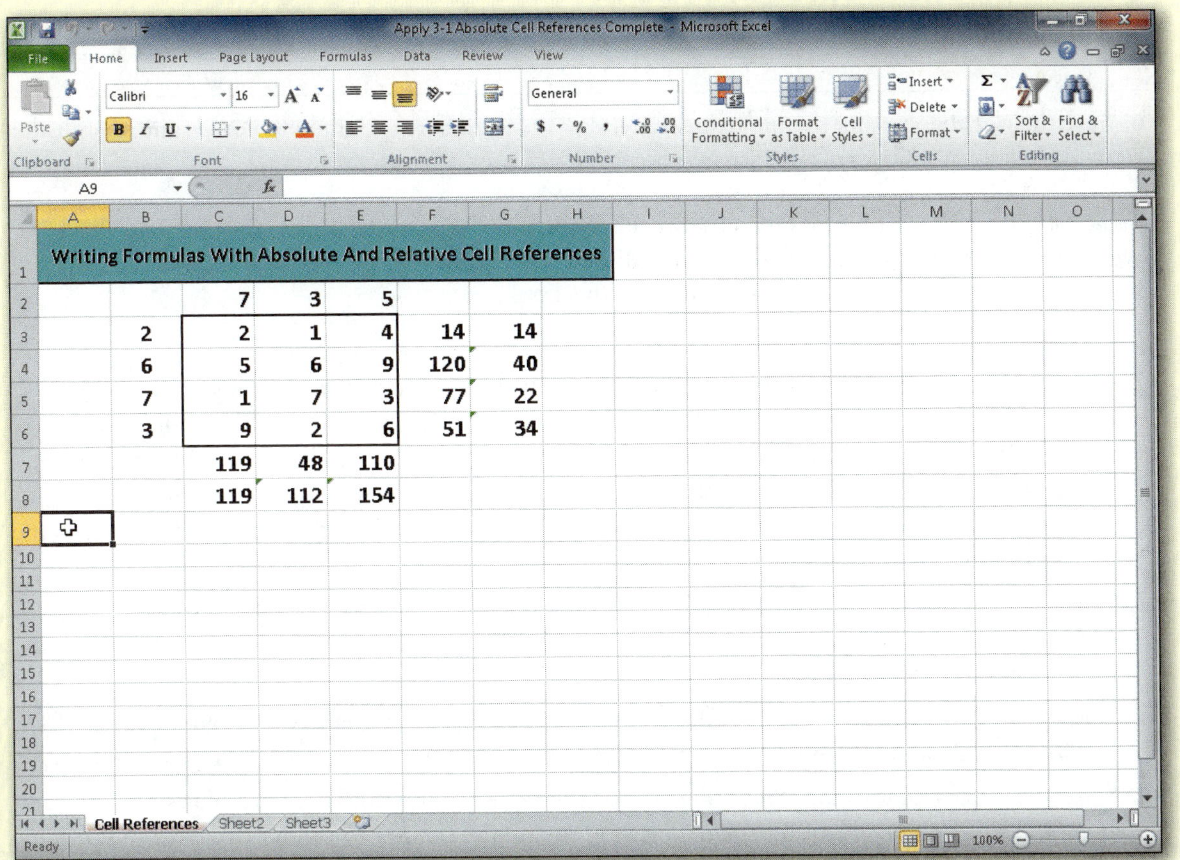

Figure 3–84

Extend Your Knowledge

Extend the skills you learned in this chapter and experiment with new skills. You may need to use Help to complete the assignment.

Nested IF Functions and More About the Fill Handle

Instructions Part 1: Start Excel. You will use nested IF functions to determine values for sets of data.

1. Using the Insert Function dialog box, enter the following IF function in cell B1:

   IF(A1="TX", "Central", "Time Zone Error")

2. Select cell B1, select the text "Time Zone Error" in the Formula Bar, click the Logical button (Formulas tab | Function Library group), click IF, and enter the following IF function:

   IF(A1="OR", "Pacific", "Time Zone Error")

3. Select cell B1, select "Time Zone Error" in the Formula Bar, click Logical button (Formulas tab | Function Library group), click IF, and enter the following IF function:

   IF(A1="VA", "Eastern", "Time Zone Error")

4. Verify that the formula in cell B1 appears as follows:

   =IF(A1="TX","Central", IF(A1="OR","Pacific", IF(A1="VA","Eastern","Time Zone Error")))

5. Use the fill handle to copy the nested IF function down through cell B6. Enter the following data in the cells in the range A1:A6 and then write down the results that display in cells B1 through B6 for each set. Set 1: A1 = TX; A2 = NY; A3 = OR; A4 = MI; A5 = TX; A6 = VA. Set 2: A1= WI; A2 = OR; A3 = IL; A4 = VA; A5 = NJ; A6 = TX.

Set 1 Results: ____

Set 2 Results: ____

6. Save the workbook using the file name, Extend 3-1 Create Series Complete Part 1, and submit the workbook as specified by your instructor.

Instructions Part 2: Start Excel. Open the workbook Extend 3-1 Create Series. See the inside back cover of this book for instructions for downloading the Data Files for Students, or see your instructor for information on accessing the files required in this book.

Perform the following tasks:

1. Use the fill handle on one column at a time to propagate the twelve series through row 14, as shown in Figure 3–85. For example, in column A, select cell A2 and drag the fill handle down to cell A14. In column C, hold down the CTRL key to repeat Saturday through cell C14. In column D, select the range D2:D3 and drag the fill handle down to cell D14. Likewise, in columns G through L, select the two adjacent cells in rows 2 and 3 before dragging the fill handle down to the corresponding cell in row 14.
2. Select cell D19. While holding down the CTRL key, one at a time drag the fill handle three cells to the right, to the left, up, and down to generate four series of numbers beginning with zero and incremented by one.
3. Select cell H19. Point to the cell border so that the mouse pointer changes to a plus sign with four arrows. Drag the mouse pointer down to cell H21 to move the contents of cell H19 to cell H21.
4. Select cell H21. Point to the cell border so that the mouse pointer changes to a plus sign with four arrows. While holding down the CTRL key, drag the mouse pointer to cell K21 to copy the contents of cell H21 to cell K21.

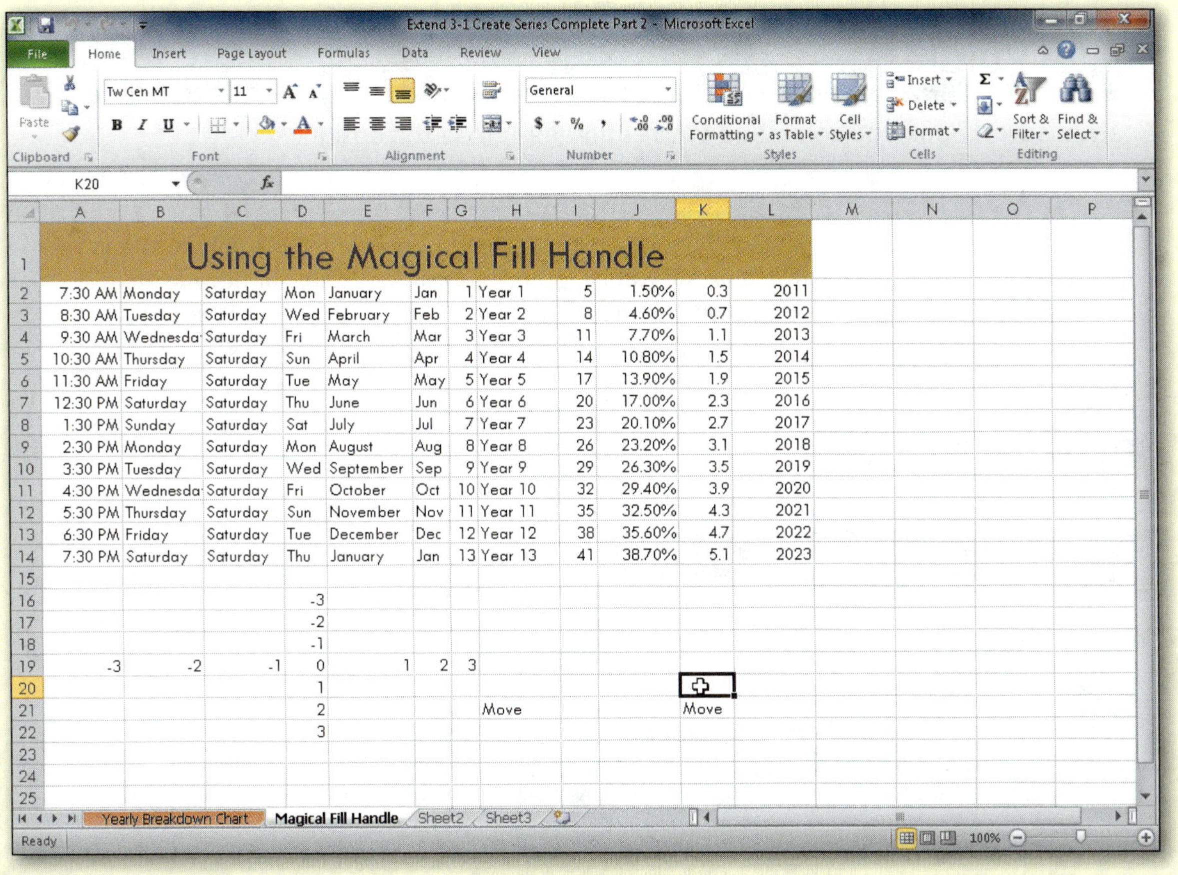

Figure 3–85

5. Select cell K19. Drag the fill handle in to the center of cell K19 so that the cell is shaded and the cell contents are deleted.
6. Apply a worksheet name to the sheet tab and apply a color of your choice to the sheet tab.
7. Select cell range H2:I14, click the Pie button (Insert tab | Charts group) to display the Pie gallery, click Pie in 3-D chart in the Pie gallery, click the Move Chart button (Chart Tools Design tab | Location group), click the New sheet option button (Move Chart dialog box), and then click the OK button (Move Chart dialog box) to move the 3-D Pie chart to a new worksheet.
8. Click the Chart Title button (Chart Tools Layout tab | Labels group), click Above Chart in the Chart Title gallery, select the title, and change the chart title to “Yearly Breakdown”.
9. Click the Data Labels button (Chart Tools Layout tab | Labels group), click Outside End in the Data Labels gallery to add data points to the chart.
10. Apply a chart sheet name to the sheet tab and apply a color of your choice to the tab.
11. Change the document properties, as specified by your instructor. Change the worksheet header with your name, course number, and other information as specified by your instructor. Save the workbook using the file name, Extend 3-1 Create Series Complete Part 2, and submit the workbook as specified by your instructor.

STUDENT ASSIGNMENTS

Make It Right

Analyze a workbook and correct all errors and/or improve the design.

Inserting Rows, Moving a Range, and Correcting Formulas in a Worksheet

Instructions: Start Excel. Open the workbook Make It Right 3-1 SpeedyOfficeSupply.com Annual Projected Net Income. See the inside back cover of this book for instructions for downloading the Data Files for Students, or see your instructor for information on accessing the files required for this book. Correct the following design and formula problems (Figure 3–86a) in the worksheet.

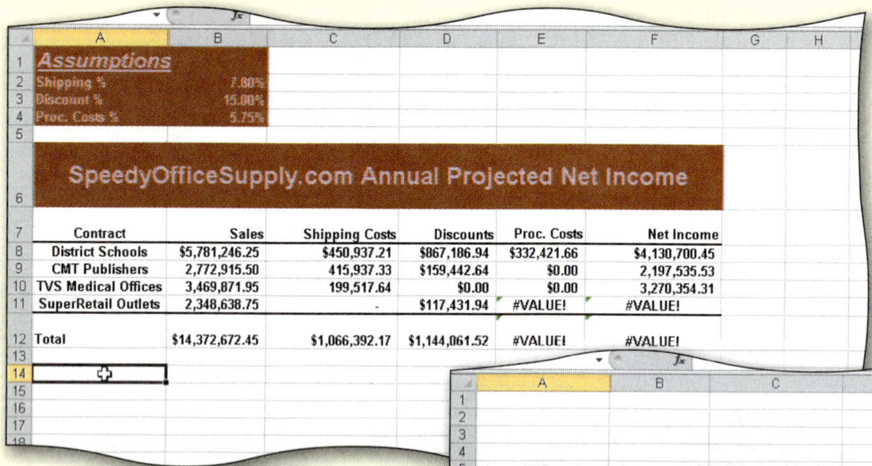

Figure 3–86 (a) Before

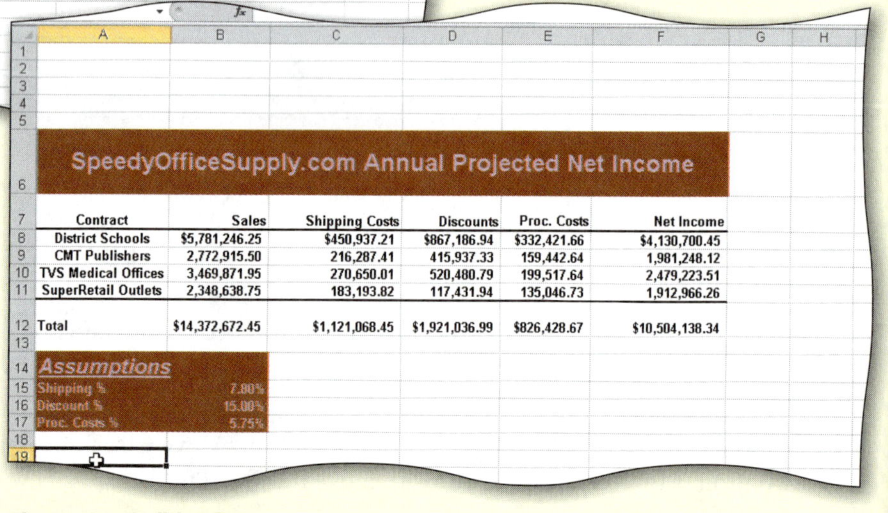

Figure 3–86 (b) After

1. The Shipping Cost in cell C8 is computed using the formula =B2*B8 (Shipping % × Sales). Similar formulas are used in cells C9, C10, and C11. The formula in cell C8 was entered and copied to cells C9, C10, and C11. Although the result in cell C8 is correct, the results in cells C9, C10, and C11 are incorrect. Edit the formula in cell C8 by changing cell B2 to an absolute cell reference. Copy the corrected formula in cell C8 to cells C9, C10, and C11. After completing the copy, click the Auto Fill Options button arrow that is displayed below and to the right of cell C11 and choose Fill Without Formatting.

2. The Discount amounts in cells D8, D9, D10, and D11 are computed using the IF function. The Discount amount should equal the amount in cell B3*B8 (Discount % × Sales) if the corresponding Sales in column B is greater than or equal to $2,500,000. If the corresponding Sales in column B is less than $2,500,000, then the Discount amount is 5%*B8 (5% × Sales). The IF function in cell D8

was entered and copied to cells D9, D10, and D11. The current IF functions in cells D8, D9, D10, and D11 are incorrect. Edit and correct the IF function in cell D8. Copy the corrected formula in cell D8 to cells D9, D10, and D11. After completing the copy, click the Auto Fill Options button arrow that is displayed below and to the right of cell D11 and choose Fill Without Formatting.

3. The Processing Costs in cell E8 is computed using the formula =B4*B8 (Proc. Costs % × Sales). The formula in cell E8 was entered and copied to cells E9, E10, and E11. Although the result in cell E8 is correct, the results in cells E9, E10, and E11 are incorrect. Edit and correct the formula in cell E8 by changing cell B4 to an absolute cell reference. Copy the corrected formula in cell E8 to cells E9, E10, and E11. After completing the copy, click the Auto Fill Options button arrow that displays below and to the right of cell E11 and choose Fill Without Formatting. Ensure that the range B9:E11 is formatted with the Accounting Number format.
4. Change the design of the worksheet by moving the Assumptions table in the range A1:B4 to the range A14:B17, as shown in Figure 3–86b. To complete the move drag the Assumptions table to the range A14:B17. Use Figure 3–86b to verify that Excel automatically adjusted the cell references based on the move. Use the Undo button and Redo button on the Quick Access Toolbar to move the Assumptions table back and forth while the results of the formulas remain the same.
5. Apply a worksheet name to the sheet tab and apply the Orange, Accent 3 color to the sheet tab.
6. Change the document properties, as specified by your instructor. Change the worksheet header with your name, course number, and other information as specified by your instructor. Save the workbook using the file name, Make It Right 3-1 SpeedyOfficeSupply.com Annual Projected Net Income Complete, and submit the revised workbook as specified by your instructor.

In the Lab

SAM

Create a workbook using the guidelines, concepts, and skills presented in this chapter. Labs are listed in order of increasing difficulty.

Lab 1: Six-Year Financial Projection

Problem: Your supervisor in the Finance department at Med Supply Online Warehouse has asked you to create a worksheet that will project the annual gross margin, expenses, total expenses, operating income, income taxes, and net income for the next six years based on the assumptions in Table 3–9. The desired worksheet is shown in Figure 3–87 on the following page. In Part 1 you will create the worksheet. In Part 2 you will create a chart to present the data, shown in Figure 3–88 on page EX 213. In Part 3 you will use Goal Seek to analyze three different sales scenarios.

Table 3–9 Med Supply Online Warehouse Financial Projection Assumptions

Units Sold in Prior Year	1,589,712
Unit Cost	$59.50
Annual Sales Growth	4.50%
Annual Price Decrease	3.80%
Margin	38.80%

Continued >

In the Lab *continued*

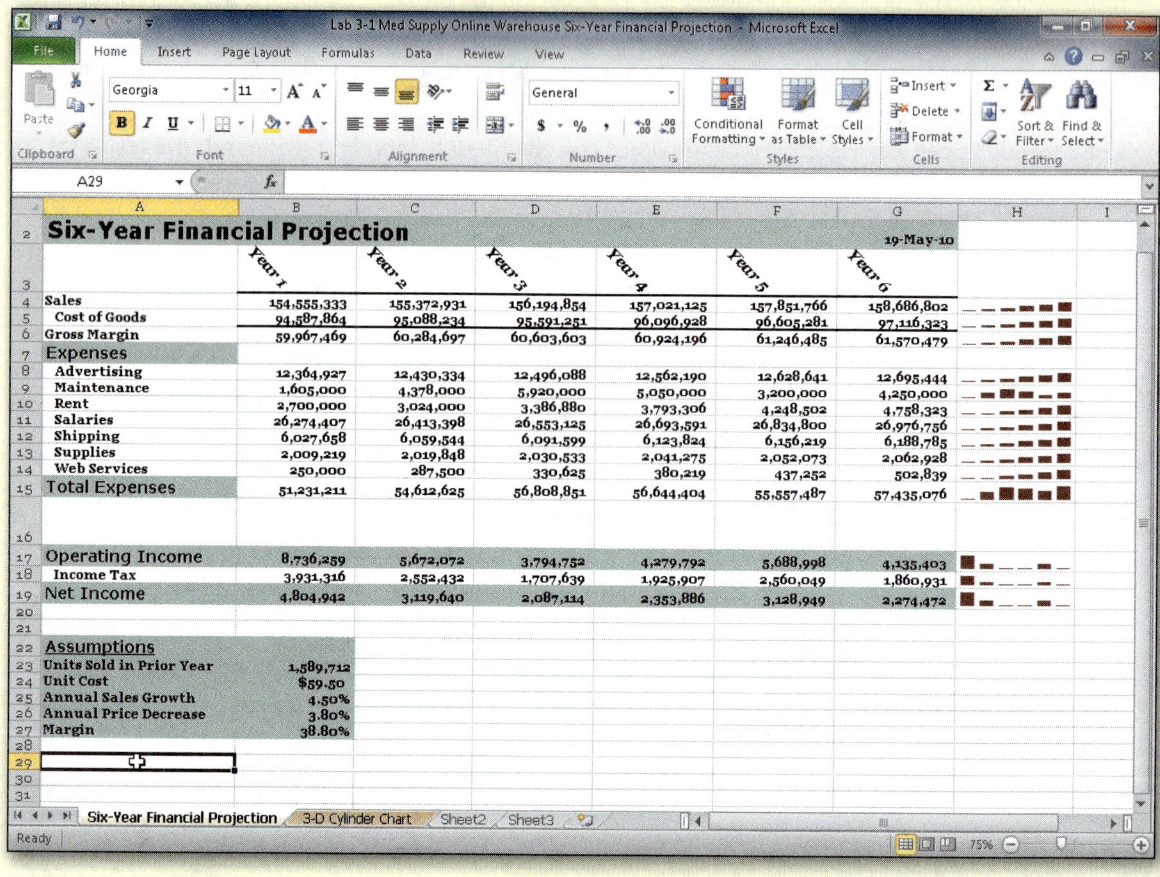

	Year 1	Year 2	Year 3	Year 4	Year 5	Year 6
Six-Year Financial Projection						19-May-10
Sales	154,555,333	155,372,931	156,194,854	157,021,125	157,851,766	158,686,802
Cost of Goods	94,587,864	95,088,234	95,591,251	96,096,928	96,605,281	97,116,323
Gross Margin	59,967,469	60,284,697	60,603,603	60,924,196	61,246,485	61,570,479
Expenses						
Advertising	12,364,927	12,430,334	12,496,088	12,562,190	12,628,641	12,695,444
Maintenance	1,605,000	4,378,000	5,920,000	5,050,000	3,200,000	4,250,000
Rent	2,700,000	3,024,000	3,386,880	3,793,306	4,248,502	4,758,323
Salaries	26,274,407	26,413,398	26,553,125	26,693,591	26,834,800	26,976,756
Shipping	6,027,658	6,059,544	6,091,599	6,123,824	6,156,219	6,188,785
Supplies	2,009,219	2,019,848	2,030,533	2,041,275	2,052,073	2,062,928
Web Services	250,000	287,500	330,625	380,219	437,252	502,839
Total Expenses	51,231,211	54,612,625	56,808,851	56,644,404	55,557,487	57,435,076
Operating Income	8,736,259	5,672,072	3,794,752	4,279,792	5,688,998	4,135,403
Income Tax	3,931,316	2,552,432	1,707,639	1,925,907	2,560,049	1,860,931
Net Income	4,804,942	3,119,640	2,087,114	2,353,886	3,128,949	2,274,472
Assumptions						
Units Sold in Prior Year	1,589,712					
Unit Cost	$59.50					
Annual Sales Growth	4.50%					
Annual Price Decrease	3.80%					
Margin	38.80%					

Figure 3–87

Instructions Part 1:

1. Start Excel. Apply the Civic theme to the worksheet by using the Themes button (Page Layout tab | Themes group). Bold the entire worksheet by selecting the entire worksheet and using the Bold button (Home tab | Font group).
2. Enter the worksheet title `Med Supply Online Warehouse` in cell A1 and the subtitle `Six-Year Financial Projection` in cell A2. Format the worksheet title in cell A1 to 36-point Copperplate Gothic Bold (or a similar font). Format the worksheet subtitle in cell A2 to 20-point Verdana (or a similar font). Enter the system date in cell G2 using the NOW function. Format the date to the 14-Mar-01 style.
3. Change the following column widths: A = 25.00 characters; B through H = 15.00 characters. Change the heights of rows 7, 15, 17, 19, and 22 to 18.00 points.
4. Enter the six column titles Year 1 through Year 6 in the range B3:G3 by entering Year 1 in cell B3 and then dragging cell B3's fill handle through the range C3:G3. Format cell B3 as follows: (a) increase the font size to 14; (b) center and italicize it; and (c) angle its contents clockwise. Use the Format Painter button (Home tab | Clipboard group) to copy the format assigned to cell B3 to the range C3:G3.

5. Enter the row titles in the range A4:A19. Change the font in cells A7, A15, A17, and A19 to 14-point Verdana (or a similar font). Add thick bottom borders to the ranges B3:G3 and B5:G5. Use the Increase Indent button (Home tab | Alignment group) to increase the indent of the row titles in cell A5, the range A8:A14, and cell A18.
6. Enter the table title **Assumptions** in cell A22. Enter the assumptions in Table 3–9 on page EX 209 in the range A23:B27. Use format symbols when entering the numbers. Change the font size of the table title in cell A22 to 14-point Verdana and underline it.
7. Select the range B4:G19 and then click the Format Cells: Number Dialog Box Launcher (Home tab | Number group) to display the Format Cells dialog box. Use the Number category (Format Cells dialog box) to assign the Comma style with no decimal places and negative numbers enclosed in parentheses to the range B4:G19.
8. Complete the following entries:
   a. Year 1 Sales (cell B4) = Units Sold in Prior Year * (Unit Cost / (1 – Margin)) or = B23*(B24/(1-B27))
   b. Year 2 Sales (cell C4) = Year 1 Sales * (1 + Annual Sales Growth) * (1 – Annual Price Decrease) or =B4*(1+$B$25)*(1-$B$26)
   c. Copy cell C4 to the range D4:G4.
   d. Year 1 Cost of Goods (cell B5) = Year 1 Sales * (1 – Margin) or =B4 * (1 - $B$27)
   e. Copy cell B5 to the range C5:G5.
   f. Gross Margin (cell B6) = Year 1 Sales - Year 1 Cost of Goods or =B4 – B5
   g. Copy cell B6 to the range C6:G6.
   h. Year 1 Advertising (cell B8) = 500 + 8% * Year 1 Sales or =500+8%*B4
   i. Copy cell B8 to the range C8:G8.
   j. Maintenance (row 9): Year 1 = 1,605,000; Year 2 = 4,378,000; Year 3 = 5,920,000; Year 4 = 5,050,000; Year 5 = 3,200,000; Year 6 = 4,250,000
   k. Year 1 Rent (cell B10) = 2,700,000
   l. Year 2 Rent (cell C10) = Year 1 Rent + (12% * Year 1 Rent) or =B10*(1+12%)
   m. Copy cell C10 to the range D10:G10.
   n. Year 1 Salaries (cell B11) = 17% * Year 1 Sales or =17%*B4
   o. Copy cell B11 to the range C11:G11.
   p. Year 1 Shipping (cell B12) = 3.9% * Year 1 Sales or =3.9%*B4
   q. Copy cell B12 to the range C12:G12.
   r. Year 1 Supplies (cell B13) = 1.3% * Year 1 Sales or =1.3%*B4
   s. Copy cell B13 to the range C13:G13.
   t. Year 1 Web Services (cell B14) = 250,000
   u. Year 2 Web Services (cell C14) = Year 1 Web Services + (15% * Year 1 Web Services) or =B14*(1+15%)
   v. Copy cell C14 to the range D14:G14.
   w. Year 1 Total Expenses (cell B15) = SUM(B8:B14)
   x. Copy cell B15 to the range C15:G15.
   y. Year 1 Operating Income (cell B17) = Year 1 Gross Margin - Year 1 Total Expenses or =B6-B15
   z. Copy cell B17 to the range C17:G17.

Continued >

In the Lab *continued*

aa. Year 1 Income Taxes (cell B18): If Year 1 Operating Income is less than 0, then Year 1 Income Taxes equal 0; otherwise Year 1 Income Taxes equal 45% * Year 1 Operating Income or =IF(B17 < 0, 0, 45%*B17)

bb. Copy cell B18 to the range C18:G18.

cc. Year 1 Net Income (cell B19) = Year 1 Operating Income – Year 1 Income Taxes or = B17-B18

dd. Copy cell B19 to the range C19:G19.

ee. In cell H4, insert a Sparkline Column chart (Insert Tab | Sparklines group) for cell range B4:G4

ff. Repeat step ee for the ranges H5:H6, H8:H15, and H17:H19

9. Change the background colors as shown in Figure 3–87. Use Teal, Accent 3, Lighter 40% for the background colors.
10. Zoom to: (a) 200%; (b) 75%; (c) 25%; and (d) 100%.
11. Change the document properties, as specified by your instructor. Change the worksheet header with your name, course number, and other information as specified by your instructor. Save the workbook using the file name, Lab 3-1 Med Supply Online Warehouse Six-Year Financial Projection.
12. Preview the worksheet. Use the Orientation button (Page Layout tab | Page Setup group) to fit the printout on one page in landscape orientation. Preview the formulas version (CTRL+`) of the worksheet in landscape orientation using the Fit to option. Press CTRL + ` to instruct Excel to display the values version of the worksheet. Save the workbook again and close the workbook.
13. Submit the workbook as specified by your instructor.

Instructions Part 2:

1. Start Excel. Open the workbook Lab 3-1 Med Supply Online Warehouse Six-Year Financial Projection.
2. Use the nonadjacent ranges B3:G3 and B19:G19 to create a 3-D Cylinder chart. Draw the chart by clicking the Column button (Insert tab | Charts group). When the Column gallery is displayed, click the Clustered Cylinder chart type (column 1, row 3). When the chart is displayed, click the Move Chart button to move the chart to a new sheet.
3. Select the legend on the right side of the chart and delete it. Add the chart title by clicking the Chart Titles button (Chart Tools Layout tab | Labels group). Click Above Chart in the Chart Title gallery. Format the chart title as shown in Figure 3–88.
4. To change the color of the cylinders, click one of the cylinders and use the Shape Fill button (Chart Tools Format tab | Shape Styles group). To change the color of the wall, click the wall behind the cylinders and use the Shape Fill button to change the chart wall color. Use the same procedure to change the color of the base of the wall.
5. Rename the sheet tabs Six-Year Financial Projection and 3-D Cylinder Chart. Rearrange the sheets so that the worksheet is leftmost and color their tabs as shown in Figure 3–88.
6. Click the Six-Year Financial Projection tab to display the worksheet. Save the workbook using the same file name (Lab 3-1 Med Supply Online Warehouse Six-Year Financial Projection) as defined in Part 1. Submit the workbook as requested by your instructor.

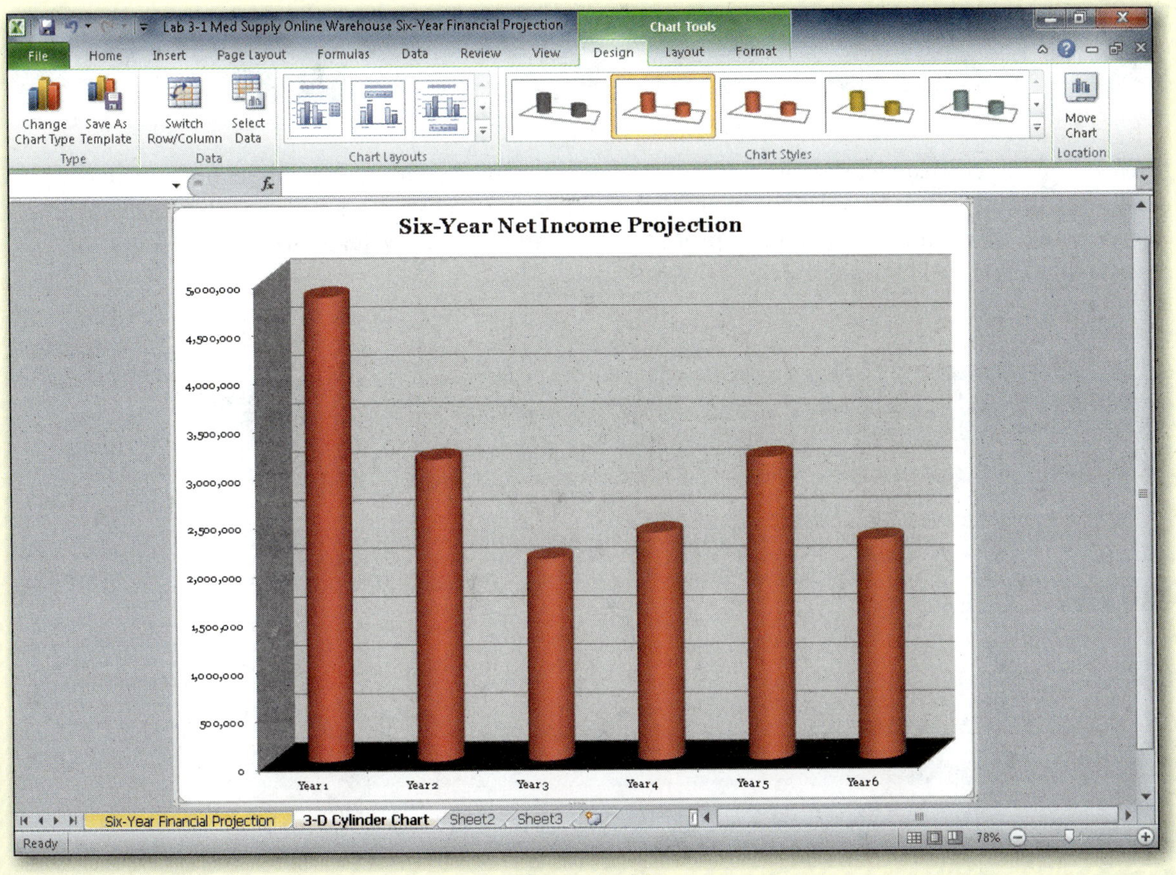

Figure 3–88

Instructions Part 3:

1. Start Excel. Open the workbook Lab 3-1 Med Supply Online Warehouse Six-Year Financial Projection. Do not save the workbook in this part of the In the Lab exercise. Divide the window into two panes by dragging the horizontal split box between rows 6 and 7. Use the scroll bars to show both the top and bottom of the worksheet. Using the numbers in columns 2 and 3 of Table 3–10, analyze the effect of changing the annual sales growth (cell B25) and annual price decrease (cell B26) on the net incomes in row 19. The resulting answers are in column 4 of Table 3–10. Submit the workbook or results of the what-if analysis for each case as requested by your instructor.

Table 3–10 Med Supply Online Warehouse Data to Analyze and Results

Case	Annual Sales Growth	Annual Price Decrease	Year 6 Resulting Net Income in Cell G19
1	8.45%	5.75%	2,925,008
2	14.75%	23.00%	(2,353,532)
3	25.50%	2.65%	14,668,149

2. Close the workbook without saving it, and then reopen it. Use the What-If Analysis button (Data tab | Data Tools group) to goal seek. Determine a margin (cell B27) that would result in a Year 6 net income of $4,000,000 (cell G19). You should end up with a margin of 40.49% in cell B27. Submit the workbook with the new values or the results of the goal seek as requested by your instructor. Do not save the workbook with the latest changes.

STUDENT ASSIGNMENTS

In the Lab

Lab 2: Analysis of Indirect Expense Allocations

Problem: Your classmate works part time as an advisor for the ReachOut Neighbors not-for-profit group. She has asked you to assist her in creating an indirect expense allocation worksheet (Figure 3–89) that will help the not-for-profit administration better evaluate the branch offices described in Table 3–11.

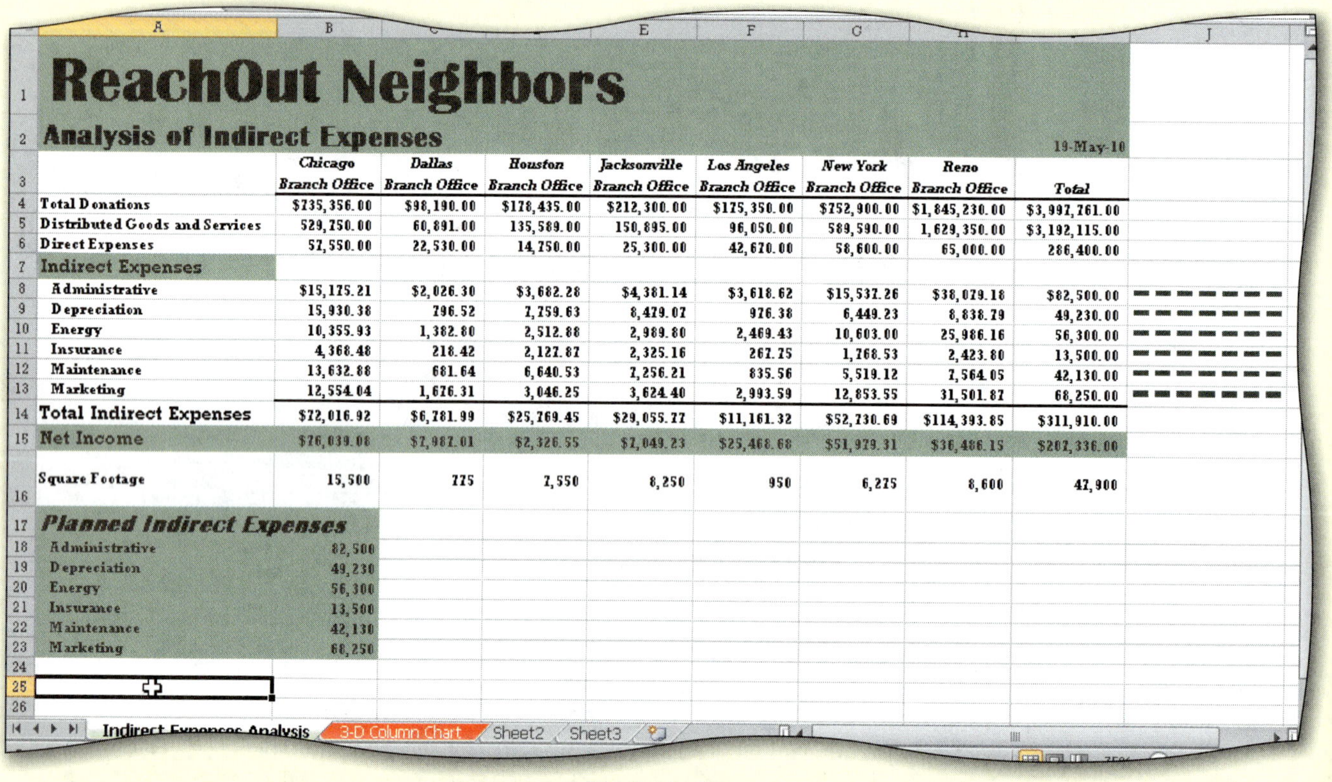

ReachOut Neighbors

Analysis of Indirect Expenses 19-May-10

	Chicago Branch Office	Dallas Branch Office	Houston Branch Office	Jacksonville Branch Office	Los Angeles Branch Office	New York Branch Office	Reno Branch Office	Total
Total Donations	$735,356.00	$98,190.00	$178,435.00	$212,300.00	$175,350.00	$752,900.00	$1,845,230.00	$3,997,761.00
Distributed Goods and Services	529,750.00	60,891.00	135,589.00	150,895.00	96,050.00	589,590.00	1,629,350.00	$3,192,115.00
Direct Expenses	57,550.00	22,530.00	14,750.00	25,300.00	42,670.00	58,600.00	65,000.00	286,400.00
Indirect Expenses								
Administrative	$15,175.21	$2,026.30	$3,682.28	$4,381.14	$3,618.62	$15,537.26	$38,079.18	$82,500.00
Depreciation	15,930.38	796.52	7,759.63	8,479.07	976.38	6,449.23	8,838.79	49,230.00
Energy	10,355.93	1,382.80	2,512.88	2,989.80	2,469.43	10,603.00	25,986.16	56,300.00
Insurance	4,368.48	218.42	2,127.87	2,325.16	267.75	1,768.53	2,423.80	13,500.00
Maintenance	13,632.88	681.64	6,640.53	7,256.21	835.56	5,519.12	7,564.05	42,130.00
Marketing	12,554.04	1,676.31	3,046.25	3,624.40	2,993.59	12,853.55	31,501.87	68,250.00
Total Indirect Expenses	$72,016.92	$6,781.99	$25,769.45	$29,055.77	$11,161.32	$52,730.69	$114,393.85	$311,910.00
Net Income	$76,039.08	$7,987.01	$2,326.55	$7,049.23	$25,468.68	$51,979.31	$36,486.15	$202,336.00
Square Footage	15,500	775	7,550	8,250	950	6,275	8,600	47,900

Planned Indirect Expenses	
Administrative	82,500
Depreciation	49,230
Energy	56,300
Insurance	13,500
Maintenance	42,130
Marketing	68,250

Figure 3–89

Table 3–11 ReachOut Neighbor Worksheet Data

	Chicago Branch Office	Dallas Branch Office	Houston Branch Office	Jacksonville Branch Office	Los Angeles Branch Office	New York Branch Office	Reno Branch Office
Total Donations	735356	98190	178435	212300	175350	752900	1845230
Distributed Goods and Services	529750	60891	135589	150895	96050	589590	1629350
Direct Expenses	57550	22530	14750	25300	42670	58600	65000
Square Footage	15500	775	7550	8250	950	6275	8600

Instructions Part 1: Do the following to create the worksheet shown in Figure 3–89.

1. Apply the Foundry theme to the worksheet. Bold the entire worksheet by selecting the entire worksheet and using the Bold (Home tab | Font group).
2. Change the following column widths: A = 30.00; B through I = 13.00; J = 20.00.
3. Enter the worksheet titles in cells A1 and A2 and the system date in cell I2. Format the date to the 14-Mar-01 style.

4. Enter the column titles, row titles, and the first three rows of numbers in Table 3–11 in rows 3 through 6. Add the column heading Total to cell I3. Center and italicize the column headings in the range B3:I3. Add a thick bottom border to the range B3:I3. Sum the individual rows 4, 5, and 6 in the range I4:I6.
5. Enter the Square Footage row as shown in Table 3–11 with the comma format symbol in row 16. Sum row 16 in cell I16. Use the Format Painter button (Home tab | Clipboard group) to format cell I16. Change the height of row 16 to 42.00. Vertically center the range A16:I16 through the use of the Format Cells dialog box.
6. Enter the remaining row titles in the range A7:A17 as shown in Figure 3–89. Increase the font size in cells A7, A14, and A15 to 14 point.
7. Copy the row titles in range A8:A13 to the range A18:A23. Enter the numbers shown in the range B18:B23 of Figure 3–89 with format symbols.
8. The planned indirect expenses in the range B18:B23 are to be prorated across the branch office as follows: Administrative (row 8), Energy (row 10), and Marketing (row 13) on the basis of Total Donations (row 4); Depreciation (row 9), Insurance (row 11), and Maintenance (row 12) on the basis of Square Footage (row 16). Use the following formulas to accomplish the prorating:
   a. Chicago Branch Office Administrative (cell B8) = Administrative Expenses * Chicago Branch Office Total Donations / ReachOut Neighbors Total Donations or =$B$18*B4/$I$4
   b. Chicago Branch Office Depreciation (cell B9) = Depreciation Expenses * Chicago Branch Office Square Footage / Total Square Footage or =$B$19*B16/$I$16
   c. Chicago Branch Office Energy (cell B10) = Energy Expenses * Chicago Branch Office Total Donations / ReachOut Neighbor Total Donations or =$B$20*B4/$I$4
   d. Chicago Branch Office Insurance (cell B11) = Insurance Expenses * Chicago Branch Office Square Footage / Total Square Footage or =$B$21*B16 /$I$16
   e. Chicago Branch Office Maintenance (cell B12) = Maintenance Expenses * Chicago Branch Office Square Footage / Total Square Footage or =$B$22*B16/$I$16
   f. Chicago Branch Office Marketing (cell B13) = Marketing Expenses * Chicago Branch Office Total Donations / ReachOut Neighbor Total Donations or =$B$23*B4/$I$4
   g. Chicago Branch Office Total Indirect Expenses (cell B14) = SUM(B8:B13)
   h. Chicago Branch Office Net Income (cell B15) = Total Donations - (Distributed Goods and Services + Direct Expenses + Total Indirect Expenses) or =B4-(B5+B6+B14)
   i. Copy the range B8:B15 to the range C8:H15.
   j. Sum the individual rows 8 through 15 in the range I8:I15.
9. Add a thick bottom border to the range B13:I13. Assign the Currency style with two decimal places and show negative numbers in parentheses to the following ranges: B4:I4; B8:I8; and B14:I15. Assign the Comma style with two decimal places and show negative numbers in parentheses to the following ranges: B5:I6 and B9:I13.
10. Change the font in cell A1 to 48-point Britannic Bold (or a similar font). Change the font in cell A2 to 22-point Britannic Bold (or a similar font). Change the font in cell A17 to 18-point italic Britannic Bold.
11. Use the background color Green, Accent 1, Lighter 40% and the font color Tan, Background 2, Darker 75% for cell A7 and the ranges A1:I2; A15:I15; and A17:B23 as shown in Figure 3–89.
12. Insert a Sparkline Win/Loss chart for the range B8:H8 in cell J8. Copy the cell J8 to the cell range J9:J13.

Continued >

In the Lab *continued*

13. Rename the Sheet1 sheet as Indirect Expenses Analysis and color its tab green.
14. Update the document properties with your name, course number, and name for the workbook. Change the worksheet header with your name, course number, and other information as specified by your instructor. Save the workbook using the file name, Lab 3-2 ReachOut Neighbor Analysis of Indirect Expenses.
15. Preview the worksheet. Use the Orientation button (Page Layout tab | Page Setup group) to fit the printout on one page in landscape orientation using the Fit to option. Preview the formulas version (CTRL+`) of the worksheet in landscape orientation using the Fit to option. Press CTRL+` to instruct Excel to display the values version of the worksheet. Save the workbook again and close the workbook.
16. Divide the window into four panes and show the four corners of the worksheet. Remove the four panes. Close the workbook but do not save the workbook.

Instructions Part 2: Start Excel. Open Lab 3-2 ReachOut Neighbor Analysis of Indirect Expenses. Draw a 3-D Column Chart (Figure 3–90) on a separate sheet that shows the contribution of each category of indirect expense to the total indirect expenses. That is, chart the nonadjacent ranges A8:A13 (category names) and I8:I13 (data series). Show labels that include value of the column. Do not show the legend. Format the 3-D Column Chart as shown in Figure 3–90. Rename the chart sheet 3-D Column Chart and color the sheet tab red. Move the chart tab to the right of the worksheet tab. Save the workbook using the file name, Lab 3-2 ReachOut Neighbor Analysis of Indirect Expenses. Submit the workbook as specified by your instructor.

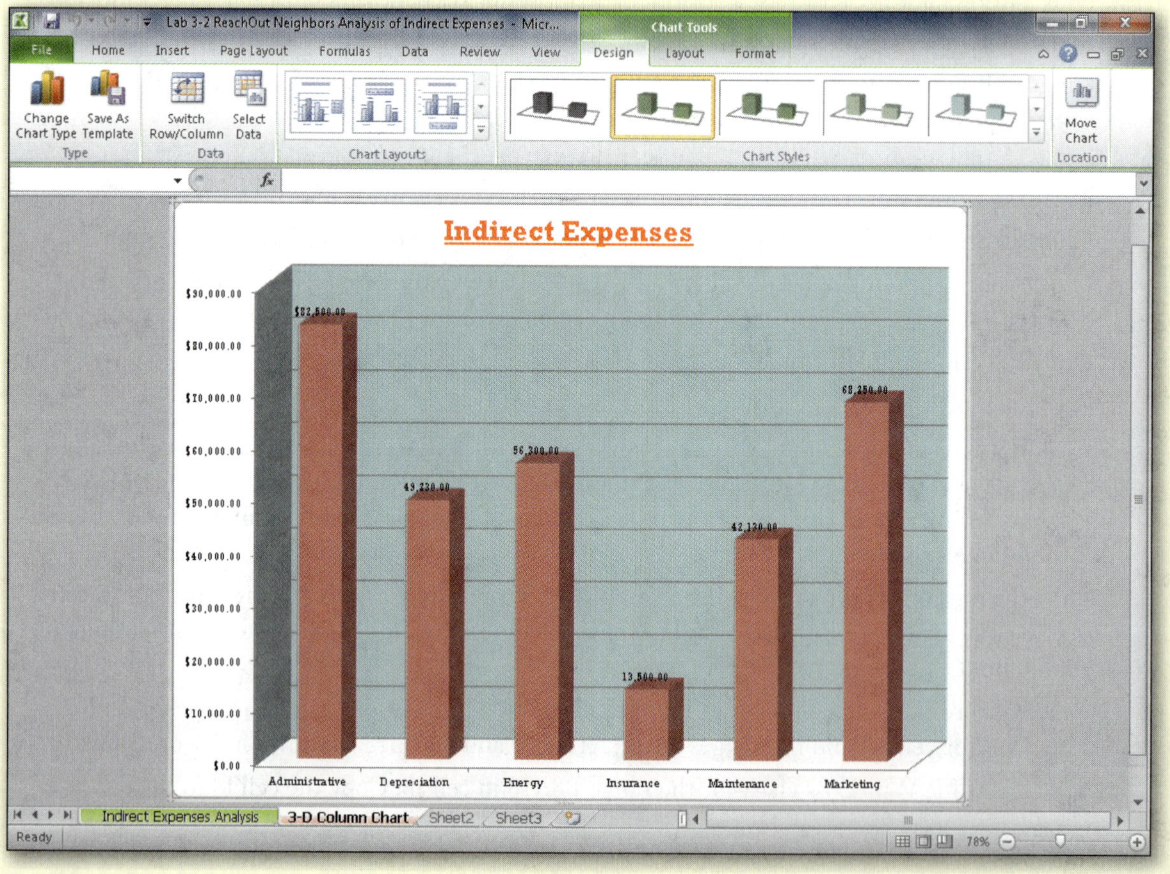

Figure 3–90

Instructions Part 3: Start Excel. Open Lab 3-2 ReachOut Neighbor Analysis of Indirect Expenses.

1. Using the numbers in Table 3–12, analyze the effect of changing the planned indirect expenses in the range B18:B23 on the net incomes for each branch office. You should end with the following totals in cell I15: Case 1 = $5,846.00 and Case 2 = $124,346.00. Submit the workbook or results for each case as requested by your instructor.
2. Use the What-If Analysis button (Data tab | Data Tools group) to goal seek. Determine a planned indirect Marketing expense (cell B23) that would result in a total net income of $50,000 (cell I15). You should end up with a planned indirect Marketing expense of $225,586 in cell B23. Submit the workbook with the new values or the results of the goal seek as specified by your instructor.

Table 3–12 ReachOut Neighbor Indirect Expense Allocations What-If Data

	Case 1	Case 2
Administrative	124000	66500
Depreciation	156575	75000
Energy	72525	56000
Insurance	46300	67000
Maintenance	75000	48000
Marketing	39000	82400

In the Lab

Lab 3: Modifying a Weekly Inventory Worksheet

Problem: As a summer intern at Dinah's Candle Depot, you have been asked to modify the weekly inventory report shown in Figure 3–91a on the following page. The workbook, Lab 3-3 Dinah's Weekly Inventory Report, is included with the Data Files for Students. See the inside back cover of this book for instructions for downloading the Data Files for Students, or see your instructor for information on accessing the files required for this book.

The major modifications to the payroll report to be made in this exercise include: (1) reformatting the worksheet; (2) adding computations of quantity to order based on reorder level and weeks to arrive; (3) adding calculations to suggest changes in ordering; (4) adding current and last month sales for inventory items; (5) adding and deleting inventory items; and (6) changing inventory item information. The final inventory report is shown in Figure 3–91b on the following page.

Continued >

In the Lab *continued*

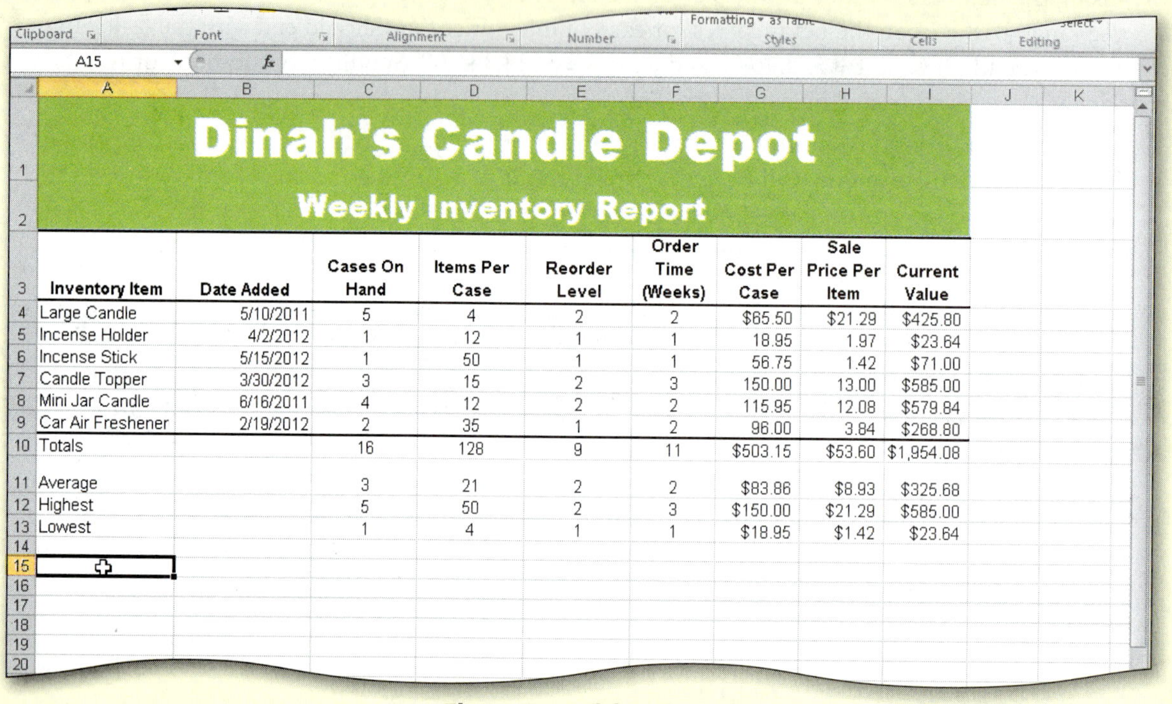

Dinah's Candle Depot

Weekly Inventory Report

Inventory Item	Date Added	Cases On Hand	Items Per Case	Reorder Level	Order Time (Weeks)	Cost Per Case	Sale Price Per Item	Current Value
Large Candle	5/10/2011	5	4	2	2	$65.50	$21.29	$425.80
Incense Holder	4/2/2012	1	12	1	1	18.95	1.97	$23.64
Incense Stick	5/15/2012	1	50	1	1	56.75	1.42	$71.00
Candle Topper	3/30/2012	3	15	2	3	150.00	13.00	$585.00
Mini Jar Candle	6/16/2011	4	12	2	2	115.95	12.08	$579.84
Car Air Freshener	2/19/2012	2	35	1	2	96.00	3.84	$268.80
Totals		16	128	9	11	$503.15	$53.60	$1,954.08
Average		3	21	2	2	$83.86	$8.93	$325.68
Highest		5	50	2	3	$150.00	$21.29	$585.00
Lowest		1	4	1	1	$18.95	$1.42	$23.64

Figure 3–91 (a) Before

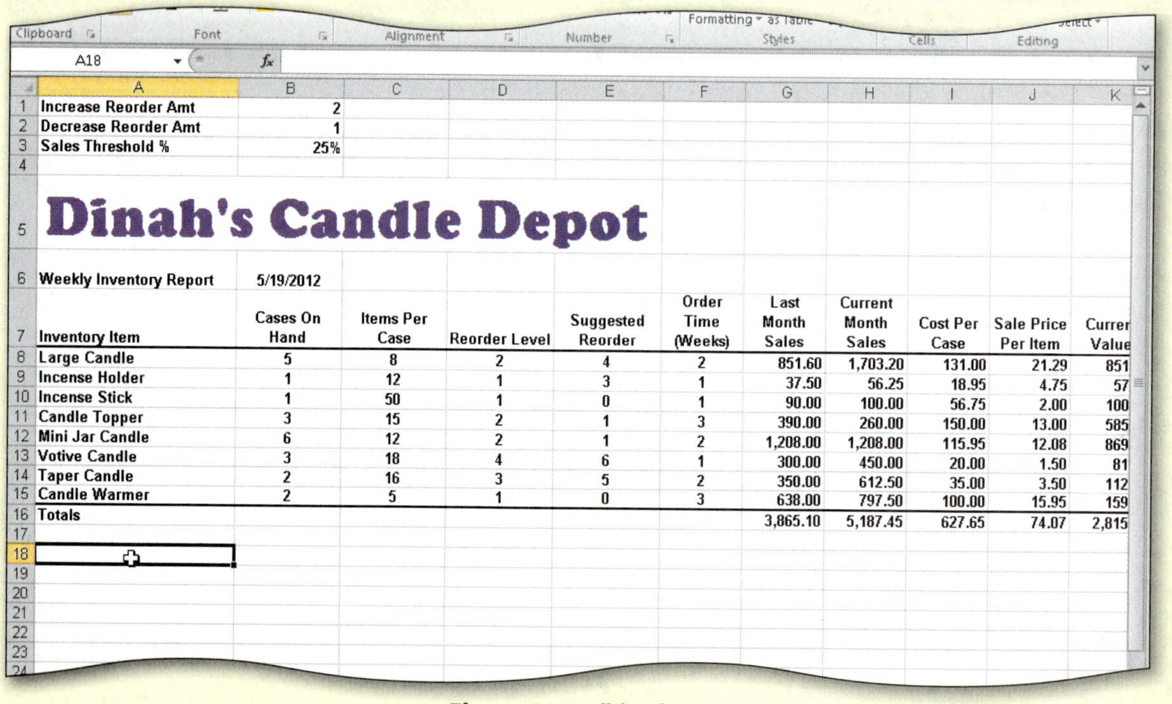

Increase Reorder Amt	2
Decrease Reorder Amt	1
Sales Threshold %	25%

Dinah's Candle Depot

Weekly Inventory Report 5/19/2012

Inventory Item	Cases On Hand	Items Per Case	Reorder Level	Suggested Reorder	Order Time (Weeks)	Last Month Sales	Current Month Sales	Cost Per Case	Sale Price Per Item	Curren Value
Large Candle	5	8	2	4	2	851.60	1,703.20	131.00	21.29	851
Incense Holder	1	12	1	3	1	37.50	56.25	18.95	4.75	57
Incense Stick	1	50	1	0	1	90.00	100.00	56.75	2.00	100
Candle Topper	3	15	2	1	3	390.00	260.00	150.00	13.00	585
Mini Jar Candle	6	12	2	1	2	1,208.00	1,208.00	115.95	12.08	869
Votive Candle	3	18	4	6	1	300.00	450.00	20.00	1.50	81
Taper Candle	2	16	3	5	2	350.00	612.50	35.00	3.50	112
Candle Warmer	2	5	1	0	3	638.00	797.50	100.00	15.95	159
Totals						3,865.10	5,187.45	627.65	74.07	2,815

Figure 3–91 (b) After

Instructions Part 1:

1. Start Excel. Open the workbook, Lab 3-3 Dinah's Weekly Inventory Report and then save the workbook using the file name Lab 3-3 Dinah's Weekly Inventory Report Complete.
2. Select the worksheet by clicking the Select All button. Click the Clear button (Home tab | Editing group) and then click Clear Formats on the Clear menu to clear the formatting. Bold the entire worksheet.

3. Delete rows 11 through 13 to remove the statistics below the Totals row. Change all the row heights back to the default height (12.75).
4. Insert four rows above row 1 by selecting rows 1 through 4, right-clicking the selection, and clicking Insert on the shortcut menu.
5. Change the row heights as follows: row 5 = 48.00; row 6 = 25.50; and 7 = 38.25. For the range B7:I7, change the format so that the text wraps. Center the range B7:I7.
6. Delete column B by right-clicking the column heading and clicking Delete on the shortcut menu.
7. Insert a new column between columns D and E. Change the column widths as follows: A = 25.00; E = 13.00; and F through I = 9.71. Enter the new column E title `Suggested Reorder` in cell E7.
8. Insert two new columns between columns F and G. Enter the new column G title `Last Month Sales` in cell G7. Enter the new column H title `Current Month Sales` in cell H7.
9. Enhance the worksheet title in cell A5 by using a 36-point purple Cooper Black (or a similar font) font style as shown in Figure 3–91b.
10. Assign the NOW function to cell B6 and format it to the 3/14/2001 style.
11. Delete item Car Air Freshener (row 13). Change Mini Jar Candle's (row 12) cases on hand to 6. Change Large Candle's (row 8) items per case to 8 and cost per case to $131.00. Change Incense Stick's (row 10) sale price per item to $2.00 and Incense Holder's (row 9) sale price per item to $4.75.
12. Freeze column A and rows 1 through 7 by selecting cell B8, clicking the Freeze Panes button (View tab | Window group), and then clicking Freeze Panes on the Freeze Panes gallery.
13. In columns G and H, enter the current month and last month sales values listed in Table 3–13.
14. Insert three new rows immediately above the Totals row. Add the new items data as listed in Table 3–14.

Table 3–13 Dinah's Candle Depot Monthly Sales Values

Inventory Item	Last Month Sales	Current Month Sales
Large Candle	851.6	1703.2
Incense Holder	37.5	56.25
Incense Stick	90	100
Candle Topper	390	260
Mini Jar Candle	1208	1208

Table 3–14 Dinah's Candle Depot New Items

Inventory Item	Cases On Hand	Items Per Case	Reorder Level	Order Time (Weeks)	Last Month Sales	Current Month Sales	Cost Per Case	Sale Price Per Item
Votive Candle	3	18	4	1	300	450	20	1.5
Taper Candle	2	16	3	2	350	612.5	35	3.5
Candle Warmer	2	5	1	3	638	797.5	100	15.95

15. Center the range B8:F15. Use the Currency category in the Format Cells dialog box to assign a Comma style (no dollar signs) with two decimal places and negative numbers within parentheses to the range G8:K16. Draw a thick bottom border in the ranges A7:K7 and A15:K15.
16. As shown in Figure 3–91b, enter and format the Increase Reorder Amt (2), the Decrease Reorder Amt (1), and the Sales Threshold % (25%) information in the range A1:B3. Use format symbols where applicable.

Continued >

In the Lab *continued*

17. Remove any Totals in the range B16:F16. Update and add totals as necessary so that totals appear in the range G16:K16.
18. In cell E8, enter an IF function that applies the following logic and then copy it to the range E9:E15. If (Current Month Sales – Last Month Sales) / Current Month Sales >= Sales Threshold %, then Reorder Level + Increase Reorder Amt, otherwise Reorder Level – Decrease Reorder Amt or =IF((H8-G8)/H8 >= $B$3, D8+$B$1,D8-$B$2).
19. In cell L8, insert a Sparkline Line chart for range G8:H8. Copy cell L8 to the range L9:L16.
20. Unfreeze the worksheet by clicking the Freeze Panes button (View tab | Window group), and then clicking Unfreeze Panes on the Freeze Panes gallery.
21. Preview the worksheet. Use the Orientation button (Page Layout tab | Page Setup group) to fit the printout on one page in landscape orientation.
22. Change the document properties, as specified by your instructor. Change the worksheet header, adding your name, course number, and other information as specified by your instructor. Save the workbook.
23. Use the Zoom button (View tab | Zoom group) to change the view of the worksheet. One by one, select all the percents on the Zoom dialog box. When you are done, return the worksheet to 100% magnification.
24. Preview the formulas version (CTRL+`) in landscape orientation. Close the worksheet without saving the latest changes.
25. Submit the workbook as specified by your instructor.

Instructions Part 2: Start Excel. Open Lab 3-3 Dinah's Weekly Inventory Report Complete. Do not save the workbook in this part. Using the numbers in Table 3–15, analyze the effect of changing the Sales Threshold in cell B3. The first case should result in a Suggested Reorder in cell E15 of 0. The second case should result in a Suggested Reorder in cell E15 of 3. Close the workbook without saving changes. Submit the results of the what-if analysis as specified by your instructor.

Table 3–15 The Dinah's Candle Depot's Sales Threshold Cases

Case	Sales Threshold
1	30%
2	15%

Instructions Part 3: Submit results for this part as requested by your instructor.

1. Start Excel. Open Lab 3-3 Dinah's Weekly Inventory Report Complete. Select cell E8. Write down the formula that Excel displays in the formula bar. Select the range D8:D15. Point to the border surrounding the range and drag the selection to the range E17:E24. Click cell E8, and write down the formula that Excel displays in the formula bar below the one you wrote down earlier. Compare the two formulas. What can you conclude about how Excel responds when you move cells involved in a formula? Click the Undo button on the Quick Access Toolbar.
2. Right-click the range D8:D15 and then click Delete on the shortcut menu. When Excel displays the Delete dialog box, click Shift cells left and then click the OK button. What does Excel display in cell D8? Click cell D8 and then point to the Trace Error button that is displayed to the left of the cell. Write down the ScreenTip that is displayed. Click the Undo button on the Quick Access Toolbar.
3. Right-click the range D8:D15 and then click Insert on the shortcut menu. When Excel displays the Insert dialog box, click 'Shift cells right' and then click the OK button. What does Excel display in the formula bar when you click cell F8? What can you conclude about how Excel responds when you insert cells next to cells involved in a formula? Close the workbook without saving the changes.

Cases and Places

Apply your creative thinking and problem solving skills to design and implement a solution.

1: Bachelor Degree Expense and Resource Projection

Academic

Attending college with limited resources can be a trying experience. One way to alleviate some of the financial stress is to plan ahead. Develop a worksheet following the general layout in Table 3–16 that shows the projected expenses and resources for four years of college. Use the formulas listed in Table 3–17 and the concepts and techniques presented in this chapter to create the worksheet.

Table 3–16 Bachelor Degree Expense and Resource Projection

Expenses	Freshman	Sophomore	Junior	Senior	Total
Room & Board	$12,550.00	Formula A →			—
Tuition & Books	16,450.00	Formula A →			—
Clothes	785.00	Formula A →			—
Entertainment	1,520.00	Formula A →			—
Miscellaneous	936.00	Formula A →			—
Total Expenses	—	—	—	—	—
Resources	**Freshman**	**Sophomore**	**Junior**	**Senior**	**Total**
Savings	Formula B →				
Parents	Formula B →				—
Job	Formula B →				—
Loans	Formula B →				—
Scholarships	Formula B →				—
Total Resources	—	—	—	—	—
Assumptions					
Savings	10.00%				
Parents	12.00%				
Job	11.00%				
Loans	35.00%				
Scholarships	32.00%				
Annual Rate Increase	8.25%				

Table 3–17 Bachelor Degree Expense and Resource Projection Formulas

Formula A = Prior Year's Expense * (1 + Annual Rate Increase)
Formula B = Total Expenses for Year * Corresponding Assumption

After creating the worksheet: (a) perform what-if analysis by changing the percents of the resource assumptions; (b) perform a what-if analysis to determine the effect on the resources by increasing the Annual Rate Increase to 9.95% (answer = $149,520.41); and (c) with the original assumptions, goal seek to determine what the Annual Rate Increase would be for the total expenses to be $175,000 (answer = 20.77%). Submit the workbook and results of the what-if analysis as specified by your instructor.

Continued >

Cases and Places *continued*

2: Fuel Cost Analysis

Personal

You are thinking about buying a new vehicle, and you want to make sure that you get the most fuel savings you can find. You know that there are hybrid vehicles available and so you decide to research them as well as gas-only cars. Your friends also are interested in the results. Together, you decide to research the fuel costs associated with various types of vehicles. Research the gas mileage for six vehicles: three should run only on gas, and the others should be hybrid vehicles, combining gas and battery power. After you find the gas mileage for each vehicle, you will use formulas to calculate the fuel cost for 1 month, 1 year, and three years. Assume that in a typical month, you will drive 400 miles and that the average price of gas is $2.69 per gallon. Develop a worksheet following the general layout in Table 3–18 that shows the fuel cost analysis. Use the formulas listed in Table 3–19 and the concepts and techniques presented in this chapter to create the worksheet. Add a 3-D line chart showing the cost comparisons as an embedded chart.

Table 3–18 Fuel Cost Analysis

Vehicle	Miles Per Gallon	1 Month	1 Year	3 Year
Ford Expedition	17	Formula A	Formula B	Formula C
Dodge RAM 1500	20	---	---	---
Honda Civic	31	---	---	---
Chevy Silverado Hybrid	21	---	---	---
Ford Fusion Hybrid	41	---	---	---
Honda Civic Hybrid	45	---	---	---
Assumptions				
Distance per Month	400			
Price of Gas	$2.69			

Table 3–19 Fuel Cost Analysis Formulas

Formula A = (Distance per Month / Miles per Gallon)*Price of Gas
Formula B = ((Distance per Month / Miles per Gallon)*Price of Gas)*12
Formula C = ((Distance Per Month / Miles per Gallon)*Price of Gas)*36

3: Quarterly Income Projections

Professional

Notable Web Site Design is one of the largest Web site design and Web site hosting companies in the Midwest. The company generates revenue from Web site design and selling Web site hosting space on their Web servers. A fixed percentage of the total net revenue is spent on administrative, equipment, marketing, payroll, and production expenses. A bonus is expensed if the total net revenue for the quarter exceeds $14,000,000. The company's projected receipts and expenditures for the next four quarters are shown in Table 3–20.

With this data, you have been asked to prepare a worksheet similar to Figure 3–87 on page EX 210 for the next management team meeting. The worksheet should show total net revenues, total expenditures, and operating income for each quarterly period. Include a 3-D Pie chart on a separate sheet that shows the quarterly income contributions to the annual operating income. Use the concepts and techniques presented in this chapter to create and format the worksheet and chart.

During the meeting, one manager lobbied to reduce marketing expenditures by 1.25% and payroll costs by 2.75%. Perform a what-if analysis reflecting the proposed changes in expenditures. The changes should result in an operating income of $22,425,581 for the year. Using the original assumptions shown in Table 3–20, another manager asked to what extent marketing would have to be reduced to generate an annual operating income of $21,000,000. Marketing would to be reduced from 13.50% by 1.92% to 11.58%.

Submit the workbook and results of the what-if analysis as specified by your instructor.

Table 3–20 Notable Website Design Operating Income Projection by Quarter

Revenues	Quarter 1	Quarter 2	Quarter 3	Quarter 4
Site Design	12,247,999	15,234,813	16,567,102	10,619,201
Web Hosting	1,678,153	5,901,988	4,718,231	1,569,378
Expenditures				
Administrative	10.50%			
Bonus	250,000.00			
Equipment	17.75%			
Marketing	13.50%			
Payroll	22.50%			
Production	6.30%			
Revenue for Bonus	14,000,000.00			

1 Databases and Database Objects: An Introduction

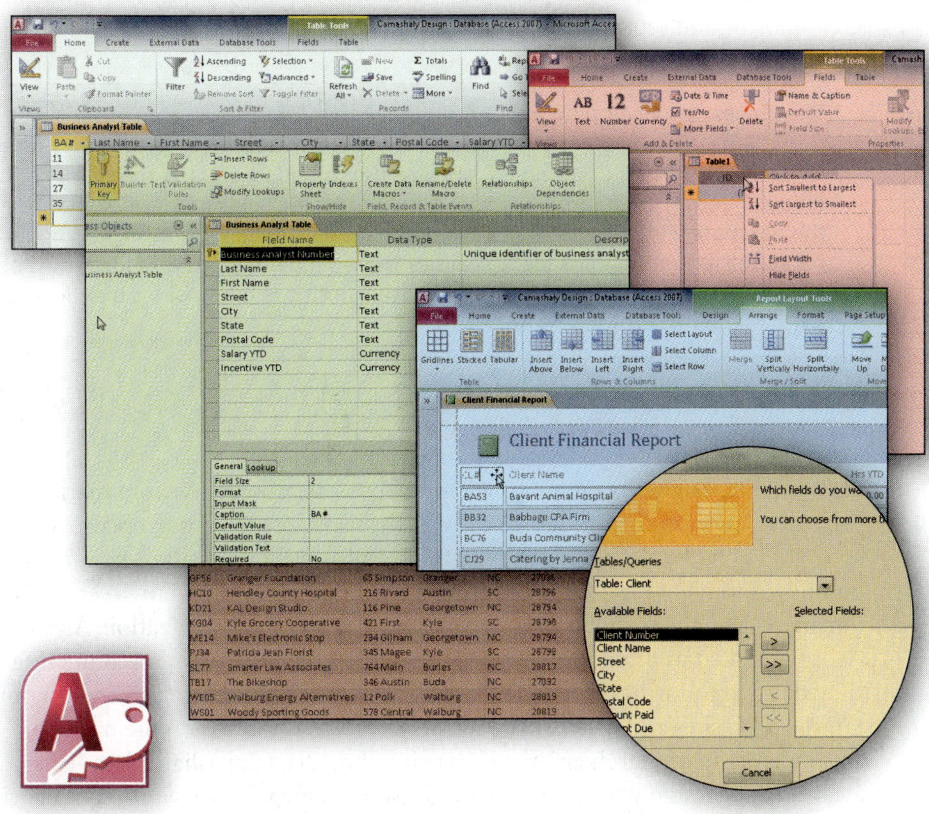

Objectives

You will have mastered the material in this chapter when you can:

- Design a database to satisfy a collection of requirements
- Describe the features of the Access window
- Create a database
- Create tables in Datasheet and Design views
- Add records to a table
- Close a database
- Open a database
- Print the contents of a table
- Create and use a query
- Create and use a form
- Create and print custom reports
- Modify a report in Layout view

1 Databases and Database Objects: An Introduction

Introduction

The term **database** describes a collection of data organized in a manner that allows access, retrieval, and use of that data. Microsoft Access 2010, usually referred to as simply Access, is a database management system. A **database management system**, such as Access, is software that allows you to use a computer to create a database; add, change, and delete data in the database; ask and answer questions concerning the data in the database; and create forms and reports using the data in the database.

Project Planning Guidelines

The process of developing a database that communicates specific information requires careful analysis and planning. As a starting point, establish why the database is needed. Once the purpose is determined, analyze the intended users of the database and their unique needs. Then, gather information about the topic and decide what to include in the database. Finally, determine the database design and style that will be most successful at delivering the message. Details of these guidelines are provided in Appendix A. In addition, each project in the Office chapters in this book provides practical applications of these planning considerations.

Project — Database Creation

Camashaly Design Group is a small company that provides custom marketing solutions for the service, nonprofit, and retail sectors. Alyssa Morgan, Camden Scott, and Ashton James started the business after they graduated from a local university. The three owners, all computer graphics design majors and business minors, worked on a service learning project during college that produced a Web site for a nonprofit organization. Alyssa, Camden, and Ashton worked well together. Upon researching the local area for competing businesses, they decided to form their own company. The company specializes in designing and maintaining Web sites and using social networking Web sites for online marketing. They also conduct market research and develop printed media. Camashaly already has received one award for its design work. Camashaly is also recognized for its efforts in providing work opportunities to individuals who want flexible schedules and to student interns.

BTW

BTWs
For a complete list of the BTWs found in the margins of the Office and Windows chapters in this book, visit the Microsoft Office and Concepts CourseMate Web site at www.cengagebrain.com and then navigate to the BTW resource for this book.

Camashaly uses business analysts to work collaboratively with clients. Business analysts are employees who translate business requirements into marketing specifications and serve as the interface between clients and Camashaly. Business analysts are paid a base salary and can earn incentive pay for maintaining and expanding client relationships.

Camashaly charges a one-time fee for Web site development. Clients can pay for Web site maintenance by contracting for a specified number of hours or can pay for maintenance on an hour-by-hour basis. Other fees vary depending on the specific scope of work.

To ensure that operations run smoothly, Camashaly organizes data on its clients and business analysts in a database managed by Access. In this way, Camashaly keeps its data current and accurate while the owners can analyze the data for trends and produce a variety of useful reports. In this chapter, you will create the Camashaly database.

In a **relational database** such as those maintained by Access, a database consists of a collection of tables, each of which contains information on a specific subject. Figure 1–1 shows the database for Camashaly Design. It consists of two tables: the Client table (Figure 1–1a) contains information about the clients to whom Camashaly provides services, and the Business Analyst table (Figure 1–1b) contains information about the business analysts to whom these clients are assigned.

caption for Client Number field

fields

Client

CL #	Client Name	Street	City	State	Postal Code	Amount Paid	Current Due	Hrs YTD	BA #
BA53	Bavant Animal Hospital	134 Main	Burles	NC	28817	$0.00	$7,500.00	0.00	11
BB32	Babbage CPA Firm	464 Linnell	Austin	SC	28796	$1,500.00	$500.00	5.00	14
BC76	Buda Community Clinic	867 Ridge	Buda	NC	27032	$2,500.00	$750.00	2.50	11
CJ29	Catering by Jenna	123 Second	Granger	NC	27036	$3,000.00	$1,000.00	15.50	27
GA74	Grant Antiques	78 Catawba	Georgetown	NC	28794	$5,500.00	$3,200.00	34.50	14
GF56	Granger Foundation	65 Simpson	Granger	NC	27036	$0.00	$6,500.00	0.00	11
HC10	Hendley County Hospital	216 Rivard	Austin	SC	28796	$3,100.00	$1,200.00	12.00	27
KD21	KAL Design Studio	116 Pine	Georgetown	NC	28794	$6,000.00	$3,200.00	30.50	14
KG04	Kyle Grocery Cooperative	421 First	Kyle	SC	28798	$3,200.00	$0.00	5.00	11
ME14	Mike's Electronic Stop	234 Gilham	Georgetown	NC	28794	$2,500.00	$1,500.00	8.50	27
PJ34	Patricia Jean Florist	345 Magee	Kyle	SC	28798	$0.00	$5,200.00	0.00	27
SL77	Smarter Law Associates	764 Main	Burles	NC	28817	$3,800.00	$0.00	10.50	11
TB17	The Bikeshop	346 Austin	Buda	NC	27032	$2,750.00	$1,200.00	14.00	27
WE05	Walburg Energy Alternatives	12 Polk	Walburg	NC	28819	$4,500.00	$1,450.00	19.50	14
WS01	Woody Sporting Goods	578 Central	Walburg	NC	28819	$2,250.00	$1,600.00	18.50	14

records

BA # (Business Analyst Number) is 11

(a) Client table

caption for Business Analyst Number field

Business Analyst Table

BA #	Last Name	First Name	Street	City	State	Postal Code	Salary YTD	Incentive YTD
11	Kerry	Cordelia	251 Painter	Georgetown	NC	28794	$3,200.00	$3,450.00
14	Martinez	Manuel	3125 Steel	Kyle	SC	28797	$3,100.00	$2,430.00
27	Liu	Jan	265 Marble	Byron	SC	28795	$3,400.00	$2,280.00
35	Scott	Jeff	1925 Pine	Georgetown	NC	28794	$500.00	$0.00

BA # (Business Analyst Number) for Cordelia Kerry is 11

(b) Business Analyst table

Figure 1–1

The rows in the tables are called **records**. A record contains information about a given person, product, or event. A row in the Client table, for example, contains information about a specific client, such as the client's name, address information, and other data.

The columns in the tables are called fields. A **field** contains a specific piece of information within a record. In the Client table, for example, the fourth field, City, contains the name of the city where the client is located.

The first field in the Client table is CL #, which is an abbreviation for Client Number. Camashaly Design assigns each client a client number. As is common to the way in which many organizations format client numbers, Camashaly Design calls it a number, although it actually contains letters. The Camashaly client numbers consist of two uppercase letters followed by a two-digit number.

The client numbers are unique; that is, no two clients are assigned the same number. Such a field can be used as a **unique identifier**. A unique identifier, as its name suggests, is a way of uniquely identifying each record in the database. A given client number will appear only in a single record in the table. Only one record exists, for example, in which the client number is BB32. A unique identifier also is called a **primary key**. Thus, the Client Number field is the primary key for the Client table.

The next eight fields in the Client table are Client Name, Street, City, State, Postal Code, Amount Paid, Current Due, and Hrs YTD, which is an abbreviation for Contract Hours YTD. YTD is an abbreviation for year to date. The Amount Paid column contains the amount that the client has paid Camashaly Design YTD prior to the current period. The Current Due column contains the amount due to Camashaly for the current period. The Hrs YTD column contains the number of hours the client has contracted for Web site maintenance so far this year. For example, client BB32 is Babbage CPA Firm. The address is 464 Linnell in Austin, South Carolina. The postal code is 28796. The client has paid $1,500.00 for services so far this year. The amount due for the current period is $500.00. The client has contracted for 5.00 hours of Web site maintenance.

Camashaly assigns a single business analyst to work with each client. The last column in the Client table, BA #, which is an abbreviation for Business Analyst Number, gives the number of the client's business analyst.

The first field in the Business Analyst table is also BA #, an abbreviation for Business Analyst Number. The business analyst numbers are unique, so the Business Analyst Number field is the primary key of the Business Analyst table.

The other fields in the Business Analyst table are Last Name, First Name, Street, City, State, Postal Code, Salary YTD, and Incentive YTD. The Salary YTD field gives the salary paid to the analyst thus far this year. The Incentive YTD gives the incentive for which the analyst qualified thus far this year. For example, business analyst 14 is Manuel Martinez. His address is 3125 Steel in Kyle, South Carolina. The Postal Code is 28797. So far this year, he has been paid $3,100.00 in salary. He has earned $2,430.00 in incentive pay.

The business analyst number appears in both the Client table and the Business Analyst table, and relates clients and business analysts. For example, in the Client table, you see that the business analyst number for client Babbage CPA Firm is 14. To find the name of this business analyst, look for the row in the Business Analyst table that contains 14 in the BA # column. After you have found it, you know the client is assigned to Manuel Martinez. To find all the clients assigned to Cordelia Kerry, you would first look in the Business Analyst table to find that her number is 11. You would then look through the Client table for all the clients that contain 11 in the BA # column. Her clients are BA53 (Bavant Animal Hospital), BC76 (Buda Community Clinic), GF56 (Granger Foundation), KG04 (Kyle Grocery Cooperative), and SL77 (Smarter Law Associates).

The last business analyst in the Business Analyst table, Jeff Scott, has not been assigned any clients yet; therefore, his business analyst number, 35, does not appear on any row in the Client table.

Overview

As you read this chapter, you will learn how to create the database shown in Figure 1–1 by performing these general tasks:

- Design the database.
- Create a new blank database.
- Create a table and add the records.
- Preview and print the contents of a table.
- Create a second table and import the records.
- Create a simple query.
- Create a simple form.
- Create and modify a report.

Plan Ahead

Database Design Guidelines

Database design refers to the arrangement of data into tables and fields. In the example in this chapter, the design is specified, but in many cases, you will have to determine the design based on what you want the system to accomplish.

When designing a database to satisfy a given set of requirements, the actions you take and the decisions you make will determine the tables and fields that will be included in the database. As you create a database, such as the one shown in Figure 1–1 on page AC 3, you should follow these general guidelines:

1. **Identify the tables.** Examine the requirements for the database to identify the main objects that are involved. There will be a table for each object you identify.

   In one database, for example, the main objects might be departments and employees. Thus, there would be two tables: one for departments and the other for employees. In another database, the main objects might be clients and business analysts. In this case, there also would be two tables: one for clients and the other for business analysts. In still another database, the main objects might be books, publishers, and authors. This database would require three tables: one for books, a second for publishers, and a third for authors.

2. **Determine the primary keys.** Recall that the primary key is the unique identifier for records in the table. For each table, determine the unique identifier. In a Department table, for example, the unique identifier might be the Department Code. For a Book table, the unique identifier might be the ISBN.

3. **Determine the additional fields.** The primary key will be a field or combination of fields in a table. A table typically will contain many additional fields, each of which contains a type of data. Examine the project requirements to determine these additional fields. For example, in an Employee table, the additional fields might include such fields as Employee Name, Street Address, City, State, Postal Code, Date Hired, Salary, and so on.

4. **Determine relationships between the tables.** Examine the list of tables you have created to see which tables are related. When you determine that two tables are related, include matching fields in the two tables. For example, in a database containing employees and departments, there is a relationship between the two tables because one department can have many employees assigned to it. Department Code could be the matching field in the two tables.

5. **Determine data types for the fields.** For each field, determine the type of data the field can contain. One field, for example, might contain only numbers. Another field might contain currency amounts, while a third field might contain only dates. Some fields contain text data, meaning any combination of letters, numbers, and special characters (!, ;, ', &, and so on). For example, in an Employee table, the Date Hired field would contain dates, the Salary field would contain currency amounts, and the Hours Worked field would contain numbers. The other fields in the Employee table would contain text data, such as Employee Name and Department Code.

6. **Identify and remove any unwanted redundancy.** Redundancy is the storing of a piece of data in more than one place. Redundancy usually, but not always, causes problems, such as wasted space, difficulties with update, and possible data inconsistency. Examine each table you have created to see if it contains redundancy and, if so, determine whether the redundancy causes the problems described. If it does, remove the redundancy by splitting the table into two tables. For example, you might have a single table of employees. In addition to typical employee data (name, address, earnings, and so on), the table might contain Department Number and Department Name. If so, the Department Name could repeat multiple times. Every employee whose department number is 12, for example, would have the same department name. It would be better to split the table into two tables: one for Employees and one for Department. In the Department table, the Department Name is stored only once.

7. **Determine a storage location for the database.** The database you have designed will be stored in a single file. You need to determine a location in which to store the file.

8. **Determine additional properties for fields.** Before creating the database, determine any other properties you should specify for the fields. These could include a field size, which is

(continued)

Plan Ahead

(continued)

the maximum number of characters that can be stored in the field. If you want something other than the field name to appear at the top of a column (such as an abbreviation), you can change the caption to the desired heading. You also can add a description, which is a message that appears on the screen concerning a field whenever the field is selected.

9. **Determine the best method for distributing the database objects.** The traditional method of distributing database objects uses a printer to produce a hard copy of a table or report on paper. You also can distribute the table as an electronic image that mirrors the original table's appearance.

When necessary, more specific details concerning the above guidelines are presented at appropriate points in the chapter. The chapter also will identify the actions performed and decisions made regarding these guidelines during the creation of the database shown in Figure 1–1 on page AC 3.

Designing a Database

This section illustrates the database design process by showing how you would design the database for Camashaly Design from a set of requirements. In this section, you will use commonly accepted shorthand to represent the tables and fields that make up the database as well as the primary keys for the tables. For each table, you give the name of the table followed by a set of parentheses. Within the parentheses is a list of the fields in the table separated by columns. You underline the primary key. For example,

Product (<u>Product Code</u>, Description, On Hand, Price)

represents a table called Product. The Product table contains four fields: Product Code, Description, On Hand, and Price. The Product Code field is the primary key.

BTW

Determining Database Requirements
The determination of database requirements is part of a process known as systems analysis. A systems analyst examines existing and proposed documents, and examines organizational policies to determine exactly the type of data needs the database must support.

Database Requirements

The Camashaly Design database must maintain information on both clients and business analysts. The business currently keeps this data in two Word tables and two Excel workbooks, as shown in Figure 1–2. They use Word tables for address information and Excel workbooks for financial information.

Client Number	Client Name	Street	City	State	Postal Code
BA53	Bavant Animal Hospital	134 Main	Burles	NC	28817
BB32	Babbage CPA Firm	464 Linnell	Austin	SC	28796
BC76	Buda Community Clinic	867 Ridge	Buda	NC	27032
CJ29	Catering by Jenna	123 Second	Granger	NC	27036
GA74	Grant Antiques	78 Catawba	Georgetown	NC	28794
GF56	Granger Foundation	65 Simpson	Granger	NC	27036
HC10	Hendley County Hospital	216 Rivard	Austin	SC	28796
KD21	KAL Design Studio	116 Pine	Georgetown	NC	28794
KG04	Kyle Grocery Cooperative	421 First	Kyle	SC	28798
ME14	Mike's Electronic Stop	234 Gilham	Georgetown	NC	28794
PJ34	Patricia Jean Florist	345 Magee	Kyle	SC	28798
SL77	Smarter Law Associates	764 Main	Burles	NC	28817
TB17	The Bikeshop	346 Austin	Buda	NC	27032
WE05	Walburg Energy Alternatives	12 Polk	Walburg	NC	28819
WS01	Woody Sporting Goods	578 Central	Walburg	NC	28819

Figure 1–2 (a) Client Address Information (Word Table)

	A	B	C	D	E	F	G	H
1	Client Number	Client Name	Amount Paid	Current Due	Contract Hours YTD			
2	BA53	Bavant Animal Hospital	0.00	7,500.00	0			
3	BB32	Babbage CPA Firm	1,500.00	500.00	5			
4	BC76	Buda Community Clinic	2,500.00	750.00	2.5			
5	CJ29	Catering by Jenna	3,000.00	1,000.00	15.5			
6	GA74	Grant Antiques	5,500.00	3,200.00	34.5			
7	GF56	Granger Foundation	0.00	6,500.00	0			
8	HC10	Hendley County Hospital	3,100.00	1,200.00	12			
9	KD21	KAL Design Studio	6,000.00	3,200.00	30.5			
10	KG04	Kyle Grocery Cooperative	3,200.00	0.00	5			
11	ME14	Mike's Electronic Stop	2,500.00	1,500.00	8.5			
12	PJ34	Patricia Jean Florist	0.00	5,200.00	0			
13	SL77	Smarter Law Associates	3,800.00	0.00	10.5			
14	TB17	The Bikeshop	2,750.00	1,200.00	14			
15	WE05	Walburg Energy Alternatives	4,500.00	1,450.00	19.5			
16	WS01	Woody Sporting Goods	2,250.00	1,600.00	18.5			

Figure 1–2 (b) Client Financial Information (Excel Worksheet)

Business Analyst Number	Last Name	First Name	Street	City	State	Postal Code
11	Kerry	Cordelia	251 Painter	Georgetown	NC	28794
14	Martinez	Manuel	3125 Steel	Kyle	SC	28797
27	Liu	Jan	265 Marble	Byron	SC	28795
35	Scott	Jeff	1925 Pine	Georgetown	NC	28794

Figure 1–2 (c) Business Analyst Address Information (Word Table)

	A	B	C	D	E	F	G	H	I
1	Business Analyst Number	Last Name	First Name	Salary YTD	Incentive YTD				
2	11	Kerry	Cordelia	3,200.00	3,450.00				
3	14	Martinez	Manuel	3,100.00	2,430.00				
4	27	Liu	Jan	3,400.00	2,280.00				
5	35	Scott	Jeff	500.00	0.00				

Figure 1–2 (d) Business Analyst Financial Information (Excel Worksheet)

For clients, Camashaly needs to maintain address data. It currently keeps this address data in a Word table (Figure 1–2a). It also maintains financial data for each client. This includes the amount paid, current amount due, and contract hours YTD for the client. It keeps these amounts, along with the client name and number, in the Excel workbook shown in Figure 1–2b.

Camashaly keeps business analyst address data in a Word table, as shown in Figure 1–2c. Just as with clients, it keeps financial data for business analysts, including their salary YTD and incentive YTD, in a separate Excel workbook, as shown in Figure 1–2d.

Finally, it keeps track of which clients are assigned to which business analysts. Each client is assigned to a single business analyst, but each business analyst might be assigned many clients. Currently, for example, clients BA53 (Bavant Animal Hospital), BC76 (Buda Community Clinic), GF56 (Granger Foundation), KG04 (Kyle Grocery Cooperative), and SL77 (Smarter Law Associates) are assigned to business analyst 11 (Cordelia Kerry). Clients BB32 (Babbage CPA Firm), GA74 (Grant Antiques), KD21 (KAL Design Studio), WE05 (Walburg Energy Alternatives), and WS01 (Woody Sporting Goods) are assigned to business analyst 14 (Manuel Martinez). Clients CJ29 (Catering by Jenna), HC10 (Hendley County Hospital), ME14 (Mike's Electronic Stop), PJ34 (Patricia Jean Florist), and TB17 (The Bikeshop) are assigned to business analyst 27 (Jan Liu). Camashaly has an additional business analyst, Jeff Scott, whose number has been assigned as 35, but who has not yet been assigned any clients.

BTW

Additional Data for Camashaly

There are many other types of data that Camashaly could include in a database. For example, they might keep all employee information in a database as well as information on client contracts and an inventory of hardware and software.

Naming Tables and Fields

BTW **Naming Files**
The following characters cannot be used in a file name: question mark (?), quotation mark ("), slash (/), backslash (\ ), colon (:), asterisk (*), vertical bar (|), greater than symbol (>), and less than symbol (<).

In designing your database, you must name the tables and fields. Thus, before beginning the design process, you must understand the rules Access applies to table and field names. These rules are:

1. Names can be up to 64 characters in length.
2. Names can contain letters, digits, and spaces, as well as most of the punctuation symbols.
3. Names cannot contain periods (.), exclamation points (!), accent graves (`), or square brackets ([ ]).
4. The same name cannot be used for two different fields in the same table.

The approach to naming tables and fields used in this text is to begin the names with an uppercase letter and to use lowercase for the other letters. In multiple-word names, each word begins with an uppercase letter, and there is a space between words (for example, Client Number). You should know that other approaches exist, all of which are acceptable in Access. Some people omit the space (ClientNumber). Still others use an underscore in place of the space (Client_Number). Finally, some use an underscore in place of a space, but use the same case for all letters (CLIENT_NUMBER or client_number).

Identifying the Tables

BTW **Naming Fields**
Access 2010 has a number of reserved words, words that have a special meaning to Access. You cannot use these reserved words as field names. For example, Name is a reserved word and could not be used in the Client table to describe a client's name. For a complete list of reserved words in Access 2010, consult Access Help.

Now that you know the rules for naming tables and fields, you are ready to begin the design process. The first step is to identify the main objects involved in the requirements. For the Camashaly Design database, the main objects are clients and business analysts. This leads to two tables, which you must name. Reasonable names for these two tables are:

Client
Business Analyst

Determining the Primary Keys

The next step is to identify the fields that will be the unique identifiers, or primary keys. Client numbers uniquely identify clients, and business analyst numbers uniquely identify business analysts. Thus, the primary key for the Client table is the client number, and the primary key for the Business Analyst table is the business analyst number. Reasonable names for these fields would be Client Number and Business Analyst Number, respectively. Adding these primary keys to the tables gives:

Client (<u>Client Number</u>)
Business Analyst (<u>Business Analyst Number</u>)

Determining Additional Fields

After identifying the primary keys, you need to determine and name the additional fields. In addition to the client number, the Client Address Information shown in Figure 1–2a on page AC 6 contains the client name, street, city, state, and postal code. These would be fields in the Client table. The Client Financial Information shown in Figure 1–2b also contains the client number and client name, which are already included in the Client table. The financial information also contains the amount paid, current due, and contract hours YTD. Adding the amount paid, current due, and contract hours YTD fields to those already identified in the Client table and assigning reasonable names gives:

Client (<u>Client Number</u>, Client Name, Street, City, State, Postal Code, Amount Paid, Current Due, Contract Hours YTD)

Similarly, examining the Business Analyst Address Information in Figure 1–2c adds the last name, first name, street, city, state, and postal code fields to the Business Analyst table. In addition to the business analyst number, last name, and first name, the Business Analyst Financial Information in Figure 1–2d would add the salary YTD and Incentive YTD. Adding these fields to the Business Analyst table and assigning reasonable names gives:

Business Analyst (<u>Business Analyst Number</u>, Last Name, First Name, Street, City, State, Postal Code, Salary YTD, Incentive YTD)

Determining and Implementing Relationships Between the Tables

Plan Ahead

Determine relationships between the tables.

The most common type of relationship you will encounter between tables is the **one-to-many relationship**. This means that each row in the first table may be associated with many rows in the second table, but each row in the second table is associated with only one row in the first. The first table is called the "one" table and the second is called the "many" table. For example, there may be a relationship between departments and employees, in which each department can have many employees, but each employee is assigned to only one department. In this relationship, there would be two tables, Department and Employee. The Department table would be the "one" table in the relationship. The Employee table would be the "many" table.

To determine relationships between tables, you can follow these general guidelines:

- Identify the "one" table.
- Identify the "many" table.
- Include the primary key from the "one" table as a field in the "many" table.

According to the requirements, each client has one business analyst, but each business analyst can have many clients. Thus, the Business Analyst table is the "one" table, and the Client table is the "many" table. To implement this one-to-many relationship between business analysts and clients, add the Business Analyst Number field (the primary key of the Business Analyst table) to the Client table. This produces:

Client (<u>Client Number</u>, Client Name, Street, City, State, Postal Code, Amount Paid, Current Due, Contract Hours YTD, Business Analyst Number)
Business Analyst (<u>Business Analyst Number</u>, Last Name, First Name, Street, City, State, Postal Code, Salary YTD, Incentive YTD)

BTW
Database Design Language (DBDL)
DBDL is a commonly accepted shorthand representation for showing the structure of a relational database. You write the name of the table and then within parentheses you list all the columns in the table. If the columns continue beyond one line, indent the subsequent lines.

Determining Data Types for the Fields

Each field has a **data type**. This indicates the type of data that can be stored in the field. Three of the most commonly used data types are:

1. **Text** — The field can contain any characters. A maximum number of 255 characters is allowed in a field whose data type is Text.
2. **Number** — The field can contain only numbers. The numbers either can be positive or negative. Fields are assigned this type so they can be used in arithmetic operations. Fields that contain numbers but will not be used for arithmetic operations (such as postal codes) usually are assigned a data type of Text.
3. **Currency** — The field can contain only monetary data. The values will appear with currency symbols, such as dollar signs, commas, and decimal points, and with two digits following the decimal point. Like numeric fields, you can use currency fields in arithmetic operations. Access assigns a size to currency fields automatically.

Table 1–1 shows the other data types that are available in Access.

BTW
Data Types
Different database management systems have different available data types. Even data types that are essentially the same can have different names. The Currency data type in Access, for example, is referred to as Money in SQL Server.

Table 1–1 Additional Data Types

Data Type	Description
Memo	Field can store a variable amount of text or combinations of text and numbers where the total number of characters may exceed 255.
Date/Time	Field can store dates and times.
AutoNumber	Field can store a unique sequential number that Access assigns to a record. Access will increment the number by 1 as each new record is added.
Yes/No	Field can store only one of two values. The choices are Yes/No, True/False, or On/Off.
OLE Object	Field can store an OLE object, which is an object linked to or embedded in the table.
Hyperlink	Field can store text that can be used as a hyperlink address.
Attachment	Field can contain an attached file. Images, spreadsheets, documents, charts, and so on can be attached to this field in a record in the database. You can view and edit the attached file.
Calculated	Field specified as a calculation based on other fields. The value is not actually stored.

In the Client table, because the Client Number, Client Name, Street, City, and State can all contain letters, their data types should be Text. The data type for Postal Code is Text instead of Number because postal codes are not used in arithmetic operations; you do not add postal codes or find an average postal code, for example. The Amount Paid and Current Due fields both contain monetary data, so their data types should be Currency. The Contract Hours YTD field contains a number that is not a currency amount, so its data type should be Number.

Similarly, in the Business Analyst table, the data type for the Business Analyst Number, Last Name, First Name, Street, City, State, and Postal Code fields all should be Text. The Salary YTD and Incentive YTD fields both contain monetary amounts, so their data types should be Currency.

Fields whose data type is Number often require you to change the field size, which is the storage space assigned to the field by Access. Table 1–2 shows the possible field sizes for Number fields. If the size were Byte, Integer, or Long Integer, for example, only integers could be stored. If you try to store a value that has decimal places, such as 2.50, the portion to the right of the decimal point would be removed, giving a result of 2. To address this problem, you would change to a size such as Single.

Table 1–2 Field Sizes for Number Fields

Field Size	Description
Byte	Integer value in the range of 0 to 255
Integer	Integer value in the range of –32,768 to 32,767
Long Integer	Integer value in the range of –2,147,483,648 to 2,147,483,647
Single	Numeric values with decimal places to seven significant digits — requires 4 bytes of storage
Double	Numeric values with decimal places to more accuracy than Single — requires 8 bytes of storage
Replication ID	Special identifier required for replication
Decimal	Numeric values with decimal places to more accuracy than Single or Double — requires 12 bytes of storage.

Identifying and Removing Redundancy

Redundancy means storing the same fact in more than one place. It usually results from placing too many fields in a table — fields that really belong in separate tables — and often causes serious problems. If you had not realized there were two objects, clients and business analysts, for example, you might have placed all the data in a single Client table. Figure 1–3 shows an example of a table that includes both client and business analyst information. Notice that the data for a given business analyst (number, name, address, and so on) occurs on more than one record. The data for analyst 11, Cordelia Kerry, is repeated in the figure.

Client Table

Client Number	Client Name	Street	...	Business Analyst Number	Last Name	First Name	...
BA53	Bavant Animal Hospital	134 Main	...	11	Kerry	Cordelia	...
BB32	Babbage CPA Firm	464 Linnell	...	14	Martinez	Manuel	...
BC76	Buda Community Clinic	867 Ridge	...	11	Kerry	Cordelia	...
...	...	...	...	...	...	...	...

business analyst numbers are 11

name of business analyst 11 appears more than once

Figure 1–3

Storing this data on multiple records is an example of redundancy, which causes several problems, including:

1. Wasted storage space. The name of business analyst 11, Cordelia Kerry, for example, should be stored only once. Storing this fact several times is wasteful.
2. More difficult database updates. If, for example, Cordelia Kerry's name is spelled wrong and needs to be changed in the database, her name would need to be changed in several different places.
3. A possibility of inconsistent data. Nothing prohibits the business analyst's last name from being Kerry on client BA53's record and Bronson on client BC76's record. The data would be inconsistent. In both cases, the business analyst number is 11, but the last names are different.

The solution to the problem is to place the redundant data in a separate table, one in which the data no longer will be redundant. If, for example, you place the data for business analysts in a separate table (Figure 1–4), the data for each business analyst will appear only once.

Client Table

Client Number	Client Name	Street	...	Business Analyst Number
BA53	Bavant Animal Hospital	134 Main	...	11
BB32	Babbage CPA Firm	464 Linnell	...	14
BC76	Buda Community Clinic	867 Ridge	...	11
...	...	...		

business analyst numbers are 11

Business Analyst Table

Business Analyst Number	Last Name	First Name	...
11	Kerry	Cordelia	...
14	Martinez	Manuel	...
...	...		...

name of business analyst 11 appears only once

Figure 1–4

BTW

Postal Codes
Some organizations with customers throughout the country have a separate table of postal codes, cities, and states. When placing an order, you typically are asked for your postal code (or ZIP code), rather than city, state, and postal code. You then are asked to confirm that the city and state correspond to that postal code.

Notice that you need to have the business analyst number in both tables. Without it, there would be no way to tell which business analyst is associated with which client. The remaining business analyst data, however, was removed from the Client table and placed in the Business Analyst table. This new arrangement corrects the problems of redundancy in the following ways:

1. Because the data for each business analyst is stored only once, space is not wasted.
2. Changing the name of a business analyst is easy. You have only to change one row in the Business Analyst table.
3. Because the data for a business analyst is stored only once, inconsistent data cannot occur. Designing to omit redundancy will help you to produce good and valid database designs.

You should always examine your design to see if it contains redundancy. If it does, you should decide whether you need to remove the redundancy by creating a separate table.

If you examine your design, you'll see that there is one area of redundancy (see the data in Figure 1–1 on page AC 3). Cities and states are both repeated. Every client whose postal code is 28794, for example, has Georgetown as the city and NC as the state. To remove this redundancy, you would create a table whose primary key is Postal Code and that contains City and State as additional fields. City and State would be removed from the Client table. Having City, State, and Postal Code in a table is very common, however, and usually you would not take such action. No other redundancy exists in your tables.

For an introduction to Windows 7 and instruction about how to perform basic Windows 7 tasks, read the Office 2010 and Windows 7 chapter in this book, where you can learn how to resize windows, change screen resolution, create folders, move and rename files, use Windows Help, and much more.

To Start Access

If you are using a computer to step through the project in this chapter and you want your screens to match the figures in the Office and Windows chapters in this book, you should change your screen's resolution to 1024 × 768. For information about how to change a computer's resolution, refer to the Office 2010 and Windows 7 chapter in this book.

The following steps, which assume Windows 7 is running, start Access based on a typical installation. You may need to ask your instructor how to start Access for your computer. For a detailed example of the procedure summarized below, refer to the Office 2010 and Windows 7 chapter.

1. Click the Start button on the Windows 7 taskbar to display the Start menu.
2. Type `Microsoft Access` as the search text in the 'Search programs and files' text box and watch the search results appear on the Start menu.
3. Click Microsoft Access 2010 in the search results on the Start menu to start Access and display the Backstage view for Access.
4. If the Access window is not maximized, click the Maximize button next to the Close button on its title bar to maximize the window.

Creating a Database

In Access, all the tables, reports, forms, and queries that you create are stored in a single file called a database. Thus, you first must create the database to hold the tables, reports, forms, and queries. You can use either the Blank database option or a template to create a new database. If you already know the tables and fields you want in your database, you would use the Blank database option. If not, you can use a template. Templates can guide you by suggesting some commonly used databases.

Plan Ahead

Determine a storage location for the database.

When creating a database, you must decide which storage medium to use.

If you always work on the same computer and have no need to transport your database to a different location, then your computer's hard drive will suffice as a storage location. It is a good idea, however, to save a backup copy of your database on a separate medium in case the file becomes corrupted or the computer's hard drive fails.

If you plan to work on your database in various locations or on multiple computers, then you can consider saving your projects on a portable medium, such as a USB flash drive or CD. The projects in the Office chapters in this book are stored on a USB flash drive, which saves files quickly and reliably and can be reused. CDs are easily portable and serve as good backups for the final versions of projects because they generally can save files only one time.

For an introduction to Office 2010 and instruction about how to perform basic tasks in Office 2010 programs, read the Office 2010 and Windows 7 chapter in this book, where you can learn how to start a program, use the Ribbon, save a file, open a file, quit a program, use Help, and much more.

To Create a Database

Because you already know the tables and fields you want in the Camashaly Design database, you would use the Blank database option rather than using a template. The following steps assume you already have created folders for storing your files, for example, a CIS 101 folder (for your class) that contains an Access folder (for your assignments). Thus, these steps save the document in the Access folder in the CIS 101 folder on a USB flash drive using the file name, Camashaly Design. For a detailed example of the procedure summarized below, refer to the Office 2010 and Windows 7 chapter in this book.

1. With a USB flash drive connected to one of the computer's USB ports, ensure the New tab is selected in the Backstage view and that Blank database is selected in the New gallery.
2. Click the Browse button in the right pane of the New gallery to display the File New Database dialog box.
3. Type `Camashaly Design` in the File New Database dialog box to change the file name. Do not press the ENTER key after typing the file name.
4. Navigate to the desired save location (in this case, the Access folder in the CIS 101 folder [or your class folder] on the USB flash drive).
5. Click the OK button, which returns you to the New gallery. (Your screen may show Camashaly Design.accdb.)
6. Click the Create button in the right pane of the New gallery to create the database on the selected drive with the entered file name (Figure 1–5).

BTW

Q&As

For a complete list of the Q&As found in many of the step-by-step sequences in the Office and Windows chapters in this book, visit the Microsoft Office and Concepts CourseMate Web site at www.cengagebrain.com and then navigate to the Q&A resource for this book.

Q&A The title bar for my Navigation Pane contains All Tables rather than All Access Objects, as in the figure. Is that a problem?

It is not a problem. The title bar indicates how the Navigation Pane is organized. You can carry out the steps in the text with either organization. To make your screens match the ones in the text, click the Navigation Pane arrow and then click Object Type.

Q&A I do not have the Search bar that appears on the figure. Is that a problem?

It is not a problem. If your Navigation Pane does not display a Search bar and you want your screens to match the ones in the text, right-click the Navigation Pane title bar arrow to display a shortcut menu, and then click Search Bar.

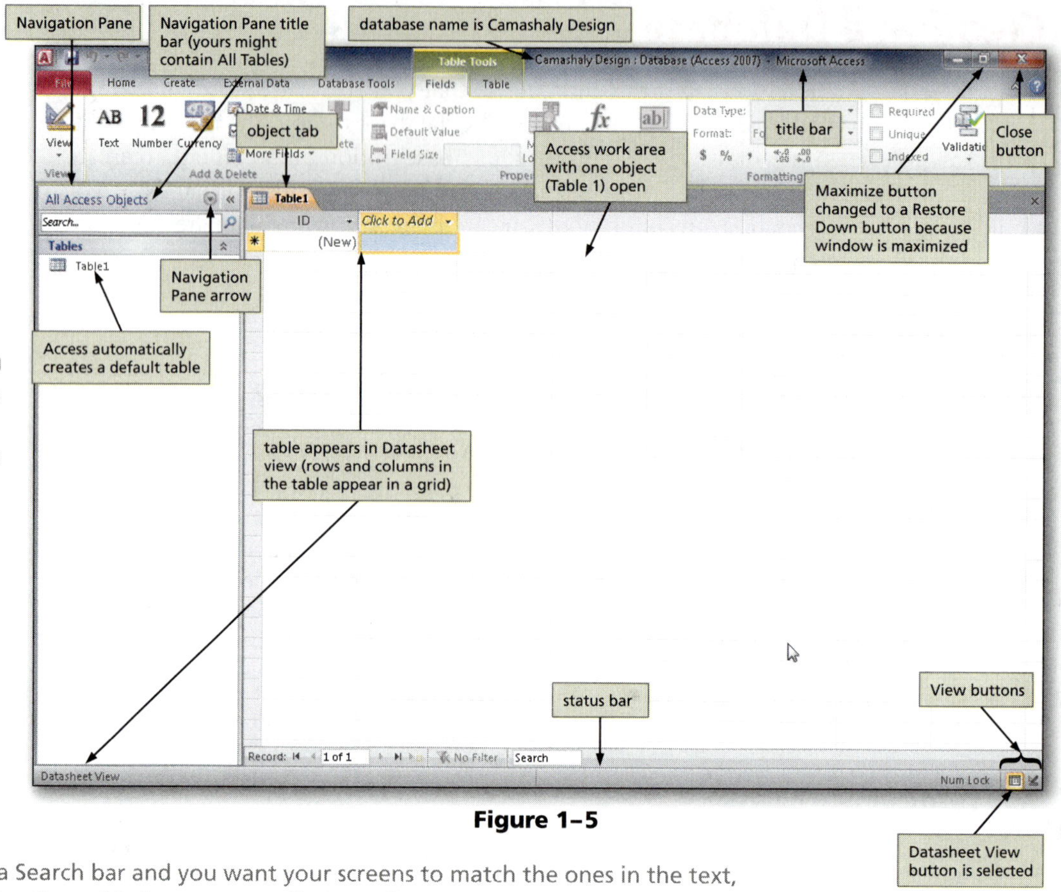

Figure 1–5

To Create a Database Using a Template

Ideally, you will design your own database, create a blank database, and then create the tables you have determined that your database should contain. If you are not sure what database design you will need, you could use a template. Templates can guide you by suggesting some commonly used databases. To create a database using a template, you would use the following steps.

1. After starting Access, be sure the Backstage view is open. If it is not, click File on the Ribbon to open it.
2. Click the New tab if it is not already selected.
3. Click Sample templates to display a list of templates stored locally or search Microsoft Office online for additional templates.
4. Click the template you want to use.
5. Enter a file name (or accept the suggested file name) and select a location for the database.
6. Click the Create button to create the database or the Download button to download the database and create the database, if necessary.

BTW **Available Templates**
The Blank web database button on the New tab in the Backstage view allows you to create a database that you can publish to a SharePoint server running Access Services. Access 2010 also includes five Web-based templates. To display previously used templates, click the My templates button.

The Access Window

The Access window consists of a variety of components to make your work more efficient and documents more professional. These include the Navigation Pane, Access work area, Ribbon, shortcut menus, and Quick Access Toolbar. Some of these components are common to other Microsoft Office 2010 programs; others are unique to Access.

Navigation Pane and Access Work Area

You work on objects such as tables, forms, and reports in the **Access work area.** In the work area in Figure 1–5, a single table, Table1, is open in the work area. **Object tabs** for the open objects appear at the top of the work area. If you have multiple objects open at the same time, you can select one of the open objects by clicking its tab. To the left of the work area is the Navigation Pane. The **Navigation Pane** contains a list of all the objects in the database. You use this pane to open an object. You also can customize the way objects are displayed in the Navigation Pane.

The **status bar**, located at the bottom of the Access window, presents information about the database object, the progress of current tasks, and the status of certain commands and keys; it also provides controls for viewing the object. As you type text or perform certain commands, various indicators may appear on the status bar. The left edge of the status bar in Figure 1–5 shows that the table object is open in Datasheet view. Toward the right edge are View buttons, which you can use to change the view that currently is displayed.

Creating a Table

To create a table, you must describe the structure of the table to Access. That is, you must describe all the fields that make up the table and their characteristics. You must also indicate the primary key.

BTW

The Ribbon and Screen Resolution

Access may change how the groups and buttons within the groups appear on the Ribbon, depending on the computer's screen resolution. Thus, your Ribbon may look different from the ones in the Office and Windows chapters in this book if you are using a screen resolution other than 1024 × 768.

In Access, you can use two different views to create a table: Datasheet view and Design view. In **Datasheet view**, the data in the table is presented in rows and columns, similar to a spreadsheet. Although the main reason to use Datasheet view is to add or update records in a table, you can also use it to create a table or to later modify its structure. The other view, **Design view**, is only used to create a table or to modify the structure of the table.

As you might expect, Design view has more functionality for creating a table than Datasheet view. That is, there are certain actions that can only be performed in Design view. If creating your table requires such actions, you must use Design view. If not, you can choose either view. In this chapter, you will create the first table, the Business Analyst table, in Datasheet view. You will create the second table, the Client table, in Design view.

Whichever view you choose to use, before creating the table, you need to determine the names and data types of the fields that will make up the table. You already have determined the types for the Camashaly fields. You also need to determine additional properties for the fields.

Plan Ahead

Determine additional properties for fields.

- **Determine if a special caption is warranted.** Normally, the field name will appear as the label for a field on a form or report and as the column name in Datasheet view. If you would rather have a different name appear, you can change the field's caption to the desired name. One common use of captions is to shorten the column heading. If the data in a column is considerably shorter than the column heading, you could change the caption to a shorter heading. This would enable you to reduce the width of the column and yet still be able to see the entire column heading.
- **Determine if a special description is warranted.** Determine whether to include a description that would appear in the status bar whenever the field is selected.
- **Determine field sizes.** For Text fields, determine the field size; that is, the maximum number of characters that can be entered in the field. Users will be prohibited from entering a value that has more characters than the field size.
- **Determine formats.** Determine whether the data in the field should be formatted in any particular way. You could, for example, specify that a number field is to be formatted with precisely two decimal places.

BTW

Naming Tables
Database users typically have their own guidelines for naming tables. Some use the singular version of the object being described while others use the prefix tbl with a table name. The Access chapters in this book use the singular version of the object (Client, Business Analyst) but add the word Table to the name for the Business Analyst table to illustrate another possible approach. Including the word Table can assist visually impaired users when viewing the Navigation Pane.

The results of these decisions for the fields in the Business Analyst table are shown in Table 1–3. The table also shows the data types and field sizes of the fields as well as any special properties that need to be changed. The Business Analyst Number field has a caption of BA #, enabling the width of the Business Analyst Number column to be reduced in the datasheet.

Table 1–3 Structure of Business Analyst Table

Field Name	Data Type	Field Size	Description
Business Analyst Number	Text	2	**Primary Key** **Description:** Business Analyst Number **Caption:** BA #
Last Name	Text	15	
First Name	Text	15	
Street	Text	15	
City	Text	15	
State	Text	2	
Postal Code	Text	5	
Salary YTD	Currency		
Incentive YTD	Currency		

To Modify the Primary Key

When you first create your database, Access automatically creates a table for you. You can immediately begin defining the fields. If, for any reason, you do not have this table or inadvertently delete it, you can create the table by clicking Create on the Ribbon and then clicking the Table button (Create tab | Tables group). In either case, you are ready to define the fields.

The following steps define the first field, the Business Analyst Number field, which is the primary key. Access has already created a primary key field, which it has named ID. Thus, the steps will change the name, data type, and other properties of this field to match the Business Analyst field in Table 1–3.

1

- Right-click the column heading for the ID field to display a shortcut menu (Figure 1–6).

Q&A

Why does my shortcut menu look different?

You right-clicked within the column instead of right-clicking the column heading.

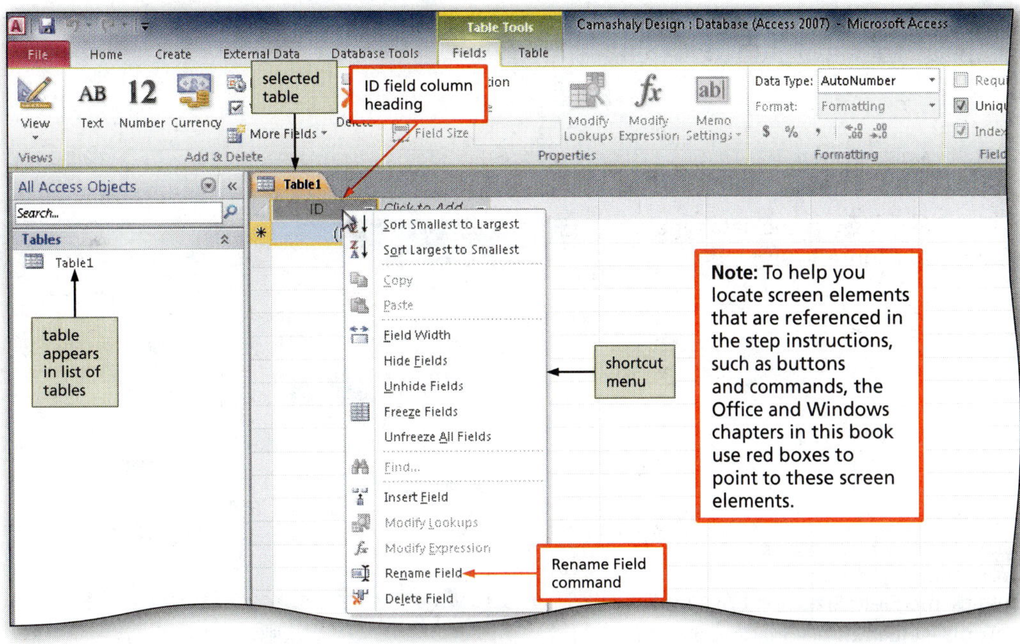

Figure 1–6

2

- Click Rename Field on the shortcut menu to highlight the current name.
- Type **Business Analyst Number** to assign a name to the new field.
- Click the white space immediately below the field name to complete the addition of the field (Figure 1–7).

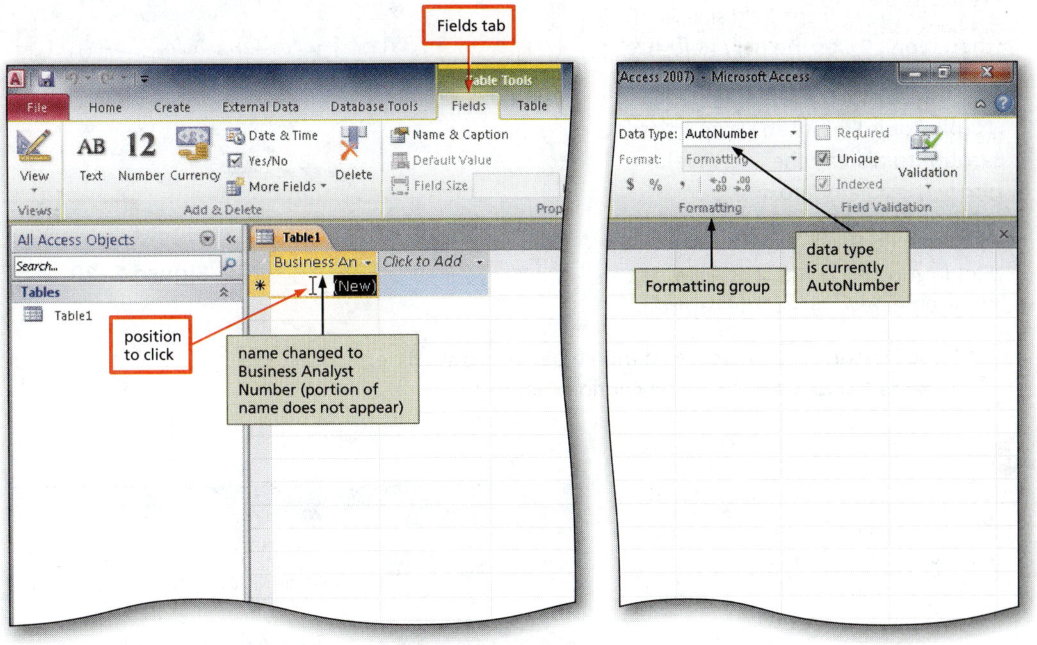

Figure 1–7

Q&A

Why does the name not appear in its entirety?

The default column size is not large enough for Business Analyst Number to appear in its entirety. You will address this issue in later steps.

3

- Because the data type needs to be changed from AutoNumber to Text, click the Data Type box arrow (Table Tools Fields tab | Formatting group) to display a menu of available data types (Figure 1–8).

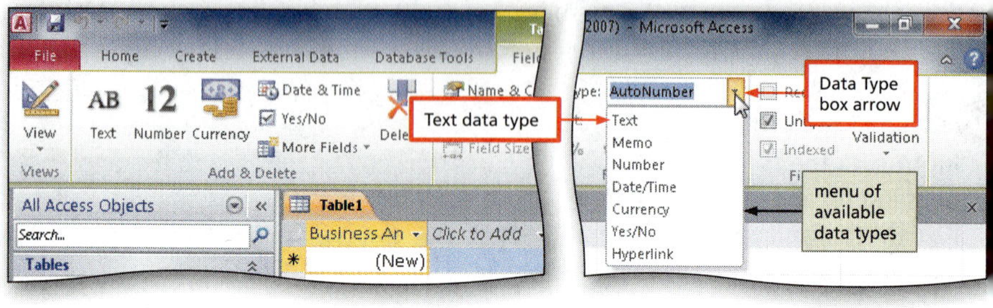

Figure 1–8

4

- Click Text to select the data type for the field (Figure 1–9).

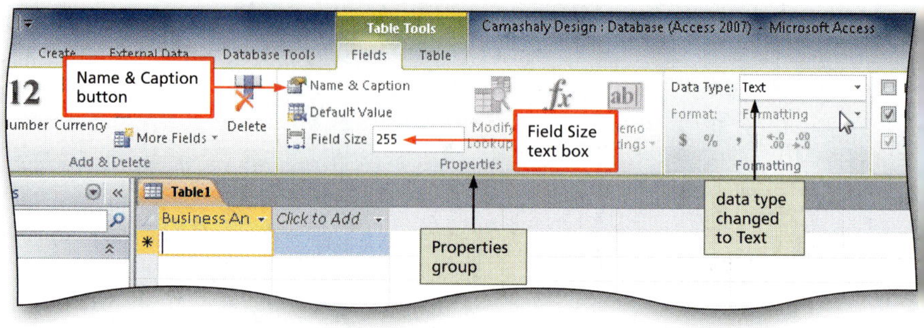

Figure 1–9

5

- Click the Field Size text box (Table Tools Fields tab | Properties group) to select the current field size, use either the DELETE or BACKSPACE keys to erase the current field size, and then type **2** as the new field size.
- Click the Name & Caption button (Table Tools Fields tab | Properties group) to display the Enter Field Properties dialog box.
- Click the Caption text box (Enter Field Properties dialog box), and then type **BA #** as the caption.
- Click the Description text box, and then type **Unique identifier of business analyst** as the description (Figure 1–10).

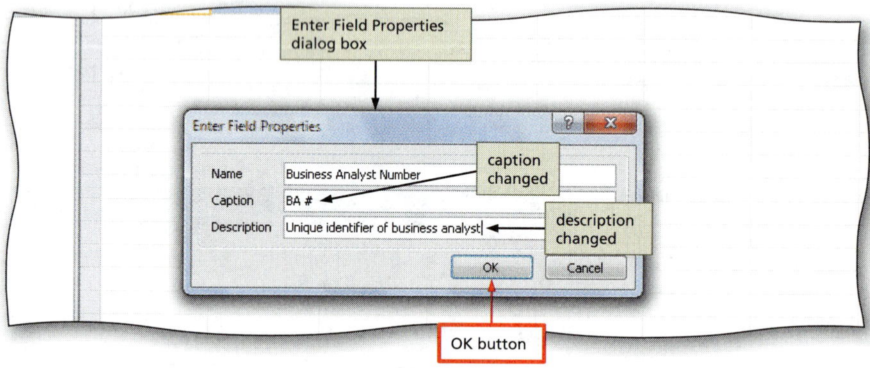

Figure 1–10

6

- Click the OK button (Enter Field Properties dialog box) to change the caption and description (Figure 1–11).

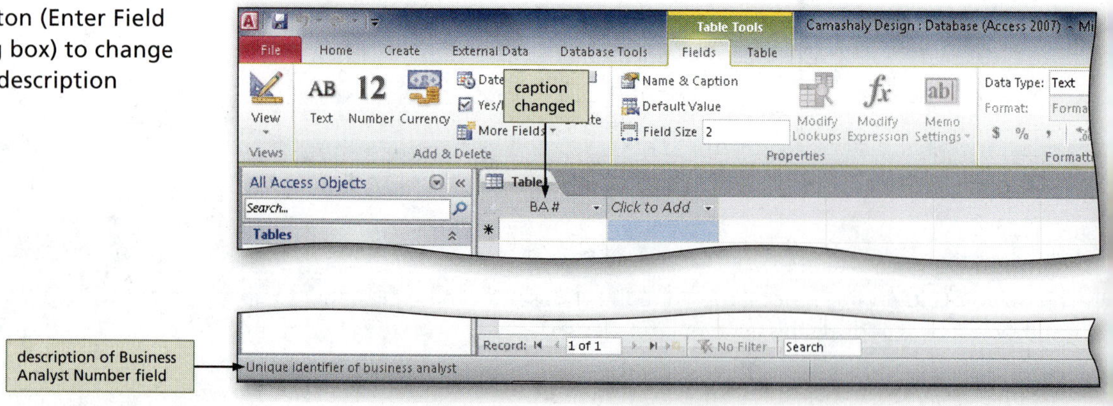

Figure 1–11

To Define the Remaining Fields in a Table

To define an additional field, you click the Click to Add column heading, select the data type, and then type the field name. This is different from the process you used to modify the ID field, which was an existing field. The following steps define the remaining fields shown in Table 1–3 on page AC 16.

1

- Click the Click to Add column heading to display a menu of available data types (Figure 1–12).

Q&A Why did I follow a different process when I renamed this field?

The ID field was an existing field, created automatically by Access. For a new field, you need to click the Click to Add heading.

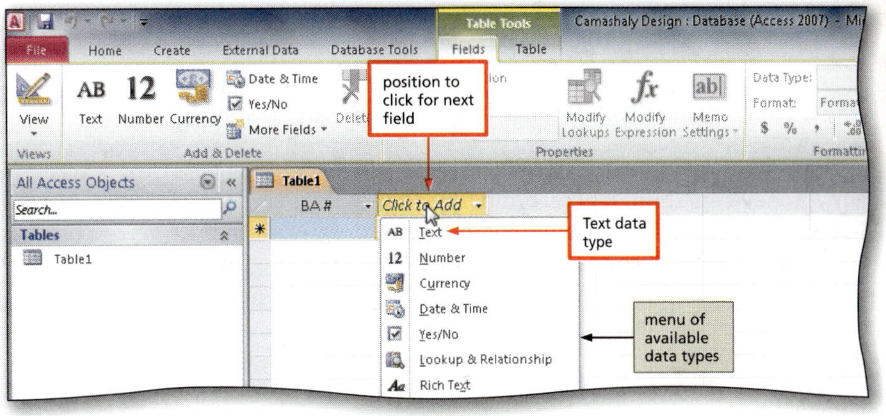

Figure 1–12

2

- Click Text in the menu of available data types to select the Text data type.
- Type Last Name to enter a field name.
- Click the white space below the field name to complete the change of the name. Click the white space a second time to select the field (Figure 1–13).

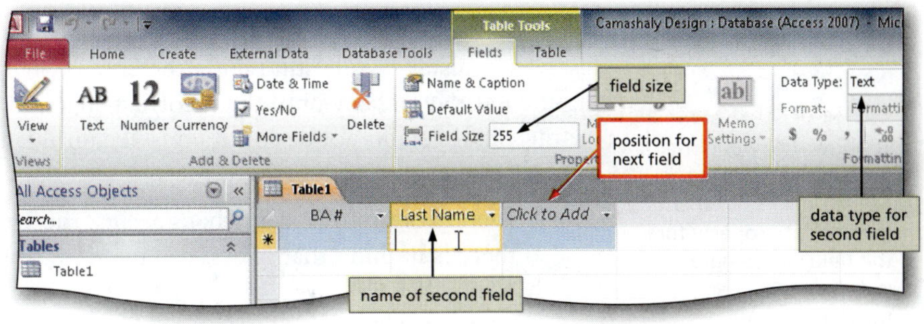

Figure 1–13

Q&A I realized after I entered the field name that I selected the wrong data type. How can I correct it?

Click the Data Type box arrow and then select the correct type.

Q&A I inadvertently clicked the white space before entering the field name. How can I correct the name?

Right-click the field name, click Rename Field on the shortcut menu, and then type the new name.

3

- Change the field size to 15 just as you changed the field size of the Business Analyst Number field.
- Using the same technique, add the remaining fields in the Business Analyst table. For the First Name, Street, City, State, and Postal Code fields, the Text data type is correct, but you will need to change the field size to match Table 1–3. For the Salary YTD and Incentive YTD fields, you need to change the data type to Currency. Before defining the Incentive YTD field, you may need to click the right scroll arrow to bring the column for the field to the screen (Figure 1–14).

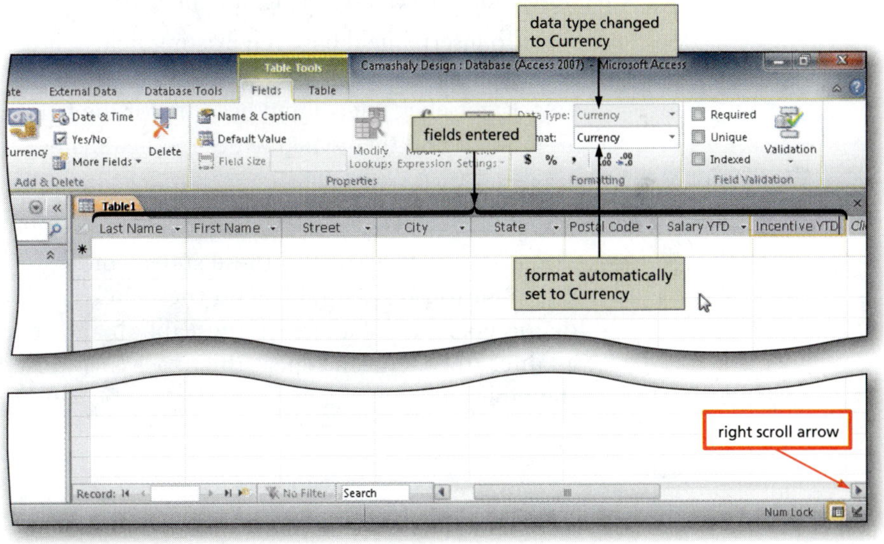

Figure 1–14

Q&A

Why does Currency appear twice?

The second Currency is the format, which indicates how the data will be displayed. For the Currency data type, Access automatically sets the format to Currency, which is usually what you would want. You could change it to something else, if desired, by clicking the arrow and selecting the desired format.

Q&A

I have an extra row between the row containing the field names and the row that begins with the asterisk. What happened? Is this a problem? If so, how do I fix it?

You inadvertently added a record to the table by pressing some key. Even pressing the SPACEBAR would add a record. You now have a record you do not want. To fix it, you need to delete the record, which you will do in Step 4.

4

- If you have an additional record between the field names and the asterisk, click the record selector (the box at the beginning of the record), press the DELETE key, and then click the Yes button when Access asks you if you want to delete the record.

Making Changes to the Structure

When creating a table, check the entries carefully to ensure they are correct. If you discover a mistake while still typing the entry, you can correct the error by repeatedly pressing the BACKSPACE key until the incorrect characters are removed. Then, type the correct characters. If you do not discover a mistake until later, you can use the following techniques to make the necessary changes to the structure:

- To undo your most recent change, click the Undo button on the Quick Access Toolbar. If there is nothing that Access can undo, this button will be dim, and clicking it will have no effect.
- To delete a field, right-click the column heading for the field (the position containing the field name), and then click Delete Field on the shortcut menu.
- To change the name of a field, right-click the column heading for the field, click Rename Field on the shortcut menu, and then type the desired field name.
- To insert a field as the last field, click the Click to Add column heading, click the appropriate data type on the menu of available data types, type the desired field name, and, if necessary, change the field size.
- To insert a field between existing fields, right-click the column heading for the field that will follow the new field, and then click Insert Field on the shortcut menu. Right-click the column heading for the field, click Rename Field on the shortcut menu, and then type the desired field name.
- To move a field, click the column heading for the field to be moved to select the field, and then drag the field to the desired position.

As an alternative to these steps, you may want to start over. To do so, click the Close button for the table, and then click the No button in the Microsoft Access dialog box. Click Create on the Ribbon and then click the Table button to create a table. You then can repeat the process you used earlier to define the fields in the table.

BTW

Currency Symbols
To show the symbol for the Euro (€) instead of the dollar sign, change the Format property for the field whose data type is currency. To change the default symbols for currency, change the settings in the operating system using the control panel.

To Save a Table

The Business Analyst table structure now is complete. The final step is to save the table within the database. As part of the process, you will give the table a name. The following steps save the table, giving it the name, Business Analyst Table.

1

- Click the Save button on the Quick Access Toolbar to display the Save As dialog box (Figure 1–15).

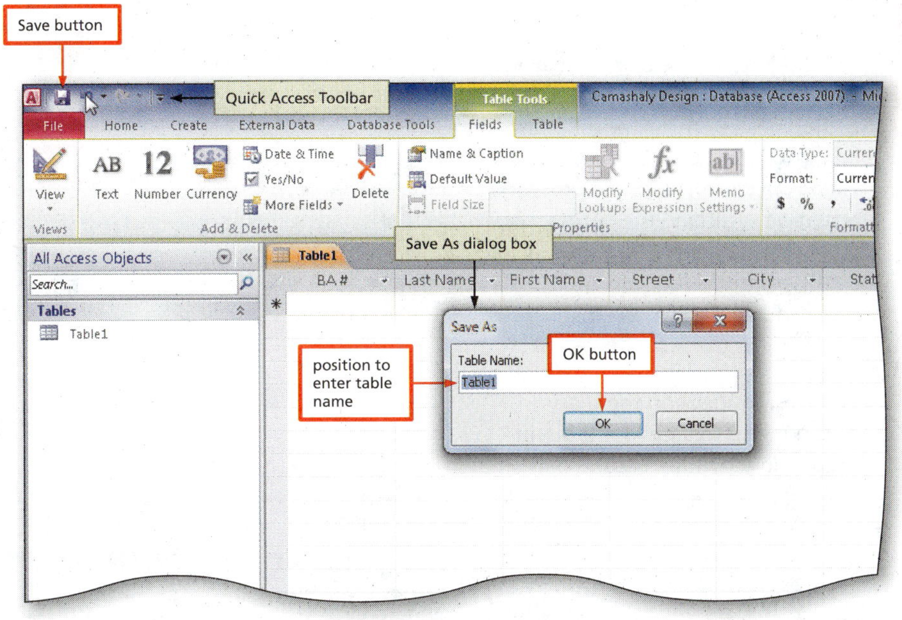

Figure 1–15

2

- Type **Business Analyst Table** to change the name to be assigned to the table.
- Click the OK button (Save As dialog box) to save the table (Figure 1–16).

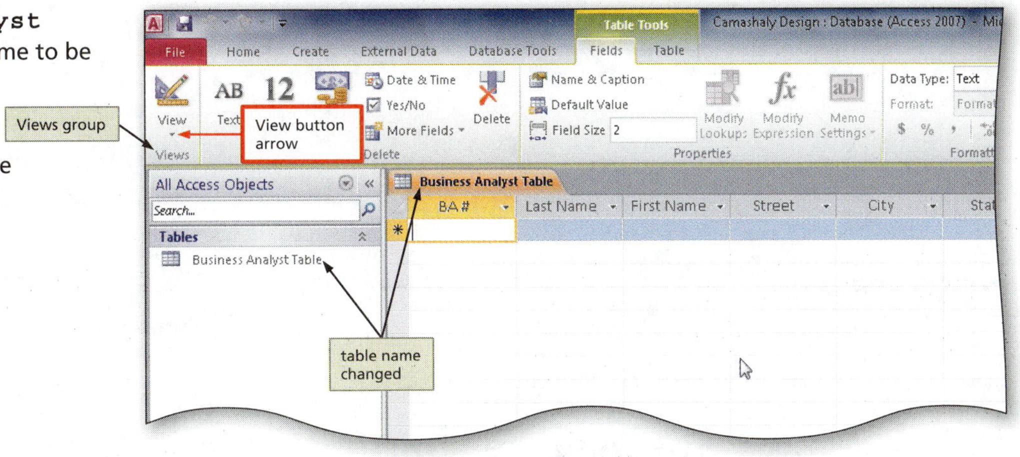

Figure 1–16

Other Ways

1. Click File on the Ribbon, click Save in the Backstage view
2. Right-click tab for table, click Save on shortcut menu
3. Press CTRL+S

To View the Table in Design View

Even when creating a table in Datasheet view, Design view can be helpful. You should view the fields, data types, and properties to ensure you have entered them correctly. This viewing is easier to do in Design view. It is also easier to determine the primary key in Design view. The following steps view the structure of the Business Analyst Table in Design view so that you can verify the design is correct.

1

- Click the View button arrow (Table Tools Fields tab | Views group) to display the View button menu (Figure 1–17).

Q&A

Could I just click the View button rather than the arrow?

Yes. Clicking the button is equivalent to clicking the command represented by the icon currently appearing on the button. Because the icon on the button in Figure 1–17 is the icon for Design view, clicking the button would display the table in Design view. If you are uncertain, you can always click the arrow and select from the menu.

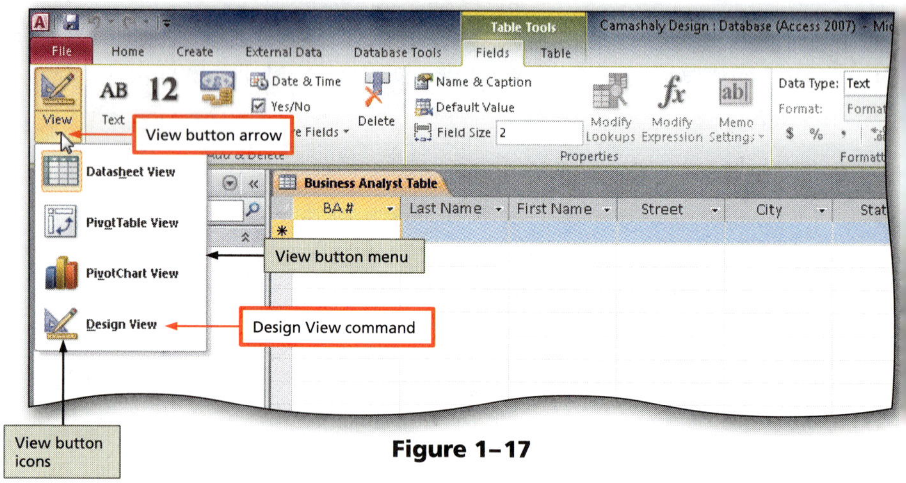

Figure 1–17

2

- Click Design View on the View button menu to view the table in Design view (Figure 1–18).

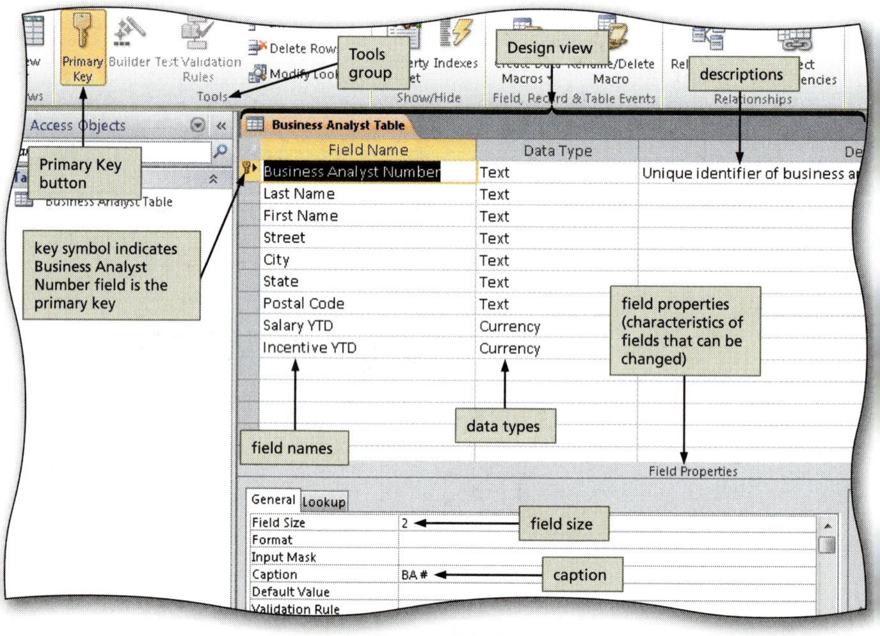

Figure 1–18

Other Ways

1. Click Design View button on status bar

Checking the Structure in Design View

You should use Design view to carefully check the entries you have made. In Figure 1–18, for example, you can see that the Business Analyst Number field is the primary key of the Business Analyst Table by the key symbol in front of the field name. If your table does not have a key symbol, you can click the Primary Key button (Table Tools Design tab | Tools group) to designate the field as the primary key. You also can check that the data type, the description, the field size, and the caption are all correct.

For the other fields, you can see the field name, data type, and description without taking any special action. To see the field size and/or caption for a field, click the field's **row selector**, the small box that precedes the field. Clicking the row selector for the Last Name field, for example, displays the field properties for the field (Figure 1–19). You then can check to see that the field size is correct. In addition, if the field has a caption, you can check to see if that is correct as well. If you find any mistakes, you can make the necessary corrections on this screen. When you have finished, you would click the Save button to save your changes.

To Close the Table

Once you are sure that your entries are correct and you have saved your changes, you can close the table. The following step closes the table.

1

- Click the Close button for the Business Analyst Table to close the table (Figure 1–19).

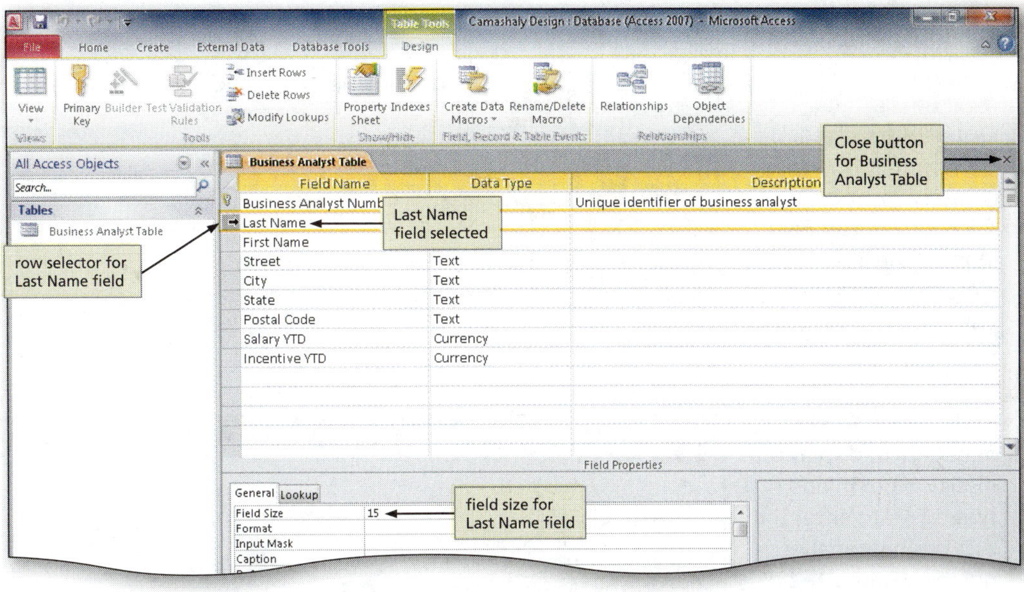

Figure 1–19

Other Ways

1. Right-click tab for table, click Close on shortcut menu

To Add Records to a Table

Creating a table by building the structure and saving the table is the first step in a two-step process. The second step is to add records to the table. To add records to a table, the table must be open. When making changes to tables, you work in Datasheet view. In Datasheet view, the table is represented as a collection of rows and columns called a **datasheet**.

You often add records in phases. For example, you might not have enough time to add all the records in one session. The following steps open the Business Analyst Table in Datasheet view and then add the first two records in the Business Analyst Table (Figure 1–20).

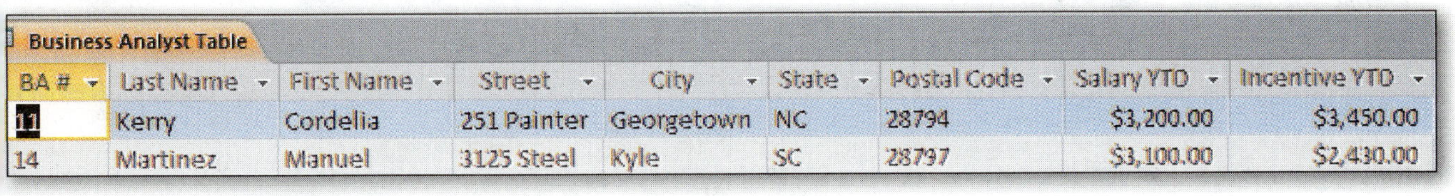

Figure 1–20

1

- Right-click the Business Analyst Table in the Navigation Pane to display the shortcut menu (Figure 1–21).

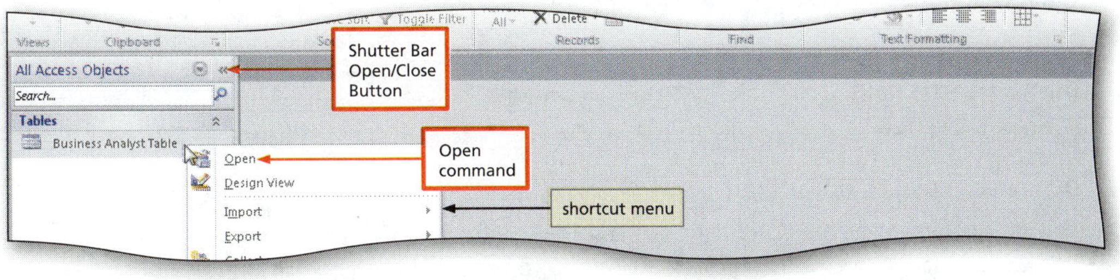

Figure 1–21

2

- Click Open on the shortcut menu to open the table in Datasheet view.

Q&A What if I want to return to Design view?

You can open Design view by clicking Design View on the shortcut menu.

- Click the Shutter Bar Open/Close Button to close the Navigation Pane (Figure 1–22).

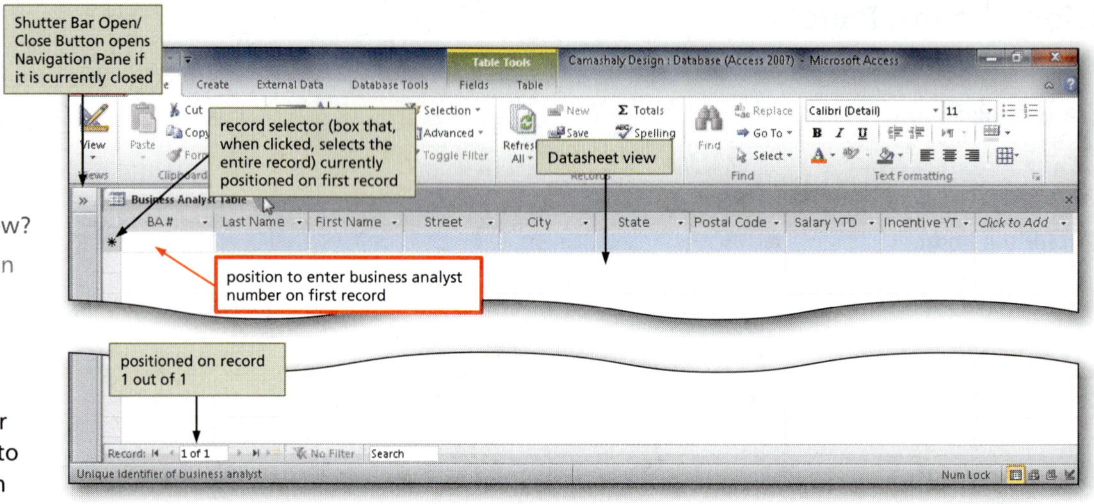

Figure 1–22

3

- Click the BA # field if necessary to display an insertion point, and type `11` to enter the first business analyst number (Figure 1–23).

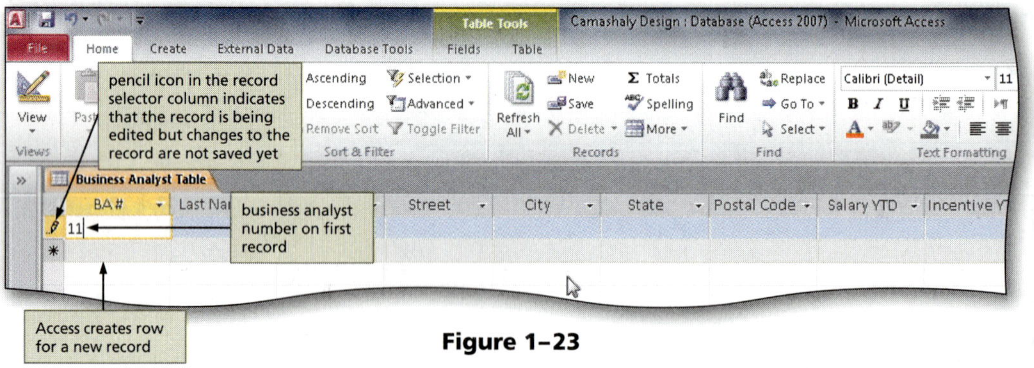

Figure 1–23

4

- Press the TAB key to move to the next field.
- Enter the last name, first name, street, city, state, and postal code by typing the following entries, pressing the TAB key after each one: `Kerry` as the last name, `Cordelia` as the first name, `251 Painter` as the street, `Georgetown` as the city, `NC` as the state, and `28794` as the postal code.
- Type `3200` in the Salary YTD field (Figure 1–24).

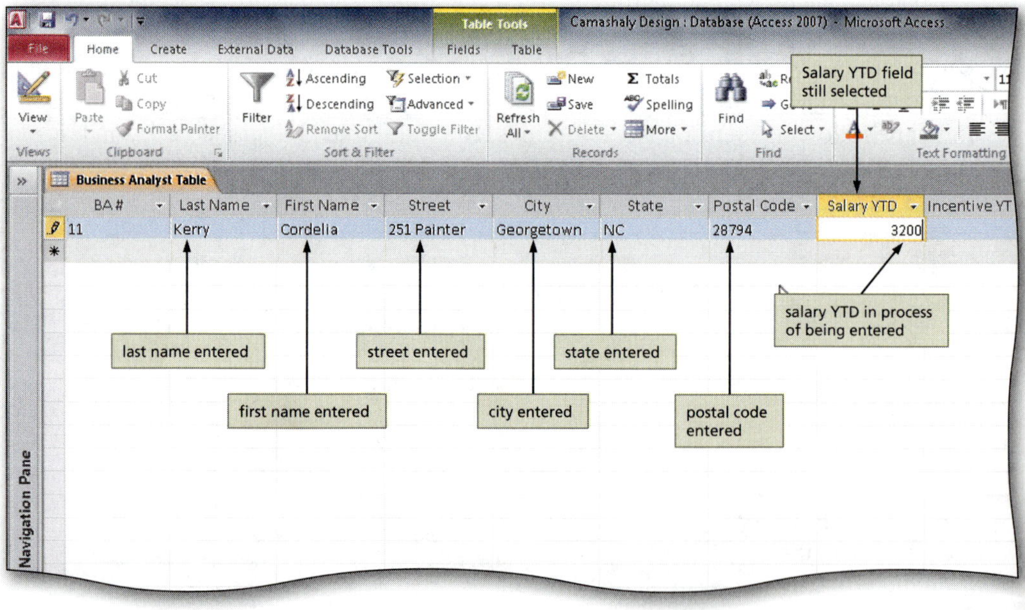

Figure 1–24

Q&A Do I need to type a dollar sign?

You do not need to type dollar signs or commas. In addition, because the digits to the right of the decimal point are both zeros, you do not need to type either the decimal point or the zeros.

5

- Press the TAB key to complete the entry for the field.
- Type `3450` in the Incentive YTD field, and then press the TAB key to complete the entry of the first record (Figure 1–25).

Q&A How and when do I save the record?

As soon as you have entered or modified a record and moved to another record, the original record is saved. This is different from other applications. The rows entered in an Excel worksheet, for example, are not saved until the entire worksheet is saved.

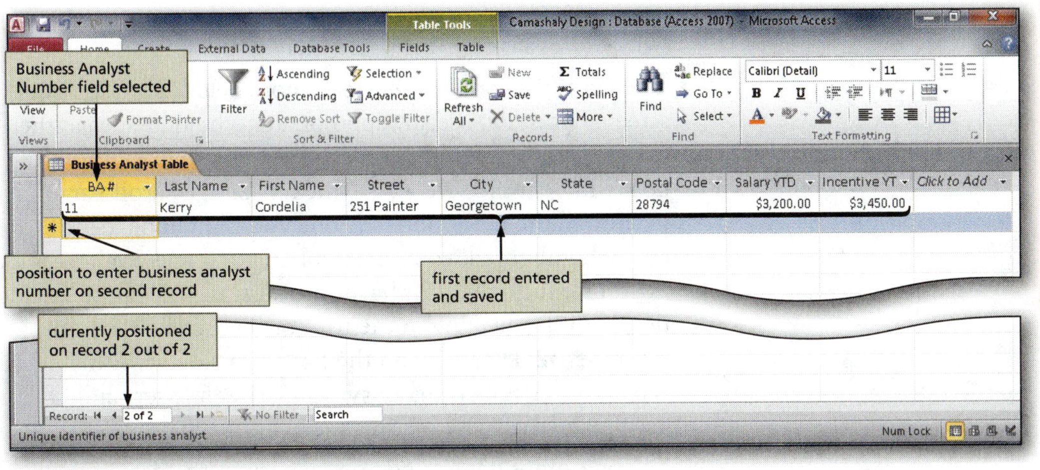

Figure 1–25

6

- Use the techniques shown in Steps 3 through 5 to enter the data for the second record (Figure 1–26).

Experiment

- Click the Salary YTD field on either of the records. Be sure the Table Tools Fields tab is selected. Click the Format box arrow and then click each of the formats in the Format box menu to see the effect on the values in the Salary YTD field. When finished, click Currency in the Format box menu.

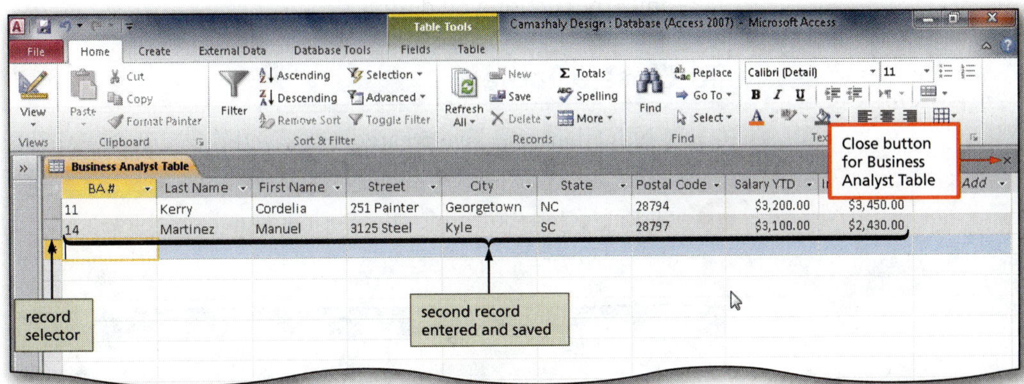

Figure 1–26

Making Changes to the Data

As you enter data, check your entries carefully to ensure they are correct. If you make a mistake and discover it before you press the TAB key, correct it by pressing the BACKSPACE key until the incorrect characters are removed, and then type the correct characters. If you do not discover a mistake until later, you can use the following techniques to make the necessary corrections to the data:

- To undo your most recent change, click the Undo button on the Quick Access Toolbar. If there is nothing that Access can undo, this button will be dimmed, and clicking it will have no effect.
- To add a record, click the New (blank) record button, click the position for the Business Analyst Number field on the first open record, and then add the record. Do not worry about it being in the correct position in the table. Access will reposition the record based on the primary key, in this case, the Business Analyst Number.

BTW **Adding Records**
You can add records in any order. When you close a table and reopen it, the records will be in order by primary key.

- To delete a record, click the record selector, shown in Figure 1–26, for the record to be deleted. Then press the DELETE key to delete the record, and click the Yes button when Access asks you to verify that you do indeed want to delete the record.
- To change the contents of one or more fields in a record, the record must be on the screen. If it is not, use any appropriate technique, such as the UP ARROW and DOWN ARROW keys or the vertical scroll bar, to move to it. If the field you want to correct is not visible on the screen, use the horizontal scroll bar along the bottom of the screen to shift all the fields until the one you want appears. If the value in the field is currently highlighted, you can simply type the new value. If you would rather edit the existing value, you must have an insertion point in the field. You can place the insertion point by clicking in the field or by pressing F2. You then can use the arrow keys, the DELETE key, and the BACKSPACE key for making the correction. You also can use the INSERT key to switch between Insert and Overtype mode. When you have made the change, press the TAB key to move to the next field.

If you cannot determine how to correct the data, you may find that you are "stuck" on the record, in which case Access neither allows you to move to another record nor allows you to close the table until you have made the correction. If you encounter this situation, simply press the ESC key. Pressing the ESC key will remove from the screen the record you are trying to add. You then can move to any other record, close the table, or take any other action you desire.

To Close a Table

Now that you have created and saved the Business Analyst Table, you can close it. The following step closes the table.

1. Click the Close button for the Business Analyst Table, shown in Figure 1–26, to close the table (Figure 1–27).

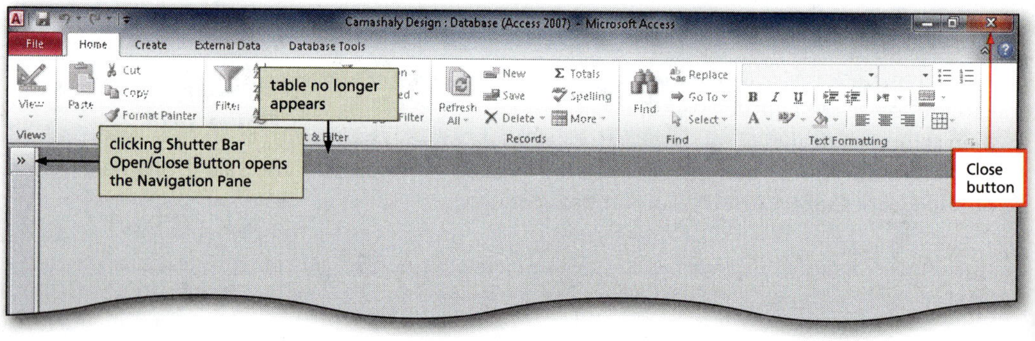

Figure 1–27

To Quit Access

The following steps quit Access. For a detailed example of the procedure summarized below, refer to the Office 2010 and Windows 7 chapter in this book.

1. Click the Close button on the right side of the title bar to quit Access.
2. If a Microsoft Access dialog box appears, click the Save button to save any changes made to the object since the last save.

Break Point: If you wish to take a break, this is a good place to do so. To resume at a later time, continue following the steps from this location forward.

Starting Access and Opening a Database

Once you have created and later closed a database, you will need to open it in the future in order to use it. Opening a database requires that Access is running on your computer.

To Start Access

1. Click the Start button on the Windows 7 taskbar to display the Start menu.
2. Type **Microsoft Access** as the search text in the 'Search programs and files' text box and watch the search results appear on the Start menu.
3. Click Microsoft Access 2010 in the search results on the Start menu to start Access.

To Open a Database from Access

Earlier in this chapter, you saved your database on a USB flash drive using the file name, Camashaly Design. The following steps open the Camashaly Design database from the Access folder in the CIS 101 folder on the USB flash drive. For a detailed example of the procedure summarized below, refer to the Office 2010 and Windows 7 chapter in this book.

BTW

Organizing Files and Folders
You should organize and store files in folders so that you easily can find the files later. For a discussion of folders and detailed examples of creating folders, refer to the Office 2010 and Windows 7 chapter in this book.

1. With your USB flash drive connected to one of the computer's USB ports, click File on the Ribbon to open the Backstage view, if necessary.
2. Click Open in the Backstage view to display the Open dialog box.
3. Navigate to the location of the file to be opened (in this case, the USB flash drive, then to the CIS 101 folder [or your class folder], and then to the Access folder).
4. Click Camashaly Design to select the file to be opened.
5. Click the Open button (Open dialog box) to open the selected file and display the opened database in the Access window.
6. If a Security Warning appears, click the Enable Content button (Figure 1–28).

Q&A

When would I not want to enable the content?

You would want to disable the content if you suspected that your database might contain harmful content or damaging macros. Because you are the one who created the database and no one else has used it, you should have no such suspicions.

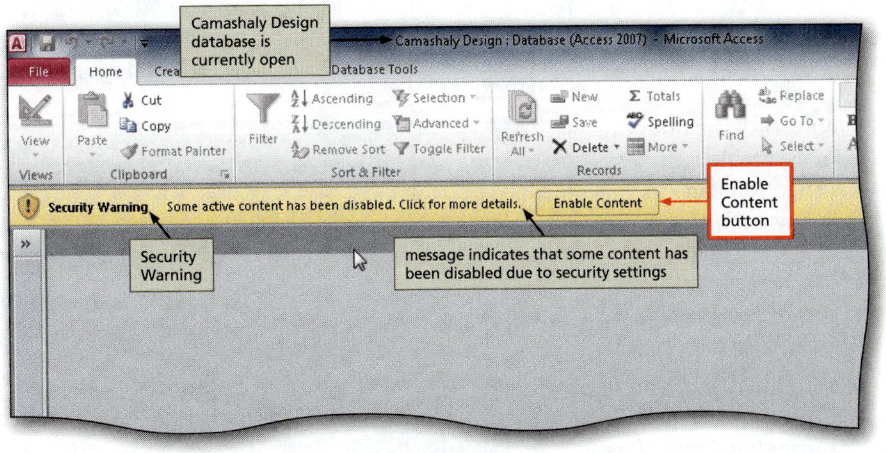

Figure 1–28

Other Ways

1. Click File on the Ribbon, click Recent in the Backstage view, click file name

To Add Additional Records to a Table

You can add records to a table that already contains data using a process almost identical to that used to add records to an empty table. The only difference is that you place the insertion point after the last record before you enter the additional data. To do so, use the **Navigation buttons**, which are buttons used to move within a table, found near the lower-left corner of the screen when a table is open. The purpose of each of the Navigation buttons is described in Table 1–4.

Table 1–4 Navigation Buttons in Datasheet View

Button	Purpose
First record	Moves to the first record in the table
Previous record	Moves to the previous record
Next record	Moves to the next record
Last record	Moves to the last record in the table
New (blank) record	Moves to the end of the table to a position for entering a new record

The following steps add the remaining records (Figure 1–29) to the Business Analyst table.

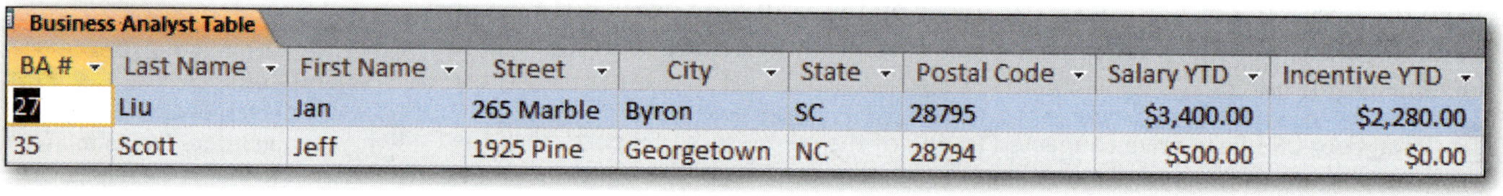

BA #	Last Name	First Name	Street	City	State	Postal Code	Salary YTD	Incentive YTD
27	Liu	Jan	265 Marble	Byron	SC	28795	$3,400.00	$2,280.00
35	Scott	Jeff	1925 Pine	Georgetown	NC	28794	$500.00	$0.00

Figure 1–29

1

- If the Navigation Pane is closed, click the Shutter Bar Open/Close Button, shown in Figure 1–27, to open the Navigation Pane (Figure 1–30).

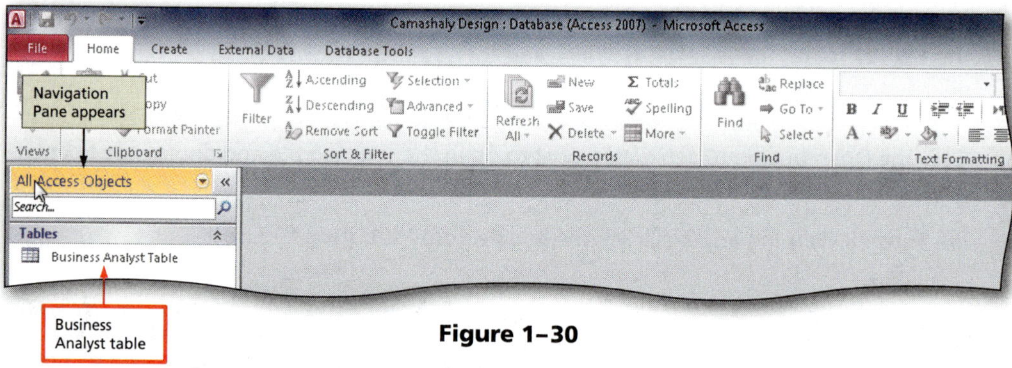

Figure 1–30

2

- Right-click the Business Analyst table in the Navigation Pane to display a shortcut menu.
- Click Open on the shortcut menu to open the table in Datasheet view.
- Close the Navigation Pane by clicking the Shutter Bar Open/Close Button (Figure 1–31).

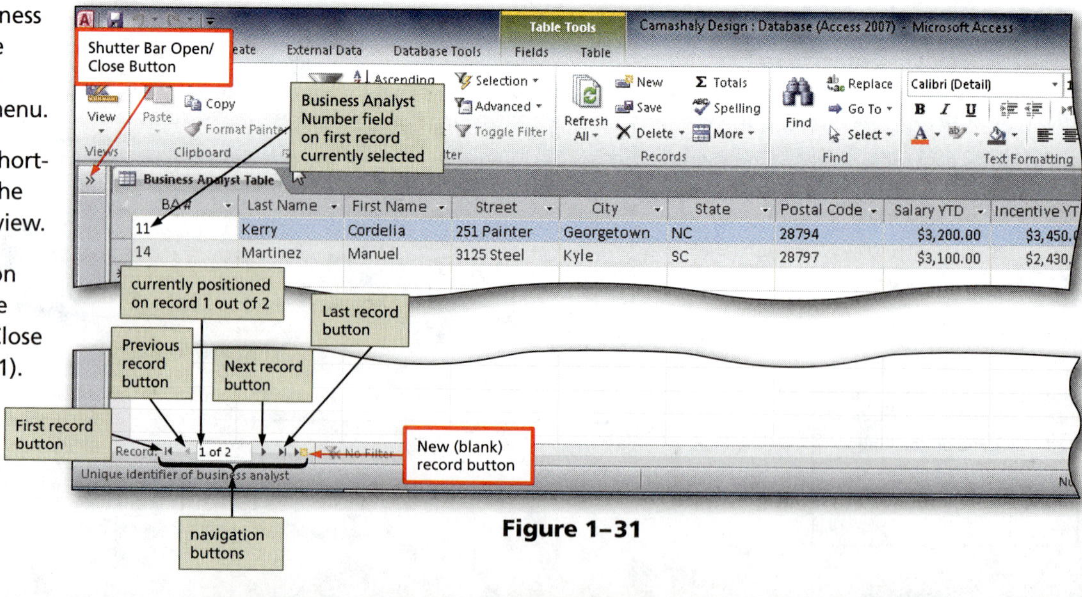

Figure 1–31

3

- Click the New (blank) record button to move to a position to enter a new record (Figure 1–32).

Q&A Could you just click the Business Analyst Number (BA #) on the first open record and then add the record?

Yes, but it's a good habit to use the New (blank) Record button. Once a table contains more records than will fit on the screen, it is easier to click the New (blank) record button.

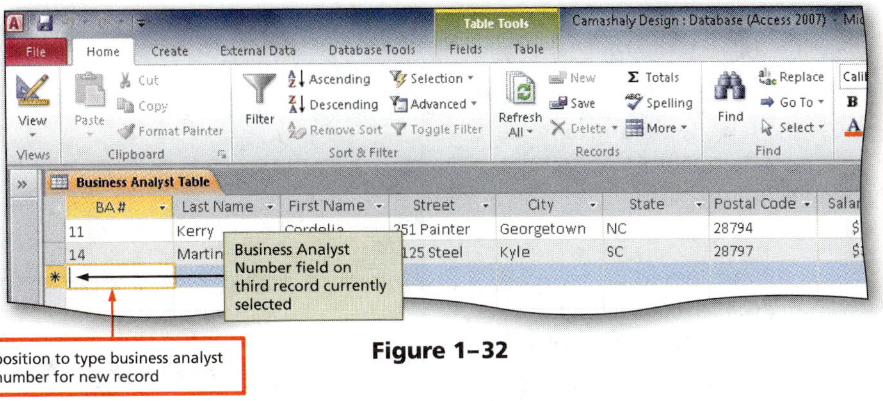

Figure 1–32

4

- Add the records shown in Figure 1–29, using the same techniques you used to add the first two records (Figure 1–33).

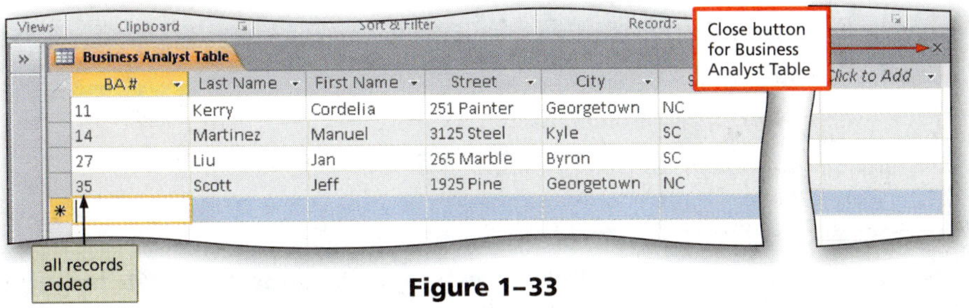

Figure 1–33

Other Ways
1. Click New button (Home tab | Records group)
2. Press CTRL+PLUS SIGN (+)

To Resize Columns in a Datasheet

Access assigns default column sizes, which do not always allow all the data in the field to appear. In some cases, the data might appear but not the entire field name. You can correct this problem by **resizing** the column (changing its size) in the datasheet. In some instances, you may want to reduce the size of a column. The State field, for example, is short enough that it does not require all the space on the screen that is allotted to it. Changing a column width changes the **layout**, or design, of a table.

The following steps resize the columns in the Business Analyst table and save the changes to the layout.

1

- Point to the right boundary of the field selector for the Business Analyst (BA #) field (Figure 1–34) so that the mouse pointer becomes a two-headed arrow.

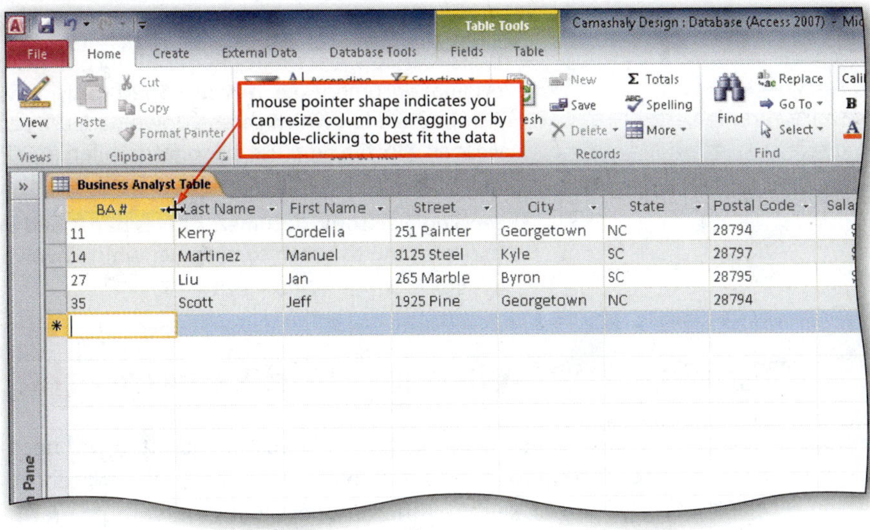

Figure 1–34

2

- Double-click the right boundary of the field selector to resize the field so that it best fits the data.
- Use the same technique to resize all the other fields to best fit the data (Figure 1–35).

3

- Save the changes to the layout by clicking the Save button on the Quick Access Toolbar (Figure 1–35).
- Click the table's Close button (shown in Figure 1–33) to the table.

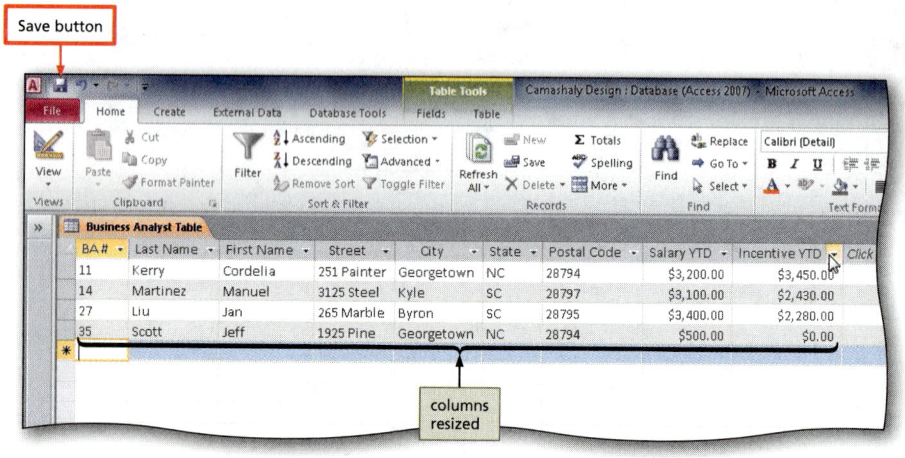

Figure 1–35

Q&A What if I closed the table without saving the layout changes?

You would be asked if you want to save the changes.

Other Ways

1. Right-click field name, click Field Width

Plan Ahead

Determine the best method for distributing the database objects.

The traditional method of distributing database objects uses a printer to produce a hard copy of a table. A **hard copy** or **printout** is information that exists on a physical medium such as paper. For users who can receive fax documents, you can elect to print a hard copy on a remote fax machine. Hard copies can be useful for the following reasons:

- Many people prefer proofreading a hard copy of a document rather than viewing it on the screen to check for errors and readability.
- Hard copies can serve as reference material if your storage medium is lost or becomes corrupted and you need to re-create the document.

Instead of distributing a hard copy, users can choose to distribute the document as an electronic image that mirrors the original document's appearance. The electronic image of the document can be e-mailed, posted on a Web site, or copied to a portable medium such as a USB flash drive. Two popular electronic image formats, sometimes called fixed formats, are PDF by Adobe Systems and XPS by Microsoft. In Access, you can create PDF and XPS files through the External Data tab on the Ribbon. Electronic images of documents, such as PDF and XPS, can be useful for the following reasons:

- Users can view electronic images of documents without the software that created the original document (i.e., Access). Specifically, to view a PDF file, you use a program called Acrobat Reader, which can be downloaded free from Adobe's Web site. Similarly, to view an XPS file, you use a program called an XPS Viewer, which is included in the latest versions of Windows and Internet Explorer.
- Sending electronic documents saves paper and printer supplies. Society encourages users to contribute to **green computing**, which involves reducing the environmental waste generated when using a computer.

BTW **Changing Printers**
To change the default printer that appears in the Print dialog box, click File on the Ribbon, click the Print tab in the Backstage view, click Print in the Print gallery, then click the Name box arrow and select the desired printer.

Previewing and Printing the Contents of a Table

When working with a database, you often will need to print a copy of the table contents. Figure 1–36 shows a printed copy of the contents of the Business Analyst table. (Yours may look slightly different, depending on your printer.) Because the Business Analyst table is substantially wider than the screen, it also will be wider than the normal printed page in portrait orientation. **Portrait orientation** means the printout is across the width of the page. **Landscape orientation** means the printout is across the height of the page. Thus, to print the wide database table, you might prefer to use landscape orientation. A convenient way to change to landscape orientation is to preview what the printed copy will look like by using Print Preview. This allows you to determine whether landscape orientation is necessary and, if it is, to change the orientation easily to landscape. In addition, you also can use Print Preview to determine whether any adjustments are necessary to the page margins.

Business Analyst Table 4/12/2012

BA #	Last Name	First Name	Street	City	State	Postal Code	Salary YTD	Incentive YTD
11	Kerry	Cordelia	251 Painter	Georgetown	NC	28794	$3,200.00	$3,450.00
14	Martinez	Manuel	3125 Steel	Kyle	SC	28797	$3,100.00	$2,430.00
27	Liu	Jan	265 Marble	Byron	SC	28795	$3,400.00	$2,280.00
35	Scott	Jeff	1925 Pine	Georgetown	NC	28794	$500.00	$0.00

Figure 1–36

To Preview and Print the Contents of a Table

The following steps use Print Preview to preview and then print the contents of the Business Analyst table.

1

- If the Navigation Pane is closed, open the Navigation Pane by clicking the Shutter Bar Open/Close Button.
- Be sure the Business Analyst table is selected.

Q&A Why do I have to be sure the Business Analyst table is selected? It is the only object in the database.

When the database contains only one object, you don't have to worry about selecting the object. Ensuring that the correct object is selected is a good habit to form, however, to make sure that the object you print is the one you want.

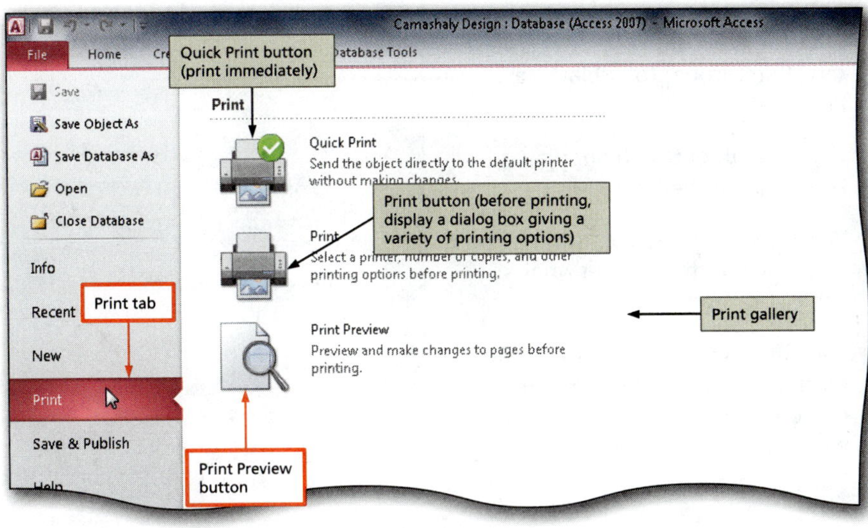

Figure 1–37

- Click File on the Ribbon to open the Backstage view.
- Click the Print tab in the Backstage view to display the Print gallery (Figure 1–37).

2

- Click the Print Preview button in the Print gallery to display a preview of what the table will look like when printed.
- Close the Navigation Pane to free up more of the screen for the preview (Figure 1–38).

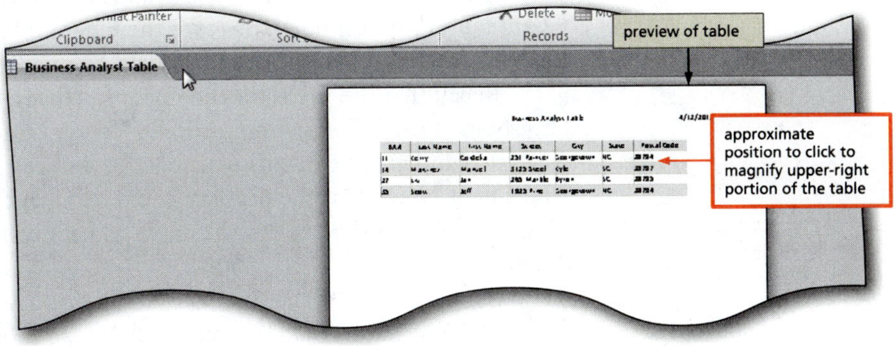

Figure 1–38

Q&A I cannot read the table. Can I magnify a portion of the table?

Yes. Point the mouse pointer, whose shape will change to a magnifying glass, at the portion of the table that you want to magnify, and then click. You can return the view of the table to the one shown in the figure by clicking a second time.

3

- Click the mouse pointer in the position shown in Figure 1–38 to magnify the upper-right section of the table (Figure 1–39).

Q&A My table was already magnified in a different area. How can I see the area shown in the figure?

One way is to use the scroll bars to move to the desired portion of the table. You also can click the mouse pointer anywhere in the table to produce a screen like the one in Figure 1–38, and then click in the location shown in the figure.

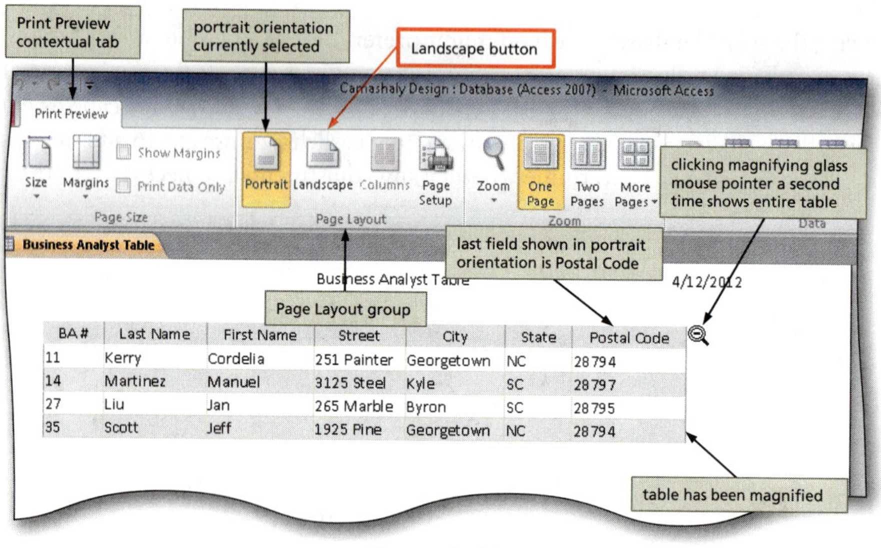

Figure 1–39

4

- Click the Landscape button to change to landscape orientation (Figure 1–40).
- Click the Print button (Print Preview tab | Print group) to display the Print dialog box.
- Click the OK button (Print dialog box) to print the table.
- When the printer stops, retrieve the hard copy of the Business Analyst Table.
- Click the Close Print Preview button (Print Preview tab | Close Preview group) to close the Print Preview window.

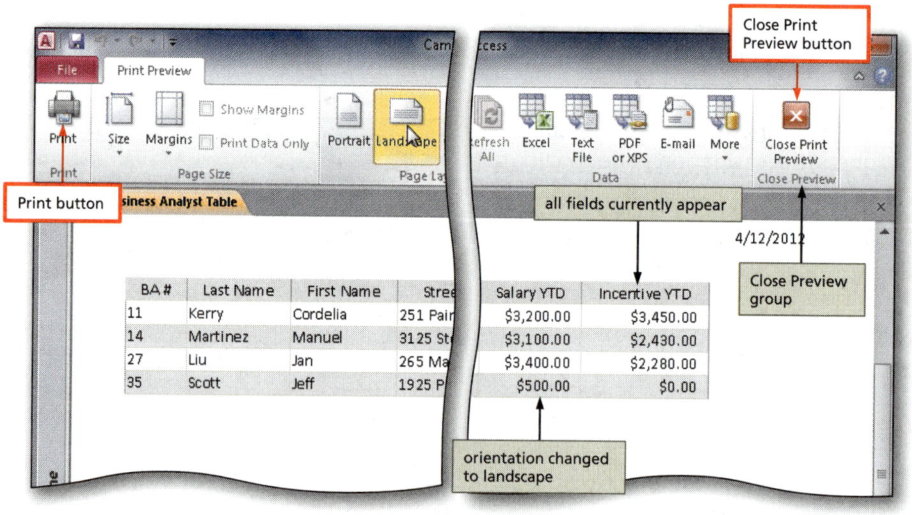

Figure 1–40

Other Ways

1. Press CTRL+P, click OK button (Print dialog box)

Creating Additional Tables

The Camashaly Design database contains two tables, the Business Analyst table and the Client table. You still need to create the Client table and add records to it. You created the Business Analyst table in Datasheet view. You will create the Client table in Design view.

Recall that the fields for the Client table are Client Number, Client Name, Street, City, State, Postal Code, Amount Paid, Current Due, Contract Hours YTD, and Business Analyst Number. The details that must be entered for these fields are shown in Table 1–5. The Client Number is the primary key. The Client Number field and the Business Analyst Number fields have both descriptions and captions. The Contract Hours YTD has a caption.

Because the values in the Contract Hours YTD field have decimal places, only Single, Double, or Decimal would be possible field size choices. (See Table 1–2 on Page AC 10 for a description of the possible field sizes for Number fields.) The difference between these choices concerns the amount of accuracy. Double is more accurate than Single, for example, but requires more storage space. Because the rates are only two decimal places, Single is a perfectly acceptable choice.

In addition to changing the field size for the Contract Hours YTD, you will also change the format to Fixed (a fixed number of decimal places) and the number of decimal places to 2.

Table 1–5 Structure of Client Table

Field Name	Data Type	Field Size	Notes
Client Number	Text	4	**Primary Key** **Description:** Client Number (two uppercase letters followed by 2-digit number) **Caption:** CL #
Client Name	Text	30	
Street	Text	15	
City	Text	15	
State	Text	2	
Postal Code	Text	5	
Amount Paid	Currency		
Current Due	Currency		
Contract Hours YTD	Number	Single	**Caption:** Hrs YTD **Format:** Fixed **Decimal Places:** 2
Business Analyst Number	Text	2	**Caption:** BA # **Description:** Business Analyst Number (number of business analyst for client)

To Create a Table in Design View

The next step in creating the table is to define the fields by specifying the required details in Design view. You will make entries in the Field Name, Data Type, and Description columns and enter additional information in the Field Properties box in the lower portion of the Table window. As you define the fields, the row selector (Figure 1–19 on page AC 23) indicates the field you currently are describing. Clicking the row selector selects the entire row. It is positioned on the first field, indicating Access is ready for you to enter the name of the first field in the Field Name column.

The following steps use Design view to define the fields in the table.

1

- Open the Navigation Pane.
- Click Create on the Ribbon to display the Create tab (Figure 1–41).

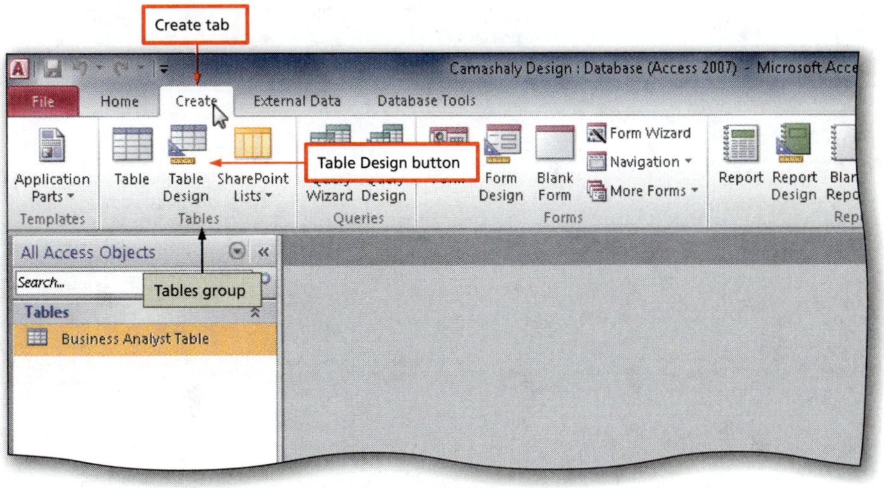

Figure 1–41

2

- Click the Table Design button (Create tab | Tables group) to create a new table in Design view (Figure 1–42).

Q&A

Could I save the table now so I can assign it the name I want, rather than Table1?

You certainly could. Be aware, however, that you will still need to save it again once you have added all your fields.

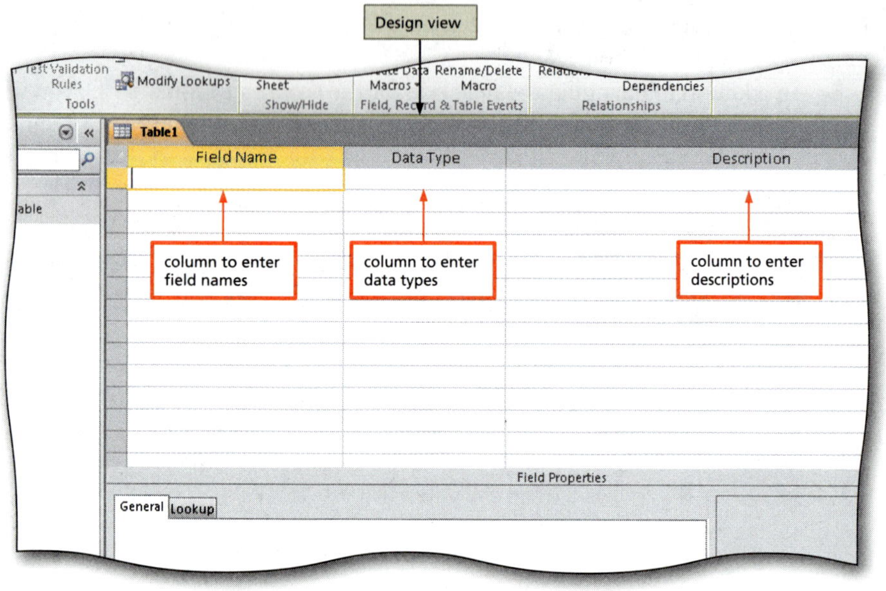

Figure 1–42

3

- Type `Client Number` (the name of the first field) in the Field Name column and then press the TAB key to accept the field name and move to the Data Type column (Figure 1–43).

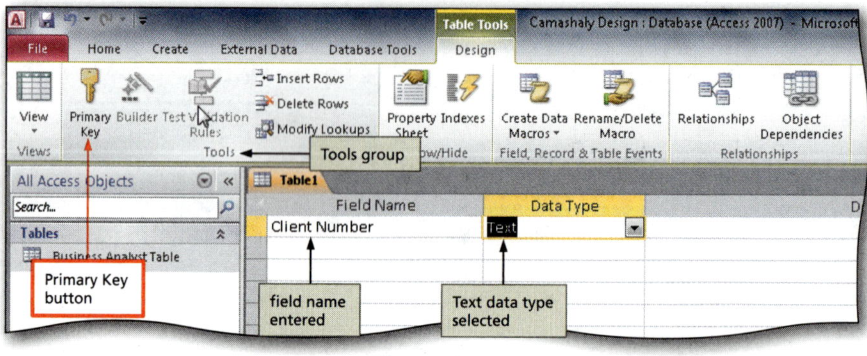

Figure 1–43

4

- Click the Primary Key button (Table Tools Design tab | Tools group) to designate the Client Number field as the primary key (Figure 1–44).

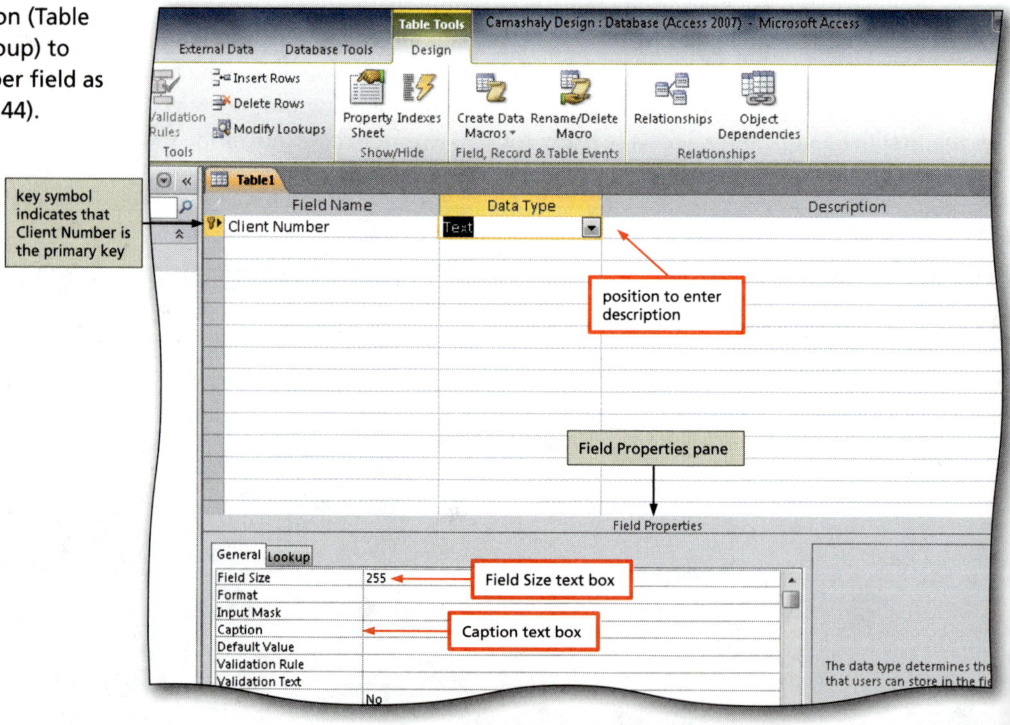

Figure 1–44

5

- Press the TAB key to move to the Description column, and then type `Client Number (two uppercase letters followed by a two-digit number)` as the description.
- Click the Field Size text box in the Field Properties pane to produce an insertion point, use either the BACKSPACE or DELETE key as necessary to erase the current entry (255), and then type `4` to change the field size.
- Click the Caption text box to produce an insertion point, and then type `CL #` to enter a caption (Figure 1–45).

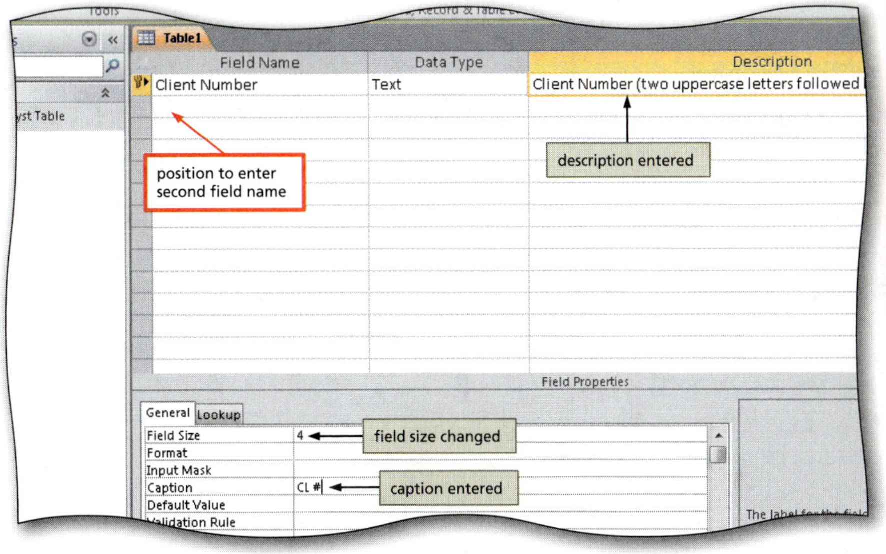

Figure 1–45

6

- Click the Field Name column on the second row to produce an insertion point and then make the entries for the Client Name field.
- Use the techniques illustrated in Steps 1 through 5 to make the entries for the remaining fields in the Client table structure, shown in Table 1–5 on page AC 33, up through and including the name of the Amount Paid field.
- Click the Data Type box arrow to display a menu of available data types (Figure 1–46).

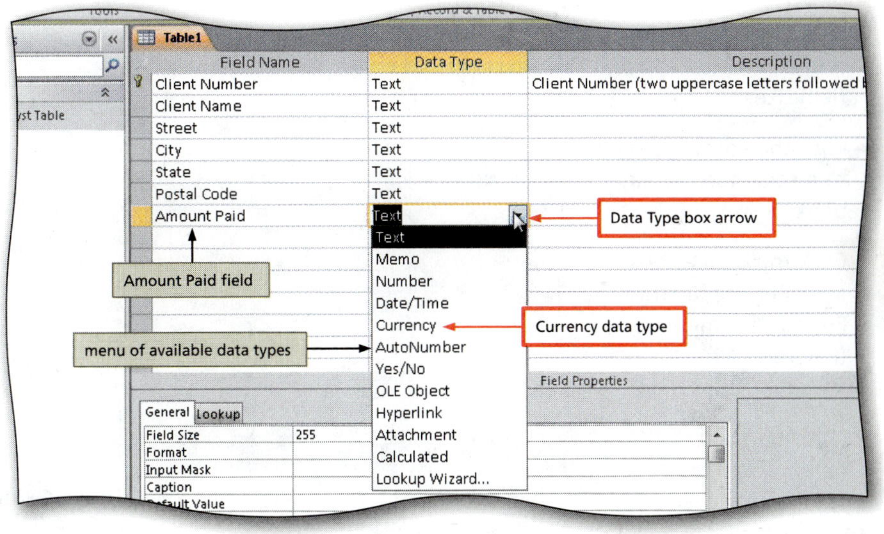

Figure 1–46

7

- Click Currency to select the data type.
- Enter the Current Due field and select the Currency data type.
- Enter the Contract Hours YTD field and select the Number data type (Figure 1–47).

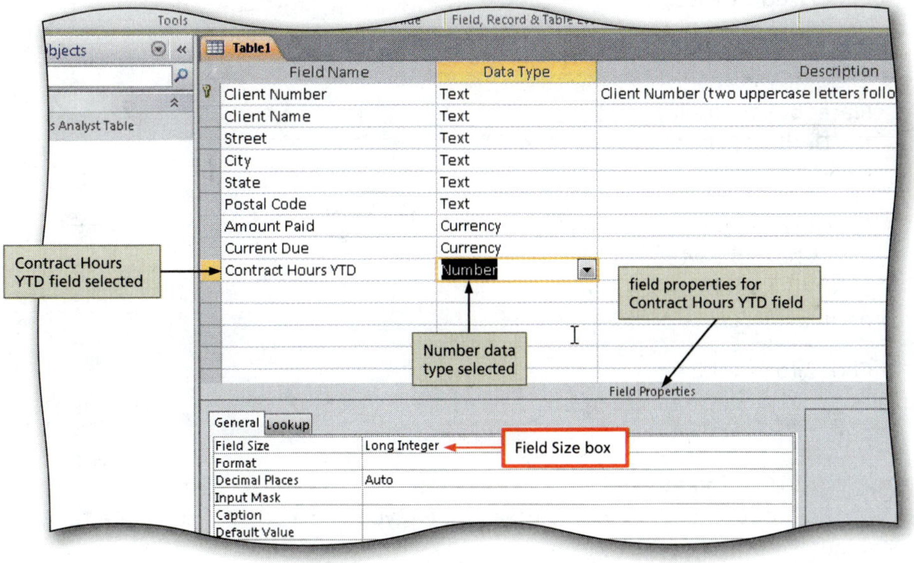

Figure 1–47

8

- Click the Field Size box to display the Field Size box arrow.
- Click the Field Size box arrow to display the Field Size box menu (Figure 1–48).

Q&A What would happen if I left the field size set to Integer?

If the field size is Integer, no decimal places can be stored. Thus a value of 2.50 would be stored as 2. If you enter your hours and none of the values have decimal places, probably you did not change the field size.

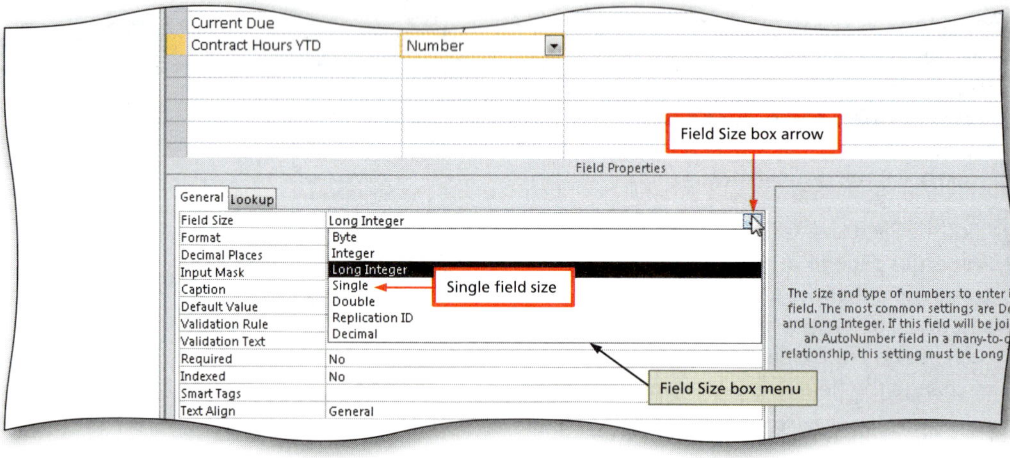

Figure 1–48

9

- Click Single to select single precision as the field size.
- Click the Format box to display the Format box arrow.
- Click the Format box arrow to display the Format box menu (Figure 1–49).

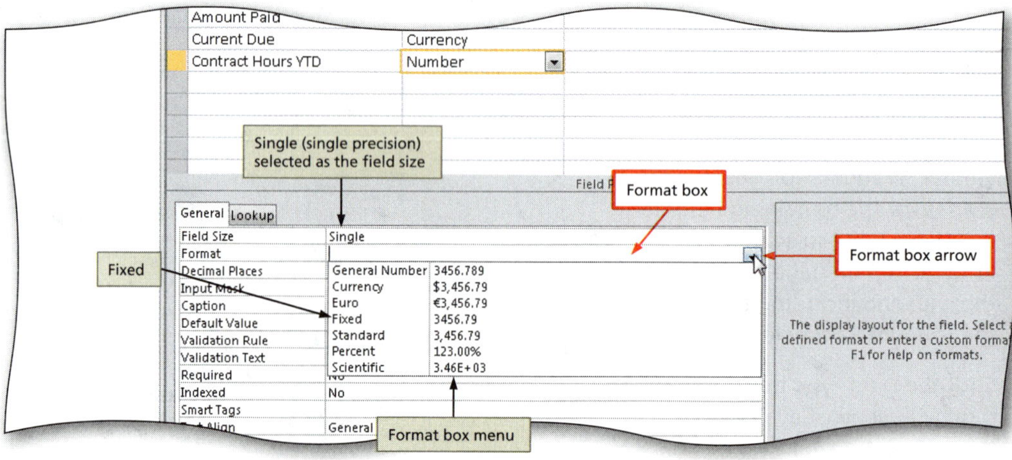

Figure 1–49

10

- Click Fixed to select fixed as the format.
- Click the Decimal Places box to display the Decimal Places box arrow.
- Click the Decimal Places box arrow to enter the number of decimal places.
- Click 2 to select 2 as the number of decimal places.
- Click the Caption text box to produce an insertion point, and then type `Hrs YTD` to enter a caption (Figure 1–50).

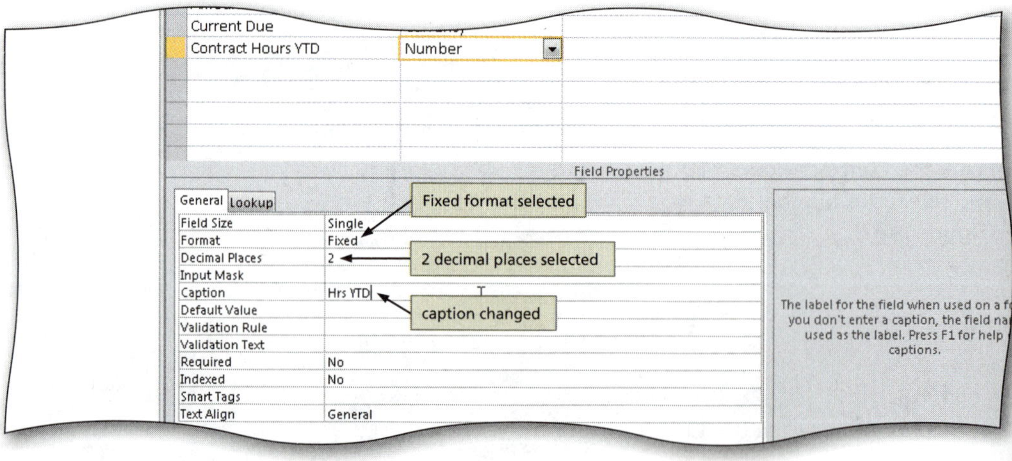

Figure 1–50

11

- Enter the Business Analyst Number field from Table 1–5. Be sure to change the description, field size, and caption to the ones shown in the table.
- Click the Save button on the Quick Access Toolbar to display the Save As dialog box, type Client as the name of the table, and then click the OK button (Save As dialog box) to save the table (Figure 1–51).

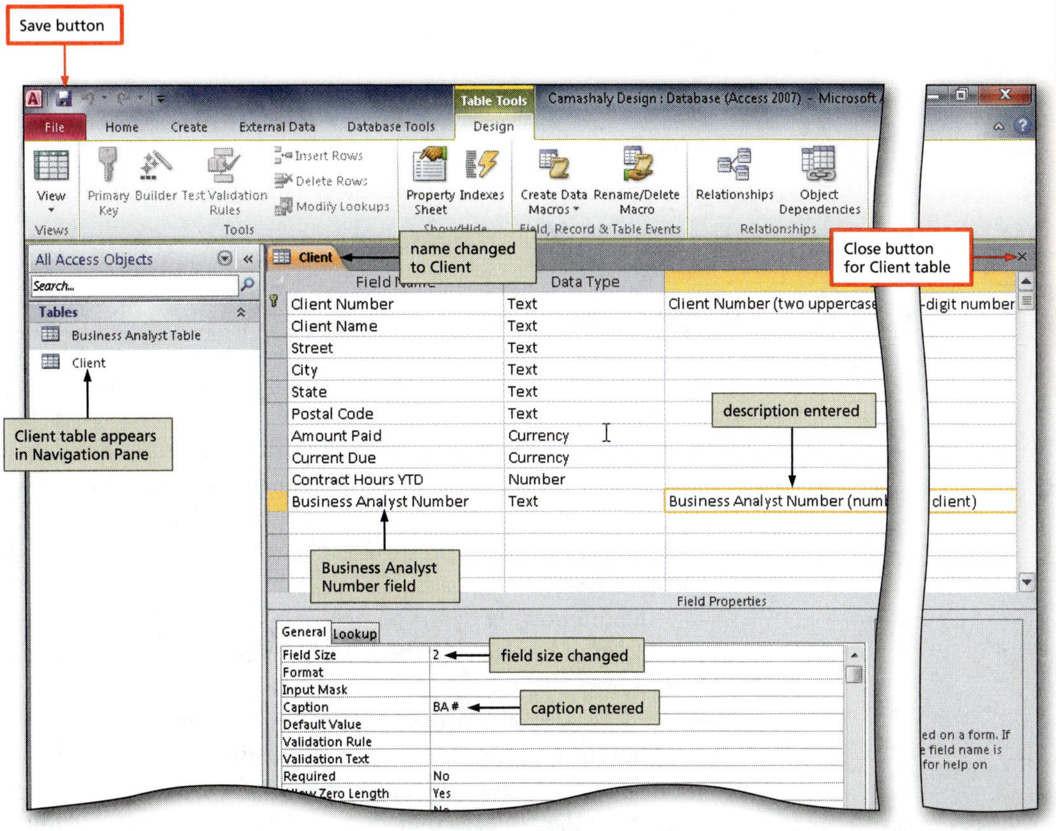

Figure 1–51

Other Ways

1. Press F6 to move between the upper pane and the lower pane in the Table Design window

Correcting Errors in the Structure

When creating a table, check the entries carefully to ensure they are correct. If you make a mistake and discover it before you press the TAB key, you can correct the error by repeatedly pressing the BACKSPACE key until the incorrect characters are removed. Then, type the correct characters. If you do not discover a mistake until later, you can click the entry, type the correct value, and then press the ENTER key. You can use the following techniques to make changes to the structure:

- If you accidentally add an extra field to the structure, select the field by clicking the row selector (the leftmost column on the row that contains the field to be deleted). Once you have selected the field, press the DELETE key. This will remove the field from the structure.
- If you forget to include a field, select the field that will follow the field you want to add by clicking the row selector, and then press the INSERT key. The remaining fields move down one row, making room for the missing field. Make the entries for the new field in the usual manner.
- If you made the wrong field a primary key field, click the correct primary key entry for the field and then click the Primary Key button (Table Tools Design tab | Tools group).
- To move a field, click the row selector for the field to be moved to select the field, and then drag the field to the desired position.

As an alternative to these steps, you may want to start over. To do so, click the Close button for the window containing the table, and then click the No button in the Microsoft Access dialog box. Click Create on the Ribbon and then click the Table Design button to create a table. You then can repeat the process you used earlier to define the fields in the table.

BTW

AutoCorrect Feature

The AutoCorrect feature of Access corrects common mistakes when entering text in a cell. AutoCorrect corrects two capital letters by changing the second letter to lowercase and capitalizes the first letter in the names of days. It also corrects more than 400 commonly misspelled words.

BTW

Other AutoCorrect Options

Using the Office AutoCorrect feature, you can create entries that will replace abbreviations with spelled-out names and phrases automatically. To specify AutoCorrect rules, click File on the Ribbon to open the Backstage view, click Options, and then click Proofing in the Access Options dialog box.

To Close the Table

Now that you have completed and saved the Client table, you can close it. The following step closes the table.

1. Click the Close button for the Client table (see Figure 1–51) to close the table.

Importing Data from Other Applications to Access

Now that you have created the Client table, you could add the records to it just as you did with the Business Analyst table. Access provides an alternative, however, that is available because Camashaly Design has already stored the necessary data in an Excel workbook (Figure 1–52). The data is stored in the form of an Excel **list**; that is, the first row contains column headings describing the data in each of the columns, and the remaining rows contain the data. Camashaly can **import** the data, which means to make a copy of the data in a table in the Access database.

When importing data, you have two choices. You can create a new table, in which case the column headings in the worksheet become the field names in the table. Access will attempt to assign appropriate data types. You would need to review the data types, adjust field sizes, captions, descriptions, and formats after the data was imported. The other option is to add the records to an existing table. This method is appropriate if you have already created the table, provided the column headings in the worksheet match the field names in the table, as they do in the case of the Client table.

	A	B	C	D	E	F	G	H	I	J	K
1	Client Number	Client Name	Street	City	State	Postal Code	Amount Paid	Current Due	Contract Hours YTD	Business Analyst Number	
2	BA53	Bavant Animal Hospital	134 Main	Burles	NC	28817	$0.00	$7,500.00	0.00	11	
3	BB32	Babbage CPA Firm	464 Linnell	Austin	SC	28796	$1,500.00	$500.00	5.00	14	
4	BC76	Buda Community Clinic	867 Ridge	Buda	NC	27032	$2,500.00	$750.00	2.50	11	
5	CJ29	Catering by Jenna	123 Second	Granger	NC	27036	$3,000.00	$1,000.00	15.50	27	
6	GA74	Grant Antiques	78 Catawba	Georgetown	NC	28794	$5,500.00	$3,200.00	34.50	14	
7	GF56	Granger Foundation	65 Simpson	Granger	NC	27036	$0.00	$6,500.00	0.00	11	
8	HC10	Hendley County Hospital	216 Rivard	Austin	SC	28796	$3,100.00	$1,200.00	12.00	27	
9	KD21	KAL Design Studio	116 Pine	Georgetown	NC	28794	$6,000.00	$3,200.00	30.50	14	
10	KG04	Kyle Grocery Cooperative	421 First	Kyle	SC	28798	$3,200.00	$0.00	5.00	11	
11	ME14	Mike's Electronic Stop	234 Gilham	Georgetown	NC	28794	$2,500.00	$1,500.00	8.50	27	
12	PJ34	Patricia Jean Florist	345 Magee	Kyle	SC	28798	$0.00	$5,200.00	0.00	27	
13	SL77	Smarter Law Associates	764 Main	Burles	NC	28817	$3,800.00	$0.00	10.50	11	
14	TB17	The Bikeshop	346 Austin	Buda	NC	27032	$2,750.00	$1,200.00	14.00	27	
15	WE05	Walburg Energy Alternatives	12 Polk	Walburg	NC	28819	$4,500.00	$1,450.00	19.50	14	
16	WS01	Woody Sporting Goods	578 Central	Walburg	NC	28819	$2,250.00	$1,600.00	18.50	14	
17											

Figure 1–52

The process of importing into an Access database uses a wizard. Specifically, if the data is imported from an Excel worksheet, the process will use the Import Spreadsheet Wizard. The wizard takes you through some basic steps, asking a few simple questions. After you have answered the questions, the wizard will import or link the data.

To Import an Excel Worksheet

To import the data in the Camashaly Client Data workbook, you use the Import Spreadsheet Wizard to place the rows from an Excel worksheet into an existing table. The following steps import the Camashaly Client Data Excel workbook, which is provided as a data file. See the inside back cover of this book for instructions on downloading the Data Files for Students, or contact your instructor for more information about accessing the required files.

1

- Click External Data on the Ribbon to display the External Data tab (Figure 1–53).

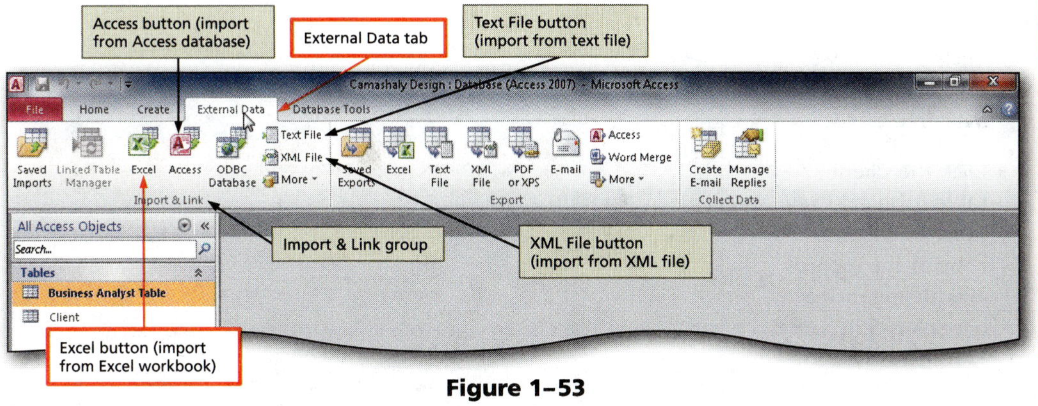

Figure 1–53

2

- Click the Excel button (External Data tab | Import & Link group) to display the Get External Data – Excel Spreadsheet dialog box.
- Click the Browse button (Get External Data – Excel Spreadsheet dialog box) to display the File Open dialog box.
- Navigate to the USB flash drive (or the location of your data files).
- Double-click your USB flash drive, and then click Camashaly Client Data to select the file to be opened.
- Click the Open button (File Open dialog box), which will return you to the Get External Data dialog box with the Camashaly Client Data workbook selected.

3

- Click the option button to append a copy of records to a table (Figure 1–54).

What happens if I select the option button to import records into a new table?

Instead of the records being added to an existing table, they will be placed in a new table. Access will assign all the data types. You would then need to ensure they are correct. You also would need to change any field sizes, descriptions, captions, formats, or number of decimal places to the ones you want.

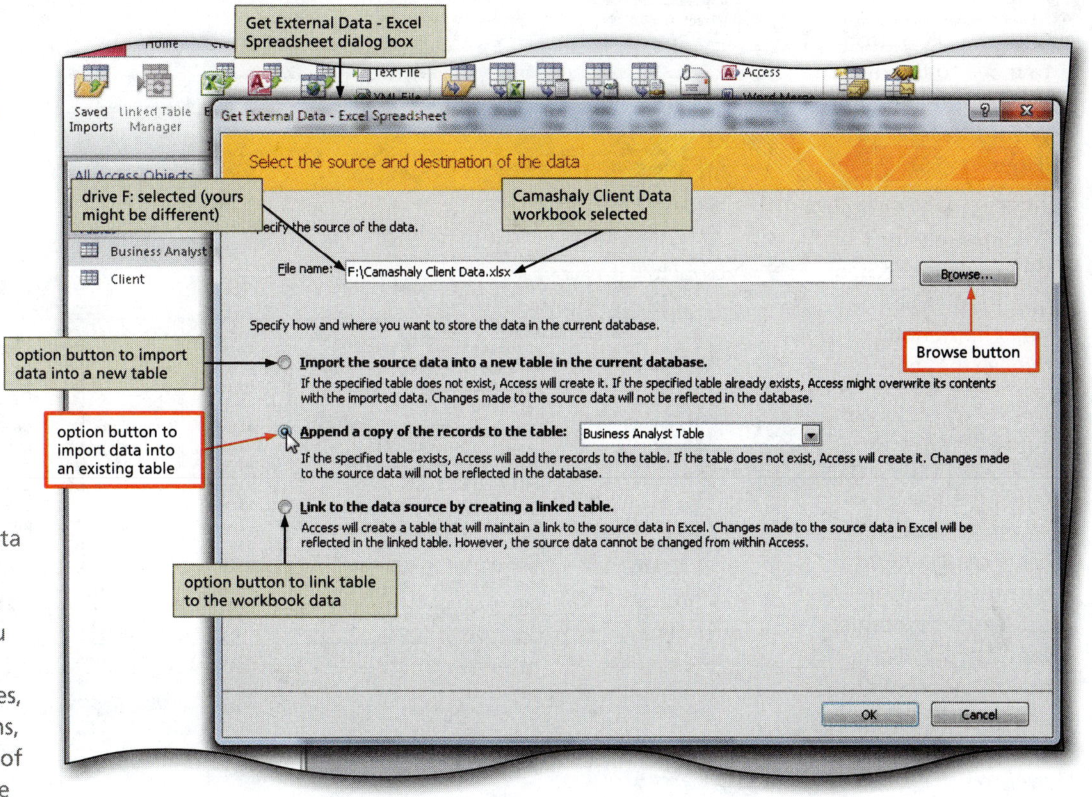

Figure 1–54

4

- Click the arrow to produce a menu of available tables.
- Click the Client table to select the table to which a copy of the records will be appended (Figure 1–55).

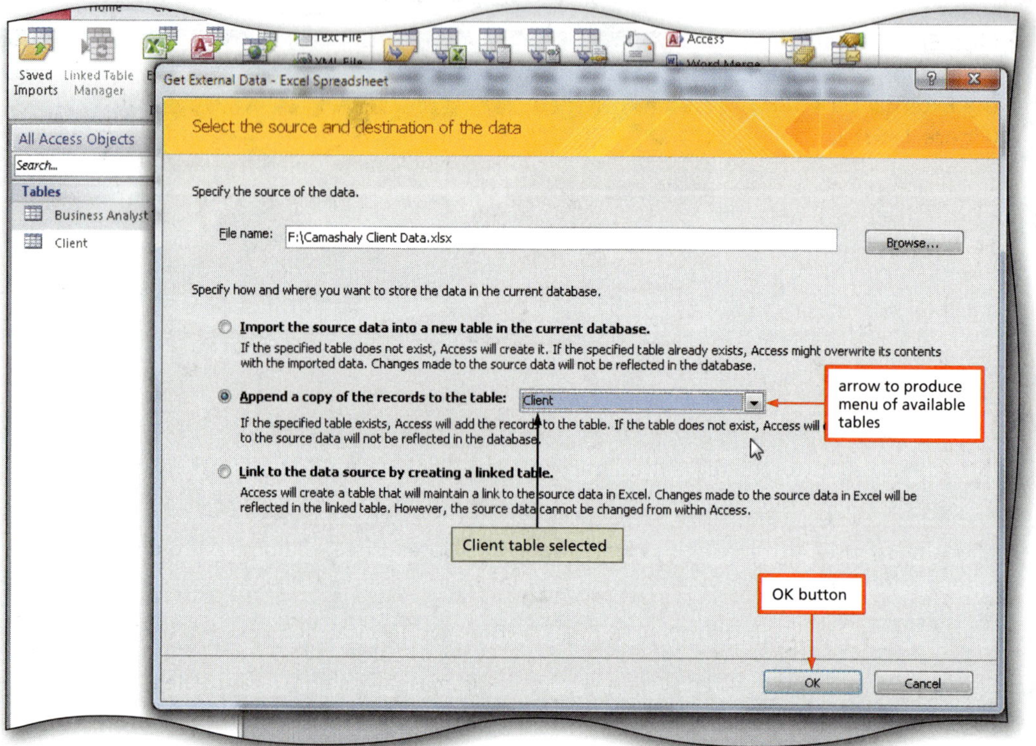

Figure 1–55

5

- Click the OK button to move to the next Import Spreadsheet Wizard screen (Figure 1–56).

Q&A

The First Row Contains Column Headings check box is checked, but it is dimmed. What if I want to remove the check mark?

When you are appending records to an existing table, the first row must contain column headings. If instead you were creating a new table, the first row might not contain column headings. In that case, you would have control over this check box.

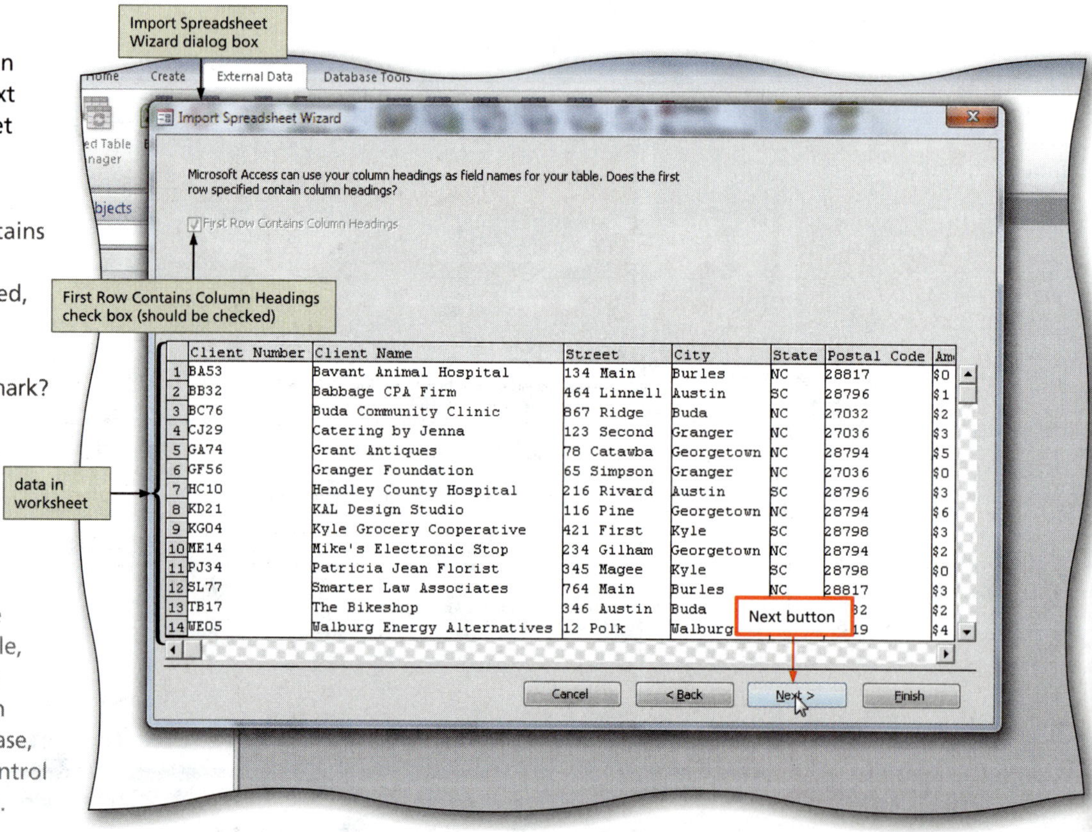

Figure 1–56

6

- Click the Next button to move to the next Import Spreadsheet Wizard screen (Figure 1–57).

Q&A What happens if I later realize I have selected the wrong table?

If you have not yet clicked the Finish button, you can click the Back button to return to the screen where you selected the table, and then select the correct table.

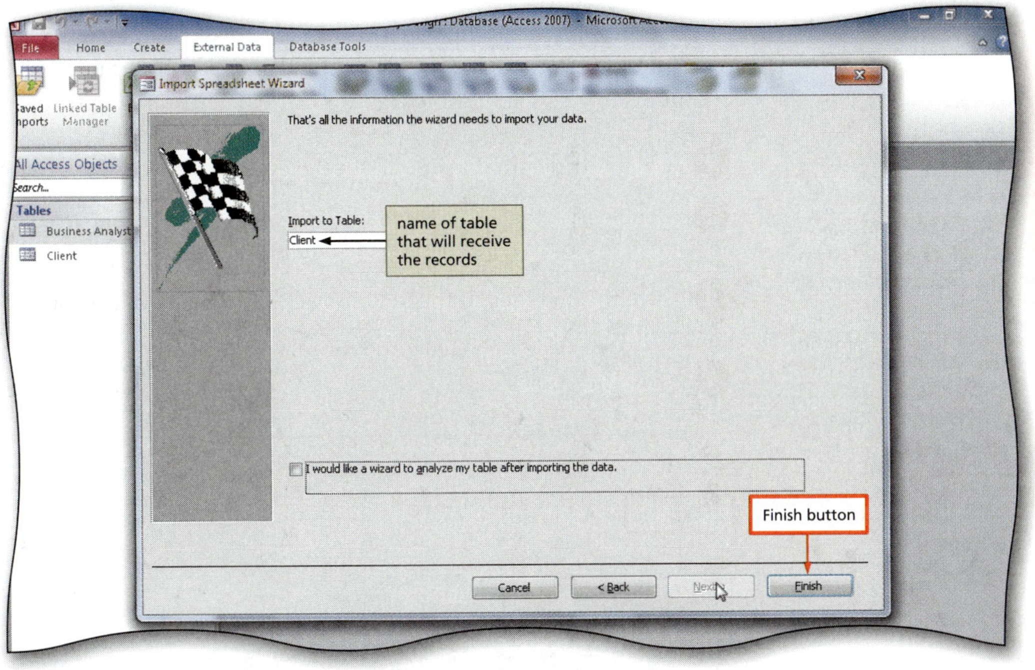

Figure 1–57

7

- Because the table name is correct, click the Finish button to import the data (Figure 1–58).

Q&A I got an error message that stated that a particular field did not exist in the Client table. What did I do wrong? How do I fix it?

When you created the table, you did not name that particular field correctly. Open the table in Design view and change the field name to the correct name. Check other field names as well. When you are done, save and close the table. Then, repeat the import process.

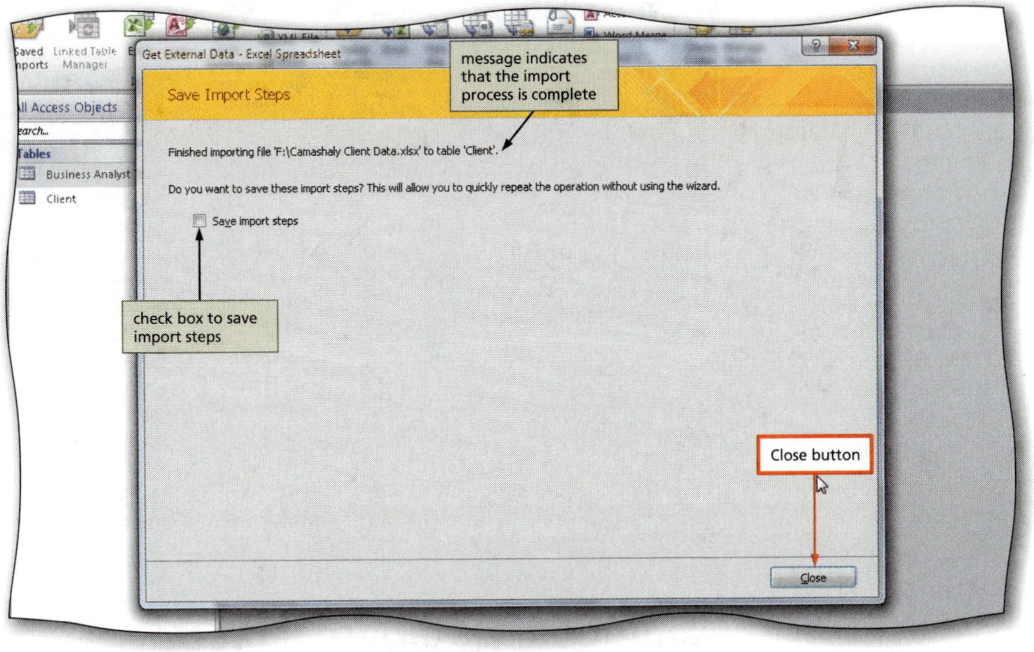

Figure 1–58

8

- Because you will not save the import steps, click the Close button.

Q&A When would I save the import steps?

If you think you might need to repeat these steps in the future, you can save time by saving the steps.

Other Ways

1. Right-click table in Navigation Pane, click Import on shortcut menu

To Resize Columns in a Datasheet

You can resize the columns in the datasheet for the Client table just as you resized the columns in the datasheet for the Business Analyst table. The following steps resize the columns in the Client table to best fit the data.

BTW

Resizing Columns
To resize all columns in a datasheet to best fit simultaneously, select the column heading for the first column, hold down the SHIFT key and select the last column in the datasheet. Then, double-click the right boundary of any field selector.

1. Open the Client table in Datasheet view and then close the Navigation Pane.
2. Double-click the right boundary of the field selectors of each of the fields to resize the columns so that they best fit the data.
3. Save the changes to the layout by clicking the Save button on the Quick Access Toolbar (Figure 1–59).
4. Close the table.

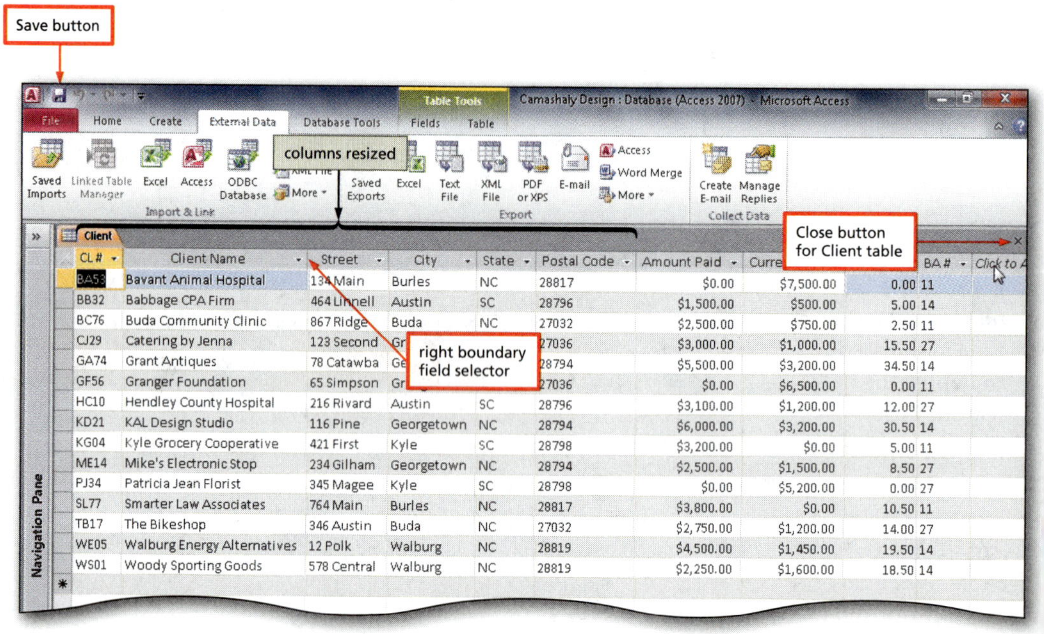

Figure 1–59

Break Point: If you wish to take a break, this is a good place to do so. You can quit Access now. To resume at a later time, start Access, open the database called Camashaly Design, and continue following the steps from this location forward.

Additional Database Objects

A computerized database such as Access contains many types of objects. Tables are the objects you use to store and manipulate data. Access supports other important types of objects as well; each of these objects has a specific purpose that assists in maximizing the benefits of a database. Through queries (questions), Access makes it possible to ask complex questions concerning the data in the database and then receive instant answers. Access also allows the user to produce attractive and useful forms for viewing and updating data. Additionally, Access includes report creation tools that make it easy to produce sophisticated reports for presenting data.

To Use the Simple Query Wizard to Create a Query

Queries are simply questions, the answers to which are in the database. Access contains a powerful query feature that helps you find the answers to a wide variety of questions. Once you have examined the question you want to ask to determine the fields involved in the question, you can begin creating the query. If there are no restrictions involved in the query, nor any special order or calculations, you can use the Simple Query Wizard.

The following steps use the Simple Query Wizard to create a query that Camashaly Design might use to obtain financial information on its clients. The query displays the number, name, amount paid, current due, contract hours YTD, and business analyst number of all clients.

1

- If the Navigation Pane is closed, click the Shutter Bar Open/Close Button to open the Navigation Pane.
- Be sure the Client table is selected.
- Click Create on the Ribbon to display the Create tab.
- Click the Query Wizard button (Create tab | Queries group) to display the New Query dialog box (Figure 1–60).

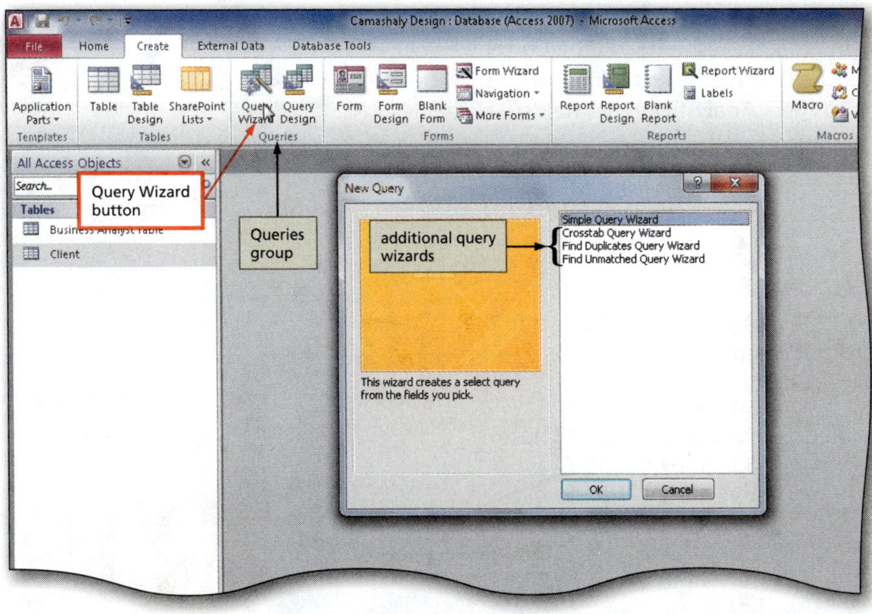

Figure 1–60

2

- Be sure Simple Query Wizard is selected, and then click the OK button (New Query dialog box) to display the Simple Query Wizard dialog box (Figure 1–61).

What would happen if the Business Analyst Table were selected instead of the Client table?

The list of available fields would contain fields from the Business Analyst Table rather than the Client table.

If the list contained Business Analyst Table fields, how could I make it contain Client table fields?

Click the arrow in the Tables/Queries box and then click the Client table in the list that appears.

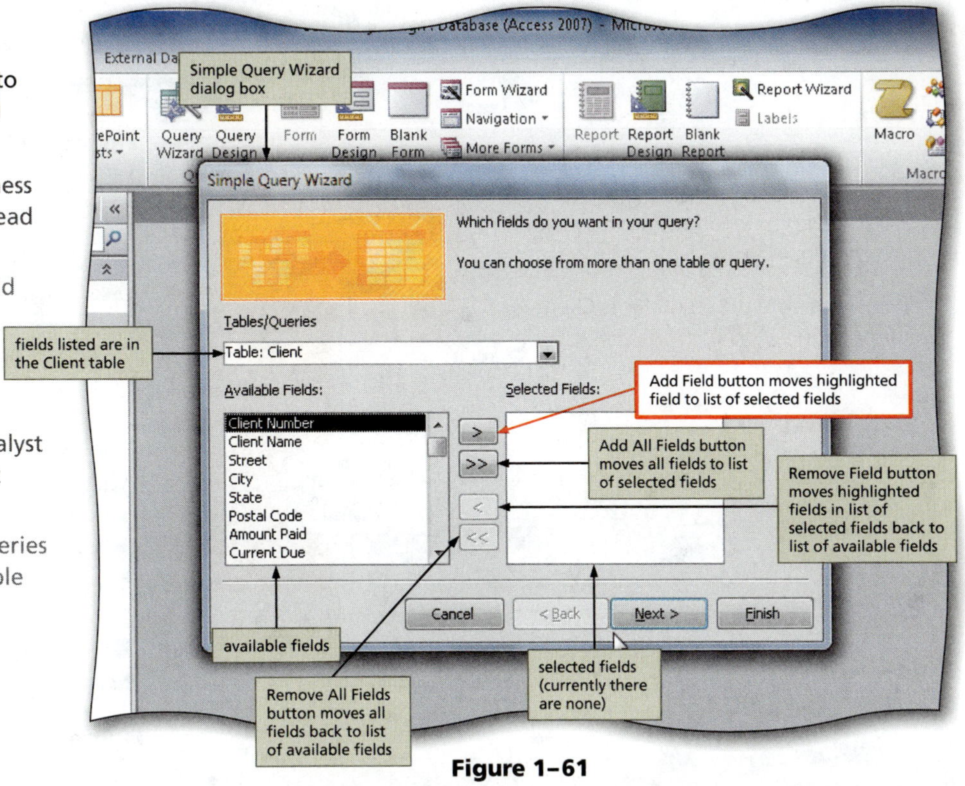

Figure 1–61

3

- With the Client Number field selected, click the Add Field button to add the field to the query.
- With the Client Name field selected, click the Add Field button a second time to add the field.
- Click the Amount Paid field, and then click the Add Field button to add the field.
- In a similar fashion, add the Current Due, Contract Hours YTD, and Business Analyst Number fields (Figure 1–62).

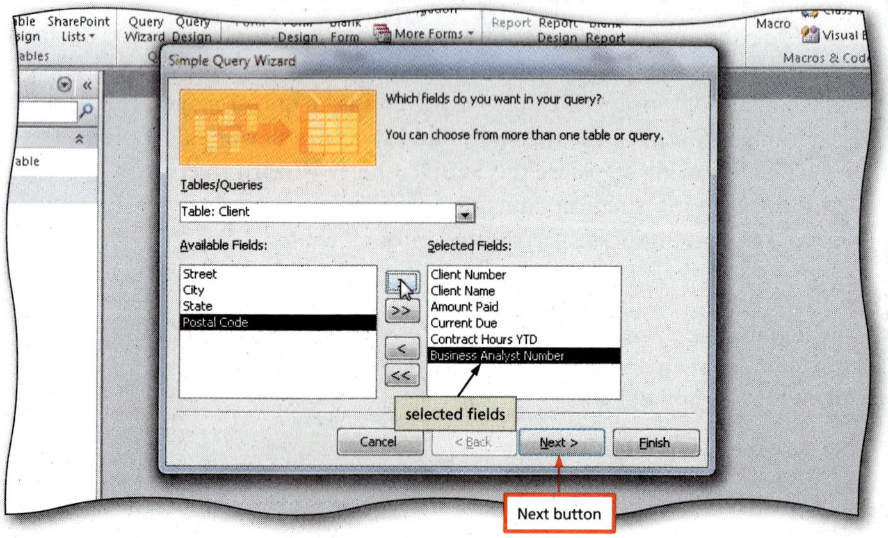

Figure 1–62

4

- Click the Next button to move to the next screen.
- Ensure that the Detail (shows every field of every record) option button is selected (Figure 1–63).

Q&A What is the difference between Detail and Summary?

Detail shows all the records and fields. Summary only shows computations (for example, the total amount paid).

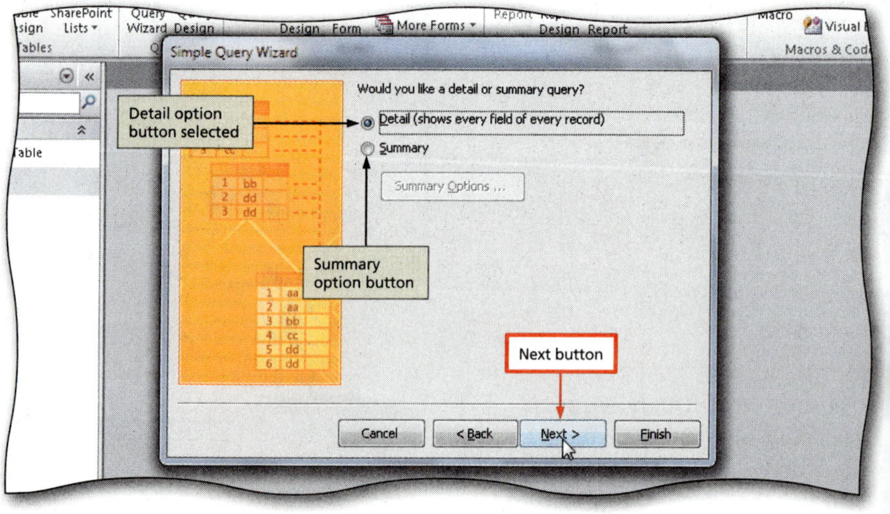

Figure 1–63

5

- Click the Next button to move to the next screen.
- Ensure the title of the query is Client Query (Figure 1–64).

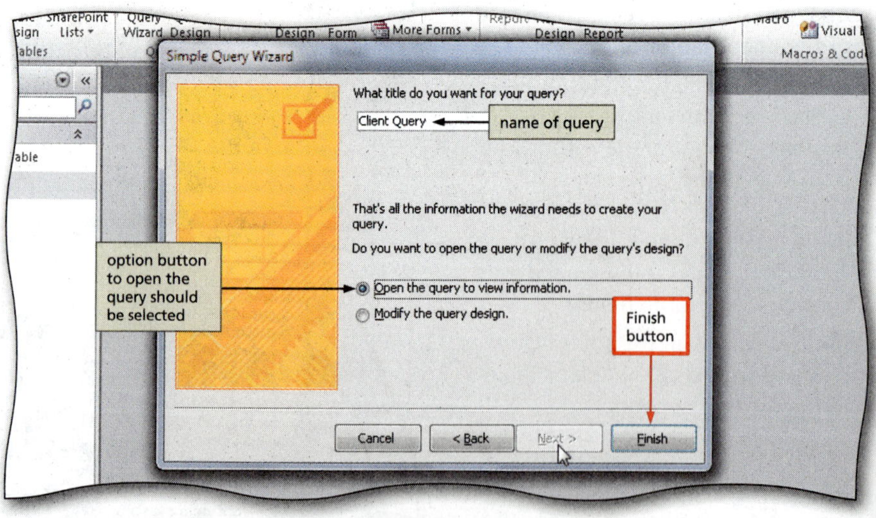

Figure 1–64

6

- Click the Finish button to create the query (Figure 1–65).
- Click the Close button for the Client Query to remove the query results from the screen.

Q&A If I want to use this query in the future, do I need to save the query?

Normally you would. The one exception is a query created by the wizard. The wizard automatically saves the query it creates.

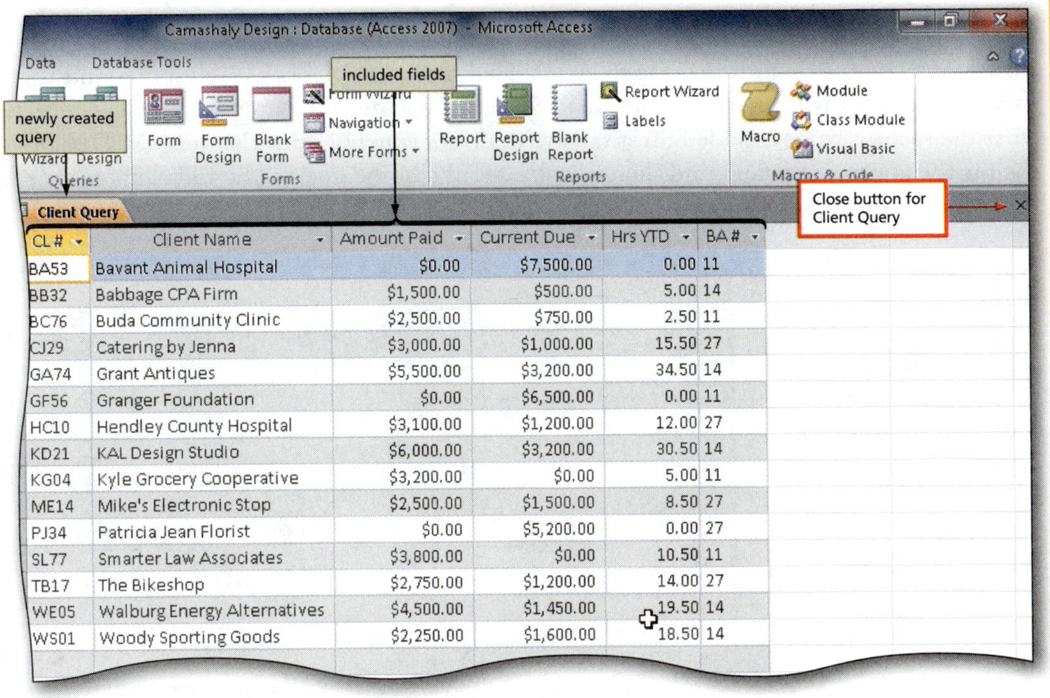

Figure 1–65

Using Queries

After you have created and saved a query, Access stores it as a database object and makes it available for use in a variety of ways:

- To view the results of the query, open it by right-clicking the query in the Navigation Pane and clicking Open on the shortcut menu.
- To print the results with the query open, click File on the Ribbon, click the Print tab, and then click either Print or Quick Print.
- If you want to change the design of the query, right-click the query in the Navigation Pane and then click Design View on the shortcut menu to open the query in Design view.
- To print the query without first opening it, be sure the query is selected in the Navigation Pane and click File on the Ribbon, click the Print tab, and then click either Print or Quick Print.

You can switch between views of a query using the View button (Home tab | Views group). Clicking the arrow in the bottom of the button produces the View button menu. You then click the desired view in the menu. The two query views you will use in this chapter are Datasheet view (see the results) and Design view (change the design). You also can click the top part of the View button, in which case, you will switch to the view identified by the icon on the button. In the figure, the button contains the icon for Design view, so clicking the button would change to Design view. For the most part, the icon on the button represents the view you want, so you can usually simply click the button.

To Use a Criterion in a Query

After you have determined the fields to be included in a query, you will determine whether there are any restrictions on the records that are to be included. For example, you might only want to include those clients whose business analyst number is 14. In such a case, you need to enter the 14 as a **criterion**, which is a condition that the records to be included must satisfy. To do so, you will open the query in Design view, enter the criterion below the appropriate field, and then view the results of the query. The following steps enter a criterion to include only the clients of business analyst 14 and then view the query results.

1

- Right-click the Client Query in the Navigation Pane to produce a shortcut menu (Figure 1–66).

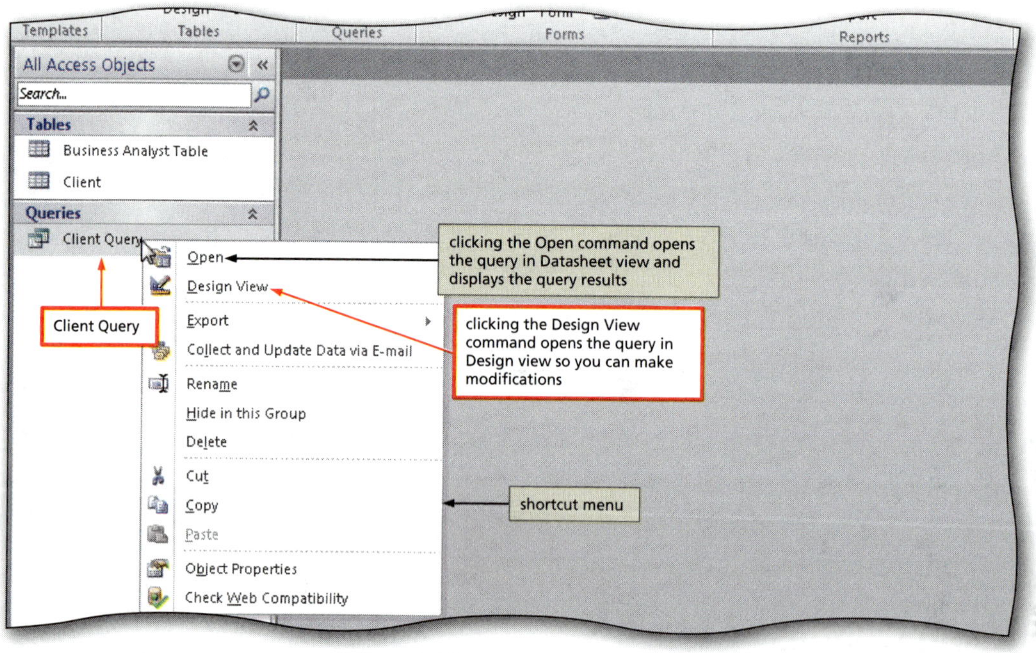

Figure 1–66

2

- Click Design View on the shortcut menu to open the query in Design view (Figure 1–67).

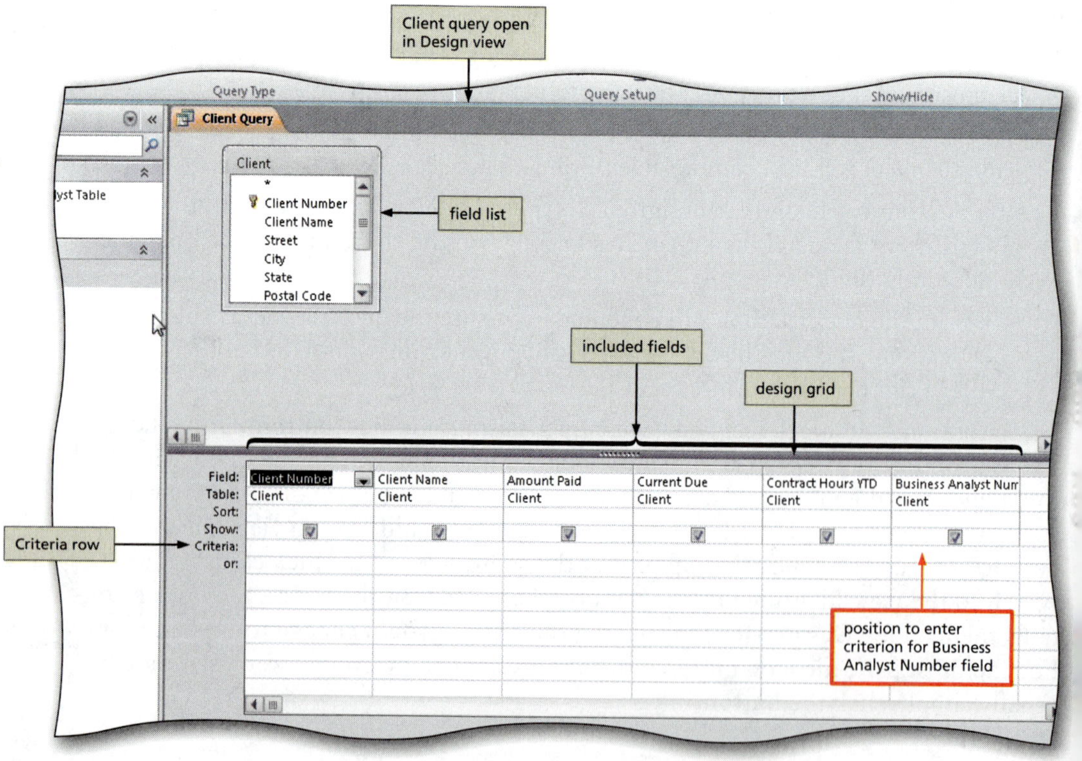

Figure 1–67

3

- Click the Criteria row in the Business Analyst Number column of the grid, and then type **14** as the criterion (Figure 1–68).

Q&A The Business Analyst Number field is a text field. Do I need to enclose the value for a text field in quotation marks?

You could, but it is not necessary, because Access inserts the quotation marks for you automatically.

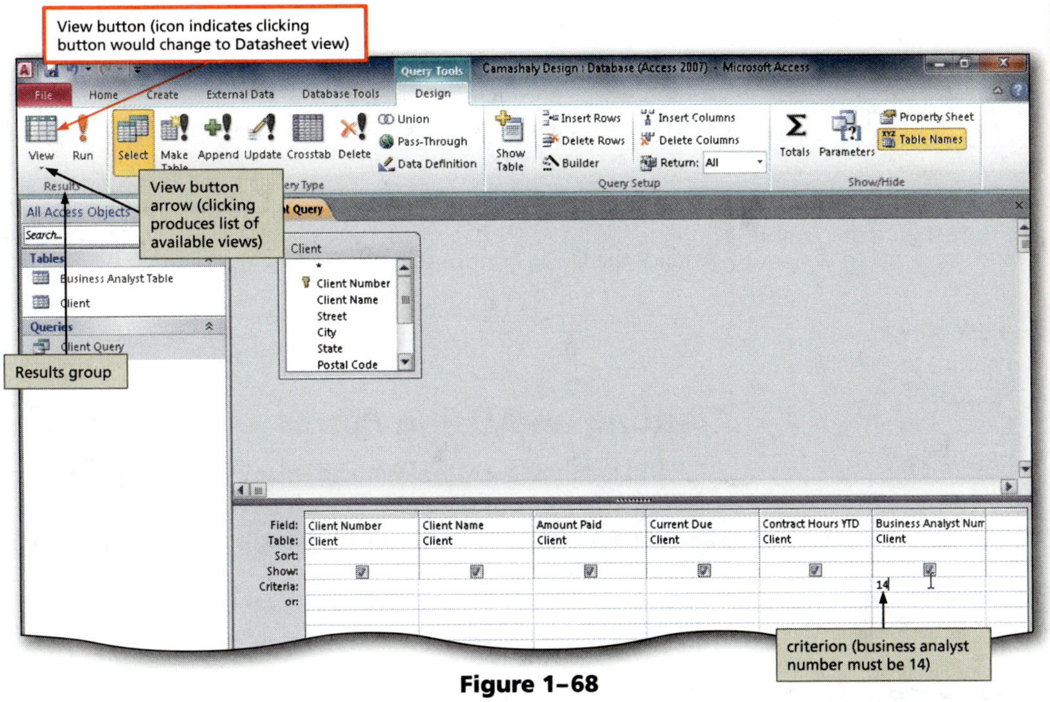

Figure 1–68

4

- Click the View button to display the query results in Datasheet view (Figure 1–69).

Q&A Could I click the View button arrow and then click Datasheet view?

Yes, if the icon representing the view you want appears on the View button; however, it is easier just to click the button.

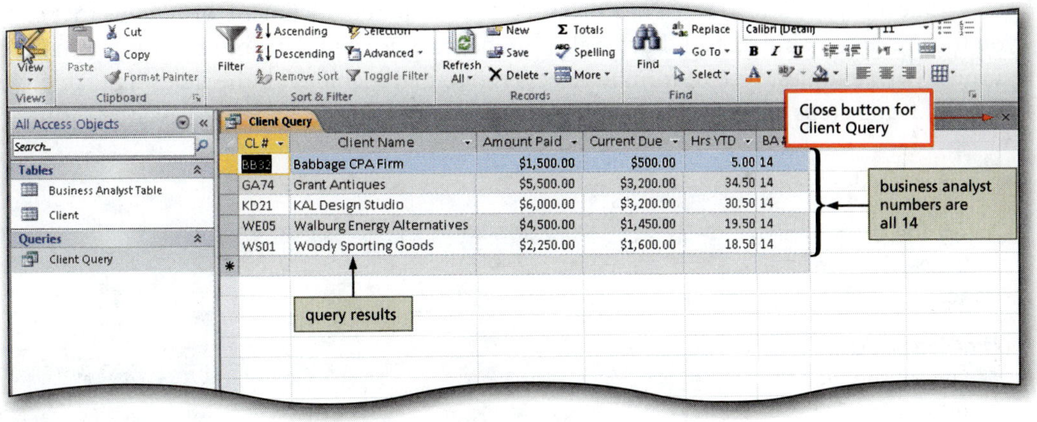

Figure 1–69

5

- Click the Close button for the Client Query to close the query.
- When asked if you want to save your changes, click the No button.

Q&A If I saved the query, what would happen the next time I ran the query?

You would see only clients of business analyst 14.

Q&A Could I save the query with another name?

Yes. To save the query with another name, click File on the Ribbon, click Save Object As, enter a new file name in the Save As dialog box and click the OK button (Save As dialog box).

Other Ways

1. Click Run button (Query Tools Design tab | Results group)
2. Click Datasheet View button on status bar

To Print the Results of a Query

The following steps print the results of a saved query.

1. With the Client Query selected in the Navigation Pane, click File on the Ribbon to open the Backstage view.
2. Click the Print tab in the Backstage view to display the Print gallery.
3. Click the Quick Print button to print the query.

Creating and Using Forms

In Datasheet view, you can view many records at once. If there are many fields, however, only some of the fields in each record might be visible at a time. In **Form view**, where data is displayed in a form on the screen, you usually can see all the fields, but only for one record.

To Create a Form

Like a paper form, a **form** in a database is a formatted document with fields that contain data. Forms allow you to view and maintain data. Forms also can be used to print data, but reports are more commonly used for that purpose. The simplest type of form in Access is one that includes all the fields in a table stacked one above the other. The following steps create a form, use the form to view records, and then save the form.

1

- Select the Client table in the Navigation Pane.
- If necessary, click Create on the Ribbon to display the Create tab (Figure 1–70).

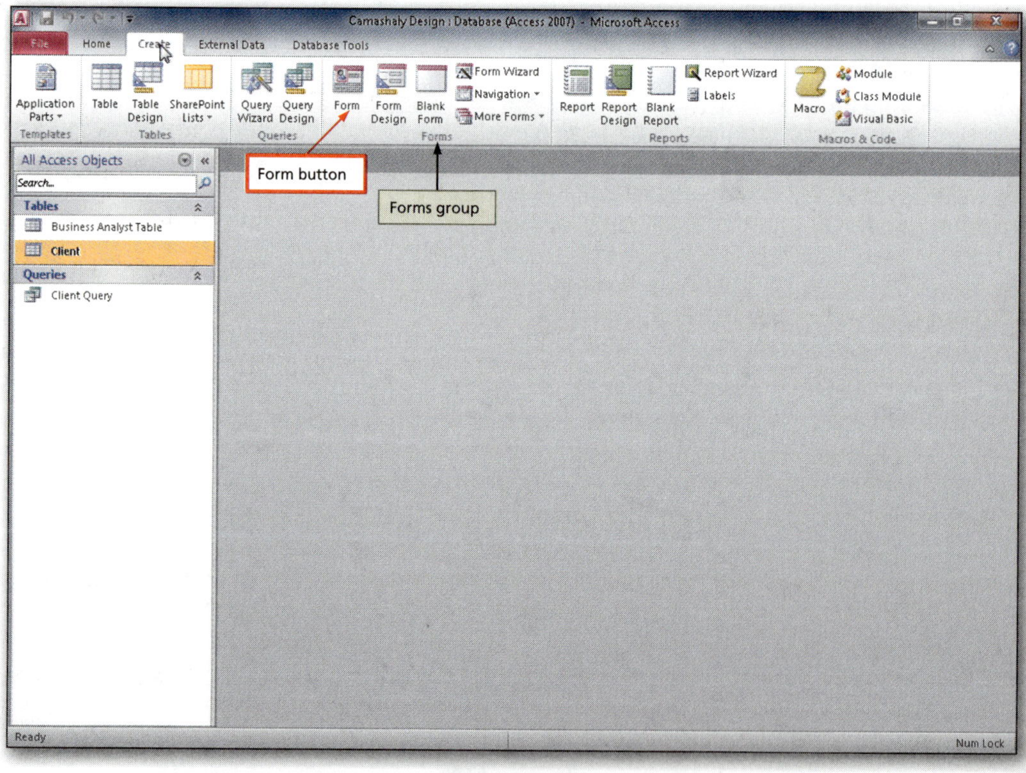

Figure 1–70

2

- Click the Form button (Create tab | Forms group) to create a simple form (Figure 1–71).

Q&A A Field list appeared on my screen. What should I do?

Click the Add Existing Fields button (Form Layout Tools Design tab | Tools group) to remove the Field list from the screen.

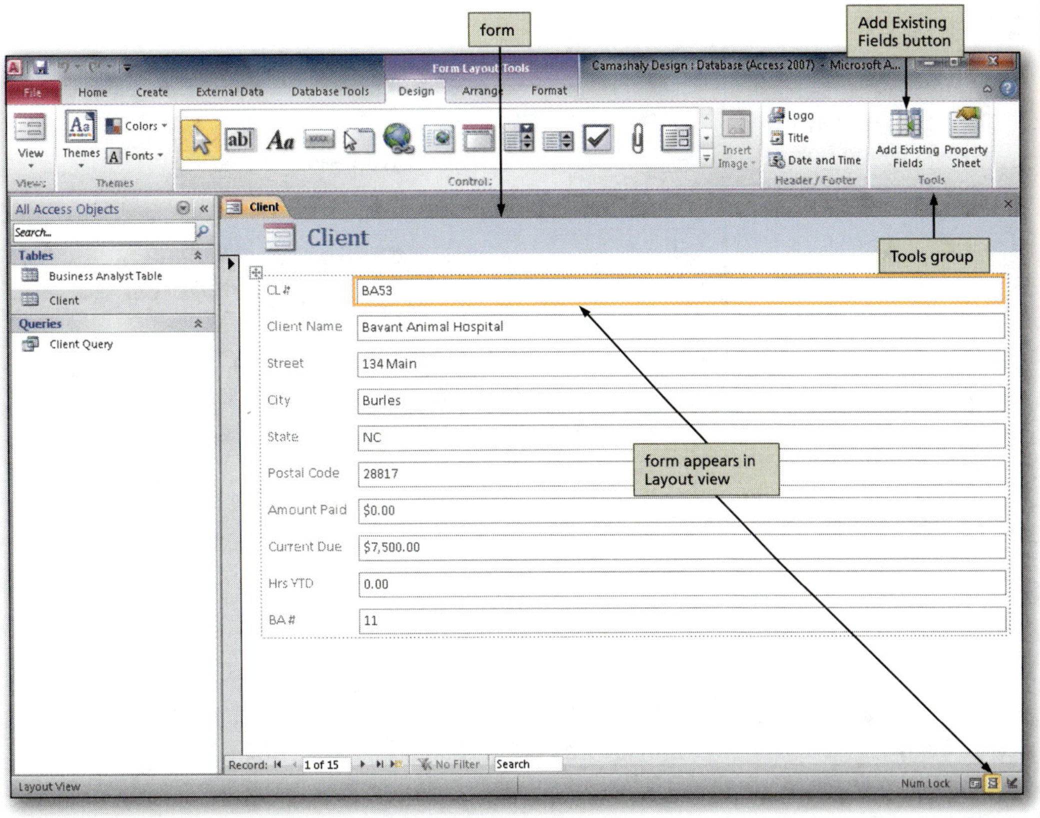

Figure 1–71

3

- If the form appears in Layout view, click the Form View button on the Access status bar to display the form in Form view.

Q&A How can I recognize Layout view?

Access identifies Layout view in three ways. The left side of the status bar will contain the words Layout View; there will be shading around the outside of the selected field in the form; and the Layout View button will be selected on the right side of the status bar.

- Click the Next Record button three times to move to record 4 (Figure 1–72).

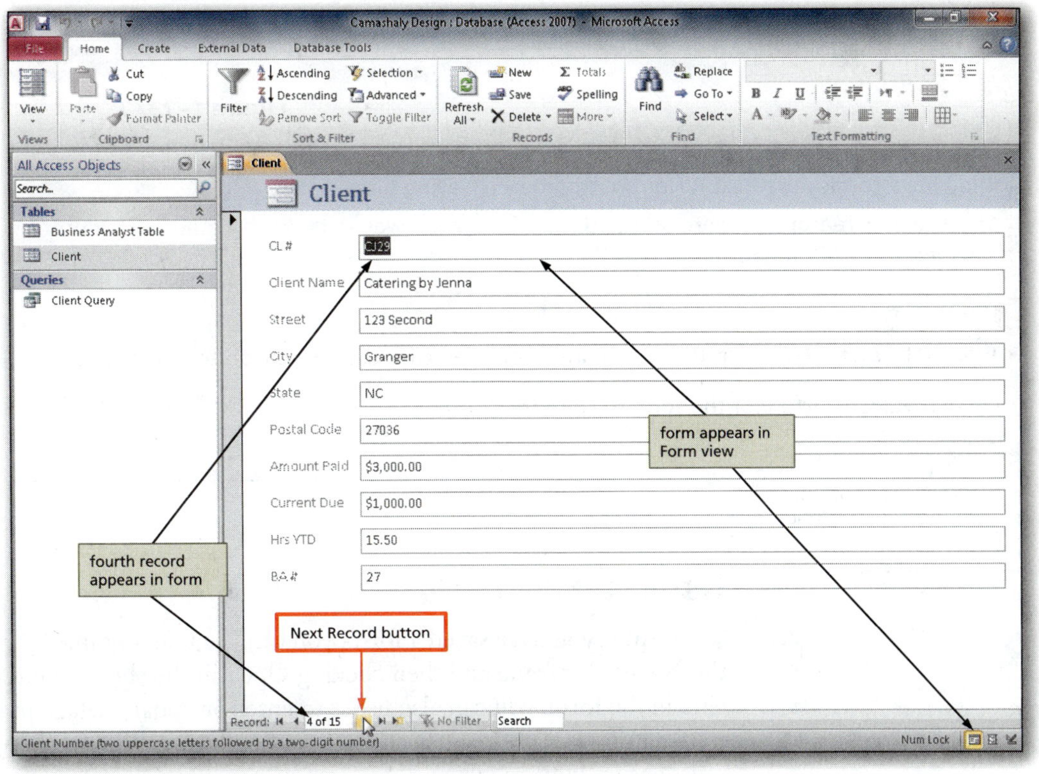

Figure 1–72

4

- Click the Save button on the Quick Access Toolbar to display the Save As dialog box (Figure 1–73).

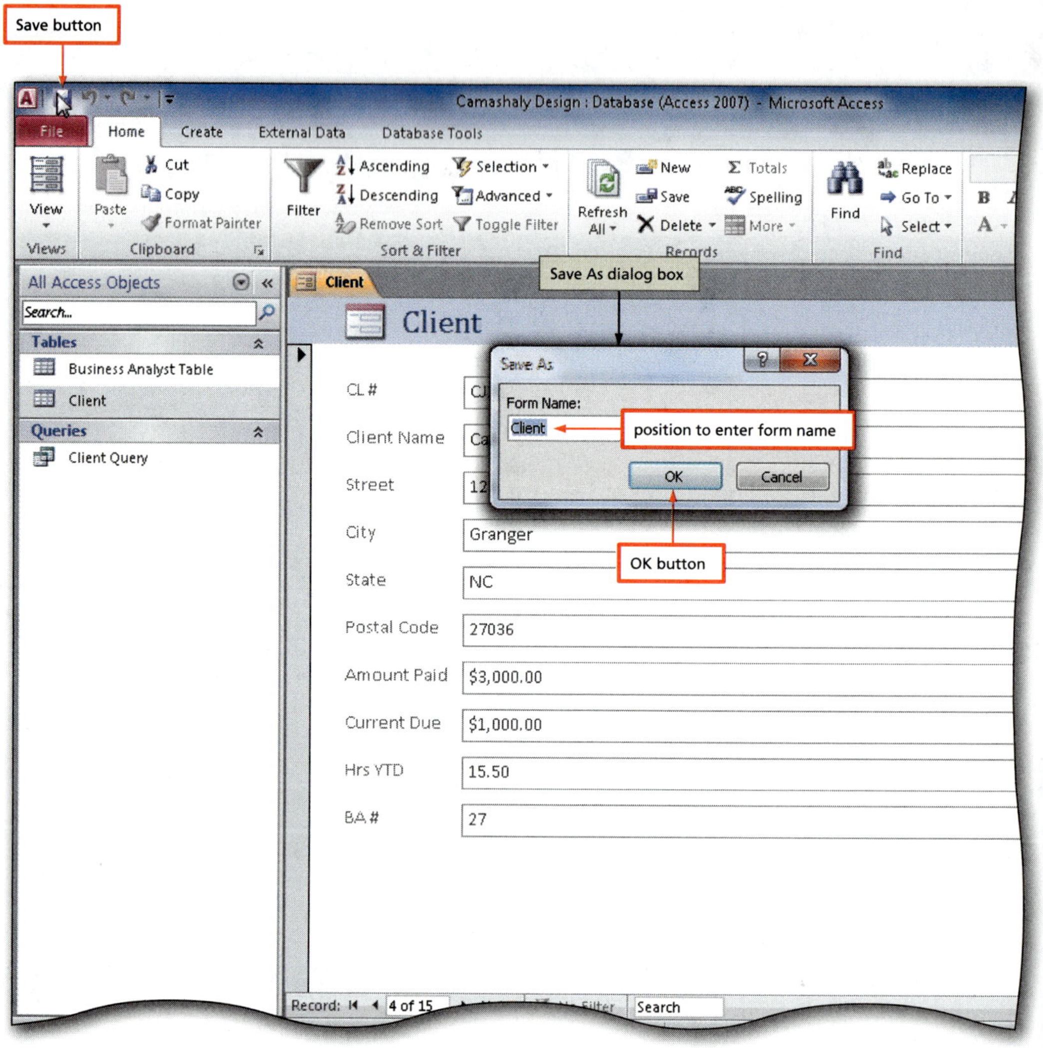

Figure 1–73

Q&A

Did I have to click the Next Record button before saving?

No. The only reason you were asked to click the button was so that you could experience navigation within the form.

5

- Type `Client Form` as the form name, and then click the OK button to save the form.
- Click the Close button for the form to close the form.

Other Ways

1. Click View button (Form Layout Tools Design tab | Views group)

Using a Form

After you have saved a form, you can use it at anytime by right-clicking the form in the Navigation Pane and then clicking Open in the shortcut menu. In addition to viewing data in the form, you can also use it to enter or update data, a process that is very similar to updating data using a datasheet. If you plan to use the form to enter or revise data, you must ensure you are viewing the form in Form view.

Break Point: If you wish to take a break, this is a good place to do so. You can quit Access now. To resume at a later time, start Access, open the database called Camashaly Design, and continue following the steps from this location forward.

Creating and Printing Reports

Camashaly Design wants to create the Client Financial Report shown in Figure 1–74. Just as you can create a form containing all fields by clicking a single button, you can click a button to create a report containing all the fields. Doing so will not match the report shown in Figure 1–74, however, which does not contain all the fields. Some of the column headings are different. In addition, some of the headings in the report in Figure 1–74 are split over multiple lines, whereas the ones in the report created by clicking the button will not be split. Fortunately, you can later modify the report design to make it precisely match the figure. To do so, you use Layout view for the report.

Client Financial Report

Thursday, April 12, 2012
5:17:00 PM

Client Number	Client Name	Amount Paid	Current Due	Hrs YTD	Business Analyst Number
BA53	Bavant Animal Hospital	$0.00	$7,500.00	0.00	11
BB32	Babbage CPA Firm	$1,500.00	$500.00	5.00	14
BC76	Buda Community Clinic	$2,500.00	$750.00	2.50	11
CJ29	Catering by Jenna	$3,000.00	$1,000.00	15.50	27
GA74	Grant Antiques	$5,500.00	$3,200.00	34.50	14
GF56	Granger Foundation	$0.00	$6,500.00	0.00	11
HC10	Hendley County Hospital	$3,100.00	$1,200.00	12.00	27
KD21	KAL Design Studio	$6,000.00	$3,200.00	30.50	14
KG04	Kyle Grocery Cooperative	$3,200.00	$0.00	5.00	11
ME14	Mike's Electronic Stop	$2,500.00	$1,500.00	8.50	27
PJ34	Patricia Jean Florist	$0.00	$5,200.00	0.00	27
SL77	Smarter Law Associates	$3,800.00	$0.00	10.50	11
TB17	The Bikeshop	$2,750.00	$1,200.00	14.00	27
WE05	Walburg Energy Alternatives	$4,500.00	$1,450.00	19.50	14
WS01	Woody Sporting Goods	$2,250.00	$1,600.00	18.50	14
		$40,600.00	$34,800.00	176.00	

Figure 1–74

To Create a Report

You will first create a report containing all fields. The following steps create and save the initial report. They also modify the report title.

1

- Be sure the Client table is selected in the Navigation Pane.
- Click Create on the Ribbon to display the Create tab (Figure 1–75).

Q&A Why do I need to select the Client table prior to clicking Create on the Ribbon?

You do not need to select it at that point. You do need to select it prior to clicking the Report button at the next step because Access will include all the fields in whichever table or query is currently selected.

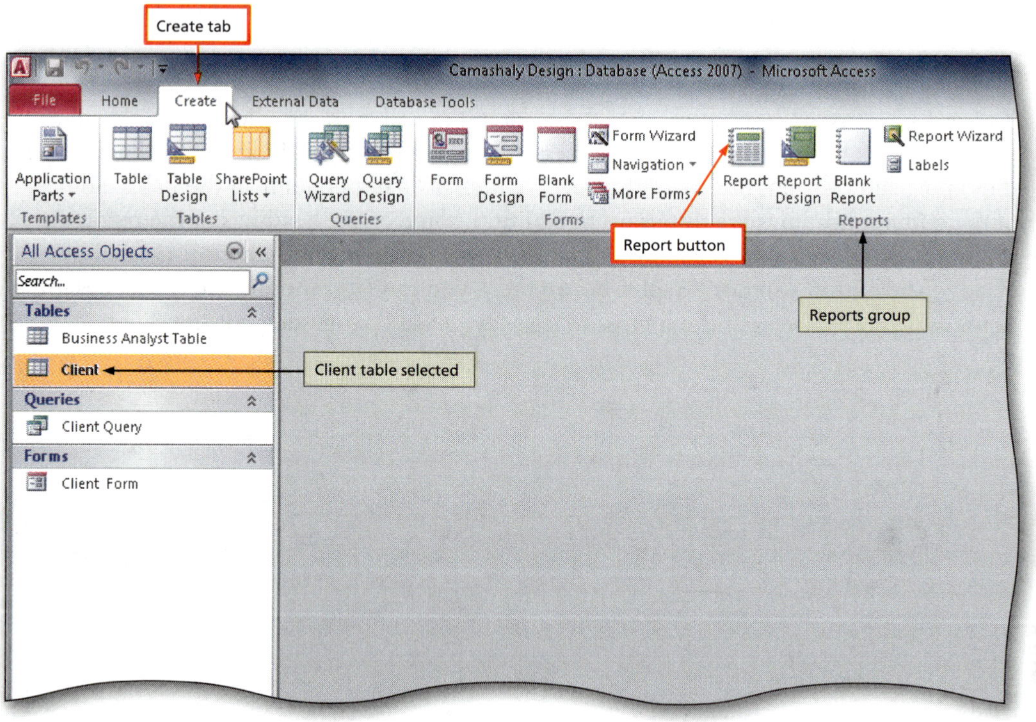

Figure 1–75

2

- Click the Report button (Create tab | Reports group) to create the report (Figure 1–76).

Q&A Why is the report title Client?

Access automatically assigns the name of the table or query as the title. It also automatically includes the date. You can change either of these later.

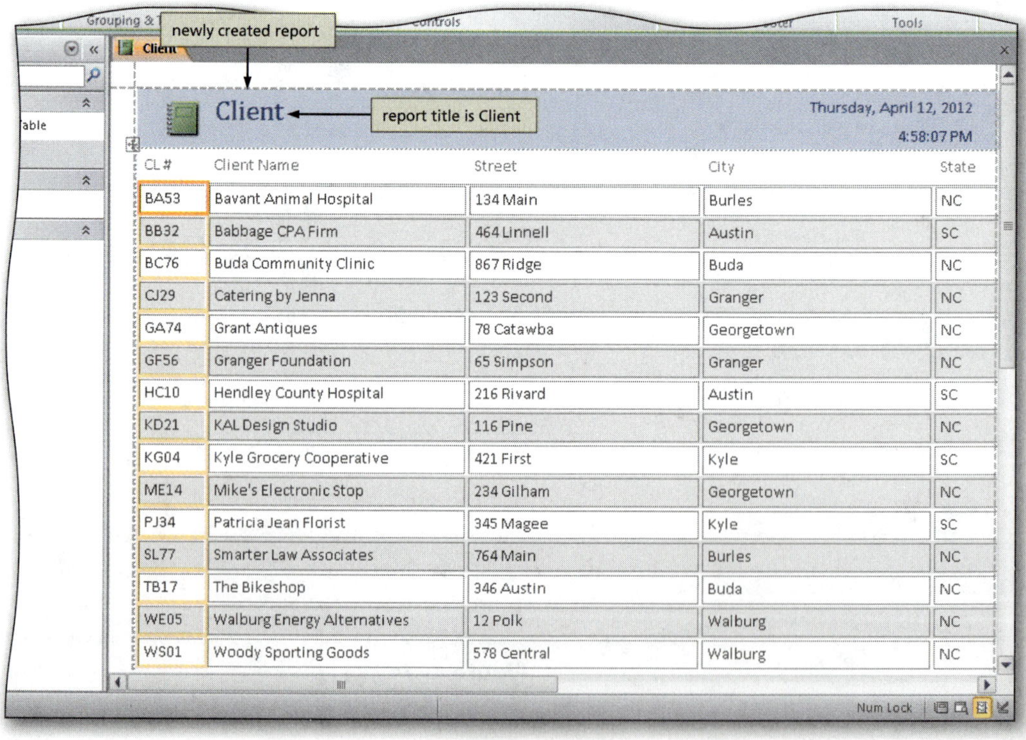

Figure 1–76

3

- Click the Save button on the Quick Access Toolbar to display the Save As dialog box and then type `Client Financial Report` as the name of the report (Figure 1–77).

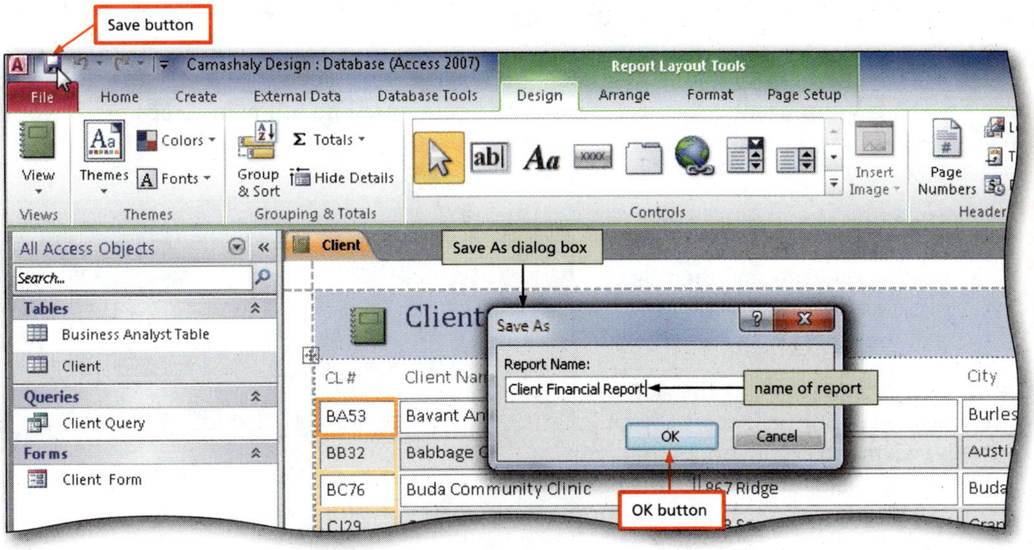

Figure 1–77

4

- Click the OK button (Save As dialog box) to save the report (Figure 1–78).

Q&A The name of the report changed. Why did the report title not change, too?

The report title just happens to begin with the same name as the report. If you change the name of the report, Access will not change the report title. You can change it at any time to any title you like.

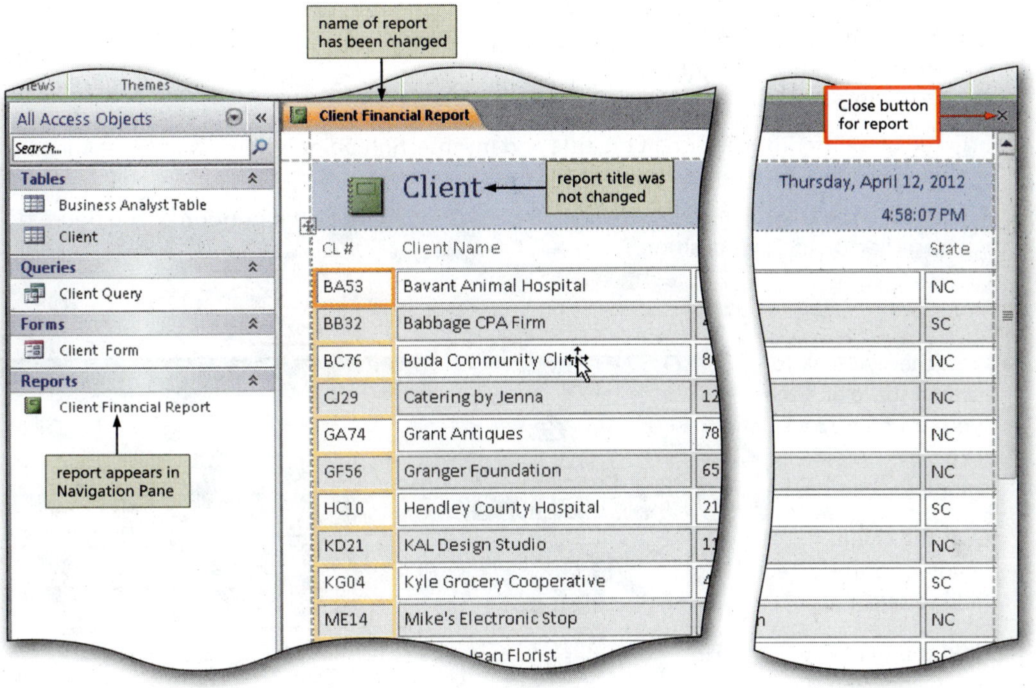

Figure 1–78

5

- Close the report by clicking its Close button.

Using Layout View in a Report

When working with a report in Access, there are four different ways to view the report. They are Report view, Print Preview, Layout view, and Design view. Report view shows the report on the screen. Print Preview shows the report as it will appear when printed. Layout view is similar to Report view in that it shows the report on the screen, but it also allows you to make changes to the report. It is usually the easiest way to make such changes. Design view also allows you to make changes, but it does not show you the actual report. It is most useful when the changes you need to make are especially complex. In this chapter, you will use Layout view to modify the report.

To Modify Column Headings and Resize Columns

To make the report match the one in Figure 1–74, you need to change the title, remove some columns, modify the column headings, and also resize the columns. The following steps use Layout view to make the necessary modifications to the report.

1

- Right-click Client Financial Report in the Navigation Pane, and then click Layout View on the shortcut menu to open the report in Layout view.
- If a Field list appears, click the Add Existing Fields button (Report Layout Tools Design tab | Tools group) to remove the Field list from the screen.
- Close the Navigation Pane.
- Click the report title once to select it.
- Click the report title a second time to produce an insertion point (Figure 1–79).

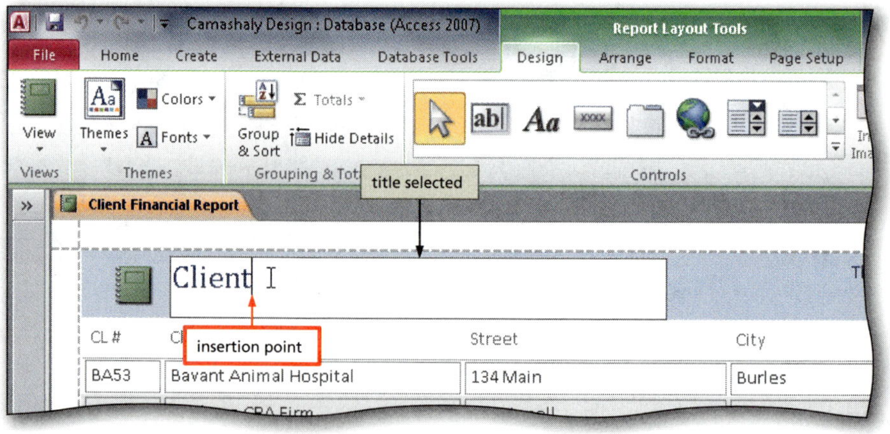

Figure 1–79

Q&A

I clicked at a different position in the title and my insertion point is in the middle of Client. How do I produce an insertion point at the position shown in the figure?

You can use the RIGHT ARROW key to move the insertion point to the position in the figure or you can click the desired position.

2

- Press the SPACEBAR to insert a space and then type `Financial Report` to complete the title.
- Click the column heading for the Street field to select it.
- Hold the SHIFT key down and then click the column headings for the City field, the State field, and the Postal Code fields to select multiple column headings.

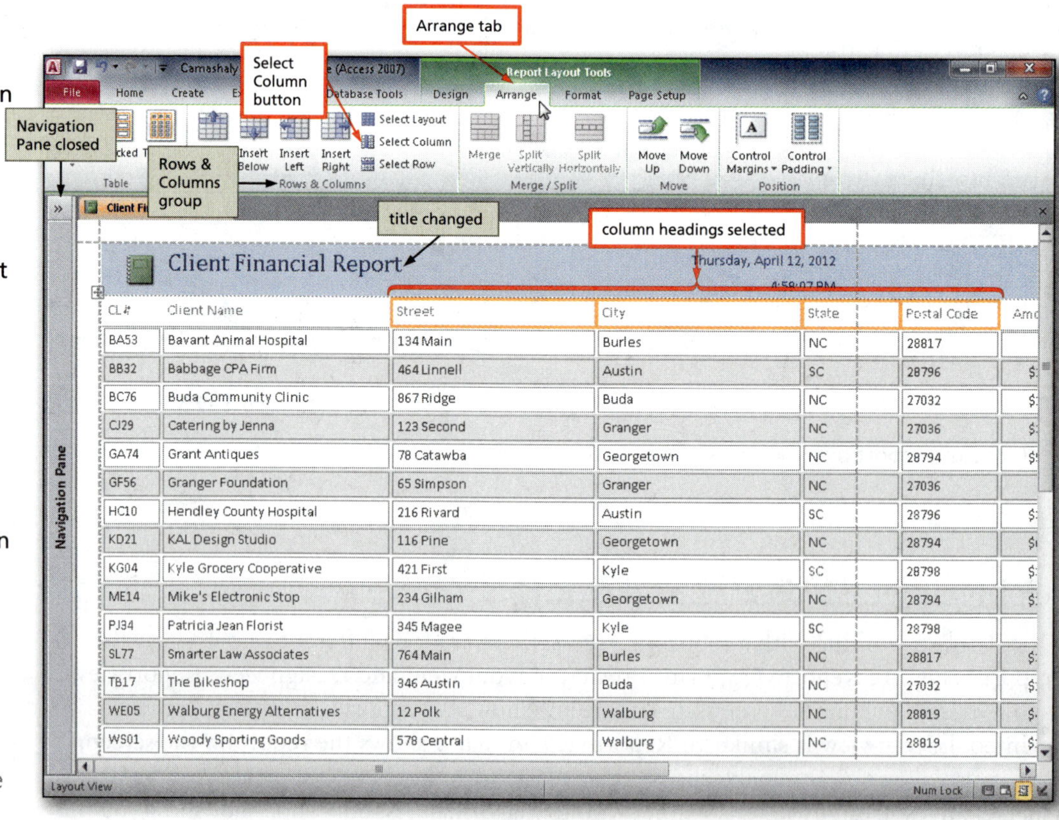

Figure 1–80

Q&A

What happens if I do not hold down the SHIFT key?

As soon as you click the column heading, it will be the only one that is selected. To select multiple objects, you need to hold the SHIFT key down for every object after the first one.

Q&A

I selected the wrong collection of objects. What should I do?

You can click somewhere else on the report so that the objects you want are not selected, and then begin the process again. Alternatively, you can repeatedly click the Undo button on the Quick Access Toolbar to undo your selections. Once you have done so, you can select the objects you want.

- Click Arrange on the Ribbon to display the Arrange tab (Figure 1–80).

3

- Click the Select Column button (Report Layout Tools Arrange tab | Rows & Columns group) to select the entire columns corresponding to the column headings you selected in the previous step.
- Press the DELETE key to delete the columns.
- Click the column heading for the Client Number field twice, once to select it and the second time to produce an insertion point (Figure 1–81).

Q&A

I inadvertently selected the wrong field. What should I do?

Click somewhere outside the various fields to deselect the one you have selected. Then, click the Client Number field twice.

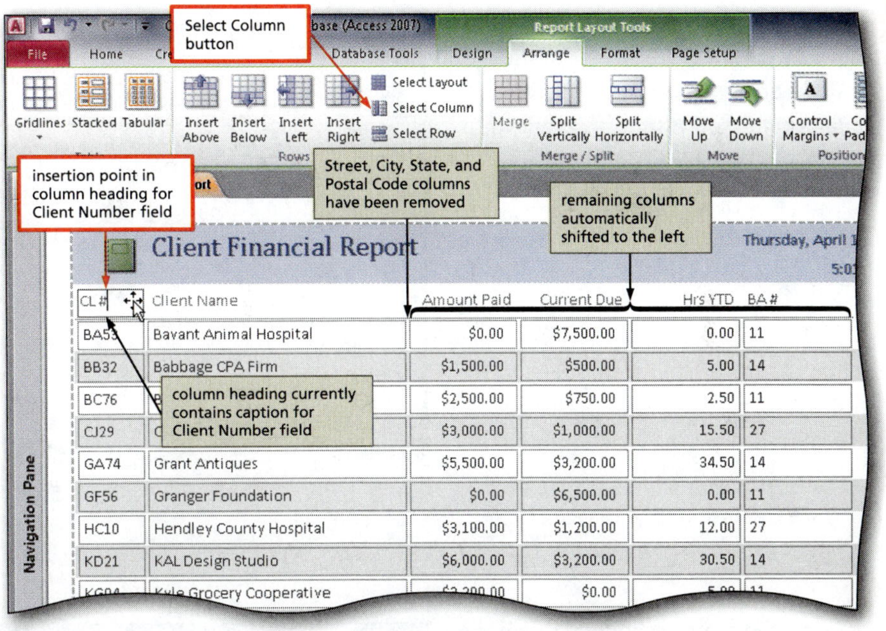

Figure 1–81

4

- Use the DELETE or BACKSPACE keys as necessary to erase the current entry and then type **`Client Number`** as the new entry.
- Click the heading for the Business Analyst Number field twice, erase the current entry, and then type **`Business Analyst Number`** as the new entry.
- Click the Client Number field heading to select it, point to the lower boundary of the heading for the Client Number field so that the mouse pointer changes to a two-headed arrow and then drag the lower boundary to the approximate position shown in Figure 1–82 to expand the column headings.

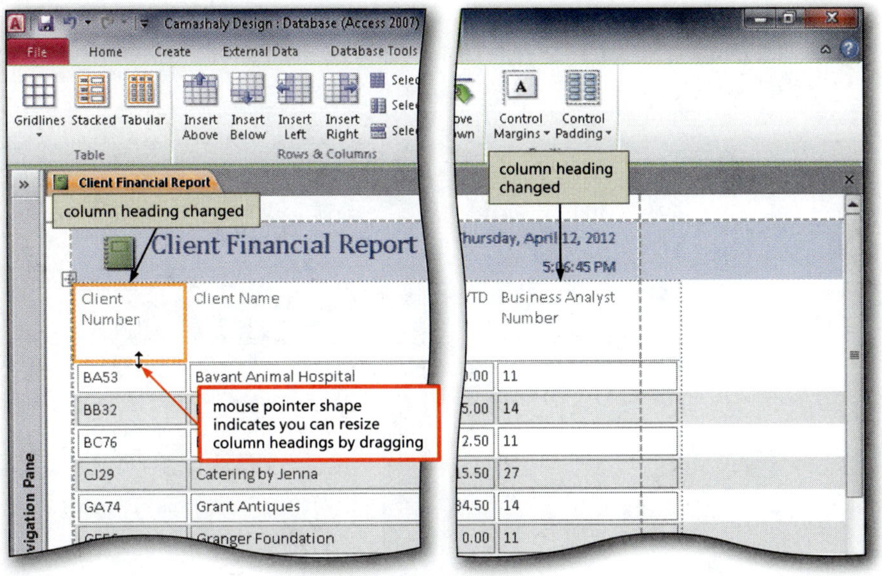

Figure 1–82

Q&A

Do I have to be exact?

No. If you are in a slightly different position, your report would look a little different from the one in the figure, but the difference would not be significant.

5

- Point to the right boundary of the heading for the Client Number field so that the mouse pointer changes to a two-headed arrow and then drag the right boundary to the approximate position shown in Figure 1–83 to reduce the width of the column.

Q&A

Do I have to be exact?

No. Again, if you are in a slightly different position, the difference between your report and the one in the figure would not be significant.

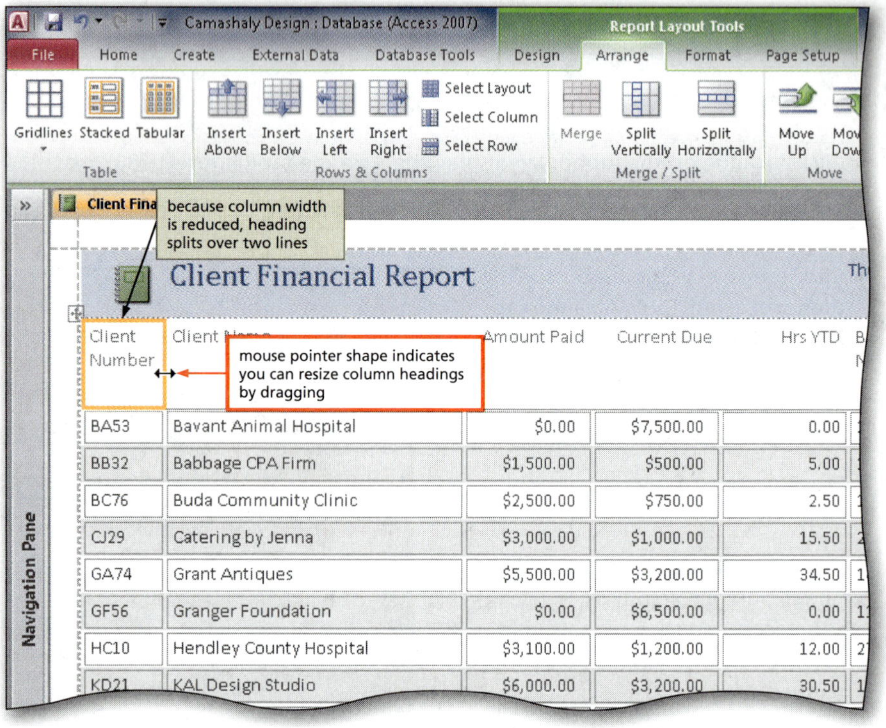

Figure 1–83

6

- Using the same technique, resize the other columns to the sizes shown in Figure 1–84.

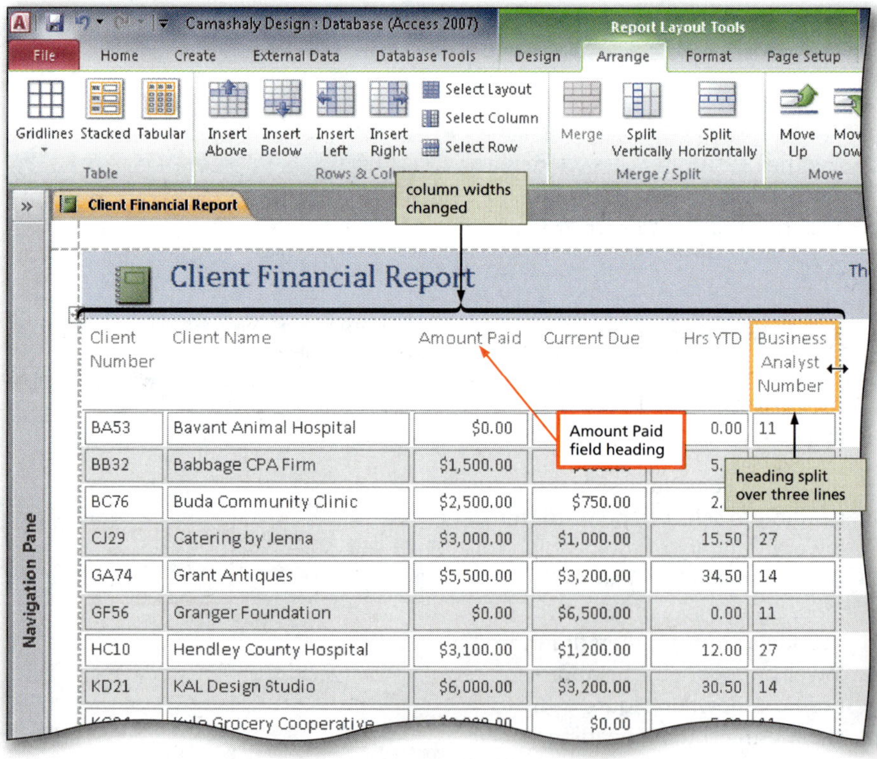

Figure 1–84

To Add Totals to a Report

The report in Figure 1–74 contains totals for the Amount Paid, Current Due, and Hrs YTD columns. You can use Layout view to add these totals. The following steps use Layout view to include totals for these three columns.

1

- Click the Amount Paid field heading (shown in Figure 1–84) to select the field.

Q&A Do I have to click the heading? Could I click the field on one of the records?

You do not have to click the heading. You also could click the Amount Paid field on any record.

- Click Design on the Ribbon to display the Design tab.
- Click the Totals button (Report Layout Tools Design tab | Grouping & Totals group) to display the list of available calculations (Figure 1–85).

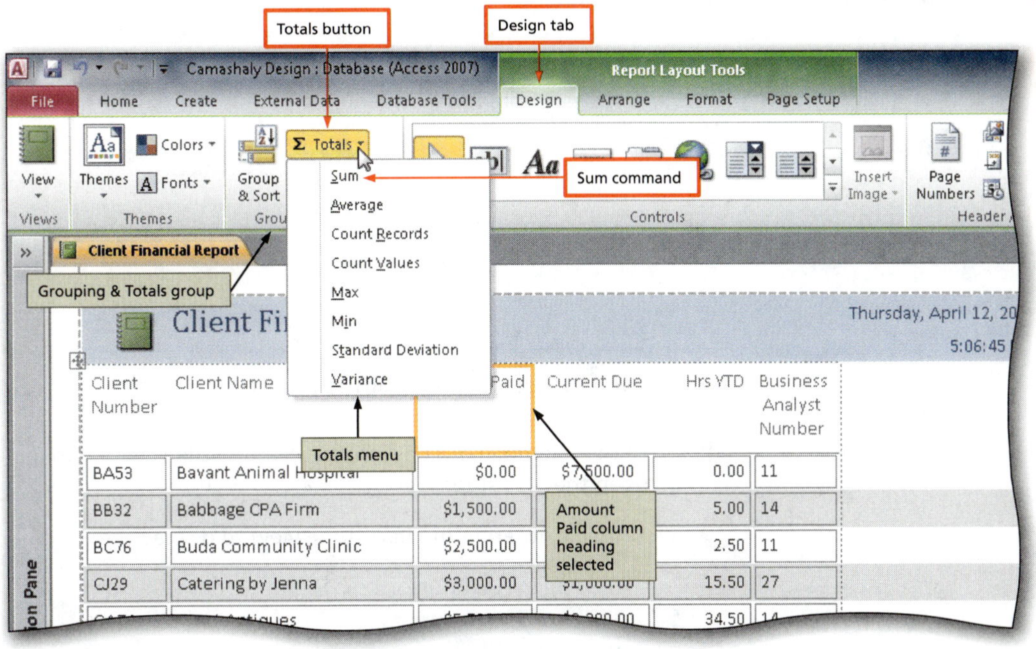

Figure 1–85

2

- Click Sum to calculate the sum of the amount of paid values.

Q&A Is Sum the same as Total?

Yes.

- Using the same technique, add totals for the Current Due and Hrs YTD columns.
- Scroll down to the bottom of the report to verify that the totals are included. If necessary, expand the size of the total controls so they appear completely.
- Click the Page number to select it and then drag it to the approximate position shown in Figure 1–86.

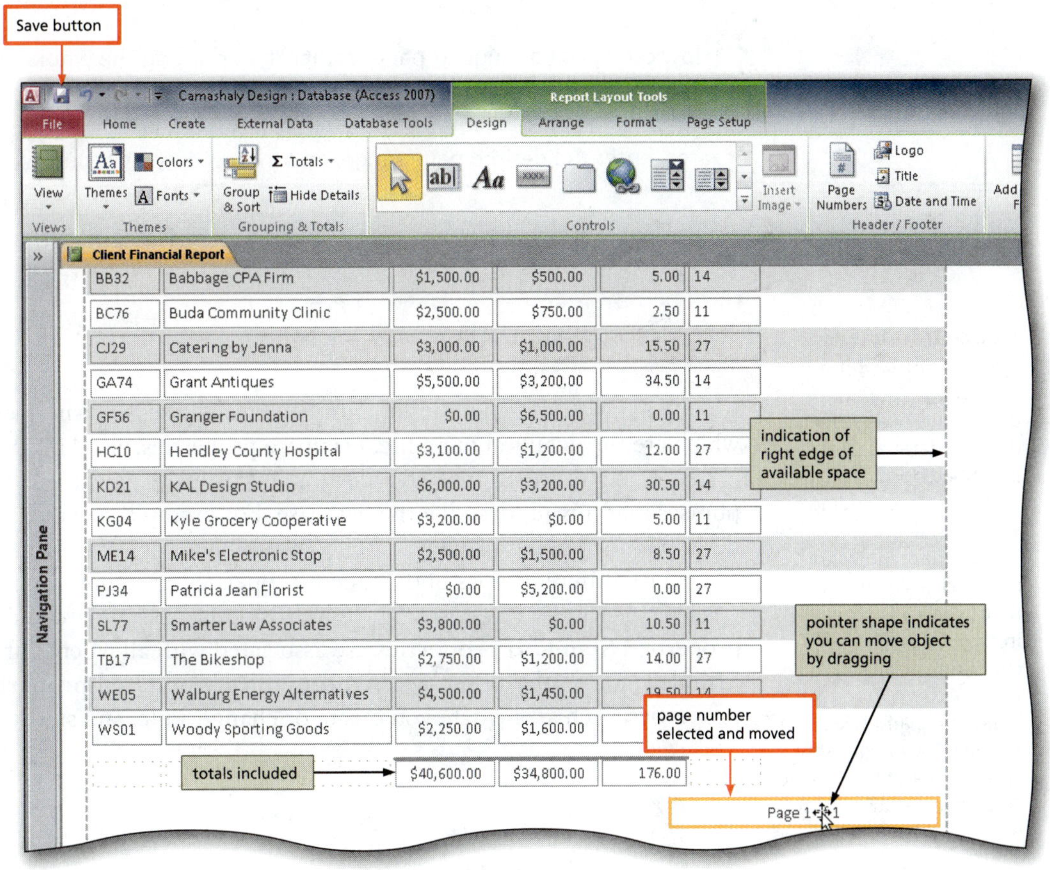

Figure 1–86

Q&A

Why did I need to move the page number?

The dotted line near the right-hand edge of the screen indicates the right-hand border of the available space on the printed page, based on whatever margins and orientation are currently selected. A portion of the page number extends beyond this border. By moving the page number, it no longer extends beyond the border.

3

- Click the Save button on the Quick Access Toolbar to save your changes to the report layout.
- Close the report.

To Print a Report

The following steps print the report.

1. With the Client Financial Report selected in the Navigation Pane, click File on the Ribbon to open the Backstage view.
2. Click the Print tab in the Backstage view to display the Print gallery.
3. Click the Quick Print button to print the report.

Q&A

How can I print multiple copies of my report?

Click File on the Ribbon to open the Backstage view. Click the Print tab, click Print in the Print gallery to display the Print dialog box, increase the number in the Number of Copies box, and then click the OK button (Print dialog box).

Q&A

How can I print a range of pages rather than printing the whole report?

Click File on the Ribbon to open the Backstage view. Click the Print tab, click Print in the Print gallery to display the Print dialog box, click the Pages option button in the Print Range area, enter the desired page range, and then click the OK button (Print dialog box).

BTW

Tabbed Documents Versus Overlapping Windows

By default, Access 2010 displays database objects in tabbed documents instead of overlapping windows. If your database is in overlapping windows mode, click File on the Ribbon, click Options in the Backstage view, click Current Database in the Access Options dialog box, and select the Display Document Tabs check box and the Tabbed Documents option button.

Database Properties

Access helps you organize and identify your databases by using **database properties**, which are the details about a file. Database properties, also known as **metadata**, can include such information as the file's author, title, or subject. **Keywords** are words or phrases that further describe the database. For example, a class name or database topic can describe the file's purpose or content.

Five different types of document properties exist, but the more common ones used in the Office and Windows chapters in this book are standard and automatically updated properties. **Standard properties** are associated with all Microsoft Office documents and include author, title, and subject. **Automatically updated properties** include file system properties, such as the date you create or change a file, and statistics, such as the file size.

To Change Database Properties

The Database Properties dialog box contains areas where you can view and enter database properties. You can view and change information in this dialog box at anytime while you are working on your database. It is a good idea to add your name and class name as database properties. You also can add keywords that further describe your database. The following steps use the Properties dialog box to change database properties.

1

- Click File on the Ribbon to open the Backstage view.
- If necessary, click the Info tab in the Backstage view to display the Info gallery (Figure 1–87).

How do I close the Backstage view?

Click File on the Ribbon or click the preview of the document in the Info gallery to return to the Access database window.

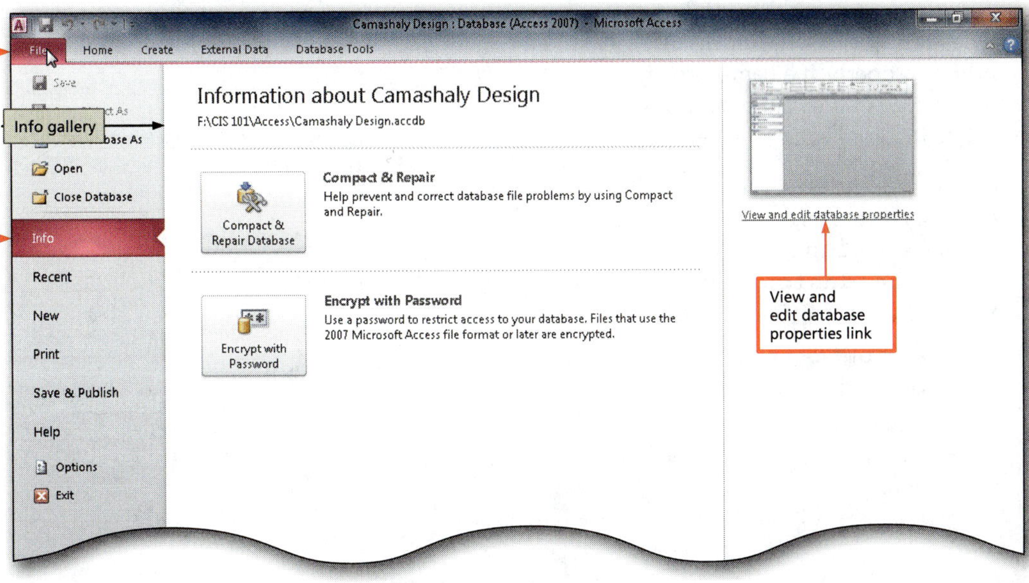

Figure 1–87

2

- Click the 'View and edit database properties' link in the right pane of the Info gallery to display the Camashaly Design.accdb Properties dialog box (Figure 1–88).

Why are some of the database properties in my Properties dialog box already filled in?

The person who installed Microsoft Office 2010 on your computer or network may have set or customized the properties.

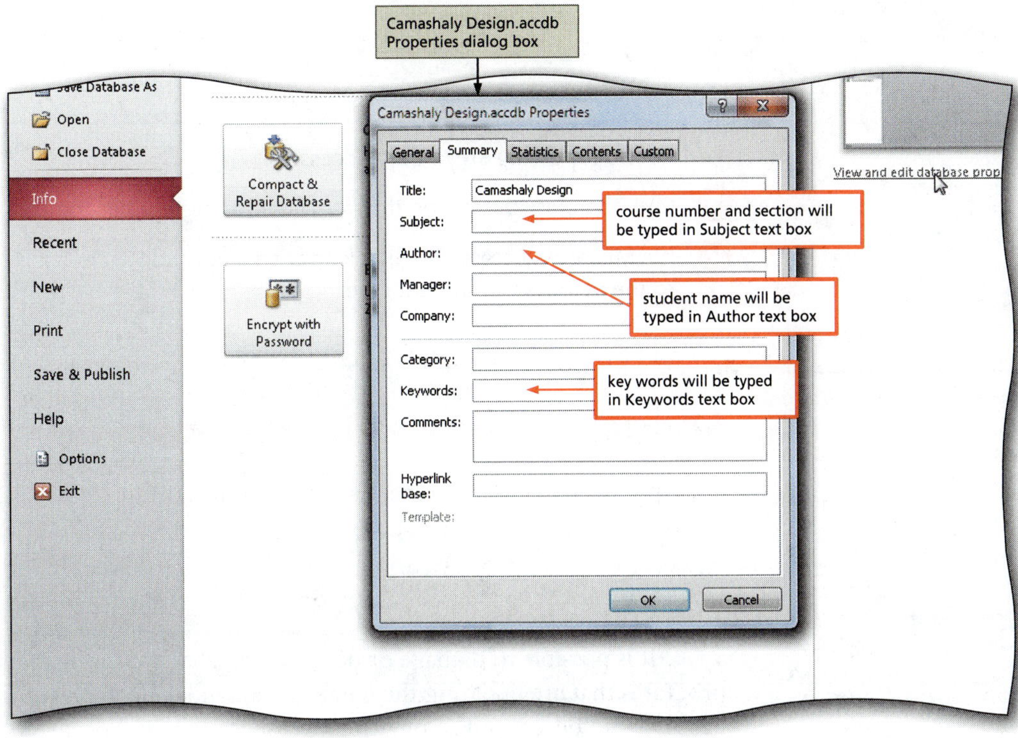

Figure 1–88

3

- If necessary, click the Summary tab.
- Click the Subject text box, if necessary delete any existing text, and then type **`CIS 101, Section 20`** as the Subject property.
- Click the Author text box and then type **`Trevor Wilkins`** as the Author property. If a name already is displayed in the Author text box, delete it before typing the new name.
- Click the Keywords text box, if necessary delete any existing text, and then type **`online marketing, Web site design`** as the Keywords property (Figure 1–89).

Q&A What types of properties does Access collect automatically?

Access records such details as when the database was created, when it was last modified, total editing time, and the various objects contained in the database.

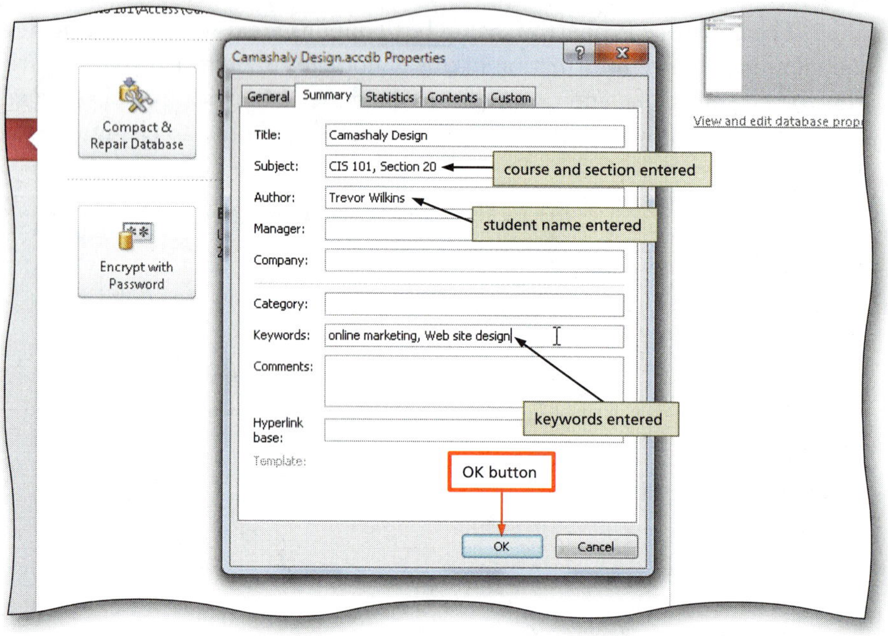

Figure 1–89

4

- Click the OK button to save your changes and remove the Camashaly Design.accdb Properties dialog box from the screen.

To Quit Access

The following steps quit Access.

1. Click the Close button on the right side of the title bar to quit Access.
2. If a Microsoft Access dialog box appears, click the Save button to save any changes made to the object since the last save.

Special Database Operations

The special operations involved in maintaining a database are backup, recovery, compacting a database, and repairing a database.

Backup and Recovery

It is possible to damage or destroy a database. Users can enter data that is incorrect; programs that are updating the database can end abnormally during an update; a hardware problem can occur; and so on. After any such event has occurred, the database may contain invalid data. It even might be totally destroyed.

Obviously, you cannot allow a situation in which data has been damaged or destroyed to go uncorrected. You must somehow return the database to a correct state. This process is called recovery; that is, you **recover** the database.

The simplest approach to recovery involves periodically making a copy of the database (called a **backup copy** or a **save copy**). This is referred to as **backing up** the database. If a problem occurs, you correct the problem by copying this backup copy over the actual database, often referred to as the **live database**.

To back up the database that is currently open, you use the Back Up Database command on the Save & Publish tab in the Backstage view. In the process, Access suggests a name that is a combination of the database name and the current date. For example, if you back up the Camashaly Design database on April 20, 2012, Access will suggest the name, Camashaly Design_2012-04-20. You can change this name if you desire, although it is a good idea to use this name. By doing so, it will be easy to distinguish between all the backup copies you have made to determine which is the most recent. In addition, if you discover that a critical problem occurred on April 18, 2012, you may want to go back to the most recent backup before April 18. If, for example, the database was not backed up on April 17 but was backed up on April 16, you would use Camashaly Design_2012-04-16.

To Back Up a Database

You would use the following steps to back up a database to a file on a hard disk or high-capacity removable disk.

1. Open the database to be backed up.
2. Click File on the Ribbon to open the Backstage view, and then click the Save & Publish tab.
3. With Save Database As selected in the File Types area, click Back Up Database in the Save Database As area, and then click the Save As button.
4. Selected the desired location in the Save As box. If you do not want the name Access has suggested, enter the desired name in the File name text box.
5. Click the Save button to back up the database.

Access creates a backup copy with the desired name in the desired location. Should you ever need to recover the database using this backup copy, you can simply copy it over the live version.

Compacting and Repairing a Database

As you add more data to a database, it naturally grows larger. When you delete an object (records, tables, forms, or queries), the space previously occupied by the object does not become available for additional objects. Instead, the additional objects are given new space; that is, space that was not already allocated. To remove this wasted space from the database, you must **compact** the database. The same option that compacts the database also repairs problems that might have occurred in the database.

To Compact and Repair a Database

You would use the following steps to compact and repair a database.

1. Open the database to be compacted.
2. Click File on the Ribbon to open the Backstage view, and then, if necessary, select the Info tab.
3. Click the Compact & Repair Database button in the Info gallery to compact and repair the database.

The database now is the compacted form of the original.

BTW

Access Help
At any time while using Access, you can find answers to questions and display information about various topics through Help. Used properly, this form of assistance can increase your productivity and reduce your frustrations by minimizing the time you spend learning how to use Access. For instruction about Access Help and exercises that will help you gain confidence in using it, read the Office 2010 and Windows 7 chapter in this book.

Additional Operations

Additional special operations include opening another database, closing a database without quitting Access, and saving a database with another name. They also include deleting a table (or other object) as well as renaming an object. Finally, you can change properties of a table or other object, such as the object's description.

When you open another database, Access will automatically close the database that previously was open. Before deleting or renaming an object, you should ensure that the object has no dependent objects; that is, other objects that depend on the object you want to delete.

To Open Another Database

To open another database, you would use the following steps.

1. Click File on the Ribbon to open the Backstage view.
2. Click Open.
3. Select the database to be opened.
4. Click the Open button.

To Close a Database without Quitting Access

You would use the following steps to close a database without quitting Access.

1. Click File on the Ribbon to open the Backstage view.
2. Click Close Database.

To Save a Database with Another Name

To save a database with another name, you would use the following steps.

1. Click File on the Ribbon to open the Backstage view, and then select the Save & Publish tab.
2. With Save Database As selected in the File Types area and Access Database selected in the Save Database As area, click the Save As button.
3. Enter a name and select a location for the new version.
4. Click the Save button.

To Delete a Table or Other Object in the Database

You would use the following steps to delete a database object.

1. Right-click the object in the Navigation Pane.
2. Click Delete on the shortcut menu.
3. Click the Yes button in the Microsoft Access dialog box.

BTW

Quick Reference
For a table that lists how to complete the tasks covered in the Office chapters in this book using the mouse, Ribbon, shortcut menu, and keyboard, see the Quick Reference Summary at the back of this book, or visit the Microsoft Office and Concepts CourseMate Web site at www.cengagebrain.com and then navigate to the Quick Reference resource for this book.

To Rename an Object in the Database

You would use the following steps to rename a database object.

1. Right-click the object in the Navigation Pane.
2. Click Rename on the shortcut menu.
3. Type the new name and press the ENTER key.

Chapter Summary

In this chapter you have learned to design a database, create an Access database, create tables and add records to them, print the contents of tables, create queries, create forms, and create reports. You also have learned how to change database properties. The items listed below include all the new Access skills you have learned in this chapter.

1. Start Access (AC 12)
2. Create a Database (AC 13)
3. Create a Database Using a Template (AC 14)
4. Modify the Primary Key (AC 16)
5. Define the Remaining Fields in a Table (AC 19)
6. Save a Table (AC 21)
7. View the Table in Design View (AC 21)
8. Close the Table (AC 23)
9. Add Records to a Table (AC 23)
10. Quit Access (AC 26)
11. Open a Database from Access (AC 27)
12. Add Additional Records to a Table (AC 28)
13. Resize Columns in a Datasheet (AC 29)
14. Preview and Print the Contents of a Table (AC 31)
15. Create a Table in Design View (AC 33)
16. Import an Excel Worksheet (AC 38)
17. Use the Simple Query Wizard to Create a Query (AC 43)
18. Use a Criterion in a Query (AC 46)
19. Print the Results of a Query (AC 48)
20. Create a Form (AC 48)
21. Create a Report (AC 52)
22. Modify Column Headings and Resize Columns (AC 54)
23. Add Totals to a Report (AC 57)
24. Change Database Properties (AC 59)
25. Back Up a Database (AC 61)
26. Compact and Repair a Database (AC 61)
27. Open Another Database (AC 62)
28. Close a Database without Quitting Access (AC 62)
29. Save a Database with Another Name (AC 62)
30. Delete a Table or Other Object in the Database (AC 62)
31. Rename an Object in the Database (AC 62)

SAM

If you have a SAM 2010 user profile, your instructor may have assigned an autogradable version of this assignment. If so, log into the SAM 2010 Web site at www.cengage.com/sam2010 to download the instruction and start files.

Learn It Online

Test your knowledge of chapter content and key terms.

Instructions: To complete the Learn It Online exercises, visit the Microsoft Office and Concepts CourseMate Web site at www.cengagebrain.com, navigate to the Access Chapter 1 resources for this book, click the link for the exercise you want to complete, and then read the instructions.

Chapter Reinforcement TF, MC, and SA

A series of true/false, multiple choice, and short answer questions that test your knowledge of the chapter content.

Flash Cards

An interactive learning environment where you identify chapter key terms associated with displayed definitions.

Practice Test

A series of multiple choice questions that test your knowledge of chapter content and key terms.

Who Wants To Be a Computer Genius?

An interactive game that challenges your knowledge of chapter content in the style of a television quiz show.

Wheel of Terms

An interactive game that challenges your knowledge of chapter key terms in the style of the television show *Wheel of Fortune.*

Crossword Puzzle Challenge

A crossword puzzle that challenges your knowledge of key terms presented in the chapter.

Apply Your Knowledge

Reinforce the skills and apply the concepts you learned in this chapter.

Adding a Caption, Creating a Query, Creating a Form, and Creating a Report

Instructions: Start Access. Open the Babbage CPA Firm database. See the inside back cover of this book for instructions for downloading the Data Files for Students, or see your instructor for information on accessing the files required in this book.

The Babbage CPA Firm employs bookkeepers who maintain the books for those clients who need bookkeeping services. The Babbage CPA Firm has a database that keeps track of its bookkeepers and clients. Each client is assigned to a single bookkeeper, but each bookkeeper may be assigned many clients. The database has two tables. The Client table contains data on the clients who use the bookkeeping services of the Babbage CPA Firm. The Bookkeeper table contains data on the bookkeepers employed by Babbage CPA Firm.

Perform the following tasks:

1. Open the Bookkeeper table in Design view and add BKR # as the caption for Bookkeeper Number. Save the changes to the table.
2. Open the Bookkeeper table in Datasheet view and resize all columns to best fit the data. Save the changes to the layout of the table.
3. Use the Simple Query Wizard to create a query for the Client table that contains the Client Number, Client Name, Amount Paid, and Balance Due. Use the name, Client Query, for the query.
4. Create a simple form for the Bookkeeper table. Use the name, Bookkeeper, for the form.
5. Close the Bookkeeper form.
6. Create the report shown in Figure 1–90 for the Client table. The report includes totals for both the Amount Paid and Balance Due fields. Be sure the totals appear completely. You might need to expand the size of the controls. Move the page number so that it is within the margins.
7. Compact the database.
8. Back up the database.
9. Change the database properties, as specified by your instructor. Submit the revised database in the format specified by your instructor.

Client Financial Report

Thursday, April 12, 2012
8:38:16 PM

Client Number	Client Name	Amount Paid	Balance Due	Bookkeeper Number
A54	Afton Mills	$575.00	$315.00	22
A62	Atlas Suppliers	$250.00	$175.00	24
B26	Blake-Scripps	$875.00	$250.00	24
D76	Dege Grocery	$1,015.00	$325.00	22
G56	Grand Cleaners	$485.00	$165.00	24
H21	Hill Shoes	$0.00	$285.00	34
J77	Jones Plumbing	$685.00	$0.00	22
M26	Mohr Crafts	$125.00	$185.00	24
S56	SeeSaw Industries	$1,200.00	$645.00	22
T45	Tate Repair	$345.00	$200.00	34
W24	Woody Sporting Goods	$975.00	$0.00	34
C29	Catering by Jenna	$0.00	$250.00	34
		$6,530.00	$2,795.00	

Figure 1–90

Extend Your Knowledge

Extend the skills you learned in this chapter and experiment with new skills. You may need to use Help to complete the assignment.

Using a Database Template to Create a Students Database

Instructions: Access includes a number of templates that you can use to create a beginning database that can be modified to meet your specific needs. You will create a Students database using the Students template. The database includes sample tables, queries, forms, and reports. You will change the database and create the Student Birthdays Query, shown in Figure 1–91.

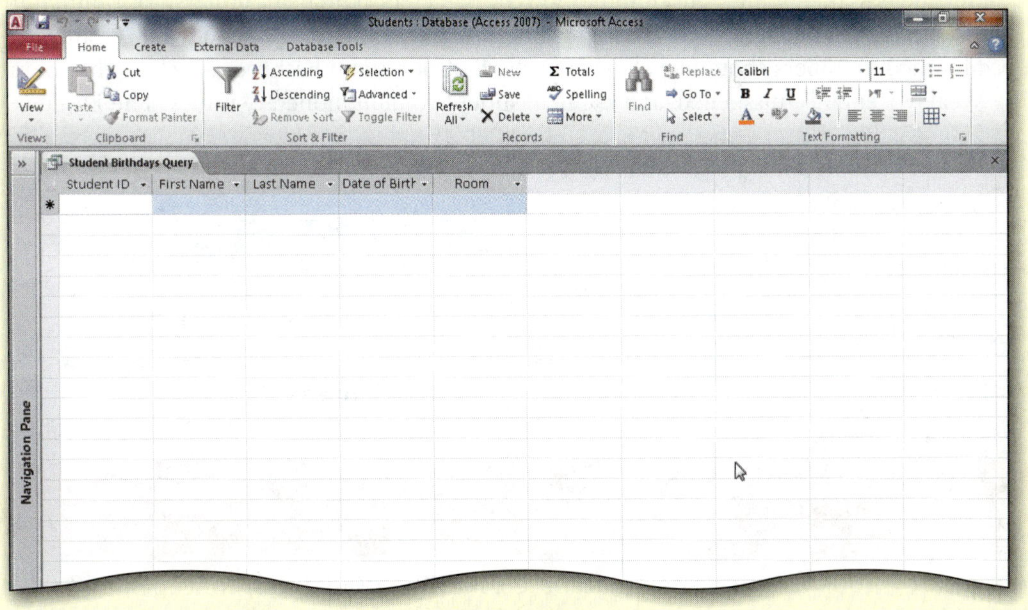

Figure 1–91

Perform the following tasks:

1. Start Access.
2. With a USB flash drive connected to one of the computer's USB ports, ensure the New tab is selected in the Backstage view and select Sample templates in the New gallery.
3. Select the Students template and create a new database on your USB drive with the file name, Students.
4. Close the Student List form and change the organization of the Navigation Pane to Tables and Related Views .
5. Delete the Student Details form.
6. Use the Query Wizard to create the query shown in Figure 1–91. Save the query as Student Birthdays Query.
7. Open the Student Phone List in Layout view and use the tools on the Format tab to make the Student Phone List title bold and change the font size to 24. Delete the control containing the time.
8. Save your changes to the report.
9. Compact the database.
10. Change the database properties, as specified by your instructor. Submit the revised database in the format specified by your instructor.

Make It Right

Analyze a database and correct all errors and/or improve the design.

Correcting Errors in the Table Structure

Instructions: Start Access. Open the Beach Rentals database. See the inside back cover of this book for instructions for downloading the Data Files for Students, or see your instructor for information on accessing the files required in this book.

Beach Rentals is a database containing information on rental properties available at a beach resort. The Rentals table shown in Figure 1–92 contains a number of errors in the table structure. You are to correct these errors before any additional records can be added to the table. The Rental Code field is a Text field that contains a maximum of three characters. The field Address was omitted from the table. The Address field is a Text field with a maximum of 20 characters. It should appear after Rental Code. Only whole numbers should be allowed in the Bedrooms and Bathrooms fields. The column heading Weakly Rental is misspelled, and the field should contain monetary values. The Distance field represents the walking distance from the beach; the field should display two decimal places. The table name should be Rental Units, not Rentals.

Change the database properties, as specified by your instructor. Submit the revised database in the format specified by your instructor.

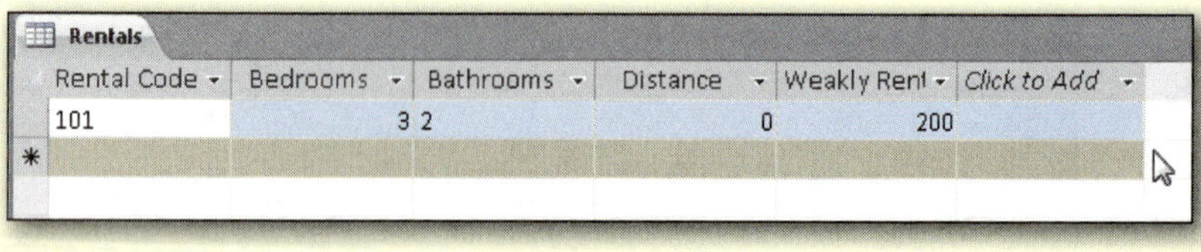

Figure 1–92

In the Lab

Design, create, modify, and/or use a database using the guidelines, concepts, and skills presented in this chapter. Labs are listed in order of increasing difficulty.

Lab 1: Creating Objects for the ECO Clothesline Database

Problem: ECO Clothesline is a local company that designs and manufactures eco-friendly casual wear, yoga clothing, and fitness apparel. All clothes are made from earth-friendly fabrics, such as bamboo, hemp, organic cotton, and natural silk. The company recently decided to store its customer and sales rep data in a database. Each customer is assigned to a single sales rep, but each sales rep may be assigned many customers. The database and the Customer table have been created, but there is no data in the Customer table. The Sales Rep table has not been created. The company plans to import the Customer data from an Excel workbook, shown in Figure 1–93a. The other Excel workbook (Figure 1–93b) contains information on the sales representatives that ECO employs. ECO would like to finish storing this data in a database and has asked for your help.

Instructions: Perform the following tasks: Start Access and open the ECO Clothesline database. See the inside back cover of this book for instructions for downloading the Data Files for Students, or see your instructor for information on accessing the files required in this book.

1. Import the Lab 1-1 Customer Data workbook into the Customer table.
2. Add the captions Cust # to the Customer Number field and SR # to the Sales Rep Number field in the Customer table and save the changes.
3. Open the Customer table in Datasheet view and resize the columns to best fit the data. Save the changes to the layout of the table.
4. Use Datasheet view to create a table in which to store the data related to sales reps. Use the name Sales Rep for the table. The fields and the data for the Sales Rep table are shown in Figure 1–93b.

Customer Number	Customer Name	Street	City	State	Postal Code	Balance	Amount Paid	Sales Rep Number
AM23	Amy's Store	223 Johnson	Oxford	TN	37021	195.00	1,695.00	44
BF34	Barbara's Fashions	1939 Jackson	Lowton	TN	37084	150.00	0.00	51
BL15	Blondie's on Main	3294 Main	Oxford	TN	37021	555.00	1,350.00	49
CM09	Casual by Marie	3140 Halsted	Ashton	VA	20123	295.00	1,080.00	51
CY12	Curlin Yoga Studio	1632 Clark	Georgetown	NC	28794	145.00	710.00	49
DG14	Della's Designs	312 Gilham	Granger	NC	27036	340.00	850.00	44
EC07	Environmentally Casual	1805 Broadway	Pineville	VA	22503	0.00	1,700.00	44
FN19	Fitness Counts	675 Main	Oxford	TN	37021	345.00	1,950.00	51
JN34	Just Natural	2200 Lawrence	Ashton	VA	20123	360.00	700.00	49
LB20	Le Beauty	13 Devon	Lowton	TN	37084	200.00	1,250.00	49
NC25	Nancy's Place	1027 Wells	Walburg	NC	28819	240.00	550.00	44
RD03	Rose's Day Spa	787 Monroe	Pineville	VA	22503	0.00	975.00	51
TT21	Tan and Tone	1939 Congress	Ashton	VA	20123	160.00	725.00	44
TW56	The Workout Place	34 Gilham	Granger	NC	27036	680.00	125.00	51
WS34	Woody's Sporting Goods	578 Central	Walburg	NC	28819	1,235.00	0.00	49

(a) Customer Data (Excel Workbook)

Sales Rep Number	Last Name	First Name	Street	City	State	Postal Code	Base Pay YTD	Comm Rate
44	Jones	Pat	43 Third	Oxford	TN	37021	13,000.00	0.05
49	Gupta	Pinn	678 Hillcrest	Georgetown	NC	28794	15,000.00	0.06
51	Ortiz	Gabe	982 Victoria	Ashton	VA	20123	12,500.00	0.05
55	Sinson	Terry	45 Elm	Walburg	NC	28819	500.00	0.04

(b) Sales Rep Data (Excel Workbook)

Figure 1–93

The primary key for the Sales Rep table is Sales Rep Number. Assign the caption SR # to the Sales Rep Number field. Comm Rate is a Number field, and Base Pay YTD is a Currency data type. The field size for Sales Rep Number is 2. The State field size is 2, and the Postal Code field size is 5. All other text fields have a field size of 15.

5. Open the Sales Rep table in Design view and change the field size for the Comm Rate field to Single, the format to Fixed, and the Decimal Places to 2.
6. Add the data shown in Figure 1–93b to the Sales Rep table. Resize the columns to best fit the data. Save the changes to the layout of the table.
7. Create a query using the Simple Query Wizard for the Customer table that displays the Customer Number, Customer Name, Balance, Amount Paid, and Sales Rep Number fields. Use the name Customer Query.
8. Create and save the report shown in Figure 1–94 for the Customer table. The report should include Customer Number, Customer Name, Balance, and Sales Rep Number fields. Include a total for the Balance field.
9. Change the database properties, as specified by your instructor. Submit the revised database in the format specified by your instructor.

Customer Balance Report
Thursday, April 12, 2012
8:55:32 PM

Customer Number	Customer Name	Balance	Sales Rep Number
AM23	Amy's Store	$195.00	44
BF34	Barbara's Fashions	$150.00	51
BL15	Blondie's on Main	$555.00	49
CM09	Casual by Marie	$295.00	51
CY12	Curlin Yoga Studio	$145.00	49
DG14	Della's Designs	$340.00	44
EC07	Environmentally Casual	$0.00	44
FN19	Fitness Counts	$345.00	51
JN34	Just Natural	$360.00	49
LB20	Le Beauty	$200.00	49
NC25	Nancy's Place	$240.00	44
RD03	Rose's Day Spa	$0.00	51
TT21	Tan and Tone	$160.00	44
TW56	The Workout Place	$680.00	51
WS34	Woody's Sporting Goods	$1,235.00	49
		$4,900.00	

Figure 1–94

STUDENT ASSIGNMENTS

In the Lab

Lab 2: Creating the Walburg Energy Alternatives Database

Problem: Walburg Energy Alternatives is a nonprofit organization that promotes the use of energy alternatives such as solar power and wind power. The organization provides a variety of services and funds itself through donations. Recently, the organization decided to sell a small number of items in its education center to help fund programs. The store purchases the items from vendors that deal in energy-saving products. Currently, the information about the items and vendors is stored in the Excel workbook shown in Figure 1–95. Each item is assigned to a single vendor, but each vendor may be assigned many items. You volunteer part-time at the store, and the store manager has asked you to create a database that will store the item and vendor information. You have already determined that you need two tables in which to store the information: an Item table and a Vendor table.

Instructions: Perform the following tasks:

1. Design a new database in which to store all the objects related to the items for sale. Call the database Walburg Energy Alternatives.
2. Use the information shown in the Excel workbook in Figure 1–95 to determine the primary keys and determine additional fields. Then, determine the relationships between tables, the data types, and the field sizes.
3. Create the Item table using the information shown in Figure 1–95.
4. Create the Vendor table using the information shown in Figure 1–95. Be sure that the field size for the Vendor Code in the Item table is identical to the field size for the Vendor Code in the Vendor table. Add the caption, Phone, for the Telephone Number field.

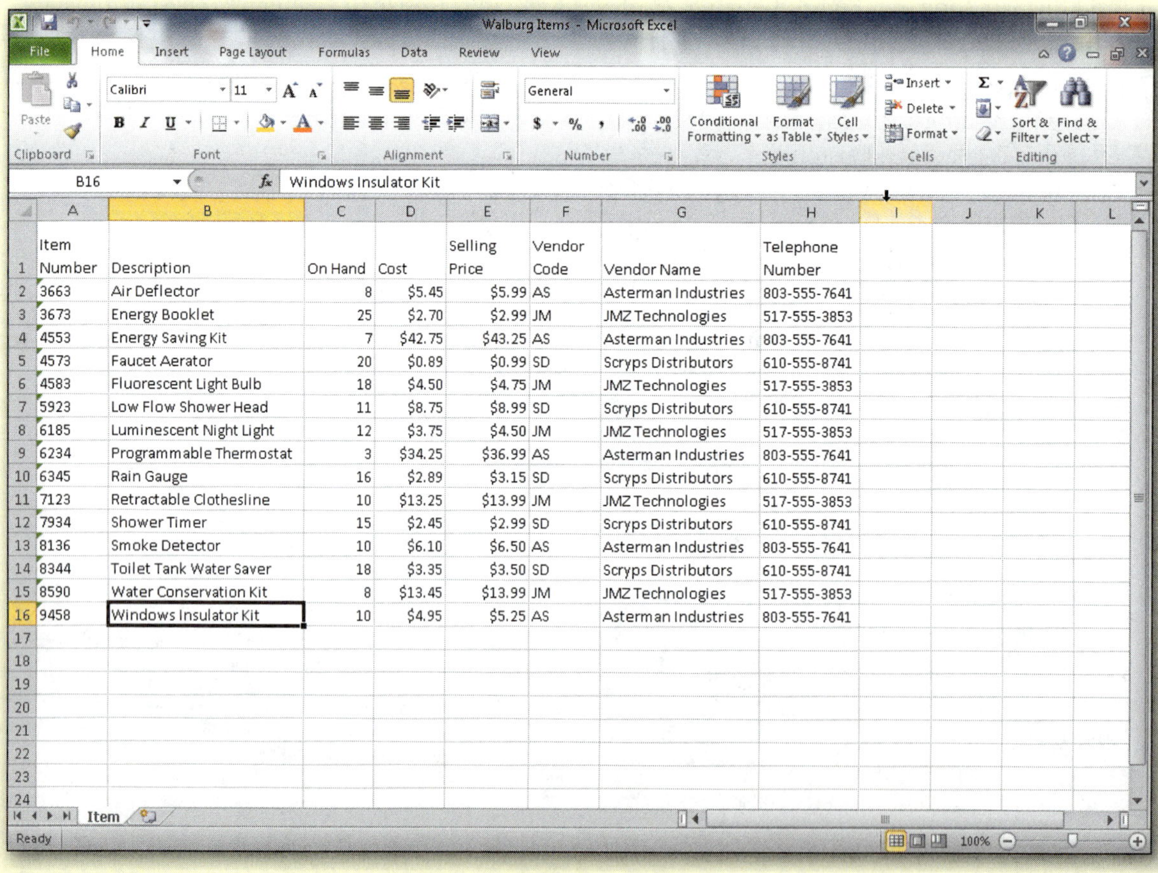

Item Number	Description	On Hand	Cost	Selling Price	Vendor Code	Vendor Name	Telephone Number
3663	Air Deflector	8	$5.45	$5.99	AS	Asterman Industries	803-555-7641
3673	Energy Booklet	25	$2.70	$2.99	JM	JMZ Technologies	517-555-3853
4553	Energy Saving Kit	7	$42.75	$43.25	AS	Asterman Industries	803-555-7641
4573	Faucet Aerator	20	$0.89	$0.99	SD	Scryps Distributors	610-555-8741
4583	Fluorescent Light Bulb	18	$4.50	$4.75	JM	JMZ Technologies	517-555-3853
5923	Low Flow Shower Head	11	$8.75	$8.99	SD	Scryps Distributors	610-555-8741
6185	Luminescent Night Light	12	$3.75	$4.50	JM	JMZ Technologies	517-555-3853
6234	Programmable Thermostat	3	$34.25	$36.99	AS	Asterman Industries	803-555-7641
6345	Rain Gauge	16	$2.89	$3.15	SD	Scryps Distributors	610-555-8741
7123	Retractable Clothesline	10	$13.25	$13.99	JM	JMZ Technologies	517-555-3853
7934	Shower Timer	15	$2.45	$2.99	SD	Scryps Distributors	610-555-8741
8136	Smoke Detector	10	$6.10	$6.50	AS	Asterman Industries	803-555-7641
8344	Toilet Tank Water Saver	18	$3.35	$3.50	SD	Scryps Distributors	610-555-8741
8590	Water Conservation Kit	8	$13.45	$13.99	JM	JMZ Technologies	517-555-3853
9458	Windows Insulator Kit	10	$4.95	$5.25	AS	Asterman Industries	803-555-7641

Figure 1–95

5. Add the appropriate data to the Item table. Resize the columns to best fit the data and save the changes to the layout.
6. Add the appropriate data to the Vendor table. Resize the columns to best fit the data and save the changes to the layout.
7. Create a query for the Item table. Include the Item Number, Description, Cost, Selling Price, and Vendor Code in the query. Save the query as Item Query.
8. Open the Item Query and add a criterion to limit retrieval to those items supplied by Scryps Distributors. Save the query as Item-Scryps Query.
9. Create a simple form for the Item table. Use the name, Item, for the form.
10. Create the report shown in Figure 1–96 for the Item table. Do not add any totals.
11. Change the database properties, as specified by your instructor. Submit the database in the format specified by your instructor.

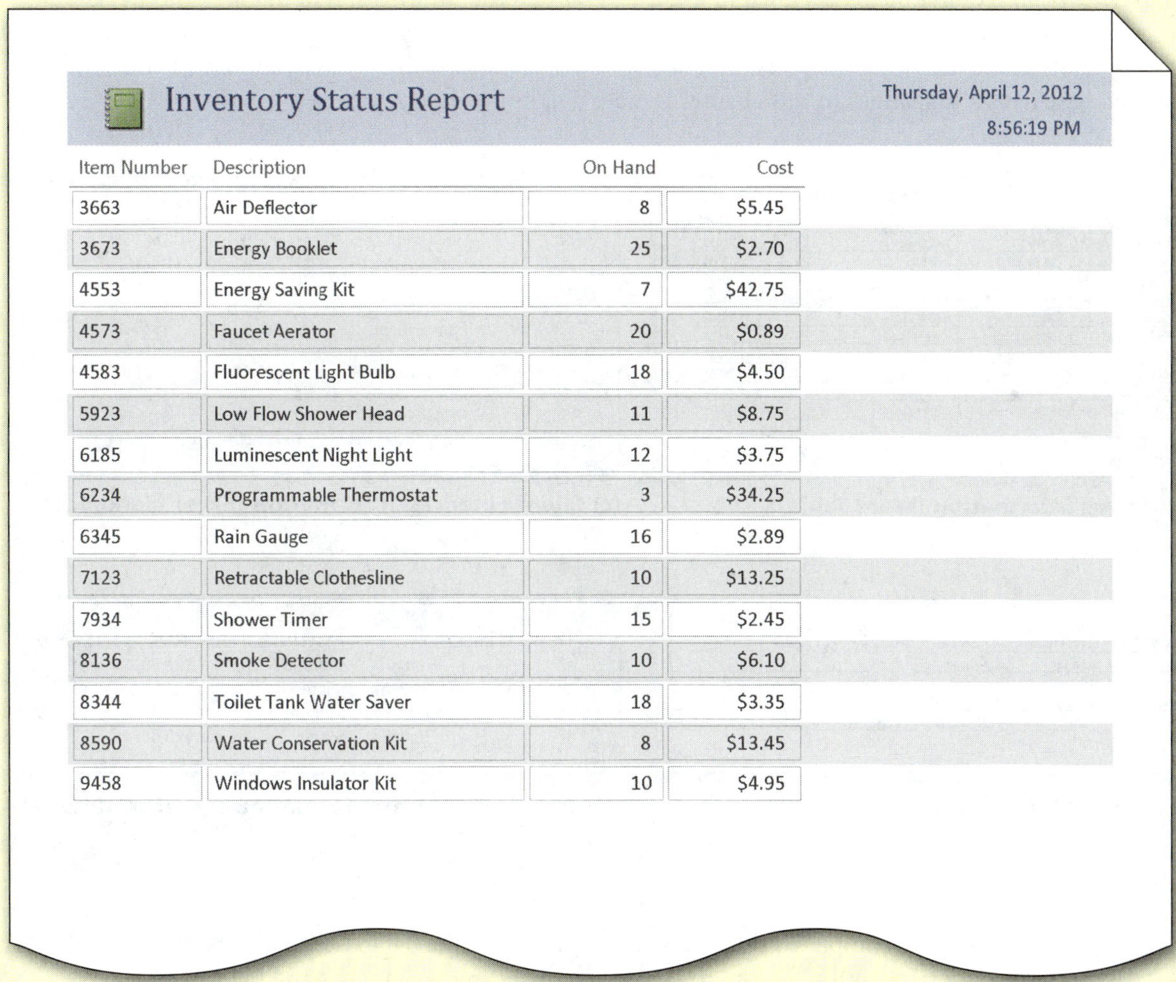

Inventory Status Report

Thursday, April 12, 2012
8:56:19 PM

Item Number	Description	On Hand	Cost
3663	Air Deflector	8	$5.45
3673	Energy Booklet	25	$2.70
4553	Energy Saving Kit	7	$42.75
4573	Faucet Aerator	20	$0.89
4583	Fluorescent Light Bulb	18	$4.50
5923	Low Flow Shower Head	11	$8.75
6185	Luminescent Night Light	12	$3.75
6234	Programmable Thermostat	3	$34.25
6345	Rain Gauge	16	$2.89
7123	Retractable Clothesline	10	$13.25
7934	Shower Timer	15	$2.45
8136	Smoke Detector	10	$6.10
8344	Toilet Tank Water Saver	18	$3.35
8590	Water Conservation Kit	8	$13.45
9458	Windows Insulator Kit	10	$4.95

Figure 1–96

In the Lab

Lab 3: Creating the Philamar Training Database

Problem: Philamar Training provides business processes and information technology training to various companies and organizations. Philamar employs trainers who work with individual companies to determine training needs and then conduct the training. Currently, Philamar keeps data on clients and trainers in two Word documents and two Excel workbooks. Philamar also keeps track of which clients are assigned to which trainers. Each client is assigned to a single trainer, but each trainer might be assigned many clients. Currently, clients BS27, FI28, and MC28 are assigned to trainer 42, Belinda Perry. Clients CE16, CP27, FL93, HN83, and TE26 are assigned to trainer 48, Michael Stevens. Clients EU28 and PS82 are assigned to trainer 53, Manuel Gonzalez. Philamar has an additional trainer, Marty Danville, who has been assigned trainer number 67, but who has not yet been assigned any clients.

Instructions: Using the data shown in Figure 1–97 and the information in the previous paragraph, design the Philamar Training database. The data shown in Figure 1–97 is included in the Data Files for Students in the following files: Lab 1-3a.docx, Lab 1-3b.docx, Lab 1-3c.xlsx, and Lab 1-3d.xlsx. Use the database design guidelines in this chapter to help you in the design process.

Client Number	Client Name	Address	City	State	Postal Code
BS27	Blant and Sons	4806 Park	Kingston	TX	76653
CE16	Center Services	725 Mitchell	San Rita	TX	78364
CP27	Calder Plastics	7300 Cedar	Kingston	TX	76653
EU28	Elba's Furniture	1445 Hubert	Tallmadge	TX	77231
FI28	Farrow-Idsen	829 Wooster	Cedar Ridge	TX	79342
FL93	Fairland Lawn	143 Pangborn	Kingston	TX	76653
HN83	Hurley National	3827 Burgess	Tallmadge	TX	77231
MC28	Morgan-Alyssa	923 Williams	Crumville	TX	76745
PS82	PRIM Staffing	72 Crestview	San Rita	TX	78364
TE26	Telton-Edwards	5672 Anderson	Dunston	TX	77893

(a) Client Address Information (Word Table)

	A	B	C	D	E
1	Client Number	Client Name	Amount Paid	Current Due	
2	BS27	Blant and Sons	$11,876.00	$892.50	
3	CE16	Center Services	$12,512.00	$1,672.00	
4	CP27	Calder Plastics	$5,725.00	$0.00	
5	EU28	Elba's Furniture	$3,245.00	$202.00	
6	FI28	Farrow-Idsen	$8,287.50	$925.50	
7	FL93	Fairland Lawn	$976.00	$0.00	
8	HN83	Hurley National	$0.00	$0.00	
9	MC28	Morgan-Alyssa	$3,456.00	$572.00	
10	PS82	PRIM Staffing	$7,500.00	$485.00	
11	TE26	Telton-Edwards	$6,775.00	$0.00	
12					

(c) Client Financial Information (Excel Workbook)

Trainer Number	Last Name	First Name	Address	City	State	Postal Code
42	Perry	Belinda	261 Porter	Burdett	TX	76734
48	Stevens	Michael	3135 Gill	Rockwood	TX	78884
53	Gonzalez	Manuel	265 Maxwell	Camino	TX	76574
67	Danville	Marty	1827 Maple	Dunston	TX	77893

(b) Trainer Address Information (Word Table)

	A	B	C	D	E
1	Trainer Number	Last Name	First Name	Hourly Rate	YTD Earnings
2	42	Perry	Belinda	$23.00	$17,620.00
3	48	Stevens	Michael	$21.00	$13,567.50
4	53	Gonzalez	Manuel	$24.00	$19,885.00
5	67	Danville	Marty	$20.00	$0.00
6					

(d) Trainer Financial Information (Excel Workbook)

Figure 1–97

When you have completed the database design, create the database, create the tables, and add the data to the appropriate tables. Be sure to determine the correct data types and field sizes.

Finally, prepare the Client Query shown in Figure 1–98 and the Client Status Report shown in Figure 1–99. The report does not include totals. Change the database properties, as specified by your instructor. Submit the database in the format specified by your instructor.

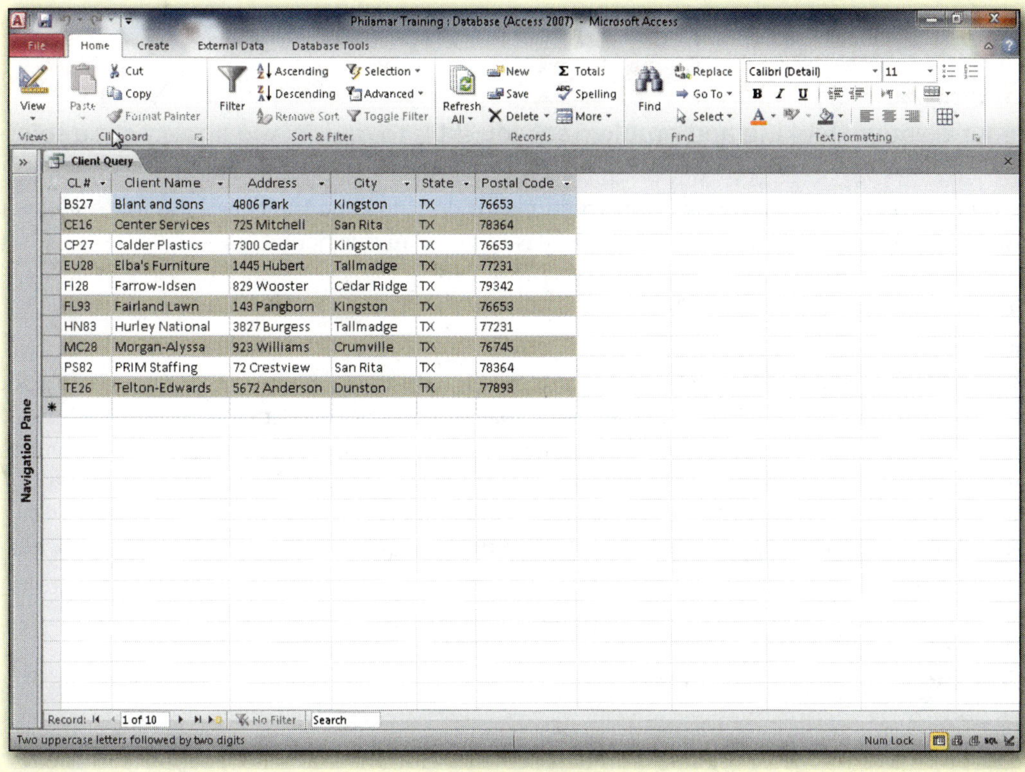

Figure 1–98

Client Status Report

Thursday, April 12, 2012
8:57:10 PM

Client Number	Client Name	Amount Paid	Current Due	Trainer Number
BS27	Blant and Sons	$11,876.00	$892.50	42
CE16	Center Services	$12,512.00	$1,672.00	48
CP27	Calder Plastics	$5,725.00	$0.00	48
EU28	Elba's Furniture	$3,245.00	$202.00	53
FI28	Farrow-Idsen	$8,287.50	$925.50	42
FL93	Fairland Lawn	$976.00	$0.00	48
HN83	Hurley National	$0.00	$0.00	48
MC28	Morgan-Alyssa	$3,456.00	$572.00	42
PS82	PRIM Staffing	$7,500.00	$485.00	53
TE26	Telton-Edwards	$6,775.00	$0.00	48

Figure 1–99

Cases and Places

Apply your creative thinking and problem solving skills to design and implement a solution.

See the inside back cover of this book for instructions for downloading the Data Files for Students, or see your instructor for information on accessing the files required in this book.

1: Design and Create an Advertising Database

Academic

You are a Marketing major currently doing an internship with the Chamber of Commerce in a local city. The Chamber publishes a Newcomer's Guide that contains advertisements from local businesses. Ad reps contact the businesses to arrange for advertising. Each advertiser is assigned to a single ad rep, but each ad rep may be assigned many advertisers. The Chamber would like your help in creating a database of advertisers and advertising representatives.

Based on the information in the Case 1-1 Chamber of Commerce workbook, use the concepts and techniques presented in this chapter to design and create a database to store the data that the Chamber needs. Submit your assignment in the format specified by your instructor.

2: Design and Create a Consignment Database

Personal

You are involved in a volunteer organization that provides clothing and school supplies to needy children. Recently, the Board of Directors decided to open a consignment shop as a way to raise additional funds. In a consignment shop, individuals bring in unwanted items, and the shop sells the items. Proceeds are split between the seller and the shop. The database must keep track of the items for sale in the shop as well as maintain data on the sellers. Each item is assigned to a single seller, but each seller may be assigned many items. The Board has asked you to create a database to store information about the consignment items.

Use the concepts and techniques presented in this chapter to design and create a database to store the consignment data. Then create the necessary tables and enter the data from the Case 1-2 Consignment workbook. Create an Available Items Report that lists the item number, description, price, and seller code. Submit your assignment in the format specified by your instructor.

3: Design and Create a Senior Care Database

Professional

You are co-owner of a company, Senior Care, that provides nonmedical services to older adults who need assistance with daily living. Helpers will drive individuals to appointments, do the grocery shopping, fill prescriptions, help with personal care, and provide companionship. Each client is assigned to a single helper, but each helper may be assigned many clients. The other owners have asked you to create a database of clients and helpers. Use the concepts and techniques presented in this chapter to design and create a database to meet Senior Care needs. Then create the necessary tables and enter the data from the Case 1-3 Senior Care workbook. Create a Client Report that lists each client's client number, client last name, client first name, balance, and helper number. Submit your assignment in the format specified by your instructor.

2 Querying a Database

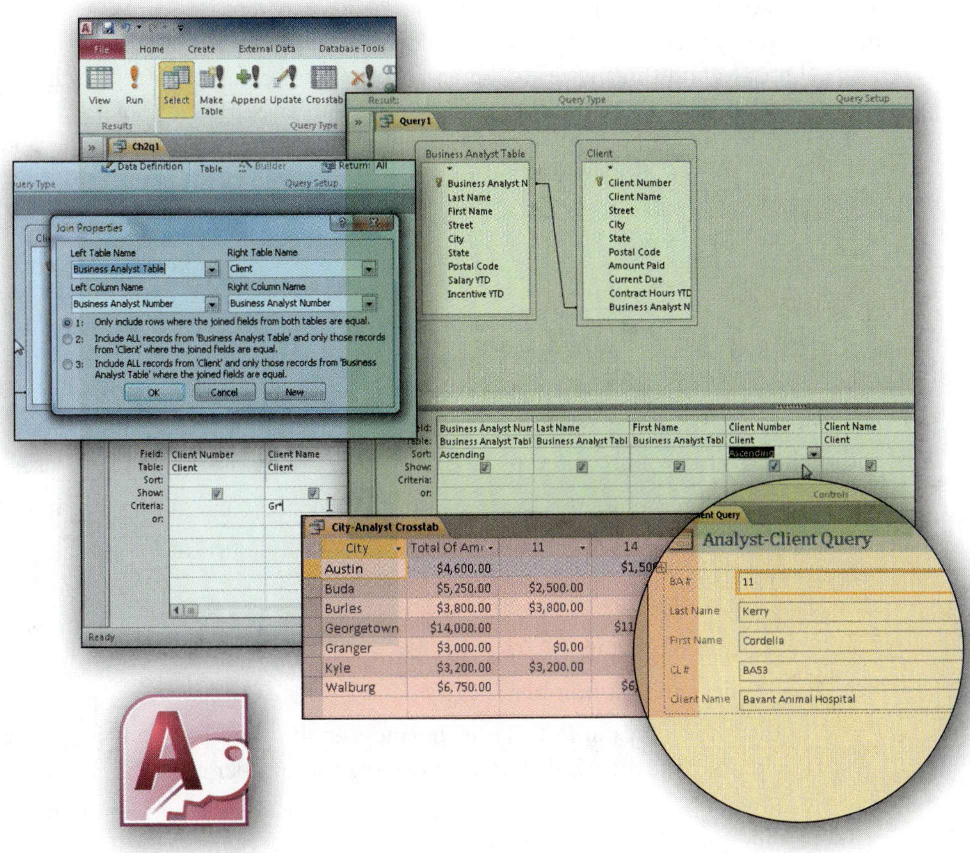

Objectives

You will have mastered the material in this chapter when you can:

- Create queries using Design view
- Include fields in the design grid
- Use text and numeric data in criteria
- Save a query and use the saved query
- Create and use parameter queries
- Use compound criteria in queries
- Sort data in queries
- Join tables in queries
- Create a report and a form from a query
- Export data from a query to another application
- Perform calculations and calculate statistics in queries
- Create crosstab queries
- Customize the Navigation Pane

2 | Querying a Database

Introduction

One of the primary benefits of using a database management system such as Access is the ability to find answers to questions related to data stored in the database. When you pose a question to Access, or any other database management system, the question is called a query. A **query** is simply a question presented in a way that Access can process.

Thus, to find the answer to a question, you first create a corresponding query using the techniques illustrated in this chapter. After you have created the query, you instruct Access to display the query results, that is, to perform the steps necessary to obtain the answer. Access then displays the answer in Datasheet view.

Project — Querying a Database

Organizations and individuals achieve several benefits from storing data in a database and using Access to manage the database. One of the most important benefits is the capability of easily finding the answers to questions and requests such as those shown in Figure 2–1 and the following, which concern the data in the Camashaly Design database:

1. What are the number, name, amount paid, and current due for client BC76?
2. What are the number, name, amount paid, and current due for all clients whose name starts with Gr?
3. Give me the number, name, amount paid, current due, and business analyst number for all clients whose amount paid is more than $3,000 and whose business analyst number is 11.
4. List the client number, name, business analyst number, and amount paid for all clients. Sort the results by business analyst number and amount paid.
5. For each business analyst, list the number, last name, and first name. Also, list the client number and name for each of the business analyst's clients.
6. List the client number, client name, amount paid, current due, and the total amount (amount paid plus current due) for each client.
7. Give me the average amount paid by clients of each business analyst.
8. Summarize the total amount paid by city and by business analyst.

In addition to these questions, Camashaly Design managers need to find information about clients located in a specific city, but they want to enter a different city each time they ask the question. The company can use a parameter query to accomplish this task. Camashaly Design managers also want to summarize data in a specific way, and they can use a crosstab query to present the data in the desired form.

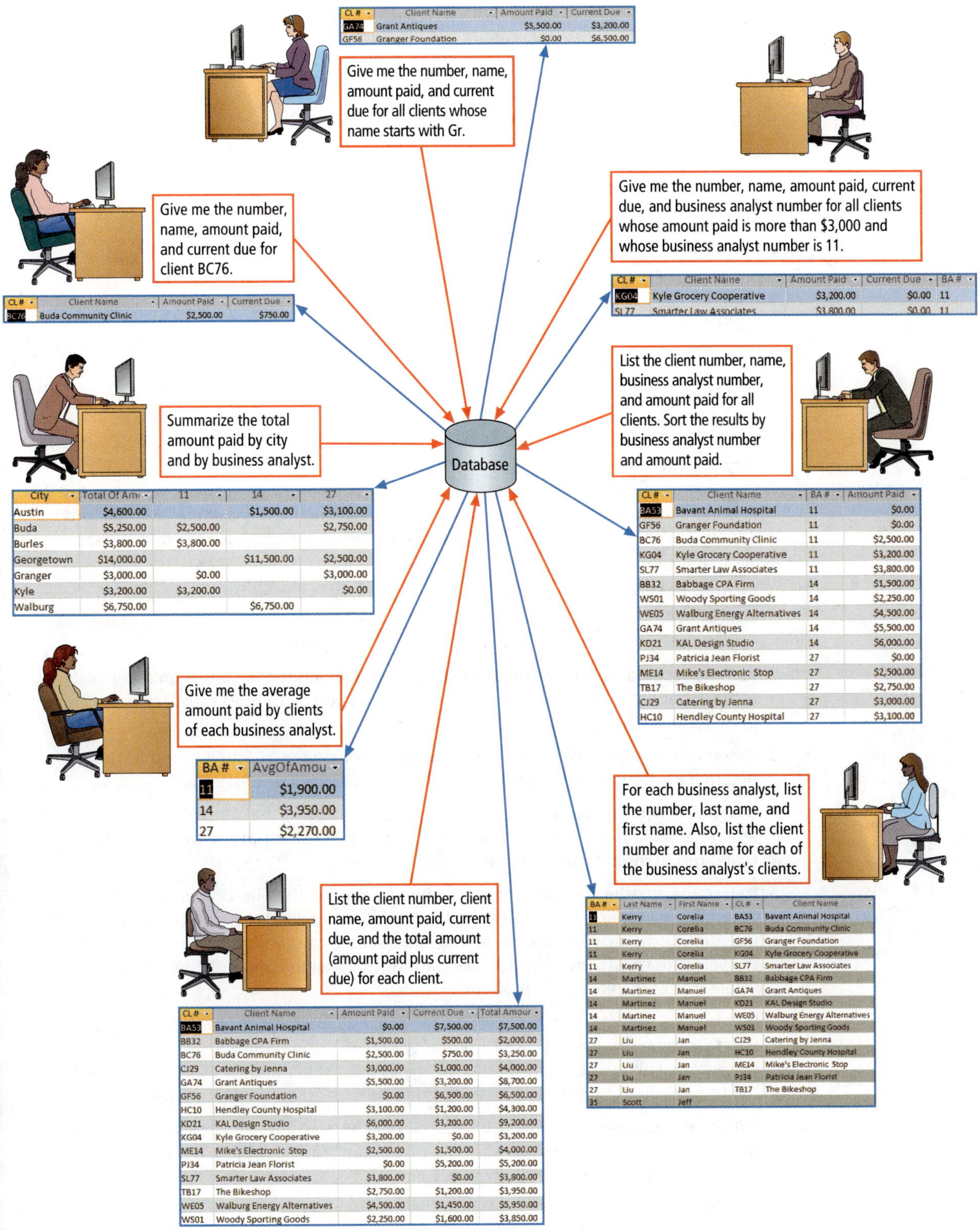

CL #	Client Name	Amount Paid	Current Due
GA74	Grant Antiques	$5,500.00	$3,200.00
GF56	Granger Foundation	$0.00	$6,500.00

CL #	Client Name	Amount Paid	Current Due
BC76	Buda Community Clinic	$2,500.00	$750.00

CL #	Client Name	Amount Paid	Current Due	BA #
KG04	Kyle Grocery Cooperative	$3,200.00	$0.00	11
SL77	Smarter Law Associates	$3,800.00	$0.00	11

City	Total Of Am	11	14	27
Austin	$4,600.00		$1,500.00	$3,100.00
Buda	$5,250.00	$2,500.00		$2,750.00
Burles	$3,800.00	$3,800.00		
Georgetown	$14,000.00		$11,500.00	$2,500.00
Granger	$3,000.00	$0.00		$3,000.00
Kyle	$3,200.00	$3,200.00		$0.00
Walburg	$6,750.00		$6,750.00	

CL #	Client Name	BA #	Amount Paid
BA53	Bavant Animal Hospital	11	$0.00
GF56	Granger Foundation	11	$0.00
BC76	Buda Community Clinic	11	$2,500.00
KG04	Kyle Grocery Cooperative	11	$3,200.00
SL77	Smarter Law Associates	11	$3,800.00
BB32	Babbage CPA Firm	14	$1,500.00
WS01	Woody Sporting Goods	14	$2,250.00
WE05	Walburg Energy Alternatives	14	$4,500.00
GA74	Grant Antiques	14	$5,500.00
KD21	KAL Design Studio	14	$6,000.00
PJ34	Patricia Jean Florist	27	$0.00
ME14	Mike's Electronic Stop	27	$2,500.00
TB17	The Bikeshop	27	$2,750.00
CJ29	Catering by Jenna	27	$3,000.00
HC10	Hendley County Hospital	27	$3,100.00

BA #	AvgOfAmou
11	$1,900.00
14	$3,950.00
27	$2,270.00

BA #	Last Name	First Name	CL #	Client Name
11	Kerry	Corelia	BA53	Bavant Animal Hospital
11	Kerry	Corelia	BC76	Buda Community Clinic
11	Kerry	Corelia	GF56	Granger Foundation
11	Kerry	Corelia	KG04	Kyle Grocery Cooperative
11	Kerry	Corelia	SL77	Smarter Law Associates
14	Martinez	Manuel	BB32	Babbage CPA Firm
14	Martinez	Manuel	GA74	Grant Antiques
14	Martinez	Manuel	KD21	KAL Design Studio
14	Martinez	Manuel	WE05	Walburg Energy Alternatives
14	Martinez	Manuel	WS01	Woody Sporting Goods
27	Liu	Jan	CJ29	Catering by Jenna
27	Liu	Jan	HC10	Hendley County Hospital
27	Liu	Jan	ME14	Mike's Electronic Stop
27	Liu	Jan	PJ34	Patricia Jean Florist
27	Liu	Jan	TB17	The Bikeshop
35	Scott	Jeff		

CL #	Client Name	Amount Paid	Current Due	Total Amour
BA53	Bavant Animal Hospital	$0.00	$7,500.00	$7,500.00
BB32	Babbage CPA Firm	$1,500.00	$500.00	$2,000.00
BC76	Buda Community Clinic	$2,500.00	$750.00	$3,250.00
CJ29	Catering by Jenna	$3,000.00	$1,000.00	$4,000.00
GA74	Grant Antiques	$5,500.00	$3,200.00	$8,700.00
GF56	Granger Foundation	$0.00	$6,500.00	$6,500.00
HC10	Hendley County Hospital	$3,100.00	$1,200.00	$4,300.00
KD21	KAL Design Studio	$6,000.00	$3,200.00	$9,200.00
KG04	Kyle Grocery Cooperative	$3,200.00	$0.00	$3,200.00
ME14	Mike's Electronic Stop	$2,500.00	$1,500.00	$4,000.00
PJ34	Patricia Jean Florist	$0.00	$5,200.00	$5,200.00
SL77	Smarter Law Associates	$3,800.00	$0.00	$3,800.00
TB17	The Bikeshop	$2,750.00	$1,200.00	$3,950.00
WE05	Walburg Energy Alternatives	$4,500.00	$1,450.00	$5,950.00
WS01	Woody Sporting Goods	$2,250.00	$1,600.00	$3,850.00

Figure 2–1

Overview

As you read this chapter, you will learn how to query a database by performing these general tasks:

- Create queries using Design view.
- Use criteria in queries.
- Create and use parameter queries.
- Sort data in queries.
- Join tables in queries.
- Create reports and forms from a query.
- Export data from a query.
- Perform calculations in queries.
- Create crosstab queries.

Plan Ahead

Query Design Decisions

When posing a question to Access, you must design an appropriate query. In the process of designing a query, the decisions you make will determine the fields, tables, criteria, order, and special calculations included in the query. To design a query, you can follow these general guidelines:

1. **Identify the fields.** Examine the question or request to determine which fields from the tables in the database are involved. Examine the contents of these fields to make sure you understand the data type and format for storing the data.
2. **Identify restrictions.** Unless the question or request calls for the inclusion of all records, determine the restrictions or the conditions records must satisfy to be included in the results.
3. **Determine whether special order is required.** Examine the question or request to determine whether the results must appear in some specific order.
4. **Determine whether more than one table is required.** If all the fields identified in Step 1 are in the same table, no special action is required. If this is not the case, identify all tables represented by those fields.
5. **Determine whether calculations are required.** Examine the question or request to determine whether, in addition to the fields determined in Step 1, calculations must be included. Such calculations include individual record calculations (for example, adding the values in two fields) or group calculations (for example, finding the total of the values in a particular field for all the records).
6. **If data is to be summarized, determine whether a crosstab query would be appropriate.** If data is to be grouped by two different types of information, you can use a crosstab query. You will need to identify the two types of information. One of the types will form the row headings and the other will form the column headings in the query results.

When necessary, more specific details concerning the decisions and/or actions are presented at appropriate points in the chapter. The chapter also will identify the use of these guidelines in creating queries such as those shown in Figure 2–1.

BTW

Designing Queries

Before creating queries, examine the contents of the tables involved. You need to know the data type for each field and how the data for the field is stored. If a query includes a state, for example, you need to know whether state is stored as the two-character abbreviation or as the full state name.

To Start Access

The following steps, which assume Windows 7 is running, start Access based on a typical installation. You may need to ask your instructor how to start Access for your computer. For a detailed example of the procedure summarized below, refer to the Office 2010 and Windows 7 chapter in this book.

1. Click the Start button on the Windows 7 taskbar to display the Start menu.
2. Type `Microsoft Access` as the search text in the 'Search programs and files' text box and watch the search results appear on the Start menu.
3. Click Microsoft Access 2010 in the search results on the Start menu to start Access.
4. If the Access window is not maximized, click the Maximize button next to the Close button on its title bar to maximize the window.

For an introduction to Windows 7 and instruction about how to perform basic Windows 7 tasks, read the Office 2010 and Windows 7 chapter in this book, where you can learn how to resize windows, change screen resolution, create folders, move and rename files, use Windows Help, and much more.

To Open a Database from Access

In the previous Access chapter, you saved your database on a USB flash drive using the file name, Camashaly Design. The following steps open the Camashaly Design database from the Access folder in the CIS 101 folder on the USB flash drive. For a detailed example of the procedure summarized below, refer to the Office 2010 and Windows 7 chapter in this book.

1. With your USB flash drive connected to one of the computer's USB ports, click File on the Ribbon to open the Backstage view, if necessary.
2. Click Open in the Backstage view to display the Open dialog box.
3. Navigate to the location of the file to be opened (in this case, the USB flash drive, then to the CIS 101 folder [or your class folder], and then to the Access folder).
4. Click Camashaly Design to select the file to be opened.
5. Click the Open button (Open dialog box) to open the selected file and display the opened database in the Access window.
6. If a Security Warning appears, click the Enable Content option button.

For an introduction to Office 2010 and instruction about how to perform basic tasks in Office 2010 programs, read the Office 2010 and Windows 7 chapter in this book, where you can learn how to start a program, use the Ribbon, save a file, open a file, quit a program, use Help, and much more.

Creating Queries

Queries are simply questions, the answers to which are in the database. Access contains a powerful query feature. Through the use of this feature, you can find the answers to a wide variety of complex questions.

BTW

Q&As

For a complete list of the Q&As found in many of the step-by-step sequences in the Office and Windows chapters in this book, visit the Microsoft Office and Concepts CourseMate Web site at www.cengagebrain.com and then navigate to the Q&A resource for this book.

Note: In this chapter, you will save each query example. When you use a query for another task, such as to create a form or report, you will assign a specific name to a query; for example, Analyst-Client Query. In situations in which you will not use the query again, you will assign a name using a convention that includes the chapter number and a query number; for example, Ch2q1. Queries are numbered consecutively.

To Create a Query in Design View

Most of the time, you will use Design view to create queries. Once you have created a new query in Design view, you can specify fields, criteria, sorting, calculations, and so on. The following steps create a new query in Design view.

1

- Close the Navigation Pane.
- Click Create on the Ribbon to display the Create tab.
- Click the Query Design button (Create tab | Queries group) to create a new query (Figure 2–2).

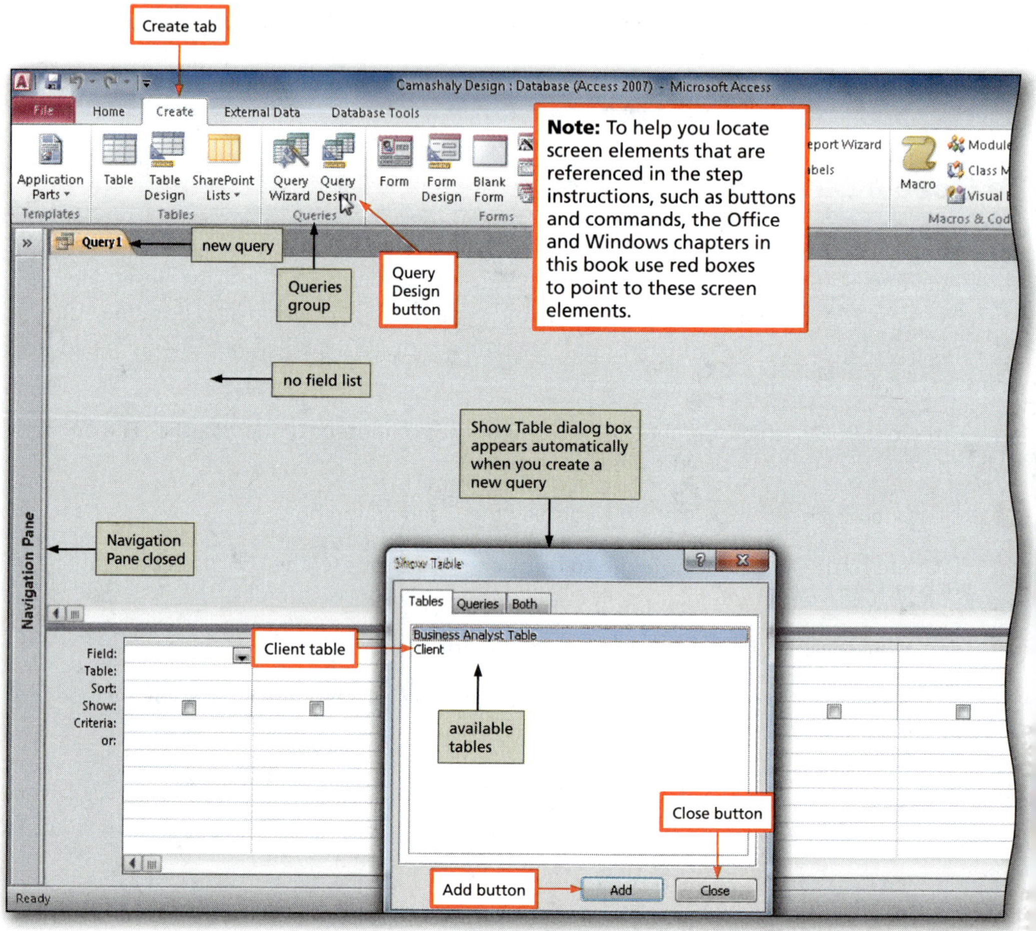

Figure 2–2

Q&A Is it necessary to close the Navigation Pane?

No. It gives you more room for the query, however, so it is usually a good practice to hide it.

2

- Click the Client table (Show Table dialog box) to select the table.
- Click the Add button to add the selected table to the query.
- Click the Close button to remove the dialog box from the screen.

Q&A What if I inadvertently add the wrong table?

Right-click the table that you added in error and click Remove Table on the shortcut menu. You also can just close the query, indicate that you don't want to save it, and then start over.

- Drag the lower edge of the field list down far enough so all fields in the table appear (Figure 2–3).

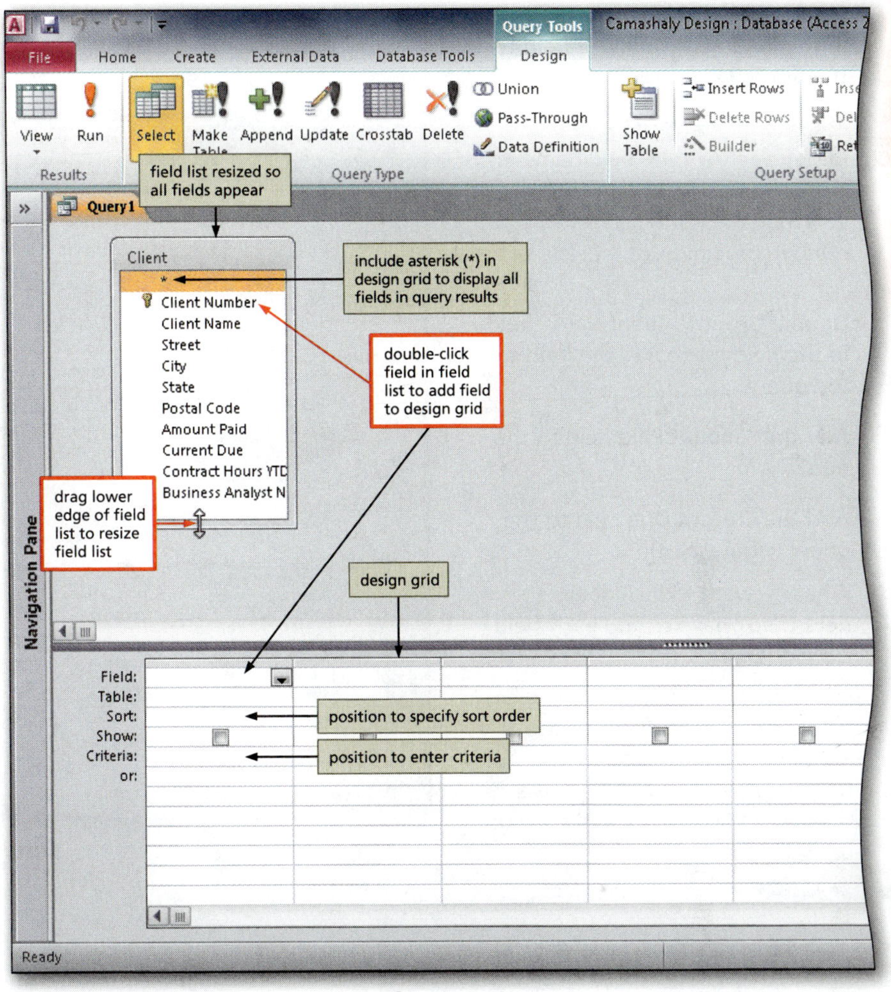

Figure 2–3

Q&A How do I drag the lower edge?

Point to the lower edge, press and hold the left mouse button, move the mouse pointer to the new position for the lower edge, and then release the left mouse button. While the mouse pointer points to the lower edge of the field list, its shape changes to a two-headed arrow.

Q&A Is it essential that I resize the field list?

No. You can always scroll through the list of fields using the scroll bar. It is usually more convenient to resize the field list so all fields appear.

To Add Fields to the Design Grid

Once you have a new query displayed in Design view, you are ready to make entries in the design grid, located in the lower pane of the window. You add the fields you want included in the query to the Field row in the grid. Only the fields that appear in the design grid will be included in the results of the query. The following steps begin the creation of a query that Camashaly Design might use to obtain the client number, client name, amount paid, and current due for a particular client. The following step selects the appropriate fields for the query.

1

- Double-click the Client Number field in the field list to add the field to the query.

Q&A What if I add the wrong field?

Click just above the field name in the design grid to select the column and then press the DELETE key to remove the field.

- Double-click the Client Name field in the field list to add the field to the query.
- Add the Amount Paid field to the query.
- Add the Current Due field to the query (Figure 2–4).

Q&A What if I want to include all fields? Do I have to add each field individually?

No. Instead of adding individual fields, you can double-click the asterisk (*) to add the asterisk to the design grid. The asterisk is a shortcut indicating all fields are to be included.

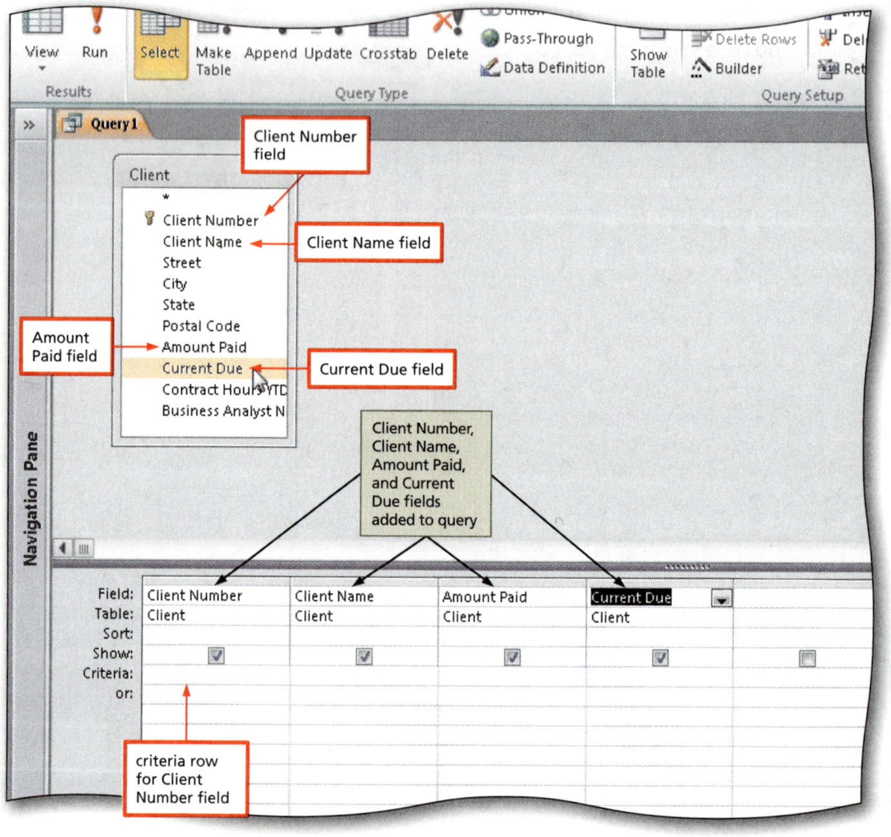

Figure 2–4

BTW **The Ribbon and Screen Resolution**

Access may change how the groups and buttons within the groups appear on the Ribbon, depending on the computer's screen resolution. Thus, your Ribbon may look different from the ones in the Office and Windows chapters in this book if you are using a screen resolution other than 1024 × 768.

Determining Criteria

When you use queries, usually you are looking for those records that satisfy some criterion. In the simple query you created in the previous Access chapter, for example, you entered a criterion to restrict the records that were included to those on which the business analyst number is 14. In another query, you might want the name, amount paid, and current due amounts of the client whose number is BC76, for example, or of those clients whose names start with the letters, Gr. You enter criteria in the Criteria row in the design grid below the field name to which the criterion applies. For example, to indicate that the client number must be BC76, you first must add the Client Number field to the design grid. You then would type BC76 in the Criteria row below the Client Number field.

To Use Text Data in a Criterion

To use **text data** (data in a field whose data type is Text) in criteria, simply type the text in the Criteria row below the corresponding field name. The following steps finish the creation of a query that Camashaly Design might use to obtain the client number, client name, amount paid, and current due amount of client BC76. These steps add the appropriate criterion so that only the desired client will appear in the results. The steps also save the query.

1

- Click the Criteria row for the Client Number field to produce an insertion point.
- Type `BC76` as the criterion (Figure 2–5).

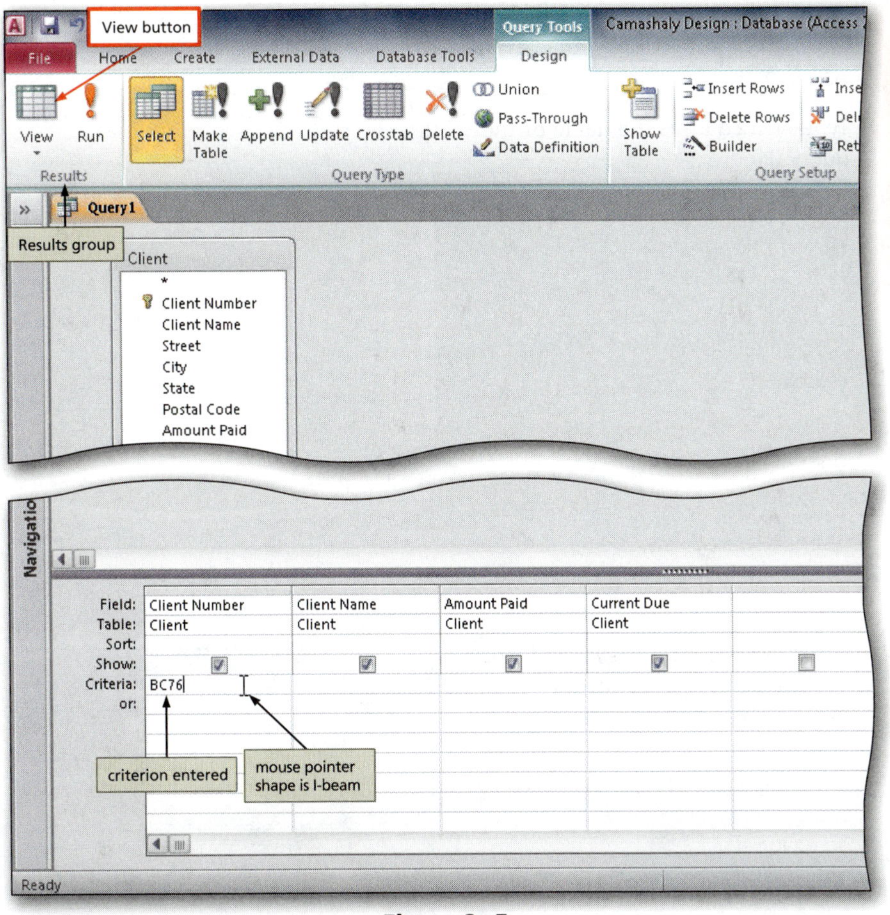

Figure 2–5

2

- Click the View button (Query Tools Design tab | Results group) to display the query results (Figure 2–6).

Q&A

I noticed that there is a View button on both the Home tab and the Design tab. Do they both have the same effect?

Yes. Use whichever one you find most convenient.

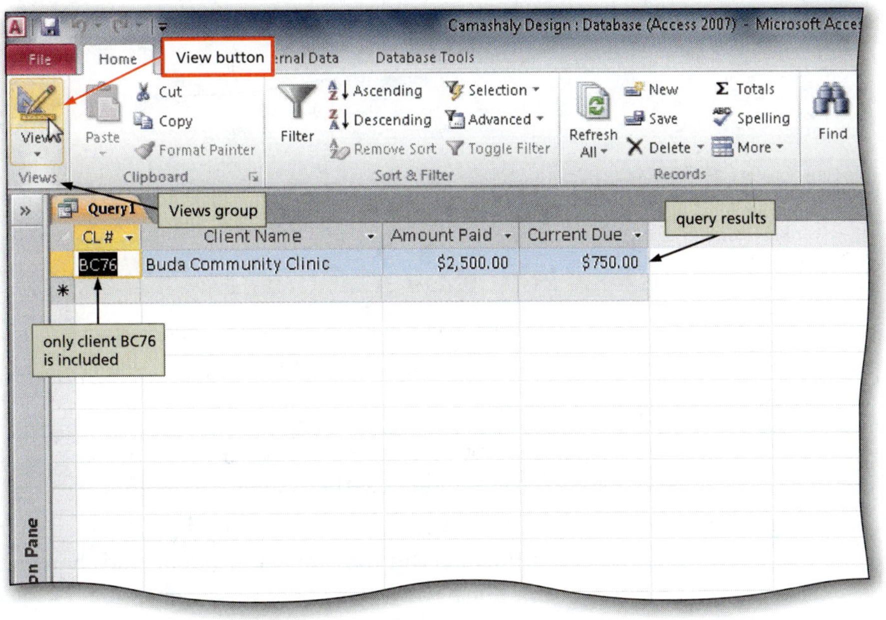

Figure 2–6

3

- Click the Save button on the Quick Access Toolbar to display the Save As dialog box.
- Type `Ch2q1` as the name of the query (Figure 2–7).

Q&A Can I also save from Design view?

Yes. You can save the query when you view it in Design view just as you can save the query when you view the query results in Datasheet view.

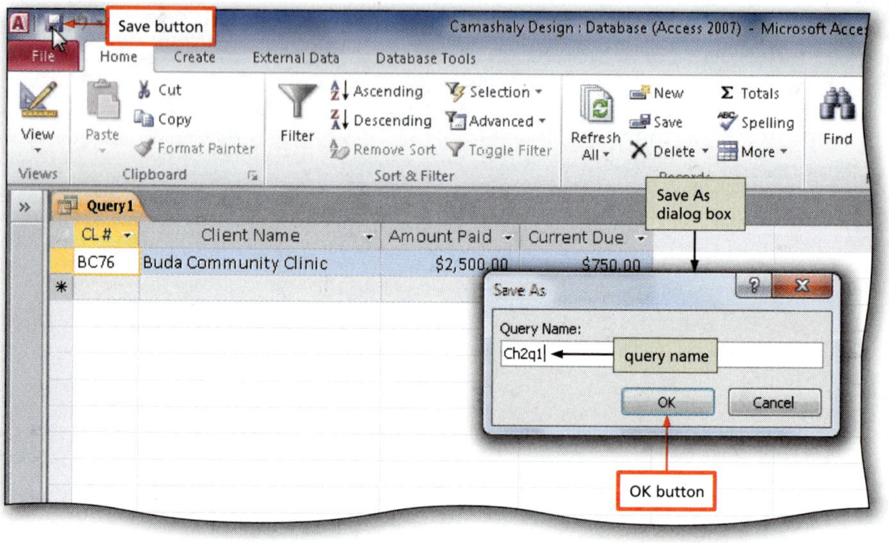

Figure 2–7

4

- Click the OK button (Save As dialog box) to save the query (Figure 2–8).

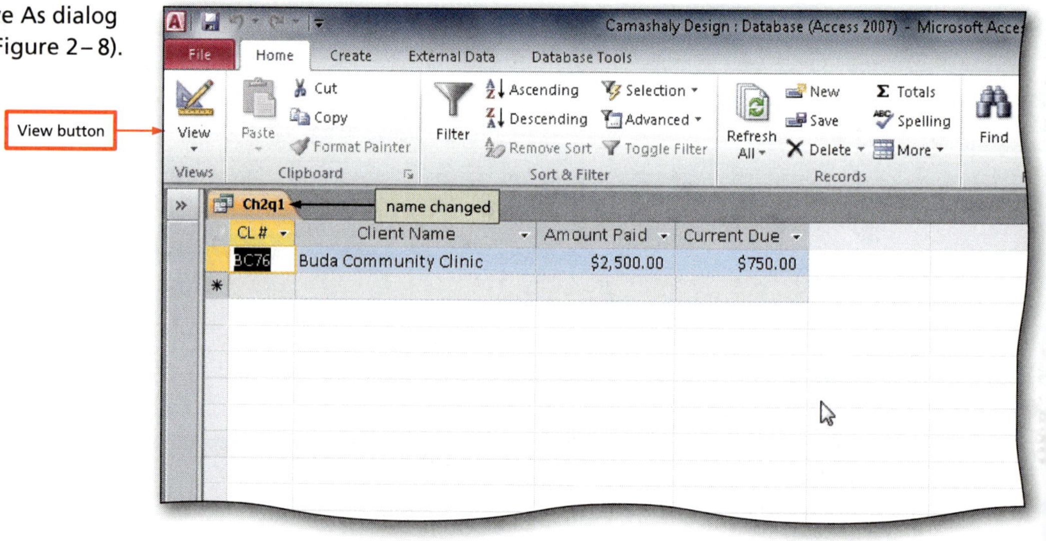

Figure 2–8

Other Ways

1. Right-click query tab, click Save on shortcut menu

Using Saved Queries

After you have created and saved a query, you can use it in a variety of ways:

- To view the results of the query that is not currently open, open it by right-clicking the query in the Navigation Pane and clicking Open on the shortcut menu.
- If you want to change the design of the query that is already open, return to Design view and make the changes.
- If you want to change the design of the query that is not currently open, right-click the query in the Navigation Pane and then click Design View on the shortcut menu to open the query in Design view.
- To print the results with the query open, click File on the Ribbon, click the Print tab in the Backstage view, and then click Quick Print.

- To print the query without first opening it, be sure the query is selected in the Navigation Pane and click File on the Ribbon, click the Print tab in the Backstage view, and then click Quick Print.
- You can switch between views of a query using the View button (Home tab | Views group). Clicking the arrow at the bottom of the button produces the View button menu. You then click the desired view in the menu. The two query views you use in this chapter are Datasheet view (see the results) and Design view (change the design). You can click the top part of the View button, in which case, you will switch to the view identified by the icon on the button. In the figure, the button contains the icon for Design view, so clicking the button would change to Design view. For the most part, the icon on the button represents the view you want, so you can usually simply click the button.

BTW

BTWs
For a complete list of the BTWs found in the margins of the Office and Windows chapters in this book, visit the Microsoft Office and Concepts CourseMate Web site at www.cengagebrain.com and then navigate to the BTW resource for this book.

To Use a Wildcard

Microsoft Access supports wildcards. **Wildcards** are symbols that represent any character or combination of characters. One common wildcard, the **asterisk** (*), represents any collection of characters. Thus Gr* represents the letters, Gr, followed by any collection of characters. Another wildcard symbol is the **question mark** (?), which represents any individual character. Thus T?m represents the letter, T, followed by any single character, followed by the letter, m; a search might return the names Tim or Tom.

The following steps modify the previous query so that Camashaly Design can select only those clients whose names begin with Gr. Because you do not know how many characters will follow the Gr, the asterisk wildcard symbol is appropriate. The steps also save the query with a new name using the Save As command.

1

- Click the View button (Home tab | Views group) to return to Design view.
- If necessary, click the Criteria row below the Client Number field to produce an insertion point.

Q&A The text I entered now has quotation marks surrounding it. What happened?

Criteria for text data needs to be enclosed in quotation marks. You do not have to type the quotation marks; Access adds them automatically.

- Use the DELETE or BACKSPACE key as necessary to delete the current entry.
- Click the Criteria row below the Client Name field to produce an insertion point.
- Type `Gr*` as the criterion (Figure 2–9).

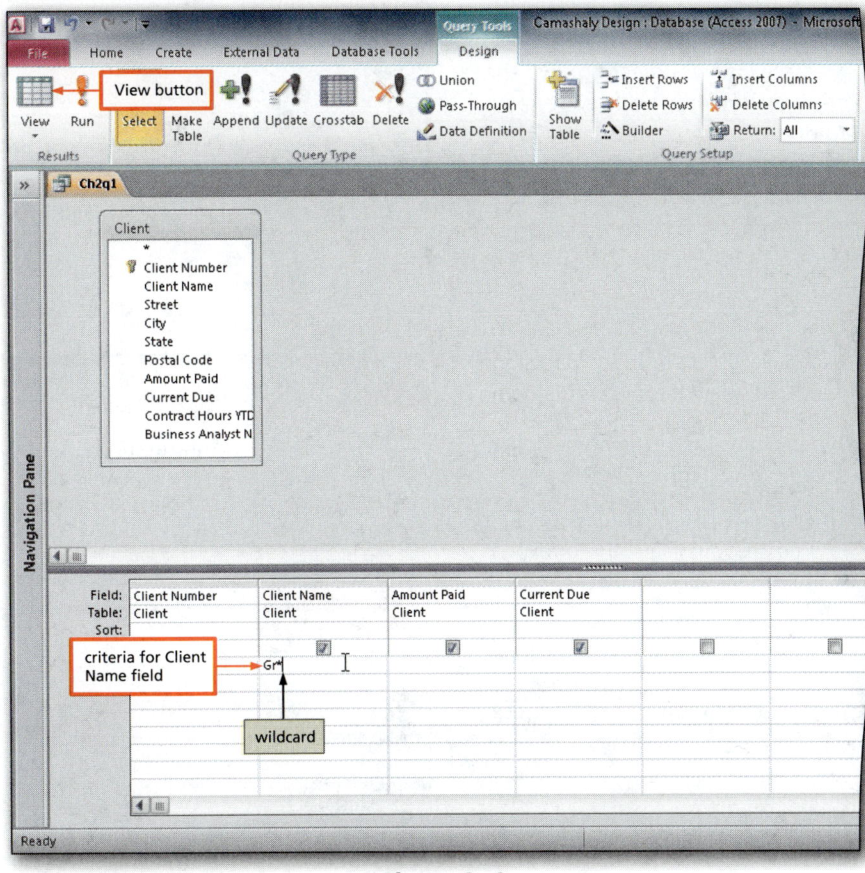

Figure 2–9

2

- View the query results by clicking the View button (Query Tools Design tab | Results group) (Figure 2–10).

Experiment

- Vary the case of the letters in the criteria and view the results to determine whether case makes a difference when entering a wildcard.

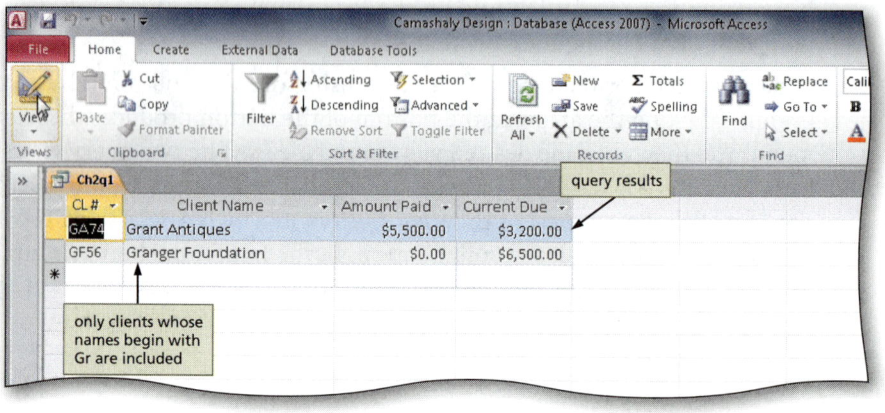

Figure 2–10

3

- Click File on the Ribbon to open the Backstage view (Figure 2–11).

Q&A Why can I not just click the Save button on the Quick Access Toolbar like I did when I saved the previous query?

If you did, you would replace the previous query with the version you just created. Because you want to save both the previous query and the new one, you need to save the new version with a different name. To do so, you must use Save Object As, which is available through the Backstage view.

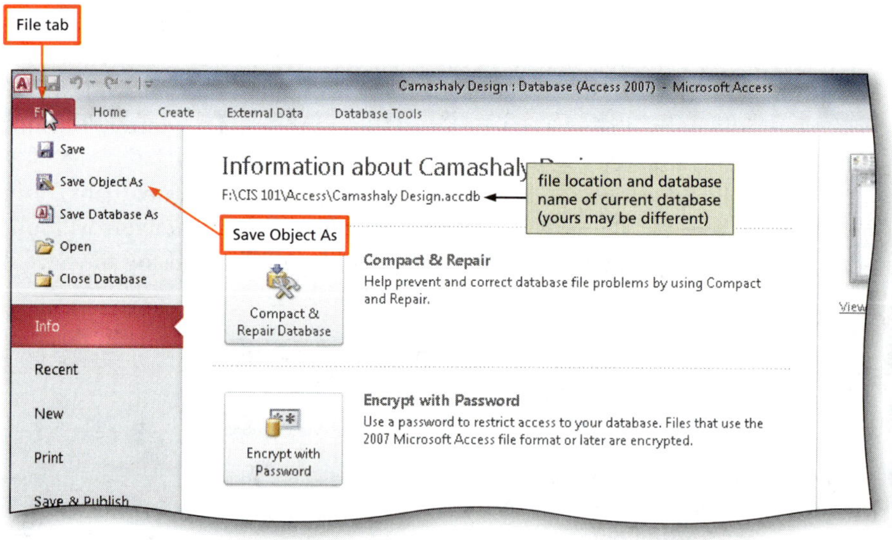

Figure 2–11

4

- Click Save Object As in the Backstage view to display the Save As dialog box.
- Type **Ch2q2** as the name for the saved query (Figure 2–12).

Q&A The current entry in the As text box is Query. Could I save the query as some other type of object?

Although you usually would want to save the query as another query, you also can save it as a form or report by changing the entry in the As text box. If you do, Access would create either a simple form or a simple report for the query.

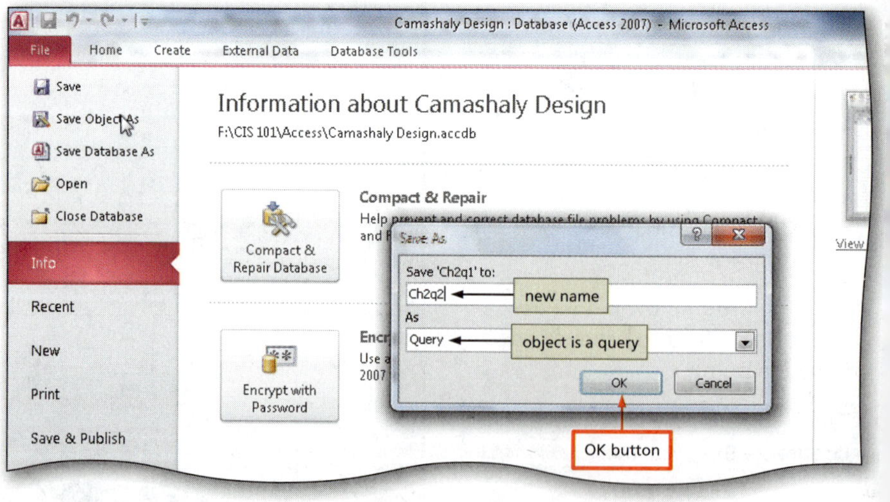

Figure 2–12

5

- Click the OK button (Save As dialog box) to save the query with the new name, and then click File on the Ribbon to close the Backstage view (Figure 2–13).

Q&A How can I tell that the query was saved with the new name?

The new name will appear on the tab.

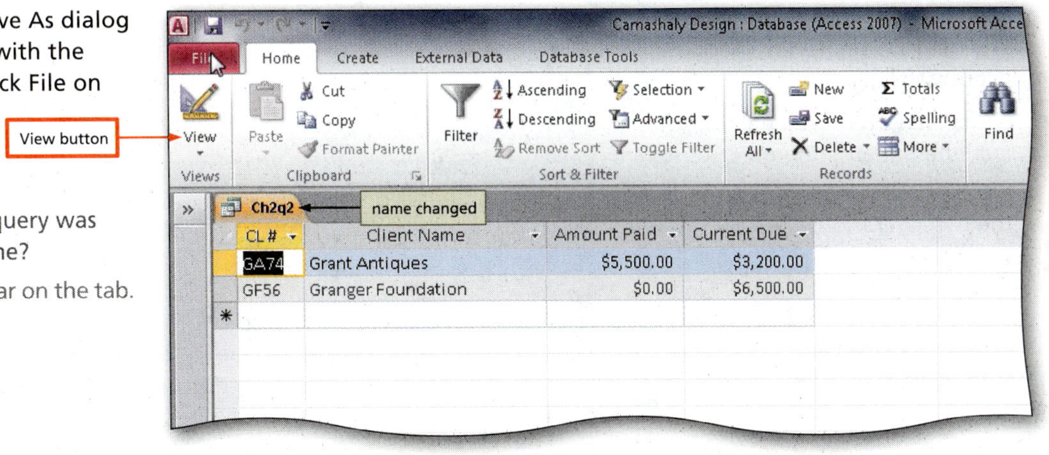

Figure 2–13

To Use Criteria for a Field Not Included in the Results

In some cases, you might require criteria for a particular field that should not appear in the results of the query. For example, you may want to see the client number, client name, address, and amount paid for all clients located in Georgetown. The criteria involve the City field, but you do not want to include the City field in the results.

To enter a criterion for the City field, it must be included in the design grid. Normally, this also would mean it would appear in the results. To prevent this from happening, remove the check mark from its Show check box in the Show row of the grid.

The following steps modify the previous query so that Camashaly Design can select only those clients located in Georgetown. Camashaly does not want the city to appear in the results, however. The steps also save the query with a new name.

1

- Click the View button (Home tab | Views group), shown in Figure 2–13, to return to Design view.

Q&A The text I entered is now preceded by the word, Like. What happened?

Criteria including wildcards need to be preceded by the word, Like. You do not have to type the word, Like, however. Access adds it automatically to any criterion involving a wildcard.

- Erase the criterion in the Client Name field.
- Add the City field to the query.
- Type **Georgetown** as the criterion for the City field (Figure 2–14).

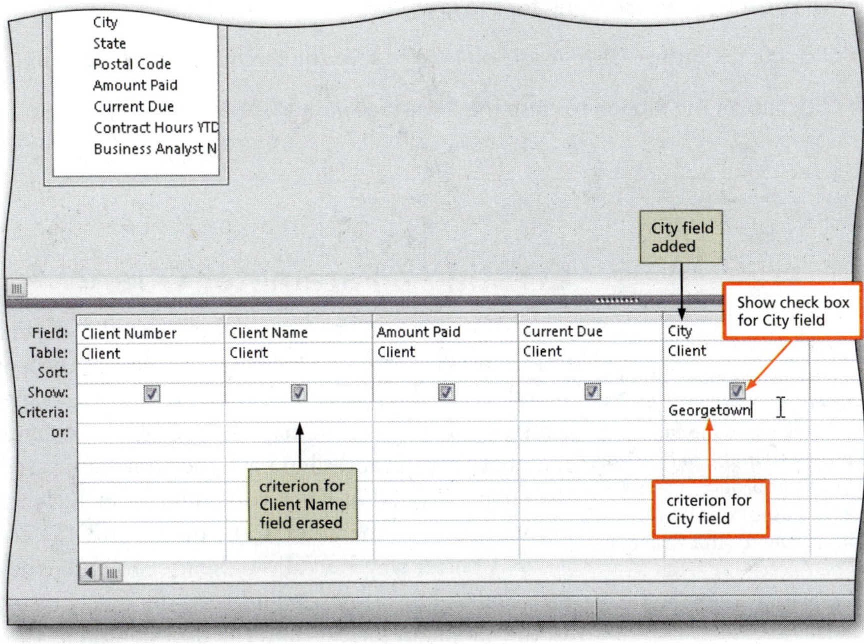

Figure 2–14

2

- Click the Show check box for the City field to remove the check mark (Figure 2–15).

Q&A

Could I have removed the check mark before entering the criterion?

Yes. The order in which you perform the two operations does not matter.

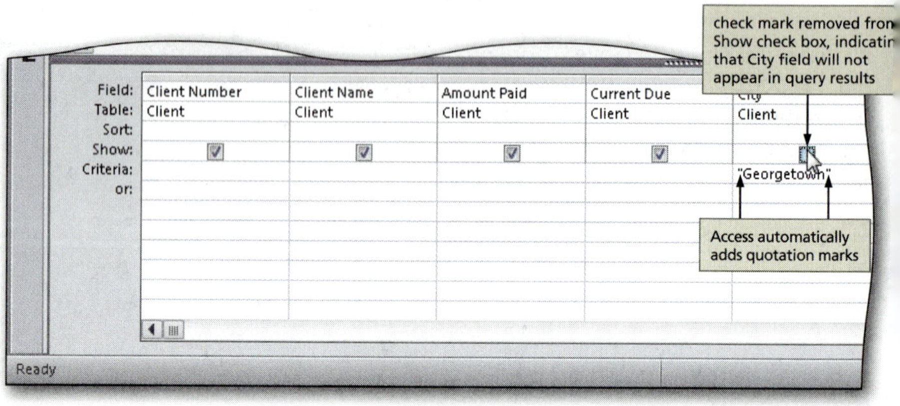

Figure 2–15

3

- View the query results (Figure 2–16).

Experiment

- Click the View button to return to Design view, enter a different city name, and view the results. Repeat this process with a variety of city names, including at least one city name that is not in the database. When finished, change the criterion back to Georgetown.

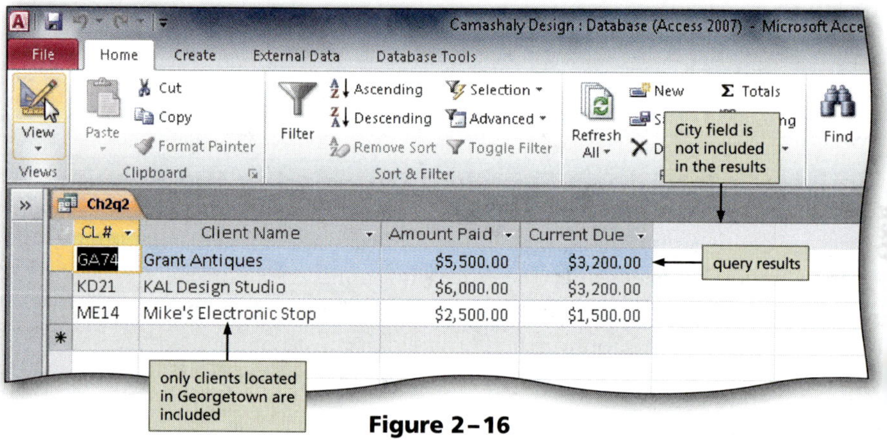

Figure 2–16

4

- Click File on the Ribbon to open the Backstage view.
- Click Save Object As in the Backstage view to display the Save As dialog box.
- Type `Ch2q3` as the name for the saved query.
- Click the OK button (Save As dialog box) to save the query with the new name.
- Click File on the Ribbon to close the Backstage view.

BTW

Queries: Query-by-Example
Query-By-Example, often referred to as QBE, was a query language first proposed in the mid-1970s. In this approach, users asked questions by filling in a table on the screen. The Access approach to queries is based on Query-By-Example.

Creating a Parameter Query

If you wanted to find clients located in Kyle instead of Georgetown, you would either have to create a new query or modify the existing query by replacing Georgetown with Kyle as the criterion. Rather than giving a specific criterion when you first create the query, on occasion, you may want to be able to enter part of the criterion when you view the query results and then have the appropriate results appear. For example, to include all the clients located in Kyle, you could enter Kyle as a criterion in the City field. From that point on, every time you ran the query, only the clients in Kyle would appear.

A better way is to allow the user to enter the city at the time the user wants to view the results. Thus, a user could view the query results, enter Kyle as the city, and then see all the clients in Kyle. Later, the user could use the same query but enter Georgetown as the city, and then see all the clients in Georgetown.

To enable this flexibility, you create a **parameter query**, which is a query that prompts for input whenever it is used. You enter a parameter (prompt for the user), rather than a specific value as the criterion. You create one by enclosing a value in a criterion in square brackets. It is important that the value in the brackets does not match the name of any field. If you enter a field name in square brackets, Access assumes you want that particular field and does not prompt the user for input. To prompt the user to enter the city name as the input, you could place [Enter City] as the criterion in the City field.

To Create and View a Parameter Query

The following steps create a parameter query that will prompt the users at Camashaly to enter a city, and then display the client number, name, address, and amount paid for all clients located in that city. The steps also save the query with a new name.

1

- Return to Design view.
- Erase the current criterion in the City column, and then type `[Enter City]` as the new criterion (Figure 2–17).

Q&A What is the purpose of the square brackets?

The square brackets indicate that the text entered is not text that the value in the column must match. Without the brackets, Access would search for records on which the city is Enter City.

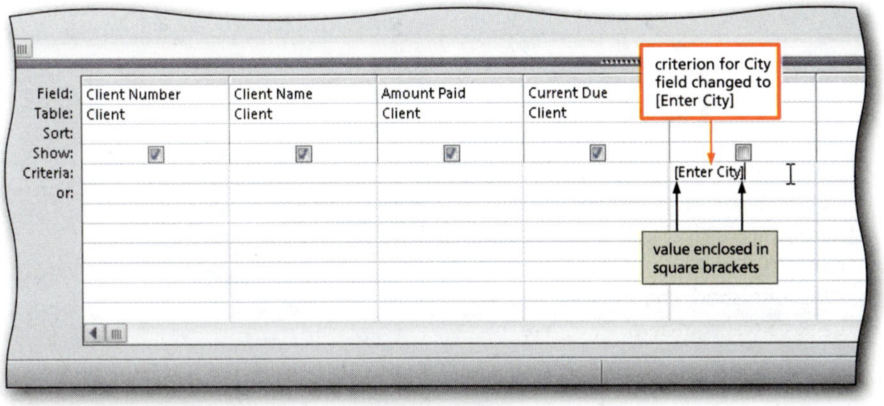

Figure 2–17

Q&A What if I typed a field name in the square brackets?

Access would simply use the value in that field. To create a parameter query, you must not use a field name in the square brackets.

2

- Click the View button (Query Tools Design tab | Results group) to display the Enter Parameter Value dialog box (Figure 2–18).

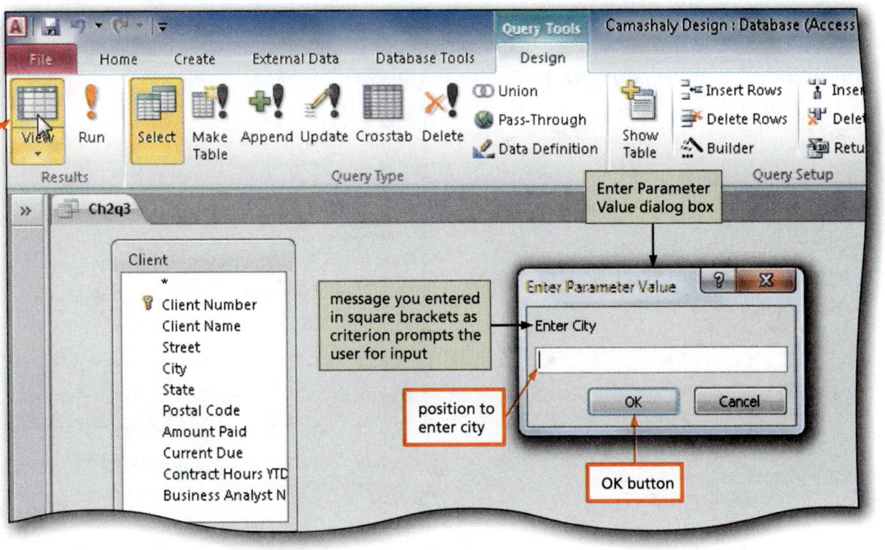

Figure 2–18

3

- Type **Kyle** as the parameter value in the Enter City text box and then click the OK button (Enter Parameter Value dialog box) to close the dialog box and view the query (Figure 2–19).

Experiment

- Try other characters between the square brackets. In each case, view the results. When finished, change the characters between the square brackets back to Enter City.

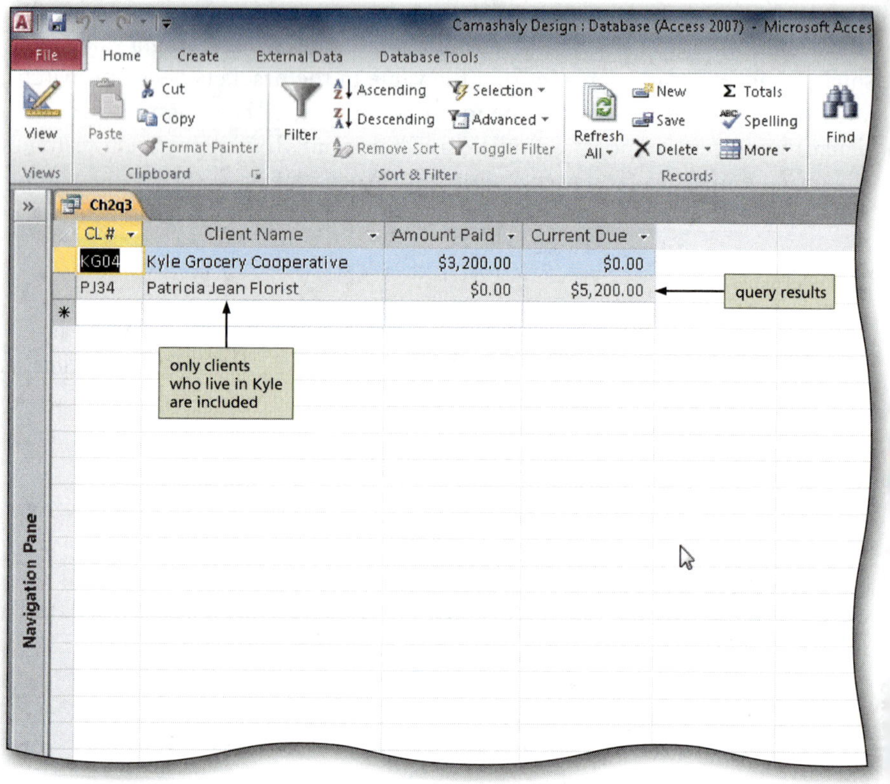

Figure 2–19

4

- Click File on the Ribbon to open the Backstage view.
- Click Save Object As in the Backstage view to display the Save As dialog box.
- Type **Client-City Query** as the name for the saved query.
- Click the OK button (Save As dialog box) to save the query with the new name and then click File on the Ribbon (Figure 2–20).

5

- Click the Close button for the Client-City query to close the query.

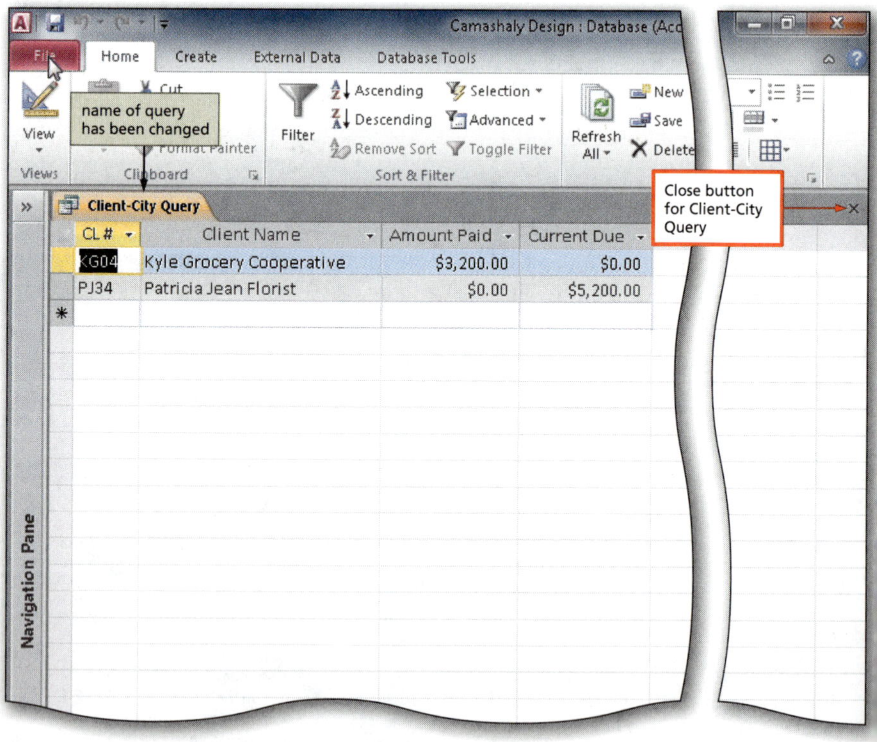

Figure 2–20

Break Point: If you wish to take a break, this is a good place to do so. You can quit Access now. To resume at a later time, start Access, open the database called Camashaly Design, and continue following the steps from this location forward.

To Use a Parameter Query

You use a parameter query like any other saved query. You can open it or you can print the query results. In either case, Access prompts you to supply a value for the parameter each time you use the query. As with other queries, the query always uses the data that is currently in the table. Thus, if changes have been made to the data since the last time you ran the query, the results of the query may be different, even if you enter the same value for the parameter. The following steps use the parameter query named Client-City Query.

1

- Open the Navigation Pane.
- Right-click the Client-City Query to produce a shortcut menu.
- Click Open on the shortcut menu to open the query and display the Enter Parameter Value dialog box (Figure 2–21).

Q&A

The title bar for my Navigation Pane contains Tables and Related Views rather than All Access Objects as it did in Access Chapter 1. What should I do?

Click the Navigation Pane arrow and then click All Access Objects.

Q&A

I do not have the Search bar at the top of the Navigation Pane that I had in Access Chapter 1. What should I do?

Right-click the Navigation Pane title bar arrow to display a shortcut menu, and then click Search Bar.

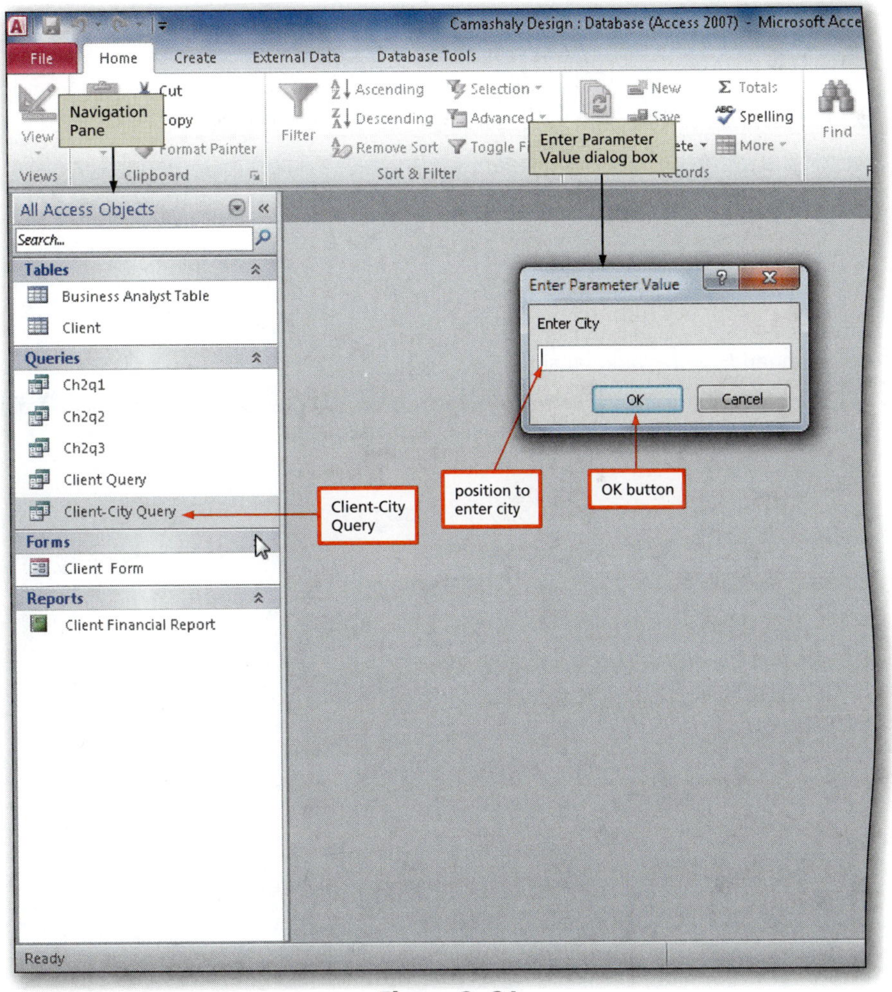

Figure 2–21

2

- Type `Kyle` in the Enter City text box, and then click the OK button (Enter Parameter Value dialog box) to display the results using Kyle as the city, as shown in Figure 2–20.
- Close the query.

To Use a Number in a Criterion

To enter a number in a criterion, type the number without any dollar signs or commas. The following steps create a query that Camashaly Design might use to display all clients whose current due amount is $0. The steps also save the query with a new name.

1

- Close the Navigation Pane.
- Click Create on the Ribbon to display the Create tab.
- Click the Query Design button (Create tab | Queries group) to create a new query.
- Click the Client table (Show Table dialog box) to select the table.

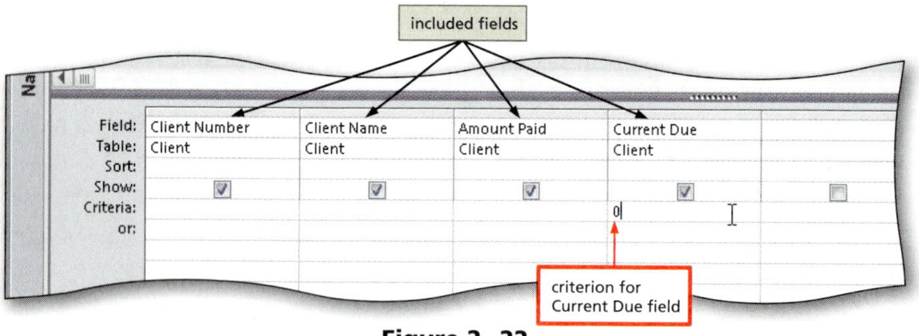

Figure 2–22

- Click the Add button to add the selected table to the query.
- Click the Close button to remove the dialog box from the screen.
- Drag the lower edge of the field list down far enough so all fields in the field list are displayed.
- Include the Client Number, Client Name, Amount Paid, and Current Due fields in the query.
- Type 0 as the criterion for the Current Due field (Figure 2–22).

Q&A Do I need to enter a dollar sign and decimal point?

No. Access will interpret 0 as $0 because the data type for the Current Due field is currency.

2

- View the query results (Figure 2–23).

Q&A Why did Access display the results as $0.00 when I only entered 0?

Access uses the format for the field to determine how to display the result. In this case, the format indicated that Access should include the dollar sign, decimal point, and two decimal places.

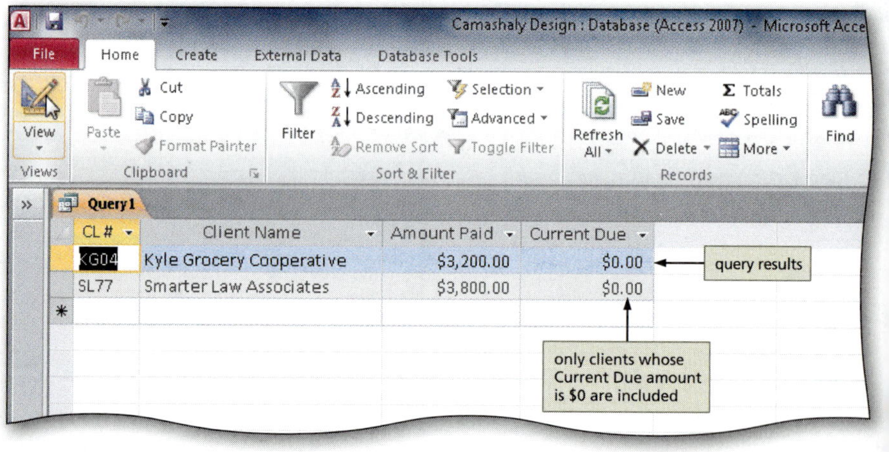

Figure 2–23

3

- Save the query as Ch2q4.

Q&A How do I know when to use the Save button to save a query or use the Backstage view to perform a Save As?

If you are saving a new query, the simplest way is to use the Save button on the Quick Access Toolbar. If you are saving changes to a previously saved query but do not want to change the name, use the Save button. If you want to save a previously saved query with a new name, you must use the Backstage view and perform a Save Object As.

To Use a Comparison Operator in a Criterion

Unless you specify otherwise, Access assumes that the criteria you enter involve equality (exact matches). In the last query, for example, you were requesting those clients whose current due amount is equal to 0 (zero). If you want something other than an exact match, you must enter the appropriate **comparison operator**. The comparison operators are > (greater than), < (less than), >= (greater than or equal to), <= (less than or equal to), and NOT (not equal to).

The following steps use the > operator to create a query that Camashaly Design might use to find all clients whose amount paid is more than $3,000. The steps also save the query with a new name.

1

- Return to Design view.
- Erase the 0 in the Current Due column.
- Type **>3000** as the criterion for the Amount Paid field (Figure 2–24).

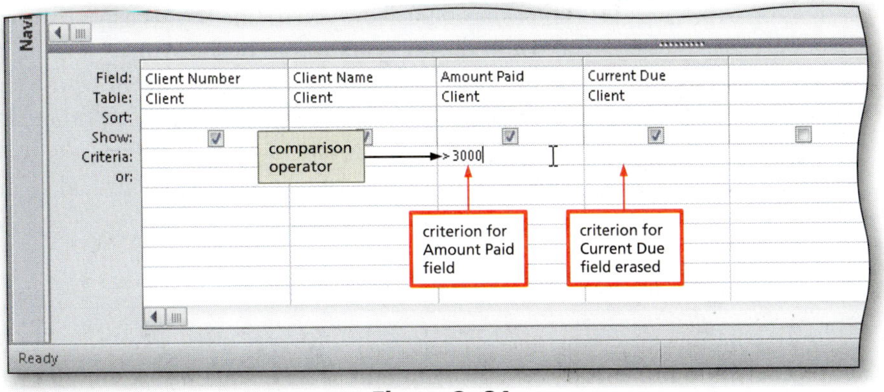

Figure 2–24

2

- View the query results (Figure 2–25).

Experiment

- Return to Design view. Try a different criterion involving a comparison operator in the Amount Paid field and view the results. When finished, return to Design view, enter the original criterion (>3000) in the Amount Paid field, and view the results.

3

- Save the query as Ch2q5.

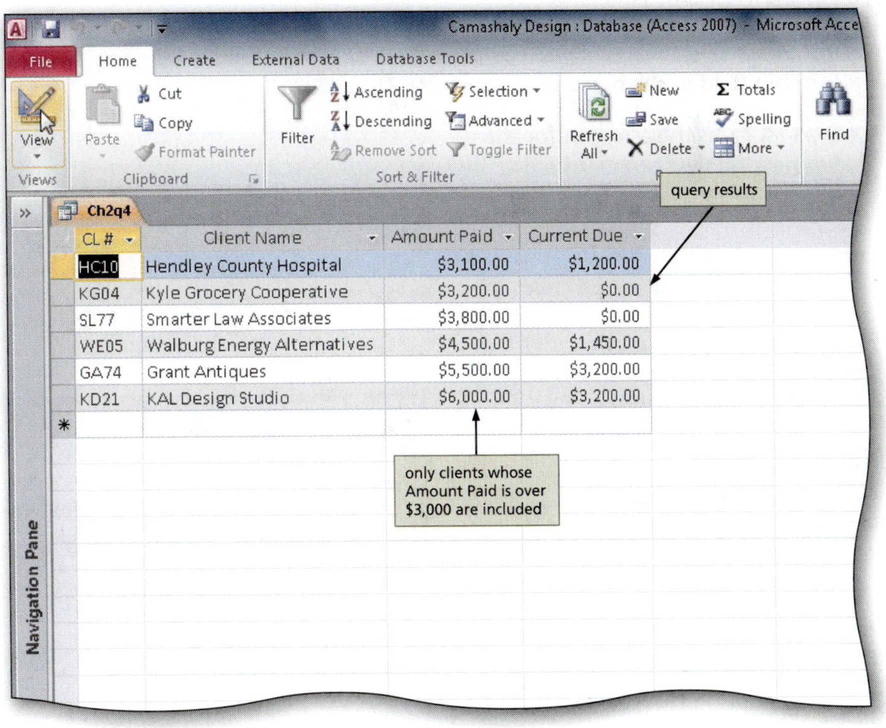

Figure 2–25

Using Compound Criteria

Often you will have more than one criterion that the data for which you are searching must satisfy. This type of criterion is called a **compound criterion**. Two types of compound criteria exist.

In an **AND criterion**, each individual criterion must be true in order for the compound criterion to be true. For example, an AND criterion would allow you to find those clients that have an amount paid greater than $3,000 and whose business analyst is business analyst 11.

Conversely, an **OR criterion** is true provided either individual criterion is true. An OR criterion would allow you to find those clients that have an amount paid greater than $3,000 and also those clients whose business analyst is business analyst 11 — either one criterion or the other is true. In this case, any client whose amount paid is greater than $3,000 would be included in the answer, regardless of whether the client's business analyst is business analyst 11. Likewise, any client whose business analyst is business analyst 11 would be included, regardless of whether the client had an amount paid greater than $3,000.

To Use a Compound Criterion Involving AND

To combine criteria with AND, place the criteria on the same row of the design grid. The following steps use an AND criterion to enable Camashaly to find those clients whose amount paid is greater than $3,000 and whose business analyst is analyst 11. The steps also save the query with a new name.

1

- Return to Design view.
- Include the Business Analyst Number field in the query.
- Type `11` as the criterion for the Business Analyst Number field (Figure 2–26).

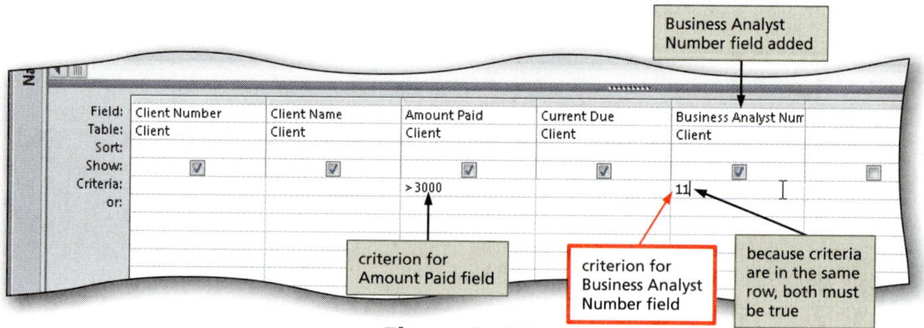

Figure 2–26

2

- View the query results (Figure 2–27).

3

- Save the query as Ch2q6.

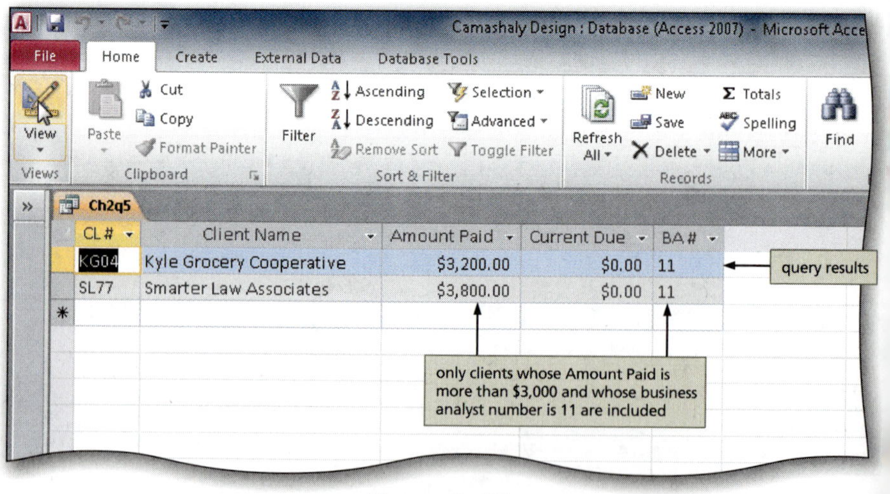

Figure 2–27

To Use a Compound Criterion Involving OR

To combine criteria with OR, the criteria must go on separate rows in the Criteria area of the grid. The following steps use an OR criterion to enable Camashaly to find those clients whose amount paid is greater than $3,000 or whose business analyst is analyst 11 (or both). The steps also save the query with a new name.

1

- Return to Design view.
- If necessary, click the Criteria entry for the Business Analyst Number field and then use the BACKSPACE key or the DELETE key to erase the entry ("11").
- Click the or row (the row below the Criteria row) for the Business Analyst Number field and then type `11` as the entry (Figure 2–28).

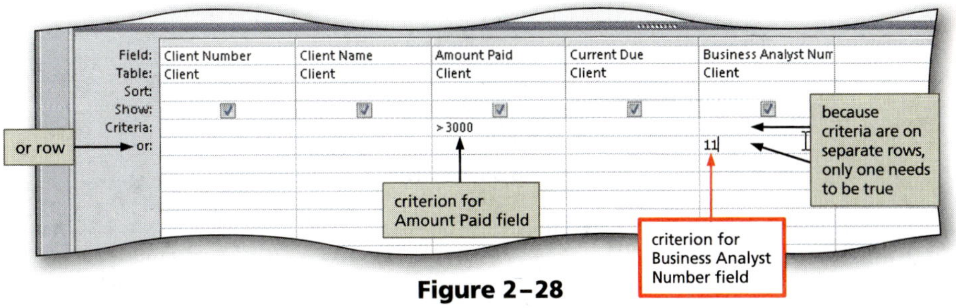

Figure 2–28

2

- View the query results (Figure 2–29).

3

- Save the query as Ch2q7.

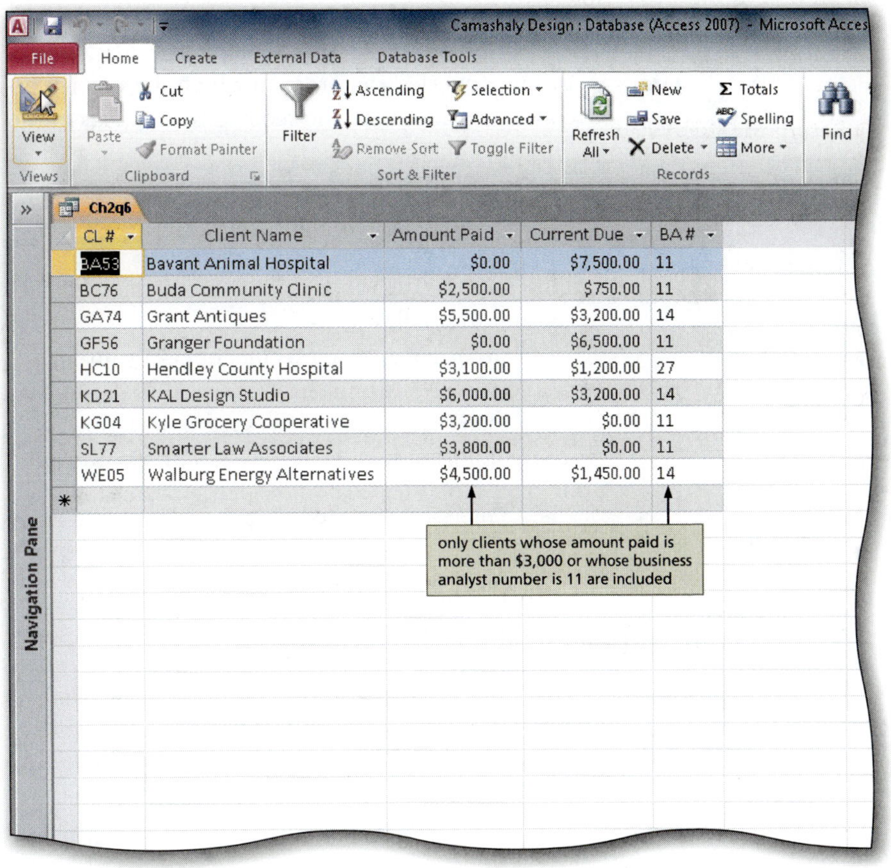

Figure 2–29

Special Criteria

There are three special criteria you can use in queries:

1. If you want to create a criterion involving a range of values in a single field, you can use the **AND operator**. You place the word AND between the individual conditions. For example, if you wanted to find all clients whose amount paid is >= $1,000 and <= $4,000, you would enter `>= 1000 AND <= 4000` as the criterion in the Amount Paid column.
2. You can select values in a given range by using the **BETWEEN operator**. This is often an alternative to the AND operator. For example, to find all clients whose amount paid is between $1,000 and $4,000, inclusive, you would enter `BETWEEN 1000 AND 4000` as the criterion in the Amount Paid column.
3. You can select values in a list by using the **IN operator**. You follow the word IN with the list of values in parentheses. For example, to find clients whose business analyst number is 11 or 14 using the IN operator, you would enter `IN ("11","14")` as the criterion in the Business Analyst Number column. Unlike when you enter a simple criterion, you must enclose text values in quotation marks.

Sorting

In some queries, the order in which the records appear is irrelevant. All you need to be concerned about are the records that appear in the results. It does not matter which one is first or which one is last.

In other queries, however, the order can be very important. You may want to see the cities in which clients are located and would like them arranged alphabetically. Perhaps you want to see the clients listed by business analyst number. Further, within all the clients of any given business analyst, you might want them to be listed by amount paid from largest amount to smallest.

To order the records in a query result in a particular way, you **sort** the records. The field or fields on which the records are sorted is called the **sort key**. If you are sorting on more than one field (such as sorting by amount paid within business analyst number), the more important field (Business Analyst Number) is called the **major key** (also called the **primary sort key**) and the less important field (Amount Paid) is called the **minor key** (also called the **secondary sort key**).

To sort in Microsoft Access, specify the sort order in the Sort row of the design grid below the field that is the sort key. If you specify more than one sort key, the sort key on the left will be the major sort key, and the one on the right will be the minor key.

The following are guidelines related to sorting in queries.

BTW

Sorting Data in a Query
When sorting data in a query, the records in the underlying tables (the tables on which the query is based) are not actually rearranged. Instead, the DBMS determines the most efficient method of simply displaying the records in the requested order. The records in the underlying tables remain in their original order.

Determine whether special order is required.
Examine the query or request to see if it contains words, such as order or sort, that would imply that the order of the query results is important. If so, you need to sort the query.

- **Determine the sort key(s).** If sorting is required, identify the field or fields on which the results are to be sorted. In the request, look for language such as ordered by or sort the results by, both of which would indicate that the specified field is a sort key.
- **If using two sort keys, determine major and minor key.** If you are using two sort keys, determine which one is the more important, or the major key. Look for language such as sort by amount paid within business analyst number, which implies that the overall order is by business analyst number. Thus, the Business Analyst Number field would be the major sort key and the Amount Paid field would be the minor sort key.
- **Determine sort order.** Words such as increasing, ascending, or low-to-high imply Ascending order. Words such as decreasing, descending, or high-to-low imply Descending order. Sorting in alphabetical order implies Ascending order. If there are no words to imply a particular order, you would typically use Ascending.
- **Determine restrictions.** Examine the query or request to see if there are any special restrictions. One common restriction is to exclude duplicates. Another common restriction is to list only a certain number of records, for example, to list only the first five records.

Plan Ahead

To Clear the Design Grid

If the fields you want to include in the next query are different from those in the previous query, it is usually simpler to start with a clear grid, one with no fields already in the design grid. You always can clear the entries in the design grid by closing the query and then starting over. A simpler approach to clearing the entries is to select all the entries and then press the DELETE key. The following steps return to Design view and clear the design grid.

1

- Return to Design view.
- Click just above the Client Number column heading in the grid to select the column.

Q&A

I clicked above the column heading, but the column is not selected. What should I do?

You did not point to the correct location. Be sure the mouse pointer changes into a down-pointing arrow and then click again.

- Hold the SHIFT key down and click just above the Business Analyst Number column heading to select all the columns (Figure 2–30).

2

- Press the DELETE key to clear the design grid.

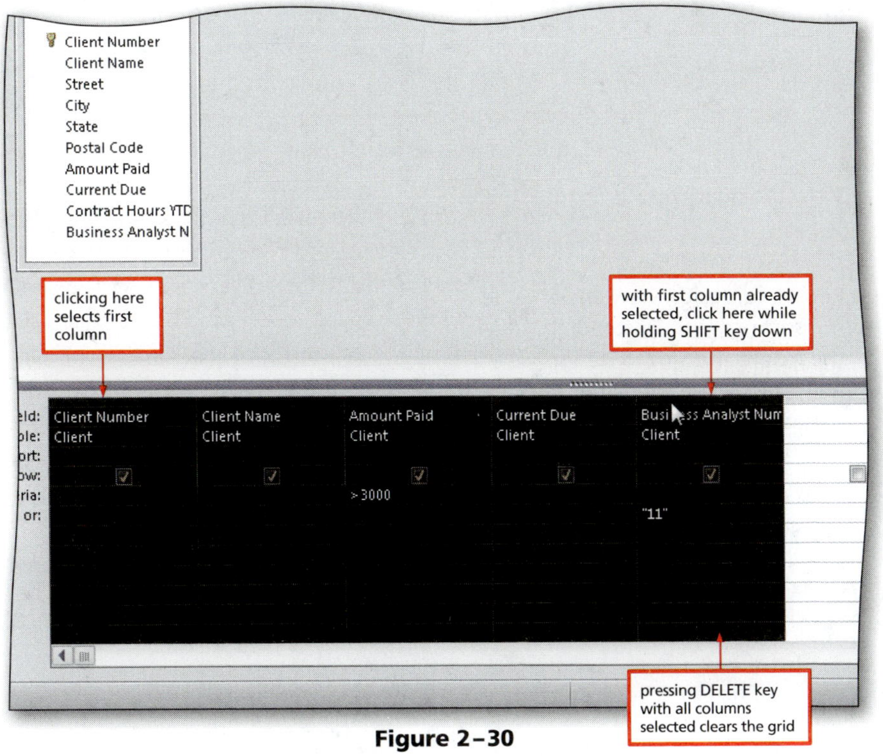

Figure 2–30

To Sort Data in a Query

After determining in the design process that a query is to be sorted, you will need to specify the sort key to Access. The following steps sort the cities in the Client table by indicating that the City field is to be sorted. The steps specify Ascending sort order.

1

- Include the City field in the design grid.
- Click the Sort row below the City field, and then click the Sort row arrow to display a menu of possible sort orders (Figure 2–31).

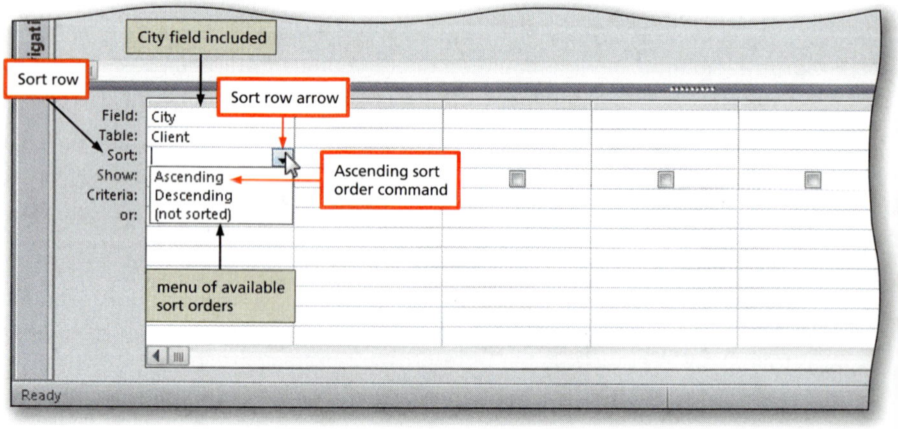

Figure 2–31

2

- Click Ascending to select the sort order (Figure 2–32).

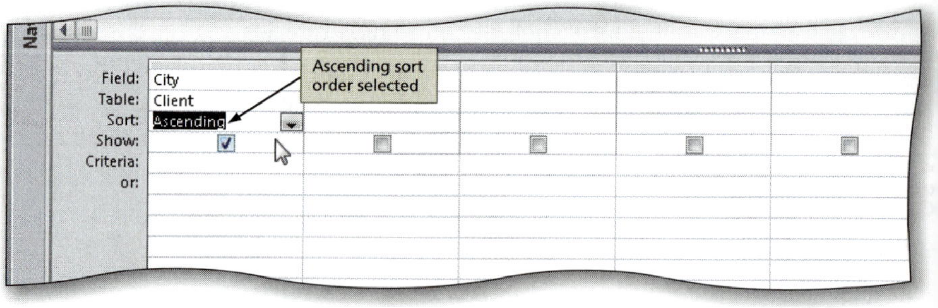

Figure 2–32

3

- View the query results (Figure 2–33).

Experiment

- Return to Design view and change the sort order to Descending. View the results. Return to Design view and change the sort order back to Ascending. View the results.

Q&A Why do some cities appear more than once?

More than one client is located in those cities.

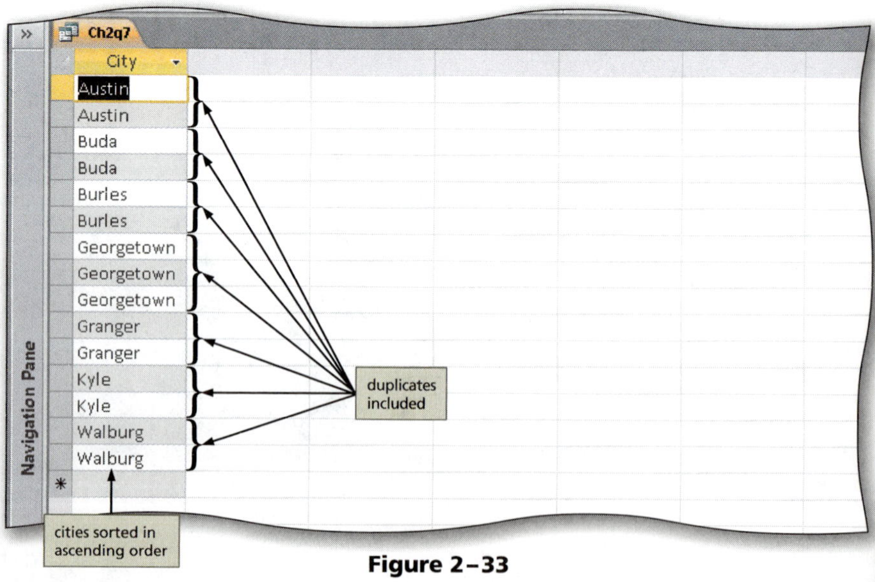

Figure 2–33

To Omit Duplicates

When you sort data, duplicates normally are included. In Figure 2–33, for example, Austin appeared twice, as did Buda, Burles, Granger, Kyle, and Walburg. Georgetown appeared three times. These duplicates do not add any value, so you should eliminate them from the results. To eliminate duplicates, display the query's property sheet. A **property sheet** is a window containing the various properties of the object. To omit duplicates, you will use the property sheet to change the Unique Values property from No to Yes.

The following steps create a query that Camashaly Design might use to obtain a sorted list of the cities in the Client table in which each city is listed only once. The steps also save the query with a new name.

1

- Return to Design view.
- Click the second field (the empty field to the right of City) in the design grid.
- If necessary, click Design on the Ribbon to display the Design tab.
- Click the Property Sheet button (Query Tools Design tab | Show/Hide group) to display the property sheet (Figure 2–34).

Q&A My property sheet looks different. What should I do?

If your sheet looks different, you clicked the wrong place and will have to close the property sheet and repeat this step.

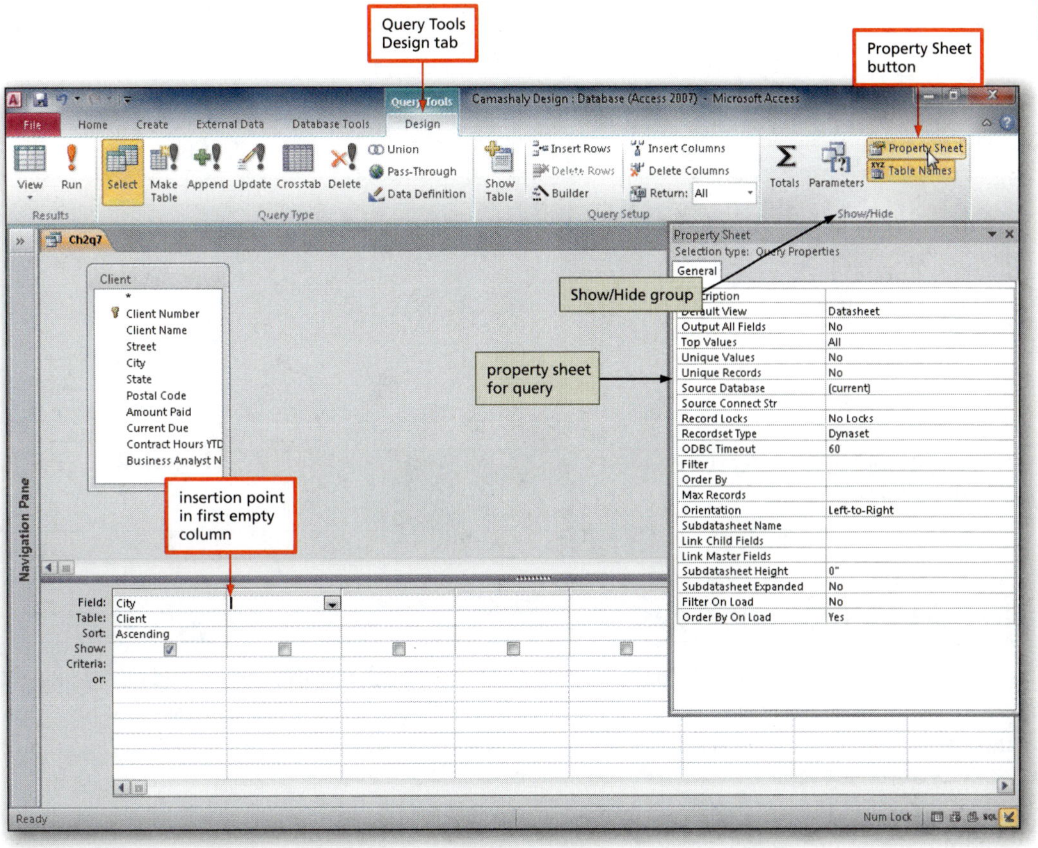

Figure 2–34

2

- Click the Unique Values property box, and then click the arrow that appears to produce a list of available choices (Figure 2–35).

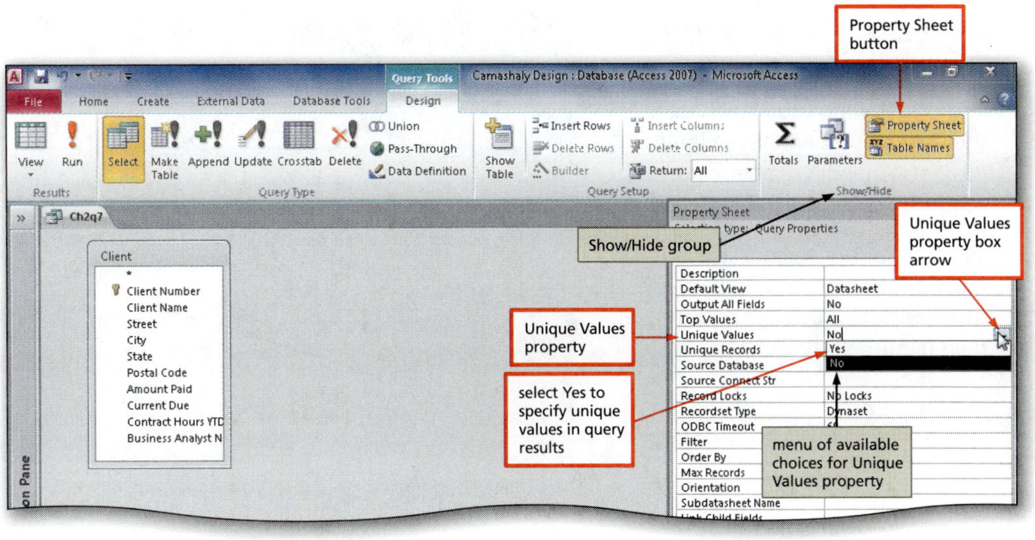

Figure 2–35

3

- Click Yes and then close the Query Properties property sheet by clicking the Property Sheet button (Query Tools Design tab | Show / Hide group) a second time.
- View the query results (Figure 2–36).

4

- Save the query as Ch2q8.

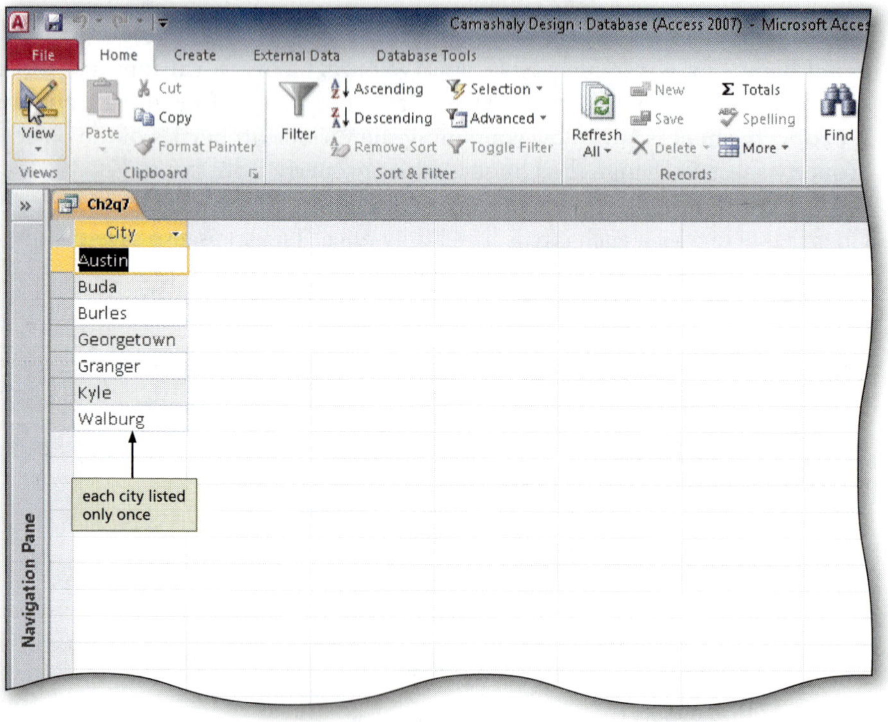

Figure 2–36

Other Ways
1. Right-click second field in design grid, click Properties on shortcut menu

To Sort on Multiple Keys

The following steps sort on multiple keys. Specifically, Camashaly needs the data to be sorted by amount paid (low to high) within business analyst number, which means that the Business Analyst Number field is the major key and the Amount Paid field is the minor key. The steps also save the query with a new name.

1

- Return to Design view. Clear the design grid by clicking the first column in the grid, and then pressing the DELETE key to clear the design grid.
- In the following order, include the Client Number, Client Name, Business Analyst Number, and Amount Paid fields in the query.
- Select Ascending as the sort order for both the Business Analyst Number field and the Amount Paid field (Figure 2–37).

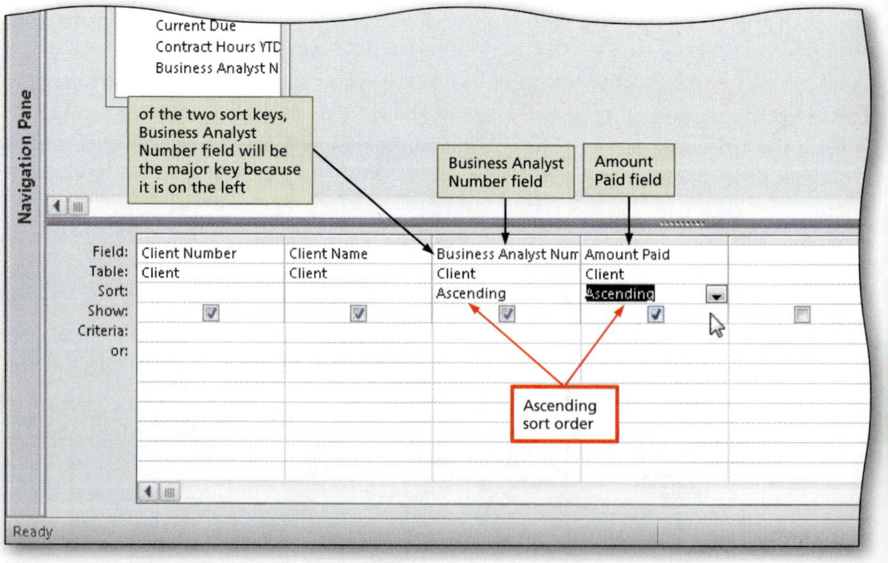

Figure 2–37

2

- View the query results (Figure 2–38).

Experiment

- Return to Design view and try other sort combinations for the Business Analyst Number and Amount Paid fields, such as Ascending for Business Analyst Number and Descending for Amount Paid. In each case, view the results to see the effect of the changes. When finished, select Ascending as the sort order for both fields.

Q&A What if the Amount Paid field is to the left of the Business Analyst Number field?

It is important to remember that the major sort key must appear to the left of the minor sort key in the design grid. If you attempted to sort by amount paid within business analyst number, but placed the Amount Paid field to the left of the Business Analyst Number field, your results would be incorrect.

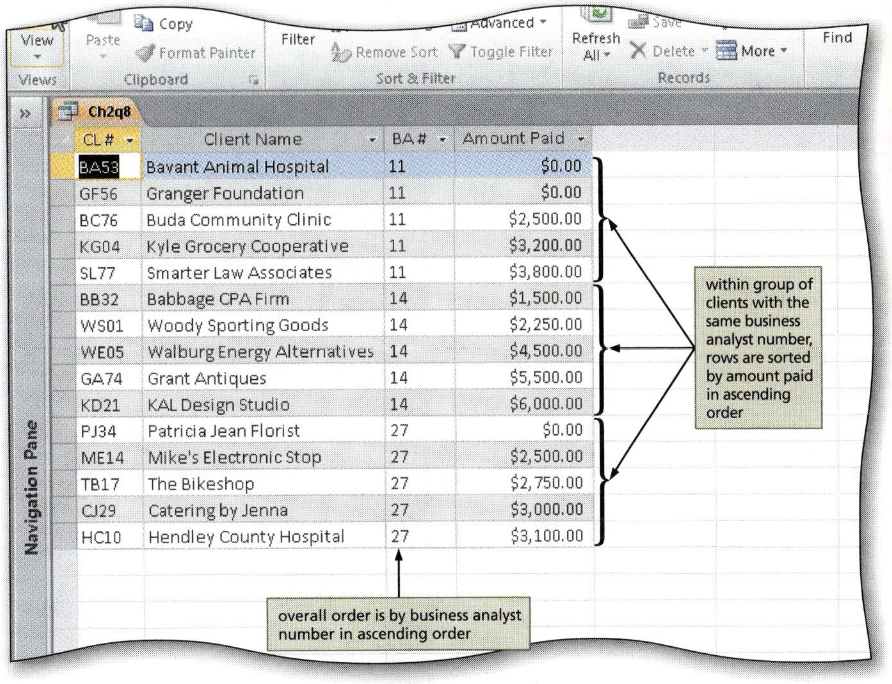

Figure 2–38

3

- Save the query as Ch2q9.

To Create a Top-Values Query

Rather than show all the results of a query, you may want to show only a specified number of records or a percentage of records. Creating a **top-values query** allows you to quantify the results. When you sort records, you can limit results to those records having the highest (descending sort) or lowest (ascending sort) values. To do so, first create a query that sorts the data in the desired order. Next, use the Return box on the Design tab to change the number of records to be included from All to the desired number or percentage. The following steps create a query for Camashaly Design that shows only the first five records that were included in the results of the previous query. The steps also save the resulting query with a new name.

1

- Return to Design view.
- If necessary, click Design on the Ribbon to display the Design tab.
- Click the Return box arrow (Query Tools Design tab | Query Setup group) to display the Return box menu (Figure 2–39).

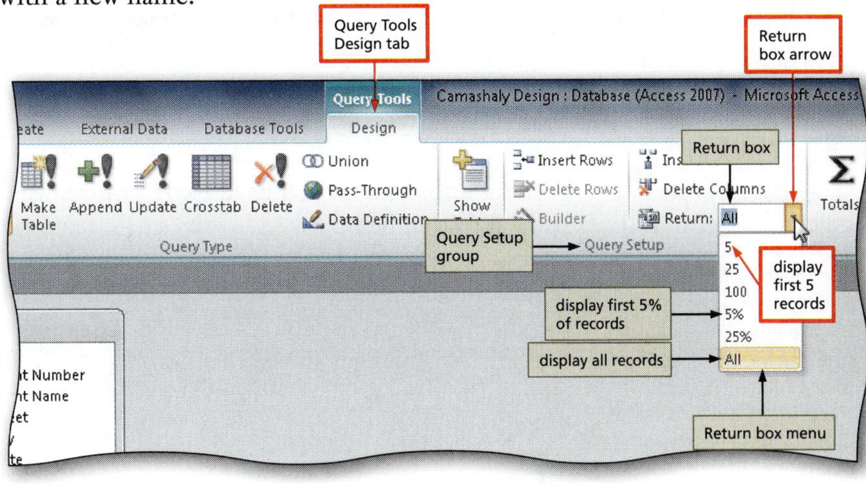

Figure 2–39

2

- Click 5 in the Return box menu to specify that the query results should contain the first five rows.

Q&A Could I have typed the 5? What about other numbers that do not appear in the list?

Yes, you could have typed the 5. For numbers not appearing in the list, you must type the number.

- View the query results (Figure 2–40).

3

- Save the query as Ch2q10.
- Close the query.

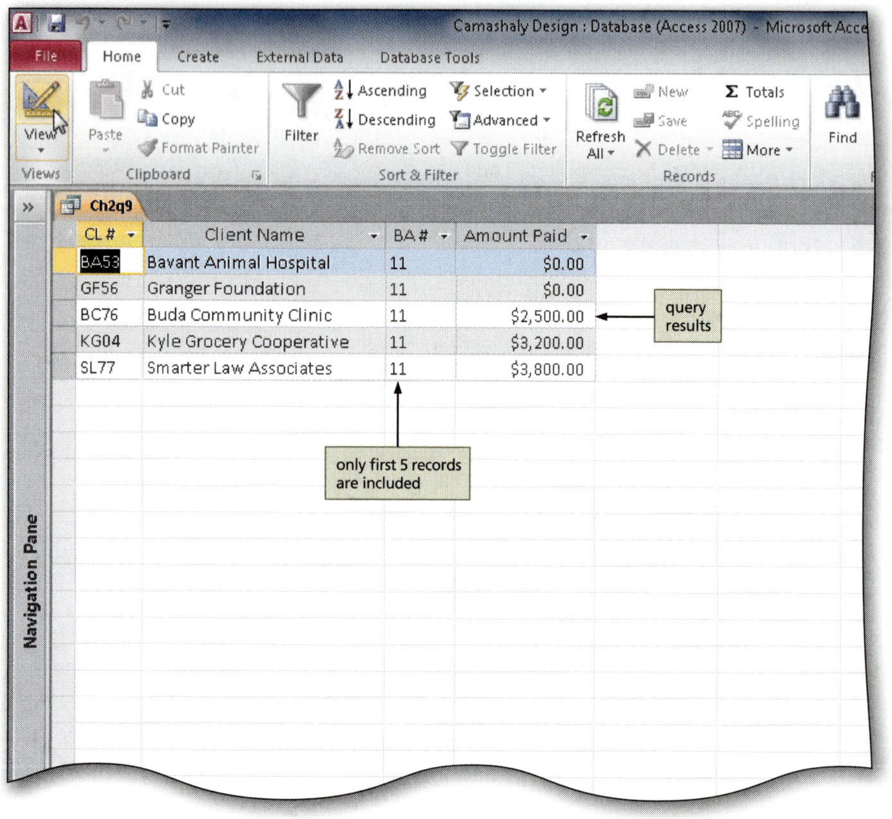

Figure 2–40

Q&A Do I need to close the query before creating my next query?

Not necessarily. When you use a top-values query, however, it is important to change the value in the Return box back to All. If you do not change the Return value back to All, the previous value will remain in effect. Consequently, you might not get all the records you should in the next query. A good practice whenever you use a top-values query is to close the query as soon as you are done. That way, you will begin your next query from scratch, which guarantees that the value is reset to All.

Break Point: If you wish to take a break, this is a good place to do so. You can quit Access now. To resume at a later time, start Access, open the database called Camashaly Design, and continue following the steps from this location forward.

BTW **Join Line**
If you do not get a join line automatically, there may be a problem with one of your table designs. Open each table in Design view and make sure that the data types are the same for the matching field in both tables and that one of the matching fields is the primary key in a table. Correct these errors and create the query again.

Joining Tables

In designing a query, you need to determine whether more than one table is required. If the question being asked involves data from both the Client and Business Analyst tables, for example, both tables are required for the query. For example, a query may require listing the number and name of each client along with the number and name of the client's business analyst. The client's name is in the Client table, whereas the business analyst's name is in the Business Analyst Table. Thus, this query cannot be completed using a single table; both the Client and Business Analyst tables are required. You need to **join** the tables; that is, to find records in the two tables that have identical values in matching fields (Figure 2–41). In this example, you need to find records in the Client table and the Business Analyst table that have the same value in the Business Analyst Number fields.

Client Table

CL #	Client Name	...	BA #
BA53	Bavant Animal Hospital	...	11
BB32	Babbage CPA Firm	...	14
BC76	Buda Community Clinic	...	11
CJ29	Catering by Jenna	...	27
GA74	Grant Antiques	...	14
GF56	Granger Foundation	...	11
HC10	Hendley County Hospital	...	27
KD21	KAL Design Studio	...	14
KG04	Kyle Grocery Cooperative	...	11
ME14	Mike's Electronic Stop	...	27
PJ34	Patricia Jean Florist	...	27
SL77	Smarter Law Associates	...	11
TB17	The Bikeshop	...	27
WE05	Walburg Energy Alternatives	...	14
WS01	Woody Sporting Goods	...	14

Give me the number and name of each client along with the number and name of the client's analyst.

Business Analyst Table

BA #	Last Name	First Name	...
11	Kerry	Cordelia	...
14	Martinez	Manuel	...
27	Liu	Jan	...
35	Scott	Jeff	...

Client Table

CL #	Client Name	...	BA #	Last Name	First Name	...
BA53	Bavant Animal Hospital	...	11	Kerry	Cordelia	...
BB32	Babbage CPA Firm	...	14	Martinez	Manuel	...
BC76	Buda Community Clinic	...	11	Kerry	Cordelia	...
CJ29	Catering by Jenna	...	27	Liu	Jan	...
GA74	Grant Antiques	...	14	Martinez	Manuel	...
GF56	Granger Foundation	...	11	Kerry	Cordelia	...
HC10	Hendley County Hospital	...	27	Liu	Jan	...
KD21	KAL Design Studio	...	14	Martinez	Manuel	...
KG04	Kyle Grocery Cooperative	...	11	Kerry	Cordelia	...
ME14	Mike's Electronic Stop	...	27	Liu	Jan	...
PJ34	Patricia Jean Florist	...	27	Liu	Jan	...
SL77	Smarter Law Associates	...	11	Kerry	Cordelia	...
TB17	The Bikeshop	...	27	Liu	Jan	...
WE05	Walburg Energy Alternatives	...	14	Martinez	Manuel	...
WS01	Woody Sporting Goods	...	14	Martinez	Manuel	...

Figure 2–41

BTW

Join Types

The type of join that finds records from both tables that have identical values in matching fields is called an inner join. An inner join is the default join in Access. Outer joins are used to show all the records in one table as well as the common records; that is, the records that share the same value in the join field. In a left outer join, all rows from the table on the left are included. In a right outer join, all rows from the table on the right are included.

The following are guidelines related to joining tables.

Plan Ahead

Determine whether more than one table is required.
Examine the query or request to see if all the fields involved in the request are in one table. If the fields are in two (or more) tables, you need to join the tables.

- **Determine the matching fields.** If joining is required, identify the matching fields in the two tables that have identical values. Look for the same column name in the two tables or for column names that are similar.
- **Determine whether sorting is required.** Queries that join tables often are used as the basis for a report. If this is the case, it may be necessary to sort the results. For example, the Analyst-Client Report is based on a query that joins the Business Analyst and Client tables. The query is sorted by business analyst number and client number.
- **Determine restrictions.** Examine the query or request to see if there are any special restrictions. For example, the user may only want clients whose current due amount is $0.00.
- **Determine join properties.** Examine the query or request to see if you only want records from both tables that have identical values in matching fields. If you want to see records in one of the tables that do not have identical values, then you need to change the join properties.

To Join Tables

If you have determined in the design process that you need to join tables, you will first bring field lists for both tables to the upper pane of the Query window while working in Design view. Access will draw a line, called a **join line**, between matching fields in the two tables, indicating that the tables are related. You then can select fields from either table. Access joins the tables automatically.

The first step is to create a new query and add the Business Analyst Table to the query. Then, add the Client table to the query. A join line will appear, connecting the Business Analyst Number fields in the two field lists. This join line indicates how the tables are related, that is, linked through these matching fields. If the names of the matching fields differ from one table to the other, Access will not insert the line. You can insert it manually, however, by clicking one of the two matching fields and dragging the mouse pointer to the other matching field.

The following steps create a query that Camashaly Design might use to display information from both the Client table and the Business Analyst Table.

1

- Click Create on the Ribbon to display the Create tab.
- Click the Query Design button (Create tab | Queries group) to create a new query.
- If necessary, click the Business Analyst Table (Show Table dialog box) to select the table.
- Click the Add button (Show Table dialog box) to add a field list for the Business Analyst Table to the query (Figure 2–42).

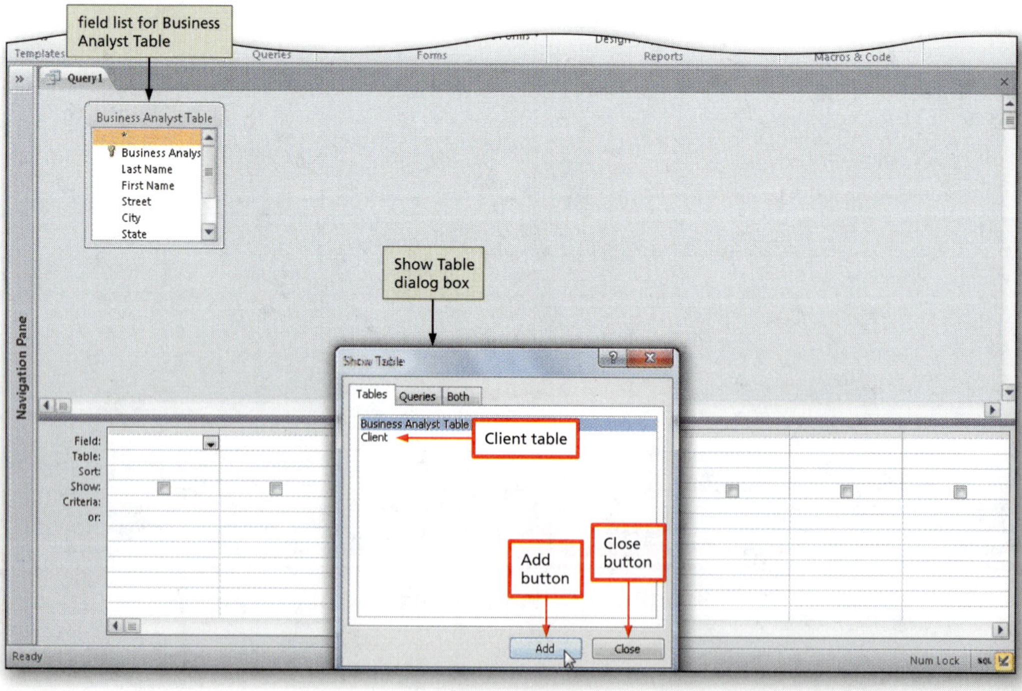

Figure 2–42

2

- Click the Client table (Show Table dialog box).
- Click the Add button (Show Table dialog box) to add a field list for the Client table.
- Close the Show Table dialog box by clicking the Close button.
- Expand the size of the two field lists so all the fields in the Business Analyst and Client tables appear (Figure 2–43).

Q&A

I did not get a join line. What should I do?

Ensure that the names of the matching fields are exactly the same, the data types are the same, and the matching field is the primary key in one of the two tables. If all of these are true and you still don't have a join line, you can produce one by pointing to one of the matching fields, pressing the left mouse button, dragging to the other matching field, and releasing the left mouse button.

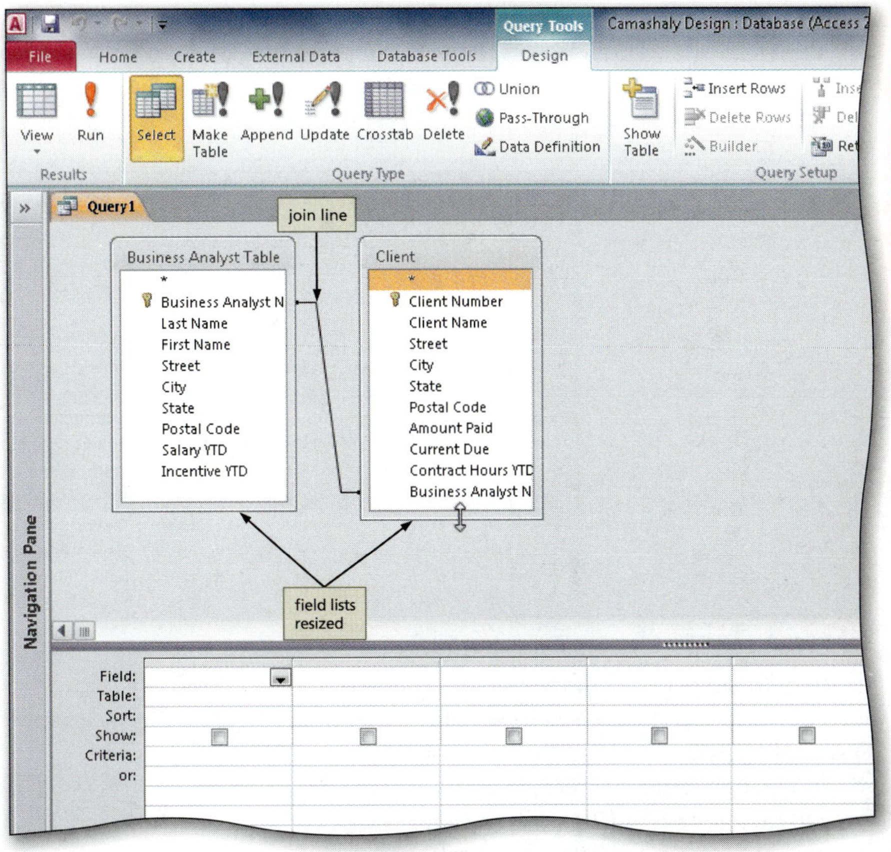

Figure 2–43

3

- In the design grid, include the Business Analyst Number, Last Name, and First Name fields from the Business Analyst Table as well as the Client Number and Client Name fields from the Client table.
- Select Ascending as the sort order for both the Business Analyst Number field and the Client Number field (Figure 2–44).

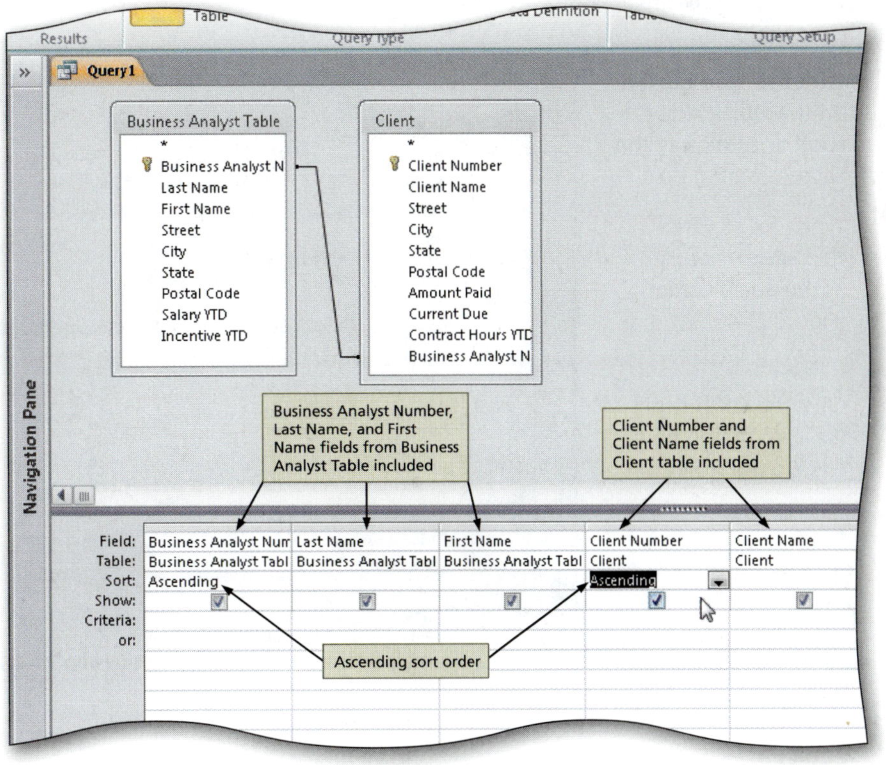

Figure 2–44

4

- View the query results (Figure 2–45).

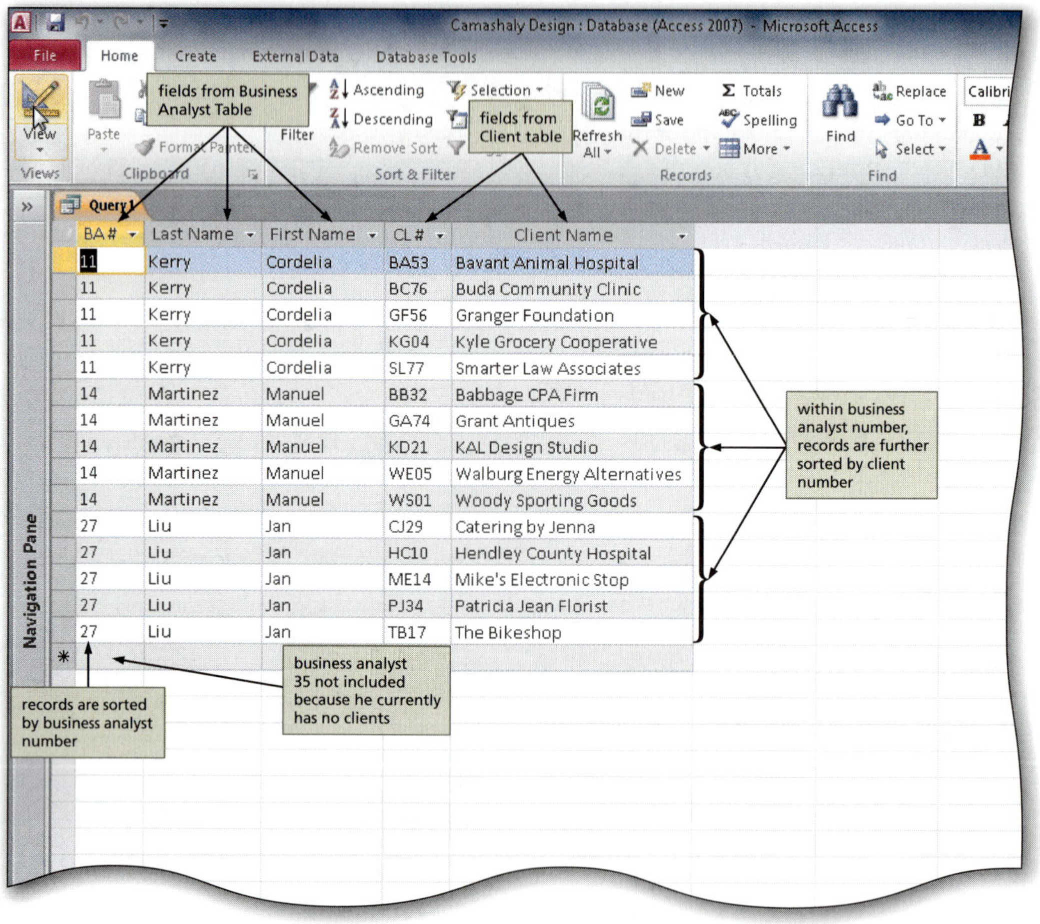

Figure 2–45

5

- Click the Save button on the Quick Access Toolbar to display the Save As dialog box.
- Type `Analyst-Client Query` as the query name (Figure 2–46).

6

- Click the OK button (Save As dialog box) to save the query.

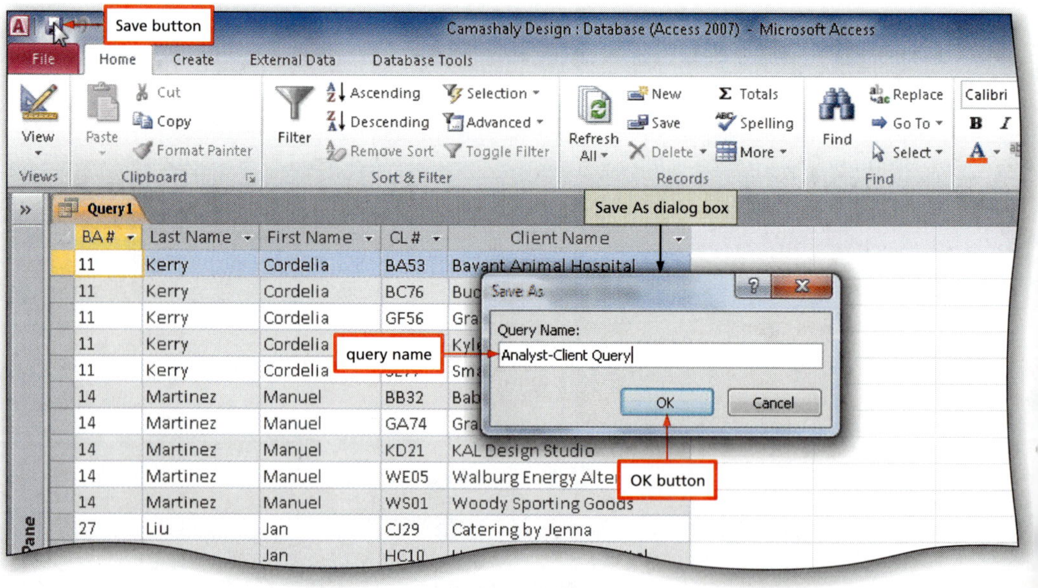

Figure 2–46

To Change Join Properties

Normally, records that do not match do not appear in the results of a join query. For example, a business analyst such as Jeff Scott, for whom no clients currently exist, would not appear in the results. To cause such a record to be displayed, you need to change the **join properties**, which are the properties that indicate which records appear in a join. The following steps change the join properties of the Analyst-Client Query so that Camashaly can include all business analysts in the results, rather than only those analysts who have already been assigned clients.

1

- Return to Design view.
- Right-click the join line to produce a shortcut menu (Figure 2–47).

Q&A

I do not see Join Properties on my shortcut menu. What should I do?

If Join Properties does not appear on your shortcut menu, you did not point to the appropriate portion of the join line. You will need to point to the correct (middle) portion and right-click again.

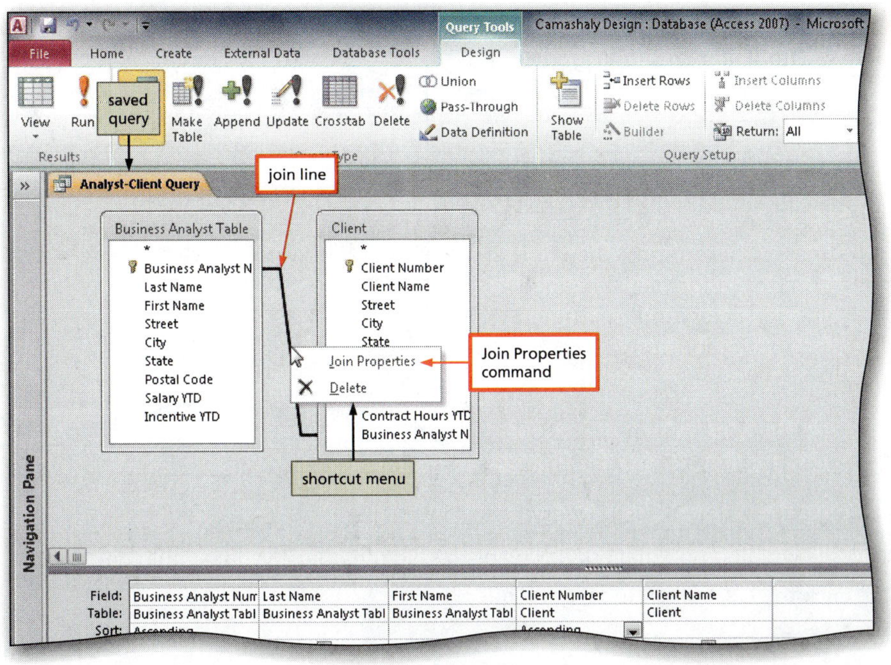

Figure 2–47

2

- Click Join Properties on the shortcut menu to display the Join Properties dialog box (Figure 2–48).

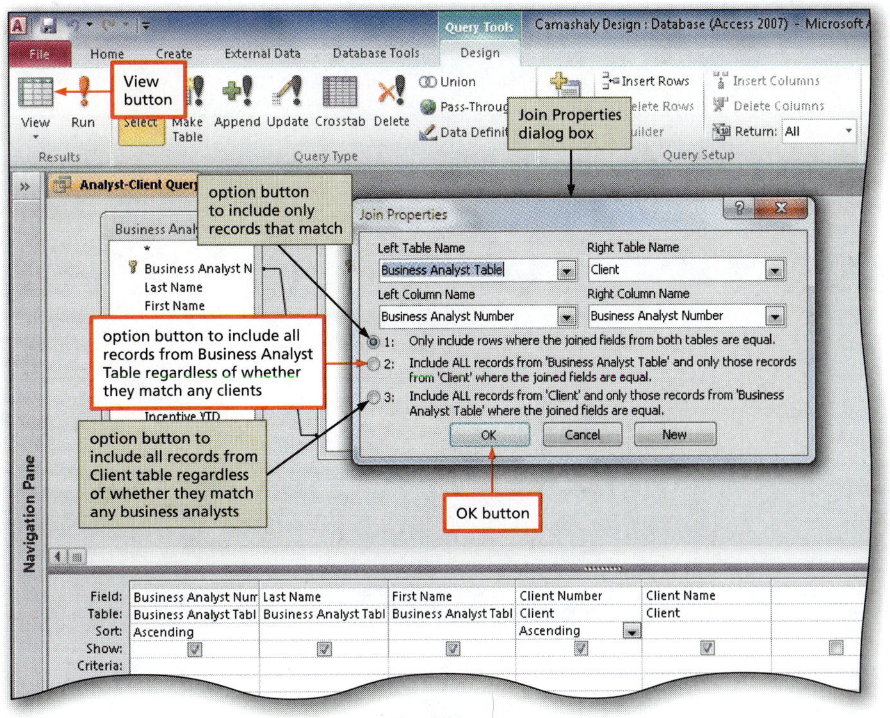

Figure 2–48

3

- Click option button 2 (Join Properties dialog box) to include all records from the Business Analyst Table regardless of whether they match any clients.
- Click the OK button (Join Properties dialog box) to modify the join properties.
- View the query results (Figure 2–49).

Experiment

- Return to Design view, change the Join properties, and select option button 3. View the results to see the effect of this option. When done, return to Design view, change the Join properties, and once again select option button 2.

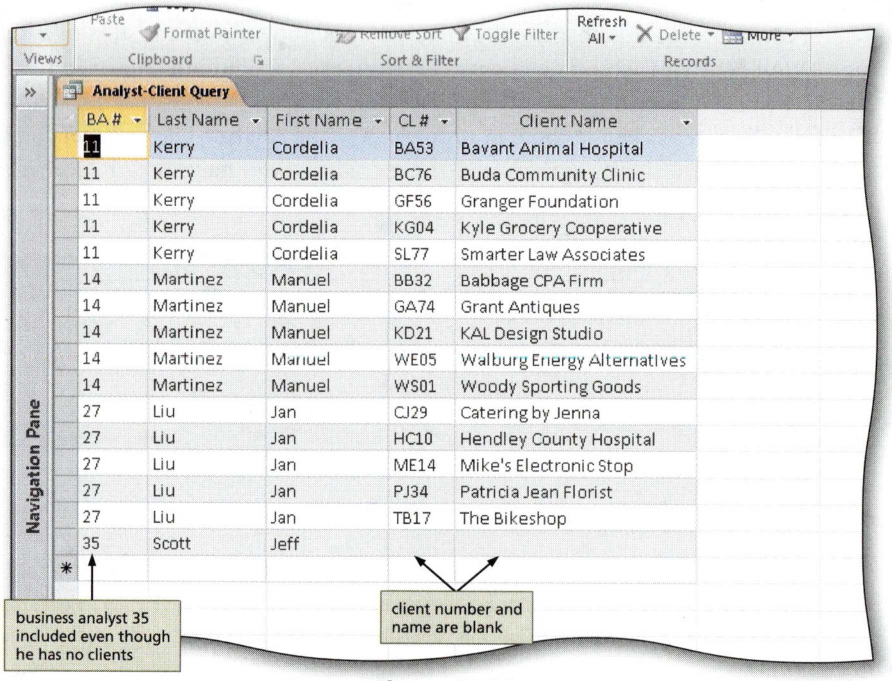

BA #	Last Name	First Name	CL #	Client Name
11	Kerry	Cordelia	BA53	Bavant Animal Hospital
11	Kerry	Cordelia	BC76	Buda Community Clinic
11	Kerry	Cordelia	GF56	Granger Foundation
11	Kerry	Cordelia	KG04	Kyle Grocery Cooperative
11	Kerry	Cordelia	SL77	Smarter Law Associates
14	Martinez	Manuel	BB32	Babbage CPA Firm
14	Martinez	Manuel	GA74	Grant Antiques
14	Martinez	Manuel	KD21	KAL Design Studio
14	Martinez	Manuel	WE05	Walburg Energy Alternatives
14	Martinez	Manuel	WS01	Woody Sporting Goods
27	Liu	Jan	CJ29	Catering by Jenna
27	Liu	Jan	HC10	Hendley County Hospital
27	Liu	Jan	ME14	Mike's Electronic Stop
27	Liu	Jan	PJ34	Patricia Jean Florist
27	Liu	Jan	TB17	The Bikeshop
35	Scott	Jeff		

Figure 2–49

4

- Click the Save button on the Quick Access Toolbar to save the changes to the query.
- Close the Analyst-Client Query.

Q&A I see a dialog box that asks if I want to save the query. What should I do?

Click the OK button to save the query.

To Create a Report Involving a Join

The following steps use the Report Wizard to create the report for Camashaly Design that is shown in Figure 2–50.

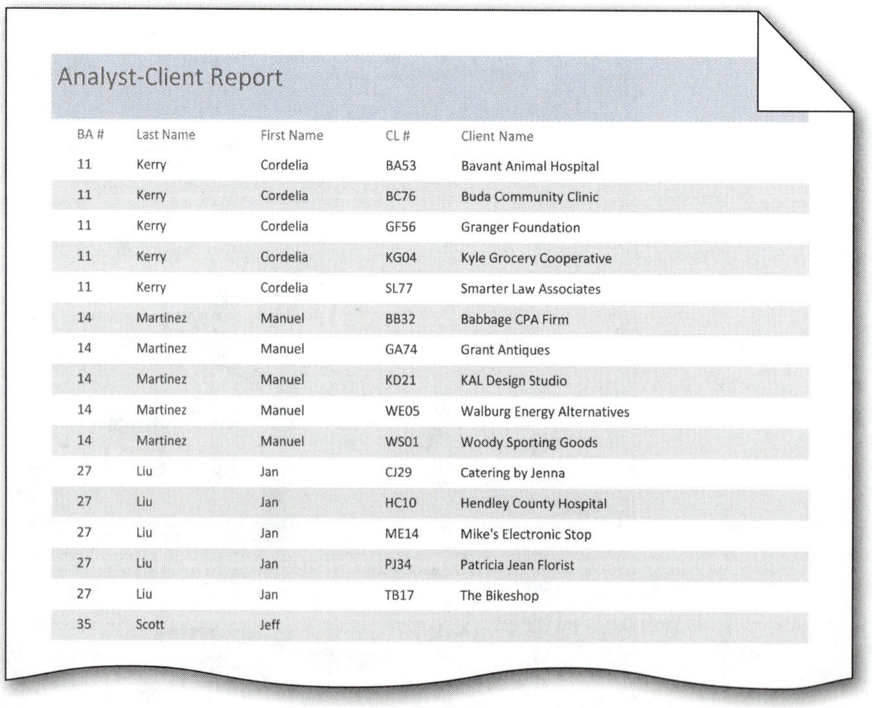

Analyst-Client Report

BA #	Last Name	First Name	CL #	Client Name
11	Kerry	Cordelia	BA53	Bavant Animal Hospital
11	Kerry	Cordelia	BC76	Buda Community Clinic
11	Kerry	Cordelia	GF56	Granger Foundation
11	Kerry	Cordelia	KG04	Kyle Grocery Cooperative
11	Kerry	Cordelia	SL77	Smarter Law Associates
14	Martinez	Manuel	BB32	Babbage CPA Firm
14	Martinez	Manuel	GA74	Grant Antiques
14	Martinez	Manuel	KD21	KAL Design Studio
14	Martinez	Manuel	WE05	Walburg Energy Alternatives
14	Martinez	Manuel	WS01	Woody Sporting Goods
27	Liu	Jan	CJ29	Catering by Jenna
27	Liu	Jan	HC10	Hendley County Hospital
27	Liu	Jan	ME14	Mike's Electronic Stop
27	Liu	Jan	PJ34	Patricia Jean Florist
27	Liu	Jan	TB17	The Bikeshop
35	Scott	Jeff		

Figure 2–50

1

- Open the Navigation Pane, and then select the Analyst-Client Query in the Navigation Pane.
- Click Create on the Ribbon to display the Create tab.
- Click the Report Wizard button (Create tab | Reports group) to display the Report Wizard dialog box (Figure 2–51).

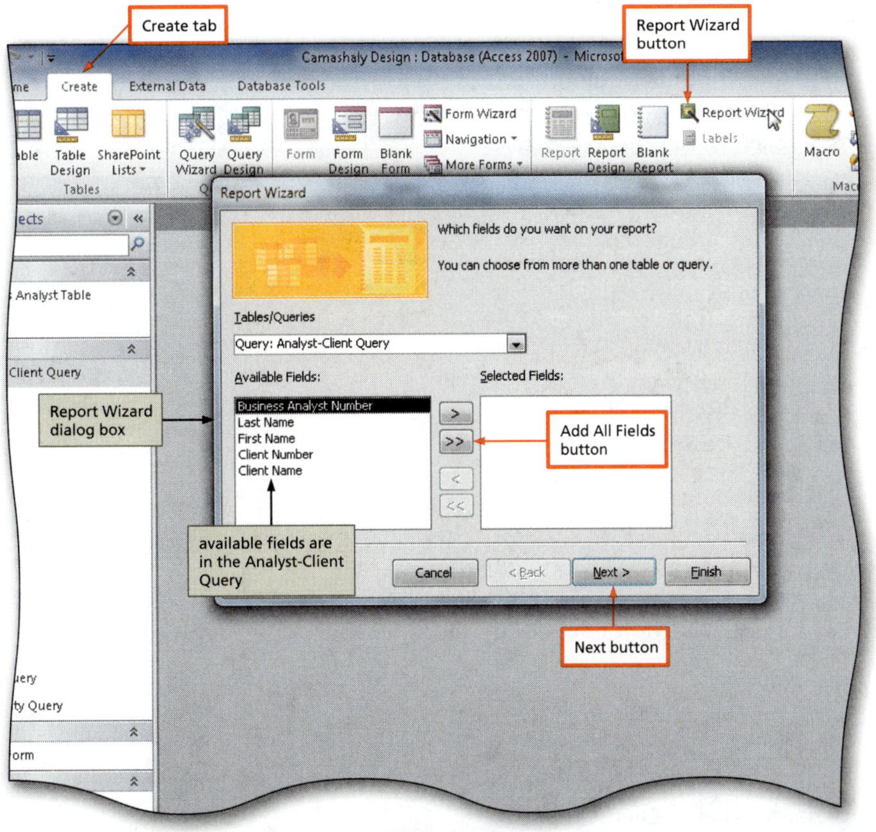

Figure 2–51

2

- Click the Add All Fields button (Report Wizard dialog box) to add all the fields in the Analyst-Client Query.
- Click the Next button to display the next Report Wizard screen (Figure 2–52).

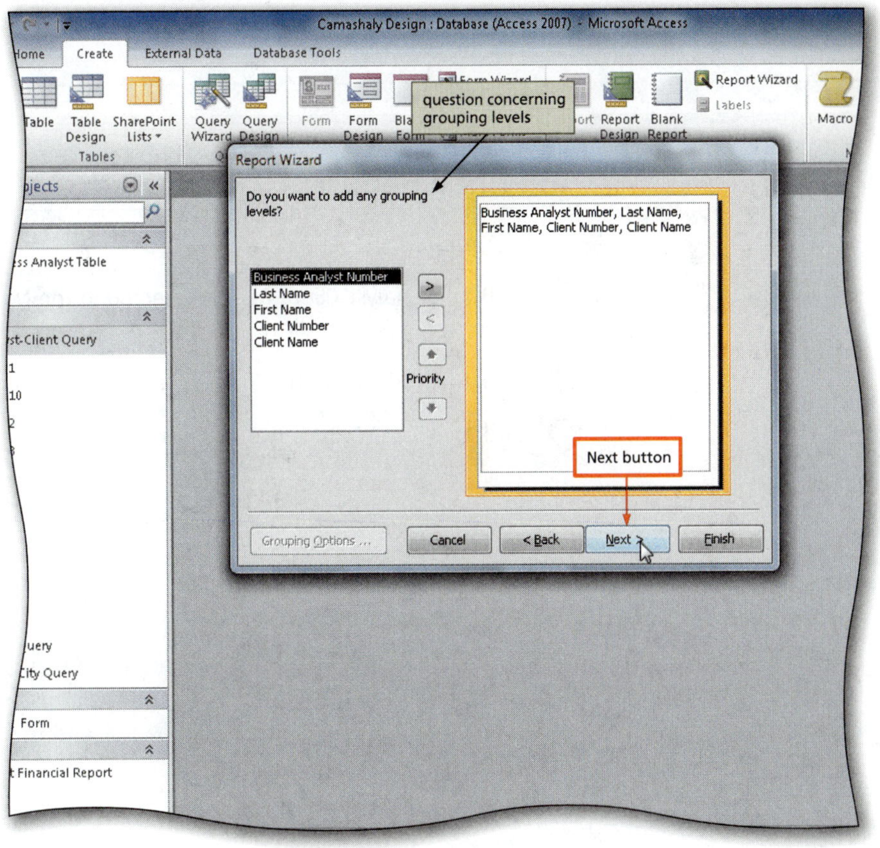

Figure 2–52

3

- Because you will not specify any grouping, click the Next button in the Report Wizard dialog box to display the next Report Wizard screen.
- Because you already specified the sort order in the query, click the Next button again to display the next Report Wizard screen.
- Make sure that Tabular is selected as the Layout and Portrait is selected as the Orientation.
- Click the Next button to display the next Report Wizard screen.
- Erase the current title, and then type **`Analyst-Client Report`** as the new title.
- Click the Finish button to produce the report (Figure 2–53).

4

- Close the Analyst-Client Report.

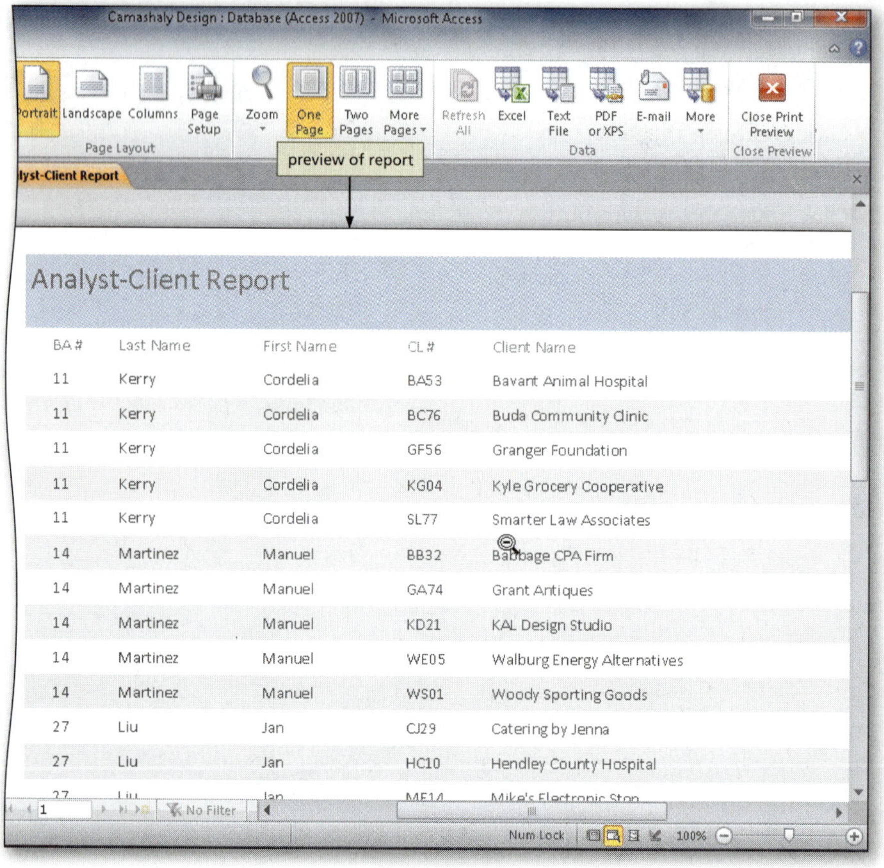

Figure 2–53

To Print a Report

The following steps print a hard copy of the report.

1. With the Analyst-Client Report selected in the Navigation Pane, click File on the Ribbon to open the Backstage view.
2. Click the Print tab in the Backstage view to display the Print gallery.
3. Click the Quick Print button to print the report.

Creating a Form for a Query

In the previous Access chapter, you created a form for the Client table. You also can create a form for a query. Recall that a **form** in a database is a formatted document with fields that contain data. Forms allow you to view and maintain data.

To Create a Form for a Query

The following steps create a form and then save the form.

1

- If necessary, select the Analyst-Client Query in the Navigation Pane.
- Click Create on the Ribbon to display the Create tab (Figure 2–54).

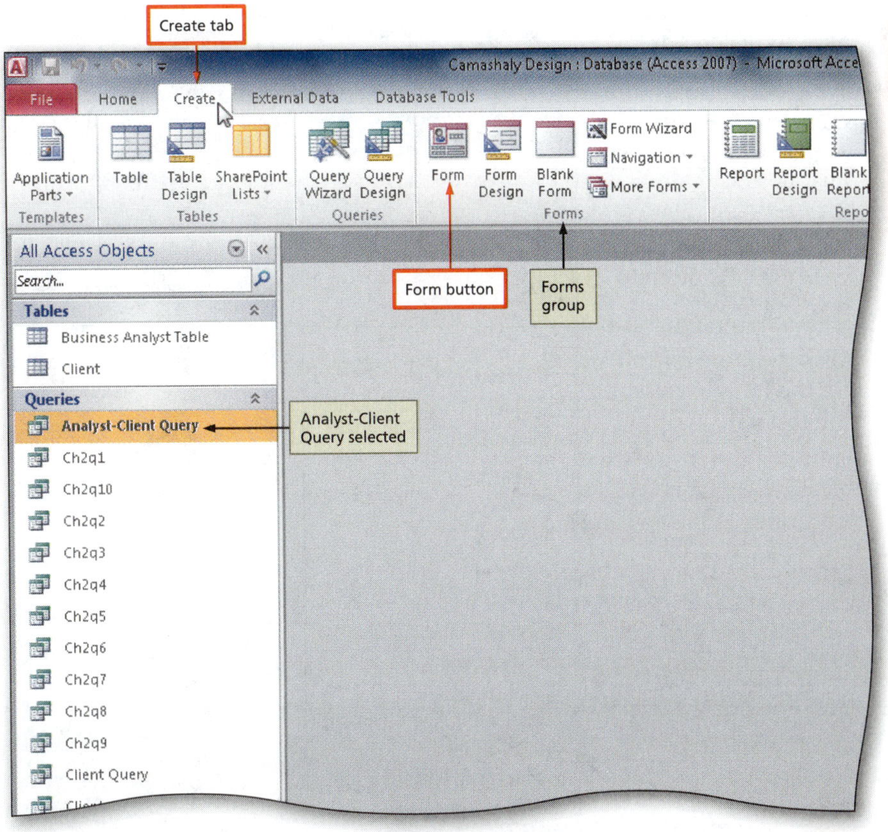

Figure 2–54

2

- Click the Form button (Create tab | Forms group) to create a simple form (Figure 2–55).

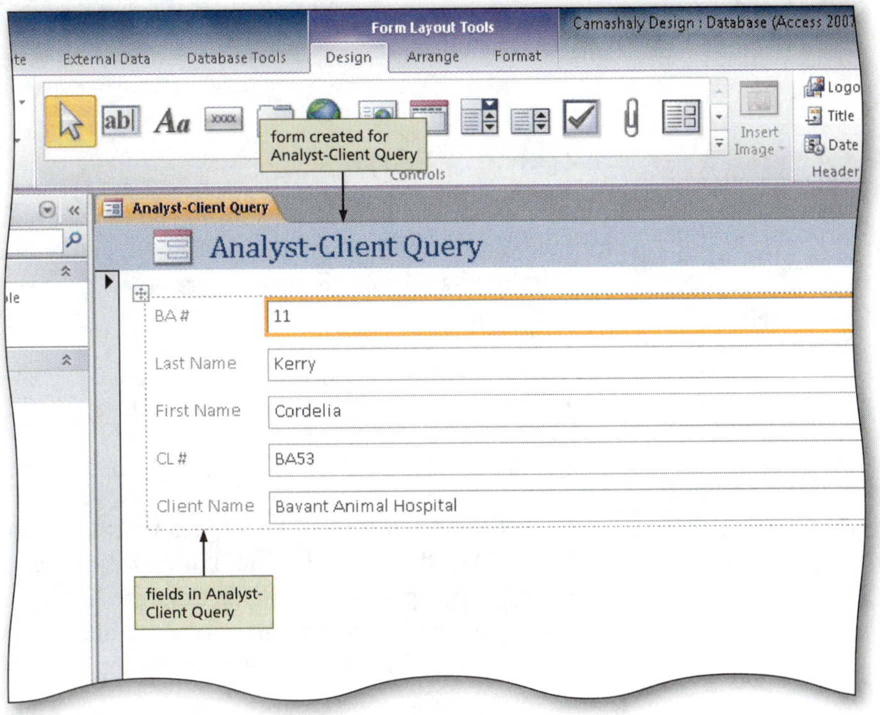

Figure 2–55

3

- Click the Save button on the Quick Access Toolbar to display the Save As dialog box.
- Type `Analyst-Client Form` as the form name (Figure 2–56).

4

- Click the OK button to save the form.
- Click the Close button for the form to close the form.

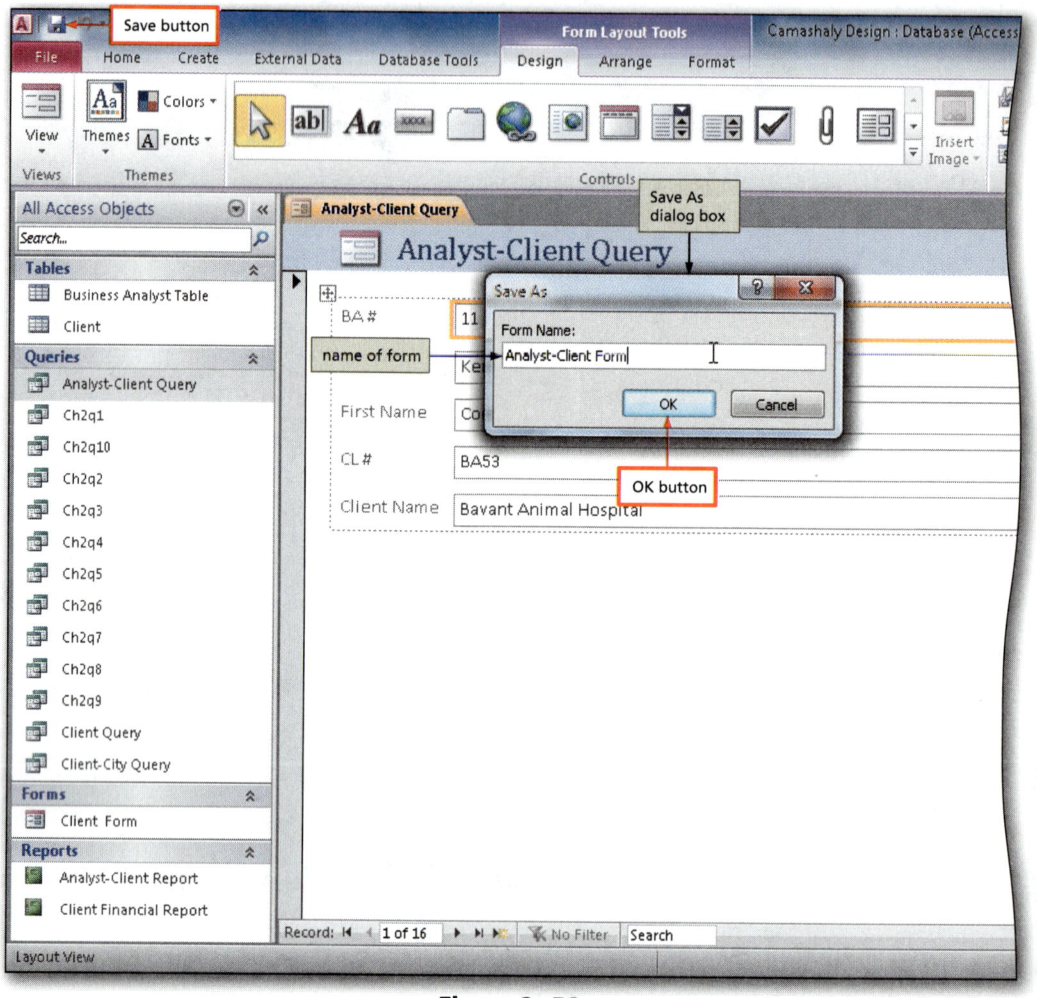

Figure 2–56

BTW

Exporting Data
You frequently need to export data so that it can be used in other applications and by other users in an organization. For example, the Accounting department might require financial data in an Excel format to perform certain financial functions. Marketing might require a list of client names and addresses in Word or RTF format for sales purposes.

Using a Form

After you have saved a form, you can use it at any time by right-clicking the form in the Navigation Pane and then clicking Open on the shortcut menu. If you plan to use the form to enter data, you must ensure you are viewing the form in Form view.

Exporting Data from Access to Other Applications

You can **export**, or copy, data from an Access database so that another application (for example, Excel or Word) can use the data. The application that will receive the data determines the export process to be used. You can export to text files in a variety of formats. For applications to which you cannot directly export data, you often can export an appropriately formatted text file that the other application can import. Figure 2–57 shows the Analyst-Client Query exported to Excel.

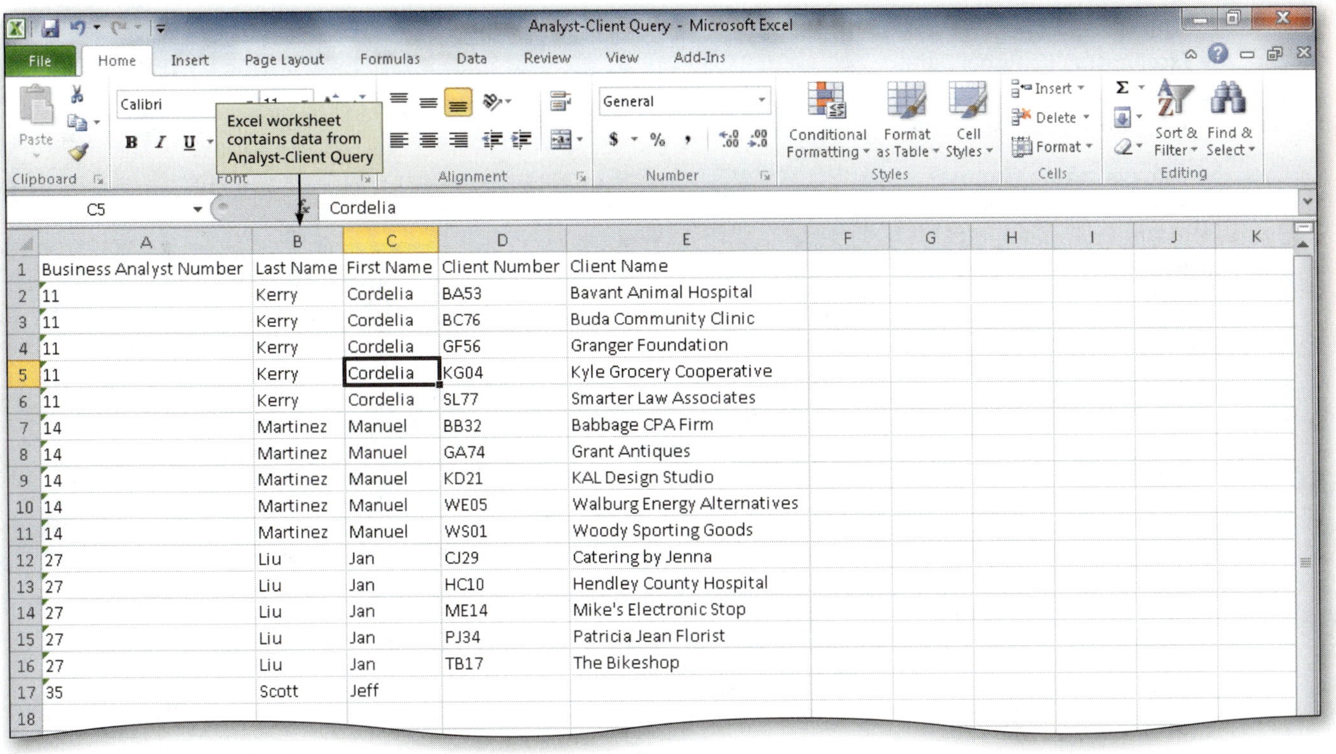

Figure 2–57

To Export Data to Excel

For Camashaly Design to make the Analyst-Client Query available to Excel users, it needs to export the data. To export data to Excel, select the table or query to be exported, and then click the Excel button in the Export group on the External data tab. The following steps export the Analyst-Client Query to Excel and save the export steps. By saving the export steps, you could easily repeat the export process whenever you like without going through all the following steps. You would use the saved steps to export data in the future by clicking the Saved Exports button (External Data tab | Export group) and then selecting the steps you saved.

1

- Click the Analyst-Client Query in the Navigation Pane to select it.
- Click External Data on the Ribbon to display the External Data tab (Figure 2–58).

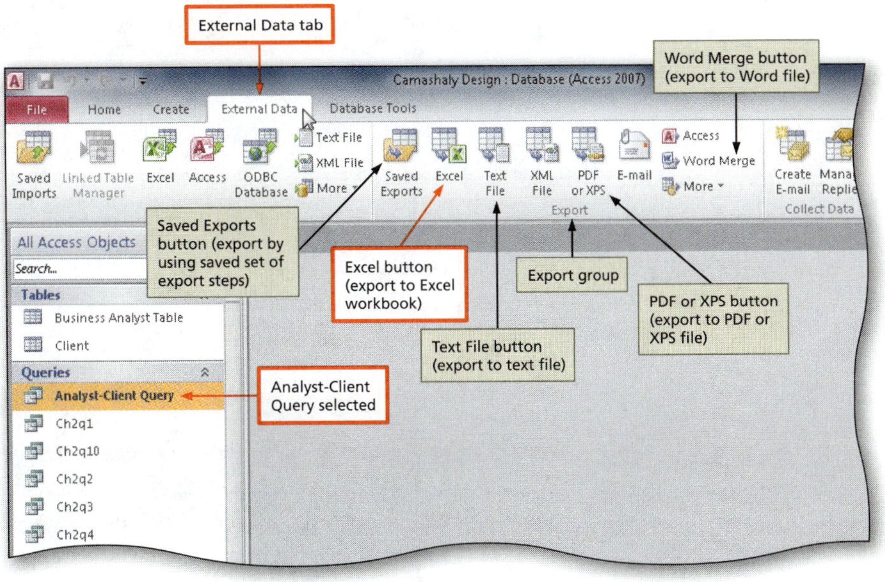

Figure 2–58

2

- Click the Excel button (External Data tab | Export group) to display the Export - Excel Spreadsheet dialog box.
- Click the Browse button (Export - Excel Spreadsheet dialog box) to display the File Save dialog box, and select your USB flash drive as the file location.
- Be sure the file name is Analyst-Client Query and then click the Save button (File Save dialog box) (Figure 2–59).

Q&A Did I need to browse?

No. You could type the appropriate file location.

Q&A Could I change the name of the file?

You could change it. Simply replace the current file name with the one you want.

Q&A What if the file I want to export already exists?

Access will indicate that the file already exists and ask if you want to replace it. If you click the Yes button, the file you export will replace the old file. If you click the No button, you must either change the name of the export file or cancel the process.

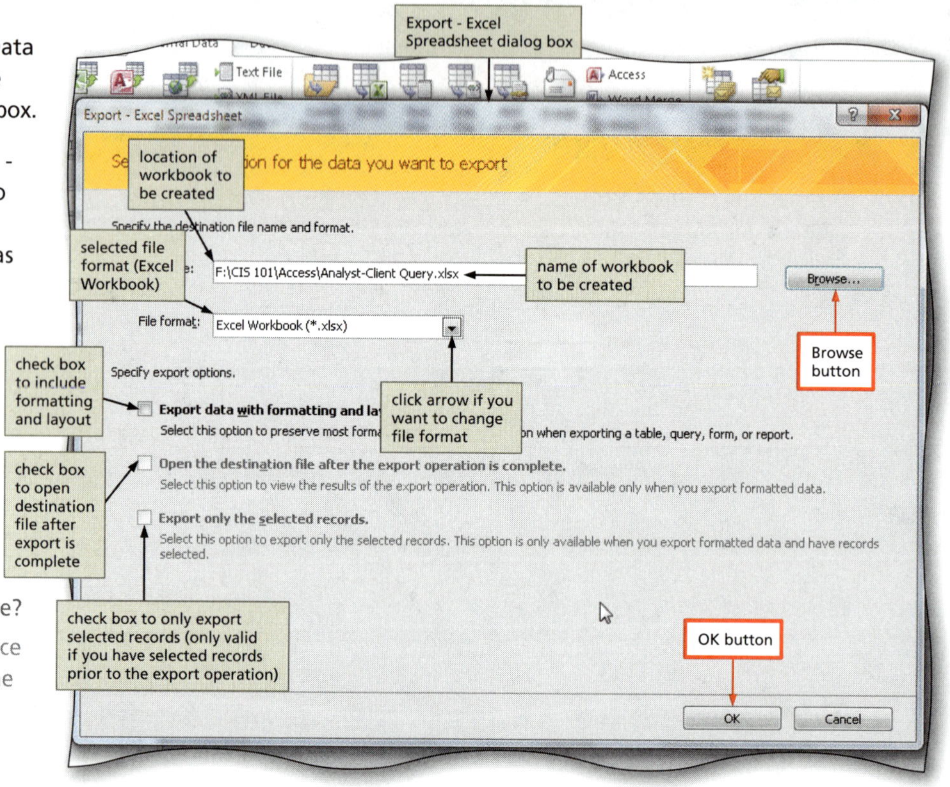

Figure 2–59

3

- Click the OK button (Export - Excel Spreadsheet dialog box) to export the data (Figure 2–60).

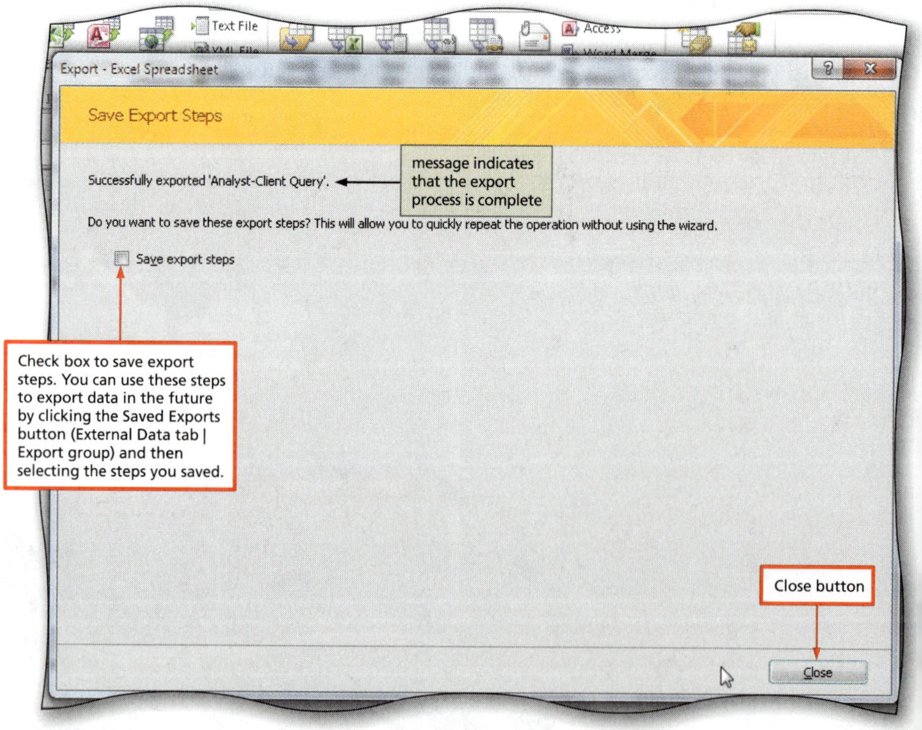

Figure 2–60

4

- Click the 'Save export steps' check box (Export - Excel Spreadsheet dialog box) to display the Save export steps options.
- If necessary, type **`Export-Analyst-Client Query`** in the Save as text box.
- Type **`Export the Analyst-Client Query without formatting`** in the Description text box (Figure 2–61).

5

- Click the Save Export button (Export - Excel Spreadsheet dialog box) to save the export steps.

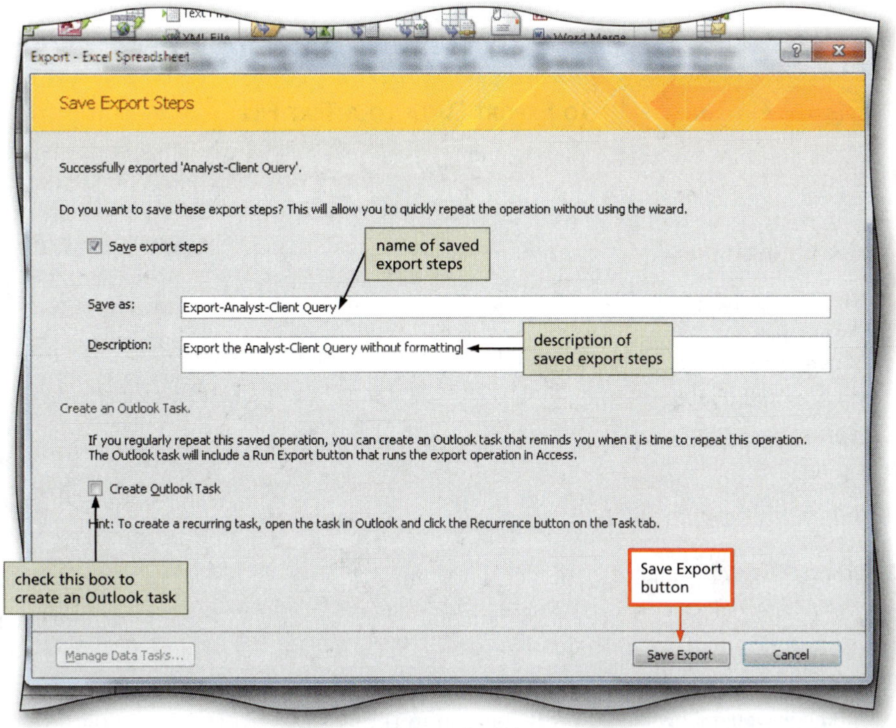

Figure 2–61

Other Ways

1. Right-click database object in Navigation Pane, click Export

To Export Data to Word

It is not possible to export data to the standard Word format. It is possible, however, to export the data as a rich text format (RTF) file, which Word can access. To export data from a query or table to an RTF file, you would use the following steps.

1. With the query or table to be exported selected in the Navigation Pane, click the More button (External Data tab | Export group) and then click Word on the More menu to display the Export - RTF File dialog box.
2. Select the name and location for the file to be created.
3. Click the Save button, and then click the OK button to export the data.
4. Save the export steps if you want, or simply click the Close button in the Export - RTF File dialog box to close the dialog box without saving the export steps.

Text Files

You also can export to text files. Text files contain unformatted characters, including alphanumeric characters, and some special characters, such as tabs, carriage returns, and line feeds.

In **delimited files**, each record is on a separate line, and the fields are separated by a special character, called the **delimiter**. Common delimiters are tabs, semicolons, commas, and spaces. You also can choose any other value that does not appear within the field contents. The comma-separated values (CSV) file often used in Excel is an example of a delimited file.

In **fixed-width files**, the width of any field is the same on every record. For example, if the width of the first field on the first record is 12 characters, the width of the first field on every other record also must be 12 characters.

To Export Data to a Text File

When exporting data to a text file, you can choose to export the data with formatting and layout. This option preserves much of the formatting and layout in tables, queries, forms, and reports. For forms and reports, this is the only option.

If you do not need to preserve the formatting, you can choose either delimited or fixed-width as the format for the exported file. The most common option, especially if formatting is not an issue, is delimited. You can choose the delimiter and also whether to include field names on the first row. In many cases, delimiting with a comma and including the field names is a good choice.

To export data from a table or query to a comma-delimited file in which the first row contains the column headings, you would use the following steps.

1. With the query or table to be exported selected in the Navigation Pane, click the Text File button (External Data tab | Export group) to display the Export - Text File dialog box.
2. Select the name and location for the file to be created.
3. If you need to preserve formatting and layout, be sure the 'Export data with formatting and layout' check box is checked. If you do not need to preserve formatting and layout, make sure the check box is not checked. Once you have made your selection, click the OK button in the Export - Text File dialog box.
4. To create a delimited file, be sure the Delimited option button is selected in the Export Text Wizard dialog box. To create a fixed-width file, be sure the Fixed Width option button is selected. Once you have made your selection, click the Next button.
5. a. If you are exporting to a delimited file, choose the delimiter that you want to separate your fields, such as a comma. Decide whether to include field names on the first row and, if so, click the Include Field Names on First Row check box. If you want to select a text qualifier, select it in the Text Qualifier list. When you have made your selections, click the Next button.

   b. If you are exporting to a fixed-width file, review the position of the vertical lines that separate your fields. If any lines are not positioned correctly, follow the directions on the screen to reposition them. When you have finished, click the Next button.
6. Click the Finish button to export the data.
7. Save the export steps if you want, or simply click the Close button in the Export - Text File dialog box to close the dialog box without saving the export steps.

BTW

Saving Export Steps
Because query results are based on the data in the underlying tables, a change to an underlying table would result in a new query answer. For example, if the last name for business analyst 11 changed from Kerry to Smith, the change would be made in the Business Analyst Table. If you run the Analyst-Client Query again and export the query using the saved export steps, the Excel workbook would show the changed name.

Adding Criteria to a Join Query

Sometimes you will want to join tables, but you will not want to include all possible records. For example, you would like to create a report showing only those clients whose amount paid is greater than $3,000. In such cases, you will relate the tables and include fields just as you did before. You also will include criteria. To include only those clients whose amount paid is more than $3,000.00, you will include >3000 as a criterion for the Amount Paid field.

To Restrict the Records in a Join

The following steps modify the Analyst-Client Query so that the results for Camashaly Design only include those clients whose amount paid is more than $3,000.

1

- Open the Analyst-Client Query in Design view and close the Navigation Pane.
- Add the Amount Paid field to the query.
- Type >3000 as the criterion for the Amount Paid field (Figure 2–62).

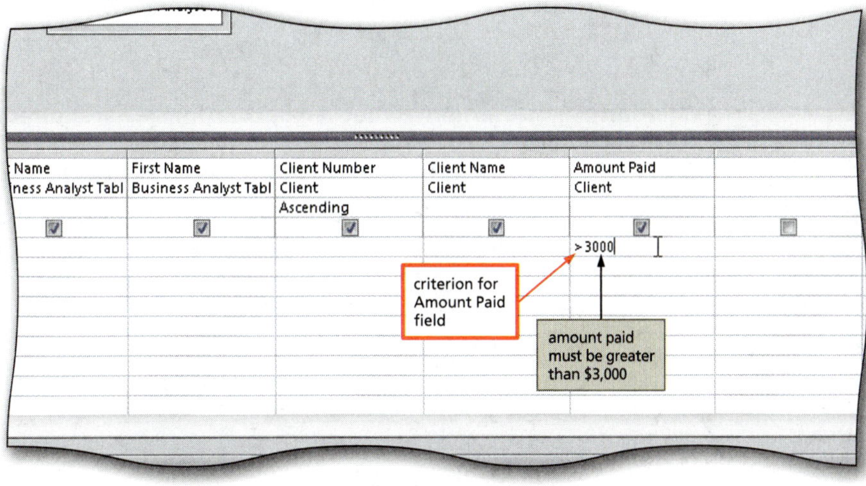

Figure 2–62

2

- View the query results (Figure 2–63).

3

- Close the query.
- When asked if you want to save your changes, click the No button.

What if I saved the changes?

The next time you used this query, you would only see clients whose amount paid is more than $3,000.

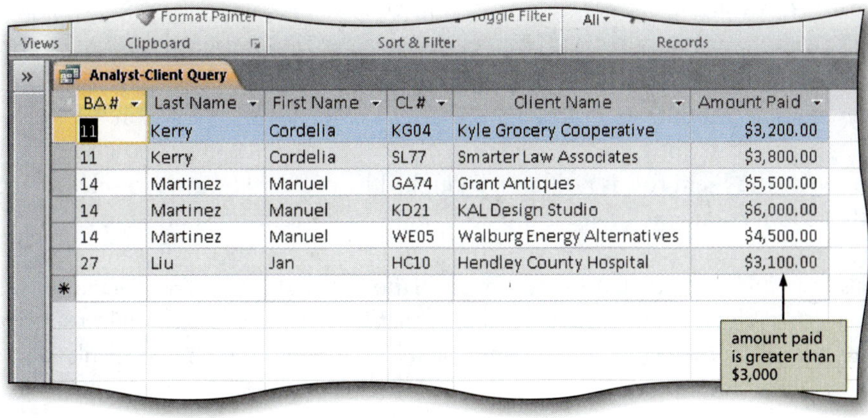

Figure 2–63

Calculations

If you have determined that a special calculation is required for a query, you then need to determine whether the calculation is an individual record calculation (for example, adding the values in two fields) or a group calculation (for example, finding the total of the values in a particular field on all the records).

Camashaly Design may want to know the total amount (amount paid and current due) from each client. This would seem to pose a problem because the Client table does not include a field for total amount. You can calculate it, however, because the total amount is equal to the amount paid plus the current due. A field that can be computed from other fields is called a **calculated field** or a **computed field**. A calculated field is an individual record calculation because each calculation only involves fields in a single record.

BTW

Expression Builder
Access includes a tool to help you create complex expressions. If you click Build on the shortcut menu (see Figure 2–64), Access displays the Expression Builder dialog box, which includes an expression box, operator buttons, and expression elements. You can type parts of the expression directly and paste operator buttons and expression elements into the box. You also can use functions in expressions.

Camashaly also may want to calculate the average amount paid for the clients of each business analyst. That is, they may want the average for the clients of business analyst 11, the average for the clients of business analyst 14, and so on. This type of calculation is called a **group calculation** because each calculation involves groups of records. In this example, the clients of business analyst 11 would form one group, the clients of business analyst 14 would be a second group, and the clients of business analyst 27 would form a third group.

The following are guidelines related to calculations in queries.

Plan Ahead

Determine whether calculations are required.
Examine the query or request to see if there are special calculations to be included. Look for words such as total, sum, compute, or calculate.

- **Determine a name for the calculated field.** If calculations are required, decide on the name for the field. Assign a name that helps identify the contents of the field. For example, if you are adding the cost of a number of items, the name Total Cost would be appropriate. The name, also called an **alias**, becomes the column name when the query is run.
- **Determine the format for the calculated field.** Determine how the calculated field should appear. If the calculation involves monetary amounts, you would use the currency format. If the calculated value contains decimals, determine how many decimal places to display.

To Use a Calculated Field in a Query

If you have determined that you need a calculated field in a query, you enter a name, or alias, for the calculated field, a colon, and then the calculation in one of the columns in the Field row of the design grid for the query. Any fields included in the expression must be enclosed in square brackets ([ ]). For example, for the total amount, you will type Total Amount:[Amount Paid]+[Current Due] as the expression.

You can type the expression directly into the Field row. You will not be able to see the entire entry, however, because the Field row is not large enough. The preferred way is to select the column in the Field row and then use the Zoom command on its shortcut menu. When Access displays the Zoom dialog box, you can enter the expression.

You are not restricted to addition in calculations. You can use subtraction (–), multiplication (*), or division (/). You also can include parentheses in your calculations to indicate which calculations should be done first.

The following steps create a query that Camashaly Design might use to obtain financial information on its clients, including the total amount (amount paid + current due), which is a calculated field.

1

- Create a query with a field list for the Client table.
- Add the Client Number, Client Name, Amount Paid, and Current Due fields to the query.
- Right-click the Field row in the first open column in the design grid to display a shortcut menu (Figure 2–64).

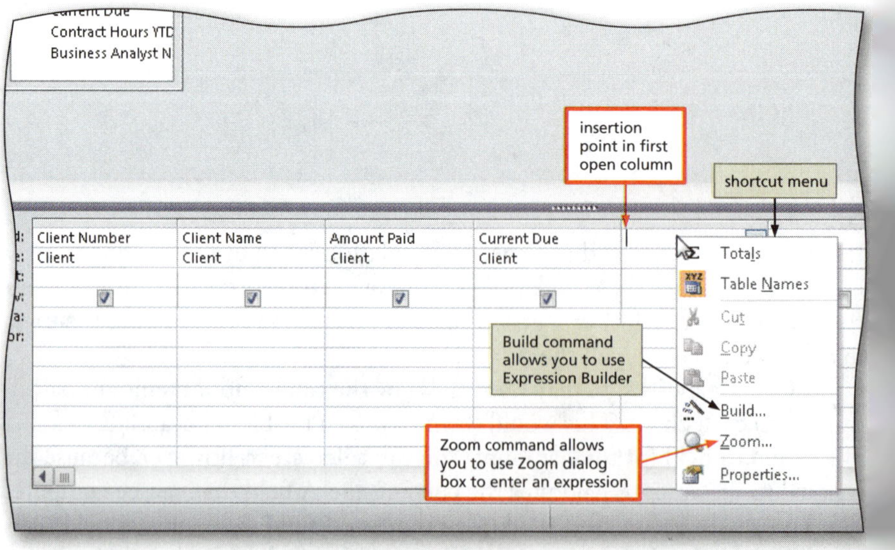

Figure 2–64

2

- Click Zoom on the shortcut menu to display the Zoom dialog box.
- Type `Total Amount: [Amount Paid]+ [Current Due]` in the Zoom dialog box (Figure 2–65).

Q&A Do I always need to put square brackets around field names?

If the field name does not contain spaces, square brackets are technically not necessary, although it is still acceptable to use the brackets. It is a good practice, however, to get in the habit of using the brackets.

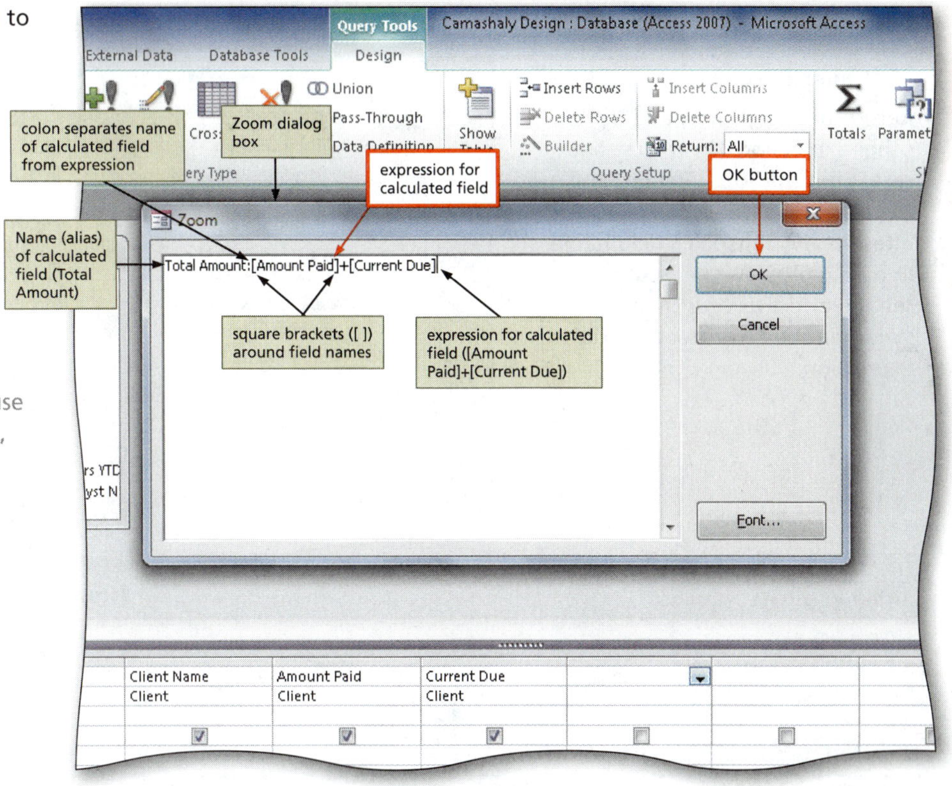

Figure 2–65

3

- Click the OK button (Zoom dialog box) to enter the expression (Figure 2–66).

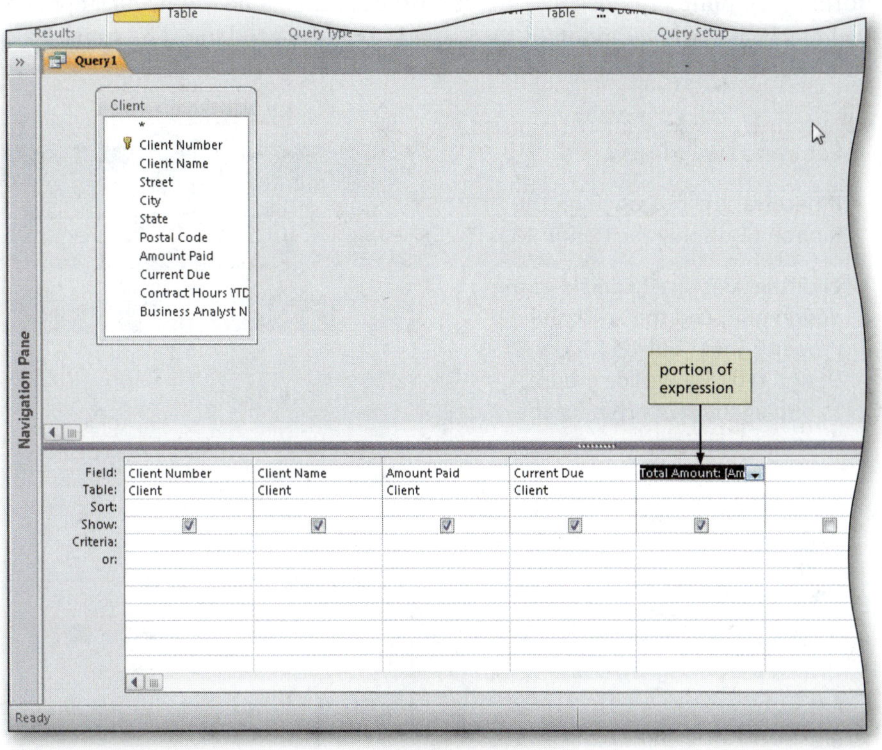

Figure 2–66

4

- View the query results (Figure 2–67).

Experiment

- Return to Design view and try other expressions. In at least one case, omit the Total Amount and the colon. In at least one case, intentionally misspell a field name. In each case, view the results to see the effect of your changes. When finished, reenter the original expression.

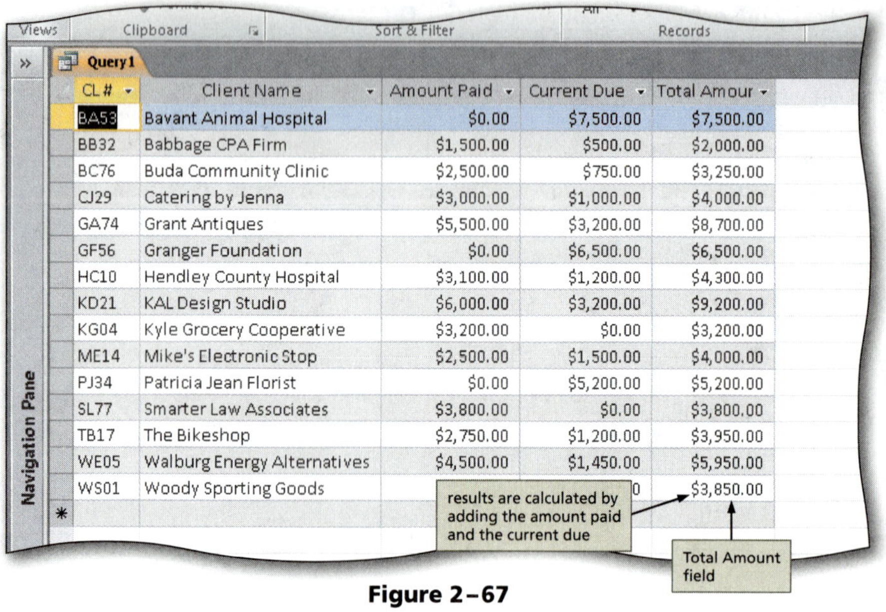

CL #	Client Name	Amount Paid	Current Due	Total Amour
BA53	Bavant Animal Hospital	$0.00	$7,500.00	$7,500.00
BB32	Babbage CPA Firm	$1,500.00	$500.00	$2,000.00
BC76	Buda Community Clinic	$2,500.00	$750.00	$3,250.00
CJ29	Catering by Jenna	$3,000.00	$1,000.00	$4,000.00
GA74	Grant Antiques	$5,500.00	$3,200.00	$8,700.00
GF56	Granger Foundation	$0.00	$6,500.00	$6,500.00
HC10	Hendley County Hospital	$3,100.00	$1,200.00	$4,300.00
KD21	KAL Design Studio	$6,000.00	$3,200.00	$9,200.00
KG04	Kyle Grocery Cooperative	$3,200.00	$0.00	$3,200.00
ME14	Mike's Electronic Stop	$2,500.00	$1,500.00	$4,000.00
PJ34	Patricia Jean Florist	$0.00	$5,200.00	$5,200.00
SL77	Smarter Law Associates	$3,800.00	$0.00	$3,800.00
TB17	The Bikeshop	$2,750.00	$1,200.00	$3,950.00
WE05	Walburg Energy Alternatives	$4,500.00	$1,450.00	$5,950.00
WS01	Woody Sporting Goods		0	$3,850.00

Figure 2–67

Other Ways

1. Press SHIFT+F2

To Change a Caption

You can change the way items appear in the results of a query by changing their format. You also can change a query result's heading at the top of a column by changing the caption. Just as when you omitted duplicates, you will make this change by using a property sheet. In the property sheet, you can change the desired property, such as the format, the number of decimal places, or the caption. The following steps change the caption of the Amount Paid field to Paid and the caption of the Current Due field to Due. The steps also save the query with a new name.

1

- Return to Design view.
- If necessary, click Design on the Ribbon to display the Design tab.
- Click the Amount Paid field in the design grid, and then click the Property Sheet button (Query Tools Design tab | Show/Hide group) to display the properties for the Amount Paid field.
- Click the Caption box, and then type **Paid** as the caption (Figure 2–68).

Q&A My property sheet looks different. What should I do?

If your sheet looks different, you clicked the wrong place and will have to close the property sheet and repeat this step.

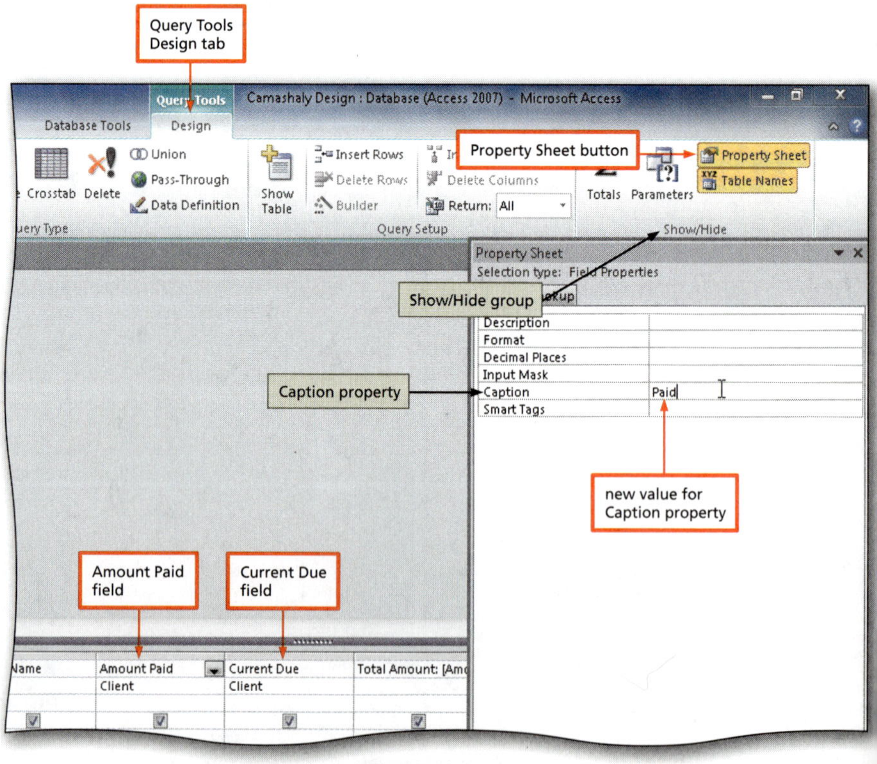

Figure 2–68

2

- Close the property sheet by clicking the Property Sheet button a second time.
- Click the Current Due field in the design grid, and then click the Property Sheet button (Query Tools Design tab | Show/Hide group).
- Click the Caption box, and then type `Due` as the caption.
- Close the Property Sheet by clicking the Property Sheet button a second time.
- View the query results (Figure 2–69).

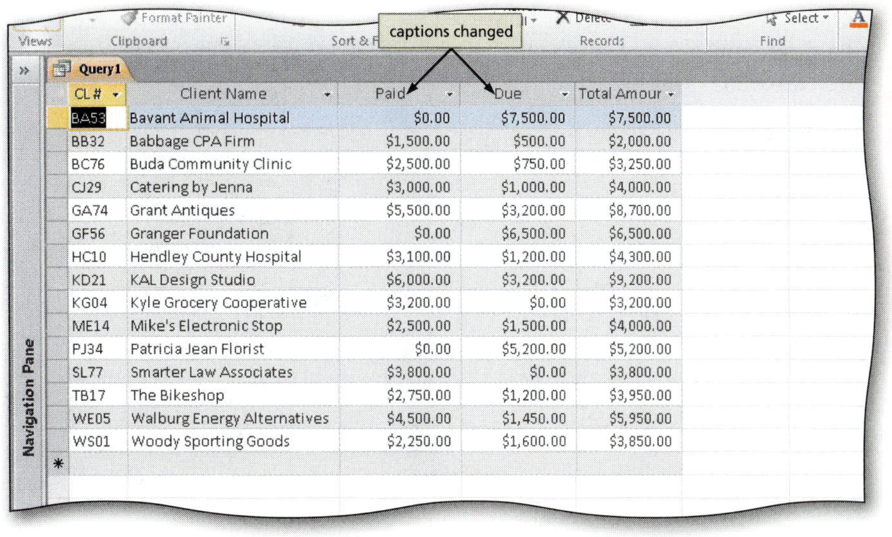

Figure 2–69

3

- Save the query as Ch2q11.
- Close the query.

Other Ways

1. Right-click field in design grid, click Properties on shortcut menu

To Calculate Statistics

For group calculations, Microsoft Access supports several built-in statistics: COUNT (count of the number of records), SUM (total), AVG (average), MAX (largest value), MIN (smallest value), STDEV (standard deviation), VAR (variance), FIRST (first value), and LAST (last value). These statistics are called aggregate functions. An **aggregate function** is a function that performs some mathematical function against a group of records. To use any of these aggregate functions in a query, you include it in the Total row in the design grid. The Total row usually does not appear in the grid. To include it, click the Totals button on the Design tab.

The following steps create a new query for the Client table. The steps include the Total row in the design grid, and then calculate the average amount paid for all clients.

1

- Create a new query with a field list for the Client table.
- Click the Totals button (Query Tools Design tab | Show/Hide group) to include the Total row in the design grid.
- Add the Amount Paid field to the query (Figure 2–70).

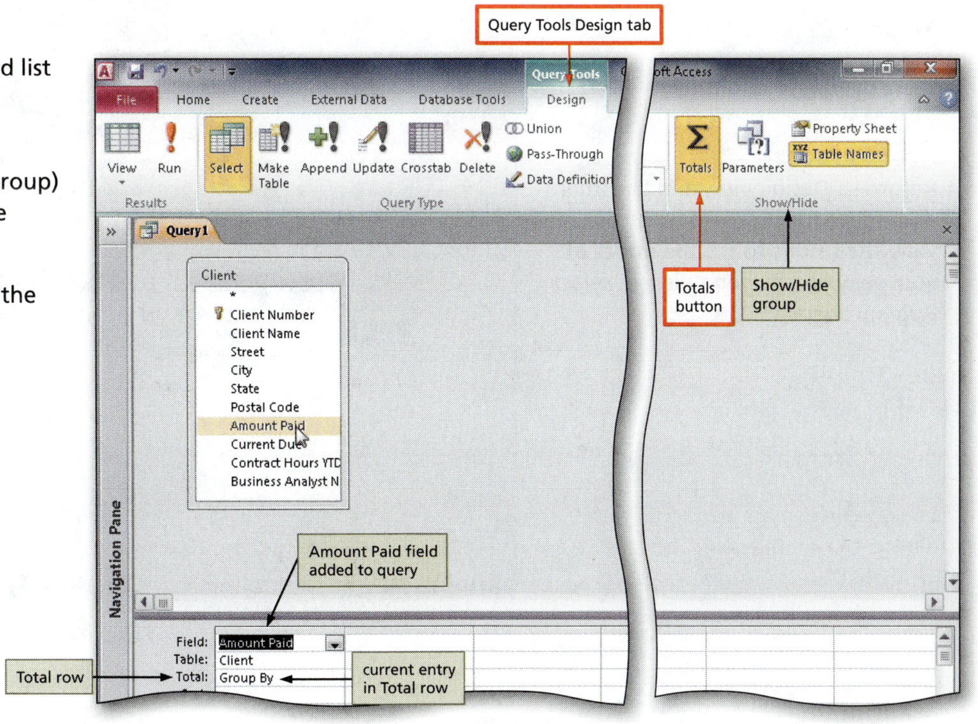

Figure 2–70

2

- Click the Total row in the Amount Paid column to display the Total box arrow.
- Click the Total box arrow to display the Total list (Figure 2–71).

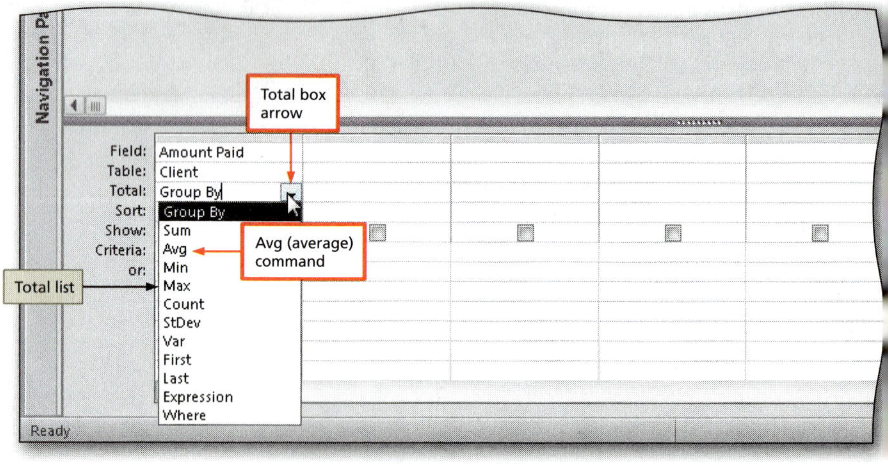

Figure 2–71

3

- Click Avg to select the calculation that Access is to perform (Figure 2–72).

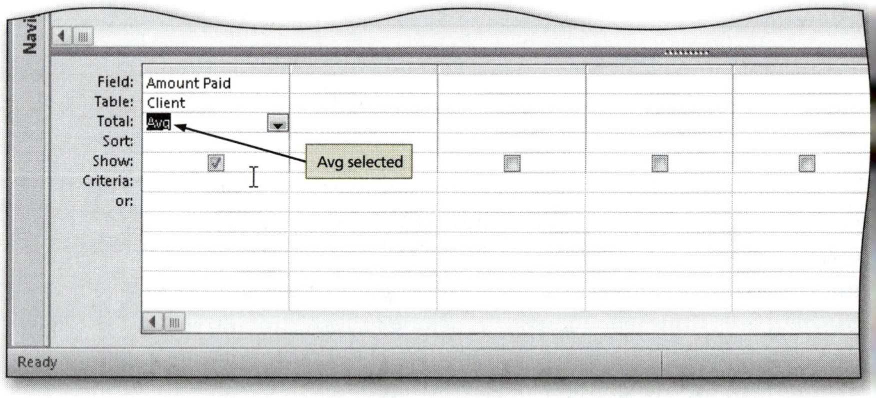

Figure 2–72

4

- View the query results (Figure 2–73).

Experiment

- Return to Design view and try other aggregate functions. In each case, view the results to see the effect of your selection. When finished, select Avg once again.

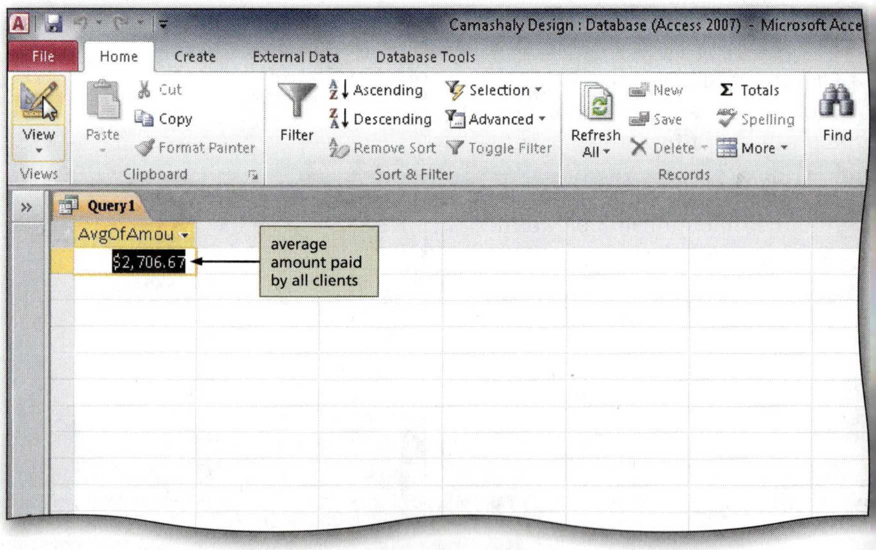

Figure 2–73

To Use Criteria in Calculating Statistics

Sometimes calculating statistics for all the records in the table is appropriate. In other cases, however, you will need to calculate the statistics for only those records that satisfy certain criteria. To enter a criterion in a field, first you select Where as the entry in the Total row for the field, and then enter the criterion in the Criteria row. The following steps use this technique to calculate the average amount paid for clients of business analyst 11. The steps also save the query with a new name.

1

- Return to Design view.
- Include the Business Analyst Number field in the design grid.
- Click the Total box arrow in the Business Analyst Number column to produce a Total list (Figure 2–74).

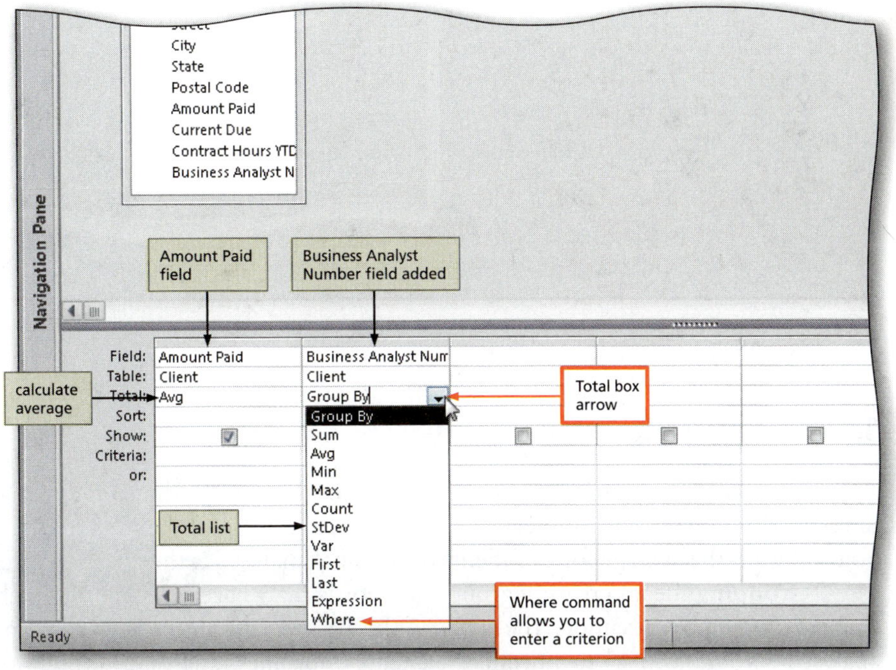

Figure 2–74

2

- Click Where.
- Type `11` as the criterion for the Business Analyst Number field (Figure 2–75).

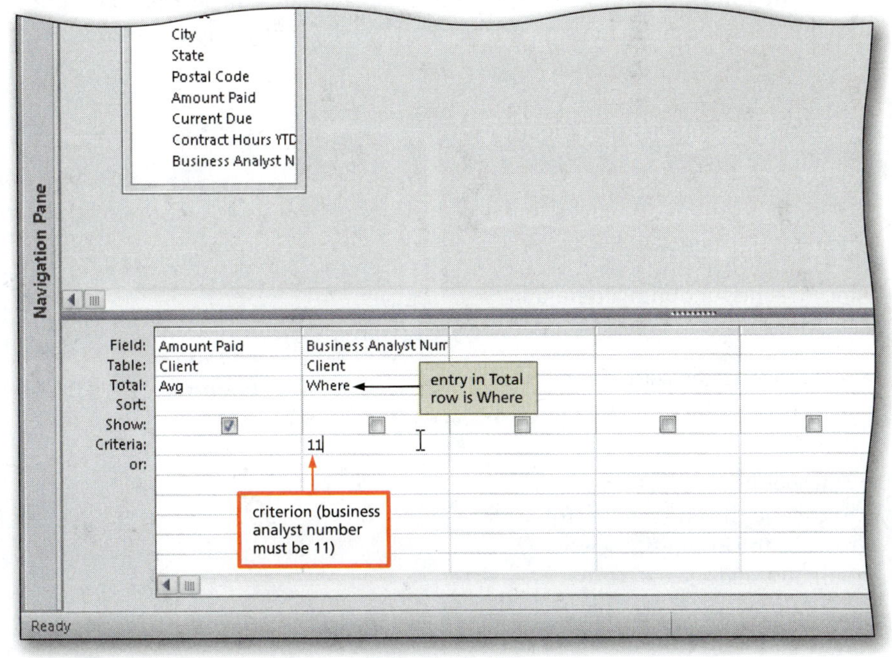

Figure 2–75

3
- View the query results (Figure 2–76).

4
- Save the query as Ch2q12.

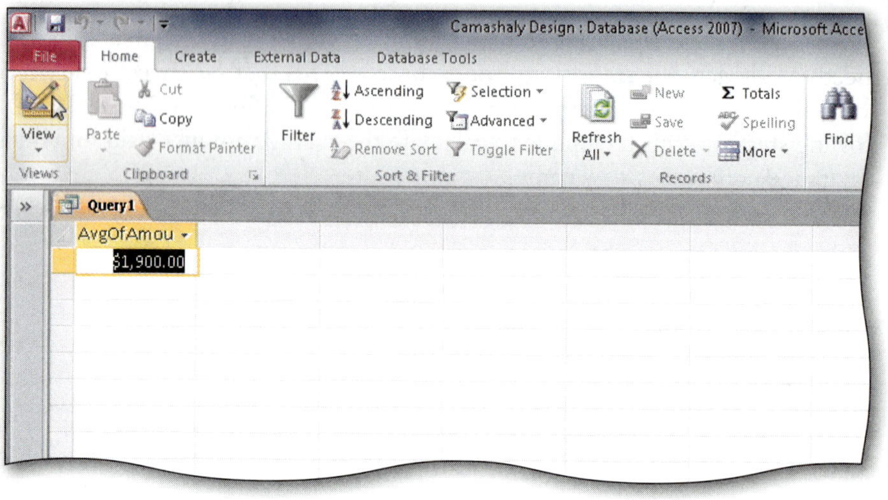

Figure 2–76

To Use Grouping

Another way statistics often are used is in combination with grouping; that is, statistics are calculated for groups of records. You may, for example, need to calculate the average amount paid for the clients of each business analyst. You will want the average for the clients of business analyst 11, the average for clients of business analyst 14, and so on.

Grouping means creating groups of records that share some common characteristic. In grouping by Business Analyst Number, for example, the clients of business analyst 11 would form one group, the clients of business analyst 14 would form a second, and the clients of business analyst 27 would form a third group. The calculations then are made for each group. To indicate grouping in Access, select Group By as the entry in the Total row for the field to be used for grouping.

The following steps create a query that calculates the average amount paid for clients of each business analyst at Camashaly Design. The steps also save the query with a new name.

1
- Return to Design view and clear the design grid.
- Include the Business Analyst Number field in the query.
- Include the Amount Paid field in the query.
- Select Avg as the calculation in the Total row for the Amount Paid field (Figure 2–77).

Q&A

Why was it not necessary for me to change the entry in the Total row for the Business Analyst Number field?

Group By, which is the initial entry in the Total row when you add a field, is correct. Thus, you did not need to change the entry.

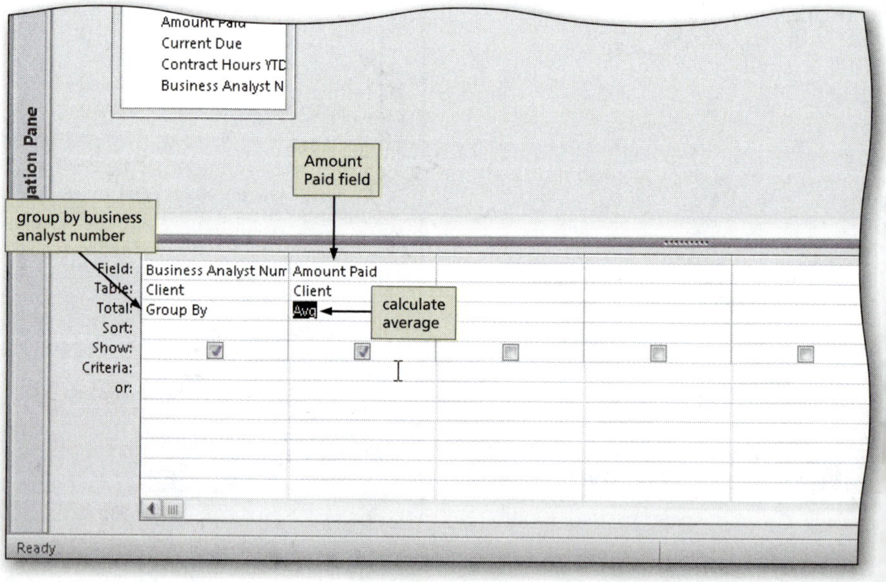

Figure 2–77

2

- View the query results (Figure 2–78).

3

- Save the query as Ch2q13.
- Close the query.

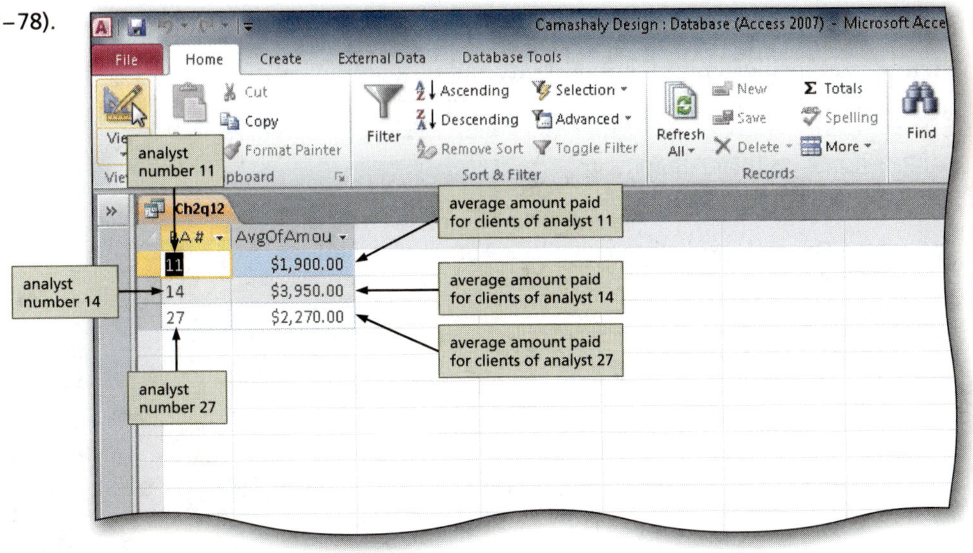

Figure 2–78

Crosstab Queries

A crosstab query calculates a statistic (for example, sum, average, or count) for data that is grouped by two different types of information. One of the types will appear down the side of the resulting datasheet, and the other will appear across the top. Crosstab queries are useful for summarizing data by category or group.

For example, if you have determined that a query must summarize the sum of the amounts paid grouped by both city and business analyst number, you could have cities as the row headings, that is, down the side. You could have business analyst numbers as the column headings, that is, across the top. The entries within the datasheet represent the total of the amounts paid. Figure 2–79 shows a crosstab in which the total of amount paid is grouped by both city and business analyst number with cities down the left side and business analyst numbers across the top. For example, the entry in the row labeled Georgetown and in the column labeled 14 represents the total of the amount paid by all clients of business analyst 14 who are located in Georgetown.

BTW

Quick Reference
For a table that lists how to complete the tasks covered in the Office chapters in this book using the mouse, Ribbon, shortcut menu, and keyboard, see the Quick Reference Summary at the back of this book, or visit the Microsoft Office and Concepts CourseMate Web site at www.cengagebrain.com and then navigate to the Quick Reference resource for this book.

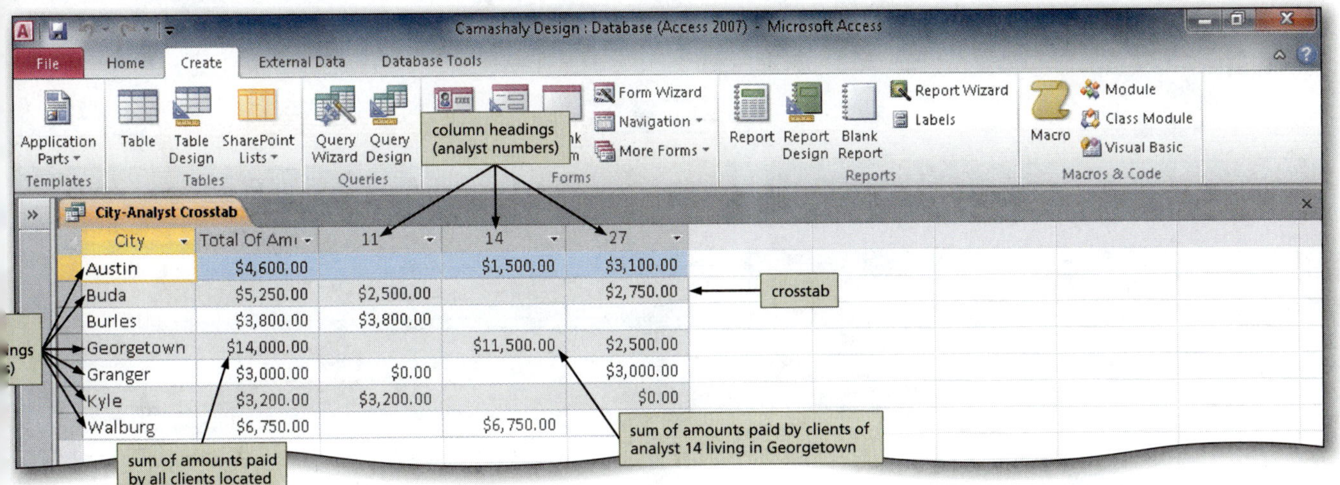

Figure 2–79

To Create a Crosstab Query

The following steps use the Crosstab Query Wizard to create a crosstab query for Camashaly Design that summarizes financial information by city and business analyst.

1

- Click Create on the Ribbon to display the Create tab.
- Click the Query Wizard button (Create tab | Queries group) to display the New Query dialog box (Figure 2–80).

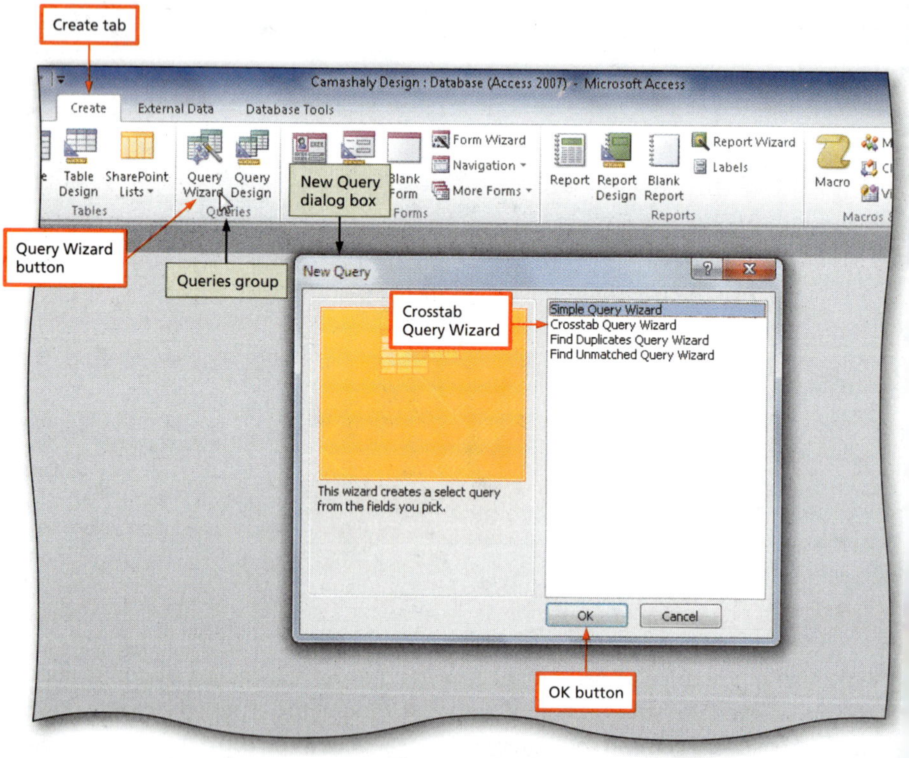

Figure 2–80

2

- Click Crosstab Query Wizard (New Query dialog box).
- Click the OK button to display the Crosstab Query Wizard dialog box (Figure 2–81).

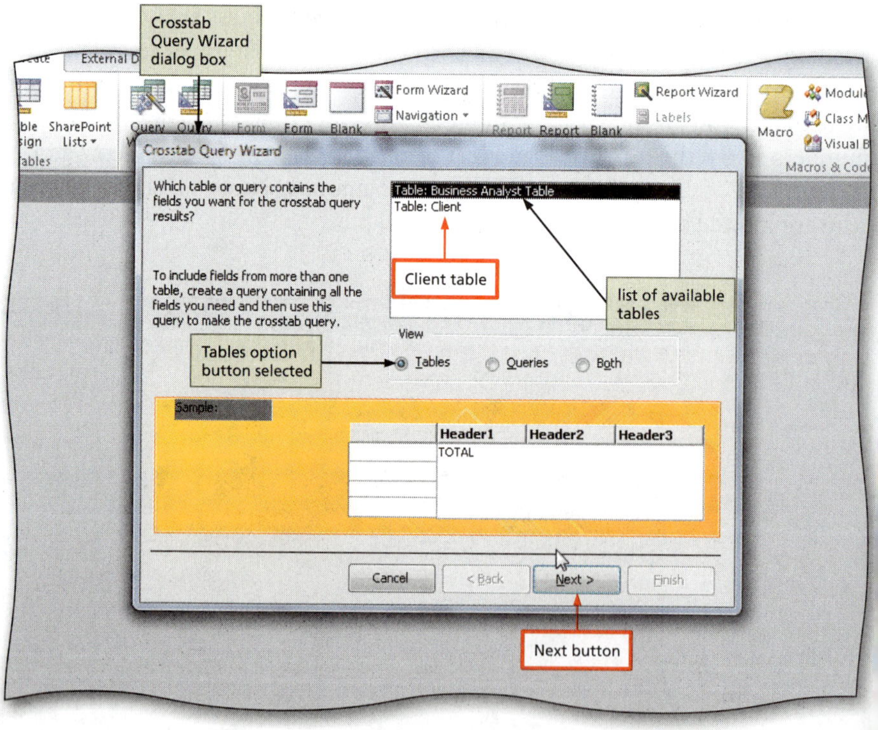

Figure 2–81

3

- With the Tables option button selected, click Table: Client to select the Client table, and then click the Next button to display the next Crosstab Query Wizard screen.
- Click the City field, and then click the Add Field button to select the City field for row headings (Figure 2–82).

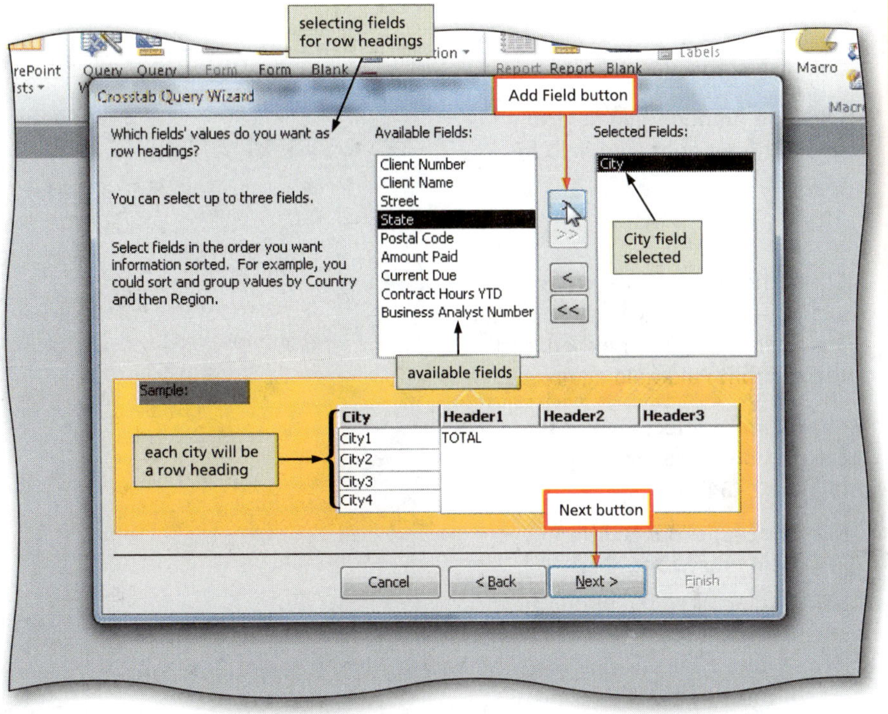

Figure 2–82

4

- Click the Next button to display the next Crosstab Query Wizard screen.
- Click the Business Analyst Number field to select the Business Analyst Number field for column headings (Figure 2–83).

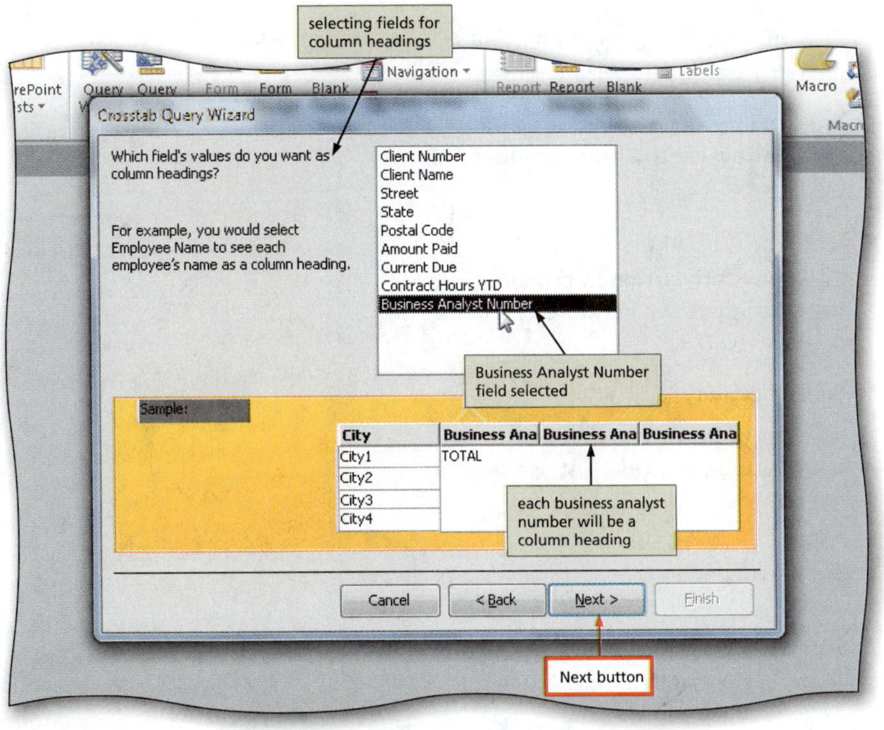

Figure 2–83

5

- Click the Next button to display the next Crosstab Query Wizard screen.
- Click the Amount Paid field to select the Amount Paid field for calculations.

Experiment

- Click other fields. For each field, examine the list of calculations that are available. When finished, click the Amount Paid field again.
- Click Sum to select Sum as the calculation to be performed (Figure 2–84).

Q&A My list of functions is different. What did I do wrong?

Either you clicked the wrong field, or the Amount Paid field has the wrong data type. For example, if you mistakenly assigned it the Text data type, you would not see Sum in the list of available calculations.

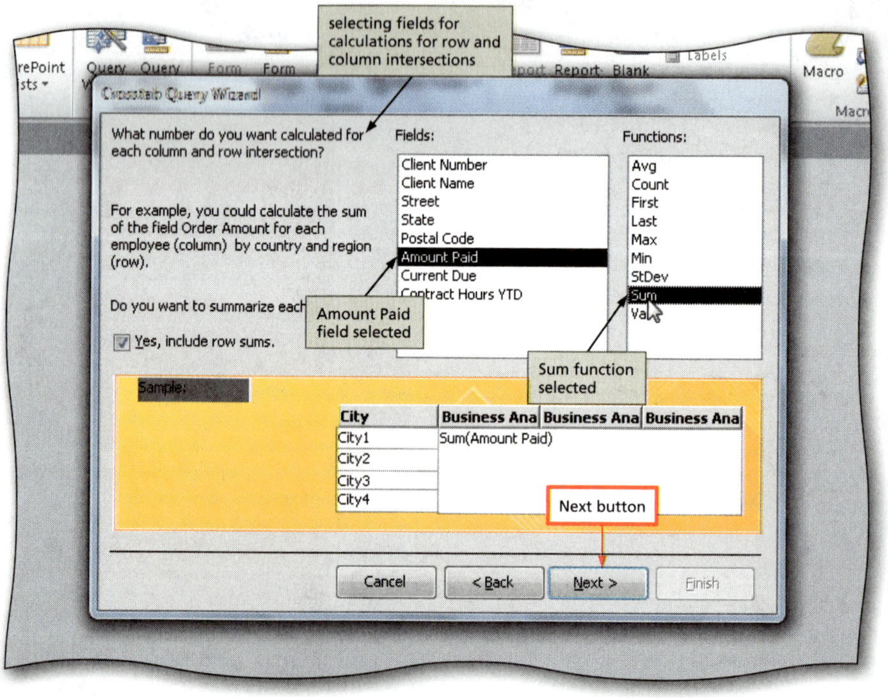

Figure 2–84

6

- Click the Next button to display the next Crosstab Query Wizard screen.
- Type `City-Analyst Crosstab` as the name of the query (Figure 2–85).

7

- Click the Finish button to produce the crosstab shown in Figure 2–79 on Page AC 123.
- Close the query.

Q&A If I want to view the crosstab at some future date, can I just open the query?

Yes.

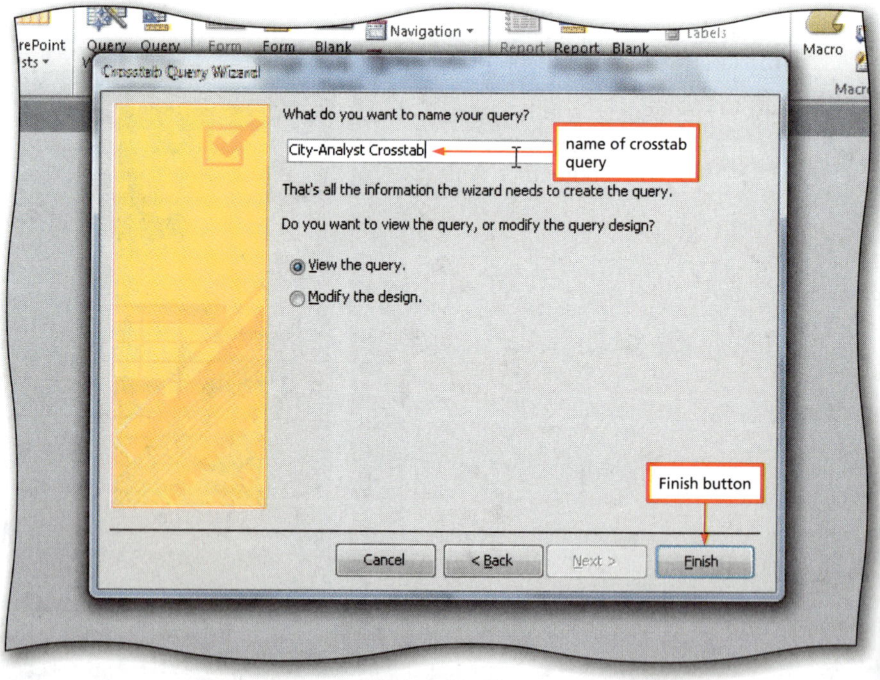

Figure 2–85

To Customize the Navigation Pane

Currently, the entries in the Navigation Pane are organized by object type. That is, all the tables are together, all the queries are together, and so on. You might want to change the way the information is organized. For example, you might want to have the Navigation Pane organized by table, with all the queries, forms, and reports associated with a particular table appearing after the name of the table. You also can use the Search bar to restrict the objects that appear to only those that have a certain collection of characters in their name. For example, if you entered the letters, Cl, only those objects containing Cl somewhere within the name will be included.

The following steps change the organization of the Navigation Pane. They also use the Search bar to restrict the objects that appear.

1

- If necessary, click the Shutter Bar Open/Close Button to open the Navigation Pane.
- Click the Navigation Pane arrow to produce the Navigation Pane menu (Figure 2–86).

2

- Click Tables and Related Views to organize the Navigation Pane by table rather than by the type of object (Figure 2–87).

3

- Click the Navigation Pane arrow to produce the Navigation Pane menu.
- Click Object Type to once again organize the Navigation Pane by object type.

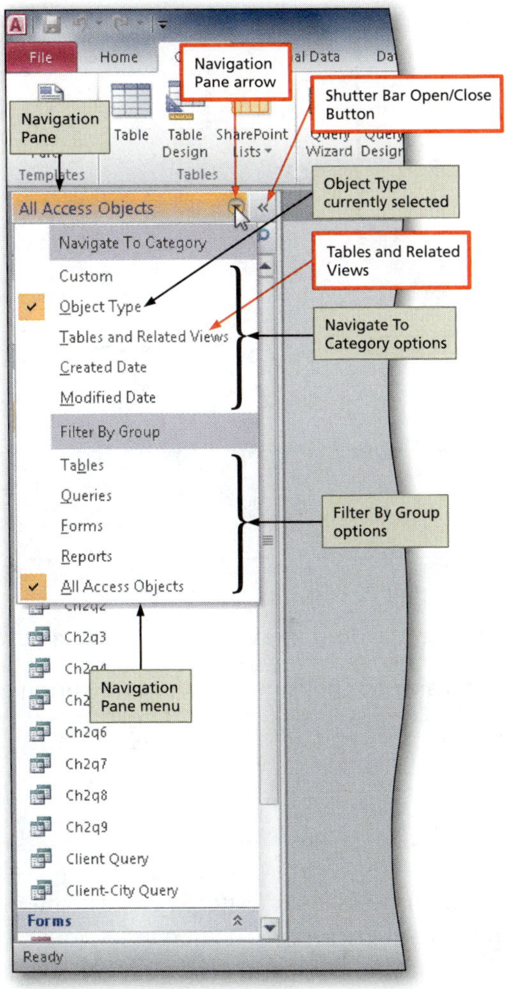

Figure 2–86

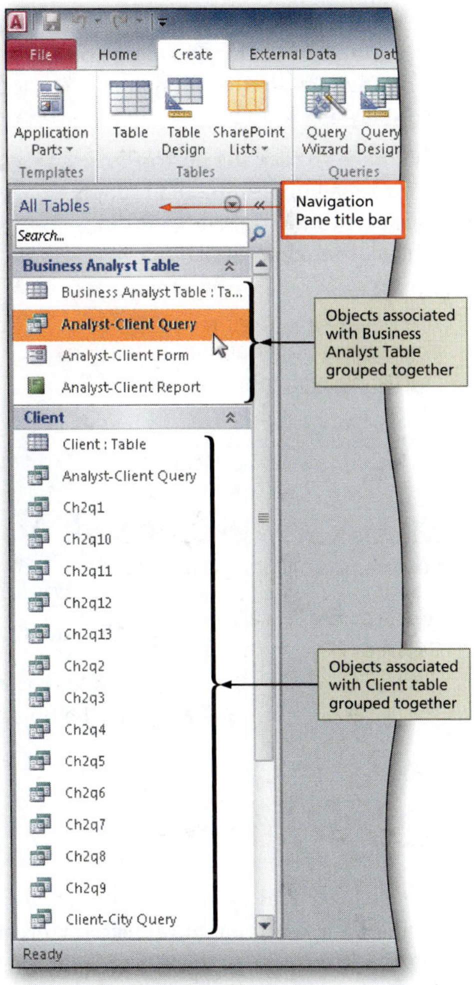

Figure 2–87

Experiment

- Select different Navigate To Category options to see the effect of the option. With each option you select, select different Filter By Group options to see the effect of the filtering. When you have finished experimenting, select the Object Type Navigate To Category option and the All Access Objects Filter By Group option.

4

- If the Search bar does not appear, right-click the Navigation Pane and click Search Bar on the shortcut menu.
- Click in the Search bar box to produce an insertion point.
- Type `Cl` as the search string to restrict the objects displayed to only those containing the desired string (Figure 2–88).

5

- Click the Clear Search String button to remove the search string and redisplay all objects.

Q&A Did I have to click the button to redisplay all objects? Could I simply have erased the current string to achieve the same result?

You did not have to click the button. You could have used the DELETE or BACKSPACE keys to erase the current search string.

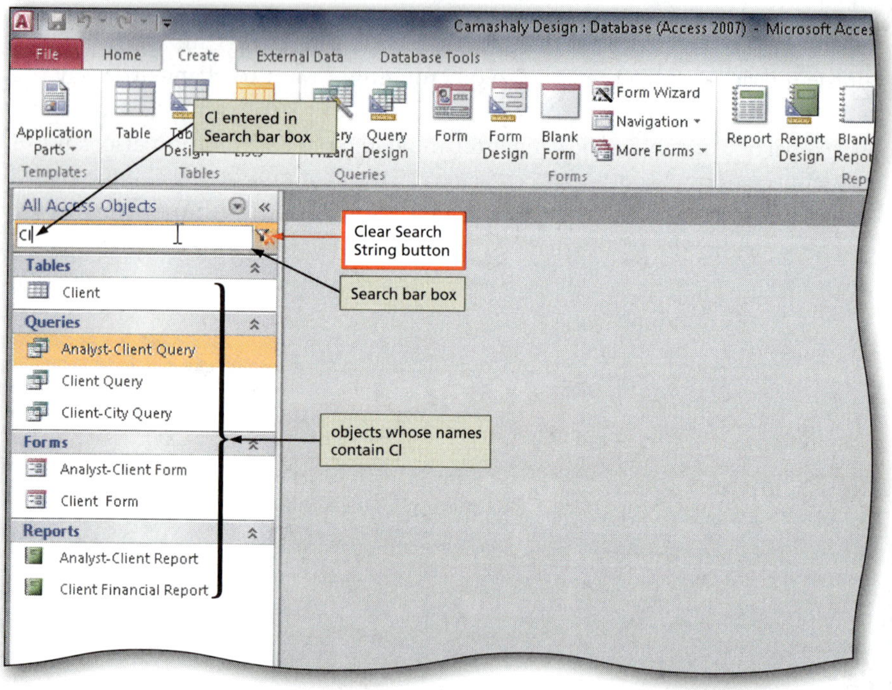

Figure 2–88

To Quit Access

The following steps quit Access.

1. Click the Close button on the right side of the title bar to quit Access.
2. If a Microsoft Access dialog box appears, click the Save button to save any changes made to the object since the last save.

Chapter Summary

In this chapter you have learned to create queries, enter fields, enter criteria, use text and numeric data in queries, use wildcards, use compound criteria, create parameter queries, sort data in queries, join tables in queries, perform calculations in queries, and create crosstab queries. You also learned to create a report and a form that used a query, to export a query, and to customize the Navigation Pane. The items listed below include all the new Access skills you have learned in this chapter.

1. Create a Query in Design View (AC 78)
2. Add Fields to the Design Grid (AC 79)
3. Use Text Data in a Criterion (AC 80)
4. Use a Wildcard (AC 83)
5. Use Criteria for a Field Not Included in the Results (AC 85)
6. Create and View a Parameter Query (AC 87)
7. Use a Parameter Query (AC 89)
8. Use a Number in a Criterion (AC 90)
9. Use a Comparison Operator in a Criterion (AC 91)
10. Use a Compound Criterion Involving AND (AC 92)
11. Use a Compound Criterion Involving OR (AC 93)
12. Clear the Design Grid (AC 95)
13. Sort Data in a Query (AC 96)
14. Omit Duplicates (AC 97)
15. Sort on Multiple Keys (AC 98)
16. Create a Top-Values Query (AC 99)
17. Join Tables (AC 102)
18. Change Join Properties (AC 105)
19. Create a Report Involving a Join (AC 106)

20. Create a Form for a Query (AC 109)
21. Export Data to Excel (AC 111)
22. Export Data to Word (AC 113)
23. Export Data to a Text File (AC 114)
24. Restrict the Records in a Join (AC 115)
25. Use a Calculated Field in a Query (AC 116)
26. Change a Caption (AC 118)
27. Calculate Statistics (AC 119)
28. Use Criteria in Calculating Statistics (AC 121)
29. Use Grouping (AC 122)
30. Create a Crosstab Query (AC 124)
31. Customize the Navigation Pane (AC 127)

SAM If you have a SAM 2010 user profile, your instructor may have assigned an autogradable version of this assignment. If so, log into the SAM 2010 Web site at www.cengage.com/sam2010 to download the instruction and start files.

Learn It Online

Test your knowledge of chapter content and key terms.

Instructions: To complete the Learn It Online exercises, visit the Microsoft Office and Concepts CourseMate Web site at www.cengagebrain.com, navigate to the Access Chapter 2 resources for this book, click the link for the exercise you want to complete, and then read the instructions.

Chapter Reinforcement TF, MC, and SA
A series of true/false, multiple choice, and short answer questions that test your knowledge of the chapter content.

Flash Cards
An interactive learning environment where you identify chapter key terms associated with displayed definitions.

Practice Test
A series of multiple choice questions that test your knowledge of chapter content and key terms.

Who Wants To Be a Computer Genius?
An interactive game that challenges your knowledge of chapter content in the style of a television quiz show.

Wheel of Terms
An interactive game that challenges your knowledge of chapter key terms in the style of the television show *Wheel of Fortune*.

Crossword Puzzle Challenge
A crossword puzzle that challenges your knowledge of key terms presented in the chapter.

Apply Your Knowledge

Reinforce the skills and apply the concepts you learned in this chapter.

Using Wildcards in a Query, Creating a Parameter Query, Joining Tables, and Creating a Report

Instructions: Start Access. Open the Babbage CPA Firm database that you modified in Apply Your Knowledge in Access Chapter 1 on page AC 64. (If you did not complete this exercise, see your instructor for a copy of the modified database.)

Perform the following tasks:

1. Create a query for the Client table and add the Client Number, Client Name, City, and Amount Paid fields to the design grid. Find all clients who live in cities that start with Bu. Save the query as Apply 2 Step 1 Query.

Continued >

Apply Your Knowledge *continued*

2. Create a query for the Client table and add the Client Number, Client Name, Bookkeeper Number, and Balance Due fields to the design grid. Sort the records in descending order by Balance Due. Add a criterion for the Bookkeeper Number field that allows the user to enter a different bookkeeper each time the query is run. Save the query as Apply 2 Step 2 Query.
3. Create a query that joins the Bookkeeper and the Client tables. Add the Bookkeeper Number, First Name, and Last Name fields from the Bookkeeper table and the Client Number and Client Name fields from the Client table. Sort the records in ascending order by Bookkeeper Number and Client Number. All bookkeepers should appear in the result, even if they currently have no clients. Save the query as Bookkeeper-Client Query.
4. Create the report shown in Figure 2–89. The report uses the Bookkeeper-Client Query.

Bookkeeper-Client Report

BKR #	First Name	Last Name	CL #	Client Name
22	Johanna	Lewes	A54	Afton Mills
22	Johanna	Lewes	D76	Dege Grocery
22	Johanna	Lewes	J77	Jones Plumbing
22	Johanna	Lewes	S56	SeeSaw Industries
24	Mario	Rodriguez	A62	Atlas Suppliers
24	Mario	Rodriguez	B26	Blake-Scripps
24	Mario	Rodriguez	G56	Grand Cleaners
24	Mario	Rodriguez	M26	Mohr Crafts
34	Choi	Wong	C29	Catering by Jenna
34	Choi	Wong	H21	Hill Shoes
34	Choi	Wong	T45	Tate Repair
34	Choi	Wong	W24	Woody Sporting Goods
38	Theresa	Sinthin		

Figure 2–89

5. Submit the revised database in the format specified by your instructor.

Extend Your Knowledge

Extend the skills you learned in this chapter and experiment with new skills. You may need to use Help to complete the assignment.

Creating Crosstab Queries, Creating Queries Using Criteria, and Exporting a Query

Instructions: Start Access. Open the Natural Earthscapes database. See the inside back cover of this book for instructions for downloading the Data Files for Students, or see your instructor for information on accessing the files required in this book.

Natural Earthscapes is a small landscaping company that specializes in landscaping with native plants. The owners have created an Access database in which to store information about the customers they serve and the workers they employ. You will create the crosstab shown in Figure 2–90. You also will query the database using specified criteria.

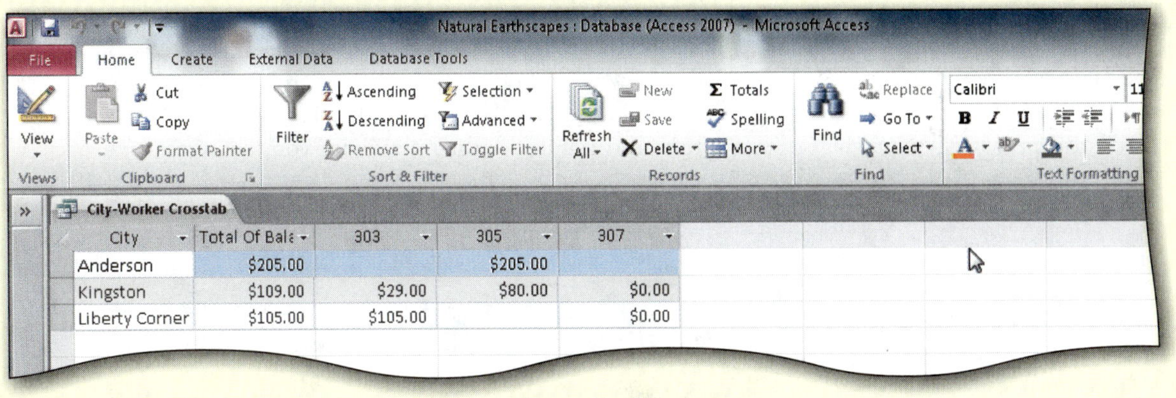

Figure 2–90

Perform the following tasks:

1. Create the crosstab query shown in Figure 2–90. The crosstab query groups the total of customers' balances by city and worker number.
2. Create a query to find all customers who do not live in Kingston. Include the Customer Number, Last Name, Balance, and Amount Paid fields in the design grid. Save the query as Extend 2 Step 2 Query.
3. Create a query to find all customers where the customer's first name is either Frances or Francis. Include the Customer Number, Last Name, First Name, Street, and City fields in the query results. Save the query as Extend 2 Step 3 Query.
4. Create a query to find all customers where the worker number is 303 or 305 and the balance is greater than $40.00. Include the Customer Number, Last Name, First Name, Balance, and Worker Number fields in the design grid. Use the IN operator in your query design. Save the query as Extend 2 Step 4 Query.
5. Export the City-Worker Crosstab as a Word file with the name City-Worker Crosstab.rtf and save the export steps.
6. Open the Customer table and change the balance for AB10 to $90.
7. Use the saved export steps to export the City-Worker Crosstab again. When asked if you want to replace the existing file, click Yes.
8. Change the database properties, as specified by your instructor. Submit the revised database and the exported RTF file in the format specified by your instructor.

Make It Right

Analyze a database and correct all errors and/or improve the design.

Correcting Errors in the Query Design

Instructions: Start Access. Open the Retired Pet Sitters database. See the inside back cover of this book for instructions for downloading the Data Files for Students, or see your instructor for information on accessing the files required in this book.

Continued >

Make It Right *continued*

Retired Pet Sitters is a database maintained by a small pet-sitting business. The queries shown in Figure 2–91 contain a number of errors that need to be corrected before the queries run properly. The query shown in Figure 2–91a displays the query results in the proper order (Last Name, First Name, Balance, Sitter Number), but it is sorted incorrectly. The query results should be sorted by last name within sitter number in ascending order. Also, the caption for the Balance field should be Owed. Save the query with your changes.

When you try to run the query shown in Figure 2–91b, you get 0 results. You are trying to find all customers who live on Magee. Correct the error and save the query with your changes.

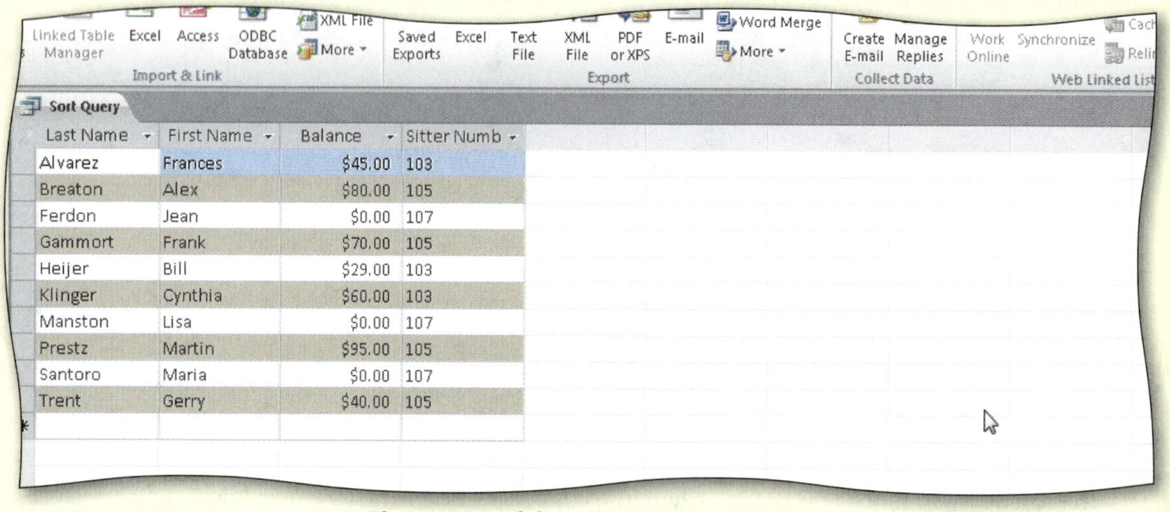

Figure 2–91 (a) Incorrect Sort Query

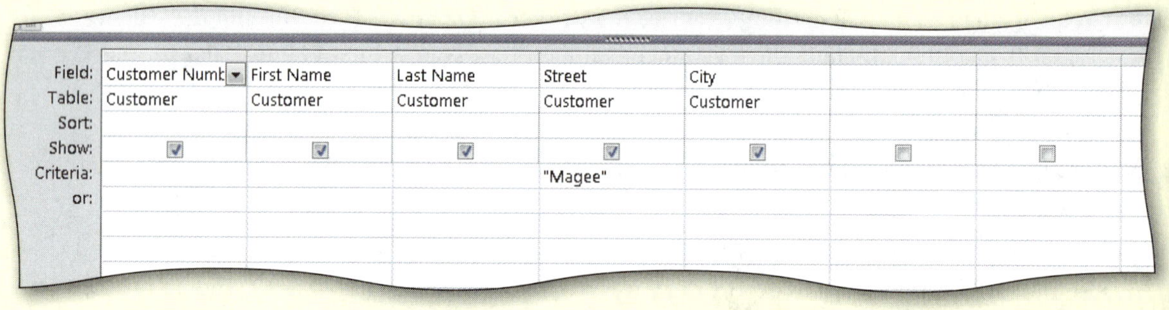

Figure 2–91 (b) Incorrect Criteria Query

Change the database properties, as specified by your instructor. Submit the revised database in the format specified by your instructor.

In the Lab

Design, create, modify, and/or use a database following the guidelines, concepts, and skills presented in this chapter. The assignments are listed in order of increasing difficulty.

Lab 1: Querying the ECO Clothesline Database

Problem: The management of ECO Clothesline has determined a number of questions it wants the database management system to answer. You must obtain answers to the questions posed by management.

Instructions: Use the database modified in the In the Lab 1 of Access Chapter 1 on page AC 66 for this assignment, or see your instructor for information on accessing the files required for this book.

Perform the following tasks:

1. Open the ECO Clothesline database and create a new query for the Customer table that includes the Customer Number, Customer Name, Amount Paid, and Sales Rep Number fields in the design grid for all customers where the sales rep number is 49. Save the query as Lab 2-1 Step 1 Query.
2. Create a query that includes the Customer Number, Customer Name, and Amount Paid fields for all customers located in Virginia (VA) with a paid amount greater than $1,000.00. Save the query as Lab 2-1 Step 2 Query.
3. Create a query that includes the Customer Number, Customer Name, Street, and City fields for all customers whose names begin with T. Save the query as Lab 2-1 Step 3 Query.
4. Create a query that lists all cities in ascending order. Each city should appear only once. Save the query as Lab 2-1 Step 4 Query.
5. Create a query that allows the user to enter the city to search when the query is run. The query results should display the Customer Number, Customer Name, Balance, and Amount Paid fields. Test the query by searching for those records where the client is located in Ashton. Save the query as Lab 2-1 Step 5 Query.
6. Include the Customer Number, Customer Name, and Balance fields in the design grid. Sort the records in descending order by the Balance field. Display only the top 25 percent of the records in the query result. Save the query as Lab 2-1 Step 6 Query.
7. Join the Sales Rep and the Customer table. Include the Sales Rep Number, First Name, and Last Name fields from the Sales Rep table. Include the Customer Number, Customer Name, and Balance from the Customer table. Sort the records in ascending order by sales rep's last name and customer name. All sales reps should appear in the result even if they currently have no customers. Save the query as Lab 2-1 Step 7 Query.
8. Open the Lab 2-1 Step 7 Query in Design view and remove the Sales Rep table. Add the Amount Paid field to the design grid. Calculate the total of the balance and amount paid amounts. Assign the alias Total Amount to the calculated field. Change the caption for the Balance field to Due. Save the query as Lab 2-1 Step 8 Query.
9. Create a query to display the average balance amount for all customers. Save the query as Lab 2-1 Step 9 Query.
10. Create a query to display the average balance amount for sales rep 51. Save the query as Lab 2-1 Step 10 Query.
11. Create a query to display the average balance amount for each sales rep. Save the query as Lab 2-1 Step 11 Query.
12. Create the crosstab shown in Figure 2–92. The crosstab groups the total of customers' amount paid amounts by state and sales rep number. Save the crosstab as State-Sales Rep Crosstab.
13. Submit the revised database in the format specified by your instructor.

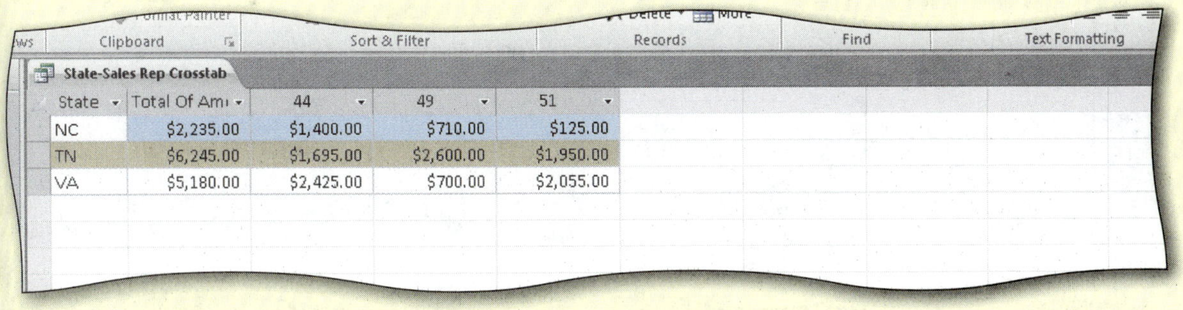

State	Total Of Ami	44	49	51
NC	$2,235.00	$1,400.00	$710.00	$125.00
TN	$6,245.00	$1,695.00	$2,600.00	$1,950.00
VA	$5,180.00	$2,425.00	$700.00	$2,055.00

Figure 2–92

In the Lab

Lab 2: Querying the Walburg Energy Alternatives Database

Problem: The manager of the Walburg Energy Alternatives store has determined a number of questions he wants the database management system to answer. You must obtain answers to the questions posed by the manager.

Instructions: Use the database created in the In the Lab 2 of Access Chapter 1 on page AC 67 for this assignment, or see your instructor for information on accessing the files required for this book.

Perform the following tasks:

1. Open the Walburg Energy Alternatives database and create a query that includes all fields and all records in the Item table. There should be only one column in the design grid. Name the query Lab 2-2 Step 1 Query.
2. Create a query that includes the Item Number, Description, Cost, and Vendor Code fields for all items where the vendor code is JM. Save the query as Lab 2-2 Step 2 Query.
3. Create a query that includes the Item Number and Description fields for all items where the description starts with the letters, En. Save the query as Lab 2-2 Step 3 Query.
4. Create a query that includes the Item Number and Description fields for all items with a cost less than $4.00. Save the query as Lab 2-2 Step 4 Query.
5. Create a query that includes the Item Number and Description fields for all items with a selling price greater than $20.00. Save the query as Lab 2-2 Step 5 Query.
6. Create a query that includes all fields for all items with a vendor code of AS and where the number on hand is fewer than 10. Save the query as Lab 2-2 Step 6 Query.
7. Create a query that includes all fields for all items that have a selling price greater than $10.00 or a vendor code of JM. Save the query as Lab 2-2 Step 7 Query.
8. Join the Vendor table and the Item table. Include the Vendor Code and Vendor Name fields from the Vendor table and the Item Number, Description, On Hand, and Cost fields from the Item table. Sort the records in ascending order by item number within vendor code. Save the query as Vendor-Item Query.
9. Create the form shown in Figure 2–93. The form uses the Vendor-Item Query.

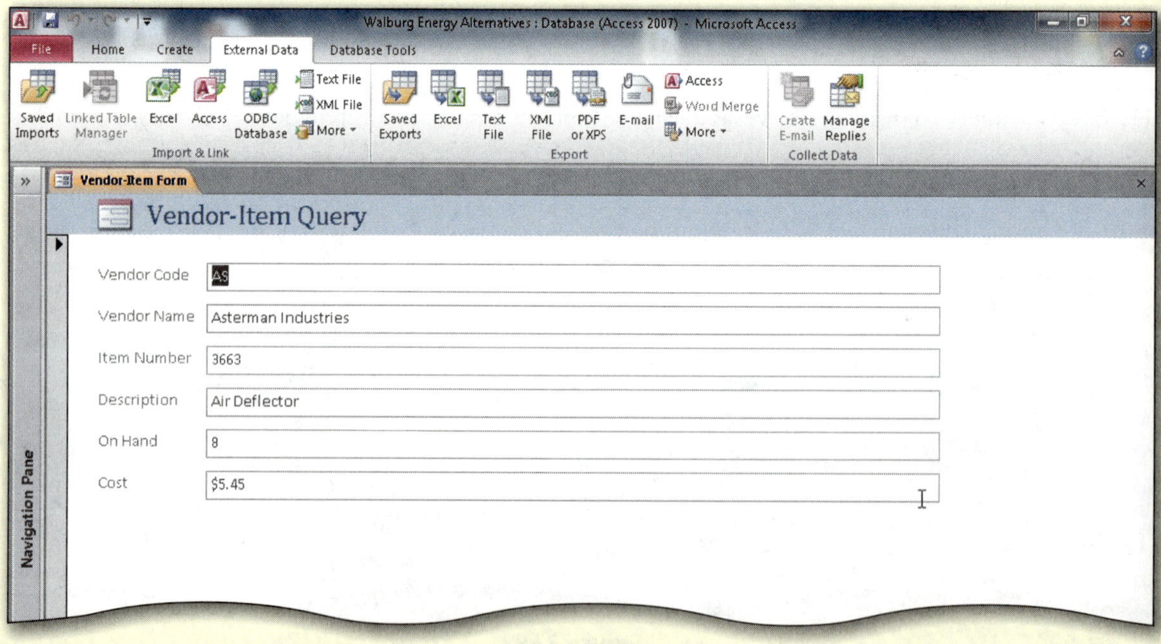

Figure 2–93

10. Create a query that includes the Item Number, Description, On Hand, and Cost fields. Calculate the inventory value (on hand*cost) for all records in the table. Assign the alias Inventory Value to the calculated field. Change the caption for the On Hand column to In Stock. Format the Inventory Value field as currency with two decimal places. Sort the records in descending order by inventory value. Save the query as Lab 2-2 Step 10 Query.
11. Create a query that calculates and displays the average cost of all items. Save the query as Lab 2-2 Step 11 Query.
12. Create a query that calculates and displays the average cost of items grouped by vendor code. Save the query as Lab 2-2 Step 12 Query.
13. Submit the revised database in the format specified by your instructor.

In the Lab

Lab 3: Querying the Philamar Training Database

Problem: The management of Philamar Training has determined a number of questions it wants the database management system to answer. You must obtain answers to the questions posed by management.

Instructions: Use the database created in the In the Lab 3 of Access Chapter 1 on page AC 70 for this assignment, or see your instructor for information on accessing the files required for this book. For Part 1 and Part 3, save each query using a format similar to the following: Lab 2-3 Part 1a Query, Lab 2-3 Part 3a Query, and so on. Submit the revised database and the Trainer-Client Query.xlsx file in the format specified by your instructor.

Instructions Part 1: Create a new query for the Client table and include the Client Number, Client Name, Amount Paid, and Current Due fields in the design grid. Create queries that answer the following questions: (a) Which clients' names begin with F? (b) Which clients are located in Kingston? (c) Which clients have a current due amount of $0.00? (d) Which clients have an amount paid amount between $5,000.00 and $10,000.00? (e) Which two clients have the highest current due amounts? (f) For each client, what is the total of the current due and amount paid?

Instructions Part 2: Join the Trainer and the Client table. In the design grid, include the Trainer Number, First Name, and Last Name from the Trainer table and the Client Number, Client Name, and Amount Paid from the Client table. Sort the records in ascending order by trainer number and client number. All trainers should appear in the result, even if they currently have no clients. Save the query as Trainer-Client Query. Export the query to Excel and save the export steps.

Instructions Part 3: Create queries to calculate the following statistics: (a) What is the average current due amount for clients assigned to trainer 42? (b) What is the total current due amount for all clients? (c) What is the total amount paid for each trainer?

Cases and Places

Apply your creative thinking and problem solving skills to design and implement a solution.

Note: To complete these assignments, you may be required to use the Data Files for Students. See the inside back cover of this book for instructions on downloading the Data Files for Students, or contact your instructor for information about accessing the required files.

1: Querying the Chamber of Commerce Database

Academic

Use the Chamber of Commerce database you created in Cases and Places 1 in Access Chapter 1 on page AC 72 for this assignment. Use the concepts and techniques presented in this chapter to create queries for the following:

a. Find the advertiser name and address of all advertisers located on Main.

Continued >

Cases and Places *continued*

b. Find the advertiser number, advertiser name, balance, and amount paid for all advertisers whose balance is greater than $300 or whose amount paid is $0.00.

c. Find the total of the balance and amount paid amounts for each advertiser. Show the advertiser number, advertiser name, and total amount. Sort the results in descending order by total.

d. Find the advertiser number, advertiser name, balance, and amount paid for all advertisers whose balance is between $200 and $500.

e. Create a parameter query for the Advertiser table that will allow the user to enter a different postal code each time the query is run. The user should see all fields in the query result.

f. Find the ad rep for each advertiser. List the ad rep number, last name, first name, advertiser number, advertiser name, and balance. Sort the results in ascending order by ad rep number and advertiser number.

g. Determine the total of the balance amounts and amount paid amounts for all advertisers.

Submit the revised database in the format specified by your instructor.

2: Querying the Consignment Database

Personal

Use the Consignment database you created in Cases and Places 2 in Access Chapter 1 on page AC 72 for this assignment. Use the concepts and techniques presented in this chapter to create queries for the following:

a. Find the item number and description of all items that contain the word, Table.

b. Find the item number, description, condition, and date of the item that has the earliest posting date.

c. Find the total price (price*quantity) of each item available for sale. Show the item number, item description, and total price.

d. Find the seller of each item. Show the seller's first name and last name as well as the item description, price, quantity, and date posted. Sort the results by item description within seller last name.

e. Create a report based on the query you created in Step d. Include all fields in the report.

f. Modify the query you created in Step d to restrict retrieval to those items with a price greater than $50.00.

g. Find all items posted between March 1, 2012, and March 4, 2012. The user should see all fields in the query result.

Submit the revised database in the format specified by your instructor.

3: Querying the Senior Care Database

Professional

Use the Senior Care database you created in Cases and Places 3 in Access Chapter 1 on page AC 72 for this assignment. Use the concepts and techniques presented in this chapter to create queries for the following:

a. Find the first name, last name, and address of all clients where the street name begins with the letter U.

b. Find the client number, last name, first name, balance, and amount paid for all clients whose balance is $0.00 or whose amount paid is $0.00.

c. Find the total of the balance and amount paid amounts for each client. Show the client number, client last name, client first name, and total amount. Sort the results in descending order by total.

d. Find the helper for each client. List the helper number, helper last name, helper first name, client number, client last name, and client first name. Sort the results in ascending order by helper number and client number.

e. Create a report for the query created in Step d. Include all fields except the helper first name in the report. Create a form for the query created in Step d.

f. Export the query created in Step d as a text file.

g. Find the highest and lowest balances.

Submit the exported text file and revised database in the format specified by your instructor.

Appendix A

Project Planning Guidelines

Using Project Planning Guidelines

The process of communicating specific information to others is a learned, rational skill. Computers and software, especially Microsoft Office 2010, can help you develop ideas and present detailed information to a particular audience.

Using Microsoft Office 2010, you can create projects such as Word documents, PowerPoint presentations, Excel spreadsheets, and Access databases. Productivity software such as Microsoft Office 2010 minimizes much of the laborious work of drafting and revising projects. Some communicators handwrite ideas in notebooks, others compose directly on the computer, and others have developed unique strategies that work for their own particular thinking and writing styles.

No matter what method you use to plan a project, follow specific guidelines to arrive at a final product that presents information correctly and effectively (Figure A–1). Use some aspects of these guidelines every time you undertake a project, and others as needed in specific instances. For example, in determining content for a project, you may decide that a chart communicates trends more effectively than a paragraph of text. If so, you would create this graphical element and insert it in an Excel spreadsheet, a Word document, or a PowerPoint slide.

Determine the Project's Purpose

Begin by clearly defining why you are undertaking this assignment. For example, you may want to track monetary donations collected for your club's fund-raising drive. Alternatively, you may be urging students to vote for a particular candidate in the next election. Once you clearly understand the purpose of your task, begin to draft ideas of how best to communicate this information.

Analyze Your Audience

Learn about the people who will read, analyze, or view your work. Where are they employed? What are their educational backgrounds? What are their expectations? What questions do they have?

PROJECT PLANNING GUIDELINES

1. DETERMINE THE PROJECT'S PURPOSE
Why are you undertaking the project?

2. ANALYZE YOUR AUDIENCE
Who are the people who will use your work?

3. GATHER POSSIBLE CONTENT
What information exists, and in what forms?

4. DETERMINE WHAT CONTENT TO PRESENT TO YOUR AUDIENCE
What information will best communicate the project's purpose to your audience?

Figure A–1

Design experts suggest drawing a mental picture of these people or finding photos of people who fit this profile so that you can develop a project with the audience in mind.

By knowing your audience members, you can tailor a project to meet their interests and needs. You will not present them with information they already possess, and you will not omit the information they need to know.

Example: Your assignment is to raise the profile of your college's nursing program in the community. How much do they know about your college and the nursing curriculum? What are the admission requirements? How many of the applicants admitted complete the program? What percent pass the state board exams?

Gather Possible Content

Rarely are you in a position to develop all the material for a project. Typically, you would begin by gathering existing information that may reside in spreadsheets or databases. Web sites, pamphlets, magazine and newspaper articles, and books could provide insights of how others have approached your topic. Personal interviews often provide perspectives not available by any other means. Consider video and audio clips as potential sources for material that might complement or support the factual data you uncover.

Determine What Content to Present to Your Audience

Experienced designers recommend writing three or four major ideas you want an audience member to remember after reading or viewing your project. It also is helpful to envision your project's endpoint, the key fact you wish to emphasize. All project elements should lead to this ending point.

As you make content decisions, you also need to think about other factors. Presentation of the project content is an important consideration. For example, will your brochure be printed on thick, colored paper or posted on the Web? Will your PowerPoint presentation be viewed in a classroom with excellent lighting and a bright projector, or will it be viewed on a notebook computer monitor? Determine relevant time factors, such as the length of time to develop the project, how long readers will spend reviewing your project, or the amount of time allocated for your speaking engagement. Your project will need to accommodate all of these constraints.

Decide whether a graph, photo, or artistic element can express or emphasize a particular concept. The right hemisphere of the brain processes images by attaching an emotion to them, so audience members are more apt to recall these graphics long term rather than just reading text.

As you select content, be mindful of the order in which you plan to present information. Readers and audience members generally remember the first and last pieces of information they see and hear, so you should place the most important information at the top or bottom of the page.

Summary

When creating a project, it is beneficial to follow some basic guidelines from the outset. By taking some time at the beginning of the process to determine the project's purpose, analyze the audience, gather possible content, and determine what content to present to the audience, you can produce a project that is informative, relevant, and effective.

Appendix B

Publishing Office 2010 Web Pages Online

With Office 2010 programs, you use the Save As command in the Backstage view to save a Web page to a Web site, network location, or FTP site. **File Transfer Protocol (FTP)** is an Internet standard that allows computers to exchange files with other computers on the Internet.

You should contact your network system administrator or technical support staff at your Internet access provider to determine if their Web server supports Web folders, FTP, or both, and to obtain necessary permissions to access the Web server.

Using an Office Program to Publish Office 2010 Web Pages

When publishing online, someone first must assign the necessary permissions for you to publish the Web page. If you are granted access to publish online, you must obtain the Web address of the Web server, a user name, and possibly a password that allows you to connect to the Web server. The steps in this appendix assume that you have access to an online location to which you can publish a Web page.

To Connect to an Online Location

To publish a Web page online, you first must connect to the online location. To connect to an online location using Windows 7, you would perform the following steps.

1. Click the Start button on the Windows 7 taskbar to display the Start menu.
2. Click Computer in the right pane of the Start menu to open the Computer window.
3. Click the 'Map network drive' button on the toolbar to display the Map Network Drive dialog box. (If the 'Map network drive' button is not visible on the toolbar, click the 'Display additional commands' button on the toolbar and then click 'Map network drive' in the list to display the Map Network Drive dialog box.)
4. Click the 'Connect to a Web site that you can use to store your documents and pictures' link (Map Network Drive dialog box) to start the Add Network Location wizard.
5. Click the Next button (Add Network Location dialog box).
6. Click 'Choose a custom network location' and then click the Next button.
7. Type the Internet or network address specified by your network or system administrator in the text box and then click the Next button.
8. Click 'Log on anonymously' to deselect the check box, type your user name in the User name text box, and then click the Next button.
9. If necessary, enter the name you want to assign to this online location and then click the Next button.
10. Click to deselect the Open this network location when I click Finish check box, and then click the Finish button.

11. Click the Cancel button to close the Map Network Drive dialog box.
12. Close the Computer window.

To Save a Web Page to an Online Location

The online location now can be accessed easily from Windows programs, including Microsoft Office programs. After creating a Microsoft Office file you wish to save as a Web page, you must save the file to the online location to which you connected in the previous steps. To save a Microsoft Word document as a Web page, for example, and publish it to the online location, you would perform the following steps.

1. Click File on the Ribbon to display the Backstage view and then click Save As in the Backstage view to display the Save As dialog box.
2. Type the Web page file name in the File name text box (Save As dialog box). Do not press the ENTER key because you do not want to close the dialog box at this time.
3. Click the 'Save as type' box arrow and then click Web Page to select the Web Page format.
4. If necessary, scroll to display the name of the online location in the navigation pane.
5. Double-click the online location name in the navigation pane to select that location as the new save location and display its contents in the right pane.
6. If a dialog box appears prompting you for a user name and password, type the user name and password in the respective text boxes and then click the Log On button.
7. Click the Save button (Save As dialog box).

The Web page now has been published online. To view the Web page using a Web browser, contact your network or system administrator for the Web address you should use to connect to the Web page.

Appendix C

Saving to the Web Using Windows Live SkyDrive

Introduction

Windows Live SkyDrive, also referred to as **SkyDrive**, is a free service that allows users to save files to the Web, such as documents, presentations, spreadsheets, databases, videos, and photos. Using SkyDrive, you also can save files in folders, providing for greater organization. You then can retrieve those files from any computer connected to the Internet. Some Office 2010 programs including Word, PowerPoint, and Excel can save files directly to an Internet location such as SkyDrive. SkyDrive also facilitates collaboration by allowing users to share files with other SkyDrive users (Figure C–1).

Figure C–1

Note: An Internet connection is required to perform the steps in this appendix.

To Save a File to Windows Live SkyDrive

You can save files directly to SkyDrive from within Word, PowerPoint, and Excel using the Backstage view. The following steps save an open Word document (Koala Exhibit Flyer, in this case) to SkyDrive. These steps require you to have a Windows Live account. Contact your instructor if you do not have a Windows Live account.

1

- Start Word and then open a document you want to save to the Web (in this case, the Koala Exhibit Flyer).
- Click File on the Ribbon to display the Backstage view (Figure C–2).

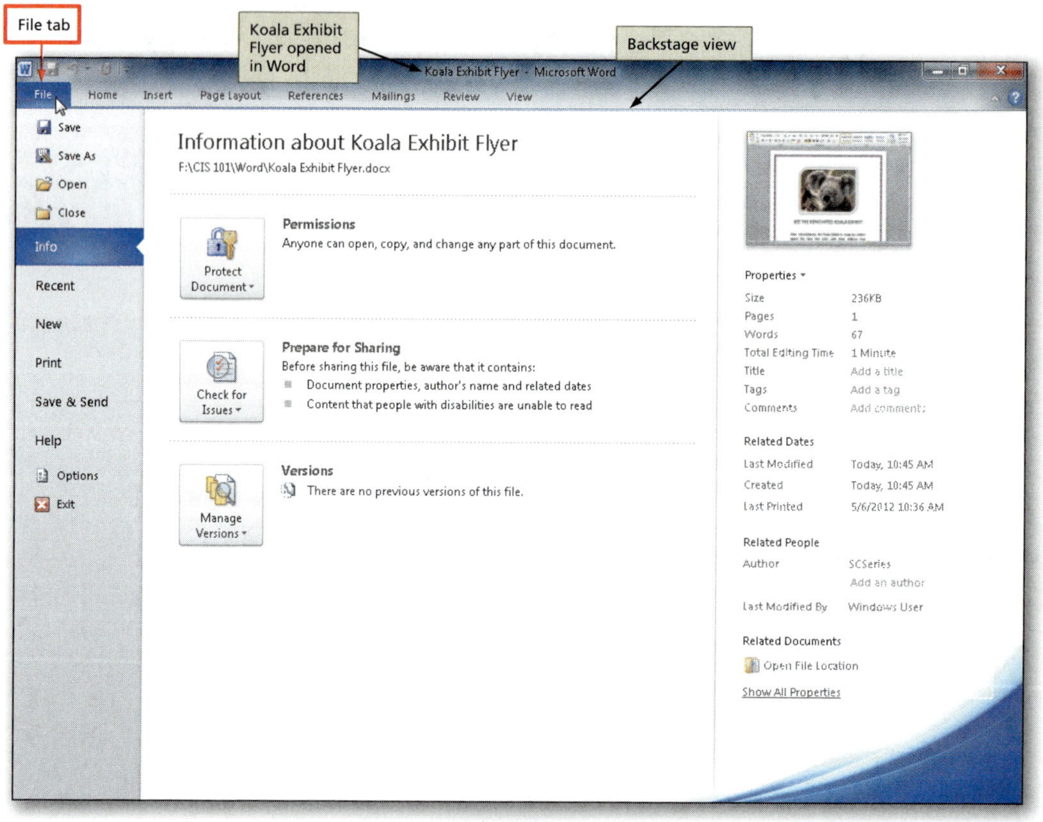

Figure C–2

2

- Click the Save & Send tab to display the Save & Send gallery (Figure C–3).

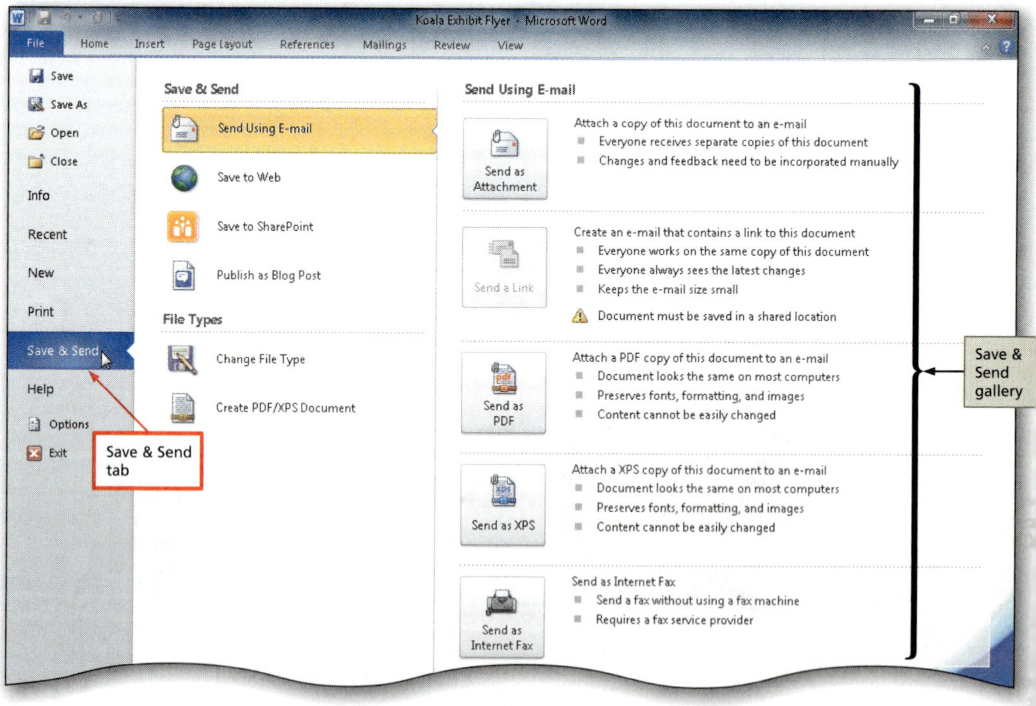

Figure C–3

3

- Click Save to Web in the Save & Send gallery to display information about saving a file to the Web (Figure C–4).

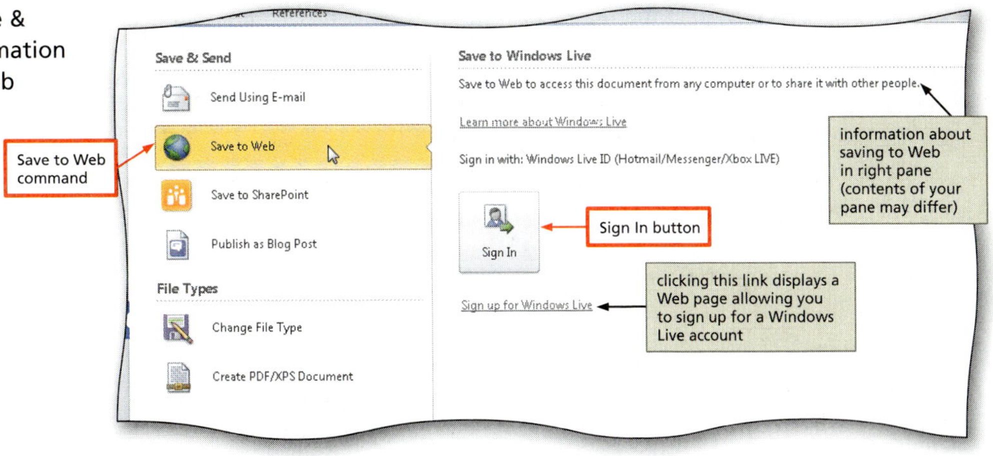

Figure C–4

4

- Click the Sign In button to display a Windows Live login dialog box that requests your e-mail address and password (Figure C–5).

Q&A What if the Sign In button does not appear?

If you already are signed into Windows Live, the Sign In button will not be displayed. Instead, the contents of your Windows Live SkyDrive will be displayed. If you already are signed into Windows Live, proceed to Step 6.

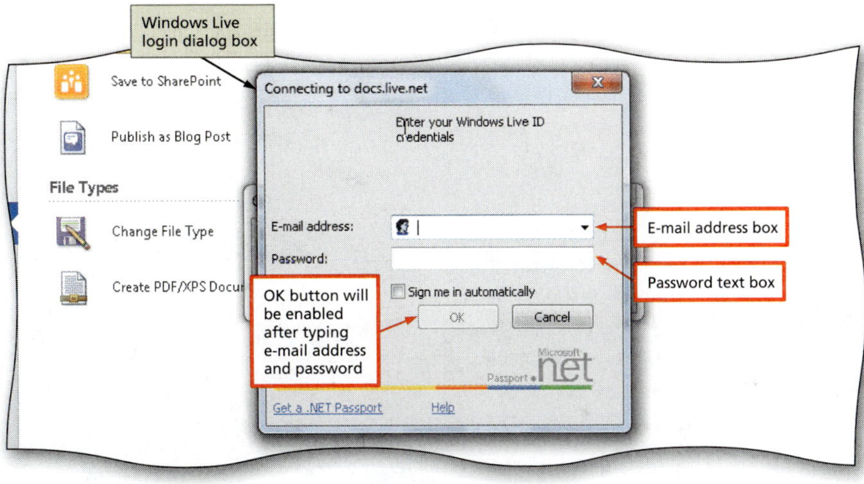

Figure C–5

5

- Enter your Windows Live e-mail address in the E-mail address box (Windows Live login dialog box).
- Enter your Windows Live password in the Password text box.
- Click the OK button to sign into Windows Live and display the contents of your Windows Live SkyDrive in the right pane of the Save & Send gallery.
- If necessary, click the My Documents folder to set the save location for the document (Figure C–6).

Q&A What if the My Documents folder does not exist?

Click another folder to select it as the save location. Record the name of this folder so that you can locate and retrieve the file later in this appendix.

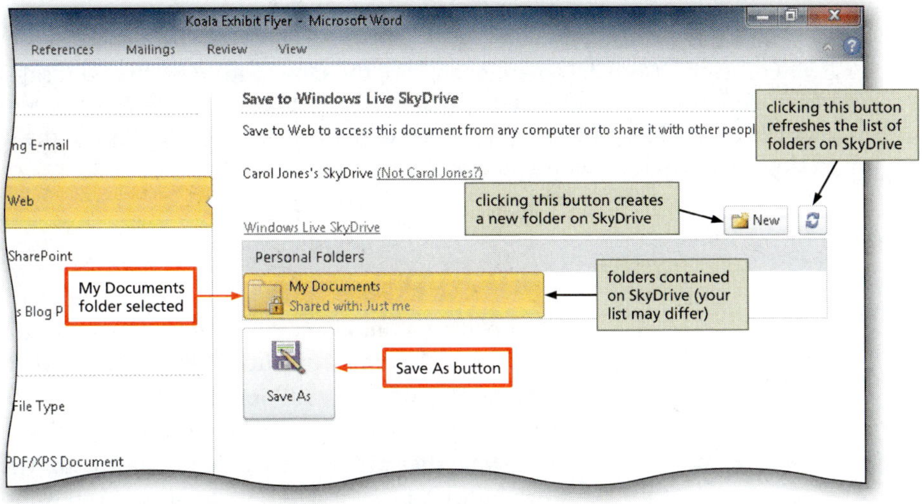

Figure C–6

Q&A My SkyDrive shows personal and shared folders. What is the difference?

Personal folders are private and are not shared with anyone. Shared folders can be viewed by SkyDrive users to whom you have assigned the necessary permissions.

6

- Click the Save As button in the right pane of the Save & Send gallery to contact the SkyDrive server (which may take some time, depending on the speed of your Internet connection) and then display the Save As dialog box (Figure C–7).

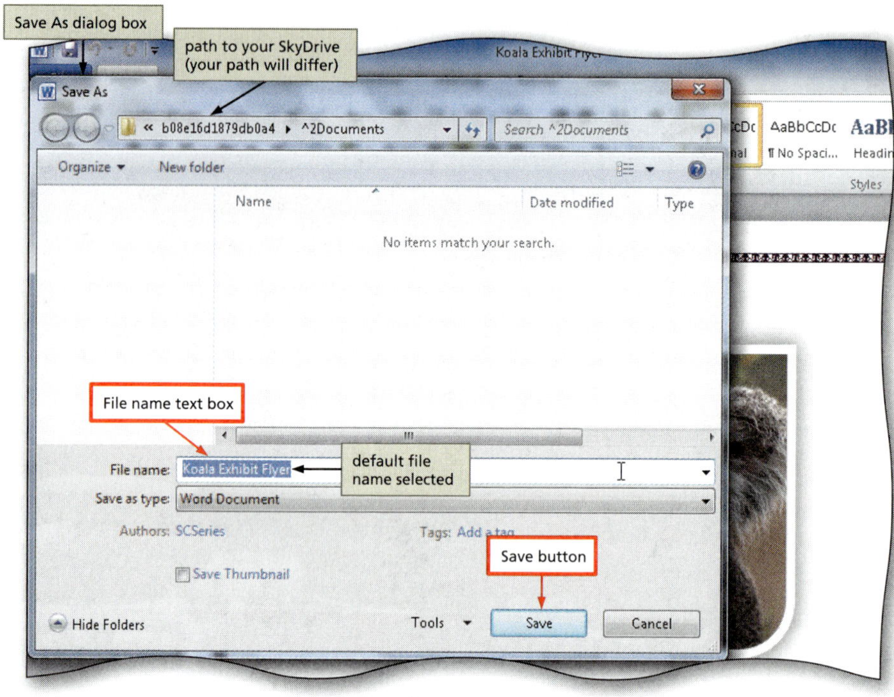

Figure C–7

7

- Type **Koala Exhibit Web** in the File name text box to enter the file name and then click the Save button (Save As dialog box) to save the file to Windows Live SkyDrive (Figure C–8).

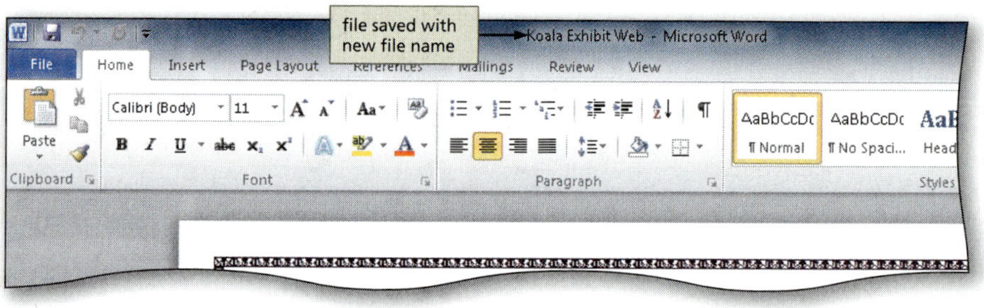

Figure C–8

Q&A

Is it necessary to rename the file?

It is good practice to rename the file. If you download the file from SkyDrive to your computer, having a different file name will preserve the original file.

8

- If you have one Word document open, click the Close button on the right side of the title bar to close the document and quit Word; or if you have multiple Word documents open, click File on the Ribbon to open the Backstage view and then click Exit in the Backstage view to close all open documents and quit Word.

Web Apps

Microsoft has created a scaled-down, Web-based version of its Microsoft Office suite, called **Microsoft Office Web Apps**, or **Web Apps**. Web Apps contains Web-based versions of Word, PowerPoint, Excel, and OneNote that can be used to view and edit files that are saved to SkyDrive. Web Apps allows users to continue working with their files even while they are not using a computer with Microsoft Office installed. In addition to working with files located on SkyDrive, Web Apps also enables users to create new Word documents, PowerPoint presentations, Excel spreadsheets, and OneNote notebooks. After returning to a computer with the Microsoft Office suite, some users choose to download files from SkyDrive and edit them using the associated Microsoft Office program.

Note: As with all Web applications, SkyDrive and Office Web Apps are subject to change. Consequently, the steps required to perform the actions in this appendix might be different from those shown.

To Download a File from Windows Live SkyDrive

Files saved to SkyDrive can be downloaded from a Web browser using any computer with an Internet connection. The following steps download the Koala Exhibit Web file using a Web browser.

1

- Click the Internet Explorer program button pinned on the Windows 7 taskbar to start Internet Explorer.
- Type **skydrive.live.com** in the Address bar and then press the ENTER key to display a SkyDrive Web page requesting you sign in to your Windows Live account (Figure C–9). (If the contents of your SkyDrive are displayed instead, you already are signed in and can proceed to Step 3 on the next page.)

Q&A Why does the Web address change after I enter it in the Address bar?

The Web address changes because you are being redirected to sign into Windows Live before you can access SkyDrive.

Q&A Can I open the file from Microsoft Word instead of using the Web browser?

If you are opening the file on the same computer from which you saved it to the SkyDrive, click File on the Ribbon to open the Backstage view. Click the Recent tab and then click the desired file name (Koala Exhibit Web, in this case) in the Recent Documents list, or click Open and then navigate to the location of the saved file (for a detailed example of this procedure, refer to the Office 2010 and Windows 7 chapter at the beginning of this book).

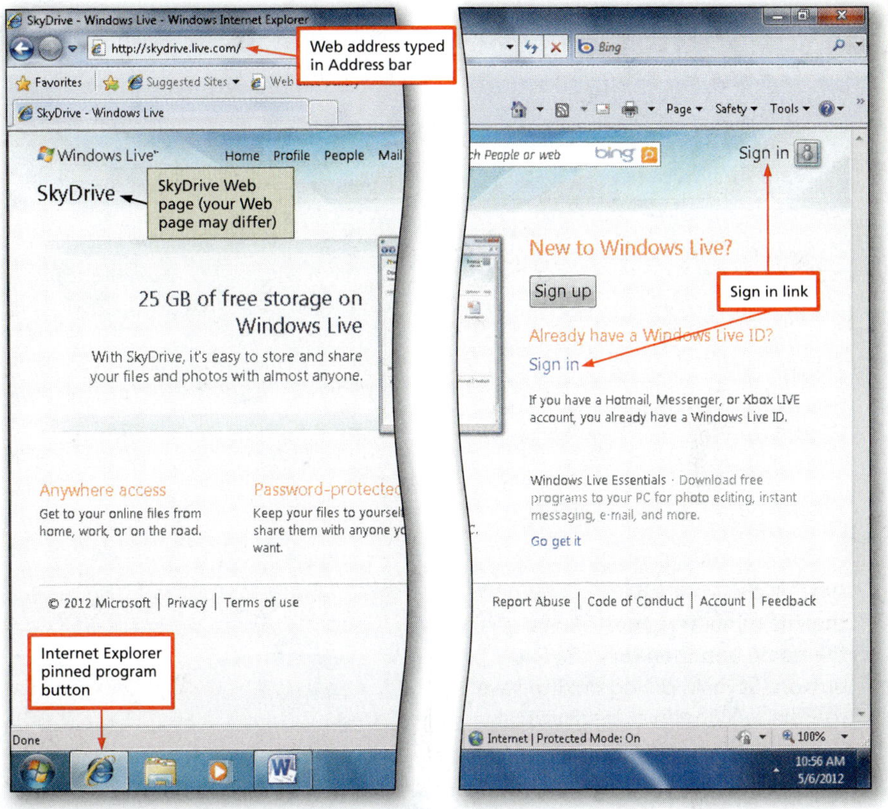

Figure C–9

2

- Click the Sign in link to display the Windows Live ID and Password text boxes (Figure C–10).

Q&A Why can I not locate the Sign in link?

If your computer remembers your Windows Live sign in credentials from a previous session, your e-mail address already may be displayed on the SkyDrive Web page. In this case, point to your e-mail address to display the Sign in button, click the Sign in button, and then proceed to Step 3. If you cannot locate your e-mail address or Sign in link, click the Sign in with a different Windows Live ID link and then proceed to Step 3.

Figure C–10

3

- If necessary, enter your Windows Live ID and password in the appropriate text boxes and then click the Sign in button to sign into Windows Live and display the contents of your SkyDrive (Figure C–11).

Q&A

What if my screen shows the contents of a particular folder, instead of all folders?

To display all folders on your SkyDrive, point to Windows Live in the upper-left corner of the window and then click SkyDrive on the Windows Live menu.

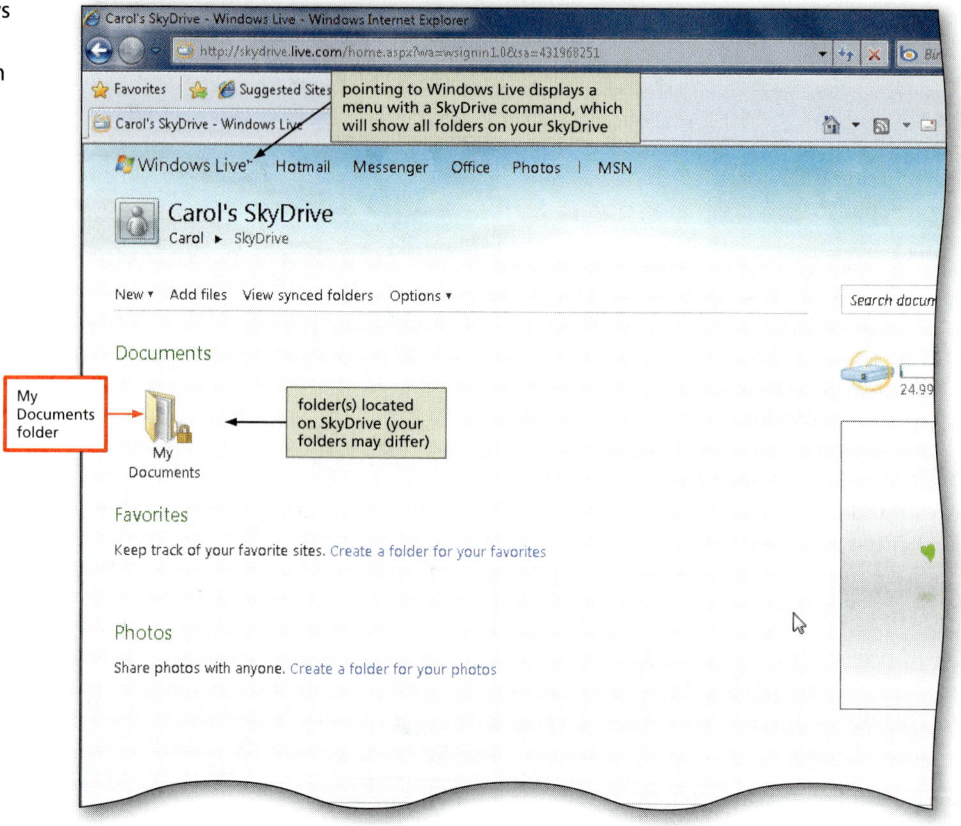

Figure C–11

4

- Click the My Documents folder, or the link corresponding to the folder containing the file you wish to open, to select the folder and display its contents (Figure C–12).

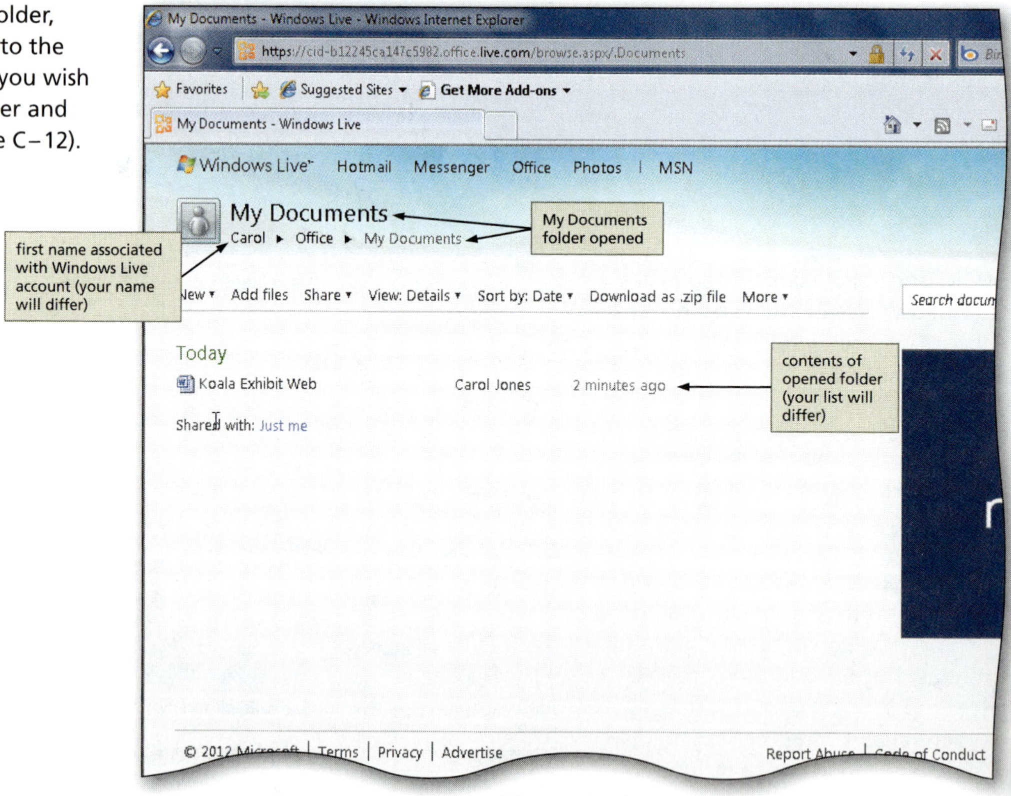

Figure C–12

5

- Point to the Koala Exhibit Web file to select the file and display commands associated with the file.
- Click the More link to display the More menu (Figure C–13).

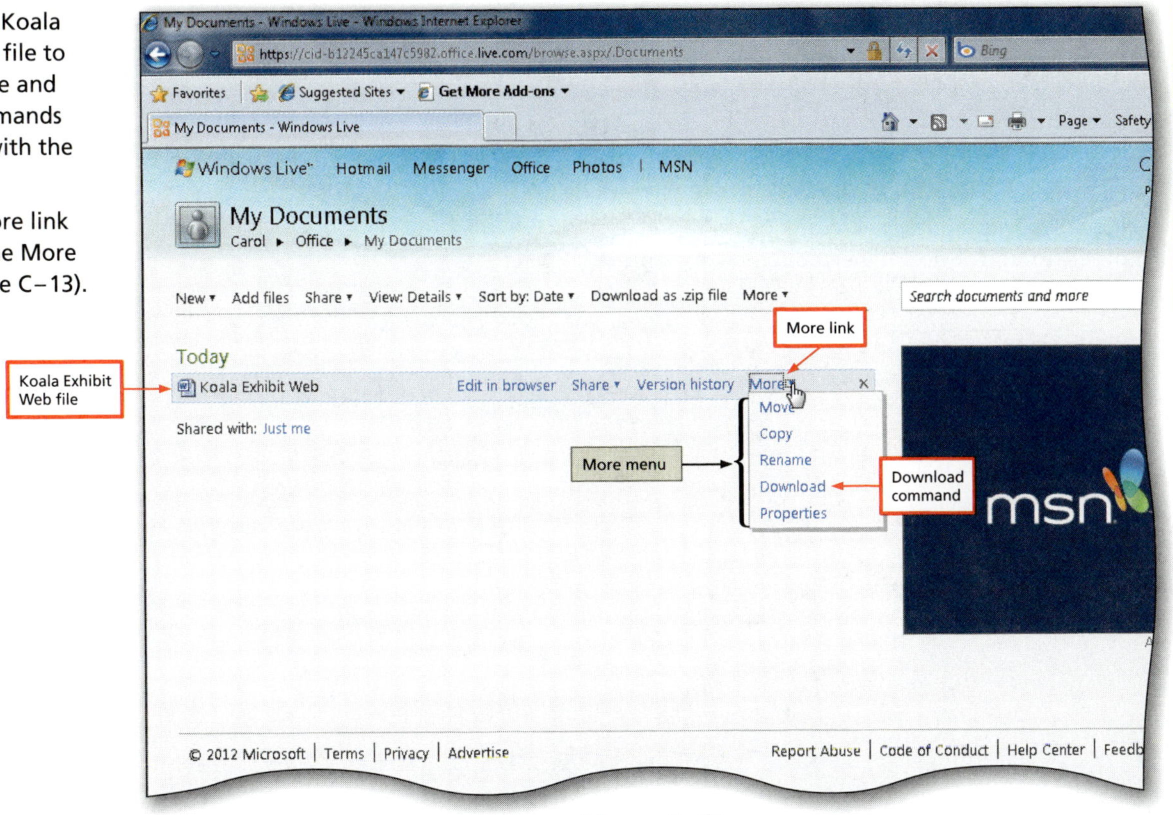

Figure C–13

6

- Click Download on the More menu to display the File Download dialog box (Figure C–14).

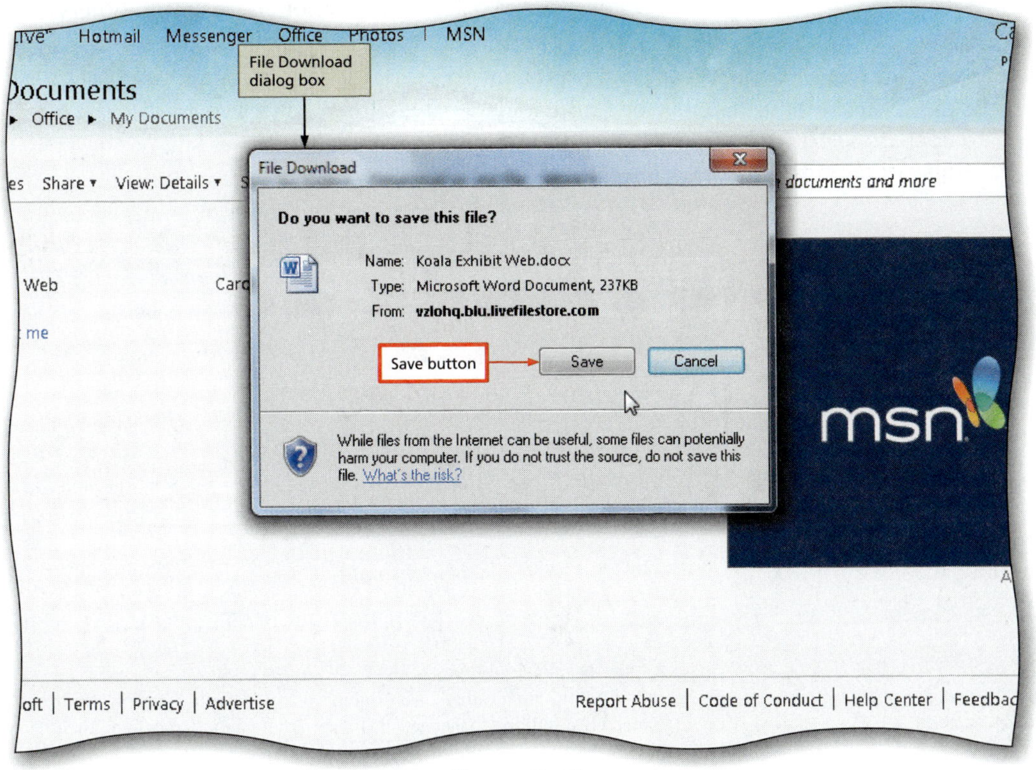

Figure C–14

7

- Click the Save button (File Download dialog box) to display the Save As dialog box (Figure C–15).
- Navigate to the desired save location.
- Click the Save button to save the file on your computer's hard disk or other storage device connected to the computer.

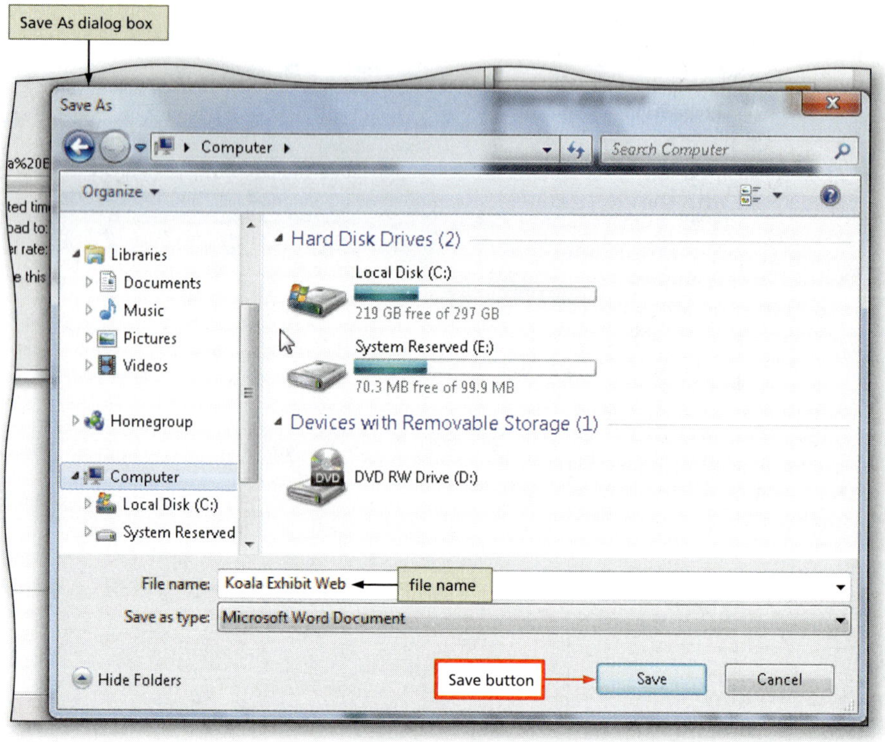

Figure C–15

Collaboration

In today's workplace, it is common to work with others on projects. Collaborating with the members of your team often requires sharing files. It also can involve multiple people editing and working with a certain set of files simultaneously. Placing files on SkyDrive in a public or shared folder enables others to view or modify the files. The members of the team then can view and edit the files simultaneously using Web Apps, enabling the team to work from one set of files (Figure C–16). Collaboration using Web Apps not only enables multiple people to work together, it also can reduce the amount of time required to complete a project.

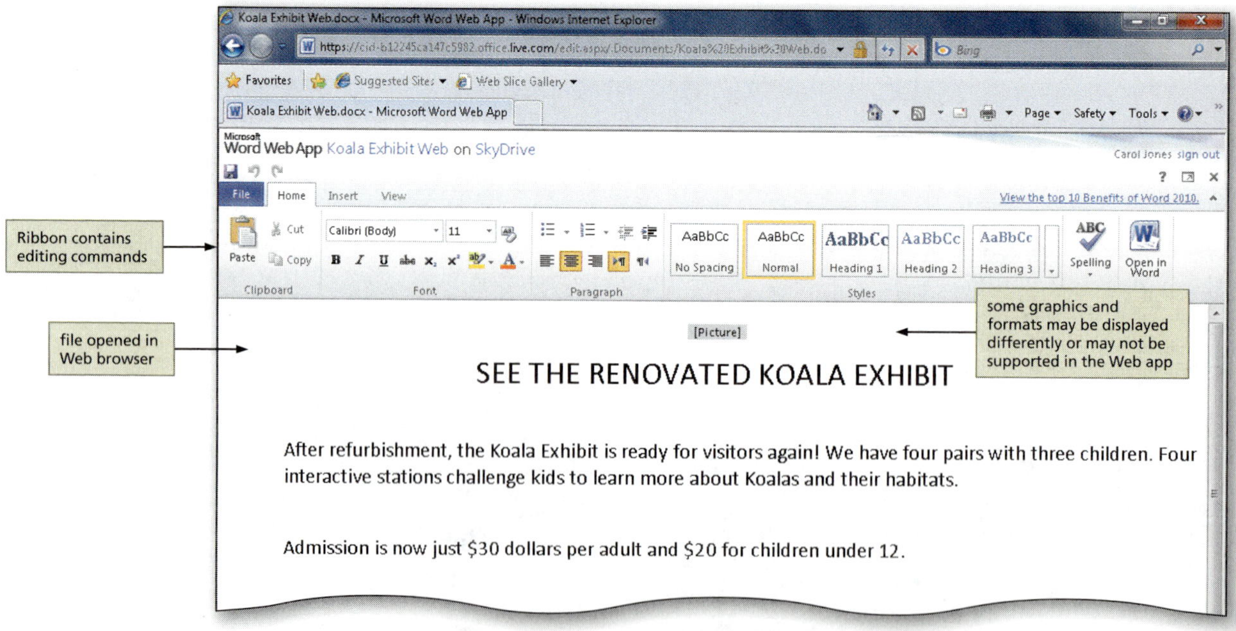

Figure C–16

Index

3D pie charts, EX 141, EX 180–192
3-D visual effects, 39, EX 188–190
802.11i, **197**

A

absolute cell references, **EX 162**
copying formulas with, EX 168
entering formulas using, EX 162–164
absoluters Web site, 94
accent colors, PPT 80
Access, OFF 8, **OFF 53**
See also databases
exporting data from, AC 110
exporting data to Excel, AC 111–113
exporting data to Word, AC 113
features and operations, OFF 54–56
Help, AC 62
importing data from other applications into, AC 38–41
overview of, OFF 53–56
quitting, OFF 58, AC 26, AC 60
starting, OFF 53, AC 12
Access control: Security measure that defines who can access a computer, when they can access it, and what actions they can take while accessing the computer. **189**
Access provider: Business that provides individuals and companies access to the Internet free or for a fee. 10, **46**
Access window, AC 15
Access work area, **OFF 54, AC 15**
Accounting Number format, EX 32–33, EX 100, EX 103
Accounting software: Software that helps companies record and report their financial transactions. 100, **107**
Accounting Style button, EX 174
Acrobat Reader, 61
actions, undoing, WD 23, EX 51
active cell (Excel), **OFF 49**
active tabs, **OFF 16**
active window, **IE 40**
adding
3-D pie charts to workbooks, EX 180–192
borders to pages, WD 41–43
borders to pictures, PPT 90–92
Clustered Cylinder charts to worksheets, EX 38–41
content to Title Slide, OFF 40, OFF 43
media to slides, PPT 163–176
notes to slides, PPT 179
records to database tables, AC 23–25, AC 28–29
shapes, PPT 106–107, PPT 109–110
slide transitions, PPT 43–45, PPT 119–120
slides to presentations, PPT 14–15, PPT 21–24
Sparkline charts to worksheets, EX 170–172
text to documents, OFF 20
text to shapes, WD 145–146, PPT 112
totals to reports, AC 57–58
video styles, PPT 172–173
Web sites to list of installed services, WD 122
words to dictionary, EX 113
addition operator (+), EX 76
Add-on: Program that extends the capability of a browser; often used to enhance multimedia. *See also* **plug-in. 61**
Address bar, **OFF 24, IE 14**
Address bar list, **IE 21–22**
Address book: List of names and e-mail addresses, created and stored by a user. **65**
addresses
Internet, 48
IP (Internet Protocol), IE 8
searching Web for street, 76–77
Web, **IE 7**, IE 16
addressing, absolute vs. relative, EX 162–163
Adjust to box, Page Setup dialog box, EX 121
adjustment handles, **WD 144**
Administrator account: Computer account held by computer and network administrators that enables them to access all files and programs on the computer or network, install programs, and specify settings that affect all users on a computer or network. **144**
Adobe Reader, 107, 121
Adobe Systems company profile, 121
advocacy Web sites, 57
Adware: Program that displays an online advertisement in a banner or pop-up window on Web pages, e-mail, or other Internet services. **155, 204, IE 6**, IE 7
Adware remover: Program that detects and deletes adware from a user's computer. **155**
Aero
described, OFF 2–3
switching between programs, OFF 27
aggregate functions, **AC 119**
airbag systems, 20
AirData Web site, 85
alias, **AC 116**
aligning
data in table cells, WD 182
paragraph text, PPT 150–151
text using tab stops, WD 168–170
All Caps effect, PPT 79
All Programs list, OFF 10
Allen, Paul, 29
alternate text, IE 19
Amazon, 29
American Psychological Association. *See* APA
analog formats, **130**
AND criterion, **AC 92**
AND operator, EX 164, **AC 94**
Anderson, Tom, 29
animated GIF files, PPT 175
Animation: Appearance of motion created by displaying a series of still images in sequence. **59, PPT 122**
anti-spam filtering, **205**
Anti-spam program: Program that attempts to remove spam before it reaches a user's inbox. **155, 205**
Antivirus program: Program that protects a computer against viruses by identifying and removing any computer viruses found in memory, on storage media, or on incoming files. **154, 186**
antivirus software, **IE 7**
APA (American Psychological Association), **WD 66**, WD 69
Apple
company profile, 29
iMovie, QuickTime format, 134
iPods, 38
vs. PCs in popularity, 15
Steve Wozniak, 159

Application software: Program designed to make users more productive and/or assist them with personal tasks. **12, 96**
area charts, EX 36
arguments, EX 75
arithmetic operations (table), EX 75
ARPANET, 44
arranging slides, PPT 39–40
art Web sites, 94
artistic effects, adding to pictures, PPT 144–146
assumptions, EX 138
asterisks (*)
converting to bullets, WD 187
and file names, OFF 28
and folder names, OFF 22
multiplication operator, EX 75, EX 76
using in searches, 55
wildcards, AC 83
attaching files to e-mail messages, 76
auction Web sites
described, 88
and pirated software sales, 194
audience, analyzing, APP 1–2
Audio: Music, speech, or any other sound. **60**
adding options, PPT 170–171
inserting files, PPT 167–172
Living Digitally (feature), 38
playing continuously, PPT 171
using in presentations, PPT 138
Audio editing software: Application software that allows a user to modify audio clips, produce studio-quality soundtracks, and add audio to video clips. **110**
Audit trail: Computer file that records both successful and unsuccessful access attempts. **189**
Auto Fill Options button, EX 18, EX 147, EX 148
AutoCalculate area, using, EX 48–49
AutoCorrect, **WD 84**, WD 87–88, PPT 180, EX 9, AC 37
vs. building blocks, WD 174
checking spelling and, EX 113
creating entries, WD 86–87
AutoCorrect Options button, **WD 84–85**
AutoFormat As You Type options (table), WD 162
automatic page breaks, **WD 101**
Automatic update: Operating system feature that automatically provides updates to a program. **143**, 164–165, **IE 7**
automatically updated properties, **WD 49, PPT 45, EX 43, AC 58**
AutoPlay window, opening, OFF 22
AVERAGE function, EX 75, EX 84–85, **EX 89–90**

B

Back button, IE 22–24
Back door: Program or set of instructions in a program that allow users to bypass security controls when accessing a program, computer, or network. **188**
Back up: To make a copy of a file. **196**
files on offsite Internet server, 214
background colors, PPT 80, EX 96–98
background programs, 140
background repagination, **WD 101**
background styles, **PPT 99–101**
backgrounds
formatting slide, PPT 95–101
resetting, PPT 95
backing up, **AC 61**
backslash (\)
and file names, OFF 28
and folder names, OFF 22
BACKSPACE key, correcting mistakes using, PPT 8, EX 8
Backstage view, **OFF 35**
closing, WD 49, EX 43
closing Office files using, OFF 44
creating new Office documents from, OFF 41–43
opening recent Office files using, OFF 45
saving files to SkyDrive from, APP 6–8
Backup: Duplicate or copy of a file, program, or disk that can be used if the original is lost, damaged, or destroyed. **196**
and recovery of databases, AC 60–61
backup copy, **AC 61**
Backup utility: Utility program that allows users to copy, or back up, selected files or an entire hard disk to another storage medium, such as another hard disk, optical disc, USB flash drive, or tape. **152**
bar charts, 104
Basic, Windows 7, OFF 2–3
Berners-Lee, Tim, 49, 71
best fit, **EX 107**
BETWEEN operator, **AC 94**
bevel effects, PPT 90
bibliographical lists
creating, **WD 108**
updating, WD 109–110
bibliography, **WD 106**
bibliography style, changing, WD 89
Bing Maps, 84
Biometric device: Device that authenticates a person's identity by translating a personal characteristic, such as a finger print, into a digital code that then is compared with a digital code stored in a computer verifying a physical or behavioral characteristic. **191**
Biometric payment: Payment method where the customer's fingerprint is read by a fingerprint reader that is linked to a payment method such as a checking account or credit card. **191**
black slides, **PPT 38**
BlackBerry operating system, 149
blank cell, **EX 83**
Blank Database option, OFF 55
blank lines, inserting, WD 7
block letter style, WD 168
Blog: Informal Web site consisting of time-stamped articles, or posts, in a diary or journal format, usually listed in reverse chronological order. Blog is short for Web log. **10, 56**
blogger Web sites, 82
Bloglines, 82
Blogosphere: Worldwide collection of blogs. **56**, 82
Bluetooth, 41
body copy, **WD 5**
bold
cell entries, EX 25, **EX 25**
text, **WD 28**, PPT 19–20
book Web sites, 88
Bookmark: Saved Web address that you access by clicking its name in a list. *See also* **favorite. 51**
Booting: Process of starting or restarting a computer. **138**
borders, **WD 160**
adding to pages, WD 41–43
adding to paragraphs, WD 160
adding to pictures, PPT 90–92
adding to video styles, PPT 173
adding to worksheet cells, EX 97

changing graphic's, WD 154
troubleshooting printing, WD 53
Botnet: Group of compromised computers connected to a network such as the Internet that is used as part of a network that attacks other networks, usually for nefarious purposes. **187**
brain waves and law enforcement, 192
Bricklin, Dan, 121
brightness, adjusting picture, WD 153, **PPT 86–87**
Brin, Sergey, 71
Bring Forward, Bring to Front commands, **PPT 146**
Broadband: High-speed Internet connection provided through cable, DSL, fiber, radio signals, or satellite. **45**, 221
Browser: Application software that allows users to access and view Web pages. *See also* **Web browser**. **49**
browsing the Web, 49–50, IE 15–26
bubble charts, EX 37
Buffer: Segment of memory or storage in which items are placed while waiting to be transferred from an input device or to an output device. **141**
building blocks, **WD 171**
vs. AutoCorrect, WD 174
creating, WD 171–172
inserting, WD 174
modifying, WD 173
bulleted lists, **PPT 15**
creating multi-level, PPT 15–20
formatting paragraphs as, WD 22–23
removing bullets from, WD 23
using, WD 13, PPT 14–15
bullets
applying to paragraphs, WD 186–187
converting asterisks to, WD 187
deleting from slides, PPT 18
burning files to optical discs, 164
business
application software, 96
perspective in digital communications, 168–179
business letters, WD 140, WD 164–188
Business software: Application software that assists people in becoming more effective and efficient while performing their daily business activities. **100**
business/marketing Web sites, 56
business-to-consumer (B2C) e-commerce, 62
Button: Graphical element that is activated to cause a specific action to take place. **98**
See also specific button
Option, EX 82
removing from Quick Access toolbar, OFF 19
on Ribbon, PPT 15
buyer's guide
desktop computers, 222–225
digital cameras, 227–228
notebook computers, 222–225
portable media players, 226–227
smart phones, 225–226

C

Cable Internet service: High-speed Internet access provided through the cable television network via a cable modem. **45**
calculated fields, **AC 115**
calculating
automatic recalculation, EX 75
statistics, AC 119–122
sums, EX 15–16
using AutoCalculate area, EX 48–49
work days, EX 177
calculations
in queries, AC 115–122
in spreadsheets, 103
Calibri font, 102
Cambria theme, WD 17, 102
Camera phone: Phone that can send picture messages. **17**
camera pills, 26
cameras
See also digital camera
digital, 18
selecting and using video, 130–134
Cancel button, OFF 35
capitalization
changing case, WD 18
PowerPoint defaults, PPT 78
CAPTCHA: Completely Automated Public Turing test to tell Computers and Humans Apart; program used by some Web sites to provide further protection for a user's password by verifying that user input is not computer generated. **190**
captions
changing, AC 118
field, AC 16
card readers/writers, 219
careers Web sites, 93
caret (^), exponentiation operator, EX 76
carpal tunnel syndrome (CTS), 198
cars
buying blogs, 128
embedded computers in, 20
sensors in, 115
case, changing, WD 18
cast, color, **PPT 142**
category axis, **EX 40**
category names, **EX 181**
cell, table, **WD 176**
cell phones, personal and business perspectives, 172–173
cell reference (Excel), **OFF 49**
cell references
adding to formulas, EX 80
and assumptions, EX 138
automatic adjustment of, EX 155
copying, EX 81
#REF! error message, EX 156
relative, EX 81
using, EX 90
cell styles, EX 98, EX 177
Cell Styles gallery, EX 52
cells, active (Excel), OFF 49
cells, table
aligning data in, WD 182
end-of-row, end-of-cell marks, **WD 177**
merging, WD 185–186
splitting, WD 186
cells, worksheet
blank cell, **EX 83**
bolding, EX 25
bordering, EX 97
centering data in, EX 98–100
changing style, EX 22–23
clearing, EX 52
copying, moving, EX 153
copying formats, EX 178–179
copying range, across columns, EX 89–90
copying range to nonadjacent destination, EX 151–152
copying to adjacent cells, EX 16–18
correcting errors, EX 49–51
dates, formatting, EX 98–100
described, EX 7
fitting entries in, EX 151
in-cell editing, EX 50
increasing font size, EX 26
indenting text in, EX 150
inserting, EX 154–155

merging, EX 28–29
rotating text in, EX 148
selecting, EX 34–35
spell-checking, EX 194
text alignment in, EX 12
undoing last entry, EX 51–52
values, and charting, EX 37
wrapping text in, EX 72
Cellular radio network: High-speed Internet connection for devices with built-in compatible technology or computers with wireless modems. **46**
centered, **WD 14**
centering
cell entries, EX 28–29
page contents vertically, WD 40
paragraphs, WD 14
tables, WD 183
text, WD 107
Certificate authority: Authorized person or company that issues and verifies digital certificates. **195–196**
changes, undoing, AC 20, AC 25
changing
background colors, EX 96–97
bibliography style, WD 89
color schemes, WD 28–29
currency symbols, AC 20
custom dictionary entries, WD 120
database properties, AC 58–60
document properties, WD 164, PPT 46–50, PPT 120, EX 43–44, EX 73
file names, OFF 52
font color, EX 27
font size, WD 21–22
fonts, WD 17, PPT 101–102, EX 24–25
line spacing, WD 73–74
presentation theme colors, PPT 81
print scaling option, EX 120–121
printers, AC 30
screen resolution, OFF 33–34
slide layouts, PPT 21–24
sources, WD 109
stacking order of objects, PPT 146–147
styles, WD 70–72
text colors, PPT 13
theme colors, WD 141
views, PPT 153–154
WordArt shapes, PPT 115–116
workbook themes, EX 94–95
worksheet names, EX 42–43
character formatting, **WD 12**
characters
bolding, WD 28
inserting special, WD 159
italicizing, WD 24
nonprinting, WD 7
overflow, EX 9
in presentations, formatting, PPT 10–14
shortcut keys for formatting (table), WD 81
tab, WD 168
underlining, WD 27
width, WD 10
chart sheets, **EX 181**
Chart Tools contextual tabs, EX 39
charting
Excel feature, **OFF 46**
PowerPoint feature, OFF 36
and spreadsheet software, 104
charts
embedded, **EX 36**
inserting titles, data labels, EX 183–186
items, EX 181
legends, **EX 41**
planning, EX 5
resizing, EX 40–41
rotating, EX 186–187
zooming, EX 196–198
Chat: Real-time typed conversation that takes place on a computer. **67**
Chat room: Location on an Internet server that permits users to chat with each other. 10, **67**, 118, 176–177
Check Point's ZoneAlarm, 153
Chess Titans, 140
children and the Internet, IE 7
chumby, 42
circle sizing handles, PPT 148, PPT 158
circular references, **EX 75**
citations
described, WD 88
editing, WD 91–92, WD 99, WD 104
editing sources, WD 97–98
inserting, WD 90–91
inserting placeholder for, WD 94, WD 102
Word's resources for, WD 88–89
clear formatting, **WD 161**
clearing
design grid, AC 95
History List, IE 26
worksheets, cell entries, EX 52
Click: To move the mouse pointer to a button or link on the computer screen, and then to press and release the left mouse button. **52, 98**
Click and Type feature, **WD 80**
Clickjacking: Scam in which an object that can be clicked on a Web site, such as a button, image, or link, contains a malicious program. **205**
clip art, **101**, **WD 148**
See also clips, graphics
inserting, WD 148–150
resizing, PPT 33–36
"today's clip" (Microsoft), PPT 26
Clip Art task pane, **PPT 26–30**
Clip art/image gallery: A collection of clip art and photos included with application software. 111, **114**
clip collections, **PPT 27**
Clip Organizer, **WD 148**, WD 154
Clipboard, **IE 39**
clips, **PPT 26**
copying, PPT 154–155
copyright regulations, PPT 27
deleting, PPT 161
inserting into content placeholders, PPT 30–31
modifying, PPT 154–162
moving, PPT 36–37
properties, PPT 29
recoloring, PPT 158–160
Close button, OFF 35
closing
Backstage view, WD 49, EX 43
database tables, AC 23
Database view, AC 59
databases, AC 62
headers, WD 78
Office files, OFF 56
Office files using Backstage view, OFF 44
programs, OFF 35
slides, PPT 38
cloud storage, 196
Clustered Cylinder charts, EX 37
codec (compressor/decompressor), **131–132**, PPT 164
Cold boot: Process of turning on a computer that has been powered off completely. **138**
collaboration using SkyDrive, Web Apps, APP 12
collapsing folders, OFF 26
collections, PPT 26–27

colons (:)
and file names, OFF 28
and folder names, OFF 22
in formulas, EX 85
color, **PPT 10**, EX 27
adjusting picture, PPT 142–144
adjusting video, PPT 164
applying to pie chart slices, EX 190–192
applying to text, WD 25
background. *See* background colors
changing clip object's, PPT 158–160
changing graphic's, WD 151
changing graphic's border, WD 154
changing picture border, PPT 92
changing text, PPT 13
changing theme, WD 141
changing WordArt, PPT 118–119
effects of different, EX 96
font. *See* font color
formatting text, PPT 12
hyperlink, PPT 80
meanings of different, WD 24
setting transparency, WD 152
sheet tabs, EX 193
using in presentations, PPT 139
color cast, **PPT 142**
color saturation, **PPT 142**
color schemes, **WD 28**, **PPT 80**
changing, WD 28–29
template, PPT 80–81
color tone, **PPT 142**
color wheel, using, PPT 142
coloring pictures, PPT 143–144
column boundary, **WD 181**
column charts, 104, EX 37
column heading (Excel), **OFF 49**
columns
adjusting width, EX 33–34, EX 149–150
changing width, EX 107–110
entering titles, EX 10–12, EX 71
formatting, EX 99
inserting in tables, WD 185
report, AC 54–56
resizing datasheet, AC 29–30, AC 42
unhiding, EX 107
Comma Style format, EX 32, EX 100–101
Command: Instruction on a menu that causes a program to perform a specific action. **98**, **OFF 10**
See also specific command
Command bar, **OFF 24**, **IE 14**
commands on, IE 14–15
Home button, IE 32
Command-line interface: Type of user interface in which a user types commands or presses special keys on the keyboard (such as function keys or key combinations) to enter data and instructions. **139**
adding to Quick Access Toolbar, OFF 19
AutoCalculate shortcut menu, EX 48
cell selection (table), EX 35
Command bar, IE 15
Help menu, IE 51
on Ribbon, OFF 14–15
toggle, EX 177
commas (,)
in Excel, EX 13
format symbol, EX 156
comma-separated values (CSV) files, AC 113
common dialog boxes, **OFF 8**
Communications device: Hardware component that enables a computer to send (transmit) and receive data, instructions, and information to and from one or more computers. **6**
compact (database), **AC 61**
company information Web sites, 93
comparison operators, EX 165, **AC 91**
complimentary close (business letter), **WD 167**
compound criterion, AC **92–93**
compressing file size, PPT 31, 126–127
computed fields, **AC 115**
Computer: Electronic device, operating under the control of instructions stored in its own memory, that can accept data, process the data according to specified rules, produce results, and store the results for future use. **3**
Computer addiction: Growing health problem that occurs when the computer consumes someone's entire social life. 7, **199**
Computer crime: Any illegal act involving a computer. **182**
Computer ethics: Moral guidelines that govern the use of computers and information systems. **199**
See also ethics
Computer literacy: Having a current knowledge and understanding of computers and their uses. *See also* **digital literacy**. **3**
computer role-playing game (CRPG), 41
Computer security risk: Any event or action that could cause a loss of or damage to computer hardware, software, data, information, or processing capability. **182**
Internet and network attacks, 184–189
computer software, 11–13
computer virus, 98, 184, **IE 7**
Computer vision syndrome: Eyestrain due to prolonged computer usage. **198**
Computer-aided design (CAD) software: Sophisticated type of application software that assists a professional user in creating engineering, architectural, and scientific designs. **109**, 120
Computer-aided manufacturing (CAM): Use of computers to assist with manufacturing processes such as fabrication and assembly. **27**
Computer-based training (CBT): Type of education in which students learn by using and completing exercises with instructional software. Also called computer-aided instruction. **115**
computers
advantages and disadvantages, 7–8
applications in society, 24–28
buyer's guide, 217–225
categories of, 13–20
changing screen resolution, OFF 31–35
components of, 4–7
and construction industry, 120
coordinating tasks, 141–142
embedded, 19
examples of usage, 20–24
health. *See* health
information accuracy, 200
logging on to, OFF 6–7
preventing virus infections, 154
security. *See* security
starting, shutting down, 138
use generally, 2–4
computing, green, **PPT 51**, **AC 30**
conditional formatting
applying, EX 104–105
operators, EX 107
rules for, EX 104
configuring devices, 142

connecting
 to online location, APP 3–4
 to the Internet, 45–48, **142**
conserving ink, toner, EX 45
constants, replacing formulas with, EX 165
construction industry, and computers, 120
consumer-to-consumer (C2C) e-commerce, 63
contact lenses monitor glaucoma, 143
Content aggregator: Business that gathers and organizes Web content and then distributes, or feeds, the content to subscribers for free or a fee. **58**
Content filtering: Process of restricting access to certain material on the Web. **207**
content placeholders
 inserting clips into, PPT 30–31
 inserting pictures into, PPT 84–85
content sharing, personal and business perspective, 178–179
contrast (in pictures), adjusting, WD 153, **PPT 86–87**
Convergence: Term used to refer to the trend of manufacturers offering computers and devices with technologies that overlap. **14**
converting
 asterisks (*) to bullets, WD 187
 colors to hues, grayscale, PPT 142
 fields to regular text, WD 110
 hyperlinks to regular text, WD 163
Cookie: Small text file that a Web server stores on a computer. **203–204**
cooking Web sites, 90
copied, **IE 39**
copy and paste method, **IE 39**
copy area, **EX 17**
copying, **WD 113**
 cell's format, EX 178–179
 cells to adjacent cells, EX 16–18
 clips, PPT 155–156
 formatting using Format Painter, PPT 105
 formulas using fill handles, EX 80–81
 formulas with absolute cell references, EX 168
 graphics, WD 155
 and pasting from other programs, EX 153
 and pasting shapes, PPT 108–109, PPT 112
 and pasting text, IE 39, WD 113–114
 pictures from Web pages, IE 44–45
 range of cells across columns, EX 89–90, EX 151–152
 slides, PPT 38–39
 Sparkline charts, EX 171–172
 text from Web pages, IE 42–43
 worksheet cells, EX 153
copyleft, 209
Copyright: Exclusive rights given to authors and artists to duplicate, publish, and sell their materials. **201**, PPT 84
copyright regulations, IE 36, PPT 27, PPT 76, PPT 83
corporate blogs, 82
correcting
 automatically, and undoing, WD 87
 errors, EX 49–51
 mistakes while typing, PPT 8
 pictures, PPT 86–87
COUNT function, AC 119
counting words, WD 101
CPU (central processing unit): Electronic component on a computer's motherboard that interprets and carries out the basic instructions that operate the computer. *See also* **processor**. **6**
Cracker: Someone who accesses a computer or network illegal with the intent of destroying data, stealing information, or other malicious action. **182**
Create: To enter text or numbers, insert images, and perform other tasks with a document using an input device such as a keyboard, mouse, or digital pen. **102**
creating
 AutoCorrect entries, WD 86–87
 backgrounds from pictures, PPT 97–98
 bibliographical lists, WD 108–109
 building blocks, WD 171–172
 business letters, WD 164–188
 crosstab queries, AC 123–126
 database records, AC 29–30
 database tables, AC 32–37
 databases, OFF 55–56, AC 13–14
 documents, OFF 20
 file from existing file, WD 165–166
 folders, OFF 22–23
 folders within folders, OFF 24–25
 footers, WD 77
 forms, AC 48–50
 forms for queries, AC 108–110
 letterhead, WD 142–164
 logos, PPT 113
 new paragraphs, OFF 20
 Office documents, OFF 41–43, OFF 47
 paragraphs, WD 6
 parameter queries, AC 86–89
 Publisher documents, OFF 60–61
 queries, AC 77–82
 reports, AC 51–53
 series of month names, EX 145–148
 Sparkline charts, EX 170–171
 text slide with multi-level bulleted list, PPT 15–20
 Title Slides, PPT 77–80
 top-values queries, AC 99–100
criteria
 determining query, AC 80–82
 using in queries, AC 85–86
criterion, **AC 46**
 adding to join queries, AC 114–115
 special, AC 94
 using compound, AC 92–93
 using in calculating statistics, AC 121–122
 using in queries, AC 46–47
 using numbers in, AC 90
crosstab queries, creating, AC 123–126
CTS (carpal tunnel syndrome), 198
Currency data type, **AC 9**, AC 20
Currency Style format, EX 102–103, EX 174, EX 179
currency symbols, AC 20
current date
 inserting in documents, WD 170–171
 inserting in handouts, PPT 184
custom dictionary, WD 120, **PPT 180**
custom layouts, **PPT 21**
Custom software: Software that performs functions specific to a business or industry, developed by a user or at a user's request. **96**
customer behavior and conversations, monitoring, 202
customizing
 home pages, IE 10
 Navigation Pane, AC 127
 Quick Access Toolbar, OFF 19
 Ribbon, OFF 49
 tab stops, WD 169–170
cutting
 cells, ranges, EX 154
 described, **WD 113**
cyberbullying, 69

Cybercrime: Online or Internet-based illegal acts. **182**
Cyberextortionist: Someone who uses e-mail as a vehicle for extortion. **182**
Cyberterrorist: Someone who uses the Internet or network to destroy or damage computers for political reasons. **183**
cylinder charts, EX 37

D

Data: Collection of unprocessed items, which can include text, numbers, images, audio, and video. **4**
aligning in table cells, WD 182
centering in cells, EX 98–100
deleting table, WD 185
entering in tables, WD 177–179
exporting from Access, AC 110
exporting to text files, AC 114
importing into Access, AC 38–41
sorting in queries, AC 94
in what-if analyses, EX 200
data types, AC 5, **AC 9**
Database: Collection of data organized in a manner that allows access, retrieval, and use of that data. **104, OFF 53, AC 2**
backup and recovery of, AC 60–61
changing structure, AC 20–26
closing, AC 62
compacting, repairing, AC 61
correcting structure errors, AC 37
creating, OFF 55–56, AC 13–15
database requirements, AC 6–7
design guidelines, AC 5–6
forms, using, AC 48–51
opening, AC 27, AC 62
opening existing, OFF 57
queries, using, AC 43–48
relational, **AC 3**
storage location for, AC 13
tables. *See* database tables
Database Design Language (DBDL), **AC 9**
database management systems (DBMSs), **OFF 53**
database management systems (DMBSs), **AC 2**
database objects, renaming, AC 62
database properties, **AC 58–60**
Database software: Application software used to create, access, and manage a database; add, change, and delete data in the database; sort and retrieve data from the database; and create forms and reports using the data in the database. **104**
overview, 104–105
database tables
adding records to, AC 23–25, AC 28–29
closing, AC 23
creating, AC 15–20, AC 32–37
defining fields in, AC 16–20
joining, AC 100–108
naming, AC 16
printing, AC 31–32
removing from queries, AC 79
saving, AC 21
Database view, **AC 15**, AC 59
datasheets, **AC 23**, AC 29–30, AC 42
date formats, EX 72
date line (business letter), **WD 167**
date stamps, **EX 159**
dates
cell formats, EX 93
entering system, EX 159–160
formatting, EX 98–100, EX 161
inserting current, in documents, WD 170–171
inserting current, in handouts, PPT 184
MLA format, WD 79
two-digit years, EX 72
work days calculations, EX 177
debugging, **EX 119**
decision-making using IF function, EX 164–166
Decrypt: Process of deciphering encrypted data into a readable form. **195**
definition updates, **IE 7**
Defragmenting: Reorganizing a disk so that the files are stored in contiguous sectors, thus speeding up disk access and the performance of the entire computer. **152**
deleting
AutoCorrect entries, WD 87
bullets on slides, PPT 18
clip objects, PPT 161
databases, AC 62
fields (database), AC 20
files, folders, OFF 64–65
notes, WD 100
placeholder text, PPT 41–42
placeholders, PPT 149
records (database), AC 26
shapes, WD 144
slides, PPT 152
table data, WD 185
text, WD 47, PPT 41
worksheet cells, EX 154–155
delimited files, **AC 113**
delimiter, **AC 113**
demoting text, **PPT 17–18**
Denial of service attack: Assault on a computer or network whose purpose is to disrupt computer access to an Internet service such as the Web or e-mail. *See also* **DoS attack. 187**
Department of Homeland Security, 208
design
aesthetics vs. function, EX 66
database, AC 5–6
grid, clearing, AC 95
Modernism's influence upon graphic, PPT 84
page enhancements, WD 40
workplace, and ergonomics, 199
Design view, **AC 15**
adding fields to design grid, AC 79–80
checking database structure in, AC 22
creating database tables in, AC 33–37
creating queries in, AC 78–79
opening, AC 24
viewing tables in, AC 21–22
Desktop: On-screen work area that has a graphical user interface. **98,** OFF 7
Desktop computer: Computer designed so the system unit, input devices, output devices, and any other devices fit entirely on or under a desk or table. **16,** 20, **98**
Desktop publishing (DTP) software: Application software used by professional designers to create sophisticated documents that can contain text, graphics, and many colors. **109**
destination area, **EX 17**, EX 151–152
developer, **13**
development cycle, worksheet, EX 4
devices, configuring, 142
DeWolfe, Chris, 29
Dialog Box Launcher, **OFF 15**
dialog boxes
common, **OFF 8**
navigating, OFF 30

Dial-up access: Internet access that takes place when the modem in your computer connects to the Internet via a standard telephone line that transmits data and information using an analog (continuous wave pattern) signal. **46**, 221
dictionaries
 adding words to, EX 113
 main and custom, WD 120–121
Digital camera: Mobile device that allows users to take pictures and stores the photographed images digitally, instead of on traditional film. **18**, 20
 buyer's guide, 227–228
Digital certificate: A notice that guarantees a user or a Web site is legitimate. **195**
digital communications (feature), 167–180
Digital forensics: The discovery, collection, and analysis of evidence found on computers and networks. **192**
digital formats, **130**
Digital literacy: Having a current knowledge and understanding of computers and their uses. *See also* **computer literacy. 3**
Digital rights management: Strategy designed to prevent illegal distribution of movies, music, and other digital content. **201**
Digital signature: Encrypted code that a person, Web site, or organization attaches to an electronic message to verify the identity of the message sender. **195**
digital video capture devices, 219
digital video technology, 39, **129**, 130–134
dimension (of table), **WD 176**
disabling database content, AC 27
Disc burning software: Utility program that writes text, graphics, audio, and video files to a recordable or rewritable CD, DVD, or Blu-ray Disc. **157**
Disk cleanup: Utility that searches for and removes unnecessary files. **152**
Disk defragmenter: Utility that reorganizes the files and unused space on a computer's hard disk so that the operating system accesses data more quickly and programs run faster. **152**
Disney.com, IE 6
display area, **IE 12**
displaying
 Document Information Panel, EX 44
 formatting marks, WD 7, WD 70, WD 140
 hidden windows, OFF 67
 home pages, IE 32
 Paste Options menu, WD 114
 Picture Tools Format tab, PPT 89
 Ribbon, OFF 16–17
 rulers, WD 5, WD 82
 shortcut menus, OFF 18
 Start menu, OFF 10–11
 user icons, OFF 6
 values as percentages, EX 103
 Web pages, IE 41
 Web pages in full screen mode, IE 12
 Web pages using Favorites Center, IE 33
 Web pages using History List, IE 26–30
Distance learning: Delivery of education at one location while the learning takes place at other locations. **119**
distributing
 database objects, AC 30
 video, 134
 worksheets, EX 45
division operator (/), EX 76
Document Information Panel, **WD 49, PPT 46–47,** EX 43–44
Document management software: Application software that provides a means for sharing, distributing, and searching through documents by converting them into a format that can be viewed by any user. **107**
document properties, **WD 49, PPT 45, EX 43**
 changing, WD 49–50, WD 164, PPT 46–47, PPT 120, EX 73
 collected automatically, EX 44
 printing, WD 123, EX 45, EX 117
document themes, **PPT 5**
 choosing, PPT 5–6
 formatting specific elements, PPT 9
document window
 components, OFF 12–16
 described, **OFF 12**
 opening new blank document in, WD 166
documents, OFF 20
 See also publications, text
 changing settings, WD 69
 creating from Backstage view, OFF 41–43
 creating new, OFF 20
 creating Publisher, OFF 60–61
 developing, 102
 entering text in, WD 5–8
 grammar-checking, WD 9–10
 inserting current date in, WD 170–171
 inserting pictures into, WD 31–32
 inserting text in, WD 46
 margin settings, WD 141
 navigating, WD 11
 opening from PowerPoint, PPT 50–51
 printing, WD 51–52
 printing as XPS files, WD 52
 quitting Office program with open, OFF 35
 requirements, **EX 3**
 revising, WD 44–48
 saving, WD 12
 saving, organizing, OFF 21–30, OFF 51–52
 saving with same name, PPT 95
 saving WordPad, IE 46–47
 scrolling through, WD 112
 spell-checking, WD 9–10
 tabbed vs. overlapping windows, AC 58
 WordPad. *See* WordPad
 zooming, WD 33, WD 36
.docx files, OFF 21, WD 14
Dolby, Ray, 38
dollar signs ($)
 in Excel, EX 13
 fixed and floating, **EX 100**
 format symbol, EX 156–157
domain highlighting, **IE 14**
Domain name: Text version of an IP address. **48, IE 8**
 organizations, and their extensions, IE 8
Do-Not-Track lists, 53
Doors transition, PPT 43–44
DoS attack: Assault on a computer or network whose purpose is to disrupt computer access to an Internet service such as the Web or e-mail. *See also* **denial of service attack. 187**
double-space, **WD 72**
doughnut charts, EX 37
download, **WD 31**

Downloading: Process of a computer receiving information, such as a Web page, from a server on the Internet. **50**
files from SkyDrive, APP 9–12
government's taxing of media, 157
drag and drop, **PPT 39–40**, **EX 153**
drag-and-drop
dragging ranges, EX 156
moving, copying cells with, EX 153
moving, resizing windows, OFF 66–67
drag-and-drop editing, **WD 47**, WD 48
drawing
PowerPoint feature, OFF 36
shapes, PPT 112
tables, WD 177
drawing objects, **WD 142**
Driver: Small program that tells an operating system how to communicate with a specific device. **142**
drives, organizing files and folders on, OFF 21–30
driving directions, searching Web for, 76
DSL: Type of digital technology that provides high-speed Internet connections using regular copper telephone lines. **45**

E

Ease of Access Center, OFF 6
eBay, 71, 194
E-book: Electronic version of a printed book, readable on computers and other digital devices. Also called a digital book. **17**
E-book reader: Short for electronic book reader; handheld device that is used primarily for reading e-books. **17**
E-commerce: Short for electronic commerce; a business transaction that occurs over an electronic network such as the Internet. 23, **62**
Edit: To make changes to the existing content of a document. **102**
Edit mode, **EX 50**
editing
citations, WD 91–92, WD 99, WD 104
drag-and-drop, **WD 47**, WD 48
headers, WD 76
in-cell, EX 50
and processing digital video, 129–134
sources, WD 92, WD 97–98, WD 103
videos, 132–133
education
application software, 96, 111
computer applications in, 24–25
computers and, 158
word processing programs, and laziness, 101
Educational software: Application software that teaches a particular skill. **115**
educational Web sites, 57, 86
effects, **PPT 113**
See also specific effect
fill, **PPT 99**
picture, PPT 89–91
text, WD 19
selecting options, PPT 119
E-learning: Short for electronic learning; delivery of education via some electronic method such as the Internet, networks, or CDs/DVDs. **119**, 158
electronic mail, **OFF 58**
electronic profiles, 203
Electronic storefront: Online business a customer visits that contains product descriptions, graphics, and a shopping cart. **62–63**
electronics Web sites, 88
e-mail, 63, 118, **OFF 58**
attaching files to messages, 76
business perspective, 169
personal perspective, 168
sending message using Outlook, 64
and viruses, 65
E-mail address: Combination of a user name and a domain name that identifies a user so he or she can receive Internet e-mail. **64**
E-mail filtering: Service that blocks e-mail messages from designated sources. **205**
e-mail messages, and viruses, 185
E-mail program: Software used to create, send, receive, forward, store, print, and delete e-mail messages. **63**–64
e-mailing pictures, IE 37
e-mailing PowerPoint presentations, OFF 36
embedded charts, **EX 36**
Embedded computer: Special-purpose computer that functions as a component in a larger product. 15, **19**–20
Embedded Linux, 149
Embedded operating system: The operating system that resides on a ROM chip inside most PDAs and small devices. 145, **149**
embedding videos within PowerPoint, PPT 138
Emoticons: Symbols used on the Internet to express emotion. **69, 76–77**
Employee monitoring: The use of computers to observe, record, and review an employee's use of a computer, including communications such as e-mail messages, keyboard activity (used to measure productivity), and Web sites visited. **207**
Encryption: Process of converting readable data into unreadable characters to prevent unauthorized access. 144, **195**
Encryption algorithm: Set of steps that can convert readable plaintext into unreadable ciphertext. **195**
Encryption key: Set of characters that the originator of the encrypted data uses to encrypt the plaintext and the recipient of the data uses to decrypt the ciphertext. **195**
endnotes, **WD 93**, WD 100–101
end-of-cell mark, **WD 177**
end-of-row mark, **WD 177**
end-user license agreement (EULA), 194
ENERGY STAR program: Program developed by the United States Department of Energy (DOE) and the United States Environmental Protection Agency (EPA) to help reduce the amount of electricity used by computers and related devices. **201**
energy-saving tips, PPT 2
Enhanced ScreenTips, **OFF 15**
Enter box, EX 9
Enterprise computing: Term large companies use to refer to the use of a huge network of computers that meets their diverse computing needs. **23, 24**
Enterprise user: Computer user working for a business that has hundreds or thousands of employees or customers that work in or do business with offices across a region, the country, or the world. **23**

Entertainment software: Application software, such as interactive games, videos, and other programs designed to support a hobby or provide amusement and enjoyment. **116**
envelopes, addressing and printing, WD 189
Environmental Defense Fund Web site, 85
environmental Web sites, 85
equal sign (=) in formulas, EX 75, EX 76
e-retail, example, 62
ergonomics, **199**, OFF 4
error messages
  interpreting, EX 169
  #REF!, EX 156
errors
  See also mistakes
  correcting, EX 49–51
  correcting text input, OFF 20, WD 6
  correcting while typing, PPT 8
  misspellings, EX 112–116
  mistyped Web addresses, IE 17
  spelling, automatic correction, WD 9
  undoing actions, WD 23
Ethical Hacker, The, 128
Euro symbol (€), AC 20
evaluating presentations, PPT 189
Excel, **OFF 46**
  See also worksheets
  creating documents from Windows Explorer, OFF 47
  features and operations, OFF 49–52
  Help, EX 51
  Option buttons, EX 82
  quitting, EX 47, EX 53
  saving files to SkyDrive from, APP 6–8
  spreadsheets, 117
  starting, EX 70
  Web App, APP 8
Excel window, OFF 49–50
Execute: Process of a computer carrying out the instructions in a program. **12**
expanding folders, OFF 26
exploded Pie charts, **EX 181**, EX 190–191
Explorer bar, IE 28
exponentiation operator (^), EX 76
export, **AC 110**
exporting
  data from Access, AC 110
  favorites, IE 31
  to text files, AC 113–114
Expression Builder, using, AC 115–116
extensions, **IE 8**
external hard disks, 219

F

Facebook, 71
FAQ: List that helps a user find answers to commonly asked questions. **11**
Favorite: Saved Web address that you access by clicking its name in a list. *See also* **bookmark. 51, IE 30**
  importing, exporting, IE 31
  keeping track of, IE 30–35
Favorites area, **OFF 24**
Favorites bar, **IE 13**
Favorites Center, IE 30–31, IE 33
Fiber to the Premises (FTTP): Technology that uses fiber-optic cable to provide high-speed Internet access to home and business users. **45**
fields (database), **AC 3**
  calculated, computed, **AC 115**
  defining, AC 16–20
  determining, AC 8–9
  planning, AC 5
fields, converting to regular text, WD 110
File: Named collection of stored data, instructions, or information. **98–99, OFF 7, EX 29, AC 13**
  attaching to e-mail messages, 76
  backing up on offsite Internet server, 214
  burning to optical discs, 164
  closing, OFF 56
  compressing size of, PPT 31
  creating new, from existing, WD 165–166
  creating through Backstage view, OFF 42
  deleting, OFF 64–65
  downloading from SkyDrive, APP 9–12
  exporting, AC 110–113
  fixed-width, AC 114
  inserting audio, PPT 167–170
  inserting video, PPT 163–164
  locating deleted, 150
  moving, OFF 64
  opening existing Office, OFF 57
  opening recent Office, using Backstage view, OFF 45
  organizing, WD 12, PPT 14, EX 20, AC 27
  renaming, OFF 63
  saving, organizing, OFF 21–30
  saving in application software, 126
  saving in folders, OFF 27–28
  saving presentation, OFF 41
  saving to SkyDrive, APP 6–8
  zipped, 126–127, **156**
File compression utility: Utility program that shrinks the size of a file(s), so the file takes up less storage space than the original file. **156**
file format, **131**
  .docx files, OFF 21, WD 14
  recognized by PowerPoint (table), PPT 31
file management, 143, **OFF 62**, OFF 63–65
File manager: Utility that performs functions related to file and disk management. **151**
file names, **OFF 21**, OFF 52
file specification, **IE 9**
File Transfer Protocol (FTP), **APP 3**
Fill Color button, EX 177
fill effects, **PPT 99**
fill handles, **EX 17**, EX 148
  clearing cell entries using, EX 52
  copying cells using, EX 16–18
  copying formulas using, EX 80–81
  copying functions using, EX 89–90
  creating series using, EX 145–148
fills, **PPT 95**
  applying WordArt text, PPT 117
  custom sequences, EX 149
  inserting texture, PPT 95–97
finance
  computer applications in, 25
  software, personal, 112
  Web sites, 86
Find and Replace dialog box, WD 117–118
Find Next button, Find and Replace dialog box, WD 117
finding
  See also searching
  formatting, WD 117
  previously displayed Web pages, IE 21–26
  and replacing text, WD 115–116, PPT 176–177
fingerprint readers, 191, 219, 225
Firewall: Hardware and/or software that protects a network's resources from intrusion by users on another network such as the Internet. 153, 186, **188–189**

fireworks software, 108
FIRST function, AC 119
First Line Indent marker, **WD 83**
first-line indent, **WD 83**
fixed dollar signs, **EX 100**
Fixed wireless: High-speed Internet connection that uses a dish-shaped antenna on a house or business to communicate with a tower location via radio signals. **45**
fixed-width files, exporting, AC 114
Flash Player, 61
Flesch-Kincaid Grade Level score, WD 120
flipping graphics, WD 157
floating dollar signs, **EX 100**, EX 102–103, EX 174
floating objects, **WD 147**
flyers, 113, WD 2
Folder: Specific named location on a storage medium that contains related documents. **151, OFF 10**
  creating, OFF 22–25
  deleting, OFF 65
  expanding, collapsing, navigating, OFF 26
  Microsoft Office, OFF 11
  OneNote, **OFF 62**
  organizing, WD 12, PPT 14, EX 20, AC 27
  saving, organizing files in, OFF 21–30, OFF 41, OFF 44
  SkyDrive, APP 7
folder windows, **OFF 24**
Font: Name assigned to a specific design of characters. **102, WD 12, PPT 10, EX 22**
  bold, PPT 19–20
  changing, WD 17, WD 147, EX 24–25
  changing caption, PPT 101–102
  increasing size, PPT 20
  themes and, EX 22
  using in worksheets, EX 22
font color, **EX 22**, EX 27
Font Color button, EX 177
Font Color gallery, EX 27
Font size: Size of the characters in a particular font. **102, WD 12, EX 22**
  changing, WD 16, WD 21–22
  decreasing, PPT 104, EX 96
  increasing, WD 146, PPT 11, EX 26
Font style: Font design, such as bold, italic, and underline, that can add emphasis to a font. **102, EX 34**
Fonts gallery, EX 24
Food Network Web site, 90
footers, **WD 75**
footnotes, **WD 93**, WD 100–101
foreground programs, 140
foreign languages, inserting synonyms, PPT 178
Format: To change a document's appearance. **102, WD 12, PPT 10, EX 20**
  analog and digital, 130
  assigning to nonadjacent ranges, EX 174–175
  date, EX 72
  selecting appropriate, EX 102
  style, WD 70
Format Background dialog box, PPT 97
Format Cells dialog box, EX 174, EX 175
format described, **PPT 10, EX 20**
Format Painter, **PPT 101**
  copying cell formats using, EX 178–179
  formatting nonadjacent ranges, EX 179
  using, PPT 105
Format Shape dialog box launcher, PPT 111
format symbols, EX **156**–157
formatting
  AutoFormat As You Type options (table), WD 162
  background picture, text fill transparency, PPT 98
  characters in presentations, PPT 10–14
  clearing, WD 161
  conditional. *See* conditional formatting
  dates, EX 161
  error checking, EX 113
  finding specific, WD 117
  numbers in worksheets, EX 31–33
  numbers using Ribbon, EX 100–103
  paragraphs, WD 12–30
  paragraphs as bulleted lists, WD 22–23
  picture, discarding, WD 38
  slide backgrounds, PPT 95–101
  Sparkline charts, EX 171–172
  text colors, PPT 12
  text using Format Painter, PPT 105
  text using Mini toolbar, WD 26
  title and content text, PPT 101–104
  words, PPT 20
  works cited page to MLA style, WD 111
  worksheets, EX 20–34, EX 92–99
formatting marks, displaying, **WD 7**, WD 70, WD 140
forms, **AC 48, AC 108**
  creating and using, AC 48–50
  for queries, AC 108–110
Formula AutoComplete list, EX 84
formula bar (Excel), EX 8, **OFF 50**, OFF 51
formulas, **EX 74**
  with absolute cell references, copying, EX 168
  adding cell references to, EX 80
  assumptions, EX 138
  checking for correctness, EX 170
  copying, EX 80–81
  entering, EX 74–80
  error checking, EX 113
  error messages, EX 169
  examples of (table), EX 77
  and goal seeking, EX 200–202
  replacing with constants, EX 165
  using absolute cell references, EX 162–164
formulas version of worksheets, **EX 119**
  printing, EX 119–120
  switching to values version, EX 167
Forward button, **IE 13**, IE 22–24
frame rate correction, **132**
Freeware: Copyrighted software provided at no cost to a user by an individual or a company that retains all rights to the software. **97**
freeze the titles, **EX 157–159**
Fry's Web site, 88
FTP: Internet standard that permits file uploading and downloading with other computers on the Internet. **68**, 118

G

galleries, **OFF 14**
Game console: Mobile computing device designed for single-player or multiplayer video games. 15, **18, 41**
game software, 116
gaming, 41
Gates, Bill, 29
Geschke, Charles, 121
GIF (Graphics Interchange Format), 59, PPT 163, PPT 175
glaucoma monitored by contact lenses, 143

glow effects, PPT 89–90
GNU/Linux Project, 209
Go To list, **IE 21**
goal seeking, **EX 200**, EX 200–202
Google, 54, 71
Google Android, 149
Google Checkout, 63
Google Docs, 57, 117
Google Earth, 117
government
computer applications in, 25
and Do-Not-Track lists, 53
laws concerning privacy (fig.), 206
security. *See* security
taxing downloads, 157
Web sites, 87
gradient fills, **PPT 95**
grammar-checking documents, WD 9–10, WD 118–119
Graphic: Digital representation of nontext information such as a drawing, chart, or photo. *See also* **graphical image. 58**
graphic design, Modernism's influence upon, PPT 84
Graphical user interface (GUI): Type of user interface that allows a user to interact with software using text, graphics, and visual images, such as icons. **11, 139**
graphics
application software, 96
changing border color, WD 154
changing color of, WD 151
copying, WD 155
flipping, WD 157
moving, WD 155, WD 156
planning, WD 31
resizing, WD 34–36, WD 150–151, PPT 93–94
rotating, PPT 86
selection rectangle, sizing handles, WD 32
setting transparent color in, WD 152
graphics software, 108–110
grayscale, **PPT 142**
Great Outdoors Web site, IE 15
greater than symbol (>)
and file names, OFF 28
and folder names, OFF 22
Green computing: Computer usage that reduces the electricity and environmental waste involved in using a computer. **7**, 128, 166, **201**, 216, PPT 51 , AC 30
gridlines (Excel), **OFF 49**
group calculation, **AC 116**
grouping, **AC 122**
and ungrouping clips, PPT 157–158
using in queries, AC 122–123
groups
on Ribbon, **OFF 14**, OFF 17, PPT 15
selecting word, PPT 19
Grow Font button, WD 146
guidelines, project planning, APP 1–2

H

Hacker: Someone who accesses a computer or network illegally. **182**
Handheld computer: Computer small enough to fit in one hand. *See also* **Ultra-Mobile PC (UMPC). 17**
handheld game consoles, 41
handouts
previewing, printing, PPT 184–186
using, PPT 139
Hanging Indent marker, **WD 109**
hanging indents, **WD 109**
hard copy, **IE 47**
hard disks, 219
hard page breaks, **WD 106**
hardcopy, **WD 51**
Hardware: Electric, electronic, and mechanical components contained in a computer. **4**
Hardware theft: The act of stealing computer equipment. **193**
Hardware vandalism: The act of defacing or destroying computer equipment. **193**
headers, **WD 75**, **EX 114**
closing, WD 78
inserting page numbers, WD 77
worksheet, EX 115–116
headings
cell style, EX 30
report column, AC 54–56
worksheet column, row, OFF 49
headlines, **WD 5**
head-mounted display (HMD), 39
health
See also medicine
concerns of computer use, 198–199
preventing wrist injuries, OFF 4
health care, computer applications in, 25–26
health Web sites, 92
healthfinder.gov Web site, 92
Help
Access, AC 62
Excel, EX 51
Internet Explorer (IE), IE 49–51
obtaining, PPT 45
obtaining using links, OFF 70
searching for, OFF 68–70
Table of Contents, OFF 71
Windows 7, OFF 5
Windows Help and Support, OFF 73–74
Word, OFF 66, WD 35
Hibernate: Operating system function that saves any open documents and programs to a hard disk before removing power from the computer. **138**
hiding
formatting marks, WD 7, WD 156
Mini toobar, OFF 15
rows, EX 111
rulers, WD 18
highlighting, domain, **IE 14**
History List
described, **IE 26**
displaying Web pages using, IE 27–30
home application software, 96, 111
Home button, Command bar, IE 32
Home design/landscaping software: Application software that assists users with the design, remodeling, or improvement of a home, deck, or landscape. 111, **115**
Home page: First page that a Web site displays. **50, IE 10**
Home user: User who spends time on a computer at home. **20, 21**
how data travels the Internet, 47
living digitally, 42
horizontal ruler, **WD 82**
Hot spots: Public locations, such as airports, hotels, schools, and coffee shops, that provide Wi-Fi Internet connections to users with mobile computers or devices. **46**
HowStuffWorks Web site, 90
HTML (Hypertext Markup Language), **IE 9**
HTTP (Hypertext Transfer Protocol), **IE 8**
HTTPS (HTTP secure), IE 8
Hubble Space Telescope, 59
Hyperlink: Built-in connection to another related Web page or part of a Web page. *See also* **link. 52, IE 5**
color, PPT 80
converting to regular text, WD 163
described, **IE 5**
hypermedia, **IE 5**

Hypertext Markup Language (HTML), **IE 9**
Hypertext Transfer Protocol (HTTP), **IE 8**
hyphens, nonbreaking, **WD 175**

I

Icon: Small image displayed on a computer screen that represents a program, a document, or some other object. **98**
See also specific icon
identifiers, unique, **AC 3**
identify theft, 10, 192
identifying and removing redundancy, AC 10–11
IE. *See* Internet Explorer (IE)
IF function
described, **EX 164**
nested, **EX 170**
using, EX 164–166
IFERROR function, EX 170
illustration software, 109
Image editing software: Application software that provides the capabilities of paint software and also includes the capability to enhance and modify existing images and pictures. **109**
Image viewer: Utility program that allows users to display, copy, and print the contents of a graphics file. **151**
images, accuracy of, 200
iMovie, 134
importing, **AC 38**
data into Access, AC 38–41
favorites, IE 31
IN operator, **AC 94**
inactive window, **IE 40**
in-cell editing, **EX 50**, EX 51
indents
first-line paragraph, WD 83
hanging, WD 109
text in cells, EX 150
industry information Web sites, 93
Information: Processed data that conveys meaning and is useful to people. **4**
accuracy of, 200
safeguarding personal, 203
information literacy, 79
Information privacy: Right of individuals and companies to deny or restrict the collection and use of information about them. **202**
Information processing cycle: Series of input, process, output, and storage activities performed by a computer. **4**
Information theft: Computer security risk that occurs when someone steals personal or confidential information. **195**
informational Web sites, 56
ink, conserving printer, WD 51, WD 122, WD 188
inline objects, **WD 147**
Input device: Any hardware component that allows users to enter data and instructions into a computer. **4**
Insert Function box, EX 86–87, EX 89
Insert mode, **WD 46**, **EX 50**
Insert Options button, EX 159
inserting
audio files, PPT 167–170
blank line, WD 7
building blocks, WD 174
citation placeholders, WD 94
citations, WD 90–91
clip art, WD 148–150
clips into content placeholders, PPT 30–31
clips into slides, PPT 29–30
columns in tables, WD 185
current date in documents, WD 170–171
fields (database), AC 20
footnote reference marks, WD 93
movie clips, PPT 174–175
multimedia into presentations, PPT 162
page numbers, WD 77
photographs into slides, PPT 32
pictures in documents, WD 31–32
pictures in presentations, PPT 82–86
pictures into slides, PPT 141–142
pictures to creating backgrounds, PPT 97–98
rows in tables, WD 184
shapes, WD 142–144
slide numbers, PPT 182–184
special characters, WD 159
symbols, WD 158–159
synonyms, WD 118, PPT 178
tables, WD 176–177
text boxes into slides, PPT 141
text in documents, WD 46
texture fills, PPT 95–97
video files, PPT 163–164
watermarks, PPT 82
WordArt, PPT 114
worksheet cells, EX 154–155
insertion point, OFF 20, WD 11, EX 8
inside address (business letter), **WD 167**, WD 171
installed services, adding Web sites to list of, WD 122
Installing: Process of setting up software to work with the computer, printer, and other hardware components. **12**–13
Instant message: Real-time Internet communication where you exchange messages with other connected users. **17**
Instant messaging (IM): Real-time Internet communications service that notifies a user when one or more people are online and then allows the user to exchange messages or files or join a private chat room with those people. 10, **66**, 67, 118, 170–171
Intellectual property rights: Rights to which creators are entitled for their work. **201**
Internet: Worldwide collection of networks that connects millions of businesses, government agencies, educational institutions, and individuals. **8**, **44**, **IE 3**, IE 4
attacks, 184–189
connecting to, 45–48, 142
and cyberbullying, 69
how home user's data travels the, 47
overview, 8–11, 44–45
popularity of, 21
security concerns, IE 6–7
traffic effects from social networking sites, Internet video, 61
usage guidelines, IE 2–3
viruses on the, 98
Internet backbone: Major carriers of network traffic on the Internet. **47**, **IE 4**
Internet Explorer (IE), **IE 10**, 121
Help, IE 49–51
market share, 49
printing Web pages in, IE 47–49
quitting, IE 52
saving information obtained with, IE 35–38
starting, IE 11–12
Suggested Sites feature, IE 30
Internet Explorer menu icon, **IE 13**
Internet Explorer window, IE **12**–14

Internet Protocol (IP) address, IE 8
Internet Public Library, 90
Internet-enabled: Technology that allows mobile devices to connect to the Internet wirelessly. **16**
Intrusion detection software: Program that automatically analyzes all network traffic, assesses system vulnerabilities, identifies any unauthorized intrusions, and notifies network administrators of suspicious behavior patterns or system breaches. **189**
IP address: A number that uniquely identifies each computer or device connected to the Internet. *See also* **Internet Protocol address. 48, IE 8**
iPhone OS, 149
iPods, 38, 41
ISP (Internet service provider): Regional or national Internet access provider. **46**
italicized (text), **WD 24**, **PPT 11**, EX 180
iTunes, purchasing and downloading music, 60

J

Java, 61
job search Web sites, 93
join line, **AC 102**, AC 103
join properties, **AC 105–106**
join queries, adding criterion to, AC 114–115
join types, AC 101
joining database tables, AC 100–108
joins
 creating reports involving, AC 106–108
 restricting records in, AC 115
Joint Photographic Experts Group (JPEG), **IE 37**
joysticks, 219
JPEG graphics format, 59
justified, **PPT 150**

K

key symbol (primary key), AC 22
keyboard
 choosing your, 223
 entering formulas using, EX 75–76
 moving insertion point with (table), WD 11
 shortcuts, **OFF 4–5**
keyboard shortcuts, **IE 13**
keyboards, 219
KeyTips, **OFF 16**
keywords, **WD 49**, **PPT 45**, **EX 43**, **AC 58**
 adding to document properties, PPT 47
 video properties, PPT 169

L

labels
 inserting data, EX 183–186
 printing mailing, WD 189–190
landscape orientation, **OFF 39**, **PPT 7**, PPT 22, EX 46–47, EX 118, **AC 30–31**
Laptop computer: Portable, personal computer often designed to fit on your lap. *See also* **notebook computer. 16**
LAST function, AC 119
last mile, the, **IE 4**
law enforcement
 See also security
 computer crime, 182
 digital forensics, 192
 privacy laws (fig.), 206
Layout gallery, **PPT 21**
Layout view, AC 49, AC 53–58
layouts, **OFF 39**, **PPT 21**
 adding slide with Title Only, PPT 21–22
 datasheet, AC 29
 Title Only, PPT 21–22
learning tools for application software, 119
learning Web sites, 90
Left Indent marker, **WD 83**
left-align, **PPT 150**
 paragraphs, WD 14, WD 76
 text in cells, EX 12
Legal software: Application software that assists in the preparation of legal documents and provides legal information to individuals, families, and small businesses. **113**
legends, chart, **EX 41**
less than symbol (<)
 and file names, OFF 28
 and folder names, OFF 22
letterhead, **WD 140**
 creating, WD 142–164
 saving as a template, WD 164
levels (paragraph), **PPT 8**
libraries, **OFF 24**
Libraries area, **OFF 24**
Library of Congress Web site, 87
License agreement: An agreement issued by a software manufacturer that gives the user the right to use the software. **194**
line charts, EX 36, 104
line spacing, **WD 72**, WD 73–74
lines
 inserting blank, WD 7
 join, AC 101
 selecting, WD 15, WD 21
LinkedIn, 126–127
Link: Built-in connection to another related Web page or part of a Web page. Short for hyperlink. **52, IE 5**
 Help, OFF 70
 Internet Explorer home page, IE 13
 printing list of, IE 49
 underlining of, IE 18
Linux: Popular, multitasking UNIX-type operating system. **148**, 159
lists
 bulleted. *See* bulleted lists
 creating bibliographical, WD 108
 Excel, **AC 38**
literature Web sites, 94
live database, **AC 61**
live preview, **OFF 14**, OFF 27
Living Digitally (feature), 37–42
Lock aspect ratio check box, Layout dialog box, WD 151
log on, **144**
logging on, **OFF 5**–7
logical operators in IF functions, EX 164
logos, creating, PPT 113
Louvre Museum Web site, 94

M

Mac OS X: Multitasking operating system that is the latest version of the Macintosh operating system. **147**
Macintosh operating system: Operating system for Apple's Macintosh computer. **147**
magnifying. *See* zooming
mailing labels, printing, WD 189–190
Mailing list: Group of e-mail names and addresses given a single name. Also called an e-mail list or a distribution list. **66**
main dictionary, WD 120
Mainframe: Large, expensive, powerful computer that can handle hundreds or thousands of connected users simultaneously, storing tremendous amounts of data, instructions, and information. 15, **19**

major key, **AC 94**, AC 99
Malware: Short for malicious software; programs that act without a user's knowledge and deliberately alter a computer's operations. **98, 184**
manual page breaks, **WD 106**
manufacturing, computer applications in, 27
margins, **EX 114**
  changing settings, WD 141
  changing worksheet's, EX 114–115
markup languages, **IE 10**
Masayoshi, Son, 121
massively multiplayer online games (MMOGs), 41
matte bevel style, PPT 114
MAX function, EX 84, **EX 86**–87, EX 89–90
Maximize button, **IE 13**
maximizing windows, **OFF 12**
McAfee antivirus program, 186
McAfee company profile, 209
media
  adding to slides, PPT 163–176
  running slide shows with, PPT 189
Media player: Program that allows you to view images and animation, listen to audio, and watch video files on your computer. **156**
Media sharing Web site: Specific type of online social network that enables members to share media such as photos, music, and videos. **57**, 83, 134, 178–179
medicine
  contact lenses monitor glaucoma, 143
  health care computer applications, 25–26
  Wii as medical skill builder, 18
Memory: Electronic components in a computer that store instructions waiting to be executed and data needed by those instructions. **6**
  virtual, **141**
Memory management: Operating system activity that optimizes the use of random access memory (RAM). **141**
Menu: Item on the computer screen that contains a list of commands from which a user can make selections. **98, OFF 10**
merging
  cells, **EX 28–29**
  table cells, WD 185–186
message (business letter), **WD 167**
Message board: Popular Web-based type of discussion group that does not require a newsreader. **69**, 118
metadata, **WD 49, PPT 45, EX 43, AC 58**
Microblog: Blog that allows users to publish short messages, usually between 100 and 200 characters, for others to read. **10, 56**
microphones, 219
Microsoft, 29, 71
  See also specific products
  company profile, 121
  "todays clip," PPT 26
Microsoft Access 2010
  See also Access
  described, OFF 8, **OFF 53**
Microsoft Clip Organizer, **PPT 26**–29, PPT 35, PPT 160
  animated GIF files in, PPT 175
  photographs and, PPT 31–32
  sound files in, PPT 163, PPT 167
Microsoft Communicator, **OFF 8**
Microsoft Excel 2010, **OFF 8**
  See also Excel
  new features, EX 4
Microsoft InfoPath 2010, **OFF 8**
Microsoft Office 2010, **OFF 7**
  See also Office programs, suites
  programs, OFF 8
Microsoft Office and Concepts CourseMate Web site, 221
Microsoft Office folder, OFF 11
Microsoft Office suites, OFF 8–9
Microsoft Office Web Apps, **APP 8**
Microsoft OneNote 2010, **OFF 8**
Microsoft Outlook 2010
  described, OFF 8, **OFF 58**
  sending e-mail message using, 64
Microsoft PowerPoint 2010
  See also PowerPoint
  described, **OFF 8**
Microsoft Publisher 2010
  creating documents, OFF 60–61
  described, **OFF 8**, OFF 59–60
Microsoft SharePoint Workspace 2010, **OFF 8**
Microsoft Web Apps, **OFF 8**
Microsoft Windows
  establishing Internet connections using, 142
  keeping up-to-date, 164–165
  Windows 7. *See* Windows 7
Microsoft Windows Internet Explorer 8, **IE 10**
Microsoft Word 2010
  See also Word
  described, **OFF 8**
MIN function, EX 84, **EX 89–90**, AC 119
Mini toolbar, using, **OFF 15**, WD 16, WD 26
minimalist design, PPT 35
Minimize button, **IE 13**
minimized windows, **OFF 30**
minimizing
  Ribbon, OFF 17
  windows, OFF 30–31
minor key, **AC 94**, AC 99
minus sign (–), subtraction operator, EX 77, EX 79
mistakes
  and AutoCorrect feature, EX 9
  correcting while typing, PPT 8
mixed cell reference, **EX 162**, EX 163
MLA (Modern Language Association of America), **WD 66**
  bibliography style, WD 89, WD 108
  citations style, WD 91
  date format, WD 79
  document style described, WD 68
  documentation style, WD 110
  footnote style, WD 95
  style for notes, WD 93
  works cited page, creating, WD 105–111
Mobile computer: Personal computer that a user can carry from place to place. 15, **16**
Mobile device: Computing device small enough for a user to hold in his or her hand. 15, **16**
Mobile users: Users who work on a computer while away from a main office, home office, or school. **22–23**
modems, 219
Modern Language Association of America. *See* MLA
Modernism's influence upon graphic design, PPT 84
Modify Style dialog box, WD 70–72
modifying
  See also changing
  building blocks, WD 173
  styles, WD 70–72
monitoring
  computer performance, 143
  customer behavior, conversations, 202
  employees, 207
monitors, 219, 223

Morris Worm, 209
mouse, 219
crosshair pointer, WD 143
drag and drop, **PPT 39–40**
navigating documents using, WD 11
operations (table), OFF 4
using, OFF 2, OFF 49
movie clips
See also video
inserting, PPT 174–175
previewing, PPT 173
movies, streaming, 42
moving
to another slide in Normal view, PPT 25–26
clips, PPT 36–37
fields (database), AC 20
files, OFF 64
graphics, WD 155, WD 156
insertion point with keyboard, WD 11
manually through slides in slide shows, PPT 49
placeholders, PPT 148–149
tables, WD 185
text, WD 47–48
windows, OFF 66–67
worksheet cells, EX 153
MP3: Format that reduces an audio file to about one-tenth of its original size, while preserving much of the original quality of the sound. **60**
MP4: Current version of a popular video compression standard. **61**
MSN Money Web site, 86
multi-level bulleted list slide, **PPT 15**–20
Multimedia: Any application that combines text with graphics, animation, audio, video, and/or virtual reality. **58**
and viruses, 185
See also specific media
application software, 96
inserting using PowerPoint, OFF 36
software, 108–110
using selectively, PPT 162
virus-infected files, 185
Multimedia authoring software: Software that allows users to combine text, graphics, audio, video, and animation in an interactive application and that often is used for computer-based training and Web-based presentations. **110**
multiplication operator (*), EX 75, EX 76
Multiprocessing: In reference to operating systems, supports two or more processors running programs at the same time. **141**
Multiuser: In reference to operating systems, enables two or more users to run programs simultaneously. **141**
Museum of Online Museums, 94
music
and computers, 70
downloading services, 38
purchasing and downloading iTunes, 60
Web sites, 88
My Collections, **PPT 26**
MySpace, 29

N

Name box
formula bar, **OFF 50**
selecting cells using, EX 34–35
names
category (pie chart), EX 181
domain, **48**
file, **OFF 21**, OFF 52
folder, OFF 22–23
menu, **IE 13**
tag, **WD 94**
user, **OFF 5, 65**
worksheet, changing, EX 42–43
naming
database tables, fields, AC 8, AC 16
databases, AC 62
files, OFF 27–28
worksheets, EX 42, EX 193
National Parks Service Web site, 51
National Press Photographers Association, 200
navigating, **OFF 30**
dialog boxes, OFF 30
documents, WD 11
with mouse, OFF 2–4
scrolling through documents, WD 112
Web pages, 52
navigation buttons, **IE 13**
Navigation buttons, **AC 28**
navigation pane, **OFF 24**
Navigation Pane, OFF 54, **WD 115**, WD 117, **AC 15**, AC 127
n.d. (no date), WD 108
negation operator (-), EX 76, EX 77
negative numbers, EX 102, EX 174
Nero disc burning software, 40, 157
nested IF function, **EX 170**
Net: Worldwide collection of networks that links millions of businesses, government agencies, educational institutions, and individuals. *See also* **Internet. 44**
Net Nanny, 207
Netbook: Type of notebook computer that is smaller, lighter, and often not as powerful as a traditional notebook computer. **16**, 224
Netiquette: Short for Internet etiquette, the code of acceptable behaviors users should follow while on the Internet. **69**
Network: Collection of computers and devices connected together, often wirelessly, via communications devices and transmission media, allowing computers to share resources. **8, IE 3**
connecting to, 142
controlling, 143–144
New Scientist Web site, 91
news Web sites, 55, 89
Newsgroup: Online area in which users have written discussions about a particular subject. **68**, 118
Next Record button, AC 50
Nintendo Wii, 18, 41
No Spacing style, WD 166–167
nonbreaking hyphens, **WD 175**
nonbreaking spaces, inserting, **WD 175**
nonprinting character, **WD 7**
Normal style, WD 5, **WD 70**
Normal view, PPT 21, **PPT 24**, PPT 25–26, PPT 153–154, **EX 114**
Norton System Works, 157
NOT operator in IF functions, EX 164
note reference marks, **WD 93**
Note taking software: Application software that enables users to enter typed text, handwritten comments, drawings, or sketches anywhere on a page. **106**
note text, **WD 93**
Notebook computer: Portable, personal computer often designed to fit on your lap. *See also* **laptop computer. 16**
buyer's guide, 222–225
safeguarding, 193
notebooks (OneNote), **OFF 62**
notes
See also footnotes, endnotes
printing speaker, PPT 187–188

Notes Page view, **PPT 24**
notes pages, **PPT 179**
Notes pane, **PPT 24**, **PPT 179**, PPT 183
note-taking program (OneNote), OFF 61–62
NOW function, **EX 159**, EX 160
number data type, **AC 9**
Number Dialog Box launcher, EX 102
numbers
entering in ranges, EX 74
entering in worksheets, EX 13–14, EX 71
entering text as, EX 16
entering with format symbols, EX 156–157
Excel limitations, EX 13
formatting in worksheets, EX 31–33
formatting using Ribbon, EX 100–103
inserting slide, PPT 182–184
negative, EX 102
using in criterion, AC 90

O

object tabs, **OFF 54**, **AC 15**
objects
changing stacking order, PPT 146–147
changing text wrapping, WD 148
distributing database, AC 30
drawing, **WD 142**
grouping, ungrouping, PPT 157
inline, and floating, **WD 147**
positioning, WD 147
possessed, 191
regrouping, PPT 162
rotate handles, WD 144
saving, AC 84
selecting nonadjacent, WD 15
Office 2010, publishing Web pages online, APP 3–4
Office Clipboard, **WD 113**, **PPT 156**
Office Collections, **PPT 26**
Office programs, suites
See also specific program
described generally, OFF 8–9
obtaining Help, OFF 68–72
starting from Windows Explorer, OFF 48
Windows Help and Support, OFF 73–74
Office theme, **PPT 5**, EX 22, EX 95
offsets, **PPT 95**
OneNote
described, OFF 61–62
Web App, APP 8
one-to-many relationship, **AC 9**
Online: Describes the state of a computer when it is connected to a network. **8**
Online auction: E-commerce method that allows consumers to bid on an item being sold by someone else. **63**
and pirated software, 194
Online banking: Online connection to a bank's computer to access account balances, pay bills, and copy monthly transactions to a user's computer. **25**, **112**
Online Help: Electronic equivalent of a user manual that usually is integrated in a program. **119**
Online investing: Use of a computer to buy and sell stocks and bonds online, without using a broker. **25**
online mapping services, 117
online mapping services, 117
Online service provider (OSP): Company that provides internet access as well as many members-only features. **46**
online shopping, 204
Online social network: Web site that encourages members in its online community to share their interests, ideas, stories, photos, music, and videos with other registered users. *See also* **Social networking Web site. 10**, **57**
personal and business perspective, 176–177
popular (fig.), 83
Open source software: Software provided for use, modification, and redistribution. **97**
opening
AutoPlay window, OFF 22
Backstage view, OFF 42
databases, AC 27, AC 62, AC 77
Design view, AC 24
documents, WD 70, PPT 50–51
existing files, OFF 57
workbooks, EX 47–48
Operating system: Set of programs that coordinates all the activities among computer hardware devices. **11**, **97**
buyer's guide, 218
closed source vs. open source, 148
overview, 136–138
Operating system (OS): Set of programs that work together to coordinate all the activities among computer hardware resources. **137**, **OFF 2**
functions, 138–144
types of, 145–149
operations
arithmetic (table), EX 75
order of, EX 76
operators
comparison, EX 165
conditional formatting, EX 107
logical, in IF functions, EX 164
optical disc creation software, 134
optical disc drives, 219, 223
optical discs, burning files to, 40, 164
Option buttons, EX 82
OR criterion, **AC 92**, AC 93
OR operator, EX 164, **AC 94**
order of operations, **EX 76**
organizations, and domain name extensions, IE 8
organizing
files, folders, OFF 21–30, WD 12, PPT 14, EX 20, AC 27
spreadsheets, 103
Oriel theme, PPT 8, PPT 15, PPT 81
orphan control, WD 102
OSP (online service provider), 46
Outline tab, **PPT 24**
outlines, **PPT 113**
outlining (PowerPoint feature), OFF 36
Outlook
described, **OFF 58**
sending e-mail message using, 64
Outlook window, OFF 58–59
Output device: Any hardware component that conveys information to one or more people. **5**
overflow characters, EX 9
overlapping windows vs. tabbed documents, AC 58
Overtype mode, **EX 50**

P

Packed software: Mass-produced, copyrighted retail software that meets the needs of a wide variety of users, not just a single user or company. **96**
Page, Larry, 71
page breaks
automatic and soft, **WD 101**
manual and hard, **WD 106**

Page Layout view, **EX 114**
page numbers
in citations, WD 91
inserting, WD 77
pages
adding borders to, WD 41–43
centering contents vertically, WD 40
going to, WD 117
landscape vs. portrait orientation, PPT 22, EX 46–47, EX 118
notes, **PPT 179**
in OneNote, **OFF 62**
viewing one, WD 40–41
Paint software: Application software that allows users to draw pictures, shapes, and other graphical images with various onscreen tools. **109**
Palm OS, 149
panes, **OFF 10**, WD 149
navigation, OFF 24
splitting windows into, EX 198–199
task, **OFF 15**
paragraph formatting, **WD 12**
paragraph mark (¶)
and formatting marks, WD 7
and paragraphs, WD 12
paragraph spacing, **WD 72**
paragraphs, **PPT 8**
aligning text, PPT 150–151
applying bullets to, WD 186–187
bottom bordering, WD 160
bulleting lists of, WD 21–22
centering, WD 14
creating new, OFF 20, WD 6
hanging indents, WD 109
indent first line, WD 83
right-aligning, left-aligning, WD 76
selecting, PPT 10
shortcut keys for formatting (table), WD 81
spacing, WD 43, **WD 72**
parameter queries, **AC 87**–88
Parental Control button, WD 122
parenthetical references, **WD 69**
Password: Private combination of characters associated with a user name that allows access to certain computer resources. **144, 190, OFF 5**
and user accounts, OFF 6–7
paste area, **EX 17**
Paste Options button, WD 48, EX 82
Paste Options gallery, WD 156, EX 152
Paste Options menu, WD 114, EX 152–153
pasted, **IE 39**
pasting, **WD 113**
with Clipboard, IE 39
copying and, WD 113–114
from other programs, EX 153
Paste Options gallery, WD 156
shapes, PPT 108–109, PPT 112
patches, **IE 7**
paths, **OFF 21**–22, **IE 9**
Payload: Destructive event or prank a malicious-logic program is intended to deliver. **184**
PayPal, 63, 71
PDA: Lightweight mobile device that provides personal information management functions such as a calendar, appointment book, address book, calculator, and notepad. *See also* **personal digital assistant. 17**
PDF: Portable Document Format; a popular file format used by document management software to save converted documents. **107**
printing documents as, AC 30
viewing, 107
percent sign (%) format symbol, EX 156
Percent Style format, EX 103
percentage operator (%) EX 76, EX 77
performance, monitoring, 143
Performance monitor: Operating system program that assesses and reports information about various computer resources and devices. **143**
personal application software, 96, 111
Personal computer: Computer that can perform all of its input, processing, output, and storage activities by itself and contains a processor, memory, one or more input and output devices, and storage devices. **15**
vs. Apple in popularity, 15
Personal computer maintenance utility: Utility program that identifies and fixes operating system problems, detects and repairs disk problems, and includes the capability of improving a computer's performance. **157**
Personal DTP software: Application software that helps home and small office/home office users create newsletters, brochures, advertisements, postcards, greeting cards, letterhead, business cards, banners, calendars, logos, and Web pages. **113**
Personal finance software: Simplified accounting program that helps home users or small office/home office users manage finances. **112**
Personal firewall: Utility program that detects and protects a personal computer and its data from unauthorized intrusions. **153, 189**
Personal identification number (PIN): Numeric password, either assigned by a company or selected by a user. **191**
Personal information manager (PIM): Application software that includes features to help users organize personal information. **106**
Personal paint/image editing software: Application software that provides an easy-to-use interface, usually with more simplified capabilities that allows users to draw pictures, shapes, and other images. **114**
Personal photo editing software: Application software that allows users to edit digital photos by removing red-eye, erasing blemishes, restoring aged photos, adding special effects, enhancing image quality, or creating electronic photo albums. 111, **114**
personal Web sites, 58
Phanfare Web site, 83
Pharming: Scam, similar to phishing, where a perpetrator attempts to obtain your personal and financial information, except they do so via spoofing. **205**
Phishing: Scam in which a perpetrator sends an official looking e-mail that attempts to obtain your personal and financial information. 10, **156, 205**
Phishing filter: Program that warns or blocks you from potentially fraudulent or suspicious Web sites. **156, 205**
phishing scams, **IE 7**
phones
business software for, 100, 106–107
digital voice communications, 172–173
smart. *See* smart phone
Photo management software: Application software that allows users to view, organize, sort, catalog, print, and share digital photos. **114**

Picture message: Photo or other image, sometimes along with sound and text, sent to or from a smart phone or other mobile device. **17**, 118
photographs
digitally altering, 201
inserting into slides, PPT 32
and the Microsoft Clip Organizer, PPT 31–32
resizing, PPT 35–36
picture effects, applying, WD 38–39, PPT 89–91
picture fills, **PPT 95**, PPT 97–98
picture message, **17**, 118
picture styles, applying, WD 37, PPT 87–88
Picture Styles gallery, PPT 88
Picture Tools Format tab, OFF 14, PPT 34, PPT 89
pictures
See also clip art, images, photographs
adding artistic effects to, PPT 144–146
adding borders to, PPT 90–92
adjusting color, PPT 142–144
coloring, PPT 143–144
copying and pasting from Web pages, IE 44–45
correcting, PPT 86–87
inserting in documents, WD 31–32
inserting in presentations, PPT 82–86
inserting into slides, PPT 141–142
inserting to create backgrounds, PPT 97–98
resizing, PPT 141–142
on Web pages, saving, IE 37–38
wrapping text around, PPT 32
Pictures library, IE 37, IE 38
picture/video messaging, 170–171
pie charts, EX 36, EX 37, 104, EX 139, **EX 180**
adding 3-D, to workbooks, EX 180–192
applying 3-D format to, EX 188–190
exploding, EX 190–191
rotating, EX 186–187
Piracy: Unauthorized and illegal duplication of copyrighted material. **193**, 201
pixels
described, **EX 107**
screen resolution, OFF 31–32
placeholders, **OFF 39**, **PPT 7**
content. *See* content placeholders
deleting text in, PPT 41–42
inserting citation, WD 94, WD 102
resizing, moving, deleting, PPT 148–149
reusing, PPT 149
selecting text, PPT 16
plagiarize, **WD 67**, WD 79
Play button, PPT 165
Player: Software used by a person to listen to an audio file on a computer. **60**
Plug and Play: Technology that gives a computer the capability to configure adapter cards and other peripherals automatically as a user installs them. **142**
Plug-in: Program that extends the capability of a browser; often used to enhance multimedia. *See also* **add-on. 61**
popular (fig.), 61
plus sign (+)
addition operator, EX 76
and shortcut keys, OFF 5
Podcast: Recorded audio stored on a Web site that can be downloaded to a computer or a portable media player such as an iPod. **10**, **60**
Point mode
described, **EX 76**, EX 85
entering formulas using, EX 76–80
point size, **EX 22**
Pointer: Small symbol displayed on a computer screen whose location and shape changes as a user moves a pointing device. **98**
points, **WD 12**, **PPT 10**
Pop-up blocker: Filtering program that stops pop-up ads from displaying on Web pages. **156**
Portable media player: Mobile device on which you can store, organize, and play digital media. **17**, 20, 226–227
Portal: Web site that offers a variety of Internet serves from a single, convenient location. **55**
portrait orientation, **OFF 39**, PPT 22, **AC 30–31**
ports, 220
positioning
footnotes, endnotes, WD 100
objects, WD 147
WordArt, PPT 115–116
Possessed object: Any item that a user must carry to gain access to a computer or computer facility. **191**
postage Web sites, 87
postal codes, AC 12
power supply, uninterruptible (UPS), 196
Power user: User who requires the capabilities of a workstation or other powerful computer, typically working with multimedia applications and using industry-specific software. **23**
PowerPoint, 140, **OFF 36–38**
Help, PPT 45
Office suites (table), **OFF 9**
quitting, PPT 50, PPT 54
saving files in folders, OFF 41
saving files to SkyDrive from, APP 6–8
saving in previous format, PPT 47
starting, OFF 37–38, PPT 4–5, PPT 50, PPT 76–77
views, PPT 24–25
Web App, APP 8
window, Ribbon, OFF 39–40, PPT 48
Presentation software: Application software that allows a user to create visual aids for presentations to communicate ideas, messages, and other information to a group. **105**
presentations, **OFF 36–37**, **PPT 2**, PPT 101
See also slides, slide shows
adding slides to, PPT 14–15, PPT 21–24
document themes, PPT 5–6
evaluating, PPT 189
formatting characters in, PPT 10–14
inserting multimedia into, PPT 162
inserting pictures into, PPT 31, PPT 82–86
planning, PPT 2
printing, PPT 51–53, PPT 120–121
saving, PPT 14, PPT 82
saving with same name, PPT 47, PPT 121–122
spell-checking, PPT 180–182
preventing
botnets, DoS attacks, back doors, spoofing, 188–189
computer virus infections, 154
computer-related aliments, 198
hardware theft, vandalism, 193
identify theft, 203
software theft, 193–194
unauthorized use, access, 189–192
virus and malware infections, 185–187, 187
preview, live, OFF 14

previewing
documents before printing, WD 124
handouts, PPT 184–186
movie clips, PPT 173
workbooks, EX 195–196
Previous Locations button, **OFF 24**
primary keys, **AC 4**
determining, AC 8–9
modifying, AC 16–18
planning, AC 5
primary sort key, **AC 94**, AC 95
Print: Placing the copy of a document on paper or some other medium. **102**
Print Layout view, **OFF 12**, WD 5
printers
buyer's guide, 220
changing, AC 30
printing, EX 118
borders, WD 53
conserving ink, toner, WD 51, WD 122, WD 188
database tables, AC 31–32
document properties, WD 49, WD 123, EX 45, EX 117
documents as XPS files, WD 52
envelopes, WD 189
formulas version of worksheets, EX 119–120
handouts, PPT 184–186
mailing labels, WD 189–190
presentations, PPT 51–53, PPT 120–121
queries, AC 45
query results, AC 48
reports, AC 108
scaling option, changing, EX 120–121
speaker notes, PPT 187–188
Web pages, IE 47–49
workbooks, EX 195–196
worksheet sections, EX 118
worksheets, EX 45–47, EX 117–118
printouts, **IE 47**
described, **WD 51**
reducing or enlarging, EX 121
privacy, 7
information, **202**
and online mapping services, 117
U.S. government laws concerning (fig.), 206
Processor: Electronic component on a computer's motherboard that interprets and carries out the basic instructions that operate the computer. *See also* **microprocessor**. **6**, 220
Product activation: Process that attempts to prevent software piracy by requiring users to provide a software product's 25-character identification number in order to receive an installation identification number. **194**
Professional photo editing software: Type of image editing software that allows photographers, videographers, engineers, scientists, and other high-volume digital photo users to edit and customize digital photos. **109**
Program: Series of related instructions that tells a computer what task(s) to perform and how to perform them. *See also* **software**. **11, OFF 8**
See also specific program
copying and pasting from other, EX 153
Help, obtaining, OFF 72
importing data from other applications into Access, AC 38–41
installing and running, 12–13
managing, 139–141
Office suites, **OFF 8**
panes, OFF 10
publishing Web pages from Office, APP 3–4
quitting, OFF 45, OFF 52
quitting with document open, OFF 35
starting and interacting from Windows, 99
starting and using, OFF 9–11
starting using search box, OFF 37–38
switching between, OFF 27
tabs in, OFF 14
Programmer: Person who writes and modifies computer programs. *See also* **developer**. **13**
Project management software: Application software that allows a user to plan, schedule, track, and analyze the events, resources, and costs of a project. **106**
projects
business letter, letterhead, and table, WD 138–140
database creation, AC 2–4
financial projection worksheet with what-if analysis, chart, EX 138–141
flyer with pictures, WD 2–4
planning guidelines, APP 1–2
presentation with bulleted lists, clip art, PPT 2–4
presentation with pictures, shapes, WordArt, PPT 74–76
presentation with video, audio, pictures with effects, PPT 138–140
querying a database, AC 74–76
research paper, WD 66–68
worksheet with embedded chart, EX 2–6
worksheet with formulas, functions, EX 66–69
promoting text, **PPT 17–18**
proofreading, **WD 112**
options, WD 87
and revising, WD 113
properties, PPT 46–47
automatically updated, **WD 49, PPT 45**
clips, PPT 29
database, changing, AC 58–60
document. *See* document properties
standard, **WD 49, PPT 45**
property sheets, **AC 97**, AC 118–119
protocols, **IE 8**
publication types, **OFF 60**
Public-domain software: Free software that has been donated for public use and has no copyright restrictions. **97**
Publisher
creating documents, OFF 60–61
described, **OFF 59–60**
publishing
computer applications in, 27
Office 2010 Web pages online, APP 3–4
punctuation, in MLA style, WD 98

Q

Quarantine: Separate area of a hard disk that holds the infected file until a virus can be removed. **186**
queries, 105, **AC 43**, **AC 74**, **AC 77**
creating, AC 43–45, AC 77–82
creating forms for, AC 108–110
criterion, using, AC 46–47, AC 85–86
crosstab, AC 123–126
designing, AC 76
determining criteria, AC 80–82
grouping, using, AC 122–123
omitting duplicates from, AC 97–98
parameter, AC 86–89
printing, AC 45
printing results, AC 48
query-by-example, AC 86

saving, AC 47, AC 82, AC 85, AC 90
sorting data in, AC 96
sorting records in, AC 94–96
top-values, AC 99–100
using, AC 45–48, AC 82–83
using calculated fields in, AC 116–118
question marks (?)
and file names, OFF 28
and folder names, OFF 22
wildcards, **AC 83**
Queue: Lineup of multiple print jobs within a buffer. **142**
Quick Access Toolbar, **OFF 16**
customizing, OFF 19
using shortcut menus, OFF 18
Quick Parts gallery, WD 172, WD 173
Quick Styles, applying, WD 166–167
QuickTime, 61, 134
quitting
Access, AC 26, AC 60
Excel, EX 47, EX 53
Internet Explorer (IE), IE 52
Office program with open document, OFF 35
Office programs, OFF 45, OFF 52
PowerPoint, PPT 50, PPT 54
quotation marks (")
and file names, OFF 28
and folder names, OFF 22
text field values, AC 47, AC 83

R

RAM (random access memory), 220
Range Finder, using, **EX 91**
ranges, **EX 15**
assigning formats to nonadjacent, EX 174–175
clearing, EX 52
copying across columns, EX 89–90
cutting, EX 154
determining highest number in, EX 86–87
determining lowest number in, EX 87–88
dragging, EX 156
entering numbers in, EX 74
selecting, EX 82, EX 180
readibility statistics, WD 120
Real time: Describes users and the people with whom they are conversing being online at the same time. **66**
Real time location system (RTLS): Safeguard used by some businesses to track and identify the location of high-risk or high-value items. **193**
RealPlayer, 61
recalculation, automatic, EX 75
Recent Documents list, WD 45
Recent Pages list, **IE 21**, IE 25–26
recolor, **PPT 142**
recording videos, 40, 130
records (database), **AC 3**
adding to database tables, AC 23–25, AC 28–29
creating new, AC 29–30
deleting, AC 26
saving, AC 25
sorting in queries, AC 94–96
recover, **AC 61**
recovering databases, AC 60–61
Recycle Bin, **OFF 7**
recycling of electronics, 14
Redo command, OFF 19
redundancy
described, AC 5
identifying and removing, AC 10–11
removing, AC 5
#REF! error message, **EX 156**
Reference software: Application software that provides valuable and thorough information for all individuals. 111, **115**
references
cell. *See* cell references
circular, **EX 75**
relative, **EX 17**
Refresh button, **OFF 24, IE 20**
refreshing Web pages, IE 20–21
regrouping objects, PPT 162
relational databases, **AC 3**
relationships, AC 9
relative cell references, **EX 81**, **EX 162**
relative references, **EX 17**
removing
See also deleting
bold format, WD 28
borders from paragraphs, WD 160
bullets, WD 23
duplicates from queries, AC 97–98
headers, WD 75
hyperlinks, WD 163
italic formatting, WD 24
KeyTips from screen, OFF 16
redundancies from databases, AC 5, AC 10–11
shadowing, PPT 103
space after paragraphs, WD 74
styles, PPT 11
tables from queries, AC 79
Web pages from Favorites Center, IE 34–35
renaming
See also naming
database objects, AC 62
fields (database), AC 19
files, OFF 63
worksheets, EX 193
repairing databases, AC 61
Repetitive strain injury (RSI): Injury or disorder of the muscles, nerves, tendons, ligaments, and joints. **198**, WD 43
Replace All button, Find and Replace dialog box, WD 117
Replace dialog box, using, PPT 176–177
reports
creating, AC 51–53
involving joins, AC 106–108
modifying in Layout view, AC 53–58
printing, AC 108
titles, AC 52
totals, adding, AC 57–58
views, AC 53
requirements, database, AC 6–7
requirements documents, **EX 3**
Research in Motion (RIM), 159
research papers, WD 66–68
planning, WD 78–79
proofing and revising, WD 112–124
Research task pane, WD 118
setting options, WD 122
using, WD 120–121
research Web sites, 81
resetting backgrounds, PPT 95
resizing, **WD 34**, **PPT 33**
See also sizing
charts, EX 40–41
clip art, PPT 33–36
datasheet columns, AC 29–30, AC 42
graphics, WD 34–36, WD 150–151, PPT 93–94
photographs, PPT 35–36
pictures, PPT 141–142
placeholders, PPT 148
report columns, AC 54–56
table columns to fit content, WD 180–181
video, PPT 174
windows, OFF 66–67
resolution
screen, and Ribbon, PPT 15, PPT 80, EX 6
screen, OFF 31–34
Resources: Hardware, software, data, and information shared using a network. **8**
Restart command, **OFF 6**

Restore: To copy backed up files by copying them to their original location on the computer. **196**
Restore button, **IE 13**
Restore utility: Program that reverses the backup process and returns backed up files to their original form. **152**
restoring
 Ribbon, OFF 17
 windows, OFF 30–31
reusing placeholders, PPT 149
Ribbon, **OFF 14–15**
 Access, OFF 54
 and computer screen resolution, PPT 15, EX 6
 customizing, OFF 49
 displaying tabs, minimizing, restoring, OFF 16–17
 Excel, OFF 49
 formatting numbers using, EX 100–103
 PowerPoint, **OFF 40**
 and various screen resolutions, OFF 32–33, WD 8, PPT 80
right-align, **PPT 150**
 numbers in cells, EX 14
 paragraphs, WD 76
RIM (Research in Motion), 159
Rock and Roll Hall of Fame and Museum Web site, 80
Rootkit: Program that hides in a computer and allows someone from a remote location to take full control of the computer. **184**
rotate handles, **WD 144**, PPT 86
rotating
 charts, EX 186–187
 graphics, WD 157, PPT 86
 text, EX 144–146
row boundary, **WD 181**
row heading (Excel), **OFF 49**
row selector, **AC 22**
rows
 assigning cell styles to nonadjacent, EX 177
 changing width, EX 107, EX 110–111
 entering titles, EX 10–12, EX 72, EX 150
 hiding, unhiding, EX 107, EX 111
 inserting, EX 154–155, EX 156
Royal Institute of Technology Web site, 85
RSS 2.0: Really Simple Syndication. Specification that content aggregators use to distribute content to subscribers. **58**
RSS aggregator, 118
RTF (rich text format) files, AC 113
rulers, **WD 83**
 displaying, WD 5, WD 82
 hiding, WD 18
rules, conditional formatting, EX 104–105
Run: Process of using software. **12**

S

safeguarding personal information, 203
salutation (business letter), **WD 167**
Satellite Internet service: Provides high-speed Internet connections via satellite to a satellite dish that communicates with a satellite modem. **46**
saturation, color, **PPT 142**
Save: To transfer a document from a computer's memory to a storage medium. **102**
Save As command, APP 3
Save As dialog box, OFF 51–52
Save command, OFF 19
save copy, **AC 61**
Save Picture dialog box, IE 38
saving
 changes to building blocks, WD 172
 database tables, AC 21
 databases, OFF 55, AC 62
 documents, WD 12
 export steps, AC 114
 files in application software, 126
 files in folders, OFF 27–29, OFF 41
 files in Office programs, **OFF 8**
 files to SkyDrive, APP 6–8
 import steps, AC 41
 information obtained with Internet Explorer, IE 35–38
 Office documents with same file name, OFF 51
 and organizing files, OFF 21–30
 pictures on Web pages, IE 37–38
 presentations, PPT 14, PPT 82
 presentations in previous PowerPoint format, PPT 47
 presentations with same name, PPT 47, PPT 95, PPT 121–122
 queries, AC 45, AC 47, AC 82, AC 90
 records (database), AC 25
 templates, WD 164
 Web pages, IE 36–37
 Web pages to online location, APP 3–4
 WordPad documents, IE 46–47
 workbooks, EX 20, EX 91
scaling, printing option, EX 120–121
scanners, 220
scatter charts, EX 36
schemes, color, **WD 28–29**, **PPT 80**
science
 computer applications in, 26–27
 Web sites, 91
Science.gov Web site, 91
screen resolution
 changing, OFF 33–34
 described, **OFF 31–32**
Screen saver: Utility program that causes a display device's screen to show a moving image or blank screen if no mouse activity occurs for a specified time. **153**
ScreenTips, Enhanced, **OFF 15**
Script kiddie: Someone who accesses a computer or network illegal with the intent of destroying data, stealing information, or other malicious action but does not have the technical skills and knowledge. **182**
scroll arrows, **OFF 4**, **PPT 24**
scroll bars
 described, using, **OFF 4**
 Word window, OFF 12–13
scroll box, **OFF 4**
scroll boxes, **PPT 24**
scrolling
 through documents, WD 112
 through folder contents, OFF 26
Search bar, AC 127–128
search box
 described, **OFF 24**
 starting programs using, OFF 37–38
Search engine: Program that finds Web sites, Web pages, images, videos, news, and other information related to a specific topic. **53**
 using, 54–55
Search text: Word or phrase entered in a search engine's text box that describes the item you want to find. **54**
search tools, widely used (table), 53
Search utility: Program that attempts to locate a file on your computer based on criteria you specify. **151**
searching
 See also finding
 for deleted files, 150
 for driving directions, addresses, telephone numbers, 76–77
 finding and replacing text, PPT 176–177

Help topics, IE 49–51
for Help topics, OFF 68–70
for jobs, 93
tips for, 55
the Web, 53–55, 81
secondary sort key, **AC 94**, AC 95
sections (OneNote), **OFF 62**
sections, printing worksheet, EX 118
Secure site: Web site that uses encryption techniques to secure its data. **195**
security
administering, 144
browser control of personal information, 52
computer risks, 182–183
computers and privacy, public safety, 7
Internet issues, IE 6–7
national and local, 208
and online mapping services, 117
wireless, 197
selecting
cells, EX 7, EX 34–35
graphics, WD 150
items in tables, WD 181
lines, WD 15
multiple lines, WD 21
nonadjacent items, WD 15
paragraphs, PPT 10
passwords, 144
ranges, EX 82, EX 180
shapes, WD 145
text (table), WD 30
text placeholders, PPT 16
word groups, WD 27, PPT 19
words, PPT 12
selection rectangle, **WD 32**, **PPT 33**, **PPT 84**
Semantic Web, 49
Send Backward command, **PPT 146**, PPT 147
Send to Back command, **PPT 146**, PPT 147
sensitivity analysis, **EX 199**
sepia, **PPT 142**
series
examples of, using fill handles (table), EX 149
of values, creating, EX 145–148
Server: Computer that controls access to the hardware, software, and other resources on a net-work and provides a centralized storage area for programs, data, and information. *See also* **host computer**. 15, **19**
backing up files on offsite Internet, 214
Server operating system: Operating system that organizes and coordinates how multiple users access and share resources on a network. **143**, 145, 148–149
overview, 148–149
servers, Web, **IE 5**
Service pack: Free downloadable software updates provided by the software manufacturer to users who have registered and/or activated their software. **143**, **IE 7**
service packs, **IE 7**
shade described, **WD 20**
shading text, WD 20
shadow, **PPT 102**, PPT 103
Shape Fill button, PPT 159–160
shape styles, PPT 113
shapes
See also graphics
adding, PPT 106–107, PPT 109–110
adding text to, WD 145–146, PPT 112
changing WordArt, PPT 115–116
copying and pasting, PPT 108–109, PPT 112
drawing, PPT 112
inserting, WD 142–144
sizing, PPT 106–108
Shapes gallery, PPT 106–107
Shared Collections, **PPT 26**
Shareware: Copyrighted software that is distributed at no cost for a trial period. **97**
sheet tab (Excel), **OFF 49**
sheet tabs, coloring and recoloring, EX 193–194
Shockwave Player, 61
Shopping cart: Element of an electronic storefront that allows a customer to collect purchases. **63**
shopping Web sites, 88
shortcut keys, **OFF 4–5**, **WD 81**
shortcut menus, **OFF 18**
modifying styles using, WD 95–97
using, OFF 18, OFF 33–34
Show/Hide ¶, WD 70
Shrink Font button, WD 146
Shut down command, **OFF 6**
Shutter Bar Open/Close button, OFF 54
shutting down Windows 7 and computer, OFF 6
signature block (business letter), **WD 167**
signature lines, **WD 5**
Silverlight, 61
Simple Query Wizard, AC 43–45
size, **PPT 10**
best fit, **EX 107**
font. *See* font size
compressing file, PPT 31
decreasing font, PPT 104
increasing font, PPT 11, PPT 20
Size and Position dialog box launcher, PPT 94
sizing
See also resizing
shapes, PPT 106–108
sizing handles, OFF 40, **WD 32**, **PPT 33**, **PPT 84**, PPT 148
SkyDrive, **APP 5**
collaboration using, APP 12
downloading files from, APP 9–12
introduction to, APP 5
saving files to, APP 6–8
Web Apps, APP 8
slash (/)
division operator, EX 76
and file names, OFF 28
Sleep command, **OFF 6**
Sleep mode: Operating system function that saves any open documents and programs to RAM, turns off all unneeded functions, and then places the computer in a low-power state. **138**
slide indicator, **PPT 25**
Slide pane, **PPT 24**, PPT 183
Slide Show toolbar, PPT 49
Slide Show view
described, **PPT 47**
using, PPT 47–48
slide shows, **OFF 36–37**, **PPT 2**
See also presentations
moving manually through slides in, PPT 49
running with media, PPT 189
Title Slide, OFF 39–40
Slide Sorter view, PPT 153–154
slide transitions, **PPT 43**
adding, PPT 119–120
adding between slides, PPT 43–45
selecting effect options, PPT 119
sliders, using, **OFF 34**
slides, **OFF 39**
adding, PPT 21–24
adding media to, PPT 163–176
adding shapes, PPT 106–107, PPT 109–110
adding to presentations, PPT 14–15
arranging, PPT 39–40
backgrounds. *See* backgrounds

black, **PPT 38**
bullets, deleting, PPT 18
closing, PPT 38
copying, PPT 38–39
copying clips between, PPT 155–156
creating Title, PPT 77–80
deleting, PPT 152
increasing transition time, PPT 44–45
inserting numbers, PPT 182–184
inserting photographs into, PPT 32
moving manually through slide shows, PPT 49
moving to another in Normal view, PPT 25–26
multi-level bulleted list, **PPT 15**
planning title text, PPT 7–8
printing, PPT 52
reviewing and revising, PPT 176–184
text, replacing or deleting, PPT 41–42
text content, PPT 776–777
zooming, PPT 156
Slides tab, **PPT 24**
Slingbox, 39
Small office/home office (SOHO): Describes any company with fewer than 50 employees, as well as the self-employed who work from home. **22**
Smart phone: Internet-enabled telephone that usually also provides personal information management functions. **17**, 172–173
buyer's guide, 225–226
and embedded operating systems, 149
SmartScreen filter, **IE 7**
Social engineering: Gaining unauthorized access or obtaining confidential information by taking advantage of the trusting human nature of some victims and the naivety of others. **205**
Social networking Web site: Web site that encourages members in its online community to share their interests, ideas, stories, photos, music, and videos with other registered users. *See also* **Online social network. 10, 57**, 61
Soft Edge Rectangle style, PPT 88–189
soft page breaks, **WD 101**
Softbank, 121
Software: Series of related instructions that tells a computer what task(s) to perform and how to perform them. *See also* **program. 11**
See also specific program or type
computer, 11–13
development, 13
for home, personal, educational use, 111–116
pirated, 194
product activation, 194
selecting for your computer, 218
updating automatically, 143
software firewall, **IE 7**
software forensics, 209
Software suite: Collection of individual programs available together as a unit. Business software suites typically include word processing, spreadsheet, e-mail, and presentation graphics software. **106**
Software theft: Computer security risk that occurs when someone (1) steals software media, (2) intentionally erases programs, (3) illegally copies a program, or (4) illegally registers and/or activates a program. **193**
solid fill, **PPT 95**
Sony's PlayStation 3, 18
sort, **AC 94**
sort key, **AC 94**, AC 95, AC 98–99
sorting
on multiple keys, AC 98–99
records, data in queries, AC 94–96
sound cards, 220
sounds
See also audio
in slide transitions, PPT 43
using in slides, PPT 163
source area, **EX 17**
sources
and bibliographies, WD 106
citing Web pages as, IE 36
creating for citations, WD 90–91
editing, WD 92, WD 97–98, WD 103
spacing
line, WD 72–74
nonbreaking spaces, WD 175
paragraph, WD 43, **WD 72**
after punctuation, WD 88
Spafford, Gene, 209
Spam: Unsolicited e-mail message or newsgroups posting sent to many recipients or newsgroups at once. **155, 204**
Sparkline charts, EX 141, **EX 170**–171
speaker notes
described, PPT 179
printing, PPT 187–188
speakers, 220
special characters, inserting, WD 159
spell checker
described, **EX 112**
using, EX 113–116
spell-checking
with AutoCorrect, PPT 180
documents, WD 9–10
and grammar-checking, WD 118–119
presentations, PPT 180–182
slide text, PPT 40
worksheets, EX 112–116, EX 194
as you type, WD 84
Spelling and Grammar Check icon, WD 6
Spelling dialog box, PPT 180–182, EX 113
splitter bar, **PPT 24**
splitting
merged cells, EX 29
table cells, WD 186
windows into panes, EX 198–199
Spoofing: Technique intruders use to make their network or Internet transmission appear legitimate to a victim computer or network. **188**
Spooling: Operating system process that sends documents to be printed to a buffer instead of sending them immediately to the printer. The buffer then holds the information waiting to print while the printer prints from the buffer at its own rate of speed. **141**
and printing, 141–142
sports Web sites, 89
Spreadsheet software: Application software that allows a user to organize data in rows and columns and to perform calculations on the data. **100, 103**
Spyware: Program placed on a computer without the user's knowledge that secretly collects information about the user. **155, 204, IE 6**
Spyware remover: Program that detects and deletes spyware and similar programs on a user's computer. **155**
square brackets ([])
and field names, AC 117
in parameter queries, AC 87–88
square sizing handles, PPT 148, PPT 158
stacking order, changing, PPT 146–147

Stallman, Richard, 209
Stand-alone operating system: Complete operating system that works on a desktop computer, notebook computer, or mobile computing device and that also works in conjunction with a network operating system. 145, **146**
standard properties, **WD 49**, **PPT 45**, **EX 43**, **AC 58**
Start button, **OFF 10**
Start menu, **OFF 10**–11
starting
- Access, AC 12
- computers, 138
- Excel, EX 70
- Excel from Windows Explorer, OFF 48
- Internet Explorer, IE 11–12
- PowerPoint, PPT 4–5, PPT 50, PPT 76–77
- programs using search box, OFF 37–38
- Publisher, OFF 60
- Slide Show view, PPT 47–48
- and using programs, OFF 9–11
- Windows 7, OFF 5–7
- Windows Help and Support, OFF 73–74
- Word, WD 4–5
- WordPad, IE 39

statistical functions, EX 84
statistics, calculating, AC 119–120
status bar, **OFF 13**, **AC 15**
STDEV function, AC 119
stock charts, EX 36–37
stock market Web sites, 86
Stop button, IE 20
Storage device: Hardware used to record (write and/or read) items to and from storage media. **6**
Storage media: The physical material on which a computer keeps data, instructions, and information. **6**
Streaming: Process of transferring data in a continuous and even flow. **60**
Subject directory: Search tool that classifies Web pages in an organized set of categories and subcategories. **53**, 55
style formats, WD 70
styles, **WD 37**, **WD 70**, **PPT 10**, **PPT 87**
- *See also specific style*
- adding video, PPT 172–173
- applying, WD 106–107
- applying picture, WD 37, PPT 87–88
- applying shape, PPT 110–111, PPT 113
- applying table, WD 178–179
- background. *See* background styles
- bibliography, changing, WD 89
- capitalization, when to use, PPT 78
- changing cell, EX 22–23
- font, **EX 22**
- guidelines, PPT 76
- MLA and APA, **WD 66**
- modifying, WD 70–72
- modifying using shortcut menus, WD 95–97
- Quick Styles, applying, WD 166–167
- updating to match selections, WD 74
- worksheet cell, EX 52

Styles Dialog Box Launcher, WD 70
subject directory, **53**, 55
Subscribe: Process of a user adding his or her e-mail name and address to a mailing list. **66**
subtitles, worksheet, EX 4, EX 7–8
subtraction operator (-), EX 77, EX 79
Suggested Sites feature, IE 30
suites, 100, **OFF 8**
Sum button menu, EX 87
SUM function, **EX 15**, EX 18–19, EX 82
sums
- calculating, EX 15–16
- determining multiple totals, EX 18–19

Supercomputer: Fastest, most powerful, and most expensive computer, capable of processing more than 135 trillion instructions in a single second. 15, **19**
surface charts, EX 37
Surfing the Web: Activity of using links to explore the Web. **52**
Surge protector: Device that uses special electrical components to smooth out minor noise, provide a stable current flow, and keep an overvoltage from reaching the computer and other electronic equipment. **196**
S-video, **131**
switching between programs, OFF 27
Symantec company profile, 209
Symbian OS, 149
Symbol dialog box, WD 158
Symbol gallery, WD 158–159
symbols
- currency, AC 20
- inserting, WD 158–159

synonyms, finding and inserting, **WD 118**, **PPT 178**
system date, entering, EX 159–160
System failure: Prolonged malfunction of a computer. **196**
System software: Programs that control or maintain the operations of a computer and its devices. **11**, **97**, **136**
System unit: Case that contains the electronic components of a computer that are used to process data. **6**

T

tab characters
- described, **WD 168**
- in tables, WD 181

tab row, **IE 15**
tab stops, **WD 168**
- aligning text using, WD 168–170
- setting custom, WD 169–170

Tabbed browsing: Web browser feature where the top of the browser displays a tab (similar to a file folder tab) for each Web page you open. **52**
tabbed documents vs. overlapping windows, AC 58
table resize handle, **WD 181**
table styles, applying, WD 179–180
tables, **WD 176**
- aligning data in cells, WD 182
- centering, WD 183
- database. *See* database tables
- deleting data in, WD 185
- determining relationships between, AC 9
- entering data in, WD 177–179
- Excel, **OFF 46**
- inserting, WD 176–177
- inserting columns in, WD 185
- inserting rows in, WD 184
- moving, WD 185
- resizing columns to fit content, WD 180–181
- selecting items in, WD 181
- splitting cells, WD 186
- tab characters in, WD 181

Tablet PC: Special type of notebook computer that you can interact with by touching the screen with your finger or a digital pen. **16**, 224, 225
tabs on Ribbon, **OFF 14**, OFF 16–17, OFF 49
Tabs dialog box, WD 168
tag names, **WD 94**
task panes, **OFF 15**, WD 149

tasks, in-cell editing (table), EX 51
Tax preparation software: Application software that is used to guide individuals, families, or small businesses through the process of filing federal taxes. **113**
taxes Web sites, 86
Telecommuting: Work arrangement in which employees work away from a company's standard workplace and often communicate with the office through the computer. **24**
Telemedicine: Form of long-distance health care where health-care professionals in separate locations conduct live conferences on the computer. **26**
telephone numbers, searching Web for, 76–77
Telesurgery: Surgery in which a surgeon performs an operation on a patient who is not located in the same physical room as the surgeon. **26**
templates
 color schemes, PPT 80–81
 creating databases using, AC 15
 publication types, OFF 60
 saving, WD 164
 Web-based, AC 15
testing workbooks, EX 113
text
 See also characters, paragraphs, words
 adding to shapes, WD 145–146, PPT 112
 aligning paragraph, PPT 150–151
 aligning using tab stops, WD 168–170
 alternate, IE 19
 bolding, WD 28, PPT 19–20
 capitalization, WD 18
 centering, WD 107
 changing font, WD 147
 changing font size, WD 16
 changing object's wrapping, WD 154
 color, formatting, PPT 12
 coloring, WD 25, PPT 13, PPT 80
 converting fields to regular, WD 110
 converting hyperlinks to regular, WD 163
 counting words, WD 101
 deleting, WD 47, PPT 41
 demoting, and promoting, PPT 17–18
 effects. *See* text effects
 entering in documents, OFF 20, WD 5–8
 entering numbers as, EX 16
 in Excel, **OFF 50**
 finding and replacing, WD 115–116, PPT 176–177
 formatting elements of, WD 13
 formatting using Format Painter, PPT 105
 formatting using Mini toolbar, WD 26
 indenting in cells, EX 150
 inserting in documents, WD 46
 inserting nonbreaking spaces, hyphens, WD 175
 inserting synonyms, PPT 178
 italicizing, WD 24, PPT 11
 matching case, PPT 176
 moving, WD 47–48
 orphan, widow control, WD 102
 replacing in slides, PPT 41
 revising your, PPT 176
 rotating, EX 144–146, EX 148
 selecting (table), WD 30
 shading, WD 20
 shadowing, PPT 102
 spell-checking, PPT 40
 underlining, WD 27
 using in worksheets, EX 7–9
 wordwrapping, WD 8
 wrapping around pictures, PPT 32
 wrapping in cells, EX 72
 wrapping options, WD 147
text boxes
 described, OFF 6
 inserting into slides, PPT 141
text data, **AC 80**–82
text data type, **AC 9**
text effects, applying, WD 19
text files, exporting to, AC 113–114
text fills, applying WordArt, PPT 117
Text message: Short note, typically fewer than 300 characters, sent to or from a smart phone or other mobile device. **17**, 118
 personal and business perspective, 170–171
 privacy of, 207
 and typing skills, 118
text placeholders, selecting, PPT 16
texture fills, **PPT 95**
 formatting background transparency, PPT 99
 inserting, PPT 95–97
theme colors, changing, WD 141
Theme Colors gallery, PPT 81
Theme Fonts area, EX 24
themes, EX 24, **EX 93**
 changing workbook, EX 94–95
 choosing document, PPT 5–6
 document, **WD 12**
 fonts and, EX 22
 planning, PPT 4
thesaurus, **WD 118**, **PPT 178**
Thumbnail: Small version of a larger graphic. **59**
tiling options, **PPT 95**
time
 adjusting video start, end, PPT 165
 setting slide transition, PPT 44–45
Title bar: Horizontal space, located at the top of a window, that contains the window's name. **98**, **OFF 11**, **IE 13**
Title Slide, **PPT 7**
 creating, PPT 77–80
 entering content in, OFF 40, OFF 43
 layout described, **OFF 39**
titles
 chart, EX 183–186
 entering row, EX 150
 entering slide, PPT 16
 formatting worksheet, EX 176
 freezing worksheet, EX 157–159
 presentation, entering, PPT 7–8
 report, AC 52
 unfreezing worksheet, EX 169
 worksheet, OFF 49–51, EX 4, EX 7–12, EX 29–31,
 worksheet columns, rows, EX 71–72
TiVo, 39
to select a cell, EX 7
toggle commands, EX 177
tone, color, **PPT 142**
toner, conserving printer, WD 51, WD 122, WD 188
tool tabs, **OFF 14**
toolbars
 Mini toolbar, **OFF 15**
 Quick Access Toolbar, **OFF 16**
 Slide Show, PPT 49
Top-level domain (TLD): Identifies the type of organization associated with the domain. **48**
 examples of generic (table), 48
top-values queries, **AC 99**–100
Torvalds, Linus, 159
totals
 See also sums
 adding to reports, AC 57–58
 determining multiple, at same time, EX 18–19
trailing zeros, EX 13
Transitions gallery, PPT 43–44
transparency, **PPT 95**
 formatting background picture, PPT 98–99
 setting color, WD 152

Transparency slider, **PPT 99**, PPT 99
transportation, computer applications in, 28
travel, computer applications in, 27
Travel and mapping software: Application software that enables users to view maps, determine route directions, and locate points of interest. 111, **115**
travel Web sites, 84
Trek theme, EX 92, EX 95, EX 107
Trim Video, **PPT 164**
trimming video files, PPT 164–165
Trojan horse: Malicious-logic program named after the Greek myth that hides within or looks like a legitimate program. **154, 184**
trusted source: Company or person a user believes will not send a virus-infected file knowingly. **185**
Turbo Tax Online, 57
two-digit years, EX 72
'Type words to search for' text box, obtaining Help, OFF 68–70

U

UBS hubs, 220
Ultra-Mobile PC (UMPC): Computer small enough to fit in one hand. *See also* **handheld computer. 17**
Unauthorized access: Use of a computer or network without permission. **189**
Unauthorized use: Use of a computer or its data for unapproved or possibly illegal activities. **189**
Uncompress: To restore a compressed, or zipped, file to its original form. **156**
underline format, EX 180
underlined (text), **WD 27**
underlining
  of links, IE 18
  spelling and grammar errors, WD 9
Undo button, PPT 8, PPT 99, PPT 177
Undo command, OFF 19
undoing
  actions, WD 23, PPT 8
  changes, AC 20, AC 25
  last cell entry, EX 51–52
unfreezing worksheet titles, EX 169
ungrouping clips, **PPT 157**–158
unhiding rows and columns, EX 107
Uninstaller: Utility program that removes a program, as well as any associated entries in the system files. **151**
Uninterruptible power supply (UPS): Device that contains surge protection circuits and one or more batteries that can provide power during a temporary or permanent loss of power. **196**
unique identifiers, **AC 3**
UNIX: Multitasking operating system that now is available for most computers of all sizes. **147**
Unsubscribe: Process of a user removing his or her e-mail name and address from a mailing list. **66**
updates, definition, **IE 7**
updating
  antivirus program, 186
  bibliographical lists, WD 109–110
  current computer date, WD 170–171
  styles to match selections, WD 74
  Windows, 164–165
Uploading: Process of transferring documents, graphics, and other objects from a computer to a server on the Internet. **68**
URL: Uniform Resource Locator. Unique address for a Web page. *See also* **Web address. 51**
U.S. Dept. of Energy's Web site, PPT 2
U.S. Environmental Protection Agency (EPA) Web site, 85
USAJOBS Web sites, 93
USB flash drives, 220
  saving documents on, WD 12
  saving files on, OFF 21–22, OFF 27–29, OFF 44
  saving presentations to, PPT 14, PPT 82
  storing files, folders on, OFF 22–23
User: Anyone who communicates with a computer or utilizes the information it generates. **7**
user accounts, 189–190, **OFF 5**
user icons, OFF 6
User ID: Unique combination of characters, such as letters of the alphabet and/or numbers, that identifies a specific user. *See also* **user name. 144**
User interface: The portion of software that defines how a user interacts with a computer, including how the user enters data and instructions and how information is displayed on the screen. **138–139**
User name: Unique combination of characters, such as letters of the alphabet and/or numbers, that identifies a specific user. *See also* **user ID. 65, 144, 190, OFF 5**
Utility: Type of system software that allows a user to perform maintenance-type tasks, usually related to managing a computer, its devices, or its programs. **150**
Utility program: Type of system software that allows a user to perform maintenance-type tasks usually related to managing a computer, its devices, or its programs. **12**, 98, 143

V

values, creating series of, EX 145–148
values version of worksheets, **EX 119**, EX 167
VAR function, AC 119
verifying
  formulas using Range Finder, EX 91
  saved files, OFF 30
VeriSign, 159
vertical bar (|) and file, folder names, OFF 22, OFF 28
vertical ruler, **WD 82**
Verve theme, PPT 79, PPT 81
Video: Images displayed in motion. **61**
  addng styles, PPT 172–173
  adjusting color, PPT 164
  digital technology, 129–134
  distributing, 134
  editing, 132–133
  inserting files, PPT 163–164
  inserting movie clips, PPT 174–175
  Living Digitally (feature), 39
  playing and displaying options, PPT 166
  PowerPoint 2010 enhancements, PPT 138
  recording, 40, 130
  resizing, PPT 174
  streaming devices, 39
  trimming files, PPT 164–165
Video blog: A blog that contains video clips. **56**
video cards, 220
video conferencing, 118
Video editing software: Application software that allows a user to modify a segment of video, called a clip. **110**, 132–133

Video message: Short video clip, usually about 30 seconds, sent to or from a smart phone or other mobile device. **17**, 118
Video phone: Phone that can send video messages. **17**
video projectors, 225
viewing
custom dictionary entries, WD 120
database tables in Design view, AC 21–22
one page, WD 40–41
parameter queries, AC 87–88
query results, AC 45
views
See also specific view
Access, AC 15
changing, PPT 153–154
changing worksheet, EX 196–198
PowerPoint, PPT 24–25
query, AC 45
report, AC 53
Virtual memory: A portion of a storage medium, usually the hard disk, that the operating system allocates to function as additional RAM. **141**
Virtual reality (VR): Computers used to simulate a real or imagined environment that appears as a three dimensional (3-D) space. **61**
Virus: Potentially damaging computer program that affects, or infects, a computer negatively by altering the way the computer works without the user's knowledge or permission. **154, 184, WD 131**
and e-mail, 65
on the Internet, 98
preventing, 185–187
signs of infection (fig.), 154
spreading through e-mail, 185
Virus definition: Known specific pattern of virus code. *See also* **virus signature. 186**
Virus hoax: E-mail message that warns users of a nonexistent virus or other malware. **187**
Virus signature: Known specific pattern of virus code. *See also* **virus definition. 186**
VisiCalc, 121
Vlog: Short for video blog. **56**
Vlogosphere: All vlogs worldwide. **56**
voice communications, digital, 172–173
VoIP: Voice over IP, or Internet Protocol; technology that allows users to speak to other users over the Internet (instead of the public switched telephone network). **68**, 118, 172–173

W

WAP (wireless access point), 197
War driving: Intrusion technique in which an individual attempts to detect wireless networks via their notebook computer or mobile device while driving a vehicle through areas they suspect have a wireless network. **197**
Warm boot: Process of using the operating system to restart a computer. **138**
Warnock, John, 121
watermarks, inserting, PPT 82
.wav files, PPT 168
Weather Channel Web site, 89
weather Web sites, 89
Web: Worldwide collection of electronic documents called Web pages, the Web is one of the more popular services on the Internet. *See also* **World Wide Web. 10, 49, IE 5**
browsing the, 79–94, IE 15–26
Excel support, OFF 46
multimedia on the, 58
searching the, 53–55, 81
Web 2.0: Term used to refer to Web sites that provide a means for users to share personal information, allow users to modify Web site content, and have application software built into the site for visitors to use. **10**, 59
Web 3.0, 49
Web address: Unique address for a Web page. *See also* **URL (Uniform Resource Locator). 51, IE 7–9**
browsing the Web using, IE 16
copying and pasting, IE 39
Web app: Web site that allows users to access and interact with software from any computer or device that is connected to the Internet. *See also* **Web application. 57, 116**
Web application: Web site that allows users to access and interact with software from any computer or device that is connected to the Internet. *See also* **Web app. 10, 57, 96**
and cookies, 203
popular (fig.), 117
Web Apps, **APP 8**, APP 12
Web browser: Application software that allows users to access and view Web pages. *See also* **browser. 49**, 118, **IE 10**
how they display home page, 50
Web cam Web sites, 80
Web cams, 220
Web Collections, **PPT 26**
Web conferencing, personal and business perspective, 176–177
Web filtering software: Program that restricts access to certain material on the Web. **156, 207**
Web page: Electronic document on the Web, which can contain text, graphics, audio, and video and often has built-in connections to other documents, graphics, Web pages, or Web sites. **10, 49, IE 5**
accuracy of, 200
adding to Favorites Center, IE 30–31
copying and pasting pictures from, IE 44–45
copying and pasting text from, IE 42–43
displaying, IE 41
displaying in full screen mode, IE 12
displaying using History List, IE 26–30
file specification, IE 9
finding previously displayed, IE 21–26
keeping track of favorites, IE 30–35
navigating, 52
printing in Internet Explorer, IE 47–49
publishing Office 2010 online, APP 3–4
refreshing, IE 20–21
removing from Favorites Center, IE 34–35
saving, IE 36–37
saving pictures on, IE 37–38
stopping transfer of, IE 20
Suggested Sites feature, IE 30
and Web publishing, 62
Web page authoring software: Software used to create Web pages that include graphical images, video, audio, animation, and other special effects with interactive content. **110**, IE 10
Web publishing: Development and maintenance of Web pages. **62**
Web server: Computer that delivers requested Web pages to a computer. **49, IE 5**

Web site: Document on the Web that contains text, graphics, animation, audio, and video. **10, 49, IE 5**
Web site: Collection of related Web pages and associated items, such as documents and pictures, stored on a Web server. **10, 49, IE 5**
Web-based training (WBT): Computer-based training that uses Internet technology and consists of application software on the Web. **119**
weight, **PPT 118**
Welcome screen, **OFF 5–6**
what-if analysis
 generally, EX 199–200
 goal seeking, EX 200–202
wheels, 219
widow control, WD 102
Wi-Fi: Network that uses radio signals to provide Internet connections to wireless computers and devices. **45**
Wi-Fi Protected Access (WPA): Security standard that improves on older security standards by authenticating network users and providing more advanced encryption techniques. **197**
Wii, 18, 41
Wiki: Collaborative Web site that allows users to create, add to, modify, or delete the Web site content via their Web browser. **56, 174–175**
Wikipedia, 56
wildcards, **AC 83**
Window: Rectangular area of a computer screen that displays data or information. **98, OFF 11**
 Access, AC 15
 active and inactive, **IE 40**
 Excel, OFF 49–50
 folder, OFF 24–25
 Internet Explorer (IE), IE 12–14
 maximizing, **OFF 12**
 minimizing, restoring, OFF 30–31
 moving, OFF 66–67
 OneNote, OFF 62
 opening new document, WD 166
 Outlook, OFF 58–59
 overlapping, vs. tabbed documents, AC 58
 PowerPoint, OFF 39–40, PPT 48
 Publisher, OFF 60
 resizing, OFF 66–67
 splitting into panes, EX 198–199
 Word, WD 5–6
Windows 7: Microsoft's fastest, most efficient operating system to date, offering quicker program start up, built-in diagnostics, automatic recovery, improved security, enhanced searching and organizing capabilities, and an easy-to-use interface. **146**
 introduction to, **OFF 2**
 starting, logging on, OFF 5–7
 Windows Help and Support, **OFF 73–74**
Windows 7 Aero, OFF 2–3
Windows 7 Basic, OFF 2–3
Windows Aero: Windows interface used by computers with more than 1 GB of RAM. **139**
Windows application software, starting and interacting with, 99
Windows Defender, IE 6
Windows desktop, OFF 7
Windows Embedded CE, 149
Windows Explorer
 creating Office document from, OFF 47
 moving, renaming, deleting files, OFF 62–65
 starting Office program using, OFF 48
Windows Help and Support, **OFF 73–74**
Windows Live Hotmail, 57
Windows Live Movie Maker, 140
Windows Live SkyDrive
 See also SkyDrive
 described, **APP 5**
Windows Media Player, 61, 140
Windows Phone 7, 149
Windows ReadyBoost: Windows feature that can allocate available storage space on removable flash memory devices as additional cache. **141**
Windows waveform (.wav), **PPT 168**
wireless
 connections for notebooks, 224
 fixed, **45**
 modems, 46
wireless access point (WAP), 197, 220
wireless chumby, 42
Wireless Internet service provider: Type of Internet service provider that provides wireless Internet access to computers and mobile devices, such as smart phones and PDAs, with built-in wireless capability or to computers with wireless modems or wireless access devices. **46**
wireless security, 197
Word, OFF 9
 Help, OFF 66, OFF 68–72, WD 35
 Office suites (table), **OFF 9**
 saving files to SkyDrive from, APP 6–8
 starting, WD 4–5
 Web App, APP 8
 window, WD 5–6
word processing
 PowerPoint feature, OFF 36
 Word. *See* Word
Word processing software: One of the more widely used types of application software; allows a user to create and manipulate documents containing mostly text and sometimes graphics. Sometimes called a word processor. **101**
Word window, components of, OFF 12–16
WordArt, **PPT 113**
 applying text fill, PPT 117
 changing outline weight, PPT 118
 changing shape, PPT 115–116
 inserting, PPT 114
WordPad, **IE 39**
 copying and pasting text into documents, IE 42–45
 quitting, IE 47
 saving documents, IE 46–47
words
 See also characters, paragraphs, text
 adding to dictionary, EX 113
 counting, WD 101
 finding whole, PPT 176
 formatting, PPT 20
 selecting, PPT 12
 selecting groups, WD 27, PPT 19
wordwrap, 101, **WD 8**
 changing text wrapping, WD 148, WD 154
 text wrapping options, WD 147
workbooks, **OFF 46**
 adding 3-D pie charts to, EX 180–192
 changing themes, EX 94–95
 opening, EX 47–48
 reordering worksheets, sheet tabs, EX 194
 saving, EX 20
works cited, **WD 69**
works cited page, **WD 105**
 creating, WD 106–111
 formatting to MLA style, WD 111

Worksheet: Rows and columns used to organize data in a spreadsheet. **103, OFF 45, EX 7**
adding charts to, EX 36
adding Clustered Cylinder charts to, EX 36, EX 38–41
assigning cell styles to nonadjacent rows, EX 177
cells. *See* cells, worksheet
changing names, EX 42–43
clearing cells, ranges, EX 52
column width, adjusting, EX 33–34
components, navigation of, OFF 49
copying cells to adjacent cells, EX 16–18
correcting errors, EX 49–51
correctness of, EX 140
design, aesthetics vs. function, EX 66
development cycle, EX 4
entering column, row titles, EX 10–12
error checking, EX 113
fill colors, EX 93
formatting, EX 20–34, EX 92–99
formatting numbers in, EX 31–33
formatting titles, EX 176
formulas. *See* formulas
formulas version, printing, EX 119–120
freezing titles, EX 157–159
functions. *See* functions
headers, EX 115–116
importing into Access, AC 38–41
margins, EX 114–115
numbers, entering, EX 13–14
planning, EX 2, EX 5
printing, EX 45–47, EX 117–118
printing sections of, EX 118
projects. *See* projects
renaming, EX 193
skipping rows vs. using white space, EX 73
Sparkline charts, adding and formatting, EX 170–172
spell-checking, EX 112–116, EX 194
summing columns of numbers, EX 15–16
text, entering, EX 7–9
titles, EX 95–96
titles, entering, EX 71
titles, subtitles, EX 4, EX 7–8, OFF 50–51
unfreezing titles, EX 169
zooming, EX 196–198
World Wide Web, **IE 5**
See also Web
overview, 49–63
World Wide Web Consortium (W3C), 45
World Wide Web (WWW): Worldwide collection of electronic documents. *See also* **Web. 49, IE 5**
Worm Program that copies itself repeatedly, using up system resources and possibly shutting down the system. **154, 184**
Wozniak, Steve, 159
wrapping
text around pictures, PPT 32
text in cells, EX 72
wrist injuries, avoiding, WD 11

X

X Y (scatter) charts, EX 36
x-axis, **EX 40**
Xbox 360, 18
XPS files
printing documents as, WD 52, EX 47, AC 30
printing presentations as, PPT 53

Y

Yellowstone National Park Web page, IE 41
yoga, PPT 74
YouTube, 61, 83, 134

Z

Zipped files: Type of compressed files that usually have a .zip extension. **156,** 126–127
Zombie: Compromised computer whose owner is unaware the computer is being controlled remotely by an outsider. **187**
zooming
documents, WD 5, WD 33, WD 36
slides, PPT 156
worksheets, charts, EX 196–198
Zuckerberg, Mark, 71

Credits

Chapter 1: Opener © Mark Scott/Getty Images; Collage: Courtesy of SanDisk Corporation; PRNewsFoto/Apple; Courtesy of Logitech; Courtesy of Apple; Courtesy of Hewlett-Packard Company; PRNewsFoto/Polaroid Corporation; © Oleksiy Maksymenko Photography / Alamy; Courtesy of Nokia; © Hugh Threlfall/Alamy; PRNewsFoto/Nintendo; 1-1 © Noel Hendrickson/Getty Images; PRNewsFoto/Apple; © David L. Moore - Lifestyle/Alamy; © Jupiterimages/Comstock Images/Alamy; © curved-light/Alamy; © Brad Wilson/Getty Images; © Jupiterimages/Thinkstock/Alamy; Courtesy of Adobe Systems, Inc; Adobe product screenshot(s) reprinted with permission from Adobe Systems Incorporated; 1-3 Courtesy of Hewlett-Packard Company; Courtesy of Logitech; Courtesy of Logitech; Courtesy of Kingston Technology Corporation; Courtesy of NETGEAR; Courtesy of SanDisk Corporation; Courtesy of SanDisk Corporation; Courtesy of LaCie; Courtesy of Hewlett-Packard Company; Courtesy of Hewlett-Packard Company; Figure 1-4 Courtesy of Seagate Technology; 1-5 © Wm. Baker/GhostWorx Images/Alamy; © Jupiterimages/Thinkstock/Alamy; 1-6 PRNewsFoto/Verizon Wireless, Achille Bigliardi; Courtesy of Dell, Inc; PRNewsFoto/VerizonWireless; Courtesy of Hewlett-Packard Company; Courtesy of Nokia; © Oleksiy Maksymenko Photography / Alamy; Courtesy of Hewlett-Packard Company; Courtesy of Microsoft Corporation; Courtesy of Hewlett-Packard Company; 1-9 © Tony Freeman/PhotoEdit; 1-10 Courtesy of Hewlett-Packard Company; Courtesy of Hewlett-Packard Company; Courtesy of Kingston Technology Corporation; Courtesy of Corel Corporation; Courtesy of Hewlett-Packard Company; 1-13 Courtesy of Dell, Inc; 1-14 Courtesy of Apple; 1-15 © Dmitry Bomshtein/iStockphoto; 1-16 © PSL Images / Alamy; 1-17 (top) © Oleksiy Maksymenko Photography; (bottom) Courtesy of Nokia; 1-18 © Yunus Arakon/iStockphoto; 1-19 Courtesy of Apple; 1-20 Courtesy of Sony Electronics Inc; © eva serrabassa/iStockphoto; 1-21 © Ian Leonard/Alamy; © ST-Images/Alamy; © Graham Hebditch/Alamy; 1-22 Courtesy of Hewlett-Packard Company; 1-23 Courtesy of IBM Corporation; 1-24 Courtesy of IBM Corporation; 1-25 Courtesy of Toyota; Courtesy of Daimler Mercedes-Benz; © Jupiterimages; 1-26 Courtesy of Intuit; © Kin Images/Getty Images; Courtesy of Apple; © Editorial Image, LLC/Alamy; 1-27 © Dwayne Newton/PhotoEdit; 1-28 © Lester Lefkowitz/Getty Images; © iStockphoto; © Myrleen Ferguson Cate/PhotoEdit; © blue jean images/Getty Images; 1-29 © Darryl Bush/San Francisco Chronicle/Corbis; 1-30 © Justin Pumfrey/Getty Images; 1-31 © Thomas Barwick/Getty Images; 1-33 AP Photo/The Post-Tribune, Leslie Adkins; 1-34 © Pigeon Productions SA/Getty Images; 1-35 AP Photo; Reza Estakhrian/Getty Images; 1-37 Courtesy of Garmin Ltd; Looking Ahead 1-1 iStockphoto; Innovative Computing 1-1 Courtesy of Banner Health; Innovative Computing 1-2 © Stockbyte/Getty Images; Computer Usage @ Work © Digital Vision; Trailblazer 1 © Justin Sullivan/Getty Images; Trailblazer 2 © Rob Kim/Landov. **Special Feature 1:** © Synthetic Alan King/Alamy; © Kevork Djansezian/Getty Images; Courtesy of Microsoft Corporation; AP Photo/Mark Lennihan; Tomohiro Ohsumi/Bloomberg via Getty Images; © Lightly Saled/Alamy; PRNewsFoto/JVC Company of America; PRNewsFoto/Verizon Wireless; Courtesy of Cakewalk; Courtesy of Nero AG; Courtesy of Iomega; Courtesy of Barco; © Roca/Shutterstock.com; © N_design/iStockphoto; Courtesy of Sling Media, Inc; AP Photo/Shizuo Kambayashi; AP Photo/Akira Suemori; Courtesy of Apple; PRNewsFoto/TiVo Inc; © Markos Dolopikos/Alamy; PRNewsFoto/Logitech; PRNewsFoto/Sony Electronics, Inc; AP Photo/Paul Sakuma; Courtesy of Chumby Industries; Exceptional Innovation, maker of Life|ware™; PRNewsFoto/Memorex; AP Photo/Joerg Sarbach; Figure 1 PRNewsFoto/Cambridge SoundWorks; Figure 3 © Chris Polk/FilmMagic/Getty Images; Courtesy of Activision Publishing, Inc; Figure 4 © Judith Collins/Alamy; Figure 5 Courtesy of Apple; Figure 6 PRNewsFoto/Myvu Corporation; Figure 7 Courtesy of Sling Media, Inc; Figure 8 (top) Yoshikazu Tsuno/AFP/Getty Images; Figure 8 (bottom); Courtesy of Physical Optics Corporation; Figure 9 PRNewsFoto/TiVo Inc; Figure 10 (left) Courtesy of LaCie; Figure 10 (right) Courtesy of Nero AG; Figure 11 Courtesy of Facebook; © Colin Young-Wolff/PhotoEdit; PRNewsFoto/JVC Company of America; Figure 12 Courtesy of Cakewalk; Figure 13 PRNewsFoto/SANYO Fisher Company; Figure 14 (left) © Lightly Salted/Alamy; Figure 14 (middle) Courtesy of Microsoft Corporation; Figure 14 (right); John MacDougall/AFP/Getty Images; Figure 15 (top) © Juice Images/Alamy; Figure 15 (bottom) Daniel Acker/Bloomberg via Getty Images; Figure 16 AP Photo/Eckehard Schulz; Figure 17 (left) © jamalludin/Shutterstock.com; Figure 17(middle) © Kevork Djansezian/Getty Images; Figure 17 (right) © Hugh Threfall/Alamy; Figure 18 AP Photo/The Lawrence Journal-World, Scott McClurg; Figure 19 PRNewsFoto/TiVo Inc; Figure 20 (top & bottom lower right) Exceptional Innovation, maker of Life|ware™; Figure 20 (bottom left) Courtesy of NuVo Technologies Inc; Figure 21 Copyright © Lucid Design Group www.luciddesigngroup.com; Figure 22 Courtesy of ViewSonic Corporation; Figure 23 Courtesy of Chumby Industries. **Chapter 2:** Opener © John-Francis Bourke/Getty Images; Opening Collage © ST-Images/Alamy; Courtesy of Cisco; 2-1 Courtesy of Microsoft Corporation; 2-2 Step 1 © ngirish/iStockphoto; 2-2 Step 2 © blue_Iq/iStockphoto; 2-2 Step 3 ARRIS C4® CMTS Courtesy of Arris Systems, Inc; 2-2 Step 4 © Stephen Chernin/Getty Images; 2-2 Step 6 Courtesy of Fujitsu Technology Solutions; 2-14 Courtesy of Hewlett-Packard Company; © titi matei/iStockphoto; © Glowimages/Getty Images; Courtesy of Hewlett-Packard Company; 2-16 Step 1, © Colin Young-Wolff/PhotoEdit; 2-16 Step 2, © Mark Evans/iStockphoto; 2-16 Step 3, © Andrew Lewis/iStockphoto; 2-16 Step 4, © Alexander Hafemann/iStockphoto; 2-16 Step 5, Courtesy of Fujitsu Technology Solutions; 2-16 Step 6, © Ed Hidden/iStockphoto; 2-16 Step 7, © Oksana Perkins/iStockphoto; 2-16 Step 8, © Bill Aron/PhotoEdit; 2-18 Step 1 Courtesy of Hewlett-Packard Company; 2-18 Step 2 Courtesy of Hewlett-Packard Company; 2-18 Step 3, Courtesy of Juniper Networks, Inc; 2-18 Step 4 Courtesy of Hewlett-Packard Company; 2-19 Step 2 Courtesy of Fujitsu Technology Solutions; 2-19 Step 3 Courtesy of Microsoft Corporation; 2-19 Step 4 Courtesy of Acer America, Inc; 2-19 Courtesy of Hewlett-Packard Company; 2-19 Step 5 Courtesy of Hewlett-Packard Company; 2-20 Courtesy of Sony Electronics Inc; Courtesy of Hewlett-Packard Company; (center) © Blend Images/Alamy; 2-21 Courtesy of Cisco; Courtesy of Siemens; © Argunova/Shutterstock.com; Courtesy of Logitech; Courtesy of Hewlett-Packard Company; Computer Usage @ Work © Picture Contact/Alamy; Trailblazer 1 © EPA/Landov; Trailblazer 2 AP Photo/Craig Ruttle; Looking Ahead 2-1 Courtesy of W3C; Innovative Computing 2-1 Courtesy of Microsoft Corporation; **Special Feature 2:** © Photodisc/Alamy; © iStockphoto; © Digital Vision/Alamy; © Digital Vision/Alamy; © Alex Segre/Alamy **Chapter 3:** Opener moodboard/Alamy; Collage © Getty Images; Courtesy of Corel Corporation; Courtesy of Microsoft Corporation; Courtesy of Microsoft Corporation; Courtesy of Microsoft Corporation; Courtesy of Nokia; Pinnacle Systems, Inc., a part of Avid

Technology, Inc; Courtesy of Cakewalk Inc; Courtesy of Intuit Inc; 3-1 Courtesy of Microsoft Corporation; Courtesy of Adobe Systems Incorporated; Courtesy of Corel Corporation; 3-2 © Brooke Slezak/Getty Images; Courtesy of Hewlett-Packard Company; Courtesy of Hewlett-Packard Company; 3-11 Courtesy of Microsoft Corporation; 3-12 Courtesy of Computer Systems Odessa Corporation; 3-13 Courtesy of Microsoft Corporation; 3-16 © Artiga Photo/Corbis; 3-17 Courtesy of Quark Inc; 3-18 © Picture Contact/Alamy; 3-19 Courtesy of Cakewalk Inc; 3-20 Courtesy of SumTotal Systems Inc; 3-22 Courtesy of Intuit Inc; © Digital Vision/Getty Images; 3-23 Courtesy of Nolo; 3-24 Courtesy of 2nd Story Software, Inc; 3-26 Courtesy of Corel Corporation; 3-27 Courtesy of Encore, Inc., a Navarre Corporation Company; 3-28 Pinnacle Systems, Inc., a part of Avid Technology, Inc; 3-29 Courtesy of IMSI/Design; 3-30 Courtesy of Microsoft Corporation; 3-31 Courtesy of Encore Software, Inc. a Navarre Corporation Company; 3-32 © Bernhard Classen/Alamy; © Lon C. Dhiel/PhotoEdit; © Fred Prouser/Reuters/Corbis; 3-37 Courtesy of Moodle; Computer Usage @ Work © iStockphoto; Trailblazer 1 AP Photo/Steven Senne; Trailblazer 2 © Tom Wagner/Corbis; Looking Ahead 3-1 Courtesy of Microsoft Corporation; Innovative Computing 3-1 © Tetra Images/Getty Images; Innovative Computing 3-2 © Wave Royalty Free/Alamy; Web Research © Brian Stablyk/Getty Images. **Special Feature 3:** Figure 1 © Balázs Őcsi/iStockphoto; Courtesy of JVC U.S.A.; PRNewsFoto/VIZIO; Courtesy of Sony Electronics Inc; © Alex Slobodkin/iStockphoto; Courtesy of Microsoft Corporation; © Silvrshootr/iStockphoto; Figure 2 Courtesy of Sony Electronics Inc; © Royalty-Free/CORBIS; Courtesy of JVC U.S.A.; Figure 3 Courtesy of Hewlett-Packard Company; © mbirdy/iStockphoto; Courtesy of JVC U.S.A.; screenshot photo © Ben Blankenburg/iStockphoto; Figure 4 © zoomstudio/iStockphoto; Courtesy of Hewlett-Packard Company; Courtesy of Pinnacle Systems Inc; Courtesy of Pinnacle Systems Inc; © Matej Pribelsky/iStockphoto; Courtesy of Sony Electronics Inc; screenshot photo © Pete Saloutos/GettyImages; Figure 5 Courtesy of Microsoft Corporation; Figure 7 Courtesy of Pinnacle Systems Inc; Figure 8 Courtesy of Pinnacle Systems Inc; Figure 9 Courtesy of Pinnacle Systems Inc. **Chapter 4:** Opener © Stuart O'Sullivan/Getty Images; Collage: Courtesy of Microsoft Corporation; © Jason Brindel Commercial/Alamy; Courtesy of Research In Motion; Courtesy of Symantec Corp; PRNewsFoto/ RealNetworks, Inc; 4-1 © Valeriy Kryvsha/iStockphoto; Courtesy of Dell Inc; Courtesy of Hewlett-Packard Company; 4-5 Courtesy of Hewlett-Packard Company; Courtesy of Western Digital Corporation; Courtesy of Printronix; 4-7 Courtesy of Microsoft Corporation; 4-10 AP Photo/Peter Zschunke; 4-11 Courtesy of KDE e.V; 4-13 Courtesy of Research In Motion; 4-19 Courtesy of Check Point Software Technologies Ltd; 4-21 Courtesy of Symantec Corp; 4-22 Courtesy of Rhapsody International, Inc; 4-23 Courtesy of Nero AG; 4-24 Courtesy of Symantec Corp; Computer Usage @ Work © Keith Morris/Alamy; Trailblazer 1 Photo © Tony Avelar/Bloomberg via Getty Images; Trailblazer 2 © Kim Kulish/CORBIS; Innovative Computing 4-1 © Ingram Publishing/Superstock Limited/Alamy; Looking Ahead 4-1 Tingrui Pan/UC Davis photo; Web Research © Jurgen Reisch/Getty Images. **Special Feature 4:** Figure 1 Courtesy of Microsoft Corporation; Courtesy of Verizon Wireless; © Alex Slobodkin/iStockphoto; © Image Source Black/Alamy; © iStockphoto; © David Hancock/Alamy; Courtesy of Skype; © CostinT/iStockphoto; Figure 3 Courtesy of Microsoft Corporation; © Stephen Wilkes/Getty Images; Figure 5 © CAP/Getty Images; Figure 7 © Picturenet/Getty Images; Courtesy of Research In Motion; © Gary Corbett/Alamy; Courtesy of Microsoft Corporation; Figure 9 Courtesy of Jive Software; © Jeff Greenberg/Alamy; Figure 11 © David R. Fraizer/PhotoEdit; © Jochen Tack/Alamy; Courtesy of Parliant Corporation; Figure 13 Courtesy of Cisco Systems, Inc; © Alex Slobodkin/iStockphoto; Courtesy of Zoom Technologies; Figure 15 © Reggie Casagrande/Getty Images; Figure 17 Courtesy of NASA; © PhotoAlto/Alamy; Figure 18 AP Photo/Screenshot, Peter Zschunke; Figure 21 Courtesy of Microsoft Corporation; p 180 (top left) © John Lund/Drew Kelly/Sam Diephuis/Getty Images; p 180 (bottom left) © Photodisc/Alamy; p 180 (top right) © MIXA/Getty Images; **Chapter 5:** Opener © Mark Scott/Getty Images; Collage: © Peter Macdiarmid/Getty Images; © TM_Design/Alamy; Courtesy of Microsoft Corporation; Courtesy of Symantec Corp; Newscom; © Tomasz Piotrowski/Alamy; Courtesy of Tripp Lite; 5-1 Courtesy of Hewlett-Packard Company; © imagebroker/Alamy; © Mustafa Deliormanli/iStockphoto; © PhotoAlto/Alamy; © blickwinkel/Alamy; © avatra images/Alamy; © Ingvald Kaldhussæter/iStockphoto; © Jupiterimages/BrandX/Alamy; 5-2 Step 3a © Christoph Weihs/iStockphoto; Step 3b © Ruslan Dashinsky/Shutterstock.com; 5-3 Courtesy of McAfee, Inc; 5-5 Courtesy of SonicWALL, Inc; Courtesy of Check Point Software Technologies Ltd; Courtesy of Fujitsu Technology Solutions; Courtesy of Hewlett-Packard Company; 5-8 © Paulo Whitaker/Reuters/Landov; 5-9 Courtesy of Kensington Computer Products Group; 5-13 © David Young-Wolff/PhotoEdit; 5-14 Courtesy of APC by Schneider Electric; 5-15 © Marcela Barsse/iStockphoto; © Krystian Nawrocki/iStockphoto; 5-16 Courtesy of Hewlett-Packard Company; © Daniel Laflor/iStockphoto; 5-17 © C Squared Studios/Getty Images; 5-19 ©Paramount/Courtesy Everett Collection; 5-22 Courtesy of Hewlett-Packard Company; 5-26 Courtesy of ContentWatch Inc; Innovative Computing 5-1 © Andrew Olney/Getty Images; Looking Ahead 5-1 © Ann Cutting/Getty Images; Computer Usage @ Work © Ben Edwards/Getty Images; Trailblazer 1 Courtesy of Dr. Eugene Spafford/Purdue University; Trailblazer 2 REUTERS/Simon Kwong; Web Research © Trevor Fisher/iStockphoto. **Special Feature 5:** Figure 1 © Heidi Kristensen/iStockphoto; Courtesy of Dell, Inc; © Tony Tremblay/iStockphoto; Courtesy of Apple; Courtesy of FUJIFILM USA; AP Photo/Paul Sakuma; Courtesy of Apple; Courtesy of Dell, Inc; p 218 Courtesy of Hewlett-Packard Company; Figure 2 Courtesy of SanDisk Corporation; Courtesy of Avid Technology; Courtesy of Seagate Technology LLC; Courtesy of Microsoft Corporation; Courtesy of Hewlett-Packard Company; Courtesy of Logitech; Courtesy of Microsoft Corporation; Courtesy of Logitech; Courtesy of US Robotics; ©Alex Slobodkin/iStockphoto; Courtesy of Microsoft Corporation; Courtesy of Sony Electronics Inc; Courtesy of Hewlett-Packard Company; Courtesy of Hewlett-Packard Company; Courtesy of Intel Corporation; Courtesy of Kingston Technology Corporation; Courtesy of UMAX; Courtesy of Creative Technology Ltd; Courtesy of Logitech; Courtesy of SanDisk Corporation; Courtesy of Belkin International Inc; Courtesy of Advanced Micro Devices, Inc; Courtesy of Logitech; © Norman Chan/iStockphoto; p 222 Courtesy of Dell, Inc; Courtesy of Hewlett-Packard Company; Courtesy of Hewlett-Packard Company; Figure 5 PRNewsFoto/Mindjet LLC; Figure 6 Courtesy of Fujitsu Technology Solutions; Figure 7 © MadTatyana/Shutterstock.com; Figure 8 Courtesy of Motion Computing; p 225 Courtesy of Nokia; Figure 9 Courtesy of Verizon Wireless; PRNewsFoto/Verizon Wireless; PRNewsFoto/Verizon Wireless; p 226 Courtesy of Microsoft Corporation; Figure10 Courtesy of Apple; p 227 Courtesy of FUJIFILM USA; Figure 11 Courtesy of SanDisk Corporation; © Muhammad Khairul Syahir Bin Abd Haki/iStockphoto; © SasPartout/Shutterstock.com

Quick Reference Summary

Table 1: Microsoft Word 2010 Quick Reference Summary

Task	Page Number	Mouse	Ribbon	Shortcut Menu	Keyboard Shortcut
All Caps	WD 81		Change Case button (Home tab | Font group), UPPERCASE		CTRL+SHIFT+A
AutoCorrect Entry, Create	WD 86		Options (File tab), Proofing (Word Options dialog box)		
AutoCorrect Options button, Use	WD 85	Point to AutoCorrect Options button in flagged word			
Bibliographical List, Create	WD 108		Bibliography button (References tab | Citations & Bibliography group)		
Bibliography Style, Change	WD 89		Bibliography Style box arrow (References tab | Citations & Bibliography group)		
Bold	WD 28	Bold button on Mini toolbar	Bold button (Home tab | Font group)	Font, Font tab (Font dialog box)	CTRL+B
Border Paragraph	WD 160		Border button arrow (Home tab | Paragraph group)		
Building Block, Create	WD 171		Quick Parts button (Insert tab | Text group)		ALT+F3
Building Block, Insert	WD 174		Quick Parts button (Insert tab | Text group		F3
Building Block, Modify	WD 173		Quick Parts button (Insert tab | Text group), right-click building block, Edit Properties		
Bullets, Apply	WD 22		Bullets button (Home tab | Paragraph group)	Bullets	* (ASTERISK), SPACEBAR
Center	WD 14	Center button on Mini toolbar	Center button (Home tab | Paragraph group)	Paragraph, Indents and Spacing tab (Paragraph dialog box)	CTRL+E
Change Case	WD 18		Change Case button (Home tab | Font group)	Font, Font tab (Font dialog box)	SHIFT+F3
Change Spacing before or after Paragraph	WD 43		Spacing Before or Spacing After box arrow (Page Layout tab | Paragraph group)	Paragraph, Indents and Spacing tab (Paragraph dialog box)	

Table 1: Microsoft Word 2010 Quick Reference Summary *(continued)*

Task	Page Number	Mouse	Ribbon	Shortcut Menu	Keyboard Shortcut
Citation Placeholder, Insert	WD 94		Insert Citation button (References tab | Citations & Bibliography group), Add New Placeholder		
Citation, Edit	WD 91	Click citation, Citations Options box arrow, Edit Citation			
Citation, Insert	WD 90		Insert Citation button (References tab | Citations & Bibliography group), Add New Source		
Clear Formatting	WD 161		Clear Formatting button (Home tab | Font group)		CTRL+SPACEBAR, CTRL+Q
Click and Type	WD 80	Position mouse pointer until desired icon appears, then double-click			
Clip Art, Insert	WD 148		Clip Art button (Insert tab | Illustrations group)		
Color Text	WD 25	Font Color button arrow on Mini toolbar	Font Color button arrow (Home tab | Font group)		
Copy	WD 113		Copy button (Home tab | Clipboard group)	Copy	CTRL+C
Count Words	WD 101	Word Count indicator on status bar	Word Count button (Review tab | Proofing group)		CTRL+SHIFT+G
Custom Dictionary, Set Default, View or Modify Entries	WD 120		Options (File tab), Proofing (Word Options dialog box), Custom Dictionaries button		
Date, Insert Current	WD 170		Insert Date and Time button (Insert tab | Text group)		
Document Properties, Change	WD 49		Properties button (File tab | Info tab)		
Document Properties, Print	WD 123		File tab | Print tab, first button in Settings area		
Double-Space	WD 73		Line and Paragraph Spacing button (Home tab | Paragraph group)	Paragraph, Indents and Spacing tab (Paragraph dialog box), Line spacing box arrow, 2.0	CTRL+2
Double-Underline	WD 81		Underline button arrow (Home tab | Font group)	Font, Font tab (Font dialog box), Underline style box arrow	CTRL+SHIFT+D
Envelope, Address and Print	WD 189		Create Envelopes button (Mailings tab | Create group), Envelopes tab (Envelopes and Labels dialog box)		
Field, Convert to Regular text	WD 110				Click field, CTRL+SHIFT+F9
Find Text	WD 115	Select Browse Object button on vertical scroll bar, Find button	Find button (Home tab | Editing group)		CTRL+F
Font Size, Change	WD 16	Font Size box arrow on Mini toolbar	Font Size box arrow (Home tab | Font group)	Font, Font tab (Font dialog box)	CTRL+D
Font Size, Decrease	WD 81	Shrink Font button on Mini toolbar	Shrink Font button (Home tab | Font group)		CTRL+SHIFT+<

Table 1: Microsoft Word 2010 Quick Reference Summary *(continued)*

Task	Page Number	Mouse	Ribbon	Shortcut Menu	Keyboard Shortcut
Font Size, Decrease 1 point	WD 81				CTRL+[
Font Size, Increase	WD 146	Grow Font button on Mini toolbar	Grow Font button (Home tab | Font group)		CTRL+SHIFT+>
Font Size, Increase 1 point	WD 81				CTRL+]
Font, Change	WD 17	Font box arrow on Mini toolbar	Font box arrow (Home tab | Font group)	Font, Font tab (Font dialog box)	CTRL+D
Footnote, Insert	WD 93		Insert Footnote button (References tab | Footnotes group)		
Formatting Marks	WD 7		Show/Hide ¶ button (Home tab | Paragraph group)		CTRL+SHIFT+*
Go to a Page	WD 117	'Browse the pages in your document' tab in Navigation Pane	Find button arrow (Home tab | Editing group)		CTRL+G
Graphic, Adjust Brightness and Contrast	WD 153		Corrections button (Picture Tools Format tab | Adjust group)	Format Picture, Picture Corrections button (Format Picture dialog box)	
Graphic, Change Border Color	WD 154		Picture Border button arrow (Picture Tools Format tab | Picture Styles group)		
Graphic, Change Color	WD 151		Color button (Picture Tools Format tab | Adjust group)	Format Picture, Picture Color button (Format Picture dialog box)	
Graphic, Flip	WD 157		Rotate button (Picture Tools Format tab | Arrange group)		
Graphic, Move	WD 155	Drag graphic			
Graphic, Resize	WD 34	Drag sizing handle	Shape Height and Shape Width text boxes (Picture Tools Format tab | Size group)	Size and Position, Size tab (Layout dialog box)	
Graphic, Set Transparent Color	WD 152		Color button (Picture Tools Format tab | Adjust group)		
Hanging Indent, Create	WD 81	Drag Hanging Indent marker on ruler	Paragraph Dialog Box Launcher (Home tab or Page Layout tab | Paragraph group), Indents and Spacing tab (Paragraph dialog box)	Paragraph, Indents and Spacing tab (Paragraph dialog box)	CTRL+T
Hanging Indent, Remove	WD 81, 109	Drag Hanging Indent marker on ruler	Paragraph Dialog Box Launcher (Home tab or Page Layout tab | Paragraph group), Indents and Spacing tab (Paragraph dialog box)	Paragraph, Indents and Spacing tab (Paragraph dialog box)	CTRL+SHIFT+T
Header and Footer, Close	WD 78	Double-click dimmed document text	Close Header and Footer button (Header & Footer Tools Design tab | Close group)		
Header, Switch to	WD 75	Double-click dimmed header	Header button (Insert tab | Header & Footer group)		
Hyperlink, Convert to Regular Text	WD 163	Undo Hyperlink (AutoCorrect Options menu)	Hyperlink button (Insert tab | Links group)	Remove Hyperlink	
Indent, Decrease	WD 81	Drag First Line Indent marker on ruler	Decrease Indent button (Home tab | Paragraph group) or Paragraph Dialog Box Launcher (Home tab | Paragraph group), Indents and Spacing tab (Paragraph dialog box)	Paragraph, Indents and Spacing tab (Paragraph dialog box)	CTRL+SHIFT+M

Table 1: Microsoft Word 2010 Quick Reference Summary *(continued)*

Task	Page Number	Mouse	Ribbon	Shortcut Menu	Keyboard Shortcut
Indent, First-Line	WD 83	Drag First Line Indent marker on ruler	Paragraph Dialog Box Launcher (Home tab or Page Layout tab | Paragraph group), Indents and Spacing tab (Paragraph dialog box)	Paragraph, Indents and Spacing tab (Paragraph dialog box)	TAB
Indent, Increase	WD 81		Increase Indent button (Home tab | Paragraph group)		CTRL+M
Insertion Point, Move Down/Up One Line	WD 11				DOWN ARROW/ UP ARROW
Insertion Point, Move Down/Up One Paragraph	WD 11				CTRL+DOWN ARROW/ CTRL+UP ARROW
Insertion Point, Move Down/Up One Screen	WD 11				PAGE DOWN/ PAGE UP
Insertion Point, Move Left/ Right One Character	WD 11				LEFT ARROW/ RIGHT ARROW
Insertion Point, Move Left/ Right One Word	WD 11				CTRL+LEFT ARROW/ CTRL+RIGHT ARROW
Insertion Point, Move to Beginning/End of Document	WD 11				CTRL+HOME/ CTRL+END
Insertion Point, Move to Beginning/End of Line	WD 11				HOME/ END
Insertion Point, Move to Bottom of Document Window	WD 11				ALT+CTRL+PAGE DOWN/ ALT+CTRL+PAGE UP
Italicize	WD 24	Italic button on Mini toolbar	Italic button (Home tab | Font group)	Font, Font tab (Font dialog box)	CTRL+I
Justify Paragraph	WD 81		Justify button (Home tab | Paragraph group)	Paragraph, Indents and Spacing tab (Paragraph dialog box)	CTRL+J
Left-Align Paragraph	WD 81		Align Text Left button (Home tab | Paragraph group)	Paragraph, Indents and Spacing tab (Paragraph dialog box)	CTRL+L
Line Spacing, Change	WD 73		Line and Paragraph Spacing button (Home tab | Paragraph group)	Paragraph, Indents and Spacing tab (Paragraph dialog box)	CTRL+[number of desired line spacing, i.e., 2 for double-spacing]
Mailing Label, Print	WD 190		Create Labels button (Mailings tab | Create group)		
Margin Settings, Change	WD 141	Drag margin boundary on ruler	Margins button (Page Layout tab | Page Setup group)		
Move Text	WD 47	Drag and drop selected text	Cut button (Home tab | Clipboard group); Paste button (Home tab | Clipboard group)	Cut; Paste	CTRL+X; CTRL+V
New File, Create from Existing	WD 165		'New from existing' button (File tab | New tab)		

Table 1: Microsoft Word 2010 Quick Reference Summary *(continued)*

Task	Page Number	Mouse	Ribbon	Shortcut Menu	Keyboard Shortcut
Nonbreaking Space, Insert	WD 175		Symbol button (Insert tab | Symbols group), More Symbols, Special Characters tab (Symbol dialog box)		CTRL+SHIFT+ SPACEBAR
Normal Style, Apply	WD 106		Normal in Quick Style gallery (Home tab | Styles group)		CTRL+SHIFT+S
Normal Style, Modify	WD 71		Styles Dialog Box Launcher (Home tab | Styles group), style box arrow, Modify	Right-click style (Home tab | Styles group), Modify	
Open a Document	WD 45		Open (File tab)		CTRL+O
Page Border, Add	WD 41		Page Borders button (Page Layout tab | Page Background group)		
Page Break, Insert	WD 106		Page Break button (Insert tab | Pages group)		CTRL+ENTER
Page Number, Insert	WD 77		Insert Page Number button (Header & Footer Tools Design tab | Header & Footer group)		
Paste	WD 113		Paste button (Home tab | Clipboard group)	Paste	CTRL+V
Paste Options	WD 156		Paste button arrow (Home tab | Clipboard group)		
Paste Options Menu, Display	WD 114	Paste Options button by moved/copied text			
Picture Style, Apply	WD 37		More button in Picture Styles gallery (Picture Tools Format tab | Picture Styles group)		
Picture Effects, Apply	WD 38		Picture Effects button (Picture Tools Format tab | Picture Styles group)	Format Picture	
Picture, Insert	WD 31		Insert Picture from File button (Insert tab | Illustrations group)		
Preview a Document	WD 124		File tab | Print tab, Next Page and Previous Page buttons		CTRL+P, ENTER
Print Document	WD 51		Print button (File tab | Print tab)		CTRL+P
Quick Style, Apply	WD 166		[style name] in Quick Style gallery (Home tab | Styles group)		CTRL+SHIFT+S, Style Name box arrow
Quit Word	WD 44	Close button on title bar	Exit (File tab)		ALT+F4
Redo	WD 23	Redo button on Quick Access Toolbar			CTRL+Y
Remove Character Formatting	WD 81				CTRL+SPACEBAR
Remove Paragraph Formatting	WD 81				CTRL+Q
Remove Space after Paragraph	WD 74		Line and Paragraph Spacing button (Home tab | Paragraph group)	Paragraph, Indents and Spacing tab (Paragraph dialog box)	

Table 1: Microsoft Word 2010 Quick Reference Summary *(continued)*

Task	Page Number	Mouse	Ribbon	Shortcut Menu	Keyboard Shortcut
Replace Text	WD 116	Select Browse Object button on vertical scroll bar, Find button, Replace tab (Find and Replace dialog box)	Replace button (Home tab | Editing group)		CTRL+H
Research Task Pane, Look Up Information	WD 120	ALT+click desired word	Research button (Review tab | Proofing group)		
Right-Align	WD 76		Align Text Right button (Home tab | Paragraph group)	Paragraph, Indents and Spacing tab (Paragraph dialog box)	CTRL+R
Rulers, Display	WD 82	View Ruler button on vertical scroll bar	View Ruler check box (View tab | Show group)		
Save New Document	WD 12	Save button on Quick Access Toolbar	Save or Save As (File tab)		CTRL+S
Save Document, Same File Name	WD 30	Save button on Quick Access toolbar	Save (File tab)		CTRL+S
Scroll, Page by Page	WD 112	Previous Page/Next Page button on vertical scroll bar			CTRL+PAGE UP or CTRL+PAGE DOWN
Scroll, Up/Down One Line	WD 11	Click scroll arrow at top/bottom of vertical scroll bar			UP ARROW/DOWN ARROW
Scroll, Up/Down One Screen	WD 11	Click above/below scroll box on vertical scroll bar			PAGE UP/PAGE DOWN
Select Block of Text	WD 30	Click beginning, SHIFT-click end			
Select Character(s)	WD 30	Drag through characters			SHIFT+RIGHT ARROW or SHIFT+LEFT ARROW
Select Entire Document	WD 30	In left margin, triple-click	Select button arrow (Home tab | Editing group)		CTRL+A
Select Graphic	WD 30	Click graphic			
Select Group of Words	WD 27	Drag mouse pointer through words			CTRL+SHIFT+RIGHT ARROW
Select Line	WD 15	Click in left margin			SHIFT+DOWN ARROW
Select Multiple Lines	WD 21	Drag mouse pointer in left margin			SHIFT+DOWN ARROW
Select Nonadjacent Items	WD 15	Select first item, hold down CTRL key while selecting additional item(s)			
Select Paragraph	WD 30	Triple-click paragraph			CTRL+SHIFT+DOWN ARROW or CTRL+SHIFT+UP ARROW
Select Sentence	WD 30	CTRL-click			
Select Word	WD 30	Double-click word			CTRL+SHIFT+RIGHT ARROW or CTRL+SHIFT+LEFT ARROW
Shade Paragraph	WD 20		Shading button arrow (Home tab | Paragraph group)		
Shape, Add Text	WD 145			Add Text	

Table 1: Microsoft Word 2010 Quick Reference Summary *(continued)*

Task	Page Number	Mouse	Ribbon	Shortcut Menu	Keyboard Shortcut
Shape, Apply Style	WD 144		More button in Shape Styles gallery (Drawing Tools Format tab | Shape Styles group)	Format Shape, Color button in left pane (Format Shape dialog box)	
Shape, Insert	WD 142		Shapes button (Insert tab | Illustrations group)		
Single-Space Lines	WD 81		Line and Paragraph Spacing button (Home tab | Paragraph group)	Paragraph, Indents and Spacing tab (Paragraph dialog box)	CTRL+1
Small Caps	WD 81		Font Dialog Box Launcher (Home Tab | Font group), Font tab (Font dialog box)		CTRL+SHIFT+K
Source, Edit	WD 97		Click citation, Citation Options box arrow, Edit Source		
Source, Modify	WD 109		Manage Sources button (References tab | Citations & Bibliography group), Edit button		
Spelling and Grammar, Check at Once	WD 118	Spelling and Grammar check icon on status bar, Spelling	Spelling & Grammar button (Review tab | Proofing group)	Spelling	F7
Spelling, Check as You Type	WD 9	Click word, Spelling and Grammar Check icon on status bar		Right-click error, click correct word on shortcut menu	
Style, Update to Match Selection	WD 74		Right-click style in Quick Style gallery (Home tab | Styles group)	Styles	
Subscript	WD 81		Subscript button (Home tab | Font group)	Font, Font tab (Font dialog box)	CTRL+EQUAL SIGN
Superscript	WD 81		Superscript button (Home tab | Font group)	Font, Font tab (Font dialog box)	CTRL+SHIFT+PLUS SIGN
Symbol, Insert	WD 158		Insert Symbol button (Insert tab | Symbols group)		
Synonym, Find and Insert	WD 118		Thesaurus (Review tab | Proofing group)	Right-click word, click desired synonym on Synonym submenu	SHIFT+F7
Tab Stops, Set Custom	WD 169	Click desired tab stop on ruler	Paragraph Dialog Box Launcher (Home tab or Page Layout tab | Paragraph group), Tabs button (Paragraph dialog box)		
Table Columns, Resize to Fit Table Contents	WD 180	Double-click column boundary	AutoFit button (Table Tools Layout tab | Cell Size group)	AutoFit	
Table, Align Data in Cells	WD 182		Align [location] button (Table Tools Layout tab | Alignment group)		
Table, Apply Style	WD 179		More button in Table Styles gallery (Table Tools Design tab | Table Styles group)		
Table, Center	WD 183	Select table, Center button on Mini toolbar	Select table, Center button (Home tab | Font group)		
Table, Delete Cell Contents	WD 185		Cut button (Home tab | Clipboard group)		Select cell contents, DELETE or CTRL+X

Table 1: Microsoft Word 2010 Quick Reference Summary *(continued)*

Task	Page Number	Mouse	Ribbon	Shortcut Menu	Keyboard Shortcut
Table, Delete Entire	WD 185		Delete button (Table Tools Layout tab | Rows & Columns group)		
Table, Delete Row or Column	WD 185		Delete button (Table Tools Layout tab | Rows & Columns group)	Select row/column, Delete Rows or Delete Columns	
Table, Insert	WD 176		Table button (Insert tab | Tables group)		
Table, Insert Column	WD 185		Insert Columns to the Left/Right button (Table Tools Layout tab | Rows & Columns group)	Insert	
Table, Insert Row	WD 184		Insert Rows Above/Below button (Table Tools Layout Tab | Rows & Columns group)	Insert	
Table, Merge Cells	WD 185		Merge Cells button (Table Tools Layout tab | Merge group)	Merge Cells	
Table, Select Cell	WD 181	Click left edge of cell	Select button (Table Tools Layout tab | Table group)		
Table, Select Column	WD 181	Click top border of column	Select button (Table Tools Layout tab | Table group)		
Table, Select Entire	WD 181	Click table move handle	Select button (Table Tools Layout tab | Table group)		
Table, Select Multiple Cells, Rows, or Columns, Adjacent	WD 181	Drag through cells, rows, or columns			
Table, Select Next Cell	WD 181				TAB
Table, Select Previous Cell	WD 181				SHIFT+TAB
Table, Select Row	WD 181	Click to left of row	Select button (Table Tools Layout tab | Table Group)		
Table, Split Cells	WD 186		Split Cells button (Table Tools Layout tab | Merge group)	Split Cells	
Text Effect, Apply	WD 19		Text Effects button (Home tab | Font group)		
Text Wrapping, Change	WD 148		Wrap Text button (Drawing Tools format tab | Arrange group)	Wrap Text	
Theme Colors, Change	WD 28		Change Styles button (Home tab | Styles group)		
Underline	WD 27	Underline button on Mini toolbar	Underline button (Home tab | Font group)	Font, Font tab (Font dialog box)	CTRL+U
Underline Words, Not Spaces	WD 81		Font Dialog Box Launcher (Home tab | Font group), Font tab (Font dialog box), Underline style box arrow		CTRL+SHIFT+W
Undo	WD 23	Undo button on Quick Access Toolbar			CTRL+Z
Zoom Document	WD 33	Zoom Out or Zoom In button on status bar	Zoom button (View tab | Zoom group)		
Zoom One Page	WD 41		One Page button (View tab | Zoom group)		

Table 2: Microsoft PowerPoint 2010 Quick Reference Summary

Task	Page Number	Mouse	Ribbon	Shortcut Menu	Keyboard Shortcut
Animated GIF (Movie), Insert	PPT 174		Picture button (Insert tab | Images group)		
Audio File, Insert	PPT 167		Insert Audio button (Insert tab | Media group)		
Audio Options, Add	PPT 170		Audio Tools Playback tab | Audio Options group		
Clip Art, Insert	PPT 27	Clip Art icon in slide	Clip Art button (Insert tab | Images group)		
Clip Art, Photo, or Shape, Move	PPT 36	Drag			ARROW KEYS move selected image in small increments
Clip Art, Regroup	PPT 162		Group button, Regroup command (Drawing Tools Format tab | Arrange group)	Group, Regroup	
Clip Art, Ungroup	PPT 157		Group button, Ungroup command (Picture Tools Format tab | Arrange group), click Yes to convert to Microsoft Office drawing, click Drawing Tools Format tab, Group button, Ungroup		
Clip Object, Recolor	PPT 158		Shape Fill button (Drawing Tools Format tab | Shape Styles group)	Format Shape, Color button (Format Shape dialog box)	
Copy	PPT 108, 155		Copy button (Home tab | Clipboard group)	Copy	CTRL+C
Document Properties, Change	PPT 46		Properties button (File tab | Info tab)		
Document Theme, Change Color	PPT 81		Colors button (Design tab | Themes group)		
Document Theme, Choose	PPT 5		More button (Design tab | Themes group)		
Font Size, Decrease	PPT 104	Decrease Font Size button or Font Size box arrow on Mini toolbar	Decrease Font Size button or Font Size box arrow (Home tab | Font group)		CTRL+SHIFT+<
Font Size, Increase	PPT 11	Increase Font Size button or Font Size box arrow on Mini toolbar	Increase Font Size button or Font Size box arrow (Home tab | Font group)		CTRL+SHIFT+>
Font, Change	PPT 102	Font box arrow on Mini toolbar	Font box arrow (Home tab | Font group)	Font, Font tab (Font dialog box)	CTRL+SHIFT+F
Font, Change Color	PPT 13	Font Color button or Font Color button arrow on Mini toolbar	Font Color button or Font Color button arrow (Home tab | Font group)	Font, Font tab (Font dialog box)	CTRL+SHIFT+F
Format Painter, Use	PPT 105	Format Painter button on Mini toolbar	Double-click Format Painter button (Home tab | Clipboard group), select text with format you want to copy, select text to apply previously selected format; press ESC to turn off Format Painter		

Table 2: Microsoft PowerPoint 2010 Quick Reference Summary *(continued)*

Task	Page Number	Mouse	Ribbon	Shortcut Menu	Keyboard Shortcut
Handout, Print	PPT 184		Print button (File tab | Print tab)		
List Level, Increase	PPT 17	Increase List Level button on Mini toolbar	Increase List Level button (Home tab | Paragraph group)		TAB or ALT+SHIFT+RIGHT ARROW
List Level, Decrease	PPT 18	Decrease List Level button on Mini toolbar	Decrease List Level button (Home tab | Paragraph group)		SHIFT+TAB or ALT+SHIFT+LEFT ARROW
Next Slide	PPT 25	Next Slide button on vertical scroll bar or next slide thumbnail on Slides tab			PAGE DOWN
Normal View	PPT 153	Normal button at lower-right PowerPoint window	Normal View button (View tab | Presentation Views group)		
Open Presentation	PPT 50		Open (File tab)		CTRL+O
Paste	PPT 109		Paste button (Home tab | Clipboard group)	Paste	CTRL+V
Photo, Insert	PPT 32, 83	Insert Picture from File icon on slide or Insert Clip Art icon on slide	Picture button or Clip Art button (Insert tab | Images group)		
Picture, Add an Artistic Effect	PPT 145		Artistic Effects button (Picture Tools Format tab | Adjust group)	Format Picture, Artistic Effects (Format Picture dialog box)	
Picture, Add Border	PPT 91		Picture border button (Picture Tools Format tab | Picture Styles group)		
Picture, Correct	PPT 87		Corrections button (Picture Tools Format tab | Adjust group)	Format Picture, Picture Corrections (Format Picture dialog box)	
Picture, Recolor	PPT 143		Color button (Picture Tools Format tab | Adjust group)	Format Picture, Picture Color (Format Picture dialog box)	
Picture Border, Change Color	PPT 92		Picture border button (Picture Tools Format tab | Picture Styles group)		
Picture Effects, Apply	PPT 89		Picture Effects button (Picture Tools Format tab | Picture Styles group)	Format Picture	
Picture Style, Apply	PPT 87		More button (Picture Tools Format tab | Picture Styles group)		
Placeholder, Delete	PPT 149				Select placeholder, DELETE
Placeholder, Move	PPT 148	Drag			
Placeholder, Resize	PPT 148	Drag sizing handles			
Previous Slide	PPT 26	Previous Slide button on vertical scroll bar or click previous slide thumbnail on Slides tab			PAGE UP

Table 2: Microsoft PowerPoint 2010 Quick Reference Summary *(continued)*

Task	Page Number	Mouse	Ribbon	Shortcut Menu	Keyboard Shortcut
Print a Presentation	PPT 51		Print button (File tab | Print tab)		CTRL+P
Quit PowerPoint	PPT 50	Close button on title bar	Exit (File tab)	Right-click Microsoft PowerPoint button on taskbar, click Close window	ALT+F4
Reading View	PPT 154	Reading View button at lower-right PowerPoint window	Reading View button (View tab | Presentation Views group)		
Resize	PPT 33, 93, 148	Drag sizing handles	Enter height and width values (Picture Tools Format tab | Size group or Drawing Tools Format tab | Size group)	Format Picture or Format Shape, Size tab; or enter height and width in Shape Height and Shape Width boxes	
Save a Presentation	PPT 14	Save button on Quick Access Toolbar	Save or Save As (File tab)		CTRL+S or F12
Shape, Apply Style	PPT 110		More button or Format Shape Dialog Box Launcher in Shapes Style gallery (Drawing Tools Format tab | Shape Styles group)	Format Shape	
Shape, Insert	PPT 106		Shapes button (Home tab | Drawing group); More button (Drawing Tools Format tab | Insert Shapes group)		
Slide, Add	PPT 14		New Slide button (Home tab | Slides group)		CTRL+M
Slide, Arrange	PPT 39	Drag slide in Slides tab or Outline tab to new position, or in Slide Sorter view drag to new position			
Slide, Delete	PPT 152			Delete Slide	DELETE
Slide, Duplicate	PPT 38		New Slide arrow (Home tab | Slides group), Duplicate Selected Slides		
Slide, Format Background	PPT 95		Background Styles button (Design tab | Background group)	Format Background	
Slide, Insert Picture as Background	PPT 97		Background Styles button (Design tab | Background group)	Format Background, Picture or Texture Fill, Insert from File (Format Background dialog box)	
Slide, Select Layout	PPT 21		Layout button or New Slide arrow (Home tab | Slides group)		

Table 2: Microsoft PowerPoint 2010 Quick Reference Summary *(continued)*					
Task	**Page Number**	**Mouse**	**Ribbon**	**Shortcut Menu**	**Keyboard Shortcut**
Slide Number, Insert	PPT 182		Insert Slide Number button (Insert tab | Text group) or Header & Footer button (Insert tab | Text group), click Slide number check box		
Slide Show View	PPT 47	Slide Show button at lower-right PowerPoint window	Slide Show button (Slide Show tab | Start Slide Show group)		F5
Slide Show, End	PPT 49	Click black ending slide		End Show	ESC or HYPHEN
Slide Sorter View	PPT 153	Slide Sorter button at lower-right PowerPoint window	Slide Sorter button (View tab | Presentation Views group)		
Speaker Notes, Add	PPT 179	In Normal view, click Notes pane and type notes			
Speaker Notes, Print	PPT 187		File tab, Print tab, click Notes Pages (Print Layout area), click Print button		
Spelling, Check	PPT 181		Spelling button (Review tab | Proofing group)	Spelling (or click correct word on shortcut menu)	F7
Stacking Order, Change	PPT 146		Bring Forward or Send Backward button (Picture Tools Format tab | Arrange group)	Send to Back or Bring to Front	
Synonym, Find and Insert	PPT 178		Thesaurus button (Review tab | Proofing group)	Right-click word, click desired synonym on Synonym submenu	SHIFT+F7
Text, Add Shadow	PPT 103		Text Shadow button (Home tab | Font group)		
Text, Align Horizontally	PPT 150	Align Text buttons on Mini toolbar	Align Text buttons (Home tab | Paragraph group)	Paragraph, Alignment box (Paragraph dialog box)	CTRL+R (right), CTRL+L (left), CTRL+E (center)
Text, Bold	PPT 20	Bold button on Mini toolbar	Bold button (Home tab | Font group)	Font, Font tab (Font dialog box)	CTRL+B
Text, Change Color	PPT 13	Font Color button or Font Color button arrow on Mini toolbar	Font Color button or Font Color button arrow (Home tab | Font group)	Font, Font tab (Font dialog box)	
Text, Delete	PPT 41		Cut button (Home tab | Clipboard group)	Cut	DELETE or CTRL+X or BACKSPACE
Text, Find and Replace	PPT 176		Replace button (Home tab | Editing group)		CTRL+H
Text, Italicize	PPT 11	Italic button on Mini toolbar	Italic button (Home tab | Font group)	Font, Font tab (Font dialog box)	CTRL+I
Text, Select Paragraph	PPT 10	Triple-click paragraph			SHIFT+DOWN ARROW or SHIFT+UP ARROW
Text, Select Word	PPT 12	Double-click word			CTRL+SHIFT+RIGHT ARROW or CTRL+SHIFT+LEFT ARROW

Table 2: Microsoft PowerPoint 2010 Quick Reference Summary *(continued)*

Task	Page Number	Mouse	Ribbon	Shortcut Menu	Keyboard Shortcut
Transition, Add	PPT 43		Transitions tab | Transition to This Slide group		ALT+A , T
Transparency, Change	PPT 98		Background Styles button (Design tab | Background group), Format Background, move Transparency slider	Format Background, Transparency slider	
Video File, Insert	PPT 163		Insert Video button (Insert tab | Media group)		
Video File, Trim	PPT 165		Trim Video button (Video Tools Playback tab | Editing group), drag video start/end points or edit Start Time and End Time boxes		
Video Options	PPT 166		Video Tools Playback tab | Video Options group		
Video Style, Add	PPT 172		More button (Video Tools Format tab | Video Styles group)		
WordArt, Add Text Effects	PPT 115		Text Effects button (Drawing Tools Format tab | WordArt Styles group)		
WordArt, Insert	PPT 114		WordArt button (Insert tab | Text group)		
Zoom for Viewing Slides	PPT 156	Drag Zoom slider on status bar; click Zoom In or Zoom Out button on Zoom slider; change percentage in Zoom level box on left side of slider	Zoom button (View tab | Zoom group)		

Table 3: Microsoft Excel 2010 Quick Reference Summary

Task	Page Number	Mouse	Ribbon	Shortcut Menu	Keyboard Shortcut
Accounting Number Format, Apply	EX 100		Accounting Number Format button (Home tab | Number group)		
All data in a cell, Select	EX 51	Double-click if there are no spaces in data			
Auto Fill	EX 18	Drag fill handle	Auto Fill Options button (Home tab | Editing group)		
AutoCalculate	EX 48	Select range | right-click AutoCalculate area | click calculation			
Average Function	EX 84	Insert Function box in formula bar | AVERAGE in Select a function list | OK | range | OK	Sum button arrow (Home tab | Editing group) or Sum button arrow (Formulas tab | Function Library)		Type =av | press DOWN ARROW | ENTER

Table 3: Microsoft Excel 2010 Quick Reference Summary *(continued)*

Task	Page Number	Mouse	Ribbon	Shortcut Menu	Keyboard Shortcut
Background Color, Change	EX 96		Format Cells Dialog Box Launcher (Home tab | Font group) | Fill tab | click color | click OK	Format Cells on shortcut menu	CTRL+1
Best Fit	EX 107	Select columns | point to boundary until arrow is split double arrow | double-click			
Bold	EX 25	Bold button on Mini toolbar	Bold button (Home tab | Font group)	Format Cells on shortcut menu | Font tab | Bold	CTRL+B
Cell Entries, Clear Selected	EX 52	Drag fill handle from empty cell through cells with entries	Clear button (Home tab | Editing group) | Clear Contents	Clear Contents on shortcut menu	DELETE
Cell Reference, Add	EX 78	Click cell			
Cell Style, Change	EX 52		Cell Styles button (Home tab | Styles group)		
Cell, Highlight	EX 19	Drag mouse pointer			
Cell, Select	EX 34	Click cell or click Name box, type cell reference, press ENTER			Use arrow keys
Cells, Merge and Center	EX 28	Merge & Center button on Mini toolbar	Merge & Center button (Home tab | Alignment group)	Format Cells on shortcut menu | Alignment tab	
Characters to left of insertion point, Delete	EX 50				BACKSPACE
Characters to right of insertion point, Delete	EX 50				DELETE
Characters, Highlight	EX 51	Drag through adjacent characters			SHIFT+RIGHT ARROW or SHIFT+LEFT ARROW
Chart, Add	EX 38		Charts group | Insert tab		
Color Text	EX 27	Font Color button on Mini toolbar	Font Color button arrow (Home tab | Font group)		
Column Width	EX 33	Drag column heading boundary		Column Width on shortcut menu	
Comma Style Format, Apply	EX 100		Comma Style button (Home tab | Number group)		
Complete an Entry	EX 8	Click Enter box			Press ENTER
Conditional Formatting	EX 104		Conditional Formatting button (Home tab | Styles group)		
Copy Range of Cells	EX 80	Select range | drag fill handle |	Copy button (Home tab | Clipboard group) |	Copy on shortcut menu	CTRL+C
Currency Style Format, Apply	EX 100		Format Cells: Number Dialog Box Launcher (Home tab | Number group)		CTRL+1 OR CTRL+SHIFT+ DOLLAR SIGN ($)

Table 3: Microsoft Excel 2010 Quick Reference Summary *(continued)*

Task	Page Number	Mouse	Ribbon	Shortcut Menu	Keyboard Shortcut
Date, Format	EX 98		Format Cells: Number Dialog Box Launcher on Home tab	Format Cells on shortcut menu | Number tab (Format Cells dialog box)	
Document Properties, Change	EX 43		Properties button (File tab | Info tab)		
Document Properties, Print	EX 45		File tab | Print tab, first box arrow (Settings area)		
Document Properties, Set or View	EX 43		File | Info tab		
Entry, Complete	EX 8	Click Enter box			Press ENTER
Font Color	EX 27	Font Color box arrow on Mini toolbar	Font Color button arrow (Home tab | Font group)	Format Cells on shortcut menu | Font tab	
Font Size, Decrease	EX 26	Font Size box arrow on Mini toolbar	Decrease Font Size button (Home tab | Font group)	Format Cells on shortcut menu | Font tab	
Font Size, Increase	EX 26	Font Size box arrow on Mini toolbar	Increase Font Size button (Home tab | Font group)	Format Cells | Font Tab	
Font Type	EX 24	Font box arrow on Mini toolbar	Font box (Home tab | Font group)	Format Cells | Font tab	
Font, Change	EX 24	Font Size box arrow on Mini toolbar	Font box arrow (Home tab | Font group)	Format Cells | Font tab	
Formulas Version	EX 119				CTRL+ACCENT MARK (`)
Highlight Cells	EX 18	Drag mouse pointer			SHIFT+ARROW KEY
In-Cell Editing	EX 50	Double-click cell			F2
Insert and Overtype modes, Toggle between	EX 50				INSERT
Insertion point, Move	EX 8	Click			Use arrow keys
Insertion point, move to beginning of data in cell	EX 51	Point to left of first character and click			HOME
Insertion point, move to ending of data in cell	EX 51	Point to right of last character and click			END
Margins, Change	EX 114	Page Layout button on status bar | Page Layout tab | Margins button	Page Setup Dialog Box Launcher | Margins tab (Page Layout tab | Page Setup group)		
Max Function	EX 86	Insert Function box in formula bar | MAX in Select a function list | OK | range | OK	Sum button arrow (Home tab | Editing group) or Sum button arrow (Formulas tab | Sum group)		
Min Function	EX 87	Insert Function box in the formula bar | MIN in Select a function list | OK | range | OK	Sum button arrow (Home tab | Editing group) or Sum button arrow (Formulas tab | Sum group)		
New Line in Cell, Start	EX 71				ALT+ENTER

Table 3: Microsoft Excel 2010 Quick Reference Summary *(continued)*

Task	Page Number	Mouse	Ribbon	Shortcut Menu	Keyboard Shortcut
Numbers, Format	EX 31	Accounting Number Format, Percent Style, or Comma Style button on Mini toolbar	Cell Styles button (Home tab | Styles group) or Accounting Number Format, Percent Style, or Comma Style button (Home tab | Number group), or Format Cells: Number dialog box launcher | Accounting, or Percentage or Number Format list arrow | Accounting or Percentage		
Open a Workbook	EX 48		Open or Recent (File tab)		CTRL+O
Percent style format	EX 103		Percent Style button (Home tab | Number group)	Format Cells on shortcut menu | Number tab | Percentage (Format Cells dialog box)	CTRL+SHIFT+ percent sign (%)
Print Scaling Option	EX 120		Page Setup Dialog Box Launcher (Page Layout tab | Page Setup group)		
Print Section of Worksheet	EX 118		File | Print tab | Print Active Sheets or Print Area button (Page Layout tab | Page Setup group)		
Print Worksheet	EX 46		File tab | Print tab		CTRL+P
Quit Excel	EX 47	Close button on right side of title bar	Exit (File tab)		
Range Finder	EX 91	Double-click cell			
Range, Deselect	EX 18	Click outside range			
Range, Select	EX 28	Drag fill handle through range			
Redo	EX 51	Redo button on Quick Access Toolbar			CTRL+Y
Row Height	EX 110	Drag row heading boundary		Row Height on shortcut menu	
Save Workbook	EX 20	Save button on Quick Access Toolbar	Save (File tab | Save button)		CTRL+S
Save Workbook, New Name	EX 20	Save button on Quick Access Toolbar			
Save Workbook, Same Name	EX 20	Save button on Quick Access Toolbar	Save (File tab | Save button)		CTRL+S
Select Cell	EX 7	Click cell or click Name box, type cell reference, press ENTER			Use arrow keys
Select Entire Worksheet	EX 52	Click Select All button			CTRL+A
Select Nonadjacent Cells	EX 100	Select first cell, hold down CTRL key while selecting second cell			
Selected characters, Delete	EX 50		Cut button (Home tab | Clipboard group)		DELETE

Table 3: Microsoft Excel 2010 Quick Reference Summary *(continued)*

Task	Page Number	Mouse	Ribbon	Shortcut Menu	Keyboard Shortcut
Selected Chart, Delete	EX 53				DELETE
Sheet Name, Change	EX 42	Double-click type name		Rename on shortcut menu	
Spelling	EX 112		Spelling button (Review tab | Proofing group)		F7
Sum	EX 15	Click Insert Function button in formula bar | SUM in Select a function list | OK | range | OK	Sum button (Home tab | Editing group)		ALT+EQUAL SIGN (=) twice
Text, Delete after typing but before pressing the ENTER key	EX 8	Click Cancel box in formula bar			Press ESC
Text, Delete while typing	EX 8				Press BACKSPACE
Undo	EX 51	Undo button on Quick Access Toolbar			CTRL+Z
Workbook Theme, Change	EX 94		Themes button (Page Layout tab | Themes group)		
Worksheet Name, Change	EX 42	Double-click sheet tab, type name		Rename on shortcut menu	
Worksheet, Clear	EX 52		Select All button | Clear button (Home tab | Editing group)		CTRL A, press DELETE
Worksheet, Preview	EX 46		File tab | Print tab		CTRL+P

Table 4: Microsoft Access 2010 Quick Reference Summary

Task	Page Number	Mouse	Ribbon	Shortcut Menu	Keyboard Shortcut
All Fields in Query, Include	AC 79, AC 80	Double-click asterisk			
Calculated Field in Query, Use	AC 116			Right-click field row, Zoom	
Caption, Change in Query	AC 118		Property Sheet button (Query Tools Design Tab | Show/Hide group), Caption box	Right-click field in design grid, click Properties on shortcut menu, Caption box	
Close Object	AC 23	Close button for object		Right-click item, Close	
Column Headings, Modify	AC 54			Right-click field name, Rename Field	
Column, Resize	AC 54, AC 55	Double-click right boundary of field selector in datasheet		Right-click field name, Field Width	
Comparison Operator, Use	AC 91	Create query, enter comparison operator in criterion			

Table 4: Microsoft Access 2010 Quick Reference Summary *(continued)*

Task	Page Number	Mouse	Ribbon	Shortcut Menu	Keyboard Shortcut
Compound Criterion Involving AND, Use	AC 92				Place criteria on same line
Compound Criterion Involving OR, Use	AC 93				Place criteria on separate lines
Criteria, Use in Calculating Statistics	AC 121		Totals button (Query Tools Design Tab | Show/Hide group), Total box arrow, click calculation		
Criterion, Use	AC 46	Right-click query, Design View, Criteria row			
Crosstab Query, Create	AC 124		Query Wizard button (Create tab | Queries group), Crosstab Query Wizard		
Data, Export to Excel	AC 111		Excel button (External Data tab | Export group)	Right-click object, click Excel on Export menu	
Data, Import	AC 38		Button for imported data format (External Data tab | Import & Link group)	Right-click object, click selected format on Import menu	
Data, Sort in Query	AC 96		Select field in design grid, click Sort row, click Sort row arrow, select order		
Database Properties, Change	AC 59		View and edit database properties link (File tab | Info tab)		
Database, Create	AC 13		Blank database button (File tab | New tab)		
Design Grid, Clear	AC 95	In Design view, select all columns, DELETE			
Duplicates, Omit	AC 97		In Design view, click first empty field, Property Sheet button (Query Tools Design tab | Show/Hide group), click Yes in Unique Values property box	Right-click first empty field, click Properties on shortcut menu, click Yes in Unique Values property box	
Field in Query, Add	AC 79	Double-click field in upper pane			
Form for Query, Create	AC 109		Select query, Form button (Create tab | Forms group)		
Form, Create	AC 48		Form button (Create tab | Forms group)		
Grouping, Use	AC 122	Create query, select Group By in Total row, select field to group by			
Join Properties, Change	AC 105			In Design view, right-click join line	
Multiple Keys, Sort on	AC 98	Assign two sort keys in design grid			

Table 4: Microsoft Access 2010 Quick Reference Summary *(continued)*

Task	Page Number	Mouse	Ribbon	Shortcut Menu	Keyboard Shortcut
Navigation Pane, Customize	AC 127	Navigation Pane arrow			
Number Criterion, Use	AC 90	Create query, select table, enter criterion in field grid			
Open Database	AC 27		Open button (File tab)		
Open Table	AC 24	Double-click table in Navigation Pane		Right-click table in Navigation Pane, click Open in shortcut menu	
Parameter Query, Create	AC 87		In Design view, type parameter in square brackets in criterion row of field grid, View button (Query Tools Design tab | Results group)		
Preview or Print Object	AC 31		Print or Print Preview button (File tab | Print tab)		CTRL+P, ENTER
Query, Create in Design View	AC 78		Query Design button (Create tab | Queries group)		
Query, Create using Simple Query Wizard	AC 43		Query Wizard button (Create tab | Queries group)		
Query, Export	AC 111, AC 113, AC 114		Select query in Navigation Pane, application button (External Data tab | Export group)	Right-click query in Navigation Pane, click Export	
Record, Add	AC 28	New (blank) record button in Navigation buttons	New button (Home tab | Records Group)		CTRL+PLUS SIGN (+)
Records in a Join, Restrict	AC 115	In Design view, enter criterion for query			
Remaining Fields in Table, Define	AC 19	In Datasheet view, click Click to Add field (Fields tab)			
Report, Create	AC 52		Report button (Create tab | Reports group)		
Report, Create Involving Join	AC 106		Select query, Report Wizard button (Create tab | Reports group)		
Save Object	AC 21	Save button on Quick Access Toolbar	File tab, Save		CTRL+S
Statistics, Calculate	AC 119		Create query, Totals button (Query Tools Design tab | Show/Hide group), click Total row in design grid, click Total box arrow, select calculation		
Table, Create in Design View	AC 33		Table Design button (Create tab | Tables group)		
Table, View in Design View	AC 21		View button arrow (Table Tools Fields tab | Views group), Design View		

Table 4: Microsoft Access 2010 Quick Reference Summary *(continued)*

Task	Page Number	Mouse	Ribbon	Shortcut Menu	Keyboard Shortcut
Tables, Join	AC 102		Query Design button (Create tab | Queries group), add field lists for tables to join, add desired fields to design grid, view query		
Text Data Criterion, Use	AC 80	Enter text as criterion in Criteria row of design grid			
Top Values Query, Create	AC 99		In Design view, Return box arrow (Query Tools Design tab | Query Setup group)		
Totals, Add to a Report	AC 57		Totals button (Report Layout Tools Design tab | Grouping & Totals group)		
Wildcard, Use	AC 83	In Design view, click Criteria row in design grid, type criterion including wildcard			